Encyclopedia of Fluid Mechanics

VOLUME 3

Gas-Liquid Flows

Gulf Publishing Company
Book Division
Houston, London, Paris, Tokyo

Encyclopedia

of

Fluid Mechanics

VOLUME 3

Gas-Liquid Flows

N. P. Cheremisinoff, Editor

in collaboration with—

T. W. Abou-Arab
M. E. Abou-El-Hassan
G. R. Assar
C. T. Avedisian
B. J. Azzopardi
D. Barnea
F. V. Bracco
R. W. Burley
F. Castiglia
J. Cermak
J. J. J. Chen
H. C. Cheng
R. P. Chhabra
D. Chisholm
D. E. Dietrich
J. Drahos
M. P. Dudukovic
T. Z. Fahidy
A. J. M. Foussat
D. Gaudin
J. K. Gehlawat
S. P. Godbole
J. A. Golding
J. R. Grace
P. F. Greenfield
K. Hertwig

J. P. Hulin
J. B. Joshi
V. Kadambi
R. Kern
H. A. Khater
M. Kielkiewicz
M. Kosinski
W. Krug
J. Lach
Z. H. Lin
J. C. Merchuk
R. Mesler
P. L. Mills
K. Nakamura
M. Nakamura
G. S. R. Narasimhamurty
T. E. Natan, Jr.
D. Niebuhr
E. Oliveri
A. B. Pandit
A. Purushothaman
M. S. Quraishi
N. Rabiger
K. S. M. S. Raghav Rao
F. Rehman
R. D. Reitz

J. F. Richardson
D. S. Rowe
M. Sadatomi
M. E. Salcudean
A. S. Sangani
Y. Sato
Y. T. Shah
Y. L. Sinai
K. Sivaji
R. V. Smith
H. M. Soliman
P. L. Spedding
G. S. Strumolo
D. Sudarmana
K. Suzuki
S. Taibi
Y. Taitel
H. Tsuge
H. E. A. van den Akker
G. Vella
K. Viswanathan
A. Vogelpohl
T. Wairegi
T. Watanabe
S. W. Webb
W. S. Yeung

Encyclopedia of Fluid Mechanics

VOLUME 3

Gas-Liquid Flows

Library of Congress Cataloging-in-Publication Data

(Revised for vol. 3)
Main entry under title:

Encyclopedia of fluid mechanics.

Includes indexes.
Contents: v. 1. Flow phenomena and measurement—
—v. 3. Gas-liquid flows.
1. Fluid mechanics—Dictionaries. I. Cheremisinoff,
Nicholas P.
TA357.E53 1985   620.1′06   85-9742

ISBN 0-87201-515-7 (v. 3)

ISBN 0-87201-515-7

CONTENTS

SECTION II: FLOW REGIMES, HOLD-UP, AND PRESSURE DROP

SECTION III: REACTORS AND INDUSTRIAL APPLICATIONS

CONTRIBUTORS TO THIS VOLUME

T. W. Abou-Arab, Mechanical Power Department, Cairo University, Cairo, Egypt.

M. E. Abou-El-Hassan, Department of Chemical Engineering, University of Qatar, Doha, Qatar.

G. R. Assar, Department of Chemical & Process Engineering, Heriot-Watt University, Edinburgh, Scotland.

C. T. Avedisian, Sibley School of Mechanical and Aerospace Engineering, Cornell University, Ithaca, New York, USA.

B. J. Azzopardi, Engineering Sciences Division, AERE Harwell, Didcot, Oxfordshire, United Kingdom.

D. Barnea, Faculty of Engineering, Tel-Aviv University, Tel-Aviv, Israel.

F. V. Bracco, Mechanical and Aerospace Engineering Department, Princeton University, Princeton, New Jersey, USA.

R. W. Burley, Department of Chemical & Process Engineering, Heriot-Watt University, Edinburgh, Scotland.

F. Castiglia, Instituto Di Applicazioni e Impianti Nucleari, Facolta di Ingegneria, University di Palermo, Palermo, Italy.

J. Cermak, Institute of Chemical Process Fundamentals, Czechoslovak Acadamy of Science, Prague, Czechoslovakia.

J. J. J. Chen, Department of Chemical and Materials Engineering, University of Auckland, New Zealand.

H. C. Cheng, Department of Applied Science, Brookhaven National Laboratory, Upton, New York, USA.

N. P. Cheremisinoff, Exxon Chemical Company, Linden, New Jersey, USA.

R. P. Chhabra, Department of Chemical Engineering, University College of Swansea, Singleton Park, Swansea, United Kingdom.

D. Chisholm, Department of Mechanical and Civil Engineering, Glasgow College of Technology, Cowcaddens Rd., Glasgow, Scotland.

D. E. Dietrich, Technadyne Engineering Consultants, Inc., Albuquerque, New Mexico, USA.

J. Drahos, Institute of Chemical Process Fundamentals, Czechoslovak Acadamy of Science, Prague, Czechoslovakia.

M. P. Dudukovic, Department of Chemical Engineering, Washington University in St. Louis, St. Louis, Missouri, USA.

T. Z. Fahidy, Department of Chemical Engineering, University of Waterloo, Waterloo, Ontario, Canada.

A. J. M. Foussat, Physics Engineering Department, Etudes et Productions Schlumberger, Clamart Cedex, France.

D. Gaudin, Physics Engineering Department, Etudes et Productions Schlumberger, Clamart Cedex, France.

J. K. Gehlawat, Indian Institute of Technology, Kanpur, India.

S. P. Godbole, Petroleum Engineering Department, University of Alaska, Fairbanks, Alaska, USA.

J. A. Golding, Department of Chemical Engineering, University of Ottawa, Ottawa, Canada.

J. R. Grace, Department of Chemical Engineering, University of British Columbia, Vancouver, Canada.

P. F. Greenfield, Department of Chemical Engineering, University of Queensland, St. Lucia, Australia.

K. Hertwig, Engineering College, Koethen, German Democratic Republic.

J. P. Hulin, Physics Engineering Department, Etudes et Productions Schlumberger, Clamart Cedex, France.

J. B. Joshi, Department of Chemical Technology, University of Bombay, Bombay, India.

V. Kadambi, General Electric Company, Research & Development Center, Schenectady, New York, USA.

R. Kern, Hoffmann-LaRoche, Inc., Nutley, New Jersey, USA.

H. A. Khater, Nuclear Products Department, Westinghouse Canada, Inc., Hamilton, Ontario, Canada.

M. Kielkiewicz, Institute of Heat Engineering, Warsaw Technical University, Warsaw, Poland.

M. Kosinski, Institute of Heat Engineering, Warsaw Technical University, Warsaw, Poland.

W. Krug, Engineering College, Koethen, German Democratic Republic.

J. Lach, Department of Reactor Engineering, Institute of Atomic Energy, Otwock-Swierk, Poland.

Z. H. Lin, Xian Jiao-Tong University, Xian, The Peoples' Republic of China.

J. C. Merchuk, Department of Chemical Engineering, Ben-Gurion University of the Negev, Beer Sheva, Israel.

R. Mesler, Department of Chemical and Petroleum Engineering, University of Kansas, Lawrence, Kansas, USA.

P. L. Mills, Corporate Research Laboratories, Monsanto Co., St. Louis, Missouri, USA.

K. Nakamura, Anan Technical College, Minobayashi-Cho, Anan City, Japan.

M. Nakamura, Department of Chemical Engineering, Nagoya University, Nagoya, Japan.

G. S. R. Narasimhamurty, Gadepally Bio-Industries, Bombay, India.

T. E. Natan, Jr., Department of Chemical and Nuclear Engineering, University of Cincinnati, Cincinnati, Ohio, USA.

D. Niebuhr, Institut fur Thermische Verfahrenstechnik, Technische Universitat Clausthal, German Democratic Republic.

E. Oliveri, Instituto di Applicazioni e Impianti Nucleari, Facolta di Ingegneria, University di Palermo, Palermo, Italy.

A. B. Pandit, Department of Chemical Technology, University of Bombay, Bombay, India.

A. Purushothaman, Gadepally Bio-Industries, Bombay, India.

M. S. Quraishi, Department of Chemical Engineering, University of Waterloo, Waterloo, Ontario, Canada.

N. Rabiger, Institut fur Thermische Verfahrenstechnik, Clausthal-Zellerfeld, Federal Republic of West Germany.

K. S. M. S. Raghav Rao, Department of Chemical Technology, University of Bombay, Bombay, India.

F. Rehman, Department of Mechanical Engineering, Wichita State University, Wichita, Kansas, USA.

R. D. Reitz, Fluid Mechanics Department, General Motors Research Laboratories, Warren, Michigan, USA.

J. F. Richardson, Department of Chemical Engineering, University College of Swansea, Singleton Park, Swansea, United Kingdom.

D. S. Rowe, Rowe and Associates, Bellevue, Washington, USA.

M. Sadatomi, Department of Mechanical Engineering, Kumamoto University, Kumamoto, Japan.

M. E. Salcudean, Department of Mechanical Engineering, University of British Colombia, Vancouver, Canada.

A. S. Sangani, Department of Chemical Engineering and Materials Science, Syracuse University, Syracuse, New York, USA.

Y. Sato, Department of Mechanical Engineering, Kumamoto University, Kumamoto, Japan.

Y. T. Shah, Department of Chemical and Petroleum Engineering, University of Pittsburgh, Pittsburgh, Pennsylvania, USA.

Y. L. Sinai, National Nuclear Corporation, Ltd., Risley, Warrington-Cheshire, United Kingdom.

K. Sivaji, Regional Research Laboratories, Hyderabad, India.

R. V. Smith, Department of Mechanical Engineering, Wichita State University, Wichita, Kansas, USA.

H. M. Soliman, Department of Mechanical Engineering, University of Manitoba, Winnipeg, Manitoba, Canada.

P. L. Spedding, Department of Chemical Engineering, Queens University of Belfast, Belfast, Northern Ireland.

G. S. Strumolo, Schlumberg-Doll Research, Ridgefield, Connecticut, USA.

D. Sudarmana, Department of Chemical Engineering, University of Queensland, St. Lucia, Australia.

K. Suzuki, Department of Mechanical Engineering, Kyoto University, Kyoto, Japan.

S. Taibi, Instituto di Applicazioni e Impianti Nucleari Facolta di Ingegneria, University di Palermo, Palermo, Italy.

Y. Taitel, Faculty of Engineering, Tel-Aviv University, Tel-Aviv, Israel.

H. Tsuge, Department of Applied Chemistry, Keio University, Yokohama, Japan.

H. E. A. van den Akker, Koninklijke/Shell Laboratorium, Amsterdam, The Netherlands.

G. Vella, Instituto di Applicazioni e Impianti Nucleari, Facolta di Ingegneria, University di Palermo, Palermo, Italy.

K. Viswanathan, Particle Technology Consultants Research Centre, New Delhi, India.

A. Vogelpohl, Institut fur Thermische Verfahrenstechnik, Clausthal-Zellerfeld, Federal Republic of West Germany.

T. Wairegi, Shell Canada Limited, Calgary, Canada.

T. Watanabe, Faculty of Engineering, Tokushima University, Minamijosanjima-Cho, Tokushima City, Japan.

S. W. Webb, Gilbert Associates Inc., Reading, Pennsylvania, USA.

W. S. Yeung, Mechanical and Energy Engineering Department, University of Lowell, Lowell, Massachusetts, USA.

ABOUT THE EDITOR

Nicholas P. Cheremisinoff heads the product development group in the Elastomers Technology Division of Exxon Chemical Company. Previously, he led the Reactor and Fluid Dynamics Modeling Group at Exxon Research and Engineering Company. He received his B.S., M.S., and Ph.D. degrees in chemical engineering from Clarkson College of Technology, and he is also a member of a number of professional societies including AIChE, Tau Beta Pi, and Sigma Xi.

PREFACE

Problems in the hydrodynamics and mass and heat transfer processes of two-phase (gas-liquid) flows have perhaps been the most extensively studied subjects in chemical engineering over the past thirty years. The extent of literature embracing this class of flows is staggering. Researchers and practitioners have long recognized the need to organize this vast body of research and design-oriented literature and several excellent texts have appeared over the past decade that attempt to establish a bridge between single-phase flow theory and the flow of complex mixtures. Despite these attempts, state-of-the-art design procedures are few and even conflicting.

Volume III addresses this class of flow problems in three sections. Section I, "Properties of Dispersed and Atomized Flows," contains 15 chapters. Initial chapters discuss characteristics and physical property estimation of various two-phase systems such as foams, bubbly flows, and dispersed particle flows. Single droplet and bubble dynamics are rigorously outlined along with the treatment of bubble-formation phenomenon. Treatment is extended to the hydrodynamic aspects of mass bubbling with presentations based on the theory of isotropic turbulence and more traditional empirical approaches. In addition, the phenomena of bubble nucleation and bubble dynamics in superheated liquid droplets are treated. Several chapters describe the formation of dynamic two-phase flows, provide design estimations of entrainment, and treat the process of liquid atomization.

Section II, "Flow Regimes, Hold-up, and Pressure Drop," contains 16 chapters which discuss complex gas-liquid flows in all tube-flow orientations. The subject of interface instability is treated in depth, and state-of-the-art flow regime maps are presented. Design procedures for predicting two-phase pressure drop and hold-up are given along with illustrative examples. Subjects not normally covered in standard texts that are included in this section are two-phase flows in non-circular channels, and through junctions, effects of flow obstructions on flow transitions and pressure drop, and experimental techniques. Sections I and II also provide insight into modeling these complex flows.

Section III, "Reactors and Industrial Applications," attempts to provide a unified approach to the design and scale-up of industrial reactors. Topics of industrial importance covered in depth include trickle-bed reactors, packed-bed reactor systems, bubble column design, sieve plate columns, extraction columns, thin film evaporators, hydraulics of distillation columns, air-lift reactors, and nuclear reactor channels. Many of these chapters contain extensive design data and scale-up methodology.

This volume represents the efforts of 78 experts. Additionally, it brings the experience and opinions of scores of engineers and researchers who aided with advice and suggestions in reviewing and refereeing the material presented. Each contributor is to be regarded as responsible for the statements and recommendations in his chapter. These individuals are to be congratulated for devoting their time and efforts to producing this volume. Without their efforts this work could not have become a reality. Special thanks is also expressed to Gulf Publishing Company for the production of this series.

Nicholas P. Cheremisinoff

ENCYCLOPEDIA OF FLUID MECHANICS

VOLUME 1: FLOW PHENOMENA AND MEASUREMENT

Transport Properties and Flow Instability
Flow Dynamics and Frictional Behavior
Flow and Turbulence Measurement

VOLUME 2: DYNAMICS OF SINGLE-FLUID FLOWS AND MIXING

Channel and Free Surface Flows
Mixing Phenomena and Practices
Fluid Transport Equipment

VOLUME 3: GAS-LIQUID FLOWS

Properties of Dispersed and Atomized Flows
Flow Regimes, Hold-Up, and Pressure Drop
Reactors and Industrial Applications

VOLUME 4: SOLIDS AND GAS-SOLIDS FLOWS

Properties of Particulates and Powders
Particle-Gas Flows
Fluidization and Industrial Applications
Particulate Capture and Classification

VOLUME 5: SLURRY FLOW TECHNOLOGY

Slurry and Suspension Flow Properties
Unit Operations of Slurry Flows

VOLUME 6: COMPLEX FLOW PHENOMENA AND MODELING

Special Topics in Complex and Multiphase Flows
Transport Phenomena in the Environment
Flow Simulation and Modeling

SECTION I

PROPERTIES OF DISPERSED AND ATOMIZED FLOWS

CONTENTS

CHAPTER 1

MEASUREMENT AND PHYSICAL PROPERTIES OF FOAM

Hsing C. Cheng

Department of Applied Science
Brookhaven National Laboratory
Upton, New York, USA

Thomas E. Natan, Jr.

Department of Chemical and Nuclear Engineering
University of Cincinnati
Cincinnati, Ohio, USA

CONTENTS

INTRODUCTION

A foam is a dispersion of gas in a liquid with the liquid as the continuous phase. Generally speaking, foams are relatively unstable. The instability is connected with the increase of surface free energy associated with an extended gas-liquid interface. From the thermodynamic point of view, the spontaneous decrease of interfacial area to decrease the free energy will tend to collapse a foam soon after it is formed. Accordingly, this chapter will describe the present state of knowledge regarding the various irreversible processes occurring in the collapsing of foam and the experimental measurements of the physical properties of foam which appear in these processes.

First, the physical structure, which includes bubble size, shape, and fit, of foam is described and methods for measuring foam liquid content and film thickness are discussed. A description of the different methods now available for studying the mechanical properties of foams is presented. This is followed by an examination of the differences between the true bubble-size frequency distribution in the bulk foam and the apparent distribution at the containing wall. Models for interstitial liquid drainage of foams are summarized, and finally the stability of foams is discussed. Two types of coalescence are described: rupture of the bubble walls and interbubble gas diffusion.

FORMATION AND STRUCTURE OF FOAM

A liquid foam is simply a dispersion of gas in a liquid, although to be called a foam the volume concentration of the gas should be greater than 90%. With this high volume concentration of gas, the system will consist of dispersed gas bubbles whose size will be greater than the average distance between them. Thus a liquid foam may be viewed as a two-phase system with a three-dimensional structure of thin liquid films acting as individual compartments for the gas. These foams are certainly agglomerations of individual bubbles, but they also have a definite structure of thin liquid lamellae.

Foams can be produced either by condensation or dispersion. With condensation, the gas is already in the liquid in individual molecules. When these molecules combine, as in the release of dissolved gas, or in gas production by reaction, foams may be formed. In the production of foams by dispersion, the gas and liquid are initially separate. Foam is produced when the two are mixed; by shaking or by bubbling the gas through the liquid. The resulting bubble sizes depend on complex mixing and interaction factors. The ability to produce foam and measurements of foaminess have been discussed thoroughly by Bikerman, [1].

Foams can be classified as either wet or dry [2, 3]. Both types are shown in Figure 1. The wet foams, or "kugelschaums," have spherical bubbles with large amounts of liquid between bubbles. This high liquid content means there is little contact between bubbles and poor packing, so slip can occur. Too high a liquid content allows the bubbles complete freedom of movement, and the dispersion is no longer a "foam" but a "gas emulsion." The dry foams, or "polyederschaums," are polyhedral in shape. A wet foam can become a dry foam, if it is stable enough to allow drainage of liquid. Likewise, a dry foam can behave like a wet foam if a wide range of bubble sizes are well dispersed. A greater number of smaller bubbles in between larger ones will prevent the larger bubbles from flattening out and increase bubble mobility.

Dry foams have a definite structure, as shown in Figure 2. The interbubble films intersect in the plane at plateau borders, or PBs, with dihedral angles of 120° each. Four PBs intersect at angles of 109°28′ to form a tetrahedral structure in space. Stable foams do not have interactions of more than four PBs, and each PB will have no more than three faces.

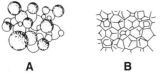

A

(a)

B

(b)

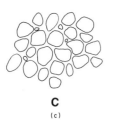

C

(c)

Figure 1. Illustration of foams: (A) kugelschaum; (B) polyeiderschaum (C) real foam.

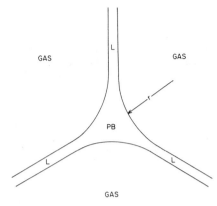

GAS

L

GAS

PB

L

L

GAS

Figure 2. Plateau border, PB, with lamellae, L, showing radius of curvature, r.

Polyhedral foams have been modeled as regular dodecahedrons—twelve-sided figures with congruent pentagonal faces. This model is appropriately called the dodecahedral model. Although these regular dodecahedrons do not fit together exactly, the residual volume is only about 3% of the total volume [3]. Thus the plateau borders are the channels formed where the edges of the pentagonal faces meet. In real polydispersed foams, the bubble sizes can vary tremendously and the shapes will not be uniform, but the PB angle of 120° appears to hold fairly well for polyhedral foams once they pass an initial period where unstable bubbles disappear.

The curvature of the plateau border walls produces a pressure difference across the walls, as shown by the equation of Laplace and Young.

$$\Delta P = \gamma \left(\frac{1}{r_1} + \frac{1}{r_2} \right) \tag{1}$$

where ΔP = the pressure difference across the wall
     γ = the surface tension
   r_1 and r_2 = the radii of curvatures of the interface

For a straight PB, $r_2 = \infty$, so $\Delta P = \gamma/r_1$. The pressure difference causes a capillary suction which keeps most of the liquid of the foam in the capillaries between the bubbles. It also pulls at the bubble walls and creates complicated patterns of movement in the walls during foam drainage.

According to Equation 1, if the bubbles are uniform in curvature (such as spheres), the gas pressure in the bubble will be greater than the average pressure in the surrounding liquid. Ross [4] derived an equation of state for foam, assuming the foam to be a congregation of cells. Each cell contains gas at some excess pressure, which corresponds to some equivalent sphere of a certain radius. In this equation,

$$n_m RT = P_a V_g + \tfrac{2}{3} rA \tag{2}$$

where n_m = number of moles of gas in the foam
    P_a = average hydrostatic pressure of the liquid
    V_g = volume of gas in the foam
    R = gas constant
    T = absolute temperature

From Equation 2, one can see that bubble coalescence will result in a decrease of the total interfacial area, A, and that there should be a small increase in V_g.

ELECTRICAL PROPERTIES

Generally speaking, the gas phase of foam does not conduct electricity; only the liquid phase does. Therefore, the electrical conductivity can serve as a measure of the liquid content in the foam, and many investigators have employed it as a measure of bulk density in foams. Theoretical analyses have been reviewed and developed by Chang and Lemlich [5] and by Agnihotri and Lemlich [6]. These cover high density foams of spherical bubbles as well as low density foams of nearly poly-hedral bubbles. Since the liquid in foams is in both the lamellae and the plateau borders, the properties of polyhedral foams are greatly influenced by the relative distribution of liquid in these two areas. Thus, the examination of electrical conductivity of a foam should give useful information on the liquid distribution.

Conduction in polyhedral foams occurs mostly in the plateau borders, since most of the liquid is drawn there, as previously described. For the theoretical limiting case in which all the interstitial liquid is in the PBs, Lemlich [7] obtained

$$D = 3K \tag{3}$$

where D = the volume fraction of liquid in the foam

K = the ratio of the conductivity of the bulk foam to the conductivity of the liquid used to generate the foam.

Equation 3 is approximated by real foams of extremely low liquid density.

For the complimentary limiting case, where the liquid is exclusively in the lamellae, Agnihotri and Lemlich [6] obtained

$$D = 1.4K \tag{4}$$

Since the lamellae and plateau borders form complex networks in both series and parallel arrangements, they found

$$2.625(D/K)^{-1} - 0.875 < F < 1.875 - 0.625D/K \tag{5}$$

where F is the fraction of interstitial liquid residing in the lamellae, hence $1 - F$ is the fraction in the plateau borders. Taking an average of the two bounds for F, for lack of specific knowledge of the network configuration, they obtained

$$F = 1.3125(D/K)^{-1} - 0.3125(D/K) + 0.5 \tag{6}$$

as an approximation for F.

Meredith and Tobias [8] used two bubble sizes in their theory, and Chang and Lemlich [5] extended this approach to any number of bubble sizes, yielding Equation 7

$$K = 2^n \prod_{i=1}^{n} \frac{D \sum_{i=1}^{n} x_i r_i^3 + (1 - D) \sum_{i=1}^{i-1} x_i r_i^3}{2D \sum_{i=1}^{n} x_i r_i^3 + 2(1 - D) \sum_{i=1}^{i-1} x_i r_i^3 + 3(1 - D)x_i r_i^3} \tag{7}$$

where x_i is the fraction of the total number of bubbles which have a given radius r_i. The relationship between K and D can be obtained by means of a computer calculation, as shown in Figure 3. Equation 7 offers a realistic approach to foams since it can include so many bubble sizes, and yields closer agreement with experimental results than the work of Meredith and Tobias.

The early experimental work of Miles et al. [9] was succeeded by Clark's [10] classical study where he used foams of five different surfactant solutions moving in plug flow through a horizontal tube. Measurements of liquid content of the foam were done by weighing small foam samples. His results show a unique relationship between D and K regardless of the system. Two problems with

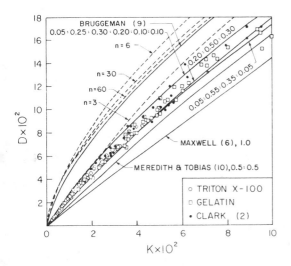

Figure 3. Theoretical results together with experimental results and one earlier related theoretical relationship shown for comparison. Solid curves are based on the respective volumetric size distributions indicated [5].

the study are that no measurements were made for D ≤ 0.04, and the relationship between D and K may differ if the bubbles in the foam are uniformly spherical. Jashnani and Lemlich [11] and Chistyakov and Chernin [12] have summarized their own work, as well as the work of others.

Recently, a "snatching" technique was devised by Chang and Lemlich [5] in which foam was passed up through a column with a removable "test section," as shown in Figure 4. The conductivity cell was in this test section, and after the conductivity was measured, the section was removed and quickly weighed to get the bulk foam density. This technique was used on foam of nonionic Triton X-100 for D up to 0.2. The results are shown in Figure 3. There appears to be a unique relationship between K and the bulk density of polydisperse foam. The theoretical prediction by Lemlich in Equation 3 that D approaches 3.0K as the bulk density of the foam approaches zero agrees well with experimental results.

The independence of the D–K relationship and the nature of the surfactant was confirmed by Dayte and Lemlich [13] by bubbling nitrogen through different solutions; sodium laurel sulfate, which is anionic; hexadecyltrimethylammonium bromide, which is cationic; and Triton X-100,

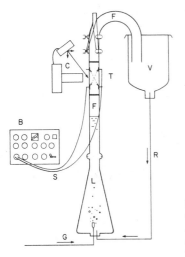

Figure 4. Apparatus (not to scale) for electrical conductivity measurements of foam: B—bridge; C—camera and flash; F—foam; G—gas; L—liquid; R—return; S—shilded cables; T—test section; V—collection vessel [5].

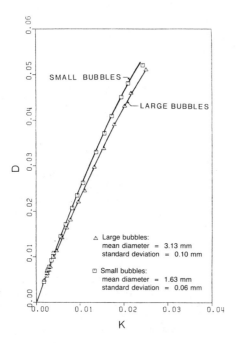

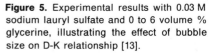

Figure 5. Experimental results with 0.03 M sodium lauryl sulfate and 0 to 6 volume % glycerine, illustrating the effect of bubble size on D-K relationship [13].

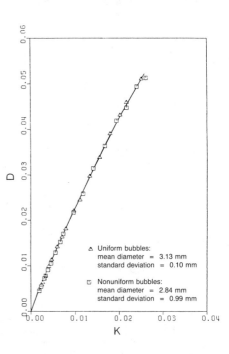

Figure 6. Experimental results with 0.03 M sodium lauryl sulfate and 0 to 6 volume % glycerine, illustrating the lack of effect of polydispersity on D-K relationship [13].

Table 1
Typical Results for the Fraction of Interstitial Liquid*

Sparger	Mean Bubble Diameter ±Standard Deviation, mm	F, % D = 0.01	D = 0.05
0.73 mm I.D. tubes	3.13 ± 0.10	22 < 30 < 38	39 < 48 < 58
0.15 mm I.D. tubes	1.63 ± 0.06	14 < 20 < 26	28 < 36 < 45
Sintered glass	0.95 ± 0.33	9 < 14 < 18	26 < 34 < 42

* *Interstitial liquid is effectively in the lamellae, F, as a function of bubble size and volumetric foam density, D. Surfactant systems: 0.03 M sodium lauryl sulfate with 0 to 6 volume % glycerine.*

which is nonionic. By employing the snatching technique, they found that K increases monotonically with D. Thus the D-K relationship is independent of the ionic nature of the liquid and the degree of nonuniformity of bubble size, at least for the range of investigation. The experimental results with a glass sparger agree well with the corresponding results of Chang and Lemlich, and thus Figure 3 can be used to correlate D and K for that purpose.

The relationship between D and K does depend somewhat on the mean bubble size. For a given K, where the bubbles are of a uniform size, the foam density increases with a decrease in bubble size, as shown in Figure 5. This is confirmed by Figure 6 where results of the uniformly sized bubbles are compared with those of nonuniform foam having almost the same mean bubble size.

A probable explanation is the drawing of more and more liquid from the lamellae into the plateau borders as the bubbles become smaller, thus increasing the conductance of the plateau borders at the expense of the lamellae. Since the plateau borders have a greater influence on K than the lamellae do, as can be seen by comparing Equations 3 and 4, the net result is a higher D for a given K for the smaller bubbles, as already reported.

The effective redistribution of interstitial liquid is presented in Table 1, with some typical approximate values for F from Equation 6. The upper and lower bounds on F from Equation 5 are also given. Clearly, for a given D, as the mean bubble size decreases, F decreases and 1 − F increases. Thus for foams of a given bulk density, more of the interstitial liquid resides in the plateau borders for foams composed of smaller bubbles. Table 1 also confirms that the decrease in F with decreasing D agrees with Equation 3. This approach to Equation 3 is clearly illustrated in Figure 7 which shows results at low D for the three previously mentioned surfactants.

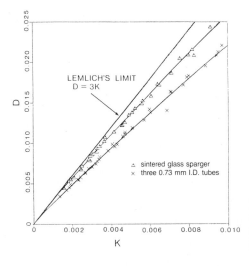

Figure 7. Experimental results at low density with all three surfactant systems, showing the approach to Lemlich's limit [7] as the density decreases [13].

In a recent paper, Sharovarnikov [14] did not present values of K, but did show by absolute resistance measurements on foam that D/K decreases as D decreases. He attributed this trend to surface conductance along the lamellae. However, as may be seen in Figures 3, 5, 6, and 7, D/K increases as D decreases, even for the low D of Figure 7, comparable to Sharovanikov's low range. Nevertheless, for an ionic surfactant in the absence of significant added electrolytes, the surface conduction can be theoretically increased by adsorption at sufficiently low D.

While Sidorova et al. [15] used electrical conductivity to discuss the structural analogies between the bulk properties of highly concentrated surfactant solutions and black foam films, Kato et al. [16] recently reported that the foamability of heat denatured ovalbumins or 11 native proteins is proportional to the initial conductivity. In addition, they reported that the stability of protein foams can also be measured from changes in the conductivity of foams with time.

OPTICAL PROPERTIES

Transmission of light is a popular technique for measuring particle sizes in dispersions [17–19], and it has also been used for measurement of interfacial area in liquid-gas dispersions [20–22]. Clark and Blackman [21] have developed a theory which predicts a linear relationship between the reciprocal of the light received and the interfacial area of the foam. The theory also predicts that the ease of transmission increases with increasing average bubble size. This method is not actually used for estimating bubble size, however, since other factors, such as the number of lamellae per unit length, affect the transmission of light. Similar measurements have been performed by Ross and Cutillas [22], relating the increase in the intensity of transmitted light to the decrease in interfacial area. These results were then used for estimating the rate of decay of various foams due to inter-bubble gas diffusion.

Movement in a bubble wall can be tracked by observing the colored patterns resulting from the interference of light reflected off of two bubble interfaces, and the progression of colors, taken in reverse order, can be used to determine the film thickness as a function of time [1, 23]. When the foam is thoroughly drained, the color by daylight is silver-white corresponding to a film thickness of 10^{-5} cm. Bits of black film may then appear, of a thickness of 10^{-6} cm. Since it is thinner and therefore lighter in weight the black film rises within the bubble face. As it rises, it experiences a viscous drag, due in large part to the surface viscosity, μ_s. By observing the rate of rise of the black film, and comparing it with a two-dimensional model for transverse drag around a cylinder, μ_s in the bubble wall can be estimated. For example, μ_s for the nonionic surfactant Triton X-100 in water was found to be 10^{-4} dyne sec/cm by Leonard and Lemlich [24]. Not all bubble walls are this mobile; however, protein films can be particularly rigid.

MECHANICAL PROPERTIES

The work done to date on measuring the mechanical properties of foams concentrates on two areas: investigation of foam formation and stability, and study of the behavior of foams subjected to applied forces or gravity. Most of the work was quantitative in nature, and has been reviewed by Bikerman [1]. No foam has had all four of its main mechanical constants (bulk modulus, shear modulus, Poisson ratio, and modulus of elasticity) measured and related in the classical manner of theories of elasticity.

The quantitative measurements of the mechanical properties of foam have been primarily through sensory evaluations. Clark and others carried out investigations of such properties as viscosity and elasticity of foam during World War II. They found that these mechanical properties depend heavily on the specific surface area and foam density; specific surface area is defined as the total interfacial area per unit volume of foam. A review of Clark's work has been completed by Matalon [25].

The adsorption and accumulation of surface-active material at liquid-gas interfaces results in increased resistance to flow. Surface viscosity is a measure of this resistance and is defined as the ratio of the interfacial shear stress to the interfacial shear strain, in units of grams per second, or surface poise. Plateau originated the concept of surface viscosity over 100 years ago [26], and the measurement of surface viscosity has since received considerable attention. Earlier observations of surface viscosity dealt mainly with insoluble monomolecular films at liquid-gas interfaces, as detailed by Gains [27] and Joly [28–30]. In recent years, reliable techniques for measuring surface viscosity have been developed by Mannheimer [31, 32] and Wasan [33, 34]. Using a deep-channel viscous traction interfacial measurement technique, they found that relatively insoluble substances will usually cause significant surface viscosity at liquid-gas interfaces.

Osipow [35] has detailed the various methods available for accurate measurement of surface tension. Surface tension affects the stability of thin films through capillary pressure, the radius of the lamellae, and the critical thickness of the lamellae. At low surfactant concentrations on the surface, the surface tension is a major factor in the stability of foam films.

Through use of an oscillating coil spring damped by soap films, Komatsu [36] has found that the shear stress of foam increases from 500 to 850 dyne/cm as foam density decreases from 0.1 to 0.04 gm/cm³. Viscosity, however, was not much affected by changes in foam density, varying between 15 and 20 poise. A similar set of experiments revealed that the elasticity of the foam decreases as the viscosity of the surfactant solution increases and it also increases with decreasing bubble size [37].

Sibree [38] reported that the apparent viscosity of foam is higher than that of each of its constituents, and it decreases with increasing shear rate. Friedrich [39] reported that the apparent viscosity of foam increased with increasing concentration of surfactant. On the other hand, Clark [40] found that only some foams behave as Friedrich described; others show only a minor dependence on solute concentration. Clark also found that the apparent viscosity of some foams increases with temperature; others are unaffected.

Penny and Blackman [41] assumed that above a certain yield stress, the apparent viscosity of foam measured between two plates can be defined in the same manner as liquid viscosity and therefore follows a Bingham relationship

$$(\tau - \tau_y) = -\mu(dV/dr) \tag{8}$$

where
τ = shear stress
τ_y = yield stress
μ = viscosity
V = foam velocity

With a friction-factor-versus-Reynolds-number plot, Grove [42] measured the apparent viscosities of fire-fighting foams as a function of the expansion ratio (the reciprocal of foam density relative to liquid density), pressure, and shear rate. The results indicate that at high shear rate, the apparent viscosity is independent of the shear rate, although the apparent viscosities varied widely over the range of the experiments (foams of density between 15 and 46 lb/ft³).

Other fire-fighting foam experiments were carried out by Wise [43]. He studied resistance to flow through commercial iron pipe, ½ or 1 inch I.D., and 18 feet long. Rheology shear diagrams failed to show Bingham yield values and demonstrated that these foams behave as pseudoplastic fluids. The apparent viscosity of aqueous foam was also studied by Fried [44]. His results with a rotational viscometer indicate that the apparent viscosities of most of his foams fall between 100 and 200 cp, and decreases with increasing shear rate. The surfactant concentration has a very small effect, but, the apparent viscosity increases with liquid drainage.

Fried also used a capillary tube viscometer to study the steady-state apparent viscosities of foams. Using Poiseuille's law, he found that apparent viscosity increased with the expansion factor and varied almost directly with the diameter of the flow channel. It appears that apparent viscosity varies widely with the investigator, and the variations may well be due to different shear stresses produced by the different instruments used.

The flow of foam through porous media has been extensively studied [44–47]. The flow through capillaries has also been widely studied [48–50]. Wise [43] and Wenzel [51] studied the flow of foam through pipes. Some investigators have concluded that foam behaves as a non-Newtonian pseudoplastic fluid with a non-zero yield stress; others have concluded that the yield stress is zero; still others have characterized foam behavior as Bingham plastic.

Recently, Thondavadi and Lemlich [52] carried out experiments on the flow of aqueous foam through acrylic and galvanized steel pipes. The results indicate that such foams flow with a completely flat profile through the acrylic pipes, but behave as a pseudoplastic in the steel pipes. A flow model is suggested which assumes a thin liquid film of the order of a few microns in thickness existing along the acrylic surface, which causes the foam to slide. The foam does not slip along the steel walls, probably because of wetting and surface roughesss.

Thordavadi and Lemlich also incorporated solid particulates with foams and found that the foam can carry up to 35% by weight of coal or sand particles with wide size ranges, such as 80–15 mesh, 115–150 mesh, and finer than 150 mesh without discernable changes in flow properties. This rheological insensitivity to the presence of particulates is believed to be partly due to the apparent aggregation of particles in the plateau borders rather than in the lamellae.

BUBBLE SIZE MEASUREMENT

It is possible to calculate the average bubble volume of a generated foam if the gas flow rate is known and the frequency of bubble generation is measured by means of a strobe light. To record individual bubble sizes, however, photography is the most popular technique. Under suitable magnification, film and plateau border dimensions can also be measured.

The foam to be photographed can be frozen and then sliced if it is to be used for nothing other than determining the size of its bubbles. It is often desirable, however, to photograph the foam without disturbing it; this is possible at a free surface, or through the walls of a transparent container. It has been reported that the distribution of bubble sizes in a surface layer is almost the same as the distribution in the bulk foam [53]. This is not to say that the photographic determination of foam bubble size is free of error, and several sources of error are outlined below.

1. *Statistical sampling bias.* The plane (or other surface) viewed through the camera tends to discriminate against smaller bubbles; that is, the foam will appear to consist of many more larger bubbles than it actually contains. This bias can be corrected by weighing the distribution inversely with the bubble radius [54, 55]. The final result can be expressed as

$$F(r) = \left[\int_0^\infty \frac{f(r)\, dr}{r} \right]^{-1} \frac{f(r)}{r} \tag{9}$$

where $F(r)$ is the corrected size frequency distribution of bubble sizes, and $f(r)$ is the apparent distribution at any surface, which would be recorded by the camera. Equation 10 expresses the relationship between mean radii calculated by the moments j and k:

$$r_{j,k} = r'_{j-1, k-1} \tag{10a}$$

where the prime on the mean radius indicates the sampling bias from measuring at the surface, and the unprimed mean radius indicates the actual mean radius in the bulk of the foam. Thus,

$$r_{j,k} = \left[\frac{\int_0^\infty r^j F(r)\, dr}{\int_0^\infty r^k F(r)\, dr} \right]^{1/(j-k)} \tag{10b}$$

and

$$r'_{j-1, k-1} = \left[\frac{\int_0^\infty r^{j-1} f(r)\, dr}{\int_0^\infty r^{k-1} f(r)\, dr} \right]^{1/(j-k)} \tag{10c}$$

This analysis can be generalized to include sampling by a line or a group of random points, as well as the sampling of a plane [56]. Equation 10 then becomes $r_{j,k} = r'_{j-1,k-1} = r''_{j-2,k-2} = r'''_{j-3,k-3}$, where the single prime indicates the surface, the double prime indicates the line, and the triple prime indicates the point.

2. *Bubble distortion.* Bubbles are distorted along the walls of a container or column. To study bubble distortion, Jashnani and Lemlich [58] attached a small number of free bubbles to each other on a wet flat glass plate. They found that for this sample (bubbles approximately 0.6 cm. in diameter), the span across the contact face at the plate for a bubble completely surrounded by other bubbles is approximately the same as the diameter of the same bubble freely suspended in air. However, it is not certain that this also applies to the case of a large number of combined bubbles of many different sizes.

Recently, Cheng and Lemlich [59] determined the characterization of foam bubble size in heterogeneous new foam by planimetric measurement of the area of the contact face at the wall of a glass column yielded excellent agreement with the *a priori* bubble size. Furthermore, this method proved to be more reliable than measurements based on either the longest chord or the longest median of the contact face. However, for highly heterogeneous new foam, all three methods underestimated the true mean bubble size.

3. *Bubble segregation.* Leonard [57] reported that in a column of liquid foam, the smaller bubbles wedge the larger bubbles away from the wall. This discrimination against large bubbles may even override the statistical planar sampling bias against small bubbles. Cheng and Lemlich [59] provide correlations for the approximate prediction of bubble segregation effects, provided conditions are not too different from those presented.

4. *Differences in stability.* As a result of interbubble gas diffusion large bubbles grow larger with gas from the smaller bubbles. The rate and manner of the change in bubble size depends on bubble curvature, which itself depends on bubble size distribution and distortion. As previously stated, the column wall can cause both distortion and segregation; in addition, the wall restricts gas diffusion through the bubble face. As the foam ages, further error may develop in bubble sizes as measured at a surface. These errors can also be compounded if the rate of rupture of the lamellae between bubbles is different at the surface than it is in the bulk.

FOAM DRAINAGE

As soon as foam is generated, it undergoes drainage by gravitational forces and capillary forces which cause suction at the plateau borders. The interstitial liquid flows down through the foam, causing thinning of the lamellae.

Various investigators have tried to formulate a theory to predict the rate of foam drainage. The earlier works employed simplistic models of flow through vertical circular channels or parallel plates, subject to a Hagen-Poiseulle type of analysis [60–65]. The actual cross-sectional geometry of the channels, the mobility of their walls, and the variation in their inclinations were not included in a quantitative manner. Accordingly, these equations contain many adjustable empirical constants, which limit their usefulness.

Leonard and Lemlich [66] developed a more realistic model. They considered that drainage takes place primarily through the plateau borders, at least for dry foams, and the plateau borders are essentially random in orientation and have a curved triangular cross section (see Figure 2). The walls of the plateau borders are subject to a finite surface viscosity. Regular dodecahedra of equal size were used as the model for the bubbles. The appropriate form of the Navier-Stokes equation for incompressible rectilinear steady flow was solved for a general plateau border, and the resulting local velocities were combined vectorially with any upward movement of the foam as a whole. The resultant velocities were then integrated with respect to the horizontal cross section of the vertical column to give the rate of steady drainage for the foam in the column. The analysis does not include bubble coalescence, and so is applicable only to stable foams, or foams for which the extent of coalescence is known.

Steady drainage of a stationary foam in a column can be accomplished by feeding a constant amount of liquid to the top of the foam. For such a system, the theory relates the drainage rate to the liquid content of the foam [67]. Combination with an unsteady-state mass balance over a differential horizontal element can extend the theory to unsteady drainage of a stable foam, at least in principle.

The theory also relates the rate of foam overflow in a column to its various independent parameters through two dimensionless groups, L and N. L is defined as $4QAg\rho d^2/G^2\mu$, or its equivalent, $4u_Qgd^2/u_G^2v$. Q is the volumetric rate of foam overflow on a gas-free basis (in other words, just the liquid), A is the horizontal cross-sectional area of the column, g is the acceleration of gravity, G is the volumetric rate of gas flow, and μ is the liquid viscosity. u_Q is the superficial linear velocity of collapsed (gas-free) foam overflow, u_G is the superficial linear velocity of the gas, and v is the liquid kinematic viscosity, μ/ρ. The other group, N, is defined as $\mu^3G/\mu_s^2g\rho A$, or its equivalent, u_Gv^3/gv_s^2, where v_s is the kinematic surface viscosity, μ_s/ρ.

The theory has been tested by Fanlo and Lemlich [67], Leonard and Lemlich [24], Hoffer and Rubin [68], and Lemlich [69], utilizing the data of Rubin et al. [70] and Shih and Lemlich [71, 72] with data from several investigators. As shown in Figures 8–10, for steady drainage through standing foam and for overflow, the agreement between theory and experiments has generally been good, provided a proper effective μ_s can be found for the surfactant involved. For systems of high μ_s, the μ_s can be considerably lower than expected. Joly [28] discussed surface viscosity and pointed out that the surface viscosity in a foam can be smaller than that measured at the surface of a pool of liquid with a surface viscometer. Furthermore, a surface viscometer is usually used on surfaces which are minutes old, while the time of travel in a foam capillary is typically less than one second.

The shaded region in Figure 8 represents the bands of data of Rubin et al. [70] with the amniotic surfactant Areseket 300 (monobutylbiphenyl sodium monosulfonate) in water, as discussed by Lemlich. The correlations of Hass and Johnson [65] appear as a horizontal dashed line because they make no allowances for changes in surface viscosity.

For wetter foam, the theoretical results are more complicated, but can be adjusted by multiplying Q obtain from Figure 8 by $1 + 3Q/G$ to give a revised Q. To compensate for variation in bubble sizes, d should be replaced by $d_{3,1}$.

Hartland and Barber [73] were the first to consider the thinning of lamellae with time, which is an essential part of foam behavior, but achieved only partial agreement with experimental data because of simplifying assumptions. Steiner [74] removed some of those simplifications and pro-

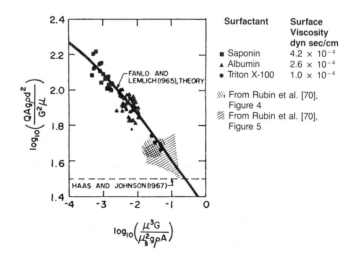

Figure 8. Comparison of theory for the rate of steady foam overflow against experimental results [72].

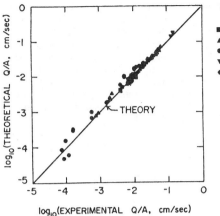

Surfactant	Surface Viscosity dyn sec/cm
■ Saponin	4.2×10^{-4}
▲ Albumin	2.6×10^{-4}
● Triton X-100	1.0×10^{-4}
▼ Areskit 300	1.8×10^{-4}
◆ NADBS	0.82×10^{-4}

Figure 9. Test of the theoretical prediction of Fanlo and Lemlich [67] for the rate of steady foam overflow [72].

posed three models which considered the walls of the plateau borders and the film surface as mobile. Of the three models, the experimental data was best fit by the model assuming gravity flow through the lamellae.

Recently, Desai and Kumar [75] confirmed experimentally that it is necessary to account for film surface mobility when analyzing the flow through plateau borders as had been done by Leonard

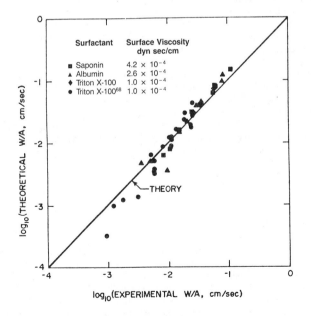

Figure 10. Test of the theory of Leonard and Lemlich [66] for the rate of steady drainage through a stationary foam. W is the volumetric rate of liquid draining through the foam, cc/sec [72].

and Lemlich [66]. They also proposed that the velocities of the plateau border walls be estimated by the surface viscosity of the system. Plateau border walls are only rigid when μ_s is below a certain value. Beyond that value, the pliability of the wall must be considered. These results were also used to present a model for predicting liquid holdup in nonrecirculating semi-batch cellular foam [76].

The work of Ruckenstein and Jain [77] shows that the increase of μ_s due to the presence of surfactants causes a decrease in a film's drainage, and greatly increases the rupture time of the film. Shah et al. [78] studied mixed surfactant systems, and determined that the molecular interaction causes a reduction in the average area per molecule in a mixed monolayer and also causes the maximum in surface viscosity. This in turn causes the minimum in foam drainage and the maximum in foam stability. They proposed the following relationship:

constituents of
surfactants in solution $\longrightarrow$ surface viscosity $\longrightarrow$ rate of drainage $\longrightarrow$ foam stability.

FOAM STABILITY

Foams coalesce from instability by two processes. The first is the rupture of the films which separate bubbles. The second is the growth of large bubbles due to interbubble gas diffusion from the smaller bubbles.

Film Rupture

The rupture of bubble walls may occur with an external disturbance, such as vibration, thermal fluctuation, cosmic radiation, and spontaneous vapor nucleation. It is well known, however, that the tendency of lamellae to rupture increases with thinner lamellae.

Before film ruptures, it first stretches and thins locally, this action increases the local surface area, which decreases the concentration of surfactant adsorbed at the surface of the bubble. This decrease occurs because the supply of surfactant in the film is limited, and also because the surfactant needs a finite amount of time to diffuse to the surface. The lower surfactant concentration causes an increase in surface tension, which in turn tends to draw the film together again. This phenomenon is called the Gibbs effect when the limited supply of surfactant predominates, and the Marangoni effect when the diffusion lag predominates.

With ionic surfactants, the electrostatic repulsion between the parallel surfaces of the film opposes thinning and contributes to stability. High surface viscosity and high liquid viscosity also promote stability by damping local disturbances and slowing drainage.

Although nothing is certain about the initial stage of the rupture process, the formation of a hole seems to be a necessary condition for rupture to occur. By converting the surface free energy released during growth of the hole into the kinetic energy of the receding liquid at the rim of the hole, Culick [79] proposed an expression for the linear velocity of hole propagation, which was later modified by Frankel and Mysel [80].

$$u = (2\gamma/\theta\rho)^{1/2} \tag{11}$$

where ρ = the density of the liquid
θ = the film thickness

u approaches 10^3 cm/sec for film thicknesses of the order of 10^{-4} cm, which means that film rupture is complete within milliseconds of initiation. This observation agrees with cinematographic measurements [54]. Thus, it may be said that initiation is the rate-determining step in the rupture process. However, Bikerman [1] points out that the preceding analysis cannot be completely correct since gas-phase kinetic energy and liquid-phase viscous drag around the hole are neglected. De Vries [55] considered that the number of ruptures per unit time follows first-order kinetics with respect to the number of bubbles present.

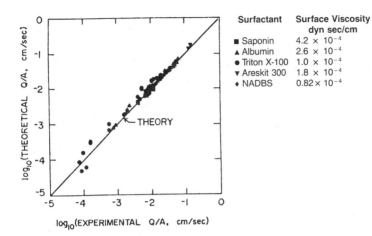

Figure 9. Test of the theoretical prediction of Fanlo and Lemlich [67] for the rate of steady foam overflow [72].

posed three models which considered the walls of the plateau borders and the film surface as mobile. Of the three models, the experimental data was best fit by the model assuming gravity flow through the lamellae.

Recently, Desai and Kumar [75] confirmed experimentally that it is necessary to account for film surface mobility when analyzing the flow through plateau borders as had been done by Leonard

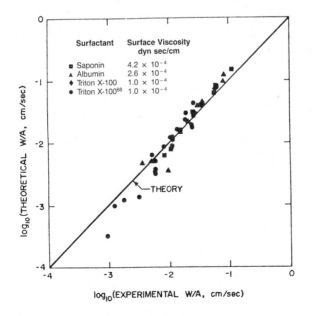

Figure 10. Test of the theory of Leonard and Lemlich [66] for the rate of steady drainage through a stationary foam. W is the volumetric rate of liquid draining through the foam, cc/sec [72].

and Lemlich [66]. They also proposed that the velocities of the plateau border walls be estimated by the surface viscosity of the system. Plateau border walls are only rigid when μ_s is below a certain value. Beyond that value, the pliability of the wall must be considered. These results were also used to present a model for predicting liquid holdup in nonrecirculating semi-batch cellular foam [76].

The work of Ruckenstein and Jain [77] shows that the increase of μ_s due to the presence of surfactants causes a decrease in a film's drainage, and greatly increases the rupture time of the film. Shah et al. [78] studied mixed surfactant systems, and determined that the molecular interaction causes a reduction in the average area per molecule in a mixed monolayer and also causes the maximum in surface viscosity. This in turn causes the minimum in foam drainage and the maximum in foam stability. They proposed the following relationship:

constituents of
surfactants in solution $\longrightarrow$ surface viscosity $\longrightarrow$ rate of drainage $\longrightarrow$ foam stability.

FOAM STABILITY

Foams coalesce from instability by two processes. The first is the rupture of the films which separate bubbles. The second is the growth of large bubbles due to interbubble gas diffusion from the smaller bubbles.

Film Rupture

The rupture of bubble walls may occur with an external disturbance, such as vibration, thermal fluctuation, cosmic radiation, and spontaneous vapor nucleation. It is well known, however, that the tendency of lamellae to rupture increases with thinner lamellae.

Before film ruptures, it first stretches and thins locally, this action increases the local surface area, which decreases the concentration of surfactant adsorbed at the surface of the bubble. This decrease occurs because the supply of surfactant in the film is limited, and also because the surfactant needs a finite amount of time to diffuse to the surface. The lower surfactant concentration causes an increase in surface tension, which in turn tends to draw the film together again. This phenomenon is called the Gibbs effect when the limited supply of surfactant predominates, and the Marangoni effect when the diffusion lag predominates.

With ionic surfactants, the electrostatic repulsion between the parallel surfaces of the film opposes thinning and contributes to stability. High surface viscosity and high liquid viscosity also promote stability by damping local disturbances and slowing drainage.

Although nothing is certain about the initial stage of the rupture process, the formation of a hole seems to be a necessary condition for rupture to occur. By converting the surface free energy released during growth of the hole into the kinetic energy of the receding liquid at the rim of the hole, Culick [79] proposed an expression for the linear velocity of hole propagation, which was later modified by Frankel and Mysel [80].

$$u = (2\gamma/\theta\rho)^{1/2} \tag{11}$$

where ρ = the density of the liquid
θ = the film thickness

u approaches 10^3 cm/sec for film thicknesses of the order of 10^{-4} cm, which means that film rupture is complete within milliseconds of initiation. This observation agrees with cinematographic measurements [54]. Thus, it may be said that initiation is the rate-determining step in the rupture process. However, Bikerman [1] points out that the preceding analysis cannot be completely correct since gas-phase kinetic energy and liquid-phase viscous drag around the hole are neglected. De Vries [55] considered that the number of ruptures per unit time follows first-order kinetics with respect to the number of bubbles present.

Investigations of foam film rupture have thus far yielded inconclusive results. It appears that a reclassification of foams into two types is necessary to help account for contradictory observations. Accordingly, these two types are transient and metastable foams [81].

In transient foams, the rapid thinning of foam can be explained by the action of van der Waals forces, which drive the liquid from thinner to thicker portions of the film. Rupture occurs instantaneously after the film reaches a critical thickness. In the absence of any long-range repulsive forces, such as the electrostatic repulsion with ionic surfactants, the van der Waals forces are strong enough to cause rapid thinning after a critical thickness of 5×10^{-6} cm is reached. The exact value of the critical thickness depends on the local surface tension gradient and geometric considerations. Ruckenstein and Jain [77] found that amount and nature of surface active agents influence the compositional elasticity of the film, as well as its surface dilational viscosity, which is associated with the change in surface tension. Recently, researchers have indicated the importance of surface dilational viscosity in foam film stability [82, 83].

Vrij and Overbeek [84] proposed a theory for fluctuations in film thickness which produce a thinning process ending in rupture. Detailed experimental data from Sheludko and Manev [85] on the critical thickness of lamellae is in fair agreement with the theory, particularly the prediction of the independence of critical thickness to variations in viscosity and surface tension.

In metastable foams, collapse often occurs in a very irregular manner even if the foam is protected from external disturbances [61]. Even reaching the critical thickness does not ensure immediate rupture. The liquid films can survive for long periods of time even at the critical thickness. Vrij [86] measured light-scattering intensity fluctuations to study long-range interactions that occur in thin films, including electrical repulsion and van der Waals forces. Ingram [87] made similar studies using different methods.

Interbubble Gas Diffusion

It may be that a foam will resist film rupture, but it will still undergo interbubble gas diffusion. It is rare that a foam will be produced with bubbles exactly equal in size. As long as the bubbles show even a small difference in radius, spontaneous interbubble gas diffusion will occur, in which gas diffuses from the smaller bubbles into the larger bubbles. The distribution of bubble sizes will continually change with time, and the small bubbles will eventually disappear. De Vries [54, 55], New [88], Clark and Blackman [89], and Lemlich [90] have proposed theories for interbubble gas diffusion.

Lemlich's theory begins with the difference in pressure between bubbles of different sizes as the driving force for gas diffusion. The gas diffuses into the interstitial liquid, which is represented as having a gas pressure equivalent to that inside a bubble of radius ρ. Using the equation of Laplace and Young, Lemlich proves that the rate of change of the size of any bubble is

$$\frac{dr}{dt} = k\left(\frac{1}{r_{2,1}} - \frac{1}{r}\right) \tag{12}$$

where $k = 2J\gamma RT/P_a$

where J = the effective permeability of transfer
P_a = the liquid pressure (usually atmospheric)
R = the gas constant
T = the absolute temperature

It turns out that the critical radius is $r_{2,1}$ (see Equation 10b). Bubbles will grow if their radii are greater than $r_{2,1}$, and shrink if their radii are less than $r_{2,1}$.

Figures 11 and 12 show the results of computer solutions to dimensionless forms of Equation 12. R is the dimensionless radius r/r_0, where r_0 is the initial mean bubble radius. Υ is dimensionless time. $\psi(R, \Upsilon)$ is the dimensionless frequency distribution function and is based on the number of

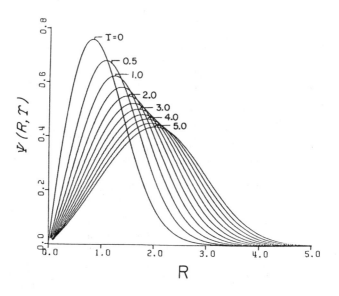

Figure 11. Distributions of dimensionless radii of bubbles computed from theory at various successive dimensionless times based on the number of bubbles present at each such time starting initially with the distribution of Lemlich.

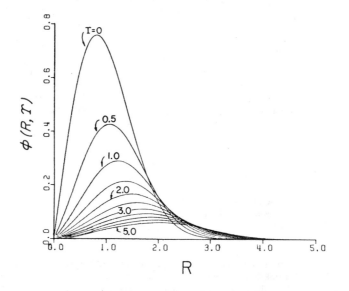

Figure 12. Distributions of dimensionless radii of bubbles computed from theory at various successive dimensionless times based on the number of bubbles present at zero time starting initially with the distribution of Lemlich.

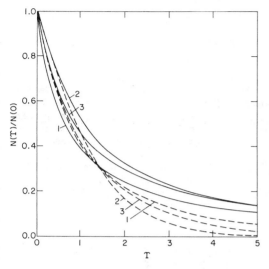

Figure 13. Fractional number of bubbles remaining as a function of dimensionless time starting with the initial distributions of (1) De Vries, (2) Bayens (Gal-Or and Hoelscher), and (3) Lemlich. The broken curves are based on an extension of De Vries theoretical approach. The solid curves are based on Lemlich's theoretical approach.

bubbles present at time Υ. $\phi(R, \Upsilon)$ is the dimensionless frequency distribution function based on the number of bubbles present initially, at $\Upsilon = 0$. Figure 11 shows that the bubbles remaining clearly have a larger size distribution as time goes on, and Figure 12 shows that the number of bubbles decreases with time. The initial dimensionless bubble size distribution, $\phi(R, 0)$ in Figures 11 and 12, was calculated by an equation proposed by Lemlich [91]:

$$\phi(R, 0) = \pi/2 \ R \ \exp(-\pi R^2/4) \tag{13}$$

Additional distributions have been proposed by de Vries [54, 55]:

$$\phi(R, 0) = \frac{2.082R}{(1 + 0.347R^2)^4} \tag{14}$$

and Bayens [92]:

$$\phi(R, 0) = 32/\pi^2 \ R^2 \ \exp(-4R^2/\pi) \tag{15}$$

De Vries's equation was derived for foam produced by a high-speed mixer; Bayen's equation follows a Maxwell-Boltzman-like distribution, and Lemlich's equation follows a simple Boltzmann-like distribution.

Cheng and Lemlich [93] examined the three equations and plotted the numbers of bubbles remaining as a function of time, as shown in Figure 13, using Equations 13–15 as the starting distributions. The dashed-line curves were calculated as suggested by De Vries [54, 55]. The solid curves were generated using Lemlich's derivation, based on Equation 12. As Υ increases, the solid curves decline less rapidly than the dashed curves, and show the influence of the growth of intermediate-sized bubbles in Lemlich's theory. These intermediate-sized bubbles eventually shrink and disappear. De Vries' theory, on the other hand, has gas from very small bubbles diffusing into very large bubbles, with none in between.

Figure 14 shows that for each of the initial distributions, the various $r_{j,k}$ (see Equation 10) all increase with Υ, and also how the $R_{r,k}$ from each distribution behave. The right-hand vertical axis shows the decrease in $S(\Upsilon)/S(0)$, which is the ratio of the total bubble surface area at time Υ to the initial total bubble surface. The choice of initial bubble size distribution has less effect here than

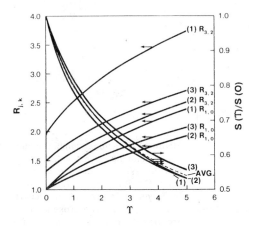

Figure 14. Progressive increase in key dimensionless mean bubble radii (left ordinate) and progressive decrease in relative total surface area (right ordinate), all as computed from theory, starting with the initial size distribution of (1) De Vries, (2) Bayens (Gal-Or and Hoelscher), and (3) Lemlich.

on the other size parameters. Total bubble surface is an important property in many industrial applications of foam and so this relative insensitivity is noteworthy.

With this in mind, the average decrease in $S(\Upsilon)/S(0)$ can be expressed as

$$S(\Upsilon)/S(0) = (1 + 0.77\Upsilon)^{-0.39} \tag{16}$$

This analysis was performed for a distribution of bubbles ranging in size all the way to zero. An initial bubble size distribution which does not go down to zero can behave quite differently.

De Vries reported reasonably good agreement between the predicted and photographically observed change in the number of bubbles in a foam generated by high-speed mixing. The permeability was assumed to follow Fickean diffusion. His theory, however, is rather too limited for general use.

Nishioka and Ross [94, 95] compared their experimental data with theoretical results based on Equation 12 in dimensionless form. The initial distribution used was Equation 14. Based on this comparison, they concluded that a fast draining foam has a highly effective permeability J, due in part to the accumulation of liquid in the plateau borders. This accumulation, in conjunction with unreplaced foam drainage thins the lamellae, which are then prone to rupture; a phenomenon not included in the theory. Slow draining foams, on the other hand, showed a low J, due to greater foam stability and surface resistance.

In another set of experiments, Cheng and Lemlich [96] sought to investigate J. In spite of the problems inherent in photographing a foam through a cylindrical column, they used the technique to investigate foams containing just two, three, or four different bubble sizes. The bubbles in the field of view were taken as an isolated system, thus requiring no correction for sampling area, although the bubbles were not truly isolated. They calculated values of J on the order of 10^{-12} to 10^{-11} sec/cm.

Assuming negligible surface resistance to diffusion, and expressing the remaining resistances as those of a stagnant film of average thickness of the lamellae for the foam of spherical bubbles,

$$J = \frac{3\mathscr{D}(1 - D)}{HDr_{3,2}} \tag{17}$$

where $\mathscr{D}$ = the gas diffusivity
   D = the liquid volume fraction of the foam
   H = the Henry's Law constant
   $r_{3,2}$ = the Sauter mean bubble radius (see Equation 10b)

This equation, however, underestimates J, because of the accumulation of liquid in the plateau borders, thus thinning the lamellae. Accordingly, Equation 17 was modified by dividing the right-hand side by the fraction of interstitial liquid residing in the lamellae, as determined by Agni-hotri and Lemlich [6] from electrical conductivity of the foam and liquid. The constant 3, which represents spheres, was changed also to the dodecahedral constant of 3.3. The modifications produce values of J on the order of 10^{-2} sec/cm.

Acknowledgment

The authors thank Dr. Robert Lemlich, Professsor of Chemical Engineering at the University of Cincinnati, for making his files available to them, and Mr. Vale P. Myles for stimulating discussions.

NOTATION

A	interfacial area	n_m	number of moles of gas in foam
D	volume fraction of liquid in foam	P	pressure
$\mathscr{D}$	gas diffusivity	P_a	average hydrostatic pressure
F	fraction of interstitial liquid residing in lamellae	Q	volumetric rate of foam overflow
		R	universal gas law constant
$F(r)$	corrected size frequency distribution of bubble size	r	radius of curvature
		S	surface area
$f(r)$	apparent bubble size distribution at any surface	T	dimensionless time; also absolute temperature
G	volumetric rate of gas flow	t	time
g	acceleration due to gravity	u_G	gas superficial velocity
H	Henry's law constant	u_Q	superficial linear velocity of collapsed foam overflow
J	effective permeability of transfer		
K	conductivity ratio	V	foam velocity; also volume
k	parameter in Equation 12	x_i	fraction of bubbles having radius r_i

Greek Symbols

γ	surface tension	τ	shear stress
θ	film thickness	τ_y	yield stress
μ	viscosity	$\phi(\Delta)$	dimensionless bubble size distribution
ν	kinematic viscosity	$\psi(\Delta)$	dimensionless frequency distribution function
ρ	density		

REFERENCES

1. Bikerman, J. J., *Foam*, New York: Springer-Verlag, 1973.
2. Adamson, A. W., *Physical Chemistry of Surfaces*, 3rd Ed., New York: Wiley Interscience, 1976.
3. Manegold, E., *Schaum*, Heidelberg: Strassenbau, Chemie and Technik Verlag, 1953.
4. Ross, S., "Bubbles and Foam," *Ind. Eng. Chem.*, Vol. 61, No. 10 (1969), pp. 48–57.
5. Chang, K. S., and Lemlich, R., "A Study of the Electrical Conductivity of Foam," *J. Coll. Interface Sci.*, Vol. 73 (1980), pp. 224–232.
6. Agnihotri, A. K., and Lemlich, R., "Electrical Conductivity and the Distribution of Liquid in Polyhedral Foam," *J. Coll. Interface Sci.*, Vol. 84 (1981), pp. 42–46.
7. Lemlich, R., "A Theory for the Limiting Conductivity of Polyhedral Foam at Low Density," *J. Coll. Interface Sci.*, Vol. 64 (1978), pp. 107–110.
8. Meredith, R. E., and Tobias, C. W., "Conductivities in Emulsions," *J. Electrochem. Soc.*, Vol. 108 (1961), pp. 286–290.
9. Miles, G. D., et al., "Foam Drainage," *J. Phys. Chem.*, Vol. 49 (1945), pp. 93–107.

10. Clark, N. O., "The Electrical Conductivity of Foam," *Trans. Faraday Soc.*, Vol. 44 (1948), pp. 13–15.
11. Jashnani, I. L., and Lemlich, R., "Coalescence and Conductivity in Dynamic Foam," *Ind. Eng. Chem. Fundam.*, Vol. 14 (1975), pp. 131–134.
12. Chistyakov, B. E., and Chernin, V. N., "Electrical Conductivity of Higher Aerated Foams," *Kolloid Zh.*, Vol. 39 (1977), pp. 1005–1007 (1978 English translation, pp. 890–893).
13. Datye, A. K., and Lemlich, R., "Liquid Distribution and Electrical Conductivity in Foam," *Int. J. Multiphase Flow*, Vol. 9 (1983), pp. 627–636.
14. Sharovarnikov, A. F., "Experimental Investigation of Electrical Conductivity in Foams with High Aeration Ratios," *Kolloid. Zh.*, Vol. 43 (1981), pp. 1194–1197 (1982 English translation, pp. 988–991).
15. Sidorova, M., et al., "High Concentrated Solutions of Surfactants and Nature of the Black Foam Films. A Study of Electroconductivity." *Colloid Polymer Sci.*, Vol. 254 (1976), pp. 45–49.
16. Kato, A., et al., "Determination of Foaming Properties of Proteins by Conductivity Measurements," *J. of Food Science*, Vol. 48 (1983), pp. 62–65.
17. Rose, H. E., and Lloyd, H. B., "On the Measurement of the Size Characteristics of Powders by Photo-Extinction Method, I. Theoretical Considerations," *J. Soc. Chem. Ind.*, Vol. 65 (1946), pp. 52–58.
18. Boll, R. H., and Sliepcevich, C. M., "Evaluation of Errors of Optical Origin Arising in the Size Analysis of a Dispersion by Light Transmission," *J. Opt. Soc. Am.*, Vol. 46 (1956), p. 200.
19. Dobbins, R. A., and Jizmagian, G. S., "Optical Scattering Cross Sections for Polydispersions of Dielectric Spheres," *J. Opt. Soc. Am.*, Vol. 56 (1966), p. 1345.
20. Calderbank, P. H., "Physical Rate Processes in Industrial Fermentation, Part I: The Interfacial Area in Gas-Liquid Contacting with Mechanical Agitation," *Trans. Inst. Chem. Engrs.*, Vol. 36 (1958), p. 443.
21. Clark, N. O., and Blackman, M., "The Transmission of Light Through Foams." *Trans. Faraday Soc.*, Vol. 44 (1948), pp. 7–13.
22. Ross, S., and Cutillas, M. J., "The Transmission of Light by Stable Foams." *J. Phys. Chem.*, Vol. 59 (1955), pp. 863–866.
23. Mysels, K. J., et al., *Soap Films.* New York: Pergamon, 1959.
24. Leonard, R. A., and Lemlich, R., "A Study of Interstitial Liquid Flow in Foam. Part II. Experimental Verification and Observations," *AIChE J.*, Vol. 11 (1965), pp. 25–29.
25. Matalon, R., "Foam," in *Flow Properties of Disperse Systems*, J. J. Hermans (Ed.) New York: Interscience Publishers, Inc., pp. 323–343.
26. Plateau, J., *Mem. Acad. Roy. Sci. Belgigue*, Vol. 37 (1869), p. 49.
27. Gaines, G. L., *Insoluble Monolayers at Liquid-Gas Interfaces*, New York: Wiley-Interscience, 1972.
28. Joly, M., "Surface Viscosity," in *Recent Progress in Surface Science*, Vol. 1, J. F. Danielli et al., (Eds.) New York: Academic Press, 1964, Chapter 1.
29. Joly, M., "Rheological Properties of Monomolecular Films. Part I: Basic Concepts and Experimental Methods," in *Surface and Colloid Science*, Vol. 5, E. Matijevic (Ed.) New York: Wiley Interscience, 1972, p. 34.
30. Joly, M., "Rheological Properties of Monomolecular Films. Part II: Experimental Results, Theoretical Interpretation-Applications," in *Surface and Colloid Science*, Vol. 5, E. Matijevic (Ed.) New York: Wiley-Interscience, 1972.
31. Mannheimer, R. J., "Surface Rheological Properties of Foam Stabilizers in Non-Aqueous Liquids," *AIChE J.*, Vol. 15 (1969), pp. 88–93.
32. Mannheimer, R. J., and Schechter, R. S., "An Improved Apparatus and Analysis for Surface Rheological Measurements," *J. Colloid Interface Sci.*, Vol. 32 (1970), pp. 195–211.
33. Gupta, L., and Wasan, D. T., "Surface Shear Viscosity and Related Properties of Adsorbed Surfactant Films," *Ind. Eng. Chem. Fundam.*, Vol. 13 (1974), pp. 26–33.
34. Djabbarah, N. F., and Wasan, D. T., "Foam Stability-I. Effect of Surface Composition and Surface Rheological Properties on the Thinning of Foam Films," presented at the AIChE 86th National Meeting, Houston, Texas, April 1–5, 1979.

35. Osipon, L. I., *Surface Chemistry*, New York: Reinhold, 1962, pp. 18–21.
36. Komatsu, H., et al., "Rheological Properties of Soap; Foam: 1. Apparatus for Viscoelastic Measurement on Foam," *J. Soc. Cosmet. Chem.*, Vol. 29 (1978), pp. 237–246.
37. Yamada, H., et al., "Influence of Bubble Size on Rheological Properties of Soap Foam," *J. Soc. Cosmet Chem.*. Vol. 33 (1982), pp. 131–140.
38. Sibree, J. O., "The Viscosity of Froth," *Trans. Farad. Soc.*, Vol. 30 (1934), pp. 325–331.
39. Friedrich, K., Foam Conference Report, Apolda, June 2, 1943.
40. Clark, N. O., Special Report No. 6, D.S.I.R., Home Ministry Stationary Office, London, 1947.
41. Penny, W. G., and Blackman, M., "The Mechanical Properties of Foam and the Flow of Foam Through Pipes," Ministry of Home Security (Britain), Note 282, 1943.
42. Grove, C. S., et al., "Viscosity of Fire Fighting Foam," *Ind. Eng. Chem.*, Vol. 43 (1951), pp. 1120–1122.
43. Wise, G. E., "Fluid Dynamics and Other Studies of Mechanical Fire Fighting Foams," Ph.D. Dissertation, 1951, Syracuse University.
44. Fried, A. N., "The Foam Drive Process for Increasing the Recovery of Oils," USBM Report, No. 5866, 1961.
45. Badalov, A. A., and Khasen, A. M., "Izv Vysshikh Uchebn Zavadenii," *Neft i Gaz*, Vol. 5 (1966), p.32.
46. Abernathy, C. K., and Eerligh, J. J. P., "An Investigation of Several Properties of Foam in Flow Through Short Connected Porous Media," M.S. thesis, 1966, Stanford University.
47. Sharma, S. K., "The Study of Microscopic Behavior of the Foam Drive Method," M. S. thesis, 1965, Stanford University.
48. Marden, S. S., and Kahn, S. A., "The Flow of Foam. II. Flow Through Short Porous Media and Apparent Viscosity," presented at the Regional Meeting of the AIME, Bakersfield, California, 1965.
49. David, A., "The Rheology of Foam," Ph.D. thesis, 1968, Stanford University.
50. Raza, S. H., and Marsden, S. S., "The Streaming Potential and the Rheology of Foam," *Soc. Pet. Eng. J.*, Vol. 7 (1967), p. 4.
51. Wenzel, H. G., et al., "Flow of High Expansion Foams in Pipes," *J. Eng. Mech. Proc. of ASCE*, Vol. 6 (1967), p. 153.
52. Thondavadi, N. N., and Lemlich, R., "Flow Properties of Foam With and Without Solid Particulates," presented at A.I.Ch.E. Annual Meeting, Washington, D.C., Oct. 30–Nov. 4, 1983.
53. Chang, R. C., et al., "Bubble Size and Bubble Size Determination," *Ind. Eng. Chem.*, Vol. 48 (1956), pp. 2035–2039.
54. De Vries, A. J., *Foam Stability*, Defft: Rubber Stichting, 1957.
55. De Vries, A. J., "Morphology, Coalescence and Size Distribution of Foam Bubbles," in *Adsorptive Bubble Separation Techniques*, R. Lemlich (Ed.) New York: Academic Press, 1972, Chapter 2.
56. Cheng, H. C., "Bubble Size Determination and Interbubble Gas Diffusion," Ph.D. Dissertation, 1980, University of Cincinnati.
57. Leonard, R. A., "A Theoretical and Experimental Study of Interstitial Liquid Flow in Foam Fractionation," Ph.D. dissertation, 1965, University of Cincinnati, p. 83.
58. Jashnani, I. L, and Lemlich, R., "Transfer Units in Foam Fractionation," *Ind. Eng. Chem. Process Des. Dev.*, Vol. 12 (1973), pp. 312–321.
59. Cheng, H. C., and Lemlich, R., "Errors in the Measurement of Bubble-Size Distribution in Foam," *Ind. Eng. Chem. Fundam.*, Vol. 22 (1983), pp. 105–109.
60. Ross, S., "Foam and Emulsion Stabilities," *J. Phys. Chem.*, Vol. 47 (1943), pp. 266–277.
61. Brady, A. P., and Ross, S., "The Measurement of Foam Stability," *J. Am. Chem. Soc.*, Vol. 66 (1944), pp. 1348–1356.
62. Miles, G. D., et al., "Foam Drainage," *J. Phys. Chem.*, Vol. 49 (1945), pp. 93–107.
63. Jacobi, W. M., et al., "Theoretical Investigation of Foam Drainage," *Ind. Eng. Chem.*, Vol. 48 (1956), pp. 2046–2051.
64. Hass, P. A., and Johnson, H. F., "Foam Columns for Countercurrent Surface-Liquid Extraction of Surface Active Solutes," *AIChE J.*, Vol. 11 (1965), pp. 319–324.

65. Hass, P. A., and Johnson, H. F., "A Model and Experimental Results for Drainage of Solution Between Foam and Bubbles," *Ind. Eng. Chem. Fundamen.*, Vol. 6 (1967), pp. 225–233.
66. Leonard, R. A., and Lemlich, R., "A Study of Interstitial Liquid Flow in Foam. Part I. Theoretical Model and Application to Foam Fractionation," *AIChE J.*, Vol. 11 (1965), pp. 18–25.
67. Fanlo, S., and Lemlich, R., "Predicting the Performance of Foam Fractionation Columns," *AIChE-Inst. Chem. Eng. (London) Symp. Ser.*, Vol. 9 (1965), pp. 75–78, 85–86.
68. Hoffer, M. S., and Rubin, E., "Flow Regimes of Stable Foams," *Ind. Eng. Chem. Fundam.*, Vol. 8 (1969), pp. 483–490.
69. Lemlich, R., "Foam Overflow Rate: Comparison of Theory with Experiments," *Chem. Eng. Sci.*, Vol. 23 (1968), pp. 932–933.
70. Rubin, E., et al. "Properties of Dynamic Foam Column," *Chem. Eng. Sci.*, Vol. 22 (1967), pp. 1117–1125.
71. Shih, F. S., and Lemlich, R., "A Study of Interstitial Liquid Flow in Foam. Part III. Test of Theory," *AIChE J.*, Vol. 13 (1967), pp. 751–754.
72. Shih, F. S., and Lemlich, R., "Continuous Foam Drainage and Overflow," *Ind. Eng. Chem. Fundam.*, Vol. 10 (1971), pp. 254–259.
73. Hartland, S., and Barber, A. D., "A Model for a Cellular Foam," *Trans. Instn. Chem. Engrs.*, Vol. 52 (1974), pp. 43–52.
74. Steiner, L., et al., "Behavior of Dynamic Cellular Foams," *Trans. Instn. Chem. Engrs.*, Vol. 55 (1977), pp. 153–163.
75. Desai, D., and Kumar, R., "Flow Through a Plateau Border of Cellular Foam." *Chem. Eng. Sci.*, Vol. 37 (1982), pp. 1361–1370.
76. Desai, D., and Kumar, R., "Liquid Holdup in Semi-Batch Cellular Foams," *Chem. Eng. Sci.*, Vol. 38 (1983), pp. 1525–1534.
77. Ruckenstein, E., and Jain, R. K., "Spontaneous Rupture of Thin Liquid Films," *J. of Chem. Soc., Faraday Trans. II*, Vol. 70 (1974), pp. 132–147.
78. Shah, D. O., et al., "A Correlation of Foam Stability with Surface Shear Viscosity and Area per Molecule in Mixed Surfactant Systems," *Colloid Polymer Sci.*, Vol. 256 (1978), pp. 1002–1008.
79. Culick, F. E. C., "Comments on a Ruptured Soap Film," *J. Appl. Phys.*, Vol. 31 (1960), pp. 1128–1129.
80. Frankel, S., and Mysel, K. J., "The Bursting of Soap Films II. Theoretical Considerations," *J. Phys. Chem.*, Vol. 73 (1969), pp. 3028–3038.
81. Kitchener, J. A., "Foams and Free Liquid Films," in *Recent Progress in Surface Science*, Vol. 1, J. F. Danielli et al., (Eds.), New York: Academic Press, 1964, pp. 68–71.
82. Prins, A., "Dynamic Surface Properties and foaming Behavior of Aqueous Surfactant Solutions," in *Foams*, R. J. Akers (Ed.) New York: Academic Press, 1976, pp. 51–60.
83. Wasan, D. T., and Mohan, V., "Interfacial Rheological Properties of Fluid Interfaces," in *Improved Oil Recovery by Surfactant and Polymer Flooding*, D. O. Shah and R. S. Schechter (Eds.), New York: Academic Press, 1977, pp. 161–203.
84. Vrij, A., and Overbeek, J. Th. G., "Rupture of Thin Liquid Films Due to Spontaneous Fluctuations in Thickness," *J. Am. Chem. Soc.*, Vol. 90, (1968), pp. 3074–3078.
85. Sheludko, A., and Manev, E., "Critical Thickness of Rupture of Chlorobenzene and Aniline Films," *Trans. Faraday Soc.*, Vol. 64 (1968), pp. 1123–1134.
86. Vrij, A., et al., "Interaction Forces in Soap Films," in *Foams*, R. J. Akers Ed. New York: Academic Press (1976), pp. 91–108.
87. Ingram, B. T., "Equilibrium Soap Films," in *Foams*, R.J. Akers (Ed.) New York: Academic Press (1976), pp. 61–72.
88. New, G. E., "Kinetics of Foam Breakdown," Proc. Int. Congr. Surface Active Substances 4th Brussels 1964, Vol. 2 (1967), pp. 1167–1177.
89. Clark, N. O., and Blackman, M., "The Degree of Dispersion of the Gas Phase in Foam," *Trans. Faraday Soc.*, Vol. 44 (1948), pp. 1–7.
90. Lemlich, R., "Prediction of Changes in Bubble Size Distribution Due to Interbubble Gas Diffusion in Foam," *Ind. Eng. Chem. Fundam.*, Vol. 17 (1978), pp. 89–93.
91. Lemlich, R., "A Boltzmann-Like Model for the Size Distribution of Bubbles or Droplet in a Well-Mixed Dispersion," *Chem. Eng. Commun.*, Vol. 16 (1982), pp. 153–157.

92. Gal-Or, B., and Hoelscher, H. E., "A Mathematical Treatment of the Effect of Particle Size Distribution on Mass Transfer in Dispersions," *AIChE J.*, Vol. 12 (1966), pp. 499–508.
93. Cheng, H. C., and Lemlich, R., "Comments on: Prediction of Changes in Bubble Size Distribution Due to Interbubble Gas Diffusion in Foam," *Ind. Eng. Chem. Fundam.*, Vol. 19 (1980), p. 133.
94. Nishioka, G., and Ross, S., "A New Method and Apparatus for Measuring Foam Stability," *J. of Colloid and Interface Sci.*, Vol. 81 (1981), pp. 1–7.
95. Nishioka, G., and Ross, S., "The Stability of Detergent Foams: Comparison of Experimental Data and Computed Results," presented at 56th Colloid and Surface Science Symp., Virginia Polytechnic INst., Blacksburg, Virginia, June 13–16, 1982.
96. Cheng, H. C., and Lemlich, R., "Theory and Experiment for Interbubble Gas Diffusion in Foam," *Ind. Eng. Chem. Fundam.*, Vol. 24 (1985), pp. 44–49.

CHAPTER 2

HYDRODYNAMICS OF FOAM FLOW IN PIPES, CAPILLARY TUBES, AND POROUS MEDIA

G. R. Assar and R. W. Burley

Department of Chemical & Process Engineering
Heriot-Watt University
Edinburgh, Scotland

CONTENTS

INTRODUCTION

Description of Foam

Foam is generally defined as the dispersion of a gas in a liquid containing one or more surface active agents with bubble sizes ranging from several microns (fine foam) to several millimeters (coarse foam).

Surfactants are chemical compounds which when dissolved in a liquid alter the surface tension of the solvent or the interfacial tension between gas and liquid, liquid and liquid, or solid and liquid, usually by decreasing the interfacial tension value. They possess both polar and nonpolar segments in their molecular structures and depending on the nature of the hydrophilic group (polar), they are classified into four groups, e.g., anionic, cationic, nonionic, and amphoteric.

The presence of surfactants in the foaming solution permits the formation of stable foam bubbles with resilient bubble walls or lamellae. Pure liquids with low surface tension exhibit high vapor pressures causing the thin liquid lamellar walls of which the bubbles are formed to evaporate too quickly to form and sustain a foam. Conversely, liquids with low vapor pressures have high surface tensions, a condition not favorable for the formation of resilient foam bubbles. Low surface tension and vapor pressure are therefore essential fluid properties for the development of foam-generating processes.

The concentration of surfactants at interfaces determines their performance in many interfacial processes, e.g., foaming, detergency, wetting, and emulsification, and their orientation at the interface determines how the interface will be affected during the adsorption process, i.e., whether it will become more hydrophilic or hydrophobic [1, 2].

The foam-producing ability increases with an increase in the concentration of surfactant up to a critical concentration (critical micelle concentration, CMC). At higher concentrations the foaming ability diminishes. The relationship between foaming ability and surface tension is also lost at higher concentrations. Thus, neither pure nor saturated solutions foam, while dilute solutions may foam. This is an indication that foaming may be considered as an evidence of lack of equilibrium at the gas-liquid interface of a system [3].

Very often, it is not a simple matter to distinguish between a system described as foam and other systems such as froth and emulsion. As described earlier, a foam is a two-phase system comprising a discontinuous phase (gas) and a continuous phase (liquid) which is maintained by monolayers of a soluble surfactant, adsorbed and oriented at the gas–liquid interface. When foam breaks there is no resultant scum.

A froth is also a two-phase system, comprising a gas and a liquid. Froths are characterised by the fact that they are stabilized by potentially insoluble monolayers at the interface. These are too minute to be visible, but when a froth collapses the molecules at the interface agglomerate and after the complete breakage, a residuum of visible particles is left on the surface, which may be in the form of small crystals or as a scum [4].

Valentine [5] describes froth and foam this way: "A froth is a layer of liquid agitated by the passage through it of a large volume of gas bubbles with a gas hold-up of up to about 50%. A foam on the other hand, often has a hold-up of 90% or more, and the liquid is present largely in the form of bubble surface films, i.e., it is largely immobile apart from some bubble motion and film drainage." The most important distinction between froth and foam, therefore, lies in the mobility of the liquid.

Foams are often considered as concentrated emulsions, having a gas ($>90\%$ $^v/_v$) instead of a liquid as the dispersed phase. In their studies of foams and emulsions, Berkman et al. [6] show that the formation of an emulsion is often accompanied by the formation of foam, which is an indication that at least in these cases, foam systems originate under the same conditions as emulsion systems.

Bikerman [7] argues that those gas dispersions in a liquid, in which the total gas volume is markedly smaller than the total liquid volume must be considered as gas-emulsions not as foams. It is common to speak of foam when the volume of liquid in a gas-emulsion is less than 10% $^v/_v$ and of emulsion, when this figure exceeds 90% $^v/_v$. The intermediate region is known as "gray-zone" [8].

General Properties of Foam

Like all colloidal solutions and dispersions, foam properties vary markedly from the properties of either of its constituents, i.e., gas and liquid. In his studies of colloidal solutions, Shaw [9] concluded that when colloidal particles are dispersed in a liquid, the flow of liquid is disturbed and the viscosity tends to be higher than that of the pure liquid. There has also been extensive experimental investigation and theoretical consideration attemping to relate the viscosities of colloidal dispersions, especially when dilute, to the nature and concentration of the dispersed phase [10–12]. It has been concluded that the increase in viscosity of a simple fluid as a result of the presence of the dispersed phase may be considered to be related, in some mathematical form, to the number of interfaces resulting from the dispersed phase or to the volume fraction of the dispersed phase.

Morphological studies of foam have revealed two distinct types of bubbles shapes [13]: the first, designated as "kugelschaum" (sphere-foam), consists of widely separated spherical bubbles; the second, named "polyeiderschaum" (polyhedron-foam), consists of bubbles that are nearly polyhedral in shape, within plane films of liquid, or at least films of very low curvature between them. A finely divided "kugelschaum" has also been named as "micro-foam" by Sebba [14]. However, these two forms are interchangeable depending on the conditions surrounding the foam.

Kugelschaum consists of spheres of different sizes, changing in size due to gas diffusion from smaller to larger bubbles and any coalescence of bubbles [15].

The pressure inside a bubble is always greater than the pressure outside as expressed in the Young-Laplace equation:

$$\Delta P = \sigma \left(\frac{1}{r_1} + \frac{1}{r_2} \right)$$

where ΔP = the pressure differential
  σ = the surface tension
  r_1 and r_2 = the principle radii of curvature

For a perfect sphere

$$\Delta P = \frac{4\sigma}{r}$$

Thus, if a small bubble is adjacent to a larger one, the pressure inside the smaller exceeds the pressure inside the larger, resulting in a net flow of gas into the larger bubbles. This flow reduces the size of the smaller bubble and increases the pressure gradient even more, until the small bubble completely disappears [16]. The transfer of gas from a small bubble to a neighboring larger bubble will occur through a dissolution into the liquid phase of the film between the bubbles and has been discussed in detail by Clark and Blackman [17].

There is also a hydrodynamical outflow of liquid from the foam caused by the buoyancy of bubbles during which all the bubbles expand while the total area of liquid also expands [13].

Kugelschaum is not always a rapidly passed transitional stage in the life of a foam. It can be made to persist for an appreciable length of time before the "polyeiderschaum" is stabilized [18–22]. It is also of higher density than polyhedral-foam and is therefore preferred in fire-fighting foams (where higher water content allows greater absorption of heat before it releases CO_2) in rubber foams and in shaving foams.

Conversely, in polyeiderschaum there is no significant diffusion of gas between the foam bubbles, as the films separating them are almost planar, thus maintaining almost equal pressures within contiguous foam cells, (note that when $r \to \infty$, ΔP will approach zero in Young-Laplace equation).

The relative stability of polyhedral-foam is also believed to be due to the loss of fluidity in the lamellae [13].

Methods of Foam Generation

Foams exhibit a high surface-area-to-liquid-volume ratio and are always thermodynamically unstable with respect to separation into liquid and gas phases. Foams are dynamic systems and their physico-chemical description involves specification of their history (i.e., method of formation), their observable behavior (i.e. properties), and their likely further behavior (i.e. stability).

Foam can be prepared using a variety of energy input processes differing in efficiency and foam property development. Like all two-phase colloidal systems, foam can also be generated by either decreasing the dimensions of a larger bulk phase or by increasing the aggregation of molecularly dispersed components [23].

Some of the conventional methods of generation of dispersion foam in a reproducible manner may be classified as: agitation, pneumatic, pour test, and packed-bed methods.

In all agitation methods, the first step involves forcing the gas into the liquid, and the degree of mixing achieved depends upon numerous external conditions (e.g., rate of shaking, shape of paddle). The volume of gas incorporated in a liquid by agitation varies not only with the kind and intensity of mixing, but also with certain properties of the liquid phase such as viscosity and density.

Some examples of the agitation methods are [24]: shaking a solution with air in a closed vessel, whipping a solution, beating in air as by rotating stirrers, and moving a perforated plate up and down in a cylinder partly filled with a foaming solution.

Pneumatic methods of producing foam may also be divided into methods involving passage of a gas into a liquid through a single orifice [25], multiple orifices [6, 26, 27] or dynamic methods [8, 27–32] in which the foam height or the foam volume is measured while the gas continues to produce bubbles through the foaming solution.

In the pour test method [33–37] the solution to be examined is poured from a pipette into a receiver which contains the same foaming solution, and the foam height generated is measured.

The method of generating foam in packed beds was first employed in the study of the operation of laboratory compressed air generators for generating fire-fighting foams. Here, the gas and liquid were allowed to expand rather slowly in intimate contact as they passed through a long column packed with metal turnings [38].

Raza [39] has also designed a novel foam generator using graded sand, and this has been extensively employed by workers investigating the application of foam in petroleum production [38–45], where, as will be described, it is of increasing significance in enhanced oil recovery.

Other methods of generating foam have been employed by workers investigating the various properties and application of foam, each with varying degrees of sophistication and reproducibility. These include:

- Spraying the foam solution through a nozzle onto a wire gauze and at the same time forcing air through it, causing foam to exit from the downstream face [46, 47].
- Using a venturi to entrain liquid. As the air jet passes through the venturi section, violent agitation with the foam solution causes very small bubbles to form [48].
- Using a pump and air injection into the liquid stream to create foam [14].
- Use of equipment employed for aeration in biological treatment processes [49] (e.g. orifice aerator, surface aerator, mechanical shear aerator, hydraulic shear aerator, and high-pressure aerator).

The quality (gas volume/foam volume) and texture (bubble size and shape) of foam is determined by the gas/liquid ratio, foaming agent concentration, the size and shape of the particles constituting the porous medium, or size of the orifice, and the operating pressure and temperature of the appropriate foam generator (see "Appendix").

Foamability and Foam Stability

The production of foam may be considered to depend upon two factors, namely the foam-producing power (foamability) and the duration of the lifetime of foam (foam stability) [28]. The concepts of "foamability" and "foam stability" has been described by several authors on foam [8, 13, 28, 33, 50], and have been shown to measure quite different foam properties.

Liquids that are able to sustain a stable foam are characterized in terms of the relative ease of foam formation using a given mode of foam production, and by the stability of the foam formed. The relative ease of foam formation, known as "foamability," depends on viscosity, surface tension, and perhaps other physical properties of the foaming solution [13]. A more fundamental measure of foamability would be the net increase in potential energy acquired by the gas plus the liquid when it is converted into foam, and a fundamental measure of the stability of foam would be the rate of dissipation of this potential energy. Thus foamability and foam stability would be expressed in the same arbitrary units. Among other suggested measures of foam stability are the average lifetime of a bubble in a dynamic foam; the average lifetime of unit volume of gas in a foam; the rate of disappearance of the interfacial area; the rate of disappearance of bubbles, as well as other variables that are dependent on the apparatus used.

Rheology and Flow of Foam

Many flow models have been proposed to describe the flow behavior of rheologically complex fluids through capillaries, pipes, and porous media. Both the complex geometry of porous media and the rheologically complex behavior of some non-Newtonian fluids introduce severe difficulties in a proper mathematical description of the flow. Savins [51] reviewed the current state of the art in flow of non-Newtonian fluids through porous media and concluded how complex and varied the flow behavior of these fluids were.

The rheology of foam is complex. Foams exhibit greater levels of viscosity than is exhibited by the separate gaseous and liquid phases of which they are constituted [53].

The flow of foam in a petroleum reservoir is believed to be by means of a large number of tenacious and resilient liquid interfaces (continuous phase) interspersed with gas slugs and fluid lamellae (discontinuous phase). The interfaces are considered to exert a piston-like force on the discontinuous oil phase, remaining after water flooding in the interstices. The multiplicity of mobile interfaces of various sizes and curvature greatly increase the probability that the force or combination of forces required to move most of the entrapped static oil will be developed, so that in this case, foam has the properties of a mobility control agent.

During the foam flow through porous media, the gas bubbles within the foam are deformed as they pass through the constrictions and the degree of deformation of lamellar interfaces from the static pentagonal dodecahedra structure will depend on the flow rate, pressure gradient, and the dimensions of the constrictions.

The high pressure required to move the foam both into and within a porous medium is a function of the shear force between the foam bubbles and the particle walls, the shear of the fluid between the gas bubbles, and the energy required to deform the gas bubbles as they pass through the constrictions. In addition, the rate of adsorption of surfactant and bubble retention in the media will also need to be accounted for in the interpretation of any flow-pressure drop results.

Rheological Methods

The application of capillary viscometers for the measurements of rheological properties of non-Newtonian fluids is well established. Flow equations of fluids in capillaries have produced accurate empirical correlations to describe the fluid flow [52, 55].

The basic rheology of foam in porous media is believed to be related to measurements of its apparent viscosity in capillaries. Thus, quantitative experimental studies in fine capillaries (representative of a continuous-pore channel) of the flow of lamellae is fundamental in establishing basic rheology.

In order to describe the complex flow behavior of foam, it is useful to take note of simplifying assumptions used in the rheology of related systems. There exist several mathematical studies of different types of fluid systems [56–59] as well as flow studies in capillary tubes of dimensions comparable with pore sizes. In most cases, they are physiological studies on blood flow [60–63], but there are also available techniques for visual observation of flow through microporous structures and fine capillaries [64–66] which would assist in elucidating more realistic flow models for foam.

An early paper due to Grove et al. [67] contained information from an investigation into the viscosity of fire-fighting foam. They measured the effects of pressure, rate of shear, and foam quality on the apparent viscosity in a flow-type viscometer, (essentially a rotameter). Other variables considered were the Reynold's number, and friction factors. The study was carried out at room temperature. They found that foam viscosities were nearly independent of the rate of flow of foam and that foams of the same density had equal viscosities, although confining pressures varied over a wide range. They also found that turbulent foam flow was independent of shear rate and that viscosity depended largely and varied directly with the quality of the foam.

Sibree [11] was one of the first to show that the viscosity of foam became constant for all shear rates above a critical value, using shear-force and shear-rate data from a rotating cylinder viscometer. He also investigated foam bubble size distribution at ambient conditions.

It is interesting to note that Sibree also found that the Hatschek [68] formula (see "Appendix") that may be used to predict viscosities of coarse emulsions could not be applied to foam. However, he concluded that the apparent foam viscosity asymptotically approached a limiting value as shear rate increased in a similar way. He also demonstrated that foam followed Newtonian behavior below a critical shear stress and plug-like flow above the critical shear stress.

Khan and Marsden [69] working at room temperature and atmospheric pressure with foam qualities in the range $0.7 < \Gamma < 0.96$, showed that the apparent viscosity of foam decreased with increasing shear rate. They also reported that at a given shear rate, apparent viscosity increased linearly with foam quality. Measurements of kinematic apparent viscosity with a vibrating viscometer were found to be independent of foam quality, whereas the apparent viscosity increased with foam quality. The results of their measurements with a capillary viscometer were not, however, reported.

Raza and Marsden [52] measured viscosities and electrical potentials that developed while foams flowed through capillary tubes of radius 1.5 mm. In their investigation of viscosities, they reported that foam flow could be described as pseudoplastic. They also reported that below a critical flow rate, which was dependent on foam quality, the flow was Newtonian, and above the critical flow rate, foam passed through the capillary in plug flow with the most highly shear region occurring as the walls were approached.

As would be expected at room temperature and 100 psig, they reported that foam was compressible and that Boyle's law could be applied directly to foam, neglecting gas solubility in the solution and liquid expansion.

Mitchell [53] carried out viscosity studies on drilling foams in large steel tubes at high pressures. He concluded that the viscosity varied directly with the quality at any single value of shear rate, but was independent of shear rate in the foam quality range $0 < \Gamma < 0.54$ (i.e., Newtonian) and dependent upon both foam quality and shear rate for qualities greater than 0.54.

He also concluded that foam viscosity depended only on the quality for all values of quality as shear rates approached large values. At variance with other investigators, however, he concluded that the viscosity did not change with the internal diameter of capillaries. This might have been due to the type of foam used or other influences, but no reason was given for this important divergence of view from comparable studies. However, in agreement with others, he stated that foam was Newtonian at higher shear rates and pseudoplastic at lower rates. However, he did not notice any slippage of the foam at the walls.

The work of Fried [70] agrees with that of Raza and Marsden [52], who all concluded that viscosity increased with tube diameter and quality. As well as the visual observations that he made, he carried out measurements of bulk viscosity by means of a rotational viscometer and carried out apparent viscosity measurements in capillary flow tubes. He also found that the flow behavior was in accordance with Poiseuille's law in the range of qualities investigated.

The phenomenon of viscosity varying directly with both flow-channel diameter and foam quality appears from the literature to be the most agreed conclusion made on foam rheology arrived at by many authors [22, 69, 71–73].

David and Marsden [74] considered foam as semi-compressible, and by taking into account slippage that occurs at the wall, they came to the conclusion that the apparent viscosity of foam was independent of foam quality, in comparison with other investigators. However, they found that the apparent viscosity was still dependent on tube diameter.

It is known that slip will cause a shift in the rheological properties with capillary diameter. David and Marsden [74] were not able to eliminate the capillary diameter effect, even after correcting for slip. They suggested that bubble size and size distribution could be responsible for the capillary effect remaining even after correction for slip.

Marsden and Khan [75] have concluded that the apparent foam viscosity decreased with increasing shear rate but usually fell within the range $50 < \mu_{app} < 500$ cp. They also found that at a given shear rate the apparent viscosity increased almost linearly with foam quality. They also showed that foam was a compressible non-Newtonian fluid such that the quality Γ at any given pressure P, depended upon the quality Γ_a measured at atmospheric pressure P_a. This leads to the following relationship for foam quality as a function of properties at atmospheric pressure.

$$\Gamma = \frac{1}{1 + \dfrac{P}{P_a}\left(\dfrac{1}{\Gamma_a} - 1\right)}$$

Application of Foam

Foam, in one form or another, is frequently encountered in chemical technology. Sometimes it is beneficial, but more often than not its presence heralds difficulties in process and equipment operation. As a result, many studies of foam have been devoted either to preventing its formation, or destroying it once formed [76]. Recently, however, interest in the more useful aspects of foam has been on the increase. One very useful application of foam is undoubtedly in fire extinguishing materials. Foam has also been used for foam fractionation [77–83], and also for effluent treatment [84–86]. Haas and Johnson [87] have applied foam to countercurrent extraction. Foam has also been used for removal of small particles [88–92] and dust from gas flows. In a more unusual application, foams of gelatine, citrus pectin, and starch phosphate have found application in protecting plants from cold weather [48].

The petroleum industry has developed an increased interest in foam and foam properties due to the possible application of foam in the field of oil and gas production. These properties are being studied extensively, and an increasing amount of experimental work has been carried out in the past 10–20 years. The application of foam by petroleum and natural gas industries began in the 1950s [93]. Foam has been successfully used as a drilling fluid [94–97], and sand cleanout fluid [98], with high apparent viscosity and low density. The resulting low mobility arising from its unique rheological properties and improved sweep efficiency in porous media has led to its application as an oil displacing medium [70]. The use of foam has also been extended to work-over and remedial well operations [99]. Since foam decreases gas permeability considerably, it has been used in several situations as a means of impeding or blocking gas flow [40, 100] thus limiting well head gas production and keeping the gas in situ. Foam has also been used to plug leaking cap-rock in underground natural gas storage reservoirs [101], as well as being applied as an agent for the removal of brine which accumulates in shallow, low-pressure gas wells [102, 103].

FOAM FLOW IN CAPILLARIES AND POROUS MEDIA

A literature survey reveals a lack of consensus on the rheology and flow behavior of foam in porous media, particularly in heterogeneous oil reservoirs. The shear-rate/viscosity relationships, determined by several types of viscometers, are unlikely to give appropriate governing relationships for flow in porous media. A viscometer operating under steady-state conditions is unlikely to give a shear rate comparable to that appropriate to unstable flow in porous media. Many previous investigators have based their conclusions on studies of a single foaming agent whose identity and commercial availability was often not disclosed, and frequently the choice of the foaming agent was arbitrary and lacked comparison with other agents [53, 69, 74, 75].

In his pioneering studies of the foam-drive process, Fried [70] observed that flow of foam through porous media occurred primarily by the progressive breakage and reformation of the foam structure; the faster the foam moved through the medium, the greater the degree of reformation. He also noted that a certain minimum pressure drop was required across the foam bank to move foam through a porous medium and that the critical pressure drop was determined primarily by the particle size distribution of sand and foam bubble sizes. This was found to be the same for a particular porous system and foam, irrespective of the viscous nature of the oil it was displacing.

According to Marsden and Khan [75], even though in a porous medium some of the liquid may flow independently of the gas, the dominant flow regime was as an intimate gas–liquid mixture. They argued further that since the gas and liquid were intimately mixed and flowed simultaneously through the same pore channel in the form of bubbles or froth, it would be inappropriate to consider them as a separate independent fluid and use their own viscosities to calculate individual effective permeabilities as did Bernard et al. [104].

Perhaps the most crucial departure from the preceding views stated are those due to Holm [105] who investigated the mechanism of gas and liquid flow through porous media in the presence of foam. He reported that the liquid and the gas formed foam separately as the foam films or lamellae broke and reformed successively in the medium. He also considered that the movement of liquid through the porous medium was via the film network of bubbles and gas that moved through the system by breaking and reforming bubbles along the length of the flow path [105].

In an attempt to offer an explanation for this flow mechanism, Albrecht and Marsden [40] suggested that although foam bubbles may break and reform as the foam moved through a porous medium, they considered that both components of the foam would flow in the same channel at about the same average velocity, except possibly in the case of the most dilute foamer solutions, which indicated the effect of the interface stability.

An early attempt to determine a mathematical model to describe the flow of foam in a porous medium was due to the work of Aizad and Okandan [71]. The flow was modeled by applying the power-law equation (see "Appendix") for the flow of an incompressible non-Newtonian fluid in a porous medium. They calculated the flow-behavior index to be less than unity in all cases which indicated that the foam behaved as a pseudoplastic fluid in unconsolidated porous media—a view held by many other investigators. It is their opinion that it would be inappropriate to consider foam, especially dry foams of quality $0.75 < \Gamma < 0.96$, as incompressible, since the presence of gas bubbles will evidently give an elastic capacity to the whole of the liquid system which will result in behavior much as if the liquid phase itself were appreciably compressible.

The flow of foam in capillary tubes and pipes has also been studied by a number of investigators under various conditions of pressure and foam quality [52–54]. The fluid behavior has been variously modeled as pseudoplastic [52], Bingham plastic [53], and Bingham fluid [54].

Work initiated by Anwar Rajah [23] showed that even at low flow rates in capillaries the pressure drop along the tube was not a linear function of flow rate of foam.

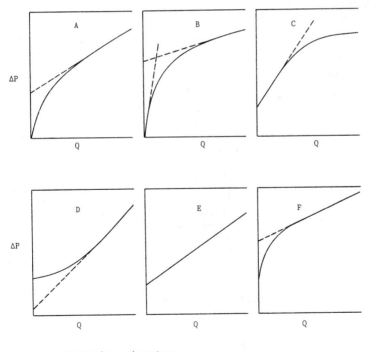

ΔP = pressure drop or shear stress
Q   = flow rate

Figure 1. A selection of non-Darcian type flows [109].

The variation of pressure-flow rate characteristics with foam quality was explained in terms of the increase in bubble size with quality and the different bubble-size orientation and distribution for various different-quality foams. His work also showed that bubble size increased with increase in the quality of foam.

Pressure-drop/flow-rate curves obtained by Ali [106] from experiments conducted in porous media show deviation from Darcy flow behavior, the deviation being either of the two main types:

1. A threshold gradient exists that must be exceeded before flow occurs (Bingham).
2. Increasing hydraulic gradient causes either an increase or a decrease in the flow rate.

Figure 1 shows a summary and Table 1 demonstrates the types of results obtained for foam flow in porous media and capillary tubes. Referring to this table and the non-Darcian flow behavior, it is apparent that no unique pressure/flow-rate curve describes all the results obtained for foam. Indeed, in some cases, the flow behavior is a hybrid of Bingham and pseudo-plastic flow. While in general the flow in pipes and capillaries is Bingham, the flow in porous media is Bingham-pseudoplastic or pseudoplastic, as shown by Gogarty and Poettman [107] in their studies of the rheology of foam in a capillary viscometer.

This apparent anomalous behavior of foam may be due to the influence of other porous particles on flow in porous media, causing a progressive breaking and reforming of the bubbles. On the other hand, the flow of foam in pipes and capillary tubes may be more easily linked to the flow of a single fluid where bubble size and orientation remains unchanged during the flow. It is indeed still a matter of speculation whether the idea of a homogeneous bubble is correct for application in porous media studies.

Table 1
A Review of Experiments on Foam Flow in Pipes, Capillaries and Porous Media

Author	Medium	Γ	Type of Curve (Refer Fig. 1)
Raza and Marsden [52]	1.50 mm radius tube.	0.75–0.93	A
Aizad and Okandan [71]	Unconsolidated sand pack (3.8 cm dia. and 10 cm long). 44–60 mesh packed to $\phi = 0.45$ and $K = 40$ Darcy.	0.70–0.94	B
Evgen'ev and Turnier [108]	Unconsolidated sand pack (3.7 cm dia. and 60 cm long). $\phi = 40$ and $K = 3.1$ Darcy.	N/A	C Thixotropic Bingham body
Mitchell [53]	Capillary tubes.	0.52–0.96	D Bingham-plastic
Starkey [54]	Pipes.	0.23–0.83	E Bingham-fluid
Ali [106]	Unconsolidated sand pack (2.7 cm dia. and 69.3 cm long). $\phi = 0.39$ and $K = 15.0$ Darcy. ϕ—voidage K—permeability	0.75–0.95	F pseudoplastic-Bingham

From Ali [106].

The lack of agreement on the nature of the flow foam in porous media coupled with the varied number of flow-rate/pressure-drop curves obtained for foam has hampered the development of a flow equation that will describe foam flow in linear systems of pipes, capillary tubes, or the complicated networks in porous media. The effects of pore dimensions and orientation on the rheological behavior of foam is therefore one of the utmost importance in considering systems of this sort.

FOAM IN ENHANCED OIL RECOVERY

An enhanced oil recovery (EOR) process refers to the technology that aims at increasing the recovery of oil above that which may be obtained through primary recovery. Primary oil recovery relies on formation pressure in the reservoir for oil production. It may also include natural water-drive, expansion of free gas, oil, water and solution gas, and capillary and gravitational forces. The difference between EOR and primary recovery therefore is that enhanced oil recovery involves the introduction of artificial forces or energy into a reservoir system for the purpose of providing or supplementing the displacing force inherent in the reservoir system.

In general, when a fluid is injected to provide supplementary drive energy, the EOR process is termed a secondary recovery operation (e.g. by water or gas).

When fluid is injected with the main purpose of introducing a new form of energy into the reservoir, the EOR process is referred to as a tertiary recovery process.

The main enhanced oil recovery methods lie in three basic categories:

- *Miscible and chemical methods:* These are aimed at reducing the interfacial tension forces between the oil and driving fluid to very low levels, (chemical flooding).
- *Thermal methods:* These are aimed at reducing the oil viscosity.
- *Viscous fluid flooding:* These are methods which aim to improve oil recovery by providing a favorable mobility ratio and by reducing fluid flow through high permeability channels.

The foam-drive process, which comes under the last category, is one of the enchanced oil recovery methods that promise significant recovery of oil not recoverable by means of water-flooding and immiscible gas injection.

The application of foam in enhanced oil recovery arose from the realization that its viscosity could be altered as the situation demanded, by adjusting its quality.

It has been observed that foam may behave as a Newtonian or non-Newtonian fluid according to its quality and flow conditions [110]. For high quality foams, it exhibits a high apparent viscosity and non-Newtonian flow behavior in porous media. This is coupled with an ability to preferentially block flow in highly permeable strata, which bestows a property on the foam/porous media system that is fundamental to its application in EOR.

The characteristics of foam point to three potential applications:

- Improving the sweep efficiency (the fraction of oil recovered within the totally swept volume) of other fluid injection processes (mobility control) and impeding the flow of in-situ fluids, which is due to an increased viscosity ratio between displacing and displaced phases favoring the formation of an oil bank.
- Improving the displacement efficiency of gas drive processes (mobility control).
- Restricting the flow of undesired fluids, leakage and plugging of high permeable zones [40, 100], and retaining gas in the porous media for later production.

The first disclosure which described how a foam flooding process could be practised was given in the patent granted to Bond and Holbrook [111] in 1958. This described the application of surfactants having foam-producing characteristics in gas-drive secondary recovery methods. According to their method, an aqueous solution of a water-soluble surfactant having foam-producing characteristics was initially introduced into the reservoir. A drive gas was then injected into the reservoir to produce a foam bank ahead of the gas-drive interface.

A further patent was also granted to Holbrook and Bernard [112] in 1965 which described the application of foam for plugging gas-producing strata. Their method consisted of injecting sufficient solution of a high-foaming agent in a liquid miscible with the formation brine in order to penetrate the formation. A foam was then generated in substantial amounts in situ only in the portion of the formation from which gas was being produced, thus reducing by plugging, gas production. A variant of the principle of using foam to plug formations was also described by Raza [113].

Studies by Nutt, Burley, and Bayat [114] of displacement of oil and water by gas and foam in sand-packs showed that foam:

- Flowed in a piston-like manner in a porous medium.
- Stopped channeling and early breakthrough by blocking more permeable layers.
- Enhanced the efficiency of a gas drive process.

This study was aimed at evaluating the efficiency of the foam drive process for application in North Sea oil wells.

Bayat's work [115] also demonstrated, by means of a limited number of experiments with only one surfactant (TRITON X-100®) as a foamer, the potential of foam in recovering oil from a water-flooded porous medium. He compiled data which determined the optimum conditions for the foam drive oil recovery process.

The behavior of a range of surfactants has also been studied by Ali [106] in order to select those which would be most suitable technically and economically for large-scale operations. Some 36 commercially available foaming agents consisting of 23 anionics, 6 nonionics, and 7 amphoterics were studied and their behavior in relation to the following objectives was evaluated.

- Screening individual surfactants for foam stability.
- Determination of foaming effectiveness of each surfactant in model sand-packs.
- Assessment of the effect of each surfactant on the production of residual oil using a foam drive.
- To determine the stability of generated foams with respect to the process variables.
- Static and dynamic adsorption data for flow of surfactant solution through sand-packs and porous media.

For the purpose of the work, foam was regarded as a compressible fluid which flowed as a non-Newtonian single-body pseudo-plastic fluid [106].

SUMMARY AND CONCLUSIONS

A fundamental assumption in most of the work on foam rheology in defined geometries has been that foam is incompressible with no consideration given to slippage between the relative velocity of gas-to-liquid phase, which occurs due to the confining boundary. The general conclusion, however, is that foam is compressible, but in order to perform simple studies this fact is ignored. Foam has been considered in this way in order to describe its rheological properties using equations of motion developed for incompressible fluids. Of course, this is an over-simplification of the real situation; however, a completely rigorous mathematical analysis of the flow of foam seems unlikely even in well-defined geometries.

Detailed and precise information on rheology and flow behavior of foam is difficult to obtain, and it is this information more than any other that is required in order to devise meaningful model systems for the simulation of oil recovery and other processes employing foam flows. To date, all rheological studies have been carried out in capillary tubes of at least > 200 μm, although in one case, Holbrook and Patton [72] studied the flow of foam in such capillaries but extrapolated the data to predict the apparent viscosity of foam in capillaries of about 17–70 μm.

The study of foam flow in capillaries of < 100 μm in diameter is clearly important as this is the order of magnitude of flow channels present in porous media. So although foam rheology has been studied, to date, in relatively large capillaries, that is not to say that such findings are indicative of rheological behavior in small capillaries, where pore diameters vary from 0.1–100 μm, and the concept of a bubble may not be appropriate to the description of the body of the fluid.

Table 2

Summary of the Works on the Rheological Studies of Foam

Author(s)	Pseudoplastic	Bingham	Newtonian	Non-Newtonian	Compressible	Incompressible	Slip	Comments
Minssieux [22]	X			X		X		μ increases with increasing Γ
David and Marsden [74]	X			X	Semi-		Considered	μ independent of Γ
Raza and Marsden [52]	X		X*	X				μ increases with increasing Γ
Khan and Marsden [75]	X			X		X		μ increases with increasing Γ
Fried [70]	X							μ increases with increasing D
Sibree [11]			X*					μ increases with increasing Γ
Evgen'ev and Turner [108]		X						
Gogarty and Poettman [107]	X	X**						μ decreases with increasing γ
Aizad and Okandan [71]	X					X		μ increases with increasing Γ
Raza [43]						X		
Holbrook and Patton [72, 73]	X			X		X		μ increases with increasing Γ
Blauer and Holcomb [116]		X						μ increases with increasing D
Bullen and Bartrud [117]		X						
Mitchell [53]	X at low shear rate		X+					μ increases with increasing Γ (for $\Gamma > 0.54$) μ independent of D

*   *Newtonian behavior below critical flow rate and plug-like flow above it.*
**   *Measurable shear stress at zero shear rate (Bingham plastic behavior).*
+   *In the range $0 < \Gamma < 0.54$.*
μ *Apparent foam viscosity.*
Γ *Foam quality [gas volume/(gas + liquid volume)]*
γ *Shear rate*
D   *Capillary diameter*

By treating foam as a single fluid, it would be possible to consider some simple established rheological model and apply the appropriate equations (e.g., assuming incompressibility) directly. There is little doubt that foams at least appear to behave as non-Newtonian fluids in a variety of circumstances and exhibit apparent viscosities considerably higher than those of either constituent phases. Their viscosities increase with increasing quality up to an undefined critical flow rate, and also with capillary diameter. They also show Newtonian behavior below a critical flow rate and plug flow behavior above it.

A foam bank which is generated in a formation of porous media first penetrates into the largest pore channels. The resistance to flow in the largest pore channels is greater because of the effective viscosity which gives rise to pore blocking. The higher injection pressures, which are developed, will force the foam into the smaller and unflushed channels. This demonstrates that foams flow as a multiplicity of liquid interfaces interspersed with gas slugs which are able to exert a piston-like force on the discontinuous oil globules left trapped in the interstices of the porous media. As far as the mode of propagation is concerned, although foam moves as a single body overall, the gas flows as a discontinuous phase by breaking and reforming lamellae, while the liquid flows as a free phase.

The effectiveness of foam as a potential improved oil recovery agent has been demonstrated.

There is also a distinct lack of literature on the quantitative rheology and flow behavior of foam. Such literature as exists shows a lack of consensus on the rheology of foam which is detailed in Table 2, which presents a summary of rheological studies carried out to date.

The lack of overall consensus cannot be considered surprising, however, when the number of variables which are likely to affect the flow of foam, or successive interfacial lamellae in pipes, capillaries, and porous media are considered. The basic rheological curve itself showing the non-linear variation of apparent viscosity with quality indicates a change in flow mechanism as the quality increases, and the ability of gas to slip relative to the fluid becomes curtailed.

From the studies so far carried out there is a clear need to quantify more precisely the apparent viscosity of foam in systems of pipes, capillaries, and porous media, particularly in identifying the most important variables in this multivariant problem. Many laboratories are continuing to study these fundamental aspects of foam rheology, particularly with reference to flows in porous structures and small diameter capillaries.

APPENDIX

- Foam quality, Γ

$$\Gamma = \frac{V_{g(P,T)}}{V_{l(P,T)} + V_{g(P,T)}}$$

where $V_{g(P,T)}$ = the volume of gas
$V_{l(P,T)}$ = the volume of liquid at a particular pressure and temperature

- Hatschek's formula [68] as modified by Sibree [11] describing the viscosity of foam at atmospheric pressure, valid for $0.515 \leq \Gamma \leq 0.73$;

$$\mu_f = \mu_0 \left[\frac{1}{1 - (2.3\Gamma)^{1/3}} \right]$$

where Γ = foam quality
μ_0 = the viscosity of the base liquid
μ_f = apparent foam viscosity

- Details of various models of foam rheology.

1. pseudoplastic model: $\mu_{app} = K(\dot{\gamma})^n$, n < 1
2. Bingham model: $\mu_{app} = \mu_0 + K(\dot{\gamma})^n$, n = 1, Bingham plastic

where $\dot{\gamma}$ = shear rate, i.e. dv/dr
   n = flow index
   μ_0 = apparent foam viscosity at $\dot{\gamma} = 0$
   K = apparent foam consistency
   μ_{app} = apparent foam viscosity at given shear rate

REFERENCES

1. Rosen, M. J., *Surfactants and Interfacial Phenomena*, Wiley, New York, 1978.
2. Bikerman, J. J., *Foams*, Springer-Verlag, New York, 1973.
3. Gaudin, A. M., *Floatation*, McGraw-Hill, 2nd Ed., pp. 328.
4. Sebba, F., "Ion Floatation," Elsevier Monograph, Elsevier Publishing Co., N.Y., 1962.
5. Valentine, F. H. H., "Absorption in Gas–Liquid Dispersions: Some Aspects of Bubble Technology," SPON's Chem. Eng. Series, London (1967).
6. Berkman, S., and Egloff, G., "Emulsions and Foams," Reinhold Publishing Corp., N.Y., 1941.
7. Bikerman, J. J., *Physical Surfaces*, Academic Press, N.Y., 1970.
8. Bikerman, J. J., Foams, Springer-Verlag. N.Y., 1973.
9. Shaw, D. J., *Introduction to Colloid and Surface Chemistry*, Butterworths, London, 2nd Ed., 1970.
10. Einstein, A., "Investigation on the Theory of Brownian Movement," Methuen, 1926 (Dover, 1956).
11. Sibree, J. O., "The Viscosity of Froth," *Faraday Soc. Trans.*, Vol. 30 (1934).
12. Hatschek, E., "The General Theory of Viscosity of Two-Phase Systems," *Faraday Soc. Trans.*, Vol. 9:80 (1913–1915).
13. Ross, S., "Bubbles and Foams," *Ind. Eng. Chem.*, Vol. 61(10) (1969).
14. Sebba, F., "Microfoams—An Unexploited Colloid System," *J. Colloid & Interface Science*, Vol. 35(4) (1971).
15. De Vries, A. J., *Morphology, Coalescence and Size Distribution of Foam in Bubbles, in Adsorptive Bubble Separation Technique*, Ed. R. Lemlich. Acad. Press. N.Y. (1972), pp. 7–13.
16. Bendure, R. L., "Introduction to Foam and their Physical-Chemical Properties," *TAPPI*. Vol. 58(2):83–87 (1975).
17. Clark, N. O., and Blackman, M., "The Degree of Dispersion of the Gas Phase in Foam," *Trans. Farad. Soc.*, Vol. 44 (1948).
18. De Vries, A. J., *Foam Stability*, Rubber-Stichting, Delft, 1957.
19. New, G. E., "Kinetics of Foam Breakdown," Proc. Int. Cong. Surface Active Subs. 4th Brussels. Vol. 2:1167–1177 (1964).
20. Kitchener, J. A., et al., "Current Concepts in the Theory of Foaming," *Quarterly Review*, Vol. 13:71–97 (1959).
21. New, G. E., "Techniques of Foam Measurements," *J. Soc. Cosmet. Chem.*, Vol. 11:390–414 (1960).
22. Minssieux, L., "Oil Displacement by Foam in Relation to their Physical Properties in Porous Media," *J. Pet. Tech.*, pp. 100–108 (Jan. 1974).
23. Anwar Rajah, D. M., "Study of Foam Generation in Porous Media," M.Sc. Thesis, Heriot-Watt Univ (July 1977).
24. Bikerman, J. J., *Surface Chemistry Theory and Application*, Academic Press, 2nd Ed., N.Y., (1958).
25. Jackson, R., "The Formation and Coalescence of Drops and Bubbles in Liquids," Industrial Research Fellow Report No. 1., Inst. Chem. Eng., London.
26. Astm. "Foaming Characteristics of Lubricating Oils," ASTM Standard Methods. D892–63.
27. Bikerman, J. J., "The Unit of Foaminess," *J. Trans. Farad. Soc.*, Vol. 34:634–38 (1938).
28. Sasaki, T., "On the Nature of Foam. Stability of Foam Produced by Aqueous Solution of Alcohols and Acids," *Bull. Chem. Soc. Japan.*, Vol. 13:517–26 (1938).
29. Baxter, R. T., et al., "Transition in Bubble Formation Made of a Submerged Porous Disc," *Chem. Eng. Sci.*, Vol. 25:1244–47 (1970).

30. Bowonder, B., et al., "Studies of Bubble Formation—Bubble Formation at Porous Discs," *Chem. Eng. Sci.*, Vol. 25:25–32 (1970).
31. Rubin, E., et al., "Properties of Dynamic Foam Columns," *Chem. Eng. Sci.*, Vol. 22:1117–1125 (1967).
32. Hoffer, M. S., et al., "Flow Regimes of Stable Foams," *Ind. Eng. Chem. Fund.*, Vol. 8(3):483–90 (1969).
33. Ross, J., et al., "An Apparatus for Comparison of Foaming Properties of Soaps and Detergents," *Oil and Soap*, Vol. 18:99–102 (1941).
34. ASTM, "Foaming Properties of Surface-Active Agents," ASTM Standard Method D1173-53 (Reapproved 1970).
35. Kelly, W. R., et al., "Foam Test Method," *J. Amer. Chem. Soc.*, Vol. 43:364–5 (1966).
36. Reich, H. E., et al., "New Dynamic Method of Detergent Foam Measurement," *Soap and Chem. Specialities*, Vol. 37:55–57, 104 (Apr. 1961).
37. Bayat, M. Gh., "Report of Study of Triton X-100 Surface Active Agent as Foaming Agent for Foam Drive Oil Recovery," (Report No. 2). Dept. of Chem. & Proc. Eng., Heriot-Watt Univ. (Apr. 1975).
38. Peterson, H. B., et al., "Research Studies in Foam-Generating Equipments," *Ind. Eng. Chem.*, Vol. 48(11):2031–2034 (1956).
39. Raza, S. H., "The Streaming Potential of Foam," Ph.D. thesis, Standord Univ (May 1965).
40. Albrecht, R. A., et al., "Foam as Blocking Agents in Porous Media," *Soc. Pet. Eng. J.*, 51–55 (Mar. 1970).
41. David, A., et al., "The Rheology of Foam," SPE paper No. 2544 (1969).
42. Marsden, S. S., et al., "The Flow of Foam Through Short Porous Media and Apparent Viscosity Measurements," *Soc. Pet. Eng. J.*, 17–25 (Mar. 1966).
43. Raza, S. H., "Foam in Porous Media—Characteristics and Potential Application," *Soc. Pet. Eng. J.*, 328–36 (Dec. 1970).
44. Abernathy, C. K., et al., "An Investigation of Several Properties of Foam in Flow Through Short Connected Porous Media," M.Sc. dissertation, Stanford Univ. (1966).
45. Marsden, S. S., et al., "Use of Foam in Petroleum Operations," 7th World Petroleum Congress. Proc., Mexico, Vol. 3:253–242.
46. Wenzel, H. G., et al., "Flow of High Expansion Foam in Pipes," *J. Eng. Mech. Proc. of ASCE*, Vol. 6:153–165 (1967).
47. Wenzel, H. G., et al., "The Viscosity of High Expansion Foams," *J. Mat.*, Vol. 5:396–412 (1970).
48. Brand, H. J., et al., "Physical Properties of Foam for Protecting Plants Against Cold Weather," *Trans. ASAE.*, Vol. 13(1):1–5 (1970).
49. Walden, C. C., et al., "Study of Foam Separation as a Means of Detoxifying Bleached Draft Mill Effluents," CPAR Project Rept. 232–3 (Mar. 31, 1975).
50. Sisley, J. P., et al., "New Methods for Determination of Foaming Power," *Soap Chem. Specialities*, Vol. 31(4):44, 66, 99 (1955).
51. Savins, J. G., "Non-Newtonian Flow Through Porous Media," *Ind. Eng. Chem.*, Vol. 61(10) (Oct. 1969).
52. Raza, S. H., et al., "The Streaming Potential and Rheology of Foam," SPEJ., 359–66 (Dec. 1967).
53. Mitchell, B. J., "Viscosity of Foam," Ph.D. thesis, Univ. of Oklahoma (1969).
54. Starkey, P. E., "The Flow Properties of Foam," Ph.D. thesis, Univ. of London, (Nov. 1975).
55. Eakin, B. E., et al., "Improved High Pressure Capillary Tube Viscometer," *Petroleum Transactions*, *AIME*, Vol. 216:85–91 (1959).
56. Cross, M. M., "Rheology of non-Newtonian Fluids—A New Flow Equation for Pseudoplastic Systems," *J. of Colloid & Interface Sci.*, Vol. 20:417 (1965).
57. Savins, J. G., "Non-Newtonian Flow Through Porous Media," *Ind. Eng. Chem.*, Vol. 61(10) (Oct. 1969).
58. Savins, J. G., et al., "The Differential Methods in Rheology, I, II, III, IV," SPEJ (Sept. 1962), (Dec. 1962), (Mar. 1963), (June 1963).
59. Whorlow, R. W., *Rheological Techniques*, Ellis Horwood Pub. (1980).

60. Merril, E. W., et al., "Pressure-Flow Relations of Human Blood in Hollow Fibres at Low Flowrates," *J. Appl. Physiology*, Vol. 20:954–967 (1965).
61. Barbee, C., et al., "Prediction of Blood Flow in Tubes with Diameters as Small as $29\mu m$," Microvascular Research, 13 (1971).
62. Barbee, C., et al., "The Fahraeus Effect," Microvascular Research, 3 (1971).
63. Fahraeus, R., et al., "The Viscosity of Blood in Narrow Capillary Tubes," *Amer. J. Physiology*, Vol. 96:562–568 (1931).
64. Tempelton, T., "A Study of Displacement in Microscopic Capillaries," TP3804, *AIME*, Vol. 201 (1954).
65. Van Meures, P., "The Use of Transparent 3-D Models for Study of the Mechanism of Flow Processes in Oil Reservoirs," *Trans. AIME.* (1957).
66. Wang, W., "Microscopic Investigation of CO_2 Flooding Process," *J. P. T.* (Aug. 1982).
67. Grove, C. S., et al., "Viscosity of Fire Fighting Foam," *Ind. Eng. Chem.*, Vol. 43:1120 (1951).
68. Hatschek, E., "The General Theory of Viscosity of Two Phase Systems," *The Faraday Soc. Tran.*, Vol. 9:80 (1913–1915).
69. Khan, S. A., and Marsden, S. S., "The Flow of Foam," unpublished dissertation, Stanford Univ. (1965).
70. Fried, A. N., "The Foam Drive Process for Increasing the Recovery of Oil," USBM Report No. 5866 (1961).
71. Aizad, T., et al., "Flow Equation for Foam Flowing Through Porous Media and its Application as a Secondary Recovery Fluid," SPE, 6599 (1976).
72. Holbrook, S.T., et al., "Rheology of Mobility Control Foams," SPE/DOE, 9809 (1981).
73. Patton, J. T., et al., "Enhanced Oil Recovery by CO_2 Foam Flooding," DOE/MC/03259-15 (1982).
74. David, A., and Marsden, S. S., "The Rheology of Foam," SPE, 2544 of AIME (1969).
75. Marsden, S. S., and Khan, S. A., "The Flow of Foam Through Short Porous Media and Apparent Viscosity Measurements," SPEJ, 17–25 (Mar. 1966).
76. Gaden, E. L., et al., "Foam in Chemical Technology," *Chem. Eng.*, Vol. 63(10):173–84 (1956).
77. Brunner, C. A., et al., "Foam Fractionation," *Ind. Eng. Chem.*, Vol. 57(5):40–48 (1965).
78. Lemlich, R., "Foam Fractionation," *Chem. Eng.*, Vol. 75:95–102 (1968).
79. Skomoroski, R. M., "Separation of Surface Active Compounds by Foam Fractionation," *J. Chem. Educ.*, Vol. 40(9):470–71 (1963).
80. Lemlich, R., "Principles of Foam Fractionation," *Progress in Separation and Purification*, Vol. 1:1–56, E. S. Perry (ED.), Interscience (1968).
81. Lemlich, R., "Adsorptive Bubble Separation Methods. Foam Fractionation and Allied Techniques," *Ind. Eng. Chem.*, Vol. 60(10):16–19 (1968).
82. Rose, J. L., et al., "Treatment of Waste Waters by Foam Fractionation," *TAPPI*, Vol. 51(7):314–321 (1968).
83. Jenkins, D., "Application of Foam Fractionation to Waste Water Treatment," *J. WPCF.*, Vol. 38(11):1737–66 (1966).
84. Rubin, E., et al., "Sewage Plant Effluent Contaminant Removal by Foaming," *Ind. Eng. Chem. Fund.*, Vol. 55(10):44–48 (1963).
85. Ng, K. S., et al., "Foam Separation. A Technique for Water Pollution Abatement," *Water and Sewage Works*, Vol. 122:48, 52–55 (June 1975).
86. Ng, K. S., et al., "Detoxification of Kraft Mill Effluents by Foam Separation," Pulp and Paper Mag. of Canada, Vol. 74(5):119–23 (1973).
87. Haas, P. A., et al., "Foam Columns for Counter-Current Surface-Liquid Extraction of Surface-Active Solutes," *AIChEJ*, Vol. 11(2): 319–24 (1965).
88. Pozin, M. E., et al., "Effect of Properties of Dust Upon Dust-Removal from Gas by the Foam Method," *J. Appl. Chem.*, (USSR), Vol. 28:805–811 (1955).
89. Pozin, M. E., et al., "Removal of Dust from Gases by the Foam Method," *J. Appl. Chem.*, (USSR), Vol. 30:297–302 (1957).
90. Mukhlenov, I. P., et al., "Effects of Properties of Scrubbing Liquid on Removal of Dust from Gas by the Foam Method," *J. Appl. Chem.* (USSR), Vol. 28:877–80 (1955).
91. Zemskov, I. F., et al., "Use of Foam Absorber for Removal of Toxic Carbon Dust from Air

Leaving an Absorber, with Fluidised Beds of Absorbent," *J. Appl. Chem.* (USSR), Vol. 35:2367–77 (1962).

92. Taheri, M., et al., "Removal of Small Particles from Air by Foam in Sieve Plate Column," *J. Air Pollution Control Assoc.*, Vol. 18(4):240–5 (1968).

93. Dunning, H. N., et al., "Foaming Agents are Low Cost Treatment for Tired Gassers," *Oil and Gas J.*, Vol. 57:108–110 (Feb. 1959).

94. Goins, W. C., et al., "How to Use Foaming Agents in Air and Gas Drilling," *World Oil.*, Vol. 152(4):59–64 (Mar. 1961).

95. Christensen, R. J., et al., "Application of Stable Foam in Canada," *Oil Week*, 30–35 (Sept. 20, 1971).

96. Murray, A. S., et al., "Foam Agents and Foam Drilling," *Oil and Gas J.*, Vol. 59:125–9 (Feb. 1961).

97. Lummus, J. L., et al., "How New Foaming Agents are Aiding Air/Gas Drilling," *World Oil*, Vol. 153:57–62 (July 1961).

98. Anderson, G. W., et al., "The Use of Stable Foam as a Low Pressure Completion and Sand-Cleanout Fluid," API Meeting in Los Angeles, 7–13 (May 1966).

99. Hutchison, S. O., "Foam Workovers Cuts Costs 50%," *World Oil*, Vol. 73:94 (Nov. 1969).

100. Bernard, G. G., et al., "Model Study of Foam as a Sealant for Leaks in Gas Storage Reservoirs," *Soc., Pet. Eng. J.*, 9–15 (Mar. 1970).

101. Albrecht, R. A., et al., "Sealing Gas Storage Reservoirs with Foam," SPE Paper No. 2357 (1968).

102. Eakin, J. L., et al., "Foams Purge Well Bore and Formation Work," *Pet. Eng.*, 71 (July 1966).

103. Eakin, J. L., et al., "Foam Removes Brine from Deep Texas Wells," *Oil and Gas J.*, Vol. 58(33):162 (Aug. 15, 1960).

104. Bernard, G. G., et al., "Effect of Foam on Trapped Gas Saturation and on Permeability of Porous Media to Water," SPEJ (Dec. 1965).

105. Holm, L. W., "The Mechanism of Gas and Liquid Flow Through Porous Media in the Presence of Foam," *SPEJ*, 359–69 (Dec. 1968).

106. Ali, J. K., "Foam in Enhanced Oil Recovery," Ph.D. thesis, Dept. of Chem. & Proc. Eng., Heriot-Watt Univ., Edinburgh (1982).

107. Gogarty, W. B., et al., "The Use of Non-Newtonian Fludis in Oil Recovery," 8th World Petroleum Congr., Vol. 3 (1971).

108. Evgen'ev, A. E., et al., "Rheological Properties of Foam in a Porous Medium," translated from Russian by Associated Technical Services Inc., New Jersey, RJ-5545 (1967).

109. Kutilek, M., "Non-Darcian Flow of Waters in Soils Laminar Region," in *Fundamentals of Transport Phenomena in Porous Media*, Elsevier, 327–37 (1972).

110. Amiel, D., "The Rheology of Foam," unpublished dissertation, Stanford Univ. (1968).

111. Bond, D. C., et al., "Gas-Drive Oil Recovery Processes," U.S. Patent No. 2,866,507 (1958).

112. Holbrook, O. C., et al., "Use of Foam for Plugging Gas Producing Strata," U.S. Patent No. 3,207,218 (1965).

113. Raza, S. H., "Plugging Formations with Foam," U.S. Patent No. 3,491,832 (1970).

114. Nutt, C. W., et al., "Foam as an Agent for the Enhanced Oil Recovery of Oil from Stratified Formations," European Symp. on EOR (1978).

115. Bayat, M. Gh., "Foam as an Agent for Enhanced Oil Recovery," Ph.D. thesis, Dept. of Chem. & Proc. Eng., Heriot-Watt Univ., Edinburgh (1977).

116. Blauer, R. E., et al., "Foam Fracturing Shows Success in Gas, Oil Formations," *Oil & Gas J.* (Aug. 1975).

117. Bullen, R. S., et al., "Fracturing with Foam," *J. Canadian Petroleum Tech.*, 32–27 (April–June 1976).

CHAPTER 3

PROPERTIES AND CHARACTERISTICS OF DROPS AND BUBBLES

John R. Grace

Department of Chemical Engineering
University of British Columbia
Vancouver, Canada

and

Tom Wairegi

Shell Canada Limited
Calgary, Canada

CONTENTS

INTRODUCTION

This chapter covers some of the principal properties of gas bubbles in liquids, liquid drops in immiscible liquids, and liquid drops in gases. We consider only the steady motion of already-formed drops and bubbles in Newtonian fluids, since formation processes, break-up, and swarms in bubble columns and dispersions are treated in other chapters.

BUBBLES AND DROPS IN IMMISCIBLE LIQUIDS

Shape Regimes

A useful starting point for describing the behavior of bubbles and drops in liquids is the regime diagram developed by Grace and coworkers [1–3] shown in Figure 1. Here the fluid particle *Reynolds number*, $Re = \rho d_e U_T/\mu$, is plotted against a dimensionless fluid particle size, the *Eötvös*

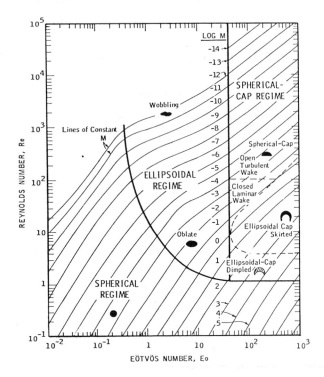

Figure 1. Regime diagram for drops and bubbles in free and steady motion through an immiscible liquid showing boundaries between regimes (heavy lines) and subregimes (dashed lines).

number, $Eo = \Delta\rho g d_e^2/\sigma$, where $\Delta\rho$ is the magnitude of the difference in densities between the continuous (unsubscripted) phase and the dispersed (subscript d) phase. The volume-equivalent sphere diameter, d_e, is conventionally used to provide a linear measure of the size of the bubble or drop. A family of lines of positive slope, each characterized by a constant value of a *fluid property group*, $M = g\mu^4 \, \Delta\rho/\rho^2\sigma^3$, independent of the fluid particle size and velocity, are plotted in Figure 1. For any dispersed-fluid/continuous-liquid system, increasing drop or bubble size causes a movement along a line of constant M upwards and to the right. For low-viscosity, high-surface tension (or interfacial tension) systems, such as for bubbles or drops in water or liquid metals, M is of the order of 10^{-10} or smaller, whereas M can be of order 100 or more for very viscous continuous phases.

Figure 1 shows that there are three principal shape regimes for drops and bubbles in liquids. At low Eo and/or at low Re, bubbles and drops are closely *spherical.* As they grow in size, there is a region called the *ellipsoidal* regime where the time-averaged shape of the fluid particle has the appearance of an oblate ellipsoid of revolution with its minor axis in the vertical direction. As shown in Figure 1 this regime is bypassed for fluid-liquid systems of $M > 10^2$. For $Eo > 40$ and $Re > 1.2$, the bubbles and drops are described as being in the *spherical-cap* regime, the leading edge appearing to be like the front edge of a complete sphere while the back may be flat, jagged, or indented.

Both the ellipsoidal and spherical-cap regimes may be divided into subregimes, as shown in Figure 1. For low M systems, ellipsoidal bubbles and drops can be described as "wobbling," with instantaneous shapes which deviate widely from the ellipsoidal form. In the spherical-cap regime with viscous liquids ($M > 10^{-1}$) the leading edge is oblate spheroidal, rather than spherical, so that the fluid particles are best described as "ellipsoidal-caps": for these cases, the rear surface is indented or dimpled, and if Re > 4, the bubble or drop may trail a "skirt" of the dispersed phase fluid from its corners [4]. For lower M systems, the wake behind the drop or bubble is closed only if Re < 100, otherwi.e it is open and turbulent [5].

The transitions between these regimes are generally gradual rather than as sharp as the boundary lines in Figure 1 might imply. This regime diagram is successful, however, in showing the key regimes for all bubbles and drops in Newtonian liquids. It covers cases where bubbles or drops move upwards ($\rho_d < \rho$) or where drops move downwards in liquid-liquid systems ($\rho_d > \rho$). Except for the appearance of the dispersed phase density in $\Delta\rho$, the density and viscosity of the dispersed phase do not appear and are not required to predict the shape regime. The presence or absence of surface-active impurities may, however, lead to slight displacement of curves for low M systems [2].

Terminal Rising or Settling Velocities

The regime plot, Figure 1, described in the previous section may also be used to provide an estimate of terminal rising or settling velocities for bubbles and drops since it amounts to a plot of $d_e U_T$, made dimensionless, versus d_e^2, also in dimensionless form, for given values of the fluid property group M. However, more accurate methods are generally available once the general regime of motion has been determined.

Spherical Regime

For drops and bubbles with Re < 0.2, the terminal velocity in the total absence of surface-active impurities is given [6, 7] by

$$U_{T\infty}^o = \frac{gd^2 \, \Delta\rho}{6\mu} \left\{ \frac{\kappa + 1}{3\kappa + 2} \right\} \tag{1}$$

where $\kappa = \mu_d/\mu$ is the viscosity ratio. In practice, few systems are sufficiently pure that they follow Equation 1. Instead, surface-active impurities accumulate at the interface between the dispersed fluid and the outer liquid where they are swept preferentially to the rear of the fluid particle, establishing a gradient in the surface tension or interfacial tension which impedes the tendency of the dispersed fluid to circulate. The damping of the internal motion causes the drop or bubble to behave as if it has a large value of κ. The terminal velocity at Re < 0.2 can then most often be predicted from the limiting case where $\kappa \to \infty$, i.e.

$$U_{TS} = \frac{gd^2 \, \Delta\rho}{18\mu} \tag{2}$$

This expression is readily recognized as the Stokes expression [8] for solid spheres. There are a number of equations in the literature (see Clift et al. [3] and Harper [9] for reviews) which give expressions intermediate between Equations 1 and 2 for cases of intermediate purity where surface-active impurities reduce, but do not completely eliminate, internal circulation. However, these expressions are of limited utility for practical cases because the nature and concentration of impurities is seldom known. Even minute traces of surface-active materials, such as may be found in tap water or in beakers previously washed with detergents, can have a significant influence. The ratio of the terminal velocity for a perfectly pure system to that in a totally contaminated system is obtained from Equations 1 and 2:

$$U_{T\infty}^o/U_{TS} = 3(\kappa + 1)/(3\kappa + 2) \tag{3}$$

The maximum increase in velocity over the Stokes terminal velocity at low Re therefore occurs for bubbles as $\kappa \to 0$ where there is a 50% increase in velocity due to circulation. The enhancement is lower as κ increases and negligible at large κ. As a simple criterion based on Bond and Newton [10], we may assume that $U_T \to U_{T\infty}^o$ for Eo > 4 while $U_T \to U_{TS}$ for Eo < 4 at low Re. In practice the transition between these two limits is more gradual than this criterion would imply.

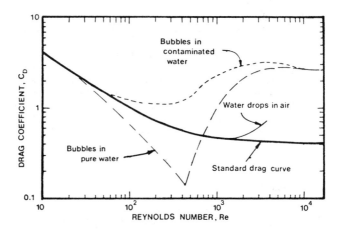

Figure 2. Drag coefficient vs. Reynolds number curve for air bubbles in water and water drops in air in comparison with standard drag curve.

At higher values of the drop or bubble Reynolds number, numerical solutions have been carried out for specific cases, e.g. for air bubbles in water and $\kappa = 1$, 3, and 10. An expression proposed by Rivkind and Ryskin [11],

$$C_D^\circ = \frac{4}{3}\frac{\Delta\rho}{\rho}\frac{gd_e}{(U_{T\infty}^\circ)^2} = \frac{1}{\kappa+1}\left[\kappa\left(\frac{24}{Re} + \frac{4}{Re^{1/3}}\right) + \frac{14.9}{Re^{0.78}}\right] \tag{4}$$

allows the terminal velocity to be calculated for spherical drops and bubbles in pure systems. Equation 4 provides a good fit for the numerical predictions of drag on spherical drops and bubbles in pure systems at all κ for $Re > 1$. For $0.2 < \kappa < 1$ it is reasonable to interpolate between the results of Equations 1 and 4.

The presence of surface-active contaminants results in actual terminal velocities which are less than those predicted from Equation 4, just as for the creeping flow regime. The changes in terminal velocity in this case can be even larger than the 50% maximum already discussed. The minimum value of the terminal velocity can be predicted from the revised standard drag curve for rigid spheres and procedures given by Clift et al. [3]. Some values of the drag coefficient for pure and contaminated air bubbles in water appear in Table 1 together with those for rigid spheres and water drops in air. Drag coefficients are also plotted in Figure 2.

Ellipsoidal Regime

For bubbles and drops in liquids where some surface-active contamination is present, there are a number of empirical equations for predicting terminal velocities. The most successful equation was proposed by Grace et al. [2] as an extension to that of Johnson and Braida [12], itself an extension of the correlation of Hu and Kintner [13]. The correlation is:

$$Re = \frac{\rho d_e U_{T\infty}}{\mu} = (J - 0.857)M^{-0.149} \tag{5}$$

$$\text{where} \quad J = 0.94N^{0.757} \quad (2 < N \le 59.3) \tag{6}$$
$$J = 3.42N^{0.441} \quad (59.3 < N) \tag{7}$$
$$N = (4/3)EoM^{-0.149}(\mu/0.0009)^{-0.14} \tag{8}$$

Table 1
Drag Coefficients for Drops and Bubbles at Different Reynolds Numbers

System	Re = 0.1	Re = 1.0	Re = 10	Re = 100	Re = 1000
Standard drag curve, solids spheres [3]	244.1	27.32	4.29	1.096	0.471
Stokes drag [8]	240.0	(24.0)	N.A.	N.A.	N.A.
Hadamard-Rybczynsky drag, $\kappa = 0$ [6, 7]	160.0	16.0	N.A.	N.A.	N.A.
Air bubble in water, pure system	191.8	18.3	2.64	0.405	0.093
Air bubble in water, contaminated system	244	27.3	4.3	1.2	2.3
Water drop in air, pure system	239	27	4.23	1.08	0.51

The continuous-phase liquid viscosity, μ, must have SI (i.e., Ns/m^2) units. The transition between the two expressions for J, Equations 6 and 7, at N = 59.3 corresponds approximately to the transition between drops or bubbles which travel in rectilinear paths and those that oscillate from side to side or those with spiral trajectories.

If great care is taken to eliminate surface-active impurities, the terminal velocity of drops and bubbles in liquids can exceed that given by Equation 5 because free circulation of the dispersed fluid leads to delayed boundary-layer separation, smaller wakes, and a delay in the onset of secondary (e.g. wobbling or helical) motion. Figure 3 shows a graphical correlation of the increase in terminal

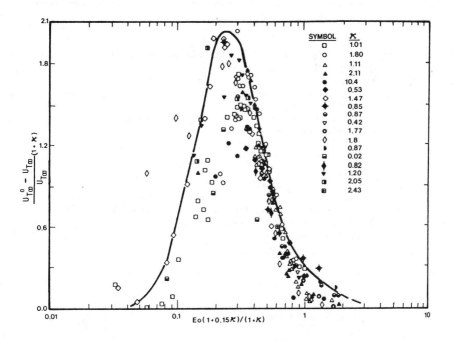

Figure 3. Graphical correlation [2] showing the increase in terminal velocity for bubbles and drops in pure systems relative to that for normal systems.

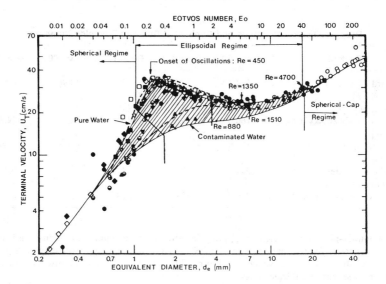

Figure 4. Experimental and predicted terminal velocities of air bubbles in water at 20°C. Experimental values are derived from 14 different studies [3]. Shaded region is the envelope plotted by Gaudin [37] for grossly contaminated systems. The broken curves are predictions from the correlations recommended in this chapter for mildly contaminated (lower curve) and pure systems (upper curve).

velocity which is achieved for purified systems. The envelope drawn can be used to estimate the maximum enhancement in the terminal velocity for completely pure systems. Results of these approaches for air bubbles in water and for carbon tetrachloride drops falling through water, together with experimental results, appear in Figures 4 and 5, respectively. The envelope between the curves predicted for pure and mildly contaminated systems is seen to give a good description of the reported scatter in data, with workers whose results approach the upper curve showing greater care in achieving or maintaining freedom from surface-active agents.

Spherical-Cap Regime

This regime is encountered by large bubbles and drops. For a spherical-cap, the velocity is derived by assuming that the pressure distribution near the leading edge is that for potential flow past a complete sphere and balancing pressures on the inside and outside of the fluid particle in that vicinity. The resulting expressions [4, 14] are

$$U_{T\infty} = \frac{2}{3}\sqrt{\frac{\Delta\rho}{\rho}\,gR} \tag{9}$$

where R is the radius of curvature of the leading edges. Extension of this equation to the case where the front edge is oblate spheroidal leads [4] to

$$U_{T\infty} = \left\{ \frac{\sin^{-1}e - e\sqrt{1 - e^2}}{e^3} \right\}\sqrt{\frac{\Delta\rho}{\rho}\,gb} \tag{10}$$

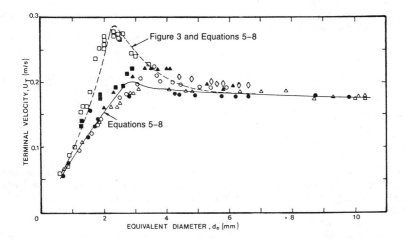

Figure 5. Experimental and predicted terminal velocities for carbon tetrachloride drops falling through water. Experimental points are derived from results of seven different studies [3].

where $e = \sqrt{(a^2 - b^2)/a^2}$ is the eccentricity and a and b are the horizontal and vertical semi-axes, respectively. Equation 10 can be shown to reduce to Equation 9 in the limit as $e \to 0$. An analogous expression for prolate spheroidal-cap bubbles or drops, observed when a vertical tube or rod is enclosed by a large fluid particle, has been derived by Grace and Harrison [15]. For spherical-cap fluid particles, where the wake angle tends towards 50° at high Re (see Equation 17 below), the drag coefficient approaches a value of 2.67 as shown in Figure 2.

Wall Effects

The expressions given above are for bubbles and drops in containing vessels of cross-sectional dimensions much greater than d_e. In vessels of finite dimensions, wall effects may lead to elongation in the vertical direction and to retardation in the terminal velocity. Typical shapes for large bubbles are shown in Figure 6. For a given value of d_e/D, where D represents the diameter or hydraulic diameter of the containing vessel, wall effects show the greatest retarding influence at low Re.

For a spherical drop of diameter d at low Re behaving as a rigid sphere on the axis of a cylindrical column, the terminal velocity can be estimated from the empirical equation of Francis [16],

$$U_T = U_{TS}\{(D - d)/(D - 0.475d)\}^4 \qquad (\text{Re} \overset{<}{\sim} 0.2, d < 0.3D) \qquad (11)$$

Somewhat smaller corrections are applicable if the bubble or drop is circulating, whereas larger corrections may be required for fluid particles at radial positions displaced from the axis. In the latter case, there is a tendency for the fluid particle to migrate radially towards the axis or wall of the containing tube. At higher Re, but with the fluid particles still in the spherical regime and $d_e < 0.3D$, correction factors derived empirically for rigid spheres [3, 17] may be employed.

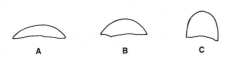

Figure 6. Shapes of large gas bubbles of equal volume, 92.6 cm³, in columns of different diameter: (A) $d_e/D = 0.19$, Re = 370; (B) $d_e/D = 0.39$, Re = 3110; (C) $d_e/D = 0.80$, Re = 210. Tracings from photographs obtained by Bhaga [36], M = 1.6×10^{-3} in each case.

A   B   C

For drops and bubbles in the ellipsoidal regime with Re > 200 and $d_e \leq 0.6D$, the wall effect correction can be estimated [3] from

$$U_T = U_{T\infty}\{(D^2 - d_e^2)/D^2\}^{1.5} \tag{12}$$

For bubbles and drops in the spherical-cap regime, retardation can be neglected for D > $8d_e$, while for $0.125 \leq d_e/D \leq 0.6$ the wall correction can be estimated from a correlation given by Wallis [18]

$$U_T = 1.13U_{T\infty} \exp[-d_e/D] \tag{13}$$

Slug Flow Regime

For $d_e \geq 0.6D$, the influence of the containing wall on the terminal velocity becomes dominant. The fluid particle then is elongated in the vertical direction having a bullet-like shape as shown in Figure 6C and is called a slug, slug-flow bubble or drop, or Taylor bubble. Figure 7, derived from the results of White and Beardmore [19] shows the terminal velocity of slugs, expressed in dimensionless Froude number form, as a function of Eo_D and M. Note that once d_e has exceeded 0.6D, further additions of displaced phase fluid to the bubble or drop merely extend the length of the slug and do not appreciably affect the terminal velocity.

Limiting expressions for slug terminal velocities are often useful. For $Eo_D > 100$ and $M \leq 10^{-6}$ viscous forces and surface tension effects are negligible and the slug terminal velocity is [14, 20]

$$U_T = 0.35\sqrt{gD\, \Delta\rho/\rho} \tag{14}$$

The coefficient 0.35 can be replaced by $(0.23 + 0.13\, l/w)$ for a rectangular cross-section of length l and width w, and by $(0.35 + 0.06D_I/D_O)$ for an annular channel having inner and outer diameters

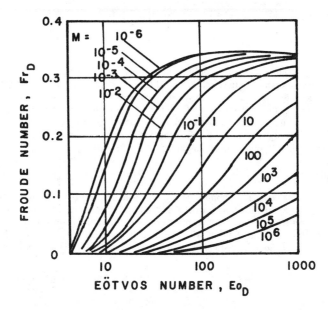

Figure 7. Graphical correlation derived from White and Beardmore [19] showing the terminal velocity of gaseous or liquid slugs in immiscible liquids.

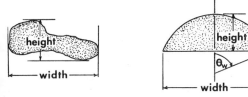

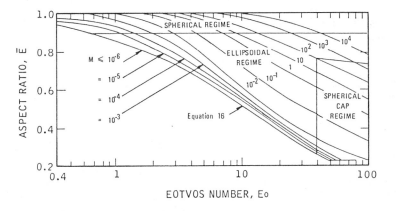

Figure 8. Determination of aspect ratio, E, and wake angle θ_w, for fluid particles of different shapes.

D_I and D_O, respectively. For $Eo_D >$ and $Fr_D = U_T/\sqrt{gD\,\Delta\rho/\rho} < 0.05$, the slug terminal velocity is given [21] by

$$U_T = g\,\Delta\rho D^2/102\mu \tag{15}$$

Finally, for $Eo_D < 3.4$ the slug remains motionless, i.e. $U_T = 0$.

Slugs rising in obliquely inclined tubes tend to travel along the underside of the top of the tube and commonly have higher terminal velocities than for vertical tubes. The maximum Fr_D is achieved for an inclination of about 55° to the vertical [22].

Shape Parameters

For high M systems and Re of order unity, small deformations from the spherical have been predicted based on matched asymptotic expansions [23–25]. For small We, the deformation leads to oblate spheroidal shapes for physically realistic cases, in accord with experimental results. There are few analytical results for higher Re and lower M systems. However, Wairegi [26] was able to obtain a reasonable description of the relative fore and aft deformation at Re > 100 by assuming the front and rear portions to be semi-spheroids of different eccentricity; the eccentricities were chosen to minimize deviations in a balance of hydrostatic, inertial, and interfacial tension forces.

For practical systems, it is often sufficient to be able to estimate an overall aspect ratio, E, defined as the time-mean ratio of the maximum vertical to maximum horizontal dimension as shown in Figure 8. An empirical correlation for unpurified systems appears in Figure 9. For E > 0.9 the deformation is small enough that the bubbles and drops are still described as belonging to the spherical regime. For $M \leq 10^{-6}$ and $Eo < 40$ the time-mean aspect ratio can be estimated from

Figure 9. Graphical correlation [2] showing time-mean aspect ratio of drops and bubbles in liquids for systems of normal degree of contamination.

a relationship proposed by Wellek et al. [27]:

$$E = [1 + 0.163Eo^{0.757}]^{-1} \tag{16}$$

Deformations tend to be larger (and hence E lower) for fluid particles in very pure systems because of the larger terminal velocities which lead to increased inertial forces.

For spherical-cap bubbles and drops, the shape is often described more usefully by a "wake angle" measured from the vertical axis through the center of curvature to the outer edge as indicated in Figure 8. An empirical equation describing this angle [3], expressed in degrees, is:

$$\theta_w = 50 + 190 \exp[-0.62Re^{0.4}] \tag{17}$$

Internal Circulation

It is very difficult in practice to predict the extent of internal circulation in a rising bubble or in a rising or falling drop. In the absence of surface-active impurities, the dispersed fluid should circulate for all bubbles and drops, small and large. In practice, the degree of circulation decreases with an increasing accumulation of surfactants at the interface, with increasing κ and with decreasing fluid particle size. In the limit internal circulation may cease altogether, and in intermediate cases a stagnant cap may form at the rear of the bubble or drop. The extent of internal circulation influences mass and heat transfer to or from the fluid particle as well as terminal velocities and wake behavior [3].

Wake Behavior and Secondary Motion

For rigid spheres in steady motion, the onset of boundary-layer separation, leading to the occurrence of an attached wake, occurs at a Reynolds number of about 20. The wake grows in size as the Reynolds number increases until fragments are shed periodically when Re reaches a critical value of the order of 270 [13]. For fluid particles, similar events occur, but the corresponding Reynolds number may differ from the preceding values. When internal circulation occurs, especially for low values of κ and pure systems, wake formation and shedding tend to be delayed. On the other hand, deformation into oblate shapes, presenting maximum area normal to the direction of motion, promotes earlier boundary-layer separation and wake instability. For fluid particles in pure systems which retain near-spherical shapes, the Re values for wake formation and shedding may be as high as about 200 and 800, respectively [28]. For spherical-cap bubbles on the other hand, wakes begin as soon as the spherical-cap form is adopted (Re as low as about 1.2, see Figure 1) and transition from an attached laminar to a turbulent wake occurs for $Re \approx 110$ [5]. In the closed wake region the wake volume is given approximately [5] by

$$V_w = 0.37Re^{1.4}V \tag{18}$$

where V is the volume of the fluid particle. When skirts are trailed by the fluid particles (see Figure 1), the skirt thickness is of order

$$t_{skirt} = \sqrt{6\mu_d U_T/g \, \Delta\rho} \tag{19}$$

The skirt appears to have little influence on the forward portion of the ellipsoidal-cap drop or bubble, although it shields the wake somewhat and probably weakens circulation there.

The onset of wake shedding can have a profound effect on the subsequent motion of the drop or bubble. Shedding tends to lead to oscillations, which may take the form of dilations, causing the instantaneous value of E to vary from the time-averaged value, or to wobbling from side to side, or to a helical trajectory. These forms of secondary motion can have a profound influence on mass or heat transfer processes.

When shape dilations do occur, they tend to have a highly irregular amplitude, but to be periodic in nature. The frequency is typically about 10%–20% less than the frequency derived by Lamb

[29] for small oscillations of a neutrally buoyant drop in the absence of viscous effects,

$$f = \frac{4}{\pi}\sqrt{\frac{3\sigma}{(2\rho + 3\rho_d)d_e^3}} \tag{20}$$

Schroeder and Kintner [30] have attempted to correlate the amplitude of the shape oscillations.

LIQUID DROPS IN GASES

Shape Regimes

The same dimensionless groups used to characterize bubbles and drops in liquids (i.e. Re, Eo, and M) are again useful in describing the behavior of drops in gases. In this case, however, the range of shapes which are observed under steady-state conditions is smaller. As shown in Figure 10 for water drops of different sizes falling freely in air, small drops in gas are spherical; with increasing drop volume, flattening occurs, especially at the leading (lower) edge. Significant deviation from the spherical occurs for drops of approximately 1 mm equivalent diameter or larger.

Terminal Settling Velocities

For drops for which Eo $\leq$ 0.15, terminal velocities are given closely by expressions for rigid spheres of the same density falling in the same gas [3]. For larger drops,

$$Re = 1.62 Eo^{0.755} M^{-0.25} \qquad (0.5 \leq Eo \leq 1.84) \tag{21}$$

$$Re = 1.83 Eo^{0.555} M^{-0.25} \qquad (1.84 \leq Eo \leq 5.0) \tag{22}$$

$$Re = 2.0 Eo^{0.5} M^{-0.25} \qquad (Eo \geq 5.0) \tag{23}$$

This piece-wise fit was proposed by Clift et al. [3] based on data for drops of various liquids falling in air. As shown in Table 1 and Figure 2, drag coefficients for pure water drops are initially slightly less than those for rigid spheres at low Re due to internal circulation, while for larger drops deformation leads to significantly higher drag coefficients. There is a lack of data for drops falling in gases other than air and even for air at temperatures and pressures widely removed from atmospheric conditions. For drops in the small range (0.15 < Eo < 0.5) not covered by the preceding recommendations and correlation, we suggest interpolation via

$$Re = Re_{Eo=0.15} + \frac{(Eo - 0.15)}{0.35}[Re_{Eo=0.5} - Re_{Eo=0.15}] \tag{24}$$

For larger drops (Eo $\geq$ 5.0), Equation 23 suggests that the terminal velocity reaches an upper limit, independent of the drop diameter and of the viscosities of both the liquid and gas, given by

$$U_T = 2.0(g\sigma \,\Delta\rho/\rho^2)^{0.25} \tag{25}$$

Except for drops composed of liquids of very high viscosity, drops falling in gases become unstable and break up for Eo $\geq$ 16. Hence the effective range of application of Equations 23 and 25 is 5.0 $\leq$ Eo $\leq$ 16.

Figure 10. Shapes of water drops of different size falling freely through air [31]: (A) d_e = 0.262 mm, U_T = 0.98 m/s; (B) d_e = 3.45 mm, U_T = 8.46 m/s; (C) d_e = 5.8 mm, U_T = 9.17 m/s; (D) d_e = 8.0 mm, U_T = 9.20 m/s.

A   B   C   D

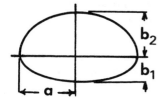

Figure 11. Double semi-ellipsoid approximate shape adopted by liquid droplets falling steadily through gases.

Wall effects are rarely of concern for drops falling in gases. Corrections for solid spheres of diameter = d_e may be employed as a first approximation for cases where d_e/D is sufficiently large that wall effects influence terminal velocities significantly.

Shape Parameters

The shape of liquid drops falling steadily in gases can be approximated as that of two adjoined semi-spheroids (see Figure 11) each having a common horizontal semi-major axis a, while the leading (lower) one has a semi-minor axis b_1 and the corresponding axis for the rear (upper) one is b_2. The overall aspect ratio can then be correlated [3] by

$$E = (b_1 + b_2)/2a = 1.0 \qquad (Eo \le 0.4) \tag{26}$$

$$E = (b_1 + b_2)/2a = [1.0 + 0.18(Eo - 0.4)^{0.8}]^{-1} \qquad (Eo > 0.4) \tag{27}$$

In the prediction of mass and heat transfer rates, it is helpful to be able to estimate the surface areas separately of the fore and aft semi-spheroids. Data obtained by Finlay [32] have been fitted [3] by the relationships:

$$b_1/(b_1 + b_2) = 0.5 \qquad (Eo \le 0.5) \tag{28}$$

$$b_1/(b_1 + b_2) = 0.5[1.0 + 0.12(Eo - 0.5)^{0.8}]^{-1} \qquad (Eo > 0.5) \tag{29}$$

Since the volume of the drop is given by

$$V = \frac{\pi}{6} d_e^3 = \frac{2}{3} \pi a^2 (b_1 + b_2), \tag{30}$$

each of the preceding lengths (a, b_1, and b_2) can be estimated for a drop of known volume, V, or equivalent diameter, d_e, from the preceding relationships.

Internal Circulation

The external flow past the drop falling in a gas induces an internal circulation pattern in the direction tending to diminish the velocity gradient across the interface. Because the internal fluid (liquid) generally has a much higher viscosity than the external fluid (gas), the internal circulation tends to be relatively weak.

Some predictions of surface velocities for rain drops in air, obtained by numerical solution of the governing equations of motion, are shown in Figure 12. Note that the velocity at the surface of the drop relative to the terminal velocity of the drop increases with increasing Re, while the angle at which the maximum occurs moves forward of the equator for finite Re. The curves indicate that separation should occur at Re ≈ 100 in the absence of surface contamination. However, surface contamination in real systems is responsible (as for fluid particles in liquids discussed earlier) for damping of internal circulation and premature boundary-layer separation. In practice, for water

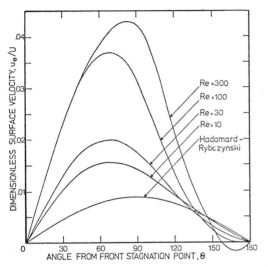

Figure 12. Surface velocity for water drops falling through air as predicted numerically by LeClair et al. [33] and by Hadamard [6].

drops in air under many conditions, separation and wake formation occur for Re ≈ 20 as for rigid spheres. For systems of intermediate purity, separation may occur for Re between 20 and 100.

Wake Behavior and Secondary Motion

Because of the large ratio of internal to external fluid densities and viscosities, liquid drops falling in gases show less secondary motion than bubbles or drops in liquids. Experimental observations may be influenced by the considerable distance required for initial oscillations, caused by the release of drops, to be damped out. Several investigators [32, 34, 35] have reported oscillations, probably associated with wake shedding. As d_e increases in the range 3–6 mm, the amplitude of oscillation increases while the frequency is of the order of that predicted by Equation 20.

NOTATION

A	horizontal semi-major axis of oblate spheroid	e	eccentricity of oblate spheroid, $\sqrt{(a^2 - b^2)/a^2}$
b	vertical semi-minor axis of oblate spheroid	Fr_D	Froude number, $U_T/\sqrt{gD\,\Delta\rho/\rho}$
b_1, b_2	vertical semi-minor axes of fore and aft sections (Figure 11)	f	frequency of oscillation
		g	acceleration due to gravity
C_D	drag coefficient, $4\,\Delta\rho g d_e/(3\rho U_T^2)$	J	dimensionless group defined by Equations 6 and 7
D	diameter or hydraulic diameter of containing vessel	l	length (longer side) of column of rectangular cross section
D_I, D_O	inner and outer diameter of annular channel	M	dimensionless fluid property group, $g\mu^4\,\Delta\rho/\rho^2\sigma^3$
d	sphere diameter	N	dimensionless group defined by Equation 8
d_e	volume-equivalent sphere diameter of fluid particle	R	radius of curvature of spherical-cap
E	aspect (height-to-width) ratio of fluid particle	Re	Reynolds number, $\rho d_e U_T/\mu$
Eo	Eötvös number, $\Delta\rho g d_e^2/\sigma$	t_{skirt}	thickness of annular skirt trailed behind bubble or drop
Eo_D	Eötvös number based on D, $\Delta\rho g D^2/\sigma$	U_T	terminal rising or settling velocity

U_{TS} Stokes terminal velocity, Equation 2
$U_{T\infty}$ terminal velocity in a column of large cross section
$U_{T\infty}^{o}$ value of $U_{T\infty}$ in the absence of surface active impurities

V   volume of fluid particle
V_w wake volume
w   width of column of rectangular cross section

Greek Symbols

$\Delta\rho$ absolute value of density difference between phases
θ_w wake angle (see Figure 8)
κ viscosity ratio, μ_d/μ
μ viscosity of continuous phase

μ_d viscosity of dispersed phase
ρ density of continuous phase
ρ_d density of dispersed phase
σ surface or interfacial tension

REFERENCES

1. Grace, J. R., "Shapes and Velocities of Bubbles Rising in Infinite Liquids," *Trans. Instn. Chem. Engrs.*, Vol. 51 (1973), pp. 116–120.
2. Grace, J. R., Wairegi, T., and Nguyen, T. H., "Shapes and Velocities of Single Drops and Bubbles Moving Freely through Immiscible Liquids," *Trans. Instn. Chem. Engrs.*, Vol. 54 (1976), pp. 167–173.
3. Clift, R., Grace, J. R., and Weber, M. E., *Bubbles, Drops and Particles*, New York: Academic Press, 1978.
4. Wairegi, T., and Grace, J. R., "The Behaviour of Large Drops in Immiscible Liquids," *Intern. J. Multiphase Flow*, Vol. 3 (1976), pp. 67–77.
5. Bhaga, D., and Weber, M. E., "Bubbles in Viscous Liquids: Shapes, Wakes and Velocities," *J. Fluid Mechanics*, Vol. 105 (1981), pp. 61–85
6. Hadamard, J. S., "Mouvement Permanent Lent d'une Sphère Liquide et Visqueuse dans un Liquide Visqueux," *Compt. Rend. Acad. Sci.*, Vol. 152 (1911), pp. 1735–1738.
7. Rybczynski, W., "Uber die Fortschreitende Bewegung einer Flussigen Kugel in einem Zahen Medium," *Bull. Int. Acad. Sci. Cracovie*, Ser. A (1911), pp. 40–46.
8. Stokes, G. G., "On the Effect of the Internal Friction of Fluids on the Motion of Pendulums," *Trans. Cambridge Phi. Soc.*, Vol. 9 (1851), pp. 8–27.
9. Harper, J. F., "The Motion of Bubbles and Drops through Liquids," *Adv. in Appl. Mech.*, Vol. 12 (1972), pp. 59–129.
10. Bond, W. N., and Newton, D. A., "Bubbles, Drops and Newton's Law," *Phil. Mag.*, Vol. 5 (1928), pp. 794–800.
11. Rivkind, V. Y., and Ryskin, G. M., "Flow Structure in Motion of a Spherical Drop," *Fluid Dynamics*, Vol. 1 (1976), pp. 5–12.
12. Johnson, A. I., and Braida, L., "The Velocity of Fall of Circulating and Oscillating Liquid Drops through Quiescent Liquid Phases," *Can. J. Chem. Eng.*, Vol. 35 (1957), pp. 165–172.
13. Hu, S., and Kintner, R. C., "The Fall of Single Liquid Drops through Water," *A.I.Ch.E.J.*, Vol. 1 (1955), pp. 42–50.
14. Davies, R. M., and Taylor, G. I., "The Mechanics of Large Bubbles Rising through Extended Liquids and through Liquids in Tubes," *Proc. Roy. Soc.*, Ser. A, Vol. 200 (1950), pp. 375–390.
15. Grace, J. R., and Harrison, D., "The Influence of Bubble Shape on the Rising Velocities of Large Bubbles, *Chem. Eng. Sci.*, Vol. 22 (1967), pp. 1337–1347.
16. Francis, A. W., "Wall Effect in a Falling Ball Method for Viscometry," *Physics*, Vol. 4 (1933), pp. 403–406.
17. Fidleris, V., and Whitmore, R. L., Experimental Determination of the Wall Effect for Spheres Falling Axially in Cylindrical Vessels, *Brit. J. Appl. Phys.*, Vol. 12 (1961), pp. 490–494.
18. Wallis, G. B., *One-Dimensional Two-Phase Flow*, New York: McGraw Hill, 1969.
19. White E. T., and Beardmore, R. H., "The Velocity of Rise of Single Cylindrical Air Bubbles through Liquids Contained in Vertical Tubes," *Chem. Eng. Sci.*, Vol. 17 (1962), pp. 351–361.

20. Dumitrescu, D. T., Strömung an einer Luftblase in Senkrechten Rohr, *Z. Angew. Math. Mech.*, Vol. 23 (1943), pp. 139–149.
21. Goldsmith, H. L., and Mason, S. G., The Movement of Single Large Bubbles in Closed Vertical Tubes, *J. Fluid Mechanics*, Vol. 14 (1962), pp. 42–58.
22. Zukowski, S. S., "Influence of Viscosity, Surface Tension and Inclination Angle on Motion of Long Bubbles in Closed Tubes," *J. Fluid Mechanics*, Vol. 25 (1966), pp. 821–837.
23. Taylor, T. D., and Acrivos, A., "On the Deformation and Drag of a Falling Viscous Drop at Low Reynolds Number," *J. Fluid Mechanics*, Vol. 18 (1964), pp. 466–476.
24. Pan, F. Y., and Acrivos, A., "Shape of a Drop or Bubble at Low Reynolds Number," *Ind. Eng. Chem. Fundamentals*, Vol. 7 (1968), pp. 227–232.
25. Brignell, A. S., The Deformation of a Liquid Drop at Small Reynolds Number," *Quart. J. Mech. & Appl. Math.*, Vol. 26 (1973), pp. 99–107.
26. Wairegi, T., "The Mechanics of Large Bubbles and Drops Moving through Extended Liquid Media," *Ph.D. dissertation*, Montreal: McGill University, 1974.
27. Wellek, R. M., Agarwal, A. K., and Skelland, A. H. P., "Shape of Liquid Drops Moving in Liquid Media," *A.I.Ch.E. Journal*, Vol. 12 (1966), pp. 854–862.
28. Winnikow, S., and Chao, B. T., "Droplet Motion in Purified Systems," *Phys. Fluids*, Vol. 9 (1966), pp. 50–61.
29. Lamb, H., *Hydrodynamics*, 6th Ed. Cambridge: Cambridge Univ. Press, 1932.
30. Schroeder, R. R., and Kintner, R. C., "Oscillations of Drops Falling in a Liquid Field," *A.I.Ch.E. Journal*, Vol. 11 (1965), pp. 5–8.
31. Pruppacher, H. R., and Beard, K. V., "A Wind Tunnel Investigation of the Internal Circulation and Shape of Water Drops Falling at Terminal Velocity in Air," *Quart. J. Roy. Meteor. Soc.*, Vol. 96 (1970), pp. 247–256.
32. Finlay, B. A., "A Study of Liquid Drops in an Air Stream," *Ph.D. dissertation*, Birmingham: Univ. of Birmingham, 1957.
33. LeClair, B. P., et al., "A Theoretical and Experimental Study of the Internal Circulation in Water Drops Falling at Terminal Velocity in Air," *J. Atmos. Sci.*, Vol. 29 (1972), pp. 728–740.
34. Magono, C., "On the Shape of Water Drops Falling in Stagnant Air," *J. Meteorology*, Vol. 11 (1954), pp. 77–79.
35. Yao, S.-C., and Schrock, V. E., "Heat and Mass Transfer from Freely Falling Drops, *J. Heat Transfer*, Vol. 98 (1976), pp. 120–125.
36. Bhaga, D., "Bubbles in Viscous Liquids: Shapes, Wakes and Velocities," *Ph.D. dissertation*, Montreal: McGill University, 1976.
37. Gaudin, A. M., *Flotation*, 2nd Ed., New York: McGraw-Hill, 1957.

CHAPTER 4

BUBBLE FORMATION AND ITS MOVEMENT IN NEWTONIAN AND NON-NEWTONIAN LIQUIDS

N. Räbiger and A. Vogelpohl

Institut fur Thermische Verfahrenstechnik
Clausthal-Zellerfeld, Fed. Rep. West Germany

CONTENTS

INTRODUCTION

For mass-transfer processes in gas-liquid systems, the gas is frequently dispersed in the liquid by means of static devices, such as sieve plates or perforated plates. It is thereby endeavored to achieve an interfacial area between the phases which is as large as possible. The generation of the interface can be subdivided into partial processes:

- Bubble formation at the gas distributor.
- Coalescence and redispersion processes during the ascent.

In spite of their great practical importance, the calculation of these partial processes in advance remains essentially an unsolved problem. Consequently, empirical or semiempirical relationships are employed for the calculation of the interfacial area. These relationships are often based on the laws of single-bubble formation.

In the literature, the process of bubble formation is consistently subdivided into a bubble regime and a jet regime. The bubble regime is described in terms of the periodic formation of single bubbles, or of double bubbles in the range of transition to the jet regime [1]. For this regime, models have been developed for describing the process of bubble formation on the basis of comprehensive investigations in stagnant Newtonian liquids [2, 3]. An extension of these models to bubble formation in the presence of a superimposed liquid motion [4] and for non-Newtonian liquids [5 to 11] has been carried out in the work described in References 50 to 52.

For the jet regime, a different mechanism of bubble formation has been assumed. A gas jet thereby forms in the liquid [1] and disintegrates into single bubbles at its upper contour. On the basis of results obtained by Leibson [12] as well as by Hallensleben and Schügerl [13], which partially contradict the proposed mechanism, Räbiger and Vogelpohl [50 to 52] have proved that single or double bubbles are always formed at the dispersing orifice in the so-called jet regime, too. Thus, a unified description of the bubble formation process is possible over the entire range of gas throughout.

EXPERIMENTAL RESULTS AND DISCUSSION

Bubble Formation at Capillaries

Qualitative Description of the Bubble Formation Process

In the literature a distinction is made between a bubble regime and a jet regime. Accordingly, bubbles are formed at the capillary orifice in the former regime (primary bubbles), whereas they are supposed to form at the upper contour of a connected gas jet in the latter regime (secondary bubbles). The gas throughput at which the change in the mechanism of bubble formation occurs is designated as "critical" throughput. The secondary bubbles of the jet regime are considerably smaller than the primary bubbles of the bubble regime [1, 14]. More recent investigations with the use of high speed movies in conjunction with the synchronous measurement of the bubble formation pressure do not support the view that such a transition occurs in the bubble formation mechanism. On the contrary, an evaluation of the high speed movies and pressure recordings indicates the formation of single and double bubbles at capillary orifices over the entire gas throughput range, as observed by Hallensleben and Schügerl [13].

Similar results are shown by the microphotographs in Figures 1 and 2 for bubble formation at various values of the gas throughput. It is evident that no change in the mechanism of primary

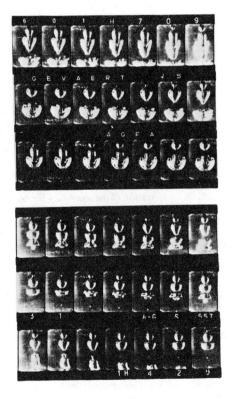

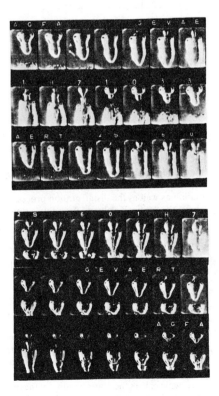

Figure 1. Microphotographs of bubble formation in bubble regime: $V_g = 68.6$ l/h, We $= 1.23$, and stagnant liquid (water).

Figure 2. Microphotographs of bubble formation in jet regime: $V_g = 119$ l/h, We $= 3.7$, and stagnant liquid (water).

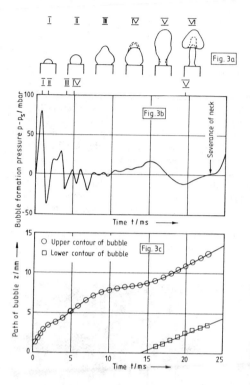

Figure 3. Bubble formation process at $\dot{V}_g = 101$ l/h, $w_k = 0$ cm/s, $d = 2$ mm.

bubble formation occurs with increasing volume flow of gas; single or double bubbles are always formed. The recorded pressure also does not indicate any fundamental change of the characteristic spectra with increasing throughput. Even though jet formation has not been observed anywhere in the entire range investigated, the term "jet regime" will still be employed for denoting the range in which the secondary bubbles are smaller than the primary bubbles. The mechanism of bubble formation as well as the disintegration process which leads to the formation of the secondary bubbles above the "critical" value of the volume flow rate of gas are described in the following with the use of Figure 3. The overall formation process is thereby subdivided into six stages.

Stage I. During the formation of the upper bubble contour, the bubble pressure passes through a maximum upon attainment of the hemispherical shape. The maximum increases linearly with augmenting gas throughput.

Stages II to IV. After vigorous initial expansion associated with a pronounced pressure drop, intermittent expansion interrupted by slight compression of the gas occurs repeatedly. The inertial force due to the vigorous liquid motion induced by the preceding bubble affects the formation process. As a result of this inertia, the bubble tends to expand. In the range where the inertial force acts, a small upper contour first arises at the edge of the bubble. This is associated with a pronounced decrease in pressure. As soon as a certain underpressure has been attained, and the neighboring liquid layers at the bubble surface have consequently decelerated, the subsequent increase in pressure once again causes the upper contour of the bubble to become uniform. This proceeds until an—albeit weaker—inertial force becomes effective (Figures 3b and 3c).

Phase V. As soon as the detaching forces are sufficiently strong, the bubble ascends with constant velocity (Figure 3c) above the orifice. However, it remains connected with the orifice through a neck. Since the volume increase exceeds the volume of the gas supplied, the pressure in the bubble decreases to a value below the pressure of the system, until equilibrium between the gas and liquid pressure acting on the neck has been established. The neck subsequently constricts, and the pressure in the capillary correspondingly rises until the system pressure has been reached.

The severed bubble tends to assume the least possible surface area; this results in motion of the neck toward and into the bubble. Liquid from the surroundings is thereby entrained and drawn into the bubble. Disintegration of the primary bubble occurs if the acceleration of this liquid is so high that it is transported beyond the upper contour of the bubble.

Stage VI. As can be seen from the movies and pressure recordings, the motion of the neck becomes especially violent when a "critical" value of the throughput is exceeded; that is, when the so-called jet regime is attained. Consequently, a second, smaller bubble with a correspondingly smaller pressure maximum is drawn out of the capillary orifice and collides with the lower contour of the primary bubble. As a result of the neck and liquid motion into the bubble, as described in conjunction with Stage V, disintegration of the bubble and thus the generation of secondary bubbles occurs.

Bubble Formation in Stagnant Liquids

Bubble formation in Newtonian liquids. In Figure 4, the measured values of the diameter of primary bubbles (open symbols) and secondary bubbles (filled symbols) are plotted as functions of the gas volume flow for the water-air system. It is evident that the diameter of the primary bubbles increases continuously with the volume flow rate of the gas. Moreover, the observed dependence is thoroughly reproduced by the plotted curve, which corresponds to a correlation given by Mersmann [16] for the bubble diameter at low gas throughput [1].

The diameter of the bubbles at a height of about 100 mm above the capillary orifice (i.e., the diameter of the secondary bubbles) is designated by the filled symbols. For a gas volume flow rate less than 70 l/h, the diameter of the primary bubbles concurs with that of the secondary bubbles. Above this "critical" throughput, however, the secondary bubbles are considerably smaller and behave in accordance with a correlation given by Brauer [1] and based on values measured by Siemes [14]. This "critical" gas throughput is employed as boundary criterion for the "jet regime" in the literature [1, 14, 16–18]. The Weber number, which results from the "critical" throughput found in this investigation, is We = 1.3 and is in agreement with the literature data compiled by Ruff [18].

As described later, Stage VI, the liquid motion induced by the neck above the "critical" throughput is capable of causing disintegration of the primary bubble. The length of the neck is thereby decisive. In Figure 5, the measured length of the neck is plotted as a function of the volume flow rate of gas. In the evaluation of microphotographs (Figures 1 and 2), the distance between the site of severance for the neck and the lower contour of the bubble has been employed as neck length. It

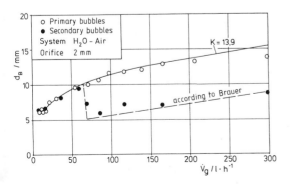

Figure 4. Bubble diameter vs. gas flow rate.

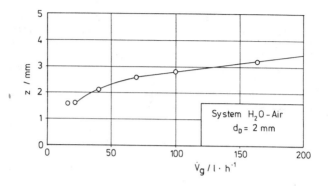

Figure 5. Length of neck at severance point in liquid at rest.

can be recognized that the neck steadily becomes longer with increasing gas throughput; the disintegrating action augments correspondingly.

The inclusion of the neck motion and of the liquid motion thus induced into the description of the bubble formation mechanism offers the possibility of coherently explaining the bubble formation process over the entire throughput range and for varied material data for the first time. Thus, a bubble formation mechanism similar to that for the water-air system is also observed in liquids of higher viscosity. In this case too, the liquid motion induced by the neck tends to draw a second bubble out of the capillary. In accordance with the formation mechanism described earlier, Stage V, however, progressively shorter connecting necks are formed with increasing viscosity and for constant throughput, since the pressure in the liquid layers near the neck increases with viscosity as a result of the decreasing share of gas in the flow channel. Consequently, the gas throughput must be increased with augmenting viscosity in order to draw a second, smaller bubble with a smaller pressure maximum from the capillary.

The process of primary bubble disintegration is affected by the viscosity similarly to the way the bubble formation is affected by pressure. However, the decisive resistance is situated in the annular flow between the phase boundaries of two successive bubbles. As indicated in Figure 6, the neck motion is capable of drawing a second, smaller bubble from the capillary, above certain values of the gas throughput. This bubble subsequently penetrates into the upper bubble from below, under the promoting influence of the liquid motion which it has induced.

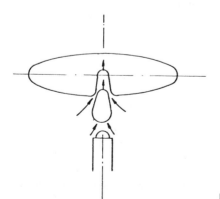

Figure 6. Annular flow between two bubbles.

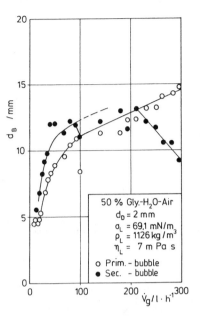

Figure 7. Bubble diameter in glycerol water system vs. gas flow rate.

An annulus is formed between the two bubbles; liquid is entrained through this annulus as a result of the neck motion. With augmenting viscosity, however, the neck motion no longer suffices for generating the required pressure difference, and the bubbles therefore coalesce.

In Figure 7 the measured values of the diameter are plotted as functions of the gas volume flow rate for primary bubbles (open symbols) and secondary bubbles (filled symbols), for a 50-50 mixture of glycerol and water. Here, too, it is evident that the diameter of the primary bubbles increases with augmenting gas volume flow, as in the case of the water-air system. However, a sudden change in diameter is observed at a gas throughput of 100 l/h. This is explained by a transition from double-bubble formation to multiple-bubble formation.

The diameter of the bubbles at a height of about 100 mm above the capillary orifice (i.e., that of the secondary bubbles) is designated by the filled symbols. Double bubbles are formed even at low values of the gas throughput; they subsequently coalesce as a result of the neck motion. Hence, the diameter of the secondary bubbles is larger than that of the primary bubbles. Smaller secondary bubbles do not occur again until a gas volume flow of 100 l/h has been attained, since not all of the bubbles coalesce after multiple-bubble formation. With a further increase of the gas volume flow, the neck motion becomes more vigorous; consequently, coalescence no longer occurs, and thus the diameter of the primary bubbles concurs with that of the secondary bubbles. If the "critical" throughput is exceeded, the liquid motion induced by the neck causes the primary bubble to disintegrate, and the secondary bubbles become considerably smaller.

The influence exerted by the viscosity on the disintegration process, and thus on the beginning of the "jet regime," is shown in Figure 8, in which the Weber number at the "critical" gas throughput is plotted against the dynamic viscosity. The effect of the viscosity on the neck motion is clearly evident from this result too.

Bubble formation in non-Newtonian liquids. In the course of investigations with structurally viscous $CMC\text{-}H_2O$ solutions and viscoelastic $PAA\text{-}H_2O$ solutions, the formation of a jet is likewise not observed. Instead, the bubble formation mechanism previously described has been confirmed here, too. A difference in behavior, as opposed to Newtonian liquids, can be recognized only in the rheological effect on the neck motion and on the liquid motion induced by the neck [52].

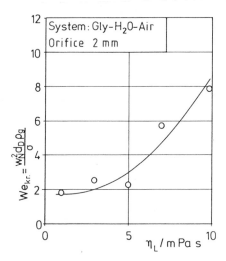

Figure 8. Critical gas flow rate at onset of jetting.

● *Structurally viscous liquids.* Liquids whose viscosity decreases with increasing shear stress are designated as structurally viscous. An example is presented by the CMC-H_2O solution whose behavior is illustrated in Figure 9. The solution is characterized by time-independent, non-Newtonian behavior. The increased viscosity at low shear stress is attributed to the cross-linkage of the long CMC molecules [20]. At a shear rate of $\dot{D} \geq 70$ s^{-1}, a high viscosity of the solution no longer results from cross-linkage of the CMC molecules, and the solution exhibits Newtonian flow behavior. As far as the bubble formation process is concerned, this implies that the formation mechanism can be influenced by non-Newtonian behavior only at a shear rate of $\dot{D} \leq 70$ s^{-1}

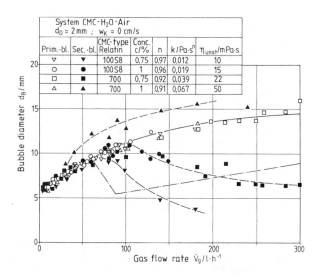

Figure 9. Bubble diameter in CMC solutions vs. gas flow rate.

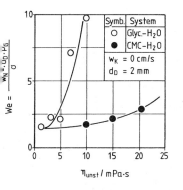

Figure 10. Critical gas flow rate at the onset of jetting.

In Figure 9 the measured diameter of the primary bubbles (open symbols) and secondary bubbles (filled symbols) is plotted as a function of the gas throughput for CMC solutions. It can be seen that the diameter of the primary bubbles steadily increases with augmenting volume flow rate of gas, just as for Newtonian liquids, and is of the same magnitude as for the water-air system. As opposed to the results for the glycerol-water system (Newtonian liquid), for which the viscosity exerts a considerable influence on the size of the primary bubbles at values beyond 30 mPa·s, no change in diameter is observed as far as a lower Newtonian viscosity of 60 mPa·s. However, the viscosity, and thus the rheological behavior of the liquid exerts a decisive influence on the secondary bubble formation. It can be seen from the results (filled symbols in Figure 9) that the dispersion of the primary bubbles is favoured by the induced liquid motion and by the non-Newtonian flow behavior. In contrast to Newtonian liquids (Figure 7), the so-called "jet regime" commences sooner for structurally viscous liquids, and the tendency toward coalescence occurs only at higher viscosities. The cause for this observation is the alteration of the flow profile for the induced liquid motion as well as the reduction of the frictional resistance to the annular flow by the altered rheology.

The result is a more thorough dispersion of the primary bubbles, and thus earlier inception of the "jet regime" (Figure 10). Moreover, coalescence of the two bubbles does not set in until a higher value of the viscosity has been reached.

During the formation of primary bubbles, vigorous motion of the liquid causes deformation of the upper contour of the bubble, as described earlier, since stronger inertial forces act on the bubble during the first stage of formation. Consequently, longer bubbles are formed. The buoyant force on the bubble does not change during this process (Figures 1 and 2; and see Figure 11 for bubble size) since a corresponding portion is covered by the capillary orifice. This process is especially evident in the case of viscoelastic liquids.

Viscoelastic liquids. Viscoelastic liquids are media which exhibit time-dependent flow behavior. They are characterized by viscous behavior as well as deformational elasticity. Thus, the stress state of a viscoelastic medium at a given time depends on the prehistory of deformation. For example, see Reference 22. The elastic behavior of the liquid is of particular importance during the formation of secondary bubbles, since the liquid is thereby subject to periodic stress as a result of the neck motion.

As described earlier for structurally viscous liquids, the altered rheological behavior leads to an increase in the motion of the liquid induced by the neck for viscoelastic liquids, too. In this case, the cause of the phenomenon is associated with the deformation of the elements of liquid. After the severance of the neck from the capillary orifice, the elements of liquid are strongly deformed in the direction of motion, as a result of the subsequent acceleration of the neck end. This causes a pronounced increase in the so-called elongational viscosity, according to Durst [21]. The resistance due to the deformation of the liquid elements dominates over that due to the shear viscosity and is perpendicular to the direction of motion [21]. Hence, this rheological

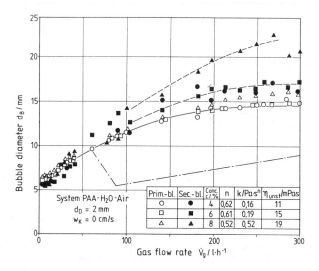

Prim.-bl.	Sec.-bl.	Conc. c/%	n	k/Pa·s^n	η_{unst}/mPas
O	●	4	0,62	0,16	11
□	■	6	0,61	0,19	15
△	▲	8	0,52	0,52	19

System PAA-H_2O-Air
d_D = 2 mm
w_K = 0 cm/s

Figure 11. Bubble diameter in PAA solutions vs. gas flow rate.

behavior of the liquid causes the subsequent bubbles to be elongated, as a result of the stronger suction (Figure 12). Since the bubble shape, and especially the lower contour of the bubble, is also altered as a consequence, the detachment process is decisively affected during primary bubble formation.

As has been shown for structurally viscous liquids, the effect of the liquid motion induced by the neck is equivalent to that of the motion during detachment on the primary bubble. No deviation in diameter of the primary bubbles has been observed, as compared to the air-water

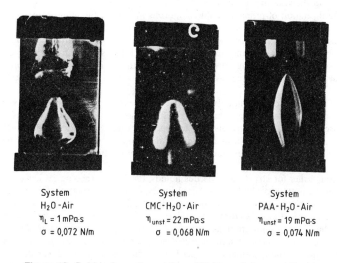

System	System	System
H_2O-Air	CMC-H_2O-Air	PAA-H_2O-Air
η_L = 1 mPa·s	η_{unst} = 22 mPa·s	η_{unst} = 19 mPa·s
σ = 0,072 N/m	σ = 0,068 N/m	σ = 0,074 N/m

Figure 12. Bubble formation at V_g = 126 l/h and stagnant liquid.

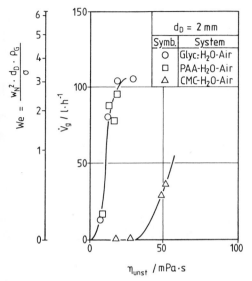

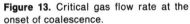

Figure 13. Critical gas flow rate at the onset of coalescence.

system with altered rheological behavior of the liquid. In Figure 11, the measured diameter has been plotted as a function of the gas throughput for primary bubbles (open symbols) and secondary bubbles (filled symbols). For viscoelastic liquids, too, the diameter of the primary bubbles is in agreement with the results for the water-air system, with the exception of the values for the 8% PAA solution at high gas throughput and the correspondingly higher resistance. For the diameter of the secondary bubbles, in contrast, considerable differences are observed. These are due to the more pronounced effect exerted on the subsequent bubble by the liquid motion induced by the severance of the neck, as in the case of structurally viscous liquids. Hence, for viscoelastic liquids too, the pressure maximum which must be overcome is smaller than that for Newtonian liquids. In comparison with corresponding, structurally viscous liquids, however, it is also evident that a stronger inertial force acts on the newly forming bubble because of the elasticity in viscoelastic liquids. Thus, even longer bubbles are created at equilibrium (Figure 12). This bubble shape persists after their severance, too, because of the properties of the liquid already described. Hence, these results confirm the eccentricity measurements performed by Acharya [23] during bubble ascent.

The occurrence of longer primary bubbles exerts a decisive influence on the secondary bubble formation. After the induction of liquid motion by the neck, liquid penetrates into the primary bubble and draws a second, smaller bubble from the capillary orifice. Since the pressure in the primary bubble thereby increases, the neck decelerates, and the liquid tends to recover the energy expended in deforming the liquid elements. Precisely this amount of energy must again be consumed for overcoming the resistance of the annular flow between the two bubbles, in order to generate the deformation of the liquid elements there during the development of this flow. Consequently, the bubbles coalesce because of the increase in pressure predetermined by the bubble shape, since this pressure cannot be overcome. The tendency toward coalescence must be similar to that for Newtonian liquids, since the decreasing deformation in the neck is compensated by the augmenting deformation of the liquid elements in the annular flow. As in the case of Newtonian liquids, therefore, the coalescence is affected only by the friction of the annular flow. In Figure 13, the values of the gas throughput and Weber number determined in the present investigation are plotted as functions of the steady-state, lower Newtonian viscosity of the liquid; for these values, the corresponding resistance of the annular flow is so high that the bubbles coalesce.

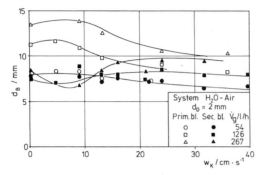

Figure 14. Bubble diameter in cocurrent flow vs. superficial liquid velocity.

Bubble Formation in Liquids Subject to Forced Motion

A liquid in forced motion influences the process of bubble formation in a way similar to that for the viscosity; the direction of motion thereby exerts the decisive influence [50].

Bubble formation in Newtonian liquids.

• *Cocurrent liquid motion.* For cocurrent motion of gas bubbles and liquid, only the length of the neck is affected by the superimposed flow. In Figure 14, the measured bubble size is plotted against the velocity of the liquid for cocurrent motion. A weakly defined maximum of the primary bubble diameter can be recognized in the range of low velocity; the diameter also decreases with increasing velocity.

The maximum is attributed to a rearrangement of the flow profile. If the rearrangement of the flow profile has been completed and the forced liquid motion dominates, the rate of bubble detachment also augments with increasing velocity, while the neck becomes smaller. This implies a corresponding decline in the neck motion, until the detached bubble finally can no longer disintegrate.

These results also explain a maximum in the relative gas content of the bubble column observed by Otake [24] for cocurrent motion of the liquid and low flow velocity in a recent investigation.

• *Countercurrent liquid motion.* For countercurrent motion of gas bubbles and liquid, the mechanism of bubble formation is affected chiefly by the resistance induced by the flow of liquid. In Figure 15, the measured diameter of the primary and secondary bubbles is plotted as a function of the average liquid velocity in the flow channel. A weakly defined maximum of the primary bubble diameter can be recognized at low velocity. The cause of this phenomenon is the low detachment rate of the bubble, which results in the formation of a longer neck. The lengthening of the neck

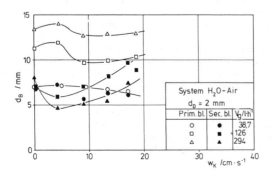

Figure 15. Bubble diameter in countercurrent flow vs. superficial liquid velocity.

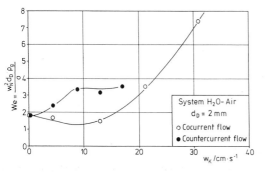

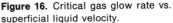

Figure 16. Critical gas glow rate vs. superficial liquid velocity.

favors the process of disintegration, and thus results in the generation of smaller secondary bubbles.

With the generation of progressively smaller secondary bubbles, and thus an increase in the share of gas above the capillary orifice, the liquid can no longer act without disturbance on the primary bubble which is being formed as the velocity increases further. Consequently, the primary bubble diameter decreases again. At a velocity higher than about 0.1 m/s, shield-shaped primary bubbles are formed. These bubbles in turn shield the succeeding five or six bubbles from the liquid flow. Hence, the latter bubbles form without disturbance and have correspondingly shorter necks. Thus, the process of disintegration is impeded.

With increasing velocity of the liquid, the shielding bubbles are generated at progressively shorter intervals. Hence, the diameter of the primary bubbles augments slightly once again, whereas the disintegration process is progressively impeded.

● *Comparison of bubble formation for cocurrent and countercurrent liquid motion.* The effect of the direction and velocity of liquid motion on the disintegration process is illustrated in Figure 16. The required "critical" gas throughput is thereby plotted in terms of the critical Weber number, as a function of the liquid velocity.

As already described in the preceding section, the shape of the primary bubble changes from the spherical shape for liquid at rest to a shield shape at a liquid velocity exceeding 0.1 m/s. At a lower flow velocity of the liquid and for an approximately spherical shape of the bubble, the flow causes an additional resistance to the liquid motion induced by the neck. Hence, a higher gas throughput is necessary, in order to effect disintegration of the bubble. That is, the "inception of the jet regime" is shifted to higher values of the Weber number with increasing liquid velocity. If, however, primary, shield-shaped bubbles are formed ($w_K \geq 0.1$ m/s), the gas content in the liquid above the capillary is so high that the liquid flow can no longer influence the bubble being formed without disturbance. Correspondingly, the resistance, and thus the "critical" gas through-put, remain constant.

These results explain the required critical Weber number of 4, as reported by Gerstenberg [25] for a liquid in cocurrent and countercurrent motion, with the use of perforated plates. This value is necessary in order to achieve uniform flow through the holes, and thus bubble formation in the "jet regime" [26, 27].

Bubble formation in non-Newtonian liquids.

● *Cocurrent liquid motion.* As already described for Newtonian liquids, a cocurrently moving non-Newtonian liquid affects only the formation of the neck, and thus the liquid motion thereby induced.

● *Structurally viscous liquid.* For structurally viscous liquids, too, a weakly defined maximum of the primary bubble diameter at low liquid velocity and a decrease in diameter with augmenting velocity can be recognized in Figure 17. As in the case of Newtonian liquids, the result for the

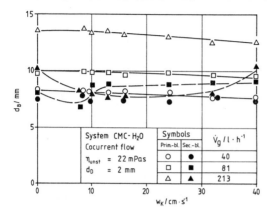

Figure 17. Bubble diameter in co-current flow vs. superficial liquid velocity.

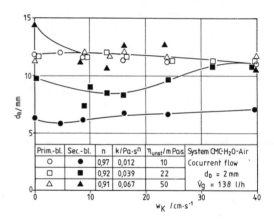

Figure 18. Bubble diameter in co-current flow vs. superficial liquid velocity.

secondary bubbles can be attributed to the rearrangement of the flow profile at low velocity here, too. The resulting longer neck induces a more pronounced motion of the liquid after severance of the bubble than would be the case in a liquid at rest. Consequently, the primary bubbles are more effectively dispersed. With increasing liquid velocity in the channel, the forced motion of the liquid dominates over the rearrangement of the flow profile, and the neck becomes shorter once again. Hence, a higher liquid velocity is necessary for influencing the so-called jet regime for structurally viscous liquids (Figures 17 and 18). The cause of this observation is the decrease in resistance of the annular flow due to the altered rheological behavior, as already described. As a result, a shorter neck is better for maintaining the annular flow in structurally viscous liquids than in Newtonian liquids. This conclusion is confirmed by the plot of the required critical gas throughput as a function of the liquid velocity in Figure 19.

- *Viscoelastic liquid.* In the case of viscoelastic liquids, it is difficult to describe the influence of cocurrent liquid motion on the bubble formation process, since the additional effect of a rearrangement of the flow profile at the capillary orifice on the rheological behavior is not known. In Figures 20 and 21, the measured bubble size is plotted as a function of the liquid velocity. As for Newtonian and structurally viscous liquids, a weakly defined maximum of the primary bubble diameter at low velocity, and a decrease in diameter with increasing velocity can be recognized.

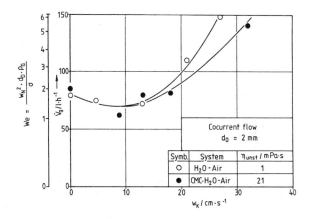

Figure 19. Critical gas flow rate at the onset of jetting.

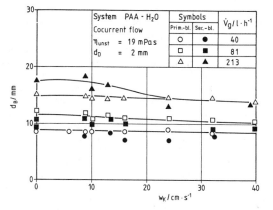

Figure 20. Bubble diameter in co-current flow vs. superficial liquid velocity.

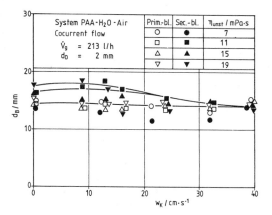

Figure 21. Bubble diameter in co-current flow vs. superficial liquid velocity.

As already described, the cause of this observation is a rearrangement of the flow profile at the capillary orifice. The velocity component which thereby becomes effective and is directed toward the bubble gives rise to the formation of longer necks and larger primary bubbles. Because of the deformational elasticity of the liquid already described, the shape of the primary bubble persists after its severance. Hence, for the reasons already known, the neck is not capable of causing the primary bubble to disintegrate, and the two bubbles created during double-bubble formation coalesce. If however, the superimposed liquid motion dominates, the detachment velocity of the bubbles augments, and the neck becomes shorter. As a result, the effect of the liquid motion induced by the neck becomes weaker, and the distance between the two bubbles generated during double-bubble formation increases. This is the cause of the decrease in the tendency toward coalescence with increasing velocity.

- *Countercurrent liquid motion.*
  1. *Structurally viscous liquid.* The effect of liquid flow which is countercurrent to the bubble motion operates essentially through an increased resistance on the detachment motion of the bubble and on the liquid motion induced by the neck. This results in slower detachment motion and the formation of longer necks than those formed in liquids at rest. After severance of the bubble, the more vigorous liquid motion induced by the neck causes a more effective disintegration of the primary bubbles and a decrease in the secondary bubble diameter at lower liquid velocity. The associated increase of the gas content in the channel no longer permits direct action of the liquid flow on the process of primary bubble formation. Hence, the primary bubbles again become smaller with augmenting liquid velocity, while the disintegrating effect of the induced liquid motion becomes less pronounced.

     In Figure 22, the measured diameter is plotted as a function of the liquid velocity. The formation mechanism already described occurs only in the case of a structurally viscous liquid with a viscosity of 10 mPa·s. At a higher viscosity of the liquid, such a maximum of the primary bubble diameter and minimum of the secondary bubble diameter are no longer observed. Instead, the diameter of the primary bubble remains constant with augmenting liquid velocity, and the disintegrating action of the induced liquid motion steadily declines (Figure 23).
  2. *Viscoelastic liquid.* The effect of countercurrent motion of a viscoelastic liquid on the process of primary bubble formation is similar to that described for low gas throughput in structurally viscous liquids. The cause of this effect is the persistence of the bubble shape due to the deformational elasticity of the liquid, and thus the resulting coalescence of the primary bubbles. The higher the liquid velocity the more primary bubbles coalesce, since the motion of the ascending bubble decelerates and the subsequent bubbles can move faster in the flow zone of the lower bubble contour. The distance between the bubbles thereby becomes so large that the liquid flow can act without hindrance on the primary bubble formation (Figures 24 and 25).

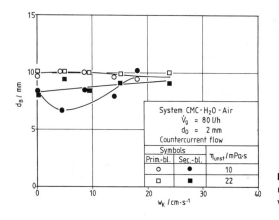

Figure 22. Bubble diameter in countercurrent flow vs. superficial liquid velocity.

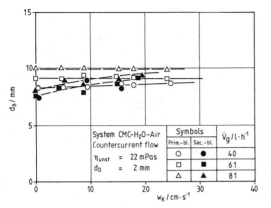

Figure 23. Bubble diameter in countercurrent flow vs. superficial liquid velocity.

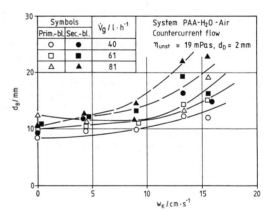

Figure 24. Bubble diameter in countercurrent flow vs. superficial liquid velocity.

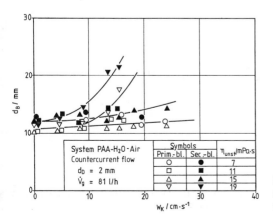

Figure 25. Bubble diameter in countercurrent flow vs. superficial liquid velocity.

Bubble Motion

As already implied in the preceding sections, knowledge of the process of bubble ascent and of the associated processes of coalescence and redispersion are a prerequisite for a hydrodynamic interpretation of bubble columns. On the basis of results concerning the bubble formation process at capillaries and single-hole plates, Klug [28] has successfully described the redispersion process and thus the stable bubble diameter with the use of sieve plates. Hence, the determination of the velocity of ascent for the bubble swarm is of decisive importance. Despite its great practical importance, a theoretical description of the swarm behavior remains an essentially unsolved problem. Therefore, empirical or semiempirical relationships based on the laws of motion for single bubbles must be employed for the purpose of predictions. This important process for single bubbles moving in Newtonian and non-Newtonian liquids is analyzed more closely in the following.

Bubble Motion in Newtonian Liquids

Very many publications concerning the motion of single bubbles in Newtonian liquids exist [1, 26, 32, 33, etc.]. The decisive influence exerted on the motion is attributed to the mobile interface [1, 32, 33] and/or to the change in the resistive force due to the bubble shape [1, 29, 30, 31]. The effect of bubble deformation on the velocity of ascent, and the less pronounced alteration of the bubble shape with increasing viscosity of the liquid have been demonstrated especially during the investigations of bubble formation in various viscous liquids by Tapucu [34] and Tadaki [35]. From [26, 32, 33, 36, 37], it is also evident that the bubble motion already changes at a viscosity of about 7 mPa·s for the liquid and that the motion then differs from that of rigid spheres only in the mobility of the interface. In Figure 26, the velocity of ascent for a single bubble is plotted as a function of the bubble diameter for a sphere of equal volume. It can be seen that a decrease in the velocity of ascent, as described by Brauer [1], for a certain range of bubble diameter occurs only up to a viscosity of 7 mPa·s in glycerol-water mixtures. Although such a change in the bubble shape also occurs in liquids of higher viscosity, it does not exert any decisive influence on the path of motion of the bubble, which describes a helical path in liquids of lower viscosity. Consequently, a continuous increase in the velocity of ascent with. augmenting bubble diameter is ob-

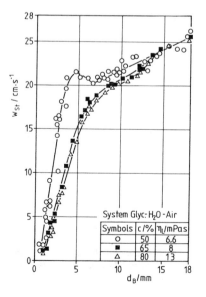

Figure 26. Bubble-rise velocity of air bubbles in Newtonian liquids.

served when the viscosity is higher than 7 mPa·s. Moreover, after the completion of deformation of the bubble to a shield shape, the velocity of bubble ascent has been observed to be independent of the viscosity of the liquid in the present investigation, too. This concurs with the results from the publications already cited.

Bubble Motion in Non-Newtonian Liquids

The motion of bubbles in non-Newtonian liquids has been considered in only a very few investigations [7–10, 42–47], in contrast to that in Newtonian liquids. This is due to the insufficient knowledge of the rheological behavior of the liquids and its effect on the bubble motion.

The first investigation of bubble motion in structurally viscous CMC-H_2O solutions and viscoelastic PAA-H_2O solutions has been conducted by Astarita and Apuzzo [9]. In contrast to CMC-H_2O solutions, a discontinuity in the velocity of ascent as a function of the bubble volume has been observed for the viscoelastic liquids investigated. This has been confirmed by subsequent investigations by other authors [8, 38, 39]. The sudden increase in velocity of ascent up to a value higher by a factor of 5 to 10 [9, 38, 39] is ascribed to a change in the interface from a rigid to mobile state. On the other hand, Acharya, Mashelkar, and Ulbrecht [8] have observed a considerably smaller increase in the velocity of ascent for all liquids employed during a comprehensive study of the bubble motion and of the deformation in non-Newtonian liquids. In the course of this investigation, it has also been suggested that a change in the state of motion of the interface cannot be the sole cause of the sudden change in the velocity of ascent, since this results in only a rather slow increase in the latter. In agreement with the results of other investigations involving the influence of surfactants, it is supposed that the sudden increase in the velocity of ascent is due to a surfactant effect exerted by the polymer molecules of the non-Newtonian liquids employed. In this case, the resulting gradient of interfacial tension for bubbles of diameter less than a certain critical diameter would give rise to a higher resistance. Above this critical value, the liquid continually renews the bubble surface, and thus renders possible the sudden increase in the velocity of ascent. According to Reference 8, the ratio of velocity of ascent before and after the increase can be computed as a function of the liquid index n for viscoelastic and structurally viscous liquids.

Results and discussion. A prerequisite for the investigation of bubble motion is the generation of single-bubble motions corresponding to those in a bubble swarm. For Newtonian and structurally viscous liquids which exhibit time-independent rheological behavior without differences in normal stress, it can be assumed that this condition is almost always satisfied. That is, after the generation of the bubble (whether at capillaries or at oscillating spoons) it is deformed as a result of the pressure and force conditions which prevail during the ascent until an equilibrium shape is established. In contrast, the difference in normal stress is effective in the case of viscoelastic liquids. Hence, the generation of bubbles can occur only at capillaries, in order that real conditions be simulated, and the mutual interaction between the bubbles govern the bubble shape (refer to Figure 13). A circulation of liquid around the bubble thereby sets in during and after the bubble formation. Because of the elastic properties of the liquid, this circulation gives rise to the establishment of normal stress differences, as a result of which the bubble shape created during the formation persists during the ascent, too. As explained, earlier, this behavior of the liquid also appears to be the cause of the differing and contradictory results presented in the literature.

• *Structurally viscous liquids.* Because of the situation already described, the motion of bubbles in structurally viscous CMC-H_2O solutions is nearly independent of the type of bubble generation. In Figure 27, the velocity of ascent measured in various CMC-H_2O solutions is plotted as a function of the bubble diameter. A definitely larger, discontinuous increase in the velocity of ascent is evident with decreasing flow index n. Only in the case of a CMC-H_2O solution which exhibits approximately Newtonian flow behavior does such a discontinuity not occur. Once the development of the bubble shape has been completed, the velocity of ascent again increases continuously.

For a different type of CMC, or for a more highly concentrated CMC-H_2O solution with a lower flow index n, the same alteration in the bubble shape occurs; however, in this case the

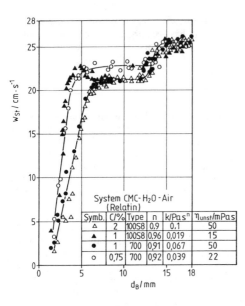

Figure 27 legend table:

Symb.	C/%	Type	n	$k/Pa \cdot s^n$	$\eta_{unst}/mPa \cdot s$
△	2	100S8	0,9	0,1	50
▲	1	100S8	0,96	0,019	15
●	1	700	0,91	0,067	50
○	0,75	700	0,92	0,039	22

System CMC-H_2O-Air (Relatin)

d_B/mm

Figure 27. Bubble rise velocity of air bubbles in CMC solutions.

bubbles move only with a slight oscillating motion and with a constant velocity, as opposed to Newtonian liquids. In the range of small bubble diameter, too, the magnitude of the measured velocity of ascent is greater than that for comparable Newtonian liquids (Figure 19). It is therefore concluded that the motion of the bubbles is more vigorous in CMC-H_2O solutions, for which the bubble motion is hindered by a surfactant effect of the adjacent CMC molecules in the range of larger bubble diameter. Thus, the resistance augments, and the velocity of ascent remains constant. The creation of a gradient of surface tension due to the adjacent CMC molecules is influenced by the concentration and length of the CMC molecules; for the shortest CMC molecules employed, the hindrance of the interfacial motion exerts no visible influence.

With a further increase in bubble diameter, a discontinuous increase in the velocity of ascent finally occurs. The cause for this observation, according to Acharya et al. [8], is a purifying effect on the interface due to the augmenting circulation around the bubble, whereby the adjoining CMC molecules are removed. Thus, a vigorous motion of the interface is suddenly initiated, and the resistance is reduced. This concept is confirmed in Figure 28, in which the average resistance coefficient c_w is plotted as a function of a modified Reynolds number. In the range of low Reynolds number, the decrease in the resistance coefficient due to the addition of CMC can clearly be seen, as compared to Newtonian liquids. Furthermore, the results show that the resistance coefficient becomes larger with decreasing flow index n, because of the presumed surfactant effect of the CMC molecules in the range of bubble deformation from an ellipsoidal to a shield shape, that is, in the range $1 \leq Re \leq 10$. If the bubble diameter, and thus the Reynolds number, increases further, the discontinuous decrease in the resistance coefficient can be recognized. This is attributed by Acharya [8] to the removal of CMC molecules from the interface, or to the elimination of the gradient of surface tension by some other mechanism. A conspicuous feature is the fact that the function resumes its general course after the discontinuous change in the resistance coefficient with increasing Reynolds number. This result suggests that the discontinuous increase in the velocity of ascent is caused not only by the removal of surface-active substances from the bubble surface, but rather that the bubble shape and path of motion also exert a considerable influence.

A comparison of all results of measurements performed on CMC-H_2O solutions with those from the literature for other CMC solutions is feasible only provided the liquid index n, as determined from the model of Ostwald-de Waele, deviates only slightly from unity. For liquids with

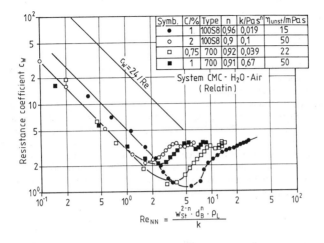

Figure 28. Resistance coefficient for air bubbles in CMC-solutions.

a greater deviation, the solution becomes viscoelastic, thus giving rise to different rheological behavior. For this reason, a comparison with the few data available from the literature is not feasible. The data hitherto published have resulted exclusively from measurements performed on CMC solutions which exhibit Newtonian [9] or viscoelastic flow behavior [8].

● *Viscoelastic liquids.* As already described in the introduction to this section, the generation of bubbles as occurs in practice is a prerequisite for a measurement of the velocity of ascent of air bubbles in viscoelastic liquids. For the aeration of bubble columns by means of static dispersion units such as sieve plates, this implies the generation of bubbles at a comparable gas throughput. This is necessary for ensuring the mutual interaction between the bubbles, which is decisive for the bubble shape. Thus, bubble shapes relevant to practice are created; as can be seen from Figure 12, the bubbles usually exhibit an elongated shape. The circulation of liquid around the bubble after its severance, as occurs in the case of viscoelastic liquids, does not cause a change in the bubble shape, since differences in normal stress arise because of the elastic properties of the liquid. This results in preservation of the bubble shape. In contrast, the bubbles generated at an oscillating spoon with a diameter of $d_B = 8$ mm assume an ellipsoidal shape; thus the conditions which actually prevail in bubble columns are not correctly reproduced.

THEORETICAL DESCRIPTION AND DISCUSSION OF THE BUBBLE FORMATION MECHANISM

Survey of the Literature

The large number of publications on the subject of formation and motion of bubbles in liquids have been reviewed in detail by Beer [40]. Therefore, only the essential developments which have led to a description of the bubble formation process are considered here.

The formation of bubbles in liquids is a dynamic process in which the shape and size of the bubbles vary continuously. In order to gain preliminary insight into the formation mechanism and to permit a calculation, the formation process is viewed as quasistatic.

Siemes [15] has described this process under the assumption of very long times of formation, with the application of the theory of capillarity. The equilibrium of forces thus derived for the element of interfacial area dA is given by

$$dF_p = dF_H + dF_\sigma \tag{1}$$

The solution of this equation yields the pressure at the summit of the upper contour of the bubble. After further transformation, it also yields information on the bubble shape and bubble volume during quasistatic bubble formation.

The approximate solutions derived by Siemes, as well as by Durst [41] and Poutanen [42] do not allow any predictions concerning the size of the bubbles upon detachment, since the theory of capillarity is applicable only to equilibrium states, whereas the detachment process is of dynamic nature.

For the purpose of calculating the bubble size at the point of severance, Mersmann [16] has postulated a model for the equilibrium of forces during bubble formation. By definition, this is valid only for small volume flow rates of gas. Here, too, the inertial force is neglected; only the buoyant force F_A, the resistant force F_W, and the force due to surface tension F_σ are taken into consideration.

$$F_A = F_W + F_\sigma \tag{2}$$

For Newtonian liquids and with the assumption of a constant coefficient of resistance, this relation leads to the following equation

$$d_B = \sqrt[3]{\frac{3\sigma d_D}{\rho_L g} + \sqrt{\left(\frac{3\sigma d_D}{g\rho_L}\right)^2 + \frac{K\dot{V}_g^2 d_D}{g}}} \tag{3}$$

The constant K, which includes the resistance coefficient and a shape factor for the geometrical deviation of the bubble from a spherical shape, has been adjusted by Mersmann to fit the measured values. From the results of Davidson [2] and five other authors, as well as Siemes [15] and Leibson [12], he thereby obtained numerical values of 13, 9, 15, and 10, respectively. Although Equation 3 is valid only for small gas volume flow rates, it includes all decisive parameters required for describing bubble formation, according to Brauer [1].

In the opinion of Kumar and Kuloor [3, 43], however, the inertial force and viscosity must also be taken into account in describing the bubble formation process in the "jet regime." In order to correctly describe the influence of these parameters, they have set up a bubble formation model [43], which comprises an expansion step and a detachment step. It is thereby assumed that the liquid is displaced from the bubble which is forming (refer to Figure 29).

During the expansion step, the bubble adheres to the capillary orifice, since the retaining forces are stronger than the detaching forces. As soon as the equilibrium of forces has been attained, the bubble becomes detached, but remains linked to the capillary through a neck. The bubble is severed when the neck attains a length which corresponds to the radius of the bubble at the conclusion of the "expansion step."

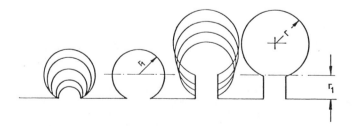

Figure 29. Bubble formation according to Kumar and Kuloor [43].

Accordingly, the gas volume of the bubble is the sum of the volume at the end of the expansion phase and that due to the influx during the detachment step

$$V_B = V_{GL} + \dot{V}_g t \tag{4}$$

Since the time of detachment in Equation 4 is not known, Kumar and Kuloor make use of the equation of motion for the center of the bubble for describing the bubble formation. This is established on the basis of a balance of forces

$$F_K + F_A - F_\sigma - F_W = F_T \tag{5}$$

With the assumption of the condition for severance just described, the equation of motion can be solved iteratively. Thus, the process of bubble formation can be described for both Newtonian and non-Newtonian liquids. However, attention must thereby be paid to the fact that the bubble diameter calculated from Equation 4 depends strongly on the selected severance condition. Only Stölting has attempted to physically describe the severance process on the basis of drop formation in a more recent publication [49], without regard to the work of Kumar and Kuloor, including the criterion which they had adapted to the measured data. For this purpose, Stölting assumes a parabolic velocity profile in the capillary and postulates that only the fluid elements which move faster than the particle base, v_B, can enter the drop (discussed later with Figure 31). Thus, the particle base must be severed at twice the average velocity of the capillary flow.

$$v_B = 2w_N = 2\frac{\dot{V}_g 4}{d_D^2 \pi} \tag{6}$$

The application of the severance condition in the equation of motion for the particle from Equation 6 yields satisfactory agreement between calculated and experimental results for bubble formation in the "jet regime" and in a Newtonian liquid at rest.

An extension of the equation of motion from Equation 6 to the bubble formation process in a cocurrently or countercurrently moving liquid has not yet been attempted. Preliminary results on the formation of air bubbles in water flowing cocurrently have been published by Sada et al. [4]. The effect of countercurrent motion of the liquid on bubble formation is hitherto not known to have been investigated.

For the "jet regime," the process of bubble formation is described as the formation of a gas jet [1, 14, 19, 26, 44] which disintegrates into small bubbles at its upper contour. Attempts to comprehensively describe this bubble formation process have been unsuccessful so far, because of the complexity involved [45–48]. Hence, a computation of the bubble size has hitherto been feasible only through a correlation given by Brauer [1] and based on values measured by Siemes and Günther [14].

Thus, it has been possible to calculate the bubble size only during its generation at single orifices in a liquid at rest and at low values of the gas volume flow [26]. A generally valid description of the bubble formation process over the entire range of gas throughput has previously not existed.

Model Concept of Räbiger and Vogelpohl

By means of high-speed movies and synchronized recording of the bubble formation pressure, it has been demonstrated that single and double bubbles are always generated at the capillary orifice over the entire investigated range of gas throughput, for both Newtonian [50, 51] and non-Newtonian liquids [52]. The formation of a gas jet thereby does not occur.

The values measured for the water-air system are well reproduced by the correlation due to Mersmann; this is an indication that the bubble formation process is not subject to any acceleration during its final phase, (i.e., during the detachment step) and thus that the inertial force can be neglected.

Stölting [49] has also arrived at this result with the use of the equation of motion due to Kumar and Kuloor for drop formation in Newtonian liquids at rest. For their model concept, however, Kumar and Kuloor assume that the bubble being formed displaces the surrounding liquid, and that the bubble is subject to continuous acceleration after detachment [43]. This assumption, which has also been applied by Ruff [19], contradicts the results presented in Figure 3, since it does not take into account the effect of the liquid motion induced by the neck of the preceding bubble on the formation process for the bubble being generated.

The detachment of the bubble from the capillary orifice begins as soon as the equilibrium between the detaching and retaining forces has been established. That is, the inertial force due to the induced liquid motion is still present, even though it is weak; in combination with the buoyant force, it suffices to overcome the adhesive force at the capillary orifice, and thus causes the detachment of the bubble. The bubble moves uniformly and at about the velocity of ascent (Figure 3) away from the capillary. This consideration is confirmed by the experimental results presented in Figures 3 and 31.

Just as for the calculation of the pressure maximum for bubble formation [50], the computation of the size of the primary and secondary bubbles formed in accordance with the bubble formation model presented earlier requires a determination of the effect exerted by the neck motion on the subsequent bubble, as well as the time of severance for the bubble.

Severance Condition

As described in the preceding sections and in Reference 51, the process of primary and secondary bubble formation is decidedly influenced by the formation and motion of the neck. Hence, the condition for bubble severance is of decisive importance for a description of the bubble-formation mechanism. The severance condition corresponding to Equation 6 according to Stölting [44] is the only one which has hitherto been physically justified; it involves the assumption that the bubble is severed at twice the average velocity of the capillary flow. Such a criterion is rather surprising, since it implies that the bubble is severed at a velocity far higher than the measured values, which indicate that the bubble is detached at approximately the velocity of ascent. This discrepancy persists even if a turbulent velocity profile is assumed to prevail in the capillary. An explanation may be as follows: On the one hand, the model of Kumar and Kuloor takes into account inertial forces, which should be neglected in accordance with the present results. On the other hand, Stölting assumes that the decrease of pressure in the neck, and thus the constriction process is caused exclusively by the increase in volume of the neck. In fact, however, the total increase in volume of the bubble must be taken into consideration. (See Figure 30.)

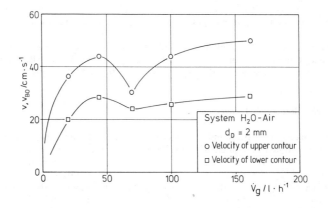

Figure 30. Velocity of severance of bubbles in stagnant liquid at rest.

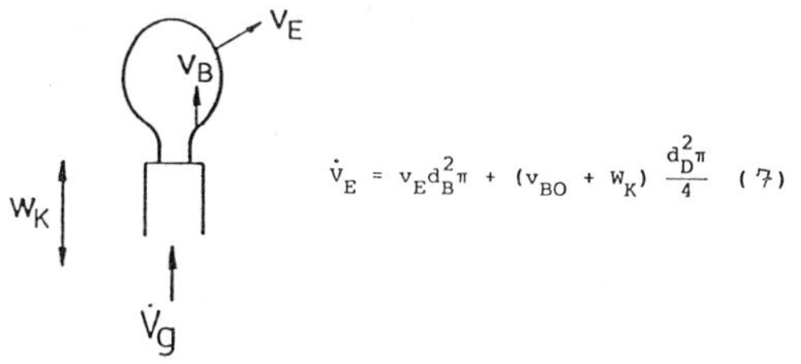

$$\dot{V}_E = v_E d_B^2 \pi + (v_{BO} + w_K) \frac{d_D^2 \pi}{4} \quad (7)$$

Figure 31. Volume increase of bubble.

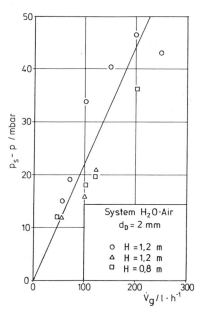

Figure 32. Underpressure in the bubble at detachment from orifice vs. gas flow rate.

In Figure 31, therefore, the total increase in volume is subdivided into components due to growth of the sphere and to that of the neck [52]. Because of this motion by the lower contour of the bubble and sustained expansion of the spherical bubble, liquid from the layers in the vicinity of the neck is entrained. The decline in pressure which thus results is depicted in Figure 32. If the pressure in the neck becomes less than that in the surrounding liquid during the further course of the formation process, the neck constricts, and the bubble is severed. As can be seen in Figure 32, the pressure in the bubble drops below that of the system; hence, for constant flow conditions in the capillary, the rate of volume increase $\dot{V}_E$ for the bubble must exceed the volume flow rate of gas. Therefore,

$$\dot{V}_E > \dot{V}_g = w_N \frac{d_D^2 \pi}{4} \quad (8)$$

or, with the use of Equation 7

$$v_E > (w_N - (v_{BO} + w_K)) \left(\frac{d_D}{2d_B}\right)^2. \quad (9)$$

The velocity of the lower bubble contour can be viewed as approximately constant and is neglected in the following. With the further assumption that underpressure in the bubble causes immediate detachment, Equation 9 yields the following severance criterion, in good agreement with the measured data [52]:

$$v_E = (w_N - w_K)\left(\frac{d_D}{2d_B}\right)^2 \tag{10}$$

Calculation of the Primary Bubble Diameter

In contrast to the model of Kumar and Kuloor, the results of recent investigations [52] show that the influence of the inertial force of the surrounding liquid on the overall motion of the bubble during the detachment step can be neglected for describing the process of primary bubble formation. On the basis of this conclusion and of the assumption that the kinetic force of the gas flowing into a bubble is negligible, it can be assumed that the bubble formation model corresponding to Equation 2 according to Mersmann [16] is applicable to the *entire* range of gas throughput. However, Equation 3 derived by Mersmann for computing the bubble diameter is valid only for liquids of low viscosity.

The model due to Mersmann, according to Equation 2, can be improved by deriving the resistive force F_W with the use of the severance condition, and considering only the corresponding partial volume of the bubble for the same equilibrium of forces [52]. This modification of the forces which act during the bubble formation process is implemented with the use of the new results. Thus, it is possible to calculate the size of the primarily formed bubble iteratively from

$$\frac{g\,\Delta\rho d_B^3 \pi}{12}\left(2 - 3\left(\frac{d_D}{d_B}\right)^2\right) = d_D\sigma\cdot\pi + c_w\rho_L K\,\frac{d_B^2\pi}{8}\left(2\left(\frac{\dot{V}_g 4}{d_D^2\pi} - w_K\right)\left(\frac{d_D}{2d_B}\right)^2 + v_{BO}\right)^2 \tag{11}$$

The accuracy of the bubble diameter computed with the use of Equation 11 has been checked by comparison with 700 values measured during the present investigation, or taken from the literature (refer to Figure 33). A constant correction for the velocity of ascent calculated from the resistance law for rigid spheres has been employed for all values of the viscosity. For $K = 1.4$, 95% of the

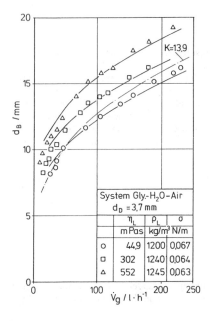

Figure 33. Comparison of experimental results of Rama-krishna et al. [3] with theory of Mersmann.

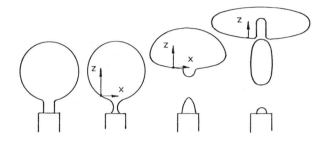

Figure 34. Secondary bubble formation.

measured data thereby used for the comparison have been reproduced within an error limit of 8% [52].

On the other hand, the effect of a superimposed liquid flow on the formation process can be qualitatively reproduced with the use of Equation 11; however, substantial quantitative deviations thereby occur. The reason for this observation is the still unknown influence of liquid flow superimposed on the bubble motion, which is exerted on the resistance during bubble formation, as well as the rheology. Especially the rearrangement of the flow profile at the capillary orifice due to the velocity and direction of the superimposed liquid flow thereby appears to be decisive [52].

Hence, the elucidation and physical description of the effect of direction and velocity of a superimposed liquid flow, as well as of rheology and resistive force, during the bubble formation process should be the subject of further investigations.

In summary, it can be concluded that the agreement between the values of the bubble diameter calculated with the use of Equation 11 and those determined experimentally is excellent (Figure 33). This result shows that the newly developed model for bubble formation correctly describes the formation process during the decisive detachment step; hence, valuable insight into this complicated process has been achieved. For the purpose of further improvement, the detachment step and the influence exerted thereon by a superimposed liquid motion must be more accurately investigated.

Calculation of the Secondary Bubble Diameter in the So-Called Jet Regime

Description of the neck motion. As described earlier and illustrated in Figure 34, the formation of secondary bubbles in the "jet regime" [52] is initiated by the motion of the neck and of the liquid which surrounds same.

After the severance of the bubble due to the constriction of the neck, the bubble tends to assume the shape with the least surface area. Hence, the neck moves toward the bubble, thus causing the entrainment of liquid and an increase of pressure in the bubble. Because of the inertia of the entrained liquid, it continues to move into the bubble and simultaneously draws a new bubble from the capillary (Figure 35). For effecting distintegration of the primary bubble, the penetrating

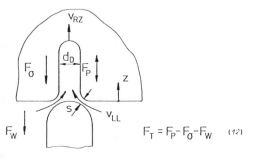

$$F_T = F_P - F_\sigma - F_W \qquad (12)$$

Figure 35. Balance of forces during secondary bubble formation.

liquid must overcome the increasing pressure in the bubble, the force due to surface tension, and the resistive force due to the annular flow.

By means of a determination of the forces affecting the neck motion and through the use of physically sensible assumptions, the neck motion itself and the influence exerted thereon, as well as the neck length during formation, can be successfully calculated [52].

Boundary conditions for the so-called jet regime. As already described, the formation of secondary bubbles is caused mainly by the liquid which penetrates into the primary bubble. For the disintegration of the primary bubble, the liquid motion induced by the neck must still possess sufficient kinetic energy upon reaching the upper contour of the bubble. The force thus exerted, in combination with the resistive force, must suffice for overcoming the force due to surface tension (Figure 36).

Insertion of the forces into Equation 13 yields an expression for the critical velocity of liquid motion [52]

$$v_{Rzkrit} = \frac{2}{d_D} \sqrt{\frac{2d_B}{\rho_L}(\sigma - 3\eta_L w_{St})} \tag{14}$$

Hence, the "jet regime" is attained, and the primary bubble disintegrates if the motion of the neck is sufficiently vigorous to induce liquid motion which still possesses the critical velocity upon reaching the upper interface.

Determination of the bubble diameter in the so-called jet regime. With the assumption that the condition for equilibrium according to Equation 13 is satisfied, the upper interface of the primary bubble expands because of the momentum of the induced liquid motion and is separated from the primary bubble [52]. The remaining portion of the primary bubble constitutes the part which is stable under the corresponding stresses. This is taken into account by the bubble diameter d_B in the boundary condition given in Equation 14. From high-speed movies, it can be recognized that the two secondary bubbles arising from the primary bubble are of about the same size at higher values of the gas throughput [50, 52]. The bubble size in the "jet regime" is thus determined.

With the assumption of this model concept, and upon insertion of the boundary condition into Equation 12, this equilibrium of forces can be satisfied only if the process of primary bubble disintegration is initiated. If the corresponding forces and boundary conditions are inserted, the equation for determining the secondary bubble diameter results from Equation 12

$$A = \sqrt{2\left(d_B g + \frac{K_4}{\sqrt{\dot{V}_g}}\sqrt{\frac{K_1 \dot{V}_g}{1 + w_K/w_{St}}} - 2v_{Rzkrit}^2\right) + 1} \tag{15}$$

and

$$B = \left(gH - \frac{K_1 \dot{V}_g}{1 + w_K/w_{St}}\right)\left(1 + \frac{2d_B}{d_D}\right) \tag{16}$$

$$0,25v_{Rzkrit}^2 = B + \frac{4\sigma}{d_D\rho_L} + \frac{4}{d_D\rho_L}(12\eta_L(K_2 - K_3 v_{Rzkrit}) + 0,1\rho_L d_D v_{Rzkrit}) \cdot A \tag{17}$$

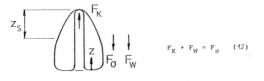

$$F_K + F_W = F_\sigma \qquad (13)$$

Figure 36. Balance of forces during division of a primary bubble.

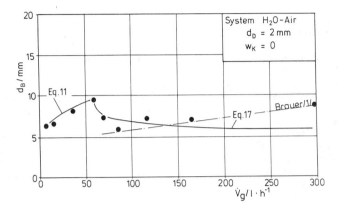

Figure 37. Comparison of own experimental results (●) and those of Siemes (correlation by Brauer [1]) for secondary bubble diameter with present theory (————).

The determination of the secondary bubble diameter from Equation 17 is at present possible only iteratively. If Equation 17 is not satisfied, it is assumed that the process of disintegration has not yet been initiated, and that the secondary bubble diameter must be computed from Equation 11.

An adaptation of the values obtained from Equation 17 to fit the results of measurements performed on the water-air system for liquid at rest has yielded the following values for the coefficients: $K_1 = 20,000$, $K_2 = 265$, $K_3 = 650$, and $K_4 = 0.8$. The corresponding results are presented in Figure 37; the solid curve thereby represents the secondary bubble diameter determined from Equations 17 and 11.

In this calculation, only the determination of a secondary bubble diameter corresponding to that from Equation 11 proved to be feasible for the critical gas throughput from Equation 17. For a smaller gas throughput, the equilibrium of forces no longer prevails; hence, Equation 17 did not yield any solution. This confirms the preceding assumption and shows that the physical process which occurs during secondary bubble formation in the "jet regime" is correctly described qualitatively by Equation 17.

A similar statement is valid for the calculation of the secondary bubble diameter with a superimposed liquid motion. In this case, however, agreement can be ascertained only qualitatively [52] because of the lack of sufficient knowledge concerning the effect of liquid lamellae formed as a result of superimposed liquid flow. For the present state of knowledge, therefore, a further adaptation does not appear reasonable, since a definite physical meaning has been ascribed to the coefficients K_1 to K_4 in the derivation of Equation 17. Hence, it must first be clarified to which extent a superimposed liquid flow and/or the viscous behavior of the liquid influence these coefficients.

NOTATION

c	concentration	F_K	kinetic force (N)
c_w	drag coefficient	F_p	pressure force (N)
$\dot{D}$	shear rate (s^{-1})	F_T	inertia force (N)
d_B	bubble diameter (m)	F_W	resistance force (N)
d_D	capillary diameter (m)	F	surface tension force (N)
F_A	buoyancy force (N)	g	gravitational acceleration (m/s^2)
F_H	hydraulic compressive force (N)	H	liquid height (m)

K   constant

k   flow consistency factor, according to Ostwald-de Waele (Pa s^n)

K_1 coefficient in Equation 15 ((m·s)$^{-1}$)

K_2 coefficient in Equation 17

K_3 coefficient in Equation 17 ((m/s)$^{-1}$)

K_4 coefficient in Equation 15 (m$^{5/2}$/s$^{3/2}$)

n   flow index, according to Ostwald-de Waele

p   pressure in the bubble (N/m^2)

p_S system pressure (N/m^2)

r_1 radius of equilibrium (m)

s   width of annular gap (m)

t   time (s)

V_B bubble volume (m^3)

v   velocity of bubble top (m/s)

v_B velocity of bubble base (m/s)

v_{BO} velocity of bubble base in stagnant liquid (m/s)

V_E volume flow rate during bubble expansion (m^3/s)

v_E expansion velocity of bubble (m/s)

$\dot{V}_g$ volumetric gas flow rate (m^3/s)

V_{GL} volume at equilibrium (m^3)

v_{LL} velocity of liquid in annular gap (m/s)

v_{RZ} relative velocity of filament end (m/s)

V_{Rzkrit} critical velocity of filament end at dispersion point of primary bubble (m/s)

w_K mean velocity of forced liquid flow (m/s)

w_N mean velocity of gas in the capillary (m/s)

w_{St} bubble rise velocity (m/s)

x, z, r   spatial coordinates

z_s extension of upper interface (m)

Greek Symbols

η viscosity (Pa s)

η_{unst} lower newtonian shear viscosity (Pa s)

ρ density (kg/m^3)

σ surface tension (N/m)

Subscripts

L   liquid

g   gas

st   stationary

Dimensionless Numbers

$Re = (v \cdot d_B \cdot \rho_L)/\eta_L$, Reynolds number

$Re_{NN} = (w_{st}^{2-n} \cdot d_B^n \cdot \rho_L)/k$, Reynolds number

$We = w_N^2 \cdot d_D \cdot \rho_g/\sigma$, Weber number

REFERENCES

1. Brauer, H., "Grundlagen der Einphasen- und Mehrphasenströmung," Sauerländer, Aarau and Frankfurt a.M., 1971.
2. Davidson, L., and Amick, E. H., "Formation of Gas Bubble at Horizontal Orifices," *AIChE Journal*, 2 (1956) 3, 337–342.
3. Ramakrishna, S., Kumar, R., and Kuloor, N. R., "Studies in Bubble Formation—I: Bubble Formation Under Constant Flow Conditions," *Chem. Engng. Sci.*, 24 (1969), 731–747.
4. Sada, E., et al., "Bubble Formation in Flowing Liquid," *Can. J. of Chem Engng.* 56 (1978), 669–672.
5. Buchholz, H., et al., "Bubble Swarm Behaviour and Gas Absorption in Non-Newtonian Fluids in Sparged Columns," *Chem. Engng. Sci.*, 33 (1978) 8, 1061–1070.
6. Acharya, A., Mashelkar, R. A., and Ulbrecht, J. J., "Bubble Formation in Non-Newtonian Liquids," *Ind. Eng. Chem. Fundam.*, 17 (1978) 3, 230–232.
7. Carreau, P. J., Devic, M., and Kapellas, M., "Dynamique des bulles en milieu viscoélastique," *Rheol. Acta*, 13 (1974), 477–489.
8. Acharya, A., Mashelkar, R. A., and Ulbrecht, J. J., "Mechanics of Bubble Motion and Deformation in Non-Newtonian Media," *Chem. Engng. Sci.*, 32 (1977), 863–872.

9. Astarita, G., and Apuzzo, G., "Motion of Gas Bubbles in Non-Newtonian Liquids," *AIChE Journal*, 11 (1965) 5, 815–820.
10. Macedo, I. C., and Yang, W. J., "The Drag of Air Bubbles-Rising in Non-Newtonian Liquids," *Jap. J. App. Phys.*, 13 (1974) 3, 529–533.
11. Costes, J., and Alran, C., "The Formation of Bubbles in a Non-Newtonian Liquid," *Chem. Eng.*, 3 (1978), 191–197.
12. Leibson, I., et al., "Rate of Flow and Mechanics of Bubble Formation from Single Submerged Orifices,"*AIChE Journal*, 2 (1956), 296–306.
13. Hallensleben, J., et al., "Blasenbildung und -verhalten im dynamischen Bereich," *Chem.-Ing.-Techn.*, 49 (1977) 663 and MS 510/77.
14. Siemes, W., and Günther, K., "Gasdispergierung in Flüssigkeiten durch Düsen bei hohen Durchsätzen," *Chem.-Ing.-Techn.*, 28 (1956), 389–395.
15. Siemes, W., "Gasblasen in Flüssigkeiten Teil I: Entstehung von Gasblasen an nach oben gerichteten kreisförmigen Düsen," *Chem.-Ing.-Techn.*, 26 (1954) 8/9, 479–496.
16. Mersmann, A., "Druckverlust und Schaumhöhen von gasdurchströmten Flüssigkeitsschichten auf Siebböden," VDI-Forschungsheft 491, Ausgabe B, Band 28 (1962).
17. Ruff, K., Pilhofer, T., and Mersmann, A., "Vollständige Durchströmung von Lochböden bei der Fluid-Dispergierung," *Chem.-Ing.-Techn.*, 48 (1976) 9, 759–764.
18. Ruff, K., "Grenze zwischen Blasengasen und Strahlgasen bei niedrigviskosen Flüssigkeiten und konstantem Gasvolumen-Durchsatz," *Chem.-Ing.-Techn.*, 46 (1974) 18, 769–771.
19. Ruff, K., "Bildung von Gasblasen an Düsen bei konstantem Volumendurchsatz," *Chem.-Ing.-Techn.*, 44 (1972) 24, 1360.
20. Ebert, F., "Strömung nicht-newtonscher Medien," Verlag Fr. Vieweg & Sohn, Braunschweig-Wiesbaden 1980.
21. Durst, F., et al., "Polymerwirkung in Strömungen-Mechanismen und praktische Anwendung," *Chem.-Ing.-Techn.*, 54 (1982) 3, 213–221.
22. Boehme, G., "Strömung nicht-newtonscher Flüssigkeiten," *Z. angew. Mathe. und Mech.*, 62 (1982) T3–T17.
23. Acharya, A., Mashelkar, R. A., and Ulbrecht, J., "Mechanics of Bubble Motion and Deformation in Non-Newtonian Media," *Chem. Engng. Sci.*, 32 (77) 863–872.
24. Otake, T., Tone, S., and Schinohara, K., "Gas Holdup in the Bubble Column with Cocurrent and Countercurrent Gas Liquid Flow," *J. Engng. Japan*, 14 (1981) 4, 338–340.
25. Gerstenberg, H., "Blasensäulen-Reaktoren," *Chem.-Ing.-Techn.*, 51 (1979) 3, 208–216.
26. Mersmann, A., "Auslegung und MaßstabsvergröBerung von Blasensäulen," *Chem.-Ing.-Techn.*, 49 (1977) 9, 679–691.
27. Neubauer, G., and Pilhofer, T., "Auslegung von Lochböden bei der Begasung von Flüssigkeiten unter Druck," *Chem.-Ing.-Techn.*, 50 (1978) 2, 115–116.
28. Klug, P., and Vogelpohl, A., "Bubble Formation with Superimposed Liquid Motion at Single-hole Plates and Sieve Plates," *Ger. Chem. Eng.* 6 (1983) 311–317.
29. Tsuge, H., and Hibino, S., "Bubble Formation from a Submerged Orifice in Liquids," Proceedings Volume V, 2nd World Congress of Chemical Engineering, Montreal, Canada 1981.
30. Takahashi, T., and Miahara, T., "Volume of Bubble Formed at a Single Circular, Submerged Orifice," *Effect of the Volume of the Gas Chamber*, International Chemical Engineering, 21 (1981) 2, 224–228.
31. Tadaki, T., and Maeda, S., "The Size of Bubble from Perforated Plates, *Kagaku Kogaku*, (1963) 1, 106.
32. Siemes, W., "Gasblasen in Flüssigkeiten Teil II: Der Aufstieg von Gasblasen in Flüssigkeiten," *Chem.-Ing.-Techn.*, 26 (1954) 11, 614–630.
33. Haas, U., Schmidt-Traub, H., and Brauer, H., "Umströmung kugelförmiger Blasen mit innerer Zirkulation," *Chemie-Ing.-Techn.*, 44 (1972) 18, 1060–1068.
34. Tapucu, A., "Viscosity Effect on the Motion of Gas Bubbles Rising through Stagnant Liquids," *Trans. of the CSME*, 2 (1973–74) 3, 151–159.
35. Tadaki, T., and Maeda, S., "On the Shape and Velocity of Single Air Bubbles Rising in Various Liquids," *Chem. Engng. (Japan)*, 25 (1961), 254–264.

36. Bryn, T., "Steiggeschwindigkeit von Luftblasen in Flüssigkeiten" *Forsch.-Gebiete Ingenieurwesen,* 4 (1931) 1, 27–30.
37. Habermann, W. L., and Morton, R. K., "An Experimental Study of Bubbles Moving in Liquids," *Trans. Amer. Soc. Civil Engr.,* 121 (1954) 227–253.
38. Calderbank, P. H., Johnson, D. S. L., and Loudon, J., "Mechanics and Mass Transfer of Single Bubbles in Free Rise through Some Newtonian and Non-Newtonian Liquids, *Chem. Engng. Sci.,* 25 (1970), 235–256.
39. Leal, L. G., Skoog, J., and Acrivos, A., "On the Motion of Gas Bubbles in a Viscoelastic Liquid," *Can. J. Chem. Engng.,* 49 (1971), 569–575.
40. Beer, W. F., "Größe fluider Partikel bei ihrer Entstehung an Einzelbohrungen und Lochplaten," *Dipl.-Arbeit,* TU München, 1975.
41. Durst, F., and Beer, H., "Blasenbildung an Düsen beim Gasdispergiere in Flüssigkeiten," *Chem.-Ing.-Techn.,* 41 (1969) 18, 1000–1006.
42. Poutanen, A. A., and Johnson, A. I., "Studies of Bubble Formation and Rise," *Can. J. Chem. Engng.,* 38 (1960) 4, 93–103.
43. Kuma, R., and Kuloor, N. R., "Blasenbildung in nichtviskosen Flüssigkeiten unter konstanten Fließbedingungen," *Chem.-Techn.,* 19 (1967) 11, 657–660.
44. Stölting, M., "Bildung und Bewegung von Einzeltropfen in einer rotierenden Flüssigkeit," Dissertation, TU München, 1979.
45. Meister, B. J., and Scheele, G. F., "Generalization of Solution of the Tomotika Stability Analysis for a Cylindrical Jet," *AIChE J.,* 13 (1976) 7, 682–688.
46. Scheele, G. F., and Meister, B. J., "Drop Formation at Low Velocities in Liquid-Liquid Systems," *AIChE J.,* 14 (1968) 1, 9–19.
47. Meister, B. J., and Scheele, G. F., "Prediction of Jet Length in Immiscible Liquid Systems," *AIChE J.,* 15 (1969) 5, 689–706.
48. Perrut, M., and Loutaty, R., "Drop Size in a Liquid-Liquid Dispersion: Formation in Jet Break-up," *Chem. Eng. J.,* 3 (1972), 268–293.
49. Stölting, M., "Partikelbildung unterhalb des Strahlbereichs bei konstantem Volumenstrom," *Chemie-Ing.-Techn.,* 52 (1980) 7, MS 817/80.
50. Räbiger, N., and Vogelpohl, A., "Blasenbildung in ruhenden und bewegten newtonschen Flüssigkeiten," *Chem.-Ing.-Techn.,* 53 (1981) 12, 976–977.
51. Räbiger, N., and Vogelpohl, A., "Berechnung der Blasengröße im Bereich des Blasen- und Strahlgasens bei ruhender und bewegter newtonscher Flüssigkeit," *Chem.-Ing.-Techn.,* 54 (1982) 11, 1082–1083.
52. Räbiger, N., "Blasenbildung an Düsen sowie Blasenbewegung in ruhenden und strömenden newtonschen und nichtnewtonschen Flüssigkeiten," *VDI-Forschungsheft,* (October 1984).

CHAPTER 5

CREEPING FLOW AROUND BUBBLES

Ashok S. Sangani

Department of Chemical Engineering
and Materials Science
Syracuse University
Syracuse, New York, USA

CONTENTS

INTRODUCTION

In this chapter we shall consider creeping motion of incompressible fluids past bubbles. The first part of this chapter deals with the flow past a single bubble, the second with the calculation of the terminal velocity of a swarm of gas bubbles and the last part with the deformation and breakup of bubbles. Although the main thrust in the chapter is towards the flow past bubbles, the results are often presented for drops of arbitrary viscosity. For this reason, the terms bubbles, drops, and particles are used interchangeably throughout the chapter. The results for bubbles could, of course, be obtained from those of drops by setting the viscosity inside the drops to zero.

There has been extensive work on the subject and some of the results presented here may be found in standard texts on fluid mechanics. A recent book by Clift, Grace, and Weber [1] deals extensively with flows past bubbles, drops, and particles and provides an excellent reference for a large number of results presented here.

RISE VELOCITY OF A SINGLE BUBBLE

The velocity of a bubble rising under the influence of gravity through a pool of viscous fluid under a low Reynolds number condition depends, in general, on several variables, such as the concentration and nature of impurities, the surface tension, and the size of the bubble and the surrounding vessel. If the surface tension forces are much larger than the viscous forces and if the size of the bubble is much smaller than the vessel, the bubble will remain spherical. Therefore, we shall study first a simple case of a spherical bubble rising through a contaminant-free unbounded fluid. A rather surprising result of this study is that a spherical bubble will retain its shape even when the surface tension forces are small!

Impurity-Free Fluids: The Hadamard-Rybczynski Solution

The problem of determining the terminal velocity of a bubble or drop in an infinite fluid medium is equivalent to determining the drag force exerted by a fluid moving with a uniform velocity U on a drop fixed at the origin. An analytical solution of this problem was obtained independently by Hadamard [2] and Rybczynski [3]. We shall present their results in terms of a stream function ψ defined by

$$u_r = \frac{1}{r^2 \sin \theta} \frac{\partial \psi}{\partial \theta} \tag{1a}$$

$$u_\theta = -\frac{1}{r \sin \theta} \frac{\partial \psi}{\partial r} \tag{1b}$$

where r = the radial distance measured from the origin
θ = the angle measured from the front stagnation point
u_r and u_θ = the radial and angular components of the velocity, respectively

For creeping flows ψ satisfies the biharmonic equation

$$\left[\frac{\partial^2}{\partial r^2} + \frac{1-\eta^2}{r^2} \frac{\partial^2}{\partial \eta^2} \right] \psi = 0 \qquad (\eta \equiv \cos \theta) \tag{2}$$

with the boundary conditions

$$\psi \to \tfrac{1}{2} r^2 U \sin^2 \theta \qquad \text{as } r \to \infty \tag{3}$$

$$\psi = \hat{\psi} = 0 \qquad \text{at } r = a \tag{4}$$

$$\frac{\partial}{\partial r} \left(\frac{1}{r^2} \frac{\partial \psi}{\partial r} \right) = \kappa \frac{\partial}{\partial r} \left(\frac{1}{r^2} \frac{\partial \hat{\psi}}{\partial r} \right) \qquad \text{at } r = a \tag{5}$$

$$p - 2\mu \frac{\partial}{\partial r} \left(\frac{1}{r^2 \sin \theta} \frac{\partial \psi}{\partial \theta} \right) + \frac{2\gamma}{a} = \hat{p} - 2\hat{\mu} \frac{\partial}{\partial r} \left(\frac{1}{r^2 \sin \theta} \frac{\partial \hat{\psi}}{\partial \theta} \right) \qquad \text{at } r = a \tag{6}$$

where the quantities designated with a hat, "$\hat{\ }$", refer to those inside the drop, p is the pressure, γ is the interfacial tension, a is the radius of the drop, and $\kappa = \hat{\mu}/\mu$ is the ratio of viscosities. Equation 3 is the uniform flow condition of infinity; Equation 4 is the zero normal velocity condition at the interface; and Equations 5 and 6 are, respectively, the tangential and normal force balances at the interface. The surface tension forces are assumed to be large so that the drop remains spherical. As we shall see presently this assumption, however, is unnecessary. Equations 3–6 are often referred to as Hadamard-Rybczynski conditions. They are valid for pure isothermal fluids for which the interfacial tension is uniform. It should be noted here that an additional term representing the tangential forces due to nonuniform interfacial tension must be included in Equation 5 for fluids containing surface-active impurities. We shall discuss this at length in the next section. But first, we continue with the solution of the Hadamard-Rybczynski problem. Equation 2 with the conditions of Equations 3–5 yields (see, for example, Reference 4)

$$\psi = \tfrac{1}{2}Ur^2 \sin^2 \theta \left[1 - \frac{a}{2r}\left(\frac{2 + 3\kappa}{1 + \kappa}\right) + \frac{a^3}{2r^3}\left(\frac{\kappa}{1 + \kappa}\right) \right] \tag{7}$$

$$\hat{\psi} = \frac{Ur^2 \sin^2 \theta}{4(1 + \kappa)}\left[1 - \frac{r^2}{a^2} \right] \tag{8}$$

The normal force balance Equation 6 can be simultaneously satisfied provided that

$$p = p_o - \frac{Ua \cos \theta}{r^2}\left(\frac{2 + 3\kappa}{1 + \kappa}\right) \tag{9}$$

$$\hat{p} = p_o + \frac{2\gamma}{a} + \frac{5\mu Ur \cos \theta}{a^2}\left(\frac{\kappa}{1 + \kappa}\right) \tag{10}$$

Equations 7–10 thus represent an exact solution of Equations 1–6, and therefore, a spherical drop would retain its shape for all values of γ. In other words, when the creeping flow approximations are valid, it is not necessary to assume that the surface tension forces are much larger than the viscous forces for a drop to remain spherical. Also this implies that a spherical drop rising through a pool of liquid would deform only when the inertia terms in the equation of motion become important. We may also note here that the presence of surface-active contaminants may cause marked changes in the internal circulation and hence the rise velocity of the drop. Its effect on the shape, however, is negligible at low Reynolds numbers.

The drag force F exerted by the fluid on the bubble, the drag coefficient C_D, and the vorticity ω at the interface can be readily evaluated from Equations 7–10:

$$F = 2\pi\mu aU(2 + 3\kappa)/(1 + \kappa) \tag{11}$$

$$C_D = \frac{2F}{\pi\rho U^2 a^2} = \frac{2}{Re}\frac{2 + 3\kappa}{1 + \kappa} \tag{12}$$

$$\omega = -\frac{U \sin \theta}{2a}\frac{2 + 3\kappa}{1 + \kappa} \tag{13}$$

where $Re \equiv \rho Ua/\mu$ is the Reynolds number and ρ is the density of the fluid. For a drop rising through a pool of liquid, the drag force must equal the buoyancy force and hence the magnitude of the terminal velocity is

$$U = \frac{2a^2}{3\mu}\left(\frac{1 + \kappa}{2 + 3\kappa}\right)(\rho - \hat{\rho})g \tag{14}$$

where g is the gravitational acceleration. The corresponding expressions for inviscid gas bubbles ($\hat{\mu}/\mu \ll 1$) may be obtained by substituting $\kappa = 0$ in the preceding expressions and for future reference we list them here.

$$\left.\begin{aligned} U &= \frac{a^2}{3\mu}(\rho - \hat{\rho})g \\[1em] F &= 4\pi\mu Ua \\[1em] C_D &= 4/Re \end{aligned}\right\} \kappa = 0 \tag{15}$$

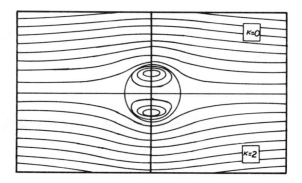

Figure 1. Streamlines relative to spherical bubble ($\kappa = 0$) at low Reynolds number: Hadamard-Rybczynski solution [1].

Similarly the results for the rigid spheres, often referred to as Stokes' expressions, are derived by substituting $\kappa = \infty$. They are

$$
\left.
\begin{aligned}
U &= 2a^2(\rho - \hat{\rho})g/9\mu \\[6pt]
F &= 6\pi\mu aU \\[6pt]
C_D &= 6/Re
\end{aligned}
\right\} \quad \kappa = \infty
\tag{16}
$$

Figure 1 illustrates the streamlines both inside and outside the bubble and clearly shows a Hill's spherical vortex with its center on the equatorial plane, as required by the symmetry of the governing equations (cf. Equations 2–6) about the mid-plane $\theta = \pi/2$.

The prior results for the inviscid bubbles (cf. Equation 15) are strictly valid for contaminant-free fluids. It is well known that traces of surface-active impurities usually present in the fluids adsorb at the interface and may, depending on the size of the bubble, profoundly affect the circulation, and hence, the drag force on the bubble. Thus, for example, the drag coefficient predicted by the Hadamard-Rybczynski theory (cf. Equation 15) may be as much as 50% lower than its actual value for small bubbles. In other words, the drag coefficient for small bubbles obey Stokes' law (cf. Equation 16) for rigid spheres. Systems which exhibit high interfacial tensions such as air-water and liquid-metal-air are most affected by the presence of the contaminants. Since in practice most systems contain surface-active contaminants, the Hadamard-Rubczynski theory is not often obeyed. It, however, serves as an important limiting case.

Effect of Surface-Active Impurities

As mentioned in the previous section, traces of impurities usually present in the fluid adsorb on the surface of the bubble and thereby reduce the degree of internal circulation, increase the drag, and lower the heat and mass transfer rates. Thus sufficiently small gas bubbles undergo a gradual transition as the bubble volume is increased from a noncirculating regime in which Stokes' drag law (Equation 16) is applicable to a freely circulating regime in which Hadamard-Rybczynski's drag law (Equation 15) is applicable.

Accounting for the influence of surface-active contaminants is complicated by the fact that both the amount and the nature of the impurity are important in determining its effect. A considerable amount of work has been done on the subject, and this has been reviewed by a number of authors (see, for example, Harper [5] and Clift, Grace, and Weber [1]). Impurities which are soluble in either phase have the greatest retarding effect. Also bubbles may be relatively impurity-free when they are injected into a system, but the internal circulation and hence, the rise velocity will decrease with time as the impurities accumulate at the interface [6–8]. Most studies on the subject deal with non-ionic impurities and hence, we shall restrict our discussion to this kind of impurities. The reader interested in systems containing ionic impurities is referred to Davis and Rideal [9] and Parsons [10].

The concentration of surface-active impurity (henceforth also referred to as surfactant) at the bubble surface and hence the retardation in the internal circulation is primarily governed by three rate processes: Diffusion of surfactant from the bulk phases to the interface; adsorption-desorption kinetics at the interface; and diffusion of surfactant along the interface. Thus the important parameters under low Reynolds number conditions are the Peclet numbers based on the diffusion coefficients of the surfactants in the bulk phases and at the interface, and the constants describing the absorption-desorption kinetics of the surfactant at the interface. The definitions of these parameters and a complete set of governing equations have been given by Sadhal and Johnson [11]. Since there is no theory at present to predict the dependence of the rise velocity for the entire range of values of these parameters, we shall restrict our discussion to two limiting cases in which the Peclet number is either small or large.

Savic [12], Davis and Acrivos [13], Harper [5], and most recently Sadhal and Johnson [11] have treated the case of large Peclet numbers which is applicable to surfactants whose solubility in both phases is very small. The phenomenon in this limiting case has been described by Davis and Acrivos [13]. A clean bubble rising through a fluid containing a dissolved surfactant will soon get contaminated due to the adsorption of the surfactant on the interface. The surfactant, being relatively insoluble, will be convected to the rear where it will accumulate, producing a surface-tension gradient (γ being a function of concentration of the surfactant) which in turn will oppose the tangential shear stress and thereby stop the surface flow over the rear portion of the bubble. As more surfactant is adsorbed, the cap will grow as long as the surface tension at the rear continues to decrease, but when the latter reaches its minimum value (γ_{min}), corresponding to a monolayer saturation, any further accumulation of surfactants cannot bring about a corresponding increase in the cap size since the existing surface tension gradient will then not be able to support the additional shear along the surface of the cap. Accordingly, if the bubble is small enough, the cap will cover the entire surface owing to the effectiveness of the surface tension forces, while, for a large bubble the surface film will collapse when the cap angle is very small. In short, the cap angle over which surfactant is collected at the rear (see Figure 2) should be determined by a dimensionless group containing the difference between the surface tension of a clean interface, (γ_{max}) and the value of the surface tension at the point of monolayer saturation (γ_{min}). This is in agreement with the experimental observations made by a number of investigators [12, 14–19] who also observed that the velocity on each side of the

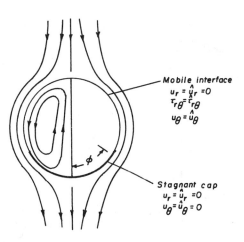

Mobile interface
$u_r = \hat{u}_r = 0$
$\tau_{r\theta} = \hat{\tau}_{r\theta}$
$u_\theta = \hat{u}_\theta$

Stagnant cap
$u_r = \hat{u}_r = 0$
$u_\theta = \hat{u}_\theta = 0$

Figure 2. A typical flow pattern in the presence of low solubility surfactants. The spherical cap having a no-slip condition is denoted by a heavy line.

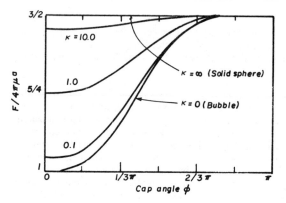

Figure 3. The drag force in the limit of large Peclet numbers as a function of the cap angle ϕ for various values of $\kappa = \hat{\mu}/\mu$ [11].

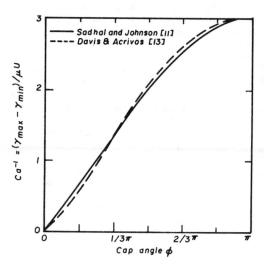

Figure 4. The reciprocal of the capillary number as a function of the cap angle ϕ [11].

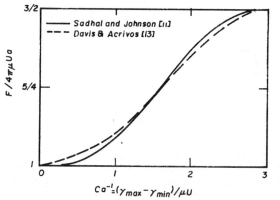

Figure 5. The drag force in the limit of large Peclet numbers [13].

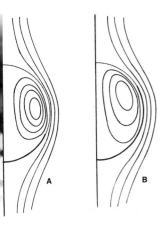

Figure 6. Streamlines (A) $\phi = \frac{1}{3}\pi$ and (B) $\phi = \frac{2}{3}\pi$, with $\kappa = \frac{1}{2}$, Pe $\gg 1$. The no-slip interface is indicated by a heavy line [13].

cap vanishes. In the limit of large Peclet numbers, therefore, the tangential force balance at the bubble surface (r = a) is (see, for example, Reference 11).

$$\frac{\partial}{\partial r}\left(\frac{1}{r^2}\frac{\partial \psi}{\partial r}\right) = \kappa \frac{\partial}{\partial r}\left(\frac{1}{r^2}\frac{\partial \hat{\psi}}{\partial r}\right) \qquad \phi < \theta \leq \pi \tag{17a}$$

$$\frac{\partial \psi}{\partial r} = \frac{\partial \hat{\psi}}{\partial r} = 0 \qquad 0 \leq \theta < \phi \tag{17b}$$

The creeping flow equation (Equation 2) with the boundary conditions (Equations 3, 4, 6, and 17) has been solved by Davis and Acrivos [13] using an approximate numerical method and, recently, by Sadhal and Johnson [11] via an exact analytical method. Their results, which are summarized in Figures 3–6, are in good agreement. In Figure 3 the drag force is plotted as a function of the cap angle for various viscosity ratios. As seen from this figure, the drag force on the bubble ($\kappa = 0$) increases from $4\pi\mu Ua$ to $6\pi\mu Ua$ as the cap angle is increased from 0 to π. In Figure 4, $Ca^{-1} \equiv (\gamma_{max} - \gamma_{min})/\mu U$ is plotted as a function of the cap angle. As expected, the cap angle increases with Ca^{-1}. Finally, since the drag force must equal the buoyancy force, the velocity and hence the drag coefficient must be a function of bubble size. This is shown in Figure 5 where the drag coefficient is seen to decrease by 50% as the nondimensional group $a\sqrt{(\rho - \hat{\rho})g/(\gamma_{min} - \gamma_{max})}$ is increased from approximately 1 to 3. The streamlines for $\phi = 1/3\pi$ and $2/3\pi$ are shown in Figure 6. This shows the reduction in internal circulation and a shift in the vortex from the equatorial plane. In addition to the preceding results, Sadhal and Johnson [11] have computed the amount of surfactant at the interface and asymptotic results for small cap angles.

In the other limit of low Peclet numbers, which is applicable to highly soluble surfactants, there is a nonzero velocity over the entire surface. The surface-diffusion and adsorption-desorption processes in this limit counteract the convection of surfactant to the rear resulting in a uniform concentration of the surfactant along the interface. Such flows have been studied by a number of investigators including Levich [20], Schechter and Farley [21], Newman [22], Wasserman and Slattery [23], Harper [5, 24], Saville [25], Lucassen and Giles [26] and Levan and Newman [27]. The resulting internal flow in this limit is symmetric about the equatorial plane, exactly as in the Hadamard-Rybczynski theory, with the surfactant producing merely a general reduction of the overall circulation rate, and hence the reduction in drag coefficient with increase in the nondimensional bubble size $a\sqrt{(\rho - \hat{\rho})g/\gamma}$ is not as dramatic as was the case with large Peclet numbers. The terminal velocity of a drop is given by

$$U = \frac{2}{3}\frac{ga^2(\rho - \hat{\rho})}{\mu}\left[\frac{1 + \kappa + C/\mu}{1 + 3(\kappa + C/\mu)}\right] \tag{18}$$

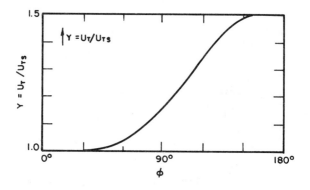

Figure 7. Savic's [12] result for the terminal velocity of bubbles or drops.

where the constant C, which corresponds to an apparent increase in the viscosity of the drop, depends on the nondimensional groups involving the adsorption-desorption kinetic parameters, solubility of the surfactant, diffusion coefficients, and the radius of the drop.

Levan and Newman [27] have derived stream functions for an arbitrary variation of interfacial tension along the bubble surface. Their results could be employed to calculate the drag coefficient or the rise velocity if the concentration distribution of the surfactant at the bubble surface and the concentration-interfacial tension equilibrium data are available.

Finally, when the information on the type of contaminant is unavailable, the Savic's [12] curve (Figure 7), which is based on the assumption of variation of the interfacial tension from its value for a clean interface (γ) at the front to a zero value at the rear of the bubble, is useful. Y in that figure is related to the terminal velocity of the drop by

$$U = \frac{4ga^2(\rho - \hat{\rho})}{3\mu} \left(\frac{1 + \kappa}{2 + 3\kappa} \right) [Y - 1] \tag{19}$$

Wall Effects

The analytical solutions presented in the previous sections are applicable to a single bubble or drop rising through an unbounded fluid. Since most fluids are bounded by some container walls, it is necessary to examine its influence on the shape and the rise velocity of bubbles or drops. We shall limit our discussion to cylindrical container walls (see Figure 8).

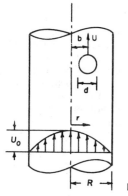

Figure 8. A bubble rising through a fluid in laminar flow.

A bubble rising through a fluid bounded by a circular tube will, in general, deviate from its spherical shape but not drift from its radial position when the creeping flow approximations are valid. This follows from the principle of reversibility for creeping flows. In other words, the motion of bubble will be parallel to the axis of the tube. We shall first consider the case of a bubble rising along the axis of the tube ($b = 0$) with a velocity U in an impurity-free fluid which is at rest ($U_0 = 0$) far upstream and downstream of the bubble. Haberman and Sayre [28] have obtained an approximate expression for the drag force for this situation:

$$F = 2\pi\mu a U K(2 + 3\kappa)/(1 + \kappa); \qquad (b = U_0 = 0) \tag{20a}$$

where K, the correction factor to the Hadamard-Rybczynski theory, is given by

$$K = \left[1 + 2.2757\lambda^5\left(\frac{1 - \kappa}{2 + 3\kappa}\right)\right]\Bigg/\left[1 - 0.7017\left(\frac{2 + 3\kappa}{1 + \kappa}\right)\lambda\right.$$
$$\left. + 2.0865\left(\frac{\kappa}{1 + \kappa}\right)\lambda^3 + 0.5689\left(\frac{2 - 3\kappa}{1 + \kappa}\right)\lambda^5 - 0.72603\left(\frac{1 - \kappa}{1 + \kappa}\right)\lambda^6\right] \tag{20b}$$

In the prior equations a is an equivalent (spherical) radius of the drop and $\lambda \equiv a/R$, R being the radius of the tube. Equation 20 for the drag force is in good agreement with the experimental data for small λ and relatively large aqueous glycerine or silicone oil drops falling through castor oil [28]. As λ increases, the presence of the walls causes the drop to deform from a spherical to an approximately prolate ellipsoidal shape. Although significant droplet deformation occurs for large λ, the preceding expression gives an accurate estimate of the drag force for λ up to about 0.5.

The preceding approximate analysis has also been extended to the case of a parabolic velocity profile of the fluid far upstream and downstream of the drop (cf. Figure 8). The drag force in this case is

$$F = 2\pi\mu a[(2 + 3\kappa)/(1 + \kappa)][KU - K'U_0] \tag{21a}$$

where K is given by Equation 20 and

$$K' = \frac{1 - \left(\frac{2\kappa}{2 + 3\kappa}\right)\lambda^2 + 0.60651\left(\frac{1 - \kappa}{2 + 3\kappa}\right)\lambda^5}{1 + 2.2757\left(\frac{1 - \kappa}{2 + 3\kappa}\right)\lambda^5} \tag{21b}$$

The prior results give good estimates for the drag force and hence the rise velocity provided that λ is less than about 0.5, the Reynolds number is less than unity, and the particle is near the axis of the tube ($b \ll R$). More work is required to estimate the dependence of K and K' on b/R. When λ exceeds 0.5, the bubble deviates significantly from the spherical shape, and in the limit of large λ, the bubbles tend to be bullet shaped as shown in Figure 9. Such bubbles are often referred to

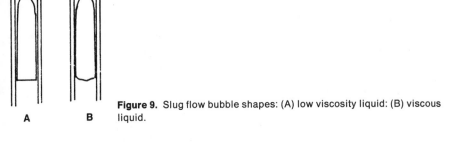

Figure 9. Slug flow bubble shapes: (A) low viscosity liquid: (B) viscous liquid.

A   B

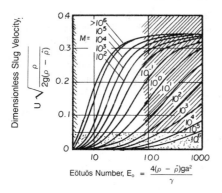

Eötuös Number, $E_o = \dfrac{4(\rho - \hat{\rho})ga^2}{\gamma}$

Figure 10. General correlation for the rise velocity of slug flow bubbles [31].

as slugs or Taylor bubbles. The slug can be considered to be composed of two parts, a rounded nose region whose shape and dimensions are independent of the overall slug length and a cylindrical section surrounded by an annular film of the continuous fluid. Wallis [29] and Govier and Aziz [30] have reviewed various theoretical and experimental studies on the behavior of slugs. A useful correlation due to White and Beardmore [31] to estimate the rise velocity of the slug is given in Figure 10. The parameter M in that figure is the Morton number, i.e.

$$M = g\mu^4(\rho - \hat{\rho})/\rho^2\gamma^3 \qquad (22)$$

Expressions for the drag force in various regimes such as the surface-tension-forces dominant and the viscous-forces-dominant regimes have been obtained and may be found in White and Beardmore [31] or Clift, Grace, and Weber [1]. These authors have also given results for the slug behavior in circular tubes inclined with respect to the gravitational vector and in noncircular container walls.

The preceding discussion for clean interface is generally applicable to relatively large bubbles or drops, i.e. when the Eötvös numbers $E_o \equiv a^2(\rho - \hat{\rho})g/\gamma$ is greater than approximately 20. When the surface-active contaminants are present and the Eötvös number is small, the bubble interface is stagnant, i.e. bubble behaves like a rigid particle. The case of a rigid particle moving through a viscous-bounded fluid has been studied extensively and the results are summarized by Happel and Brenner [32] and Leal [33]. We summarize here some of the important results.

For a rigid sphere moving through an otherwise undisturbed fluid, without rotation and with translational velocity U parallel to a principle axis of the container wall,

$$K = F/6\pi\mu Ua = [1 - Ca/l + 0(a/l)^3]^{-1} \qquad (23)$$

Table 1
Wall Correction Coefficient C in Equation 23 for Rigid Boundaries

Boundary	Location of Particle	Direction of Motion	C
Circular cylinder	Axis	Axial	2.10444
	Eccentric	Axial	Figure 11
Parallel plane walls	Midplane	Parallel to walls	1.004
	$\frac{1}{4}$ distance across channel	Parallel to walls	0.6526
Single plane wall		Parallel to wall	$\frac{9}{16}$
		Normal to wall	$\frac{9}{8}$
Spherical	Center		$\frac{9}{4}$

From Clift, Grace, and Weber [1].

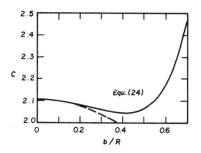

Figure 11. Wall correction coefficient [C in Equation 23] for a rigid particle moving eccentrically in a circular cylinder [1].

where l is the shortest distance from the center of the sphere to the wall and C depends on the geometry of the container wall. Table 1 lists C for various situations. For a rigid sphere moving eccentrically in a cylinder, C depends upon distance from the axis as shown in Figure 11 where it is also compared with the asymptotic result for small b/R:

$$C = 2.1044 - 0.6977(b/R)^2 + 0(b/R)^4 \tag{24}$$

It is interesting and perhaps significant to note that K is relatively insensitive to position provided that b/R is less than 0.6.

Equation 23 is an exact analytical result for small a/l. Experimental determination of K reported by Fidleris and Whitemore [34] agrees within 1% for $\lambda \le 0.6$ with an approximate expression due to Haberman and Sayre [28]:

$$K = \frac{1 - 0.75857\lambda^5}{1 - 2.1050\lambda + 2.0865\lambda^3 - 1.7068\lambda^5 + 0.72603\lambda^6} \tag{25}$$

Finally, K can also be estimated from an empirical correlation due to Francis [35]:

$$K = \left[\frac{1 - 0.475\lambda}{1 - \lambda}\right]^4 \tag{26}$$

For a rigid sphere on the axis of a tube through which a fluid moves in laminar flow (cf. Figure 8 with b = 0), Haberman and Sayre [28] obtained

$$F = 6\pi\mu aK(U - K'U_0)$$

where

$$K' = \frac{1 - 2\lambda^2/3 - 0.20217\lambda^5}{1 - 0.75857\lambda^5} \tag{27}$$

It should be noted that Equations 23–27 are strictly applicable to rigid spheres and hence are useful only for small Eötvös numbers (Eo < 1) at which the internal circulation in the bubble vanishes.

Non-Newtonian Effects

The transition from a freely circulation Hadamard-Rybczynski's regime to a noncirculating Stokes' regime as the bubble volume is decreased below some critical range has also been observed for non-Newtonian fluids [36].

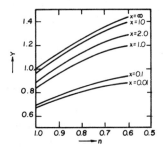

Figure 12. The correction factor Y (cf. Equation 29) as a function of the power-law index n [37].

The drag force exerted by a power-law fluid, whose constitutive relation is given by

$$\underset{\approx}{\tau} = -K(\tfrac{1}{2}\underset{\approx}{e}:\underset{\approx}{e})^{(n-1)/2}\underset{\approx}{e} \tag{28}$$

—$\underset{\approx}{\tau}$ and $\underset{\approx}{e}$ being, respectively, the stress and deformation tensors defined in the usual way, on a freely circulating Newtonian fluid sphere has been computed via an approximate collocation method by Nakano and Tien [37]. Their results for various viscosity ratios $X = \hat{\mu}a^{n-1}/KU^{n-1}$ are shown in Figure 12 in terms of a correction factor Y for the drag coefficient C_D:

$$C_D = \frac{24Y}{2^n Re_0} \tag{29a}$$

$$Re_0 \equiv \frac{\rho U^{2-n}a^n}{K} \tag{29b}$$

An asymptotic expression valid for n close to unity and a freely circulating bubble ($X = 0$) has been obtained by Hirose and Moo-Young [38]. Their results can be expressed as

$$Y = \frac{2^n 3^{(n-3)/2}(13 + 4n - 8n^2)}{(2n+1)(n+2)} \qquad (x = 0, |n-1| \ll 1) \tag{30}$$

From the prior results we see that a freely circulating drop moving in a pseudoplastic fluid (n < 1) experiences less drag as compared to that in a Newtonian fluid. Nakano and Tien's [37] results for $X = \infty$, on the other hand, can be used to estimate drag on a bubble in a noncirculating Stokes' regime. Alternatively, their results can be expressed in terms of a ratio of drag forces in two regimes:

$$C = \left(\frac{Y_{\text{rigid sphere}}}{Y_{\text{fluid sphere}}}\right)^{1/n} \tag{31}$$

As shown in Figure 13, C is greater than a Newtonian value 1.5 for all values of n less unity, thereby indicating an increase in drag coefficients for pseudoplastic fluids as the bubble interface changes its characteristics from a freely circulating to a noncirculating one. This is in agreement with the experimental observations of Astarita and Apuzzo [36] and Fararoui and Kintner [39]. The case of a viscoelastic suspending fluid is even more interesting. Here the experimental observations [36, 40–42] have shown that the transition from a freely circulating to a noncirculating regime as the bubble volume is decreased is very sharp, and occurs at relatively larger gas bubble volumes. Moreover, the ratio of correction factors Y in the two regions has been found to be of $0(10)$ compared with $\frac{3}{2}$ for a Newtonian suspending fluid. Although an exact quantitative treatment

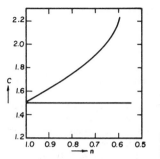

Figure 13. C (cf. Equation 31) versus the power-law index n [37].

for the range of parameters employed in the experiments is still lacking, it is believed that the elastic behavior of the suspending fluid is primarily responsible for the observed large difference in the drag coefficients in the two regimes.

RISE VELOCITY OF A SWARM OF GAS BUBBLES

Dispersion of gases in liquids is widely employed in many processes and it is often desirable to estimate the terminal velocity of a swarm of gas bubbles rising through a pool of liquid. In addition to the variables discussed in the preceding section for isolated bubbles, the terminal velocity will depend on the geometry and the size distribution of the bubbles. Since there are no systematic experimental investigations examining the effect of these parameters, we shall restrict our discussion to theoretical investigations of the problem. Although the results presented here are derived for limiting cases corresponding either to small bubble volume fractions or to specific geometrical configurations of swarms, they are useful in estimating the rise velocity of swarms encountered in practice. All the investigations deal with infinitely extended swarms, i.e. they neglect the wall effects. The results would therefore be applicable to dispersions whose average bubble-bubble separation is much smaller compared to the dimensions of the vessel.

Wacholder [43] employed a statistical averaging technique [44] to estimate the terminal velocity of bubbles or drops when their volume fraction c is small. His analysis has been corrected recently by Haber and Hetsroni [45], who gave the following expression for the terminal velocity of identical-sized drops:

$$\frac{U_c}{U} = 1 - \left[\frac{4 + 5\kappa}{1 + \kappa} + \frac{(2 + 3\kappa)(8 + 15\kappa)}{24(1 + \kappa)^2} - \frac{(17 + 2\kappa)(2 + 3\kappa)^2}{384(1 + \kappa)^2}\right]c + 0(c^2) \tag{32}$$

where U_c is a velocity of any representative drop in the dispersion (or swarm) and U is the corresponding Hadamard-Rybczynski velocity (cf. Equation 14) for an isolated drop. For a special case of gas bubbles ($\kappa = 0$), the previous expression reduces to

$$\frac{U_c}{U} = 1 - 4.49c + 0(c^2) \tag{33}$$

In addition, Haber and Hetsroni [44] have also presented, in their paper, the results for the 0(c) coefficients in the preceding equation for bidispersed system, i.e. the dispersions consisting of drops of two different sizes.

The foregoing results are valid for clean interfaces. If the surface-active impurities are present in the system, the circulation inside a relatively small drop may be significantly affected. For dispersions of small noncirculating drops (Eo < 1), an estimate for the velocity may be obtained by substituting $\kappa = \infty$ in Equation 32. In this noncirculating regime, Batchelor [45] obtained

$$\frac{U_c}{U} = 1 - 6.55c + 0(c^2) \tag{34}$$

which has an $0(c)$ coefficient slightly different from -6.59 given by Equation 32 with $\kappa = \infty$ owing to an approximation employed in Haber and Hetsroni's [44] analysis.

The preceding theory determines the density probability function specifying the location of drops from purely hydrodynamic forces and hence the results are applicable to systems with relatively weak Brownian forces—a condition satisfied by most dispersions except those whose drops are in the colloidal size range. Sirkar [46] assumed that the problem of determining the terminal velocity is equivalent to the calculation of pressure drop in fluid moving with a steady velocity through a dispersion whose drops have fixed locations with a uniform probability density function. Since the location of drops during settling is affected by the flow, Sirkar's results for the fixed drops are invalid except for the initial settling of a well-stirred dispersion or the Brownian-force-dominated systems.

Determination of the coefficient of $0(c^2)$ in Equations 32–34 using the statistical techniques is extremely difficult and has not met with much success to date. Hence these techniques have been limited to dilute dispersions ($c \ll 1$). There is no completely acceptable theory at present to predict the terminal velocity of nondilute dispersions; two approaches have, however, gained some acceptance.

The first approach employs a unit cell model. This model was applied for rigid particles by Kuwabara [47] and for drops by Gal-Or and Waslo [48]. According to this model the influence of neighboring particles is taken into account by assuming sufficient boundary conditions on a finite boundary (usually a sphere of radius $ac^{-1/3}$) enclosing the particle under consideration. The results obtained by this approach obviously depend on the choice of boundary conditions. For example, Kuwabara's [47] results, which were obtained by assuming vanishing normal components of velocity and vorticity at the cell boundary, are different from those of Gal-Or and Waslo [48], who assumed vanishing components of velocity at the boundary. This approach has been, therefore, criticized for its ad hoc nature implied in the choice of the shape of the cell and boundary conditions there.

The second approach overcomes this criticism by dealing with specific geometrical arrangements of the particles. Sangani and Acrivos [49] have considered the case of dispersion whose particle centers coincide with the lattice points of a periodic array. Since the particles initially in a periodic array continue to remain so as they rise through the fluid, this choice of geometrical arrangement avoids the difficulty experienced in Sirkar's [46] investigation described earlier for small c. Sangani and Acrivos [49] employed a method of multipole expansions and obtained the terminal velocities of freely circulating gas bubbles ($\kappa = 0$). Their results are presented in Table 2 in terms of a hindrance factor Y_H defined by

$$U_c = \frac{a^2}{3\mu}(\rho - \hat{\rho})g/Y_H \tag{35}$$

χ in that table is defined as

$$\chi \equiv \left(\frac{c}{c_{max}}\right)^{1/3} \tag{36}$$

where c_{max} is the maximum volume fraction, i.e. the volume fraction of bubbles when they are touching each other, whose value equals $\pi/6 = 0.5236$, $\sqrt{3}\,\pi/8 = 0.6802$, and $\sqrt{2}\,\pi/6 = 0.7405$, respectively for a simple, body-centered, and face-centered cubic arrays. These results are also plotted in Figure 14 where we see that Y_H and hence the terminal velocity is relatively insensitive to the geometry of the array provided that $c < 0.3$. Sangani and Acrivos also gave asymptotic results for small

Table 2
The Hinderance Factor Y_H (cf. Equation 35) for Freely Circulating and Noncirculating Bubbles ($\kappa = 0$) in Simple Cubic (SC), Body-Centered Cubic (BCC) and Free-Centered Cubic (FCC) Arrays

χ	Y_H freely circulating			Y_H noncirculating		
	SC	BCC	FCC	SC	BCC	FCC
0.1	1.140	1.117	1.121	1.747	1.779	1.789
0.2	1.233	1.266	1.276	2.082	2.173	2.200
0.3	1.396	1.460	1.480	2.250	2.750	2.811
0.4	1.609	1.724	1.760	3.228	3.635	3.765
0.5	1.898	2.101	2.168	4.263	5.830	5.362
0.6	2.315	2.678	2.808	5.961	7.662	8.306
0.7	2.967	3.650	3.927	9.006	13.297	14.575
0.8	4.11	5.54	6.26	15.09	25.35	31.3
0.85	5.06	7.29	8.59	20.46	38.7	51.9
0.9	6.51	10.26	13.01	28.74	64.2	97.6
0.95	8.84	15.99	23.34	41.85	118.0	228
1.0	12.8	28.7	59.0	63.1	243 ± 3	657 ± 15

volume fractions:

$$Y_H^{-1} = \begin{cases} 1 - 1.1734c^{1/3} - 0.1178c^2 + 0(c^{8/3}) & \text{(simple cubic)} \\ 1 - 1.1946c^{1/3} + 0.3508c^2 + 0(c^{8/3}) & \text{(body-centered cubic)} \\ 1 - 1.1945c^{1/3} + 0.3611c^2 + 0(c^{8/3}) & \text{(face-centered cubic)} \end{cases} \quad (37)$$

These results agree with the numerical results presented in Table 2 to within 5% for $\chi < 0.6$ for all the three cubic arrays.

The preceding results for freely circulating bubbles are expected to apply to relatively large bubbles ($E_o \gg 1$). Small bubbles ($E_o \ll 1$), as discussed earlier, would tend to behave like rigid

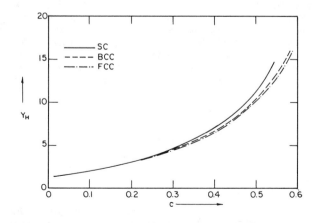

Figure 14. Y_H (cf. Equation 35) as a function of volume fraction of freely circulating bubbles in simple cubic (SC), body-centered cubic (BCC), and face-centered cubic (FCC) arrangements [49].

particles. Sangani and Acrivos [50] have also computed the terminal velocities of rigid particles and their results are presented in Table 2 along with those of freely circulating particles. From these results we note that the hindrance to the rise velocity of a bubble due to the presence of other bubbles is much more pronounced in case of rigid interfaces.

DEFORMATION AND BREAKUP OF SINGLE BUBBLES OR DROPS

In this section we shall consider deformation and breakup of a single drop or bubble placed in fluid undergoing a steady shear. The results are important in the design of mixing devices for dispersing one phase into another [51] and in understanding the rheological behavior of emulsions [52].

A drop placed in a shear field tends to rotate and deform. If the velocity gradients are large enough, interfacial tension forces are no longer able to maintain the fluid particle, and it ruptures into two or more smaller particles [53–56]. Figure 15 shows tracings of photographs showing the effect of increasing shear rate. Observations of drop and bubble breakup have also been obtained in hyperbolic flows [54, 55]. Those experiments suggest that the behavior of the drop, under creeping flow conditions, depends in a rather complicated manner on the nature of flow generated in the experimental apparatus and on the two dimensionless groups: κ, the ratio of viscosities and $N \equiv G\mu a/\gamma$ where G is the magnitude of the applied rate of strain, $a \equiv (3v/4\pi)^{1/3}$ with v the volume of the drop, γ is the interfacial tension and μ is the viscosity of the suspending medium. For example, it was found that in a simpler shear, drop with viscosity ratio κ greater than approximately 4 retained a steady shape even when N was increased seemingly without bound, whereas in a hyperbolic flow the same drops broke up when N exceeded a value of about 0.4. On the other hand, when $\kappa \ll 1$, the drops became long and slender prior to breakup for both types of shear. This required relatively large strain rates, the critical value of N being proportional to $\kappa^{-0.55}$ in a simple shear and proportional to $\kappa^{-0.16}$ in a hyperbolic flow [51]. And finally, the mode of breakup was found to depend upon the rate at which the strain is applied [56]. If dG/dt was too large, drops with κ less than about 0.2 developed pointed ends and fragments broke off both ends. On the other hand, if G was increased gradually, necking occurred in the center until rupture produced two large drops of nearly equal size separated by tiny satelite drops (cf. Figure 15A). With large dG/dt and $0.2 < \kappa < 3$, drops were pulled out into a long and slender thread which eventually broke up due to hydrodynamic instabilities (cf. Figure 15B). No corresponding experiments appear to have been performed in which the applied shear is of a more general type.

A considerable insight into the phenomenon of deformation and breakup has been gained by a number of theoretical studies on the subject. These studies have dealt with two limiting cases in which the deformation from a spherical shape is either small [56–61] or large (so that the drop is long and slender and hence the slender-body theory is applicable to predict the flow) [62–67]. Exceptions are the investigations of Youngren and Acrivos [68] and Rallison and Acrivos [69] who obtained numerically the shape and transient response of bubbles and drops placed in viscous extensional flows. Their numerical results shall be presented later along with the asymptotic results to be described next.

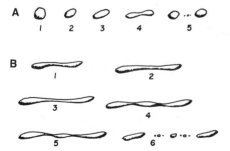

Figure 15. Breakup of liquid drops in a simple shear. Velocity gradient G increases in each sequence: (A) Rumscheidt and Mason [54]: $\kappa = 1.1, \gamma = 4.8$ dynes/cm; (B) Torza, Cox and Mason [56]: $\kappa = 1.1, \gamma = 1.3$ dynes/cm.

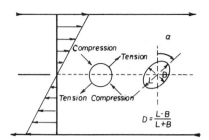

$$D = \frac{L-B}{L+B}$$

Figure 16. Deformation a spherical drop in a simple shear.

Small Deformations

Taylor [57] showed that a drop placed in a steady shear flow as shown in Figure 16 deforms into an ellipsoid when $G\mu a/\gamma \ll 1$. In terms of a shape parameter D and an orientation angle α defined in Figure 16, his results are

κ fixed, $N \to 0$

$$\alpha \simeq \pi/4, \quad D = N\left(\frac{19\kappa + 16}{16\kappa + 16}\right) \tag{38}$$

and

$\kappa \to \infty$, N fixed

$$\alpha \simeq \pi/2, \quad D = \frac{5}{4\kappa} \tag{39}$$

Inspection of the preceding equation suggests that the deformation parameter D is small in both cases; however, one would also expect that $D \to 0$ when $N \to 0$ and $K \to \infty$ simultaneously, suggesting the possibility of a more general treatment in which the only limitation is that $D \ll 1$. This general theory was developed by Cox [60], who also determined the transient response of an initially spherical drop freely suspended in a simple shear or hyperbolic flow. In case of a simple shear, the deformation and orientation undergo damped oscillations with a relaxation time given by

$$\tau_r = a\mu\kappa/\gamma \tag{40}$$

and at very large times

$$D = \frac{5(19\kappa + 16)}{4(1 + \kappa)\sqrt{(19\kappa)^2 + (20/N)^2}} \tag{41}$$

$$\alpha = \frac{\pi}{4} + \frac{1}{2}\tan^{-1}\left(\frac{19N\kappa}{20}\right) \tag{42}$$

Equations 41 and 42 are valid for all values of κ and N which yield $D \ll 1$ and, in particular, reduce to Equations 38 and 39 for, respectively, $N \to 0$ and $\kappa \to \infty$. Barthés-Biesel and Acrivos [61] extended the preceding analysis by including $0(N^2)$ terms for fixed κ (or, equivalently, $0(\kappa^{-2})$ terms with fixed N) in their calculations and employed a linear stability theory to determine the onset of droplet bursting for extensional, shear, and hyperbolic flows. According to this analysis, the phenomenon of breakup is identified with the nonexistence of a steady state when N exceeds a critical value, rather than as is commonly the case in many branches of fluid mechanics with the instability

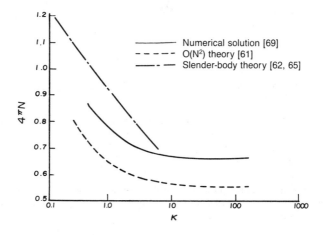

Figure 17. Critical value of N for bursting as a function of κ for extensional flows.

of the solution to the corresponding steady-state problem when the value of the appropriate dimensionless group N lies beyond the critical point. Barthés-Biesel and Acrivos' predictions for the limiting deformation as well as critical value of N at breakup, which are listed in their paper for various flows, are generally in good agreement with the experimental data referred to earlier provided that κ is not too small. For this reason Barthés-Biesel and Acrivos' criterion for low viscosity drops with κ less than approximately 0.2 should be treated with caution. In Figure 17, the predictions of Barthés-Biesel and Acrivos' $O(N^2)$ theory for critical values of N as a function of κ are compared with the exact numerical calculations of Rallison and Acrivos [69] for extensional flows. As seen from this figure, they agree within about 20% for $\kappa \gtrsim 0.5$. For small values of κ, Taylor's [62] analysis for slender drops, to be discussed in the next section, appears to be in a good agreement with the exact numerical results. Finally, as mentioned earlier, the small deformation theories would be inapplicable for the case of inviscid gas bubble ($\kappa = 0$). In Figure 18, D calculated from

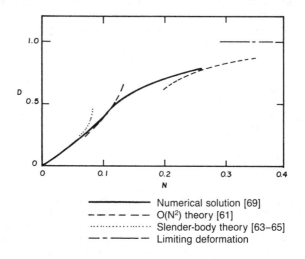

Figure 18. Deformation of an inviscid gas bubble in an extensional flow.

0(N) and 0(N^2) theories is compared with the exact numerical calculations of Youngren and Acrivos [68] for an inviscid gas bubble placed in an extensional flow. As seen in this figure, the 0(N) and 0(N^2) theories agree with the numerical results only for N less than approximately 0.08 and 0.12, respectively.

Long and Slender Drops

As mentioned earlier, drops with small κ tend to deform into long and slender threads prior to their breakup due to the applied shear. In this case, rather than extending small deformation theories discussed in the previous section, it would seem more appropriate to employ a slender-body theory to describe the deformation and breakup of drops. This was first perceived by Taylor [62] who by means of an approximate analysis obtained a quantitative criterion for the maximum value of N for which a steady slender drop can exist under creeping flow conditions; specifically, for the case of extensional flow, he predicted that a droplet would break up when N is increased beyond $0.148\kappa^{-1/6}$. Buckmaster [63, 64] and Acrivos and Lo [65] presented a mathematically systematic treatment and confirmed Taylor's findings. Buckmaster found that there were an infinite number of possible steady shapes of the droplet—all of which satisfied the appropriate governing equations within the order of approximation considered in the analysis—while Acrivos and Lo showed that all of these except one were unstable and hence only one steady shape would be observed under experimental conditions. The predictions of Taylor's theory for the critical value of N at breakup and the deformation of an inviscid gas bubble are compared with the exact numerical results for extensional flows in Figures 17–18. As seen from these figures, they are in good agreement for $\kappa < 0.1$ and N > 0.3. Figure 19 shows numerical results [68] for the steady shapes of an inviscid gas bubble symmetrically placed in an extensional flow as a function of N^{-1}. We see that the shape predicted by the slender-body theory is approached when N is approximately 0.2.

Buckmaster's [63, 64] and Acrivos and Lo's [65] studies were, like Taylor's, confined to the axisymmetric extensional flow; Hinch and Acrivos [66] extended their analysis to the case of a drop placed in a hyperbolic flow—the experimentally used flow field—and showed that the criterion for breakup is virtually identical with that given by Taylor (the critical value of $N\kappa^{1/6}$ being 0.145 as opposed to 0.148). This is in reasonably good agreement with experimental data of Torza, Cox, and Mason [56], Grace [51], and Yu [70], who found that drop breakup occurs at $N\kappa^{0.16} > 0.12$. Finally, the case of long slender drops in simple shear has been studied theoretically by Hinch and Acrivos [68] whose prediction that breakup would occur at $N\kappa^{2/3} > 0.0541$ is in fair agreement with the relation $N\kappa^{0.55} > 0.17$ obtained by fitting Grace's [51] experimental data for $\kappa < 0.1$. In summary, the asymptotic theories for small and large deformations seem to generally agree well with the available experimental and numerical results.

The above results—theoretical as well as experimental—apply to systems relatively free of surface-active contaminants. When the Reynolds number is small, care must be exercised in applying these results to drops under other conditions.

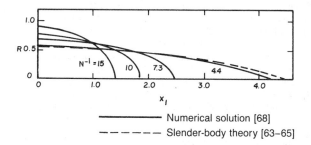

Figure 19. Steady shapes of an inviscid gas bubble symmetrically placed in an extensional flow.

NOTATION

a	drop radius	M	Morton number
C_D	drag coefficient	P	pressure
C	parameter defined by Equation 24; also	Re	Reynolds number
	a constant	r	radical distance
c	volume fraction	U	velocity
D	shape parameter	u_r, u_θ	radial and angular velocity compo-
E_o	Eötvös number		nents, respectively
e	deformation tensor	Y	terminal velocity parameter in Equa-
F	drag force		tion 19
g	acceleration due to gravity	Y_H	hindrance factor
K	correction factor		

Greek Symbols

γ	interfacial tension	τ	stress tensor
θ	angle	τ_r	relaxation time
κ	viscosity ratio	ϕ	angle
λ	ratio of drop to tube radii	χ	volume fraction parameter defined by
μ	viscosity		Equation 36
ρ	density	ψ	stream function

REFERENCES

1. Clift, R., Grace, J. R., and Weber, M. E., "Bubbles, Drops, and Particles," Academic Press, New York, 1978.
2. Hadamard, J. S., *C. R. Acad. Sci.*, 152:1735 (1911).
3. Rybczynski, W., Bull. Int. Acad. Pol. Sci. Lett., Cl. Sci. Math. Nat., Ser. A, 40 (1911).
4. Batchelor, G. K., "An Introduction to Fluid Dynamics," Cambridge University Press, London, 1967.
5. Harper, J. F., *Adv. Appl. Mech.* 12:59 (1972).
6. Garner, F. H., and Skelland, A. H. P., *Chem. Engng. Sci.*, 4:149 (1955).
7. Linton, M., and Sutherland, K. L., Proc. Int. Congr. Surf. Act., 2nd, London, 1:494 (1957).
8. Robinson, J. V., *J. Phys. Colloid Chem.*, 51:431 (1947).
9. Davies, J. T., and Rideal, E. K., "Interfacial Phenomena," Academic Press, New York, 1963.
10. Parsons, R., *Modern Aspects of Electrochemistry*, Vol. 1, 103, Butterworth, London, 1954.
11. Sadhal, S. S., and Johnson, R. E., *J. Fluid Mech.*, 126:237 (1983).
12. Savic, P., Nat. Res. Counc. Can., Div. Mech. Engng. *Rep.*, MT-22 (1953).
13. Davis, R. E., and Acrivos, A., *Chem. Engng. Sci.*, 21:681 (1966).
14. Garner, F. H., and Skelland, A. H. P., *Chem. Engng. Sci.*, 4:149 (1955).
15. Elzinga, E. R., and Banchero, J. T., *A.I.Ch.E.J.*, 7:394 (1961).
16. Griffith, R. M., *Chem. Engng. Sci.*, 17:1057 (1962).
17. Horton, T. J., Fritsch, T. R., and Kintner, R. C., *Can. J. Chem. Engng.*, 43:143 (1965).
18. Huang, W. S., and Kintner, R. C., *A.I.Ch.E.J.* 15:735 (1969).
19. Beitel, A., and Heideger, W. J., *Chem. Engng. Sci.*, 26:711 (1971).
20. Levich, V. G., *Physiochemical Hydrodynamics*, 395, Prentice-Hall, 1962.
21. Schechter, R. S., and Farley, R. W., *Can. J. Chem. Engng.*, 41:103 (1963).
22. Newman, J., *Chem. Engng. Sci.*, 22:83 (1967).
23. Wasserman, M. L., and Slattery, J. C., *A.I.Ch.E.J.*, 15:533 (1969).
24. Harper, J. F., *Appl. Sci. Res.*, 38:343 (1982).
25. Saville, D. A., *Chem. Engng. J.*, 5:251 (1973).
26. Lucassen, J., and Giles, D., *J. Chem. Soc. Faraday Trans.*, 171:217 (1975).
27. Levan, and Newman, J., *A.I.Ch.E.J.*, 72:695 (1976).

28. Haberman, W. L., and Sayre, R. M., David Taylor Model Basin Rep. No. 1143 (1958).
29. Wallis, G. B., "One-Dimensional Two-Phase Flow," McGraw-Hill, New York, 1969.
30. Govier, G. W., and Aziz, K., *The Flow of Complex Mixtures in Pipes*. Van Nostrand-Reinhold, New York, 1972.
31. White, E. T., and Beardmore, R. H., *Chem. Engng. Sci.*, 17:351 (1962).
32. Happel, J., and Brenner, H., *Low Reynolds Number Hydrodynamics*, 2nd ed. Noordhoff, Leyden, Netherlands, 1973.
33. Leal, L. G., *Ann. Fluid Mech.*, 12:435 (1980).
34. Fidleris, V., and Whitemore, R. L., *Br. J. Appl. Phys.* 12:490 (1961).
35. Francis, A. W., *Physics*, 4:403 (1933).
36. Astarita, G., and Apuzzo, G., *A.I.Ch.E.J.*, 11:815 (1965).
37. Nakano, Y., and Tien, C., *A.I.Ch.E.J.*, 14:145 (1968).
38. Hirose, T., and Moo-Young, M., *Can. J. Chem. Engng.*, 47:265 (1969).
39. Fararoui, A., and Kintner, R. C., *Trans. Soc. Rheol.*, 5:369 (1961).
40. Calderbank, P. H., Johnson, D. S. L., and London, J., *Chem. Engng. Sci.*, 25:235 (1970).
41. Leal, L. G., Skoog, J., and Acrivos, A., *Can. J. Chem. Engng.*, 49:569 (1971).
42. Zana, E., and Leal, L. G., *Int. J. Multiphase Flow*, 4:237 (1978).
43. Wacholder, E., *Chem. Engng. Sci.*, 28:1447 (1973).
44. Batchelor, G. K., *J. Fluid Mech.*, 52:245 (1972).
45. Haber, S., and Hetsroni, G., *J. Colloid Interface Sci.*, 79:56 (1981).
46. Sirkar, K. K., *Chem. Engng. Sci.*, 32:1127 (1977).
47. Kuwabara, S., *J. Phys. Soc. Japan*, 14:527 (1959).
48. Gal-Or, G., and Waslo, S., *Chem. Engng. Sci.*, 23:1431 (1968).
49. Sangani, A. S., and Acrivos, A., *Int. J. Multiphase Flow*, 9:181 (1983).
50. Sangani, A. S., and Acrivos, A., *Int. J. Multiphase Flow*, 8:343 (1982).
51. Grace, H. P., Engng. Found. 3rd Res. Conf. Mixing, Andover, New Hampshire (1971).
52. Barthés-Biesel, D., and Acrivos, A., *Int. J. Multiphase Flow*, 1:1 (1973).
53. Karam, H. J., and Bellinger, J. C., *Ind. Engng. Chem. Fundam.* 7:576 (1968).
54. Rumscheidt, F. D., and Mason, S. G., *J. Colloid Sci.*, 16:238 (1961).
55. Taylor, G. I., *Proc. R. Soc. London*, A146:501 (1934).
56. Torza, S., Cox, R. G., and Mason, S. G., *J. Colloid Interface Sci.*, 38:395 (1972).
57. Taylor, G. I., *Proc. R. Soc.* A138:41 (1932).
58. Chaffey, C. E., Brenner, H., and Mason, S. G., *Rheol. Acta*, 4:56 (1965).
59. Buckmaster, J. D., *J. Appl. Mech.*, 95:18 (1973).
60. Cox, R. G., *J. Fluid Mech.*, 37:601 (1969).
61. Barthés-Biesel, D., and Acrivos, A., *J. Fluid Mech.*, 61:1 (1973).
62. Taylor, G. I., Proc. 11th Int. Cong. Appl. Mech., Munich (1964).
63. Buckmaster, J. D., *J. Fluid Mech.*, 55:385 (1972).
64. Buckmaster, J. D., *J. Appl. Mech.*, E40:18 (1973).
65. Acrivos, A., and Lo, T. S., *J. Fluid Mech.*, 56:641 (1978).
66. Hinch, E. J., and Acrivos, A., *J. Fluid Mech.*, 91:401 (1979).
67. Hinch, E. J., and Acrivos, A., *J. Fluid Mech.*, 98:305 (1980).
68. Youngren, G. K., and Acrivos, A., *J. Fluid Mech.*, 76:433 (1976).
69. Rallison, J. M., and Acrivos, A., *J. Fluid Mech.*, 89:191 (1978).
70. Yu, K. L., Ph.D. thesis, University of Houston (1974).

CHAPTER 6

CORRELATIONS FOR BUBBLE RISE IN GAS-LIQUID SYSTEMS

M. E. Abou-El-Hassan

Department of Chemical Engineering
University of Qatar
Doha, Qatar

CONTENTS

IMPORTANCE AND SCOPE

Gas-liquid contact operations play an important role in many industrial chemical processes (e.g. hydrogenation, oxidation, aerobic biological processes, flotation, boiling, air-lifting, absorption, and distillation). It is evident that accurate information about bubble rise phenomena will help in the proper design and operation of process equipment.

The problem of bubble rise in liquids has been addressed since the beginning of this century. A tremendous amount of published work appeared about studies of:

- Bubble formation, shape, geometry, and mode of rise.
- Single bubbles rising in Newtonian and non-Newtonian fluids, pure and impure liquids, fluids contaminated with surface-active agents, liquid metals, and fluidized beds. The effect of the diameter of the container (wall effect), and the effect of the presence of bubble swarms have been considered. Comparison is always done with single, isolated bubbles rising in stagnant infinite liquids.
- Mass transfer from bubbles, bubble age, and dissolution rates.

Theoretical developments of bubble-rise correlations have been done on the basis of the continuity equation, the boundary-layer theory, and dimensional analysis for creeping, intermediate, and potential flow around spheres of rigid and mobile interfaces.

The results from both theoretical and experimental work are usually graphically represented as drag coefficient (C_D) versus Reynolds number on log-log coordinates (Figure 1). Comparison with solid-sphere settling and Stokes law has been always done. Attempts have been made to develop analytical forms of bubble-rise correlations which are in all cases subjected to regime and bubble shape limitations.

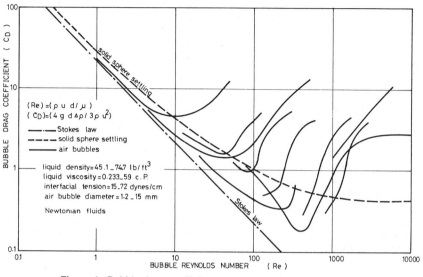

Figure 1. Bubble drag coefficients vs. bubble Reynolds number.

Grace [1] has developed a generalized graphical correlation for different bubble shapes and regimes, using three dimensionless numbers: Reynolds (Re), Eötvös (Eö), and Morton (M) numbers.

The only generalized analytical correlation has been developed by the Author [2] on the basis of new dimensionless groups: flow (F) and velocity numbers (V). The developed correlation is not sensitive to regime limitations or bubble shape, and is valid for a wide range of conditions. Agreement with previous investigators is noticeable for bubble rising in Newtonian and pseudoplastic (non-Newtonian) fluids.

DIMENSIONLESS PARAMETERS USED

Among the dimensionless parameters used to correlate bubble rise in liquids, the following are the most common:

$$\text{Reynolds number (Re)} = (\rho u d / \mu) \tag{1}$$

$$\text{Drag coefficient (C}_\text{D}) = (4gd(\Delta\rho)/\rho u^2) \tag{2}$$

$$\text{Eötvös number (Eö)} = (gd^2(\Delta\rho)/\sigma) \tag{3}$$

$$\text{Morton number (M)} = (g\mu^4(\Delta\rho)/\rho^2\sigma^2) \tag{4}$$

where ρ = liquid density
$(\Delta\rho)$ = difference between liquid and gas densities
u = bubble rise velocity
d = bubble equivalent spherical diameter
μ = liquid viscosity
g = gravitational acceleration
σ = surface (interfacial) tension

A graphical correlation based upon a dimensionless velocity (K_1) and the inverse of viscosity (N_f), and the Archimedes (Ar) number is proposed by Wallis [3] for bubble-rise velocity in slug flow, where:

$$K_1 = \left(u \middle/ \sqrt{gD \frac{\Delta\rho}{\rho}} \right) \tag{5}$$

$$N_f = \sqrt{\frac{gD^3\rho(\Delta\rho)}{\mu^2}} \tag{6}$$

and

$$A_r = \sqrt{(\rho^2\sigma^3/g\mu^4(\Delta\rho))} \tag{7}$$

where   D = tube diameter

White and Beardmore [4] presented another graphical correlation for cylindrical bubbles (slug flow) using dimensionless velocity (K_1) (Equation 5) and the Eötvös number (Eö) (Equation 3), with the Morton number (M) (Equation 4) as a parameter.

BUBBLE-RISE CORRELATIONS AND LIMITS OF APPLICATION

The analytical forms of bubble-rise correlations developed from either theoretical analysis or experimental work are:

1. For bubble Reynolds numbers <0.2 and all values of Eötvös number (Eö), bubbles are spherical and their velocities are bounded by the Stokes [5] and Hadamard-Rybczynski [6] equations. The Stokes law applies to a bubble with a rigid interface, when surface-active impurities are present in amounts sufficient to prohibit internal circulation. The Hadamard-Rybczynski equation applies to a bubble with a completely mobile interface, corresponding to very pure systems.
    In equation form the bubble-rise correlations become:

$$Re = [(E\ddot{o})^{1.5}/K'M^{0.5}] \qquad (Re < 0.2) \tag{8}$$

where $K' = 18$,   for rigid interface
         $K' = 12$,   for mobile interface

Alternative forms of Equation 8 are

$$C_D = (4K'/3Re) \tag{9}$$

$$C_D = \frac{24}{Re} \quad \text{for rigid interface} \tag{10}$$

$$C_D = \frac{16}{Re} \quad \text{for mobile interface} \tag{11}$$

The theoretical development for a spherical bubble rising in straight motion with a wake behind it in streamline creeping flow (Re ≪ 1) gives:

$$C_D = \frac{24}{Re} \cdot \frac{3K'' + 2}{3K'' + 3} \tag{12}$$

where $K'' = $ (gas viscosity/liquid viscosity)

Equation 12 is similar to Equation 10 when K'' is very large, and to Equation 11, if $K'' \cong 0$.

Bubbles smaller than 1 mm in diameter are approximately spherical and rise in straight vertical lines [7]. Bubbles of spherical shapes were observed by Peebles and Garber [8] for the range of Re < 400. This corresponds to a bubble diameter between 0.8 and 0.9 mm for air bubbles rising in water at room temperature. Photographs by Pattle [9] show that air bubbles of diameters of 2 mm rising in water are very seldom symmetrical spheroids.

2. For bubble Reynolds number ranges of 5,000 > Re > 400, which corresponds to equivalent bubble diameter ranges of 18 > d > 2 mm, the bubbles assumed an oblate spheroid or ellipsoidal shape. The motion is not straight and may assume either an helical or a zig-zag path.

The following formula is proposed by Taylor and Acrivos [10] for the rise of ellipsoidal bubbles, for the range: Re < 2 and M $\cong 10^2 - 10^5$

$$C_D = \frac{16}{Re} + 2 + \frac{2}{5} Re \ln\left(\frac{Re}{2}\right) + 1.33 \frac{We}{Re} \tag{13}$$

The Mendelson [11] formula is applicable for ellipsoidal bubbles with: M = 10^{-10}

$$C_D = \frac{8}{3} - \frac{16}{3We} \tag{14}$$

Calderbank and Lochiel [12] proposed an approximate correlation for ellipsoidal bubbles of air and CO_2 rising in water at room temperature based upon the characteristic length which define oblate spheroids: (2a) and (2b), i.e.

$$C_D' = 1.4 \tag{15}$$

For the range of 8,000 > Re > 1,000

$$C_D' = \frac{8gb \, \Delta\rho}{3\rho u^2} \tag{16}$$

and

$$Re' = \frac{2au\rho}{\mu} \tag{17}$$

This also means that

$$U \infty \sqrt{b} \tag{18}$$

$$U \infty \sqrt{d} \tag{19}$$

This result is in agreement with spherical-cap bubbles correlations:

$$C_D = \text{constant} \tag{20}$$

for spherical-cap bubbles rising in inviscid fluids. Davies and Taylor [13] assumed a constant of 2.63; Haberman and Morton [14] assumed a constant of 2.6. The experimental value of the constant is in the range of 2.6 to 2.7.

For spherical-cap bubbles rising in viscous fluids at high Morton numbers, and for Re > 1.2 and Eö > 40, Darton and Harrison [15] proposed the correlation:

$$C_D = 2.7 + \frac{16}{Re} \tag{21}$$

The correlation has been verified by the data of Jones [16] and Kojima et al. [17]. The ranges of spherical-cap bubbles are:

d > 18 mm

Re > 5,000

bubble volume > 3 cm³

Generally for spherical-cap bubbles and cylindrical bubbles, the velocity of rise is found to be:

$$U \propto \sqrt{gd} \qquad \text{spherical-caps} \tag{22}$$

or

$$U \propto \sqrt{gD} \qquad \text{cylindrical (slugs)} \tag{23}$$

where   d = equivalent spherical bubble diameter
         D = tube diameter

The constant of proportionality of Equation 22 is around 0.7 for air bubbles in water at room temperature, and the constant of Equation 23 is around 0.328–0.351 from the work of Davies and Taylor [13], Dumitrescu [18], and Harmathy [19]. This means that

$$C_D = 2.6 \sim 2.7 \tag{24}$$

and

$$(d/D) \cong 0.25$$

from comparison.

3. For bubble Reynolds numbers: Re > 5,000, the bubble rise velocity is no longer dependent upon equivalent diameter or liquid viscosity, and the following correlation is obtained:

$$U \propto \left(\frac{g \, \Delta\rho\sigma}{\rho^2} \right)^{0.25} \tag{25}$$

which is proposed by Harmathy [19] and corresponds to regime 4 of the work of Peebles and Garber [8]. The Harmathy proportional constant for Equation 25 is 1.53, and that of Peebles and Garber is 1.18. If Equation 25 is rearranged we arrive at:

$$\frac{We}{C_D} = \text{constant} \tag{26}$$

or

$$C_D \infty \, We \tag{27}$$

The limit proposed by Peebles and Garber [8] for such a regime is:

$$Re^4 M > 92 \tag{28}$$

DEVELOPING A GENERALIZED BUBBLE-RISE CORRELATION

To develop a generalized correlation for bubble-rise velocity, the effect of the interaction of various forces (buoyancy, viscous, inertial, and interfacial tension forces) must be included in the correlating parameters. The direct use of simple parameters such as density (ρ), density difference ($\Delta\rho$), viscosity (μ), equivalent spherical diameter (d), gravity (g), and velocity (u) will lead to the drag coefficient (C_D) and the Reynolds number (Re).

Since it is common to use dimensionless parameters as force ratios (e.g., the Reynolds number is the ratio of inertial to viscous forces) and since the buoyancy force is the only force responsible for bubble (drop or solid bodies) motion in fluids, therefore the following force ratios will be considered: (buoyancy/viscous), (buoyancy/inertia), and (buoyancy/interfacial tension). As a result of force interaction a measure of interaction may be taken as the geometric mean of the above three ratios, i.e. ((buoyancy/viscous) (buoyancy/inertia) (buoyancy/interfacial tension))$^{1/3}$ and in equation form it is:

$$[g(\Delta\rho)d^{5/3}/u(\rho\mu\sigma)^{1/3}] \tag{29}$$

In order to select the basic parameters associated with bubble motion, the work appearing in the literature was examined and the following parameters selected:

1. The bubble equivalent spherical diameter (d).
2. The kinematic viscosity of the continuous liquid phase (v)
3. A proposed physical parameter ($\sigma\mu^2$) developed from the Mendelson wave analog (11) and the Stokes law of settling to include the interaction of the effect of interfacial tension (σ) and viscosity (μ) at the upper and lower limits of the Reynolds number.
4. The buoyancy force per unit volume (g $\Delta\rho$) as the driving force for bubble motion.
5. The momentum per unit volume (ρu) associated with the motion of bubble.

The preceding arrangement of the selected parameters has a logical sequence of events associated with bubble motion and may be introduced as such for dimensional analysis, i.e.

$$\phi(d, v, \sigma\mu^2, g, \rho u) = 0 \tag{30}$$

and the Pi-theorem of dimensional analysis, when used, gives the following dimensionless numbers:

$$\text{flow number (F)} = (gd^{8/3}(\Delta\rho)\rho^{2/3}/\mu^{4/3}\sigma^{1/3}) \tag{31}$$

and

$$\text{velocity number (V)} = (ud^{2/3}\rho^{2/3}/\mu^{1/3}\sigma^{1/3}) \tag{32}$$

The developed flow and velocity numbers may be written in terms of bubble Reynolds number (Re), drag coefficient (C_D), and the term of interaction (Equation 29) as:

$$F = Re \text{ (interaction term, Equation 29)} \tag{33}$$

$$V = (4/3C_D) \text{ (interaction term, Equation 29)} \tag{34}$$

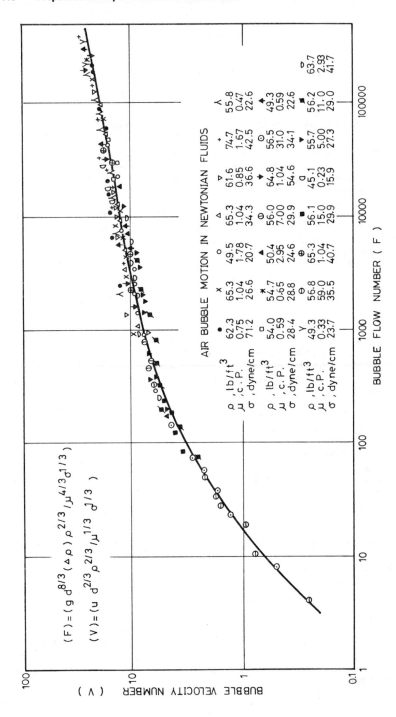

Figure 2. The bubble velocity number vs. the flow number.

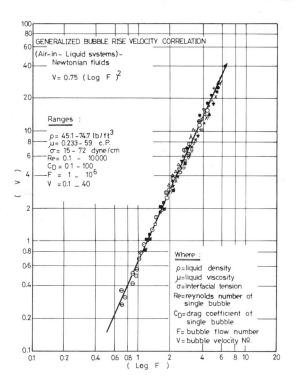

Figure 3. Generalized bubble-rise velocity correlation.

where $Re = (\rho u d/\mu)$
$C_D = (4gd\,\Delta\rho/3u^2\rho)$

The flow and velocity numbers were calculated from the data of the literature for the ranges:

liquid phase density $(\rho) = 45.1 - 74.7$ lb/ft^3

liquid phase viscosity $(\mu) = 0.233 - 59$ centiPoise

interfacial tension $(\sigma) = 15 - 72$ dynes/cm

The gas phase is air, and the bubble size ranges from 1.2 to 1.5 mm. The bubble shapes are spherical, oblate spheroids, and mushroom-like with a spherical cap. The bubble size (diameter) is taken as the equivalent spherical diameter d $= [(6/\pi)(\text{bubble volume})]^{1/3}$. The results are plotted on a log-log paper (Figure 2), and the data fall on a single curve. The analytical form of a generalized correlation (Figure 3) is:

$$V = 0.75\,(\log F)^2 \tag{35}$$

for the preceding range of physical parameters $(\rho, \mu, \sigma,$ and d) and for $Re = 0.1 - 10^4$, $C_D = 0.1 - 10^2$, $F = 1 - 10^6$, and $V = 0.1 - 40$.

COMPARISON WITH PREVIOUSLY DEVELOPED CORRELATIONS

In order to compare with previous investigations, a power-law equation between the flow and the velocity numbers is assumed, i.e.

$$V \propto F^n \tag{36}$$

or after resolving the F and V number into the basic parameters (g, $\Delta\rho$, ρ, u, μ, σ, d) (Equations 31 and 32), we get:

$$u \propto (g \, \Delta\rho)^n \mu^{(1-4n)/3} \sigma^{(1-n)/3} \rho^{(2n-2)/3} d^{(8n-2)/3} \tag{37}$$

The exponent (n) may be regarded as an index for flow regime (e.g. if n = 1, this corresponds to the laminar (viscous) regime where the effect of viscosity is appreciable and of interfacial tension is negligible), and Equation 37 reduces to Stokes law of settling. If n = 0.25, this corresponds to the turbulent regime where the effect of viscosity becomes negligible, and Equation 37 becomes:

$$u \propto (g \, \Delta\rho\sigma/\rho^2)^{0.25} \tag{38}$$

If n = 0.4375, i.e. an intermediate value between 1 and 0.25, this corresponds to a transition regime, where Equation 37 gives: $u \propto \sqrt{d}$, a result in agreement with Haberman and Morton [14], Maneri and Mendelson [20], and Davidson [21], and is also predictable from the Mendelson wave analogy [11] and the Davies-Taylor theory [13].

To compare the results of air bubble motion in non-Newtonian (pseudoplastic) fluids [22], equation [37], may be used and the viscosity (μ) is replaced by

$$KF(n')(u/d)^{n'-1}$$

where   K = consistency
         n′ = pseudoplasticity index
         F(n′) = a correction term

Equation 37 is then rearranged to give:

$$u \propto (g \, \Delta\rho)^A [KF(n')]^B (\sigma)^C (\rho)^D (d)^E \tag{39}$$

$$A = (3n/(3 + (4n - 1)(n' - 1))$$

$$B = -(4n - 1)/(3 + (4n - 1)(n' - 1))$$

$$C = -(n - 1)/(3 + (4n - 1)(n' - 1))$$

$$D = 2(n - 1)/(3 + (4n - 1)(n' - 1))$$

$$E = (4n - 1)(n' + 1)/(3 + (4n - 1)(n' - 1))$$

If n′ = 1, Equation 39 reduces to Equation 37 applicable for bubble motion in Newtonian fluids. If n = 1, Equation 39 becomes:

$$u \propto (g \, \Delta\rho)^{1/n'} [KF(n')]^{-1/n'} (d)^{(n'+1)/n'} \tag{40}$$

Equation 40 when rearranged reduces to the Stokes-drag formula for the non-Newtonian fluid behavior, i.e.

$$C_D \propto F(n')(\rho u^{2-n'} d^{n'}/K) \tag{41}$$

At large Reynolds numbers the bubble velocity (u) becomes less sensitive to fluid rheology and for n = 0.4375, and $1 \geqq n' \geqq 0.5$, Equation 41 gives u ∞ $\sqrt{gd}$, approximately, a result supported by the Mendelson wave analogy [11] and the Davies-Taylor theory [13].

EXTENSION TO DESCRIBE OTHER RELATIVE MOTIONS

The preceding treatment, although derived by trial and error, provides good correlation [23]:

1. Settling of solid spheres in Newtonian fluids.
2. Drop motion in liquids and gases.
3. Pipeline flow.
4. Flow of single-phase, Newtonian fluids in porous media.
5. Power of agitation (Newtonian).
6. Blending time in agitated vessels (Newtonian).

In all the preceding cases only two correlating parameters are used, the flow and the velocity numbers, and the corresponding generalized analytical form of correlations are developed covering the whole range of data, regardless of any flow regime.

CONCLUSIONS

A generalized analytical correlation of bubble-rise velocity is developed to cover the range of conditions:

liquid-phase density = 45.1 to 74.7 lb/ft^3

liquid-phase viscosity = 0.233 to 59 cP

interfacial tension = 15 to 72 dynes/cm

The gas-phase is air, and the bubble size ranges from 1.2 to 15 mm.

The developed correlation is based upon new dimensionless groups which contain the parameters affecting bubble-rise velocity as well as their interaction. The correlation is independent of flow regimes or bubble shape and is applicable for Reynolds numbers from 0.1 to 10^4 (i.e. from the Stokes law to the Newton's law regions). It is in good agreement with work appearing in the literature.

NOTATION

Ar	Archimedes number	K'	correction factor in Equation 8
C_D	drag coefficient	K''	ratio of gas and liquid viscosities
D	tube diameter	M	Morton number
d	bubble equivalent spherical diameter	N_f	inverse of viscosity
Eö	Eötvös number	Re	Reynolds number
F	flow number	u	rise velocity
g	gravitational acceleration	V	velocity number
K_1	dimensionless velocity	We	Weber number

Greek Symbols

μ	viscosity	ρ	density
ν	kinematic viscosity	σ	surface tension

REFERENCES

1. Grace, J. R., *Trans. Instn. Chem. Engrs.*, London, 51:116 (1973).
2. Abou-El-Hassan, M. E., *Chemical Engineering Communications*, 22 (3–4): 243 (1983).
3. Wallis, G. B., *One-Dimensional Two-Phase Flow*, McGraw-Hill Book Company, pp. 289 (1969).
4. White, E. T., and Beardmore, R. H., *Chem. Eng. Science*, 17:351 (1962).
5. Stokes, G. D., *Math. and Phys. Papers.*, 1 (1880), Cambridge University Press.
6. Hadamard, J., *Compt. Rond*, 152:1735 (1911).
7. Garner, F. H., and Hammerton, D., *Chem. Engng. Science*, 3:1 (1954).
8. Peebles, F. N., and Garber, H. J., *Chem. Engng. Progress*, 49:88 (1953).
9. Pattle, R. E., *Trans Instn. Chem. Engrs.*, 28:27 (1950).
10. Taylor, T. D., and Acrivos, A., *J. Fluid Mech.*, 18:466 (1964).
11. Mendelson, H. D., *A.I. Ch E. Jl.*, 13:250 (1967).
12. Calderbank, P. H., and Lochiel, A. C., *Chem. Engng. Science*, 19:485 (1964).
13. Davies, R. M., and Taylor, G. I., *Proc. Roy. Soc.* (London), A-200, 375 (1950).
14. Haberman, W. L., and Morton, R. K., *Trans. Amer. Soc.*, Civil Engrs., 121:227 (1956).
15. Darton, R. C., and Harrison, D., *Trans. Instn. Chem. Engrs.*, 52:301 (1974).
16. Jones, D. R., Ph.D. thesis, University of Cambridge, (1965).
17. Kojima, E., Akehata, T., and Shirai, T.; *J. Chem. Engng. (Japan)*, 1:45 (1968).
18. Dumitrescu, D. T., *Z. Angew, Math. Mech.*, 23:139 (1943).
19. Harmathy, T. Z., *A.I. Ch. Eng. Jl.*, 6:281 (1960).
20. Maneri, C. C., and Mendelson, H. D., *A.I. Ch. E. Jl.*, 14:295 (1968).
21. Davison, J. F., *Trans. Instn. Chem. Engrs.* (London), 39:230 (1981).
22. Acharya, A., Mashelkar, R. A., and Ulbrecht, J., *Chem. Engng. Science*, 32:872 (1977).
23. Abou-El-Hassan, M. E., The First Conference on Applied Modelling and Simulation (ASME), Lyon, France, Sept. (1981).

CHAPTER 7

BUBBLE NUCLEATION

Russell Mesler

Department of Chemical and Petroleum Engineering
University of Kansas
Lawrence, Kansas, USA

CONTENTS

INTRODUCTION

A liquid, either pure or containing a gas in solution, can be made to produce a bubble within itself by either increasing the temperature or by decreasing the pressure or by some combination. Increasing the temperature of a liquid increases the gas or vapor pressure exerted by the liquid. The amount this pressure must exceed the ambient pressure depends upon the bubble nuclei that exist in the liquid.

The production of a bubble in a liquid begins with such small dimensions that direct observation of the first stages is not usually feasible. The existence of a bubble only becomes apparent after some initial growth. Bubbles are said to grow from nuclei that are inferred to exist in the liquid. Being small, a bubble nucleus that is not associated with any solid foreign substance must be spherical because of the action of surface tension. Surface tension, γ, acting on a small spherical bubble of radius, r, increases the pressure by $2\gamma/r$. For the nucleus to grow the total pressure exerted by gases or vapor escaping from the liquid must exceed the ambient pressure and the increased pressure due to surface tension.

Nuclei are usually presumed to be very small bubbles existing in the liquid. Numerous experiments point to the existence of nuclei, but it is difficult to understand their existence for two reasons. First, any bubble larger than a few micrometers in size should, given adequate time, rise to the surface and disappear. Second, the high pressure in small bubbles should lead in time to their complete solution. The high pressure within the nucleus forces gas into solution decreasing the radius. Thus, for the nucleus hypothesis to be tenable it must suggest how the nucleus is able to survive buoyancy and solution.

INDUCED NUCLEATION

Under some circumstances a superheated or supersatured liquid can be maintained until nucleation is induced by some independent process or event. Three causes have been identified: ionizing radiation, friction, and entrainment.

The discovery that ionizing radiation induced nucleation was reported by Glaser [1] in 1953. The discovery led to the development of the bubble chamber that has proved a useful tool in the study of nuclear reactions. In a bubble chamber a large bath of liquid is suddenly made superheated by lowering the chamber pressure just prior to the expected arrival of a nuclear particle. The tracks of the particles participating in a reaction become visible by the nucleation of bubbles along the tracks. After the tracks are photographed the chamber pressure is raised preparatory to the next experiment.

Friction has been shown to induce nucleation and the process called tribonucleation. Tribonucleation is well known in crystallization, but not until 1967 was evidence of it recognized in bubble nucleation by Hayward [2]. Nucleation was induced in denucleated water by rubbing with a variety of both hard and soft materials at only modest superheats. Very soft silicone rubber rubbed gently against glass produced nucleation.

Tribonucleation occurred just as readily in de-aerated liquids as in liquid saturated at one atmosphere with dissolved air. It was observed in water and a variety of organic liquids.

An obvious source of bubble nucleation would be the entrainment of small quantities of gas or vapor into the liquid by some process. A drop of liquid striking a liquid entrains tiny bubbles. These are potential nuclei and the evidence for such nucleation is discussed later under secondary nucleation.

NUCLEI REMOVAL AND HOMOGENEOUS NUCLEATION

Three general means have been found effective in at least partially removing nuclei from a liquid, and these methods suggest that the nuclei that are removed are initially very small gas bubbles. First, nuclei can be removed by subjecting a liquid to a high pressure for just a short while. Second, nuclei can be removed by degasing a liquid under a vacuum and allowing it to stand for a few minutes at atmospheric pressure. Third, filtration has been demonstrated to remove bubble nuclei. Subjecting a liquid to high pressure apparently increases the solubility of the gas in any gas nuclei, tending to further dissolve the gas and thus eliminate some nuclei [3–5]. Filtering water through a filter with a pore size of 0.2 micrometers allows the water to sustain a negative pressure greater than 50 atm. At least the larger bubble nuclei are unable to pass the filter [6, 7]. Degasing apparently allows at least the larger nuclei to serve as nucleation sites and create larger bubbles that rise to an interface and disappear thus removing the nucleus [2, 3, 8].

Great effort has been expended in attempts to eliminate all extraneous nuclei to study homogeneous nucleation. Homogeneous nucleation is defined as spontaneous nucleation caused by random thermal motions of the molecules creating a microbubble large enough to grow. Homogeneous nucleation is important in determining the maximum tensile strength of a liquid or determining the maximum limit of superheat. Spontaneous nucleation is not cited as an important source of nucleation in engineering technology. Skripov [9] treats the subject thoroughly.

MODELS FOR NUCLEI STABILIZATION

Several hypotheses have been proposed to explain the stabilization of gas nuclei in liquids. Four are:

- The crevice model.
- An ionic skin model.

● A rigid organic skin model.
● Varying permeability skin model.

Crevice Model

This model depends upon the surface of either solid particles in suspension or solid walls of the container being incompletely wet by the liquid. Surfaces are known to have imperfections. The crevice model proposed by Harvey et al. [10, 11, 12] visualizes a conical cavity with an acute apical angle. Gas is trapped at the apex. With the liquid pushing into a cavity with unwet walls the liquid interface would be curved toward the apex. The action of surface tension in this tight curvature is to help hold back the liquid and keep the gas from being completely dissolved by reducing the pressure in the gas below the liquid pressure. Harvey proposed that one test of this hypothesis would be to subject water to a high enough pressure so as to force the meniscus far enough into the cavity so that no gas remained.

Ionic Skin Model

This model postulates that negative ionic charges accumulate on the wall of a bubble. The repulsion of these like charges then tends to prevent total collapse of the bubble and prevent complete solution of the gas in the bubble thus stabilizing the nucleus.

Rigid Organic Skin Model

This model proposed that nuclei may be stabilized by organic skins that mechanically prevent the loss of gas by diffusion. When subjected to a high external pressure the skin would crumble and the nucleus would disappear. A sufficient decrease in ambient pressure would rupture the skin, initiating bubble growth. Not long after the rigid skin model was proposed by Fox and Herzfeld [13] experiments showed that the application of even small increases in ambient pressure reduce the number of nuclei. Since the rigid skin model predicted a threshold, the rigid skin model was soon rejected by Herzefeld [14], but it did lay a foundation for a model with a skin of varying permeability.

Varying Permeability Skin Model

Another hypothesis is that bubble nuclei are stabilized by a skin of varying permeability. This hypothesis depends upon the presence of surfactants forming a skin on the bubble nucleus. This skin is assumed to be permeable to gases until the ambient pressure is suddenly increased by a threshold amount. When the pressure is suddenly increased above this threshold the skin becomes impermeable to further diffusion and remains so until the pressure is later lowered. The gas trapped within the nucleus is assumed to behave as an ideal gas. Compression of the gas in the nucleus retards further decrease in the size of the nucleus. Since the skin is impermeable the gas cannot be dissolved.

HYPOTHESIS TESTING

Crevice Model Tests

The crevice model was the first of the hypotheses advanced and was the first to be tested experimentally. Harvey et al. [10] cited as support of the hypothesis an experiment in which water was subjected to a pressure of 1,090 atm for 15 minutes. The water then could be heated to at least 202°C before bursting into vapor. This was explained with the crevice model by noting that the pressure had forced most of the gas nuclei stabilized by crevices into solution.

Knapp [4, 5] investigated the behavior of bubble nuclei in water subjected to various pressure treatments. Three different methods were used to measure the difficulty of inducing bubbles to form in the treated water. Two static tests were used in which the temperature was either increased or the pressure decreased until bubbles formed. The third test was a dynamic test in which the liquid was subjected to the low pressure as it flowed through a nozzle.

Water in carefully cleaned glass vessels was exposed to pressures up to 1,300 atm. Both multiple distilled and airsaturated tap water containing relatively high concentrations of dissolved and suspended material were examined. All three methods gave consistent results, but the results of the second static test had to be interpreted in view of the higher pressure subjected to the liquid in administering the test.

Knapp found that pressures of 20 to 30 atm produced a definite increase in the effective tensile strength but pressures above 135 to 200 atm caused no further increase. The duration of the treatment produced little effect whether it was one minute or several days. Once treated the effect lasts at least for several weeks if the sample is protected from contamination. The purity of the water had no effect. In flowing through the nozzle the liquid was exposed to a low pressure for only a few milliseconds but results were comparable to those of the static test. Knapp concluded that his results were consistent with the crevice model of Harvey.

Ionic Skin Model Tests

Sirotyuk [8] investigated high-purity water for evidence of gas-bubble stabilization. To test for bubble nucleation he used an ultrasonic apparatus to measure the cavitation threshold. The apparatus had a sensitive zone far from the walls so wall nuclei were not measured. The high-purity water was prepared by multiple distillation in a stream of purified inert gas. The water was tested for purity by use of conductivity measurements aand absorption polarographic analysis was used to detect trace amounts of surface-active agents. The conductivity was varied over 1,000-fold in some experiments. The conductivity was varied for a test of the ionic skin model.

Samples of distilled and tap water gave the same cavitation strength despite disparities in conductivity and surface-active substances content. Water with suspended particles removed gave an increase by a factor of 1.3 in the cavitation strength. Very pure water distilled with a helium stream showed an increase by over a factor of two in the cavitation strength, while that distilled with an oxygen stream showed little difference from distilled or tap water. High-purity water with the least surface-active substances as revealed by a polaragraphic analysis showed an increase of about four in cavitation strength.

Sirotyuk concluded that his results failed to show any support for the ionic skin model. He claimed that mere traces of surface-active impurities were enough to stabilize bubble nuclei.

Varying Permeability Skin Model Tests

Research on the topic of decompression sickness has recently led Strauss [15–17] to develop a new technique for studying bubble nucleation. Samples of gelatin are saturated with nitrogen. The pressure is then suddenly lowered to some final pressure and the number of bubbles produced are counted. To analyze the results of these experiments Yount [18] has proposed a new varying permeability model. Many aspects of the work with gelatin to develop and test the varying permeability model give further insight into vapor bubble nucleation and are therefore worth reviewing.

A large batch of gelatin was prepared and measured into 10-ml samples that were kept frozen until needed. This method was adopted to reduce the variability of results obtained when individual samples were prepared separately. The solution concentration was 25 gm of Knox unflavored gelatin per liter. The gel changed to sol at about 25°C. Three or four containers filled with gelatin to a depth of 4 mm were placed in a temperature-controlled water bath at 21°C inside a pressure vessel. Pure nitrogen was admitted to a maximum pressure of 20 atm. A window in the vessel permitted observations of the samples. A microscope permitted bubbles with radii larger than 10 micrometers to be counted, but few bubbles were so small. A grid scored on each container provided a reference for filling and counting bubbles.

In a typical run the pressure in the chamber was held constant at p_s for 5.25 hrs to allow samples to become saturated, and then the pressure was lowered suddenly to the final pressure, p_f. The bubbles became visible within seconds after rapid decompression and grew for some minutes before stabilizing. Bubbles in the lower 3 mm of the container were of uniform radius and distribution, while those in the upper 1 mm were noticeably smaller and appeared to be more numerous than elsewhere. Only the bubbles in the lower 3 mm were counted.

When the chamber pressure was 20 atm and the final pressure was atmospheric about 400 bubbles were counted. It was demonstrated that almost all nuclei could be removed by first subjecting a sample to hydrostatic pressures of 100 atm in a centrifuge prior to testing. This was interpreted as a specific test for gas nuclei and it was concluded that 99.9% of the bubbles formed in gelatin were gas nuclei.

As a further test of the origin of nuclei in the gelatin samples additional samples were prepared using distilled water that had been centrifuged. Three samples were prepared with this water and tested, similarly producing an average of 28 bubbles per sample. This was interpreted as indicating 93% of the nuclei were already present in the water with which the gelatin was prepared. Additional tests produced no evidence that any of the procedures used in preparing the samples such as stirring, heating, cooling, freezing, or melting introduced nuclei.

Samples exposed to a higher gage pressure (p_m) of 20 atm for a short time and then for the remaining 5.25 hrs at a lower gage pressure of 10 atm demonstrated that the brief exposure influenced the subsequent nucleation. Exposures of one second reduced nucleation by 75%. After 10 min nucleation was reduced by 97% but no further decrease occurred with longer times. The interpretation here is that the high pressure crushes the nuclei quickly long before the sample can become saturated.

During rapid decompression the pressure was lowered from p_s to p_f in about 10 s. The difference is the supersaturation pressure, p_{ss}. With this difference and the surface tension (γ) the smallest nuclear radius that can grow is $r_c = 2\gamma/p_{ss}$. With a p_{ss} of 20 atm r_c is 0.049 micrometers using the measured surface tension of 51 dynes/cm. When the pressure was lowered on saturated samples from 1 atm the average pressure required to produce nucleation was 19 kPa, and this gives a radius of 1.24 micrometers.

The rate at which pressure is applied to a sample is important in determining the subsequent nucleation that occurs on rapid decompression. This was revealed in a series of tests where pressure was applied rapidly in one series and slowly in another. After allowing time for saturation the pressure was rapidly released to 1 atm. Rapid compression produced much less nucleation for the same supersaturation pressure, p_{ss}. The number of bubbles increased sharply with supersaturation pressure for the rapid compression series, beginning at a threshold near 100–130 kPa and continuing until an apparent maximum was observed in the vicinity of 14 atm. Apparently slow compression permits some diffusion of gas into nuclei, allowing nuclei to resist crushing.

In additional tests the effect of saturation pressure was investigated as supersaturation pressure was varied. A new variable $p_{crush} = p_m - p_o = p_s - p_o$ was found useful in analyzing the results. In these test p_{crush} was held constant at three different values, 8.2, 14.3, and 20.4 atm.

From a plot of N vs. p_{ss} on the abscissa with p_{crush} as a parameter it was possible to replot the results as p_{ss} vs. p_{crush} on the abscissa with N as a parameter. Two lines seem to represent each value of N with the slope on the right being less than the slope on the left. The intersection occurred at $p_{crush} = p^* - p_o$ and p^* was important in the hypothesis that was formulated. The predictions of the model are not very sensitive to the p^*, and for simplicity a smooth curve was drawn so as to represent $p^* - p_o$ at various values of N. $p^* - p_0$ was 8.2, 8.3, 8.4, 8.6, 9.6, and 12 atm for N of 1, 3, 10, 30, 100, and 200, respectively.

The hypothesis begins by observing that a distribution of nuclei sizes can account for increased nucleation that occurs with decompression to a lower final pressure. It is assumed that a change in pressure changes the size of these nuclei but not the number. One now inquires how the size would change with a series of changes in pressure. It is assumed that the manner by which nuclei radii change with an increase in pressure changes at pressures above p^*. Below p^* it is assumed that the skin around the nucleus is permeable, but above p^* the skin becomes impermeable. Further decreases in the nucleus radius with a pressure increase above p^* is resisted by the compression of the gas assumed to behave ideally and trapped within the nucleus. When the pressure release begins, the skin is again assumed permeable. This leads to predictions of supersaturation pressures, p_{ss}. For a specified value of N there is a corresponding value for r_0.

$$2(\gamma_c - \gamma)[(1/r) - (1/r_0)] = p - p_0 \qquad p < p^*$$

is used to predict r^* at p^*.

$$2(\gamma_c - \gamma)[(1/r_m) - (1/r^*)] = p_m - p^* + p_0[1 - (r^*/r_m)^3] \qquad p > p^*$$

is used to predict r_m at p_m. Then

$$p_{ss} = [2\gamma(\gamma_c - \gamma)/r_0\gamma_c]\{[p_m - p_0(r^*/r_m)^3](\gamma - \gamma_c)\}$$

gives the value of p_{ss} corresponding to the original value of N.

The parameter γ_c in the equation was found to vary with r_0 and was given by the equation

$$\gamma_c/\gamma = 1.00 + 1.40r_0$$

where r_0 must be expressed in micrometers.

In a more recent test of the varying permeability model [19] the effect of varying the manner in which the pressure is applied was investigated. Only in one step was the pressure changed substantially, and the difference in pressure in this step was taken as p_{crush}. All other steps to achieve the saturation pressure were less. Some time was allowed at each step, and 5.25 hrs were allowed for the final step. Maximum pressure was 20 atm. By this procedure it was possible to achieve values of p_{ss} greater than p_{crush}.

A new batch of gelatin was prepared. The batch was especially formulated to give a low yield of nuclei to avoid producing too many bubbles in some experiments.

Numerous experiments were run to obtain a plot of N vs. p_{ss} with p_{crush} as a parameter. Values of p_{crush} were 2.0, 6.7, 8.2, 12.2, 16.3, and 20.4. In a cross plot of p_{ss} vs. p_{crush} with N as a parameter it was found the straight lines approximated the values at constant N except for the values at p_{crush} of 2.0 atm. There was no change in slope that would indicate p^* had been exceeded. The anomalous behavior at $p_{crush} = 2$ was attributed to a different type of nucleus to which the usual model equations do not apply. These nuclei were easily crushed and perhaps were due to gas-filed crevices in suspended dust particles or some other type of surfactant nuclei.

Discrepancies between the model and experiment at larger N were attributed to skin thickness effects at small nuclei radii. A skin thickness was incorporated into a revised model.

For this new sample of gelatin it was necessary to revise the relation between γ_c/γ and r_0 to

$$\gamma_c/\gamma = 1.0 + 7.5r_0$$

with r_0 in micrometers. More specifically, it appears that the low-yield gelatin crystals may contain substances which alter the relevant chemical potentials for surfactant molecules in the nuclear skin.

CHARACTERIZING NUCLEI DISTRIBUTIONS

The presence of bubble nuclei in different flow situations is now well established, but the steps necessary to chacterize the nuclei have yet to be standardized. Several detection and observation techniques are under development [20]. Included among these are microscopic observations of water samples, use of light scattering as in the Coulter counter [21], acoustic methods [6, 8, 22], holograms with microscopic observations of the reconstructed image [23], and the use of a venturi flow device [4, 24].

An example of the importance of nuclei is provided by Katz and Acosta [23]. They provide a summary of nuclei distributions in water from a variety of sources. The nuclear radii of interest are principally between 10 and 100 micrometers, and the number density varies over 4 orders of magnitude.

Using holography the bubble population in the neighborhood of a step in the flow prior to the appearance of macroscopic cavitation was shown to vary significantly at different locations. They demonstrate that the history of the experiment prior to making a specific test can influence the distribution and number of nuclei. Free stream nuclei population are an important scaling factor and their control is an essential part of any cavitation test.

There are very few undistrubed messurements of bubble nuclei population in natural waters or even in the circuits of large hydraulic testing structures. The need for further research on bubble nuclei characterization is critical to future progress in cavitation research.

SECONDARY NUCLEATION

The possible creation of nuclei as a process occurs has received little consideration in vapor bubble nucleation even though it occurs prominently in crystallization [25]. Crystal nuclei are produced profusely by the fragmentation of larger crystals in industrial crystallizers, and the process is called secondary nucleation.

The increase of the free stream nuclei population with the operation of a water tunnel indicates some mechanism for the creation of nuclei. Numerous reports of hysteresis effects in cavitation are evidence of nuclei creation. In nucleate boiling evidence of a specific mechanism by which vapor bubble nuclei are produced by the boiling process itself has been presented.

The excellence of nucleate boiling in transferring heat depends upon bubbles and consequently upon bubble nucleation. The crevice model for nucleation is extensively used to explain nucleation in boiling [26]. The crevice model is easily demonstrated by the use of boiling chips used to reduce the superheat of liquids boiled in glass vessels. Bubbles grow rapidly from the boiling chips because the chips provide a profusion of nucleation sites.

Recently it has been recognized that boiling from a thin liquid film offers even more efficient heat transfer than boiling larger quantities of liquid. Furthermore, as the liquid level on a boiling surface is lowered nucleation increases. High speed motion pictures show that when a bubble bursts from a liquid film new bubbles appear where the bubble has just burst [27]. High speed motion pictures also show that when a bubble bursts on the surface of superheated water, clusters of bubble nuclei appear a few milliseconds later and a few millimeters beneath the surface [28]. The pictures also show that when a bubble bursts the top film collect into drops which are drawn back to the surface. This evidence suggests that the drops entrain vapor bubbles with them. Any vapor bubbles entrained in this manner could serve as bubble nuclei.

With proper lighting it is easy to demonstrate that drops do entrain bubbles when they strike a liquid surface [29]. A beam of light directed from the side shows that small water drops can entrain hundreds of bubbles.

A surprising result is that many of the bubbles are entrained in a vortex ring which a drop forms when it strikes the surface. The vortex ring rapidly penetrates the liquid carrying the entrained bubbles with it. Figure 1 shows examples of the vortex ring carrying the larger bubbles, and Figure 2 is a sketch of the entrainment.

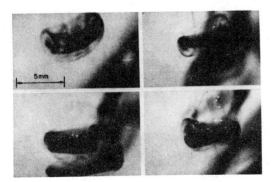

5mm

Figure 1. Examples of a drop-formed vortex ring entraining bubbles

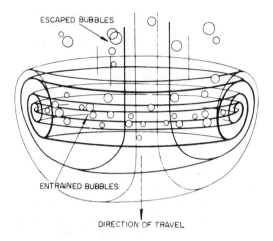

ESCAPED BUBBLES

ENTRAINED BUBBLES

DIRECTION OF TRAVEL

Figure 2. Sketch of a drop-formed vortex ring showing entrained and escaped bubbles.

The ability of drops to entrain bubbles and form vortex rings has been known since the last century when it was reported in 1858 by W. B. Rogers [30], the founder of the Massachusetts Institute of Technology.

REFERENCES

1. Glaser, D. A., *Phys. Rev.*, 91:762 (1953).
2. Hayward, A. T. J., *Brit. J. Appl. Phys.*, 18:641 (1967).
3. Harvey, E. N., Barnes, D. K., McElroy, W. D., Whitely, A. H., and Peace, D. C., *J. Amer. Chem. Soc.*, 67:156 (1945)
4. Knapp, R. T., *Trans. ASME*, 80:1315 (1958).
5. Knapp, R. T., Daily, J. W., and Hammitt, F. G., *Cavitation*, McGraw-Hill, New York, 1970.
6. Greenspan, M., and Tschiegg, C. E., *J. Res. Natl. Bur. Std.*, 71C:299 (1967).
7. Yount, D. E., and Yeung, C. M., *J. Acoust. Soc. Am.*, 65:1440 (1979).
8. Sirotyuk, M. G., *Soviet Physics—Acoustics*, 16:237 (1970).
9. Skripov, V. P., *Metastable Liquids*, John Wiley, New York (1974).
10. Harvey, E. N., Barnes, K. K., McElroy, W. D., Whitely, A. H., Pease, D. C., and Cooper, K. W., *J. Cell Comp. Physiol.*, 24:1 (1944).
11. Winterton, R. H. S., *J. Phys. D: Appl. Phys.*, 10:2041 (1979).
12. Crum, L. A., *Appl. Sci. Res.*, 38:101
13. Fox, F. F., and Herzfeld, K. F., *J. Acoust. Soc. Am.*, 26:984 (1954).
14. Herzfeld, K. F., *Proc. First Symposium Naval Hydrodynamics*, Nat. Acad. Sci., Washington, D.C., Pub. 515:319 (1957).
15. Strauss, R. H., *Undersea Biomedical Res.*, 1:169 (1974).
16. Yount, D. E., and Strauss, R. H., *J. Appl. Phys.*, 47:5081 (1976).
17. Yount, D. E., Kunkle, T. D., D'Arrigo, J. S., Ingle, F. W., Yeung, C. M., and Beckman, E. L., *Aviation and Environmental Med.*, 48:185 (1977).
18. Yount, D. E., *J. Acoust. Soc. Am.*, 65:1429 (1978).
19. Yount, D. E., and Yeung, C. M., *ibid*, 69:702 (1981).
20. Hammitt, F. G., *Cavitation and Multiphase Flow Phenomena*, McGraw Hill, New York, 1980.
21. Pyun, J., Hammitt, F. G., and Keller, A., *Trans. ASME, J. Fluids Engr.*, 98:87 (1976).
22. Medwin, H., *J. Geophysical Res.*, 82:921 (1977).
23. Katz, J., and Acosta, A., *Appl. Sci. Res.*, 38:123 (1982).

24. Oldenziel, D. M., Measurements on the Cavitation Susceptability of Water, 5th Conf. on Fluid Machinery, Budapest, 1975 (Delft Hydraulics Laboratory, Pub. 153).
25. Mesler, R., *Chem. Engr. Education*, XVI:152 (1982).
26. Cole, R., *Advances in Heat Transfer*, 10:85 (1974).
27. Mesler, R., and Mailen, G., *AIChE J.*, 23:954 (1977).
28. Bergman, T., and Mesler, R., *ibid*, 27:851 (1981).
29. Carroll, K., and Mesler, R., *ibid*, 27:853 (1981).
30. Rogers, W. B., *Amer. J., Sci. and Arts, 2nd ser.*, 26:246 (1858).

CHAPTER 8

BUBBLE GROWTH IN SUPERHEATED LIQUID DROPLETS

C. T. Avedisian

Sibley School of Mechanical and Aerospace Engineering
Cornell University
Ithaca, New York, USA

CONTENTS

INTRODUCTION

If two immiscible liquids of different volatility are mixed such that one of the liquids (the volatile one, hereafter referred to as liquid 1) is dispersed in the other (liquid 2) in the form of droplets, the droplets may be heated by direct contact heat transfer across the liquid/liquid interface. This heat may be transferred by

1. Conduction or convection
2. Nucleate boiling
3. Film boiling

In the absence of preferred nucleation sites, single-phase conduction or convection could exist far beyond the normal saturation state of liquid 1. In this event liquid 1 is said to become superheated. The stable, superheated state can exist as long as the droplet does not come in contact with a vapor phase with which it is in equilibrium. An upper limit to the temperature any liquid can sustain at a given pressure (or a lower limit of pressure at a given temperature) exists at which a phase change must occur. This temperature is called the *superheat limit*. At this temperature an intrinsic phase transition is initiated by the molecular processes of homogeneous nucleation within the bulk of the encapsulated droplet. These processes are characterized by creation of a vapor phase within bulk liquid in the form of tiny (~ 10 Å diameter) bubbles (critical size nuclei) such that they are in metastable equilibrium with the surrounding liquid. Subsequent growth of these initial bubbles completes the phase transition process and is manifested by the boiling-up of the superheated liquid droplet. Two steps in the phase change process relevant to superheated liquid droplets are therefore

1. An initial stage during which microscopic bubbles form within the droplet by molecular processes.
2. A second or bubble growth stage during which the initial microscopic bubbles grow as the liquid droplet vaporizes.

Detailed discussions of both stages are given in this chapter.

Bubble growth beyond the critical size is governed by, in turn, the effects of molecular evaporation across the phase boundary, surface tension, liquid inertia, and thermal diffusion. The compendium of these processes is manifested by the macroscopic behavior of the droplets when they vaporize. Superheated droplets may vaporize in an explosive-like manner and generate blast waves in the surrounding liquid, or boil quiescently as characterized by a comparatively gradual disappearance of the liquid phase and a concomitant emergence of a vapor bubble within the droplet. What little is known about the intensity of vaporization of droplets at their superheat limit suggests that boiling intensity is influenced by such factors as ambient pressure in the field liquid, and physical properties.

This chapter reviews the processes of initial bubble formation and growth within liquid droplets at the superheat limit. The essential configuration considered is that of droplets of a pure volatile liquid (liquid 1) encapsulated in an ambient nonvolatile field liquid (liquid 2) of infinite extent. A summary of applications in which this configuration may be encountered in industrial settings is given in the next section. The problem is then formulated in more formal terms in the following section. A review of the mechanism by which bubbles are created within superheated liquids is presented in the next section, and the bubble growth problem is then discussed. Those aspects of bubble growth in infinite media related to the present problem are reviewed and modifications to the classical theories required by the finite mass of the vaporizing liquid are discussed. Finally, experimental methods used to provide the foundation of our understanding of bubble nucleation and growth within superheated liquid droplets are described in the final section.

APPLICATIONS

The energy released by a liquid at its limit of superheat is approximately equivalent to the sensible heat above normal saturation. If a significant fraction of this energy appears in the form of a thermal detonation wave, or if bubbles grow at a rate which exceeds the ability of the surrounding liquid to acoustically respond, the resulting phase transition is called a "vapor explosion." This energy is orders of magnitude less than that typical of chemical explosions. However, the destructive capability of vapor explosions, produced when a hot nonvolatile liquid comes into intimate contact with a cold volatile liquid, is well documented in the literature [1–3].

To bring a liquid to a state at which there is a high probability for the type of phase transition characteristic of a vapor explosion, the liquid must be devoid of any extraneous nucleation aids. This requirement will most readily (though not always) be satisfied when one liquid is dispersed in another relatively nonvolatile liquid with which it is immiscible. In this case, the "container" for the volatile liquid is the liquid/liquid interface. As the structure of such an interface is not fundamentally different from that of the bulk, the only way for a phase change to occur would be by the same molecular processes as that under which critical size nuclei form. The attendant liquid state will correspond to the deepest possible penetration of the liquid into the domain of metastable states (due account being taken of the effect of the interface)—the limit of superheat—and therefore create the possibility for a vapor explosion. The precise mechanism of vapor-explosive boiling is not well understood due to a lack of fundamental experiments. Our observations and understanding of the phenomenon are at present rather qualitative. Vapor explosive boiling has been observed during spillage of liquified natural gases on water, preparation and burning of certain alternative fuels, melt-down of nuclear reactor fuel rods in a (as yet hypothetical) nuclear reactor accident, mixing of water and molten metal during the cold mold arc-melting and casting processes, and dissolving of molten salt in water during paper pulping operations. The effect of these explosions have ranged from detrimental, creating a hazard to life and property [3] to potentially beneficial in the case of burning alternative fuels [4, 5].

Conditions which must be satisfied for vapor explosions to occur vary widely and defy generalizations. Though several reviews have recently appeared on the subject [1, 3, 6, 7] no unique mechanism has yet been formulated which can explain all observed phenomena. At present, two necessary conditions for a vapor explosion appear to have received general agreement:

1. A volatile and nonvolatile liquid must come into intimate contact.
2. The temperature of the nonvolatile liquid must be heated to some well defined minimum value which is greater than the boiling point of the volatile liquid—below the threshold temperature, or well above it, vapor explosions will not occur.

The potential for vapor explosions appears to be influenced as much by the way the two liquids are brought together as it is by the heating requirements of the volatile liquid: even if the requisite temperatures are achieved, the method of mixing apparently influences the ability of the volatile liquid to vapor explode.

Other factors such as ambient pressure [8–11], liquid phase composition [12–15], and wetting characteristics of the two liquids [16, 17] have been observed to effect the intensity of boiling after the triggering mechanism of homogeneous nucleation has occurred. Thus by itself, more information must supplement the preceding necessary conditions in order to provide a complete account of the potential for vapor explosions in any interaction between two liquids of different volatilities. The missing information is provided by the dynamics of growth of the initial bubble. These dynamics are influenced by precisely those factors which have been observed to influence the intensity of boiling of a liquid at its superheat limit. Thus we may conjecture a third condition for a vapor explosion which involves bubble growth:

3. Growth of the initial bubble must be sufficiently rapid so as to produce shock waves in the surrounding liquid.

The production of shock or blast waves will usually require a high pressure source (vapor in the bubble itself) and rapid expansion of the liquid/vapor interface. Experimental evidence is suggestive of the necessity of a large enough pressure initially existing in the bubble to support such a shock wave [11, 18].

The necessity to consider the dynamics of bubble growth in connection with vapor explosion has been recognized [e.g. 2, 3, 6, 8, 19]. Little work has, however, been done to quantify the dynamics and heat transfer of bubble growth for the configuration most typical of that encountered as a result of the type of mixing processes already outlined—droplets of one liquid in another. Most previous work in connection with the vapor explosion problem has simplified the problem by not considering the finite extent of the vaporizing liquid-droplet, and has, instead, drawn on results for bubble growth in infinite media to explain qualitative expectations for phenomenon associated with droplets [e.g. 2, 3, 20]. This extension can be valid for certain ranges of the important parameter which will be shown to govern bubble growth in the fifth section. In the general case, however, discrepancies in the growth rate and therefore in the expectations one is likely to predict pertaining to the rate at which the liquid phase vaporizes may be expected.

Finally, the emphasis in this section has been on problems associated with the vapor explosion phenomenon. The present work is, however, not about vapor explosions, but about bubble growth in droplets. The perspective of vapor explosions is convenient to show the importance of the essential configuration considered in this chapter—droplets of a volatile liquid encapsulated in a nonvolatile liquid of infinite extent. In other respects, the subsequent discussions are not restricted to any unique application.

DESCRIPTION OF THE PROBLEM

Figure 1 illustrates the basic geometry of interest in this chapter. A spherical droplet of a volatile liquid (liquid 1) is suspended in a nonvaporizing nonvolatile liquid of infinite extent (liquid 2). The two liquids are mutually immiscible. The nonvolatility of liquid 2 is such that the potential exists for altering its thermodynamic state to induce intrinsic bubble formation within the bulk of the liquid 1 droplet without jeopardizing the stability of its stable state. This requirement means that the normal saturation temperature of liquid 2 is higher, at a given ambient pressure, than the limit of superheat of liquid 1 at the same pressure. Both liquids are assumed to be free of any extraneous nucleation aids which would tend to initiate a phase transition at conditions less extreme than would be realized in the presence of such aids. Thus we assume an absence of any dissolved gases, unwetted solid particles, or minute gas bubbles in both liquids. In this event the present work will be distinguished from previous studies of phase change in droplets suspended in immiscible liquids [e.g. 21–26] in that the droplets considered here remain liquid at reduced temperatures typically greater than 0.9 corresponding to reduced pressures greater than about 0.04 before boiling.

The problem considered is as follows. At time t = 0 a vapor bubble (created by the process of homogeneous nucleation) appears within the bulk of the liquid 1 droplet. The initial temperatures of liquids 1 and 2 are the same and there is no relative motion between the droplet and the field liquid. The unstable equilibrium of the bubble is then perturbed in such a manner that the bubble starts to grow. This perturbation may be an incremental increase in bubble size beyond the initial value corresponding to static equilibrium, and be brought about by a slight reduction of ambient pressure, P_o, or increase in ambient temperature, T_o. Subsequent growth of the bubble consumes the volatile liquid 1 until the initial mass of the droplet is entirely vaporized, after which a vapor

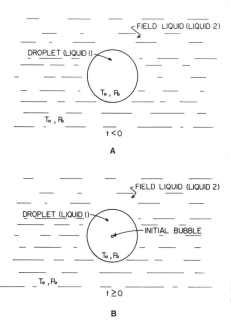

Figure 1. Schematic of droplet/field liquid system illustrating appearance of initial bubble (t ≥ 0).

bubble of finite size in static equilibrium with liquid 2 remains. The radius of this final bubble is

$$R_f = (1 - \varepsilon)^{-1/3} S_o \tag{1}$$

At this radius, liquid 1 has completely vaporized. For a bubble growing in an infinite medium of liquid 1 (i.e., $S_o \to \infty$), the vapor bubble in principle grows to infinite size.

We now proceed to a discussion of the two main developments pertinent to the present work:

1. The initial conditions for bubble growth characterized by formation of critical size nuclei within the bulk of the droplet.
2. Growth of the initial bubble within the droplet.

A review of those aspects of nucleation theory relevant to predicting the initial conditions for bubble growth is given in the fourth section. A discussion of the bubble growth problem itself is presented in the fifth section.

INITIAL CONDITIONS FOR BUBBLE GROWTH

Superheated Liquids

The terms "superheated liquids" and "limit of superheat" have been used in connection with the initial liquid droplet state at which vaporization is initiated. In this section we wish to more precisely define these terms and to present useful methods for quantitative prediction.

The essential requirement of a superheated liquid is transgression of its normal or saturation phase boundary. "Normal" in this sense is rather arbitrarily defined. By convention the term refers to a special case of equilibrium across a flat-phase boundary, $r \to \infty$ where r is the radius of curvature of the phase boundary.

Figure 2 illustrates two of a possible infinity of paths a pure liquid may follow to transgress its normal-phase boundary. The illustration is made on conventional pressure-temperature and pressure-volume projections on a phase diagram. The two paths illustrated are isobaric heating (a-c) and isothermal decompression (b-c). The latter path is more commonly associated with cavitation processes. The solid line illustrated in Figure 2A which separates the stable liquid and stable vapor regions corresponds to the normal equilibrium boundary. Transgression of this phase boundary implies an absence of a planar interface between the two phases. Hence any vapor present within the superheated liquid regions shown in Figure 2 must be in the form of bubbles ($r < \infty$). The radii of curvature of these bubbles defines the depth of penetration of the liquid in the metastable region.

The initial bubbles are in mechanical equilibrium. Hence,

$$P + \vec{n} \cdot \vec{P}_o = \frac{2\sigma_1}{r} > 0 \tag{2}$$

where $\vec{n}$ is the outward normal to the bubble surface.

The gas pressure, P, is not precisely the same as the equilibrium vapor pressure, $P_s(r \to \infty)$ at temperature T. This is seen by considering the consequences of phase equilibrium across flat and curved phase boundaries illustrated in Figure 3. In both configurations, equality of chemical potentials defines equilibrium. For the planar inteface in Figure 3A

$$\mu'(P_s, T) = \mu''(P_s, T) \tag{3a}$$

while for equilibrium between the gas in the bubble and the surrounding liquid (Figure 3B) at the same temperature,

$$\mu'(P_o, T) = \mu'' (P, T) \tag{3b}$$

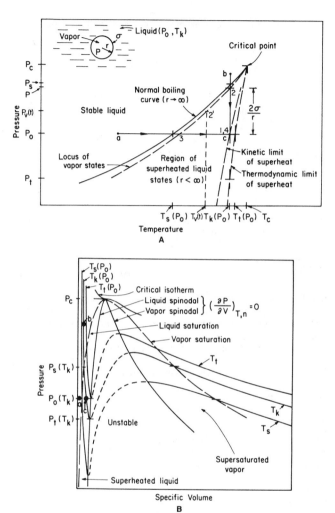

Figure 2. Phase diagram of a pure substance on pressure/temperature (A) and pressure volume (B) projections illustrating the domain of stable, superheated liquid, and unstable states.

Figure 3. (A) Equilibrium across a flat phase boundary at temperature T; (B) equilibrium across a curved phase boundary (bubble) of radius r and temperature T.

Assuming, for simplicity, the liquid to be incompressible and the gas phase to be ideal, it can be shown that

$$\mu'(P_s, T) - \mu'(P_o, T) = v'(P_s - P_o) \tag{4}$$

and

$$\mu''(P_s, T) - \mu''(P, T) = \mathscr{R}T \ln \frac{P_s}{P} \tag{5}$$

Combining Equations 2–5 yields the desired result:

$$P \simeq P_s \exp\left[\frac{v'}{\mathscr{R}T}(P_o - P_s)\right] \tag{6a}$$

For multicomponent mixtures a similar expression applies where P is the partial pressure of component i in the ideal gas mixture within the bubble [29]

$$P_i \simeq P_s y_{is} \exp\left[\frac{v'_i}{\mathscr{R}T}(P_o - P_s)\right] \tag{6b}$$

P_s is the mixture bubble point pressure of gas-phase composition y_{is}, and v'_i is the corresponding liquid partial molar volume of component i. The exponential terms in Equations 6 are usually very close to one for liquids at the superheat limit. Figure 2 schematically illustrates the locus of vapor states defined by Equation 6a for a pure liquid.

The external liquid pressure, P_o, may be either compressive on the bubble wall or extensive (as in the case of tensile strength measurements [30–32]). In the present discussion we shall be concerned primarily with compressive ambient liquid pressures so that

$$P - P_o = \frac{2\sigma_1}{r} \tag{7}$$

defines the initial equilibrium state of the bubble.

For a vapor bubble $P > P_o$ and $r < \infty$. As a consequence $T(P_o) > T_s(P_o)$. In principle all allowable liquid states are those for which $T(P_o) < T_c$.

Thermodynamic Limit of Superheat

There is an absolute limit to the extent to which a liquid droplet can be isobarically heated. At this limit the liquid is inherently unstable with respect to any small perturbation in its thermodynamic state. The system comprising the liquid then breaks up into two or more portions, the separation being called a phase transition [33].

The limit of stability, or so-called *thermodynamic limit of superheat*, is defined by the basic extreme principle of thermodynamics which asserts that the entropy of an isolated system is a maximum in a stable equilibrium state with respect to small variations of its natural variables, $U, V, n_1, n_2 \ldots$ [34]. Alternatively, the Helmholtz function, F, assumes a minimum value in a stable equilibrium state for an open system with respect to variations of $T, V, n_1, n_2 \ldots$. For variations from a stable state (i.e., virtual processes),

$$\Delta F > 0 \tag{8}$$

To explore the consequences of Equation 8, ΔF is expanded in a series about a stable equilibrium state. Such an expansion will accurately represent ΔF if enough terms are retained. Thus, for variations from a stable state

$$\Delta F = \delta F + \frac{1}{2!} \delta^2 F + \frac{1}{3!} \delta^3 F + \cdots \geq 0 \tag{9}$$

For simplicity we consider the stability of states along an isotherm ($\delta T = 0$). Only small variations in the natural variables are considered such that the first nonvanishing term in Equation 9 is also the largest. The vanishing of certain of these terms defines several thermodynamic states of interest. For systems in a stable state

$$\delta F = 0 \tag{10a}$$

and

$$\delta^2 F \geq 0 \tag{10b}$$

defines stability of this equilibrium. At the thermodynamic limit of superheat equality of Equation 10b applies,

$$\delta^2 F = 0 \tag{11a}$$

and

$$\delta^3 F \geq 0 \tag{11b}$$

defines the stability of states at this limit. A critical point is defined such that

$$\delta^3 F = 0 \tag{12a}$$

and its stability is determined by

$$\delta^4 F \geq 0 \tag{12b}$$

Interest here is in exploring the consequences of Equations 10 and 11 for a liquid not at its critical point (Equation 12). States defined by Equation 11a correspond to the deepest possible penetration of a liquid in the domain of metastable states.

For $F(T, V, n_1, n_2, \ldots)$ Equation 10b can be written ($\delta T = 0$)

$$\delta^2 F = F_{vv}(\delta V)^2 + F_{n_1 n_1}(\delta n_1)^2 + F_{n_2 n_2}(\delta n_2)^2 + \cdots + 2[F_{vn_1}\delta V \delta n_1 + F_{vn_2}\delta V \delta n_2 + \cdots$$
$$+ F_{n_1 n_2}\delta n_1 \delta n_2 + F_{n_1 n_3}\delta n_1 \delta n_3 + \cdots$$
$$\vdots$$
$$> 0 \tag{13}$$

Subscripts denote differentiation with respect to the indicated variable:

$$F_v = \frac{\partial F}{\partial V}\bigg|_{T,n_j} = -P \tag{14a}$$

$$F_{n_i} = \frac{\partial F}{\partial n_j}\bigg|_{T,V,n_j} = \mu_i \tag{14b}$$

$$F_{vn_i} = \frac{\partial^2 F}{\partial V \partial n_i}\bigg|_{T,P,n_j} \tag{14c}$$

Equation 13 is a homogeneous quadratic form. The requirement that it be positive (hence that the state be stable) is equivalent to the requirement that discriminants of the matrix

$$
\bar{\bar{A}} \equiv
\begin{bmatrix}
F_{vv} & F_{vn_1} & F_{vn_2} & \cdots & F_{vn_n} \\
F_{vn_1} & F_{n_1n_1} & F_{n_1n_2} & \cdots & F_{n_1n_n} \\
F_{vn_2} & F_{n_1n_2} & F_{n_2n_2} & \cdots & F_{n_2n_n} \\
\vdots & \vdots & \vdots & & \vdots \\
F_{vn_n} & F_{n_1n_n} & F_{n_2n_n} & & F_{n_nn_n}
\end{bmatrix}
\tag{15}
$$

all be positive [35]. Hence,

$$
F_{vv} > 0
$$

$$
\begin{vmatrix}
F_{vv} & F_{vn_1} \\
F_{vn_1} & F_{n_1n_1}
\end{vmatrix} > 0
\tag{16}
$$

$$
\vdots
$$

$$
|\bar{\bar{A}}| > 0
$$

From the Gibbs-Duhem equation we can write that

$$
\bar{\bar{A}} \cdot
\begin{bmatrix}
V \\
n_1 \\
n_2 \\
\vdots
\end{bmatrix} = 0
\tag{17}
$$

Thus,

$$
|\bar{\bar{A}}| = 0
\tag{18}
$$

whether or not the state under consideration is stable. The limit of stability is then defined by the discriminant which first vanishes from those constructed from the first $n - 1$ rows and columns of the $n \times n$ matrix $\bar{\bar{A}}$. It can be shown that this discriminant will always be the determinant of the $(n - 1) \times (n - 1)$ matrix of $\bar{\bar{A}}$ [34]. Therefore, at the thermodynamic limit of superheat

$$
\begin{vmatrix}
F_{vv} & F_{vn_1} & \cdots & F_{vn_{n-1}} \\
F_{vn_1} & F_{n_1n_1} & \cdots & F_{n_1n_{n-1}} \\
\vdots & & & \\
F_{vn_n} & F_{n_1n_n} & \cdots & F_{n_{n-1}n_{n-1}}
\end{vmatrix} = 0
\tag{19}
$$

To illustrate, for a pure substance $F(T, V, n)$. Along an isotherm, Equation 19 yields

$$
F_{vv} = -\frac{\partial P}{\partial V}\bigg|_{T,n} = 0
\tag{20}
$$

For a binary mixture, $F(T, V, n_1, n_2)$. From Equation 19 the thermodynamic limit of superheat is defined by

$$
F_{vv}F_{n_1n_1} - F_{vn_1}^2 = 0
\tag{21}
$$

with

$$F_{vv} = \frac{\partial P}{\partial V}\bigg|_{T,n_1,n_2} > 0$$

Equation 21 may be cast in a more useful form by using the definition of an ideal gas limit where $V \to \infty$ and

$$\mu_1 = \mu_1^o(T) + RT \ln \frac{n_1 \mathcal{R}T}{V} + \int_\infty^V \frac{\partial \mu_1}{\partial V}\bigg|_{T,n_1,n_2} dV \tag{22}$$

Combining Equations 14 and 22, performing the indicated differentiations in Equation 21, and taking $n = n_1 + n_2 = 1$ yields

$$\left\{ \int_V^\infty \frac{\partial^2 P}{\partial n_1^2}\bigg|_{T,V,n_2} \cdot dV + \frac{\mathcal{R}T}{x_1} \right\} \cdot \frac{\partial P}{\partial V}\bigg|_{T,n_1,n_2} + \left[\frac{\partial P}{\partial n_1}\bigg|_{T,V,n_2} \right]^2 = 0 \tag{23}$$

This procedure may be extended to higher order mixtures using the Legendre transform theory [36].

The loci of states defined by Equation 19 in the general case (Equation 20 for a pure substance or Equation 23 for a binary mixture) defines the so-called "spinodal" curve of a substance. The characteristic form of this curve for a pure substance is shown in Figure 2B. Thermodynamic states outside the domain of unstable states defined by the spinodal curve are theoretically accessible.

States on the spinodal curve define the deepest possible transgression of the normal-phase boundary a liquid droplet can sustain before it must change phase. Prediction of these states requires a pressure-explicit equation of state applicable in the metastable region. Unfortunately, no such equation of state currently exists (except possibly for water [37]). One is then forced to rather arbitrarily extrapolate existing equations of state into the region of metastable states; there is a paucity of physical property data for superheated liquids. This fact puts a limitation on the ability to predict the thermodynamic limit of superheat.

For example consider the simple van der Waals equation of state for a pure substance,

$$\left(P + \frac{a}{V^2} \right)(V - b) = \mathcal{R}T \tag{24}$$

where a and b are constants (determined from the critical point definition, Equation 12a). This equation is known to inaccurately represent the saturation state of most substances. It will, however, serve a useful purpose in the present discussion. The spinodal curve (Equation 20) for the van der Waals equation of state is

$$P = \frac{a}{V^2} - \frac{2ab}{V^3} \tag{25}$$

Given a pressure P, V may be eliminated between Equations 24 and 25 to yield the thermodynamic limit of superheat, $T \to T_t$. This procedure generally requires an iterative solution (except when $P \to 0$ in which case Equations 24 and 25 yield $T = \frac{27}{32}T_c$ [38]). A simple correlation of T_t corresponding to Equations 24 and 25 which obviates this iterative procedure is [39]

$$T_t \simeq T_c \left[\frac{27}{32} + \frac{5}{32} \cdot \left(\frac{T_s}{T_c} \right)^{5.16} \right] \tag{26}$$

Table 1 lists the thermodynamic limit of superheat for six pure substances at 0.101 MPa calculated from Equation 26 (T_t). These temperatures are substantially above the normal boiling points of

Table 1
Thermodynamic Limit of Superheat of Some Pure Liquids at Atmospheric Pressure

Substance	T_s	T_{t_1}	T_{t_2}	T_m	T_c	$J(T_{t_2})$
n-pentane	309	405	431	426	470	8×10^{24}
n-heptane	372	468	499	494	540	8×10^{26}
n-octane	399	494	525	514	569	2×10^{26}
methanol	338	442	477	466	513	10^{29}
ethanol	352	447	482	472	516	10^{30}
water	373	552	596	575	647	9×10^{28}

T_s—*Normal boiling point (K) at 0.101 MPa.*
T_{t_1}—*Calculated thermodynamic limit of superheat (K) at 0.101 MPa using the van der Waals equation of state.*
T_{t_2}—*Calculated thermodynamic limit of superheat (K) at 0.101 MPa using the Peng-Robinson equation of state.*
T_m—*Highest measured liquid phase temperature (K) at 0.101 MPa [64].*
J—*Nucleation rate (nuclei/cm^3-s) at T_{t_2} and .101 MPa.*

the respective liquids, thus indicating that in principle the liquid phase could sustain significant superheating. This is confirmed by experiment. However, the spinodal curve is a second-law defined limit. The best experiments may thus be expected to yield maximum temperatures (or minimum pressures) such that

$$T_t(P_o) > T_m(P_o) \tag{27}$$

(rather like the inability to precisely reach 0 K). Calculated values using the van der Waals limit must therefore be rejected because measured superheat limits would then fall in the region of unstable states and thus constitute a violation of the second law. A different result is obtained if the Peng-Robinson equation of state is used to predict the thermodynamic limit of superheat. This equation [40],

$$P = \frac{\mathscr{R}T}{(v - b)} - \frac{a}{v^2 + 2bv - b^2} \tag{28}$$

(a and b are constants and v is molar volume) yields for the spinodal curve (Equation 20)

$$\frac{\mathscr{R}T}{(v - b)^2} - \frac{2a(v + b)}{(v^2 + 2bv - b^2)^2} = 0 \tag{29}$$

Equation 27 is now satisfied as shown in Table 1. However, using another equation of state would yield yet a third value of T_t. This fact illustrates a dilemma one faces when attempting to calculate the thermodynamic limit of superheat.

The situation for mixtures is even more tenuous owing to increased difficulty in accurately representing mixture properties. Figure 4 illustrates the variation of thermodynamic limit of superheat with mole fraction at 0.101 MPa for ethane/n-propane mixtures [41] using the Peng-Robinson equation of state in Equation 23. Results reveal the expected over-prediction of measurement. In view of the somewhat arbitrary value of predicted mixture thermodynamic superheat limits (different equations of state yield different predictions), it is not known if the dashed line in Figure 4 actually constitutes a true upper boundary of measured limits of superheat.

Assuming T_t predicted from the Peng-Robinson equation of state yields correct values (a tenuous assumption), differences between T_t and T_m are outside the range of the experimental uncertainty of the measurements reported in Table 1 and Figure 4. The approach to the thermodynamic

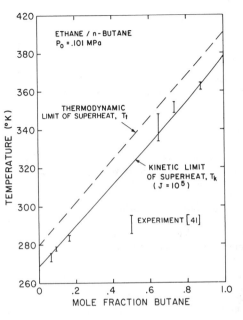

Figure 4. Comparison between highest measured liquid state temperatures (T_k) for various ethane/propane mixtures [41] and thermodynamic limits of superheat (T_t) calculated using the Peng-Robinson equation of state at 0.101 MPa.

limit of superheat then evidently triggers other phenomenon within the liquid whereby the liquid becomes "aware" of an impending violation of the second law. This conjecture forms the foundation for a mechanistic viewpoint of a phase transition which yields a practical upper limit on the superheat a liquid droplet can sustain. This mechanism defines the initial, realizable, condition for bubble growth within a droplet.

Kinetic Limit of Superheat

Introduction

A superheated liquid droplet (indeed any macroscopic liquid mass) is not quiescent on the microscopic level. Incessant random molecular motion creates local density variations. These density fluctuations in turn create "holes" or "nuclei" within which the molecules may be gas like in terms of their molecular spacing and potential energy. These nuclei grow or decay by the acquisition or loss of individual molecules until a certain size nucleus is produced such that it is in unstable equilibrium with the surrounding liquid. These bubbles are known as critical size nuclei: their appearance defines the initial condition for bubble growth within a liquid droplet.

Homogeneous nucleation theory provides a means for predicting the rate of formation of critical size nuclei at a given temperature, pressure, and composition. The mean rate of forming nuclei which continue to grow to macroscopic size is called the nucleation rate (units of nuclei/volume-time or nuclei/area-time for nucleation within the bulk of a liquid or at a surface, respectively.)

Kinetic theory [42] provides a mechanistic viewpoint for critical nucleus formation. From this theory the steady-state nucleation rate is proportional to the exponential of the energy of forming the nucleus:

$$J = \Gamma k_{f(n^*)} N_o \exp\left[-\frac{\Delta\Phi^*}{KT}\right] \tag{30}$$

or in terms of T

$$T \equiv T_k = \frac{\Delta\Phi^*}{K}\left[\ln\left(\frac{\Gamma k_{f(n^*)}N_o}{J}\right)\right]^{-1} \tag{31}$$

The temperature T_k in Equation 31 is called the *kinetic limit of superheat*. $\Delta\Phi^*$ is the minimum energy of forming a critical size nucleus and is given by the following well-known expression [43]

$$\Delta\Phi^* = \frac{16\pi\sigma_1^3}{3(P^* - P_o)^2} \tag{32}$$

where P^* is given by Equation 6 ($P \rightarrow P^*$). Γ is a factor which takes into account the detailed mechanism by which critical size nuclei form within the molecular network of the liquid. In the process of determining an explicit expression for Γ, three problems must be solved:

1. The energy of a nucleus of any size must be determined as a function of the number of molecules it contains.
2. The origin of the exponential dependence of J on $\Delta\Phi^*$ must be determined.
3. The mechanism by which the component molecules form critical size nuclei must be described.

Thermodynamics of Bubble Formation

The following assumptions are made to assist in determining the energy required to form a bubble within a superheated liquid droplet:

1. The temperature and pressure of the droplet in which the bubble forms is constant and uniform.
2. The bubble is bulk-like in terms of its thermophysical properties.
3. The bubble does not rotate, translate, or vibrate.
4. The gas within the bubble is ideal.

The so-called "capillarity approximation" which constitutes the second assumption is justified on the grounds that experimentally measured properties at the high liquid superheats typical of those characteristic of homogeneous nucleation (i.e., $T_r \gtrsim 0.9$ at $P_r > 0.04$) are in excellent agreement with predicted bulk values [44, 45].

The minimum work to form a nucleus within a homogeneous liquid under pressure P_o and temperature T is equal to the change in availability $\Delta\Phi$:

$$W = -\Delta\Phi$$

where in general [46]

$$\Phi \equiv V(P_o - P) + \sum_i \mu_i n_i + \sigma\mathscr{S} \tag{33}$$

Consider the homogeneous liquid system shown in Figure 5A, composed of a solution of n components at pressure P_o and temperature T (essentially a droplet which, relative to the bubble, appears to be of infinite extent). From Equation 33, the availability is

$$\Phi_A = \sum_i \mu_{i1}' n_{i'} \tag{34}$$

For the system in Figure 5B which includes a vapor bubble,

$$\Phi_B = \sum_i \mu_{i2}' n_{i2}' + \sum_i \mu_i'' n_i + V(P_o - P) + \sigma\mathscr{S} \tag{35}$$

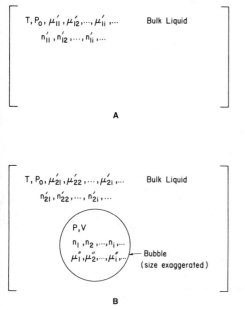

Figure 5. (A) Bulk multicomponent liquid without a vapor nucleus at indicated temperature (T), pressure (P_o), composition (n'_{ij}), and species chemical potentials (μ'_{ij}); (B) bulk liquid with vapor nucleus at indicated compositions and chemical potentials.

where n_i is the number of molecules in the vapor nucleus. Conservation of species requires that

$$n'_{i1} = n'_{i2} + n_i = \text{constant}$$

Also, since $n'_{i2} \gg n_i$ is reasonable to assume

$$\mu'_{i1} \simeq \mu'_{i2} \equiv \mu'_i(T, P_o, n'_1, n'_2, \ldots, n'_n) \tag{36}$$

Hence,

$$\Delta\Phi = \Phi_B - \Phi_A = V(P_o - P) + \sum_i n_i(\mu''_i - \mu'_i) + \sigma\mathscr{S} \tag{37}$$

In view of the ideal gas approximation, and assuming an incompressible liquid, the chemical potential difference in Equation 37 may be written as

$$\mu''_i(P_i, T) - \mu'_i(P_o, T, n'_1, n'_2, \ldots, n'_n) = KT \ln \frac{P}{P^*} + KT \ln \frac{y_i}{y_i^*} \tag{38}$$

For a spherical bubble, $V = \frac{4}{3}\pi r^3$ and $\mathscr{S} = 4\pi r^2$. Equations 37 and 38 may then be combined to give

$$\Delta\Phi = \frac{4}{3}\pi r^3 \left(P_o - P + P \ln \frac{P}{p^*} \right) + 4\pi r^2\sigma + KT \sum_i n_i \ln \frac{y_i}{y_i^*} \tag{39}$$

Equation 39 is an expression for the minimum energy required to form a bubble of radius r with gas phase composition y_i in the superheated droplet.

It has been argued [47, 48] that nucleus formation will proceed in a manner which maintains the gas composition close to the value it would have at the critical size. Hence $y_i \to y_i^*$ and $P \to P^*$

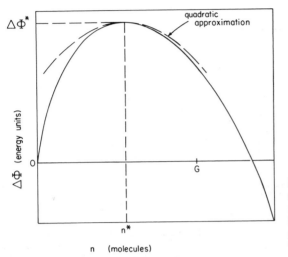

Figure 6. Typical variation of energy of forming a nucleus with number of molecules it contains. Dashed line shows representative quadratic approximation around the critical nucleus state.

(though Equation 2 will not apply for subcritical nuclei because such nuclei are not in static mechanical equilibrium). This assumption, though strictly valid only for a critical size bubble, introduces little error because its effect on the final result is only to alter the expression for Γ. In view of the ideal gas approximation

$$PV = \sum_i n_i KT \tag{40}$$

Equation 39 becomes

$$\Delta\Phi(n) = \left[36\pi\left(\frac{KT}{P^*}\right)^2\right]^{2/3} n^{2/3} - \left[KT\frac{P^* - P_o}{P^*}\right]n \tag{41a}$$

The qualitative variation of $\Delta\Phi$ with n is shown in Figure 6. The maximum in $\Delta\Phi$ depicted in Figure 6 defines the critical nucleus state. For this nucleus Equations 2 (with $P \rightarrow P^*$), 40, and 41 may be combined to yield Equation 32.

The stability of a critical size nucleus can be examined by twice differentiating Equation 41 $(d\Delta\Phi/dn|_{n=n^*} = 0)$

$$\Phi_{nn} \equiv \frac{d^2\Delta\Phi}{dn^2}\bigg|_{n=n^*} = -\left(\frac{KT}{P^*}\right)^2\frac{(P^* - P_o)^4}{32\pi\sigma^3} < 0 \tag{41b}$$

Thus, $\Delta\Phi$ does indeed exhibit a maximum at the critical size as expected. Such a nucleus is therefore in unstable equilibrium with the surrounding liquid; Equation 32 represents an effective energy barrier to bubble nucleation, and hence to bubble growth.

Kinetic Mechanism of Bubble Formation

The mechanistic view to nucleation yields a means by which nuclei may overcome the energy barrier defined by Equation 32. Among the first to propose such mechanisms were Frenkel [42], Volmer [49], and Reiss [50]. Additional theoretical work (e.g., [51–59]) has formalized the theory. Vapor nuclei are considered to grow or decay by a series of single molecule reactions. A molecule entering the nucleus results in its incremental growth; its escape causes an incremental decrease in size (recent modifications of the classical theory accounting for nuclei-nuclei interactions are not considered here [60]).

Following the classical line of reasoning, the primitive steps in nucleus formation may be modeled by the following set of "reactions"

$$E_n + E_1 \underset{k_{r(n+1)}}{\overset{k_{f(n)}}{\rightleftharpoons}} E_{n+1} \tag{42}$$

where $n = 1, 2, \ldots, n^*, \ldots, G - 2$ and E_n refers to a bubble containing n molecules. There is one such reaction for each class of nucleus. The set terminates when $n > G - 2$ where $G \geq n^*$ [42, 52, 53], and the reaction in the set of Equation 42 for which $n = G - 1$ is irreversible. The forward and reverse "rate constants," $k_{f(n)}$ and $k_{r(n+1)}$, are molecular evaporation and condensation rates, respectively. For an ideal gas, the condensation rate is approximated by the ideal gas collision frequency,

$$k_{r(n)} = \frac{P}{\sqrt{2\pi KT}} \sum_i \frac{y_i}{\sqrt{m_i}} S_i(n) \tag{43}$$

where $S_i(n)$ is the surface area to which the species i has access for condensation, and an accommodation coefficient of unity has been assumed. The molecular evaporation rate is not known *a priori*, but may be related to $k_{r(n)}$ as discussed in the following.

The nucleation rate $I_{n,t}$ in the reaction sequence of Equation 42 is the following:

$$I_{n,t} = k_{f(n-1)}f_{n-1,t} - k_{r(n)}f_{n,t} \tag{44}$$

$f_{n,t}$ is the number of nuclei at time t in a unit volume which contain n molecules. The subscript, t, reflects the possibility that this distribution may be time dependent. A quasi-steady assumption for nucleus formation is commonly invoked. In this assumption, the time to establish a steady state nucleation rate ($I_{n,t} \rightarrow I_n$) is much shorter than the characteristic experimental time required to bring the liquid droplet into the metastable state at which the probability for formation of a critical size nucleus would be likely [59, 61]. Thus

$$\frac{\partial f_{n,t}}{\partial t} = I_{n-1,t} - I_{n,t} = 0 \tag{45}$$

Hence,

$$\cdots = I_n = I_{n+1} = \cdots = I_G \equiv J = \text{constant} \tag{46}$$

where J is the steady-state nucleation rate. This rate represents the net rate at which nuclei overcome the energy barrier to nucleation and continue to grow. This is also the rate of forming nuclei containing G molecules. For such nuclei, the corresponding reaction in the set of Equation 42 is irreversible.

The specific form of f_n is unknown. It can, however, be related to an analogous distribution conceived to exist in either

1. A superheated liquid constrained to be in hypothetical equilibrium such that $J = 0$ [e.g., 42, 52, 53].
2. In the reference normal phase equilibrium state corresponding to $r \rightarrow \infty$ [57] and $J \rightarrow 0$.

The latter approach avoids the artifice of an equilibrium distribution in a metastable liquid, while the former assumption requires some means whereby such a hypothetical equilibrium could be created. In either approach, $f \rightarrow N$ so that Equation 44 with $I = 0$ yields

$$k_{r(n+1)} = k_{f(n)} \frac{N_n}{N_{n+1}} \tag{47}$$

Equation 44 can then be written $(I \rightarrow J)$

$$J = k_{f(n)}N_n\left[\frac{f_n}{N_n} - \frac{f_{n+1}}{N_{n+1}}\right] \tag{48}$$

Assuming that

$$f_n \rightarrow N_n \quad \text{as } n \rightarrow 1$$

(the population of nuclei containing the smallest number of molecules is effectively the same as the equilibrium population) and

$$f_n \rightarrow 0 \quad \text{as } n \rightarrow G$$

(there are no large nuclei present in the steady-state population), the device of summing Equation 48 from $n = 1$ to $n = G$ yields

$$J = \frac{1}{\displaystyle\sum_{n=1}^{G-1} \frac{1}{k_{f(n)}N_n}} \tag{49}$$

The constrained equilibrium distribution, N_n, is classically determined by assuming the outwardly homogeneous superheated liquid droplet is an ideal dilute solution of vapor bubbles as solute and single molecules as solvent. On minimizing the availability of mixing such a solution it can be shown that

$$N_n \simeq N_o \exp\left[-\frac{\Delta\Phi(n)}{KT}\right] \tag{50}$$

Figure 7 illustrates the qualitative variation of N_n with n (consistent with Equation 41). Equation 50 should be regarded more as a mathematical identity than as an expression for a distribution of nuclei which could actually occur in a superheated liquid droplet. This distribution is meaning-

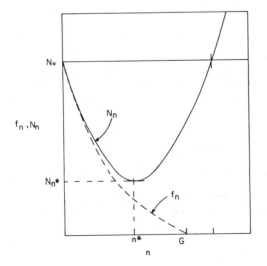

Figure 7. Schematic variation of hypothetical equilibrium (N_n) and actual (f_n) distributions of nuclei with n. Starred quantities represent the critical nucleus state.

less if n is large enough such that $N_n > N_o$. However, $f_G \rightarrow 0$ before this happens (provided G is not chosen too large).

If Equation 48 is partially summed from n = 1 to some n < G and the result combined with Equation 49, we find that

$$\frac{f_n}{N_n} < 1$$

This inequality, together with the boundary conditions on f_n, define the qualitative variation of f_n with n. This variation is shown in Figure 7. The device of summing Equation 48 [53] has obviated the need to determine a precise form of the actual distribution function f_n. Whether the equilibrium distribution is defined in the classical manner [42, 52, 53, etc.] or identified with a real distribution which exists in a saturated liquid [57] is unimportant with respect to predicting the superheat limit: differences in the two approaches will translate to minimal differences in the limiting liquid state at which a critical size nucleus is most likely to form in a liquid superheated droplet.

The present interest is in determining the thermodynamic state at which a critical size nucleus will form at the rate J in a droplet. Liquid properties appear in the distribution N_n and $k_{f(n)}$ (as yet unspecified). Equation 49 may of course be solved by iteration by including as many terms in the series as would be required to achieve a specified accuracy. This is a cumbersome approach. By treating n as a continuous rather than a discrete variable [62, 63] the summation can be converted to an integral [53]. Furthermore, the dominant contribution to this integral will occur in a region around the critical nucleus state. The consequences of this fact are two-fold:

1. A series expansion for $\Delta\Phi(n)$ truncated after the first nonzero term—a quadratic approximation (Figure 6)—is sufficiently accurate to represent the true behavior of the integral over the span of n.
2. The limits of integration may be extended from $-\infty$ to ∞ because the exponential term (Equation 50) behaves like a delta function [54]. Equation 49 then reduces to Equation 30 with

$$\Gamma = \left[\int_{-\infty}^{\infty} \exp\left[\frac{1}{2} \Phi_{nn} \cdot \frac{1}{KT} \cdot (n - n^*)^2 \right] dn \right]^{-1} \tag{51}$$

The continuous approximation for n also yields a more illuminating relation between $k_{r(n+1)}$ and $k_{f(n)}$ than given by Equation 47. In view of Equation 50 and the definition of a derivative, Equation 47 in the continuous approximation ($\Delta n = \pm 1 \rightarrow dn$ and $n \gg 1$) becomes

$$k_{f(n)} \simeq k_{r(n)} \exp\left[-\frac{\Phi_n}{KT} \right] \tag{52}$$

where $\Phi_n \equiv d\Delta\Phi/dn$. With reference to Figure 6 and Equation 41, for n < n*, $\Phi_n > 0$ so that $k_{f(n)} < k_{r(n)}$. Subcritical nuclei will degenerate because of the propensity for molecular condensation over evaporation; the opposite is true when n > n* because $\Phi_n < 0$. The relative values of $k_{f(n)}$ and $k_{r(n)}$ are fundamental manifestations of the tendency for molecular transfer to or from the nuclei and can be considered a measure of the difference in chemical potential between liquid and vapor. Integrating Equation 51, noting that $k_{f(n^*)} = k_{r(n^*)}$ (Equation 52), and combining the result with Equations 42 and 43 gives

$$\Gamma k_{f(n^*)} = \left[\frac{2\sigma}{\pi} \right]^{1/2} \sum_i \frac{y_i}{\sqrt{m_i}} \tag{53}$$

(For a pure substance, $y_i \rightarrow 1$, and $m_i \rightarrow m$).

Equation 31 may now be solved for the kinetic limit of superheat, T_k ($= T$), given a nucleation rate. Because $\Gamma k_f N_o = 10^{35}$, a precise value of J need not be known to estimate T_k. In this respect,

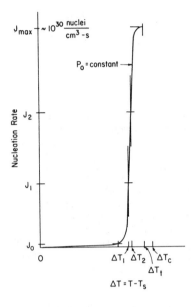

Figure 8. Variation of nucleation rate with temperature (not to scale). Peak rate ($\sim 10^{30}$ nuclei/cm^3-s) is shown corresponding to the thermodynamic limit of superheat.

T_k is a very weak function of J as schematically illustrated in Figure 8. Table 2 illustrates in numbers what Figure 8 schematically displays (using water as an example substance), and Figure 9 shows the variation of liquid temperature (Equation 31) at which critical size nuclei would form at rates $J = 1$, 10^5, 10^{10}, and 10^{20} nuclei/cm^3-s in n-octane (C_8H_{18}) at various pressures P_0. The range in nucleation rates shown in Figure 9 is typical of all experimental methods thus far used to measure the limit of superheat of liquids [64]. Several facts are worth noting about the kinetic limit of superheat.

The initial condition for bubble formation within a liquid droplet is not a precise value. This fact reflects the statistical nature of nucleation, yet it is usually within experimental error and thus undetectable except in the most precise measurements.

The limit of superheat increases as pressure increases. This is in agreement with experimental facts. The variation of T_k with J is not generally experimentally detectable.

Table 2
Limit of Superheat and Nucleation Rate of Water at Atmospheric Pressure

T	P	P_s	r × 10^7	J	Waiting time/cm^3 ($\sim 1/J$)
500	25.8	25.2	25.2	$< 10^{-99}$	$> 10^{91}$ years
550	59.1	61.0	6.76	$< 10^{-99}$	$< 10^{91}$ years
560	68.3	71.0	5.2	1.7×10^{-76}	1.2×10^{68} years
570	78.5	82.0	3.9	8.5×10^{-20}	3.7×10^{11} years
575	83.9	88.0	3.4	5.7×10^{-3}	1.8×10^2 sec
580	89.6	94.4	2.9	4.3×10^9	2.3×10^{-10} sec
590	101.6	108.9	2.1	4.3×10^{23}	2.3×10^{-24} sec

T—temperature (K)
P—pressure in vapor nucleus (atm)
P_s—equilibrium vapor pressure (atm)
r—radius of critical size nucleus (cm)
J—nucleation rate (nuclei/cm^3-sec)

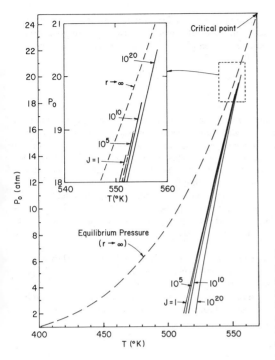

Figure 9. Calculated variation of liquid temperature with pressure at the superheat limit for n-octane corresponding to various nucleation rates. Dashed line is normal saturation curve for n-octane. Inset depicts limiting states above which no solution exists at indicated J, P_0, and T.

For constant J, the variation of T_k with P_0 (solid line) appears to approach the critical point. However a solution could not be extended to the critical state while maintaining J constant in Equations 31, 32, and 53 for the n-octane properties used: $P_0 \rightarrow P^*$ for some $P^* < P_c$. This fact may reflect inaccuracies in physical property prediction (most notably σ_1 and P_s) near the critical point. Another reason could be the existence of a limiting pressure above which homogeneous nucleation would not be possible at a given rate J. Above this limiting liquid pressure, $P_0 > P$ and a bubble could not exist in equilibrium with a superheated liquid. This conjecture could provide a practical restriction on the ambient pressure at which a bubble could form within a superheated liquid droplet. The increasing difficulty of detecting the macroscropic manifestation of critical nucleus formation within a superheated liquid droplet (droplet vaporization) as ambient pressure is increased [29, 65] has been experimentally observed. Part of the reason for this is undoubtedly a decrease in the bubble growth rate as pressure is increased. For example, above $P_r \sim 0.75$, it is not possible to observe any outward changes of n-heptane droplets initially about 1 mm diameter in an immiscible field liquid of glycerine when the droplets are heated close to their critical point when $J < 10^{10}$ nuclei cm^3-s [29]. Calculations for several other liquids did not exhibit the limitations shown in Figure 9.

The kinetic limit of superheat at a given pressure must be lower than the thermodynamic limit of superheat. This fact creates a consistency test for calculated thermodynamic and kinetic superheat limits. Better agreement is also obtained between the kinetic superheat limit and measurement, as shown, for example in Figure 4.

Given that $T_t < T_c$ and that J increases with T_k, some range of pressures and temperatures over which the solution to Equations 31, 32, and 53 is carried must be rejected; otherwise the state so calculated would fall in the domain of unstable states (Equation 19) in Figure 2B. These boundary states imply the existence of a maximum nucleation rate for $T_s < T < T_t$ ($J \rightarrow 0$ as $T \rightarrow T_s$ and

$T \rightarrow T_c$ so that it must pass through a maximum). Table 1 lists nucleation rates at 0.101 MPa corresponding to thermodynamic superheat limits calculated from the Peng-Robinson equation of state. The orders of magnitude of J_{max} listed in Table 1 conform to values suggested in the literature [66–68] which fix this maximum at about 10^{28} to 10^{30} nuclei/cm^3-s.

Approximate Methods

The motivation for seeking approximate methods for predicting the kinetic superheat limits of liquids resides in the difficulty of accurately predicting the relevant physical properties required to solve for T_k. The most difficult property to predict, and coincidently the one on which the superheat limit exhibits the greatest sensitivity, is surface tension. (This problem is particularly severe for mixtures.) A successful method for predicting the superheat limit, and therefore the initial condition for bubble growth within a superheated liquid droplet, should obviate the need for surface tension data. A number of successful approaches have recently appeared which satisfy this intent.

One such approximation has already been presented as Equation 26 [39]. However, this approximation represents the thermodynamic limit of superheat corresponding to the van der Waals equation of state and therefore is not relevant to the present study. A more useful approach must be based on the kinetic superheat limit.

The reduced superheat limits (T/T_c) of a large number of substances have been shown to be quite close to one another at the same reduced pressure [68, 69] as illustrated in Figure 10 [68]. This fact is suggestive of a method based on corresponding states theory [70, 71]. This theory assumes that an intrinsic property of a substance, α (such as the limit of superheat corresponding to a pressure P_o and rate J), may be expressed in terms of a universal function of reduced temperature and pressure as

$$\alpha = \alpha_o(T_r, P_r)$$

Lienhard [72] recently explored this approach for the limit of superheat of pure substances by correlating reduced nucleation pressure, $P_r \equiv P_o/P_c$, in terms of both acentric factor

$$\omega \equiv -1 - \log_{10} P_r|_{T_r = 7}$$

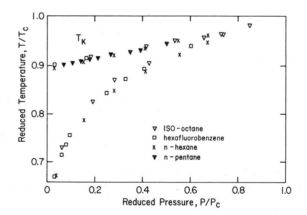

Figure 10. Reduced temperature and pressure for several substances indicating correlation of both saturation and limiting superheated liquid states [68].

and reduced superheat limit, T_r. Guided by the result from homogeneous nucleation theory, Equation 30, written in terms of pressure, is

$$P_o = P - \left(\frac{16}{3}\pi\right)^{1/2} \frac{\sigma^{3/2}}{\sqrt{kT_a}\sqrt{\ln(C/J)}} \tag{54}$$

where $T_a = T_k$ and $C = \Gamma k_{f(n\bullet)} N_o$. Lienhard and Karimi [66] argued the substitution of T_a by T_c, and a successful correlation was then obtained in the form [72]

$$P_{roi} = P_{rsi} - \frac{f_i}{\sqrt{-\beta}}(1 - T_{roi})^{1.83} \tag{55a}$$

where

$$f_i = 112.82 + 224.42\omega_i \tag{55b}$$

and

$$\beta = \ln(J) - C \tag{55c}$$

$$P_{roi} = P_{oi}/P_{ci}$$

$$P_{rsi} = P_{si}/P_{ci}$$

$$T_{roi} = T_{ki}/T_{ci}.$$

The term in temperature on the right-hand side of Equation 55a conforms to the classical expectation $\sigma \sim (1 - T_{roi})^{11/9}$ [71]. Fortunately C is nearly constant for a wide range of substances: $45 < C < 85$ [68, 73, 74]. The utility of Equation 55 resides both in relative accuracy and simplicity; no surface tension data are required. (In view of this accuracy, surface tension of a superheated liquid may actually be calculated by combining Equations 54 and 55 and solving for σ.) Figure 11 illustrates calculated (Equation 55) and measured superheat limits of a number of pure liquids. The data are predicted within a pencil width [72] and no surface tension data are explicitly required in the calculation.

A recent extension of the corresponding states methods for the superheat limit of a pure liquid has been made to mixtures [74]. The reduced mixture superheat limit was shown to be a mole fraction weighted average of the reduced limits of superheat of the individual components in an n-component mixture

$$T_{rm} = \sum_{i=1}^{n} x_i T_{roi} \tag{56}$$

where $T_{rm} = T_k/T_{cm}$ and the T_{roi} ($=T_{ki}/T_{ci}$) are evaluated at the same reduced pressure P_{rm} ($=P_o/P_{cm}$) as the mixture. Thus these quantities are themselves implicit functions of mole fraction through the variation of P_{cm} with x_i. The T_{ki} must be evaluated independently. This may be done by direct measurement or by using Equations 31 or 55 (depending on the availability of physical property data for the mixture in question). They are relatively constant over the range of critical pressures corresponding to $0 \le x_i \le 1$ at constant P_o for many substances, so the T_{ki} may be determined at only one reduced pressure and then constrained to be constants in Equation 56 over the span of x_i with little loss of accuracy [74]. The variation of T_k with x_i for the mixture is then carried entirely in T_{cm} and the explicit linear relation with the x_i. It should be noted that while the reduced superheat limits calculated from Equation 56 exhibit a linear variation with mole fraction,

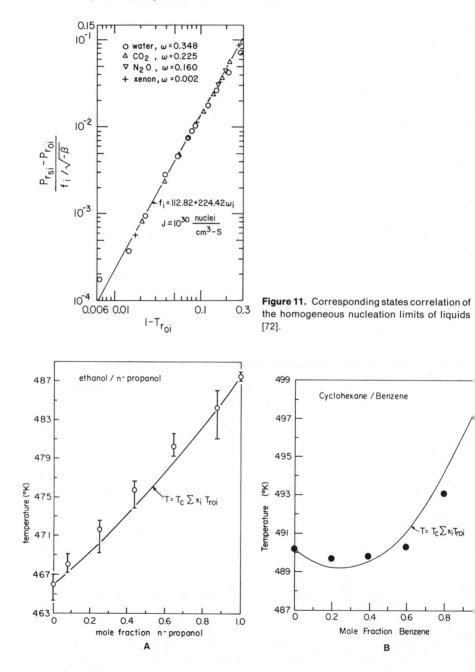

Figure 11. Corresponding states correlation of the homogeneous nucleation limits of liquids [72].

Figure 12. Comparison between measured kinetic limits of superheat of several ethanol-n -propanol (A) and cyclohexane/ benzene (B) mixtures [48] with predictions of the generalized corresponding states method at various mixture compositions [74].

the superheat limit itself will not generally vary linearly with x_i. Only when

$$T_{cm} = \sum_{i=1}^{n} x_i T_{ci}$$

and the T_{roi} are all the same over the span of x_i for constant P_o does Equation 56 yield the often quoted result

$$T_k = \sum_{i=1}^{n} x_i T_{ki} \tag{57}$$

Figures 12A and B illustrate the variation of T_k with x_i for two binary mixtures. It is evident that inaccurate predictions may generally be expected if Equation 57 is assumed to be universally valid.

Conclusions

The practically attainable superheat limit of a liquid corresponds to the kinetic limit of superheat. This limit may be either measured or predicted using the approach based on classical homogeneous nucleation theory or from one of the recent approximate corresponding states methods. Though this discussion has been in the context of liquid droplets, the results are independent of droplet volume as long as the liquid state is not appreciably altered from the ambient by the droplet/field liquid interfacial tension. In any case, the result gives the thermodynamic state—pressure, temperature, and composition—at which super-critical nuclei (the initial bubbles) form within the bulk of the droplet at a particular nucleation rate. However, merely defining the thermodynamic state for initial bubble formation does not provide information concerning the dynamics of phase change.

BUBBLE GROWTH IN DROPLETS

Introduction

Critical size nuclei are in static (unstable) equilibrium and would remain in this state unless perturbed by a change in pressure, temperature, or composition. Such a perturbation is inherent in the nucleation process itself in that the nucleation rate prescribes the rate of forming supercritical nuclei (containing $n > n^*$ molecules). These nuclei are not in static equilibrium in as much as $k_{f(G)} > k_{r(G)}$ (Equation 52). Inherent in the nucleation process is thus the further growth of supercritical nuclei. The process of homogeneous nucleation itself is considered to end with the appearance and subsequent growth of these nuclei.

As the initial bubble grows both its pressure P and temperature T_v decrease (path 2 → 2' in Figure 2A). Growth continues until $P \to P_o$ and $T_v \to T_s$. Finally, when liquid 1 completely vaporizes, the final vapor bubble at T_v must be reheated to T_o to regain thermal equilibrium. These aspects of bubble growth are well documented with reference to bubbles growing in infinite media (see, for example, the excellent reviews in References 75 and 76).

The dynamics of growth within a droplet may be affected from the beginning by the finite mass of vaporizing liquid. For both small liquid/liquid interfacial tensions and differences between the two fluid densities, the initial bubble exhibits a growth similar to its growth in an infinite media ($S \to \infty$). The initially isothermal field within the droplet is perturbed due to expansion of the bubble. A thermal boundary layer is created at the evaporating boundary which may initially be far removed from the boundary of the droplet (depending, of course, on the physical location of the initial bubble in the droplet; regardless of this location there will be *some* period of growth. that is, the boundary layer does not penetrate into the field liquid). Figure 13 illustrates the qualitative picture. As the bubble grows and its temperature continues to drop, the thermal boundary layer propagates progressively farther into the vaporizing liquid and eventually reaches the droplet

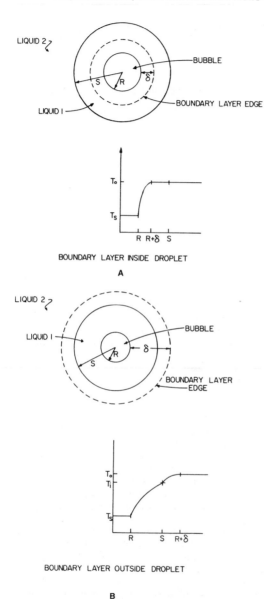

Figure 13. Schematic illustration of bubble growth in a droplet suspended in an immiscible liquid: (A) early stage where thermal boundary layer (δ) is within the droplet; (B) later stage where boundary layer extends into liquid 2.

boundary (Figure 13B). Until that time growth will be very similar to that which would occur in an infinite medium, as the temperature field in liquid 2 remains unperturbed. The conservation equations governing bubble growth in a droplet will then be identical to those for bubble growth in an infinite media. When the thermal boundary layer extends into liquid 2 the temperature and pressure fields in both liquids must be determined at each instant of time, as well as the radial history of the bubble.

Review of Bubble Growth in Stationary Infinite Media

Governing Equations

Consider an isolated bubble expanding in a pure inviscid constant property uniformly super-heated liquid at temperature T_o and pressure P_o. We shall utilize all assumptions made in an earlier study of this problem [77]. Viscous effects are also neglected [76]. For a stationary spherical bubble growing in a stagnant inviscid liquid the velocity field is [77, 78]

$$v = \varepsilon \frac{R^2}{r^2} \dot{R} \tag{58}$$

where $\varepsilon = 1 - \rho_v/\rho_1$. When Equation 58 is combined with the inviscid momentum equation,

$$\frac{D\bar{v}_i}{Dt} = -\frac{1}{\rho_i} \bar{\nabla} P_i \tag{59}$$

(where $i = 1$ denotes the droplet and $i = 2$ is the immiscible field liquid) and integrated

$$\int_R^S \left\{ \frac{\varepsilon}{r^2} [\ddot{R} R^2 + 2\dot{R}^2 R] - 2\varepsilon \frac{R^2 R^4}{r^3} \right\} dr = -\frac{1}{\rho_i} \int_R^S dP_i \tag{60}$$

the classical Rayleigh equation emerges when $S \to \infty$ and Equation 2 is used to replace interfacial pressure in the liquid with surface tension and radius [76, 77, 79]:

$$R\ddot{R} + \dot{R}^2 \left(2 - \frac{\varepsilon}{2} \right) = \frac{P - P_o}{\varepsilon \rho_1} - \frac{2\sigma_1}{\varepsilon \rho_1 R} \tag{61}$$

The energy equation governing the temperature field in liquid 1 (which is effectively infinite during the time for which $\delta < S - R$) is

$$\frac{\partial T_i}{\partial t} + \bar{v}_i \cdot \bar{\nabla} T_i = \alpha_i \bar{\nabla}^2 T_i \tag{62}$$

(where $i = 1$). The boundary and initial conditions are the following:

$$r = R: \qquad T_1 = T_v(t) \tag{63a}$$

$$k_1 \frac{\partial T_1}{\partial r} \bigg|_{r=R} = \rho_v h_{fg} \dot{R} \tag{63b}$$

$$r \to \infty: \qquad T_1 \to T_o \tag{63c}$$

$$t = 0: \qquad T_1 = T_o \tag{63d}$$

$$R = R_o \tag{63e}$$

$$\dot{R} = 0 \tag{63f}$$

The phase equilibrium condition which couples Equations 61–63, neglecting nonequilibrium effects [80, 81], is

$$P = P(T_v(t)) \tag{63g}$$

The specific form of this relation depends on the fluid under consideration. In general the often used linearized Clausius/Clapeyron equation (e.g., [82, 83])

$$P[T_v(t)] \simeq P_o + \rho_1 \mathscr{A}[T_v(t) - T_s(P_o)] \tag{64}$$

where $\mathscr{A}$ is a constant dependent on the specific fluid, will not generally be accurate at the high liquid superheats of interest here ($T_o - T_s > 100$ K at $P_r \sim 0.04$) except when $P_r \to 1$.

The unknowns in Equations 61–63 are $T_1(r, t)$, $P(t)$, $T_v(t)$, and $R(t)$. A rather large number of solutions to this set of equations has appeared in the literature, which range from approximate analytical solutions to fully numerical treatments that involve no further approximations than are already incorporated in the governing equations as written. These solutions may be divided into three classes:

1. Solutions in which only the momentum equation (Equation 61) is solved.
2. Solutions in which the full set of Equations 61–63 is solved simultaneously.
3. Solutions for which only the energy equation is solved.

Approximate Solutions

Inertia controlled growth. The initial temperature field is isothermal so that growth is controlled by the difference in pressure which exists across the liquid/vapor interface ($\Delta P \equiv P - P_o$). This pressure difference may be large for a droplet at its superheat limit. For example, for critical size nuclei $R_o \sim 10^{-7}$ cm and $\sigma \sim 3$ dyne/cm (typical of many organic liquids at $T_r \sim 0.9$). Therefore, $\Delta P \sim (10$ atm).

The solution of Equation 61 yields a bubble growth rate in the form

$$\dot{R} = C_1$$

where [76, 79, 83, 84]

$$C_1 = \left\{ \frac{2}{3} \frac{P - P_o}{\varepsilon \rho_1} \left[1 - \left(\frac{R_o}{R} \right)^3 \right] - \frac{2\sigma_1}{\varepsilon \rho_1 R} \left[1 - \left(\frac{R_o}{R} \right)^2 \right] \right\}^{1/2} \tag{65a}$$

When $R \gg R_o$ and the surface tension term is neglected, C_1 becomes independent of R such that

$$C_1 \simeq \left\{ \frac{2}{3} \frac{P - P_o}{\varepsilon \rho_1} \right\}^{1/2} \tag{65b}$$

The evolution of bubble radius then takes the form

$$R \simeq C_1 t^q \tag{66}$$

where $q = 1$.

Immediately after the bubble starts to expand, the gas pressure as well as both the gas temperature and temperature of the liquid adjacent to the bubble wall begin to drop. Eventually, $T_v \to T_s$ and $P \to P_o$ (though in fact ΔP is never identically zero). The temperature gradient at the bubble wall then controls growth (Equation 63b) and this gradient is determined by solving the energy equation (Equation 62); the momentum equation is not now needed.

Heat transfer controlled growth. Various analytical solutions to Equations 62 and 63b yield a bubble growth law of the same form as Equation 66 with

$$q = \tfrac{1}{2} \tag{67}$$

[77, 83–86]. The solutions differ in the growth constant C_1. Scriven [77] discovered a similarity variable for Equation 62 and showed that C_1 is obtained by numerically solving

$$Ja = 2\beta^3 \exp[\beta^2 + 2\varepsilon\beta^2] \int_\beta^\infty X^{-2} \exp[-X^2 - 2\varepsilon\beta^3 X^{-1}] \, dX \tag{68}$$

where the Jakob number is defined as

$$Ja = \frac{\rho_1 C_{p1}(T_o - T_s)}{\rho_v h_{fg}} \tag{69}$$

and

$$\beta = \frac{C_1}{2\alpha_1^{1/2}} \tag{70}$$

(The Jakob number has also been found to be an important parameter for defining the intensity of vaporization of droplets [27].) Birkhoff et al. [86] used the same similarity variable as Scriven and arrived at a similar result.

Approximate solutions to Equation 62 were obtained by Plesset and Zwick [83] and Forster and Zuber [85] in the form

$$C_1 = Ja \cdot (C\alpha_1)^{1/2} \tag{71a}$$

where

$$C = \pi \, [85] \tag{71b}$$

or

$$C = \frac{12}{\pi} \, [84] \tag{71c}$$

Plesset and Zwick employed the assumption of a "thin" thermal boundary layer in their analysis. This assumption requires that $Ja \gg 1$ [76]. At lower superheats wherein this approximation is no longer valid, the growth constant must be determined by numerically solving Equations 68–70.

An approximate analytical expression for C_1 was presented by Moalem-Maron and Zijl [87] (for $R \gg R_o$) which agrees with the limiting values for small ($Ja \ll 1$) [77] and large ($Ja \gg 1$) [77, 83] Jakob number:

$$C_1 \simeq \left(\frac{3\alpha_1}{\pi}\right)^{1/2} Ja \left\{ 1 + \sqrt{1 + \frac{2\pi}{3Ja}} \right\} \tag{72}$$

The growth law expressed by Equation 66 with $q = \frac{1}{2}$ exhibits a singularity as $t \to 0$. This fact does not usually cause difficulties. When fluid conditions are such as to render valid the assumption of heat-transfer-controlled growth, the size range of visible bubbles is usually large enough that this initial velocity singularity has a minimal effect on predicted bubble radii.

Growth in the intermediate region. The full set of equations (Equations 61–63) must be solved when the already mentioned asymptotic approximations are not valid. There is no closed-form analytical solution to this set of equations. Either fully numerical procedures [88–90] or approximate analytical/numerical methods must be used (e.g., [83, 85, 91, 92]). A review of some of these solutions is given in Reference 76.

The simplest of the approximate solutions and one which also yields limits of validity of the asymptotic solutions previously discussed was obtained by Mikic et al. [82] and later modified by

Theofanous and Patel [93]. Their approach was to solve the asymptotic expressions for bubble growth given by Equation 66 with $q = 1$ (Equation 65b) and $q = \frac{1}{2}$ (Equation 71c) for $T_v(t)$, and then eliminate $T_v(t)$ between the two equations. Only small superheats were considered such that $(T_v - T_s)/(T_o - T_s) \sim 1$ and the linearized Clausius-Clapeyron equation was used to replace P by $T_v(t)$ in Equation 65b. The result was the following:

$$R^+ = \frac{2}{3}[(t^+ + 1)^{3/2} - t^{+3/2} - 1] \tag{73a}$$

where

$$R^+ = \frac{A}{C_1^2} R \tag{73b}$$

$$t^+ = \frac{A^2}{C_1^2} t \tag{73c}$$

$$A = \left(\frac{2}{3} \frac{h_{fg}\rho_v(T_o - T_s)}{\rho_1 T_s}\right)^{1/2} \tag{73d}$$

The utility of Equation 73 lies in its simplicity. It facilitates calculating the temporal variation of R which spans the range of controlling mechanisms for bubble growth.

The real time domain over which the approximate asymptotic solutions thus far considered may be valid can be estimated from Equation 73. When $t^+ \ll 1$, Equation 73 yields the correct limit for inertia controlled bubble growth, while for $t^+ \gg 1$, the correct limit for heat-transfer-controlled growth is recovered. At the superheat limit corresponding to $P_r \sim 0.04$ for many organic liquids, $200 < Ja < 300$ (Figure 14) which, unfortunately, is outside the range of validity of Equation 73a. We only intend to use Equation 73 here to establish approximate limits for the validity of the various asymptotic solutions. The order of magnitude of relevant properties of many organic liquids at $T_r \sim 0.9$ is the following: $Ja \sim 10^2$, $h_{fg} \sim 10^3$ cal/g, $\alpha_1 \sim 10^{-4}$ cm^2/s, $T_s \sim 10^2$ K, $\Delta T \sim 10^2$ K, $\rho_1 \sim 0.1$ g/cm^3, and $\rho_v \sim 10^{-2}$ g/cm^3. From Equation 73c $t^+ \sim 10^3 t$. The temperature field will then essentially be isothermal for times $t \ll 1$ ms. As pressure increases, Ja decreases (Figure 14) and the time domain for isothermal growth becomes progressively shorter.

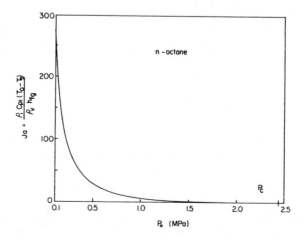

Figure 14. Typical variation of Jakob number (Ja) with pressure (P_0) at its superheat limit using properties of n-octane for illustration.

Experimentally accessible times for bubble growth measurements within superheated liquid droplets have, with one exception [18], been on the order of 1 ms [11, 27, 28]. The available data are
thus representative of phase change dominated by heat transfer processes.

Bubble Growth in Finite Media—Droplets

Introduction

The application of an analysis for bubble growth in an infinite medium to growth in a liquid of
finite extent (i.e., a droplet) requires that the thermal boundary layer does not penetrate into the
region outside of the droplet boundary (Figure 13A). As the bubble grows and the droplet evaporates, the bubble wall approaches the liquid/liquid interface, and clearly the thermal boundary layer
must eventually extend into the field liquid (Figure 13B). In this event, the temperature field is a
two-domain problem and the full set of Equations 61–63 must be solved simultaneously to determine the temporal variation R, T_v, P, and S. A number of solutions to this set of equations have
been obtained which involve various approximations which we shall review here. As a prelude, we
first provide criteria which will ensure that the initial bubble forms within the bulk of the droplet
and not at the liquid 1/liquid 2 interface. Then we shall define an appropriate geometrical configuration for the two-phase droplet.

The liquid 1/liquid 2 interface represents an ideal smooth container for a droplet. The process
of homogeneous nucleation may equally occur at this interface as in the bulk of the droplet. The
relative value of the nucleation rate determines the location of bubble formation, with nuclei forming in the region where J is highest. For most purposes, this requirement is equivalent to determining
where ΔΦ (Equation 32) is lowest. Exceptions are sometimes encountered for nuclei forming at solid
surfaces [94]. Five possible locations for nuclei formation may be identified (Figure 15):

1. Completely within the bulk of the droplet (position 1).
2. At the liquid 1/liquid 2 interface but resting entirely within liquid 1 (position 2 in Figure 15):
3. Between liquid 1 and liquid 2 (position 3):
4. At the liquid 1/liquid 2 interface but resting entirely within (position 4):
5. Completely within liquid 2 (position 5):

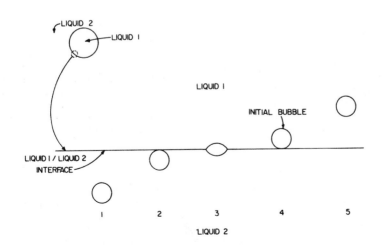

Figure 15. Possible locations of initial bubble appearance within a superheated droplet (liquid
1) relative to interface between droplet and field liquid (liquid 2).

The basis for expecting nucleation to occur at the liquid 1/liquid 2 interface is determined by the interfacial forces acting on the vapor lens (position 3) and the energy of the critical size bubble. If a lenticular nucleus (position 3) is to be stable, then we must assure that [16, 73, 95–97]

$$\sigma_{12} = |\sigma_1 - \sigma_2| \tag{74a}$$

Otherwise, if

$$\sigma_1 \geq \sigma_2 + \sigma_{12} \tag{74b}$$

or

$$\sigma_2 \geq \sigma_1 + \sigma_{12} \tag{74c}$$

the nucleus forms in the liquid with the lower surface tension. This latter possibility is of interest in the present discussion and corresponds to the tendency of liquid 1 to spread on liquid 2 [98]. The bubble will then remain within the boundaries of the droplet and liquid 2 will serve only as a medium for heating the droplet and will not itself affect the ability of the droplet to be heated to its limit of superheat. Liquid 2 will, of course, affect the bubble growth process when the thermal boundary layer penetrates into it. If Equations 74a or 74b were satisfied, a bubble might leave the droplet before all of liquid 1 vaporizes [16, 17, 24, 99]. In the present work the bubble is considered to remain entirely within the boundary of the droplet and does not penetrate the liquid 1/liquid 2 interface during its growth. The surface tension of the vaporizing liquid is then low compared to the liquid 2 surface tension and Equation 74c is satisfied.

Geometry of the Two-Phase Droplet

The spatial location of the initial bubble within an isothermal droplet will be random unless temperature gradients exist within the droplet. A simple mass balance on the droplet reveals that this initial location is unimportant during evaporation of most of the liquid mass of the droplet. A mass balance shows that the ratio of bubble radius R to droplet radius, S, is

$$\frac{R}{S} = \left[\frac{\chi}{1 - \varepsilon(1 - \chi)} \right]^{1/3} \tag{75}$$

where χ is the mass fraction of liquid evaporated. For many liquids, $\varepsilon > 0.9$ at $T_r \sim 0.9$. When as little as 10% of liquid is evaporated, $R/S \sim 0.8$; when 50% of the liquid in the droplet has evaporated, $R/S \sim 0.97$. In either case the unevaporated liquid will essentially exist as a relatively thin film around the bubble. This fact has been observed experimentally [11, 21]. Effects due to eccentricity of the vapor bubble (Figure 16A) will be minimal after this initial evaporation. The salient features of evaporation of a bubble within a droplet were therefore examined with the aid of the model shown in Figure 16B—a vapor bubble growing from the center of a liquid droplet.

Approximations and Previous Work

The equations governing bubble growth in a droplet are Equations 59, 62, and 63 with i = 1, 2. The problem requires solving both the momentum and energy equations simultaneously within liquids 1 and 2, taking due account of their coupling at the liquid/liquid interface. We first review here simplifications to this problem which have appeared in the literature.

Main simplifications involved neglect of detailed dynamics and heat transfer processes within the droplet. Sideman and Taitel [21] and Tochitani et al. [100] assumed the two-phase droplet was a rigid sphere to determine both the temperature field in the ambient liquid (i.e., the temperature adjusts instantaneously to changes in droplet radius) and average Nusselt number around the droplet when

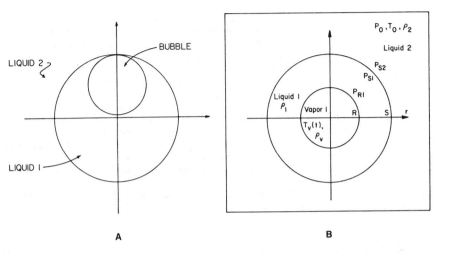

A   B

Figure 16. Geometric model for bubble growth in a liquid droplet. (A) bubble geometry as determined by photographs from several experiments; (B) simplified geometric model used in present analysis (pressures correspond to values at indicated interfaces).

heat transfer occurred over part of the surface of the droplet. The remainder of the boundary was considered insulated. Sideman and Isenberg [22] later used this Nusselt number to determine the temporal variation of droplet radius using the two-phase droplet model shown in Figure 17. A similar model was used by Moalem-Maron et al. [101] except heat transfer was accounted for over the entire surface of the droplet. Selecki and Gradon [25] extended this model to an evaporating (nonrigid) droplet and used the result for bubble growth in an infinite medium (Equation 71) to describe the temporal variation of droplet radius. Detailed account of the external flow field for both an expanding and translating droplet was included in the analysis of Mokhtarzadeh and El-Shirbini [26], while the droplet interior was considered to be at a uniform temperature with an average heat transfer coefficient used to determine heat transfer to the droplet. An analysis of bubble growth in droplets when Equation 74b is satisfied (liquid 2 now spreads on liquid 1) has also been reported such that the bubble was either considered to leave the droplet as soon as it formed [24] or after moving through the liquid 1/liquid 2 interface [99]. This latter study [99] utilized a modification of Equations 66, 67, and 71 and included vapor density variations with temperature, while the former work [24] obtained the temperature and velocity fields within the droplet only for those periods between departure of the nucleus from the droplet to its subsequent formation (i.e., for a single-phase droplet exposed to a liquid 2 in uniform motion).

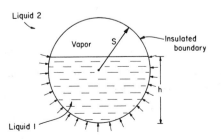

Figure 17. Model for quasi-steady vaporization of a droplet in an immiscible liquid when thermal boundary layer extends well into liquid 2 and the vapor/liquid 2 boundary is assumed insulated [22].

The solutions referred to previously employed various approximations including neglect of radial liquid motion, dominant axial convection (i.e., moving droplets), quasi-steady heat transfer, or taking full account of the transient temperature field. The importance of translatory motion resides in the fact that experimental methods often involve moving droplets. The quasi-steady approximation involves certain assumptions about the characteristic times for heat transport and bubble expansion. Delineation of the important characteristic parameters which govern these approximations will aid in both classifying the various solutions presented and in establishing the most simplified form of the equations governing bubble growth in a liquid droplet at the superheat limit. For this purpose we will initially consider an isolated expanding bubble in uniform motion in a static liquid. Whether we consider this configuration or focus attention on an internal bubble within a droplet is unimportant with regard to the present intent. The droplet may expand at about the same rate as the internal bubble during most of the evaporation. It is only desired here to estimate the standard order of magnitude of the terms in the energy equation to ascertain which terms are important and which are not.

For a translating and expanding droplet the velocity field, Equation 58, must be modified. We follow previous work and neglect viscous effects around the droplet. The velocity field is then [102, 103]

$$V_r = U_\infty \left(1 - \frac{R^3}{r^3} \right) \cos \theta + \varepsilon \frac{R^2}{r^2} \dot{R} \tag{76a}$$

$$V_\theta = U_\infty \left(1 + \frac{R^3}{2r^3} \right) \sin \theta \tag{76b}$$

where θ is measured from the vertical. Equations 62 and 76 are combined and nondimensionalized to yield

$$\underbrace{\frac{\partial \bar{T}}{\partial \tau}}_{\text{(A)}} + \underbrace{\left[\varepsilon \frac{\bar{R}^2}{\bar{r}^2} \dot{\bar{R}} - Pe \left(1 - \frac{\bar{R}^3}{\bar{r}^3} \right) \right]}_{\text{(B)}} \underbrace{\frac{\partial \bar{T}}{\partial \bar{r}}}_{\text{(C)}} + \underbrace{Pe \left(1 + \frac{\bar{R}^3}{\bar{r}^3} \right) \frac{\sin \theta}{\bar{r}} \frac{\partial \bar{T}}{\partial \bar{r}}}_{\text{(D)}}$$

$$= \underbrace{\frac{1}{\bar{r}^2} \frac{2}{\partial \bar{r}} \left(\bar{r}^2 \frac{\partial \bar{T}}{\partial \bar{r}} \right)}_{\text{(E)}} + \underbrace{\frac{1}{\bar{r}^2} \frac{1}{\sin \theta} \frac{\partial}{\partial \theta} \left(\sin \theta \frac{\partial \bar{T}}{\partial \theta} \right)}_{\text{(F)}} \tag{77}$$

where the Peclet number is defined as

$$Pe = \frac{U_\infty S_0}{\alpha_1} \tag{78a}$$

$$\tau = \frac{\alpha_1 t}{S_0^2} \tag{78b}$$

$$\bar{T} = \frac{T - T_s}{T_0 - T_s} \tag{78c}$$

$$\bar{r}, \bar{R} = r, R/S_0 \tag{78d}$$

The boundary conditions are approximately given by Equation 63. Translational convection (terms (C) and (D)) may be neglected in comparison with radial convection (B) if

$$Pe \ll \frac{Ja}{\bar{\delta}^2} \tag{79}$$

where from Equation 63b, $\bar{R} \sim Ja/\bar{\delta}$ has been used; $\bar{\delta}$ is the nondimensional boundary layer thickness ($= \delta/R$). Now, in analogy with bubble growth in an infinite medium, $\bar{\delta}$ is approximated as [76]

$$\bar{\delta} \sim 1/Ja \tag{80}$$

Equation 79 is then

$$Pe \ll Ja^3 \tag{81}$$

On the other hand if

$$Pe \gg Ja^3 \tag{82}$$

translational convection dominates.

The validity of the quasi-steady approximation resides in the relative values of characteristic time for thermal diffusion in the liquid surrounding the bubble, and the characteristic bubble expansion time. If Equation 81 is satisfied the characteristic time for heat diffusion in the liquid surrounding the bubble is

$$t_H \sim \frac{R^2}{\alpha_1} \tag{83a}$$

If radial convection is of negligible importance and translational motion of the droplet dominates (Equation 82), then approximately

$$t_H \sim \frac{R}{U_\infty} \tag{83b}$$

In either case, the characteristic bubble expansion time is estimated from Equations 63b ($\partial T/\partial r \sim \Delta T/\delta$) and 80 as

$$t_R \sim \frac{R^2}{\alpha_1 Ja^2} \tag{84}$$

When Equation 82 applies,

$$\frac{t_R}{t_H} \sim \frac{Pe}{Ja^2} \gg 1 \tag{85a}$$

so unsteady heat transfer in the liquid surrounding the bubble may also be neglected (i.e., the time-dependent term in Equation 62 may be dropped and the quasi-steady approximation is reasonable). When radial motion dominates (in the limit, $Pe \to 0$)

$$\frac{t_R}{t_H} \sim \frac{1}{Ja^2} \tag{85b}$$

The quasi-steady approximation will then be reasonable only for low Jakob number. For many liquids heated to their superheat limits, $Ja \sim \theta(10^2)$ at $P_r \sim 0.04$ (Figure 14). The quasi-steady approximation is then not valid as the thermal boundary layer remains close to the bubble. The time-dependent term in Equation 62 must be retained in the solution. When $T_r \to 1$ ($P_r \to 1$ in view of the fact that the limit of superheat is not independent of pressure) $Ja \to 0$ and the thermal boundary layer is thick relative to the droplet radius. Liquid phase quasi-steadiness may then be assumed.

(Near the critical pressure, though, gas phase unsteadiness becomes increasingly important to consider.) The fact that this approximation has been used at much lower superheats in previous work (e.g., [104]) is indicative of extraneous nucleation aids suppressing homogeneous nucleation.

Quasi-Steady Solutions

The quasi-steady approximation has led to a number of approximate analytical solutions for the temporal variation of droplet radius, which do not involve the equation of motion. In the extreme case of negligible radial convection (Equation 82) the droplet is considered a rigid sphere and viscous effects are neglected. Sideman and Taitel [21] and Sideman and Isenberg [22] considered a two-phase droplet to be a spherical shell of vapor with a puddle of liquid at the bottom (Figure 18A). Heat transfer over the upper portion of the droplet—the liquid 2/vapor interface—was neglected. The average Nusselt number characterizing heat transfer to the liquid sheath in a potential flow field was obtained as [21]

$$Nu = \frac{h \cdot 2R}{k_1} = 2\left(\frac{Pe}{\pi} \cdot \left[\frac{1 - (1 - \varepsilon)\bar{S}^3}{\varepsilon \bar{S}^4}\right]\right)^{1/2} \tag{86}$$

where $\bar{S} \equiv S/S_o$. Using Equation 86 in an energy balance at the liquid 1/liquid 2 interface, $\bar{S}$ was determined as [22]

$$\bar{S} = (1 - \varepsilon)^{-1/3}\left\{1 - \varepsilon\left[\left(\frac{9}{2\pi}\right)^{1/2}(1 - \varepsilon)JaPe^{1/2}\tau - 1\right]^2\right\}^{1/3} \tag{87}$$

The variations of $\bar{S}$ with τ is shown in Figure 18 for one particular set of conditions corresponding to pentane droplets in water with Pe = 5,000, Ja = 4.3, $\Delta T = 5°K$, and $S_o = 1.5$ mm [22]. Conditions of their data were such that the origin of the initial bubble was not homogeneous nucleation, but extraneous nucleation aids of the type not of principle interest here: deliberately introduced air bubbles or solid particles. The corresponding superheats were far lower than values characteristic of homogeneous nucleation.

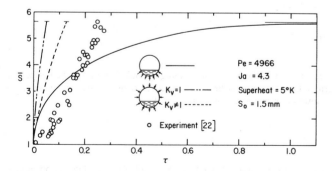

Figure 18. Comparison between predicted and observed droplet radii at various times (τ) and low superheats. Data from Reference 22 and simplified analyses from References 22 (Equation 87) and 101 (Equation 91).

Viscous effects in the flow field around the droplet were accounted for in an ad-hoc manner by Moalem-Maron et al. [101]. The viscous flow Nusselt number around a rigid sphere

$$Nu = \frac{2}{\pi^{1/2}}(0.25Pr^{-1/3}Pe)^{1/2} \tag{88}$$

was written in a form analogous to the potential flow solution,

$$Nu = \frac{2}{\pi^{1/2}} Pe^{1/2}$$

by defining [101, 105]

$$k_v = 0.25Pe^{-1/3} \tag{89}$$

k_v was considered a correction by which the inviscid flow solution around a rigid sphere would be transformed to yield the average heat flux around an expanding sphere in a viscous flow field. Hence,

$$Nu \simeq 2\left(\frac{Pe}{\pi}k_v\right)^{1/2} \tag{90}$$

Considering heat transfer to occur over the entire surface of the droplet (a more reasonable assumption when liquid 1 spreads on liquid 2), a heat balance yielded

$$\bar{S} = \left[1 + \frac{3}{2}Ja\frac{\zeta}{\gamma}Pe^{1/2}\left(\frac{k_v}{\pi}\right)^{1/2}\tau\right]^{2/3} \tag{91}$$

Figure 18 illustrates the variation of $\bar{S}$ with τ for the same approximate set of conditions as reported by Sideman and Isenberg [22].

Dominant Radial Convection

Equations. All experimental methods used to create superheated liquid droplets involved slowly moving droplets. With characteristic velocities of all methods on the order of $U_\infty \sim 1$ cm/s, droplet diameters in the range of 0.5 m and $\alpha_1 \sim 10^{-4}$ cm^2/s, Pe ~ 500 while Ja $\sim \theta(100)$ for droplets at the superheat limit. Translational effects are neglected (Equation 81). Also, $t_R/t_H \gg 1$ may not be satisfied so that the time-dependent term in the energy equation must be retained. As a result the energy (Equation 62) and momentum (Equation 59) equations must be solved simultaneously to describe the full evolution of the thermal boundary layer as it moves from the liquid 1/vapor interface out into liquid 1, and eventually penetrates into liquid 2.

The finite mass of vaporizing liquid is accounted for in two ways. First, the equation of motion (Equation 59) is integrated twice: first from R to S, and then from S to ∞. This yields two equations for the evolution of the pressure fields within the droplet and liquid 2. These equations are coupled by matching the radial velocities at the liquid 1/liquid 2 interface (viscous effects are neglected). Since there is no mass transfer across the liquid 1/liquid 2 boundary, the radial velocity is continuous across it. The velocity field within liquid 2 is then also described by Equation 58 (for the droplet geometry shown in Figure 16B). Combining Equations 58 and 59 integrating from R to S and again from S to ∞ yields

$$[\ddot{R}R + 2\dot{R}^2]\left(1 - \frac{R}{S}\right) - \varepsilon\frac{\dot{R}^2}{2}\left(1 - \frac{R^4}{S^4}\right) = \frac{1}{\rho_1\varepsilon}(P_{R1} - P_{S1}) \qquad R < r < S \tag{92}$$

$$[\ddot{R}R + 2\dot{R}^2]\frac{R}{S} - \varepsilon\frac{\dot{R}^2}{2}\frac{R^4}{S^4} = \frac{1}{\rho_2\varepsilon}(P_{S2} - P_o) \qquad S < r < \infty \tag{93}$$

Where P_{R1}, P_{S1}, and P_{S2} are defined in Figure 16B. These pressures are related to radius as

$$P - P_{R1} = \frac{2\sigma_1}{R} \tag{94}$$

$$P_{S1} - P_{S2} = \frac{2\sigma_{12}}{S} \tag{95}$$

where σ_{12} is the liquid 1/liquid 2 interfacial tension. Combining Equations 92–95 yields the equation of motion for a spherical bubble growing from the center of a spherical droplet:

$$[R\ddot{R} + 2\dot{R}^2]\left(1 - \bar{\varepsilon}\frac{R}{S}\right) - \varepsilon\frac{\dot{R}^2}{2}\left(1 - \bar{\varepsilon}\frac{R}{S}\right) = \frac{P - P_o}{\varepsilon\rho_1} - \frac{2\sigma_1}{\varepsilon\rho_1 R}\left(1 + \frac{\sigma_{12}}{\sigma_1}\frac{R}{S}\right) \tag{96}$$

where $\bar{\varepsilon} \equiv 1 - \rho_2/\rho_1$. When $S \to \infty$, or in the early stages of growth when $R \ll S$ and if the last term in Equation 96 is negligible, Equation 96 reduces to the classical Rayleigh equation (Equation 61). At later times when $R \to S$ the importance of dynamic effects resides in $\bar{\varepsilon}$; as $\bar{\varepsilon} \to 1$, dynamic effects will be unimportant when $R \to S$. In general, the time domain over which Equation 96 has to be included in the analysis may be small—less than the first few milliseconds after nucleation.

Secondly, the temperature field is a two-domain problem. The energy equations for liquids 1 and 2 (Equation 62 with i = 1, 2) are coupled by interface matching conditions. These equations are the following:

$$\frac{\partial T_1}{\partial t} = \frac{\alpha_1}{r^2}\frac{\partial}{\partial r}\left(r^2\frac{\partial T_1}{\partial r}\right) - \varepsilon\frac{\dot{R}R^2}{r^2}\frac{\partial T_1}{\partial r} \qquad R < r < S \tag{97}$$

and

$$\frac{\partial T_2}{\partial t} = \frac{\alpha_2}{r^2}\frac{\partial}{\partial r}\left(r^2\frac{\partial T_2}{\partial r}\right) - \varepsilon\frac{\dot{R}R^2}{r^2}\frac{\partial T_2}{\partial r} \qquad S < r < \infty \tag{98}$$

The interface boundary conditions are the following:

$$T_1(r, 0) = T_2(r, 0) = T_o \tag{99a}$$

$$T_1(R, t) = T_v \tag{99b}$$

$$T_1(S, t) = T_2(S, t) \tag{99c}$$

$$k_1\frac{\partial T_1}{\partial r}(S, t) = k_2\frac{\partial T_2}{\partial r}(S, t) \tag{99d}$$

$$T_2(\infty, t) = T_o \tag{99e}$$

where T_o is the kinetic limit of superheat corresponding to the applied pressure P_o. An energy balance applied to the vapor/liquid 1 interface with spherical symmetry yields again Equation 63b. This equation relates the bubble growth rate to the temperature field, while the momentum equation, Equation 96, relates P to t.

The statement of the problem is made more general by introducing the following nondimensional quantities:

$$\bar{T} = \frac{T - T_s}{T_o - T_s} \qquad \bar{r} = \frac{r}{S_o} \qquad \bar{R} = \frac{R}{S_o}$$

$$\dot{\bar{R}} = \frac{RS_o}{\alpha_1} \qquad \tau = \frac{t\alpha_1}{S_o^2} \qquad \gamma = \frac{\alpha_2}{\alpha_1}$$

$$\zeta = \frac{k_2}{k_1} \qquad Ja = \frac{\rho_1 C_{\rho 1}(T_o - T_s)}{\rho_v h_{fg}} \qquad \bar{\sigma}_{12} = \frac{2\sigma_{12}S_o}{\alpha_1^2 \rho_1 \varepsilon}$$

$$a_p = \frac{S_o^2}{\alpha_1 \rho_1 \varepsilon}\{P(T_o) - P_o\} \qquad \bar{P} = \frac{P(T_v) - P_o}{P(T_o) - P_o} \qquad \bar{\sigma}_1 = \frac{2\sigma_1 S_o}{\alpha_1^2 \rho \varepsilon}$$

Equations 96–98 then become

$$[\ddot{\bar{R}}\bar{R} + 2\dot{\bar{R}}^2]\left(1 - \bar{\varepsilon}\frac{\bar{R}}{\bar{S}}\right) - \frac{\varepsilon\dot{\bar{R}}^2}{2}\left(1 - \bar{\varepsilon}\frac{\bar{R}^4}{\bar{S}^4}\right) = a_p\bar{P} - \frac{\bar{\sigma}_1}{\bar{R}}\left[1 + \frac{\bar{\sigma}_{12}}{\bar{\sigma}_1}\frac{\bar{R}}{\bar{S}}\right], \qquad R < r < \infty \qquad (100)$$

$$\frac{\partial\bar{T}_1}{\partial\tau} = \frac{1}{\bar{r}^2}\frac{\partial}{\partial\bar{r}}\left(\bar{r}^2\frac{\partial\bar{T}_1}{\partial\bar{r}}\right) - \frac{\varepsilon\bar{R}\dot{\bar{R}}^2}{\bar{r}^2}\frac{\partial\bar{T}_1}{\partial\bar{r}}, \qquad \bar{R} < \bar{r} < \bar{S} \qquad (101)$$

and

$$\frac{\partial\bar{T}_2}{\partial\tau} = \frac{1}{\bar{r}^2}\frac{\partial}{\partial\bar{r}}\left(\bar{r}^2\frac{\partial\bar{T}_2}{\partial\bar{r}}\right) - \frac{\varepsilon\dot{\bar{R}}\bar{R}^2}{\bar{r}^2}\frac{\partial\bar{T}_2}{\partial\bar{r}} \qquad \bar{S} \leq \bar{r} < \infty \qquad (102)$$

subject to the following initial and boundary conditions

$$\bar{T}_1(\bar{r}, 0) = \bar{T}_2(\bar{r}, 0) = 1 \qquad (103a)$$

$$\bar{T}_1(\bar{R}, \tau) = \bar{T}_v \qquad (103b)$$

$$\bar{T}_1(\bar{S}, \tau) = \bar{T}_2(\bar{S}, \tau) \qquad (103c)$$

$$\frac{\partial\bar{T}_1}{\partial\bar{r}}(\bar{S}, \tau) = \zeta\frac{\partial\bar{T}_2}{\partial\bar{r}}(\bar{S}, \tau) \qquad (103d)$$

$$\bar{T}_2(\infty, \tau) = 1 \qquad (103e)$$

Equation 63b is nondimensionalized to:

$$Ja\frac{\partial\bar{T}}{\partial\bar{r}}\bigg|_{\bar{r}=\bar{R}} = \dot{\bar{R}} \qquad (104)$$

No known analytical solution to Equations 100–104 exists so numerical methods must be employed. The main difficulty with a numerical solution is the existence of two moving boundaries: at the liquid 1/vapor interface, and at the liquid 1/liquid 2 interface. A coordinate system which immobilizes these boundaries facilitates a solution. Such a coordinate transformation was first utilized by Duda et al. [106] in connection with analyzing growth of a single vapor bubble in an unbounded atmosphere (in which there is only one moving boundary), and later generalized by Saitoh [107] to boundaries of arbitrary shape. This transformation is illustrated in Figure 19 and

Co-ordinate Transformation:

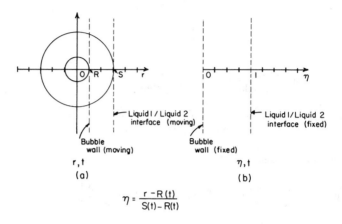

$$\eta = \frac{r - R(t)}{S(t) - R(t)}$$

Figure 19. Coordinate transformation to immobilize moving boundaries in a bubble/droplet system.

expressed as

$$\eta = \frac{\bar{r} - \bar{R}}{\bar{S} - \bar{R}} \tag{105}$$

Time is untransformed. Introducing this transformation into Equations 101 and 102 yields

$$A_i(\eta, \tau) \frac{\partial \bar{T}_i}{\partial \tau} = \frac{\partial}{\partial \eta} \left[B_i(\eta, \tau) \frac{\partial \bar{T}_i}{\partial \eta} \right] - D_i(\eta, \tau) \frac{\partial \bar{T}_i}{\partial_\eta} \tag{106}$$

with

$$A_i(\eta, \tau) = \bar{r}^2 (\bar{S} - \bar{R})/d_i$$

$$B_i(\eta, \tau) = \bar{r}^2 /(\bar{S} - \bar{R})$$

$$D_i(\eta, \tau) = \left[\varepsilon \bar{R}^2 + \frac{\bar{r}^3 (\bar{S}^2 - \varepsilon \bar{R}^2) - \bar{r}^2}{\bar{S}^2 (\bar{S} - \bar{R})^2} \right] \dot{\bar{R}}/d_i \tag{107}$$

where i = 1, 2

$$d_1 = 1 \qquad (0 \le \eta < 1) \tag{108a}$$

$$d_2 = \gamma \qquad (0 \le \eta < \infty) \tag{108b}$$

and

$$\bar{r} = \eta(\bar{S} - \bar{R}) + \bar{R} \tag{108c}$$

The transformed initial and boundary conditions are:

$$\bar{T}_1(\eta, 0) = \bar{T}_2(\eta, 0) = 1 \tag{109a}$$

$$\bar{T}_1(0, \tau) = 0 \tag{109b}$$

$$\bar{T}_1(1, \tau) = \bar{T}_2(1, \tau) \tag{109c}$$

$$\left.\frac{\partial \bar{T}_1}{\partial \eta}\right|_{\eta=1} = \zeta \left.\frac{\partial \bar{T}_2}{\partial \eta}\right|_{\eta=1} \tag{109d}$$

$$\bar{T}_2(\infty, \tau) = 1 \tag{109e}$$

Finally, the interface heat balance is transformed to

$$\bar{R} = \frac{\text{Ja}}{(\bar{S} - \bar{R})} \left.\frac{\partial \bar{T}_1}{\partial \eta}\right|_{\eta=0} \tag{110}$$

The momentum equation (Equation 100) is independent of r and unaffected by this variable transformation.

The transformation of Equation 105 makes the transformed energy equation much more complicated. This is more than compensated by the ability to apply the boundary conditions simply and accurately in the numerical scheme. No assumptions regarding the thickness of the thermal boundary layer or neglect of thermal resistance of liquid 1 have been made in Equation 106–110.

A Crank-Nicholson method was used to solve Equations 100 and 106–110 simultaneously at each time step [108]. The initial bubble size was perturbed by 10^{-4} to 10^{-5} to start the computations. The radius of the droplet, $\bar{S}$, is related to the bubble radius, $\bar{R}$, at any time by

$$\bar{S} = (1 + \varepsilon \bar{R}^3)^{1/3} \tag{111}$$

Computations were terminated when liquid 1 was completely vaporized (Equation 1). The final bubble is not in thermal equilibrium with liquid 2 and restoration of equilibrium requires a further expansion of the bubble beyond $\bar{R}_f$ attendant to its temperature increasing from T_v to T_o. This expansion is very small and was neglected.

Four nondimensional groups control the radius-time history of the bubble: Ja, $\bar{\varepsilon}$, γ, and ζ. Calculations were performed for values of these parameters typical of hydrocarbon (liquid 1)/glycerine (liquid 2) and hydrocarbon/water combinations.

The solution may be broadly divided into two regions:

1. A period during which the thermal boundary layer resides in liquid 1 and growth is similar to growth in an infinite medium.
2. A later stage of growth characterized by thermal boundary-layer penetration into liquid 2.

Early stages of growth. Several aspects of bubble growth in the early stages wherein the thermal boundary layer resides entirely in the droplet are identical to bubble growth in an infinite medium. This is illustrated in Figure 20 which shows the evolution of P, T_v, and $\bar{R}$ for a bubble growing in an n-octane droplet in glycerine (liquid 2) at Ja = 10. The initial state of the droplet (T_o and $P(T_o)$) corresponds to the limit of superheat as calculated by methods described earlier. The asymptotic temperatures and pressures ($T_v(P_o)$ and $P(T_s)$) correspond to saturation conditions. The results shown in Figure 20 are identical to what would be obtained if the n-octane droplet were considered to be of infinite radius and $\bar{\varepsilon} \sim 1$.

Figure 21 illustrates the variation of bubble radius during this very early period. The initial radius ($\bar{R}_o$ in Figure 21) corresponds to the unstable state of the critical nucleus. The characteristic

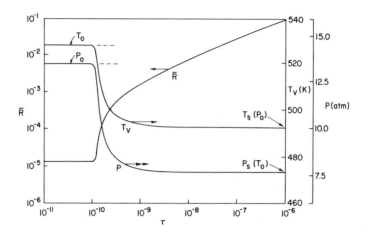

Figure 20. Early time variation of vapor pressure, and vapor temperature, and radius of a bubble growing in a superheated n-octane droplet using model shown in Figure 16B. Initial conditions correspond to kinetic limit of superheat of octane at indicated pressure.

delay period is shown, followed by relaxation of surface tension and attendant rapid increase in growth rate. These characteristics are similar to those for growth in an infinite medium (e.g., [76]).

The temperature field within the droplet during this early period is shown in Figure 22 for the special case Ja = 10. The evolution of both the thermal boundary layer ($\bar{\delta}$ where $\bar{T} \rightarrow 1$) and vapor temperature $\bar{T}$ ($\eta = 0$) are indicated. For $\tau > 5 \times 10^{-8}$, $\bar{T}$ ($\eta = 0$) $\rightarrow 0$ and the analysis becomes a purely thermal problem; the thermal boundary layer is still close to the bubble wall ($\bar{\delta} \sim 10^{-4}(\bar{S} - \bar{R})$). The bubble itself, though, is still quite small at this time (Figure 22).

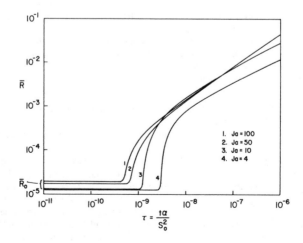

Figure 21. Variation of bubble radius with time at various Jakob numbers (ie., superheats) during early stages of bubble growth in an n-octane droplet.

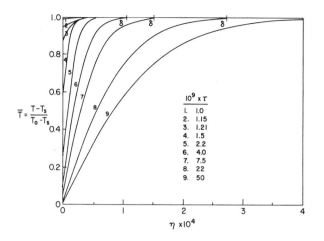

Figure 22. Variation of liquid temperature with position in a droplet at various early times such that thermal boundary layer (δ) is still within the droplet and vapor temperature is changing with time ($\bar{T} > 0$ at $\eta = 0$) [108]. Ja $= 10$, $\varepsilon = 0.995$, $\zeta = 5$, and $\gamma = 1$.

Later stages of growth. Eventually the thermal boundary layer will extend into liquid 2 before liquid 1 completely evaporates and the energy equation for liquid 2, and associated matching conditions at the interface (Equation 109) must be included in the analysis. Figure 23 illustrates calculated temperature fields at various times for Ja $= 10$, $\varepsilon = 0.995$ (a hypothetical value), $\zeta = 5$, and $\gamma = 1$. For $\tau > 0.006$ the thermal boundary layer extends into liquid 2. The essentially linear temperature profile in liquid 1 for $\tau > 0.01$ shown in Figure 23 could lead to simplifications in the

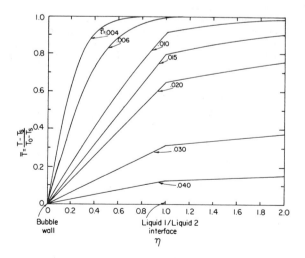

Figure 23. Variation of liquid temperature with position in a droplet showing evolution of temperature field T $\rightarrow$ 0 at $\eta = 0$. For $\tau \gtrsim 0.006$ boundary layer enters liquid 2. Ja $= 10$, $\varepsilon = 0.995$, $\zeta = 5$, and $\gamma = 1$.

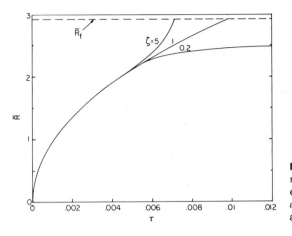

Figure 24. Evolution of bubble radius ($\bar{R}$) with time (τ) showing effect of ζ for $\gamma = 1$, Ja $= 10$, and $\varepsilon = 0.96$. (Properties of n-octane at its superheat limit.)

analysis which have not been fully explored. The corresponding simplification associated with condensation of vapor on an immiscible liquid droplet has been previously studied [109].

The effect of thermal boundary-layer penetration in liquid 2 on bubble growth rate is shown in Figures 24 and 25 for the indicated ranges of Ja, γ, and ζ. Growth is independent of liquid 2 properties up to some time, after which the bubble (and droplet) growth rate undergo rather dramatic changes, depending on the values of ζ and γ. This initial period where liquid 2 does not effect growth reflects the fact that the thermal boundary layer is still within liquid 1. $\zeta > 1$ implies a less steep temperature gradient in liquid 2 than in liquid 1. This in turn creates a gradient in liquid 1 at $\eta = 1$ larger than would be realized if $\zeta = 1$ (i.e., when properties of liquids 1 and 2 are identical). This increased temperature gradient at $\eta = 1$ translates into a larger temperature gradient at $\eta = 0$ (the bubble wall). The bubble then experiences an increase in its growth rate. This behavior cannot be predicted from an analysis which (1) neglects the thermal resistance of liquid 1, and/or (2) assumes results from growth in an infinite medium apply to this problem.

Similar effects occur when γ varies while ζ is fixed. This is illustrated in Figure 26 for Ja $= 10$. The bubble grows faster as γ decreases. For example, a lowering of γ means that the heat capacity per unit volume of liquid 2, $\rho_2 Cp_2$, is increased. The ability of liquid 2 to supply more heat to

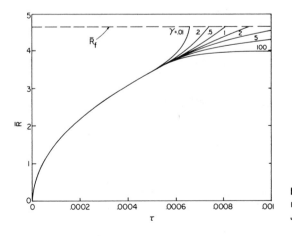

Figure 25. Evolution of bubble radius showing effect of γ for $\zeta = 1$, Ja $= 10$, and $\varepsilon = .96$.

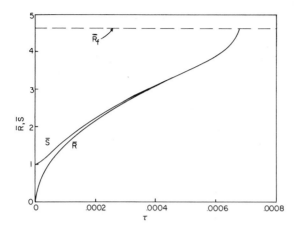

Figure 26. Evolution to both bubble ($\bar{R}$) and droplet ($\bar{S}$), radii for Ja $= 50$ and $\zeta = 5.0$. Curves terminate when $\bar{R} \rightarrow \bar{S} = \bar{R}_f$ and the droplet is completed evaporated.

liquid 1 is then increased as γ decreases, and the growth rate correspondingly increases when the thermal boundary layer enters liquid 2.

The very early period of growth wherein the momentum equation is needed to describe the evolution of pressure field is undetectable on the scale of Figures 24 and 25 (cf., Figure 22). For the time scales in these figures P $\simeq$ P$_o$ and $\bar{T}(\eta = 0) \simeq 0$, though there will always (at least numerically) be a nonzero difference in pressure across the evaporating boundary. The effect of this small pressure difference on growth rate is negligible for conditions of the calculations appearing in Figures 24 and 25.

As liquid 1 evaporates, both the internal vapor bubble and the droplet as a whole expand. Figure 26 illustrates a typical evolution of $\bar{S}$ and $\bar{R}$ for Ja $= 50$ for one representative set of conditions. When $\bar{R} \rightarrow \bar{S}$, the droplet is completely vaporized. It is worth noting that the droplet is almost completely taken up by vapor with just a thin layer of liquid 1 around it when $\tau \geq 2 \times 10^{-4}$.

As the Jakob number increases, the time for which liquid 2 effects growth (i.e., when $\bar{\delta} > \bar{S} - \bar{R}$) increases and the characteristic "fanning" of the growth curves shown in Figures 24 and 25 originates at progressively larger times. For sufficiently high Jakob number the thermal boundary layer remains within liquid 1 throughout nearly the entire period of evaporation, except when $\bar{S} \rightarrow \bar{R}$ at which time the boundary layer must contact the droplet boundary. Growth is then independent of liquid 2 properties. Figure 27 illustrates this for Ja $= 100$. At this high Jakob number, $\bar{T}(\eta = 0) \rightarrow 0$ at times much shorter than indicated in Figure 27.

For purely heat-transfer-controlled growth, a simplified analysis similar to that formulated by Sideman and Isenberg [22] (in which they used the quasi-steady approximation) has recently been presented [11] based on the droplet geometry shown in Figure 28. Thermal boundary layers were assumed to be close to the bubble (Ja $\gg 1$) over the time domain characteristic of the experiments reported in Reference 11 (< 100 ms). These boundary layers were approximated as growing according to the classic planar variation of

$$\delta_i \sim (c_i \alpha_i t)^{1/2}$$

A simple energy balance around the two-phase droplet yields

$$\frac{d\bar{S}}{d\tau} = \frac{Ja\varepsilon}{4c_1}(2 - Z)\left[Z + \zeta\left(\frac{c_1}{c_2} \cdot \frac{1}{\gamma}\right)^{1/2}\right]\tau^{-1/2} \tag{112}$$

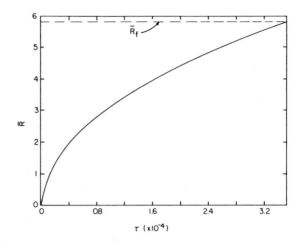

τ $(\times 10^{-4})$

Figure 27. Evolution of bubble radius within a droplet when thermal boundary layer resides within droplet throughout its entire evaporation. Ja $= 100$ and $\varepsilon = 0.995$.

where Z (a geometrical factor) is given by

$$Z = 2 \cos\left[\frac{1}{3}\cos^{-1}\left\{1 - \frac{1 - (1 - \varepsilon)\bar{S}^3}{\varepsilon\bar{S}^3}\right\} + \frac{4\pi}{3}\right] + 1 \tag{113}$$

The constants c_1 and c_2 were essentially considered as empirical values. Equations 111 and 112 provide an alternative to Equations 66 or 87 for correlating bubble growth data in liquid droplets by judiciously selecting c_1 and c_2 when growth is heat-transfer-controlled. However, numerical integration will be required which may make such efforts cumbersome.

It is interesting to explore the similarity of heat-transfer-controlled bubble growth in a droplet to the bubble growth law characteristic of an infinite medium (Equation 66 with $q = \frac{1}{2}$. For this purpose calculations for Ja $= 10$, $\zeta = 1$, and $\varepsilon = 0.9995$ (a hypothetical value chosen so that $\bar{S} \to \bar{R}_f$ at a time large enough to clearly illustrate the similarity) are displayed in Figure 29 on a logarithmic scale for three values of γ. When $\gamma = 1$ the indicated line is identical to the asymptotic heat transfer limit of Equations 66 and 67–70 [77] regardless of placement of the thermal boundary layer. For general γ and $\tau \gtrsim 1.1 \times 10^{-2}$ in Figure 29 the thermal boundary layer extends into liquid 2. q may

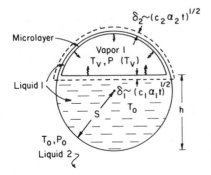

Figure 28. Model for heat-transfer-controlled growth when thermal boundary layer remains close to the evaporating boundary [11].

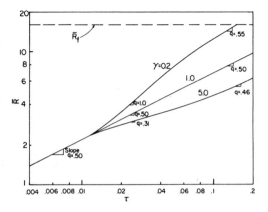

Figure 29. Effect of time (τ) on bubble growth exponent (Equation 66) for heat transfer controlled growth of a bubble in a droplet at various γ and $\zeta = 1$, Ja $= 10$, and $\varepsilon = 0.9995$ (a hypothetical value). Thermal boundary layer penetrates into liquid 2 at $\tau \lesssim .011$.

then be larger or smaller than $\frac{1}{2}$. When $\gamma > 1$, the temperature gradient in liquid 2 is larger than the corresponding gradient in liquid 1. The growth rate decreases compared to the infinite medium case and $q < \frac{1}{2}$. The opposite is true when $\gamma < 1$. Eventually as $\bar{\delta} \gg \bar{S} - \bar{R}$, the thermal resistance of liquid 1 becomes of negligible importance, and the temperature field resembles that which would exist for a bubble growing in an infinite medium of liquid 2 (through ρ_v and h_{fg} would be that corresponding to liquid 1); again $q \to \frac{1}{2}$. In general q will be a function of the depth of penetration of the thermal boundary layer into liquid 2. This fact could be useful in correlating experimental bubble growth data in a liquid droplet, using Equation 66, similar to its utility in correlating bubble growth in an infinite medium (eg., [110]).

Exploding Droplets

The present discussion has not specifically addressed the origin of vapor explosions of droplets commonly observed in the experimental methods discussed in the next section. Such explosions are defined by the appearance of shock blast waves of such a magnitude as to create an audible sound when the droplet vaporizes. The origin of these waves is evidently the very rapid movement and high mass flux at the bubble wall. The theory outlined in the preceding discussion requires modification in light of some recent experiments.

A mechanism to explain explosive growth of bubbles in liquid droplets has been offered by Shepherd and Sturtevant [18] which is a significant departure from the classical approach previously discussed. Under certain conditions (low ambient pressures and high superheats for many organic liquids), the bubble surface is not smooth (such as occurs at high pressures [11]), but rather rough and appears wrinkled thus giving the appearance of waves. The mass evaporative flux across such wrinkled evaporating boundaries was estimated to be two orders of magnitude greater than that calculated from knowledge of just the bubble radius history, ρ_v dR/dt where ρ_v is effective vapor density inside the bubble and R is bubble radius.

Figure 30 shows that measured bubble growth data [18] obtained under explosive conditions are actually bounded by the classical theory—corresponding to bubble growth in an infinite media (relevant in view of the very early times at which the indicated data were obtained—the first few *micro* seconds after nucleation). This similarity between predicted and observed bubble radii is probably fortuitous. The presence of comparatively large observed evaporative mass fluxes during explosive vaporization of droplets at the superheat limit (i.e., a vaporization generating blast waves in the surrounding liquid) led Shepherd and Sturtevant to conjecture the existence of an instability at the interface driven by mass transfer which effectively wrinkles and distorts it. Similar to the inertial instability first introduced by Landau [111] in connection with the instability of laminar flames, this kind of instability may now also be present in the vapor explosion of liquid droplets at their superheat limit [18]. At elevated pressures, or for certain miscible mixtures which contain

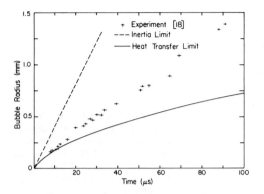

Figure 30. Variation of bubble radius with time during the first few microseconds after homogeneous nucleation in an n-butane droplet at 0.101MPa. Calculations correspond to purely thermally or dynamically driven growth [18].

a nonvolatile component, the interfacial instability at the bubble surface is not present [11, 15], and vaporization is not explosive. Further work is needed to explore in greater depth this interesting new idea.

EXPERIMENTAL METHODS

The principle experimental method used to study superheated liquid droplets involves encapsulating a droplet of the volatile liquid (liquid 1) in another immiscible field liquid (liquid 2), and then subjecting the field liquid to such conditions as to bring the encapsulated droplet into the metastable state. These conditions have consisted of isobarically heating the field liquid [11, 15, 16, 18, 28, 29, 41, 48, 65, 74, 97, 112–122] or isothermally decompressing it [30, 95, 123, 124]. The corresponding loci of states the test droplet experiences as it approaches its limit of superheat are illustrated by paths a-c and b-c in Figure 2A. When the droplet vaporizes, the ambient pressure and temperature are inferred from corresponding measurements in liquid 2 (due account being taken of any droplet underheating). This method, coupled with high speed cine [11, 27, 28, 125] or spark gap [18] photography, has yielded essentially all the information which forms the foundation of our understanding of bubble growth within liquid droplets at the superheat limit. The first demonstration of the existence of superheated liquids was made over 100 years ago by a variant of this "floating droplet" method [126, 127].

The chief advantage of heating droplets suspended in immiscible liquids resides in the fact that the liquid 1/liquid 2 interface constitutes a hypothetically ideal smooth surface free of any solid motes or trapped gases which would tend to initiate a phase transition. This interface has essentially a similar microscopic structure as the bulk of the droplet. Any phase transition at this interface would therefore have to occur by essentially the same mechanism as in the bulk of the test droplet.

The key to successful use of this method is to carefully select the liquid 1/liquid 2 combination to satisfy the following criteria:

1. The field liquid must have a boiling point higher than the limit of superheat of the most nonvolatile component within the liquid 1 droplet over the entire range of ambient pressures at which the limit of superheat is to be measured.
2. Both liquids must have low mutual solubility.
3. The physical properties of both liquids should be available (or predictable).
4. The probability for nucleation within the bulk of the test droplet must be higher than at the droplet/field liquid interface.

As we have seen from Equation 74c, this latter requirement dictates that liquid 2 has a relatively high surface tension. Otherwise, measured phase transition states will essentially have characterized the interface between the two liquids rather than the test liquid itself. Such temperatures (at a given pressure) are generally far below those indicative of homogeneous nucleation in the bulk of the test droplet. This fact limits the extent of the various liquids which can be tested by floating droplet methods. Nevertheless, the method, when the preceding criteria are satisfied, has yielded some of the most reproducible and accurate superheat limit (and all bubble growth) data thus far reported.

Two principal variants of the suspended droplet method have been used. The first involves droplets moving through a static field liquid, and the second involves levitating the droplets in either a moving field liquid or via imposing a standing acoustic wave on a static field liquid (e.g., see Reference 64).

In the first method, the field liquid is usually heavier than the droplet, though experiments with heavy droplets heated in light field liquids have also been performed [17, 95]. A schematic diagram of a typical apparatus of this genre is shown in Figure 31. The first to use a variant of this apparatus were Wakeshima and Takata [121] and Moore [95]. The essential components consist of a vertical tube (called a "bubble column") which contains the field liquid on which a stable temperature gradient is imposed (e.g., hot at the top of the tube and cold at the bottom for light droplets), a droplet injector, and instrumentation to measure the temperature and pressure in the field liquid at which the droplets vaporize. The bubble column itself is glass with inside diameters which have ranged from as small as 1.3 cm [74] to over 6 cm [18]. Tube length has ranged from 100 cm [112] down to 35 cm [121, 122]. Temperature gradients imposed on the field liquid have been effected by heating nichrome wire wrapped around the tube with varying pitch, a metal sleeve fitted around the tube with attached electrical heater, or commercially available rope heaters. Temperature gradients have ranged from 0.03 K/cm [48] to 10 K/cm [119]. For typical rise velocities of 1 cm/s to 5 cm/s, test droplets are heated at rates ranging from 0.03 K/s to 50 K/s.

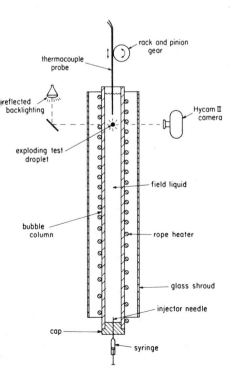

Figure 31. Schematic illustration of a typical bubble column apparatus for superheating liquid droplets by isobaric heating.

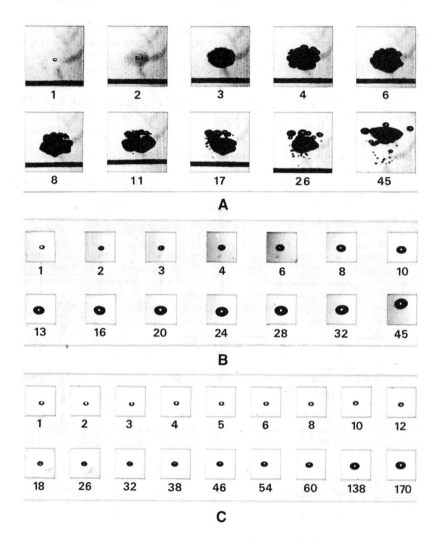

Figure 32. High speed motion picture sequence of n-octane droplets boiling in glycerine. Number of frame in the motion picture sequence is shown below each photograph [11]:
(A) $P_0 = 0.101$ MPa, $T_0 \simeq 514$ K, $S_0 \simeq 0.05$ mm, framing rate = 1,033 frames/s;
(B) $T_0 = 0.687$ MPa, $T_n \simeq 525$ K, $S_0 \simeq 0.6$ mm and framing rate = 933 frames/s;
(C) $P_0 = 1.22$ MPa, $T_0 \simeq 531$ K, $S_0 = 0.5$ mm and framing rate = 900 frames/s.

The use of high-speed cine photography with this method to measure droplet expansion rates [11, 27, 28] requires proper synchronization between the emergence of the moving droplet in the field of view of the (stationary) camera and activation of the camera. This fact limits the usefulness of this photographic technique for recording the dynamics of vaporization, inasmuch as some luck is involved with synchronizing the activation of the camera with the start of boiling. The maximum camera framing rate is limited to that which will yield a high probability of recording vaporization.

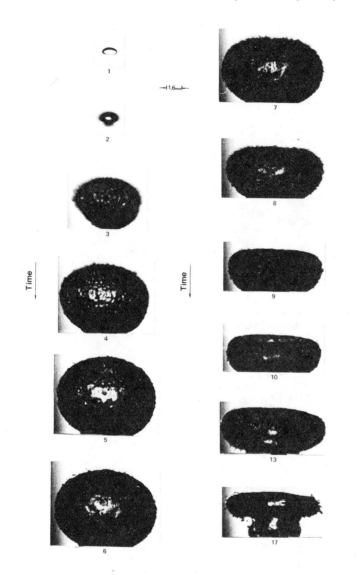

Figure 33. Motion picture sequence of n-butanol droplet boiling in Krytox 143AD (DuPont). $P_0 = 0.101$ MPa, T = 512 K, and framing rate = 2,000 frames/s.

Framing rates corresponding to effective observation times on the order of a millisecond are typical. (Figures 32–34 illustrate the kind of photographic quality of droplets evaporating at their superheat limit one may expect from this method. More will be said about these photographs later.)

Schematic diagrams of two methods used for levitating droplets are shown in Figures 35 and 36 [28, 30, 123, 124]. Droplets were superheated by isothermal decompression (path b-c in Figure 2A) in these apparatuses. The first method (Figure 35) consists of a test section in the shape of a diverging channel placed in a flow loop of liquid 2 driven by an impeller pump. By adjusting the liquid 2

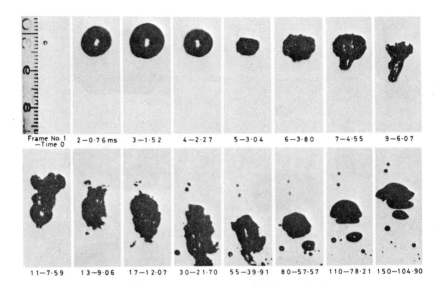

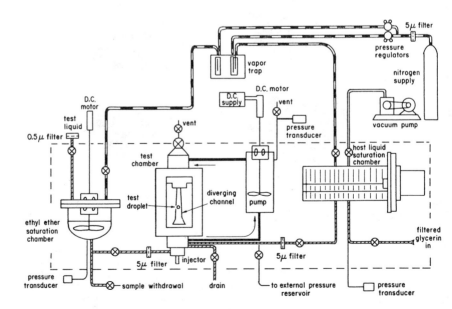

Figure 34. Motion picture sequence of an ether droplet boiling in glycerine. Number below each photograph indicates time elapsed after frame no. 1. $P_0 = 0.101$ MPa, T = 421 K, and $S_0 = 0.55$ mm [125].

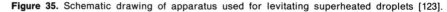

Figure 35. Schematic drawing of apparatus used for levitating superheated droplets [123].

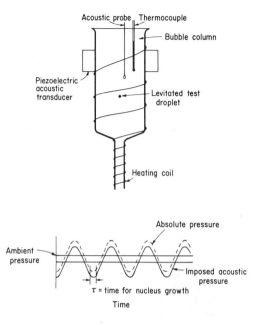

Figure 36. Schematic illustration of apparatus (A) which levitates superheated droplets by exposure to a standing acoustic wave. Thypical wave form shown in (B) [30].

flow rate, a light test droplet injected at the bottom of the test chamber could be levitated. The experiment as illustrated was designed to study the effect of a dissolved gas (nitrogen) on the superheat limit of a single component fluid (ether) over a range of pressures. Droplet vaporization was not photographically documented. The droplet levitation method employed by Apfel [28, 30] (Figure 36) consisted of imposing a standing acoustic wave on liquid 2 (by a piezoelectric transducer cemented to the walls of the bubble column) of such a magnitude that the force of the acoustic pressure just balanced the buoyancy force of the droplet. With the droplet levitated, it was stressed for those periods of exposure to the negative parts of the acoustic cycle (Figure 36B). When the magnitude of the negative pressure is high enough and of long enough duration, any cavities formed by homogeneous nucleation will grow to observable size; otherwise the bubble will collapse as the acoustic pressure becomes positive. Measured tensile strengths were found to be in excellent agreement with predicted values for several organic liquids. This was the first such agreement using any experimental method for measuring tensile strengths of liquids. Apfel and Harbison [28] later used high-speed (3,500 frames/s) cine photography to measure expansion rates of ether droplets at atmospheric pressure. The same problem of synchronizing camera activation with initiation of vaporization apparently existed with this levitation method as with the rising droplet method.

Basic information obtained from the previously mentioned experiments consisted of temperature and pressure of liquid 2 at which droplets were observed to vaporize; when photographic methods were employed to record vaporization of the test droplets, droplet radius as a function of time was also measured (the methods employed were sufficiently imprecise to resolve the evolution of internal bubble radii (R) so that only overall droplet radii (S) could accurately be measured).

Figures 32–34 illustrate a series of photographs of n-octane, n-butanol, and ether droplets, respectively, boiling in various field liquids. The droplets are at their (approximate) superheat limits at pressures ranging from atmospheric to about 12 atm. It is evident that vaporization at atmospheric pressure occurred at a time between the first two frames of the motion picture sequences shown in Figures 32A–34, and thus in less than 1 ms. For the vaporization shown in these pictures the droplets vaporized with an audible sound and resembled a kind of mini explosion. Subsequent events illustrate droplets which have completely vaporized inasmuch as the bubble shown in the second or third frame in Figures 32A–34 either corresponds to that predicted by Equation

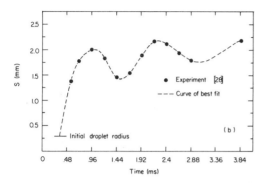

Figure 37. Measured temporal variation of radius of an ether droplet vaporizing in glycerine at its superheat limit. $P_0 \simeq -0.8$ MPa and $T \simeq 413$ K [28].

1 or is larger. For this kind of explosive vaporization, the final bubbles were always observed to oscillate. Such oscillations are believed to be a result of the kinetic energy stored in the outward motion of the vapor/liquid interface moving the interface beyond its final equilibrium size, and then contracting as the ambient liquid pressure counterbalances the reduction in gas pressure due to this expansion [18, 28]. Some measurements of droplet radii during oscillatory motion of an ether bubble during this oscillatory motion are shown in Figure 37 [28]. A theory to explain and predict the origin of these oscillations has not yet been developed. The line shown in Figure 37 is a best fit through the data; the analysis of the previous section does not account for bubble oscillations.

A unique improvement of the method of photographically recording rapid (explosive) evaporation of droplets at the superheat limit has recently been developed by Shepherd and Sturtevant [18]. This method resolves the early time domain (<1 ms) which is inaccessible using conventional high speed cine photography. The technique consists of using the pressure signal generated on a piezoelectric pressure transducer (immersed in liquid 2) by the blast wave created by an exploding droplet to trigger a spark gap light source with a variable time delay. Effective observation times are thus on the order of *microseconds*. The evolution of phase change of a single droplet is pieced together from individual observations of a number of droplets, each of which is photographed at progressively later times in the vaporization process. Fortunately, the vaporization process is sufficiently repeatable that this does not create problems.

Figure 38 illustrates several photographs of n-butane droplets vaporizing in glycerine at atmospheric pressure which were taken using this technique. Times range from 9 μs to about 70 μs after homogeneous nucleation. It is clear that the detail depicted in these photographs is completely missed using photographic methods which operate on a millisecond time scale. This detail also permits direct measurement of bubble radius (R) in addition to overall droplet radius (S). The results are suggestive of only one bubble having been nucleated within the initial butane droplet (1 mm diameter). This bubble apparently nucleates at a more or less random location at the droplet boundary (where the temperature is highest due to droplet underheating). As is shown in Figure 38, the evaporating boundary is apparently wrinkled and wave-like. This nonsmooth surface persists well into the oscillatory phase after complete evaporation (cf., Figure 33). The origin of this wrinkling requires further investigation. Several other salient features of explosive vaporization of droplets are discussed in Reference 18.

At sufficiently high pressures, droplets at the superheat limit do not vapor explode inasmuch as

- No audible sound is generated on vaporization.
- No oscillations occur.
- The evaporating boundary is smooth.

Figures 32B and 32C clearly illustrate this for n-octane droplets in glycerine at 0.687 MPa and 1.22 MPa [11] (the indicated temperature is the n-octane superheat limit). As noted in these figures,

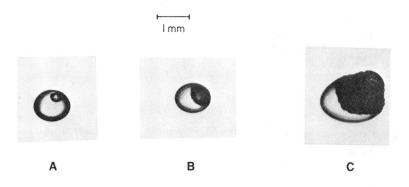

|←—————→|
I mm

A   **B**   **C**

Figure 38. Photographic sequence of an n-butane droplet boiling in glycerine during the first few microseconds after nucleation at $P_0 = 0.101$ MPa and $T \simeq 378$ K: (A) $9\mu s < t < 12 \mu s$, (B) $17\mu s < t < 34 \mu s$, (C) $55 \mu s < t < 65 \mu s$ [18].

the time for complete evaporation progressively increases with pressure. Evaporation of a ~ 1 mm-diameter droplet takes about four times longer at 1.22 MPa than 0.687 MPa. This fact reflects a strong effect of pressure on bubble growth. The origin of this effect is a combination of reduced influence of dynamic-inertia effects on growth and a decrease in Jakob number, hence temperature difference and heat supply to the bubble, as pressure increases. This reduced growth rate with increasing pressure will also bear on the utility of the spark-gap method of Shepherd and Sturtevant [18] at high pressures. Just how high a pressure the method can be employed before the blast wave intensity created by rapid movement of the bubble boundary diminishes to a value which cannot be detected by the transducer requires further investigation. The precise pressure at which a transition from explosive to nonexplosive vaporization occurs is not known in general, but for n-octane droplets ~ 1 mm in diameter it appears to be about 4 atm to 6 atm (P_r from 0.24 to 0.33).

The model for bubble growth in droplets developed in the previous section applies under the nonexplosive condition depicted in Figure 32B and C in which the evaporating boundary is also smooth and the bubble does not oscillate. These observations may provide a test of the usefulness of the model presented. Figure 39 shows a comparison between measured [11] and predicted (Section 5) droplet radii ($\bar{S}$) for n-octane. The measurements were sufficiently imprecise to create some

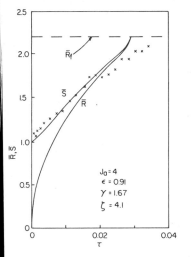

Figure 39. Comparison between calculated [108] and measured [11] droplet radii for an n-octane droplet boiling in glycerine at $P_0 = 1.22$ MPa, $T = 531$ K, and indicated parameters.

Figure 40. Photograph of an n-butane droplet boiling in water at $P_0 = 0.101$ MPa and a few degrees superheat [128].

uncertainty about the initial droplet size (which enters in the analysis in the definition of τ). Also shown in Figure 39 is the evolution of internal bubble radius ($\bar{R}$), which was not measured. The time domain for the development of a steady vapor temperature and pressure was sufficiently small on the scale of Figure 39 to be undetectable; the data shown correspond to heat-transfer-controlled growth.

Droplets vaporizing at conditions far from their superheat limit occasionally exhibit similarities to high pressure evaporation at the superheat limit. This is shown in Figure 40 which shows evaporation of an n-pentane droplet in water at 0.101 MPa, but only a few degrees superheat [128]. For the droplet nucleation was apparently induced by introducing small gas bubbles or allowing minute amounts of air to dissolve in the droplet. By contrast, the effect of such impurities on an n-octane droplet was minimal (Figures 32b and 32c). It may be noted that the two-phase droplet geometry illustrated in Figure 32 does not correspond to the concentric sphere model which formed the basis of the analysis discussed in the previous section. However, this photograph was taken from the 18th (out of 170) of the sequence illustrated in Figure 32C and corresponded to a time such that only about 10% of the liquid had evaporated. Beyond this time, the liquid sheath becomes increasingly difficult to discern and the assumed geometry provides a better approximation.

CONCLUDING REMARKS

Bubble growth in a liquid droplet at its superheat limit has been reviewed. The problem was divided into two parts:

1. An initial phase during which bubbles form by homogeneous nucleation.
2. A later stage characterized by growth of the initial bubble.

Methods were reviewed for predicting the superheat limits of liquids. This information yields the thermodynamic state of a droplet (its pressure, temperature, and composition) at which the initial bubble is formed in the absence of any extraneous nucleation aids. Subsequent growth of the bubble was analyzed by extending the conventional conservation equations which govern bubble growth in an infinite medium to account for the finite mass of vaporizing liquid. It was shown that the time domain of dynamic effects wherein the bubble gas pressure is still significantly different from the ambient pressure is usually less than a millisecond. Classical analysis will have to be modified to account for bubble oscillations and the wrinkled, nonsmooth, liquid/vapor interface characteristic of explosive boiling.

At present, our understanding of nucleation phenomena outweighs our understanding of the dynamics and heat transfer of bubble growth in droplets. Reliable methods are available for predicting the thermodynamic state of a droplet at which bubbles will form by homogeneous nucleation. A comparatively large data base also exists on the limits of superheat of liquids which forms the foundation of our confidence in predictive methods. By contrast, a paucity of data exist relating to bubble growth in liquid droplets at the superheat limit. As such, more experiments need to be performed to provide a firmer foundation for more detailed analysis. It is hoped this review stimulates further work on this fundamental and important problem.

Acknowledgments

The author would like to thank Dr. Robert M. Wellek., program director of the Thermodynamics and Transport Phenomenon Program of the National Science Foundation, and Dr. Oscar P. Manley, head of the Engineering Research Program, Office of Basic Energy Sciences of the Department of Energy for their support of this work through grant No. CPE-8106348 and contract No. DE-AC02-83ER13092, respectively.

NOTATION

a	equation of state constant defined by Equation 64	P_{cm}	mixture critical pressure
b	equation of state constant	Pe	Peclet number (Equation 78a)
C_1	bubble growth constant (Equation 65a)	P_o	ambient (or nucleation) pressure
c_i	empirical constants defined by Equation 112 ($i = 1, 2$)	Pr	Prandtl number
		P_r	reduced pressure ($= P/P_c$)
C_{pi}	liquid i ($i = 1, 2$)	r	radius
E_n	symbol for a vapor nucleus containing n molecules	$\bar{r}$	$= r/R_o$
		R	bubble radius
F	Helmholtz function	R_f	final bubble radius (Equation 1)
$f_{n,t}$	number density of vapor nuclei containing n molecules at time t	$\mathscr{R}$	gas constant
		$\dot{R}$	bubble wall velocity
h	heat transfer coefficient	$\bar{R}$	$= R/R_o$
h_{fg}	latent heat of vaporization of liquid 1	$\bar{R}_f$	$= R_f/R_o$
$I_{n,t}$	nucleation rate of a nucleus containing n molecules at time t	R_o	initial bubble radius
		S	overall droplet radius
$k_{f(n)}$	molecular evaporation rate in a nucleus containing n molecules	S_o	initial overall droplet radius
		$\bar{S}$	$= S/S_o$
$k_{r(n)}$	molecular condensation rate in a nucleus containing n molecules	$\mathscr{S}$	bubble surface area
		t	time
k_i	thermal conductivity of liquid i ($i = 1, 2$)	T	temperature
		T_c	critical temperature
		T_{cm}	mixture critical temperature
k_v	velocity factor (Equation 89)	T_k	kinetic limit of superheat
K	Boltzmann constant	T_m	measured kinetic limit of superheat
m_i	molecular mass of liquid i ($i = 1, 2$)	T_o	ambient (or nucleation) temperature
n	number of molecules	T_r	reduced temperature ($= T/T_c$)
n_i	number of molecules of component i in a vapor mixture	T_{roi}	$= T_{ki}/T_{ci}$
n_i^1	number of liquid molecules	T_t	thermodynamic limit of superheat
n^*	number of molecules in a critical size nucleus	T_v	temperature of vapor in bubble
		U	internal energy
N_n	number density of nuclei in a hypothetical equilibrium state (Equation 50)	U_∞	free stream velocity of liquid 1
		V	volume
N_o	number density of molecules	v'	liquid specific volume
Nu	Nusselt number	x_i	liquid mole fraction of component i in a mixture
P	pressure of vapor in bubble	y_i	vapor mole fraction of component i
P^*	pressure of vapor in a critical size nucleus	y_i^*	vapor mole fraction of component i in a critical size nucleus
P_c	critical pressure		

Greek Symbols

α_i	thermal diffusivity of liquid i (i = 1, 2)	μ'_{ij}	chemical potential of component i in a liquid mixture in system j
γ	$= \alpha_2/\alpha_1$		
Γ	defined by Equations 30 and 51	μ''_i	chemical potential of component i in a vapor mixture
δ	thermal boundary layer thickness		
ΔF	change in Helmholtz function	ρ_i	density of liquid i (i = 1, 2)
$\Delta\Phi$	minimum energy to form a vapor nucleus	ρ_v	vapor density in bubble
		σ_i	surface tension of liquid i (i = 1, 2)
$\Delta\Phi^*$	energy of a critical size nucleus	σ_{12}	liquid 1/liquid 2 interfacial tension
ε	$= 1 - \rho_v/\rho_1$	v	velocity of liquid
$\bar\varepsilon$	$= 1 - \rho_1/\rho_2$	Φ	availability (Equation 33)
ζ	$= k_2/k_1$	ω	acentric factor
η	transformed coordinate variable (Equation 105)		

Subscripts

i	liquid i (i = 1, 2)	s	condition at saturation (r → ∞)

REFERENCES

1. Bankoff, S. G., "Vapor Explosions: A Critical Review." *Proc. 6th Int. Heat Transf. Conf.*, Aug. 7–11 (1978).
2. Henry, R. E., and Fauske, H. K., "Nucleation Processes in Large Scale Vapor Explosion," *J. Heat Transf.*, 101:280 (1979).
3. Reid, R. C., "Rapid Phase Transitions from Liquid to Vapor," in *Advances in Chemical Engineering*, Vol. 12, Academic Press, New York (1983).
4. Lasheras, J. C., Fernandez-Pello, A. C., and Dryer, F. L., "On the Disruptive Burning of Free Droplets of Alcohol/n-Paraffin Solutions and Emulsions" *18th Symp. (Int.) Comb.*, 293 (1981).
5. Dryer, F. L., "Water Addition to Practical Combustion Systems-Concepts and Applications" *16th Symp. (Int.) Comb.*, 279 (1976).
6. Fauske, H. K., "The Role of Nucleation in Vapor Explosions," *Trans. Am. Nuc. Soc.*, 15:813 (1974).
7. Anderson, R. P., and Armstrong, D. P., "R-22 Vapor Explosions," ASME Winter Annual Meeting, Atlanta, Ga, 31 (1977).
8. Buchanan, D. J., and Dullforce, T. A., "Mechanism for Vapour Explosions," *Nature*, 245:32 (1973).
9. Peckover, R. S., Buchanan, D. J., and Ashby, D.E.T.F., "Fuel-Coolant Interactions inSubmarine Vulcanism," *Nature*, 245:307 (1973).
10. Nelson, L. S., and Duda, P. M., "Steam Explosions of Molten Iron Oxide Drops: Easier Initiation at Small Pressurizations," *Nature*, 296:844 (1982).
11. Avedisian, C. T., "Effect of Pressure on Bubble Growth Within Liquid Droplets at the Super heat Limit," *J. Heat Transfer.*, 104:750 (1982).
12. Yang, K., "Explosive Interaction of Liquified Natural Gas and Organic Liquids," *Nature*, 243:221 (1973).
13. Porteous, W. M., and Reid, R. C., "Light Hydrocarbon Vapor Explosions," *Chem. Eng. Prog.*, 72(5):83 (1976).
14. Nakanishi, E., and Reid, R. C., "Liquid Natural Gas-Water Reactions." *Chem. Eng. Prog.*, 67(12):36 (1971).
15. Blander, M., Henstenberg, D., and Katz, J. C., "Bubble Nucleation in n-Pentane, n-Hexane, n-Pentane + n-Hexadecane Mixtures, and Water," *J. Phys. Chem.*, 75:3613 (1971).

16. Jarvis, T. J., Donohue, M. D., and Katz, J. L., "Bubble Nucleation Mechanisms of Liquid Droplets Superheated in Other Liquids," *J. Coll. Inter. Sci.*, 50(2):359 (1975).

17. Avedisian, C. T., and Glassman, I., "Superheating and Boiling of Water in Hydrocarbons at High Pressures," *Int. J. Heat Mass Transf.*, 24(4):695 (1981).

18. Shepherd, J. E., and Sturtevant, B., "Rapid Evaporation at the Superheat Limit," *J. Fluid Mech.*, 121:379 (1982).

19. Buchanan, D. J., "Fuel-Coolant Interaction Theory," *Proc. 4th Int. Heat Transf. Conf.*, 270 (1970).

20. Lasheras, J. C., Yap, L. T., and Dryer, F. L., "The Effect of Ambient Pressure on the Disruptive Vaporization and Burning of Emulsified and Multicomponent Fuel Droplets," Paper No. WSCI 82–94, Western States Section Meeting, Combustion Insitute, Los Angeles, October 11–12, 1982.

21. Sideman, S., and Taitel, Y., "Direct-Contact Heat Transfer with Change of Phase: Evaporation of Drops in an Immiscible Liquid Medium," *Int. J. Heat Mass Transf.*, 7:1273 (1964).

22. Sideman, S., and Isenberg, J., "Direct Contact Heat Transfer with Change of Phase: Bubble Growth in Three-Phase Systems," *Desalination*, 2:207 (1967).

23. Simpson, H. C., Beggs, G. C., and Sohal, M. S., "Nucleation of Butane Drops in Flowing Water," *Proc. 6th Int. Heat Trans. Conf.*, Paper No. PI-10 (1978).

24. Gradon, L., and Selecki, A., "Evaporation of a Liquid Drop Immersed in Another Immiscible Liquid. The case of $\sigma_c < \sigma_d$," *Int. J. Heat Mass Transf.*, 20:459 (1977).

25. Selecki, A., and Gradon, L., "Equation of Motion of an Expanding Vapour Drop in an Immiscible Liquid," *Int. J. Heat Mass Transfer*, 19:925 (1976).

26. Mokhtarzadeh, M. R., and El-Shirbini, A. A., "A Theoretical Analysis of Evaporating Droplets in an Immiscible Liquid," *Int. J. Heat Mass Transf.*, 22:27 (1979).

27. Mori, Y. H., and Komotori, K., "Boiling Modes of Volatile Liquid Drops in an Immiscible Liquid Depending on Degree of Superheat," ASME paper No. 76-HT-13 (1976).

28. Apfel, R. F., and Harbison, J. P., "Acoustically Induced Explosions of Superheat Liquids," *J. Acoust. Soc. Amer.*, 57(6):1371 (1975).

29. Avedisian, C. T., and Glassman, I., "High Pressure Homogeneous Nucleation of Bubbles Within Superheated Binary Liquid Mixtures," *J. Heat Transf.*, 103:272 (1981).

30. Apfel, R. F., "Vapor Cavity Formation in Liquids," Tech. Memo. No. 62, Acoustics Research Laboratory, Harvard University, Cambridge, Mass. (1970).

31. Beams, J. W., "Tensile Strength of Liquid Argon, Helium, Nitrogen, and Oxygen," *Phys. Fluids.*, 2(1):1 (1959).

32. Briggs, L. J., "The Limiting Negative Pressure of Acetic Acid, Benzene, Aniline, Carbon Tetrachloride, and Chloroform," *J. Chem. Phys.*, 19(7):970 (1951).

33. Callen, H. B., *Thermodynamics*, John Wiley, New York, 1960, Chapter 8.

34. Modell, M., and Reid, R. C., *Thermodynamics and Its Applications*, Prentice-Hall, Englewood Cliffs, 1974, Chapter 7.

35. Hildebrand, F. B., *Methods of Applied Mathematics*, Prentice-Hall, Englewood Cliffs, 1965, p. 52.

36. Beegle, B. L., Modell, M., and Reid, R. C., "Thermodynamic Stability Criterion for Pure Substances and Mixtures," *AIChEJ.*, 20(6):1200 (1974).

37. Karimi, A., and Lienhard, J. H., "A Fundamental Equation Representing Water in the Stable Metastable and Unstable States," Electric Power Research Institute Report No. EPRI NP-3328, Project 1438-2, Final Report, December (1983).

38. Temperley, H. N. V., "The Behaviour of Water Under Hydrostatic Tension: III," *Proc. Phys. Soc. Lond.*, 58:199 (1947).

39. Lienhard, J. H., "Correlation for the Limiting Liquid Superheat," *Chem. Eng. Sci.*, 31:847 (1976).

40. Peng, D. Yu, and Robinson, D. B., "A New Two-Constant Equation of State," *Ind. Eng. Chem. Fundam.*, 15(1):59 (1976).

41. Porteous, W., and Blander, M., "Limits of Superheat and Explosive Boiling of Light Hydrocarbons, Halocarbons, and Hydrocarbon Mixtures," *AIChEJ* 21(3):560 (1975).

42. Frenkel, J., *Kinetic Theory of Liquids*, Oxford U. P., Oxford, 1946, pp. 382–400.

43. Gibbs, J. W., *Collected Works*, Vol. 1, Longmans, Green, New York, 1928.
44. Skripov, V. R., and Sinitsyn, E. N., "Nucleation in Superheated Liquids and Surface Tension," 42:167 (1968).
45. Katz, J. L., "Condensation of A Supersaturated Vapor. I. The Homogeneous Nucleation of the n-Alkanes," *J. Chem. Phys.*, 52(9):4733 (1970).
46. Keenan, J. H., *Thermodynamics*, John Wiley, New York, 1941, Chapter 17.
47. Pinnes, E. C., and Mueller, W. K., "Homogeneous Vapor Nucleation and Superheat Limits of Liquid Mixtures," *J. Heat Transf.*, 101:617 (1979).
48. Holden, B. C., and Katz, J. C., "The Homogeneous Nucleation of Bubbles in Superheated Binary Liquid Mixtures," *AIChEJ*, 24(2):260 (1978).
49. Volmer, M., *Kinetics of Phase Formation*, translated by Intelligence Department, ATI No. 81935 (F-TS-7068-RE) from the clearinghouse for Federal and Technical Information.
50. Reiss, H., "The Kinetics of Phase Transitions in Binary Systems," *J. Chem. Phys.*, 18(6):840 (1950).
51. Turnbull, D., and Fisher, J. C., "Rate of Nucleation in Condensed Systems," *J. Chem. Phys.*, 17(1):71 (1949).
52. Farley, F. J. M., "The Theory of the Condensation of Supersaturated Ion-Free Vapour," *Proc. Roy. Soc. Lond.*, A212:530 (1952).
53. McDonald, J. E., "Homogeneous Nucleation of Vapor Condensation. II, Kinetic Aspects," *Am. J. Phys.*, 31:31 (1963).
54. Katz, J. L., Saltsburg, H., and Reiss, H., "Nucleation in Associated Vapors," *J. Coll. Inter. Sci.*, 21:560 (1966).
55. Hirschelder, J. O., "Kinetics of Homogeneous Nucleation on Many-Component Systems," *J. Chem. Phys.*, 61(7):2690 (1974).
56. Stauffer, D., "Kinetic Theory of Two-Component ("Hetero-Molecular") Nucleation and Condensation," *J. Aerosol. Sci.*, 7:319 (1976).
57. Katz, J. L., and Wiedersich, H., "Nucleation Theory without Maxwell Demons," *J. Coll. Inter. Sci.*, 61(2):351 (1977).
58. Katz, J. L., and Donohue, M. D., "A Kinetic Approach to Homogeneous Nucleation Theory," in *Advances in Chemical Physics*, 40:137 (1979).
59. Springer, G. S., "Homogeneous Nucleation," in *Advances in Heat Transfer*, 14:281 (1978).
60. Vega, E., and Peters, L. K., "Dynamics of Cluster Growth During Homogeneous Nucleation of Supersaturated Vapors," *Aerosol. Sci. Tech.*, 2:513 (1983).
61. Andres, R. P., and Boudart, M., "Time Lag in Multistate Kinetics: Nucleation," *J. Chem. Phys.*, 42(6):2057 (1965).
62. Cohen, E. R., "The Accuracy of the Approximations in Classical Nucleation Theory," *J. Stat. Phys.*, 2(2):147 (1970).
63. Katz, J. L., "The Critical Supersaturations Predicted by Nucleation Theory," *J. Stat. Phys.*, 2(2):137 (1970).
64. Avedisian, C. T., "The Homogeneous Nucleation Limits of Liquids," *J. Phys. Chem. Ref. Data*, 14(3):695 (1985).
65. Skripov, V. P., and Erinakov, F. C., "Pressure Dependence of the Limiting Superheating of a Liquid," *Russ. J. Phys. Chem.*, 38(2):208 (1964).
66. Lienhard, J. H., and Karimi, A., "Homogeneous Nucleation and the Spinodal Line," *J. Heat Transf.*, 103:61 (1981).
67. Pavlov, P. A., and Skripov, V. P., "Kinetics of Spontaneous Nucleation in Strongly Heated Liquids," *High Temp.*, 8:540 (1970).
68. Skripov, V. P., *Superheated Liquids*, John Wiley, New York, 1974.
69. Lienhard, J. H., and Karimi, A., "Corresponding States Correlations of the Liquid and Vapor Spinodal Lines," ASME Paper No. 77-HT-20. (1977).
70. Prausnitz, J. M., *Molecular Thermodynamics of Fluid-Phase Equilibration*, Prentice-Hall, Englewood Cliffs, 1969, pp. 69–73.
71. Guggenhiem, E. A., "The Principle of Corresponding States," *J. Chem. Phys.*, 13(7):253 (1945).

72. Lienhard, J. H., "Corresponding States Correlations of the Spinodal and Homogeneous Nucleation Limits," *J. Heat Transf.*, 104:379 (1982).
73. Apfel, R. E., "Vapor Nucleation at a Liquid-Liquid Interface," *J. Chem. Phys.*, 54(1):62 (1971).
74. Avedisian, C. T., and Sullivan, J. R., "A Generalized Corresponding States Method for Predicting the Limits of Superheat of Mixtures: Application to the Normal Alcohols," *Chem. Eng. Sci.*, 39(6):1033–1042 (1984).
75. Bankoff, S. G., "Diffusion Controlled Bubble Growth," in *Advances in Chemical Engineering*, Vol. 6, Academic Press, New York (1966).
76. Prosperetti, A., and Plesset, M., "Vapour-Bubble Growth in a Superheated Liquid," *J. Fluid Mech.*, 85(2):349 (1978).
77. Scriven, L. E., "On the Dynamics of Phase Growth," *Chem. Eng. Sci.*, 10:1 (1959).
78. Chambré, P. L., "On the Dynamics of Phase Growth," *Quart. J. Mech. Appl. Math.*, 9(2):224 (1956).
79. Rayleigh, Lord, "On the Pressure Developed in a Liquid During the Collapse of a Spherical Cavity," *Philos. Mag.*, 34:94 (1917).
80. Bornhorst, W. J., and Hatsopoulos, G. N., "Bubble Growth Calculation Without Neglect of Interfacial Discontinuities," *J. Appl. Mech.*, 34:847 (1967).
81. Theofanous, T. G., et al., "A Theoretical Study on Bubble Growth in Constant and Time Dependent Pressure Fields," *Chem. Eng. Sci.*, 24:885 (1969).
82. Mikic, B. B., Rohsenow, W. M., and Griffith, P., "On Bubble Growth Rates," *Int. J. Heat Mass Transf.*, 13:657 (1970).
83. Plesset, M. S., and Zwick, S. A., "The Growth of Vapor Bubbles in Superheated Liquids," *J. Appl. Phys.*, 25(4):493 (1954).
84. Plesset, M., and Prosperetti, A., "Bubble Dynamics and Cavitation," *Ann. Rev. Fluid. Mech.*, 9:145 (1977).
85. Forster, H. K., and Zuber, N., "Growth of a Vapor Bubble in a Superheated Liquid," *J. Appl. Phys.*, 25(4):474 (1954).
86. Birkhoff, G., Margulies, R. S., and Horning, W. A., "Spherical Bubble Growth," *Phys. Fluids*, 1:201 (1958).
87. Moalem-Maron, D., and Zijl, W., "Growth, Condensation, and Departure of Small and Large Vapour Bubbles in Pure and Binary Systems," *Chem. Eng. Sci.*, 33:1339 (1978).
88. Saitoh, T., and Shima, A., "Numerical Solution for the Spherical Bubble Growth Problem in a Uniformly Ultraheated Liquid," *J. Mech. Eng. Sci.*, 19(3):101 (1977).
89. Aguila, F., and Thompson, S., "Nonequilibrium Flashing Model for Rapid Pressure Transients," ASME Paper No. 81-HT-35 (1981).
90. Dalle-Donne, M., and Ferranti, M. P., "The Growth of Vapor Bubbles in Superheated Sodium," *Int. J. Heat Mass Transf.*, 18:901 (1975).
91. Bankoff, S. G., and Choi, H. K., "Growth of a Bubble at a Heated Surface in a Pool of Liquid Metal," *Int. J. Heat Mass Transf.*, 19:87 (1976).
92. Cha, Y. S., and Henry, R. E., "Bubble Growth During Decompression of a Liquid," *J. Heat Transf.*, 103:56 (1981).
93. Theofanous, T. G., and Patel, P. D., "Universal Relations for Bubble Growth," *Int. J. Heat Mass Transf.*, 19:425 (1976).
94. Van Stralen, S. J. D., and Cole, R., *Boiling Nucleation*, Vol. 1, Hemisphere, New York, 1979, Chapter 3.
95. Moore, G. R., "Vaporization of Superheated Drops in Liquids," *AIChEJ.*, 5(4):458 (1959).
96. Blander, M., and Katz, J. L., "Bubble Nucleation in Liquids," *AIChEJ.* 21(5):833 (1975).
97. Avedisian, C. T., and Andres, R. P., "Bubble Nucleation in Superheated Liquid-Liquid Emulsions," *J. Coll. Interf. Sci.*, 64(3):438 (1978).
98. Burdon, R. S., *Surface Tension and the Spreading of Liquids*, Cambridge U. P., Cambridge, 1949.
99. Jongenelen, F. C. H., Groeneweg, F., and Gouda, J. H., "Effects of Interfacial Forces on the Evaporation of a Superheated Water Droplet in a Hot Immiscible Oil," *Chem. Eng. Sci.*, 33:777 (1978).

100. Tochitani, Y., et al., "Vaporization of Single Liquid Drops in an Immiscible Liquid Part II: Heat Transfer Characteristics," *Wärme-und Stoffübertragung*, 10:71 (1977).
101. Moalem-Maron, D., Skolov, M., and Sideman, S., "A Closed Periodic Condensation-Evaporation Cycle of an Immiscible, Gravity Driven Bubble," *Int. J. Heat Mass Transf.*, 23:1417 (1980).
102. Tokuda, N., Yang, W. J., and Clark, J. A., "Dynamics of Moving Gas Bubbles in Injection Cooling," *J. Heat Transf.*, 90:371 (1968).
103. Ruckenstein, E., and Davis, E. J., "The Effects of Bubble Translation on Vapor Bubble Growth in a Superheated Liquid," *Int. J. Heat Mass Transf.*, 14:939 (1971).
104. Sidman, D., "Direct Contact Heat Transfer Between Immiscible Liquid Drops," in *Advances in Chemical Engineering*, Vol. 6, Academic Press, New York.
105. Isenberg, J., and Sideman, S., "Direct Contact Heat Transfer with Change of Phase" Bubble Condensation in Immiscible Liquid," *Int. J. Heat Mass Transf.*, 13:997 (1970).
106. Duda, J. L., Malone, M. F., and Notter, R. H., "Analysis of Two-Dimensional Diffusion-Controlled Moving Boundary Problems," *Int. J. Heat Mass Transf.*, 18:901 (1975).
107. Saitoh, T., "Numerical Method for Multidimensional Freezing Problems in Arbitrary Domains," *J. Heat Mass Transf.*, 100:294 (1978).
108. Suresh, K., "Vaporization of a Superheated Liquid Drop," M.S. thesis, Cornell University (1984).
109. Jacobs, H. R., and Cook, D. S., "Direct Contact Condensation on a Non-Circulating Drop," *Proc. 6th Int. Heat Transf. Conf.*, paper No. CS-2 (1978).
110. Strenge, P. H., Orell, A., and Westwater, J. W., "Microscopic Study of Bubble Growth During Nucleation Boiling," *AIChEJ.*, 7(4):579 (1961).
111. Landau, L. D., "On the Theory of Slow Combustion," *Acta Physioch.*, 19:77 (1974).
112. Apfel, R. E., "Water Superheated to 279.5°C at Atmospheric Pressure," *Nature Phys. Sci.*, 238:63 (1972).
113. Apfel, R. E., "Tensile Strength of Superheated n-Hexane Droplets," *Nature Phys. Sci.*, 233:119 (1971).
114. Ermakov, G. V., and Skripov, V. P., "Experimental Test of the Theory of Homogeneous Nucleus Formation in Superheated Liquids," *Russ. J. Phys. Chem.*, 43(9):1242 (1969).
115. Ermakov, G. V., and Skripov, V. P., "Saturation Five, Critical Parameters, and the Maximum Degree of Superheating of Perfluoro-Paraffins, " *Russ. J. Phys. Chem.*, 41(1):39 (1967).
116. Eberhart, J. G., Kremsner, W., and Blander, M., "Metastability Limits of Superheated Liquids: Bubble Nucleation Temperatures of Hydrocarbons and their Mixtures," *J. Coll. Interf. Sci.*, 50(2):369 (1975).
117. Renner, T. A., Kucera, G. H., and Blander, M., "Explosive Boiling in Light Hydrocarbons and their Mixtures," *J. Col. Interf. Sci.*, 52(2):391 (1975).
118. Patrick, J. R., and Reid, R. C., "Superheat-Limit Temperatures of Polar Liquids," *Ind. Eng. Chem. Fundam.*, 20(4):315 (1981).
119. Skripov, V. P., and Ermakov, G. V., "The Limit of Superheating of Liquids," 37(8):1047 (1963).
120. Patrick-Yeboah, J. R., "Superheat Limit Temperatures for Nonideal Liquid Mixtures and Pure Components," Ph.D. Thesis, Massachusetts Institute of Technology (1979).
121. Wakeshima, H., and Takata, K., "On the Limit of Superheat," *J. Phys. Soc. Japan*, 13(11):1398 (1958).
122. Skripov, V. P., and Kukushkin, V. I., "Apparatus for Observing the Superheating Limits of Liquids," *Russ. J. Phys. Chem.*, 35(12):1393 (1961).
123. Forest, T. W., and Ward, C. A., "Effect of a Dissolved Gas on the Homogeneous Nucleation Pressure of a Liquid," *J. Chem. Phys.*, 66(6):2322 (1977).
124. Forest, T. W., and Ward, C. A., "Homogeneous Nucleation of Bubbles in Solutions at Pressures above the Vapor Pressure of the Pure Liquid," *J. Chem. Phys.*, 69(5):2221 (1978).
125. Mori, Y. H., and Komotori, K., "Boiling of Single Superheated Drops in an Immiscible Liquid," *Heat Transf-Japanese Res.*, 5(3):75 (1976).
126. Dufour, L., "Sur L'Ebullition des Liquides," *Comptes Rendus*, 52:986, Jan.-June (1861).
127. Dufour, L., "Sur L'Ebullition des Liquides," *Comptes Rendus*, 53:846, July-Dec. (1861).
128. Sideman, S., "Photography of Drops in Liquid Media," 19(6):426 (1966).

CHAPTER 9

HYDRODYNAMICS OF BUBBLE FORMATION
FROM SUBMERGED ORIFICES

Hideki Tsuge

Department of Applied Chemistry
Faculty of Science and Technology
Keio University
Yokohama, Japan

CONTENTS

INTRODUCTION

The dispersion of gas bubbles in liquids plays an important role in many physical and chemical processes in order to bring about efficient mass transfer and heat transfer between the two phases. One of the common dispersion methods is gas bubbling through orifices submerged in a liquid. In the design of gas-liquid contacting equipment it is very essential to clarify the effects of the various factors on the volume of bubbles formed from an orifice horizontally submerged in a liquid, especially under the condition of relatively low liquid height so that the coalescence and breakdown of bubbles are not serious.

Many works have been made of bubble formation from a submerged single orifice in a liquid, and summaries of literatures have been presented by Siemes [1], Jackson [2], Kumar et al. [3] and Clift et al. [4]. Previous experimental and theoretical works may be classified into three bubble formation conditions; (i.e., constant-flow, constant-pressure, and the intermediate condition [3]). Much work has been done under constant-flow conditions in which the gas flow rate through an orifice is constant throughout the bubble formation. On the other hand, bubble formations in the presence of pressure fluctuations in the gas chamber (i.e., under intermediate conditions and constant pressure conditions) are so complex that it is not easy to calculate the bubble volume by simple explicit equations based on the bubble formation model. This chapter will summarize previous works and correlate the bubble volume by the dimensionless groups, discuss the bubble formation models and the hydrodynamics used in these models and compare the experimental results with the results computed by these models, and discuss effects of various factors on bubble formation, such as the velocity of surrounding liquid, column diameter, physical properties of the gas, orifice orientation, and nonwettability of the orifice.

SUMMARY OF THE PREVIOUS WORKS (CORRELATIONS OF BUBBLE VOLUME)

The following variables are considered representative of ones affecting the volume of bubbles, V_b, formed at a wetted orifice under the constant-flow condition (orifice inside diameter, D_i; gas superficial velocity through orifice, u_o; liquid density, ρ_1; liquid viscosity, μ_1; surface tension, σ; and gravitational acceleration, g).

A dimensional analysis of these factors produces the following functional relationship for the bubble volume:

$$\bar{V}_b = \text{function (Fr, Bo, Ga)} \tag{1}$$

where
$$\bar{V}_b = V_b/D_i^3$$
$$Fr = u_o^2/D_i g$$
$$Bo = \rho_1 D_i^2 g/\sigma$$
$$Ga = \rho_1^2 D_i^3 g/\mu_1^2$$

Referring to the previous works, it might be adequate to use $\bar{V}_b Bo$ as the dimensionless bubble volume and $N_w = Bo\, Fr^{0.5}$ as the dimensionless gas flow rate.

In cases of intermediate and constant pressure conditions, $N'_c = 4V_c g(\rho_1 - \rho_g)/\pi D_i^2 \rho_g c$ and $N_c = 4V_c g \rho_1/\pi D_i^2 p_h$ were proposed as the dimensionless capacitance number by Hughes et al. [5] and Tadaki et al. [6], where c is the sound velocity in the gas whose density is ρ_g so that $c = \sqrt{\gamma p_c/\rho_g}$. If $\rho_1 \gg \rho_g$ and $p_c \cong p_h$, N_c is equal to $\gamma N'_c$, where γ is the specific heat ratio of gas. N_c is used in the following.

By using these dimensionless groups, the previous experimental equations or bubble formation models for bubble volumes are classified into groups shown in Table 1, where the capacitance number N_c is divided into three ranges, namely:

A. Constant-flow condition.
B. Intermediate condition.
C. Constant-pressure condition.

The ranges are as follows for air (Tadaki et al. [6]):

A. $N_c < 1$
B. $1 < N_c < 9$
C. $9 < N_c$

In Table 1, gas flow rate number N_w is also divided into three ranges—I, II, and III as follows:

I. When N_w is small, uniform bubbles are formed.
II. The bubble volume increases with the increase of N_w.
III. When N_w increases further, the bubbles break down after detachment at the orifice and the distributions of bubble volume are produced.

Tadaki et al. [6] determined experimentally that for liquids of relatively low viscosity when $N_c > 1$, these ranges correspond to (I) $N_w < 2.4(N_c - 1)$, (II) $2.4(N_c - 1) < N_w < 16$, and (III) $16 < N_w$. In the following sections, the bubble formation models and the hydrodynamics of bubble formation are discussed for cases where the orifice plates are completely wetted by the liquids. Cases of nonwettability of the orifice are discussed later.

BUBBLE FORMATION IN THE REGION A-I

When $N_c < 1$ and N_w is small, bubbles are formed statically. In the case of a submerged single nozzle, Takahashi et al. [7] experimentally observed that constant-flow conditions are attained using the nozzle with length L long enough to be compared with the nozzle inside diameter D_i, such that $L/D_i^4 > 10^6$ in cgs units.

Force Balance Model (Statical Bubble Formation Model)

The force balance between the buoyancy and the surface tension is assumed for the spherical bubble [8].

$$(\rho_1 - \rho_g)V_b g = \pi D_i \sigma \cos \theta_c \tag{2}$$

when the contact angle $\theta_c = 0$ and $\rho_1 \gg \rho_g$,

$$\rho_1 V_b g = \pi D_i \sigma \tag{3}$$

Table 1
Summary of the Previous Works for Volume of an Air Bubble Formed from a Single Orifice

N_w / N_c	I	II	III
A	Mair [8]: $\bar{V}_b Bo = \pi$ (T1) Siemes [1]: $\bar{V}_b Bo = 0.79\pi$ (T2) Takahashi et al. [7]: $\bar{V}_b Bo = 0.89\pi(\mu_1/\mu_w)^{0.15}$ (T3)	• For liquids of relatively low viscosity Davidson et al. [12]: $\bar{V}_b Bo = 1.03 N_w^{1.2}/Bo^{0.2}$ (T7) Tadaki et al. [6]: $N_w < 16$, $\quad \bar{V}_b Bo = \pi + 1.31 N_w$ (T8) Mersmann [57]: $\bar{V}_b Bo = \dfrac{\pi}{2} + \dfrac{\pi}{6}\left(9 + K\left(\dfrac{\pi N_w}{4}\right)^2\right)^{0.5}$ (T9) (K = 10 – 26) Bhavaraju et al. [52]: $\bar{V}_b Bo = 13.0 N_w^{0.96}/Bo^{0.96} Ga^{0.15}$ (T10)	• Formation at the orifice Wraith [35]: $N_w > 140$, $\bar{V}_b Bo = 0.816 N_w^{1.2}/Bo^{0.2}$ (T13) Wraith et al. [37]: $\bar{V}_b Bo = 1.15 N_w^{1.2}/Bo^{0.2}$ (T14) Calderbank [53]: $V_b = 0.05 Q_g$ (T15) (Constant frequency chain bubbling) • After breakdown of the primary bubble formation at the orifice

	• For viscous liquids Davidson et al. [11]: $\bar{V}_b Bo = 5.41 N_w^{0.75} Bo^{0.25}/Ga^{0.375}$ (T11) Models for constant flow condition [3, 7, 11, 12, 15, 16, 35–37, 55]	Leibson et al. [54]: $Re_o = \rho_g D_o u_o/\mu_g > 1.10^4,$ $d_{vs} = 0.28 Re_o^{-0.05}$ (T16) Tadaki et al. [6]: $N_w > 16,$ $\bar{V}_b Bo = 906 N_w^{-1.3}$ (T17) Models for high gas flow rate [32–37]
B	Tadaki et al. [6]: $\bar{V}_b Bo = \pi N_c$ (T4) Park et al. [18]: $\bar{V}_b Bo = \pi N_c/\gamma$ (T5)	Tadaki et al. [6]: $2.4(N_c - 1) < N_w < 16,$ $\bar{V}_b Bo = \pi + 1.31 N_w$ (T12)
	Models for intermediate condition [18–22, 24–26, 29, 30, 41, 48, 49, 56]	
C	Tadaki et al. [6]: $N_w < 16,$ $\bar{V}_b Bo = 28.8$ (T6)	
	Models for constant pressure condition [11, 12, 14, 17, 45]	

so that

$$\bar{V}_b Bo = \pi \tag{4}$$

In practice, Equation 4 is rewritten as

$$\bar{V}_b Bo = C_c \pi \tag{5}$$

where C_c was determined experimentally by Siemes [1] and Takahashi et al. [7] as follows:

$$C_c = 0.79 \tag{6}$$

$$C_c = 0.89(\mu_1/\mu_w)^{0.15} \tag{7}$$

where μ_w is the viscosity of water at the liquid temperature.

Quasi-Statical Bubble Formation Model

For a very small flow rate, the force balance exerted at the gas-liquid interfacet as shown in Figure 1 is written as follows [1]:

$$p_b = p_\sigma + p_{hz} \tag{8}$$

where p_b, p_σ, and p_{hz} are the pressure in the bubble, the surface tension pressure and the pressure at a liquid height of hz. When the bubble apex is taken as the origin, the hydrostatic pressure is given by

$$p_{hz} = p_{h0} + \rho_1 gz \tag{9}$$

p_σ is written by the radii of curvature of the interface R_1 and R_2 as follows:

$$p_\sigma = \sigma(1/R_1 + 1/R_2) \tag{10}$$

Therefore

$$p_b = \sigma(1/R_1 + 1/R_2) + \rho_1 gz + p_{h0} \tag{11}$$

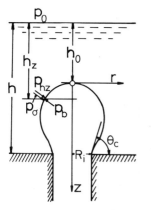

Figure 1. Cross section of gas bubble at a circular orifice [1].

At the apex of the bubble (z = 0), the radius of curvature of bubble is assumed to be R_0,

$$p_b = 2\sigma/R_0 + p_{h0} \tag{12}$$

From Equations 11 and 12,

$$\sigma(1/R_1 + 1/R_2) = 2\sigma/R_0 - \rho_1 gz \tag{13}$$

where R_1 and R_2 are given by,

$$R_1 = [1 + (dz/dr)^2]^{1.5}/(d^2z/dr^2) \tag{14}$$

$$R_2 = r[1 + (dz/dr)^2]^{0.5}/(dz/dr) \tag{15}$$

Therefore, the following ordinary differential equation for the bubble profile is written in terms of the dimensionless coordinates $\bar{z}\ (= z/R_0)$ and $\bar{r}\ (= r/R_0)$:

$$(d^2\bar{z}/d\bar{r}^2)/[1 + (d\bar{z}/d\bar{r})^2]^{1.5} + (d\bar{z}/d\bar{r})/\bar{r}[1 + (d\bar{z}/d\bar{r})^2]^{0.5} = 2 - \beta\bar{z} \tag{16}$$

where

$$\beta = \rho_1 g R_0^2/\sigma \tag{17}$$

The bubble size and bubble profile are determined by R_0 and the dimensionless parameter β, respectively.

Numerical solutions were obtained for various values of β by Hartland and Hartley [9] and the analytical solution for small β has been obtained by Chesters [10].

BUBBLE FORMATION IN THE REGION A-II

One-Stage Model by Davidson and Schüler

In this model [11, 12] the surface tension force is neglected.

For Viscous Liquids [11]

Small flow rate. The model is based on the following assumptions:

1. The bubble is spherical throughout formation.
2. The liquid surrounding the orifice is at rest when the bubble starts to form.
3. The motion of the bubble is not affected by the presence of another bubble immediately above it.
4. The momentum of the gas is negligible.
5. The bubble is moving at the Stokes' velocity.

Consider the motion of a bubble forming at a point source in an infinite liquid under the above conditions as shown in Figure 2. The velocity of the bubble center, v at time t after the start will be given by the force balance between the buoyancy force and the viscous drag while neglecting the inertia term:

$$ds/dt = v = 2\rho_1 R^2 g/9\mu_1 = (2\rho_1 g/9\mu_1)(3Q_g t/4\pi)^{2/3} \tag{18}$$

where s is the distance between the center of the bubble and the point of gas supply. By integrating

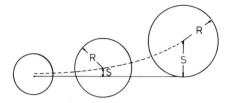

Figure 2. Idealized one-stage model [11].

Equation 18 under the condition that the bubble will detach when s = R,

$$V_b = (4\pi/3)^{0.25}(15\mu_1 Q_g/2\rho_1 g)^{0.75} \tag{19}$$

Then

$$\bar{V}_b Bo = 5.41(Bo^{0.25}/Ga^{0.375})N_w^{0.75} \tag{20}$$

Large flow rate. Equation of motion of the bubble is written by considering the buoyancy, the inertia, and viscous forces:

$$Mg = (11/16)(d(Mv)/dt) + 6\pi\mu_1 Rv \tag{21}$$

$$M = \rho_1 Q_g t \tag{22a}$$

where the virtual mass is considered as follows: If a sphere moves in a direction perpendicular to a wall, the virtual mass of the sphere is given by $M_s + M/2 + MR^3/16s^3$ for the completely invisid liquid [13]. When the sphere is a bubble ($M_s = 0$) and R = s, the virtual mass is 11M/16, and this is taken as an average value of the virtual mass for a bubble forming above a horizontal plate for an inviscid liquid. For viscous liquids this virtual mass gives only the order of magnitude of the effect due to inertia. Equation 21 is solved under the condition that the bubble detaches when s = R. When the orifice diameter is large, the detachment condition is assumed to be s = R + R_i. In this case, Equation 22a is modified to allow for the initial volume of the bubble V_0 as follows:

$$M = \rho_1 Q_g t + V_0 \tag{22b}$$

For Inviscid Liquids [12]

When the liquids are inviscid, the assumptions in deriving the equation of motion of bubble are:

1. The flow around the bubble is assumed to be irrotational. When a solid sphere or cylinder is accelerated from rest in a fluid, the initial motion is practically irrotational, and the wake is not fully established until the body has moved an appreciable distance. It seems likely that the flow around the accelerating bubble will be similar, and consequently the drag coefficient is likely to be negligible until after the bubble has detached from the orifice. Hayes et al. [14], however, assigned a drag coefficient to a forming bubble, thereby assuming that there is a fully established wake behind each bubble as it forms.
2. The upward momentum of the gas is neglected.

The force balance is set up between the buoyancy force and the inertial force of the liquid surrounding the bubble.

$$\rho_1 V_b g = d(11\rho_1 V_b v/16)/dt \tag{23}$$

The bubble is assumed to detach when $s = R + R_i$. When $R_i \cong 0$, the final bubble volume is:

$$V_b = 1.378Q_g^{1.2}/g^{0.6} \tag{24}$$

Therefore

$$\bar{V}_b Bo = 1.03N_w^{1.2}/Bo^{0.2} \tag{25}$$

Two-Stage Model

The bubble formation is assumed to take place in two stages [7, 15, 16], that is, the first or expansion stage, and the second or detachment stage. During the first stage the spherical bubble expands while its base remains attached to the orifice, whereas in the second stage the bubble base moves away from the orifice, while the bubble itself remains in contact with the orifice through a neck as shown in Figure 3.

The first stage is assumed to end when the downward forces (i.e., the viscous drag force, the surface tension force, and the inertial force) are equal to the upward force, namely, the buoyancy force, so that Newton's second law of motion is used as follows:

$$d(M'v)/dt = \rho_1 V_b g - C_D(\pi D_b^2/4)(\rho_1 v^2/2) - C_c \pi D_i \sigma \tag{26}$$

where $M' = 11\rho_1 V_b/16$ was used as the virtual mass of the bubble [12]. The bubble volume at the end of the first stage, V_f, is obtained by solving Equation 26. As the drag coefficient in Equation 26, Stokes' equation for a solid sphere (Equation 27) was used by Ramakrishnan et al. [15], the modified Stokes' equation (Equation 28) by Ruff [16] and the Hadamard-Rybczynski equation for fluid sphere, (Equation 29), by Takahashi et al. [7].

$$C_D = 24/Re \tag{27}$$

$$C_D = 24/Re + 4/Re^{0.5} + 0.4 \tag{28}$$

$$C_D = 16/R_e \tag{29}$$

The correction factor for surface tension, C_c, is normally taken as unity, but Takahashi et al. [7] proposed the use of Equation 7 for C_c.

FIRST STAGE   SECOND STAGE   CONDITION OF DETACHMENT

Figure 3. Two-stage model [15].

The bubble movement during the second stage is expressed also by Newton's second law of motion:

$$d(M'v')/dt = (V_f + Q_g t)\rho_1 g - C_D(\pi D_b^2/4)(\rho_1 v'^2/2) - C_c \pi D_i \sigma \tag{30}$$

where $v' = ds/dt$

The same virtual mass, drag coefficient, and correction factor of surface tension in the second stage have been used as those in the first stage [15, 16], while Takahashi et al. [7] assumed C_c in the second stage is half of C_c in the first stage. The condition for detachment is when the distance between the bubble center and the orifice plate is equal to the bubble radius at the end of the first stage such that the subsequent expanding bubble does not coalesce with it.

$$s - R = R_f = (3V_f/4\pi)^{1/3} \tag{31}$$

BUBBLE FORMATION IN THE REGIONS C-I and C-II

When the gas passes into the bubble formed from an infinite gas chamber at near-constant pressure, the model must be modified to allow for the change in gas flow rate.

One-Stage Model by Davidson and Schüler

The gas flow rate into the forming bubble through an orifice is given approximately by the orifice equation [11, 12]:

$$Q_0 = dV_b/dt = k_0(p_c - p_0 - \rho_1 gh - 2\sigma/R + \rho_1 gs)^{0.5} \tag{32}$$

where P_c is the pressure in the gas chamber and k_0 is an orifice constant. In deriving Equation 32, the effects of the kinetic energy of liquid and the viscosity of liquid on the pressure within the bubble are neglected.

For a large flow rate, the inertia terms become important and must be allowed for the equation of motion of the bubble:

$$\rho_1 V_b g = (11/16)\rho_1(d(V_b v)/dt) + C_D(\pi D_b^2/4)(\rho_1 v^2/2) \tag{33}$$

The two simultaneous equations, Equations 32 and 33, are solved numerically. Initial conditions are as follows: $s = 0$, $V = V_0 = \pi D_i^3/6$, and $v = 0$ at $t = 0$. The volume of the bubble moving away from the orifice is taken to be the total volume at $s = R + R_i$ minus the initial volume V_0. For an inviscid liquid the viscous drag in the right-hand side of Equation 33 is neglected.

One-Stage Model by Hayes et al. [14]

The growth of a spherical bubble at an orifice may be represented as shown in Figure 4. To obtain the velocity of a point on the surface of a bubble at any instant during its formation, the bubble formation process is considered to be composed of two steps: first, that the center of a given bubble is fixed and the bubble expands, and second, that each point on the surface of the bubble is displaced vertically. Thus when the actual bubble is replaced by one moving with the instantaneous velocity and with the same set of forces acting on its external surface, Newton's second law is applied:

$$u_0 \, dm/dt + \rho_1 V_b g + \pi D_i^2(p_b - p_h)/4 - \pi D_i \sigma - F_D - M' \, dv/dt = d(mv)/dt \tag{34}$$

where $u_0 \, dm/dt$ is the force exerted when the mass traveling with the velocity u_0 is added at the rate dm/dt; $\rho_1 g V_b$ is the net buoyancy force; $(\pi D_i^2/4)(p_b - p_h)$ is the excess pressure force; $\pi D_i \sigma$ is the surface tension force; $F_D = C_D(\pi D_b^2/4)(\rho_1 v^2/2)$ is the drag force; and $M' \, dv/dt$ is the force re-

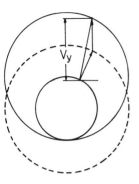

Figure 4. Idealized two step model [14].

quired to overcome the inertia of the liquid surrounding the bubble. M' equals one half of the mass of the displaced fluid in the case of irrotational motion. By solving Equation 34, it was found that at small flow rates the bubble volume is essentially constant, whereas at high flow rates the bubble frequency remains constant.

Two-Stage Model by Satyanarayan et al.

These researchers [17] assumed that the spherical bubble is formed in the same two stages as shown under the constant flow condition. The variation of the gas flow rate through the orifice to the forming bubble during the first stage can be expressed by the orifice equation Equation 32. At the end of the first stage, the upward buoyancy force is equal to the sum of the downward force, which is expressed by Equation 26. During the second stage the gas flow rate is assumed to be constant and equal to the flow rate at the end of the first stage. The bubble motion during the second stage can be also expressed by Newton's second law of motion Equation 30. The detachment condition is the same as that described by Equation 31.

BUBBLE FORMATION IN THE REGIONS B-I AND B-II

In these intermediate regions, the gas chamber volume plays a significant part. Both the pressure inside the gas chamber and flow rate into the bubble are time dependent.

A typical pressure-time trace for this gas chamber region is shown in Figure 5, which illustrates the practically linear buildup of pressure during which the interface remains within the orifice, followed by the rapid depressurization, which is the characteristic of spontaneous growth until the instant of the detachment of the bubble.

The coordinate system moving with the bubble is shown in Figure 6.

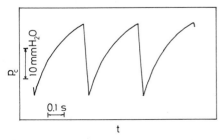

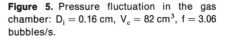

Figure 5. Pressure fluctuation in the gas chamber: $D_i = 0.16$ cm, $V_c = 82$ cm^3, $f = 3.06$ bubbles/s.

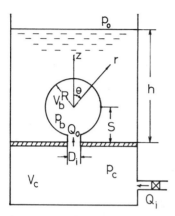

Figure 6. Coordinate system of moving with bubble.

Simplified Material Balance Model

Tadaki et al. [6] and Park et al. [18] applied a material balance to the gas in the chamber

$$V_c(d\rho_c/dt) = Q_i\rho_i - Q_0\rho_0 \tag{35}$$

where Q is the gas flow rate and subscripts c, i, and 0 mean the values in the gas chamber, inflowing gas into the chamber, and outflowing gas from the chamber. By the ideal gas law:

$$(V_cT_i/p_i)d(p_c/T_c)/dt = Q_i - (p_cT_i/T_cp_i)Q_0 \tag{36}$$

If the pressure fluctuations in the system are so rapid as to be adiabatic, Equation 36 becomes:

$$(V_cT_i/np_iT_c)(dp_c/dt) = Q_i - (p_cT_i/T_cp_i)Q_0 \tag{37}$$

where n is a polytropic index. By assuming $Q_0 \gg Q_i$ during bubble formation and $p_cT_i/p_iT_c \cong 1$, Equation 37 reduces to:

$$Q_0 = dV_b/dt = -(V_c/np_c)(dp_c/dt) \tag{38}$$

By integrating over the depressurization step in Figure 5:

$$V_b - V_0 = (V_c/n) \ln(p_{max}/p_{min}) \tag{39}$$

Equation 39 can be rewritten without any significant loss in accuracy:

$$V_b = (V_c/np_{av})(p_{max} - p_{min}) \tag{40}$$

Assuming that a bubble detaches when the minimum chamber pressure becomes equal to the hydrostatic liquid pressure at the orifice, the term $(p_{max} - p_{min})$ is equal to $2\sigma/R_i$:

$$V_b = 2\sigma V_c/nR_ip_{av} \tag{41}$$

Tadaki and Maeda [6] derived the dimensionless gas chamber volume N_c by comparing the bubble volume in Equation 41 for n = 1 and the static bubble volume given by Equation 3.

One-Stage Force Balance Model by Swope

Swope [19] solved Newton's second law, Equation 34 given by Hayes et al. [14], for slow bubble formation in viscous liquids with pressure fluctuation in the gas chamber. For the gas flow rate into the bubble, the average gas flow rate into the chamber is modified by multiplying the ratio of the bubbling time with the sum of bubbling and nonbubbling times.

Two-Stage Model by Khurana and Kumar

These authors [20] considered that the bubble is formed in the same two stages as under the constant flow condition and the constant pressure condition. At the end of the first stage, a force balance equation is obtained by equating the buoyancy force with the sum of the inertial force, surface tension, and the viscous drag:

$$\rho_1 V_b g = d(M'v)/dt + \pi D_i \sigma \cos \theta_c + C_D(\pi D_b^2/4)(\rho_1 v^2/2) \tag{42}$$

For the second stage, Newton's second law of motion is applied, neglecting the surface tension force:

$$d(M'v')/dt = \rho_1 V_b g - C_D(\pi D_b^2/4)(\rho_1 v'^2/2) \tag{43}$$

By the electrical analogy of bubble formation, they obtained the gas flow rate into the bubble as a function of time to solve Equation 43. The bubble detaches at $s - R = R_f$, where R_f is the bubble radius at the end of the first stage.

Two-Stage Model by Takahashi et al.

Takahashi et al. [21] assumed that the bubble volume in the low gas flow rate region is evaluated on the assumption that the pressure fluctuation in the chamber is so rapid that the process is adiabatic as given by Equation 41, and the bubble volume in the high gas flow rate is calculated by modifying the model [7] obtained for the constant gas flow rate. The final bubble volume can be obtained by adding both bubble volumes in low and high gas flow rates, and the correlation by this model is experimentally confirmed at least approximately.

Two-Stage Model by Potential Flow Theory (Kupferberg and Jameson Model)

The idealized stages for the formation of a spherical bubble are illustrated in Figure 7 [22].

1. *First stage.* The bubble grows while remaining at the orifice. This stage terminates when the upward force on the bubble becomes equal to the downward force so that the bubble begins to rise.
2. *Second stage.* The bubble continues growing while moving away from the orifice plate but is still connected to the orifice by a neck. This stage ends when the neck has elongated to such an extent that it breaks off and the bubble continues to accelerate away from the plate.

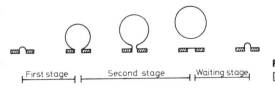

First stage | Second stage | Waiting stage

Figure 7. Idealized two-stage model [22].

3. *Waiting stage.* After the detachment of a bubble from the orifice, there is no outflow of gas from the chamber hence the pressure in the chamber increases and the next bubble begins to form. During a part of this stage weeping through the orifice might occur.

In each of these stages the calculations of the velocity and pressure fields around the bubble are made under the following assumptions:

1. The bubble is spherical throughout formation and its motion is not affected by the preceding bubble.
2. The effect of viscosity may be ignored so that the flow around the bubble is assumed to be at a high Reynolds number. Also since the bubble starts practically from rest, the motion is taken to be irrotational.
3. The liquid is very deep compared to the diameter of the bubble.
4. The momentum of the gas is ignored.

Evaluation of motion of a growing, translating bubble. Applying the continuity equation, the velocity potential must satisfy Laplace's equation:

$$\nabla^2\phi = 0 \tag{44}$$

The pressure in the liquid, p, may be found from the unsteady form of Bernoulli's equation:

$$p/\rho_1 = \partial\phi/\partial t - q^2/2 - g(s + R\cos\theta) + p_h/\rho_1 \tag{45}$$

In a liquid of infinite extent the potential flow field around a translating and expanding spherical bubble would be:

$$\phi = \phi_T + \phi_P = (R^3/2r^2)(ds/dt)\cos\theta + (R^2/r)(dR/dt) \tag{46}$$

On the other hand, the presence of the wall near the bubble was taken into account by using Lamb's method of images [23]:

$$\phi = (ds/dt)(R^3/2r^2 + R^3r/8s^3 + R^6/16s^3r^2 + R^6r/64s^6 + R^9/128r^2s^6 + \cdots)\cos\theta$$
$$+ (dR/dt)[R^2/r + (R^2r/4s^2 + R^5/8s^2r^2 + R^5r/32s^5 + R^8/64s^5r^2 + \cdots)\cos\theta] \tag{47}$$

This equation holds providing $s \geq R$, so it can be used for both the first and second stages.

Here

$$q^2 = (\partial\phi/\partial r)^2 + (1/r)(\partial\phi/\partial\theta)^2 \tag{48}$$

Substituting for q and ϕ in Equation 45:

$$(p - p_h)/\rho_1 = R(d^2R/dt^2) + 1.5(dR/dt)^2 - gs + \text{function}(\cos\theta, R, s) \tag{49}$$

The net upward force on the bubble boundary due to fluid pressure is found by integrating the vertical component of pressure over the surface of the bubble:

$$F_n = \int_0^\pi (2\pi R^2 p \sin\theta \cos\theta)_{r=R} \, d\theta \tag{50}$$

During the first stage, this force acts downwards, and since the bubble is in direct contact with the plate, s is equal to R. The condition for the termination of the first stage is that F_n should just equal zero. From Equations 49 and 50, with s = R, this will occur when:

$$gR = 1.13R(d^2R/dt^2) + 2.13(dR/dt)^2 \tag{51}$$

For the second stage the buoyancy force is equal to the inertial force but $s \geq R$. Substituting Equation 49 into Equation 50 with $F_n = 0$:

$$d^2s/dt^2 = [g - (0.375R^2/s^2 + 0.047R^5/s^5)(d^2R/dt^2) - (1.125R^2/s^2 + 0.282R^5/s^5)(1/R)(dR/dt)^2$$
$$+ (0.563R^4/s^4 + 0.141R^7/s^7)(1/R)(ds/dt)^2$$
$$- (1.5 - 0.070R^6/s^6)(1/R)(dR/dt)(ds/dt)/(0.5 + 0.188R^3/s^3 + 0.023R^6/s^6)] \tag{52}$$

Equation for radial expansion of the bubble. The equation for radial expansion is obtained from a set of three equations which describe the relation between the pressure in the gas chamber, p_c, and the pressure in the bubble, p_b. The initial conditions for bubble growth are:

1. The bubble radius is equal to the inside radius of the orifice:

$$R = R_i \tag{53}$$

2. The growth rate is zero:

$$dR/dt = 0 \tag{54}$$

3. The pressure in the gas chamber is equal to the sum of the hydrostatic pressure at the orifice and the surface tension pressure:

$$p_c|_{t=0} = p_0 + \rho_1 gh + 2\sigma/R_i \tag{55}$$

The pressure drop across the orifice is given by an orifice equation:

$$(p_c - p_b)/\rho_g = k_1 u_o^2 \tag{56}$$

where k_1 is an orifice constant and equal to $\pi D_i^4/\rho_g k_o^2$, and u_o is the gas velocity through the orifice.

By assuming adiabatic behavior in the chamber volume, V_c, the pressure in the gas chamber during the first and second stages is:

$$p_c - p_c|_{t=0} = -(c^2\rho_g/V_c)[(V_b - V_0) - Q_i t] \tag{57}$$

This indicates that a difference between inflowing and outflowing gas rates corresponds to the pressure change in the chamber.

The pressure inside the bubble is assumed to be independent of θ, which follows from the assumption that the bubble remains spherical during formation. These assumptions will only be reasonable if the surface tension pressure $2\sigma/R$ dominates over the hydrostatic and inertial pressures. Disregarding the θ-dependent terms in Equation 49, the pressure in the bubble is then:

$$p_b = p_0 + \rho_1 gh + \rho_1[R(d^2R/dt^2) + 1.5(dR/dt)^2 - gs] + 2\sigma/R \tag{58}$$

For the first stage, Equations 56, 57, and 58 are solved simultaneously, whereas Equations 52, 56, 57, and 58 are solved for the second stage.

They found experimentally that the end of the second stage is approximately when $s = R + R_i$ for the $\frac{1}{4}$-in. orifice and $s = R + D_i$ for the $\frac{1}{8}$-in. orifice.

Two-Stage Model by Potential Flow Theory (McCann and Prince Model)

Independently with Kupferberg et al. [22], McCann and Prince [24] derived a potential flow theory to describe the flow of gas from the gas chamber into an expanding, rising spherical bubble forming at the orifice, by considering the wake behind the bubble. They assumed the effect of the orifice plate on the motion of the bubble may be ignored. The potential function for a rising, expanding bubble Equation 46 and the liquid velocity (Equation 48) are substituted in the generalized Bernoulli's equation (Equation 45). By setting $F_n = 0$ in Equation 50,

$$V_b g = 0.5 d(V_b(ds/dt))/dt \tag{59}$$

This is the same equation as that derived by a force balance between the buoyancy and the inertial force with the virtual mass associated with a spherical bubble in an unbounded liquid, namely $M' = 0.5M$. The chamber pressure is given as follows:

$$dp_c/dt = (c^2 \rho_g/V_c)(Q_i - Q_0) \tag{60}$$

The pressure inside the bubble is obtained as follows:

For $s < R$

$$p_b = \rho_1[R(d^2R/dt^2) + 1.5(dR/dt)^2 - gs] - [\rho_1(ds/dt)^2 R/4(s + R)](1 + 2.5s/R - 1.5s^3/R^3)$$
$$+ p_0 + \rho_1 gh + 2\sigma/R \tag{61a}$$

For $s > R$

$$p_b = \rho_1[R(d^2R/dt^2) + 1.5(dR/dt)^2 - gs] - \rho_1(ds/dt)^2/4 + p_0 + \rho_1 gh + 2\sigma/R \tag{61b}$$

The orifice equation is given as:

$$dV_b/dt = k_2(p_c - p_b - p_w)^{0.5} \tag{62}$$

The pressure field in the wake of a rising bubble will affect the motion of the next bubble, which is calculated as a pressure p_w exerted at $\theta = \pi$ at the mean height of the forming bubble:

$$p_w = (\rho_1 R_d^3(v_d + 2gt_w)^2/r_w^3)(1 - R_d^3/2r_w^3) - \rho_1 g R_d^3/r_w^2 \tag{63}$$

where r_w = distance between one bubble and its follower

$$r_w = s_d + v_d(t + t_D) + g(t + t_D)^2 - s_m \tag{64a}$$

and s_m is mean height

$$s_m = s \qquad \text{for } s > R \tag{64b}$$

$$s_m = (s + R)/2 \qquad \text{for } s < R \tag{64c}$$

Subscript d shows the value at detachment. t_w and t_D show the time during weeping, and the sum of the briding and weeping times. This correction of the wake to the bubble motion is very small at low flow rates where the distance between successive bubbles is large. The effect becomes more pronounced with increasing flow rates and is greatest at the weep point where the spacing between bubbles is small.

Equations 59, 60, 61, and 62 are solved numerically. The bubble detaches at $s = R$ if $p_{OR} > p_c$ or at $s > R$ when $p_{OR} = p_c$, where p_{OR} is equal to p at $\theta = \pi$ and $r = s$, and shows the liquid pressure behind the bubble at the orifice.

Two-Stage Model by Modified Potential Flow Theory (Tsuge and Hibino [25, 26])

The flow rate of gas through the orifice, Q_o, is assumed to be given by the orifice equation

$$|p_c - p_b| = (Q_o/k_o)^2 = (4\pi R^2/k_o)^2 (dR/dt)^2 \tag{65}$$

Assuming adiabatic behavior in the gas chamber, the pressure change during the first and second stages is expressed as:

$$dp_c/dt = (\gamma p_c/V_c)(Q_i - Q_o) = (\gamma p_c/V_c)(Q_i - 4\pi R^2 \, dR/dt) \tag{66}$$

where Q_i is the inflowing rate of gas into the chamber.

When the pressure inside the bubble becomes greater than the sum of the average hydrostatic pressure and the surface tension pressure, the bubble expands by this pressure difference. The equation of the radial bubble expansion is written as:

$$p_b - p_s = \phi(d^2R/dt^2, dR/dt, \rho_1, \mu_1) + 2\sigma/R \tag{67}$$

The average hydrostatic pressure, p_s, at the bubble surface is approximately expressed as:

$$p_s = p_0 + \rho_1 gh - \rho_1 g(R - R_i) \tag{68}$$

where R_i is the radius of the orifice. In the right-hand side of Equation 68, R_i is included to meet the initial condition that when $t = 0$, $R = R_i$ and $p_s = p_0 + \rho_1 gh$.

For the ideal liquid, Kupferberg et al. [22] and McCann et al. [24] have derived the functional form of ϕ from the potential flow theory, but for a real liquid it is difficult to derive theoretically the concrete form of ϕ in Equation 67. Hence, it is assumed that ϕ is expressed as the product of the inertial term for the ideal liquid and a factor α which is a function of dimensionless liquid physical property, $M_o = g\mu_1^4/\rho_1\sigma^3$. Then ϕ becomes:

$$\phi = \alpha\rho_1(R(d^2R/dt^2) + 1.5(dR/dt)^2) \tag{69}$$

where

$$\alpha = 8.6 + 0.425 \log M_o \qquad (1.6 \cdot 10^{-11} < M_o < 1.5 \cdot 10^{-4}) \tag{70}$$

The equations for the first stage, Equations 65, 66, 67, and 69, are solved simultaneously under the initial conditions $R = R_i$, $dR/dt = 0$, and $p_c = p_h + 2\sigma/R_i$.

The termination of the first stage is the time when the following force balance equation holds:

$$\rho_1 V_b g = d[M'(dR/dt)]/dt + 2\pi R_i \sigma + 0.5 C_D \rho_1 (dR/dt)^2 \pi R^2 \tag{71}$$

where M' is the virtual mass for the ascending motion of the bubble and is assumed to be $11\rho_1 V_b/16$ [13].

By considering the inertial force, the net buoyancy force, and the viscous drag force on the bubble, the equation of motion for the bubble in the second stage is written as follows:

$$d(M'(ds/dt))/dt = \rho_1 V_b g - 0.5 C_D \rho_1 (ds/dt)^2 \pi R^2 \tag{72}$$

where s is the vertical distance of the center of the bubble from the orifice plate. The equations for the second stage, Equations 65, 66, 67, 69, and 72 are solved by using the final values of the first stage as the initial conditions. The detachment condition is found experimentally to be approximately when the length of the bubble neck becomes equal to the orifice diameter D_i.

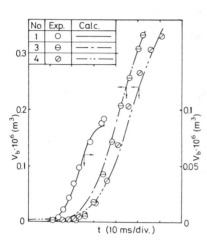
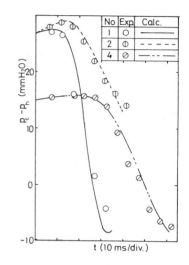

Figure 8. Changes of bubble volume with time [26].

Figure 9. Pressure fluctuation in the gas chamber [26].

For C_D in Equations 71 and 72, it is appropriate to use the drag coefficient of a bubble sphere rather than that of a solid sphere, so that the C_D-Re relations of Tadaki et al. [27] and Kubota et al. [28] for a single bubble rising in a pure liquid apply for $0.7 < $ Re. This gives the following approximate relations for C_D:

For Re < 0.7

$$C_D = 16/Re \qquad (29)$$

For 0.7 < Re < 1500

$$\log C_D = 1.2672 - 0.7165 \log Re + 0.0149(\log Re)^2 - 0.0778(\log Re)^3 + 0.0223(\log Re)^4 \qquad (73a)$$

For Re > 1,500

$$C_D = 0.087 \qquad (73b)$$

Figures 8 and 9 show examples of bubble volume and pressure in the gas chamber, respectively, as a function of growing time under the conditions shown in Table 2. In these figures, the experimental

Table 2
Conditions of Bubble Formation

Run No.	$D_i \cdot 10^3$ [m]	$V_c \cdot 10^6$ [m³]	N_c [—]	$Q_i \cdot 10^6$ [m³/s]
1	1.11	32.3	3.17	0.257
2	1.11	187	18.3	2.61
3	1.45	200	11.4	0.698
4	1.99	187	5.70	0.803

points are taken from the analysis of high-speed films and the curved lines show the calculated results from the model. It may be said that the model describes the bubble formation mechanism rather well.

Nonspherical Model by Marmur and Rubin [29]

The models just described have assumed the spherical shape of the bubble and have been forced to use an empirical or semi-empirical criterion for determining the instant of detachment. Whereas their model enables to continuous computation of the instantaneous shape of the bubble during its formation, using the equations of motion for the liquid and the thermodynamic relationships for the gas in the bubble and the gas chamber. There is no need for the empirical detachment criteria because the instant of detachment comes naturally at the time when the neck, which develops during formation, attains zero width.

This model is based on the following assumptions:

1. The bubble is a volume of revolution around the axis of the orifice.
2. The gas-liquid interface is acted upon by the pressure difference between the gas and the liquid and by the surface tension force. It is assumed that the influence of the liquid viscosity is negligible, except for the immediate vicinity of the orifice plate.
3. An inertial mass is assigned to the bubble interface, which equals the instantaneous mass of liquid being accelerated. This mass is computed using the virtual mass in the inviscid liquids.
4. The volume of the liquid around the bubble is very large compared to the volume of the bubble.
5. The gases in the bubble and the chamber flow and expand adiabatically.
6. A pressure difference exists across the orifice, which determines the rate of gas flow into the bubble.
7. The pressures in the bubble and the gas chamber are uniform.
8. The momentum of the gas is negligible.
9. The formation of the bubble is unaffected by the presence of other bubbles.
10. Bubble detachment occurs when the neck narrows to zero at one of its points.

Based on the previously mentioned assumptions, the approximate equations of motion for the gas-liquid interface were developed. Figure 10 shows a differential element of this interface and the forces acting on it. The surface force is due to the pressure difference between the gas in the bubble and the liquid, and the line forces are due to surface tension. For a static interface these forces are in equilibrium, but in dynamic formation the resultant of these forces is equal to the rate of change in the liquid momentum. In order to avoid the complicated solution of the Navier-Stokes equations

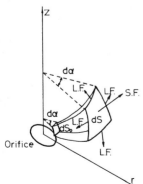

Figure 10. Interface element and forces acting on it [29]: L.F. = line force, S.F. = surface force [29].

for the motion of the liquid, it was assumed that the momentum of the liquid may be calculated using the virtual mass and the velocity of the interface. As shown in Figure 10, an initial differential interface element dS_0 grows to dS after time t. The mathematical formulation of this physical assumption leads to the following equations of motion:

$$r \, \Delta p - \sigma \partial(r \sin \psi)/\partial r = (1/u_r) d(u_z(d\bar{m}/dt))/dt \tag{74}$$

$$r \, \Delta p + \sigma[\partial(r \cos \psi)/\partial z - 1/\sin \psi] = (1/u_z) d(u_r(d\bar{m}/dt))/dt \tag{75}$$

where

$$r = r(r_0, z_0, t) \tag{76}$$

$$z = z(r_0, z_0, t) \tag{77}$$

$$u_r = dr/dt \tag{78}$$

$$u_z = dz/dt \tag{79}$$

$$\sin \psi = \pm(\partial z/\partial r)/[1 + (\partial z/\partial r)^2]^{0.5} \tag{80}$$

$$\Delta p = p_b - p_o - p_h + \rho_1 gz + \rho_1(u_r^2 + u_z^2)/2 \tag{81}$$

The pressure difference Δp is computed using Bernoulli's equation, neglecting the term which accounts for time derivatives. The differential mass $d\bar{m}$ assigned to the interface element per unit angle $d\alpha$ is defined by:

$$d\bar{m} = \max\left[d\bar{m}_1 = \rho_1\chi \int_0^t df(t) \, dt; |d\bar{m}_2| = \rho_1\chi \left|\int_0^t dS(t)u(t) \, dt\right|\right] \tag{82}$$

$$df(t) = dS(t)u(t) \qquad \text{(if } u > 0 \text{ and } d\bar{m}_1 = d\bar{m}_2\text{)} \tag{83a}$$

$$= 0 \qquad \text{(otherwise)} \tag{83b}$$

where χ is the virtual mass coefficient and can be taken as 0.85, and ψ is the angle between the interface and the horizontal plane. Equations 74–83 are integro-differential equations of one independent variable t. If the right-hand sides of Equations 74 and 75 are zero, (i.e., there is no motion), they reduce to the equilibrium equations for the interface. The boundary conditions are as follows:

1. Symmetry at the top of the bubble at $t > 0$ and $r_0 = 0$

$$\partial z/\partial r = 0 \tag{84}$$

where r_0 is the radial Lagrangian coordinate.
2. Three-phase point at the edge of the orifice at $t > 0$, $r_0 = R$ and $z_0 = 0$

$$r = R_0 = R, \qquad z = z_0 = 0 \tag{85}$$

The initial bubble is approximated by a spherical segment of height H:

at $t = 0$

$$z_0 = H - R_0 \pm \sqrt{R_0^2 - r_0^2} \tag{86}$$

$$R_0 = (1 + H^2)/2H \qquad (87)$$

$$u_r = u_z = 0 \qquad (88)$$

$$d\bar{m}_0 = d\bar{m}_0(r_0, z_0) \qquad (89)$$

As the gas in the system behaves adiabatically, the following equation is obtained from the first law of thermodynamics:

$$V_c \, dp_c/dt + V_b \, dp_b/dt + n(p_b \, dV_b/dt - p_A Q_g) = 0 \qquad (90)$$

where p_A is the pressure at which the gas flow rate Q_g is specified and n is the polytropic index.
Writing the first law of thermodynamics for the gases in the bubble and in the chamber which will enter the bubble during the time interval dt:

$$V_b \, dp_b/dt + n(p_b \, dV_b/dt - p_c Q_o) = 0 \qquad (91)$$

where Q_o is the rate of gas flow into the bubble.
The orifice equation is written as:

$$Q_o = k_3 \pi R_i^2 \sqrt{(|p_c - p_b|)/\rho_g} \qquad (92)$$

where k_3 is the orifice coefficient.
Equations 74–92 were solved numerically, using a finite difference method, and Figure 11 shows the typical sequences of the computed bubble formation.

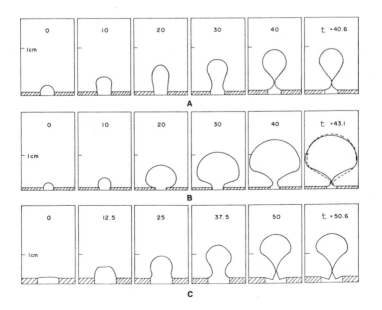

Figure 11. Typical sequences of computed bubble formulation [29]: (A) $R_i = 0.16$ cm, $Q_i = 2.0$ cm³/s, $V_c = 10$ cm³; (B) $R_i = 0.16$ cm, $Q_i = 16.7$ cm³/s, $V_c = 2250$ cm³; (C) $R_i = 0.48$ cm, $Q_i = 20.0$ cm³/s, $V_c = 22$ cm³.

Nonspherical Model by Pinczewski

The nonspherical bubble growth model, which takes into account the effect of gas momentum, was proposed [30] to be applicable to a wider range of gas flow rates and system pressures than existing models.

The gas circulation for a spherical bubble is approximated by a Hills' spherical vortex [13]

$$\phi_{GC} = u_o(1 - r^2/R^2)r^2 \sin^2 \theta/2 \quad \text{for } r \leq R \tag{93}$$

where ϕ_{GC} = the velocity potential for the flow
   u_o = the orifice velocity
   θ = the angle between the position vector r and the vertical axis of symmetry

Combining this stream function with Bernoulli's equation at the interface (r = R) results in an expression for the pressure at bubble surface due to gas motion:

$$p_{GC} = 0.5\rho g u_o^2 \cos^2 \theta \tag{94}$$

For the case of a spherical bubble growing in an incompressible liquid of infinite extent and negligible gas momentum, the motion of the gas-liquid interface is governed by the modified Rayleigh equation [31]:

$$p_b - p_h = \rho_1(R(d^2R/dt^2) + 1.5(dR/dt)^2) + 2\sigma/R + (4\mu_1/R)(dR/dt) \tag{95}$$

where the three terms on the right-hand side represent the inertia, surface tension, and viscous forces, respectively. Equation 95 is assumed to be equally valid for any point on a nonspherical surface where R becomes the equivalent radius of the surface as defined in the following equation:

$$2\sigma/R = \sigma(1/R_1 + 1/R_2) \tag{96}$$

The effect of gas momentum is modeled by simply including the gas circulation term:

$$p_b - p_h = \rho_1(R(d^2R/dt^2) + 1.5(dR/dt)^2) + 2\sigma/R + (4\mu_1/R) \, dR/dt - 0.5\rho_g u_o^2 \cos^2 \theta \tag{97}$$

The liquid-phase pressure at any point on the bubble surface, p, is related to the pressure within the bubble by:

$$p = p_b - 2\sigma/R \tag{98}$$

and the net upward force on the bubble, F_n, is obtained by integrating the vertical component of this pressure over the surface of the bubble. When F_n is negative, the bubble grows while it remains at the orifice. When F_n becomes positive, the bubble lifts off the plate and the motion consists of both radial expansion and vertical translation. Following Davidson and Schüler [11], the equation for vertical translation is:

$$F_n = d((11V_b\rho_1/16)(ds/dt))/dt \quad \text{for } F_n > 0 \tag{99}$$

The gas velocity through the orifice is given by the usual orifice equation, Equation 56:

$$p_c - p_b = \rho_g k_1 u_o^2 \tag{56}$$

where

$$u_o = (dV_b/dt)/(\pi R_i^2) \tag{100}$$

Assuming adiabatic behavior in the chamber, the chamber pressure, p_c, at time t, is given by:

$$p_c = p_c|_{t=0} - (c^2\rho_g/V_c)((V_b - V_0) - Q_i t) \tag{57}$$

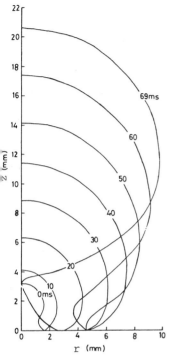

Figure 12. Computed sequence of bubble shapes [30]: $R_i = 0.16$ cm, $Q_i = 16.7$ cm^3/s, $V_c = 2250$ cm^3.

Equations 97–100, 56 and 57 describe the dynamics of the bubbling system and are solved by the finite-difference method. Figure 12 shows a sequence of computed bubble shape.

BUBBLE FORMATION IN THE REGIONS A-III, B-III AND C-III

In these regions the effect of the gas chamber volume on the bubble volume is relatively small and the gas flow rate through an orifice is assumed to be constant. At high gas flow rates, the coalescence between the growing bubble and the detached bubble at the orifice occurs. The coalescence is repeated approximately twice and the cycle of coalescence goes to completion. Coalescence between detached bubbles at the orifice becomes more or less continuous at very high gas flow rates, namely a gas jet is formed [32], although Räbiger and Vogelpohl [33, 34] claimed that a gas jet does not occur.

Two-Stage Model by Wraith

The two-stage model of bubble formation at a plate orifice submerged in an inviscid liquid at a high gas flow rate was proposed by Wraith [35]. The following assumptions are made:

1. The liquid is inviscid and of large extent.
2. Surface tension may be neglected.
3. The gas is incompressible, and the gas density is neglected.
4. The gas bubble surface is spherical.

Consider the expansion of a gas bubble from a point source, which is equivalent to a zero orifice radius. The pressure in the liquid associated with the expansion is given by the generalized

Bernoulli's equation:

$$p/\rho_1 = \partial\phi/\partial t - q^2/2 + F(t) \tag{101}$$

For a stationary expanding sphere of radius R,

$$\phi = (R^2/r)\,dR/dt \tag{102}$$

$$q = (R^2/r^2)\,dR/dt \tag{103}$$

When the source has a constant flow rate Q_g

$$\phi = Q_g/4\pi R^2 \tag{104}$$

and

$$\partial\phi/\partial t = (R^2/r)(d^2R/dt^2) + 2(R/r)(dR/dt)^2 = 0 \tag{105}$$

Substituting into Equation 101, the pressure at $R < r$ is

$$p/\rho_1 + (R^4/2r^4)(dR/dt)^2 = F(t) \tag{106}$$

Assuming that the pressure at infinity may be neglected,

$$p/\rho_1 + (R^4/2r^4)(dR/dt)^2 = 0 \tag{107}$$

Figure 13 shows the configuration of an expanding hemispherical bubble. The radial velocity of a semispherical envelope is

$$da/dt = Q_g/2\pi a^2 \tag{108}$$

where a is the hemisphere radius. The pressure p_c due to expansion at the hemispherical surface, $r = a$, is given by substituting Equation 108 in Equation 107:

$$p_c/\rho_1 + Q_g^2/8\pi^2a^4 = 0 \tag{109}$$

An equilibrium equation for the expanding hemisphere can be obtained by setting equal to zero the sum of the reactive force F_R due to the plate, and the force on the expanding surface due to the components of surface pressure, p_θ, in the liquid, whence

$$F_R - 2\pi a^2 \int_0^{\pi/2} p_\theta \cos\theta \sin\theta = 0 \tag{110}$$

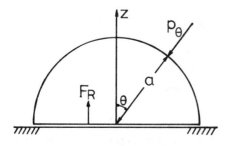

Figure 13. Idealized expanding hemispherical bubble [35].

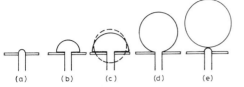

Figure 14. Idealized two-stage model [35]. (Figure C shows the transition from hemispherical, first stage to the spherical, second stage).

(a)   (b)   (c)   (d)   (e)

p_θ has two components, that is, the pressure due to expansion and the hydrostatic pressure at (a, θ).

$$p_\theta = \rho_1 Q_g^2/8\pi^2 a^4 + p_h - \rho_1 ga \cdot \cos \theta \qquad (111)$$

Substituting into Equation 110, integration gives

$$F_R - \rho_1 Q_g^2/8\pi a^2 - \pi a^2 p_h + 2\pi a^3 \rho_1 g/3 = 0 \qquad (112)$$

If F_R becomes less than the hydrostatic force on the basal surface, the bubble will start to move upwards so that the maximum radius attained by a stable hemispherical expanding bubble is

$$a_h = 0.453 Q_g^{0.4} g^{-0.2} \qquad (113a)$$

Therefore the bubble volume in the first stage is

$$V_f = 0.194 Q_g^{1.2} g^{-0.6} \qquad (113b)$$

Suppose now the bubble becomes spherical about the center of mass of a hemispherical envelope at the end of the first stage. Figure 14 shows the two successive stages schematically. In the second stage, the force balance equation for a spherical bubble growing at the orifice is assumed to be given by the Davidson and Schüler model [11, 12] (Equation 21), with neglecting the viscous force

$$\rho_1 V_b g = d((11\rho_1 V_b/16)(ds/dt))/dt \qquad (114)$$

The bubble volume in the second stage is

$$V_b = V_f + Q_g t \qquad (115)$$

As the center of mass of a hemisphere is located at a polar height $3a/8$ above the base, by integrating Equation 114, setting s equal to the bubble radius at detachment so that the bubble volume at detachment is

$$V_b = 1.090 Q_g^{1.2} g^{-0.6} \qquad (116)$$

Walters and Davidson [36] used $\rho_1 V_b/2$ as the virtual mass for the spherical bubble formed at the free-standing nozzle, assuming the hypothetical point gas source, and obtained

$$V_b = 1.378 Q_g^{1.2} g^{-0.6} \qquad (117)$$

Potential Flow Theory by Wraith and Kakutani

Wraith and Kakutani [37] derived the equation of motion and the associated pressure field on the basis of the potential flow theory for a growing spherical gas bubble rising in an inviscid liquid from an orifice or a free-standing nozzle. With a constant gas flow rate, the dimensionless pressure

$(p_N - p_h)/\rho_1 gR$ rises sharply to a maximum when the bubble center has risen to a position 1.55R above an orifice plate, while for a free standing nozzle the maximum occurs at a displacement of 1.38R, where p_N is the pressure with liquid motion at the orifice or nozzle. These positions of maximum pressure correspond well to experimentally observed positions of bubble detachment. The bubble volumes at this instant are predicted by the potential flow theory as follows:

For an orifice plate

$$V_b = 1.54Q^{1.2}g^{-0.6} \tag{118a}$$

For a nozzle

$$V_b = 1.39Q^{1.2}g^{-0.6} \tag{118b}$$

Two-Stage Model for the Noncoalesced First Bubble by Miyahara et al.

These researchers [32] assumed for the formation of the noncoalesced first bubble the following:

1. The effect of the gas chamber volume is negligible.
2. The change of the gas flow rate into the forming bubble is small compared to the absolute value of the gas flow rate so that the constant flow rate assumption into the bubble is satisfied.
3. The effect of the surface tension term is negligible.

By introducing the gas momentum term into the two-stage model for the constant-flow condition (discussed earlier) at the end of the first stage:

$$d[(11\rho_1 V_f v)/16]/dt = \rho_1 V_f g - C_D(\pi R_f^2/4)(\rho_1 v^2/2) + 4\rho_g Q_g^2/\pi D_i^2 \tag{119}$$

The equation of motion at the second stage is:

$$d[11(V_f + Q_g t_s)\rho_1(v + v_n)/16]/dt_s$$
$$= \rho_1(V_f + Q_g t_s)g - C_D(\pi D_b^2/4)[\rho_1(v + v_n)^2/2] + 4\rho_g Q_g^2/\pi D_i^2 \tag{120}$$

The growing rate of the neck is

$$V_n = d(s - R)/dt_s \tag{121}$$

The bubble detaches at $s = R + R_f$.

The calculated diameter of the first bubble, D_c, do not agree with the experimental value, D_E, because the effect of the preceding bubble is neglected in the model. They obtained experimentally

$$D_E/D_C = 1.4Fr^{-0.042} \tag{122}$$

The appearance of the coalescence depends on the gas chamber volume. When the gas chamber volume is small, "double bubbling" will occur (i.e., the spacing between bubbles is decreased and bubbles coalesce at the orifice). On the other hand, "pairing" occurs at large gas chambers (i.e., after the bubble has detached, the smaller second bubble grows very rapidly and elongates into a closed-tail shape). This tail subsequently breaks at the orifice and moves into the first bubble. These pairing and double bubbling phenomena were at first recognized by McCann and Prince [24]. The critical points for transition to the occurrence of coalescence and gas jet have been correlated empirically.

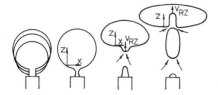

Figure 15. Bubble formation model [34] (v_{RZ}: relative velocity of filament end).

Force Balance Model by Räbiger and Vogelpohl

These researchers' [33, 34] basic principles of the model are as follows:

1. Single or double bubbles (primary bubbles) are always formed at the mouth of a nozzle also in the jetting regime. A gas jet does not occur.
2. In the detachment step, the bubbles move at a constant velocity, which roughly corresponds to their rise velocity.
3. The disintegration of the primary bubble in the jetting regime is caused by the induction of liquid flow into the bubble by the severance of the neck connecting the bubble to the nozzle as shown in Figure 15. Above a critical gas flow rate, this liquid flow breaks up the bubble head and thus initiates the disintegration of the bubble into secondary bubbles.

Calculation of the Primary Bubble Diameter

The formation of primary bubbles is described by a force balance, namely, the buoyancy force is equal to the sum of the surface tension force and resistance force. Excluding the neck from contributing to the buoyancy, the buoyancy force is:

$$F_B = (\Delta\rho g \pi D_b^3/12)(2 - 3D_i^2/D_b^2) \tag{123}$$

The resistance force F_D is defined as follows:

$$F_D = C_D(\pi D_b^2/4)(\rho_1 v_R^2/2) \tag{124}$$

The relative bubble velocity v_R is influenced by a superimposed liquid flow only through the expansion velocity v_E and the bubble base velocity v_B in the stagnant liquid

$$v_R = 2v_E + v_B \tag{125}$$

and

$$v_E = (u_o - U_1)(D_i/2D_b) \tag{126}$$

where u_o and U_1 are the mean velocity of gas in the nozzle and the mean velocity of forced liquid flow. Assuming spherical bubbles attached to the nozzle by a neck, the resistance law for the motion or rigid spheres is applied to the bubble formation. Hence the drag coefficient is given by [58]:

$$C_D = 24/Re + 4/Re^{0.5} + 0.4 \tag{127}$$

and the velocity of the bubble base is

$$v_B = \sqrt{4gD_b/3C_D} \tag{128}$$

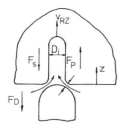

Figure 16. Force balance during secondary bubble formation [34] (v_{RZ}: relative velocity of filament end).

The force balance is written as follows:

$$(g \, \Delta\rho\pi D_b^3/12)(2 - 3(D_i/D_b)^2)$$
$$= \pi D_i\sigma + C_D\rho_1 K(\pi D_b^3/8)[2(4Q_g/\pi D_i^2 - U_1)(D_i^2/2D_b)^2 + v_B)^2 \quad (129)$$

where K is a constant. The bubble diameter is obtained by solving Equation 129 by iteration.

Filament Motion

The force balance is considered for the description of the filament motion as shown in Figure 16:

$$F_I = F_P - F_S - F_D \quad (130)$$

where F_I, F_P, F_S, and F_D are the inertial force, pressure force, surface tension force, and resistance force, respectively.

The neck length on detachment can be calculated from Equation 130 with forces affecting the filament motion.

Calculation of the Secondary Bubble Diameter

The formation of secondary bubbles is caused chiefly by the liquid penetrating into the primary bubble. For disintegration of the primary bubble to occur, this liquid motion, which is induced by the filament, must still possess a sufficiently large kinetic force on reaching the bubble head, to overcome the surface tension force and the resistance force as shown in Figure 17. By the force balance

$$F_K + F_D = F_S \quad (131)$$

The kinetic force of the liquid motion is:

$$F_K = (\rho_1 v_{RC}^2/2)(\pi D_i^2/4) \quad (132)$$

The resistance force is given by Stokes's law:

$$F_D = 3\mu_1 v D_b \quad (133)$$

Figure 17. Force balance during disintegration of a primary bubble [34].

If these forces are substituted into Equation 131, the critical velocity of the liquid motion is given by:

$$v_{RC} = (2/D_i)\sqrt{2D_b(\sigma - 3\mu_1 v)/\rho_1} \tag{134}$$

If the motion of the filament is strong enough to generate liquid motion which still exhibits the critical velocity on reaching the top interface, the jetting regime sets in and the primary bubble undergoes disintegration when

$$v_{RC} = 0.5v_{RM} \tag{135}$$

where v_{RM} is the maximum relative velocity of filament end.

On substitution of the corresponding forces and of the boundary conditions, Equation 130 yields an equation for the determination of the secondary bubble diameter:

$$0.25v_{RC}^2 = B + 4\sigma/D_i\rho_1 + 4[12\mu_1(K_4 - K_5v_{RC}) + 0.1\rho_1 D_i v_{RC}]A/D_i\rho_1 \tag{136}$$

The calculated values of the bubble diameter by this model are in relatively good agreement with the experimental ones, whereas four experimentally determined parameters, K_4, K_5, A, B, are included in Equation 136.

FORMATION OF BUBBLES IN FLOWING LIQUIDS

The bubble formations in the cocurrent, countercurrent, and crosscurrent flowing liquids have been investigated.

Cocurrent and Countercurrent Flows

In these cases the bubble formations have been made under the constant gas flow condition.

One-Stage Model

The force balance at the bubble detachment in cocurrent flow is obtained by Chuang and Goldschmidt [38] as follows

$$F_I = F_B + F_D - F_S \tag{137}$$

namely,

$$0.5 \, d(M(ds/dt))/dt = \pi\rho_1 D_b^3/6 + C_D(\pi\rho_1(D_b^2 - D_i^2)/4)(\rho_1(U_1 - D_b f_b/6))/2 - \pi D_i \sigma \tag{138}$$

where U_1 = liquid flow velocity
                f_b = the bubble formation frequency

The bubble volumes are obtained from Equation 138 or its dimensionless form.

Sada et al. [39] assumed that the total force acting on the bubble at the nozzle, F, is the sum of the buoyance force and the drag force:

$$F = \pi D_b^3 \rho_1/6 + C_D(\pi D_b^2/4)(\rho_1 U_1^2/2) \tag{139}$$

By using the modified Froude number ($Fr' = u_o^2/(gD_b + 0.33U_1^2)$), they obtained the dimensionless correlation.

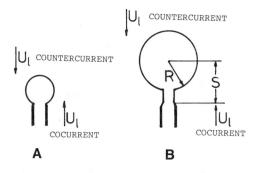

Figure 18. Two-stage model in cocurrent and countercurrent flows [40]: (A) first stage; (B) second stage.

Two-Stage Model

Takahashi et al. [40] assumed that spherical bubbles are formed by the two stages as shown in Figure 18. Newton's second law was applied at the end of the first stage:

$$d[(11\rho_1 V_f/16)(v \mp U_1)]/dt_f = \rho_1 V_f g - C_D(\pi D_f^2/4)(\rho_1/2)(v \mp U_1)|v \mp U_1| - C_C \pi D_i \sigma \tag{140}$$

where the upper and lower signs show the cocurrent and countercurrent flows. As the drag coefficient C_D, they used:

$$C_D = 1 + 16/Re \tag{141}$$

Newton's second law is applied to the second stage:

$$d[(11\rho_1 V_b/16)(v' \mp U_1)]/dt_s$$
$$= \rho_1(V_f + Q_g t_s)g - C_D(\pi D_b^2/4)(\rho_1/2)(v' \mp U_1)|v' \mp U_1| - C_C N \pi D_i \sigma \tag{142}$$

where

$$v' = ds/dt \tag{143}$$

Equations 142 and 143 are solved by assuming that the bubble detaches at $s = [3V_f/(4\pi)]^{1/3} + R$, where V_f is the volume at the end of the first stage.

Crosscurrent Flow

Constant Pressure Condition

Sullivan, Hardy, and Holland [59] assumed a three-steps process as shown in Figure 19. The first two steps are the same as those used by Hayes et al. [14] in an earlier section. The liquid velocity U_1 is superimposed upon the model of Hayes et al. [14], namely each point on the surface of the bubble has its horizontal component of velocity increased by U_1.

When the forces are summed in the vertical direction, Newton's second law of motion gives:

$$u_o \, dm/dt + \rho_1 V_b g + \pi D_i^2(p_b - p_h)\cos\theta_C/4 - \pi D_i \sigma \cos\theta_C - F_D - F_I = d(mv_y)/dt \tag{144}$$

where the drag force

$$F_D = C_D(\rho_1 v_y^2/2)(\pi D_b^2/4) \tag{145}$$

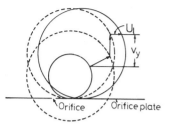

Figure 19. Three-steps bubble formation model [59].

and the force required to overcome the inertia of the liquid is given by:

$$F_I = (\chi \rho_1 V_b) \, dv_y/dt \tag{146}$$

When the forces are summed in the horizontal direction, Newton's second law of motion gives:

$$\pi D_i^2 (p_b - p_h) \sin \theta_C/4 - \pi D_i \sigma \sin \theta_C = d(mv_x)/dt \tag{147}$$

From Equations 144–147, the following equation is obtained:

$$\Delta \rho V_b g(1 - \psi) = (\pi D_i \sigma \sec \theta_C)(1 - D_i/D_b) - \xi \tag{148}$$

where

$$\psi = (3\rho_1/4 \, \Delta \rho)(Q_g^2/(\pi^2 D_b^5 g))(C_D - 16\chi/3) \tag{149}$$

$$\xi = (4Q_g^2 \rho_g/\pi D_i^2)[1 - (1/12)(D_i/D_b)^2] - U_1 \rho_g Q_g \tan \theta_C \tag{150}$$

$$\theta_C = \tan^{-1}(U_1 V_b/Q_g)/(D_b/2) \tag{151}$$

The flow region was divided into two regions:

Constant-volume region:

$$(\pi D_i \sigma \sec \theta_C)(1 - D_i/D_b) > \xi \tag{152}$$

Constant-frequency region:

$$(\pi D_i \sigma \sec \theta_C)(1 - D_i/D_b) < \xi \tag{153}$$

In the constant-volume region, the volume of the bubbles varied little, but the frequency of formation varied considerably with the air flow rate. In the constant-frequency region, the situation was reversed.

Constant-Flow Condition

Takahashi et al. [40] modified their two-stage model for cocurrent and countercurrent flow by considering that the bubbles are formed at a given inclination angle θ' to the vertical line as shown in Figure 20. θ' is given by the force balance between the buoyancy force at the end of the first stage and the drag force exerted by the liquid velocity.

Morgenstern and Mersmann [41] also presented the two-stage model. Figure 21 shows the balance of forces for the first stage, namely buoyancy F_B, surface tension F_S, drag force F_D, inertial force F_I, and a force which the flowing liquid exerts on the bubble F_L.

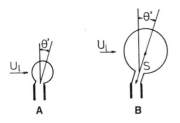

Figure 20. Two-stage model in crosscurrent flow [40]: (A) first stage; (B) second state.

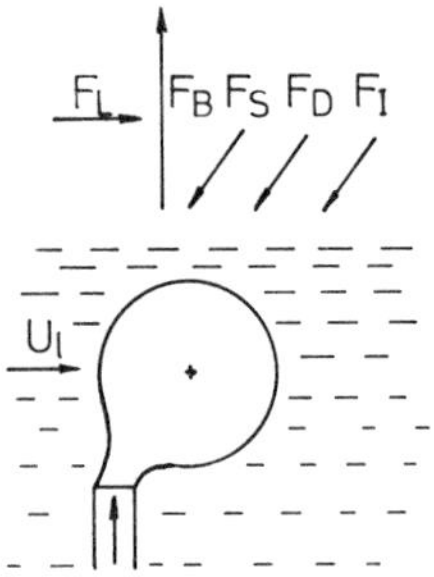

Figure 21. Force balance for flowing liquid [41].

$$\sqrt{F_L^2 + F_B^2} = F_S + F_D + F_I \tag{154}$$

On introducing expressions for individual forces:

$$[(10/Re + 0.1)(\rho_1 U_1^2/2)(\pi D_f^2/4) + (\Delta\rho V_f g)] = \pi D_i \sigma + C_D(\rho_1 v^2/2)(\pi D_f^2/4) + d(mv)/dt \tag{155}$$

The total dimensionless volume V_b^* is the sum of the dimensionless first stage volume V_f^* and second stage volume V_s^*. V_s^* is obtained experimentally:

$$V_b^* = V_b g^{0.6}/Q_g^{1.2} = V_f^* + V_s^* = V_f g^{0.6}/Q_g^{1.2} + [1 + 4.7(\mu_1/g^{0.2}Q_g^{0.6}\,\Delta\rho) - Fr^{*-1/3}] \tag{156}$$

where Fr^* is the modified Froude number.

Kawase and Ulbrecht [42] used Equation 24 in the Davidson and Schüler model [12] for very low velocities of liquid. For very high velocities of liquid, they assumed that the center of the bubble is displaced horizontally by an amount U_1 in unit time and the detachment takes place when the center of the bubble is displaced by a distance equal to the sum of the radius of the bubble and the radius of the nozzle. Formation time, t_2, at high liquid velocities is given by:

$$U_1 t_2 = D_i/2 + D_b/2 = D_i/2 + (6Q_g t_2/\pi)^{1/3}/2 \tag{157}$$

Usually the first term of the right-hand side of Equation 157 is negligible compared with the second term. An exponential interpolation formula, which is applicable for the entire liquid flow rate range, is:

$$V_b = V_1(1 - e^{-a'/U_1^{b'}}) + V_2 e^{-a'/U_1^{b'}} \tag{158}$$

where V_1 and V_2 are the bubble volumes for very low velocities and for very high velocities of liquid, and a' and b' were determined experimentally ($a' = 1.00$ and $b' = 0.242$).

Figure 22. Geometric configuration of bubble in flowing liquid [43].

Intermediate Condition

Tsuge, Nojima, and Hibino [43] investigated the effect of the crosscurrent flow on the size and the mechanism of formation of a bubble formed at an orifice as the pressure inside the gas chamber is varied. From the generalized Bernoulli's equation, which has been obtained by integrating Euler's equation for an ideal liquid

$$p/\rho_1 + \partial\phi/\partial t + q^2/2 + gs = p_s/\rho_1 \tag{159}$$

The velocity potential ϕ around a spherical bubble which is expanding and floating upward in a uniform flow can be expressed as the sum of the potential ϕ_T for flow around a translating sphere, the potential ϕ_P associated with the expansion and contraction of the bubble, and the potential ϕ_L due to the uniform liquid flow. Therefore, using the geometrical configuration shown in Figure 22, and ignoring all terms of higher order than $(R/s)^4$:

$$\phi = \phi_T + \phi_P + \phi_L = (ds/dt)(R^3/2r^2 + R^3r/8s^3 + R^6/16s^3r^2)\cos\theta$$
$$+ (dR/dt)[R^2/r + (R^2r/4s^2 + R^5/8s^2r^2)\cos\theta] + U_1r \tag{160}$$

Now,

$$q^2 = (\partial\phi/\partial r)^2 + [(1/r)(\partial\phi/\partial\theta)]^2 \tag{161}$$

Substituting Equations 160 and 161 into Equation 159 and rearranging give the following equation for the expansion of the bubble, wherein it is assumed that the pressure inside the bubble is uniform at every point of its surface and is independent of θ:

$$p_b - p_s = \rho_1[R(d^2R/dt^2) + 1.5(dR/dt)^2 + U_1^2/2] + 2\sigma/R \tag{162}$$

This equation can be considered as being the same as Equations 67 and 69, which are the expressions for the expansion of the bubble in the quiescent liquid, but with the addition of the term $\rho_1 U_1^2/2$ to the group of inertial terms of the right-hand side. Then, if it is assumed that the effect of the liquid viscosity expressed in terms of α in a quiescent liquid is the same as to the case of a flowing liquid, and if the factor α' is introduced to account for the deviation of the actual flow away from ideal flow, it follows that:

$$p_b - p_p = \alpha\rho_1[R(d^2R/dt^2) + 1.5(dR/dt)^2 + d'U_1^2/2] + 2\sigma/R \tag{163}$$

where $\alpha' = 1.2$ was obtained from their experimental results. Their two-stage model described earlier was solved numerically by using Equation 163 and the final condition for the second stage, as determined by analysis of the high-speed photographs:

$$s \geq [R + (1 - 0.02U_1)D_i][1 - (C_D\rho_1U_1^2R^2/2D_i\sigma)]^{0.5} \tag{164}$$

It is confirmed as shown in Figure 23 that the bubble volume decreases as the liquid velocity increases at the same gas flow rate. The experimental results and the calculated results agree qualitatively well when N_c is smaller than 25.

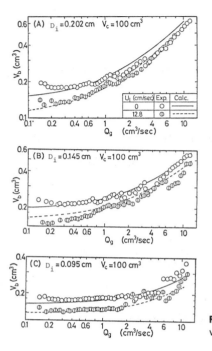

Figure 23. Effect of liquid velocity on the bubble volume [43].

WALL EFFECT ON THE BUBBLE FORMATION

The models described above have not taken into account the dimensions of the bubble column. Provided the column is large enough, the effect on the bubble volume of any upward motion of the liquid, which is brought about as a result of the bubble formation, can be ignored. If the column is of smaller dimensions, however, it would seem reasonable to assume that the effect of inertia of the upward-moving liquid will have to be taken into account. Potter [44] has pointed out that, when a bubble is being formed at a single orifice under the constant-pressure condition, it is unreasonable to disregard the inertial force of the upward-moving liquid. Lanauze and Harris [45] investigated the effect on the bubble volume of the inertial term due to the movement of the liquid, using the empirical data of Davidson and Schüler [12]. No reports have come to our notice, however, in relation to the formation of a bubble under conditions where the pressure in the gas chamber is fluctuating.

When bubbles are being formed under fluctuating pressure in the gas chamber in a bubble column of small dimensions, the inertial force due to the movement of the liquid will be closely dependent on the pressures in the gas chamber and in the bubble. It will therefore be advisable in the first and second stages to introduce a term which accounts for the effect of inertial forces into ϕ in Equation 69, (corresponding to the expansion of the bubble in an infinite medium). Tsuge and Hibino [46] therefore multiply the inertia term that has been proposed by Potter [44] by a constant ε, which will be determined experimentally, and add the result to the right hand side of Equation 69 as follows:

$$\phi = \alpha\rho_1[R(d^2R/dt^2) + 1.5(dR/dt)^2] + \varepsilon(16\rho_1 h/D_T^2)[R^2(d^2R/dt^2) + 2R(dR/dt)^2] \qquad (165)$$

where h and D_T are the liquid height and column diameter, and the value of ε was found to be

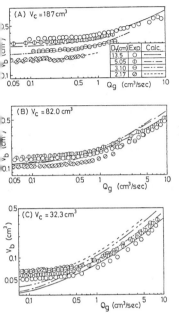

Figure 24. Wall effect on the bubble volume in distilled water [46]: $D_i = 0.199$ cm.

0.5. They solved the two-stage model in an earlier section by using Equation 165. The experimental results and the calculated results agree qualitatively well as shown in Figure 24.

EFFECT OF THE PHYSICAL PROPERTIES OF GAS

Few studies have been carried out on the effect of the physical properties of gas on bubble volume. Davidson et al. [11] showed that a 2% difference in bubble volume should result from the formation of air and CO_2 bubbles for high gas flow rate at atmospheric pressure, under the constant-flow condition, owing to the difference of the gas momentum, namely the gas density.

Kling [47] observed the formation of N_2, Ar, and He gas bubbles in water at system pressures from atmospheric to 8.2 MPa. He found that smaller bubbles were formed under increasing pressure, although no bubble formation mechanism to quantify the effect was attempted.

LaNauze et al. [48] showed experimentally that by increasing the system pressure of CO_2 up to 2.0 MPa, the gas density affected the gas momentum and the capacity of the gas chamber, and presented a model of bubble growth to explain the experimental results.

Pinczewski [30] calculated the experimental conditions of LaNauze et al. [48] and showed that their computed results are in rather good agreement with the experimental results.

On the other hand, in most published experimental work, only air or nitrogen has been used as the gas, and Kumar and Kuloor [3] claimed in their review that the effects of the gas density and viscosity on the bubble volume could be neglected under atmospheric pressure.

Tsuge, Tanaka, and Hibino [49] have taken into account the effects of the gas properties and modified the two-stage model for the intermediate condition described earlier. The orifice constant k_o is generally considered to be a function of gas flow rate; gas density, ρ_g; gas viscosity, μ_g; and the thickness of orifice plate, L, so that by taking into account the pressure drop by sudden enlargement and contraction at the orifice and the frictional head loss

$$k_o = \kappa (2/\rho_g C_g)^{0.5} (\pi D_i^2/4) \tag{166}$$

where

$$C_g = 0.4(1.25 - \delta) + 4fL/D + (1 - \delta)^2 \qquad (167)$$

As the free area of the orifice plate $\delta \cong 0$ holds to a fairly good approximation in Equation 167,

$$C_g = 1.5 + 4fL/D_i \qquad (168)$$

Assuming that the gas flow through the orifice is laminar so that friction factor $f = 16/Re$ and that the bubble is spherical,

$$C_g = 1.5 + 4\mu_g L/[\rho_g R^2(dR/dt)] \qquad (169)$$

k_o, obtained from Equations 166 and 169, is substituted in the orifice Equation 65. The parameter κ in Equation 166 was determined to be 0.83, which shows the deviation between the experimental and the calculated values of k_o.

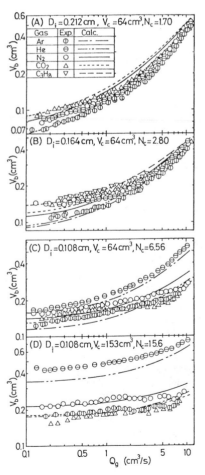

Figure 25. Effect of gas properties on the relation between bubble volume and gas flow rate [49].

Table 3
Physical Properties of Gases

Gas	$T_g(°C)$	$\rho_g(kg/m^3)$	$\mu_g(Pa \cdot s)$	$\gamma(-)$
Ar	19.7	1.664	$2.22 \cdot 10^{-5}$	1.67
He	20.4	0.1661	$1.96 \cdot 10^{-5}$	1.67
N_2	20.2	1.164	$1.75 \cdot 10^{-5}$	1.40
CO_2	21.6	1.829	$1.48 \cdot 10^{-5}$	1.30
C_3H_8	19.9	1.867	$0.80 \cdot 10^{-5}$	1.13

Since the instantaneous rate of gas momentum is written as $4\rho_g Q_g^2/\pi D_i^2$, as shown by Davidson et al. [11] and LaNauze et al. [48], the termination of the first stage is the time when the sum of the buoyancy and the rate of gas momentum is larger than the sum of the inertial force, the surface tension, and the viscous force. Therefore:

$$(\rho_1 - \rho_g)V_b g + 4\rho_g Q_g^2/\pi D_i^2 \geq d(M'(dR/dt))/dt + \pi D_i \sigma + C_D \rho_1 (dR/dt)^2 \pi R^2/2 \qquad (170)$$

where M' is the virtual mass for the ascending motion of bubble and is given by $(\rho_g + 11\rho_1/16)V_b$ [13].

When s is the distance between the center of the bubble and the orifice plate, by considering the rate of gas momentum, the equation of motion in the detachment stage will be as follows:

$$d[M'(ds/dt)]/dt = (\rho_1 - \rho_g)V_b g + 4\rho_g Q_g^2/\pi D_i^2 - C_D \rho_1 (ds/dt)^2 \pi R^2/2 \qquad (171)$$

The simultaneous differential equations described earlier are solved numerically by the Runge-Kutta-Gill method so that the bubble volume can be calculated.

For large $N_c(N_c > 9)$, the bubble volume decreases with the increase of gas density and the effect of the specific heat ratio becomes small as shown in Figure 25. The physical properties of gases are summarized in Table 3. The reason is considered from the model as follows: When the gas density is small in large N_c, the orifice constant k_o in Equation 166 becomes large so that the gas flow rate through the orifice and then the bubble volume increase. The experimental and calculated results agree qualitatively well.

EFFECT OF ORIFICE ORIENTATION

Kumar and Kuloor [3] extended their models for the constant-flow condition and constant-pressure condition discussed earlier. The first stage is assumed to end when the vertical components of the expansion drag and the surface tension force together become equal to the buoyancy. The second stage commences, and its characteristics in the present model are the same as before, except for the condition for detachment which occurs when the bubble has covered a distance equal to $R_f \cos \omega + (D_i \sin \omega)/2$, where ω is the angle between the orifice plate and the horizontal. In the case of the constant-flow condition, the increase in ω tends to reduce the first-stage volume because of the smaller net downward force, whereas it increases the second stage volume because of the distance covered by the bubble base. The final volume is the result of both these conflicting factors. The results obtained for constant-pressure conditions exhibit the same kind of irregular behavior as observed for constant-flow conditions.

Takahashi et al. [50] measured the bubble volumes formed at a single circular hole drilled in a pipe and found experimentally that the bubble volume is affected by the inclined angle of orifice in the low gas flow rate region. For low-viscosity liquids under the critical value of the chamber

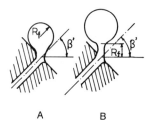

A   B

Figure 26. Formation model at inclined orifice [50]: (A) first stage; (B) second state.

number, a model for bubble formation at an inclined orifice is shown in Figure 26. Both the expansion and the movement of bubble are essentially in the vertical direction for all orifice orientations. Therefore the surface tension force in the vertical direction is given by the following equation:

$$F_S = C_p S \sigma \tag{172}$$

where C_p = the correction factor depending upon the inclined angle of the orifice, the physical properties of the liquid, and the dimensionless gas chamber volume

   S = peripheral length of orifice hole

The computed results were obtained by extending their two-stage model for the constant-flow condition described earlier. The experimental values agree well with the calculated results. This model of bubble formation is applicable to the bubble formation at the inclined-flat plate orifice.

THE NONWETTABILITY OF THE ORIFICES

The models just presented are derived for cases of wetted orifices. On the other hand, in cases of the gas bubble formation in liquid metals, the nonwettability of the orifices must be taken into account.

Sano and Mori [51] obtained the size of the bubble formed at the nozzle in molten metals for relatively wider gas flow rates by using the outer diameters of the nozzle D_o as follows:

$$D_b = [(\alpha^* \sigma D_o / \Delta \rho g)^2 + 9.5(Q_g^2 D_o / g)^{0.867}]^{1/6} \tag{173}$$

where

$$N_c^* < 1: \alpha^* = 6$$

$$1 < N_c^* < 9: \alpha^* = 6N_c^*$$

$$9 < N_c^*: \alpha^* = 55$$

and

$$N_c^* = 4T_B \left[\int_0^{V_c} (1/T) \, dV_c(T) \right] \Delta \rho g \cdot \sin \theta_c / \pi D_i D_o P_h \tag{174}$$

T and T_B are the gas temperature and the bubble temperature. The experimental and the calculated results agree well.

CONCLUSIONS

The bubble formation from a submerged single orifice has been the subject of many experimental and theoretical works. A number of bubble-formation models has been developed to estimate the volume of bubbles formed or to make clear the effects of various factors on the bubble volume. In this chapter, the existing theoretical bubble formation studies were classified into three ranges by the dimensionless gas chamber volume and also in three ranges by the dimensionless gas flow rate. By discussing the bubble formation mechanisms and hydrodynamics in each region, the following may be concluded:

1. The spherical bubble formation processes under the constant-flow condition in inviscid liquids are well described by the two-stage models.
2. The bubble-formation processes under cconstant-pressure and intermediate conditions in inviscid liquids are rather well described by the two-stage models by potential flow theory, while in a strict sense the nonspherical bubble-formation models are more adequate for estimating the bubble shape and the instant of bubble detachment. The modeling of the weeping phenomena in these conditions will be important in order to extend these models for a single orifice to the multiple orifice systems such as sieve plates.
3. The formation mechanisms concerning the coalescence and disintegration of bubbles at the orifice or nozzle in high gas flow rate have been studied and the models have been presented recently. These phenomena have to receive considerable attention for the design of gas-liquid contactors and performance estimation of industrial equipment.
4. Few bubble formation models in viscous liquids have been derived by modifying the theories in inviscid or ideal liquids. In addition to this, the bubble formation in non-Newtonian liquids, which remains untouched here, is important. Hydrodynamics of bubbles formed in viscous Newtonian and non-Newtonian liquids has to be made clear to present more appropriate bubble-formation models.
5. The effects of various factors on bubble formation, namely the velocity of surrounding liquids, column diameter, physical properties of gas, orifice orientation and nonwettability have been extensively studied. Modified versions of the bubble-formation models in quiescent fluids are shown to explain the bubble phenomena rather well.

NOTATION

a	hemisphere radius in Figure 13 (m)	D_T	column diameter (m)
Bo	Bond number (—)	d_{vs}	volume-surface diameter (m)
C_c	Correction factor in Equation 5 (—)	f	friction factor (—)
		f_b	bubble formation frequency (1/s)
C_D	drag coefficient of bubble (—)	F	total force (N)
C_g	coefficient given by Equation 167 (—)	F_B	buoyancy force (N)
		F_D	drag force (N)
C_p	correction factor in Equation 172 (—)	F_I	inertial force (N)
		F_K	kinetic force (N)
c	sound velocity (m/s)	F_L	force exerted by the flowing liquid (N)
D_b	equivalent spherical diameter of bubble (m)	F_n	net upward force due to fluid pressure (N)
D_f	bubble diameter at the end of the first stage (m)	F_p	pressure force (N)
		F_R	reactive force (N)
D_i	inside diameter of orifice or nozzle (m)	F_S	surface force (N)
		Fr	Froude number (—)
D_o	outside diameter of orifice or nozzle (m)	g	gravitational acceleration (m/s^2)
		Ga	Galilei number (—)

h   liquid height (m)

k_o orifice constant in Equation 65 $(m^{3.5}/kg^{0.5})$

k_1 orifice constant in Equation 56 (—)

k_2 orifice constant in Equation 62 $(m^{3.5}/kg^{0.5})$

k_3 orifice constant in Equation 92 (—)

L   thickness of orifice plate or nozzle length (m)

M   mass of liquid displaced by bubble (kg)

M_o dimensionless physical property of liquid (—)

M'   virtual mass of bubble (kg)

m   mass of the bubble (kg)

N_c, N_c' capacitance number (—)

N_w dimensionless gas flow rate (—)

n   polytropic index (—)

p   pressure in the liquid (Pa)

p_b pressure in bubble (Pa)

p_c pressure in gas chamber (Pa)

p_{GC} pressure due to gas circulation (Pa)

p_h pressure at orifice plate (Pa)

p_{hz} pressure at a liquid height of h_z (Pa)

p_{max} maximum pressure in gas chamber (Pa)

p_{min} minimum pressure in gas chamber (Pa)

p_N pressure at the orifice or nozzle with liquid motion (Pa)

p_{OR} liquid pressure behind the bubble at orifice (Pa)

p_s average pressure on the bubble surface (Pa)

p_w pressure in the wake of a rising bubble (Pa)

p_0 atmospheric pressure (Pa)

p_σ surface tension pressure (Pa)

Q_g average gas flow rate (m^3/s)

Q_i inflowing rate of gas into gas chamber (m^3/s)

Q_o outflowing rate of gas from gas chamber (m^3/s)

q   liquid velocity defined by Equation 48 (m/s)

R   equivalent spherical radius of bubble (m)

R_f bubble radius at the first stage (m)

R_i inside radius of orifice or nozzle (m)

R_0, R_1, R_2 radius of curvature of bubble (m)

Re   Reynolds number (—)

r   Eulerian radial coordinate

r_0 Lagrangian radial coordinate

$\bar{r}$ dimensionless coordinate

r_w distance between bubbles (m)

s   distance between bubble center and orifice plate (m)

T   gas temperature (K)

T_B bubble temperature (K)

t   bubbling time (s)

t_s bubbling time in second stage (s)

U_1 liquid velocity at orifice (m/s)

u_o gas superficial velocity through orifice (m/s)

V_b bubble volume (m^3)

$\bar{V}_b$ dimensionless bubble volume (—)

V_b^* dimensionless bubble volume in Equation 156 (—)

V_c gas chamber volume (m^3)

V_f bubble volume at the end of the first stage (m^3)

V_0 initial bubble volume (m^3)

v   velocity of bubble (m/s)

v_f velocity of bubble at the first stage (m/s)

v'   velocity of bubble at the second stage (m/s)

v_B bubble base velocity (m/s)

v_E bubble expansion velocity (m/s)

v_R relative velocity of bubble (m/s)

z   Eulerian axial coordinate

z_0 Lagrangian axial coordinate

$\bar{z}$ dimensionless coordinate

Greek Symbols

α parameter in Equation 69

α' parameter in Equation 163

α^* parameter in Equation 173

β dimensionless parameter defined by Equation 17

γ specific heat ratio (—)

δ free area of the orifice plate (—)

ε correction factor in Equation 165

θ angle shown in Figure 6 (rad)

θ_c contact angle in Figure 1 (rad)

θ' angle in Figure 20 (rad)

κ constant in Equation 166

μ viscosity (Pa·s)

ρ density (kg/m^3)

$\Delta\rho$ density difference (kg/m^3)

σ surface tension (N/m)

ϕ velocity potential (m^2/s)

ϕ_{GC} velocity potential for the gas circulation (m^2/s)

ϕ_L velocity potential for the flowing liquid (m^2/s)

ϕ_P velocity potential for expanding bubble (m^2/s)

ϕ_T velocity potential for translating bubble (m^2/s)

χ virtual mass coefficient in Equation 82 (—)

ω angle between the orifice plate and the horizontal (rad)

Subscripts

b   bubble

c   gas chamber

d   detachment

f   first stage

g   gas

i   inner or inflowing

l   liquid

o   outer, orifice or outflowing

s   second stage

w   wake

REFERENCES

1. Siemes, W., *Chem. Ing. Techn.*, 26:479 (1954).
2. Jackson, R., *Chem. Eng.*, CE107 (1964).
3. Kumar, R., and Kuloor, N. R., *Advances in Chemical Engineering*, Vol. 8, Academic Press Inc. (1970).
4. Clift, R., Grace, J. R., and Weber, M. E., *Bubbles, Drops, and Particles*, Academic Press Inc. (1978).
5. Hughes, R. R., et al. *Chem. Eng. Progr.*, 51:557 (1955).
6. Tadaki, T., and Maeda, S., *Kagaku Kogaku*, 27:147 (1963).
7. Takahashi. T., and Miyahara, T., *Kagaku Kogaku Ronbunshu*, 2:138 (1976).
8. Maier, C. G., U.S. Bur. Mines Bull., 260 (1927).
9. Hartland, S., and Hartley, R. W., *Axisymmetric Fluid-Fluid Interfaces*, Elsevier, Amsterdam (1976).
10. Chesters, A. K., *J. Fluid Mech.*, 81:609 (1977).
11. Davidson, J. F., and Schüler, B. O. G., *Trans. Instn. Chem. Engrs.*, 38:144 (1960).
12. Davidson, J. F., and Schüler, B. O. G., *Trans. Instn. Chem. Engrs.*, 38:335 (1960).
13. Milne-Thomson, L. N., *Theoretical Hydrodynamics*, 3rd. Ed., Macmillan and Co., Ltd., London (1955).
14. Hayes, W. B., Hardy, B. W., and Holland, C. D., *AIChE J.*, 5:319 (1959).
15. Ramakrishnan, S., Kumar, R., and Kuloor, N. R., *Chem. Eng. Sci.*, 24:731 (1969).
16. Ruff, K., *Chem. Ing. Techn.*, 44:1360 (1972).
17. Satyanarayan, A., Kumar, R., and Kuloor, N. R., *Chem. Eng. Sci.*, 24:749 (1969).
18. Park, Y., Tyler, A. L., and Nevers, N., de., *Chem. Eng. Sci.*, 32:907 (1977).
19. Swope, R. D., *Can. J. Chem. Eng.*, 49:169 (1971).
20. Khurana, A. K., and Kumar, R., *Chem. Eng. Sci.*, 24:1711 (1969).
21. Takahashi, T., and Miyahara, T., *Kagaku Kogaku Ronbunshu*, 5:453 (1979).
22. Kupferberg, A., and Jameson, G. J., *Trans. Instn. Chem. Engrs.*, 47:241 (1969).
23. Lamb, H., "Hydrodynamics" 6th Ed., The University Press, Cambridge (1932).
24. McCann, D. J., and Prince, R. G. H., *Chem. Eng. Sci.*, 24:801 (1969).
25. Tsuge, H., and Hibino, S., *J. Chem. Eng. Japan*, 11:173 (1978).
26. Tsuge, H., and Hibino, S., *Chem. Eng. Commun.*, 22:63 (1983).
27. Tadaki, T., and Maeda, S., *Kagaku Kogaku*, 25:254 (1961).
28. Kubota, M., Akehata, T., and Shirai, T., *Kagaku Kogaku*, 31:1074 (1967).
29. Marmur, A., and Rubin, E., *Chem. Eng. Sci.*, 31:453 (1976).

30. Pinczewski, W. V., *Chem. Eng. Sci.*, 36:405 (1981).
31. Scriven, L.E., *Chem. Eng. Sci.*, 10:1 (1959).
32. Miyahara, T., Haga, N., and Takahashi, T., *Kagaku Kogaku Ronbunshu*, 8:18 (1982).
33. Räbiger, N., and Vogelpohl, A., *Ger. Chem. Eng.*, 5:314 (1982).
34. Räbiger, N., and Vogelpohl, A., *Ger. Chem. Eng.*, 6:173 (1983).
35. Wraith, A. E., *Chem. Eng. Sci.*, 26:1659 (1971).
36. Walters, J. K., and Davidson, J. F., *J. Fluid Mech.*, 17:321 (1963).
37. Wraith, A. E., and Kakutani, T., *Chem. Eng. Sci.*, 29:1 (1974).
38. Chaung, S. C., and Goldschmidt, V. M., *Trans. of ASME, J. Basic Eng.*, 705 (1970).
39. Sada, E., et al., *Can. J. Chem. Eng.*, 56:669 (1978).
40. Takahashi, T., et al., *Kagaku Kogaku Ronbunshu*, 6:563 (1980).
41. Morgenstern, I. B., and Mersmann, A., *Ger. Chem. Eng.*, 5:374 (1982).
42. Kawase, Y., and Ulbrecht, J. J., *Ind. Eng. Chem. Process Des. Dev.*, 20:636 (1981).
43. Tsuge, H., Nojima, S., and Hibino, S., *Kagaku Kogaku Ronbunshu*, 6:136 (1980).
44. Potter, O. E., *Chem. Eng. Sci.*, 24:1733 (1969).
45. LaNauze, R. D., and Harris, I. J., *Chem. Eng. Sci.*, 27:2102 (1972).
46. Tsuge, H., and Hibino, S., *Kagaku Kogaku Ronbunshu*, 5:361 (1979).
47. Kling, G., *Int. J. Heat Mass Transfer*, 5:211 (1962).
48. LaNauze, R. D., and Harris, I. J., *Trans. Instn. Chem. Engrs.*, 52:337 (1974).
49. Tsuge, H., Tanaka, Y., and Hibino, S., *Can. J. Chem. Eng.*, 59:569 (1981).
50. Takahashi, T., Miyahara, T., and Komoto, I., *Kagaku Kogaku Ronbunshu*, 2:602 (1976).
51. Sano, M., and Mori, K., *Tetsu to Hagane*, 60:348 (1974).
52. Bhavaraju, S. M., Russell, T. W. F., and Blanch, H. W., *AIChE J.*, 24:456 (1978).
53. Calderbank, P. H., *Trans. Instn. Chem. Engrs.*, 34:79 (1956).
54. Leibson, I., et al., *AIChE J.*, 2:296 (1956).
55. Stölting, M., *Chem. Ing. Techn.*, 52:598 (1980).
56. Davidson, L., and Amick, E. H., *AIChE J*, 2:337 (1956).
57. Mersmann, A., *Forschungsheft V. D. I.*, 491:1 (1962).
58. Brauer, H., *Grundlagen der Einphasen- und Mehrphasenströmung*, Sauerlander, Aaran-Frankfurt/M (1971).
59. Sullivan, S. L., Hardy, B. W., and Holland, C. D., *AIChE J.*, 10:848 (1964).

CHAPTER 10

MECHANISMS OF BREAKUP OF ROUND LIQUID JETS

R. D. Reitz

Fluid Mechanics Department
General Motors Research Laboratories
Warren, Michigan, USA

and

F. V. Bracco

Mechanical and Aerospace Engineering Department
Princeton University
Princeton, New Jersey, USA

CONTENTS

INTRODUCTION

The mechanisms of jet breakup discussed here result from the steady injection of a liquid through a single-hole nozzle into a quiescent gas. The complexity of the breakup process is due to the unusually large number of parameters which influence it, including the details of the design of the nozzle, the jet's velocity and turbulence, and the physical and thermodynamic states of both liquid and gas. In this work we discuss a framework by means of which some of the underlying mechanisms of breakup can be organized and, eventually, be better understood.

The approach followed is to divide the jet breakup phenomena of interest into various breakup regimes. These regimes reflect differences in the appearance of the jet as the operating conditions are changed. We then attempt to relate these regimes to limiting cases of a stability analysis of liquid jets. The analysis considers the growth of initial perturbations of the liquid surface and includes the effects of liquid inertia, surface tension, viscous and aerodynamic forces on the jet. The theory is found to offer a reasonably complete description of the breakup mechanisms of low speed jets. For high-speed liquid jets however, the initial state of the jet appears to be progressively more important and less understood. We will summarize the results of recent research aimed at closing this gap.

It should be pointed out that we consider only fluid-dynamic instabilities and that there are other causes of breakup such as superheating [1], electrostatic charge [2], acoustical excitation [3], and chemical reactions. Even in the field of fluid-dynamic instabilities there are difficulties: many parameters influence the outcome; the magnitude of these parameters vary over broad ranges; there are no generally accepted theories, regimes, or even terminology. Thus even comparisons of results and statements of various authors are complicated. But when conditions are properly identified and nomenclature difficulties are overcome, the framework to be presented in this work is found to be compatible with much of the published work.

The Jet Breakup Regimes

If all other parameters are kept constant, the jet velocity becomes a convenient quantity to introduce various regimes.

Grant and Middleman [4] reviewed the behavior of low-speed jets and reported the results in the form of a breakup curve (Figure 1) which describes the unbroken length of the jet, L_1, as a function of the jet velocity, U. Once a jet is formed (point C, Figure 1) the jet breakup length at first increases linearly with increasing jet velocity. Thereafter it reaches a maximum (point E) and then decreases. These first two breakup regimes are reasonably well understood, as will be seen later, and here are called the Rayleigh (CD) and first wind-induced breakup (EF) regimes. A feature of breakup in these two regimes is that drops are pinched off from the end of the jet and their sizes are comparable to that of the jet (see also Figures 5A and 5B).

For higher velocity jets beyond the point F there still remains some confusion over the true shape of the breakup curve. Haenlein [5] reported that the breakup length remains constant or decreases slightly with increasing velocity (curve FG, Figure 1) and then it abruptly reduces to near zero beyond point G. This suggests the existence of at least two more breakup regimes, each causing new features in the breakup curve. However, McCarthy and Malloy [6] and Grant and Middleman [4] report that the breakup length initially increases (curve FH).

It should be noted that the definition and measurement of the intact length becomes increasingly difficult as U is increased, as pointed out also by Grant and Middleman [4]. At sufficiently high velocities, the jet surface is disrupted prior to the breakup of the jet core and the use of only one breakup length is no longer a complete measure of the jet stability. Thus we distinguish between the intact-surface length, L_1, and the intact-core length, L_2. In the Rayleigh and first wind-induced regimes the jet breaks up simultaneously over the entire cross-section and the two lengths coincide.

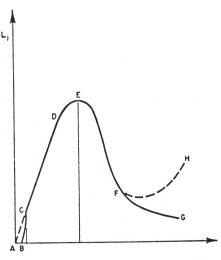

Figure 1. Jet surface breakup length L_1 as a function of jet velocity: ABC—drip flow; CD—Rayleight breakup regime; EF-first wind-induced breakup regime; FG (FH)—second wind-induced breakup regime; beyond G (H)—atomization regime.

In the second wind-induced and atomization regimes which will be described next, the disruption starts at the jet surface and eventually reaches the jet axis so that at least two lengths are necessary to identify the gross features of the breakup.

We call the atomization regime that regime in which the intact-surface length is zero (but the intact-core length is not necessarily zero) so that L_1 versus U follows the trend suggested by Haenlein [5], viz. the breakup length goes to zero beyond the point G (H) in Figure 1. Here the jet surface appears to break up immediately at the nozzle exit and drops are formed that are much smaller than the nozzle diameter (see Figure 5D described later). Although we find this definition of the atomization regime unequivocal and useful, we must point out that the term atomization has also been used by other authors in a variety of different contexts. This regime is of interest in many fuel-injection applications.

For breakup in the second wind-induced regime (curve FG or FH, Figure 1), both the intact-surface length and the intact-core length are finite and drops are formed with sizes also much smaller than the nozzle diameter (see Figure 5C described later).

To introduce the four regimes, we have used the injection velocity as a parameter and have kept all other parameters constant. Actually dimensionless numbers separate the various regimes as will be discussed in the following sections. Indeed the high-velocity jets in jet cutting applications, for example, exhibit long intact-surface lengths even though they are faster than atomizing fuel jets, but the two families of jets differ in nozzle design, gas density, surface tension, and liquid viscosity.

Attempts have been made by various authors to offer criteria with which to demarcate breakup regimes. For example, Miesse [7] correlated breakup regime data and presented the results in a form suggested by Ohnesorge [8] as shown in Figure 2. The boundaries of the regimes are represented by oblique straight lines on a graph of ln Z (a function of the physical properties of the liquid and the nozzle diameter alone) versus ln Re_1. Unfortunately, this method of correlation does not include the effect of the initial state of the jet (that is influenced, for example, by the nozzle design) nor the effect of the ambient gas density (pressure), which according to Torda [9] modifies the graph as shown by the dashed lines. These modified boundary curves show, for example, that atomization can be achieved at lower injection velocities by injecting into a compressed gas.

The effect of ambient gas density on jet breakup regimes was discussed by Ranz [10] who argued that the Weber number We_2 should be a controlling parameter. He offered the criterion $We_2 > 13$

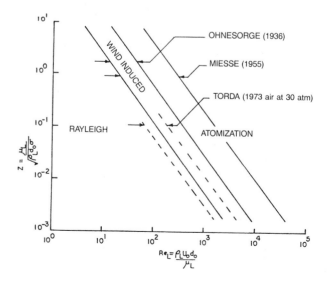

Figure 2. Jet breakup regime boundaries of Miesse [7], Ohnesorge [8], and Torda [9].

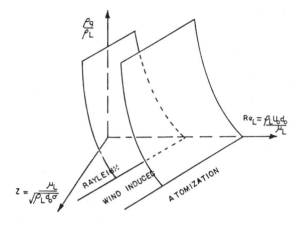

Figure 3. Schematic chart of influence of gas density on breakup regime boundaries [11].

for the onset of atomization. However, it should be noted again that his definition of the term atomization differs from ours—he does not refer to the state of the jet itself but instead refers to the process of disintegration of already-formed droplets during their flight within a spray. He argued that the criteria for the formation and the subsequent further breakup of the droplets should be the same since when the inertial stresses developed by the surrounding gas exceed the surface tension stresses opposing the deformation sufficiently, the liquid drop (or ligament in the formation process) will subdivide into smaller units. But a Weber number correlation by itself is still incomplete since now the liquid viscosity is not accounted for.

This latter objection can be removed (at least conceptually) by combining Figure 2 with a gas density parameter as is shown qualitatively in Figure 3, taken from Reitz [11]. Still, different sets of surfaces should be given in Figure 3 to account for the effects of different initial states of the jet. Thus completely satisfactory correlations for the regime boundaries are not yet available. Indeed many authors do not even distinguish between the two wind-induced regimes as can be seen in Figure 2. Finally, as previously stated, we feel that part of the difficulty in interpreting published results is due to a lack of agreed upon terminology in the field, and insufficient characterization of the injection system and the nozzle geometry.

LINEAR STABILITY ANALYSIS

We consider a cylindrical liquid jet issuing from a circular orifice into a stationary incompressible gas. The stability of the liquid surface to perturbations is examined using a first-order linear theory which ultimately leads to a dispersion equation (Equation 5). This equation relates the growth rate, ω, of an initial perturbation of infinitesimal amplitude, η_0, to its wavelength λ (wavenumber k = $2\pi/\lambda$). The relationship also includes the physical and dynamical parameters of the liquid jet and the surrounding gas. The present treatment will be seen to unify the results of Levich [12], Stirling and Sleicher [13] and other authors who have treated individual jet breakup regimes.

The column of liquid is assumed to be infinite in the axial direction and a cylindrical polar coordinate system is used which moves with the jet velocity, U. Imposed on the initially steady motion is an infinitesimal axisymmetric surface displacement, one Fourier component of which has the form

$$\eta = \mathcal{R}(\eta_0 e^{ikz + \omega t})$$

The linearized hydrodynamical equations are

$$\frac{\partial u_1}{\partial z} + \frac{1}{r}\frac{\partial}{\partial r}(rv_1) = 0$$

$$\frac{\partial u_1}{\partial t} = -\frac{1}{\rho_1}\frac{\partial p_1}{\partial z} + v_1\left\{\frac{\partial^2 u_1}{\partial z^2} + \frac{1}{r}\frac{\partial}{\partial r}\left(r\frac{\partial u_1}{\partial r}\right)\right\}$$

$$\frac{\partial v_1}{\partial t} = -\frac{1}{\rho_1}\frac{\partial p_1}{\partial r} + v_1\left\{\frac{\partial^2 v_1}{\partial z^2} + \frac{\partial}{\partial r}\left(\frac{1}{r}\frac{\partial}{\partial r}rv_1\right)\right\}$$ (1)

where u_1, v_1, and p_1 are small axisymmetric velocities and pressure. With the assumption that $\eta \ll a$, the kinematic, tangential stress, and normal stress equations are to first order

$$v_1 = \frac{\partial \eta}{\partial t}$$

$$\frac{\partial u_1}{\partial r} = -\frac{\partial v_1}{\partial z}$$ (2)

$$-p_1 + 2\mu_1\frac{\partial v_1}{\partial r} - \frac{\sigma}{a^2}\left(\eta + a^2\frac{\partial^2 \eta}{\partial z^2}\right) + p_2 = 0$$

The inertial effects of the gas enter through the gas pressure p_2. This is found from the linearized inviscid equations of motion for the gas

$$\frac{\partial u_2}{\partial z} + \frac{1}{r}\frac{\partial}{\partial r}(rv_2) = 0$$

$$\frac{\partial u_2}{\partial t} + U(r)\frac{\partial u_2}{\partial z} + \frac{dU}{dr}v_2 = -\frac{1}{\rho_2}\frac{\partial p_2}{\partial z}$$ (3)

$$\frac{\partial v_2}{dt} + U(r)\frac{\partial v_2}{\partial z} = -\frac{1}{\rho_2}\frac{\partial p_2}{\partial r}$$

where the mean gas motion above the liquid surface is given by $U(r)$. The boundary conditions are

$$v_2 = \frac{\partial \eta}{\partial t} + U\frac{\partial \eta}{\partial z} \quad \text{at} \quad r \cong a$$

$$u_2, v_2, P_2 \to 0 \quad \text{as} \quad r \to \infty$$

Equation 1 is solved by introducing a stream function ψ_1, and a velocity potential ϕ_1 and by seeking wave solutions of the form

$$\phi_1 = \Phi_1(r)e^{ikz+\omega t} \quad \text{and} \quad \psi_1 = \Psi_1(r)e^{ikz+\omega t}$$

Solutions free from singularities on the axis $r = 0$ are found to be $\Phi_1 = C_1 I_0(kr)$ and $\Psi_1 = C_2 r I_1(\ell r)$, where C_1 and C_2 are arbitrary constants, and the liquid pressure can then be found from the relation $p_1 = -\rho_1 \partial\phi_1/\partial t$.

For the gas flow, Equation 3 can be simplified by defining a stream function $\psi_2 = (U - i\omega/k)\eta f(r)$. This leads to an Orr-Sommerfeld equation

$$\frac{d^2f}{dr^2} + \left(\frac{2U'r}{U - i\omega/k} - 1\right)\frac{d(f/r)}{dr} - k^2f = 0$$

with $f(r = a) = 1$, and $f(r \to \infty) = 0$. The equation for the gas pressure is

$$P_2 = -\rho_2\eta\left(U - i\frac{\omega}{k}\right)^2\left(\frac{df}{dr} - \frac{f}{r}\right) \tag{4}$$

Here the arbitrary constant of integration has been set equal to zero. If the gas velocity profile $U(r)$ is known, the gas pressure at the jet surface can be determined from Equation 4 for use in Equation 2. For the special case of slip at the gas-liquid interface, $U(r) = U = $ constant, and the gas surface pressure is

$$p_2 = -\rho_2\left(U - i\frac{\omega}{k}\right)^2 k\eta\frac{K_0(ka)}{K_1(ka)}$$

Finally, substituting these relationships into Equation 2 yields

$$\omega^2 + 2\nu_1k^2\omega\left[\frac{I_1'(ka)}{I_0(ka)} - \frac{2k\ell}{k^2 + \ell^2}\frac{I_1(ka)}{I_0(ka)}\frac{I_1'(\ell a)}{I_1(\ell a)}\right]$$

$$= \frac{\sigma k}{\rho_1a^2}(1 - k^2a^2)\left(\frac{\ell^2 - k^2}{\ell^2 + k^2}\right)\frac{I_1(ka)}{I_0(ka)} + \frac{\rho_2}{\rho_1}(U - i\omega/k)^2k^2\left(\frac{\ell^2 - k^2}{\ell^2 + k^2}\right)\frac{I_1(ka)K_0(ka)}{I_0(ka)K_1(ka)} \tag{5a}$$

which is the governing dispersion relationship. Equation 5a may for brevity be written in non-dimensional form as

$$\beta^2 + 2Zk^2a^2F_1\beta = ka(1 - k^2a^2)F_2 + We_2k^2a^2F_3 \tag{5b}$$

where
$$\beta = \omega\sqrt{\rho_1a^3/\sigma}$$
$$Z = \mu_1/\sqrt{\rho_1\sigma d}$$
$$We_2 = \rho_2U^2d/\sigma$$

and the F's are dimensionless ratios of Bessel functions and wavenumbers.

BREAKUP REGIMES AND THE DISPERSION EQUATION

In this section we attempt to relate the mechanisms of breakup in the four jet breakup regimes to limiting cases of the linear stability analysis of the previous section. This theory offers a unified approach for the organization of the jet breakup phenomena but is not complete mostly because it does not account explicitly for different initial states of the jet.

Rayleigh Breakup Regime

Rayleigh [14] made substantial contributions to the understanding of the stability of low-speed jets. He obtained a dispersion equation for the growth of axisymmetric surface disturbances by equating the potential and kinetic energies of an inviscid jet. With the hypothesis that that disturbance with the maximum growth rate would lead to the destruction of the jet, he also obtained an

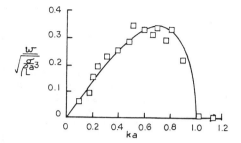

Figure 4. Wave growth rate with wave number for jets in Rayleigh breakup regime: line—theory Equation 6; Symbols—measured wave growth rates of Donnely and Glaberson [15].

expression for the droplet size, assuming that it would be of the order of the wavelength of this disturbance.

For the special case $Z = 0$ and $We_2 = 0$ (inviscid liquid jet at low velocity) the dispersion Equation 5a (cf. also Equation 5b) becomes

$$\omega^2 = \frac{\sigma k}{\rho_1 a^2}(1 - k^2 a^2)\frac{I_1\{ka\}}{I_0\{ka\}} \tag{6}$$

which is the same as Rayleigh's result. This equation predicts that the jet surface is unstable for all wavenumbers with $ka < 1$ and the corresponding wavegrowth curve is given in Figure 4.

This wavegrowth curve can be found experimentally by vibrating low speed jets at various frequencies and by measuring the growth rate of the axisymmetric surface oscillations. The corresponding measurements of Donnely and Glaberson [15] given in Figure 4 show excellent agreement with the first-order theory. Differentiating Equation 6 shows that the maximum growth rate is

$$\omega_m \cong 0.34\left(\frac{\sigma}{\rho_1 a^3}\right)^{1/2} \quad \text{at} \quad k \cong 2\pi/9.02a$$

and if the initial disturbance η_0 of the most unstable wave grows exponentially to a magnitude "a" in time T, it follows that the breakup length of the jet (the position of the point of droplet formation) then on average will be

$$L_1 = UT = U\ln(a/\eta_0)/\omega_m \tag{7}$$

This linear dependence of L_1 on U was seen in Figure 1 for low-velocity jets in the Rayleigh breakup regime.

The parameter $\ln(a/\eta_0)$ has been determined experimentally. It lies in the range 11–16 [16], but it has been found to be weakly related to the Ohnesorge number Z [17]. The theoretical influence of the liquid viscosity is found by retaining the term involving Z in Equation 5b. For large Z (high liquid viscosity) the maximum wavegrowth rate is

$$\omega_m = \frac{1}{2\sqrt{2}}\left(\frac{\sigma}{\rho_1 a^3}\right)^{1/2}\frac{1}{1+3Z} \quad \text{at} \quad k = \frac{1}{a\sqrt{(Z+2)}}$$

where ka has been assumed to be small and the Bessel functions and their arguments have been replaced by their asymptotic values. This relationship was first obtained by Weber [18]. His analysis showed that the effect of the increased liquid viscosity is to move the most unstable wave to longer wavelengths without altering the value of the stability boundary, ka = 1. The jet breakup agency remains the destabilizing combination of surface tension and inertia forces on the jet.

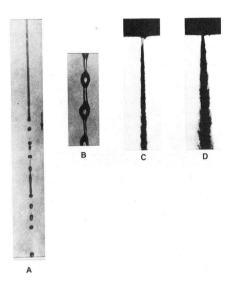

Figure 5. Examples of jets in the four break-up regimes [11, 19]. (A) Jet breakup in the Rayleigh regime. Droplet sizes of the order of the jet diameter and breakup occurs many nozzle diameters downstream of the nozzle. (B) Jet breakup in the first wind-induced regime. Droplet sizes are still of the order of the jet diameter and breakup occurs many nozzle diameters downstream of the nozzle. (C) Jet breakup in the second wind-induced regime. Droplet sizes much smaller than the jet diameter and the breakup starts some distance downstream of the nozzle. (D) Jet breakup in the atomization regime. Droplet sizes much smaller than the jet diameter and the breakup starts at the nozzle exit.

The preceding analysis predicts that the jet breakup yields droplets many nozzle diameters downstream of the nozzle. The drop diameters are larger than that of the jet and a photograph typical of jet breakup in this regime is shown in Figure 5A, taken from Lee and Spencer [19].

To estimate the droplet size, Rayleigh assumed that all of the liquid enclosed within the wave forms the volume of the newly created drop when the surface wave amplitude equals the jet radius. However, as pointed out by Wang [20] when the wave amplitude becomes comparable to the jet radius, the surface deformation is observed to be nonsinusoidal due to nonlinear effects. Also, mass is only conserved to first-order in the first-order stability analysis. Yuen [21] and Nayfey [22] retained higher order terms in their jet stability analysis and Rutland and Jameson [23] demonstrated that this improved theory also predicts the existence of satellite droplets formed between the primary drops. Interestingly, LaFrance [24] showed that the drop sizes are not influenced by the magnitude of the initial disturbances to the jet.

First Wind-Induced Breakup Regime

The second term on the right-hand side of Equation 5 becomes important when the jet velocity (for example) is increased. In this case the inertial effects of the surrounding gas can no longer be neglected and the Weber number We_2 becomes a controlling parameter in the dispersion equation. Weber [18] showed that the effect of the environment on the jet is to enhance the growth rate of disturbances, leading to earlier breakup of the jet. He obtained the result

$$\omega^2 + 3v_1 k^2 \omega = \frac{\sigma}{2\rho_1 a^3}(1 - k^2 a^2)k^2 a^2 + \frac{\rho_2}{\rho_1}\frac{U^2 k^3 a^3}{2a^2}\frac{K_0(ka)}{K_1(ka)} \tag{8}$$

which can also be found from Equation 5 in the limit $ka < 1$. Computations of the maximum wave-growth rate now show that the jet breakup length equation, Equation 7, becomes a nonlinear formula which must be solved numerically. It indeed predicts that the breakup length L_1 decreases with increasing jet velocity (Figure 1, curve EF). However the predicted value of the maximum in the breakup curve Figure 1, point E) fails to agree with experimental results, since Weber's theory is found to overestimate the aerodynamic effect of the gas. This has led many investigators to attempt modifications to Equation 8.

Fenn and Middleman [25] argued that the viscosity of the gas should also be considered in a more complete analysis. The effect of the gas viscosity enters through the normal and tangential stress boundary conditions Equation 2 and was neglected by Weber (also in the linear stability analysis described earlier). The inviscid gas approximation implies slip at the gas liquid interface.

Benjamin [26] showed that if the gas boundary layer is thin compared to the surface wave wavelength (high gas Reynolds numbers) then the energy transmitted between the gas and the liquid by normal stresses (aerodynamic effect) is large compared to that transmitted by shear stresses (viscous effect), and their ratio is independent of the Reynolds number. However, for finite Reynolds numbers the magnitude of the fluctuating pressure component p_2 which is in phase with the wave elevation (the part responsible for energy transfer) becomes reduced. Based on these results, Sterling and Sleicher [13] introduced an attenuation coefficient C, multiplying p_2 with $C = 1 - h(ka, Re_2)$. The function, h, increases as k increases and decreases to zero as the Reynolds number becomes large. They found that C could be replaced by a constant, noticing that the wavenumber and the Reynolds number move in opposite directions as the aerodynamic effects increase.

This modification of Weber's theory with $C = 0.175$ multiplying the second term on the right-hand side of Equation 5 agrees well with experimental results. The numerical results of Sterling and Sleicher [13] then show that the point E in Figure 1 is reached when $We_2 = 1.2 + 3.41Z^{0.9}$. In this regime the jet breakup still occurs many nozzle diameters downstream of the nozzle and produces droplets whose diameters are still comparable to that of the jet as was seen in Figure 5A for jets in the Rayleigh breakup regime (see Figure 5B). The breakup is still due to the destabilizing influence of surface tension, but it is now augmented by the aerodynamic interaction between the liquid and gas.

Sterling and Sleicher [13] also pointed out that relaxation of the jet's exit velocity profile to a uniform flow beyond the nozzle can influence the jet breakup process. In their analysis (which was quoted above) they considered the case where l_r/L is small (l_r is the jet profile relaxation length). For large l_r/L they suggest that jet instability could be enhanced by velocity profile rearrangement effects, but they offered no details of the mechanism by which this would occur. The profile relaxation phenomenon was also alluded to by Grant and Middleman [4] who found a dependence of L_1 on the nozzle passage length. In particular, nozzles of short length produced more stable jets than those produced from long tubes. They argued that this implies a coupling between the velocity profile and the mechanism of instability in this breakup regime. Parenthetically, their experiments also showed that the breakup length in the Rayleigh regime is not influenced by nozzle design details.

Another example of the influence of the initial state of the jet is discussed by Phinney [27] who proposed that liquid turbulence also enhances the jet breakup process. He reasoned that the effect of the jet turbulence is to increase the initial disturbance level η_0. He noted that, even in the absence of aerodynamic effects, the jet breakup length L_1 is reduced once a critical value of the jet Reynolds number is reached. Furthermore, this critical Reynolds number is of the same order as that for transition to turbulence in the nozzle. However the influence of jet turbulence on the magnitude of the initial disturbance level is still quantitatively unclear.

Second Wind-Induced Breakup Regime

With further increases in We_2, Equation 8 predicts that the maximum wavegrowth rate occurs at progressively larger wavenumbers (shorter wavelengths). An inspection of Equation 8 (or Equation 5), shows that the first term on the right-hand side changes sign at $ka = 1$, after which the surface tension forces oppose the breakup process. Jet breakup is now due to the unstable growth of short wavelength surface waves ($ka > 1$) which are induced by the relative motion between the jet and the ambient gas. An analysis of Equation 8 shows that the maximum wavegrowth rate occurs at $ka = 1$ when $We_2 \cong 12$ for inviscid jets. This estimate was made using the numerical results of Sterling and Sleicher [13]. The estimate also agrees well with the experimentally obtained criterion of Ranz [10], $We_2 = 13$, for the onset of short wavelength waves.

An expression for the growth rate of short wavelength surface waves was presented by Levich [12] and Levich and Krylov [28], who examined Equation 5 in the limit $ka \gg 1$ and deduced, neglecting the liquid viscosity, that

$$\omega^2 = (\rho_2 k^2 U^2 - \sigma k^3)/\rho_1 \tag{9}$$

This result implies the existence of unstable surface waves when $k < \rho_2 U^2/\sigma$. The maximum growth rate is given by

$$\omega_m \cong 0.4 \frac{U^3}{\sigma} \left(\frac{\rho_2^3}{\rho_1}\right)^{1/2}$$

Equation 9 shows that the dispersion relation Equation 5 becomes independent of the jet radius in this limit. Consequently, for $ka \gg 1$ jet curvature effects are unimportant. Similarly, the Weber number We_2 can no longer appear as a controlling parameter.

The influence of the liquid viscosity is seen by retaining the second term on the left-hand side of Equation 5. In the limit $ka \to \infty$ this reduces to

$$(\omega + 2v_1 k^2)^2 + \sigma k^3/\rho_1 - 4v_1^2 k^3 \sqrt{(k^2 + \omega/v_1)} + (\omega + iUk)^2 \rho_2/\rho_1 = 0$$

This result is identical to that of Taylor [29] who performed an analysis of the unstable growth of two-dimensional planar surface waves due to the relative motion between a liquid and a gas. He considered the limit $ka \gg 1$ and, assuming $\rho_2 \ll \rho_1$ he found that the wavegrowth rate is

$$\omega/kU = 2\left(\frac{\rho_1}{\rho_2}\right)^{1/2} xg(\Gamma, x)$$

The function g is a correction to the result of Levich [12] which now accounts for the effect of the liquid viscosity. It is shown as a function of the new parameter

$$\Gamma = \frac{\rho_1}{\rho_2} \frac{\sigma^2}{\mu_1^2 U^2} = \frac{\rho_1}{\rho_2} \left\{\frac{Re_1}{We_1}\right\}^2$$

and the nondimensional wavelength $x = \rho_2 U^2/\sigma k$ from Taylor's work in Figure 6. The figure shows that the disturbance growth rate increases with increasing Γ, and that the maximum growth rate occurs at larger wavenumbers (shorter wavelengths) as Γ increases.

Taylor [29] also estimated the intact-core length, L_2, by computing the rate at which droplets remove mass from the liquid core. Here the droplet sizes were assumed to be proportional to the unstable surface wave wavelengths. This analysis gives (see also Reitz and Bracco [30])

$$L_2 = B_1 a \left(\frac{\rho_1}{\rho_2}\right)^{1/2} \Big/ f(\Gamma) \tag{10a}$$

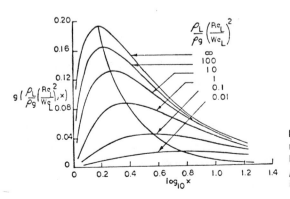

Figure 6. Theoretical wave growth rate as a function of dimensionless wave length parameter, $x = \rho_2 U^2/\sigma k$ for jets in the second wind-induced breakup regime [29].

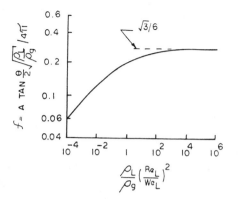

Figure 7. Dependence of the maximum growth rates in Figure 6 on Taylor's parameter $\Gamma = (\rho_1/\rho_2) \{Re_1/We_1\}^2$.

where B_1 is a constant of order unity. The function $f(\Gamma)$ corresponds to the maximum wavegrowth rates of Figure 6, and it is shown in Figure 7. The intact-surface length L_1 can be estimated using similar arguments to those which led to the development of Equation 7 (where the jet radius "a" is replaced by some characteristic wave height at breakup, say). In this case we find that

$$L_1 = B_2 L_2/We_2 \qquad (10b)$$

where B_2 is another constant which would be dependent weakly (logarithmically) on drop size.

Equation 10a predicts that the intact-core breakup length L_2 remains constant with increasing jet velocity until the parameter Γ becomes small (i.e., for high velocity jets). L_2 then decreases with increasing jet velocity. The intact-surface length L_1 from Equation 10b is predicted to decrease as the inverse square of the velocity and then to decrease even faster when Γ becomes small. This prediction is not inconsistent with the form of breakup curve of Haelein [5] for jets in the second wind-induced regime and, possibly, even in the atomization regime once L_1 becomes of the order of the wavelength of the surface waves. A photograph typical of jet breakup in this regime is shown in Figure 5C from Reitz [11]. The photograph shows that the jet breakup starts some distance downstream of the nozzle exit and yields droplets whose average diameters are much less than the jet diameter. Droplet formation results from the unstable growth of short wavelength surface waves on the jet. This wavegrowth is caused by the relative motion between the jet and the ambient gas, and surface tension forces oppose the wavegrowth process.

Atomization Regime

In this regime the breakup appears to commence at the nozzle exit (see Figure 5D). The spray takes the form of a cone with its vertex within the nozzle. Various authors have suggested possible jet breakup agencies for jets in the atomization regime, and some of these are considered below, but a complete and tested theory is not yet available.

Experiments were made to study atomization in Reitz and Bracco [31, 32] and Wu et al. [1, 33]. The range of conditions of these studies has been extensive and includes the operating conditions of fuel injection systems in diesel and stratified charge internal combustion engines. The experiments were made under steady conditions with injections into a semi-infinite gas. The test conditions include constant liquid injection pressures in the ranges 3.4–17.0 MPa [31] and 10.8–90.5 MPa [33]; constant gas pressures in the range 0.1 – 4.1 MPa with air, nitrogen, helium, and xenon (different molecular weights to isolate effects of gas density and pressure [31]); water and water + glycerol injections (10^3 range in liquid viscosity [31]); hexane, water, and tetradecane (factor of 10 in viscosity, 4 in surface tension, 1.5 in liquid density [33]); pentane, hexane, and ethanol (factor of 3 surface tension, 1.5 liquid density [1]); 21 nozzles—sharp edge inlet tube nozzles (length-to-diameter ratio range 0.5–85.0 (diameter 0.35 mm), rounded inlet [31] and rounded exit nozzles, and cavitation-free nozzles; and a factor of 2.5 in nozzle exit diameter [33, 1]; liquid temperature—room temperature [31, 33], 100–200°C [1]. Certain trends were found from photographs of jet breakup in the experiments. For example, the spray angle (divergence angle of the jet) was found to increase with increasing (isothermal) gas compression. Moreover, it was established that this is due to increases in the gas density, not pressure [31]. The spray angle was also found to increase with decreasing liquid viscosity.

Another trend concerns the boundary between the atomization and the second wind-induced regimes. It was found that the breakup starts progressively closer to the nozzle exit as the gas density is increased, until it reaches the exit with no evidence of an abrupt change. This trend is also shown in Figure 8 in which the measured spray angle is plotted against the gas–liquid density ratio for sharp edge inlet nozzles with a length-to-diameter ratio of 4.0. The solid data points are in the second wind-induced regime—jets intact before diverging. The open points show atomizing jets—divergence begins at the nozzle exit. It was also found that atomization is reached once the liquid viscosity is decreased below a certain level, again with no abrupt change in the appearance of the jet.

Other results were: The spray angle decreases with increased nozzle passage length for nozzle-length-to-diameter ratios greater than 10 or 20. (For shorter nozzles there is more scatter in the results, and the trends are not yet fully established [33]). For the same length, rounded inlet nozzles produce less divergent jets than sharp edge inlet nozzles. Atomization commences at different gas density and liquid viscosity levels as the nozzle design is changed.

With these results it is possible to examine previously proposed theories for atomization in detail. For example, DeJuhasz [34] and Schweitzer [35] proposed that liquid turbulence causes atomization. But if pipe turbulence were the *only* mechanism, turbulent jets (from the nozzles with large length-to-diameter ratios [36]) would have been the most unstable flows—contrary to the experiments. Similarly, cavitation phenomena were proposed Bergwerk [37] to lead to atomization. But jets were found to atomize even when the cavitation-free nozzles of Wu et al. [33] were used.

In fact, an evaluation of other proposed atomization mechanisms has revealed that none of the theories take *alone*, is able to explain the results fully [31]. These theories include proposals that atomization is caused by: aerodynamic surface wavegrowth [38, 39]—the results would be independent of the nozzle geometry; rearrangement of the jet's velocity profile [40]—the high viscosity jets would be the most unstable; liquid supply pressure oscillations [41]—atomization would not have occurred since the pressure was constant in the experiments; and wall boundary-layer velocity profile relaxation [42]—atomization would have been independent of the gas density; all of these contrary to the experiments.

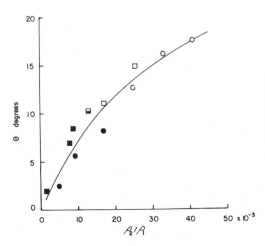

Figure 8. Measured spray angle versus gas-liquid density ratio for nozzle-length-to-diameter ratio of 4 [11, 33]. Nozzle diameter—0.34 mm. Nozzle $\Delta P = 10.0$–14.0 mPa. Liquid—water. Gas—nitrogen. Solid symbols—jets intact before diverging (second wind-induced regime). Open symbols—jet divergence starts at the nozzle exit (atomization regime). Partially solid symbols—marginal breakup at the nozzle exit. Line—aerodynamic theory prediction Equation 11 with $A = 4.0$.

However, the aerodynamic surface wavegrowth theory was found to predict many of the trends in tests with a given nozzle. Thus it is useful to consider its predictions in more detail. In this case, the appropriate limit of the dispersion Equation 5 is ka → ∞, as in the foregoing second wind-induced regime. Ranz [43] argued that the spreading angle of the atomizing jet could be predicted by combining the radial velocity of the fastest growing of the unstable surface waves with the axial injection velocity:

$$\tan(\theta/2) = \frac{v}{U} = \frac{2\pi\omega}{AkU} m = 4\pi(\rho_2/\rho_1)^{1/2}f(\Gamma)/A \tag{11}$$

where the proportionality constant A is obtained from experiment.

In Equation 11 the spray angle increases with increasing gas density and decreases with increasing liquid viscosity and increasing velocity. This is consistent with tests with a given nozzle. Notice also from Figure 7 that for $\Gamma > 1$ the function $f(\Gamma)$ becomes asymptotically equal to $\sqrt{3}/6$. Equation 11 then predicts that the spray angle depends only on the gas-liquid density ratio—which is surprising considering the many parameters that could effect it. This behavior is also generally borne out by the measurements with a given nozzle.

Ranz [43] determined that A ≃ 18 or 20, but he pointed out that the data of Schweitzer [44] give A ≃ 3. Results given in Reitz and Bracco [31] indicate that the predicted variation of the spray angle with gas density is followed if A has a different value for each different nozzle. Also other results show that agreement is found with respect to liquid viscosity variations by using (for each nozzle) the same value of A as that obtained from the gas density best fit. Figure 9 shows spray angle measurements and the predictions of Equation 11 with respect to gas density and jet velocity

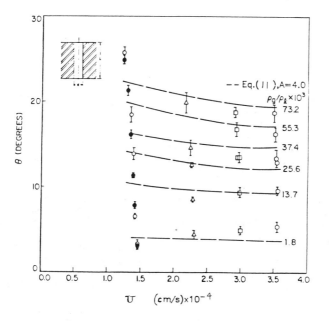

Figure 9. Measured spray angle versus liquid jet velocity for different gas-liquid density ratios [33]. Liquid—n-hexane. Gas—nitrogen. Straight tube nozzle-length-to-diameter ratio—4. Open symbols—data at ΔP = 15.3, 38.0, 64.9, and 91.8 mPa (U = 1.5, 2.3, 3.0, and 3.6 × 10⁴ cm/s, respectively). Closed symbols—repeated measurements at ΔP = 15.3 mPa made after the high injection pressure (ΔP = 91.8 mPa) runs.

variations. Again the measurements follow the predicted trend, but the results do exhibit a mild opposite trend at low gas densities, indicating that the theory only complies with the most pronounced, and practically important, of the measured trends.

There is additional evidence in support of the aerodynamic theory. For example, the data of Hiroyasu et al. [45] agree with the prediction of the intact-core length of Equation 10a with respect to injection velocity and gas density changes. Their experiments were based on measurements of electrical resistance between the nozzle and a screen that could be moved axially within the spray; thus detecting any continuous liquid connection between the nozzle and the screen. However, a connected ligament could give the same signal as a solid liquid core free of gas. Consequently there is still some uncertainty about the structure of the core.

Drop sizes have been measured at the edge of the spray in the vicinity of the nozzle exit [46]. In the surface wave growth theory the drop size would be related to the wavelength of the unstable surface waves, i.e.

$$r \simeq c2\pi\sigma x/\rho_2 U^2 \tag{12}$$

where c is a constant of order unity. The predictions of Equation 12 with regard to liquid properties, jet velocity, and lack of sensitivity to nozzle design are found to be in agreement with experiment. However a discrepancy has been found with the dependence on gas density but it appears that a reasonable explanation for this disagreement exists [47].

Based on the definition that atomization occurs when the intact surface length approaches zero, Equation 10a can be used to predict that atomization occurs if:

$$(\rho_1/\rho_2)^{1/2} < K \quad \text{for} \quad \Gamma > 1$$

and

$$\left(\frac{\rho_1 We_1}{\rho_2 Re_1}\right)^{1/3} < K \quad \text{for} \quad \Gamma < 1 \tag{13}$$

where the constant, K, depends on the nozzle geometry. For the nozzles in Figure 8 (length-to-diameter ratio = 4), K is found empirically to be equal to 9.2.

The stability analysis does not include the details of the flow field within the nozzle. This shortcoming was also mentioned earlier for the first and second wind-induced breakup regimes. Thus, it appears that the stability analysis can explain many of the experimental results in the atomization regime (and also in the second wind-induced regime) if it is supplemented by additional information pertaining to the initial state of the jet, since such information is not included explicitly in the theory. In particular, the nozzle geometry obviously effects the initial state of the jet. The simplest way of accounting for the initial state of the jet is through the magnitude of the initial perturbation η_0 which could have a different value for different nozzle geometries, for example. However, even if this is eventually found to be a sufficient modification, the magnitude of the perturbation is known at best only empirically. All that can be said at present is that η_0 depends in some complex manner on the details of the initial jet flowfield that in turn is influenced by the nozzle geometry and possibly by other parameters, such as the flowfield just upstream of the nozzle.

However, a physical picture of the atomization process can now be proposed which is consistent with the available data. The surface of the liquid jet emerges from the nozzle already perturbed by events that occur within the nozzle itself and are affected by its geometry. The perturbations are rapidly and selectively amplified by aerodynamic interaction with the gas until the outer surface of the jet breaks into drops. The size of the drops and the intact-surface length is much smaller than the diameter of the nozzle. The depth from the surface of the jet to which the above drop formation mechanism would apply is not known. But the core eventually breaks up too since only isolated drops are found far downstream.

Other aspects of atomization still remain unresolved besides the influence of the nozzle. Not predicted by the stability theory, and therefore unknown, are the size and size distribution of the unstable waves at the moment of breakup and also the time between successive ruptures. Away from the nozzle exit, as the generating surface regresses towards the axis of the jet, there are questions as to what gas velocities are seen by the liquid surface. The velocity of the entrained gas certainly approaches that of the liquid surface. Thus the breakup process should be coupled with the two-phase flow field that exists between the presumed intact-core and the unperturbed outer gas. As the relative velocity between the liquid and gas decreases inside the jet, larger drops or ligaments or blobs should be formed; just as larger drops are found when the injection velocity is decreased, as in going from Figure 5D to Figure 5A.

An additional factor to be considered is coalescence of the liquid fragments which can be expected where locally large values of the liquid volume fraction exist. In fact, the net outcome of atomization may be the result of a small difference between large droplet formation and coalescence rates [48]. Thus it is clear that Equations 10 to 13 may provide some information about the outcome of the breakup, but in no way do they give all that is necessary.

Acknowledgments

This work was supported under grants NSF-RANN, AER 75-09538, and ARO DAAG 29-77-G-0146.

NOTATION

a	liquid jet or nozzle exit radius	K	nozzle constant, Equation 13
A	nozzle constant Equation 11	ℓ	wavenumber ($\sqrt{k^2 + \omega/v_1}$)
$B_{1,2}$	breakup length constants, Equation 10	l_r	velocity profile relaxation length
c	drop size constant Equation 12	L_1	intact-surface breakup length
$C_{1,2}$	constants of integration in stability analysis	L_2	intact-core breakup length
		p	pressure
C	attenuation coefficient	r	radial coordinate, drop radius
d	nozzle exit diameter ($= 2a$)	$\mathscr{R}$	real part of a complex quantity
f	Orr-Sommerfeld parameter, Equation 4	Re	Reynolds number ($\rho Ud/\mu$)
		t	time
f	maximum growth rate parameter, Equation 10 and Figure 7	T	jet breakup time
		u	axial velocity component
$F_{1,2,3}$	dimensionless ratios of Bessel functions in Equation 5b	U	jet exit velocity (averaged over jet cross-section)
g	Taylors wavegrowth function Figure 6	v	radial velocity component
i	$\sqrt{-1}$	We	Weber number ($\rho U^2 d/\sigma$)
I_n	n-th order modified Bessel function of the first kind	x	dimensionless wavelength $\rho_2 U^2/\sigma k$
k	wavenumber $2\pi/\lambda$	z	axial coordinate
K_n	n-th order modified Bessel function of the second kind	Z	Ohnesorge number ($\mu_1/\sqrt{(\rho_1 \sigma d)}$)

Greek Symbols

β	dimensionless wavegrowth ($\omega\sqrt{(\rho_1 a^3/\sigma)}$)	μ	kinematic viscosity
		v	dynamic viscosity (μ/ρ)
Γ	Taylor parameter ($\rho_1\sigma^2/(\rho_2\mu_1^2 U^2)$)	ρ	fluid density
ΔP	effective injection pressure ($P_1 - P_2$)	σ	surface tension coefficient
η	surface wave amplitude	ϕ	velocity potential
θ	jet divergence or spray angle	ψ	stream function
λ	wavelength	ω	wavegrowth rate ($\mathscr{R}(\omega)$)

Subscripts

1, L   liquid phase
2, g   gas phase
m   maximum value

REFERENCES

1. Wu, K.-J., Steinberger, R. L., and Bracco, F. V., "On the Mechanism of Breakup of Highly Superheated Liquid Jets," The Combustion Institute Central States Meeting, March 23–24, General Motors Research Laboratories, Warren, Michigan, 1981.
2. Kelly, A. J., "The Electrostatic Atomization of Hydrocarbons," Proceedings of the Second International Conference on Liquid Atomization and Spray Systems, June 20–24, Maidison, Wisconsin, 1982.
3. Topp, M. N., "Ultrasonic Atomization—A Photographic Study of the Mechanism of Disintegration," *J. Aerosol Sci.*, Vol. 4 (1973), p. 17.
4. Grant, R. P., and Middleman, S., "Newtonian Jet Stability," *A.I.Ch.E.*, Vol. 12 (1966), p. 669.
5. Haenlein, A., "Uber den Zerfall eines Flussigkeitsstrahls" ("On the disruption of a Liquid Jet"), *N.A.C.A.*, TM 659, 1932.
6. McCarthy, M. J., and Malloy, N. A., "Review of Stability of Liquid Jets and the Influence of Nozzle Design," *The Chem. Eng. J.*, Vol. 7 (1974), p. 1.
7. Miesse, C. C., "Correlation of Experimental Data on the Disintegration of Liquid Jets," *Indust. Engng. Chem.*, Vol. 47 (1955), p. 1690.
8. Ohnesorge, W. von, "Die Bildung von Tropfen an Dusen und die Auflosung Flussiger Stralen" ("Formation of Drops by Nozzles and the Breakup of Liquid Jets"), *Z, Angew. Math. Mech.*, Vol. 16 (1936), p. 355.
9. Torda, T. P., "Evaporation of Drops and the Breakup of Sprays," *Astronautica Acta.*, Vol. 18 (1973), p. 383.
10. Ranz, W. E., "On Sprays and Spraying," *Dept. Engng. Res. Penn. State University*, Bulletin 65, 1956.
11. Reitz, R. D., "Atomization and Other Breakup Regimes of a Liquid Jet," Ph.D. thesis, AMS Department, Princeton University, 1978.
12. Levich, V. G., *Physicochemical Hydrodynamics*, Prentice-Hall, New Jersey, 1962.
13. Stirling, A. M., and Sleicher, C. A., "The Instability of Capillary Jets," *J. Fluid Mech.*, Vol. 68 (1975), p. 477.
14. Rayleigh, W. S., "On the Instability of Jets," *Proc. Lond. Math. Soc.*, Vol. 4 (1878), p. 10.
15. Donnely, R. J., and Glaberson, W., "Experiments on the Capillary Instability of a Liquid Jet," *Proc Royal Society London A*, Vol. 290 (1965), p. 547.
16. Meister, B. J., and Scheele, G. F., "Prediction of the Jet Length in Immiscible Systems," *A.I.Ch.E. J.*, Vol. 15 (1969), p. 689.
17. Phinney, R. E., "Stability of a Laminar Viscous Jet—The Influence of the Initial Disturbance Level," *A.I.Ch.E. J.*, Vol. 18 (1972), p. 432.
18. Weber, C., "On the Breakdown of a Fluid Jet," *Z.A.M.P.*, Vol. 11 (1931), p. 136.
19. Lee, D. W., and Spencer, R. C., "Photomicrographic Studies of Fuel Sprays," *N.A.C.A. TR.* 454 (1933).
20. Wang, D. P., "Finite Amplitude Effect on the Stability of a Jet of Circular Cross-section," *J. Fluid Mech.*, Vol. 34 (1968), p. 299.
21. Yuen, M. C., "Non-linear Capillary Instability of a Liquid Jet," *J. Fluid Mech.*, Vol. 33 (1968), p. 151.
22. Nayfey, A. H., "Capillary Jet Instabilities," *The Physics of Fluids*, Vol. 13 (1968), p. 841.
23. Rutland, D. F., and Jameson, G. J., "Theoretical Prediction of the Size of Drops Formed in the Breakup of Capillary Jets," *Chem. Eng. Science.*, Vol. 25 (1970), p. 1689.
24. LaFrance, P., "Non-linear Breakup of a Liquid Jet," *The Physics of Fluids*, Vol. 18 (1975), p. 428.

25. Fenn, R. W., and Middleman, S., "Newtonian Jet Stability—The Role of Air Resistance," *A.I.Ch.E. J.*, Vol. 15 (1969), p. 379.

26. Benjamin, T. B., *J. Fluid Mech.*, Vol. 6 (1959), p. 161.

27. Phinney, R. E., "The Breakup of a Turbulent Liquid Jet in a Gaseous Atmosphere," *J. Fluid Mech.*, Vol. 60 (1973), p. 689.

28. Levich, V. G., and Krylov, V. S., "Surface Tension Driven Phenomena," *Annual Review of Fluid Mech.*, Vol. 1 (1969), p. 293.

29. Taylor, G. I., "Generation of Ripples by Wind Blowing over a Viscous Fluid," Collected Works of G. I. Taylor, Vol. 3 (1940).

30. Reitz, R. D., and Bracco, F. V., "On the Dependence of Spray Angle and Other Spray Parameters on Nozzle Design and Operating Conditions," SAE paper 790494, 1979.

31. Reitz, R. D., and Bracco, F. V., "Mechanism of Atomization of a Liquid Jet," *The Physics of Fluids*, Vol. 25 (1982), p. 1730.

32. Reitz, R. D., and Bracco, F. V., "Ultra High Speed Filming of Atomizing Jets," *The Physics of Fluids*, Vol. 22 (1979), p. 1054.

33. Wu, K. J., et al., "Measurements of the Spray Angle of Atomizing Jets," *J. Fluids Engng.*, Vol. 105 (1983), p. 406.

34. DeJuhasz, K. J., "Dispersion of Sprays in Solid Injection Oil Engines," *Trans. A.S.M.E. (OGP)*, Vol. 53 (1931), p. 65.

35. Schweitzer, P. H., "Mechanism of Disintegration of Liquid Jets," *J. Applied Physics*, Vol. 8 (1937), p. 513.

36. Hinze, J. O., *Turbulence*, McGraw Hill, New York, 1st Ed. (1959), p. 514.

37. Bergwerk, W., "Flow Pattern in Diesel Nozzle Spray Holes," *Proc. Instn. Mech. Engrs.*, Vol. 173 (1959), p. 655.

38. Castleman, R. A., "Mechanism of Atomization Accompanying Solid Injection," *N.A.C.A. Report*, 440 (1932).

39. Castleman, R. A., "Mechanism of Atomization of Liquids," *U.S. Natl. Bureau Std. J. Res.*, Vol. 6 (1931), p. 281.

40. Rupe, J. H., "On the Dynamic Characteristics of Free-Liquid Jets and a Partial Correlation with Orifice Geometry," *J.P.L. Tech. Report*, No. 32 (1962), p. 207.

41. Giffen, E., and Muraszew, A., *The Atomization of Liquids Fuels*, John Wiley, New York, 1953.

42. Shkadov, V. Ya., "Wave Formation on the Surface of a Viscous Liquid due to Tangential Stress," *Fluid Dynamics*, Vol. 5 (1970), p. 473.

43. Ranz, W. E., "Some Experiments on Orifice Sprays," *Canad. J. Chem. Engng.*, Vol. 36 (1958), p. 175.

44. Schweitzer, P. H., "On the Formation and Dispersion of Oil Sprays," *Penn. State University*, Bulletin 40, 1932.

45. Hiroyasu, H., Shimizu, M., and Arai, M., "The Breakup of a High Speed Jet in a High Pressure Gaseous Atmosphere," Proceedings of the Second International Conference on Liquid Atomization and Spray Systems, June 20–24, Maidison, Wisconsin, 1982.

46. Wu, K.-J., "Atomizing Round Jets." Ph.D. thesis, MAE Department, Princeton University, 1983.

47. Wu, K.-J., Reitz, R. D., and Bracco, F. V., "Drop Sizes of Atomizing Jets," to be published.

48. O'Rourke, P. J., and Bracco, F. V., "Modeling of Drop Interactions in Thick Sprays and Comparisons with Experiments," *Proc. Instn. Mech. Engrs.*, Publication No. 085298-469, 1980.

CHAPTER 11

HYDRODYNAMICS OF LIQUID DROPS IN AIR

G. S. R. Narasimhamurty and **A. Purushothaman**

Gadepally Bio Industries
Bombay, India

and

K. Sivaji

Regional Research Laboratories
Hyderabad, India

CONTENTS

INTRODUCTION

The familiar phenomena of rainfall consists of the fall of water droplets in the air. During the fall of water droplets, some evaporation takes place. The evaporation from and condensation on water droplets in air is made use of in humidification/dehumidification operations used as part of air conditioning. Spray drying of milk and various food products involves evaporation of moisture from solutions sprayed in drop form to get solid particles. Spraying not only helps in moisture removal but also produces particles or granules of small size. The formation of ammonium nitrate in spray towers not only makes use of evaporation combined with chemical reaction but also avoids the hazardous operation of grinding ammonium nitrate. Atomization and combustion inside furnaces and internal combustion engines are other familiar examples of the production of liquid drops in a gaseous atmosphere to enhance combustion.

In all these operations, liquid drops formed by natural or artificial means travel through a certain distance in a gaseous medium and help to quicken heat and mass transfer through evaporation or chemical reaction. The increase in surface area obtained by causing a liquid to form drops helps obtain faster rates of mass transfer and/or chemical reaction. The breakup of liquid into drops is much more energy efficient than the grinding of solid matter and as such is to be preferred whenever process conditions permit.

In view of the common occurrence of liquid drops in gases, a knowledge of the hydrodynamics of liquid droplets in air should precede any study of heat and mass transfer or chemical reaction of such systems. Because of the simplicity and the basic nature of single-drop systems, more studies have been carried out on single-drop systems than on multidrop systems.

The pertinent literature on the subject is summarized in Table 1.

DROP FORMATION

Slow Drop Formation

If a drop is allowed to form at a very slow rate in air so that the kinetic energy of inflow of liquid to the drop is negligible, the drop will grow slowly and finally break off from the tip of the nozzle or tube from which it is formed when the gravitational force on the drop just exceeds the surface tension that holds it to the tip. If the tip is a sharp circular one, we can write the force balance equation thus:

$$2\pi R\sigma = mg \qquad (1)$$

where R = radius of the circular tip at which the drop is formed
σ = surface tension of the liquid
m = mass of the drop
g = acceleration due to gravity

Equation 1 is used for the determination of the surface tension of liquids.

The drop formation goes through the stages of slow growth of the drop below the tip, followed by elongation of the drop leading to neck formation and breakup. During the drop detachment from the nozzle, sometimes one or more small droplets, generally called tail drops or satellite drops, are formed just behind the main drop. The tail drops may sometimes coalesce with the main drop or travel separately by themselves.

After the drop is detached from the tip, the drop tries to regain an equilibrium shape according to the equation

$$1/r_1 + 1/r_2 = (P_i - P_o)/\sigma \qquad (2)$$

where r_1, r_2 = principal radii at any point on drop surface
P_i, P_o = pressures inside and outside the drop
σ = surface tension

For a spherical drop of small size the equation becomes

$$2/r = (P_i - P_o)/\sigma \qquad (3)$$

The property of surface tension tries to make the drop attain the minimum surface area as in a sphere. As the drop was originally elongated and deformed during the drop formation and detachment stage, the effort of the drop to attain the minimum surface area leads to oscillations in shape. These oscillations die down for small drops but not so for large drops.

Table 1
Summary of Literature

Sl. No.	Authors	Subject	Systems Studied and Other Features
1.	Merrington and Richardson [1]	Breakup of liquid jets.	Jets of liquids such as zinc chloride, soap solution, titanium tetrachloride, methylene chloride, methyl salicylate, chlorosulfonic acid, water, glycerine, glycerine + 20% water, aniline, mercury, carbon tetrachloride; ρ_l: 1.0 to 1.77 gm/cm^3; μ_l/ρ_l: 0.004 to 10 cm^2/sec; σ: 25 to 73 dynes/cm; Re: 10^2 to 10^5; drop diameter: 0.2 to 10 mm.
2.	Rayleigh [2]	Breakup of low viscosity liquid jet.	Equation for ideal drop diameter in terms of jet diameter for low viscosity liquid jet.
3.	Brodkey [3]	Drop formation, drop motion, and breakup.	Review.
4.	Marshall [4]	Atomization and spray drying.	Review.
5.	Weber [5]	Breakup of high-viscosity liquid jet.	Equation for ideal drop diameter in terms of jet diameter and liquid properties.
6.	Ohnesorge [6]	Liquid jets.	Criteria for transformation from varicose to sinuous region and also from sinuous to atomization region. Re$_j$—1 to 10^6, We$_j$—10^2 to 10^6.
7.	Duffie and Marshall [7]	Drop-size distribution.	Size distribution in varicose region. Nozzle diameter—145 to 300 micron (1 mm); d_G—276 to 647 micron; μ_l—0.836 to 36 Cp; ρ_l—0.996 to 1.2699 gm/cm^3; Re—23 to 2220; flow rate—3.12 to 18.87 cc/min.
8.	Orr [8]	Spraying and atomizing.	Review on size distributions, nozzle, and atomization characteristics, spray evaluation, evaporation, and combustion.
9.	Masters [9]	Spray drying.	Review on sprays, size distributions, spray evaluation, heat and mass transfer.
10.	Pilcher and Thomas [10]	Size distribution.	Normal distribution function.
11.	Lewis et al. [11]	Size distribution.	Log-normal and Nukiyama-Tanasawa distributions for pneumatic atomization.
12.	Mugele and Evans [12]	Size distribution.	Review of size distribution functions and application of upper limit equation to spray data.
13.	Mache [13]	Shape and terminal velocity.	Photographs of rain drops. Data on terminal velocity agreed with that of Lenard.

No.	Author	Topic	Description
14.	Edgerton and Killian [14]	Shape.	Photograph of water drop.
15.	Sutton [15]	Terminal velocity.	Water drops, diameter—1.0 to 12 mm; terminal velocity—400 to 920 cm/s.
16.	Magono [16]	Shape and terminal velocity.	Water drops, diameter—2.8 to 6.5 mm; terminal velocity—680 to 890 cm/s.
17.	Magono [17]	Shape.	Photograph of water drop.
18.	Saito [18]	Equilibrium shape.	Mathematical expression for equilibrium shape.
19.	Best [19]	Shape.	Estimation of eccentricity of water drops.
20.	Best [20]	Shape.	Drop size measurement from photographs of Sutton [15].
21.	Henrickson [21]	Shape and terminal velocity.	Water, nitrobenzene, and n-propanol. For water drops, diameter—1.0 to 6.0 mm; terminal velocity—400 to 879 cm/s.
22.	Srikrishna [23]	Size, shape, oscillation, terminal velocity and evaporation.	Water, n-heptane, acetone, tetrachloroethylene, toluene, xylene, methyl ethyl ketone, tertiary butyl alcohol, chlorobenzene, ethylene glycol, bromoform, nitrobenzene, eugenol, dibutyl phthalate, tetra-bromoethene, isopropyl alcohol. Drop diameter—2.0 to 8.4 mm; ρ_l—0.6 to 3 gm/cm³; μ_l—0.3 to 20 cp; σ—18 to 73 dynes/cm; Re—628 to 4,271; We—1.532 to 9.632; drag coefficient—0.8228 to 3.824; Sc—0.6099 to 2.503; Sh—3.26 to 100.14.
23.	Rayleigh [24]	Oscillation.	A mathematical expression for small oscillations in shape for liquid drops.
24.	Blanchard [26]	Size, shape, and oscillation.	Water drops; diameter—5 to 10 mm; data on major and minor axes of water drops and oscillation frequency.
25.	Gunn [27]	Oscillation and drift.	Transverse drift of 2 to 3 ft in a fall of 50 ft for droplets of mass greater than 0.5 mg.
26.	Lane [28]	Shape and breakup.	Water drops: diameter—0.5 mm to 5.0 mm; equation for maximum stable drop size.
27.	Garner and Lane [29]	Oscillation size, and shape.	Glycerol, monoethanol amine, propylene glycol, ethylene glycol, water, transformer oil, mentor-28, dekaline drops in air and in 50-50 mixture of air and carbon dioxide. Oscillation frequencies—23.7 to 26.2 cycles/s; drop diameter—2.74 to 5.85 mm equation for average value of a/b, circulation velocity—0 to 18 cm/s.

(Continued)

Table 1 Continued

SI. No.	Authors	Subject	Systems Studied and Other Features
28.	Constan and Calvert [30]	Oscillation and internal circulation.	Drops of glycerine, propylene glycol, ethylene glycol, 80% propylene glycol, 80% glycerol, water in sulfur dioxide. Diameter—2 to 2.87 mm; air velocity—216.4 to 874.8 cm/s; circulation velocity—0.11 to 6.4 cm/s; frequency of oscillation—19 to 75 cycles/s; amplitude—0.004 to 0.042 cm.
29.	Finlay [31]	Oscillation terminal velocity and evaporation.	Water, 98% glycerol, 78% glycerol, tetrabromoethane, isobutanol, n-heptane, isooctane: drop diameter—1.97 to 8.5 mm; terminal velocity—674 to 890 cm/s.
30.	Srikrishna, Sivaji and Narasimhamurty [32]	Oscillation, shape, and evaporation.	Water, n-heptane, acetone, tetrachloroethylene, toluene, xylene, methyl ethyl ketone, n-hexane, isopropyl alcohol, tertiary butyl alcohol, chlorobenzene, ethylene glycol, bromoform, nitrobenzene eugenol, dibutyl phthalate and tetrabromoethane. Drop diameter—2.0 to 8.4 mm; ρ_1—0.66 to 3.0 gm/cm³; μ_1—0.30 to 20 cp; σ—18 to 73 dynes/cm; Re—628 to 4271; Sc—0.6099 to 2.503; Sh—3.26 to 100.
31.	Hadamard [33] and Rybczynski [34]	Terminal velocity, drag coefficient, and internal circulation.	Mathematical expression for terminal velocity of a fluid sphere moving in another fluid for Re < 1.
32.	McDonald [35]	Shape, terminal velocity, and internal circulation.	Rain drops.
33.	Pruppacher and Pitter [36]	Shape, internal circulation.	Rain drops, semiempirical treatment.
34.	Green [37]	Shape, internal circulation.	Rain drops.
35.	Flower [38]	Distance of fall, terminal velocity.	Drops of water and methyl salicylate: drop diameter—2.26 to 5.48 mm; terminal velocity—556.7 to 810.7 cm/s.
36.	Laws [39]	Distance of fall, terminal velocity.	Water drops; distance of fall—0.5 to 20 m; drop diameter—2.0 to 6.0 mm; terminal velocity—670 to 930 cm/s.
37.	Best [40]	Distance of fall, terminal velocity.	Water drops.
38.	Harilal [41]	Height of fall and fall velocity.	Drops of distilled water, benzene, toluene, carbon tetrachloride. Drop diameter—2.47 to 5.45 mm; height of fall—0.4 to 86.05 cm; velocity—105 to 402 cm/s, ρ_1—0.866 to 1.58 gm/cm³; μ_1—0.585 to 1.068 cp, σ—23.2 to 72.6 dynes/cm.

No.	Reference	Type	Description
39.	Gillapsy and Hoffer [42]	Terminal velocity and drag coefficient.	Ethylene glycol, propylene glycol isobutyl ether, dipropylene glycol, methyl ether DPM, glycerol, Newtonian thickened DPMs and non-Newtonian thickened DPMs. ρ_l—0.951 to 1.253 gm/cm³; μ_l—3.41 to 300 cp; σ—26.8 to 63 dynes/cm; Re—100 to 2,000, Cd: 0.3 to 1.2.
40.	Bond and Newton [43]	Terminal velocity.	Criteria for solid-like behavior of liquid drops.
41.	Lenard [44]	Terminal velocity.	Water drops: drop diameter—1.5 to 5.5 mm; terminal velocity—570 to 800 cm/s.
42.	Schmidt [45]	Terminal velocity.	Empirical equation for terminal velocity. Water drops: diameter—1.5 to 3.5 mm; terminal velocity—496 to 740 cm/s.
43.	Meinzer [46]	Terminal velocity.	Water drops.
44.	Gunn and Kinzer [47]	Terminal velocity.	Water drops: diameter—2.0 to 5.4 mm; terminal velocity—649 to 914 cm/s.
45.	Spilhaus [48]	Terminal velocity.	Water drops, equation for terminal velocity.
46.	Hitschfeld [49]	Terminal velocity.	Expression for time of fall and distance of fall using Schmidt's equation.
47.	Imai [50]	Terminal velocity.	Correlations for terminal velocity.
48.	Hughes and Gilliland [51]	Terminal velocity.	Plots of (1) drag coefficient as a function of Reynolds number with surface tension group as parameter; C_d—0.1 to 10; Su—10^4 to 10^6; Re—10 to 10^4. (2) Terminal velocity group as a function of gravity group with surface tension-size group as parameter: Tv—1 to 100; Wt—10 to 500; Sd—10^2 to 10^6.
49.	Narasimhamurty [52]	Terminal velocity.	Generalized correlation for terminal velocity of liquid drops in fluids and bubbles in liquids: Re—10^{-3} to 10^5; We—10^{-6} to 10^3.
50.	Lane and Green [53]	Breakup.	Stages of breakup: flattening, torus formation, increasing bag size, bursting of the film and breakup of torus ring into droplets.
51.	Hinze [54]	Breakup.	Weber number and viscosity group as parameters determining the conditions of drop breakup.
52.	Hinze [55]	Breakup.	Review.
53.	Haas [56]	Breakup.	Mercury drops; We_{crit}—11.2; We—6.72 to 75; Re—1,440 to 8,800.
54.	Hanson et al. [57]	Breakup.	Water, methyl alcohol and silicon oil; drop diameter—0.1 to 1 mm; ρ_l—0.787 to 0.978 gm/cm³; σ—20.14 to 71.97 dynes/cm; We_{crit}—4.79 to 7.94; Re_{crit}—317 to 661.

(Continued)

Table 1 Continued

Sl. No.	Authors	Subject	Systems Studied and Other Features
55.	Wolfe and Andersen [58]	Breakup.	"Bag" breakup and "stripping" breakup.
56.	Lehrer [60]	Breakup.	Equation for critical diameter.
57.	Sarjeant [61]	Breakup.	Review.
58.	Marshall [62]	Heat and mass transfer.	Re—1 to 100; drop diameter—1 to 1,000 microns.
59.	Froessling [63]	Mass transfer.	Equation for Sherwood number; Re—2 to 1,300.
60.	Ranz and Marshall [64]	Heat and mass transfer.	Water, aniline, naphthalene, nitrobenzene and benzene drops in air: Nu—2 to 10; Sh—2 to 10.
61.	Hsu, Sato, and Sage [65]	Mass transfer.	n-heptane drops: diameter—1.7 mm; Re—50 to 350; Sh—2 to 20.
62.	Manning and Gauvin [66]	Mass transfer.	Re—1 to 20.
63.	Pritchard and Biswas [67]	Evaporation.	Drops of benzene, acetone, carbon tetrachloride, ethyl alcohol, methyl alcohol.
64.	Ahmadzadeh and Harker [68]	Evaporation.	Drops of acetone-water mixture; nozzle diameter—1.07 to 3.13 mm; Sh—2 to 25.
65.	Duffie and Marshall [69]	Spray drying.	Spray drying of ammonium nitrate, sodium sulfate, potassium nitrate, dye AQD 585A, corn syrup, whole milk, gelatin, sodium nitrate, sodium silicate, potassium sulfate, sodium chloride, and marasperse-C.
66.	Dennis [70]	Growth rate of hygroscopic liquid drops.	Sulfuric acid, calcium chloride, ammonium nitrate, sodium chloride solutions: drop diameter—0.35 to 1.08 mm; air velocity—75 to 480 cm/s; relative humidity—73 to 97%.
67.	Ray and Davis [71, 72]	Evaporation.	Single and multiple drops.
68.	Labowsky [73]	Evaporation.	Mathematical treatment.
69.	Danckwerts [74]	Absorption by diffusion and chemical reaction.	Mathematical expressions for absorption by diffusion and chemical reaction for $Re < 1.0$.

70.	Johnstone and Coughanowr [75]	Absorption, chemical reaction.	Absorption of sulfur dioxide by liquid drops (700 to 900 micron diameter) containing manganese sulfate.
71.	Plit [76]	Mass transfer.	Theoretical study.
72.	Abdul-Rahman and Crosby [77]	Mass transfer with chemical reaction.	Reaction of drops of orthophosphoric acid with ammonia and sulfuric acid with ammonia.
73.	Gal-or, Klinzing and Tavlarides [78]	Drop phenomena.	Review.
74.	Tavlarides et al. [79]	Drop phenomena.	Review.
75.	Sivaji [80]	Mass transfer with chemical reaction.	Absorption of oxygen in air by liquid drops containing sodium sulfite and cobaltous sulfate. Terminal velocity—625 to 852 cm/s; μ_f—0.54 to 0.87 cp.
76.	Sivaji and Narasimhamurty [81]	Mass transfer with chemical reaction.	Review.
77.	Sivaji and Narasimhamurty [82]	Mass transfer with chemical reaction.	Reaction kinetics of sulfite oxidation.
78.	Charlesworth and Marshall [83]	Evaporation.	Review.
79.	Angus et al. [84]	Laser Doppler technique for motion measurement.	Review.
80.	Golovin et al. [85]	Laser techniques.	Review.
81.	Kintner et al. [86]	Photographic techniques.	Review.
82.	Berger et al. [87]	Optical techniques.	Review.
83.	Deich, Shanin and Karyshev [88]	Drop size determination.	Optical techniques.
84.	Tate [89]	Drop size determination.	Immersion sampling up to 500 micron.
85.	Adler [90]	Drop size determination.	Scanning device: scanning rate—10,000 drops in 15 minutes.
86.	Pye [91]	Drop size determination.	Pulse counting—15 micron to 1 mm drop size.
87.	Soo [92]	Drop size determination.	Light diffraction, gas absorption, and electrical methods.

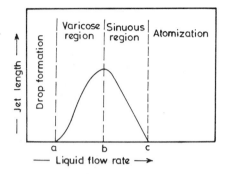

Figure 1. Jet length as a function of liquid flow rate.

Fast Drop Formation

When the inlet velocity of the liquid from the nozzle to the drop increases, the kinetic energy is no more negligible, and Equation 1 does not apply. At low velocities we can get individual drops of reasonably uniform size formed at the tip of the nozzle but as the velocity increases the flow will be in the form of a jet which breaks down into drops. The phenomena of drop and jet formation may be represented as shown in Figure 1. The jet length increases to a maximum and then decreases to zero when a spray of liquid takes place at the tip of the nozzle. This phenomenon is also called atomization. The jetting region in the range up to the maximum jet length formation was called varicose (due to the occasional lumps in the jet) and the region after the maximum jet length to the onset of atomization was called sinuous (because of irregular weaving of the jet) by Merrington and Richardson [1].

For the breakup of a low viscosity liquid jet, Rayleigh [2] predicted the drop size:

$$d = 1.89d_j \tag{4}$$

where d = drop diameter
        d_j = jet diameter

The idealized breakup and actual breakup of a water jet are shown in Figure 2.
Weber [5] proposed a correction factor for the breakup of a high viscosity liquid jet:

$$d = 1.88d_j[1 + (3\mu_l/\sqrt{\sigma\rho_l d_j})]^{1/2} \tag{5}$$

Figure 2. (A) idealized jet breakup showing uniform drop diameter; (B, C) actual breakup of a water jet.

where d = drop diameter
d_j = jet diameter
μ_l = liquid viscosity
ρ_l = liquid density
σ = surface tension

This type of breakup of liquid jets predicts uniform size drops.
A criterion for transition from sinuous to atomization region was suggested by Ohnesorge [6]:

$$We_j = 10^6 Re_j^{-0.45} \tag{6}$$

where We_j = jet Weber number, $(d_n u_j^2 \rho_l)/\sigma$
Re_j = jet Reynolds number, $(d_n u_j \rho_l)/\mu_l$
d_n = nozzle diameter
u_j = jet velocity
ρ_l = liquid density
μ_l = liquid viscosity
σ = surface tension

The drop size distribution in the varicose region, also called the Rayleigh breakup region was studied by Duffie and Marshall [7]. Using their experimental data they correlated the geometric mean diameter of drops with nozzle diameter and jet Reynolds number thus:

$$d_G = 36 d_n^{0.56} Re_j^{-0.10} \tag{7}$$

Equation 7 has a maximum deviation of 18% and an average deviation of 7.3%.
Since a spray from any nozzle consists of a large number of droplets of varying sizes, distribution functions are necessary to express the spread of droplet sizes. Some of the frequently used distributions are normal, log-normal, Rosin-Rammler, and Nukiyama-Tanasawa distribution functions as summarized by Brodkey [3], Orr [8] and Masters [9].
The normal distribution function is given by

$$N = (\sum N/(s\sqrt{2\pi})) \exp[-(d - d_m)^2/(2s^2)] \tag{8}$$

where N = frequency of observation of the diameter d
$\sum N$ = total number of observations
d_m = mean diameter
s = standard deviation

According to Pilcher and Thomas [10] droplets produced by condensation, precipitation, and chemical reaction are represented by normal distribution functions.
The log-normal distribution is given by

$$N = (\sum N)/(\log s_g \sqrt{2\pi} \exp[-(\log d - \log d_{gm})^2/2(\log s_g)^2] \tag{9}$$

where $\log d_{gm} = \sum(N\log d)/\sum N$, log-geometric mean diameter
$\log s_g = \sqrt{\sum N(\log d - \log d_{gm})^2/\sum N}$, log-standard geometric deviation

The log-normal distribution was found to describe the droplet sizes produced by rotary atomizers and pneumatic atomization (Masters [9] and Lewis et al. [11]).
The Rosin-Rammler distribution applicable to nozzle sprays [9] is expressed as

$$P_v = 100 \exp -(d/d_{RR})^x \tag{10}$$

where P_v = percent of spray by volume, existing as droplets with sizes greater than diameter d
d_{RR} = Rosin-Rammler mean
x = dispersion exponent having values between 2 and 4

For pneumatic atomization, Lewis et al., [11] found that the Nukiyama-Tanasawa distribution was suitable. The expression is given as

$$\log(1/d^2)(N/\Delta d) = \log k_1 - (k_2 d)^k 3/2.303 \qquad (11)$$

where d = droplet diameter
         N = number of droplets in diameter range Δd
k_1, k_2, k_3 = constants

Mugele and Evans [12] studies the application of Rosin-Rammler, Nukiyama-Tanasawa, and log-probability distribution functions for spray data. They proposed the upper-limit function where the parameter $y = \ln[(qd)/(d_{max} - d)]$ follows the normal distribution given by Equation 8. Mugele and Evans [12] found that drop size data from sprays can be represented by the upper-limit equation accurately.

The distribution parameters should be correlated with the physical characteristics of the spray-generating system. These include the physical properties of the fluids, nozzle geometry, nozzle velocity and other operating conditions. Brodkey [3], Orr [8], and Masters [9] presented reviews of such correlations for sprays.

SHAPES AND OSCILLATIONS OF DROPS

Small size drops below 1 mm diameter seem to be nearly spherical but the larger drops deviate from spherical shape. They generally attain an ellipsoidal shape with a certain amount of flattening on the bottom side while falling in air. This led to the belief that drops have an equilibrium shape. Snapshots of water drops falling in air were taken by Mache [13], Edgerton and Killian [14], Sutton [15], and Magono [16]. These photographs were single images. Magono's photograph of a water drop falling in air as given by McDonald [17] is reproduced in Figure 3.

Assuming the drop to have an equilibrium shape, Saito [18] proposed a criterion for the drop to be an oblate spheroid or a prolate spheroid. Best [19] compared the terminal velocity of a liquid drop with that of an equivalent sphere and estimated the eccentricity of drops. Based on measurements of drop sizes from the photographs of single water drops supplied by Sutton [15], Best [20] postulated that the drop could be assumed to be two half ellipsoids of revolution. The deformations of water, nitrobenzene, and n-propanol drops were observed by Henrickson [21]. Photographic

Diameter = 4·35mm

Figure 3. Water drop falling in air, photograph by Magono [17].

Figure 4. Acetone drops in air [23].

studies especially of multiple pictures of the same liquid drop in air revealed that drops during their fall in air do not have any particular equilibrium shape but show oscillations in shape and even rotations. Srikrishna's [23] photograph for acetone drops in air is reproduced in Figure 4.
A mathematical expression for the frequency of oscillations of a small liquid drop was given by Rayleigh [24]:

$$\omega^2 = (8\sigma)/(\rho_1 r^3) \tag{12}$$

where ω = angular frequency
      σ = surface tension
      ρ_1 = density of liquid
      r = radius of liquid drop

The derivation is referred to by Lamb [25]. Since $\omega = 2\pi f$ where f is the frequency in cycles/sec and $m = \frac{4}{3}\pi r^3$ where m is the mass of the liquid drop, Equation 12 can be written in the form

$$f = [(8\sigma)/(3\pi m)]^{0.5} \tag{13}$$

Blanchard [26] studied the shapes and oscillations of water drops in air by taking stroboscopic pictures. He presented average values of major and minor axes. Blanchard [26] observed that for water drops having less than a 5-mm diameter, the ratio of the major and minor axes is close to 1, while as drop diameter approaches 9 mm, the ratio is close to 2. According to Blanchard [26] oscillation frequencies decreased with an increase in drop diameter. Gunn [27] found that freely falling water drops possessed a natural frequency of oscillation as given by Equation 13. Lane [28] discussed the shapes of water drops in a vertical air stream. Garner and Lane [29] determined experimentally the frequency of oscillation of water and seven organic liquids and found that the values agreed with those calculated by using Equation 13. The oscillation frequencies reported by Gonstan and Calvert [30] for drops of water and three organic liquids did not agree with the theoretical values obtained using Equation 13. The shapes and oscillation frequencies of drops of water and seven organic liquids were determined by Finlay [31]. Srikrishna [23] studied the shapes and oscillations of liquid drops in air. Besides Blanchard [26], Srikrishna [23] also found that oscillation frequencies of liquid drops in air decreased with an increase in drop diameter. Figure 5 shows the data on the oscillation frequencies of water drops reported by Srikrishna [23] and

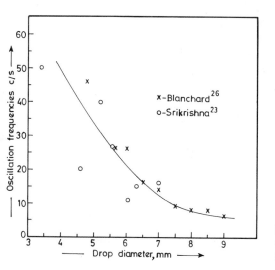

Figure 5. Comparison of data on oscillation frequencies of water drops.

Blanchard [26]. For some drop sizes Srikrishna [23] observed more than one frequency. Srikrishna proposed a correlation

$$f = [(8\sigma)/(3\pi m)]^{0.48} \tag{14}$$

based on his experimental data. The exponent of the group $(8\sigma)/(3\pi m)$ is close to the theoretical value 0.5 as in Equation 13. For drops of fourteen liquids falling in air, Srikrishna, Sivaji, and Narasimhamurty [32] reported that Equation 13 is satisfactory with about 20% maximum deviation.

The data reported on the average values of the major and minor axes of the ellipse for water drops are shown in Figure 6. (Blanchard [26], Finlay [31], and Srikrishna [23]). Garner and Lane [29] correlated the mean values of the ratio of the major and minor axes (a/b) with the group $(g \Delta\rho d^2)/\sigma$ and gave the following correlation:

$$(a/b) = 0.12(g \Delta\rho d^2)/\sigma + 1.0 \tag{15}$$

where   a = semi-major axis of the drop
         b = semi-minor axis of the drop
         g = acceleration due to gravity
         $\Delta\rho = \rho_l - \rho_a$, difference in densities of liquid and air
         σ = surface tension

Srikrishna [23] proposed the following correlation for the mean value of (a/b):

$$(a/b) = i(g \Delta\rho d^2)/\sigma + 1 \tag{16}$$

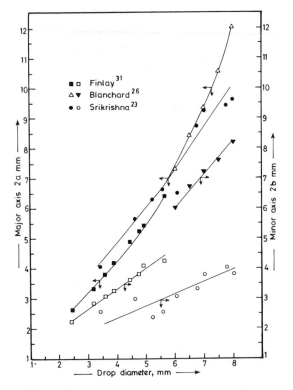

Figure 6. Comparison of data on shapes of water drops.

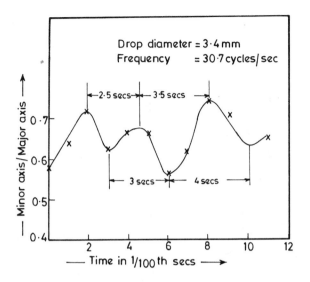

Figure 7. Deformation of n-heptane drops with time.

Using his data on drops of fifteen liquids Srikrishna [23] tabulated the values of i and l for each liquid. A general correlation for the mean value of (a/b),

$$(a/b) = 0.146(g \, \Delta\rho d^2)/\sigma + 1.0 \tag{17}$$

was proposed by Srikrishna, Sivaji, and Narasimhamurty [32]. This equation was found to fit the data with a standard deviation of 0.18 and a correlation coefficient of 0.84.

Srikrishna [23] presented curves for instantaneous values of the ratio of the minor axis to major axis with time. A typical curve for an n-heptane drop in air is shown in Figure 7. Srikrishna [23] also obtained data on the amplitude of oscillation of liquid drops. These curves were sinusoidal in shape. Figure 8 shows the curve for n-heptane drops in air.

The surface areas of water drops and n-heptane drops in air reported by Finlay [31] and Srikrishna [23] are shown in Figure 9. Photographs taken by Srikrishna [23] showed a large variation of surface area from image to image of a single drop indicating continuous generation of new surface area.

A transverse drift in the vertical free fall of water drops having weight more than 0.5 mg. was reported by Gunn [27]. No other researcher seems to have mentioned drift.

Only Blanchard [26] reported rotations of water drops.

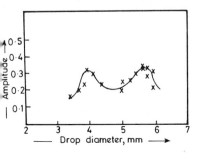

Figure 8. Amplitude of oscillations of n-heptane drops [23].

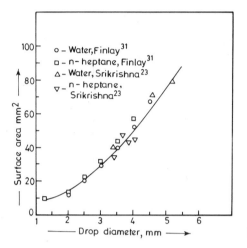

Drop diameter, mm ⟶

Figure 9. Surface area of liquid drops.

The phenomenon of internal circulation occurring in liquid drops falling in air interested several research workers. A mathematical expression relating the internal circulation, denoted by the ratio of viscosities μ_a/μ_l, to the drag coefficient for Stokes region (Reynolds number less than 1) was derived by Hadamard [33] and Rybczinski [34]:

$$C_d = C_{ds}[1 + \tfrac{2}{3}(\mu_a/\mu_l)]/[1 + (\mu_a/\mu_l)] \tag{18}$$

$$C_d = C_{ds}[1 - \tfrac{1}{3}(\mu_a/\mu_l)] \qquad \text{if } \mu_a/\mu_l \ll 1 \tag{19}$$

where C_d = drag coefficient for fluid sphere
        C_{ds} = drag coefficient for equivalent solid sphere
        μ_a = viscosity of air
        μ_l = viscosity of liquid

According to Equation 19 the drag coefficient is linearly related to internal circulation. For liquid drops in air the factor $(3\mu_l + 2\mu_a)/(3\mu_l + 3\mu_a)$ is nearly equal to 1. Garner and Lane [29] tried to measure circulation velocities of drops falling in gases by observing movement of aluminium particles inside the drop. The measured circulation velocities were found to be of the same order as those calculated by using Rybczinski-Hadamard equation. Immediately after detachment, the drops were found to have a high rate of internal circulation. These were rapidly damped out and the natural circulation rate caused by the drop motion was found to predominate. Garner and Lane [29] reported that surface-active agents reduced the circulation velocities. Constan and Calvert [30] also reported circulation velocities of liquid drops. Blanchard [26], Finlay [31], McDonald [35], Pruppachar and Pitter [36], and Green [37] suggested that internal circulation does not affect drop shape significantly.

More experimental information is necessary on drift, rotation and internal circulation of liquid drops falling in air before any conclusions can be drawn.

MOTION OF DROPS

A force balance around a liquid drop falling in air may be written as follows:

$$V(\rho_l - \rho_a)g = C_d A_F(\rho_a u^2/2) + V\rho_l(du/dt) \tag{20}$$

where   V = drop volume
ρ_l = liquid density
ρ_a = air density
g = acceleration due to gravity
C_d = drag coefficient
A_F = frontal area
u = drop velocity
t = time
du/dt = acceleration of the drop

The velocity of fall increases and attains a maximum value called terminal velocity. For very small liquid drops (diameter less than 0.1 mm) it is found that the terminal velocity is equal to that of a solid sphere. The larger liquid drops attain terminal velocities much faster than rigid spheres of equal volume, due to the deformation as well as oscillations of the drops. Also the terminal velocities of liquid drops are lower than those of rigid spheres of equal volume. Comparatively, more information is available on terminal velocities of drops than on their velocities in the accelerating region.

Flower [38], Laws [39], Best [40], and Harilal [41] reported fall velocities of liquid drops in air for different heights of fall. Flower [38] developed an empirical equation connecting height of fall required by a drop of a particular volume to attain terminal velocity and the volume of the drop. Best [40] developed an empirical relationship for the terminal velocity of water drops in terms of heights of fall and drop diameter. Gillaspy and Hoffer [42] gave an empirical equation for velocity:

$$u = u_t \exp(-c/t) \tag{21}$$

where   u = velocity of liquid drop
u_t = terminal velocity
t = time of fall
c = constant

The terminal velocity of a solid sphere at Reynolds number less than unity is given by the Stokes formula:

$$u_{ts} = d^2(\rho - \rho_a)g/18\mu_a \tag{22}$$

where u_{ts} = terminal velocity of solid sphere

The Rybczinski-Hadamard [33, 34] formula for terminal velocity of a fluid sphere in Stokes region is

$$u_t = u_{ts}(3\mu_l + 2\mu_a)/(3\mu_l + 3\mu_a) \tag{23}$$

where u_t = terminal velocity of fluid sphere
μ_l = viscosity of liquid
μ_a = viscosity of air

Since the factor $(3\mu_l + 2\mu_a)/(3\mu_l + 3\mu_a)$ is very nearly equal to 1 for liquid drops in air, Equation 23 gives $u_t = u_{ts}$. Even though the terminal velocity of liquid drops deviates from Stokes law, it still follows the solid sphere curve till a diameter of 1 mm, corresponding to a Reynolds number of approximately 300 (Brodkey [3]). Bond and Newton [43] suggested an approximate criterion for deviation from the solid sphere curve:

$$(\rho_l - \rho_a)d^2g/\sigma = 0.4 \tag{24}$$

For water drops in air Equation 24 gives d = 1.7 mm.

Lenard [44] reported data on fall velocities of water drops in air (diameter 1.28 mm to 6.36 mm). The velocities were less than those of rigid spheres of equal volume. The fall velocity increased to a maximum as drop size increased and leveled off asymptotically with further increases in drop size. Mache's [13] data agreed with that of Lenard [44]. Schmidt [45] reported data on fall velocities of water drops in air and suggested the following equation for terminal velocity:

$$u_t = a_1 r^2/(b_1 + c_1 r^{1.5})$$ (25)

where r = drop radius
$a_1 = 10^6$
$b_1 = 0.83$
$c_1 = 454$

Laws [39] and Meinzer [46] reported fall velocities of water drops (1 mm to 6.1 mm diameter). Gunn and Kinzer [47], after studying terminal velocity of water drops falling in air (weight 0.2 μg to 1,000 μg) observed that the same drag relationships as rigid spheres are valid upto a Reynolds number of 500 corresponding to a drop diameter of 1.6 mm. This is comparable to the value 1.7 mm obtained from Equation 24.

A correlation connecting drop size, surface tension, and terminal velocity was proposed by Spilhaus [48], assuming that drag coefficient for a liquid drop is intermediate between that of a flat plate and a sphere. The equations are:

$$C_d = C_o(\gamma - h(\gamma - 1))$$ (26)

$$u_t^2/r_p = (4\rho_l g)/(3\rho_a C_o)[\gamma - h(\gamma - 1)]^{-1} h^{2/3}$$ (27)

where C_d = drag coefficient
$\gamma = C_{fp}/C_o$
C_{fp} = drag coefficient for a flat plate
C_o = drag coefficient for a sphere of same volume
$h = a/b$, ratio of semi-major and semi-minor axes
r_p = radius of spherical drop of equivalent volume

For drops having less than 1.3 mm diameter Spilhaus [48] assumed that the shapes were spherical. For larger drops he assumed constant values for C_{fp} (= 0.6) and C_o (= 0.21). Using Schmidt's [45] relation, Hitschfeld [49] developed expressions for time of fall and distance of fall as functions of fall velocity.

Imai [50] suggested a fall velocity correlation considering surface tension:

$$r = [(3\mu_l C_d Re^2)/(32\rho_a g)]^{1/3}$$ (28)

$$u_t = [(\mu_l Re)/(2\rho_l r)][1 - 3\mu_l Re^2)/(128r\sigma\rho_l)]$$ (29)

The expression predicted velocity of water drops up to 2 mm diameter and the values compared well with the experimental data of Gunn and Kinzer [47].

Hughes and Gilliland [51] developed plots of C_d vs. Reynolds number with $Su = (du_t \rho_a/\mu_a)$ [$(\sigma/(\mu_a u_t)]$ as a parameter. They also plotted the terminal velocity group $T_v = (C_d/Re)^{-1/3} = u_t[(3\rho_a^2)/(4g\mu_a(\rho_1 - \rho_a)]^{1/3}$ vs. $Wt = (C_d Re^2)^{1/3} = (4/3)^{1/3}(g\rho_a(\rho_1 - \rho_a)/\mu_a^2)^{1/3}d$ with $Sd = (\sigma/\mu_a) \cdot [(3\rho_a^2)/(4g\mu_a(\rho_1 - \rho_a))]^{1/3}$ as parameter.

These graphs were tested by using the limited data of Laws and Weston only.

Narasimhamurty [52] developed a generalized correlation for the motion of liquid drops in gases and immiscible liquids and also for gas bubbles in liquids:

$$We = C(Re)^n$$ (30)

where $We = (du_t^2 \rho_a/\sigma)$
$Re = (du_t \rho_a/\mu_a)$

Equation 30 is valid for We $\leq$ 1.0 and We $\geq$ 4.0. For We $\leq$ 1.0 the values of C and n were correlated by

$$We = 0.252(M)^{0.338}Re^{1.602} \tag{31}$$

where $M = (g\mu_a^4)/(\sigma^3 \rho_a)$

Finlay [31] proposed an equation of the type

$$C_d We\, p^{0.13} = \alpha(Re/p^{0.13})^n \tag{32}$$

where C_d = drag coefficient
  p = property group, $\rho_a^2\sigma^3/(g\mu_a^4(\rho_l - \rho_a))$
  n = 1.26 for water
  n = 1.55 for other liquids
  α = proportionality constant

Srikrishna [23] found that terminal velocity of liquid drops increased with increasing diameter. His data for water drops compared well with those of Flower [38], Lenard [44], and Schmidt [45]. The data reported by Sutton [15], Magono [16], Laws [39], Henrickson [21], Gunn and Kinzer [47] and Finlay [31] were higher when compared to Srikrishna's [23] data. This may be due to the higher temperature of air in Srikrishna's experiments. Figure 10 shows terminal velocity

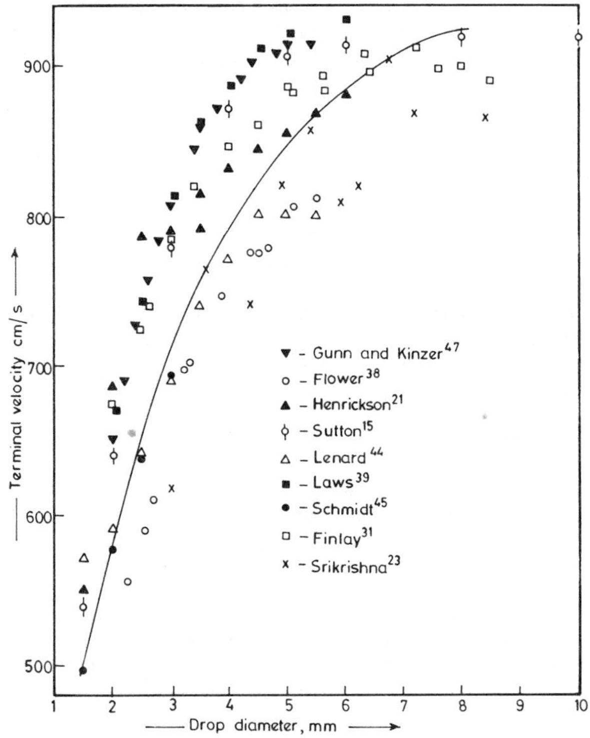

Figure 10. Terminal velocity of water drops in air.

Table 2
Values of α and n in Equation 32

Group of liquids	α	n	Deviation
Water	0.1814	1.551	-6.7% to 21%
Isopropyl alcohol, n-hexane, methyl ethyl ketone	0.5627	1.50	-17.4% to 29%
n-heptane; acetone, toluene, xylene, tetracholoethylene	1.269	1.220	-34% to 13%

From Srikrishna [23].

of water drops reported by Flower [38], Lenard [44], Sutton [15], Schmidt [45], Laws [39] Henrickson [21], Gunn and Kinzer [47], Finlay [31], and Srikrishna [23]. Srikrishna's [23] equa- tions of the type of Equation 32 had three sets of values for the proportionality constant and the exponent n as given in Table 2.

Gillaspy and Hoffer [42] measured the drag coefficients of Newtonian as well as non-Newtonian liquid drops in air. They proposed an equation of the type:

$$C_d = C_d(\text{Re}, \mu_l = \infty)(1 - (\mu_a/\mu_l)B\phi(\text{Re}))$$ (33)

valid for $800 \le \text{Re} \le 2{,}000$ and $\mu_l > 3.0$ cp. (B = a constant and $\phi(\text{Re})$ = a function of Reynolds number).

For estimation of terminal velocity of liquid drops in air, it appears that the same relationships applicable for solid spheres are valid till a Reynolds number of about 500. For Reynolds number greater than 500, a correlation of the form of Equation 32 is applicable. The constants proposed by Srikrishna [23], given in Table 2 may be used for design purposes for the Reynolds number range of about 600 to 4,300. Besides Reynolds number and drag coefficient, the correlation involves Weber number as well as the property group.

DROP BREAKUP

New surface area is created by breakup of large drops. Lenard [44] considered large free falling drops in air and noted that some drops were blown inside out. Lane and Green [53] described the breakup of a drop wherein the drop passed through stages of increasing flattening, torus formation, increasing bag size, bursting of the film and breakup of torus rim-producing droplets. Lane [28] considered the flattening type of deformation of water drops (diameter 0.5 mm to 5 mm). The dif- ference between velocity of air stream required to break the drop and the velocity of the drop at the instant of breaking was measured by Lane [28]. He reported

$$u_c^2 d_{max} = 612 \times 10^3 \text{ cm}^3/\text{sec}^2$$ (34)

where u_c = difference in velocity between the drop and its surroundings at breakup conditions
       d_{max} = diameter of the largest stable drop

The stages of breakup of a drop of water given by Lane [28] as photographed by Hoch schwender are shown in Figure 11.

Another kind of breakup where the drop was subjected to a transient pulse of air was also reported by Lane [28]. The drop presented a convex surface to the flow of air and the breakup was a chaotic disintegration. Hinze [54] presented a review of breakup of drops where he de- scribed three kinds of deformation: flattening type, cigar-shaped deformation as a jet, and a bulgy deformation.

Several studies of drop breakup concentrated on defining conditions under which a drop will break (or determining the largest stable drop size). The stability criterion is generally given by

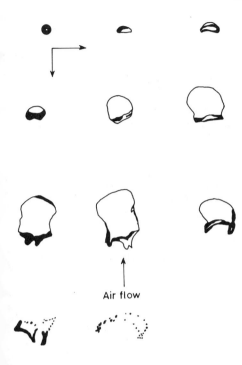

Air flow

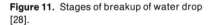

Figure 11. Stages of breakup of water drop [28].

the Weber number

$$We = u^2 \rho_a d_{max}/\sigma \tag{35}$$

Using the data of Merrington and Richardson [1], Hinze [55] estimated the critical Weber number as 13 for low-viscosity liquids. The value obtained from Equation 34 is approximately 10. Haas [56] reported a Weber number of 11.2 for mercury drops in air. Hanson and coworkers [57] studied liquid drops in the range of 0.1 mm to 1 mm diameter and reported the following equations:

$$u_c^2 d_{max} = 576.9 \times 10^3 \qquad \text{for water drops} \tag{36}$$

$$u_c^2 d_{max} = 251.8 \times 10^3 \qquad \text{(methyl alcohol)} \tag{37}$$

$$u_c^{1.8} d_{max} = 45.5 \times 10^3 \qquad \text{(silicon oil, 10 centistokes)} \tag{38}$$

$$u_c^{1.62} d_{max} = 17.3 \times 10^3 \qquad \text{(silicon oil, 50 centistokes)} \tag{39}$$

$$u_c^{1.36} d_{max} = 2.41 \times 10^3 \qquad \text{(silicon oil, 100 centistokes)} \tag{40}$$

Using $\rho_a = 1.18 \times 10^{-3}$ gm/cm^3 and the values of surface tension given by Hanson and coworkers [57], a critical Weber number of 9.5 is obtained for water, and 13.4 for methyl alcohol.

Hinze [54] proposed that the critical Weber number also depends on liquid viscosity and the relative velocity history. He suggested that the change in Weber number for high viscosity fluids may be expressed as:

$$We_{crit} = (We_{crit})_{\mu_l = 0}[1 + \phi(\mu_l/\sqrt{\rho_l d_{max}\sigma})] \tag{41}$$

Brodkey [3] gave an empirical equation

$$We_{crit} = (We_{crit})_{\mu_1=0} + 14(\mu_1/\sqrt{\rho_1 d_{max}\sigma})^{1.6} \tag{42}$$

where $\quad (We_{crit})_{\mu_1=0} = 4$ to 20 $\tag{43}$

Equation 42 was found to have about 20% maximum deviation.

Wolfe and Andersen [58] proposed an equation correlating their data on drop breakup for volume median diameter:

$$d_{vm} = [136(\mu_1\sigma^{3/2}d_i^{1/2})/(\rho_a\rho_1^{1/2}u^4)]^{1/3} \tag{44}$$

where $\quad d_{vm}$ = volume mean drop diameter (midpoint of cumulative volume plot
giving the largest size of various average sizes)

$\quad\quad\quad d_i$ = initial droplet diameter

$\quad\quad\quad u$ = drop velocity

Lehrer [60] proposed an equation for the critical diameter of a droplet before it breaks up:

$$d_{max} = [(16\sigma)/(\rho_1 - \rho_a)g]^{1/2} \tag{45}$$

Using Equation 45 Lehrer [60] obtained $d_{max} = 10.8$ mm for drops of distilled water which compares very well with the observed value of 10 mm reported by Merrington and Richardson [1]. A review on the critical conditions of breakup of liquid drops in gases was presented by Sarjeant [61].

HEAT AND MASS TRANSFER

The rate of heat and mass transfer from or to the drop depends on droplet diameter, drop velocity, temperature, humidity, and the transport properties. For heat transfer to a spherical droplet in still air, the Nusselt number is given by

$$Nu = h_c d/k = 2.0 \tag{46}$$

where $\quad h_c$ = heat transfer coefficient
$\quad\quad\quad d$ = drop diameter
$\quad\quad\quad k$ = thermal conductivity of air

according to Marshall [62]. By analogy, for mass transfer, the Sherwood number is given by

$$Sh = k_m d/D = 2.0 \tag{47}$$

where $\quad k_m$ = mass transfer coefficient
$\quad\quad\quad D$ = diffusivity

For moving drops, the Nusselt number and Sherwood number are expressed by

$$Nu = 2 + k_4(Re)^{p_1}(Pr)^{q_1} \tag{48}$$

and

$$Sh = 2 + k_5(Re)^{p_2}(Sc)^{q_2} \tag{49}$$

where k_4 and k_5 = constants
$\quad\quad$ Re = Reynolds number
$\quad\quad$ Pr = Prandtl number, $C_p\mu_a/k$
$\quad\quad$ Sc = Schmidt number, $\mu_a/(\rho_a D)$
p_1, p_2, q_1, q_2 = constants

Froessling [63] studied mass transfer from drops for Reynolds numbers in the range of 2 to 1,300 and proposed

$$Sh = 2.0 + 0.552Re^{0.5}Sc^{0.33} \tag{50}$$

Ranz and Marshall [64] suggested

$$Sh = 2.0 + 0.6Re^{0.5}Sc^{0.33} \tag{51}$$

Hsu, Sato, and Sage [65] studied evaporation from n-heptane drops in the Reynolds number range of 50 to 350. The constant k_5 was found to be 0.54, as compared to 0.6 in Ranz and Marshall's [64] study. For lower Reynolds numbers in the range of 1 to 20, Manning and Gauvin [66] obtained the same relationship as suggested by Ranz and Marshall [64]. Constan and Calvert [30] studied mass transfer from drops under oscillation and internal circulation. They proposed that effective diffusivities were 2 to 8 times greater than the theoretically calculated values. Pritchard and Biswas [67] developed equations describing evaporation of pure liquid droplets in free fall and found that the penetration theory gave a better fit to the experimental data. Finlay [31] found significant deviation from the Ranz and Marshall equation [64] for evaporation of liquid drops. He attributed the higher rates of evaporation to the oscillation and circulation within the drops. Srikrishna [23] studied evaporation rates of nine liquids in air and found that in all cases the rates were higher than those given by Ranz and Marshall [64]. Srikrishna [23] proposed equations of the form

$$Sh = k_6 + k_5Re^{1/2}Sc^{1/3} \tag{52}$$

where k_6 and k_5 are constants, for each of the nine liquids. Ahmadzadeh and Harker [68] studied evaporation rates from drops of acetone-water mixture and proposed

$$Sh = 3(0.345d_e - 0.744)Re \tag{53}$$

where d_e = equivalent spherical droplet diameter

Srikrishna, Sivaji, and Narasimhamurty [32] developed an equation for the Sherwood number:

$$Sh = 2 + 0.37Re^{0.577}Sc^{0.333} \tag{54}$$

For Equation 54, which is applicable for a Reynolds number range of 628 to 4,271 and Schmidt numbers varying from 0.61 to 2.5, the deviations were found to be within 18%.

Duffie and Marshall [7, 69] presented equations for calculating the time for complete evaporation of liquid drops in air, using the Ranz and Marshall Equation [64], for the Reynolds number range of 0.2 to 500. Dennis [70] studied the effect of relative humidity and air velocity on the growth rate of hygroscopic liquid drops such as sulfuric acid and ammonium nitrate solution. A summary of methods for estimating the evaporation rates of liquid drops containing dissolved and insoluble solids is given by Masters [9].

Ray and Davis [71, 72] evaluated the evaporation rate of a single droplet and the evaporation rate of a droplet surrounded by a finite array of droplets. These results were compared with the numerical results of Labowsky [73]. Ray and Davis [71, 72] neglected the interfacial movement and considered the case where rate of diffusion is higher than the rate of decrease of drop size.

For estimating mass transfer coefficients, Equation 54, which is applicable for a Reynolds number range of 628 to 4,271 can be used.

CHEMICAL REACTION

Simultaneous heat and mass transfer along with chemical reaction and production of liquid drops in gases is important in the design of spray reactors and absorption towers. Danchwerts [74] presented expressions for absorption rates of gas into a falling liquid droplet. For studying the absorption rate of sulfur dioxide, Johnstone and Coughanowr [75] suspended a liquid droplet (700 to 900 micron diameter) containing manganese sulfate. Plit [76] derived an expression for average concentration of dissolved gas in a small diameter drop in terms of Fourier number:

$$(A^* - A_{ave})/(A^* - A_o) = (6/\pi^2)[\exp(-\pi^2 Fo) + (1/2^2)\exp - [(2\pi)^2 Fo] + (1/3^2)\exp - [(3\pi)^2 Fo]]$$

where A^* = equilibrium concentration of gas at the surface
A_o = concentration at any instant i
A_{ave} = average concentration reached during a definite time of phase interaction
Fo = Fourier number, Dt/r^2
D = diffusity
t = time
r = drop radius

Abdul-Rahman and Crosby [77] studied the reaction of single drops of aqueous orthophosphoric acid with a flowing mixture of dry nitrogen and ammonia. They also studied the reaction of sulfuric acid drops with ammonia. Gal-or, Klinzing, and Tavlarides [78] and Tavlarides et al. [79] reviewed the work on mass transfer, and heat transfer with and without chemical reaction in bubbles and drops. Sivaji [80], and Sivaji and Narasimhamurty [81] also reviewed the literature on mass transfer with chemical reaction. Sivaji [80] and Sivaji and Narasimhamurty [82] studied the absorption of oxygen in air by liquid drops, suspended freely in air. The liquid drops contained sodium sulfite and cobaltous sulfate was used as catalyst. They found that the absorption rate was independent of the sulfite concentration.

EXPERIMENTAL TECHNIQUES

The mechanics of liquid drops in air can be studied using the following methods:

1. Observing the drop falling freely in stagnant air from high fall distances.
2. Suspending drops from thin fibers.
3. Suspending drops aerodynamically in an upward current of air.

Lenard [44], Schmidt [45], Flower [38], Laws [39], and Gunn [27] are some of the researchers who used the first method. The drop has to fall through 10 to 15 meters before attaining terminal velocity. Since terminal velocities of liquid drops in air are in the range of 4 to 10 m/s, very little time is available for observing the drop behavior. High-speed photographic techniques are necessary in such cases. Since time of contact is very small, it is difficult to study evaporation rates and absorption rates. Great care should be taken in the experimental set up as well as measuring techniques.
    The second method involves suspending liquid drops from thin fibers. Ranz and Marshall [64] and Charlesworth and Marshall [83] employed this method. This may involve errors due to heat conduction through supporting material and also may influence the internal circulation within the drop. Further, this technique is useful for studying very small droplets of the size of microns.
    Blanchard [26], Srikrishna [23], Sivaji [80], and other researchers used the third method where the drop was suspended at a point in an upward current of air. In this method, when the air veloc-

ity equals the terminal velocity of the drop, the drop gets suspended in the air steam. The contact times are much longer and it is much easier to use photographic techniques to study the details of shapes and oscillation frequencies of liquid drops. Using suspension techniques a tall tower is not needed as in the case of a falling drop.

Angus et al. [84] and Golovin [85] discussed the application of laser Doppler technique for the measurement of the velocity of liquid drops. The technique involves the Doppler shift of laser light scattered by moving particles. This technique has advantages of flow pattern determination of fluid, instantaneous response, and measurement of velocity in the range of 10^{-3} cm/s to 2,500 m/s.

High speed photography is used for determining the shape, size, evaporation rate, and terminal velocity of liquid drops. Kintner et al. [86] reviewed the application of high-speed photography in drop and bubble phenomena. Blanchard [26], Srikrishna [23], and Sivaji [80] used high-speed photography. Berger et al. [87], and Deich, Shanin, and Karyshev [88] discussed the application of optical methods in the determination of droplet sizes. Tate [89] described the immersion sampling method for determination of droplet size distribution. Adler et al. [90], used a scanning instrument for measuring droplet size distribution. Pye [91] developed an apparatus using a pulse technique which could determine drop sizes in the range of 15 micron to 1.0 mm. Light diffraction, gas absorption, and electrical methods were discussed by Soo [92] for droplet-size determination.

DESIGN APPLICATIONS

Determination of surface tension of liquids by using Equation 1

$$2\pi R\sigma = mg \tag{1}$$

is one of the early applications of the formation of liquid drops at a very slow rate. In the initial stages of jetting region, where the drops formed are fairly uniform in size, Equation 4

$$d = 1.89d_j \tag{4}$$

proposed by Rayleigh [2] and Equation 5

$$d = 1.88d_j[1 + (3\mu_1/\sqrt{\sigma d_j\rho_1})]^{1/2} \tag{5}$$

proposed by Weber [5] may be used. As the jet length increases, the drops formed have a size distribution and the appropriate distribution functions given by Equations 8 to 11 should be used. A summary of correlations where the distribution parameters are correlated with the features of the system generating the spray are given by Brodkey [3], Orr [8], and Masters [9].

Below 1 mm diameter the drops may be assumed to be spherical in shape. Larger drops oscillate and the oscillation frequency can be estimated by using Equation 13:

$$f = [8\sigma/(3\pi m)]^{0.5} \tag{13}$$

The mean values of the major and minor axes of liquid drops may be calculated using Equation 17 proposed by Srikrishna, Sivaji, and Narasimhamurty [32]:

$$a/b = 0.146(g \, \Delta\rho d^2/\sigma) + 1.0 \tag{17}$$

Upto a Reynolds number of 500 terminal velocity of liquid drops may be estimated by using the same equations for solid spheres. For Reynolds numbers greater than 500

$$C_d We \, p^{0.13} = \alpha(Re/p^{0.13})^n \tag{32}$$

along with the constants given by Srikrishna [23] can be used.

The critical diameter of a drop before it breaks up can be calculated by using the Equation 45 suggested by Lehrer [60]:

$$d_{max} = [(16\sigma)/(\rho_l - \rho_a)g]^{1/2} \tag{45}$$

For estimation of Sherwood numbers Equation 54 developed by Srikrishna, Sivaji, and Narasimhamurty [32] is useful:

$$Sh = 2 + 0.37Re^{0.577}Sc^{0.333} \tag{54}$$

Masters [9] gave an extensive summary of equations for calculating evaporation rates of liquid drops.

A generalized correlation has yet to be developed for heat and mass transfer with chemical reaction for liquid drops. Reviews on the topic are given by Gal-or, Klinzing, and Talvarides [78], Talvarides et al., [79] and Sivaji and Narasimhamurty [81].

SUMMARY

The literature on hydrodynamics of liquid droplets in air has been reviewed in the present work. Determination of surface tension of liquids is facilitated by the slow drop formation method. As liquid velocity to the nozzle increases a jet is formed which breaks down to form drops of varying sizes. The jet length increases, reaches a maximum and then decreases, resulting in atomization. The common distribution functions applicable to the droplet sizes are described in the chapter.

It is found that small drops below 1 mm diameter are nearly spherical in shape. Larger drops do not have any equilibrium shape and they show oscillations in shape. The frequency of oscillation can be estimated knowing the surface tension and mass of the drop. The frequency of oscillation decreases as drop diameter increases. Equations for calculating the mean value of the ratio of the major and minor axes of the ellipsoid are presented.

Liquid drops behave as solid spheres upto a Reynolds number of about 500, and hence the same equations for estimating the terminal velocity of solid spheres may be used in this region. Larger liquid drops are found to attain terminal velocities in a shorter time than solid spheres of equal volume. Also beyond a Reynolds number of 500 the terminal velocity of liquid drops is less than that of solid spheres of equal volume. This is mainly due to the deformations and oscillations in shape. The terminal velocity increases with increasing drop diameter and approaches an asymptotic value. Correlations involving drag coefficient, property group, Weber number, and Reynolds number are used for estimating terminal velocities.

The factors controlling the breakup of liquid drops are discussed and methods for calculating the maximum stable size of a liquid drop are indicated.

Correlations for the Sherwood number are summarized in the article. Studies on chemical reaction with liquid drops in gases are briefly discussed. Various experimental techniques used for studying the mechanics of liquid drops are summarized and their relative merits are examined. The design applications are also mentioned.

Further work is necessary in the following areas:

1. Drop size distribution in the varicose and sinuous region and also for atomization.
2. Development of generalized design equations correlating size-distribution parameters with features of spray-generation system.
3. Further work on drop behavior in the accelerating region.
4. Generalized equations for estimating terminal velocity of liquid drops.
5. Phenomena of internal circulation, drift and rotation—more experimental information is necessary.
6. Correlation of drop phenomena such as oscillation and internal circulation to the rate of heat and mass transfer and also to chemical reaction.
7. Quantitative information on drop coalescence.

8. Studies on the mechanics of multidrop systems and drop interactions.
9. Hydrodynamics of non-Newtonian liquid drops.

NOTATION

A_F	frontal area	N	number of drops having diameter d
A^*	equilibrium concentration of the gas at the surface	Nu	Nusselt number
A_o	concentration at any instant	n	exponent
A_{ave}	average concentration reached during a definite time of phase interaction	Pr	Prandtl number
		P_v	percent of spray by volume existing as droplets with sizes greater than diameter d
a	semi-major axis		
a_1	a constant in Equation 25	p	property group in Equation 32
B	constant in Equation 33	P_i, P_o	pressures inside and outside the drop
b	semi-minor axis		
b_1	constant in Equation 25	P_1, P_2	exponents
C	constant in Equation 30	q	constant
C_d	drag coefficient for fluid sphere	q_1, q_2	exponents
C_o	drag coefficient for a sphere	R	radius of circular tip at which drop is formed
C_p	specific heat at constant pressure		
C_{ds}	drag coefficient for solid sphere	Re	Reynolds number
C_{fp}	drag coefficient for flat plate	Re_j	jet Reynolds number
c	constant in Equation 21	r	drop radius
c_1	constant in Equation 25	r_1, r_2	principal radii at any point on the surface of the drop
D	diffusivity		
d	drop diameter	r_p	radius of spherical drop of equivalent volume
d_e	equivalent diameter of a spherical droplet		
		s	standard deviation
d_G	geometric mean diameter of the drops	s_g	standard geometric mean deviation
d_i	initial droplet diameter	Sc	Schmidt number
d_j	jet diameter	Sd	surface tension-size group used in Hughes and Gilliland's plots
d_m	mean diameter		
d_n	nozzle diameter	Sh	Sherwood number
d_{gm}	geometric mean diameter	Su	surface tension group used in Hughes and Gilliland's plots
d_{vm}	volume mean drop diameter		
d_{RR}	Rosin-Rammler mean diameter	T_v	terminal velocity group used in Hughes and Gilliland's plots
d_{max}	diameter of largest stable drop		
du/dt	acceleration of the drop	t	time
Fo	Fourier number, Dt/r^2	u	drop velocity
f	oscillation frequency	u_c	difference in velocity between drop and surroundings at breakup
g	acceleration due to gravity		
h	ratio of semimajor and semiminor axes, a/b	u_j	jet velocity
		u_t	terminal velocity of drop
h_c	heat transfer coefficient	u_{ts}	terminal velocity of solid sphere
i	constant in Equation 16	V	drop volume
k	thermal conductivity of air	We	Weber number
k_m	mass transfer coefficient	We_j	jet Weber number
k_1, k_2, k_3	constants in Equation 11	We_{crit}	critical Weber number
k_4, k_5, k_6	constants	Wt	gravity group used in Hughes and Gilliland's plots
l	constant in Equation 16		
M	property group in Equation 31	x	exponent
m	mass of the drop		

Greek Symbols

α	symbol for proportionality	ρ_a	density of air
γ	ratio of drag coefficients	ρ_l	density of liquid
Δ	difference	$\sum$	summation
μ_a	viscosity of air	σ	surface tension of liquid
μ_l	viscosity of liquid	ϕ	symbol for function
π	3.1416 . . .	ω	angular frequency of oscillation

REFERENCES

1. Merrington, A. C., and Richardson, E. G., "The Breakup of Liquid Jets," *The Proceedings of the Physical Society*, Vol. 59, Part I, No. 331 (Jan. 1947), pp. 1–13.
2. Rayleigh, Lord, *The Proceedings of London Mathematical Society*, Vol. 10, No. 4 (1878), pp. 4, cited in R. S. Brodkey [3].
3. Brodkey, R. S., *The Phenomena of Fluid Motions*, Reading, Massachusetts: Addison-Wesley Publishing Company, 1967, pp. 539–618.
4. Marshall, W. R., Jr., *Atomisation and Spray Drying*, Chemical Engineering Progress Monograph Series, No. 2, New York: American Institute of Chemical Engineers, 1954.
5. Weber, C., *Z. Angew. Math. Mech.*, Vol. 11 (1931), pp. 136–154, cited in R. S. Brodkey [3].
6. Ohnesorge, G., *Z. Angew. Math. Mech.*, Vol. 16 (1936), pp. 355, cited in R. S. Brodkey [3].
7. Duffie, J. A., and Marshall, W. R., Jr., "Factors Influencing the Properties of Spray-Dried Materials Part I," *Chemical Engineering Progress*, Vol. 49, No. 8 (Aug. 1953), pp. 417–423.
8. Orr, C., Jr., *Particulate Technology*, New York: The Macmillan Company, 1966.
9. Masters, K., *Spray Drying Handbook*, 3rd Ed., London: George Godwin Limited, 1979.
10. Pilcher, J. M., and Thomas, R. E., "Drop-Size Distributions of Fuel Sprays," *Advances in Chemistry*, Series 20, 1958, pp. 155–165.
11. Lewis, H. C., et al., "Atomisation of Liquids in High Velocity Gas Streams," *Industrial and Engineering Chemistry*, Vol. 40, No. 1 (Jan. 1948), pp. 67–74.
12. Mugele, R. A., and Evans, H. D., "Droplet Size Distribution in Sprays," *Industrial and Engineering Chemistry*, Vol. 43, No. 6 (June 1951), pp. 1317–1324.
13. Mache, H., *Met. Zeit.*, Vol. 39 (1904) pp. 378, cited in M. Srikrishna [23].
14. Edgerton, E. K., and Killian, A. R., *Flash: Seeing the Unseen by Ultra High Speed Photography*, Hale Publishing Company, 1939.
15. Sutton, O. G., cited in M. Srikrishna [23].
16. Magono, C., *Journal of Meteorology*, Vol. 11 (1954), pp. 77, cited in M. Srikrishna [23].
17. McDonald, J. E., *Theoretical Cloud Physics Studies Final Report*. Project NR082093, Office of Naval Research, U.S. Navy Dept., pp. 72, cited in G. S. R. Narasimhamurty [22].
18. Saito, S., *Sci. Repts. Tohoku Imp. Univ.*, Vol. 2 (1914), pp. 179–201, cited in Harilal [41].
19. Best, A. C., *M.R.P.*, 227 (1946), cited in M. Srikrishna [23].
20. Best, A. C., *M.R.P.* 330 (1947), cited in M. Srikrishna [23].
21. Henrickson, F., Jr., *S. M. Thesis in Ch. E. Pract.*, Massachusetts Institute of Technology, 1941, cited in G. S. R. Narasimhamurty [22].
22. Narasimhamurty, G. S. R., *Studies on the Rate of Fall of Liquid Droplets*, Ph.D. thesis, University of Cincinnati, 1954.
23. Srikrishna, M., *Motion of Liquid Drops in Gases (Effect of Physical Properties of Liquids on the Mechanics of Drops in Air)*, Ph.D. thesis, Indian Institute of Technology, Bombay, 1968.
24. Rayleigh, Lord, cited in H. Lamb [25].
25. Lamb, H., *Hydrodynamics*, 6th Ed., Cambridge: University Press 1959, pp. 473–475.
26. Blanchard, D. C., *PROJECT CIRRUS on Observations on the Behaviour of Water Drops at Terminal Velocity in Air*, Occasional Report No. 7, Schenectady, New York: General Electric Research Laboratory, 1 Nov. 1948.
27. Gunn, R., *J. Geophysics Res.*, Vol. 54 (Dec. 1949), pp. 383–385, cited in M. Srikrishna [23].

8. Lane, W. R., "Shatter of Drops in Streams of Air," *Industrial and Engineering Chemistry*, Vol. 43, No. 6 (June 1951), pp. 1312–1317.

9. Garner, F. H., and Lane, J. J., "Mass Transfer to Drops of Liquid Suspended in a Gas Stream Part II—Experimental Work and Results," *Transactions of Institution of Chemical Engineers (London)*, Vol. 37 (1959), pp. 162–172.

30. Constan, G. L., and Calvert, S., "Mass Transfer in Drops Under Conditions that Promote Oscillation and Internal Circulation" *AIChE Journal*, Vol. 9, No. 1 (Jan. 1963), pp. 109–115.

31. Finlay, B. A., *A Study of Liquid Drops in an Air Stream*, Ph.D. thesis, University of Birmingham, 1957.

32. Srikrishna, M., Sivaji, K., and Narasimhamurty, G. S. R., "Mechanics of Liquid Drops in Air," *The Chemical Engineering Journal*, Vol. 24 (1982), pp. 27–34.

33. Hadamard, M. J., *Compt. Rend.*, Vol. 152 (1911), pp. 1735 and Vol. 154 (1912), pp. 107, cited in R. S. Brodkey [3].

34. Rybczybski, D. P., *Bull. Intern. Acad. Sci.* Cracovie, A403, 1911, pp. 40, cited in R. S. Brodkey [3].

35. McDonald, J. E., "The Shape and Aerodynamics of Large Raindrops," *Journal of Meteorology*, Vol. 11 (1954), pp. 478, cited in P. H. Gillaspy and T. E. Hoffer [42].

36. Pruppacher, H. R., and Pitter, R. L., "A Semi-empirical Determination of the Shape of Cloud and Rain Drops," *J. Atmos. Science*, Vol. 28 (1971), p. 86, cited in P. H. Gillaspy and T. E. Hoffer [42].

37. Green, A. W., "An Approximation for the Shapes of Large Rain Drops," *J. Applied Meteor.*, Vol. 14 (1975), pp. 1578 cited in P. H. Gillaspy and T. E. Hoffer [42].

38. Flower, W. D., "The Terminal Velocity of Drops," *Proceedings of the Physical Society*, Vol. 40 (1928), pp. 167, cited in M. Srikrishna [23].

39. Laws, J. O., "Measurments of Fall Velocities of Water Drops and Rain Drops," *Transactions of American Geophysical Union*, Vol. 22 (1941), pp. 709, cited in M. Srikrishna [23].

40. Best, A. C., "Empirical Formulae for the Terminal Velocity of Drops Falling Through the Atmosphere," *Quarterly Journal of the Royal Meteorological Society*, 1950, cited in M. Srikrishna [23].

41. Harilal, *Motion of Liquid Drops in Gases*, M. Tech Thesis, Indian Institute of Technology, Bombay, 1962.

42. Gillaspy, P. H., and Hoffer, T. E., "Experimental Measurments of the Effect of Viscosity on Drag for Liquid Drops," *AIChE Journal*, Vol. 29, No. 2 (March 1983), pp. 229–236.

43. Bond, W. N., and Newton, D. A., *Phil. Mag.*, Vol. 5 (1928), pp. 794–800, cited in R. S. Brodkey [3].

44. Lenard, P., *Met. Zeit.*, Vol. 39 (1904), pp. 209, cited in M. Srikrishna [23].

45. Schmidt, *W. Akad. Wiss. Wien. Sitz. Ber.*, Vol. 118, (1909) pp. 71, cited in M. Srikrishna [23].

46. Meinzer, O. E., *Hydrology (Physics of the Earth IX)*. New York: McGraw Hill Book Company, 1942, pp. 40.

47. Gunn, R., and Kinzer, G. D., "The Terminal Velocity of Fall for Water Droplets in Stagnant Air," *Journal of Meteorology*, Vol. 6 (1949), pp. 243–248.

48. Spilhaus, A. F., *Journal of Meteorology*, Vol. 5 (1948), pp. 108, cited in M. Srikrishna [23].

49. Hitschfeld, W., "Free Fall of Drops Through Air," *Transactions of American Geophysical Unions*, Vol. 32, No. 5 (1951), pp. 697.

50. Imai, I., *Journal of Meteorological Society of Japan*, Series 2, Vol. 28, No. 4 (April 1950), pp. 113, cited in G. S. R. Narasimhamurty [22].

51. Hughes, R. R., and Gilliland, E. R., "The Mechanics of Drops," *Chemical Engineering Progress*, Vol. 48, No. 10 (Oct. 1952), pp. 497–504.

52. Narasimhamurty, G. S. R., "The Motion of Deformable Bodies in Fluids," *Transactions of the Indian Institute of Chemical Engineers*, Vol. 7, Part II (1954–1955), pp. 123–128.

53. Lane, W. R., and Green, H. L., in *Surveys in Mechanics*, G. K. Batchelor and R. M. Davies (Eds.), New York: Cambridge University Press, 1956, pp. 162–215.

54. Hinze, J. O., "Fundamentals of the Hydrodynamic Mechanism of Splitting in Dispersion Processes," *AIChE Journal*, Vol. 1 No. 3 (Sept. 1955), pp. 289–295.

55. Hinze, J. O., *Appl. Sci. Res.* Al (1948), pp. 263–273, cited in R. S. Brodkey [3].
56. Haas, F. C., "Stability of Droplets Suddenly Exposed to a High Velocity Gas Stream," *AIChE Journal*, Vol. 10, No. 6 (Nov. 1964), pp. 920–924.
57. Hanson, A. R., Domich, E. G., and Adams, H. S., "Shock Tube Investigation of the Breakup of Drops by Air Blasts," *The Physics of Fluids*, Vol. 6, No. 8 (Aug. 1963), pp. 1070–1080.
58. Wolfe and Andersen, *Proc. 5th Intern. Shock Tube Symp.*, April 1965, pp. 1145–1969, cited in R. H. Perry and C. H. Chilton [59].
59. Perry, R. H., and Chilton, C. H., *Chemical Engineering Handbook*, 5th Ed., Tokyo; Mc Graw-Hill Kogakusha Ltd, 1973, pp. 18/58–18/67.
60. Lehrer, I. H. "On Bubble and Drop Deformation and Breakup," *Israel Journal of Technology*, Vol. 13, No. 4 (1975), pp. 246–252.
61. Sarjeant, M., "Drop Breakup by Gas Streams," *Proceedings of IIIrd Eur. Conf. Mixing.*, Vol. 1 (1979), pp. 255–268 cited in *Chemical Abstracts*, 93:116516x, 1980.
62. Marshall, W. R., Jr., "Heat and Mass Transfer in Spray Drying," *Transactions of the ASME*, Vol. 77, No. 11 (Nov. 1955), pp. 1377–1385.
63. Froessling, N., *Gerlands. Beits. Geophysik*, Vol. 52 (1938), pp. 170, cited in M. Srikrishna [23].
64. Ranz, W. E., and Marshall, W. R., "Evaporation from Drops. Part II," *Chemical Engineering Progress*, Vol. 48, No. 4 (April 1952), pp. 173–180.
65. Hsu, N. T., Sato, K., and Sage, B. H., "Material Transfer in Turbulent Gas Streams," *Industrial and Engineering Chemistry*, Vol. 46, No. 5 (May 1954), pp. 870–876.
66. Manning, W. P., and Gauvin, W. H., "Heat and Mass Transfer to Decelerating Finely Atomised Sprays" *AIChE Journal*, Vol. 6, No. 2 (June 1960), pp. 184–190.
67. Pritchard, C. L., and Biswas, S. K., "Evaporation of Drops in Free Fall," *Transactions of Indian Chemical Engineer*, Vol. 8, No. 4 (Oct. 1966), pp. 93–97.
68. Ahmadzedeh, J., and Harker, J. H., "Evaporation of Liquid Droplets in Free Fall" *The Transactions of Institution of Chemical Engineers*, Vol. 52, No. 1 (Jan. 1974), pp. 108–111.
69. Duffie, J. A., and Marshall, W. R., Jr., "Factors Influencing the Properties of Spray-Dried Materials Part II," *Chemical Engineering Progress*, Vol. 49, No. 9 (Sept. 1953), pp. 480–486.
70. Dennis, W. L., "The Growth of Hygroscopic Drops in a Humid Air Stream," *Discussions of the Faraday Society*, No. 30 (1960), pp. 78–85.
71. Ray, A. K., and Davis, E. J., "Heat and Mass Transfer with Multiparticle Interactions Part I Droplet Evaporation," *Chemical Engineering Communications*, No. 6 (1980), pp. 61–79.
72. Ray, A. K., and Davis, E. J., "Heat and Mass Transfer with Multiparticle Interactions Part II Surface Reaction," *Chemical Engineering Communications*, No. 10 (1981), pp. 81–102.
73. Labowsky, M., "The Effects of Nearest Neighbour Interactions on the Evaporation Rate of Cloud Particles," *Chemical Engineering Science*, Vol. 31, No. 9 (1976), pp. 803–813.
74. Danckwerts, P. V., "Absorption by Simultaneous Diffusion and Chemical Reaction into Particles of Various Shapes and into Falling Drops," *Transactions of the Faraday Society*, Vol. 47 (1951), pp. 1014–1023.
75. Johnstone, H. F., and Coughanowr, D. R., "Absorption of Sulfur Dioxide from Air (Oxidation in Drops Containing Dissolved Catalysts)," *Industrial and Engineering Chemistry*, Vol. 50, No. 8 (Aug. 1958), pp. 1169–1172.
76. Plit, I. G., "Theory of Mass Transfer in Drops of Small Diameter in Contact with Gas of Constant Concentration," *Journal of Applied Chemistry of U.S.S.R.* Vol. 38, No. 1 (Jan. 1965), pp. 125–132.
77. Abdul-Rahman, Y. A. K., and Crosby, E. J., "Direct Formation of Particles from Drops by Chemical Reaction with Gases," *Chemical Engineering Science*, Vol. 28, No. 6 (June 1973), pp. 1273–1284.
78. Gal-or, B., Klinzing, G. E., and Tavlarides, L. L., "Bubble and Drop Phenomena," *Industrial and Engineering Chemistry*, Vol. 61, No. 2 (Feb. 1969), pp. 21–34.
79. Tavlarides, L. L., et al., "Bubble and Drop Phenomena," *Industrial and Engineering Chemistry*, Vol. 62, No. 11 (Nov. 1970), pp. 6–27.
80. Sivaji, K., "Absorption Accompanied by Chemical Reaction in Single Liquid Drops," Ph.D. thesis, Indian Institute of Technology, Bombay, 1977.

81. Sivaji, K., and Narasimhamurty, G. S. R., "Mass Transfer with Chemical Reaction in Drops and Bubbles," *Indian Chemical Journal*, Vol. 8 (1974), pp. 8–15.

82. Sivaji, K., and Narasimhamurty, G. S. R., "Kinetics of Sulfite Oxidation," *Industrial and Engineering Chemistry Fundamentals*, Vol. 24 (1982), pp. 344–352.

83. Charlesworth, D. H., and Marshall, W. R., Jr., "Evaporation of Drops Containing Dissolved Solids," *AIChE Journal*, Vol. 6 (1960), pp. 9–23.

84. Angus, J. C., et al., "Motion Measurement by Laser Doppler Techniques," *Industrial and Engineering Chemistry*, Vol. 61, No. 2 (Feb. 1969), pp. 8–20.

85. Golovin, V. A., et al., "Model of a Two-phase Flow Studied Using a Laser," *Teplofiz. Vys. Temp.*, Vol. 9, No. 3 pp. 606–610, cited in *Chemical Abstracts*, 74: 153346, r, 1971.

86. Kintner, R. C. et al., "Photography in Bubble and Drop Research," *Canadian Journal of Chemical Engineering*, Vol. 39, No. 6 (Dec. 1961), pp. 235–241.

87. Berger, J. E., et al., "Miscellaneous Applications of Optics," *Optical Transforms* (1972), pp. 401–422, cited in *Chemical Abstracts*, 77:119049, c, 1972.

88. Deich, M. E., Shanin, V. K., and Karyshev, A. K., "Determination of the Spectrum of Water Drop Dimensions in Two-phase Flows by Optical Methods," *Teploenergitika*, *(Moscow)*, Vol. 3 (1980), pp. 30–32.

89. Tate, R. W., "Immersion Sampling of Spray Droplets," *IAChE Journal*, Vol. 7, No. 4 (Dec. 1961), pp. 574–577.

90. Adler, C. R., et al., "A Scanning Device for Determining the Size Distribution of Spray Droplet Images," *Chemical Engineering Progress*, Vol. 50, No. 1 (Jan. 1954), pp. 14–23.

91. Pye, J. W., "Droplet Size Distribution in Sprays Using Pulse Counting Technique," *Journal of Institute of Fuel*, Vol. 44, No. 364 (May 1971), pp. 253–256.

92. Soo, S. L., *Fluid Dynamics of Multiphase Systems*. Waltham, Massachusetts: Blaisdell Publishing Company, 1967.

CHAPTER 12

DYNAMICS OF GAS-LIQUID SPRAY SYSTEMS

Woon-Shing Yeung

Mechanical and Energy Engineering Department
University of Lowell
Lowell, Massachusetts, USA

CONTENTS

INTRODUCTION

When a liquid first emerges through a pressure-atomizing nozzle it is in the form of a jet or a sheath. This liquid jet or sheath quickly disintegrates into droplets of various sizes due to aerodynamic instabilities. We shall call the region where the liquid jet or sheath has not completely disintegrated the near region, and the region where the liquid exists as droplets the far region. A schematic diagram of a liquid spray is shown in Figure 1.

The dynamics of the near region, or the atomization region [1], depends on the various mechanisms of the atomization process. These mechanisms are discussed in Chapter 11. Of particular

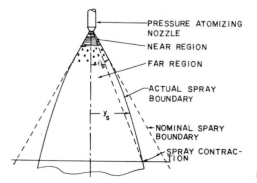

Figure 1. Notations of a liquid spray.

interests in the near region are the break up length; the spray angle; the velocity of the liquid sheath; drop size distribution; and the droplet velocity at the break-up point. These parameters serve as initial conditions on the dynamics of the liquid spray in the far region. We shall now proceed to describe the behavior of the far region.

As the droplets travel downstream in the far region, they entrain the ambient gas and consequently set up an overall induced gas flow field. This induced gas motion in turn modifies the droplet trajectories. The subsequent behavior of the far region is then governed by the interaction between the droplet and the gas phases.

This chapter discusses the fluid dynamics of the liquid spray in the far region. Information requiring the consideration of the near region will be assumed known or determined from available correlations.

LITERATURE REVIEW

Numerous analytical and experimental studies have been made on the aerodynamics of liquid sprays. These studies can be divided into two main categories: one that considers the induced gas motion only and the other considers the droplet trajectories only.

In the former category, Briffa and Dombrowski [2] investigated the rate of air entrainment for a plane spray while Benatt and Eisenklam [3] considered that for hollow cone sprays. Measurements of air velocity inside conical sprays were made by Rasbash and Stark [4] and by Gluckert [5]. They found that the induced air motion is dynamically similar to that of a turbulent gas jet. A small-scale experiment was conducted by Chuah et al. [6] to measure the induced air velocity inside several small plane sprays, using a probe introduced by Rasbash et al. [4].

In the latter category, the trajectories of the droplets are calculated given a particular ambient gas motion. In principle, it involves the integration of the Lagrangian equations of motion of the droplets. Heat and mass transfer are usually coupled with the hydrodynamics in this category. For example, Gauvin et al. [7] calculated the trajectories of evaporating droplets in a rotating flow field of a spray dryer. Sandoz and Sun [8] studied the effects of the ambient gas motion on spray trajectories taking into account condensation. Recent progress has also been made in computing the spray trajectories with droplet-droplet interactions included [9].

Analyses of the interaction between the induced gas motion and the droplet trajectories are relatively scarce. This may be attributed to the necessity of solving the gas and droplet flow fields simultaneously. One of the interesting phenomena that results from the gas-droplet interaction is the contraction of the spray from its nominal spray envelope, as shown in Figure 1. This downward bending of the spray is partly due to gravity and interfacial drag of the entrained gas. Experimentally, the spray contraction is found to increase with increasing ambient pressure [10, 11].

Rothe and Block [12] presented a mechanistic one-dimensional model to calculate the gas and droplet flow fields. Boysan and Binark [13] gave a three-dimensional numerical solution for the hollow cone spray. A more comprehensive numerical solution for the steady, turbulent, axisymmetric spray was later given by Alpert and Mathews [14]. The transient development of subcooled water spraying into a saturated steam environment was numerically studied by Chan et al. [15]. Recently, Yeung presented an integral analysis [16] and a similarity solution [17] of gas-liquid sprays based on a simplified set of governing equations.

THEORY

We consider three common types of pressure-atomizing nozzles. They are the plane (or flat, or fan) spray, the solid (or full) cone spray, and the hollow cone spray. The physical system is shown in Figure 1. A nozzle discharges liquid vertically downwards into a quiescent region of ambient gas. To maintain generality, we assume the gas medium can be

1. Entirely the vapor phase of the liquid substance.
2. A mixture of a noncondensible gas and the liquid vapor.
3. Entirely a noncondensible gas.

Practical situations include spray dryers in which water droplets are vaporized in a hot humid air stream [7]; the nuclear reactor emergency core cooling (ECC) spray system in which subcooled water is used to condense the large amount of steam generated during an accident situation [15]; sprinkler systems for fire extinguishment [14]; and fuel injection systems in internal combustion engines.

The basic assumptions are:

1. The spray is dilute, i.e., the volume occupied by the droplets is negligible.
2. The ambient temperature is constant at T_v, even though heat and mass transfer may occur.
3. In the case of the ambient being a mixture of a noncondensible gas and vapor, the properties such as viscosity, conductivity, etc. of the ambient region are taken as those of the non-condensible gas.
4. The flow field is two-dimensional for the plane spray, and axisymmetric for the solid and hollow cone sprays.

In the following discussion, we shall refer to the ambient as the gas field or phase and the droplet as the droplet field or phase. The gas field can contain at most two species or components: a noncondensible gas and the vapor of the liquid substance issuing from the nozzle. The droplet field contains only the liquid species or component. All equations and variables are pertinent to the fields or phases, not the individual species or component, unless otherwise stated.

Two subregions can be distinguished in the far region. Inside the spray envelope there is a dispersed mixture of droplets and gas. Outside the spray envelope, only gas is present. We shall discuss these two subregions separately.

Denote x as the distance vertically downward from the nozzle and y as the normal distance from the spray axis. The velocity components of either the droplet or the gas phase are denoted by u and v in the directions of increasing x and y, respectively. Inside the spray envelope, the common two-fluid formulation for two-phase flows is applicable [18]. Thus, for the gas phase, we have

$$\partial \rho/\partial t + \partial(\rho u)/\partial x + 1/y^\sigma \, \partial(\rho v y^\sigma)/\partial y = \Gamma \tag{1}$$

$$\partial(\rho u)/\partial t + \partial(\rho u^2)/\partial x + 1/y^\sigma \, \partial(\rho u v y^\sigma)/\partial y = -\partial P/\partial x + \rho g + A_x + B_x - D_x \tag{2}$$

$$\partial(\rho v)/\partial t + \partial(\rho u v)/\partial x + 1/y^\sigma \, \partial(\rho v^2 y^\sigma)/\partial y = -\partial P/\partial y + A_y + B_y - D_y \tag{3}$$

where ρ = the density

P = the pressure

A = the viscous force per unit volume

B = the momentum transfer rate per unit volume due to mass transfer

D = the interphase drag per unit volume

Γ = the mass generation (depletion) rate per unit volume due to evaporation of droplets (condensation of vapor)

Subscripts x and y, respectively, denote the x and y components of the quantity. σ is a geometrical factor given by

$$\sigma = 0 \quad \text{plane sprays}$$
$$\sigma = 1 \quad \text{axisymmetric sprays} \tag{4}$$

The use of σ conveniently combines the two-dimensional and axisymmetric formulations. If the gas phase is a mixture of a noncondensible gas and vapor, Equations 1 to 3 will be applied to the entire mixture, as mentioned before. Also, an additional equation is needed for the mass concentration,

X, of the vapor component. This is given by the diffusion equation:

$$\rho(\partial X/\partial t) + \rho u(\partial X/\partial x) + \rho v(\partial X/\partial y) = \Gamma \tag{5}$$

We have neglected the Fick's diffusional term in Equation 5.

The last terms in Equations 2 and 3 represent the aerodynamic drag force per unit volume due to the droplet phase. In general, the drag force due to a swamp of droplets is difficult to evaluate, because of droplet-droplet interactions [9, 19]. Ishii and Zuber [20] provided drag coefficients for dispersed flow systems over a wide range of Reynolds number and hold-up. Since the present discussion assumes a dilute spray, droplet interactions are correspondingly small. Hence, the drag force per unit volume can be approximated by summing over the drag force of all droplets contained in the unit volume. Assuming that each droplet behaves as a rigid sphere, the drag coefficient, C_D, can be taken as [21]:

$$C_D = 24/|Re|(1 + 0.15|Re|^{0.687}) \qquad |Re| \leq 1,000$$
$$\tag{6}$$
$$C_D = 0.44 \qquad |Re| > 1,000$$

where Re is the droplet Reynolds number which depends on the magnitude of the relative velocity between the gas and the droplet phase. Thus,

$$Re = \rho(\bar{u} - \bar{u}_d)d/\mu$$

or

$$Re = \rho\sqrt{[(u - u_d)^2 + (v - v_d)^2]}\,d/\mu \tag{7}$$

where   d = the droplet diameter
        μ = the gas dynamic viscosity

Subscript d refers to the droplet phase. The drag force due to one droplet is then given by

$$F_D = m_d(u - u_d)/\tau_m$$

where m_d is the mass of a droplet and τ_m is given by

$$\tau_m = (\rho_f d^2/18\mu)(24/|Re|)(1/C_D) \tag{8}$$

τ_m is called the momentum equilibrium time [19]. It physically indicates how fast a droplet adjusts to the ambient gas motion. ρ_f is the liquid density in Equation 8. The total drag force per unit volume experienced by the gas phase is then

$$D_x = nm_d(u - u_d)/\tau_m \tag{9a}$$

where n is the number of droplets contained per unit volume of the gas phase. Similarly,

$$D_y = nm_d(v - v_d)/\tau_m \tag{9b}$$

n is determined by considering the motion of the droplet phase. We shall return to it later.

The viscous force per unit volume can be written as

$$A_x = \partial(\mu_{eff}\,\partial u/\partial x)/\partial x + 1/y^\sigma\,\partial(\mu_{eff}\,y^\sigma\,\partial u/\partial y)/\partial y + \{\partial(\mu_{eff}\,\partial u/\partial x)/\partial x + 1/y^\sigma\,\partial(\mu_{eff}\,\partial vy^\sigma/\partial x)/\partial y\}$$
$$- \{\tfrac{2}{3}\,\partial[\mu_{eff}(\partial u/\partial x + 1/y^\sigma\,\partial(vy^\sigma)/\partial y)]/\partial x\} \tag{10}$$

and

$$A_y = \partial(\mu_{eff} \, \partial v/\partial x)/\partial x + 1/y^\sigma \, \partial(\mu_{eff} y^\sigma \, \partial v/\partial y)/\partial y - \sigma\mu_{eff} v/y^2$$
$$- \{\tfrac{2}{3} \, \partial[\mu_{eff}(\partial u/\partial x + 1/y^\sigma \, \partial(vy^\sigma)/\partial y)]/\partial y\} + \{\partial(\mu_{eff} \, \partial u/\partial y)/\partial x + 1/y^\sigma \, \partial(\mu_{eff} y^\sigma \, \partial v/\partial y)/\partial y\} \quad (11)$$

Equations 10 and 11 have been obtained by expressing the derivatives of the stress tensor of a Newtonian fluid in cylindrical polar coordinates [22]. We have replaced the molecular viscosity by an effective viscosity, μ_{eff}, suitable for turbulent flow.

The quantities A_x and A_y are considerably simplified in the case of an incompressible gas medium with negligible mass transfer. In this case, Equation 1 is reduced to

$$\partial u/\partial x + 1/y^\sigma \, \partial(vy^\sigma)/\partial y = 0 \tag{12}$$

Hence, the last two bracketed terms in Equations 10 and 11 vanish by virtue of Equation 12, and A_x and A_y become

$$A_x = \partial(\mu_{eff} \, \partial u/\partial x)/\partial x + 1/y^\sigma \, \partial(\mu_{eff} y^\sigma \, \partial u/\partial y)/\partial y \tag{13}$$

and

$$A_y = 1/y^\sigma \, \partial(\mu_{eff} y^\sigma \, \partial v/\partial y)/\partial y + \partial(\mu_{eff} \, \partial v/\partial x)/\partial x - \sigma\mu_{eff} v/y^2 \tag{14}$$

Finally, the momentum transfer per unit volume due to mass transfer is generally formulated as

$$B_x = u_I \Gamma \tag{15}$$

$$B_y = v_I \Gamma \tag{16}$$

where (u_I, v_I) is a phenomenological interface velocity. The interface velocity is commonly written as [21]

$$(u_I, v_I) = \delta(u, v) + (1 - \delta)(u_d, v_d) \tag{17}$$

where δ is an empirical factor. δ is usually taken as zero for positive Γ (i.e., evaporation of droplets) and unity for negative Γ (i.e., condensation of vapor). In the absence of evaporation or condensation, B_x and B_y vanish.

Having discussed the gas conservation equations, we turn to the droplet-phase conservation equations. In dispersed flow, we can either use the Lagrangian or Eulerian formulation to describe the droplet motion. Both formulations are being used in the literature.

In the Lagrangian formulation, the motion of each droplet (or a discretized number of droplets [23]) is followed. Each droplet is characterized by its coordinates (x_d, y_d), velocity (u_d, v_d), mass m_d, volume ϑ_d, diameter d, and temperature T_d. The Lagrangian equations of motion of a droplet is then given by

$$d(m_d u_d)/dt = -\vartheta_d \, \partial P/\partial x + m_d g(1 - \rho/\rho_f) + m_d(u - u_d)/\tau_m + u_I \dot{m}_d \tag{18}$$

$$d(m_d v_d)/dt = -\vartheta_d \, \partial P/\partial y + m_d(v - v_d)/\tau_m + v_I \dot{m}_d \tag{19}$$

In general, the equation of motion of a droplet is far more complicated than Equation 18 or 19. Among the forces neglected in Equations 18 and 19 are: the lift force due to rotation of the droplet, the force due to virtual mass, and the Basset force [24]. The significance of the various terms in Equation 18 is as follows: The left-hand side is simply the material time rate of change of x-momentum. The right-hand side represents the force due to the pressure gradient in the gas medium, the weight of the droplet less the buoyance force, the drag force, and the force imparted to the droplet due to mass transfer. $\dot{m}_d$ denotes the time rate of change of the droplet mass. (u_l, v_l) is given by Equation 17. One can include the effect of mass transfer in the drag force term by modifying the standard drag coefficient, C_D. In that case, the last terms in Equations 18 and 19 are omitted [23]. The trajectory of the droplet can be found from the following kinematic relations:

$$dx_d/dt = u_d \tag{20}$$

$$dy_d/dt = v_d \tag{21}$$

We now determine the time rate of change of the droplet mass, $\dot{m}_d$. Notice that $\dot{m}_d$ is positive for condensation of the ambient vapor, and negative for evaporation of droplets. There exist two approaches to determine $\dot{m}_d$: one for condensation and one for evaporation. First, we consider the case of condensation.

As mentioned earlier, condensation of the ambient vapor phase occurs when a subcooled liquid is sprayed into a region of saturated vapor of the same substance as the liquid. The case of super-heated liquid sprayed into a saturated vapor region is unimportant from a practical viewpoint, and will not be discussed here. We assume that the droplet has initial diameter, d_0, initial tempera-ture, T_0, and vapor temperature, T_v. By treating the process of vapor condensation as unsteady-state heat transfer to a rigid sphere of constant diameter with negligible resistance at the interface [8], the average temperature of the droplet can be found as [25]:

$$T_d(t) = T_v - 6(T_v - T_0)/\pi^2 \cdot \sum_{n=1}^{\infty} (e^{-4\alpha n^2 \pi^2 t/d_0^2})/n^2 \tag{22}$$

where α is the thermal diffusivity of the droplet. The corresponding droplet diameter can then be calculated as [15]

$$d(t) = d_0 \left\{ 1 + C_p(T_v - T_0)/h_{fg} \cdot \left[1 - 6/\pi^2 \sum_{n=1}^{\infty} (e^{-4\alpha n^2 \pi^2 t/d_0^2})/n^2 \right] \right\}^{1/3} \tag{23}$$

where c_p = the specific heat of the condensing steam
         h_{fg} = the latent heat of condensation

Therefore, the instantaneous droplet mass and the time rate of increase of droplet mass are respec-tively given by [15]

$$m_d = (1/6)\rho_f \pi d_0^3 \left\{ 1 + C_p(T_v - T_0)/h_{fg} \cdot \left[1 - 6/\pi^2 \sum_{n=1}^{\infty} (e^{-4\alpha n^2 \pi^2 t/d_0^2})/n^2 \right] \right\} \tag{24}$$

and

$$\dot{m}_d = 4\pi d_0 K_d (T_v - T_0)/h_{fg} \sum_{n=1}^{\infty} e^{-4\alpha n^2 \pi^2 t/d_0^2} \tag{25}$$

where K_d is the thermal conductivity of the droplet. Ford and Lekic [26] proposed a semi-empirical expression for the instantaneous droplet diameter, as follows:

$$d = d_0 \{ 1 + E\sqrt{[1 - e^{-4\alpha \pi^2 t/d_0^2}]} \} \tag{26}$$

where

$$E = \sqrt[3]{(1 + c_p(T_v - T_0)/h_{fg})} - 1 \tag{27}$$

Corresponding m_d and $\dot{m}_d$ can be easily determined.

Next, we consider the case of evaporation from the droplets. One important industrial application is the performance of spray dryers. Consider a water droplet which is injected into a region of hot air with a certain relative humidity. Water at the droplet surface will evaporate and diffuse into the air environment due to water vapor concentration gradient between the droplet surface and the air. The rate of evaporation depends upon the concentration gradient and the heat transfer rate. The following analysis is adapted from Crowe et al. [23]. The rate of decrease of droplet mass due to evaporation is given by

$$\dot{m}_d = -Sh(\rho \mathscr{D})\pi d(X_v - X) \tag{28}$$

where   Sh = the Sherwood number
$\mathscr{D}$ = the diffusion coefficient
X_v = the mass concentration of vapor at the interface
X = the mass concentration of vapor in the ambient governed by Equation 5.

Hence, the instantaneous droplet diameter satisfies the following equation:

$$d(d)/dt = -2Sh(\rho \mathscr{D})(X_v - X)/\rho_f d \tag{29}$$

The mass concentration of vapor at the interface is given by

$$X_v = P_v/[\lambda P - (\lambda - 1)P_v] \tag{30}$$

where λ is the ratio of the gas to vapor molecular weight. For the common case of air-water vapor mixture, λ equals 1.608. P_v is the vapor partial pressure at the interface. In general, P_v can be approximated by the saturation pressure corresponding to the temperature of the droplet.

Thus, it remains to calculate the temperature history of the droplet along its trajectory. Assuming the droplet temperature is uniform at any instant, the energy equation for the droplet can be written as

$$m_d c_d \, dT_d/dt = h\pi d^2(T_v - T_d) + h_{fg}\dot{m}_d \tag{31}$$

where c_d is the specific heat of the droplet and h is the heat transfer coefficient. Substituting Equation 28 into Equation 31, one obtains

$$dT_d/dt = 6Nu \, K/(\rho_f d^2 c_d) \cdot \{(T_v - T_d) - h_{fg}Sh(\rho \mathscr{D})(X_v - X)/(Nu \, K)\} \tag{32}$$

where Nu is the Nusselt number defined as

$$Nu = hd/K$$

and K is the thermal conductivity of the ambient gas. The Sherwood number and Nusselt number can be found from existing empirical correlations, such as [27]:

$$Sh = 2 + 0.6Re^{0.5}Sc^{0.33} \tag{33}$$

$$Nu = 2 + 0.6Re^{0.5}Pr^{0.33} \tag{34}$$

where Re is the Reynolds number defined in Equation 8, Sc is the Schmidt number

$$Sc = \mu/\rho\mathscr{D} \tag{35}$$

and Pr is the Prandtl number

$$Pr = \mu/\rho K \tag{36}$$

For example, for water vapor diffusing into air at atmospheric pressure conditions, Sc is about 0.6 and Pr is about 0.7. Since the Reynolds number depends on both the droplet diameter and velocity, and P_v depends on T_d, Equations 32, 29, and 28 must be solved simultaneously with the droplet equations of motion. The dependence of P_v on T_d can be obtained from the appropriate thermodynamic table for the liquid substance. For water, empirical correlations are also available [28].

This completes the discussion on the Lagrangian formulation. In summary, the Lagrangian formulation focuses on the motion of a droplet. The approximate equations of motion are given by Equations 18 and 19. The droplet mass, and hence its diameter and volume, changes along its trajectory due to any evaporation of the droplet or condensation of the ambient vapor. For the case of condensation, approximate analytical expressions for the instantaneous droplet mass, diameter, and temperature are available and are given by Equations 24, 23, and 22, respectively. These expressions can be substituted into Equations 18 and 19. The resulting equations can then be integrated simultaneously with the solution procedure of the ambient flow field. For evaporation, approximate differential equations are derived for the time rate of change of the droplet mass, diameter, and temperature in Equations 28, 29, and 32, respectively. These equations must be integrated simultaneously with Equations 18 and 19. Again, the droplet trajectories must be found in conjunction with the solution procedure of the gas flow field.

The other common formulation for the droplet motion is the Eulerian formulation. The basic assumption is to treat the droplet phase as a continuum. Conservation equations similar to those of the gas phase can be formally written for the droplet phase. In view of the assumption of negligible droplet interactons (i.e., negligible 'viscous force' of the droplet phase), we have [18]

$$\partial \rho_d / \partial t + \partial(\rho_d u)/\partial x + 1/y^\sigma \ \partial(\rho_d v_d y^\sigma)/\partial y = -\Gamma \tag{37}$$

$$\partial(\rho_d u_d)/\partial t + \partial(\rho_d u_d^2)/\partial x + 1/y^\sigma \ \partial(\rho_d u_d v_d y^\sigma)/\partial y$$
$$= -(\rho_d/\rho_f) \ \partial P/\partial x + (1 - \rho/\rho_f)\rho_d g + \rho_d(u - u_d)/\tau_m - u_I\Gamma \tag{38}$$

$$\partial(\rho_d v_d)/\partial t + \partial(\rho_d u_d v_d)/\partial x + 1/y^\sigma \ \partial(\rho_d v_d^2 y^\sigma)/\partial y = -(\rho_d/\rho_f) \ \partial P/\partial y + \rho_d(v - v_d)/\tau_m - v_I\Gamma \tag{39}$$

By virtue of the continuum approximation, we can define a macroscopic phase density, ρ_d, for the droplet phase. ρ_d formally represents the mass of the droplet phase per unit volume of the dispersed mixture. All other variables have been previously defined. Equations 37 to 39 are written for a unit volume of the gas-droplet mixture inside the spray envelope. One should not confuse the phase density, ρ_d, with the liquid density, ρ_f, of the droplet phase. Indeed, ρ_d and ρ_f are related by the following

$$\rho_d = \beta \rho_f \tag{40}$$

where β is the volume fraction of the droplets inside the spray. Since β is small for a dilute spray, ρ_d is small compared to ρ_f.

Expanding the left-hand sides of Equations 38 and 39, and using the continuity equation, Equation 37, we obtain

$$\partial u_d/\partial t + u_d(\partial u_d/\partial x) + v_d(\partial u_d/\partial y) = (1 - \rho/\rho_f)g - (1/\rho_f) \ \partial P/\partial x + (u - u_d)/\tau_m + (u_d - u_I)\Gamma/\rho_d \tag{41}$$

$$\partial v_d/\partial t + u_d(\partial v_d/\partial x) + v_d(\partial v_d/\partial y) = -(1/\rho_f) \ \partial P/\partial y + (v - v_d)/\tau_m + (v_d - v_I)\Gamma/\rho_d \tag{42}$$

Equations 37, 41, and 42 are the Eulerian equations of motion for the droplet phase. At this point, let us compare the Lagrangian and Eulerian formulations. Firstly, there is no continuity equation in the Lagrangian formulation. Secondly, the motion of a droplet is formulated in the Lagrangian description, whereas the average motion of a swamp of droplets per unit mixture volume is formulated in the Eulerian description. Thirdly, ρ_d replaces m and Γ replaces $\dot{m}_d$ in the Eulerian description.

The phase density of the droplet phase provides a convenient mean to calculate the mass generation rate and the interfacial drag force. As mentioned before, the interfacial drag per unit volume experienced by the gas phase can be approximated by summing over the drag forces of all droplets contained in a unit volume of the mixture. Rewrite Equation 8 here

$$D_x = nm_d(u - u_d)/\tau_m$$

where n is the number of droplets per unit volume. In this regard, n is the number density of the droplet phase. The product nm_d is simply the mass of droplet per unit volume, which is ρ_d. Thus,

$$\rho_d = nm_d \tag{43}$$

Equations 8 and 9 can be rewritten as

$$D_x = \rho_d(u - u_d)/\tau_m \tag{44}$$

$$D_y = \rho_d(v - v_d)/\tau_m \tag{45}$$

Similarly, the mass source (or sink) term, Γ, can be evaluated by summing over the evaporation from (or condensation on) all the droplets in a unit mixture volume. Thus,

$$\Gamma = -n\dot{m}_d \tag{46}$$

The minus sign is needed since Γ is taken positive for evaporation of droplets in which $\dot{m}_d$ is negative. Remember $\dot{m}_d$ is the time rate of change of the droplet mass, which is negative for evaporation and positive for condensation. Using Equation 43 in 46, we obtain

$$\Gamma = -\rho_d\dot{m}_d/m_d \tag{47}$$

Equations 44, 45, and 47 amply indicate the role of the Eulerian variable ρ_d in the calculation of the interfacial mass and momentum coupling between the gas and droplet flow fields. In this regard, the Eulerian formulation is convenient because ρ_d is part of the solution of the Eulerian droplet equations of motion. The Lagrangian formulation only models the motion of a single droplet. In order to evaluate the interfacial mass and momentum transfer terms in the gas-phase equations, one must somehow estimate the number of droplets per unit volume, n. A particular procedure is discussed in Crowe and Stock [29]. The drawback of the Eulerian formulation is that it consists of a system of partial differential equations. This generally makes the Eulerian formulation mathematically unattractive versus the Lagrangian formulation which involves only ordinary differential equations.

In summary, we have presented the governing equations for the dispersed region within the spray envelope. We have adapted a two-fluid formulation widely used in multiphase flow research. The flow field is composed of the gas field and the droplet field. The gas field is taken either as entirely vapor or a mixture of a noncondensible gas and vapor. Separate governing equations are written for each field. These field equations are coupled by interfacial mass and momentum transfer. Heat transfer is decoupled by assuming isothermal ambient conditions. Both the Lagrangian and Eulerian formulations have been discussed for the droplet phase.

Outside the spray envelope, we assume no droplets are present. The gas field equations are given by

$$\partial\rho/\partial t + \partial(\rho u)/\partial x + 1/y^\sigma\, \partial(\rho vy^\sigma)/\partial y = 0 \tag{48}$$

$$\partial(\rho u)/\partial t + \partial(\rho u^2)/\partial x + 1/y^\sigma\, \partial(\rho uvy^\sigma)/\partial y = -\partial P/\partial x + \rho g + A_x \tag{49}$$

$$\partial(\rho v)/\partial t + \partial(\rho uv)/\partial x + 1/y^\sigma\, \partial(\rho v^2 y^\sigma)/\partial y = -\partial P/\partial y + A_y \tag{50}$$

where A_x and A_y are the viscous force components previously given.

The final relation required for the gas field is the equation of state. In most gas-liquid spray systems, the induced gas flow field in the far region is subsonic enough to neglect any density change due to dynamic effects. Also, changes of density due to gravity can be safely neglected. Since we have also assumed that the gas field temperature remains constant, the change in the gas-phase density is due only to changes in the composition of the gas phase, if there is any.

When the ambient contains entirely vapor, its composition remains unchanged and hence the gas-phase density would be constant. When the ambient is a mixture of a noncondensible gas and vapor, and if evaporation of the droplets occurs, the gas-phase density will be increased due to the additional vapor evaporated from the droplets. Assuming a perfect gas mixture, the gas-phase density can be estimated from

$$\rho/\rho_0 = [(\lambda - 1)X_0 + 1]/[(\lambda - 1)X + 1] \tag{51}$$

where subscript 0 denotes the initial, reference state of the gas phase without the spray. λ is the molecular weight ratio and previously appears in Equation 30.

To complete the formulation, appropriate boundary and initial conditions must be imposed on both the gas and droplet fields. In general, the boundary conditions are given on, and far away from, the axis of symmetry. Thus, for the gas field, we have

$$\left.\begin{array}{l} v = 0 \\ \partial u/\partial y = \partial X/\partial y = 0 \end{array}\right\}, \quad y = 0 \tag{52}$$

due to symmetry; and

$$\left.\begin{array}{l} u, v \to 0 \\ X \to X_0 \end{array}\right\}, \quad y \to \infty \tag{53}$$

due to the initially quiescent atmosphere. Additional boundary conditions are needed above and below the spray nozzle [13, 14]. For the droplet field, initial droplet velocity, (u_{do}, v_{do}); droplet diameter, d_0; droplet temperature, T_0; and droplet injection angle, θ, must be supplied. In the Eulerian formulation, the following symmetry conditions are also needed:

$$\left.\begin{array}{l} v_d = 0 \\ \partial u_d/\partial y = \partial \rho_d/\partial y = 0 \end{array}\right\}, \quad y = 0 \tag{54}$$

Finally, the initial conditions correspond to those of a quiescent atmosphere:

$$u = 0, \quad v = 0, \quad P = P_0, \quad X = X_0, \quad t = 0 \tag{55}$$

everywhere within the domain of interest.

PARAMETER EVALUATION

Various parameters appear in the mathematical model in the previous section. They include, for instance, the droplet diameter, droplet velocity from the nozzle, and the effective viscosity for the gas field. These parameters must be determined before numerical solutions can be obtained.

We first consider the gas field. All physical and transport properties of the gas field can be obtained from standard handbooks. The effective viscosity, μ_{eff}, is evaluated using the mixing length theory [30]. The effective viscosity is written as

$$\mu_{eff} = \rho\varepsilon + \mu \tag{56}$$

where ε is called the virtual, or apparent, kinematic viscosity. In the mixing length theory, ε is given by

$$\varepsilon = \ell^2 |\partial u/\partial y|$$

where ℓ is the mixing length. More sophisticated turbulence models have also been used for spray system analyses [13, 14]. In a turbulent gas jet, the mixing length is proportional to the width of the jet. We have also mentioned that the induced gas flow in a liquid spray is dynamically similar to a turbulent gas jet [4]. Thus, we shall write ℓ as

$$\ell = \kappa y_s \tag{58}$$

where κ is an empirical coefficient and y_s is the width of the spray envelope. Experimental evidence [3] indicates that the turbulence level inside the spray is considerably higher than that outside the spray. Thus, the empirical coefficient in Equation 58 should be given a higher value inside the spray envelope.

For the droplet field, all physical properties associated with the liquid substance are easily obtainable. The difficult task is to evaluate the initial drop size, velocity, and injection angle. All these depend on the near field dynamics. A liquid spray nozzle usually produces a range of drop sizes. Empirical correlations are available for predicting the droplet size distribution [31]. If, on the other hand, one assumes a monodispersed spray, the initial average droplet diameter can be calculated from [32]

$$d_0(m) = 4.075 \times 10^{-8} \dot{W}_L^{1/3} \, \Delta P_n^{-1/2} \tag{59}$$

where $\dot{W}_L$ is the liquid volumetric flow rate in m^3/s through the nozzle, and ΔP_n is the pressure difference in N/m^2 across the nozzle. The initial droplet speed is given by

$$V_0 = C_v \sqrt{[2\Delta P_n/\rho_f]} \tag{60}$$

where C_v is an empirical coefficient, akin to a discharge coefficient. The initial droplet velocity components are then given by

$$u_{d0} = V_0 \cos \theta \tag{61}$$

$$v_{d0} = V_0 \sin \theta$$

where θ is the angle of the velocity vector measured from the spray axis. θ ranges from zero to the spray half angle, θ_s. We assume that the droplets emanate from a point source (i.e., the nozzle) as

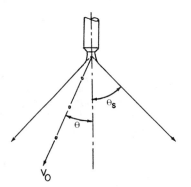

Figure 2. Droplet velocity vector at nozzle exit.

shown in Figure 2. The spray half angle can be determined from photographs of the spray or empirical correlations [10, 33].

NUMERICAL AND ANALYTICAL SOLUTIONS OF THE GOVERNING EQUATIONS

Numerical solutions to the governing equations of a gas–liquid spray system can be obtained by finite difference methods. Computer codes are available for the general numerical solution of multiphase flows. The domain of interest is divided into a finite number of computational cells, or grids. Equations 1 to 3, or Equations 48 to 50, for the gas phase, and Equations 37 to 39 for the droplet phase are represented in a finite difference manner over each cell. The final results are a system of algebraic equations, usually linearized in a certain manner, relating the unknowns at each computational cell. These algebraic equations are then solved to give the flow field of each phase. Notice that the gas and droplet field are obtained simultaneously. A general study describing in detail the preceding numerical procedure is contained in Harlow and Amsden [18].

Another common technique is given by Crowe et al. [23], known as the PSI-CELL method. The PSI-CELL method has been used in recent numerical studies of gas-liquid sprays [13–15]. The method solves iteratively the gas and droplet flow fields. The droplet field is treated as sources of mass and momentum for the gas field in each computational cell. The numerical technique used for the gas field equations is usually a standard code, such as the TEACH program [34] or the ICE method [35]. Initially, the gas flow field is solved assuming no droplets are present. Using this flow field, Equations 18 and 19 are integrated together with the other necessary equations for condensation or evaporation. The mass and momentum source terms for each computational cell are then determined, using Equations 9a, 9b, and 46. The gas flow field is solved again, incorporating these source terms. The new gas flow field is used to determine the new droplet flow field, and hence new source terms for the next iteration of the gas flow field. The procedure is repeated until the results converge to within a prescribed tolerance.

An integral analysis was proposed by Yeung [16] for the case of negligible mass transfer and incompressible gas phase. Additional assumptions were made regarding the gas field:

1. The flow is steady.
2. The pressure is solely hydrostatic. It follows then

$$\partial P/\partial x = \rho g \quad \text{and} \quad \partial P/\partial y = 0 \tag{62}$$

3. The normal velocity component is small compared to the axial velocity component.
4. Axial diffusion (i.e., $\partial^2 u/\partial x^2$) is small compared to normal diffusion (i.e., $\partial^2 u/\partial y^2$) and can be neglected.

In view of Assumption 4, Equation 13 becomes

$$A_x = 1/y^\sigma \ \partial(\mu_{eff} y^\sigma \ \partial u/\partial y)/\partial y \tag{63}$$

Equation 3 can be neglected due to Assumption 3. Using Equations 62 and 63, the governing equations for the gas field, Equations 1 to 3, reduce to the following [16]:

$$\partial(uy^\sigma)/\partial x + \partial(vy^\sigma)/\partial y = 0 \tag{64}$$

$$u(\partial u/\partial x) + v(\partial u/\partial y) = 1/y^\sigma \ \partial(v_{eff} y^\sigma \ \partial u/\partial y)/\partial y - (\rho_d/\rho)(u - u_d)/\tau_m \tag{65}$$

where v_{eff} is the effective kinematic viscosity:

$$v_{eff} = \mu_{eff}/\rho \tag{66}$$

Equations 64 and 65 are essentially those describing a turbulent gas jet [30] with an additional interfacial drag term due to the presence of the droplets. As mentioned earlier, the induced gas flow field is dynamically similar to that of a turbulent gas jet [4, 5]. This justifies to a certain extent the aforementioned assumptions.

For the droplet phase, the Eulerian formulation was used. In this case, Equations 37, 41, and 42 become

$$\partial(\rho_d u_d y^\sigma)/\partial x + \partial(\rho_d v_d y^\sigma)/\partial y = 0 \tag{67}$$

$$u_d(\partial u_d/\partial x) + v_d(\partial u_d/\partial y) = (u - u_d)/\tau_m + g(1 - 2\rho/\rho_f) \tag{68}$$

$$u_d(\partial v_d/\partial x) + v_d(\partial v_d/\partial y) = (v - v_d)/\tau_m \tag{69}$$

Since ρ/ρ_f is usually of order 10^{-3}, we shall assume $(1 - 2\rho/\rho_f) \approx 1$ in Equation 68.

Outside the spray, Equations 67 to 69 are no longer needed, and ρ_d is identically zero in Equation 65. Equation 64 remains unchanged. The appropriate boundary conditions are reduced to

$$u = 0, \qquad y \to \infty \tag{70}$$

and

$$\partial u/\partial y = \partial u_d/\partial y = \partial \rho_d/\partial y = v = v_d = 0, \qquad y = 0 \tag{71}$$

Following Yeung [16], Equations 64 and 65 are combined and the resulting equation is integrated with respect to y from $y = 0$ to $y = \infty$. The result is the momentum integral equation for the gas field, appropriately nondimensionalized:

For $0 < \zeta < 1$

$$d/d\xi \int_0^1 U_i^2 \zeta^\sigma \, d\zeta - (\bar{y}_s'/\bar{y}_s)U_e^2 + (\sigma + 1)(\bar{y}_s'/\bar{y}_s)\int_0^1 U_i^2 \zeta^\sigma \, d\zeta + V_e U_e/\bar{y}_s$$
$$= (1/\bar{y}_s^2 Re_{eff})(\partial U/\partial \zeta)_e - \int_0^1 \zeta^\sigma I(U_i - U_d) \, d\zeta \tag{72}$$

and for $\zeta > 1$,

$$d/d\xi \int_1^\infty U_0^2 \zeta^\sigma \, d\zeta + (\bar{y}_s'/\bar{y}_s)U_e^2 + (\sigma + 1)(\bar{y}_s'/\bar{y}_s)\int_1^\infty U_0^2 \zeta^\sigma \, d\zeta - V_e U_e/\bar{y}_s$$
$$= -(1/\bar{y}_s^2 Re_{eff})(\partial U/\partial \zeta)_e \tag{73}$$

where U_i denotes the velocity profile inside the spray, U_0 denotes the velocity profile outside the spray, and subscript e refers to the value at the spray boundary. The nondimensional variables are defined as follows:

$$U = u/V_0, \quad V = v/V_0, \quad \xi = x/D_s, \quad \zeta = y/y_s, \quad \bar{y}_s = y_s/D_s \tag{74}$$

where D_s is an equivalent diameter of the spray nozzle, usually supplied by the nozzle manufacturer, V_0 is the initial droplet speed, and y_s is the width of the spray at distance x measured from the nozzle. The prime denotes total differentiation with respect to ξ.

In addition, Re_{eff} is the effective Reynolds number given as

$$Re_{eff} = V_0 D_s/\nu_{eff} \tag{75}$$

and I is defined as

$$I = \rho_d/(\rho \tilde{L}_m) \tag{76}$$

where

$$\tilde{L}_m = V_0 \tau_m / D_s \tag{77}$$

$\tilde{L}_m$ is called the nondimensional momentum equilibration length. The normal gas velocity at $\zeta = 1$ can be formally calculated from the continuity Equation 64 as

$$V_e = \bar{y}_s' U_e - (\sigma + 1)\bar{y}_s' \int_0^1 \zeta^\sigma U_i \, d\zeta - \bar{y}_s d/d\xi \int_0^1 \zeta^\sigma U_i \, d\zeta \tag{78}$$

Similarly, the droplet equations, Equations 67 to 69, can be nondimensionalized as

$$U_d(\partial R/\partial \xi) + R(\partial U_d/\partial \xi) - \{\zeta U_d \bar{y}_s' \, \partial R/\partial \zeta - V_d \, \partial R/\partial \zeta\}/\bar{y}_s - (\bar{y}_s'/\bar{y}_s)\zeta R(\partial U_d/\partial \zeta)$$
$$+ (R/\bar{y}_s)(\partial V_d/\partial \zeta + \sigma V_d/\zeta) = 0 \tag{79}$$

$$U_d(\partial U_d/\partial \xi - \zeta(\bar{y}_s'/\bar{y}_s) \, \partial U_d/\partial \zeta) + (V_d/\bar{y}_s) \, \partial U_d/\partial \zeta = (U - U_d)/\tilde{L}_m + 1/Fr \tag{80}$$

$$U_d(\partial V_d/\partial \xi - \zeta(\bar{y}_s'/\bar{y}_s) \, \partial V_d/\partial \zeta) + (V_d/\bar{y}_s) \, \partial V_d/\partial \zeta = (V - V_d)/\tilde{L}_m \tag{81}$$

where Fr is the Froude number, defined as

$$Fr = V_0^2/(gD_s) \tag{82}$$

The nondimensional variables are:

$$U_d = u_d/V_0, \qquad V_d = v_d/V_0, \qquad R = \rho_d/\rho \tag{83}$$

The droplet variables, namely, U_d, V_d, and R, are evaluated along two droplet streamlines or trajectories. Their variations at a given downstream station are then approximated by interpolation functions between the two trajectories. For example, evaluating Equations 79 to 81 at the spray axis ($\zeta = 0$) and spray boundary ($\zeta = 1$), we obtain

$$dR_e/d\xi = -(R_e/U_{de})\{dU_{de}/d\xi - (\sigma + 1)U_{de}/\xi - \bar{y}_s'/\bar{y}_s(\partial U_d/\partial \zeta)_e + (1/\bar{y}_s)[\sigma V_{de} + (\partial V_d/\partial \zeta)_e]\} \tag{84}$$

$$dU_{de}/d\xi = (1/U_{de})\{(U_e - U_{de})/\tilde{L}_m + 1/Fr\} \tag{85}$$

$$dV_{de}/d\xi = (1/U_{de})(V_e - V_{de})/\tilde{L}_m \tag{86}$$

at $\zeta = 1$, and

$$dR_c/d\xi = -(R_c/U_{dc})\{dU_{dc}/d\xi - (\sigma + 1)U_{dc}/\xi + (\sigma + 1)/\bar{y}_s(\partial V_d/\partial \zeta)_c\} \tag{87}$$

$$dU_{dc}/d\xi = (1/U_{dc})\{(U_c - U_{dc})/\tilde{L}_m + 1/Fr\} \tag{88}$$

at $\zeta = 0$. Subscript c refers to the value at $\zeta = 0$. All the ζ-derivatives can be evaluated once the interpolation functions are specified. Equations 72, 73, 84–88 constitute a set of coupled ordinary differential equations in ξ, which can be integrated given sufficient initial conditions. Details concerning profile representations and initial conditions for the three common sprays are discussed in reference [16].

Figure 3 shows the comparison of numerical prediction and experimental data for the rate of air entrainment. The predicting capability of the simplified integral analysis is comparable to the full numerical treatment of the basic governing equations. The integral analysis has also been used to predict the experimental spray contraction data of DeCorso and Kemeny [10]. Figure 4 shows the comparison. Substantial disagreement between theory and experiment exists at high ambient pressures. It is plausible that contraction occurs mainly in the near region where the liquid has not yet broken up. The results of Chan et al. [15] appear to support the preceding conjecture. They [15]

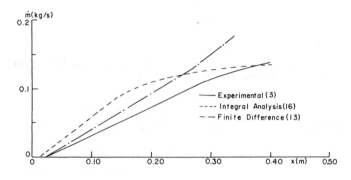

Figure 3. Rate of air entrainment in a hollow cone spray: comparison of experimental data [3] and numerical results [13, 16].

have calculated the flow of liquid through the nozzle, and found that the liquid jet or sheath bends substantially at high ambient pressures before breaking up into droplets. Figure 5 illustrates the shape of the sheath in the near region. It is more appropriate to use θ_s, instead of the actual spray half angle, θ_s, for the calculation of the spray development in the far region. The total contraction should then be calculated as that due to the bending of the liquid sheath and that due to the bending of the droplet trajectory. The latter can be calculated from the present formulation.

Finally, we mention that a detailed similarity analysis was given by Yeung [16, 17] for the simplified formulation represented by Equations 64, 65, and 67–69. A streamfunction, ψ, is defined for the gas field, such that

$$u = 1/y^\sigma(\partial\psi/\partial y), \qquad v = -1/y^\sigma(\partial\psi/\partial x) \tag{89}$$

Equation 64 is then identically satisfied. In the initial development of the spray, the droplet motion is inertia dominated. The influence of drag and gravity forces is minimal. In this case, the droplet speed remains constant at V_0 and the droplet trajectories are straight lines. A realistic similarity solution for the plane spray system is possible if we define the following

$$\psi = xV_0 f(\eta) \tag{90}$$

$$v_{eff} = \kappa_1 x \tag{91}$$

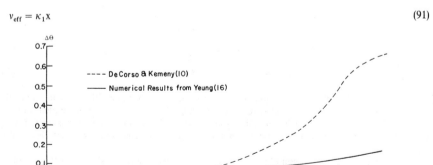

Figure 4. Spray contraction: comparison of experimental results [10] and numerical results [16].

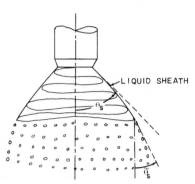

Figure 5. Schematic representation of the shape of the liquid sheath in the near region.

where η is the similarity variable

$$\eta = y/x \tag{92}$$

Equation 65 is reduced to an ordinary differential equation of the following form [17]:

$$-\tilde{f}(\tilde{\eta})f''(\tilde{\eta}) = \kappa_1/V_0(\tilde{f}''(\tilde{\eta})/\tan^2 \theta_s) - F_1(\tilde{\eta})[F_2(\tilde{\eta})\tilde{f}(\tilde{\eta}) - 1] \tag{93}$$

where

$$\tilde{f}(\tilde{\eta}) = f(\eta)/\tan \theta_s, \qquad \tilde{\eta} = \eta/\tan \theta_s \tag{94}$$

The known functions $F_1(\tilde{\eta})$ and $F_2(\tilde{\eta})$ can be evaluated from the droplet phase density, ρ_d, and axial velocity, u_d. The boundary conditions for f are, from Equations 70 and 71,

$$\tilde{f}(0) = \tilde{f}'(0) = 0, \qquad \tilde{f}''(\infty) = 0 \tag{95}$$

Equation 93 can be numerically integrated subject to the preceding boundary conditions. Figure 6 shows typical similarity velocity profiles for the gas and droplet phases and the corresponding

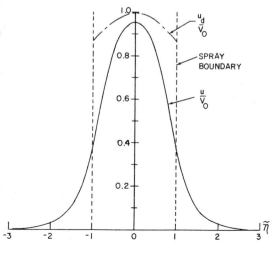

Figure 6. Similarity velocity profiles [17].

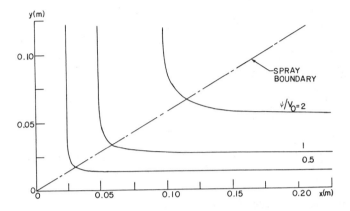

Figure 7. Gas streamlines pattern corresponding to the similarity solution [17].

gas streamlines are shown in Figure 7. The similarity solution has been verified against experimental data [17]. Figure 8 shows a typical comparison between the similarity and experimental results.

CONCLUSION

In conclusion, we have given a rather general formulation for the dynamics of a liquid spray, under several simplifying assumptions. In essence, it is a two-fluid formulation commonly used in multiphase flow studies. Similar formulations have been used in the literature for spray analyses, and have been shown to be capable of capturing the basic characteristics of the spray dynamics.
The most important assumptions used in the present discussion are

- Negligible volume occupied by the droplets.
- Isothermal gas phase
- Negligible drop interactions.

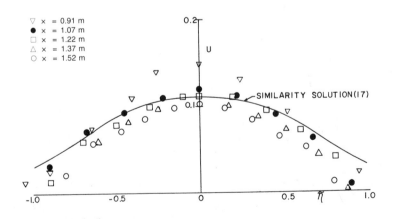

Figure 8. Comparison of the similarity solution with experimental results [17].

The first assumption removes the need to treat the void fraction, or hold-up, of the dispersed flow region as an additional unknown. The second assumption does away with the energy equation for the gas phase. Both of these assumptions can be easily included in our formulation if necessary. Indeed, neither assumptions are made in many numerical studies of two-phase flow. In contrast, the third assumption is made mainly due to the fact that little is known concerning drop interactions. To the author's knowledge, a rigorous formulation for drop collisions, attrition, and coalesence is not yet possible. Droplets can combine to form bigger droplets, or split to form smaller droplets. The initial drop size distribution from the atomization process most likely will change downstream of the spray. Existing studies on dispersed flow which take into account droplet coalesence and attrition [36] seem to indicate that drop interaction can considerably affect the behavior of the two-phase flow field.

Recent advance of efficient numerical schemes for single and multiphase flows [18, 35, 37] and continuous development of high-speed computers have made it possible to quantitatively study the interaction between the spray and the induced gas motion. From a numerical viewpoint, one is no longer limited to study the motion of one field given that of the other, as most authors of earlier spray analyses were. Nor is it necessary to invoke any one-dimensional assumption. The major difficulty is to determine the various physical parameters that appear in the basic formulation, as mentioned earlier. Part of the difficulty is due to the considerable empiricism in models of interfacial phenomena and turbulence. These issues are long-standing subjects of research and are relevant to general two-phase flows. Part of the difficulty, which is pertinent to spray systems, is due to the complexity of the atomization process. Accurate evaluation of the various parameters, such as drag coefficients, effective viscosity, initial droplet speed, initial drop size distribution, etc., will undoubtedly improve the predicting capability of the present state-of-the-art spray models, such as the one given herein.

Further understanding of the atomization process is also necessary for studying the dynamics of the near region. Analyses of the liquid motion through the nozzle and in the near region, incorporating the atomization mechanism, can help study the effects of nozzle geometry, ambient conditions, mass transfer, etc., on the shape of the liquid jet or sheet. The author does not know of any theoretical study in this aspect. A very idealized study is available [15]. More research is warranted in this area. The study of gas-liquid spray systems is not complete, unless the near region can be modeled adequately.

Finally, the present discussion is for a single spray nozzle. Most industrial applications involve an array of nozzles. If the distance between one nozzle and another is large, one may neglect the interaction between sprays. In this case, single-spray analyses can be extended to the spray array [38]. If interaction between sprays is not negligible, the analysis will be very complicated. In particular, one must now deal with the difficult process of drop collisons.

NOTATION

A	viscous force per unit volume of the gas phase	$\tilde{L}_m$	nondimensional momentum equilibration length
B	momentum transfer rate per unit volume due to mass transfer	P	pressure of the gas field
C_D	drag coefficient of a single droplet	Pr	Prandtl number
C_v	velocity coefficient of the spray nozzle	R	nondimensional droplet phase density
D	drag force per unit volume	Re	Reynolds number
D_s	equivalent nozzle diameter	Re_{eff}	effective Reynolds number
E	coefficient defined in Equation 27	Sc	Schmidt number
F_1	function in Equation 93	Sh	Sherwood number
F_2	function in Equation 93	T	temperature
F_D	drag force for a single droplet	U	nondimensional axial velocity component
Fr	Froude number		
I	parameter defined in Equation 76	V	nondimensional normal velocity component
K	thermal conductivity	V_0	droplet speed leaving the nozzle

$\dot{W}_L$ liquid volumetric flow rate through the nozzle

X   mass concentration of vapor in the gas field

c_d specific heat of the droplet

c_p specific heat of the vapor

d   droplet diameter

$\underline{f}$ nondimensional streamfunction

$\tilde{f}$ defined as $f(\eta)/\tan\theta_s$

g   acceleration due to gravity

h   heat transfer coefficient

h_{fg} latent heat of vaporization or condensation

m_d droplet mass

$\dot{m}_d$ time rate of change of droplet mass

$\dot{m}$ rate of air entrainment into the liquid spray

n   number density of droplets

t   time variable

u   axial velocity component

v   normal velocity component

x   axial distance from spray nozzle

y   normal distance from spray axis

y_s width of the spray region

$\bar{y}_s$ nondimensional spray width

Greek Symbols

Γ mass generation rate per unit volume

α thermal diffusivity

β hold-up, or volumetric fraction of droplets

δ parameter in Equation 17

ε apparent kinematic viscosity

ζ nondimensional normal distance

η similarity variable

θ angle of droplet velocity vector at nozzle exit

θ_s spray half angle

κ empirical coefficient in mixing length theory

κ_1 empirical coefficient in Equation 91

λ molecular weight ratio

μ dynamic viscosity

μ_{eff} effective, or turbulent, viscosity

ν_{eff} effective kinematic viscosity

ξ nondimensional axial distance

ρ density

ρ_f liquid density

σ geometrical factor defined in Equation 4

τ_m momentum equilibration time

ψ gas streamfunction

l   mixing length

ϑ_d droplet volume

$\mathscr{D}$ diffusion coefficient

ΔP_n pressure difference across the nozzle

$\Delta\theta$ spray contraction

Subscripts

c   Spray axis

d   Droplet phase

e   Spray boundary

v   Vapor

x   x component

y   y component

o   initial value

Superscript

total differentiation with respect to ξ

REFERENCES

1. Reitz, R. D., and Bracco, F. V., "Mechanisms of Atomization of a Liquid Jet," *Physics of Fluid,* Vol. 25, No. 10, pp. 1730–1742 (1982).
2. Briffa, F. E. F., and Dombrowski, N., "Entrainment of Air into a Liquid Spray," *AIChE Journal,* Vol. 12, No. 4, pp. 708–717 (July 1966).
3. Benatt, F. G. S., and Eisenklam, P., "Gaseous Entrainment into Axisymmetric Liquid Sprays," *Journal of the Institute of Fuel,* pp. 309–315 (Aug. 1969).
4. Rasbash, D. J., and Stark, G. W. V., "Some Aerodynamics Properties of Sprays," *The Chemical*

Engineer, in Transaction of the Institution of Chemical Engineers, No. 164, pp. A83–A88 (Dec. 1962).

5. Gluckert, F. A., "A Theoretical Correlation of Spray-Dryer Performance," *AIChE Journal*, Vol. 8, No. 4, pp. 460–466 (1962).

6. Chuah, Y. K., Yeung, W.-S., and Fisher, E. N., *Measurement of Air Velocity in a Plane Turbulent Spray*, Report, Thayer School of Engineering, Dartmouth College, Hanover, NH 03755 (Dec. 1980).

7. Gauvin, W. H., Katta, S., and Knelman, F. H., "Drop Trajectory Predictions and their Importance in the Design of Spray Dryers," *International Journal of Multiphase Flow*, Vol. 1, pp. 793–816 (1975).

8. Sandoz, S. A., and Sun, K. H., "Modeling Environmental Effects on Nozzle Spray Distribution," ASME Paper No. 76-WA/FE-39 (1976).

9. O'Rourke, P. J., and Bracco, F. V., "Modeling of Drop Interactions in Thick Sprays and Comparison with Experiments," *Proceeding of the Stratified Charge Automative Engine Conference*, The Institute of Mechanical Engineers, London, England, Publication 085298-469 (Nov. 1980).

10. DeCorso, S. M., and Kemeny, G. A., "Effect of Ambient and Fuel Pressure on Nozzle Spray Angle," *Transactions of the ASME*, pp. 607–615 (1957).

11. Nakakuki, A., "Properties of Sprays Injected into Compressed Atmospheres," ASME Paper No. 73-WA/FE-18 (1973).

12. Rothe, P. H., and Block, J. A., "Aerodynamic Behavior of Liquid Sprays," *International Journal of Multiphase Flow*, Vol. 3, pp. 263–272 (1977).

13. Boysan, F., and Binark, H., "Predictions of Induced Air Flows in Hollow Cone Sprays," *ASME Journal of Fluids Engineering*, Vol. 101, pp. 312–318 (Sept. 1979).

14. Alpert, R. L., and Mathews, M. K., "Calculation of Large-Scale Flow Fields induced by Droplet Sprays," in R. A. Bajura (Editor), *Polyphase Flow and Transport Technology*, ASME, pp. 115–127 (1980).

15. Chan, W. K., et al., *Single-Nozzle Spray Distribution* Analysis, Report EPRI NP-1344, Electric Power Research Institute, Palo Alto, California 94303, (Feb. 1980).

16. Yeung, W.-S., *Air-Water Spray Analysis*, Report EPRI NP-1879, Electric Power Research Institute, Palo Alto, California 94303 (June 1981).

17. Yeung, W.-S., "Similarity Analysis of Gas-Liquid Spray Systems," *ASME Journal of Applied Mechanics*, Vol. 49, pp. 687–690 (Dec. 1982).

18. Harlow, F. H., and Amsden, A. A., "Numerical Calculation of Multiphase Fluid Flow," *Journal of Computational Physics*, Vol. 17, pp. 19–52 (1975).

19. Soo, S. L., *Fluid Dynamics of Multiphase Flow*, Blaisdell, Waltham, MA. (1967).

20. Ishii, M., and Zuber, N., "Drag Coefficient and Relative Velocity in Bubbly, Droplet or Particulate Flows," *AIChE Journal*, Vol. 25, pp. 843–855 (1979).

21. Wallis, G. B., *One Dimensional Two Phase Flow*, McGraw Hill Book Co. (1969).

22. Spencer, A. J. M., *Continuum Mechanics*, Longman, London, New York (1980).

23. Crowe, C. T., Sharma, M. P., and Stock, D. E., "The Particle-Source-In Cell (PSI-CELL) Model for Gas-Droplet Flows," *ASME Journal of Fluids Engineering*, Vol. 99, pp. 325–332 (June 1977).

24. Zuber, N., "On the Dispersed Two-Phase Flow in the Laminar Flow Regime," *Chemical Engineering Science*, Vol. 19, pp. 897–917 (1964).

25. Carslaw, H. S., and Jaeger, J. C., *Conduction of Heat in Solids*, Oxford University Press, 2nd Edition (1959).

26. Ford, J. D., and Lekic, A., "Rate of Growth of Drops During Condensation," *International Journal of Heat and Mass Transfer*, Vol. 16, pp. 61–64 (1973).

27. Bird, R. B., Stewart, W. E., and Lightfoot, E. N., *Transport Phenomena*, Wiley (1960).

28. Bridgeman, O. C., and Aldrich, E. W., "Vapor Pressure Tables for Water," *ASME Journal of Heat Transfer*, Vol. 86, No. 2, pp. 279–286 (May 1964).

29. Crowe, C. T., and Stock, D. E., "A Computer Solution for Two-Dimensional Fluid-Particle Flows," Paper Presented at the International Symposium on Finite Element Methods in Flow Problems, Swansen, Wales, January 7–11, 1974.

30. Schlichting, H., *Boundary Layer Theory*, 7th Edition, McGraw Hill Book Co. (1979).

31. Lekic, A., Kajramovic, R., and Ford, J. D., "Droplet Size Distribution: An Improved Method for Fitting Experimental Data," *Canadian Journal of Chemical Engineering*, Vol. 54, pp. 399–40? (1976).
32. Dombrowski, N., and Wolfsohn, D. L., "The Atomization of Water by Swirl Spray Pressure Nozzle," *Institution of Chemical Engineers*, Transactions, Vol. 50, pp. 259–269 (1972).
33. Wu, K.-J., et al., "Measurements of the Spray Angle of Atomizing Jets," ASME Paper 83 WA/FE-10, (Nov. 1983).
34. Gosman, A. D., and Pun, W. M., *Lecture Notes for course entitled "Calculation of Recirculating Flows*," Imperial College of Science and Technology, London, England, (Dec. 1973).
35. Harlow, F. H., and Amsden, A. A., "A Numerical Fluid Dynamics Calculation Method for Al Flow Speeds," *Journal of Computational Physics*, Vol. 8, No. 2 (1971).
36. Jiricny, V., Kratky, M., and Prochazka, J., "Counter-Currrent Flow of Dispersed and Continuous Phase-I," *Chemical Engineering Science*, Vol. 34, pp. 1141–1149 (1979).
37. Spalding, D. B., "Numerical Computation of Multi-phase Fluid Flow and Heat Transfer," in EPRI Workshop Proceedings: Basic Two-Phase Flow Modeling in Reactor Safety and Performance, Volume 2, Report EPRI WS-78-143, Volume 2, WS 78–143 Workshop Proceedings pp. 9–220 to 9–275 (Mar. 1980).
38. Heskestad, G., Kung, H. C., and Todtenkopf, N. F., "Air-Entrainment into Water Sprays and Spray Curtains," ASME Paper 76-WA/FE-40 (1976).

CHAPTER 13

HYDRODYNAMIC MIXING OF DISPERSED AND ATOMIZED FLOWS

Nicholas P. Cheremisinoff

Exxon Chemical Company
Linden, NJ

CONTENTS

INTRODUCTION

In many industrial applications the various types of dispersed flows described in the previous chapters are desirable for promoting effective contacting between heterogeneous fluids. Effective contacting or mixing is aimed at one or more of the following objectives:

The exchange of heat
The exchange of mass
The promotion of chemical reactions
Homogenization

This chapter relates the hydrodynamics of dispersed flows to the practical problems of mixing gas-liquid systems. Three general areas are covered, namely—general concepts of fluid-fluid mixing, atomization processes, and gas-in-liquid dispersions. Detailed treatment of contacting in specific industrial reactors are given in Section 3 of this volume.

CONCEPTS OF SINGLE-FLUID MOTION AND MIXING

Flow Behavior

Before discussing the complex subject of forced mixing between gas and liquid phases, a general review of hydrodynamic principles is warranted. These initial remarks will help to establish terminology used not only in this chapter, but in subsequent chapters as well.

Fluid motion is produced by external forces acting upon the system. There are in principle two types of forces acting on a fluid particle, namely, pressure forces and mass forces. Consider an infinitesimal volume of fluid with pressure forces acting at right angles upon its surface. The fluid volume can be considered to have the shape of a cube with the edges dx, dy, and dz (Figure 1) with its respective face subjected to the pressure p in the direction of the x-axis while the opposite face is acted upon by the pressure $p + \partial p/\partial x \, dx$ and in the opposite direction. The term $\partial p/\partial x$ represents the relative pressure increment in the direction of the x-axis. The resultant pressure force in this direction is given by:

$$P_x = \left(p - p - \frac{\partial p}{\partial x} dx\right) dy \, dz = -\frac{\partial p}{\partial x} dx \, dy \, dz = -\frac{\partial p}{\partial x} dV \qquad (1)$$

The resultant force P, acting upon the entire fluid element is:

$$P = -\left(\frac{\partial p}{\partial x} + \frac{\partial p}{\partial y} + \frac{\partial p}{\partial z}\right) dV \qquad (2)$$

Expressing this in vectorial form,

$$P = -\nabla p \, dV \qquad (2a)$$

where the operator ∇ denotes the symbol of a vector such that·in the product with the scalar function forms its gradient. Force P represents the influence of the static pressure upon the moving element.

Mass forces are proportional to the mass of the moving particle and to the particle's acceleration (e.g., gravitational, centrifugal). In this case, the magnitude of the mass force is the product of the mass of the considered elementary volume and the mass acceleration.

$$G = \rho \, dx \, dy \, dz \, a = dV \, a \qquad (3$$

where ρ = the density
        V = the volume
        a = the vector of mass acceleration
        G = the vector of mass force

The *resistance* to the motion of the element is due to internal friction within the fluid, commonly known as viscosity.

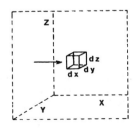

Figure 1. Flow of fluid through an elementary fluid particle.

Viscosity may be explained on the basis of the kinetic theory. When a fluid element moves in the flow, its constituent molecules move in two ways: first, in the direction of the motion of the element as its parts, and second, irregularly in all directions in consequence of Brownian movement. Despite the fact that the mean free paths of the molecules are insignificant, molecules of the moving element penetrate into the surrounding layers by Brownian movement, and conversely. The molecules diffused from the moving element collide with molecules in the surrounding fluid. In this collision, molecules transmit to each other part of their momentum. This also applies to entire moving layers of the fluid. The layers of the fluid adjacent to the flowing layer are likewise set into motion by the penetrating molecules, but at a lower velocity. The molecules from the layer moving more slowly, pass into the faster-moving layer and, by the influence of their smaller momentum, decrease the velocity of its motion. Mutual penetration of the molecules from the individual layers, moving at different velocities, then manifests itself as if there were a shear stress in the boundary layer, thus producing a resistance.

The term *dynamic viscosity* is defined as the ratio between the shear stress τ, related to unit area, and the shear rate between adjacent layers, a distance by apart.

$$\eta = \frac{\tau}{\dfrac{du}{dy}} \tag{4}$$

where u = the velocity normal to the direction of y
  du/dy = the shear rate
  η = the coefficient of dynamic viscosity
  τ = the shear stress per unit area

The coefficient of dynamic viscosity is commonly expressed in units of poises (g cm^{-1} sec^{-1}).

In the technical system the unit of dynamic viscosity is kg$_f$ m^{-2} sec, which is often encountered in mixing problems. Other magnitudes in the calculation of mixers are usually given in the technical system. For converting viscosity values between the absolute and the technical systems the following relation applies:

$$\eta_{\text{tech}} = 0.012 \cdot \eta_{\text{abs}} \tag{5}$$

For Newtonian fluids in laminar flow and at constant temperature, viscosity is a physical constant.

The coefficient of dynamic viscosity η depends on temperature, because it is a function of the mean free path of the molecules, which increases with temperature. The dependence of viscosity on temperature is expressed by various semi-empirical formulae found in standard textbooks on physical chemistry.

Viscosity is sometimes expressed by the coefficient of kinematic viscosity v, which expresses the ratio between dynamic viscosity and density:

$$v = \frac{\eta}{\rho} \tag{6}$$

The unit of kinematic viscosity in the absolute system is termed the Stoke (St = cm^2 sec^{-1}). A hundredth part of this unit is the centistoke (cSt).

The laws governing fluid flow are expressed by three fundamental equations; the continuity equation—expressing the principle of conservation of mass in the fluid system; the equation of motion—which is the application of Newton's second law to the motion of a moving elementary fluid particle; the energy balance equation—expressing the principle of conservation of energy in fluid flow.

The *continuity equation* can be derived from examination of the flow of the fluid through the described infinitesimal volume in the form of a cube with the edges dx, dy, and dz. The mass of the fluid in the considered infinitesimal volume is ρ dx dy dz $= \rho$ dV.

Generally, the change of mass in the considered infinitesimal volume in the time interval dt can be represented by the relation:

$$\frac{\partial \rho}{\partial t} \, dV \, dt = -\frac{\partial \rho u_x}{\partial x} \, dV \, dt - \frac{\partial \rho u_y}{\partial y} \, dV \, dt - \frac{\partial \rho u_z}{\partial z} \, dV \, dt \tag{7}$$

The differentials dV dt cancel out and by arranging the signs, we then obtain the continuity equation:

$$\frac{\partial \rho}{\partial t} = -\left\{ \frac{\partial \rho u_x}{\partial x} + \frac{\partial \rho u_y}{\partial y} + \frac{\partial \rho u_z}{\partial z} \right\} \tag{8}$$

or

$$\frac{\partial \rho}{\partial t} = -(\nabla \rho u) \tag{9}$$

The continuity equation expresses the conservation of matter. It is inapplicable in this form if a chemical reaction occurs.

The *equation of motion* for fluid flow is based upon Newton's second law of motion, which states that the change of momentum with time is proportional to the acting force and of the same direction as this force. The equation of motion may be resolved according to the individual coordinate axes in the following manner:

$$\varrho\left(\frac{\partial u_x}{\partial \tau} + \frac{\partial u_x}{\partial x} u_x + \frac{\partial u_x}{\partial y} u_y + \frac{\partial u_x}{\partial z} u_z\right) = -\frac{\partial p}{\partial x} + \varrho a_x \tag{10}$$

$$\varrho\left(\frac{\partial u_y}{\partial \tau} + \frac{\partial u_y}{\partial x} u_x + \frac{\partial u_y}{\partial y} u_y + \frac{\partial u_y}{\partial z} u_z\right) = -\frac{\partial p}{\partial y} + \varrho a_y \tag{10a}$$

$$\varrho\left(\frac{\partial u_z}{\partial \tau} + \frac{\partial u_z}{\partial x} u_x + \frac{\partial u_z}{\partial y} u_y + \frac{\partial u_z}{\partial z} u_z\right) = -\frac{\partial p}{\partial z} - \varrho a_z \tag{10b}$$

Nonideal fluids exhibit internal friction and are considered to be compressible. The equation of motion for nonideal fluids has therefore an additional expression on the right-hand side defining the influence of viscosity, and another expression for the compressibility. The equations then become:

$$\varrho\left(\frac{\partial u_x}{\partial \tau} + \frac{\partial u_x}{\partial x} u_x + \frac{\partial u_x}{\partial y} u_y + \frac{\partial u_x}{\partial z} u_z\right) = -\frac{\partial p}{\partial x} - \varrho a_x + \eta\left(\frac{\partial^2 u_x}{\partial x^2} + \frac{\partial^2 u_x}{\partial y^2} + \frac{\partial^2 u_x}{\partial z^2}\right)$$
$$+ \frac{1}{3}\eta\frac{\partial}{\partial x}\left(\frac{\partial u_x}{\partial x} + \frac{\partial u_y}{\partial y} + \frac{\partial u_z}{\partial z}\right) \tag{11}$$

$$\varrho\left(\frac{\partial u_y}{\partial \tau} + \frac{\partial u_y}{\partial x} u_x + \frac{\partial u_y}{\partial y} u_y + \frac{\partial u_y}{\partial z} u_z\right) = -\frac{\partial p}{\partial y} + \varrho a_y + \eta\left(\frac{\partial^2 u_y}{\partial x^2} + \frac{\partial^2 u_y}{\partial y^2} + \frac{\partial^2 u_y}{\partial z^2}\right)$$
$$+ \frac{1}{3}\eta\frac{\partial}{\partial y}\left(\frac{\partial u_x}{\partial x} + \frac{\partial u_y}{\partial y} + \frac{\partial u_z}{\partial z}\right) \tag{11a}$$

$$\varrho\left(\frac{\partial u_z}{\partial \tau} + \frac{\partial u_z}{\partial x} u_x + \frac{\partial u_z}{\partial y} u_y + \frac{\partial u_z}{\partial z} u_z\right) = -\frac{\partial p}{\partial z} + \varrho a_z + \eta\left(\frac{\partial^2 u_z}{\partial x^2} + \frac{\partial^2 u_z}{\partial y^2} + \frac{\partial^2 u_z}{\partial z^2}\right)$$
$$+ \frac{1}{3}\eta\frac{\partial}{\partial z}\left(\frac{\partial u_x}{\partial x} + \frac{\partial u_y}{\partial y} + \frac{\partial u_z}{\partial z}\right) \tag{11b}$$

where a_x, a_y, a_z are the components of mass acceleration in the direction of the individual coordinate axes and η is the coefficient of dynamic viscosity (assumed to be constant). Equations 11–11b are the *Navier-Stokes equations*.

The *energy balance equation* for a fluid in motion expresses the law of conservation of energy and is called *Bernoulli's equation*. Its differential form for ideal fluids is:

$$g\,dz + \frac{dp}{\rho} + d\left(\frac{u^2}{2}\right) = 0 \tag{12}$$

The Bernoulli equation may also be stated as:

$$z_1 + \frac{P_1}{\gamma} + \frac{u_1^2}{2g} = z_2 + \frac{P_2}{\gamma} + \frac{u_2^2}{2g} \tag{13}$$

All terms in Equation 13 have the dimension of length and are called *heads*. The term z represents the *potential head* (H_{pot}), the term p/γ the *pressure head or static head* (H_p), and the term $u^2/2g$ the *kinetic* or *velocity head* (H_{kin}). The sum of all these three heads is the *hydrodynamic head*, H. The Bernoulli equation can also be written in the form:

$$H = H_{pot} + H_p + H_{kin} \tag{14}$$

For nonideal fluids the head loss (H_ℓ) is also included in the equation. The head loss represents the energy expended for overcoming the internal friction of the fluid.

$$H = H_{pot} + H_p + H_{kin} + H_\ell \tag{14a}$$

The nature or characteristic of the flow system is of great importance. It depends on the velocity of the flow, the kinematic viscosity of the fluid, and the geometric arrangement of the space through which the fluid moves. The two basic types of flow are *laminar* and *turbulent*.

Laminar flow is a hydrodynamic process in which the fluid particles move along streamlines parallel to the direction of the flow. The mean velocity of the fluid along a given streamline is equivalent to the instantaneous velocity. In such a flow, only molecules pass between adjacent layers of the flow due to Brownian motion which is also the case for a fluid at rest. The fluid elements contain many molecules and do not penetrate from one layer of the fluid into another, but slide parallel to the direction of the flow.

In contrast, *turbulent flow* is characterized by the presence of eddies. The elements moved not only in parallel layers, but also along erratic paths. Not only molecules but also fluid elements pass from individual layers into other ones, whereby mixing is effected. Fluid motion becomes turbulent at higher velocities and the boundary between a laminar and a turbulent process is represented by the critical velocity of the flow for given conditions.

From similarity theory, the criterion known as the *Reynolds number* was developed. It permits prediction as to whether the process in question will be laminar or turbulent. The Reynolds number is expressed as:

$$Re = \frac{uL}{v} \tag{15}$$

where u = the velocity of the fluid

   v = the kinematic viscosity

and L = a characteristic length (e.g. for flow through a pipe, L is the inner diameter; for sedimentation it is the diameter of the particle)

In mixing with rotating mechanical impellers the velocity is expressed as the linear speed of the tip of the impeller, so that $\omega = \pi nd$, where n is the number of revolutions per second and d the diameter of the impeller. The characteristic length is usually considered to be the impeller diameter; from whence the Reynolds number is:

$$Re = \frac{\pi n d^2}{\nu} \tag{16}$$

The more common expression for Re is as follows:

$$Re = \frac{nd^2}{\nu} = \frac{nd^2 \rho}{\eta} \tag{17}$$

where the constant π is omitted.

The transition from laminar to turbulent flow at increasing velocity does not occur as soon as the Reynolds number attains the critical value. Turbulence first appears in a restricted section of the fluid. Newly formed eddies are immediately dispersed, and others are produced in the same place. However, if the velocity is further increased, the entire region assumes the character of turbulent flow. Thus, a transitional zone exists between laminar and turbulent flow.

The Reynolds numbers defining the limit of laminar flow have been determined experimentally for various hydrodynamic systems. The maximum value for laminar motion in flow through pipes is Re = 2,000, in sedimentation Re = 1, in liquid mixing by mechanical mixers Re = 10 to 20.

Under turbulent conditions the fluid moves in the mean direction of the flow but with varying instantaneous velocities. The instantaneous velocity of the fluid u may be assumed to be the resultant of the translatory or mean flow velocity $\bar{u}$ and the secondary velocity u' due to oscillations of relatively high frequency. The dependence of u on the individual velocity components can be expressed as follows:

$$u = \bar{u} + u' \tag{18}$$

The secondary velocity u' is the instantaneous value of the eddy motion and can be resolved in the directions of the individual coordinate axes into the components u'_x, u'_y, u'_z. The translatory flow velocity $\bar{u}$ is considered to be the velocity at which the eddy proceeds from the place in which it has been observed.

There are two principal types of turbulence: isotropic and nonisotropic.

In *isotropic* turbulence the secondary velocities are of equal probability in all directions. Each of these velocities have in any given time the same number of positive and negative values. There are three basic characteristics of isotropic turbulence [1]:

1. The mean value of a component of the secondary velocity in the direction of one of the coordinate axes (i.e., the algebraic sum of its positive and negative partial values) is within a certain interval equal to zero. Thus, we introduce the root mean square velocity, $\sqrt{u'^2}$. This eliminates the changes of the sign and represents the secondary velocity in absolute magnitude. For simplification, the expression $\sqrt{u'^2}$ is replaced by $\bar{u}'$, and the components of the root mean square are denoted by the secondary velocity in the direction of the individual coordinate axes by $\bar{u}'_x$, $\bar{u}'_y$, $\bar{u}'_z$.
2. The components of the root mean square secondary velocity in the direction of the individual coordinate axes have the same value, i.e., $\bar{u}'_x = \bar{u}'_y = \bar{u}'_z$.
3. The mean values of the product of two different secondary components are zero. If the components of the mean square secondary velocity in the direction of the individual coordinate axes have the same value within the entire system under consideration, then *homogeneous isotropic* turbulence exists.

Nonisotropic turbulence is a state in which the secondary velocities are neither equally probable nor of equal magnitude in all directions.

In turbulent flow, the kinetic head in the Bernoulli equation (Equation 3) may be regarded as being composed of a term representing the translatory velocity and a term corresponding to the secondary velocity. Substituting for u from Equation 1, gives the total kinetic head as:

$$\frac{u^2}{2g} = \frac{\bar{u}^2}{2g} + \frac{u'^2}{2g}$$ (19)

The term $u'^2/2g$ represents the part of the energy expended in turbulence. The higher the degree of turbulence, the larger is the magnitude of this term because of the higher values of u'.

Prandtl proposed a measure of turbulence by introducing the *mixing length* L_p. The mixing length L_p is the distance which an eddy travels in turbulent flow from a moving layer into the surrounding fluid before it has equalized its velocity with the surroundings and thus lost its identity. When the mixing length L_p is larger, the more intense is the turbulence. It is not constant within the entire region of the flowing fluid. In the center of the flow, where velocity and turbulence are highest, the Prandtl mixing length is also largest, whereas towards the wall its value decreases. Prandtl [2] defined the mixing length by the following equation:

$$\tau = \rho L_p^2 \left(\frac{du}{dy}\right)^2$$ (20)

where τ = the shear stress
  ρ = the density
  du/dy = the shear rate (velocity gradient) in the considered region

Under turbulent conditions the shear stress is much higher than in the laminar region. In this case, the ratio between shear stress and shear rate cannot be expressed only as the coefficient of internal friction or viscosity η. Its value must be increased by the *coefficient of turbulent friction* or *eddy viscosity* ε.

Hence, for turbulent conditions, the shear rate is:

$$\tau = (\eta + \varepsilon)\frac{du}{dy}$$ (21)

The eddy viscosity is not constant for a fluid at a given temperature, and it is not constant in all parts of the fluid. Rather, it varies with regard to the fluctuating character of the shear rate from small values at the wall to relatively high values in the center of the flow.

For fully developed turbulence the influence of laminar friction may be neglected and the resultant shear stress can be expressed as follows:

$$\tau = \varepsilon\frac{du}{dy}$$ (22)

In addition to internal friction, the rate of diffusion also increases, as the flow becomes more turbulent. For a binary system, the *molar rate of diffusion* of the component A into component B (termed N_A) represents the quantity of the substance A in moles passing in unit time through unit surface area. For molecular diffusion the molar rate is:

$$N_A = -\mathscr{D}\frac{dC_A}{dy}$$ (23)

where $\mathscr{D}$ = the coefficient of molecular diffusion
  C = the concentration
  y = the distance in the direction of diffusion

Assuming miscibility, elementary particles of the component A penetrate by turbulent diffusion into the component B, and conversely. To obtain an expression for the molar rate of diffusion in a turbulent medium, it can be assumed that the fluid flows in the x-axis direction. The transfer of elementary particles along the y-axis by turbulent diffusion is then:

$$\bar{u}'_y C_A \, dt - \bar{u}'_y (C_A + dC_A) \, dt = -\bar{u}'_y \, dC_A \, dt \tag{24}$$

Since the algebraic sum of the secondary velocities at a given time equals zero, the component of the secondary velocity u'_y has within a certain time interval equal numbers of positive and negative values. Thus, if according to Equation 24 the total transfer of elementary particles along the y-axis within the time dt equals $\bar{u}'_y C_A \, dt$, its value in the positive direction of the y-axis will amount to half this quantity.

The molar rate of diffusion under turbulent conditions is given (analogously to molecular diffusion) by the expression:

$$N_A = \mathscr{D}_{turb} \frac{dC_A}{dy} \tag{25}$$

where $\mathscr{D}_{turb}$ is the *coefficient of turbulent diffusivity* (same dimensions as the coefficient of molecular diffusion). As with the eddy viscosity or eddy diffusivity ε, the coefficient of turbulent diffusivity is not a physical constant.

The distance dy along which the elementary particle of the fluid advances under turbulent conditions into the surroundings may be regarded as equal to the mixing length. The coefficient of turbulent diffusivity is given by the relation:

$$\mathscr{D}_{turb} = \tfrac{1}{2}\bar{u}'_y L_p \tag{26}$$

Note that the mixing length L_p cannot be estimated, and neither can the coefficient of turbulent diffusion. This follows from the definition of the mixing length, which is a variable quantity, dependent on the intensity of turbulence.

In contrast, with molecular diffusion, the mass transfer rate by fully developed turbulent diffusion is very large.

If the diffusing component A is not replenished, its concentration decreases as the diffusion process proceeds. However, in the direction of diffusion the concentration of the component A increases and the rate of diffusion depends on the concentration gradient. Therefore Equations 23 and 25 do not give the overall rate of diffusion when the concentration gradient is not constant. The progress of molecular diffusion in a stagnant fluid under conditions involving changes of the concentration gradient by the diffusion process itself is expressed as follows:

$$\frac{\partial C_A}{\partial t} = \mathscr{D}\left(\frac{\partial^2 C_A}{\partial x^2} + \frac{\partial^2 C_A}{\partial y^2} + \frac{\partial^2 C_A}{\partial z^2}\right) \tag{27}$$

For diffusion in turbulent flow, replace the term $\partial C_A/d\tau$ in Equation 27 and express the change of the concentration in a small element of fluid in the time dt, by the group $\partial C_A/\partial t + \partial(\bar{u}_x C_A)/\partial x + \partial(\bar{u}_y C_A)/\partial y + \partial(\bar{u}_z C_A)/\partial z$.

Replacing the coefficient of molecular diffusion by the sum of the coefficients of molecular and turbulent diffusion, i.e., by $\mathscr{D} + \mathscr{D}_{turb}$, the equation becomes:

$$\frac{\partial C_A}{\partial t} + \frac{\partial(\bar{u}_x C_A)}{\partial x} + \frac{\partial(\bar{u}_y C_A)}{\partial y} + \frac{\partial(\bar{u}_z C_A)}{\partial z} = (\mathscr{D} + \mathscr{D}_{turb})\left(\frac{\partial^2 C_A}{\partial x^2} + \frac{\partial^2 C_A}{\partial y^2} + \frac{\partial^2 C_A}{\partial z^2}\right) \tag{28}$$

Equation 28 defines the time-dependence of the change of concentration in a turbulent medium.

From the preceding it follows that molecular diffusion always effects slow mixing. The rate of technical mixing operations is increased by the penetration of fluid elements into each other by he action of turbulent diffusion. A properly designed mixing system is one that achieves the optimum conditions for this penetration. We shall now consider several common methods for producing adequate turbulent action for mixing, namely, mixing in a pipe, jet mixing, and liquid mixing by gases.

Mixing in Pipe Flow

The simplest mixing process is that taking place during the transport of miscible fluids through a pipe. Mixing is mainly effected by turbulent diffusion in this case. The fluid is generally pumped under turbulent conditions. This method of mixing is suitable for both gases and low viscosity liquids. It can be employed in cases where the pipe through which the fluid passes is sufficiently long. The length of the pipe is of special importance in the case of liquids since mixing proceeds more slowly.

In contrast, liquids are more frequently mixed in vessels than directly in pipes. Mixing vessels may be designed either for *continuous* or for batch operations. In either case, mixing is usually achieved by forced convection. Hence, the motion of the liquid produced in the vessel must be intense enough to bring about turbulence and thus turbulence diffusion. Note that it is not possible to attain the same intensity of turbulence throughout the entire contents of the vessel. This is specially true at the walls of the vessel where the turbulence is less intense. It is common practice then to periodically force all the liquid in the vessel through regions of highly developed turbulence. This is achieved by circulation of the liquid in the vessel.

Mixing in a vessel is therefore influenced by two important factors:

1. The degree of turbulence.
2. The rate of circulation, which is best expressed by the time required for one passage of the entire contents through a given area (usually the peripheral surface described by the mixer blades or the orifice of a jet).

Jet Mixing

Jet mixing is applied to both gases and liquids. The jet is usually employed for the mixing of liquids in combination with a pump which withdraws part of the liquid from the tank and recycles it through a pipe terminated by the submerged nozzle into the tank. The fluid discharging from a nozzle into a large space assumes the shape of a cone enlarging with the distance from the orifice. The flow of the fluid discharging from the nozzle displaces the fluid in the vessel in front of the orifice. The layers of the fluid adjacent to the stream of the jet are then entrained into a motion parallel to the flow. This action is caused by the transfer of part of the momentum of the jet to the surrounding fluid. The transfer of momentum is effected by the shear stress between the fast moving and the stagnant (or more slowly moving) fluid layers and by the turbulent penetration of elementary particles from the jet into the the surrounding fluid. The product of mass and velocity of the moving fluid is constant (neglecting the losses due to internal friction), hence:

$$\sum M_0 u_0 = \sum M_1 u_1 \tag{29}$$

The velocity of the fluid entrained into the moving stream is smaller than the velocity of this stream. Thus each layer of the fluid set in motion entrains the adjacent stagnant layers. The cross section of the flow consequently becomes larger the farther it is from the orifice of the nozzle, and its velocity decreases. In any cross section perpendicular to the flow direction, the velocity decreases towards the periphery of the cone.

When surrounding fluid is entrained into the stream a decrease in pressure occurs in its original place. This pressure loss causes additional fluid to be rapidly sucked into this space and likewise put in motion by momentum transfer from the jet. Under steady-state conditions this cycle is steadily repeated.

The entrainment of fluid into the moving stream results in the formation of a turbulent boundary layer at the periphery of the cone, whereby mixing takes place.

The *boundary-layer thickness* increases proportionally to the distance from the orifice. This consumes some of the momentum of the fluid in the core of the jet. The gradual increase of the boundary layer results in an enlargement of the cone and a constriction of the core, which finally disappears at a certain distance from the orifice (as illustrated in Figure 2).

Folsum and Fergusson [3] give the following empirical formula for the case of a water jet into water:

$$Q_E = \left[0.23 \left(\frac{x}{d} - 1 \right) \right] Q_0 \tag{30}$$

where Q_E = the volumetric or mass rate of entrainment in the cone cross section perpendicular to the direction of the flow

Q_0 = the volumetric or mass rate of flow in the nozzle

d = the diameter of the orifice

x = the distance on the axis of the jet from the nozzle to the cross section where the flow rate is measured

Rushton [4] has shown that the utilization of the kinetic energy of the flow, manifesting itself by entrainment of the fluid from the surroundings, is highest for $x/d = 17.1$. Note, however, that this does not imply that beyond this distance the jet has entirely lost its entraining effect, instead the most economical conditions are encountered at a distance equalling 17:1 times the nozzle diameter. The distance up to which the jet is still capable of entraining fluid from the surroundings varies between 80 and 100 times the nozzle diameter depending on th initial velocity of the outflow (see Volume 2).

Kristmanson and Danckwerts [5] give the following correlaton for the concentration for liquid injected through a nozzle into another liquid:

$$\bar{C} = 4.78 \frac{d}{x} \exp - \left(\frac{r}{0.135x} \right)^2 \tag{31}$$

where $\bar{C}$ = the average concentration within a time interval in the region x, r
d = the diameter of the nozzle
x = the distance from it on the flow axis
r = the perpendicular distance from the flow axis

(Volume 2 of the Encyclopedia treats this subject in detail.)

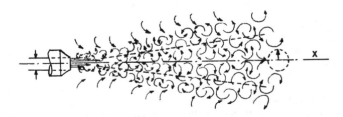

Figure 2. Shows a submerged jet nozzle.

Liquid Mixing by Gases

In contrast, gas mixing of liquids in vessels is accomplished in two ways; by free airlift, and by airlift controlled by a draft tube.

Mixing by free airlift is similar to that by a submerged nozzle. A cone of turbulent liquid rises vertically in the liquid, starting at the inlet of the gas into the vessel and resembling a jet brought about by the submerged nozzle. To include the largest possible volume of liquid into the cone, the gas outlet is usually located at the bottom of the vessel. Vessels designed for mixing liquids by means of free airlift must be capable of containing high liquid columns.

As gas disperses through the liquid in the form of bubbles, the liquid is, displaced and thrown upwards and to the sides. When a bubble ascends slowly the streamlines in the liquid are laminar in nature (refer to Figure 3). With increasing velocity an eddy is formed behind the bubble (Figure 3B), and the liquid in its immediate vicinity is entrained by the action of the shear stress between the surface of the bubble and the liquid. A pressure loss occurs behind the rising bubble and is immediately equalized by entrainment of the surrounding liquid into this space.

The size of the bubble results from the equilibrium between the gas pressure within the bubble and the outer hydrostatic head which corresponds to the height of the liquid column above the bubble. In the direction of the free surface the hydrostatic head steadily reduces, so that the volume of the bubble increases during its upward flow. This expansion results in the generation of additional eddies in the surrounding liquid. The paths of the individual bubbles become erratic because of more frequent collisions. The formation of eddies by the expansion of bubbles and their collisions enhance turbulent diffusion and mixing.

Mixing intensity does not decrease with increasing distance from the air inlet towards the free surface. Bubble expansion promotes additional turbulence. Lamont [7] has observed that the intensity of mixing increases in the direction to the level. In this respect air agitation differs from both that by means of a submerged nozzle and that produced by means of mechanical impellers.

Rising bubbles tend to entrain large amounts of liquid towards the free surface and so the cone of the fast-moving stream expands in the upward direction. In the region of the upper limitation of the cone the liquid level appears convex, as shown in Figure 4. As gas escapes from the surface, the liquid raised by it flows to the wall of the vessel and descends to the bottom from where it is again entrained into the cone of the main stream. Consequently, the contents of the vessel are circulated through the turbulent region of the cone. Hence, air agitation produces motion by transfer of the momentum of the gas bubbles to the surrounding liquid. The required energy is supplied by compression of the air prior to its introduction into the vessel. Naturally, the gas pressure must be higher than the hydrostatic head of the liquid at the gas inlet.

The energy transmitted to the surrounding liquid by the expanding bubbles is the energy that would be required for isothermal compression of the gas from the volume and pressure at the free

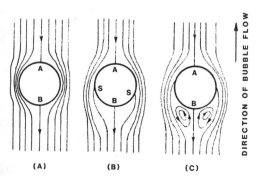

(A)   **(B)**   **(C)**

DIRECTION OF BUBBLE FLOW

Figure 3. Typical flow patterns of bubbles rising in a liquid.

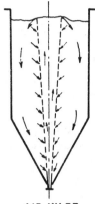

AIR INLET   **Figure 4.** Flow pattern in a vessel mixed by a free air-lift [7].

surface to the volume and pressure of the gas entering at the bottom [7]. That is:

$$N = P_1 Q_1 \ln \frac{P_2}{P_1} \tag{32}$$

where   N = the power transmitted by the gas
P_1 = the gas pressure at the free surface
P_2 = the gas pressure at the bottom of the vessel
Q_1 = the volumetric flow rate of the gas at the free surface

The gas pressure at the inlet orifice must be greater than the gas pressure at the level at least by the liquid head in the vessel. This last expression may also be written as [7]:

$$N = P_1 Q_1 \ln \frac{P_1 + \gamma H}{P_1} \tag{32a}$$

where γ = the specific weight of the liquid
H = the effective depth of the vessel

Note that the ascent of a given volume of gas from the bottom to the surface must be equivalent to the descent of an equal liquid volume from the level to the bottom. The potential energy of the liquid volume at the surface is expressed by the product of the volume of the liquid, its specific weight and the depth of the liquid at rest. The transformation of potential energy into mechanical energy along the path h is [7]:

$$\frac{dN}{dh} = \frac{P_1 Q_1 \gamma}{P + \gamma(H - h)} \tag{33}$$

where h is the height of the point under observation from the bottom.

The gas pressure in the bubble is higher by the partial pressure of the liquid that has vaporized into the bubble of the agitating gas. Equation 33 can also be expressed as follows:

$$\frac{dN}{dh} = \left\{ \frac{P_1 Q_0 \gamma}{(P_1 - p) - \gamma(H - h)} \right\} \left\{ 1 + \frac{p}{(P_1 - p) + \gamma(H - h)} \right\} \tag{33a}$$

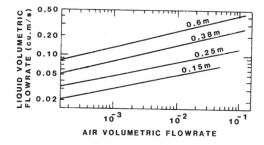

Figure 5. Plot of volumetric liquid flow vs. volumetric air flow in mixing by air-lift with draft tube (liquid density $\simeq 1.6$) [8].

where p is the partial pressure of the liquid in the gas and Q_0 is the volumetric flow rate of the gas without vapors of the liquid. A draft tube is often used in mixing systems that are airlift controlled. The tube prevents entrainment of the liquid from the remaining volume of the vessel, because liquid can only enter the draft tube at the bottom. The flow velocity in the draft tube is thus higher than in the cone of flow produced by a free air lift and, moreover; increases toward the surface under the influence of the energy released by the expansion of the bubbles. As such, the intensity of turbulence in the liquid streaming through the draft tube also increases in the direction to the surface, which in this case, too, is convex at the end of the draft tube. The liquid at the surface flows to the walls of the vessel and descends to the bottom, where it is entrained into the draft tube.

The liquid's circulation rate in the vessel depends on the diameter of the draft tube and on the flow rate of the entering gas. The relationships are shown graphically in Figure 5. For a constant air flow rate, circulation increases with the diameter of the draft tube; at the same time, however, the intensity of turbulence of the liquid streaming through the draft tube decreases. Thus, an optimum ratio between the given flow rate of air and the draft tube diameter for attaining the turbulent flow in the tube necessary for mixing, and the highest possible degree of circulation of the liquid in the vessell must be determined.

The homogenization process in the draft tube was studied by Siemes and Weiss [9]. In this work, changes in concentration of a solution were evaluated in a narrow draft tube in the direction of its vertical axis during air agitation. The rate of homogenization was expressed by the "mixing coefficient," which corresponds to the coefficient of turbulent diffusion in the direction of the vertical axis, as defined by Equation 26:

$$\frac{\partial C_A}{\partial t} = K_{mix} \frac{\partial^2 C_A}{\partial y^2} \tag{34}$$

where K_{mix} is the mixing coefficient.

Figure 6 shows the dependence of the mixing coefficient on the air velocity.

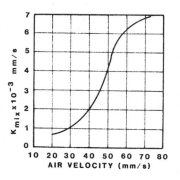

Figure 6. Shows the dependence of the mixing coefficient on the velocity of air introduced into a draft tube [9].

Closure

The subject of mixing is considerably complex and extends well beyond the discussions in this chapter. In general, the formation of heterogeneous fluid systems may be classified as follows:

- Immiscible liquids.
- Solid-in-liquid dispersions.
- Liquid-in-gas dispersions.
- Gas-in-liquid dispersions.

The first two subjects are covered in Volume 2 of this Encyclopedia. In addition, References 10 through 36 provide introductory readings on these subjects.

LIQUID-IN-GAS DISPERSIONS

As described in the previous chapter, dispersion of a liquid into a gas requires a certain amount of work to overcome surface tension forces, in which the liquid must take on a form occupying the smallest possible surface area. By droplet generation, the overall surface of the original amount of liquid is increased, and the required work to be expended for this purpose is:

$$dW = \sigma \, dA \tag{35}$$

where W = the work
σ = the surface tension
A = the overall surface area of the liquid

Because the specific gravity of the droplets is greater than that of the gas, settling occurs. For small droplets in the Stokes' region, the free-fall velocity is:

$$u_s = \frac{d_0^2(\gamma_1 - \gamma_2)}{18\mu} \tag{36}$$

where d_0 = the diameter of the droplet
γ_1 = the density of the liquid
γ_2 = the density of the gas
μ = the viscosity of the gas

The settling of droplets can be counteracted by a gas flow in the opposite direction.

Atomization of a liquid jet being discharged from a given orifice into gas-filled space is the result of the interaction of the liquid stream and the gaseous environment. This intervention is extremely complex since not only does the jet itself break up but also the independent primary droplets.

The initial conditions for the stream are the conditions for its discharge from the spray nozzle. These conditions are determined by the geometric configuration of the chamber, the spray-nozzle orifice, and the discharge velocity of the jet.

As for any flow in a gas-liquid system, mathematical description is by the equations of motion of the phases and by the conditions for their interaction at the boundaries. Here, because of considerable velocities of the liquid jet, gravitational forces can be considered small in comparison with inertia.

In the region where breakup takes place, the liquid-phase flow establishes strong turbulent perturbations in the surrounding gas. As such, the forces of molecular friction in the gas phase can also be disregarded.

The fundamental equations describing the breakup of a simple jet are:

$$-\operatorname{grad} p' + \mu \nabla^2 \vec{w} = \rho' \frac{D\vec{w}}{d\tau};$$

$$\operatorname{div} \vec{w}' = 0;$$

$$-\operatorname{grad} p'' = \rho'' \frac{D\vec{w}''}{d\tau};$$

$$\operatorname{div} \vec{w}'' = 0; \tag{37}$$

$$\mu \left(\frac{\partial w'_i}{\partial x_k} + \frac{\partial w'_k}{\partial x_i} \right)_b = -\rho \, \overline{(v'_i v''_k)_b};$$

$$p' - 2\mu' \left(\frac{\partial w'_k}{\partial x_k} \right)_b = P'' - \rho''(v''^2_k)_b + \sigma \left(\frac{1}{R_1} + \frac{1}{R_2} \right);$$

$$\vec{w}'_b = \vec{w}''_b$$

where, v_i and v_k are the fluctuating velocity components.

These equations can be reduced to the following primary similarity criteria.

$$\left\{ \frac{\Delta p}{\rho' w'^2}; \frac{w'\ell}{v'}; \frac{\Delta p}{\rho'' w''^2}; \frac{p'' w''^2 \ell}{\mu' w'}; \frac{\Delta p \ell}{\sigma}; \frac{w'}{w''} \right\} \tag{38}$$

And considering that

$$\frac{\Delta p}{\rho' w'^2} \cdot \frac{\rho'' w''^2}{\Delta p} = \frac{\rho'' w''^2}{\rho' w'^2} \tag{39}$$

and

$$\frac{\rho'' w''^2 \ell}{\mu' w'} = \frac{\rho'' w''^2}{\rho' w'^2} \cdot \frac{w'\ell}{v'} \tag{40}$$

we can write a system of criteria, strictly equivalent to Equation 38 but containing one less criterion:

$$\left\{ \frac{\Delta p}{\rho' w'^2}; \frac{w'\ell}{v'}; \frac{\rho'' w'^2}{\rho' w'^2}; \frac{\Delta p!}{z}; \frac{w'}{w''} \right\} \tag{41}$$

The primary conditions which uniquely define the examined process are the geometric dimensions of the spray nozzle, flow velocities of the phases, and the physical constants in Equation 37. We now form combinations from the criteria in Equation 41 so as to isolate the maximum number of groups composed only of quantities that are among the conditions uniquely defining the system.

$$\frac{\Delta p \ell}{\sigma} \cdot \frac{\rho'' w''^2}{\rho' w'^2} \cdot \frac{\rho' w'^2}{\Delta \rho} = \frac{\rho'' w''^2 \ell}{\sigma}$$

$$\frac{\Delta p \ell}{\sigma} \cdot \frac{\rho' w'^2}{\Delta p} \left(\frac{v'}{w'\ell} \right) = \frac{\mu'^2}{\sigma \rho' \ell} \tag{42}$$

Consequently, the following is equivalent to the system described by Equation 41:

$$\left\{ \frac{\Delta p}{\rho' w'^2}; \frac{\mu^2}{\sigma \rho' \ell}; \frac{\rho'' w''^2 \ell}{\sigma}; \frac{\rho'' w''^2}{\rho' w'^2}; \frac{w'}{w''} \right\} \tag{43}$$

Four of these criteria are determining.

The higher the rate of the breakup process, the greater the dynamic interaction between the jet and the gas. This interaction depends on their relative velocity. Therefore, it is expedient to introduce the relative velocity of the gas into the criteria in Equation 43 rather than its absolute velocity:

$$w = w'' - w'$$

Taking this into account, any determinable criterion for the atomization process in geometrically similar spray nozzles is thus a certain function of the following determining dimensionless parameters:

$$\left\{ \frac{\rho'' w^2 \ell}{\sigma}; \frac{\mu'^2}{\sigma \rho' \ell}; \frac{\rho'' w^2}{\rho' w'^2}; \frac{w'}{w} \right\} \tag{44}$$

As a liquid jet discharges, it begins to oscillate, interacts with the surrounding gas, and breaks up into drops. The greater the gas density, the more complete is the disruption of the jet. The jet has an extremely pronounced wave character. The waves originate at the exit of the nozzle, and are gradually damped as they move away from the orifice. Once these waves have been completely damped, unstable waves develop whose amplitude continually increases along the jet and finally causes it to break up into drops.

The theory of jet breakup [40–42] is based on the concept that the jet breaks up as a result of a disturbance of the equilibrium of the free surface of liquid under the effect of surface tension. The insignificant initial perturbations promote the formation of waves with spontaneously increasing amplitude. This process is accelerated by additional perturbations due to the relative motion of the liquid and the gas.

The equations of motion and continuity for the jet can be expressed in terms of the corresponding fluctuating components of velocity and pressure. In cylindrical coordinates, these equations are:

$$\left. \begin{array}{l} \rho' \dfrac{Du}{d\tau} = -\dfrac{\partial x'}{\partial z} + \mu' \left(\dfrac{\partial^2 u}{\partial z^2} + \dfrac{\partial^2 u}{\partial R^2} + \dfrac{1}{R} \cdot \dfrac{\partial u}{\partial R} \right) \\[12pt] \rho \dfrac{Dv}{d\tau} = -\dfrac{\partial \pi'}{\partial R} + \mu' \left(\dfrac{\partial^2 v}{\partial z^2} + \dfrac{\partial^2 v}{\partial R^2} + \dfrac{1}{R} \cdot \dfrac{\partial v}{\partial R} - \dfrac{v}{R^2} \right) \\[12pt] \dfrac{\partial u}{\partial z} + \dfrac{\partial v}{\partial R} + \dfrac{v}{R} = 0 \end{array} \right\} \tag{45}$$

where   v, u = the fluctuating velocities in the radial and axial directions
         π' = the fluctuating pressure in the jet

The boundary conditions are given by Equation 37. These conditions can be expressed in a simpler form. Specifically, the tangential stresses on the jet surface are assumed to equal zero, from whence we have:

$$
\left.
\begin{aligned}
\frac{dR}{d\tau} &= v_b \\[2mm]
\mu'\left(\frac{\partial u}{\partial R} + \frac{\partial v}{\partial z}\right)_b &= 0 \\[2mm]
\pi' + 2\mu'\left(\frac{\partial v}{\partial R}\right)_b &= \pi'' + \pi_\sigma
\end{aligned}
\right\}
\tag{46}
$$

where π'' = the fluctuating pressure in the gas
π_σ = the fluctuating pressure caused by the forces of surface tension

A solution of this system of equations for the time changes in the amplitude of oscillations has the form:

$$
\delta = F\left(\frac{R}{R_0}; \zeta\,\frac{z}{R_0}\right)e^{\pi'}
\tag{47}
$$

where q is the increment of oscillations in the jet, determined approximately by the following equation:

$$
q^2 + q\,\frac{3\mu}{\rho'R_0^2}\,\xi^2 = \frac{\sigma}{2\rho'R_0^3}\,(1 - \xi^2)\xi^2 + \frac{\rho''w^2\xi^3}{2\rho'R_0^2}\,f_0(\xi)
\tag{48}
$$

where R_0 = the mean radius of the jet

$\xi = \dfrac{2\pi R}{\lambda}$ = the wave number (λ is the wavelength of the oscillations)

Oscillations resulting in the breakup of the jet occur at $q > 0$. Upon examining Equation 48, it becomes apparent that two determining criteria corresponding to the first two criteria of the system of Equation 44 materialize. Moreover, Equation 48 gives nondetermining criteria containing the increment and the wave number of the oscillation which leads to the breakup of the jet.

Breakup of a Single Drop

The behavior of a single drop entrained by a gas stream is a function of the interaction between the dynamic effect which the stream has on the drop and the "strength" of the drop, which depends on the surface tension and the viscosity of the liquid. The interaction of the liquid and gas is generally described by the system of Equations 37. Four determining criteria in Equation 44 result. For a single drop entrained by a stream, the velocity w' drops out of the conditions which uniquely define the process. Thus, the last two criteria of the system of Equation 44 cease to be determining.

For a drop of known size, breakup initiates at a specific velocity of the entraining stream. This velocity, denoted as w''_{cr}, is a function of conditions which uniquely define the breakup process. It is assumed that

$$
We = \frac{\rho''w''^2_{cr}r_0}{\sigma} = f\left(\frac{\mu'^2}{\rho'\sigma r_0}\right)
\tag{49}
$$

where r_0 is the initial drop radius.

For low-viscosity liquids (when breakup does not depend on μ'), it follows from Equation 49:

$$We = \frac{\rho'' w''^2_{cr} r_0}{\sigma} = \text{const.} \tag{50}$$

where

$$w''_{cr} = \text{const} \sqrt{\frac{\sigma}{\rho'' r_0}} \tag{51}$$

The Weber number (Equation 49) is one of the more significant parameters which is a measure of the ratio of the disruptive aerodynamic forces to the surface tension forces acting on a drop. When a certain value of We is exceeded, the aerodynamic forces are sufficient to overcome the surface tension forces and the drop deforms and breaks up into smaller drops. As the Weber number increases, the time to break up and the size of the droplets decrease. According to the experiments of Lane [43], the interval where the drops become unstable is determined by the inequality:

$$7 > \frac{\rho'' w''^2 r_0}{\sigma} > 5.3 \tag{52}$$

Lane [43] examined the breakup of water drops ranging from 0.5 to 5.0 mm in diameter both when falling down the axis of a small vertical wind tunnel and when exposed to a transient blast at the end of a shock tube. For the drops falling down the wind tunnel, he found the critical Weber number was 5.4.

From an examination of some data of Merrington and Richardson [44] for drops of various liquids allowed to fall down a tall tower, Hinze [45] reconciled and $We_{gc} \simeq 10$, individual results ranging from 7 to 15. He deduced $We_{sc} \simeq 6$ for $\mu^2 d/\rho \, d\sigma r \ll 1$, a condition for the effect of viscosity to be negligible. These results are about a factor of two greater than Lane's.

Hanson et al. [46] studied the breakup of drops of water, methyl alcohol, and three grades of silicone oil with diameters between 100 and 1,000 μm in a shock tube. They compared the critical velocities for water and methyl alcohol drops for a number of diameters, concluding that their ratio was closer to the cube root than the square root of the surface-tension ratio. As the combination of liquid properties and drop sizes used produced values of $\mu^2/\rho\sigma r$ ranging from 2×10^{-4} to 10, they were able to demonstrate the effect of this nondimensional group on breakup. For those combinations where $\mu^2/\rho\sigma r < 0.1$, they found We_{sc} was in the range 3.6 to 8.4. They further observed that We_{sc} increased as the drop diameter decreased.

One must conclude that there are two limiting cases for the variation of relative velocity with time that have been studied. For the case of suddenly applied relative velocity, the critical Weber numbers range from 2.25 to 8.4 while for gradually applied relative velocities they range from 5.4 to 15. In practical situations, sudden relative velocity changes are rare. However, if the rise time of the relative velocity is short compared with a drop's breakup time, it is reasonable to assume that a relative velocity has been suddenly applied.

A commercial oil burner is an example where the aerodynamic break up of a drop is important. A 100 μm residual fuel oil (r.f.o.) drop exposed to a gas stream at a relative dynamic pressure of 1 kN m^{-2} has a We of 4, both the drop diameter and the dynamic pressure being typical of those found in power station oil burners. Various studies [47–49] show that the critical Weber numbers vary from 2 to 18 [47–49]. If the lower value of 2 is applicable to r.f.o. drops, then a substantial proportion of the larger drops produced by atomizers in power station oil burners will be unstable in the combustion air stream and will experience secondary atomization. In contrast, a value in the region of 18 is applicable, then only the relatively large drops, of which there are few, if any, will be unstable. An examination of critical Weber numbers is therefore required to determine the degree of secondary atomization occurring.

In other systems where the objective is to break up drops by relative gas motion, a knowledge of the time to break up and the size of the residual droplets is needed before optimizing the system.

As an example, consider a system in which drops are projected transversely across an air jet, the aim being to produce droplets less than a specified size. Knowledge of breakup time would allow the minimum width of the air jet to be estimated while a knowledge of droplet diameters would allow the minimum jet velocity to be calculated. These parameters together define the minimum power supply to the jet.

Quantitative conclusions on how breakup time and droplet size vary with ε' ($= \rho_s/\rho_d$—density ratio where subscripts s and d related to surrounding gas and drop, respectively) are difficult. The following parameters and dimensionless groups appear to describe the dominant forces in atomization [50]; Reynolds number Re, Ma (Mach number) Ma $= U/C$ (where U is the initial relative velocity between drop and stream and C is the speed of sound in the surrounding fluid); Hinze number Hi ($= \mu_d/\rho_d\sigma r_0 = Hi^2$).

From an incompressible fluid analysis, the effect of drop acceleration appears to be small for ε' less than about 0.001. For ε' greater than 0.001, all that can be concluded is that breakup time might be expected to change and droplet size to increase. Baines and Buttery [51] provide some data for mercury drops in water ($\varepsilon' = 0.073$). Their study indicates that changes in ε' appear to principally affect droplet size for ε' greater than about 0.001.

For the Reynolds number, the only available indicators of the regimes in which it is likely to have an effect are the sphere drag coefficient and We_{sc}; where We_{sc} is the critical Weber number for a suddenly applied relative velocity. Since the drag coefficient is constant over the range of Re from 10^3 to 10^5 for incompressible flow, it would be reasonable to expect the break up of drops with We of the order of 10 to be little affected over this range as well. With increasing We and the finer liquid structures produced during breakup there is likely to be a corresponding increase in the value of Re below which breakup is affected. At Ma less than 0.6, the variations in drag coefficient suggest correspondingly little variation in breakup [52].

For Hi, the effects on breakup are likely to occur above a limiting value which decreases with We. For low values of We, the limiting value of Hi is probably in the range 0.01 to 0.05. In general, increasing Hi will lead to an increased maximum droplet size [53]. When Hi is increased to about 0.2, the photographs of Hanson, Domich, and Adams [46] show that the thickness of the bag's rim is reduced, resulting in a smaller maximum droplet size. Droplet size in this case has been found to correlate the terms of a nondimensional breakup time T, defined as $\sqrt{\rho_s/\rho_d}(Ut/r)$.

Mean Drop Size

Atomization can be characterized by the fractional composition of the drops and the spray density distribution throughout the cross section of the atomized jet. The mean drop diameter is determined from the property of weight as:

$$\bar{d} = \frac{\sum_n G_i d_i}{\sum_n G_i} \tag{53}$$

where G_i is the total weight of drops of diameter d_i. This indicates to some extent the nature of liquid atomization by a given spray nozzle. In the immediate discussions we shall outline the characteristics of pneumatic-type spray nozzles.

Figure 7 shows the relationship [54] between the relative mean drop diameter d/D_0 (where D_0 is the diameter of the spray-nozzle orifice) and the first group of Equation 44. In these experiments, the air velocity changed over the range of 43 to 121 m/sec., and the liquid velocity over 0.55 to 2.3 m/sec. No influence of the relative flow rate of the phases w'/w'' was observed. As shown in Figure 7, the experimental points correlate as a straight line having slope n $= -0.45$ on logarithmic scales. At the same time the distance of the drops from the spray nozzle orifice has no noticeably appreciable influence on the mean drop diameter. The proportionality factor in the relation is:

$$\frac{\bar{d}}{D_0} = A_0\left(\frac{\sigma}{\rho''w^2D_0}\right)^{0.45} \tag{54}$$

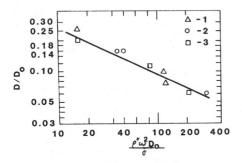

Figure 7. Plot of $\bar{D}/D_0$ vs. $\rho''\omega^2 D_0/\sigma$ from experiments with pneumatic spray nozzles [54].

This relationship varies for different liquids. This difference is determined only by the viscosity of the liquid and is characterized by the second criterion of Equation 44.

The data of Figure 8 show the following relationship:

$$\frac{\bar{d}}{D_0}\left(\frac{\rho''w^2 D_0}{\sigma}\right)^{0.45} = f\left(\frac{\mu'^2}{\rho'\sigma D_0}\right) \tag{55}$$

The viscosity of the atomized liquids varied in these experiments from 0.067×10^{-3} to 54.4×10^{-3} kg · sec/m². These data reveal that the effect of viscosity on drop size is only significant when

$$\frac{\mu'^2}{\rho'\sigma D_0} > 0.1 \tag{56}$$

Experiments with a number of other spray nozzles have confirmed the indicated laws. The working formulas proposed by Vitman, et. al. [54] have the form:

at $\dfrac{\mu'^2}{\rho'\sigma D_0} > 0.5$

$$\frac{\bar{D}}{D_0}\left(\frac{\rho''w^2 D_0}{3}\right)^{0.45} = A_0 + 0.94\left(\frac{\mu'^2}{\rho'\sigma D_0}\right)^{0.28} \tag{57}$$

at $\dfrac{\mu'^2}{\rho'\sigma D_0} < 0.5$

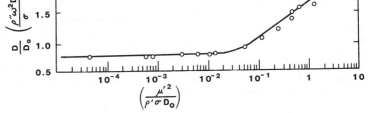

Figure 8. Generalized relationship between $(\bar{D}/D_0)\,[(\rho''\omega^2 D_0)/\sigma]^{0.45}$ and $[(\mu'^2)/\rho'\sigma D_0]$ [54].

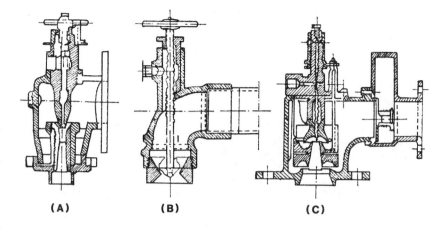

Figure 9. Sectional views of different spray nozzles: (A) STS-FDM-1; (B) STS-FOB-2; (C) STS-FDB-1.

$$\frac{\bar{D}}{D_0}\left(\frac{\rho''w^2D_0}{3}\right)^{0.45} = A_B + 1.24\left(\frac{\mu'^2}{\rho'\sigma D_0}\right)^{0.63} \tag{58}$$

The quantity A_0 depends on the design of the spray nozzle. Various nozzle configurations to which these correlations apply are shown in Figure 9. We conclude that the fineness of liquid atomization by pneumatic sprayers is approximately inversely proportional to the square root of the kinetic energy of the gas.

The relative velocity of the gas-liquid stream for the case when primary and secondary air are fed to the spray nozzle can be calculated as follows:

$$w = \sqrt{\frac{w_{10}^2 G_1'' + w_{20}^2 G''}{G_1'' + G_2''}} \tag{59}$$

where w_{10} = the initial relative velocity between the primary air and the liquid jet
w_{20} = the relative velocity of the gas liquid stream encountering the secondary air
G_1'' = the mass flow rate of primary air
G_2'' = the mass flow rate of the secondary air

It should be noted that most pneumatic-type spray nozzles actually produce a bimodal drop size distribution. Figure 10 shows drop size distributions as measured by a laser interferometer (see Chapter 38 in Volume 1 for a description of the measuring principle). As shown, a secondary, smaller distribution of satellite droplets which are broader in size exists. Experiments by the author with air-water flow generally show the satellites to comprise less than 10% of the droplet population on an estimated mass basis. This does, however, suggest that careful measurements of nozzles contemplated for critical operations, should be made and that the distribution as well as mean size, be quantified prior to operation.

Drop size can be represented by a distribution function, which can be stated as a normalized number distribution function:

$$\frac{dn}{dd_p} = f_n(d_p) \tag{60a}$$

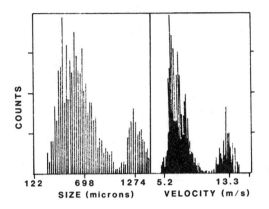

Figure 10. Bimodal drop size distribution measured for air-water flows through a pneumatic nozzle.

Hence

$$\int_0^\infty f_n(d_p)\, dd_p = 1 \tag{60b}$$

This expression can be interpreted as giving the fraction of the drops having diameters between d_p and $d_p + dd_p$. In lieu of sophisticated instruments such as an interferometer, it is not always convenient to measure f_n because of the larger number of fine droplets. With less sophisticated techniques such as photography or light obscuration (see Volume 1) a normalized volume distribution function may be more conveniently defined:

$$\frac{dv}{dd_p} = f_v(d_p)$$

$$\int_0^\infty f_v(d_p)\, dd_p = 1 \tag{61}$$

This gives the fraction of the volume comprised of droplets between d_p and $d + dd_p$.

Note that the volume distribution function and the number distribution function are not independent methods of representing drop sizes. They are, in fact, related through the following expression:

$$f_v(d_p) = \frac{d_p^3 f_n(d_p)}{\int_0^\infty d_p^3 f_n(d_p)\, dd_p} \tag{62}$$

The volume of particles varies as the cube of diameter, and hence, the larger particles contribute much more to the total volume than the smaller drops. Thus, the volume distribution function is skewed more in the direction of large d_p than is the number distribution function. This means that the volume median diameter ($d_{v\mu}$) is much larger than the number median diameter ($d_{n\mu}$).

A generalized definition for average size is:

$$\bar{d}_{qm}^{q-m} \int_0^\infty d^m f_n\, dd_p = \int_0^\infty d^q f_n\, dd_p \tag{63}$$

Based on this definition, the arithmetic average and volume average diameters are $\bar{d}_{10}$ and $\bar{d}_{30}$, respectively. Obviously, these sizes give different values, and characterization of atomized liquid by an average particle diameter depends on the application. In some applications, for example, as in using atomized water to "wash-down" entrained solid particles in a stack, the volume medium diameter, $d_{v\mu}$, might be the most appropriate definition of particle diameter. However, in mass or heat transfer from the gas to liquid droplets, the area/volume ratio of the droplets is most important, and the Sauter mean diameter d_{32} is a more appropriate definition of the average droplet diameter. Note that $\bar{d}_{32}$ represents a droplet having a surface-to-volume ratio equivalent to the quotient of the total surface area of the spray and the total volume of the spray.

The relative magnitudes of the different average diameters are illustrated by the plots in Figure 11. Figures 11A and 11B show the volume distribution and number distribution function obtained

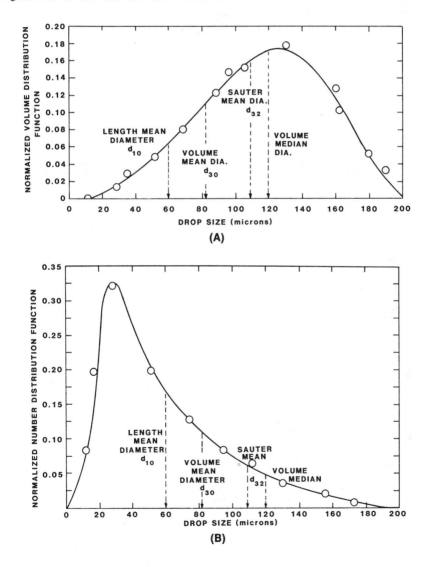

Figure 11. (A) Volume distribution data; (B) number distribution data; (C) cumulative distribution of all drops; (D) cumulative volume distributions.

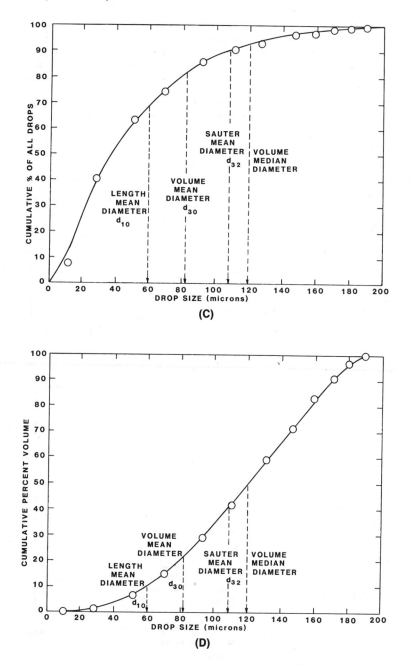

Figure 11. (Continued)

from drop size measurements for air-water flow through a converging-diverging nozzle (see Figure 12). The cumulative distribution functions are defined as the fraction of the particles with diameters less than d_p:

$$F(d_p) = \int_0^{d_p} f(d_p)\, dd_p \tag{64}$$

These have been computed from the data and are shown in Figures 11C and 11D. The volume median diameter is the value of d_p for which $F(d_p) = 0.5$. As shown by these plots

$$d_{10} < d_{30} < d_{32} < d_{v\mu}$$

In the example of Figure 10 the median diameter is nearly twice as great as the number average diameter.

Several definitions of the distribution function can be used to describe drop size. The most frequently used definition is the log-normal distribution given as:

$$\frac{dV}{dy} = \frac{\bar{\delta}}{\sqrt{\pi}}\, \ell^{-\bar{\delta}^2 y^2} \tag{65}$$

or

$$\frac{dn}{dy} = \frac{\bar{\delta}}{\sqrt{\pi}}\, \ell^{-(\bar{\delta}y + 3/2\bar{\delta})^2} \tag{66}$$

where

$$y = \ln(d_p/\bar{d})$$

Parameters $\bar{d}$ and $\bar{\delta}$ represent the magnitude and the spread of particle sizes, respectively. The mean particles defined by Equation 66 can be related to $\bar{d}$ through:

$$\bar{d}_{pq} = \bar{d}\left[\exp\left(\frac{p + q - \delta}{4\delta^2}\right) \right] \tag{67}$$

A simple modification of the log-normal distribution enables more degrees of freedom in correlating data. Equations 65 and 66 can be used with the following definition of y:

$$y = \ln\left(\frac{1}{a}\right)\left(\frac{d_p}{d_m - d_p}\right) \tag{68}$$

where d_m = maximum droplet diameter. This provides three adjustable parameters, a, d_m, and δ to provide a better fit of experimental data compared to two parameters for the log-normal distribution.

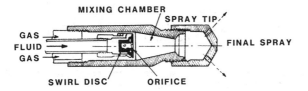

Figure 12. Nozzle configuration studied by author.

Substituting this last expression into Equation 65 yields the upper limit log-normal distribution:

$$\frac{dV}{dd_p} = \frac{\delta d_m}{\sqrt{\pi}\, d_p(d_m - d_p)} \exp\left[-\delta^2\left(\ln\frac{d_p}{d_m - d_p} - \ln a'\right)^2\right] \tag{69}$$

where $a' = \dfrac{d_{v\mu}}{d_m - d_{v\mu}}$

$d_{v\mu}$ = volume medium diameter

For approximations of the volume surface diameter for pneumatic and hydraulic type nozzles the Nukiyama-Tanasawa correlation [55] can be used:

$$d_{32} = \frac{585\sqrt{\sigma}}{V_r\sqrt{\rho}} + 597\left(\frac{\mu}{\sqrt{\sigma\rho}}\right)^{0.45}\left(\frac{1,000Q_\ell}{Q_g}\right)^{1.5} \tag{70}$$

where $\bar{d}_{32}$ = average volume surface drop size (microns)
   σ = surface tension (dynes/cm)
   ρ = liquid density (g/cc)
   μ = liquid viscosity (poise)
   Q_ℓ, Q_g = volumetric liquid and gas flow rates, respectively
   V_r = relative velocity of the liquid

Figure 13 compares the measured mean volume surface diameter for a two-phase nozzle with the predictions of Equation 70. The two-phase nozzle is designed to generate liquid droplets by imping-

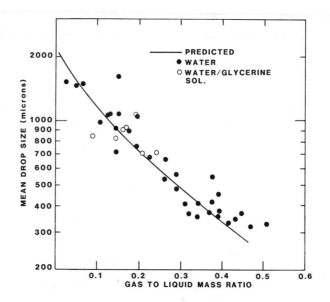

Figure 13. Comparison of measured mean drop diameters to predictions of the Nukiyama-Tanasawa correlation. Data are for air-water and air-water/glycerine solutions (viscosity 20 cp). Measurements were made using a laser interferometer operated in the 30° forward scattering mode.

g a high-velocity gas jet onto a liquid stream. The predicted curve in Figure 13 was obtained by sing the measured mean drop velocity for V_r in the calculations. Hence, when the proper velocity known, Equation 70 provides reasonable predictions.

For an impinging-type nozzle just described, an estimate of V_r can be made from an appropriately fined two-phase slip velocity. The ability to properly estimate the mean drop velocity depends n the accuracy of holdup estimates for the nozzle. Chisholm [56] describes several methods for stimating liquid holdup and two-phase density needed for the relative velocity estimate. Among e most widely used methods, drop velocities can be predicted based on either a mixture volume finition or an effective volume definition. The two-phase (emulsion) velocity is defined as:

$$U_{tp} = \tilde{G}\dot{v} \qquad (71)$$

here $\tilde{G}$ is the gas mass flow rate per unit area of nozzle discharge and $\dot{v}$ is either the effective or ixture specific volume. The slip velocity is then defined as

$$U_{slip} = U_{tp} - U_{\ell} \qquad (72)$$

here U_{ℓ} is the superficial liquid velocity at the nozzle discharge.

Figure 14 compares predicted mean drop velocities to measured for both a mixture volume and fective volume definition. The velocity data are shown to be well represented by an effective olume calculation with an exponential correction term n. That is,

$$V_r = U_{slip}^n \qquad (73)$$

here n = 2/3.

The following relations can be used to estimate the effective mixture volume and two phase slip elocity. The superficial velocity ratio is:

$$K = C_D U_g/U_{\ell} \qquad (74)$$

here U_g and U_{ℓ} = the superficial gas and liquid phase velocities at the nozzle inlet region
C_D = a discharge coefficient (for the test nozzle $C_D \simeq 0.6$).

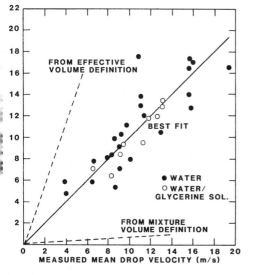

Figure 14. Droplet velocity data correlated by corrected effective volume definition.

The dryness fraction in the nozzle is:

$$x = \rho_g Q_g/(\rho_g Q_g + \rho_\ell Q_\ell) \tag{75}$$

The mixture volume is:

$$V_m = \{x/\rho_g + k(1 - x)/\rho_\ell\}/\{x + k(1 - x)\} \tag{76}$$

And liquid holdup can be approximated by:

$$\alpha_\ell = (1 - x)\sqrt{1/\rho_\ell V_m} \tag{77}$$

We now define an effective two-phase volume:

$$\dot{v}_e = V_m\{x + k(1 - x)\}\{x + (1 - x)/k\} \tag{78}$$

The two-phase emulsion velocity is:

$$U_{tp} = \tilde{G}\dot{v}_e \tag{79}$$

The relative slip velocity is then

$$U_{slip} = U_{tp} - U_\ell \tag{80}$$

where U_ℓ is the liquid's superficial velocity at the nozzle exit.

As an aside, a practical exercise is to model the drop behavior for a mass-transfer or heat-transfer related problem. For example, consider a stack in which we desire to cool the gases down to some desired temperature. A simple evaporation model would provide guidance in selecting a nozzle that produces the proper initial mean drop size based on the constraints of flue gas temperature and the available residence time in the stack. Considering such a problem, where the driving force for evaporation is the difference in liquid vapor concentration between the drop surface and the external flue gas stream, we develop the following model.

First, the rate of mass transfer is governed by a relationship similar in form to a heat transfer rate expression, but with concentration substituted for temperature, and a mass transfer coefficient replacing the heat transfer coefficient.

$$\dot{m} = kA(Y_s - Y_\infty) \tag{81}$$

where $\dot{m}$ = rate of mass transfer (kg/sec)
         k = mass transfer coefficient (kg/sec m^2)
         A = surface area (m^2)
         Y_s = mass fraction of liquid vapor at the drop surface ($-$)
         Y_∞ = mass fraction of liquid vapor in the gas ($-$)

The mass transfer coefficient, k, is related to the stream conditions by

$$\frac{kd}{\rho_f \mathscr{D}_f} = Sh \tag{82}$$

where d = drop diameter (m)
         ρ_f = density of vapor in the film (kg/m^3)
         $\mathscr{D}_f$ = vapor diffusivity in the film (m^2/sec)
         Sh = Sherwood number ($-$)

A Sherwood number of 2 corresponds to a zero-slip condition between the gas and liquid droplets (i.e., the drops have the same velocity as the gas stream). In this limiting case of pure diffusion mass transfer, Equation 82 may be restated as:

$$k = \frac{2.0 \rho_f \mathscr{D}_f}{d} \tag{83}$$

The concentration of the liquid vapor at the drop surface, Y_s, can be assumed constant and equal to unity. This assumption introduces some nonconservativism into the solution, because in reality the vapor concentration at the drop surface is a function of the drop temperature. A more rigorous solution would allow the water vapor concentration at the drop surface to vary as a function of the heat transfer. As the drop evaporates, the concentration of the vapor in the gas stream, Y_∞, increases. Thus, the driving force for the evaporation process (i.e., the difference in vapor concentration between the drop surface and the gas stream) decreases with time.

A computer program can be written to allow the vapor concentration in the gas phase to increase with droplet evaporation. Such a code can be used to determine the time required to evaporate droplets of a given size.

The effects of a droplet size distribution on the liquid evaporation rate can be investigated by using, for example, a Rosin-Rammler type distribution,

$$V = \exp\left[-3.0 \left(\frac{d}{d_{95}} \right)^{2.5} \right] \tag{84}$$

where V = cumulative volume fraction of particles with diameters greater than d
d_{95} = particle diameter corresponding to 95 vol % of particles smaller than d_{95}
d = particle diameter

The predictions of such a model are compared against measured mean drop sizes in Figure 15. The drop-size measurements were made at the nozzle discharge and at the end of an environmental

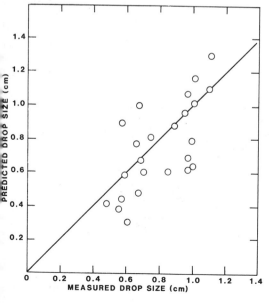

Figure 15. Comparison of predicted drop size to measured drop size for evaporating flows.

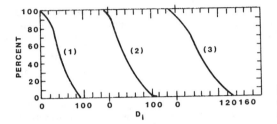

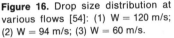

Figure 16. Drop size distribution at various flows [54]: (1) W = 120 m/s; (2) W = 94 m/s; (3) W = 60 m/s.

chamber using a laser interferometer, where droplets had approximately 10 sec of residence time in which to fractionally evaporate.

Spray Densities from Pneumatic Nozzles

The term "spray density" refers to the flow rate of liquid through a unit of jet cross-section. The process of liquid breakup continues after a continuous jet has broken up into single drops. The resultant appearance of a complex breakup mechanism in a jet dissolving into a number of drops has a probabilistic character. Experimental curves of fractional distribution have precisely such a shape. For fractional (drop-size) distribution of an atomized liquid, the following formula is applicable:

$$v = \exp\left\{ -\left[G\left(1 + \frac{1}{m'}\right)\frac{d_i}{\bar{d}} \right]^m \right\} \tag{85}$$

where v = the fraction of liquid consisting of drops of diameter greater than d_1
   m' = a parameter characterizing the drop-size distribution

Experimental results [54] are shown in Figures 16 and 17. The experimental points for a given type of spray nozzle are satisfactorily correlated by the relation:

$$v = v\left(\frac{d_1}{\bar{d}}\right) \tag{86}$$

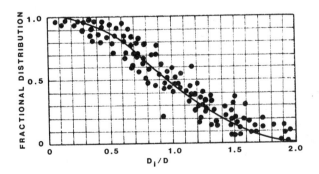

Figure 17. Character of drop distribution by fractions when atomized by spray nozzles [54].

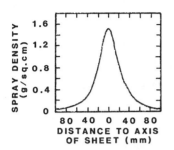

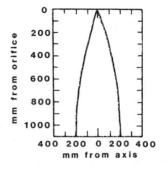

Figure 18. Spray density throughout the cross-section of a sheet from a pneumatic spray nozzle [54].

Figure 19. The shape of the sheet for the STS-FOB-2 spray nozzle [54].

Values of parameter m' are dependent upon the specific spray nozzle configuration. Figure 18 shows a typical spray density distribution for pneumatic spray nozzles.

The shape of the atomized jet characteristic of noncentrifugal spray nozzles is shown in Figure 19.

Liquid Motion in a Centrifugal Spray Nozzle

The conditions which promote jet atomization in mechanical spray nozzles are first established in the chamber preceding the spray nozzle orifice. The theory of the motion of a liquid in the chamber of a centrifugal spray nozzle was developed by Abramovich [57]. Figure 20 illustrates the major features of a centrifugal spray nozzle. Liquid is fed into the nozzle's chamber tangentially, as a consequence of which the stream acquires a twisted motion. The nozzle orifice is located in the front wall of the spray nozzle. When this twisted jet discharges from the spray nozzle, the effect of centripetal forces from the rigid walls ceases and the jet breaks down due to nonsteady-state oscillations. Drops are thus scattered in a pattern of rectilinear streams, tangent to the cylindrical surfaces coaxial with the spray nozzle orifice. This action is illustrated in Figure 21.

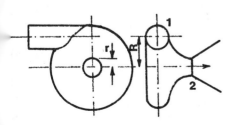

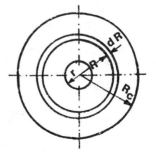

Figure 20. Illustrates a centrifugal swirl nozzle.

Figure 21. Cross-section of the sprayer exit orifice.

The angle α, between the lines of atomization and the spray-nozzle axis, is determined by the ratio of the tangential velocity w_t' to the translational velocity w_n' in the exit cross section of the nozzle orifice:

$$\alpha = \tan^{-1} \frac{w_t'}{w_n'} \tag{87}$$

Ignoring friction, the momentum of a liquid particle moving relative to the spray axis is constant. Hence,

$$w_{in}'R' = w_t'R \tag{88}$$

where w_{in}' = the velocity of the liquid entering the spray nozzle

R' = the radial distance from the spray-nozzle axis to the liquid particle in the entrance orifice of the spray nozzle

w_t' = the tangential component of the liquid velocity in the spray-nozzle exit orifice

R = the radial distance from the spray nozzle axis to the liquid particle in the exit orifice

Assuming the difference in the entrance and exit orifice levels is negligible in comparison with the head, the Bernoulli equation is:

$$\frac{p_{in}}{\gamma'} + \frac{w_{in}^2}{2g} = \frac{p}{\gamma'} + \frac{w_t'^2}{2g} + \frac{w_n'^2}{2g} = \text{const.} \tag{89}$$

Rearranging terms and including Equation 88:

$$\frac{p}{\gamma'} = H - \frac{w_n'^2}{2g} - \frac{w_{in}'^2}{2g}\left(\frac{R'}{R}\right)^2 \tag{90}$$

where H is the total head defined as:

$$H = \frac{p_{in}}{\gamma'} + \frac{w_{in}'^2}{2g}$$

From Equation 90 we note that at the limits of the spray-nozzle axis ($R = 0$) the flow velocity goes to infinity and the pressure goes to minus infinity. Obviously this is physically impossible, and hence there must be a mechanism maintaining a certain pressure at the spray-nozzle axis. This pressure cannot be noticeably below the pressure in the gas since the axial area of the stream is in contact with the gaseous medium outside the spray nozzle.

The central part of the spray nozzle cannot be filled with liquid. Therefore, a gaseous vortex with a pressure equal to the gas pressure outside the spray nozzle will develop in that central region. The liquid is discharged from the spray nozzle through an annular cross section of area:

$$\Omega = \pi(R_0^2 - R_0''^2) \tag{91}$$

where R_0 = the radius of the spray-nozzle orifice

R_0'' = the radius of the gas vortex

The filled fraction of the nozzle (referred to as the coefficient of the effective nozzle cross section) is

$$\psi = 1 - \left(\frac{R_0''}{R_0}\right)^2 \tag{92}$$

Consider an elementary annular plane $2\pi R\, dR$ in the nozzle-exit cross section. The change in pressure along the nozzle radius is proportional to the centrifugal force

$$\frac{dp}{dR} = \frac{\gamma' w_t'^2}{gR} \tag{93}$$

And from Equation 88:

$$R = \frac{w_{t,0}' R_0''}{w_t'} \tag{94}$$

where $w_{t,0}'$ is the tangential velocity at the surface of the gas vortex.
Differentiating this expression and substituting the obtained value of dR into Equation 93, and integrating, we get:

$$\frac{p}{\gamma'} = -\frac{w_t'^2}{2g} + c \tag{95}$$

In the gas vortex, the excess pressure is

$$-\frac{w_{t,0}'^2}{2g} + c = 0 \tag{96}$$

Hence,

$$\frac{p}{\gamma'} = \frac{w_{t,0}'^2}{2g} - \frac{w_t'^2}{2g}$$

Combining Equations 96 and 90 we obtain:

$$\frac{w_0'^2}{2g} = H - \frac{w_{t,0}'^2}{2g} \tag{97}$$

That is, the translational velocity at the exit of the spray nozzle is constant.
The volumetric liquid flow rate through the spray nozzle is:

$$Q_\ell = w_0 \pi R_0^2 \tag{98}$$

where $w_0' = w_n'$ is a reference velocity of the liquid discharge from the nozzle orifice.
Note that,

$$Q_\ell = w_{in}' \pi R_{in}^2 n \tag{99}$$

where R_{in} = the radius of the orifices through which the liquid is fed to the spray nozzle
n = the number of orifices

Combining Equations 98 and 99, and accounting for Equation 88, we obtain:

$$\left. \begin{aligned} n w_{in}' &= w_0' \left(\frac{R_0}{R_{in}}\right)^2; \\ n w_i' &= w_0' \frac{R'}{R} \left(\frac{R_0}{R_{in}}\right)^2 \end{aligned} \right\} \tag{100}$$

Abramovich [57] applies the approximation $R' = R_{ch} - R_{in}$, where R_{ch} is the radius of the vortex chamber.

The tangential velocity near the chamber wall is

$$w'_{i,ch} = w'_0 \frac{(R_{ch} - R_{in})R_0}{nR_{in}^2}$$

(101)

On the boundary of the air vortex

$$w'_{t,0} = w'_0 \frac{(R_{ch} - R_{in})R_0^2}{R_{in}^2 R'_0}$$

(102)

And from Equation 92, we obtain.

$$w'_{t,0} = w'_0 \frac{(R_{ch} - R_{in})R_0}{nR_{in}^2} \cdot \frac{1}{\sqrt{1 - \psi}}$$

(103)

Substituting the value of $w'_{t,0}$ from Equation 103 into 97 and solving the obtained equation for the total head H

$$H = \frac{w'^2_0}{2g}\left(\frac{1}{\psi^2} + \frac{A_0^2}{1 - \psi}\right)$$

(104)

where A_0 is the geometric characteristic of the spray nozzle defined as:

$$A_0 = \frac{(R_{ch} - R_{in})R_0}{nR_{in}^2}.$$

(105)

Hence,

$$w'_0 = \xi\sqrt{2gH}$$

(106)

where

$$\xi = \frac{1}{\sqrt{1/\psi^2 + \dfrac{A_0^2}{1 - \psi}}}$$

(107)

is the spray-nozzle coefficient of discharge.

Abramovich [57] introduces the condition for maximum rate of discharge of the liquid through the spray nozzle

$$\frac{d\xi}{d\psi} = 0$$

(108)

with this condition

$$A = (1 - \psi)/\sqrt{\psi^3/2}$$

$$\xi = \psi\sqrt{\frac{\psi}{2 - \psi}}$$

(109)

The volumetric rate of discharge of the liquid through the spray nozzle, according to Equations 98 and 106 is:

$$Q = \xi \pi R_0^2 \sqrt{2gH} \tag{110}$$

Figure 22 shows the relationship of the coefficient of effective cross section of the spray nozzle orifice and the geometric characteristic A_0, calculated from Equation 109.
Introducing w_t' into Equation 87, we obtain:

$$R_{av} = \frac{R_0 + R_0'}{2} \tag{111}$$

$$w_{t,av}' = \frac{w_{t,0}' R_0}{R_{av}} \tag{112}$$

And finally

$$\tan \alpha = \frac{(1 - \psi)\sqrt{8}}{(1 + \sqrt{1 - \psi})\sqrt{\psi^3}} \tag{113}$$

Figure 23 shows the relationship between $\tan \alpha$, α, and A_0, as computed from Equation 113.
In general, the quantity ξ in Equation 110, is a function of the geometric parameters of the spray nozzle and of the criterion of hydrodynamic similarity:

$$Re' = \frac{w_0' D_0}{v'} \tag{114}$$

where $D_0 = 2R_0$ is the diameter of the spray-nozzle orifice

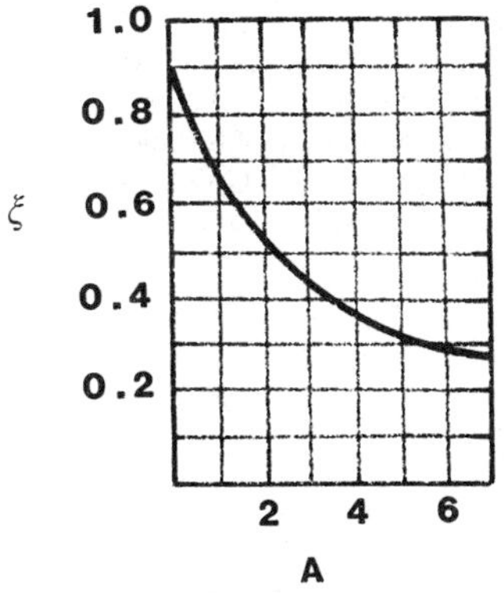

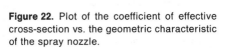

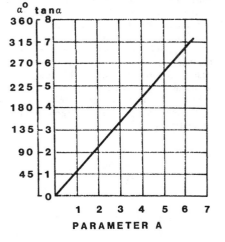

Figure 22. Plot of the coefficient of effective cross-section vs. the geometric characteristic of the spray nozzle.

Figure 23. Plot of tan α and α vs. A.

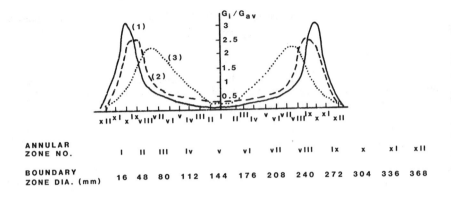

ANNULAR ZONE NO.	I	II	III	Iv	v	vI	vII	vIII	Ix	x	xI	xII
BOUNDARY ZONE DIA. (mm)	16	48	80	112	144	176	208	240	272	304	336	368

Figure 24. Relative spray density distribution for low-viscosity liquid (water) atomization by a mechanical spray nozzle: A = 5.38: (1) p = 20 atm. abs.; (2) p = 29 atm. abs.; (3) p = 5 atm. abs.

Abramovich [57] and others have shown that:

$$\xi = \xi\left(A; \frac{D_{ch}}{D_0}; Re'\right) \tag{115}$$

In the region $Re' < 1.6 \times 10^4$

$$\xi = \psi \sqrt{\frac{\psi}{2 - \psi}} (13)\left(\frac{\sqrt{D_{ch}/D_0}}{\sqrt[3]{Re'}}\right) \tag{116}$$

where ψ is taken as a function of A from the curve in Figure 22.

At $Re' > 1.6 \times 10^4$, the coefficient of discharge, for practical purposes, depends neither on viscosity nor, apparently, on D_{ch}/D_0. The gas vortex in the centrifugal spray nozzle and the rotational motion of the jet being discharged cause the jet to acquire the shape of a hollow rotational body. For these type nozzles a density distribution is typical in which the central region of the sheet (the atomized jet) is filled with a small quantity of liquid, and at some distance from the axis the spray density reaches its maximum. The presence of a certain amount of liquid in the central zone is due to the fact that individual droplets are carried away from the jet because of turbulent fluctuations.

Figures 24 and 25 show the distribution curves for relative spray density $\tilde{G}/\tilde{G}_{av}$ from experiments by Vitman et al. [54]. Here $\tilde{G}_\ell$ (kg/m² sec) is the local spray density; $\tilde{G}_{av}$ (kg/m² sec) is the average spray density.

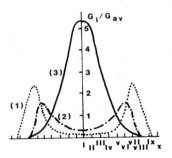

Figure 25. Effect of viscosity on the relative spray density in atomization by a mechanical spray nozzle. A = 4.4. (1) water (p = 8.5 atm.; $\mu' = 1 \times 10^{-4}$ kg-s/m²; $\sigma = 7.3 \times 10^{-3}$ kg/m); (2) kerosene (p = 9.5 atm, $\mu' = 3.08 \times 10^{-4}$ kg-s/m²; $\sigma = 2.8 \times 10^{-3}$ kg/m); (3) gas-oil (p = 6 atm.; $\mu' = 7.84 \times 10^{-4}$ kg-s/m²; $\sigma = 3.6 \times 10^{-3}$ kg/m).

The plots suggest that the structure of the sheet varies depending on the viscosity, the rate of liquid discharge, and the nozzle-orifice diameter. For moderately viscous liquids, the angle of spray remains constant when the rate of liquid discharge varies. Only the character of the spray density distribution curve changes. With viscous liquids, the rate of discharge affects the angle of spray. Furthermore, the influence of frictional forces increases, and a maximum spray density builds up in the center of the sheet.

Vitman et al. [54] give the following empirical formula for estimating average drop diameter in the sheet projected from a centrifugal spray nozzle

$$\frac{\bar{d}}{D_0} = 47.8A^{-0.6}\left(\frac{\rho'\sigma D_0}{\mu'^2}\right)^{0.1}\left(\frac{v'}{w_0'D_0}\right)^{0.7} \tag{117}$$

The fractional composition of the sheet can be determined from Equation 85, wherein, for the previously mentioned spray nozzles, m = 2 to 2.5.

Equation 117 is applicable for practically all low-viscosity liquids. According to these same data, the angle of spray at $Re' > 3.5 \times 10^3$ and $\mu'^2/(\sigma\rho'D_0) > 3 \times 10^{-5}$ is determined by the formula

$$\tan \alpha = (\tan \alpha_A)3.05 \times 10^{-2}\left(\frac{D_0}{D_{ch}}\right)^{0.4}\left(\frac{\sigma\rho'D_0}{\mu'^2}\right)^{0.33} \tag{118}$$

where $\tan \alpha_A$ is obtained from Equation 113.

At $Re' < 3.5 \times 10^3$ and $\mu'^2/(\sigma\rho'D_0) > 3 \times 10^4$, $\tan \alpha$ depends also on Re'. For this region, the following relationship was developed for a spray nozzle of $A_0 = 4.4$.

$$\tan \alpha = (\tan \alpha_A)1.88 \times 10^{-3}\left(\frac{\mu'^2}{\rho'\sigma D_0}\right)^{0.25}\left(\frac{w_0 D_0}{v'}\right)^{0.9} \tag{119}$$

GAS-IN-LIQUID DISPERSIONS

There are many operations requiring the contact of gases and liquids where the liquid is the continuous phase. There are three main objectives in these operations:

● Gas-liquid contacting to promote absorption or stripping, with or without chemical reaction.
● Agitation of the liquid.
● Foam or froth production.

A gas may be dispersed in a liquid by

1. Vaporizing a volatile liquid by either decreasing the system pressure or increasing its temperature.
2. Producing gas from a chemical reaction.
3. Introducing the gas bubbles directly into the liquid.
4. Disintegrating a massive bubble or stream of gas by a mixer (shear and/or turbulence in the liquid).

Only methods 3 and 4 are discussed here.

Gas Sparging

When a gas is mixed with a liquid, at sufficiently high flow rates of both phases a mass motion of gas bubbles is produced, which in turn, gives rise to an intensive mixing of the liquid. Depending on the flow rates of the gas and liquid in the mixture, different hydrodynamic regimes arise, and consequently, changes in the structure of the mixture occur. This structure can be characterized by its hydraulic resistance, which for the particular case of gas being forced into a liquid through an array of orifices depends on the height of the liquid column in the chamber and also on the surface contact area, defined in terms of the bubble size, gas content, and liquid column height.

At low flow rates, the gas passes through the liquid mixture at regular intervals in the form of bubbles generated from the orifices [58–63]. Under this condition a layer of cellular foam, consisting of greatly enlarged bubbles that are close-packed and deformed, is formed on the free surface of the liquid. As the superficial gas velocity is increased, this layer of cellular foam thickens and finally, at a certain ratio of gas and liquid flow rates, the entire bubbling mixture is transformed into cellular foam.

The mode of gas injection into the liquid is also changed when we increase the gas flow rate. Instead of bubbles, the orifices produce gas jets, which are broken up into bubbles as a result of the dynamic influence of the liquid [58, 64–66]. Increasing the gas flow rate retards the circulatory downflow of liquid, and at a certain critical gas velocity the amount of liquid descending to the orifices is insufficient to generate new bubbles, at which point the height of the cellular foam layer reaches its maximum and the foam starts to disintegrate [58–67]. At still higher superficial gas velocities (to about 1.0 m/s) there is an abrupt change in the structure of the mixture, from the cellular foam regime to a regime of developed turbulence. In this regime, the bubbling process is accompanied by liquid breaking up into drops. As the superficial gas velocity increases (to about 3.0 m/s) the bubbling mixture is totally destroyed and liquid is completely transformed into drops entrained by the gas flow.

The regimes arising after destruction of the cellular foam condition are of practical importance [67]. The lower gas flow limit of these regimes is characterized by the Froude number being greater than unity (Fr $= v_s^2/gh > 1$, where v_s is the superficial gas velocity, h the height of the liquid column, and g acceleration due to the gravity) and transition from one regime to the other is, as already qualitatively described, defined by the gas and liquid flow rates and geometric properties of the flow system.

The mass bubbling regime can be described by the theory of homogeneous and isotropic turbulence, since the motion of a large swarm of bubbles through a liquid produces complete mixing. That is, a regime of developed turbulence is created, and it can be assumed that the energy of the gas passing into the liquid is transmitted to the liquid and dissipated by its turbulent behavior.

The turbulent eddies associated with flows of large Reynolds numbers, are usually classified by their size. Much of the energy of the flow is contained in large-scale eddies, this scale having an order of magnitude comparable to the largest dimension of the flow system (e.g., the diameter of a tank or a pipe). Also, the velocity of these large-scale eddies is comparable to the mean velocity occurring in the system, so that the Reynolds number of these motions is therefore of the same order of magnitude as the Reynolds number of the mean or time-averaged flow.

Kinetic energy is continuously being transferred from large eddies to eddies of smaller sizes until it is dissipated in the smallest eddies, where the liquid motion has a viscous character.

From the theory of homogeneous isotropic turbulence [68], all eddies, the scales of which are significantly less than the large-scale eddies, are statistically independent of the larger ones, and the properties of these smaller eddies are defined solely by the local energy dissipation. This homogeneous isotropic turbulence exists only in a small region of the flow, much smaller than the volume of the enclosing system. In contrast, large-scale turbulent motion is obviously far from being isotropic as it is influenced by wall effects. Liquid viscosity is significant only for small-scale motion, and conversely, quantities describing large-scale motion are independent of liquid viscosity.

The dissipation energy is defined by properties of the large-scale motion, and the relationship between the dissipation and these properties can be expressed [69, 70] by the following equation:

$$\varepsilon' \simeq U^3/\ell \tag{120}$$

where ε' = the energy dissipation per unit mass and time
U = the characteristic (or typical) velocity of the large eddies
ℓ = the characteristic size of the large eddies

The characterizing pressure difference in turbulent motions is defined as [69]:

$$\Delta p \simeq \rho_f U^2 \tag{121}$$

The velocity U_t, defines the motion of the turbulent liquid itself, and can be expressed as the change of velocity of an element of liquid in a (small) time, t. It is dependent on local properties of the turbulence and the time interval; and can be written as:

$$U_t \simeq (\varepsilon t)^{1/2} \tag{122}$$

As noted earlier, the size of large eddies is comparable with the largest dimension of the flow system, either the height of the gas-liquid mixture or the diameter of the liquid chamber [70]. The characteristic velocity of the large eddies can be estimated from a consideration of the work done by the gas during the bubbling process. This loss of energy consists of work done against gravity and surface forces. The work against surface forces during intensive bubbling is so small that it can be ignored. The total kinetic energy, E, of the gas injected into the liquid is converted into potential energy of the liquid, which, in turn, is transformed into kinetic energy of the descending flow of liquid. Azbel [58] and Azbel and Cheremisinoff [71] have shown that the work done by the gas during its passage through the fluid medium can be expressed as:

$$E = \rho_f Q_\ell g h \left(\frac{\phi}{1 - \phi} \right) \tag{123}$$

where Q_ℓ is the volume of liquid and ϕ the gas void fraction (defined as the ratio of gas volume to total volume). When this work is divided by the volume of gas in the chamber it is numerically equal to the liquid static pressure in the chamber, Δp.

From Equation 121, the velocity of large-scale eddies is

$$U = \text{const.} \left(\frac{\Delta p}{\rho_f} \right)^{1/2} = \text{const.}(gh)^{1/2} \tag{124}$$

Now that we have defined various quantities characterizing turbulent flows, we are in a position to study the effect of liquid turbulence on bubble motion.

Maximum Bubble Velocity in Turbulent Flow

Large-scale eddies may entrain a bubble suspended in the turbulent flow, but because the density of a bubble differs significantly from the density of the liquid, the inertia forces are of different magnitudes, and this entrainment cannot be complete. At the other extreme the small-scale eddies cannot entrain a bubble, and in relationship to these eddies the bubble may be considered to be an immobile body. Liquid taking part in this small-scale motion will flow around the surface of the gas bubble. Hence, we need to determine the intermediate scale that is capable of entraining bubbles.
The equation of motion determining the scale of eddies that can entrain a rising bubble can be written [72]:

$$(\rho g + k\rho_f)V \frac{dv_r}{dt} = (\rho_f - \rho_g)V \frac{dv_t}{dt} - F_D \tag{125}$$

where ρ_f = the liquid density
   ρ_g = the gas density
   V = the volume of a bubble
   v_r = the velocity of the bubbles relative to the liquid
   F_D = the drag force
   v_t = the liquid velocity
   k = the coefficient of "apparent additional mass" (for spherical bubbles $k = 1/2$)

Here, the left-hand side of the equation is the inertia force of the bubble; the first term on the right-hand side of the equation expresses the inertial effect of the surrounding turbulent liquid; and the last term is the drag force. Usually, this force F_D is taken to be equal to the drag of a free-rising bubble of a moderate size (Re $\simeq$ 800); in other words,

$$F_D = 12\pi\mu_f r_b v_r \qquad (126)$$

where μ_f = the dynamic viscosity of the liquid
          r_b = the radius of the bubble

However, in mass-bubbling operations, where the turbulent motion is generated by the bubbly flow, each bubble is influenced by other bubbles, both close to it and farther removed from it, and it is obvious that in such a case the drag of a bubble must differ from the drag of a single free-rising bubble.

The estimation of the drag exerted on an individual bubble in a swarm of bubbles is very difficult [73–78] and cannot be accomplished without the use of some simplifying assumptions. Let us assume a uniform bubble distribution in the volume of liquid [79–81]. In this case, we shall suppose that every bubble is located in the center of a *spherical compartment* formed by adjacent bubbles, so using this model we can use spherical coordinates and consider the motion to be equivalent to that of liquid between two concentric spheres, the inner surface being the bubble and the outer constituting a *free-surface* boundary condition.

For this flow system, the radial and tangential velocity components of the enclosed liquid can be written as follows [73, 81]:

$$v_R = \frac{v_r}{1-\phi}\left(1 - \frac{r_b^3}{r^3}\right)\cos\theta \qquad (127a)$$

$$v_\theta = \frac{v_r}{1-\phi}\left(1 + \frac{r_b^3}{2r^3}\right)\sin\theta \qquad (127b)$$

where ϕ = the gas void fraction
          r = the radial coordinate
          θ = the polar angle
          r_b = the bubble radius

Azbel [58] has estimated the drag from knowledge of the energy dissipation in the flowing liquid obtaining

$$\frac{dE}{dt} = 9\mu_f\left(\frac{v_r}{1-\phi}\right)^2 r_b^6 \int_0^\pi \int_{r_b}^{r_b/\phi^{(1/3)}} \frac{1 + 2\cos^2\theta}{r^8} 2\pi r^2 \sin\theta\, d\theta\, dr \qquad (128)$$

Note that as an upper boundary condition on the radial coordinate r, we have $r = r_b/\phi^{1/3}$, so that the volume of integration and the volume of the bubble are consistent with the flow system void fraction. After integrating, we find that

$$\frac{dE_f}{dt} = 12\pi\mu_f v_r^2 r_b \frac{1 - \phi^{5/3}}{(1-\phi)^2}$$

and therefore, the drag force is simply

$$F_D = 12\pi\mu_f v_r r_b \frac{1 - \phi^{5/3}}{(1-\phi)^2} \qquad (129)$$

Thus the expression for the drag on a bubble in a swarm of bubbles, given by Equation 129, differs from the drag on a single free-rising bubble, given by Equation 126, by a factor that takes into account the flow system void fraction.

Now, using the value of the drag force, F_D, from Equation 129 and v_t from Equation 123 in Equation 125, we obtain an expression that can be solved for v_r.

$$v_r = \frac{\rho_f - \rho_g}{\rho_f}(\varepsilon t)^{1/2}\left\{k + \frac{9v_f t}{r_b^2}\left[\frac{1 - \phi^{5/3}}{(1 - \phi)^2}\right]\right\}^{-1} \tag{130}$$

where v_f is the liquid kinematic viscosity. Here we have said that $\rho_g/\rho_f \ll 1$.

The characteristic period of the liquid motion, t, can be expressed by the scale of entraining eddies, λ, and the energy dissipation of the turbulent flow ε in the form:

$$t = \left(\frac{\lambda^2}{\varepsilon}\right)^{1/3} \tag{131}$$

Now, the velocity of the bubbles is a maximum when we have eddies of size λ obtained by the following condition:

$$\frac{dv_r}{d\lambda} = 0$$

or its equivalent by Equation 131,

$$\frac{dv_r}{dt} = 0$$

Performing the differentiation on Equation 130 and using the foregoing condition, with the assumption that $\rho_g \ll \rho_f$ gives the time duration for maximum bubble velocity,

$$t = \frac{kr_b^2(1 - \phi)^2}{9v_f(1 - \phi^{5/3})} \tag{132}$$

The maximum velocity of the bubbles is obtained by substituting the values of ε and t from Equations 120 and 132 into Equation 130

$$v_{r_{max}} = \text{const.}\frac{U^{3/2}r_b}{(\ell v_f)^{1/2}}\frac{1 - \phi}{(1 - \phi^{5/3})^{1/2}} \tag{133}$$

Size of Bubbles in Mass Bubbling

In intensive mass-bubbling operations, bubbles of a fairly uniform size are formed in a gas-liquid mixture, this being a result of the breaking up and coalescing of bubbles, which in turn is due to the dynamic interaction between the liquid and gas. It has been shown experimentally that the size of a bubble depends on surface tension [82–87] and the viscosity of the liquid [88–92], but that the physical properties of the gas [82] have no significant influence on the size of the bubble. At low gas flow rates the bubble radius increases with an increase in viscosity [88]. For example, at a superficial velocity of gas of 4 mm/s (0.16 in./s), the bubble radius is double with an increase in viscosity from 5×10^{-2} to 1 g/cm·s.

In mass bubbling the bubble radius is practically independent of the geometric characteristics of the flow system (e.g., the diameter of the orifice in a gas-distributing device [93]), so, for example, increasing the diameter of the orifice 100 times increases the bubble diameter only twice for an air-water system [94]. On the other hand, the *wall effect* has some influence on bubble size when the diameter of an apparatus is less than 200 mm (8 in.).

In a mass-bubbling process, bubbles have an oblate ellipsoid shape (refer to Chapter 3)whose short axis is parallel with the direction of motion [87, 88], and the rise of velocity of such bubbles has been estimated by equating drag to buoyancy force [72]:

$$v_c \simeq \left(\frac{\sigma^2 g}{3\pi\mu_f \rho_f} \right)^{1/5} \tag{134}$$

where v_c is the velocity of the center of the bubble. Note that the surface tension, σ, contributes to this equation insofar as it affects the shape of the bubble and hence the drag force [72]. This equation can be used to obtain a rough estimate of the bubble velocity.

We are interested in obtaining information about bubble size in mass bubbling, and Equation 134 is of use in this quest, as it defines a dynamic property of the bubbles, the velocity, in terms of system properties. Now, it is known [95–99] that viscous liquid moving under the action of constant forces has an unambiguous potential, and in this case the velocity distribution is such that it gives a minimum of dissipative energy.

During the motion of sufficiently large single bubbles, they are not only deformed but also break up, and the condition for breakup of bubbles may be written as:

$$\frac{\rho_g v_r^2}{2} \geq \frac{3\sigma^3}{r_b^3 \rho_f^2 v_r^4}$$

The left-hand side of the foregoing equation represents the kinetic energy of the flow per unit volume, and the right-hand side expresses the surface-tension energy of th bubble (the surface tension σ is to the third power because of its effect on the bubble shape, the details of which have been described elsewhere [72]). The equation states that if the kinetic energy of the flow id greater than the energy of surfae tension, the bubblel is likely to break up. This equation can be rewritten as

$$r_c = \frac{6^{1/3}\sigma}{v_r^2 (\rho_f^2 \rho_g)^{1/3}} \tag{135}$$

where r_c is now the critical bubble size for breakup. Now, the velocity of the liquid changes from place to place in turbulent flow, and thus different dynamic heads are present in the flow, leading, by acting on the bubble surface in successive instants, to the deformation and rupture of the bubble, as represented by Equation 135.

Large-scale eddies hardly change their velocity from one end of a bubble to the other, and thus have no influence on the bubble, so that deformation and breakup of a bubble is caused by comparatively small turbulent eddies whose characteristic velocity may written as:

$$v_e \simeq (\varepsilon\lambda)^{1/3} \tag{136}$$

where $\varepsilon = $ the energy dissipation
       $\lambda = $ the scale of eddies capable of breaking up the bubbles

We can say that this scale will be approximately that of the critical bubble diameter, so that $\lambda = 2r_c$. Further, we can say that the relative velocity of the bubble is approximately the same as the eddy velocity, $v_r \simeq v_e$, which means that we are assuming that the absolute velocity of the bubble is small. Using this in Equation 136 and taking into account Equations 120 and 135, we find that:

$$r_c = c \left(\frac{\sigma}{\rho_f} \right)^{3/5} \frac{\ell^{2/5}}{U^{6/5}} \left(\frac{\rho_f}{\rho_g} \right)^{1/5} \tag{137}$$

where ℓ and U are the scale and velocity of large-scale motions, and c is a dimensionless constant. Equation 137 is an expression for the average bubble size in terms of known quantities.

Now, if we assume that the tangential stress as a result of turbulence is:

$$\tau_s = c_1 \rho_f (\varepsilon r_c)^{2/3} \tag{138}$$

where c_1 is a constant, and we note that the stress of surface forces is proportional to σ/r_c, then the critical bubble size is also determined by the ratio of tangential stress to the surface force stress. This ratio of stresses gives the Weber number,

$$We = \frac{\tau_s r_c}{\sigma} \qquad (139)$$

The Weber number is constant for a given steady-state flow. Therefore, substituting a constant for We along with the value of the tangential stress from Equation 138 into Equation 139, we obtain:

$$r_c = c_2 \left(\frac{\sigma}{\rho_f}\right)^{3/5} \frac{\ell^{2/5}}{U^{6/5}} \qquad (140)$$

where c_2 is a constant. Note that the most probable bubble size, r_c, given in Equation 140 that we have obtained by considering tangential and surface tension stresses is very similar to Equation 137. The latter expression was derived by considering the condition of bubble breakup by a critical balance of dynamic pressure and surface tension forces. The velocity, U, and length, ℓ, are taken from the overall flow system; for instance, U may be taken to be the gas superficial velocity, v_s, and ℓ might be the disturbed liquid level in the chamber, $h/(1 - \phi)$. We can rewrite this expression in the form:

$$r_c = c_3 \left[\frac{(\sigma/\rho_f g)^3}{h(1 - \phi)^2}\right]^{1/5} \qquad (141)$$

In actual flows, because of the "wall effect," coalescence, and viscous effects, the average bubble radius may differ from its value determined by Equation 140, which was derived from breakup conditions. Analysis of experimental data on bubbles of differing sizes in systems with differing physical properties has shown that Equation 141 does not correlate the experimental data correctly within a constant. Therefore, we introduce into the equation factors ϕ^n and $(\mu_g/\mu_f)^n$, which take into account the influence of coalescence and viscosity.

Experimental data [101, 102, 75] of the specific surface area for flows under various conditions, and the average bubble diameter was then estimated from the average void fraction and the specific phase contact area. This made it possible to obtain experimental data on bubble size not only in the region near the wall but also in the bulk of the gas-liquid flow. From such an analysis the following equation was derived by Azbel [58] for calculating the average radius of a bubble in mass-bubbling operations:

$$r_c = 2.56 \left(\frac{\sigma}{\rho_f g}\right)^{0.6} h^{-0.2} \left(\frac{\mu_g}{\mu_f}\right)^{0.25} \frac{\phi^{0.65}}{(1 - \phi)^{0.4}} \qquad (142)$$

where σ = the surface tension
ρ_f = the liquid density
g = the acceleration due to gravity
h = the height of the liquid column
μ_g and μ_f = the dynamic viscosity of the gas and liquid, respectively

Gas Void Fraction

The gas void fraction, ϕ, is defined as the ratio of gas volume to total volume. We will obtain the void fraction as a function of system properties for the case of rapid bubbling of gas in liquid when the viscosity of the liquid is negligible (i.e., an ideal liquid).

For moderate and large values of the Reynolds number, which is typical of bubbling processes utilized in commercial equipment, the viscous forces, being small compared to the inertia forces, have little influence on the hydrodynamics of the gas-liquid mixture and therefore may be ignored in a study of such flows. Theoretical [69] and experimental studies [55, 119, 120] concerning the influence of viscosity on the behavior of the two-phase flow in a bubbling process confirm this conclusion, giving validity to our assumption of an ideal liquid.

There have been many detailed experimental studies [121–145] on mass-bubbling operations, where three groups of parameters influencing the gas-liquid flow are apparent:

1. Geometrical characteristics of the flow system.
2. Physical properties of the gas and liquid.
3. Dynamic factors.

To the first group, for example, belong the height of the liquid in a flow system where the liquid is static, the diameter of the equipment, and the geometry of the gas-distributing device (e.g., the orifices). To the second group belong the viscosity and surface tension of the gas and liquid, and to the third group belong the gas and liquid flow rates.

Consider a two-phase flow that is non-wall controlled and is not influenced by the gas-distribution devices.

We can then take the two-phase flow to be one-dimensional, and at a distance a from the gas inlet we consider a differential layer located perpendicular to the direction of motion of the gas stream, with thickness dx. The fraction of the volume of this differential layer occupied by the gas is:

$$\phi = \tfrac{4}{3}\pi r_b^3 n' \tag{143}$$

where r_b = the mean radius of the bubbles
         n' = the number of bubbles per unit volume

Let us make an energy balance of a unit cross section of the differential layer during the bubbling process:

$$dE = dE_1 + dE_2 + dE_3 \tag{144}$$

where dE = the total energy of the layer
         dE_1 = the potential energy of the liquid
         dE_2 = the kinetic energy of the layer
         dE_3 = the energy of surface tension of the bubbles in the layer

Taking into account the fact that buoyancy forces are balanced by the resistance forces, we will assume that the potential energy of the gas does not change during the motion of a bubble. If we substitute into Equation 144 the expressions for dE_1, dE_2, and dE_3 we obtain:

$$dE = \left[(1 - \phi)\rho_f g x + \left(\rho_g + \frac{\rho_f}{2} \right) \frac{v_f^2}{2\phi} + \frac{3\sigma}{r_b}\phi \right] dx \tag{145}$$

As shown by Azbel [58] and Azbel and Cheremisinoff [71], the total energy of a two-phase mixture of height x_1 is

$$E = \int_0^{x_1} \left[(1 - \phi)\rho_f g x + \left(\rho_g + \frac{\rho_f}{2} \right) \frac{v_f^2}{2\phi} + \frac{3\sigma}{r_b}\phi \right] dx \tag{146}$$

It is a fundamental axiom of physical theory that for any system, the steady state of the system is that for which the available energy of the system is at a minimum. Hence, the steady-state distribution of the gas void fraction ϕ occurs when this energy is at a minimum. Thus to find ϕ it is necessary to determine the minimum of the integral in Equation 146. This problem [146] can be reduced to that of finding the minimum of the integral E under the condition of invariability of the amount of liquid in the system, in other words with:

$$h = \int (1 - \phi) \, dx = \text{const.} \tag{147}$$

where h is the static liquid height. Equation 147 is a boundary condition on the variation of Equation 146.

When we apply the method of calculus of variation to Equation 146 with the constraint Equation 147, we find that:

$$f(\phi, \phi'; x) = (1 - \phi)\rho_f g x + \left(\rho_g + \frac{\rho_f}{2}\right) \frac{v_s^2}{2\phi} + \frac{3\sigma}{r_b} \phi$$

$$\psi(\phi, x) = 1 - \phi$$

and for the Euler equation, we obtain:

$$-\rho_f g x - \left(\rho_g + \frac{\rho_f}{2}\right) \frac{v_s^2}{2\phi^2} + \frac{3\sigma}{r_b} - \lambda = 0 \tag{148}$$

We have ignored the variation due to the unknown upper limit, x_1, in the calculus of variation analysis given above. This upper limit is the point where the two-phase nature of the flow breaks down, in other words, when $\phi = 1$. We now show that it is acceptable to ignore the variation due to x_1. We find from Equation 148 that

$$\phi(x) = \left[\frac{v_f^2(\rho_g + \rho_f/2)}{2[(3\sigma/r_b) - \rho_f g x - \lambda]} \right]^{1/2}$$

Further, since the derivative $\phi(x)$ does not appear in Equation 147, we cannot impose any additional conditions on the values of $\phi(x)$ at the limits of the interval 0 to x_1, and therefore this function may become discontinuous at the ends of the interval. However, from physical considerations it must be the case that the function $\phi(x)$ is continuous at all values of x between the limits, and therefore can be determined from Equation 148. The value of x_1 can now be determined from the equality

$$1 = \left[\frac{v_f^2(\rho_g + \rho_f/2)}{2[(3\sigma/r_b) - \rho_f g x_1 - \lambda]} \right]^{1/2} \tag{149}$$

We still have to eliminate the undetermined Lagrange multiplier λ, and to do this we use ϕ from Equation 148 in the constraint Equation 147; integrate the resultant expression and eliminate λ using Equation 149 to give:

$$h = x_1 + \frac{\rho_g + \rho_f/2}{\rho_f} \frac{v_f^2}{g} - \frac{2}{\rho_f g} \left\{ \left[\frac{(\rho_g + \rho_f/2)v_f^2}{2} \right] \left[\rho_f g x_1 + \frac{(\rho_g + \rho_f/2)v_s^2}{2} \right] \right\}^{1/2} \tag{150}$$

After some manipulation and assuming $\rho_R \ll \rho_f$, the height of the dynamic two-phase mixture in terms of the static liquid level will be:

$$x_1 = \left(\frac{v_f^2 h}{g} \right)^{1/2} + h = h(\text{Fr}^{1/2} + 1) \tag{151}$$

where Fr is the Froude number. It follows that the height of the dynamic two-phase mixture varies linearly with the superficial velocity of the gas, v_s.

From Equation 149 we can write:

$$\lambda = \frac{3\sigma}{r_b} - \rho_f g \left[x_1 + \frac{v_s^2}{4g} \right]$$

where we have again used the inequality $\rho_g \ll \rho_f$. If we substitute the value of x_1 from Equation 151, we get:

$$\lambda = \frac{3\sigma}{r_b} - \rho_f g \left(hFr^{1/2} + h + \frac{v_s^2}{4g} \right)$$

Taking into consideration that:

$$\frac{hv_s^2}{4gh} = \frac{h}{4} Fr$$

we can write:

$$\frac{3\sigma}{r_b} \lambda = \rho_f gh \left(Fr^{1/2} + \frac{Fr}{4} + 1 \right)$$

and using this in Equation 149,

$$\phi(x) = \left[\frac{Fr}{4[Fr^{1/2} + (Fr/4) + 1 - (x/h)]} \right]^{1/2} \qquad (152)$$

If we designate $Fr/4$ by F and substitute F in Equation 152, we finally have:

$$\phi(x) = \left[\frac{F}{(1 + F^{1/2})^2 - x/h} \right]^{1/2} \qquad (153)$$

This gives the local gas void fraction $\phi(x)$ solely in terms of the Froude number, Fr, and the location, x, for the case of an ideal liquid Equation 153 is illustrated [147] for a particular flow configuration in Figure 26. The limitation of this analysis is that of ideal-fluid conditions, which is found to give good results for tests in equipment that have typical dimensions less than 20 cm. It follows that the gas content (or void fraction) does not depend on the form and size of the bubbles of gas, since the bubble radius does not enter into the equation. Consequently, this equation can be used for calculations over a broad range of velocities of the gas.

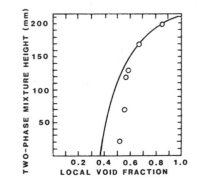

Figure 26. Void fraction plotted against height.

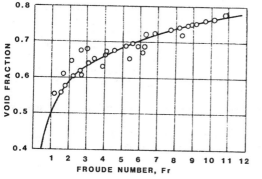

Figure 27. Mean void fraction vs. Froude number for air-water flow.

The average gas content (or void fraction) of the two-phase mixture:

$$\phi_{av} = \frac{1}{1 + (1/Fr^{1/2})} \tag{154}$$

We obtain the result that the average void fraction in a rapidly bubbling flow, with an ideal liquid, is given by a very simple function of the Froude number alone. Equation 154 is shown in Figure 27.
The average relative density of the gas liquid mixture (the specific gravity of the foam) is determined by the formula:

$$\psi = \frac{h}{x_1} \tag{155}$$

where ψ is now the average relative density. This can be written as:

$$\psi = \frac{1}{1 + Fr^{1/2}} \tag{156}$$

Liquid Agitation by Gas Sparging

A special application worth noting is liquid agitation by gas sparging which is sometimes used to handle corrosive fluids, and in operations at high temperatures and pressures. In metallurgy, it is employed in leaching operations as well as for handling thick solid slurries in the inorganic chemicals industry.

Oyama et al. [154] have studied gas blowing into liquids from a single nozzle. They observed the mechanism of generation and state of movement of gas bubbles, and the flow pattern of liquid. From this study, three steps are characterized by the increase in discharge flow rates which depend on the difference in density and interfacial tension.

1. Gas bubbles show the shape of distinct spheres.
2. Time intervals of generation of gas bubbles become short and groups of bubbles rise apparently composing a cylindrical column in the liquid.
3. Gas bubbles discharged from a nozzle break up further into smaller bubbles and rise in the liquid in turbulent motion.

Step 1 corresponds to the state of bubble formation in a period of 0.6 sec. In Step 2, bubbles appear as flattened mushrooms. The ascending velocity of bubbles increases gradually, and tends to a constant value, 0.43 m/sec, when the bubbles rise 7 cm or more away from the nozzle.

This terminal velocity is approximately 4 times as large when compared with that of a single bubble. When the discharge gas flow rate is increased further, gas bubbles begin to split and Step 3 takes place. The transition from Step 2 to 3 takes place abruptly with a small difference in pressure.

The relationship between air flow rates (Q) and pressure drop (P) at the discharge nozzle is shown in Figure 28. In the range AB, splitting of the gas bubbles does not occur (Steps 1 and 2). Range BC corresponds to Step 3. Nozzles of smaller diameter require larger pressure to discharge an equal volume of air, but the discharge flow rate (Q_c) at the critical point (B) from the Region 2 to 3 is small when the nozzle diameter is small.

Quantity Q_c is not affected as much by the fluid density and viscosity, and is almost determined by the nozzle diameter, d_0(m).

The Reynolds number ($Q_c/d_0 v_{air}$) at this critical air flow rate is between 210–250.

The air discharge flow rate (important for the design of gas absorbers) is calculated from the following equation for the region of gas splitting.

For high viscosity liquids:

$$Q/D_0 v = 10.5(\sigma \cdot g_c \cdot D_0/\rho v^2)^{0.48}(\Delta P D_0/\sigma)^{0.75} \tag{157}$$

For low viscosity liquids:

$$Q/D_0 v = 21(\sigma \cdot g_c \cdot D_0/\rho v^2)^{0.48}(\Delta P \cdot D_0/\sigma)^{0.65} \tag{158}$$

where ΔP = pressure drop across the nozzle (kg/m^2)
 σ = surface tension (kg/m)
 Q = gas discharge flow rate (m^3/sec)
 ρ = density (kg/m^3)
 d_0 = nozzle diameter (m)
 v = kinematic viscosity (m^2/sec)

Rearranging these expressions, it is found that Q is proportional to $D_0^{0.2}\Delta P^{0.75\sim0.65}\rho^{-0.48}v^{0.04}/\sigma^{0.27\sim0.17}$, that is surface tension and viscosity have little effect on gas discharge flow rates.

Lamont [155] has analyzed the mixing energy of air agitation. A given volume of air under pressure contains an amount of energy from which useful work may be derived. Gas bubbles expand during their ascent through the liquid and in doing so, give their energy to the surrounding liquids.

Two common assumptions applied to analyzing this case are:

1. The expansion of the air in a vessel of fluid is isothermal.
2. The analysis may reasonably start with air at the tank bottom.

Nozzle and jet effects and the kinetic energy of the entering air are ignored.

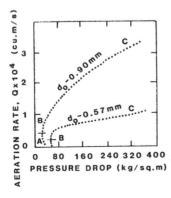

Figure 28. Air pressure and rate of aeration [154].

The work performed W(lb · ft/min) in the course of isothermal expansion is given by the following expression assuming the gas to be ideal.

$$W = 144P_1Q_1 \ln \frac{P_2}{P_1} \tag{159}$$

where   P = the absolute pressure in lb/in.²
Q = air volume rate in ft³/min

Subscripts 1 and 2 refer to the top and bottom of the tank, respectively.
The work expression may also be expressed as follows:

$$W = 144P_1Q_1 \ln \frac{P_1 + (\rho/144)H}{P_1} \tag{160}$$

where ρ = the density
H = the depth at which air is released into the tank in ft

In a mechanically agitated tank, the mechanical energy is transferred from the impeller to the tank contents, but is restricted to the vicinity of the impeller, while in a vessel agitated by air, energy input diffuses throughout the depth of the tank.

As gas bubbles pass through a volume of liquid, a portion of their energy potential is lost because of bubble slip. As the bubbles rise, fluid is displaced from ahead of them to behind them. This results in the production of small-scale turbulence and eddying. Depending upon the geometric relationships of the tank and the air current, another portion of the energy potential may be converted to gross fluid flow. The proportionate amounts of the energy potential that are lost in turbulence and that produce gross flow can readily be determined. Denoting the relative velocity of bubbles and slurry by u(ft/sec) and the velocity of the slurry in which bubbles move by v ft/sec, the time required for the bubbles to rise through a height dh ft is:

$$d\theta = dh/u_{ap} = dh(u + v) \tag{161}$$

The slip distance dh' between bubbles and the liquid during time dθ is:

$$dh' = u \, d\theta = \{u/(u + v)\} \, dh \tag{162}$$

Therefore, the energy loss by the slippage of bubbles (i.e., the energy lost to turbulence W_T (lb·ft/min)) is:

$$\frac{dW_T}{dh'} = \frac{dW}{dh} \left(\frac{u}{u + v} \right) \tag{163}$$

Hence, a fraction of the potential energy of the air is lost to small-scale turbulence. This lost fraction is $1(1 + v/u)$ of the total energy transfer. If there is no gross slurry flow (v = 0), the fraction becomes unity, and the whole of the energy potential is converted to minor eddy currents. The higher the slurry flow rate is, the lower is the fraction of the energy lost to slip. The other factor affecting the fraction is the rate of bubble size. The loss fraction is about 15% in Pachuca tanks with no center draft column; however, this can be reduced by producing finer bubbles.

Regarding the required air to produce various degrees of agitation, Kauffman [155] recommends the values given in Table 1 for a liquid depth of 9 ft.

When gases are introduced at the bottom of a vessel, the liquid in the vessel is drawn upwards accompanied by the rise of bubble swarms and then flows down along the vessel wall and is sucked into the column of bubbles again. If the amount of discharged air is not large, liquid circulation

Table 1
Degree of Agitation by Air Blown in Tanks per Sq. Ft of Cross-Sectional Area

Moderate agitation	0.65 ft³ free air/min
Complete agitation	1.3 ft³ free air/min
Violent agitation	3.1 ft³ free air/min

From Lamont [155].

around the column of bubbles predominates, while in an increased rate the column of air behaves as a jet and the liquid is induced into the bubble swarms so that the circulation is greatly promoted. At still further increases in aeration, the liquid surface becomes violent until finally liquid splashing into the air takes place.

In a liquid of low viscosity, there may be a horizontal circulation flow generated by ascending flow of bubbles in a helical path in addition to vertical circulation flow patterns.

Three types of Pachuca tanks are shown in Figure 29. The original design has in it a central column for almost the full tank depth (A). Air is introduced at the bottom of the column, causing pulp to rise in the column, and developing circulation in the tank. The second type is described in detail by von Bernewitz [155]. The third type of tank is that used almost universally in the South African uranium plants.

A standard Pachuca tank is 22.5 ft in diameter, with a 60° cone at the bottom containing a 45 ft depth of pulp of sp. gr. 1.6 and would normally use about 300 ft³/min of free air [155]. Figure 30 shows that the pumping head is made up of a combination of velocity head and pressure head.

The mechanism of the transfer of energy from air to slurry can be assumed at all levels in the tank. This further implies that the terminal bubble velocities are established immediately at the tank bottom. The assumption of uniform upward slurry velocity on any given axis may then be applied. It follows that slurry flow at any level is proportionate to the energy transfer to that level.

Assuming that the velocity distribution in the bubble column changes linearly from the velocity at the center, $v_{max} = 8$ ft/sec to that at the boundary (1) of rising stream $v = 0$, an average rising velocity to $v_{max}/3 = 2.67$ ft/sec can be assumed. The energy loss of the rising flow accompanied by

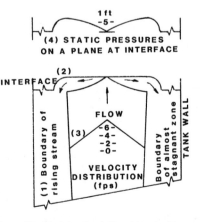

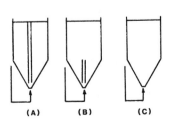

Figure 29. Types of Pachuca tanks: (A) Komata reefs tank; (B) stub-column tank; (C) free-airlift tank.

Figure 30. Sketch of relationships in the release area of a free air lift.

the change to radial flow may be negligible. Therefore, the difference in total energy minus energy loss due to the slip of bubbles is consumed to the rising flow of the slurry.

For a velocity head of 1.0 ft on the central axis, the corresponding velocity is obtained $v_{max} = 8$ ft/sec from the relation $v^2/2g = 1$, and the average velocity, one-third of v_{max} or 2.67 ft/sec. For a relative bubble velocity $u = 0.5$ ft/sec ($d_p = 2$ mm), the energy loss due to slip of bubbles is estimated $u/(u + v) = 0.5/(0.5 + 2.67) = 0.16$ or 16% of the available energy. For an energy transfer rate of 726,000 lb·ft/min per 300 ft³/min of air, the full flow q developed in the air lift is then estimated as follows:

$$q = \frac{W\left\{1 - \dfrac{u}{u + v}\right\}}{\rho(v^2/2g)} = \frac{726,000 \times 0.84}{1.0} = 610,000 \text{ lb/min}$$

or 6,100 ft³/min.

The area of the rising stream at the top of the tank is then 38 ft² and the diameter 7 ft.

Air lift tubes are employed in cases where the rising flow is too low to fluidize solid particles by air sparging at the vessel bottom. Energy transferred to the liquid from air in the air lift tube may be consumed to produce entrance, friction and velocity heads. Each of these hydraulic heads is a function of the fluid velocity, v, with the following values:

- Entrance head, for a Borda-type entry $= 0.83v^2/2g$
- Friction head, for a friction factor of 0.03, a tube length of 45 ft and a tube diameter of 1.5 ft $= 0.03 \times \dfrac{45}{1.5} v^2/2g$
- Velocity head $= 1.0v^2/2g$
- Total hydraulic head, the sum of entrance, velocity, and friction heads $= 2.76v^2/2g$

Gas Dispersion by a Mechanical Mixer

In agitated vessels without baffles, the vortex is generated at the central part of the liquid surface. The free surface is isobaric, and many other isobaric faces exist parallel to the free surface. Gas bubbles blown into the liquid near the bottom are subject to buoyance perpendicular to these isobaric faces and gather around the agitator axis. As such, the contacting efficiency of gas and liquid is poor under unbaffled conditions. This can be avoided by suppressing the tangential flow and maintaining a horizontal surface contour. In this respect, vertical baffles are generally used on the side wall of the vessel equally spaced.

The second emphasis is to disperse gas bubbles blown into the liquid by an impeller. The major factors in order to apply shear forces effectively on to the bubbles are:

1. Gas inlet pipe should be set close to impeller blades.
2. Gas should be blown from many holes bored in a ring sparger than from a single nozzle.
3. The loop diameter (D_s) of discharge hole arrangement is chosen to be 80% of the impeller diameter. However, when the impeller speed is large, shear stress due to the impeller action becomes controlling and no significant difference is observed due to these factors.

For generating a proper gas dispersion in a tank, a specific superficial gas velocity is needed. The superficial gas velocity is defined as the average volumetric gas-fluid rate in and out of the vessel divided by the tank's cross-sectional area at the midpoint.

Minimum dispersion occurs at a point where the energy content of the mixer and gas stream are almost equal. This usually results in a gas-controlled flow pattern in which uniform bubble dispersion

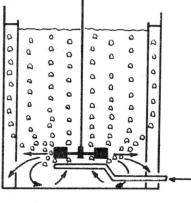

LOW MIXER HP

Figure 31. Typical flow pattern of gas bubbles for relatively low mixer horsepower compared to gas rate.

leaves the area of the impeller. However, the overall flow pattern is governed by the rising expanding gas stream. Below that point are the areas where gas tends to form geysers and large splashing brings bursts of liquid to the surface.

The flow pattern from axial-flow impellers is controlled by the upward velocity of the gas stream. Thus, axial-flow impellers do not operate satisfactorily unless their energy input is five to ten times higher than that of the gas stream.

Radial-flow impellers and disk-type impellers are most commonly used. The latter prevent the gas from rising through the low shear zone around the hub.

Sparge rings or open inlets permit the admission of the gas at a somewhat smaller diameter than the impeller periphery below. Thus, the gas can rise into the maximum impeller-zone shear rate. However, the question of what speed is needed for an impeller to disperse a given quantity of gas does not have a unique answer [156]. For example, assume that a certain volume of gas is being bubbled through a tank from a sparge ring and impeller speed is increased from zero up to a higher value. If the gas streams out of the sparge ring and the impeller is at zero speed, the gas flow pattern predominates. The horsepower transmitted to the liquid by the expanding gas, hp_G, is estimated from the pressure change in the expanded gas.

Figure 31 shows a typical flow pattern for a relatively low mixer horsepower compared to gas rate. Referring to Table 2 we note that as the mixer speed increases to a point where the power input from the mixing impeller equals the horsepower transmitted by the gas, the mixer can disperse the gas stream, causing the majority of the gas to escape with relatively "small" bubbles at the surface. There can be some gas bubbles that erupt as geysers. The liquid motion in the tank is still determined predominantly by the upward gas velocity.

Table 2
Liquid Surface Appearance at Various Mixer Power Levels
(Constant Gas-Rate Conditions)

Mixer power	Surface structure	Type dispersion
Low	Small to large eruptions	Gas rises unhindered
Low-moderate	Uniform	Gas distributes to vessel walls
Moderate	Uniform	Mixer flow pattern predominates
High	Uniform	Gas holdup plateau

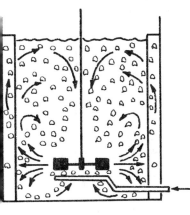

HIGH MIXER HP

Figure 32. Typical gas bubble flow pattern for relatively high mixer horsepower for a given gas rate.

When the mixer power level is increased to a level several times higher than the gas horsepower, the gas is dispersed out to the side walls of the tank and then on up to the surface. The mixer flow pattern now predominates, giving the typical flow pattern of the radial flow turbine illustrated in Figure 32. The mixer power level must be increased higher than this to drive the gas down into the bottom areas of the tank to provide an even greater intimate dispersion of the gas.

At extremely high power levels from the impeller the gas holdup reaches a plateau of about 20% to 30% by volume when in a nonfoaming liquid.

Any increment of impeller power increases the absorption rate from the gas stream. At about equal gas power and mixer power [157], the maximum absorption rate per unit total gas and mixer horsepower is often achieved, but at relatively low absorption rates per unit volume of liquid as shown by Figure 33. At higher mixer power levels, there are much higher gas absorption rates per unit volume of liquid, but at a decreased absorption rate per unit of total horsepower of gas and mixer.

The minimum agitator speed for dispersing gas bubbles (n_0) was observed by Van Dierendonck et al. [158]. As shown in Figure 34, gas hold-up (ϕ) is increased with increasing agitator speed.

At low superficial gas velocity (v_s), n_0 can be approximated by extrapolation towards $\phi = 0$ of the line indicating the empirical relation between gas hold-up ϕ agitator speed n.

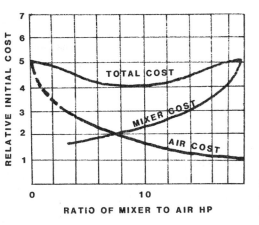

RATIO OF MIXER TO AIR HP

Figure 33. Total cost of air system and mixer for various rates of mixer horsepower and air horsepower [157].

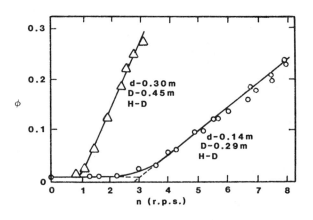

Figure 34. Agitated gas-liquid reactor system. n_0 = minimum agitator speed required for bubble dispersion. Data for aminocaprolactam solution in water.

The minimum agitator speed for dispersing gas bubbles (n_0) is correlated as follows:

For pure liquids:

$$\left(\frac{n_0 d^2}{D}\right)\bigg/(gD)^{1/2} = 0.07, \quad \text{if } D < 1.0 \text{ m} \tag{164}$$

and

$$\left[\frac{\mu n_0 d^2}{D\sigma}\right]\left[\frac{\rho\sigma^3}{g\mu^4}\right]^{1/4} = 2.0\left[\frac{H-C}{D}\right]^{1/2}, \quad \text{if } D > 1.0 \text{ m} \tag{165}$$

independent of v_s for $v_s < 0.03$ m/sec, $0.1 < (H - C)/D < 0.6$.
For electrolyte solutions:

$$\left[\frac{\mu n_0 d^2}{D\sigma}\right]\left[\frac{\rho\sigma^3}{g\mu^4}\right]^{1/4} = A\left(\frac{d}{D}\right) - B \tag{166}$$

In most of the cases investigated [158], A appeared to be very small and $B \simeq 1$.
Westerterp et al. [159] proposed the following equation to estimate the minimum agitator speed n_0 at which dispersion of gas bubbles takes place.

$$\frac{n_0 d}{(\sigma g/\rho_c)^{1/4}} = A + B\left(\frac{D}{A}\right) \tag{167}$$

where   A = 1.22 and B = 1.25 for turbines
         A = 2.25 and B = 0.68 for paddles

The distribution of gas bubbles is not uniform throughout agitated liquids. Calderbank [160] observed the interfacial area of air in agitated water by a light transmission technique. Figure 35 shows the distribution of specific interfacial area (a) in the vertical direction of a mixing vessel agitated in 200–400 rpm under aeration Q = 1 ft^3/min. There are two maxima of interfacial area in the vicinity of an impeller and in the middle height between the impeller and the free surface.

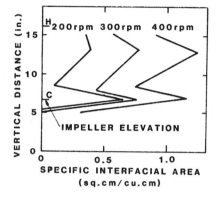

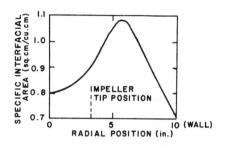

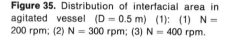

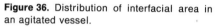

Figure 35. Distribution of interfacial area in agitated vessel (D = 0.5 m) (1): (1) N = 200 rpm; (2) N = 300 rpm; (3) N = 400 rpm.

Figure 36. Distribution of interfacial area in an agitated vessel.

Bubble Diameter and Interfacial Area of Gas Bubbles in an Agitated Tank

The forces acting on gas bubbles are: shear stress, τ, and surface tension, σ/d_p (where d_p is the gas bubble diameter). When these two forces are equal, bubbles are in equilibrium in size. Therefore the maximum diameter of bubbles is determined by the ratio of these forces (i.e., the Weber number) (see Figure 36):

$$\frac{\tau d_p}{\sigma} = We \tag{168}$$

For bubbles ascending or descending in liquids, the ratio of lifting or settling force $((1/6)d_p \, \Delta\rho g)$ and surface tension is involved, and We is:

$$We = \frac{d_p^2 \, \Delta\rho g}{6\sigma} \tag{169}$$

With the dispersion of gases in mixing vessels, the shear stress due to turbulence is important. The primary eddies produced by impellers have a wavelength or scale (L) of similar magnitude to the dimension of the main flow. The large primary eddies are unstable and disintegrate into smaller eddies until finally their energy is dissipated into heat by viscous flow. According to Kolmogoroff's theory [161] on the local isotropy, the scale (η') of the smallest eddies where energy dissipation may occur is expressed by:

$$\eta' = \frac{\mu_c^{3/4}}{\rho_c^{1/2}} (P_v)^{-1/4} \tag{170}$$

where $P_v = P/V$, i.e., power input per unit volume of tank

The mean square fluctuation velocity $\bar{u}^2$ over a distance, s, in a turbulent flow field where $L \gg s \gg \eta'$ (L being the scale of the primary eddies and η' that of the smallest eddies) is expressed as:

$$\bar{u}^2 \propto p^{2/3} \left(\frac{s}{\rho_c}\right)^{2/3} \tag{171}$$

Mass and heat transfer from gas bubbles and the degree of dispersion are controlled by turbulence. The shear stress τ caused by turbulence is:

$$\tau = c_1 \rho_c \left(P_v \frac{d_p}{\rho_c} \right)^{2/3} \tag{172}$$

where c_1 is a dimensionless number.
Using Equations 168 and 172 and taking We as a constant, we have:

$$d_p \propto \frac{\sigma^{0.6}}{P_v^{0.4} \rho_c^{0.2}} \tag{173}$$

Transforming this by using the power number N_P, and the Weber number $(We)_I$ for mixing impellers,

$$\frac{d_p}{d} \propto (We)_I^{-3/5} N_P^{-2/5} (d^3/V)^{-2/5} \tag{174}$$

$$N_p = \frac{P}{\rho_c n^3 d^5}, \qquad (We)_I = \frac{d^3 n^2 \rho_c^*}{\sigma} \tag{175}$$

For geometrically similar vessels, d^3/V is equal and N_P is also fixed for a fully baffled condition, therefore,

$$\frac{d_p}{d} \propto (We)_I^{-3/5} \tag{176}$$

Vermeulen [34] presented the following from his experiments:

$$\frac{d_p}{d} \propto (2.5\phi + 0.75)(We)_I^{-3/5} \tag{177}$$

Calderbank [160] studied the bubble size in solutions of electrolytes agitated by six-bladed turbines and obtained Equation 178 which is similar to Equation 173 in functional form:

$$d_{SM} = 2.25 \left[\frac{\sigma^{0.6}}{P_v^{0.4} \rho_c^{0.2}} \right] \phi^{0.4} \left(\frac{\mu_d}{\mu_c} \right)^{0.25} \tag{178}$$

where d_{SM} is the Sauter mean diameter defined as follows:

$$d_{SM} = \frac{\sum n_i d_i^3}{\sum n_i d_i^2} = \frac{6\phi}{a} \tag{179}$$

where n_i is the number of bubbles having spherical diameter d_i of equivalent volume.
This relation is similar to that derived by Hinze [45] for the maximum bubble diameters in turbulent liquids.

$$d_{max} = k \left(\frac{\sigma^{0.6}}{P_v^{0.4} \rho_c^{0.2}} \right) \tag{180}$$

Solutions containing electrolytes or alcohols experience smaller diameter gas bubbles than in pure water. Apparently those additives hinder the coalescence of gas bubbles. Vermeulen et al. [34] derived Equation 181 after rearranging their experimental data on interfacial area obtained by a light transmission technique.

$$\frac{d_p dn^{1.5}\rho_c^{0.5}\mu_d^{0.75}}{\sigma \bar{f}_\phi \mu_c^{0.25}} = 4.3 \times 10^{-3} \tag{181}$$

Equation 181 is transformed to an equation expressing a specific interfacial area (a), a being equal to $6\phi/d_{SM}$.

$$a = \frac{1,400n^{1.5}d\rho_c^{0.5}\mu_d^{0.75}\phi}{\sigma\mu_c^{0.25}\bar{f}_\phi} \tag{182}$$

where $\bar{f}_\phi$ is a correction factor for gas hold-up. Further rearrangement produces the following dimensionless expression:

$$aD \propto \left(\frac{D^3n^2\rho_c}{\sigma}\right)\left(\frac{D^2n\rho_c}{\mu_c}\right)^{-0.5}\left(\frac{\mu_d}{\mu_c}\right)^{0.75} \tag{183}$$

Calderbank [160] studied the interfacial area of gas bubbles in liquids agitated by six-bladed turbines of d = D/3 in vessels, D = 50.8 cm, and 18.4 cm and proposed the following correlation:

$$a = 1.44\left(\frac{P_v^{0.4}\rho_c^{0.2}}{\sigma^{0.6}}\right)\left(\frac{v_s}{v_t}\right)^{0.5} \tag{184}$$

where v_t = terminal velocity of bubbles in free rise
         v_s = superficial gas velocity in mixing vessels

Equation 184 is applicable in the range $(d^2n\rho_c/\mu_c)^{0.7}(dn/V_s)^{0.3} < 20,000$.

When V_s or n is changed to give $(d^2n\rho_c/\mu_c)^{0.7}(dn/v_s)^{0.3} > 20,000$, a is increased, because suction of air takes place from the free surface. Interfacial area in this region is denoted by a' and is estimated from:

$$\log\frac{2.3a'}{a} = 1.95 \times 10^{-5}\left(\frac{d^2n\rho_c}{\mu_c}\right)^{0.7}\left(\frac{dn}{v_s}\right)^{0.3} \tag{185}$$

Still another correlation is given by Reith and Beek [162] who measured the interfacial area in geometrically similar mixing vessels with diameters of D = 19, 45, and 120 cm. These measurements were performed at one superficial gas velocity, v_s = 4.7 cm/sec.

Experimental results are shown in Figure 37. A reasonable correlation is obtained by using n^3d^2 as the independent parameter, which has the dimension of power input per unit volume. The ordinate shows the specific interfacial area per unit volume of liquid $a(1 - \phi)$.

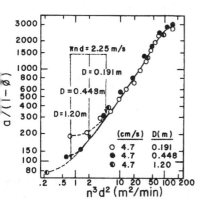

Figure 37. $a(1 - \phi)$ as a function of n^3d^2 in three agitated vessel gas-liquid contactors.

At the left-hand side of this graph, we see that the curves deviate from the solid line at low agitator speeds as the vessel diameter increases. In the region, $\pi nd < 2.25$ m/sec, the curves for the three vessels differ considerably, giving lower values of $a/(1 - \phi)$ with increasing vessel diameters. Van Dierendonck et al. [158] proposed the following correlation for all the gas-liquid systems investigated:

$$Eo = \frac{d_{SM}^2 \rho g}{\sigma} = \left[1.2 + 260 \frac{\mu(n - n_0)d}{\sigma} \right]^{-2} \tag{186}$$

provided that $0 < (n - n_0)d < 1.5$ m/sec; $n > n_0$. Eo is called the Eötvös number.
In the region $n > 2n_0$ for pure liquids, we have:

$$Eo = \frac{d_{SM}^2 \rho g}{\sigma} = 0.45 \tag{187}$$

where n_0 is the agitator speed at which dispersion of gas bubble takes place.
Calderbank [160] proposed the following equation for gas hold-up ϕ in aerated vessels agitated by six-bladed turbines:

$$\phi = \left(\frac{v_s \phi}{v_t} \right)^{1/2} + 0.0216 \left(\frac{P_v^{0.4} \rho_c^{0.2}}{\sigma^{0.6}} \right) \left(\frac{v_s}{v_t} \right)^{1/2} \tag{188}$$

This equation is applicable in the range $(d^2 n \rho_c/\mu_c)^{0.7}(dn/v_s)^{0.3} < 20{,}000$.
In Equation 188 when P_v tends to zero, ϕ is equal to v_s/v_t. This result is explained by the relation as follows, H' being the liquid depth under aeration:

$$\phi = \frac{\theta v_s}{H'} = \frac{(H'/v_t)v_s}{H'} = \frac{v_s}{v_t} \tag{189}$$

When P_v becomes larger, the first term is negligible and Equation 190 is obtained.

$$\phi \propto P_v^{0.4} v_s^{0.5} \tag{190}$$

This relation agrees fairly well with the experimental result obtained by Rushton et al. [163]:

$$\phi = K P_v^{0.47} v_s^{0.53} \tag{191}$$

The distribution of gas hold-up in a mixing vessel is also nonuniform. An example of observed distribution data is shown in Figure 38. Gas hold-up shows a maximum value at an intermediate

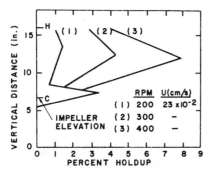

Figure 38. Typical vertical distributions of gas holdup in a 100 ℓ tank.

height between the impeller and the free surface. Gas hold-up seems to be independent of agitator speed and is held almost constant in the vicinity of and underneath the impeller. The contact time of gas with liquid (θ) is estimated from gas hold-up. Denoting the average liquid depth as H'(ft), the mean residence time of gas bubbles as θ(sec), and superficial gas velocity as v_s(ft/sec), we have $\theta = (\phi/v_s)H'$ from Equation 189 and the contact time per unit depth of liquids $\theta'(=\theta/H')$ is obtained by substituting Equation 191 in the above relation.

$$\theta = \frac{\phi}{v_s} = K \left(\frac{P_v}{v_s}\right)^{0.47} \tag{192}$$

Values of the proportional constant K depend on the vessel's design and range from 1.3 to 1.6. As can be seen from Equations 191 and 192, gas hold-up is increased by the increase of aeration velocity, while the contact time θ' is decreased. For example, 50% increase in v_s causes 25% increase in hold-up (ϕ), and 17% decrease in contact time per unit depth of liquids (θ). The following relationships were derived by Van Dierendonck [158]

For pure liquids:

$$\phi = 0.31 \left[\frac{\mu V_s}{\sigma}\right]^{2/3} \left[\frac{\rho\sigma^3}{g\mu^4}\right]^{1/6} + 0.45 \frac{(n - n_0^*)d^2}{D(gD)^{1/2}} \tag{193}$$

if $\phi \leq 0.2$; $n \geq n_0^*$; $0 < V_s < 0.05$ m/sec and H/D = 1.

For electrolyte solutions:

$$\phi = 0.075 \left[\frac{\mu(n - n_0)d^2}{D\sigma}\right] \left[\frac{\rho\sigma^3}{g\mu^4}\right]^{1/4} \tag{194}$$

if $\phi \leq 0.3$ and $0.003 < V_s < 0.03$ m/sec; $n \geq n_0$; H/D = 1.

NOTATION

A	area	G	mass force vector
A_0	nozzle flow factor in Equation 54	G_i	weight of drops having diameter d_i
a	mass acceleration vector	$\tilde{G}$	mass flow per unit area
a'	diameter ratio parameter defined in Equation 69	g	gravitational acceleration
		H	head
C	constant of integration (Equation 95); also concentration	Hi	Hinze number
		h	height
C_D	discharge coefficient	K_{mix}	mixing coefficient
$\bar{C}$	average concentration	K	velocity ratio (see Equation 74)
c	speed of sound	k	coefficient of apparent additional mass; also mass transfer coefficient
D_0	nozzle diameter		
$\mathscr{D}$	coefficient of molecular diffusion	L	length
d	diameter	L_p	mixing length
$\bar{d}$	mean drop diameter	ℓ	characteristic size of eddies
d_0	droplet diameter	M	mass
$\bar{d}_{32}$	Sauter mean diameter	Ma	Mach number
E	energy	$\dot{m}$	rate of mass transfer
Eo	Eötvös number	m'	drop side distribution parameter (Equation 85)
F_D	drag force		
Fr	Froude number	N	power

N_A	molar diffusion of component A	U	initial relative velocity between drop
n	number of revolutions per unit time;		and stream
	also number of drops	U_{tp}	two-phase velocity
n_0	agitator speed	u	normal direction velocity
n'	number of bubbles per unit volume	u'	instantaneous velocity of eddy motion
P	pressure force	u_s	settling velocity
p	pressure	u, v	fluctuating velocities in axial and ra-
Q	volumetric flow rate		dial directions, respectively
Q_E	volumetric rate of entrainment	V	volume
q	increment of oscillations in jet	V_r	relative velocity
R_0	mean jet radius	V_s	superficial gas velocity
Re	Reynolds number	W	work
r	radial distance	We	Weber number
r_b	bubble radius	w	jet velocity
r_0	initial drop radius	x	dryness fraction
Sh	Sherwood number	x, y, z	coordinates
T	dimensionless drop break-up time	Y	mass fraction
t	time	y	parameter defined by Equation 68

Greek Symbols

α	angle	π_σ	fluctuating pressure due to surface
α_1	liquid holdup		tension forces
γ	specific gravity	π'	fluctuating jet pressure
$\bar{\delta}$	spread of drop sizes	π''	fluctuating gas pressure
ε	coefficient of eddy viscosity; energy	ρ	density
	dissipation term	σ	surface tension
ε'	density ratio of gas and liquid	τ	shear stress
η	coefficient of dynamic viscosity	τ'	time constant
θ	polar angle	ϕ	gas void fraction
λ	scale of entraining eddies in mass bub-	ψ	filled fraction of nozzle
	bling; also wavelength	Ω	annular cross-section for centrifugal
μ	viscosity		nozzle
$\dot{v}$	specific volume	ω	rotational velocity of a mixer's
v	kinematic viscosity		impeller
ζ	nozzle discharge coefficient defined by		
	Equation 107; also wave number		

REFERENCES

1. Beranek, J., "Theorie Turbulentniho Proudeni Tekutin," NCSAV (Theory of Turbulent Fluid flow, Czechoslovak Academy of Sciences), Prague, 1954.
2. Kozeny, J., *Hydraulik*, Springer, Wien, 1953.
3. Folsum, R. G., and Fergusson, C. K., *Trans. ASME*, 71:73 (1949).
4. Rushton, J. H., *Pet. Refiner*, 33(8); 101 (1954).
5. Kraussold, D., and Danckwerts, P. V., *Chem. Eng. Sci.*, 16:267 (1961).
6. Garner, F. H., *Trans. Inst. Chem. Engrs.*, 28:88 (1956).
7. Lamont, A. G. W., *Can. J. Chem. Eng.*, 36:153 (1958).
8. Lamont, A. G. W., *Mines Mag.*, 10:10 (1958).
9. Siemes, W., and Weiss, W., *Chem. Ing. Technik*, 26:479 (1954).
10. Peck, W. C., *Industrial Chemist*, 31:12, 505 (1955).
11. Sterbacek, Z., and Tausk, P., *Mixing in Chemical Industry*, Pergamon Press, NY, 1965.
12. Nagata, S., et al., *Met. Fac. Eng.*, Kyoto Univ., XXII(1):68 (1960).
13. Sachs, J. P., and Rushton, J. H., *Chem. Eng. Prog.*, 50:597 (1954).

14. Bissell, et al., *Chem. Eng. Prog.*, 43:649 (1947).
15. Lyons, E. J., *Chem. Eng. Prog.*, 44:545 (1948).
16. Brown, D. E., and Pitt, K., "Effect of Impeller Geometry on Drop Break-Up in a Stirred Liquid-Liquid Contactor," *Chem. Eng. Sci.*, 29(2):345–348 (1974).
17. Ramkrishna, D., "Drop Breakage in Agitated Liquid-Liquid Dispersions," *Chem. Eng. Sci.*, 29(4):987–992, (1974).
18. Mlynck, Y., and Resnick, W., "Drop Sizes in Agitated Liquid-Liquid System," *A.I.Ch.E.J.*, 18(1):122–127 (1972).
19. Endoh, K., and Ovama, Y., "On the Size of Droplet Disintegrated in Liquid-Liquid Contacting," Sci. papers of Inst. of Phy. and Chem. Res., 53(1486):131–142 (1958).
20. Sprow, F. B., "Drop Size Distributions in Strongly Coalescing Agitated Liquid-Liquid Systems," *A.I.Ch.E.J.*, 13(5):995–998 (1967).
21. Chen, H. T., and Middleman, S., "Drop Size Distribution in Agitated Liquid-Liquid Systems," *A.I.Ch.E.J.*, 13(5):989–995 (1967).
22. Weinstein, B., and Treybal, R. E., "Liquid-Liquid Contacting in Unbaffled, Agitated Vessels," *A.I.Ch.E.J.*, 19(2):304–312 (1973).
23. Madden, A. J., and Damerell, G. L., "Coalescence Frequencies in Agitated Liquid-Liquid Systems," *A.I.Ch.E.J.*, 8(2):233–239 (1962).
24. Howarth, W. J., "Measurment of Coalescence Frequency in an Agitated Tank," *A.I.Ch.E.J.*, 13(5):1007–1013 (1967).
25. Valentas, K. J., and Amundsen, N. R., "Analysis of Breakage in Dispersed Phase System," *Ind. Eng. Chem. Funds.*, 5(2):271–279 (1966).
26. Valentas, K. J., Amundsen, N. R., and Bilous, O., "Breakage and Coalescence in Dispersed Phase Systems," *Ind. Eng. Chem. Funds.*, 5(2):533–541 (1966).
27. Gal-or, B., and Walatka, V., "A Theoretical Analysis of Some Interrelationships and Mechanisms of Heat and Mass Transfer in Dispersions," *A.I.Ch.E.J.*, 13(4):650–657 (1967).
28. Rodriguez, F., Grotz, L. C., and Engle, D. I., "Interfacial Area in Liquid-Liquid Mixing," *A.I.Ch.E.J.*, 7(4):663–665 (1961).
29. Garner, F. H., and Skelland, A. H. P., "Liquid-Liquid Mixing as Affected by the Internal Circulation Within Droplets," *Trans. Inst. Chem. Engrs.*, 29(3):315–321 (1951).
30. Quinn, J. K., and Sigloh, D. B., "Phase Inversion in the Mixing of Immiscible Liquids," *Con. J. Che. Engrg.*, 41(1):15–18 (1963).
31. Selker, A. H., and Sleicher, C. A., "Factors Affecting Which Phase will Disperse When Immiscible Liquids are Stirred Together," *Can. J. Ch. Engrg.*, 43(6):298–391 (1965).
32. Miller, S. A., and Mann, C. A., "Agitation of Two-Phase Systems of Immiscible Liquids," *A.I.Ch.E.J.*, 40(6):709–745, (1944).
33. Trayball, P. I., and Bartlett, P. D., *Tetrahedron Lett.*, 30 (24) (1960).
34. Vermeulen, T., Williams, G. M., and Langlois, G. F., "Interfacial Areas in Liquid-Liquid and Gas-Liquid Agitation," *Chem. Eng. Progr.*, 51(2):85F–94F (1955).
35. Olney, R. B., and Carlson, G. J., "Tower Absorption in Mixers Correlations with Equipment Dimensions and Fluid Properties," *Chem. Eng. Progr.*, 43(9):473–480 (1947).
36. Esch, D. D., D'Angelo, P. J., and Pike, R. W., *Can. J. Chem. Engrg.*, 49(6):812 (1971).
37. Hinze, J., *A.I.Ch.E.J.*, 1:289 (1955).
38. Rodger, W. A., Trice, V. G., Rushton, J. H., *Chem. Eng. Progr.*, 52:515 (1956).
39. Misek, "Hydrodynamic Behaviour of Agitated Liquid Extractors," Diss. Inst. Chem. Technol., Prague, 1960.
40. Rayleigh, I. W., *Theory of Sound*, Dover Pub., N.Y. 1954.
41. Weber, K., Break-Up of Liquid Jet, Symposium: Internal Combustion Engines, V. I.
42. Kolmogorov, A. N., DAN SSR, Vol. 66, N.5 (1949).
43. Volynskiy, M. S., DAN SSR, Vol. 68, N.2 (1949).
44. Merrington, A. C., and Richardson, E. G., *Proc. Phys. Soc.*, 59(1):1 (1947).
45. Hinze, J. O., *Appl. Sci. Res.*, Al, 263 (1948).
46. Hanson, A. R., Domich, E. G., and Adams, H. S., *Phys. Fluids*, 6(8):1070 (1963).
47. Putnam, A. A., et al.: "Injection and Combustion of Liquid Fuels," USAF WADC Technical Report 56–344, p. 5–41 (March, 1957).

48. Habler, G.: "Break-Up of Large Water Drops Under the Influence of Aerodynamic Forces in a Steady Stream of Steam at Subsonic Velocities," Proc. 3rd Int. Conf. Rain Erosion and Associated Phenomena, A. A. Fyall and R. B. King (Eds.) pp. 707–725, organized by RAE Farnborough (1970).

49. Dyner, H. B., and Hill, J. A. F.: "Drop Break-Up in Accelerating and Decelerating Air Streams," Proc. 3rd Int. Conf. Rain Erosion and Associated Phenomena, A. A. Fyall and R. B. King (Eds.) pp. 669–690, organized by RAE Farnborough (1970).

50. Sargeant, M., Proc. Third Europ. Conf. on Mixing, April 4–6, 1979, Vol. 1, held at the Univ of York, England, B.H.R.A. Fluid Engineering, p. E2.

51. Baines, M., and Buttery, N. E.: "The Hydrodynamics of Large Scale Fuel/Coolant Interactions," Paper presented to the International Meeting on Nuclear Power Reactor Safety, Am. Nuc Soc. and Euro. Nuc. Soc. Joint Conf. (16–19th October, 1978).

52. Bailey, A. B., "Sphere Drag Coefficient for Subsonic Speeds in Continuum and Free-Molecule Flows," *J. Fluid Mech.*, 65(2):401–410 (1974).

53. Dodd, K. N., "On the Disintegration of Water Drops in an Air Stream," *J. Fluid Mech.* 9:175–182 (1960).

54. Vitman, et al., *Sb. Nauchnyth Rabot Inzh.*, F-ta Leningrad. Inst. Mekhnizatsii Sel'skogo Khozyaystva,Vol. X (1953).

55. Nukiyama and Tanasawa, *Trans. Soc. Mech. Engrs.*, Japan, 6(22):S7–S8 (1940).

56. Chisholm, D., Chapt. 18, pp. 483–513, in *Handbook of Fluids in Motion*, N. P. Cheremisinoff and R. Gupta (Eds.), Ann Arbor Science Pub., Ann Arbor, MI (1983).

57. Abramovich, G. N., Prikladnaya Gazovaya Dinamika (Applied Gas Dynamics), Gostekhizdat, Moscow 1953.

58. Azbel, D., *Two-Phase Flow in Chemical Engineering*, Cambridge Univ. Press, N.Y. 1981.

59. Akselrod, L. S., and Dilman, V. V., *Zh. Prikl. Khim.* (Moscow), 29(12):1803 (1956).

60. Davidson, L., and Amick, E. E., *A.I.Ch.E.J.*, 2(2):337 (1956).

61. Jackson, I. R. W., *Ind. Chem.*, 28(3):68 (1952).

62. Siemes, W., and Kauffmann, J. F., *Chem. Eng. Sci.*, 5:127 (1956).

63. Chang, R. C., Schoen, H. M., and Grove, C. S., *Ind. Eng. Chem.*, 48(11):2035 (1956).

64. Spells, K. B., *Trans. Inst. Chem. Eng.*, 32:167 (1954).

65. Stabnikov, V. N., *Khim. Mashinostr.* (Moscow), No. 1, 17 (1938).

66. Shabalin, K. N., *Gas Friction Against Liquid in Absorption Processes*, Metallurgizdat, Moscow, 1943.

67. Ramm, V. M., *Absorption of Gases*, Chimia, Moscow, 1966. (In Russian).

68. Kolmogoroff, A. N., *Dokl. Acad. Nauk SSSR*, 31(2):99 (1941).

69. Landau, L. D., and Lifshitz, E. M., *Fluid Mechanics*, Pergamon Press, London, (1959).

70. Hinze, I. O., *Turbulence*, McGraw-Hill, NY 1959.

71. Azbel D. and N. P. Cheremisinoff, "Mathematical Model of a Mass Bubbling Fluid Bed," Intl. Conf. of Mathematicians, Zurich, Switzerland (1983).

72. Levich, V. G., *Physiochemical Hydrodynamics*, Prentice-Hall, Englewood Cliffs, NJ (1962).

73. Lamb, G., *Hydrodynamics*, Dover Publications, NY 1945.

74. Golovin, A. M., Levich, V. G., and Tolmachev, *Prikl. Mat. Teor. Fiz.*, 2:63 (1966).

75. Golovin, A. M., *Prikl. Mat Teor. Fiz.*, 6 (1967).

76. Miasnikov, V. P., and Levich, V. G., *Khim. Prom.* (Moscow), No. 6 (1966).

77. Gupalo, Yu. P., *Inzh.-Fiz. Zh.*, 1:16 (1962).

78. Leva, M., *Fluidization*, McGraw-Hill, NY 1959.

79. HaOple, J., *A.I.Ch.E.J.*, 4:197 (1958).

80. Uchida, S., *Ind. Eng. Chem.*, 46:1194 (1958).

81. Marrucci, G., *Ind. Eng. Chem. Fund.*, 2:224 (1965).

82. Halberstadt, S., and Praussnitz, P. H., *Angew. Chem.*, 2(43):970 (1940).

83. Praussnitz, P. H., *Kolloid-Z.*, 50:183 (1930).

84. Praussnitz, P. H., *Kolloid-Z.*, 76:227 (1936).

85. Praussnitz, P. H., *Kolloid-Z.*, 104:246 (1943).

86. Rudolph, H., *Kolloid-Z.*, 60:308 (1932).

87. Siemes, W., and Borchers, E., *Chem. Eng. Sci.*, 12(2):77 (1960).

88. Kolber, H., Borchers, E., and Langemann, H., *Chem-Ing.-Tech.*, 33(10):668 (1961).

89. Siemes, W., and Borchers, E., *Chem.-Ing.-Tech.*, 28:783 (1956).
90. Houghton, G., McLean, P., and Ritchie, D., *Chem. Eng. Sci.*, 7:40 (1957).
91. Schnurmann, R., *Z. Phys. Chem.*, 14:456 (1929).
92. Schnurmann, R., *Kolloid-Z.*, 80:148 (1937).
93. Aizenbud, M. B., Candidate's dissertation, Moscow Institute of Chemical Engineers, 1961. (In Russian).
94. Smirnov, N. I., and Poluta, S. E., *Zh. Fiz. Khim.*, 22(11):1208 (1949).
95. Helmholtz, H. L. F. von, *Verh. Naturhist. Med. Vereins.* (Oct. 30, 1868).
96. Reyleigh, Lord, *Phil. Mag.*, 26:776 (1913).
97. Sterman, L. S., *Zh. Tekh. Fiz.*, 26(7):1512 (1956).
98. Sterman, L. S., and Surnov, A. B., *Teploenergetika*, 8:39 (1955).
99. Vinokur, Ya. G., and Dil'man, V. V., *Khim. Prom.* (Moscow), No. 7, 619 (1959).
100. Radikovskii, V. M., Candidate's dissertaion, D. I. Mendeleev Moscow Institute of Chemical Technology, 1965. (In Russian.)
101. Kashnikov, A. M., Candidate's dissertation, D. I. Mendeleev Moscow Institute of Chemical Technology, 1965. (In Russian.)
102. Calderbank, P. H., and F. Rennie, *Trans. Inst. Chem. Eng.*, 40:1, 3 (1962).
103. Siemes, W., *Chem.-Ing.-Tech.*, 26(11):639 (1954).
104. Viviorovski, M. M., Dil'man, V. V., and Aizenbud, M. B., *Khim. Prom.* (Moscow), (3):204 (1965).
105. Gnedenko, V. V., *Treatise of Probability Theory*, Fizmatgis, Moscow, 1961. (In Russian.)
106. Siemes, W., and Ganther, K., *Chem.-Ing.-Tech.*, 28(6):389 (1956).
107. Koto, T., *Kagaku Kogaku [Chem. Eng. (Jap.)]*, 26(11):114 (1962). Abstracted in *Ref. Zh. Khim.*, (16):110 (1963).
108. Rodionov, A. I., Kashnikov, A. M., and Radikovskii, V. M., *Khim. Prom. (Moscow)*, (10):17 (1964).
109. Radionov, D. A., *Distribution Functions of the Contest of Elements and Minerals in Igneous Rocks*, Nauka, Moscow, 1964. (In Russian.)
110. Thornton, J. D., *Ind. Chem.*, 39(12):632 (1963).
111. Kagan, S. Z., Doctoral dissertation, D. I. Mendeleev Moscow Institute of Chemical Technology, 1965. (In Russian.)
112. Yamaguchi, I., Kabuta, S., and Nagata, S., *Chem. Eng. (Jap.)*, 27(8):576 (1963).
113. Babanov, B. M., Candidate's dissertation, D. I. Mendeleev Moscow Institute of Chemical Technology, 1960. (In Russian.)
114. Bezemer, C., and Schwarz, N., *Kolloid-Z.*, 146(1-3):145 (1956).
115. Avdeev, N. Ya., *Analytical Method for Sedimentometric Dispersion Analysis Calculations*, Rostov University, Rostov-on-Don, 1964. (In Russian.)
116. Gel'perin, N. I., Sklokin, L. I., and Assmus, M. G., *Teor. Osn. Khim. Tekhnol.*, 1(4):463 (1967).
117. Gal-or, B., and Hoelscher, H. E., *AIChE J.*, 12(3):499 (1966).
118. Levich, V. G., *K teorii poverkhnostnykh yavlenii (Theory of Surface Phenomena)*, Izdatelstvo Sov. Nauka, Moscow (1941).
119. Akselrod, L. S., and Dilman, V. V., *Zh. Prikl. Khim (Moscow)*, 29(12):1803 (1956).
120. Kasatkin, A. G., Dyinerskii, Yu. I., and Popov, D. M., *Khim. Prom. (Moscow)*, (7):482 (1961).
121. Akselrod, L. S., and Dilman, V. V., *Zh. Prikl. Khim. (Moscow)*, 27:5 (1954).
122. Chhabra, P. S., and Mahajan, S. P., *Indian Chem. Eng.*, 16(2):16 (1974).
123. Bhaga, D., and Weber, M. E., *Can. J. Chem. Eng.*, 50(3):323 (1972).
124. Bhaga, D., and Weber, M. E., *Can. J. Chem. Eng.*, 50(3):329 (1972).
125. Pruden, B. B., and Weber, M. E., *Can. J. Chem. Eng.*, 48:162 (1970).
126. Pozin, M. E., Mukhlenov, I. P., and Tarat, E. Ya., *Zh. Prikl. Khim. (Moscow)*, 30(1):45 (1957).
127. Zuber, N., and Finlay. J. A., *J. Heat Trans. ASME*, C87:453 (1965).
128. Chekhov, O. S., Candidate's dissertation, Moscow Institute of Chemical Engineers, 1960. (In Russian.)
129. Solomakha, G. P., Candidate's dissertation, Moscow Institute of Chemical Engineers, 1957. (In Russian.)
130. Artomonov, D. S., Candidate's dissertation, Moscow Institute of Chemical Engineers, 1961. (In Russian.)
131. Brown, R. W., Gomezplata, A., and Price, J. D., *Chem. Eng. Sci.*, 24:1483 (1969).

132. Ribgy, G. R., and Capes, C. E., *Can. J. Chem. Eng.*, 48:343 (1970).
133. Gomezplata, A., Munson, R. E., and Price, J. D., *Can. J. Chem. Eng.*, 50:669 (1972).
134. Gomezplata, A., and Sung, P. T., *Chem. Eng. Sci.*, 48:336 (1970).
135. Koide, K., Hirahara, T., and Kubota, H., *Kogaku Kogaku*, 5(1):38 (1967).
136. Stepanek, J., *Chem. Eng. Sci.*, 25:751 (1970).
137. Pruden, B. B., Hayduk, W., and Laudie, H., *Can. J. Chem. Eng.*, 52:64 (1974).
138. Laudie, H. A., M.A.Sc. thesis, University of Ottawa, 1969.
139. Bell, R. L., *AIChE J.*, 18(3):498 (1972).
140. Kuz'minykh, I. N., and Koval', G. A., *Zh. Prikl. Khim. (Moscow)*, 28(1):21 (1955).
141. Noskov, A. A., and Sokolov, V. N., *Tr. Leningr. Tekhnol. Inst. Lensoveta*, 39:110 (1957).
142. Pozin, M. E., *Sb. Vopr. Massoperedachi*, p. 148 (1957).
143. Sherherd, E. B., *Ind. Chem.*, (4):175 (1956).
144. Jackson, R., *Ind. Chem.*, (336):16; (338):109 (1953).
145. Hyghes, R. R., *Chem. Eng. Prog.*, 51(12):555 (1955).
145a. Loitsyanskii, L. G., *Mekhanika zhidkosti i gaza*, Gostekhizdat, Moscow, 1957.
146. Smirnov, V. I., *Kurs vysshey matematiki*, Vol. 4, Gostekhizdat, Moscow, 1941.
147. Vinokur, Ya. G., and Dilman, V. V., *Khim. Prom. (Moscow)*, (7):619 (1959).
148. Kashnikov, A. M., Candidate's dissertation, D. I. Mendeleev Moscow Institute of Chemical Technology, 1965. (In Russian.)
149. Rodionov, A. I., Kashnikov, A. M., and Radikovsky, V. M., *Khim. Prom. (Moscow)*, (10):17 (1964).
150. Lavrent'ev, M. A., and Luysternak, L. A., *A Course of Variation Calculus*, Gosizdat (state publishing house) of Theoretical and Technical Literature, Moscow, 1950. (In Russian.)
151. Aizenbud, M. B., and Dilman, V. V., *Khim. Prom. (Moscow)*, (3):199 (1961).
152. Artomonov, D. S., Candidate's dissertation, Moscow Insitute of Chemical Engineers, 1961. (In Russian.)
153. Popov, D. M., Candidate's dissertation, D. I. Mendeleev Moscow Institute of Chemical Technology, 1960. (In Russian.)
154. Oyama, Y., and Yamaguchi, K., Report of Scientic Research Institute, 21:916 (1942).
155. Lamont, A. G. W., *Canad. J. Chem. Eng.*, 36:153 (1958).
156. Oldshue, T. Y., *Ind. Eng. Chem.*, 61(9):79 (1969).
157. Oldshue, T. Y., Proc. 10th Annual Waste Treatment Conf., Ext. Bul. 89, Purdue Univ., Lafayette, IN (1955).
158. Van Dierendonck, L. L., et al., Chem. React. Eng. Symp., (1968), p. 205.
159. Westerterp, K. R., et al., *Chem. Eng. Sci.*, 18:157 (1963).
160. Calderbank, P. H., *Trans. Inst. Chem. Engrs., (London)*, 36:443 (1958).
161. Kolmogoroff, A. N., *Compt. Rend. Acad. Sci.*, USSR, 30:301 (1941).
162. Reith, T., and Beek W. J., Chem. Reaction Eng. Symp., 1968, p. 191.
163. Rushton, J. H., et al., *Ind. Eng. Chem.*, 52(9):799 (1960).
164. Weisman, J. J., Eflerding, L. E., *AIChE J.*, 6(3):419 (1960).
165. Zweitering, T. N., *Chem. Eng. Sci.*, 8:244 (1958).
166. Christiansen, E. B., Pettyjohn, E. S., *Chem. Eng. Prog.*, 44(2):157 (1948).
167. Narayaran, S., et al., *Chem. Eng. Sci.*, 24:223 (1969).
168. Holmes, D. B., et al., *Chem. Eng. Sci.*, 19(3):201 (1964).
169. Porcelli, J. V., *Ind. Engrg. Chem. Fund.*, 1(3):176 (1962).
170. Kolar, V., *Collection Czechoslov. Chem. Communs*, 26:613 (1961).
171. Rao, S. R., Mukheji, B. K., *Trans. Indian Instr. Chem. Engrs.*, 7:63 (1954–1955).
172. Weisman, J., Efferding, L. E., *AIChE J.*, 6:419 (1955).
173. Nagata, et al., *Mem. Fac. Eng.*, Kyoto Univ. XX, (1):72 (1958).

CHAPTER 14

MECHANICS AND DESIGN OF CENTRIFUGAL SWIRL NOZZLES

D. E. Dietrich

Technadyne Engineering Consultants, Inc.
Albuquerque, New Mexico, USA

CONTENTS

INTRODUCTION

Many nozzles have been designed for producing small, essentially spherical, drops from a bulk liquid entering through one or more nozzle inlets. This process is called atomization. Various nozzle designs are described by Simmons [1], including a very commonly used type, the swirl atomizer. In some swirl atomizers, air is also injected into the nozzle, and its energy further aids the atomization process. Here, we discuss fluid mechanisms involved in this process, with application to the design of swirl nozzles.

Atomization can be interpreted as a special form of mixing, whereby a bulk liquid deforms into drops by mixing with a bulk gas. The drops produced have more surface area (and, therefore, surface energy) per unit volume than the bulk liquid entering the nozzle. The extra surface energy comes from the combined kinetic and pressurization energy of the liquid and, sometimes, the gas entering the nozzle. Energy must also be supplied to overcome viscous dissipation. Thus, the mechanics of the atomization process depends on the ratio of the surface tension to viscous forces.

FLUID MECHANISMS IN SWIRL ATOMIZERS

An effective means of atomizing is to use swirl to produce a thin annular sheet of liquid flow through a nozzle orifice into a passive external gas medium (which moves mainly by interaction with the moving liquid). This is a simplex swirl atomizer nozzle (Figure 1). Such thin liquid sheets are unstable and are observed to deform into ligaments, which then separate and deform into one or more quasi-spherical drops.

The initial occurrence of ligaments suggests that fluid dynamic forces other than surface tension are significant, not only in sheet formation, but also in the early part of the atomization process. This could be associated with centrifugal Taylor instabilities leading to Gortler vortices [2] in the boundary shear layer inside the nozzle and/or similar instabilities associated with liquid-air shears near the orifice. Indeed, Taylor [3] suggests that viscous forces might be very important inside swirl chambers.

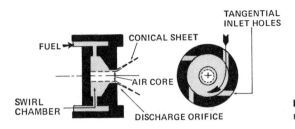

TANGENTIAL
INLET HOLES

CONICAL SHEET

FUEL→

AIR CORE

SWIRL
CHAMBER

DISCHARGE ORIFICE

Figure 1. Simplex swirl chamber nozzle [1].

As noted by Simmons [1], the drop size is closely related to the sheet thickness in simplex (not air-assisted) swirl nozzles. Since the drop size is difficult to measure, theoretical approaches have been developed, which relate sheet thickness to more readily measured quantities. Early theories are discussed by Giffen and Muraszew [4]. A recent theory by Simmons and Harding [5] assumes the liquid trajectory approximates a straight line after leaving the orifice. (This is reasonable, especially after a short turn-on transient, during which the passive air medium accelerates to near the liquid stream velocity, thereby reducing air-liquid shear forces.) The readily measured spray angle (θ), orifice discharge coefficient (c), and orifice diameter (d) can then be combined to get the following approximate sheet thickness formula:

$$t = cd/[4 \cos(\theta)] \tag{1}$$

This formula is useful for simplex swirl nozzles. However, it does not necessarily apply to air-assisted swirl nozzles, because high-velocity air is used to strongly accelerate the liquid sheet material. Such rapid acceleration could produce air-sheet interface instabilities whose scale is rather unrelated to sheet thickness, but perhaps related to the thickness of an unstable shear layer near the air-sheet interface. This possibility is discussed by Dietrich [6], and is to be discussed further later. Such high velocities also reduce the effect of surface tension compared to viscous effects, as indicated by the non-dimensional ratio of surface tension to viscous forces:

$$e = \sigma/(\nu U) \tag{2}$$

where σ is the surface tension coefficient, ν is the viscosity coefficient, and U is the relative air-liquid velocity. Dietrich [6] further noted that, from energy balance considerations, the average drop size from a given nozzle should be the following function of relative liquid-air velocity:

$$d = C_1/U + C_2/U^2 \tag{3}$$

C_1 and C_2 are coefficients that depend on nozzle design, fluid properties, and gas-to-liquid flow ratio (for air-assisted nozzles). For large velocity differences, and corresponding large Reynolds numbers and small σ (Equation 2), it is reasonable to assume a Bernoulli relation, so that Equation 3 predicts that drop size is proportional to $P^{-0.5}$, where P is the pressure drop. As noted by Dietrich [6], this is consistent with observations.

FLUID MECHANISMS IN AIR-ASSISTED SWIRL NOZZLES

In air-assisted swirl nozzles, it is desirable to inject air with swirl in the opposite direction to the swirl of the liquid, with the optimum condition being such that the swirl angular momentum injection rate for the air balances the swirl angular momentum injection rate for the liquids. Two designs for opposed swirl injection are shown in Figure 2. The Figure 2B (with throat) design has been found to be more effective and stable than the Figure 2A design.

The balanced swirl condition can be verified by measuring the mixture swirl in the orifice region. As will be seen later, this swirl should be very small under balanced injection conditions. A mini-

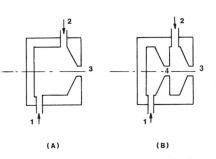

(A)   (B)

Figure 2. Opposed swirl nozzles: (A) *single-chamber design.* Fluid A enters upstream end · of axisymmetric chamber through inlet(s) 1, which are arranged to produce a vortex. Fluid B enters downstream end through inlet(s) 2, which are arranged to produce a vortex with opposite rotation to that of fluid A. Fluid A interacts with fluid B before leaving with fluid B through orifice 3. (B) *Two-chamber design.* Similar to single chamber design except for throat 4, through which fluid A passes before interacting with fluid B in chamber downstream from throat.

mum spray angle should correspond to approximately balanced injection conditions. In single-phase mixing, balanced swirl conditions are theoretically achieved (based on a Bernoulli relation) when the injector pressures and cross-sections are equal, and the swirl injection angles are opposed but equal in magnitude. This also gives equal mass flow rates for the injected materials. If unequal mass flow rates are desired, the injection angles, areas, and pressure drops can be adjusted, but when strongly contrasting and/or wide ranges of mass flow ratio are desired, the Figure 2B design (with throat) is more stable than the Figure 2A design.

The fluid mechanics of such balanced swirl nozzles is particularly interesting. During a turn-on transient, the pressure field adjusts to the swirl distribution, which is governed by approximate conservation of angular momentum in the region "upstream" (for both injected fluids) from the mixing region, although some angular momentum can be lost in boundary layers, especially if boundary layer Gortler vortices develop through Taylor instabilities. (Taylor instability, an important air-assisted swirl nozzle mechanism, will be discussed further later.) The result is a generally inward pressure force. This force drives the generally inward flow against the generally outward centrifugal acceleration occurring in the nozzle. (The work performed modifies the swirl velocity such that angular momentum is conserved.) However, it is most effective in accelerating fluid with lower swirl velocity and, therefore, fluid that has decreased its angular momentum magnitude by mixing with fluid with the opposite swirl angular momentum. (This is analogous to the teacup effect, in which low angular momentum fluid in the bottom boundary layer converges toward the middle of a stirred cup of tea, bringing tea leaves with it.) On the other hand, the centrifugal acceleration of fluid with larger swirl velocity opposes the inward pressure force, so that it tends not to move closer to the centerline. Thus, the natural background pressure gradient selectively accelerates well mixed fluid toward the nozzle centerline, while the unmixed fluid remains "trapped" inside the nozzle, since the orifice is near the centerline. Indeed, it is extremely difficult for any unmixed fluid to exit through an orifice near the centerline, because of the exceptionally high swirl velocities that would occur through conservation of angular momentum (figure skater effect) as it moves toward the centerline, thereby requiring exceptionally large pressure forces to approach the orifice. Only by reducing this angular momentum by mixing with the other injected fluid material, can the fluids approach the orifice with available pressure forces.

Since it appears so difficult for the separately injected fluids to leave the nozzle before mixing, a natural question is "by what mechanism is the required mixing achieved?" The answer appears to be that the injection conditions force a basic (time averaged) flow that is very unstable to eddy disturbances. These disturbances grow rapidly, at the expense of basic flow energy, leading to very turbulent flow that accomplishes the mixing. Specifically, the injection conditions force a basic flow in which the swirl velocity changes sign near the interface between the separately injected fluids. Since the interface cannot feasibly be normal to the nozzle centerline, this implies that swirl velocity, multiplied by the radial distance from the centerline, must decrease in magnitude as radial position increases in a region just inside the interface. Such shears are unstable, and the instability is called Taylor (or centrifugal) instability. This instability occurs near the ideal location for the resulting turbulent eddies to efficiently accomplish mixing: near the interface and away from the influence of rigid boundary constraints that would tend to inhibit the growth of turbulent eddies. This instability is intensified when the fluid inside the interface is more dense than the fluid outside the interface.

It is interesting to speculate on the details of the instability dynamics. It is quite likely that the fluid swirling in the left chamber (Figure 2B) passes through the throat in a thin layer, just as in simplex swirl nozzles. This thin layer immediately experiences large shearing forces from fluid injected with opposite swirl into the right chamber. The shearing forces are very large just downstream from the throat, but the unstable shear layer is also very thin, probably thinner than the total thickness of the axial fluid mass transport layer in the throat. The thickness of the unstable shear layer is likely to be closely related to the scale of the most rapidly growing eddies. Further downstream, the unstable shear layer is thicker due to diffusion and mixing already accomplished by finite amplitude counterparts of the initial unstable eddies. Thus, larger scale eddies probably grow fastest, leading to the formation of larger drops as the bulk liquid material moves downstream. Thus, this unstable shear layer thickening could contribute to the range of drop sizes typically produced by nozzles. Finally, although the mass transport layer thickness in the throat probably puts an upper limit on the drop size, the drop sizes produced could be well below this upper limit.

Another interesting characteristic of the opposed swirl nozzle is that balanced swirl angular momentum injection rate assures that the swirl energy will be entirely eliminated when the fluids become well-mixed which, as previously noted, occurs naturally before the fluid leaves through any opening near the centerline (i.e., an orifice). Thus, if injection conditions put most of the energy into the swirl component, a substantial portion of this energy must be converted to eddies that mix the injected fluids, leading to deformations that produce drops if one of the injected fluids is a liquid. Also, the loss of swirl energy leads to a "full-cone" spray pattern, in contrast to the hollow cone patterns that occur when the swirl is not balanced. Alternatively, the absence of swirl in the spray allows one to shape the spray pattern without substantially deteriorating the spray quality.

One of the many appealing potential applications of opposed swirl nozzles is the atomization of abrasive materials such as slurries, because the largest slurry swirl velocity occurs away from rigid boundaries. Further, the aforementioned overstable shear layer outside the slurry-gas interface tends to not only inhibit turbulent heat transport, as previously noted, but also inhibits turbulent transport of slurry material across the overstable layer, toward the nozzle walls.

In general, opposed swirl nozzles are multi-purpose fluid systems components that can be used for a variety of mixing, atomization, and emulsification applications. They can be used either to premix reactive materials, or as reactors (with reactions occurring together with mixing inside the nozzle—see Figure 2). More specific applications include liquid and slurry fuel injection, agricultural and paint spraying, spray drying, and artificial snow making.

THE IMPORTANT TAYLOR INSTABILITY

It appears that the success of opposed swirl nozzles is partly due to the unstable eddy scales being smaller than for similar conditions (i.e., similar pressure drops) in other types of nozzles. This is apparently related to the Taylor instability occurring at lower Reynolds number than other fluid dynamic instabilities. It therefore appears that better understanding of swirl nozzle dynamics could be obtained from studies of Taylor instability in the unique basic flow configurations occurring in opposed swirl nozzles.

The Taylor instability is perhaps the most widely investigated instability in fluid dynamics. The simplest configuration for this instability is the classical Taylor-Couette problem in which a fluid is contained between two concentric cylinders, with the inner one rotating and the outer one fixed. This is "one of the best-known problems in the whole field of fluid mechanics; indeed, it is so well documented as to be a useful testing ground for many new techniques, both theoretical and experimental" [2]. Although the flow configuration in the balanced swirl nozzle is quite different from the classical Taylor-Couette problem, the wealth of observations and data from that problem might shed light on the dynamics of balanced swirl nozzles. One example is that observations indicate a preference for elongated quasi-toroidal vortices. One would expect that surface tension effects, which apparently have not been investigated in the classical problem, would tend to de-

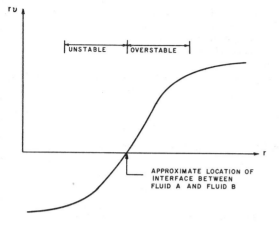

Figure 3. Schematic swirl distribution in opposed swirl nozzle. Distribution of time-averaged swirl along radial line just downstream from throat (see Figure 2B). The radius-weighted swirl velocity, rv, is approximately constant away from the interface, reflecting approximate conservation of angular momentum.

crease the scale of angular variations in these vortices, with the ratio of the angular scale to the radial and axial scales related to the ratio of surface tension to viscous forces. Thus, as previously noted, this ratio is probably quite important in atomization dynamics.

In contrast to the classical Taylor-Couette problem, the unstable layer in the balanced swirl nozzle is a free shear layer (a thin layer away from rigid boundaries). Outside this thin unstable shear layer, the swirl shears are moderately to strongly overstable, with the strongly stable region just outside the strongly unstable region (Figure 3). Just how strongly the eddy energy is concentrated in the unstable free shear layer appears relevant to the eddy and drop sizes expected, and to the degree of turbulent heat and liquid material transport to the wall region.

RELEVANT PRACTICAL CONSIDERATIONS REGARDING THE DESIGN AND OPTIMIZATION OF SWIRL NOZZLES

A rather important performance criterion of nozzles in general is their efficiency in producing small drops from a given bulk liquid. A good measure of this efficiency is the ratio of compression and pumping power to the liquid mass flow rate in producing a given average drop size. Although drop size measurements have demonstrated the superior efficiency of opposed swirl nozzles, as expected from the previous discussions, it is desirable to optimize the design of the opposed swirl nozzle for its many applications. Another important feature in some applications is the uniformity of drops produced. For example, in agricultural spraying, large drops do not coat effectively, while small drops tend to blow away and/or vaporize in the wind. In combustors, large drops can leave the system before complete combustion.

Some general questions of practical and scientific interest include:

1. Does single-phase mixing have a substantially different optimum design from atomization (two-phase mixing)?
2. Does compressibility substantially affect optimum design for one- and two-phase mixing processes? How about shock formation?
3. Does surface tension substantially affect the optimum design under typical operating conditions?
4. Can the optimum design for axisymmetric nozzles be determined by axisymmetric models, or is it necessary to consider three-dimensional fluid instabilities?
5. Is it better to premix and prevaporize, as in a fuel injector nozzle, thereby producing a relatively uniform full-cone flame, or is it better to use the opposed swirl concept directly in the combustor design (internal combustion nozzle) thereby reducing convective heat loss to the walls?
6. Does combustion substantially affect the optimum design for internal combustion nozzles?
7. Is the optimum nozzle a strong function of Reynolds number? Mach number? Weber number?

Addressing such questions will improve our basic understanding of atomization/vaporization/ mixing/combustion processes, including the fundamental Taylor (centrifugal) instability and how it works in opposed swirl nozzles to atomize and mix injected materials. As noted by Dietrich [6], this nozzle is an ideal candidate for computer-aided design, due to its good mixing/atomization performance at relatively low pressure drops, which is related to the fact that its primary performance mechanism, Taylor instability, can occur at lower Reynolds number than other turbulence-generating instabilities.

Acknowledgment

It is a pleasure to acknowledge my father, Dr. Verne E. Dietrich, and Harold C. Simmons for valuable information used in preparing this article.

REFERENCES

1. Simmons, H. C., "The Atomization of Liquids," Report #7901/2, Parker Hannifin Corporation, Gas Turbine Fuel Systems Division, 1979.
2. Barcilon, A., Brindley, J., Lessen, M., and Mobbs, F. R., "Marginal Instability in Taylor-Couette Flows at Very High Taylor Numbers," *J. Fluid Mech.*, 94, pp. 453–463, 1979.
3. Taylor, G. I., "The Mechanics of Swirl Atomizers," Seventh International Congress of Fluid Mechanics, Vol 2, Part I, p. 280, 1948.
4. Giffen, E., and Muraszew, A., *The Atomization of Liquid Fuels*, John Wiley & Sons, New York, 1953.
5. Simmons, H. C., and Harding, C. F., "Some Effects of Using Water as a Test Fluid in Fuel Nozzle Spray Analysis," ASME Paper No. 80-GT-90, 1980.
6. Dietrich, D. E., "Theory, Observation, and Model Design for Nozzles with Application to a Balanced Swirl Nozzle," Second International Conference on Liquid Atomization and Spray Systems (Proceedings), Madison, WI, 20–24 June, 1982, pp. 161–168.

CHAPTER 15

MOMENTUM EQUATIONS IN DISPERSED TWO-PHASE FLOWS

H. E. A. van den Akker

Koninklijke/Shell Laboratorium
Amsterdam, The Netherlands

CONTENTS

INTRODUCTION

This chapter, which is devoted to dispersed two-phase flow, presents a derivation of the momentum balances for the two separate phases. The method adopted is that proposed recently by Rietema and Van den Akker and, hence, many ideas and views presented in this chapter have been taken straight from their paper [1]. The actual derivation, which is presented later is preceded by several introductory sections.

The following section describes the concept of dispersed two-phase flow, presents an overview of a wide variety of types of dispersed two-phase flow, and mentions some historical developments and trends.

While the derivation of the momentum balances to be presented in this chapter applies to dispersed two-phase flow in particular, a completely different, indirect approach is also thinkable: first, the momentum balances are derived for two-phase flow in general, i.e. without the restriction that one of the two phases is dispersed; subsequently, they are simplified and restricted in view of the dispersion of one of the two phases. The next section therefore summarizes the various ways in which momentum balances for two-phase flows may be derived. This also provides an opportunity to comment on mathematical properties and numerical exercises reported on in the literature relating to momentum balances.

Next, this chapter discusses some basic concepts of averaging that are usually used to derive two-phase flow momentum balances. In addition, it explains how to apply the balancing method of the cubic volume element that is well-known from single-phase flow theory [2, pp. 71–81] to dispersed two-phase flow. In particular, two methods are introduced for dealing with the so-called boundary particles, i.e. the particles that are intersected by the flat faces of the above cubic volume element.

Definitions and considerations are then presented relating to pressures and stress tensors that are encountered in the description of dispersed two-phase flow. The relations between local flow phenomena on either side of particle boundaries and continuum variables as occurring in momentum balances are the subject of extensive discussion. In this context the interaction force between the two phases is also defined by means of a very elementary expression. A summary of the constitutive relations expressing part of this interaction force in terms of phase velocities according to familiar concepts (such as drag force and added mass) concludes this section.

The next section comprises the actual derivation of the momentum balances of the two separate phases. The two methods for dealing with the boundary particles (introduced earlier) prove to lead to equal final formulations of these balances, although some intermediate results for several terms of the balances are different.

Finally, two items are discussed that in recent years gave rise to lively debates in the literature, viz. the final formulations of the pressure gradient terms in the two momentum balances, and the requirement of well-posedness (hyperbolicity) of the full set of conservation equations upon which the formulation of the two momentum balances has a great impact.

DISPERSED TWO-PHASE FLOW

In dispersed two-phase flow one of the two phases, the dispersed phase is made up by segregated, individual particles (gas bubbles, liquid droplets, solid particulates) in the midst of a continuous (gas or liquid) phase. A continuous phase is characterized by the fact that any arbitrary point lying in the space occupied by this particular phase can be connected with any other point in this space by means of a continuous line in such a way that all points of this line are also within this same space. On the other hand, any particle of the dispersed phase has a closed interface or boundary (almost) completely surrounded by the continuous phase. Now, it is impossible to connect a point in some particle with a point in another particle without crossing the boundaries of these particles. Generally, in doing so one will pass through the continuous phase as well; in certain cases, however, some particles might be in mutual contact—temporarily or continuously—so that the connecting line could comprise the contact point of these particles without passing through the continuous phase. The swarm of dispersed-phase particles move through or are suspended more or less freely in the continuous phase.

This description covers a wide gamut of phase combinations in a variety of equipment used for divergent purposes. An incomplete catalogue of dispersed two-phase flows comprises rocket nozzle flow with droplets or solid particles, fuel spray nozzles, steam jets, water sprays, spray driers, cyclones, gas-fluidized and liquid-fluidized beds, bubble columns, liquid-liquid spray columns, and hydraulic and pneumatic transport lines for solids. In all these examples of dispersed two-phase flow the individual particles often maintain their own identity, while either their volume fraction or their mass fraction is essentially constant over the piece of equipment involved. In some examples coalescence of fluid particles and redispersion may take place. A somewhat different category of dispersed two-phase flow is formed by a limited range of vapor-liquid flows as occur in (nearly) horizontal natural gas transmission lines, in vertical risers near natural gas production platforms, in hypothetical loss-of-coolant accidents in nuclear reactor coolant systems, and during blowdowns and ventings of pressurized storage vessels and chemical reactors. In this category, phase transition processes (flashing, evaporation, condensation) play a dominant role, resulting in varying proportions of vapor and liquid, and in various flow patterns. Two of these flow patterns are dispersed droplet flow and dispersed bubbly flow.

In view of this wide spectrum of dispersed two-phase flows, each with its own inherent properties and problems, it is not surprising that in each field specific approaches and techniques have been developed for describing properties and solving problems. This can nicely be illustrated by the use of different terms (void fraction, hold-up, porosity, quality, loading ratio) for denoting the relative proportions in which the two phases are present, and of different concepts (slip velocity, slip or velocity ratio, two-fluid approach) for taking into account the unequal velocity fields of the two phases.

While some types of dispersed two-phase flow have received more or less continuous attention (such as bubble columns and pneumatic transport of solids), other types were studied or modeled over a limited number of years, in close relation to specific applications. In the early 1960s a large effort was dedicated to gas-particle nozzle flow: at the dawn of the era of astronautics there was a need to predict performance losses in liquid rocket nozzles due to condensed-phase combustion products, and to evaluate the effects of inclusion of metallic powder in solid rockets [3]. At about the same time many investigators [4, 5] were fascinated by the hydrodynamic stability of gas-fluidized beds and the related occurrence of gas bubbles in these beds, i.e. by the distinction between uniform, homogeneous fluidization (without bubbling) and aggregative, heterogeneous fluidization (with gas bubbles), though fluidization had developed into a wide-spread technology for catalytic cracking since World War II. Recently, fluidization research received a new stimulus from processes such as fluidized bed combustion and fluidized bed coal gasification and liquefaction, catching on after the two world energy crises of 1973/74 and 1979/80. Due to these developments, in many countries nuclear energy assumed a more pronounced role in policies of energy supply as well; as a result, many national research programs were undertaken to model, among other things, the phenomena and processes pertinent to a so-called loss-of-coolant accident in a nuclear reactor coolant system. These studies were based on the work on steam-water flows performed in the early 1960s in view of the emergence of the first commercial nuclear reactors.

In general, however, only limited cross-fertilization between the various fields of (dispersed) two-phase flow took place. Hence, even recent reviews are still restricted to one specific field, such as gas-liquid pipe flows [6, 7], dilute gas-particle flows [8–10], bubble columns [11, 12], fluidized beds [13], and choked vapor-liquid pipe flows [14, 15]. Reference 16, too, presents separate reviews on the various topics by different authors. Only very few authors [17–19] observe analogies in flow behavior and flow phenomena between different examples of dispersed two-phase flow, while this very approach is able to bring out the aspects common to the various fields of dispersed two-phase flow.

It should be realized that in many types of two-phase flow the motion of the two phases need not be considered separately and that a mixture description suffices. This can be illustrated by several examples. In all these examples the equations describing the mixture behavior are postulated on the basis of empiricism and intuition. A priori information on the flow pattern (slug flow, annular flow, dispersed flow, etc.) plays a dominant role.

The first example relates to steady-state vapor-liquid pipe flow as encountered in natural gas transportation through pipelines. Here, pressure drop prediction is the item of interest. Actually, the pressure drop equation is a simple momentum balance for the mixture equating the pressure gradient to the sum of three terms, viz. an acceleration (or expansion) term, a gravity term (for non-horizontal flow) and a wall friction term [20–22]. The dependence of the friction pressure gradient and the liquid hold-up on the phase velocities is related to the prevailing flow pattern. Separate criteria have therefore been developed for deciding, prior to the pressure drop calculation, which flow pattern prevails [23–25].

In the second example, choked two-phase flow, on account of the high velocities involved the gravity term may be deleted from the pressure drop equation as well. A radical, but disputed simplification of this type of two-phase flow is the assumption of homogeneous flow, i.e. of equal velocities of the two phases [14, 15, 26, 27].

In gas-liquid bubble columns [28, 29] and liquid-liquid spray columns [30–32] exhibiting large-scale circulatory behavior, a simplified momentum balance for the mixture equates the vertical pressure gradient to the sum of the gravity term and a wall friction term. Without the recognition at the onset of these analyses that the circulatory behavior could give rise to high velocities in the near-wall region, this wall friction term would have been ignored as well.

These examples illustrate how important physical intuition and experimental information are in formulating the (momentum) equations governing two-phase flow behavior. While in the previous examples a rather superficial approach focusing on the mixture behavior may be sufficient, in many other types of two-phase flow, however, the description or the analysis of the (dynamic) flow behavior of the system requires a detailed modeling of the motion of the separate phases. This is the subject of the remainder of this chapter.

VARIOUS WAYS OF DERIVING CONSERVATION EQUATIONS

In describing the hydrodynamic behavior of many two-phase flow systems the equations of conservation of mass and momentum, the so-called continuity equations and momentum balances for the separate phases, are essential. There is an extensive bibliography on momentum balances of two-phase flow, their derivation and applications. In particular, correct modeling of the mechanisms by which, at the phase interface, momentum can be transferred between the phases proves to be extremely difficult. At this stage a general discussion of the basic concepts used in the formulation of conservation equations for two-phase systems seems appropriate.

Soo [33-35] and co-workers [36, 37] adopted the fundamental postulate that the formulation of the conservation equations for multiphase systems should begin with the mixture. The basic reasoning for such a choice stems from their observation that all experimental evidence supports the use of the Navier-Stokes equation for describing air motion, despite the fact that air is a mixture of nitrogen and oxygen*. Consequently, the authors of this school believe that the global momentum and energy equations for the mixture of the multiphase system assume the same form as those for a homogeneous medium, when viewed within the context of continuum mechanics. On this basis these authors [33-37] extended the continuum mechanics of a single-phase multicomponent fluid to a suspension of solid particles in a gas. Particles of different size ranges are conceived as constituting different phases from the point of view of continuum mechanics [33, 34]. This approach leads to the presence of so-called inertial coupling terms in the momentum balances of the individual phases due to the different velocities of the center-of-mass of the dispersed phase and the center-of-mass of the mixture [35, 37]. In addition, much attention has been devoted by Soo [34, 43, 44] to the equation of motion of a discrete solid particle suspended in a fluid.

This multiphase fluid mechanics approach has not found wide acceptance so far. Instead, most of the derivations of the momentum equations for two-phase flow systems start from considering the motion of the individual phases. At least in principle, the motion of a fluid phase in two-phase flow is determined by the Navier-Stokes equation to be satisfied at each point of that phase, while each particle of a particulate phase obeys the Newtonian equation of motion. Solution of these locally valid equations provided with appropriate boundary and initial conditions would yield a complete description of the two-phase flow in question. However, when the system of interest comprises, for instance, a large number of interacting particles, the problem is far too complicated to permit a direct solution along the previously mentioned line. The problem must be simplified by replacing the point mechanical and point fluid mechanical variables by smoothed variables obtained by averaging over space and time. The resulting equations then describe the motion of the two phases as though they were interpenetrating and interacting continua. The necessarily more

---

* The concept that air motion can be described by a single equation is not generally valid: under certain conditions separation of gas mixtures such as air is possible. In a Ranque-Hilsch vortex tube [38] the oxygen content of the cooler central exit stream is higher than that of the warmer outer annular exit stream [39]; in the atmosphere, gravity acting over very long distances accomplishes an uneven distribution of nitrogen and oxygen; high-speed centrifuging is an old, familiar technique [40, 41] for separating gases and vapors into their constituents (isotopes) that, for instance, is used in the Kistemaker ultracentrifuging process for the enrichment of urane. These examples illustrate that a mixture description by means of a single equation is only valid if, as a consequence of the prevalent forces, the velocities of the constituents of that mixture are exactly equal [42].

superficial view provided by the continuum models leads to interaction forces between the phases and to viscous forces appearing as formal terms in the momentum equations. The form of these terms must be determined empirically and thus there is ample scope for differences of opinion about the final form of the equations describing a two-phase flow of specific interest.

Standart [45], Anderson and Jackson [46], Vernier and Delhaye [47] and Whitaker [48] were among the first to present a rigorous treatment on how to obtain from the local instantaneous conservation equations for the individual phases and particles the macroscopic, averaged, equations describing the average motions of the two phases. Much attention has since been paid to averaging techniques [49–59] and to the treatment of the phase interface [60–63]. Rigorous and impressive mathematical formulations of the conservation equations for two-phase flow are now available [63–66]. Eventually, however, when employing these "exact" conservation equations for the description of specific examples of two-phase flow, constitutive relations are required for expressing the contributions to the conservation equations from the stress tensors of the two phases and from the interphase phenomena in terms of the primary variables, such as velocities and volume fractions of the two phases. These constitutive equations are still based on physical intuition and experience. This implies that the mathematical rigor of the derivation of the equations cannot be fully fulfilled in describing two-phase flows of practical interest. Gross simplifications to the general concepts used in the derivations, not seldom based on an a priori identification of the flow pattern involved, must smooth the way to a useful set of equations of motion for the two-phase flow of interest [6, 67–71]. Eventually, the resulting set of equations is often indistinguishable from what would have been generated from a much less sophisticated starting point [7, 68].

A disadvantage of this continuum approach is that so much attention is given to mathematics, that little scope is left for physical arguments and considerations. As a result, a number of controversies have arisen on the meaning and correctness of various terms in the "exact" conservation equations. An example of such a controversy [72–80] is the question whether the volume fraction of each phase should occur either *in* the gradient of pressure or as a multiplier *on* the pressure gradient. Mention can also be made of various views on the use of different pressures for the two phases and of an interfacial pressure [65, 69, 81, 82].

A completely different approach of the conservation equations has been pursued in the field of transient vapor-liquid flow analyses in view of nuclear engineering applications (loss-of-coolant accidents, LOCAs). Usually these analyses started by simply postulating a set of two-phase conservation equations without viscous stress terms and with a simple drag term as the only interaction force between the two phases. After Gidaspow [83] had noticed that such a set possesses complex-valued characteristics and hence does not represent a well-posed initial-value problem (discussed later), a spirited dialogue ensued on the possible causes of these complex characteristics, the seriousness of their existence in view of numerical calculations and hydrodynamic stability analyses, and possible cures to eliminate their occurrence [69, 72, 81, 84, 85].

As the nature of the characteristics is not affected by the non-homogeneous terms in the differential equations, i.e. by the so-called source and sink terms (such as the simple drag term), some authors even considered momentum balances consisting of three terms only, viz. the partial derivative to time, a convective term and a pressure gradient term. But gradually the insight has grown that these strongly simplified balance equations must be incomplete or incorrect in some essential physical respect [81, 85]. The various authors arrive at different suggestions for eliminating the complex characteristics; most of these suggestions relate to the interaction force between the two phases which—as far as particles are concerned—has been the subject of many studies in other fields [34, 46, 86–88]. This again illustrates how slowly insights gained in one type of two-phase flow find their way to another field.

In none of the three mentioned types of analyses, viz. the two-continua approach and the analyses focusing on well-posedness of the set of differential equations, interest was focused on deriving the correct formulation of the separate momentum balances for two-phase flow *in general*. The remainder of this chapter is devoted to a fourth way of deriving the separate momentum balances which, however, will only be valid for *dispersed* two-phase flow. In this derivation use is made, from the very beginning, of the information that one of the two phases is in a dispersed form. This approach has been common in fields of two-phase flow in which solid particles are present, such as in gas-solids flows [3, 4, 10, 89] and in fluidization [46, 88, 90–96]. A further restriction to the derivation to be presented is that phase transition and redistribution processes as well as chemical reactions are not considered. In addition, coalescing of fluid particles and/or redispersion are left out, as is also done with processes involving (solid) particle size reduction. Finally, the densities of the phases are assumed to be constant.

AVERAGING AND BALANCING IN DISPERSED TWO-PHASE FLOW

In the preceding section the concept of treating the two phases as though they were two inter-penetrating and interacting continua has already been mentioned. This concept will be applied throughout the remainder of this chapter. Some averaging procedure may be required to obtain the conservation equations describing the motion of the two continua, since for either phase the local instantaneous values of the flow variables must be averaged because each phase is only inter-mittently present at each point. In an analysis restricted to dispersed two-phase flow it is possible to make rather detailed assumptions on the stochastic fluctuations typifying this type of flow. Thus, the averaging procedure can be held rather straightforward and simple. This is the subject of this section.

The Length Scales of Interest and Their Use in Averaging

Two length scales are of relevance in dispersed two-phase flow. First, there is the scale L of the apparatus, equipment, or natural ambience in which the two-phase flow of interest comes about. Secondly, the so-called scale of dispersion l_d is important. This latter scale may be defined as the average size of a volume element containing only one discrete particle of the dispersed phase. It is assumed that l_d is at least three orders of magnitude smaller than L.

For engineering purposes a detailed description of the flow behavior of the two individual phases at the level of l_d may be redundant, and a description in terms of length scales only one order smaller than L may suffice. When for this purpose—starting from the instantaneous local flow variables such as velocity and pressure—manageable mass and momentum balances are to be derived, some averaging procedure has to be introduced. Averaging should be such as to retain the flow variables varying on the scale of L, and to smooth the more or less stochastic irregularities and fluctuations at the scale of l_d. It seems therefore appropriate to assume that the momentary local or point variables are the resultants of two types of variations, one at the scale of L and the other at the scale of l_d. The L-scale variations determine the overall behavior of the two-phase flow; the l_d-scale fluctuations arise from the distortion of the fluid streamlines around and between the dispersed-phase particles and from the complicated paths of individual particles responding to the variations in the fluid velocity field and influenced by adjacent particles. Hence, any instantaneous point property a′ may be conceived as a superposition of its mean value a (varying at the L-scale) and a fluctuation a″ which at the l_d-scale varies in time and in space:

$$a' = a + a'' \tag{1}$$

Note that the fluctuation a″ is not the result of macroscopic turbulence, which will be ignored in this chapter. This concept [46, 50] implies that on averaging a′ according to the previous requisites, the second term of the right-hand side of Equation 1 should yield zero. However, averaging the product of two point properties, such as $v'_{cx}v'_{cy}$, results in two non-zero terms, viz. $v_{cx}v_{cy}$ and $\overline{v''_{cx}v''_{cy}}$.

This concept sets bounds to the size of the control volume element V_0, the control surface element S_0 and the period of time t_0 over which averaging is to be performed. The size r_0 of V_0 or S_0 should be large compared to l_d and small with respect to L. In other words, V_0 or S_0 should comprise many particles, but may still be small in a macroscopic sense. In addition, the integration time t_0 should be long compared to the passage time t_p of a specific particle ($t_p = l_d/v_p$) and short with respect to the relaxation time T of the L-scale variations.

In most averaging techniques the flow variations in the whole averaging volume or surface area all equally contribute to the averaged value of the variable of interest at some specific location r_1. It seems physically plausible to take into account that variations close to r_1 may have a greater impact on the averaged value at r_1 than variations at remote locations. In view of this, Anderson and Jackson [46] introduced some weighting function which on multiplication attributes a greater impact to nearby variations than to variations at larger distances. This weighting function was then used in averaging, term after term, the locally valid flow equations for the individual phases. Unfortunately, in the elaboration of the many complicated integrals, the elegance of this averaging technique could not be maintained, because many approximations could not be circumvented [64]. The contradictory nature of some of these approximations has already been discussed [1, 97]. In view of these deficiencies a weighting function for averaging purposes will not be used in this chapter, though there have been some authors [50, 52, 94, 98] who adopted it.

The Cubic Volume Element Method

Instead of an averaging technique that should be applied to each term of the locally valid flow equations, a method well-known from single-phase flow theory [2, pp. 71–81] can also be used for deriving the balance equations of momentum (and mass and energy) in the case of dispersed two-phase flow. The method in question [1] involves balancing over a cubic volume element of edge r_0, meeting the qualifications as set out earlier. The separate contributions to the balance equations are found by integration of flow variables over the cubic volume element or over its faces.

If this method is applied in single-phase flow, concentrations are averaged over the volume of the element, e.g. for the momentum concentration (in the constant-density case):

$$\frac{1}{\Delta x\,\Delta y\,\Delta z}\int_{\Delta x,\Delta y,\Delta z}\rho v_x'\,dx\,dy\,dz = \rho v_x \tag{2}$$

while fluxes are averaged over the faces of the cubic volume element, e.g. over the face $x = x_1$:

$$\frac{1}{\Delta y\,\Delta z}\int_{\Delta y,\Delta z} v_x'(x_1, y, z)\,dy\,dz = v_x(x_1, y, z) \tag{3}$$

Note that the fluctuations at the l_d-scale, i.e. in the previous examples v_x'', vanish on averaging, due to the concept underlying Equation 1. Indeed, the condition $r_0 \gg l_d$ forbids us to take the limit of $\Delta x, \Delta y, \Delta z$ approaching to zero. While at the same time $r_0 \ll L$, it may be reasonable to assume that within the volume element all variables change linearly so that, e.g. for the plane at $x = x_1 + \Delta x$:

$$v_x(x_1 + \Delta x, y, z) = v_x(x_1, y, z) + \left(\frac{\partial v_x}{\partial x}\right)_{x_1}\Delta x \tag{4}$$

In the case of a dispersed two-phase system the previous method must consider that each phase is not present everywhere all the time. Hence, first of all the volume fractions of the continuous phase and of the dispersed phase, to be denoted by ε and $1 - \varepsilon$, respectively, must be defined. Such definitions make sense only at a scale that is large compared to l_d, since at the scale of l_d the volume fraction of each phase is either one or zero. Thus, there is no sense in defining a point value ε', as is done for all remaining flow variables. A satisfactory definition of ε might run as

$$\varepsilon = \frac{1}{\Delta x\,\Delta y\,\Delta z}\int_{\substack{\Delta x,\Delta y,\Delta z \\ \text{cont. ph.}}} dx\,dy\,dz \tag{5}$$

where the integration is to be performed over all points in the cubic volume element that are occupied by the continuous phase. When averaging fluxes through the boundary planes of a cubic volume element, however, Equation 5 is not adequate, since it does not allow ε to vary over the size of the control volume element. Instead, suppose the control volume element to be split up into a large number of thin slabs parallel to the plane $x = x_1$ where the thickness of these slabs is small compared to the size of the dispersed particles (see Figure 1). The intersection of these slabs by the dispersed particles can then be conceived as being constant, i.e. independent of x, over this thickness.

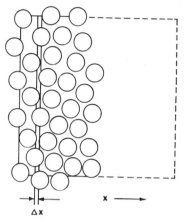

Figure 1. Control volume split into a number of thin slabs parallel to the plane $x = x_1$. Thickness of slabs is small in comparison to the dispersed particles.

Consequently the value of ε is not affected by the following manipulation:

$$\varepsilon = \frac{1}{\Delta x} \int_{\Delta x} \left\{ \frac{1}{\Delta y \, \Delta z} \int_{\substack{\Delta y, \Delta z \\ \text{cont. ph.}}} dy \, dz \right\} dx = \frac{1}{\Delta y \, \Delta z} \int_{\substack{\Delta y, \Delta z \\ \text{cont. ph.}}} dy \, dz \tag{6}$$

Of course, similar expressions can be derived for slabs in the remaining directions.

Let us now consider the remaining flow variables in dispersed two-phase flow. A flux a'_c of the continuous phase through the plane $\Delta y \, \Delta z$ at $x = x_1$ will be averaged on the analogy of Equation 3; hence,

$$\frac{1}{\Delta y \, \Delta z} \int_{\substack{\Delta y, \Delta z \\ \text{cont. ph.}}} a'_c(x_1, y, z) \, dy \, dz = \varepsilon a_c(x_1, y, z) \tag{7}$$

Similarly, for a flux of the dispersed phase:

$$\frac{1}{\Delta y \, \Delta z} \int_{\substack{\Delta y, \Delta z \\ \text{disp. ph.}}} a'_d(x_1, y, z) \, dy \, dz = (1 - \varepsilon) a_d(x_1, y, z) \tag{8}$$

For the extrema $\varepsilon = 0$, i.e. no continuous phase present, and $\varepsilon = 1$, i.e. no dispersed phase present, Equations 7 and 8 reduce to Equation 3; in the case of a'_c being constant in the plane $\Delta y \, \Delta z$ at $x = x_1$, Equation 7 yields Equation 6 again. As discussed earlier, averaging the product of two point flow variables over a face of a cubic volume element yields two non-zero terms; e.g.,

$$\frac{1}{\Delta y \, \Delta z} \int_{\substack{\Delta y, \Delta z \\ \text{cont. ph.}}} a'_c(x_1, y, z) a'_c(x_1, y, z) \, dy \, dz = \varepsilon(a_c a_c + \overline{a''_c a''_c}) \tag{9}$$

Finally, a concentration in the continuous phase or a body force I' acting upon this phase will be averaged according to

$$\frac{1}{\Delta x \, \Delta y \, \Delta z} \int_{\substack{\Delta x, \Delta y, \Delta z \\ \text{cont. ph.}}} I' \, dx \, dy \, dz = \varepsilon I \tag{10}$$

which for a constant value of I' again reduces to Equation 5.

METHOD II |←———————— r_0 ————————→| METHOD I

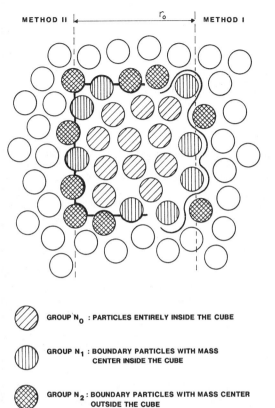

⊘ GROUP N_0 : PARTICLES ENTIRELY INSIDE THE CUBE

⊟ GROUP N_1 : BOUNDARY PARTICLES WITH MASS
CENTER INSIDE THE CUBE

⊠ GROUP N_2 : BOUNDARY PARTICLES WITH MASS CENTER
OUTSIDE THE CUBE

Figure 2. Particles contained in a cubic volume element with edge r_0.

The Boundary Particles of the Cubic Volume Element

One aspect of the cubic volume element balancing method applied to dispersed two-phase flow has not yet been considered so far, viz. the problem how to treat the so-called boundary particles, i.e. the particles that are intersected by the faces of the cubic volume element. This difficulty seems too serious to be ignored, as was done by several authors [91, 99]. Some authors [3, 100] considered explicitly how to take the intersected boundary particles into account. When setting up the balance, in the presence of intersected boundary particles, between all momentum flows and pertinent forces, intra-particle flow variables will appear. As will be discussed later, however, intra-particle flow variables are not directly related to the motion of the dispersed phase. Hence, eliminating them from the balance requires special care. Rietema and Van den Akker [1] dodged the problem of intersected particles by means of two different methods, which are discussed below.

Prior to that discussion a closer look at the particles contained in a cubic volume element with edge r_0 is desirable (Figure 2). First of all, the particles of the largest group, denoted by N_0, are completely inside the cubic volume element. In addition, there are two types of boundary particles that protrude through the faces of the cubic volume element: the group N_1 comprising all boundary particles with their center-of-mass lying within the cubic volume element; and the group N_2 composed of all boundary particles having their center-of-mass outside the cubic volume element. It can be shown that the ratio n_1/n_2, n_1 and n_2 being the numbers of particles in the groups N_1 and N_2, respectively, is approximated by

$$\frac{n_1}{n_2} = 1 - \frac{2d}{r_0} + 2\left(\frac{d}{r_0}\right)^2 \tag{11}$$

Due to the averaging concept used (d ≪ r_0), it follows from Equation 11 that the difference between the integers n_1 and n_2 tends to zero.

Method I

Now the boundary planes of the cubic volume element are conceived to be flexible and to pass through the continuous phase in between the boundary particles in such a way that the particles of group N_1 are entirely inside the volume element and those of group N_2 entirely outside (Figure 2, right-hand side). External forces (except body forces) are now all acting upon the continuous phase only. It is obvious, however, that this method can be applied only if the volume concentration of the dispersed phase is low, and that it certainly cannot be applied if there is permanent contact between particles.

Method II

As in Method I, the volume element contains the particles of the groups N_0 and N_1, and it does not contain those of group N_2. The boundary planes of the volume element, however, are now different—they coincide with the flat faces of the cubic volume element as long as the latter are in the continuous phase, and they coincide with the outward-facing boundaries* of the particles of group N_1 and with the inward-facing boundaries* of the particles of group N_2 (Figure 2, left-hand side). In Method II the boundary particles (of both groups N_1 and N_2) are subject to internal forces as well as to external forces.

The position of the flexible boundary planes in both Methods I and II does not remain unchanged with time, because of the motion of the particles with respect to the framework of the cubic volume element. It is supposed that a flexible boundary plane leaps a particle for enclosing it as soon as it approaches the cubic volume element closely enough, whereas a boundary will retreat from particles when they are about to leave the cubic volume element. This implies that all the previously mentioned averaging procedures (Equations 6–10) should also extend over the previously mentioned period t_0. By virtue of this averaging in time and owing to d ≪ r_0, the averaged positions of the flexible boundary planes are identical to the positions of the flat faces of the cubic volume element.

Before the balancing method itself is presented, an introduction to the pressures and the stresses in the two phases as well as on the interaction force between the phases would seem to be appropriate.

PRESSURES, STRESSES, AND THE INTERACTIONS BETWEEN THE PHASES

This section considers the pressures and (shear) stresses in the immediate vicinity of the particle boundaries. The local flow phenomena on either side of the particle boundary are discussed first, and attention is restricted to the interactions between pressure and stress fields inside and outside the particles over distances comparable to l_d. The next sub-section deals with the way in which the pressure and shear stress distributions around any particle, integrated over the whole particle boundary, result in a force between fluid and particle. Part of this force depends on the slip velocity,

---

* The terms "outward-facing" and "inward-facing" should be understood with respect to the cubic volume element.

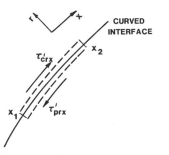

Figure 3. Illustration of how the internal stress tensor relates to the stress tensor of the continuous phase at the curved interface between two fluid phases.

i.e. the difference in velocity between the particle and the fluid. Contrary to the flow phenomena inside a particle, the so-called interaction force between particles and continuous phase significantly contributes to the momentum balances of the two phases. This difference between internal particle dynamics and interaction force is noteworthy, particularly in view of their common source, viz. the pressure and stress fields around any particle. An extensive discussion on the interaction force is appropriate here, since in the literature there is no unanimity as to this force.

Pressures and Stresses

At the interface of two fluid phases, pressure and stresses are not necessarily continuous functions of the spatial coordinates; they may exhibit jumps. In the case of fluid particles these jumps are related to the action of the interfacial or surface tension γ. It is this very tension that causes each fluid particle to retain its identity so that each individual particle has its own specific velocity with which it moves with respect to the surrounding continuous phase. On the contrary, this tension γ does allow a particle to respond to pressure and stress fluctuations in the surrounding fluid by means of continuous adjustments of its shape. In addition, the tension γ does not prohibit that inside a fluid particle a velocity distribution, e.g. a vortex ring, may arise as a result of the shear stresses exerted upon the interface.

For a spherical particle the relation between the internal pressure p'_p and the (external) pressure p' of the continuous phase is represented by the equation of Laplace:

$$p'_p = p' + 4\gamma'/d \tag{12}$$

where d denotes the particle diameter. Let us now consider a thin slice in a dispersed two-phase flow that is normal to the direction of flow and contains fluid particles of varying size, the densities of the two phases being equal. As a matter of fact, pressure p of the continuous phase, being the average of p' (Equation 7), is a constant in that plane. Application of Equation 12 to particles of unequal size in that plane, however, reveals that such particles have varying internal pressures p'_p. Evidently, p'_p has no relation at all to the flow of the dispersed phase.* In addition, only the pressure p of the continuous phase can be measured by sensors.

How the internal stress tensor $\underline{\tau}'_p$ relates to the stress tensor $\underline{\tau}'_c$ of the continuous phase can be found by considering in more detail a very thin slice, Δx in length and with essentially no dimensions in the remaining directions, that contains part of the curved interface between two fluid phases (Figure 3). Balancing the local tangential forces acting on this slice in the x-direction yields

$$(\tau'_{crx} - \tau'_{prx})\,\Delta x + \gamma'(x_2) - \gamma'(x_1) = 0 \tag{13}$$

---

* This significant feature of dispersed two-phase flow has not generally been appreciated [69, 135].

or, with Δx approaching zero:

$$\tau'_{crx} - \tau'_{prx} = -\frac{\partial \gamma'}{\partial x} \tag{14}$$

Equation 14 is illustrative of the coupling of the various components of the stress tensors $\underline{\tau}'_p$ and $\underline{\tau}'_c$ of the two phases. These two tensors prescribe the local flow fields on either side of the interface. The tensor $\underline{\tau}'_p$ may be connected to the internal circulation within a particle, but is obviously not related to the average motion of the individual particles. Whether or not a fluid particle in response to the surrounding $\underline{\tau}'_c$-field is circulating internally, or is being deformed, or oscillates, has some slight effect on its relative velocity; this, however, is usually allowed for by means of a correction to the pertinent drag coefficient [101, 102]. Equations 12–14 show the dependence of internal fluid particle dynamics on surface tension; hence, surfactants are able to change both the form and the internal flow behavior of a fluid particle and therefore the pertinent drag coefficient [103].

It should be added that $\underline{\tau}'_p$ is not to be confused with the particle stress tensor $\underline{\sigma}_d$ that arises from interaction and exchange of momentum between separate individual particles, either by permanent contact [104–107] or by collisions [91, 108] due to attractive and repulsive interparticle forces [10, 46]. Hence, as opposed to $\underline{\tau}'_p$, the tensor $\underline{\sigma}_d$ does affect the overall motion of the dispersed phase particles and the dynamics of the dispersed two-phase flow as a whole [93–96, 98, 106, 107]. It is further noted that $\underline{\sigma}_d$ differs from the tensors $\underline{\tau}'_p$ and $\underline{\tau}'_c$ in comprising the isotropic interparticle pressure p_d, which may be equivalent to the continuous phase pressure p.

In the case of solid particles making up the dispersed phase, the concepts of an internal pressure p'_p, an internal stress tensor $\underline{\tau}'_p$ and an interfacial tension γ have no practical meaning. As the solid may safely be assumed to be incompressible, a solid particle may only be able to respond to local differences or variations in the tangential components of the stress tensor of the surrounding fluid: it has the potential to rotate. If the variations in the components of $\underline{\tau}'_c$ actually are more or less stochastic fluctuations with time, the possibly resulting particle rotations and similar motions are secondary local effects restricted to individual particles that do not give rise to a separate term in the momentum balances. Under very specific conditions, however, such as in shear flows (i.e. in cases of non-uniform velocity profiles due to non-zero $\underline{\tau}'_c$-components) and particularly near solid walls, the rotations can occur systematically and are then symptomatic; in such cases a separate term in the momentum balances might be essential.

The presence and the relative motion of dispersed phase particles within the continuous phase contributes to an increased transport of momentum in the continuous phase. This effect is usually taken into account by the introduction of a correction factor to the viscosity coefficient of the continuous phase. Internal circulations in and deformations or oscillations of fluid particles, as well as rotations of solid particles are among the secondary phenomena affecting the degree to which the momentum transport within the continuous phase is increased. For a more detailed discussion on these effects the reader is referred to more specific literature [19, 32, 102, 109].

The Interaction Force Between the Phases

Let us consider for a while a single particle suspended in some steady-state condition in a flowing fluid. It is commonly known [2, pp. 56–60 and 190–194] that the pressure and stress distributions around such a particle are such that the fluid exerts a drag force upon the particle. This drag force can be split up into two components. First there is the *form drag*, which is the result of the local pressure distribution around the particle, an essential feature being that the pressure in the wake behind the particle is lower than the pressure at the stagnation point at the nose. Secondly, there is the *viscous drag* due to the local viscous friction forces in the boundary layer around the particle. The resulting drag force may balance the remaining forces exerted upon the particle (such as the gravity force), and contributes to the eventual behavior of the particle considered. In the case of a particle accelerating or decelerating with respect to the surrounding fluid, the prevailing pressure and shear stress distributions around such a particle will be different and will change with time; hence, the interaction force between particle and fluid will be different from that in a steady-state situation. These considerations sufficiently substantiate the following definition [2, 46, 99, 100] of the local force exerted by a single particle upon the surrounding fluid:

$$F'_{pc} = \int_{S_p} \mathbf{n} \cdot (p' \underline{\delta} + \underline{\tau}'_c) \, dS \tag{15}$$

where S_p and $\mathbf{n}$ denote the particle boundary and the outward normal to the surface element dS, respectively. A single prime is attached to p', $\underline{\tau}'_c$, and F'_{pc}, since they are all defined at the scale of the particle, i.e. at the scale of 1_d.

The averaging concept that is concisely expressed in Equation 1 makes it possible to rewrite Equation 15 as

$$F'_{pc} = \int_{S_p} \mathbf{n} \cdot (p \underline{\delta} + \underline{\tau}_c) \, dS + \int_{S_p} \mathbf{n} \cdot (p'' \underline{\delta} + \underline{\tau}''_c) \, dS \tag{16}$$

Due to a well-known theorem by Gauss the first term of the right-hand side of Equation 16 can be transformed into an integral over the particle volume V_p. This transformation is permitted in the case of this first term, since p and $\underline{\tau}_c$ are continuum properties defined at the scale of L and therefore also defined within V_p at any moment.* As ∇p and $\nabla \cdot \underline{\tau}_c$ are essentially constant at the scale of a particle, Equation 16 can be rewritten as

$$F'_{pc} = (\nabla p + \nabla \cdot \underline{\tau}_c) V_p + F'_s \tag{17}$$

where

$$F'_s = \int_{S_p} \mathbf{n} \cdot (p'' \underline{\delta} + \underline{\tau}''_c) \, dS \tag{18}$$

The term F'_s obviously arises from the local distortions of the fluid streamlines around a particle.

In summing up the forces F'_{pc} exerted by all n particles within a cubic volume element the boundary particles need specific consideration. The two methods dedicated to dealing with them lead to different results of this summation and are therefore treated separately. The number n of particles within the cubic volume element ($n = n_0 + n_1$) is independent of the method adopted for dealing with the boundary particles. In the concept of Method I, each of these n particles exerts a force F'_{pc} on the continuous phase *within* the volume element. If, on the other hand, Method II is followed, the n_1 boundary particles, though completely contained within the control volume element, only partly contribute to the total interaction force exerted on the continuous phase *within* the volume element: as far as their boundaries coincide with the flexible faces of the volume element, they exert a force F'_{pe} upon the continuous phase *outside* the volume element. Summation of these local boundary forces F'_{pe} yields the force F_{be} on the continuous phase outside. Hence, the interaction force $F_{dc(II)}$ (i.e. the interaction force on the continuous phase within the control volume element in case Method II is adopted for dealing with the boundary particles) differs from $F_{dc(I)}$ according to Method I merely by the force F_{be}:

$$F_{dc(II)} = F_{dc(I)} - F_{be} \tag{19}$$

The force F_{be} is considered in more detail later. First, the interaction force $F_{dc(I)}$ is discussed.

Method I

If Method I is adopted for dealing with the boundary particles, the interaction force $F_{dc(I)}$ exerted by all n particles inside the control volume element upon the continuous phase within the same volume element is obtained by simply summing up over all n particles, viz.

---

* Note that $\underline{\tau}_c$ within a particle fundamentally differs from $\underline{\tau}'_p$. Perhaps this is best illustrated by means of the example of gas bubbles dispersed in a flowing liquid: here $\underline{\tau}'_p$ approaches zero, while $\underline{\tau}_c$ does not necessarily do so.

$$\mathbf{F}_{dc(l)} = \frac{1}{r_0^3} \sum_n \mathbf{F}'_{pc} \tag{20}$$

Substituting Equations 17 and 18 into Equation 20 leads to

$$\mathbf{F}_{dc(l)} = (1 - \varepsilon)(\nabla p + \nabla \cdot \underline{\underline{\tau}}_c) + \mathbf{F}_s \tag{21}$$

where $\quad \mathbf{F}_s = \dfrac{1}{r_0^3} \sum_n \int_{S_p} \mathbf{n} \cdot (p'' \underline{\underline{\delta}} + \underline{\underline{\tau}}''_c) \, dS \tag{22}$

In a slightly variant derivation Equation 16 is substituted into Equation 20; application of Gauss' theorem, along with averaging on the analogy of Equation 10, yields Equation 21 as well. The advantage of this variant is that the assumption that ∇p and $\nabla \cdot \underline{\underline{\tau}}_c$ are essentially constant over the size of a particle is avoided.

The previous derivations are not exactly equal to that by Rietema and Van den Akker [1, 19]; the result, however, is very similar. Anderson and Jackson [46] derived an expression for $\mathbf{F}_{dc}$ that, apart from the use of a weighting function, is equivalent to the present Equations 21 and 22. In defining the interaction force $\mathbf{F}_{dc}$ some authors [65, 69, 110] explicitly consider some interfacial pressure p'_i being different from the bulk pressure p. The difference $p - p'_i$ may be equal to p'' of the present concept. However, maintaining p'_i in the momentum balances along with introducing the concept of an interaction force due to slip is considered to be too much of the same, since it conflicts with the definition of $\mathbf{F}_s$ as given in Equation 22.

Equation 21 expresses, as indeed it should do, that the interaction force $\mathbf{F}_{dc(l)}$ is composed of various contributions. That the pressure gradient partly belongs to $\mathbf{F}_{dc(l)}$ has been appreciated already by several authors [10, 46, 88, 111]. The first term of the right-hand side of Equation 21 denotes the well-known Archimedes force and allows for the buoyant force acting on a particle owing to the unequal pressure distribution around it; it even exists in the case of a stationary particle in a stagnant fluid due to the hydrostatic head only. For that reason, some authors [90–92] may have expressed the buoyancy effect in terms of a fluid density times the gravitational acceleration constant.

The second term of the right-hand side of Equation 21 plays a similar role, but only when the continuous phase velocity $\mathbf{v}_c$ is not uniform, i.e. when there are non-zero velocity gradients at the scale of L. Hence, this second term of $\mathbf{F}_{dc(l)}$ might explain a phenomenon observed in the case of particles dispersed in a non-uniform shear flow (i.e. in a flow with e.g., a parabolic velocity profile), viz. the sideward drift towards some preferential radial or transverse position in the flow field [112–115]. In addition, several authors [114–116] derived that in the case of Poiseuille flow neutrally buoyant particles lag behind the fluid; this effect could also be explained by means of the second term of $\mathbf{F}_{dc(l)}$ involving $\nabla \cdot \underline{\underline{\tau}}_c$.

The third contribution in Equation 21 to $\mathbf{F}_{dc(l)}$ stems from the p'' and $\underline{\underline{\tau}}''_c$ variations resulting from the distortions of the flow field due to the presence of the particles themselves, as is shown by Equation 22. These distortions may depend on the momentary difference between particle velocity and fluid velocity. Hence, most authors conclude that the force $\mathbf{F}_s$ in its turn consists of two components at least, viz. the *drag force* that is some function of the steady-state slip velocity $\mathbf{v}_s (= \mathbf{v}_d - \mathbf{v}_c)$, and the *added mass force* for a particle that accelerates or decelerates relative to the fluid. More detailed discussions on both the drag force and the added mass concept are available [19, 46, 71].

Second-order effects related to the surface tension of bubbles and drops that occur as formal terms in the momentum balances as derived by some authors [64, 81], are more conveniently taken into account by adjusting the drag coefficient [19, 101, 102]. In addition to the drag force and the added mass force, some more contributions to $\mathbf{F}_s$ have been discerned by some authors. Drew and Lahey [71] and Immich [117] mention a *lift force* due to the interaction of a relative velocity and the shear field of the continuous phase. It must be added, however, that these authors do not mention the second contribution to $\mathbf{F}_s$ due to $\nabla \cdot \underline{\underline{\tau}}_c$ (Equation 21). Di Giacinto et al. [10] refers to a lift force resulting from particle rotation and becoming relevant in shear flows, particularly near solid walls, but he ignores it in his analysis. Finally, the so-called *Basset force* allows for memory effects in the instantaneous fluid velocity field around a particle [46, 71, 86, 117].

Method II

If Method II is chosen for dealing with the boundary particles, the interaction force $F_{dc(II)}$ exerted by the particles inside the control volume element upon the continuous phase contained within the same volume element, follows from Equation 19, where F_{be} is to be elaborated further. Consider for this purpose the reaction force $-F_{be}$, i.e. the force exerted by the fluid outside the control volume element directly upon the boundary particles of group N_1 (Figure 2). This force $-F_{be}$ follows from balancing the pressure and stress forces acting on these n_1 boundary particles, i.e. on the local proportions $(1 - \varepsilon)$ of the faces of the control volume element. As $(1 - \varepsilon)$ may vary over distances of the order of r_0, the linear size of the control volume element, it is found that

$$-F_{be} = -V(1 - \varepsilon)p - V \cdot (1 - \varepsilon)\underline{\tau}_c \tag{23}$$

Substituting Equations 21 and 23 into Equation 19 then results in

$$F_{dc(II)} = pV\varepsilon + \underline{\tau}_c \cdot V\varepsilon + F_s \tag{24}$$

where F_s is still given by Equation 22. All remarks on F_s made earlier therefore still apply. A somewhat different derivation of Equation 24 has been presented [1, appendix 2]. Several authors [64, 65, 69, 75, 93, 98, 118] arrived at expressions for the interaction force that are quite similar to Equation 24 indeed. The present derivation clearly indicates how the terms $pV\varepsilon$ and $\underline{\tau}_c \cdot V\varepsilon$ come about in Equation 24. These terms are the subject of a more detailed discussion later in this chapter.

THE DERIVATION OF THE MOMENTUM BALANCES

General Aspects

The separate momentum balance equations for the two phases are derived by balancing over a cubic volume element $\Delta x \, \Delta y \, \Delta z$ (of size r_0^3) as dealt with earlier. The present method differs from the familiar technique as presented by Bird et al. [2] only in the two-phase nature of the flow. Thus, the momentum balance states, on the basis of the principle of conservation of momentum, that the rate of momentum accumulation in the cubic volume element is the resultant of the net momentum flows and the sum of the forces acting; applied to either phase:

$$\left\{\begin{array}{c} \text{rate of} \\ \text{momentum} \\ \text{accumulation} \end{array}\right\} = \left\{\begin{array}{c} \text{rate of} \\ \text{momentum} \\ \text{in} \end{array}\right\} - \left\{\begin{array}{c} \text{rate of} \\ \text{momentum} \\ \text{out} \end{array}\right\} + \left\{\begin{array}{c} \text{sum of forces} \\ \text{acting} \\ \text{on the phase of} \\ \text{interest} \end{array}\right\} \tag{25}$$

Momentum flows into and out of the cubic volume element by two mechanisms: by convection (that is, by virtue of the bulk fluid flow) and by molecular transfer (that is, by virtue of the velocity gradients). The forces acting on the volume element are first those arising from the pressure p of the continuous phase and the body force due to gravity, just as in single-phase flow [2]. In addition, inherent in two-phase flow there is a third force, viz. the interaction force experienced by either phase due to the presence and the relative motion of the companion phase. The latter force should occur with opposite sign in both momentum balances. On summation of the two separate balances the momentum balance of the two-phase flow as a whole is obtained, in which the interaction force no longer should occur. The early models developed for describing dilute gas-particle flows, however, were based on so-called one-way coupling: the gas flow field was not supposed to be affected by the presence and the motion of the particles, while, on the other hand, particle trajectories were determined by the motion of the supporting fluid [8–10]. The consequence of one-way coupling is that the balance equation for the total two-phase flow comprises the interaction force. This is obviously incorrect. Two further remarks on the concept of one-way coupling have to be added.

First of all, it has always been postulated to be valid for low solids loadings only. In addition, however, it violates Newton's law of action and reaction. Instead, the two-way physical coupling—from fluid to particles and vice versa—has now found general acceptance.

In balancing over the cubic volume element, Methods I and II for dealing with the boundary particles (Figure 2) have to be distinguished. The intermediate results in the derivation of the momentum balances, i.e. the terms representing the various contributions, are allowed to be different; the final formulation, the sum of all contributions, however, should be independent of the method by which the boundary particles have been treated.

As an illustration of the balancing method the derivation of the net convective momentum flow of phase k in the x-direction into the cubic volume element will now be presented. A constraint applied throughout the chapter is that the two phases are assumed to have constant densities. The actual convective momentum flow rate in, represented by

$$\left\{ \iint_{\substack{\Delta y, \Delta z \\ \text{at } x = x_1 \\ \text{phase k}}} \rho_k v'_{kx} v'_{kx} \, dy \, dz + \int_{\substack{\Delta x, \Delta z \\ \text{at } y = y_1 \\ \text{phase k}}} \rho_k v'_{kx} v'_{ky} \, dx \, dz + \int_{\substack{\Delta x, \Delta y \\ \text{at } z = z_1 \\ \text{phase k}}} \rho_k v'_{kx} v'_{kz} \, dx \, dy \right\} \Delta t \tag{26}$$

minus the actual rate out, represented by

$$\left\{ \iint_{\substack{\Delta y, \Delta z \\ \text{at } x = x_1 + \Delta x \\ \text{phase k}}} \rho_k v'_{kx} v'_{kx} \, dy \, dz + \int_{\substack{\Delta x, \Delta z \\ \text{at } y = y_1 + \Delta y \\ \text{phase k}}} o_k v'_{kx} v'_{ky} \, dx \, dz + \int_{\substack{\Delta x, \Delta y \\ \text{at } z = z_1 + \Delta z \\ \text{phase k}}} \rho_k v'_{kx} v'_{kz} \, dx \, dy \right\} \Delta t \tag{27}$$

makes the net rate in:

$$-\rho_k \left\{ \frac{\partial}{\partial x} \left(\alpha_k v_{kx} v_{kx} + \alpha_k \overline{v''_{kx} v''_{kx}} \right) + \frac{\partial}{\partial y} \left(\alpha_k v_{kx} v_{ky} + \alpha_k \overline{v''_{kx} v''_{ky}} \right) \right.$$
$$\left. + \frac{\partial}{\partial z} \left(\alpha_k v_{kx} v_{kz} + \alpha_k \overline{v''_{kx} v''_{kz}} \right) \right\} \Delta x \, \Delta y \, \Delta z \, \Delta t \tag{28}$$

in which α_k denotes the volume fraction of phase k. In deriving Expression 28 use has been made of the Equations 4 and 9. The volume fraction α_k reflects the number of times in the period of time Δt (of order t_0, see "The Length Scales of Interest and Their Use in Averaging") the flexible faces of the volume element have leapt particles approaching or leaving the volume element (see "The Boundary Particles of the Cubic Volume Element"). The products of the velocity fluctuations contribute to the total convective momentum transport in a way completely comparable to the role of Reynolds stresses in turbulent transport [87], in spite of the completely different origin. After introducing

$$\underline{R}_k = \alpha_k \rho_k \overline{v''_k v''_k} \tag{29}$$

the expression (28) for the net convective momentum influx of phase k in the x-direction can be rewritten as

$$-\left\{ \rho_k [\nabla \cdot \alpha_k v_k v_k]_x + [\nabla \cdot \underline{R}_k]_x \right\} \Delta x \, \Delta y \, \Delta z \, \Delta t \tag{30}$$

The Momentum Balance of the Continuous Phase

Whichever of Methods I and II for dealing with the boundary particles is adopted, three terms of the momentum balance of the continuous phase can immediately be written, since they are independent of that choice, viz.

$$\left\{ \begin{array}{c} \text{gain of} \\ \text{accumulation} \end{array} \right\} = \frac{\partial}{\partial t} \int_{\substack{\Delta x \, \Delta y \, \Delta z \, \Delta t \\ \text{cont. ph.}}} \rho_c v'_c \, dx \, dy \, dz \, dt = \rho_c \frac{\partial}{\partial t} (\varepsilon v_c) \, \Delta x \, \Delta y \, \Delta z \, \Delta t \tag{31}$$

$$\begin{Bmatrix} \text{net gain} \\ \text{due to convection} \end{Bmatrix} = -\{\rho_c \nabla \cdot \varepsilon v_c v_c + \nabla \cdot \underline{\underline{R}}_c\} \, \Delta x \, \Delta y \, \Delta z \, \Delta t \tag{32}$$

and

$$\begin{Bmatrix} \text{gain due to} \\ \text{body force} \end{Bmatrix} = \int_{\substack{\Delta x \, \Delta y \, \Delta z \, \Delta t \\ \text{cont. ph.}}} \rho_c g \, dx \, dy \, dz \, dt = \varepsilon \rho_c g \, \Delta x \, \Delta y \, \Delta z \, \Delta t \tag{33}$$

The three remaining terms of the momentum balance of the continuous phase, viz. the momentum flow by molecular transport, the pressure gradient term and the interaction force between the phases, differ accordingly as Method I or Method II is used for dealing with the boundary particles.

Method I

As in this method the flexible boundaries of the volume element are completely within the continuous phase at any instant during the period Δt, the net momentum flow by molecular transfer (shear) takes place within this phase. Hence, the volume fraction ε will not come into the expression for this net gain due to shear. For the rest, the derivation of the pertinent expression is analogous to that presented earlier for the convective momentum contribution; thus,

$$\begin{Bmatrix} \text{net gain} \\ \text{due to shear} \end{Bmatrix} = -\{\nabla \cdot \underline{\underline{\tau}}_c\} \, \Delta x \, \Delta y \, \Delta z \, \Delta t \tag{34}$$

Similarly, the force due to the pressure acts upon the full boundaries; hence,

$$\begin{Bmatrix} \text{gain due to} \\ \text{pressure force} \end{Bmatrix} = -(\nabla p) \, \Delta x \, \Delta y \, \Delta z \, \Delta t \tag{35}$$

without volume fraction ε having entered. Finally, the interaction force $\mathbf{F}_{dc(I)}$ has already been considered.

Equating, according to Equation 25, Equation 31 to the sum of Equations 32–35, dividing by $\Delta x \, \Delta y \, \Delta z \, \Delta t$, and adding $\mathbf{F}_{dc(I)}$ yields

$$\rho_c \left\{ \frac{\partial}{\partial t} \varepsilon v_c + \nabla \cdot \varepsilon v_c v_c \right\} = -\nabla \cdot \underline{\underline{R}}_c - \nabla \cdot \underline{\underline{\tau}}_c - \nabla p + \varepsilon \rho_c g + \mathbf{F}_{dc(I)} \tag{36}$$

Use of the continuity equation for the continuous phase and substitution of Equation 21 into Equation 36 finally lead to

$$\varepsilon \rho_c \frac{D}{Dt} v_c = \varepsilon \rho_c \left\{ \frac{\partial}{\partial t} v_c + v_c \cdot \nabla v_c \right\} = -\nabla \cdot \underline{\underline{R}}_c - \varepsilon \nabla \cdot \underline{\underline{\tau}}_c - \varepsilon \nabla p + \varepsilon \rho_c g + \mathbf{F}_s \tag{37}$$

where $\mathbf{F}_s$ is still given by Equation 22 and comprises at least the familiar drag force and the added mass force.

Method II

In this method the flexible boundaries of the control volume element touch on the boundary particles. As far as the continuous phase is concerned, the momentum flows due to molecular transfer (shear) take place through parts ε of the boundaries of the volume element only. Hence,

$$\begin{Bmatrix} \text{net gain} \\ \text{due to shear} \end{Bmatrix} = -\{\nabla \cdot \varepsilon \underline{\underline{\tau}}_c\} \, \Delta x \, \Delta y \, \Delta z \, \Delta t \tag{38}$$

Similarly, pressure contributes to the momentum balance of the continuous phase again via the parts ε of the volume element boundaries only. Hence,

$$\left\{ \begin{array}{l} \text{gain due to} \\ \text{pressure force} \end{array} \right\} = -(\nabla \varepsilon p)\, \Delta x\, \Delta y\, \Delta z\, \Delta t \tag{39}$$

Finally, the interaction force $\mathbf{F}_{dc(II)}$ was discussed earlier and now needs no further discussion.
Equating Equation 31 now to the sum of Equations 32, 33, 38, and 39, dividing them by $\Delta x\, \Delta y\, \Delta z\, \Delta t$, and adding $\mathbf{F}_{dc(II)}$ results in

$$\rho_c \left\{ \frac{\partial}{\partial t}\, \varepsilon \mathbf{v}_c + \nabla \cdot \varepsilon \mathbf{v}_c \mathbf{v}_c \right\} = -\nabla \cdot \underline{\underline{R}}_c - \nabla \cdot \varepsilon \underline{\underline{\tau}}_c - \nabla \varepsilon p + \varepsilon \rho_c \mathbf{g} + \mathbf{F}_{dc(II)} \tag{40}$$

Substituting Equation 24 into Equation 40 and using the continuity equation yields exactly the same final expression for the momentum balance of the continuous phase as found in the framework of Method I, viz. Equation 37. This identical result has been obtained in spite of the differences between separate Equations 21, 34, and 35 on the one hand and separate Equations 24, 38, and 39 on the other. Obviously, the sum of the three terms involved does not depend on the method adopted for dealing with the boundary particles.

The Momentum Balance of the Dispersed Phase

Again, three terms of the momentum balance of the dispersed phase are independent of the method adopted for dealing with the boundary particles, viz.

$$\left\{ \begin{array}{l} \text{gain of} \\ \text{accumulation} \end{array} \right\} = \rho_d \frac{\partial}{\partial t} \{(1 - \varepsilon)\mathbf{v}_d\}\, \Delta x\, \Delta y\, \Delta z\, \Delta t \tag{41}$$

$$\left\{ \begin{array}{l} \text{net gain} \\ \text{due to convection} \end{array} \right\} = -\{\rho_d \nabla \cdot (1 - \varepsilon)\mathbf{v}_d \mathbf{v}_d + \nabla \cdot \underline{\underline{R}}_d\}\, \Delta x\, \Delta y\, \Delta z\, \Delta t \tag{42}$$

and

$$\left\{ \begin{array}{l} \text{gain due to} \\ \text{body force} \end{array} \right\} = (1 - \varepsilon)\rho_d \mathbf{g}\, \Delta x\, \Delta y\, \Delta z\, \Delta t \tag{43}$$

The number and form of the remaining terms contributing to the momentum balance of the dispersed phase depend on whether Method I or Method II is used for dealing with the boundary particles.

Method I

As the flexible faces of the control volume element are completely within the continuous phase, there are no flows of momentum due to stresses and there are no pressure forces acting on the dispersed phase via its boundary particles. The only force being relevant is the interaction force $\mathbf{F}_{dc(I)}$ exerted by the particles within the control volume element upon the continuous phase. Equating Equation 41 to the sum of Equations 42 and 43, dividing them by $\Delta x\, \Delta y\, \Delta z\, \Delta t$, and subtracting $\mathbf{F}_{dc(I)}$ yields

$$\rho_d \left\{ \frac{\partial}{\partial t}(1 - \varepsilon)\mathbf{v}_d + \nabla \cdot (1 - \varepsilon)\mathbf{v}_d \mathbf{v}_d \right\} = -\nabla \cdot \underline{\underline{R}}_d + (1 - \varepsilon)\rho_d \mathbf{g} - \mathbf{F}_{dc(I)} \tag{44}$$

It has been argued before [1] that in the framework of Method I the tensor $\underline{R}_d$ should contain zero elements only, since in the framework of Method I the particles never touch and hence there is no mechanism for direct exchange of momentum between particles as would be required by non-zero elements of $\underline{R}_d$. The absence of a particle stress tensor $\underline{\sigma}_d$ can be explained in the same way. Remember that it has already been stated that Method I is only applicable in cases where $1 - \varepsilon$ has low values. Ignoring $\underline{R}_d$, employing the continuity equation of the dispersed phase, and substituting Equation 21 into Equation 44 eventually results in

$$(1 - \varepsilon)\rho_d \frac{D}{Dt} \mathbf{v}_d = (1 - \varepsilon)\rho_d \left\{ \frac{\partial}{\partial t} \mathbf{v}_d + \mathbf{v}_d \cdot \nabla \mathbf{v}_d \right\}$$

$$= -(1 - \varepsilon)\nabla \cdot \underline{\tau}_c - (1 - \varepsilon)\nabla p + (1 - \varepsilon)\rho_d \mathbf{g} - \mathbf{F}_s \qquad (45)$$

Method II

This method does allow for permanent or incidental contact between particles. This implies that, as far as the particles within the control volume element are concerned, $\underline{R}_d$ does not necessarily contain zero elements only and, hence, can no longer be ignored a priori. In addition, the particles outside the control volume element, in particular the boundary particles of group N_2 (Figure 2), might exert stresses on the particles within the control volume element via the boundary particles of group N_1. These stresses in the dispersed phase, along with the terms of $\underline{R}_d$, make up the particle stress tensor $\underline{\sigma}_d$. The total effect of this tensor on the motion of the dispersed phase is then represented by

$$\left\{ \begin{array}{l} \text{net gain due to} \\ \text{interparticle} \\ \text{forces and stresses} \end{array} \right\} = -\{\nabla \cdot (1 - \varepsilon)\underline{\sigma}_d\} \, \Delta x \, \Delta y \, \Delta z \, \Delta t \qquad (46)$$

which strongly resembles Equation 38, except that $\underline{\sigma}_d$ comprises $\underline{R}_d$, and $\underline{\tau}_c$ does not contain $\underline{R}_c$.

Further, there is a net gain of momentum by virtue of the pressure experienced by the boundary particles of group N_1 from the continuous phase outside the control volume element. These boundary particles occupy the part $1 - \varepsilon$ of the boundaries; hence,

$$\left\{ \begin{array}{l} \text{net gain due to} \\ \text{pressure forces} \end{array} \right\} = -\{\nabla(1 - \varepsilon)p\} \, \Delta x \, \Delta y \, \Delta z \, \Delta t \qquad (47)$$

Similarly, there is transfer of momentum due to stresses exerted by the continuous phase outside the control volume element upon the parts $1 - \varepsilon$ of the boundaries of the control volume element which are occupied by the boundary particles of group N_1. Hence,

$$\left\{ \begin{array}{l} \text{net gain due to} \\ \text{shear from} \\ \text{continuous phase} \end{array} \right\} = -\{\nabla \cdot (1 - \varepsilon)\underline{\tau}_c\} \, \Delta x \, \Delta y \, \Delta z \, \Delta t \qquad (48)$$

Note that the sum of the Equations 47 and 48 has already been encountered in the form of the force $-\mathbf{F}_{be}$, as represented by Equation 23. Finally, there is the force $\mathbf{F}_{dc(II)}$ exerted by the particles inside the control volume element upon the continuous phase contained.

Equating now Equation 41 to the sum of Equations 42, 43, 46, 47, and 48, dividing them by $\Delta x \, \Delta y \, \Delta z \, \Delta t$, and subtracting $\mathbf{F}_{dc(II)}$ yields

$$\rho_d \left\{ \frac{\partial}{\partial t} (1 - \varepsilon)\mathbf{v}_d + \nabla \cdot (1 - \varepsilon)\mathbf{v}_d \mathbf{v}_d \right\} = -\nabla \cdot (1 - \varepsilon)\underline{\sigma}_d - \nabla \cdot (1 - \varepsilon)\underline{\tau}_c - \nabla(1 - \varepsilon)p$$

$$+ (1 - \varepsilon)\rho_d \mathbf{g} - \mathbf{F}_{dc(II)} \qquad (49)$$

where $\underline{R}_d$ is contained within $\underline{\underline{\sigma}}_d$. Using again the continuity equation, and substituting Equation 24 into Equation 49 eventually results in the final formulation of the momentum balance of the dispersed phase, viz.

$$(1 - \varepsilon)\rho_d \frac{D}{Dt} \mathbf{v}_d = (1 - \varepsilon)\rho_d \left\{ \frac{\partial}{\partial t} \mathbf{v}_d + \mathbf{v}_d \cdot \nabla \mathbf{v}_d \right\}$$

$$= -\nabla \cdot (1 - \varepsilon)\underline{\underline{\sigma}}_d - (1 - \varepsilon)\nabla \cdot \underline{\underline{\tau}}_c - (1 - \varepsilon)\nabla p + (1 - \varepsilon)\rho_d \mathbf{g} - \mathbf{F}_s \qquad (50)$$

which, of course, differs from Equation 45 by the first term of the right-hand side only. Equation 50 is more generally valid, since, when adopting Method II to deal with the boundary particles, no restrictive assumptions are made as to the volume fraction of the dispersed phase, or with respect to particle-particle interactions.

CONCLUSION

The Final Results

After basic ideas of averaging and balancing, and working concepts of pressures, stresses, and interaction force had been dealt with, the momentum balances for the separate phases of dispersed two-phase flow were derived. For easy reference, the final formulations of the respective momentum balance equations are repeated here. For the continuous phase:

$$\varepsilon\rho_c\left(\frac{\partial}{\partial t} + \mathbf{v}_c \cdot \nabla\right)\mathbf{v}_c = -\nabla \cdot \underline{\underline{R}}_c - \varepsilon\nabla \cdot \underline{\underline{\tau}}_c - \varepsilon\nabla p + \varepsilon\rho_c \mathbf{g} + \mathbf{F}_s \qquad (37)$$

For the dispersed phase:

$$(1 - \varepsilon)\rho_d\left(\frac{\partial}{\partial t} + \mathbf{v}_d \cdot \nabla\right)\mathbf{v}_d = -\nabla \cdot (1 - \varepsilon)\underline{\underline{\sigma}}_d - (1 - \varepsilon)\nabla \cdot \underline{\underline{\tau}}_c - (1 - \varepsilon)\nabla p + (1 - \varepsilon)\rho_d \mathbf{g} - \mathbf{F}_s \qquad (50)$$

while

$$\mathbf{F}_s = \frac{1}{r_0^3}\sum_n \int_{S_p} \mathbf{n} \cdot (p''\underline{\underline{\delta}} + \underline{\underline{\tau}}_c'') \, dS \qquad (22)$$

$\mathbf{F}_s$ has to be conceived as comprising at least the drag force and the added mass force. Note that, while $\underline{R}_d$ is contained in the particle stress tensor $\underline{\underline{\sigma}}_d$, the tensor $\underline{\underline{R}}_c$ cannot be combined with the fluid stress tensor $\underline{\underline{\tau}}_c$. The main reason is that $\underline{\underline{R}}_c$ occurs in the momentum equation of the continuous phase only, whereas $\underline{\underline{\tau}}_c$ also plays a part in the dispersed phase momentum equation. This argument does not apply to $\underline{R}_d$ and $\underline{\underline{\sigma}}_d$. Some authors [46, 135], however, did combine $\underline{\underline{R}}_c$ and $\underline{\underline{\tau}}_c$ into a single stress tensor; this is now felt to be incorrect.

The previous results have been obtained for the specific case of dispersed two-phase flow. This very restriction made it possible to decompose flow variables into contributions related to two distinct length scales, as was expressed by means of Equation 1. This procedure was successfully employed in the elaboration of the interaction force (Equations 15 and 16), and in the interpretation of the resulting terms. A further characteristic feature of the present derivation is the use of flexible volume element faces in balancing over a cubic volume element. The striking advantage of flexible faces is that intersected boundary particles can be avoided. Two related methods of employing flexible faces have been adopted; both of them yield the same final formulation of the momentum balance equation for the continuous phase, viz. Equation 37. The most generally valid formulation of the dispersed phase momentum balance equation, viz. Equation 50, however, can only be obtained by means of Method II, in which the element faces coincide with particle boundaries as much as possible.

Summing up Equations 37 and 50 results in the momentum balance equation for dispersed two-phase flow as a whole:

$$\varepsilon\rho_c\left(\frac{\partial}{\partial t} + \mathbf{v}_c \cdot \nabla\right)\mathbf{v}_c + (1 - \varepsilon)\rho_d\left(\frac{\partial}{\partial t} + \mathbf{v}_d \cdot \nabla\right)\mathbf{v}_d$$

$$= -\nabla \cdot \underline{\mathbf{R}}_c - \nabla \cdot (1 - \varepsilon)\underline{\sigma}_d - \nabla \cdot \underline{\tau}_c - \nabla p + \bar{\rho}\mathbf{g} \qquad (51)$$

in which

$$\bar{\rho} = \varepsilon\rho_c + (1 - \varepsilon)\rho_d \qquad (52)$$

As a matter of fact, the interaction force $\mathbf{F}_s$ no longer occurs in overall momentum balance Equation 51.

It would be an enormous task to compare the present balance Equations 37 and 50 with the manifold formulations available in the literature. Earlier, several frameworks within which two-phase flow momentum balances were derived and applied have already been discussed. Various comments have already been presented on several aspects of momentum equations in order to rectify confusion in the literature. (A comparison of Equations 37 and 50 with the balance equations presented by Drew [135] clearly illustrates several misunderstandings.) At the end of this chapter only two further points deserve separate discussion, viz. first the correct formulation of the pressure gradient terms in the momentum equations, and secondly the question of well-posedness and real characteristics of the whole set of conservation equations. A separate discussion seems appropriate, since both items are the subject of spirited controversies in the literature.

The Pressure Gradient Terms in the Momentum Balances

The debate on the correct formulation of the pressure gradient terms in the momentum equations is concerned with the question as to whether in the continuous phase balance the pressure term should read as $\varepsilon\nabla p$ or as $\nabla\varepsilon p$, and in the dispersed phase balance as $(1 - \varepsilon)\nabla p$ or as $\nabla(1 - \varepsilon)p$. A related item is the physical significance of the term $p\nabla\varepsilon$: while it has been referred to as a diffusive force [35] or as a force due to volumetric displacement [34], other authors [119, 100] reject it as being physically unrealistic. In the present derivation [1] it has been found that the introduction of terms such as $p\nabla\varepsilon$ and $\underline{\tau}_c \cdot \nabla\varepsilon$ is only related to the way in which boundary particles are dealt with. Also, these terms do not occur in the final formulations of the balances, Equations 37 and 50, irrespective of the method adopted in dealing with the boundary particles.

In the light of the derivations presented in this chapter, the various formulations of the pressure gradient terms in the momentum balances as occurring in the literature are now discussed. In doing so, only the continuous phase balance will be considered, though all remarks made also apply to the dispersed phase balance (replacing ε by $1 - \varepsilon$).

It is obvious from the expressions for the interaction force $\mathbf{F}_{dc}$, viz. Equations 21 and 24, that pressure gradient terms and the forces $\mathbf{F}_{dc}$ and $\mathbf{F}_s$ are related. This is due to the decomposition of the interaction force $\mathbf{F}_{dc}$, as defined by Equation 15, into two contributions, one of which proves to be related to the continuum properties of pressure and stress, while the other one, denoted by $\mathbf{F}_s$, is argued to be dependent on the local instantaneous flow field disturbances connected to the presence and the motion of the individual particles. Hence, pressure gradient terms and interaction force must be considered together. This illustrates once more the statement by Bouré [76] that there should not be any controversy on the pressure gradient terms, provided these terms are considered in close connection with the remaining terms in the momentum balances.

First of all, Van Deemter and Van der Laan [99] arrived at a momentum balance for the continuous phase containing $-\nabla p + \mathbf{F}$. As no explicit statement has been made by these authors as to $\mathbf{F}$, i.e. as to whether $\mathbf{F}$ denotes $\mathbf{F}_{dc}$ or $\mathbf{F}_s$, no particular comment can be made. However, the formulations presented by Rudinger and Chang [89], Murray [91], Gidaspow et al. [74, 77–80], Di Giacinto et al. [10], and Needham and Merkin [108], comprising $-\nabla p + \mathbf{F}_s$ in the continuous phase balance, are obviously incorrect: these formulations do not reflect that part of the pressure gradient is directly acting on the dispersed phase particles (see Equation 21). This fact of physical reality was appreciated by several authors [35, 92, 107, 119–123] who, without giving detailed derivations or arguments, presented the correct result $-\varepsilon\nabla p + \mathbf{F}_s$ for the continuous phase balance. More recently, quite a few authors [64, 71, 93, 98, 117, 118, 124] arrived in the course of their derivations at the term $p\nabla\varepsilon$, but ultimately still found the correct final result $-\varepsilon\nabla p + \mathbf{F}_s$ for the continuous phase balance. Some authors [65, 69, 110] suggest that interfacial pressure plays a role and arrive at $-\nabla\varepsilon p + p_i\nabla\varepsilon + \mathbf{F}_s$ in the continuous phase balance. This concept has already been discussed.

Unfortunately, several researchers [72–74] reported $-\nabla\varepsilon p + \mathbf{F}_s$ in the continuous phase balance and $-\nabla(1 - \varepsilon)p - \mathbf{F}_s$ in the dispersed phase momentum balance (with $\mathbf{F}_s$ conceived as a simple drag force only) to render the set of conservation equations well-posed. The confusion that resulted may perhaps best be illustrated by means of a series of papers to which the names of Soo et al. are connected: Soo [35] first argued $-\varepsilon\nabla p + \mathbf{F}_s$ to be correct, but he changed his mind to arrive at $-\nabla\varepsilon p + \mathbf{F}_s$ [37, 125, 126]. This latter formulation was also adopted or derived by some other authors [3, 127, 128], while many papers [72–80, 84] are explicitly dealing with the dilemma: $\varepsilon\nabla p$ or $\nabla\varepsilon p$. Sha et al. [36, 75, 129] even introduced $\nabla\varepsilon p - Bp\nabla\varepsilon$, in which the so-called displacement factor B (with $0 \leq B \leq 1$) was assumed to be some function of particle size, fluid properties, and flow characteristics (flow patterns). Various views were presented giving support to all potential values of B between zero and unity [75], but none of them was sufficiently convincing. The present author judges that the dilemma substantially stems from the deficient and hazy analogy between the behavior of single-phase mixtures and two-phase flows that has been employed in deriving the two-phase momentum balances [34, 36, 37, 75]. The decisive argument as to the dilemma can only be found on the basis of a transparent derivation that encompasses all terms of the momentum balances, including $\mathbf{F}_{dc}$ [76].

It is hoped that the derivations in this chapter, though, strictly speaking, restricted to dispersed two-phase flow systems, confirm that the correct final formulation should read $-\varepsilon\nabla p + \mathbf{F}_s$ for the continuous phase and $-(1 - \varepsilon)\nabla p - \mathbf{F}_s$ for the dispersed phase, and that there is no physical basis for deviatory formulations, at least in dispersed two-phase flows.

Well-Posedness of the Set of Conservation Equations

This sub-section widens the scope of the discussion to comprise the whole set of conservation equations, viz. with respect to mass, momentum, and energy. Such a set of partial differential equations can be classified by using the method of characteristics [72, 81, 84, 85, 130, 131]. A set of partial differential equations is said to be hyperbolic whenever the characteristics are real-valued. Together with initial and boundary conditions a hyperbolic set of partial differential equations forms a well-posed initial-value problem. Complex characteristics are connected with ill-posedness of the set of partial differential equations.

In recent years there has been much confusion about the occurrence and significance of complex characteristics in two-phase flow equation systems. This issue first received wide-spread attention following early attempts to obtain numerical solutions to two-phase flow problems in nuclear reactor safety analyses. In these attempts unexpected stability difficulties were encountered that at first appeared to be numerical in nature. Subsequent analysis, however, showed that the differential equations being solved had complex characteristic roots [72, 83, 119] and therefore constituted an ill-posed initial-value problem.

It is generally believed [72, 81, 85, 132] that in two-phase flow, as in many other areas of physics and engineering science, physical phenomena should find their mathematical expression in terms of properly posed problems. It then follows that a set of partial differential equations possessing complex-valued characteristics must be incomplete or incorrect in some essential physical respect [72, 81, 84, 85]. This is not very surprising, since the momentum balances used in early times for describing the transient two-phase flows in nuclear reactor safety analyses (hypothetical loss-of-coolant accidents) were very rudimentary, as has been discussed already. Non-hyperbolicity in such cases implies that important physical effects have not been properly considered in the conservation equations. Various authors have therefore made suggestions as to the incorporation of additional terms and/or the modification of existing terms in the momentum balances, attempting to render the governing set of equations well-posed, i.e. to eliminate the complex characteristics. These suggestions comprise the added mass or relative acceleration contribution to the interaction force F_s [72, 133, 135], deviating formulations of the pressure gradient terms [72–74, 77–80, 125], viscous dissipation terms [84, 94, 134, 135], so-called inertial coupling terms [35–37, 75, 125, 136], transverse distribution parameters for phase fractions and axial velocities [132, 137], interfacial pressure forces [69, 110] and surface tension effects [81].

It is clear at the end of this chapter that the Equations 37 and 50 represent complete momentum balances that embody all essential features of dispersed two-phase flows. From the earlier discussions it follows that unequal phase pressures, interfacial pressure forces, and surface tension effects cannot play a part in dispersed two-phase flow as long as the concept of F_s as represented by Equation 22 is employed. In addition, the derivation presented earlier has undoubtedly pointed out that the pressure gradient term in the continuous phase momentum balance should read $-\varepsilon\nabla p$, provided that the interaction force is expressed as F_s. Hence, the conclusion drawn by Bouré [76] that incorporation of a $p\nabla\varepsilon$ term into the momentum balances (resulting in a $\nabla\varepsilon p$-term) along with F_s has no physical basis, is correct. Weisman and Tentner [85] have also queried whether pressure drop should occur in the continuous phase only, as suggested in several papers [10, 74, 77–80, 89, 91, 108]. All this implies that, in view of the well-posedness of the set of conservation equations, in the momentum equations as derived in this chapter the added mass contribution to F_s and the shear stress terms may be of paramount importance [135]. This also explains the attention recently paid in the literature to the added mass concept [46, 71, 72, 133, 135, 138, 139].

For reasons of completeness and clarity it should be added that generally the question of well-posedness and real characteristics bears no relation to the hydrodynamic stability of some flow condition with respect to disturbances of any wavelength. While the former question refers to mathematical properties relevant to numerical calculations, the latter point denotes a physical feature of the flow condition of interest. Therefore, flows described by means of equation systems with real characteristics can indeed exhibit physical instabilities, and complex characteristics are by no means required for describing such behavior. This has not only been proven in a formally mathematical sense [81, 84, 85], but also follows from the analyses by Rietema et al. [106, 107] and, after them, by other investigators [94–96, 98, 124]. All these authors found homogeneously fluidized beds to be unstable with respect to disturbances under many but not all conditions, notwithstanding the real characteristics of the set of conservation equations. Essential in their analyses is a term comprising a $\nabla\varepsilon$-component that represents some kind of elasticity of the particle assembly, making it stable to disturbances in a restricted domain of flow variables. The statement due to Lyczkowski et al. [72] that ill-posedness "manifests itself as instability of the differential equations to disturbances of all wavelengths" is therefore generally incorrect. It is only valid in the absence of so-called source and sink terms in the set of first-order differential equations [81, 84, 85], i.e. in the absence of terms without derivatives. Actually, such terms denote dissipative effects due to which physical disturbances are damped [81, 84, 94, 134]. Characteristics and hydrodynamic stability indeed refer to two distinct concepts that should not be confused.

NOTATION

a	arbitrary variable, some flux	n_0, n_1, n_2	number of particles in groups N_0, N_1, N_2
B	displacement factor		
d	particle diameter, L	N_0, N_1, N_2	groups of particles with different position with respect to control volume boundaries (Figure 2)
F	force, ML/t^2		
g	gravitational acceleration, L/t^2		
I	some concentration or force	p	pressure, M/Lt^2
l_d	scale of dispersion, L	r	radius, radial coordinate, L
L	scale of apparatus, equipment, etc., L	r_0	edge of control surface or volume element, L
n	normal to surface element	$\underline{\underline{R}}$	stress tensor due to velocity fluctuations, M/t^2L
n	number of particles in control volume element	S	surface or boundary area, L^2

t   time, t
t_p passage time of particle, t
T   relaxation time of L-scale variations, t

v   velocity, L/t
V   volume, L^3
x, y, z   rectangular coordinates, L

Greek Symbols

α volume fraction of phase k, L^3/L^3
γ surface or interfacial tension, M/t^2
Δ difference
$\underline{\delta}$ unit tensor

ε volume fraction of continuous phase, L^3/L^3
ρ density, M/L^3
$\underline{\sigma}$ pressure tensor $(= p\underline{\delta} + \underline{\tau})$, M/t^2L
$\underline{\tau}$ viscous stress tensor, M/t^2L

Superscripts

$'$ local point value
$''$ fluctuation around averaged value

Subscripts

b   at boundary of control volume element
c   continuous phase
d   dispersed phase
e   acting on continuous phase outside control volume element
i   interfacial

k   phase k
p   particle
s   slip between the two phases
r, x, y, z   in direction of r,x,y,z-coordinates
0   control surface area or volume or time (for averaging purposes)
I, II   according to Methods I, II

REFERENCES

*1. Rietema, K. and Van den Akker, H. E. A., "On the Momentum Equations in Dispersed Two-Phase Systems," *Int. J. Multiphase Flow*, vol. 9, no. 1 (1983). pp. 21–36.
*2. Bird, R. Byron, Stewart, Warren E. and Lightfoot, Edwin N., *Transport Phenomena*, John Wiley, 1960.
3. Panton, Ronald, "Flow Properties for the Continuum Viewpoint of a Non-Equilibrium Gas-Particle Mixture," *J. Fluid Mech.*, vol. 31 (1968). pp. 273–303.
4. Rowe, P. N., "A Personal View of Fluidization in 1967," in Drinkenburg, A. A. H., ed., *Proceedings of the International Symposium on Fluidization* (Eindhoven), Netherlands University Press, Amsterdam, 1967. pp. 11–20.
5. Van Deemter, J. J., "Report on Instabilities," in *ibid.*, pp. 91–98.
*6. Delhaye, J. M., "Two-Phase Pipe Flow," *Intern. Chem. Eng.*, vol. 23, no. 3 (July, 1983). pp. 385–410. Translation from French: "Les écoulements diphasiques gaz-liquide en conduite," *Entropie*, vol. 17, no. 99 (1981). pp. 3–25.
7. Wallis, G. B., "Review—Theoretical Models of Gas-Liquid Flows," *ASME J. Fluids Eng.*, vol. 104 (Sept., 1982). pp. 279–283.

* Denotes authoritative reviews and key references containing pioneering/original material.

8. Sharma, M. P. and Crowe, C. T., "A Novel Physico-Computational Model for Quasi One-Dimensional Gas-Particle Flows," *ASME J. Fluids Eng.*, vol. 100 (Sept., 1978). pp. 343–349.

9. Crowe, C. T., "Review—Numerical Models for Dilute Gas-Particle Flows," *ASME J. Fluids Eng.*, vol. 104 (Sept., 1982). pp. 297–303.

10. Di Giacinto, M., Sabetta, F. and Piva, R., "Two-Way Coupling Effects in Dilute Gas-Particle Flows," *ASME J. Fluids Eng.*, vol. 104 (Sept., 1982). pp. 304–312.

11. Joshi, J. B. and Shah, Y. T., "Hydrodynamic and Mixing Models for Bubble Column Reactors," *Chem. Eng. Commun.*, vol. 11 (1981). pp. 165–199.

12. Walter, James F. and Blanch, Harvey W., "Liquid Circulation Patterns and Their Effect on Gas Hold-up and Axial Mixing in Bubble Columns," *Chem. Eng. Commun.*, vol. 19 (1983). pp. 243–262.

13. Krishna, R., "Design and Scale-Up of Gas Fluidized Bed Reactors," in Rodrigues, A. E., Calo, J. M., and Sweed, N. H., eds., *Multiphase Chemical Reactors*, vol. 2, *Design Methods*, Sijthoff and Noordhoff, 1981.

14. Weisman, Joel and Tentner, Adrian, "Models for Estimation of Critical Flow in Two-Phase Systems," *Progr. Nucl. Energy*, vol. 2 (1978). pp. 183–197.

15. Wallis, G. B., "Critical Two-Phase Flow," *Int. J. Multiphase Flow*, vol. 6 (1980). pp. 97–112.

16. Hetsroni, Gad, ed., *Handbook of Multiphase Systems*, Hemishere, 1982.

17. Miyauchi, T., Furusaki, S., Morooka, S. and Ikeda, Y., "Transport Phenomena and Reaction in Fluidized Catalyst Beds," in Drew, Thomas B., Cokelet, Giles R., Hoopes, John W., and Vermeulen, Theodore, eds., *Advances in Chemical Engineering*, vol. 11, Academic Press, 1981. pp. 275–448.

18. Krishna, R., "Analogies in Multi-Phase Hydrodynamics" (in Dutch), *De Ingenieur*, vol. 93, no. 17 (23 Apr., 1981). pp. 8–11.

19. Rietema, K., "Science and Technology of Dispersed Two-Phase Systems—I and II," *Chem. Eng. Sci.*, vol. 37 (1982). pp. 1125–1150.

20. Beggs, H. Dale and Brill, James P., "A Study of Two-Phase Flow in Inclined Pipes," *J. Pet. Techn.*, (May, 1973). pp. 607–617.

21. Gould, Thomas L., "Compositional Two-Phase Flow in Pipelines," *J. Pet. Techn.*, (March, 1979). pp. 373–384.

22. Oliemans, R. V. A., "Two-Phase Flow in Gas-Transmission Pipelines," ASME paper No. 76-Pet.-25 presented at Joint Petr. Mech. Eng. & Press. Vessels and Piping Conf., 1976, Mexico City.

23. Taitel, Y. and Dukler, A. E., "A Model for Predicting Flow Regime Transitions in Horizontal and Near Horizontal Gas-Liquid Flow," *AIChE Journal*, vol. 22 (1976). pp. 47–55.

24. Taitel, Yehudah, Lee, Naugab and Dukler, A. E., "Transient Gas-Liquid Flow in Horizontal Pipes: Modeling the Flow Pattern Transitions," *AIChE Journal*, vol. 24 (1978). pp. 920–934.

25. Taitel, Yehuda, Bornea, Dvora and Dukler, A. E., "Modeling Flow Pattern Transitions for Steady Upward Gas-Liquid Flow in Vertical tubes," *AIChE Journal*, vol. 26 (1980). pp. 345–354.

26. Richter, H. J., "Separated Two-Phase Flow Model: Application to Critical Two-Phase Flow," *Int. J. Multiphase Flow*, vol. 9 (1983). pp. 511–530.

27. Van den Akker, H. E. A. and Bond, W. M., "Discharges of Saturated and Superheated Liquids from Pressure Vessels. Prediction of Homogeneous Choked Two-Phase Flow Through Pipes," Symp. on The Protection of Exothermic Reactors and Pressurised Storage Vessels (Chester), *IChemE Symp. Series No.* 85 (1984). pp. 91–108.

28. Rietema, K. and Ottengraf, S. P. P., "Laminar Liquid Circulation and Bubble Street Formation in a Gas-Liquid System," *Trans. I. Chem. Engrs.*, vol. 48 (1970). pp. T54–62.

29. Hills, J. H., "Radial Non-Uniformity of Velocity and Voidage in a Bubble Column," *Trans. I. Chem. Engrs.*, vol. 52 (1974). pp. 1–9.

30. Wijffels, J.-B. and Rietema, K., "Flow Patterns and Axial Mixing in Liquid-Liquid Spray Columns," Parts I and II, *Trans. I. Chem. Engrs.*, vol. 50 (1972). pp. 224–232 and pp. 233–239.

31. Anderson, W. J. and Pratt, H. R. C., "Wake Shedding and Circulatory Flow in Bubble and Droplet-Type Contactors," *Chem. Eng. Sci.*, vol. 33 (1978). pp. 995–1002.

32. Van den Akker, H. E. A. and Rietema, K., "Flow Patterns and Axial Mixing in Liquid-Liquid Spray Columns," Parts III and IV, *Trans. I. Chem. Engrs.*, vol. 57 (1979). pp. 84–93 and pp. 147–155.

33. Soo, S. L., "Dynamics of Multiphase Flow Systems," *IEC Fundamentals*, vol. 4 (1965). pp. 426–433.

34. Soo, S. L., *Fluid Dynamics of Multiphase Systems*, Blaisdell, 1967.

35. Soo, S. L., "On One-Dimensional Motion of a Single Component in Two Phases," *Int. J. Multiphase Flow*, vol. 3 (1976). pp. 79–82.

36. Sha, William T. and Soo, S. L., "Multidomain Multiphase Fluid Mechanics," *Int. J. Heat Mass Transfer*, vol. 21 (1978), pp. 1581–1595.

37. Chao, B. T., Sha, W. T. and Soo, S. L., "On Inertial Coupling in Dynamic Equations of Components in a Mixture," *Int. J. Multiphase Flow*, vol. 4 (1978). pp. 219–223.

38. Van Deemter, J. J., "On the Theory of the Ranque-Hilsch Cooling Effect," *Appl. Sci. Res. A*, vol. 3 (1952). pp. 174–196.

39. Tollert, H., "Die Wirkung der Magnuskraft in laminaren Strömungen-2. Teil. Der Quertrieb in Lösungen und Gasgemischen," *Chemie-Ing.-Technik*, vol. 26 (1954). pp. 270–278 (in German)

40. Beams, J. W. and Haynes, F. B., "An Ultracentrifuge for Gases and Vapors," *Phys. Rev.*, vol. 49 (1936). p. 644.

41. Beams, J. W., "High-Speed Centrifuging," *Rev. Mod. Physics*, vol. 10, no. 10 (1938). pp. 245–263.

42. No, Hee Cheon, "On Soo's Equations in Multidomain Multiphase Fluid Mechanics," *Int. J Multiphase Flow*, vol. 8 (1982). pp. 297–299.

43. Soo, S. L., "Equation of Motion of a Solid Particle Suspended in a Fluid," *Phys. Fluids*, vol 18, no. 2 (Feb., 1975). pp. 263–264.

44. Soo, S. L., "Net Effect of Pressure Gradient on a Sphere," *Phys. Fluids*, vol. 19, no. 5 (May 1976). p. 757.

45. Standart, G., "The Mass, Momentum, and Energy Equations for Heterogeneous Flow Systems," *Chem. Eng. Sci.*, vol. 19 (1964). pp. 227–236.

*46. Anderson, T. B. and Jackson, Roy, "A Fluid Mechanical Description of Fluidized Beds," *I&EC Fundamentals*, vol. 6, no. 4 (Nov., 1967). pp. 527–539.

47. Vernier, Philippe and Delhaye, Jean-Marc, "Equations générales des écoulements diphasiques appliqués à la thermohydrodynamique des réacteurs nucléaires à eau bouillant," *Acta Technica Belgica* EPE, vol. 4, no. 1–2 (1968). pp. 5–46. (in French).

48. Whitaker, Stephen, "The Transport Equations for Multiphase Systems," *Chem. Eng. Sci.*, vol 28 (1973). pp. 139–147.

49. Gray, William G., "A Derivation of the Equations for Multiphase Transport," *Chem Eng Sci.*, vol. 30 (1975). pp. 229–233.

50. Blake, Thomas R. and Garg, Sabodh K., "On the Species Transport Equation for Flow in Porous Media," *Water Resour. Res.*, vol. 12, no. 4 (Aug., 1976). pp. 748–750.

51. Gray, W. G. and Lee, P. C. Y., "On the Theorems for Local Volume Averaging of Multiphase Systems," *Int. J. Multiphase Flow*, vol. 3 (1977). pp. 333–340.

52. Gray, William G. and O'Neill, Kevin, "Comment on 'On the Species Transport Equation for Flow in Porous Media' by Thomas R. Blake and Sabodh K. Garg," *Water Resour. Res.*, vol 13, no. 3 (June, 1977). pp. 695–696.

53. Blake, T. R. and Garg. S. K., "Reply" (to Ref. 52), Water Resour. Res., vol. 13, no. 3 (June 1977). p. 697.

54. Tosun, Ismail and Willis, Max S., "Deviation Representation for the Volume Averaging Technique," *Chem. Eng. Sci.*, vol. 36 (1981). pp. 781–782.

55. Gray, William G., "On the Need for Consistent Manipulation in Volume Averaging," *Chem. Eng. Sci.*, vol. 37 (1982). pp. 121–122.

56. Tosun, Ismail and Willis, Max S., "Consistent Deviation Representations in Volume Averaging," *Chem. Eng. Sci.*, vol. 37 (1982). pp. 801–802.

57. Van den Akker, H. E. A., "Deviation Representations," *Chem. Eng. Sci.*, vol. 37 (1982). p. 803

58. Tosun, Ismail and Willis, Max. S., "Multiphase Deviations," *Chem. Eng. Sci.*, vol. 37 (1982). p. 804.

59. Gray, William G., "Local Volume Averaging of Multiphase Systems Using a Non-Constant Averaging Volume," *Int. J. Multiphase Flow*, vol. 9 (1983). pp. 755–761.

60. Slattery, John C., "General Balance Equation for a Phase Interface," *I&EC Fundamentals*, vol. 6, no. 1 (Feb., 1967). pp. 108–115.

61. Delhaye, J. M., "Jump Conditions and Entropy Sources in Two-Phase Systems. Local Instant Formulation," *Int. J. Multiphase Flow*, vol. 1 (1974). pp. 395–409.

62. Deemer, Arthur R. and Slattery, John C., "Balance Equations and Structural Models for Phase Interfaces," *Int. J. Multiphase Flow*, vol. 4 (1978). pp. 171–192.

63. Drew, Donald A., "Averaged Field Equations for Two-Phase Media," *Studies in Appl. Math.*, vol. L, no. 2 (June, 1971). pp. 133–168.

*64. Drew, Donald A. and Segel, Lee A., "Averaged Equations for Two-Phase Flows," *Studies in Appl. Math.*, vol. L, no. 3 (Sept., 1971). pp. 205–231.

65. Ishii, M., *Thermo-Fluid Dynamic Theory of Two-Phase Flow*, Eyrolles, Paris, 1975.

66. Hughes, E. D., "Macroscopic Balance Equations for Two-Phase Flow Models," *Nucl. Engng. Des.*, vol. 54 (1979). pp. 239–259.

67. Drew, Donald A. and Segel, Lee A., "Analysis of Fluidized Beds and Foams Using Averaged Equations," *Studies in Appl. Math.*, vol. L, no. 3 (Sept., 1971). pp. 233–257.

68. Yadigaroglu, G. and Lahey, R. T., Jr., "On the Various Forms of the Conservation Equations in Two-Phase Flow," *Int. J. Multiphase Flow*, vol. 2 (1976). pp. 477–494.

69. Stuhmiller, J. H., "The Influence of Interfacial Pressure Forces on the Character of Two-Phase Flow Model Equations," *Int. J. Multiphase Flow*, vol. 3 (1977). pp. 551–560.

70. Delhaye, J. M., "Two-Phase Flow Fundamentals," Seminar on Momentum, Heat and Mass Transfer in Two-Phase Energy and Chemical Systems; Interphase Phenomena in Two-Phase Flows, Dubrovnik (Yugoslavia), 1978.

*71. Drew, Donald A. and Lahey, Richard T., Jr., "Application of General Constitutive Principles to the Derivation of Multidimensional Two-Phase Flow Equations," *Int. J. Multiphase Flow*, vol. 5 (1979). pp. 243–264.

*72. Lyczkowski, Robert W., Gidaspow, Dimitri, Solbrig, Charles W. and Hughes, E. D., "Characteristics and Stability Analyses of Transient One-Dimensional Two-Phase Flow Equations and Their Finite Difference Approximations," *Nucl. Sci. Engng.*, vol. 66 (1978). pp. 378–396.

73. Gidaspow, D., "Fluid-Particle Systems," in: Kakac, S. and Mayinger, F., eds., *Two-Phase Flow and Heat Transfer*, Hemisphere Publishing Corp., 1977, vol. I, pp. 115–128.

74. Arastoopour, Hamid, "Hydrodynamic Analysis of Solids Transport," Ph. D. thesis, Illinois Inst. of Technology, Chicago, 1978.

75. Sha, W. T. and Soo, S. L., "On the Effect of $p\nabla\alpha$ Term in Multiphase Mechanics," *Int. J. Multiphase Flow*, vol. 5 (1979). pp. 153–158.

*76. Bouré, J. A., "On the Form of the Pressure Terms in the Momentum and Energy Equations of Two-Phase Flow Models," *Int. J. Multiphase Flow*, vol. 5 (1979), pp. 159–164.

77. Arastoopour, Hamid and Gidaspow, Dimitri, "Vertical Pneumatic Conveying Using Four Hydrodynamic Models," *I&EC Fundamentals*, vol. 18, no. 2 (1979). pp. 123–130.

78. Arastoopour, Hamid and Gidaspow, Dimitri, "Vertical Countercurrent Solids Gas Flow," *Chem. Eng. Sci.*, vol. 34 (1979). pp. 1063–1066.

79. Shih, Yang T., Arastoopour, Hamid and Weil, Sanford A., "Hydrodynamic Analysis of Horizontal Solids Transport," *I&EC Fundamentals*, vol. 21 (1982). pp. 37–43.

80. Arastoopour, Hamid, Lin, Shaw-Chan and Weil, S. A., "Analysis of Vertical Pneumatic Conveying of Solids Using Multiphase Flow Models," *AIChE Journal*, vol. 28 (1982). pp. 467–473

*81. Ramshaw, John D. and Trapp, John A., "Characteristics, Stability and Short-Wavelength Phenomena in Two-Phase Flow Equation Systems," *Nucl. Sci. Engng.*, vol. 66 (1978). pp. 93–102.

82. Rousseau, J. C. and Ferch, R. L., "A Note on Two-Phase Separated Flow Models," *Int. J. Multiphase Flow*, vol. 5 (1979). pp. 489–493.

83. Gidaspow, Dimitri, Introduction to "Modeling of Two-Phase Flow," Round Table Discussion (RT-1-2), *Proc. 5th Int. Heat Transfer Conference*, vol. VII (1974). p. 163.

*84. Arai, Masahiko, "Characteristics and Stability Analyses for Two-Phase Flow Equation Systems with Viscous Terms," *Nucl. Sci. Engng.*, vol. 74 (1980). pp. 77–83.

*85. Weisman, Joel and Tentner, Adrian, "Application of the Method of Characteristics to Solution of Nuclear Engineering Problems," *Nucl. Sci. Engng.*, vol. 78 (1981). pp. 1–29.

86. Corrsin, S. and Lumley, J., "On the Equation of Motion for a Particle in Turbulent Fluid," *Appl. Sci. Res. A*, vol. 6 (1956). pp. 114–116.

87. Hinze, J. O., *Turbulence*, McGraw-Hill, 1959. p. 460.

88. Hinze, J. O., "Momentum and Mechanical-Energy Balance Equations for a Flowing Homogeneous Suspension with Slip Between the Two Phases," *Appl. Sci. Res. A*, vol. 11 (1961). pp 33–46.

89. Rudinger, George and Chang, Angela, "Analysis of Nonsteady Two-Phase Flow," *Phys. Fluids*, vol. 7, no. 11 (Nov., 1964). pp. 1747–1754.

*90. Jackson, R., "The Mechanics of Fluidized Beds: Part I: The Stability of the State of Uniform Fluidization," *Trans. Instn. Chem. Engrs.*, vol. 41 (1963). pp. 13–21.

91. Murray, J. D., "On the Mathematics of Fluidization. Part 1: Fundamental Equations and Wave Propagation," *J. Fluid Mech.*, vol. 21 (1965). pp. 465–493.

92. Ruckenstein, E. and Tzeculescu, M., "On the Hydrodynamics of the Fluidized Bed," in Drinkenburg, *Eindhoven Symposium*, 1967. pp. 180–188. (see above Ref. 4).

93. Garg, S. K. and Pritchett, J. W., "Dynamics of Gas-Fluidized Beds," *J. Appl. Phys.*, vol. 46, no. 10 (Oct., 1975). pp. 4493–4500.

94. Blake, T. R., Garg, S. K., Levine, H. B. and Pritchett, J. W., "Computer Modeling of Coal Gasification Reactors. Year 1," Systems, Science and Software, La Jolla (Ca.), July 1976, Report FE-1770-15.

95. Gidaspow, Dimitri, Seo, Y. C. and Ettehadieh, Bozorg, "Hydrodynamics of Fluidization: Experimental and Theoretical Bubble Sizes in a Two-Dimensional Bed with a Jet," *Chem. Eng. Commun.*, vol. 22 (1983). pp. 253–272.

96. Gidaspow, Dimitri and Ettehadieh, Bozorg, "Fluidization in Two-Dimensional Beds with a Jet. 2: Hydrodynamic Modeling," *I&EC Fundamentals*, vol. 22 (1983). pp. 193–201.

97. Van den Akker, H. E. A., "Liquid-Liquid Spray Columns. Hydrodynamic Stability and Reduction of Axial Mixing," Ph. D. thesis, Eindhoven University of Technology, Netherlands, 1978. pp. 94–96.

98. Pritchett, John W., Blake, Thomas R. and Garg, Sabodh K., "A Numerical Model of Gas Fluidized Beds," *AIChE Symp. Series*, no. 176, vol. 74 (1978). pp. 134–148.

*99. Van Deemter, J. J. and Van der Laan, E. T., "Momentum and Energy Balances for Dispersed Two-Phase Flow," *Appl. Sci. Res. A*, vol. 10 (1960). pp. 102–108.

100. Crowe, C. T., "On the Dispersed Phase Flow Equations," *Seminar MHM Transfer, Dubrovnik*, 1978 (see above Ref. 70).

*101. Wallis, G. B., "The Terminal Speed of Single Drops or Bubbles in an Infinite Medium," *Int. J. Multiphase Flow*, vol. 1 (1974). pp. 491–511.

*102. Barnea, E. and Mizrahi, J., "A Generalized Approach to the Fluid Dynamics of Particulate Systems. Part 2: Sedimentation and Fluidization of Clouds of Spherical Liquid Drops," *Can. J. Chem. Engng.*, vol. 53 (1975). pp. 461–468.

103. LeVan, M. Douglas and Newman, J., "The Effect of Surfactant on the Terminal and Interfacial Velocities of a Bubble or Drop," *AIChE Journal*, vol. 22 (1976). pp. 695–701.

104. Massimilla, L., Donsi, G. and Zucchini, C., "The Structure of Bubble-Free Gas-Fluidized Beds of Fine Fluid Cracking Catalyst Particles," *Chem. Eng. Sci.*, vol. 27 (1972). pp. 2005–2015.

*105. Rietema, K., "The Effect of Interparticle Forces on the Expansion of a Homogeneous Gas-Fluidized Bed," *Chem. Eng. Sci.*, vol. 28 (1973). pp. 1493–1497.

106. Rietema, K. and Mutsers, S. M. P., "The Effect of Interparticle Forces on the Expansion of a Homogeneous Gas-Fluidized Bed," *Proc. Int. Symp. on Fluidization and Its Applications*, Toulouse, 1973. pp. 28.

*107. Mutsers, S. M. P. and Rietema, K., "The Effect of Interparticle Forces on the Expansion of a Homogeneous Gas-Fluidized Bed," *Powder Technology*, vol. 18 (1977). pp. 239–248.

108. Needham, D. J. and Merkin, J. H., "The Propagation of a Voidage Disturbance in a Uniformly Fluidized Bed," *J. Fluid Mech.*, vol. 131 (1983). pp. 427–454.

*109. Barnea, E. and Mizrahi, J., "A Generalized Approach to the Fluid Dynamics of Particulate Systems. Part 1: General Correlation for Fluidization and Sedimentation in Solid Multiparticle Systems," *Chem. Eng. J.*, vol. 5 (1973). pp. 171–189.

110. Nguyen, Hung, "One-dimensional Models for Transient Two-Phase Separated Flow," in Plesset, M. S. and Zuber, N., eds., *Proc. 3rd CSNI Specialist Meeting on Transient Two-Phase Flow (Pasadena, 1981)*, Hemisphere, 1983. pp. 389–402.

111. Pai, S. I., "A Critical Review of the Fundamental Equations of a Mixture of Gas and Small Solid Particles," *Z. Flugwiss.*, vol. 19 (1971). pp. 353–360.

112. Segré, G. and Silberberg, A., "Behavior of Macroscopic Rigid Spheres in Poiseuille Flow. Part 2: Experimental Results and Interpretation," *J. Fluid Mech.*, Vol. 14 (1962). pp. 136–157.

113. Oliver, D. R., "Influence of Particle Rotation on Radial Migration in the Poiseuille Flow of Suspensions," *Nature*, vol. 194 (1962). pp. 1269–1271.

114. Brenner, H., "Hydrodynamic Resistance of Particles at Small Reynolds Numbers," in Drew, T. B., Hoopes, J. W., Jr., and Vermeulen, T., eds., *Advances in Chemical Engineering*, vol. 6, Academic Press, 1966. pp. 287–438.

115. Ho, B. P. and Leal, L. G., "Inertial Migration of Rigid Spheres in Two-Dimensional Unidirectional Flows," *J. Fluid Mech.*, vol. 65 (1974). pp. 365–400.

116. Simha, R., "Untersuchungen über die Viskostät von Suspensionen and Lösungen," *Kolloid-Z.*, vol. 76 (1936). pp. 16–19 (in German).

117. Immich, Hans, "Impulsive Motion of a Suspension: Effect of Antisymmetric Stresses and Particle Rotation," *Int. J. Multiphase Flow*, vol. 6 (1980). pp. 441–471.

118. Pai, S. I. and Hsieh, T., "Interaction Terms in Gas-Solid Two-Phase Flows," *Z. Flugwiss.*, vol. 21 (1973). pp. 442–445.

119. Harlow, Francis H. and Amsden, Anthony A., "Numerical Calculation of Multiphase Fluid Flow," *J. Computational Phys.*, vol. 17 (1975). pp. 19–52.

*120. Pigford, Robert L. and Baron, Thomas, "Hydrodynamic Stability of a Fluidized bed," *I&EC Fundamentals*, vol. 4, no. 1 (Feb., 1965). pp. 81–87.

121. Sparenberg, J. A., "On the Equations of Motion of a Fluid with Suspended Particles or Gas Bubbles," *Appl. Sci. Res. A*, vol. 15 (1965). pp. 221–231.

122. Mecredy, R. C. and Hamilton, L. J., "The Effects of Nonequilibrium Heat, Mass, and Momentum Transfer on Two-Phase Sound Speed," *Int. J. Heat Mass Transfer*, vol. 15 (1972). pp. 61–72.

123. Crowe, Clayton T., "On Soo's Equations for the One-Dimensional Motion of Single-Component Two-Phase Flows," *Int. J. Multiphase Flow*, vol. 4 (1978). pp. 225–229 and 231.

124. Fanucci, Jerome B., Ness, Nathan and Yen, Ruey-Hor, "On the Formation of Bubbles in Gas-Particulate Fluidized Beds," *J. Fluid Mech.*, Vol. 94 (1979). pp. 353–367.

125. Soo, S. L., "Multiphase Mechanics of Single Component Two-Phase Flow," *Phys. Fluids*, vol. 20 (1977). pp. 568–570.

126. Soo, S. L., "Reply to Professor Crowe" (Ref. 123 above), *Int. J. Multiphase Flow*, vol. 4 (1978) pp. 229–231.

127. Deich, M. E. et al., "Critical Conditions in Two-Phase Flows with a Continuous Vapor or Gas Flow," *High Temperature*, vol. 12, no. 2 (1974). pp. 299–307.

128. Kim, J. M. and Seader, J. D., "Pressure Drop for Cocurrent Downflow of Gas-Solids Suspensions," *AIChE Journal*, vol. 29 (1983). pp. 353–360.

129. Chao, B. T., Sha, W. T. and Soo, S. L., "In Response to Discussions of G. B. Wallis (1978) and J. A. Bouré (1979)," *Int. J. Multiphase Flow*, vol. 6 (1980). pp. 383–384.

130. Trimble, G. D. and Turner, W. J., "Characteristics of Two-Phase One-Component Flow with Slip," *Nucl. Eng. Des.*, vol. 42 (1977). pp. 287–295.

131. Tentner, A. and Weisman, J., "The Use of the Method of Characteristics for Examination of Two-Phase Flow Behavior," *Nucl. Tech.*, vol. 37 (Jan., 1978). pp. 19–28.

132. Roy, R. P. and Ho, S., "Influence of Transverse Intraphase Velocity Profiles and Phase Fraction Distributions on the Character of Two-Phase Flow Equations," *Int. J. Heat Mass Transfer*, vol. 23 (1980). pp. 1162–1167.

133. Gidaspow, Dimitri, "A set of Hyperbolic Incompressible Two-Phase Flow Equations for Two Components," *AIChE Symp. Series No. 174*, vol. 74 (1978). pp. 186–190.

134. Travis, John R., Harlow, Francis H. and Amsden, Anthony A., "Numerical Calculation of Two-Phase Flows," *Nucl. Sci. Eng.*, vol. 61 (1976). pp. 1–i0.
135. Drew, D. A., "Mathematical Modeling of Two-Phase Flow," in Van Dyke, Milton, Wehausen, J. V. and Lumley, John L., *Annual Review of Fluid Mechanics*, vol. 15 (1983). pp. 261–291
136. Wallis, G. B., Discussion of the paper "On Inertial Coupling . . . " (Ref. 37 above), *Int. J. Multi phase Flow*, vol. 4 (1978). pp. 585–586.
137. Roy, Ramendra P. and Ho, S. Allen, "An Unequal Velocity, Unequal Temperature Two-Fluid Description of Transient Vapor-Liquid Flow in Channels," *Nucl. Sci. Eng.*, vol. 81 (1982). pp. 459–467.
138. Drew, D., Cheng, L. and Lahey, R. T., Jr., "The Analysis of Virtual Mass Effects in Two-Phase Flow," *Int. J. Multiphase Flow*, vol. 5 (1979). pp. 233–242.
*139. Lahey, R. T., Jr., Cheng, L. Y., Drew, D. A. and Flaherty, J. E., "The Effect of Virtual Mass on the Numerical Stability of Accelerating Two-Phase Flows," *Int. J. Multiphase Flow*, vol. ((1980). pp. 281–294.

SECTION II

FLOW REGIMES, HOLD-UP, AND PRESSURE DROP

CHAPTER 16

FLOW PATTERN TRANSITION IN TWO-PHASE GAS-LIQUID FLOWS

Dvora Barnea and **Yehuda Taitel**

Faculty of Engineering
Tel-Aviv University
Tel-Aviv, Israel

CONTENTS

INTRODUCTION

Gas-liquid two-phase flow in horizontal, vertical, and inclined pipes occurs in a wide variety of industrial applications such as petroleum industry, chemical plants, heat transfer equipment with change of phase, nuclear reactors, and geothermal energy production.

In gas-liquid flow the two phases can be distributed in the conduit in many configurations called flow regimes or flow patterns differing from each other in the spatial distribution of the interface. The flow pattern depends on the operational variables, physical properties of the fluids, and geometrical variables of the system. Hydrodynamics of the flow, as well as the mechanisms of momentum, heat and mass transfer, change significantly from one flow regime to another. As a result, accurate understanding of any process in two-phase flow depends on the knowledge of the existing flow pattern, and determining the flow pattern is the first step for developing techniques to accurately predict pressure drop, heat and mass transfer, and liquid holdup, etc.

This chapter describes and classifies the various flow patterns in horizontal, vertical, and inclined gas liquid flow in pipes and examines the conditions under which transitions among flow patterns occur.

FLOW PATTERN CLASSIFICATION

The flow observed in two-phase gas liquid flow may take many different configurations with respect to the distribution of the gas-liquid interface. Some of the configurations are chaotic and difficult to classify, whereas others can be clearly defined. Transitions between the various configurations are usually gradual with respect to the flow rate changes or the pipe inclination, but sometimes may be quite sharp.

The main task in classifying the flow patterns is to group together flow configurations that have common character according to some defined definitions. The designation of the flow pattern should be based on the flow configuration that has basically the same character, pertaining to the distribution of the interfaces and the mechanisms dominating pressure drop and heat and mass transfer. This task is not easy nor unique. It depends largely on the individual interpretation of the different researchers. Some researchers detailed as many basic configurations as possible while others try to group the flow patterns to the minimum essentials.

Unfortunately, up to now the designation of flow patterns has not yet been accurately standardized and in many cases the flow pattern definition is quite loose allowing a considerable freedom and overlap of the boundaries that separate the flow patterns.

Recent attitudes of most researchers is to minimize the number of the flow patterns. It is, however, still desired to reach standardization, so that data from different laboratories could be correctly interpreted and compared. It seems that recent work indicates a tendency to reach an agreed standard. Barnea et al. [1] proposed the following definitions, which are fairly close to the recent trend.

Horizontal Pipes (Figure 1)

Stratified (S). Liquid flows at the bottom of the pipe with gas at the top. The stratified pattern is subdivided into stratified smooth (SS) where the liquid surface is smooth, and stratified wavy (SW) where the interface is wavy.

Intermittent (I). In this flow pattern the liquid inventory in the pipe is non-uniformly distributed axially. Plugs or slugs of liquid that fill the pipe are separated by gas zones that contain a stratified liquid layer flowing along the bottom of the pipe. The liquid may be aerated by small bubbles, which are concentrated at the front of the liquid slug and the top of the pipe. The intermittent pattern is usually subdivided into slug and elongated bubble flow patterns. The elongated bubble pattern is considered the limiting case of slug flow when the liquid slug is free of entrained gas bubbles. With this criterion the elongated bubble-slug transition is quite sharp and easy to identify.

Annular (A). The liquid flows as a film around the pipe wall. A liquid film surrounds a core of high-velocity gas that may contain entrained liquid droplets. The film at the bottom is normally thicker

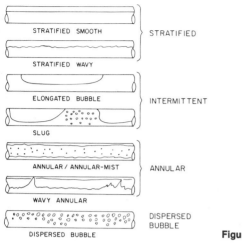

STRATIFIED SMOOTH   } STRATIFIED

STRATIFIED WAVY

ELONGATED BUBBLE   } INTERMITTENT

SLUG

ANNULAR / ANNULAR-MIST   ANNULAR

WAVY ANNULAR

DISPERSED BUBBLE   DISPERSED BUBBLE

Figure 1. Flow pattern in horizontal pipe flow.

than at the top depending on the flow rates of liquid and gas. At low gas rates at which transition to annular from slug flow or stratified flow is observed, most of the liquid flows at the bottom of the pipe. The upper walls are intermittently wetted by large aerated, unstable waves sweeping through the pipe. This is not slug flow, which requires a competent bridge of liquid, nor is it fully developed annular flow, which requires a stable film over the entire pipe perimeter. Thus, it is designated as the wavy annular pattern. Nicholson, Aziz, and Gregory [2] also recognized the existence of this hybrid pattern between annular and slug flow and designated it as "proto-slug" flow.

Dispersed bubble (DB). The gas phase is distributed as discrete bubbles within a continuous liquid phase. At the transition boundary most bubbles are located near the top, as the liquid rate increases, the bubbles are dispersed more uniformly.

Vertical Pipes (Figure 2)

Bubble flow. The gas phase is approximately uniformly distributed in the form of small discrete bubbles in a continuous liquid phase. The flow is designated as bubble flow (B) at low liquid flow

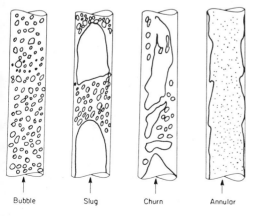

Bubble   Slug   Churn   Annular

Figure 2. Flow pattern in vertical pipe flow.

rate and as dispersed bubble (DB) at high liquid rate in which case the bubbles are finely dispersed in the liquid. This distinction, however, is not always clearly separable.

Slug flow (SL). Most of the gas is located in large bullet-shaped bubbles that have a diameter almost equal to the pipe diameter and move upward. These bubbles are sometimes designated as "Taylor bubbles." The Taylor bubbles are separated by slugs of continuous liquid that bridges the pipe and usually contains small gas bubbles. Between the Taylor bubbles and the pipe wall, liquid flows downwards in the form of a thin falling film. This flow pattern is sometimes designated as plug flow or piston flow. When the flow is relatively slow, has well-defined gas–liquid boundaries, and the liquid slug is free of bubbles, the term plug is sometimes used. When the flow is faster, boundaries are not very clearly discerned and froth is generated, the term slug flow is used.

Churn flow (CH). This is similar to slug flow, but is much more chaotic, frothy, and disordered. The bullet-shaped Taylor bubble becomes narrow and its shape is distorted. The continuity of the liquid in the slug between successive Taylor bubbles is destroyed by a high gas concentration in the slug, and as this happens the liquid slug falls. This liquid accumulates, forms a bridge, and is again lifted by the gas. Thus, typical to churn flow is the oscillatory motion of the liquid slug. For higher rates the flow is even more disordered and is sometimes called froth flow.

Annular flow (A). This flow is characterized by the continuity of the gas phase along the pipe in the core. Liquid phase moves upwards partially as wavy liquid film and partially in the form of drops entrained in the gas core. The annular flow is termed wispy annular when the entrained phase is in the form of large lumps or "wisps." The terms froth, mist, or semi-annular flow have been used to describe conditions between churn and annular.

In vertical downward flow as well as in upward and downward inclined flows the flow patterns observed are essentially similar to those described previously and are covered by the aforementioned definitions.

Published work introduced many terms related to the flow pattern classification, usually without exact definition. Those are repeated here for the sake of generality.

For horizontal flow the following terminology has been used [1–7]: Stratified flows were designated as stratified, stratified smooth, stratified wavy, laminar stratified, stratified + ripple, stratified + roll waves, stratified + inertial waves and separated flow. For intermittent flows the terms used were: Plug, bubble, elongated bubble, slug, slug and froth, proto slug, and intermittent. Annular type flow was designated as: Annular, annular + slug, annular + droplets, annular + blow through, droplets, froth, pulsating froth, wavy annular, semi-annular, mist, annular mist, and spray. Dispersed bubble flow was termed as bubble flow, dispersed bubble, and homogeneous flow.

For vertical flow the distinction among the flow patterns is not always clear and the following terms have been used to classify upward flow patterns [4, 7–16]: Bubble, dispersed bubble, homogeneous, slug, bubble or slug, plug, piston, slug annular, slug and semi-annular, quiet slug, frothy slug, dispersed slug, churn, froth, annular, pulsating annular, froth at wall, wispy annular, liquid phase continuous, alternating phases, both phases continuous, gas phase continuous, and choked flow.

FLOW PATTERN DETECTION

Experimental detection of the flow pattern and of the transition boundaries separating the various flow patterns is based on the predetermined definitions of the flow patterns. But even where clear definitions exist the flow pattern determination from the experimental results is not obvious [17a]. The flow for a large range of operating conditions is fast and chaotic and the experimental observations cannot be correctly interpreted. In addition the transition between flow patterns is usually a gradual process and the exact transition boundary is not always determined sharply. A brief review of accepted methods that have been used for the detection of the flow patterns is given herewith.

Visual Observation and Photography

Flow pattern information in gas-liquid flow is usually obtained by visual observation of the flow in transparent pipes. Clear observation is not possible at high liquid and gas flow rates, and high-speed photography must be used. Photographic studies were performed by Hewitt and Roberts [12], Bergles and Sue [18], Raisson [19] and Hsu and Graham [20]. If the fluids on the pipe walls are opaque, X-rays techniques can be employed [12, 21].

Conductance Probe

The visual observation technique is often criticized as being subjective, so more objective devices for determining flow pattern were developed. The most popular and simple of these is the conductance probe technique. Needle probes are inserted into the flow and the current from the needle tip is measured. The time trace of the current represents the distribution of the phases and the flow pattern [22–27]. This technique was in many instances not specific for all flow patterns.

Recently, Barnea et al. [1] used an improved set of conductance probes and were able to obtain fingerprints that characterize all flow patterns satisfactorily. The basic probe design for application to horizontal and inclined tubes is shown in Figure 3. Three probes designated as A, B, and C were used at different locations to detect flow patterns in horizontal and slightly inclined pipes. The flat large electrode E or D is located in this case at the bottom of the pipe.

Probes A and B are teflon-coated electrodes with exposed stainless steel tips. Probe B is designed to detect bubbles at about 3 mm below the top of the pipe. Since the probe is quite small, it can easily detect even small gas bubbles yielding zero voltage during a bubble passage. The fall, as well as the rise, of the voltage has been found immediate and the voltage fluctuates from zero to maximum. Probe A is flat with the upper part of the wall. It is designed to detect any surface wetness around the inner tube periphery. Even thin liquid films present in annular flow or the remaining film after the passage of the liquid slug in intermittent flow causes a voltage output of this probe.

Probe C is designed to detect the liquid level under stratified conditions. It is constructed of a non-isulated needle that is inserted vertically along the pipe diameter and almost reaches (about 3-mm gap) the bottom flat electrode. A change of the liquid level interface is easily detected by this probe.

In vertical upflow, the flow is symmetrical and from this point of view, less complicated; two probes were sufficient to detect the flow patterns. Probe A was used for the same purpose as in the horizontal case. Probe B was extended to the center of the pipe to detect bubbles at the tube centerline.

Stratified flow was detected by zero voltage output from probes A and B. In this case probe C was used to distinguish between stratified smooth and stratified wavy, where the wavy flow was indicated by the wavy shaped signal. Figure 4A shows a sequence of three traces of stratified flow that were taken as the gas flow rate increased gradually from stratified smooth to stratified wavy. The middle trace corresponds to the transition boundary itself.

A voltage output from probe A while probe B is dry, except possibly for short and infrequent pulses, indicates annular flow. A wavy output from probe A indicates "normal" annular flow (Figure 4D). When probe A shows large pulses with a tendency to drain and dryout as indicated by the smooth decaying signal after the pulse (as in intermittent flow), the flow is wavy annular (Figure 4E).

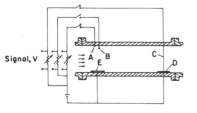

Signal, V

Figure 3. Electrode configuration for conductance method.

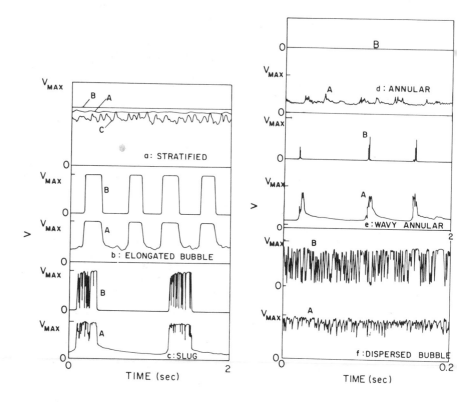

Figure 4. Time traces from conductance probes—horizontal air/water flow.

A voltage output from both probes A and B indicates intermittent or dispersed bubble flow. The exact pattern is detected by probe B alone. Dispersed bubble flow is characterized by uniform, high-frequency, crowded pulses of magnitude zero to maximum voltage (Figure 4F). Intermittent flow is characterized by the intermittent, rectangular, long pulses separated by zero voltage. Slug flow is distinguished from elongated bubble flow when bubbles are detected within the liquid slug zone (Figures 4B and C).

For vertical upflow the exact flow pattern is detected by probe B alone. Dispersed bubble flow is indicated by short abrupt fall of the output voltage. Typical for both slug and churn flow is the intermittent appearance of slug and gas zones. In churn flow the slug zone is short and the output trace is pointed at the top separated by long zero output of the gas zone, whereas the trace for slug flow has a rectangular characteristic, "flat" at top, and normally contains gas bubbles (Figure 5). In annular flow the output of probe B is zero while probe A output is a wavy signal.

This present method is limited to electrically conducting liquids. The actual results were obtained for water-air systems only, and the applicability of this method for non air-water systems remains to be determined.

Hot Wire Probe

Another probe technique is the hot wire anemometry, which has been used by Hsu et al. [28]. In this technique the rate of heat dissipation from a hot wire probe, exposed alternately to liquid

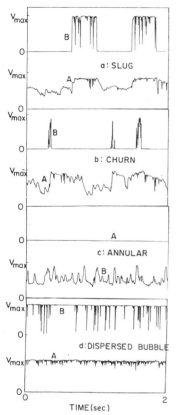

Figure 5. Time traces from conductance probes—vertical air/water flow.

and gas, is measured. Since the physical properties of the liquid and gas are very different the variations due to change of phase are not confused with that due to velocity fluctuations.

Photon Attenuation Technique

This is another technique that has been extensively used for flow pattern detection. In this technique absorption of x-rays or γ-rays by the liquid phase is used to measure the void fraction along either a single beam or an array of multiple beams across the flow path [29–33]. Jones and Zuber [29] used the probability density function (PDF) of the void fraction fluctuation to discriminate between flow patterns in upwards vertical flow. Figure 6 shows typical results of the PDF for bubbly slug and annular flows. Vince and Lahey [32] used x-rays to measure a series of chordal average void fractions and generate probability density function and power spectral density function. They pointed out that the moments of the PDF indicate the various flow regime transitions.

Pressure Fluctuations

Analysis of the pressure fluctuations to identify flow pattern was used by Hubbard and Dukler [34] who measured the pressure fluctuations in horizontal air-water flows and developed a method to determine the flow pattern from the spectral distribution of the wall pressure fluctuations. The

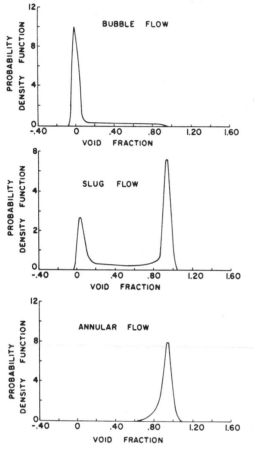

Figure 6. Probability density function of void fraction [29].

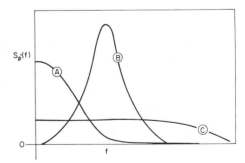

Figure 7. Power spectral density of wall pressure fluctuations [34].

A = SEPARATED FLOWS

B = INTERMITTENT

C = DISPERSED

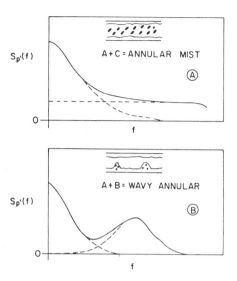

$S_{p'}(f)$

A+C = ANNULAR MIST

(A)

0

f

$S_{p'}(f)$

A+B = WAVY ANNULAR

(B)

0

f

Figure 8. Superposed spectra [34].

three basic types of spectra observed are shown in Figure 7. Type A spectra corresponds to separated flows, namely stratified flow and annular flow with low entrainment, and its spectra is characteristic of turbulent flow with a maximum at zero frequency. Type B spectra corresponds to intermittent flow and is typical of a periodic process. Type C spectra corresponds to dispersed flows namely bubble or spray flows and its spectra is typical to white noise. Figure 8 shows that superposition of two basic patterns is observed as a superposition of their spectra. Hubbard and Dukler [34], however, could not discriminate by their method between stratified and annular flows or between the dispersed liquid and dispersed gas flows.

Weisman et al. [6] attempted to develop relatively simple criteria that could be readily applied to the oscillograph trace of the pressure drop measured between two pressure taps 15 cm apart. They developed a set of criteria based primarily on the ratio of amplitude of the trace to the amplitude of a "standard slug." Their results are summarized in Table 1.

Recently, Tutu [35] pointed out that for vertical flow and widely different gas and liquid densities the variation of the local pressure drop with time can be used as a diagnostic tool.

Summary

There are two basic flow pattern identifications. The first is based on void fraction detection. This category covers most of the aforementioned techniques such as conductance probe, hot wire probe, and photon attenuation technique. Note that also visual observation and photographic techniques are essentially based on visual evaluation of the void fraction. The second method is based on the experimental observation that the pressure fluctuations along a pipe seem to depend on the flow pattern.

The void detection method seems to be superior to the pressure detection method because void detection is more closely related to the fluids distribution.

The void fraction signal and the pressure signal can be interpreted by three basic ways:

1. Direct readout of the trace.
2. Spectral density function (based on frequency domain).
3. Probability density function or average amplitude (based on amplitude domain).

Obviously, the latter methods are more complex, yet, so far no real advantage has been proven compared to the direct readout of the trace.

Table 1
Criteria for Determining Flow Patterns on Basis of ΔP Fluctuations [6]

Amplitude ratio* = R	Frequency = F		Range of applicability in horizontal air-water flow	
		Flow Pattern	$G_{water} \dfrac{kg}{hr\text{-}m^2}$	$G_{air} \dfrac{kg}{hr\text{-}m^2}$
$R \geq 2.5$		Homogeneous	$5 \times 10^5 \leq G_w \leq 5 \times 10^7$	$3 \times 10^4 \leq G_a \leq 2 \times 10^5$
$R \leq 2.5$		Annular	$5 \times 10^5 \leq G_w \leq 5 \times 10^7$	$3 \times 10^4 \leq G_a \leq 2 \times 10^5$
Pressure fluctuation trace characterized by a pressure peak followed by a quiescent region whose length is at least twice the length of the peak		Slug	$5 \times 10^5 \leq G_w \leq 5 \times 10^6$	$5 \times 10^3 \leq G_a \leq 5 \times 10^4$
$R \geq 0.75$		Annular	$5 \times 10^4 \leq G_w \leq 5 \times 10^5$	$5 \times 10^4 \leq G_a$
$R \leq 0.75$ V 4 cycles/sec		Wavy	$5 \times 10^6 \leq G_w \leq 5 \times 10^5$	$1.5 \times 10^4 \leq G_a \leq 5 \times 10^4$
$F \geq 7$ cycles/sec		Homogeneous	$5 \times 10^6 \leq G_w \leq 5 \times 10^7$	$5 \times 10^2 \leq G_a \leq 5 \times 10^3$
$F \leq 6.5$ cycles/sec		Plug	$5 \times 10^6 \leq G_w \leq 5 \times 10^7$	$5 \times 10^2 \leq G_a \leq 5 \times 10^3$
$R \geq 0.2$		Wavy	$5 \times 10^4 \leq G_w \leq 5 \times 10^5$	$1.5 \times 10^4 \leq G_a \leq 5 \times 10^4$
$R \leq 0.2$		Stratified	$5 \times 10^4 \leq G_w \leq 5 \times 10^5$	$5 \times 10^2 \leq G_a \leq 1.5 \times 10^4$

* *Amplitude ratio based on the ratio of amplitude of the trace to the amplitude of the standard slug flow at fixed G_w and G_a:*

$$G_w \simeq 1.1 \times 10^6 \, kg/hr \, m^2$$

$$G_a \simeq 1.5 \times 10^4 \, kg/hr \, m^2$$

FLOW PATTERN PREDICTION

Experimental data on flow patterns and the transition boundaries are usually mapped on a two-dimensional plot. Two basic types of coordinates were used for this mapping—one that uses dimensional coordinates such as superficial velocities, mass superficial velocities, or momentum flux; and another that uses dimensionless coordinates in which some kind of dimensionless groups are used as coordinates.

The dimensional coordinates maps are inherently limited to the range of data and flow conditions under which the experiments were conducted. In spite of this limitation, it is widely used because of its simplicity and ease of use. Figure 9 shows an example of such a map [5].

Maps based on dimensionless coordinates were suggested using coordinates such as the Froude number, gas volumetric ratio, Reynolds number, liquid, and gas mass flow rate ratio. Figure 10 shows a map by Spedding and Nguyen [7], who used as coordinates $(V_T/\sqrt{gD})^{1/2}$ vs. Q_L/Q_G. Q_L and Q_G are the liquid and gas volumetric flow rates, respectively, and V_T is the average total velocity in the pipe. D is the pipe diameter and g the acceleration of gravity.

Some used a mixed coordinate system. For example, the well known Baker map (Figure 11) [3] uses G/λ vs. $L\lambda\psi/G$, where G is the gas mass velocity (a dimensional coordinate) and L/G is a ratio of liquid and gas mass flow rates. The fluid properties enter as the dimensionless correction

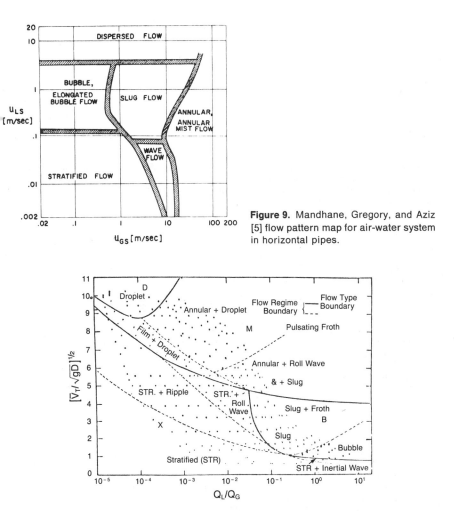

Figure 9. Mandhane, Gregory, and Aziz [5] flow pattern map for air-water system in horizontal pipes.

Figure 10. Spedding and Nguyen [7] flow regime map for horizontal flow (D—droplet; X—stratification; M—mixed; B—bubble)

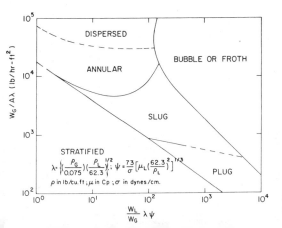

$$\lambda = \left\{ \left(\frac{\rho_G}{0.075} \right) \left(\frac{\rho_L}{62.3} \right) \right\}^{1/2}; \; \psi = \frac{73}{\sigma} \left[\mu_L \left(\frac{62.3}{\rho_L} \right)^2 \right]^{1/3}$$

ρ in lb/cu.ft ; μ in Cp ; σ in dynes/cm.

Figure 11. Baker [3] flow pattern map.

factors defined as

$$\lambda = \left[\left(\frac{\rho_G}{0.075}\right)\left(\frac{\rho_L}{62.3}\right)\right]^{1/2}$$

$$\psi = \frac{73.0}{\sigma}\left[\left(\frac{\mu_L}{1.0}\right)\left(\frac{62.3}{\rho_L}\right)^2\right]^{1/3}$$

where ρ_G and ρ_L are the gas and liquid densities in lb/ft^3, μ_L is the liquid viscosity (centipoise), and σ is the surface tension expressed in (dyne/cm).

Maps that are based on dimensionless coordinates carry more weight as being more general since, if properly constructed, they should be universally correct and independent of fluid properties and pipe size. Unfortunately, determining the "correct" dimensionless coordinates for flow pattern is not at all trivial. There is also no guarantee that two dimensionless coordinates are sufficient to determine the flow pattern boundaries.

Dimensionless analysis is the straightforward approach to select the proper dimensionless coordinates. It is applied by "guessing" the physical variables that affect the flow patterns. Under isothermal incompressible condition these are the liquid and gas flow rates (or the superficial velocities u_{LS} and u_{GS}), the liquid and gas densities and viscosities (ρ_L, ρ_G, μ_L and μ_G), pipe diameter (D), pipe roughness (ε), pipe inclination angle (β), acceleration of gravity (g), liquid surface tension (σ), and solid liquid gas contact wetting angle (γ).

The flow pattern transition boundaries should be a function of all these variables. Note that this is already a reduced set of variables as it is assumed that the entrance geometry has no influence on the steady state flow pattern.

Using Buckingham π method one can show that the flow pattern boundaries depend on the following dimensionless parameters:

$$\frac{u_{LS}\rho_L D}{\mu_L}, \quad \frac{u_{GS}\rho_L D}{\mu_L}, \quad \frac{g\rho_L^2 D^3}{\mu_L^2}, \quad \frac{\rho_G}{\rho_L}, \quad \frac{\mu_G}{\mu_L}, \quad \frac{\sigma\rho_L D}{\mu_L^2}, \quad \beta, \quad \frac{\varepsilon}{D}, \quad \gamma \tag{1}$$

Note that this list of dimensionless parameters is by no means unique. A set of variables in which each variable in the new set is a combination of the abovementioned set is also permissible and is in principle completely equivalent to the original set. In fact, an infinite number of sets of the dimensionless parameters exist, each of which could be justified as the "original" set.

The normal approach at this point is to find an explicit functional relation among one set of variables based on experimental data. Clearly, to find the relation among nine parameters based only upon experimental data is impractical. Furthermore, the rigorous result is not a two-dimensional map but rather a nine-dimensional map.

In order to reduce the number of dimensionless groups one tries to distinguish among the important and non-important variables, the correlation of the data is performed with relation only to the important variables in the hope that the number of important parameters will be only two or three so that the result could be plotted on a two-dimensional map. Note that the number of important parameters depends also on the choice of the dimensionless set of variables. An alternative set of parameters, for example, is

$$\frac{(u_{LS} + u_{GS})}{\sqrt{gD}}, \quad \frac{u_{LS}}{u_{GS}}, \quad \frac{g\rho_L^2 D^3}{\mu_L^2}, \quad \frac{\rho_G}{\rho_L}, \quad \frac{\mu_G}{\mu_L}, \quad \frac{\sigma\rho_L D}{\mu_L^2}, \quad \beta, \quad \frac{\varepsilon}{D}, \quad \gamma \tag{2}$$

One may also notice that in this set, the first two variables are identical to the coordinates chosen by Spedding and Nguyen [7] to plot their flow pattern map. It means that only the first two variables (in addition to the inclination angle) were considered important in this set of variables and that the effect of six variables was neglected. This is a dangerous path to take since neglecting six groups within a set of nine based essentially on physical intuition and limited experimental data may result in erroneous answers. A further complication is that since different transition boundaries are caused by different mechanisms, it is quite possible, and in fact probable, that different dimensionless parameters will be important for different transition boundaries. Thus, the practical implementation of using dimensionless analysis to correlate the experimental results correctly requires enormous efforts and vast experimental data that makes this "straightforward" approach unrealistic and, in fact, impossible. Therefore, up to now, the usual experimental approach has been to guess the important variables (usually two for a specific angle of inclination) and apply them to all transitions. The chance of this approach being correct, outside the specific range of operating conditions that has been used to correlate the data, is very slim.

A different logical method of solving problems as complex as flow pattern transition is by understanding and identifying the important physical mechanisms underlying each transition. Once this is done, a mathematical model that describes each transition can be formulated. This leads to a mathematical determination of the transition boundaries which also yields, as part of the solution, the minimum important dimensionless coordinates (provided the model is basically correct). The chance of this approach yielding correct results is certainly better than just a coordinating data, and it could more confidently be extrapolated to conditions for which no data exist.

The works of Taitel and Dukler [36], Taitel et al. [16], and Barnea et al. [37–40] are a step in this direction. It yields generalized maps where the coordinates are based solely on physical modeling of the transition mechanisms. The aforementioned predictive models of Taitel et al. as well as others will be reviewed in detail in the next chapters.

HORIZONTAL FLOW

Since the earliest two-dimensional flow pattern map proposed by Baker [3] (Figure 11), many have been suggested [5, 7, 41–46] (Figures 9 and 10).

Almost exclusively, past efforts were based on extensive reliance on data, mostly in the form of a data bank [5, 47]. The results of the experimental data were correlated on a two-dimensional map using two coordinate systems. Al-Sheikh et al. [47] defined a variety of dimensionless groups in their efforts to find the appropriate dominant dimensionless groups that control the flow pattern. They concluded that no two groups characterize all transitions. They used an approach that uses several maps and concluded that if a single flow pattern is predicted by all the maps, then one can be relatively confident of that flow pattern. Unfortunately, this is seldom the case and, generally, various maps will conflict each other and the usefulness of such predictive scheme is doubtful.

More recently, Weisman et al. [6] examined the effect of fluid properties and developed flow pattern maps and algebraic correlations for the flow pattern transitions. They used two experimental loops: (1) air-water, 6.1 m long, 1.2 cm, 2.5 cm, and 5.1 cm I.D.; (2) vapor-liquid Freon 113 system, 1.52 m long, 2.45 cm I.D. The effect of fluid properties was examined. Liquid viscosity was changed by using water-glycerol solutions. The surface tension was changed in the range of 60 to 38 dyne/cm. The effect of liquid density was examined using potassium carbonate solutions and the effect of vapor density was checked in their Freon system loop. Based on their own data, as well as data in the literature, they correlated their results considering the following transition boundaries:

Separated-intermittent transition

$$(Fr_G)^{1/2} \equiv \frac{u_{GS}}{\sqrt{gD}} = 0.25\left(\frac{u_{GS}}{u_{LS}}\right)^{1.1} \tag{3}$$

Transition to annular flow

$$1.9\left(\frac{u_{GS}}{u_{LS}}\right)^{1/8} = \left\{\frac{u_{GS}\rho_G^{1/2}}{[g(\rho_L - \rho_G)\sigma]^{1/4}}\right\}^{0.2}\left(\frac{u_{GS}^2}{gD}\right)^{0.18} = Ku^{0.2}Fr_G^{0.18} \tag{4}$$

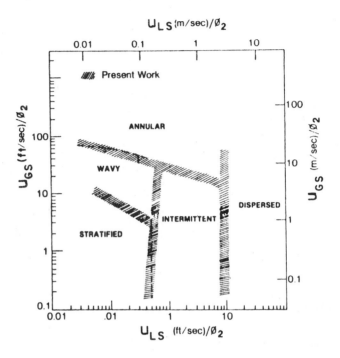

Figure 12. Weisman et al. [6] flow pattern map for horizontal flow.

Transition to dispersed bubble

$$\left[\frac{(dP/dx)_{LS}}{(\rho_L - \rho_G)g}\right]^{1/2}\left[\frac{\sigma}{(\rho_L - \rho_G)gD^2}\right]^{-1/4} = 1.7 \tag{5}$$

Stratified smooth-stratified wavy transition

$$\left[\frac{\sigma}{gD^2(\rho_L - \rho_G)}\right]^{0.2}\left(\frac{Du_{GS}\rho_G}{\mu_G}\right)^{0.45} = 8\left(\frac{u_{GS}}{u_{LS}}\right)^{0.16} \tag{6}$$

Noticing that the major influence on the flow pattern are the superficial gas and liquid velocities, Weisman et al. [6] followed Mandhane et al. [5] suggestion and presented a generalized map using u_{LS}/ϕ_2 and u_{GS}/ϕ_1 as coordinates. The properties correction ϕ_1 and ϕ_2 equal unity under "standard" conditions, which were taken for air-water at room temperature in a 2.54-cm diameter pipe. Equations 3–6 are presented in Figure 12 in the form of a flow pattern map while the properties corrections are summarized in Table 2.

Experimental flow regime maps for air-water flow in inclined pipes at angles from vertically upward to vertically downward was recently reported by Spedding and Nguyen [7]. The maps are based on data collected in a 6-m-long perspex pipe with an inner diameter of 4.55 cm. Their map for horizontal flow is given in Figure 10. The authors suggested four basic flow patterns: X type flow regime, in which both phases are continuous, including the stratified and annular regimes; B type flow regime, in which the liquid phase is continuous, including slug flow and bubble flow; D type flow regime, in which the gas phase is continuous and the liquid phase is distributed as droplets; and finally M type mixed flow regime, in which both phases are discontinuous including

Table 2

Property and Pipe Diameter Corrections to Overall Flow Map [70]

Flow orientation		ϕ_1	ϕ_2
Horizontal, Vertical and Inclined Flow	Transition to dispersed flow	1.0	$\left(\dfrac{\rho_L}{\rho_{sL}}\right)^{-0.33}\left(\dfrac{D}{D_s}\right)^{0.16}\left(\dfrac{\mu_{sL}}{\mu_L}\right)^{0.09}\left(\dfrac{\sigma}{\sigma_s}\right)^{0.24}$
	Transition to annular flow	$\left(\dfrac{\rho_{sG}}{\rho_G}\right)^{0.23}\left(\dfrac{\Delta\rho}{\Delta\rho_s}\right)^{0.11}\left(\dfrac{\sigma}{\sigma_s}\right)^{0.11}\left(\dfrac{D}{D_s}\right)^{0.415}$	1.0
Horizontal and Slightly Inclined Flow	Intermittent-separated transition	1.0	$\left(\dfrac{D}{D_s}\right)^{0.45}$
Horizontal Flow	Wavy-stratified transition	$\left(\dfrac{D_s}{D}\right)^{0.17}\left(\dfrac{\mu_G}{\mu_{sG}}\right)^{1.55}\left(\dfrac{\rho_{sG}}{\rho_G}\right)^{1.55}\left(\dfrac{\Delta\rho}{\Delta\rho_s}\right)^{0.69}\left(\dfrac{\sigma_s}{\sigma}\right)^{0.69}$	1.0
Vertical and Inclined Flow	Bubble-intermittent transition	$\left(\dfrac{D}{D_s}\right)^{n} (1 - 0.65\cos\beta)$ $n = 0.26e^{-0.17(V_{SL}/V_{sL}^S)}$	1.0

"s" denotes standard conditions

$D_s = 1.0\ in. = 2.54\ cm$ $\mu_{sL} = 1\ centipoise$
$\rho_{sG} = 0.0013\ kg/l$ $\sigma_s = 70\ dynes/cm$
$\rho_{sL} = 1.0\ kg/l$ $V_{sL} = 1.0\ ft/sec = 0.305\ m/sec$

all other flow patterns, such as film plus droplets or annular plus droplets. Spedding and Nguyen [7] present the result on flow pattern maps using two dimensionless coordinates, $(u_M/\sqrt{gD})^{1/2}$ and u_{LS}/u_{GS}. A partial explanation for the choice of these particular coordinates is given by an analysis of the transition mechanism from stratified to slug flow.

Although empirical correlations for flow pattern prediction are still in use, efforts have been made in the last years to develop analytical models for the prediction of the regimes. Following is Taitel and Dukler's [36] development of flow patterns transition based on physical modeling.

Modeling Flow Pattern Transitions in Horizontal and Slightly Inclined Pipes

Taitel and Dukler [36] suggested a mechanistic model, which is a basis for an unambiguous analytical prediction of transition between flow patterns. The analysis considers the conditions for transition between five basic flow regimes: stratified smooth (SS), stratified wavy (SW), intermittent(I) (slug and elongated bubbles), annular and annular with dispersed liquid (A), and dispersed bubble (DB).

Analyzing the transitions between flow regimes starts from the condition of stratified flow. The approach is to visualize a stratified liquid and then to determine the mechanism by which a change from stratified flow can be expected to occur, as well as the flow pattern that can be expected to result from the change. In many cases stratified flow is seen to actually exist in the entry region of the pipe. However, the fact that stratified flow may not actually exist is not important, since it is well established that the existence of a specific flow pattern at specified gas and liquid rates is independent of the path used to arrive at that state.

Since the condition of stratified flow is central to this analysis, the initial step is to develop a generalized relationship for stratified flows.

Equilibrium Stratified Flow

Consider smooth, equilibrium stratified flow as shown in Figure 13. A momentum balance on each phase yields

$$-A_L\left(\frac{dP}{dx}\right) - \tau_L S_L + \tau_i S_i + \rho_L A_L g \sin \beta = 0 \tag{7}$$

$$-A_G\left(\frac{dP}{dx}\right) - \tau_G S_G - \tau_i S_i + \rho_G A_G g \sin \beta = 0 \tag{8}$$

Equating pressure drop in the two phases gives

$$\tau_G \frac{S_G}{A_G} - \tau_L \frac{S_L}{A_L} + \tau_i S_i \left(\frac{1}{A_L} + \frac{1}{A_G}\right) + (\rho_L - \rho_G)g \sin \beta = 0 \tag{9}$$

The shear stresses are evaluated in a conventional manner:

$$\tau_L = f_L \frac{\rho_L u_L^2}{2} \qquad \tau_G = f_G \frac{\rho_G u_G^2}{2} \qquad \tau_i = f_i \frac{\rho_G(u_G - u_i)^2}{2} \tag{10}$$

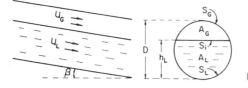

Figure 13. Equilibrium stratified flow.

with the liquid and gas friction factors evaluated from

$$f_L = C_L \left(\frac{D_L u_L}{\nu_L}\right)^{-n} \qquad f_G = C_G \left(\frac{D_G u_G}{\nu_G}\right)^{-m} \tag{11}$$

where D_L and D_G are the hydraulic diameter evaluated in the manner as suggested by Agrawal et al. [48]:

$$D_L = \frac{4A_L}{S_L} \qquad D_G = \frac{4A_G}{S_G + S_i} \tag{12}$$

This implies that the wall resistance of the liquid is similar to that for open-channel flow and that of the gas to closed-duct flow. It has been established that for smooth stratified flow, $f_i \simeq f_G$ [49]. Even though many of the transitions considered here occur in stratified flow with a wavy interface, the error incurred by making this assumption is small. At flow rates conditions, where transitions are observed to take place, $u_G \gg u_i$. Thus, the gas side interfacial shear stress is evaluated with the same equation as the gas wall shear. In this work, the following coefficients were utilized: $C_G = C_L = 0.046$, $n = m = 0.2$ for the turbulent flow and $C_G = C_L = 16$, $n = m = 1.0$ for laminar flow.

It is useful to transform these equations to dimensionless form. The reference variables are: D for length, D^2 for area, and the superficial velocities, u_{LS} and u_{GS} for the liquid and gas velocities, respectively. By designating the dimensionless quantities by a tilde ($\sim$), Equation 9 with Equations 10 and 11 takes the form

$$X^2 \left[(\tilde{u}_L \tilde{D}_L)^{-n} \tilde{u}_L^2 \frac{\tilde{S}_L}{\tilde{A}_L} \right] - \left[(\tilde{u}_G \tilde{D}_G)^{-m} \tilde{u}_G^2 \left(\frac{\tilde{S}_G}{\tilde{A}_G} + \frac{\tilde{S}_i}{\tilde{A}_L} + \frac{\tilde{S}_i}{\tilde{A}_G} \right) \right] - 4Y = 0 \tag{13}$$

$$\text{where} \quad X^2 = \frac{\dfrac{4C_L}{D}\left(\dfrac{u_{LS}D}{\nu_L}\right)^{-m}\dfrac{\rho_L u_{LS}^2}{2}}{\dfrac{4C_G}{D}\left(\dfrac{u_{GS}D}{\nu_G}\right)^{-m}\dfrac{\rho_G u_{GS}^2}{2}} = \frac{\left|\left(\dfrac{dP}{dx}\right)_{LS}\right|}{\left|\left(\dfrac{dP}{dx}\right)_{LS}\right|} \tag{14}$$

$$Y = \frac{(\rho_L - \rho_G)g \sin \beta}{\dfrac{4C_G}{D}\left(\dfrac{u_{GS}D}{\nu_G}\right)^{-m}\dfrac{\rho_G u_{GS}^2}{2}} = \frac{(\rho_L - \rho_G)g \sin \beta}{|(dP/dx)_{GS}|} \tag{15}$$

$|(dP/dx)_S|$ designates the pressure drop of one phase flowing alone in the pipe. Thus, X is recognized as the parameter introduced by Lockhart and Martinelli [50] and can be calculated unambiguously with the knowledge of flow rates, fluid properties, and tube diameter. Y is zero for horizontal tubes and represents the relative forces acting on the liquid in the flow direction due to gravity and pressure drop. It too can be calculated directly. All dimensionless variables with the superscript $\sim$ depend only on $\tilde{h}_L = h_L/D$, as can be seen from

$$\tilde{A}_L = 0.25[\pi - \cos^{-1}(2\tilde{h}_L - 1) + (2\tilde{h}_L - 1)\sqrt{1 - (2\tilde{h}_L - 1)^2}] \tag{16}$$

$$\tilde{A}_G = 0.25[\cos^{-1}(2\tilde{h}_L - 1) - (2\tilde{h}_L - 1)\sqrt{1 - (2\tilde{h}_L - 1)^2}] \tag{17}$$

$$\tilde{S}_L = \pi - \cos^{-1}(2\tilde{h}_L - 1) \tag{18}$$

$$\tilde{S}_G = \cos^{-1}(2\tilde{h}_L - 1) \tag{19}$$

$$\tilde{S}_i = \sqrt{1 - (2\tilde{h}_L - 1)^2} \tag{20}$$

$$\tilde{u}_L = \tilde{A}/\tilde{A}_L \tag{21}$$

$$\tilde{u}_G = \tilde{A}/\tilde{A}_G \tag{22}$$

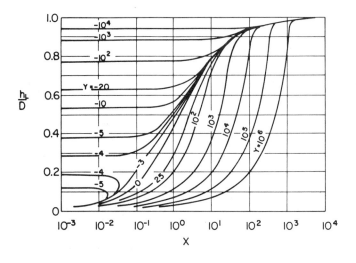

Figure 14. Equilibrium liquid level.

Thus, each X-Y pair corresponds (usually) to a unique value of h_L/D for all conditions of pipe size, fluid properties, flow rates, and pipe inclinations for which stratified flow exists. The solution of Equation 13 has been executed for turbulent flow of both phases, which is clearly the case of greatest practical interest (n = m = 0.2, $C_G = C_L = 0.046$). The results are shown as the solid curves in Figure 14. Other situations may be readily solved from Equation 13 by utilizing the applicable coefficients. The case for turbulent liquid with laminar gas flow can occur in practice for transitions that occur at low gas rates. The solution for n = 0.2, m = 1, $C_L = 0.046$, $C_G = 16$ is remarkably close to the turbulent/turbulent case. It should be noted that the decision on whether laminar or turbulent flow occurs in each phase should be based on the Reynolds number calculated by using the actual velocity and hydraulic diameter of this phase, not the superficial velocity and diameter.

Transition Between Stratified (S) and Intermittent (I) or Annular (A) Regimes

Extensive experimental and analytical studies [51] have shown that for the range of flow conditions over which intermittent flow is observed, the flow at the inlet of the pipe is, at first, stratified. As the liquid rate is increased, the liquid level rises and a wave is formed, which grows rapidly, tending to block the flow. At lower gas rates, the blockage forms a competent bridge, and slug or plug flow ensues. At higher gas rates, there is insufficient liquid flowing to maintain or, in some cases, even to form, the liquid bridge, and the liquid in the wave is swept up and around the pipe to form an annulus with some entrainment, if the gas rate is high enough. Butterworth [52] has demonstrated this mechanism for annular film formation. Thus, this transition can be defined as that from stratified flow to either intermittent or annular flow. It occurs when the conditions are such that a finite amplitude wave on the stratified surface will grow. This transition can be expected to be sharply defined as observed in practice.

Consider stratified flow with a wave existing on the surface over which gas flows. As the gas accelerates, the pressure in the gas phase over the wave decreases owing to the Bernoulli effect, and this tends to cause the wave to grow. The force of the gravity acting on the wave tends to make it decay. The Kelvin-Hemlholtz theory [53] provides a stability criteria for waves of infinitesimal amplitude formed on a flat sheet of liquid flowing between horizontal parallel plates. According to

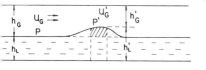

Figure 15. Instability of a solitary wave.

this theory, waves will grow when

$$u_G > \left[\frac{g(\rho_L - \rho_G)h_G}{\rho_G}\right]^{1/2} \tag{23}$$

where h_G is the distance between the upper plate and the equilibrium liquid level.

This type of stability analysis is now extended in a rather elementary manner, first to the case of a finite wave on a flat liquid sheet between parallel plates and then to finite waves on stratified liquid in an inclined pipe. Consider a finite solitary wave on a flat horizontal surface, as shown in Figure 15, having a peak height h'_L and a gas gap dimension h'_G. The equilibrium dimensions are h_L and h_G. If the motion of the wave is neglected, the condition for wave growth is

$$P - P' > (h_G - h'_G)(\rho_L - \rho_G)g \tag{24}$$

with $P - P' = \frac{1}{2}\rho_G(u'^2_G - u^2_G)$ \hfill (25)

The criterion for instability then becomes

$$u_G > C_1 \left[\frac{g(\rho_L - \rho_G)h_G}{\rho_G}\right]^{1/2} \tag{26}$$

where C_1 depends on the size of the wave:

$$C_1 = \left[\frac{2}{(h_G/h'_G)(h_G/h'_G + 1)}\right]^{1/2} \tag{27}$$

For infinitesimal disturbance, $h_G/h'_G \rightarrow 1.0$, $C_1 \rightarrow 1.0$, and Equation 26 reduces to Equation 23. However, a comparison of these two equations shows that finite disturbances are less stable than infinitesimal ones, since for a finite disturbance C_1 is less than unity.

Wallis and Dobson [54] arrived at Equation 26 with $C = 0.5$ from observation of experimental data. Using qualitative arguments, they extended Benjamin's [55, 56] work for flow of liquid around a gas cavity to the idea of a flow of gas over a wave to attempt to justify this value of the coefficient. However, their arguments are questionable for this application because the inversion of gas and liquid has little theoretical basis in this procedure.

This simple analysis can be easily extended to the round pipe geometry and to inclined pipes to give

$$u_G > \left[\frac{2(\rho_L - \rho_G)g \cos \beta(h'_L - h_L)}{\rho_G} \frac{A'^2_G}{A^2_G - A'^2_G}\right]^{1/2} \tag{28}$$

For small, though finite, disturbances, A'_G can be expanded in a Taylor Series around A_G to yield

$$u_G > C_2 \left[\frac{(\rho_L - \rho_G)g \cos \beta \, A_G}{\rho_G \, dA_L/dh_L}\right]^{1/2} \tag{29}$$

where $C_2 = \left[2\frac{(A'_G/A_G)^2}{1 + A'_G/A_G}\right]^{1/2}$

C_2 is seen to be unity for the infinitesimal disturbance where $A'_G \rightarrow A_G$. When the equilibrium liquid level approaches the top of the pipe and A_G is small, any wave of finite amplitude which appears will cause C_2 to approach zero. Conversely, for low levels the appearance of a small finite amplitude wave will have little effect on the air gap size, and C_2 approaches 1.0. For this reason Taitel and Dukler [36] speculate that C_2 can be estimated as follows:

$$C_2 = 1 - \frac{h_L}{D} \tag{30}$$

Note that for $h_L/D = 0.5$, C_2 equals 0.5, and this is consistent with the result of Wallis and Dobson [54]. Kordyban and Ranov [57] analyzed the transition from stratified to slug flow for water and air between horizontal parallel plates. Their data for air velocity to effect transition as a function of the channel air and water gaps gives close agreement with Equation 26, using C_1 given by Equation 30. Thus, it is suggested that Equations 29 and 30 describe the conditions for the transition in pipes from stratified (S) to intermittent (I) and to annular (A) flow.

In dimensionless form the criterion becomes

$$F^2 \left[\frac{1}{C_2^2} \frac{\tilde{u}_G^2 \, d\tilde{A}_L/d\tilde{h}_L}{\tilde{A}_G} \right] \geq 1 \tag{31}$$

where F is a Froude number modified by the density ratio:

$$F = \left[\frac{\rho_G}{\rho_L - \rho_G} \right]^{1/2} \frac{u_{GS}}{\sqrt{Dg \cos \beta}} \tag{32}$$

Note that all terms in the square brackets of Equation 31 are functions of h_L/D which is, in turn, a unique function of the dimensionless groups X and Y as shown in Figure 14. Thus, this transition is uniquely determined by three dimensionless groups X, Y, and F. For any specified value of Y, the transition is uniquely determined by X and F and can be represented on a generalized two-dimensional map. For example, for horizontal flow a series of values of X were selected, and the corresponding values of h_L/D were determined from Figure 14. The bracketed term in Equation 31 can then be calculated by each h_L/D by using Equations 17, 22, and 30 and the following expression.

$$\frac{d\tilde{A}_L}{d\tilde{h}_L} = \sqrt{1 - (2\tilde{h}_L - 1)^2} \tag{33}$$

Then the value of F required to satisfy the equality in Equation 31 can be calculated. The curve describing the relation between X and F that satisfies Equation 31 for horizontal flow is designated as boundary A in Figure 16. The region to the left of this curve represents stratified flow. Although not presented here, it is a simple matter to repeat the calculation previously described for inclined pipes by specifying other values of Y and by using the corresponding curve in Figure 14.

Transition Between Intermittent (I) and Annular (A) Regimes

Equation 31 presents the criteria under which finite waves that appear on the stratified liquid can be expected to grow. Two events can take place when such a growth is observed. A stable slug can form when the supply of liquid in the film is large enough to provide the liquid needed to maintain such a slug. When the level is inadequate, the wave is swept up around the wall, as described by Butterworth [52], and annular or annular mist flow occurs. This suggests that whether intermittent or annular flow will develop depends uniquely on the liquid level in the stratified equilibrium flow. It is suggested that when the equilibrium liquid level in the pipe is above the pipe centerline, intermittent flow will develop, and if $h_L/D < 0.5$, annular flow will result. This choice of $h_L/D = 0.5$ can be explained as follows. When a finite amplitude wave begins to grow as a result of the suction over the crest of the wave, liquid must be supplied from the fluid in the film adjacent to the wave.

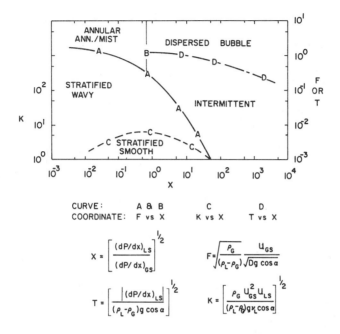

CURVE :   A & B   C   D
COORDINATE: F vs X   K vs X   T vs X

$$X = \left[\frac{(dP/dx)_{LS}}{(dP/dx)_{GS}}\right]^{1/2}$$

$$F = \sqrt{\frac{\rho_G}{(\rho_L - \rho_G)}} \frac{u_{GS}}{\sqrt{Dg \cos a}}$$

$$T = \left[\frac{|(dP/dx)_{LS}|}{(\rho_L - \rho_G)g \cos a}\right]^{1/2}$$

$$K = \left[\frac{\rho_G \, u_{GS}^2 \, u_{LS}}{(\rho_L - \rho_G)g \nu_L \cos a}\right]^{1/2}$$

Figure 16. General flow pattern map for horizontal tubes.

and a depression or trough forms there. Picture the wave as a sinusoid. If the level is above the centerline, the peak of the wave will reach the top before the trough reaches the bottom of the pipe, and then blockage of the gas passage and slugging results. When the liquid level is below the centerline, the inverse will be true, which will make slugging impossible.

In the previous analysis the slug liquid holdup was considered unity. For liquid slug holdup less than unity Barnea et al. [38] suggested that $h_L/D = 0.5\phi$ should be used in order to satisfy the inventory of liquid in the slug. Typically, the liquid holdup within the liquid slug near transition is about 0.7 resulting $h_L/D \simeq 0.35$ as the criteria for transition to annular flow. It will be shown however (Figure 18, 19) that the transition is not very sensitive to the equilibrium level in this range and in fact the transition zone is essentially bounded by $h_L/D = 0.35$ to 0.5.

Since transition occurs at a constant value of h_L/D, a single value of X characterizes the change in regime for any value of Y (Figure 14). For horizontal tubes and $h_L/D = 0.35$ this value is X = 0.6, and this is plotted in Figure 16 as boundary B. Note that the location of this curve now defines two possible transitions as one moves across boundary A: from stratified to intermittent (S/I) for values of X greater than X = 0.6 and stratified to annular flow (S/A) for values of X less than X = 0.6.

Unlike the transition between stratified and intermittent flow for which the mechanism suggests a sharp, well-defined change, this transition is a gradual one since it is difficult to distinguish between a high aerated slug and wavy annular flow or annular flow with large roll waves.

Transition Between Stratified Smooth (SS) and Stratified Wavy (SW) Regimes

The region designated as a stratified regime includes two subregions: stratified smooth (SS) and stratified wavy (SW). These waves are caused by the gas flow under conditions where the velocity of the gas is sufficient to cause waves to form but slower than that needed for the rapid wave growth, which causes transition to intermittent or annular flow.

The phenomenon of wave generation is quite complicated and not completely understood. It is generally accepted that waves will be initiated when pressure and shear work on a wave can overcome the viscous dissipation in the waves. However, there is considerable controversy over the mechanism by which the energy transfer occurs. A good summary is provided by Stewart [58].

Taitel and Dukler [36] use the ideas introduced by Jeffreys [59, 60], who suggested the following condition for wave generation:

$$(u_G - c)^2 c > \frac{4 v_L g (\rho_L - \rho_G)}{s \rho_G} \qquad (34)$$

In this equation s is a sheltering coefficient that Jeffreys suggested should be about 0.3. However, based on theory as well as on experimental result for flow and fixed wavy surfaces, Benjamin [56] indicated much smaller values for this coefficient ranging from 0.01 to 0.03. For this work the value of s = 0.01 is used.

c is the velocity of propagation of the waves. For most conditions where transition is expected, $u_G \gg c$. Theories concerning these waves suggest that the ratio of the wave velocity to the mean of the film velocity c/u_L decreases with increasing Reynolds number of the liquid, and the data of Fulford [61], Brock [62], and Chu [63] confirm this. At the high Reynolds numbers associated with turbulent liquid flow taking place near these transitions, the ratio approaches 1.0 to 1.5. For simplicity, and because a precise location of this transition boundary is not important, the relation $u_L = c$ is used.

These approximations substituted into Equation 34 give the criterion for this transition:

$$u_G \geq \left[\frac{4 v_L (\rho_L - \rho_G) g \cos \beta}{s \rho_G u_L} \right]^{1/2} \qquad (35)$$

In dimensionless form this can be expressed as

$$K \geq \frac{2}{\sqrt{\tilde{u}_L}\, \tilde{u}_G \sqrt{s}} \qquad (36)$$

where K is the product of the modified Froude number and the square root of the superficial Reynolds number of the liquid:

$$K^2 = F^2 Re_{LS} = \left[\frac{\rho_G (u_{GS})^2}{(\rho_L - \rho_G) D g \cos \beta} \right] \left[\frac{D u_{LS}}{v_L} \right] \qquad (37)$$

Since $\tilde{u}_L$ and $\tilde{u}_G$ depend only on h_L/D (see Equations 21 and 22), they are determined once X and Y are specified. Thus, this transition between smooth and stratified wavy flow depends on the three parameters K, X, and Y. For any fixed inclination, this becomes a two-parameter dependence on X and K. The relationship that satisfies the equality of Equation 36 can conveniently be mapped in Figure 16 by designating a differently scaled ordinate than that which applies to the two transitions discussed previously. Curve C shows the results for Y = 0 (s = 0.01).

While the location of this transition curve is approximate, it is important to note that it is based on a physically realistic model. Should it be necessary to locate the curve more accurately, this would be possible once additional data on c/u_L and s are available. However, the result depends on each of these quantities to the one-half power and thus is relatively insensitive to changes.

Transition Between Intermittent (I) and Dispersed Bubble (DB) Regimes

For values of X in Figure 16 to the right of boundaries A and B, waves will tend to bridge the pipe forming a liquid slug and an adjacent gas bubble. At high liquid rates and low gas rates, the equilibrium liquid level approaches the top of the pipe, as is apparent from Figure 14. With such a fast running liquid stream the gas tends to mix with the liquid, and it is suggested that the transition to dispersed bubble flow occurs when the turbulent fluctuations are strong enough to overcome the buoyant forces tending to keep the gas at the top of the pipe.

The force of buoyancy per unit length of the gas region is

$$F_B = g \cos \beta (\rho_L - \rho_G) A_G \tag{38}$$

In a manner used by Levich [64], the force acting because of turbulence is estimated to be

$$F_T = \tfrac{1}{2} \rho_L \overline{v'^2} s_i \tag{39}$$

where v' is the radial velocity fluctuation whose root-mean-square is estimated to be approximately equal to the friction velocity. Thus

$$\overline{v'^2}^{1/2} = u_* = u_L \left(\frac{f_L}{2} \right)^{1/2} \tag{40}$$

Dispersion of the gas is visualized as occurring when $F_T \ge F_B$, or

$$u_L \ge \left[\frac{4 A_G}{S_i} \frac{g \cos \beta}{f_L} \left(1 - \frac{\rho_G}{\rho_L} \right) \right]^{1/2} \tag{41}$$

In a dimensionless form, Equation 41 takes the form

$$T^2 \ge \left[\frac{8 \tilde{A}_G}{\tilde{S}_i \tilde{u}_L^2 (\tilde{u}_L \tilde{D}_L)^{-n}} \right] \tag{42}$$

where $\quad T = \left[\dfrac{\dfrac{4 C_L}{D} \left(\dfrac{u_{LS} D}{\nu_L} \right)^{-n} \dfrac{\rho_L u_{LS}^2}{2}}{(\rho_L - \rho_G) g \cos \beta} \right]^{1/2} = \left[\dfrac{|(dP/dx)_{LS}|}{(\rho_L - \rho_G) g \cos \beta} \right]^{1/2} \tag{43}$

T can be considered as the ratio of turbulence to gravity forces acting on the gas.

The terms in the square bracket in Equation 42 are again dependent only on h_L/D and thus on X and Y. For any specific value of Y, a two-dimensional representation for this transition is possible, with X and T used as the dimensionless coordinates. It is possible to map this transition on Figure 16 by using the common X abscissa and T as an ordinate as shown by curve D calculated for Y = 0.

Generalized Flow Regime Map

Figure 16 shows the generalized flow regime map for the case of horizontal tubes (Y = 0). Curve A represents the transition from stratified (S) to intermittent (I) or annular (A) flows, with the coordinates for curve A being F vs. X. The curve gives the locus of the F-X pairs, which satisfies Equation 31 and results from the argument that waves of finite size will grow and tend to block or sweep around the pipe when the force due to the Bernoulli effect above the wave is greater than gravity force acting on the wave. Thus, all values of X to the left of the curve represent conditions under which stratified flow will exist.

Curve B locates the transition between intermittent (I) or dispersed bubble (DB) and annular (A) flow. This occurs at a constant value of X resulting from the argument that the growing waves will have sufficient liquid supply to form a slug only when $h_L/D \ge 0.35$, and below that value they will be swept around the pipe into an annular configuration.

Curve C represents the transition between stratified smooth (SS) and stratified wavy (SW) flow. It is plotted in the K-X plane and locates the K-X pairs, which satisfy Equation 36. The model is based on the assumption that the Jeffreys model is valid for describing the condition for transfer of

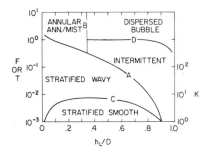

Figure 17. General flow pattern map.

energy to the liquid in order to create waves, with the wave velocity estimated from the mean velocity of the liquid film and the sheltering coefficient determined from an analysis of Benjamin [56]. Any value of K lower than curve C in the K-X plane will provide insufficient gas flow to cause waves to form.

Curve D indicates the transition between intermittent and dispersed bubble flow. It represents an identification of conditions where the turbulent fluctuations in the liquid become equal to the buoyant forces, which tends to make the gas rise to the top of the pipe. This curve gives the locus of the T-X pairs, which satisfies Equation 42. All values of T below the curve represent conditions where turbulence is insufficient to keep the gas mixed, and the elongated gas bubbles characteristic of intermittent flow will form. The set of transition curves for other values of Y can easily be calculated from Figure 14 and the defining transition equations.

The effect of pipe roughness on these transitions is not specifically considered in the development. However, subject to experimental demonstration, it is suggested that if the $(dp/dx)_S$ values are calculated by using known roughness parameters, the transition boundaries of Figure 16 will continue to apply [65].

It is, of course, not necessary to use a flow regime map at all. Given any one set of flow conditions (rates, pressure, line size, and inclination), the flow pattern that exists for that condition can be determined rather simply by using Equations 31, 36, and 42 with the help of Figure 14.

Figure 16 is a generalized map applicable only for the horizontal case. By recognizing that the flow pattern is a direct function of h_L/D it is possible to provide a generalized map applicable for slightly inclined pipes if the intrinsic variable h_L/D is used instead of X on the abscissa. Figure 17 provides such a map. The use of the generalized map in Figure 17 is preceeded by calculating the equilibrium level h_L/D using Figure 14. Since Figure 14 is applicable for inclined pipes so is the generalized map of Figure 17. Thus, a convenient use of two figures can be used to calculate the flow pattern for horizontal and slightly inclined pipes.

Transition Between Slug (SL) and Elongated Bubble (EB)

Taitel and Dukler [36] did not differentiate between the slug and the elongated bubble flow patterns and considered them as the intermittent flow pattern. Recently, Barnea and Brauner [39] proposed a physical model for the prediction of gas holdup within the liquid slug (α_s). This model can be also used to yield the transition between elongated bubbles and slug within the intermittent flow pattern. It was suggested that the gas within the developed liquid slug behave as dispersed bubbles and thus the liquid slug will accommodate the same gas holdup as the fully dispersed bubble flow on the transition boundary with the same mixture velocity (u_S). Therefore, curves of constant $u_S = u_{LS} + u_{GS}$ represent the locus where the gas holdup within the liquid slug (α_s) is constant and is equal to the holdup of the dispersed bubble pattern at the transition boundary. The special case of $\alpha_s \rightarrow 0$, namely that the liquid slug is almost free of entrained gas bubbles can be considered as the elongated bubble-slug transition.

To obtain the elongated bubble-slug transition boundary one has to locate a point on the transition to the dispersed bubble phase where $\alpha \rightarrow 0$ [note that $\alpha = u_{GS}/(u_{LS} + u_{GS})$ on this transition] and

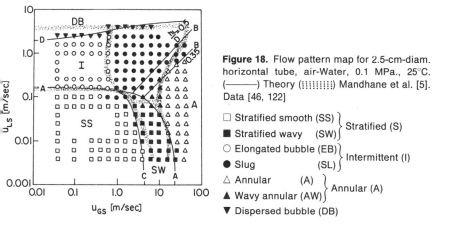

Figure 18. Flow pattern map for 2.5-cm-diam. horizontal tube, air-Water, 0.1 MPa., 25°C. (————) Theory (⋮⋮⋮⋮⋮⋮⋮) Mandhane et al. [5]. Data [46, 122]

□ Stratified smooth (SS) ⎫
■ Stratified wavy   (SW) ⎬ Stratified (S)

○ Elongated bubble (EB) ⎫
● Slug   (SL) ⎬ Intermittent (I)

△ Annular   (A) ⎫
▲ Wavy annular (AW) ⎬ Annular (A)

▼ Dispersed bubble (DB)

then plot a curve of constant $u_{LS} + u_{GS}$ that passes through this point. Using the transition boundary to the dispersed bubble-D, the case where $\alpha = 1\%$ is mapped on Figures 18 and 19 as transition N.

Comparison with Data

The results of the water-air system theory were compared to experimental data of Shoham [46] and the proposed transition boundaries suggested by Mandhane et al. [5] as shown in Figures 18 and 19. As seen, the agreement between the experiments and the theory is satisfactory. There is some discrepancy between the predicted transition lines and the proposed map of Mandhane et al. The difference may arise because Mandhane obtained the average map based on data bank results applicable for conditions not exclusive to water-air in 2.5- and 5.1-cm diameter pipes. Discrepancies may also result from ambiguous definitions of the flow patterns especially near transition boundaries. For example, the wavy annular flow pattern can be interpreted easily as slug or stratified wavy. Also the location of the elongated bubble-dispersed bubble transition boundary may be determined differently by different people. Nevertheless, also the map proposed by Mandhane et al. is in reasonable agreement with the proposed theory and the data.

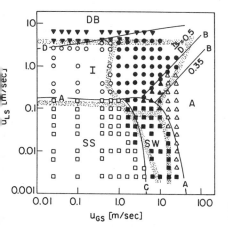

Figure 19. Flow pattern map for 5.1-cm-diam. horizontal tube air-Water, 0.1 MPa., 25°C. (————) Theory (⋮⋮⋮⋮⋮⋮⋮) Mandhane et al. [5]. (See Figure 18 for legend.)

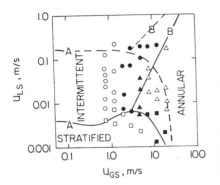

Figure 20. Flow patterns for 165 Cp glycerine/ water and air in a horizontal, 3.8-cm-diam pipe (———) Theory for 165 Cp, (----) Theory for 1.0 Cp (See Figure 18 for legend.)

It is also interesting to compare the results of Weisman et al. [6] with Taitel and Dukler model, which predicts that the stratified-intermittent transition is controlled by F (modified Froude number) and X (Lockhart-Martinelli parameter). For the case of turbulent flow where the friction factors are only weakly dependent on the liquid and gas Reynolds numbers the theory shows that the transition boundary is given by

$$\sqrt{\frac{\rho_G}{\rho_L - \rho_G}} \frac{u_{GS}}{\sqrt{gD}} = f\left(\sqrt{\frac{\rho_G}{\rho_L}} \frac{u_{GS}}{u_{LS}}\right) \tag{44}$$

Weisman's results (Equation 3) are quite similar if the gas density is neglected relative to the liquid density and the exponent of u_{GS}/u_{LS} is taken as unity. Indeed, for turbulent flows and horizontal pipes both approaches yield fairly comparable results.

For high-viscosity liquids, however, the results are drastically different. The Taitel and Dukler model predicts a considerable effect of the liquid viscosity, whereas Weisman's correlation backed by his data is unaffected by the liquid viscosity. To check this discrepancy Weisman's experiments were repeated [66] in a 14-meter, 3.81-cm-diameter pipe, using glycerol-water solution of 90% (viscosity about 165 cp) and 85% (viscosity about 90 c.p.). The results are shown in Figure 20 while Weisman's results are represented by the air-water system. The effect of viscosity is indeed substantial and is predicted very reasonably by Taitel and Dukler model. The discrepancy can partially be explained by the different interpretation of wavy-annular flow for high gas flow rates. It seems that Weisman considered this region as wavy flow. Indeed the lower film in annular flow looks wavy while the upper film is very thin. At lower gas flow rates where transition to slug flow occurs (Figure 20), the discrepancy is probably due to a relatively short pipe used by Weisman with L/D = 120, (Taitel and Dukler used a pipe with L/D = 360), as a result the viscous liquid was driven by gravity to the pipes exit not allowing an equilibrium stratified flow to develop. In the latter experiment it was clearly seen that transition to intermittent flow is caused by the unstable high liquid level that is developed near the entrance section typical of a high viscous liquid as viewed by the analytical model.

Other correlations suggested by Weisman et al. (Equations 4, 5, and 6) do not seem to be comparable to Taitel and Dukler results since some of the dimensionless variables are not the same. Noteworthy is that only viscosity was the property that was checked over a wide range. Surface tension as well as liquid densities can be experimentally varied only in a relatively narrow range. As a result, the effect of these properties on the correlations cannot be adequately tested.

Comparing the results [36, 46] for air-water with Weisman's correlations indicates reasonable agreement for most of the transition boundaries except for the slug-annular transition. This discrepancy is attributed to the different experimental data for slug-annular transition obtained by Weisman. Weisman's data for the transition shows opposite trend. It seems that this apparent contradiction results from the difficulty in the experimental interpretation of the slug-annular transition at high liquid and gas flow rate. Weisman's et al. results show that the slug-annular transition boundary "bends" to the left with increasing liquid flow rate (Figure 12), which is in conflict with other data (Figures 18 and 19) as well as Taitel and Dukler model. Clearly, this conflict invites future clarification of this particular transition line.

Transient Flow in Horizontal Pipes

The prediction of the flow pattern under steady state conditions leads to transition boundaries that depend on the flow rates provided the flow rates are kept constant. In many applications the flow rates may change, resulting in a change in the flow patterns. If a change in the flow rates is infinitesimally slow, it is expected that transition from one flow regime to another will occur as predicted by the steady flow map.

The question arises, What is the effect of a finite change of liquid or gas rates (or both) on the location of the transition boundaries? This problem is treated by Taitel, et al. [67].

The approach to modeling the flow pattern transitions under transient flow conditions parallels that for steady flow. First, the stratified liquid level is predicted, but in this case this level varies with position along the pipe, x, and the time, t. The stability of this level to the disturbances that underlie the transitions is explored as the flow transient proceeds according to the criteria previously stated. As seen, these criteria all depend on the liquid level. Under steady conditions, this level is invariant with time. Under transient conditions, the liquid level as well as the fluid velocities are time dependent. Thus, under conditions of transient flow and depending on the nature of the transient, flow pattern transition will occur at flow rates different from those expected for steady, equilibrium conditions. This happens because the liquid level during a transient is such that the transition can be satisfied at different rates than for equilibrium conditions. Furthermore, under certain conditions, in moving from one flow condition to another, flow regimes will appear that would not exist if the flow changes along this path were executed slowly.

Figure 21 shows the geometry of stratified flow. Liquid and gas enter the pipe at x = 0, both flowing in the positive x direction. Under transient flow conditions, the gas-liquid interface is, in general, not parallel to the x axis; thus, the liquid level h_L, average liquid velocity u_L, and average gas velocity u_G are all functions of x and t. Likewise, the liquid and gas cross-sectional areas A_L and A_G and the contact perimeter between the liquid and wall S_L gas and wall S_G and liquid gas interface S_i are all functions of the local liquid level h_L and thereby also depend on time and position.

The momentum and continuity equations for the liquid phase are given by

$$\rho_L \frac{\partial(u_L A_L)}{\partial t} + \rho_L \frac{\partial(u_L^2 A_L)}{\partial x} = -\tau_L S_L + \tau_i S_i - A_L \rho_L g \frac{\partial h_L}{\partial x} - A_L \frac{\partial P}{\partial x} \tag{45}$$

$$\frac{\partial A_L}{\partial t} + \frac{\partial(u_L A_L)}{\partial x} = 0 \tag{46}$$

Since the cross-sectional area of the liquid film depends on the level of the liquid in the pipe, $A_L = A_L(h_L)$. Thus, Equations 45 and 46 take the form

$$g \frac{\partial h_L}{\partial x} + \frac{\partial u_L}{\partial t} + u_L \frac{\partial u_L}{\partial x} = -\frac{\tau_L S_L}{\rho_L A_L} + \frac{\tau_i S_i}{\rho_L A_L} - \frac{1}{\rho_L} \frac{\partial P}{\partial x} \tag{47}$$

$$\frac{\partial h_L}{\partial t} + u_L \frac{\partial h_L}{\partial x} + \frac{A_L}{A_L'} \frac{\partial u_L}{\partial x} = 0 \tag{48}$$

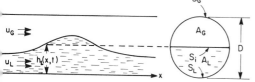

Figure 21. Non-equilibrium stratified flow.

Next, consider the equations of motion for the gas phase. The pressure gradient in the liquid and the gas is assumed to be equal, and Equations 45 and 46 with suitable subscripts are equally valid for the flow of the gas. The gas velocity is much greater than that of the liquid, and since gas flow rate changes are propagated down the pipe very rapidly compared to the liquid, a quasi steady state is assumed with respect to any time interval in which changes in liquid flow or level are significant:

$$\rho_G \frac{\partial(u_G^2 A_G)}{\partial x} = -\tau_G S_G - \tau_i S_i - A_G \frac{\partial P}{\partial x} \tag{49}$$

$$A_G u_G \rho_G = W_G = \text{const} \tag{50}$$

Substitution of Equations 49 and 50 into 47 yields

$$\left[g - \frac{\rho_G}{\rho_L} \left(\frac{W_G}{\rho_G A_G} \right)^2 \frac{A_L'}{A_G} \right] \frac{\partial h_L}{\partial x} + \frac{\partial u_L}{\partial t} + u_L \frac{\partial u_L}{\partial x} = -\frac{\tau_L S_L}{\rho_L A_L} + \frac{\tau_i S_i}{\rho_L} \left(\frac{1}{A_L} + \frac{1}{A_G} \right) + \frac{\tau_G S_G}{\rho_L A_G} \tag{51}$$

$$\frac{\partial h_L}{\partial t} + u_L \frac{\partial h_L}{\partial x} + \frac{A_L}{A_L'} \frac{\partial u_L}{\partial x} = 0 \tag{52}$$

Equations 51 and 52 are two simultaneous partial differential equations for $h_L(x, t)$ and $u_L(x, t)$. Note that the right-hand side of Equation 51 is a known function of h_L and u_L. Also note that for steady equilibrium conditions, namely, the case where the liquid level is constant, the left-hand side of Equation 51 is identically zero, and Equation 51 becomes identical to Equation 9.

Equations 51 and 52 predict the transient variation of the local liquid level and local average velocity as the flow conditions are varied from one state to another. Knowing the instantaneous liquid level and applying the mechanisms for transition as previously discussed indicate when transition will occur.

Equations 51 and 52 are two hyperbolic, partial differential equations provided

$$g \gg \frac{\rho_G}{\rho_L} \left(\frac{W_G}{\rho_G A_G} \right)^2 \frac{A_L'}{A_G} \tag{53}$$

Unless Equation 53 is satisfied, a unique solution to these equations does not exist [68]. Calculations show that even at flow rates closely approaching these for instability of the stratified flow, the Bernoulli term is, in fact, negligible compared to gravity. But neglecting this term can also be justified on a physical basis as well. Physically, the right-hand side of Equation 53 describes the Bernoulli forces opposing gravity that act on the fluid when the gas is accelerated to high velocity over the crest of a wavy interface. To avoid this mathematical problem, the approach to solving Equations 51 and 52 is to predict the variation of smooth liquid level profile and velocity with time in the absence of local waves. At each point in space and time, the local stability of the surface to wave growth due to Bernoulli forces is explored using the criteria of Equation 29. Consistent with this approach, the Bernoulli term is neglected in Equation 51. While this approach provides a device to overcome mathematical difficulties, it is also consistent with the physical behavior as observed near the entry where the liquid level is stratified. Waves formed on this surface travel and grow as they move downstream as if superimposed on a smooth stratified surface.

Once the Bernoulli term in Equation 51 is neglected, Equations 51 and 52 take the form

$$\frac{\partial u_L}{\partial t} + u_L \frac{\partial u_L}{\partial x} + g \frac{\partial h_L}{\partial x} + E = 0 \tag{54}$$

$$\frac{\partial h_L}{\partial t} + u_L \frac{\partial h_L}{\partial x} + H \frac{\partial u_L}{\partial x} = 0 \tag{55}$$

where $H = H(h_L) = A_L/A'_L$ and $E = E(h_L, u_L)$ is minus the right-hand side of Equation 51. Using standard methods [69] Equations 54 and 55 can be converted to

$$\left[(u_L + c)\frac{\partial}{\partial x} + \frac{\partial}{\partial x}\right]u_L + \sqrt{\frac{g}{H}}\left[(u_L + c)\frac{\partial}{\partial x} + \frac{\partial}{\partial t}\right]h_L + E = 0 \qquad (56)$$

$$\left[(u_L - c)\frac{\partial}{\partial x} + \frac{\partial}{\partial t}\right]u_L - \sqrt{\frac{g}{H}}\left[(u_L - c)\frac{\partial}{\partial x} + \frac{\partial}{\partial t}\right]h_L + E = 0 \qquad (57)$$

where $c = \sqrt{gH}$ is the critical velocity.

Equations 56 and 57 were solved using the finite-difference technique described by Stoker [69]. In this method, explicit forward finite differences are used with respect to time, whereas the spacial derivative is replaced by either forward or backward finite differences depending on the direction of the characteristic lines. Equation 56 is associated with the forward characteristic, which has a slope of $dx/dt = 1/(u_L + c)$, and thus backward finite differences are used. Equation 57 is associated with the characteristics having the slope $dx/dt = 1/(u_L - c)$. When, at a given x and t, $u_L > c$, or the flow is supercritical, the direction of the characteristic associated with Equation 57 is positive, and a backward finite spacial differentiation is used. At subcritical conditions when $u_L < c$, forward differentiation is used.

In the numerical scheme, each point is checked to determine whether the flow is sub or supercritical and the appropriate forward or backward numerical scheme selected. In order to ensure stability, the time increment Δt is limited by $\Delta t < \Delta x/(u_L + c)$.

The boundary conditions needed for the solution of Equations 56 and 57 depend on whether the local conditions are sub or supercritical. For the supercritical case $h_L(x, 0)$, $u_L(x, 0)$, $u_L(0, t)$, and $h_L(0, t)$ are required as boundary and initial conditions. When the flow is subcritical, only $h_L(0, t)$ or $u_L(0, t)$ can be assumed, since they are related through Equation 57 and are associated with the backward characteristics. In this case, however, the flow rate is specified, and for the subcritical case both $u_L(0, t)$ and $h_L(0, t)$ are determined by the flow rate.

A variety of solutions for $h_L(x, t)$ can be generated by this technique and the local flow pattern is determined using the steady state criteria which are only a function of h_L/D.

Consider equilibrium stratified flow. Increasing the liquid rate very slowly will result in transition to slug flow as predicted by the equilibrium flow pattern map (Figures 18 and 19). The results of a fast change of the liquid flow rate are demonstrated in Figure 22 where typical results of the profile of $h_L(x, t)/D$ for a fast increase of the liquid flow rate (for a constant gas flow rate) are shown. The initial condition corresponding to Figure 22A is $u_{GS} = 7.8$ m/sec and $u_{LS} = 0.03$ m/sec (water-air, 3.81-cm pipe, 25°C at 1 atm). An increase of the liquid rate from 0.03 to 0.1 m/sec linearly over 1.0 sec is applied where 0.1 m/sec is exactly on the stratified-intermittent transition boundary. The variation of the liquid level with time is shown and it is observed that the local level reaches conditions for transition at $u_{LS} = 0.081$ m/sec namely the transition occurs at a lower liquid rate than for the quasi steady state process. Notice that the condition of Figure 22A corresponds to supercritical flow. For subcritical flow (Figure 22B) the behavior is quite different as the local "hamp" occurs at the entrance of the pipe. In Figure 22B the liquid rate is increased from 0.03 m/sec to 0.3 m/sec while the steady state transition boundary is at $u_{LS} = 0.14$ m/sec. The results show that conditions for transition are reached at $u_{LS} = 0.2$ m/sec, namely the transition is delayed. Thus the results of the analysis show that a fast increase of the liquid flow rate may cause transition at a higher liquid flow rate when the stratified flow is subcritical (transition is delayed) and at lower liquid flow rate when the flow is supercritical. When the initial steady state is intermittent, the opposite effect occurs for decreasing liquid flow rate. Under subcritical conditions the transition is faster, while for supercritical conditions the transition is delayed.

Characteristic to transient changes of gas flow rates is that the liquid levels and velocities are very slow to respond to changes in gas rate. This allows one to simplify the prediction method by assuming that the liquid level does not change when the gas flow rate is changed. As a result, this transition can be predicted by a simple graphical procedure using the equilibrium map. Furthermore, the time

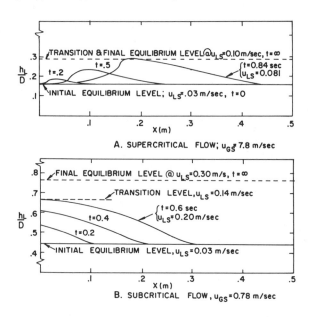

Figure 22. Increasing liquid rate at constant gas rate total transient time 1.0 sec.

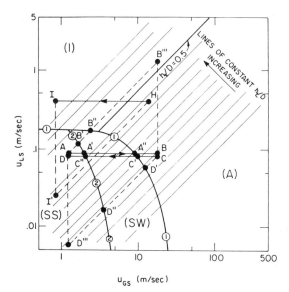

Figure 23. Gas flow transient.

and the gas flow rate at which each transition will occur can be calculated. The method can be understood by reference to Figure 23. Consider the path A to B, where the gas rate is increased. If the process is carried out very slowly, the system will pass through a series of quasi equilibrium states along A-B, and transition will be observed at each flow rate where the line A-B crosses a transition curve. Superimposed on this curve are a series of lines of constant equilibrium level h_L/D. That such lines are straight with a slope of $45°$ on log-log coordinates follows from Taitel and Dukler [36] for the case when both gas and liquid are in turbulent flow. A fast gas transient is one in which the initial level remains unchanged until the gas rate has reached its final value. Thus, the level remains constant at its initial value along the line AB′B″B‴ as the gas rate changes. But the intersection of this constant level line with the transition curves indicates the gas flow rates that satisfy each transition criterion.

Thus, transition to stratified wavy and intermittent occur at gas flow rates corresponding to those at B′ and B″, respectively. This method provides a visual display of the true path to be expected during a fast transient.

Under steady state conditions (very slow transient) path A-B is expected. During the fast transient path A-B′-B″-B‴-B, the transition to stratified wavy occurs "earlier" and unexpected temporary slug flow appears (this flow pattern is not expected at all in the A-B path). If decrease of the gas velocity from point C to D is considered, the true transient path will be C-D′-D″-D‴-D. Path H-I′-I shows that transition from annular to intermittent flows passed via a quiescent temporary stratified-smooth pattern. Thus, fast changes in the gas flow rate have a more substantial effect on the transient behavior on the two-phase system than the change of liquid rate.

VERTICAL UPWARD FLOW

Upward two-phase flow is often very chaotic and difficult to describe, so there are many flow pattern maps based largely on experimental data that do not agree very well with each other.

Some investigators used dimensional coordinates, such as superficial velocities u_{GS} and u_{LS} [10, 11] or superficial momentum flux $\rho_G u_{GS}^2$ [12]. Govier and Aziz [4] attempted to modify these dimensional coordinates for systems other than air-water by considering property ratios between the fluids of interest and that of air-water.

Others represented the results by dimensionless coordinates. The dimensionless groups selected by Duns and Ros [9] ($u_{LS}(\rho_L/g\sigma)^{1/4}$ vs. $u_{GS}(\rho_L/g\sigma)^{1/4}$) and also used by Gould [15] seem arbitrary. Griffith and Wallis [8] attempted to invoke theory to arrive at suitable coordinates. They showed that the dimensionless coordinates u_S^2/gD and u_{GS}/u_S control the transition from the slug to annular pattern. The theory was not completed sufficiently to provide an analytical expression for the transition curve, and experimental data were used to provide the unknown constants. A similar coordinate system was presented by Oshinowo and Charles [13]. The abscissa chosen was $u_S^2/gD\sqrt{\Lambda}$ where $\Lambda = \Gamma_s(S_s\sigma_s^3)^{1/4}$ is a property effect modification. Γ_s, S_s, σ_s are specific viscosity, specific gravity and specific surface tension of the liquid, each relative to the water. The ordinate is $(u_{GS}/u_S)^{1/2}$, which is similar in principle to Griffith and Wallis' [8] ordinate u_{GS}/u_S.

Spedding and Nguyen's [7] recent upward flow pattern map for air-water in a 4.35-cm-diameter pipe is shown in Figure 24. They followed Griffith and Wallis' suggestion and used the coordinates $[u_S/\sqrt{gD}]^{1/2}$ vs. u_{LS}/u_{GS}. Spedding and Nguyen [7] used a non-conventional method for classifying the flow pattern.

Weisman and Kang [70] investigated upward flow patterns in Freon 113 vapor-liquid system in a 2.5-cm-diameter tube. They also used the air-water data of Hewitt and Roberts [12] and the high-pressure (33.5 and 67 bars) data of Bennett et al. [71]; and they considered four flow patterns—intermittent, annular, bubble, and dispersed flows.

Weisman and Kang [70] concluded that the transition to annular flow and to dispersed bubble flow (dispersed flow) is unaffected by the inclination angle and is the same as for horizontal flow (Equations 4 and 5). A somewhat simplified version for the transition to annular flow was suggested by using the same exponent for the Froude and the Kutateladze numbers

$$Fr_G Ku = 25\left(\frac{u_{GS}}{u_{LS}}\right)^{5/8}$$

(58)

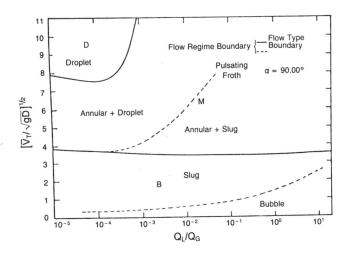

Figure 24. Spedding and Nguyen [7] flow regime map for vertical upwards. (D—droplet; M— mixed; B—bubble)

Thus, the intermittent-bubble transition is the only new transition introduced for vertical upward flow:

$$\frac{u_{GS}}{\sqrt{gD}} = 0.45 \left[\frac{u_{GS} + u_{LS}}{\sqrt{gD}}\right]^{0.78} \tag{59}$$

Based on Equations 58, 59, and 5 Weisman suggested a generalized map (Figure 25) in the form of u_{LS} vs. u_{GS} for standard conditions modified for variable properties by the factors ϕ_1 and ϕ_2 as given in Table 2. Note that since Equation 59 cannot be directly placed on the proposed map, an approximation for the bubble intermittent transition is used (Table 2).

Comparison among the various flow pattern maps for vertical upward flow shows considerable scatter and lack of agreement. This is partially due to difficulty in discriminating between flow regimes as well as the lack of consistent flow regime definitions.

It seems important to place a theoretical basis for the conditions of transition from one flow pattern to another in order to improve the generality of the mapping and to prevent conflicting experimental observations.

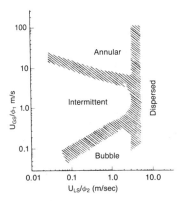

Figure 25. Weisman and Kang [70] overall flow pattern map for vertical and sharply inclined pipes.

Taitel, Barnea, and Dukler [16] developed physically-based transition criteria for the prediction of the upward vertical flow pattern boundaries. Their approach is detailed in the next section.

Modeling Flow Pattern Transitions for Vertical Upward Flow

Taitel et al. [16] proposed a model for the prediction of flow pattern transitions in upward vertical flow. They considered four basic flow patterns: bubble flow, slug flow, churn flow, and annular flow. Transition boundaries are given in the form of algebraic equations that can be easily used.

Bubble—Slug Transition

When gas is introduced at low flow rates into a large diameter vertical column of liquid (flowing at low velocity), the gas phase is distributed into discrete bubbles. Many studies of bubble motion demonstrated that if the bubbles are very small, they behave as rigid spheres rising vertically in rectilinear motion. However, above a critical size (about 0.3 cm for air-water at low pressure) the bubbles begin to deform, and the upward motion is a zig-zag path with considerable randomness. The bubbles randomly collide and coalesce, forming a number of somewhat larger individual bubbles with a spherical cap similar to the Taylor bubbles of slug flow, but with diameters smaller than the pipe. Thus, even at low gas and liquid flow rates, bubble flow is characterized by an array of smaller bubbles moving in zig-zag motion and the occasional appearance of larger, Taylor-type bubbles. The Taylor bubbles are not large enough to occupy the cross section of the pipe so as to cause slug flow in the manner previously described. Instead they behave as free rising spherically-capped voids, in the manner originally described by Taylor. With an increase in gas flow rate, at these low liquid rates, the bubble density increases and a point is reached where the dispersed bubbles become so closely packed that many collisions occur and the rate of agglomeration to larger bubbles increases sharply. This results in a transition to slug flow.

Experiments suggest that the bubble void fraction at which this happens is around 0.25 to 0.30 [72]. A semi-theoretical approach to this problem considers a cubic lattice in which the individual bubble fluctuates [73]. They [73] postulated that the maximum void fraction is reached when the frequency of collision is very high, and it was shown that this happens around void fraction of 0.30.

An alternative approach is to consider this problem from the viewpoint of maximum allowable packing of the bubbles. If we consider the bubbles to be spherical and arranged in a cubic lattice, the void fraction of the gas can be, at most, 0.52. However, as a result of their deformation and random path, the rate of collision and coalescence will increase sharply at void fractions well below this lattice spacing at which they touch. Therefore, the closest distance between the bubbles before transition must be the one that permits some freedom of motion for each individual bubble. If the spacing between the bubbles at which coalescence begins to increase sharply is assumed to be approximately half their radius, this corresponds to about 25% voids. While this approach is not a prediction of the void fraction at transition from first principles, it does provide a reasonable interpretation of the experimental data. Published data agree in that the void fraction in bubbly flow rarely exceeds 0.35, whereas for void fractions less than 0.20 coalescence is rarely observed [8]. Thus, at liquid rates low enough, so that bubble breakup due to turbulence is small, the criteria for transition from bubbly to slug flow is that the void fraction reaches 0.25.

If the gas bubbles rise at a velocity u_G this velocity is related to the superficial gas velocity u_{GS} by

$$u_G = \frac{u_{GS}}{\alpha} \tag{60}$$

where α is the void fraction. Likewise, the average liquid velocity is given in terms of the liquid superficial velocity as

$$u_L = \frac{u_{LS}}{1 - \alpha} \tag{61}$$

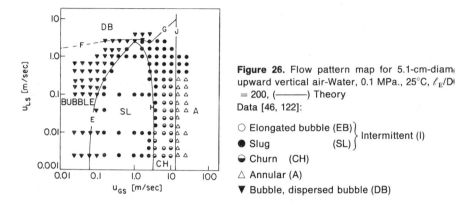

Figure 26. Flow pattern map for 5.1-cm-diam, upward vertical air-Water, 0.1 MPa., 25°C, ℓ_E/D = 200, (————) Theory

Data [46, 122]:

○ Elongated bubble (EB) ⎫
● Slug (SL) ⎬ Intermittent (I)
◑ Churn (CH)
△ Annular (A)
▼ Bubble, dispersed bubble (DB)

Designating u_0 as the rise velocity of the gas bubbles relative to the average liquid velocity, Equations 60 and 61 yield

$$u_{LS} = u_{GS} \frac{1 - \alpha}{\alpha} - (1 - \alpha)u_0 \qquad (62)$$

The rise velocity u_0 of relatively large bubbles has been shown by Harmathy [74] to be quite insensitive to the bubble size and is given by the relation

$$u_0 = 1.53 \left[\frac{g(\rho_L - \rho_G)\sigma}{\rho_L^2} \right]^{1/4} \qquad (63)$$

Substituting Equation 63 into Equation 62 and considering the transition to slug flow to occur when $\alpha = \alpha_T = 0.25$ results in an equation characterizing this transition for conditions where the dispersion forces are not dominant:

$$u_{LS} = 3.0u_{GS} - 1.15 \left[\frac{g(\rho_L - \rho_G)\sigma}{\rho_L^2} \right]^{1/4} \qquad (64)$$

Once fluid properties are designated, the theoretical transition curve can be plotted on u_{LS} vs. u_{GS} coordinates and will remain invariant with tube size. Such a curve is shown in Figure 26 for the water-air system at 25°C and 10 N/cm² where it is designated as curve E. At higher gas and liquid flow rates, where the bubble rise velocity relative to the liquid velocity is negligible, the theoretical transition curve is linear, with a slope of unity in these log coordinates. On the other hand, at low liquid rates where liquid velocity is negligible, the boundary of the bubble region is controlled by the free rise velocity of the bubbles and is essentially independent of liquid rate.

This method for predicting the bubble-slug transition is similar in principle to that of Griffith and Wallis [8]. They used $\alpha = 0.18$ as a criterion for maximum packing and set u_0 equal to a constant of 0.24 m/sec, which is the rise velocity predicted from Equation 63 for an air-water system. The results were, therefore, not general for fluids other than air-water.

At higher liquid flow rates, turbulent forces act to break and disperse the gas phase into small bubbles even for gas void fractions higher than 0.25. The theory of breakup of immiscible fluid phases by turbulent forces was given by Hinze [75] and recently confirmed by Sevik and Park [77]. Hinze determined that the characteristic size of the dispersion results from a balance between surface tension forces and those due to turbulent fluctuations. His study led to the following relationship for the maximum stable diameter of the dispersed phase, d_{max}

$$d_{max} = k \left(\frac{\sigma}{\rho_L} \right)^{3/5} (\varepsilon)^{-2/5} \qquad (65)$$

where ε is the rate of energy dissipation per unit mass. Hinze's investigation explored dispersion under non-coalescing conditions that can be realized only at very low concentrations of the dispersed phase. He applied his formula to the data of Clay [76] for droplet breakup at low concentration of dispersed phase and found k to be equal to 0.725. Sevik and Park [77] developed theoretical values of k by considering the natural frequency of a bubble or drop in its lowest order mode of vibration and found k to be equal to 1.14.

The rate of energy dissipation per unit mass for turbulent pipe flow, ε, is

$$\varepsilon = \left|\frac{dP}{dx}\right| \frac{u_M}{\rho_M} \tag{66}$$

where

$$\frac{dP}{dx} = \frac{2f}{D} \rho_M u_M^2 \tag{67}$$

If the bubble size produced by the breakup process is large enough to permit deformation, then at values of α approaching 0.25 the large Taylor bubbles characteristic of slug flow again are formed by the process of coalescence. Thus, the turbulent breakup process can prevent agglomeration only if the bubble size produced is small enough to cause the bubbles to remain spherical. The bubble size at which this occurs is given by Brodkey [78] as

$$d_{crit} = \left[\frac{0.4\sigma}{(\rho_L - \rho_G)g}\right]^{1/2} \tag{68}$$

Once turbulent fluctuations are vigorous enough to cause the bubbles to break into this small critical size, coalescence is suppressed and the dispersed bubble flow pattern must exist even for $\alpha > 0.25$. From Equations 65 to 68, the conditions for this transition can be found. Note that in this region of high flow rate the slip velocity can be neglected and the gas holdup is calculated simply by

$$\alpha = \frac{u_{GS}}{u_{GS} + u_{LS}} \tag{69}$$

The friction factor needed in Equation 67 can be predicted by the Blasius equation based on the superficial mixture velocity and the liquid kinematic viscosity, namely

$$f = C\left(\frac{u_M D}{\nu_L}\right)^{-n} \tag{70}$$

where C and n are taken as 0.046 and 0.2, respectively. Combining Equations 66–70 results in a dimensionless expression relating the flow rates, properties, and pipe size at which turbulent induced dispersion occurs

$$u_{LS} + u_{GS} = 4.0 \left\{ \frac{D^{0.429}(\sigma/\rho_L)^{0.089}}{\nu_L^{0.072}} \left[\frac{g(\rho_L - \rho_G)}{\rho_L}\right]^{0.446} \right\} \tag{71}$$

An improvement of this transition line was recently suggested by Barnea et al. [37] by including the effect of the gas holdup on the process of coalescence and breakup and on the resulting bubble size.

Calderbank [79] investigated the interrelation between coalescence, breakup, and bubble size in a gas-liquid system and found that the critical bubble diameter increases in proportion to the square root of the gas holdup. Considering that at negligible gas holdup Hinze's [75] correlation is valid and based on Calderbank's measurements the following correlation evolves, which includes the effect of the void fraction on the bubble size:

$$\frac{d_{max}}{(\sigma/\rho_L)^{3/5}\varepsilon^{-2/5}} = 4.15\alpha^{1/2} + 0.725 \tag{72}$$

In addition, d_{crit} is taken as the diameter at which the distortion from spherical shape starts to occur. This is estimated, based on data [80] to be twice the value given by Equation 68. Using the aforementioned modification the transition boundary is calculated to yield

$$2\left[\frac{0.4\sigma}{(\rho_L - \rho_G)g}\right]^{1/2}\left(\frac{\rho_L}{\sigma}\right)^{3/5}\left[\frac{2}{D}C_L\left(\frac{D}{\nu_L}\right)^{-n}\right]^{2/5}u_S^{2(3-n)/5} = 0.725 + 4.15\left(\frac{u_{GS}}{u_S}\right)^{0.5} \tag{73}$$

Once the fluid properties and pipe size are set, Equation 73 defines the relationship between the values of u_{GS} and u_{LS} above which slug flow cannot exist. For air-water at 25°C and 10 N/cm² pressure this result is shown in Figure 26 for a 5.0-cm-diameter pipe and is designated as curve F. However, regardless of how much turbulent energy is available to disperse the mixture, bubble flow cannot exist at packing densities above $\alpha = 0.52$. Thus, the F curve delimiting dispersed bubble flow must terminate at the curve G, which relates u_{LS} and u_{GS} for $\alpha = 0.52$ in Equation 69.

Thus, the bubble flow pattern can be seen to exist in two zones as shown in Figure 26. In the zone to the left of curve E and below F, one predicts the presence of deformable bubbles that move upward with a zig-zag motion with Taylor-type bubbles occasionally appearing in the liquid. In the second zone above curve F and to the left of G, one observes a more finely dispersed bubble system without any Taylor bubbles. To the right of E and below F, one expects to see the slug pattern.

Still a different transition mechanism comes into play in the special case of tubes of small diameter. Consider the zone to the left of curve E and below F in Figure 26 where one observes discrete deformable bubbles rising in zig-zag paths and the occasional appearance of a Taylor bubble. The velocity of rise of the deformable bubbles relative to the liquid u_0 is given by Equation 63 and depends only on the properties of the fluids. The rise velocity of the Taylor bubbles relative to the mean velocity of the liquid on the other hand is given by [81, 82].

$$u_G \simeq 0.35\sqrt{gD} \tag{74}$$

and is property independent. Whenever $u_0 > u_G$ the rising bubbles approach the back of the Taylor bubble coalescing with it and increasing its size. Under these conditions bubbly flow cannot exist in this zone. On the other hand, when $u_0 < u_G$ the Taylor bubble rises through the array of distributed bubbles and the relative motion of the liquid at the nose of the Taylor bubble sweeps the small bubbles around the larger one, and coalescence does not occur. The properties of air-water at low pressure are such that $u_0 \simeq u_G$ at $D \simeq 5.0$ cm. Thus, for tubes smaller than 5 cm in diameter, no bubbly flow can exist below the curve F and the entire zone is in slug flow. Only at high liquid rates, above F and G, can bubbly flow exist for small tubes where dispersion occurs due to turbulence. The flow pattern map for 2.5-cm-diameter tubes and air-water is shown in Figure 27. A

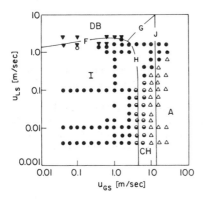

Figure 27. Flow pattern map for 2.54-cm-diam upward vertical air-Water, 0.1 MPa., 25°C, $\ell_E/D = 400$, (———) Theory. (See Figure 26 for legend.)

system having a small diameter satisfies the criterion:

$$\left[\frac{\rho_L^2 g D^2}{(\rho_L - \rho_G)\sigma} \right]^{1/4} \leq 4.36 \tag{75}$$

It is of interest that the range of diameters used in most laboratory air-water experiments, i.e., 2–6 cm, spans this critical diameter of 5.0 cm. This accounts for the apparent differences in reported observations. It also shows that for this particular transition, experimental data taken on small pipes cannot be scaled to larger diameters. It is only through an understanding of mechanism, as discussed here, that rational size scaling can be accomplished.

Slug-Churn Transition

The slug flow pattern develops from a bubbly pattern when the gas flow increases to such an extent that it forces the bubbles to become closely packed and coalesce. At this point Taylor type bubbles are formed which, if the process of coalescence continues, occupy most of the pipe cross-sectional area and are axially separated by a liquid slug in which small bubbles are dispersed. The liquid confined between the bubble and the pipe wall flows around the bubble as a falling film.

As the gas flow rate is increased still more, a transition to churn flow occurs. There is a considerable difficulty in accurately identifying the slug-churn transition because there is a confusion as to the description of the churn flow itself. Some identify churn flow on the basis of the froth that appears within the gas region, and these investigations describe the pattern as frothy. Others associate churn flow with the instability of the liquid film adjacent to the Taylor bubble. The churn flow pattern is characterized here as that condition where oscillatory motion of the liquid is observed, contrary to slug flow where the liquid between two Taylor bubbles moves at a constant velocity and its front as well as its tail have constant speed.

There have been several mechanisms proposed for transition to the churn pattern. Nicklin and Davidson [82] suggested that the transition to churn flow occurs when the gas velocity relative to the falling liquid film around the Taylor bubble approaches the condition of flooding. Moissis [83] attributed this transition to Helmholtz instability of the liquid film bounding the Taylor bubble. The Helmholtz instability criterion was applied for an infinitely thick gas region and very thin liquid film using Feldman's [84] result that the wavelength is 10 times the film thickness. The analysis is inconsistent since Feldman's theory is not based on Helmholtz type analysis. Griffith and Wallis [8] suggested that transition from slug to annular flow occurs when the individual Taylor bubbles become very (infinitely) long. Their predicted transition to annular flow occurs at much lower gas rates than indicated by experiment, which suggests that this mechanism might account for the slug-churn transition instead. No predictive model was presented, and their transition curve was finally obtained solely from experimental data.

Careful and repeated observations of the slug-churn flow patterns on 2.5- and 5.0-cm-diameter test sections in our laboratories suggest a rather different mechanism than any of the above. These observations indicate that the churn flow pattern is an entry region phenomenon associated with the existence of slug flow further along the pipe. That is, whenever one observes slug flow, the condition near the entry appears to be churning. Furthermore, the entry length, or the distance that such churning can be observed before stable slug flow takes place, depends on the flow rates and pipe size.

The process of developing a stable slug near the entrance section can be described as follows: at the inlet the gas and liquid, which are introduced, form short liquid slugs and Taylor bubbles. A short liquid slug is known to be unstable and it falls back and merges with the liquid slug coming from below causing it to approximately double its length. In this process, the Taylor bubble following the liquid slug overtakes the leading Taylor bubble and coalesces with it as the slug between the two bubbles collapses. This process repeats itself and the length of the liquid slugs as well as the length of the Taylor bubbles increase as they move upwards, until the liquid slug is long enough to be stable and form a competent bridge between two consecutive Taylor bubbles. Between the inlet and the position at which a stable slug is formed, the liquid slug alternately rises and falls, and this is precisely the condition of churn flow. As the gas rate increases, it is evident that the length of this entrance region increases to the extent that it can occupy the entire length of any test section. Thus, one should think of churn flow as an entrance phenomenon. Since, in practice, all pipes are of finite length, it would be useful to provide some estimates of the lengths over which churn flow is the predominant mode. With this objective, a method was developed for calculating the entry length required to develop stable slug flow. The distance from the entrance to that length will be observed to be in the churn flow pattern.

The rise velocity of a Taylor bubble can be estimated [81, 82]

$$u_G \simeq 1.2u_M + 0.35\sqrt{gD} \tag{76}$$

In this equation the second term on the right-hand side describes the rise velocity of a large bubble in stagnant liquid. It was derived theoretically by Davies and Taylor [85] and by Dumitrescu [86]. The first term on the right side adds the liquid velocity at the centerline, since 1.2 is approximately the ratio of centerline to average velocity in fully developed turbulent flow.

Consider two consecutive Taylor bubbles as shown in Figure 28. The first (top) bubble moves at a velocity given by Equation 76. The second (lower) bubble will move at the same speed when the slug length ℓ_s is long enough so that the velocity profile in the liquid at the front of the second bubble will be the same as that at the front of the first bubble, namely, the average velocity is u_M and the centerline velocity is $1.2u_M$. This is the situation to be expected when the slugs are long enough so that the turbulent velocity distribution in the liquid can be fully reestablished before the next Taylor bubble appears. Then the velocity of the two consecutive Taylor bubbles is the same, the length of the liquid slug will remain constant with time and position in the direction of flow and stable slug flow exists.

But since the liquid slugs are shorter in the developing region, the velocity distribution in the liquid can be severely distorted by the flow reversal near the wall as a result of the falling film. Consider the velocity distributions in the planes A-A and B-B behind the leading Taylor bubble shown in Figure 28. If the liquid slug is long, far enough behind the trailing edge of the bubble (plane B-B), the velocity becomes that typical of turbulent flow. However, at A-A the flow is downward near the wall as a result of the falling film around the bubble. In order to maintain mass continuity, the velocity at the centerline must increase. Since the velocity of a Taylor bubble depends on the centerline velocity plus its rise velocity, it is clear that for liquid slugs too short to reestablish the turbulent velocity distribution, the second bubble will overtake the first [87]. As a result, the two bubbles will coalesce, the liquid bridge between them will disintegrate, and fall to a lower level creating churn flow.

Experimental observations for water-air systems suggest that the length of a stable slug relative to its diameter, ℓ_s/D is fairly constant and independent of gas and liquid flow rates [4, 88]. The

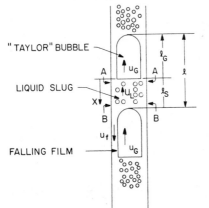

Figure 28. Slug flow geometry.

minimum value of ℓ_s/D reported was 8. Studies in our laboratory, using very long 2.5 and 5.0-cm-diameter tubes, showed stable slug lengths approach 16D. The earlier observations can be considered the result of two slugs, each not quite of stable length, $\ell_s/D = 8$, which approach each other so slowly that they would never coalesce except in a long tube. By use of the following very approximate argument, it is possible to show that this stable length, $\ell_s/D = 16$, observed for air-water, should be essentially independent of fluid properties or pipe diameter.

The liquid falling along the Taylor bubble has an average velocity u_f and velocity relative to the liquid at plane A-A behind the bubble of $(u_f + u_G)$. Consider this liquid sheet as a two-dimensional jet that enters a stagnant pool of liquid (the slug) at a uniform velocity, $(u_f + u_G)$. The axial velocity, u, in the liquid induced by the jet will depend on the distance x in the direction of the jet and y, the normal distance from the jet centerline. Both experimental and theoretical studies have shown that the ratio of $u(x, y)$ to $u_{max}(x, 0)$ varies as

$$\frac{u}{u_{max}} = 1 - \tanh^2\left(\gamma\,\frac{y}{x}\right) \tag{77}$$

where γ is a universal constant approximately equal to 7.67 [89]. A stable slug is one long enough that the jet has been absorbed by the fluid and the velocities have slowed to that of the surroundings. In this case, we explore the distance $x = \ell_s$ which at the centerline, $y = D/2$, the velocity profile is essentially flat, say $u/u_{max} \geq 0.95$, and thus the normal turbulent distribution in the liquid slug is undistorted. Equation 77 shows that this occurs at $\ell_s/D \simeq 16$. This is, of course, only an approximate argument because the falling film is a wall jet, not a free jet and the fluid is confined, not of infinite extent. However, Patel [90] showed that the velocity distributions in a wall jet on the side of the velocity maximum away from the wall can be estimated as in a free jet. Since the falling film is so thin, the approximations previously used become quite reasonable.

Entry length for churn flow. Designate ℓ_E as the entry length of pipe required to establish stable slug flow and therefore the region that one would observe churning. Consider a coordinate x pointing downward from the trailing edge of the leading Taylor bubble as in Figure 28. The velocity at the center of the pipe, u_C varies from u_G at $x = 0$ to $1.2u_M$ at $x = \ell_s$. Assume exponential variation with x as

$$u_C = u_G e^{-\beta x/\ell_s} + 1.2u_M(1 - e^{-\beta x/\ell_s}) \tag{78}$$

The constant β determines the decay rate and was chosen at $\beta = \ln 100 = 4.6$ so that at $x = \ell_s$ the decay will be 1%. The final results are not sensitive to the particular choice of β, or to the particular profile assumed as long as $u_C(x = 0) = u_G$ and $u_C(x = \ell_s) = 1.2u_M$. Designating the leading bubble as the first and the trailing bubble as the second and using Equation 76 for calculating the velocities of the two consecutive bubbles, we obtain an approach velocity between two bubbles, $-\dot{x}$, as

$$-\dot{x} = u_{G2} - u_{G1} = (u_G - 1.2u_M)e^{-\beta x/\ell_s} = 0.35\sqrt{gD}\,e^{-\beta x/\ell_s} \tag{79}$$

In calculating the entry length or length for churn flow, it is assumed that near the gas liquid inlet, coalescence is instantaneous and short Taylor bubbles as well as short liquid slugs are formed The merging of the Taylor bubbles to larger gas bubbles and larger liquid slugs occurs when the second bubble overtakes the leading bubble. When they combine the volume, as well as the length, of the newly created Taylor bubble is doubled. Likewise, the liquid slug behind the leading bubble falls and merges with the liquid slug behind the second bubble to create a slug twice as long. At approximately the same time, the third and fourth bubbles will combine and again create a new bubble and new liquid slug of double length. This process will go on, and pairs of bubbles will coalesce as they move upward, doubling their length each time until a stable liquid slug of length $\ell_s/D \simeq 16$ is formed. The term ℓ_s designates the length of a stable slug while ℓ_L is the length of a slug formed during the period of coalescence. Because the last merger of two slugs of length $\ell_L = 8D$ is quite slow, we consider the entrance of churning length to exist up to the point where $\ell_L = 8D$ or $(\ell_L = \ell_s/2)$, the region of churn flow.

Integrating Equation 79 gives the time needed for each merger as a function the distance, ℓ_{Li}, between two consecutive bubbles

$$t_i = \frac{\ell_s}{0.35\beta\sqrt{gD}} \left[e^{\beta\ell_{Li}/\ell_s} - 1\right] \tag{80}$$

where i takes successive values of 0, 1, 2, 3, ... Letting ℓ_{Li} take the sequence from 0 to $\ell_s/4$, namely, $\ell_{Li} = \ell_s/4, \ell_s/8, \ell_s/16, \ldots, 0$ yields an infinite series for t_i whose sum multiplied by u_G yields the estimated entrance length ℓ_E.

$$\ell_E = \frac{\ell_s u_G}{0.35\beta\sqrt{gD}} \sum_{n=2}^{\infty} (e^{\beta/2^m} - 1) \tag{81}$$

or considering $\beta = 4.6$ and $\ell_s = 16D$ yields

$$\frac{\ell_E}{D} = 35.5 \frac{u_G}{\sqrt{gD}} \tag{82}$$

$$\frac{\ell_E}{D} = 40.6\left(\frac{u_M}{\sqrt{gD}} + 0.22\right) \tag{83}$$

where $u_M = u_{GS} + u_{LS}$. This shows that the dimensionless entry length for churning depends on one parameter, namely, $u_M/\sqrt{gD}$. The solution to this equation for a low pressure air-water system and a pipe length of $\ell = 10$ m is shown in Figures 26 and 27 for 5.0- and 2.5-cm-diameter tubes where these curves are designated as "H."

Transition to Annular Flow

For high gas flow rates the flow becomes annular. The liquid film flows upwards adjacent to the wall, and gas flows in the center carrying entrained liquid droplets. The upward flow of the liquid film against gravity results from the forces exerted by the fast moving gas core. This film has a wavy interface and the waves tend to shatter and enter the gas core as entrained droplets. Thus, the liquid moves upwards, due to both interfacial shear and form "drag" on the waves and drag on the droplets. Based on the idea by Turner et al. [91] applied to gas lift operations, it is suggested that annular flow cannot exist, unless the gas velocity in the gas core is sufficient to lift the entrained droplets. When the gas rate is insufficient, the droplets fall back, accumulate, form a bridge, and churn or slug flow takes place.

The minimum gas velocity required to suspend a drop is determined from the balance between the gravity and drag forces acting on the drop:

$$\tfrac{1}{2}C_d(\pi d^2/4)\rho_G u_G^2 = (\pi d^3/6)g(\rho_L - \rho_G) \tag{84}$$

or

$$u_G = \frac{2}{\sqrt{3}} \left[\frac{g(\rho_L - \rho_G)d}{\rho_G C_d}\right]^{1/2} \tag{85}$$

The drop size is determined by the balance between the impact force of the gas that tends to shatter the drop and surface tension forces that hold the drop together. Hinze [75] showed that the maximum stable drop size will be $d = K\sigma/\rho_G u_G^2$ where K is the critical Weber number and takes a value between 20 and 30 for drops that are gradually accelerated. Substituting into Equation 85 yields

$$u_G = \left(\frac{4K}{3C_d}\right)^{1/4} \frac{[\sigma g(\rho_L - \rho_G)]^{1/4}}{\rho_G^{1/2}} \tag{86}$$

As suggested by Turner et al. [91] values of K = 30 and C_d = 0.44 were selected. Note that K and C_d appear in the power of 1/4. Thus, the result for u_G is quite insensitive to their exact values. The gas velocity given by Equation 86 predicts the minimum value below which stable annular flow will not exist. While this analysis is applied to the droplets within the gas core, the same treatment can be used for the crests of the waves on the rising film, which are pictured as being supported by the gas stream in a manner similar to the support of the liquid droplets.

Characteristic of annular flow is that the film thickness is quite low even for relatively high liquid flow rates. As a result the true gas velocity u_G can be replaced by the superficial rate u_{GS} and the final transition boundary is given by

$$\frac{u_{GS}\rho_G^{1/2}}{[\sigma g(\rho_L - \rho_G)]^{1/4}} = 3.1 \tag{87}$$

This simple criterion shows the transition to the annular pattern is independent of liquid flow rate and pipe diameter. For water-air at 25°C, 10 N/cm² this velocity is calculated to be about 15 m/sec, and the transition boundary is plotted as a vertical line in Figures 26 and 27 designated as curve J. The dimensionless group in Equation 87 is recognized as the Kutateladze number.

Equation 87 is almost identical to the empirical results of Pushkina and Sorokin [92], who determined the air velocity necessary to lift the liquid film for flooding experiments in tubes varying from 6 to 309 mm in diameter. They correlated their experimental results in terms of the Kutateladze number, except the constant 3.1 is replaced by the constant 3.2. While Pushkina and Sorokin arrived at their result by dimensional analysis and experiment, this development places a theoretical basis under the result.

Conclusion

The predicted transition boundaries for vertical upward flow are represented by simple algebraic equations. For given operational conditions and fluids properties these transitions criteria can readily be drawn on a u_{LS}-u_{GS} coordinates map. Comparisons of the theoretically predicted transitions with data taken in 2.5 and 5.0-cm-diameter tubes [40] show good agreement.

Previously published data on vertical upflow show a considerable scatter and disagreement both among themselves as well as in comparison to the present theory. This results from the difficulty of defining and observing the flow pattern boundaries for upward flow which is usually fast and chaotic. Nevertheless, it seems the theory presents a reasonable average of the previously published results.

VERTICAL DOWNWARD FLOW

Downward flow received less attention than upward flow, and there are relatively few investigations of gas liquid mixtures in downward flow. Golan and Stenning [93] considered downward flow in an inverted U tube consisted of a vertical riser followed by a vertical downcomer. In the downcomer they identified the transition from slug and bubble flow to annular flow. In between the two boundaries they found an oscillatory regime that results probably because of the U type configuration of the pipe. Martin [94] investigated the transition from bubble to slug flow in downward flow of air-water in a 14-cm-diameter pipe. The data was correlated on a map of "flowing volumetric concentration" versus Froude number and on a map of gas flux versus liquid flux. Martin [95] investigated experimentally vertical downward slug flow of air-water mixtures in pipes and measured the terminal velocity of descending, stationary, and ascending bubbles in downward flows. Kulov et al. [96] measured pressure drop, film thickness, and entrainment in downward two-phase flow, and proposed relationships for calculating the measured parameters as a function of gas and liquid flow rates. An experimental study on downward vertical flow in an air-water system was carried out by Yamazaki and Yamaguchi [97] on flow regimes, holdup, and pressure drop. Spedding and Nguyen [7] published a flow regime map for vertical downward flow using their own classification that has been presented previously (Figure 29).

The data of Barnea et al. [37] as well as the predicted flow pattern boundaries are shown in Figures 30 and 31, for pipe diameters of 2.5 and 5.1 cm, respectively. Three flow regimes were

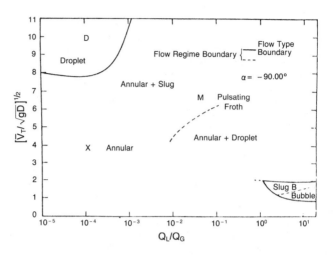

Figure 29. Spedding and Nguyen [7] flow regime map for vertical downwards (D—droplet; B—bubble; both X and M regimes are in the annular flow region.)

observed: annular flow, slug flow, and dispersed bubble flow. The most "natural" regime in vertical downward flow is the annular flow, which takes the form of falling film at low gas rate and typical annular flow for high gas flow rates.

At high liquid flow rates of about 0.6 cm/sec the annular-to-slug-flow transition is observed. This transition occurs at relatively constant liquid flow rate. At very high gas flow rates the transition line to slug flow moves slightly towards higher liquid flow rates.

As the liquid rate is increased still further a transition to dispersed bubble is observed. For the 2.54-cm-diameter pipe (Figure 30) this transition is almost at the same position as in vertical upflow, while in the 5.1-cm-diameter pipe the transition to dispersed bubble occurs at relatively lower liquid flow rates and the slug flow regime shrinks somewhat (Figure 31).

Modeling Flow Pattern Transitions for Vertical Downward Flow

Barnea et al. [37] modeled the transition mechanisms in vertical downward flow. The process of analyzing transition between flow regimes in downward flow starts from the condition of annular flow that can be expected at low liquid flow rates. The approach is to determine the mechanism

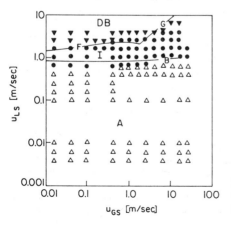

Figure 30. Flow pattern map for 2.54-cm-diam vertical downward air-Water, 0.1 MPa., 25°C, (———) Theory. (See Figure 18 for legend.)

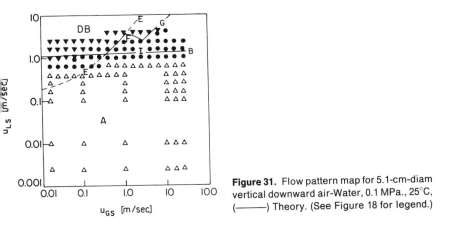

Figure 31. Flow pattern map for 5.1-cm-diam vertical downward air-Water, 0.1 MPa., 25°C, (———) Theory. (See Figure 18 for legend.)

by which a change from annular to slug flow is expected to occur and then determine the mechanism for the slug-dispersed bubble transition. The first step is to develop the relationship between the film thickness and the flow parameters.

Consider an equilibrium annular (or falling film) flow, as shown in Figure 32, a momentum balance on each phase yields

$$-A_L\left(\frac{dP}{dx}\right) - \tau_L S_L + \tau_i S_i + \rho_L A_L g = 0 \tag{88}$$

$$-A_G\left(\frac{dp}{dx}\right) - \tau_i S_i + \rho_G A_G g = 0 \tag{89}$$

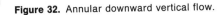

Figure 32. Annular downward vertical flow.

Equating pressure drop in the two phases yields

$$\tau_i S_i \left(\frac{1}{A_L} + \frac{1}{A_G} \right) + g(\rho_L - \rho_G) - \tau_L \frac{S_L}{A_L} = 0 \tag{90}$$

Substituting

$$S_L = \pi D \qquad\qquad S_i = \pi(D - 2\delta)$$

$$A_L = \pi(D\delta - \delta^2) \qquad A_G = \pi \left(\frac{D}{2} - \delta \right)^2 \tag{91}$$

yields

$$\tau_i \frac{1}{D(\tilde{\delta} - \tilde{\delta}^2)(1 - 2\tilde{\delta})} + g(\rho_L - \rho_G) - \tau_L \frac{1}{D(\tilde{\delta} - \tilde{\delta}^2)} = 0 \tag{92}$$

where $\tilde{\delta} = \delta/D$.
The shear stresses are evaluated in the conventional manner

$$\tau_L = f_L \frac{\rho_L u_L^2}{2} \qquad \tau_i = f_i \frac{\rho_G(u_G - u_L)^2}{2} \tag{93}$$

with the liquid and the interfacial friction factors evaluated from

$$f_L = C_L \left(\frac{D_L u_L}{\nu_L} \right)^{-n} \qquad f_i \simeq f_G = C_G \left(\frac{D_G u_G}{\nu_G} \right)^{-m} \tag{94}$$

where $\quad D_L = \dfrac{4A_L}{S_L} = 4D(\tilde{\delta} - \tilde{\delta}^2) \qquad D_G = \dfrac{4A_G}{S_G} = (1 - 2\tilde{\delta})D \tag{95}$

$$u_L = \frac{u_{Ls}}{4(\tilde{\delta} - \tilde{\delta}^2)} \qquad\qquad u_G = \frac{u_{Gs}}{1 - 4\tilde{\delta} + 4\tilde{\delta}^2} \tag{96}$$

The following coefficients were used: $C_G = C_L = 0.046$, $n = m = 0.2$ for the turbulent flow and $C_G = C_L = 16$, $n = m = 1.0$ for laminar flow.

A solution of Equation 92 yields the film thickness as a function of the superficial liquid and gas velocities, the physical properties of the fluids and the pipe diameter.

The criterion for transition between annular and slug flow is based on the same concept as in Taitel and Dukler [36]. A stable slug will be formed when the supply of liquid in the film is large enough to provide the liquid needed to maintain such a slug. When the liquid holdup within the liquid slug is twice the liquid holdup in annular flow then transition to slug flow occurs. It is visualized that such a slug is formed when, because of waves, an axial transfer of fluid from the wave trough is transferred to the wave crest. When enough liquid is present at the crest cross section, a blockage occurs, which leads to transition to slug flow.

Assuming the liquid holdup within the liquid slug is 0.7, the transition to slug flow will take place at

$$\frac{A_L}{0.7A} = 0.5 \quad \text{or} \quad \frac{A_L}{A} = 0.35 \tag{97}$$

The transition line based on this criterion is plotted in Figures 30 and 31 as transition B and show a good agreement with the experimental data for $D = 2.5$ cm and somewhat higher values, but still acceptable, for $D = 5.1$ cm.

The mechanism of transition from slug to dispersed bubble flow is the same as in upward vertical flow, transition F. This transition occurs when turbulent forces overcome interfacial tension to disperse the gas phase into small bubbles and is not affected by gravity. Thus, the result given by Equation 73 is applicable here. Transition F can be used up to gas holdup of $\alpha = 0.52$ where a maximum "packing" of gas bubbles is reached. For $\alpha > 0.52$ transition to dispersed bubble is given by transition G (Equation 69).

Similar to the case of vertical upward flow the bubble flow pattern can exist below the aforementioned transition line provided (a) the pipe diameter is larger than (Equation 75)

$$D > 19\left[\frac{(\rho_L - \rho_G)\sigma}{\rho_L^2 g}\right]^{1/2} \tag{98}$$

and (b) the gas holdup is below $\alpha = 0.25$

Conditions (a) and (b) represent the situation where coalescence is negligible and bubbles keep their separate identity even under relatively low liquid rate.

Condition (a) is associated with the difference between the rise velocity of Taylor bubbles and small spherical bubbles. A necessary condition for bubble flow to exist is that whenever a random Taylor type agglomeration is formed, its upward velocity should exceed the bubbles velocity. This condition is satisfied for pipe diameters given by Equation 98. In the case of smaller pipe diameters the faster rising bubbles approach the back end of the Taylor bubble coalescing with it and increasing its size. Under these conditions bubbly flow cannot exist.

Condition (b) states that at low liquid rates and low density of bubbles coalescence is not likely in pipe diameters larger than those given by Equation 98. Thus for large pipe size the value of $\alpha = 0.25$ was chosen as the transition line separating slug and bubbly flow. This transition line is given by

$$u_{LS} = 3u_{GS} + 1.15[g(\rho_L - \rho_G)\sigma/\rho_L^2]^{1/4} \tag{99}$$

which corresponds to Equation 64 for down flow.

Thus, for a pipe size of 5 cm the transition to dispersed bubble is composed of four different sections depending on the mechanism of transition. Proceeding from right to left (see Figure 31) the first section is transition G line of $\alpha = 0.52$ (Equation 69) below which bubbles cannot exist because of their high density. The second section is the transition F caused by turbulent breakup (Equation 73). The third section is the transition E of $\alpha = 0.25$ for which, as discussed, bubbles can exist even at low turbulent conditions provided $\alpha < 0.25$ and coalescence is negligible (Equation 99). Finally, the fourth section is the extension of the transition to annular flow that for low gas flow rate represents annular-dispersed bubble transition while for higher gas flow rate it is for annular-slug transition line (transition B).

For a pipe diameter of 2.54 cm the transition to dispersed bubble is shown in Figure 30 to consist of only two sections: transition G and transition F. As mentioned for small diameter pipes, bubbles cannot exist at liquid flow rates below transition F.

As seen in Figures 30 and 31, the experimental results show a considerable different trend of the transition to dispersed bubble for 2.54 and 5.1-cm pipes, which follows reasonably well the trend predicted by the theory.

UPWARD INCLINED FLOW

Most of the data reported on flow pattern transitions have dealt with either horizontal or vertical tubes with only limited results reported for inclined pipes. Several investigators have considered only one transition for inclined pipes while others have performed experiments only over a limited range of inclination angles.

Singh and Griffith [98a] investigated slug flow in an air-water system at shallow upward inclination and developed simple correlations for pressure drop and holdup. Slug flow in inclined pipes was also treated by Bonnecaze et al. [99] who reported data for air-water at angles ranging over $\pm 10°$ from the horizontal. Beggs and Brill [100] developed a model for the prediction of pressure drop and holdup in inclined pipes based on the use of holdup correlations for horizontal flow to which a correction factor for the inclination angle is applied. Although data was taken systematically in the full range of $\pm 90°$ inclination angles, no flow pattern maps were reported. Gould et al. [14] published flow pattern maps for pipes that were horizontal and vertical, and for inclined upward flow at 45°. They concluded that the location of the transition boundaries for the dispersed bubble and annular flow pattern does not vary significantly with inclination.

Experimental flow regime maps for air-water flow in inclined pipes at angles from vertically upward to vertically downward were recently reported by Spedding and Nguyen [7]. The maps are based on data collected in a 6-m-long perspex pipe with an inner diameter of 4.55 cm. Their map for 45° upward inclination is given in Figure 33.

Weisman and Kang [70] present data for air-water and air-glycerol systems in slightly inclined pipes and for freon liquid-vapor system at inclination angles of 30°, 45°, and 90°. Based on their own data, and those reported by Spedding and Nguyen [7], the authors proposed empirical correlations for the transition boundaries to annular flow, to dispersed bubble flow and between intermittent and bubble flow. Their overall flow pattern map constructed for vertical and sharply inclined pipes is given in Figure 25 in u_{LS}, u_{GS} coordinates. ϕ_1 and ϕ_2 are correction factors for physical properties and geometry (Table 2).

Shoham [46] and Barnea et al. [39] reported new data on flow pattern transition for gas-liquid flow in upward inclined flow that cover the whole range of inclination. The experimental apparatus consisted of air and water supply systems and test sections made of two transparent plexiglass tubes with I.D. of 2.55 and 5.1 cm. The tubes that were 10 m long were supported on a steel frame capable of varying the angle of inclination continuously in the full range from horizontal to vertical. The flow patterns were determined by visual observation and by oscilloscope display using conductivity probes as suggested by Barnea et al. [1].

The effect of the inclination angle on the flow pattern transition boundaries was examined by varying the inclination angle in small steps in the range of 0° to 90°. Some of the flow pattern data are presented in Figures 18, 19, 26, 27, and 34–41.

Small inclinations from the horizontal have a major effect on the transition from stratified to intermittent or annular pattern. Such inclinations cause intermittent flow to take place over a much

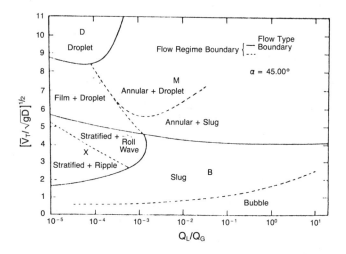

Figure 33. Spedding and Nguyen [7] flow regime map for upward inclined flow $\beta = 45°$ (D—droplet; X—stratification; M—mixed; B—bubble.)

wider range of flow rates (Figures 34–41). The stratified-intermittent transition is very sensitive to the angle of inclination. Even for upward slopes of less than 1° the regime of stratified flow shrinks into a small dome shaped region (see Figures 34 and 35). The stratified smooth pattern is not observed except for angles of less than 0.25°. For values of $u_{LS} > 0.001$ stratified flow is not observed at all at angles greater than about 20°.

For these small angles the intermittent-annular transition passes to the left of the dome (see Figures 34–37). Thus, there exists a range of liquid rates for which, as gas rate is increased, the pattern changes from intermittent to stratified and then to annular.

Studies in vertical tubes showed that at low liquid rates bubbly flow could exist only in pipes large enough to satisfy a diameter criterion (Equation 75). However, as these "large" pipes are

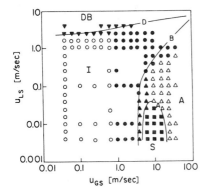

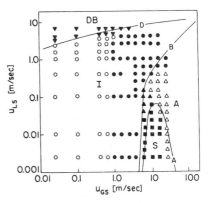

Figure 34. Flow pattern map for 2.54-cm-diam, 0.5° upward inclination air-Water, 0.1 MPa., 25°C, (———) Theory. (See Figure 18 for legend.)

Figure 35. Flow pattern map for 5.1-cm-diam, 0.5° upward inclination air-Water, 0.1 MPa., 25°C, (———) Theory. (See Figure 18 for legend.)

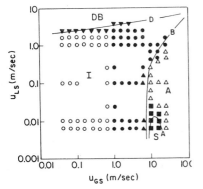

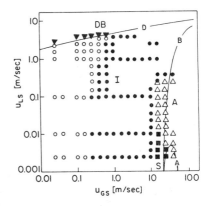

Figure 36. Flow pattern map for 2.54-cm-diam, 2° upward inclination air-Water, 0.1 MPa., 25°C. (———) Theory. (See Figure 18 for legend.)

Figure 37. Flow pattern map for 5.1-cm-diam, 10° upward inclination air-Water, 0.1 MPa., 25°C, (———) Theory. (See Figure 18 for legend.)

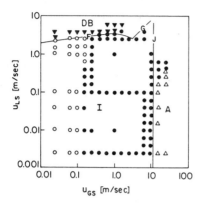

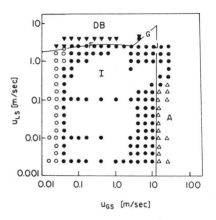

Figure 38. Flow pattern map for 5.1-cm-diam, 20° upward inclination air-Water, 0.1 MPa., 25°C, (———) Theory. (See Figure 18 for legend.)

Figure 39. Flow pattern map for 5.1-cm-diam, 50° upward inclination air-Water, 0.1 MPa., 25°C, (———) Theory. (See Figure 26 for legend.)

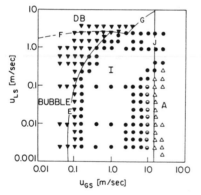

Figure 40. Flow pattern map for 5.1-cm-diam, 70° upward inclination air-Water, 0.1 MPa., 25°C, (———) Theory. (See Figure 26 for legend.)

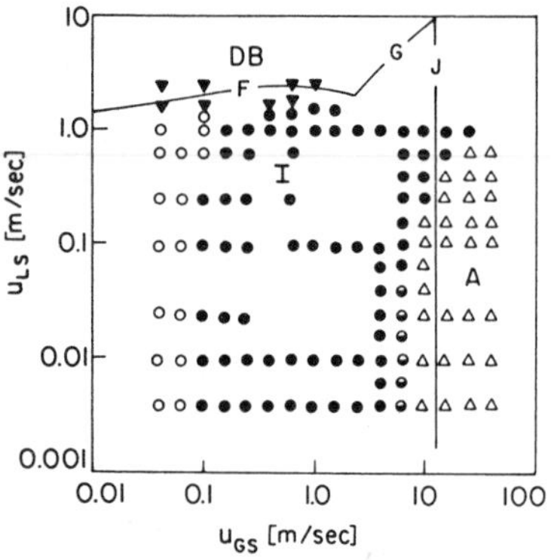

Figure 41. Flow pattern map for 2.5-cm-diam, 70° upward inclination air-Water, 0.1 MPa., 25°C, (———) Theory. (See Figure 26 for legend.)

inclined off the vertical, the data presented here (compare Figures 26, 39, and 40) show that the region of bubbly flow observed at low liquid rates disappears. Then only at high liquid rates where turbulent forces cause breakup is the dispersed bubble pattern observed. In these experiments the angle below which the bubbly flow vanishes is between 50°–70°.

The churn flow pattern is typical of vertical upward flow. It persists in off-vertical inclination angles down to 70° where it shrinks into a very small region on the flow pattern map (Figures 40 and 41).

In summary, small deviations from the horizontal have profound effects on the flow pattern map while small deviations from the vertical have little effect on the flow patterns. At large angles from the vertical significant changes in flow patterns are observed.

Modeling Flow Pattern Transitions for Upward Inclined Flow

The objective in developing flow pattern transition boundaries is to propose models that will apply to all angles of inclination; namely, that the effect of inclination will be incorporated in the model in such a way that the same model will apply for horizontal, vertical up, vertical down, and all angles of inclination.

Such an aim seems to be too ambitious at the present. So far the models proposed apply either to the horizontal or the vertical case; namely, mechanisms of transition or accuracy of the model in the horizontal case could be different from the vertical case. Simplicity requires that only few mechanisms be considered and those that are important for horizontal flow do not apply for vertical flow and vice versa. As a result, we presently have different models for horizontal and vertical flows.

Owing to this limitation, a natural approach to treat the inclined flow is to extend the vertical models to include the steep inclination while the shallow inclination could be treated via extension of the horizontal and slightly inclined model.

This is the approach implemented here while the terms "shallow inclination" and "steep inclination" may however apply to a different inclination angle for each transition boundary, depending on the range of applicability of the modified horizontal and vertical models.

The Shallow Inclination Model

The previously published model [36] applies in principle to horizontal and "slightly" inclined pipes, yet the term "slightly" is not defined. As the angle of inclination increases, the accuracy of the model is expected to be affected. For example, in upward inclination τ_i is expected to increase with the angle of inclination and this is not considered by the model. In addition, the mechanism of transition to bubble flow, which is based on the buoyancy effect, becomes invalid at high inclinations. Therefore, the accuracy of the horizontal model is limited to shallow inclination, however, the angle at which the model is not applicable can be different for each transition boundary.

Presently, the applicability of the horizontal and "slightly" inclined model will be based on experimental results.

Steep Inclination Model

The model for vertical upward flow is modified to include the off vertical inclination.

Bubble-to-slug transitions. Taitel et al. [16] showed that three transition mechanisms are operative for vertical tubes.

At high liquid rates, the turbulence causes the bubbles to break. Thus, coalescence to form the large Taylor bubbles required for slug flow cannot take place. This transition to dispersed bubble flow was given by Equation 73 (the F curve), which is valid for $0 \leq \alpha \leq 0.52$. At the higher limit the packing density makes it impossible to maintain discrete bubbles. The curve on a flow pattern map characterizing the condition of $\alpha = 0.52$ is

$$u_{LS} = u_{GS} \frac{1 - \alpha}{\alpha} \tag{100}$$

where $\alpha = 0.52$ (curve G).

At low liquid rates where turbulence does not cause bubble breakup but coalescence is negligible, bubble flow can exist provided two conditions are met: (a) pipe diameter is large

$$D > 19 \left[\frac{(\rho_L - \rho_G)\sigma}{\rho_L^2 g} \right]^{1/2} \tag{101}$$

(b) the bubbles void fraction is less then $\alpha \simeq 0.25$. For inclined pipes this condition is given by Equation 62 modified for inclined tubes

$$u_{LS} = \frac{1 - \alpha}{\alpha} u_{GS} - 1.53(1 - \alpha)\left[\frac{g(\rho_L - \rho_G)^\sigma}{\rho_L^2}\right]^{1/4} \sin \beta \qquad (102)$$

where $\alpha = 0.25$.

This transition was observed only in vertical upward flow and in steep upward inclinations. However, when the tube is inclined below a specific angle, bubbly flow no longer exists (compare Figures 26, 39, and 40). This can be explained by the fact that as the angle decreases the bubbles tend to migrate to the top wall of the pipe. High local voids result and a transition to slug flow occurs even when the cross-sectional average voidage is less than 0.25. An estimate of the angle below which bubbly flow cannot exist can be developed as follows. Miyagi [80] investigated the motion of large bubbles in still water in vertical tubes. He indicated that the shape of a bubble changes as it moves upwards in a zig-zag path as described schematically in Figure 42. The bubble flattens in the direction of motion and its zig-zag path consists of oblique legs where the bubbles accelerate as they move away from the wall and decelerate as they approach the opposite wall. The forces that act on the bubble near the wall (see Figure 42) are buoyancy F_B, drag F_D, and "lift" F_L. When the tube is slightly inclined from the vertical, the buoyancy force can be resolved into a component parallel to the pipe axis (F_{Ba}) and a component normal to the pipe wall (F_{Br}). F_{Br} tends to keep the dispersed bubbles at the upper part of the pipe and enhance the transition to intermittent flow. On the other hand, the "lift" force tends to disperse the bubble maintaining the bubble pattern. The condition for the existence of the dispersed bubbles at low liquid flow rates is thus

$$F_B \cos(\beta) < F_L \qquad (103)$$

where β is the angle of inclination below which bubbly flow cannot exist due to high local voids at the upper wall.

$$F_B = \frac{1}{6}d^3(\rho_L - \rho_G)g \qquad (104)$$

$$F_L = C_L A_n \frac{\rho_L(u_0 \sin \beta)^2}{2} \qquad (105)$$

where A_n is the projected area of the bubble in the flow direction, C_L is the lift coefficient and $u_0 \sin \beta$ is the axial component of the bubble rise velocity relative to the liquid.

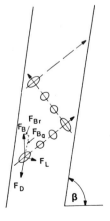

Figure 42. Zig zag motion of bubbles.

Assuming the zig-zag bubble path is at $45°$ to the pipe axis, A_n is approximated equal to $(\gamma d)^2 \pi/4) \cos 45°$ where γ is the distortion coefficient of the bubble. Substituting Equations 104 and 105 in Equation 103 yields

$$\frac{\cos \beta}{\sin^2 \beta} = \frac{3}{4} \cos 45° \frac{u_0^2}{g} \left(\frac{C_L \gamma^2}{d} \right) \tag{106}$$

This equation predicts the inclination angle below which the bubble pattern cannot exist even at low liquid rates.

In order to test this equation we estimate the variables for the conditions of the experiments described here. The rise velocity, u_0, is known to be about 0.25 m/s. The other quantities can only be approximated to range within these bounds: bubble size d, between 4 and 10 mm; C_L between 0.4 and 1.2 [101] and γ between 1.1 to 1.5. Substituting into Equation 106 shows that β falls in the range $55–70°$, which compares well with the data (see Figures 39 and 40).

At high liquid rates turbulence results in a breakup of large gas pockets and causes a transition to the dispersed bubble pattern. Equation 73 results from the model for vertical flow. It is independent of the angle of inclination and thus applies also for "steep inclination" angles.

Transition to annular flow. The mechanism for the transition as originally proposed by Taitel et al. [16] is based on the idea that the gas velocity must be large enough to lift the largest stable drop out of the pipe in order to maintain annular flow (Equation 87). For an inclined pipe this becomes

$$u_{GS} = 3.1 \left[\frac{\sigma g(\rho_L - \rho_G) \sin \beta}{\rho_G^2} \right]^{1/4} \tag{107}$$

Slug-churn transition. There is little of a quantitative nature that can be stated on how this transition depends on inclination angle. Even small derivations from the vertical tend to enhance the separation between the gas and the liquid phases, thus suppressing the chaotic nature of the churn flow pattern. As a result the region of flow rate space over which churn flow occurs shrinks and becomes insignificant at angles between $70–80°$.

Intermediate Upward Inclinations

As previously mentioned, a unique model for the prediction of flow pattern transitions in the whole range of inclination is not available at the present. The approach here is to use the horizontal and slightly inclined model for shallow inclination and the steep inclined model for steep inclination. One should switch from one model to the other as the angle of inclination varies.

For the shallow inclinations one has the following transition boundaries:

A—stratified to nonstratified
B—annular to slug
C—stratified smooth to wavy
D—intermittent to dispersed bubble
N—elongated bubble to slug

The transitions for steep inclinations are:

E—bubble to intermittent
F & G—intermittent to dispersed bubble
H—slug to churn
J—annular to slug (or churn)

Starting from horizontal flow and changing the angle of inclination the following is occurring: The stratified region shrinks as the angle of inclination increases and practically vanishes at intermediate angles of inclination. This observation is predicted very well by transition A; namely, transition A can be also used to predict the angle at which stratified flow disappears (at the specified region of flow rates).

Transition C seems to be important only for the horizontal and very close to the horizontal case (up to 0.25° for air water). For larger angles of inclination the region of stratified flow is wavy (transition C is external to this region).

The transition to annular flow shifts slightly toward higher gas flow rates as the angle of inclination increases and the stratified region disappears. This is predicted quite well by the shallow inclination model—transition B (Figures 34–37). For an inclination angle larger than about 10° (for air-water system) the experimental results show that the transition to annular flow is almost unaffected by inclination while transition B over-predicts the shift toward high gas flow rates. This is probably due to the increase in the interfacial shear with inclination, which is not incorporated in the model. Transition J to annular flow (the steep inclination model) seems to agree with experiment even at this shallow inclination angle. Therefore, use transition B up to 10° inclination and transition J for inclination angles higher than 10°.

The observed transition to dispersed bubble is very little affected by the angle of inclination and for small diameter pipes (Equation 75) the transition is almost the same for the horizontal and the vertical cases. Transition D (turbulent vs. buoyancy forces) predict well the transition to dispersed bubble in horizontal and slightly inclined pipes. Transition F & G (turbulent vs. surface tension forces) does not consider gravity effects and gives a good prediction even at shallow inclination. Thus, the angle at which one has to switch from the shallow model to the steep inclination model is somewhat arbitrary. It is suggested to use 10° for this angle consistent with the transition to annular flow.

Transition N is valid from all angles of inclination. It depends, however, on the transition mechanism to dispersed bubble and is calculated using an applicable transition to dispersed bubble.

Thus, from 10° and up the steep inclination model is valid for all transition boundaries. Obviously, however, the approach taken here is somewhat tentative and the matter of predicting flow pattern transitions is still in the developing stage.

DOWNWARD INCLINATION

Very little work is directly related to the problem of flow patterns in down sloping pipe lines. Singh and Griffith [98b] investigated flow patterns in downward slightly inclined pipes (0° to 9°) and attempted to find the transition boundaries through a match of the holdup correlations of the annular, stratified and slug flows. The flow regime map shown in Figure 43 is given in terms of the dimensionless volumetric fluxes of the two phase coordinates, as used in flooding correlations

$$u_{LS}^* = \frac{u_{LS}}{\sqrt{\dfrac{\rho_L - \rho_G}{\rho_L}} \sqrt{gD \sin \beta}} \tag{108}$$

$$u_{LS}^* = \frac{u_{GS}}{\sqrt{\dfrac{\rho_L - \rho_G}{\rho_G}} \sqrt{gD \sin \beta}} \tag{109}$$

The problem of pressure drop as well as holdup received somewhat more attention and has been studied by Savigny [102] and Begges and Brill [100].

Recently, Barnea et al. [37] focused attention on the transition mechanisms in downward two-phase inclined pipe flow. The transition boundaries were modeled using similar approaches presented by Taitel and Dukler [36] for horizontal flow and Taitel et al. [16] for vertical flow. The analytical results are compared with data collected for air-water in 10 m long 2.55 and 5.1 cm

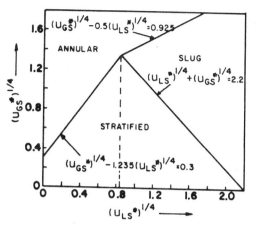

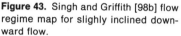

Figure 43. Singh and Griffith [98b] flow regime map for slighly inclined downward flow.

diameter pipes in the range of 0 to 90° downward inclination angles. Figures 44–49 show representative data for angles from 0 to 90°. Superimposed on the data are the theoretical transition boundaries.

A change to downward inclination has a major effect on the stratified flow regime. In downward stratified flow the liquid moves more rapidly than in the horizontal case and has a lower level in the pipe owing to the downward gravity force. As a result, higher gas and liquid flow rates are required to cause transition from stratified flow, and the stratified flow region is considerably expanded as the angle of inclination increases. This change occurs primarily at the lower angles of inclination from 0 to about 10°, whereas from 10° to 60° the region of stratified flow is almost unchanged (Figures 46 and 47). From about 60° downward inclination and up, stratified flow changes gradually to annular flow. Thus, annular flow is expanded at the expense of the stratified flow, which shrinks until it disappears completely at vertical downward flow (Figures 30, 48, and 49).

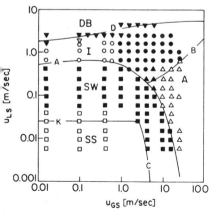

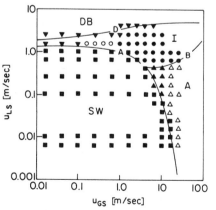

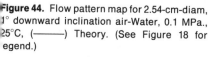

Figure 44. Flow pattern map for 2.54-cm-diam, 1° downward inclination air-Water, 0.1 MPa., 25°C, (———) Theory. (See Figure 18 for legend.)

Figure 45. Flow pattern map for 2.54-cm-diam, 5° downward inclination air-water, 0.1 MPa., 25°C, (———) Theory. (See Figure 18 for legend.)

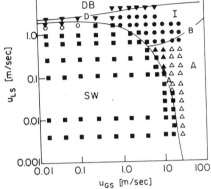

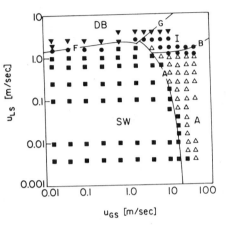

Figure 46. Flow pattern map for 2.54-cm-diam, 10° downward inclination air-Water, 0.1 MPa., 25°C, (————) Theory. (See Figure 18 for legend.)

Figure 47. Flow pattern map for 2.54-cm-diam, 50° downward inclination air-Water, 0.1 MPa., 25°C, (————) Theory. (See Figure 18 for legend.)

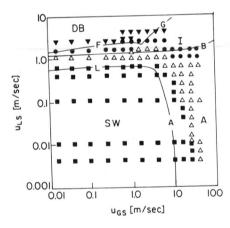

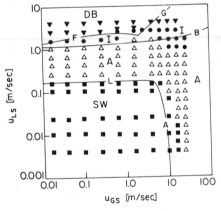

Figure 48. Flow pattern map for 2.54-cm-diam, 70° downward inclination air-Water, 0.1 MPa., 25°C. (————) Theory. (See Figure 18 for legend.)

Figure 49. Flow pattern map for 2.54-cm-diam, 80° downward inclination air-Water, 0.1 MPa., 25°C, (————) Theory. (See Figure 18 for legend.)

Stratified smooth flow was not observed in downward inclinations above about 5° (in the reported range of flow rates). For downward flow, contrary to the case of horizontal and slightly upward flow where waves are generated owing to the gas action on the interface, natural instability of the interface occurs for almost pure gravity downward flow. The transition for negligible gas flow rate from smooth to wavy interface depends only on the liquid rate and is independent of the gas flow rate (Figure 44). The stratified flow for downward inclination was always wavy or ripply for an inclination above 1° for the 2.5 cm diameter pipe, or 5° for the 5.1-cm-diameter pipe (Figures 45–49).

The transition to annular flow up to about 70° downward inclination occurs at high gas flow rates (Figures 44–47). At downward inclination about 70° and up, annular flow appears also at low gas flow rates at the expense of the stratified flow and the region of annular flow is considerably expanded (Figures 48 and 49).

The intermittent region shrinks considerably as inclination increases. Above 10° the region of intermittent flow was observed only at very high liquid and gas flow rates (Figures 47 and 49).

The transition to dispersed bubble flow is insensitive to the angle of inclination. At high liquid rates the gas is dispersed into small bubbles owing to the turbulent forces and thus is almost unaffected by gravity (Figures 18, 30, 44–49).

Modeling Flow Pattern Transitions for Downward Inclined Flow

Stratified—Nonstratified Transition

The stratified—nonstratified transition predicted by Taitel and Dukler [36] (transition A) is applicable in the whole range of inclination. However, the boundary curve may be terminated by either the transition to dispersed bubble (transition F & G) (Figure 47) or by the stratified-annular boundary (transition L) for pipes of high inclinations (Figures 48 and 49). Transition L is a new transition mechanism that occurs in steep downward flow at relatively low gas flow rates.

Stratified to Annular Transition

The transition between stratified and annular flow in horizontal or moderate inclined tubes results from the instability of stratified flow due to the high gas flow rate over the liquid layer (transition A). At steep downward inclination another mechanism, typical to low gas flow rates, arises. The mechanism by which stratified flow is seen to change into annular flow, at low gas flow rates, is through liquid lumps that are torn away from a wavy turbulent interface and are thrown towards the unwetted tube walls. Once the energy is sufficient to throw the liquid lumps all the way to the top of the pipe then the condition for annular flow is reached. Note that when this energy is not sufficient, at low liquid flow rate or at shallow inclination, this phenomenon causes the stratified interface to become concave such that the concaved wedges climb the tube periphery as the liquid flow rate or inclination increases. Finally, the tube periphery is continuously wetted and annular flow ensues.

Referring to Figure 50 one may visualize a liquid particle at the interface that is thrown radially with a velocity v' while having an axial velocity u_L (the film velocity). The trajectory made by this

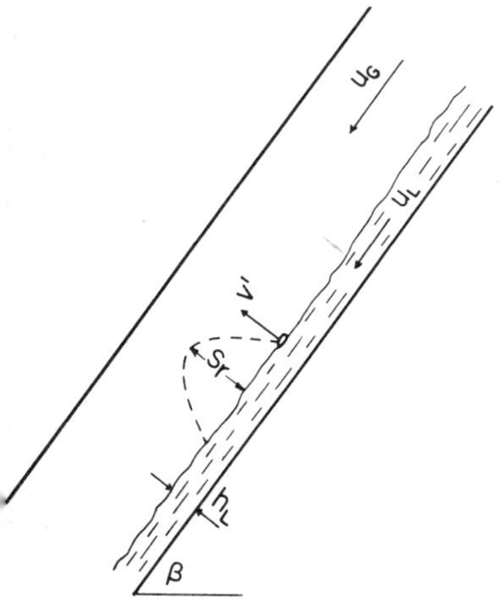

Figure 50. Trajectory of a torn away liquid particle in downwards stratified flow.

particle is shown in Figure 50. The radial distance that the particle passes depends only on its initial radial velocity and the radial component of the acceleration of gravity. v' is assumed to be of the order of the radial turbulent velocity fluctuation that can be estimated [64] by

$$\bar{v}' = \sqrt{(\bar{v}')^2} = u_* = u_L \sqrt{\left(\frac{f_L}{2}\right)} \tag{110}$$

The maximum radial velocity is assumed to be twice the average velocity thus

$$v' = 2\bar{v}' = 2 \sqrt{\left(\frac{f_L}{2}\right)} u_L \tag{111}$$

The radial distance that the particle moves against gravity is

$$S_r = \frac{v'^2}{2g \cos \beta} \tag{112}$$

The condition for annular flow to occur (at low gas flow rate) is $S_r > D - h_L$, namely

$$u_L^2 > \frac{gD\left(1 - \dfrac{h_L}{D}\right) \cos \beta}{f_L} \tag{113}$$

u_L, f_L, and h_L/D for given flow conditions can be calculated by the method presented earlier.

This transition criterion is mapped on Figures 48 and 49 as the boundary L and shows good agreement with the experimental results.

For small angles of inclination the result of transition L is above the transition to dispersed bubble and therefore is not applicable. For the limiting case of $\beta = 90°$ stratified flow disappears completely and the model presented previously for vertical downward flow is used.

The stratified-annular transition is composed of two boundaries that represent the two different mechanisms. Transition L, which originates as a result of liquid flow at steep angles, and transition A, which is caused by instability of stratified flow due to the high gas flow rate over the liquid layer.

Stratified Smooth to Stratified Wavy Transition

Another new mechanism that should be considered when dealing with downward inclined flow is the transition from stratified smooth to stratified wavy that may result from gravity rather than the action of the "wind." As well known for the liquid flow in downward slopes, waves can be developed also for negligible or no gas flow rate. The existence of these waves depends on the liquid flow rate and the level of the interface that changes significantly with inclination.

For turbulent flow in smooth and relatively wide channels, a simple criterion for the condition at which waves will appear has been proposed:

$$F_r = \frac{u_L}{\sqrt{gh_L}} \geq 1.5 \tag{114}$$

The values of u_L and h_L for given gas and liquid rates, fluid properties, inclination angle and pipe size are calculated by the method presented by Taitel and Dukler [36]. The predicted transition line is designated as curve K in Figure 44 and compares well with the experimental results. Note that at large gas flow rates this transition boundary is terminated by boundary C, which represents the condition where waves are formed by interfacial shear. At larger inclination angles both theory and experiment show that smooth interface is not observed.

Intermittent-Annular Transition

The slug-annular transition (transition B) is applicable only when stratified flow is unstable. Therefore, it is terminated by the stratified-nonstratified boundary A at small and moderate inclinations (Figures 44–47). At steep angles of inclination where annular flow appears at low gas flow rates, the annular-intermittent transition B as given by $h_L/D = 0.35$ is extended to very low gas flow rates (Figures 48 and 49).

Transition to Dispersed Bubbles

The prediction of the transition to dispersed bubbles using the horizontal and slightly inclined model (transition D) becomes unacceptable for angles of inclination above 10°. Thus, for steeper angles it is proposed to use the "vertical model," which is unaffected by the angle of inclination (transitions F & G). In fact, transition F & G, based on the vertical model, is applicable in the whole range of inclination and could be used also at small angles of inclination (less than 10°).

Summary

For downward inclination two new transition boundaries are introduced:

K—transition to wavy flow for gravity flow down an incline.
L—transition to annular flow owing to high turbulence associated with fast downward flow.

Typical of these transitions is that they result in, due to the inclination effect, and are not influenced by the gas flow. Both also are applicable in the whole range of inclination, namely valid for shallow as well as steep inclination.

Transitions A, B, and C are also valid for the whole range of inclination.

Transition D, however, was found to be valid up to about 10° and for larger inclination transition F & G should be used.

Note that all transition boundaries for the shallow inclination model, excluding transition D (the transition to dispersed bubble) are valid for shallow, intermediate, and steep inclination.

FLOW PATTERNS IN SMALL DIAMETER PIPES

Most of the flow regime studies on two-phase gas-liquid flow have been performed in large diameter tubes. Very few experimental results on two-phase flow in small diameter pipes are reported. Marchessault and Mason [103] studied the flow of air bubbles through a capillary tube. They measured the film thickness surrounding moving air and liquid bubbles in glass capillary tubes containing wetting liquids. Drainage of films surrounding the bubbles was also studied. Sue and Griffith [104] studied the flow of gas and liquid in horizontal tubes of capillary diameter (1 mm diameter) in the slug flow regime. They correlated the density and film thickness of the liquid film around the bubbles. Oya [105] investigated experimentally the flow patterns in upward two-phase flow in tubes of 2, 3 and 6 mm diameters. He studied the effects of the entrance section and the type of liquid on the flow pattern transitions. The experiments concerned the undeveloped flow in tubes that have shorter length than required for fully developed flow. Oya [106] also measured the pressure drop in upward two-phase flow in small diameter tubes. For each flow pattern a semi-empirical equation for pressure drop was obtained.

Barnea et al. [122] reported on two-phase horizontal and vertical upward flow of air-water in tubes with diameters of 4.0, 6.0, 8.15, 9.85, and 12.3 mm. The validity of the models, for very small diameter pipes where surface tension might occur, was tested against data.

Figure 51 shows the experimental results for the transition boundaries in horizontal two-phase flow. The results are compared with the Taitel and Dukler model [36] plotted as the solid line. The stratified-nonstratified transition boundary A (Equation 13) predicted by the model deviates

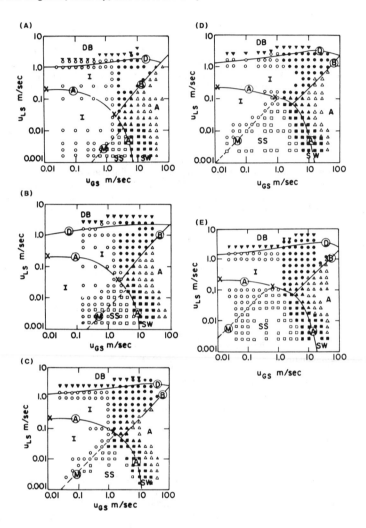

Figure 51. Flow pattern map in small diameter pipes, horizontal, air-Water, 0.1 MPa., 25°C, (———) Theory [36] not valid between the x signs; (– – – –) Present modification. (A) 4 mm pipe; (B) 6 mm pipe; (C) 8.15 mm pipe; (D) 9.85 mm pipe; (E) 12.3 mm pipe. (See Figure 18 for legend.)

considerably from the experimental results. The smaller the pipe diameter the larger is the deviation from the model. All other transition boundaries agree quite well with the model.

Wetting liquid has a tendency to wet and climb the tube wall. In small diameter horizontal pipes it is observed that as a result of this capillary force the climbing liquid forms a complete liquid bridge and as a result intermittent flow is initiated. This phenomenon is typical of low liquid and gas flow rates and small diameters. With larger diameters under these conditions the flow pattern is stratified smooth.

The model of Taitel and Dukler [36] for horizontal flow does not consider the effect of surface tension on the stratified-nonstratified transition boundary. Transition to slug flow caused by surface tension forces at low liquid and gas flow rates is modeled by considering gravity and surface tension forces.

Consider liquid and gas flow in stratified flow as shown in Figure 52 by the solid line. Due to surface tension effects the liquid at an arbitrary location, climbs to the upper level, thereby reducing partially the liquid level in the layer. The new local level profile is shown schematically by the broken line in Figure 52. This transfer of liquid requires that $v_1 = v_2$ (Figure 52). In order for slug flow to develop in this process, the surface tension forces that pull the liquid upward must overcome gravity.

The following simplified analysis can be used to give an estimate of the transition criterion. The flow is treated as two-dimensional and the curved bubble shape (Figure 52) is assumed to be a circle with radius y. Equating v_1 and v_2 yields

$$y = \frac{4}{\pi} h_G \qquad (115)$$

where h_G is the equilibrium gas layer thickness in stratified flow. h_G, as a function of flow rates, fluid properties, and pipe geometry is obtained via a solution of the momentum balance on the liquid and gas phases. The method was described earlier.

A static force balance on the fluid element ABC, equating upward surface tension forces (2σ) vs. gravity ($\rho g v_{ABC}$) (see Figure 52) yields

$$\sigma = \rho_L g \left(y^2 - \frac{\pi}{4} y^2 \right) \qquad (116)$$

which leads to

$$h_G \leq \frac{\pi}{4} \sqrt{\frac{\sigma}{\rho_L g \left(1 - \frac{\pi}{4} \right)}} \qquad (117)$$

which is the condition for intermittent flow.

Note that Equation 117 predicts a constant minimum gas gap (for specific fluids). For small pipe size, one may reach the point at which $y = D$, which is the upper possible limit for y. For smaller pipe size (Equation 117) is always satisfied and transition will occur whenever the liquid level will be high enough to satisfy mass balance (Equation 115 for $y = D$), namely, whenever

$$h_G \leq \frac{\pi}{4} D \qquad (118)$$

h_G as a function of u_{GS} and u_{LS} for a given flow system is calculated using Equations 9 or 13. Thereafter, the transition boundary given by Equations 117 and 118 can be calculated and plotted on u_{LS} vs. u_{GS} coordinates as shown in Figure 51 by the broken lines (transition M). This line is terminated by the stratified-nonstratified transition A (the solid line). Above the broken line the flow pattern is intermittent flow generated by surface tension while above the solid line the intermittent flow is generated by Helmholtz instability (transition A). For pipe diameters of 25 mm and

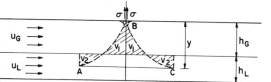

Figure 52. Liquid level caused by surface tension—schematic representation.

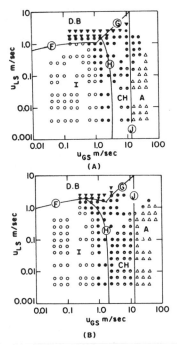

Figure 53. Flow pattern map in small diameter pipes, upward vertical, air-Water, 0.1 MPa, 25°C, (‒ ‒ ‒ ‒) Theory [16]. (A) 4 mm pipe; (B) 12.3 mm pipe. (See Figure 26 for legend.)

greater the broken line presented by Equation 117 is located outside the boundary A and the effect of surface tension can be ignored.

Thus, the flow pattern prediction by Taitel and Dukler [36] is modified by a new transition boundary M that considers the surface tension effect valid only in small diameter pipes. Comparison with the data shows good agreement between the present theory and the experimental results, with the exception of the stratified annular transition at very low liquid flow rates and small pipe size (4 and 6 mm). No explanation is given for this deviation. It should be mentioned, however, that at this region the so-called stratified flow takes the form of very narrow surface-tension-dominated rivulets that prevent the formation of annular flow.

Figure 53 shows the results for vertical upward flow, where the solid lines represent the theoretically predicted transition boundaries for upward two-phase flow as described earlier.

The effect of pipe diameter was found to be small both in the experiments and from the theory. Therefore, although measurements for all 5 pipe diameters were made, only the results for the smallest and largest diameter are presented. The agreement between experiment and theory has been found to be good. Note that this theory, which has been shown to agree well for large diameter pipes [16], is shown here to be valid also for small pipe size. The predicted slug-churn transition line deviates from the experimental data at high liquid flow rates, but at high liquid velocities it is extremely difficult to discriminate between churn and slug especially in very small diameter pipes.

COUNTER-CURRENT GAS-LIQUID VERTICAL FLOW

Counter-current flow has been studied primarily in connection with flooding and flow reversal as well as in connection with bubble columns. The flooding phenomenon is associated with the limit of counter-current flow; namely, the limit of liquid flow rate downward under gravity caused by gas flowing upwards driven by pressure difference. Some of the most recent work on this topic is by Wallis et al. [107] and Taitel et al. [108], who suggested a film model to predict the flooding limit. Richter [109] suggested that flooding occurs due to unstable waves and developed a theory for predicting the flooding limit. Tien et al. [110] developed new correlations of the Wallis-Kutateladze type. Their derivation is based on modeling using the concept of interfacial instability coupled with kinematic wave theory and the critical wavelength concept. Wallis et al. [111] considered the case of flooding in many parallel vertical tubes. In spite of the progress achieved in understanding the flooding process [112–116], it is far from being well understood and prediction techniques rely heavily on experimental correlations.

The most successful correlation [11] (Equation 119) relates the superficial velocities of the liquid and gas to the flooding point. Also of special interest is the correlation that correlates the gas flow rate at the zero liquid penetration point [92]. Note that Pushkina and Sorokin's [92] result is in contradiction to Wallis' [11] correlation, and it is believed [109] that the Wallis correlation applies to small diameter pipes whereas the latter to large diameter pipes. In all the aforementioned studies, the flow pattern associated with this process is counter-current annular flow.

Counter-current flow is closely associated with bubble columns, which are widely used as gas liquid reactors where questions like holdup, pressure drop, and interfacial area are important. A thorough review on bubble columns is presented by Shah et al. [117] and covers all types of gas liquid reactors. A fairly recent work on gas holdup in bubble columns is given by Hikita et al. [118]. Vermeer and Krishna [119] considered the performance of bubble columns in the range of slug-bubble flow at superficial gas velocity above 0.1 m/s.

The performance of bubble flow can be treated by the drift flux model since, to a good approximation, the drift flux in bubble flow is a function only of the gas holdup. The classical analysis given by Wallis [11] shows that there are three possible situations for counter-current bubble flow: (a) condition of no solution, namely, the bubble column cannot operate in a steady state fashion for the liquid and gas flow rate in this region; (b) condition of two solutions, namely, the bubble column can operate in two values of void fraction; and (c) where only one solution exists. The latter occurs on the exact boundary between the condition of no solution and two solutions. This approach, however, is valid only in a bubble flow regime that cannot exist at high void fraction (considering non-foaming systems).

In spite of the extensive work on counter-current annular flow (flooding) and bubble flow, no experimental work has been focused on the conditions under which either of the flow patterns exists, nor on mapping the flow pattern boundaries.

Recently, Taitel and Barnea [120], modeled the various flow patterns and the transition boundaries in counter-current vertical flow as well as the pressure drop.

The flow patterns that can be observed in vertical counter-current flow are bubble flow, slug flow, and annular flow. However, unlike co-current flow (either upward or downward) where the flow pattern is a fairly unique function of the flow rates, multiple solutions for the flow patterns can occur in counter-current flow. Furthermore, counter-current flow may not exist for certain values of liquid and gas flow rates, again contrary to the case of co-current flow.

Figure 54 shows three cases of the typical counter-current flow patterns that may exist at the same gas and liquid flow rates. Intuitively one may realize that annular flow will exist when the bottom of the column is wide open. On the other hand, bubble or slug flow will occur when the liquid valves are only slightly open. Clearly, the latter is associated with much higher pressure drop owing primarily to the hydrostatic head.

Modeling

Depending on the operating conditions, i.e., gas and liquid flow rates, pipe diameter, entrance and exit conditions, as well as physical properties, three flow patterns may be observed: annular flow, bubble flow, and slug flow.

The possible existence of each of the flow patterns is modeled and criteria for transitions from one flow pattern to another are developed. In addition, the pressure drop is calculated for each flow pattern since it has an influence on the flow pattern map in the case where multiple solutions exist.

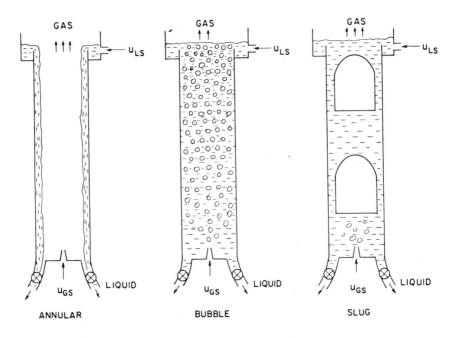

ANNULAR   BUBBLE   SLUG

Figure 54. Flow patterns in vertical countercurrent two-phase flow.

Annular Flow

This seems to be the "most natural" flow pattern of counter-current flow. It is the only flow pattern obtained for open exit lower end. The liquid is in the form of falling film for a wide range of gas flow rates up to the flooding point at which the downcoming liquid is swept upward. The flooding phenomenon is the limiting possible solution for counter-current flow. Thus, the flooding line is the transition boundary from annular flow to "no solution." There is no acceptable theory for an accurate prediction of the flooding process. For the purposes of this study we will use Wallis'

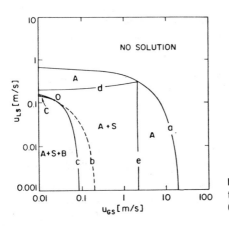

Figure 55. Flow pattern map for vertical countercurrent pipes. 5 cm diam, air-water at 25°C, 0.1 MPa. (A—annular; S—slug; B—bubble)

correlation of the form

$$\left[\frac{u_{GS}\rho_G^{1/2}}{\sqrt{gD(\rho_L - \rho_G)}}\right]^{1/2} + \left[\frac{u_{LS}\rho_L^{1/2}}{\sqrt{gD(\rho_L - \rho_G)}}\right]^{1/2} = C \tag{119}$$

where C is an empirical constant of the order of unity. The transition line with C = 1 is shown in Figure 55 for air-water in a 5 cm diameter pipe by transition a.

Since Wallis' correlation is supported by data, so is transition a. Note, however, that no attempt to be very accurate was made here, and the transition line may shift somewhat if more up-to-date and possibly more accurate correlations are used.

Bubble Flow

The next flow pattern considered is bubble flow, which may exist within the region bounded by "a" under certain conditions.

For counter-current bubble flow the liquid flows downwards while the gas bubble rise upwards. The relation between the liquid and gas superficial velocities and the liquid holdup ϕ is given by

$$u_{LS}(1 - \phi) + \phi u_{GS} = u_0\phi(1 - \phi) \tag{120}$$

where u_0 is the relative rise velocity of the bubbles, namely, $u_0 = u_L - u_G$ ($u_L = u_{LS}/\phi$ and $u_G = u_{GS}/(1 - \phi)$). Although the rise velocity u_0 is a complex function of the bubble diameter, pipe diameter, and void fraction, it can be considered approximately constant for "large" bubbles and low void fraction and is given by Equation 63 [74]. For air-water at about 25°C and atmospheric pressure $u_0 \simeq 0.25$ m/sec. Equation 120 is a quadratic equation yielding two, one or no solution for ϕ. The case of no solution is given by

$$u_{LS} > u_{GS} + u_0 - \sqrt{4u_{GS}u_0} \tag{121}$$

This curve is shown in Figure 55 by the boundary b. Bubble flow cannot exist for liquid and gas flow rates above this line.

At $\phi < 0.7$ (gas void fraction greater than 0.3) bubbles tend to coalesce and form Taylor bubbles [72]. Thus, within the region of solution defined by Equation 121 bubble flow can exist only in the subregion where $\phi > 0.7$ in Equation 120. The line $\phi = 0.7$ is shown in Figure 55 by transition c. As seen, transition c is tangent to the boundary b at a single point 0. The region to the left of c corresponds to two possible solutions, one of which is for $\phi > 0.7$ and the other for $\phi < 0.7$. The latter is unacceptable and therefore this region corresponds to a single solution of bubble flow. The region to the right of c and left of b, up to the point 0, is the region where both solutions yield $\phi < 0.7$ and therefore do not exist. Thus, the boundary b to the "right" of 0 is "imaginary" and is plotted as a broken line. The small shaded region above transition c and below b is a region where both solutions for ϕ are between 0.7 to 1. Thus, in this region two solutions of bubble flow exist. As seen, however, this region is quite small (in the range of flow rates shown in Figure 55). The limiting boundary for bubble flow consists of transition c up to point 0 (the solid line) and transition b to the left of point 0.

Notice that both annular flow and bubble flow can exist for this region. The factor that will determine the actual flow pattern is the pressure drop as provided by the boundary conditions.

For very low liquid flow rates the liquid is almost stagnant and transition c in this region is the same as bubble-slug transition for co-current flow (transition E). Thus, transition c in this range is supported by data that was found valid for upward co-current flow. Note also the observation by Vermeer and Krishna [119] for stagnant liquid systems that small bubble flow changes to "large, fast rising bubbles," namely, to slug flow (for D < 10 cm) or churn-turbulent flow (for D > 10 cm) above $u_{GS} \simeq 0.1$ m/sec. This agrees also quite well with transition c at low liquid flow rates.

Slug Flow

Bubble flow develops into slug flow beyond transitions c and b as previously mentioned. Slug flow consists of long Taylor type bubbles separated by slugs of liquid. The term slug flow used here is an idealization of all types of intermittent flows including churn-turbulent that has been observed in large diameter pipes. The liquid slugs may or may not contain small bubbles. For the purpose of this analysis the liquid slug will be assumed to be free of gas bubbles. The Taylor bubble has a characteristic spherical cap with a cylindrical body having a cross-sectional area close to that of the pipe. The liquid confined between the bubble and the pipe flows around the bubble in the form of a falling film.

Counter-current slug flow is not possible for either high liquid or high gas flow rates, where transition to annular flow must occur. Increasing liquid flow rate decreases the upward velocity of the Taylor bubbles until a limiting point is reached where gas mass balance cannot be satisfied. On the other hand, increasing the gas flow rate causes flooding conditions to be reached in the liquid film adjacent to the Taylor bubble that limits the possible counter-current liquid flow rate. As a result, again, slug flow is not possible beyond this point.

The velocity of the Taylor bubble u_G is given quite accurately by the relation [81]:

$$u_G = 1.2u_L + 0.35\sqrt{gD} \tag{122}$$

Equation 122 was proposed for co-current flow, however, it has no restriction to counter-current application. Continuity considerations require that

$$u_L = u_{GS} - u_{LS} \tag{123}$$

and

$$u_G - u_L = 4\frac{\delta}{D}(u_G + u_f) \tag{124}$$

where u_f is the film average downward velocity and δ is the film thickness.

Equation 124 is a mass balance relative to the moving gas bubble. Note also that in Equation 124, δ/D is assumed small such that the cross-sectional area of the liquid film is $\pi D\delta$. Since the liquid film adjacent to the gas bubble is in the form of a free falling film, its average velocity u_f is related to its thickness by [11]

$$\frac{\delta}{D} = B\left[\frac{\mu_L^2}{D^3 g(\rho_L - \rho_G)\rho_L}\right]^p \left[\frac{4\rho_L u_f D}{\mu_L}\right]^q \tag{125}$$

where B, p, and q equal to 0.00448, $\frac{5}{6}$, and $\frac{3}{2}$ for turbulent flow and 0.8667, $\frac{1}{2}$, and $\frac{1}{2}$ for laminar flow, respectively. The determination of laminar or turbulent flow in the film is based, as suggested by Wallis [11], on the film Reynolds number $Re_f = \rho_L u_f \delta/\mu_L$. Thus, the film flow is turbulent for $Re_f > 1,000$ and laminar for $Re_f < 1,000$.

Substituting Equations 122 and 123 into Equation 124 yields

$$u_L = u_{GS} - u_{LS} = \frac{4\frac{\delta}{D}u_f - 0.35\sqrt{gD}\left(1 - 4\frac{\delta}{D}\right)}{0.2 - 4.8\frac{\delta}{D}} \tag{126}$$

For given u_{GS} and u_{LS} Equations 125 and 126 can be solved for u_f and δ/D.

The relative length of the gas bubble ℓ_G/ℓ can be derived from a simple mass balance on the gas that leaves the upper end of the pipe or alternatively on the liquid that leaves the bottom of the pipe, assuming the gas bubble is a cylinder of constant cross sectional area. This yields

$$\frac{\ell_G}{\ell} = \frac{u_{GS}}{4\dfrac{\delta}{D}u_f + (u_{GS} - u_{LS})} \tag{127}$$

For a physical solution that satisfies mass balance ℓ_G/ℓ should be always less than unity. Therefore,

$$4\frac{\delta}{D}u_f > u_{LS} \tag{128}$$

limits the possibility of the slug flow pattern. Equation 128 is plotted in Figure 55 by the boundary d, which limits the region of slug flow as liquid flow rate is increased.

A different boundary limits slug flow when gas flow rate is increased. This limit is reached when the relative velocity between the Taylor bubble and the liquid film adjacent to it reaches the condition of flooding. Equation 119 can be used for this purpose when u_{GS} is replaced by $(1 - 4(\delta/D))u_G$ and u_{LS} by $4(\delta/D)u_f$. The final results, using also Equations 122 and 123 for u_G, yield

$$u_{GS} - u_{LS} \leq \frac{\left\{C[gD(\rho_L - \rho_G)]^{1/4} - \left[4\dfrac{\delta}{D}u_f\rho_L^{1/2}\right]^{1/2}\right\}^2}{1.2\left(1 - 4\dfrac{\delta}{D}\right)\rho_G^{1/2}} - 0.292\sqrt{gD} \tag{129}$$

Thus, Equation 129 has to be satisfied for slug flow to exist. Equation 129 is plotted in Figure 55 as transition e. Notice that transitions d, e and a intersect at a common point, since at this point transition d represents the case when ℓ_G/ℓ approaches unity and the slug flow approaches annular flow.

Results and Discussion

Figure 55 shows a typical flow pattern map obtained using the aforementioned models for air-water system in a 5 cm pipe at 25°C and atmospheric pressure. Transition a separates the flow region into "no solution zone" and a zone where solution is possible. The region of possible solution is subdivided into three zones:

1. Region A where only annular flow exists (above transition d and to the right of e).
2. Region A + S where only annular and slug flow can exist (left to boundary.e, below d and to the right of c).
3. Region A + S + B where annular, slug and bubble flow can exist. This region is bounded on the right by boundary c up to the point 0 and at the top, to the left of the point 0, by boundary b.

Note that in the small shaded area bounded by c and b two solutions for bubble flow exist; namely, two possibilities for void fraction for the same flow rates.

Annular flow is the dominant flow pattern that can exist in the whole range of possible solutions. It is, therefore, being considered here as the "most natural" flow pattern for counter-current flow.

Slug flow can exist in the A + S region and the A + S + B region. Bubble flow can exist only in the A + S + B zone.

The question that arises is what determines the actual flow pattern that takes place in a zone where multiple solutions are possible.

The pressure drop associated with annular flow is about two to three orders of magnitude lower than for slug and bubble flow (except for very high gas flow rates) [120]. Therefore, annular flow will result when low pressure exit boundary condition is imposed at the lower end of the tube. In other words, when the liquid can flow with minimal restriction at the liquid exit (Figure 54). When the liquid flow is restricted, the liquid will accumulate in the pipe until the static head is sufficient to force out the liquid at a comparable rate to the annular flow pattern with no restriction. In the latter case bubble on slug flow will result.

The pressure drop in slug and bubble flow is primarily the result of the hydrostatic head. Both flow patterns have about the same order of pressure drop in the region where both patterns can exist (the A + S + B zone). As mentioned in Taitel et al. [16], slug flow is unstable for pipes where the free rise velocity of a Taylor bubble in slug flow exceeds the rise velocity of the bubbles, namely when

$$0.35\sqrt{gD} > 1.53\left[\frac{g(\rho_L - \rho_G)\sigma}{\rho_L^2}\right]^{1/4} \tag{130}$$

The mechanistic explanation is as follows: Slug flow is generated through spontaneous agglomeration of bubbles. In slug flow, however, bubbles are torn away from the back end of the Taylor bubble owing to the vigorous mixing of the free falling film that penetrates the liquid slug. If the bubbles move slower than the Taylor bubble they are left behind and eventually the slug flow pattern is destroyed, maintaining the bubble flow pattern. Thus, the region A + S + B will result in bubble flow in large diameter pipes and slug flow in small diameter pipes. For air-water this occurs at pipe diameter of about 5 cm. In spite of the aforementioned, bubble flow can exist also in small diameter pipe if special efforts are taken to introduce the bubbles at a small diameter. Bubbles of small size tend to behave as rigid spheres and resist agglomeration and, therefore, can exist also in small diameter pipes. Thus, it is estimated that when the bubble diameter is less than [78]

$$d < \left[\frac{0.4\sigma}{(\rho_L - \rho_G)g}\right]^{1/2} \tag{131}$$

the bubbles will not coalesce to form slugs.

Summary

Transition a is the result of flooding in annular flow beyond which no possible solution can exist. Transitions b and c limit bubble flow. The former to the region where bubble flow can exist while the latter to the region where the void fraction is less than 0.3. Thus, the bubble flow pattern is bounded by a section of transition c (at lower liquid flow rate) and a section of transition b.

Transitions d and e limit the region of slug flow. Transition d is caused by the inability of flow rates above d to satisfy mass balance for slug flow. Transition e is caused by reaching flooding condition.

The question of multiple solution for the flow pattern can be summarized as follows:

1. Annular flow can exist in the whole range and will occur in the case where the liquid outlet is not restricted (open exit).
2. Bubble flow will occur in the A + S + B zone in pipes of large diameter as given by Equation 130. Also, bubble flow will occur if the bubbles, introduced into the column, are very small (Equation 131).

The aforementioned theory is based on a mechanistic approach that puts together known experimental observations and correlations in order to construct a complete picture of the flow pattern map. The accuracy of the approach relies also on the correlations used. However, as has been demonstrated so many times in the past, accuracy in flow pattern transitions is impossible and usually not necessary.

Experimental evidence is provided to confirm the validity of some of the transition lines. This applies to transitions a and c (at low liquid flow rates). More experimental work is needed to verify the complete theory.

NOTATION

A	pipe cross-sectional flow area; annular flow pattern
AW	wavy annular flow pattern
B	bubble flow pattern
c	wave velocity
C	constant in the friction factor correlation
CH	churn flow pattern
C_d	drag coefficient
C_L	lift coefficient
d	bubble or drop diameter
D	pipe diameter
DB	dispersed bubble flow pattern
f	friction factor
F	modified Froude number (Equation 32); force
Fr	Froude number
g	acceleration of gravity
h	liquid or gas level
H	A_L/A_L'
I	intermittent (slug and elongated bubble) flow pattern
k	constant (Equation 114)
K	dimensionless wavy flow parameter (Equation 37); critical Weber number
Ku	Kutateladze number
ℓ	length

L	length of pipe
m	exponent (Equation 11)
n	exponent (Equation 11)
P	pressure
Q	volumetric flow rate
Re	Reynolds number
s	Jeffreys' sheltering coefficient
S	perimeter; stratified flow pattern
SL	slug flow pattern
SS	stratified smooth flow pattern
SW	stratified wavy flow pattern
t	time
T	dimensionless dispersed bubble flow parameter (Equation 43)
u	velocity in the x-direction
u_0	free rise velocity
u_*	frictional velocity
v	velocity perpendicular to the x-direction
V	voltage
W	mass flow rate
x	coordinate in the downstream direction
X	Lockhart Martinelli parameter (Equation 14)
Y	dimensionless inclination parameter (Equation 15)

Greek Symbols

α	gas holdup
β	angle of inclination, positive for downward flow; decay rate (Equation 78)
γ	wetting angle; shape factor for a bubble
δ	film thickness
Δ	small increment
ε	pipe roughness; energy dissipation per unit mass

μ	dynamic viscosity
ν	kinematic viscosity
ρ	density
σ	interfacial tension
τ	shear stress
ϕ	liquid holdup; properties correction factor

Subscripts

C	center
E	entry length
f	film
G	gas
i	interface
L	liquid; lift

M	mixture
s	slug
S	superficial
$\sim$	dimensionless
$'$	fluctuation

REFERENCES

1. Barnea, D., Shoham, O., and Taitel, Y., "Flow Pattern Characterization for Two-Phase Flow by Electrical Conductance Probe," *Int. J. Multiphase Flow*, 6, 387–397 (1980).
2. Nicholson, M. K., Aziz, K., and Gregory, G. A., "Intermittent Two Phase Flow in Horizontal Pipes, Predictive Models," Can. J. Chem. Eng., 56, 653–663 (1978).

3. Baker, O., "Simultaneous Flow of Oil and Gas," *Oil and Gas J.*, 53, 185 (1954).
4. Govier, G. W., and Aziz, K., "The Flow of Complex Mixtures in Pipes," Van Nostrand Reinhold Co. (1972).
5. Mandhane, J. M., Gregory, G. A., and Aziz, K., "A Flow Pattern Map for Gas Liquid Flow in Horizontal Pipes," *Intern. J. Multiphase Flow*, 1, 537–553 (1974).
6. Weisman, J., Duncan, D., Gibson, J., and Crawford, T., "Effect of Fluid Properties and Pipe Diameter on Two-Phase Flow Pattern in Horizontal Lines," *Int. J. Multiphase Flow*, 5, 437 (1979).
7. Spedding, P. L., and Nguyen, V. T., "Regime Maps for Air-Water Two-Phase Flow," *Chem. Eng. Sci.*, 35, 779–793 (1980).
8. Griffith, P. and Wallis, G. B., "Two-Phase Slug Flow," *J. Heat Transfer*, 83, 307–320 (1961).
9. Duns, Jr., H., and Ros, N. C. J., "Vertical Flow of Gas and Liquid Mixtures from Boreholes," *Proc. 6th World Petroleum Contress*, Frankfurt (June 1963).
10. Sternling, V. C., "Two-Phase Flow Theory and Engineering Decision," *Award Lecture Presented at AIChE Annual Meeting* (1965).
11. Wallis, G. B., *One Dimensional Two-Phase Flow*, McGraw-Hill (1969).
12. Hewitt, G. F., and Roberts, D. N., "Studies of Two-Phase Flow Patterns by Simultaneous X-Rays and Flash Photography," *AERE Report* M-2159 (1969).
13. Oshinowo, T., and Charles, M. E., "Vertical Two-Phase Flow: Part I: Flow Pattern Correlations and Part II: Holdup and Pressure Drop," *Can. J. Chem. Eng.*, 52, 438–448 (1974).
14. Gould, T. L., Tek, M. R., and Katz, D. L., "Two-Phase Flow through Vertical Inclined or Curved Pipe," *J. Pet. Techn.*, 914–926 (1974).
15. Gould, T. L., "Vertical Two-Phase Stream Water Flow in Geothermal Wells," *J. Pet. Tech.*, 833–842 (1974).
16. Taitel, Y., Barnea, D., and Dukler, A. E., "Modeling Flow Pattern Transitions for Steady Upward Gas-Liquid Flow in Vertical Tubes," *AIChE J.*, 26, 345 (1980).
17a. Hewitt, G. F., *Measurement of Two-Phase Flow Parameters*, Academic Press (1970).
17b. Hewitt, G. F., and Hall-Taylor, N. S., *Annular Two-Phase Flow*, Pergamon Press (1970).
18. Bergles, A. E., and Sue, M., "Investigation of Boiling-Water Flow Regimes at High Pressure," *Dynatech Report* No. NYO-3304-8, HTFS 1909 (1966).
19. Raisson, C., "Flow Regime Studies Up to Critical Heat-Flux Conditions at 80 kg/cm²," *CEN Grenoble*, Report No. TT62 (1965).
20. Hsu, Y. Y., and Graham, R. W., "A Visual Study of Two-Phase Flow in a Vertical Tube with Heat Addition," *NASA Tech. Note D-1564* (1963).
21. Derbyshire, R. T. P., Hewitt, G. F., and Nicholls, B., "X-Radiography of Two-Phase Gas-Liquid Flow," *AERE Report M-1321* (1969).
22. Solomon, J. V., "Construction of a Two-Phase Flow Regime Transition Detector," M.Sc. thesis, Mech. Eng. Dept., MIT (1962).
23. Griffith, P., "Two-Phase Flow Regime Detection," ASME Paper, 64-WA/HT-43 (1963).
24. Bergles, A. E., Lopina, R. F., and Fiori, M. P., "Critical Heat Flux and Flow Pattern Observation for Low-Pressure Water Flowing in Tubes," *J. Heat Transfer*, 89, 69–74 (1967).
25. Ryan, J. T., and Vermeulen, L. R., "A Slug Flow Transducer," *Review Sci. Insrt.*, 39, 1756–1757 (1971).
26. Bergles, A. E., "Electrical Probes for Study of Two-Phase Flows," Eleventh Nat. ASME/ AIChE Heat Transfer Conference, Minneapolis, 70–81 (1969).
27. Reimann, J., and John, H., "Measurements of the Phase Distribution in Horizontal Air-Water and Steam Water Flow," Paper presented at CNSI Meeting on Transient Two-Phase Flow, Paris (June 1978).
28. Hsu, Y. Y., Simon, F. F., and Graham, R. W., "Applications of Hot Wire Anemometry for Two-Phase Flow Measurements," Paper presented at the ASME Winter Meeting, Philadelphia, PA (1963).
29. Jones, Jr., O. C., and Zuber, N., "The Interrelation Between Void Fraction Fluctuations and Flow Pattern in Two-Phase Flow," *Int. J. Multiphase Flow*, 2, 273 (1975).
30. Smith, A. V., "Fast Response Multi-Beam X-Ray Absorption Technique for Identifying Phase Distributions During Steam Water Blowdowns," *J. Br. Nucl. Ener. Soc.*, 14(3), 227–235 (1975).

31. Wesley, R. D., "Performance of Drag-Disc Turbine and Gamma Densitometer in LOFT," US Nuclear Regulatory Commission, Proceeding of Meeting of Review Group on Two-Phase Flow Instrumentation, NUREG-0375 (Paper No. I.5) (Jan. 1977).

32. Vince, M. A., and Lahey, R. T., Jr., "On the Development of an Objective Flow Regime Indicator," *Int. J. Multiphase Flow*, 8, 93–124 (1982).

33. Lubbesmeyer, D., and Leoni, B., "Fluid Velocity Measurements and Flow-Pattern Identification by Noise-Analysis of Light-Beam Signals," *Int. J. Multiphase Flow*, 9, 665–679 (1983).

34. Hubbard, M. G., and Dukler, A. E., "The Characterization of Flow Regimes for Horizontal Two-Phase Flow," Proc. Heat Transfer and Fluid Mechanics Institute (edited by Saad, M. A., and Moller, J. A.), Stanford University Press Ca., (1966).

35. Tutu, N. K., "Pressure Fluctuations and Flow Pattern Recognition in Vertical Two-Phase Gas-Liquid Flows," *Int. J. Multiphase Flow*, 8, 443 (1982).

36. Taitel, Y., and Dukler, A. E., "A Model for Prediction Flow Regime Transition in Horizontal and Near Horizontal Gas-Liquid Flow," *AIChE J.*, 22, 47 (1976).

37. Barnea, D., Shoham, O., and Taitel, Y., "Flow Pattern Transition for Vertical Downward Two-Phase Flow," *Chem. Eng. Sci.*, 37, 741–746 (1982).

38. Barnea, D., Shoham, O., and Taitel, Y., "Flow Pattern Transition for Downward Inclined Two-Phase Flow: Horizontal to Vertical," *Chem. Eng. Sci.*, 37, 735–740 (1982).

39. Barnea, D., and Brauner, N., "Holdup of the Liquid Slug in Two-Phase Intermittent Flow," *Int. J. Multiphase Flow*, 11, 43–49 (1985).

40. Barnea, D., Shoham, O., Taitel, Y., and Dukler, A. E., "Gas Liquid Flow in Inclined Tubes: Flow Pattern Transition for Upward Flow," *Chem. Eng. Sci.*, 40, 131–136 (1985).

41. White, P. O., and Huntington, R. L., "Horizontal Co-Current Two-Phase Flow of Fluids in Pipe Lines," *Petro. Eng.*, 27, 9 D40 (August 1955).

42a. Hoogendorn, C., "Gas-Liquid Flow in Horizontal Pipes," *Chem. Eng. Sci.*, 9, 205–207 (1959).

42b. Hoogendorn, C., and Buitelaar, A. A., "The Effect of Gas Density and Gradual Vaporization on Gas-Liquid Flow in Horizontal Pipes," *Chem. Eng. Sci.*, 16, 208 (1961).

43. Govier, G. W., and Omer, M. M., "The Horizontal Pipeline Flow of Air Water Mixtures," *Can. J. Chem. Eng.*, 40, 93–104 (1962).

44. Eaton, B. A., Andrews, D. E., Knowles, C. R., Silberberg, I. H., and Brown, K. E., "The Prediction of Flow Patterns, Liquid Holdup and Pressure Losses Occurring During Continuous Two-Phase Flow in Horizontal Pipeline," *J. Petrol. Tech.*, 19, 815–828 (1967).

45. Simpson, H. C., Rooney, D. H., Grattan, E., and Al-Samarrae, F., "Two-Phase Flow in Large Diameter Horizontal Lines," Paper A6, European Two Phase Flow Group Meeting, Grenoble (June 1977).

46. Shoham, O., "Flow Pattern Transitions and Characterization in Gas-Liquid Two-Phase Flow in Inclined Pipes," Ph.D. dissertation, Tel Aviv University (1982).

47. Al-Sheikh, J. N., Saunders, D. E., and Brodkey, R. S., "Prediction of Flow Patterns in Horizontal Two-Phase Flow," *Can. J. Chem. Eng.*, 48, 21 (1970).

48. Agrawal, S. S., Gregory, G. A., and Govier, G. W., "An Analysis of Horizontal Stratified Two-Phase Flow in Pipes," *Can. J. Chem. Eng.*, 51, 280–186 (1973).

49. Gazley, C., "Interfacial Shear and Stability in Two-Phase Flow," Ph.D. dissertation, Univ. of Delaware, Newark (1949).

50. Lockhart, R. W., and Martinelli, R. C., "Proposed Correlation of Data for Isothermal Two-Phase, Two-Component Flow in Pipes," *Chem. Eng. Prog.*, 45, 38–49 (1949).

51. Dukler, A. E., and Hubbard, M. G., "A Model for Gas-Liquid Slug Flow in Horizontal Tubes," *Ind. Eng. Chem. Fundamentals*, 14, 337–347 (1975).

52. Butterworth, D., "A Visual Study of Mechanism in Horizontal Air Water Flow," *AERE Report M2556*, Harwell, England (1967).

53. Milne-Thomson, L. M., *Theoretical Hydrodynamics*, The MacMillan Co., NY (1960).

54. Wallis, G. B., and Dobson, J. E., "The Onset of Slugging in Horizontal Stratified Air-Water Flow," *Int. J. Multiphase Flow*, 1, 173 (1973).

55. Benjamin, T. B., "Gravity Currents and Related Phenomena," *J. Fluid Mech.*, 31, 209–248 (1968).

56. Benjamin, T. B., "Shearing Flow Over a Wavy Boundary," *J. Fluid Mech.*, 6, 161 (1959).

57. Kordyban, E. S., and Ranov, T., "Mechanism of Slug Formation in Horizontal Two-Phase Flow," Trans. ASME, J. Basic Engineering, 92, Series D., No. 4, 85 (1970).
58. Stewart, R. W., "Mechanics of the Air Sea Interface, Boundary Layers and Turbulence," Phys. Fluids, 10, 547 (1967).
59. Jeffreys, H., "On the Formation of Water Waves by Wind," Proc. Royal Soc., A107, 189 (1925).
60. Jeffreys, H., "On the Formation of Waves by Wind," Proc. Royal Soc., A110, 241 (1926).
61. Fulford, G. D., "The Flow of Liquids in Thin Films," Advan. Chem. Eng., 5, 151 (1964).
62. Brock, R. R., "Periodic Permanent Roll Waves," Proc. Am. Soc. Civil Engrs., 96, HYD 12, 2565 (1970).
63. Chu, K. T., "Statistical Characteristics and Modeling of Way Liquid Film in Vertical Two-Phase Flow," Ph.D. dissertation, Univ. Houston, TX (1973).
64. Levich, V. G., Physiochemical Hydrodynamics, Prentice-Hall, Englewood Cliffs, NJ (1962).
65. Taitel, Y., "Flow Pattern Transition in Rough Pipes," Int. J. Multiphase Flow, 3, 597 (1977).
66. Taitel, Y., and Dukler, A. E., "Effect of Pipe Length on the Transition Boundary for High Viscous Liquids," in preparation.
67. Taitel, Y., Lee, N., and Dukler, A. E., "Transient Gas-Liquid Flow in Horizontal Pipes-Modeling Flow Pattern Transitions," AIChE J., 24, 920 (1978).
68. Taitel, Y., and Dukler, A. E., "A Model for Slug Frequency During Gas Liquid Flow in Horizontal and Near Horizontal Pipes," Int. J. Multiphase Flow, 3, 585 (1977).
69. Stoker, J. J., Water Waves, Interscience, NY (1957).
70. Weisman, J., and Kang, S. Y., "Flow Pattern Transitions in Vertical and Upwardly Inclined Lines," Int. J. Multiphase Flow, 7, 271 (1981).
71. Bennett, A. W., Griffith, G. F., Kearsy, H. A., Keeys, R. K. F., and Lacey, P. M. C., "Flow Visualization Studies of Boiling at High Pressure," Proc. Inst. Mech. Eng., Part 3C, 1, (1965–1966).
72. Griffith, P., and Synder, G. A., "The Bubbly-Slug Transition in a High Velocity Two-Phase Flow," MIT Report 5003-29 (TID-20947) (1964).
73. Radovicich, N. A., and Moissis, R., "The Transition from Two-Phase Bubble Flow to Slug Flow," MIT Report 7-7673-22 (1962).
74. Harmathy, T. Z., "Velocity of Large Drops and Bubbles in Media of Infinite or Restricted Extent," AIChE J., 6, 281 (1960).
75. Hinze, J. O., "Fundamentals of the Hydrodynamic Mechanism of Splitting in Dispersion Processes," AIChE J., 1, 289 (1955).
76. Clay, P. H., "The Mechanism of Emulsion Formation in Turbulent Flow," Part I, Proc. Roy. Acad. Sci. (Amsterdam), 43, 852 (1940).
77. Sevik, M., and Park, S. H., "The Splitting of Drops and Bubbles by Turbulent Fluid Flow," Trans. ASME J., Fluid Eng., 95, 53 (1973).
78. Brodkey, R. S., The Phenomena of Fluid Motion, Addison-Wesley Press (1967).
79. Calderbank, P. H., "Physical Rate Processes in Industrial Fermentation: Part I: The Interfacial Area in Gas-Liquid Contacting with Mechanical Agitation," Trans. Inst. Chem. Eng., 36, 443 (1958).
80. Miyagi, O., "On Air Bubbles Rising in Water," Phil. Mag., 50, No. 295 (1925).
81. Nicklin, D. J., Wilkes, J. O., and Davidson, J. F., "Two-Phase Flow in Vertical Tubes," Trans. Inst. Chem. Eng., 40, 61 (1962).
82. Nicklin, D. J., and Davidson, J. F., "The Onset of Instability on Two-Phase Slug Flow," Inst. Mech. Eng. (London), Proc. of Symp. on Two-Phase Flow, Paper 4 (1962).
83. Moissis, R., "The Transition from Slug to Homogeneous Two-Phase Flow," J. Heat Transfer, 85, 366 (1963).
84. Feldman, S., "On the Hydrodynamics Stability of Two Viscous Incompressible Fluids in Parallel Uniform Shearing Motion," J. Fluid Mech., 1, 343 (1957).
85. Davis, R. M., and Taylor, G. I., "The Mechanism of Large Bubbles Rising Through Liquids in Tubes," Proc. of Roy. Soc. (London), 200, Ser. A, 375 (1950).

86. Dumitrescu, D. T., "Stromung and Einer Luftblase in Senkrechten Rohr, ZAMM, 23, 139 (1943).
87. Moissis, R., and Griffith, P., "Entrance Effects in a Two-Phase Slug Flow," *J. Heat Transfer*, 84, 29 (1962).
88. Akagawa, K., and Sakaguchi, T., "Fluctuation of Void Ratio in Two-Phase Flow," *Bulletin of JSMA*, 9, 104–120 (1966).
89. Schlichting, H., *Boundary Layer Theory*, McGraw-Hill (1968).
90. Patel, R. P., "Turbulent Jets and Wall Jets in Uniform Streaming Flow," *Aeron Q.*, 23, 311 (1971).
91. Turner, R. G., Hubbard, M. G., and Dukler, A. E., "Analysis and Prediction of Minimum Flow Rate for the Continuous Removal of Liquid from Gas Wells," *J. Petroleum Tech.*, 21, 1475 (1969).
92. Pushkina, O. L., and Sorokin, Y. L., "Breakdown of Liquid Film Motion in Vertical Tubes," *Heat Trans. Soviet Res.*, 1, 56–64 (1969).
93. Golan, L. P., and Stenning, A. H., "Two-Phase Vertical Flow Maps," *Proc. Instn. Mech. Engrs.*, 184, Part 3C, 108–114 (1969–1970).
94. Martin, C. S., "Transition from Bubble to Slug Flow of a Vertically Downward Air-Water Mixture," *ASME Symposium*, Atlanta (June 1973).
95. Martin, C. S., "Vertically Downward Two-Phase Slug Flow," *J. Fluids Eng.*, 98, 715–722 (1976).
96. Kulov, N. N., Maksimov, V. V., Mal-usov, V. A., and Zhavoronkov, N. M., "Pressure Drop Mean Film Thickness and Entrainment in Downward Two-Phase Flow," *Chem. Eng. J.*, 18, 183–188 (1979).
97. Yamazaki, Y., and Yamaguchi, K., "Characteristics of Cocurrent Two-Phase Downflow in Tubes," *J. Nuclear Sci. and Tech.*, 16, 245–255 (1979).
98a. Singh, G., and Griffith, P., "Determination of the Pressure Drop Optimum Pipe Size for a Two-Phase Slug Flow in an Inclined Pipe," *J. Eng. Ind. Trans.*, *ASME*, 92 717–726 (1970).
98b. Singh, G., and Griffith, P., "Down Sloping Inclined Pipe Flow Regime Transitions," ASME Publication, Paper 76-Pet-30, Petroleum Mech. Eng. and Pressure Vessels and Piping Conference, Mexico City (Sept. 1976).
99. Bonnecaze, R. H., Erskine, W., and Greskovich, E. J., "Holdup and Pressure Drop for Two-Phase Flow in Inclined Pipe Lines, *AIChE J.*, 17, 1109 (1971).
100. Beggs, H. D., and Brill, J. P., "A Study of Two-Phase Flow in Inclined Pipes," *J. Pet. Techn.*, 606–617 (1973).
101. Streeter, V. L., *Handbook of Fluid Dynamics*, McGraw-Hill (1961).
102. Savigny, R., "Investigation of Isothermal Co-Current Two Fluid, Two-Phase Flow in an Inclined Tube," PhD. dissertation, University of Rochester, Rochester, NY (1962).
103. Marchessault, R. N., and Mason, S. G., "Flow of Entrapped Bubbles Through a Capillary," *Industrial and Engineering Chemistry*, 52, 79–84 (1960).
104. Sue, M., and Griffith, P., "Two-Phase Flow in Capillary Tubes," *Transaction of the ASME J. of Basic Engineering*, 576–582 (1964).
105. Oya, T., "Upward Liquid Flow in Small Tube into Which Air Streams" (1st report, experimental apparatus and flow patterns), *Bulletin of the JSME*, 14, No. 78, 1320–1329 (1971).
106. Oya, T., "Upward Liquid Flow in Small Tube into Which Air Streams" (2nd report, pressure drop at the confluence), *Bulletin of the JSME*, 14, No. 78, 1330–1339 (1971).
107. Wallis, G. B., Richter, H. J., and Bharathan, D., "Air-Water Counter-Current Annular Flow in Vertical Tubes," EPRI Rep. NP-786 (1978).
108. Taitel, Y., Barnea, D., and Dukler, A. E., "A Film Model for the Prediction of Flooding and Flow Reversal for Gas-Liquid Flow in the Vertical Tubes," *Int. J. Multiphase Flow*, 8, 1–10 (1982).
109. Richter, H. J., "Flooding in Tubes and Annuli," *Int. J. Multiphase Flow*, 7, 647–658 (1981).
110. Tien, C. L., Chung, K. S., and Liu, P. C., "Flooding in Two-Phase Countercurrent Flows," *EPRI Rep. NP-1283 (1979).

111. Wallis, G. B., Karlin, A. S., Clard, III, C. R., Bharathan, D., Hagi, V., and Richter, H. J., "Countercurrent Gas-Liquid Flow in Parallel Vertical Tubes," *Int. J. Multiphase Flow*, 7, 1–19 (1981).
112. Shearer, C. J., and Davidson, J. F., "The Investigation of a Standing Wave Due to Gas Blowing Upwards Over a Liquid Film: Its Relation to Flooding in Wetted Wall Columns," *J. Fluid Mech.*, 22, 321–335 (1965).
113. Centinbudaklar, A. G., and Jameson, G. J., "The Mechanism of Flooding in Vertical Counter Current Two-Phase Flow," *J. Fluid Mech.*, 22, 1669–1680 (1969).
114. Imura, H., Dusuda, H., and Funatsu, S., "Flooding Velocity in a Counter-Current Annular Two-Phase Flow," *Chem. Engng. Sci.*, 32, 79–87 (1977).
115. Dukler, A. E., and Smith, L., "Two-Phase Interactions in Counter-Current Flow Studies of the Flooding Mechanism," U.S. Nuclear Regulatory Agency Rep. NUREG/CR-0617 (1977).
116. Suzuki, S., and Ueda, T., "Behavior of Liquid Films and Flooding in Counter-Current Two-Phase Flow—1. Flow in Circular Tubes, *Int. J. Multiphase Flow*, 3, 517–532 (1977).
117. Shah, Y. T., Stiegel, G. J., and Sharma, M. M., "Backmixing in Gas-Liquid Reactors," *AIChE J.*, 24, 369–400 (1978).
118. Hikita, H., Asai, S., Tanigawa, K., Segawa, K., and Kitao, M., "Gas Hold-Up in Bubble Columns," *Chem. Engng. J.*, 20, 59–67 (1980).
119. Vermeer, D. J., and Krishna, R., "Hydrodynamics and Mass Transfer in Bubble Columns Operating in the Churn-Turbulent Regime," *I&EC Process Design & Devel.*, 20, 475–482 (1981).
120. Taitel, Y., and Barnea, D., "Counter-Current Gas Liquid Vertical Flow—Model for Flow Pattern and Pressure Drop," *Int. J. Multiphase Flow*, 9, 637–648 (1983).
121. Greskovich, E. H., "Holdup Prediction for Stratified Downflow of Gas-Liquid Mixtures," *Ind. and Eng. Chem. Process Design Development*, 11, 81 (1972).
122. Barnea, D., Luninski, Y., and Taitel, Y., "Flow Pattern in Horizontal and Vertical Two-Phase Flow in Small Diameter Pipes," *Canadian J. Chem. Eng.*, 61, 617–620 (1983).

CHAPTER 17

INTERFACIAL PHENOMENA OF FULLY-DEVELOPED, STRATIFIED, TWO-PHASE FLOWS

Y. L. Sinai

National Nuclear Corporation, Ltd.
Risley, Warrington
Cheshire, England

CONTENTS

INTRODUCTION

Stratified, near-horizontal, internal, two-phase flows arise in a broad range of situations in the process, oil and power-generation industries, among others. Two important examples relevant to the nuclear reactor industry concern postulated loss-of-coolant-accidents (LOCA's) in pressurized-water reactors. In the first example, during a "small" LOCA, condensed steam drains backward from the steam generators, along the horizontal hot legs toward the core, and is impeded in its progress by the steam emanating from the core. The rate of condensate drain-back influences the cooling of the core. The second example arises in designs having hot-leg injection of emergency cooling water (ECW), and here condensation of steam by the ECW, as well as momentum transfer, influences the ECW effectiveness and system dynamics. Realistic predictions of pressure drop and holdup are clearly needed for all of these events.

Frequently, the processes at a gas/liquid interface involve coupled momentum and heat and mass transfer [1], but in this chapter focuses on independent momentum transfer; the interested reader may, as a first step, proceed to estimate heat and mass transfer by utilizing the analogies for Stanton and Sherwood numbers [2, 3, 4], or preferably, exploit the extensive literature available on this topic.

When a gas flows sufficiently slowly over a liquid, the interface remains smooth. However, as the gas speed increases, interfacial waves are excited, propagate, and influence the gas flow. The gross surface conditions are conveniently characterized in terms of the gas-phase friction velocity U_{G_r}, and over a certain value of U_{G_r} the flow above the interface has been observed to correspond to that over an aerodynamically rough surface. Charnock [5] used dimensional arguments to propose an algebraic relation between U_{G_r} and a roughness scale ε, as elaborated in the literature survey below in this chapter, Charnock's relation has been widely applied in oceanography, where it predicts interfacial stress in terms of the air speed at a reference height when used in conjunction with the logarithmic profile of aerodynamically rough turbulent flows. As regards internal flows, its use has been restricted to identifying the roughness elements from measurements of the shear stress, and it has been ignored as a predictive tool because the roughness ε has been considered to be unknown. Recently, Sinai [6, 7] investigated the viability of a technique that is exactly analogous to the external-flow one, with the logarithmic profile being replaced by the classical relation between *mean* flow and roughness scale; relating roughness, and hence interfacial drag, to mean flow rates renders the procedure a candidate for internal flow computations. A tentative comparison with Wallis and Dobson's [8] experiments showed excellent agreement near wave inception, but discrepancies appeared under smooth conditions and near the stratified-slug transition. This is not surprising, since Charnock's relation applies to rough flow and to roughness that is small on the scale of the mean water depth. Furthermore, the comparison was indirect since Wallis and Dobson did not report values of interfacial stress or pressure gradient, and my [6] experimental values of the stress were *deduced* from the channel inclinations reported by Wallis and Dobson [8]. Nevertheless, the comparisons were sufficiently promising to encourage refinements of the modeling, and in this chapter incorporates the Colebrook-White formula [9] in order to encompass the complete turbulent range in the gas phase, from smooth to fully-rough flows. An optional, empirical correction factor is also presented in order to reduce the contradiction near transition, but it is emphasized that this factor is provisional, and it will only be worthwhile to improve upon it when additional direct comparisons can be made with data for fully-developed, rather than developing flows.

If the voidage is too high for slugging to occur, a suggestion is made, albeit on an intuitive basis, for bridging the gap between the univeral stress relation presented herein and the stratified-annular transition.

The appeal of the technique in this chapter lies in its physical basis, as opposed to the purely empirical nature of alternative schemes, and this facilitates assessment of the likely shortcomings, as well as the advantages of the method. It is not expected to apply to thin-film phenomena, but it should succeed in co-current and counter-current flows, as well as flows over nominally stagnant liquid. The difficult subject of spray and bubble generation at the interface is ignored, and the flow is assumed to be near-horizontal; the concepts supporting the proposed models are inappropriate for vertical channels and are therefore expected to break down at some intermediate inclination where new mechanisms come into play.

LITERATURE REVIEW

A huge source of information on phenomena near the interface between two fluids exists in the literature, so the present survey will, perforce, be perfunctory. Understanding and describing general laminar and turbulent transport at plane surfaces can be difficult enough but one manifestation of gas/liquid coupling that adds another dimension to the level of complexity is the occurrence of interfacial waves.

The book by Davies and Rideal [10] deals with the physics and chemistry of clean and "contaminated" interfaces, and other notable books are those by Levich [3] and Davies [4].

Analyses of laminar interactions may be found in [11, 12, 13]. Helpful surveys of the literature on turbulent exchange, both at solid boundaries and fluid interfaces, are provided [14, 15]. There are two fundamental approaches to predictive estimates in turbulent exchange, with some degree of overlap—"quasi-laminar" and "eddy" diffusion. Recent advances in flow visualization at solid walls have highlighted coherent "hairpin" structures [16] that are associated with intermittency and bursting characteristic of the surface-renewal concept, which is categorized under the "quasi-laminar" approach [17–20].

The propagation of surface gravity waves in a liquid, without the influence of gas above the surface, is a subject in its own right and is still an area of active research. Wind-wave interactions and their influences on interfacial transport are even more complex, and most of the published material in this area has been contributed by workers in oceanography, geophysical fluid dynamics, and civil engineering. Excellent accounts are available [1, 21–27] and illustrate some of the experimental and theoretical procedures [28–31] adopted by workers in these fields when dealing with specialized aspects of this broad-ranging topic. In the geophysical context, thermal stability of the gas, embodied in the Richardson number, is important, but will be ignored here.

The process is unsteady not only because of turbulent fluctuations but also because of the interfacial waves. It should be noted that generally the interface will exhibit a broad spectrum of wavelengths, and in the range of wavelengths that are smaller than the mean liquid depth the wave components are dispersive, even in the absence of gas/liquid coupling, and will therefore travel at different speeds. A prime objective is the prediction of τ, the time-mean interfacial stress, whether in developing or saturated conditions. Incidentally, some researchers have reported an inequality of the Reynolds stresses, $\rho_j u'v'$, on the two sides of the interface and have ascribed it to mechanical energy transfer in a developing situation; but whether this is true or not, this chapter only considers fully-developed regimes. Oceanographers normally use a simple correlation,

$$\tau = \rho_G U_{10}^2 C_{10}; \qquad C_{10} = fn(U_{10}) \tag{1}$$

where U_{10} is the wind speed at a height of 10 meters above the mean liquid position. Equation 1 is, of-course, meaningless for internal flow. As mentioned, the time-mean horizontal velocity profile has been observed in the laboratory and the field to be similar to that over a rigid, rough boundary, with a (normally small) correction for the surface drift current [24, 28–33]:

$$U_G/U_{G_\tau} \cong 2.5 \ln(z/z_0), \qquad z_0 \cong \varepsilon/30 \tag{2}$$

Here ε is a mean roughness height. About thirty years ago, Charnock [5] argued, on dimensional grounds subsequently supported by theoretical considerations [24], that under saturated conditions

$$z_0 = \gamma U_{G_\tau}^2/g, \qquad \gamma = \text{constant} \tag{3}$$

Substitution of Equation 3 in Equation 2 yields an algebraic equation for U_τ in terms of U_{10} [24, 34]:

$$U_{10}/U_{G_\tau} = 2.5 \ln(10g/\gamma U_{G_\tau}^2) \tag{4}$$

Wu [29] has manipulated Equation 3 into the form

$$U_\tau \cong (g/k)^{1/2} \tag{5}$$

where k is the wavenumber of the element; the right-hand side is the linear phase speed of the element on deep water, and Wu therefore identifies the elements as those components that possess phase speeds smaller than U_τ and over which the flow will separate. In the field, the roughness elements appear as ripples on the large "significant" waves, whereas in the laboratory the significant waves themselves normally act as the roughness elements. Many of the laboratory tests have been conducted at scales that are comparable to those encountered in typical engineering situations, although the flows have frequently been evolutionary so that the inferred "constant" γ has been a function of fetch (distance along the surface).

It is worth pointing out that Equation 3 has not remained unchallenged [35, 36], but the evidence in its support appears overwhelming, at least for water that is deep relative to the roughness wavelength. If the concepts underlying Equation 5 are true, an iterative algorithm for water that is not deep may be feasible.

Attention is now turned to internal, near-horizontal flows that are more closely allied to the configurations in the chemical and nuclear industries. A brief review covering most of the material until 1977 may be found in [37]. In these industries the gas velocities can be greater than those encountered in the field, and the far broader range of relative flow rates of gas and liquid imply that several flow "regimes" are possible: stratified (smooth or wavy), intermittent (slug or plug), dispersed bubble, and annular droplet. Gross flow properties like pressure loss and heat transfer are naturally critically dependent on the flow regime, and several regime maps are currently available. The simpler maps use only two independent variables for all the transitions, but the more sophisticated maps [38] employ a different pair of coordinates for each transition, as is to be expected.

The transitions of concern in this chapter are the smooth/wavy, stratified/annular, and stratified/slug. The first has of course been extensively, but not exhaustively, studied by oceanographers, and the three predictive methods are those of Jeffreys, Miles, and Phillips [21, 24, 27]. Hanratty and Engen [39] observed three fundamental types of waves in the rough domain: two-dimensional, three-dimensional ("squalls"), and roll waves, which would form slugs if the voidage is not high.

Two important papers on slugging are those by Kordyban and Ranov [40] and by Wallis and Dobson [8]. Both papers note a sensitivity of the stratified/slug transition to small changes in the channel slope, but Wallis and Dobson appear to have been the only workers who have adjusted the channel inclination to ensure constant time-mean voidage along the duct length. This facility is important if a validation of a theory for fully-developed conditions is to be performed. For the common situations in which $U_G \gg U_L$, Wallis and Dobson's correlation for the stratified/slug transition is

$$V_G^* = 0.5\alpha^{3/2} \tag{6}$$

or, for a rectangular channel,

$$U_{G_T} = 0.5[gh_G(\rho_L - \rho_G)/\rho_G]^{1/2} \tag{7}$$

There is a sizeable source of information on thin films, corresponding to voidages that are very close to 1, with application, for example to blade erosion by liquid droplets in steam turbines [41–43]. Very thin films can only disintegrate into rivulets and entrained droplets. The work of Hanratty et al. [39, 44] appears to cover an intermediate range of thicknesses (Table 1).

Some of the work on continuously-stratified flows is relevant [45–48]. The Lockhart-Martinelli [49] approach has been extended but interfacial phenomena have been ignored. Most of those authors who have considered the influence of τ on pressure drop have assumed

$$\tau = \tfrac{1}{2}\rho_G f_G(U_G - U_L)^2 \tag{8}$$

where f_G is the smooth turbulent friction factor. Kadambi [48] appears to have obtained very good agreement for gross flow properties with other theoretical and experimental data. He used Pai's [50] exact solution of the Reynolds equations, but while suggesting that the interface can be represented in terms of an equivalent roughness, he applied Pai's solution to a smooth interface; it is possible that several assumptions in that theory have conspired beneficially to yield such promising agreement. Akai et al. [51] have considered interfacial roughness in some detail and used the k-ε turbulence model for numerical computations. However, the paper is made conspicuous by the absence of even a single reference to material originating in oceanography, and moreover, the authors claim to have introduced the idea of wave-induced shear stress when in fact researchers have been aware of it for many years [52]. The paper [51] gives an experimental correlation of interfacial roughness as a function of the gas-phase Reynolds number for the air/mercury pair; the roughness size was identified as a wave amplitude.

In considering condensation during counter-current flow, Bankoff and Kim [53] quote Linehan's correlation of interfacial stress for *co-current* flow. Such a correlation is useful, of course, but is not as general in its applicability as one would wish; for example, the interfacial friction factor should

Table 1
Measurements of Hanratly, Engen, and Cohen [39, 44] in Terms of $\hat{U}_G$ and $\hat{U}_\tau$

Re_G	U_G (ft/s)	U_τ (ft/s)	$\hat{U}_G$	$\hat{U}_\tau$
8,440	18.2	1.47	1.41	0.114
12,800	29.7	2.19	2.48	0.183
13,900	31.8	2.28	2.65	0.189
14,250	31.6	1.88	2.58	0.153
19,200	41.2	2.29	3.31	0.184

depend on the *gas* speed when the liquid is nominally stagnant (e.g., zero mean liquid flow), whereas Linehan's correlation [53] depends solely on the *liquid* Reynolds number.

I [6, 7] investigated the possibility of applying a procedure, a analogous to the solution of Equations 2 and 3 in oceanography, to internal flows, with Equation 2 replaced by the classical relation between mean flow and roughness, under *fully* rough conditions [9]:

$$U_G/U_\tau \cong 2.5 \ln(R/\varepsilon) + 4.73 \tag{9}$$

ε is the equivalent sand roughness, which depends in a complicated manner on the roughness geometry.

It transpires that Equations 3 and 9 do not possess a solution above a critical value of U_G, and the mathematical breakdown was interpreted as slug transition [6]; a direct comparison of the prediction of U_{G_c} (viz. U_G at slug transition) with Equation 7 then fixed a disposable parameter introduced earlier into Charnock's relation and a single, universal stress curve was proposed. Unfortunately, Wallis and Dobson reported neither the interfacial shear stress nor the axial pressure gradient, so only qualitative similarities could be discerned in [6]. However, Wallis and Dobson's shear stress was *deduced* in [7], albeit indirectly from their reported values of channel inclination, and the agreement was very encouraging except in the smooth regime and near transition. More details are to be found in the next section.

Finally, some comments about statements made in [15] are appropriate. The authors discard Charnock's relation for two reasons: (1) They claim that existing data does not support the relation. (2) The roughness is unknown and the relation therefore cannot be utilized as a predictive tool for internal flows. As previously pointed out, however, there is widespread support for the Charnock relation, except that allowance must be made for variation of the "constant" γ with distance under developing conditions. This is only to be expected since in developing flows the local roughness is unlikely to depend solely on the local shear stress, and is affected by conditions upstream and by wave propagation phenomena in the water. As regards the second point, the technique investigated by the author evaluates both the stress and the roughness, so that objection is no longer a valid one.

THEORY AND COMPARISON WITH EXPERIMENT

As described in the introduction, the starting point is the pair of Equations 3 and 9. As a first approximation [6], when the interface is rough and $\tau \gg \tau_{w_G}$, only the contribution of the interface to the pressure loss need be considered, so that one may introduce an "effective" roughness ε_e (see Figure 1),

$$\varepsilon_e = 0.33\xi U_\tau^2/g; \quad \xi = \eta C_i/(C_G + C_i) \tag{10}$$

Here, the ratio $C_i/(C_G + C_i)$ accounts for the fact that the roughness is not uniformly distributed around the perimeter; alternatively, its introduction into Equation 9 is equivalent to employing a

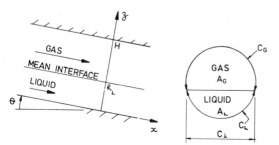

Figure 1. The configuration.

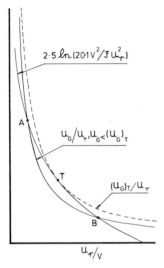

u_τ/v **Figure 2.** A sketch of the terms in Equation 11.

mean hydraulic radius of $2A_G/C_i$ instead of $2A_G/(C_G + C_i)$. η is a constant yet to be determined, and is expected to include the phase densities so that buoyancy forces are manifested. The algebraic equation may be written as

$$\hat{U}_G = -5\hat{U}_\tau \ln \hat{U}_\tau \tag{11}$$

where U_G and U_τ have been non-dimensionalized with respect to $V^{-1}(\xi/20.1)^{1/2}$, and $V^2 = gR_G$. The constant 5 could be absorbed into the definition of U_G but is retained in this form in order to use the same coordinates as [6]. For U_G greater than a certain critical value, denoted by U_{G_T}, Equation 11 does not possess a solution, as illustrated in Figure 2. In that sketch, the point marked A is the relevant solution when $\hat{U}_G < \hat{U}_{G_T}$, since point B implies that the stress decreases as U_G increases. The mathematical "breakdown" occurs at point C, where

$$\hat{U}_{G_T} = 5_e^{-1} \cong 1.839 \tag{12}$$

$$\hat{U}_{\tau_T} = e^{-1} \cong 0.368 \tag{13}$$

In dimensional terms, Equation 12 reads

$$\hat{U}_{G_T} \cong 11.66\left(\frac{gA_G}{\eta C_i}\right)^{1/2} \tag{14}$$

Note the similarity with [38] when the voidage is 0.5. Indeed, as a rough estimate one may modify the gravitational term in Equation 14 to $g \cos \theta$, as suggested by [38] and by the argument regarding the role of buoyancy forces. When confined to a rectangular channel, Equation 14 is seen to possess the same functional dependence as Equation 7, and η may be fixed as

$$\eta \cong \frac{545\rho_G}{\rho_L - \rho_G} \tag{15}$$

As it stands, the model has been forced to predict transition in agreement with [8], and the result is portrayed in Figure 3. If the voidage is sufficiently high [38] no slugs occur, and significantly

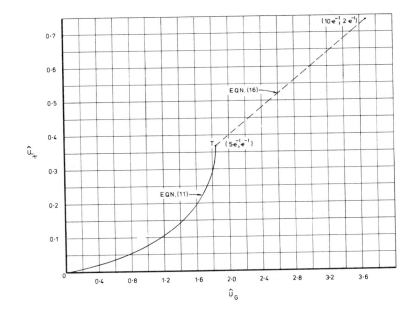

Figure 3. The first model—fully rough, uncorrected. If no slug transition occurs, C_f is assumed constant for $\hat{U}_G$ lying between $\hat{U}_{G_T}$ and the transition to annular flow.

higher gas flows can be achieved before the next transition is reached. The hypothesis is made here that in such cases the interfacial drag coefficient remains constant, at the value which is predicted by Equation 13 or its correction described in the following section. On Figure 3, this region would appear as a straight line

$$\hat{U}_\tau = \left(\frac{\hat{U}_\tau}{\hat{U}_G}\right)_T \hat{U}_G \tag{16}$$

emanating from, and lying to the right of the "transition" point T. Taitel and Dukler's model [38] implies that the maximum value attainable by $\hat{U}_G$ before the transition to annular flow is $10e^{-1}$.

In a subsequent paper [7], I considered rectangular channels and carried out a mixing-length calculation of single-phase fully-developed, turbulent channel flow with an arbitrary arrangement of (two) smooth or rough walls and with an allowance for relative motion between the walls. The calculation was aimed at the liquid phase in the present case, with one rough, moving wall representing the gas/liquid interface, and the other wall representing the floor of the channel. Only one of the results in that paper will be quoted here, namely the relation between the mean liquid flow rate and the other flow parameters when the interfacial stress is significant.

First, define the following quantities:

$$\hat{\chi} = \tau/\tau_0, \qquad \Psi = 1 - \hat{\chi}, \qquad \phi = -\Psi$$

$$\tau_0 = h_L\left(\rho_L g \sin\theta - \frac{dp}{dx}\right) \tag{17}$$

The convention used in that paper is such that τ is positive when U_G is negative, and vice versa. Ignoring transverse pressure gradients [50], the shear stress in the fluid is

$$\tau_L/\tau_0 = \Psi - z/h_L, \qquad \tau = \tau_0\Psi \tag{18}$$

The types of flows may be categorized as follows:

$\hat{\chi} > 0$, Poiseuille; $\qquad \hat{\chi} = 0$, open-channel; $\qquad \hat{\chi} < 0$, Couette

Co-current flows: $\Psi < 0$

$$\frac{KU_L}{U_{\tau_0}} = (\hat{\chi}^{1/2} + \phi^{1/2}) \ln \left| \frac{\hat{\chi}^{1/2} + \phi^{1/2}}{\hat{\chi}^{1/2} - \phi^{1/2}} \right| - 2(\hat{\chi}^{1/2} - \phi^{1/2}) - \hat{\chi}^{1/2} \ln \left| \frac{4x}{\eta_I} \right| - \phi^{1/2} \ln \left| \frac{4\phi}{\eta_B} \right| \tag{19}$$

Here the quantity η is given by

$$\eta_B = e^{-A} v_L/U_{\tau_B} h_L, \text{ smooth bed, } A \cong 2.3 \tag{20}$$

$$\eta_B = e^{-A} \varepsilon_B/h_L, \text{ rough bed, } A \cong 3.4 \tag{21}$$

Similarly, η_I is a "false origin" of the velocity profile at the liquid/gas interface, and under rough conditions the analogue of Equation 21 applies.

Counter-current flow: $\psi > 0$

$$\frac{KU_L}{U_{\tau_0}} = U_\Psi - 2(\hat{\chi}^{1/2} + \Psi^{1/2}) + 2\hat{\chi}^{1/2} \tan^{-1} \left(\frac{\Psi}{\hat{\chi}}\right)^{1/2} + 2\Psi^{1/2} \tan^{-1} \left(\frac{\hat{\chi}}{\Psi}\right)^{1/2} \tag{22}$$

where $\quad U_\Psi = \Psi^{1/2} \ln \left| \frac{\Psi^{1/2} + (\Psi - \eta_B)^{1/2}}{\Psi^{1/2} - (\Psi - \eta_B)^{1/2}} \right| - 2\hat{\chi}^{1/2} \tan \left(\frac{\Psi - \eta_B}{\hat{\chi}}\right) \tag{23}$

These two relations for U_L, together with Equations 11 and 16, make up a model that is analogous to the triangular relationship available for annular vertical flow [54, 55]. Actually, one should also account for wall friction of the gaseous phase, but this will sometimes be negligible in its influence on the pressure drop when compared with the contribution of the interface.

The detailed analysis presented in [7] is useful because it permits calculations of a wide range of conditions, including those where the liquid velocity is positive over part of the liquid depth and negative elsewhere. The latter situation arises when U_L is small or zero, for example in currents driven by wind in lakes or shallow basins. Indeed, Wallis and Dobson [8] reported the channel slope versus gas speed with zero mean liquid flow, and the analysis in [7] facilitated an estimation of their interfacial stress.

One can deduce from Equation 22 that when $U_L = 0$, Ψ must be small (this has been observed experimentally [56]. If one assumes that the interfacial stress is much greater than that at the channel roof, then

$$dp/dx \cong \tau/h_G \tag{24}$$

and it follows from Equation 17 that

$$\rho_L g H\alpha(1 - \alpha) \sin \theta \cong \tau \tag{25}$$

$\hat{U}_G$ and $\hat{U}_\tau$ for rectangular geometry are now related to the variables plotted by Wallis and Dobson, V_G^* and θ:

$$(1 - \alpha) \sin \theta \cong 0.0738\hat{U}_\tau^2, \qquad \alpha^{3/2}U_G \cong 3.68V_G^* \tag{26}$$

substituting in Equation 11,

$$V_G^* \cong -5[\alpha^3(1-\alpha)\theta]^{1/2} \ln[3.68(1-\alpha)^{1/2}\theta^{1/2}] \tag{27}$$

The comparison, reproduced in Figure 4, is gratifying, except near transition, where the model is suspect anyway. A discrepancy is also apparent under smooth conditions, because the model as embodied in Equation 11 applies only to fully-rough flows. Remember also that as smooth conditions are approached, Equation 24 will become spurious.

The coupling between the phases is "limited" in the sense that is independent of U_L. If, however, J_L is comparable to U_G, one may, as a first approximation, replace U_G in Equation 2 by $U_G - U_L$, and the algebraic coupling is then a stronger one. Reference 7 provides an estimate of the interfacial drift velocity.

One useful way of solving these equations is to regard θ as an unknown, and this can form the basis of a computational procedure for slowly-varying flows where θ is the inclination of the interface, even for horizontal ducts. This complies with the hydrostatic approximation for flows in which the vertical acceleration is small.

It is now possible to outline the first of the two techniques presented in this chapter for general duct geometry. After making the common (but strictly untrue) assumption that the shear stresses τ_i, τ_{W_L}, and τ_{W_G} are constant over C_i, C_L and C_G (see Figure 1), and equating the pressure gradients of the two phases appearing in the integral momentum conservation relations [38],

$$\tau_{W_G}\frac{C_G}{A_G} - \tau_{W_L}\frac{C_L}{A_L} + \tau_i C_i(A_L^{-1} + A_G^{-1})\,\text{sgn}(U_G - U_L) + (\rho_L - \rho_G)g\sin\theta = 0 \tag{28}$$

Here $\text{sgn}(x) = \pm 1$ for $x \gtrless 0$; this formalism allows for co- and counter-current flows. The wall stresses are estimated in the customary way, using a general correlation that can describe either laminar or turbulent flows:

$$\tau_{W_j} = \tfrac{1}{2}\rho_j U_j |U_j| f_j \tag{29}$$

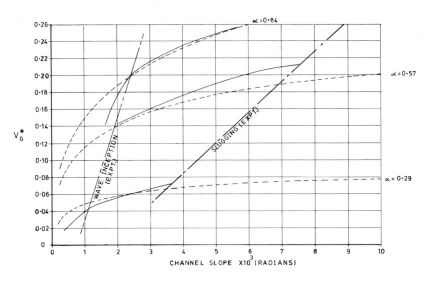

Figure 4. Gas flow versus channel slope needed to maintain uniform time-mean liquid depth, $J_L = 0$. (————), Experiment [8]; (— — — —) Theory [7].

$$f_G = B_G |D_G U_G / v_G|^{-m}, \qquad f_L = B_L |D_L U_L / v_L|^{-n} \tag{30}$$

D_G and D_L are phase hydraulic diameters, and Agrawal et al. [46] recommend the usual definition for D_G, but the open-channel form for D_L. Equation 28 is non-dimensionalized slightly differently to [38]: Phase velocities, areas, and lengths with respect to the respective phase superficial velocities V_j, channel area A, and channel mean hydraulic diameter D. Together with the definition of $\hat{U}_\tau$ and ξ, Equation 28 reads (dimensionless quantities are denoted by tilde)

$$\chi^2 |\tilde{D}_L \tilde{U}_L|^{-n} \tilde{U}_L |\tilde{U}_L| \tilde{C}_L / \tilde{A}_L - |\tilde{D}_G \tilde{U}_G|^{-m} \tilde{U}_G |\tilde{U}_G| \tilde{C}_G / \tilde{A}_G$$

$$- Z \tilde{A}_G \hat{U}_\tau^2 \left(\frac{1}{\tilde{A}_L} + \frac{1}{\tilde{A}_G} \right) \text{sgn}(U_G - U_L) - Y = 0 \tag{31}$$

where $\quad \chi^2 = \dfrac{(dp/dx)_L}{(dp/dx)_G}; \quad Z = \dfrac{160.8 \rho_G gA}{\eta D^2 (dp/dx)_G}; \quad Y = \dfrac{C(\rho_L - \rho_G)g \sin\theta}{D(dp/dx)_G} \tag{32}$

Here $(dp/dx)_{G,L}$ denotes the pressure gradient of the respective phase flowing alone in the channel, and x^2 is the Lockhart-Martinelli parameter [37]. The quantities $\hat{U}_G$ and $\tilde{U}_G$ are related by

$$\hat{U}_G = \left(\frac{\eta D \tilde{C}_i V_G^2}{40.2 gA \tilde{A}_G} \right)^{1/2} \tilde{U}_G \tag{33}$$

Thus, Equation 31, together with Equation 11 and its extension, Equation 16, if slugging does not occur, constitute a determinate system for the voidage in terms of the volumetric flow rates (all non-dimensional quantities with a tilde are functions of the voidage alone). This completes the first model, represented by the unmodified stress relation (Equation 11).

Attention is now focused on the second model proposed in this chapter, in which two modifications are knitted into Equation 11: (1) Generalization of Equation 2 to allow for smooth interfaces; and (2) a provisional, empirical correction to Equation 13 based on a comparison [7] with the experimental results [8].

The first modification is effected with the aid of the Colebrook-White formula encompassing the complete range of smooth and rough turbulent flow [9]:

$$f^{-1/2} = -0.86 \ln \left(\frac{\varepsilon}{3.7D} + \frac{2.51}{R_e \sqrt{f}} \right)$$

After invoking Equation 10 and altering the numerical constants slightly in order to guarantee the same definitions of $\hat{U}_G$ and $\hat{U}_\tau$ as follow from Equation 2, one can express this formula as

$$\hat{U}_G = -2.5 \hat{U}_\tau \ln\{\hat{U}_\tau^2 + 0.89 v_G / [\hat{U}_\tau (gR_G^3)^{1/2}]\} \tag{34}$$

The second modification is an empirical one following from Equation [7], and the pertinent graph is reproduced in Figure 5. Write Equation 34 as

$$\hat{U}_G = F(\hat{U}_\tau); \qquad F = -2.5 \hat{U}_\tau \ln(\hat{U}_\tau^2 + a/U_\tau)$$

$$a = 0.89 v_G / (gR_G^3)^{1/2} \tag{35}$$

Then formally,

$$\hat{U}_\tau = G(\hat{U}_G) \tag{36}$$

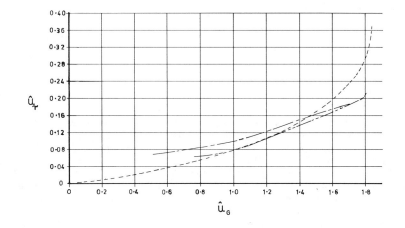

Figure 5. Interfacial friction velocity versus mean gas flow, deduced from experiments [8]. (———) $\alpha = 0.29$; (— — —) $\alpha = 0.57$; (— — — —) $\alpha = 0.84$; (— — — —) Theory [6].

where G is the inverse function of F. The indication from Figure 5 is that overestimates U_τ near transition, so Equation 36 is changed to

$$\hat{U}_\tau = J(\hat{U}_G)G(\hat{U}_G) \tag{37}$$

where J is an arbitrary function yet to be chosen. Since

$$G(\hat{U}_G) = \hat{U}_\tau/J(\hat{U}_G)$$

it follows that

$$\hat{U}_G = F(\chi); \qquad \chi = \hat{U}_\tau/J(\hat{U}_G) \tag{38}$$

Noting that

$$[1 + \hat{U}_\tau J'(\hat{U}_G)F'(\chi)/J^2]\,\frac{d\hat{U}_G}{d\hat{U}_\tau} = F'(\chi)/J$$

it is also clear that, provided the term in square brackets on the left-hand side does not vanish, stratified-slug transition occurs when

$$F'(\chi_T) = 0 \tag{39}$$

or $\quad \ln(\chi_T^2 + a/\chi_T) + (2\chi_T^2 - a/\chi_T)/(\chi_T^2 + a/\chi_T) = 0 \tag{40}$

(here a dash denotes differentiation with respect to the argument). One boundary condition on J is therefore

$$J(\hat{U}_{G_T}) = \hat{U}_{\tau T}/\chi_T < 1 \tag{41}$$

Another obvious boundary condition is

$$J(0) = 1 \tag{42}$$

The provisional form of J chosen is

$$J(U) = \lambda_1 + \lambda_2 U^{0.7} \tag{43}$$

Applying Equations 41 and 42

$$J(\hat{U}_G) = 1 - (1 - \hat{U}_{\tau\tau}/\chi_T)(\hat{U}_G/\hat{U}_{G_T})^{0.7} \tag{44}$$

It must be emphasized that this is only a tentative empiricism, but a refinement will only be justified when a more reliable, *direct* comparison of interfacial stresses can be made with experimental results from a facility such as the one used in [8]. Be that as it may, the procedure recommended at present is the following: (a) solve Equation 41 for χ_T; (b) determine $\hat{U}_{G_T}$ from Equation 38; (c) specify $\hat{U}_{\tau\tau}$ (Figure 5 suggests that a value of about 0.2 is reasonable.) The function J is now determined from Equation 44 and the (implicit) stress relation, Equation 38, is complete. It only remains to repeat the hypothesis reflected in Equation 16, whereby the interfacial friction coefficient is assumed constant above "transition" if the voidage is too high for slugs to occur.

The results using Equations 38 and 44 are set out in Figure 6, together with some of Wallis and Dobson's experimental measurements transformed via Equation 26. The latter equation(s) is also used for expressing the results as V_G^* versus θ, and it is apparent that while improvements have been attained below wave inception and near transition, some accuracy has been sacrificed between these two conditions. The discrepancy increases with voidage, but it should be remembered that it is just when the voidage is high that the contribution of the wall stresses to the pressure gradient become significant, and the approximation inherent in Equation 24 is no longer valid. This point serves to re-emphasize the need for a measurement of, rather than an indirect deduction of τ or dp/dx. Nevertheless, the technique allows a continuous sweep between smooth and rough flows and still offer potential improvements via the function J. The reader may have noticed that the curves in Figure 6 do not pass through the origin; this reflects the assumptions of turbulent conditions and its rectification is reported elsewhere; in most cases this flaw will hardly be noticeable.

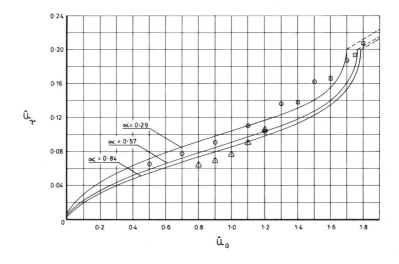

Figure 6. The second model—full range of smooth and rough conditions, Equation 38 with an empirical correction, Equation 44. Comparison with some values deduced from [8]. ($\bigcirc$) $\alpha = 0.29$; ($\square$) $\alpha = 0.57$; ($\triangle$) $\alpha = 0.84$. Assumptions; $U_{\tau\tau} = 0.2$, and Equation 16 for $\hat{U}_G > \hat{U}_{G_T}$.

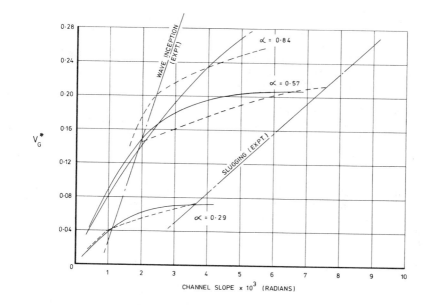

Figure 7. Gas flow versus channel slope needed to maintain uniform time-mean liquid depth, $U_L = 0$. (———) Theory, second model; (– – – –) Exerpiment [8].

Finally, consideration is now given to the experimental results of Hanratty et al. [39, 44]. Their facility for co-current flows has a wide aspect ratio (12 ins × 1 in) simulating two-dimensional conditions, and they assert that the flows are fully developed near the end of its 21-foot length. Table 1 lists some of their data, transformed to the present coordinates. Their voidages were in the region of 0.9 so that slug transition did not occur, and it is interesting to note that $\hat{U}_r$ varies little for $\hat{U}_G > \hat{U}_{G_T}$, where $\hat{U}_{G_T}$ is about 1.8. This conflicts with Equation 16, but may be attributable to significant coupling between the phases manifesting as noticeable interfacial drift velocities. Incidentally, the parameters during the previously mentioned experiments were such that

$$(\zeta/20.1V^2)^{1/2} \cong 0.0225A_G^{-1/2}$$

CONCLUSION

Two Charnock-based relations for the interfacial stress have been proposed. The first, consisting of Equations 11 and 16 and shown in Figure 3, is a slightly extended version of the formula presented in [6]. Strictly, it should only be applied when the gas flow near the interface is in the fully rough regime.

The second relation, embodied in Equations 16 and 38, is a generalized version of the first, and encompasses the complete range of "turbulent" smooth and rough interfaces. A tentative comparison with the experimental results of [8] has also led to an empirical correction J given in Equation 44. However, the comparison is indirect because Wallis and Dobson did not report interfacial stress or pressure gradient, and several assumptions lie behind the expressions (Equation 26) relating channel inclination to interfacial stress. The assumption underlying Equation 24 is that the interfacial stress dominates the gas-phase pressure gradient and may be expected to be reasonable when the voidage is low. The formula (Equation 25) is in turn based on the two-dimensional calculation in [7], applied to the liquid phase, and is therefore expected to be sound when the voidage is high for the square channel of [8].

In any case, the current comparison indicates that $U_{\tau\tau} \cong 0.2$. Either of the stress relations can be used in conjunction with Equation 31 to calculate the voidage and pressure drop given the volumetric flow rates, for co- or counter-current configurations. Equation 31 is similar to that of Taitel and Dukler [38] except for the interfacial term, the definition of D_L and the use of a different reference area in the definition of non-dimensional quantities.

The gas/liquid coupling implied by Equation 11 and 38 is "weak" in the sense that $|U_G|$ is assumed to be so much greater than $|U_L|$ that U_L may be ignored. However, if stronger coupling is anticipated U_G may be replaced in those two equations by $U_G - U_L$; no general technique appears to be available at present for calculating the interfacial drift velocity, although that velocity has been calculated for two-dimensional flows under smooth conditions [48] and for smooth and rough conditions [7].

Acknowledgments

My thanks to the staff at the NNC library for their extensive assistance and to Mrs. G. M. Cook for the typing. This chapter is published by permission of the National Nuclear Corporation. Some figures from References 6 and 7 have been reproduced by permission from Pergamon Press Ltd. and the American Nuclear Society.

NOTATION

a	$0.89 v_G/(gR_G^3)^{1/2}$	K	von-Karman's constant, $\cong 0.4$
A	$A_G + A_L$	m, n	friction law exponents, Equation 30
A_j	cross-sectional area of phase j	Q_j	phase volumetric flow rate
B_j	constants, Equation 31	Re_j	$D_j U_j / v_j$
C	$C_G + C_L$, Figure 1	R_j	$\frac{1}{2}D_j$
C_f	$\tau/\frac{1}{2}\rho_G U_G^2$	U_i	mean interface velocity
C_i	length of time-mean interface, Figure 1	U_j	phase velocity
C_j	length of perimeter between phase j and the wall	U_{j_τ}	phase interfacial friction velocity, $(\tau/\rho_j)^{1/2}$
D	channel mean hydraulic diameter, 4A/C	U_τ	U_{G_τ}
		$U_{\tau 0}$	$(\tau_0/\rho_L)^{1/2}$
D_j	phase mean hydraulic diameter, $4A_j/(C_j + C_i)$	$U_{\tau B}$	$(\tau_L/\rho_L)^{1/2}$ at $z = 0$
f_j	wall friction coefficient of phase j, Equation 29	$\hat{U}_G$	$U_G/\hat{V}$
		$\hat{U}_\tau$	$U_\tau/\hat{V}$
F	Equation 35	V	$(gR_G)^{1/2}$
g	gravitational acceleration	V_j	phase superficial velocity, Q_j/A
G	Equation 36	V_j^*	$V_j[\rho_G/gH(\rho_L - \rho_G)]^{1/2}$
h_j	height of phase j	$\hat{V}$	$(20.1V^2/\xi)^{1/2} \equiv 6.34(A_G/\eta C_i)^{1/2}$
H	$h_G + h_L$	x, y, z	coordinates (Figure 1)
J	Equation 37	X	Lockhart-Martinelli parameter

Greek Symbols

α	voidage	τ, τ_i	Time-mean interfacial stress (assumed constant along C_i)
γ	Charnock's "constant", Equation 3		
ε	physical roughness length	τ_0	Equation 17
η	constant, Equations 10 and 15	$\tau_j(y, z)$	shear stress in phase j
θ	channel slope (+ve downwards)	τ_{w_j}	wall shear stress of phase j (assumed constant along C_i)
μ_j	phase dynamic viscosity		
v_j	phase kinematic viscosity	χ	Equation 38
ξ	$\eta C_i/(C_G + C_i)$, Equation 10	$\hat{\chi}$	Equation 17
ρ_j	phase density (assumed constant)	Ψ	$1 - \hat{\chi}$

ubscripts

B	at channel bed	L	liquid
G	gas	T	at stratified-slug transition
j	G or L	w	at a wall

REFERENCES

1. Coantic, M. "Mass Transfer Across the Ocean-Air Interface: Small Scale Hydrodynamic and Aerodynamic Mechanisms," *Physico Chemical Hydrodynamics*, vol. 1, pp. 249–279 (1980).
2. Knudsen, J. G. and Katz, D. L. *Fluid Dynamics and Heat Transfer*, McGraw-Hill, New York, 1958.
3. Levich, V. G. *Physiochemical Hydrodynamics*, Prentice-Hall, Englewood Cliffs, New Jersey, 1962.
4. Davies, J. T. *Turbulence Phenomena*, Academic, New York, 1972.
5. Charnock, H. "Wind Stress on Water Surface," *Quar. J. Roy. Met. Soc.*, vol. 81, p639, 1955.
6. Sinai, Y. L. "A Charnock-Based Estimate of Interfacial Resistance and Roughness for Internal Fully-Developed, Stratified, Two-Phase Horizontal Flow," *Int. J. Mult. Flow*, vol. 9, pp. 13–19, 1983.
7. Sinai, Y. L. "The Application of a Charnock-Based Estimate of Interfacial Stress to Some Near-Horizontal, Stratified Two-Phase Flows," *Thermal Hydraulics of Nuclear Reactors*, M. Merilo ed. Proceedings of the Second International Topical Meeting on Nuclear Reactor Thermal-Hydraulics, Santa Barbara, USA, January 1983. American Nuclear Society, LaGrange Park, vol. 1, pp. 226–234, 1983.
8. Wallis, G. B. and Dobson, J. E. "The Onset of Slugging in Horizontal Stratified Air-Water Flow," *Int. J. Multiphase Flow*, vol. 1, pp. 173–193, 1973.
9. Streeter, V. L. and Wylie, E. B. *Fluid Mechanics*, McGraw-Hill Kogakusha, Tokyo, 1979.
0. Davies, J. T. and Rideal, E. K. *Interfacial Phenomena*, Academic, New York, 1963.
1. Kotake, S. "Heat Transfer and Skin Friction of a Phase-Changing Interface of Gas-Liquid Laminar Flows," *Int. J. Heat Mass Transfer*, vol. 16, pp. 2165–2176, 1973.
2. Kotake, S. "Gas-Liquid Laminar Boundary-Layer Flows With a Wavy Phase-Changing Interface," *Int. J. Heat Mass Transfer*, vol. 17, pp. 885–897, 1974.
3. Boyadjiev, C., Mitev, P. and Beshkov, V. "Laminar Boundary Layers at a Moving Interface Generated by a Counter-Current Gas-Liquid Stratified Flow," *Int. J. Multiphase Flow*, vol. 3, pp. 61–66, 1976.
4. Wengefeld, P. "Impuls-, Wärme- und Wasserdampftransport an der Oberfläche ines offenen Gerinnes unter dem Einflub des Windes." Communications of the Institute of Hydraulic Engineering, University of Karlsruhe, vol. 12, 1978.
5. Jensen, R. J. and Yuen, M. C. "Interphase Transport in Horizontal Stratified Co-Current Flow," NUREG/CR-2334, U.S. Nuclear Regulatory Commission, Washington, 1982.
6. Head, M. R. and Bandyopadhyay, P. "New Aspects of Turbulent Boundary-Layer Structure," *J. Fluid Mech.*, vol. 107, pp. 297–338, 1981.
7. Einstein, H. A. and Li, H. "The Viscous Sublayer Along a Smooth Boundary," *Proc. A.S.C.E. J. Eng. Mech. Div.* vol. 82, pp. 1–27, 1956.
8. Hanratty, T. J. "Turbulent Exchange of Mass and Momentum with a Boundary," *A.I.Ch.E. Journal*, vol. 2, pp. 359–362, 1956.
9. Thomas, L. C. "A Turbulent Burst Model of Wall Turbulence for Two-Dimensional Turbulent Boundary Layer Flow," *Int. J. Heat Mass Transfer*, vol. 25, pp. 1127–1136, 1982.
0. Cohen, Y. "Mass Transfer Across a Sheared, Wavy Air-Water Interface," *Int. J. Heat Mass Transfer*, vol. 26, pp. 1289–1297, 1983.
1. Ursell, F. "Wave Generation by Wind". In *Surveys in Mechanics*, G. K. Batchelor and R. M. Davies (eds.), Cambridge, 1956.
2. Kinsman, B. *Wind Waves*. Prentice-Hall, Englewood Cliffs, New Jersey, 1965.
3. Dukler, A. E. "Characterization, Effects and Modeling of the Wavy Gas-Liquid Interface." *Proceedings of the International Symposium on Two-Phase Systems*, Haifa (1971). *Progress in Heat and Mass Transfer*, vol. 6, pp. 207–234, 1972.

24. Phillips, O. M. *The Dynamics of the Upper Ocean*. Cambridge University Press, 2nd Edition, 1977.
25. Favre, A. and Hasselmann, K. (eds), *Turbulent Fluxes Through the Sea Surface, Wave Dynamics, and Prediction*. Plenum, 1978.
26. Hsu, C-T. et al., "Momentum and Energy Transfer in Wind Generation of Waves," *J. Phys. Oceanog.* vol. 12, pp. 929–951, 1982.
27. Ewing, J. A. "Wind Waves: A Review of Research During the Last Twenty-Five Years," *Geophys. J.R. Astr. Soc.*, vol. 74, pp. 313–329, 1983.
28. Wu, J. "Laboratory Studies of Wind-Wave Interactions," *J. Fluid Mech.*, vol. 34, pp. 91–111, 1968.
29. Wu, J. "Wind-Stress Coefficients over Sea Surface near Neutral Conditions—A Revisit," *J. Phys. Oceanog.*, vol. 10, 727–740, 1980.
30. Street, R. L. "Turbulent Heat and Mass Transfers Across a Rough, Air-Water Interface; A Simple Theory," *Int. J. Heat Mass Transfer*, vol. 22, pp. 885–899, 1979.
31. Howe, B. M. et al., "Comparison of Profiles and Fluxes of Heat and Momentum Above and Below an Air-Water Interface," *J. Heat Transfer*, vol. 104, pp. 34–39, 1982.
32. Hidy, G. M. and Plate, E. J. "Wind Action on Water Standing in a Laboratory Channel," *J. Fluid Mech.*, vol. 26, pp. 651–687, 1966.
33. Shaw, Y. C. and Lee, Y. "Wind-Induced Turbulent Heat and Mass Transfer over Large Bodies of Water," *J. Fluid Mech.*, vol. 77, pp. 645–664, 1976.
34. Hsu, S. A. "A Dynamic Roughness Equation and Its Application to Wind Stress Determination at the Air-Sea Interface," *J. Phys. Oceanog.*, vol. 4, pp. 116–120, 1974.
35. Kraus, E. B. *Atmosphere-Ocean Interactions*. Clarendon, Oxford, 1972.
36. Monin, A. S. and Yaglom, A. M. *Statistical Fluid Mechanics*, vol. 1. M.I.T. Press, Cambridge, 1979.
37. Butterworth, D. and Hewitt, G. F. *Two-Phase Flow and Heat Transfer*. Oxford University Press, 1979.
38. Taitel, Y. and Dukler, A. E. "A Model for Predicting Flow Regime Transitions in Horizontal and Near-Horizontal Gas-Liquid Flow," *A.I.Ch.E. Journal*, vol. 22, pp. 47–55, 1976.
39. Hanratty, T. J. and Engen, J. M. "Interaction Between a Turbulent Air Stream and a Moving Water Surface," *A.I.Ch.E. Journal*, vol. 3, pp. 299–304, 1957.
40. Kordyban, E. S. and Ranov, T. "Mechanism of Slug Formation in Horizontal Two-Phase Flow," *Trans. ASME, J. Basic Engng.*, vol. 92, pp. 857–864, 1970.
41. Van Rossum, J. J. "Experimental Investigation of Horizontal Liquid Films," *Chem. Eng. Sci.*, vol 11, pp. 35–52, 1959.
42. Craik, A. D. D. "Wind-Generated Waves in Thin Liquid Films," *J. Fluid Mech.*, vol. 26, pp. 369–380, 1966.
43. Ryley, D. J. and Small, J. "Re-Entrainment of Deposited Liquid from Simulated Steam Turbine Fixed Blades," in *Proceedings of the Conference on Heat and Fluid Flow in Steam and Gas Turbine Plant*, April 1973. Inst. Mech. Engrs., London, 1973.
44. Cohen, L. S. and Hanratty, T. J. "Effect of Waves at a Gas-Liquid Interface on a Turbulent Air Flow," *J. Fluid Mech.*, vol. 31, pp. 467–479, 1968.
45. Yih, C-S. "Stratified Flows," in *Annual Rev. Fluid Mech.* vol. 1, pp. 73–109, 1969.
46. Agrawal, S. S., Gregory, G. A. and Govier, G. W. "An Analysis of Horizontal Stratified Two-Phase Flow in Pipes," *Can. J. Chem. Eng.*, vol. 51, pp. 280–286, 1973.
47. Davis, E. J., Cheremisinoff, N. P. and Guzy, C. J. "Heat Transfer with Stratified Gas-Liquid Flow," *A.I.Ch.E. Journal*, vol. 25, pp. 958–966, 1979.
48. Kadambi, V. "Void Fraction and Pressure Drop in Two-Phase Stratified Flow," *Can. J. Chem. Eng.*, vol. 59, pp. 584–589, 1981.
49. Chen, J. J. J. and Spedding, P. L. "An Extension of the Lockhart-Martinelli Theory of Two-Phase Pressure Drop and Holdup," *Int. J. Multiphase Flow*, vol. 7, pp. 659–675, 1981.
50. Pai, S-I. *Viscous Flow Theory*, vol. 2, Van Nostrand, Princeton, New Jersey, 1957.
51. Akai, M. Inoue, A. and Aoki, S. "The Prediction of Stratified Two-Phase Flow with a Two Equation Model of Turbulence," *Int. J. Multiphase Flow*, vol. 7 pp. 21–39, 1981.
52. Townsend, A. A. "Flow in a Deep Turbulent Boundary Layer Over a Surface Distorted by Water Waves," *J. Fluid Mech.*, vol. 55, pp. 719–735, 1972.

53. Bankoff, S. G. and Kim, H. J. "Local Condensation Rates in Nearly Horizontal Stratified Counter-Current Flow of Steam and Cold Water," in *Proceedings of Heat Transfer—21st National Conference*, Seattle, USA, July 1983. A.I.Ch.E Symposium Series, vol. 79, No. 225, pp. 209–223, 1983.

54. Hewitt, G. F. and Hall-Taylor, N. S. *Annular Two-Phase Flow*, Pergamon, Oxford, 1970.

55. Yaitel, Y. Barnea, D. and Dukler, A. E. "A Film Model for the Prediction of Flooding and Flow Reversal for Gas-Liquid Flow in Vertical Tubes," *Int. J. Multiphase Flow*, vol. 8, pp. 1–10, 1982.

56. Baines, W. D. and Knapp, D. J. "Wind Driven Water Currents," *Proc. A.S.C.E., J. Hydraulics Div.*, vol. 91, pp. 205–221, 1965.

CHAPTER 18

HOLD-UP IN MULTIPHASE FLOW

P. L. Spedding

Department of Chemical Engineering
Queen's University of Belfast
Northern Ireland

and

J. J. J. Chen

Department of Chemical and Materials Engineering
University of Auckland
New Zealand

CONTENTS

INTRODUCTION

Hold-up is one of the three major characteristics associated with two-phase flow; the other two being flow regime and pressure loss. Hold-up is the relative proportion of space occupied by a phase in a flow conduit. It can be expressed on a time or space average basis, with the actual method chosen depending on the use of the hold-up value and the measurement method available. There are at least 22 methods of measuring hold-up with varying degrees of accuracy and reliability. The quick-closing-valve technique generally is accepted as the most accurate of the techniques and has been used in many investigations. Perhaps the most widely used method of hold-up measurement is the beam or ray attenuation technique. While its accuracy varies with the design of equipment, it can certainly be as accurate as the quick-closing-valve technique. Of course, the accuracy depends not only on the technique of measurement but also on the design and operation of the experimental apparatus. While it is not the intention to deal with the subject of accuracy in detail, it is important to point out that data must be checked carefully before they are used as a basis for comparison with a theory or correlation because it is possible to obtain data containing significant errors either inherent or otherwise.

GENERAL TWO-PHASE THEORIES AND CORRELATIONS

Many theories and correlations were developed for two-phase parameter predictions without any consideration of the actual flow pattern formed in the conduit. Since experimental data were inevitably used to obtain the correlation, it is hoped that effects due to the flow patterns were incorporated inherently. In fact, changes in flow patterns sometimes can result in correlation curves that behave in a rather unusual manner, so much so that is has led Weisman and Choe [1] to refer to the unusual behavior as "vagaries." Such behavior implies that the particular correlation is forced in some manner usually by ignoring fundamental aspects of the general phenomena, thus compelling the correlation to depart from the ordered pattern normally expected from most natural phenomena.

Many of these types of correlations are based on a pressure drop-hold-up relation. Armand [2] derived the following relationship from semi-empirical analyses:

$$(dP/dL)_F/(dP/dL)_{SL} = \frac{a}{(1 - \bar{R}_G)^b} = \phi_L^2 \tag{1}$$

The ratio $(dP/dL)_F/(dP/dL)_{SL}$ was plotted against $(1 - \bar{R}_G)$ and the data fell into three distinct ranges shown in Figure 1 where the values of the constants a and b are as indicated. However, Armand [2] pointed out that the three ranges corresponded approximately to the bubble-slug, the stratified, and the annular regimes, respectively.

Formulas to calculate $\bar{R}_G$ for substitution into Equation 1 were, however, not strictly flow pattern dependent. For $\beta \geq 0.9$.

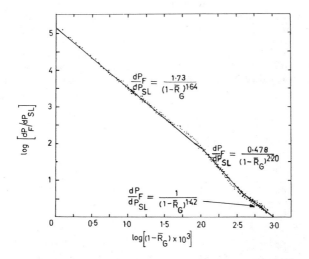

Figure 1. Pressure loss vs hold-up after Armand [2].

$$(1 - \bar{R}_G) = \frac{4 + \frac{8}{7}d_1}{5 + d_1\left(\frac{\beta}{1 - \beta} + \frac{8}{7}\right)} \tag{2}$$

where $d_1 = 4[0.69 + (1 - \beta)(4 + 21.9(\bar{V}_{LS}/\sqrt{gD})] \, Re_{SL}^{1/8}\sqrt{\rho_G/\rho_L}$ \hfill (3)

and for $\beta < 0.9$

$$(1 - \bar{R}_G) = \left(1 - \frac{\beta}{C}\right) \tag{4}$$

Equation 4 is of course a modification of the homogeneous model to which a term C has been incorporated. The equation with $C = 1.2$ has gained wide acceptance in two-phase flow studies, while Equations 2 and 3 for $\beta \geq 0.9$ may be too complex since they have not gained popularity except in the Russian literature. Alad'yev et al. [3] reported than Equation 2 gave good agreement ($\pm 8\%$) with extensive steam-water data over a wide range of variables (P = 1 to 120 bar; $G_T = 50$ to 2,500 kg m^{-2} s^{-1}, D = 7 to 70 mm). In addition, the relation followed within $\pm 4\%$, vertical two-phase flow data for potassium (P = 1 bar, $G_T = 49$ to 488 kg m^{-2} s^{-1}, D = 5.4 to 12 mm). Extensive liquid hold-up data for stratified, annular, and droplet flow regimes in the co-current air-water system (P = 1 bar, $G_T = 10$ to 1,127 kg m^{-2} s^{-1}, D = 45.4 mm) had an error range of $+138\%$ to -87%, and therefore strictly do not fit the relation. Of course, the gas hold-up data easily fit the relation ($\pm 4\%$) because with $\beta > 0.9$ the actual gas hold-up values were close to unity. This is why the Russian data gave acceptable agreement.

Actually, Nicklin et al. [4] showed that Equation 4 was a special case of a correlation derived for upward vertical two-phase flow, while Scott [5] demonstrated that Equation 4 was not general but only applied to the slug, plug, and bubble flow regimes. Chen and Spedding [6] later confirmed this latter observation and subsequently showed that Equation 4 held for data drawn from a wide variety of sources [7] only for the slug and bubble regimes. Figures 2-4 detail the method of presentation that was used to help overcome any tendency for C to exhibit a weak function of properties. Various investigators [8-11] have reported slightly different values for C and that it was a weak function of pressure, β, Reynolds and Froude numbers. However, the variation suggested in the value of C was well within experimental error. For example, Brown and Kranich [8] found that for bubble flow a 4.3% error existed between experimental data and Equation 4 with $C = 1.15$. Even then there was a weak mass velocity effect. Hughmark [11] reported that voidage data were consistently above the Armand relation of Equation 4 when the Froude number was less than 150. However, in this flow regime the data tend to be more scattered since the voidage has in general a low absolute value. Indeed, Nguyen and Spedding [12] report voidage data that tend on average

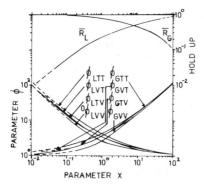

Figure 2. The Lockhart and Martinelli relations.

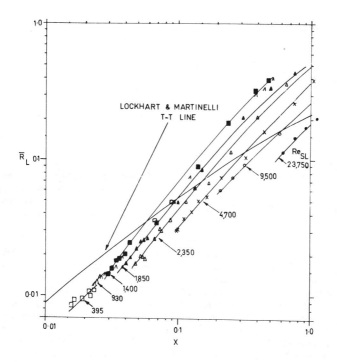

Figure 3. The effect of liquid Reynolds number on the Lockhart and Martinelli hold-up relation.

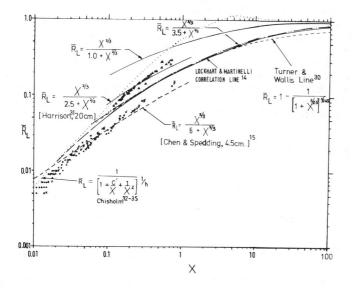

Figure 4. Comparison of various hold-up correlations with the data from Chen and Spedding [15] and Harrison [31].

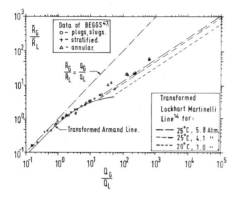

Figure 5. Horizontal pipe data for plug, slug and annular flows from Beggs [47] compared with Armand [2] and Lockhart and Martinelli [14] correlations transformed into the form of Equation 12.

to be below the Armand relation of Equation 4 in this regime while Spedding and Chen [13] report data that show a slight tendency in the opposite direction and this on the same apparatus.

Lockhart and Martinelli [14] derived a semi-empirical relation linking both the hold-up and the pressure loss factor, ϕ^2, with a parameter X, the square root of the ratio of superficial liquid to gas pressure drop. The correlation exhibited a continuous curve, as shown in Figure 2, on which no effect of flow patterns could be distinguished. Many workers have shown that there is a mass velocity effect not accounted for by the Lockhart and Martinelli correlation. For example, data of Chen and Spedding [15] given in Figure 3 detail the actual effect of liquid Reynolds number, which is more pronounced than for the corresponding pressure loss case. In addition, the liquid hold-up often is overpredicted by the Lockhart and Martinelli correlation [16]. Actually, there is approximately a ±75% spread in the data used to establish the correlation. But there is another aspect to the derivation of the correlation that must be kept in perspective. Some of the data used was for liquids with viscosities well above 0.02 kg m^{-1} s^{-1}. Experience has shown [17] that below this value viscosity has little effect on two-phase phenomena. However, when the viscosity limit is exceeded it would be expected that the liquid hold-up would increase for the same flow rates. Thus in general it would be expected that the correlation would tend to overpredict liquid hold-up for conditions where the viscosity is below 0.02 kg m^{-1} s^{-1}, and tend to predict more accurately when the viscosity was above this value as indeed Rosehart et al. [18] reported. Various attempts have been made to improve the effectiveness of the Lockhart and Martinelli correlation. For example McMillan et al. [19] incorporated the effect of interfacial roughness while Chenoweth and Martin [20] included the volumetric input ratio β in their version of the correlation. Baker [21] modified the correlation for the case of large diameter pipes while Gloyer [22] rederived the basis equation in order to include all the possible flow conditions in a more general way. These modification were reported to lead to improved accuracy but in general the results were not satisfactory. It re

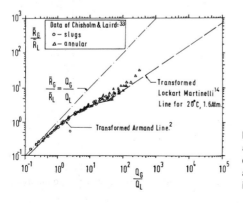

Figure 6. Horizontal pipe data for slug and annular flows from Chisholm and Laird [33] compared with the Armand [2] and Lockhart and Martinelli [14] correlations transformed into the form of Equation 12.

nained for others to show later that the general derivation could be extended to handle particular low regimes such as separated flows [15]. Stratified flow can to predicted accurately using the Taitel and Dukler [23] approach, but the case of annular flow does not give a satisfactory result and empirical solutions are sought [15].

Styushin and Dyorina [24] used the Chenoweth and Martin [20] form of the correlation to obtain a relation from steam-water data of the form,

$$\phi_{LO}^2 = \frac{(1-x)^{1.75}}{(1-\bar{R}_G)^{1.875}} \tag{5}$$

or pressures ranging from 1 to 200 atmospheres. Baroczy [25, 26] attempted a general correlation using data for steam, water-air, and mercury-nitrogen for a wide range of qualities and mass velocities. The two-phase pressure multiflow ϕ_{LO} was plotted for a standard mass flux as a function of a property index $(\rho_G/\rho_L)(\mu_L/\mu_G)^{0.2}$ with quality as a parameter. Corrections for other fluxes were obtained by introduction of very complex correction factors, which also were shown to be a function of the property index and quality. The correlation has been shown to give moderately good agreement with experimental data [1, 27], but it is difficult to use, particularly when employing a computer. Besides, the inclusion of liquid metal data in the correlation could lead to errors as will be discussed later.

Levy [28] applied Prandtl's mixing length to two-phase flow. It was claimed that the model inherently took account of the local flow structure. Charts were presented for prediction of velocity and density distributions in two-phase flow. The method also allowed the prediction of pressure drop. However, the results were not in good agreement with experimental data. Moreover, the calculation procedures prove to be difficult to implement. Beattie [29] later used this type of approach but was forced to apply empirical correlations that showed definite links with flow patterns.

Turner and Wallis [30] used a separate-cylinder model in conjunction with horizontal flow. A general equation was derived but the spatial distribution determined from the flow pattern was required in order to arrive at a solution. An empirical equation was then recommended for prediction of void fraction and pressure drop in preliminary design calculations, without consideration of flow pattern,

$$\bar{R}_G = (1 + X^{1/1.25})^{-1/2.65} \tag{6}$$

The equation matches the Lockhart and Martinelli correlation up to a value of about X = 10.0 and therefore suffers from the same criticisms as that correlation. Chen and Spedding [15] used an empirical extension of the Lockhart and Martinelli theory, which gave good agreement with a wide range of experimental data over the complete range of hold-up values.

$$\bar{R}_L = \frac{X^{2/3}}{6 + X^{2/3}} \tag{7}$$

Of course, the number 6 in the denominator of Equation 7 can be altered to fit most data as shown in Figure 4. For example, 3.5 will enable the relation to follow the Lockhart and Martinelli correlation, which 2.5 will give a fit of other data.

Chisholm et al. [32-34] attempted to curve fit the Lockhart and Martinelli correlation by employing the following equation,

$$(1 - \bar{R}_G) = \frac{1}{\left(1 + \dfrac{'C}{X} + \dfrac{1}{X^2}\right)^{1/h}} \tag{8}$$

where $h = 1.8 - \left[\dfrac{2.5 \times 10^{-5}}{(\mu_G/\mu_L)^{0.2}(\rho_L/\rho_G)(X + 0.06)}\right]$ (9)

$$'C = \sqrt{(\mu_L/\mu_G)^{0.2}(\rho_G/\rho_L)} + 0.5 \tag{10}$$

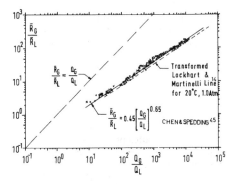

Figure 7. Horizontal data for annular flow of Chen and Spedding [15] compared with the Lockhart and Martinelli [14] correlation.

Some theoretical justification was given for the form of these equations but some empiricism also was involved [35]. Chisholm and Sutherland [34] used other equations to represent the Baroczy curves in much more concise form, but Equation 8 was shown to compare satisfactorily with the Baroczy hold-up correlation and therefore presumably has a similar accuracy. Figure 4 gives some idea of the worth of the method. The equation tends to give results that are 40-60% higher than data but when X > 3.0 anomalous results are obtained. Other data by Heywood and Richardson [36] gave a variation of +13% to −17% (air-water, PVC pipe, d = 4.2 cm). Chisholm [37] also gave a modified form of the Armand Equation 4 in which the coefficient was given as a function of β and ρ_L/ρ_G. The relation was shown to represent experimental data reasonably well. Chawla [38, 39] developed a model that included the effect of momentum transfer between the two phases. The basic correlating factor was ε the momentum exchange parameter,

$$\varepsilon \simeq \left(\frac{1-x}{x}\right)\left(\frac{\rho_L}{\rho_G}\right)^{0.9}\left(\frac{\mu_L}{\mu_G}\right)^{-0.5}(Re_L Fr_L)^{-1/6} \tag{11}$$

The constant of proportionality and the indices were obtained from experimental data. The general method of correlation was not successful in the sense that the proportionality only could be maintained constant for values of ε under about 10^{-2}. Chawla reported large errors with this system, which have been confirmed by other workers [40].

Butterworth [41] showed that the hold-up equations from the homogeneous model, the Zivi model [42], the Turner and Wallis [30] model, the Lockhart and Martinelli [14] correlation, the Thom correlation [43], and the Baroczy correlation [25, 26] all may be cast in the general form,

$$\frac{\bar{R}_L}{\bar{R}_G} = A'\left(\frac{1-x}{x}\right)^p\left(\frac{\rho_G}{\rho_L}\right)^q\left(\frac{\mu_L}{\mu_G}\right)^r \tag{12}$$

Harrison [31] used the method to correlate hold-up data for steam-water flow in a 20-cm diameter pipe. Spedding and Chen [44, 45] gave a theoretical basis for the correlation method and pointed out that the general picture could be best expressed by reference to the actual flow patterns involved. Also the proposed correlation method fit other general models, for example for thoose by Armand [2] and Smith [46], and models developed for specific flow regimes. Figures 5–7 give a wide range of experimental data plotted in the more simple form of $\bar{R}_G/\bar{R}_L$ vs. $\bar{Q}_G/\bar{Q}_L$ and show the general reliability of the Armand relation for bubble and slug flow.

Hoogendoorn [48] developed a correlation for hold-up that was based on the slip velocity between the phases. The basic principle was drawn from work done in vertical flow, but it was claimed that the general scheme of correlation worked well for horizontal use with no significant effect of flow pattern, diameter (2.4-, 5.0-, 9.1-, and 14.0-cm pipes) or liquid viscosity (0.0010, 0.0024,

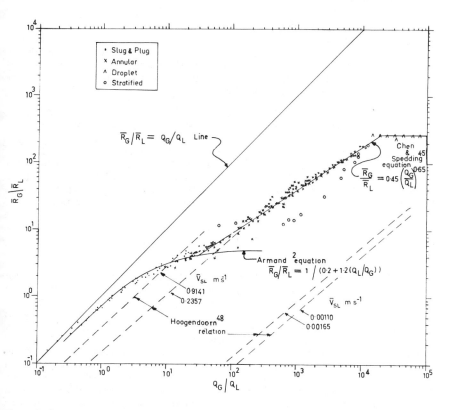

Figure 8. Comparison of data with the models lof Hoogendoorn [48] and Chen and Spedding [15].

$0.0208 \text{ kg m}^{-1} \text{ s}^{-1}$). The general equation was:

$$\frac{\bar{R}_G}{\bar{R}_L} = e_1 \left[\bar{V}_{SG} - \frac{\bar{R}_G}{\bar{R}_L} \bar{V}_{SL} \right]^{0.85} \tag{13}$$

where $e_1 = 0.6$ if the phase velocities were in m s^{-1}. Figure 8 shows that data do not support the theory particularly for the cases of stratified, droplet, bubble, and slug flows. At best, Equation 13 gives a reasonable correlation for some annular flow data. In addition, Hoogendoorn [48] showed that the Lockhart and Martinelli correlation did not coincide with much of the experimental data particularly for the slug flow regime.

Levy [49] used a momentum exchange theory based on the premise that each phase satisfied the Bernoulli equation. The momentum equations of the phases, when subtracted one from the other gave a general equation for gas holdup. A simplified version of the equation was integrated to yield a relation involving the density ratio the gas mass fraction and gas hold-up. However, the equation showed the opposite trend to the Lockhart and Martinelli correlation and tests against experimental data gave predicted values of hold-up which were 50% above to 40% below measured values.

Mamaev [50] attempted to correlate hold-up data by using input conditions and the Froude number as the variables. Greskovich et al. [51, 52] followed along similar lines for slug flow as did

Beggs [47] for general flow conditions. Eaton et al. [53] used the results of Ros' [54] dimensiona analysis to give another type of general correlation for the horizontal condition, which employe different dimensionless numbers as the correlating parameters. Later the work was extended b Andrews et al. [55]. Stepanek and Kasturi [56] also derived a general correlation of hold-up base on separated flow assumptions but then applied in a general manner. All these latter correlation showed a wide variation in accuracy as detailed in Table 1.

GENERAL THEORIES AND CORRELATIONS FOR OTHER GEOMETRIES

Many theories and correlations have been reported for hold-up in vertically upward flow i tubes [57–77] and channels [78]. Vertical downward flow [79–83] also has been handled as well a inclined flow [13, 47, 84–88]. Other work has been reported on coils [89–91], annuli [92] an tube or rod bundles [93]. We do not intend to cover these areas in this work except to point ou that many theories and correlations developed for horizontal two-phase flow have been applied t other geometries and vice versa.

FLOW PATTERN MODELS

The inadequacy of general models such as the Lockhart and Martinelli approach indicates tha at least one other parameter, namely the flow pattern, was not considered. It is obvious that differen forces are dominant in different flow patterns [94, 95] and hence, it is unlikely that one singl correlation should apply to all flow regimes. Therefore, it is really quite surprising that correlation such as the Lockhart and Martinelli model are able to predict results for such a wide range c conditions to the degree of accuracy that is obtained.

Armand [2] pointed out that different correlation curves correspond approximately to differen flow patterns. Baker [21] recognized the dependence of the Lockhart and Martinelli correlatio on flow pattern and suggested modifications for different flow patterns. The effect of flow patter on pressure drop and hold-up in vertical flow has been illustrated by Govier et al. [62]. Hoogendoor [48] showed that for a fixed value of the Lockhart and Martinelli X parameter, there may be two-fold variation in the value of ϕ_G^2 as a result of a change in flow pattern. He proposed separat correlations for the different flow patterns. Ros [54] gave separate correlations of hold-up an friction factor for the different flow patterns. Rippel et al. [90] while studying flow in a coiled tub also found a strong flow pattern dependence in their results and proposed different pressure dro correlations for the annular, bubble and slug, and stratified flow patterns based on a consideratio of the difference in drag forces occurring in the separate flow patterns.

Eaton et al. [53, 55, 96] found that their "energy loss factor" exhibited a strong dependence o flow pattern while Beattie [97], by using the Colebrook equation, defined different friction factor and Reynolds numbers for the different conditions and flow patterns. Nevstrueva and Tyntyae [98] observed that a transition in flow pattern resulted in a quantitative change in both the tota pressure drop and its components. More recently, Solbrig et al. [95] analyzed two-phase flow base upon unequal phase velocities with interphase interaction terms that require different correlation or models for the different flow regimes. Many other workers have recognized the importance o flow pattern on hold-up and pressure drop leading to the development of flow pattern models These are discussed under the following headings: homogeneous model, annular flow, plug anc slug flow, stratified flow, and bubbly flow. Droplet flow is dealt with under the homogeneous mode or as a special section of the annular flow regime.

The Homogeneous Model

This is the simplest approximation of a two-phase flowing mixture where the phases are treated as homogeneously mixed and flowing at the same velocity. With this assumption, the individual terms in the pressure drop equation as derived from momentum and energy consideration are

Table 1

Hold-up Theories and Correlations

Reference	Relation	Application	Accuracy
Armand [2]	Equation 1, Figure 1	B + S[St, A as separate equations]	±13%
Armand [2]	Equations 2, 3	$\beta \geq 0.9$	$\bar{R}_L$ + 138% to −87%
Armand [2]	Equation 4	$\beta < 0.9$	$\bar{R}_L$ + 5% B, ±11% S.
Lockhart-Martinelli [14]	Figure 2	All regimes	Accuracy varies widely e.g. $\bar{R}_L$ = −13% to −32% [31] $\bar{R}_L$ = +40% to 60% [33]
Styushin-Dyorina [24]	Equation 5	All regimes	$\bar{R}_L$ varies widely
Baroczy [25, 26]	Correlations	All regimes	$\bar{R}_L$ varies widely, eg. ±50%
Levy [28]	Theory	All regimes	Inaccurate
Turner-Wallis [30]	Equation 6	All regimes	Similar to Lockhart-Martinelli + 60%
Chisholm [32–34]	Equations 8–10	All regimes	
Chawla [38, 39]	Equation 11	All regimes	Inaccurate
Hoogendoorn [48]	Equation 13	All regimes	Inaccurate except for A
Levy [49]	Theory	All regimes	$\bar{R}_L$ = +50% to −40%
Mamaev [50]	Correlation	All regimes	$\bar{R}_L$ = +30% to −50%
Greshovich [51, 52]	Correlation	All regimes	$\bar{R}_L$ = +250% to −60%
Beggs [47]	Correlation	All regimes	$\bar{R}_L$ = +150% to −60%
Eaton [53, 55]	Correlation	All regimes	$\bar{R}_L$ = +270% to −80%
Stepanek [56]	Correlation	All regimes	Inaccurate
Homogeneous	Theory	G_T > 2, > 10 kg m^{-2} s^{-1}	±1%
Levy [128]	Theory	A	+100% approx.
Zivi [42]	Equations 33, 34	A, A + D	$\bar{R}_G$ = +3.5% to −13%

A-annular, B-bubble, D-droplet, S-slug, St-stratified

(Continued)

Table 1 (Continued)

Smith [46]	Equation 37	A	$\bar{R}_G = +0.5\%$ to -50%
Nishino [159]	Equation 38	A	$\bar{R}_G = +15\%$ to -60%
Thom [43]	Equation 39	All regimes	$\bar{R}_G = +60\%$ to -50%
Fujie [160]	Equation 40	A	$\bar{R}_G = +10.0\%$ to -4%
Levy-Wallis [164, 165]	Theory	A	$\bar{R}_L = +60\%$ to -43%
Harrison [31]	Equation 41	A	$\bar{R}_G = \pm14\%$
Chen-Spedding [45]	Equation 42	A, A + D	$\bar{R}_G = \pm10\%$
Bankoff [9]	Correlation	B, A,	$\bar{R}_G = +5.0\%$ to -20%
Hughmark [11]	Correlation	B, all regimes	$\bar{R}_G = +25\%$ to -45%
Brown [224]	Correlation	B, all regimes	$\bar{R}_G$ error 11 to 25%
Von Glahn [119]	Correlation	B, all regimes	$\bar{R}_G = +25\%$ to -15%
Taitel-Dukler [23]	Theory	St,	$\pm10\%$
Chen-Spedding [15]	Theory	St. if X $\geq$ 0.08	$\pm10\%$
Spedding-Chen [13]	Theory	D	$\pm10\%$

identical. In two-phase flow, as in single-phase flow, the total pressure drop may be written as,

$$\left[\frac{dP}{dL}\right]_T = \left[\frac{dP}{dL}\right]_A + \left[\frac{dP}{dL}\right]_H + \left[\frac{dP}{dL}\right]_F \tag{14}$$

$[dP/dL]_A$ and $[dP/dL]_H$ are the pressure drop terms due to acceleration and hydrostatic head respectively, and are commonly termed the reversible components, while the frictional term, $[dP/dL]_F$, is the irreversible component.

There is a slight difference in the absolute values of the terms given in the total pressure drop of Equation 14, depending on whether an energy or a momentum consideration had been used on its derivation. For example, an energy consideration would give $[dP/dL]_H$ as

$$\left[\frac{dP}{dL}\right]_{HE} = \left[\frac{\rho_G \rho_L}{\rho_L x + \rho_G(1-x)}\right] \sin \theta \tag{15}$$

$$= [\rho_G \beta + \rho_L(1-\beta)] \sin \theta = \rho_H \sin \theta \tag{16}$$

while a momentum consideration would yield,

$$\left[\frac{dP}{dL}\right]_{HM} = [\rho_L(1-\bar{R}_G) + \rho_G \bar{R}_G] \sin \theta \tag{17}$$

Equations 15–17 have been used widely by different researchers. The term in square brackets in Equations 15 and 16 is commonly termed the homogeneous density ρ_{HO}, while the corresponding term in Equation 17, is termed the two-phase mixture density ρ_{TP}. There are corresponding variations in the terms $[dP/dL]_A$ and $[dP/dL]_F$; while $[dP/dL]_{FE}$ refers to the total mechanical energy, $[dP/dL]_{FM}$ refers to the wall shear stress. Details may be found in the literature [99–102]. The corresponding terms are, however, exactly identical irrespective of whether the derivation had been based on the energy or the momentum equation if homogeneous flow had been assumed.

Methods of calculating $[dP/dL]_A$ have been given by Butterworth and Hewitt [100], Wallis [103], etc. [8, 33, 74, 104–106] while the experimental measurements of this quantity have been reported by Rose and Griffith [74], etc. [107, 108]. Generally, for the case of adiabatic, steady-state flow in a pipe of constant cross section, $[dP/dL]_A$, is small and is usually ignored. However, in cases of flow with heat transfer, changing flow cross-sectional area, large variations in pressure along the flow line, or when the flow is not fully developed, $[dP/dL]_A$ must be considered. Natrually, when $[dP/dL]_A$ is significant variations in hold-up can be expected.

The irreversible term, $[dP/dL]_F$, is the subject of most studies [109–110]. In horizontal flow, if $[dP/dL]_A$ is negligible,

$$\left[\frac{dP}{dL}\right]_F = \left[\frac{dP}{dL}\right]_T$$

In vertical flow, $[dP/dL]_F$ is obtained from $[dP/dL]_T$ through Equation 14. The techniques commonly used in single-phase flow may be applied to two-phase flow by using similar parameters, e.g., the use of a two-phase friction factor, f_{TP}. Govier and Omer [111] discuss the use of the homogeneous model in some detail. The voidage is given as,

$$\bar{R}_G = \beta = Q_G/(Q_G + Q_L) \tag{18}$$

and the two-phase friction factor as

$$f_{TP} = \left[\frac{dP}{dL_F}\right] \bar{D}\rho_H/(2G_T^2) \tag{19}$$

where ρ_H, the homogeneous density is given in Equation 16 as the ratio of the total mass to volume rate.

The two-phase friction factor f_{TP} is related to a two-phase Reynolds number Re_{TP} thus,

$$f_{TP} = f_{TP}(Re_{TP}) = f_{TP}\left[\frac{G_T\bar{D}}{\mu_{TP}}\right] \tag{20}$$

To solve for f_{TP}, two alternative approaches are possible: To define a new relationship between f_{TP} and Re_{TP} or to define a μ_{TP} such that the Moody chart used commonly for single-phase flow may also be applied. The first alternative was commonly used in early studies of gas-oil mixture flow in the oilfields. Poettman and Carpenter [112] using data from flowing oil wells and gas-lift wells attempted a correlation of f_{TP} as a function of $G_T\bar{D}$, but the correlating parameter was in fact Re_{TP} without the term μ_{TP}. Bertuzzi, et al. [113] used horizontal flow data to correlate f_{TP} against the gas and liquid superficial Reynolds number,

$$f_{TP} = \text{function } (Re_G \times Re_L^{'b}) \tag{21}$$

where $\quad 'b = e^{-0.1(x/(1-x))}$ \tag{22}

Fancher and Brown [114], extended this correlation to cover a wider range of flow conditions with the inclusion of the gas-liquid ratio as a parameter. They noted the effect of changing flow pattern on the accuracy of the correlation. Hagedorn and Brown [64] attempted to incorporate the effect of viscosity into the correlation because it was found that when liquid viscosity was in excess of $0.012 \text{ kg m}^{-1}\text{s}^{-1}$, deviations occurred. Their new correlation is of the same form as Equation 20 but with,

$$\mu_{TP} = \mu_L^{z_4}\mu_G^{z_3} \tag{23}$$

where $\quad z_4 + z_3 = 1.0$ \tag{24}

for $\quad \mu_L < 0.012 \text{ kg m}^{-1}\text{s}^{-1}, \quad z_4 = 0 \quad$ and $\quad z_3 = 1.0$

for $\quad \mu_L > 0.012 \text{ kg m}^{-1}\text{s}^{-1}, \quad z_4 = 0.25 \quad$ and $\quad z_3 = 0.75$

It is quite obvious that this type of correlation is not universal and is of rather limited application. In the second alternative, it is necessary to define μ_{TP}. Some of those used are

$$\mu_{TP} = \mu_L \qquad\qquad \text{Owens [115] Shiba and Yamazaki [116]} \tag{25}$$

$$\mu_{TP} = \mu_G x + \mu_L(1-x) \qquad\qquad \text{Cicchetti et al. [117]} \tag{26}$$

$$\frac{1}{\mu_{TP}} = \frac{x}{\mu_G} + \frac{1-x}{\mu_L} \qquad\qquad \text{McAdams et al. [118]} \tag{27}$$

$$\mu_{TP} = (1-x)\frac{\rho_H}{\rho_L}\mu_L + x\frac{\rho_H}{\rho_G}\mu_G \qquad\qquad \text{Dukler et al. [27]} \tag{28}$$

$$\mu_{TP} = \mu_L^{\bar{R}_{PL}}\mu_G^{\bar{R}_{PG}} \qquad\qquad \text{Hagedorn and Brown [64]} \tag{29}$$

Hagedorn and Brown [64] defined μ_{TP} in terms of some correlated value of pseudo-hold-up $\bar{R}_{PL}$, which might not necessarily correspond to the actual holdup $\bar{R}_L$. The calculated values of $\bar{R}_{PL}$ were correlated with the dimensionless groupings suggested by Ros [54].

$$D\sqrt{\rho_L g/\sigma}, \quad \bar{V}_{SG}\left[\frac{\rho_L}{g\sigma}\right]^{1/4}, \quad \bar{V}_{SL}\left[\frac{\rho_L}{g\sigma}\right]^{1/4}, \quad \mu_L\left[\frac{g}{\rho_L\sigma^3}\right]^{1/4} \tag{30}$$

The accuracy of the homogeneous model in predicting two-phase flow data has been found to increase with the intermixing of the phases, such as is found in mist or fog flow. When the phases are clearly separated, e.g., stratified or annular flow, the predictions deviate as expected. Collier [92] checked the homogeneous model using the methods of Owens [115] and McAdams et al. [118] and found that both were in poor agreement with the experimental results obtained from annular flow. Hewitt, King, and Lovegrove [105] also arrived at the same conclusions. Von Glahn [119] found that the homogeneous model overpredicts the void fraction in steam-water flow by about 10%.

Larson [120], and Isbin et al. [121, 122] compared results using the homogeneous model with steam-water data at pressures of 27, 41, 54, and 68 atmospheres. The model was found to over predict $\bar{R}_G$ and total pressure drops. Further comparison of data against the homogeneous model may be found in Friedel [123], Dukler et al. [27, 124], and Gould [125].

More recently, Husain et al. [126] suggested that flow patterns observed in co-current gas-liquid flow may be classified as either homogeneous, including froth and mist flow, or non-homogeneous, i.e., intermittent (including bubble, slug, and plug flow) and separated flow. The transition from non-homogeneous to homogeneous took place when $Q_G/Q_L > 140{,}000$ and $G_T > 2{,}710 \, \mathrm{kg \, m^{-2} \, s^{-1}}$, while the dependence of the transition on flow regime was rather small. They reported that when $G \geq 2{,}710 \, \mathrm{kg \, m^{-2} \, s^{-1}}$, the use of either Dukler's or McAdam's definition of μ_{TP} gave excellent agreement with results from a very wide range of conditions.

The homogeneous model has also been used in the study of geothermal steam-water flow by Gould [125] and Harrison [31] with reasonable success.

Annular Flow

The annular flow regime has received the most attention both analytically and experimentally because of its practical importance and the relative ease with which analytical treatment may be applied. The actual flow regime is composed of a flowing central gas core with or without entrained droplets, and an annulus of liquid adjacent to the channel wall. Hence, annular flow can be classified as a separated flow model since the liquid and gas flows are confined to definite regions of the total flow area. The gas-liquid interface between the phases is covered with either ripples or waves [127]. Annular-mist flow is the pattern normally encountered in practice except when the liquid rate is below a critical value.

The annular flow pattern is employed in film heating and cooling processes particularly in power generation especially in nuclear power reactors. Many of the two-phase transportation process found in the gas-oil industry and geothermal steam-water production occur in the annular flow regime. Of course, there are obvious differences between vertical and horizontal annular flow. The film thickness and velocity profiles are essentially symmetric in the case of vertical flow but for horizontal flow gravity causes the film thickness to be greatest along the base of the conduit.

Levy [128] analyzed ideal horizontal annular flow by assuming that gravity does not distort the concentric annular liquid film. The liquid and gas velocity distributions were obtained by using the Navier-Stokes equation in the case of laminar flow and seventh power law in the case of turbulent flow. Continuity of velocity and shear stress were assumed at the interface. The result was cast in the Lockhart and Martinelli form but, while it was perhaps the first attempt to justify the approach analytically, it gave liquid hold-ups that were a factor of two above experimental data. The development did allow the derivation of the following useful relation for the case when the quality is small,

$$\phi_L^2 = \frac{1}{(1 - \bar{R}_G)^2} \tag{31}$$

Chisholm and Laird [33] gave empirical correlations based on Equation 31 for smooth and rough tubes but the accuracy of the correlations was $\pm 20\%$. Isbin et al. [121] detailed other similar types of correlations. There have been quite a few analyses of horizontal annular flow in which uneven film thickness were considered. McManus [104, 129–131] studied the film thickness in horizontal annular flow and found that variation in the input liquid rate only affected the film depth in the lower half of the tube. The film thickness in the upper half of the tube was found to vary as an inverse function of the air rate.

Symmetry of the flow profiles occurred about a vertical plane passing through the axis of the pipe. This was confirmed by Butterworth [132]. McManus further showed that the maximum wave height varied with the mean film thickness and that it tended to an upper value. The liquid film was found to be a monotonically increasing function of circumferential position (with $0°$ at the top of the pipe). The variable liquid surface roughness is believed to cause a skewing in the velocity profile and secondary flow. McManus reported that the ratio of maximum to minimum film thickness was of the order of 10. Allen [133] suggested that this ratio may be as high as 50 in large diameter (> 20 cm) pipes, giving a feasible explanation to the observation made by Anderson and Russel [134, 135] that the ratio of the droplet interchange at the bottom of the pipe to that at the top is about 10.

McManus [129–131] also gave a correlation for the film thickness as:

$$\frac{\delta_L}{D} = j \frac{Re_L^i}{Re_G^u} \left[\frac{\rho_G}{\rho_L} \right]^w \left[\frac{\mu_L}{\mu_G} \right]^o \tag{32}$$

where parameters j, i, w, o, and u were given values that were dependent on the circumferential position. The relation was found to be unsatisfactory by Butterworth [132] who tested it using data for an air-water system flowing in a 3.2-cm diameter pipe. Jacowitz and Brodkey [136], by assuming isothermal conditions, zero entrainment and no mass transfer formulated a model to account for the various forces that acted upon the gas and liquid phases. The annular flow pattern was partitioned into a series of wedge-shaped elements for solving force balances due to body forces (gravity, centrifugal, and coriolis) and surface forces (wave drag, wave lift, wall friction, surface tension, pressure, and viscous forces). Given the inlet conditions, the film geometry and pressure were traced stepwise downstream using a numerical technique. These workers treated the friction at the gas-liquid interface as being due to frictional drag and profile drag. However, the practical application of such a model is rather limited since the use of a computer is essential. Moreover, the model gave only moderate agreement with results for 2.5-cm and 5.08-cm diameter pipes. With the latter the solution became divergent due to a high circumferential gradient in the film thickness.

The results of Russell and Lamb [137] agreed qualitatively with those of McManus in that a plane of symmetry was found to exist. The mechanism they proposed was that the liquid film drained in the direction of the gravitational force. The model was justified by using a salt solution and measuring the circumferential variation of concentration. Dye and short nylon threads were also used to enable visual observation to be made. The circumferential film velocity was determined as a function of the circumferential position and showed a maximum of about $6–12$ cm s^{-1} at about halfway up the side of the tube. This result is many orders higher than the value of 0.1 cm s^{-1} estimated by Jacowitz and Brodkey [136]. To maintain steady state annular flow, it is necessary that all parts of the liquid film are replenished continuously. This could be accomplished by the impingement of droplets on the upper portion of the pipe or by the flow processes associated with disturbance or roll waves. Russell and Lamb [137] analyzed the interchange of droplets with the aid of a circumferential diffusivity term and claimed that the model was in agreement with data obtained from salt concentration measurements.

Butterworth [132] suggested that there is a unique relationship between the film thickness and the wave structure similar to that found by Hewitt [138] for the case of vertical flow. Butterworth [132] gave a simple analysis of the circumferential variation of shear stress showing that at the bottom of the tube it is about three times that at the top. According to Lee and Bryce [139] the figure is high since secondary flow and circumferential momentum transfer will reduce the value by an unknown amount. Butterworth [132] also discussed and analyzed the various mechanisms for maintaining the film in horizontal annular flow. He argued that since the action of gravity is to induce breakdown of the film at the top of the tube, there must be forces for maintaining or a mechanism for replenishing it. Four highly simplified models were considered: The first was the *surface tension model*. It was shown that for the model to be feasible a surface tension of the order of 10 kg s^{-2} was necessary. Since this value is well beyond that normally encountered it may be inferred that the surface tension effect is too small to maintain the liquid film. The second model was the *entrainment-droplet deposition model*, which postulated that there was a net entrainment from the bottom of the tube and a net deposition at the top of the tube. Studies of the entrainment-deposition model had been carried out by many investigators [134, 135, 140–150]. But by considering a simplified model without entrainment at the top of the tube Butterworth [132] showed that the calculated deposition rate required to maintain the liquid film at the top of the tube is 10 times that actually measured. Inception criteria for entrainment [151–155] and correlations for entrainment may be found in the literature [80, 156–158].

The third model is termed the *secondary flow model*. There exists a circumferential variation of roughness of the surface because the film thickness is greater at the bottom than at the top of the tube and there is a relationship between wave amplitude and film thickness. As a result, secondary flow in the gas phase occurs and introduces an interfacial shear in the circumferential direction. Calculations show that the predicted circumferential shear is smaller than, but of the same order of magnitude as, the typical peripheral shear induced by secondary flow. Therefore, secondary flow may provide a feasible mechanism for maintaining the annular film.

The final mechanism is the *wave spreading model*. Due to the uneven thickness of the liquid film, a wave formed at the entrance of the conduit will move further at the center of the tube than at the side. Consequently, it will result in the development of a distorted wave in the conduit itself. This distortion together with the impact pressure of the gas will induce a component of force in the circumferential direction so as to transfer liquid in that direction. While surface ripples were observed to behave in the manner described, disturbance waves did not. However, the latter did promote mixing, some of which was in the circumferential direction. Thus this mechanism also was shown to be feasible. McManus [131] also had suggested that waves at the bottom of the tube were relatively tall, slender, and sharp crested, while at the top of the tube they were short and smooth crested. Such observations support the wave spreading model in addition to the entrainment-deposition model and the secondary flow model.

Zivi [42] equated the minimum entropy production to the minimum kinetic energy flux to give for annular-droplet flow

$$\frac{\bar{V}_G}{\bar{V}_L} = \left[\frac{\rho_L}{\rho_G}\right]^{1/3} \left[\frac{1 + \frac{\rho_G}{\rho_L} E_D\left(\frac{1-x}{x}\right)}{1 + E_D\left(\frac{1-x}{x}\right)}\right]^{1/3}. \tag{33}$$

For ideal annular flow the result was

$$\bar{R}_G = \frac{1}{1 + \left(\frac{1-x}{x}\right)\left(\frac{\rho_G}{\rho_L}\right)^{2/3}} \tag{34}$$

Zivi [42] showed that most experimental results lay between the equation for ideal annular flow and the homogeneous model. Figure 9 shows that the model gives reasonable agreement with data for the annular flow regime ($+0.7\%$), but best results were obtained for low liquid flow rates ($+5.3\%$ to -0.3%).

Smith [46] used the concept of equal velocity heads in the two phases of the flowing system; the basic assumption being that there was a homogeneous mixture in the core of the conduit and a liquid film on the wall.

The analysis led to,

$$\bar{R}_G = \left\{1 + \frac{Q_L}{Q_G} E_D + \frac{Q_L}{Q_G}(1 - E_D)\left[\frac{\frac{\rho_L}{\rho_G} + \frac{W_L}{W_G} E_0}{1 + \frac{W_L}{W_G} E_D}\right]^{1/2}\right\}^{-1} \tag{35}$$

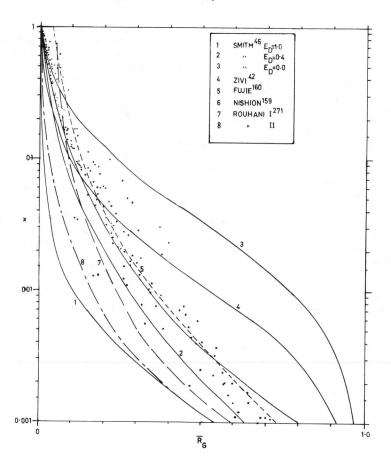

1	SMITH[46]	$E_D=1.0$
2	"	$E_D=0.4$
3	"	$E_D=0.0$
4	ZIVI[42]	
5	FUJIE[160]	
6	NISHION[159]	
7	ROUHANI I[271]	
8	" II	

Figure 9. Comparison of the models of Zivi [42], Smith [46], Nishino and Yamazaki [159], Thom [43] and Fugi [160] with experimental data.

When the flow was misty, $E_D = 1.0$ and

$$\bar{R}_G = \frac{x}{x + (1 - x)\dfrac{\rho_G}{\rho_L}} \tag{36}$$

For annular flow $E_D = 0$ and

$$\bar{R}_G = \frac{x}{x + (1 - x)\left(\dfrac{\rho_G}{\rho_L}\right)^{1/2}} \tag{37}$$

Droplet and annular flow data gave an overall deviation of -6.5% for the model while at low liquid flows an error of $+3.2\%$ to -13.1% was in evidence. The approach does not agree well with data for other flow regimes, despite the claim that by using $E_D = 0.4$ the model predicted within $\pm 10\%$ data for horizontal and vertical flow, regardless of pressure, mass velocity, input ratio etc. Figure 9 does not support the claim and, in fact, it exhibits a mass velocity effect. Of course, Smith [46] does not imply that all flows have an entrainment of 0.4, but is simply attempting to use a correlation factor to make a general hold-up correlation from a derivation that obviously is dependent on flow regime as well as mass velocity. Nishino and Yamazaki [159] used the empirical relation,

$$\bar{R}_G = 1 - \sqrt{\frac{(1 - x)\rho_G}{x\rho_L + (1 - x)\rho_G}} \tag{38}$$

to obtain hold-up but the result did not aline well with data. Michiyoshi et al. [69] later extended the model and applied it to vertical flow but again with limited success.

Thom [43] proposed the empirical relation,

$$\bar{R}_G = \frac{\gamma x}{1 + x(\gamma - 1)} \tag{39}$$

for the steam-water system where γ depended on operating pressure of the system.

Fujie [160] carried out an analytical treatment of the annular flow regime, which was based on dividing the system into three distinct regions of flow: liquid, gas, and mixture. Different equations were obtained from a consideration of the force balances depending on angle of conduit inclination. For horizontal flow.

$$x = \frac{\rho_G \bar{R}_G}{\rho_L(1 - R_G)} \left[1 + \frac{\bar{R}_G^{0.25}}{1 - \sqrt{R_G}} \sqrt{\frac{10}{P}} \right] \tag{40}$$

Figure 9 shows that the equation gives a better overall correlation than the Smith [46] correlation of Equation 35 but registers consistently low readings in the annular flow regime. Cravarolo and Hussid [161] attempted to derive a correlation along the same general lines, which included the effects of mass velocity, diameter, gas density, and surface tension. In general the resulting complex correlation gave results that were high ($+0.5$ to 80%). Later, Madsen [162] sought to extend the correlations of Zivi [42] and Smith [46] by including a variable exponent for the $(1 - x)/x$ term. However, the result was of little improvement. Further, the correlation gave consistently high values of void fraction for the annular regime and the deviation became even larger when an attempt was made to extend the use of the correlation to other flows, such as the bubble and slug regimes.

Friedel [163] mentions several correlations of a similar type to those of Zivi [42] and Smith [46] but the overall result obtained was not too dissimilar to that shown in Figure 9.

Levy [164] used mixing length theory to obtain a general relation for the ratio of film thickness to pipe radius. The amount of entrainment was accounted for in the treatment by using data to give an empirical correlation. The overall result was almost identical to the simpler approach by Wallis [165]. Referring to Figure 4 the analysis gives a result that is -43% at the top end of the X scale and $+60\%$ at the lower end.

Harrison [31] suggested a correlation for annular steam-water data in large diameter pipes,

$$\bar{R}_G = \frac{1}{1 + \left(\dfrac{1 - x}{x}\right)^{0.8} + \left(\dfrac{\rho_G}{\rho_L}\right)^{0.515}} \tag{41}$$

which is given in Figure 10. The Harrison correlation obviously possesses limitations, but it does give reasonable agreement with a wide variety of data despite being formulated from large diameter pipe conditions.

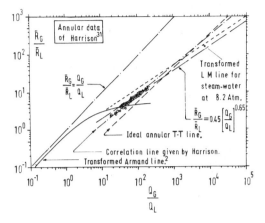

Figure 10. Hold-up relations compared with steam water data of Harrizon [31] for large diameter pipes.

Chen and Spedding [45] developed a more general correlation for the annular type flow regime.

$$\frac{\bar{R}_G}{\bar{R}_L} = 0.45 \left[\frac{Q_G}{Q_L}\right]^{0.65} \tag{42}$$

This relation when used in conjunction with the Armand equation (4) and stratified flow relations [13] enables calculations of hold-up to the performed over the complete range of flow rates and regimes. The particular relation is shown among other places in Figure 8.

Annular Flow Models for Other Geometries

The analysis of vertical annular flow has received considerably more attention than the horizontal case and the equations obtained often have been applied to the case of horizontal flow and in some instances found to give a reasonable treatment. There are several approaches used in the vertical geometry. The first can be called the rough wall method in which a gas core is considered to be flowing in a tube with rough walls due to the presence of the wavy gas-liquid interface. Since the gas velocity usually is very large compared with the interfacial velocity, the rough surface may be assumed to be stationary. However, the correlations derived have been found to depend on the conditions at the interface [60, 65–78, 127, 131, 136, 139, 141, 144, 154, 165–177]. The second approach is sometimes termed the triangular relationship since it is involved with the film thickness-shear stress-film flow rate inter-relation. The method has been used by many workers for many geometries employing either a theoretical or semi-empirical approach [58, 78, 154, 156–158, 170, 171, 178–189].

Slug Flow

Slug flow is of importance in the study of oil wells, geothermal systems, furnace heat transfer, gas lifts etc. It also is important in chemical reactors, since very often the optimal operating conditions are in the slug flow regime. On the other hand, the presence of high-speed slugs of liquid causes vibrations in pipelines and other equipment, which may damage pumps, pipelines, valves, and other fittings.

Many slug flow models have been developed in conjunction with upward flow particularly vertical upward flow where the regime is the predominant flow pattern. Behringer [190], Griffith and Wallis [191], Nicklin et al. [192], and various other workers [69, 193–198] have used bubble rise theory and semi-empirical techniques in order to derive gas hold-up relations for use in vertical flow. Hughmark [199] applied the development to the horizontal situation and derived a result that corresponded to the Armand relation of Equation 4. Hughmark [199] also showed that the relation only applied to the slug, plug, and bubble flow regimes.

Singh and Griffith [87] and Bonnecaze et al. [84] applied the development to the case of upward inclined flows, while Gomezplata et al. [197] and Martin [198] applied it to the case of downward flows. Dukler and Hubbard [200, 201] developed a slug flow model that was expanded by others [51, 52, 202] but only could be used when a detailed knowledge was available of the hold-up and slug length and frequency. These data on slug characteristics were in the main supplied by empirical correlations [36, 198, 203, 204]. Even data for the non-Newtonian situation [205-207] has been found to be applicable. On the other hand, Taitel and Dukler [208] presented a model of slug flow that enabled certain slug characteristics to be calculated and gave substantial agreement with experiment. Kobayashi et al. [209] gave details of the void profiles exhibited by the slug flow regime. Sakagachi et al. [210] studied slug flow and developed a mechanistic model based on mass and momentum balances, which agreed with data and was applicable to the solution of the Dukler-Hubbard model [200, 201]. However, Hubbard's earlier contribution showed that the translational velocity of a liquid slug was proportional to the total velocity. The constant of proportionality was determined by experiment as having a value of 1.25. The true average gas velocity was then given by,

$$\bar{V}_G = \bar{V}_{SG}\bar{R}_G = 1.11\bar{V}_T \tag{43}$$

Gregory and Scott [204] found that the constant in the equation was too low and suggested a value of 1.19.

Gregory et al. [211] correlated the liquid volume fraction of the slug as,

$$\bar{R}_L = \frac{1}{1 + \left[\dfrac{\bar{V}_T}{8.66}\right]^{1.39}} \tag{44}$$

with $\bar{V}_T$ in m s^{-1}. Although the correlation was developed for two diameters—2.58 and 5.12 cm— it was suggested that it must be modified to include the effect of geometry and possibly fluid properties.

Kordyban [212] derived a model for horizontal slug flow by considering that the portion of the liquid flowing in the lower part of the tube obeyed the laws of open channel flow while the remainder of the liquid flows in disc-shaped slugs, which alternate with vapor in the top portion of the tube. However, Kordyban and Ranov [213] found the model did not describe satisfactorily the behavior of slug flow and gave data that disagreed with the theory. Despite this, Vermeulen and Ryan [214] extended the theory to inclined flows. However, Chen and Spedding [215] later showed that the flow in the lower section of the tube does not follow the open channel theory in a satisfactory manner and considerable modification is required before agreement with experimental data can be obtained.

Bubble Flow

Bubble flow generally covers the situation when the gas phase is dispersed in the form of small bubbles that may not be uniform in shape or size but are small in comparison to the pipe size. Its study is important in many industrial processes, e.g., in agitated vessels, waste water treatment, mass transfer processes. It also is involved in controlling the sound produced by propellors of both surface and submerged vessels due to their accoustical properties [216-218]. The dynamic behavior of bubbly mixture is of importance in the design of devices to propel high-speed water-born craft such as hydrofoils and air-cushion vehicles [219]. The study of flowing bubbly mixtures also has been carried out in relation to blood flow by Sakao and Sueda [220] and to model tests in the hypersonic range as mentioned by Weinig [221].

Very often the bubbly flow regime is associated with the slug and plug flow patterns and some of the correlations and theories outlined for these latter regimes are intended to include at least some portion of the bubbly flow regime as well [222]. A second approach is to invoke the homogeneous model [223] which assumes that the velocity of the gas bubbles is the same as that of the surrounding liquid phase.

Bankoff [9] suggested a theory of hold-up based on the assumption that the two phase mixture could be treated as a single phase with a variable local density. The equivalent fluid density varied with radial position due to the uneven distribution of bubbles in the mixture. The local velocities of the two phases also were assumed to be equal to the mixture velocity while a typical power law distribution was used to describe the local velocity and voidage profiles.

$$\frac{V_T}{V_{T_m}} = \left[\frac{y}{D/2} \right]^{1/m} \tag{45}$$

$$\frac{'r_G}{'r_{Gm}} = \left[\frac{y}{D/2} \right]^{1/n} \tag{46}$$

By performing a materials balance and integrating the local velocity and voidage profiles it was possible to obtain an expression for the input mass fraction.

$$\frac{W_T}{W_G} = \frac{1}{x} = 1 - \frac{\rho_L}{\rho_G} \left(1 - \frac{K}{\bar{R}_G} \right) \tag{47}$$

$$\text{where} \quad K = \frac{2(m + n + mn)(m + n + 2mn)}{(m + 1)(2n + m)(m + 1)(2m + 1)} \tag{48}$$

An empirical approach was used to assign a value to K but the results according to Von Glahn [119] were not as good as the Martinelli approach. Zuber [10] showed that

$$\bar{R}_G = \beta K = \frac{Q_G}{Q_T} K \tag{49}$$

However, these equations are inconsistent in the limit when $W_G \rightarrow 0$ if K has a real value.

Despite the problems, the approach of Bankoff [9] was used as a basis for general hold-up correlations by Hughmark [11], Brown et al. [224], Von Glahn [119], Petrick and Kudirka [225], and Stepanek [226]. Basically the Bankoff model is equivalent to the Armand relation of Equation 4 in which form Zuber [10] and Rose and Griffith [74] showed that with suitable empirical constants it can be made to adequately fit the data for bubbly flow in both one and two component systems.

Two approaches followed these developments. First, several workers attempted to correlated the bubble flow regime by either directly applying existing slug flow models or slightly modifying such models to fit into the particular situation presented by bubbly flow. The second development was to measure voidage profiles and other two-phase phenomena and seek to use the results to test the various models such as those by Bankoff [9] and Zuber and Findlay [227].

Ueda [77] applied the Nicklin-Griffith type flow model developed for slug flow to the vertical bubbly flow regime. Gomezplata et al. [197] extended the work to the case of downward flow while Holmes and Russel [228] did a similar thing with horizontal flow. Arosio et al. [229] used the Lockhart and Martinelli [14] approach for the case of downward bubbly flow.

Measurements of voidage and velocity profiles were performed by various workers [9, 106, 209, 221, 228–234]. St. Pierre and Bankoff [235] showed that in a vertical rectangular channel the measured voidage distribution compared favourably with the Bankoff [9, 236] and Zuber and Findlay [227] models. Beattie [29] later showed that the mixing length concepts also could handle the situation. However, Kabayashi et al. [209] reported a peak in the voidage profile close to the channel wall, which could not be accounted for by any of these theories.

Michiyoshi et al. [69] carried out an analysis of bubbly flow in the steam-water system in which a force balance was performed assuming the bubbles acted as rigid spheres. The final equation required correlation but was in the form of Equations 34–39 except that some cognizance was given to the effect of mass velocity and other variables. Generally, agreement with data was poor. Yamazaki and Yamaguchi [237] correlated vertical flow data for boiling and non-boiling conditions using the same parameters. Also Moussalli and Chawla [238] modified their theory to suit the bubble flow regime and again the correlation technique was not successful.

Chen and Spedding [215] showed that in general bubbly flow followed the Armand relation of Equation 4 except for the situation of non-slip between phases when the homogeneous model applied.

Downward bubble flow was studied by Lorenzi and Satgia [82], Arosio et al. [229], Martin [198] and Griffith [194].

Annular Bubble and Slug Flows

The formulation by Bankoff [9] for bubbly flow was widened later by Neil and Bankoff [236] to include a wider range of flow regimes by using a model that was a closer approach to the actual conditions found in the conduit. It was assumed that at any position in the conduit three average quantities existed: time-average, cross-sectional average, and space average for the velocity, voidage, and density of the system. The analysis resulted in the following equation by taking voidage at the pipewall equal to zero.

$$\frac{\bar{R}_G Q_T}{Q_G} = \bar{R}_G \left(1 - \frac{v_{Lm}}{(v_{Gm})C_1} + \frac{(v_{Lm})C_2}{(v_{Gm}C_1)} \right) \tag{50}$$

where C_1 and C_2 are constants that are functions of the exponents in the power-law distribution equations of velocity and voidage across the conduit. Because the velocity maximum ratio of the phases were unknown, an empirical approach was necessary.

$$\frac{\bar{R}_G}{Q_G} = 1.25 \left[\frac{Q_G}{Q_T} \right]^{0.88} \left[\frac{\bar{V}_{SL}^2}{gD} \right]^{0.2} \tag{51}$$

Zuber and Findlay [227] used the principle of flux concentration to derive,

$$\bar{V}_G = \frac{\bar{V}_{SG}}{\bar{R}_G} = C_0 \bar{V}_T + \frac{\bar{r}_G \bar{v}_{DG}}{\bar{R}_G} \tag{52}$$

where the last term was the weighted mass drift velocity and,

$$C_0 = \frac{\frac{1}{A} \int_A v_G v_T \, dA}{\left[\frac{1}{A} \int_A v_T \, dA \right] \left[\frac{1}{A} \int_A r_G \, dA \right]} \tag{53}$$

was termed the distribution parameter. Plots of $\bar{V}_G$ against $\bar{V}_T$ were indeed straight lines for certain patterns. The weighted mass drift velocity was constant with $C_0 = 1.2$ for slug flow and $C_0 = 1.0$ for annular and homogeneous bubble flow.

The constant C_0 was in fact first derived by Neal [196] as the inverse of the Bankoff flow parameter K when there was no slip between phases. Simpson and Rooney [239] proposed a similar development for vertical flow but based on the relative or slip velocity between the phases.

$$\frac{Q_G}{Q_T \bar{R}_G} = 1 + \frac{\bar{V}_R}{\bar{V}_T} \tag{54}$$

The slip velocity was correlated as Q_G/Q_{TG} against $(\sigma g \Delta \rho/\rho_L)^{1/4}/\bar{V}_T$ and prediction was claimed to have an accuracy of $\pm 10\%$ for a wide pressure range regardless of pipe diameter and inclination. However, the correlation did not give such good accuracy when compared with the data of other workers. Brown and Govier [195] Gomezplata et al. [224], Stepanek [226], and Bhaga and Weber [240] modified the development in several ways so as to include the effect of other variables such as counter-current flow and multiphase systems.

However, the basic equation is mathematically inconsistent. For example, in the case of two phase flow when $Q_G \to 0$ and $Q_L \neq 0$ then the hold-up possesses a positive value depending on the liquid flow rate. Thus,

$$\frac{Q_L}{A_T} = -\frac{r_G v_{DG}}{\bar{R}_G C_0} \tag{55}$$

which gives a constant value on the right-hand side while Q_L can vary at will.

To overcome these problems Nguyen and Spedding [12] derived a similar but more fundamental equation by applying the conservation of mass to a field theory concept of heterogeneous mixed flow.

$$\left[\frac{Q_G/Q_T - Q_3/Q_T}{\bar{R}_G - A_3/A_T}\right]\bar{V}_T = C_0\left[\frac{Q_S A_T}{Q_T A_S}\right]V_T + B \tag{56}$$

where

$$C_0 = \frac{\frac{1}{A_S}\int_{A_S} r_G(\rho_L - \rho_G)v_T \, dA}{(\rho_L - \hat{\rho}_G)\bar{R}_{G_S}} \tag{57}$$

the initial function

$$B = -\frac{1}{A_S}\int_{A_S}\frac{\rho' v_T \, dA}{(\rho_L - \rho_G)\bar{R}_{G_S}} \tag{58}$$

and the prime refers to the point value.

The form of Equation 56 was shown to be mathematically consistent. For example, the initial function was found to approach the free velocity of a gas bubble when the gas and liquid rates were reduced to zero [241] and the equation reduced to zero when the mixtures region was not present, that is when separated flow occurred. In fact, it was shown from experimental data that suitable relationships agreeing with theory only could be obtained for bubble, slug, plug, and annular flow. However, the equations were shown to apply to all geometries and are not just restricted to vertical co-current flow as suggested by Bankoff [236]. The general form of the equation was shown by Chen and Spedding [45] to be in accord with those proposed by other workers including most empirical correlations such as the Armand [2] relation. The original derivation by Nguyen and Spedding [12] was deficient, however, and Spedding and Chen [242] justified the derivation by using a process based on integration by parts. In applying the theory Nguyen and Spedding [12] assigned values to C_0 and B based on data, except where the theory does not apply in the stratified regimes i.e., horizontal and downward flow with Q_G in the lower range. Equation 56 thus predict that no one general correlation can be formulated that will correlate holdup over the entire range of flow regimes and geometries. However, correlations can be developed for the individual flow patterns and geometries. Oliver and Young Hoon [243] besides showing that pseudo-plastic and Newtonian fluid behaved differently in two-phase flow situations, clearly demonstrated that there are marked differences between flow regimes that do not allow the use of a general theory.

In addition Nguyen and Spedding [244] showed that the general theory was of wider applicability in that it applied to all types of two and three phase systems.

Stratified Flow

A considerable amount of attention has been directed towards this flow regime because its simple geometry provides a means of obtaining a fundamental understanding of two-phase flow. The stratified flow regime occurs only in the horizontal and negatively inclined orientations [245].

Theoretical studies of two-phase stratified flow first received attention through its importance in relation to atmospheric conditions and the movement of large bodies of water in oceans and rivers. Lord Rayleigh [246] and Lamb [247] analyzed two-phase stratified flow using the classical hydrodynamic theories. More recent investigations relating to such phenomena include those of Benjamin [248], Hanratty [249–250], etc. [251–255].

Analysis of stratified flow in a conduit is a more recent matter [256]. Its analysis generally is related to the transport phenomena [257], although it has been studied in relation to other applications such as mass transfer or the co-extrusion of molten plastics to form bicomponent fibers. Yu and Sparrow [258] considered analytically laminar two-phase stratified flow and obtained solutions relating volumetric flow rate and pressure drop for various equilibrium liquid levels, i.e. hold-ups. Greskovich [81] suggested that hold-up in downward inclined stratifies flow may be accurately predicted by using open channel flow equations. Spedding and Nguyen [259] demonstrated that while there was a parallel between the two cases, considerable difficulties existed in matching the theory to experimental data. Later analysis by Chen and Spedding [215] showed that the open channel theory could be used to predict hold-up in the horizontal (and downward) geometries for stratified flow.

Russel et al. [260] considered the case of laminar liquid-turbulent gas two-phase stratified flow. The equation of motion was solved by taking into account the interfacial shear. In many ways the procedure was similar to that suggested by Chisholm [35] and later by Buffham [261], Agrawal et al. [262]. Good agreement was reported with experimental results but an iterative method was necessary in order to obtain a solution. Thus, any design procedure was not practical unless computer methods were adopted. These authors recognized the limitations of the method and suggested that under laminar conditions the procedure of Yu and Sparrow [258] be used and to resort to the use of a standard correlation if one or both phases were turbulent.

Cheremisinoff and Davis [263] recently analyzed turbulent gas-liquid stratified flow. Eddy viscosity expressions developed for single phase flow were applied to the turbulent liquid phase. Different expressions were used to calculate the interfacial shear depending on the type of intefacial disturbance present. The expressions developed by Cohen and Hanratty [250] for roll waves and ripples were used. The method of solution involved an iterative calculation until the pressure drop in both the gas and liquid phases coincided.

These iterative methods are in no way superior to those of Johannessen [264], Taitel and Dukler [23], and Chen and Spedding [15], which are in fact basically an extension of the Lockhart and Martinelli analytical method. Johannessen [264] formulated momentum flux equations separately for the gas and liquid phases based on work of Chisholm [35]. Hydraulic diameters were employed by assuming the gas phase flowed in a conduit and the liquid phase in an open channel. The parameters ϕ and $\bar{R}_L$ were solved in terms of X and the solution presented in graphical form. But Johannessen [264] considered only the case of both phases flowing turbulently and ignored interfacial shear. Chen and Spedding [15] extended the Lockhart and Martinelli derivation for the case of separated flow.

Close agreement was registered with the results of the analysis of Johannessen [264] which, while not starting from the same basis, was similar in that the effects of interfacial shear were ignored.

Taitel and Dukler [23] followed closely the approach of Johannessen [264] but included the effects of interfacial shear and all possible flow regimes for the two phases. The result from their analysis showed excellent agreement with experimental data [48, 111, 262, 265], as shown in Figures 11 and 12, while the analyses of Johannessen [264] and Chen and Spedding [15] only predict accurately in the region of high values X above 0.08 where interfacial shear is negligible. However, the method of Chen and Spedding [15] is extremely simple to use and can be applied rapidly to any particular situation. It is interesting to note that the annular flow theory of Zivi [42] applies to the same region giving a result that is about 0.5% high.

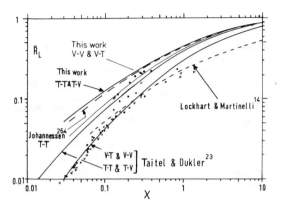

Figure 11. Hold-up relations as derived by Lockhart and Martinelli [14], Johannessen [264]. Taitel and Dukler [23] and Chen and Spedding [15] for stratified two-phase flow compared to data from various sources [48, 111, 262, 266].

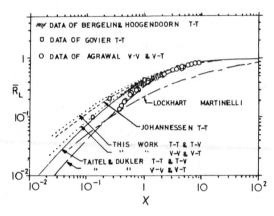

Figure 12. Comparison of the hold-up relations as derived by Lockhart and Martinelli [14], Johannessen [264], Taitel and Dukler [23], and Chen and Spedding [15], for stratified two-phase flow compared to data. [48, 111, 262, 265].

Droplet Flow

Strictly, this flow regime would follow the homogeneous model in a manner previously mentioned. However, Spedding and Chen [13] point out that with steadily increasing β the annular droplet regime develops into a flow condition where the hold-up remains constant over a considerable range of flow conditions. The annular film reduces asympotically to a constant value that remains until the film is ruptured and stripped from the conduit wall. There after the hold-up climbs rapidly to the homogeneous conditions. The constant hold-up regime is well illustrated in Figure 8, and its value can be calculated by the method given by Spedding and Chen [13]. In essence, it is assumed the film thickness on the inner wall of the conduit is 0.083 mm at $Q_G/Q_L = 15,000$ to approximately 85,000. Eventually, at $Q_G/Q_L = 140,000$ the flow is homogeneous.

TESTS OF MODELS USING EXPERIMENTAL DATA

Several attempts have been made to test independently the various theories and correlations that have been developed. Dukler [27, 124, 266] was perhaps the first to systematically attempt to use "discriminated" data for testing of hold-up correlations. Three models were checked, the Lockhart and Martinelli [14], Hoogendoorn [48] and that of Hughmark [11]. The latter was found to give the best result but in general, agreement with data was poor for all the correlations. In the test procedure the use of the error or root mean square error as the criterion is misleading

Table 2
Recommended Hold-Up Correlations

	Flow Regime	Hold-up Correlation	Average Deviation %	Range %
M [270]	Bubble-Plug	Hughmark [11]	1.8	+27 to −31
A	Stratified	Agrawal et al. [262]	26.8	+68 to −28
N	Stratified + wave	Chawla [38, 39]	30.2	+40 to −45
D	Slug	Hughmark [11]	4.4	+25 to −53
H	Annular	Lockhart-Martinelli [14]	−0.2	+50 to −86
A	Bubble	Beggs-Brill [268]	0.4	+14 to −7
N				
E				
F [163]	Single Component	Hughmark [11]	4.5	+60 to −20%
R	"	Rouhani I [271]	−4.8	+63 to −17%
I	"	Rouhani II [271]	−4.6	+61 to −22%
E	Two Component	Hughmark [11]	2.5	+64 to −49%
D	"	Rouhani I [271]	−5.2	+60 to −31%
E	"	Rouhani II [271]	4.1	+58 to −59%
L				

since positive and negative deviations cancel out. No matter which experimental method of hold-up measurement was used it was noted that the error became larger as $\bar{R}_L$ wne down in value.

Vohra et al. [267] used the data of Beggs [47] and Eaton [96] to compare the correlations of Beggs and Brill [268], Dukler [266], Eaton et al. [53], Guzhov et al. [269], Hughmark [11], and Lockhart and Martinelli [14]. Overall the Eaton [53] correlation proved to be best followed by that of Beggs and Brill [268]. Mandhane et al. [270] also compared these correlations plus those of Hoogendoorn [48], Chawla [38, 39], Scott [5] (and Hughmark [199]), Agrawal et al. [262] and Levy [28, 49]. Recommendations were as set out in Table 2, but again the use of percentage error gave no real idea of the spread of the actual error values. These latter are detailed in Table 2 where it can be seen that the only correlations that gave reasonable agreement are the Beggs and Brill [268] and the Hugmark [11] models.

Friedel [163] compared eighteen different correlations but only reported on three for the one component and two component conditions. Generally, the range of the predictions was better for the one component system but still it was unacceptably high.

Recommendations

Detailed checking of the various models has led to the following tentative conclusions:

1. There is no general correlation that consistently predicts the hold-up within a reasonable accuracy for all flow conditions.
2. Indeed, the recommended method of hold-up prediction is to use models developed for particular flow patterns. The expected flow patterns are detailed out in Figure 13.
3. Since it is not possible to test any model to a degree of accuracy greater than the experimental technique used to collect data, it should be assumed that in general ±10% is the best order of accuracy to be expected from any model.
4. For bubble, slug, and plug flow the Armand [2] relation of Equation 4 adequately predicts hold-up.

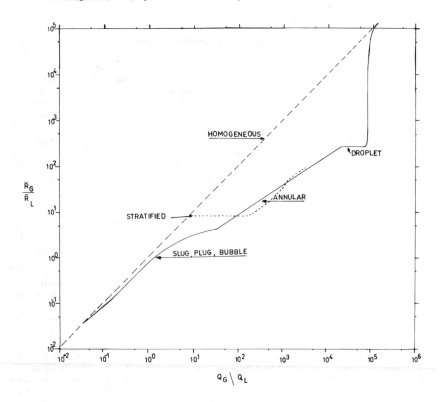

Figure 13. Hold-up regimes across the complete range of flows.

5. There is, however, a weak effect of pressure, β, Re, and Fr that is particularly noticeable with the single component system. As a result the order of accuracy of the model is $\pm 13\%$.
6. The stratified flow regime is predicted by the Taitel and Dukler [23] theory over the complete stratified flow regime.
7. However, the model is complex and requires iterative methods of calculation. A simpler model by Chen and Spedding [15] gives predictions when X > 0.08; that is when waves are not present on the liquid surface.
8. The Zivi [42] model of Equations 33–34 actually predicts the same conditions within $\pm 0.5\%$ despite it being developed for the annular flow regime.
9. The annular flow regime is best predicted by the Chen and Spedding [45] correlation of Equation 42.
10. Equation 42 does exhibit a weak liquid mass velocity effect but adequately describes both single and two component conditions for a wide range of pipe geometries.
11. The droplet flow regime often is associated with annular flow, but a situation does arise where basically the hold-up does not alter with β over a considerable range. The condition is best predicted by the method of Spedding and Chen [13].
12. For the flow conditions $G_T > 2, > 10\,\text{kg}\,\text{m}^{-2}\text{s}^{-1}$, $Q_T/Q_L > 140,000$ or $Q_G/Q_L < 10^{-2}$ the homogeneous model applies.
13. In general, the Zuber and Findlay [227] model or the more basic extension by Nguyen and Spedding [12] applies to the bubble, slug, and annular flow regimes.

APPENDIX

The study of two-phase gas-liquid metal flow has gained importance due to its use as a heat transfer media particularly in compact nuclear power systems for both terrestrial and space applications. There is a large difference in density ratio between the metallic system and the air-water and steam-water systems. This has raised the question whether the air-water correlations can be applied to the liquid metal system. It is known, for example, that if the liquid phase has a viscosity in excess of $0.02 \text{ kg m}^{-1} \text{s}^{-1}$, the liquid hold-up is increased for similar flow conditions in the non-metallic system. It would, therefore, not be unreasonable to expect a significant difference to exist between the metallic and air-water systems.

Indeed, Neal [196, 236] showed that the gas hold-up profiles in a two-phase Hg-N$_2$ system were substantially flatter than in the corresponding air-water system. Visual observation suggested that the reason was that mercury was non-wetting. Both Smith et al. [272] and various Russian workers [50] attempted to correlate hold-up for metallic systems using Fr as the parameter. However, Smith et al. [273] found that data for K/8% Na did not respond to the suggested method of correlation. Indeed, the metallic data gave $\bar{R}_L$ values that were some 200% higher than the corresponding values for the air-water system. Again, it was suggested that the difference may be due to differences in wettability.

Data for Na/K-N$_2$ and Hg-N$_2$ two-phase flow did not give good agreement with the correlation of Barozy [25, 26] even though metallic two-phase flow data were used in the development of the correlation [274]. Alad'yev et al. [3], on the other hand, reported that potassium two-phase flow data agreed with the Armand relation of Equation 4. Fauske [275] was in agreement with this observation.

Thus, it would appear that metallic two-phase flow hold-up data do not follow the models developed for the air-water system except perhaps in the case of the Armand relation of Equation 4.

Of course, it should be pointed out that the two-phase flow hold-up correlations will not hold when conditions are not steady, for example, in the case of a heated evaporating system. The Johnson and Abou-Sabe [276] data illustrates this point where $\bar{R}_L$ is shown to increase over the heated surface, i.e., as Q_G/Q_L rises.

NOTATION

a	constant, Equation 1	j	constant, Equation 32
A'	constant, Equation 12	K	constant, Equation 47
A	area, m^2	L	length of conduit, m
b	exponent, Equation 1	m	exponent, Equation 45
'b	exponent, Equation 21	n	exponent, Equation 46
C	constant, Equation 4	o	exponent, Equation 32
'C	constant, Equation 10	p	index, Equation 12
C$_1$, C$_2$	constants, Equation 50	P	pressure, kg m^{-1} s^{-2}
C$_0$	constant, Equation 53	'p	pressure, psia., Equation 40
d$_1$	constant, Equation 2	q	exponent, Equation 12
D	diameter, m	Q	volumetric flow rate, m^3 s^{-1}
D̄	hydraulic diameter, 4 times flow area over wetted parameter	r	exponent, Equation 12
		'r	local time average hold-up
e$_1$	factor, Equation 13	R̄	time average, volume average hold-up
E$_D$	fractional weight of liquid entrained as droplets	Re	Reynolds number
		u	exponent, Equation 32
f	friction factor	v	local velocity, m s^{-1}
Fr	Froude number, $\bar{V}^2/gD$	'v	fluctuation component of velocity, m s^{-1}
G	mass velocity, kg m^{-2} s^{-1}		
g	gravitational acceleration, m s^{-2}	V̄	average velocity, m s^{-1}
h	constant, Equation 9	W	mass flow rate, kg s^{-1}
i	exponent, Equation 32	w	exponent, Equation 32

x   dryness function, W_G/W_T
X   Lockhart-Martinelli parameter
$= \sqrt{(\Delta P/\Delta L)_{SL}/(\Delta P/\Delta L)_{SG}}$

y   distance from wall, m
z   exponent, Equation 23

Greek Symbols

β input volumetric ratio, Q_G/Q_T
γ factor, Equation 39
δ film thickness, m
θ angle of inclination, degrees
μ viscosity, $\text{kg m}^{-1}\,\text{s}^{-1}$
ε momentum exchange parameter, Equation 11

$\bar{\rho}$ average gas density, kg m^{-3}
ρ density, kg m^{-3}
$'\rho$ fluctuating component of density kg m^{-3}
σ surface tension, m s^{-2}
ϕ Lockhart-Martinelli factor, Equation 1

Subscripts

A	acceleration	m	maximum
D	drift	M	momentum
E	energy	P	pseudo
F	frictional	S	superficial
G	gas phase	T	total
H	hydrostatic	TP	two-phase
HO	homogeneous	3	all gas
L	liquid phase	4	all liquid
LO	all mass flux treated as if liquid	5	mixture

REFERENCES

1. Weisman, J., and Choe, W. G. "Methods for Calculation of Pressure Drop in Co-current Gas-Liquid flow." in *Two-Phase Transport and Reactor Safety*. Veziroglu. T. N. and Kakac, S (eds.) 1 193–224, Hemisphere, 1976.
2. Armand, A. A. "The Resistance during the Movement of a Two-Phase System in Horizontal Pipes." Izv. V.T.I. 1 16–23 (1946) also AERE Trans. 828 (1959).
3. Alad'yev, I. T., Gavrilova, N. D., and Dodonov, L. D. "Hydrodynamics of a Two-Phase Flow of Potassium in Tubes." ASME, Heat Transf. Soviet Research 1 (4) 1–13 (1969).
4. Nicklin, D. J., Wilkes, J. O., and Davidson, J. F. "Two-Phase Flow in Vertical Tubes." *Trans. Inst. Chem. Eng.* 40 61–68 (1962).
5. Scott, D. S. "Void Fractions in Horizontal Cocurrent Gas-Liquid Flow. Can. J. Chem. Eng 40 224–225 (1962).
6. Chen, J. J. J., and Spedding, P. L. "Correlation of Holdup in Two-Phase Flow." *ANZAAS* 49 (1) 16 (1979).
7. Chen, J. J. J. "Two-Phase Gas-Liquid Flow with Particular Emphasis on Hold-up Measurement and Predictions." Ph.D. dissertation, Univ. of Auckland (1979).
8. Brown, F. C., and Kranich, W. L. "A Model for the Prediction of Velocity and Void Fraction Profiles in Two-Phase Flow." *A.I.Ch.E.J.* 14 (5) 750–758 (1968).
9. Bankoff, S. G. "A Variable Density Single Fluid Model for Two-Phase Flow with Particular Reference to Steam-Water Flow." *J. Heat Trans.* 82C 265–272 (1960).
10. Zuber, N. "On the Variable Density Single-Fluid Model for Two-Phase Flow." TASME *J. Heat Trans.* 82C 255–258 (1960).
11. Hughmark, G. A. "Hold-up in Gas-Liquid Flow." *Chem. Eng. Prog.* 58 (4) 62–65 (1962).
12. Nguyen, V. T., and Spedding, P. L. "Hold-Up in Two-Phase, Gas-Liquid Flow. A. Theoretical Aspects. B. Experimental Results." *Chem. Eng. Sci.* 32 1003–1021. (1977).

13. Spedding, P. L., and Chen, J. J. J. "Hold-up in Inclined Tubes." *Int. J. Multiphase Flow.* 10 307–341 (1984).

14. Lockhart, R. W., and Martinelli, R. C. "Proposed Correlation of Data for Isothermal Two-Phase, Two-Component Flow in Pipes." *CEP* 45 (1) 39–48 (1949).

15. Chen, J. J. J., and Spedding, P. L. "An Extension of the Lockhart-Martinelli Theory of Two-Phase Pressure Drop and Hold-up." *Int. J. Multiphase Flow.* 7 (6) 659–675 (1981).

16. Hewitt, G. F., King, I., and Lovegrove, P. C. "Hold-up and Pressure Drop Measurements in the Two-Phase Annular Flow of Air-Water Mixtures." *British Chem. Eng.* 8 (5) 311–318 (1963). Also AERE-R 3764 (1961).

17. Spedding, P. L., Chen, J. J. J., and Nguyen, V. T. "Pressure Drop in Two-Phase Gas-Liquid Flow in Inclined Pipes. *Int. J. Multiphase Flow* 8 (4) 407–431 (1982).

18. Rosehart, R. G., Rhodes, E., and Scott, D. S. "Studies of Gas-Liquid (Non-Newtonian) Slug Flow: Void Fraction Meter, Void Fraction and Slug Characteristics." *Chem. Eng. J.* 10 57–64 (1975).

19. McMillan, H. K., Fontaine, W. E., and Chaddock, J. B. "Pressure Drop in Isothermal Two-Phase Flow—A Modification of the Lockhart-Martinelli Correlation." ASME 64-WA/FE-4 (1964).

20. Chenoweth, J. M., and Martin, M. W. "Turbulent Two-Phase Flow," *Pet. Ref.* 34 (10) 151–155 (1955).

21. Baker, O. "Simultaneous Flow of Oil and Gas." *Oil & Gas J.* 185–195 July 1954.

22. Gloyer, W. "A New Look at Two-Phase Flow." *Chem. Eng.* 75 (1) 93–95 (1968).

23. Taitel, Y., and Dukler, A. E. "A Theoretical Approach to the Lockhart-Martinelli Correlation for Stratified Flow." *Int. J. Multiphase Flow.* 2 591–595 (1976).

24. Styushin, N. G., and Dyorina, G. M. "Slip Effect and Flow Friction in an Adiabatic Vapor-Liquid Mixture Flowing in Tubes." *Int. J. Heat Mass Trans.* 9 1227–1232 (1966).

25. Baroczy, C. J. "Correlation of Liquid Fraction in Two-Phase Flow with Application to Liquid Metals" *A.I.Ch.E. Symp.* 61 (57) 179–191 (1965).

26. Baroczy, C. J. "A Systematic Correlation for Two-Phase Pressure Drop." *CEP Symp. Ser.* 62 (64) 232–249 (1966).

27. Dukler, A. E., Wicks, M., III, and Cleveland, R. L. "Frictional Pressure Drop in Two-Phase Flow: (A) A Comparison of Existing Correlations for Pressure Loss and Hold-Up." *A.I.Ch.E.J.* 10 (1) 38–43 (1964).

28. Levy, S. "Prediction of Two-Phase Pressure Drop and Density Distribution from Mixing Length Theory." *Trans. A.S.M.E. J. Heat Transfer* 85c 137–152 (1963).

29. Beattie, D. R. H. "Two-Phase Flow Structure and Mixing Length Theory." *Nucl. Eng. and Des.* 21 46–64 (1972).

30. Turner, J. M., and Wallis, G. B. "The Separate-Cylinder Model of Two-Phase Flow." Rept. NYO-3114-6 Thayer College Eng. Dartmouth College (1965).

31. Harrison, R. F. "Methods for the Analysis of Geothermal Two-Phase Flow." M. E. thesis Univ. Auckland. (1975).

32. Chisholm, D. "Note on Relationships Between Friction and Liquid Cross Sections During Two-Phase Flow." *J. Mech. Eng. Sci.* 8 (1) 107–109 (1966). Also NEL Rept. 232 (1966).

33. Chisholm, D., and Laird, A. D. K. "Two-Phase Flow in Rough Tubes." *Trans. A.S.M.E.* 80 276–286 (1958).

34. Chisholm, D. and Sutherland, L. A. "Prediction of Pressure Gradients in Pipeline Systems during Two-Phase Flow." *Proc. I. Mech. E.* 184 (3C) 24–32 (1969–70).

35. Chisholm, D. "A Theoretical Basis for the Lockhart-Martinelli Correlation for Two-Phase Flow." *Int. J. Heat Mass Transfer* 10 1767–1778 (1967).

36. Heywood, N. Y., and Richardson, J. F. "Slug Flow of Air-Water Mixtures in a Horizontal Pipe. Determination of Liquid Hold-up by X-ray Absorption." *Chem. Eng. Sci.* 34 17–30 (1979).

37. Chisholm, D. "Research Note: Void Fraction during Two-Phase Flow." *J. Mech. Eng. Sci.* 15 (3) 235–236 (1973).

38. Chawla, J. M. "Frictional Pressure Drop on the Flow of Liquid/Gas Mixtures in Horizontal Pipes." *For. Ing. Wes.* 34 (2) 47–54 (1968). Chem. Ing. Tech. 44 58–63 (1972).

39. Chawla, J. M. "Hold-up in Pipe for Liquid/Gas Mixtures in Two Phase Flow." *Chem. Ing Tech.* 41 (5/6) 328–330 (1969).

40. Hewitt, G. F., and Boure, J. A. "Some Recent Results and Development in Gas-Liquid Flow A Review." *Int. J. Multiphase Flow.* 1 139–171 (1973).

41. Butterworth, D. "A Comparison of Some Void-Fraction Relationships for Cocurrent Gas Liquid Flow." *Int. J. Multiphase Flow.* 1 845–850 (1975). Also AERE M2619 (1974).

42. Zivi, S. M. "Estimation of Steady State Steam Void Fraction by Means of the Principle c Mininum Entropy Production." *J. Heat Transfer.* 86C 247–252 (1964).

43. Thom, J. R. S. "Prediction of Pressure Drop During Forced Circulation Boiling of Water.' *Int. J. Heat Mass Transfer* 7 709–724 (1964).

44. Spedding, P. L., and Chen, J. J. J. "Correlation and Estimation of Hold-up in Two-Phase Flow." *N.Z. Geothermal Workshop* 1 (1) 180–199 (1979).

45. Chen, J. J. J., and Spedding, P. L. "An Analysis of Hold-up in Horizontal Two-Phase Gas Liquid Flow." *Int. J. Multiphase Flow* 9 (2) 147–159 (1983).

46. Smith, S. L. "Void Fractions in Two-Phase Flow. A Correlation Based Upon an Equal Ve locity Head Model." *Heat and Fluid Flow* 1 (1) 22–39 (1971).

47. Beggs, H. D. "An Experimental Study of Two-Phase Flow in Inclined Pipe." Ph.D. disserta tion, Univ. Tulsa (1972).

48. Hoogendoorn, C. J. "Gas-Liquid Flow in Horizontal Pipes." *Chem. Eng. Sci.* 9 205–21' (1959).

49. Levy, S. "Steam Slip-Theoretical Prediction from Momentum Model." *T. ASME* 82C 113–12 (1960).

50. Mamaev, V. "Some Problem in the Hydrodynamics of Joint Transport of Gas and Liquid.' *Int. Chem. Eng.* 5 (2) 318 (1965).

51. Greskovich, E. J., Shrier, A. L., and Bonnecaze, R. H. "True Gas Content for Horizontal Gas Liquid Flow." *IEC Fund* 8 (3) 591–593 (1969).

52. Greskovich, E. J., and Shrier, A. L. "Pressure Drop and Hold-Up in Horizontal Slug Flow." *A.I.Ch.E.J.* 17 (5) 1214–1219 (1971).

53. Eaton, B. A., Andrews, D. E. Knowles, C. R., Silberberg, I. H., and Brown, K. E. "The Pre diction of Flow Patterns, Liquid Hold-up and Pressure Losses Occurring during Continuous Two-phase Flow in Horizontal Pipelines." *J. Pet. Tech.* 19 (6) 815–828 (1967).

54. Ros, N. C. J. "Simultaneous Flow of Gas and Liquid as Encountered in Well Tubing." *J. Pet Tech.* 13 1037–1049 (1961).

55. Andrews, D. E., Knowles, C. R., Eaton, B. A., Silberberg, I. H., and Brown, K. E. "Prediction of Pressure Loss During Two-Phase Horizontal Flow in Two-Inch Pipe." *T.ASME* 89B 44–52 (1967).

56. Stepanek, J. B., and Kasturi, G. "Two-Phase Flow—Part II Parameters for Void Fraction and Pressure Drop Correlations." *Chem. Eng. Sci.* 27 1881–1891 (1972).

57. Alia, P. et al. "Liquid Volume Fraction in Adiabatic Two-Phase Vertical Upflow-Round Conduit." *CISE R* 105 (1965).

58. Anderson, G. H., and Mantzouranis, B. G. "Two-Phase (Gas Liquid) Flow Phenomena I Pres sure Drop and Hold-up for Two-Phase Flow in Vertical Tubes." *Chem. Eng. Sci.* 12 109–126 (1960).

59. Brown, R. A. S., Sullivan, G., and Govier, G. W. "The Upward Vertical Flow of Air-Water Mixtures III Effect of Gas Phase Density on Flow Pattern, Hold-Up and Pressure Drop.' *Can. J. Chem. Eng.* 62–66 (1960).

60. Friedel, L. "Mean Void Fraction and Friction Pressure Drop: Comparison of Some Correla tions with Experimental Data." European Two-Phase Flow Group Meeting, Paper A7 Grenoble, June (1977).

61. Gill, L. E., and Hewitt, G. F. "Further Data on the Upwards Annular Flow of Air-Water Mixtures." *AERE R* 3935 (1962).

62. Govier, G. W., Radford, B. A., and Dunn, J. S. C. "The Upward Vertical Flow of Air-Water Mixtures I. Effect of Air and Water Rates on Flow Pattern, Hold-up and Pressure Drop.' *Can. J. Chem. Eng.* 35 58–70 (1957).

3. Govier, G. W., and Short L. W. "The Upward Vertical Flow of Air-Water Mixtures II. Effect of Tubing Diameter on Flow Pattern, Holdup and Pressure Drop." *Can. J. Chem. Eng.* 34 195–202 (1956).

4. Hagedorn, A. R., and Brown, K. E. "Experimental Study of Pressure Gradients Occurring During Continuous Two-Phase Flow in Small Diameter Vertical Conduits." *J. Pet. Tech.*, 17, 475–484 (1965).

5. Hagedorn, A. R., and Brown, K. E. "The Effect of Liquid Viscosity in Two-Phase Vertical Flow." *J. Pet. Tech.* 16 203–210 (1964).

6. Hsu, Y. C., and Dudukovic, M. P. "Gas Hold-up and Liquid Recirculation in Gas-Lift Reactors." *Chem. Eng. Sci.* 35 135–141 (1980).

7. Hughmark, G. A., and Pressburg, B. S. "Hold-up and Pressure Drop with Gas-Liquid Flow in a Vertical Pipe." *A.I.Ch.E.J.* 7 (4) 677–682 (1961).

8. Keeys, R. K. F., Ralph, J. C., and Roberts, D. N. "Liquid Entrainment in Adiabatic Steam-Water Flow at 500 and 1,000 p.s.i.a. (3.447 and 6.894 × 10^6 N m^{-2}). *AERE R6293* (1970).

9. Michiyoshi, I., Shirataki, K., and Takitani, K. "The Steam Volume Fraction in Two-Phase Flow." *Int. Chem. Eng.* 7 (1) 159–167 (1967).

0. Moore, T. V., and Wilde, H. D. "Experimental Measurement of Slippage in Flow Through Vertical Pipes." *T.AIME* Pet. Division 92 296–313 (1931).

1. Neusen, K. F. "Void Fractions in a Developing Two-Phase Flow System with Flowing and Non-Flowing Liquid Phase." ASME-A.I.Ch.E. Heat Transfer Conference, Los Angeles Aug. (1965).

2. Oshinowo, T., and Charles M. E. "Vertical Two-Phase Flow Part II Hold-up and Pressure Drop." *Can. J. Chem. Eng.* 52 438–448 (1974).

3. Premoli, A. et al. "An Empirical Correlation for Evaluating Two-Phase Mixture Density Under Adiabatic Conditions." European Two-Phase Flow Group Meeting, Milano (1970).

4. Rose, S. C., and Griffith, P. "Flow Properties of Bubbly Mixture." ASME-AIChE Heat Transfer Conf., Los Angeles Aug. (1965).

5. Tomida, T., Yamamoto, T., Takebayashi, T., and Okazaki, T. "Correlation of Data on the Apparent Friction Coefficient in Upward Two-Phase Flow of Air-Liquid Mixtures." *J. Chem. Eng. Japan* 8 (2) 113–118 (1975).

6. Ueda, T. "Studies on the Flow of Air-Water Mixtures—The Upward Flow in a Vertical Tubes." *Bull J.S.M.E.* 1 (2) 139–145 (1958).

7. Ueda, T. "On Upward Flow of Gas-Liquid Mixtures in Vertical Tubes." *Bull JSME* 10 (42) 989–1015 (1967).

8. Quandt, E. R. "Measurement of Some Basic Parameters in Two-Phase Annular Flow." *A.I.Ch.E.J.* 11 (2) 311–318 (1965).

9. Bergelin, O. P., Carpenter, F. G., Kegel, P. K., and Gazley, C. "*Heat Trans. Fluid Mech. Inst.*" 19 (1949).

0. Webb, D. R. and Hewitt, G. F. "Downwards Co-current Annular Flow," *Int. J. Multiphase Flow*, 2, 35–49 (1975).

1. Greskovich, E. J. "Hold-up Predictions for Stratified Down Flow of Gas-Liquid Mixtures." *I.E.C. Proc. Des. Dev.* 11 (1) 81–85 (1972).

2. Lorenzi, A., and Sotgia, G. "Downward Two-Phase Flow Experimental Investigation" *Eng. Nucl.* 23 (7) 396–401 (1976).

3. Nencetti, G. F., Zanelli, S., and Bitossi Coronedi, G. "Two-Phase Co-Current Downward Flow in a Vertical Tubes. Experimental Apparatus and Methods of Measuring Head Loss, Hold-up, the Liquid Entrainment and Liquid Film Thickness on the Walls. Calore (12) 621–629 (1968).

4. Bonnecaze, R. H., Erskine, W., and Greskovich, E. J. "Hold-up and Pressure Drop for Two-Phase Slug Flow in Inclined Pipelines. *A.I.Ch.E.J.* 17 (5) 1109–1113 (1971).

5. Greskovich, E. J. "Prediction of Gas-Liquid Hold-up for Inclined Flows." *A.I.Ch.E.J.* 19 1060 (1973).

6. Greskovich, E. J., and Cooper, W. T. "Correlation and Prediction of Gas-Liquid Hold-ups in Inclined Up Flows." *A.I.Ch.E.J.* 21 (6) 1189–1192 (1975).

87. Singh, G., and Griffith, P. "Determination of the Pressure Drop Optimum Pipe Size for Two-Phase Slug Flow in an Inclined Pipe." TASME-*J. Eng. Ind.* 92, 717–725 (1970).
88. Gregory, G. A. "Comments on the Prediction of Liquid Hold-up for Gas-Liquid Flow i Inclined Pipes." *Can. J. Chem. Eng.* 52 463 (1974).
89. Banerjee, S., Rhodes, E., and Scott, D. S. "Studies on Cocurrent Gas-Liquid Flow in Helicall Coiled Tubes. I. Flow Patterns, Pressure Drop and Hold-Up." *Can. J. Chem. Eng.* 47 445–45 (1969).
90. Rippel, G. R., Eidt, C. M., and Jordan, H. B. "Two-Phase Flow in a Coiled Tube." *IE(Process Design and Devel.* 5 (1) 32–39 (1966).
91. Unal, H. C. "Determination of Void Fraction, Incipient Point of Boiling, and Initial Point c Net Vapor Generation in Sodium-Heated Helically Coiled Steam Generator Tubes." *Tran ASME* 100 268–274 (1978).
92. Collier, J. G. "Pressure Drop Data for the Forced Convective Flow of Steam/Water Mixture in Vertical Heated and Unheated Annuli." *AERE R* 3808 (1962).
93. Beattie, D. R. H. "Two-Phase Pressure Loss and Void Fraction Characteristics in Rod Bundl Geometries." *IAHR Congress* 18 Cagliari, Italy Sept. (1979).
94. Beattie, D. R. H., "Two-Phase Pressure Losses—low Regime Effects and Associated Phenom ena." AAEC/TM589 May (1971).
95. Solbrig, C. W., McFadden, J. R. I., Lyczkowski, R. W., and Hughes, E. D. "Heat Transfer an Friction Correlation Required to Describe Steam-Water Behavior in Nuclear Safety Studies. *A.I.Ch.E. Symp. Ser.* 74 (174) 100–128 (1978).
96. Eaton, B. A. "The Prediction of Flow Patterns, Liquid Hold-up, and Pressure Losses." Ph.C dissertation Univ. Texas (1966).
97. Beattie, D. R. H. "A note on the Calculation of Two-Phase Pressure Losses." *Nucl. Eng. an Des.* 25 395–402 (1973).
98. Nevstrueva, E. I., and Tyutyaev, V. V. "Inter-relationship Among Two-Phase Pressure Dror Steam Void Fraction and Flow Patterns." *Int. Sem. Future Energy Prod. and Heat Transfe Problems.* Dubrovnik 225–232 Aug. 25–30 (1975).
99. Silvestri, M. "Fluid Mechanics and Heat Transfer of Two-Phase Annular Dispersed Flow. *Adv. Heat Trans.* 1 355–455 (1964).
100. Butterworth, D., and Hewitt, G. F. *Two-Phase Flow and Heat Transfer.* Oxford (1977).
101. Ginoux, J. J. (ed.) *Two-Phase Flow and Heat Transfer with Application to Nuclear Reactc Design Problems.* Hemisphere (1978).
102. Lombardi, C., and Pedrochi, E. "A Pressure Drop Correlation in Two-Phase Flow." *Eng. Nuc* 19 (2) 91–99 (1972).
103. Wallis, G. B. *One-Dimensional Two-Phase Flow.* McGraw-Hill (1968).
104. McManus, H. N. "Local Liquid Distribution and Pressure Drop in Annular Two-Phase Flow. *ASME* 61-HYD-20 (1961).
105. Hewitt, G. F., King, I., and Lovegrove, P. C. "Techniques for Liquid Film and Pressure Dro, Studies in Annular Two-Phase Flow." *CEP* 60 191–200 (1964).
106. Magiros, P. G., and Dukler, A. E. "Entrainment and Pressure Drop in Concurrent Gas-Liqui(Flow II Liquid Properties and Momentum Effects." *Dev. in Mech.* 1 532–553 (1961).
107. Andeen, G. B., and Griffith, P. "Momentum Flux in Two-Phase Flow." *TASME J. Hea Transfer,* 90C, 211–222 (1968).
108. Baumeister, K. J., Graham, R. W., and Henry, R. E. "Momentum Flux in Two-Phase Two Component Low Quality Flow." *CEP Symp.,* 69 (131) 46–54 (1973).
109. Idsinga, W., Todreas, N., and Brwring, R. "An Assessment of Two-Phase Pressure Drop Cor relation for Steam-Water Systems." *Int. J. Multiphase Flow* 3 401–413 (1977).
110. Shilimkan, R V., and Stepanek, J. B., "Interfacial Area in Co-current Gas Liquid Upward Flov in Tubes of Various Size." *Chem. Eng. Sci.* 32 149–154 (1977).
111. Govier, G. W., and Omer, M. M. "The Horizontal Pipeline Flow of Air-Water Mixtures." *Can. J. Chem. Eng.* 40 93–104 (1962).
112. Poettmann, F. H., and Carpenter, P. G. "The Multiphase Flow of Gas, Oil and Water throug! Vertical Flow Strings with Application to Design of Gas Lift Installations." *Drill and Proc Pract.* API N257 (1952).

13. Bertuzzi, A. F., Tek, M. R., and Poettmann, F. H., "Simultaneous Flow of Liquid and Gas through Horizontal Pipe." *Pet. Div.* TAIME 207 17–24 (1956).
14. Fancher, G. H., and Brown, K. E. "Production of Pressure Gradients for Multiphase Flow in Tubings." *Soc. Pet. Eng. J.* 59–69 (1963).
15. Owens, W. L. "Two-Phase Pressure Gradient." *Int. Dev. Heat Transfer Inst. Mech. Eng.* 2 Paper 41 361–368 (1961).
16. Shiba, M., and Yamazaki, Y. "A Comparative Study on the Pressure Drop of Air-Water Flow." *Bull. J.S.M.E.* 10 (38) 290–298 (1967).
17. Cicchetti, A., Lombard, C., Silvestri, M., Soldaini, G., and Zavattarell, R. "Two-Phase Cooling Experiments-Pressure Drop, Heat Transfer and Burnout Measurements." *Eng. Nucl.* 7 407–425 (1960).
18. McAdams, W. H., Woods, W. K., and Heroman, L. C. "Vaporization Inside Horizontal Tubes—II Benzene-Oil Mixtures." *Trans. ASME* 64, 193–200 (1942).
19. Von Glahn, V. H. "An Empirical Relation for Predicting Void Fraction with Two-Phase, Steam-Water Flow." NASA TND 1189 (1962).
20. Larson, H. C. "Void Fractions of Two-Phase Steam Water Mixture." M.S. thesis, Univ. of Minnesota (1957).
21. Isbin, H. S., Rodriguez, H. A., Larson, H. C., and Pattie, B. D. "Void Fractions in Two-Phase Flow." *A.I.Ch.E.J.* 5 (4) 427–432 (1959).
22. Isbin, H. S., Sher, N. C., and Eddy, K. C. "Void Fractions in Two-Phase Steam-Water Flow." *A.I.Ch.E.J.* 3 (1) 136–142 (1957).
23. Friedel, L. "Momentum Exchange and Pressure Drop in Two-Phase Flow." NATO Adv. Study Inst. Two-Phase Flow and Heat Transfer. Istanbul 16–27 Aug. (1976).
24. Dukler, A. E., Baker, O., Cleveland, R. L., Hubbard, M. G., and Wicks, M., III. "Gas-Liquid Flow in Pipe Lines-Part I. Research Results." NX-28 Univ. Houston (1969).
25. Gould, T. L. "Vertical Two-Phase Steam-Water Flow in Geothermal Wells." *J. Pet. Tech.* 26 833–842 (1974).
26. Husain, A., Choe, W. G., and Weisman, S. "Applicability of the Homogeneous Flow Model to Two-Phase Pressure Drop in Straight Pipe and Across Area Changes." *A.I.Ch.E. Sym. Ser.* 74 (174) 205–214 (1978).
27. Hewitt, G. F., and Roberts, D. N. "Investigation of Interfacial Phenomena in Annular Two-Phase Flow by Means of the Axial View Technique." *AERE*-R6070 (1969).
28. Levy, S. "Theory of Pressure Drop and Heat Transfer for Annular Steady-State Two-Phase Two Component Flow in Pipes." *Proc. Mid-Western Conf. Fluid Mech.* 2 337–348 (1952).
29. McManus, H. N. "An Experimental Investigation of Film Establishment, Film Profile Dimensions, Pressure Drop, and Surface Conditions in Two-Phase Annular Flow." Ph.D. dissertation Univ. Minnesota (1956).
30. McManus, H. N. "An Experimental Investigation of Film Characteristics in Horizontal Annular Two-Phase Flow." *ASME* 57-A-144.
31. McManus, H. N. "Film Characteristics and Dimensions in Annular Two-Phase Flow." Mid-Western Conf. *Fluid Mech.* 6 292–302 (1957).
32. Butterworth, D. "Air-Water, Annular Flow in a Horizontal Tube." *Prog. Heat Mass Transfer* 6 235–251 (1972).
33. Allen, M. D. "Geothermal Two-Phase Flow. A Study of the Annular Dispersed Flow Regime." Ph.D. dissertation, Univ. Auckland (1977).
34. Anderson, R. J., and Russell, T. W. F., "Circumferencial Variation of Interchange in Horizontal Annular Two-Phase Flow." *IEC Fund.* 9 (3) 340–344 (1970).
35. Anderson, R. J., and Russell, T. W. F., "Film Formation in Two-Phase Annular Flow." *A.I.Ch.E.J.* 16 (4) 626–633 (1970).
36. Jacowitz, L. A., and Brodkey, R. S. "An Analysis of Geometry and Pressure Drop for the Horizontal, Annular, Two-Phase Flow of Water and Air in the Entrance Region of a Pipe." *Chem. Eng. Sci.* 19 261–274 (1964).
37. Russell, T. W. F., and Lamb, D. E. "Flow Mechanism of Two-Phase Annular Flow." *Can. J. Chem. Eng.* 43 (5) 237–245 (1965).

138. Hewitt, G. F. "Disturbance Waves in Annular Two-Phase Flow." *Proc. Inst. Mech. Eng.* 18 (C) 142–150 (1969/1970).
139. Lee, D. H., and Bryce, W. M. "European Two-Phase Flow RDD Group Meeting," Grenobl June (1977). RDD Note 305 (HTFS25276).
140. Ganic, E. N., and Rohesnow, W. M. "On the Mechanism of Liquid Drop Deposition in Two Phase Flow." *ASME* 76-WA/HT-18 (1976).
141. Ovchinniko, Y. U., and Khoze, A. N. "Heat and Mass Transfer in Two Component Two-Phas Flow Inside Cylinders." *Heat Trans. Sov. Res.* 2 (6) 130–135 (1970).
142. Farmer, R., Griffith, P., and Rohsenow, W. M. "Liquid Droplet Deposition in Two-Phas Flow." *TASME J. Heat Transfer*, 587–594 (1970).
143. Paul, H. I., and Sleicher, C. A. "Maximum Stable Drop Size in Turbulent Flow. Effect of Pip Diameter." *Chem. Eng. Sci.* 20 57–59 (1965).
144. Moeck, E. O., and Stachiewicz, J. W. "A Droplet Interchange Model for Annular Disperse Two-Phase Flow." *Int. J. Heat Mass Transfer* 15 637–653 (1972).
145. Alexander, L. G., and Coldren, C. L. "Droplet Transfer from Suspending Air to Duct Walls. *IEC* 43 (6) 1325–1331 (1951).
146. Cousins, L. B., and Hewitt, G. F. "Liquid Phase Mass Transfer in Annular Two-Phase Flow Droplet Deposition and Liquid Entrainment." *AERE* R-5657 (1968).
147. McCoy, D. D., and Hanratty, T. J. "Rate of Deposition of Droplets in Annular Two-Phas Flow." *Int. J. Multiphase Flow* 3 319–331 (1977).
148. Longwell, J. P., and Weiss, M. A. "Mixing and Distribution of Liquids in High Velocity Ai Streams." *IEC* 45 (3) 667–677 (1953).
149. James, P. W., and Hutchinson, P. "Droplet Deposition in an Annular Geometry." *AERE* R9008 (1978).
150. Hewitt, G. F., and Hutchinson, P. "A Mathematical Model of Two-Phase Annular Flow." A Union Conf. Heat Mass Transfer 5 May 1976 Paper 3.79 (HTFS 22524).
151. Ishii, M., and Grolmes, M. A. "Inception Criteria for Droplet Entrainment in Two-Phas Concurrent Film Flow." *A.I.Ch.E.J.* 21 (2) 308–318 (1975).
152. Abramson, A. E. "Investigation of Annular Liquid Flow with Co-current Air Flow in Hori zontal Tubes." *J. Appl. Mech.* 19 267–274 (1952).
153. Kinney, G. R., Abramson, A. E., and Sloop, J. L. "Internal Liquid Film Cooling Experiment with Air-Steam Temperatures to 2,000°F in 2- and 4-Inch Diameter Horizontal Tubes." *NACA* 1087 (1952).
154. Hughmark, G. A. "Film Thicknesss, Entrainment, and Pressure Drop in Upward Annula and Dispersed Flow." *A.I.Ch.E.J.* 19 (5) 1062–1065 (1973).
155. Tatterson, D. F., Dallman, J. D. and Hanratty, T. J. "Drop Sizes in Annular Gas-Liqui Flows." *A.I.Ch.E.J.* 23 (1) 68–76 (1977).
156. Troung, Q. M., and Huyghe, J. D. "Some Hydrodynamical Aspects of Annular Disperse Flow. Entrainment and Film Thickness." Symp. Two-Phase Flow, Univ. Exeter 1 C201–C21 June (1965).
157. Wicks, M., and Dukler, A. E. "Entrainment and Pressure Drop in Concurrent Gas-Liquic Flow: (I) Air-Water in Horizontal Flow." *A.I.Ch.E.J.* 6 (3) 463–468 (1960).
158. Collier, J. G., and Hewitt, G. F. "Data on the Vertical Flow of Air-Water Mixtures in the Annular and Dispersed Flow Regimes P + II." *Trans. Int. Chem. Eng.* 39 127–144 (1961).
159. Nishino, H., and Yamazaki, Y. *J. Soc. Atom. Energy Japan* 5 (1) 39 (1963).
160. Fujie, H. "A Relation Between Steam Quality and Void Fraction in Two-Phase Flow." *A.I.Ch.E.J.* 10 (2) 227–232 (1964).
161. Cravarolo, L., and Hassid, A. "Liquid Volume Fraction in Two-Phase Adiabatic Systems." *Energia Nucleare* 12 (11) 569–577 (1965).
162. Madsen, N. "A Void-Fraction Correlation for Vertical and Horizontal Bulk-Boiling of Water." *A.I.Ch.E.J.* 21 (3) 607–8 (1975).
163. Friedel, L. "Pressure Drop During Gas/Vapour-Liquid Flow in Pipes." *Chem. Ing. Tech.* 50 (3) 167–180 (1978).
164. Levy, S. "Prediction of Two-Phase Annular Flow with Liquid Entrainment." *Int. J. Heat Mass Transfer* 9 171–188 (1966).

165. Wallis, G. B. "Annular Two-Phase Flow: Pt. I, A Simple Theory; Pt. II, Additional Effects." *T.ASME J. Basic Eng.* 59–72, 73–81 (1970).

166. Udea, T., and Tanaka, T. "Studies of the Liquid Flow in Two-Phase Annular and Annular-Mist Flow Regions Part I, Down Flow in a Vertical Tube." *Bull. J.S.M.E.* 17 (107) 603–613 (1974).

167. Sekoguchi, K., Hori, K., Nakazatomi, M., and Nishikawa, K. "On Ripples of Annular Two-Phase Flow II Characteristics of Wave and Interfacial Friction Factor." *Bull. J.S.M.E.* 21 (152) 279–286 (1978).

168. Dukler, A. E. "Hydrodynamics of Liquid Films in Single and Two-Phase Flow." Ph.D. dissertation, Univ. of Delaware (1951).

169. Chien, S. F., and Ibele, W. "Pressure Drop and Liquid Film Thickness of Two-Phase Annular and Annular-Mist Flows." *T.ASME J. Heat Transfer*, 89–96 (1964).

170. Shearer, C. J., and Nedderman, R. M. "Pressure Gradient and Liquid Film Thickness in Co-current Upward Flow of Gas/Liquid Mixtures. Application to Film Cooler Design." *Chem. Eng. Sci.* 20 671–683 (1965).

171. Wrobel, J. R., and McManus, H. N. "An Analytical Study of Film Depth, Wave Height and Pressure Drop in Annular Two-Phase Flow." *Devel. in Mech.* 1 578–587 (1961).

172. Gill, L. E., Hewitt, G. F., and Lacey, P. M. C. "Sampling Probe Studies of the Gas Core in Annular Two-Phase Flow II Studies of the Effect of Phase Flow Rates on Phase Velocity Distribution." *Chem. Eng. Sci.* 19 665–682 (1964).

173. Willis, I. J. "Upward Annular Two-Phase Air/Water Flow in Vertical Tubes." *Chem. Eng. Sci.* 20 895–902 (1965).

174. Hikita, H., Ishimi, K., and Ikeki, H. " Frictional Pressure Drop for Turbulent Gas Steams in Wetted Wall Columns with Co-Current and Counter-Current Gas-Liquid Flow." *J. Chem. Eng. Japan* 10 (5) 375–379 (1977).

175. Sekoguchi, K., Hori, K. and Nakazatomi, M. et al. "On Ripples of Annular Two-Phase Flow. I Statistical Characteristics of Ripples." *Bull. J.S.M.E.* 20 (145) 844–851 (1977).

176. Chien, S. F., and Ibele, W. "A Literary Survey: The Hydrodynamic Stability of the Liquid Film in Falling Film Flow in Vertical Annular Two-Phase Flow." *Int. J. Mech. Sci.* 9 547–557 (1967).

177. Fulford, G. D. "The Flow of Liquids in Thin Films." *Adv. Chem. Eng.* 6 151–236 (1964).

178. Dukler, A. E. "Fluid Mechanics and Heat Transfer in Vertical Falling-Film Systems." *CEP Symp. Ser.* 56 (30) 1–10 (1959).

179. Hewitt, G. F. "Analysis of Annular Two-Phase Flow: Application of the Dukler Analysis to Vertical Upflow in a Tube." *AERE* R3680 (1961).

180. Pogson, J. T. Roberts, J. H., and Waibler, P. J. "An Investigation of the Liquid Distribution in Annular-Mist Flow." *J. Heat Transfer* 92C 651–658 (1970).

181. Kosky, P. G. "Thin Liquid Films Under Simultaneous Shear and Gravity Forces." *Int. J. Heat Mass Transfer* 14 1220–1224 (1971).

182. Van Rossum, J. J. "Experimental Investigation of Horizontal Liquid Films, Wave Formation, Atomization, Film Thickness." *Chem. Eng. Sci.* 11 35–52 (1959).

183. Traviss, D. P., Baron, A. B., and Rohsenow, W. M. "Forced-Convection Condensation Inside Tubes." Rept. DSR 72591–74 MIT Heat Transfer Lab. (1971).

184. Butterworth, D. "An Analysis of Film Flow and its Application to Condensation in a Horizontal Tube." *Int. J. Multiphase Flow* 1 671–682 (1974).

185. Henstock, W. H., and Hanratty, T. J. "The Interfacial Drag and the Height of the Wall Layer in Annular Flows." *A.I.Ch.E.J.* 22 (6) 990–1000 (1976).

186. Anderson, G. H., and Mantzouranis, B. G. "Two-Phase (Gas/Liquid) Flow Phenomena. II Liquid Entrainment." *Chem. Eng. Sci.* 12 (4) 233–242 (1960).

187. Kunz, H. R., and Yerazunis, S. "An Analysis of Film Condensation, Film Evaporation and Single-Phase Heat Transfer for Liquid Prandtl Numbers from 10^{-3} to 10^4." *T. ASME J. Heat Transfer* 91C 413–420 (1969).

188. Biasi, L., Clerici, G. C., Sala, R., and Tozzi, A. "A Theoretical Approach to the Analysis of an Adiabatic Two-Phase Annular Dispersed Flow." *Eng. Nucl.* 15 (6) 384–405 (1968).

189. Ghosal, S. K. "Estimation of Frictional Loss in Gas-Liquid Two-Phase Flows: An Analysis Approach." *Indian Chem. Eng.* 16 T87–T89 (1974).
190. Behringer, H. "The Flow of Liquid-Gas Mixtures in Vertical Tubes." *Zeit. Ges. Kalte-Ind.* 43 55–70 (1936).
191. Griffith, P., and Wallis, G. B. "Two-Phase Slug Flow." *J. Heat Transfer* 83C 307–320 (1961).
192. Nicklin, D. J. "Two-Phase Bubble Flow." *Chem. Eng. Sci.* 17 693 (1962).
193. Moissis, R., and Griffith, P. "Entrance Effects in a Two-Phase Slug Flow." T.ASME *J. Heat Transfer.* 84C 29–39 (1962).
194. Griffith, P. "The Prediction of Low-Quality Boiling Voids." *J. Heat Trans.* 86C 327–333 (1964).
195. Brown, R. A. S., and Govier, G. W. "The Mechanics of Large Gas Bubbles in Tubes II. The Prediction of Voidage in Vertical Gas-Liquid Flow." *Can. J. Chem. Eng.* 43 217–230 (1965).
196. Neal, L. G. "An Analysis of Slip in Gas-Liquid Flow Applicable to the Bubble and Slug Flow Regimes." KR-62 Norway (1963).
197. Gomezplata, A., Munson, R. E., and Price, J. D. "Correlation of Two-Phase Void Fraction Data." *Can. J. Chem. Eng.* 50 (10) 669–671 (1972).
198. Martin, C. S. "Characteristics of an Air-Water Mixture in a Vertical Shaft." Hyd. Eng. & Env. *Proc. Hyd. Div. Spec. Cong.,* Bozeman, Montana. Aug. 15–17 (1973).
199. Hughmark, G. A. "Holdup and Heat Transfer in Horizontal Slug Gas Liquid Flow." *Chem. Eng. Sci.* 20 1007–1010 (1965).
200. Hubbard, M. G. "An Analysis of Horizontal Gas-Liquid Slug Flow." Ph.D. thesis Univ. Houston (1965).
201. Dukler, A. E., and Hubbard, M. G. "A Model for Gas-Liquid Slug Flow in Horizontal and Near Horizontal Tubes." *IEC Fund.* 14 (4) 337–347 (1975).
202. Nicholson, M. K., Aziz, K., and Gregory, G. A. "Intermittent Two-Phase Flow in Horizontal Pipes-Productive Model." *Can. J. Chem. Eng.* 56 653–663 (1978).
203. Suo, M., and Griffith, P. "Two-Phase Flow in Capillary Tubes". *J. Basic Eng.* 86D 576–582 (1964).
204. Gregory, G. A., and Scott, D. S. "Correlation of Liquid Slug Velocity and Frequency in Horizontal Co-current Gas-Liquid Slug Flow." *A.I.Ch.E.J.* 15 (6) 933–935 (1969).
205. Greskovick, E. J., and Shrier, A. L. "Slug Frequency in Horizontal Gas-Liquid Slug Flow." *IEC Process Des. Dev.* 11 (2) 317–318 (1972).
206. Rosehart, R. G., Scott, D. S. and Rhodes, E. "Gas-Liquid Slug Flow with Drag-Reducing Polymer Solutions." *A.I.Ch.E.J.* 18 (4) 744–750 (1972).
207. Otten, L., and Fayed, A. S. "Pressure Drop and Drag Reduction in Two-Phase Non-Newtonian Slug Flow." *Can. J. Chem. Eng.* 54 111–114 (1976).
208. Taitel, Y., and Dukler, A. E. "A Model for Slug Frequency During Gas-Liquid Flow in Horizontal and Near-Horizontal Pipes." *Int. J. Multiphase Flow* 3 585–596 (1977).
209. Kobhyashi, K., Yoshihiro, I., and Naomichi, K. "Distribution of Local Void Fraction of Air-Water Two-Phase Flow in a Vertical Channel." *Bull J.S.M.E.* 13 (62) 1005–1012 (1970).
210. Sakaguchi, T., Akagawa, K., Hamaguchi, H., Arima, H., and Takaoka, T. "Water-Air Two-Phase Flow in Horizontal Tubes." *Int. Ass. Hyd. Res.* 17 387–394 (1977).
211. Gregory, G. A., Nicholson, M. K., and Aziz, K. "Correlation of the Liquid Volume Fraction in the Slug for Horizontal Gas Liquid Slug Flow." *Int. J. Multiphase Flow* 4 33–39 (1978).
212. Kordyban, E. S. "A Flow Model for Two-Phase Slug Flow in Horizontal Pipes." *J. Basic Eng.* 83D 613–618 (1961)
213. Kordyban, E. S., and Ranov, T. "Experimental Study of the Mechanism of Two-Phase Slug Flow in Horizontal Tubes." Multiphase Flow Symp. ASME Philadelphia Nov. 17–22 p. 1–6 (1963).
214. Vermeulen, L. R., and Ryan, J. T. "Two-Phase Slug Flow in Horizontal and Inclined Tubes." *Can. J. Chem. Eng.* 49 195–201 (1971).
215. Chen, J. J. J., and Spedding, P. L. "Hold-Up in Horizontal Gas-Liquid Flow." Multiphase Flow Heat Transfer Symp.-Workshop Florida (1983).
216. Carstensen, E. L., and Foldy, L. L. "Propagation of Sound Through a Liquid Containing Bubbles." *J. Acoust. Soc. Am.* 19 (3) 481–501 (1947).

217. McWilliam, D., and Duggins, R. K. "Speed of Sound in Bubbly Liquids". *Proc. I. Med. Eng.* 184 Pt 3C 102–107 (1969/1970.)
218. Radovskii, I. S., and Droban, N. V. "Velocity and Damping Decrement of Sound in a Stream Mixture of Bubble Structure." *High Temp.* 16 (2) 239–243 (1978).
219. Van Wijngaarden, K. "One-Dimensional Flow of Liquids Containing Small Gas Bubbles." *Ann. Rev. Fluid Mech.* 4 369–396 (1972).
220. Sakao, F., and Sueda, Y. "Measurement of Effective Viscosity of Two-Phase (gas-liquid) Fluid in a Laminar Pipe Flow I." *Fac. Eng. Memoir*, Hiroshima Univ. 5 (2) 45–58 (1974).
221. Weinig, F. S., "Some Properties of Foam and the Possible Use of Foam for Model Test Especially in Hypersonic Range." *Proc. Mid-West Conf. Fluid Mech.* 3 515–527 (1953).
222. Kopalinsky, E. M., and Bryant, R. A. A. "Friction Coefficients for Bubbly Two-Phase Flow in Horizontal Pipes." *A.I.Ch.E.J.* 22 (1) 82–86 (1976).
223. Serizawa, A., Kataoka, I., and Michiyoshi, I. "Turbulent Structure of Air-Water Bubbly Flow-I. Measuring Techniques." *Int. J. Multiphase Flow* 2 235–246 (1975).
224. Brown, R. W., Gomezplata, A. S., and Price, J. D. "A Model to Predict Void Fraction in Two-Phase Flow." *Chem. Eng. Sci.* 24 1483–1489 (1969)
225. Petrick, M., and Kudirka, A. A. "On the Relationship Between the Phase Distributions and Relative Velocities in Two-Phase Flow." *Proc. Int. Heat Trans. Conf.* 3 (4) 184–192 (1966).
226. Stepanek, J. B., "A Model to Predict Void-Fraction in Two-Phase Flow." *Chem. Eng. Sci.* 25 751–752 (1970).
227. Zuber, N., and Findlay, J. A. "Average Volumetric Concentration in Two-Phase Flow Systems." *J. Heat Trans.* 87C 453–468 (1965).
228. Holmes, T. L., and Russell, T. W. F. "Horizontal Bubble Flow." *Int. J. Multiphase Flow.* 2 51–66 (1975).
229. Arosio, S., Bartoloni, R., Lorenzi, A., and Sotgia, G. "Two-Phase Downward Flow in Large Diameter Ducts—Preliminary Results." *Eng. Nucl.* 23 (4) 224–232 (1976).
230. Herringe, R. A., and Davis, M. R. "Flow Structure and Distribution Effects in Gas-Liquid Mixture Flows." *Int. J. Multiphase Flow* 4 461–486 (1978).
231. Hinata, S., Kuga, O., and Kobayashi, K. "Diffusion of Bubbles in Two-Phase Flow." *Bull. JSME* 20 (148) 1299–1305 (1977).
232. Sekoguchi, K., and Fukai, H. et al. "Investigation into the Statistical Characteristics of Bubble Two-Phase Flow." *Trans. JSME* 40 (336) 2295–2301 (1974).
233. Nassos, G. P., and Bankoff, S. G. "Slip Velocity Ratios in An Air-Water System Under Steady-State and Transient Conditions." *Chem. Eng. Sci.* 22 661–668 (1967).
234. Sato, Y., and Sekoguchi, K. "Liquid Velocity Distribution in Two-Phase Bubble Flow." *Int. J. Multiphase Flow.* 2 79–95 (1975).
235. St. Pierre, C. C., and Bankoff, S. G. "Vapor Volume Profiles in Developing Two-Phase Flow." *Int. J. Heat Mass Trans.* 10 237–249 (1967).
236. Neal, L. G., and Bankoff, S. G. "Local Parameters in Co-Current Mercury-Nitrogen Flows." *A.I.Ch.E.J.* 11 (4) 624–635 (1965).
237. Yamazaki, Y., and Yamaguchi, K. "Void Fraction Correlation for Boiling and Non-Boiling Vertical Two-Phase Flow in Tubes." *J. Nucl. Sci. and Tech.* 13 (12) 701–707 (1976).
238. Moussalli, G., and Chawla, J. M. "Void Fraction and Pressure Drop in Bubble Flow." *For. Ing. Wes.* 42 (5) 149–153 (1976).
239. Simpson, H. C., and Rooney, D. H. "Design for Two-Phase Flow-Part II: Void Fraction Prediction Under Saturated Conditions." *NEL Rept.* 386 (1969).
240. Bhaga, D., and Weber, M. E. "Hold-Up in Vertical Two- and Three-Phase Flow." *Can. J. Chem. Eng.* 50 (3) 323–329 (1972).
241. Spedding, P. L., and Nguyen, V. T. "Bubble Rise and Liquid Content in Horizontal and Inclined Tubes." *Chem. Eng. Sci.* 33 987–994 (1978).
242. Spedding, P. L., and Chen, J. J. J. "Verification of a Two-Phase Hold-Up Relation." *Chem. Eng. Sci.* 33 403–4 (1978).
243. Oliver, D. R., and Young Hoon A. "Two-Phase Non-Newtonian Flow. Part I: Pressure Drop and Hold-Up." *Trans. Inst. Chem. Eng.* 46 T106–T115 (1968).

244. Nguyen, V. T., and Spedding, P. L. "Hold-Up in Fluid-Solid Two-Phase Flow I. Theoretical II. Experimental Development." *Chem. Eng. J.* 15 (2) 131–146 (1978).
245. Spedding, P. L., and Nguyen, V. T. "Regime Maps for Air Water Two Phase Flow." *Chem Eng. Sci.* 35 779–793 (1980).
246. Rayleigh Lord, J. W. S. *Theory of Sound*, 2 Dover (1945).
247. Lamb, H. *Hydrodynamics*, 6th ed., Dover (1945).
248. Benjamin, T. B. "Wave Formation in Laminar Flow Down as Inclined Plane." *J. Fluid Mech.* 2 554–574 (1957).
249. Hanratty, T. J., and Engen, J. M. "Interaction Between a Turbulent Air Stream and a Moving Water Surface." *A.I.Ch.E.J.* 3 (3) 299–304 (1957).
250. Cohen, L. S., and Hanratty, T. J. "Generation of Waves in the Co-Current Flow of Air and a Liquid." *A.I.Ch.E.J.* 11 (1) 138–144 (1965).
251. Yih, C. S. "Stability of Parallel Laminar Flow with a Free Surface." *Proc. U.S. Natl. Cong. Appl. Mech.* 2 Ann Arbor (1954).
252. Yih, C. S. *Dynamics of Non-Homogeneous Fluids*. McMillan (1965).
253. Craik, A. D. D. "Wind-Generated Waves in Thin Liquid Films." *J. Fluid Mech.* 26 369–392 (1966).
254. Lin, S. P. "Finite Amplitude Stability of a Parallel Flow with a Free Surface." *J. Fluid Mech.* 36 (1) 113–126 (1969).
255. Belafoutos, G. J., and Abbott, M. B. "Two Dimensional Model for Two-Layer Flow." *J. Eng. Mech. Div. Proc. ASCE* 103 789–806 (1977).
256. White, J. L., and Lee, D. L. "Theory of Interfacial Distortion in Stratified Two-Phase Flow." *Trans. Soc. Rheology* 19 (3) 457–479 (1975).
257. Pimsner, V., and Toma, P. "The Wavy Aspect of a Horizontal Co-Current Air-Water Film Flow and the Transport Phenomena." *Int. J. Multiphase Flow.* 3 273–283 (1977).
258. Yu, H. S., and Sparrow, E. M. "Stratified Laminar Flow in Ducts of Arbitrary Shape." *A.I.Ch.E.J.* 13 (1) 10–16 (1967).
259. Spedding, P. L., and Nguyen, V. T. "Bubble Rise and Liquid Content in Horizontal and Inclined Tubes." *Chem. Eng. Sci.* 33 987–994 (1978).
260. Russel, T. W. F., Etchells, A. W., Jensen, R. H., and Arruda, P. J. "Pressure Drop and Hold-Up in Stratified Gas-Liquid Flow." *A.I.Ch.E.J.* 20 (4) 664–669 (1974).
261. Buffham, B. A. "Laminar Flow in Open Circular Channels and Symmetrical Lenticular Tubes." *Trans. Inst. Chem. Eng.* 46 T153–T160 (1968).
262. Agrawaal, S. S., Gregory, G. H., and Govier, G. W. "An Analysis of Horizontal Stratified Two-Phase Flow in Pipes." *Can. J. Chem. Eng.* 51 280–286 (1973).
263. Cheremisinoff, N. P., and Davis, E. J. "Stratified Turbulent-Turbulent Gas-Liquid Flow." *A.I.Ch.E.J.* 25 (1) 48–56 (1979).
264. Johannessen, T. "A Theoretical Solution to the Lockhart and Martinelli Flow Model for Calculating Two-Phase Flow Pressure Drop and Hold-Up." *Int. J. Heat Mass Transfer* 15 1443–1449 (1972).
265. Bergelin, O. P., and Gazley, C. "Co-Current Gas-Liquid Flow: Flow in Horizontal Tubes." *Heat Transfer and Fluid Mech.*, Inst. California Meeting ASME (1949).
266. Dukler, A. E. "Research Results Gas-Liquid Flow in Pipelines." AGA and API (1969).
267. Vohra, I. R., Marcano, N., and Brill, J. P. "Comparison of Liquid Hold-up Correlations for Gas-Liquid Flow in Horizontal Pipes." SPE-AIME Annual Meeting 48 SPE4690 (1973).
268. Beggs, H. D., and Brill, J. P. "A Study of Two-Phase Flow in Inclined Pipes." *J. Pet. Tech.* 25 607–617 (1973).
269. Guzhov, A. I., Mamaev, V. A., and Odishariya, G. E. "A Study of Transportation in Gas-Liquid Systems." *Int. Gas. Conf.* 10 (1967).
270. Mandhane, J. M., Gregory, G. A., and Aziz, K. "Critical Evaluation of Hold-Up Prediction Methods for Gas-Liquid Flow in Horizontal Pipes." *J. Pet. Tech.* 27 1017–1026 (1975).
271. Rouhawi, Z. AE-RTV-841 (1969).
272. Smith, C. R., Tang, Y. S., and Walker, C. L. "Measurement of Slip Velocity in Two-Phase Mercury Flow." *A.I.Ch.E.J.* 10 (4) 586–588 (1964).

273. Smith, L. R., Tek, M. R., and Balzhiser, R. E. "Pressure Drop and Void Fractions in Horizontal Two-Phase Flows of Potassium." *A.I.Ch.E.J.* 12 (1) 50–58 (1966).

274. Baroczy, C. J. "Pressure Drop for Two-Phase Potassium Flowing Through a Circular Tube and an Orifice." *A.I.Ch.E. Sym.* 64 (82) 12–25 (1968).

275. Fauske, H. R. "Transient Liquid-Metal Boiling and Two-Phase Flow." *Prog. Heat Mass Trans.* 7 451–465 (1973).

276. Johnson, H. A., and Abou-Sube, A. H. "Heat Transfer and Pressure Drop for Turbulent Flow of Air-Water Mixtures in a Horizontal Pipe." *TASME* 74 977–987 (1952).

CHAPTER 19

PREDICTING TWO-PHASE FLOW PRESSURE DROP

D. Chisholm[†]

Department of Mechanical and Civil Engineering
Glasgow College of Technology
Glasgow, Scotland

CONTENTS

[†] Presently with Heat Transfer Research Inc (HTRI), Alhambra, California.

INTRODUCTION

This chapter presents methods for predicting pressure gradients and pressure changes during the flow of gas-liquid and vapor-liquid mixtures in pipelines and heat exchangers. It does not attempt to present a general review of the various methods available, but aims to provide a coherent set of practical equations.

CONTINUITY EQUATIONS AND OTHER RELATIONSHIPS

The total mass flow rate and the phase mass flow rates are related

$$\dot{m} = \dot{m}_G + \dot{m}_L \tag{1}$$

The void fraction, the fraction of the flow cross-section occupied by the gas phase, is

$$\alpha = \frac{A_G}{A} \tag{2}$$

The gas continuity equation is

$$\dot{m}_G = \alpha A u_G / v_G \tag{3}$$

and that of the liquid component

$$\dot{m}_L = (1 - \alpha) A u_L / v_L \tag{4}$$

The mass dryness fraction is

$$x = \frac{\dot{m}_G}{\dot{m}} \tag{5}$$

It is convenient to use a mass velocity or flux

$$G = \frac{\dot{m}}{A} \tag{6}$$

The phase velocity ratio is

$$K = \frac{u_G}{u_L} \tag{7}$$

and the void fraction using the previous equations is

$$\alpha = x v_G / [x v_G + K(1 - x) v_L] \tag{8}$$

The gas velocity is

$$u_G = G[x v_G + K(1 - x) v_L] \tag{9}$$

and the homogeneous velocity, the velocity when $K = 1$, is

$$u_H = G[x v_G + (1 - x) v_L] \tag{10}$$

As in single-phase flow, the total pressure gradient is due to gravity, momentum change, and friction. This is expressed

$$Dp = Dp_g + Dp_M + Dp_F \tag{11}$$

The derivative of pressure with respect to displacement in the flow direction is represented, fo convenience, by D.

A physical property parameter is defined [1, 2]

$$\Gamma = \left(\frac{Dp_{Go}}{Dp_{Lo}}\right)^{1/2} = \left(\frac{v_G}{v_L}\right)^{1/2} \left(\frac{\mu_G}{\mu_L}\right)^{n/2} \tag{12}$$

where Dp_{Lo} and Dp_{Go} are the pressure gradients, due to either momentum change or friction, if the mixture mass flow rate flows as liquid or as gas, respectively. The viscosity ratio is appropriate to gradients associated with friction; for momentum changes, n, the Blasius exponent, would be zero.

The Lockhart-Martinelli parameter [3] is

$$X = \left(\frac{Dp_L}{Dp_G}\right)^{1/2} = \left(\frac{1-x}{x}\right)^{2-n/2} \cdot \frac{1}{\Gamma} \tag{13}$$

where Dp_L and Dp_G are the pressure gradients if the phases flowed alone.

PRESSURE GRADIENT DUE TO GRAVITY

The pressure gradient due to gravity and the specific volume of the mixture are related

$$-Dp_g = \frac{g \sin \theta}{v_m} \tag{14}$$

where θ is the angle of the tube to the horizontal; the sign corresponds to upflow. Using Equation 8, the mixture specific volume is

$$v_m = \left[\frac{\alpha}{v_G} + \frac{1-\alpha}{v_L}\right]^{-1} = [xv_G + K(1-x)v_L]/[x + K(1-x)] \tag{15}$$

The homogeneous specific volume ($K = 1$) is

$$v_H = xv_G + (1-x)v_L \tag{16}$$

Over a wide range of conditions [4, 5] the following formulas can be used for the velocity ratio:

$$X > 1 \quad K_0 = \left(\frac{v_H}{v_L}\right)^{1/2} \tag{17}$$

$$X \leq 1 \quad K_0 = \left(\frac{v_G}{v_L}\right)^{1/4} \tag{18}$$

The subscript 0 has been used here to distinguish values of K evaluated by these equations.

Figure 1 compares void fraction predictions using Equations 8, 17, and 18 with experimental data.

With decreasing mixture velocity in vertical pipes, the velocity ratio will gradually increase above values given by K_0. Labuntsov's [7] version of drift flux theory [8] can be stated

$$u_G = u_H + u_{wD} \tag{19}$$

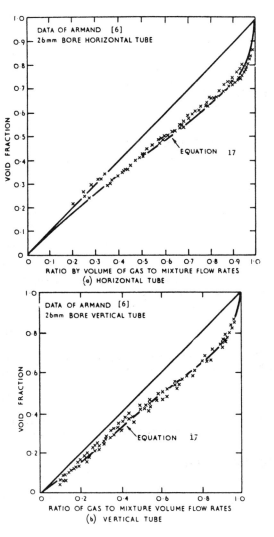

Figure 1. Void fraction to a base of the ratio of gas to mixture volume flow rates. (Air-water mixtures at atmospheric pressure.)

where the weighted drift flux, for small bore pipes, is

$$u_{wD} = 0.35w_D \left[gd\left(1 - \frac{v_L}{v_G}\right) \right]^{1/2} \tag{20}$$

and for large bore pipes

$$u_{wD} = 1.5w_D \left[\sigma \cdot g \cdot v_L \left(1 - \frac{v_L}{v_G}\right) \right]^{1/4} \tag{21}$$

The term

$$w_D = 1.4\left(\frac{v_G}{v_L}\right)^{1/5}\left(1 - \frac{v_L}{v_G}\right)^5 \tag{22}$$

The transitional diameter is obtained by equating Equations 20 and 21. Equation 19 should be used when evaluating u_G using Equations 17 and 18,

$$u_H > (u_G - u_{wD}) \tag{23}$$

Using Equations 8 and 18, the liquid cross-section can be expressed

$$(1 - \alpha) = \frac{1}{\dfrac{1}{1 - x}\left(\dfrac{v_H}{v_L}\right)^{1/2} + 1 - \left(\dfrac{v_L}{v_H}\right)^{1/2}} \tag{24}$$

This can be approximated

$$(1 - \alpha) = (1 - x)\left(\frac{v_L}{v_H}\right)^{1/2} \tag{25}$$

This expression will be used in considering friction. It is also useful in that it can be integrated to give an estimate of the average liquid cross-section along a pipe.

For flow in inclined pipes, Beggs [9] has developed an equation that can be written

$$\alpha = \alpha_h + (\alpha_v - \alpha_h)f(\theta) \tag{26}$$

where the subscripts h and v indicate flow in the horizontal and vertical plane, respectively. For downward flow a negative sign should be used in Equation 19. The function is

$$f(\theta) = 3.333[\sin(1.8\theta) + 0.333\sin^3(1.8\theta)] \tag{27}$$

where θ is the angle of the pipe to the horizontal, assumed positive reqardless of the flow direction. A statistical assessment of the accuracy of these and other methods is given in Reference 10.

PRESSURE GRADIENT DUE TO MOMENTUM CHANGE

Using a separated flow model, the momentum flux of the mixture can be expressed as

$$MF = xGu_G + (1 - x)Gu_L$$

$$= G^2[xv_G + K(1 - x)v_L]\left[x + \frac{1 - x}{K}\right] \tag{28}$$

Define [11] an effective specific volume v_e by the equation

$$MF = G^2v_e \tag{29}$$

Then

$$\frac{v_e}{v_L} = \frac{1}{v_L}[xv_G + K(1 - x)v_L]\left[x + \frac{1 - x}{K}\right]$$

$$= 1 + \left(\frac{v_G}{v_L} - 1\right)[Bx(1 - x) + x^2] \tag{30}$$

where the B-coefficient [12] is

$$B = \frac{\frac{1}{K}\left(\frac{v_G}{v_L} - 1\right) + K - 2}{\frac{v_G}{v_L} - 1} \tag{31}$$

Provided $\frac{v_G}{v_L} \gg 1$, then, approximately

$$B = \frac{1}{K} \tag{32}$$

It should be noted that

$$\frac{v_e}{v_m} = [x + K(1 - x)]\left[x + \frac{1 - x}{K}\right] \tag{33}$$

Thus, the effective volume, v_e, and that based on the content of the tube, v_m, can be significantly different.

Define now an effective mixture velocity

$$u_e = Gv_e \tag{34}$$

From Equation 29

$$MF = \frac{u_e^2}{v_e} \tag{35}$$

and

$$MF = Gu_e \tag{36}$$

The momentum flux if the mixture flows as liquid is

$$MF_{Lo} = Gu_L \tag{37}$$

By defining

$$\psi_M = \frac{\frac{MF}{MF_{Lo}} - 1}{\frac{v_L}{v_G} - 1} \tag{38}$$

then from Equations 29, 30, 37 and 38

$$\psi_M = Bx(1 - x) + x^2 \tag{39}$$

The group ψ_M [13] has been referred to as the "normalized two-phase multiplier."

Andeen and Griffith [14] and Wiafe [15] have measured the momentum flux during two-phase flow. Wiafe's measurements are shown in Figure 2 in the form of a ψ-x plot. In these tests the void

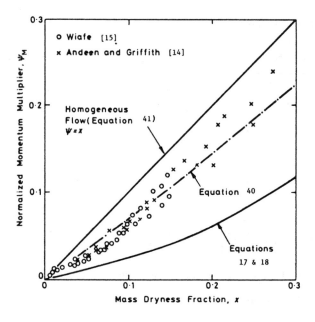

Figure 2. Normalized two-phase multiplier, ψ_M, to a base of mass dryness fraction x. (Air-water mixtures at atmospheric pressure).

fractions were measured and were well represented by K_0; however the momentum flux measurements were more closely represented by a velocity ratio

$$K_e = K_0^{0.28} \tag{40}$$

The subscript e is used to indicate an "effective" velocity ratio in the momentum equation. Figure 2 compares prediction with experiment. For homogeneous conditions (K = 1.0) Equation 39 reduces to

$$\psi = x \tag{41}$$

This line is also shown in Figure 2.

It is understood that the effective velocity ratio is given by Equation 40, rather than by K_0, due to the large radial variation in liquid velocity. The liquid momentum is considerably greater than

$$MF = (1 - x)Gu_L \tag{42}$$

The pressure gradient due to momentum changes is, using Equation 36,

$$A\,d(p_M) = d(Mu_e) \tag{43}$$

Alternatively

$$dp_M = G\,du_e \tag{44}$$

and

$$v_e \, dp_M = u_e \, du_e \tag{45}$$

For a constant flow cross-section

$$dp_M = G^2 \, dv_e \tag{46}$$

FRICTION IN TURBULENT FLOW

In this section equations are given for predicting the pressure gradient due to friction in turbulent flow. For single-phase flow

$$-Dp_F = \frac{\lambda G^2 v}{2d} \tag{47}$$

where the friction factor, in terms of Reynolds number, can be represented using the Blasius equation

$$\lambda = \frac{c}{Re^n} \tag{48}$$

The simplest model, for two-phase flow, is the "homogeneous" model

$$-Dp_F = \frac{\lambda G^2 v_H}{2d} \tag{49}$$

For the case of rough tubes (n = 0), this can be transformed [16] to

$$\frac{Dp_F}{Dp_{FL}} = \phi_{FL}^2 = \left[1 + \frac{C}{X} + \frac{1}{X^2} \right] \tag{50}$$

where [17]

$$C = \left(\frac{v_G}{v_L} \right)^{1/2} + \left(\frac{v_L}{v_G} \right)^{1/2} \tag{51}$$

Equation 50 introduces the concept of the "two-phase multiplier" ϕ^2 [3]. For vertical flow, in certain conditions, Equations 50 and 51 give satisfactory agreement with experiment, as can be seen [5] in Figure 3. The experimental conditions corresponded to C-coefficients in the range 24 to 29, compared with the experimental value of 26. When Equation 51 is applied to smooth tubes, it is referred to as the "psuedo-homogeneous" equation.

For turbulent flow the pressure gradient due to friction tends to be least with flow in horizontal tubes, except at very low mass velocities. For the conditions of the tests shown in Figure 3, the C-coefficient for horizontal flow [16] had a value

$$C = 21 \tag{52}$$

Sadatomi et al. [18] has shown that these equations are applicable to flow in ducts of annular and triangular cross-section. Equation 50 can be transformed [13] to

$$\frac{Dp_F}{Dp_{FL_o}} = \phi_{FL_o}^2 = 1 + (\Gamma^2 - 1)\left[Bx^{(2-n)/2}(1 - x)^{(2-n)/2} + x^{2-n} \right] \tag{53}$$

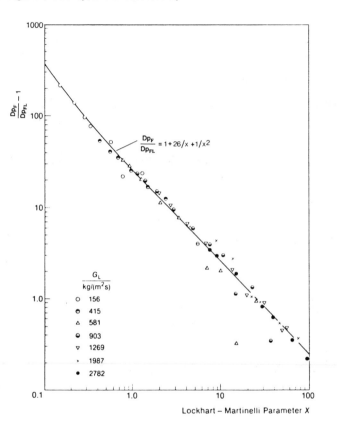

Figure 3. $(\phi_{FL}^2 - 1)$ to a base of the Lockhart-Martinelli parameter X. (Air-water mixtures in a vertical smooth 27 mm bore tube.)

where

$$B = \frac{C\Gamma \mp 2^{2-n} + 2}{\Gamma^2 - 1} \tag{54}$$

There is a remainder to the transformation that is negligible in practice. For flow in rough tubes (n = 0) homogeneous theory corresponds to

$$B = 1.0 \tag{55}$$

Stratified flow [19] and conditions at the thermodynamic critical point [20] approximate to

$$B = \frac{2^{2-n} - 2}{\Gamma + 1} \tag{56}$$

For annular flow (with full entrainment in horizontal flow), intermittent flow, and dispersed bubble flow, recommended values of the B-coefficient are given in Table 1. Coefficients from this table are denoted by B_A.

Table 1
Values of B for Fully Developed Flow in Smooth Tubes (B$_A$)

Γ	$\dfrac{G}{kg/(m^2 \cdot s)}$	B
9.5	≤ 500 $500 < G < 1,900$ $\geq 1,900$	4.8 2,400/G $55/G^{0.5}$
$9.5 < \Gamma < 28$	≤ 600 > 600	$520/(\Gamma G^{0.5})$ $21/\Gamma$
≥ 28	—	$\dfrac{15,000}{\Gamma^2 G^{0.5}}$

Define now

$$\psi_F = \frac{\dfrac{Dp_F}{Dp_{FLo}} - 1}{\Gamma^2 - 1} \tag{57}$$

This group is analagous to ψ_M defined by Equation 38. From Equations 53 and 57

$$\psi = Bx^{(2-n)/2}(1 - x)^{(2-n)/2} + x^{2-n} \tag{58}$$

In horizontal flow, friction, during the transition from stratified flow to annular flow with full entrainment, is predicted [21, 22] using

$$\psi = Rx^{2-n} \tag{59}$$

where, for d $\leq$ 50 mm,

$$R = 1 + 0.001223\Gamma G \tag{60}$$

The coefficient R for larger diameter tubes is discussed below. Define a flow pattern parameter

$$e = \frac{\psi - \psi_S}{\psi_A - \psi_S} \tag{61}$$

where ψ_S is the value during stratified flow, and ψ_A the value obtained using B$_A$.
From Equations 58, 59, and 61

$$e = \frac{R - 1}{B_A - B_S}\left(\frac{x}{1 - x}\right)^{(2-n)/2} - \frac{B_S}{B_A - B_S} \tag{62}$$

or, using Equation 60

$$e = \frac{0.001223\Gamma G}{B_A - B_S}\left(\frac{x}{1 - x}\right)^{(2-n)/2} - \frac{B_S}{B_A - B_S} \tag{63}$$

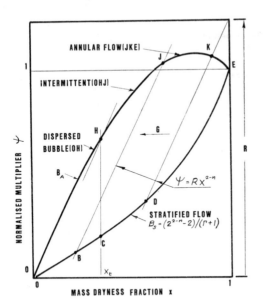

ANNULAR FLOW(JKE)

INTERMITTENT(OHJ)

DISPERSED
BUBBLE(OH)

$\psi = R x^{2-n}$

STRATIFIED FLOW
$B_s = (2^{2-n}-2)/(n+1)$

NORMALISED MULTIPLIER ψ

MASS DRYNESS FRACTION x

Figure 4. The normalized two-phase multiplier, ψ_F, to a base of mass dryness fraction.

Figure 4 shows schematically the manner in which ψ varies. When $e = 0$, from Equations 13 and 63

$$G_S = \frac{B_S X}{0.001223} = 818 B_S X \qquad (64)$$

and, when $e = 1$,

$$G_A = \frac{B_A X}{0.001223} = 818 B_A X \qquad (65)$$

When $0 < e < 1$, Equation 59 is used to predict the friction pressure gradient, or Equation 53 with

$$B = B_e = B_S + e(B_A - B_S) \qquad (66)$$

One method [23] assumes that the stratified-spray transition only occurs when the void fraction is greater than

$$\alpha = 0.72 \qquad (67)$$

This is slightly in excess of the void fraction corresponding to a regular packing of spheres. The value of the Lockhart-Martinelli parameter corresponding to this voidage, when the velocity ratio is taken as K_0, is denoted by X_t. It follows that the maximum mass flux for which stratified flow will occur is

$$G_t = 818 B_S X_t \qquad (68)$$

For air-water mixtures at atmospheric pressure this gives $G \doteq 210 \text{ kg}/(m^2 s)$, which is in line with experiment (24, 25). A more detailed procedure would allow for the effect of diameter on this transition. The B-coefficients for horizontal flow are therefore as shown in Table 2. For rough tubes

Table 2
Values of B for Horizontal Turbulent Flow

G kg/(m$^2 \cdot$s)	e	B
	$\leqslant 0$	B_S
$< 818 B_S X_L$	$0 < e < 1.0$	B_e
	$\geqslant 1.0$	B_A
$\geqslant 818 B_S X_t$	—	B_A

B_A should be modified (26), as follows, to

$$B_R = 0.5 B_A \left[1 + \left(\frac{\mu_G}{\mu_L} \right)^2 + 100^{-600\varepsilon/d} \right]^{(0.25-n)/0.25} \tag{69}$$

where ε/d is the surface roughness ratio.

The experiments of Simpson et al. [27] with tubes of 127 mm and 215 mm bore suggest that at these larger diameter the general form of Equation 59 applies at higher mass velocities than given by Equation 68. When applied to larger tubes these methods will tend to overestimate the pressure drop. The influence of diameter is an aspect requiring further study.

For flow in vertical and inclined tubes the B-coefficients in Table 1 should be used. This will tend to overestimate friction at low mass velocities. A statistical comparison of prediction with experiment, for both vertical and horizontal flow, using Table 1 and other methods is given in Reference 10.

Before concluding this discussion of friction during two-phase flow, the relationship of annular flow theory [28], homogeneous theory, and K_0 as defined by Equation 17 will be shown. Wallis [29] has shown that for annular flow, approximately,

$$\frac{Dp_F}{Dp_{FL}} = \frac{1}{(1 - \alpha)^2} \tag{70}$$

Also

$$\frac{Dp_F}{Dp_{FLo}} = \frac{Dp_F}{Dp_{FL}} \cdot \frac{Dp_{FL}}{Dp_{FLo}}$$

$$= \frac{Dp_F}{Dp_{FL}} \cdot (1 - x)^{2-n}$$

$$\doteqdot \frac{Dp_F}{Dp_{FL}} \cdot (1 - x)^2 \tag{71}$$

Combining Equations 25, 70, and 71 gives homogeneous Equation 49. Thus, K_0 derived from Equation 17 is the velocity ratio which [28] will result in annular flow theory and homogeneous theory giving similar predictions for friction.

FRICTION IN LAMINAR FLOW

For the case in which one or other of the components, or both, would flow laminarly, if they flowed alone, the C-coefficients shown in Table 3 have been recommended [30].

Table 3
C-Coefficient for Flow With Laminar Component

Laminar-Gas	C	m Equation 75
Turbulent-Laminar	12	0.345
Laminar-Turbulent	10	0.310
Laminar-Laminar	5	0.160

Kubie and Oates [31] simulated conditions near the thermodynamic critical point, using two liquids of similar densities but immiscible. For each of the three mechanisms in Table 3 it was found that

$$C = 2 \tag{72}$$

This is illustrated in Figure 5. This is a surprising conclusion; from Equations 54 and 56, at the thermodynamic critical point

$$C = 2^{2-n} - 2 \tag{73}$$

which gives the C-coefficient zero, when $n = 1$ as with laminar flow. In contrast to the findings of Kubie and Oates [31] the data of Charles and Lillelehet [32], for two immiscible liquid where one flowed laminarly, were well represented by

$$C = 0.8 \tag{74}$$

As an interim measure, the following equation is recommended

$$C = 1 + \left(\frac{v_G}{v_L}\right)^m \tag{75}$$

The value of m is obtained from Table 3.

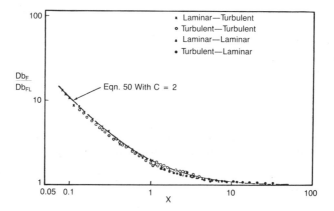

Figure 5. Comparison of the theoretical prediction with experimental data for all flow mechanisms [31].

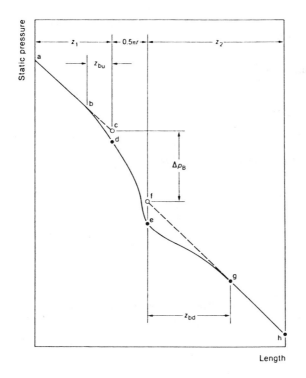

Figure 6. Pressure distribution over a 90° bend.

BENDS

In discussing the static pressure change in pipe fittings in the following sections, the change attributable to the device generally is considered; downstream effects are included. The pressure change attributable to a bend is specified in Figure 6. Where the bend is in the vertical plane, part of the change will be due to gravitational effects; the discussion here is concerned primarily with pressure change due to friction and momentum effects. Gravitational effects are estimated using equilibrium values of the velocity ratio, although undoubtedly the bend will influence the velocity ratio.

For simplicity, therefore, consider a bend in the horizontal plane. For single-phase flow, define a single-phase pressure drop coefficient

$$k_B = -\frac{\Delta p_B}{G^2 v/2} \tag{76}$$

Define

$$\Gamma_B = \left[\frac{k_{BGo}}{k_{BLo}} \cdot \frac{v_G}{v_L}\right]^{1/2} \tag{77}$$

It has been shown [33] for 90° bends that

$$B = 1 + \frac{2.2}{k_{BLo}(2 + R_B/d)} \tag{78}$$

where R_B is the radius of the bend, and d the pipe bore. For bends other than 90°, the following formula is recommended

$$B_{B\theta} = 1 + (B_{B90} - 1)\frac{k_{B90}}{k_{B\theta}} \tag{79}$$

CHANGES OF SECTION

Incompressible Flow

For the case of an incompressible flow, where the velocity ratio does not change along the flow path, from Equation 45

$$-\Delta p = \left[\frac{u_{e2}^2}{2} - \frac{u_{e1}^2}{2}\right]\frac{1}{v_e} = \frac{G_1^2}{2}v_e\left[\frac{1}{\sigma^2} - 1\right] \tag{80}$$

where

$$\sigma = \frac{A_2}{A_1} \tag{81}$$

The subscripts 1 and 2 refer to upstream and downstream points respectively.
Also, for single-phase flow of the mixture,

$$-\Delta p_{Lo} = \frac{G_1^2}{2}v_L\left[\frac{1}{\sigma^2} - 1\right] = k \cdot \frac{G_1^2}{2} \cdot v_L \tag{82}$$

Hence, using Equations 30, 81, and 82

$$\frac{\Delta p}{\Delta p_{Lo}} = 1 + \left[\frac{v_G}{v_L} - 1\right]\left[Bx(1 - x) + x^2\right] \tag{83}$$

where B varies along the flow path, the path can be divided into steps of approximately constant B. The overall B coefficient can be shown [5, 12] to be

$$B = \frac{\sum\limits_{1}^{n} kB/\sigma^2}{\sum\limits_{1}^{n} k/\sigma^2} \tag{84}$$

where σ is defined

$$\sigma = \frac{A_i}{A_1} \tag{85}$$

and k is defined with respect to the velocity at cross-section A_i, and A_1 is the overall reference cross-section. Where all k values are based on A_1, Equation 84 reduces to

$$B = \frac{\sum\limits_{1}^{n} kB}{\sum\limits_{1}^{n} k} \tag{86}$$

The velocity ratio at points along a complex flow path can be approximated as follows:

For a round inlet, to and at the throat [34]

$$B = \frac{1}{K_0^{0.4}} \tag{87}$$

For a sharp inlet, to and at the throat [5]

$$B = \frac{1}{K_0} \tag{88}$$

Through a Venturimeter [35]

$$B = \frac{1}{K_0} \tag{88}$$

Equilibrium flow, using Equations 32 and 40,

$$B = \frac{1}{K_0^{0.28}} \tag{89}$$

Using Equations 84 to 89 leads to the following equations, when the contraction coefficient is C_c.

Sudden expansion

$$B = \frac{1}{K_0^{0.28}} \tag{89}$$

Sudden contraction (sharp inlet)

$$B = \frac{\left[\left(\dfrac{1}{C_c\sigma}\right)^2 - 1\right]\dfrac{1}{K_0} - \dfrac{2}{C_c\sigma^2 K_0} + \dfrac{2}{\sigma^2 K_0^{0.28}}}{\left(\dfrac{1}{C_c\sigma}\right)^2 - 1 - \dfrac{2}{C_c\sigma^2} + \dfrac{2}{\sigma^2}} \tag{90}$$

Thin plate (sharp inlet)

$$B = \frac{\left[\left(\dfrac{1}{C_c\sigma}\right)^2 - 1\right]\dfrac{1}{K_0} - \dfrac{2}{C_c\sigma K_0} + \dfrac{2}{K_0^{0.28}}}{\left(\dfrac{1}{C_c\sigma}\right)^2 - 1 - \dfrac{2}{C_c\sigma} + 2} \tag{91}$$

Thick plate (sharp inlet)

$$B = \frac{\left[\left(\dfrac{1}{C_c\sigma}\right)^2 - 1\right]\dfrac{1}{K_0} - \dfrac{2}{C_c\sigma K_0} + \dfrac{2}{\sigma^2 K_0^{0.28}} - \dfrac{2}{\sigma K_0^{0.28}} + \dfrac{2}{K_0^{0.28}}}{\left(\dfrac{1}{C_c\sigma}\right)^2 - 1 - \dfrac{2}{C_c\sigma^2} + \dfrac{2}{\sigma^2} - \dfrac{2}{\sigma} + 2} \tag{92}$$

The equation for a thin plate is compared with experiment in Figure 7.

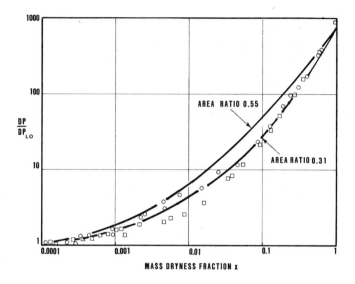

Figure 7. Two-phase multiplier to a base of mass dryness fraction form orifices. (Air-water mixture at atmospheric pressure. Area ratios: (□) 0.31; (○) 0.55.) [37].

One important point to note is that for a thin plate $B < 1.0$, while for a thick plate $B > 1.0$; this is confirmed by experiment [36]. Data for the flow of air-water mixtures through gate valves indicates that they behave essentially as thin plates [37]. It has been suggested [5] that where the valve seat length (z) is greater than 0.5 of the equivalent aperture diameter, the gate valve will behave as a thick plate. Globe valves can also be approximated by thin plates (37).

Compressible Flow

For compressible flow, using Equation 45,

$$\int_1^2 v_e \, dp = \frac{u_{e2}^2}{2} - \frac{u_{e1}^2}{2} = \frac{G_2^2}{2}\left[v_{e2}^2 - v_{e1}^2\left(\frac{A_1}{A_2}\right)^2\right] \tag{93}$$

This can be solved for the pressure change by numerical integration, evaluating v_e using Equation 30. The B-coefficient along the flow path is evaluated as for incompressible flow conditions. For sudden contractions it has proved satisfactory [34, 35] to assume the gas expands isentropically, according to the law

$$pv^n = \text{constant} \tag{94}$$

where n is taken as the ratio of the specific heats.

If it is assumed that during the expansion the gas and liquid remain at the same temperature, the following equation for the expansion exponent [38] in Equation 94 is obtained

$$n = \frac{(1 - x)C_{pL} + xC_{pG}}{(1 - x)C_{pL} + xC_{vG}} \tag{95}$$

In using the isentropic value, it is being assumed that the flow over the change of section is too rapid for the gas to be in equilibrium with the liquid.

For sharp inlet the contraction coefficient was [35] evaluated from

$$C_c = \frac{xv_G + K(1-x)v_L}{\dfrac{xv_G}{C_G} + \dfrac{K(1-x)v_L}{C_L}} \tag{96}$$

where C_G and C_L are the contraction coefficients for the gas and liquid respectively, if they flowed alone. The contraction coefficients for the gas were evaluated using an equation by Jobson [39].

Flashing Flow

With vapor-liquid mixtures, for small pressure changes over the device, effects of phase change and compressibility can be ignored [4]. For larger pressure drops compressibility effects must be introduced, and it may be necessary then to allow for phase change; Equation 93 can be used, evaluating the mass dryness fraction along the flow path on the basis of thermodynamic equilibrium.

However, in an expanding vapor-liquid flow the expansion may not be in thermodynamic equilibrium; "metastable" flow may occur where the liquid becomes superheated to a temperature above the saturation temperature and the mass dryness fraction is less than the equilibrium value.

Metastable conditions are particularly significant where the fluid is initially a saturated liquid, or at low mass dryness fraction, due to the small number of nucleation sites.

Define [40, 41]

$$N = \frac{x_N}{x} \tag{97}$$

where x_N is the actual mass dryness fraction, and x is the thermodynamic equilibrium value. Equation 30 can be written

$$\frac{v_e}{v_L} = 1 + \left(\frac{v_G}{v_L} - 1\right)\left[\frac{x_N}{K}(1 - x_N) + x_N^2\right] \tag{98}$$

Non-equilibrium effects, as already mentioned, occur at low values of x, hence [5], approximately

$$\frac{v_e}{v_L} = 1 + \left(\frac{v_G}{v_L} - 1\right)\left[\frac{N}{K}x(1 - x) + x^2\right] \tag{99}$$

This is, of course, Equation 30 with

$$B = \frac{N}{K} \tag{100}$$

The problem reduces once more to evaluating the coefficient B. Thermodynamic equilibrium corresponds to $N = 1.0$.

Examination of experimental data suggests the following equations:

$$X \leq 1 \quad B = \frac{1}{K} \tag{101}$$

$$X > 1 \quad B = \frac{1}{K}\frac{x_N}{x} \tag{102}$$

The mass dryness fraction corresponding to $X = 1.0$ is

$$X_t = \frac{1}{\left(\dfrac{v_G}{v_L}\right)^{1/2} + 1} \tag{103}$$

For isentropic flow a recommended [5] equation for the metastable mass dryness fraction is

$$x_N = x_0 + \left(\frac{x - x_0}{x_t - x_0}\right)^2 (x - x_0) \tag{104}$$

where x_0 is the stagnation mass dryness fraction. For flashing pipe flow x_0 should be replaced by the initial mass dryness fraction. For the case where the fluid is initially saturated liquid Equation 104 reduces to [42]

$$X_N = \left(\frac{x}{x_t}\right)^2 \cdot x \tag{105}$$

The velocity ratio is evaluated using x_N.

This procedure parallels that developed by Henry and Fauske [40, 41]. For pipes they recommended

$$x < 0.05 \qquad N = \frac{x}{0.05} \tag{106}$$

$$x \geq 0.05 \qquad N = 1.0 \tag{107}$$

For nozzles and short pipes they recommended

$$x < 0.14 \qquad N = \frac{x}{0.14} \tag{108}$$

$$x \geq 0.14 \qquad N = 1.0 \tag{109}$$

For the flow of vapor-liquid mixtures through valves it is recommended that they be modeled as a thin plate, and the previous equations used to evaluate the pressure change.

CROSSFLOW

Horizontal Flow

Pressure drop during crossflow over tube banks can be predicted [5, 22, 43–46] in a manner analogous to that used for predicting pressure gradients due to friction in tubes. In horizontal crossflow the flow patterns [43] are as follows:

Bubble: bubbles of gas in a liquid continuum.
Bubble-spray: the transition from bubble to spray flow.
Spray: the majority of the liquid is carried as droplets in the gas. The walls remain wetted.
Stratified: the liquid flows along the bottom of the duct with the gas above.
Stratified-spray: liquid flows along the bottom of the duct, with spray flow above.

The pressure drop in the bubble flow regime is approximately represented using Equation 53 with

$$B_b = \left(\frac{v_L}{v_H}\right)^{1/2} \tag{110}$$

The spray regime is well represented on the basis of pseudo-homogeneous theory, Equation 51. Combining Equations 51 and 54 gives the B-coefficient as approximately

$$B_f = \left(\frac{\mu_L}{\mu_G}\right)^{n/2} \tag{111}$$

The stratified pattern again corresponds to a B-coefficient given by

$$B_S = \frac{2^{2-n} - 2}{\Gamma + 1} \tag{56}$$

The pressure drop in the stratified-spray regime is given [45] by

$$\psi = Rx^{2-n} \tag{59}$$

where [46], with horizontal tubes,

$$R = 1.3 + 0.09N^2 Fr_{Lo}\left(\frac{\mu_L}{\mu_G}\right)^n \tag{112}$$

The number of tubes normal to the flow is N, and the Froude number is

$$Fr_{Lo} = \frac{G^2 v_L}{gd} \tag{113}$$

The mass velocity is based on the minimum flow cross-section. As for tube flow, the entrainment parameter is

$$e = \frac{R - 1}{B_f - B_S}\left(\frac{x}{1 - x}\right)^{(2-n)/2} - \frac{B_S}{B_f - B_S} \tag{62}$$

Substituting Equation 112 gives, for the stratified-spray transition

$$e = \frac{0.3 + 0.09N^2 Fr_{Lo}\left(\frac{\mu_L}{\mu_G}\right)^n}{B_f - B_S}\left(\frac{x}{1 - x}\right)^{(2-n)/2} - \frac{B_S}{B_f - B_S} \tag{114}$$

For the bubble-spray transition

$$e = \frac{0.3 + 0.09N^2 Fr_{Lo}\left(\frac{\mu_L}{\mu_G}\right)^n}{B_f - B_b}\left(\frac{x}{1 - x}\right)^{(2-n)/2} - \frac{B_b}{B_f - B_b} \tag{115}$$

In the stratified-spray and bubble-spray transitions Equation 59 can be used. Alternatively for the stratified-spray transition

$$B_e = B_S + (B_f - B_S)e \tag{116}$$

and for the bubble-spray transition

$$B_{be} = B_b + (B_f - B_b)e \tag{117}$$

The maximum void fraction for bubble flow was assumed [5]

$$\alpha = 0.75 \tag{118}$$

as compared with 0.72 for pipe flow. The corresponding value of mass dryness fraction, evaluated assuming the velocity ration is given by Equation 17, is denoted by x_t.

The maximum value of Froude number for stratified flow is then, using Equations 110 and 115 with e = 0,

$$Fr_{Lot} = \frac{\left(\dfrac{v_L}{v_H}\right)^{1/2}\left(\dfrac{1-x_t}{x_t}\right)^{(2-n)/2} - 0.3}{0.09N^2\left(\dfrac{\mu_L}{\mu_G}\right)^n} \tag{119}$$

The subscript t associated with v_L/v_H indicates that the ratio is evaluated using x_t.

The flow patterns are identified by the values of e, α (or x), and Fr_{Lo} as indicated in Table 4; the table also summarizes the B-coefficients.

The table recommends that the upper limit of void fraction is 0.67, as compared to 0.75 recommended by Chisholm [5]; this is to provide consistency with the following sections. It is a matter requiring further study.

Figure 8 compares predictions by these methods with experiments for air flowing horizontally over a horizontal tube bundle. There were 8 tubes normal to the flow, and bypass effects were prevented by the use of half tubes at the walls.

Table 4
B-Coefficients for Crossflow

	e	α	Fr_{Lo}		B	(Equation)
A. Horizontal flow						
bubble	—	<0.67	>Fr_{Lot}	(119)	B_b	(110)
stratified	≤0		<Fr_{Lot}		B_S	(56)
bubble-spray	0 < e < 1.0		>Fr_{Lot}		B_{be}	(117)
stratified-spray	0 < e < 1.0		<Fr_{Lot}		B_e	(66)
spray	>1.0		—		B_f	(111)
B. Vertical upflow						
bubble		<0.67			3.0	(120)
bubble-spray		0.67			$\psi = f(x_t)$	(122)
intermittent	<0				B_f	(111)
spray		>0.67			B_f	(111)
C. Vertical downflow						
bubble	—	<0.67			B_b	(110)
separated	≤0				B_S	(56)
separated-spray	0 < e < 1.0				B_e	(66)
spray	>1.0				B_f	(111)

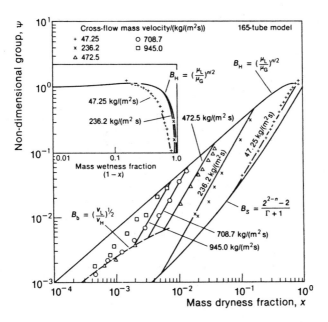

Figure 8. Nomalized two-phase multiplier to a base of mass dryness fraction for crossflow. (Air-water mixtures at atmospheric pressure.) [46]

Vertically Up

Where a two-phase mixture flows vertically upward through a bank of horizontal tubes, the flow patterns are as follows [47]:

Bubble: as for horizontal flow.
Bubble-spray: the transition from bubble to spray flow.
Intermittent: alternately bubble and spray.
Spray: as for horizontal flow.

For vertical flow there is limited information on the factors influencing flow patterns. The use of the e-parameter, calculated as for horizontal flow, has been found to be useful in predicting the approximate magnitude of the flow pattern boundaries.

In vertical flow the flow regimes are a function of e and α, independent, it it believed, of the Froude number.

For bubble flow the B-coefficient is based on the experimental data in Reference 47. The B-coefficient is approximately

$$B = 3.0 \tag{120}$$

and bubble flow ceases at a void fraction

$$\alpha = 0.67 \tag{121}$$

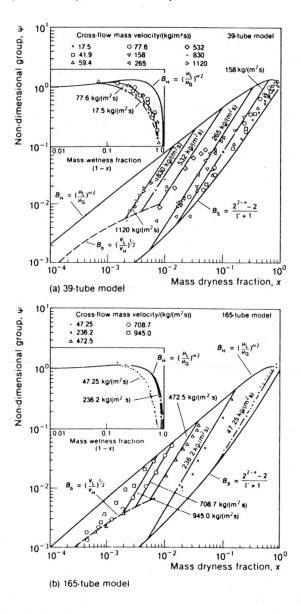

(a) 39-tube model

(b) 165-tube model

Figure 9. Two-phase pressure drop in vertically upward crossflow.

The pressure drop in the bubble-spray transition is given by

$$\psi = 3x_t^{(2-n)/2}(1 - x_t)^{(2-n)/2} + x_t^{2-n} \tag{122}$$

where x_t is the mass dryness fraction corresponding to $\alpha = 0.67$. Intermittent flow is assumed to occur at conditions, which in horizontal flow, would cause stratified flow; hence intermittent flow occurs when $e < 0$. The B-coefficient is approximately that for spray flow, which is given by Equation 111. Table 4 summarizes these recommendations.

Vertically Down

For the downward flow of a two-phase mixture through a bank of horizontal tubes the flow patterns are as follows:

Bubble: as for horizontal flow.
Separated: the liquid flows on the walls.
Separated-spray: liquid flows on the walls, spray in the core.
Spray: as for horizontal flow.

The pressure drop in bubble and spray flow are evaluated as for horizontal flow. Separated and separated-spray are evaluated on the same basis as for stratified and stratified-spray flow. Table 4 summarizes these recommendations.

VERTICAL CROSSFLOW IN BAFFLED HEAT EXCHANGERS

In baffled shell-and-tube heat exchangers, where vertical flow occurs in the crossflow zones, the flow direction changes in each successive pass. Grant and Murray [48] measured the pressure drop over two successive passes, attributing the pressure drop to friction and form drag. Their data can be approximated [44] by

$$B = 1.0 \tag{55}$$

The procedure assumes that the pressure drop due to gravity cancels in successive passes; this is not entirely valid due to changes in velocity ratio with flow direction. Inclusion of this differential slip effect would lower the value of B. Equation 55 gives a B value lower than given by Table 4; a possible explanation is that in the second pass the pressure drop is affected by the presence of the baffle "window" upstream. In the case of horizontal flow [46], however, the window did not appear to have a significant effect.

ENTRAINMENT AND SUBMERGENCE

For horizontal crossflow the entrainment of the liquid in the gas or vapor, and the submergence, the cross-section occupied by the separated liquid using the previous equations. Considering the separated liquid flow, the pressure gradient [49] is

$$Dp = Dp_{FLo}[(1 - w)(1 - x)]^{(2-n)} \tag{123}$$

where w is the entrainment, defined

$$w = \frac{\dot{m}_L - \dot{m}_{SL}}{\dot{m}_L} \tag{124}$$

The fraction of the flow cross-section occupied by the separated liquid is α_{SL}, the liquid mass flow rate is $\dot{m}_L$, and the flow rate of the separated liquid $\dot{m}_{SL}$.

For the gas with the entrained liquid, assuming a common pressure gradient

$$Dp = Dp_{FLo}[x + w(1 - x)]^{(2-n)} \frac{\phi_{FLoe}^2}{(1 - \alpha_{SL})^{2-n}} \tag{125}$$

where

$$\phi_{FLoe}^2 = 1 + [\Gamma^2 - 1][B_f x_e^{(2-n)/2}(1 - x_e)^{(2-n)/2} + x_e^{2-n}] \tag{126}$$

The mass dryness fraction of the spray is

$$x_e = \frac{x}{x + w(1 - x)} \tag{127}$$

Equations 125–127 illustrate the application of the spray flow equation; B_f is obtained from Equation 111.

These equations can be combined to give

$$\alpha_{SL} = (1 - \omega)(1 - x)/[(1 - w)(1 - x) + \{[x + w(1 - x)]^{2-n} + (\Gamma^2 - 1)[B_f w^{(2-n)/2} x^{(2-n)/2}(1 - x)^{(2-n)/2} + x^{2-n}]\}^{1/(2-n)}] \tag{128}$$

Equations 53, 66, 123, and 128 can be solved simultaneously, numerically, to give related values of e and w. On this basis Grant and other [49] obtained

$$w = e^{1.35} \tag{129}$$

BYPASS

Bypass effects at the wall can have major effects on the pressure drop in crossflow. The three studies reported in the literature relate to vertical upflow through banks of horizontal tubes. In the experiments reported [47], bypass reduces the value of B by about three-fold.

Three models of the bypass process have been examined; they all assume the pressure gradient is the same in each phase. The key assumptions in each model are as follows:

1. The vapor contains 10% of the liquid flow [47].
2. The separated liquid flows along the walls, and the liquid entrainment is that which minimizes the pressure drop [50].
3. At low mass dryness fractions the separated liquid fills the bypasses, the remaining liquid and the gas forming a two-phase mixture. At high mass dryness fractions, a two-phase mixture occupies the bypass, and gas the bundle [51].

The analytical procedure parallels that described earlier under "Entrainment and Submergence."

WINDOW PRESSURE DROP

The strong flow pattern dependency of pressure drop in crossflow is also to be found in horizontal flow around baffle windows in shell-and-tube heat exchangers. The pressure drop is that between inlet and outlet of the window; downstream effects are included in the crossflow correlation

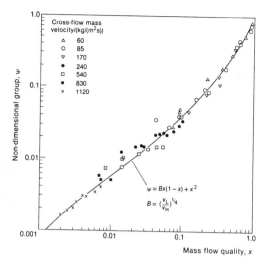

Figure 10. Nomalized two-phase multiplier to a base of mass dryness fraction for a baffle window with a vertical up-down flow. (Air-water mixtures at atmospheric pressure.) [44].

tions. Equation 53 is again used. The coefficients are those recommended for crossflow except for the spray regime, where [46]

$$B = \left(\frac{v_L}{v_H}\right)^{1/4}$$
(130)

The relevant mass velocity is the maximum value in the window. The bubble flow pattern is assumed to exist up to a void fraction of 0.8.

For the case of vertical flow, for all the flow patterns, the B-coefficient was found to be given by Equation 130. Figure 10 demonstrates the agreement between experiment and prediction.

MOMENTUM AND GRAVITATIONAL EFFECTS IN CROSSFLOW

It is recommended that the momentum flux is evaluated as for flow in a tube, as discussed previously, using for the effective velocity ratio

$$K_e = K_0^{0.28}$$
(40)

This is likely to overestimate momentum effects for stratified flow, where the velocity ratio associated with the void fraction is given by [43]

$$K = \frac{v_G}{v_L} \cdot \frac{1}{\Gamma^{2/(2-n)}}$$
(131)

Nevertheless, due to the low mass velocities associated with stratified flow, this will not introduce unacceptable errors. Void fraction in vertical two-phase flow has not yet been the subject of systematic study. It is recommended that the equations recommended for tube flow be used. Where it is relevant to evaluate a mass velocity, in void fraction estimation, it should be based on the average flow cross-section in the bank. In momentum calculations within the bank this should also be the basis of calculation; in calculating the overall momentum change the flow areas before and beyond the bank should be used.

SUMMARY

Friction in tubes. For turbulent flow use Equation 53. For horizontal flow obtain B using Equation 66 and Tables 1 and 2. For vertical flow obtain B from Table 1. For laminar flow of one or other component, use Equations 50 and 75.

Void fractions in tubes. Obtain the velocity ratio using Equations 17 to 23.

Momentum flux in tubes. Use Equations 29, 30, and 32, evaluating the effective velocity ratio using Equation 40.

Bends. Evaluate the B-coefficient using Equations 78 and 79.

Change of section. For incompressible flow obtain B from Equations 84, 87 to 89. For compressible flow conditions use Equation 93. For flashing flow use either Equation 98 or 99 in evaluating the effective specific volume.

Crossflow friction and form drag. Use Equation 53 and the B-coefficients in Table 4. See section on "Bypass" for discussion of effects.

Window pressure drop. Evaluate, using Equation 53, with crossflow B-coefficients, except for the spray pattern, where the value of B is given by Equation 130. Bubble flow is assumed to exist up to a void fraction of 0.8.

Crossflow momentum and gravitational effects. Use the methods recommended for tubes.

NOTATION

A	flow cross section	k_B	pressure drop coefficient for a bend, Equation 76
A_G	flow cross section occupied by gas		
B	coefficient defined by Equation 53	MF	momentum flux, Equation 28
B_A	coefficient evaluated using Table 1	$\dot{m}_G$	mass flow rate of gas
B_e	coefficient evaluated using Equation 66	$\dot{m}_L$	mass flow rate of liquid
		N	Henry's metastability ratio, Equation 97
B_f	coefficient for spray flow, Equation 111		
B_R	coefficient for rough tubes, Equation 69	n	Blasius exponent, Equation 48
		n	expansion exponent, Equations 94 and 95
B_S	coefficient for stratified flow, Equation 56		
		p	static pressure
C	coefficient, Equation 50	R	coefficient, Equation 59
C_c	contraction coefficient, Equation 96	Re	Reynolds number
C_G	contraction coefficient for gas	u_e	effective velocity, Equation 34
C_L	contraction coefficient for liquid	u_G	velocity of gas, Equation 9
c	Blasius coefficient, Equation 48	u_H	homogeneous velocity, Equation 10
Cp	specific heat; at constant pressure	u_L	velocity of liquid
Cv	specific heat at constant volume	u_{wD}	velocity of weighted drift, Equation 19
D	derivative with respect to displacement in flow direction	w	entrainment, Equation 124
		w_D	correction factor to drift velocity, Equation 20
d	bore		
e	entrainment parameter, Equation 61	v	specific volume
Fr	Froude number, Equation 113	v_e	effective specific volume, Equation 29
G	mass flux	v_G	specific volume of gas
G_A	mass flux defined by Equation 65	v_H	homogeneous specific volume, Equation 16
G_s	mass flux defined by Equation 64		
g	gravitational acceleration	v_L	specific volume of liquid
K	phase velocity ratio, u_G/u_L	v_m	specific volume of mixture, Equation 15
K_0	phase velocity ratio evaluated using Equations 17 and 18	X	Lockhart-Martinelli parameter, Equation 13
k	pressure drop coefficient, Equation 82	x	mass dryness fraction, Equation 5

Greek Symbols

α void fraction, Equation 8

Γ physical property parameter, Equation 12

ε surface roughness, Equation 69

θ inclination of tube to horizontal

λ friction factor, Equation 47

μ dynamic viscosity

σ flow area ratio, A2/A1, Equation 81

ϕ^2 two-phase multiplier, Equations 50 and 53

ψ normalized two-phase multiplier, Equa-

tions 38 and 57

ψ_A normalized two-phase multiplier evaluated using Table 1

ψ_b normalized two-phase multiplier for bubble flow

ψ_F normalized two-phase multiplier for friction

ψ_M normalized two-phase multiplier for moment flux change

ψ_S normalized two-phase multiplier for stratified flow

Subscripts

B	bend	L	liquid
be	bubble-spray	Lo	mixture flows as liquid
F	friction	M	momentum
G	gas	N	thermodynamic equilibrium
Go	mixtures flows as gas	SL	separated liquid
g	gravity	t	transaction from bubble flow

REFERENCES

1. Baroczy, C. J. "A Systematic Correlation for Two-Phase Pressure Drop." *Chem. Engng. Prog. Symp. Ser.* 1966, 62(44), 232–49.
2. Chisholm, D., and Sutherland, L. A. "Prediction of Pressure Changes in Pipeline Systems During Two-Phase Flow." Paper No. 4. I. Mech. E./I. Chem. E. Joint Symp. on Fluid Mechanics and Measurements in Two-Phase Systems, 24–25 September 1969, University of Leeds.
3. Lockhart, R. W., and Martinelli, R. C. "Proposed Correlation of Data for Isothermal Two-Phase Two-Component Flow in Pipes." *Chem. Engng. Progr.,* 1949, 45(1), 39–48.
4. Chisholm, D. "Two-Phase Flow Through Sharp-Edged Orifices." *J. Mech. Engng. Sci.,* 1977, 19(3), 128–30.
5. Chisholm, D. *Two-phase Flow in Pipelines and Heat Exchangers.* Harlow, Essex, England: George Godwin/I. Chem. E., 1983.
6. Armand, A. A. "Resistance to Two-Phase Flow in Horizontal Tubes." (In Russian). Izv. VII, 1946, 15(1), 16–23. English translation NLL. M882, Boston Spa, Yorks: National Lending Library.
7. Labuntsov, D. A. et al. "Vapor Concentration of a Two-Phase Adiabatic Flow in Vertical Ducts." *Thermal Engng.,* 1968, 15(4), 62–7.
8. Zuber, N., and Findlay, J. A. "Average Volumetric Concentration in Two-Phase Flow Systems." *Trans. ASME J. Heat Transfer,* 1965, 87, 453–68.
9. Beggs, H. D. "An Experimental Study of Two-Phase Flow in Inclined Pipes." Ph.D. thesis, Univ. of Tulsa, 1972. Order No. 72-21-615. Ann Arbor, Michigan: Univ. Microfilms, 1972.
10. Friedel, L. "Mean Void Fraction and Friction Pressure Drops: Comparison of Some Correlations with Experimental Data." European Two-Phase Flow Group Meeting, Grenoble, 6–9 June 1977. Paper A7.
11. Chisholm, D. "Critical Conditions During Flow of Two-Phase Mixtures Through Nozzles." Thermodynamic and Fluid Mechanics Group Convention, Bristol, 27–29 March 1968. *Inst.*

of Mech. Engrs. Proceedings 1967–68, 182(3H), 145–51. London: Institution of Mechanical Engineers, 1968.

12. Chisholm, D. "Prediction of Pressure Drop at Pipe Fittings During Two-Phase Flow." 13th Int. Inst. of Refrig. Cong., Washington, 27 August–3 September 1971, 2, 781–9.

13. Chisholm, D. "Pressure Gradients Due to Friction During the Flow of Evaporating Two-Phase Mixtures in Smooth Tubes and Channels. *Int. J. Heat Mass Transfer*, 1973, 16(2), 347–58.

14. Andeen, G. B., and Griffith, P. "Momentum Flux in Two-Phase Flow." *Trans. A.S.M.E. J. Heat Transfer*, Paper No. 67-HT-32, August, 1967.

15. Wiafe, F. "Two-Phase Flow in Rough Tubes." Ph.D. thesis, University of Strathclyde, Glasgow, 1970.

16. Chisholm, D., and Laird, A. D. M. "Two-Phase Flow in Rough Tubes, *Trans. Amer. Soc. Engrs.* 1958, 80(2), 276–86.

17. Chisholm, D. "Pressure Gradients During Flow in Incompressible Two-Phase Mixtures Through Pipes, Venturis, and Orifice Plates. *Brit. Chem. Engng.*, 1967, 12(9), 1368–71.

18. Sadatomi, M., Sato, Y., and Saruwatari, S. "Two-Phase Flow is Vertical Noncircular Channels." *Int. J. Multiphase Flow*, 1982, 8(6), 641–655.

19. Chisholm, D. Discussion of paper by Johannessen, T. A.,"Theoretical Solution of the Lockhart and Martinelli Flow Model for Calculating Two-Phase Flow Pressure Drop and Hold-Up." *Int. J. Heat Mass Transfer*, 1972, 15, 1443–9. Discussion: 1973, 16, 225–6.

20. Chisholm, D. "The Pressure Gradient Due to Friction During the Flow of Boiling Water." *Eng. and Boiler House Rev.*, 1963, 78(9), 287–9.

21. Chisholm, D. "The Turbulent Flow of Two-Phase Mixtures in Horizontal Pipes at Low Reynolds Number." *J. Mech. Engng. Sci.*, 1980, 22(4), 199–202.

22. Chisholm, D. "The Transition from Stratified Flow in Tubes and Crossflow." *European Two-Phase Meeting*, University of Strathclyde, 3–4 June 1980.

23. Chisholm, D. "Flow Pattern Maps in Horizontal Two-Phase Flow." *Paper F1. Int. Conf. on the Modeling of Multiphase Flow*, 19–21 April 1983. Bedford, England; BHRA, 1983.

24. Weisman, J. et al. "Effects of Fluid Properties and the Pipe Diameter on Two-Phase Flow Patterns in Horizontal Pipes." *Int. J. Multiphase Flow*, 1979, 5, 437–62.

25. Weisman, J. "Two-Phase Flow Patterns," Chapter 15. In: *Handbook of Fluids in Motion.* Cheremisinoff, N. P. and Gupta, R. (eds.) Ann Arbor, Michigan: Ann Arbor Sciences, 1983.

26. Chisholm, D. "Influence of Pipe Surface Roughness on Friction Pressure Gradient During Two-Phase Flow. *J. Mech. Engng. Sci.*, 1978, 20(6), 353–4.

27. Simpson, H. C., Rooney, D. H., Grattan, E., and Al-Sammarrae, F. A. A. "Two-Phase Flow Studies in Large Diameter Horizontal Tubes." NEL Report No 677. East Kilbride, Glasgow: National Engineering Laboratory, 1981.

28. Chisholm, D. Void Fraction During Two-Phase Flow. *J. Mech. Engng. Sci.*, 1973, 15(3), 235–6.

29. Wallis, G. B. *One-Dimensional Two-Phase Flow.* New York: McGraw-Hill, 1969.

30. Chisholm, D. "Gas-Liquid Flow in Pipeline Systems." Chapter 18. In: *Handbook of Fluids in Motion.* Cheremisinoff, N. P. and Gupta, R. (eds.) Ann Arbor, Michigan: Ann Arbor Sciences, 1983.

31. Kubie, H., and Oates, H. S. "Aspects of Two-Phase Frictional Pressure Drop in Tubes. *Trans. Inst. Chem. Eng.*, 1978, 56, 205–9.

32. Charles, M. E., and Lillelehet, L. U. "Correlation of Pressure Gradients for Stratified Laminar-Turbulent Flow of Two Immiscible Liquids." *Can. J. Chem. Eng.*, 1966, 44(1), 47–9.

33. Chisholm, D. "Two-Phase Pressure Drop in Bends. *Int. J. Multi-Phase Flow*, 1980, 6, 363–367.

34. Chisholm, D. "Flow of Compressible Two-Phase Mixtures Through Orifices and Nozzles." Paper No. C101/83. *Heat and Fluid Flow in Nuclear and Process Plant Safety.* London: I. Mech. E. Conf. Publications 1983–84.

35. Chisholm, D. "Flow of Compressible Two-Phase Mixtures Through Throttling Devices." *Chem. Process Engng.*, 1967, 48(12), 73–8.

36. Janssen, E. "Two-Phase Pressure Loss a Cross Abrupt Contractions and Expansion, Steam-Water at 600 and 1,400 lb/in². *Proc. Third Int. Heat Transfer*, 1965, 5, 13–25, New York American Inst. Chem. Engrs. 1966.

37. Fairhurst, C. P. "Component Pressure Loss During Two-Phase Flow." *Paper A1. Int. Conf. on the Physical Modeling of Multi-phase Flow*, 19–21 April 1983. Coventry, England: BHRA Fluid Engineering, 1983.

38. Tangren, R. F., Dodge, C. H., and Seifert, H. S. "Compressibility Effects in Two-Phase Flow." *J. Appl. Phys.* 1949, 20(7), 47–55.

39. Jobson, D. A. "On the Flow of Compressible Fluids Through Orifices." *Proc. Instn. Mech. Engrs*, 1955, 169(37), 767–76.

40. Henry, R. E. "A Study of One and Two-Component Two-Phase Flows at Low Qualities." *Report No ANL-7430*. Argonne, Illinois: Argonne National Laboratory, 1968.

41. Henry, R. E., and Fauske, H. K. "Two-Phase Critical Flow of One Component Mixtures in Nozzles, Orifices, and Short Tubes." ASME, *Trans., Series C-J. Heat Transfer*, 1971, 93, 179–87.

42. Chisholm, D. "Mass Velocities Under Choked Flow Conditions in Two-Phase Flashing Pipe Flow." *J. Mech. Engng. Sci.*, 1981, 23(6), 309–11.

43. Grant, I. D. R. "Two-Phase Flow and Pressure Drop on the Shell-Side of Shell-and-Tube Heat Exchangers." *Heat and Fluid Flow in Steam and Gas Turbine Plant*, Univ. of Warwick, Coventry, 3–5 April, 1973. CP3, pp. 244–251. London: I. Mech. E., 1973.

44. Grant, I. D. R., and Chisholm D. "Two-Phase Flow on the Shell-Side of a Segmentally Baffled Shell-and-Tube Heat Exchanger." *Trans.* ASME, 1979, 101, 38–42.

45. Grant, I. D. R., and Chisholm, D. "Horizontal Two-Phase Flow Across Tube Banks." *Int. J. Heat and Fluid Flow.* 1980, 2(2), 97–100.

46. Grant, I. D. R., Chisholm, D., and Cotchin, C. D. "Shell-side Flow in Horizontal Condensers." Joint ASME/AIChE National Heat Transfer Conference, Orlando, Florida, July 27–30, 1980, ASME *Preprint No 80-HT-52*.

47. Grant, I. D. R., Finlay, I. C., and Harris, D. "Flow and Pressure Drop During Vertically Upward Two-Phase Flow Past a Tube Bundle With and Without Bypass Leakage." I. Chem. E./I. Mech. E. Joint Symp. on Multiphase Flow Systems, Univ. of Strathclyde Glasgow, 2–4 April, 1974, 2, *Paper 17*. London: The Institution of Chemical Engineers, 1974.

48. Grant, I. D. R., and Murray, I. "Pressure Drop on the Shell-Side of a Segmentally Baffled Shell-and-Tube Heat Exchanger with Vertical Two-Phase Flow." *NEL Report No 500*. East Kilbride, Glasgow: National Engineering Laboratory, 1972.

49. Grant, I. D. R., Cotchin, C., and Chisholm, D. "Tube Submergence and Entrainment on the Shell-side of Heat Exchangers." Heat and Mass Transfer Conference, Dubrovnik, September, 1981.

50. Polley, G. T., and Grant, I. D. R. "Pressure Drop Prediction for Two-Phase Upward Flow Through a Tube Bundle with Bypassing." Assoc. Engrs. Grad. Univ. Liege (A.I.Ig.) *Proc. Int. Meeting. Industrial Heat Exchangers and Heat Recovery*, Liege, 14–16 November 1979. *Paper A10*. Liege, Belgium: A.I.Ig., 1979.

51. Chisholm, D. "Two-Phase Vertical Upflow Through Tube Banks with Bypass Lanes." *Int. J. Heat and Fluid Flow*, at press.

CHAPTER 20

CO-CURRENT HORIZONTAL AND VERTICAL UPWARD FLOW
OF GAS AND NON-NEWTONIAN LIQUID

R. P. Chhabra and **J. F. Richardson**

Department of Chemical Engineering
University College of Swansea
Swansea, United Kingdom

CONTENTS

INTRODUCTION

The simultaneous two-phase flow of gases and liquids is encountered in many chemical and processing industries. The three most important hydrodynamic features of such systems during pipe flow are the flow pattern, the hold up of the two phases, and the frictional pressure drop. The fluid mechanics of such systems must be fully understood before other transport processes such as heat and mass transfer can be modeled.

During the last three decades or so, there have been many studies of the co-current flow of gases and Newtonian liquids and most of these have been described by Hewitt [1]. The work has been summarized in several books [2, 3] and in the three preceding chapters of this volume.

In recent years it has been recognized that in many engineering applications in petroleum exploration, polymer and food processing, biochemical operations etc., the liquid phase exhibits complex non-Newtonian behavior. The primary objective in this chapter is to provide an up-to-date and critical assessment of the information that has become available during the last ten years or so. The treatment is presented in three main sections, namely, flow patterns, average hold-up and pressure drop. In each of these sections, there is a brief review of the current status on work with Newtonian liquids because, in general, the correlations presented for materials exhibiting non-Newtonian behavior are based on those for the much simpler case of the Newtonian liquid.

No consideration is given to problems involving phase change, and throughout attention has been confined to steady-state isothermal situations and conditions where the effects of expansion of the gas are small.

FLOW PATTERNS

An important feature of two-phase co-current gas-liquid flow—horizontal as well as upward vertical—is the wide variety of possible flow patterns governed by the physical properties and input fluxes of the two phases and the size and orientation of the pipe. Since the mechanisms responsible for momentum transfer (or frictional loss) vary from one flow pattern to another, it is essential to know which flow pattern is occurring in any instance before attempting to model a two-phase flow system. In this section, our primary concern is to formulate schemes that would enable a priori prediction of the flow pattern likely to prevail in a given situation. Although this chapter relates mainly to the flow of gases with non-Newtonian liquids, it is necessary first to discuss the well established schemes proposed for Newtonian liquids, because these will be extended to cover non-Newtonian behavior. Furthermore, as there are inherent differences between horizontal and vertical flow, the two cases are dealt with separately.

Horizontal Flow

It is now generally agreed that the classification proposed by Alves [4] encompasses all the major and easily recognizable flow patterns encountered in horizontal pipes. These are sketched in Figure 1 and are defined below.

Bubble flow. This flow pattern, sometimes referred to as dispersed bubble flow, is characterized by a train of discrete gas bubbles moving predominantly close to the upper wall of the pipe at almost the same velocity as the liquid. As the liquid flow rate is increased, the bubbles become more evenly dispersed throughout the liquid.

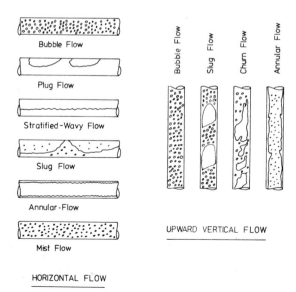

Figure 1. Flow patterns in horizontal and vertical two-phase flow.

Plug flow. At increased gas rates bubbles coalesce to give rise to large bullet-shaped bubbles occupying most of the pipe cross section.

Stratified flow. In this mode of flow the gravitational forces dominate and the gas flows in the upper section of pipe. At relatively low flowrates, the interface between the two phases is smooth, but ripply waves develop at the interface at higher gas rates to give *wavy flow.* The distinction between the smooth and wavy interface is often ill defined, and some workers [5] use the term *stratified-wavy* to cover both types.

Slug flow. In this type of flow *frothy slugs* of liquid phase carrying entrained gas bubbles alternate with gas slugs surrounded by liquid films. Although plug and slug flow are both well defined, as shown in Figure 1, it is in practice not easy to distinguish between them.

Annular flow. In this flow the drag forces at the gas-liquid interface are comparable with the gravitational forces and the liquid is carried along the inner wall of pipe as a thin film, while the gas forms a central core occupying a substantial portion of the cross section. Liquid is usually entrained as fine droplets in the gas core. Sometimes the term *film flow* is used to describe this flow pattern.

Mist flow. Mist flow is said to occur when a significant amount of liquid becomes transferred to the gas core from the annular film; at high gas rates nearly all of the liquid is entrained in the gas. In recent years, some investigators, particularly Taitel and Dukler [6] and Hewitt [5], have argued that this mode of flow is really an extreme case of annular flow.

The flow patterns just described are the principal ones currently used to classify gas-liquid horizontal flow. It is important to remember that the distinction between any two flow patterns is far from clear cut, especially in the case of bubble, plug and slug flows. Hewitt [5] and Weisman et al. [7] have combined all three and described them as *intermittent flow.* On this basis the chief flow patterns adopted in this treatment are dispersed, intermittent, stratified, wavy, and annular-mist flow. Detailed descriptions of flow patterns and of the methods by which they may be determined are contained in the chapter by Barnea and Taitel in this volume. as well as in several other books [2, 5, 8]. Although most of the information regarding flow patterns has been gathered from experiments on gas flowing co-currently with Newtonian liquids, the limited experimental work reported so far [9, 10, 17] on shear thinning liquids suggests that they give rise to qualitatively similar flow patterns and therefore the same nomenclature will be adopted here.

Background Information on Gas-Newtonian Flow

For the flow of mixtures of gas and Newtonian liquids, several, mostly empirical, attempts have been made to construct flow patterns maps. An exhaustive review will not be given here, but attention is drawn to some of the detailed descriptions of the subject that have recently appeared [5, 7, 11, 12]; these are also dealt with by Barnea and Taitel.

Although one might expect the physical properties of the two phases to play important roles in governing the transition from one flow pattern to another, it is now generally recognized that they indeed have very little influence [7, 13]. Thus, the flow pattern maps based on data obtained for air-water flow are generally adequate for most other gases and Newtonian liquids. The flow pattern map proposed by Mandhane et al. [13], though entirely empirical, has gained wide acceptance and is simple to use. It is shown in Figure 2 for the flow of air-water mixtures. Note that the coordinates have been expressed in SI units in preference to those used by the original authors. The transition bands shown in this figure correspond to $\pm 10\%$ of values of superficial velocity. This flow pattern map portrays all the flow patterns identified by Alves [4], but the boundary separating the bubble/plug/slug flow regimes has been removed in subsequent figures and the term *intermittent flow* used to cover all three patterns.

Although the physical properties of the two phases have little effect on the transition boundaries, Mandhane et al. [13] suggested the following scaling parameters (in SI units) to extend the

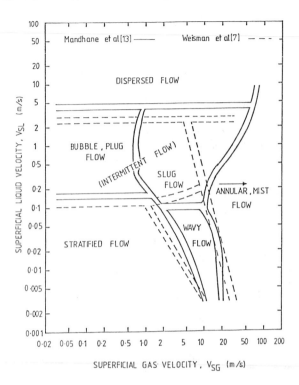

Figure 2. Comparison of the maps of Mandhane et al. [13] and Weisman et al. [7].

applicability of their map to other gas-liquid systems:

$$
X = \left(\frac{\rho_G}{1.21}\right)^{0.2} \left(\frac{\rho_L}{1,000}\right)^{0.25} \left(\frac{0.0728}{\sigma_L}\right)^{0.25} \left(\frac{\mu_G}{1.8 \times 10^{-5}}\right)^{0.2}
$$

$$
\text{and} \quad Y = \left(\frac{\mu_L}{0.001}\right)^{0.2} \left(\frac{\rho_L}{1,000}\right)^{0.2} \left(\frac{0.0728}{\sigma_L}\right)^{0.25}
$$

(1)

The method of applying these parameters to amend Figure 2 is outlined in Table 1. Both X and Y have values of unity for the flow of air-water mixtures at standard temperature and pressure. Furthermore, since pipe diameter does not appear in either X or Y, it clearly has not been found to have a significant influence on the flow pattern transitions over the range studied (12 < D < 165 mm).

Hewitt [5] has recently shown that this empirical map corresponds closely with that obtained from semi-theoretical considerations by Taitel and Dukler [6]. Weisman et al. [7], who carried out extensive experimental measurements, also found that flow patterns were little affected by the physical properties of the two phases. Their reference map for the flow of air/water mixtures in a one-inch diameter pipe at standard temperature and pressure is also shown in Figure 2. Note that in this map no distinction is made between bubble, plug, and slug flow. In view of the poor reproducibility and inherent subjectivity in this field, the agreement between the two flow

Table 1
Application of X and Y for Systems Other Than Air/Water [13]

Transition boundary	Physical property correction multiply the r.h.s. equation of transition boundary, $V_{SL} = \zeta(V_{SG})$ by
Stratified to Elongated Bubble	1/Y
Wavy to Slug	Y
Elongated bubble and slug to dispersed bubble	Y
Stratified, elongated bubble to wavy and slug	X
Wavy and slug to annular/mist	X
Dispersed bubble to annular-mist	X

pattern maps is regarded as satisfactory, except for a minor discrepancy between the slug/annular and the intermittent/annular transition boundaries.

The location of the boundary for the transition from intermittent to annular flow on the map proposed by Weisman et al. [7] has received further support from the independent study of Nguyen and Spedding [14]. Weisman et al. [7] also proposed a new set of scaling parameters to modify their map for systems other than air-water. These (ϕ_1 and ϕ_2) are given in Table 2 and the coordinates of the map now become V_{SG}/ϕ_1 and V_{SL}/ϕ_2. Here again, ϕ_1 and ϕ_2 reduce to unity for the flow of air-water mixtures in a one inch diameter pipe under standard conditions. It is of particular interest to note that in spite of the narrow range of pipe diameter (12, 25, 51 mm) employed, Weisman et al. [7] reported a marked influence of pipe diameter on the transition between flow patterns, and this is also evident from the definitions of ϕ_1 and ϕ_2, which contain the pipe diameter as a variable. This effect of pipe diameter is in accordance with the semi-theoretical analysis of Taitel and Dukler [6] but is not borne out by the experimental results of Mandhane et al. [13] whose map is based on data for pipes up to 165 mm in diameter. Conflicting evidence regarding the effect of pipe diameter can also be seen in the work of Simpson et al. [15]. Since only a very limited amount of data is available on flow patterns in large diameter pipes, no definite conclusions can be drawn at this stage. By incorporating the results of Weisman et al. [7] into the map of Mandhane et al., Chhabra and Richardson [16] have recently presented a revised map that covers a wider range of physical properties, as shown in Figure 3.

This map has then been used by Chhabra and Richardson [16] as the basis for the prediction of flow pattern for two phase flow involving shear-thinning non-Newtonian liquids.

Data Bank for Gas/Solids Non-Newtonian Liquid Systems

Chhabra and Richardson [16] also created a data base on flow patterns in two-phase gas non-Newtonian liquid systems using the results from the very few studies in which the flow patterns have been observed and actually reported. Table 3 shows the range of rheological properties and conditions studied; although there is a tenfold variation in pipe diameter the maximum value is only 42 mm, except in the work of Chhabra et al. [23] who obtained a few results on a 207-mm-diameter pipe. In most cases, the laminar flow properties of the test liquids have been approximated using the generalized two parameter power-law model $(-D \Delta P/4L) = K'(8V/D)^{n'}$; additionally some of the polymer solutions used by Chhabra et al. [24] also displayed viscoelastic effects. It is important to bear in mind that in all cases flow patterns were determined by visual observations of the test section, and hence have a degree of inherent arbitrariness and subjectivity, particularly for opaque suspensions (china clay and anthracite). The preponderance of data in intermittent flow is evident, but nevertheless they do extend to the other major flow patterns with the exception of dispersed and stratified flow. In all there are 3,652 data points distributed as follows: intermittent, 3,448; wavy, 25; annular, 176; stratified, 2; and dispersed flow, 1.

Table 2
Property and Pipe Diameter Corrections Proposed by Weisman et al. [7]

	ϕ_1	ϕ_2
Transition to dispersed flow	1.00	$\left(\dfrac{\rho_L}{\rho_{Ls}}\right)^{-0.33}\left(\dfrac{D}{D_s}\right)^{0.16}\left(\dfrac{\mu_{Ls}}{\mu_L}\right)^{0.09}\left(\dfrac{\sigma}{\sigma_s}\right)^{0.24}$
Transition to annular flow	$\left(\dfrac{\rho_{Gs}}{\rho_G}\right)^{0.23}\left(\dfrac{\Delta\rho}{\Delta\rho_s}\right)^{0.11}\left(\dfrac{\sigma}{\sigma_s}\right)^{0.11}\left(\dfrac{D}{D_s}\right)^{0.415}$	1.00
Wavy-stratified	$\left(\dfrac{D_s}{D}\right)^{0.17}\left(\dfrac{\mu_G}{\mu_{Gs}}\right)^{1.55}\left(\dfrac{\rho_{Gs}}{\rho_G}\right)^{1.55}\left(\dfrac{\Delta\rho}{\Delta\rho_s}\right)^{0.69}\left(\dfrac{\sigma_s}{\sigma}\right)^{0.69}$	1.00
Intermittent-separated	1.00	$\left(\dfrac{D}{D_s}\right)^{0.45}$

The subscript, s, denotes standard conditions:

$D_s = 25.4\ mm$; $\quad \mu_{Ls} = 1\ mPas$; $\quad \rho_{Ls} = 1,000\ kgm^{-3}$

$\rho_{Gs} = 1.3\ kgm^{-3}$; $\quad \sigma_s = 0.07\ Nm^{-1}$; $\quad \Delta\rho = (\rho_L \div \rho_G)$

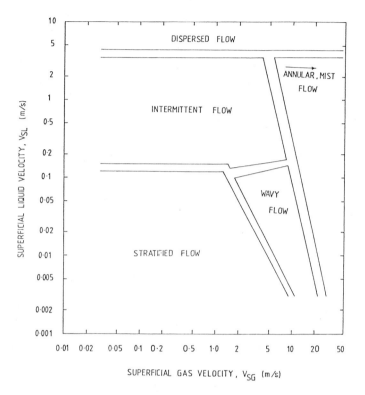

Figure 3. Modified flow pattern map [16].

Prediction of Flow Patterns for Flow of Gas/Solids Non-Newtonian Liquid Mixtures

At the outset, the relative magnitudes of the ratios of physical properties appearing in parameters X and Y are considered. In most of the investigations listed in Table 3, air or nitrogen was used as the gas at or near atmospheric pressure and ambient temperature, and hence the ratios $(\rho_G/1.21)$ and $(\mu_G/1.8 \times 10^{-5})$ would be near enough to unity. Similarly, the maximum liquid density is 1,500 kgm^{-3} [22] giving $(\rho_L/1,000)^{0.25}$ equal to 1.11, which again is close to unity. The limited information [10, 25, 26, 79] regarding the surface tension of polymer solutions similar to those listed in Table 3 suggests that the ratio $(0.0728/\sigma_L)^{0.25}$ does not exceed 1.19. The resulting shift in the transition boundary is small compared with the error in determining the transition velocities which is of the order of $\pm 10\%$. The influence of physical properties is also small, considering their effect on the scaling factors, ϕ_1 and ϕ_2 proposed by Weisman et al. [7]. Indeed the maximum values of ϕ_1 and ϕ_2 are 1.19 and 1.25, respectively, but in most cases the shift in boundaries is less than 15%. Most of the non-Newtonian materials investigated so far have apparent viscosities that are highly shear dependent and therefore the term $(\mu_L/0.001)^{0.2}$ cannot be evaluated because the shear rate (which itself would depend upon flow pattern, etc.) is varying and unknown. Rosehart [18] suggested calculating the apparent viscosity at a shear rate determined by the no-slip (mixture) velocity and reported that viscosity had very little influence on the transition boundaries. Clearly, such an approach is relevant only to the intermittent flow pattern.

Any discrepancies between the observed behavior of non-Newtonian systems and those predicted using the flow pattern map proposed (shown in Figure 3) for Newtonian systems are most likely

Table 3
Summary of Studies on Flow Patterns

Investigator	D (mm)	System used	Range of rheological properties (S.I. Units)	V_{SL} (ms^{-1})	V_{SG} (ms^{-1})	Flow patterns observed	Number of points
Oliver and Young-Hoon [17]	6.35	N$_2$ and aqueous solutions of sodium carboxy-methyl cellulose and Polyox	$0.49 < n' < 0.51$ $2.46 < K < 3.42$	0.17–0.34	0.09–16.0	Intermittent, stratified, wavy, annular	53
Rosehart [18]	25.0	Air and aqueous solutions of CMC, Polyhall and Carbopol 941	$0.39 < n' < 0.75$ $0.19 < K' < 1.58$	0.28–0.67	0.3–1.77	Intermittent	605
Mahalingam and Valle [9]	12.7	Air and aqueous solutions of Methocel, Carbopol	$0.61 < n' < 0.95$ $0.0037 < K' < 1.16$	0.124	0.011–37	Intermittent, wavy, annular	44
Eisenberg and Weinberger [19]	2.9	Air-aqueous solutions of Separan AP-30, CMC and Polyox	$0.34 < n' < 0.6$ $0.2 < K' < 10.25$	0.2–0.63	10–37	Annular	139
Heywood [20]	42	Air-aqueous anthracite and china clay suspensions	$0.10 < n' < 0.225$ $1.02 < K < 52.0$	0.25–1.5	0.2–7	Intermittent	628
Farooqi et al. [21]	42	Air-aqueous suspensions of anthracite	$0.2 < n' < 0.86$ $0.028 < K' < 25.2$	0.25–1.5	0.15–7	Intermittent	362
Farooqi and Richardson [22]	42	Air-china clay suspensions	$0.14 < n' < 0.96$ $0.02 < K < 28.6$	0.25–2.0	0.15–7	Intermittent	1,093
Chhabra et al. [23]	207	Air and aqueous suspensions of china clay	$n' = 0.103$ $18 < K' < 48.5$	0.28–1.35	0.3–3.00	Intermittent	33
Raghavan et al. [10]	12	Air and aqueous solutions of Methocel	$0.64 < n' < 0.91$ $0.0061 < K' < 0.34$	0.021–6.1	0.061–55	Intermittent, dispersed, stratified wavy, annular	17
Chhabra et al. [24]*	42	Air-aqueous solution of CMC, Natrosol, Separan AP-30	$0.28 < n' < 0.92$ $0.039 < K < 10$	0.25–2.0	0.15–7	Intermittent	678

Note: Values of K' $(Pa\,s^n)$ correspond to apparent viscosity at shear rate of $1\,s^{-1}$.
* Aqueous solutions of Separan AP-30 were viscoelastic.

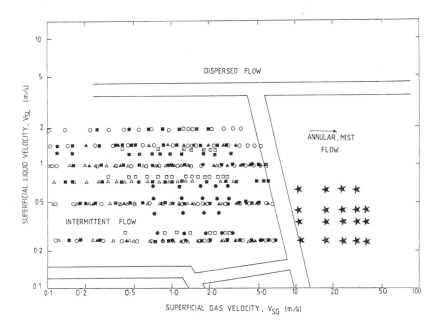

Figure 4. Map (Figure 3) showing experimental results for non-Newtonian liquids. Intermittent flow: (○) [22]; (●) (18); (△) [24]; (▲) (21); (■) [20]; (□) [23]. Annular flow: (★) [19].

to be attributable to their shear-thinning characteristics, as the other physical properties have already been shown to exert little influence. In one case the test liquids exhibited viscoelasticity [24]. The results for non-Newtonian fluids are shown on the flow pattern map in Figures 4 and 5; due to the confusion arising from overlapping data points, especially in Figure 4, the results for only one typical gas-liquid system are shown for each of the investigations. An inspection of Figure 4 clearly reveals that the data of Rosehart [18] for intermittent flow, of Eisenberg and Weinberger [19] for annular flow, and of Richardson et al. [20–24] for intermittent flow, giving a total of 3,538 data points, are in complete agreement with the flow pattern map. It is of interest to note that even though there is some uncertainty regarding the effect of pipe diameter, the limited results of Chhabra et al. [23] for a 207-mm-diameter pipe are also in excellent agreement. In addition, there are 114 data points [9, 10,17] shown in Figure 5 for which the agreement, although less good, is still seen to be reasonable. In fact, approximately 62% of the tests reported by Oliver and Young-Hoon [17], 77% of Mahalingam and Valle [9] and 80% of Raghavan et al. [10] are successfully predicted by the present scheme. Because Mandhane et al. [13] claimed a success rate of only 67% for Newtonian liquids, the comparisons depicted in Figures 4 and 5 may be regarded as satisfactory.

Thus, in short, the same flow pattern map can be used to delineate flow patterns involving both Newtonian and non-Newtonian shear-thinning liquids over a substantial range of flow conditions and rheological properties.

Vertical Upward Flow

Qualitatively similar flow patterns are observed in the vertical two-phase flow of gas and Newtonian liquids, and these are described in detail by Barnea and Taitel. The principal flow patterns are illustrated in Figure 1. In 1980, Taitel et al. [27] made a semi-theoretical study of the

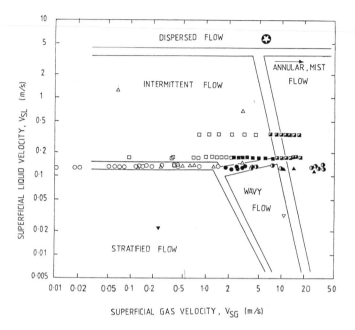

Figure 5. Map (Figure 3) showing experimental results for non-Newtonian liquids. [10]: ($\triangle$) intermittent; ($\blacktriangle$) annular; ($\triangledown$) wavy; ($\blacktriangledown$) stratified; and ($\odot$) dispersed. [9]: ($\bigcirc$) intermittent; ($\bullet$) wavy; ($\bullet$) annular. [17]: ($\square$) intermittent; ($\blacksquare$) stratified-wavy; ($\blacksquare$) annular.

fundamental mechanisms responsible for each flow pattern, and derived criteria for the transition from one to another. Their flow pattern map is reproduced in Figure 6 for the co-current upward flow of air and water mixtures in a 38-mm-diameter pipe.

The only study dealing with the vertical two-phase flow involving shear-thinning liquids is that of Khatib and Richardson [28, 29], who concluded that their results on flow patterns covering a limited range of conditions were well predicted by the map of Taitel et al. [27]. Typical experimental results are included in Figure 6. Thus, the available evidence from the so far limited number of experimental results suggests that, as for horizontal flow, the map for Newtonian liquids can be applied to shear-thinning liquids. However, further conclusions over the wide range of conditions must await additional experimental work in this area.

HOLD-UP

Because of the considerable differences in the physical properties (particularly viscosity and density) of gases and liquids, the gas always tends to flow at a higher average velocity than the liquid. Therefore, the "hold-up," α, defined as the fraction of the pipe volume occupied by a given phase will differ from the volume fraction λ of that phase in the mixture at the inlet. Furthermore, if the change in pressure along the pipeline is significant, the gas hold-up will tend to increase as a result of expansion.

If α_L and α_G are the hold-ups for liquid and gas respectively it follows that

$$\alpha_L + \alpha_G = 1 \tag{2}$$

Similarly for the input volume fractions:

$$\lambda_L + \lambda_G = 1 \tag{3}$$

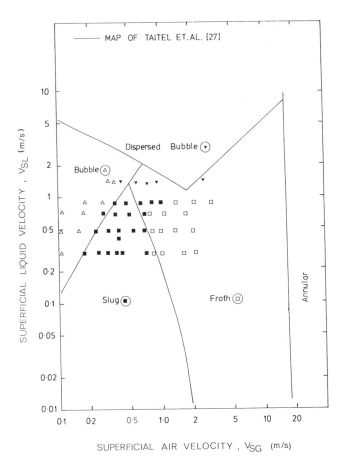

Figure 6. Experimental results [28] for upward vertical flow of shear thinning suspensions, shown on map of Taitel et al. [27].

λ_L and λ_G may be expressed as follows:

$$\lambda_L = \frac{Q_L}{Q_L + Q_G} = \frac{V_{SL}}{V_{SL} + V_{SG}} \quad \text{and} \quad \lambda_G = \frac{Q_G}{Q_L + Q_G} = \frac{V_{SG}}{V_{SL} + V_{SG}} \tag{4}$$

where Q_L and Q_G are volumetric flowrates of liquid and gas respectively. Only under limiting *no slip* conditions and when there is no measureable pressure difference will α and λ be equal. A knowledge of liquid (or gas) hold-up is needed for the calculation both of two-phase pressure drop and of the inventory present in a pipe.

The techniques presently available for measuring holdup fall into two categories, viz. direct methods and indirect methods. In the first method, after isolation, part of the pipe is emptied and the volume of each phase measured. Good reproducibility may be obtained as shown by the studies of Hewitt et al. [30] and of Chen and Spedding [31]; some measurements have been made with non-Newtonian liquids [9, 17, 32, 79]. Although the method is simple, it has two main drawbacks: first, a finite time, however small, is needed to isolate the test section of pipe, and this must, in principle, lead to certain inaccuracy in the method; and after each measurement, ample time should be allowed for the flow to reach a steady state. Second, this method is not practical where temperatures and pressures are high.

The indirect methods have the advantage of not disturbing the flow. The underlying principle is to measure a change in a physical or electrical property that is strongly dependent upon the composition of the mixture. Typical examples include the measurement of γ-ray and X-ray attenuation [33–36], of change of impedance [18, 37, 38] etc. Such methods require calibration and give average values of holdup. Richardson et al. [39, 40] have employed a modified version of the γ-ray absorption technique to obtain "instantaneous" values of hold-up, by scanning over periods as short as 0.10 s.

Detailed descriptions of each of these and other methods and their merits and demerits are available in the excellent book of Hewitt [8].

Upward Horizontal Flow

Gas/Solids Newtonian Systems

Available techniques to predict the average value of liquid hold-up can be divided into two classes: those methods based on consideration of the flow pattern, and purely empirical methods. An example of the former class of method is that of Taitel and Dukler [6] for stratified flow. A

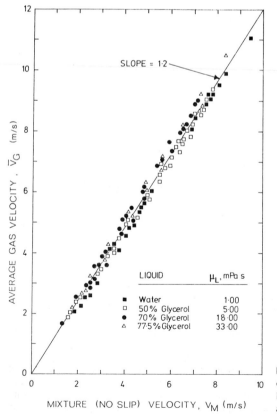

Figure 7. Relationship between average gas velocity and mixture velocity for the horizontal flow of air and Newtonian liquids [22].

further example is that of Zuber and Findlay [41] who established that the in situ (average) gas velocity should be a linear function of the no-slip (mixture) velocity. That is,

$$\bar{V}_G = C_0 V_M + V_0 \tag{5}$$

where C_0 is known as the distribution parameter and is determined by the flow pattern, and V_0 is the drift velocity, which in vertical intermittent-type flow corresponds to the rise velocity of a gas bubble in quiescent liquid. The applicability of Equation 5 may be checked simply by plotting $\bar{V}_G$ ($\equiv V_{SG}/\alpha_G$) against V_M; typical plot is shown in Figure 7 for various gas/liquid systems. Results for non-Newtonian liquids, presented here for convenience, show a similar trend (see Figure 8).

Exhaustive review articles in which theoretical developments were critically examined have been published [5] and attention is again drawn to the chapter in this volume written by Chen and Spedding.

The second category of method for predicting hold-up includes pragmatic correlations, with little or no theoretical background, which take no account of the conditions of flow but which may be

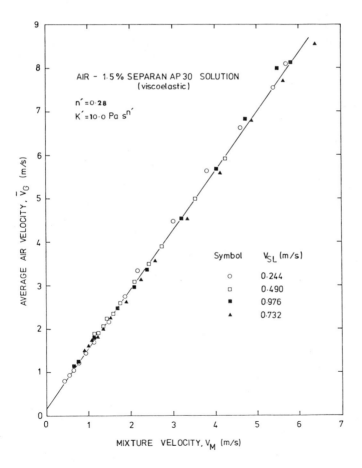

Figure 8. Relationship between average gas velocity and mixture velocity for the horizontal flow of air—1.5% Separan AP30 solution [24].

used over a wide range of the variables of practical interest. Although such an approach does not add to our understanding, it does provide the designer with vital information with an acceptable degree of reliability and accuracy. During the last thirty years or so, numerous correlations have been proposed and well summarized by Mandhane et al. [42] and Govier and Aziz [2]. Perhaps the correlation most widely referred to, and is simple to use, is that of Lockhart and Martinelli [43]. It utilizes information on single-phase flow to express the hold-up data in terms of the so-called Lockhart-Martinelli parameter χ, which is defined as

$$\chi = \sqrt{\frac{-\Delta P_L/L}{-\Delta P_G/L}} \tag{6}$$

where $(-\Delta P_L/L)$ and $(-\Delta P_G/L)$ are pressure gradients, for the flow of liquid and gas alone at the volumetric flow rates occurring in the two-phase system. The correlation is shown in Figure 9. Over the years, much experimental data has been accumulated and it is now generally recognized [17, 20, 22, 44] that the original correlation of Lockhart and Martinelli consistently overpredicts the value of liquid hold-up (α_L) in horizontal two-phase flow. This is clearly shown in Figure 10 where the data of Farooqi and Richardson [22] on the flow of mixtures of air and water and of air and water plus glycerol and the data of Chen and Spedding [31] for the air/water system are plotted along with the correlation of Lockhart and Martinelli [43]. There is some overlap in the range of variables covered in these two independent investigations. Based on their data, most of which relate to the intermittent flow pattern, Farooqi and Richardson [22] proposed the following explicit relations:

$$\left. \begin{array}{ll} \alpha_L = 0.186 + 0.0191\chi & 1 < \chi < 5 \\[2mm] \alpha_L = 0.143\chi^{0.42} & 5 < \chi < 50 \\[2mm] \alpha_L = \dfrac{1}{0.97 + 19/\chi} & 50 < \chi < 500 \end{array} \right\} \tag{7}$$

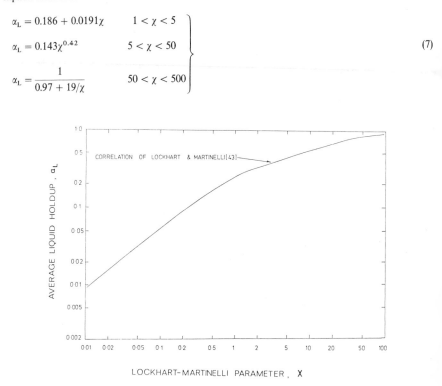

Figure 9. Correlation of Lockhart and Martinelli for average liquid hold-up.

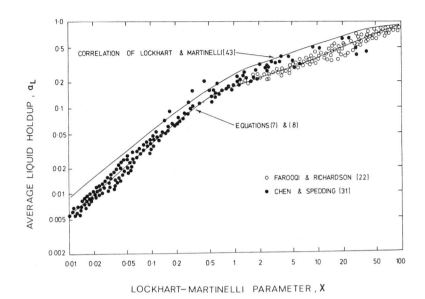

CORRELATION OF LOCKHART & MARTINELLI [43]

EQUATIONS (7) & (8)

○ FAROOQI & RICHARDSON [22]

● CHEN & SPEDDING [31]

AVERAGE LIQUID HOLDUP , α_L

LOCKHART– MARTINELLI PARAMETER , X

Figure 10. Comparison of experimental results for Newtonian liquids with the correlation of Lockhart and Martinelli [43].

Equation 7 is based on the data covering the following ranges of variables: $0.25 < V_{SL} < 2 \text{ ms}^{-1}$; $0.1 < V_{SG} < 7 \text{ ms}^{-1}$ and $1 < \mu_L < 33 \text{ mNsm}^{-2}$; it predicts the average value of hold-up with an error not exceeding $\pm 15\%$. The data of Chen and Spedding [31], on the other hand, refer to a much wider range of experimental conditions, but not of liquid viscosity nor density, and over all the major flow patterns. Thus, considering their work, Equation 7 may be slightly adjusted, to extend its range of applicability as follows

$$\left.\begin{array}{ll} \alpha_L = 0.24\chi^{0.80} & 0.01 < \chi < 0.5 \\[2mm] \alpha_L = 0.175\chi^{0.32} & 0.5 < \chi < 5.0 \end{array}\right\} \tag{8}$$

Equations 7 and 8 are compared with the original correlation of Lockhart and Martinelli [43] in Figure 11.

Other correlations that purport to have better accuracy than Equations 7 and 8 are restricted to a narrow range of conditions. Some of these, which may be regarded as derivatives of the Lockhart-Martinelli correlation, are described by Govier and Aziz [2] and Chisholm [3]. In the following section Equations 7 and 8 will be modified to extend their range of applicability firstly to purely shear-thinning liquids and then to liquids exhibiting viscoelastic effects as well.

Gas/Solids Non-Newtonian Flow

In contrast to the Newtonian case, the flow of gases and shear-thinning liquid mixtures in horizontal pipes has received very little attention. Moreover, among the various workers who have studied the hydrodynamics of such systems, only a few have reported the experimental values of average hold-up. In 1970, Rosehart [18] employed an impedance meter to measure average hold-up in a one-inch-diameter pipe during the two-phase flow of air and a series of aqueous polymer solutions exhibiting shear-thinning behavior. The test liquids were not examined for possible

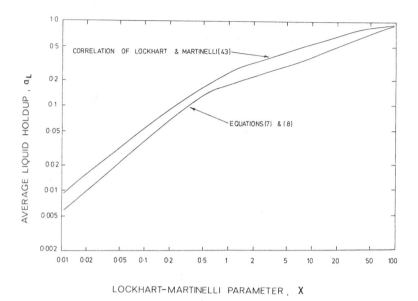

LOCKHART–MARTINELLI PARAMETER , X

Figure 11. Modified form of the correlation of Lockhart and Martinelli.

viscoelastic effects. Rosehart [18] merely demonstrated that the approach of Zuber and Findlay [41] was also applicable to these systems, but did not develop predictive correlations.

Subsequently, Richardson et al. [21, 22, 24] have made an experimental study of the influence of rheological behavior on average hold-up. Measurements were made in a $1\frac{1}{2}$-inch-(42 mm)-diameter pipe for the two-phase flow of air and flocculated aqueous suspensions of fine anthracite and kaolin in water and water-glycerol mixtures. Such suspensions are shear-thinning and do not display viscoelastic effects. The shear stress/shear rate relationship was obtained for each suspension used using a capillary viscometer over the range of shear rates likely to be encountered in the two-phase flow experiments. The aqueous suspensions of anthracite exhibited approximately Bingham Plastic behavior that could be described in terms of a yield stress τ_y and a plastic viscosity μ_p; these two quantities in turn may be related to the generalized parameters introduced by Metzner and Reed [45] viz. n' and K'. On the other hand, the laminar flow behavior of kaolin suspensions conformed more closely to a power-law model, and they were characterized by specifying the values of n and K, which again may be related to n' and K' [2]. The values of n' and K' are summarized in Table 4. Note that since the units of K' (and K) depend upon the numerical value of n' (and n), the values of K' (or K) can be compared only if the two liquids have identical values of n' (or n). Alternatively, the numerical value of K' for a liquid may be viewed as its apparent viscosity at a shear rate of unity (s^{-1}). Although Farooqi et al. [21] and Farooqi and Richardson [22] have covered a wide range of n' and K' values, their results are confined to intermittent flow because of limitations of their equipment.

When Farooqi et al. [21] examined the applicability of the Zuber-Findlay approach, they confirmed the preliminary findings of Rosehart [18] that the method was not very useful because the two constants involved, C_0 and V_0, could not be estimated independently. In the case of vertical two-phase flow involving Newtonian liquids, V_0 closely corresponds to the rise velocity of a single bubble in stationary liquid. In a recent paper, Weber [46] has advanced similar arguments for horizontal flow but available experimental evidence does not seem to support his contention. More recently, Chhabra et al. [24] have attempted, without success, to correlate V_0 and C_0 with the rheological (n', K') and physical properties of the liquid.

Table 4
Rheological Properties of the Test Fluids Used by Richardson et al. [21, 22, 24]

Liquid	Test fluid Solute and its concentration (w/w)	ρ_L kg m^{-3}	n'	K' (Pa s$^{n'}$)
Farooqi and Richardson [22]				
75% aqueous glycerol	4.1% kaolin	1,225	0.93	0.058
	13.1% kaolin	1,289	0.75	0.200
65% aqueous glycerol	2.8% kaolin	1,187	0.96	0.02
	8.3% kaolin	1,225	0.78	0.068
	15.8% kaolin	1,281	0.60	0.32
	19.6% kaolin	1,311	0.50	0.67
	24.2% kaolin	1,352	0.40	2.10
	35.0% kaolin	1,452	0.35	6.70
45% aqueous glycerol	25.7% kaolin	1,310	0.33	1.34
	30.5% kaolin	1,354	0.30	2.98
	39.8% kaolin	1,448	0.27	7.62
	46.0% kaolin	1,520	0.26	16.20
Tap water	18.3% kaolin	1,128	0.27	0.51
	29.6% kaolin	1,225	0.18	4.23
	39.0% kaolin	1,320	0.16	10.95
	46.0% kaolin	1,400	0.14	28.60
Chhabra et al. [24]				
Tap water	1.5% Separan AP30*	1,000	0.28	10.00 (m = 23.1 Pa s^p, p = 0.46)
	1.0% Separan AP30*	1,000	0.33	5.15 (m = 4.5 Pa s^p, p = 0.66)
	0.75% Separan AP30*	1,000	0.42	2.10 (m = 0.37 Pa s^p, p = 0.96)
	0.30% Separan AP30*	1,000	0.58	0.33 (m = 0.07 Pa s^p, p = 1.15)
	0.15% Separan AP30	1,000	0.70	0.10
	2% Natrosol 250L	1,000	0.79	0.15
	1.5% Natrosol 250L	1,000	0.89	0.039
	1.25% Carboxymethylcellulose	1,000	0.58	3.20
	1.00% Carboxymethylcellulose	1,000	0.72	0.56
	0.75% Carboxymethylcellulose	1,000	0.92	0.064
Farooqi et al. [21]				
Water	18.23% Anthracite	1,055	0.86	0.028
	24.82% Anthracite	1,076	0.36	0.57
	33.48% Anthracite	1,106	0.26	1.65
	35.11% Anthracite	1,111	0.19	4.20
	40.28% Anthracite	1,130	0.21	4.81
	43.21% Anthracite	1,141	0.24	8.10
	50.38% Anthracite	1,168	0.17	25.20

* Exhibited viscoelastic effects.

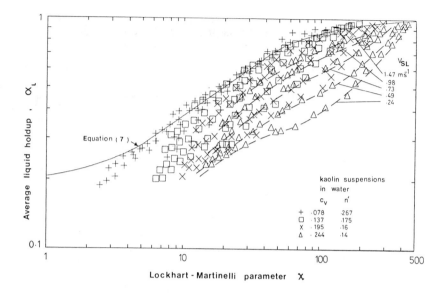

Figure 12. Hold-up as a function of the Lockhart and Martinelli parameter; typical experimental results for shear-thinning china clay suspensions.

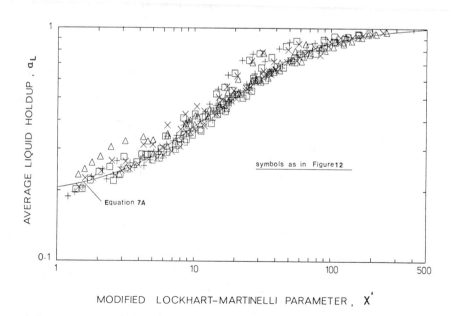

Figure 13. Liquid hold-up as a function of the modified Lockhart-Martinelli parameter (for the laminar flow of kaolin suspension).

Farooqi and Richardson [22] were more successful in using the Lockhart-Martinelli parameter χ in conjunction with Equations 7 and 8. They segregated data into two groups depending upon whether the liquid was in laminar or turbulent flow prior to the introduction of air. The transitional value of the Metzner-Reed Reynolds number Re_{MR} for non-Newtonian liquids ($Re_{MR} = (\rho_L V_{SL}^{2-n'} D^{n'})/8^{n'-1} K')$ was taken to be 2,000.

Laminar conditions ($Re_{MR} < 2,000$). By comparing the results for $Re_{MR} < 2,000$ with the amended form of the Lockhart-Martinelli correlation for Newtonian liquids given by Equation 7 and 8, it becomes apparent that this approach is not immediately applicable for shear-thinning liquids. This can be clearly seen in Figure 12, which shows average values of liquid hold-up for the simultaneous flow of air and one typical kaolin suspension. Further examination of the results shown in Figure 12 reveals that the lower is the superficial velocity of the liquid and the lower the value of n' the greater is the divergence between the experimental results and the predictions given by Equations 7 and 8. When the superficial liquid velocity approaches its critical value (corresponding to $Re_{MR} = 2,000$) the experimental values of hold-up become evenly scattered about the line representing the results for Newtonian liquids. Similar conclusions can be drawn from the results of Heywood [20], of Farooqi et al. [21] and of Chhabra et al. [24].

Farooqi and Richardson [22] suggested that the Lockhart-Martinelli parameter χ be multiplied by a dimensionless correction factor J to give a modified parameter χ', i.e.,

$$J = \left[\frac{V_{SL}}{(V_{SL})_c}\right]^{1-n'} \tag{9}$$

and $\chi' = \chi J$ (10)

In Equation 9 $(V_{SL})_c$ is the critical value of superficial liquid velocity corresponding to $Re_{MR} = 2,000$. The dimensionless correction factor J, which must always be less than unity for a shear-thinning liquid in laminar flow becomes greater as both the superficial liquid velocity and the flow behavior index n' increase; and finally when either $n' = 1$ or $V_{SL} = (V_{SL})_c$, $J = 1$ and no correction is then needed. Now, if in Equations 7 and 8 χ' is substituted for χ, we obtain Equations 7a and 8a as

$$\alpha_L = 0.24(\chi')^{0.80} \qquad 0.01 < \chi' < 0.5 \\ \alpha_L = 0.175(\chi')^{0.32} \qquad 0.5 < \chi' < 5.0 \tag{8a}$$

$$\alpha_L = 0.186 + 0.0191\chi' \qquad 1 < \chi' < 5 \\ \alpha_L = 0.143(\chi')^{0.42} \qquad 5 < \chi' < 50 \\ \alpha_L = \frac{1}{0.97 + (19/\chi')} \qquad 50 < \chi' < 500 \tag{7a}$$

In Figure 13 are plotted the experimental results for the shear-thinning materials shown in Figure 12 and these are seen to coincide remarkably well with the curve. The complete set of data (about 1,100 experimental points $3 < \chi' < 205$) calculated in this fashion is shown in Figure 14; deviations are well within the range of errors of Equations 7 and 8. The data cover a variation in χ' of three orders of magnitude.

Farooqi and Richardson [22] tested the validity of their approach further by using the data of Heywood [20] who reported extensive measurements of hold-up for the horizontal flow of air and kaolin suspensions in intermittent flow. The range of rheological properties and other variables covered is included in Table 3. A comparison between the measured values of hold-up and the predictions from Equation 7 is shown as a function of χ' in Figure 15 from which it is seen that the experimental values are consistently higher than those corresponding to Equation 7, but lie

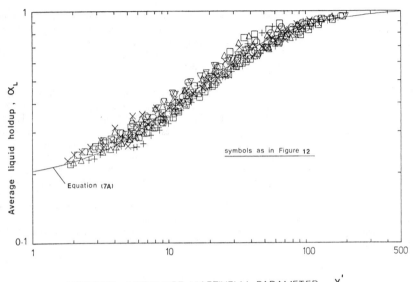

MODIFIED LOCKHART–MARTINELLI PARAMETER , X'

Figure 14. Liquid hold-up for shear thinning liquids: comparison of experimental data with Equation (7a).

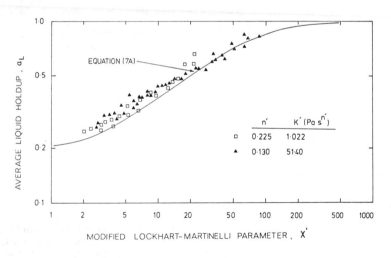

MODIFIED LOCKHART–MARTINELLI PARAMETER , X'

Figure 15. Heywood's [20] data compared with Equation (7a).

well within the error band. The limited amount of data on two-phase flow of shear-thinning liquids is summarized in Table 3 and the results have been re-examined to facilitate a direct comparison with the approach of Farooqi and Richardson [22]. These comparisons are shown in Figures 16 and 17. The data of Farooqi et al. [21] for the flow of air with aqueous suspensions of fine anthracite, of Mahalingam and Valle [9] and of Chhabra et al. [24] for inelastic polymer solutions are in good agreement with the predictions of the Farooqi-Richardson model.

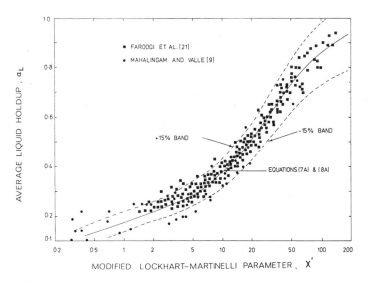

Figure 16. Comparison of experimental results [9, 21] for laminar conditions of liquid with Equations (7a) and (8a).

On the other hand, the scant results [17, 19] available for polymer solutions, which probably exhibit viscoelasticity show appreciable deviations from the predictions of equation [7]. Eisenberg and Weinberger [19] used aqueous polymer solutions of polyacrylamide (Separan AP30), which can exhibit viscoelasticity above certain concentrations [47, 48], while Oliver and Young-Hoon [17] used aqueous solutions of sodium carboxymethyl cellulose and of Polyox WSR-301, both of

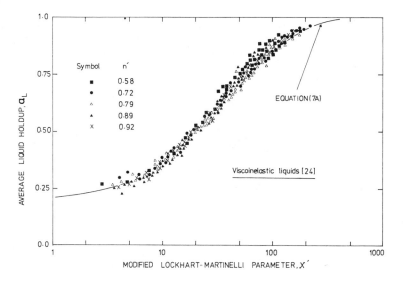

Figure 17. Comparison of experimental results [24] for laminar conditions of liquid with Equations (7a) and (8a).

which have been reported to be viscoelastic. Therefore, the divergences observed in these two cases might well be attributable to viscoelastic effects. The approach of Farooqi and Richardson therefore appears to be applicable to shear-thinning inelastic suspensions and polymer solutions but not to liquids exhibiting viscoelasticity.

More recently, Chhabra et al. [24] investigated the influence of viscoelasticity on average hold-up in a 1.5-inch-diameter pipe. Aqueous solutions of Polyacrylamide (Separan AP-30) were used as model viscoelastic liquids; these exhibited shear-thinning characteristics as well as finite values of the primary normal stress difference. Over the range of shear rate of interest, a power law type expression ($N_1 = m\dot\gamma^p$) was found to be adequate to describe the $N_1 - \dot\gamma$ data. The relevant rheological (n', K', m, p) and physical properties of the liquids employed are given in Table 4.

As previously indicated, a preliminary examination of hold-up data had shown that the approach of Farooqi and Richardson [22] consistently under-estimated the value of hold-up, and this can be seen in Figure 18 where the experimental results seem to be bounded by the correlations of Lockhart and Martinelli [43] and of Farooqi and Richardson [22]. As it was probable that the deviations apparent in Figure 18 were due to the viscoelastic nature of the test liquids, Chhabra et al. defined a Deborah number, De, to characterize viscoelasticity:

$$De = \frac{\theta V_M}{D} \tag{11}$$

where θ is a fluid characteristic time:

$$\theta = \left(\frac{m}{2K'}\right)^{1/(p-n')} \tag{12}$$

The factor of 2 in Equation 12 is quite arbitrary but is retained here to be consistent with the method of representation used by other workers [49, 50].

It is difficult to give a physical explanation of the role of viscoelasticity, but Chhabra et al. [24] empirically correlated the hold-up values using the following expression:

$$\alpha_{Lv} = \alpha_{Li}(1 + 0.56\chi'^{-0.5}De^{0.05}) \tag{13}$$

where the subscripts "v" and "i" refer respectively to viscoelastic and viscoinelastic conditions. In Figure 19, the experimental values of α_{Lv} (covering the ranges $0.3 < De < 300$; $2 < \chi' < 160$) are shown plotted against the values calculated from Equation 13; the value of α_{Li} is obtained from

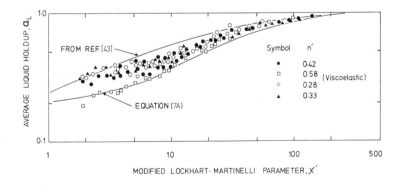

Figure 18. Average liquid hold-up as function of modified Lockhart-Martinelli parameter χ' for laminar flow of viscoelastic liquids [24].

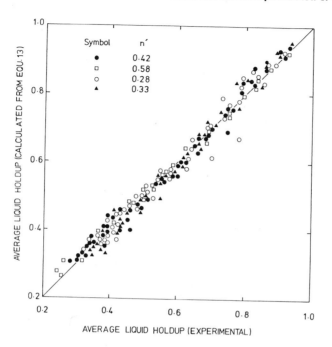

Figure 19. Comparison of experimental data (from Figure 18) for average liquid hold-up with values calculated from Equation 13 [24].

Equation 7a. The correlation in Figure 19 is seen to be satisfactory, with an average deviation of 5.4%. When the Deborah number approaches zero (i.e. $\theta \to 0$) for inelastic liquids, Equation 13 appropriately reduces to Equation 7a or 8a as the case may be.

Turbulent flow conditions ($Re_{MR} > 2,000$). When the non-Newtonian liquid into which gas is introduced is initially in turbulent flow (the value of Re_{MR} is calculated using the values of n' and K' obtained in laminar conditions), the experimental results of average liquid hold-up agree well with values predicted by Equations 7 and 8, and the original Lockhart-Martinelli parameter may therefore be used. Thus, for turbulent flow the non-Newtonian characteristics of the liquid appear to have little effect. This is consistent with the results of many experimental studies of single-phase turbulent flow of non-Newtonian liquids. The experimental data drawn from several different sources [21, 22, 24, 32], encompassing a wide range of experimental materials including polymer solutions [24], kaolin suspensions [20, 22], anthracite suspensions [21] and chalk in water suspensions [32] are shown in Figure 20. The results are seen to be well represented by the curve corresponding to Equations [7] and [8] derived for two-phase flow involving Newtonian liquids.

Vertical Upward Flow

The previous discussion on hold-up was restricted to the two-phase gas—non-Newtonian flow in horizontal pipes. The only study of vertical flow identified so far is that of Khatib and Richardson [29] who pumped mixtures of air and aqueous kaolin suspensions through a 38.8 mm smooth pipe 12 m long. The two-parameter-power-law model could satisfactorily be employed to approximate the shear-thinning characteristics of the test suspensions. The average values of liquid hold-up were

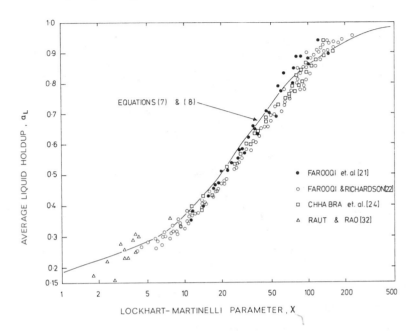

Figure 20. Experimental and predicted (from Equation 7) values of average liquid hold-up for turbulent conditions for shear thinning polymer solutions and suspensions.

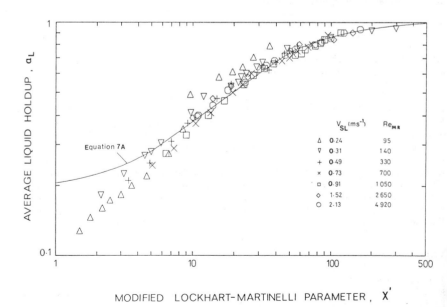

Figure 21. Average hold-up data for the co-current upward vertical flow of air and 13.7% kaolin in water suspension [51].

measured using the γ-ray attenuation technique employed by Heywood and Richardson [39] and by others [21, 22, 24]. When the results were analyzed by Farooqi and Richardson [22] and by Chhabra et al. [51], they were found to be well correlated by the method already described for horizontal flow (see Figure 21).

PRESSURE DROP

The pressure drop for flow of gas-liquid mixtures in a pipe is perhaps the most important of all the design parameters, and this is reflected in the many published models and correlations. Here only a selection of the widely used methods is described.

The experimental measurements in two-phase systems serve first to supply design information and second to provide means by which a proposed model or correlation may be validated. Because of the fluctuating nature of the flow, measurements are difficult to make and their accuracy and reproducibility are much poorer than in the case of single-phase flow. Simple U-tube manometers have been employed almost universally to record two-phase pressure drop over a pre-determined length of pipe. The pressure transmission lines may need to be flushed periodically to remove air bubbles. It may also be necessary to constrict the manometer lines so as to reduce the fluctuations that otherwise occur, especially at high flow rates of the two phases [18, 40]. Despite all these difficulties good measurements can be achieved by careful design and by making a careful choice of manometer fluid. A few investigators [18, 52] have measured pressure drop using strain gauges, which have several advantages, the output is linear and reproducible, the signal is electrically time-variant and thus can be integrated and digitized etc.

By starting with the conservation equations for mass and momentum for each phase, it can be shown that the total pressure drop is attributable to three separate components [5], that is,

$$-\Delta P_{TOTAL} = (-\Delta P)_{acc} + (-\Delta P)_{TP} + (-\Delta P)_g \qquad (14)$$

where $(-\Delta P_{acc})$ is the accelerational pressure drop, $(-\Delta P_{TP})$ is due to friction at the pipe walls and $-\Delta P_g$ is due to change in elevation. The accelerational component is usually negligible except when the ratio of the pressures at the two ends of the pipe is sufficient to cause expansion of the gas. $(-\Delta P_g)$ becomes increasingly important as the angle of the orientation of pipe to the horizontal increases. For vertical upwards flow $-\Delta P_g$ represents a major component of the overall pressure drop and will frequently exceed $(-\Delta P_{TP})$.

Gas/Newtonian Systems

The existing methods for estimating two-phase frictional pressure drop may be conveniently divided into two groups. In the first are methods based either on an idealized model or on phenomenological considerations applicable only to a specific flow pattern. All theoretical analyses involve the interfacial stresses, which cannot be simply described and which are almost impossible to measure experimentally. Invariably simplifying assumptions must be made. For example, Dukler and Hubbard [53] have analyzed the slug flow pattern in considerable detail. Starting with the conservation equations, and invoking some simplifications, they have derived formulae which can, in principle, be used to predict two phase pressure drop; however, their method is of little practical utility because many of the variables are not capable of measurement or of ready estimation. Annular flow, which is more amenable to mathematical analysis, has been a subject of detailed examination by Hewitt et al. [54]. Although their final equations are rather cumbersome to use, they provide an understanding of the relative importance of the different variables. Similarly, Taitel and Dukler [55] and Cheremisinoff and Davis [56] have derived equations for stratified flow where the gas-liquid interface is smooth. Detailed accounts of other theoretical developments in this field are available in various text books [2, 57], in review papers [5, 58] and also to a limited extent, in the accompanying chapter by Chisholm.

Methods of the second type are essentially empirical correlations based on the results of the extensive research carried out over the last three decades. One of the earliest, and probably most widely used, correlation is that of Lockhart and Martinelli [43] who expressed two-phase pressure drop in terms of a dimensionless drag ratio ϕ_L^2, which was related to the parameter, χ, defined earlier in Equation 6.

$$\phi_L^2 = \frac{-\Delta P_{TP}/L}{-\Delta P_L/L} \tag{15}$$

$$\chi = \sqrt{\frac{-\Delta P_L/L}{-\Delta P_G/L}} \tag{6}$$

Alternatively, the drag ratio ϕ_G^2 may be defined as

$$\phi_G^2 = \frac{-\Delta P_{TP}/L}{-\Delta P_G/L} \tag{16}$$

The two drag ratios ϕ_L^2 and ϕ_G^2 are inter-related by $\phi_G^2 = \chi^2 \phi_L^2$. Furthermore, Lockhart and Martinelli [43] used a flow classification scheme depending upon whether the gas/liquid are in laminar-laminar, laminar-turbulent, turbulent-laminar, or turbulent-turbulent flow. The nature of flow is ascertained by calculating the value of Reynolds number on the assumption that each phase is flowing alone and taking the laminar to turbulent transition as occurring at the value of 1,000–2,000. The original graphical representation of Lockhart and Martinelli [43] is reproduced in Figure 22. The correlation has an accuracy of $\pm 30\%$, but in some cases, errors up to 100% have been reported [15, 23]; it performs particularly poorly in stratified flow conditions [15, 23, 66]. The method is simple and no prior knowledge regarding the flow pattern is necessary; this is in contrast to the theoretical models where this information would be needed before they could be applied.

In the intervening years, several attempts were made to improve this correlation. Thus, for example, Chisholm [59] suggested the following algebraic expression for the calculation of ϕ_L^2 in terms of χ:

$$\phi_L^2 = 1 + \frac{C}{\chi} + \frac{1}{\chi^2} \tag{17}$$

where C is an empirical constant whose value depends upon the conditions of flow. The recommended values are given in Table 5.

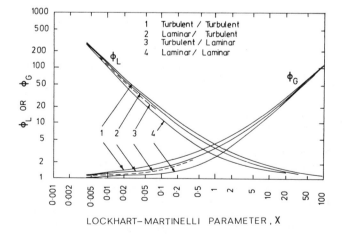

Figure 22. Two-phase pressure drop correlation of Lockhart and Martinelli.

Table 5
Values of C

Liquid	Gas	C
Laminar Re < 1,000	Laminar Re < 1,000	5
Laminar Re < 1,000	Turbulent Re > 2,000	12
Turbulent Re > 2,000	Laminar Re < 1,000	10
Turbulent Re > 2,000	Turbulent Re > 2,000	20

However, the values of C given in Table 5 are restricted to mixtures for which gas-to-liquid-density ratios correspond to those for air-to-water at atmospheric pressure. In a subsequent paper, Chisholm and Sutherland [60] have outlined a method for estimating the value of C for other density ratios.

Extensive evaluations of the different methods available have been carried out by Dukler et al. [61], by Mandhane et al. [62] and by others [63]. The Lockhart and Martinelli method is probably the most widely used. Other correlations that may have a somewhat better accuracy are restricted in application and have been reviewed by Govier and Aziz [2].

This section is concluded by presenting typical comparisons of experimental results, taken from Farooqi [40] and Farooqi and Richardson [64], with the values calculated using both Equation 17 and the original graphical correlation of Lockhart and Martinelli [43]. The data were obtained in a 42-mm-diameter horizontal pipe and the test mixtures included air/water and air/aqueous glycerol solutions. Such comparisons, shown in Figures 23 to 26, respectively for each of the four regimes

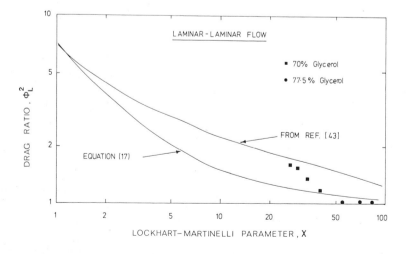

Figure 23. Comparison of typical experimental values of two-phase pressure drop with the correlations of Lockhart and Martinelli and of Chisholm for laminar-laminar conditions for Newtonian liquids.

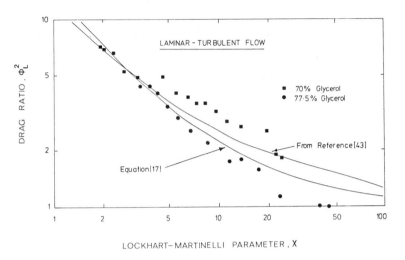

Figure 24. Comparison of typical experimental values of drag ratio with the correlations of Lockhart and Martinelli and of Chisholm for laminar-turbulent conditions for Newtonian liquids.

designated by Lockhart and Martinelli, indicate the extent of experimental errors, and provide a basis for estimating the accuracy of results for experiments on the flow of air/non-Newtonian liquid mixtures, which will be presented in the next section. Although the deviations appear to be large particularly in the case of turbulent-laminar flow, most of the experimental points lie within ± 30% of either correlation. Moreover, there is very little to choose between the original correlation of

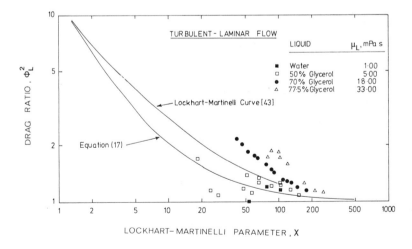

Figure 25. Comparison of typical experimental values of drag ratio with the correlations of Lockhart and Martinelli and of Chisholm under turbulent-laminar conditions for Newtonian liquids.

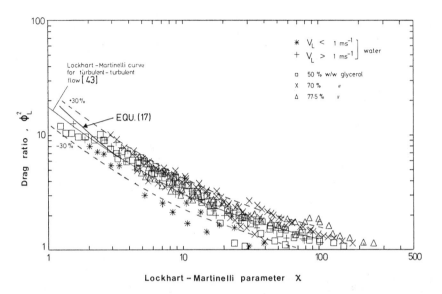

Figure 26. Comparison of typical experimental values of drag ratio with the correlations of Lockhart and Martinelli and of Chisholm under turbulent-turbulent conditions for Newtonian liquids.

Lockhart and Martinelli [43] and the explicit equation of Chisholm [59], except that the latter is more convenient to use.

Gas/Solids Non-Newtonian Systems

Horizontal Pipes

Although two-phase flow of gas and non-Newtonian shear-thinning materials occurs in several practical situations, the problem has received only scant attention both theoreticaly and experimentally. The main objective must be to devise versatile methods for estimating the frictional component ΔP_{TP} of the overall pressure drop. As in the case of Newtonian liquids, several investigators have attempted theoretical and semi-theoretical analyses based on idealized models [9, 10, 17, 19, 65, 66]. For instance, for the relatively simple annular flow pattern, Oliver and Young-Hoon [17], and subsequently others [9, 65] have carried out approximate mathematical analyses. In some of these treatments, the flow of the thin annular liquid film at the wall is assumed to be capable of being described in the same way as a laminar film between two flat plates [9], while in others [17, 65] the flow area has been taken as an annulus; in all cases the gas-liquid interface is assumed to be smooth and without the presence of ripples. These simplifications introduce considerable errors and it is therefore not surprising that the values of pressure drop so obtained differ from the corresponding experimental values by a factor of up to four. Heywood and Charles [66] and others [79] have modified the idealized model for stratified flow due to Taitel and Dukler [55] and applied it to power-law model liquids. A summary of the work in this area is given in Table 6 and a review has been presented by Mahalingam [77].

On the other hand, experimental work in this field has yielded satisfactory results. From Table 6, which gives a comprehensive summary of the investigations reported so far, the range of conditions covered and the wide variety of non-Newtonian model fluids used will be seen.

Table 6

Summary of Investigations Carried Out with the Horizontal Two-Phase Flow of Gases and Non-Newtonian Liquids

Investigator	Nature of work	Experimental materials used	Pipe diameter (mm)	Quantities measured
Ward and Dallavalle [67]	Experimental	Aqueous kaolin suspensions and air	19, 25, and 38	Two-phase pressure drop
Oliver and Young-Hoon [17]	Theoretical and experimental	Aqueous solutions of sodium carboxy-methyl cellulose and polyox in conjunction with nitrogen	6.35	Two-phase pressure drop and hold-up
Greskovich and Shrier [68]	Experimental	Polyethylene oxide in water and PIB in kerosene flowing cocurrently with nitrogen	38	Two-phase pressure drop
Mahalingam and Valle [9]	Theoretical and experimental	Air and aqueous solutions of methocel HG 90 and carbopol 934	12.7	Two-phase pressure drop and hold-up
Rosehart, Scott and Rhodes [69]	Experimental	Air-drag reducing polymer solution	25.4	Two-phase pressure drop
Srivastava and Narasimhamurthy [70]	Experimental	Air and aqueous solutions of sodium carboxy-methyl cellulose	21.7 and 36.5	Two-phase pressure drop
Cheng et al. [71]	Experimental	Air-asbestos slurry	50	Two-phase pressure drop
Carleton et al. [72]	Experimental	Air-asbestos slurry, bentonite, chalk suspension	50, 75	Two-phase pressure drop
Tyagi and Srivastava [65]	Approximate theoretical analysis	Power law model	—	Annular flow regime
Otten and Fayed [73]	Experimental	Air/drag reducing polymer solution	25	Two-phase pressure drop

Reference	Type	System		Remarks
Deshpande and Bishop [79]	Theoretical and experimental	Air and aqueous solutions of methocel and hydroxyethyl cellulose	25 and 52	Two-phase pressure drop and hold-up in stratified flow
Rosehart et al. [74]	Experimental	Air/aqueous solutions of carbopol, CMC	25	Hold-up measurements
Raut and Rao [32]	Experimental	Air flowing with aqueous chalk suspensions	19	Average pressure, drop, hold-up and heat transfer coefficients
Eisenberg and Weinberger [19]	Theoretical and experimental	Air mixed with the aqueous solutions of polyacrylamide, polyox and carboxy-methyl cellulose	2.9	Mainly pressure drop, but limited measurements of hold-up
Heywood and Richardson [75]	Experimental	Suspensions of kaolin and anthracite flowing simultaneously with air	42	Two-phase pressure drop and hold-up
Heywood and Charles [66]	Theoretical	Power law model fluid	—	Stratified flow conditions
Farooqi, Heywood and Richardson [21]	Theoretical and experimental	Aqueous suspensions of anthracite and air	42	Two-phase pressure drop and average hold-up
Farooqi and Richardson [22, 64]	Experimental	Air-kaolin suspensions	42	Two-phase pressure drop and hold-up
Mujawar and Rao [76]	Experimental	Air-aqueous polymer solutions	12.1	Two-phase pressure drop
Chhabra et al. [23]	Experimental	Air-kaolin suspensions	207	Two-phase pressure drop
Chhabra et al. [24]	Experimental	Air-aqueous solutions of high molecular weight polymers	42	Two-phase pressure drop and average hold-up
Raghavan et al. [10]	Theoretical and experimental	Aqueous solution of methocel and air	12.7	Two-phase pressure drop

The results obtained with the liquid in laminar or turbulent flow prior to the introduction of gas will be dealt with separately. The treatment is then consistent with that adopted in the preceding section for hold-up. Furthermore, shear-thinning materials exhibit completely different behavior from Newtonian liquids for laminar conditions, whereas for turbulent flow it will be seen that the non-Newtonian characteristics are of relatively minor importance. The critical value of the Metzner-Reed Reynolds number at which the flow becomes turbulent is taken to be 1,000–2,000.

Laminar conditions (Re$_{MR}$ < 2,000). When a gas is introduced into a shear-thinning liquid in laminar flow, there is a range of conditions over which the frictional pressure drop is actually reduced below the value for the liquid flowing alone at the same rate. When this drag reduction occurs, the two-phase pressure drop passes through a minimum value and then increases again as the gas flow rate is increased, eventually reaching a value higher than that for the flow of liquid alone. Ward

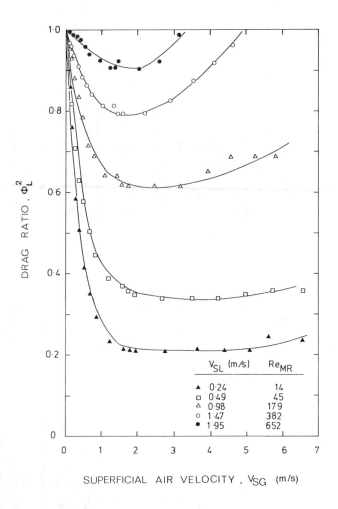

V_{SL} (m/s)	Re$_{MR}$
▲ 0·24	14
▫ 0·49	45
△ 0·98	179
○ 1·47	382
● 1·95	652

SUPERFICIAL AIR VELOCITY , V_{SG} (m/s)

Figure 27. Drag ratio for the co-current flow of air and 24.4% (by vol.) aqueous kaolin suspension in a 42-mm-diameter horizontal pipe [64].

and Dallavalle [67] who were the first to report this phenomenon worked with air and kaolin suspensions. Since then a number of investigators have reported the same effect for a variety of shear-thinning materials, including polymer solutions [9, 17, 24, 70], particulate suspensions of kaolin [20, 23, 64, 75], of anthracite [21, 78], and of asbestos [71, 72], and pastes of bentonite [72] all of which display shear thinning characteristics.

Pressure drop results are conveniently expressed in the form of a drag ratio ϕ_L^2, as defined by Lockhart and Martinelli [43]. Some typical results showing the phenomenon of drag reduction, drawn from the publications of Richardson et al [23, 24, 40, 64], are presented in Figures 27–30 for a range of materials and rheological behavior and for pipes of different diameter. In each of these figures, drag ratio that is plotted against superficial gas velocity with liquid flow rate as parameter is seen to fall below unity, (thereby denoting a decrease in two-phase pressure drop), and to pass through a minimum. Moreover, the lower is the superficial liquid velocity, the greater is the degree of drag reduction. When the superficial liquid velocity reaches the transition velocity (laminar-turbulent flow), no reduction in pressure drop is observed. This is clearly shown in Figure 28 where the range of experimental conditions is wide enough to cover both laminar and turbulent liquid flow. Furthermore, Farooqi and Richardson [64] showed that the higher the degree of shear-thinning (the smaller the value of n′) the greater was the degree of drag reduction. From a practical point of view, this finding presents interesting possibilities in the field of slurry pipelines, as either

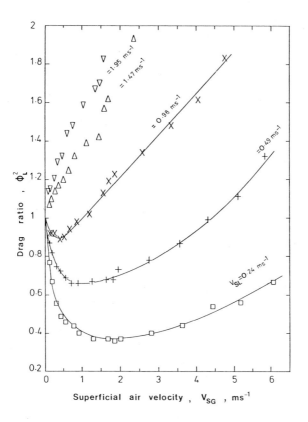

Figure 28. Drag ratio for the co-current flow of air and 13.7% (by vol.) aqueous kaolin suspension in a 42-mm-diameter horizontal pipe [51].

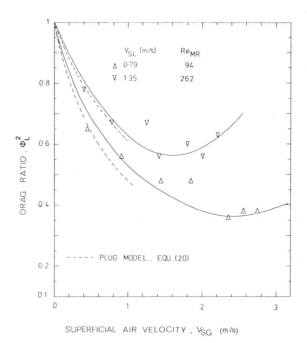

Figure 29. Drag ratio for the co-current flow of air and 36.5% (w/w) aqueous kaolin suspension in a 207-mm-diameter horizontal pipe [23].

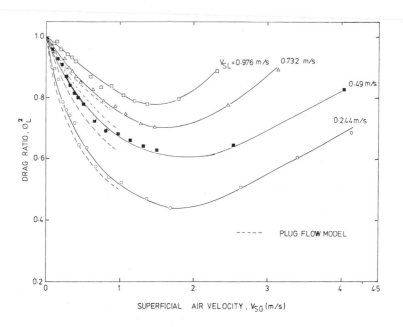

Figure 30. Drag ratio for the co-current flow of air and 1.25% aqueous solution of carboxymethyl cellulose in a 42-mm-diameter horizontal pipe [24].

the system can be designed for a lower pressure duty or greater quantities of solids can be transported for a given pressure drop.

The behavior can be explained in terms of a plug flow model, originally proposed by Carleton et al. [72], and subsequently developed by Richardson and co-workers [23, 24, 75]. Schematically the idealized model is shown in Figure 31. It postulates:

1. That the gas and liquid form discrete flat-ended plugs each filling the entire cross-section of the pipe and that there is no slip between the two phases. Furthermore, the presence of a film of liquid at the wall surrounding the gas plug is ignored.
2. That the pressure drop across a gas plug is negligible.
3. That the pressure gradient along a liquid plug is determined by the mixture or no slip velocity, $(V_M = V_{SL} + V_{SG})$, there being no flow of gas relative to the liquid.

For laminar flow, the pressure drop $(-\Delta P_L)$ for a liquid of known rheology (n', K') flowing at a velocity V_{SL} through a pipe of diameter D and length L is given as:

$$-\Delta P_L = K_1 L V_{SL}^{n'} \tag{18}$$

where K_1 is a system constant and incorporates D, K' and ρ_L.

The addition of gas has two effects: the length of pipe in contact with liquid is reduced and the velocity of the liquid plug is increased. If λ_L (defined by Equation 4) is the input volume fraction of liquid, then in the absence of slip, the length of pipe in contact with liquid is $L\lambda_L$ and the velocity of the liquid plug is V_{SL}/λ_L. Then, if the flow in the liquid plug is still laminar:

$$-\Delta P_{TP} = K_1(\lambda_L L)(V_{SL}/\lambda_L)^{n'} \tag{19}$$

Then the drag ratio ϕ_L^2 is obtained as

$$\phi_L^2 = \frac{-\Delta P_{TP}}{-\Delta P_L} = \lambda_L^{1-n'} \tag{20}$$

λ_L must be less than unity and for a shear thinning liquid n' is also less than unity. Thus, on the basis of this highly simplified model, Equation 20 predicts that drag reduction will occur. Furthermore, Equation 20 predicts an increasing degree of drag reduction both as the liquid superficial velocity decreases and as n' decreases (i.e., as the extent of shear-thinning behavior becomes greater). These predictions are in qualitative agreement with the observations of Farooqi and Richardson [64]. This model is likely to under-estimate the magnitude of two-phase pressure drop because the liquid and gas will not form idealized plugs and there will be some relative motion of the gas to the liquid.

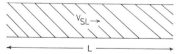

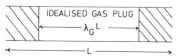

Figure 31. Idealized plug flow model.

Equation 20 predicts that the pressure drop for laminar flow of a Newtonian liquid will be unaffected by the introduction of a gas. This is contrary to experience and increased pressure drops are obtained as a result of interactions between the two phases. However, Heywood and Richardson [75] and others [40] have concluded that Equation 20 yields reasonable results provided $V_{SG} <$ 1 ms^{-1} and Re$_{MR}$ (based on no-slip velocity and properties of liquid) is less than 500. Within these limits, the values of drag ratio, calculated from Equation 20, are included as dotted lines in Figures 29 and 30. As the superficial liquid velocity is increased, the deviations from the model become progressively greater. The model does not predict a minimum value of drag ratio. One of the main virtues of this simple model is that it does offer a plausible explanation for the phenomenon of drag reduction.

In Figures 27–30, it will be noted that the minimum in the curves occurs at a progressively greater gas velocity as the liquid velocity is decreased. If the results are replotted using mixture velocity ($V_M = V_{SL} + V_{SG}$) as abscissa, in place of gas superficial velocity, it will be seen (Figures 32 and 33) that for a given liquid the minimum on each curve occurs at the same mixture velocity. Again, if the Metzner-Reed Reynolds number Re$_{MR}$ (based on the mixture velocity) is used as abscissa, all the minima occur when Re$_{MR}$ is in the region of 1,000–2,000; this suggests that the drag ratio is minimum when the flow of liquid in the plug just becomes turbulent. Based on this observa-

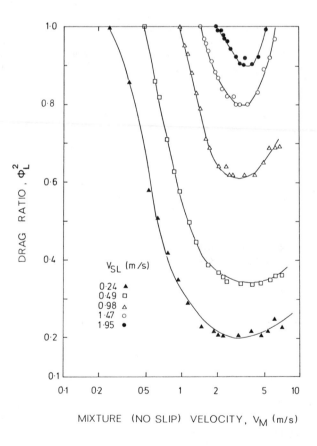

Figure 32. Drag ratio for 24.4% (by vol.) aqueous kaolin suspension as function of mixture velocity (replotted from Figure 27).

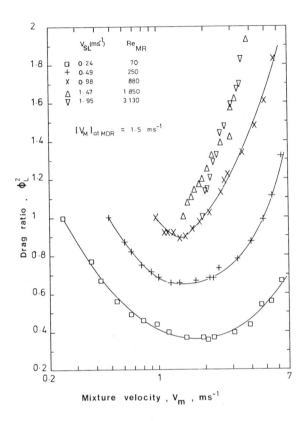

Figure 33. Drag ratio for 13.7% (by vol.) aqueous kaolin suspension as function of mixture velocity (replotted from Figure 28).

tion, Farooqi and Richardson [64] were able to correlate the minimum values of drag ratio with the dimensionless parameter J (defined by Equation 9). This relationship is shown graphically in Figure 34, where relevant data culled from other investigations are also included. The corresponding best-fit equations are:

$$
\begin{aligned}
(\phi_L^2)_{\min} &= J^{0.205} & 0.60 < J < 1.0 \\
&= 1 - 0.0315\, J^{-2.25} & 0.35 < J < 0.6 \\
&= 1.9\, J & 0.05 < J < 0.35
\end{aligned}
\tag{21}
$$

where

$$
J = \left(\frac{V_{SL}}{(V_{SL})_c} \right)^{1-n'}
\tag{9}
$$

Excellent agreement between Equation 21 and experimental data is obvious over a wide range of pipe diameters (42–207 mm).

In a more recent study, Chhabra et al. [24] used viscoelastic polymer solutions as test liquids and found that Equation 21 applied in these circumstances also. Even though in some instances the minimum value of drag ratio occurred at a rather lower value of Re_{MR} (~ 300), yet the values of $(\phi_L^2)_{\min}$ are in line with Equation 21 as shown in Figure 35. Equation 21 is particularly useful in

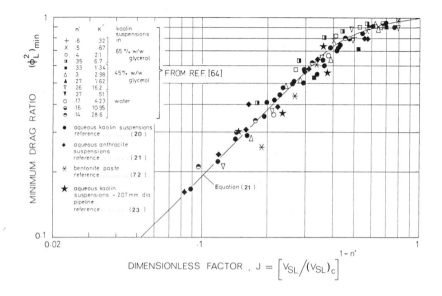

Figure 34. Relationship between minimum drag ratio and dimensionless factor $J = (V_{SL}/(V_{SL})_c)^{1-n'}$ [51].

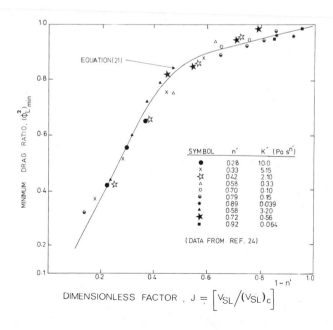

Figure 35. Comparison of experimental values of minimum drag ratio for viscoelastic and viscoinelastic polymer solutions with the values calculated from Equation 21 [24].

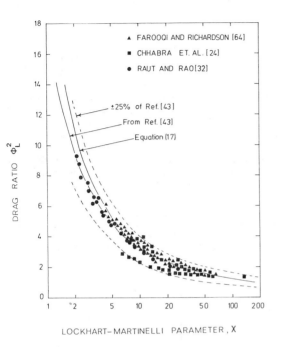

DRAG RATIO Φ_L^2

LOCKHART–MARTINELLI PARAMETER , X

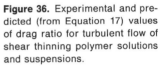

Figure 36. Experimental and predicted (from Equation 17) values of drag ratio for turbulent flow of shear thinning polymer solutions and suspensions.

estimating, a priori, the minimum achievable drag ratio as it requires a knowledge of only the properties of liquid (ρ_L, n', K'), and of the operating conditions (D, V_{SL}).

The advantage of air-injection lies in the reduction achieved in the pressure gradient and hence in the maximum pressure that the equipment must sustain. Conversely, it will allow greater flow rates of liquid in a system in which there is a fixed maximum permissible pressure at the upstream end. Whether or not there are net savings in power consumption is a complex question and will depend upon the relative magnitudes of the power saving in the liquid pump and the energy expended in compressing the air to be injected into the line. Thus, an important factor is the efficiency of the gas compressor relative to that of the liquid pump.

Until now, the consideration has been focused on intermittent (particularly plug) flow. In horizontal flow, the amount of data for other flow patterns is too meagre to warrant an analysis. Several tentative modifications [19, 76, 79] of the Lockhart-Martinelli correlation exist in the literature, but, unfortunately, are too restrictive in application to be included here. There is a real dearth of experimental data in the other flow regimes.

Turbulent flow ($Re_{MR} > 2,000$). When gas is introduced into any liquid whether Newtonian or non-Newtonian in turbulent flow, the pressure drop is increased, and thus the values of drag ratios exceed unity. This behavior is exemplified in Figure 28 where drag ratio is plotted against superficial gas velocity for a number of constant liquid velocities for the flow of mixtures of air/kaolin suspensions. When expressed in the form of the Lockhart-Martinelli parameter χ, these results are well represented by Chisholm's equation (Equation 17). Typical comparison between the experimental values of drag ratio and those calculated using Equation 17 are shown in Figure 36. Similar findings have been reported by other workers [32,67,68,70,73].

Vertical Flow

Whereas in a vertical pipe the overall pressure drop is attributable to friction and associated effects, in vertical (upward) flow the hydrostatic component may represent a significant fraction of the total pressure gradient. The interpretation of results for vertical flow is therefore more complicated.

Khatib and Richardson [28, 29], to whom reference has been made earlier, measured two-phase pressure drop for the vertical upward co-current flow of air and various liquids in a $1\frac{1}{2}$-inch-(38 mm)-diameter pipe. The experimental details are contained in a paper by Khatib and Richardson [29]. Representative results of their investigation are shown in Figures 37 and 38 respectively where the total pressure gradient is plotted against superficial air velocity. In all cases, as the air velocity is increased, the total pressure gradient falls, passes through a minimum, and then increases again. The minimum pressure drop for a given liquid seems to occur at about the same value of mixture or no slip velocity, but in this case it does not always correspond to the transition from laminar to turbulent flow. It is important to recognize that the reduction in pressure gradient here is due mainly to the reduction in hydrostatic component caused by the introduction of gas, and substantial reductions therefore occur even when the liquid is water. As the input rate of gas is increased, the hydrostatic component progressively decreases. However, at very high gas velocities, the rate of increase of the frictional pressure drop exceeds the rate of decrease of the hydrostatic component and a minimum occurs in the pressure gradient solids/gas velocity curve. In horizontal flow the minimum is associated entirely with the shear-thinning behavior of the liquid. From the measurements of liquid hold-up referred to earlier, the hydrostatic component of the pressure gradient may be calculated. If this is then subtracted from the total gradient, the frictional component may be estimated.

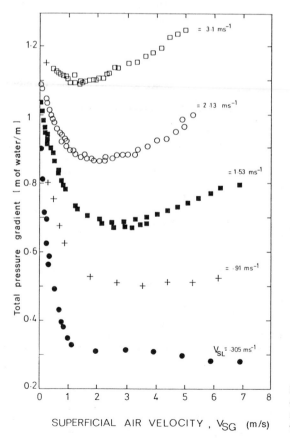

Figure 37. Total pressure gradient for the upward flow of air-water mixtures in a 38.5-mm-diameter vertical pipe [51].

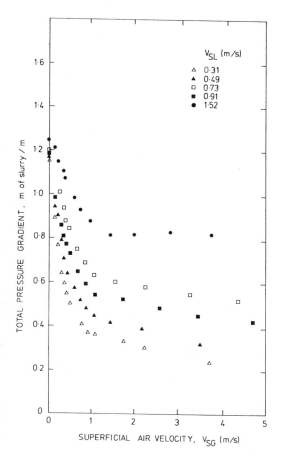

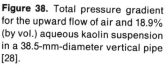

Figure 38. Total pressure gradient for the upward flow of air and 18.9% (by vol.) aqueous kaolin suspension in a 38.5-mm-diameter vertical pipe [28].

The results so obtained for the data corresponding to Figure 38 are plotted against superficial gas velocity in Figure 39. It will be seen that under certain conditions (particularly low liquid flow rates), the frictional components calculated in this way appear to approach a zero value. For the flow of air/water mixtures "negative friction losses" are well documented in the literature. This anomaly arises because not all of the liquid present in the test section of the pipe contributes to the hydrostatic pressure, because some of the liquid is present as a film near the wall and may, under some conditions, in fact be flowing downwards; most of the weight of this liquid film is then supported by the shearing force at the wall acting upward. The other upward force on the liquid is the drag exerted by the gas but this may be small compared with the force at the wall.

From the "instantaneous" values of hold-up obtained by Khatib [28] by scanning the test section for short intervals, it is possible to split the liquid hold-up into two components: that associated predominantly with the liquid slug and that surrounding the gas slug. If it is then assumed that only the liquid present in the liquid slugs contributes to the hydrostatic pressure gradient, it is possible to calculate a modified value, which may then be subtracted from the total gradient. The frictional pressure gradient calculated in this way has been plotted in Figure 40. However, the accuracy of the procedure is such that the resulting values for the frictional pressure gradients entail large errors thus making the quantitative interpretation of the results rather difficult.

The frictional pressure gradient calculated in this way includes not only a true pipe friction term but also an acceleration component attributable to the need continually to accelerate elements of

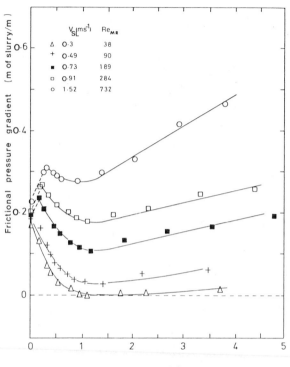

SUPERFICIAL AIR VELOCITY , V_{SG} (m/s)

Figure 39. Frictional component of pressure gradient for the results shown in Figure 38.

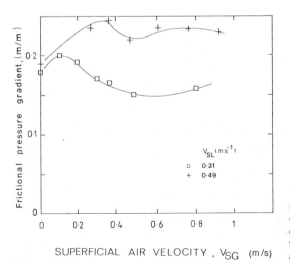

SUPERFICIAL AIR VELOCITY , V_{SG} (m/s)

Figure 40. Corrected frictional component of pressure gradient calculated using slug hold-up data for the results shown in Figures 38 and 39.

fluid. This process may be illustrated by considering what happens in the slug flow regime, where a spherical nosed gas slug forces liquid ahead of it as it rises, with some of the liquid continuously flowing back as a film at the wall to be picked up by the following slug. In the extreme case where there is no net liquid flow, the downward flow in the liquid film will be exactly equal to the upward flow in the liquid slugs. Where there is an overall upward flow of liquid, the film will be flowing downwards unless the drag force exerted by gas at the interface is sufficiently large to overcome the gravitational force. The liquid present in the film will be accelerated again each time it is picked up by the following liquid slug and this process gives rise to an important component of the energy losses in the system, and will occur even if there is no net flow of liquid.

In this chapter, the treatment has been limited to horizontal and vertical (upward) flow. However, in practice flow may take place either in inclined pipes or vertically downward, but no studies have been reported of two-phase flow of gas/non-Newtonian liquids in such geometries.

CONCLUSION

This chapter has been concerned with the hydrodynamics of two-phase gas-liquid flow both horizontally and vertically upward with special reference to liquids exhibiting non-Newtonian characteristics. In particular, the discussion has focused on the development of methods for the prediction of flow pattern, average liquid (or gas) hold-up and pressure losses due to friction. The state-of-art may be summarized as follows:

1. The available methods of predicting flow pattern, hold-up and pressure gradient for co-current flow of gas and Newtonian liquids have been examined, with a view to providing a base line for consideration of the effects of non-Newtonian behavior. Thus, two of the existing flow pattern maps have been combined to produce a modified version to delineate flow patterns. It is shown that the physical properties of the two phases do not seem to have significant influence on the transition boundaries. The correlation of Lockhart and Martinelli for hold-up has been modified and explicit expressions are presented for calculating the average value of liquid hold-up in the intermediate flow regime. For pressure drop, both Lockhart-Martinelli correlation and Chisholm's modification yield a reasonable correlation of the available experimental data, though there is a paucity of results for two-phase frictional loss in large-diameter pipes.

2. The new flow pattern map previously referred to has been shown to be applicable to horizontal two-phase flow involving shear-thinning and, to a limited extent, viscoelastic polymer solutions over a substantial range of rheological and operating conditions. In the case of upward vertical flow, only scant experimental data are available on gas/shear-thinning liquid flow, but these also are in good agreement with the flow pattern map of Taitel et al. [27] initially devised for Newtonian liquids.

3. It is shown how the correlation of hold-up based on the Lockhart-Martinelli approach can be extended to incorporate shear-thinning behavior for liquids, which would be in laminar flow in the absence of gas. By this approach it has been possible to reconcile most of the data available in the literature on purely shear-thinning fluids in both horizontal and vertical pipes. Furthermore, the effect of viscoelasticity has been considered by incorporating a Deborah number in the correlating equation. However, when the liquid is in turbulent flow before the introduction of gas, hold-up values are well correlated by expressions for Newtonian liquids (Equations 7 and 8).

4. For the horizontal laminar flow of shear-thinning materials, gas injection has the potential for reducing the pressure gradient and this effect has important applications in the field of slurry transportation. A simple plug flow model enables the magnitude of the drag reduction to be calculated over a limited range of conditions, particularly for low gas/liquid rates. The conditions for maximum drag reduction are presented in simple form. For turbulent flow of shear-thinning and viscoelastic liquids, the non-Newtonian characteristics of the liquid appear to have no appreciable effect on the pressure gradient.

Acknowledgements

Our research program on multiphase flow has been supported by the Science and Engineering Research Council of the United Kingdom, and this support is gratefully acknowledged. We would also like to express our sincere thanks to Drs. N. I. Heywood, S. I. Farooqi, and Z. Khatib, whose work, as research students, has formed such a significant part of this review.

NOTATION

C	constant, Equation 17	N_1	first normal stress difference
c_v	volume fraction of kaolin or anthracite	n'	generalised flow behaviour index
C_0	distribution parameter, Equation 5	$-\Delta P$	pressure drop
D	pipe diameter	p	index in first normal stress difference expression
De	Deborah number, Equation 11	Q	volumetric flow rate
J	dimensionless factor, Equation 9	Re_{MR}	Metzner-Reed Reynolds number
K'	generalized power law consistency index	V_M	no-slip or mixture velocity
		V_0	drift velocity, Equation 5
L	pipe length	V_s	superficial velocity
m	coefficient in first normal stress difference expression	$\bar{V}_G$	average gas velocity
		X, Y	scaling factors, Equation 1

Greek Symbols

α	hold-up	σ	surface tension
$\dot{\gamma}$	shear rate	τ_y	Bingham yield stress
θ	fluid relaxation time, Equation 12	ϕ_1, ϕ_2	scaling factors, Table 2
λ	input volume fraction	ϕ	drag ratio
μ	viscosity of Newtonian liquid	χ	Lockhart-Martinelli parameter, Equation 6
μ_p	plastic viscosity of Bingham model fluid	χ'	Modified Lockhart-Martinelli parameter, Equation 10
ρ	density		

Subscripts

L	liquid	TOTAL	total
G	gas	acc	accelerational contribution
min	minimum	TP	friction
c	critical value at $Re_{MR} = 2{,}000$	g	gravitational

REFERENCES

1. Hewitt, G. F., "Two-Phase Flow Studies in the United Kingdom," *Int. J. Multiphase Flow*, 9, 715–749 (1983).
2. Govier, G. W., and Aziz, K., *The Flow of Complex Mixtures in Pipes*. R. E. Krieger Pub. Co., FL (1982).
3. Chisholm, D., *Two-Phase Flow in Pipelines and Heat Exchangers*, George Goodwin, London (1983).
4. Alves, G. E., "Co-Current Liquid-Gas Flow in a Pipeline Contactor," *Chem. Eng. Prog.* 50, 449–456 (1954).
5. Hewitt, G. F., in *Handbook of Multiphase Systems*, edited by G. Hetsroni, McGraw-Hill (1982) p. 2–25.

6. Taitel, Y., and Dukler, A. E., "A Model for Predicting Flow Regime Transitions in Horizontal and Near Horizontal Flow," *A.I.Ch.E.J.*, 22, 47–55 (1976).
7. Weisman, J., et al., "Effects of Fluid Properties and Pipe Diameter on Two-Phase Flow Patterns in Horizontal Lines," *Int. J. Multiphase Flow*, 5, 437–462 (1979).
8. Hewitt, G. F., *Measurement of Two-Phase Flow Parameters*, Academic Press, New York (1978).
9. Mahalingam, R., and Valle, M. A., "Momentum Transfer in Two-Phase Flow of Gas-Pseudo-plastic Liquid Mixtures," *Ind. Eng. Chem. Fundam.*, 11, 470–477 (1972).
10. Raghavan, K., Mahalingam, R., and Oh, C. H., "Interfacial Interaction in Two-Phase Gas-Non-Newtonian Liquid Flow Systems," paper presented at A.I.Ch.E. Diamond Jubilee/Annual Meeting, Washington, (1983).
11. Weisman, J., "Two-Phase Flow Patterns" in *Handbook of Fluids in Motion*, N. P. Cheremisinoff and R. Gupta (eds.), Ann Arbor Science, Michigan (1983).
12. Spedding, P. L., and Nguyen, V. T., "Regime Maps for Air/Water Two-Phase Flow," *Chem. Eng. Sci.*, 35, 779–793 (1980).
13. Mandhane, J. M., Gregory, G. A., and Aziz, K., "A Flow Pattern Map for Gas-Liquid Flow in Horizontal Pipes," *Int. J. Multiphase Flow*, 1, 537–553 (1974).
14. Nguyen, V. T., and Spedding, P. L., "Hold-up in Two-Phase Gas-Liquid Flow," *Chem. Eng. Sci.*, 32, 1003–1021 (1977).
15. Simpson, H. C., et al., "Two-Phase Flow Studies in Large-Diameter Horizontal Tubes," National Engineering Laboratory Report No. 677 (1981), Glasgow.
16. Chhabra, R. P., and J. F., Richardson, "Prediction of Flow Patterns for the Co-Current Flow of Gas and Non-Newtonian Liquid in Horizontal Pipes," *Can. J. Chem. Eng.*, 62, 449–454 (1984).
17. Oliver, D. R., and Young-Hoon, A., "Two-Phase Non-Newtonian Flow," *Trans. Inst. Chem. Engrs.*, 46, T106–T115 (1968).
18. Rosehart, R. G., "Horizontal Two-Phase Non-Newtonian Slug Flow," Ph.D. dissertation, University of Waterloo (1970).
19. Eisenberg, F. G., and Weinberger, C. B., "Annular Two-Phase Flow of Gases and Non-Newtonian Liquids," *A.I.Ch.E.J.*, 25, 240–246 (1979).
20. Heywood, N. I., "Air Injection into Suspensions Flowing in Horizontal Pipelines," Ph.D. thesis, University of Wales (1976).
21. Farooqi, S. I., Heywood, N. I., and Richardson, J. F., "Drag Reduction by Air Injection for Suspension Flow in a Horizontal Pipeline," *Trans. Inst. Chem. Engrs.*, 58, 16–27 (1980).
22. Farooqi, S. I., and Richardson, J. F., "Horizontal Flow of Air and Liquid (Newtonian and Non-Newtonian) in a Smooth Pipe: Part I, A Correlation for Average Liquid Hold-up," *Trans. Inst. Chem. Engrs.*, 60, 292–305 (1982).
23. Chhabra, R. P., et al., "Co-Current Flow of Air and China Clay Suspension in Large Diameter Pipes," *Chem. Eng. Res. Des.*, 61, 56–61 (1983).
24. Chhabra, R. P., Farooqi, S. I., and Richardson, J. F., "Isothermal Two-Phase Flow of Air and Aqueous Polymer Solutions in a Smooth Horizontal Pipe," *Chem. Eng. Res. Des.*, 62, 22–32 (1984).
25. Prud'homme, R. K., and Long, R. E., "Surface Tensions of Concentrated Xanthan and Poly-acyrlamide Solutions with Added Surfactants," *J. Colloid Interface Sci.*, 93, 274–276 (1983).
26. Paul, D. D., and Abdel-Khalik, S. I., "Nucleate Boiling in Drag Reducing Polymer Solutions," *J. Rheo.*, 27, 59–76 (1983).
27. Taitel, Y., Barnea, D., and Dukler, A. E., "Modeling Flow Pattern Transitions for Steady Upward Gas-Liquid Flow in Vertical Tubes," *A.I.Ch.E.J.*, 26, 345–354 (1980).
28. Khatib, Z., "Hydraulic Transportation of Solids in Vertical Pipelines: Effect of air injection," Ph.D. dissertation, University of Wales (1981).
29. Khatib, Z., and Richardson, J. F., "Vertical Co-Current Flow of Air and Shear-Thinning Suspensions of Kaolin," *Chem. Eng. Res. Des.*, 62, 139–154 (1984).
30. Hewitt, G. F., King, I., and Lovegrove, P. C., "Hold-up and Pressure Drop Measurements in the Two-Phase Annular Flow of Air-Water Mixtures," *Brit. Chem. Eng.*, 8, 311–318 (1963).
31. Chen, J. J. J., and Spedding, P. L., "An Analysis of Hold-up in Horizontal Two-Phase Gas-Liquid Flow," *Int. J. Multiphase Flow*, 9, 147–159 (1983).

32. Raut, D. V., and Rao, M. N., "Momentum and Heat Transfer Characteristics of Air and Water Chalk Suspension in a Horizontal Pipe," *Ind. J. Tech.*, 13, 254–259 (1975).
33. Petrick, P., and Swanson, B. S., "Radiation Attenuation Method of Measuring Density of a Two-Phase Fluid," *Rev. Sci. Instru.*, 29, 1079–1085 (1958).
34. Shook, C. A., and Liebe, J. O., "Experimental Determination of Dispersed Gases in Slurries," *Can. J. Chem. Eng.*, 54, 118–120 (1976).
35. Pike, R. W., Wilkins, B., and Ward, H. C., "Measurement of the Void Fraction in Two-Phase Flow by X-Ray Attenuation," *A.I.Ch.E.J.*, 11, 794–800 (1965).
36. Miropolsky, Z. L., and Shneyerova, R. I., "Application of X-rays, Excited by β-Sources, to Studying Hydrodynamics of Two-Phase Media," *Int. J. Heat Mass Transfer*, 5, 723–728 (1962).
37. Gregory, G. A., and Mattar, L., "An In Situ Volume Fraction Sensor for Two-Phase Flows of Non-Electrolytes," *J. Can. Pet. Tech.*, 12 (2), 48–52 (1973).
38. Shu, M. T., Weinberger, C. B., and Lee, Y. H., "A Simple Capacitance Sensor for Void Fraction Measurement in Two-Phase Flow," *Ind. Eng. Chem. Fundam.*, 21, 175–181 (1982).
39. Heywood, N. I., and Richardson, J. F., "Slug Flow of Air-Water Mixtures in a Horizontal Pipe: Determination of Liquid Hold-up by γ-Ray Absorption," *Chem. Eng. Sci.*, 34, 17–30 (1979).
40. Farooqi, S. I., "The Effect of Rheological Properties on the Flow of Gas-Liquid Mixtures," Ph.D. dissertation, University of Wales (1981).
41. Zuber, N., and Findlay, J. A., "Average Volumetric Concentration in Two-Phase Flow Systems," *J. Heat Transfer, Trans. ASME.*, 87c, 453–468 (1965).
42. Mandhane, J. M., Gregory, G. A., and Aziz, K., "Critical Evaluation of Hold-up Prediction Methods for Gas-Liquid Flow in Horizontal Pipes", *J. Pet. Tech.*, 27, 1017–1027 (1975).
43. Lockhart, R. W., and Martinelli, R. C., "Proposed Correlation of Data for Isothermal Two-Phase, Two-Component Flow in Pipes," *Chem. Eng. Prog.*, 45 (1), 39–48 (1949).
44. Chisholm, D., and Laird, A. D. K., "Two-Phase Flow in Rough Tubes," *J. Heat Transf., Trans. A. S.M.E.*, 80c, 276–281 (1958).
45. Metzner, A. B., and Reed, J. C., "Flow of Non-Newtonian Fluids—Correlation of the Laminar, Transition and Turbulent Flow Regions," *A.I.Ch.E.J.*, 1, 434–440 (1955).
46. Weber, M. E., "Drift in Intermittent Two-Phase Flow in Horizontal Pipes," *Can. J. Chem. Eng.*, 59, 398–399 (1981).
47. Chang, H. D., and Darby, R., "Effect of Shear Degradation on the Rheological Properties of Dilute Drag-Reducing Polymer Solutions," *J. Rheo.*, 27, 77–88 (1983).
48. R. Brodkey, *Applied Mechanics Reviews*, 34, 137–138 (1981).
49. Grimm, R. J., "Squeezing Flow of Polymeric Liquids," *A.I.Ch.E.J.*, 24, 427–439 (1978).
50. Chhabra, R. P., Tiu, C., and Uhlherr, P. H. T., "A Study of Wall Effects on the Motion of a Sphere in Viscoelastic Fluids," *Can. J. Chem. Eng.*, 59, 771–775 (1981).
51. Chhabra, R. P., Farooqi, S. I., Khatib, Z., and Richardson, J. F., "The Co-Current Flow of Shear-Thinning Liquids and Air in Horizontal and Vertical Pipes," *J. Pipelines*, 2, 169–185 (1982).
52. Hubbard, M. G., and Dukler, A. E., "The Characteristics of Flow Regimes for Horizontal Two-Phase Flow," paper presented at Fluid Mechanics Conference, Stanford (1966).
53. Dukler, A. E., and Hubbard, M. G., "A Model for Gas-Liquid Slug Flow in Horizontal and Near Horizontal Tubes," *Ind. Eng. Chem. Fundam.*, 14, 337–347 (1975).
54. Hewitt, G. F., and Hall-Taylor, N. S., *Annular Two Phase Flow*, Pergamon Press, Oxford (1970).
55. Taitel, Y., and Dukler, A. E., "A Theoretical Approach to the Lockhart-Martinelli Correlation for Stratified Flow," *Int. J. Multiphase Flow*, 2, 591–595 (1976).
56. Cheremisinoff, N. P., and Davis, E. J., "Stratified Turbulent-Turbulent Gas-Liquid Flow," *A.I.Ch.E.J.*, 25, 48–56 (1979).
57. Wallis, G. B., *One-Dimensional Two-Phase Flow*, McGraw-Hill (1969).
58. Hewitt, G. F., and J. A., Boure, "Some Recent Results and Developments in Gas-Liquid Flow: A Review," *Int. J. Multiphase Flow*, 1, 139–171 (1973).
59. Chisholm, D., "A theoretical Basis for the Lockhart-Martinelli Correlation for Two-Phase Flow, *Int. J. Heat Mass Transfer*, 10, 1767–1778 (1967).

60. Chisholm, D., and Sutherland, L. A., "Prediction of Pressure Gradients in Pipeline Systems During Two-Phase Flow," *Proc. Inst. Mech. Engrs.*, *184* (Part 3c), 24–32 (1969–70).

61. Dukler, A. E., Wicks, M., and Cleveland, R. G., "Frictional Pressure Drop in Two-Phase Flow: A Comparison of Existing Correlations for Pressure Loss and Hold-up," *A.I.Ch.E.J.*, 10, 38–43 (1964).

62. Mandhane, J. M., Gregory, G. A., and Aziz, K., "Critical Evaluation of Friction Pressure Drop Prediction Methods for Gas-Liquid Flow in Horizontal Pipes," *J. Pet Tech.*, 29, 1348–1358 (1977).

63. *Engineering Science Data*, Vol. 5—Two Phase Flow (published by Eng. Sci. Data Unit, London (1976)).

64. Farooqi, S. I., and Richardson, J. F., "Horizontal Flow of Air and Liquid (Newtonian and Non-Newtonian) in a Smooth Pipe. Part II: Average pressure drop," *Trans. Inst. Chem. Engrs.*, 60, 323–333 (1982).

65. Tyagi, K. P., and Srivastava, R. P. S., "Flow Behavior of Non-Newtonian Liquid-Air in Annular Flow," *Chem. Eng. J.*, 11, 147–152 (1976).

66. Heywood, N. I., and Charles, M. E., "The Stratified Flow of Gas and Non-Newtonian Liquids in Horizontal Pipes," *Int. J. Multiphase Flow*, 5, 341–352 (1979).

67. Ward, H. C., and Dallavalle, J. M., "Co-Current Turbulent-Turbulent Flow of Air and Water Clay Suspensions in Horizontal Pipes," *Chem. Eng. Prog. Symp.* (Ser. 10), vol. 50, 1–14 (1954).

68. Greskovich, E. J., and Shrier, A. L., "Drag Reduction in Two-Phase Flow," *Ind. Eng. Chem. Fundam.*, 10, 646–648 (1971).

69. Rosehart, R. G., Scott, D. S., and Rhodes, E., "Gas-Liquid Slug Flow with Drag-Reducing Polymer Solutions", *A.I.Ch.E.J.*, 18, 744–750 (1972).

70. Srivastava, R. P. S., and Narsimhamurthy, G. S. R., "Hydrodynamics of Non-Newtonian Two-Phase Flow in Pipes," *Chem. Eng. Sci.*, 28, 553–558 (1973).

71. Cheng, D. C-H., et al., "The Design and Development of a Pneumatic Conveying System for an Asbestos Slurry," *Pneumotransport* 1, Paper A1, Cambridge, (1971).

72. Carleton, A. J., Cheng D. C-H., and French, R. J., "Pneumatic Transport of Thick Pastes," *Pneumotransport* 2, paper F2, Guildford, U.K. (1973).

73. Otten, L., and Fayed, A. S., "Pressure Drop and Drag Reduction in Two-Phase Non-Newtonian Slug Flow," *Can. J. Chem. Eng.*, 54, 111–114 (1976).

74. Rosehart, R. G., Rhodes, E., and Scott, D. S., "Studies of Gas-Liquid (non-Newtonian) Slug Flow: Void Fraction Meter, Void Fraction and Slug Characteristics," *Chem. Eng. J.*, 10, 57–64 (1975).

75. Heywood, N. I., and Richardson, J. F., "Head Loss Reduction by Gas Injection for Highly Shear-Thinning Suspensions in Horizontal Pipe Flow," *Hydrotransport* 5, paper C1, Hanover (1978).

76. Mujawar, B. A., and Raja Rao, M., "Gas Non-Newtonian Liquid Two-Phase Flow in a Straight Horizontal Tube," *Ind. J. Tech.*, 19, 343–348 (1981).

77. Mahalingam, R., "Two-Phase Gas Non-Newtonian Fluid Flow," *Adv. Trans. Proc.*, 1, 58–82 (1980).

78. Farooqi, S. I., "Flow of Anthracite Suspensions and the Effect of Air Injection in a Horizontal Pipe Line," M.Sc. dissertation, University of Wales (1977).

79. Deshpande, S. D., and Bishop, A. A., "Stratified Pseudoplastic Liquid-Gas Flow Through Horizontal Tubes," paper presented at A.I.Ch.E. Diamond Jubilee/Annual Meeting, Washington (1983).

CHAPTER 21

STABILITY OF ANNULAR FLOW IN HORIZONTAL TUBES

V. Kadambi

General Electric Company
Research and Development Center
Schenectady, New York, USA

CONTENTS

INTRODUCTION

In horizontal tube two-phase flows there exist several flow patterns. Alves [1] classified the observed patterns into the following categories: stratified, wavy, slug, plug, bubbly, froth flow, and annular or annular mist flow, which finally degenerates into dispersed flow. In the design of pipes that carry liquid-gas mixtures (as in the petroleum industry) and in heat exchangers where phase changes occur, it is necessary to know the pressure drop and the heat transfer, both of which are strongly dependent on the flow pattern. Hoogendoorn [21], for example, has demonstrated that for essentially similar flow conditions, slug or wave flow may be attained in air-water mixtures, resulting in changes in pressure drop by a factor of 2. The calculations of Bell et al. [3] show that the use of stratified flow correlations could result in condensation heat transfer estimates that are several orders of magnitude different from those that result from using annular flow correlations. Thus, in order to obtain an accurate estimate of the pressure drop and heat transfer in a pipe, it is necessary to know the actual flow pattern at any point in the pipe.

Several attempts have been made to predict the flow pattern for specified liquid and gas mass flow rates or superficial velocities. Kosterin [4], Alves [1], Baker [5], Krasiakova [6], and Hoogendoorn [2] were among the first few to propose maps for predicting flow patterns in adiabatic flow. These maps show various regions into which the flow patterns fall when two selected correlation parameters are plotted against each other. Several other investigators have also proposed empirical maps that are usually modifications of earlier maps based on more extensive data, e.g., Govier and Omer [7], Scott [8], Govier and Aziz [9], and Mandhane et al. [10]. In most of these maps (e.g. Figures 1 or 2), lines of demarcation among the various flow regimes are shown. In practice, however, there are no sharply distinguishable boundaries, and the type of flow changes gradually from one to another as the parameters change.

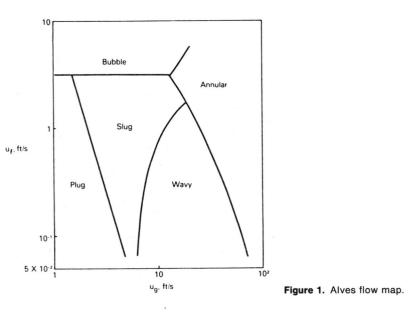

Figure 1. Alves flow map.

Empirical maps to predict transitions among the flow patterns in condensation are also available. Travies and Rohsenow [11] observed the flow regimes in horizontal two-phase flow with condensation. Soliman and Azer [12] formulated a flow pattern map based upon observations in tubes ranging from 0.476 cm to 1.59 cm.

Among the flow patterns that can exist, annular/annular-mist and stratified flow are the most important and cover a quality range between them from about 1% to 90% or more. In flows with phase changes, as much as 95% to 98% of the heat transfer can occur in these regimes. So, a considerable amount of attention has been focused on the annular stratified transition. Jaster and Kosky [13] have defined an empirical force balance parameter that represents the ratio between gravitational and shear forces. This factor is expected to define the existence of annular or stratified flow depending upon its magnitude. Wallis [14] has also defined a force balance parameter for vertical

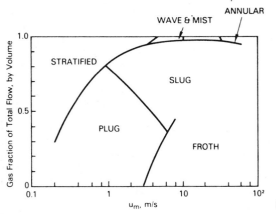

Figure 2. Hoogendoorn map.

flows. According to Palen et al. [15], the same parameter can be used to determine annular-stratified transitions in horizontal tubes as well.

In spite of all the effort expended so far, there has been no general agreement among the investigators about even the independent variables to be used in the flow pattern maps. Alves [1] used the superficial liquid and gas velocities, whereas Baker [5] used the mass flux ratio for the abscissa and the gas mass flux for the ordinate. While Govier and Omer [7] used the liquid and gas fluxes as the coordinates, Govier and Aziz [9], Mandhane et al. [10], and Dukler [16] recommend the use of superficial liquid and gas velocities. Several correction factors to account for changes in tube diameters and liquid, as well as gas properties have been proposed, based mostly on observations, without any physical basis for their selection. So far, none of the flow maps has dimensionless coordinates. Another major difficulty is that data from several sources do not necessarily agree with one another. There are strong indications that centrifugal forces, the existence of bends, heat transfer, etc., alter the flow patterns significantly [17–19]. (See also, the recent review by Rouhani and Sohal [20]). Further, as stated earlier, a mere variation in inlet conditions has produced slug as well as wave patterns at the same liquid and gas mass flow rates. It was for these reasons that Scott [8] proposed a modified Baker [5] plot showing areas of flow transition in place of lines. Even with this map, Scott recommends that further allowances be made for tube diameters 2.5 cm and lower, since the indicated areas tend to change rapidly with decreasing tube sizes. Mandhane et al. [10] have made allowances for property changes by defining a parameter, F, which is itself a function of the liquid-gas properties such as densities, viscosities, and surface tension.

Taitel and Dukler [21] have proposed a mechanistic, semi-theoretical model for flow transitions among several flow patterns. They use the Kelvin-Helmholtz condition for the stability of a wavelet to determine the criteria for transition from stratified to slug flows. They assert further that annular flow results if the stratified liquid level before transition is below the pipe centerline, while slug flow results otherwise. Even though the results obtained therefrom agree reasonably with the Mandhane et al. [10] flow map, several authors [17, 22, 23] have raised questions regarding the model on theoretical and experimental grounds. Also, their results do not agree with the Baker [5] and Scott [8] maps everywhere. Taitel and Dukler [24] have extended the model to unsteady flow with changing gas flow rates, to predict slug frequency. Niu and Dukler [25] have also presented an intermittent heat transfer calculation based on these ideas.

The mechanism that maintains a full annular film in a horizontal tube has been the subject of conjecture as well as investigation by several authors. Jacowitz [26] argues that the only stable situation is one that is dynamic, where a balance exists among the several forces (lift, surface drag, pressure, wall drag, wave formation effect, etc.), with a small but continuous downward drainage of liquid in the film. The film is expected to become thinner and thinner as the two-phase flow proceeds along the tube. Butterworth and Pulling [27, 28] have shown that waves play an important role in maintaining the film at the top of the tube. Butterworth [27] concludes that the liquid annulus can be maintained due to a continuous replenishment of the film at the top by one of two possible mechanisms. The first involves a secondary circulation in the film against gravity caused by differences in liquid film thickness between the bottom and the top [29]. The second is the action of waves that spread the liquid from the high-flow to the low-flow regions [30, 31]. A third mechanism favored by some authors is that the liquid drains continuously under gravity and is replenished purely by entrainment and redeposition of the liquid droplets due to the high-velocity gas flow. Several observations [6, 33] indicate either negligible entrainment or decreasing entrainment with increased liquid flux. It is difficult to see how entrainment can be the sole mechanism to maintain the film when annular flows have been reported with only 5% entrainment or less. What is possible is that several of these mechanisms aid one another in maintaining a stable film, with entrainment being an unimportant contributor at the start of annular flow.

Since the exact mechanisms that cause a change from stratified to annular flow are very complicated, little understood and hard to analyze, an attempt has been made here to predict the transition requirements based upon "global" considerations. It is postulated that annular flow arises when the energy exchange between the phases is sufficient to raise the liquid energy to that in annular flow. The force of interaction between phases is pictured as the agency responsible for the energy exchange between the phases. The transition criterion is based on the requirement that the gas should undergo a total energy change that is greater than the work done by the interactive forces between the gas and the liquid. Thus, the proposed criterion is completely different from that of Taitel and Dukler [21], which postulates the instability of a wavelet at the interface in stratified flow as responsible for the transition. The present postulate leads to transition condition that depends upon the specified annular and stratified void-fractions and slip, as well as on the nondimensional groups, the Froude number, Weber number, and Reynolds number. Calculations demonstrate that annular flow can occur only if the liquid Froude number is close to unity. This implies that for stability, the liquid kinetic energy in annular flow be greater than its potential energy at the center of the tube. Moreover, the stable region is shown to depend upon the inlet and the exit void-fractions utilized as the input and thus helps to explain the discrepancies among the results of various investigators as well as the necessity for establishing a fully stable flow before making measurements. A comparison with the Scott [8] version of the Baker [5] plot shows very good agreement for air-water flow in 10-cm (4-in.) diameter tubes. For 5-cm (2-in.) and 2.5-cm (1-in.) diameter tubes, the criterion specifies larger stable annular regions of flow than specified by the map.

ANALYSIS

The attempt here is to model transition between the annular and stratified flows. Even though other flow regimes like wavy, slug, bubbly, etc. exist and change to annular flow under suitable conditions, it is felt that stratified flow forms a basic pattern, while wavy and bubbly flow are merely variations in stratified flow brought about by surface tension and interfacial shear. (Note, however, that slug and plug flows are not variations of stratified flow). Moreover, the annular-stratified flow transition is the most important in the study of two-phase heat exchangers since almost 95% of the total energy exchange occurs in these flow regimes. Hence, consideration will be limited to this transition, though it is expected that the analysis will predict with reasonable accuracy, the transition boundary between annular and the rest of the patterns in its neighborhood.

Let a two-phase liquid gas mixture with a specified void fraction enter a horizontal pipe in annular flow. If the flow induced is unstable, it will change to stratified conditions over a transition zone, as shown in Figure 3. Similarly, if it is started in stratified flow, it will change into annular flow, provided annular flow is stable under the impressed conditions. Thus, the direction of flow indicated in the figure is not of much consequence in the analysis. We simply consider the flow on one side of the transition zone (indicated by subscript 1) as annular and on the other side (indicated by subscript 2) as stratified.

Let u_1 and u_g be the respective average liquid and gas velocities, flowing through a tube of radius R. The intention is to make mass and momentum balances over the transition region, assuming steady, incompressible flows coming into and going out of the control volume. In addition, heat transfer is neglected so that the present analysis applies only to adiabatic conditions. The occurrence of droplet entrainment and redeposition, commonly observed in annular flow, is neglected in this first analysis. If sufficient information on droplets is available, these effects can be included and modified results obtained.

In annular flow, the gas core has always been observed to be eccentric with respect to the pipe, resulting in a thicker liquid film at the bottom of the tube than at the top. Assume that the gas core

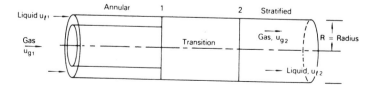

Figure 3. Annular-stratified transition.

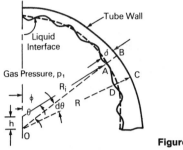

Figure 4. Annular film.

is also circular with radius, R, and its center displaced from that of the pipe, as shown in Figure 4. For given values of the eccentricity, h, and radii R, R_i, it is readily demonstrated from geometry that the liquid layer thickness is related to the angle θ at the center of the pipe by the equation:

$$\delta = (R - h\cos\theta) - (R_i^2 - h^2\sin^2\theta)^{1/2} \tag{1}$$

We now try to estimate the variation of pressure in the annular film, since this is needed later as an input to the momentum equation. Assuming the pressure exerted by the gas on the interface, p_{12} to be constant all over the boundary, the liquid pressure will clearly vary from the top to the bottom due to surface tension, waviness, shear (drag), gravity, and several other effects [26]. However, the velocities of recirculation and drainage in the film are rather small compared with the axial velocities of flow, as evidenced by Jacowitz's experiment as well as calculations. We assume that the effects of drag and shear are small in the radial direction so that the radial change in pressure may be treated as if it is caused by purely hydrostatic effects. Further, if the effect of film waviness is neglected (commensurate with the picture of a smooth average film), a force balance taking account of gravity yields

$$\frac{\partial p}{\partial r} = -\rho_1 g\cos\theta \tag{2a}$$

where p is the pressure at any point in the film located at a radius r and angle θ from the vertical. An integration subject to the condition

$$r = R - \delta: \quad p = p_i = p_1 - \sigma/R_i \tag{2b}$$

yields $\quad p - p_i = -\rho_1 g\cos\theta\{r - [h\cos\theta + (R_i^2 - h^2\sin^2\theta)^{1/2}]\} \tag{2c}$

Since the pressure at every point in the film is known, it permits us to calculate the total axial force on the film due to pressure at section 1:

$$\begin{aligned}
F_{11} &= 2\int_0^\pi \int_{R-\delta}^R pr\,d\theta\,dr \\
&= 2\int_0^\pi \int_{R-\delta}^R \{p_i - \rho_1 g\cos\theta[r - h\cos\theta + (R_i^2 - h^2\sin^2\theta)^{1/2}]\}r\,d\theta\,dr \\
&= (p_i + \rho_1 gh/2)\pi(R^2 - R_i^2) \tag{3}
\end{aligned}$$

The details of the integration have been omitted in the interest of brevity.

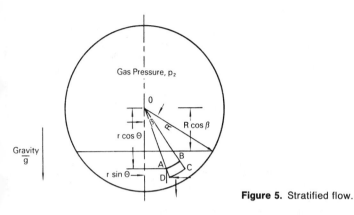

Figure 5. Stratified flow.

In order to determine the axial force on the stratified liquid section 2, consider Figure 5. Assuming a uniform gas pressure, p_2, acting on the liquid surface, the pressure on a little element ABCD becomes

$$p_1 = p_2 + \rho_1 g(r \cos \theta - R \cos \beta) \qquad (4)$$

The total axial force on the liquid due to pressure is

$$F_{12} = -2 \int_0^\beta \int_{R \cos \beta / \cos \theta}^R [p_2 + \rho_1 g(r \cos \theta - R \cos \beta)] r \, d\theta \, dr$$

$$= -2 \int_0^\beta \left[\left(p_2 \frac{R^2}{2} - \frac{\rho_1 g R^3 \cos \beta}{2} \right) \left(\frac{\cos^2 \beta}{\cos^2 \theta} - 1 \right) - \rho_1 g \frac{\cos \theta \; R^3}{3} \left(\frac{\cos^3 \beta}{\cos^3 \theta} - 1 \right) \right] d\theta$$

$$= (p_2 R^2 - \rho_1 g R^3 \cos \beta)(\beta - \sin 2\beta/2) + 2\rho_1 g R^3 \sin^3 \beta/3 \qquad (5)$$

Note that in annular flow the void-fraction is related to R_i by the relation

$$\alpha_1 = R_i^2/R^2 \qquad (6a)$$

while in stratified flow, the void fraction is related to the angle, β, by the relation

$$\alpha_2 = 1 - (\beta - \sin 2\beta/2)/\pi \qquad (6b)$$

By using Equations 4, 5, and 6a, b, and by noting that the axial forces due to pressure on the gas sections 1 and 2 are respectively

$$F_{g1} = \pi R_i^2 p_1 \quad \text{and} \quad F_{g2} = \pi R^2 \alpha_2 p_2 \qquad (7)$$

we can write the momentum equation in the axial direction in the following form:

$$F_{g1} + F_{11} + (\text{Mom})_1 = F_{g2} + F_{12} + (\text{Mom})_2 + F_s$$

i.e., $$\pi R^2 \left[p_1 \alpha_1 + \left(p_1 - \frac{\sigma}{R_i} + \frac{\rho_1 g h}{2} \right)(1 - \alpha_1) + \rho_g u_{g1}^2 \alpha_1 + \rho_1 u_{11}^2(1 - \alpha_1) \right]$$

$$= \pi R^2 [p_2 \alpha_2 + (p_2 - \rho_1 g R \cos \beta)(1 - \alpha_2) + 2\rho_1 g R \sin^3 \beta/(3\pi)$$
$$+ \rho_g u_{g2}^2 \alpha_2 + \rho_1 u_{12}^2(1 - \alpha_2)] + F_s \qquad (8)$$

Here, F_s, is the shear force due to wall effects and other dissipative forces in the transition region. Experimental observations in the previously cited literature as well as those conducted by the present author in a 1.9-cm tube (see section on Experiment), indicate that the transition region is itself short, compared with the tube length. It is likely that frictional forces that are usually of proportional length are small in this regime and may be neglected as compared with the rest of the quantities in the previous equation.

We write the continuity equations as follows:

$$u_{g1}\alpha_1 = u_{g2}\alpha_2 \qquad \text{(gas volume flow)} \tag{9a}$$

$$u_{11}(1 - \alpha_1) = u_{12}(1 - \alpha_2) \qquad \text{(liquid volume flow)} \tag{9b}$$

Equations 9a and b are based on the assumption that the gas temperature does not change appreciably during transition and that the densities of both phases may be considered as constant in view of the small pressure change, $p_1 - p_2$.

With these relations and assumptions, Equation 8 can be simplified to obtain an expression for the pressure change during transition:

$$\frac{\Delta p_R}{\rho_1 u_{11}^2} = (\alpha_2 - \alpha_1)\left[\frac{1 - \alpha_1}{1 - \alpha_2} - R_d S_1^2 \frac{\alpha_1}{\alpha_2}\right] + \frac{1}{\pi Fr^2}\left[\sin \beta \left(1 - \frac{\sin^2 \beta}{3}\right)\right.$$

$$\left. - \beta \cos \beta - \frac{\pi h(1 - \alpha_1)}{2R}\right] + \frac{(1 - \alpha_1)}{We\sqrt{\alpha_1}} \tag{9}$$

In this equation, the quantity, Δp_R, represents the pressure difference, $p_1 - p_2$, assuming frictional effects during transition to be negligible. The quantities, Fr and We, are respectively the Froude number and the Weber number, defined as follows:

$$Fr = u_{11}/(gR)^{1/2}, \qquad We = \rho_1 u_{11}^2 R/\sigma \tag{10}$$

The Froude and Weber numbers based on liquid superficial velocities and tube diameter are related to the above quantities by the respective equations

$$Fr^* = (1 - \alpha_1)Fr/\sqrt{2} = u_{1s}/(gD)^{1/2} \tag{11a}$$

$$We^* = 2(1 - \alpha_1)^2 We = \rho_1 u_{1s}^2 D/\sigma \tag{11b}$$

In these equations, u_{1s}, is the liquid superficial velocity and D is the tube diameter. For a given liquid-gas combination (air-water, for example), the Weber number is specified once the tube radius and Froude number are fixed.

For specified values of α_1, the annular void-fraction, and α_2, the stratified void-fraction, Froude and Weber numbers, the slip ratio, $S_1 = u_{g1}/u_{11}$, and annulus eccentricity, h, it is now possible to compute the pressure change, Δp_R, that will occur in the event of transition. Since the interest here is in specifying the line of stability of annular flow, computations have been carried out assuming that the eccentricity is the maximum permissible for the given value of α_1, i.e., one where the liquid-gas interface is just tangential to the tube inner surface. Then,

$$h = R - R_i = R(1 - \sqrt{\alpha_1}) \tag{12}$$

Experimentally, it should be possible to produce almost any specified void-fraction and slip-ratio, at either the inlet to the annular or the inlet to the stratified section. Indeed, Hasson and Nir [34], through a suitable combination of a nozzle and fluid flow arrangement, produced various inlet annular conditions to study the stability of such flows. Hence, one can choose any arbitrary values of α_1 and α_2 $(0 \leq \alpha_1 \leq 1, 0 \leq \alpha_2 \leq 1)$, slip, etc., and require Equation 9 to provide the pressure difference for that particular case. For calculational purposes, what has been done is to pick the void-fractions and slip for annular flow by the use of the Pai [35] velocity profiles and the Wallis [14] interfacial friction factor, given by the equation:

$$f_i/f = 151 - 150\sqrt{\alpha} \tag{13}$$

where f_i is the actual interfacial friction factor, while f is the friction factor that would exist if the same two-phase flow existed with a smooth annular interface. The details of the derivation can be found in Kadambi [36]. Similarly, for stratified flow, the curve-fits provided by Kadambi [37] and exhibited below have been utilized:

Turbulent-turbulent flow:

$$\alpha_2 = \frac{1 + 1.4133X_{tt}}{1 + 2.5315X_{tt} + 0.4403X_{tt}^2} \qquad (Re_1 \leq 2,000, Re_g > 2,000) \tag{14a}$$

Laminar-turbulent flow:

$$\alpha_2 = \frac{1 + 1.9566X_{1t}}{1 + 3.0927X_{1t} + 0.6946X_{1t}^2} \qquad (Re_g \geq 2,000, 1,200 \leq Re_1 < 2,000) \tag{14b}$$

For superficial liquid Reynolds numbers lower than 1,200 in the laminar-turbulent range, the following equations are used:

$$1 - \alpha_2 = (1 - \alpha_2')[1 + 0.161 \times 10^{-3}(Re_1 - 1,200)] \qquad (500 \leq Re_1 \leq 1,200) \tag{14c}$$

$$1 - \alpha_2 = (1 - \alpha_2')[1 + 0.246 \times 10^{-3}(Re_1 - 1,200)] \qquad (120 \leq Re_1 \leq 500) \tag{14d}$$

$$1 - \alpha_2 = (1 - \alpha_2')[1 + 0.31 \times 10^{-3}(Re_1 - 1,200)] \qquad (25 \leq Re_1 \leq 120) \tag{14e}$$

In these equations, α_2', is the void-fraction calculated from Equation 14b.

Laminar-laminar flow:

$$\alpha_2 = \frac{1 + 0.6684X_{11}}{1 + 1.2424X_{11} + 0.201X_{11}^2} \tag{14f}$$

In Equations 14a–f, the quantities X_{tt}, X_{1t}, and X_{11} are the Lockhart-Martinelli parameters defined by the following equations:

$$X_{tt} = [(1 - x)/x]^{0.9}R_d^{0.5}/M^{0.1} \tag{15a}$$

$$X_{1t} = 18.6501(Re_1)^{0.1}(R_d/Re_1)^{0.5}(1 - x)/x \tag{15b}$$

and

$$X_{11} = [(1 - x)/x]^{1/2}(R_d/M)^{1/2} \tag{15c}$$

It has been demonstrated [36, 37] that the results obtained from these equations as well as the Pai velocity profile in annular flows, are accurate and agree with data from many sources. It is therefore felt that they will produce realistic void-fractions and other values needed to study the stability of annular flow, except at very low qualities.

THE TRANSITION CRITERION

Having determined the pressure change during the expected transition, it is necessary to propose a criterion that will specify which of the two states, annular or stratified, will exist. A survey of the literature reveals that one of two propositions is usually used in similar situations: the minimum entropy production principle, and the principle of minimum energy.

For the present situation, minimum entropy production principle leads one to believe that the stable configuration is that with the lower dissipation and therefore the lower pressure drop (between annular and stratified flows) for the same liquid and gas mass fluxes. The minimum energy principle, on the other hand, leads one to believe the stable state is that with less mechanical energy between the two possible ones. However, both the criteria ignore the transition region where the liquid-gas interaction leading to the change in flow regimes occurs.

Based on energy conservation for the gas and the liquid phases and a momentum balance, Gardner [22] proposed a criterion applicable to transition between stratified and wavy flows. It requires that the stable state is that which maximizes the energy difference between two stations. It leads to the requirement that the ratio, $u_{g2}/(u_{g1} - u_{11})$, be less than 0.5 for transition.

Wallis and Dobson [38] have correlated the transition from stratified to slug flow for rectangular ducts in terms of the dimensionless gas superficial velocity, j_g^*, and the void-fraction, α, by the relation:

$$j_g^* = 0.5\alpha^{3/2} \tag{16}$$

The 3/2 power of α in the above equation has been obtained from the use of the Kelvin-Helmholtz classical theory of instability [39], while the coefficient, 0.5, is empirical. The Taitel-Dukler [21] analysis also uses a result obtained from the Kelvin-Helmholtz principle, except for a coefficient chosen in a form that meets the limiting conditions as α tends to zero or unity in stratified flow. Taitel and Dukler further asserted that annular flow occurs due to the instability if the equilibrium liquid level in stratified flow is lower than the pipe centerline. The basis for such an assertion, however, is not clear.

All of these criteria specify the existence of a final stable state, based purely on the conditions at the beginning and the end of the proposed transition. The implication is that certain forces exist and these necessarily cause momentum and energy exchanges if the conditions set forth in the criteria are satisfied. So far, experimental data in support of such assertions are not readily available, except in special circumstances.

As is generally observed in several transitions, there is a considerable amount of interaction between the phases in any liquid-gas flow. It seems logical to suppose that the interfacial energy transfer between the phases plays a key role in the transition. If this assumption is correct, any criterion that neglects the interactive forces between the phases cannot be complete and general enough to describe all the transition phenomena. This is especially true in the complicated transition pertaining to the stratified and annular flow regimes.

Based upon these considerations, we now examine the forces and the work of interaction between the phases to determine if a satisfactory criterion that will explain the stability of annular flow can be put forth. Since a combined momentum equation for the liquid and gas has already been written, we write an equation for the gas alone, to determine the interfacial forces between the gas and the liquid during the transition. By considering a differential volume element of the gas, a momentum-force balance yields

$$\dot{m}_g \, du_g = -A\alpha \, dp + dF_i \tag{17}$$

Here, dF_i is the force of interaction between the gas and the liquid element, which may ultimately cause the transition. Once again, shear and dissipative forces have been neglected as done for the overall momentum balance.

Since the void-fraction, α, varies during the transition, it will not be possible to integrate this equation exactly. An approximate result can, however, be obtained by assuming that the effect on F_i of the variation in α is not large for flows close to transition, and replace α by its mean value at its end states, i.e., by $\alpha_m = 0.5(\alpha_1 + \alpha_2)$. Then, Equation 17 can be integrated directly and leads to the result

$$F_i = -A[\alpha_m \, \Delta p_R + \dot{m}_g(u_{g1} - u_{g2})] = -A\alpha_1 \left[\frac{\alpha_m}{\alpha_1} \Delta p_R + \rho_g u_{g1}^2 \frac{(\alpha_2 - \alpha_1)}{\alpha_2} \right] \tag{18}$$

Here, Δp_R is the pressure change in a transition obtained by neglecting all dissipative effects. The force, F_i, is responsible for energy transfer between the liquid and the gas. If the flow should become annular starting from a stratified condition, it is necessary that the gas should provide the difference in liquid energies between the two regimes through the medium of this interactive force, which acts at the interface. The rate of work done by the gas on the liquid is, therefore

$$W = F_i u_i = -\dot{m}_1 \frac{\alpha_1 u_i u_{11}}{(1 - \alpha_1)} \left[\frac{\alpha_m}{\alpha_1} \frac{\Delta p_R}{\rho_1 u_{11}^2} + \frac{R_d S_1^2 (\alpha_2 - \alpha_1)}{2} \right] \tag{19}$$

where u_i is the average interfacial velocity in the transition regime.

Since the gas does work on the liquid during the transition, it suffers an energy loss between stratified and annular flows by an amount equal to

$$\Delta E_g = \dot{m}_g \left[\left(\frac{p_2}{\rho_g} + \frac{u_{g2}^2}{2} \right) - \left(\frac{p_1}{\rho_g} + \frac{u_{g1}^2}{2} \right) \right] = -\rho_g u_{g1} A \alpha_1 \left[\frac{\Delta p_R}{\rho_g} + \frac{u_{g1}^2 - u_{g2}^2}{2} \right]$$

$$= -\dot{m}_1 \frac{1}{1 - \alpha_1} u_{11} u_{g1} \left[\frac{\Delta p_R}{\rho_1 u_{11}^2} + \frac{R_d S_1^2}{2} \left(\frac{\alpha_2^2 - \alpha_1^2}{\alpha_2^2} \right) \right] \tag{20}$$

We shall now accept as a postulate that a flow transition of the type specified above will occur if the mechanical energy change experienced by the gas is greater than the work done by the interfacial forces in bringing about the transition, i.e., the proposed flow transition occurs provided the gas energy difference between the two regimes, ΔE_g, is at least as large as the energy transfer at the interface. Stable annular flow can occur only if

$$\Delta E_g \geq -F_i u_i \tag{21}$$

On substituting for ΔE_g and $F_i u_i$ respectively from Equations 20 and 19 and simplifying, we obtain

$$-u_{g1} \left[\frac{\Delta p_R}{\rho_1 u_{11}^2} + \frac{R_d S_1^2}{2} \frac{(\alpha_2^2 - \alpha_1^2)}{\alpha_2^2} \right] \geq u_i \left[\frac{\alpha_m}{\alpha_1} \frac{\Delta p_R}{\rho_1 u_{11}^2} + R_d S_1^2 \frac{(\alpha_2 - \alpha_1)}{\alpha_2} \right]$$

or

$$\frac{\Delta p_R}{\rho_1 u_{11}^2} \left[1 + \frac{\alpha_m}{\alpha_1} \frac{u_i}{u_{g1}} \right] \leq -\frac{R_d S_1^2 (\alpha_2 - \alpha_1)}{\alpha_2} \left[\frac{\alpha_m}{\alpha_2} + \frac{u_i}{u_{g1}} \right] \tag{22}$$

The quantity, u_i, the average interfacial velocity during the transition, is not easily determined. It is probably safe to assume that u_i is of the same order of magnitude as the interfacial velocities in annular and stratified flows. It is known through observations [40–42] and theoretical calculations [36, 37] that the interfacial velocities in both annular and stratified flows are quite small, being often less than 4%–5% of u_{g1}. If we therefore neglect terms containing u_i/u_{g1} compared with unity, the transition criterion reduces to the form:

$$\frac{\Delta p_R}{\rho_1 u_{11}^2} \leq \frac{R_d S_1^2 (\alpha_1^2 - \alpha_2^2)}{2\alpha_2^2} \tag{23}$$

It is thus asserted that transition to annular flow occurs and a stable flow results if the inequality in Equation 22 (or the approximate form in Equation 23) is satisfied. If not, stratified flow will be stable, since the gas does not have enough energy to bring about the transition to annular flow. Since energy exchange between the gas and the liquid is the postulated mechanism for the transition, it is clear that the gas energy in annular flow is less than that in stratified flow under the same mass flow rates and other conditions, i.e., ΔE_g must be positive. From Equation 20 it follows that:

$$\frac{R_d S_1^2(\alpha_1^2 - \alpha_2^2)}{2\alpha_2^2} - \frac{\Delta p_R}{\rho_1 u_{11}^2} \geq 0$$

This requirement is automatically satisfied if the transition criterion in Equation 23 is met. Also,

$$-F_i u_i = \frac{\dot{m}_1 \alpha_1 u_i u_{11}}{(1 - \alpha_1)} \left[\frac{\alpha_m}{\alpha_1} \frac{\Delta p_R}{\rho_1 u_{11}^2} + \frac{R_d S_1^2(\alpha_2 - \alpha_1)}{\alpha_2} \right]$$

$$\leq \frac{\dot{m}_1 \alpha_1 u_i u_{11}}{1 - \alpha_1} \left[\frac{\alpha_m^2}{\alpha_1} \frac{R_d S_1^2(\alpha_1 - \alpha_2)}{\alpha_2^2} + \frac{R_d S_1^2(\alpha_2 - \alpha_1)}{\alpha_2} \right]$$

$$\leq \frac{\dot{m}_1 \alpha_1 u_i u_{11}}{1 - \alpha_1} \frac{(\alpha_1 - \alpha_2)^3}{4\alpha_1 \alpha_2^2} R_d S_1^2 \qquad (24)$$

Since $F_i u_i$ is the energy supplied to the interface by the gas, this quantity should be positive as well. The product $u_i u_{11}$ is positive and $\alpha \leq 1$. Therefore, all the terms on the right-hand side of Equation 24 will be positive if

$$\alpha_1 > \alpha_2 \qquad (25)$$

Hence, a necessary condition for transition is that the *annular void-fraction be greater than the stratified void-fraction*. This condition ensures that the annular gas velocity is lower than that in stratified flow. The same conclusion may be reached by looking at the gas-liquid energy transfers as well. Since the liquid is lifted up in going from the stratified to the annular state, it is reasonable to suppose that the total liquid energy in the annular state is higher than that in the stratified state. The total mechanical energy of the flow can, at best, remain constant during the transition, so that an increment in liquid energy can occur only at the expense of the gas kinetic energy due to the interaction postulated earlier. Hence, the gas velocity in annular flow must be lower than that in stratified flow.

EXPERIMENT

In order to gain a qualitative understanding of annular and stratified flows, a simple experiment has been run in a 1.9-cm diameter transparent plastic tube mounted horizontally between supports, as shown in Figure 6. This is a slightly modified form of an apparatus used formerly to study slugging in horizontal tubes. Water and air are brought into the test section by means of an annular T-section arrangement, with air in the central tube and water through the tee. Fisher and Porter type flow meters and pressure gauges located upstream of the T-section were used to determine the flow rates of the fluids. The exit plenum, located 3 m from the inlet, was provided with an extra-large-sized drain valve to prevent interference between the tube flow and the liquid collected in the plenum chamber. Dye injection stations were located at two sections along the test section as shown, providing ability for food dye injection from the top, the bottom or from the side, at each station.

Experiments were run by maintaining a constant gas flow rate, as read by the flow meter on the air line and the water flow rates gradually raised from very low values. After each adjustment of flow rate, some time was allowed to ensure that the sytem reached steady state conditions be-

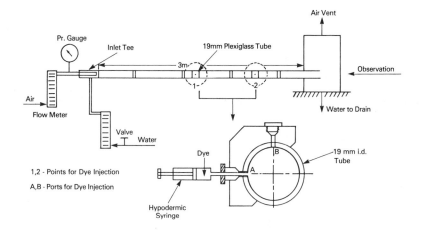

Figure 6. Schematic of test apparatus.

fore observations and dye injection were begun. The rates of air flow were such that the superficial velocities were in excess of 70 ft/s (21.5 m/s) and varied between 12 scfm (340 l/min) and 25 scfm (705 l/min). The water flow rates were varied between 0.02 ft³/min (0.55 l/min) and 12 ft³/min (260 l/min).

It was observed that for very low water flow rates with superficial velocities on the order of 0.1–0.4 ft/s (3–12 cm/s), the flow was often stratified, even though the air velocity was in excess of 70 ft/s (21.5 m/s). A rise in the rate of water flow maintaining a constant air flow brought on a gradual transition from stratified to semi-annular and, finally, annular flow, under these conditions. In order to ensure that parallax errors were not responsible for these observations, the flow at the end of the plexiglass tube was sighted axially in the direction of the arrow, near the exit chamber, which was also transparent. Before the flow became completely annular, no water could be seen emerging from the top of the tube. In semi-annular flow, a crescent shaped water line could be clearly seen at the tube end while in stratified/wavy flow a nearly flat surface was visible. These observations contradict the predictions of the Mandhane et al. [10] flow map, according to which the annular regime should prevail even at water superficial velocities below 1 ft/s, as long as the air superficial velocity exceeds 70 ft/s.

An injection of the dye at the side in fully established annular flow always showed it spreading uniformly towards the top and the bottom. There was no tendency for it to move preferentially one way or the other. Cine-camera films were also shot sequentially and observed later. These, too, indicated that the dye spread was uniform towards the top and the bottom. This observation may be interpreted in one of two ways. The first is that, in annular flow, there exist forces that oppose gravity such that there is no preferential flow downwards. The observed spread of the dye towards the top and the bottom would then be attributed to the high level of turbulence. A second interpretation is that there is a circulatory motion in the liquid film such that the liquid draining down from the sides is exactly compensated by the liquid moving towards the top. This interpretation would be supported by Darling and McManus' [29] observation of circulatory air currents in a dry tube, with varying degrees of roughness between the top and the bottom. Either of these interpretations would fit Butterworth's [31] observations, as well as estimates of film stability.

Injection of the dye into a semi-annular film always showed a greater tendency for the dye to move down under gravity rather than to move up. The higher the gas velocity for a given liquid flow rate, the more the dye spreads upwards, until the establishment of fully annular flow showed the dye spreading symmetrically upwards and downwards from the point of injection. The dye injected at the top of the tube always spread equally to both sides. Injection of the dye at the bottom of the tube also showed a symmetric dye spread to both sides of the point of injection, in every type of flow.

RESULTS AND DISCUSSION

By using equilibrium values of void-fractions in annular and stratified flows, the pressure change required for transition is obtained from Equation 9. Subsequently, the transition criterion specified by the inequality in Equation 21 has been used to predict the stability of annular flow. Most of the calculations are for air-water mixtures in 2.5-cm, 5-cm, and 10-cm tubes, though a few calculations have been carried out for gas-oil systems as well, with the properties specified by Baker [5]. Some of the calculated results as well as a comparison with those available in the literature, are presented in the following.

Figure 7 shows the input values of the void-fraction difference, $\alpha_1 - \alpha_2$, plotted against the annular void-fraction, α_1, for 2.5-cm-diameter tubes. The annular void-fractions were obtained through a complete calculation involving a velocity profile, and interfacial friction factor [36], while the stratified void-fractions were obtained from Equations 14a–f, both at the same liquid and gas mass flow rates. The Froude number specified by Equation 10 has been used as a parameter in the plot. It is seen that the stratified void-fraction is usually smaller than the annular void-fraction, the difference between the two increasing with increasing Froude numbers. In addition, for every Froude number, there exist some conditions where α_2 is greater than α_1. These observations apply to tubes of other diameters as well.

By using these void-fractions, predictions of stable annular flow regions have been made and the results are shown in Figure 8. Here, the superficial liquid and gas Reynolds numbers have been plotted, respectively, as the abscissa and the ordinate, with $FrWe^{3/2}$ as a parameter. Regions of stable annular flow are seen to depend on tube diameter and are shown by shading the inside of the curves for 2.5-cm, 5-cm, and 10.2-cm tubes. In agreement with the observations of Scott [8], the smaller diameter tubes tend to go into annular flow more easily than large diameter tubes. This trend seems to be reasonable, since the liquid undergoes less of potential energy change between stratified and annular flows in a small tube than in a large tube.

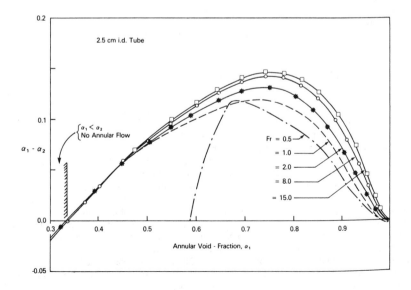

Figure 7. Void-fractions in annular and stratified flows.

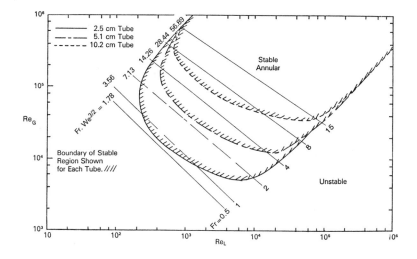

Figure 8. Predicted annular-stratified boundaries for various tube diameters.

Figure 8 also depicts that there exists a certain Froude number below which no transition can occur. This value turns out to be approximately 0.75 for the three diameters considered. Since the Froude number as defined here involves only the average liquid velocity and the tube radius, it implies that, in annular flow, the average liquid kinetic energy should at least be equal to its potential energy at the tube center. This is an observation that is amenable to experimental verification.

Since energy exchange between the liquid and the gas is the mechanism that causes annular flow, a large gas kinetic energy and a sufficiently large interfacial area are necessary for the transition. If, therefore, holding the gas velocity constant, the liquid mass flow rate and thus its superficial velocity are reduced, the interfacial area of contact between the liquid and the gas gradually decreases in stratified flow. Thus, the chances of transition to annular flow are continuously reduced with decreasing liquid flow rates. This is what is implied by the Baker plot, Figure 9, which shows larger and larger requirements of gas mass flux, G_g, with decreasing values of G_1/G_g. In Figure 8, this effect manifests itself as a limiting value of Re_1 for a given tube diameter, below which no annular flow can occur.

Figure 9 is the Scott [8] version of the Baker plot, on which the predictions of the present theory for 2.5-cm, 5.1-cm, and 10.2-cm tubes are shown for comparison. For the 10.2-cm tube, the predicted transition line agrees closely with that of the map, except near the slug-flow boundary. The predictions for the smaller sized tubes indicate larger stable regions of annular flow than the map. Moreover, this predicted diameter effect is in general agreement with the data of Weisman et al. [17]. The limited calculations carried out for oil-air two-phase flow provide similar results, though they have not been shown on the map.

The disagreement between the present theory and the map in the slug region arises partly due to the void-fractions used in the annular regime. As noted earlier, the void-fractions were calculated by using the Pai velocity profiles in turbulent flow along with Equation 13 due to Wallis [43]. This equation is valid only for large values of α. The values of f_i obtained for large liquid flow rates (small α) are inaccurate and, thus, the predicted region of stability is not accurate in the slug regime. Moreover, slug flow does not approximate stratified flow, which has been used as the model in this theory. For both these reasons, some discrepancy between the theory and observations ought to be expected at the boundary of this regime.

A comparison among some of the flow maps, as well as the Taitel-Dukler [21] and present theories, is shown in Figure 10. Here, the superficial velocities are the coordinates. The lack of agreement among the maps is evident. The Mandhane et al. [10] region of stable annular flow is

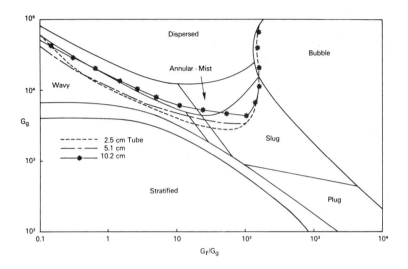

Figure 9. Comparison of predictions with Scott map.

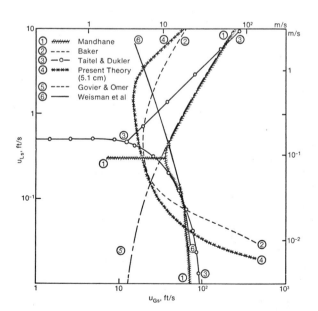

Figure 10. Comparison of predictions with Mandhane plot.

Line 1-1 and the Baker [5] region is Line 2-2. Line 3-3 is the Taitel-Dukler [21] theory, while Line 4-4 is the present prediction. For low-liquid superficial velocities, both the Mandhane line and the Taitel-Dukler line indicate the existence of stable annular flow, as long as the gas velocity is in excess of 70–80 ft/s (23–26 m/s). As already pointed out, the experimental results presented earlier seem to disagree with this prediction. Both the Baker plot and the present theory agree with experimental data since they require higher and higher gas velocities are needed to achieve annular conditions as the liquid velocity is reduced. Nevertheless, at high liquid velocities, the present theory seems to overpredict the region of stability, as already noted. If data become available regarding the void-fractions in annular flow at relatively high liquid fluxes, or if a better interfacial friction factor correlation is obtained, the results of the present prediction can be improved.

In order to see how sensitive the predicted stability is to the input variables, two sets of "experimental" calculations were attempted. In the first one, the values of α_1, S_1, etc. were all chosen as the solutions to the annular flow problem with laminar liquid and laminar gas conditions, irrespective of the Reynolds numbers. Similarly, the stratified flow void-fraction was obtained by using Equation 14f, which is valid only in laminar flow. The stability criterion then predicts a totally stratified flow, independent of the Froude and Weber numbers. A second set of "experimental" calculations involved slightly changing the values of α_1, α_2, etc., from those used in the graph, Figure 7. These indicate that annular flow stability usually improves with increasing values of $\alpha_1 - \alpha_2$, and diminishes with decreasing values when the other parameters are all fixed. Thus, the type of flow finally obtained in a given experiment for the same flow rates of liquid and gas, can depend strongly on the conditions prevailing at the test section inlet and exit. This is the likely reason for the large amount of disagreement among the several investigations exhibited in Figure 10. In accordance with the recommendations of Hewitt [44], the transition maps should therefore be used purely as guides and no reliance should be placed upon them to provide the exact regions of stability.

It is to be noted that the stability criterion developed here is independent of the procedure used to calculate the annular and stratified void-fractions. My procedures have been used to predict α_1 and α_2, simply because they have been found to agree with data from several sources, especially for air-water flows. There is no requirement or necessity to use them to determine the equilibrium void-fractions. Other procedures that predict these void-fractions can be used equally well.

Since the stability criterion provided by Equation 22 involves u_i, the interfacial transition velocity whose value is not known accurately, some calculations have also been carried out to determine the sensitivity of the results to changes in assumed values of u_i. As long as u_i is less than about 8% of u_{g1}, the predicted region of stability is almost independent of its magnitude. For all practical purposes, therefore, Equation 23 is as good as Equation 22 for transition calculations.

All the present calculations consider annular flow as complete when a liquid film of zero thickness forms at the top of the tube, with an eccentricity as specified by Equation 12. Experimental observations are, however, subject to parallax errors and it is impossible to tell when the annular film has just formed completely. Usually, a liquid film of finite thickness exists at the tube top when one recognizes the flow as annular. This results in data that tend to underestimate the range of stable annular flow, especially when transitions to the slug- and bubble-flow patterns are under investigation. Therefore, the present theory can be expected to overpredict the region of annular flow in comparison with observations. In addition, since frictional and dissipative effects have been neglected, one expects a further slight overestimation of the annular regime. If corrections are incorporated to obtain the proper value of Δp, including dissipative effects in transition, one can expect better agreement between the predictions of the present model and observations. Considering the simplifications used, the agreement between experimental observations (as specified by the flow maps) and the present theory may be considered as quite satisfactory, except near the annular-slug boundary.

It must be emphasized that the present theory is quite general and may be applied to any proposed transition, be it annular-stratified, stratified-wavy or stratified-plug, provided that the interactive forces can be calculated. It deals only with the conditions required for the existence of stable flow regimes, without considering the details of the transition process. Therefore, it does not propose a mechanism for the transition or for the causes of the instability of a given flow pattern. In this respect, it is quite different from the Taitel-Dukler [21] model, which proposes the Kelvin-Helmholtz stability criterion as the requirement for stratified flow. The present theory suggests that a transition to annular flow occurs due to an energy exchange between the liquid and the gas at the interface, without any specification of the mechanism for the transfer. This postulate has been successful in predicting transition in several situations as already shown and thus provides a new insight to the problem as a whole. It also suggests strongly that entrainment and redeposition have no influence in the film formation, since the equations used here exhibit stability with no entrainment at all. This supports the contention of Butterworth [31] that wave-spread or secondary flow maintains the annular film at the top of the tube against gravity. It is possible that both these mechanisms complement each other and are aided by entrainment at a later stage.

CONCLUSIONS

1. Based on momentum balance and energy exchange considerations, a criterion for the existence of stable annular flow has been established. This criterion predicts a line of transition between annular flow and the rest of the flow patterns that is different for different tube sizes: the smaller the tube size, the larger the range of stable annular flow.
2. The predicted range of stability is in reasonable agreement with the Baker plot. At very low liquid flow rates, it predicts results that are in better agreement with experimental observations than the Mandhane plot.
3. Stable annular flow can occur only when the liquid kinetic energy is equal to or larger than the liquid potential energy at the tube center. If it is smaller, the flow cannot be annular.
4. The two-phase flow stability is a function of the specified conditions at the entry to the test section, even when the mass flow rates and fluid properties are fixed. This explains the large degree of disagreement among the experimental data in specifying the ranges of stability of the various flow patterns.

Corrections are incorporated to obtain the proper value of Δp.

Acknowledgments

The author is grateful to Mr. Karl Hardcastle and Mr. Peter Morgan who very ably assisted him in the experimental observations as well as in the picture taking.

NOTATION

A	cross-sectional area	p	pressure
D	diameter	p_i	pressure at interface
Fr	Froude number	Re	Reynolds number
F_s	shear force	R, r	radius
F_{12}	total axial force	S_1	slip ratio
f	friction factor	u	velocity
g	gravitational acceleration	W	work
h	eccentricity	We	Weber number
j_g^*	dimensionless gas superficial velocity	X_{tt}	Lockhart-Martinelli parameter
$\dot{m}_g$	mass	x	quality

Greek Symbols

α	void fraction	θ	angle
β	angle	ρ	density
δ	film thickness	σ	surface tension

REFERENCES

1. Alves, G. E., "Co-Current Liquid-Gas Flow in a Pipeline Contactor," *Chem. Eng. Prog.*, 50, No. 9, 1954. pp. 449–456.

2. Hoogendoorn, C. J., "Gas-Liquid Flow in Horizontal Pipes," *Chem. Eng. Sci.* 9, 1959, pp. 205–217.

3. Bell, K. J. et al., "Interpretation of Horizontal In-Tube Condensation Heat Transfer Correlations with a Two-Phase Flow Regime Map," *CEP Symp. Series* 66, No. 102, 1970. pp. 150–163.

4. Kosterin, S. I., "An Investigation of the Influence of the Diameter and Inclination of a Tube on the Hydraulic Resistance and Flow Structure of Gas-Liquid Mixtures," *Izvest. Akad. Nauk. SSSR, Otdel Tekh Nauk.* 12, 1949. pp. 1824–1830. Also, ANL-6734-2684.

5. Baker, O., "Simultaneous Flow of Oil and Gas," *Oil Gas J.* 53, 1954. pp. 183–195.

6. Krasiakova, L. I., "Some Characteristic Flows of a Two-Phase Mixture in a Horizontal Pipe," *Zh. Tekh. Fiz.* 22, No. 4, 1952. p. 6 (Trans. UKAEA, 17).

7. Govier, C. W. and Omer, M. M., "The Horizontal Pipeline Flow of Air-Water Mixtures," *Can. J. Chem. Eng.* 40, 1962. pp. 93–104.

8. Scott, D. S., "Properties of Co-Current Gas-Liquid Flow," *Adv. Chem. Eng.*, Academic Press, 1963, pp. 207–214.

9. Govier, C. W. and Aziz, K., *The Flow of Complex Mixtures in Pipes*, Van-Nostrand, Reinhold, New York, 1972.

10. Mandhane, J. M. et al., "A Flow Pattern Map for Gas-Liquid Flow in Horizontal Pipes," *Int. J. Multiph. Flow* 1, 1974. pp. 537–553.

11. Travies, D. P. and Rohsenow, W. M., "Flow Regimes in Horizontal Two-Phase Flow with Condensation," *ASHRAE Cont. RP63, MIT Rept. DSR-72591-74*, Cambridge, Mass., 1971.

12. Soliman, H. and Azer, N. Z., "Visual Studies of Flow Patterns During Condensation Inside Horizontal Tubes," *5th Int. Heat Trans. Conf., Tokyo*, Vol. III, Pap. No. Cs 1.6, 1974. pp. 241–245.

13. Jaster, H. and Kosky, P. G., "Condensation Heat Transfer in the Mixed Flow Regime," *Int. J. Heat Mass Trans.*, 19, 1976. pp. 95–99.

14. Wallis, G. B., "Flooding Velocities for Air and Water in Vertical Tubes," *U.K. At. Energy Auth.*, Rept. AEEW-R-123, 1962.

15. Palen, J. W. et al., "Prediction of Flow Regimes in Horizontal Tube-Side Condensation," *Heat Tr. Eng.* 1, No. 2, 1979. pp. 47–57.

16. Dukler, A. E., "Modeling Two-Phase Flow and Heat Transfer," *Sixth Int. Heat Tr. Conf.*, Pap. No. KS-11, 1978, pp. 1–17.

17. Weisman, J., Duncan, D., Gibson, J. and Crawford, T., "Effects of Fluid Properties and Pipe Diameter on Two-Phase Flow Patterns in Horizontal Lines," *Int. J. Multiph. Flow* 5, 1979. pp.437–462.

18. Hughes, R. R. et al. "Flash Vaporization," *Chem. Eng. Prog.* 49, No. 2, 1953. pp. 78–87.

19. Isbin, H. S. "Two-Phase Steam-Water Pressure Drops," *CEP Symp. Ser.* 55, No. 23, 1959, pp. 75–84.

20. Rouhani, S. Z. and Sohal, M. S., "Two-Phase Flow Patterns: A Review of Results," *Prog. In Nucl. Energy*, 11, No. 3, 1983, pp. 219–259.

21. Taitel, Y. and Dukler, A. E., "A Model for Predicting Flow Regime Transition in Horizontal and Near Horizontal Gas-Liquid Flow," *AIChE J* 22, 1976. pp. 47–55.

22. Gardner, G. C., "Onset of Slugging in Horizontal Ducts," *Int. J. Multiph. Flow* 5, 1979. pp. 201–209.

23. Hewitt, G. F., "Liquid-Gas Systems," *Handbook of Multiphase Flow*, (ed. G. Hetsroni), Chap. 2, Hemisphere, Washington, 1981.

24. Taitel, Y. and Dukler, A. E., "A Model for Slug Frequency During Gas-Liquid Flow in Horizontal and Near Horizontal Gas-Liquid Flow," *Int. J. Multiph. Flow* 3, 1975. pp. 585–596.

25. Niu, T. and Dukler, A. L., *Proc. Specialists Meet. Trans. Two-Phase Flow*, Banerjee (ed.), Pergamon Press, 1978.

26. Jacowitz, L. A., "An Analysis of Geometry and Pressure Drop for the Annular Flow of Gas-Liquid Systems," PhD thesis, Department of Chemical Engineering, Ohio State University, 1962.

27. Butterworth, D., "Air-Water Climbing Film Flow in an Eccentric Annulus," *Co-current Gas-Liquid Flow* (E. Rhodes and D. S. Scott, eds.), Plenum Press, New York, 1969. pp. 145–201.

28. Butterworth, D., and Pulling, D. J., "RS29: A Visual Study of Mechanisms in Horizontal, Annular, Air-Water Flow," *U.K. At. Energy Auth.*, No. AERE-M2556, 1972.

29. Darling, R. S. and McManus, H. N., "Flow Patterns in Circular Ducts with Circumferential Variation of Roughness: A Two-Phase Flow Analog," *Proc. 11th Mid-Western Conf., Dev. in Mech.*, 5, 1968, pp. 153–163.

30. Butterworth, D., "Note on a Fully-Developed, Horizontal, Annular Two-Phase Flow," *Chem. Eng. Sci.* 24, 1969. pp. 1832–1834.

31. Butterworth, D., "Air-Water, Annular Flow in a Horizontal Tube," *U.K. At. Energy Auth.*, No. AERE-R6687, 1971.

32. Fisher, S. A., and Pearce, D. L., "A Theoretical Model for Describing Horizontal Annular Flows," *Int. Sem. Mom. Heat Mass Trans. Two-Phase Energy and Chem. Systems*, Dubrovnik, Pap. No. 3.3–5, Sep. 4–9, 1978.

33. Wicks, M. and Dukler, A. E., "Entrainment and Pressure Drop in Concurrent Gas-Liquid Flow: I. Air-Water in Horizontal Flow," *AIChE J.* 6, No. 3, 1960. pp. 463–468.

34. Hasson, D. and Nir, A., "Annular Flow of Two Immiscible Liquids. II Analysis of Core-Liquid Ascent," *Can. J. Chem. Eng.* 48, 1970. pp. 521–526.

35. Pai, S. I., "On Turbulent Flow in a Circular Pipe," *J. Franklin Inst.* 256, 1953. pp. 337–352.

36. Kadambi, V., "Prediction of Pressure Drop and Void-Fraction in Annular Two-Phase Flows," GE Rep. No. 80CRD156, 1980.

37. Kadambi, V., "Prediction of Void-Fraction and Pressure Drop in Two-Phase Stratified Flow," *Can. J. Chem. Eng.* 59, 1981. pp. 584–589.

38. Wallis, G. B. and Dobson, J. E., "The Onset of Slugging in Horizontal Stratified Air-Water Flow," *Int. J. Multiph. Flow* 1, 1973, pp. 173–193.

39. Milne-Thompson, L. M., *Theoretical Hydrodynamics*, McMillan, 1968.

40. Armand, A. A., "The Resistance During the Movement of a Two-Phase System in Horizontal Pipes," *AERE Transl.* 828, UKAEA Res. Group, Harwell 1959.

41. Bergelin, O. P. and Gazley, C., "Cocurrent Gas-Liquid Flow in Horizontal Tubes," *Proc. Heat Transfer Fluid Mech. Inst.* 29, Berkeley, 1949. pp. 5–18.

42. Agrawal et al., "An Analysis of Horizontal Stratified Two-Phase Flow in Pipes," *Can. J. Chem. Eng.* 1, 1973, pp. 280–286.

43. Wallis, G. B., "Annular Two-Phase Flow, Part I: A Simply Theory," *J. Basic Eng., Trans. ASME*, 1970. pp. 59–72.

44. Hewitt, G. F., "Two-Phase Flow Patterns and Their Relationship to Two-Phase Heat Transfer," *Proc. NATO Ad. Study Inst.* 1 (S. Kakac and F. Mayinger, eds.), Hemisphere, Washington, 1976. p. 21.

CHAPTER 22

FLOW PATTERN TRANSITIONS DURING HORIZONTAL IN-TUBE CONDENSATION

H. M. Soliman

Department of Mechanical Engineering
University of Manitoba
Winnipeg, Manitoba, Canada

CONTENTS

INTRODUCTION

The flow of condensing two-phase mixtures inside tubes or ducts is encountered in an increasing number of applications involving engineering equipment in the power and process industries. Process heaters, refrigeration and air conditioning systems, and steam power plant condensers are examples of such equipment. Improved design of such equipment requires full understanding of the hydrodynamic and thermal characteristics of the flow as a prerequisite for the selection or development of appropriate pressure drop and heat transfer correlations.

During horizontal intube condensation of pure vapors the ratio of vapor to liquid flow rates changes continuously along the condensation path. This is naturally accompanied by a corresponding change in the velocity of both phases and the relative magnitude of forces acting on the flow. When the dominant force acting on the flow changes, so does the flow pattern. For example, the spray and annular flow patterns would exist as long as the dominant force is vapor shear; transition to wavy and stratified flow would start when liquid gravity begins to dominate. Consequently, between the inlet of a condenser (pure vapor) and the exit (pure liquid), a succession of flow patterns is expected to exist depending on the local hydrodynamics of the flow. Figure 1 shows schematically the flow pattern progression observed in several experimental investigations for conditions of high and low mass fluxes. The major differences between the two parts of Figure 1 are the existence of spray flow in the entry part and complete condensation in the exit part at high mass fluxes, while at low mass fluxes, spray flow and probably slug flow do not appear and the flow is stratified at the exit of the condenser (as seen in many experimental arrangements). In addition, the quality at which any flow pattern exists is known to be strongly dependent on the total mass flow rate, tube diameter, and properties of the flowing mixture.

Due to the gradual nature of variation in the acting forces, the transition from one flow pattern to another is not abrupt, but rather gradual. Transitional flow patterns, such as spray-annular and

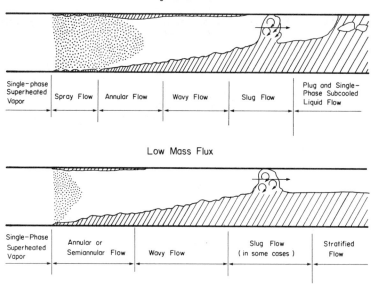

Figure 1. Flow-pattern development during horizontal intube condensation.

annular-wavy, were identified in some experimental studies. Consequently, it must be emphasized that the sharp lines defined by the different correlations of flow pattern transitions (analytical or empirical) are in fact representatives of transition zones of finite widths.

Studies of two-phase flow patterns and their transitions have gained increasing interest and importance from the well accepted view that the pressure drop and heat transfer characteristics are strongly dependent on the flow pattern. In single-phase flow, laminar and turbulent conditions have separate correlations for the calculation of the pressure drop and heat transfer rate with reasonably established and simple criteria for the laminar-turbulent transition. The situation is similar in two-phase flow, but not quite as simple. In the development of almost all the two-phase heat transfer correlations available in the literature (analytical or empirical), a certain flow pattern was assumed either explicitly or implicitly. Using a certain heat transfer correlation under operating conditions inconsistent with the flow pattern for which it was developed could lead to serious errors in magnitude and trend. This point was illustrated quantitatively for the case of horizontal intube condensation of pure vapors by Bell et al. [1]. Consequently, it is very important to know which flow pattern is expected to exist at certain flow conditions inside a condenser; this is the equivalent of knowing whether the flow is laminar or turbulent in single-phase situations.

The objective of this chapter is to provide a comprehensive and up-to-date coverage of the different methods available for predicting the flow patterns during horizontal intube condensation. Before proceeding with this task, a brief review of the available flow pattern data is presented. This is necessary since these data did and continue to serve as the basis of all empirical correlations, as well as the means of assessing the adequacy and accuracy of theoretical correlations.

FLOW PATTERN DATA

Due to the importance of the flow patterns, as previously discussed, several experimental investigations were undertaken having as major objectives the generation of information on the flow patterns expected to exist during condensation and on the operating conditions under which each pattern is supposed to exist. The first of these studies was reported in 1971 by Soliman and Azer [2] in which the flow patterns of refrigerant R-12 condensing inside a 12.7-mm I.D. horizontal tube were investigated. This study was followed by other studies [3–5] in which different tube diameters and/or different working fluids were used. The data in [2–5] constitute the bulk of data available in the open literature.

In generating these data, the test condensers used were basically double-pipe heat exchangers with the test fluid flowing in the inner pipe and cooling water in the jacket. Several visual sections were installed at fixed locations along the condenser from which the flow patterns were visually identified and recorded. Energy balances were applied to calculate the local flow conditions corresponding to each visual observation. For detailed information concerning the test systems, experimental procedure and method of data reduction the reader is referred to References [2–5].

In this chapter the data base is divided into eight sets with each set corresponding to a certain combination of tube diameter and test fluid. The ranges of operating conditions for these eight sets are listed in Table 1. In terms of diameter and fluid properties the data base listed in Table 1 encompasses a major portion of the conditions encountered in practical applications. It must be pointed out, however, that additional data points are available in other sources, e.g. [6–10]. These data are small in number (total of 72 points), and in addition, they correspond mostly to conditions falling within the range listed in Table 1, and hence will not be referred to in later sections.

Six major and three transitional flow patterns were visually identified in the nine data sets of Table 1. There is reasonable agreement among different investigators in the descriptions used for classifying these flow patterns, except for one discrepancy that will be pointed out later. The six major flow patterns were described as follows:

Spray flow. No stable liquid film was apparent. Most of the liquid phase was entrained by the vapor in the form of a mist.

Annular flow. A stable liquid film covered the entire tube wall, while the vapor flowed in the core. Part of the liquid phase was entrained by the vapor. Asymmetry was apparent in the liquid film with the maximum thickness being at the bottom of the tube.

Semi-annular flow. The flow had an appearance similar to the annular flow, except that the stable film did not cover the entire wall periphery. A small portion of the upper half of the tube appeared dry, while the liquid film thickness increased to a maximum at the bottom.

Wavy flow. The two phases were separated, with the liquid flowing at the bottom of the tube. The velocity difference between the vapor and liquid caused the liquid surface to be wavy. The wavelength increased with the decrease in quality. A draining thin film may appear on the upper half of the wall periphery.

Slug flow. The flow is basically wavy, however, surface waves grew frequently forming slugs wetting the upper tube wall. These slugs traveled at high speeds and the frequency of their occurence depended on the flow conditions.

Plug flow. The flow appeared as a single-phase liquid flow with the intermittent appearance of large vapor plugs at the upper tube wall. Vapor plugs were irregular in shape, different in size and appeared to be flowing at the same velocity of the liquid.

The three transitional flow patterns were associated with the following descriptions:

Spray-annular flow. Intermittent liquid films appeared but were swept away after their appearance to become part of the mist.

Annular-wavy flow. The flow had the annular appearance but the thickness of liquid increased at the bottom forming a thick stratum.

Table 1
Operating Conditions for Which Flow Pattern Data Is Available

Data set no.	Inside tube diameter (D, mm)	Condensing fluid	Average saturation temperature T_s °C	Density ratio ρ_ℓ/ρ_v	Viscosity ratio μ_ℓ/μ_v	Surface tension $\sigma \times 10^3$ N/m	Quality range covered x	Mass flux range $G \times 10^{-4}$ kg/hr·m²	Number of data points	Ref.
1	4.8	R-12	28.6	31.7	16.2	8.9	0.01–0.99	21–305	111	[4]
2	8.0	R-12	27.6	32.6	16.6	8.9	0.02–0.96	36–356	83	[3]
3	12.7	R-12	30.0	30.4	16.1	8.9	0.01–0.95	9–100	93	[2]
4	15.9	R-12	32.9	27.9	15.5	8.9	0.02–0.99	6–72	138	[4]
5	4.8	R-113	62.3	128	38.4	19.0	0.01–0.62	81–242	74	[4]
6	12.7	R-113	59.5	140	40.0	19.0	0.01–0.82	14–88	79	[4]
7	15.9	R-113	62.7	126	38.1	19.0	0.01–0.94	4–55	86	[4]
8	13.4	Steam	110.0	1150	20.2	56.9	0.01–0.70	15–89	174	[5]

Semi-annular-wavy flow. The flow had the semi-annular appearance but with a thick stratum flowing at the bottom of the tube. A fraction of the upper half of the tube was still covered by a stable liquid film.

Only one discrepancy exists in the flow pattern classification of the present data base. In data set no. 2, Traviss and Rohsenow [3] did not classify any of the observed flow patterns as wavy. Instead, they used the classification "semi-annular" and described this flow pattern as follows: "The liquid asymmetrically distributed as a film around the top and sides of the tube and a thick stratum at the bottom of the tube." Comparing this description with the previous list we find that it approaches the description of annular-wavy and probably wavy flow depending on the thickness of the stratum. This assumption is supported by the fact that Traviss and Rohsenow [3] considered their semi-annular flow to be gravity controlled. Since a division of the semi-annular data in [3] into wavy and annular-wavy cannot be done here with certainty, all this group of data points will be classified here as wavy (i.e. gravity controlled). Discrepancies similar to this are found in several segments of the two-phase flow literature, and will continue to occur until terminology, notation, and methods of data presentation has been standardized or commonly agreed upon; a condition not yet achieved.

FLOW PATTERN CORRELATION

General Overview

By way of introduction, one can state with absolute certainty that there is no generalized method or standard technique for presenting the two-phase flow pattern data. The question the designer needs answered is: Given the tube diameter, the fluid, and flow conditions (mass flow rate, pressure, temperature, and quality), what flow pattern is expected to exist?

Early investigations in this field used the approach of plotting the data in the form of a map with each flow pattern occupying a certain area and approximate transition lines separating the different areas. Normally, this approach was followed when the data corresponded to one combination of a tube diameter and flowing-mixture properties. Several coordinate systems were used in plotting these maps: for example, Alves [11] used the superficial gas velocity, V_{vs}, and the superficial liquid velocity, $V_{\ell s}$, for the adiabatic air-water flow patterns inside a horizontal tube; Hoogendoorn [12] used the mixture velocity, V_m, and the gas volumetric ratio, R, for the adiabatic gas-oil flow patterns inside horizontal tubes; and Hosler [13] used the total mass flux, G, and the quality, x, for the flow patterns of boiling water in a rectangular channel. The full-map approach is acceptable, irrespective of the coordinate system, as long as the resulting map is not used under conditions different from those for which it was constructed.

In engineering practice, however, it is always desirable to develop generalized correlations applicable to a wide range of design situations. The essential ingredient for the construction of a generalized map is the development of a coordinate system with which the transition lines on the map become independent of tube diameter and fluid properties. With all the coordinate systems mentioned before (V_{vs} vs. $V_{\ell s}$, V_m vs. R, and G vs. x) the transition lines were found to be sensitive to changes in tube diameter or fluid properties.

An attempt that gained wide acceptance and is still commonly used in some industries is the generalized map by Baker [14]. Basically (for an air-water mixture at 1 bar and 20°C), the coordinates of this map are the gas mass flux, G_v, and the ratio of liquid and vapor mass fluxes, G_ℓ/G_v. The coordinates were adjusted by two correction factors, λ and ψ, to account for fluid properties other than those of air-water at 1 bar and 20°C. Parameters λ and x were defined as

$$\lambda = [(\rho_v/\rho_a)(\rho_\ell/\rho_w)]^{1/2} \tag{1a}$$

and

$$\psi = (\sigma_w/\sigma)[(\mu_\ell/\mu_w)(\rho_w/\rho_\ell)^2]^{1/3} \tag{1b}$$

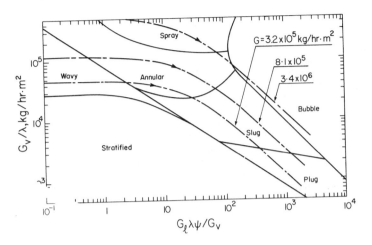

Figure 2. Condensation paths of refrigerant R-12 at different mass fluxes plotted on Baker's [14] map.

where ρ_a, ρ_w, μ_w, and σ_w are the air density, water density, water viscosity, and water surface tension, respectively, all at 1 bar and 20°C, while ρ_v, ρ_ℓ, μ_ℓ, and σ are the vapor or gas density, liquid density, liquid viscosity, and liquid surface tension, respectively, all at actual flowing conditions.

A demonstration of the possible use of Baker's map for predicting the flow patterns of a condensing fluid is shown in Figure 2. In this figure the transition lines developed by Baker are reproduced and the condensation paths of refrigerant R-12 at a saturation temperature of 25°C are plotted on the map for $G = 3.2 \times 10^5$, 8.1×10^5, and 3.4×10^6 kg/hr m². It can be seen from Figure 2 that at $G = 3.4 \times 10^6$ kg/hr m², the flow pattern in the condenser (as predicted by Baker's map) starts as spray and then changes to annular and bubble as the flow progresses along the condenser. This flow-pattern progression is consistent with the experimental results reported in [2 to 5]. However, at $G = 3.2 \times 10^5$ and 8.1×10^5 kg/hr m², the flow pattern is predicted to develop in the following order: wavy, annular, slug, plug. Experimental observations and logic do not agree with this order of flow patterns. The annular flow in the condenser was always seen to precede the wavy, not to follow it [2–10]. In addition, knowing that the flow velocities are decreasing along the condenser, it follows that annular flow controlled by vapor shear (and hence is associated with high velocities) cannot logically follow wavy flow that is gravity controlled (and hence is associated with low velocities). Observations like this one led investigators [2, 4, 15] to conclude that the well-known Baker's map that was developed for adiabatic gas-liquid flows in horizontal tubes is not adequate for predicting flow patterns during condensation. Consequently, efforts were directed towards developing generalized flow pattern maps for horizontal intube condensation of pure vapors based on the data listed in Table 1. Results of these efforts are presented and discussed in a following section.

It is seen then, that the full-map approach is based on selecting two-dimensional or dimensionless quantities as coordinates that are normally functions of the flow rates of the mixture, duct geometry, and different properties of the flowing mixture and then developing the different transition lines empirically as functions of the selected coordinates. The immediate implication of this approach is that all the transition lines on the map are expected to be influenced by the same group of parameters of which the coordinates are comprised. On the other hand, if we consider the fact that each flow pattern transition is controlled by a particular force balance that may be different from one transition to the other and hence relevant parameters differ from one transition to the other, we can logically conclude that the full-map approach cannot be generalized to apply with similar accuracy to all transitions. In a recent experimental study by Weisman et al. [16] in which fluid properties were varied in a systematic manner it was found that a particular property may have a strong influence on one or more transitions, but has a negligible effect on the other transitions. For example, gas density was found to have a strong influence on the gas mass flow rate necessary for transitions to annular and to wavy flows, while the transitions to bubble and intermittent (slug and plug) flows experienced much smaller ρ_v-influences.

Based on the preceding reasoning and experimental observations, we conclude that each flow pattern transition should be treated separately considering only the relevant forces for this transition. This approach is expected to produce correlations that include geometrical, property, and flow parameters relevant only to the transition under consideration. This individual-transition approach, due to its obvious promise of accurate results, has been used in recent investigations of both adiabatic gas-liquid and condensation flow patterns.

In the remaining part of this chapter a comprehensive review of the correlations developed for predicting the flow patterns during horizontal intube condensation of pure vapors is given. Results based on the full-map approach and the individual-transition approach are presented separately. Only correlations with claimed generality are considered.

The Full-Map Approach

In this section we will consider four maps developed empirically from a large data base, which implies some degree of generality. Data sets no. 1 to 7 constitute the main data source for these four maps. The predictions of each map will be checked against data set no. 8 in order to assess its ability to perform outside the range of parameters from which it was generated.

Maps by Soliman and Azer

The first map (shown in Figure 3) was developed using Baker's [14] coordinates. This choice of coordinates was motivated by their success in adiabatic gas-liquid flows. The transition lines shown in Figure 3 represent the best fit with data sets no. 1 to 7. In Reference [4] all the data points were

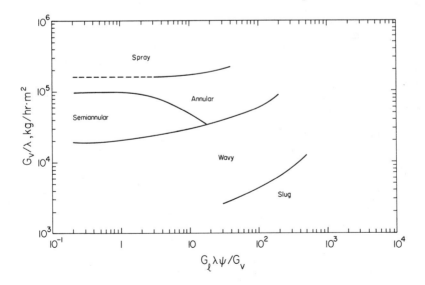

Figure 3. Modified Baker map for horizontal intube condensation, proposed by Soliman and Azer [4].

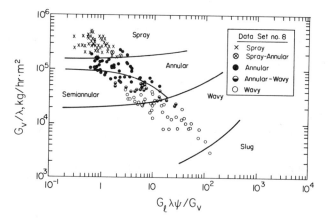

Figure 4. Comparison between data set no. 8 and the modified Baker map.

shown and the scatter around the transition lines seems reasonably acceptable. The transition line between spray and annular flows was drawn partially dashed in the region where data were sparce. The data of plug flow were found to fall outside the range of the map and hence the slug-to-plug transition line was not shown. This does not lower the value of the map since both slug and plug flows correspond to very low qualities and many investigators lump both flows in one area under the name "intermittent." This map was the first with a broad data base map for condensation and was recommended by Soliman and Azer [4] as a modification to the original Baker map.

With the availability of data set no. 8 an important test can now be performed on the generality of the transition lines in Figure 3. Data set no. 8 corresponds to a tube diameter that falls within the range covered in the first seven sets but involves markedly different fluid properties, particularly in the values of ρ_ℓ/ρ_v and σ. The comparison between set no. 8 and the map of Figure 3 is shown in Figure 4. The agreement seen in Figure 4 is quite satisfactory; actually the only area of disagreement is the apparent slight underprediction in G_v/λ of the annular-wavy transition. No slug flow data were reported in set no. 8. This flow pattern was observed but was not possible to map because it corresponded to extremely low qualities which were incalculable with accuracy [5].

Based on the results presented in [4] and the good agreement shown in Figure 4, it is proper to conclude that for the diameter and property ranges encompassed in Table 1, the modified Baker map developed by Soliman and Azer [4] can be used with reasonable confidence in predicting the flow patterns of condensing flows inside horizontal tubes.

Another generalized map is that of Soliman and Azer [4] (shown in Figure 5) using V_ℓ and $(1 - \alpha)/\alpha$ as coordinates. This map was developed because of the uncertainty about the ability of Baker's parameters in absorbing the diameter and property effects for all transitions. In selecting the coordinates of this map an attempt was made to use parameters that characterize or at least are significant for all the flow patterns. Quite clearly, the void fraction, α, is a dimensionless quantity that satisfies this selection criterion. The range of α associated with any flow pattern is characteristic in the sense that this range is independent of the tube diameter and fluid properties. On the other hand, the average velocity of the liquid phase (a dimensional quantity) was selected as a compromise due to its significance as a flow pattern parameter. This compromise was adopted because it was not possible to develop a second dimensionless group (besides α) that is characteristic to all flow pattern transitions. This difficulty is not surprising in view of the different dominant forces acting at each transition. The average velocity of the liquid phase, V_ℓ, was calculated from

$$V_\ell = (1 - x)G/[(1 - \alpha)\rho_\ell] \tag{2}$$

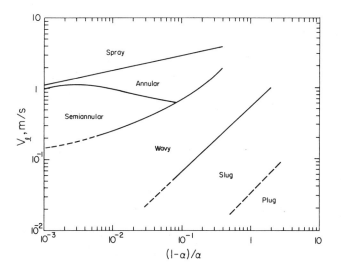

Figure 5. The V_ℓ vs. $(1 - \alpha)/\alpha$ — map proposed by Soliman and Azer [4].

Since the void fraction, α, was not measured in any of the flow pattern studies [2, 3, 4], its value was computed from the following correlation:

$$1/\alpha = 1 + (\rho_v/\rho_\ell)[(1 - x)/x][0.4 + 0.6\{[(\rho_\ell/\rho_v) + 0.4(1 - x)/x]/[1 + 0.4(1 - x)/x]\}^{0.5}] \qquad (3)$$

Equation 3 was developed by Smith [17] from a simple physical model that included a constant that was determined by comparing the prediction of the model with a large base of experimental data from different sources. Smith [17] suggested that Equation 3 is valid for all flow conditions of co-current two-phase flow irrespective of flow pattern, mass flow rate, quality, or pressure.

In preparing the map of Figure 5, Soliman and Azer [4] used $(1 - \alpha)/\alpha$ as ordinate rather than α in order to obtain a wider distribution of data points. The transition lines were shown as dashed lines in the regions where the data were sparse. These lines were developed from data sets no. 1 to 7, and it was reported in [4] that the unavoidable overlap of data points between any two adjacent flow patterns across their transition line was minimal.

A test on the performance of the map of Figure 5 under operating conditions widely different from the conditions from which it was developed is now possible with the availability of data set no. 8. The result of this comparison is presented in Figure 6 showing excellent agreement. The conclusion drawn earlier about the range of applicability of the modified Baker map would also apply to the present map.

The Map by Breber et al.

In developing this map Breber et al. [18] used a data base consisting mainly of sets no. 1 to 7 of Table 1, in addition to the flow pattern data reported in References [6–10] and some unpublished data generated at the Heat Transfer Research Institute, Alhambra, California. This data base was compared with the predictions of a theoretical flow pattern correlation proposed earlier by Taitel and Dukler [19] in which j_g^* and X were two of the major parameters developed for correlating the transition lines of adiabatic gas-liquid flows. The parameter j_g^* was defined by,

$$j_g^* = xG/[gD\rho_v(\rho_\ell - \rho_v)]^{1/2} \qquad (4)$$

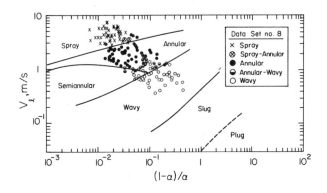

Figure 6. Comparison between data set no. 8 and the V_ℓ vs. $(1 - \alpha)/\alpha$ − map.

and the two-phase pressure drop parameter X (due to Lockhart and Martinelli [20]) reduces to X_{tt} (turbulent liquid and vapor phases) for most flows of practical interest, i.e.

$$X \cong X_{tt} = [(1 - x)/x]^{0.9}(\rho_v/\rho_\ell)^{0.5}(\mu_\ell/\mu_v)^{0.1} \tag{5}$$

Breber et al. [18] concluded that j_g^* and X were relevant for the flow patterns of condensation and proposed the following simple map (shown graphically in Figure 7) for their predictions:

Zone I: Annular and Spray-Annular
      $j_g^* > 1.5$ and $X < 1.0$
Zone II: Wavy and Stratified
      $j_g^* < 0.5$ and $X < 1.0$
Zone III: Slug and Plug
      $j_g^* < 0.5$ and $X > 1.5$
Zone IV: Bubble
      $j_g^* > 1.5$ and $X > 1.5$

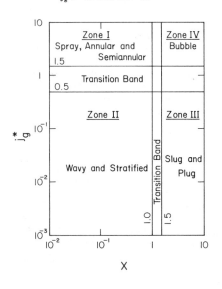

Figure 7. The map proposed by Breber et al. [18].

The regions ($(0.5 < j_g^* < 1.5, X < 1.0)$ and ($1.0 < X < 1.5, j_g^* < 0.5$) were considered transition bands between zones I and II, and zones II and III, respectively. Breber et al. [18] supported their approach by reporting the overall rate of success of their map in predicting the data base. In total terms, 84% of the data points falling in zone I were annular, semi-annular and spray, 85% of the data points falling in zone II were wavy and stratified, and 82% of the data points falling in Zone III were slug and plug.

The existence of a transition band between any two major patterns is an undeniable fact, however, the width suggested by Breber et al. is quite large (especially between zones I and II) when compared with any individual data set from Table 1. In order to clarify this point, a comparison was made between this map and the annular and wavy data points of each of the individual data sets. It was found that for small tube diameters (sets no. 1, 2, and 5), 98% of the annular data points fall above $j_g^* = 1.5$, while only 12% of the wavy data points fall below $j_g^* = 0.5$. On the other hand, for large tube diameters (sets no. 4 and 7), only 38% of the annular data points fall above $j_g^* = 1.5$, while 86% of the wavy data points fall below $j_g^* = 0.5$. This wide variation in the rate of success of this map from one data set to the other was also illustrated in a recent publication by Tandon et al. [21] who showed graphically that when data set no. 1 was plotted on the map by Breber et al. [18] none of the wavy or slug data points fell in their respective zones.

A further test was performed on this map by comparing its predictions with data set no. 8, and the results are shown in Table 2. These results indicate that the present map succeeded in providing an accurate prediction of the annular-wavy transition in data set no. 8. On the other hand, the wavy-slug transition predicted by the map does not seem to agree well with data set no. 8. Generally, for this map, the rate of success is worst at the wavy-slug transition, which seems to indicate that j_g^* and X cannot serve as the major parameters in correlating this transition.

The Map by Tandon et al.

Tandon et al. [21] worked exclusively with sets no. 1 to 7 as their data base. In justifying the need for a new map they noted the unsatisfactory performance by the map of Breber et al. [18] in predicting the data of small tube diameters (sets no. 1, 2, and 5). As well, they compared data set no. 2 (that of Traviss and Rohsenow [3]) with the V_ℓ vs. $(1 - \alpha)/\alpha$—map developed by Soliman and Azer [4] and critized the map when the entire semi-annular flow data points fell in the wavy flow region. Taking into consideration that the description of the semi-annular flow in [3] is almost identical to the descriptions of wavy or annular-wavy in [4] (as discussed earlier), the agreement between set no. 2 and the V_ℓ vs. $(1 - \alpha)/\alpha$ − map (presented in Figure 1 of Reference [21]) becomes excellent. This is pointed out as an example of misunderstanding that may result from non-uniform terminology in the literature.

Tandon et al. [21] selected j_g^* and $(1 - \alpha)/\alpha$ as coordinates for their map with the void fraction, α, being computed from Equation 3 by Smith [17]. The boundaries of their proposed flow pattern map (shown graphically in Figure 8) were given by:

$$\text{Spray:} \quad j_g^* \geq 6 \text{ and } (1 - \alpha)/\alpha \leq 0.5$$
$$\text{Annular and Semi-annular:} \quad 1 \leq j_g^* \leq 6 \text{ and } (1 - \alpha)/\alpha \leq 0.5$$
$$\text{Wavy:} \quad j_g^* \leq 1 \text{ and } (1 - \alpha)/\alpha \leq 0.5$$
$$\text{Slug:} \quad 0.01 \leq j_g^* \leq 0.5 \text{ and } (1 - \alpha)/\alpha \geq 0.5$$
$$\text{Plug:} \quad j_g^* \leq 0.01 \text{ and } (1 - \alpha)/\alpha \geq 0.5$$

With these boundaries Tandon et al. [21] obtained marginal improvements over the correlation of Breber et al. [18] in the overall prediction of the data of annular and semiannular flow (85% instead of 84%) and the data of wavy flow (88% instead of 85%). On the other hand, the success in predicting the slug flow dropped from the 82% rate with Breber et al. [18] down to a 65% rate. The problems with the small tube diameters reported in connection with the previous map still remained to some degree in this map.

A comparison between the present map and set no. 8 is shown in Table 3. Judging by the percentages of data points of each pattern that were correctly predicted we see excellent agreement at the annular-wavy transition and moderate agreement at the spray-annular transition.

Table 2
Comparison Between Data Set No. 8 and the Map of Breber et al. [18]

Area on map / Observed flow pattern	Zone I (spray, annular, and semi-annular)	Zone II (wave and stratified)	Zone III (slug and plug)	Transition between zone I and zone II	Transition between zone II and zone III	Total observations
Spray, spray-annular, annular, and semi-annular	98 (88%)			14 (12%)		112 (100%)
Wavy		12 (28%)	12 (28%)	7 (16%)	12 (28%)	43 (100%)
Annular-wavy and semi-annular-wavy				19 (100%)		19 (100%)

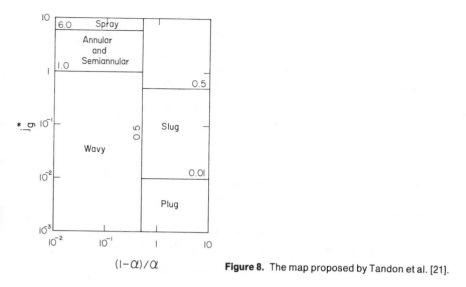

$(1-\alpha)/\alpha$ **Figure 8.** The map proposed by Tandon et al. [21].

From the previous presentation and discussion of the different maps proposed for the prediction of condensation flow patterns, the following general conclusions on the full-map approach can be drawn:

1. Since the coordinates of these maps are normally selected empirically, not as a result of rigorous analyses, there is no promise of satisfactory performance by these maps outside the range from which they were developed. Sometimes these maps do not exhibit consistency even within

Table 3
Comparison Between Data Set No. 8 and the Map of Tandon et al. [21]

Observed flow pattern / Area on map	Spray	Annular and semi-annular	Wavy	Slug	Plug	Total observations
Spray	32 (54%)	27 (46%)				59 (100%)
Annular and semi-annular		50 (100%)				50 (100%)
Wavy			43 (100%)			43 (100%)
Spray-annular		3 (100%)				3 (100%)
Annular-wavy and semi-annular-wavy		7 (37%)	12 (63%)			19 (100%)

their range of development by showing excellent agreement with the data of some fluids or some tube diameters, but moderate or poor agreement with others.

2. Since each flow pattern transition is governed by a different force balance, it it possible that parameters that are extremely significant for one transition may be totally irrelevant to another transition. Thus a given map might show significant promise in predicting one or more transitions, but give highly unacceptable performance at other transition(s).

These criticisms are not directed to one map or the other, but rather to the full-map approach, and apply irrespective of the coordinates used.

The Individual-Transition Approach

The previous drawbacks of the full-map approach motivated the more promising individual transition approach. In this approach each flow pattern transition is considered separately with the objective of developing a correlation that has a basis in theory, thus creating the potential for eliminating the diameter and property effects. The approach was probably pioneered by Quandt [22] and applied recently by Taitel and Dukler [19] for the case of adiabatic gas-liquid flow in horizontal and near horizontal ducts. Two important flow pattern transitions during horizontal intube condensation have been considered in very recent research efforts [23, 24]; the approach, resulting correlations and comparisons with the data base of Table 1 are presented next.

The Annular-Wavy Transition

This transition is extremely important since it coincides with a shift from vapor-shear controlled flow and convective-type heat transfer into gravity controlled flow and Nusselt-type heat transfer. Accurate definition of this transition has obvious consequences on the accuracy of pressure drop and heat transfer predictions. The few research efforts [3, 25] directed at the analysis of this transition had a limited amount of data available at the time of conducting the analyses. The analysis presented here is based on a recent effort by Soliman [23] who benefited from the wide data base of Table 1.

All experimental results [2–10] confirm that for a wide range of flow rates, a stable annular flow pattern exists over a certain length of any condenser tube. As we move downstream along the condensation path, we note an increase in the average liquid film thickness and a decrease in the liquid phase velocity. As a result, the gravitational force acting on the liquid film increases continuously along the condensation path, while the inertia force decreases continuously. This gradual change in forces has a reflection on the geometry of the liquid film in the form of increasing asymmetry around the axis of the tube until most of the liquid phase flows as a thick stratum at the bottom of the tube [26]. This marks the transition into wavy flow and the hypothesis [23] is that this transition occurs when the Froude number, Fr, (which is a measure of the ratio of inertia to gravitational forces) reaches a certain value, i.e. at the transition,

$$Fr = constant \tag{6a}$$

where the Froude number is defined as,

$$Fr = V_\ell / \sqrt{(g\delta)} \tag{6b}$$

In order to place Equation 6b in a usable form, the average liquid film thickness, δ, must be expressed in terms of other properties and flow parameters. The following simple expression was developed by Kosky [27] and was found to agree well with experimental results of co-current flow under simultaneous shear and gravity forces:

$$\delta^+ = 0.707 Re_{\ell s}^{0.5}, \qquad Re_{\ell s} \leq 1,250 \tag{7a}$$

and

$$\delta^+ = 0.0504 Re_{\ell s}^{0.875}, \qquad Re_{\ell s} > 1,250 \tag{7b}$$

where

$$Re_{\ell s} = G(1 - x)D/\mu_\ell \tag{8}$$

$$\delta^+ = \rho_\ell \, \delta u^*/\mu_\ell \tag{9}$$

and

$$u^* = \sqrt{(\tau_w/\rho_\ell)} \tag{10}$$

Taking into consideration the fact that the liquid film thickness is much smaller than the tube diameter, and assuming that all the liquid phase is flowing in the film (i.e. no entrainment), which is a reasonable assumption, near the transition to wavy flow, we can express the mass balance of the liquid film by the simple equation,

$$G(1 - x) = 4\rho_\ell V_\ell(\delta/D) \tag{11}$$

Substituting Equations 8, 9, and 11 into Equation 6b and rearranging we get,

$$Fr = 0.25 Re_{\ell s}(u^*/\delta^+)^{1.5}/\sqrt{(g\mu_\ell/\rho_\ell)} \tag{12}$$

Directing our attention to the frictional velocity, u^*, we find that this quantity is related to the two-phase frictional pressure gradient by,

$$u^{*2} = \tau_w/\rho_\ell = -(D/4)(dp/dz)_f/\rho_\ell \tag{13}$$

In a comprehensive review of the different methods available in the literature for the evaluation of two-phase frictional pressure drop in horizontal pipes, Mandhane et al. [28] emphasized the extreme significance of the flow pattern in the selection of proper correlations. A particular correlation may provide reasonable prediction of the pressure drop for a particular flow pattern but inadequate prediction for other flow patterns. One of the correlations recommended in [28] for annular flow is the Lockhart-Martinelli correlation [20] which involves ϕ_v, defined by,

$$(dp/dz)_f = \phi_v^2 (dp/dz)_{vs} \tag{14}$$

where the superficial vapor pressure gradient is given by

$$(dp/dz)_{vs} = -(2/D)(0.045 Re_{vs}^{-0.2})(G^2 x^2/\rho_v)$$

and the superficial vapor Reynolds number, Re_{vs}, is related to the superficial liquid Reynolds number, $Re_{\ell s}$, by the expression,

$$Re_{vs} = xGD/\mu_v = Re_{\ell s}(\mu_\ell/\mu_v)[x/(1 - x)] \tag{15}$$

Substituting Equations 13, 14 and 15 into Equation 10 and reducing results in

$$u^* = 0.15[\mu_\ell/(\rho_\ell D)](\phi_v/X_{tt})Re_{\ell s}^{0.9} \tag{16}$$

where X_{tt} is the Lockhart-Martinelli parameter [20] defined earlier by Equation 5. With Equations 16 for u^* and 7 for δ^+ now available, Equation 12 can be placed in the following final form:

$$Re_{\ell s} = 10.2 Fr^{0.63} Ga^{0.31}(\phi_v/X_{tt})^{-0.94}, \qquad Re_{\ell s} \le 1,250 \tag{17a}$$

and

$$Re_{\ell s} = 0.79Fr^{0.96}Ga^{0.48}(\phi_v/X_{tt})^{-1.44}, \quad Re_{\ell s} > 1,250 \tag{17b}$$

where Ga is the Galileo number given by

$$Ga = gD^3\rho_\ell^2/\mu_\ell^2 \tag{18}$$

Several correlations have been proposed in the literature for the two-phase pressure-drop multiplier, ϕ_v, with wide deviations in their predictions. Equation 17 is expected to be sensitive to the choice of ϕ_v—correlation. To the best of the author's knowledge, the only correlation developed from data of annular flow condensation inside a horizontal tube is the following one by Azer et al. [29]:

$$\phi_v = 1 + 1.09X_{tt}^{0.039} \tag{19}$$

With the formulation of the model now complete it is possible to test the adequacy of Equation (hypothesis) 6. This hypothesis would be true if it is possible to define a value or a narrow range of values for Fr that would make Equation 17 capable of predicting the annular wavy transition with accuracy for a wide range of tube diameters and fluid properties.

Comparing Equation 17 with data sets no. 1 to 8, Soliman [23] concluded that good agreement is possible with the value Fr = 7. Samples of these agreements with Fr = 7 are shown in Figures 9 and 10. In Reference [23] comparisons were also made between the data base and the predictions of other well known correlations for the annular-wavy transition [3, 16, 19, 30] and it was found that Equation 17 was more accurate and more consistent with the data base. Due to its theoretical

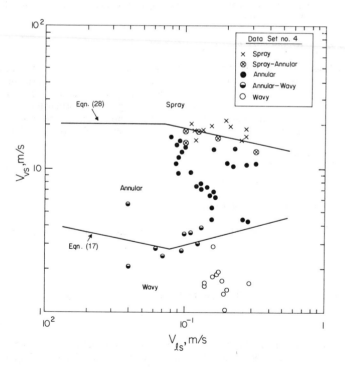

Figure 9. Comparison between data set no. 4 and correlations 17 and 28.

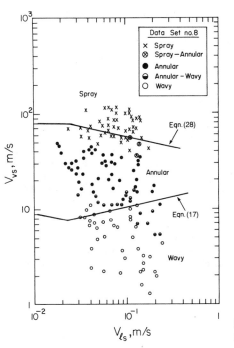

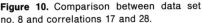

Figure 10. Comparison between data set no. 8 and correlations 17 and 28.

basis, and its capability of accurate and consistent agreement with the wide data base of Table 1, Equation 17 is recommended for the prediction of the annular-to-wavy transition during condensation inside horizontal tubes.

The Spray-Annular Transition

At sufficiently high mass fluxes, spray flow was observed in several studies [2–5] covering the entry part of the condenser. Further along the condensation path, this flow pattern was consistently followed by the annular flow pattern. The quality range over which spray flow was observed varied according to the total flow rate, tube diameter, and fluid properties. However, this range was found to be as wide as $1 > x > 0.3$ for steam condensing inside a 13.4-mm I.D. horizontal tube [5].

Spray flow is characterized by a continuous, high-speed vapor phase carrying the liquid phase in the form of droplets with no visible stable film at the wall, while annular flow includes as a main feature a stable liquid film traveling along the wall with only a fraction of the liquid phase entrained within the high-speed vapor. This difference in flow structure was found, as expected, to reflect significantly on the heat transfer and pressure drop characteristics. For example, Chien and Ibele [31] reported that an observed flow pattern transition from annular to spray-annular during air-water flow in a vertical tube coincided with a change in the slope of measured frictional pressure gradient. Groothuis and Hendal [32] obtained experimental results that indicate clearly that at any liquid flow rate the heat transfer coefficient increases as the gas flow rate increases up to a maximum beyond which the heat transfer coefficient decreases with further increase in the gas flow rate. This reversal of trend in the heat transfer data (which was confirmed in later experiments [33]) was attributed to the transition to spray-annular flow. Another important aspect relating to the modeling of flow hydrodynamics was considered by Husain and Weisman [34]. They found that the homogeneous model fits the two-phase frictional pressure drop data only at high mass flow rates and high qualities, conditions at which spray flow is expected. This suggestion of special treatment for spray flow is in line with Vijay's [35] recommendation.

These observations and trends suggest the necessity of separate treatment for the spray and annular flows and hence, the need for a correlation for the spray-annular transition. It is known that entrainment during annular flow occurs due to the removal of the tops of waves traveling on the surface of the liquid film. However, this mechanism has been difficult to model so far due to the complexity of the phenomenon itself, as well as shortage of reliable data on the entrainment rate [36].

In spite of the fact that the mechanism of entrainment still needs further study, it is apparent from the present state of knowledge that the inertia force of the vapor phase is the dominant destructive force acting on the liquid film while the surface tension and liquid viscous forces are the major stabilizing forces. A recent study [24] was successful in developing a simple, easy to use, and reasonably accurate correlation for the spray-annular transition during condensation based on a balance between the aforementioned forces. The hypothesis adopted in [24] is that the balance between destructive and stabilizing forces can be expressed in terms of the following simple ratio:

$$F^2 = [(\rho_v V_v^2)/(\sigma/D)][(\sigma/D)/(\mu_\ell V_\ell/\delta)]^b \tag{20}$$

where $(\rho_v V_v^2)$, $(\mu_\ell V_\ell/\delta)$, and (σ/D) are measures of vapor inertia, liquid viscosity, and surface tension forces, respectively. Parameters b and F are constants to be determined from the data base of Table 1. For Equation 20 to be successful in correlating the spray-annular transition with a fair deal of generality, parameters b and F must have characteristic values or fall within narrow ranges when applied to different data sets.

Equation 20 can be easily rearranged to take the form

$$F^2 = (\rho_v V_v^2 D/\sigma)[\mu_\ell^2/(\rho_\ell \sigma D)]^{-b}[\delta/D)/(\rho_\ell V_\ell D/\mu_\ell)]^b \tag{21}$$

This form brings out the interesting feature that the first two dimensionless groups in the right-hand side were used as the determining criteria in the study of interaction between gases and liquids during nozzle spraying [37].

In order to express Equation 21 in a usable form, all the variables appearing in this equation must be expressed in terms of quantities that are easy to measure or calculate. Starting with the liquid film thickness, we find that Equations 7, 9, and 16 can be combined to give,

$$\delta/D = 4.71 Re_{\ell s}^{-0.4} X_{tt}/\phi_v, \qquad Re_{\ell s} \le 1,250 \tag{22a}$$

and

$$\delta/D = 0.336 Re_{\ell s}^{-0.025} X_{tt}/\phi_v, \qquad Re_{\ell s} > 1,250 \tag{22b}$$

where $Re_{\ell s}$, X_{tt}, and ϕ_v are given by Equations 8, 5, and 19, respectively. Also, keeping in mind that the liquid film thickness, δ, is small compared with the tube diameter, D, we can equate the average velocity of the vapor phase to the superficial vapor velocity, i.e.,

$$V_v \cong V_{vs} = xG/\rho_v \tag{23}$$

Using Equations 5, 8, and 23 we can write the following expression for the quantity $(\rho_v V_v^2 D/\sigma)$ appearing in Equation 21:

$$\rho_v V_v^2 D/\sigma = [\mu_\ell^2/(\rho_\ell \sigma D)](\rho_v/\rho_\ell)^{0.11}(\mu_\ell/\mu_v)^{0.22} Re_{\ell s}^2/X_{tt}^{2.22} \tag{24}$$

One term in Equation 21, that is $\rho_\ell V_\ell D/\mu_\ell$, now remains to be determined. From Equations 8 and 11, this term can be expressed as,

$$\rho_\ell V_\ell D/\mu_\ell = 0.25 Re_{\ell s}/(\delta/D) \tag{25}$$

and with Equation 22 for δ/D, Equation 25 can be further developed to the following form:

$$\rho_\ell V_\ell D/\mu_\ell = 0.053 Re_{\ell s}^{1.4} \phi_v / X_{tt}, \qquad Re_{\ell s} \leq 1,250 \qquad (26a)$$

and

$$\rho_\ell V_\ell D/\mu_\ell = 0.744 Re_{\ell s}^{1.025} \phi_v / X_{tt}, \qquad Re_{\ell s} > 1,250 \qquad (26b)$$

On substituting Equations 22, 24, and 26 for the relevant three dimensionless quantities appearing in Equation 21 and rearranging we obtain,

$$Re_{\ell s}^{2-1.8b} = (88.7)^{-b} F^2 [\mu_\ell^2/(\rho_\ell \sigma D)]^{b-1} (\rho_\ell/\rho_v)^{0.11} (\mu_v/\mu_\ell)^{0.22} X_{tt}^{2.22-2b} \phi_v^{2b}, \qquad Re_{\ell s} \leq 1,250 \qquad (27a)$$

and

$$Re_{\ell s}^{2-1.05b} = (0.452)^{-b} F^2 [\mu_\ell^2/(\rho_\ell \sigma D)]^{b-1} (\rho_\ell/\rho_v)^{0.11} (\mu_v/\mu_\ell)^{0.22} X_{tt}^{2.22-2b} \phi_v^{2b}, \qquad Re_{\ell s} > 1,250 \qquad (27b)$$

We are now left with the task of evaluating b and F that will result in the best possible correlation between the present theory and the data base of Table 1. It is clear from Equation 27 that on an $Re_{\ell s}$ vs. X_{tt} plot, the value of b would influence the slope of the transition line. In addition, for the same value of F, the value of b determines the magnitude of shift in the transition line due to fluid properties and/or tube diameter changes. After several attempts it was found that good agreement between Equation 27 and the trend in the data base could be achieved with b = 0.4. Once this value was determined, it was easy to find that the range $20 < F < 30$ defines the transition zone between spray and annular flow patterns for data sets no. 1 to 8. All data corresponding to $F < 20$ belong to annular flow and all the data corresponding to $F > 30$ belong to spray flow. With the average value of F = 25, together with b = 0.4, Equation 27 reduces to the following final form:

$$Re_{\ell s} = 37.6 [\mu_\ell^2/(\rho_\ell \sigma D)]^{-0.47} (\rho_\ell/\rho_v)^{0.087} (\mu_v/\mu_\ell)^{0.17} X_{tt}^{1.11} \phi_v^{0.63}, \qquad Re_{\ell s} \leq 1,250 \qquad (28a)$$

and

$$Re_{\ell s} = 72.0 [\mu_\ell^2/(\rho_\ell \sigma D)]^{-0.38} (\rho_\ell/\rho_v)^{0.070} (\mu_v/\mu_\ell)^{0.14} X_{tt}^{0.90} \phi_v^{0.51}, \qquad Re_{\ell s} > 1,250 \qquad (28b)$$

A sample of the comparison between Equation 28 and the data base is shown in Figures 9 and 10 and more comparisons are available in [24]. The agreement illustrated in Figures 9 and 10 is quite satisfactory, particularly if we note the fact that the transition line shown represents a transition zone with a finite width. In addition, different investigators contributed the data sets of Table 1 and some degree of judgment is expected when visual observation is used for flow pattern identification, particularly with the difficult distinction between spray and annular flows.

Based on these comparisons and others conducted outside the range of Table 1 [24], it is fair to conclude that Equation 28, which is based on the hypothesis described at the beginning of this section, is adequate for the present transition. Thus, this correlation is recommended for the prediction of spray-annular transition during condensation inside tubes, at least for flow conditions encompassed by the range in Table 1. Further tests of this correlation, as well as Equation 17, are recommended with more data as they become available.

CONCLUSION

The objective of this chapter is to provide an up-to-date review of the different methods available in the literature for predicting the flow patterns of condensing fluids inside horizontal tubes. In achieving this objective, the available experimental data were first introduced. These data encompass a wide range of operating conditions of practical interest (Table 1) and is easily accessible.

Next, the research efforts dealing with flow-pattern correlation were presented and discussed in two separate parts based on the approach followed. These two approaches are the full-map approach and the individual-transition approach, with the latter being the more preferable one due to its promise of improved accuracy and generality. Two correlations are presented that were developed based on the individual-transition approach; these are Equation 17 for the annular-wavy transition and Equation 28 for the spray-annular transition. These correlations are recommended due to their theoretical bases, as well as accuracy and consistency with the data base.

One flow-pattern transition, the wavy-slug transition, remains without a correlation that can be recommended with confidence. This transition requires further research, and there are currently efforts in this direction.

Acknowledgments

This chapter was reviewed in draft form by Professor G. E. Sims who made several suggestions for improvement. His sincere efforts are acknowledged with deep appreciation. Thanks are also due to Mr. F. Rashwan for preparing some of the figures appearing in this chapter and Mrs. Violet Lee for typing the manuscript.

NOTATION

b	arbitrary constant in Equation 20		fined by Equation 8
D	tube diameter	Re_{vs}	vapor superficial Reynolds number defined by Equation 15
F	arbitrary constant in Equation 20		
Fr	Froude number defined by Equation 6b	T_s	average saturation temperature
		u^*	friction velocity defined by Equation 10
g	gravitational acceleration		
G	total mass flux	V_ℓ	average velocity of the liquid phase
G_ℓ	mass flux of the liquid phase, $(1 - x)G$	$V_{\ell s}$	superficial liquid velocity, $(1 - x)G/\rho_\ell$
G_v	mass flux of the vapor phase, xG	V_v	average velocity of the vapor phase
Ga	Galileo number defined by Equation 18	V_{vs}	superficial vapor velocity, xG/ρ_v
j_g^*	dimensionless vapor velocity defined by Equation 4	x	quality
		X, X_{tt}	Lockhart-Martinelli parameter defined by Equation 5
$Re_{\ell s}$	liquid superficial Reynolds number de-		

Greek Symbols

α	void fraction	ρ_ℓ	liquid density
δ	average thickness of the liquid film	ρ_v	vapor density
δ^+	dimensionless film thickness defined by Equation 9	σ	surface tension
		ψ	correction factor given by Equation 1b
λ	correction factor given by Equation 1a	τ_w	wall shear stress
μ_ℓ	liquid dynamic viscosity	ϕ_v	two-phase, pressure drop multiplier defined by Equation 14
μ_v	vapor dynamic viscosity		

REFERENCES

1. Bell, K. J., Taborek, J., and Fenoglio, F., "Interpretation of Horizontal In-Tube Condensation Heat Transfer Correlations With a Two-Phase Flow Regime Map," *AIChE Symp. Ser.* no. 102, Vol. 66, pp. 150–163 (1970).
2. Soliman, H. M., and Azer, N. Z., "Flow Patterns During Condensation Inside a Horizontal Tube," *ASHRAE Trans.*, Vol. 77, pp. 210–224 (1971).

3. Traviss, D. P., and Rohsenow, W. M., "Flow Regimes in Horizontal Two-Phase Flow With Condensation," *ASHRAE Trans.*, Vol. 79, pp. 31–39 (1973).

4. Soliman, H. M., and Azer, N. Z., "Visual Studies of Flow Patterns During Condensation Inside Horizontal Tubes," *Proceedings of the Fifth International Heat Transfer Conference*, Vol. 3, pp. 241–245 (1974).

5. Fathi, A. M., "Analysis of Two-Phase Flow Patterns of Condensing Steam Inside a Horizontal Tube," M.Sc. thesis, University of Manitoba, Winnipeg, Canada (1980).

6. Chen, J., "Condensing Heat Transfer in a Horizontal Tube," M.Sc. report, Kansas State University, Manhattan, Kansas (1962).

7. Chato, J. C., "Laminar Condensation Inside Horizontal and Inclined Tubes," *ASHRAE J.*, Vol. 4, no. 252, pp. 52–60 (1962).

8. Brauser, S. O., "Turbulent Condensation in a Horizontal Tube," Ph.D. dissertation, Kansas State University, Manhattan, Kansas (1966).

9. Calder, C. A., "Flow Regime Characterization for Horizontal Two-Phase Steam Flow," Microfiche No. UCRL—52186, Lawrence Livermore Lab., University of California (1976).

10. Fujii, T., Honda, H., Nagata, T., Fujii, F., and Nozu, S., "Condensation of R-11 Inside a Horizontal Tube," *JSME Trans.*, Vol. 42, no. 363, pp. 3541–3550 (1976).

11. Alves, G. E., "Co-Current Liquid-Gas Flow in a Pipeline Contactor," *Chem. Eng. Prog.*, Vol. 50, pp. 449–456 (1954).

12. Hoogendoorn, C. J., "Gas-Liquid Flow in Horizontal Pipes," *Chem. Eng. Sci.*, Vol. 9, pp. 205–218 (1959).

13. Hosler, E. R., "Visual Study of Boiling at High Pressure," *Chem. Eng. Prog. Symp. Ser.* no. 61, Vol. 57, pp. 269–279 (1965).

14. Baker, O., "Simultaneous Flow of Oil and Gas," *Oil and Gas J.*, Vol. 53, pp. 185–195 (1954).

15. Palen, J. W., Breber, G., and Taborek, J., "Prediction of Flow Regimes in Horizontal Tubeside Condensation," Preprints of AIChE papers, 17th National Heat Transfer Conf., pp. 38–44 (1977).

16. Weisman, J., Duncan, D., Gibson, J., and Crawford, T., "Effeects of Fluid Properties and Pipe Diameter on Two-Phase Flow Patterns in Horizontal Lines," *Int. J. Multiphase Flow*, Vol. 5, pp. 437–462 (1979).

17. Smith, S. L., "Void Fractions in Two-Phase Flow: A Correlation Based Upon an Equal Velocity Head Model," *Inst, of Mech. Eng.*, London, Vol. 184, pp. 647–657 (1969–1970).

18. Breber, G., Palen, J. W., and Taborek, J., "Prediction of Horizontal Tubeside Condensation of Pure Components Using Flow Regime Criteria," *J. Heat Transfer*, Vol. 102, pp. 471–476 (1980).

19. Tailel, Y., and Dukler, A. E., "A Model for Predicting Flow Regime Transitions in Horizontal and Near Horizontal Gas-Liquid Flow," *AIChE J.*, Vol. 22, pp. 47–55 (1976).

20. Lockhart, R. W., and Martinelli, R. C., "Proposed Correlation of Data for Isothermal Two-Phase, Two-Component Flow in Pipes," *Chem. Eng. Prog.*, Vol. 45, pp. 39–48 (1949).

21. Tandon, T. N., Varma, H. K., and Gupta, C. P., "A New Flow Regimes Map for Condensation Inside Horizontal Tubes," *J. Heat Transfer*, Vol. 104, pp. 763–768 (1982).

22. Quandt, E., "Analysis of Gas-Liquid Flow Patterns," *Chem. Eng. Prog. Symp. Ser.* no. 57, Vol. 61, pp. 128–135 (1965).

23. Soliman H. M., "On the Annular-to-Wavy Flow Pattern Transition During Condensation Inside Horizontal Tubes," *Can. J. Chem. Eng.*, Vol. 60, pp. 475–481 (1982).

24. Soliman, H. M., "Correlation of Mist-to-Annular Transition During Condensation," *Can. J. Chem. Eng.*, Vol. 61, pp. 178–182 (1983).

25. Jaster, H., and Kosky, P. G., "Condensation Heat Transfer in a Mixed Flow Regime," *Int. J. Heat Mass Transfer*, Vol. 19, pp. 95–99 (1976).

26. Soliman, H. M., and Azer, N. Z., "Analysis of the Geometry of the Liquid Film During Annular Flow Condensation Inside Horizontal Tubes," *Proceedings of the 1974 Heat Transfer and Fluid Mechanics Institute*, pp. 2–20 (1974).

27. Kosky, P. G., "Thin Liquid Films Under Simultaneous Shear and Gravity Forces," Int. J. Heat Transfer, Vol. 14, pp. 1220–1224 (1971).

28. Mandhane, J. M., Gregory, G. A., and Aziz, K., "Critical Evaluation of Frictional Pressure Drop Prediction Methods for Gas-Liquid Flow in Horizontal Pipes," *J. Pet. Tech.*, Vol. 29, pp. 1348–1358 (1977).

29. Azer, N. Z., Abis, L. V., and Soliman, H. M., "Local Heat Transfer Coefficients During Annular Flow Condensation," *ASHRAE Trans.*, Vol. 78, pp. 135–143 (1972).

30. Mandhane, J. M., Gregory, G. A., and Aziz, K., "A Flow Pattern Map for Gas-Liquid Flow in Horizontal Pipes," *Int, J. Multiphase Flow*, Vol. 1, pp. 537–553 (1974).

31. Chien, S., and Ibele, W., "Pressure Drop and Liquid Film Thickness of Two-Phase Annular and Annular-Mist Flows," *J. Heat Transfer*, Vol. 86, pp. 89–96 (1964).

32. Groothuis, H., and Hendal, W. P., "Heat Transfer in Two-Phase Flow," *Chem. Eng. Sci.*, Vol. 11. pp. 212–220 (1959).

33. Ravipudi, S. R., and Godbold, T. M., "The Effect of Mass Transfer on Heat Transfer Rates for Two-Phase Flow in a Vertical Pipe," *Proceedings of the Sixth International Heat Transfer Conference*, Vol. 1, pp. 505–510 (1978).

34. Husain, A., and Weisman, J., "Applicability of Homogeneous Flow Model to Two-Phase Pressure Drop in Straight Pipes and Across Area Changes," *AIChE Sym. Ser. no. 174*, Vol. 74, pp. 205–214 (1978).

35. Vijay, M. M., "Study of Heat Transfer in Two-Phase, Two-Component Flow in a Vertical Tube," Ph.D. dissertation, University of Manitoba, Winnipeg, Canada (1977).

36. Bergles, A. E., Collier, J. G., Delhaye, J. M., Hewitt, G. F., and Mayinger, F., *Two-Phase Flow and Heat Transfer in the Power and Process Industries*, Hemisphere Publishing Corp. (1981).

37. Paleev, I. I., and Fillippovich, B. S., "Phenomena of Liquid Transfer in Two-Phase Dispersed Annular Flow," *Int. J. Heat Mass Transfer*, Vol. 9, pp. 1089–1093 (1966).

CHAPTER 23

TWO-PHASE FLOW IN VERTICAL NONCIRCULAR CHANNELS

Y. Sato and M. Sadatomi

Department of Mechanical Engineering
Kumamoto University
Kumamoto, Japan

CONTENTS

INTRODUCTION

This chapter deals with the specific problems of pressure drop calculation and flow description of two-phase gas-liquid flows in noncircular channels. For convenience' sake, noncircular passage can be divided into two categories—a single channel and a rod bundle. Parallel flows in rod bundles or tube bundles are of particular significance in practical systems, such as water-cooled nuclear reactors and shell-and-tube heat exchangers with phase interchange process. In order to predict these flows it is important to be able to describe gas-liquid flows in any single, noncircular channel. However, most studies on two-phase flow to date have been concerned with circular pipes and there is little information about the flow characteristics in both single, noncircular channels and rod bundles. It is then desirable to obtain systematic knowledge of the flow mechanics in these channels not only for better understanding of the inherent flow behavior but also for making use of the information compiled from a lot of investigations for round tubes.

The second section of this chapter is devoted to pressure drop calculation of single-phase flows in single channels as a preliminary stage in this subject. The third section addresses two-phase flows in single channels, also pressure drop, bubble rising velocity, void fraction, and flow pattern. Finally, the last section reports observations of two-phase flows in rod bundles made by several authors.

SINGLE-PHASE FLOW

In discussing two-phase frictional pressure drop in any noncircular channel, it is important to know a reasonable method for predicting that of single-phase flow in the channel considered. A literature survey concerning fully developed single-phase flows in straight noncircular passages reveals that knowledge of the laminar flow is satisfactory at least in engineering applications [1], while that of turbulent flow in various shapes encountered in practical systems is still far from adequate.

If hydraulic equivalent diameter D_h and corresponding friction factor λ are introduced, the relation between frictional pressure gradient $\Delta p_f / \Delta x$ and mean velocity $\hat{u}$ can be written as the conventional Darcy's formula:

$$\frac{\Delta p_f}{\Delta x} = \lambda \frac{1}{D_h} \frac{\rho \hat{u}^2}{2} \tag{1}$$

As for fully developed laminar flow in a straight channel of constant cross-sectional area, the pressure gradient can be obtained from the following Navier-Stokes equation:

$$\frac{\partial^2 u}{\partial y^2} + \frac{\partial^2 u}{\partial z^2} - \frac{1}{\mu} \frac{\partial p_f}{\partial x} = 0 \tag{2}$$

where u is the velocity in the x-direction, and μ the dynamic viscosity. This equation can be solved either analytically or numerically for a given pressure gradient; i.e. the velocity profile is determined. Then, the relation between the pressure gradient and the mean velocity is obtained. Substitution of these values into Equation 1 results in the following friction factor vs Reynolds number relationship in the channel,

$$\lambda = C_\ell \text{Re}^{-1} \tag{3}$$

where

$$\text{Re} = \rho \hat{u} D_h / \mu \tag{4}$$

The proportionality constant C_ℓ is referred to as "geometry factor for laminar flow," because it is determined solely by the geometry of a channel cross section [2]. The geometry factor C_ℓ for various channels has been obtained by many investigators, and, in particular, Shah and London [1] present C_ℓ-tables for many kinds of channel geometry.

For turbulent flows, in general, the friction factor is unable to be determined by purely theoretical calculation. For this factor there is the well-known hydraulic diameter concept [3]. That is, the friction factor vs Reynolds number relationship for circular pipe may also be valid for noncircular one if the hydraulic diameter is substituted for the diameter. In recent years, however, there have been several experimental evidences that do not support this concept [4–6].

According to the reliable experimental data on noncircular, smooth channels so far made by several investigators [4–12], the friction factor for a turbulent flow can be simply correlated by

$$\lambda = C_t \text{Re}^{-0.25} \tag{5}$$

which is similar to the Blasius formula. The coefficient C_t is designated as "geometry factor for turbulent flow", analogous to C_ℓ in Equation 3. In addition, it has been indicated empirically that C_t of any channel has a unique relation with C_ℓ of the same channel, as shown in Figure 1 [12]. The dependence of C_t on C_ℓ can be approximated by

$$\frac{C_t}{C_{t0}} = \sqrt[3]{\left(0.0154 \frac{C_\ell}{C_{\ell 0}} - 0.012\right)} + 0.85 \tag{6}$$

in which C_{t0} and $C_{\ell 0}$ denote the factors of a round tube, 0.316 and 64, respectively. Hence, for a given channel geometry C_t can be estimated by Equation 6 once C_ℓ has been obtained from either available data in literature or a numerical calculation. Then, the friction factor for a turbulent flow can be determined.

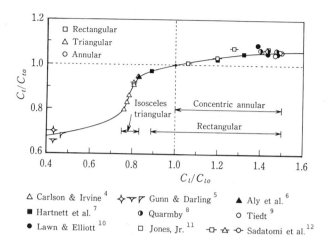

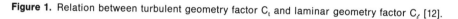

△ Carlson & Irvine [4]   ✧⊤⊦ Gunn & Darling [5]   ▲ Aly et al. [6]
■ Hartnett et al. [7]   ◑ Quarmby [8]   ○ Tiedt [9]
● Lawn & Elliott [10]   □ Jones, Jr. [11]   ⊕ ⊿ ⊙ Sadatomi et al. [12]

Figure 1. Relation between turbulent geometry factor C_t and laminar geometry factor C_ℓ [12].

TWO-PHASE FLOW

Pressure Drop

Sadatomi et al. [12] have obtained the data of pressure drop for two-phase air-water flows in an isosceles-triangular, a concentric annular channels as well as rectangular ones (Table 1). The data have been correlated by means of the Lockhart and Martinelli parameters [13]:

$$\phi_L = \sqrt{\left(\frac{(\Delta p_f/\Delta x)}{(\Delta p_f/\Delta x)_L}\right)} \tag{7}$$

$$\chi = \sqrt{\left(\frac{(\Delta p_f/\Delta x)_L}{(\Delta p_f/\Delta x)_G}\right)} \tag{8}$$

where $(\Delta p_f/\Delta x)$ is the frictional pressure gradient for two-phase flow, and $(\Delta p_f/\Delta x)_G$ and $(\Delta p_f/\Delta x)_L$ are those for the gas and liquid phases, respectively, flowing alone within the same channel. The data for the isosceles-triangular channel is presented in Figure 2 as a typical example. They have

Table 1
Dimensions of Test Sections and
Comparison Between C_1 and $u_m/\hat{u}$ at
Re = 2 × 10⁴ [12]

shape	dimension mm	A mm²	D_h mm	C_1	$u_m/\hat{u}$
▭	17×50	850	25.4	1.20	1.23
	10×50	500	16.7	1.24	1.23
	7×50	350	12.3	1.16	1.17
	7×20.6	144	10.4	1.21	1.23
◁	20°,h=55	533	16.3	1.34	1.31
◎	φ15/φ30	530	15.0	1.30	1.15

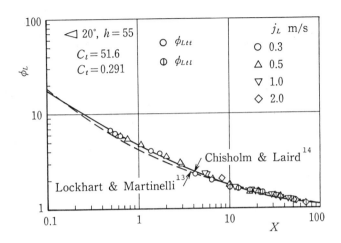

Figure 2. Two-phase frictional pressure gradient for a vertical triangular channel [12].

recommended that the Chisholm-Laird correlation [14],

$$\phi_{Ltt}^2 = 1 + \frac{21}{\chi} + \frac{1}{\chi^2} \tag{9}$$

is also applicable to the frictional pressure drop in noncircular channels. In this case it is essential to estimate an appropriate value for both $(\Delta p_f/\Delta x)_G$ and $(\Delta p_f/\Delta x)_L$, which are obtainable from the method described in the above section.

It is important to know how frictional pressure drop depends on the cross-sectional distribution of the phases in a passage. Sadatomi and Sato [15] have obtained the experimental data on pressure drop of two-phase air-water flows in a horizontal isosceles-triangular channel placed in two different

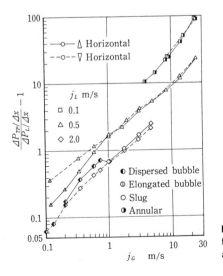

Figure 3. Comparison of pressure drop data for the two postures of a horizontal, isosceles-triangular channel [15].

ways—the apex up and down. Its apex angle and height were 20° and 55 mm, respectively. Such a horizontal triangular channel was chosen for extremely different cross-sectional distributions of the phases to occur under the same flow conditions, depending upon the channel posture alone. The results are presented in Figure 3, which makes comparisons between the aforementioned two postures, apex up and apex down. (The void fraction distributions along the bisector are shown in Figure 4, pertaining to $j_L = 1.0$ m/s.) Figure 3 shows that there is a slight difference between the two in dispersed bubble flows or elongated bubble flows. As a whole, however, it can be concluded that, even if there can be a variety of cross-sectional distribution of void fraction as seen in Figure 4, the corresponding difference in frictional pressure drop is small and remains within the experimental errors.

Bubble Rising Velocity

Solitary Gas Bubble in Moving Liquid Streams

It is to be expected that the velocity of gas bubble in a two-phase flow will be influenced by flow behavior of the liquid phase that is probably accounted for by the channel geometry. Measure-

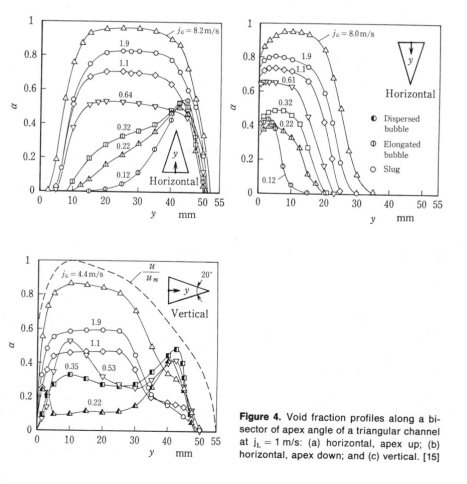

Figure 4. Void fraction profiles along a bisector of apex angle of a triangular channel at $j_L = 1$ m/s: (a) horizontal, apex up; (b) horizontal, apex down; and (c) vertical. [15]

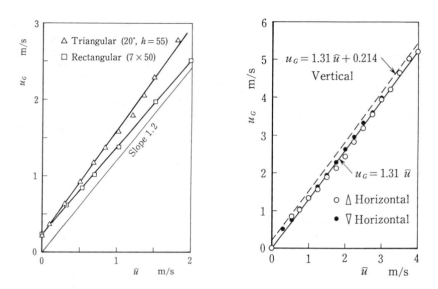

Figure 5. Rising velocity of a solitary gas bubble in moving water streams: ◁20°, h = 55 mm and □7 × 50 mm [12].

Figure 6. Rising velocity of a solitary gas bubble for a triangular channel; horizontal, apex up and apex down [15].

ments of the rising velocity of air bubble have been made by Sadatomi et al. [12] for several noncircular channels shown in Table 1.

First of all, the rising velocity of solitary air bubbles was measured. The typical results for the triangular and the 7 × 50 mm rectangular channels are shown in Figure 5. The rising velocity u_G increases linearly with mean water velocity û, and the slope varies with channel geometry; i.e. the slope for the isosceles-triangular channel is steeper than that for the rectangular one. The rising velocity of a gas bubble in a noncircular channel can therefore be correlated by

$$u_G = C_1 \hat{u} + u_{GO} \tag{10}$$

in which u_{GO} is the velocity in the stagnant liquid column. The coefficient C_1 has been found to be nearly equal to the ratio of maximum to mean liquid velocity in the cross section, $u_m/\hat{u}$, as seen in Table 1.

As an extreme case, it is of interest to examine the bubble velocity in horizontal flows though this chapter is devoted to vertical flows. Figure 6 has been prepared in this connection [15], which compares data of the horizontal triangular channel for both cases of the apex up and the apex down. The same trends are seen to hold for the horizontal flows as held for the vertical flows. The second term on the right-hand side of Equation 10 is the only difference between them.

Solitary Gas Bubble in a Stagnant Liquid Column

For a relatively large circular pipe the rising velocity of a solitary gas bubble can be formulated as $u_{GO} = 0.35\sqrt{(gD)}$ [16, 17], since only gravity and inertia forces are the dominant parameters. For a noncircular channel, however, a question has arisen as to diameter D. Sadatomi et al. [12] have suggested the correlation in terms of an equi-periphery diameter D_e, which is equivalent to the quotient of the periphery divided by π. The experimental data reported by Griffith [18] as well as

Table 2
Rising Velocity of a Solitary Gas Bubble in a Stagnant Water Column [12]

shape	dimension mm	D_e*) mm	u_{GO} m/s	$u_{GO}/\sqrt{gD_e}$	shape	dimension mm	D_e*) mm	u_{GO} m/s	$u_{GO}/\sqrt{gD_e}$
▭	7×20.6	17.6	0.142	0.34	◁	20°,h=55	41.7	0.214	0.33
	8.9×37.8+)	29.7	0.167	0.31		φ15/φ30	45.0	0.211	0.32
	7×50	36.3	0.228	0.38	◎	φ5.9/φ50.8+)	56.7	0.247	0.33
	10×50	38.2	0.204	0.33		φ12.3/φ50.8+)	63.1	0.272	0.35
	30×30	38.2	0.207	0.34		φ17.8/φ50.8+)	68.6	0.272	0.33
	17×50	42.7	0.216	0.33	⦂ tube bundle	φ3.9×7/φ50.8+)	77.8	0.267	0.31
	37.6×50.3+)	56.0	0.232	0.31		φ6.6×7/φ50.8+)	97.0	0.310	0.32
	51.6×52.1+)	66.0	0.254	0.32		φ10×7/φ50.8+)	121	0.429	0.39
	11.0×133 +)	91.9	0.292	0.31	○	φ26	26.0	0.181	0.36
	30×120	95.5	0.336	0.35		φ50.8 +)	50.8	0.240	0.34

*) equi-periphery diameter; D_e = periphery/π
+) from the measurements performed by Griffith[18]

by Sadatomi et al. are presented in Table 2. Almost all data are within the range of $u_{GO}/\sqrt{(gD_e)} = 0.31 \sim 0.36$ except for the two cases. White and Beardmore [19] showed, on the other hand, that the effect of both surface tension and viscous forces are negligible when a Eötvös number, $\rho_L g D_e^2/\sigma$, is greater than 70, as those cases in Table 2. From these facts Sadatomi et al. have concluded that, when the Eötvös number exceeds 70, the correlation

$$u_{GO} = 0.35\sqrt{(gD_e)} \tag{11}$$

is applicable to a noncircular channel.

Successive Gas Bubbles in Two-Phase Slug Flow

The results for solitary air bubbles mentioned in the preceding paragraphs suggest that the rising velocity of gas bubbles in two-phase flow can be described by

$$u_G = C_1(j_G + j_L) + u_{GO} \tag{12}$$

This is analogous to the currently used equation of Griffith and Wallis [20] and Nicklin et al. [21] for a circular pipe. In fact, the experimental data of two-phase slug flows in noncircular channels confirm Equation 12 along with $C_1 = u_m/\hat{u}$ and $u_{GO} = 0.35\sqrt{(gD_e)}$ [12].

Void Fraction

Mean Void Fraction

Relation of the mean void fraction, the superficial velocity and the gas velocity in a two-phase flow is expressed by

$$\alpha = \frac{j_G}{u_G} \tag{13}$$

Sadatomi et al. [12] reported that, when $\alpha < 0.8$, Equation 13 together with Equations 11 and 12 give agreement with their experimental data of the mean void fraction for both bubble and slug flows in vertical noncircular channels.

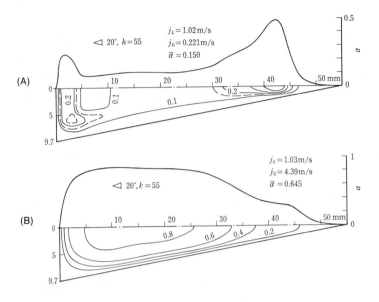

Figure 7. Equi-void-contour map for an isosceles-triangular channel: (a) bubble flow of $\hat{\alpha} = 0.150$; (b) slug flow of $\hat{\alpha} = 0.645$ [12].

Cross-Sectional Distribution of Void Fraction

Due to the laborious experiment little is known about the distribution of void fraction in noncircular channels. Sadatomi et al. [12] have presented several data for vertical two-phase air-water flows in a triangular and a rectangular channels. The local void fraction was determined by using a needle contact probe.

The typical results for the isosceles-triangular one are illustrated in Figures 7A and B, in an equi-void-contour map form, pertaining to a bubble flow and a slug flow, respectively. In a bubble flow at intermediate water velocities the local voids tend to peak near the walls and corners due to sliding bubbles [22], and there is a basin in the central region. In the vicinity of the apex the extremely low fluid velocity cuases the relatively higher local void fraction in addition to the bubble concentration. In a vertical slug flow, on the other hand, the gas phase flows in the central core while the liquid occupies the corners. The peak value of void fraction is observed near the point at which the liquid velocity in a single-phase turbulent flow has its maximum value in the cross section.

Figure 4 demonstrates the void fraction profiles along the bisector of the apex angle of this channel, and compares the profiles in vertical flows with those in horizontal flows at $j_L = 1.0$ m/s.

Flow Pattern

Figure 8 shows the flow pattern boundaries of vertical two-phase air-water flows for the six noncircular channels and a circular tube [12]. The geometries of such channels have been listed in Table 1. Flows are classified into three primary patterns—bubble flow, slug flow, and annular flow. They were determined from the slugging frequency measured by using a needle contact probe.

From a comparison of the flow pattern boundaries in this figure, there is little difference of the running among the channels, though the 7×20.6 mm rectangular one alone deviates somewhat from the others. Then, it can be said that channel geometry itself has no remarkable influence on the flow pattern transitions both from bubble to slug flow and from slug to annular flow, while channel dimension affects them in particular just above and below $D_h \simeq 10$ mm.

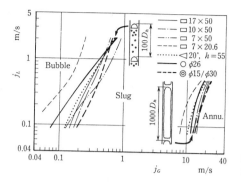

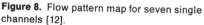

Figure 8. Flow pattern map for seven single channels [12].

Theoretical, Two-Dimensional Flow Description

Owing to complexity of both basic equations and boundary conditions, there has been essentially no previous work done on the two-dimensional analysis of gas-liquid flow in noncircular channels except for concentric annuli. Such situation seems to be unchanged in some time also in the future.

As for a concentric annular channel alone, symmetry permits analytical treatment of the flow in some extent. Saruwatari et al. [23] have proposed a model that describes the transfer process of momentum and heat in a two-phase bubble flow in concentric annuli. From this model the velocity profile and the wall shear stress for a given flow can be predicted when its void fraction profile is known. Furthermore, when a uniform heat flux is added to the system, its temperature distribution and heat transfer coefficient can be determined.

TWO-PHASE FLOW BEHAVIOR IN ROD BUNDLE

Because a topic of gas-liquid flow within a vertical rod bundle is a vast subject, this section will be limited to observation of characteristic behavior of the flow rather than analysis. As for the analytical approach there are various levels of detail, from the so-called "lumped model" to the sophisticated "subchannel analysis." In this connection several books are available particularly in the field of nuclear reactor technology [24].

Bubble Rising Velocity

Venkateswararao et al. [25] measured rising velocity of solitary air bubbles in a rod bundle consisting of 24 rod matrix in a 8.89 cm cylindrical shell containing water. The rods were 1.27 cm in diameter and were arranged in a square pitch of 1.75 cm. They observed three types of air bubble depending upon its size; (a) *small bubbles*, whose diameters are less than the characteristic spacing between the rods; (b) *cell Taylor bubbles*, which occupy a large part of the free space in a four rod cell, and whose caps are not penetrated by the rods as shown in Figure 9B; and (c) *shroud Taylor bubbles*, which occupy the large part of the cross-sectional area of the shroud, and then whose caps are penetrated by a number of rods as shown in Figure 9A. From this reference [25] the rise velocities of each type of bubbles are outlined below.

Small bubbles. As size of these bubbles increases from 2 to 8 mm in diameter, the corresponding rise velocity increases from 20 to 30 cm/s. This trend is different from that in an infinite, stagnant water reported in the literature.

Cell Taylor bubbles. The rise velocity of this type of bubbles is remarkably constant at 24 $\pm$ 1 cm/s, which is nearly equal to the value calculated by Equation 11 if D_e is substituted by four times of the rod diameter; that is, only four rods are considered to influence the behavior of a cell Taylor bubble.

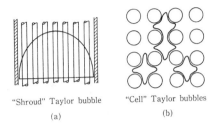

"Shroud" Taylor bubble   "Cell" Taylor bubbles
      (a)   (b)

Figure 9. Two types of Taylor bubbles [25].

Shroud Taylor bubbles. Velocities of these bubbles are shown in Figure 10 as curves 4 representing two sets of data. The spread of data between the two curves is a measure of the scatter due to the averaging of a relatively small number of bubbles. The constant curve marked 1 is the prediction of Dumitrescu [16] and Taylor [17] theory, while curve 3 shows that of Equation 11 [12]. And, the curve 2 is the prediction of the theory of Grace and Harrison [26].

Flow Pattern

Venkateswararao et al. [25] have proposed models for flow pattern transitions in a rod bundle, using an approach similar to that of Taitel et al. [27] for flow in a single, vertical tube. The applicability of the models has been examined by their own data for air-water flows in a 24-rod matrix, as well as data of Williams and Peterson [28] and Bergles et al. [29] for steam-water flows in a 4-rod array. Figure 11 shows a comparison of the predicted boundries with the observed ones in their experiment. The agreement is reasonable.

In addition to phenomena observed from one-dimensional point of view, peculiar phenomena that can hardly be observed in a single channel take place in rod bundles under some conditions. Griffith [18] has reported that in a rod bundle with relatively large diameter rods a marked channeling occurs at moderate fluid velocities, which is characterized by partition of the passage between rods into two sorts, one consisting almost entirely of gas and the rest consisting almost entirely of liquid.

Bergles [30] studied adiabatic steam-water flows at 6.9 MPa in a 4-rod square array shown in Figure 12, in which positioning of the needle contact probes for both flow pattern measurements

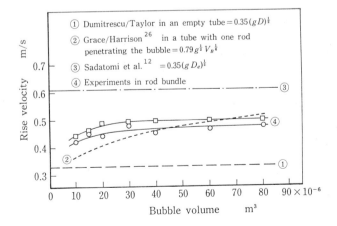

Figure 10. Rise velocity of shroud Taylor bubbles compared with other cases [25].

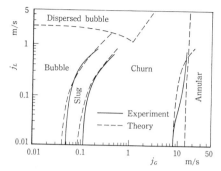

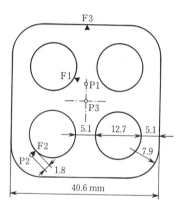

Figure 11. Flow pattern transitions for air-water in a 24 rod array [25].

Figure 12. Rod bundle geometry used by Bergles [30] for flow pattern and film thickness measurements.

(P1 ∼ P3) and film thickness measurements (F1 ∼ F3) is indicated. The resulting flow pattern map in terms of the total mass velocity and quality is reproduced in Figure 13, where the results are plotted for the three positions, for the extent of the transition regions of the bubble-to-slug and the slug-to-annular. As for the first transition (bubble-to-slug), there is little difference of the running among these three positions. However, the separation of the curves is seen as to the second transition (slug-to-annular), indicating that different flow pattern can be present in the subchannels.

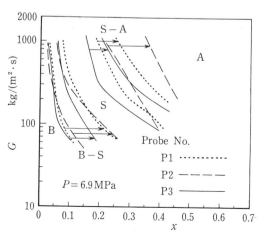

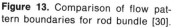

Figure 13. Comparison of flow pattern boundaries for rod bundle [30].

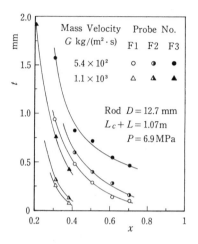

Figure 14. General survey of annular film thickness in a rod bundle [30].

As pointed out by Bergles, this flow pattern distribution over the bundle cross section will have a significant influence on film behavior in the annular flow regime. Figure 14 is represented in this connection, and shows the film thickness vs steam quality relationship obtained also from the Bergles experiment [30]. Film thickness measurements were done at the three positions, F1–F3, as shown in Figure 12. In general, the thickest films are observed at the shroud (F3). And, the rod film for the corner subchannel (F2) is somewhat thicker than the rod film for the central subchannel (F1), as might be expected from the flow pattern results.

NOTATION

A	area, m^2		j	superficial phase velocity, m/s
C_1	constant, Equation 10		P	pressure, Pa
C_ℓ	geometry factor for laminar flow		$\Delta p/\Delta x$	pressure gradient, Pa/m
C_t	geometry factor for turbulent flow		Re	Reynolds number, Equation 4
D	diameter, m		u	velocity in flow direction, m/s
D_e	equi-periphery diameter, m		x	distance in flow direction, m, or flow
D_h	hydraulic equivalent diameter, m			quality
G	mass velocity, kg/($m^2 \cdot$s)			

Greek Symbols

α	void fraction		ϕ_L	two-phase frictional multiplier,
λ	friction factor			Equation 7
μ	dynamic viscosity, Pa·s		χ	Lockhart and Martinelli parameter,
ρ	density, kg/m^3			Equation 8

Subscripts and Superscripts

f	friction		t	turbulent
G	gas phase		TP	two-phase flow
L	liquid phase			cross-sectional mean
ℓ	laminar			

REFERENCES

1. Shah, R. K. and London, A. L. *Laminar Flow Forced Convection in Ducts.* New York: Academic Press, 1978.
2. Rehme, K. "Laminarströmung in Stabbündeln." *Chemie-Ing.-Technik,* Bd. 43, 1971, pp. 962–966.
3. Nikuradse, J. "Untersuchungen über turbulente Strönmungen in nicht kreisförmigen Rohren." *Ingenieur-Archiv,* Bd. 1, 1930, pp. 306–332.
4. Carlson, L. W. and Irvine, Jr., T. F. "Fully Developed Pressure Drop in Triangular Shaped Ducts." *J. Heat Transfer, ASME Trans.,* Vol. 83, 1961, pp. 441–444.
5. Gunn, D. J. and Darling, C. W. W. "'Fluid Flow and Energy Losses in Non-Circular Conduits." *Trans. Inst Chem. Engrs.,* Vol. 41, 1963, pp. 163–173.
6. Aly, A. M. M. et al. "Measurements and Prediction of Fully Developed Turbulent Flow in an Equilateral Triangular Duct." *J. Fluid Mech.,* Vol. 85, 1978, pp. 57–83.
7. Hartnett, J. P. et al. "A Comparison of Predicted and Measured Friction Factors for Turbulent Flow through Rectangular Ducts." *J. Heat Transfer, ASME Trans.,* Vol. 84, 1962, pp. 82–88.
8. Quarmby, A. "An Experimental Study of Turbulent Flow through Concentric Annuli." *Int. J. Mech. Sci.,* Vol. 9, 1967, pp. 205–221.
9. Tiedt, W. "Berechnung des laminaren und turbulenten Reibungswiderstandes konzentrischer und exzentrischer Ringspalte." *Chem.-Ztg./Chem.,* Vol. 92, 1968, pp. 76–89.
10. Lawn, C. J. and Elliott, C. J. "Fully Developed Turbulent Flow through Concentric Annuli" *J. Mech. Engng. Sci.,* Vol. 14, 1972, pp. 195–204.
11. Jones, Jr., O. C. "An Improvement in the Calculation of Turbulent Friction in Rectangular Ducts." *J. Fluid Engineering, ASME Trans.,* Vol. 98, 1976, pp. 173–181.
12. Sadatomi, M. et al. "Two-Phase Flow in Vertical Noncircular Channels." *Int. J. Multiphase Flow,* Vol. 8, 1982, pp. 641–655.
13. Lockhart, R. W. and Martinelli, R. C. "Proposed Correlation of Data for Isothermal Two-Phase, Two-Component Flow in Pipes." *Chem. Eng. Prog.,* Vol. 45, 1949, pp. 39–48.
14. Chisholm, D. and Laird, A. D. K. "Two-Phase Flow in Rough Tubes." *ASME Trans.,* Vol. 80, 1958, pp. 276–286.
15. Sadatomi, M. and Sato, Y. "An Examination of One-Dimensional Two-Phase Flow Models Using the Data for a Horizontal Isosceles-Triangular Channel." *Technical Report of the Kumamoto University,* Vol. 32, 1983, pp. 21–28.
16. Dumitrescu, D. T. "Strömung an einer Luftblase in senkrechten Rohr." *ZAMM,* Vol. 23, 1943, pp. 139–149.
17. Davis, R. M. and Taylor, G. I. "The Mechanics of Large Bubbles Rising through Extended Liquids and through Liquids in Tubes." *Proc. Roy. Soc.,* Vol. 200, Ser. A, 1950, pp. 375–390.
18. Griffith, P. "The Prediction of Low-Quality Boiling Voids." *J. Heat Transfer, ASME Trans.,* Vol. 86, 1964, pp. 327–333.
19. White, E. T. and Beardmore, R. H. "The Velocity of Rise of Single Cylindrical Air Bubbles through Liquids Contained in Vertical Tubes." *Chem Eng. Sci.,* Vol. 17, 1962, pp. 351–361.
20. Griffith, P. and Wallis, G. B. "Two-Phase Slug Flow." *J. Heat Transfer, ASME Trans.,* Vol. 83, 1961, pp. 307–320.
21. Nicklin, D. J. et al. "Two-Phase Flow in Vertical Tubes." *Trans. Inst. Chem. Engrs.,* Vol. 40, 1962, pp. 61–68.
22. Sato, Y. et al. "An Experimental Investigation of Air Bubble Motion in Water Streams in Vertical Ducts -I. On Sliding Bubble." *Technical Report of the Kumamoto University,* Vol. 25, 1976, pp. 97–105.
23. Saruwatari, S. et al. "Momentum and Heat Transfer in Two-Phase Bubble Flow in Concentric Annuli." *Bulletin of the JSME,* Vol. 25, 1982, pp. 1746–1754.
24. Lahey, Jr., R. T. and Moody, F. J. *The Thermal-Hydraulics of a Boiling Water Nuclear Reactor.* American Nuclear Society, 1979.
25. Venkateswararao, P. et al. "Flow Pattern Transition for Gas-Liquid Flow in a Vertical Rod Bundle." *Int. J. Multiphase Flow,* Vol. 8, 1982, pp. 509–524.
26. Grace, J. R. and Harrison, D. "Influence of Bubble Shape on the Rising Velocities of Large Bubbles." *Chem. Eng. Sci.,* Vol. 25, 1967, pp. 1337–1347.

27. Taitel, Y. et al. "Modelling Flow Pattern Transitions for Steady, Upward Gas-Liquid Flow in Vertical Tubes." *AIChE J.*, Vol. 26, 1980, pp. 345–354.

28. Williams, C. L. and Peterson, Jr., A. C. "Two-Phase Flow Patterns with High-Pressure Water in a Heated Four-Rod Bundle." *Nucl. Sci. & Eng.*, Vol. 68, 1978, pp. 155–169.

29. Bergles, A. E. et al. "Investigation of Boiling Flow Regimes and Critical Heat Flux." NYO-3304-13, 1968, Dynatech Corporation, Cambridge, Massachusetts.

30. Bergles, A. E. "Two-Phase Flow Structure Observations for High Pressure Water in a Rod Bundle." *Proc. ASME Symp. Two-Phase Flow and Heat Transfer in Rod Bundles*, 1969, pp. 47–55.

CHAPTER 24

SONIC VELOCITY IN TWO-PHASE, SEPARATED FLOW

R. V. Smith and F. Rehman

Department of Mechanical Engineering
Wichita State University
Wichita, Kansas, USA

CONTENTS

INTRODUCTION

Sonic velocity in two-phase flow provides useful information in several areas. It is directly useful in "sounding devices," for example in sonar, and it provides basic information used to indicate or evaluate the flow pattern, quality, and the phase-interface transport processes of mass, energy, and momentum. Velocity of sound is also closely related to critical flow rate.

Separated Flow

Two-phase flow geometry (flow patterns) is an area where common definitions and reliable predictions have not yet been established. For this treatment the regions may be broadly defined as

1. Bubble flow (liquid continuous).
2. Intermittent flow (intermittently two-phase, liquid and vapor carriers for a given flow section).
3. Separated flow (droplet-gas flow, gas continuous).

The limits of these regions as a function of flow dynamics have been reported by, for example, Baker [1] and Griffith and Wallis, [2] and these have been widely used as a predictive guide. Both predict the limits of the separated flow region, which they call annular and mist or dispersed. This work is limited to that region because, for analysis, the gas-droplet model is generally applicable. The gas flow represents a continuum for the path of a sonic wave.

SONIC VELOCITY: GAS AND GAS-DROPLET (SEPARATED FLOW)

Sonic velocity expressions may be derived by a study of wave propagation [3] or of a strain-related velocity involving the fluid bulk modulus [4]. Both treatments yield

$$a = -\left(\frac{\partial p}{\partial \rho}\right)_{process} \tag{1}$$

where, for a gas, the process is accurately approximated as isentropic. If energy is rapidly infused during the propagation process (for example, during combustion) the process may be more closely approximated by assuming it isothermal.

For the two-phase treatment, the analysis is often more straight-forward if the sonic velocity is considered as a relaxation process. That is, for a gas, the rate of the propagation of the pressure pulse is determined by the rate of the distribution of the translational kinetic energy in the sonic-velocity direction to the various degrees of freedom of the molecules. This distribution process produces a pressure wave peak and subsequent distribution to the adjacent section in the direction of the propagation.

Figure 1 is a representation of the molecular velocity vectors in three stages during the first half of a compression wave. Figure 1A shows the element just before the pressure pulse enters the section. Molecular velocities are evenly distributed and their impact will establish a steady wall pressure. In Figure 1B the pressure pulse causes an increase in the velocity vectors in the propagation direction and that energy begins to distribute to the remaining velocity directions causing the wall pressure to begin to rise. Figure 1C shows the distribution completed and the maximum pressure of the wave is recorded at the wall.

In a kinetic-theory treatment of the gas molecules, one may divide the molecular energy coefficient, C_v, into $C_{v(TR)anslational}$ (the x, y, z components) and $C_{v(TOT)al}$ (including all degrees of freedom, translational, rotational and vibrational). Further, it may be shown that the specific heat ratio may be then expressed as

$$\gamma = \frac{C_p}{C_v} = 1 + \frac{\frac{2}{3}C_{VTR}}{C_{VTOT}} \tag{2}$$

and the gas constant as

$$R = \tfrac{2}{3}C_{VTR}$$

Then, for isentropic and equilibrium (equal partition), for an ideal gas Equation 1 becomes

$$a = \sqrt{\left[1 + \left(\frac{\frac{2}{3}C_{VTR}}{C_{VTOT}}\right)(\tfrac{2}{3}C_{VTOT})\right]T} \tag{3}$$

This expression and the figure show the sonic velocity as a function of the translational kinetic energy, and the total molecular energy. Both terms are in the coefficient for T which is a measure of the square of the molecular velocity.

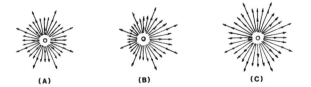

(A)   (B)   (C)

Figure 1. Molecular Velocity Vectors During the First Half of a Compression Wave.

Considerations of Non-Equilibrium Propagation Frequency

The preceding treatment assumes that there is a time period of the passing wave for an equilibrium distribution of energy to occur. This would be the case for single wave (zero frequency) wave propagation. If, however, the second wave enters the section before energy distribution has occurred, then the equilibrium distribution of the first wave will not occur and the sonic wave propagation velocity will be increased. Actually the distributions that have a slower rate will be cut-off. Thus, the distribution to rotational energy may be diminished or eliminated. This has been shown experimentally to be the case by several investigators as reported by Rossinni [5]. This change in sonic velocity, however, for a gas occurs only at a very high frequency. This is because the distribution, by molecular collisions, occurs in a shorter time than the period of most sound waves.

Two-Phase Flow Sonic Velocity

Two-phase sonic velocity in the separated (gas-droplet) region behaves as the gas-only sonic velocity except that there are additional degrees of freedom in the droplet phase. The distribution of wave energy for mixture equilibrium is affected by gas-liquid interface transport processes of momentum, energy, and mass.

The energy distribution to these additional degrees of freedom is much slower than the molecular distributions in a gas. Therefore, except for a single pulse of zero frequency, many sonic velocity frequency pulses are not likely to provide sufficient time for an equilibrium (all degrees of freedom) distribution. It follows that the two-phase, sonic velocity data will not agree with the predictions of an analytical treatment, which assumes equilibrium such as the prediction of the homogeneous, thermal equilibrium model. The two-phase sonic velocity will be frequency sensitive at much lower frequencies than those for the gas. The measured or analytically predicted sonic velocity must be accompanied by information regarding the frequency of the propagating wave. This determines the time available to allow the transport process to produce equilibrium in the mixture.

REPORTED WORK

Experimental Results

Reported experimental results for sonic velocity in the two-phase separated flow region are summarized in Figure 2 and Table 1. The fluids are flowing mixtures of air-water (two components) and steam-water (single component).

Although the experimental method showed some variation, the general system was the same for almost all of the investigators. The pressure wave was typically generated by a diaphragm rupture, perpendicular to the flow. Sound velocity data was obtained from arrival time and distance data between to axially spaced pressure pick-ups. The passage time is recorded for the first pressure pulses of the wave at the two pick-ups. Therefore, if one assumes that the diaphragm rupture creates a wave of wide range of frequencies, there will be a frequency distribution in the pressure wave. The higher frequency waves will have higher velocities. This is based on the frequency dependency (less time for equilibrium) arguments in the introduction. Thus, the preceding would indicate that the timing of the initial pressure pulse of the wave would afford a measure of sonic velocity for the highest frequency part of the wave. Continuing to follow the treatment in the introduction one would conclude that these data represent the portion of the sonic velocity data farthest from the equilibrium distribution of the wave energy among the various degrees of freedom. It would be highly likely that the distribution of the energy by the transport processes (mass, energy and momentum) may be very small and their influence on sonic velocity could not be recorded in these reported data. Therefore, the data may show behavior similar to or the same as the wave traveling through the gas.

These arguments are supported by the data reported because with one exception [6] the two-phase sonic velocity data are approximately equal to the predicted data for sonic velocity in the

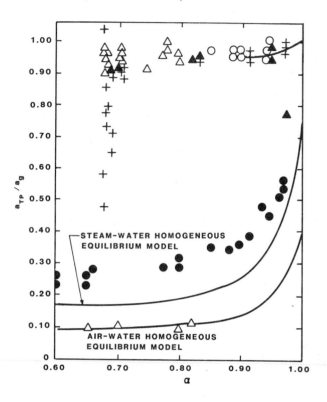

Figure 2. Experimental data for sonic velocity at high void fraction. (———) steam-water [19]. (+) air-water [7, 20]; (○) air-water [17]; (▲) [10]; (△) air-water [18]; (●) steam-water [6].

gas. Further, there are no distinct differences in the sonic data for the one-component and two-component fluid mixtures. Theoretically, the difference would indicate the influence of mass transfer (condensation or evaporation), which is not present in the two-component mixture.

This mass-transport process may be shown to be the slowest energy distribution among all the degrees of freedom. Therefore, the high frequency data would not be expected to show a distinct difference between single and two-component mixtures and the reported data supports this reasoning.

The data of Martindale and Smith [7] shows erratic behavior at a void fraction of 0.65 to 0.7. This was assumed to indicate a change from the separated flow pattern to an intermittent flow pattern. In the intermittent flow pattern region one would expect different fluid composition (liquid, gas, two-phase mixtures) for the pressure wave to travel through at different times. This causes the erratic pattern shown.

Sonic velocity is defined as the propagation of an infinitesimal pressure disturbance. In the process of rupturing the diaphragm to produce a pressure wave, the pressure differential was necessarily larger than that of a small disturbance. This larger differential was necessary to produce a good signal at the pressure pick-up points. This experimental deviation introduced by the use of a higher differential is conventionally corrected by a gas calibration of ΔP (at the diaphragm rupture) versus sonic velocity in the gas alone. This calibration curve is extrapolated to infinitesimal Δp. It is assumed that this calibration will be applicable for the two-phase mixture data.

Some further discrepancies may arise in calculating the sonic velocity in a two-phase flowing mixture because there will be an influence of the fluid (gas) velocity on the wave velocity (Doppler

Table 1

Source (Reference)	Fluids	Flow pattern	Geometry	Wave generation mechanism	Recording device and data reduction	Conclusion
[6]	Air-water and steam-water, $\alpha = 0.05 - 0.59$, $p = 143, 213,$ and 285 psia	Mixed	Vertical test section	Compression pulse was generated by the closing of a quick action valve.	Pressure pulses were picked up and fed to an oscilloscope	Agreement with homogeneous and adiabatic model (freezing the phase change) for air-water mixture
[14]	Wet steam and steam-water, steam quality 0.05 to 1.0, $p = 15.45$ psia	Annular dispersed	Vertically downward straight test section consisting largely of rubber steam hose 2 in. in diameter.	Plastic disks of various strengths were burst by the application of vacuum. The resulting rarefaction wave traveled downward through the wet steam in the test section.	Two quartz, crystal, piezoelectric pressure gages were used to determine the time taken for the wave to travel through two fixed points in the test section. The amplified signals were fed to an oscilloscope and displayed and photographed yielding the time interval taken.	Propagation speed is equal to the acoustic velocity in slightly superheated steam ($\sim$450 m/s) and is not influenced by quality.
[15]	Steam-water, steam quality 0.1 to 0.3, $p = 500, 2000$ psia	Annular-dispersed flow	The horizontal test section was 15 ft. long and 0.621 in. in diameter.	A rupture disc located at the downstream end of the test section was punctured thus resulting in a rarefaction pressure wave.	Pressure transients in the test section were measured by quartz crystal transducers and the amplified signals were recorded on a film using a cathoderay oscilloscope and camera arrangement.	Propagation speed is close to the acoustic velocity in single steam phase flow, and has the same tendency as that of low pressure systems obtained by other investigators.

(Continued)

Table 1 (Continued)

Source (Reference)	Fluids	Flow pattern	Geometry	Wave generation mechanism	Recording device and data reduction	Conclusion
[7]	Air-water, air quality 0.2 to 1.0.	Annular-dispersed flow	The vertical test section was made up of 1.5 in. in diameter plexiglass pipe 2.0 ft. long.	Pressure pulses were generated by the rupture of thin plastic and aluminum diaphragms down-stream of the test section.	The pressure pulses were picked up by quartz transducers fixed in the test section. The amplified signals were then fed to an electronic timer thus yielding the travel time of the wave.	Sonic velocity in the mixture has almost the same value as that in all-air flow up to a value of air void fraction of 0.65–0.70. For lower void fractions the data show erratic behavior indicating a change in flow pattern.
[10]	Air-water and steam-water	Annular-dispersed and mist-flow		Pressure wave		Agreement with homogeneous model. For air-water propagation speed agrees with the acoustic velocity in single gas phase flow. Propagation speed increases with bubble diameter of air-water mixture. No differ-ence of propagation speed between compression and rarefaction waves for steam-water mixtures.

Ref.	Fluid conditions	Flow regime	Test section	Wave generation	Measurement	Results
[9]	Air-water $\alpha = 0.035 - 1.0$ $p = 25$ psia Steam-water $\alpha = 0.13 - 1.0$ $p = 14.7, 50$ psia	Stratified, annular, and droplet dispersed flow	Test section was constructed of 2 in. in diameter stainless steel pipe with the mixture flowing upwards.	Compression and rarefaction pulses were generated by either pressurizing or evacuating the chamber above the diaphragm.	Quartz crystal piezo-electric transducers were used to detect the wave and the amplitude-time history of the wave was displayed on the oscilloscope. This yields in determining the time taken to travel between two fixed points.	In air-water mixtures propagation speed agrees with the acoustic velocity in gas phase. For steam-water mixture, propagation speed of rarefaction wave is slightly slower than the compression wave.
[16]	Steam-water, steam quality 0.2 to 0.5, $p = 17, 45$ psia	Mist flow	The mixture flows downward through a straight test section consisting largely of rubber steam hose 2 in. in diameter.	Rarefaction wave was generated by bursting plastic disks of various thicknesses by applying vacuum to the upper chamber.	Waves were picked up by quartz crystal piezoelectric transducers and after amplification were fed into an electronic timer which gave the time of travel.	Agreement with data of Collingham and Firey. Propagation speed decreases with decreasing quality.
[17]	Air-water, void fraction 0.565 to 0.981	Slug, annular and mist flow	The vertical test section consisted of 0.5 in. in diameter plexiglass pipe, 168 in. in length, preceded by a 36 in. air straightener. Mixture flow was upwards.	Compression waves were generated downstream of the test section by rupturing a cellophane diaphragm placed in front of a high pressure chamber.	Two piezoelectric transducers were used to sense the waves and the amplified signals were displayed on an oscilloscope and photographed thus yielding the travel time for the wave between two fixed points.	Propagation speed is about 1,100 ft/sec in the high void fraction region. The speed decreases for void fractions less than 0.5.
[18]	Air-water	Annular flow		Small amplitude pressure pulse.		Propagation speed agrees with the acoustic velocity in the air within 10% error.

effect). There are various assumptions involved in estimating this gas velocity. The effective gas-flow area must be determined from the gas void fraction (calculated or measured) and from estimates of the area of the slow-moving gas in the wakes of the droplets and waves [7].

Analytical Results

Reported analytical work in the separated flow region may be divided into two major parts. One approach uses an effective density (mixture) model. Although separated flow concepts may be employed in this development, the final expression employs a single density (or mixture) expression to describe the medium through which the sound wave travels. This treatment most often assumes homogeneous, equilibrium flow. Examples of this treatment are Henry [8, 9], and Hamilton [10].

The second approach uses a completely separated flow model studying the propagation through the continuous medium (gas in separated flow). This propagation is influenced by both transport processes in the gas (relatively rapid) and by transport processes at the liquid-gas interface (relatively slow). Clinch and Karplus [11], though they finally used effective density terms, may be said to make a major use of a separated flow model.

Clinch and Karplus [11] Analytical Model

The analysis was for a mixture of droplets suspended in a gas. Although mass transfer (condensation and vaporization) was considered in their model, the major part of their work was concerned with viscosity effects (momentum transfer) and heat transfer effects (energy transport). This suits the case for two-component flow (e.g., air-water) and for single-component flow at a mixture ratio where a pressure change will produce zero mass transfer (no condensation or vaporization).

For viscosity effects the authors followed the viscous drag analysis of Lamb [12]. The ratio of sonic velocity in the gas phase to sonic velocity in the two-phase mixture was found to be

$$\left(\frac{a_g}{a_{Tp}}\right)^2 = 1 + \left(\frac{1-q}{q}\right)\frac{\phi(1+\theta)+\theta^2}{(1+\theta)^2+\theta^2}\left(1-\frac{\rho_g}{\rho_f}\right) \tag{4}$$

where the inertial force coefficient is

$$\phi = \left(\frac{1}{2}+\frac{q}{4\beta R_f}\right)\frac{\rho_g}{\rho_f}$$

and the viscous force coefficient is

$$\theta = \frac{q}{4\beta R_f}\left(1+\frac{1}{\beta R_f}\right)\frac{\rho_g}{\rho_f}$$

where $\beta = \sqrt{\omega/2v_g}$, v is kinematic viscosity coefficient, R_f is droplet radius, q is quality, and ρ is density.

Thus, the variables are mixture quality, the viscosity parameter (β), the density ratio, and the droplet radius.

Similarly, from the analysis of Epstein and Carhart [13] the authors developed an effective specific heat ratio

$$\gamma_{eff} = \frac{q_c\gamma_\infty + \left(\dfrac{1-q_c}{C_{vg}}\right)C_{pf0}(1-I_{nRf})}{q_c + \left(\dfrac{1-q_c}{C_{vg}}\right)C_{pf0}(1-I_{nRf})} \tag{5}$$

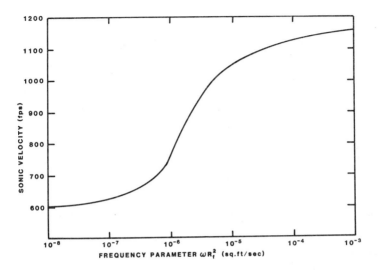

Figure 3. Sonic velocity in hydrogen mixture of quality 0.375 versus ωR_f^2.

where q_c = critical quality

C_{vg} = constant volume specific heat of gas

C_{pf0} = constant pressure specific heat of liquid at low frequencies

I_{nRf} = function that determines the influence of temperature changes
on the acoustic wave propagation

From the viscous drag analysis an expression was developed for effective mixture density

$$\rho_{eff} = \rho_g \left[1 + \left(\frac{1 - q_c}{q_c} \right) \frac{\phi(1 + \phi) + \theta^2}{(1 + \phi)^2 + \theta^2} \left(1 - \frac{\rho_g}{\rho_c} \right) \right] \tag{6}$$

Finally, the expression for sound velocity in the two-phase mixture is given by

$$a_{TP}^2 = \frac{\gamma_{eff} P}{\rho_{eff}}$$

where P is the static pressure.

Evaluations of this expression for liquid-vapor hydrogen [11] and air-water [21] mixtures are shown in Figures 3 and 4.

Henry-Analytical Model

Henry et al. [8, 9] proposed an effective density model that would account for interface momentum and energy transport processes as related to various flow patterns. They did not use a specific separated flow model but accounted for momentum transport by the use of a "virtual mass" term and for energy transport by the assumption of a rate process for the sonic wave. This assumption produced a value of dv_g/dp, and subsequently a predicted sonic velocity. The analysis considered both two-component and one-component systems.

In the separated flow region, the authors considered annular-flow (negligible liquid dispension in the gas) and mist flow.

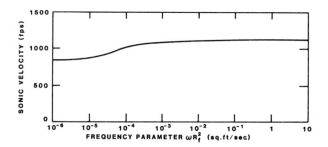

Figure 4. Sonic velocity in air-water mixture of quality 0.7 versus ωR_f^2.

In annular flow, a smooth and wavy interface between the phases was considered. Mass and energy transport between the phases was considered negligible. Therefore, one- and two-component systems produced the same predictive expressions.

For annular flow with smooth interface, the effective density behavior was assumed to be a function of the change in slip ratio.

$$\frac{dk}{dp} = -\frac{1}{a^2}\left(\frac{1}{\rho_g} - \frac{1}{\rho_f}\right) \tag{7}$$

and

$$\frac{a}{a_g} = \sqrt{1 + \frac{1-q}{q}\left(\frac{\rho_g}{\rho_f}\right)^2} \tag{8}$$

For annular flow with wavy interface, the gas flowing over a wavy interface was approximated by flow over half-cylinders. This model resulted in the expression

$$\frac{dp}{d\ell} = \rho_f u_f\left(\frac{du_f}{d\ell}\right) - \rho_g\left(u_g\frac{du_g}{d\ell} - u_f\frac{du_f}{d\ell}\right) \tag{9}$$

where the second term on the right represents the contribution of the "virtual mass."

The ratio of sonic velocity in two-phase mixture to sonic velocity in the gas is given by

$$\frac{a}{a_g} = \sqrt{\alpha} \tag{10}$$

where α is the void fraction.

For mist flow, the expressions differ between one- and two-component systems. For two-component mist flow, the momentum equation is similar to that of the wavy interface except that the liquid geometry is changed from half-cylinders to spheres. The momentum equation with the virtual mass term is

$$\frac{dp}{d\ell} = \rho_f u_f\frac{du_f}{d\ell} - \frac{\rho_g}{2}\left(u_g\frac{du_g}{d\ell} - u_f\frac{du_f}{d\ell}\right) \tag{11}$$

The sonic velocity term then becomes

$$\frac{a}{a_g} \approx \sqrt{\frac{2\alpha}{1+\alpha}} \tag{12}$$

For the one-component mist flow, the compression wave was assumed to be "frozen" (no mass transport and the expression is the same as for the two-component system). For the one-component system the rarefaction wave was assumed to allow mass transfer at a rate to produce equilibrium. For an isentropic process

$$\frac{dq}{dp} = -\frac{1-x}{S_{fg}}\frac{dS_f}{dp} \tag{13}$$

and

$$a^2 = \frac{1 + 2\alpha^2(1-\alpha)\rho_f/(1+\alpha)\rho_g}{[\alpha^2 + \alpha(1-\alpha)(\rho_f/\rho_g)]/a_g^2 + \rho_f[\alpha(1-\alpha)/qS_{fg}](dS_f/dp)} \tag{14}$$

NOTATION

a	strain—related velocity	l	length
C_p	specific heat at constant pressure	p	pressure
C_v	molecular energy coefficient (i.e., specific heat at constant volume)	q	quality
		R	universal gas constant
I_{nRF}	function that determines influence of temperature changes on acoustic wave propagation	R_f	droplet radius
		u	velocity

Greek Symbols

α	void fraction	ν	kinematic viscosity
γ	ratio of specific heats	ρ	density
γ_{eff}	effective specific heat ratio	ϕ	inertial force coefficient
θ	viscous force coefficient	ω	velocity

REFERENCES

1. Baker, O., "Simultaneous Flow of Oil and Gas," *Oil-Gas Journal*, 53(7), 1954.
2. Griffith, P., and Wallis, G., "Two-Phase Slug Flow," *Journal Heat Transfer*, 83C(3), 1961.
3. Shapiro, A. H., *Dynamics and Thermodynamics of Compressible Fluid Flow*, Vol. 1, Ronald Press, New York, 1953.
4. Wood, A. B., *A Textbook of Sound*, G. Bell, London, 1949.
5. Rossini, F. R., *Thermodynamics and Physics of Matter*, Princeton University Press, Princeton, NJ, 1955.
6. Semenov, N. I., and Kosterin, S. I., "Results of Studying the Speed of Sound in a Gas Liquid System," *Templo Energetika*, Vol. II, No. 6, 1964.
7. Martindale, W. R., and Smith, R. V., "Pressure Drop and Sonic Velocity in Separated Two-Phase Flow," *Journal of Fluids Engineering*, Vol. 102, 1980.
8. Henry, R. E., "Pressure Wave Propagation Through Annular and Mist Flows," *Chemical Engineering Progress Ser.*, 67, 113, 1971.
9. Henry, R. E., Grolmes, M. A., and Fauske, H. K., "Propagation Velocity of Pressure Waves in Gas-Liquid Mixtures," *Co-Current Gas-Liquid Flows*, Plenum Press, New York, 1969.
10. Hamilton, L. B., "Propagation of Pressure Waves in Two-Phase Media," Ph.D. dissertation, Univ. of California at Berkeley, 1968.
11. Clinch, J. M., and Karplus, H. B., "An Analytical Study of the Propagation of Pressure Waves in Liquid Hydrogen-Vapor Mixtures," NASA CR-54015, Illinois Institute of Technology Research Institute, 1964.

12. Lamb, H., *Hydrodynamics*, Dover Publications, New York, 1945.
13. Epstein, P. S., and Carhart, R. R., "Absorption of Sound in Suspensions and Emulsions," *Journal of Acoustical Society of America*, Vol. 25, 1953.
14. Collingham, C. E., and Firey, J. C., "Velocity of Sound Measurements in Wet Steam," *I&EC Process Design and Development*, 2, 197, 1963.
15. White, R. F., and D'Arcy, D. F., "Velocity of Sound and Critical Discharge Pressure in Annular Two-Phase Flow," *Symposium Fluid Mechanics and Measurements in Two-Phase Flow Systems*, Univ. of Leeds, 1969.
16. England, W. G., Firey, J. C., and Trapp, D. E., "Additional Velocity of Sound Measurements in Wet Steam," *I&EC Process Design and Development*, 5, 198, 1966.
17. Evans, R. G., Gouse, S. W., and Bergles, A. E., "Pressure Wave Propagation in Adiabatic Slug-Annular-Mist Two-Phase Gas-Liquid Flow," *Chemical Engineering Science*, 25, 1970.
18. Gerrard, C. W., Jr., "A Study of the Propagation of Small Amplitude Pressure Pulses in a Two-Phase, Two-Component Mixture with an Annular Flow Pattern," Ph.D. dissertation, Texas A&M University, 1968.
19. DeJong, V. J., and Firey, J. C., "Effect of Slip and Phase Change on Sound Velocity in Steam Water Mixtures and the Relation to Critical Flow," *I&EC Process Design and Development*, Vol. 7, 1968.
20. Smith, R. V., Martindale, W. R., Lindsted, R. D., "Two-Phase Sonic Velocity Measurements for Separated Flow," ASME, 75-WA/HT-34.
21. Rehman, F., "Sonic Velocity in Two-Phase Flow as a Function of Frequency," M.Sc. thesis, Wichita State University, 1983.

CHAPTER 25

TWO-PHASE FLOWS IN JUNCTIONS

B. J. Azzopardi

Engineering Sciences Div.
AERE Harwell
Didcot, Oxfordshire, United Kingdom

CONTENTS

INTRODUCTION

Junctions are an often necessary aspect of many pipeline systems. For single-phase flows, the present state of knowledge is sufficiently advanced to enable the majority of cases to be designed in spite of the number of the relevant variables. In the case of two-phase flow, however, the number of variables is much larger; in addition there are complicating factors in the partition and mixing of the phases. The problem is particularly acute for dividing junctions; either phase can pass preferentially into the minor branch of the junction. This preferential partition can have a significance for power or process plants far exceeding the size of the junction relative to the complete plant. In power plants there is the junction between the pressurizer and the hot leg in the primary cooling circuit of pressurized water nuclear reactors. During loss-of-coolant accidents, there can be two-phase flow in the primary circuit. If pressure is relieved, then one phase would enter the pressurizer preferentially and have significant effects on subsequent plant operation. In the process industries there are many dividing junctions (for example, in the pipework distributing two-phase flow to a bank of air-cooled condensers). Obviously maldistribution of the phases will have a direct effect on the heat exchanger performance; those receiving mainly liquid will underperform significantly because the intube heat transfer coefficients during subcooling will be much lower than the corresponding condensation coefficient. Those exchangers receiving mainly vapor will perform slightly better than expected. However this is not sufficient to compensate for the poor performers and the entire bank could behave below specification. Apart from these cases where the preferential phase partition causes problems, there are examples where the phenomenon has been used to advantage. Examples of these are given by Fryar [1] who discusses drip legs used in natural gas/condensate lines as primary separators before compressors, and by Oranje [2] considering design of slug catchers for similar lines. The difficulty in predicting the two-phase flow split has led to an attitude amongst designers that the two-phase flow should be separated and processed separately, and only recombined when totally necessary. Of course, such practice is essential in certain circumstances; in natural gas lines which contain condensate, liquid and gas must be separated and pressurized separately before being recombined.

In any calculations involving junctions the flows are governed not only by what occurs at the junction but also by the resistances in the rest of the system. Calculations must therefore be carried out over the entire system. Here we are not considering such calculations; instead the aim is to identify the contributions from a junction to such an overall calculation. Obviously for such calculations of network systems the requirement is for knowledge of the flow rates and qualities in each of the three components of the junction together with the pressure losses associated with the junction.

In this chapter the available material, both experimental data and theoretical analyses, for two-phase flow splitting are examined together with the related pressure-drop information. Factors in-

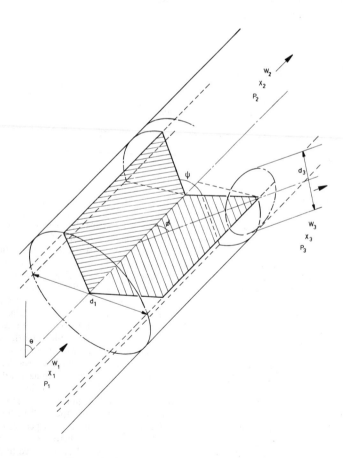

Figure 1. Geometric definition of the junction.

fluencing the flow split are discussed. Finally the information available for manifolds, (i.e., junctions close together) is presented. Combining junctions are then considered, particularly their effect on flow pattern and on mixing lengths required downstream of the junction. The chapter is completed by an examination of flow behavior and gas entrainment in combining Y junctions in gravity drainage lines.

DIVIDING JUNCTIONS

Parameters and Geometric Definition

For a junction, as shown in Figure 1, the subscripts 1, 2, and 3 usually refer to the inlet and outlet of the main tube (or header or run) and to the side arm (or branch), respectively. In most cases the main tube diameter is constant across the junction ($d_1 = d_2$), and the main tube is straight. The limited cases studied where these conditions are not met are identified later.

Flow splits at junctions, such as shown in Figure 1, are defined by eight parameters, the flow rates, and qualities in the three legs of the junction, w_1, x_1, w_2, x_2, w_3, x_3, and the two pressure drops across the junction, Δp_{12}, Δp_{13} (these are defined in detail later). Normally three of these parameters are specified, (e.g., w_1, x_1, and say Δp_{13}). Therefore there are five unknowns, and five equations are necessary to specify the problem. Four of these equations are easily obtained from total and phase mass balances and from momentum balances along the main tube and across the side arm. The fifth equation, which defines the flow split, is much more difficult to specify.

In this discussion it has been assumed that the junction is geometrically specified. This specification involves many parameters. In single-phase flow, Gardel [3] has shown that the pressure drops are affected by the angle between the main tube and the side arm, ϕ, the ratio of side arm to main tube diameters, d_3/d_1, and the degree of rounding of the corner r/d_3. In the case of two-phase flow, gravity can cause stratification, it is also necessary to specify the angle between the main tube and the vertical, θ, and the angle ϕ, between the side arm and the top of the main tube. There are a great many possible combinations of values of these parameters. In practice, however, only certain values of these parameters are used, usually $\theta = 0$ or 90, $\phi = 45$, 90, 135, and $\psi = 0$, 90, or 180, and some combinations are not possible (e.g., ψ is not relevant if $\theta = 0$). The problem thus reduces to one of potentially manageable proportions.

In the subsequent sections the available data and theories for flow split and pressure drop are considered together with suggestions made to improve the split or otherwise influence the maldistribution. Finally the problems of junctions very close together in manifolds are examined.

Experimentally Observed Parametric Dependence

The available data for two-phase flow splits in junctions and the associated pressure drops are summarized in Table 1. Inspection of the geometric parameters varied shows that most of the data is from fairly small diameter tubes and from limited values of the defining angles. These data have been studied and the range of parameters they cover and the conclusions that can be drawn from them are described here. The most striking feature of the data is shown in Figure 2 where the maldistribution (or preferential partition) of the phases can be clearly seen. As shown, either phase can emerge preferentially. In particular, in comparing the data of Azzopardi [7] (for high quality) and Hewitt and Shires [8] (for low quality) taken from junctions of identical geometry, it can be seen that in the high-quality data the liquid emerges preferentially, whereas at lower qualities it is the gas that comes out first. Similarly, the data of Hong [12] and Azzopardi [7] show the same phase emerging preferentially, though to varying degrees. These two data sets are from different geometries though similar qualities and mass fluxes (mass flow rate/cross sectional area). The preferential emergence of one phase can be explained by consideration of the flow pattern (the distribution of the phases about the cross section) in the approach to the junction.

Table 1
A Summary of Data Flow for Two-Phase Flow and Junctions

θ	ϕ	ψ	d_1 (mm)	d_3 (mm)	w_3/w_1	P bar	Split	Pressure Drop
0	90	—	38	38	0.3–0.7	1.5	Honan and Lahey [4]	
0	90	—	32	6.3 12.7 19	0–0.92	1.5	Azzopardi and Whalley [5]	
0	90	—	100 50 24	50	0.05–0.9	2.0	Zetzmann [6]	Zetzmann [6]
0	90	—	32	25 32	0–0.5	1.5	Azzopardi [7]	
0	90	—	32	32	0–1.0	3.0	Hewitt and Shires [8]	
0	45	—	38	38	0.3–0.7	1.5	Honan and Lahey [4]	
0	45	—			0.05–0.9	2.0	Zetzmann [6]	
0	135	—	38	38	0.3–0.7	1.5	Honan and Lahey [4]	
90	90	0	50	25	0.25–0.8		Fouda and Rhodes [9]	Fouda and Rhodes [9]
90	90	0	206	20 12		5.0	Reimann and Smoglie [10]	
90	90	0			0.1–0.7		Katsaounis et al [11]	Katsaounis et al [11]
90	90	0–180	32	12.7	0–0.4	2.5	Azzopardi and Whalley [5]	
90	90	0–180	9.5	9.5	0–1.0	1.6	Hong [12]	
90	90	90	38	25	0.05–0.9	3.0	Collier [13]	
90	90	90	9.5	9.5	0–1.0	1.6	Hong [12]	
90	90	90	100	20	0–0.02	1.5	Henry [14]	
90	90	90	76	76	0.05–0.6	30.0	Oranje [15]	
90	90	90	50	50	0.05–1.0	5.0		Reimann and Seeger [16]
90	90	90	38	38	0.3–0.7	1.5	Saba and Lahey [17]	Saba and Lahey [17]
90	90	90	23	23	0–1.0			Tsuyama and Taga [18]
90	90	180	206	6 12 20	0–1.0	5.0	Reimann and Khan [19]	
90	90 $\phi' = 90$	90	9.5	9.5	0–1.0	1.6	Hong [12]	

The data of Azzopardi and Whalley [5], Azzopardi [7], and Hong [12] are taken from annular flow. Here the gas occupies the center of the tube carrying with it some liquid as drops, while a substantial part of the liquid travels as a slow moving film on the channel walls. Obviously it is the liquid in the film with its lower momentum that will be diverted into the side arm, whereas the gas (and drops) will be less easily moved. Azzopardi and Whalley [5] were able to relate the fraction of liquid taken off to the liquid film flow rate. They used the observation of McNown [20] that fluid (single-phase flow) emerging from the side arm originated from the segment of the main tube

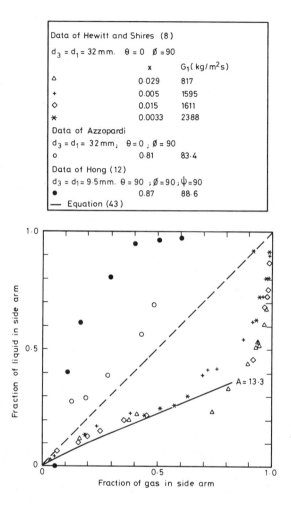

Figure 2. Examples of maldistribution of phases at a dividing junction.

cross section nearest the side arm. Assuming that both liquid from an angular portion of the film and gas from the same segment are taken off, Azzopardi and Whalley obtained

$$\frac{w_3 x_3}{w_1 x_1} = \frac{1}{2\pi} \left\{ \frac{2\pi w_3(1 - x_3)}{w_1(1 - x_1)(1 - E_1)} - \sin\left[\frac{2\pi w_3(1 - x_3)}{w_1(1 - x_1)(1 - E_1)}\right] \right\} \tag{1}$$

This was found to correlate data from a range of conditions. In the Equation 1, E_1 is the fraction of liquid traveling as drops in the center of the inlet tube. The equation can be simplified further to give a linear relationship between liquid and gas take off; this linearity was also observed by Henry [14].

At low qualities where the flow pattern is bubbly, the phases are more uniformly distributed about the cross section and velocities are more nearly equal. In this case it is the gas with its lower

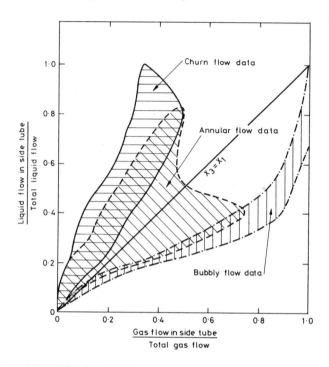

Figure 3. Flow split at a tee junction—effect of flow pattern [5].

momentum that diverts more easily and is preferentially extracted. This flow pattern dependence is shown in Figure 3 where the areas covered by data from different flow patterns are marked. This shows that even with annular flow the gas may still emerge preferentially.

An effect of inlet quality can be seen in the data of Collier [13], Figure 4, which covers a quality range of 0.021–0.5. For the vast majority of the data the gas is extracted preferentially, though the degree of phase separation depends on quality in a complex manner. It first increases and then decreases as the quality is increased. Zetzmann [6], working at higher mass fluxes (500 < G < 3,000 kg/m² s) but lower qualities (0.005 < x < 0.035) than Collier, found that for a fixed mass flux into the junction and a constant fractional total take off, the quality in the side arm was directly proportional to the inlet quality. This appears a much simpler relation than that found by Collier, though it is probable that Zetzmann was only seeing part of the complex relationship observed by Collier.

Zetzmann [6] uses alternative methods of presenting data to those already shown in Figures 2–4. The first plots the ratio of the qualities in the side arm and at inlet against the fractional total take off. For the data shown in Figure 5 the side-arm quality is greater than that at the inlet except for take off fraction <0.05 when the opposite is true. This does not always occur. Figure 6 shows the data of Hong [12], already presented in Figure 2, plotted as suggested by Zetzmann. Here the side-arm quality is almost always less than that at the inlet. The data of Collier [13], which exhibited preferential gas extraction, behaves in a manner similar to that of Zetzmann. A third way of presenting data is shown in Figures 7 and 8. Here the quality in the side arm is plotted against inlet quality for a given inlet mass flux and fractional take off. Figure 7 illustrates the effect of the angle between the main tube and the side arm, ϕ, and shows the side-arm quality increasing as the angle increases to 90°. Zetzmann attributes the difference to the fact that 45° junctions, the geometric paths along which the phases are deflected, are shorter. He suggests that the heavier liquid

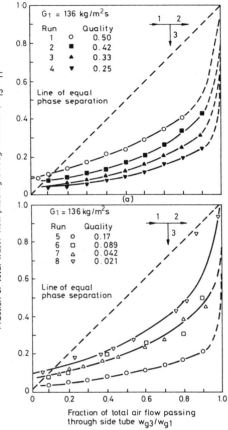

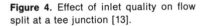

Figure 4. Effect of inlet quality on flow split at a tee junction [13].

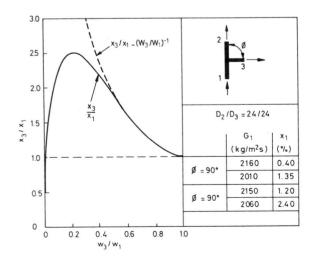

Figure 5. Variation of quality ratio with fraction taken off [6].

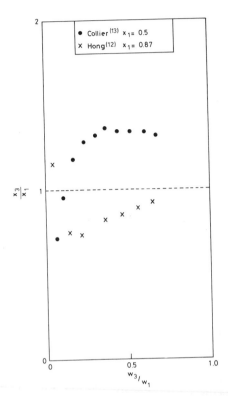

Figure 6. Effect of inlet quality on quality ratio.

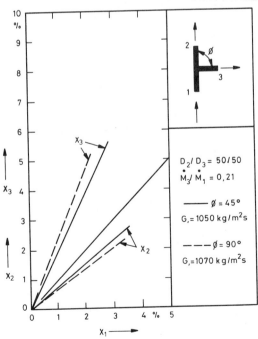

Figure 7. Effect of angle between the junction tubes on flow split [6].

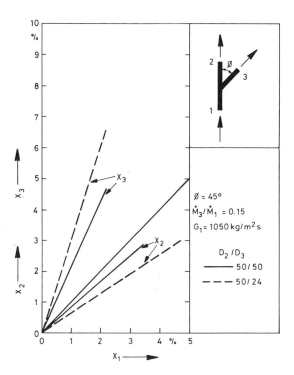

Figure 8. Effect of diameter ratio on flow split [6].

phase finds it harder to follow the 90°path. The effect could also be explained by consideration of the effective axial length of the junction. The longer the hole through which the phases have to pass, the easier it is for the less easily deflected liquid to arrive at the side of the main tube containing the hole before it has passed through the end of the junction. As the length can be expressed as

$$\frac{\ell}{d_1} = \frac{d_3}{d_1 \sin \phi} \tag{2}$$

the nearer ϕ is to 90° the smaller is the length of the junction. Figure 8 shows the effect of diameter ratio with the small side arm giving a greater side-arm quality. Zetzmann's explanation for the greater redistribution of the phases when the side-arm diameter is reduced while incoming flow parameters remain constant is that with the constant mass flow ratio w_3/w_1 a smaller cross section is offered to the same fluid throughout. Therefore the driving pressure difference must become greater and in turn may increase the zone of influence within the main tube. As there is a difference in inertia between the gas and the liquid, the gas is more preferentially extracted. An alternative explanation has been suggested by Azzopardi [7] who noted that with smaller side arms the axial distance of the take-off hole is decreased. Therefore liquid which might be dragged across to the side arm arrives at points downstream of the take off point. The effect of side-arm diameter is illustrated in Figure 9 taken from annular flow, where a small but not always clear cut effect of diameter ratio can be seen. From his extensive data set, Zetzmann found little effect of mass flux for mass fluxes greater than 500 kg/m^2 s and found no effect of diameter for geometrically similar junctions.

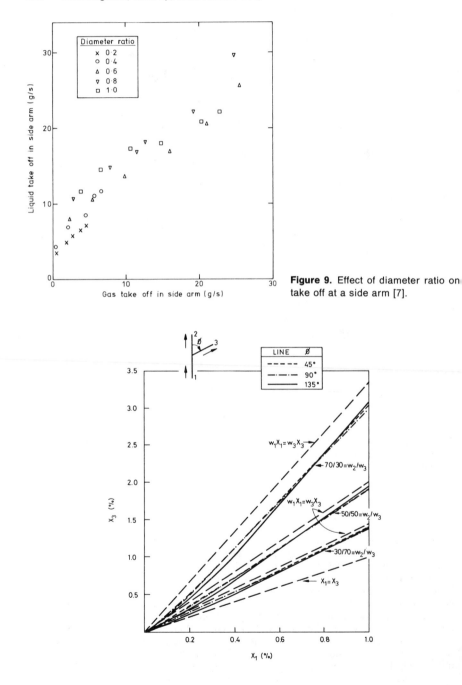

Figure 9. Effect of diameter ratio on take off at a side arm [7].

Figure 10. Effect of angle between the junction tubes at low qualities [4].

Data for very low qualities has been provided by Honan and Lahey [4] who used test sections with $\theta = 0$; $\phi = 45°, 90°, 135°$. Over their range of data $(1,357 < G < 2,714;\ 0.001 < x < 0.01)$ they found that the effect of ϕ was small and not very systematic (Figure 10). In this figure they illustrate how the data lies between limits of a perfect split $(x_3 = x_1)$ and total phase separation $(x_3 = x_1 w_1/w_3)$. They found that the greater the take off the more perfect the phase separation, an observation which can also be seen in the data of Hewitt and Shires [8] illustrated in Figure 2. Saba and Lahey [17], with a similar test section but a horizontal main tube $(\theta = 90;\ \phi = 90;\ \psi = 90)$, show very similar results, a not surprising result, as at high mass fluxes the effect of gravity is not so significant. For higher inlet qualities the total separation limit is more complex, as shown in Figure 11; for certain split ratios perfect separation would mean only gas being extracted through the side arm. Figure 11 also illustrates the complex nature of the inlet quality effect described in the data of Collier [13] shown in Figure 4. A similar maximum in x_3 has been observed by Henry [14]; the value of x_1, at which this maximum occurs, decreases as the inlet flow rate, w_1, increases.

Data at higher qualities has been presented by Azzopardi and Whalley [15], Hong [12], and Oranje [15]. The results of Azzopardi and Whalley have been correlated by Equation 1. Hong has studied the effect of gas and liquid flow rates and liquid viscosity. He finds the liquid phase is preferentially extracted over most of the ranges of his experimental variables. Increases in gas velocity and liquid viscosity both make for increased extraction of liquid. Increasing the liquid flow rate, in contrast, produces a trend towards perfect split and at the highest liquid flow rate there is preferential gas extraction (i.e., $x_3 < x_1$). The data of Oranje [15] is unique among all the available data having been taken at higher pressure (440 psig). This limited set of data, from a geometry similar to that of Hong, shows trends similar to those described earlier in the data of Hong.

The effect of the orientation of the side arm when the main tube is horizontal has been studied by Hong [12] and Azzopardi and Whalley [5]. Both worked with annular flows. Because of stratification effects, the film flow rate at the bottom of the main tube will be greater than at the top. Therefore as the side-arm position was varied from the top round to the bottom of the main tube, the amount of liquid taken off increased significantly. This was observed by both Hong and Azzopardi and Whalley and is illustrated in Figure 12. Also shown are the predictions made by

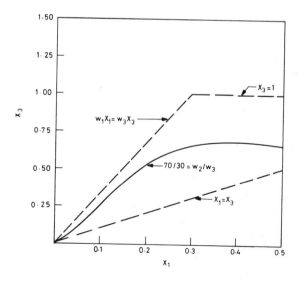

Figure 11. Effect of inlet quality on flow split [13].

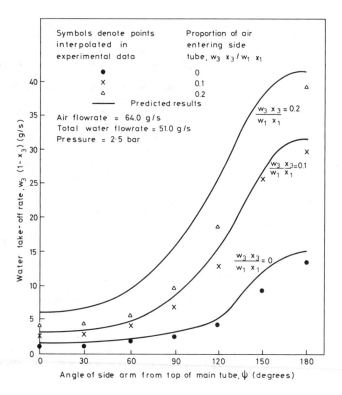

Figure 12. Effect of side-arm inclination on flow split [5].

Azzopardi and Whalley using values of local film flow rate integrated over appropriate portions of the tube periphery (this is discussed in greater detail in the next section).

The effect of side-arm orientation, when the flow in the main tube is stratified, has been studied by Reimann and Khan [19], $\psi = 180$, and Reimann and Smoglie [10] and Katsaounis et al. [11], $\phi = 0$. Reimann carried out experiments with a large-diameter main tube ($d_1 = 206$ mm) and varied the size of the side-arm diameter ($d_3 = 6, 12, 20$ mm). They found that initially only one phase was extracted; gas for $\psi = 0$, liquid for $\psi = 180°$. When the side arm was at the bottom of the main tube, Reimann and Khan observed that the surface of the liquid above the side arm became depressed and that gas was entrained into the side arm. They found that the exact behavior could be grouped into three types:

1. Where liquid is approaching the side arm from both sides.
2. Where the liquid flow rate w_{L1} is less than the possible flow rate through the side arm; such conditions exist if there is a bend up to the vertical downstream of the junction and the gas flow is not sufficient to lift the liquid up the vertical leg.
3. Where the water flow rate in the side arm is less than that entering the main tube.

Here Type 3 will be considered. Examples of such flows are shown in Figure 13 where flows with single- and two-phase flow in the side arm are illustrated. Figure 14 shows that once breakthrough has occurred and two-phase flow is emerging through the side arm, an increase in the driving force (that is the pressure drop across the side arm) has very little effect on the amount of liquid emerging.

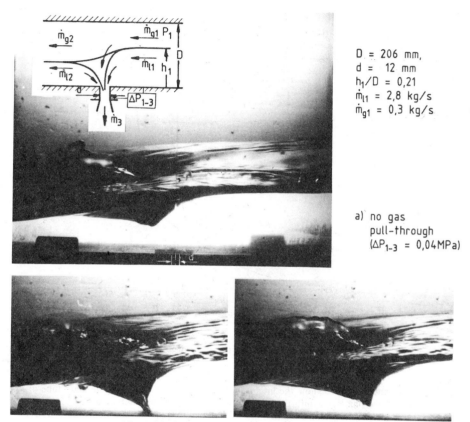

$D = 206$ mm,
$d = 12$ mm
$h_1/D = 0,21$
$\dot{m}_{l1} = 2,8$ kg/s
$\dot{m}_{g1} = 0,3$ kg/s

a) no gas
pull-through
$(\Delta P_{1-3} = 0,04$ MPa$)$

b) oscillating gas pull-through $(\Delta P_{1-3} = 0,065$ MPa$)$

c) continuous
gas pull-through
$(\Delta P_{1-3} = 0,22$ MPa$)$

Figure 13. (A) Examples of bottom exit with stratified flow [19]; (B) Vortex-free gas pull-through at stratified flow in the horizontal pipe.

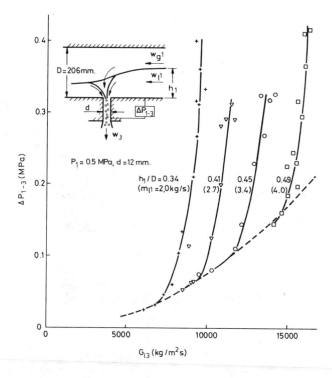

Figure 14. Effect of driving pressure drop on take off [19].

This figure and Figure 15 show the importance of the height of liquid in the main tube on the inception of two-phase flow into the side arm and on the actual quality and flow rate into that side arm. Reimann and Khan found that the point of pull through, as they termed the start of two-phase flow in the side arm, could be correlated by an equation of the form originally derived by Lubin and Hurwitz [21] for the flow of liquids out of tank drains. Equation 3

$$\frac{v_{L3}}{\sqrt{gd_3}}\left(\frac{\rho_L}{\rho_L - \rho_G}\right)^{0.5} = 0.94\left(\frac{h_B}{d_3}\right)^{2.5} \tag{3}$$

correlates the data from three side-arm diameters well. They also found that the mass flow, w_3, with two-phase flow in the side arm could be related to the mass flow at pull through by

$$\frac{w_3}{w_{3B}} = \left(\frac{h}{h_B}\right)^{1.62} \tag{4}$$

where h is the height of liquid in the main tube, and h_B is the height at pull through. Over the ranges they studied Reimann and Khan found little effect of the gas and liquid flow rates in the main tube. They also speculate about the effect of density ratios. When the side arm was at the top of the main tube, Reimann and Smoglie [10] found that for constant values of the system pressure and gas outlet flow rate and small values of the liquid level, h, only gas enters the side arm; the interface is a nearly ideal horizontal plane. (Note that in their paper Reimann and Smoglie use

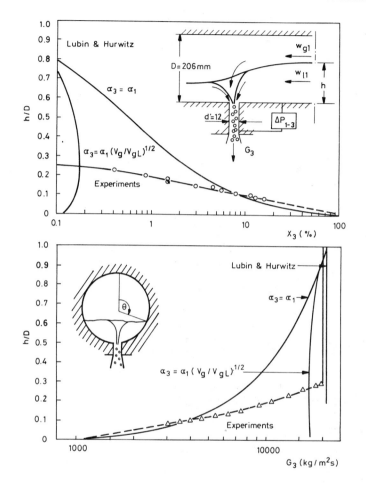

Figure 15. Effect of liquid level on flow split during stratified flow with a bottom take off [19].

h to denote the height of the pipe occupied by the gas phase, here to preserve consistency between this and the work of Reimann and Khan it is used to denote the liquid level.) As the gas enters the side arm it accelerates and the pressure on the interface just below the side arm is lowered, a manifestation of the Bernoulli effect. Once the water level reaches a particular value the pressure force due to this acceleration is able to overcome the force of gravity and the interface is raised locally (Figure 16). Droplets are broken off from the cone formed on the interface, though these do not all reach the side arm. The gas has a considerable component of swirl as it enters the side arm and in addition the distortion of the interface can be shifted from under the side-arm entrance, thus decreasing the possibility of liquid entering the side arm. The conditions for the start of entrainment have been correlated by an equation similar in form to Equation 3

$$\frac{v_{3G}}{\sqrt{gd_3}}\left(\frac{\rho_G}{\rho_L - \rho_G}\right)^{0.5} = 0.315\left(\frac{d_1 - h_B}{d_3}\right)^{2.5}$$

(5)

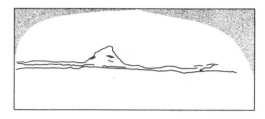

a) Stratified Flow With Horizontal Interface

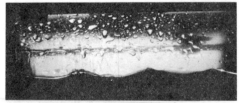

b) Stratified Flow With Wavy Interface

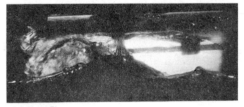

c) Slug Flow

Figure 16. (A) Example of water "lift" during stratified flow with a top take off [10]. (B) Entrainment at different flow regimes.

The flow in the side arm for two-phase flow is correlated in a manner similar to that used by Reimann and Khan; heights and flow rates are considered relative to those for the start of entrainment (Figure 17). There is considerable scatter in the data; however, certain features can be seen. The quality in the side arm, x_3, decreases slightly with decreasing $(d_1 - h)/(d_1 - h_B)$; a sudden decrease occurs when the flow regime in the main tube changes from stratified to slug flow. In the slug flow regime the liquid mainly enters the branch when the slug bridges the cross section of the main tube; the time-averaged liquid flow rate in the side arm is increased considerably. Similarly a strong increase in G_3/G_{3B} occurs in slug flow.

There is very limited data for cases when neither outlet branch is colinear with the inlet. Hong [12] presents some information for a junction where the angle between the outlet branches is 180°. He found that over the most of the range of flow splits the quality in each outlet was the same. However when most flow was going down one side, most of the liquid entered the side arm receiving most of the gas. Fouda and Rhodes [22] studied the division of annular flow in special manifolding devices. These divided the flow into three passages in directions close to that of the

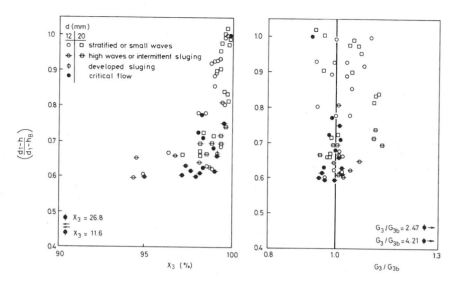

Figure 17. Effect of liquid level on flow split during stratified flow with top take off [10].

entrance pipe. Equal and nonequal divisions were both studied. They found that the liquid film is divided according to the geometry of the manifold, while the entrained droplets are divided according to the mass flow rates of the gas phase in the three side streams.

Analytical Models

In the introduction to two-phase flow division the requirement for five equations to completely specify the problem was broached. Five approaches have been suggested though not stated explicitly. These are essentially different versions for the fifth equation, that describe the physics of the split. Only Saba and Lahey [17] have expressed the problem formally, presenting the complete five equation system. None of the approaches so far presented are universally applicable. Empirical methods have been published by Hong [12], Henry [14], and Zetzmann [6]. These are, of course, limited to the ranges of the parameters of the data with which the workers operated. The approaches of Saba and Lahey [17] and Azzopardi and Whalley [5], and Azzopardi and Baker [23] are based on the physical phenomena of the split. Even these are limited in their applicability as discussed later.

From considerations of mass continuity across the junction, mass balance equations can be written for the gas and liquid phases. For the gas phase

$$w_1 x_1 = w_2 x_2 + w_3 x_3 \tag{6}$$

and for the liquid phase

$$w_1(1 - x_1) = w_2(1 - x_2) + w_3(1 - x_3) \tag{7}$$

Obviously addition of Equations 6 and 7 yields an overall mass balance. The third and fourth equations are momentum balances across the branch and along the main pipe. The momentum balance between point 1 upstream of the junction and point 3 downstream along the side arm yields

$$\Delta p_{13} = \int_0^{L_1} \frac{f_{Li}w_1^2}{2d_1\rho_L A_1^2} \phi_{\ell oi}^2 \, dz_1 + \int_0^{L_1} \bar{\rho}_i g \sin \theta_1 \, dz_1 + (\Delta p_{13})_j$$

$$+ \int_0^{L_3} \frac{f_{L3}w_3^2}{2d_3\rho_L A_3^2} \phi_{\ell o3}^2 \, dz_3 + \int_0^{L_3} \bar{\rho} g \sin \theta_3 \, dz_3 \tag{8}$$

where the first two terms are the frictional and gravitational components of pressure loss in the inlet pipe, $(\Delta p_{13})_j$ is the pressure loss due to the junction, and the last two terms are the components of pressure drop in the side arm. In Equation 8 f_{Li} is a friction factor for all of the two phases flowing as a liquid and $\phi_{\ell oi}^2$ is a two-phase multiplier which can be specified from correlations such as those of Lockhart and Martinelli [24] or Chisholm [25] or from more accurate proprietary correlations such as those of HTFS (Heat Transfer and Fluid Flow Service). $\bar{\rho}_i$ is a two-phase density which can be defined by

$$\bar{\rho}_i = \rho_L(1 - \alpha_i) + \rho_G \alpha_i \tag{9}$$

If the flow can be assumed to be homogeneous, this reduces to

$$\bar{\rho}_i = \frac{\rho_L \rho_G}{x\rho_L + (1 - x)\rho_G} \tag{10}$$

In any calculation of a network system involving junctions the $(\Delta p_{13})_j$ can be taken as belonging to the junction, while all other terms are related to the pipes linking at the junction. The momentum balance between points 1 and 2 yields

$$\Delta p_{12} = \int_0^{L_1} \frac{f_{Li}w_1^2}{2d_1\rho_L A_1^2} \phi_{\ell oi}^2 \, dz_1 + \int_0^{L_1} \bar{\rho}_i g \sin \theta_1 \, dz_1 + (\Delta p_{12})_j$$

$$+ \int_0^{L_2} \frac{f_{L2}w_2^2}{2d_2\rho_L A_2^2} \phi_{\ell o2}^2 \, dz_2 + \int_0^{L_2} \bar{\rho}_2 g \sin \theta_3 \, dz_2 \tag{11}$$

where the terms have a similar meaning to those in Equation 8. The following section discusses the different definitions of $(\Delta p_{13})_j$ and $(\Delta p_{12})_j$ that have been suggested.

Hong [12] presents a graphical correlation method; this relates the fraction of liquid in the side arm to the fraction of gas in the side arm. The correlation is derived from data from a single geometry through a range of gas velocities, liquid flow rates, and liquid viscosities. The suggested method is to calculate the superficial gas velocity and volumetric liquid fraction approaching the junction. Hong provides a graph which relates these two quantities to the equivalent experimental liquid flow rate. The fraction of liquid taken off through the side arm $w_3(1 - x_3)/w_1(1 - x_1)$ is determined in terms of the fraction of gas taken off w_3x_3/w_1x_1 from appropriate graphs for different gas velocities and liquid viscosities. The liquid flow rate is a parameter on these graphs. For values for which there are no graphs interpolation should be used. If the total split, w_3/w_1, is known and the side-arm quality, x_3, is sought, an iterative approach is employed. Hong has used this method to predict the phase distribution in a steam/water distribution system containing two junctions. These differed considerably in geometry from the experimental conditions used by Hong. Though predictions gave of the correct order of magnitude, actual errors in the liquid mass fraction were up to 50%. In addition, though Hong considered a number of geometric configurations, his approach, which mainly predicts preferential liquid extraction, would fail in those circumstances for which the gas is preferentially diverted.

Henry [14] working with a horizontal junction $\theta = \phi = \psi = 90$ observed that the liquid flow rate emerging through the side arm $G_3(1 - x_3)$ was linearly related to the gas flow rate in the side arm G_3x_3. He found that the slope and intercept values describing these lines could be related to the inlet quality and gas flow rate. His correlation can be expressed as

$$G_3(1 - x_3) = 710^{-5}\frac{(1 - x_1)}{x_1}(G_1 x_1 - 10)^3 + 8.110^{-7}(1 - x_1)G_1^3 x_1^2 G_3 x_3 \tag{12}$$

Henry found this to be a reasonable correlation and also capable of describing some of the data of Collier shown in Figure 4. As this is a correlation, it should be treated with care outside the parametric range on which it was based ($d_3/d_1 = 0.2$; $200 < G_1 < 800$ kg/m^2 s; $0.1 < x_1 < 0.4$).

Zetzmann [6] found that the parameters which most strongly affected the phase separation were the flow fraction removed through the side arm, w_3/w_1, the diameter ratio, d_3/d_1, and, for low inlet flows, the angle, ϕ, between the main tube and side arm. He presents correlating equations describing the quality in the outlet branches by:

For $0.0 \leq w_3/w_1 \leq 0.12$:

$$x_1/x_2 = b\left\{\exp\left[-4\left(\frac{w_3}{w_1}\right)^{1.75}\right] - 0.147\left(\frac{w_3}{w_1}\right)\left(1 - \frac{w_3}{w_1}\right)\right\} \tag{13}$$

$$x_1/x_3 = a\left\{1 - \left(\frac{x_2}{x_1}\right)\left(1 - \frac{w_3}{w_1}\right)\right\}\Big/\frac{w_3}{w_1} \tag{14}$$

For $0.12 < w_3/w_1 \leq 0.5$:

$$x_1/x_2 = b\left\{\exp\left[-4\left(\frac{w_3}{w_1}\right)^{1.75}\right] - 0.147\left(\frac{w_3}{w_1}\right)\left(1 - \frac{w_3}{w_1}\right)\right\} \tag{15}$$

$$x_1/x_3 = a\left\{15.64\left(\frac{w_3}{w_1}\right)^{0.75}\exp\left[-2.75\left(\frac{w_3}{w_1}\right)\right] - 2.0\left(\frac{w_3}{w_1}\right)\left(1 - \frac{w_3}{w_1}\right)\right\} \tag{16}$$

For $0.5 < w_3/w_1 \leq 1.0$:

$$x_1/x_2 = \frac{1}{(1 - w_3/w_1)}\left\{1 - \left(\frac{x_3}{x_1}\right)\left(\frac{w_3}{w_1}\right)\right\} \tag{17}$$

$$x_1/x_3 = a\left\{15.64\left(\frac{w_3}{w_1}\right)^{0.75}\exp\left[-2.75\left(\frac{w_3}{w_1}\right)\right] - 2.0\left(\frac{w_3}{w_1}\right)\left(1 - \frac{w_3}{w_1}\right)\right\} \tag{18}$$

where a and b depend on the diameter ratio d_3/d_1 and the angle ϕ is as shown in Table 2. The correlation was derived from data taken over the following ranges and conditions and should be

Table 2
Parameters a and b as Functions of Diameter Ratio

d_3/d_1	ϕ	a	b
50/100	90°	0.8	1.00
24/50	90°	1.35	0.75
24/50	45°	1.4	0.80
50/50	90°	1.05	0.90
24/24	90°	1.05	0.90
24/24	45°	0.9	0.98
50/50	45°	0.9	0.98

used with caution elsewhere

$$\theta = 0$$
$$\phi = 45, 90$$
$$24 \leq d_1 \leq 100 \text{ mm}$$
$$500 \leq G_1 \leq 3,000 \text{ kg/m}^2 \text{ s}$$
$$0.005 \leq x \leq 0.035$$
$$0.1 < w_3/w_1 < 0.8$$

In contrast to the preceding empirical approaches, Saba and Lahey [17] considered the fluid mechanics of two-phase flow. They reasoned that because of the relatively lower inertia of the gas phase it was allowed to preferentially separate at the junction. They therefore carried out a momentum balance on the gas phase, arguing that it could define the dividing streamline. Through this, a reasonable fifth equation could be obtained. The momentum balance gave

$$\alpha \rho_v u_v \frac{du_v}{dz} = -\alpha \frac{dp}{dz} - \alpha F_D - \alpha F_W - g \rho_v \sin \theta_{13} \tag{19}$$

where F_D and F_W are the volumetric interfacial drag and wall drag forces, respectively. Integrating this along the straight sections of pipe yields

$$p_1 - p_{1J} = \int_1^{1J} F_D \, d\zeta = \frac{3}{4} \rho_L \left(\frac{C_D}{D_B} \right) U_{Ri}^2 L_1 \tag{20}$$

$$p_{3J} - p_3 = \int_{3J}^3 F_D \, d\zeta = \frac{3}{4} \rho_L \left(\frac{C_D}{D_B} \right) U_{R3}^2 L_3 \tag{21}$$

where U_{Ri} is the relative velocity in section i. Many of the conditions considered can be classified as Churn-turbulent so that the Hench [26] equation can be used

$$\left(\frac{C_D}{D_B} \right) = 0.549(1 - \alpha)^3$$

Substituting into Equation 19 yields,

$$\Delta_{p13} \equiv \Delta p_{1-1J} + (\Delta p_{13})_J + \Delta p_{3J-3}$$
$$= \frac{K_1}{2} \frac{w_1^2}{\rho_L A_1^2} \phi_{\ell o1}^2 + \bar{\rho}_1 g L_1 \sin \theta_1 + (\Delta p_{13})_J + \frac{K_3}{2} \frac{w_3^2}{\rho_L A_3^2} \phi_{\ell o3}^2 + \bar{\rho}_3 g L_3 \sin \theta_3 \tag{22}$$

where

$$(\Delta p_{13})_J = \frac{3}{4} \rho_L \frac{C_D}{D_B} U_{RJ}^2 L_J + \frac{\rho_{G3}}{2} \left(\frac{w_3^2 x_3^2}{\rho_{G3}^2 A_3^2 \alpha_3^2} - \frac{w_1^2 x_1^2}{\rho_{G1}^2 A_1^2 \alpha_1^2} \right) + \frac{K_{13}}{2} \frac{w_1^2 x_1^2}{\rho_{G1}^2 A_1^2 \alpha_1^2} + g \rho_{G3} L_J \sin \sigma_{13} \tag{23}$$

where

$$U_{Rj} = u_{vj} - u_{Lj} = \frac{j_j(Co - 1) + V_{GJj}}{1 - \alpha_j} \tag{24}$$

and the mean length of the vapor streamline was determined from the data of Saba and Lahey to be

$$L_J = 2.81 D_{43} \left\{ e^{-0.12A(w_3/w_1)^{(1-x_1)^3}} \right\} (1 - x_3)^3 \tag{25}$$

where

$$A = \left(\frac{1 - x_1}{x_1} \right)^{0.15} \left(\frac{\rho_{G1}}{\rho_L} \right)^{0.5} \tag{26}$$

Saba and Lahey found that Equation 22 together with Equations 6–8 and 11 and their pressure drop descriptions (see later) gave a good description of their own data and those of Collier [13]. However they expect that this approach might fail for some flow patterns and geometries at low mass withdrawal ratios. This would be particularly true for stratified and annular flows and for mass withdrawal ratios, w_3/w_1, of less than 0.3 might be true in general.

A generalized phenomenological model for low take off has been suggested by Azzopardi and Baker [23]. For annular flow it will be shown that this reduces to the relationship involving the film flow rate derived from experimental observation by Azzopardi and Whalley [5]. Azzopardi and Baker go on to develop preliminary models which might be useful for bubbly and churn-turbulent flows. The approach employs the observation of McNown [20] that the fluid taken off comes from the segment of the main tube nearest the side arm. As the momentum fluxes of the phases differ and that of the gas is often low, the probability of the liquid will be diverted with the gas depending on the ratio of momentum fluxes. The liquid taken off is then the integral of the product of the probability times the local liquid flow rate.

$$w_3(1 - x_3) = \int_{\psi - \Phi/2}^{\psi + \Phi/2} \int_{R - r(\Phi')}^{R} P_L \rho_L u_L(r') \left[1 - \alpha(r')\right] r' \, dr' \, d\psi' \tag{27}$$

The equivalent equation for the gas can be integrated assuming a uniform gas flow rate across the cross section to yield

$$\frac{w_3 x_3}{w_1 x_1} = \frac{1}{2\pi} (\Phi - \sin \Phi) \tag{28}$$

For annular flow the probability, P_L, can be written separately for the film on the walls and for the drops.

$$P_L = \frac{K \rho_G \bar{u}_G^2}{\rho_L \bar{u}_{LF}^2} \quad \text{for} \quad R \geq r \geq R - \delta \tag{29}$$

and

$$P_L = \frac{K' \rho_G \bar{u}_G^2}{\rho_L \bar{u}_{LD}^2} \quad \text{for} \quad 0 > r > R - \delta \tag{30}$$

Assuming $K \sim K'$ and remembering $\bar{u}_G \gg \bar{u}_{LF}$ and $\bar{u}_G \sim \bar{u}_{LD}$, then

$$\frac{K \rho_G \bar{u}_G^2}{\rho_L \bar{u}_{LF}^2} \gg \frac{K' \rho_G \bar{u}_G^2}{\rho_L \bar{u}_{LD}^2} \tag{31}$$

As the maximum probability is 1.0, P_L can be approximated by

$$\left. \begin{array}{l} P_L(r > R - \delta) \simeq 0 \\ P_L(R > r > R - \delta) \simeq 1.0 \end{array} \right\} \tag{32}$$

Also $\alpha = 0$ for $R \geq r \geq R - \delta$, therefore Equation 27 becomes

$$w_3(1 - x_3) = \int_{\psi - \Phi/2}^{\psi + \Phi/2} \int_{R - \delta}^{R} \rho_L u_L(r') r' \, dr' \, d\psi' \tag{33}$$

Now $(R - \delta)/R \ll 1.0$ so the velocity $u_L(r')$ can be assumed to be equal to $\bar{u}_{LF}(\psi')$. Equation 33 can then be integrated, using the definition of the film flow rate per unit periphery $\Gamma(\psi') = \rho_L \bar{u}_{LF}(\psi') \delta(\psi')$, to yield

$$w_3(1 - x_3) = \int_{\psi - \Phi/2}^{\psi + \Phi/2} \Gamma(\psi') \, d\psi' \tag{34}$$

If $\Gamma(\psi')$ is known, the liquid taken off can be determined by integrating Equation 34 using Equation 28 to define Φ.

For cases where the main tube is vertical or for high-velocity cases in horizontal main tubes Γ is independent of ψ' so that Equation 34 can be integrated, i.e.

$$w_3(1 - x_3) = R\Gamma\Phi \tag{35}$$

The right-hand side of this equation is a definition of the film flow rate when $\Phi = 360°$,

$$w_{LF} = w_1(1 - x_1)(1 - E_1) = 360R\Gamma \tag{36}$$

Combining Equations 35 and 36 defines the liquid taken off in terms of Φ

$$\Phi = \frac{360w_3(1 - x_3)}{w_1(1 - x_1)(1 - E_1)} \tag{37a}$$

which substituted into Equation 28 yields the equation determined by Azzopardi and Whalley from experimental considerations,

$$\frac{w_3 x_3}{w_1 x_1} = \frac{1}{2\pi}\left[\frac{2\pi w_3(1 - x_3)}{w_1(1 - x_1)(1 - E_1)} - \sin\left(\frac{2\pi w_3(1 - x_3)}{w_1(1 - x_1)(1 - E_1)}\right)\right] \tag{1}$$

This constitutes a fifth equation for the system of equations. An empirical correction has been suggested by Azzopardi [7] to allow for the effect of side-arm diameter.

Equation 34 was tested by Azzopardi and Whalley [5] (Figure 12). They used a description of $\Gamma(\psi')$ determined experimentally by Butterworth and Pulling [27] and Φ defined by a linear equivalent to Equation 28.

$$\Phi = 35 + 450\frac{w_3 x_3}{w_1 x_1} \tag{37b}$$

As seen in Figure 12, this approach can well describe experimental data.

The suitability of Equation 1 for vertical flow can be seen in Figure 18 where it can be seen reasonably to correlate data from a number of inlet conditions.

The general approach has been applied by Azzopardi and Baker [23] to bubbly flows (this can include churn flows). For the liquid phase, the liquid mass rate going into the side arm is given by

$$w_3(1 - x_3) = \int_{\psi - \Phi/2}^{\psi + \Phi/2} \int_{r(\Phi')}^{R} P_L \rho_L u_L(r', \psi')[1 - \alpha(r', \psi')]r' \, dr' \, d\psi' \tag{38}$$

and for the gas phase

$$w_3 x_3 = \int_{\psi - \Phi/2}^{\psi + \Phi/2} \int_{R(\psi')}^{R} \rho_G u_G(r', \psi')\alpha(r',\psi')r' \, dr' \, d\psi' \tag{39}$$

For cylindrical symmetry, such as in vertical flows, u_G, u_L, and α are functions of r' only. Azzopardi and Baker reasoned that the probabilities could be expressed by

$$P_L = \frac{A\rho_G u_G^2(r')}{\rho_L u_L^2(r')} \tag{40}$$

In Equation 40 $\rho_G u_G^2(r')$ is the local momentum flux of the bubbles. From the bubbly flow measurements of Serizawa [28], Azzopardi and Baker found $u_G(r') \simeq 2\bar{u}_L$. Thus Equation 40 becomes

$$P_L = \frac{4A\rho_G \bar{u}_L^2}{\rho_L u_L^2(r')} \tag{41}$$

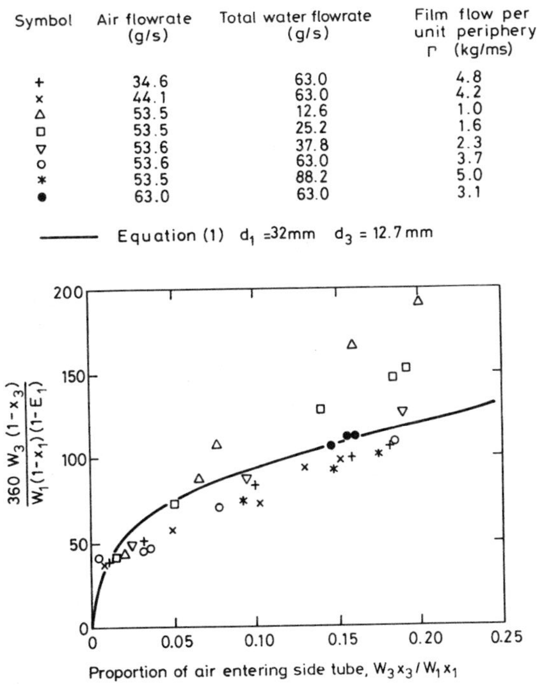

Symbol
Air flowrate (g/s)
Total water flowrate (g/s)
Film flow per unit periphery Γ (kg/ms)
+ 34.6 63.0 4.8
× 44.1 63.0 4.2
△ 53.5 12.6 1.0
□ 53.5 25.2 1.6
▽ 53.6 37.8 2.3
○ 53.6 63.0 3.7
* 53.5 88.2 5.0
● 63.0 63.0 3.1
Equation (1) d1 =32mm d3 = 12.7 mm
360 W3 (1-x3) / W1(1-x1)(1-E1)
200
150
100
50
0
0.05
0.10
0.15
0.20
0.25
Proportion of air entering side tube, W3x3/W1x1

Figure 18. Comparison of prediction of Equation 1 with data [5].

Substituting into Equation 39 and describing $u_L(r')$ and $\alpha(r')$ by power laws yields

$$w_3(1 - x_3) = \frac{4n^2 A\rho_G \bar{u}_L}{m^2(n+1)(2n+1)} \int_{\psi-\Phi/2}^{\psi+\Phi/2} \int_{r(\psi')}^{R} \left[\frac{r'}{(1 - r'/R)^{1/n}}\right] \times [2m^2 - (m+1)(2m+1)]\bar{\alpha} \times \left[1 - \frac{r'}{R}\right]^{1/n} dr'\, d\psi' \tag{42}$$

which can be integrated with respect to r′

$$\begin{aligned} w_3(1 - x_3) = {} & \frac{8n^3 A\rho_G \bar{u}_L}{R^{1/n}(n+1)(2n+1)} \int_{\psi-\Phi/2}^{\psi+\Phi/2} \left[\frac{R(R - r(\psi'))^{(n-1)/n}}{n-1} - \frac{(R - r(\psi'))^{(2n-1)/n}}{2n-1}\right] d\psi' \\ & - \frac{4n^3 A\rho_G \bar{u}_L \bar{\alpha}(m+1)(2m+1)}{R^{1/n} m(n+1)(2n+1)} \int_{\psi-\Phi/2}^{\psi+\Phi/2} \left[\frac{R(R - r(\psi'))^{(mn+n-m)/mn}}{(mn+n-m)} \right. \\ & \left. - \frac{(R - r(\psi'))^{(2mn+n-m)/mn}}{(2mn+n-m)}\right] d\psi' \end{aligned} \tag{43}$$

As $r(\psi') = R\cos(\Phi/2)/\cos(\psi')$, Equation 43 must be integrated numerically. Azzopardi and Baker assumed $\bar{\alpha} = 0$, $n = 7$. In addition they assumed $u_G(r)$ to be a constant, thence Equation 39 can be nondimensionalized with respect w_1, x_1 to yield

$$\frac{w_3 x_3}{w_1 x_1} = \frac{1}{2\pi}(\Phi - \sin\Phi) \tag{28}$$

Using the preceding simplications these equations have been found to describe the data of Hewitt and Shires [8] with $A = 13.3$ (see Figure 2). This method, however, does not apply for $w_3 x_3 / w_1 x_1 > 0.8$.

Junction Pressure Drops

There is much less data on pressure drops across the junction than on flow splits. Among these data some cannot be abstracted as it is presented in terms of derived variables. The physical significance of these pressure drops can best be seen in the pressure profiles measured by Saba and Lahey [17] and reproduced in Figure 19. This data is represented by Equations 8 and 11, the linear portions being the terms corresponding to pipes. The pressure changes across the actual junction can be fairly complicated with over and under shoots. It is therefore most convenient to determine them as the values between the lines extrapolated from the pressure gradients far from the junction. The presence of the under and over shoot make it important that the pressure drops be determined in this way, as those obtained from point values taken from tappings close to the junction might include part of the under/over shoot and thus not give a true representation of the pressure drop.

The lack of available data is complicated by the variety of methods used for correlation. In order to clarify the picture the various equations are provided here in full and their inter-relation clearly shown,

$$(\Delta p_{1i})_J = \frac{\rho u_1^2}{2} - \frac{\rho u_i^2}{2} + K_A \frac{\rho u_1^2}{2} \tag{44}$$

$$(\Delta p_{1i})_J = \frac{\rho u_1^2}{2} - \frac{\rho u_i^2}{2} + K_B \frac{\rho u_i^2}{2} \tag{45}$$

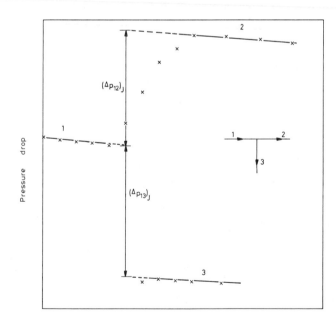

Figure 19. Pressure profiles about a dividing junction.

$$(\Delta p_{1i})_J = K_C \frac{\rho u_1^2}{2} \tag{46}$$

$$(\Delta p_{1i})_J = K_D \frac{\rho u_1^2}{2} \tag{47}$$

$$(\Delta p_{1i})_J = K_E(\rho u_1^2 - \rho u_i^2) \tag{48}$$

where ρ and u are the two-phase density and velocity. Using the definition $q = u_i/u_1$, the various loss coefficients can be inter-related.

$$K_A = q^2 K_B = K_C - 1 + q^2 = (K_D + 1)q^2 - 1 = (K_E - 1)(1 - q^2) \tag{49}$$

In Equations 44 and 45 the pressure drop is taken as the sum of a reversible and an irreversible pressure drop. Equations 46 and 47 use forms of discharge coefficients. Equation 48 considers the pressure drop as a modified form of momentum change.

For $(\Delta p_{13})_J$ three approaches have been presented in a usable manner and present a definition of loss coefficient based on Equation 44 where the velocity is obtained from a homogeneous density and $K_A = K_{1-3}$ is taken from single-phase correlations such as those of Gardel [3]. This is known as the homogeneous model (HM). Chisholm [33] has suggested a different approach, describing the irreversible term in Equation 44 by the equivalent single-phase pressure drop times a two-phase multiplier,

$$(\Delta p_{13})_{Jirr} = K_{1-3} \frac{G_1^2}{2\rho_L} \left[(1 - x_1)^2 \left(1 - \frac{C_{1-3}}{X_{tt}} + \frac{1}{X_{tt}^2} \right) \right] \tag{50}$$

where K_{1-3} is taken from single-phase data and X_{tt}, the Lockhart-Martinelli parameter, is defined as

$$\frac{1}{X_{tt}} = \left(\frac{x_1}{1 - x_1} \right) \left(\frac{\rho_L}{\rho_G} \right)^{0.5} \tag{51}$$

and

$$C_{1-3} = \left[1 + (C_3 - 1) \left(\frac{\rho_L - \rho_G}{\rho_L} \right)^{0.5} \right] \left[\left(\frac{\rho_L}{\rho_G} \right)^{0.5} + \left(\frac{\rho_G}{\rho_L} \right)^{0.5} \right] \tag{52}$$

where $C_3 = 1.0$ for homogeneous flow and 1.75 for flow with slip between the phases. Saba and Lahey [17], who use this approach, suggest

$$K_{1-3} = \left[1.18 + \left(\frac{w_3}{w_1} \right)^2 - 0.8 \left(\frac{w_3}{w_1} \right) \right] \left(\frac{1_1}{A_3} \right) \tag{53}$$

For the reversible part Saba and Lahey recommend the use of the "energy" density. An extension of the preceding models has been presented by Reimann and Seeger [16]. They state briefly that the assumption is made of a reversible pressure drop between the inlet pipe and the vena contracta just in the side arm. Beyond the vena contracta can be considered as a sudden expansion. A generalized model with slip can be defined. Reimann and Seeger have only presented the homogeneous version of their model. In this the irreversible component of pressure drops becomes,

$$(\Delta p_{13})_{Jirr} = \frac{\rho_{h3}}{\rho_{h1}} K_{1-3} \frac{G_1^2}{2\rho_{h1}} \tag{54}$$

where $K_{1-3} = 1.0117 - 0.7478\left(\dfrac{G_3}{G_1}\right) + 1.175\left(\dfrac{G_3}{G_1}\right)^2$ (55)

Reimann and Seeger suggest K_{1-3} is best defined in terms of $f(\dot{v}_3/\dot{v}_1)$, where $\dot{v}_3$ and $\dot{v}_1$ are volumetric flow rates. Figure 20, taken from Reimann and Seeger, shows that Equations 54 and 55 give a better prediction of data than the homogeneous model, particularly at take off fractions below 0.3.

Data in a less usable form has been presented by Tsuyama and Taga [18] in the form of K_A and K_B. Because they used experimental values of void fraction to define the two-phase density and velocity, it is difficult to compare their data with those of other workers or to derive a correlation from this data.

Fouda and Rhodes [9] present definitions of K_D. However their data base is limited so it is not certain how widely applicable are their correlations. Collier [13] suggests the use of Equation 44 employing separated flow definitions of the densities and velocities. Values of $K_{14} = K_{13}$ are given as 1.0 for $A_3/A_1 = 1.0$ increasing to 1.5 as A_3/A_1 is reduced below 0.2. Katsaounis et al [11] suggest an approach similar to that of Reimann and Seeger [16]. They also indicate that the approaches of Fouda and Rhodes [9] and Chisholm [32] can represent their data.

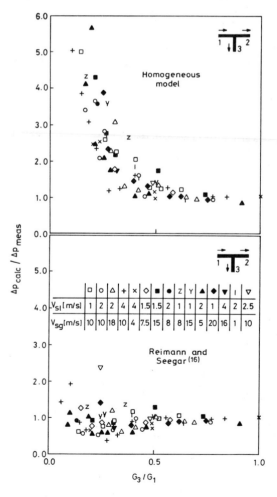

Figure 20. Accuracy of correlations in prediction of $(\Delta p_{13})_j$[16].

For $(\Delta p_{12})_J$, Tsuyama and Taga [18] have presented data in the form of K_A and K_B. As they use experimentally derived void fractions to determine the two-phase density and velocity, the use of their data is limited. It does serve, however, to show that the two-phase pressure drop would be reasonably represented by the single-phase value times a two-phase multiplier (Figure 21), the two-phase values appearing to be multiples of the single-phase data. Both the remaining sources of $(\Delta p_{12})_J$ data are correlated by means of the loss coefficient defined in Equation 48. Fouda and Rhodes [9] present an equation with slip

$$(\Delta p_{12})_J = \frac{K_{12S}}{A_1^2}\left(\frac{w_1^2 x_1^2}{\alpha_1 \rho_G} + \frac{w_1^2(1-x_1)^2}{\alpha_1 \rho_L} - \frac{w_2^2 x_2^2}{\alpha_2 \rho_G} - \frac{w_2^2(1-x_2)^2}{\alpha_2 \rho_L}\right) \tag{56}$$

and a homogeneous equation

$$(\Delta p_{12})_J = K_{12H}\left[\left(\frac{G_1^2}{\rho_{H1}}\right) - \left(\frac{G_2^2}{\rho_{H2}}\right)\right] \tag{57}$$

They suggest values of 0.53, 0.35 for K_{12S}, K_{12H}. Better agreement with the data can be obtained by use of

$$K_{12S} = 4.55643 x^{0.410645} \tag{58}$$

$$K_{12H} = 2.04814 x^{0.564571} \tag{59}$$

Saba and Lahey [17] suggest

$$K_{12H} = 0.11 + \frac{5.0}{Re_1^0.17} \tag{60}$$

where $Re_1 = \frac{w_1 d_1}{A_1 \mu_L}$ \hfill (61)

and μ_L is the liquid viscosity. In this case Saba and Lahey recommend the momentum density be used in Equation 57.

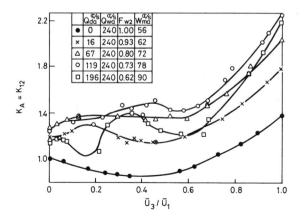

Figure 21. Effect of two-phase flow on main tube loss coefficients.

Split Modifiers

The realization that the split was almost always imperfect has led to suggestions for geometric modifications to lessen the imperfection or to increase it in order to separate the phases. Fouda and Rhodes [9] experimented with a number of baffles at the junction ($\frac{1}{4}, \frac{1}{2}, \frac{3}{4}d_1$). These were intended to homogenize the flow as their earlier studies had shown the liquid in the film and the drops in annular flow could divide in entirely different proportions. Only the $\frac{3}{4}d_1$ baffle had a significant effect (Figure 22) bringing the phase split ratio, x_3/x_1, closer to 1.0; the effect of the smaller baffles is felt downstream of the junction. An orifice plate placed upstream of the junction produced a noticeable effect. It is not known how these devices would affect other flow patterns. Butterworth [29] has studied junctions in which the side arm extends into the main tube, as shown in Figure 23A and B. In the first case the protrusion acts as a scoop and gathers liquid into the side arm (Figure 23C). When the protrusion is on the leading edge of the side arm, it acts as a break water and liquid is diverted past the side arm; air is then preferentially extracted. This behavior is in keeping with the explanation for phase separation in annular flow (studied by Butterworth) given previously. However, as if to illustrate the complexity of the problem, Butterworth found that when he altered his inlet conditions both versions of the protrusion encouraged gas to emerge from the side arm. This indicates that scoop-type devices should be used with caution.

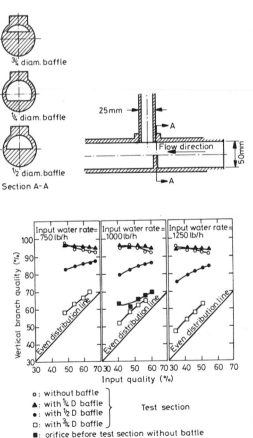

o: without baffle
▲: with ¼ D baffle
•: with ½ D baffle   Test section
□: with ¾ D baffle
■: orifice before test section without baffle

Figure 22. Effect of baffles and homogenizing orifice on flow split [9].

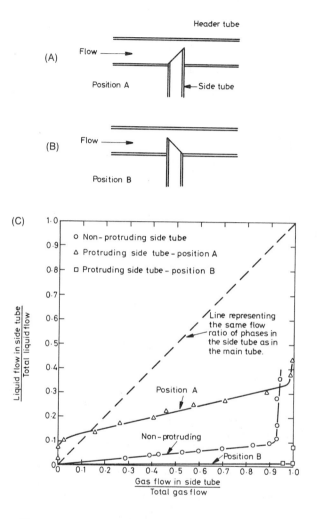

Figure 23. Effect of side-arm protrusions on flow split [29].

Manifolds

Manifolds, junctions close together on a main pipe, have been studied by Collier [13] and Coney [30]. Miller [31] notes that for single-phase flow interaction between junctions can be expected if the interjunction distance is less than three main tube diameters. No equivalent information is available for two-phase flow.

Collier [13] describes part of a wider unpublished study undertaken by HTFS at Harwell. A horizontal system of form tubes linked by inlet and outlet headers was used (see Figure 24). Void fractions (measured using quick closing valves) and pressure drops were used to determine the flow rates and qualities in each tube. The results obtained were similar to those for single junctions already described; the gas was preferentially diverted. It follows that there was the accumulation of liquid

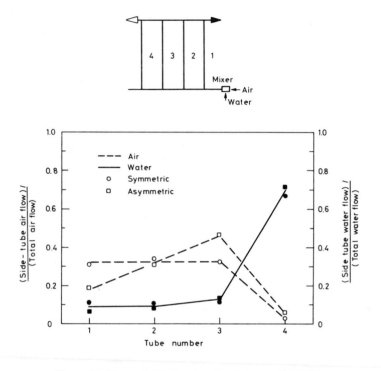

Figure 24. Phase distribution in a four-tube manifold [13].

in the fourth tube (Figure 24). Collier comments that the manifold results were consistent with the measurements taken on equivalent single junctions. The second study of manifolds [30] was on a vertical manifold (or main tube) with horizontal side arms each linked to a cyclone which separated the phases. The emerging phase flow rates were then measured. These results show a good deal of similarity to those of Collier at equivalent qualities (Figure 25). At lower qualities there was less accumulation of liquid at the fourth tube. Coney found that for a constant inlet gas flow rate, $G_1 x_1$, the fractions were insensitive to the inlet water flow rate $G_1(1 - x_1)$ above a minmum value of $350 \text{ kg/m}^2 \text{ s}$. He also observed that a frothy plug of liquid was present in the main tube. This oscillated between tubes at low gas rates. Tubes adjacent to this plug received the most water. At higher gas flow rates the plug is pushed to the end of the manifold, and it is the end tube that receives the most water. The intermittent nature of the flow, represented by the frothy plug, is probably due to the way the two-phase flow is introduced to the main tube, through four combining junctions. The following discussion on combining junctions considers the effect of combining junctions on flow pattern.

COMBINING JUNCTIONS

Pressure Drops

In the case of combining junctions, the problem is usually much more specified. Two streams of known flow rate and qualities combine to give a well-defined third stream. For calculations in network systems pressure drop $(\Delta p_{21})_j$, $(\Delta p_{31})_j$ are required. There is less published information on these than for the equivalent pressure drops for dividing flow. Equations similar to Equations 44–48 have been used. For the pressure drop along the main tube, Collier [13] suggests values of

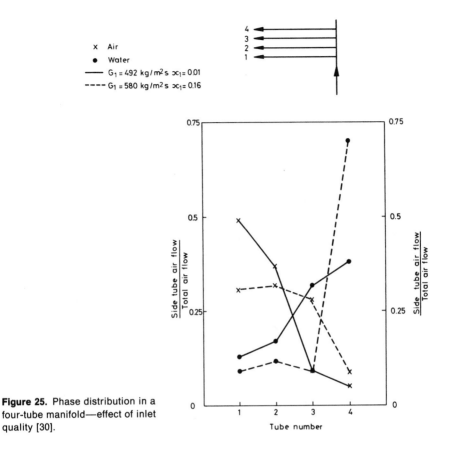

Figure 25. Phase distribution in a
four-tube manifold—effect of inlet
quality [30].

K'_E (for an equation similar to Equation 48) increasing from 1 to 2 as the intake from the side arm increases. He notes that stratified flow in the main tube can increase K'_E to as high as 5 for low A_3/A_1 values. For the side-arm pressure drop, Collier suggests a homogeneous model with values of K_{31} ($= K_A$) as suggested by a single-phase correlations (for example, Gardel [3]). Kubo and Ueda [33] also present data on loss coefficients for combining junctions.

Flow Patterns and Mixing

Flow patterns can be influenced by the way the phases are combined. If gas and liquid are combined at a junction then slug flow will occur at conditions where other flow patterns would normally be present. The same would probably apply when higher and lower quality two-phase flows are similarly combined at a junction. Consideration should therefore be given to the implications of such combination.

It is also known that long entrance or development lengths can be necessary in two-phase flow. Brown [34] reports that some cases of annular flow only achieved quasi-equilibrium after 600 diameters. Similar considerations apply to combining flows in junctions and the implications of this should be thought about.

Combining Y Junctions in Drainage Systems

In process plants, the discharge of liquid under gravity through pipework is common often simply because it is desired to keep the vessel, through which the liquid flows, drained. The layout and sizing of pipework joining vessels can lead to problems if proper design is not employed. Simpson [35] has discussed these matters and indicated how this design should be approached so as to avoid unfavorable flow regimes and minimize or eliminate problems such as pressure surging and cavitation. In some vessels it is appropriate to use more than one bottom exit, particularly in vessels with large horizontal dimensions where these multiple exits are used to ensure uniform drainage. Often two exits are connected to a common vertical limb by a Y junction. Here the problems relating to such junctions are considered, particularly those of vapor/gas entrainment and hence two-phase flow. In particular, when the fluids considered are vapor and liquid near saturation phase, change can occur; this can take the form of the explosive collapse of bubbles, causing fluctuations of pressure.

Flow behavior in such junctions has been studied for cases where there is phase change [36] and where phase change is negligible [37]. Observations, measurements and analyses are discussed together with the applicability and implications for design.

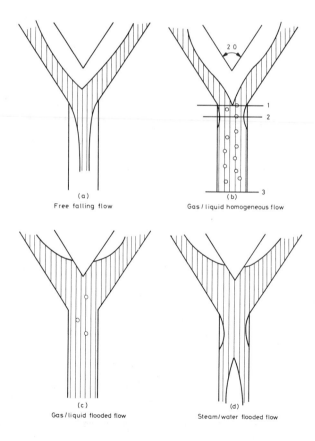

Figure 26. Flow regimes in a Y junction with gravity drainage flows: (A) free-falling flow; (B) gas/liquid homogeneous flow; (C) gas/liquid flooded flow; (D) steam/water flooded flow.

When its flow rate is low the liquid flows freely down the center of the vertical pipe (Figure 26A) through a stationary or nearly stationary gas phase. A small amount of air is entrained. Beyond a critical flow rate, the two liquid streams entering the junction mix so vigorously that there is not an easy path for the gas to flow from below to above the junctions. Homogeneous two-phase flow forms in the vertical pipe (Figure 26B) flowing downwards occupying the full pipe cross section. Under these conditions much more gas is entrained than in the previous regime. As the liquid flow rate is increased further (Figure 27) less and less gas is entrained until a point, termed flooding, is reached when liquid fills the entire junction and the lower part of the sloping pipes (Figure 26C). When this has occurred, the gas entrainment is much diminished.

When the gas/liquid comprises a liquid and its vapour close to saturation, the intermediate flow regime with higher entrainment is not present. In this case the bubbles of vapour are rapidly condensed. Either the free falling or flooded regimes can occur.

Obviously a designer would require to be able to determine the boundary between the different regimes. For the entraining regime, a prediction of the quality of entrained gas is sought. A momentum balance between points 1 and 3 (Figure 26B) can be rearranged and simplified by use of a mass balance and the assumption of $\rho_L \gg \rho_G$ to

$$\frac{A_1}{A_3} = \frac{\cos\theta}{4} \frac{1 + \left[1 + \dfrac{4}{\cos^2\theta}\dfrac{gL}{V_{1L}^2}\left(1 + \dfrac{fL}{R}\right)\right]^{1/2}}{1 + \dfrac{fL}{R}} \tag{62}$$

where A_1 and A_3 are the fractional areas occupied by the liquid and f is a friction factor. Kubie and Gardner [37] recommend a value of 0.008 for f. The liquid velocity before the branch V_{1L} can be related to the liquid mass flow

$$\frac{V_{1L}}{\sqrt{gR\cos\theta}} = 5.9\left(\frac{w_{L1}/\rho_L}{\sqrt{gR^5\cos\theta}}\right)^{0.22} \tag{63}$$

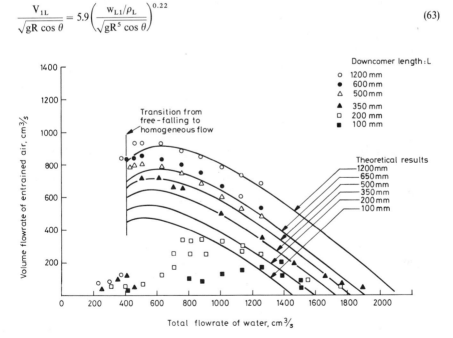

Figure 27. Entrainment rate in combining Y junction with gravity drainage flows [37].

which is derived from a balance between frictional and gravitation forces using the approximation

$$P_1 = 0.7A_1^{0.44} \tag{64}$$

where P_1 is the wetted perimeter. In the vertical pipe the two-phase flow is assumed to be homogeneous (i.e., $V_{3L} = V_{3G}$. Zuber and Finlay [38] have produced a description for two-phase bubble flow. For the conditions studied the equation is

$$w_G = \rho_G\left[0.96\left(\frac{w_G}{\rho_G} + \frac{w_L}{\rho_L}\right) - 1.53\pi R^2\left(\frac{\sigma(\rho_L - \rho_G)g}{\rho_L^2}\right)^{1/4}\right](1 - A_3) \tag{65}$$

which for homogeneous flow can be rearranged to yield

$$w_G = 1.53\frac{\rho_G\pi R^2(1 - A_3)}{0.04}\left(\frac{\sigma(\rho_L - \rho_G)g}{\rho_L^2}\right)^{1/4} \tag{66}$$

From the definition of V_{L1}, A_1 is

$$A_1 = \frac{w_{L1}}{\rho_L V_{L1}\pi R^2} \tag{67}$$

The entrained gas flow rate can therefore be determined from Equation 66 using Equations 62, 63, and 67 to determine A_3.

Experimental and theoretical considerations have shown that a suction is created at the top of the vertical pipe. Knowledge of this is essential to predict the transition between the free falling and homogeneous flow regimes. In the homogeneous flow regime there is a vena contracta just into the vertical pipe. From mass, momentum, and energy balances between points 1 and 2 (Figure 26B) and the assumption of $\rho_L \gg \rho_G$ it is possible to obtain an implicit expression for the suction pressure difference,

$$\frac{(P_1 - P_2)}{\rho_L V_{L1}^2} = 2A_1\left(\frac{1}{(1 + \gamma)^{1/2}}\left[\frac{2}{Fr} + 1 + 2\left(\frac{P_1 - P_2}{\rho_L V_{L1}^2}\right)\right]^{1/2} - \cos\theta\right.$$

$$\left. - \frac{1}{2Fr}\left\{1 + \frac{1}{(1 + \gamma)^{1/2}\left[\frac{2}{Fr} + 1 + 2\left(\frac{P_1 - P_2}{\rho_L V_{L1}^2}\right)\right]^{1/2}}\right\}\right) \tag{68}$$

where $Fr = V_{L2}^2/gL$ and γ can be taken as a loss coefficient. Experimental data has shown that γ can be represented by the values proposed by ESDU [39] for miter bends. This gave good agreement with experimentally derived pressure differences.

The transition to homogeneous flow is taken to occur when the liquid in the vertical pipe attaches to the wall instead of falling freely. This might be described by the point of equality of the pressure force and the momentum force pushing the liquid to the center

$$\rho_L V_{L1}^2 A_1\pi R^2 \sin\theta = 2(P_1 - P_2)\frac{4R^2}{\sin\theta} \tag{69}$$

The constant 2 on the right-hand side was determined experimentally. This equation can be combined with Equation 68, neglecting Fr and letting $\gamma = 0.0$ to yield the critical fractional area A_{C1}. Substituting into Equation 63 gives

$$w_C = 7.5\rho_L\left(\frac{R^5g\cos\theta}{f_1}\right)^{1/2}\left(\frac{\pi}{16}\sin^2\theta + \frac{\cos\theta}{2} - \frac{1}{\pi}\right)^{1.28} \tag{70}$$

Flooding of the junction follows the decrease entrainment with increasing liquid flow rate (Figure 27). As the entrainment rate falls to zero, a condition is reached when any more liquid cannot be accommodated and the junction floods. However, in practice there is a small residual entrainment level probably due to entrainment just above the junction. This results in a critical value of $A_3 = 0.92$. Substitution into Equation 62 and using Equation 63 yields a flooding flow rate. For saturated or nearly saturated flows a different approach is employed. From mass and momentum balances, after some rearrangement it is possible to obtain

$$\frac{h}{R} = \frac{4\cos\theta}{C_D}\left\{\frac{w_{L1}}{\rho_L\pi\sqrt{gR^5}}\right\}^2 - 2\cos\theta\frac{V_{L1}}{\sqrt{gR}}\left\{\frac{w_{L1}}{\rho_L\pi\sqrt{gR^5}}\right\} + \frac{\ell}{R}\cos\theta\left[2f\left\{\frac{w_{L1}}{\rho_L\pi\sqrt{gR^5}}\right\} - 1\right] \quad (71)$$

where   h = the subcooling pressure expressed as a height of liquid

ℓ = the distance that the entrance limbs are full of liquid

C_D = a discharge coefficient which collects together the effects of the liquid being forced to turn the corner

Values of C_D were found in the range 0.67 to 0.61, decreasing as θ increased. For saturated flows, the pressure at 1 is equal to the saturation pressure. If there are no obstructions at the junction and no additional head is required to discharge the liquid, steam spaces will be formed just below the junction, the pressure there will also be the saturation pressure. Thus h = 0. Equation 71 then can be solved together with Equation 63 to give the penetration of liquid into the entry pipes of the junction. The case of $\ell = 0$ is the start of flooding. For subcooled flow there is an increase in the apparent discharge capacity of the junction. Because subcooled liquid can be depressurized down to its saturation pressure, when this occurs below the junction it helps accelerate liquid through it. In this case h is not zero but an extra variable to be specified.

The preceding Equations have been tested Kubie and Gardner [37] and Kubie and Oates [36] against experimental data taken on 26-mm-diameter pipes. All pipes were of the same diameter. The prediction of the start of homogeneous gas/liquid flows has been found to be quite reasonably predicted for longer vertical tubes (Figure 27). The entrainment rate is also well predicted for these conditions. However Kubie et al. point out that the predictions are sensitive to the constant, set at 0.96, in Equation 65. They recommend that extrapolation be carried out with caution. The transition to flooding in gas-liquid flows (Equation 70) also gave good agreement with data. In the case of flows at saturation pressure, good agreement was found for the liquid penetration, ℓ, and for the start of flooding (Figure 28). Subcooled flows were also well predicted; in this case, however, it is much more difficult to determine the start of flooding.

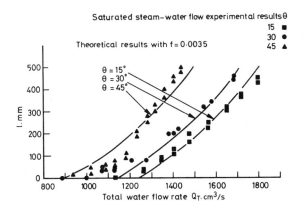

Figure 28. Effect of liquid flow rate on liquid penetration into the entrance pipes of a combining Y junction during flooded saturated steam/water flows [36].

NOTATION

A	parameter defined by Equation 26; also area	P_1	wetted perimeter
		p	pressure
d	diameter	q	velocity ratio
E_1	fraction of liquid as drops	Re	Reynolds number
Fr	Froude number	r	radius
f	friction factor	U_{Ri}	relative velocity
G	mass flux	u	velocity
g	acceleration due to gravity	V	velocity
h	height	w	mass flow
K	flow correction factor	X_{tt}	Lockhart-Martinelli parameter
L_J	mean length of vapor streamline	x	quality
l	length		

Greek Symbols

α	void fraction	θ	angle
Γ	flow rate per unit periphery	μ	viscosity
γ	loss coefficient	ρ	density
δ	film thickness	ϕ	angle

REFERENCES

1. Fryar, J. R., "Options Available for Pipeline and Compressor-Station Drip Design," *Oil Gas J.*, Vol. 78 (1980), pp. 154–161.
2. Oranje, L., "Handling Two-Phase Gas Condensate Flow in Offshore Pipeline Systems," *Oil Gas J.*, Vol. 81 (1983), pp. 128–138.
3. Gardel, A., "Les Pertes de Charge dans les Écoulements an Travers de Branchments en Te," *Bulleting Technique de la Suisse Romande*, Vol. 83 (1957), pp. 123–130 and pp. 143–148.
4. Honan, T. J., and Lahey, R. T., "The Measurement of Phase Separation in Wyes and Tees," *Nuclear Eng. and Design*, Vol. 64 (1981), pp. 93–102.
5. Azzopardi, B. J., and Whalley, P. B., "The Effect of Flow Pattern on Two Phase Flow in a T Junction," *Int. J. Multiphase Flow*, Vol. 8 (1982), pp. 491–507.
6. Zetzmann, K., "Phasen seperation und Druckelufall in Zweiphasig Durchstromen Vertikalen Rohrabzweigungen," Dr. Ing. Thesis, University of Hanover F.R.G., 1982.
7. Azzopardi, B. J., "The Effect of the Side Arm Diameter on the Two-Phase Flow Split at a T Junction," *Int. J. Multiphase Flow*, Vol. 10, pp. 509–512.
8. Hewitt, G. F., and Shires, G., unpublished information.
9. Fouda, A. E., and Rhodes, E., "The Phase Annular Flow Stream Division in a Simple Tee," *Trans. Inst. Chem. Engrs.*, Vol. 52 (1974), pp. 354–360.
10. Reimann, J., and Smoglie, C., "Flow Through a Small Pipe at the Top of a Large Pipe with Stratified Flow," European Two Phase Flow Group Meeting, Zurich, Switzerland.
11. Katsaounis, A., Furst, H. D., and Hofmann, K., "Pressure Drop Measurements of Liquid and Gas-Liquid Flow in a Tee with a Divergent Branch," European Two Phase Flow Group Meeting, Paris, 1982.
12. Hong, K. C., "Two-Phase Flow Splitting at a Pipe Tee," *J. Petroleum Technology* (1978), pp. 270–296.
13. Collier, J. G., "Single-Phase and Two-Phase Flow Behaviour in Primary Circuit Components," Proceedings of NATO Advanced Study Institute on Two Phase Flow and Heat Transfer, Istanbul, Turkey, 1976.
14. Henry, J. A. R., "Dividing Annular Flow in a Horizontal Tee," *Int. J. Multiphase Flow*, Vol. 7 (1981), pp. 343–355.

15. Oranje, L., "Condensate Behaviour in Gas Pipelines is Predictable," *Oil Gas J.*, Vol. 71 (1973), pp. 39–44.
16. Reimann, J., and Seeger, W., "Two-Phase Pressure Drop in a Dividing T Junction," Proceedings of La Méchnique des Systemes Gaz-Liquide, Grenoble, France, Sept. 1983.
17. Saba, N., and Lahey, R. T., "Phase Separation Phenomena in Branching Conduits". NUREG/CR2590, 1982. See also "The Analysis of Phase Separation Phenomena in Branched Conduits," *Int. J. Multiphase Flow*, Vol. 10 (1984), pp. 1–20.
18. Tsuyama, M., and Taga, M., "On the Flow of the Air-Water Mixture in the Branch Pipe—1. Experiment on the Horizontal Branch which is equal to the Main One in Diameter," *Bull. JSME*, Vol. 2 (1959), pp. 151–156.
19. Reimann, J., and Khan, M., "Flow Through a Small Break at the Bottom of a Large Pipe with Stratified Flow," 2nd Int. Topical Meeting on Nuclear Reactor Thermohydraulics, Santa Barbara, California, 1983.
20. McNown, J. S., "Mechanics of Manifold Flow," *ASCE Trans*, Vol. 119 (1954), pp. 1103–1142.
21. Lubin, B. and Hurwitz, M., "Vapour Pull Through at a Tank Drain with and without Dielectrophoretic Buffeting," Proc. Conf. Long Term Cryopropellant Storage in Space, NASA Marshall Space Center, Huntsville, Ala., 1966, p. 173.
22. Fouda, A. E., and Rhodes, E., "Two Phase Annular Flow Stream Division," *Trans. Inst. Chem. Engrs.*, Vol. 50 (1972), pp. 353–363.
23. Azzopardi, B. J., and Baker, S. R., "Two Phase Flow in a T Junction: The Effect of Flow Pattern in Vertical Upflow," UKAEA Report AERE-R 10174, 1981.
24. Lockhart, R. W., and Martinelli, R. C., "Proposed Correlation of Data for Isothermal Two-Phase Two-Component Flow in Pipes," *Chem. Eng. Pr.*, Vol. 45 (1949), pp. 39–48.
25. Chisholm, D., "A Theoretical Basis for the Lockhart-Martinelli Correlation for Two-Phase Flow," *Int. J. Heat Mass Transfer*, Vol. 10 (1967), pp. 1767–1778.
26. Hench, J. E., and Johnson, J. P., "Two-Dimensional Diffuser Performance with Subsonic Two-Phase Air/Water Flow," APED-5477, 1968.
27. Butterworth, D., and Pulling, D. J., "Film Flow and Film Thickness Measurements for Horizontal Annular Air-Water Flow," UKAEA Report AERER 7576, 1973.
28. Serizawa, A., "Fluid-Dynamic Characteristics of Two-Phase Flow," Ph.D Thesis, Kyoto University, 1974.
29. Butterworth, D., "Unresolved Problems in Heat Exchanger Design," Presented at Interflow 80—The Fluid Handling Conference, Harrogate, U.K., 1980.
30. Coney, M. W. E., "Two-Phase Flow Distribution in a Manifold System," European Two-Phase Flow Group Meeting, Glasgow, 1980.
31. Miller, D. S., "Internal Flow, A Guide to Losses in Pipe and Duet Systems," BHRA Cranfield, Bedford, U.K., 1971.
32. Chisholm, D., "Pressure Losses in Bends and Tees During Steam/Water Flow," NEL Report No. 318, 1967.
33. Kubo, T., and Ueda, T., "On the Characteristics of Confluent Flow of Gas Liquid Mixers in Headers," *Bull. JSME*, Vol. 16 (1973), pp. 1376–1384.
34. Brown, D. J., "Disequilibrium Annular Flow," D. Phil. Thesis, University of Oxford, 1978.
35. Simpson, L. L., "Sizing Piping for Process Plant," *Chem. Eng.*, Vol. 75 (1968), p. 192.
36. Kubie, J., and Oates, H. S., "Two-Phase Steam-Water Flow Through Y-Junctions," *I. J. Heat and Fluid Flow*, Vol. 1 (1979), pp. 161–167.
37. Kubie, J., and Gardner, G. C., "Two-Phase Gas-Liquid Flow Through Y-Junctions," *Chem. Engng. Sci.*, Vol. 33 (1978), pp. 319–329.
38. Zuber, N., and Findlay, J., "Average Volumetric Concentration in Two-Phase Flow Systems," *Trans. ASME, J. Heat Transfer*, Vol. 87, 1965, p. 453.
39. Engineering Science Data Unit Limited, "Pressure Losses in Curved Ducts: Single Bends," ESDU Report No. 77008, 1977.

CHAPTER 26

EFFECT OF FLOW OBSTRUCTIONS ON FLOW TRANSITIONS AND PRESSURE DROP IN TWO-PHASE FLOWS

Martha E. Salcudean

Department of Mechanical Engineering
University of British Columbia
Vancouver, Canada

CONTENTS

INTRODUCTION

Pressure drop in two-phase flow through different obstructions, such as orifices, valves, and bends, occurs in many industrial applications. The flow obstructions increase the hydraulic resistance, hence more power is required to maintain a given mass flow rate in the system. In addition, obstructions can also have considerable influence on the heat transfer in two-phase systems. However, two-phase flow through obstructions has been relatively little studied. This can be partly explained by the considerable difficulties encountered in theoretical approaches and the limited range of validity for correlations based on experiments.

In the following, some aspects of the effects of obstructions on two-phase flow pressure drop, flow transitions, and void distributions are presented. The discussion is not exhaustive as much work, data, and results are not discussed. The object is to describe some of the approaches by different investigators and to give a few examples of results pertinent to the problem. Discussions will be related to:

- Flow through sudden enlargement.
- Flow through sudden contraction.
- Flow through orifices.
- Effect of flow obstructions on flow pattern transitions in horizontal two-phase flow.
- Effect of flow obstructions on void distribution in horizontal two-phase flow.
- Effect of flow stratification on pressure drop through obstructions in horizontal two-phase flow.
- Two-phase pressure drop through complex shaped obstructions.

FLOW THROUGH SUDDEN ENLARGEMENT

In the case of a sudden expansion, the pipe area increases and flow separation occurs. A force balance may be written to express the pressure loss in the expansion for single-phase flow [1]. The expansion is illustrated schematically in Figure 1, and a list of symbols used is given in the following.

Notation for Figure 1

A   area, ft^2
g   conversion factor, 32.2 ft-lb (mass)/sec^2-lb (force)
K   loss coefficient, dimensionless
N   number of velocity heads, dimensionless
P   pressure, lb (force)/ft^2
V   velocity, ft/sec
v   specific volume, ft^3/lb (mass)
W   flow rate, lb (mass)/sec
x   vapor flow weight fraction, lb (vapor)/lb (mix)
α vapor volume fraction, ft^3 (vapor)/ft^3 (mix)
σ area ratio, A_1/A_2
ρ density, lb (mass)/ft^3

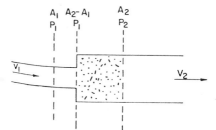

Figure 1. Sudden expansion of a flowing fluid.

Subscripts

0   refers to total mass flowing as liquid (no vapor present)
1   refers to position upstream from expansion
2   refers to position downstream from expansion
f   refers to saturated liquid
g   refers to saturated vapor

The following equation can be written

$$P_1 + \frac{1}{2}\rho V_1^2 = P_2 + \frac{1}{2}\rho V_2^2 + K\rho \frac{V_1^2}{2} \tag{1}$$

where the loss coefficient is

$$K = (1 - \sigma)^2 = \left(1 - \frac{A_1}{A_2}\right)^2 \tag{2}$$

It follows then

$$P_1 - P_2 = -\frac{1}{2}\rho V_1^2 |2\sigma(1 - \sigma)| \tag{3}$$

The pressure difference may also be written in terms of the number of velocity heads:

$$N = \frac{P_1 - P_2}{\frac{1}{2}\rho V_1^2} = -2(1 - \sigma) \tag{4}$$

The value of K is always positive and the pressure change is always negative. The maximum loss occurs when the area ratio is zero. At the condition of maximum loss, the change in static pressure is zero. The following relation can be written between K and N

$$K + N = 1 - \sigma^2 \tag{5}$$

Several methods were suggested to compute the pressure difference $P_1 - P_2$ for two-phase flows. A few of them are described in the following.

Lottes' Method

Lottes' method [1] was derived based on the assumption that all losses take place in the liquid phase only.
The force balance is written as

$$P_1 + \frac{\rho_f V_{1f}^2}{2} = P_2 + \frac{\rho_f V_{2f}^2}{2} + K\frac{\rho V_{1f}^2}{2} \tag{6}$$

where the index f refers to saturated liquid. Ignoring the gaseous mass flow $(x \ll 1)$ we can write

$$V_{1f} = \frac{V_0}{1 - \alpha_1} \tag{7}$$

and

$$V_{2f} = \left(\frac{V_0}{1 - \alpha_2}\right)\sigma \tag{8}$$

where V_0 is the velocity for the total mass flowing as liquid.

Based on the assumption that all losses occur in the liquid phase, one can write

$$K = \left| 1 - \sigma \frac{(1 - \alpha_1)}{(1 - \alpha_2)} \right|^2 \tag{9}$$

The expression $\sigma(1 - \alpha_1)/(1 - \alpha_2)$ represents the area change for the flowing liquid.

The static pressure change can then be written as

$$P_2 - P_1 = \frac{\rho_f V_0^2}{2}(2\sigma) \left| \frac{1}{(1 - \alpha_1)(1 - \alpha_2)} - \sigma\left(\frac{1}{1 - \alpha_2}\right)^2 \right| \tag{10}$$

Romie's Method

This method is based on a momentum balance across an abrupt expression [2]

$$P_1 A_2 + W_{f1} V_{f1} + W_{g1} V_{g1} = P_2 A_2 + W_{f2} V_{f2} + W_{g2} V_{g2} \tag{11}$$

The pressure P_1 is assumed to act on area A_2 just after the expansion as in the case of one-phase flow.

From continuity one can write,

$$W_{f2} = W_{f1} = W_0(1 - x) = \rho_f V_0 A_1 (1 - x) = \rho_f V_0 \sigma A_2 (1 - x)$$

$$W_{g2} = W_{g1} = xW_0 = \rho_f V_0 A_1 x = \rho_f V_0 \sigma A_2 x$$

$$V_{f1} = \frac{V_0(1 - x)}{1 - \alpha_1}$$

$$V_{g1} = V_0 \frac{x}{\alpha_1} \frac{\rho_f}{\rho_g} \tag{12}$$

$$V_{f2} = \frac{\sigma V_0(1 - x)}{1 - \alpha_2}$$

$$V_{g2} = \sigma V_0 \frac{x}{\alpha_2} \frac{\rho_f}{\rho_g}$$

One can see that in Romie's method the quality "x" is not neglected. The pressure loss can then be expressed as

$$P_2 - P_1 = \frac{\rho_f V_0^2}{2}(2\sigma) \left| x^2\left(\frac{\rho_f}{\rho_g}\right)\left(\frac{1}{\alpha_1} - \frac{\sigma}{\alpha_2}\right) + (1 - x)^2\left(\frac{1}{1 - \alpha_1} - \frac{\sigma}{1 - \alpha_2}\right) \right| \tag{13}$$

Richardson's Method

Richardson reported data on loss coefficients for air-water mixtures flowing through horizontal channels at atmospheric pressure for area ratios of 0.125 to 0.5 [3]. He found that the energy loss could be represented by

$$\frac{\Delta KE_{loss}}{\Delta KE} = 1 - \sigma \tag{14}$$

where the kinetic energy variation ΔKE was computed for liquid flow and an unchanged void fraction $\alpha_1 = \alpha_2 = \alpha$ was assumed. Richardson defined the kinetic energy as

$$\Delta KE = \frac{\rho_f(1 - \alpha)}{2}(V_{f1}^2 - V_{f2}^2) \tag{15}$$

One can write then

$$\frac{\Delta KE - (P_2 - P_1)}{\Delta KE} = 1 - \sigma$$

$$P_2 - P_1 = \frac{\rho_f V_{f1}^2}{2}(1 - \alpha)(1 - \sigma^2)\sigma \tag{16}$$

or, since

$$V_{f1} = \frac{V_0(1 - x)}{1 - \alpha}$$

$$P_2 - P_1 = \frac{\rho_f V_0^2(1 - x)^2(1 - \sigma^2)\sigma}{2g(1 - \alpha)} \tag{17}$$

While the Lottes method does not allow for the effect of the void fraction "α" the Romie and Richardson methods do. Richardson has carried out pressure variation measurements through expansions and experienced considerable difficulties, as the length over which the recovery took place was not well defined.

Figure 2 illustrates the pressure losses he correlated as a function of the parameter $G_w^2 x^{1/2}$ where G_w is given in lb/s in^2 for different area ratios. The pressure drop shows a significant influence on the area ratio. Chisholm [4] has carried out extensive work for varied pipe fittings and made recommendations for the use of two-phase flow correlation for the case of sudden expansion. As his work was more related to orifices, his correlation will be presented later.

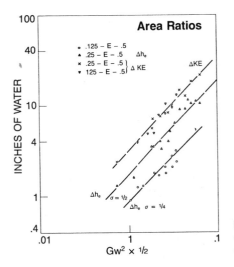

Figure 2. Correlation for two-phase pressure expressed in inches of water for sudden enlargement.

FLOW THROUGH SUDDEN CONTRACTION

As fluid passes from a larger pipe section to a smaller one it is first accelerated through the vena contracta and pressure energy is converted to kinetic energy with little or no frictional dissipation. Once passed through the vena contracta the conditions become similar to those in sudden enlargement and considerable frictional dissipation occurs [5]. G. E. Geiger and W. M. Rohrer have carried out theoretical and experimental work for water-steam systems in the pressure range of 1.379–3.447 MPa with area ratios varying from 0.144 to 0.398 kg/m² s and mass velocities from 0.42 × 10⁵ to 3.92 × 10⁵ kg/m² s [6]. The relation for the pressure drop was developed based on the continuity, momentum, and energy equations following Mendler's [7] development for sudden enlargements.

The equations were derived from the following assumptions:

1. The vapor phase may flow at a mean velocity which is different from that of the liquid phase.
2. The flow pattern before and after the sudden contraction is in a stationary pattern with time or is at least in a steady recurrent pattern.
3. The static pressure at any cross-section is uniform across the cross-section.
4. The pressure change across the sudden contraction is very small compared to the absolute pressure of the system.
5. The process is overall adiabatic.
6. There is no significant change in the weight fraction mixture (quality) in the vicinity of the sudden contraction.
7. The process is in overall thermal equilibrium.

The pressure loss was expressed as:

$$(P_1 - P_3)_{actual} = (P_1 - P_3)_{ideal} + \Delta P_{loss} \tag{18}$$

Therefore,

$$
\Delta P_{loss} = \frac{G_3^2}{2g_c\bar{\rho}}\left[\frac{2X^2\bar{\rho}}{\rho_g}\left|\frac{\gamma_{3g}}{\alpha_3} - \frac{\gamma_{2g}}{\alpha_2 C_c}\right|\right.
$$

$$
+ \frac{2(1-X)^2\bar{\rho}}{\rho_f}\left|\frac{\gamma_{3f}}{1-\alpha_3} - \frac{\gamma_{2f}}{(1-\alpha_2)C_c}\right| + \frac{X^3\bar{\rho}^2}{P_g}\left|\frac{\beta_{2g}}{R_2^2C_2^2}\frac{B_{1g}\sigma^2}{\alpha_1^2} + \frac{\sigma^2}{\alpha_1^2}\frac{1}{\alpha_3^2}\right|
$$

$$
+ \frac{(1-X)^3\bar{\rho}^2}{\rho_f^2}\left|\frac{\beta_{2f}}{(1-\alpha_2)^2C_c^2}\frac{\beta_{1f}\sigma^2}{(1-\alpha_1)^2} + \frac{\sigma^2}{(1-\alpha_1)^2}\frac{1}{(1-\alpha_3)^2}\right| \left.\right] + \frac{g}{g_c}\bar{\rho}H_{1,2} + F_{2,3}/A_3 \tag{19}
$$

where 1, 2, and 3 represent, respectively, the upstream section, the vena contracta, and the downstream section as illustrated in Figure 3. The notations used are as follows:

Notation Used in Figure 3

A   total cross-sectional flow area, ft²
A_f cross-sectional flow area occupied by liquid phase, ft²

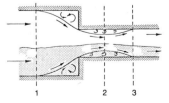

1   2   3   **Figure 3.** Sudden contraction.

A   cross-sectional flow area occupied by vapor phase, ft^2
C_c contraction coefficient of vena contracta, dimensionless
F   shear force, lb_f
G   mass velocity, $lb_m/hr \cdot ft^2$
g   gravitational acceleration, 32.2 ft/sec^2
g_c conversion factor in Newton's law, 32.2 lb_m-ft/lb_f-sec^2
$H_{1,2}$ acceleration head loss from stations 1 to 2, ft
K   contraction loss coefficient, dimensionless
$\bar{K}$ modified contraction loss coefficient, dimensionless
P_1, P_2, P_3 static pressure, psf (used with subscripts)
P   system pressure, psia (used without subscripts)
ΔP static pressure difference, upstream minus downstream, psf
ΔP_{loss} static pressure loss due to sudden contraction, psf
R   vapor volume fraction, dimensionless
V   average velocity across a given cross-section, ft/hr
V_f average velocity of liquid across a given cross-section, ft/hr
V_g average velocity of vapor across a given cross-section, ft/hr
w   mass flow rate, lb_m/hr
X   mixture quality, mass of vapor to mass of mixing flowing, dimensionless
Z   elevation, ft

Subscripts

f   liquid phase
g   vapor phase
SPC   for single-phase flow through a contraction
SEP   separated flow model
TPC   for two-phase flow through a contraction
1   at the station upstream of the area change
2   at the vena contracta station
3   at the station downstream of the vena contracta
β kinetic energy correction factor, dimensionless
γ momentum correction factor, dimensionless
ρ density of single-phase fluid, lb_m/ft^3
ρ_f density of liquid phase, lb_m/ft^3
ρ_g density of vapor phase, lb_m/ft^3
$\bar{\rho}$ density of homogeneous two-phase fluid, lb_m/ft^3
ρ_{SEP} density of Martinelli-Nelson separated flow model, lb_m/ft^3
σ area contraction ratio, A_3/A, dimensionless

The pressure loss across a sudden change in area is usually defined in single-phase flow as

$$\Delta P_{loss} = K_{SPC} \frac{\rho V_3^2}{2g_c} = K_{SPC} \frac{G_3^2}{2g_c \rho} \tag{20}$$

If one expresses the two-phase flow pressure loss in a similar way, one obtains

$$\Delta P_{loss} = K_{TPC} \frac{G_3^2}{2g_c \bar{\rho}} \tag{21}$$

In single-phase flow the pressure difference $P_1 - P_3$ is expressed as

$$\Delta P_c = (P_1 - P_3)_{actual} = \frac{G_3^2}{2g_c \bar{\rho}} |1 - \sigma^2 + K_{SPC}| \tag{22}$$

The elevation pressure is considered to be zero. By defining a $\bar{K}_{TPC}$ one can then express the two-phase pressure loss as:

$$\Delta P_c = (P_1 - P_3)_{actual} = \frac{G_3^2}{2g_c\bar{\rho}} |1 - \sigma^2 + \bar{K}_{TPC}| \qquad (23)$$

the modified $\bar{K}_{TPC}$ having the expression

$$\bar{K}_{TPC} = (\sigma^2 - 1) + \frac{2X^2\bar{\rho}}{\rho_g}\left[\frac{\gamma_{3g}}{\alpha_3} - \frac{\gamma_{2g}}{\alpha_2 C_c}\right] + \frac{2(1-X)^2\bar{\rho}}{\rho_f}\left[\frac{\gamma_{3f}}{(1-\alpha_3)} - \frac{\gamma_{2f}}{(1-\alpha_2)C_c}\right]$$
$$\frac{X^3\bar{\rho}^2}{\rho_g^2}\left[\frac{\beta_{2g}}{\alpha_2^2 C_c^2} - \frac{\beta_{1g}\sigma^2}{\alpha_1^2}\right] + \frac{(1-X)^3\bar{\rho}^2}{\rho_f^2}\left[\frac{\beta_{2f}}{(1-\alpha_2)^2 C_c^2} - \frac{\beta_{1f}\sigma^2}{(1-\alpha_1)^2}\right] \qquad (24)$$

The expression $\bar{K}_{TPC}$ was evaluated by Geiger and Rohrer for several flow models. The most often used models they considered were the homogeneous flow model and the separate flow model.

The Homogeneous Flow Model

This flow model assures a completely homogeneous mixture. The velocities of the vapor and liquid phases are then given as

$$V_g = \frac{XG}{\rho_g\alpha} \qquad (25)$$

$$V_f = \frac{(1-X)G}{\rho_f(1-\alpha)} \qquad (26)$$

If one calculates α from Equations 25 and 26 and one considers $\bar{\rho}$ as the average mixture density it results;

$$\Delta P_c = \frac{G_2^3}{2g_c\rho}(1 - \sigma^2 + K_{SPC}) \qquad (27)$$

The Martinelli-Nelson Separated Flow Model

This flow model assumes completely separated phases, with each phase having its own values of velocity, density, and enthalpy. The density becomes

$$\rho_{SEP} = \rho_f(1-\alpha) + \rho_g\alpha \qquad (28)$$

If one considers the momentum and the energy correction factors as unity, $\bar{K}_{SPC}$ is given by:

$$\bar{K}_{SPC} = \left(\frac{1}{C_c} - 1\right)^2 \qquad (29)$$

and the pressure drop has the expression

$$\Delta P_c = \frac{G_3^2}{2g_c\rho_{GEP}}(1 - \sigma^2 + \bar{K}_{SPC}) \qquad (30)$$

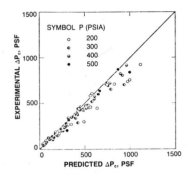

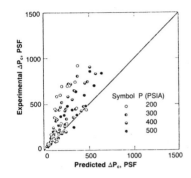

Figure 4. Comparison of data with predictions from homogeneous flow model.

Figure 5. Comparison of data with predictions from separated flow model.

One can see that the difference between the two models consists in the way of computing the two-phase density. (The constants g_c are present because the British units system was used by Mender.) Geiger and Rohrer have analyzed their experimental data and compared them against the pressure drop expressions for different flow models. They found that the homogeneous model predictions were better than those by the separated flow model. Its predictions are closer and slightly conservative, generally an advantageous feature for design purposes. The results from the two different models are shown in Figures 4 and 5.

FLOW THROUGH ORIFICES

Flow through sharp-edged orifices is particularly important as orifices are associated with throttling processes and metering of steam-water mixtures. This is what accounts for a more extensive investigation of orifices as compared with other flow obstructions. Chisholm has extensively investigated two-phase flows through orifices [4, 8]. He has derived expressions for the pressure drop through sharp orifices based on the assumption of both phases being incompressible and no evaporation during the two-phase flow through the orifice. A schematic illustration of the flow is illustrated in Figure 6. The following force balance can be written

$$(P_1 - P_2)A_{LN} + f\left(\frac{W_L^2}{g}\right)\rho_L A_{LN} + S = \frac{W_L U_L}{g} \tag{31}$$

$$(P_1 - P_2)A_{VN} + f\left(\frac{W_V^2}{g}\right)\rho_V A_{VN} - S = \frac{W_V U_V}{g} \tag{32}$$

where P_1, P_2 = upstream and downstream pressure
A_{LN}, A_{VN} = liquid and vapor cross-section at throat during two-phase flow
ρ_L, ρ_G = liquid and vapor density
f = friction coefficient
W_L, W_V = liquid and vapor flow rate by weight
U_L, U_V = liquid and vapor velocity at vena contracta during two-phase flow
S = shear force

The upstream momentum is considered as being negligible in these equations. This is an acceptable hypothesis if the orifice area is small as compared with the pipe. The phase continuity equa-

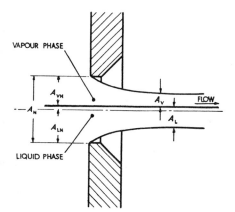

Figure 6. Two-phase flow through an orifice.

tions can be written as

$$(1 - x)W = W_L = A_L U_L \rho_L \tag{33}$$

$$xW = W_V = A_V U_V \rho_V \tag{34}$$

Assuming that each phase has the same contraction coefficient, C_c, it results

$$A_L = C_c A_{LN} \quad \text{and} \quad A_V = C_c A_{VN} \tag{35}$$

where A_L, A_V = liquid and vapor cross-sections at "vena contracta" during two-phase flow

Combining the Equations 31–35 gives

$$\frac{P_1 - P_2}{\rho_L} \left\{ 1 + \frac{SC_c}{A_L(P_1 - P_2)} \right\} = \frac{U_L^2}{2g} \tag{36}$$

and

$$\frac{P_1 - P_2}{\rho_V} \left\{ 1 - \frac{SC_c}{A_V(P_1 - P_2)} \right\} = \frac{U_V^2}{2g} \tag{37}$$

If one introduces the shear force ratio

$$S_R = \frac{SC_c}{A_V(P_1 - P_2)} \tag{38}$$

it follows

$$\frac{P_1 - P_2}{\rho_L} \left(1 + S_R \frac{A_V}{A_L} \right) = \frac{V_L^2}{2g} \tag{39}$$

and

$$\frac{P_1 - P_2}{\rho_V} (1 - S_r) = \frac{U_r^2}{2g} \tag{40}$$

Combining Equations 39 and 40 gives the phase velocity ratio in the vena contracta

$$K = \frac{U_V}{U_L} = \frac{1}{Z}\left(\frac{\rho_L}{\rho_V}\right)^{0.5} \tag{41}$$

where

$$Z = \left[\frac{1 + S_R\left(\frac{A_V}{A_L}\right)}{1 - S_R}\right]^{0.5} \tag{42}$$

The expression for Z was referred to by Chisholm as the "shear force function." The area ratio can then be expressed as:

$$\frac{A_V}{A_L} = Z \frac{x}{1-x}\left(\frac{\rho_\ell}{\rho_V}\right)^{0.5} = ZY \tag{43}$$

where

$$Y = \frac{x}{1-x}\left(\frac{\rho_\ell}{\rho_V}\right)^{0.5} \tag{44}$$

The basic relationship for flow of liquid alone through a sharp-edged orifice for negligible upstream velocity can be then written as

$$W_{LS} = C_c A_N \{2g\rho_L(P_1 - P_2)\}^{0.5} \tag{45}$$

where A_N = is the orifice throat cross-section

W_{LS}, W_{VS} = are liquid and vapor flow rates by weight during single-phase flow with two-phase pressure drop

Then,

$$W_L = A_L U_L \rho_L = A_L\left\{1 + S_R\left(\frac{A_V}{A_L}\right)\right\}^{0.5}\{2g\rho_L(P_1 - P_2)\}^{0.5} \tag{46}$$

and

$$C_c A_N = A_L + A_V$$

It follows that,

$$\frac{W_{LS}}{W_L} = \frac{1 + \dfrac{A_V}{A_L}}{\left\{1 + S_R\left(\dfrac{A_V}{A_L}\right)\right\}^{0.5}} \tag{47}$$

and

$$\frac{W_{LS}}{W_L} = \left[1 + \left(\frac{A_V}{A_L}\right)\right]^{0.5}\left[\left(\frac{A_V}{A_L}\right)\frac{1}{Z^2} + 1\right]^{0.5} \tag{48}$$

$$\frac{W_{LS}}{W_L} = (1 + ZY)^{0.5}\left(\frac{Y}{Z} + 1\right)^{0.5} \tag{49}$$

$$\frac{W_{LS}}{W_L} = (1 + CY + Y^2)^{0.5} \tag{50}$$

where $C = Z + \dfrac{1}{Z}$

In terms of the gas flow rates the equation can be written as

$$\frac{W_{VS}}{W_V} = \left(1 + \frac{C}{Y} + \frac{1}{Y^2}\right)^{0.5} \tag{51}$$

For incompressible flow it can be shown

$$Y^2 = \frac{\Delta P_V}{\Delta P_L} \tag{52}$$

where $\Delta P_L, \Delta P_V$ = pressure drop over orifice if liquid or vapor components flow alone

and

$$\left(\frac{W_{LS}}{W_L}\right)^2 = \frac{\Delta P_{TP}}{\Delta P_L} \tag{53}$$

where ΔP_{TP} = pressure drop over orifice during two-phase flow

It results

$$\frac{\Delta P_{TP}}{\Delta P_L} = 1 + C\left(\frac{\Delta P_V}{\Delta P_L}\right)^{0.5} + \frac{\Delta P_V}{\Delta P_L} = 1 + \frac{C}{X} + \frac{1}{X^2} \tag{54}$$

where   X = the Lochart-Martinelli correlating group

Figure 7 shows Murdoch's data correlated by Equation 54 with C = 2.66.
For pressure ratio P_2/P_1 near unity Chisholm and Watson have developed the correlation:

$$\frac{W_{LS}}{W_L} = 1 + aY^6 \tag{55}$$

where $a = 1.6d^{0.4}$ (where d is in inches)
          $b = 0.91 - \log a$

Chisholm uses Lottes' and Hooper's [1, 9] equation to determine the C value in the equation

$$\frac{P_{TP}}{P_L} = 1 + \frac{C}{X} + \frac{1}{X^2} \text{ *}$$

---

* Lottes and Hooper equations lead to a similar expression.

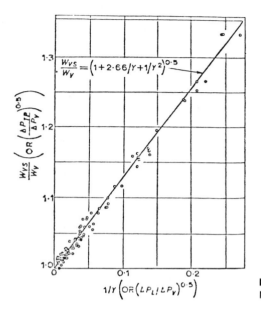

$$\frac{1}{\gamma}\left(\text{OR}\left(^{L}P_{L}/^{L}P_{V}\right)^{0.5}\right)$$

Figure 7. W_{VS}/W_V to a base of $1/Y$; Murdock's data.

and proposes the following general equation:

$$\frac{\Delta P_{TP}}{\Delta P_{LO}} = 1 + (r^2 - 1)\{B_g + (1 - B)g^2\} \tag{56}$$

where ΔP_{TP} = pressure drop due to restriction during two-phase flow
ΔP_{LO} = pressure drop due to restriction if all mixture flows as liquid
g = ratio of gas to total mass flow-rate

$$\Gamma = \left(\frac{V_g}{V_L}\right)^{0.5} \tag{57}$$

where V_G = gas specific volume
V_L = liquid specific volume

$$B = \frac{\dfrac{1}{R}\dfrac{V_G}{V_L} + K - 2}{\dfrac{V_G}{V_L} - 1} \tag{58}$$

where K = ratio of the gas to liquid velocity

Chisholm recommended the use of this equation for other obstructions with the following values for B.

Sudden contraction—The flow is assumed to be homogeneous, therefore $B = 1$.
Sudden expansion—The recommended procedure is to assume a slip ratio (K) corresponding to pipe flow conditions. A simple approximation is to consider $B = 0.5$ corresponding to $K \cong 2$.

Thin plates—Despite extensive work, there are not enough data on the pressure recovery downstream of the plate. Chisholm recommends B = 0.5 and mentions that it overestimates the pressure loss at low pressures.

Thick plates—Chisholm recommends the assumption of B = 1 for the contraction and B = 0.5 for the expansion.

The overall pressure drop is then:

$$\Delta P_{TP} = \Delta P_{LOC} + \Delta P_{LOC}(\Gamma^2 - 1)g + \Delta P_{LOE}(\Gamma^2 - 1)(0.5g + 0.5g^2) \tag{59}$$

where ΔP_{LOC} = pressure drop if all mixture flows as liquid at a contraction
ΔP_{LOE} = pressure drop if all mixture flows as liquid at an expansion

The all-liquid pressure drop over the plate is

$$\Delta P_{LO} = \Delta P_{LOC} + \Delta P_{LOE} \tag{60}$$

and

$$B = 1 - 0.5 \frac{\Delta P_{LOE}}{\Delta P_{LO}} \tag{61}$$

For single-phase flow

$$\frac{\Delta P_{LOE}}{\Delta P_{LO}} = \frac{2(\sigma - \sigma^2)}{\left(\dfrac{1}{C_c - 1}\right)^2 + (\sigma - 1)^2} \tag{62}$$

where C_c = contraction coefficient
σ = ratio of downstream to upstream flow cross-sections

Chisholm equations are recommended to be used as they encompass several types of obstructions, hence allowing for a comprehensive calculation of complex circuits. The parameters used in the equations have a sound physical basis and are similar to parameters used in two-phase flow analysis, thus facilitating the approach for engineers familiar with the field.

EFFECT OF FLOW OBSTRUCTIONS ON FLOW PATTERN TRANSITIONS IN HORIZONTAL TWO-PHASE FLOW

Flow patterns and flow-pattern transitions are of considerable importance in the design of two-phase flow systems, as they can be significant in determining the pressure drop and heat transfer characteristics.

Flow patterns occurring in horizontal gas-liquid flow have been subject to extensive investigations. As most of the classifications were based on qualitative and subjective judgment of the observer, there were a multiple of names assigned to particular phase distributions in horizontal cocurrent flow. Also, many flow regime maps based on experimental data have been proposed by different investigators; among whom are Bergelin and Gazley [10], Jenkins [11], Alves [12], Baker [13], and Mandhane [14].

Hubbard and Dukler [15] suggest the following three basic flow pattern groups:

• Separated continuous flows characterized by two phases flowing separately (e.g., stratified smooth, stratified wavy and annular flow).
• Intermittent flows characterized by discontinuity of one of the phases (e.g., plug and slug flow).

• Dispersed flows characterized by one phase being dispersed in the other phases (e.g., liquid deficient flow, bubbly flow).

The numerous flow patterns reported in the literature are basically combinations of these basic flow patterns.
A study was undertaken [16] to investigate the effect of flow obstructions on the flow pattern transitions.
The experimental work was carried out on a loop shown schematically in Figure 8. The test section consisted of a 25.4-mm ID, 3-m long horizontal plexiglass tube. The air (max. 0.2 kg/s) and water (max. 1.7 kg/s) was supplied through a honeycomb mixer and a 3-m long calming section before entering the test section.
The effect of flow obstruction was studied using the two different designs illustrated in Figure 8; each of them resulted in a flow blockage of 25% of the channel area. The effect of both obstructions was analyzed for different flow regimes. Flow regime maps were constructed for non-obstructed flows and flows with obstructions. The flow maps were constructed based on visual observations. A strobe light was used to improve visualization.
The maps for the obstructed flow were based on visual observation of the flow regime at a section 300 mm downstream from the obstruction. The length affected by the flow obstruction was found to depend on the flow regime and was longer for the dispersed flow (30 L/D where L is the length of the channel and D is its diameter) and shorter for annular (15 L/D).

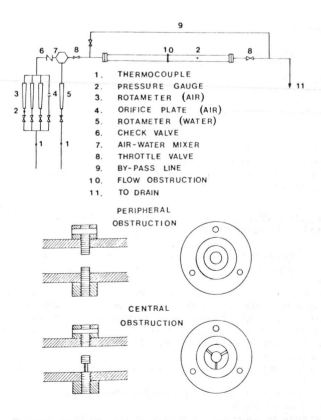

Figure 8. Schematic diagram of the loop and the obstructions.

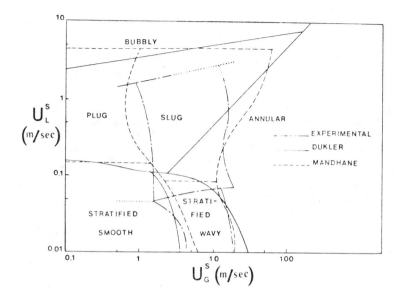

Figure 9. Flow pattern map in the unobstructed channel. Comparison with Mandhane's and Dukler's flow regime boundaries.

Unobstructed Channel Results

Figure 9 illustrates the flow-regime map of the unobstructed channel. The results are compared with Mandhane's [14] map (empirical) and the map proposed by Taitel and Dukler [17] (based on a physical model for flow regime transitions). Considering the differences between the existing flow regime maps the agreement is reasonable. The following discrepancies were noted: the transition between stratified smooth and stratified wavy to intermittent flow occurred at lower liquid velocities while the plug-slug transition occurred at higher gas velocities. Visual distinction between plug and slug flow is very subjective as they both have the same general appearance, the difference being mainly in the size and shape of the plugs and slugs.

The slug to annular transition is in fairly good agreement with Mandhane's results except for higher liquid velocities. Note that the region characterized by Mandhane [14] and the present work as slug flow is considered to be annular by Taitel and Dukler [17]. The discrepancy is due to the difficulty of observing or measuring the slug-annular transition especially for thin liquid films. Stratified smooth to stratified wavy and stratified wavy to annular transitions show good agreement with Mandhane's and Taitel-Dukler's map.

The major causes for the discrepancies between the maps are:

1. Different experimental conditions (e.g., geometry, inlet).
2. Subjective observer's judgment.

Obstructed Channel Results

Taitel and Dukler [17] have analyzed the mechanism controlling the flow regime transition from stratified flow by considering the forces acting on a growing wave. As the gas flows over the wave, the pressure decreases due to the increased velocity generating an upward force. When the upward pressure force exceeds the gravity force, conditions for wave growth are created. The obstructions decrease the area available for the gas flows, thus increasing the gas velocity. Hence, in general one expects (as was observed) that flow obstructions will cause the transition to occur at lower liquid and gas superficial velocities.

Figure 10 compares the flow regime maps in the unobstructed test section with maps for test sections with central and peripheral obstructions. The effect of the obstructions on each flow regime boundary is as follows:

- *Transition from stratified wavy to intermittent flow.* The significant disturbance caused by the flow obstruction will result in larger waves which will eventually bridge the gas phase; hence intermittent flow will occur for obstructed flow at lower liquid velocities. The observed stronger effect of the central obstruction is due to its intersecting the waves to a greater extent.
- *Transition from stratified wavy to annular flow.* The effect of the peripheral obstruction is considerably greater than that of the central one. The reason is probably due to the low ratios of h_L/D^* at which this transition occurs. The effect of the obstruction increases with decreasing liquid velocity (the ratio h_L/D decreases).
- *Transition from intermittent to annular flow.* At low liquid velocities the effect of the flow obstruction is not significant. For higher liquid velocities, this effect becomes more important. The peripheral obstruction is more effective than the central one due to the presence of the slugs primarily in the upper part of the test section.
- *Transition from stratified smooth to stratified wavy flow.* Taitel and Dukler [17] suggest this transition occurs when the pressure and shear stress forces exerted by the gas flow on the wave are greater than the viscous dissipation in the waves. Flow obstructions locally increase the vapor velocities and hence the local pressure and shear forces. Thus a transition to stratified wavy flow is expected at a lower vapor velocity. This is corroborated by Figure 10. The central obstruction intersects the vapor to a greater extent, especially at low h_L/D ratios, and hence is more effective in shifting the flow regime boundary to lower superficial vapor velocities. The central obstruction effect is considerably stronger than that of the peripheral one, because it intersects the liquid-gas interface to a greater extent.

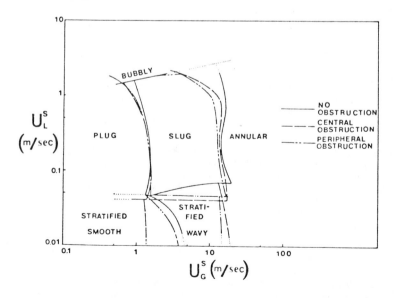

Figure 10. Comparison of the flow pattern transition boundaries; no obstruction, central obstruction, and peripheral obstruction.

In conclusion, it can be said that both central and peripheral flow obstructions affect the flow transitions. The central obstruction appears to have the strongest effect on the transition from stratified smooth to stratified wavy and from stratified wavy to intermittent flow. The peripheral obstruction has a stronger effect on the transition from intermittent to annular flow.

EFFECT OF FLOW OBSTRUCTION ON VOID DISTRIBUTION IN HORIZONTAL AIR-WATER FLOWS

In order to understand two-phase flow behavior, it is imperative to acquire information on the void distribution under the effect of obstructions.

A study was undertaken [18] using the same loop as described earlier related to flow pattern transitions.

To measure the average void fraction, quick-closing valves were located 1.22 m apart. These valves did not introduce any flow obstruction when fully opened.

To measure the local void fraction, a miniature optical probe was used in conjunction with a phase indicator and a void fraction unit. The signal provided by the probe is amplified and processed to obtain the integrated void fraction over various time intervals (0.1, 1, 10, 100 sec).

The test section can be rotated after installation thus permitting local void fraction measurements at different angular locations. Three measurement stations were located along the test section. To obtain a cross-sectional average void fraction $\bar{\alpha}$, half of the cross-section was divided into 95 segments (the void fraction distribution was assumed to be symmetric with respect to the vertical axis). In the center of each of these 95 segments, the void fraction was obtained experimentally and the value found was assumed to be representative of the void fraction in the whole segment. The cross-sectional average void fraction was approximated numerically as:

$$\alpha = \frac{\sum \alpha_i A_i}{\sum A_i} \tag{63}$$

where α_i is the measured void fraction and A_i the cross-sectional area of segment "i". This void fraction was compared with the value obtained with the quick-closing valves. An example of the void distribution is illustrated in Figure 11. The iso-voidage lines are illustrated for 0.4 kg/s water and 0.0215 kg/s air-flow rate. The mean value of 75% was obtained by the use of quick-closing

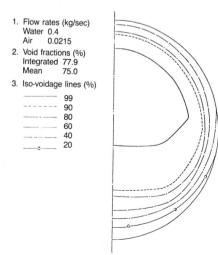

1. Flow rates (kg/sec)
   Water 0.4
   Air   0.0215
2. Void fractions (%)
   Integrated 77.9
   Mean   75.0
3. Iso-voidage lines (%)
   ——————— 99
   -------- 90
   —— —— —— 80
   —— —— 60
   —— ·· —— 40
   ——∘—— 20

Figure 11. Void fraction distribution.

valves and an integrated average value of 77.9% was obtained based on the local measurements using optical probes.

In the following, the effect of the obstructions for different flow patterns is presented.

Bubbly Flow

In bubbly flow, void distributions and the integrated void fraction were considerably changed due to the flow obstructions.

Peripheral Obstruction

Figure 12 illustrates the change of void distribution along the test section. Void distribution at Tap 1 where the flow is not yet disturbed is characterized by the air phase tending to move along the top of the channel.

As the flow approaches the obstruction, an increase of voidage can be found. This is probably due to the following mechanism; the air bubbles are slowed down by the obstruction more than the liquid phase. As a result, the slip is decreased, and the voidage is increased.

Following the obstruction, considerable flow homogenization can be observed at the bottom of the channel resulting in an increase of voidage. The change of the paths of air bubbles causes the decrease of their momenta in the direction of flow, and consequently the ratio of inertial forces to the surface tension forces is decreased. This introduces a larger number of bubbles with smaller diameters, resulting in an increase of voidage. The obstruction also introduces turbulence which is known to produce breaking up of the bubbles because of momentum redistribution.

At 12 hydraulic diameters downstream from the obstruction, the isovoidage lines become similar to those at Tap 1. However, air phase was still detected at the lower part of the channel. It could be observed that the length of disturbed flow was about 20 hydraulic diameters.

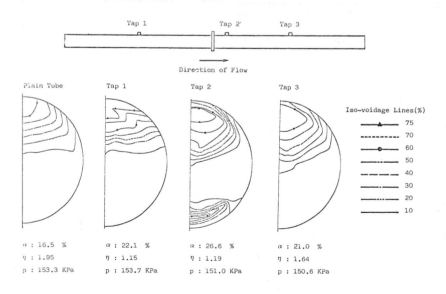

Figure 12. Change of void distribution—peripheral obstruction (bubbly flow) (water: 1.1 kg/sec; air: 0.000775 kg/sec; quality: 0.0704%).

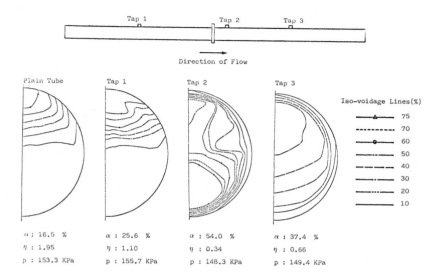

Figure 13. Change of void distribution—central obstruction (bubbly flow) (water: 1.1 kg/sec; air: 0.000775 kg/sec; quality: 0.0704%).

Central Obstruction

The general influence of the obstruction is similar to the peripheral case, but the effect is much stronger as shown in Figure 13. The area affecting the two-phase mixtures is larger in the case of the central obstruction. This caused the slowing down of bubbles, resulting in a slip ratio of less than one. Also, the central obstruction increases the bubble breakdown, therefore, smaller sizes of air bubbles were observed. In addition, three supporting bars, required to hold the obstruction, help the flow homogenization.

At Tap 3, the voidage distribution was still far from the nondisturbed distribution observed at Tap 1, since considerable flow homogenization was largely achieved by the central obstruction. The flow was recovered at about 30 hydraulic diameters downstream from the obstruction.

One can thus conclude that for bubbly flow the central obstruction has a stronger effect.

Annular Flow

The effects of flow obstruction on the annular flow were less pronounced than on the bubbly flow. However, changes of void distribution could be observed.

Peripheral Obstruction

Figure 14 shows the change of void distribution along the test section. In the undisturbed void distribution, the air phase flows in the central part of the test section and the liquid phase forms an annulus. The distribution is asymmetric, since air phase tends to move upward. Many small air bubbles were entrained in the water film at the top of the channel.

For the peripheral obstruction, two contrary trends can be considered:

1. The air phase is accelerated more rapidly through the obstruction. This increases the slip ratio and leads to a decrease of voidage. On passing the obstruction, two-phase flow also undergoes

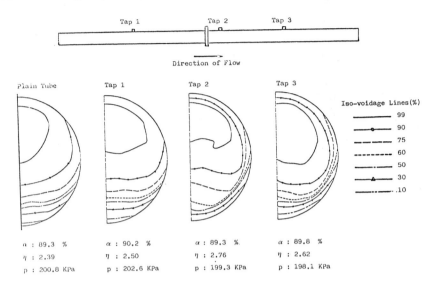

Figure 14. Change of void distribution—peripheral obstruction (annular flow) (water: 0.3 kg/sec; air: 0.0143 kg/sec; quality: 4.55%).

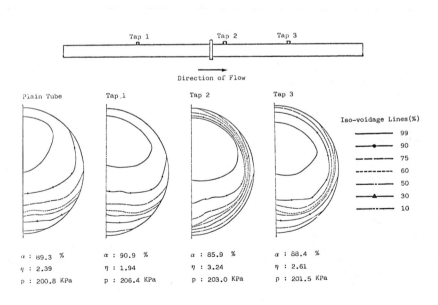

Figure 15. Change of void distribution—central obstruction (annular flow) (water: 0.3 kg/sec; air: 0.0143 kg/sec; quality: 4.55%).

mixing. As a result, a great number of small air bubbles are entrained in the water film. This decreases the area available for the flow of air in the separated central core. Hence, the voidage is decreased.
2. Air entrainment in the water film results in homogenization in the region close to the wall. Due to this homogenization, the slip is lowered and voidage is increased.

Between the two trends, the voidage decrease seems to be slightly stronger as illustrated in Figure 14.

At Tap 3, the two-phase mixture is recovering the original phase distribution. However, the water film at the top of the channel is still thicker than in the undisturbed case, resulting in a decrease of voidage. The void distribution was recovered within 15 hydraulic diameters.

Central Obstruction

Central obstruction has stronger effects on both void fraction and void distribution as shown in Figure 15.

As the obstruction is located in the middle of the channel, it introduces much stronger separation of the mixture, resulting in a decrease of voidage and more symmetric phase distribution compared to the peripheral obstruction.

Slug Flow

Figures 16 and 17 show the changes of void distribution along the test section for peripheral and central obstructions respectively. The behavior of slug flow is closer to annular flow than to bubbly flow.

As the slugs are formed in the upper part of the test section, the peripheral obstruction shows a stronger effect. On passing both obstructions, clear separation occurs. Thus, air flows in the core of the test section and water is present in the upper part of test section continuously.

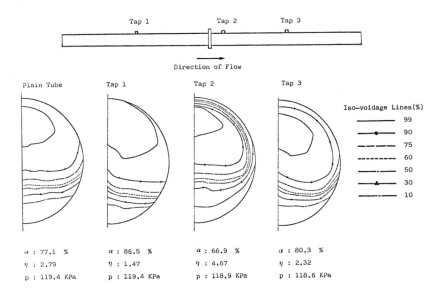

Figure 16. Change of void distribution—peripheral obstruction (slug flow) (water: 0.2 kg/sec; air: 0.00268 kg/sec; quality: 1.32%).

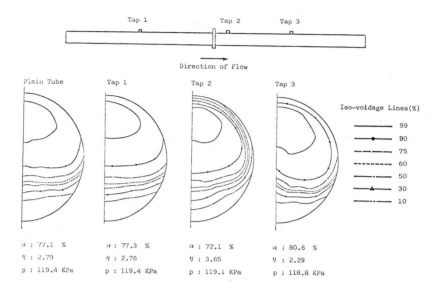

Figure 17. Change of void distribution—central obstruction (slug flow) (water 0.2 kg/sec; air: 0.00268 kg/sec; quality: 1.32%).

EFFECT OF FLOW STRATIFICATION ON PRESSURE DROP THROUGH OBSTRUCTIONS IN HORIZONTAL TWO-PHASE FLOW

Horizontal two-phase-flow pressure drop through obstructions is relevant to petroleum and nuclear industries. Examples of applications are partially closed valves in gas-liquid pipelines and rod spacing devices in nuclear fuel assemblies. Two-phase flow through horizontal channels stratifies under the action of gravitational forces, the light-phase flowing mainly at the top of the channel and the heavy phase at the bottom. This stratification is more pronounced at lower mass flow rates. The stratification affects two-phase flow behavior through obstructions as well. Salcudean et al. [21] have undertaken an investigation of the horizontal and vertical two-phase flow through obstruction of different size and shapes as illustrated in Figure 18.

Obstructions with area ratios (area of the obstructed flow/area of the unobstructed flow) of 0.25 and 0.40 were investigated.

When a fluid flows across an obstruction, separation may occur and a turbulent wake can form behind the obstacle. Some of the pressure energy is converted to kinetic energy and turbulence and is only partially recovered after the blockage. The pressure loss depends upon the size, location, and shape of the blockage.

The pressure loss due to an obstruction can be expressed as

$$\Delta P_{ob} = (f_{ob}t/D_e)_{ob})(\rho_1 v_1^2/2) - (ft/D_e)(\rho_1 v_1^2/2) + K_{LOC}(\rho_1 v_1^2/2) \tag{64}$$

where f_{ob} = the obstruction friction factor
          t = is the thickness
          $(D_e)_{ob}$ = the hydraulic diameter of the obstruction
          f = the channel friction factor
          D_e = the hydraulic diameter of the channel
          K_{LOC} = the obstruction loss coefficient
          ρ_1 = water density
          v_1 = water velocity

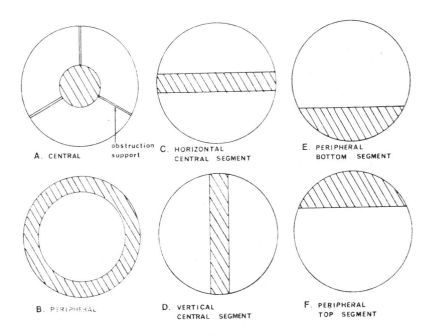

A. CENTRAL   obstruction support   C. HORIZONTAL CENTRAL SEGMENT   E. PERIPHERAL BOTTOM SEGMENT

B. PERIPHERAL   D. VERTICAL CENTRAL SEGMENT   F. PERIPHERAL TOP SEGMENT

Figure 18. Various obstructions.

For a thin obstruction the first two terms can be neglected since t is small. Hence, the general expression has the form:

$$\Delta P_{LOC} = K_{LOC} \frac{\sigma V_1^2}{2} \tag{65}$$

The pressure loss through obstructions may be expressed as the two-phase multiplier which is defined as

$$(\phi_{LO}^2)_{LOC} = (\Delta P_{TP}/\Delta P_{LO})_{LOC} \tag{66}$$

The object of the investigation was two-fold:

1. To assess the influence of the obstruction geometry in the pressure drop.
2. To evaluate the dependence of pressure drop on flow stratification.

A schematic diagram of the apparatus used is shown in Figure 19. Water was circulated by a centrifugal pump and was metered by a rotameter. Air was supplied by the central system and was metered by three rotameters in different ranges. A Bourdon gage was installed at the common outlet of the air rotameters. The two-phase mixture was stabilized in a calming section before entering the section in which the measurements were taken. After passing through the test-section, the mixture was led to a reservoir where the phases were separated. The water was recirculated in the loop and the air was exhausted to the atmosphere.

The test-section was constructed with two 0.0254-m (1 in.) ID, 1.83-m (72 in.) copper pipes. A flange was installed at the connecting ends of the two pipes. An obstruction plate was inserted

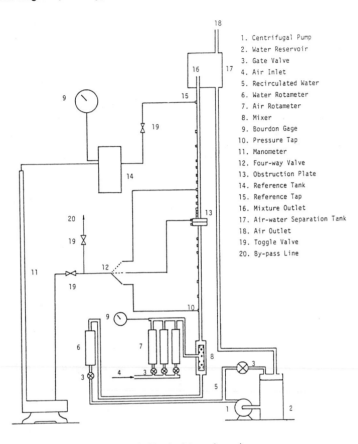

1. Centrifugal Pump
2. Water Reservoir
3. Gate Valve
4. Air Inlet
5. Recirculated Water
6. Water Rotameter
7. Air Rotameter
8. Mixer
9. Bourdon Gage
10. Pressure Tap
11. Manometer
12. Four-way Valve
13. Obstruction Plate
14. Reference Tank
15. Reference Tap
16. Mixture Outlet
17. Air-water Separation Tank
18. Air Outlet
19. Toggle Valve
20. By-pass Line

Figure 19. Vertical two-phase loop.

between the flanges. A transparent test-section was used in the horizontal flow experiments. The apparatus used for the horizontal flow was the one described earlier with adequate instrumentation for pressure drop measurements.

Six different shapes of obstruction plates (as shown in Figure 18) with two blockage area ratios (25% and 40%) were tested. The shapes were:

A: Central obstruction—a circular blockage which was supported by three steel rods (the blockage area included the obstructed area by the steel rods). It obstructed the central part of the channel.

B: Peripheral obstruction—a blockage which obstructed the circumference of the channel.

C, D: Central segment obstruction—a strip of blockage which blocked the central part of the channel.

E, F: Peripheral segment obstruction—a segment which blocked part of the circumference of the channel.

The peripheral segment and the central segment located in the vertical flow should give a pressure drop independent of its position to the axis of symmetry. In the horizontal channel due to the flow stratification one expects the pressure drop to vary as a function its location relative to the axis of symmetry.

Single-phase pressure drops were measured for a wide range of Reynolds numbers for both vertical and horizontal flows.

Figure 20 illustrates an example of the observed axial pressure distribution. Five separate regions were observed, both in single and two-phase flows. Regions I and V represent the undisturbed channel flow. Region II displays a stagnation effect of the flow obstruction, resulting in a leveling off of the pressure. Region III shows a rapid drop in pressure due to a pressure-energy conversion into increased kinetic energy and an increased turbulence level. Significant flashing may occur due to the corresponding drop in the saturation temperature for one-component two-phase flows. In Region IV, some of the pressure is recovered as the velocity drops and the turbulence level decays. (The unrecovered pressure energy is dissipated). Figure 20 also shows the obstruction pressure drop, defined usually as the decrease in pressure due to the presence of a flow obstruction. The pressure drop in one-phase flow can be approximated:

$$\Delta P_{ob} = K_{ob} \frac{\rho_L V_0^2}{2} \qquad (67)$$

where K_{ob} is an overall pressure-loss coefficient.

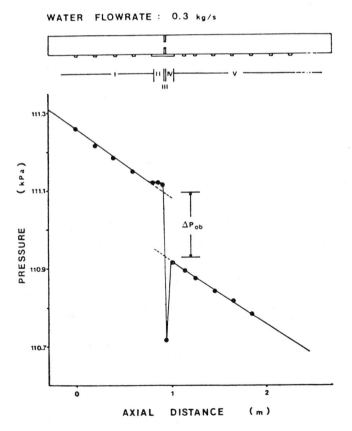

Figure 20. Pressure profile for single-phase (water) flow.

Table 1
Loss Coefficients, Momentum and Kinetic Energy Ratios in Single-Phase Flow

Obstruction shape (Figure 3)		Flow blockage (25%)			Flow blockage (40%)		
		K	r_{mom}	$r_{k.e.}$	K	r_{mom}	$r_{k.e.}$
Peripheral	B	0.30	0.10	0.06	1.80	0.18	0.12
Central	A	0.85	0.22	0.20	2.12	0.33	0.30
Central segment	C	0.74	0.16	0.16	2.14	0.29	0.25
Peripheral segment	E	0.68	0.145	0.11	2.01	0.247	0.20

The pressure-drop coefficients for the obstructions illustrated on Figure 18 are presented in Table 1. This tablle also shows the momentum and the kinetic-energy ratios of the obstructions defined as follows:

$$r_{mom} = \left(\int^{A_{ob}} V^2 \, dA \right) \Big/ \left(\int^{A_0} V^2 \, dA \right) \tag{68}$$

and

$$r_{k.e.} = \left(\int^{A_{ob}} V^3 \, dA \right) \Big/ \left(\int^{A_0} V^3 \, dA \right) \tag{69}$$

where r_{mom} = the momentum ratio
$r_{k.e.}$ = the kinetic energy ratio
A_{ob} = the obstruction area
A_0 = the channel area
V = the velocity of the flow

The momentum ratio, r_{mom}, was computed by integrating the momentum (based on the local velocity in the undisturbed fluid) over the obstructed area and over the channel area.

The kinetic energy ratio, $r_{k.e.}$, was computed by integrating the kinetic energy (based on the local velocity in the undisturbed fluid) over the obstructed area and over the channel area.

A turbulent profile with power law variation was assumed. As expected, for all obstruction shapes, the 40% obstruction produced a larger pressure drop than the 25% obstruction.

The largest pressure drops were produced by the central segments and the central obstruction for both 25% and 40% ratios.* This is in agreement with the momentum and the kinetic energy ratios and is probably due to the interception of the high velocity flow.

One can see that a large momentum and kinetic energy ratio is associated generally with larger pressure-loss coefficients. The lowest pressure-loss coefficients are due to the peripheral obstructions, as they obstruct the lower velocity region near the wall. The vertical and horizontal segments produce larger pressure drops than the peripheral segments for both 25% and 40% obstructions, since they intercept the higher velocity fluid.

It is likely that the obstruction shape influences also the turbulence generation and the re-attachment point. The influence cannot be quantified by the present kinetic energy and momentum calculations.

---

* The central obstruction including the supports block a total of 25% and respectively 40% of the channel area. Therefore, as compared with an ideal case of central obstruction, the drag is decreased due to a smaller blockage in the higher velocity central region. On the other hand, a slight increase of the drag is expected due to the effect of the supports. The calculations were carried out for the ideal geometry of a central disk.

The "K" values for horizontal flow were close to those in vertical flow. Some differences occurred due to experimental errors or slight geometry differences. The flow pattern was established in the horizontal flow through visualization and optical probe measurements. In the vertical flow there were no void measurements carried out and the flow distribution was established based on a map proposed by Hewitt and Roberts [22]. Two-phase flow pressure drop was investigated for vertical and horizontal bubbly and annular flows.

Bubbly Flow

The pressure loss is increasing with increasing flow quality as shown in Figures 21 and 22 for vertical flow upstream and downstream of the obstruction for 40% obstructed area. For upstream of the obstruction, the frictional pressure loss is not affected by the presence of the obstruction (Figure 21). It increases linearly with the flow quality and can be expressed in the form of

$$(\Delta P_F)_{TP} = 25.6x + (\Delta P_F)_L \tag{70}$$

where x is the quality, and $(\Delta P_F)_L$ is the single-phase pressure loss, within the range of study.

For downstream of the obstruction, as shown in Figure 22, similar characteristics as in the upstream are observed at low quality. As the quality increases, the effect of the obstruction becomes significant. The obstruction seems to promote the flow transition from bubbly to annular flow regimes (the trend of transition was also reported by Govier et al. [23]). Stronger effects of the obstructions on the downstream flow are observed for the central segment obstructions, with lesser effects observed for peripheral segment obstructions.

The pressure drop upstream and downstream of the obstruction for horizontal bubbly flow is presented in Figures 23 and 24. Comparison with the vertical flow shows that the pressure drop upstream of the obstruction is slightly more affected than for vertical flow. The pressure drop downstream of the obstruction is affected by the obstructions slightly less than for the vertical flow. Strongest effect is shown by the top peripheral segment. This is probably related to the void

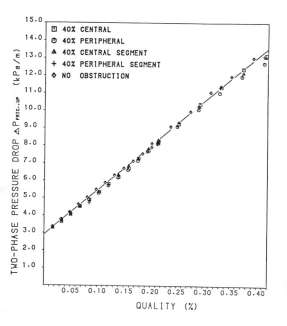

Figure 21. Two-phase frictional pressure losses for upstream of the 40% obstructions in vertical bubbly flow.

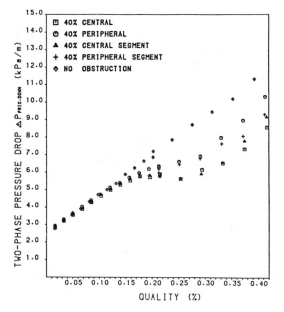

Figure 22. Two-phase frictional pressure losses for downstream of the 40% obstructions in vertical bubbly flow.

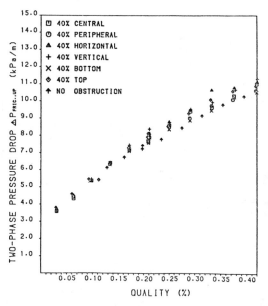

Figure 23. Two-phase frictional pressure losses for upstream of the 40% obstructions in horizontal bubbly flow.

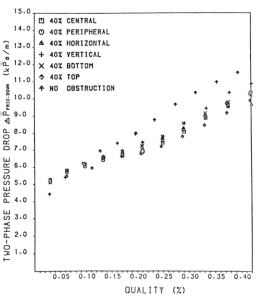

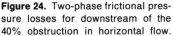

Figure 24. Two-phase frictional pressure losses for downstream of the 40% obstruction in horizontal flow.

distribution in the horizontal channel with the gaseous phase flowing mainly in the upper half of the channel due to stratification.

The pressure drop through the 25% obstruction for vertical and horizontal flow are illustrated in Figures 25 and 26. The largest pressure drop is produced in both cases for the central obstruction. This is in agreement with the discussion related to the void distribution variation due to the

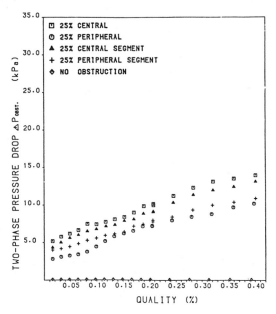

Figure 25. Two-phase local pressure losses due to the 25% obstructions in vertical bubbly flow.

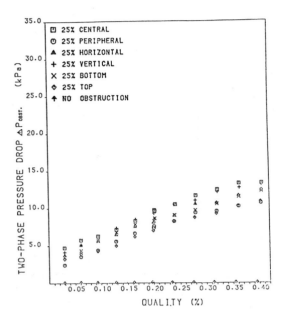

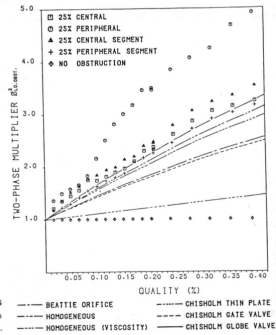

Figure 26. Two-phase local pressure losses due to the 25% obstructions in horizontal bubbly flow.

Figure 27. Two-phase multipliers for the local losses due to the 25% obstructions in vertical bubbly flow.

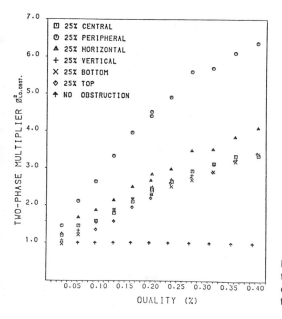

Figure 28. Two-phase multipliers for the local losses due to the 25% obstructions in horizontal bubbly flow.

obstruction effect. The liquid phase is deflected to the wall by the obstruction as shown and the gas forms a pocket in the wake generating strong turbulence and considerable pressure loss. Also, since the bubbly flow is dispersed, the central obstruction intercepts to a great extent the heavy phase thus producing significant pressure loss. In the vertical bubbly flow pressure losses are produced decreasingly by central, central segment, peripheral segment, and peripheral obstruction. The flow being dispersed behaves almost as a homogeneous one producing a similar pattern as found for single-phase flow. In horizontal flow, however, the pressure losses are produced decreasingly by the central obstruction closely followed by vertical segment, horizontal segment, bottom segment, peripheral and top segment. The bottom segment produces a consistently larger pressure loss than the top segment. This is an effect of the flow stratification which causes the bottom obstruction to intercept more of the heavy phase while the top obstruction intercepts more of the light phase.

The obstruction two-phase multipliers for the 25% obstructions for vertical and horizontal flows are illustrated on Figures 27 and 28. The two-phase multipliers are close for all obstructions other than the peripheral obstruction. This is probably due to the low pressure drop in single phase flow, resulting from the low velocity fluid intercepted by the liquid close to the wall. The same obstruction located in two-phase flow intercepts significantly the heavy phase flowing at considerably larger real velocities, as one can assume that the velocity profile would be considerably steeper for two-phase than for single-phase flow.

Comparison with two-phase multipliers in the literature shows that the correlations underpredict the pressure drop for the present experiments. This is not a surprising fact with the differences in geometry and flow parameters. The pressure drop through the 40% obstruction is shown in Figures 29 and 30 for vertical and horizontal flow. As expected, the pressure drops produced by the 40% obstructions are higher than for 25% obstructions. The order of decreasing pressure loss produced by the obstruction is the same as for 25% in vertical flow (slight differences are observed for peripheral segments and peripheral obstructions). However, for horizontal flows one can notice the effect of the flow stratification. The vertical central segment produces a larger pressure drop than the horizontal segment. Also the top peripheral segment produces a considerably lower pressure

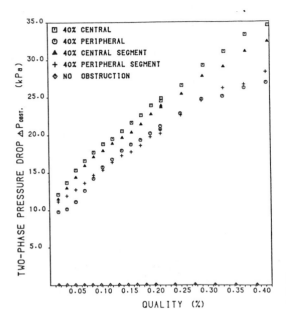

Figure 29. Two-phase local pressure losses due to the 40% obstructions in vertical bubbly flow.

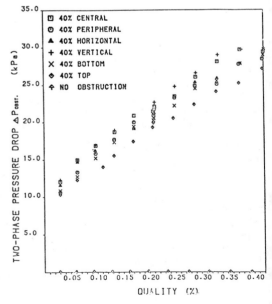

Figure 30. Two-phase local pressure losses due to the 40% obstructions in horizontal bubbly flow.

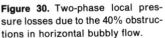

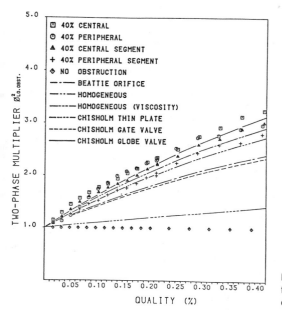

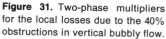

Figure 31. Two-phase multipliers for the local losses due to the 40% obstructions in vertical bubbly flow.

drop than the bottom segment as the latter intercepts mostly the heavy phase due to the flow stratification.

The corresponding two-phase multipliers are illustrated in Figures 31 and 32.

The two-phase multipliers for different obstructions are close for the vertical flow. For horizontal flow they are close except for the peripheral obstruction.

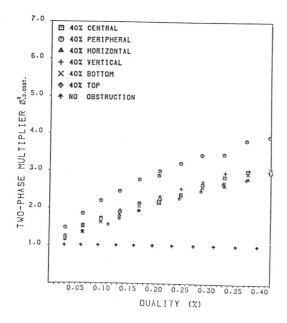

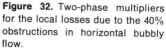

Figure 32. Two-phase multipliers for the local losses due to the 40% obstructions in horizontal bubbly flow.

Annular Flow

Measurements were carried out in vertical and horizontal annular flows. Some of the results are presented in the following.

In annular flow, the pressure drop upstream from the obstruction was slightly influenced by the obstruction.

Stronger influence was observed downstream from the obstruction. Figures 33 and 34 illustrate the downstream two-phase multipliers. The pressure drop through the 25% obstruction in vertical and horizontal flows are shown in Figures 35 and 36. One can see that in the vertical flow the pressure drops produced in decreasing order are by central, peripheral, central segment, and peripheral segment. The relatively larger pressure drop produced by the peripheral obstruction is due to the high flow velocity in the liquid annulus.

The pressure drops in the horizontal flow show the clear effect of stratification. This effect is considerably more noticeable than for bubbly flow. The lowest pressure drop is given by the top segment while the greatest is given by the bottom segment. This is clearly an effect of flow separation due to buoyancy forces. The bottom segment intercepts more of the liquid phase, while the top segment intercepts more of the gaseous phase. The peripheral obstruction, which was associated with the lowest pressure drop in single-phase flow, produces a relatively larger pressure drop as it intercepts the liquid annulus. Two-phase pressure drops for the 40% obstruction are illustrated in Figures 37 and 38. A similar effect of the obstructions on both vertical and horizontal flow pressure drops can be observed. Pressure drop for the bottom peripheral segment is considerably larger than for the top one. In order to explain the trends in a more quantitative manner, an integration of the momentum and the kinetic energy of the obstructed two-phase flow was carried out.

The calculations were based on the following assumptions:

- A turbulent profile with power-law variation was assumed in the thin liquid annulus surrounding the channel surface;

- Uniform velocity was assumed in the bulk of the liquid and gas flows, equal to the average velocity of each phase;

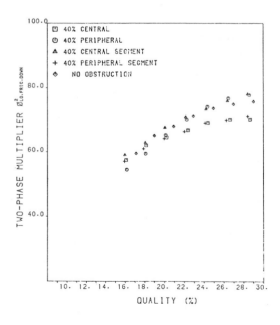

Figure 33. Two-phase downstream frictional multipliers for the 40% obstructions in vertical annular flow.

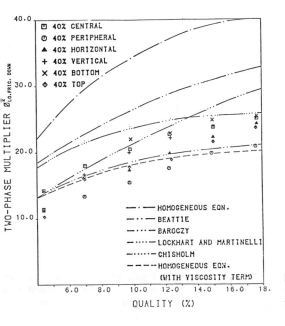

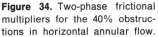

Figure 34. Two-phase frictional multipliers for the 40% obstructions in horizontal annular flow.

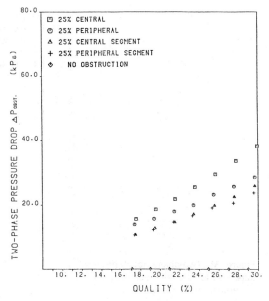

Figure 35. Two-phase local pressure loss for the 25% obstructions in horizontal annular flow.

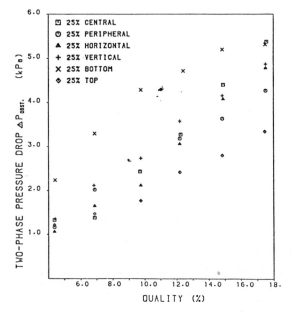

Figure 36. Two-phase local pressure loss for the 25% obstructions in horizontal annular flow.

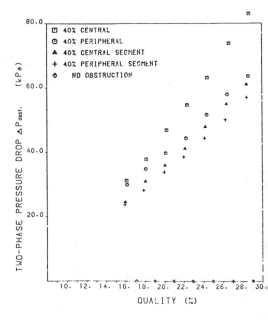

Figure 37. Two-phase local pressure loss for the 40% obstructions in vertical annular flow.

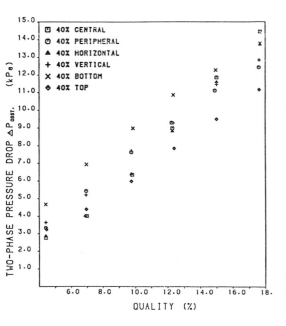

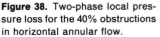

Figure 38. Two-phase local pressure loss for the 40% obstructions in horizontal annular flow.

- Along the channel axis (high void region), the entrained water was assumed to flow at the same velocity as the gas flow, an assumption which leads to an overestimation of the momentum and the kinetic energy ratio.

These assumptions are crude approximations, necessary because of the lack of knowledge of velocity distributions. Also, the phase distribution plays a considerably more important role in determining the momentum value than does the velocity distribution. This is due to the large density difference between the phases.

Table 2 presents the momentum and kinetic energy ratios computed for the different blockages. Figures 39–42 illustrate the obstruction two-phase multipliers for 20% and 40% vertical and horizontal flows, respectively. In vertical flow one observes the largest two-phase multipliers associated with the peripheral 25% obstructions. This is probably due to the interception of the liquid phase. For one-phase flow, the peripheral obstruction intercepts the lowest-velocity fluid, and thus, the pressure loss coefficient is considerably lower than for other obstruction shapes. For two-phase

Table 2
Momentum ratio, r_{mom}, and Kinetic Energy Ratio, $r_{k.e.}$, for Two-Phase Flow

Obstruction shape (Figure 3)		Flow blockage (25%)		Flow blockage (40%)	
		r_{mom}	$r_{k.e.}$	r_{mom}	$r_{k.e.}$
Peripheral	B	0.084	0.05	0.109	0.07
Central	A	0.117	0.27	0.252	0.57
Horizontal central segment	C	0.042	0.06	0.083	0.13
Vertical central segment	D	0.053	0.07	0.097	0.14
Peripheral bottom segment	E	0.086	0.07	0.11	0.09
Peripheral top segment	F	0.03	0.02	0.041	0.03

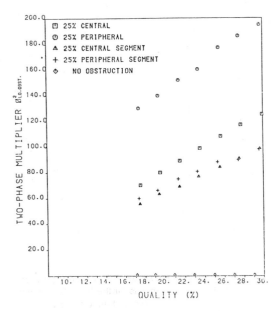

Figure 39. Two-phase obstruction multipliers for the 25% obstructions in vertical annular flow.

flow the peripheral obstruction intercepts the liquid phase, and this difference accounts for the large two-phase flow multiplier. For the 40% obstructions, as the intercepted area is larger, the relative increase of the two-phase multiplier for the peripheral obstruction is less pronounced.

In the horizontal flow the flow stratification causes the highest two-phase multiplier to appear for the peripheral bottom segment. The considerable difference between the top and the bottom obstruction multipliers are caused by the flow stratification.

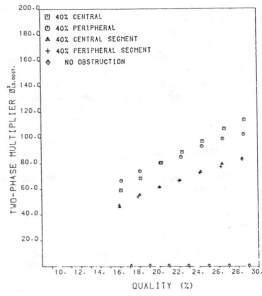

Figure 40. Two-phase obstruction multiplier for the 40% obstruction in vertical annular flow.

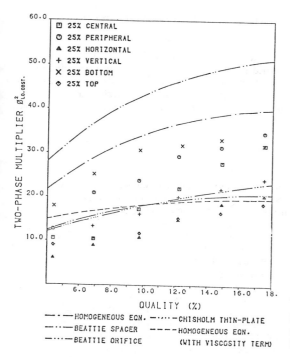

Figure 41. Two-phase obstruction multipliers for the 25% obstructions in horizontal annular flow.

One can conclude that the obstruction shape influence is more significant for annular flows than for bubbly flow. This is probably related to the separated higher quality flow associated with the annular pattern. This explains also the fact that annular flows through obstructions exhibit more dependence on the flow stratification.

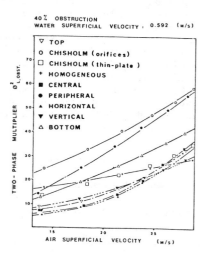

Figure 42. Two-phase obstruction pressure drop multiplier for the 40% obstruction in horizontal annular flow.

TWO-PHASE PRESSURE DROP THROUGH COMPLEX-SHAPED OBSTRUCTIONS (BUNDLES)

An understanding of two-phase flow in complex channel geometries is required because of the importance of flow boiling in water-cooled nuclear reactors. It is known that with single-phase flow, pressure equations for flow in round tubes can be extended with little loss in accuracy to complex geometries by replacing the diameter term in relevant dimensionless groups with the equivalent hydraulic diameter $D_e = 4A/P$ where A is the flow area and p is the sheared surface perimeter.

Vertical Two-Phase Flow Through Bundles

Beattie and Lowther have carried out experiments with upflow air-water mixtures through vertical seven-rod clusters at atmospheric pressure [24]. The pressure drop for the vertical flow investigated by Beattie and Lawther had two components: the frictional component and the gravitational component. The acceleration component was considered to be negligible.

Three different rod-cluster arrangements were used with upflow of air-water mixtures through vertical seven-rod clusters in a transparent shroud, 95-mm dia., 3.66-m length. Pressure tappings were located 1.97 and 2.69 m from the inlet end of the shroud.

The *first* cluster arrangement (42-mm equivalent dia. × 3.66 m) comprised a central rod (15.9-m dia.), surrounded by six equidistant rods (12.7-mm dia.) on a pitch circle (50.8-mm dia.). The rods were held in position relative to each other by seven sets of spacers made from 13 × 0.9 mm metal strip, which were placed at equal intervals along the cluster as shown in Figure 43. The cluster was held centrally in the shroud by connections screwed axially into the central rod at each end. A probe housing 2.07 m from the inlet end enabled local voidage gas bubble velocity to be measured by a double-needle conductivity probe of the type commonly used in two-phase flow experiments. The probe could be moved in both radial and circumferential directions relative to the cluster.

The *second* cluster arrangement was the same as the first except that the rod bundle was bowed into near contact with the shroud, 2.44 m from the inlet end, by means of screwed rods through the shroud. The rod cluster was thus in an extremely eccentric position in the region of the pressure tappings and the double-needle probe.

The *third* cluster arrangement (17-mm equivalent dia. × 3.66 m) comprised seven 25.4-mm dia. rods in the same shroud, six rods being equispaced on a 60-mm pitch circle diameter around the seventh. Sets of spacers, each consisting of eighteen 4.7-mm lengths of a 4.7-mm dia. threaded rod, separated the rods from each other and from the shroud, as shown in Figure 43; one of these was located 1 m below the upstream pressure tapping and another 77 mm above the downstream tapping.

Experimental data were obtained for flows of air-water mixtures with atmospheric pressure at the test section exit. The flow rates for experiments with the first two cluster arrangements correspond to gas and liquid superficial velocities ranging from 0 to 3.0 m s^{-1} for (j_G), and 0 to 2.0 m s^{-1} for (i_L). Flow rates in the third cluster arrangement correspond to gas and liquid superficial velocities ranging from 0 to 16 m s^{-1} for (j_G), and 0.08 to 2.0 m s^{-1} for (j_L).

Gas and liquid flow rates were measured separately upstream of the mixer section. For the first two cluster arrangements, local phase content and gas bubble velocity data were obtained from radial traverses at the probe housing for a number of azimuthal positions of the probe housing, relative to the cluster. The results are as follows.

42-mm Equivalent Diameter, Cluster Arrangements

Pressure gradient data. Single-phase pressure-drop measurements resulted in friction factors for the first and second cluster arrangements which are, respectively, ~30% and ~20% above those corresponding to the Nikuradse equation:

$$1/\sqrt{f} = 4 \log Re \sqrt{f} - 0.4 \tag{71}$$

AXIAL FLOW THROUGH SEVEN-ROD CLUSTERS

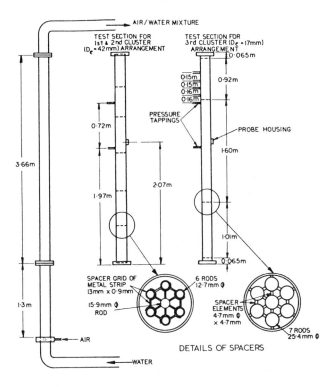

Figure 43. Test arrangements.

These are somewhat higher than expected, and apparently reflect an influence of the spacers and the probe assembly. Further evidence of this influence comes from an analysis of the two-phase voidage data discussed later. The reduction of friction factors on bowing was expected and can be explained by a decrease in effective shear surface under bowed conditions.

The two-phase flows were observed to be bubble flows, either with or without slugs. Axial pressure gradients in these flows had significant contributions from both gravity and friction for the bubble-slug flows, whereas those in the bubble flows were due predominantly to gravity. Pressure gradient data were analyzed by subtracting estimates of the frictional component and the void fraction was then derived from the gravitational component using the relation:

$$\left|\frac{dp}{dz}\right|_g = \{\rho_L(1 - \langle\alpha\rangle) + \rho_g\langle\alpha\rangle\}g \tag{72}$$

where $|dp/dz|_g$ = gravitational pressure drop
        ρ_L, ρ_g = liquid and vapor density
        $\langle\alpha\rangle$ = void fraction averaged over the cross-section

Flow structure. The double-needle conductivity probe was used to obtain local voidage and bubble velocity contour maps for selected flow conditions in both cluster arrangements. The conductivity probe measurements were confined to bubble flows because preliminary tests indicated that meaningful velocities could not be obtained if slugs were present.

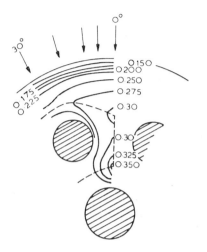

Figure 44. Void contour map for nonbowed 42-mm equivalent diameter rod cluster.

Figures 44 and 45 show typical flow structure results in which the velocity and voidage contours follow the broadly expected trends, but two points are noteworthy. The first is that the rods are not necessarily at the center of the subchannel boundaries obtained from the contours; this is relevant for rod-centered subchannel analysis studies. The second point is that secondary flows, as evidenced by irregularities in the velocity contours in the rod-free region of the bowed cluster data, play a stronger role than is the case in single-phase flows.

17-mm Equivalent Diameter, Cluster Arrangement

Pressure losses. Pressure gradients were examined upstream and downstream from one of the spacers. For superficial liquid velocities greater than $1 \mathrm{~m~s}^{-1}$, the pressure gradient was predominantly frictional, and the gravitational component was allowed for using Zuber and Findlay's equation [25].

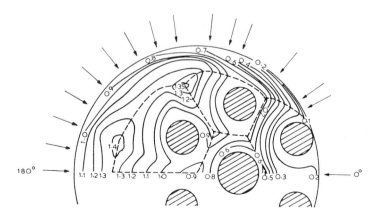

Figure 45. Bubble velocity contour map in ms^{-1} for bowed 42-mm equivalent diameter rod cluster.

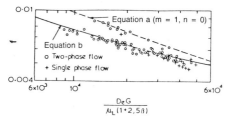

Figure 46. Bubble flow friction factors upstream of spacer of 17-mm equivalent diameter rod cluster.

The pressure gradients downstream of the spacer, determined from measurements at the four downstream pressure tappings, indicated that the effect of the spacer had largely disappeared after 5 hydraulic diameters and rarely extended to 15 diameters. Friction factors beyond 15 diameters downstream of the spacer were the same as those upstream of the spacer. The upstream and the recovered downstream axial static pressure profiles were extrapolated to determine the pressure losses associated with the spacer, and hence the spacer loss coefficients.

The friction factors upstream of the spacer are illustrated in Figure 46 as a function of the parameter $De\ G/\mu_1\ (1 + 2.5\beta)$ where De is the equivalent diameter, G is the mass flux, μ_L is the liquid viscosity and β is the volume flow fraction.

Equations a and b in Figure 46 are:

a. $\dfrac{1}{\sqrt{f}} = (\sqrt{2})^{m+4}\{\log Re\ \sqrt{f} - (0.11m + 0.5m + 1.1)\}$

b. $\dfrac{1}{f} = 4 \log Re\sqrt{f} - 0.4$

The friction data for higher voidages could not be correlated with a if m and n are integers. However, the data do agree with the equation if a half-integer value of m is used. For the general case described by a relation

$$f = \min\{f(0, -2, a), f(m, n, c)\} \tag{73}$$

all friction values for superficial velocity higher than $1\ m\ s^{-1}$ agree with:

$$f = \min\{f(0, -2, a), f(-2, -6.5, c)\} \tag{74}$$

The results are illustrated in Figure 47.

It has been suggested [26] that the single-phase-pressure-loss coefficient/Reynolds-number curves should apply to the two-phase case, provided that the two-phase Reynolds number is appropriately defined. This is the case with the present spacer loss coefficient data illustrated in Figure 48. The scatter in the data is caused by the relatively small pressure drop across the spacer, combined with the extrapolation procedure necessary to estimate this pressure drop.

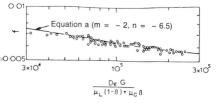

Figure 47. Annular flow friction factors upstream of spacer of 17-mm equivalent diameter rod cluster.

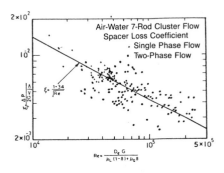

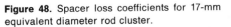

Figure 48. Spacer loss coefficients for 17-mm equivalent diameter rod cluster.

The Reynolds number was determined based on a wavy gas-liquid interface sublayer type with the viscosity μ equal to:

$$\mu = \mu_L(1 - \beta) + \mu_G\beta \tag{75}$$

The experiments have shown that the data in Beattie's experiment were consistent with the mixing length concept developed for two-phase flow in round tubes using the equivalent diameter concept. The bowing of the rod cluster resulted in a $\sim 10\%$ decrease in two-phase friction loss and no discernible effect on average void. Beattie found that pressure loss coefficients of rod spacer elements were applicable to two-phase flow conditions if the appropriate Reynolds numbers were used.

Effect of Streamlining on Bundle Pressure Drop in Horizontal Flow

Investigations were carried out to assess the influence of streamlining and bundle misalignment on the pressure drops. The experiments were carried out for horizontal configurations at low pressures.

Most of the pressure drop in the primary circuit of a nuclear reactor takes place along the fuel bundle. In the case of the horizontal CANDU-type fuel bundles, the bundle string pressure drop is composed of skin friction pressure drop, junction pressure drop*, spacer pressure drop, and acceleration pressure drop in two-phase flow.

The skin friction pressure drop for a channel is obtained by using the Darcy-Weisbach equation:

$$\Delta P_F = \frac{fL}{D_e} \frac{\rho_\ell v^2}{2} \tag{76}$$

where f = the friction factor
      L = the length of the bundle
      D_e = the equivalent hydraulic diameter
      ρ_ℓ = the density of the liquid
      v = the flow velocity

Many authors [27] recommend this equation for the bundle geometry, with the friction factor evaluated using equivalent hydraulic diameter. However, the friction factor has been found experimentally to be also affected by the channel geometry [28, 29]. Rehme [30] and Malak et al. [31]

---

* In CANDU reactors, the reactor core is made up of several hundred pressure tubes, each containing a string of twelve or thirteen 50-cm-long bundles. The junction pressure drop refers to the pressure drop at the junction of two adjacent 50-cm fuel bundles.

have studied this effect and have proposed relations which can be used to estimate the friction factor in bundle geometry.

The pressure drop at the junction of the two bundles can be written as

$$\Delta P_J = K_J \frac{\rho_\ell v^2}{2} \tag{77}$$

where K_J is the junction loss coefficient. It consists of the pressure drops because of

1. Obstructions such as an end-plate.
2. Discountinuity of fuel rods.

The pressure drop due to obstruction depends on the size, location, and shape of the blockage. For various types of obstructions, the streamlined shape has the best pressure recovery. The pressure recovery can be improved by rounding the leading edge of the obstruction [31]. The pressure drop caused by the discontinuity of the elements has been observed in both aligned bundles [29] and aligned plates [33]. It is simply an effect of flow expansion and contraction. The pressure drop can be reduced if the areas of the exit and entrance change gradually. In a string of bundles, more pressure drop can occur in the junction area if adjacent bundles are misaligned (see Figure 49) because of the increased blockage area from the misaligned downstream bundle. This additional pressure drop depends on the shape of the end-plug and can be reduced by using a shape that does not promote turbulence.

The spacer which is used to maintain the subchannel space and prevent rod vibration, also interferes with the subchannel flow and increases the overall pressure drop. The spacer pressure drop can be written as

$$\Delta P_S = K_S \frac{\rho_\ell v^2}{2} \tag{78}$$

where K_S is the spacer loss coefficient. It was found that it is not only dependent upon the size and location of the spacer, but that it is also affected by factors such as the shape of the leading edge [34] and that of the trailing edge [35], the roughness of the rod [36], and the length of the spacer [37].

The total pressure drop is the summation of the skin friction pressure drop and the local pressure drops in the junction plane and the spacer plane. It can be written as

$$\Delta P_T = \Delta P_F + \Delta P_J + \Delta P_S = \left(\frac{fL}{D_e} + K_J + K_S\right)\frac{\rho_\ell v^2}{2} = K_T \frac{\rho_\ell v^2}{2} \tag{79}$$

where K_T is the total loss coefficient.

a) ALIGNED REGULAR BUNDLES

b) 22.5° MISALIGNED REGULAR BUNDLES

c) 45° MISALIGNED STREAMLINED BUNDLES

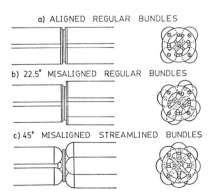

Figure 49. Change of flow blockage area in junction plane due to bundle rotation.

In two-phase flow the total pressure drop in the horizontal bundles consists of the two-phase frictional pressure drop, the two-phase accelerational pressure drop, the two-phase junction pressure drop, and the two-phase spacer drop. As the channel is horizontal gravitational components are not present. The frictional pressure drop may be expressed in terms of the single-phase pressure drop and the two-phase multiplier which is defined as

$$\phi_{LO}^2 = \frac{\Delta P_{TP}}{\Delta P_{LO}} \tag{80}$$

where ΔP_{TP} is the two-phase pressure drop, and ΔP_{LO} is the single-phase pressure drop assuming the total flow to be liquid. Two-phase multipliers as defined in Reference 31 are used also to evaluate the pressure drop through obstructions, as discussed.

The accelerational pressure drop is obtained by evaluating the change of the momentum in the axial direction by using a one-dimensional approach. It is a significant factor in two-phase flow with phase change but can be neglected when phase change does not occur since the density gradients are small in channel flow for the low pressure range investigated.

The total pressure drop is made up of the components already mentioned. It can be written as

$$(\Delta P_{TP})_T = (\Delta P_{TP})_F + (\Delta P_{TP})_J + (\Delta P_{TP})_S$$
$$= (\Delta P_{LO})_F (\phi_{LO}^2)_F + (\Delta_{LO})_J (\phi_{LO}^2)_J + (\Delta P_{LO})_S (\phi_{LO}^2)_S \tag{81}$$

where $(\Delta P_{TP})_F$, $(\Delta P_{TP})_J$, and $(\Delta P_{TP})_S$ are the two-phase pressure drop for friction, junction, and spacer, respectively; $(\Delta P_{LO})_F$, $(\Delta P_{LO})_J$, and $(\Delta P_{LO})_S$ are the single-phase pressure drop for friction, junction, and spacer, respectively; and $(\phi_{LO}^2)_F$, $(\phi_{LO}^2)_J$, and $(\phi_{LO}^2)_S$ are the two-phase multipliers for the friction, junction, and spacer, respectively.

The objective of the work which follows was to compare the single and two-phase pressure drops for the simulated regular bundle used currently in the CANDU reactor with those for the modified streamlined bundle [38, 39].

The schematic diagram of the apparatus used is shown in Figure 50. Water and air mixture was stabilized in a calming section before entering the test-section. The test-section was constructed with a 0.0381-m ID, 1.83-m long lucite tube. Twenty-three pressure taps were installed along a string of three 0.5-m long bundles. Two panels of Meriam 33KB35 well-type, multi-tube manometers were used to measure the pressure variation along the bundles. The manometric fluid used was water for the single-phase test, and mercury for the two-phase test. After passing through the test-section, the two-phase mixture was led to a reservoir where the phases were separated. The water was recirculated in the loop, and the air was exhausted to the atmosphere.

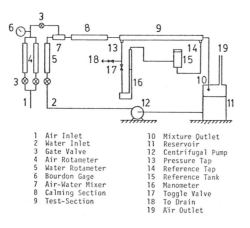

1	Air Inlet	10	Mixture Outlet
2	Water Inlet	11	Reservoir
3	Gate Valve	12	Centrifugal Pump
4	Air Rotameter	13	Pressure Tap
5	Water Rotameter	14	Reference Tap
6	Bourdon Gage	15	Reference Tank
7	Air-Water Mixer	16	Manometer
8	Calming Section	17	Toggle Valve
9	Test-Section	18	To Drain
		19	Air Outlet

Figure 50. Schematic Diagram of the loop.

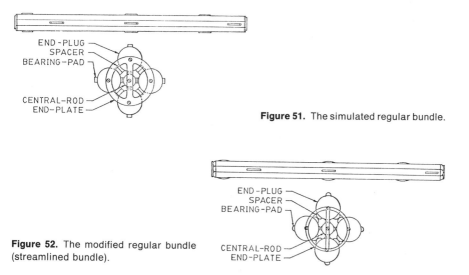

Figure 51. The simulated regular bundle.

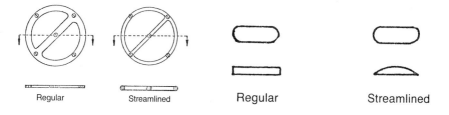

Figure 52. The modified regular bundle (streamlined bundle).

Three bundles were constructed for both the simulated regular bundles (Figure 51) and the streamlined bundles (Figure 52). Each of the three bundles was composed of four stainless-steel tubes covered with an end-plug in each end, one central rod, two end-plates, sixteen spacers, and twelve bearing pads. The end-plug was of the flat-plate type for the regular bundle, whereas it was hemispherical for the streamlined bundle. The central rod was included to obtain the same hydraulic diameter as the 37-element bundle. The shape of the end-plate is illustrated in Figure 53. It was circular with a rectangular cross-sectional area for the regular bundle and with a circular cross-sectional area for the streamlined bundle. The sizes of the spacer and bearing pad were similar for both types of bundles, but the edges of these fixtures had been smoothed and rounded for the streamlined bundle (Figure 54). The water flow rate for single-phase flow was varied from 0.44 kg/s to 1.88 kg/s.

For two-phase flow, measurements were carried out at water flow rates of 1.57, 1.26, and 0.94 kg/s, with air flow rates varying respectively between 0.00026 to 0.00744 kg/s, 0.00177 to 0.017 kg/s, and 0.00841 to 0.021 kg/s.

The measurements were performed on both types of bundle in various bundle rotations (0°, 22.5°, and 45.0°) for both single- and two-phase flows.

Single- and two-phase pressure drops were recorded, and some of the results are presented in the following.

Regular	Streamlined

Regular   Streamlined

Figure 53. End-plate comparison.   **Figure 54.** Spacer comparison.

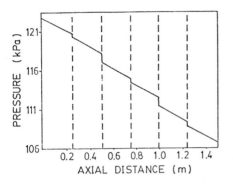

Figure 55. Single-phase pressure variation of the aligned regular bundle.

Single-Phase Pressure Drop

The single-phase pressure distribution for the aligned regular bundles is illustrated in Figure 55. The gradual decrease of pressure along the bundle is due to skin friction. The frictional pressure gradient is relatively constant throughout the test-section. The junctions and the spaces are characterized by sudden drop of pressure. The location of different planes are indicated by dotted lines. The pressure drops in the junction planes are larger than those in the spacer planes.

The frictional pressure drop can be expressed in terms of a friction factor as shown in Figure 56. Some correlations are illustrated for comparison. The friction factors are the same for both types of bundles and for various misalignments. Both predictions proposed by Rehme [30] and Malak et al. [31] have shown good agreement with the results, whereas the friction factors derived from the relations for smooth tubes are too low.

The junction loss coefficients for various bundle arrangements are shown in Figure 57. For the regular bundle, the junction loss coefficients are not affected by the change in Reynolds number, but are strongly influenced by the misalignments of the bundles. For a large misalignment, the junction loss coefficient is large. This is caused by the additional blockage from the exposed rods. In contrast, the junction loss coefficients for the streamlined bundle vary with Reynolds numbers and are not affected by misalignment. This can be explained by the precedence of friction drag (which depends on Re) over pressure drag which is reduced for the streamlined bundle.

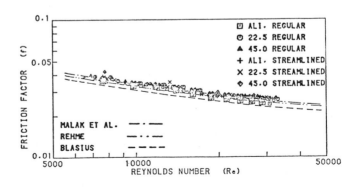

Figure 56. Friction factors for the bundles.

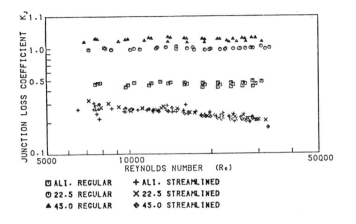

Figure 57. Junction loss coefficients for various bundle arrangements.

The spacer loss coefficients, shown in Figure 58, are only slightly affected by the Reynolds number. They are larger for the regular bundle than for the streamlined bundle. This indicates that the pressure recovery can be improved with minor modification to the shape of the obstruction. Even though bundle misalignment does not alter the spacer's blockage area, the spacer loss coefficients appear to be slightly decreased as the misalignment increases. One possible explanation would be that the spacers are located within the separation region created by the junction of misaligned bundles.

The total pressure drop is also expressed in terms of loss coefficient (Figure 59). The loss coefficient decreases as the flow rate increases. Of the total pressure drop, the frictional component contributes approximately 50% for the 45° misaligned regular bundle and 75% for the streamlined bundle. The second dominant factor is the junction pressure drop which induces the dependency of the total pressure drop upon the bundle misalignment. Streamlining the bundle junction reduces the junction pressure drop by up to 75% and decreases overall pressure drop up to about 33% (comparison is made between the streamlined bundle and the 45° misaligned regular bundle) at larger Reynolds numbers. Though improvement has been shown for the spacer pressure drop of the streamlined shape, it is not too significant in the total pressure drop. This is due to the fact that the spacer pressure drop is only about 5% of the total pressure drop.

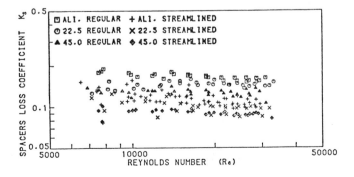

Figure 58. Spacer loss coefficients for various bundle arrangements.

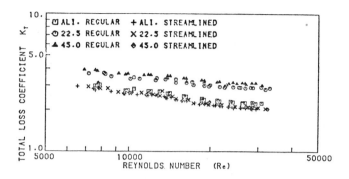

Figure 59. Total loss coefficients for various bundle arrangements.

Two-phase pressure drop. The two-phase pressure distribution for the aligned regular bundle is illustrated in Figure 60. It follows the same trend as the single phase, but the magnitude of the pressure drop is much larger. Since the two-phase mixture is water and air, the accelerational pressure drop is not significant (about 5% of the local pressure). However, it is eliminated from the pressure drop by using an estimated void fraction variation [40]. The pressure decreases because of friction, but the rate of decrease is not uniform along the string of bundles due to the presence of the flow obstructions. The mean frictional pressure drop for the last two bundles was considered in the present calculation. The local pressure drops due to the junctions and the spacers are also shown in Figure 60. As in the single-phase flow, the junction pressure drop is larger than the spacer pressure drop. These local drops are constant along the string of bundles. The small deviation might be caused by the slight changes in density and void distribution as well as experimental inaccuracy. The mean values for each type of local pressure drop were considered in the present calculation. The spacer pressure drop in the first bundle is not considered, however, because it occurs in the entrance region.

The two-phase frictional pressure gradients were measured for different flow rates. As an example, the results for a water flow rate of 1.26 kg/s are illustrated in Figure 61. The two-phase frictional pressure gradient increases with increasing quality. It is not influenced by the misalignment of the bundles. An increase of the friction pressure gradient for increasing water flow rate was also observed. The two-phase frictional multiplier is shown in Figure 62 for the same water flow rate. In the same figure. some correlations are illustrated for comparison. For low quality, all presented correlations predict reasonably well the experimental results. For increased quality, Beattie's correlation gives the best performance.

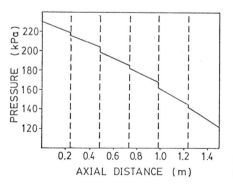

Figure 60. Two-phase pressure variation of the aligned regular bundle.

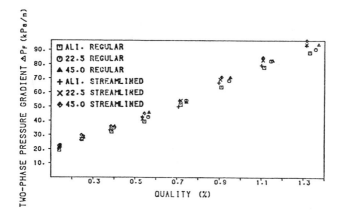

Figure 61. Two-phase frictional pressure gradient for 1.26 kg/s liquid mass flow rate.

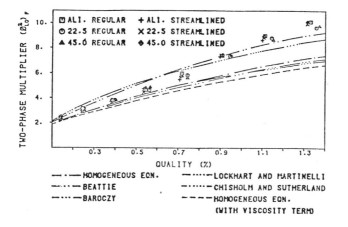

Figure 62. Two-phase frictional multiplier for 1.26 kg/s liquid mass flow rate.

The two-phase junction pressure drop for 1.26 kg/s water flow rate is shown in Figure 63. The pressure drop increases with increasing water and air flow rates. Similar to the single-phase junction pressure drop, the bundle misalignment affects the pressure drop for the regular bundle but not for the streamlined bundle. The regular bundle with 45° misalignment has the largest pressure drop, while the streamlined bundle has the smallest.

The junction two-phase multiplier is shown in Figure 64. It is dependent on the fluid flow rate. The streamlined bundle has the smallest pressure drop, yet it gives the largest two-phase multiplier. This is so because the ratio of the single-phase pressure drop of the regular bundle, and that of the streamlined bundle is larger than the same ratio in two-phase flow. That is:

$$\frac{(\Delta P_{LO})_{Reg.}}{(\Delta P_{LO})_{Str.}} > \frac{(\Delta P_{TP})_{Reg.}}{(\Delta P_{TP})_{Str.}} \tag{82}$$

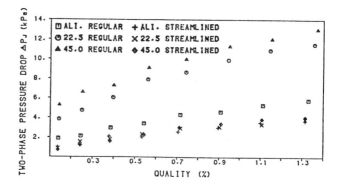

Figure 63. Two-phase junction pressure drop for 1.26 kg/s liquid mass flow rate.

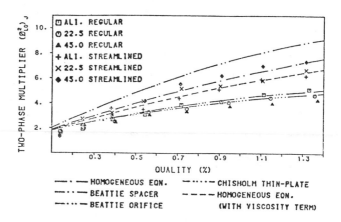

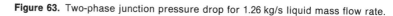

Figure 64. Two-phase junction multiplier for 1.26 kg/s liquid mass flow rate.

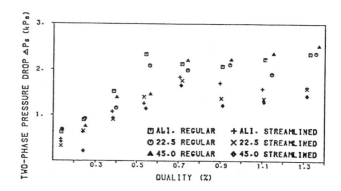

Figure 65. Two-phase spacer pressure drop for 1.26 kg/s liquid mass flow rate.

where the subscripts Reg. and Str. represent the respective pressure drop for the regular bundle and for the streamlined bundle.

Some correlations are shown in the same figure for comparison. Since the junction two-phase multipliers vary for different bundle misalignments and streamlining, none of the correlation is capable of predicting the various multipliers. Overall, the orifice correlation proposed by Beattie is the best for estimating the multiplier for the aligned regular bundle, while the homogeneous two-phase multiplier provides good agreement with the values for the streamlined bundle.

The two-phase spacer pressure drop for 1.26 kg/s water flow rate is shown in Figure 65. It is affected by the water and air flow rates, but is not significantly influenced by the bundle misalignments. Though the results are quite scattered, it can be seen that the regular bundle has caused higher pressure drop. The small variation of pressure drop between 0.5% and 1.0% quality is probably caused by the flow transition effect.

The two-phase multiplier for the spacer is shown in Figure 66. It increases with increasing quality and is not affected by the bundle misalignment. For both types of bundles, the two-phase multipliers are close. A comparison between the correlations indicates that the homogeneous theory predicts the experimental results reasonably well, but the Beattie orifice correlation tends to underestimate the results.

The total two-phase pressure drop for 1.26 kg/s water flow rate is shown in Figure 67. The first bundle was not included in order to avoid entrance effects. The pressure drop increases with increasing quality. For the regular bundle, it is larger than that for the streamlined bundle, and it is affected by the misalignment of the bundles. The 45° misaligned bundle has the largest pressure drop. The pressure drop for the streamlined bundle is not affected by the misalignment, and it is smaller than that for the regular bundle (the larger total pressure drop for the streamlined 45° bundle as compared with the aligned regular bundle is due to the difference in friction pressure loss (see Figure 61).

The two-phase multiplier for the total pressure drop is shown in Figure 68. It is larger for the streamlined bundles. This is so because the ratio of the single-phase pressure drop of the regular bundle and that of the streamlined bundle is larger than the same ratio in two-phase flow.

In conclusion, the streamlined bundle has shown a better performance than the regular bundle because the streamlined bundle causes the least pressure drops in both junction and spacer area and its pressure drops are independent of bundle misalignment.

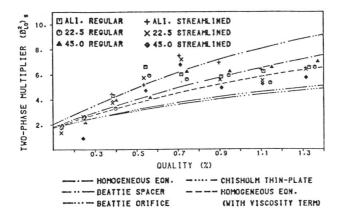

Figure 66. Two-phase spacer multiplier for 1.26 kg/s liquid mass flow rate.

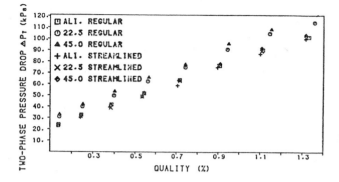

Figure 67. Total two-phase pressure drop for 1.26 kg/s liquid mass flow rate.

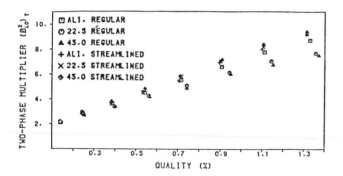

Figure 68. Total two-phase multiplier for 1.26 kg/s liquid mass flow rate.

Acknowledgments

The author wishes to acknowledge the assistance of Laurence Leung for the experimental work, Zia Abdullah for arranging the manuscript, the AECL and the National Research Council of Canada for financial support.

NOTATION

A	area	V	velocity
g	conversion factor = 32.2 ft-lb_m/s^2-lb_f	v	specific volume
K	loss coefficient	W	mass flow rate
N	number of velocity heads	x	vapor flow weight fraction
p	pressure		

Greek Symbols

α	vapor volume fraction	ρ	density
σ	area ratio		

Subscripts

0   refers to total mass flowing as liquid (no   2   refers to position downstream from
    vapor present)   expansion
1   refers to position upstream from   f   refers to saturated liquid
    expansion   g   refers to saturated vapor

REFERENCES

1. Lottes, P. A., *Expansion Losses in Two-Phase Flow Nuclear Science Engineering*, Vol. 9, pp. 26–31, 1961.
2. Romie, F., American Standard Company, private communication (1958).
3. Richardson, B. L., "Some Problems in Horizontal Two-Phase, Two-Components Flow," ANL-59YS, 1958.
4. Chisholm, D., "Prediction of Pressure Drop at Pipe Fittings During Two-Phase Flow," Proc. 13th International Inst. of Refrig. Congress, Washington, D. C., Aug. 29–Sept. 3, 2, pp. 781–789, 1971.
5. Collier, J. G., *Convective Boiling and Condensation*, Second Edition, McGraw-Hill, 1981.
6. Geiger, G. E., and Rohrer, W. M., "Sudden Contraction Losses in Two-Phase Flow," *Journal of Heat Transfer*, Trans. ASME, pp. 1–9, May 1966.
7. Mendler, O. T., "Sudden Expansion Losses in Single and Two-Phase Flow" Ph.D. dissertation, Mechanical Engineering Department, University of Pittsburgh, Pittsburgh, PA., 1963.
8. Chisholm, D., "Flow of Incompressible Two-Phase Mixtures Through Sharp-Edged Orifice," *Journal of Mechanical Engineering Science*, Vol. 3, No. 1, (1967).
9. Hoopes, J. W., "Flow of Steam-Water Mixtures in a Heated Annulus and Through Orifices," *A.I.Ch.E. J.*, 1957, 3(2), pp. 268–275.
10. Bergelin, O. P., and Gazley, C., "Cocurrent Gas/Liquid Flow: Part 1 Flow in Horizontal Tubes," Proc. Heat Transfer and Fluid Mechanics Inst., 5–18, 1949.
11. Jenkins, R., "Two-Phase, Two-Component Flow of Air and Water," M. S. thesis, University of Delaware, 1947.
12. Alves, G. E., "Co-Current Liquid/Gas Flow in a Pipeline Contractor," *Chem. Engng Prog.*, 50, pp. 449–456 (1954).
13. Baker, O., "Multiphase Flow in Pipelines," *Oil Gas J.*, Nov. 10, pp. 156–167, Progress Report, 1958.
14. Mandhane, J. M., Gregory, G. A., and Aziz, K., "A Flow Pattern Map for Gas Liquid Flow in Horizontal Pipes," *Int. J. Multiphase Flow*, 1, pp. 537–553, 1974.
15. Hubbard, M. G., and Dukler, A. E., "Characterization of Flow Regimes for Horizontal Two-Phase Flow: Statistical Analysis of Wall Pressure Fluctuations," Proc. Heat Transfer and Fluid Mechanics Conf., Santa Clara, Calif., 1966.
16. Salcudean, M., Chun, C. H., and Groeneveld, D. C., "Effect of Flow Obstructions on the Flow Pattern Transitions in Horizontal Two-Phase Flow," *Int. J. Multiphase Flow*, Vol. 9, pp. 87–90 (1983).
17. Taitel, Y., and Dukler, A. E., "A Model for Predicting Flow Regime Transitions in Horizontal and Near Horizontal Gas-Liquid Flow," *A.I.Ch.E. J.*, 22, pp. 47–55 (1976).
18. Salcudean, M., Chun, C. H., and Groeneveld, D. C., "Effect of Flow Obstructions in Void Distribution in Horizontal Air-Water Flow," *Int. Journal of Multiphase Flow*, Vol. 9, pp. 91–96 (1983).
19. Chun, C. H., M.A.Sc. thesis, Dept. of Mech. Eng., Univ. of Ottawa, 1979.
20. Leung, L., M.A.Sc. thesis, Dept. of Mech. Eng., Univ. of Ottawa, 1983.
21. Salcudean, M., Groeneveld, D. C., and Leung, L., "Effect of Flow-Obstruction Geometry in Pressure Drops in Horizontal Air-Water Flow," *Int. Journal of Multiphase Flow*, Vol. 9, No. 1, pp. 73–85 (1983).
22. Hewitt, G. F., and Roberts, D. N., "Studies of Two-Phase Flow Patterns by Simultaneous X-Ray and Flash Photography," AERE-M2159.

23. Govier, G. W., Radford, B. A., and Dunn, J. S. C., "The Upwards Vertical Flow of Air-Water Mixtures: I. The Effect of Air and Water Rates on Flow Pattern Holdup and Pressure Drop," *Can. J. Chem. Eng.*, Vol. 35, pp. 58–70 (1957).

24. Beattie, D. R. H., and Lowther, K. R., "Two-phase Hydrodynamic Experiments with Axial Flow Through Seven-rod Clusters," *Int. J. Multiphase Flow, Vol.* 7, pp. 423—437 (1981).

25. Zuber, N., and Findlay, J. A., "Average Volumetric Concentration in Two-Phase Flow Systems," *J. Heat Transfer*, 87, pp. 453–468 (1965).

26. Beattie, D. R. H., "A Note on the Calculation of Two-Phase Pressure Losses," *Nucl. Engng. Des.*, 25, pp. 395–402 (1973).

27. Tong, L. S., "Pressure Drop Performance of a Rod Bundle in Single-Phase Coolant Heat Transfer in Rod Bundles," V. E. Schrock (Ed.), pp. 57–69, ASME, New York, 1968.

28. Courtaud, M., Ricque, R., and Martinet, B., "Etude des Pertes de Charge dans des Conduites Circulaires Contenant un Faisceau de Barreaux, *Chem. Eng. Sci.*, Vol. 21, pp. 881–893 (1966).

29. Le Tourneau, B. W., Grimble, R. E., and Zerbe, J. E., "Pressure Drop for Parallel Flow Through Rod Bundles," Trans. ASME, pp. 1751–1758, Nov. 1957.

30. Rehme, K., "Simple Method of Predicting Friction Factors of Turbulent Flow in Non-Circular Channels," *Int. J. Heat Mass Transfer*, Vol. 16, pp. 993–950 (1973).

31. Malak, J., Hejna, J., and Schmid, J., "Pressure Losses and Heat Transfer in Non-Circular Channels with Hydraulically Smooth Walls," *Int. J. Heat Mass Transfer*, Vol. 18, pp. 139–149 (1975).

32. Idel'chik, I. E., *Handbook of Hydraulic Resistance*, AEC-tr-6630, 1966.

33. Cur, N., and Sparrow, E. M., "Experiments on Heat Transfer and Pressure Drop for a Pair of Colinear, Interrupted Plates Aligned with the Flow," *Int. J. Heat Mass Transfer*, Vol. 21, pp. 1069–1080 (1978).

34. Rehme, K., "The Pressure Drop of Spacer Grids in Rod Bundles of 12 Rods with Smooth and Roughened Surfaces," KFK-2697.

35. De Stordeur, A. N., "Drag Coefficient for Fuel Element Spacers," *Nucleonics*, Vol. 19, No. 6, pp. 74–79, 1961.

36. Rehme, K., "Pressure Drop of Spacer Grids in Smooth and Roughened Rod Bundles," *Nuclear Technology*, Vol. 33, pp. 314–317 (1977).

37. Grover, R. B., and Venkat Raj, V., "Pressure Drop Along Longitudinally-Finned Seven-Rod Cluster Nuclear Fuel Elements," *Nuclear Engineering and Design*, Vol. 58, pp. 79–83 (1980).

38. Leung, L., et al., "Effect of Streamlining on Bundle Pressure Drop," Proceedings of the 3rd Multiphase Flow and Heat Transfer Symposium Workshop, (18–20 Apr., 1983) (in print).

39. Messina, W. A., "Steam-Water Pressure Drop and Critical Discharge Flow-Digital Computer Program," HW-65706, June 1960.

40. Salcudean, M., and Leung, L., "Effect of Flow Obstruction on Pressure Loss in Vertical Flow," Internal report, Dept. of Mech. Eng. University of Ottawa, 1983.

41. Salcudean, M., and Leung, L., "Effect of Streamlining on Pressure Loss," Internal report, Dept. of Mech. Eng., University of Ottawa, 1982.

CHAPTER 27

VORTEX EMISSION BEHIND OBSTACLES IN TWO-PHASE FLOWS

Jean-Pierre Hulin, Andre J. M. Foussat, and Didier Gaudin

Physics Engineering Department
Etudes et Productions Schlumberger
Clamart Cedex, France

and

Gary S. Strumolo

Schlumberger-Doll Research
Ridgefield, Connecticut, USA

CONTENTS

INTRODUCTION

Vortex emission behind an obstacle lying across a flow or vortex generation inside a mixing layer are widespread phenomena. In most cases, a so-called Karman vortex street appears made up of two periodic rows of vortices with opposite circulations. This phenomenon has been known and studied for years [19, 20, 28] and vortex street sketches can even be found in Leonardo da Vinci's works.

A detailed study of vortex emission in single-phase flows can be found in Volume 1 of this Encyclopedia. The physics of vortex emission have been investigated in a large variety of gases and Newtonian or non-Newtonian liquids. However, relatively few references are available on vortex emission in two-phase flows, although such flows are more and more frequently encountered [3, 9–11, 15].

Various Origins of Two-Phase Flows

Two-phase flows can occur in several circumstances [8]:

- Simultaneous injection of two liquids or of a liquid and a gas inside a flow. This occurs, for instance, in oil wells where various reservoir rocks layers located at different depths can inject water, oil, and gas at the same time. This also occurs in chemical reactors.
- Generation of vapor in a boiling liquid often due to pressure or temperature variations (oil running up a producing well towards low pressure zones, boiling water nuclear reactors, loss of coolant accidents in a pressurized water nuclear reactor).
- Cavitation, which is just a special case for boiling occurring in high-velocity regions for liquid flows.
- Gas entrainment into liquid flows with a free surface occurring for instance in breaking waves or in hydraulic jumps close to downshafts [13].

Fundamental and Practical Questions Arising About Vortex Emission in Two-Phase Flows

We shall attempt in to answer some of the following questions:

- At high Reynolds numbers, the Karman vortex street is a coherent periodic structure superimposed on a highly turbulent flow. Can it survive to the additional disorder induced by the presence of a second phase? What is the importance of the length scale characterizing the structure of the dispersed phase?
- Vortex flowmeters are based on the linear variation of the vortex emission frequency behind sharp-edged obstacles with the fluid velocity [30]. Does this relation remain linear in two-phase flows and how is the corresponding Strouhal number modified?
- Vortex emission can have destructive effects. Those are often due to the large periodic pressure fluctuations they induce on the vortex-shedding bodies or in their wakes (for instance, collapse of bridges or cooling towers, damage to bridge piers). What is the variation of these pressure oscillations amplitude in two-phase flows?
- At high enough velocities and upstream gas contents, the obstacle can be completely surrounded by a gas pocket. What are the threshold values at which this effect occurs?

• Vortex cores and front edges of vortex-shedding obstacles are regions of high velocity gradients: there, the bubbles or droplets of the dispersed phase may be broken up into smaller ones resulting in a more homogeneous mixture. In addition, does the vortex emission also induce local variations for the mixture composition?

We shall first describe visual and quantitative experimental results on the structure of vortex streets in liquid-liquid and gas-liquid flows. Then, we present a theoretical discussion of the bubble trapping effects inside vortices as well as the results of numerical simulations of the vortex shedding process. And finally, we shall discuss observations of the vortex emission spectrum and of the amplitude of the pressure difference variations between the two sides of a vortex-shedding obstacle. Of special interest for flow-measurement applications are the variations of the Strouhal number.

ANALYSIS OF BUBBLE AND VORTEX TRAPPING INSIDE A KARMAN VORTEX STREET

Visual and Photographic Observations

Figure 1A and 1B have been obtained [10, 11] inside a cavitation tunnel. Triangular obstacles with a 22° tip angle pointing upstream were used. The tunnel speed is set so that cavitation subsists just in the low pressure zones at the vortex cores or in the regions behind the obstacle where the vortices build up before being shed away. The cavitation parameter must be high enough to allow the generation of a large number of bubbles but low enough to avoid the build-up of a continuous gas pocket behind the obstacle as occurs at high gas contents. The cavitation tunnel has flat side walls, and there is no gap between the obstacles and these walls. Figure 1A is a side view of a vortex street observed in such conditions. Figure 1B is obtained by viewing the vortex street slightly from the top.

Large clusters of bubbles mark the location of the vortex cores and of the region where the next vortex to be shed is being formed close behind the obstacle. There are two additional unexpected features:

• Curved vortex filaments perpendicular to the main vortices are observed between them.
• Small straight vortex filaments are observed right behind the rear edges of the obstacle in Figure 1B with a direction parallel to these edges.

The first result shows that the representation of a Karman vortex street as a two-dimensional flow structure of infinitely long vortex filaments is only a very coarse approximation and that three-dimensional effects play a very important role.

A first possible interpretation is that the streamwise vortices do in fact connect the main vortices: the vortex street would not then be made out of separate vortex segments but out of a single vortex with a ladder-like shape such as shown in Figure 2B. (This interpretation is perfectly compatible with the consequence of Kelvin's theorem stating that, in a perfect fluid a vortex filament must either be a closed curve or be attached to a wall.) However, in this case, the streamwise vortices should be located preferentially near the walls while, experimentally, many of them are observed in the middle of the flow. The phenomenon is therefore probably more complex and involves three-dimensional flow instabilities. The variation of the bubble cluster structure behind the obstacle (Figures 1, 2A and 2C) gives a vivid picture of the mechanism of the vortex generation process.

Instabilities of the velocity shear layer leaving the rear obstacle layers generate the small straight vortices already reported between the back of the obstacle and the vortex in formation (Figure 1B and 2C). Those vortices join the main bubble cluster and increase its vorticity until it gets shed. At times, the small filament shedding is almost symmetrical (Figure 2C), and one side serves as the nucleus of a new vortex while the order finishes up feeding the last shed one. Further away from the obstacle, the velocity field due to the vortices decreases, the pressure on the bubbles increases again, and they collapse in the end (Figure 2A). A concentration of the cavitation bubbles at the vortex cores is only clearly observed at high enough Reynolds numbers Re. When Re increases,

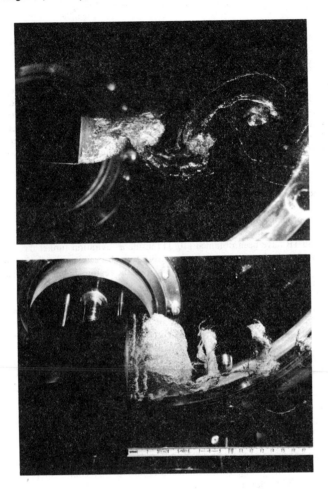

Figure 1. Visualization of the vortex emission behind a triangular obstacle (pointing upstream) in cavitating flows with a cavitation parameter v = 0,96: (A) side view, Reynolds number Re = 180,000; (B) view from above, Reynolds number Re = 210,000. (Courtesy of J. P. Franc and J. M. Michel [10, 11].)

the cavitation effect can be observed at large distances from the obstacle (up to 30 times the obstacle width). In this case, it seems that the velocity field relaxes more slowly.

A practical consequence of this cavitation effect is the generation of large pressure shocks and of a very high noise level due to the periodic collapse of the bubble structure at the vortex cores. In this case, the destructive effects of cavitation can be very much enhanced by the presence of vortex emission. Such large pressure variations have also been reported in vortices generated near hydraulic jumps, for instance in outfall down-shafts of large power generating stations [13]. These vortices appear in the submerged jet-mixing region of the plunging flow. A large part of the gas entrained inside the hydraulic jump gets trapped into these vortices resulting in large-amplitude level surges which can have extremely destructive effects on the concrete walls of the downshaft.

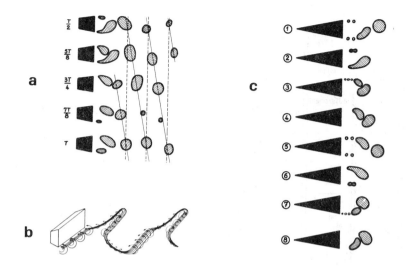

Figure 2. Side schematic view of the vortex street structure behind an obstacle in a cavitating flow: (A) side view of the time variation of the shape of the bubble cluster behind the obstacles observed experimentally (courtesy of J. P. Franc and J. M. Michel [10, 11]); (B) artist's view of a possible 3D structure of the vortex street behind the obstacles; (C) side view of the variation with time of the bubble cluster structure close behind the obstacle (courtesy of J. P. Franc and J. M. Michel [10, 11]).

In laboratory conditions, the bubble-trapping effect can also be visually observed when a non-cavitating flow containing externally injected gas bubbles impinges on an obstacle Bubble trapping inside the vortex cores is clearly observed at low upstream void fraction values for which the flow is transparent enough and no gas pocket builds up around the obstacle. In this case the observation is less clear than in cavitating flows where the view is not obscured by bubbles located outside the vortex cores. However, one can observe that the bubbles trapped inside the vortex cores are much smaller than those in the flow upstream of the obstacle. Therefore, it is necessary to use local void fraction measurement probes in order to investigate in detail the flow structure in the injected bubble case. Local probes can in addition provide quantitative void fraction measurement results.

Analysis of the Void Fraction Repartition Inside a Vortex Street for Gas-Liquid Flows Using Local Optical Probes

Experimental Procedure

A typical set-up is shown in Figure 3. Cylindrical obstacles with a trapezoidal cross-section are located along a diameter of 15-cm ID vertical flow-tube. Two parallel obstacles or just one is used. The experimental flow channel is a 12-m high vertical tube with the obstacles located 2m below the top. All flows are directed upwards. Using sharp-edged trapezoidal obstacles eliminates the instabilities of the vortex emission signal observed in the 10^4–10^5 Reynolds number range for circular cylinders; this is probably due to the fact that the boundary layer separation points are fixed at the front edges of the obstacle and do not move in the transition region from laminar to turbulent boundary layers as is the case for circular cylinders.

The mean water flow velocity is between 0.45 m/s and 1.7 m/s. Air is injected axially at the bottom of the flow-tube, the void fraction is between 0% and 25% and the typical bubble size is 2–4 mm. Air and water flow-rates are separately measured before the injection.

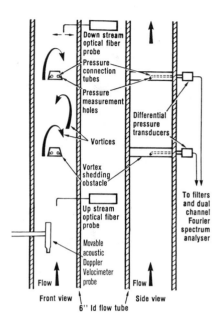

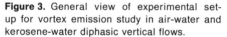

Figure 3. General view of experimental set-up for vortex emission study in air-water and kerosene-water diphasic vertical flows.

A fundamental parameter to describe the two-phase air-water flow is the percentage of volume (void fraction) occupied by gas. The void fraction in the center of the flow tube is measured by an optical fiber probe. This probe is located 30 cm upstream of the obstacles in order to avoid void fraction variations induced by them. It detects the phase (liquid or gas) surrounding a 100-μm diameter tip. An electronic circuit computes then the percentage of the total measurement time spent in air [7, 16]. In principle, it would be preferable to characterize the flow by the mean value of the void fraction over the complete cross section; this cannot be done practically using a local probe since a large number of measurements at different points across the diameter would then be necessary.

The analysis of the void fraction repartition inside the vortex street is then performed by a second optical probe (Figure 3) located at one of three different distances downstream of the obstacle (namely 17 cm or about one vortex street spatial period, 28 cm or 35 cm). The end of the probe faces the flow and can be moved along a flow tube diameter, perpendicular to the obstacle.

Figure 4A shows a direct raw recording with time of the downstream probe output. (The signal level is 1 when the probe tip is located inside an air bubble and 0 inside water.) The void fraction upstream of the obstacle is 2.8% and the probe is at 18 cm from the obstacle slightly off axis in order to be on the trajectory of the cores from one of the vortex street rows. The dotted curve is the pressure difference oscillation signal measured simultaneously on the downstream obstacle. Clearly bubbles do not reach the probe tip at random times but come by bursts nearly synchronous with the pressure oscillations. The power spectrum of the optical probe signal exhibits indeed a sharp peak at the vortex emission frequency (defined as the inverse of the time necessary to create two vortices—one on each side of the obstacle).

In order to get more quantitative results, we average many (1,000) recordings like those of Figure 4A. Each recording is triggered synchronously with the vortex-induced pressure fluctuation signal to obtain meaningful local void fraction averages inside the vortex street. (This signal is obtained by measuring the pressure difference between the two sides of the obstacle parallel to the flow.)

We obtain in this way the curve of Figure 4B which represents the average probability for detecting a bubble at given time delays after the emission of a vortex. The strong probability maxima correspond to times at which the vortex cores reach the probe tip. The time lapse between

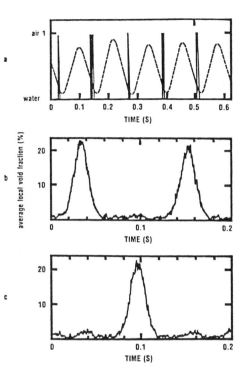

Figure 4. Time variation of the signal from an optical fiber probe located 17 cm downstream of the obstacles (liquid flow rate 80 m³/h, $Re_1 = 8-10$, upstream void fraction on tube axis $\alpha_g = 2.8\%$): (A) direct recording of the optical probe signal (solid curve). Signal level 1 corresponds to the presence of gas at the probe tip, signal level 0 to the presence of liquid. The dotted curve is a simultaneous recording of the pressure fluctuations; (B–C) averages of 1,000 recordings of the optical probe signal triggered synchronously with the vortex emission. Probe positions corresponding to the two curves are symmetrical with respect to the pipe axis.

the two maxima is indeed equal to the vortex emission period. For this probe location, only vortices belonging to one of the rows of the vortex street are clearly detected. When the probe is moved to the symmetrical position with respect to the obstacle, only vortices belonging to the other vortex street row are detected (Figure 4C). One also sees that vortex cores are detected one half period after those observed in Figure 4B (all flow conditions as well as the trigger signal have been kept identical).

The curves in Figure 4B and 4C demonstrate the existence of a very strong bubble trapping effect at the vortex cores. While the void fraction α_g on the tube axis upstream of the obstacles is only 2.8%, maximum bubble presence probabilities in excess of 20% are measured at the vortex cores. (This probability can be interpreted as a local void fraction value.) Between the vortices, this local void fraction is sometimes less than 0.5%. No such void fraction fluctuations are observed upstream of the obstacles. Clearly, the bubbles that were initially distributed rather uniformly inside the flow have been sucked inside the vortices resulting in large local void fractions at the cores.

We shall now discuss local void fraction repartition inside the vortex street and dependence on liquid flow rate, distance from the obstacle, and the upstream void fraction

By moving the probe stepwise, perpendicular to the obstacle across the probe diameter, a pseudo-two-dimensional image of the void fraction repartition in the vortex street can be obtained. At each probe location, an averaged curve similar to those in Figure 4B-C is recorded (the triggering signal remains the same).This set of curves can be stacked into a pseudo three-dimensional display (Figure 5) with the oblique axis corresponding to the local α_g value. This mode of presentation shows clearly the sharp void fraction maxima occurring on the trajectory of the vortex cores when they go past the probe.

It is more convenient, for further interpretations, to plot the lines of equal void fraction by measuring, at a given probe location the delay between the trigger signal and the times at which selected average values of the gas holdup are reached (we chose 2%, 4%, 10%, and 20%). The

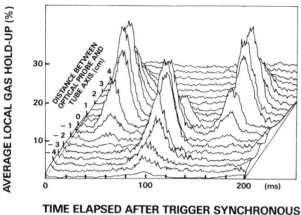

**TIME ELAPSED AFTER TRIGGER SYNCHRONOUS
WITH VORTEX EMISSION**

Figure 5. Pseudo three-dimensional map of the void fraction variation at a distance of 17 cm downflow of a vortex shedding obstacle in a gas-liquid flow with $\alpha_{gup} = 2.8\%$ and $Q_1 = 80$ m³/h. The map is obtained by associating several curves like those of Figure 4 corresponding to different positions of an optical probe across the tube diameter.

corresponding points have been plotted in Figure 6A. Let us emphasize that the horizontal scale is not a length scale but a time scale. The image corresponds to what would be seen by an observer looking at the vortex street through a fixed slot perpendicular to both the flow and the obstacle, and watching the vortices go by.

Figure 6A corresponds to the same liquid flow rate, void fraction, and probe distance from the obstacle as are in Figure 5. The total time lapse displayed is about one vortex emission period

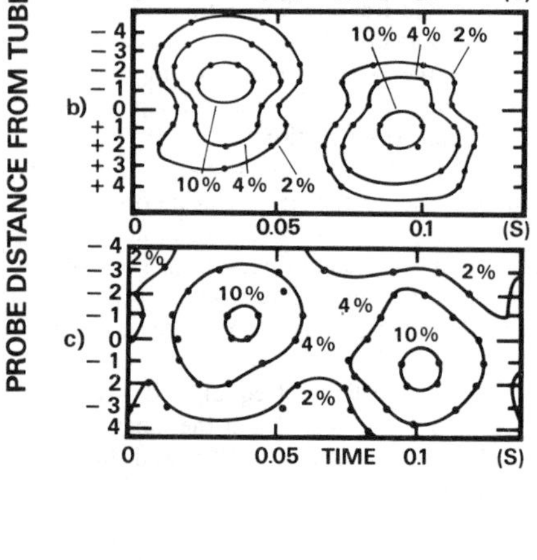

Figure 6. Pseudo two-dimensional mappings of time-averaged void fraction repartitions inside the vortex street at fixed distances downstream of the obstacles (time origins different for the three curves). Solid lines are curves of equal void fraction values (2%, 4%, 10%, 20%) drawn from the experimental points (solid dots). Upstream void fraction $\alpha_{gup} = 2.8\%$. Water flow rate $Q_1 = 80$ m³/h. (A) probe located 17 cm downstream of the obstacle (1 vortex street spatial period); (B) probe located 28 cm downstream of the obstacle; (C) probe located 35 cm downstream of the obstacle (2 vortex street spatial periods).

PROBE DISTANCE FROM TUBE AXIS (CM)

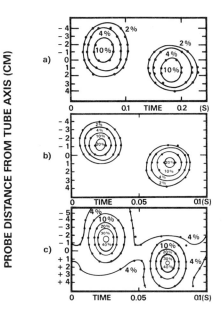

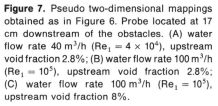

Figure 7. Pseudo two-dimensional mappings obtained as in Figure 6. Probe located at 17 cm downstream of the obstacles. (A) water flow rate 40 m³/h ($Re_1 = 4 \times 10^4$), upstream void fraction 2.8%; (B) water flow rate 100 m³/h ($Re_1 = 10^5$), upstream void fraction 2.8%; (C) water flow rate 100 m³/h ($Re_1 = 10^5$), upstream void fraction 8%.

allowing us to observe one vortex from each row. As expected, the very sharp void fraction maximum at the vortex cores is clearly marked (local void fraction larger than 20%), while outside the vortex velocity field the void fraction falls well below 2%. When a similar mapping is realized further downstream of the obstacle (28 cm in Figure 6B and 35 cm or about 2 vortex street spatial periods in Figure 6C), a smoother bubble repartition pattern is observed. The maximum local void fraction is then only 13% in Figure 6C, and bubbles tend to spread out from the vortices. This is probably caused by a damping of the vortex intensity due to viscous effects.

We have performed the same measurements as in Figure 6A at a lower liquid flow rate of 40 m³/h ($Ret = 4.10^4$) but for the same probe location and the same upstream void fraction (Figure 7A). Bubbles are less strongly concentrated at the vortex cores than in Figure 6A due to the smaller Bernoulli-type pressure gradients at this lower velocity (maximum local void fraction < 16%).

The results of Figure 7B correspond to a higher flow-rate (100 m³/h or $Re_1 = 10^5$). The equal void fraction lines are not very different from those of Figure 6A, which seems to show that the trapping effect has reached a saturation level. Another clue for explaining the vortex emission characteristics in air-water flows is given by the dependence of the probe signal on the upstream void fraction. An example is shown in Figure 7C (the flow has the same flow rate as in Figure 7B but a higher upstream void fraction (8%)). The maximum of α_g at the vortex cores rises markedly (up to 40%) but proportionally less than the upstream α_g value, while in between the vortices, α_g increases to more than 5%.

Curves 8a-b-c show analogous results obtained at a liquid flow rate $Q_1 = 80$ m³/h ($Re_1 = 8 \times 10^4$) with a fixed probe at a distance of 17 cm downflow of the obstacle and located on one of the vortex cores trajectory (as was the case in Figure 4B). For a 1% upstream void fraction α_{gup} (measured on the tube axis), the local void fraction outside the vortices is extremely low (<0.3%) but rises to 8% at the vortex cores (Figure 8A): nearly all bubbles are concentrated on the vortices.

For $\alpha_{gup} = 8.2\%$ (Figure 8B), the results are very close to those shown in Figure 7C: the bubble clusters corresponding to the vortices remain clearly defined but spread out (vortices from the second row are clearly detected). Even between the vortices, the bubble concentration rises to more than 3%; the maximum local void fraction at the cores is very high (>40%). For $\alpha_{gup} = 11.5\%$ (Figure 8C), this maximum void fraction does not become higher, but the value of α_g increases rapidly (>8%) between the bubble clusters centered at the vortex cores. The orderly pattern of bubble-filled vortices separated by a bubble-free flow has started to disappear.

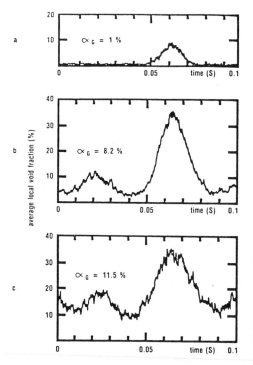

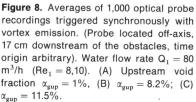

Figure 8. Averages of 1,000 optical probe recordings triggered synchronously with vortex emission. (Probe located off-axis, 17 cm downstream of the obstacles, time origin arbitrary). Water flow rate $Q_1 = 80$ m^3/h (Re$_1 = 8,10$). (A) Upstream void fraction $\alpha_{gup} = 1\%$, (B) $\alpha_{gup} = 8.2\%$; (C) $\alpha_{gup} = 11.5\%$.

These results on the magnitude of the trapping effect are summarized in Figure 9 by the variation with α_{gup} of the maximum and minimum local α_g values at two water flow rates: $Q_w = 40$ m^3/h and $Q_w = 100$ m^3/h. (The probe is at a distance of 17 cm downstream of the obstacles.) The minimum of α_g increases very slowly up to $\alpha_{gup} = 9\%$ at $Q_w = 100$ m^3/h but only up to $\alpha_{gup} = 5\%$ at 40 m^3/h. Above $\alpha_{gup} = 10\%$, the minimum of α_g increases very fast; in addition, at high velocities, a continuous

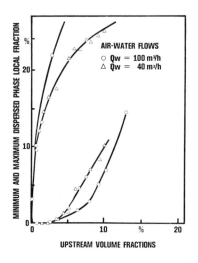

Figure 9. Maximum and minimum dispersed-phase local fraction measured on the vortex core trajectory in air-water flows.

gas pocket appears and destroys the vortex street. In the same way, the maximum of α_g saturates at a higher value ($\alpha_g = 40\%$) for $Q_w = 100 \text{ m}^3/\text{h}$ than $Q_w = 40 \text{ m}^3/\text{h}$ ($\alpha_g = 25\%$).

In conclusion, the efficiency of the bubble trapping inside the vortex street increases with the flow velocity but can only be effective to preserve the vortex individuality at moderate upstream α_g values. At α_{gup} values above 10%, the space between vortices gets filled with gas and the vortex emission almost disappears.

One may wonder why, at the high local void fractions which have been observed, air bubbles remain separated instead of gathering into large gas pockets rising very fast through the flowing fluid; this is probably due to the large velocity gradients near the vortex cores which prevent the formation of larger bubbles.

Vortex Street Structure in Liquid-Liquid Flows

Experimental Procedure

Using the same flow set-up as described before, we have performed similar local dispersed-phase volume fraction measurements in water-kerosene flows will be often referred to as oil in the following text). The total flow rates are between 10 and 40 m^3/h ($1.5 \times 10^4 < \text{Re}_t < 6 \times 10^4$). All percentages of water and kerosene can be obtained in the flowing mixture.

The optical probe is replaced by a local radiofrequency probe similar to that described by Reiman and Muller [24] and Kobori and Terada [17]. This probe is used in the same way and at the same location as the optical probe but provides a much better signal amplitude variation between oil and water.

The density contrast between oil and water is much smaller than between air and water so that the oil droplets trapping effect is weaker when water is the continuous phase. When oil is the continuous phase, water droplets are expelled from the vortices. In addition, even when a continuous oil pocket builds up around the obstacle, the vortex emission is not destroyed.

Experimental Results

Figure 10 shows averaged probe recordings similar to those of Figure 4: they were obtained with the probe tip located on the trajectory of one of the vortex cores row.

Figure 10A is a reference curve obtained for an air-water flow ($\alpha_{gup} = 2.8\%$) with a 40 m^3/h water flow-rate ($\text{Re}_t = 4 \times 10^4$). Figure 10B corresponds to a water-kerosene flow (continuous water phase) with the same velocity and upstream dispersed-phase volume fraction ($\alpha_{kup} = 2.8\%$). The trapping effect is somewhat weaker for kerosene than for gas: the maximum of α_k at the cores is only 13% instead of 16% for α_g and the minimum value between the vortices increases from .5% for α_g to 2% for α_k. At $Q_t = 15 \text{ m}^3/\text{h}$ ($\text{Re}_t = 1.5 \times 10^4$), the trapping effect is much weaker than for $Q_t = 40 \text{ m}^3/\text{h}$ ($\text{Re}_t = 4 \times 10^4$) (Figure 10C) and the separation between the minimum and maximum local values of α_k (α_{kmin} and α_{kmax}) remains smaller in the whole α_{kup} mixture concentration range (Figure 11).

When α_{kup} increases above 10%, α_{max} does not saturate but goes to very high values ($\alpha_{kmax} = 70\%$ for $\alpha_{kup} = 30\%$) and the kerosene phase becomes locally continuous near the vortex cores (the inversion transition from a continuous water phase to a continuous oil phase occurs for $\alpha_k \simeq 66\%$). Above the inversion point (Figure 11) one verifies that the water droplets get expelled from the vortex cores.

In short, both for gas-liquid and liquid-liquid flows, the light phase concentration increases markedly above the upstream value at the vortex cores:

- At high enough flow velocities and small upstream volume fractions, it can be as much as 10 times higher.
- At low total flow rates (typically 10–15 m^3/h in our set-up), the velocity and pressure gradients near the vortex cores decrease and the bubble attraction becomes almost negligible.

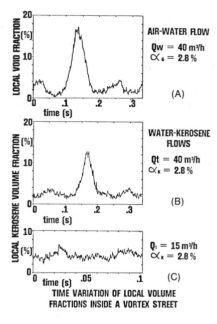

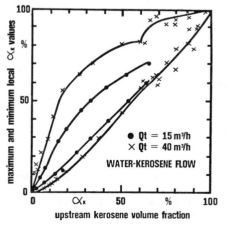

Figure 10. Averages of 1,000 RF probe recordings triggered synchronously with the vortex emission. The probe is located on one of the vortex cores trajectory 17 cm downflow of the obstacles. The time origin is arbitrary: (A) air-water flow: water flow rate 40 m³/h (Re₁ = 4 × 10⁴), upstream void fraction on tube axis g = 2.8%; (B) water-kerosene flow: total flow rate Q$_t$ = 40 m³/h (Re$_t$ = 4 × 10⁴), kerosene volume fraction 2.8%; (C) water-kerosene flow: total flow rate Q₁ = 15 m³/h (Re$_t$ = 1.5 × 10⁴), kerosene volume fraction 2.8%.

- At high upstream gas volume fractions, the maximum void fraction at the cores saturates while, for liquid-liquid flows it goes on increasing and a local inversion from a continuous oil phase may occur.
- At high velocities another effect is observed in gas-liquid flows: for α_{gup} larger than about 10%, a continuous gas pocket builds up downflow of the obstacle and destroys the vortex street.

Clearly, the light-phase attraction towards the vortex cores plays a major role in the characteristics of the vortex emission process for two-phase flows. Let us now investigate theoretically this problem.

Figure 11. Maximum and minimum local kerosene volume fractions measured in the vortex street on the vortex cores trajectory.

THEORETICAL STUDY OF THE LIGHT PHASE VOID FRACTION
REPARTITION INSIDE THE VORTEX STREET

Bubble Trapping Inside an Isolated Vortex (or an Idealized Periodic Vortex Street [2, 29])

Let us study first the interaction between a nondeforming two-dimensional "bubble" and a point
vortex in the presence of an external flow. A complex-variable analysis is used to determine the
pressure forces acting on the bubble and this leads to an ordinary differential equation for the
bubble motion. Depending upon the strength of the vortex, bubbles passing close to it are pulled
in while others escape entrainment. This attraction is due to the fact that the vortex is a low-pressure
region. Figure 12 depicts this for a sample case; the vortex here is located at the origin and the
large circle around it illustrates the size of a bubble. The lines give the trajectories of the bubble
centers (solid for those entrained and dashed for those which are not). The vortex has
counterclockwise rotation as indicated. The X mark northeast of the origin behaves as a saddle
point, i.e., bubbles near this point must either move into the vortex or away from it.

This analysis is then extended to the case of a single two-dimensional bubble and an idealized
vortex street (two rows of oppositely rotating vortices arranged so each vortex of one row is placed
over the midpoint of the two neighboring vortices on the other row). Figure 13A illustrates the
trajectories of a bubble from different initial points past a vortex street (vortices on the top row
having a clockwise rotation).

Let us emphasize that, in this model, only the relative motions of the bubbles and the vortices
are taken into account. So, what is the probability for a bubble going past the obstacle to get
trapped into the nearest vortex or into vortices located farther downstream? The trapping width
used in this discussion corresponds to the range of distances from the vortex street axis at which
a bubble gets trapped into the nearest obstacle, into the next nearest, and so on. Figure 13A shows
clearly that the trapping width is larger for the nearest vortices. We see also in Figure 13A that
there exists unstable saddle points separating the domains of attraction of each vortex. One expects
dead zones with low bubble densities to be present in these regions.

The preceding analysis is both two-dimensional and highly simplified. The more complex problem
of a spherical bubble in the presence of line vortices has been studied by Auton [2]. Figure 13B
shows the result of this analysis. As in the earlier study, we see that the trapping width for each
vortex decreases as we proceed downstream. This width has been computed for both methods in
the case of a single-bubble single-vortex interaction; a comparison between the results is shown

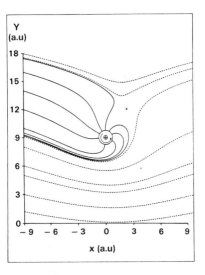

Figure 12. Computed trajectory of a "two-dimensional" bubble near a line vortex with a counterclockwise rotation.

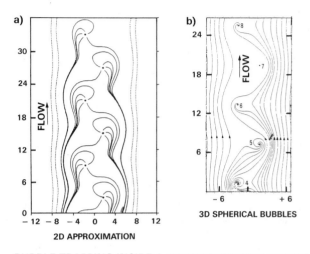

2D APPROXIMATION

3D SPHERICAL BUBBLES

BUBBLE TRAPPING INSIDE A KARMAN VORTEX STREET

Figure 13. Computed trajectories of bubbles near a periodic vortex street (two rows of line vortices with opposite circulations). The initial velocity of the bubbles is parallel to the vortex rows. (A) two-dimensional model; (B) three-dimensional bubbles from Auton [2].

in Figure 14. The original curve gives trapping width values taken at a fixed point far upstream (in the two-dimensional case): this is fine for low circulation values since in this case the trajectories are nearly horizontal there, but as the circulation increases, they become slightly inclined. After making a geometric adjustment a transformed curve is obtained (Figure 14). The curve found by Auton is labeled and drawn as a solid line. The + marker on this curve are obtained through a vertical shift of the corrected data points from the 2D model. Interestingly, both analyses appear to give the same power law exponent.

There is a considerable number of limitations to this type of analysis. First, only a single bubble is considered, and so the effects of the upstream void fraction on gas entrainment cannot be determined. Second, the effect this entrainment has on the vortex street structure is not taken into account. Finally,, the object producing the street is not modeled nor are the side walls bounding

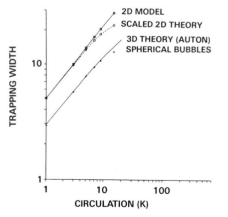

Figure 14. Variation of the trapping width for a single-bubble/single-vortex interaction; upper solid line—2D model; dashed line—2D model corrected for the effect of the inclination of the trajectories; (+)—2D corrected points shifted vertically for comparison with the 3D model; lower solid line—3D model [2].

the flow. Despite this, the high gas concentration in the cores and the depletion outside them are correctly predicted.

In order to provide a more quantitative analysis of this phenomenon, a complete two-dimensional simulation of vortex shedding in gas-liquid flows has been performed and will be now described.

Physical Theoretical Basis for the Simulation of the Karman Vortex Street in Gas-Liquid Flows

The following simulation model does not consider the gas phase as dispersed in infinitely small bubbles but makes use of such parameters as the bubble number concentration and their radius.

We begin with a three-field representation of the fluid consisting of the bulk liquid (with subscript l, superscript $'$), the gas phase (subscript 2), and an "entrapped" liquid (subscript 3). The latter liquid field is introduced to provide a virtual mass term in the equation of motion.* With this formulation, we can write the mass conservation equations as:

$$\frac{\partial \rho_1 \alpha_1'}{\partial t} + \nabla \cdot \rho_1 \alpha_1' V_1' = 0$$

$$\frac{\partial \rho_2 \alpha_2}{\partial t} + \nabla \cdot \rho_2 \alpha_2 V_2 = 0 \qquad (1)$$

$$\frac{\partial \rho_1 \alpha_3}{\partial t} + \nabla \cdot \rho_1 \alpha_3 V_3 = 0$$

where ρ = density
          α = void fraction
          V = velocity

The equation of state is simply:

$$\alpha_1' + \alpha_2 + \alpha_3 = 1 \qquad (2)$$

Momentum conservation is described by:

$$\frac{\partial \rho_1 \alpha_1' V_1'}{\partial t} + \nabla \cdot (\rho_1 \alpha_1' V_1' V_1') = -\alpha_1' \nabla P + \rho_1 \alpha_1' g + \rho_1 W_1 + K_{12}(V_2 - V_1') + K_{13}(V_3 - V_1')$$

$$\frac{\partial \rho_2 \alpha_2 V_2}{\partial t} + \nabla \cdot (\rho_2 \alpha_2 V_2 V_2) = -\alpha_2 \nabla P + \rho_2 \alpha_2 g + \rho_2 W_2 + K_{12}(V_1' - V_2) + K_{23}(V_3 - V_2)$$

and

$$\frac{\partial \rho_1 \alpha_3 V_3}{\partial t} + \nabla \cdot (\rho_1 \alpha_3 V_3 V_3) = -\alpha_3 \nabla P + \rho_1 \alpha_3 g + \rho_1 W_3 + K_{13}(V_1' - V_3) + K_{23}(V_2 - V_3) \qquad (3)$$

where W is a viscous term and the K's are momentum exchange functions. We can reduce these to a two-field set of equations with the following relations:

$$\alpha_1 = \alpha_1' + \alpha_3$$

$$\alpha_1 V_1 = \alpha_1' V_1' + \alpha_3 V_3 \qquad (4)$$

---

* This concept of an entrapped liquid is not new; Milne-Thomson [22] in his discussion on the virtual mass of a cylinder in two-dimensional flow states "thus the added mass really represents a mass of liquid entrained by the cylinder."

The latter simply states that the total momentum in the liquid phase equals the sum of the separate momenta contained in the bulk and entrapped fields. We then make the assumptions:

$$\alpha_3 = f\alpha_2$$
$$V_3 = V_2 \tag{5}$$

i.e., that the void fraction in the entrapped liquid is some fixed fraction f of the gas void fraction and the entrapped liquid moves with the velocity of the "entrapping" gas. Equation 4 then reduces to:

$$\alpha_1' = \alpha_1 - f\alpha_2$$
$$\alpha_1'V_1' = \alpha_1V_1 - f\alpha_2V_2 \tag{6}$$

and after considerable manipulations, we obtain the following momentum equations:

$$\rho_1\left[\frac{\partial\alpha_1V_1}{\partial t} + \nabla\cdot\alpha_1V_1V_1\right] - \frac{f\rho_1\alpha_1\alpha_2}{\alpha_1 - f\alpha_2}\left(\frac{\partial V_2}{\partial t} - \frac{\partial V_1}{\partial t}\right)$$
$$= -\alpha_1\nabla P + K(V_2 - V_1) + \rho_1\alpha_1 g + \rho_1W_1$$
$$- \frac{f\rho_1\alpha_1}{\alpha_1 - fd_2}\nabla\cdot\left(\frac{\alpha_1\alpha_2}{\alpha_1 - f\alpha_2}\right)(V_2 - V_1)(V_2 - V_1) + \frac{f\rho_1\alpha_1\alpha_2}{\alpha_1 - f\alpha_2}(V_2\cdot\nabla V_2 - V_1\cdot\nabla V_1)$$

$$\rho_2\left[\frac{\partial\alpha_2V_2}{\partial t} + \nabla\cdot\alpha_2V_2V_2\right] + \frac{f\rho_1\alpha_1\alpha_2}{\alpha_1 - f\alpha_2}\left(\frac{\partial V_2}{\partial t} - \frac{\partial V_1}{\partial t}\right)$$
$$= -\alpha_2\nabla P + K(V_1 - V_2) + \rho_2\alpha_2 g + \rho_2W_2$$
$$+ \frac{f^2\rho_1\alpha_2}{\alpha_1 - f\alpha_2}\nabla\cdot\left(\frac{\alpha_1\alpha_2}{\alpha_1 - f\alpha_2}\right)(V_2 - V_1)(V_2 - V_1) - \frac{f\rho_1\alpha_1\alpha_2}{\alpha_1 - f\alpha_2}(V_2\cdot\nabla V_2 - V_1\cdot\nabla V_1)$$

Coupled with these equations, is one governing bubble number transport:

$$\frac{\partial N_B}{\partial t} + \nabla\cdot V_2N_B = \omega(Ne - N_B) \tag{8}$$

Where ω is the coalescence and/or fragmentation rate and Ne is a local equilibrium number based on a Weber number criterion and defined by:

$$Ne = \frac{3\alpha_2}{4\pi\Omega_{\omega e}^3}$$
$$\Omega_{\omega e} = \frac{2We\sigma}{\rho_1|\delta V|^2} \tag{9}$$

Here We is the Weber number and σ is the surface tension. The momentum exchange function K is given by:

$$K = \frac{3\rho_1 C_D}{8r_b}\left(\frac{1}{\dfrac{1}{\alpha_1} + \dfrac{1}{\alpha_2}}\right)|\delta V| + \varepsilon \tag{10}$$

Where the coefficient Cd is determined experimentally as:

$$C_D = \begin{cases} 24Re_b^{-1} & Re_b \leq 2 \\ 18.7Re_b^{-0.68} & 2 < Re_b \leq 4.02G_1^{-0.214} \\ 0.6145r_b|\delta V| - 2 & Re_b > 4.02G_1^{-0.214} \end{cases} \tag{11}$$

and

$$Re_b = \frac{2r_b|\delta V|}{\eta_1}$$

$$G_1 = \frac{|g|\mu_1^4}{\rho_1\sigma^3}$$

$$r_b = \left(\frac{3\alpha_2}{4\pi N_B}\right)^{1/3}$$

Finally, the viscous stress term is:

$$W_j = (\nabla \cdot \eta_j\alpha_j\nabla)V_j \qquad j = 1, 2 \tag{12}$$

Numerical Simulation Results Obtained for a Gas-Liquid Flow

A computer simulation program incorporating those ideas has been developed at the Los Alamos National Laboratory. A series of runs has been performed where the upstream initial gas void fraction was varied and the subsequent aggregation of bubbles was examined [6].

The flow domain consists of a channel 15 cm wide by 42 cm high. Vortices are shed from a rectangle 3 cm by 2.25 cm by a flow rising vertically against gravity. Void fractions of 0, 3, 5, 8, 10, and 12 percent were considered. The Reynolds number for these flows is 333.

The pressure difference across the sides of the rectangle parallel to the flow is shown in Figure 15A from the initial deadstart onto a time of 2.25 seconds, at which the periodic vortex shedding is established (the upstream void fraction is 10%).

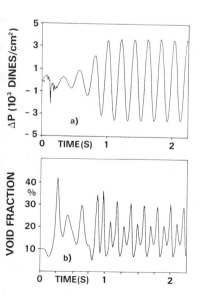

Figure 15. Numerical 2D simulation of vortex emission behind an obstacle with a rectangular cross section in an air-water flow with a 10% upstream (void) fraction (obstacle size: 3 cm wide, 2.25 cm deep): (A) time variation of the pressure difference between the two sides of the obstacle (the time scale represents the time elapsed after a dead start); (B) time variation of the local void fraction at a point 8 cm downstream of the obstacle.

Figure 15B shows the time variation of the void fraction at a fixed point in space in the same conditions as Figure 15A (the measurement point is located 8 cm downstream of the rectangle along a row of vortices). As expected, we observe a peak of the mean void fraction each time a vortex of the corresponding row goes by. The second, lower peak is due to the gas contained in the vortices of the other row. The difference in magnitude should increase with the upstream void fraction. The maximum gas concentration in the first vortex core is greater than 20% while, in the depleted zones, it is less than 2%.

Let us now look at the spatial void fraction distribution shown in Figure 16 for $\alpha_{gup} = 3\%$. Figure 16B is an equal void fraction contour map while Figure 16A shows this same map along the base of a box. Above it, is a three-dimensional representation of the contour surface. We can immediately see that the highest concentration of gas lies in the first vortex core with successively smaller amounts in subsequent cores downstream. In addition, the depletion of gas outside these cores is also evident.

Let us point out that Figures 16A and 16B differ from Figures 5–8 since the Y axis corresponds to a length scale (Figure 16) instead of a time scale as in Figures 5–8, which were obtained by using measurements performed at a fixed distance from the obstacle.

So far, we have considered only void fraction concentrations. Using the bubble number transport equation, we can obtain some information on the number and effective size of the "bubbles" composing this concentration. These results are depicted in Figure 17. They show that the vortex cores consist of very small bubbles while, outside, there are a few larger bubbles, in agreement with the observations made experimentally. The breakup of gas into small bubbles is probably due to the high velocity gradients present in the vortex cores.

Similar results for upstream void fractions of 5% and 10% are shown in Figures 18–20, respectively, for the void fraction, the bubble number, and the mean radius distributions. If we combine all our results, we can plot the maximum gas concentration in the vortex cores as a function of the upstream void fraction (solid line in Figure 21A). At this point, it may be interesting to compare our computed results with the experimental ones reported earlier.

Converting our velocity to three dimensions gives a volume flux of approximately 57 m³/h. The dotted line in Figure 21A gives the experimental results at 40 m³/h, while the dashed line corresponds to 100 m³/h. The saturation of bubble concentration appearing for α_{gup} around 8%–10% as well as the higher maximum void fraction value obtained for $Q_w = 100$ m³/h correlate very well with the results of Figure 9.

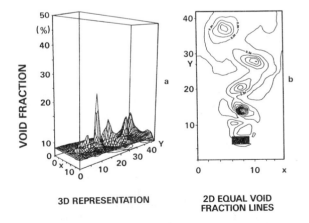

3D REPRESENTATION   2D EQUAL VOID
                           FRACTION LINES

Figure 16. Mapping of the void fraction distribution behind an obstacle in an air-water flow with a 3% upstream void fraction at time t = 2 (equivalent 3D flow rate = 57 m³/h). (A) pseudo 3D representation; (B) equal void fraction lines: void fraction variation from one line to the next = 2%. Numbered line corresponds to $\alpha_g = 4\%$.

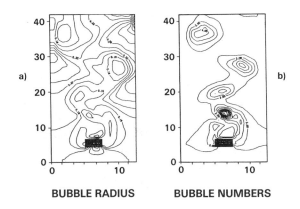

BUBBLE RADIUS   BUBBLE NUMBERS

Figure 17. Numerical 2D simulation of the vortex street structure behind a rectangular obstacle n an air-water flow (same flow rate and upstream void fraction as in Figure 16): (A) bubble mean radius repartition inside the vortex street. The equal mean radius lines are spaced by).02 (in the same units as used for the horizontal and the vertical scales). The bubble radius decreases near the obstacle and the vortex cores. The two numbered lines correspond to radii values of 0.22 and 0.18; (B) bubble number repartition. The number variation from one line to the next corresponds to 1 bubble per unit area. The numbered line corresponds to 1 bubble per unit area.

In short, the numerical simulations using the model just described predict satisfactorily the void fraction variations observed in a gas-liquid flow behind an obstacle. An interesting validity test will be the application of this model to liquid-liquid flows. A weakness of the model lies in the estimation of the vortex emission frequency: a decrease of the frequency with the void fraction is predicted (Figure 21B), while as we shall see now, experiments give exactly the opposite result.

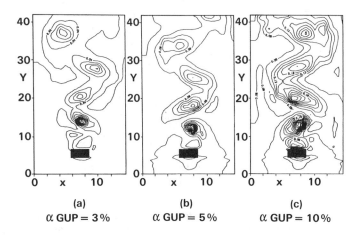

| (a) | (b) | (c) |
| α GUP = 3 % | α GUP = 5 % | α GUP = 10 % |

Figure 18. Equal void fraction line maps inside the vortex street taken at time 2 after the initial dead start (equivalent 3D flow rate 57 m³/h): (A) $\alpha_{gup} = 3\%$, spacing between equal void fraction lines = 2%, numbered line corresponds to $\alpha_g = 4\%$; (B) $\alpha_{gup} = 5\%$, spacing between equal void fraction lines = 3%, numbered line corresponds to $\alpha_g = 8\%$; (C) $\alpha_{gup} = 10\%$, spacing between equal void fraction lines = 2.5%, numbered lines correspond to $\alpha_g = 8$, 13, and 18%.

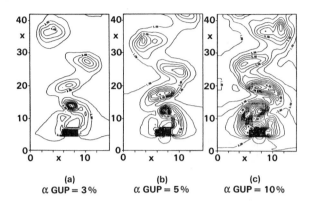

(a)
α GUP = 3%

(b)
α GUP = 5%

(c)
α GUP = 10%

Figure 19. Theoretical bubble number density map (same flow parameters as in Figure 18: the numbers used correspond to average numbers of bubbles per unit area. (A) $\alpha_{gup} = 3\%$, equal bubble number density lines are spaced by 1 (bubble per unit area). The numbered lines correspond to densities of 2 and 4 bubbles per unit area; (B) $\alpha_{gup} = 5\%$, equal bubble number density lines are spaced by 1. The numbered lines correspond to densities of 1 and 3 bubbles per unit area; (C) $\alpha_{gup} = 10\%$, equal bubble number density lines are spaced by 2. The numbered lines correspond to densities of 1, 3 and 5 bubbles per unit area.

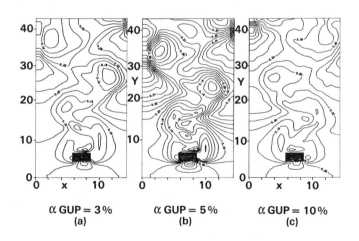

α GUP = 3%
(a)

α GUP = 5%
(b)

α GUP = 10%
(c)

Figure 20. Theoretical mean bubble radius density map obtained from the 2D numerical simulation (same flow parameters as in Figure 18). The radius scale is the same as the length scale on the map; (A) $\alpha_{gup} = 3\%$, equal bubble radius density lines are spaced by 2. Numbered lines correspond to mean radii equal to 0.18 and 0.22; (B) $\alpha_{gup} = 5\%$, equal bubble radius density lines as spaced by 1. Numbered lines correspond to mean radii equal to 0.16, 0.18, 0.20, 0.22, and 0.24; (C) $\alpha_{gup} = 10\%$, equal bubble radius density lines are spaced by 2. Numbered lines correspond to mean radii equal to .16, .20, and .24.

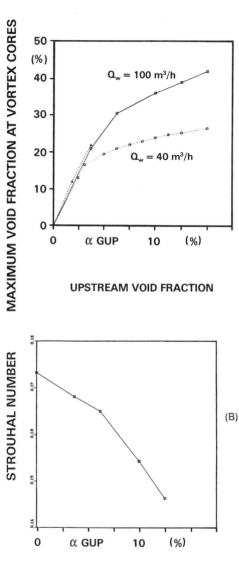

UPSTREAM VOID FRACTION

Figure 21. Theoretical results from the 2D numerical simulation: (A) Solid line; variation with the upstream void fraction of the maximum void fraction values obtained at the vortex cores (solid curve corresponding to an equivalent flow rate of 57 m^3/h). The dotted and dashed curves correspond to the experimental variations already shown in Figure 9 for $Q_w = 40$ and $100 \, m^3/h$; (B) variation with the upstream void fraction of the Strouhal number.

VARIATIONS OF THE SPECTRAL CHARACTERISTICS STABILITY AND AMPLITUDE OF THE VORTEX INDUCED PRESSURE FLUCTUATIONS ON AN OBSTACLE

This study is very important from the practical point of view:

• For flowmetering applications of the vortex emission, steady vortex emission signals with a large stable amplitude and a narrow bandwidth are needed.

- The destructive and perturbing effects of the vortex emission both on the obstacle itself and on the flow channel downstream will be largest when the vortex emission is very periodical and of large amplitude.

Experimental Procedure

The same obstacle and flow-tube set-up as in Figure 3 are used with either one or two obstacles. In the two-obstacles set-up, vortex emission on the downflow obstacle is triggered by the vortices emitted from the first one. This allows us to gain, through phase shift and coherence measurements between the signals from the two obstacles, additional information on the downflow propagation of the vortex street.

Vortex emission is detected by monitoring oscillations of the pressure difference between both sides of the obstacle: these are induced by the local velocity variations during the alternate emission of vortices on each side. This method is in fact one of the practical vortex-emission-sensing methods used in vortex flowmeters.

Several types of measurements are performed on the output of the differential pressure sensor used for detecting the vortex emission.

- Spectral analysis of the vortex emission signal using an FFT analyzer: The vortex emission frequency is taken equal to the value v_m corresponding to the maximum of the signal power spectrum $I(v)$. In monophasic flows, v_m is proportional to the flow rate and is the parameter used for its measurement.

In addition, we measure the rms time-averaged signal amplitude A (computed from the integral of the power spectrum) and its spectral width Δv. The variation of the ratio $\Delta v / v_m$ characterizes the deterioration of the signal spectral purity and of the measurement precision in diphasic flows.

In the two-obstacles set-up, only the preceding measurements corresponding to the downstream obstacle are quoted but we measure in addition the:

- Coherence and phase shift between the signals on the obstacles. This allows us to determine the variations of the spatial period λ of the Karman vortex street and to give information on the vortex street stability as it is carried away from the obstacles.
- Fluctuations of the vortex emission signal rms amplitude: The output of the pressure transducer is first fed into a bandpass amplifier selecting the vortex emission frequency and eliminating the low-frequency drifts, then into a rectifier followed by a ripple-eliminating filter. The final output follows closely the envelope of the pressure fluctuations signal. An histogram of these instantaneous amplitudes is then computed using 1,000 samples. We characterize the signal amplitude fluctuations by the ratio $\Delta A / A$ where ΔA is the rms deviation (computed from the histogram) from the mean amplitude A.

This measurement is of a great practical interest because it indicates the validity of vortex-emission-frequency measurements performed using standard zero-crossing counting circuits. In some cases, for instance, very narrow vortex emission spectra are observed, but the signal has an irregular amplitude and even vanishes occasionally. In this case, measurements with simple circuits have a poor precision and the device is of limited practical use.

Single-Phase Measurements and Determination of the Spatial Period

These measurements provide a basis for comparison with the two-phase flow experiments. They also allow to test the validity of the determination of λ using coherence and phase shift measurements.

The vortex emission frequency v is measured at average liquid velocities $\bar{V}_1$ varying between 0.3 and 1.5 m/s $\bar{V}_1$ is defined by:

$$\bar{V}_1 = \frac{Q_L}{C}. \tag{13}$$

Where Q_1 is the water flow rate and C the tube cross section. The Strouhal number S, defined as $S = Wv/\overline{V}_1$, is constant in that range and equal to $0.22 + 0.01$ (W being the obstacle width). Following Goldstein [14], we assume that the vortex street structure is carried downflow at a velocity $V_v = 0.92\overline{V}_1$, then we find that

$$\lambda = \frac{V_v}{v} = 0.92\frac{\overline{V}_1}{v} = 14.6 \text{ cm} \tag{14}$$

where λ is the wavelength or spatial period of the vortex street (distance between two consecutive vortices on one row).

Hence, $\overline{V}_1/v = $ constant means that the vortex street wavelength λ is constant and depends only on the obstacle size and geometry (However, in this estimation of λ, we have not taken into account the possible variations of either $\overline{V}_1$ or v due to the presence of the two obstacles).

Another value for λ can be estimated from measurements of the phase shift $\Delta\varphi$ between vortex-generated pressure oscillations by using the relation:

$$\Delta\varphi = 2\pi\frac{1}{\lambda} \tag{15}$$

where l is the spacing between obstacles (Figure 3). $\Delta\varphi$ is measured practically as the phase of the complex cross spectrum between signals from the two obstacles [4]. Experimentally, $\Delta\varphi = 444 +/- 3°$ in the range of $\overline{V}_1$ values explored, giving $\lambda = 14.6$ cm for $1 = 18$ cm. This surprisingly good agreement, in view of the crude approximations involved, indicates only that both procedures are physically correct for evaluating λ.

The rms amplitude of the pressure oscillations has also been measured; it is proportional to Q_1^2. Some measurement (0–40 m^3/h) with lighter kerosene of density $\rho = 0.75$ g/cm^3 verified that the amplitude is also roughly proportional to ρ.

Gas-Liquid Two-Phase Flow Measurements

General Features of Experimental Results

We analyzed pressure oscillations from both obstacles at water flow rates between 30 and 110 m^3/h (superficial velocity between 0.45 and 1.7 m/s) and void fractions α_{gup} between 0% and 25% (measured upstream of the obstacle on the axis of the flow tube). Lower velocities and higher void fractions yielded poor vortex-induced oscillation spectra.

Two different regimes can be identified after a first examination of the direct signals and their power spectra. For α_{gup} below about 10% (Figure 22), vortex-induced oscillations remain permanent;

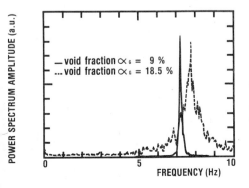

— void fraction $\alpha_G = 9\%$
··· void fraction $\alpha_G = 18.5\%$

POWER SPECTRUM AMPLITUDE (a.u.)

FREQUENCY (Hz)

Figure 22. Power spectra of vortex-induced pressure oscillations for air-water void fractions with upstream void fractions $\alpha_{gup}=9\%$ and 18.5% (the vertical scale has been multiplied by 20 for the dotted curve $\alpha_g = 18.5\%$). Water flow rate $Q_1 = 60$ m^3/h (Reynolds number $Re_1 = 6, 10$).

their amplitude is rather constant with time. Although the mean value of the amplitude decreases, the power spectra display very sharp peaks.

For higher α_g's, vortex oscillations become erratic, their amplitude fluctuates a great deal, and the power spectra display much broader peaks (Figure 22).

Vortex Emission Frequency Dependence on Gas Hold-up and Water Superificial Velocity

Figure 23 shows the variation with the void fraction α_g of a generalized Strouhal number defined as:

$$S_+(\alpha_g, Q_1) = \frac{v(1 - \alpha_g)\,CW}{Q_1} \tag{16}$$

The $(1 - \alpha_g)$ factor is used to take into account approximately the variations of the fluid velocity due to the injection of air. Several constant water flow rates have been used (30 m³/h to 120 m³/h), corresponding to mean water superficial velocities between 0.45 and 1.8 m/s.

A first important result is the increase of the Strouhal number by about 8% when the void fraction varies from 0% to 10%. At higher void fractions, $S+$ decreases slowly towards its monophasic value. As expected due to the high value of the Reynolds numbers used, the monophasic $S+$ value is constant within less than 1% when the flow rate varies ($S+ = 0.22$).

For velocities above 0.9 m/s ($Q_1 > 60$ m³/h), the Strouhal number depends only on the void fraction value upstream of the obstacle and not on the flow rate. For velocity values of 0.45 and 0.6 m/s ($Q_1 = 30$ and 40 m³/h), the Strouhal number is less than 3% lower. The Strouhal number variation shown in Figure 2 is the same whether one or two obstacles are used. This shows that the signal frequency is determined by the vortex emission on the first obstacle.

These results have important consequences for flow metering applications. They show that the vortex-emission frequency provides a precise measurement of the liquid flow rate in air-water flows if the value of α_g upstream of the obstacles is separately measured. Equation 16 and the variation of $S+$ with the gas holdup shown in Figure 23 are used to compute Q_1 from v_m and α_g. Therefore Figure 23 represents the calibration curve for the vortex flowmeter in gas-liquid flows. The precision on the determination of Q_1 is $+/- 1\%$ in the range of Q_1 and α_g values already discussed.

The variation of the Strouhal number with the void fraction previously discussed is qualitatively extremely similar to the behavior observed in cavitating flows by Franc et al. [11, 12] (Figure 24). When the cavitation parameter varies and the gas content increases inside the vortex street, the Strouhal number first increases to a value 20% higher than its monophasic value then decreases again. In these cavitation experiments, too, the behavior does not depend very fast on the Reynolds number.

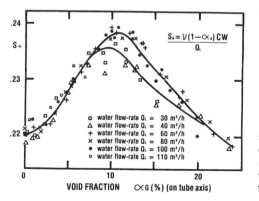

Figure 23. Variation of the vortex emission Strouhal number $S+$ for a 2-obstacles set-up. The void fraction α_g is measured upstream of the obstacle on the tube axis at several constant water flow rates.

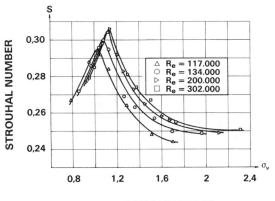

CAVITATION PARAMETER

Figure 24. Variation of the Strouhal number for vortex emission behind a triangular obstacle (pointing upstream) inside a cavitating flow at various Reynolds numbers. (Courtesy of J. P. Franc and J. M. Michel [10, 11].)

Let us not discuss the origin of this variation of the Strouhal number $S+$. We can assume that the vortex motion velocity V_v is proportional to the mean flow velocity and therefore to $Q_1(1 - \alpha_g)$; if this is the case, we find by combining Equations 16 and 14 that the number $S+$ is proportional to $\lambda = V_v/v$; and then, a variation of $S+$ should reflect a variation of the vortex street spatial period λ. Hence, we must determine the dependence of λ on the void fraction α_g. λ is itself proportional to the inverse of the phase shift $\Delta\varphi$ between the vortex emission signal from the two obstacles (Equation 15); thus $\Delta\varphi$ measurements are the practical method that we will use to study variations of λ.

Phase Shift Variations Between the Vortex-Generated Signals from the Two Obstacles

Figure 25 shows variations of the phase shift $\Delta\varphi$ with the void fraction α_g at several constant water flow rates Q_1 between 40 and 110 m³/h (corresponding to Reynolds numbers Re_1 between 4×10^4 and 11×10^5, with $Re_1 = \rho_1 Q_1 W/\eta_1 C$.

The experimental points are more scattered than in figure 23, especially for $\alpha_g > 0.08-0.1$. (The coherence between signals from the two obstacles decreases in this void fraction range.) However, several characteristics appear clearly:

- All points corresponding to $Q_1 > 60$ m³/h are located within $+7\%$ of a same mean curve ($Re_1 > 6 \times 10^4$).
- For $Q_1 = 30$ and 40 m³/h, variations are slower than at higher flow rates ($Re_1 = 3 \times 10^4$ and $= 4 \times 10^4$).
- $\Delta\varphi$ is a maximum around $\alpha_g = 0.1$. This confirms the indications of a flow regime transition around this void fraction value that were already found in the Strouhal number measurements.

We shall now compute the variations of λ (vortex street spatial period) from Figure 24 and check whether they can explain the variations of the Strouhal number $S+$. Using Equation 15, we find:

$$\frac{\lambda(Q_1, \alpha_G)}{\lambda(Q_1, 0)} = \frac{\Delta\varphi(Q_1, 0)}{\Delta\varphi(Q_1, \alpha_G)} \tag{17}$$

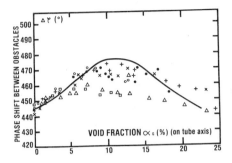

Figure 25. Variation of the phase shift $\Delta\varphi$ between vortex-induced pressure oscillations on the 2 obstacles. The variations of $\Delta\varphi$ with the upstream void fraction α_{gup} on the tube axis are displayed at several constant liquid flow rates Q_1. Symbols determining the values of Q_1 corresponding to each experimental point are the same as in Figure 23. The solid curve represents predictions for the variations obtained using Strouhal number measurements results from Figure 23.

or from Equation 14:

$$\frac{\Delta\varphi(Q_1, \alpha_G)}{\Delta\varphi(Q_1, 0)} = \frac{v(Q_1, \alpha_G)}{v(Q_1, 0)} \frac{V_v(Q_1, 0)}{V_v(Q_1, \alpha_G)} \tag{18}$$

we assume, as a first approximation, that V_v increases as Q_1, $1 - \alpha_g$. Then by using Equations 16 and 17 becomes:

$$\frac{\Delta\varphi(Q_1, \alpha_G)}{\Delta\varphi(Q_1, 0)} \simeq \frac{S(Q_1, \alpha_G)}{S(Q_1, 0)} \tag{19}$$

Therefore, the variations of the phase shift $\Delta\varphi$ should be proportional to those of the Strouhal number $S+$.

The continuous lines in Figure 25 represent the variations of $\Delta\varphi$ predicted from Equation 19. For this computation, we used the variations of $S+$ represented in Figure 23 and corresponding to $Q_1 > 60 \text{ m}^3/\text{h}$.

For $\alpha_g < 7\%$, the agreement between the experimental points and the predicted curves is very good (difference less than $5°$), the fast initial frequency increase at $\alpha_g < 7\%$ is therefore very likely due to a decrease of the vortex street spatial period λ. At larger void fractions, the experimental points are more scattered and correspond to $\Delta\varphi$ values lower than predicted (for $\alpha_g < 0.15$) and to a slower variation.

However (especially at $Q_1 = 80 \text{ m}^3/\text{h}$), the general trend of our experimental values follow the theoretical curves, and the expected maximum around $\alpha_g = 0.1$ is observed. The influence of the velocity and void fraction inhomogeneities can certainly explain part of the remaining difference. For $Q_1 = 30$ and $40 \text{ m}^3/\text{h}$ ($Re_1 = 3 \times 10^4$ and 4×10^4), both the Strouhal number $S+$ and the phase shift $\Delta\varphi$ vary slower than at higher flow rates; this result is consistent with Equation 19.

We can then conclude that the Strouhal number dependence on α_g can be explained satisfactorily by variations of the vortex street spatial period, especially for $\alpha_g < 0.1$. This result is confirmed by the direct photographic observations of Franc [10] and Franc et al. [11] who observed a similar variation of the spatial period in qualitative agreement with our determination.

Coherence Measurements

Figure 26 displays the variations with α_{gup} of the value, at the vortex emission frequency, of the coherence spectrum between the signals from the two obstacles. Coherence is very close to 1 at low void fractions (above 0.98 for $\alpha_g < 5\%$ above 0.9 for $\alpha_g < 0.1$). Then it decreases either sharply (100 m³/h curve in Figure 26) or more smoothly ($Q_1 = 60 \text{ m}^3/\text{h}$ or $Re_1 = 6 \times 10^4$).

We conclude that, at low α_g, the vortex street distorts only slowly as it drifts downflow, and the synchronization between vortex emission at the two obstacles is nearly perfect. At larger void fractions, the vortex emissions are more independent and a large random noise is present.

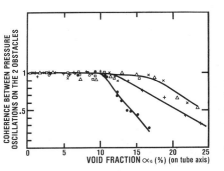

Figure 26. Variation at the vortex emission frequency, of the value of the coherence spectrum between the signals from the two obstacles. The variation with α_{gup} is shown at several constant liquid flow rates. The symbols for the values of Q_1 are the same as is Figure 23.

Vortex Emission Signal rms Amplitude Fluctuations

Figure 27 shows the variations with the void fraction of the relative amplitude $\Delta A/A$ of the vortex emission signal fluctuations for the same water flow-rates used earlier. The values plotted are obtained as previously explained from the histogram of the instantaneous amplitude of the vortex emission signal. Results for both 1 and 2 obstacles are shown (in the latter case, measurements are performed on the downflow obstacle).

In monophasic flows, $\Delta A/A$ varies little with the flow rate in the range investigated.

At high flow rates ($Q_1 > 100$ m^3/h), $\Delta A/A$ is minimum around $\alpha_g = 3\%-5\%$ and increases rapidly above $\alpha_g = 10\%$ for both 1 and 2 obstacles. A surprising fact is the very good stability of the signal rms amplitude around $\alpha_g = 6\%$ for two obstacles which is markedly better than for monophasic flows. For $\alpha_g > 11\%$ the signal is very irregular and disappears completely at some times. Measurements using simple, zero-crossing counting-type methods become almost impossible. A possible explanation for this cut-off effect may be the appearance of a large gas pocket completely surrounding the rear part of the obstacle and suppressing the transmission of the pressure fluctuations.

At lower water flow rates, the variations of $\Delta A/A$ are completely different for one and two obstacles: with one obstacle the stability of the oscillations deteriorates when Q_1 decreases at a constant α_g; with two obstacles, down to $V_1 = 45$ cm/s ($Q_1 = 30$ m^3/h), a good signal stability is retained at significantly higher α_g values than at high flow rates (up to $\alpha_g = 18\%$ at $Q_1 = 30$ m^3/h).

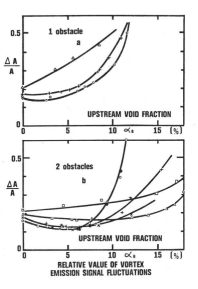

Figure 27. Variation of the fluctuations ΔA of the vortex signal rms amplitude. (ΔA is divided by the time-averaged rms amplitude A.) The symbols for the value of Q_w are the same as Figure 23.

At still lower Q_l the stability is poor even at low α_g's. These results show that using two obstacles is mandatory for obtaining an acceptable signal stability at medium gas-liquid diphasic flow rates. At high flow rates, the use of the system is limited to void fractions of about 11% above which the signal is irregular.

Variations of the Vortex Emission Signal Bandwidth

From this point on, all gas-liquid flow measurements which we shall report have been obtained using the two obstacles set-up which gives a much better signal stability.

Figure 28 shows variations of the relative bandwidth $\Delta v/v_m$ of the vortex oscillations as defined earlier. At high flow-rates ($Q_l > 60$ m^3/h), the spectral bandwidth remains at least as low as for monophasic flows up to $\alpha_g = 11\%$ and deteriorates quickly thereafter particularly for $Q_l > 100$ m^3/h ($V_1 > 1.5$ m/s). While the variation of $\Delta v/v_m$ is very similar to that of $\Delta A/A$ in this case, the behaviors are very different at lower flow rates $Q_l = 40$ m^3/h or $Q_l = 30$ m^3/h. In this case, even using two obstacles and although the signal amplitude remains very stable up to $\alpha_g = 15\%$, $\Delta v/v_m$ increases even at low α_g values and the precision of the measurement gets degraded.

Vortex Emission Signal Average rms Amplitude Measurements

Figure 29 shows the variation with α_g of the signal rms amplitude A as already defined at different water flow-rate values. $A(\alpha_g, Q_l)$ has been divided for normalization purposes by the amplitude $A(0, Q_l)$ at the same monophasic water flow rate.

Even at large Q_l, the mean rms amplitude A decrease very fast with α_g, although the fluctuations of A and the spectral bandwidth remain low. A similar amplitude variation is also observed when only one obstacle is used. This effect may be due to the high concentration of bubbles near the obstacle resulting in an anomalously low local density and small Bernoulli-type pressure fluctuations.

At lower flow rates, the relative amplitude variation is similar at low void fractions but saturates at a larger fraction of the monophasic amplitude.

Practical Applications of the Vortex Flowmeter in Gas-Liquid Flows

The previous results show that the vortex flowmeter can be used for precise measurements of the liquid flow rate in gas-liquid flows if the void fraction α_g is separately measured. The calibration constant (frequency/liquid flow rate) increases by 18% between $\alpha_g = 0$ and $\alpha_g = 10\%$ but is independent of the flow rate in the range of interest so that the correction can easily be performed if the value of α_g is known.

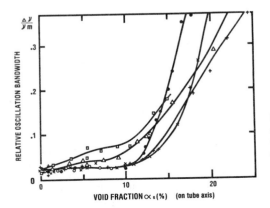

Figure 28. Variation of the relative oscillation bandwidth $\Delta v/v_m$ with the void fraction α_g at several constant liquid flow-rates Q_w (v_m = vortex induced pressure fluctuation frequency, Δv = width of the corresponding power spectrum peak).

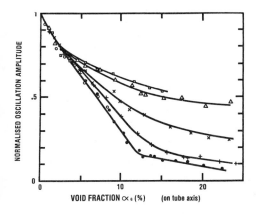

Figure 29. Variation of the time-averaged vortex emission signal rms amplitude $A(Q_w, \alpha_g)$ with the void fraction α_g. A is divided by its value $A(Q_w, 0)$ in a monophasic water flow.

At large enough flow rates above $Q_1 = 60 \text{ m}^3/\text{h}$ ($V_1 = 90$ cm/s), stable vortex emission signals with a very narrow bandwidth are obtained up to void fractions $\alpha_g = 11\%$. At higher α_g's, the signal characteristics deteriorate rapidly. At low flow rates ($Q_1 = 30$ or $40 \text{ m}^3/\text{h}$ corresponding to $V_1 = 45$ to 60 cm/s), the signal stability is greatly improved by using 2 obstacles and performing the detection on the downstream one.

In this case stable, easily analyzable signals are obtained up to $\alpha_g = 15\%$. However, the signal bandwidth deteriorates even at low gas holdups so that measurements are a little less precise.

Vortex Emission Characteristics in Liquid-Liquid Flows

Range of Measurements and Qualitative Observations

Measurements were performed on flowing mixtures of water and kerosene (density $= 0.775 \text{ g/cm}^3$, viscosity $= 1.8$ cp). The maximum total liquid flow rate is $Q_t = 40 \text{ m}^3/\text{h}$ (mean liquid superficial velocity $V_t = 60$ cm/s) due to oil-water separation problems. The kerosene volume fraction α_k varies from 0% to 100%. In favorable conditions, we could observe stable vortex emission signals down to $Q_t = 10 \text{ m}^3/\text{h}$ ($V_t = 15$ cm/s).

Figure 30 shows power spectra obtained for the vortex emission signal at a total flow rate of $15 \text{ m}^3/\text{h}$ for various kerosene volume fractions α_k.

The first spectrum obtained for a monophasic water flow shows a narrow and well-defined peak at the vortex emission frequency. The second one corresponds to $\alpha_k = 10\%$; the peak is much broader and the frequency is shifted upwards by about 10%. Visually, the vortex-induced pressure oscillations are more irregular.

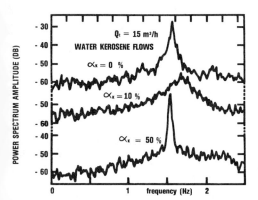

Figure 30. Power spectra of the vortex-induced pressure variations signal measured on a vortex-shedding obstacle in water-kerosene flows with various kerosene upstream volume fractions and a total flow rate $Q_t = 15 \text{ m}^3/\text{h}$ ($R_{cw} = 1.5 \times 10^4$). The amplitude scales are the same, but the spectra have been shifted for better readibility.

The last spectrum corresponds to $\alpha_k = 50\%$ with a very large number of oil droplets with a 3–6 mm diameter moving inside the water.

Surprisingly, the vortex emission signal has become extremely stable again, the frequency has come back to its original value for monophasic flows, and the spectrum is even narrower than in the monophasic case.

Vortex Emission Frequency Variation with the Flow Rate and the Oil Volume Fraction

We have plotted in Figure 31 the variation of the Strouhal number S_1, with the mean kerosene volume fraction α_k measured upstream of the obstacle for two total flow-rate values: $Q_t = Q_k + Q_w = 15 \text{ m}^3/\text{h}$ and $Q_t = 30 \text{ m}^3/\text{h}$. (Figure 31A corresponds to one obstacle and Figure 31B to two obstacles). One sees that the S_1 values obtained with one and two obstacles are identical within 1% at both flow-rate values.

At 30 m³/h, S_1 varies by less than $+/-1.5\%$ from its mean value. (At higher flow-rates such as $Q_t = 40 \text{ m}^3/\text{h}$, the variation is even smaller.) Therefore at high enough velocities, ($Q_t > 30 \text{ m}^3/\text{h}$ or $V_t > 45 \text{ cm/s}$), the vortex-emission frequency together with the monophasic calibration constant provides without correction a total liquid flow-rate value. It measures the average velocity of the mixture and not that of a particular phase (which may differ by nearly 30% in that range).

At $Q_t = 15 \text{ m}^3/\text{h}$, S_1 increases by up to 9% when α_k varies from 0 to 10–15% then drops (around $\alpha_k \simeq 20\%$) to a value closer (2%) to the monophasic Strouhal number. S_1 rises again by about 3% near the continuous water- to continuous oil-phase inversion point ($\alpha_k \simeq 66\%$). Then a symmetrical behavior is observed in the continuous oil-phase domain; S_1 increases by up to 6% at $\alpha_k = 85\%$.

At $Q_t = 10 \text{ m}^3/\text{h}$, stable oscillations are only observed for α_k between 0.2 and 0.8, and S_1 is 4% to 5% higher than in monophasic flows.

These results show that the vortex flowmeter provides basically a total flow-rate measurement in the range of flow rates and α_k values which have been investigated.

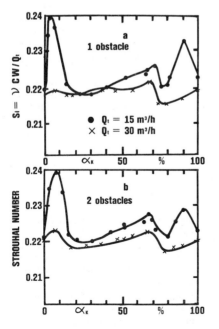

Figure 31. Variation of the Strouhal number $S_1 = \nu CW/Q_t$ with the kerosene volume fraction α_k at total liquid flow rates $Q_t = 15 \text{ m}^3/\text{h}$ and $Q_t = 30 \text{ m}^3/\text{h}$.

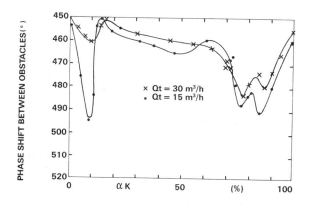

Figure 32. Variation with α_{kup} of the phase shift $\Delta\varphi$ between the signals from two obstacles in a water-kerosene flow at 2 different flow rates $Q_1 = 15\,m^3/h$ ($R_{cw} = 1.5 \times 10^4$) and $Q_t = 30\,m^3/h$ ($R_{cw} = 3 \times 10^4$).

Coherence and Phase-Shift Measurements Between the Vortex-Emission Signals on the Two Obstacles

In the two-obstacles set-up, we have performed measurements of the phase shift $\Delta\varphi$ between the signals on the two obstacles and of the value of the coherence function at the vortex emission frequency. The coherence is always very good and higher than 0.95 both at 15 and 30 m³/h.

The variations of the phase shift are shown in Figure 32. In the continuous water phase, the phase-shift variations correlate very well with those of the Strouhal number both at $Q_t = 15\,m^3/h$ and $Q_t = 30\,m^3/h$. This proves that the frequency variations observed are, also in this case, associated to corresponding changes of the wavelength of the vortex street.

In the continuous water phase, the correspondence is good at $Q_t = 15\,m^3/h$ but the variation is anomalously high at 30 m³/h (perhaps due to flow inhomogeneities).

Vortex Emission Signal rms Amplitude Fluctuations in Liquid-Liquid Diphasic Flows

Figure 33 shows the variations with α_k of the vortex-emission signal rms amplitude fluctuations. $\Delta A/A$ is defined in an earlier section; Figure 33A is obtained using one obstacle and Figure 33B corresponds to two obstacles with measurements performed on the downstream one.

At 30 m³/h, $\Delta A/A$ is always quite low and the frequency measurement is easy. The peak values are however significantly lower when two obstacles are used.

Another interesting feature is the low $\Delta A/A$ value for α_k between 0.2 and 0.7; in this domain, the amplitude fluctuations are sometimes half as large as for monophasic flows. These results are also true at higher flow-rates.

For $Q_t = 15\,m^3/h$ the variations of $\Delta A/A$ follow closely those of the Strouhal number number S_1; large amplitude fluctuations occur in the ranges of volume fractions α_k at which S_1 increases markedly above its monophasic value. Measurements become difficult with just one obstacle for $\alpha_k > 85\%$ and $< 20\%$ and also near $\alpha_k = 70\%$ where the phase inversion occurs.

When two obstacles are used , $\Delta A/A$ is much smaller even in the domains of less stable vortex emission, and the frequency measurement can be performed easily. As already observed for $Q_t = 30\,m^3/h$, amplitude fluctuations are smaller than for monophasic flows in the range $\alpha_k = 20$ to 60% with a minimum around $\alpha_k = 0.45$.

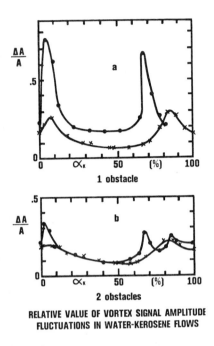

RELATIVE VALUE OF VORTEX SIGNAL AMPLITUDE
FLUCTUATIONS IN WATER-KEROSENE FLOWS

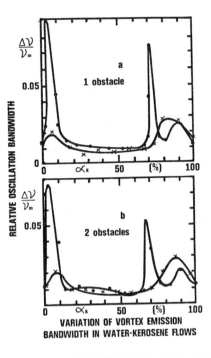

VARIATION OF VORTEX EMISSION
BANDWIDTH IN WATER-KEROSENE FLOWS

Figure 33. Variation or the fluctuations ΔA of the vortex signal rms amplitude. ΔA is divided by the time-averaged value A of this amplitude. The symbols for the values of Q_t are the same as in Figure 31.

Figure 34. Variation of the relative oscillation bandwidth $\Delta v/v_m$ with the oil fraction α_k at several constant liquid flow-rates Q_w (v_m = vortex-induced pressure fluctuations frequency, Δv = width of the corresponding power spectrum peak). The symbols for Q_t values are the same as in Figure 31.

Variation of the Vortex Emission Signal Bandwidth in Water-Kerosene Diphasic Flows

The values of $\Delta v/v_m$ are plotted in Figure 34A (1 obstacle) and Figure 34B (2 obstacles). The variations of $\Delta v/v_m$ are nearly identical in both cases; this confirms that the vortex emission spectrum is essentially determined by the upstream obstacle. Therefore, as for gas-liquid flows, while the signal analysis is often much easier with two obstacles, the errors associated with the spectral width do not get smaller.

The variations of $\Delta v/v_m$ follow closely those obtained for $\Delta A/A$ when only one obstacle was used; the spectral width increases around the phase inversion point and for $\alpha_k > 80\%$ or $< 15\%$.

Extremely sharp spectra are observed for α_k around 50% with Q factors in excess of 150 (the measurement is limited by our frequency resolution).

At 10 m^3/h, acceptable bandwidth values are only obtained for α_k between 0.25 and 0.75. For $Q_t >$ 30 m^3/h ($V_w > 0.45$ m/s) spectra are always narrow enough to provide precise measurements.

Vortex-Emission-Signal Average Amplitude Variations in Water-Kerosene Flows

The mean signal rms amplitude A is computed as described earlier from the signal spectrum at both $Q_t = 15$ m^3/h and $Q_t = 30$ m^3/h. Figure 35 shows normalized A values computed by dividing the actual amplitude by that obtained for a monophasic water flow with the same rate and for two obstacles.

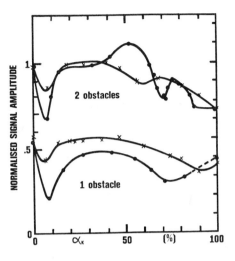

Figure 35. Variation of the time-averaged vortex emission signal rms amplitude in water-kerosene flows with the kerosene volume fraction α_k. $A(Q_t, \alpha_k)$ is divided by its value at the same monophasic water flow rate obtained using two obstacles.

A first important result observed at all flow rates is the nearly twofold amplitude increase obtained by using two obstacles instead of one. As expected, the normalized amplitude is lower in monophasic kerosene flow than in monophasic water; the ratio is very close to that of the densities.

At intermediate α_k values, the variation of A with α_k deviates strongly from the linear law which would be obtained with a homogeneous mixture. A decrease markedly in the unstable signal region, particularly for one obstacle, probably in part due to the amplitude fluctuations.

In the range $\alpha_k = 20$ to 70%, A increases and can be up to 20% higher than the value expected for a homogeneous mixture particularly for two obstacles. These large A values may be in part associated with local density variations creating an additional pressure oscillation component.

Practical Application of the Vortex Flowmeter in Liquid-Liquid Flows

The experimental results just described show that with the set-up we have used the vortex flowmeter measures directly the total volume flowrate with a precision of $+/-$ 1.5% at mean flow velocities >45 cm/s for all water and oil percentages.

The good results obtained at these flowrates are not due to an emulsification of the flowing mixture upstream of the obstacles: the flow contains indeed mostly droplets of a few mm diameter.

At lower flowrates yet, above 15 m³/h ($V_t = 0.22$ m/s), usable signals can be obtained at all fluid compositions, particularly with a two-obstacles set-up. As for gas-liquid flows, the use of two obstacles greatly improves the signal stability and the ease of measurement but does not change the spectral bandwidth or the intrinsic measurement precision.

In this flowrate range, the calibration constant V_m/Q_t increases by up to 10% for $\alpha_k < 15\%$ and by up to 5% for $\alpha_k > 80\%$ and near the phase inversion point. These large V_m/Q_t values are accompanied by an increase of the spectral bandwith and of the signal amplitude fluctuations $\Delta A/A$. For $Q_t = 10$ m³/h ($V_t = 0.15$ m/s), usable signals are only obtained for α_k between 0.25 and 0.75.

ANALYSIS OF PHYSICAL PHENOMENA DETERMINING THE CHARACTERISTICS OF THE VORTEX EMISSION IN LIQUID-LIQUID AND LIQUID-GAS FLOWS

Similarities and Differences Between Vortex Emission Characteristics in Gas-Liquid and Liquid-Liquid Flows

- A first important difference is the behavior at high dispersed-phase volume fractions. In air-water flows, the signal is nearly undetectable for $\alpha_g > 20$ or 25% at most; in water-kerosene flows, the most stable vortex emissions are observed at dispersed-phase fractions above 20%.

• A transition occurs around $\alpha_g = 10\%$ in air-water flows towards less stable vortex emissions. At high flow rates, the signal even completely disappears due to the formation of a large continuous gas pocket behind the obstacle.

• For air-water flows, the vortex frequency v_m increases by the same amount with the void fraction α_g at all flowrates above 40 m³/h. For water-kerosene flows, v_m varies slower with α_k as Q_l increases and these variations are less than 2% at $Q_l = 40$ m³/h.

• The signal amplitude stability and its mean value are improved by using two vortex-shedding obstacles both for water-air and water-kerosene flows. The spectral bandwidth and the vortex emission frequency remain unchanged.

• The flowrate threshold for useful measurements is higher for gas-liquid flows ($Q_w = 30$ m³/h) than for liquid-liquid flows ($Q_l = 15$ or even 10 m³/h). This has to be taken into account for comparing the results (in addition, the upper experimental flowrate limit is different in both cases).

Influence of Bubble Trapping on the Vortex Emission Characteristics

Vortex Emission Stability and Bandwidth in Gas-Liquid Flows

The local void fraction measurements already described show that, at low void fractions, α_{gup} upstream of the obstacle bubbles gather onto vortex cores leaving probably a relatively low void fraction in the rest of the flow. Little distortion to the velocity field between vortices occurs due to bubbles.

Thus, the process of creating a new vortex, helped by the influence of those emitted beforehand is not very perturbed and the coherence and regularity of vortex emission remains high. This explains why for $\alpha_g < 10\%$, the bandwidth of the vortex-emission signal remains very low (at large liquid velocities) indicating a well-defined emission frequency (Figure 28). At lower liquid flow rates ($Q_l < 40$ m³/h) the trapping effect is weaker and the bubble cluster near the vortices is wider (Figure 7A): we observe indeed that, for these liquid velocities, the signal bandwidth increases slightly even for α_g below 10% (Figure 28): in this case, the bubble concentration between the vortices increases faster.

Bubble trapping induces large bubble concentrations near the obstacles. This fact explains the fast decrease in amplitude of the pressure oscillations observed in Figure 29: these are of the order of $\frac{1}{2}\rho V_f^2$ where V_f is the velocity oscillation amplitude and ρ the average density near the obstacle; if ρ is anomalously low due to high bubble concentration, then the pressure oscillation amplitude $A(\alpha_g)$ will also be very low. Since the increase in local bubble density is weaker at low liquid flow rates ($Q_l < 40$ m³/h) (Figure 7A), the maximum amount of bubbles that can get trapped inside the vortices is lower in this case. This explains why the curve $A(\alpha_g)$ stops decreasing earlier for low water flow rates (Figure 29).

Bubble trapping also influences strongly the variations of the pressure drop between the upstream and downstream sides of the obstacle. A large part of the drag forces on bluff bodies is indeed associated with vortex emission. Therefore, the amplitude of vortex-induced pressure oscillations is probably closely related to the drag forces. The energy lost by the mean flow due to these forces is turned into rotational kinetic energy and carried away by the vortices. Most of this energy is stored into the high-velocity regions close to the vortex cores [18, 22]. If many bubbles get trapped inside the vortices, this rotational energy must strongly decrease. We observe indeed a fast decrease of the pressure-drop induced by the obstacles when the void fraction α_{gup} increases from 0 to 0.1. Above 0.1, the variation is much slower.

For $\alpha_{gup} > 0.1$, the vortex emission signal is weaker and very irregular. The amount of bubbles stored into the vortices has reached its limit (higher at the largest velocities), the density of bubbles in between the vortices increases (Figure 9) and they perturb the vortex-emission process. At high velocities, a continuous gas pocket builds up between the vortices and no effect is observed any more. In addition, the energy of the vortices gets lower because of the high amount of bubbles that they contain and they can easily be broken up or distorted. Even when no continuous gas pocket builds up in the wake behind the obstacle when α_{gup} increases, bubble swarms and gas pockets will appear in the flow upstream of the obstacle. They strongly distort the flow profile and stop the vortex emission as they go by.

For these reasons, vortex emission at high void fractions is rather incoherent and seems difficult to model precisely.

Origin of the Vortex Emission Frequency Variations in Air-Water Flows

Several models have been suggested to account for vortex-emission frequency values in monophasic flows [1, 5, 25–27]. Among them, vortex-emission-frequency variations due to bubble trapping in vortex cores are particularly easily explained in Birkhoff's theory. In this model, the wake behind the obstacle is pictured as a wing oscillating around the main flow direction.

The lift force, F_{lift}, on the wake is assumed to be proportional to the angle of attack, θ, and to the average fluid density in the main flow:

$$F_{lift} = -K\rho_{main\,flow}V_0^2\theta \tag{20}$$

This force induces on the wake an angular acceleration, $d^2\theta/dt^2$.

If the effective wavelength, L, is assumed to be proportional to its width, d, then:

$$\rho_{main\,flow}V_0^2\theta = -K'\rho_{wake}d^2\frac{d^2\theta}{dt^2} \tag{21}$$

After solving this differential equation, we find that the vortex-emission frequency verifies:

$$v \propto \frac{V_0}{d}\sqrt{\left(\frac{\rho_{main\,flow}}{\rho_{wake}}\right)} \tag{22}$$

In the present case, the average fluid density inside the wake is lower than in the main flow due to bubble trapping inside the vortices. Therefore, v is higher than for a monophasic flow of the same average velocity V_0; this variation, from equation 22, is mainly related to the gas holdup α_g and not to the main velocity, V_0. This is indeed verified by the experimental results (Figures 23 and 24).

It would seem, at first sight, that buoyancy forces on trapped bubbles might also play an important part in changing the vortex emission frequency. However they are constant with velocity; thus their effect on the vortices, which have a fast increasing energy should decrease at high velocities. This has not been observed in our measurements and seems to rule out that other mechanism.

In conclusion, bubble trapping appears as a dominant effect in gas-liquid flows.

Droplet Trapping in Liquid-Liquid Flows

At low liquid flow rates (15 m^3/h), the bubble trapping is not strong enough to explain the abrupt transitions observed around $\alpha_k = 10\%-15\%$. In addition, the signal stability improves as α_k increases which is the opposite of what would be expected if only trapping effects were involved.

At high flowrates (40 m^3/h) trapping gets strong and is probably a significant parameter in explaining why the signal gets better in the range $0 < \alpha_k < 15\%$. In any case, other phenomena must now be investigated.

Volume Fraction and Dispersed-Phase Velocity Profiles in Liquid-Liquid Flows

Measurement Method

We have performed dispersed-phase velocity profile measurements using an acoustic Doppler velocimeter probe inserted inside the flow tube far upstream of the obstacles (Figure 3). The probe has a 8-mm diameter and faces the flow. It can be moved all the way across the flow tube to

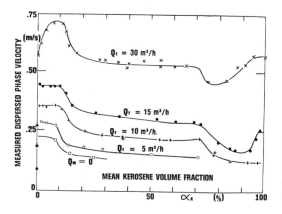

Figure 36. Variations of the dispersed-phase velocity in water-kerosene flows with the kerosene volume fraction α_k at total liquid flow rates ranging from 0 to 30 m^3/h.

measure the velocity profile. A pulsed emitter with a gated receiver is used in order to eliminate echoes originating near the surface of the probe. This probe measures selectively the velocity of dispersed bubbles and droplets in the direction of beam propagation. This measurement is associated with a volume fraction measurement performed by a local high-frequency probe at the same point.

Droplet Velocity Measurements on the Flow-Tube Axis

Figure 36 shows the variation with α_k of the dispersed-phase velocity values read by the Doppler flowmeter on the flow-tube axis; the velocity reading has been calibrated from the values read in monophasic flows assuming a standard turbulent flow profile.

At low α_k values, the velocity reading increases abruptly above the monophasic velocity by about 15–17 cm/s in good agreement with rise velocity values for isolated kerosene droplets in water [23]. (This increase is due to the transition from sound diffusion by very small emulsified droplets moving at the water velocity to scattering by the larger, faster moving injected droplets.)

Around $\alpha_k = 15\%$, the Doppler frequency reading drops abruptly to a value corresponding to a 6 cm/s rise velocity: clearly a major change in the structure of the flow occurs in this α_k range. This rise velocity variation occurs at about the same α_k value for which the vortex-emission characteristics change.

Volume Fraction and Velocity Profiles in Liquid-Liquid Flows

Since this transition occurs always at the same α_k for all flow rates, we have investigated at a given constant $Q_t = 15$ m^3/h the changes of the velocity and α_k profiles across the flow-tube diameter. These measurements (Figure 37A and 37B) show that at low α_k both the velocity and the α_k profiles are very curved; this is probably due to the effect of the wall on the bubble dynamics.

For α_k above 15%, the α_k profile becomes extremely flat except at distances of less than 10 mm from the pipe wall. The velocity profile takes a saddle-type shape with a minumum on the pipe axis corresponding to the sharp drop in the curves of Figure 36. At still higher α_k values the velocity profile becomes, too, very flat.

A possible explanation for these results is the fact that, at low α_k the droplet velocity is determined by the distance to the pipe wall, while at large α_k the interaction with the neighboring droplets becomes the dominant effect. This effect may be similar to the hindered settling effect observed above a critical concentration of solid suspensions.

For α_k above the phase inversion point (66%), a symmetrical behavior is observed with flat velocity and α_k profiles up to $\alpha_k = 85\%$ and curved profiles above that value (the high velocity value measured on the pipe axis for α_k close to 1 may be due to echoes from small dispersed droplets).

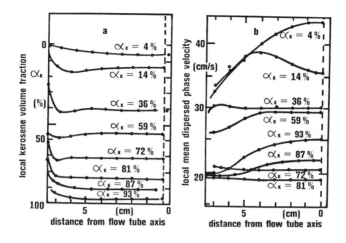

Figure 37. Variation of kerosene volume fraction profiles and dispersed-phase velocity profiles with the average kerosene volume fraction for a total flow rate of 15 m³/h.

Relation Between Flow Profile Variations and Vortex Emission Characteristics

It seems very likely that the presence of flat velocity and α_k profiles is a major factor of the sharp improvement of the vortex-emission bandwidth and stability between $\alpha_k = 20\%$ and $\alpha_k = 85\%$. Vortex emission is basically a monophasic two-dimensional phenomenon which is very disturbed by the presence of large velocity gradients across the vortex-shedding obstacle. The sharp decrease of the relative velocity of the dispersed and continuous phase (from 16 cm/s down to 6 cm/s) and of the velocity and α_k gradients around $\alpha_k = 85\%$ will then certainly be a very favorable factor for strengthening the vortex emission process.

In gas-liquid flows, transitions to slug-type flows occur before a similar effect can take place.

Vortex Emission Instabilities near the Phase Inversion Point in Liquid-Liquid Flows

They are very probably due to the overall instability of the flow in that α_k domain where large-scale flow composition inhomogeneities are seen to occur.

Dominant Physical Factors Influencing the Vortex Emission in Gas-Liquid Flows

At low void fractions the dominant effect in gas-liquid flows is bubble trapping inside the vortex cores: most bubbles get sucked into the cores and the vortex emission remains almost unperturbed.

At void fractions around 10% and above the density of gas inside the obstacle wake becomes very high: at high velocities, a continuous gas pocket abruptly builds up behind the obstacle and destroys the vortex emission. At low velocities, the vortex emission is perturbed but the degradation is more progressive.

Dominant Factors Influencing the Vortex Emission in Liquid-Liquid Flows

The droplet trapping is not strong enough to suppress the bubbles in between the vortices, particularly at low flow rates; the dominant phenomenon is the very flat velocity and α_k profiles observed in the flow for mean α_k values between 20% and 85%. In this α_k range, the droplet rise velocity becomes also very low (typically 6 cm/s instead of 17 cm/s) and the vortex emission gets extremely stable.

For α_k below 20% and above 15%, the trapping effect at low flow rates is not sufficient to influence the vortex emission which is very degraded by the presence of droplets. At higher flow-rates, the perturbation decreases partly due to the trapping effect (present only when the water phase is continuous) and partly to the lower relative value of the bubble rise or fall velocity with respect to the main flow.

Near the continuous-oil-to-continuous-water-phase transition point, large-scale flow instabilities occur which perturb the vortex emission.

CONCLUSIONS

Dominant Features of Vortex Emission in Two-Phase Flows

One of the most surprising results of this study is the fact that in some cases vortex emission in two-phase flows can be more stable and have a narrower spectrum that in single-phase flows (either due to a flattening of the flow profile or to bubble trapping at the cores). These high-stability domains correspond to the range $\alpha_g < 10\%$ for gas-liquid flows and $15\% < \alpha_k < 80\%$ for low-velocity water-kerosene flows.

In cavitating flows, large pressure pulses can therefore be induced due to the collapse of the vapor pockets generated at the cores. In vortex flows with a free surface, the entrainment of bubbles can result in large level surges. Vortex emission behind an obstacle induces often strong pressure oscillations on the sides of the obstacle parallel to the flow. In liquid-liquid flows, those oscillations remain the same or can even be enhanced. In gas-liquid flows, the pressure variations amplitude decreases due to the low mean density of the fluid near the obstacles and the drag on the obstacle also becomes smaller.

Practical Conclusions on the Performance of Vortex Flowmeters in Two-Phase Flows

The experiments just described have demonstrated that vortex flowmeters can be used in diphasic flows provided certain conditions are verified:

Gas-Liquid Flows

The vortex flowmeter can measure precisely $(+/- 1\%)$ the liquid flow rate if a separate α_g measurement is available to correct the reading. The signal amplitude is very dependent on the void fraction and can be used for that purpose in some cases.

The fluid velocity must be high enough (typically > 45 cm/s) and the void fraction must generally remain below 10% if simple, zero-crossing-type frequency-measurement methods are to be used. Using two identical obstacles instead of one greatly improves the stability of the vortex-emission signal amplitude and stability.

Measurements at higher gas holdups can be performed using more complex circuits or spectral analysis and the precision will be lower.

The trapping of most of the gas inside the vortex cores explains for a large part the good performance of the flowmeter at low void fractions.

Liquid-Liquid Flows

The vortex flowmeter measures in this case the total liquid flow rate Q_t in a large range of conditions. Easy vortex-frequency measurements can be performed for all mixture compositions when the mean flow velocity is above 40 cm/s. Above 20 cm/s the signal is very stable for kerosene volume fractions α_k between 20% and 85%. In these conditions the flowmeter measures Q_t with a 2% precision (keeping the monophasic calibration constant).

In the preceding range of α_k values, the vortex emission signal has even better characteristics than in monophasic flows; this effect is partly due to the very flat velocity and α_k profiles and to the low droplet rise velocity in that range of α_k values. At 20 cm/s for $\alpha_k > 85\%$ or $<20\%$ usable signal can still be obtained, but the measurement is less precise. In this case, too, the use of two obstacles improves markedly the signal stability.

Additional Problems to be Investigated

The above results have been obtained for obstacles with a width 10 times larger than the typical bubble size. In this case, the vortex emission is not destroyed and can even be enhanced by the presence of a dispersed phase (liquid or gas).

It is clear·that the relative size of the obstacle and of the bubble or droplets will play an important role in this phenomenon. Preliminary results performed with smaller obstacles (with a width of the order of the bubble size) show that, in this case, the vortex emission is much less stable, particularly at low velocities.

This suggests two important questions:

• Does the vortex-emission frequency depend on the bubble size at a given gas or oil volume fraction?
• What is the equilibrium size of bubbles or droplets inside the vortex cores?

On the latter aspect, photographs and visual examinations both in gas-liquid and liquid-liquid flows do show that very small bubbles can be produced at large velocities: this suggests that vortex creation can be a simple, efficient mixing and emulsification method.

From a more general point of view, the most striking results from all vortex-emission studies performed in two-phase flows is the fact that the orderly pattern of vortex emission can survive or even in favorable conditions become more periodic in extremely disordered two-phase flows.

Acknowledgment

We wish to thank R. Coudol and C. Fierfort for their active participation in many of the experiments described in References 9 and 15, and also J. P. Franc and J. M. Michel, at the Institut de Mecanique de Grenoble (B. P. 68, 38402- St Martin d'Heres Cedex) for their fruitful cooperation on cavitating flows.

REFERENCES

1. Abernathy, F. H., and Kronauer, R. E., "The Formation of Vortex Streets," *J. Fluid Mech.*, Vol. 25 (1966), pp. 1–20.
2. Auton, T. R., "On the Dynamics of Gas Bubbles in Liquids," an essay submitted in partial fulfilment of a PhD thesis DAMTP (Cambridge University), 1981.
3. Baker, R. C., and Deacon, J. E., "Tests on Turbine, Vortex, and Electromagnetic Flowmeters in Two-Phase Air-Water Upward Flow," International Conference on Physical Modelling of Multiphase Flow, Coventry, England, April 1983, paper Hl, pp. 337–352.
4. Bendat, J. S., and Piersol, A. G., *Engineering Applications of Correlation and Spectral Analysis*, Wiley and Sons, 1980.
5. Birkhoff, G., "Formation of Vortex Streets," *J. Appl. Phys.*, Vol. 24 (1953), pp. 98–103.
6. Cook, T., and Harlow, F., "Virtual Mass in Multiphase Flow," submitted to *Int. J. Multiphase Flow*.
7. Danel, F., and Delhaye, J. M., "Sonde Optique pour la, Mesure du Taux de Vide Local en Ecoulement Diphasique," Mesures, Regulation, Automatisme, Aug.–Sept. 1971, pp. 99–101.
8. Delhaye, J. M., et al. (Eds.), *Thermohydraulics of Two-Phase Systems for Industrial Design and Nuclear Engineering*, McGraw Hill, 1980.
9. Foussat, A. J. M., and Hulin, J. P., "Vertical Liquid-Liquid and Liquid-Gas Two-Phase Flow Measurements with a Vortex Flowmeter," I.U.T.A.M. Symposium on Measuring Techniques in Gas-Liquid Two-Phase Flows, Nancy, France, July 1983.

10. Franc, J. P., "Etudes de Cavitation," 3rd Cycle Thesis, Universite Scientifique et Medicale, Institut National Polytechnique de Grenoble, France, 1982.
11. Franc, J. P., et al., "Structures Rotationnelles Bi- et Tri-Dimensionnelles dasn un Sillage Cavitant," C. R. Acad. Sc. Paris, Vol. 295, (1982), pp. 773–777.
12. Gerrard, J. H., "The Mechanism of the Formation Region of Vortices Behind Bluff Bodies," J. Fluid Mech.,Vol. 25, Part 2 (1966), pp. 401–413.
13. Goldring, B. T., et al., "Level Surges in the Circulating Water Downshaft of Large Generating Stations," Third International Conference on Pressure Surges, Canterbury, England, March 1980, paper F2.
14. Goldstein, S., "Modern Developments in Fluid Dynamics," Oxford, Clarendon Press, 1950, Chap. XIII.
15. Hulin, J. P., et al., "Experimental Study of Vortex Emission Behind Bluff Obstacles in a Gas-Liquid Vertical Two-Phase Flow," Int. J. Multiphase Flow, Vol. 8 (1982), pp. 475–490.
16. Jones, O. C., and Delhaye, J. M., "Transient and Statistical Measurement Techniques for Two-Phase Flow (a Critical Review)," Int. J. Multiphase Flow, Vol. 3 (1976), pp. 89–116.
17. Kobori, T., and Terada, M., "Application of the Needle Type Void Meter to Blow-Down Test," Proceedings of the CSNI specialist meeting on transient two-phase flow, Paris, France, 1978, pp. 699–714.
18. Lamb, H., Hydrodynamics, 6th Edition, Cambridge University Press, 1975, Chap. VII.
19. Mair, W. A., and Maul, D. J., "Bluff Bodies and Vortex Shedding, a Report on Euromech 17," J. Fluid Mech., Vol 45 (1971), pp. 209–224.
20. Marris, A. W., "A Review of Vortex Streets, Periodic Wakes, and Induced Vibration Phenomena." J. Basic Eng., Vol. 86 (1974), pp. 185–196.
21. Medlock, R. S., "The Vortex Flowmeter, Its Development and Characteristics," Australian J. of Instrumentation and Control (April 1976), pp. 24–34.
22. Milne-Thomson, L. M., "Theoretical Hydrodynamics," 5th Edition, London, McMillan, 1968, Chap. XIII.
23. Nicolas, Y., and Witterholt, F. J., "Measurement of Multiphase Flow," 47th Annual Fall Meeting of the Society of Petroleum Engineers of AIME, San Antonio, Texas, Oct. 1972.
24. Reimann, J., et al., "Bestimmung der Stromungs in Horizontaler Luft-Wasser sowie Dampf-wasser Stromung mit einer Localen Impedanz Sonde," Report KFK 2527, Karlsruhe Nuclear Research Center, 1977.
25. Roshko, A., "On the Development of Turbulent Wakes from Vortex Streets," NACA TR 1191, 1954.
26. Roshko, A., "On the Wake and Drag of Bluff Bodies," J. of Aerospace Sciences, Vol. 22 (1955), pp. 124–132.
27. Schaefer, J. W., and Eskinazi, S., "An Analysis of the Vortex Street Generated by a Viscous Fluid," J. Fluid Mech., Vol. 6, Part 2 (1959), pp. 241–260.
28. Strouhal, V., "Uber eine Besondere Art der Tonerregung," Ann. Phys. Chem., Vol. 5 (1878, pp. 216–251.
29. Thomas, N. H., et al., "Entrapment and Transport of Bubbles by Transient Large Eddies in Multiphase Turbulent Shear Flows." International Conference on Physical Modelling of Multiphase Flow, Coventry, England, April 1983, Paper El, pp. 169–184.
30. White, D. F., et al., "The Vortex Shedding Flowmeter," Flow, Its Measurement and Control in Science and Industry (Instrument Society of America), Vol. 1, 1974, pp. 967–974.

CHAPTER 28

TECHNIQUES FOR FLOW PATTERN STUDIES

Mohd S. Quraishi and Thomas Z. Fahidy

Department of Chemical Engineering
University of Waterloo
Waterloo, Ontario, Canada

CONTENTS

INTRODUCTION

General

Flow visualization may be defined as the visual determination of fluid flow fields. Optimal methods for testing fluid flow are "nonintrusive" in the sense that they do not disturb flow patterns. Visualization techniques may be used for precise measurements or as a supportive tool in conjunction with other means of flow measurement. If properly employed, flow visualization can provide a true picture of complex three-dimensional flow fields.

Flow behavior was first recorded by Leonardo da Vinci, who sketched the profile of a free jet and the formation of eddies in its wake at abrupt expansions. He was also the first to propose the use of suspended particles for the observation of flow currents. The first scientific application of a flow visualization technique is credited to O. Reynolds (1883) who injected a thin thread of liquid dye into flowing water inside a long glass tube, in order to demonstrate transition from laminar to turbulent flow. During its history of about one hundred years suspended particles and dye-injection became the most popular technique, although more sophisticated methods (e.g., holographic interferometry) and the advent of lasers and microprocessors have begun to revolutionize the field of flow visualization. Automatic analysis of raw visualization data via digital image processing provides for presentation in any desired form via computer-generated color graphics. The recently developed direct decoding of binary flow-pattern signals by the so-called "solid state computer eye" eliminates the intermediate recording stage by employing still or motion photography or video cassette-disc recorders. The current "state of art" of this rapidly expanding field is well illustrated in three recent proceedings of international symposiums on flow visualizations [1-3].

Classification of Flow Visualization Techniques

Flow visualization techniques can be broadly classified into two main groups:

● Direct flow visualization.
● Indirect flow visualization.

The former includes all techniques of observing a complex flow field by the naked eye without interpretation of visual image (e.g., suspended-particle technique), while in the latter either an interpretation of flow field is required or the visual image is created at a plane outside the test area. Direct techniques are usually simple and quick but qualitative. Indirect techniques are usually complicated and slow, but they furnish accurate quantitative information.

An alternative and widely accepted classification of flow visualization techniques is based on the properties of light modified by the techniques. In this sense the following major categories can be defined:

● Fluid marker techniques (e.g., dye injection).
● Suspended-particle techniques (e.g., smoke injection).

● Surface-coating techniques.
● Tuft techniques.
● Techniques based on the shift in phase and direction of light beams (e.g., interferometry).

Further subdividing is feasible on the basis of flow containment, i.e., whether flow in the bulk or on a surface is to be visualized. Grouping of the most common techniques is as follows:

● For bulk flow study: fluid markers, suspended-particles, shadowgraphy, Schlieren methods, interferometry, speckle photography, Raman scattering, and Rayleigh scattering.
● For surface flow study: Tuft techniques, surface coating, stripped surface, electrochemical oxidation/deposition of metals, and electrochemical dye techniques.

VISUALIZATION

General

It is an a priori characteristic of every flow visualization technique to interfere with the radiative properties of the electromagnetic waves; this is manifested by a mutual interaction modifying both the electromagnetic waves and fluid flow, although a carefully designed technique minimizes flow field distortion. The most commonly employed electromagnetic waves in flow visualization are in the visible radiation range, although ultraviolet and infrared rays are also used in certain techniques. Electromagnetic waves possess wave-like and particle-like properties, both of which are utilized by visualization techniques. The wave-like property (i.e., oscillating wave of wavelength λ and frequency ν) serves the majority of techniques, such as the suspended particles, dye injection, interferometry, etc., while the particle-like property (i.e., secondary photon-emission of free electrons, excited by primary photon bombardment returning to a lower energy level) is exploited by certain techniques, e.g., the fluorescent-dye method.

Radiative Properties of Electromagnetic Waves

The interaction of light waves with a fluid is quantitatively described by their radiative properties which determine in what manner the fluid will emit (fluorescent dye technique), reflect (suspended particle technique), absorb (dye injection technique), or transmit (interferometry) radiant energy. Radiative properties are wavelength-selective, e.g., a blue solution is a good transmitter for blue light but a very poor one for red light. This selectivity depends on the monochromatic or spectral properties which are usually modified to render a flow visible.

When a beam of light strikes a fluid segment it is divided into three fractions: the absorbed, the reflected, and the transmitted portion, as shown in Figure 1A. The thermal property "absorptivity," α, is defined as the fraction of the incident energy absorbed, the "reflectivity," ρ, is defined as the fraction of energy reflected, and the "transmissivity," τ, is defined as the fraction of energy transmitted through the fluid segment. Two types of reflection phenomena may be observed when a fraction of light is reflected from the fluid segment (or suspended particle). If the angle of incidence is equal to the angle of reflection (Figure 1B), a strong light beam and a mirror image of the light source at one angle will be seen. This is "specular reflection." If the incident beam is scattered uniformly in all directions (Figure 1C), a uniformly illuminated fluid segment will be seen. This is diffused reflection, used in most flow visualization techniques.

Flow visualization techniques which use the transmissivity property of the incident light provide integrated information about the flow field along the path of the light in the fluid. The transmitted light can change its direction due to change in the refractive index of the fluid segment. Flow visualization techniques using the light scattering (reflectivity property) of the fluid or suspended particles yield local information about the flow field at the point of scattering, the intensity of the scattered light being normally much lower than the transmitted light. However, the intensity of light scattered by suspended particles is normally higher than the intensity of light scattered by fluid molecules.

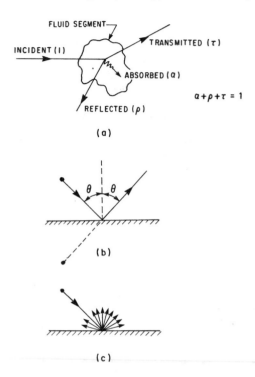

Figure 1. Radiation properties of light waves: (A) interaction of light and fluid segment; (B) specular reflection; (C) diffused reflection.

Apart from the modification of amplitude and direction of electromagnetic waves, flow methods may also rely on changes in the frequency, phase and polarization properties. The frequency of transmitted or reflected radiation can change due to the state of motion (Doppler effect). The frequency of transmitted light can also change due to a moving-phase object (Schlieren system). The frequency of the light scattered from a suspended particle can change due to the dynamic state of the scatterer (Raman effect, fluorescent tracers). The phase of a transmitted light changes according to the refractive index of the fluid; this property is the basis for visualization via interferometry. The direction of polarization of a linearly polarized light wave is changed by varying concentrations of some substance in the fluid (e.g., sugar) and can serve for visualizing mixing processes.

Light Sources

There are two types of light source used in flow visualization:

- White light—It consists of thermal radiation propagating in a wide band of frequencies. Natural light, photoflood light, movie light, strobe light, etc., are the usual white light sources.
- Monochromatic light—It consists of thermal radiation propagating in a very narrow band of frequencies, normally around a single frequency. Lasers, sodium lamps, and mercury lamps are the most important sources.

Information Storage and Data Retrieval

The whole-field and transient point information methods are usually employed.

- Whole field—This information record is continuous in fluid field but discontinuous in time. At every time step the entire flow field is recorded by a data retrieval system at equal or unequal

time steps. Still photography, movie photography, video cassette recording, and long-time exposure photography of suspended particles are major methods in this category.
- Transient point information—Information is continuous in time but obtained only at selected locations of the flow field, defined arbitrarily or forming a very closely spaced grid pattern. Optical probes using photomultipliers and advanced laser techniques are major methods in this category.

Note that the human eye is a continuous observer of the whole field or at least a good portion of it, without direct recording.

Lighting Arrangements

A variety of lighting arrangements are commonly used for flow visualization studies. Selecting the best lighting arrangement is usually a trial-and-error procedure. The most common arrangements are summarized in this section.

1. Uniform diffused light—Common for dye injection and suspended-particle studies and easily available via natural light. In a laboratory such light can be simulated by multiple light reflections from white ceilings, walls, or cardboards using special reflecting umbrellas.
2. Diffused front-lighting—This type of lighting is normally produced by placing a semi-transparent white paper in front of the light source set in front of the experimental setup. Non-reflecting background and reflecting umbrellas are commonly used.
3. Diffused back-lights—This lighting is normally produced by bouncing light from a white surface placed behind the experimental setup, or by placing a semi-transparent paper between the light source and at the back of the experimental setup.
4. Tangential lighting—A light source is placed perpendicularly to the line of observation. This lighting is favored with the suspended-particles technique, using commonly a black background.
5. Parallel (collimated) lighting—Normally this light is produced by a combination of a point light source and lenses; lamps for white light and lasers for monochromatic light are normally used. Parallel lighting is quite common in shadowgraphy and interferometry.
6. Light sheet—A special type of tangential light used to illuminate a cross section of the flow field. The light is produced either by a point source or a cylindrical lens or a glass rod, or by a sweeping laser beam; lamps and lasers are common sources. A black background and nonreflecting black surfaces to reduce the amount of stray light are usually employed.
7. Multiple (tangential) strobe lighting—A dark-room technique popular with the suspended particle approach. Recommended particularly for velocity measurements in two-dimensional laminar flow.
8. Combination lighting—The various categories described in sections 1–4 and 7 may be combined, if needed, in a specific study.

FLUID-MARKING TECHNIQUES

The oldest techniques, commonly known as dye-injection techniques, are based on the phenomenon of selective absorption of white or monochromatic lights. Absorbed light is either converted to nonvisible electromagnetic waves or re-emitted at a different frequency in the visible light range. They usually furnish integrated information in the direction of view, but this information is effected by the previous history of the marker from the time of its injection or creation.

Dye-Injection Technique

Although the injection of a dye into a flowing liquid stream appears to be deceivingly simple, care must be taken that the density be sufficiently close to the liquid density and that its injection velocity be small enough for the flow field distortion to be negligible. Dye can be injected upstream

(a)

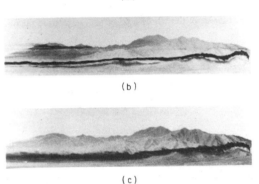

(b)

(c)

Figure 2. Simulation of a plume from a stack by dye tracer injection in a small-scale model (courtesy of Messrs. H. T. Lin and J. T. Lin, Flow Industries Inc., Kent, Washington, USA): (A) full-Scale Plumes From the Kennecott Copper Smelter, Garfield, Utah; (B) a simulated plume k ~ 2.0, Froude number ~ 1.0; (C) a simulated plume k ~ 1.0, Froude number 2.1 (k is the ratio of the effluent speed divided by the mean wind speed.)

of the apparatus in a mixing chamber, into a flow stream entering a vessel or into a flow boundary layer by using hypodermic needles. In some applications dye may be injected through small holes at solid surfaces. Colored threads of dye can be produced by injecting low miscibility dyes with properly placed hypodermic needles.

Although food-coloring agents are the most popular dyes, recorder ink, fountain pen ink, and color pigments are also widely used. Certain chemicals, e.g., potassium permanganate, have also been employed. Color pigment dissolved in organic solvents yields dyes of low miscibility to be used in aqueous media. In some applications liquid milk is used with food color in order to increase its reflectivity. Diffused white background light is normally preferred, although tangential light can also be effective if the dye has sufficient reflectivity. The technique is not recommended for flow visualization in polymer solutions where drastic changes in fluid properties can be introduced by dyes [4].

Figure 2 shows an application of blue food dye injection to study plume dispersion phenomena [5]. The study was done on a small-scale model of physical terrain in a 1.2-m wide towing tank [5–7]. Stable atmospheric conditions were simulated by stable stratification of the fluid with a constant-density gradient. Full-scale plumes (Figure 2A) released from two older stacks and two laboratory plumes released (as dye) from one of the stacks (Figure 2B and 2C) are shown. Although the observations were not made under identical conditions, both the full-scale and the laboratory plumes demonstrate (1) the cessation of the plume rise and (2) the adjustment of the mean plume trajectory to the underlying topography, the two most prominent features of plumes released into a stable environment.

Surface Coating by Dyes

To study the movement of a fluid segment coming in contact with a solid surface, the solid surface may be coated with a slowly dissolving dye, such as nigrosine [8].

The Electrochemical Indicator Technique

A colored dye can be generated at a solid-liquid interface by using electrochemical means [9, 10]. The liquid contains initially a predetermined amount of an analytical indicator, e.g., bromo-cresol green, bromo-phenol red, bromo-thymol blue, meta-cresol purple, thymol blue, etc., at an acidic pH, where the indicator color is light and transparent. The solid surface is polarized cathodically at the onset of the experiment, creating an immediate local shortage of hydronium ions at the surface, hence a sudden and strong increase in the local pH. Consequently, the indicator changes its color to a deep (opaque) hue at the polarized surface and a clear visual contrast is created. Hydrogen produced at the solid surface is dissolved in the liquid as long as the voltage drop (and current flow) between the cathode and the counterelectrode positioned outside the area of flow visualization, is sufficiently low. The aqueous solution normally contains 0.1 g/L indicator mixed with a small amount of hydrochloric acid and sodium chloride to set its pH just below the lower limit of the acid to alkaline transition range of the indicator. A few drops of dilute aqueous hydrochloric acid added to the solution after use will immediately reset the original pH and hence color. The high degree of color reversibility renders this technique particularly attractive for the study of flow propagation in closed systems.

Figure 3 shows the application of the electrochemical indicator technique to study convection patterns in flow past an obstacle [11]. The obstacles made of copper and attached to a copper rod were connected as cathode and the color change of a 0.04 g/L bromo-thymol blue solution was employed for the marking of convective flow. Typical convection patterns observed in the Reynolds number range of 800–950 are shown in Figure 3A and 3G. The flow is characterized by a linear-thread structure strongly modified by large-size eddies. In the case of a rod obstacle (Figure 3A) the marked fluid is confined to the central core near the obstacle, but slightly downstream it is broken into large patches. Similar behavior is observed for a single cone (Figure 3B). In the case of a double cone (Figure 3C) and a parallel horizontal cylinder (Figure 3D) the breakup of eddies results in an intermingling of the thread-like filaments. In the case of a sphere (Figure 3E), cross horizontal cylinder (Figure 3F), and reverse single cone (Figure 3G) the central tube section is filled with orderly arranged large eddies.

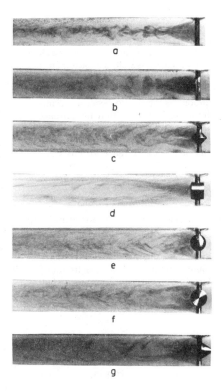

a

b

c

d

e

f

g

Figure 3. Convection patterns in flow past various obstacles inside a horizontal tube using an analytical indicator and the electrochemical technique (Re = Reynolds number based on tube diameter): (A) 3-mm cylinder Re = 859.1; (B) single cone Re = 924.3; (C) double cone Re = 888.8; (D) parallel horizontal cylinder Re = 807.4; (E) sphere Re = 891.1; (F) cross horizontal cylinder Re = 807.4; (G) reverse single cone Re = 803.5 (Authors' experimental results obtained in the Dept. Chem. Engg., University of Waterloo, Waterloo, Ontario, Canada.

Figure 4. Front view of convection pattern in a jet entering a rectangular cell via analytical indicator technique. Entry velocity = 1.2 m/s (Reynolds number ≃ 11,000) (Authors' experimental results obtained in the Dept. Chem. Engg., University of Waterloo, Waterloo, Ontario, Canada.)

The Chemical Indicator Technique

In this technique of visualizing bulk flow or mixing between different liquid streams, the analytical indicator changes its color by the addition of an alkaline solution [9], normally sodium hydroxide. The indicator concentration is 0.01–0.1 g/L, and the injected alkali contains a small amount of sodium chloride to increase its natural buoyancy. Phenolphthalein as well as indicators mentioned previously may be used. The technique is highly reversible; the alkaline color can be easily removed by adding dilute hydrochloric acid to the liquid. This technique is also well suited for closed systems inasmuch as it is as free of "color pollution" as the electrochemical variant.

Figure 4 shows the application of the chemical indicator technique to study the entrance effects in a rectangular flow vessel [12]. The working fluid is an aqueous 0.03 g/L phenolphtalein solution at pH ≅ 8. The marking solution has a pH ≅ 12. Typical convective patterns due to entrance into a rectangular cell are shown at a jet inlet velocity of 1.2 m/s (entrance Reynolds number ≃ 11,000).

Ozone

This fluid-marker technique is intended for gaseous flows and is based on the selective absorption of ultraviolet light by ozone [13]. O_3 is totally transparent to the visible light spectrum, but it is more opaque than, for example, gold to ultraviolet light (253.7 nm). In practice, an ultraviolet light source, such as a mercury vapor lamp with a black glass filter, is placed at the back of the experimental cell, and a flat glass plate painted with fluorescent material is set in front of the cell. A stream of ozone from an ozone generator is injected into the flow stream as a tracer and identified as a black area on the fluorescent screen. If minor temperature variations are not critical, ozone can be generated within a flow stream by an electric corona discharge at a desired location.

Fluorescein Dyes

Similar to the dye injection technique, the fluorescein-dye technique is based on the high absorptivity of ultraviolet light by the dye and the emission of the absorbent energy in the visible portion of the spectrum. The most commonly used fluorescein dyes are 4-methyl-umbelliferone, rhodamine-B, rhodamine-6G and fluorescein sodium (uramine). Black light fixtures and argon ion lasers are used as popular excitation sources. Sheet light from argon ion lasers with uramine dye is the most common combination; the color produced is greenish-yellow. Rhodamine dye produces a distinctive purple-red color.

Photochromic Dyes

In this technique, ultraviolet light excites the dye molecules whose color in the excited state will eventually fade away [14] as the molecules regain their original state. Normally, a narrow ultraviolet light laser beam is used to generate a colored line at time zero in a nonpolar solution of uniformly distributed photochromic dye, normally colorless in the absence of short-wavelength light. The photochromic dye 1,3,3-Trimethyl-6-nitro-indoline-2-spiro-2-2-benzopyran (TNSBP) in petroleum solvent [15] produces a bright blue color when selectively activated by an ultraviolet laser beam.

Figure 5 shows the photographic record produced by this technique for a liquid-liquid system. In this application the internal velocities of forming drops in a single nozzle, liquid-liquid spray column were measured using the photochromic dye technique [14]. A photochromic dye [15], which under normal room lighting conditions is colorless in solution, was dissolved in the dispersed-phase liquid. The dye was selectively activated using a finely focused ultraviolet pulsed laser [16] to form bright blue narrow lines in the plane of symmetry of the forming drops. Velocities were determined from high-speed cinematography of the motion of the originally straight lines. The photographs represent four frames taken from the high-speed film depicting drops formed on a 4.76-mm nozzle at a rate of 3 drops per second.

SUSPENDED-PARTICLE TECHNIQUES

Known about as long as the fluid-marker group, these techniques make use of (usually diffused) light reflected from the surface of suspended foreign particles in a fluid continuum. It is important that the particles be "buoyant," i.e., they should not sink to the bottom or float to the surface at an appreciable speed. Tangential light and lasers are the most commonly employed means of

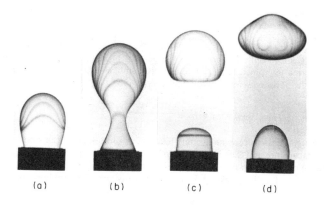

(a)   (b)   (c)   (d)

Figure 5. The distortion of a horizontal line, representing activation of a photochromic dye by an ultraviolet pulse laser, due to fluid motion inside a liquid drop. Photographs a to d are in chronological order. (Courtesy of Messrs. G. Johnson, E. Marshall and J. Hutchins, University of California, Santa Barbara, California, USA.)

illumination. Particle size may vary from a few micrometers (e.g., dust particles) to a few decimeters (balloons filled with helium), but the maximum is usually less than a centimeter. The techniques can be classified into four categories:

1. Smoke tracers.
2. Suspended solid particles.
3. Gas bubbles and liquid droplets.
4. Precipitation.

The introduction of the laser light sheet for the illumination of suspended particles is one of the most significant developments in this field during the last few years. Although various light sources may and have been used for producing a light sheet, lasers provide a very intense light at a very low level of power consumption (although at a high cost). In the simplest arrangement a laser beam is set vertically to a glass rod or a cylindrical lens in order to spread the laser beam in a plane. In a second arrangement the laser beam is guided over an oscillating mirror, and the oscillatory movement generates the light sheet. Thirdly, a laser beam may be reflected by the rotation of a multi-mirror-phase prism which may have up to sixteen faces.

Smoke-Tracer Techniques

The observation of flow by smoke visualization is the oldest technique in this category [17]. Smoke or a gas stream resembling smoke can be produced by the following commonly used methods.

Cigarette Smoke

Smoke is generated by a slowly burning cigarette in a medium moving at a low speed. The smoke is not naturally buoyant but may be used for flow visualization in areas far from the smoke source.

Incense Smoke

Smoke from burning dry incense contains particles of size less than one micrometer; this is a good flow-indication method under appropriate conditions.

Oil Vaporization

Smoke can be produced by vaporizing oils (e.g., Shell ondina oil) in an inert gas medium or in an oxidizing gas atmosphere. The size of the aerosol produced by condensing oil droplets is normally less than a micrometer and can be used as a smoke tracer. One of the best fuels for producing a nontoxic, noncorrosive, dense smoke is Type 1964 Fog Juice.

Smoke Wand, Smoke Tube, Smoke Rack

These commercial devices provide a single filament or uniformly spaced smoke line by heating oil to a high temperature and then injecting it into a flow stream. In some devices the oil feed tube leading to the smoke injection port is electrically heated. In some wands and smoke tubes only a single port is provided, while smoke racks have uniformly spaced multiple ports for the injection of heated oil [18].

Smoke Wire

The smoke wire technique, first developed in the early 1950s and much improved in later years [19], is capable of producing very fine filaments of smoke; this is one of the most widely used smoke

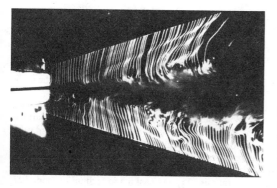

Figure 6. Visualization of the large-scale motion of a plane jet by the smoke wire technique. (Courtesy of Messrs. D. J. Shlien and A. K. M. F. Hussain, University of Houston, USA.)

tracer techniques. A chemically coated wire is suspended at the region of observation and a current is passed through an ohmic resistance to the wire, creating a sheet of smoke filaments due to resistance heating. Oil and molten paraffin are normally used as chemical coating. In the case of a vertical or an inclined wire, an oil reservoir at the top provides a continuous supply of oil to produce a continuous smoke sheet. Horizontal wires must be either coated each time or moved through the oil reservoir placed to one side. Nickel-chrome, nichrome, and Elgin alloy stainless steel wires in the size range of 0.5 mm to 0.05 mm are normally used in this method, which is limited to flows where Re < 20, based on the wire diameter.

The smoke wire technique is illustrated in Figure 6, showing the study of the large scale motion of a plane jet. The experiments were conducted in a turbulent plane air jet having a vertical slit of 1 cm width and an aspect ratio of 137:1. The two horizontal wires outside the expanded jet were viewed looking down on the plane formed by the wires. In this view the convection of the smoke threads can be followed, and their entrainment in jet can be observed by using multiple views recorded by a movie camera.

Molten Metals

In this method [20, 21] a molten metal droplet is projected across the flow field of interest and a visible trail of metal oxide is left behind in the wake of the droplet. Electromagnetic methods are used to heat and accelerate simultaneously 2-mm solder pellets producing 0.2-mm droplets. Due to its small size and high velocity, the trail left by the droplet is a straight line moving along with the flow; its displacement provides the necessary information about the flow.

Titanium Chloride

The technique is based on a particular property of $TiCl_4$, a light yellow liquid: when in contact with moist air, it develops dense white fumes of TiO_2 [22]. This liquid can be painted on a surface, or it can be projected as small droplets through the flow field leaving a trail of white lines [23]. It can also be used as a source of smoke by passing air through a jar of $TiCl_4$ and injected as a smoke threat or as a smoke sheet by means of a smoke rake. Mixing titanium tetrachloride with carbon tetrachloride prevents an early blockage of the rake [24].

Suspended Solid Particles

Strictly speaking, smoke itself is a form of suspended particles of very small diameter. This section concerns methods where flow is seeded with relatively large powders, spheres, or pellets, apart from very fine dust suspended in air [25]. Aloxite powder, about 4 μm in diameter, is a well-known gas seeder; most SSP techniques are limited to visualization of liquid bulk flow or of free flows on liquid surfaces due to the relatively high density of solids. Aluminum, in the form of dust, powder, and foil, is another commonly used agent. Not easily wettable, aluminum particles should be pasted with an aliquot of a surface wetting agent (e.g., alcohol or liquid soap) before use to provide a very good seeding agent. Particle size is limited to a few micrometers on account of high density, in an ordinary aqueous suspension. Glass beads can be used up to about 10 μm and pumice powder (density = 0.03 g/cm^3) up to 20–40 μm. For the use of larger-size particles, the density of the liquid medium must be increased.

In the case of water, glycerine, water soluble polymers, and sodium chloride are commonly used to increase its density up to about 1.2 g/cm^3. With sodium chloride solutions, polystyrene particles with a density range 1.03–1.09 and size range 0.2–3.2 mm are used; ABS plastics, nylon, and other polymer particles are also commonly employed. With glycerine and polymer solutions, amberlite ion exchange resin (crosslinked polystyrene) particles (IRA 904 Rohm and Mass Corp., PA, USA) of density 1.07 g/cm^3 are useful, the particle size varying from 40 μm to 300 μm. The density of these particles can be changed by treating with mineral oils [26] and soaking in sodium bromide [27] or sodium chloride [28] solutions. An increase in density is brought about by replacing hydroxide ions with chloride or bromide ions. The particles can be surface coated with fluorescent dyes. When ultraviolet light is used for illumination, the contrast between fluid and particles is further enhanced.

Figure 7. Visualization of the unsteady wake induced by an impulsively started translating airfoil via the suspended particle technique. (Courtesy of Mr. M. Coutanceau, Laboratoire de Mécanique des Fluides, Poitiers, France.)

For the study of very fast turbulent flows laser-induced luminescence is employed, where a beam of an N_2 pulse laser is passed through an aqueous solution of 0.05% (wt) ZnS particles and 40% (wt) glycerine [29, 30]. A line of luminescent ZnS particles is generated, and its distortion after a few microseconds represents distortion of the flow field.

Recently, a new visualization method [31] of eddy structure similar to an aluminum-flakes technique [32] has been reported. Here, TiO_2-coated mica pellets 10–20 μm in diameter and 3–4 μm thick are used as suspended particles (density = 3 g/cm^3). The pellets are aligned in the direction of the shear stress present in the fluid, and as long as the eddy size is larger than the pellet size, the regions of turbulence can be seen very clearly.

Figure 7 presents an application of the suspended particle technique to study a phase of the two-dimensional unsteady wake forming behind an impulsively accelerated translating NACA 0012 airfoil, for an angle of attack of 30°, a Reynolds number of 500, at a certain time instant. The flow is produced by abruptly causing the profiled cylinder (initially at rest in the quiescent liquid contained in a tank of rectangular cross section) to rise vertically at a constant speed in a direction perpendicular to its generators. The visualization is realized by illuminating, along a thin plane of cross section, solid tracers (rilsan powder) uniformly put in suspension in the fluid with a powerful arc-projector and by taking sequential photographs with a motorized 6 cm × 6 cm camera that accompanies the foil in its translation. It has been possible at suitable times of exposure to capture quasi-instantaneous flow fields, in a frame attached to the cylinder, showing clearly the details of the flow structure, in particular those of the recirculating zones.

From such visualizations the location of the main characteristic points (the separation and reattachment points, the center of vortices, and their closure points when they are detached from the foil) may be found, and dominant velocity profiles can be determined.

Suspended Gas Bubbles and Liquid Droplets

A change in the properties of light at bubble and drop interfaces is exploited in these methods; normally, suspended gas bubbles are used for gas flows and liquid droplets for liquid flows, although interchange is possible if the size of bubbles or droplets is very small. Water fog [33] used to seed air flows and air bubbles [34] used in water flow are such examples. In glycerine solutions air bubbles are stable and uniformly dispersed, but in water the use of a small amount of emulsifying agents is recommended.

Insoluble organic liquids are often used as suspended droplets in aqueous solutions. A reliable, naturally buoyant insoluble organic liquid for the study of water flows [35] consists of a mixture of carbon tetrachloride (density = 1.596 g/cm^3) and benzene (density = 0.881 g/cm^3) with a trace of white paint. These colorless organic liquids are mutually soluble, but they are insoluble in water. Droplets as large as 5 mm can be employed.

In the study of gas flows helium-filled soap bubbles are widely used; commercial equipment is capable [36] of producing bubble sizes from less than 5 mm up to 15 mm. The bubble size can be adjusted by the control of soap and helium-air flow. A dark background and tangential light (e.g., laser-produced light sheets) with a narrow angle of dispersion are optimal for illumination. The upper limit of air speed is 60 m/s; at higher speeds bubbles are destroyed. Mixing a fluorescent dye (e.g., Leucophor dye) with the standard bubble mixture and using an ultraviolet light source yields brightly fluorescent bubbles against a dark black background.

For use in liquids, the hydrogen bubble method [37] has received considerable attention. A fine wire placed in water with a small amount of salt or acid is used as the cathode in an aqueous electrolysis unit which generates periodic current pulses. Small-diameter hydrogen bubbles are thus produced on the wire, whose motion in the liquid provides information about fluid flow. Experiments carried out at sufficiently low Reynolds numbers can demonstrate significant buoyancy effects.

Figure 8 shows the application of the helium bubble method to study swirling flow at a burner exit [38]. If the degree of swirl is sufficiently high, recirculation or back flowing will occur which helps flame stabilization. To illustrate the burner flow patterns, the helium bubble flow visualization technique is used in scaled, cold flow models. Small, helium-filled soap bubbles are injected

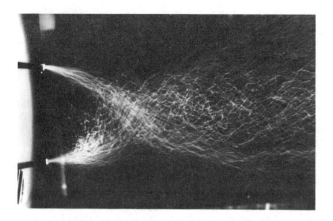

Figure 8. Visualization of swirl flow at a burner exit by the helium bubble method. (Courtesy of Messrs. C. B. Santanam and G. L. Tietbohl, Riley Stoker Corporation, Worcester, Massachusettes, USA.)

into the flow which easily follow the streamlines since they are neutrally buoyant. For better visualization, high-intensity lights are directed along the flow axis. In Figure 8, the degree of swirl is just enough to produce the onset of circulation—only a few bubbles are backward- flowing.

Precipitation

Precipitation is one means of suspending liquid droplets in a liquid medium of the same density, in a manner somewhat similar to techniques discussed earlier. The major difference is that the liquid-solid interface is generated by the precipitation of a metal hydroxide of a sufficiently small solubility product. Metal ions which are highly soluble in an acidic medium but highly

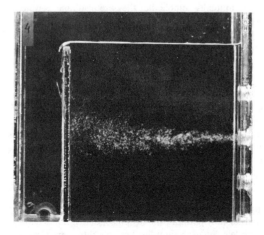

Figure 9. Front view of the convection pattern caused by a jet entering a rectangular cell, and obtained by the precipitation technique. Entry velocity = 8 cm/s (Reynolds number = 740). (Authors' experimental results obtained in the Dept. Chem. Engg., University of Waterloo, Waterloo, Ontario, Canada.)

insoluble in an alkaline medium (e.g., Fe and Al) are obvious candidates. The aqueous solution consists of sodium chloride (to increase density), a small amount of the metal salt and traces of an acid. A naturally buoyant alkaline solution of high pH and of the same density as the working solution is dispersed in the working solution. When the alkaline "blob" comes in contact with the acidic solution, a precipitate of metal hydroxide forms at the surface. The "blob" behaves as a deformable solid particle; it will gradually shrink due to hydronium ion diffusion and will disappear in time without leaving any trace of its former existence.

Figure 9 shows the visualization of a jet inlet flow in a rectangular vessel by using this technique. The working fluid is an acidic 0.3 g/L Al^{3+} solution and the alkaline solution contains about 0.1 mol/L NaOH. The alkaline solution is injected slightly before the entry point. The jet velocity at 7.8 cm/s corresponds to an entrance Reynolds number of 740. The figure shows the location of the precipitate particles eight seconds after the instant of alkali injection.

SURFACE-COATING TECHNIQUES

Surface coating techniques are widely used for the study of flow fields at a solid surface or in its vicinity. This inexpensive method can be divided into two major categories according to its application:

1. Visualization of transition from the laminar to the turbulent regime.
2. Visualization of surface flow patterns.

First, the model surface is painted and thoroughly dried; then another layer of contrasting color is painted on it. The flowing fluid selectively removes the top layer and thus provides a record of the flow on the surface. While the physical experiments are relatively easy to conduct, there are certain difficulties in interpreting the observations: much experience and good judgment with respect to flow transients is needed on the part of the experimenter.

One time-honoured approach is the oil flow technique: a white or black surface is uniformly painted with a mixture of oil and black or white pigment. The paint can also be applied as uniformly spaced dots or a long leading edges, and it flows along with the surface flow to be studied, leaving a characteristic pattern on the surface. Alternatively, the paint may be allowed to dry on the surface for a permanent record of the flow pattern. The pigments used are normally a 4:1 mixture of kerosene and lampblack [39] which leaves a dry lampblack trace: kerosene and black tempera paint, and a mixture of titanium oxide in diesel fuel with a few drops of oleic acid [40]. Colored pigments are sometimes used instead of black and white paint to facilitate pattern interpolation by applying different colors to different areas, lines, or dots. Fluorescent lacquers may replace ordinary pigment to increase the contrast in ultraviolet light. The model can be coated with a layer of fluorene or azobenzene [40] compounds; due to a more rapid sublimation under a turbulent boundary layer with respect to a laminar layer, a dark underlayer indicates the extent of turbulence. Dust deposited on the remains of a volatile liquid layer may enhance visualization of the flow pattern. The surface under study need not necessarily be coated by paint in every application inasmuch as nonadherent particle layers (or fluid layers), e.g., at horizontal surfaces may indicate correctly a flow pattern at the surface. Condensed milk, powdered milk, and dust and powdered milk dissolved in water may be spread in thin layers, depending on the application. A serious shortcoming of surface-coating techniques is their poor response to changing flow conditions, especially in the case of unsteady or cyclic flow. Eventual contamination of flow tunnels is a further disadvantage.

Figure 10 shows the application of the oil flow technique to the study of the location and size of separated and stagnant flow regions on space shuttles [41]. The complex flow field generated by the interaction of a 20-knot wind and 12-jet array around the Space Shuttle Launch configuration is clearly observable in this photograph. Only six of the jet nozzles are shown there, the other six being arranged in an almost symmetrical manner at the other side of the model. The Space Shuttle Orbiter has been removed to allow an unobstructed view of the external tank and

Figure 10. Visualization of flow regimes on space shuttle surface by the surface oil flow technique. (Courtesy of Messrs. J. L. F. Porteiro, D. J. Norton and T. C. Pollock, Texas A & M University, Texas, USA.)

the launch tower, which causes significant flow blockage, is not shown but is to the left. It is evident that jet flow does not impinge the top section of the external tank and that the flow on the lower section is also wind-dominated, the jets being unable to penetrate the 20-knot wind. (Note line on lower section of right solid stagnation/separation rocket booster.)

TUFT TECHNIQUES

Tuft techniques are similar to surface-coating techniques in many respects. An important difference is their quick response to unsteady and cyclic flows, although they do not generate a fixed pattern on the surface when the flow is stopped.

Tuft is the descriptive name for small pieces of yarn, thread, string, etc., which are taped or glued to a surface at regular distances in a predetermined pattern. The model thus prepared can be used both in gas or liquid flows. The method can be advantageously applied to visualizing flow in the vicinity of a solid surface, and if mounted on pin tips, at regions reasonably far from a surface. Since tufts have a tendency to develop a "self-excited" whipping motion, and they are difficult to photograph, the basic technique has been modified to overcome these shortcomings. In one modification small solid cones [42] are attached to the free end of the tuft: the cones are rigid, narrow, and usually hollow to minimize their mass. By applying a highly reflective coating or retroreflective tapes on them, the cones can be easily photographed even from a distance of several hundred feet. In another modification very thin tufts coated with fluorescent dye and illuminated with an ultraviolet light source are used [43, 44]. Under strong ultraviolet light, the fluorescent tuft will present a sharp contrast against the nonfluorescent surface. In a typical preparation, "fluorescent minitufts" [45] are made of 0.03-mm diameter nylon monofilament fibers. The fibers are treated with Leucophor fluorescent dye (Sandoz Corporation), a known commercial fabric brightener, then immersed into an aqueous solution of 1% dye, 2% acetic acid at 180°F for 15 minutes, and then dried.

REFRACTIVE INDEX-BASED METHODS

General

Owing to the dependence of the refractive index of a fluid on density, temperature, and concentration, optical methods which transform refractive index variations into visual images can be used for flow visualization as long as there is a known quantitative relationship between these quantities. Because of the highly indirect nature of such methods a good deal of experience and knowledge is required for the correct interpretation of experimental visualization patterns. The optical means employed are deflection of light beams (shadowgraphy, Schlieren) or the phase change in light beams (interferometry). The information obtained is always integrated over the entire flow field. .

Theoretical Background

In a single gas, the refractive index, n, defined as the speed of light in vacuum divided by the speed of light in a particular medium is correlated with density, ρ, by the Gladstone-Dale equation

$$n - 1 = k\rho \tag{1}$$

where the Gladstone-Dale constant, k, is a property of the gas and weak function of the wavelength of the light. It is virtually independent of temperature and pressure. For a mixture of two gases a and b

$$n - 1 = k_a\rho_a + k_b\rho_b \tag{2}$$

where ρ_a and ρ_b are the individual gas densities at their respective partial pressure in the gas mixture. In the case of liquids the refractive index is a function of density; the density of a mixture of gases or liquids is a function of pressure, temperature, and concentration, hence the refractive index is indirectly related to these three important quantities. When a beam of light traverses a section of a fluid it suffers deflection and its speed changes according to the index of the fluid. As shown in Figure 11, the change in optical path for the beam passing through the test fluid with respect to a reference beam may be written [46] as

$$\Delta L = L_b(n_b - n_a) \tag{3}$$

if $k_a \cong k_b = k$, and if L_b is the thickness of the test section. Equation 3 indicates interference of two beams if $\rho_b \neq \rho_a$; this interference is manifested by black-and-white fringes due to phase difference in the refracted light. The fringe shift number N defined as

$$N = \frac{\Delta L}{\lambda} = \frac{kL_b}{\lambda}(\rho_b - \rho_a) \tag{4}$$

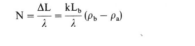

Figure 11. Basic optical effects caused by refraction in a fluid.

is the very property of the light wave on which the method of interferometry is based. If there is no density variation in fluid b, the light rays will travel in a straight line as shown by the dotted line in Figure 11, but if a density gradient exists, then an incoming light-ray will be deflected through an angle ε

$$\varepsilon = L_b \left(\frac{dn_b}{dy}\right)_{y=y_b} = L_b k_b \left(\frac{d\rho_b}{dy}\right)_{y=y_b} \tag{5}$$

This property of light rays is used in Schlieren techniques.

If a parallel beam of light enters fluid b and if there is no density gradient, no deflection will be suffered; in the presence of a uniform density gradient the uniform angle of deflection is ε; if the density gradient is nonuniform, the light rays will be deflected at various angles. The net effect of such deflections will be the appearance of highly concentrated light directions ("bright spots") and directions devoid of light rays ("dark spots"), the brightness effect depending on the relative deflection

$$\frac{d\varepsilon}{dy} = L_b k_b \left(\frac{d^2\rho_b}{dy^2}\right) \tag{6}$$

This property of light beams is employed in shadowgraphy and by stripped-background methods.

Holography

Holographic methods are used in a variety of visualization techniques based on the refractive index, especially in (holographic) interferometry and (holographic) Schlieren photography. The advantage of this method is in obtaining information at a given time in the form of a hologram; in turn, the hologram is used to find the best possible interferograms or Schlieren photographs of the flow field studied.

Holography is a three-dimensional imaging technique utilizing a coherent light (mostly laser light) as shown in Figure 12. A hologram is a photograph of the light waves arriving from an object, and *not* a photograph of the object itself. When reconstructed, the holographic image possesses physical characteristics of the object-size, dimension, volume and space, excepting mass.

Holography produces a facsimile of the object wave at one plane in space which has the same complex amplitude as the original object wave. The light propagating away from this plane is identical to the original object wave. The holograms are created by adding a coherent reference wave to the object wave (Figure 12A) and the interference patterns thus produced are recorded on a photographic plate. The reference beam is normally brought in at an angle with the object wave (off-axis holography). When illuminated from the reference beam with the same angle, the hereby produced hologram reconstructs the object wave as shown in Figure 12B. This reconstructed object wave is used, instead of the flow field itself, for analysis in holographic flow visualization techniques.

The Stripped-Background Method

In this very simple but limited method a black and white stripped background is placed on one side of the test section and is visualized from the other side. A change in the refractive index distorts the background and provides information about the flow field. The stripped background method applied to tunnel walls or outside tunnels is useful in the visualization of shockwaves [51–53]. It is particularly well suited for opaque test models when shadow or Schlieren photography is impractical due to the blockage of light beams. The technique is used mainly for studying shockwaves.

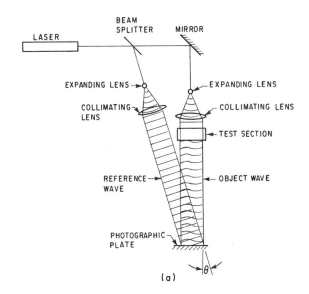

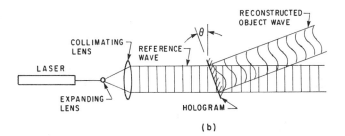

Figure 12. Off-axis holography: (A) Recording of the object wave. (B) Reconstruction of the object wave.

Shadowgraphy

In this rather simple method coherent collimated light or just a point light source may be used to cast a shadow of the test section (transparent fluid) on a screen or a photographic plate. As shown in Figure 13, high-intensity and low-intensity zones appearing on the screen and caused by spatial variations of the refractive index in the test section, are used for visualizing flow patterns. The zone distribution on the screen placed outside the test section depends on the relative deflection of light rays, i.e. $d\varepsilon/dy$. Shadowgraphy can be used even with room light and the naked eye to follow, e.g., the thermal plumes and boundary layers on a horizontal hot plate by viewing it from the edge of the plate. The technique is used mostly in shockwave and turbulent flow (wake) studies; it provides very little quantitative information.

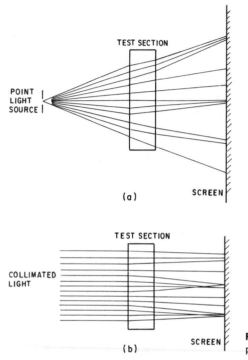

Figure 13. Shadowgraph of flow field: (A) pointlight source. (B) parallel beam.

Some commonly employed lighting arrangements are shown in Figure 14; mirrors as large as 18 inches in diameter are quite frequent.

Schlieren Photography

As shown earlier, if a collimated light beam passes through a test section of a nonuniform refractive index, the deflected light is no longer collimated. If this uncollimated light passes through a lens, some portion of it can be selectively blocked by a knife edge placed at an appropriate location in front of another lens and a screen. This is the principle of Schlieren photography, illustrated in Figure 15. The dashed lines represent light rays which would pass unhindered if the test section were absent. The black spot appearing on the screen is caused by the absence of these light rays due to the presence of the test section and the knife edge. A slit source of light is normally used, and in some applications spherical or concave parabolic mirrors replace lens L_1 and L_2 to provide a collimated beam of large cross section. In the colored version of the technique, a colored Schlieren mask [54, 55] is employed instead of the knife edge. Schlieren photography is used extensively for locating shock waves and for studying complicated boundary-layer phenomena in supersonic flow systems.

Interferometry

Interference is the reciprocal action of meeting light waves by which they reinforce or cancel each other. It is visible best in coherent light but an interferometer, the device used to superimpose light waves, also employs white light for its rainbow effect. The alternating bright and dark curves

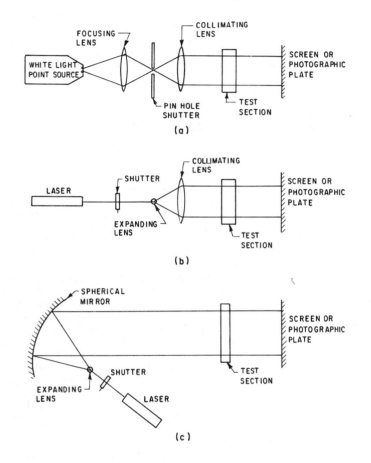

Figure 14. Common lighting arrangements for shadowgraphy: (A) non-coherent light source; (B) coherent light source with collimating lens; (C) coherent light source with spherical mirror.

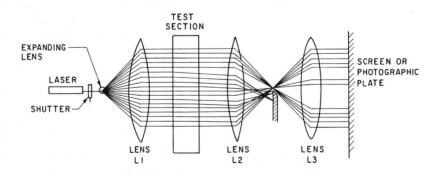

Figure 15. Schematic of a Schlieren system.

produced on a screen or film are called interference fringes. A large variety of interferometers emplo slightly different methods to achieve the same goal. A brief description of some of the importar concepts is given in this section; details of this technique are available elsewhere [50, 56, 57] Interferometers can essentially be classified as reference beam interferometers and shearing inter ferometers. In reference beam interferometry one beam passes through the test section (test beam while the other (reference beam) passes undisturbed by the flow field. In shearing interferometr both rays traverse the test field, but afterwards are separated or sheared by a small distance d. A third variation, holographic interferometry, although a class on its own, yields information simila to reference beam interferometry, the only difference being the handling of the reference beam.

Reference Beam Interferometers

As shown in Figure 16, the light beam arriving from a light source is split into two beams. Th test beam passes through the test field, while the reference beam remains undisturbed. Most inter ferometers are designed to provide an equal geometric length for both beams; when the beam coincide, the image on the screen will appear uniformly illuminated. A change in the optical pat due to a variation in the refractive index in the flow field will produce fringes: this arrangemen is called infinite fringe setting. By inserting a plane transparent wedge into the path of one ligh beam, finite fringe-width alignment can be produced, where a uniform flow field is represented b parallel black and white strips which are disturbed by a change in the refractive index.

The most common interferometer in this class is the Mach-Zehnder interferometer [58] show in Figure 16A. Light from a point source or a laser beam is converted to a collimated beam an split into two beams by a splitter. Guiding mirrors pass the test beam through the test section an the reference beam along an external path. The two beams are recombined by a second beam splitte and eventually focused on a screen. If a wedge is inserted or at least one mirror is inclined, paralle interference fringes are produced. Otherwise the arrangement will provide an infinite-width fringe In order to obtain good quality fringes a colorant should preferentially be used, and if laser light i employed, a special arrangement is necessary (Figure 16B); according to certain researchers [59] Polychromatic light can also be used, Mach-Zehnder interferometry is rather expensive because o the high quality optical components necessary, and it requires difficult adjustments. Excellent dis cussions on the construction, use, and adjustment of these interferometers are available in literatur [46, 60, 61].

The principle of double-mirror interferometry [62] is sketched in Figure 16C. Here, a partially reflecting mirror is placed in front of the test section and the beam traveling towards the test sectior is split into two beams. One passes through the test section, while the other one is reflected back to create an interference pattern at the screen.

The grating interferometer (Figure 16D) employs diffraction gratings to produce interference [63] the arrangement is similar to a Schlieren system, with gratings placed at the focal point of lense or mirrors. The gratings split the beam of light into various beams of 0, ± 1, $\pm 2 \ldots$ orders. Inter ference is established between the lights of overlapping orders if the conditions of optical coherence are fulfilled. A major drawback is the heavy loss of light intensity caused by orders of light beam not utilized.

Holographic Interferometry

Holographic interferometry [50] is very similar to reference beam interferometry, the importan difference being separation of test- and reference-beam in time but not in space. In exposur holographic interferometry two holograms are constructed on the same plate, one with a test sec tion prior to any variation in the refractive index (i.e., before starting the visualization experiment and the other one during the experiment but without moving the test section or the holographic plate. The reconstructed hologram yields a light wave pattern via superposition of the two ligh waves: the form of interference depends on the variation of the refractive index in the test cell during the time elapsed between the creation of the two holograms. There are two advantages to thi

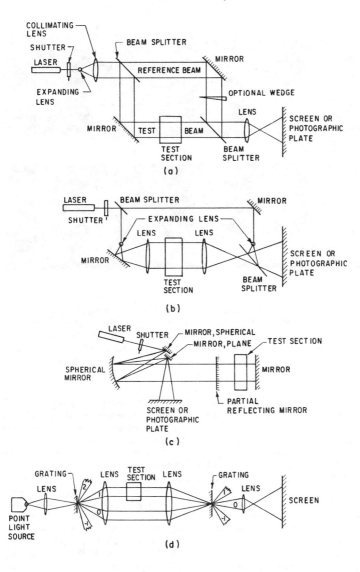

Figure 16. Reference beam interferometers: (A) Mach-Zehnder interferometer; (B) laser Mach-Zehnder interferometer; (C) double-mirror interferometer; (D) grating interferometer.

technique:

1. The effect of the imperfect test chamber window is eliminated because both beams traverse the same path, hence any ordinary transparent material can be used as a window [64].
2. A holographic interferogram created with a diffused light can be observed at various viewing directions, thus information on the three-dimensional propagation at a flow field can readily be obtained [65].

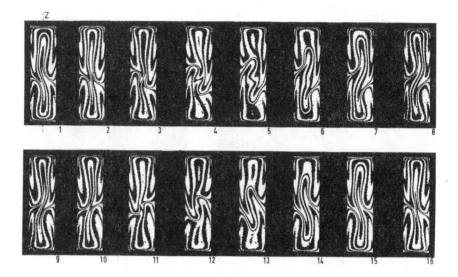

Figure 17. A single period of oscillatory convection flow in a high-conductivity Hele Shaw slot via holographic real-time interferometry. Height/width = 3.5; Ra = 5.2 × 10⁷; time interval between two interferograms = 10 s; frequency of oscillation = 6.6 mHz. (Courtesy of Messrs. J. N. Koster and V. Muller, Institut für Reaktor Bauelemente, Karlsruhe, Federal Republic of Germany; Figure 3 of "Oscillatory Convection in Vertical Slots," *J. of Fluid Mech.* (1984), Cambridge University Press.)

Finite-fringe interferograms can also be produced by this technique by tilting the holographic plate, tilting the test beam, or inserting a wedge between exposures. A variation of the theme in double-exposure holographic interferometry is real-time holographic interferometry [64, 66]. In this technique a hologram of the reference beam through the test section is made prior to the experiment. This hologram is developed and placed back at its original position; then it is adjusted to produce an infinite-width or finite-width fringe between the reconstructed beam and the beam through the nonoperating test section. During the experiment, i.e., when there is a variation in the refractive index in the test section, the screen will show an interference pattern similar to that obtained in reference beam interferometry. Thus, the hologram reconstructs the original reference beam, which is interfering with the test beam, in real time.

Figure 17 illustrates the real-time holographic technique [67] showing a complete cycle of periodic oscillatory convective flow in a high conductivity Hele-Shaw slot heated from below. The Rayleigh number is Ra = 5.2 × 10⁷; compared to the onset of oscillations $Ra/Ra_{osc} = 1.06$. The Prandtl number is $Pr \approx 38$, and the geometrical aspect ratio (height to width) is h/b = 3.5. One period is recognized by a periodically appearing pattern of the interferograms, e.g., image 1 and image 15. The time interval between two interferograms is $\Delta t = 10$ s. The frequency is f = 6.6 mHz. Lines of equal brightness correspond to lines of equal temperature. Owing to the linear vertical temperature profile in the sidewalls, each isotherm is fixed at constant height at the sidewalls. The isotherms between these points oscillate. The interferograms show an alternate release of plumes from the thermal boundary layers at the horizontal walls which rise or fall along the sidewalls and along the vertical centerlines of the slot.

Shearing Interferometry

In shearing interferometry, a coherent collimated beam of light passes through the test section, then it is sheared (or displaced over a small distance) into two beams; the interferometer compares

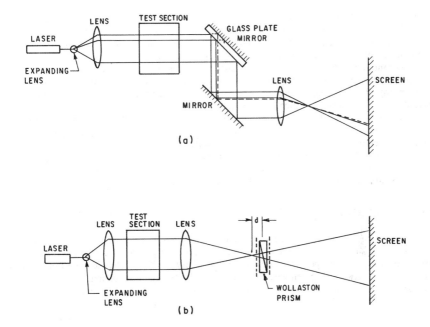

Figure 18. Shearing interferometers: (A) glass-plate Shearing interferometer, (B) Wollaston prism interferometer.

the optical paths of these two light beams. It is not necessary to use a beam splitter to separate the two beams before entering the test field.

The simplest arrangements are called plane-glass plate and glass-wedge interferometry. The incident light is reflected from the front and the rear of a glass plate or wedge. Each ray of the light beam undergoes multiple reflection at the front and the rear surface (Figure 18A). With a suitable choice of reflection coefficients and of the angle of incidence, the intensity of third and higher order reflections may be suppressed to the extent that they can be considered to be negligible.

In shearing interferometry based on optical transmission gratings [68] and holography [69] the most common method uses the Wollaston prism Schlieren interferometer [70] as shown in Figure 18B, where a Wollaston prism is placed between two polarizers instead of the knife edge used in a standard Schlieren optical system. The Wollaston prism splits every incoming light ray into two rays separated from each other by a small angle (on the order of arc minutes). The rays are polarized transversally; the polarizers on either side of the prism are oriented at 90° to each other and at 45° to the lateral axis of the prism. The distance between the focal point of the lens and the center-line of the Wollaston prism determines the fringe width: when d = 0, infinite-width fringes are produced.

SPECIAL TECHNIQUES

There are a large number of quantitatively accurate special techniques developed for the study of specific flow configurations, but of limited scope due to their complicated nature or the specific conditions required. Very recently developed techniques require further testing time, and their full scope cannot yet be fully assessed.

One special group is based on the study of scattered light from molecules. The frequency of the scattered light changes either due to the state of motion (Doppler effect) or due to the thermo-dynamic state of the molecule (Raman effect). There can be an energy exchange between incident radiation and molecule (inelastic Raman scattering) [17] or no energy exchange (elastic Rayleigh scattering) [72]. Elastic scattering from tracer particles is used in laser Doppler velocimetry [73], the laser-dual-focus method, speckle photography [74, 75], and speckle interferometry, normally used for velocity measurements for flat flow fields [76].

The second group of special techniques is particularly well suited for medical studies: X-ray angiography, nuclear magnetic resonance techniques (NMR), ultrasound (VS) and positron emission tomography (PET) are major members of this group. In the X-ray angiographic technique [77] an organic iodinated substance which absorbs X-rays is injected into blood vessels, in order to make the blood stream visible for X-ray photography. NMR techniques [78] can be used for flow rates and flow profiles within large blood vessels. Ultrasound [79] as well as flow measurements (due to Doppler effect) by reflection or scattering of sound waves provide the picture of tissue interface. The PET technique [80] is based on the detection of the movement of radioactive isotopes, generated by γ-ray emission, in blood vessels and various organs. Six specific techniques, promising in a number of application areas, are briefly discussed in this section.

Spark-Tracer Techniques

Spark-tracer techniques [81] are related to light-emitting ions which move together with a field. The operating fluid is uniformly seeded with an ion-producing material, and the seeded ions are excited by a high-voltage periodic discharge. A 20–250 kV, 1–75 kHz electric pulse train is passed for about 1 μs between tungsten wire electrodes placed a few centimeters apart. The light emitted by a sequence of discharge and photographed as a set of trails provides information about the flow field.

Fluorescent-Particle Method

A seeded fluid is exposed to an ultraviolet laser light source and fluorescence produced by the seeding material renders the flow visible. Biacetyl [82] for argon, krypton, or dye laser; sodium [83] for dye laser and iodine [84, 85] for argon or dye lasers are the usual seeders. The method has been recommended for the visualization of velocity, density, temperature, and pressure fields [86].

Electrolytic Metal Oxidation [87]

When certain metals such as titanium, niobium, tantalum, and zirconium are anodically oxidized, they are gradually covered with an oxide film whose color varies with the thickness and the nature of the oxide; there exists also a threshold voltage determining the color of the oxide scale. If a cyclic voltage, oscillating above and below the threshold value, is applied at the moment of wetting the surface with an electrolyte, a permanent record of the movement of the liquid front may be obtained. The method is particularly well suited for the study of initial transients where dissolution of a non-conducting liquid in a conducting liquid and displacement of a nonconducting liquid by a conducting liquid is taking place. It can also record surface wetting patterns at the instant of immersing a surface in a conducting liquid, and follow postincidental transitory behavior (e.g., tube rupture and runoff from rupture discs or safety valves).

Electrolytic Metal Deposition [88]

Secondary flow on surfaces, hidden by the primary flow in bulk, can be visualized by selective deposition of metal; deposition of copper from an aqueous solution of copper and sulphuric acid with [88] or without [89] gelatine have been recently used for this purpose. The voltage applied must be high enough to produce limiting (diffusion) current for the metal or even a slightly larger current. Under such conditions copper deposition is controlled by diffusion of copper ions across the boundary layer which is related to the movement of the flow field in the boundary layer.

Laser Doppler Anemometry [90]

In this method, developed for studying flow motions inside engine cylinders, two laser beams are focused into the test section and particles of 1 μm size are added to the inlet flow. The particles scatter light in the bright fringes, which is collected and measured by a photomultiplier tube. Electronic processing of the generated signal permits the determination of the time of particle traversal across a fixed number of fringes, hence velocity. With sophisticated filtering and other methods, local velocity profiles are obtained to visualize flow patterns at various crank angles.

Infrared Light Techniques

Most gases and vapors with a bipolar molecular structure absorb energy in the infrared portion of the spectrum. If such a gas is interposed between an object emitting infrared radiation and a thermocamera, the gas will absorb some of the incident infrared radiation and will create a shadow on the picture tube of the thermocamera [91]. This method of visualizing gas flow has been used to study pollution caused by anaesthetic gases [92] and vapors [93] in hospitals. In a typical application [91] an electrically heated screen is used as the infrared radiation source (temperature: 60 $\pm$ 3°C) on one side of object plane. The shade of the gray picture appearing on the monitor corresponds to the total concentration of all absorbing gases between the screen and camera ("integrated" information). The picture may be photographed or filmed or recorded on a video recorder.

CONCLUDING REMARKS

Flow visualization is a typical example of a field where the experimenter has a wide choice of techniques, ranging from the simple and inexpensive to the highly sophisticated and very expensive. As in many instances of life, a complex method will not necessarily do better than a simpler method: meticulous maintenance of proper experimental conditions and inventiveness can often yield highly reproducible quantitative results even in the case of a relatively inelegant direct visualization approach. In choosing a particular technique, carefully matched purpose and limitations may indicate the use of a less involved and less costly method in order to obtain a well-defined set of information about flow patterns. In this respect, not all techniques documented in the literature are employed to their full potential.

A major parameter to consider in selecting a flow visualization method is the extent of interference (local) velocity, density, viscosity, and temperature fields can suffer without engendering an unacceptable level of distortion of true flow patterns. Imaginative means of minimizing such interference hold much promise for classical visualization techniques which do not normally require heavy instrumentation and a back-up computer. On the other hand, recent impressive advances in microprocessor technology and instrumentation extend the scope of flow visualization into areas beyond the power of conventional techniques. Progress brings new domains of scientific and engineering endeavor into the realm of flow visualization, in addition to the classical fields of fluid mechanics and heat transmission. This chapter can offer only a summary of the current state of the art to the seriously interested reader, and a concise guide to the impressive and still rapidly growing literature.

REFERENCES

1. *International Symposium on Flow Visualization*, Univ. of Tokyo Inst. Space Aeronat. Sci., Japan, 1977; *Flow Visualization Volume I*, T. Asanuma (Ed.), Hemisphere Publishing Corp., USA, 1979.
2. *Second International Symposium on Flow Visualization*, Ruhr Univ. of Bochum, Inst. Thermo. Fluid dyn., West Germany, 1980; *Flow Visualization Volume II*, M. Merzkirch (Ed.), Hemisphere Publishing Corp., USA, 1982.
3. Young, W. J., (Ed.), *Third International Symposium on Flow Visualization*, Preprints, Ann Arbor, USA, 1983.

4. Berman, N. S., Berger, R. B., and Leis, J. R., *J. Rheol.*, 24:571 (1980).
5. Liu, H. T., "Applications of A Tow Tank For Physical Modelling of Plume Dispersion: Flow Visualization," paper presented at the Third International Symposium on Flow Visualization, Ann Arbor, Mich., USA, 1983.
6. Liu, H. T., and Lin, J. T., "Physical Modeling of Plume Dispersion In Complex Terrain With An Elevated Inversion," paper presented at the Tenth International Technical Meeting On Air Pollution Modeling and Its Application, Rome, Italy, 1979; NTIS (NATO/CCMS) Report No. 108.
7. Liu, H. T., and Lin, J. T., "Physical Modeling of Plume Dispersion In Complex Terrain: Neutral and Stable Atmosphere," paper presented at the Ninth International Technical Meeting on Air Pollution Modeling and Its Application, Toronto, Canada, 1978; NTIS (NATO/CCMS) Report No. 103.
8. Pao, H. P., *Third International Symposium On Flow Visualization*, Preprints, 274–278, Ann Arbor, USA, 1983.
9. Quraishi, M. S., and Fahidy, T. Z., *Chem. Eng. Science*, 37:775 (1982).
10. Baker, D. J., *J. Fluid Mech.*, 26:573 (1966).
11. Quraishi, M. S., and Fahidy, T. Z., *Chem. Eng. Science*, 38:1271 (1983).
12. Quraishi, M. S., and Fahidy, T. Z., *Proceedings of 2nd World Congress of Chemical Engineering*, Vol. 5, 215–218, Montreal, Canada (1981).
13. Dickerson, R. R., and Stedman, D. H., *Rev. Sci. Instrum.*, 50:88 (1979).
14. Popovich, A., and Hummel, R., *Chem. Eng. Science*, 22:21 (1967).
15. Esdorn, J., *A New Flow Visualization Technique*, Report no. USB-ME-21-1, University of California, Santa Barbara (1982).
16. Hutchins, J., et al., *Third International Symposium on Flow Visualization*, Preprints, 345–349, Ann Arbor, USA, 1983.
17. Mueller, T. J., AIAA paper No. 80-0420-CP, *AIAA 11th Aerodynamic Testing Conference*, 1980.
18. Mueller, T. J., *Third International Symposium on Flow Visualization*, Preprints, 556–566, Ann Arbor, USA, 1983.
19. Cornish, J. J., *A Device for the Direct Measurement of Unsteady Air Flows and Some Characteristics of Boundary Layer Transition*, Aerophysics Research note 24, Mississippi State University (1964).
20. Steinhoff, J., "Some Properties of Vapour Trails Left By Accelerated Metal Droplets," paper presented at APS Meeting on Fluid Dynamics, Rutgers University, 1982.
21. Steinhoff, J., *Third International Symposium on Flow Visualization*, Preprints, 88–93, Ann Arbor, USA (1983).
22. Simmons, L. F. G., and Dewey, N. S., *Repts. and Mem. Nat. Adv. Comm. Aeronautics No. 134 and 135*, London, U.K. (1931).
23. Smith, E., Reed, R. M., and Hodges, H. D., *Texas Eng. Exp. Sta. Research Rpt. 25* (1951).
24. Bienkiewicz, B., *Third International Symposium on Flow Visualization*, Preprints, 590–594, Ann Arbor, USA (1983).
25. Taylor, M. K., *NACA TN 2220* (1950).
26. Wieting, D. W., *Dynamic Flow Characteristics of Heart Valves*, Ph.D. Dissertation, The University of Texas at Austin, USA (1969).
27. Miller, V. J., Bussolari, S. R., and Shanebrook, J. R., *J. Biomech.*, 9:663 (1976).
28. Walburn, F. J., and Stein, P. D., *Third International Symposium on Flow Visualization*, Preprints, 95–99, Ann Arbor, USA (1983).
29. Nakatani, N., Fujiwara, K., and Yamada, T., *Japan J. Appl. Phys.*, 10:1748 (1971).
30. Nakatani, N., et al., *J. Phys. E. Sci. Instrum.*, 10, 172 (1977).
31. Carlson, D. R., Windal, S. E., and Peeters, M. F., *J. Fluid Mech.*, 121:487 (1982).
32. Cantwell, B., Coles, D., and Dimotakis, P., *J. Fluid Mech.*, 87:641 (1978).
33. McGregor, I., *J. Fluid Mech.*, 11:481 (1961).
34. Werle, H., *Ann. Rev. Fluid Mech.*, 5:361 (1973).
35. Ren, Z., *Third International Symposium on Flow Visualization*, Preprints, 551–555, Ann Arbor, USA (1983).
36. *Sage Action Inc.*, P. O. Box 416, Ithaca, N.Y., USA, 14850.

37. Schraub, F. A., and Kline, S. J., *ASME paper No. 64-WA/FE-20* (1964).
38. Santanam, C. B., and Tietbohl, G. L., *Third International Symposium on Flow Visualization*, Preprints, 70–75, Ann Arbor, USA (1983).
39. Settles, G. S., and Teng, H. Y., *AIAA Journal*, 21:390 (1983).
40. Maltby, R. L., (Ed.), *Flow Visualization in Wind Tunnel Using Indicators*, AGARDOGRAPH No. 70, April 1962.
41. Porleiro, J. L. F., Norton, D. J., and Pollock, T. C., Report no. TEES-TR-U587-82-01, Vol. 11, Flow Visualization, Texas A & M University (1982).
42. Crowder, J. P., and Robertson, P. E., *Third International Symposium on Flow Visualization*, Preprints, 699–703, Ann Arbor, USA (1983).
43. Crowder, J. P., et al., *AIAA paper 80-0458-CP* (1980).
44. Crowder, J. P., *Report MDCJ7374*, McDonnell Douglas (1977).
45. Stinebring, D. R., and Treaster, A. L., *Third International Symposium on Flow Visualization*, Preprints, 704–709, Ann Arbor, USA (1983).
46. Goldstein, R. J., *Optical Techniques for Temperature Measurements*, Chapter 5 of *Measurements in Heat Transfer*, E. Eckert and R. J. Goldstein (Eds.), 2nd edition, Hemisphere Publishing Corp. (1976).
47. Hauf, W., and Grigull, U., *Optical Methods in Heat Transfer* in *Advances in Heat Transfer*, J. P. Hartnett and T. F. Irvine Jr. (Eds.) Vol. 6, Academic Press (1970).
48. Gabor, D., *Proc. Roy. Soc.*, A197:454 (1949).
49. Leith, E. N., and Upatnieks, J., *J. Opt. Soc. Am.*, 52:1123 (1962).
50. Vest, C. M., *Holographic Interferometry*, John Wiley & Sons (1979).
51. Schardin, H., *Ergebn. d. Exak. Naturwis*, 20 (1942), (English N70-25586).
52. Dugger, P. H., and Hill, J. W., *AIAA Journal*, 10:1544 (1972).
53. Settles, G. S., and Tang, H. Y., *AIAA Journal*, 21:390 (1983).
54. North, R. J., *APL/AERO/266*, British National Phys. Lab. (1954).
55. Rotem, Z., Hauptman, E. G., and Classen, L., *Applied Optics*, 8:2326 (1969).
56. Steel, W. H., *Interferometry*, Cambridge University Press (1967).
57. Tolansky, S., *An Introduction to Interferometry*, Longman (1973).
58. Ladenburg, R. W., and Bershader, D., *Physical Measurements in Gas Dynamics and Combustion*, R. W. Ladenburg (Ed.), Princeton Univ. Press (1954).
59. Heilig, W., and Reichenbach, H., *15th Int. Cong. High Speed Photo and Photonics; Proc. SPIE*, Vol. 348, L. L. Endelman (Ed.), San Diego, USA (1982).
60. Hauf, W., and Grigull, U., *Advances in Heat Transfer*, 6:133 (1960).
61. Gebhart, B., and Knowles, C. P., *Rev. Sci. Instr.*, 37:12 (1966).
62. Sheng-jie, Xia, *Third International Symposium on Flow Visualization*, Preprints, 247–251, Ann Arbor, USA (1983).
63. Kraushoar, R., *J. Opt. Soc. Am.*, 40:400 (1950).
64. Koster, J. N., *Exp. Fluids*, 1:121 (1983).
65. Witte, A. B., and Wuerker, R. F., *AIAA J.*, 8:581 (1970).
66. Aung, W., and O'Regan, R., *Rev. Sci. Instr.*, 42:1755 (1971).
67. Koster, J. N., and Muller, V., *J. Fluid Mech.*, in press (1984).
68. Yokozeki, S., and Suzuki, T., *Appl. Opt.*, 10:1575 (1971).
69. Bryngdahl, O., *J. Opt. Soc. Am.*, 59:142 (1969).
70. Merzkirch, W. F., *AIAA Journal*, 3:1974 (1965).
71. Weber, B. R., Long, M. B., and Chang, R. K., *Apl. Phys. Lett*, 35:119 (1979).
72. Escoda, M. C., and Long, M. B., *AIAA Journal*, 21:81 (1983).
73. Forman, J. W., et al., *Proc. IEEE*, 54:424 (1966).
74. Simpkins, P. G., and Dudderar, T., *J. Fluid Mech.*, 89:665 (1978).
75. Meynart, R., *Appl. Opt.*, 22:535 (1983).
76. Anderson, B. H., Putt, C. W., and Giamati, C. C., *Computer Generated Color Graphic Techniques to the Processing and Display of Three-Dimensional Fluid Dynamic Data*, Winter Annual ASME Meeting, Washington, D.C., Nov. 1981.
77. Mistretta, C. A., et al., *Digital Subtraction Arteriography: An Application of Computerized Fluoroscopy*, Year Book Medical Publisher, Chicago, 1982.

78. Rartian, L., et al., *Nuclear Magnetic Resonance Imaging*, W. B. Saunders, Philadelphia, 1982.
79. Hatte, L., and Angelson, B., *Doppler Ultrasound in Cardiology: Physical Principles and Clinical Applications*, Lea and Febiger, Philadelphia, 1982.
80. Phelps, M. E., Schelbert, H. R., and Mazziotta, J. C., *Ann. Int. Med.*, 98:339 (1983).
81. Ohki, H., Yoshinaga, Y., and Tsutsumi, Y., *Third International Symposium on Flow Visualization*, Preprints, 497–501, Ann Arbor, USA (1983).
82. Epstein, A. H., *Engr. Power*, 99:460 (1977).
83. Zimmerman, M., and Miles, R. B., *Appl. Phys. Lett.*, 37:885 (1980).
84. Cekner, A. A., and Driscoll, R. J., *AIAA Journal*, 21:812 (1982).
85. McDaniel, J. C., *AIAA 21st Aerospace Science Meeting*, Paper 0049, Reno, 1983.
86. McDaniel, J. C., and Hanson, R. K., *Third International Symposium on Flow Visualization*, Preprints, 153–157, Ann Arbor, USA (1983).
87. Pedeferri, P., and Joppolo, C. M., *Third International Symposium on Flow Visualization*, Preprints, 634–639, Ann Arbor, USA (1983).
88. Huin, D., and Mallet, J., *Third International Symposium on Flow Visualization*, Preprints, 486–491, Ann Arbor, USA (1983).
89. Quraishi, M. S., and Fahidy, T. Z., *The Canadian J. of Chem. Eng.*, 60:100 (1982).
90. *American Scientist*, "The Illuminated Vortex," 71:568 (1983).
91. Carlson, P., Ljungquist, B., and Neikler, K., *British J. of Industrial Medicine*, 39:300 (1982).
92. Allandar, C., et al., *Acta Anaesthesiol. Scand.*, 25:21 (1981).
93. Carlson, P., et al., *Acta Anaesthesiol. Scand.*, 25:315 (1981).

CHAPTER 29

TWO-PHASE FLOW MEASUREMENTS WITH ORIFICES

Z. H. Lin

Xian Jiao-Tong University
Xian, The Peoples' Republic of China

CONTENTS

INTRODUCTION

Construction of an Orifice and Principle of Operation

The construction of an orifice is quite simple. It is a plate provided with a sharp-edged circular orifice fitted into a pipe between two flanges as shown in Figure 1.

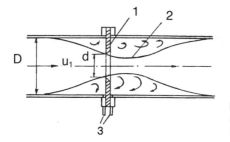

Figure 1. Pattern of a single-phase flow across an orifice: (1) orifice plate; (2) vena contracta; (3) pressure taps.

An orifice is a kind of common flow rate meter for single-phase fluid. The flow pattern of a single-phase flow across an orifice meter is also shown in Figure 1.

Upstream from the plate the stream velocity is u_1 and the pressure is P_1; downstream from the plate the minimum cross-sectional area the so-called "vena contracta," is formed. At the vena contracta the velocity attains its maximum value and the pressure decreases to P_2. Further downstream the stream gradually expands and resumes normal flow.

By using the Bernoulli equation and continuity equation a relationship between the mass flow rate or volumetric flow rate and pressure difference across orifice can be established. The equation for calculating a single-phase mass flow rate across an orifice is

$$W_{sp} = Y\psi cA\sqrt{(2\Delta P_{sp}\rho_{sp})} \tag{1}$$

or

$$\Delta P_{sp} = W_{sp}^2/[2(Y\psi cA)^2\rho_{sp}] \tag{2}$$

where W_{sp} = the mass flow rate of a single-phase fluid
ψ = the orifice thermal expansion factor
c = the orifice discharge coefficient determined experimentally
A = the orifice flow area
ΔP_{sp} = the pressure drop across an orifice for single-phase fluid flow
ρ_{sp} = the single-phase density
Y = the expansion coefficient for single phase fluid

The orifice discharge coefficient for single-phase c is a function of the Reynolds number, based on the pipe inner diameter D, the ratio of orifice diameter to the pipe inner diameter d/D, and the location of the pressure taps. Thus c is experimentally obtained.

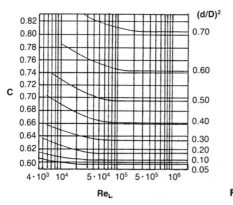

Figure 2. Discharge coefficients of VDI orifice.

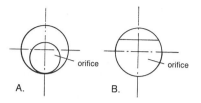

A.   B.

Figure 3. Special orifices: (A) eccentric orifice; (B) segmental orifice.

Orifices designed according to different standard methods are called standard orifices. A standard orifice can be installed in a pipe and used with sufficient accuracy without performing a calibration for obtaining coefficient c at the site. For instance, values of c for the VDI standard orifices are given in Figure 2.

In addition to standard orifices there are other kinds of special orifices, such as the orifice plate with a segmental orifice and the orifice plate with an eccentric orifice, etc. (Figure 3). Special orifices must be used when performing a calibration beforehand. Theories and experiments have shown that an orifice can also be used to measure a gas-liquid two-phase flow rate or quality. When a two-phase fluid passes through an orifice plate fitted in a pipe, the differential pressure across the orifice is measured. By assuming a flow model and conducting mathematical derivation, this differential pressure can be related to the quality for a given mass flow rate or vice versa. When the differential pressure is measured and the mass flow rate or the quality is given, from that obtained relationship the quality or the mass flow rate can be determined.

The Application of Orifices in Industrial Two-Phase Flow Measurements

Measurements of flow rate and quality of a gas-liquid (or vapor-liquid) mixture are of interest in many fields of engineering, such as power cycles, chemical, geothermal, petroleum, and refrigeration. In large-capacity once-through boilers or recirculation boilers, the quality of the wet steam at the exit of certain boiling pipes needs to be measured by a quality meter. In nuclear power plants because of the difficulties of accurate measurement of nuclear reactor channel power with a neutron flux monitor or similar instruments, it is preferable to calculate channel power from measurements of the channel flow rate and channel inlet and exit enthalpies. In a boiling water reactor, calculation of exit enthalpy will be dependent upon provision of an instrument for measurement of steam quality at the channel exit. In a geothermal area, for determining the output characteristics of boreholes, both the flow rate and quality of the steam-water mixture have to be measured. Although the methods of using a pitot-type probe to collect the sample of a two-phase flow and using beta rays to measure the quality of the two-phase fluid may be used, because of their defects, noise, precipitation, and poor accuracy, a new method must be considered. In oilfields steam-water mixtures from a steam boiler must sometimes be injected into the field for a thermal recovery operation. In this case, both the two-phase flow rate and the quality have to be measured. In addition, in the transportation of oil-gas mixtures through pipelines, the total oil mass flow rate and gas mass flow rate have to be measured. In general one needs to separate the liquid from the gas first and then to measure each phase individually by conventional methods. For this process simpler measuring devices are required. For solving all the difficulties about two-phase measurement problems mentioned previously in different industries, the orifice is always selected as one of the reasonable methods. As the orifice is a simple convenient and reliable device and has sufficient accuracy for the measurement of mass flow rate and quality, it has been receiving increasing attention in the recent two decades.

One-Parametric Measurement and Two-Parametric Measurements

For gas-liquid or vapor-liquid two-phase tubular flow generally two parameters have to be determined: the total flow rate of the two-phases and the quality (dryness fraction) of the two-phase flow. If one of the two parameters is known (for instance, if the total mass flow rate through a boiling channel is measured (from a measurement of the liquid input to the channel) or the inlet quality is given), then a single measurement may be sufficient. This case may be named as one-parametric measurement.

On the other hand, if both the total mass flow rate and quality are required, and both are unknowns, then at least two measurements are needed. This case may be defined as two-parametric measurements. In the latter case two metering devices are required for measurements. The simplest form of a metering device for quality and masss flow rate when used in combination with another measurement is an orifice.

CORRELATIONS

Up to now a considerable number of papers on the topic of two-phase flow measurements with orifices have been published, and a certain amount of correlations have been presented. Most of the proposed correlations were derived from different theoretical two-phase flow models and compared with experimental data.

In this part, flow models for gas-liquid two-phase flow across an orifice will be discussed first and then correlations will be introduced and discussed.

Flow Models

When a gas-liquid two-phase fluid flows cocurrently along a horizontal pipe, the flow pattern of the mixture depends on the proportion of gas to liquid. Under different conditions, the following main flow patterns will take place in the horizontal pipe: bubbly flow, stratified flow, slug flow, annular flow, and dispersed flow.

The flow condition of gas-liquid two-phase flow across an orifice is very complicated. Up to now, what kind of flow patterns may happen when the mixture passes through an orifice is still not clear. Thus, when establishing their correlations, some scientists consider that when a gas-liquid mixture passes through an orifice mounted in a pipe, it is possible that a relatively high degree of mixing is engendered by the orifice. Therefore they use the homogeneous model to establish their correlations. The homogeneous model (Figure 4A) considers the two phases to flow as a single phase possessing mean fluid properties, and has been in use in various forms in the steam generation, petroleum, and refrigeration industries for a long time.

The basic assumptions of this model are

1. The gas velocity is equal to the liquid velocity.
2. The thermodynamic equilibrium between two phases is attained.

From flow patterns just mentioned it might be expected that this model would be valid for the bubbly or dispersed flow patterns, particularly at high velocities and pressure.

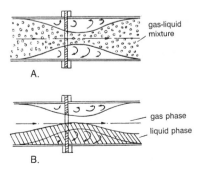

A.

B.

Figure 4. Flow models: (A) homogeneous model; (B) separated model.

Other scientists consider that because of the bend effect of the fluid stream line when the flow passes through the orifice, the two-phase mixture might flow separately. Thus the separated flow model (Figure 4B) is taken for establishing correlations.

The separated flow model has been used since 1944. The basic assumptions of this model are

1. The gas velocity is not necessarily equal to the liquid velocity.
2. The thermodynamic equilibrium between two phases is attained.

From the various flow patterns already mentioned, it would be expected that this model would be valid for the stratified flow pattern and the annual flow pattern.

Reported correlations for gas-liquid two-phase flow meters were mainly derived from these two models. However, in reality limited experiments showed that the flow at the throat of a differential pressure two-phase flowmeter was not homogeneous. Even the flow pattern upstream of the throat was bubbly flow, which is usually considered as homogeneous flow. Three-dimensional suction effects gave rise to an appreciable transverse pressure gradient at the throat section. This gradient caused a localized increase in void fraction near the wall [1]. It was not a wholly separated flow. It is found that correlations obtained from the homogeneous model or separated model without corrections are usually quite inaccurate.

Therefore more scientists choose the modified homogeneous flow model or the modified separated flow model to form their correlations. These correlations usually possess a corrective factor or corrective term determined experimentally and are more accurate than those correlations without corrections.

Methods of Derivation

After assuming a flow model, scientists may derive their correlations by different methods. In examining the expression development one may find that reported two-phase flowmeter correlations are derived from or generally related to the single-phase flowmeter expression Equation 1 or 2. The main methods that have been used to adapt this single-phase expression for the two-phase case may be listed as follows:

1. Assume the two-phase flow to be a homogeneous or a separated flow. An expression involving quality or void fraction is used to produce an effective density. Replace the single-phase density in Equation 1 or 2 by the effective density to form a flowmeter correlation for two-phase flow.
2. Assume the two-phase flow to be a homogeneous or a separated flow. Multiply Equation 1 with a correction term to form a flowmeter correlation for two-phase flow.
3. Assume the two-phase flow to be a homogeneous flow. Correct the exponent of quality in the density expression to form a flowmeter correlation for two-phase flow.
4. Assume the two-phase flow to be a separated flow. Apply the single-phase expression to both the gas stream and liquid stream. Use a Martinelli parameter and correction factors to form a flowmeter correlation for two-phase flow.
5. Assume the two-phase flow to be a separated flow. Multiply Equation 1 with a two-phase blockage factor, which accounts for the liquid blockage of gas flow, to calculate the gas flow rate. Then the two-phase flow rate may be obtained by simply dividing the gas flow rate by the quality

These methods have been employed and modified by different scientists to develop two-phase orificemeter correlations which will now be introduced.

Homogeneous Flow-Model Correlation

Two-phase orificementer correlations usually express the relationship among glow rate, pressure drop, fluid properties, and meter characteristics. Among the various reported correlations, the homogeneous model correlation is the simplest one.

The density of a homogeneous gas-liquid two-phase flow ρ_H can be expressed as follows:

$$1/\rho_H = x/\rho_G + (1 - x)/\rho_L \tag{3}$$

where   x = the mass quality

ρ_G and ρ_L = the density of gas and liquid, respectively

Assuming that the two-phase flow is a homogeneous flow and substituting the density of the homogeneous mixture, ρ_H, as an effective density, for the single-phase density ρ_{sp} in Equation 2, we may obtain the following homogeneous model correlation for a two-phase orificemeter:

$$\Delta P_{TP} = W_{TP}^2[1 + (\rho_L/\rho_G - 1)x]/[2\rho_L(Y\psi cA)^2] \tag{4}$$

Where ΔP_{TP} is the pressure drop across an orifice for two-phase flow; W_{TP} is the mass flow rate for two-phase flow and is equal to the single-phase mass flow rate when total flow is liquid or gas. Equation 4 can be rearranged as below:

$$\Delta P_{TP}/\Delta P_0 = 1 + x(v_G - v_L)/v_L \tag{5}$$

where v_L and v_G express the specific volume of liquid and gas respectively; ΔP_0 is the pressure drop across the orifice assuming total flow to be liquid and can be expressed as follows:

$$\Delta P_0 = W_{TP}^2/[2(\psi cA)^2\rho_L] \tag{6}$$

In practice, it is found that the use of Equation 4 or 5 is very inaccurate. In accordance with several author's experimental data, the two-phase pressure drop predicted by the homogeneous model correlation is considerably overestimated, particularly at low qualities and under low pressure.

Hoopes [2] found that the ratio of the two-phase pressure drop through the orifice to the pressure drop with no vaporization $\Delta P_{TP}/\Delta P_0$ was approximately a linear function of quality in the vena contracta, but was only one tenth to one third as great as would be predicted by Equation 5. Hoopes' experiments were conducted within the following range of parameters

Pressure, p—0.62–12.41 bar,
Mass velocity, G—1,300–7,000 kg/m²·S
Quality, x—up to 0.34
Pipe inner diameter, D—25.4 mm
Ratio of orifice diameter to pipe inner diameter $\beta = d/D$—0.3
Two-phase fluid—steam-water mixture

Hoopes Correlation

After considering the slip between the gas phase and liquid phase, Hoopes [2] proposed the following correlation to predict the two-phase pressure drop across an orifice:

$$\Delta P_{TP} = W_{TP}^2[(1 - x^2)/(1 - \alpha) + (\rho_L/\rho_G)(x^2/\alpha)]/[2\rho_L(\psi cA)^2] \tag{7}$$

or

$$\Delta P_{TP}/\Delta P_0 = (1 - x)^2/(1 - \alpha) + (\rho_L/\rho_G)(x^2/\alpha) \tag{8}$$

where α is the void fraction of the two-phase flow and is evaluated from a straight pipe flow correlation for conditions at the vena contracta.

Although this correlation agrees much better with Hoopes' experimental data than the homogeneous model correlation, the accuracy of prediction ($\pm 50\%$) is still rather poor.

Murdock Correlation

After considering the two-phase fluid as a separated flow, Murdock [3] correlated the experimental data obtained by the U.S. National Boiler and Turbine Laboratory and Osborne by plotting the Martinelli parameters

$$\sqrt{(\Delta P_{TP}/\Delta P_G)}$$

and

$$\sqrt{(\Delta P_L/\Delta P_G)}$$

where ΔP_{TP} = the pressure drop across the orifice for two-phase fluid flow

ΔP_G = the pressure drop across the orifice for gas or vapor phase flow alone

ΔP_L = the pressure drop across the orifice for the liquid phase flow alone

The method of least squares was used to fit the data to a linear equation as follows:

$$\sqrt{(\Delta P_{TP}/\Delta P_G)} = 1 + 1.26\sqrt{(\Delta P_L/\Delta P_G)} \tag{9}$$

The experimental constant 1.26 was derived from the analysis of 90 test points for two-phase flow of steam-water, air-water, natural gas-water, natural gas-salt water and natural gas-distillate combinations.

A final expression can be produced from Equation 9

$$W_{TP} = \psi K_G Y_G A \sqrt{(2\Delta P_{TP}\rho_G)}/[x + 1.26(1 - x)(K_G Y_G/K_L)\sqrt{(\rho_G/\rho_L)}] \tag{10}$$

where A = the orifice flow area

K_G and K_L = coefficients for the combined velocity of approach and discharge coefficient for gas flow only and for liquid flow only through orifice, respectively

Y_G = the expansion coefficient for gas

ψ = the orifice thermal expansion factor

Since both K_G and K_L appearing in Equation 10 are treated as unknown parameters, the Murdock correlation requires an iteration scheme based on initial estimates of K_G and K_L to compute values of W_{TP}.

Experimental data used by Murdock to produce his correlation ranged as follows:

Pressure, P—1–40 bar
Reynolds' number of liquid—50–50,000.
Reynolds' number of gas—15,000–1,000,000.
Quality, x—0.11–0.98
Orifice diameter, d—25.4–31.8 mm.
Pipe inner diameter, D—58.4–101.5 mm.
Ratio of orifice diameter to pipe diameter, $\beta = d/D$—0.26–0.5

Two-phase fluids—Steam-water, air-water, natural gas-water, natural gas-salt water and natural gas-distillate combinations [The accuracy of Equation 9 or 10 will be discussed in the latter part of this chapter.]

James Correlation

James [4] tried to use an orificemeter and a pressure tap at the exit to determine both the flow rate and enthalpy of a steam-water mixture passing through a pipeline to the atmosphere or to a low-pressure receiver from a borehole in a geothermal area.

He found that the homogeneous flow model was quite inaccurate except that quality x in the density expression was raised to the 1.5 power rather than the 1 power for the homogeneous density case. James' correlation is

$$\Delta P_{TP} = W_{TP}^2[1 + (\rho_L/\rho_G - 1) \times {}^{1.5}]/[2\rho_L(\psi YcA)^2] \tag{11}$$

where c is the discharge coefficient, and is equal to $0.61/\sqrt{[1 - (d/D)^4]}$. The range of his experimental parameters was:

Pressure, P—5.1–18.7 bar
Mass velocity, G—370–3447 kg/m²·S
Quality, x—0.01–0.56
Orifice diameter, d—14.2 mm and 16.8 mm
Pipe inner diameter, D—20.05 mm
Ratio of orifice diameter to pipe diameter, $\beta = d/D$—0.707 and 0.837
Two-phase fluid—steam-water mixture

The accuracy of Equation 11 will be discussed in the latter part of this chapter.

Bizon Correlation

Bizon [5] used Murdock's method to correlate his experimental data. He found the following correlation could fit his data best:

$$\sqrt{(\Delta P_{TP}/\Delta P_G)} = a + b\sqrt{(\Delta P_L/\Delta P_G)} \tag{12}$$

where a and b are coefficients which slightly depend on the ratio of orifice diameter to the pipe inner diameter d/D.
In his experiments, when d/D = 0.45, a = 1.0372 and b = 1.0789, and when d/D = 0.70, a = 1.0818 and b = 0.9999. The range of his experimental parameters was:

Pressure, P—82.8 bar.
Mass velocity, G—203, 5–524.5 kg/m²·S
Quality, x—0.5–0.50
Orifice diameter, d—11.4 and 17.8 mm.
Pipe inner diameter, D—25.4 mm.
Ratio of orifice diameter to pipe inner diameter $\beta = d/D$, 0.45 and 0.70.
Two-phase fluid—steam-water mixture.

Marriott Correlation

Marriott [6] also assumed the two-phase mixture across the orifice to be a separated flow. He used the concept of an equivalent single-phase liquid flow through the orifice to derive his correlation. The general form of the Marriott correlation is:

$$W_{TP} = c\phi^x A[(1 - \alpha)/(1 - x)]\sqrt{(2\Delta P_{TP}\rho_L)} \tag{13}$$

where ϕ = defined as a function of pressure ratio across the orifice, orifice geometry, and gas and liquid properties

           c = the discharge coefficient for liquid
           α = the void fraction
           x = the mass quality

The accuracy of Equation 13 will also be discussed later.

Collins and Gacesa Correlation

Collins and Gacesa [7] used Murdock's method to correlate their two-phase flow data from an orifice plate. The two-phase data were presented in terms of the dimensionless Martinelli parameters. They found that the following correlation could fit their experimental data best:

$$\sqrt{(\Delta P_{TP}/\Delta P_G)} = B_1 + B_2\sqrt{(\Delta P_L/\Delta P_G)} + B_3\sqrt[4]{(\Delta P_L/\Delta P_G)} \tag{14}$$

where B_1, B_2, and B_3 are empirical constants determined experimentally. Within the range of their experimental parameters

$B_1 = 0.913$

$B_2 = 0.928$

$B_3 = 0.375$

The range of their experimental parameters was:

Pressure, P—67.6 bar
Total mass flow rate, W_{TP}—1.89–12.6 kg/s
Quality, x—0.05–0.90
Orifice diameter, d—40.7–52.6 mm
Pipe inner diameter, D—63.50–76.2 mm
Ratio of orifice diamter to pipe inner diameter, $\beta = d/D$—0.62–0.75
Two-phase fluid—steam-water mixture

Comparison with other data shows that Equation 14 may be used to calculate steam qualities in the range of operating pressure 4.80–67.60 bar and in pipe sizes from 63.5–203 mm. The R.M.S. deviation of the calculated from the measured steam qualities using this correlation is about 10 percent.

Kremlevskii and Dyudina Correlation

Kremlevskii and Dyudina [8] assumed at the inlet of the orifice that gas velocity was equal to the liquid velocity, while at the vena contracta, because of the great density difference between the water droplet and steam at low pressure, the droplet velocity might be much smaller than the steam velocity. By using the energy equation and continuity equation, they obtained the following expression:

$$W_{TP} = kcY_GA\sqrt{(2\Delta P_{TP}\rho_H)} \tag{15}$$

where ρ_H = the density of the homogeneous two-phase mixture determined by Equation 3
   k = a corrective coefficient determined experimentally

Within the range of their experimental parameters, coefficient k can be predicted as follows:

$$k = 1.56 - 0.56x \tag{16}$$

The range of their experimental parameters was:

Pressure, P—1–4 bar
Quality, x—0.7–1.0
Ratio of orifice diameter to pipe diameter, $\beta = d/D$—0.316–0.633
Two-phase fluid: steam-water mixture.

Within the experimental range, the R.M.S. deviation of this correlation is about 0.6%.

Davies and Daniels Correlation

The Davies and Daniels [9] correlation for gas-liquid two-phase flow was obtained from correlating the experimental data of R-12 flowing through different sizes of orifices, the inlet and exit orifice pressures being measured at points 13 pipe diameters up and downstream of the orifice, respectively.

The correlation for two-phase flow across an orifice is

$$(M_{LS}/M_L) - 1 = a(Y'F)^b \tag{17}$$

where a and b are coefficients determined as follows:

$$a = 0.5529(d)^{-0.33013} \tag{18}$$

$$b = 0.00232(d)^{-1.602} \tag{19}$$

F is a nondimensional factor for accounting for the effect of the pressure ratio P_2/P_1 and vapor expansion (P_1 and P_2 express the inlet and exit pressure of the orifice).

$$F = 2.1 - 1.25(P_2/P_1) \tag{20}$$

Y' is a nondimensional parameter.

$$Y' = (x/(1 - x))(M_{LN}/M_{GN}) \tag{21}$$

In Equation 17 and 21 M_{LS} is the liquid flow rate by mass during single-phase flow and the normal contraction coefficient and two-phase pressure drop; M_L is the liquid flow rate by mass during two-phase flow; M_{LN} is the liquid flow rate by mass during single-phase flow with a unit contraction coefficient and two-phase pressure drop; M_{GN} is the gas flow rate by mass during single-phase flow with a unit contraction coefficient and a two-phase pressure drop.

The range of their experimental parameters was:

Pressure, P—6 bar
Orifice diameter, d—0.762–1.422 mm
Pipe inner diameter, D—9.525 mm
Quality, x—0.00017–0.18.
Ratio of orifice diameter to pipe inner diameter, $\beta = d/D$—0.08–0.149

Within the experimental range, the R.M.S. deviation is about $\pm 10\%$.

Chisholm Correlation

Chisholm et al. [10–12] considered the two-phase flow across an orifice to be a separated flow. By using the momentum equation for the more general problem of friction and acceleration pressure drops. He related the ration $\sqrt{(\Delta P_{TP}/\Delta P_L)}$ to the Martinelli parameter X

$$\Delta P_{TP}/\Delta P_L = 1 + a/X + 1/X^2 \tag{22}$$

where

$$X = \sqrt{(\Delta P_L/\Delta P_G)} \left[(1 - x)/x\right] \sqrt{(\rho_G/\rho_L)} \tag{23}$$

$$c = (1/S)\sqrt{(\rho_L/\rho_G)} + S\sqrt{(\rho_G/\rho_L)} \tag{24}$$

where s is the slip ratio and can be calculated as follows:

$$S = (1/Z)\sqrt{(\rho_L/\rho_G)} \tag{25}$$

For pressure less than 150 bar

$$Z = (0.19 + 0.92 \, P/P_c)^{-1} \tag{26}$$

For pressure above 150 bar

$$Z = (0.42 + 0.58P/P_c)^{-1} \tag{27}$$

where   P = the absolute pressure of mixture
$\quad\quad$ P_c = the critical pressure

Equation 25 only fits for high-quality conditions. For low-quality tubular two-phase flows, S should be calculated as follows:

$$S = \sqrt{(\rho_L/\rho_H)} \tag{28}$$

where ρ_H is the homogeneous density and can be determined by Equation 3.
The upper limit of quality x for which Equation 28 should be used is

$$x_u = [(1/Z)^2(\rho_L/\rho_G) - 1]/[(\rho_L/\rho_G) - 1] \tag{29}$$

Equation 28 is valid for quality $x < x_u$, while Equation 25 is valid for quality $x > x_u$.
Chisholm [12] developed his correlations for the pressure-drop across on orifice during the flow of two-phase mixtures. He proposed in Equation 22 the c value should be calculated as follows.

For X < 1

$$c = (\rho_L/\rho_G)^{1/4} + (\rho_G/\rho_L)^{1/4} \tag{30}$$

For X ≥ 1

$$c = (\rho_H/\rho_G)^{1/2} + (\rho_G/\rho_H)^{1/2} \tag{31}$$

The error of Equation 22 for low quality (x ≤ 0.1) under the pressure from 10 to 70 is about ±20%. Equation 22 agrees with Collins' and other authors' experimental data with an error of about ±12%, but disagrees with the data of James and Murdock.

Smith and Leang Correlation

Smith and Leang [13] proposed a correlation for two-phase flow across an orifice. Under the assumption of a separated flow model, they introduced a blockage factor to modify the total flow area at the orifice to an effective flow area available to the gas phase portion of the flow.
The Smith and Leang correlation is

$$W_{TP} = cY_G\psi A(BF)\sqrt{(2\Delta P_{TP}\rho_G)/x} \tag{32}$$

where   c = the discharge coefficient for gas phase

$\quad\quad$ BF = the blockage factor which accounts for the liquid blockage of the gas flow and can be determined as follows (when x > 0.1)

$$BF = 0.637 + 0.4211x - 0.00183/x^2 \tag{33}$$

The accuracy of Equation 32 will be discussed later.

Lorenzi and Muzzio Correlation

Lorenzi and Muzzio [14] applied the energy equation to the air-water two-phase flow across an orifice. Finally they obtained the following correlating for predicting the two-phase pressure drop across an orifice.

$$\phi_{Lo}^2 = \Delta P_{TP}/\Delta P_0 = [c_L/(c_{TP}Y_{TP})]^2[(\rho_L/\rho_G)^2(x^3/\alpha^2) + (1-x)^3/(1-\alpha)^2]/[(\rho_L/\rho_G)x + (1-x)] \quad (34)$$

where c_L = the discharge coefficient for liquid
c_{TP} = the discharge coefficient for two-phase flow
Y_{TP} = the expansion coefficient for two-phase flow

Let c_L equal c_{TP} and Y_{TP} equal unity. Then

$$\phi_{Lo}^2 = [(\rho_L/\rho_G)^2(x^3/\alpha^2) + (1-x)^3/(1-\alpha)^2]/[(\rho_L/\rho_G)x + (1-x)] \quad (35)$$

under their low-pressure and low-temperature experimental conditions, the void fraction α can be determined from the following empirical relationship:

$$\alpha = 1/\{(1-\beta)/\beta + \sqrt{[1 + A(1-\beta)/\beta]}\} \quad (36)$$

where β = the gas-phase volumetric flow fraction

A = a function of the ratio of orifice diameter to the pipe inner diameter d/D and can be determine from Figure 5.

Lorenzi and Muzzio's experimental pressure was from 1.41 to 1.49 bar and the temperature was from 14° to 18°C. The experimental two-phase fluid was an air-water mixture.

Matter Correlation

Matter et al. [15] tried to obtain a relationship between the orificemeter differential reading and the flow rates of two individual phases. They used an air-oil mixture as the flowing fluid, and found the following correlation:

$$Q_{TPG}/Q_G = 1 + b'Q_L/Q_G \quad (37)$$

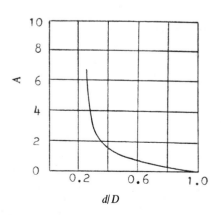

Figure 5. Value of coefficient A as a function of d/D.

where Q_{TPG} = the volumetric gas flow rate that would result in a pressure drop of ΔP_{TP}
     Q = the volumetric liquid flow rate
     Q_G = the volumetric gas flow rate
     b' = a coefficient determined experimentally

They found in spite of the wide range of orifice diameters investigated, the results were independent of the size of the orifice used.

For an oil-air ratio of less than 0.35

$$Q_{TPG}/Q_G = 1 + 50\, Q_L/Q_G \tag{38}$$

For an oil-air ratio greater than 0.35

$$Q_{TPG}/Q_G = 1 + 40\, Q_L/Q_G \tag{39}$$

Equation 37 is valid for a limited range of the liquid-to-gas ratio. In Equation 37, b' should be determined from a test at actual conditions.

The range of their experimented parameters was:

Pressure, P—2.44 $\pm$ 0.3 bar
Flow rate of gas phase—$5.10^{-4} < W_G < 0.1$ kg/s
Flow rate of liquid phase—$0.05 < W_L < 5$ kg/s
Oil/air ratio—$0.0008–9$ m^3/m^3
Orifice diameter, d—22.2–38.1 mm
Pipe inner diameter, D—52.5 mm
Ratio of orifice diameter to pipe inner diameter, $\beta = d/D$—0.423–0.726
Two-phase Fluid—air-oil mixture

Lin Correlation

Lin [16] assumed that the gas and liquid phase flow separately through an orifice; the gas phase is incompressible; the discharge coefficient c is the same for both phases; the pressure drop for each phase is the same as the pressure drop for the two-phase flow in the device; there is no evaporation during the flow. After this derivation the following equation for two-phase flow across an orifice was obtained.

$$\sqrt{(\Delta P_{TP}/\Delta P_0)} = \theta + x(\sqrt{(\rho_L/\rho_G)} - \theta) \tag{40}$$

where ΔP_{TP} is the pressure drop across an orifice for two-phase flow; θ is a corrective coefficient determined experimentally; ΔP_0 is the pressure drop across an orifice assuming total flow to be liquid, and can be calculated as follows:

$$\sqrt{(\Delta P_0)} = W_{TP}/\psi c A \sqrt{(2\rho_L)} \tag{41}$$

θ is a function of slip ratio S and density ρ_G/ρ_L. Therefore, θ reflects the influence of slip ratio S and working pressure or density ratio ρ_G/ρ_L. As the slip ratio is also a function of ρ_G/ρ_L, on the whole, θ is a function of ρ_G/ρ_L. Under given ρ_G/ρ_L, θ is a constant.

Lin used R-113 as the experimental fluid, but he showed that the coefficient θ obtained from the R-113 two-phase mixture could also be applied to a steam-water mixture, if they had the same ρ_G/ρ_L or vice versa. By correlating his own data and experimental data obtained by Murdock [3], James [4], Bizon [5], and Collins [7], Lin obtained a set of values θ for different ρ_G/ρ_L. Being plotted against ρ_G/ρ_L the corrective coefficient θ can be found from Figure 6, or calculated by the

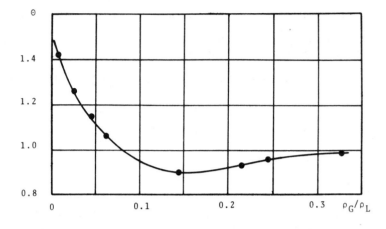

Figure 6. Variation of θ and ρ_G/ρ_L.

following correlation:

$$\theta = 1.48625 - 9.26541(\rho_G/\rho_L) + 44.6954(\rho_G/\rho_L)^2 - 60.6150(\rho_G/\rho_L)^3$$
$$-5.12966(\rho_G/\rho_L)^4 - 26.5743(\rho_G/\rho_L)^5 \tag{42}$$

Equation 40 fits for $x \geq 0.1$, when $x < 0.1$, $\sqrt{(\Delta P_{TP}/\Delta P_0)}$ can be calculated by using interpolation between the value of $\sqrt{(\Delta P_{TP}/\Delta P_0)}$ at $x = 0.1$ and the value of $\sqrt{(\Delta P_{TP}/\Delta P_0)}$ at $x = 0$, i.e. $\sqrt{(\Delta P_{TP}/\Delta P_0)} = 1.0$.

A direct equation for calculating the two-phase total mass flow rate W_{TP} is as follows:

$$W_{TP} = \psi c A \sqrt{(2\Delta P_{TP}\rho_L)}/[(1-x)\theta + x\sqrt{(\rho_L/\rho_G)}] \tag{43}$$

The range of experimental data correlated by Equation 40 was as follows,

Pressure, P—7.72–188 bar
Mass velocity, G—400–3500 kg/m²·s
Quality, x—0–1.0
Orifice diameter, d—10–142 mm
Pipe inner diameter, D—19–200 mm
Ratio of orifice diameter to pipe diameter, $\beta = d/D$—0.25–0.75.
Two-phase fluid—R-113 vapor-liquid mixture, steam-water mixture and R-11 vapor-liquid mixture.

The R.M.S. deviation of the calculated from the measured qualities using this correlation is about $\pm 12\%$.

In addition to those correlations already introduced, there were still other papers that reported useful experimental results but did not propose correlations.

For instance, Ragolin [17] conducted a series of experiments about steam-water mixture flowing across an orifice under pressure ranging from 27.3—120.6 bar. Palm et al. [18] conducted experiments about steam-water mixtures across orifices of different sizes under pressure ranging from 8.9–20.7 bar. Palm found Murdock's correlation could agree with his experimental data. Chen [19] also reported his high pressure steam-water data about two-phase flow across an orifice. These results also improved the research work in this topic.

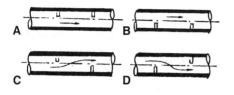

Figure 7. Different forms for orifices in series.

METHODS FOR TWO-PARAMETRIC TWO-PHASE FLOW MEASUREMENTS

In some cases, such as in oil field or geothermal areas, when a gas-oil or steam-water two-phase mixture is flowing along pipes, both the flow rate and the mass quality are unknowns. Thus, one needs to separate the liquid from gas first, and then measures the flow rate of each phase individually by conventional methods. If the two parametric two-phase flow measurements can be realized, it is possible to measure the flow rate and quality of the two-phase mixture simultaneously without having to separate the phases.

Up to now, some methods for two parametric two-phase flow measurements have been proposed and studied. However, research works on this topic are quite insufficient.

Method of Using Two Orifices in Series

Sekoguchi et al. [20] used two oriifices in series to conduct air-water two-parametric two-phase flow measurements. Two types of orifices were researched, namely, the segmental orifice and the eccentric orifice (shown in Figure 3).

Two orifices in series were mounted with four different forms (Figure 7) in the experimental pipe. Analytical and experimental results expressed that best results were obtained when two segmental orifices were mounted according to the c form in Figure 7.

The test results were plotted to give nomograms. The abscissa of the nomogram expresses the sum of the pressure drops of the two orifices in series, i.e. $(\Delta P_1 + \Delta P_2)$.

The ordinate represents the ratio of the two pressure drops $\Delta P_1/\Delta P_2$. Figure 8 is one of such nomograms. Curves in Figure 8 are drawn for different j_G and j_L. j_G is the superficial velocity of the gas phase and is defined as the rate of the volumetric flow of the gas phase divided by the total flow area. j_L is the superficial velocity of the liquid phase and is defined as the rate of volumetric flow of the liquid phase divided by the total flow area. Figure 8 should be calibrated at the site. During operation, when the two pressure drops ΔP_1 and ΔP_2 are measured, j_G and j_L can be found from Figure 8, thus, the flow rate of each phase can be determined. No analytical correlation was proposed. The error of this method is about $\pm 30\%$.

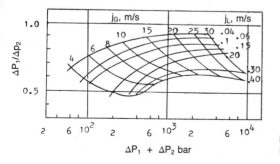

Figure 8. Nomogram for Form c in Figure 7.

Method of Using a Volumetric Flow Rate Meter and an Orifice in Series

Medvejev et al. [21, 22] used a volumetric flow rate meter and an orifice in series to conduct the air-water two-parametric two-phase flow measurements. From the experimental data, they found the volumetric flow rate of the mixture Q_{TP} could be determined as follows:

$$Q_{TP} = c_{TP}A\sqrt{(2\Delta P_{TP}/\rho_H)} \tag{44}$$

where c_{TP} = the discharge coefficient for two-phase mixture

ρ_H = the homogeneous density of the mixture and can be expressed in terms of volumetric flow fraction of gas phase β:

$$\rho_H = \rho_G\beta + \rho_L(1 - \beta) \tag{45}$$

$$c_{TP} = kc \tag{46}$$

where k is a corrective coefficient and is a function of quality and the ratio of orifice flow area to pipe flow area m when m $\geq$ 0.5 and β = 0–0.5, k is approximately equal to 1.0 and c is single-phase discharge coefficient.

The total volumetric flow rate Q_{TP} can be determined directly from the volumetric flow rate meter; the error is less than 3%.

$$Q_{TP} = Q_G + Q_L \tag{47}$$

Equation 44 can be rearranged as follows:

$$\rho_H = k'\Delta P_{TP}/Q_{TP}^2 \tag{48}$$

where $k' = 2(c_{TP}A)^2$

when these two flowmeters are arranged in series, Q_{TP} can be determined by the volumetric flow rate meter directly. ρ_H can be determined by Equation 48 since ΔP_{TP} is measured from the orifice and C_{TP} is equal to c under the condition of m $\geq$ 0.5 and β = 0–0.5. Therefore from Equation 45 β can be predicted. The volumetric flow rate of gas phase Q_G and liquid phase Q_L can be calculated as follows:

$$Q_G = Q_{TP}\beta \tag{49}$$

$$Q_L = Q_{TP}(1 - \beta) \tag{50}$$

In Medvejv's experiments, the experimental loop diameter was 50 mm. The volumetric flow fraction of the gas phase ranged from 0.2 to 0.98. The ratio of orifice flow area to the pipe flow area ranged from 0.1 to 0.5.

Chen et al. [22] conducted similar experiments to Medvejv's.

In their experiments, air-water two-phase two-parametric measurements were conducted by using an oval gear meter (type Lc-50) and a sharp-edged orifice (diameter ratio d/D = 15.84/25.4 mm/mm) in series (Figure 9).

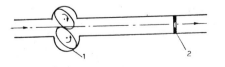

Figure 9. An oval gear meter and an orifice plate in series: (1) oval gear meter; (2) orifice plate.

The length of the straight pipe on the upstream and downstream of the orifice were 2,065 and 1,055 mm, respectively. Experiments were done at temperatures between 9.8° and 14.7°C and at an orifice inlet pressure between 0.49 and 1.53 kg/cm². The air flow rate varied from 7.23 to 30.84 m³/hr, and the water flow rate from 0.948 to 3.045 m³/hr.

The mass quality ranged from 0.0071 to 0.0562 and the respective gas-phase volumetric flow fraction β ranged from 0.707 to 0.955.

Chen et al. found that the following relationship could fit their experimental data quite well.

$$\beta_0 = 1/\{1 + [(1.34\, Q_{0G}/YcA)\sqrt{(\rho_G/2\Delta P_{TP})} - (P_0/P_{0G})]/[(1.35\, Q_{0G}/cA)\sqrt{(\rho_L/2\Delta P_{TP})} - 1]\} \quad (51)$$

where β_0 = the gas-phase volumetric flow fraction at the orifice

Q_{0G} = the volumetric flow rate of the two-phase flow passing through the oval gear meter

P_0 and P_{0G} = pressures before the orifice and the oval gear meter, respectively

ΔP_{TP} = the two-phase pressure drop across the orifice

The volumetric flow fraction at the oval gear meter β_{0G} can be determined as follows:

$$\beta_{0G} = 1/[1 + (P_{0G}/P_0)(1/\beta_0 - 1)] \quad (52)$$

The volumetric flow rate of each phase passing through the oval gear meter $(Q_{0G})_G$ and $(Q_{0G})_L$ are

$$(Q_{0G})_G = \beta_{0G}Q_{0G} \quad (53)$$

and

$$(Q_{0G})_L = (1 - \beta_{0G})Q_{0G} \quad (54)$$

Therefore when the pressure drop across the orifice, ΔP_{TP}; the total volumetric flow rate of a two-phase mixture passing through the oval gear meter, Q_{0G}; the inlet pressure of the gear meter, P_{0G}; and of the orifice, P_0, are known, β_0 can be determined from Equation 51. β_{0G} can be determined from Equation 52. Then the volumetric flow rate of each phase can be determined from Equation 53 and 54, respectively.

Within the experimental range the R.M.S. of this method for volumetric flow rate of each phase is less than $\pm 7\%$.

COMPARISONS AND RECOMMENDATIONS

Correlations for predicting the flow rate or quality of a gas-liquid two-phase flow across an orifice are semi-empirical relationships, therefore their available regions should not exceed their corresponding experimental ranges.

Under its own experimental conditions, each correlation has its own accuracy. However, when it is applied to other conditions (for instance, if the working pressure is greatly changed), the predicting error may sharply increase.

It is impossible and unnecessary to give various comparisons for each correlation in this part. Here, the comparisons among several correlations are introduced as examples.

In the low gas-(or vapor)-density-to-liquid-density-ratio region or under lower-pressure conditions, Smith and Leang [13] as well as Smith and Murdok [23] compared the two-phase flowmeter correlations of James, Marriott, Murdock, and Smith by using experimental data. The range of data used by Smith and Leang for comparisons were as follows:

Pressure, P—0.827–40.3 bar
Quality, x—0–0.9672

Pipe inner diameter, D—6.35–168 mm
Ratio of orifice diameter to pipe inner diameter, β = d/D—0.1875–0.8373
Orifice diameter, d—6.35–168 mm
Two-phase fluid—steam-water mixture

After comparison, Smith and Leang expressed the R.M.S. fractional deviation E for the four correlations as being:
For the Murdock correlation, when x < 0.1, E = 0.334; when x > 0.1, E = 0.185 (average); when x > 0.2, E = 0.126. For the Marriott correlation, for all x, E = 0.207. For the James correlation, when x < 0.1, E = 0.272; when x > 0.1, E = 0.134 (average); when x > 0.2, E = 0.063. For the Smith correlation, when x < 0.1, it can not be used; when x > 0.1, E = 0.15; when x > 0.2, E = 0.087.

Smith and Murdock also compared the same four two-phase orificemeter correlations. They evaluated these four correlations for the flow of steam-water mixtures and two-component gas-liquid mixtures through ASME-code measuring orifices. Experimental data for all evaluations were listed in Murdock's [3] and James' [4] papers.

For steam-water mixtures, the range of data used was:

Pressure, P—7.72–40.31 bar
Mass velocity, G—676–2,514 kg/m²·S
Quality, x—0.062–0.95
Pipe inner diameter—63.35 and 200.70 mm
Ratio of orifice diameter to pipe inner diameter, β = d/D—0.5 and 0.707
Two-phase fluid—steam-water mixture
Ratio of vapor density to liquid density, ρ_G/ρ_L—0.00455–0.0251

For gas-liquid mixtures, the range of data used was:

Pressure, P—1.03–63.9 bar
Mass velocity—46.5–1,002 kg/m²· S
Quality, x—0.11–0.976
Pipe inner diameter, D—75–98 mm
Ratio of diameter, β = d/D—0.26 and 0.43

Smith and Murdock expressed when the fluid was steam-water the R.M.S. fractional deviation E for the four correlations as being:
For the Murdock correlation, when x = 0.062–0.95, E = ±0.141; for the James correlation when x = 0.062 − 0.95, E = ±0.081; for the Marriott correlation, when x = 0.062 − 0.95, E = ±0.114; for the Smith Leang correlation, when x = 0.1 − 0.95, E = ±0.218.

When the fluids were two-component gas-liquid mixtures, the R.M.S deviations E for the four correlations were: For the Murdock correlation, E = ±0.074; for the James correlation, E = ±0.178; for the Marriott correlation, E = ±0.458; for the Smith and Leang correlation, E = ±0.183.

Therefore one may find that within the range of the experimental data used for comparison, for the flow of steam-water mixtures, the James correlation [4] gives the best results; for the flow of two-component gas-liquid mixtures, the Murdock correlation [3] gives the best results. The Marriott correlation cannot be used to predict the two-component gas-liquid mixture data.

In the high gas-(or vapor)-density-to-liquid-density-ratio region or under higher pressure conditions, Lin [16] compared the two-phase flowmeter correlations for the homogeneous flow model, Murdock [3], James [4], Chisholm [11], Smith [13], and Lin [16].
The range of the experiment data was:

Ratio of vapor density to liquid density, ρ_G/ρ_L—0.215–0.328
Mass velocity, G—917–1,477 kg/m²·S
Quality, x—0–1.0
Pipe inner diameter, D—32 mm
Orifice diameter, d—10–20 mm
Ratio of orifice diameter to Pipe inner diameter, β = d/D—0.312–0.624
Two-phase fluid—R-113

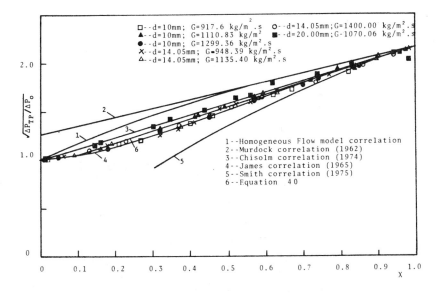

Figure 10. Comparison of experimental data with various correlations $\rho_G/\rho_L = 0.215$.

In Figures 10 and 11, these correlations are plotted at different ρ_G/ρ_L and compared with experimental data. Figure 10 is for the case of $\rho_G/\rho_L = 0.215$, while Figure 11 is for $\rho_G/\rho_L = 0.328$.

Figure 10 shows the correlation of Murdock and the correlation of Smith and Leang are not in good agreement with high ρ_G/ρ_L data. The Chisholm correlation and the James correlation are in better agreement with the experimental data of high ρ_G/ρ_L. The agreement of the Lin correlation with the high ρ_G/ρ_L data is quite good.

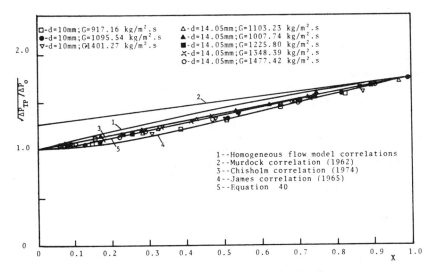

Figure 11. Comparison of experimental data with various correlations $\rho_G/\rho_L = 0.328$.

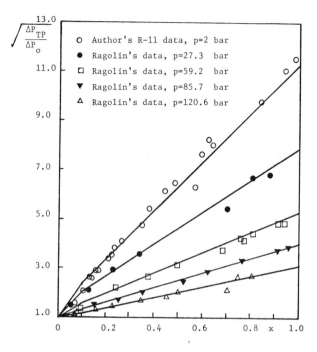

Figure 12. Comparison of Ragolin's steam-water data and author's R-11 data with Equation 40.

Figure 11 shows the similar results. In Figure 11, one may find that the predicted results of the Chisholm correlation are quite close to those of the Lin correlation and the accuracy of the homogeneous flow model correlation is getting much better at higher pressure or under higher ρ_G/ρ_L ratio condition.

The Lin correlation has also been compared with experimental data obtained under low ρ_G/ρ_L conditions and with Ragolin's steam-water data (Figure 12). Good agreements were obtained, too.

The comparison with experimental data shows the Lin correlation can be used to calculate the quality or flow rate of low-viscosity vapor-liquid or steam-water mixtures in the effective range 0.00455–0.328 of the ρ_G/ρ_L ratio. For steam-water mixtures, the corresponding effective range of the pressure is about 8–198 bar.

As a conclusion, we may say that the effective ranges of correlations mentioned in this chapter should not exceed their experimental parameter ranges. Within its own experimental range, every correlation has its own accuracy. The effective ranges of the Lin correlation and Chisholm correlation are quite wide. For two-component gas-liquid mixtures the Murdock correlation gives good results. For low ρ_G/ρ_L ratio conditions the James correlation is a good correlation. The accuracy of the homogeneous flow model correlation improves when the working pressure increases.

For the problem of two-phase measurements, on the whole, the method of using an orifice in combination with another metering device is convenient; however, investigation on this topic is quite insufficient. Much research still must be done in this area.

PROBLEMS IN APPLICATION

An orifice is a metering device that depends on the measurement of pressure drop. When it is used for measuring the gas-liquid two-phase flow, there are two main problems: the problem of pressure drop measurement and the problem of upstream flow conditions.

In two-phase flow systems, pressure drop can be measured using either manometric or pressure transducer techniques. When a U-tube manometer is used for measuring the gas-liquid two-phase flow pressure drop, for the sake of accurate measurement, it is important to know the density of the fluid in the connection lines between the manometer and pressure taps of the experimental pipeline. However, because the pressure fluctuations in the pipe cause a pumping action, there is a change of pressure drop in the manometer etc. leading to gas ingress into the taps, which produces an unknown density in the connection lines. Thus, the problem of how to control the line to be filled with single-phase fluid is very important.

For one-component vapor-liquid two-phase systems, a small cooling section just downstream of the pressure tapping point may be arranged, so that vapor entering the line can be condensed. Small separating pots may also be used in the position mentioned above. For improving the performance of liquid-filled connection lines further, a balance liquid purge system can be employed [24].

Depending on the pressure range to be measured water-mercury manometers, inverted water-mercury manometers, or water-carbon tetrachloride manometers can be used.

When a differential-pressure transducer is used, strain-gauge and reluctance transducers are more suitable, while capacitance and piezoelectric types are unsuitable.

In addition, care has to be taken to minimize the effects of pressure drop fluctuations.

Another main problem for orificemeters when used as two-phase flowmeters or quality meters is the influence of upstream flow conditions. Upstream flow disturbances caused by, the influence of components such as a valve, bend, or other device critically determines the response of the orifice. Therefore for obtaining accurate measuring results, it is necessary to conduct careful calibration of the orifice at the site.

NOTATION

A	area	P	absolute pressure
B	empirical coefficient	P_c	critical pressure
a, b	coefficients	Q	volumetric flow rate
c	discharge coefficient	Re	Reynolds number
D	inner diameter	S	slip ratio
d	orifice diameter	W	mass flow rate
F	dimensionless parameter	x	mass quality
G	mass velocity	Y	expansion coefficient
K	loss coefficient	Y'	dimensionless parameter
k	correction factor	Z	pressure loss parameter
M	mass flow rate		

Greek Symbols

α	void fraction	ρ	density
β	volumetric flow fraction; also diameter ratio	ϕ	function of pressure ratio across orifice
		ϕ_{Lo}^2	two-phase pressure drop multiplier
θ	corrective coefficient	ψ	thermal expansion factor

REFERENCES

1. Thang, N. T., and Davis, M. R., "The Structure of Bubbly Flow Through Ventures," *Int. J. Multiphase Flow*, Vol. 5, No. 1, pp. 17–37 (1979).
2. Hoopes, J. W., "Flow of Steam-Water Mixture in A Heated Annulus and through Orifices," *AIchE J.*, Vol. 3, No. 2, pp. 268–275 (1957).
3. Murdock, J. W., "Two-Phase Flow Measurement with Sharp-Edged Orifices," *J. Basic Engng*, Vol. 84, No. 4, pp. 419–433 (1962).

4. James, R., "Metering of Steam-Water Two-Phase Flow by Sharp-Edged Orifices," *Proc. Inst. Mech. Engrs.*, Vol. 180, No. 23, pp. 549–566 (1965).

5. Bizon, E., "Two-Phase Flow Measurements with Sharp-Edged Orifices and Ventures," AECL-2273 (1965).

6. Marriott, P. W., "Two-Phase Steam Water Flow through Sharp-Edged Orifices," Gen. El. Rep. NEDO 10210 (1970).

7. Collins, D. B., and Gacesa, M., "Measurements of Steam Quality in Two-Phase Upflow with Venturimeters and Orifice Plate," *ASME Sen. D.*, Vol., No. 1, pp. 11–21 (1971).

8. Kremlevskii, P. P., and Dyudina, I. A., "Measurements of Moist Vapor Discharge by Means of Gauging Diaphragms, " *Measurement Techniques*, Vol. 15, No. 5, pp. 741–744 (1972).

9. Davies, A. D., and Daniels, T. C., "Single and Two-Phase Flow of Dichlorodifluoromethane, (R-12), Through Sharp-Edged Orifice," *ASHRAE Transaction*, Vol. 79, pt. 1, pp. 109–123 (1973).

10. Chisholm, D., and Leishman, J., "The Metering of Wet Steam," *Chem. and Process Engng.* (July), pp. 103–106 (1969).

11. Chisholm, D., "Pressure Drop during Steam/Water Flows through Orifices," *J. Mech. Engng Science*, Vol. 16, No. 5, pp. 353–355 (1974).

12. Chisholm, D., "Two-phase Flow through Sharp-Edged Orifices," *J. Mech. Engng. Science*, Vol. 19, No. 3, pp. 128–130 (1977).

13. Smith, R. V., and Leang, J. T., "Evaluations of Correlations for Two-Phase Flowmeters Three Current—One New," *ASME Ser. A.*, Vol. 97, No. 4, pp. 589–593, (1975).

14. Lorenzi, A., and Muzzio, A., "Two-Phase Flow Rate Measurement with Sharp-Edged Orifices," *Jol. Termotecnics*, No. 3 (1977).

15. Matter, L., Nicholson, M., and Aziz, K., "Orifice Metering of Two-Phase Flow, "*J. of Petroleum Technology* (August), pp. 955–961 (1979).

16. Lin, Z. H., "Two-Phase Flow Measurements with Sharp-Edged Orifices," *Int. J. Multiphase Flow*, Vol. 8, No. 6, pp. 683–693 (1982).

17. Ragolin, N. V., "Measurements of Steam-Water Flow," *Teploenergetika*,Vol. 2, No. 5, pp. 51–55 (1958).

18. Palm, J. W., Kirkpatrick, J. W., and Anderson, W. H., "Determination of Steam Quality Using an Orifice Meter," *J. of Petroleum Technology* (June), pp. 587–591 (1968).

19. Chen, S. T., "The Primary Report about Using Orifice to measure the quality of Steam Water Mixture," Report of the Harbin Boiler Institute of China, CBZ-092 (1979).

20. Sekoguchi, K., "Two-Phase Flow Measurements with Orifice-Couple in Horizontal Pipe Line (1st Report),"*Trans. JSME*, Vol. 44 (April), pp. 1347–1353 (1978).

21. Medvejev, V. F., "Gas and Liquid Flow Rate Measurement in Gas-Liquid Mixture," *Instrument and Control System*, No. 10, pp. 18–20 (1972).

22. Chen, Z. H., Chen, Z. Y., and Xu, Y. L., etc. "Two Parametric Flow Measurement in Gas-Liquid Two-Phase Flow," the Proceeding of the 7th Int. Heat Transfer Conference (Sept. 1982).

23. Smith, L. T., Murdock, J. W., and Applebaum, R. S., "An Evaluation of Existing Two-Phase Flow Correlations for Use with ASME Sharp Edge Metering Orifices," *ASME Ser. A.*, Vol. 99, No. 3, pp. 343–347 (1977).

24. Hewitt, G. F., *Measurement of Two Phase Flow Parameters*, Academic Press, 1978, pp. 24–30.

CHAPTER 30

TURBULENCE MODELS FOR TWO-PHASE FLOWS

T. W. Abou-Arab

Mechanical Power Department
Faculty of Engineering
Cairo University
Cairo, Egypt

CONTENTS

INTRODUCTION

Multiphase systems occur in many practical applications such as nuclear power plants, sanitary engineering, bioengineering, fluidized beds and furnaces, crude and processed oil piping lines, pulverized-coal combustors, diesel engine sprays, aerosols, and rocket plumes. It was found that the multiphase flow differs from the single-phase one in many aspects. Thus, in order to enhance the understanding of such flows, extensive experimental and theoretical research should be continued [1].

The flow structure changes by the existence of a dispersed phase [2] in the carrying fluid. Further, heat transfer data [3, 6] and metering [3, 7, 8] of multiphase flows show discrepancy from the single-phase data. Complete understanding of the effects of the presence of suspended solid particles or liquid droplets on the structure of a turbulent flow is a formidable task [9, 10]. These particles may attenuate the turbulence intensity and the spreading rate in a jet flow. However, in pipe flows, the variation of the turbulence structure was found to depend on the particle size as well as the physical properties of the different existing phases.

A review of published experimental studies on turbulent two-phase jets is given by Danon et al [11] and for two-phase pipe flows by Lee and Durst [12], while theoretical work has been reviewed by Elghobashi and Abou-Arab [13–14] and Abou-Arab and Abou-Ellail [15]. Soo [16], Hinze [17], and Rudinger [18] gave however, an excellent analysis for the mechanics of multiphase systems. Their analyses are mainly based on available experimental observations and the physics of the interaction between mutual phases.

Although the statistical equations for multiphase turbulent flow have been derived and modeled from an exact and general conservation equation form, it should be stressed here that this form is still a very important and rich subject for future research work. Soo [16], Rudinger [18], Buyevich [19] and many others gave different forms for these equations. For example, Soo [16] introduced a factor K (effectiveness of momentum transfer) into the drag term and pressure gradient term to interpret the shock-tube data of Rudinger [20]. However, Rudinger [20] interpreted his results on the basis of the relaxation of the particles within the shock wave. Buyevich [21] introduced another concept for the formulation of multiphase systems. He proposed a model for the effect of the random motion (pseudo-turbulence) of the dispersed phase on the mean motion of the carrier fluid in laminar multiphase flows. This "pseudo turbulence" has nothing in common with conventional turbulence, and is generated by the random motion of particles with respect to the surrounding fluid. Additional terms (stresses) will thus appear in the conservation equations of the fluids. Buyevich gave, in successive publications [22–24], the method for the determination of these terms via solution of constitutive equations for these stresses. Sato et al. [25] proposed another model for estimating these additional apparent stresses in a bubbly flow. They introduced a pseudo viscosity concept. This concept is based on empirical input parameters which are not yet validated for other flows. None of these equation forms seems to be certainly convincing, either due to the lack of physical manipulation of the governing equation terms or due to the insufficiently experimental verifications. To validate a form of the multiphase equation set, a work is undertaken [26] by the present author and co-authors. These equations are namely, mass and momentum as well as energy equations. For turbulent multiphase flows, however, an extra set of equtions is needed to close the previously mentioned equations. These are, in the case of using two-equation turbulence closure, for example, the specific kinetic energy of turbulence and its dissipation rate.

The theoretical work presented here will employ the two-equation model of Elghobashi and Abou-Arab [14] for two-phase flows. Extension to the cases of multisize and evaporating sprays will be also discussed. The two-phase turbulent flows tested with our model are for round free jet [27], evaporating sprays [28] and confined pipe flows [15, 29]. The numerical prediction of the flow when compared with the experimental data show promising progress in the turbulence modeling of multiphase flows. It indicates also the advantage of the model of Elghobashi and Abou-Arab [14] over the single phase and other two-phase turbulence models [11, 30].

Compressibility, wall effects, and particle transport in addition to the turbulence closure are all topics to be partially covered by this work.

FLOW-GOVERNING EQUATIONS

The construction of the governing balance equations in differential form is often not possible because of the lack of understanding of the physical processes involved [17]. So, everyone who attempts to obtain theoretical relations for the prediction of two-phase turbulent flows is forced to introduce a number of assumptions in order to arrive at some equation form, which then has to be further simplified in order to make it tractable.

When studying the literature on turbulent two-phase flows, it is striking that not all the consequences of the simplifying assumptions have been well appreciated or even understood with respect to the applicability of theoretical results and the correct interpretation of experimental data.

Thus, we begin the formulation of such problems by stating the assumptions invoked in the derivation of the governing equations. These are:

1. Both phases behave macroscopically as a continuum, but only the carrier fluid behaves microscopically as continuum. This means that the volume-averaged equations are based on a control volume larger than the particle spacing but much smaller than the characteristic volume of the flow system. Mutual exclusion of the phases is also ensured.
2. The dispersed phase consists of particles or droplets spherical in shape and uniform in size. The uniformity of size reduces the magnitude of book-keeping at this stage of the work, and thus concentrates the effort on under-standing the mechanisms of interactions between the two phases. It should be emphasized that this assumption does not pose a fundamental restriction to the equation to be presented; extension to nonuniform size distribution is a straightforward matter.
3. The volume fraction of the dispersed phase is such that no collisions occur between the particles or the droplets. This assumption renders the equations valid only for dilute suspensions.
4. Neither the suspended matter nor the carrier fluid undergoes any phase changes. Although this assumption rules out situations of practical interest, it is necessary to investigate complexities in a stepwise manner. The extension of the derived transport equations to govern the two-phase flow with evaporation is a very simple task and will be discussed later.
5. Bouyancy force is mainly due to the density differences between the phases.
6. The flow is assumed to be vertically downward. Under these circumstances, neither gravity nor electrical forces are acting on particles in the direction of the wall, so that the deposition (if it exists) is entirely due to fluid turbulence.
7. The roughness effect is ruled out by considering the wall to be smooth. Effect of roughness on the form of the flow-governing equations is also discussed.

Thus far, most practical turbulent flows have been treated largely as incompressible flows. In fact, no fluid is incompressible, but any fluid, in some range of flow conditions, is effectively incompressible. However, in problems of turbulent combustion, in the mixing processes, high-speed flows, and many other important systems, density fluctuations at some point in the flow may be of a magnitude comparable with that of the mean density of the carrier fluid at the same location. These density fluctuations are mainly due to the variations in temperature and/or pressure. Under such circumstances, any credible turbulent flow formulation must specifically address the influence large-density fluctuations will have on the transport of mass, momentum, energy, and turbulent fluxes.

Until about 1973 nearly all computational studies of variable density flows neglected any contribution of density fluctuations to the transport processes. More recently, turbulent flow studies have tended to follow one of two routes. In the first approach, the instantaneous density is represented as the sum of mean and fluctuating parts; therefore upon averaging the convective transport terms, correlations between fluctuating density and velocity will appear in the conservation equations, in addition to the conventional Reynolds stresses. This approach has been followed by Bray [31], Donaldson and co-workers [32], Janicka and Kollmann [33] and others. Those following this approach have, implicitly, invoked the principle of receding influence, since in the modeled transport equation form, uniform density modeling aspects have been adopted. Thus, if the flow is compressible and at the same time two phase, the transport equations will contain further correlations such as $\overline{\rho'\phi}$, $\overline{\rho'\phi u}$, etc., where ϕ is the void-fraction, u is velocity fluctuations, and ρ' is the density fluctuation and will have more uncertainties. The second and increasingly followed approach, originally proposed by Favre [34], adopts a mass weighting of velocity and other dependent variables except pressure. With this arrangement the transport equations governing any flow are simple in appearance [1]. This apparent simplicity has increased the hope that turbulence closure ideas evolved from the invariant density case would be directly applicable to variable density flows; one of the referees of a recent publication of the present author [14], who cited Kent and Bilger [35] and Jones [36], suggested that a mass-weighted averaging can be used to simplify the two-phase k-ε model transport equations. The reasons that we could not apply this type of averaging are

1. The expected simplicity of the exact equations in mass-weighted coordinates gives little guidance about how to tackle the problem.
2. Most practical two-phase flows involve both density fluctuation and volume-fraction fluctuation. A direct Favre-averaging would not be appropriate. A new method of averaging [37] is thus required.
3. A direct application of Reynolds-averaged closure modeling methods to density-weighted equations without adjusting the emperical coefficients to values that would give unacceptable predictions in uniform flows [37].
4. The two- as well as multiphase-flows involve, parallel to the theoretical study, an experimental investigation whose objective is to obtain data about turbulence structure in these flows. However, in most of the recent experimental studies in this area, the laser doppler (LDA) technique is usually adopted. LDA measures unweighted quantities. Thus, in comparing measurements with theory we must determine unweighted quantities from the theoretically evaluated density-weighted quantities; this is not a straightforward task and some assumptions have to be made.

In the present work, we will also discuss the approach of Ha Minh, Launder, and Mac Innes [37] in which they refer to it as a "mixed weighting," since in the transport equations both conventional and density-weighted velocity and velocity correlations appear. We noticed that when this approach is to be extended for the case of two-phase flows, different possibilities of the final transport equation forms could be achieved. Because, of space limitations, we give here only few examples, and most of the equations will appear in the severely truncted forms.

Mean Flow Equations

The instantaneous, volume-averaged momentum equations, in cartesian tensor notations, of the carrier (lighter) fluid are thus

$$(\rho_1\phi_1 U_i)_{,t} + (\rho_1\phi_1 U_j U_i)_{,j} = -(1 - K\phi_2)P_{,j} - KF\phi_2(U_i - V_i)$$
$$+ [\mu_1\phi_1(U_{i,j} + U_{j,i})]_{,j} - \tfrac{2}{3}(\mu_i\phi_1 U_{1,1})_{,j} \tag{1}$$

The corresponding equations for the dispersed phase are

$$(\rho_2\phi_2 V_i)_{,t} + (\rho_2\phi_2 V_j V_i)_{,j} = -\phi_2 P_i + F\phi_2(U_i - V_i) + [\mu_2\phi_2[(V_{i,j} + V_{j,i})]_{,j}$$
$$- \tfrac{2}{3}(\mu_2\phi_2 V_{1,1})_i + g_i\phi_2(\rho_2 - \rho_1) + f_i \tag{2}$$

The continuity equation for the dispersed phase is

$$(\rho_2\phi_2)_{,t} + (\rho_2\phi_2 V_i)_{,i} = 0, \tag{3}$$

and the global continuity is

$$\phi_1 + \phi_2 = 1 \tag{4}$$

In Equations 1–4 and throughout the paper the subscripts 1 and 2 denote the fluid and dispersed phase, respectively. Partial derivatives are represented by a subscript consisting of a comma and an index [e.g., $(\ )_{,t} = \partial(\ )/\partial t$; $U_{i,j} = \partial U_i/\partial x_j$; $U_{i,k1} = U_{i,1k} = \partial^2 U_i/\partial x_k \partial x_1$], U_i are the velocity components of the fluid, V_i is the velocity components of the dispersed phase, ρ and μ are the material density and viscosity, P is pressure, ϕ is the volume fraction, g_i is the component of gravitational acceleration in the i direction, f_i is the component of body forces other than that due to gravity and F is the interphase friction coefficient ($= 18\mu_1/d_p^2$ for Stokes' flow around a particle of diameter d_p). K is the local effectiveness of momentum transfer from the dispersed phase to the fluid and is discussed in detail by Soo [16] and others. In general, K depends on the local properties of the fluid and turbulence, the slip velocity, and the particulate size and concentration. It suffices here to state that K equals unity for accelerated dispersed phase and assumes lower values when this phase decelerates.

The mean flow equations are now obtained from the instantaneous ones, for constant material densities and viscosities of both phases by performing the conventional Reynolds averaging of Equations 1 and 2.

The mean momentum equations of the carrier fluid are:

$$(\rho_1\Phi_1 U_i + \rho_1\overline{\phi_1 u_i})_{,t} + (\rho_1\Phi_1 U_j U_i)_{,j}$$
$$= -(1 - K\Phi_2)P_{,i} + K[\overline{\phi_2}P_{,i} - F\Phi_2(U_i - V_i) - F\overline{\phi_2(u_i - v_i)}] + [\mu_1\Phi_1(U_{i,j} + U_{j,i})$$
$$+ \mu_1\overline{\phi_1(u_{i,j} + u_{j,i})}]_{,j} - \tfrac{2}{3}(\mu_1\Phi_1 U_{\ell,\ell} + \mu_1\overline{\phi_1 u_{\ell,\ell}})_{,i}$$
$$- (\rho_1\Phi_1\overline{u_i u_j} + \rho_1 U_i\overline{\phi_1 u_j} + \rho_1 U_j\overline{\phi_1 u_i} + \rho_1\overline{\phi_1 u_i u_j})_{,j} \tag{5}$$

The mean momentum equations of the dispersed phase are

$$(\rho_2\Phi_2 V_i + \rho_2\overline{\phi_2 v_i})_{,t} + (\rho_2\Phi_2 V_j V_i)_{,j}$$
$$= -\Phi_2 P_{,i} - \overline{\phi_2}P_{,i} + F[\Phi_2(U_i - V_i) + \overline{\phi_2(u_i - v_i)}] + [\mu_2\Phi_2(V_{i,j} + V_{j,i}) + \mu_2\overline{\phi_2(v_{i,j} + v_{j,i})}]_{,j}$$
$$- \tfrac{2}{3}(\mu_2\Phi_2 V_{\ell,\ell} + \mu_2\overline{\phi_2 v_{\ell,\ell}})_{,i} - (\rho_2\Phi_2\overline{v_i v_j} + \rho_2 V_i\overline{\phi_2 v_j} + \rho_2 V_j\overline{\phi_2 v_i} + \rho_2\overline{\phi_2 v_i v_j})_{,j}$$
$$+ g_i\Phi_2(\rho_2 - \rho_1) + f_i \tag{6}$$

The mean continuity equation of the dispersed phase is

$$\Phi_{2,t} + (\phi_2 V_i)_{,i} + (\overline{\phi_2 v_i})_{,i} = 0 \tag{7}$$

the mean global continuity is

$$\Phi_1 + \Phi_2 = 1 \tag{8}$$

In Equations 5–8 (and thereafter) capital letters denote time-mean quantities, lower case letters (except g_i and f_i) designate fluctuating components, and overbars indicate Reynolds-averaged correlations. Fluctuation of the carrier-phase velocities from the mean may be split further into two parts on the assumption that there are two kinds of turbulence in the carrier phase: one is independent of and the other is dependent on the particle agitation, designated as u_i, u_i'' respectively. According to the previous studies of Buyevich [22] and Sato et al. [25], derivations of the basic relations for the correlations arising due to these fluctuations (e.g., $\overline{u_i' u_i''}$ or $\overline{u_i'' u_i''}$) are given in detail. Buyevich's constitutive relations describing these quantities are similar to those of Reynolds stress transport equations; however, the manipulation of the terms is completely different. Sato et al. [25] on the other hand, gave a very simple approach for estimating these correlations. In this approach, the shear stress τ for the carrier fluid is identified as:

$$\tau = \tau_1 + \tau_t + \tau_p \tag{9a}$$

where τ_1 and τ_t are the conventional molecular and turbulent stresses, respectively, however, τ_p is the pseudo-turbulent stress ($\tau_p = -\rho_1 u_i' u_j'$) which arises due to the existence of a secondary phase in the carrier fluid. For simple shear flows, τ_p is given by:

$$\tau_p = -\rho_1\overline{u_1'' u_2''} = \rho_1 v''\frac{dU_1}{dy} \tag{9b}$$

in which v'' is the pseudo viscosity. As for the other eddy viscosity v_e, the following formula has been proposed for its estimation:

$$v'' = k_1(1 - \phi_1)\left(\frac{dp}{2}\right)V_r \tag{10}$$

where k_1 = an empirical constant

d_p and V_r = the mean particle diameter and relative velocity of the particles

Equation 10 is similar in form to the well-known virtual viscosity equation of a free turbulent flow such as a wake behind a solid body (v_t = turbulent kinematic viscosity = $k_1 \, bU_{1 \, max.}$ where b is the width of the mixing zone and $U_{1 \, max}$ is the maximum deficit velocity [38].

The last set of equations is only valid under the assumptions stated before. However, the extension of this equation set to the case of evaporating multiphase flow is straight-forward [28]. Thus, we assume that droplets of different sizes constitute different phases. This is from the point of view of "continuum" mechanics of a cloud of droplets, apart from the obvious definition of a multiphase system (mixture of phases of liquid droplets, and gas). Therefore, the continuous droplet size distribution will be divided into n intervals; d^k is the average diameter for droplets in the k-th diameter range. If d^s and d^L are the smallest and largest droplet diameters, then the sizes are ordered as follows:

$$d^s = d^n < d^{n-1} \ldots < d^1 = d^L \tag{11}$$

Thus, n different diameter ranges constitute correspondingly n dispersed phases and the evaporated mass with the surrounding gas constitute the carrier phase. Material properties for the different phases are also assumed to be constant.

The instantaneous, volume-averaged momentum equations, in cartesian tensor notations, of the carrier (lighter) phase in the axial direction are [14–39]:

$$(\rho_1\phi_1 U_i)_{,t} + (\rho_1\phi_1 U_i U_j)_{,j} = -\phi_1 P_{,i} - \sum_k F^k\phi^k(U_i - V_i^k) - \dot{m}^k\phi^k V_i^k$$
$$+ [\mu_1\phi_1(U_{i,j} + U_{j,i})]_{,j} \tag{12}$$

The corresponding equations for the k-th dispersed phase are

$$(\rho_2\phi^k V_i^k)_{,t} + (\rho_2\phi^k V_i^k V_j^k)_{,j} = -\phi^k P_{,i} + F^k\phi^k(U_i - V_i^k) - \dot{m}^k\phi^k V_i^k$$
$$+ \mu_2\phi^k(V_{i,j}^k - V_{j,i}^k)_{,j} + g_i\phi^k(\rho_2 - \rho_1)$$

The continuity equation for the k-th dispersed phase is

$$(\rho_2\phi^k)_{,t} + (\rho_2\phi^k V_i^k)_{,i} = -\dot{m}^k\phi^k \tag{14}$$

The momentum equations of the different phases in the radial direction are similar to those in the axial direction and are not shown here.

The global continuity is

$$\phi_1 + \sum_k \phi^k = 1 \tag{15}$$

Using the continuity equations for the different phases, Equations 12 and 13 can be written as

$$\rho_1\phi_1 U_{i,t} + \rho_1\phi_1 U_j U_{i,j} = -\phi_1 P_{,i} - \sum_k \phi^k(F^k + \dot{m}^k)(U_i - V_i^k) + \mu_1[\phi_1(U_{i,j} + U_{j,i})]_{,j} \tag{16}$$

$$\rho_2\phi^k V_{i,t}^k + \rho_2\phi^k V_j^k V_{i,j}^k = -\phi^k P_{,i} + F^k\phi^k(U_i - V_i^k) + g_i\phi^k(\rho_2 - \rho_1)$$
$$+ \mu_2[\phi^k(V_{i,j}^k + V_{j,i}^k)]_{,j} \tag{17}$$

where   k = the k-th dispersed phase

U_i = the velocity components of the carrier fluid

V_i^k = the velocity components of the droplets in the k-th diameter range

$\dot{m}$ = the evaporation rate per droplet volume

The equations of motion for the mean flow are obtained from the instantaneous ones by performing the conventional Reynolds decomposition and averaging of Equations 12 and 13. This yields for the carrier fluid

$$\rho_1(\Phi_1 U_i U_j)_{,j} = -\Phi_1 P_{,i} - \overline{\phi_1 p}_{,i} - \sum_k \Phi^k F^k(U_i - V_i^k) + \sum_k \dot{m}^k \Phi^k V_i^k$$

$$- \sum_k \overline{F^k \phi^k(u_i - v_i^k)} + \sum_k \overline{\dot{m}^k \phi^k v_i^k} + \mu_1[\Phi_1(U_{i,j} + U_{j,i}) + \overline{\phi_1(u_{i,j} + u_{j,i})}]_{,j}$$

$$- \rho_1(\Phi_1 \overline{u_i u_j} + U_i \overline{\phi_1 u_j} + U_j \overline{\phi_1 u_i} + \overline{\phi_1 u_i u_j})_{,j} \tag{18}$$

and for the k-th phase

$$\rho_2(\Phi^k V_i^k V_j^k)_{,j} = -\overline{\Phi^k P}_{,i} - \overline{\phi^k p}_{,i} + F^k \Phi^k(U_i - V_i^k) - \dot{m}^k \Phi^k V_i^k$$

$$+ F^k \overline{\phi^k(u_i - v_i^k)} - \dot{m}^k \overline{\phi^k v_i^k} + \mu_2[\Phi^k(V_{i,j}^k + V_{j,i}^k) + \overline{\phi^k(v_{i,j}^k + v_{j,i}^k)}]_{,j}$$

$$- \rho_2[\Phi^k \overline{v_i^k v_j^k} + V_i^k \overline{\phi^k v_j^k} + V_j^k \overline{\phi^k v_j^k} + \overline{\phi^k v_i^k v_j^k}]_{,j} + g_i \Phi^k(\rho_2 - \rho_1) \tag{19}$$

The mean continuity equation of the k-th phase is

$$\rho_2(\Phi^k V_i^k)_{,i} + \rho_2(\overline{\phi^k v_i^k})_{,i} = \dot{m}^k \Phi^k \tag{20}$$

The mean global continuity is

$$\Phi_1 + \sum_k \Phi^k = 1 \tag{21}$$

In Equations 18–21 the overbars indicate Reynolds-averaged correlations.

The evaporated liquid will diffuse into the surrounding gas. If we define the droplet vapor concentration C as the ratio of the evaporated mass within a control volume to the mass of the carrier phase in the same volume, then the instantaneous volume-averaged concentration equation (or the mean temperature equation) for the evaporating material is

$$(\rho_1 \phi_1 C)_{,t} + (\rho_1 \phi_1 C)_{,j} = (\rho_1 \phi_1 \delta C_{,j})_{,j} + \sum_k \phi^k \dot{m}^k \tag{22}$$

where δ is the mass diffusivity of the evaporating material in air. The equation of the mean concentration is obtained by the Reynolds decomposition and time averaging of the preceding equation:

$$(\rho_1 \Phi_1 U_j C)_{,j} = [\rho_1 \delta(\Phi_1 C_{,j} + \overline{\phi_1 c}_{,j})] = \sum \Phi^k \dot{m}^k - \rho_1(\overline{\phi_1 c}U_j + C\overline{\phi_1 u_j} + \overline{\phi_1 u_j c} + \Phi_1 \overline{u_j c})_{,j} \tag{23}$$

Mixed Weighted Averaging

We note that the velocity vector in the second term on the L.H.S of Equation 1 for example plays two roles. $\rho_1 \phi_1 U_j$ represents the continuous phase mass flow rate per unit area, while U_i is the specific x_i-momentum flux. Here these separate roles are brought into prominence by defining

$$\rho_1 \phi_1 U_j = G_j. \tag{24}$$

Let us introduce Equation 24 into Equation 30 and define the mean value of a dependent variable whose instantaneous and fluctuating parts are, respectively, Ψ and ψ by

$$\Psi = \frac{1}{2\pi} \int_{-T}^{T} \psi(t) \, dt, \qquad \psi(t) = \Psi + \psi \tag{25}$$

On averaging Equation 1 in the conventional way implied by Equation 25 we obtain, for a stationary turbulent compressible two-phase flow, the following equation form:

$$G_{i,t} + (G_j U_i)_{,j} = -[1 - K\Phi_2]P_{,i} + \overline{K\phi_2 p}_{,i} - KF[\Phi_2(U_i - V_i) + \overline{\phi_2(u_i - v_i)}]$$
$$+ [\mu_1\Phi_1(U_{i,j} + U_{j,i}) + \mu_1\overline{\phi_1(u_{i,j} + u_{j,i})}]_{,j} - \tfrac{2}{3}(\mu_1\phi_1 U_{\ell,\ell} + \mu_1\overline{\phi_1 u_{\ell,\ell}})_{,i}$$
$$- (\overline{g_j u_i})_{,j} \tag{26}$$

It is evident that the averaged forms of the transport equations governing the velocity field that arise from the present decompositions are more compact than those of the corresponding Reynolds averaged two-phase incompressible flow equations. In the same time, no density fluctuation correlations appear explicitly. This compactness does not carry over to the transport equations for turbulent correlations, however. This, we would argue, is a helpful feature for, if we are fortunate, the intrinsic physical interactions giving rise to the alteration of the mean field and turbulent structure will be reflected in the additional terms of $\overline{g_j u_i}$ transport equations.

The asymmetric mixed-weighted Reynolds stress, $\overline{g_j u_i}$, is now the most important quantity for which a turbulence model must be devised and that topic will be discussed in this section. The Reynolds stress $\overline{u_i u_j}$ can be usually written in this form:

$$\overline{u_i u_j} = -2v_t S_{ij} + \tfrac{2}{3}\delta_{ij} v_t S_{ii} + \tfrac{1}{3}\delta_{ij}\overline{u_m u_m} \tag{27}$$

μ_t is the turbulent kinematic viscosity defined as ($v_t^2 = C_\mu k^2/\varepsilon$ and can be determined from $k - \varepsilon$ model [14] (see Appendices A and B). The assumption that v_t in Equation 27 is a scalar forces the principal axis of $\overline{u_i u_j}$ and the mean strain rate S_{ij} to be aligned. This is true in pure strain, but not true in any flow with mean vorticity. Saffman [40] proposed a modified constitutive equation;

$$\overline{u_i u_j} = -2v_t S_{ij} + \tfrac{2}{3}\delta_{ij} v_t S_{ii} + \tfrac{1}{3}\delta_{ij}\overline{u_m u_m} - C_{11}\ell^2(S_{i\ell}\Omega_{1j} + S_{j\ell}\Omega_{\ell i}) \tag{28}$$

where $\Omega_{ij} = \tfrac{1}{2}(U_{i,}{}^{-j}U_{j,i})$ is the rotation tensor and C_{11} is constant of order unity. In a two-equation model of turbulence, the length scale ℓ could be expressed in terms of the kinetic energy $k = \tfrac{1}{2}\overline{u_i u_i}$ and its dissipation rate $\varepsilon = v_1\overline{(u_{i,k})^2}$. Equation 28 does produce the right sort of normal stress anisotropy in shear flows, but the new terms do not alter the shear stress, and hence Equation 28 works no better [40] than Equation 27 in practice. For the mixed-weighted correlation $\overline{g_j u_i}$ we propose, however, the following definition

$$\overline{g_j u_i} = -v_t(G_{i,j} + G_{j,i}) + \tfrac{1}{3}\delta_{ij}\overline{g_i u_i} + \tfrac{1}{3}\delta_{ij}G_{i,i} \tag{29}$$

The viscosity hypothesis—or more specifically the two-equation models—fail to predict the return to isotropy after the removal of strain, or the isotropizing of grid-generated turbulence. This failure arises because of the need for a constitutive equation for $\overline{u_i u_j}$. Thus one should not really expect two-equation models to be very general. In spite of the difficulties with models based on constitutive equations, the simplicity, success, and capability of the two-equations model in predicting with sufficient accuracy many flows makes them attractive. For completeness only the exact transport equation for the second moment correlation $\overline{g_j u_i}$ will be given in this work. This equation form can be obtained by multiplying the equation of motion for U_i by g_i, averaging and then adding it to the corresponding equation for G_j multiplied by u_i and averaged. In this connection, the "corresponding" G_j equation is formed by multiplying and dividing the U_j equation by $\rho_1\Phi_1$:

$$(G_k U_j)_{,k} = (G_k G_j \rho_1 \Phi_1)_{,k} = \frac{1}{\rho_1\Phi_1}[(G_k G_j)_{,k} - G_k U_j(\rho_1\Phi_1)_{,k}] \tag{30}$$

Then by straightforward manipulation we find that the transport equation of $\overline{g_j u_i}$ is described by the form shown in Appendix C. This equation is clearly more cumbersome in appearance than its incompressible counterpart. Moreover, further unknowns (e.g., second moment tensor $\overline{g_j g_k}$) are introduced. One should therefore be able to make fairly reasonable assumptions and simplifications to this equation on the ground that certain terms, although not negligible, cannot foreseeably be responsible for the mean flow field and turbulence structure changes in the case of any two-phase flow.

Turbulence Kinetic Energy and Dissipation Rate Equations

The first step in the derivation of the equations of the carrier fluid's turbulence kinetic energy ($k = \overline{u_i u_i}/2$) and its dissipation rate ($\varepsilon = v_1 \overline{u_{i,k} u_{i,k}}$) is to obtain a transport equation for u_i by subtracting Equation 5 from Equation 1. The k equation is produced by multiplying the u_i equation throughout by u_i and then time-averaging. The ε equation is obtained by differentiating the u_i equation with respect to x_k, multiplying throughout by $v u_{i,k}$ and finally time-averaging. Following the same procedure, similar equations could be also derived for the evaporating sprays.

The resulting k and ε equations are given in the Appendices A and B; however, the closure of these equations is now discussed

Modeling Technique

Closure of the Momentum and Concentration Equations

The turbulent correlations appearing in Equations 5–6 and 18–19 are of five types:

1. Correlations of velocity fluctuations with those of the volume fraction or concentration fluctuation, e.g. $\overline{\phi_1 u_i}$.
2. The pressure interaction correlation $\overline{\phi_2 p}_{,i}$.
3. Multiple correlations among various components of velocity fluctuations with those of the volume fraction or concentration fluctuation, e.g. $\overline{\phi_1 u_i u_j}$, $\overline{c u_i u_j}$.
4. Correlations of strain rate fluctuations with those of the volume fraction, e.g. $\overline{\phi_1 u_{i,j}}$.
5. Correlations between two scalars such as $\overline{\phi_1 c}$ or $\overline{u_i \phi_1 c}$.
6. Multiple correlations of various components of velocity fluctuations, e.g. $\overline{u_i u_j}$.

The first four types occur only due to the presence of the second phase; their modeling is discussed in the following.

The simplest and most common method for evaluating $\overline{\phi_1 u_i}$ or $\overline{c u_i}$ is to assume a gradient transport which gives:

$$\overline{\phi_1 u_i} = -(v_t/\sigma_\phi)\Phi_{1,i}. \tag{31}$$

where $v_t =$ the kinematic eddy viscosity ($C_\mu k^2/\varepsilon$)
  $\sigma_\phi =$ the turbulent Schmidt number of Φ

However, simple gradient transport is strictly correct only for situations where the size of the energy-containing eddies is much smaller than the distance over which the gradient of ϕ_1 varies appreciably. When this condition is not satisfied a counter-gradient transport may occur [41]. A more general approach is to solve a transport equation for $\overline{\phi_1 u_i}$, which in turn contains higher-order correlations that require modeling. In order to avoid additional complexities at present especially when the influence of the dispersed phase on the turbulence structure is not well understood we may adopt the model developed by Lumley [42] for the turbulent flux of passive scalar in inhomogeneous flows. According to this model, $\overline{\phi_1 u_i}$ is evaluated to a first-order from:

$$\overline{\phi_1 u_i} = -(v_t/\sigma_\phi)\Phi_{1,i} - \tfrac{1}{2}\Phi_1(v_t/\sigma_\phi)_{,i} \tag{32}$$

Equation 32 states that the turbulent flux consists of gradient transport in addition to a convective transport which vanishes in homogeneous (constant v_t) flows. It is also clear that counter-gradient diffusion is allowed in this model.

The correlation $\overline{\phi_2 p}_{,i}$ is decomposed into two terms, as proposed by Lumely [43] analogous to the treatment of a pressure-strain correlation. Thus

$$\overline{\phi_2 p}_{,i} = -\overline{\phi_1 p}_{,i} = \overline{p\phi_1}_{,i} - (\overline{\phi_1 p})_{,i} \tag{33}$$

The first term on the right, which provides a limit to the growth of $\overline{u_i \phi_1}$, is approximated by four terms according to Launder [44]; the first two are functions of the turbulent fluxes $\overline{u_i \phi_1}$, and the other two depend on the mean strain [43–45]. The final form is

$$\overline{p\phi_1}_{,i} = \rho_1(\varepsilon/k)[c_{\phi 1}\overline{u_i \phi_1} - \varepsilon_{\phi 2}(\overline{u_i u_\ell}/k - 2/3\delta_{i\ell})\overline{u_\ell \phi_1}] + \rho_1[0.8\overline{u_\ell \phi_1}U_{i,\ell} - 0.2\overline{u_\ell \phi_1}U_{\ell,i}] \tag{34}$$

the values of the constants $c_{\phi 1}$ and $c_{\phi 2}$, 4.3 and -3.2, respectively, are approximate at present due to insufficient experimental data [44]. It should be noted that inherent in Equation 34 is the assumption that the velocity time-scale is proportional to that of ϕ_1. A constant time-scale ratio is not true in general; however, in order to calculate the time scale of scalar variance independently one needs to solve, at least, two additional transport equations, one for the variance and the other for the dissipation rate of that variance [46]. This task lies, at present, beyond the scope of this work.

The second term on the right of Equation 33, though it is a divergence, is not in the form of a transport term [43]. It is modeled here in a manner similar to that of the first term. Starting from the equation of u_i and taking the divergence with respect to x_i one obtains:

$$\frac{1}{\rho}p_{,ii} = -2u_{i,k}U_{k,i} - (u_iu_k)_{,ik} + (\overline{u_iu_k})_{,ik}, \tag{35}$$

Now applying Green's theorem on the fluctuating pressure, multiplying the resulting equation by ϕ_1 and finally time-averaging we get

$$\overline{\phi_1 p} = \frac{\rho_1}{4\pi}\int_{vol.}\overline{(u_m u_n)_{,nm}\phi_1}\frac{d\,vol.}{r} + \frac{\rho_1}{2\pi}\int_{vol.}U_{n,m}\overline{(u_{n,m}\phi_1)}\frac{d\,vol.}{r} + \text{wall terms} \tag{36}$$

$$\underbrace{}_{\psi_1} \qquad \underbrace{}_{\psi_2}$$

where the primes denote points at the surface of the control volume over which integration is performed. Wall terms can be modeled in a similar way [43].

Now ψ_1 and ψ_2 are approximated by

$$\psi_1 = -c_{\phi 3}\rho_1 k^{1/2}\overline{u_m \phi_1} \tag{37}$$

and

$$\psi_2 = c_{\phi 4}\rho_1 \frac{k^{3/2}}{\varepsilon}U_{n,m}\overline{u_m \phi_1} \tag{38}$$

where $k^{1/2}$ and $k^{3/2}/\varepsilon$ represent isotropic velocity and length scales appropriate for the transport process considered, and $c_{\phi 3}$ and $c_{\phi 4}$ are constants of order 1.

Now Equations 33–34 and 36–38 complete the modeling of $\overline{\phi_1 p}_{,i}$.

The correlation $\overline{\phi_2 u_i u_j}$ may be evaluated by solving its transport equation. However in order to have a consistant level of closure we will adopt Launder's proposal [43] which gives

$$\overline{\phi_1 u_i u_j} - c_{\phi 5}(k/\varepsilon)[\overline{u_i u_\ell}(\overline{u_j \phi_1})_{,\ell} + \overline{u_j u_\ell}(\overline{u_i \phi_1})_{,\ell}] \tag{39}$$

where $c_{\phi 5}$ is a constant with a value of about 0.1. Equation 39 is also valid if c replaces ϕ.

The strain-rate volume-fraction correlations of the type $\overline{\phi_1 u_{i,j}}$ appear only multiplied by the molecular viscosity of the fluid and therefore will be neglected due to their relatively small magnitude. The correlations between any two scalars will also be neglected due to their relatively small value. The last correlation to be modeled in the momentum equations is that of the form $\overline{u_i u_j}$. Again, to be consistent with the present level of closure this quantity will be calculated from

$$\overline{u_i u_j} = -v_t[U_{i,j} + U_{j,i}] + 1/3\delta_{ij}\overline{u_m u_m} - \tfrac{2}{3}v_t\delta_{ij}U_{j,j} \tag{40}$$

This completes the modeling of the momentum equations.

Closure of the Turbulence Kinetic Energy Equation

The exact equation of the turbulence kinetic energy, k, for the carrier fluid appears in Appendix A and consists of 38 terms. They are classified into groups enclosed by brackets or braces; each group is labeled according to its particular contribution to the conservation of k.

The various correlations in these groups range from second to fourth order. We decide at the outset on neglecting all fourth order correlations such as $\overline{u_i \phi_1 (u_i u_\ell)}_{,\ell}$ and $\overline{u_i u_i u_\ell \phi_1}_{,\ell}$. Also the contribution to the diffusion of turbulence energy due to the pressure interaction $\overline{(u_i p)}_{,i}$ will be neglected because of its relatively small magnitude [47]. Now the remaining terms will be modeled.

The five transient terms will be collectively approximated by $(\rho_1 \phi_1 k)_{,t}$. The convection terms require no approximation. The production group contains the correlation $\overline{\phi_1 u_i u_\ell}$ which was evaluated earlier by Equation 39.

The pressure velocity-divergence correlation $\overline{pu_{i,i}}$ in the turbulent diffusion group cannot be neglected here since $u_{i,i}$ does not vanish in two-phase flows. $\overline{pu_{i,i}}$ is evaluated following the approach of Launder et al. [48]. Thus

$$2\frac{\overline{p}}{\rho_1}u_{i,i} = -c_1(\varepsilon/k)(\overline{u_i u_i} - 2k/3) - \frac{(c_2 + 8)}{11}(P_{ii} - 2/3P) - \frac{(30c_2 - 2)}{55}(2kU_{i,i})$$

$$- \frac{(8c_2 - 2)}{11}(D_{ii} - 2/3P) \tag{41}$$

where
$$\begin{aligned}
P_{ii} &= -2(\overline{u_i u_k}U_{i,k}) \\
P &= \tfrac{1}{2}P_{ii} \\
D_{ii} &= -2(\overline{u_i u_k}U_{k,i}) \\
c_1 &= 1.5 \\
c_2 &= 0.4
\end{aligned} \tag{42}$$

The fourth term, $\overline{u_i u_i (\rho_1 \Phi_1 u_\ell)}_{,\ell}$ in the same group can be decomposed as follows:

$$\overline{u_i u_i (\rho_1 \Phi_1 u_\ell)}_{,\ell} = \rho_1 \Phi_1 \overline{u_i u_i u_\ell}_{,\ell} + \overline{u_i u_i u_\ell}(\rho_1 \Phi_1)_{,\ell} \tag{43}$$

The first term on the right of Equation 43 is written as

$$\rho_1 \Phi_1 \overline{u_i u_i u_\ell}_{,\ell} = \rho_1 \Phi_1 [\overline{(u_i u_\ell)}_{,\ell} - \overline{u_\ell (u_i^2)}_{,\ell}] \tag{44}$$

The second term on the right of Equation 43 is modeled as

$$\overline{u_i u_i u_\ell}(\rho_1 \Phi_1)_{,\ell} = (\mu_t/\sigma_k)k_{,\ell}\Phi_{1,\ell} \tag{45}$$

The fifth term, $\rho_1 \Phi_1 \overline{u_i u_\ell u_{i,\ell}}$, in the turbulent diffusion group is rewritten as

$$\rho_1 \Phi_1 \overline{u_i u_\ell u_{i,\ell}} = \rho_1 \Phi_1 [\tfrac{1}{2}\overline{(u_i^2 u_\ell)}_{,\ell} - \tfrac{1}{2}\overline{u_i^2 u_{\ell,\ell}}] \tag{46}$$

Combining Equations 44 and 46 we get

$$\rho_1\Phi_1\overline{u_iu_iu_{\ell,\ell}} + \rho_1\Phi_1\overline{u_iu_\ell u_{i,\ell}} = \rho_1\Phi_1[\overline{(u_i^2u_\ell)}_{,\ell} - \tfrac{1}{2}\overline{u_\ell(u_i^2)}_{,\ell}] \tag{47}$$

Now, adding the right sides of Equations 45 and 47 and applying Equation 32 we obtain the total contribution to the turbulent diffusion of k by both the fourth and fifth terms in this group as

$$\{\Phi_1[(\mu_t/\sigma_k)_{k,\ell} + \tfrac{1}{2}k(\nu_t/\sigma_k)_{,\ell}]\}_{,\ell}$$

There are 8 terms in the extra production and transfer group, the last two of which are neglected for being of fourth order. The remaining six terms are modeled next.

The second term, $-\rho_1\Phi_1U_i\overline{u_iu_{\ell,\ell}}$, is modeled following the proposal of Harlow-Nakayama [49] as $\rho_1\Phi_1U_i\nu_tU_{\ell,i\ell}$. The correlation of the form $\overline{u_i(\phi_1u_\ell)}_{,\ell}$, which appears in the third and fourth terms, is expanded as

$$\overline{u_i(\phi_1u_\ell)}_{,\ell} = \overline{(u_i\phi_1u_\ell)}_{,\ell} - \overline{\phi_1u_\ell u_{i,\ell}} \tag{48}$$

where the first term on the right is evaluated using Equation 39, and the second term is modeled as:

$$\overline{\phi_1u_\ell u_{i,\ell}} = -c_{\phi5}(\varepsilon/k)[(\nu_t/\sigma_\phi)\Phi_{1,\ell} + \tfrac{1}{2}\Phi_1(\nu_t/\sigma_\phi)_{,\ell}] \tag{49}$$

The correlation ϕ_1u_i in the first and fifth terms has been discussed earlier.

The sixth term is approximated by

$$\rho_1U_iU_\ell\overline{u_i\phi_1}_{,\ell} = \rho_1U_iU_\ell[\overline{(u_i\phi_1)}_{,\ell} - \overline{\phi_1u_{i,\ell}}] \tag{50}$$

where $\overline{\phi_1u_{i,\ell}}$ is neglected for being relatively smaller than $\overline{u_i\phi_1}_{,\ell}$.

The extra dissipation group contains three terms which exist only due to the slip between the two phases. We first evaluate $\overline{u_\ell(v_\ell - u_\ell)}$ by defining the fluctuating slip-velocity w_ℓ as

$$w_\ell = v_\ell - u_\ell \tag{51}$$

Thus the ratio of the mean squares $\overline{w_\ell^2}$ and $\overline{u_\ell^2}$ becomes:

$$(\overline{w_\ell^2/u_\ell^2}) = (\overline{v_\ell^2} - 2\overline{u_\ell v_\ell} + \overline{u_\ell^2})/\overline{u_\ell^2} \tag{52}$$

Now the correlation $u_\ell v_\ell$ can be obtained from

$$\overline{u_\ell v_\ell} = \tfrac{1}{2}\overline{u_\ell^2}[1 + (\overline{v_\ell^2/u_\ell^2}) - (\overline{w_\ell^2/u_\ell^2})] \tag{53}$$

In order to evaluate the right side of Equation 53 we refer to Chao's solution [50] of the linearized Lagrangian equation of motion of a spherical particle in a turbulent fluid. Chao [50] obtained the relation

$$(\overline{w_\ell^2/u_\ell^2}) = \int_0^\infty (\Omega_R/\Omega_2)f(\omega)\,d\omega \tag{54}$$

where ω is the frequency of turbulence

$$\Omega_R = [(1 - \beta)\omega/\alpha\beta]^2 \tag{55}$$

$$\Omega_2 = \beta^{-2}(\omega/\alpha)^2 + \sqrt{6}\beta^{-1}(\omega/\alpha)^{3/2} + 3(\omega/\alpha) + \sqrt{6}(\omega/\alpha)^{1/2} + 1 \tag{56}$$

$$\alpha = 12\nu_1/d^2 \text{ for stoke's drag} \tag{57}$$

$$\beta = 3\rho_1/(2\rho_2 + \rho_1) \tag{58}$$

He also evaluated $(\overline{v_\ell^2/u_\ell^2})$ as

$$(\overline{v_\ell^2/u_\ell^2}) = \int_0^\infty (\Omega_1/\Omega_2)f(\omega)\, d\omega \tag{59}$$

where

$$\Omega_1 = (\omega/\alpha)^2 + \sqrt{6}(\omega/\alpha)^{3/2} + 3(\omega/\alpha) + \sqrt{6}(\omega/\alpha)^{1/2} + 1 \tag{60}$$

Substituting from Equations 54 and 59 into Equation 53 we get:

$$\overline{u_\ell(v_\ell - u_\ell)} = -\tfrac{1}{2}\overline{u_\ell^2}\left\{1 - \int_0^\infty [(\Omega_1 - \Omega_R)/\Omega_2]f(\omega)\, d\omega\right\} \tag{61}$$

Similarly for any higher-order correlation a combination of Equations 39 and 61 will yield the required closure form.

The Lagrangian frequency function $f(\omega)$ and Taylor's autocorrelation, R, are mutually the Fourier cosine transforms of one another. Thus:

$$R = \overline{u_i(t)u_i(t + \tau)}/\overline{u_i^2} = \int_0^\infty f(\omega) \cos \omega\tau\, d\omega, \tag{62}$$

and

$$f(\omega) = [4(\pi)^{3/2}\lambda/\sqrt{(\overline{u_i^2})}]e^{-(\lambda\omega)^2/4\overline{u_i^2}} \tag{63}$$

where λ is Taylor's microscale.

The dissipative action of the correlation $\overline{u_\ell(v_\ell - u_\ell)}$ can be now examined for a few limiting cases. When the two phases have equal densities ($\beta = 1, \Omega_1 = \Omega_2$ and $\Omega_R = 0$) the correlation vanishes and the second phase has no influence on the turbulence energy. The same result can be obtained for infinitesimally small particles or droplets where

$$\alpha \to \infty, \Omega_R \to 0$$

and

$$\Omega_1 = \Omega_2 = 1$$

On the other hand, when ρ_2 is much larger than ρ_1 (heavy particles in gas) or the diameter of the particles increases considerably, the correlation approaches the value of $-\tfrac{1}{2}\overline{u_\ell^2}$. In these cases the second phase significantly reduces the kinetic energy of turbulence.

The last term in the extra dissipation group contains the triple correlation $\overline{\phi_2 u_\ell v_\ell}$ which in the absence of experimental data is modeled in a similar manner to that of calculating $\overline{\phi_1 u_i u_j}$ in Equation 39, thus:

$$\overline{\phi_2 u_\ell v_\ell} = -c_{\phi 5}(k/\varepsilon)[\overline{u_\ell v_j}(\overline{v_\ell \phi_2}) + \overline{v_\ell u_j}(\overline{u_\ell \phi_2})]_{,j} \tag{64}$$

where the double correlations on the right side have been modeled earlier. The term $\mu_1\Phi_1\overline{u_i(u_{i,\ell} + u_{\ell,i})}_{,\ell}$ constitutes the dissipation of k due to viscous action, and if Φ_1 is set to unity, the term reduces to the single-phase dissipation case. This term is modeled as:

$$\mu_1\Phi_1\overline{u_i(u_{i,\ell} + u_{\ell,i})}_{,\ell} = \mu_1\phi_1[\overline{(u_{i,\ell} + u_{\ell,i})u_i}]_{,\ell} - \mu_1\Phi_1\overline{(u_{i,\ell} + u_{\ell,i})u_{i,\ell}} = -\rho_1\Phi_1\varepsilon \tag{65}$$

The last group in the k equation describes the viscous diffusion of k and will be neglected due to its relatively small magnitude as compared to the turbulent diffusion.

Closure of the Turbulence Energy Dissipation Rate Equation

The exact equation of the dissipation rate of turbulence energy, ε, for the carrier fluid appears in Appendix A and consists of 67 terms. They are classified into groups similar to those of the k equation.

Again we neglect all fourth-order correlations as mentioned in the previous section.

All the terms in the first group labeled transient are approximated collectively by $(\rho_1 \phi_1 \varepsilon)_{,t}$.

The convection group consists of 8 terms of which only the first and the second are of higher magnitude than the other six at large Reynolds numbers. This is based on an order-of-magnitude analysis [51], which shows that the first and second terms are greater than the others by at least a factor of (ℓ/λ), which is of order $(R_\ell)^{1/2}$. Here ℓ is the length scale of the energy containing eddies, λ is Taylor's microscale, and R_ℓ is the Reynolds number based on λ.

The third term in the production group is decomposed as

$$-2\rho_1 v_1 \Phi_1 (\overline{u_i u_{\ell,k} u_{i,k}})_\ell = -2\rho_1 v_1 \Phi_1 (\overline{u_{i,\ell} u_{\ell,k} u_{i,k}} + \overline{u_i u_{\ell,k\ell} u_{i,k}} + \overline{u_i u_{\ell,k} u_{i,k\ell}}) \tag{66}$$

The third term on the right side of Equation 66 and the second term in the production group differ only in their signs and thus both vanish. The first term on the right of Equation 66, which represents the production of ε by self stretching of the vortex tubes, is the dominant one at large Reynolds numbers. It is larger than the second term by a factor of R_ℓ and the first term by a factor of $R_\ell^{1/2}$.

We therefore retain only $-2\rho_1 v_1 \Phi_1 \overline{u_{i,\ell} u_{\ell,k} u_{i,k}}$ as the main generation of ε. This term and the extra production terms are modeled collectively as

$$-2\rho_1 v_1 \Phi_1 \overline{u_{i,\ell} u_{\ell,k} u_{i,k}} + \text{extra production terms} = c_{\varepsilon 1} G_k \varepsilon/k, \tag{67}$$

Where G_k is the total production of k discussed in the previous section, and $c_{\varepsilon 1}$ is a constant of value 1.43. Total here means the production terms which are common to the single-phase and two-phase k equations in addition to the extra production and transfer terms.

The turbulent diffusion group contains six terms. At high Reynolds numbers only the last two terms in the turbulent diffusion group will be retained; they are larger by at least a factor of $R_\ell^{1/2}$ than the other terms. These two turbulent diffusion terms will be modeled collectively as

$$[\Phi_1 (v_t/\sigma_\varepsilon)\varepsilon_{,\ell} + \tfrac{1}{2}\Phi_1 \varepsilon (v_t/\sigma_\varepsilon)_{,\ell}]$$

All the terms in the extra production group except the mean pressure gradient term are smaller than the main production term, modeled in Equation 67, by at least a factor of $R_\ell^{-1/2}$ and thus can be neglected. The mean pressure gradient term is included in the production term Equation 67. The first term in the dissipation group represents the main dissipation of ε; it reduces to the single-phase form when Φ_1 equals unity. This term is larger than the other terms in the group by a factor of $R_\ell^{3/2}$, and thus it is the only one retained. Now the total dissipation of ε includes this term in addition to the extra dissipation terms. They are modeled collectively as $c_{\varepsilon 2}\Phi_1 \varepsilon_t(\varepsilon/k)$ where ε_t equals ε plus the extra dissipation terms appearing in the k equation, and $c_{\varepsilon 2}$ is a constant of a value about 1.92. The evaporating spray's exact equations show, however, no new correlation than that existing in the no-phase-change case, and thus the same modeling technique will be adopted.

WALL EFFECT

Because a wall is ever present in almost any physical applications, some understanding of its influence on two-phase turbulent motion is needed. This is particulary significant when treating transport processes other than momentum transfer. In a heat-transfer process from a wall to a two-phase stream or vice versa for example, the particle motion near the wall affects predominantly this process [16]. Most of the existing analytical work is concentrated on the empirical correlation of heating augmentation with emphasis on the incompressible flow regime. These analytical models make it possible to monitor boundary-layer structure via detailed boundary-layer profiles while making global comparisons with skin friction or heating data. However, from the point of view of the present study, one weakness in all these approaches is that they are only valid for single-phase flows with constant density. The extension of these models to the present case is rather simple, but it needs modifications to their empirical correlations developed for single-phase flows. However, a deeper understanding appears to be necessary before any extension of the single-phase models to two-phase flows can be done. Little work has been reported on the motion of bounded fluids past small suspended particles, except for creeping flow [51]. The walls were found to delay the formation of an attached wake which, in turn, affects the drag coefficients and momentum transfer [16].

In addition to the effect of the walls on the particle drag force, the particle alters the shear on the duct and can experience two kinds of transverse force, the Magnus force and the slip-shear force, due to the presence of a velocity gradient in the fluid, such as the shear layer near a wall. The particles tend to migrate across the flow due to these lift forces, which are quadratic; that is, such lift forces are associated with inertia, which is usually excluded in the Stokes regime. Hence we may expect migration only at nonnegligible relative Reynolds numbers (based on the maximum fluid speed relative to the particle surface). This sort of migration can be important in certain flows such as the pipe flow, since it may result in a reduced concentration of particles in the viscous sublayer [9]. In the turbulent part of the flow, these forces may be expected to be much smaller than the other forces producing the turbulent motion of the particle in this part. However, near the wall the migration must be balanced against the progressively weaker transport by the fluctuating velocities (including large eddies). Although these lift forces and all other forces affecting the particle motion are usually calculated according to single-particle studies and under certain circumstances, it might be pointed out first of all this is not a stumbling block to the study of multiparticle systems. For rough walls, the present study recommends the extension of the concept of single-phase flow over rough walls to evaluate the properties of two-phase in the near-wall regions [52].

The particle forces, which develop from velocity differences between the particle and gas phase, are dependent on fluctuating random components of the turbulence. These forces are discussed for example by Crowe [53]. They are rewritten here in terms of the present notations. The forces considered include drag, Magnus, and Saffman lift, in the following order:

$$F_{p,j} = (\pi d_p^2/8)C_D\rho_1|U_j - V_j|(U_j - V_j) \qquad \text{drag force}$$

$$+ \varepsilon_{ijk}(\pi d_p^2/8)\rho_1(U_j - V_j)\omega_k \qquad \text{Magnus force} \qquad (68)$$

$$+ C_2\sqrt{\mu_1}\rho_1 d_p^2(U_j - V_j)\left|\frac{\partial U_j}{\partial x_n}\right|^{1/2} \qquad \text{Saffman force}$$

Including the virtual mass effect and the Basset history term is outside the scope of the present work. However, as explained by Gitterman et al. [54], the noninstantaneous Basset history term is not important from the point of view of the force balance on the particles; it is only important for the requirements of the second fluctuation dissipation theory [55], which result in changing the equation of motion of the particles from differential form to integral-differential form via modification of drag and lift, etc. In the foregoing force relations (Equation 68) we have introduced the particle diameter d_p; the drag coefficient C_D, which is dependent on the nature of both mean and fluctuating field; the assumed particle spin angular velocity ω_k in the plane of motion i, j; dynamic gas viscosity μ_1; the gas phase density ρ_1; and the notation n representing the gradient direction normal to the particle stream primary motion.

In Nikuradse's pioneering work [56] on turbulent incompressible single-phase flows through rough pipes, he introduced the concepts of the

- Hydraulically smooth (i.e. $k^+ < 5$ where $k^+ = ku*/v_1$ and k is the roughness height)
- Transitionally rough ($5 < k^+ < 60$)
- Fully rough ($k^+ > 60$) surfaces

The important experimental observation concerning the velocity profiles is that the roughness effect is confined to the inner region of the boundary layer. In the present case we can assume that the influences of the dispersed phase on the velocity defect law are manifested by a shift in the logarithmic profile in both sub-and buffer-layer, i.e.,

$$u^* = 2.5 \log y^+ + C - \Delta u^* \tag{69}$$

$$u^* = 2.5 \log(y/k) + B(k^+) \tag{70}$$

where   B = two-phase functions

Δu^* = logarithmic velocity shift

$$k^+ = \frac{d_p u^*}{v_1}$$

B and Δu^* are deduced from experimental measurements. However, very little has been done to develop a physical model from which B or Δu^* can be achieved. Thus we proposed the more general approach, which is based on the solution of the closed set of the mass, momentum, and modeled equation forms for the turbulent correlations (i.e., $\overline{u_i u_j}$, $\overline{u_i \phi}$, ...). Therefore we need to specify the boundary conditions for the turbulent correlations. Some of these conditions are given for compressible single-phase boundary layers by Reference 57; however, following similar approach to that of Lin et al. [52] we can define these conditions for the present case as follows:

$$1 = 1_w + 0.41y + 4.85\mu_w(\exp - y^+/11.83 - 1)/\rho u^+ \tag{71}$$

$$\sqrt{k} = (\mu_t/\rho\ell)c\mu^{-1} \tag{72}$$

$$(\mu_t)_v = \mu_w/2[(1 + 4\ell_w^{+2})^{1/2} - 1] \tag{73}$$

$$\ell_w^+ = (1.28 + 0.014k^+)[1 - \exp(-k^+/37)][1 - \exp(-k^+/2]^{14} \tag{74}$$

where $u^* = \sqrt{\tau/\rho_1}$, 1_w is estimated from Dahm's correlation μ_w the carrier viscosity at the wall, and $k^+ = d_p u^*/v_1$. The differences in the present rough-wall approach are that we introduce the particle size instead of roughness height in the preceding formulation and that the wall shear stress is calculated according to the two-phase concept

$$\tau_w = \Phi_1 \rho_1 (U_{iw} - V_{ip}) C_\mu^{1/2} k_p^{1/2} K/\ln(Ey^+) \tag{75}$$

where K = 0.4187, E = 9.79, and the subscript p and w denote node p and wall condition respectively.

DIFFUSION OF SUSPENDED PARTICLES

Basic studies of the transport of solid and liquid particles by gaseous flows and the motion of solid particles and gas bubbles in liquid flows have been the subject of numerous scientific and engineering investigations [58]. In a similar manner to turbulent transport of momentum, the turbulent transport of a scalar quantity such as temperature, mass, . . . , etc. suggests that the definition of a transport coefficient (simple gradient transport),

$$\varepsilon_{\Gamma_i} = -\overline{u_i\gamma}/(\partial\Gamma/\partial x_i) \tag{76}$$

in which Γ = local time average value of any scalar and γ is the turbulent fluctuation of this scalar. It is generally accepted that in the case of homogeneous turbulence, the turbulent transport of such scalar quantities can be modeled as gradient-type (or Fickian) transport, provided the diffusion time is large when compared with an integral time scale of the turbulence, the scalar quantity is passive and conservative, and the fluid is incompressible [17]. There seems to be less unanimity as regards inhomogenous turbulence. Corrsin [41], for instance, observes that the assumption of a place-dependent turbulent diffusivity tensor, which is quite common in practical application, is not necessarily the correct generalization of the result for homogenous turbulence.

A number of authors, most recently Corrsin [59], gave a detailed comparison for the performance of five different transport models, by which the gradient term was extended, for example, with a term representing turbulent convection not accounted for by the mean Eulerian velocity [42] and other similar extension approaches. Kronenburg [60] gave also an expression for turbulent transport of a passive scalar in a way such that in addition to the gradient and turbulent convection terms [42], he introduced an extra term proportional to material derivative of the mean concentration. These added terms as derived by various authors have a theoretical basis. They account for the phenomenon of a negative diffusivity in certain (small) regions of the scalar field and the inhomogeneity of the flows. Thus, we can write the turbulent flux of any scalar as follows:

$$-\overline{u_i \gamma} = \varepsilon_{ij} \frac{\partial \Gamma}{\partial x_i} + \mu_i \frac{\partial}{\partial x_i} \cdot \varepsilon_{ij} \frac{\partial \Gamma}{\partial x_j} \tag{77}$$

where ε_{ij} = diffusion coefficient
        μ_i = integral length scale

This model of Kronenburg as well as the other models are tested by Corrsin et al. [59], and the conclusion of their study was that the simple gradient transport model is perfectly adequate with a constant diffusivity for homogeneous flows, but it cannot handle inhomogeneous flows even qualitatively. The Kronenburg model appears to work reasonably well for mixing layers. However, it seems that none of the available generalizations of the gradient transport model has had reliable success in evaluating the turbulent transport in any inhomogeneous flow. A proposal by Spalding [60] and the probability density function approach of Pope [61] seem to be the only methods available for bypassing any gradient transport assumption. The study of Corrsin et al. [59] and indirectly the work by Hutchinson et al. [62] led us to propose that a gradient transport model, by which the diffusion exchange coefficients are obtained from a large-eddy simulation approach [63], may serve as a general tool for the determination of the scalar flux in any flow situation. Clearly, the success of the last proposal is limited by the accuracy of the large-eddy simulation approach.

All the phenomenological approaches just mentioned describe diffusion by following a marked "fluid lump" which maintains its identity as it is carried along by the flow. Assuming negligible molecular exchange, any contaminant contained in the "lump" will be adequately described, whether that contaminant be heat or trace molecules. Extremely small particles, which behave just like trace molecules as the particle radius becomes infinitesimal, will also be accurately described by these theories. i.e. these investigations theoretically treat the transport of particles by turbulent flows without taking into account the density difference between the particle material and the fluid, and the limit on the smallness of these particles. However, it is clear that as the particle size increases, diffusion will be opposed by particle inertia and fall out [9] and so once some critical particle size is exceeded, discrete particle diffusion must be treated in a different manner from "fluid lump" diffusion. Chandrasekhar [64] proved that the particle diffusion equation remains identical to the usual diffusion equation form.

Having mentioned in passing a number of the difficult aspects of two-phase flows about which, at our present stage of development, little can be done, we are ready to devote a lot of time to the relatively simple case in which much of all these aspects are excluded. For most practical applications ρ_2/ρ_1 values are ranging from 10^3 to 10^{-3}. The response of the particle to the carrying fluid is controlled by the physical properties of particles and the fluid, flow characteristics [65], and any external or surface force affecting its motion [9].

The aspects of heavy and large particles diffusion [66] are different than any other scalar [67], however the correlation $\overline{u_i \gamma}$ still has meaning even in the case of the transport of discrete particles as long as the time averaging is done so as to see a continuum in the scalar phase [58]. The unsuccessful attempts at a generalized prediction for v_t have introduced a justified element of uncertainty in the hopes of solving for ε_Γ in terms of properties of the flow field.

Most engineering approximations rely on the values of turbulent kinematic viscosity v_t (either from turbulence theories or from measurements) and deduce the turbulent scalar flux by first equating ε_Γ to $v_t = \varepsilon_f$). Their ratio

$$\varepsilon_f/\varepsilon_\Gamma = Sc \tag{78}$$

is called the turbulent Schmidt number. Engineering approximations usually state that $Sc = 1$. This assumption is inconsistent with any two-phase flow measurements or analyses (e.g., Chao [50], Tchen [17], and Yun et al. [68] Peskin [69]). A fundamental result of the turbulent diffusion theory of asserting that the turbulent diffusion coefficients of the particle and fluid moles are equal for a long diffusion time is obviously incorrect if the relative motion of the particles is significant [69]. Bueyvich [22] gave expressions of ε_f and ε_Γ (Γ = particle concentration) which are based on more sophisticated semiempirical hypotheses. Unlike the usual method for estimating ε_f by length-time and/or velocity scale, Bueyvich [22] gave an expression for ε_f and ε_Γ on the basis of the energy spectrum content for both phases following a method by Monin and Yoglom [70]. Reeks [71] pointed out that in the absence of a general transport equation it is assumed on the basis of the evidence for both passive-scalar and heavy particle motion in such turbulence that Fick's law is operative throughout the entire range of particle inertia, and thus that the particle diffusion coefficient ε_Γ uniquely determines the temporal evolution of the particle concentration. His analysis incorporated both the simultaneous effects of finite particle inertia and crossing trajectories due to the action of a constant external gravitational force. In the absence of external forces he showed that in the long time limit the particle diffusion coefficient will be greater than that of the fluid. This result differs significantly from the earlier work of Tchen [17] and Peskin [69] where the long-time particle diffusion coefficient was either the same as (Tchen) or less than (Peskin) that of the fluid. Lumley [9] made a rough estimation for the effects of particle-crossing trajectories and the inertia effect on the particle-diffusion coefficient. Lumley and more recently Nir and Pismen [72] found that the inertia has a slight effect on ε_p; however, the crossing-trajectory reduces ε_p by a large direction invariant factor:

$$\varepsilon_{p_z} = \varepsilon_f/(1 + 4V_T^2/9u'^2)^{1/2} \tag{79}$$

$$\varepsilon_{p_x} = \varepsilon_f/(1 + 16V_T^2/9u'^2)^{1/2} \tag{80}$$

where V_T = the particle fall velocity
        u' = isotropic velocity scale

While Tchen's [73] results are still widely used and cited, (Kuboi, Komasawa, and Otake [74]), Levins and Glastonburg [75] attempt to improve the theory using the intuitive concept of random encounters between a moving particle and fluid elements, along with Soo [16] and the notion of crossing trajecteries proposed by Yudine [76], Csandy [77], Meek and Jones [66]. These works have elucidated two basic mechanisms for the discrepancy between the diffusivities of fluid elements and foreign particles: a trend to increasing particle diffusivity due to inertial effects and a countering trend, usually stronger, to decreasing diffusivity due to the passing of a particle from one domain of strongly correlated fluid to another.

Finally, the studies by the previously mentioned authors as well as Johnston and Friedlander [78], Davis [79], Rouhiannen and Stachiewicz [80] and many other made a significant contribution to an understanding of some of the basic mechanisms of interaction between particles and the surrounding fluid. They correctly pointed out that $\varepsilon_p = \varepsilon_f$ is reasonable in some limited cases for particles of diameter much smaller than the microscale (Kolomogrov length scale) in other words for $d_p = 1\mu$ the assumption $\varepsilon_p = \varepsilon_f$ was found to become questionable. Peskin [69], however, derived the following formula for $\varepsilon_p/\varepsilon_f$:

$$\frac{\varepsilon_p}{\varepsilon_f} = 1 - (3/2)(L_L/\lambda)^2[Q^2/(Q+2)] \tag{81}$$

where

$$Q = 2\rho_2/FT_L$$

The local Lagrangian integral time scale, T_L, is evaluated assuming isotropic turbulence [51]; thus

$$\varepsilon = 15 v_1 \overline{u^2}/\lambda^2$$

and

$$\lambda^2 = 24 v_1 T_L$$

which gives

$$T_L = (5/12)k/\varepsilon$$

The local Lagrangian length scale, L_L, and the Eulerian microscale λ are calculated from

$$L_L = \sqrt{\frac{2}{3}k} \cdot T_L$$

$$\lambda = \sqrt{10 v_1 k/\varepsilon}$$

when L_L/λ is much less than unity the fluid elements in the neighborhood of the solid particle will have similar velocities (i.e., homogeneous flow). The Gittermann et al. [54] analysis, which is based on the memory effect and the dissipation theorem, shows that the diffusivity ratio can be given as follow:

$$\frac{\varepsilon_p}{\varepsilon_f} = \left(\frac{\overline{v^2}}{\overline{u^2}} \frac{J}{a} \right)^2 \tag{82}$$

where
$$J = \frac{1}{\tau_t} = \frac{\varepsilon}{k}$$

$$a = \frac{1}{T_r} = F$$

The only difference between the formula of Gittermann and that of Peskin is the introduction of the inverse time-scale ratio, which are assumed unity in Peskin's formula.

The particle transport in any two-phase flow is found to be affected also by the presence of a wall and a model for that is proposed by Johnston et al. [81]. Recently, Ganic et al. [82] gave an extended review for most of the pioneering research in this area, and they in turn proposed a more general expression for the particle deposition in the near-wall region. It is also shown that all existing theoretical treatments, except that of Lee and Durst [12], assume that the transport of particles from the core of the flow to the near-wall region (Stokes stopping distance or viscous sublayer thickness) is entirely controlled by turbulent diffusion. Only in the immediate vicinity of the wall, in the so-called viscous sublayer, the particles are taken to directly interact with the mean flow. On the dynamic behavior of a particle in the laminar sublayer, Rouhiainess et al. [80] made the important observation that the classical concept of the Stokes stopping distance cannot be valid, especially in the case of a dense particle passing through the sublayer, due to the effect of the shear-flow-induced-transverse lift force (as first derived by Saffman [83] who showed that it is not negligible). Actually, the importance of the inclusion of this lift force had already been recognized in the laminar two-phase flow analysis by Otterman and Lee [84]. The main weakness of the analysis of Rouhiainess et al. [80] lies in its lack of a suggestion of a rational scheme to link the two distinctly different flow regions—the turbulent diffusion core and the laminar sublayer. However, Lee and Durst [12] point out that the extents of the diffusion-controlled region and the mean-flow controlled region of the particle transport in turbulent flow are entirely defined by the frequency response characteristics [85] of the particle with respect to the surrounding eddy motion. They assumed a simple step function to approximate the particle frequency response to the most energetic eddy. This approximation permits the flow regime to be subdivided according to the particle size into two regions—a central region in which the particle transport is governed by turbulent diffusion

and an annular region in which the particle transport is due to direct particle mean flow interactions. Following Hinze's approach [17], they wrote the particle equation of motion in a simplified form, neglecting the external force

$$\frac{dV}{dt} + av = aU + b\frac{dU}{dt} + c \int_0^t [(dU/dt' - dV/dt')/\sqrt{(t - t')}] \, dt' \tag{83}$$

where $a = 36\mu_1/(2\rho_2 + \rho_1) \, d_p^2$,
    $b = 3\rho_1/(2\rho_2 + \rho_1)$, and
    $c = 18\sqrt{\rho_1\mu_1/\pi}/(2\rho_2 + \rho_1) \, d_p$

Expressing U and V by their Fourier integrals

$$U = \int_0^\infty (\xi \cos \omega t + \lambda \sin \omega t) \, d\omega \tag{84a}$$

$$V = \int_0^\infty \{\eta[\xi \cos(\omega t + \beta) + \lambda \sin(\omega t + \beta)\} \, d\omega \tag{84b}$$

in Equation 83, we obtain the amplitude ratio.

$$\eta = [(1 + f_1)^2 + f_2^2]^{1/2} \tag{85}$$

and the phase angle

$$\beta = \tan^{-1} f_2/(f_1 + 1) \tag{86}$$

where $f_1 = \omega[\omega + c(\pi\omega/2)^{1/2}](b - 1)/\{[a + c(\pi\omega/2)^{1/2}]^2 + [\omega + c(\pi\omega/2)^{1/2}]^2\}$

    $f_2 = \omega[a + c(\pi\omega/2)^{1/2}](b - 1)/\{[a + c(\pi\omega/2)^{1/2}]^2 + [\omega + c(\pi\omega/2)^{1/2}]^2\}$

The amplitude ratio has been shown to be directly related to the diffusional characteristics of
particles (e.g., see Tchen [17]) through the following expression:

$$\frac{\varepsilon_p}{\varepsilon_f} = \int_0^\infty \eta^2 E_f(n) \, dn \int_0^\infty E_f(n) \, dn \tag{87}$$

where $E_f(n)$ is the Lagrangian energy spectrum as a function on n-th wave number of frequency.
The frequency-response model proposed by those authors is given by a step function (Figure 1)

    I. Turbulent diffusion controlled range
    II. Mean fluid motion controlled range

$\eta = 0$

Region I and II are brought to join each other at ω_c, the cut-off frequency, which is obtained by
putting an intermediate value for $\eta = \frac{1}{2}$ say in Equation 85. This conclusion has been reached
on the assumption that a single value of the dominate eddy frequency, ω_e, can be identified to
characterize the turbulent motion at any given point in the flow in spite of the fact that the turbulent
fluid motion is characterized by a distribution of eddy frequencies. This distribution in frequency
can be in turn related to a distribution in eddy size. The ω_e distribution is obtained from the
most energetic eddy size distribution expression l_e, given by Townsend [8] and the V' (R.M.S.
fluctuations) distribution, given by Laufer.

$$\omega_e = \frac{V'}{l_e} \tag{88}$$

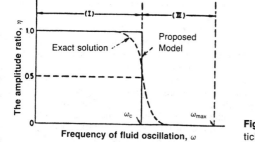

Figure 1. Model frequency response of particles.

Thus, now, Equation 85 gives ω_c for a given particle size d_p and physical properties of the particle and fluid.

The location of the joining boundary between the turbulent eddy diffusion-controlled region is then determined by the following matching condition.

$$\omega_e = \omega_c \tag{89}$$

$$\omega_e(r) = \omega_c(d_p, \rho_2/\rho_1, \mu_1)$$

Using Equation 89 a radial location is determined and defined as the cut-off radius r_c. Therefore, for a given flow system there is a fixed cut-off radius r_c $(0 \rightarrow 1)$ for a fixed particle size d_p. In the present work we proceed like Lee and Durst [12], except that

1. The assumption of equal diffusivities $\varepsilon_p = \varepsilon_f$ and the calculation of the length-scale functions from algebraic expressions are useful in many other shear flows. Thus a two-phase second-order closure similar to that of Elghobashi and Abou-Arab [11] should be used.

2. The frequency response model will be divided into three zones as in Figure 2.

Zone II at which

$$\omega_e = \frac{V'(x, r)}{1_e(x, r)} > \omega_{T2}$$

$$\omega_e \text{ from kE-model} = \frac{\varepsilon}{k}$$

when $\eta = 0$, the particle does not respond in any way to turbulent fluctuation.

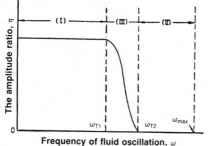

Figure 2. Model of frequency response of particles proposed by the author.

If $\omega_{T1} < \omega_e \leq \omega_{T2}$, the particle responds partially to the flow fluctuations, $\varepsilon_p \neq \varepsilon_f$, and the formulation for Schmidt number given before must be used.

In the case of $\omega_e < \omega_{T1}$ the particle completely follows the carrier fluid fluctuation. This is true according to the analysis of Tchen who showed that for infinitely long diffusion time $\varepsilon_p = \varepsilon_f$. This equality of ε_p to ε_f can be explained following Hinze [17]. According to the equation $\varepsilon_f = 1/4E_{FL}(0)$ (E_{FL} = Lagrangian energy spectrum function). The diffusion coefficient is proportional to the fractional kinetic energy contributed by the turbulent motion with zero frequency. The relations between the diffusion of fluid applications scalar are almost general (from the engineering applications point of view) and valid for both compressible and incompressible flows. However, the compressibility of the fluid affects theoretically the diffusion rates. Thus if we introduce a coefficient of diffusion to describe the diffusion process in a compressible fluid, we have to reckon with a value different from the value for an incompressible fluid. In a very recent paper by Drew and Lahey [88] it is noted that the lateral phase distribution observed in a solid-liquid system indicates that the compressibility effects cannot account completely for phase-distribution effects.

Modeled Form of the Flow Equations with No Phase Changes

The mean motion of each phase is governed by its momentum equations in the axial and radial directions and the conservation of its volume fraction. These equations were written in Cartesian tensor notations by Elghobashi and Abou-Arab [11]; they will be cast here in cylindrical coordinates for the axisymmetric flow (e.g., jet and pipe flow).

The modeled form [11] of the mean momentum equation of the carrier fluid in the axial (x) direction is:

$$\rho_1 \Phi_1 U_x U_{x,x} + \rho_1 \Phi_1 U_r U_{x,r} = -\Phi_1 p_{,x} - F\Phi_2(U_x - V_x)$$

$$+ \frac{1}{r}(\rho_1 \Phi_1 r v_t U_{x,r})_{,r} + c_{m1}\rho_1 U_{x,r}\left(\frac{v_t}{\sigma_\phi}\Phi_{1,r}\right)$$

$$+ c_{\phi 5}\frac{1}{r}\left(\frac{k}{\varepsilon}r\mu_t U_{x,r}\right)_{,r}\left(\frac{v_t}{\sigma_\phi}\Phi_{1,r}\right)_{,r}$$

$$+ c_{\phi 5}\frac{k}{\varepsilon}\mu_t U_{x,r}\left(\frac{v_t}{\sigma_\phi}\Phi_{1,r}\right)_{,rr} \qquad (90)$$

The momentum equation of the solid phase in the axial (x) direction is

$$\rho_2 \Phi_2 V_x V_{x,x} + \rho_2 \Phi_2 V_r V_{x,r} = -\Phi_2 p_{,x} + F\Phi_2(U_x - V_x) + \frac{1}{r}(\rho_2 \Phi_2 r v_p V_{x,r})_{,r}$$

$$+ (\rho_2 - \rho_1)g\Phi_2 + F_p \qquad (91)$$

where $c_{m1} = 0.4$ and $c_{\phi 5} = 0.1$.

In the preceding equations the comma-suffix notation indicates differentiation with respect to the spatial coordinates x and r. U and V are, respectively, the mean velocities of the carrier fluid and dispersed phase. The subscripts 1 and 2 denote respectively the carrier fluid and the dispersed phase. ρ is the material density, Φ the mean volume fraction, P the mean pressure, μ_t the eddy viscosity of the fluid, v_p the kinematic eddy viscosity of the dispersed phase, v_t the kinematic eddy viscosity of the fluid, σ_ϕ the turbulent Schmidt number of the volume fraction, g is the gravitational acceleration and F_p is the sum of Magnus and Saffman lift forces.

We assumed in the preceding equations that the diffusional fluxes in the radial direction are much larger than those in the axial direction for the flows considered. The momentum equations of both phases in the radial direction can be written in a similar manner and will not be presented here due to space limitation.

The quantities F and v_p are evaluated in the following section.

The Interphase Friction Factor F

The interphase friction factor F is given by

$$F = Z(18\mu_1/d_p^2) \tag{92}$$

where d_p = the particle diameter

μ_1 = the dynamic viscosity of the fluid

Z = a correction factor of the Stokes' drag law which depends on the particle Reynolds number and can be obtained from the standard drag curve of steady flow around a sphere [89] as follows

$$Z = 1 + 0.1315 \, Re(0.82 - 0.05 \log_{10} Re), \, 0.01 < Re < 20$$

and

$$Z = 1 + 0.1935 \, Re^{0.6305}, \, 20 < Re < 260$$

The particle Reynolds number Re is calculated from

$$Re = d_p|\vec{u} - \vec{v}|/v_1 \tag{93}$$

where $|\vec{u} - \vec{v}|$ is the magnitude of the total relative velocity vector between the two phases, and v_1 is the kinematic viscosity of the fluid.

Turbulent Diffusivity of Solid Particles

The turbulent diffusivity of solid particles is evaluated by introducing the particle Schmidt number σ_p defined as:

$$\sigma_p = \frac{v_t}{v_p} \tag{94}$$

Since solid particles do not in general follow the motion of the surrounding fluid from one point to another, it is expected that σ_p will be different from unity and vary with the particle relaxation time and local turbulence quantities. Alonso [90] reviewed the recent developments in evaluating σ_p and recommended the use of Peskin's [69] formula,

$$\frac{v_p}{v_t} = (1/\sigma_p) = 1 - (3/2)(L_L/\lambda)^2[Q^2/(Q + 2)] \tag{95}$$

where

$$Q = (2\rho_2/ZFT_L) \tag{96}$$

The local Lagrangian integral time scale, T_L, is evaluated assuming isotropic turbulence [91], thus

$$\varepsilon = 15v_1u^2/\lambda^2 \text{ and } \lambda^2 = 24v_1T_L \text{ which give}$$

$$T_L = (5/12)k/\varepsilon \tag{97}$$

The local Lagrangian length scale, L_L, appearing in and the Eulerian microscale λ are calculated from

$$L_L = \sqrt{\frac{2}{3}} k \cdot T_L \tag{98}$$

$$\lambda = \sqrt{10 v_1 k / \varepsilon} \tag{99}$$

When L_L / λ is much less than unity the fluid elements in the neighborhood of the solid particle will have similar velocities (i.e., homogeneous flow).

Consequently, the correlation of fluid velocities encountered by the particle will be similar to the Lagrangian fluid correlation and σ_p, from Equation 95, will approach unity. On the other hand as L_L becomes larger than λ the particle will be surrounded by random fluid velocities and its diffusivity will decrease relative to that of the fluid.

The Turbulence Model

The modeled form of the turbulence kinetic equation (k) of the carrier fluid; according to Elghobashi and Abou-Arab [11] is;

$$\rho_1 \Phi_1 U_x k_{,x} + \rho_1 \Phi_1 U_r k_{,r} = \rho_1 \Phi_1 v_t U_{x,r} U_{x,r} + \frac{4}{3} \rho_1 c_{\phi 5} \frac{v_t}{C_\mu} \left(\frac{v_t}{\sigma_\phi} \Phi_{1,r} \right)_{,r} U_{r,r}$$

$$- \rho_1 c_{\phi 5} \left(\frac{k}{\varepsilon} \right)_{v_t} \left(\frac{v_t}{\sigma_\phi} \Phi_{1,r} \right) U_{x,r} U_{x,r}$$

$$- F\Phi_2 k \left[1 - \int_0^\infty \left(\frac{\Omega_1 - \Omega_R}{\Omega_2} \right) f(\omega) \, d\omega \right] - F(U_r - V_r) \left(\frac{v_t}{\sigma_\phi} \Phi_{1,r} \right)$$

$$+ c_{\phi 5} \left(\frac{v_t}{C_\mu} \right) F \left[1 - \int_0^\infty \left(\frac{\Omega_1 - \Omega_R}{\Omega_2} \right) f(\omega) \, d\omega \right] \left(\frac{v_t}{\sigma_\phi} \Phi_{1,r} \right)_{,r} \tag{100}$$

The turbulence energy dissipation rate equation (ε) is

$$\rho_1 \Phi_1 U_x \varepsilon_{,x} + \rho_1 \Phi_1 U_r \varepsilon_{,r} = c_{\varepsilon 1} \frac{\varepsilon}{k} \left[\rho_1 \Phi_1 v_t U_{x,r} U_{x,r} + \frac{4}{3} \rho_1 c_{\phi 5} \left(\frac{v_t}{C_\mu} \right) \left(\frac{v_t}{\sigma_\phi} \Phi_{1,r} \right) U_{r,r} \right.$$

$$\left. - \rho_1 c_{\phi 5} \left(\frac{k}{\varepsilon} \right) v_t \left(\frac{v_1}{\sigma_\phi} \Phi_{1,r} \right)_{,r} U_{x,r} U_{x,r} \right]$$

$$- c_{\varepsilon 3} \frac{\varepsilon}{k} \left[F\Phi_2 k \left(1 - \int_0^\infty \left(\frac{\Omega_1 - \Omega_R}{\Omega_2} \right) f(\omega) \, d\omega \right) \right.$$

$$+ F(U_r - V_r) \left(\frac{v_t}{\sigma_\phi} \Phi_{1,r} \right)$$

$$\left. - c_{\phi 5} \left(\frac{v_t}{C_\mu} \right) F \left(1 - \int_0^\infty \left(\frac{\Omega_1 - \Omega_R}{\Omega_2} \right) f(\omega) \, d\omega \right) \left(\frac{v_t}{\sigma_\phi} \Phi_{1,r} \right)_{,r} \right]$$

$$+ \rho_1 \Phi_1 \frac{1}{r} \left(\frac{v_t}{\sigma_\varepsilon} r \varepsilon_{,r} \right)_{,r} - c_{\varepsilon 2} \frac{\varepsilon}{k} (\rho_1 \Phi_1 \varepsilon) \tag{101}$$

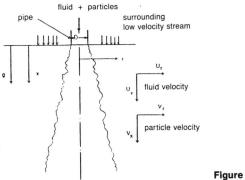

Figure 3. Flow schematic.

The items in Equations 100 and 101 involving integration in the frequency domain (ω) represent additional dissipation of k or ε due to the slip between the particles and the fluid and depend on the magnitude of correlation between their respective instantaneous velocities.

The Lagrangian frequency function $f(\omega)$ is in general affected by the presence of the dispersed phase. In the low-frequency range (inertial subrange), the modulation of the Lagrangian frequency function of the carrier fluid by the dispersed phase can be neglected. Thus in the present work the Lagrangian frequency function is given by Hinze [17].

$$f(\omega) = \left(\frac{2}{\pi}\right)\left(\frac{T_L}{1 + \omega^2 T_L^2}\right) \tag{102}$$

where ω ranges from 1 to 10^4 (sec^{-1}) and T_L is calculated from Peskin's formula [69]. The functions $\Omega_1, \Omega_2, \Omega_R, \alpha$, and β are evaluated from Equations 55 and 60.

The Flow Considered

Figure 3 shows a sketch of the two-phase turbulent jet considered in this work. Air carrying uniform-size glass beads issues vertically downwards from a cylindrical pipe of diameter D($=.02$ m). The jet is enclosed in a cylindrical container of a diameter equal to 30 D to avoid ambient disturbances. A low-velocity air stream surrounds the nozzle and extends to the container wall to provide well-defined boundary conditions. Table 1 lists the experimental conditions at 0.1 D downstream of the pipe exit.

Model Constants

The values of the coefficients appearing in Equations 100 and 101 are listed in Table 2. It is seen that three new coefficients ($\sigma_\phi, c_{\phi 5}, c_{\varepsilon 3}$) are now added to the well-established k-ε coefficients for single-phase flows, namely, $\sigma_k, \sigma_\varepsilon, c_\mu, c_{\varepsilon 1}$ and $c_{\varepsilon 2}$.

The values of the new coefficients have been optimized to produce good agreement with the data of References 92 and 93 for one particle size (200 microns) and then used to predict the data of the other size (50 microns). It should be emphasized that more validation testing is required to establish the universality of these coefficients.

Boundary Conditions

The parabolic flow considered here requires the prescription of three boundary conditions for each dependent variable. Table 1 provides these conditions at the pipe exit plane and at the jet

Table 1
Experimental Flow Conditions at 0.1D Downstream of Nozzle Exit

Phase	Quantity	Case 1	Case 2	Case 3
Gas (air)	Center line velocity $(U)_{x,c}$	12.6	12.6	13.4
	Exponent n, of power law velocity profile $(U_x/U_{x,c}) = [1 - (2r/D)]^{1/n}$	6.6	6.6	6.6
	Turbulence intensity $(u_x/U_{x,c})$		$(0.04 + 0.1\ r/D)$	
	Density, ρ_1 (kg/m^3)	1.178	1.178	1.178
	Mass flow rate $\dot{m}_1$ (kg/s) $= \rho_1(\pi/4D^2)U_x\Phi_1$	3.76×10^{-3}	3.75×10^{-3}	4×10^{-3}
	Reynolds number $Re = (4\dot{m}_1/\pi\mu_1 D)$ $= (\rho_1 U_x \Phi_1 D/\mu_1)$	13,300	13,300	14,100
	Uniform mean velocity of surrounding stream, $U_{x,s}$ (m/s)	0.05	0.05	0.05
	Intensity of turbulence in surrounding stream $(U_{xs}/U_{x,s})$	0.1	0.1	0.1
solid (glass beads)	Particle size d_p (microns)	50	50	200
	Particle density, ρ_2 (kg/m^3)	2,990	2,990	2,990
	Mass flow rate $\dot{m}_2$ (kg/s) $= \rho_2\pi/4D^2 V_{x2}$	1.2×10^{-3}	3.2×10^{-3}	3.2×10^{-3}
	Ratio of mass flow rates $(\dot{m}_2/\dot{m}_1)$	0.2	0.85	0.8
	Ratio of volumetric flow rates: Φ_2/Φ_1 $\Phi_2/\Phi_1 = (\dot{m}_2/\dot{m}_1)(\rho_1 U_{x,av}/\rho_2 V_{x,av})$	1.19×10^{-4}	2.9×10^{-4}	3.52×10^{-4}
	Centerline velocity, $V_{x,c}$ (m/s)	12.4	12.4n	10.2
	Exponent "n" of power law velocity profile	27.60	27.60	70.60

Table 2
Coefficients of the Turbulence Model

σ_ϕ	σ_k	C_μ	σ_ε	$c_{\phi 5}$	$c_{\varepsilon 1}$	$c_{\varepsilon 2}$	$c_{\varepsilon 3}$
1	1	$k - \varepsilon_1$ [91]	1.3	0.1	1.44	$k - \varepsilon_1$ [91]	1.2

boundary. At the axis of symmetry ($r = 0$) all the radial gradients are set to zero, in addition to the vanishing radial velocity of each phase.

Numerical Solution Procedure

The marching finite-difference procedure employed in this work is a modified version of that developed and described by Spalding [94] for laminar two-phase flows and thus only a brief outline is given here.

The coordinates of the expanding finite-difference grid are x and ψ, the stream function based on the mean gas-phase properties, i.e.

$$\psi = \int_0^r \rho_1 \Phi_1 U_x r dr$$

The steps followed to obtain the solution at a given axial location are:

1. Guess the downstream Φ_1^* distribution.
2. Solve for U_x downstream.
3. Solve for k and ε; obtain r's and solve for U_r's.
4. Obtain p(r) from U_r equation.
5. Solve for downstream V_x, V_r, Φ_2, and get Φ_1.
6. Compare the new Φ_1 with the guessed Φ_1^* and repeat Steps 1 through 5 until the solution converges before marching to the next station.

It was found that 3 iterations are needed at each station to achieve convergence.

RESULTS AND DISCUSSIONS

Two-Phase Jet Flow

The results presented here were obtained using 40 lateral nodes to span the flow domain between the centerline of the jet and its outer edge. Grid-dependence tests were conducted with 30, 40, and 50 lateral nodes and different axial step sizes and concluded that the 40-node grid results are virtually grid independent. In what follows we compare the predicted with the measured distributions of the mean velocities, volume fractions of the two phases, turbulence intensity, and shear stress of the gaseous phase and the jet spreading rate.

Figure 4 shows the radial profiles of the mean axial velocities of the two phases at $x/D = 20$, normalized by the centerline velocity of the single-phase jet, $U_{c,s,ph}$. The flow conditions are those of Case 3 in Table 1. Also shown is the mean velocity profile of the turbulent single-phase jet having the same Reynolds number (14,100) at the pipe exit.

It is seen that the centerline velocity of the dispersed phase is about 1.8 times that of the carrier fluid, although the latter is 1.3 times the former at the pipe exit. This can be explained by the fact that large-diameter ($> 10 \mu$) particles do not respond well to the fluid turbulent fluctuations (Equations 95 and 96), which indicate that for a fixed ρ_2 and T_L we get $v_p \ll v_t$ for small F (i.e., large

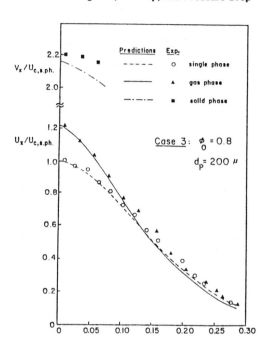

Figure 4. Mean velocity profiles at x/D = 20 for case 3.

d_p; thus the main force that accelerates a particle in the radial direction is the viscous drag exerted on the particle by the fluid having radial velocity, U_r. This drag force is proportional to $(U_r - V_r)$, and since U_r is negative in the outer region of the jet (and $V_r < U_r$), the resulting force will be directed inwards, thus limiting the radial spread of the particles. This is evident in Figure 5 where the concentration of the solid particles vanish at a radial distance of $r/x = 0.12$ while the fluid

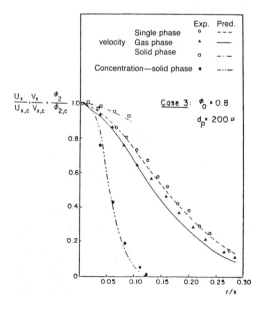

Figure 5. Normalized mean velocity at volume fraction profiles at x/D = 20 for case 3.

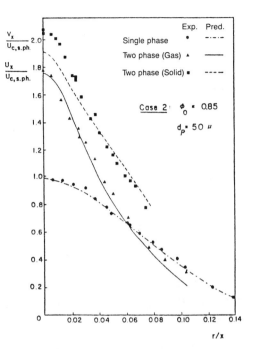

Figure 6. Mean velocity profiles at x/D = 20 for case 2.

spreads to at least three times this distance. Conservation of momentum of each phase then results in the solid-phase axial velocity being much higher than that of the fluid, and in turn the particles continue to be a source of momentum for the fluids. It is also clear from Figure 5 that the single-phase jet is wider than the particle-laden jet; this will be discussed later in this section. Both Figures 5 and 6 display in general good agreement between the measured and predicted velocity and concentration profiles.

The measured and predicted mean velocity profiles for case 2 ($d_p = 50\ \mu$, $\Phi_0 = 0.85$, Re = 13300) are shown in Figure 6. Similar qualitative behavior to that of case 3 is exhibited here except that now the ratio between the experimental velocities of the solid and the fluid is only about 1.15 instead of 1.8 in case 3 ($d_p = 200\ \mu$, $\Phi_0 = 0.8$, Re = 14,100). The main difference between the two cases is the particle diameter, and thus any quantitative change in the mean velocity profiles is attributed to the interphase surface area acted on by the viscous drag. This surface area in case 2 is four times that in case 3, since, for nearly the same loading ratio, the number of the 50 μ particles is 64 times that of the 200 μ particles. This increase in the number of particles and interphase area results in augmenting the momentum sources of the carrier fluid thus reducing the rate of decay of its centerline velocity.

The agreement is very good between the measured and predicted fluid velocity while the solid-phase velocity is underestimated by 8% in the inner region, a discrepancy well within the bounds of experimental error. Figure 7 shows the mean velocity profiles at x/D = 20 for case 1 (50 μ, Re = 13,300, $\Phi_0 = 0.32$), which has a lower loading ratio, Φ_0, than case 2; otherwise the two cases are identical. Again the behavior of the two phases is similar to that observed in the other two cases except that now the experimental ratio between the centerline velocities of the solid and the fluid is 1.2 instead of 1.15 in the higher-loading cases (case 2). This indicates that other conditions being the same higher loading reduces the rate of decay of the fluid centerline velocity. This is a result of the increase in the number of particles and hence their contribution to the fluid momentum as discussed earlier.

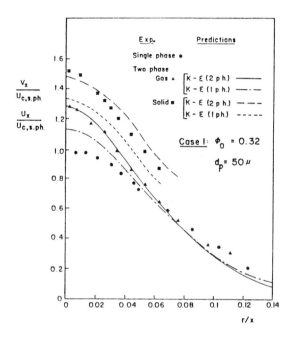

Figure 7. Mean velocity profiles at x/D = 20 for case 1.

In order to distinguish between the dispersed-phase effects on the mean motion (inertia and drag) and on turbulence (diffusion) we show Figure 7 the mean velocity profiles obtained by solving the complete two-phase momentum Equations 9 and 91 together with the single-phase k and ε Equations 100 and 101 without the additional production and dissipation terms due to the dispersed phase. We see that the resulting increase in the fluid centerline velocity, as compared to that of the single-phase jet, is only half that measured and predicted by the new k-ε model. Stated differently, the modulation of the fluid mean-velocity profile by the dispersed phase is not only due to the particles inertia and drag but equally important due to the additional turbulence dissipation. This in turn reduces the fluid momentum diffusivity with the result of a peaked velocity profile near the jet centerline. The additional turbulence dissipation is caused mainly by the fluctuating particle slip velocity and its correlation with the fluid velocity fluctuation [11]. The consequent reduction in the fluid turbulence intensity and shear stress is displayed in Figures 8 and 9 where the agreement between the measurement and prediction is good.

Figure 10 shows the effect of the dispersed phase on the spreading rate of the jet by comparing the different $Y_{1/2} \sim x$ distributions of the three cases, where $Y_{1/2}$ is the radius at which the fluid mean axial velocity is half that at the centerline. While for a turbulent single-phase jet the value of the slope $(dY_{1/2}/dx)$ is constant $(=0.08)$, that for a two-phase jet is a function of the dispersed phase properties such as particle diameter and density and loading ratio. This dependence is displayed in the figure. For case 3 ($d_p = 200\ \mu$, $\Phi_0 = 0.8$) the predicted slope value is 0.053, for case 2 ($d_p = 50\ \mu$, $\Phi_0 = 0.85$) it is 0.046, and for case 1 ($d_p = 50\ \mu$, $\Phi_0 = 0.32$) it is 0.064. Cases 2 and 3 have nearly the same loading ratio but the particle diameter in the latter is one quarter that of the former; the result being a reduction of the spreading rate by more than 13%.

Cases 1 and 2 are identical except that the loading ratio in the latter is 2.66 times that of the former; the result being a reduction of the spreading rate by 28%.

The figure also shows the discrepancy that results in predicting the spreading rate if the single-phase k-ε model is used instead of the proposed model. The former predicts for case 1 a slope of 0.072 while the latter agrees with the experimental value of 0.064. As explained earlier this is due to the fact that the additional dissipation of turbulence energy due to the dispersed phase is accounted for in the proposed model.

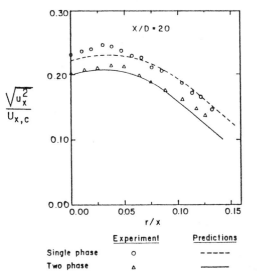

	Experiment	Predictions
Single phase	o	- - - - -
Two phase	△	———

Figure 8. Turbulence intensity profile at x/D = 20 for case 3.

Confined Two-Phase Pipe Flows

Without Heat Transfer

The numerical computations presented in this study are also carried out for an upward flow of air with dispersed glass-bead particles. To compare the prediction with the experimental data of Lee and Durst [12] four values for the particles diameter (100, 200, 400, and 800 μ) are assigned

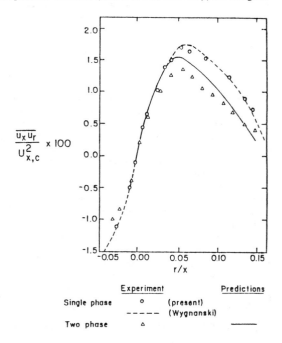

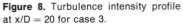

Figure 9. Turbulence shear stress profile at x/D = 20 for case 3.

	Experiment		Predictions
Single phase	o	(present)	———
	- - - -	(Wygnanski)	
Two phase	△		

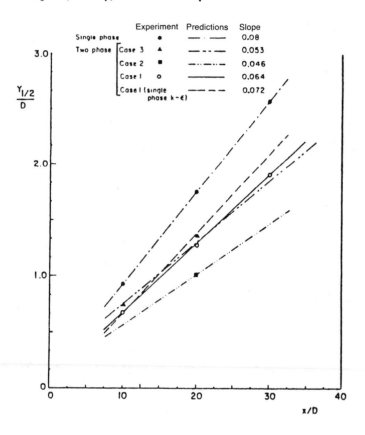

Figure 10. Jet spread rates for the three cases.

for the computations. The initial values (U_0 = initial centerline velocity, concentration kg solids/kg air, and d_p = particle diameter) are also similar to those Lee and Durst [12]. These are some comments about the data used in the present task. Moreover, it should be mentioned that in the computations, a nonuniform grid was employed in the radial direction while a uniform grid was used in the axial direction. For the domain considered, a grid having 15 nodes in the radial direction is found enough to give the grid-independent solution. Marching is however continued in the axial direction until fully developed profiles are obtained.

The measured [12] and predicted mean velocity profiles for the four particles sizes and four loading ratios considered are depicted in Figures 11–14. The agreement between the data and the computations is satisfactory in most cases. With particles the mean velocity profile flattens in the center of the pipe but becomes steeper in the region near the wall. The quantitative change in the mean velocity profiles for the four cases is probably attributed to the interface viscous drag acting over a surface area, which is proportional the particle diameter.

Although the agreement between data and predictions is excellent for the gaseous phase, the solid phase velocity profiles are overestimated 20% to 40% for larger and smaller particles, respectively. This deviation can be attributed to the assumption in the formulation of turbulent diffusivities for both phases.

Satisfactory agreement between data and fluctuation correlations can be obtained; however, excellent agreement can only be achieved if the previously mentioned interactions as well as all other

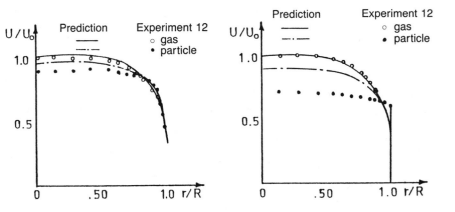

Figure 11. Radial distribution of the axial flow velocities of gas and solid phases and particle diameter 100 um, loading ratios; 58×10^{-3} kg/kg, inlet mean flow velocity $U_0 = 5.7$ m/s)

Figure 12. Radial distribution of the axial flow velocities of gas and solid phases (particle diameter 200 um loading ratio 6.63×10^{-3} kg/kg, inlet mean flow velocity $U_0 = 5.84$ m/s)

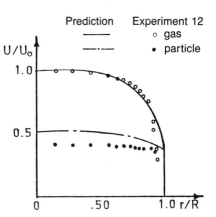

Figure 13. Radial distribution of the axial flow velocities of gas and solid phases (particle diameter 400 um, loading ratios 0.32×10^{-3} kg/kg, inlet mean flow velocity $U_0 = 5.77$ m/s)

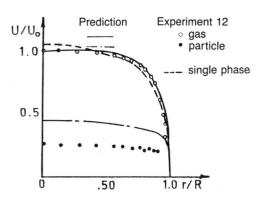

Figure 14. Radial distribution of the axial flow velocities of gas and solid phases (particle diameter 800 um, loading ratio 1.21×10^{-3} kg/kg, inlet mean flow velocity $U_0 = 5.66$ m/s)

effects are considered in the turbulence closure. The prediction shows however that the turbulence intensity for the two-phase flow can be smaller than that of a clear gas in the case of very fine suspended particles.

With Heat Transfer

The carrying gas properties were always evaluated at the mixed mean temperature T_M. This temperature was calculated from the global integral form of the energy balance at each section;

$$T_M = \frac{\int_A Cp_g r_g u_g T_g dA + \int_A Cp_p r_p v_p T_p dA}{\int Cp_g r_g u_g dA + \int_A Cp_p r_p v_p dA}$$

The Reynolds number is based only on the air flow rate W, and it is given by

$$Re = \frac{4W}{\pi D \mu}$$

where D is the pipe diameter. However the local Nusselt number is defined as

$$Nu = \frac{hD}{k_g}$$

where h is the local heat transfer coefficient given by

$$h = \frac{q_t}{T_w - T_M}$$

Also the nondimensional temperature θ is defined throughout this work for gases and solids as follow:

$$\theta_g = (T_g - T_{in}) k_g/q_t D$$

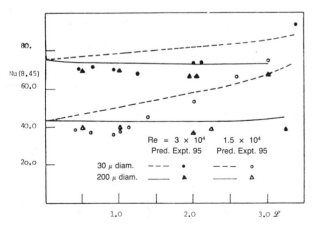

Figure 15. Nusselt number variations versus loading ratio ($\mathscr{L}$).

and

$$\theta_s = (T_s - T_{in}) \, k_g/q_t D$$

Both theoretical [29] and experimental results [95] are presented in Figures 15–20. However, because of the numerous factors affecting the rate of heat transfer from the pipe wall to both flow phases, it seems necessary to plot only the figures that illustrate efficiently the effect of each factor. The Nusselt numbers at $x/D = 8.45$ (designated by Nu (8.45)) versus loading ratios are shown in Figure 1, and those at $x/D = 46.4$ in Figure 16. These x/D stations are those at which experimental data [95] are available.

From Figure 16, it is seen that for 30-μ glass particles the Nusselt number increases as the solids rate is increased. The Nusselt number at a longer axial distance from the entrance has similar variations as shown from this figure. For any loading ratio of the 30-μm glass particles, it is noticed that Nusselt number is of higher value compared with pure air. However, for the 200-μm glass particles, a slight decrease at lower loading ratios is noticed. Summarizing the previously mentioned events, it is easily remarked that the Nusselt number decreases to a critical value as the solids rate (200 μm) is increased whatever the value of the Reynolds number. Experiment 95 shows however a decrease of the Nusselt number to a critical value as the solids rate is increased. After this point, Nu (46.4) for Re $= 1.5 \times 10^4$ begins to show a small increase with the loading ratio, while Nu (46.4) for Re $= 3 \times 10^4$ still decreases but at a lesser rate. The predictions could not obtain such a variation with the Reynolds number; however, both theory and experiment show a dominant effect of smaller-size particles than the coarser ones on the air heat transfer. This can be attributed to their higher number density, i.e., for the same loading ratio the smaller in size particles will count more than the larger. Also, the smaller particles allow larger interphase transport for both heat and

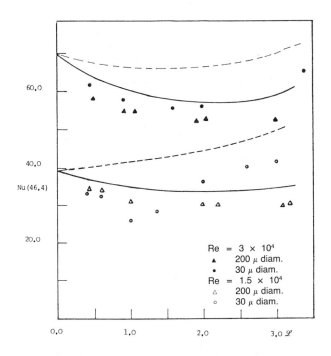

Figure 16. Fully developed Nusselt number variations versus loading ratio ($\mathscr{L}$).

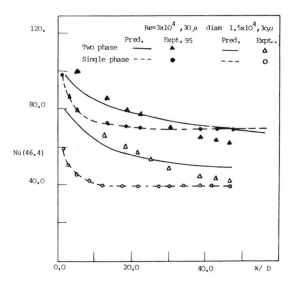

Figure 17. Fully developed Nusselt number variations at different axial stations.

momentum due to their higher surface-volume ratio and the decrease of the inverse relaxation parameters. The uncertainty in the near-wall treatment for the solid and gas phases could also contribute to differences between theory and experiment. The authors are currently considering this point, and improvement of the near-wall treatment will be separately reported. The agreement between the predictions and experimental values is fairly good.

At a Reynolds number of 3.0×10^4 the change in the heat transfer coefficient as a result of the presence of solids is smaller than at a Reynolds number of 1.5×10^4. This could be experimentally

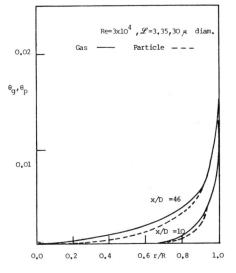

Figure 18. Radial distribution of nondimensional temperature for both phases.

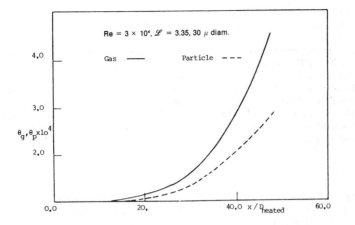

Figure 19. Axial distribution of nondimensional temperature for both phases.

as well as theoretically justified [96]. Probably, at higher Reynolds numbers the interphase coefficients have decreased effects on the heat transfer.

The variation of the local Nusselt number Nu with axial distance is depicted in Figure 17. For 30-μ glass particles, and at each Reynolds number, one curve is plotted for a loading ratio of about 3. Other curves are plotted for different loading ratios. The curve for pure air is included only for comparison. The thermal entrance length is found to become longer as more solids are added to the air stream. This finding is well supported from both the theory and experiment.

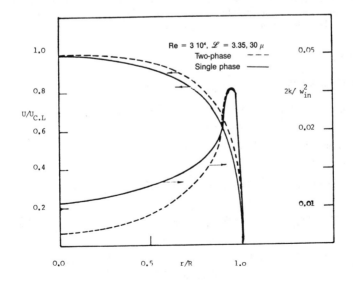

Figure 20. Radial distribution of mean flow and particle velocity and the specific kinetic energy of turbulence with and without particles.

Figures 18 and 19 depict the radial and axial distribution of nondimensional temperature distributions for both the gas and solid phase. Experimental data, with our limited knowledge of multiphase flows, are not available.

Similar to hydrodynamics, a temperature difference between the phases is built up within the core of the flow. This difference is initially smaller in value and increases with the flow development. This can be clearly shown in Figure 19. The differences in temperature between phases are mainly due to the differences in their heat capacities as well as the hydrodynamic slip between the phases and the possibility of the noncontinuum behavior of the solids in the near wall region. It is recommended that better formulation for the law of the wall is badly needed for this region. The variation of the ratio of the turbulent diffusion coefficients of both phases with the local flow properties should be also considered.

CONCLUSIONS

Existing theoretical models of turbulent multiphase flows are based on ad hoc modifications of the single-phase turbulent kinetic energy and length-scale equations. As a result, the models fail to predict the physical behavior of two-phase flows.

The present approach rests on the rigorous derivation of the turbulence kinetic energy and length-scale equations from the multiphase momentum equations and the provision of the exact and modeled form of these equations.

This work presents the Reynolds and mixed weighted-averaged set of transport equations for both incompressible and compressible turbulent dilute multiphase flow with and without evaporation. The equations are written in Cartesian-tensor notation form, making them applicable to any turbulent process satisfying the assumption embodied therein in any arbitrary geometry.

The proposed closure of the equations accounts for the interaction between the phases and its influence on the turbulence structure. The closed set of equations has been solved numerically to predict the flow of a turbulent two-phase jet with [28] and without [27] evaporation and confined two-phase pipe flow with [6] and without [15] heat transfer. Comparison of the prediction with experimental data indicates that the new turbulence model of Elghobashi and Abou-Arab predicts the significant effects of the dispersed phase on the flow and heat transfer of the carrying fluid.

However, the author recommends further testing and validation via well-defined experiments of this model to check the universality of the model coefficients.

APPENDIX A

The turbulence kinetic energy ($k \equiv \overline{u_i u_i}/2$) equation of the carrier fluid is

$$[(\rho_1 \phi_1 \overline{u_i u_i}/2)_{,t} + \overline{u_i \phi_\ell}(\rho_1 U_1)_{,t} + \rho_1 U_1 \overline{u_i \phi}_{1,t} + \rho_1 \overline{u_i(\phi_1 u_i)}_{,t} + \rho_1 \overline{u_i u_i} \Phi_{1,t/2}]$$

Transient

$$+ [(\rho_1 \Phi U_1 \overline{u_i u_i}/2)_{,\ell} + (\overline{u_i u_i}/2)(\rho_1 \Phi_1 U_\ell)_{,\ell}]$$

Convection

$$= [-\overline{u_i u_\ell}(\rho_1 \Phi_1 U_i)_{,\ell} - \overline{\phi_1 u_i u_\ell}(\rho_1 U_i)_{,\ell} - \overline{\phi_1 u_i u_i}(\rho_1 U_\ell)_{,\ell}]$$

Production

$$+ [(1 - K\Phi_2)\overline{pu}_{i,i} - (1 - K\Phi_2)(\overline{u_i p})_{,i} - K\overline{\phi_1 u_i p}_{,i} - \overline{u_i u_i(\rho_1 \Phi_1 u_\ell)}_{,\ell} - \rho_1 \Phi_1 \overline{u_i u_\ell u_{i,\ell}}]$$

Turbulent Diffusion

$$+ [-K\overline{\phi_1 u_i} P_{,i} - \rho_1 \Phi_1 U_i \overline{u_i u_{\ell,\ell}} - \rho_1 U_i \overline{u_i(\phi_1 u_\ell)}_{,\ell} - \rho_1 U_\ell \overline{u_i(\phi_1 u_i)}_{,\ell} - \rho_1 \overline{\phi_1 u_i}(U_i U_\ell)_{,\ell}]$$

Extra Production and Transfer

$$- U_i U_\ell \overline{u_i(\rho_1 \phi_1)}_{,\ell} - \rho_1 \overline{u_i \phi_1(u_i u_\ell)}_{,\ell} - \overline{u_i u_i u_\ell(\rho_1 \phi_1)}_{,\ell}]$$

$$+ \left[KF\Phi_2\overline{u_i}(v_i - u_i) + KF\overline{\phi_2 u_i}(V_i - U_i) + KF\overline{\phi_2 u_i(v_i - u_i)}\right] + \left[\mu_1\Phi_1\overline{u_i(u_{i,\ell} + u_{\ell i})}_{,\ell}\right]$$

Extra Dissipation   Dissipation

$$+ \left\{\mu_1\overline{u_i(u_{i,\ell} + u_{\ell,i})}\Phi_{1,\ell} + \overline{\phi_1 u_i}[\mu_1(U_{i,\ell} + U_{\ell,i})]_{,\ell}\right.$$

Viscous Diffusion

$$+ \mu_1\overline{u_i\phi_{1,\ell}}(U_{i,\ell} + U_{\ell,i}) + \mu_1\overline{\phi_1 u_i(u_{i,\ell} + u_{\ell,i})}_{,\ell}$$

and Dissipation

$$+ \mu_1\overline{u_i\phi_{1,\ell}}(u_{i,\ell} + u_{\ell,i}) - \tfrac{2}{3}\mu_1\left[\Phi_1\overline{u_i u_{\ell,i\ell}} + \overline{u_i u_{\ell,\ell}}\Phi_{1,i} + \overline{\phi_1 u_i U_{\ell,i\ell}} + \overline{u_i u_{\ell,\ell}\phi_1}\gamma_{i,}\right.$$

$$\left.+ \overline{\phi_1 u_i u_{\ell,i\ell}} + \overline{u_i\phi_{1,i}U_{\ell,\ell}}\right]\}.$$

The exact equation of ε is

$$\left\{(\rho_1\Phi_1\varepsilon)_{,t} + 2v_1\overline{u_{i,k}[u_i(\rho_1\Phi_1)_{,k}]}_{,t} + 2\rho_1 v_1\overline{[\phi_{1,k} U_i]_{,t} u_{i,k}} + 2\rho_1 v_1\overline{u_{i,k}[U_{i,k}\phi_1]}_{,t}\right.$$

Transient

$$+ (\rho_1 v_1\overline{\phi_1 u_{i,k}u_{i,k}})_{,t} + \rho_1 v_1\overline{u_{i,k}u_{i,k}}[\Phi_1 + \phi_1]_{,t} + 2\rho_1 v_1\overline{u_{i,k}[\phi_{1,k}u_{i,t} + u_i\phi_{1,tk}]}\} +$$

$$\left[(\rho_1\Phi_1 U_\ell\varepsilon)_{,\ell} + \varepsilon(\rho_1 U_\ell\Phi_1)_{,\ell} + 2v_1(\rho_1\Phi_1{}^1 U_i)_{,\ell}\overline{u_{\ell,k} u_{i,k}} + 2v_1(\rho_1\Phi_1 U_i)_{,k}\overline{u_{\ell,\ell} u_{i,k}}\right.$$

Convection

$$+ 2v_1(\rho_1\Phi_1 U_i)_{,\ell k}\overline{u_\ell u_{i,k}} + 2\rho_1 v_1[(\Phi_1 U_\ell)_{,k}\overline{u_{i,\ell}u_{i,k}} - (\Phi_1 U_\ell)_{,\ell k}\overline{u_i u_{i,k}}] + 2\rho_1 v_1\Phi_1 U_i\overline{u_{\ell,\ell k}u_{i,k}}\right]$$

$$= \left[-2\rho_1 v_1\Phi_1\overline{u_{i,k}u_{i,k}u_{\ell,\ell}} + 2\rho_1 v_1\Phi_1(\overline{u_i u_{\ell,k}u_{i,k\ell}}) - 2\rho_1 v_1\Phi_1(\overline{u_i u_{\ell,k}u_{i,k,k}})_{,\ell}\right] + \{2v_1 FK[\Phi_2\overline{u_{i,k}v_{i,k}}\right.$$

Production

$$+ \overline{v_i u_{i,k}}\Phi_{2,k} - \Phi_2\overline{u_{i,k}u_{i,k}} - \overline{u_i u_{i,k}}\Phi_{2,k} + \overline{\phi_2 u_{i,k}}V_{i,k} + V_i\overline{u_{i,k}\phi_{2,k}} - \overline{\phi_2 u_{i,k}}U_{i,k} - \overline{u_{i,k}\phi_{2,k}}U_i$$

Extra Dissipation

$$+ \overline{\phi_2 v_{i,k}u_{i,k}} + \overline{v_i u_{i,k}\phi_{2,k}} - \overline{\phi_2 u_{i,k}u_{i,k}} - \overline{u_i u_{i,k}\phi_{2,k}}] - 2\rho_1 v_1\overline{u_i u_\ell u_{i,k}}\Phi_{1,\ell k}$$

$$- 2\rho_1 v_1\Phi_{1,k}\overline{(u_i u_{\ell,\ell} + u_\ell u_{i,\ell})u_{i,k}} - 2\rho_1 v_1\overline{u_i u_{\ell,k}u_{i,k}}\Phi_{1,\ell} - 2v_1\overline{P_{,ki}u_{i,k}}$$

Turbulent Diffusion

$$- 2\rho_1 v_1\Phi_1\overline{u_\ell u_{i,k}u_{i,\ell k}} - 2\rho_1 v_1\overline{u_\ell u_{i,k}u_{i,k}}\Phi_{1,\ell}\} + \{2v_1\overline{(K\Phi_2 P_{,i})_{,k}u_{i,k}} - 2v_1 K\overline{\phi_1 u_{i,k}}P_{,ki}$$

$$- 2v_1\overline{u_{i,k}(K\phi_1)_{,k}}P_{,i} - 2v_1\overline{(K\phi_1 P_{,i})_{,k}u_{i,k}} - 2v_1\overline{u_{i,k}[u_{\ell,k}(\rho_1\phi_1 U_i)_{,\ell} + u_{\ell,\ell}(\rho_1\phi_1 U_i)_{,k}]}$$

$$- 2\rho_1 v_1\overline{\phi_1 U_i u_{\ell,\ell k}u_{i,k}} - 2\rho_1 v_1\overline{u_\ell(\phi_1 U_i)_{,\ell k}u_{i,k}} - 2\rho_1 v_1\overline{\phi_1 U_\ell u_{i,\ell k}u_{i,k}} - 2\rho_1 v_1\overline{u_i(\phi_1 U_\ell)_{,\ell k}u_{i,k}}$$

$$- 2\rho_1 v_1\overline{[(\phi_1 U_\ell)_{,\ell} u_{i,k}u_{i,k} + u_{i,\ell}u_{i,k}(\phi_1 U_\ell)_{,k}]} - 2\rho_1 v_1\overline{[U_i U_\ell\phi_{1,\ell k}]}$$

Extra Production

$$+ \overline{\phi_{1,k}(U_i U_{\ell,\ell} + U_\ell U_{i,\ell})]u_{i,k}} - 2\rho_1 v_1\overline{[\phi_1(U_{i,\ell}U_\ell)_{,k} + U_i U_{\ell,k}\phi_{1,\ell} + \phi_1(U_{\ell,\ell}U_i)_{,k}]}$$

$$- 2\rho_1 v_1\overline{[U_\ell U_{i,k}\phi_{1,\ell} + u_i u_\ell\phi_{1,\ell k} + \phi_{1,k}(u_i u_{\ell,\ell} + u_\ell u_{i,\ell})]u_{i,k}}$$

$$- 2\rho_1 v_1\overline{[\phi_1(u_i u_{\ell,k})_{,\ell} + u_i u_{\ell,k}\phi_{1,\ell} + \phi_1(u_\ell u_{i,k})_{,\ell} + u_\ell u_{i,k}\phi_{1,\ell}]u_{i,k}}\}$$

$$+ \{2\rho_1 v_1^2\overline{u_{i,k}[\phi_1(u_{i,\ell} + u_{\ell,i})]_{,k\ell}} + 2\rho_1 v_1^2\overline{u_{i,k}[\phi_1(U_{i,\ell} + U_{\ell,i})]}_{,k\ell} + 2\rho_1 v_1^2\overline{u_{i,k}[\phi_1(u_{i,\ell} + u_{\ell,i})]}_{,k\ell}$$

Dissipation

$$- \tfrac{4}{3}\rho_1 v_1^2\overline{[(\phi_1 u_{\ell,i\ell})_{,k}u_{i,k}} + \overline{u_{i,k}(u_{\ell,\ell}\phi_{1,i})_{,k}} + \overline{(\Phi_1 u_{\ell,i\ell})_{,k}u_{i,k}} + \overline{u_{i,k}(u_{\ell,\ell}\Phi_{1,i})_{,k}}$$

$$+ \overline{(\phi_1 U_{\ell,i\ell})_{,k}u_{i,k}} + \overline{u_{i,k}(\phi_{1,i}U_{\ell,\ell})_{,k}}]\}$$

APPENDIX B: EXACT EQUATIONS OF TURBULENCE KINETIC ENERGY AND ITS DISSIPATION RATE FOR EVAPORATING SPRAY

The equation governing the mean kinetic energy ($k = \frac{1}{2}\overline{u_i u_i}$) of turbulence is obtained from the instantaneous momentum equation of the carrier fluid Equation 16 following the same procedure as in the earlier work of Elghobashi and Abou-Arab [11]. The resulting mean kinetic energy equation then reads:

$$[\Phi_1 U_\ell(\overline{u_i u_i}/2)_{,\ell}] = [-\Phi_1 U_{i,\ell}\overline{u_i u_\ell} - U_{i,\ell}\overline{\phi_1 u_i u_\ell}]$$

Convection =   (I) Production

$$+ [\Phi_1\overline{p_{,i}u_i} - P_{,i}\overline{\phi_1 u_i} - \overline{\phi_1 u_i p_{,i}} - \Phi_1\overline{u_i u_\ell u_{i,\ell}} - \overline{\phi_1 u_i u_\ell u_{i,\ell}}]$$

(II) Turbulent Diffusion

$$+ [-U_\ell\overline{u_i \phi_1 u_{i,\ell}} - U_\ell U_{i,\ell}\overline{\phi_1 u_i}]$$

(III) Production
and Transfer

$$+ \left[\frac{1}{\rho_1}\sum_k [F^k + \dot{m}^k][\overline{\phi^k u_i}(V_i^k - U_i) + \Phi\overline{u_i(v_i^k - u_i)} + \overline{\phi^k u_i(v_i^k - u_i)}]\right]$$

(IV) Extra Dissipation (ε')

$$+ [\nu_1\overline{u_i[(u_{i,\ell} + u_{\ell,i})\Phi_1]_{,\ell}}] + [\nu_1\overline{u_i[\phi_1(U_{i,\ell} + U_{\ell,i})]_{,\ell}} + \nu_1\overline{u_i[\phi_1(u_{i,\ell} + u_{\ell,i})]_{,\ell}}]$$

(V) Viscous Diffusion   (VI) Extra Viscous Diffusion
and Dissipation   and Dissipation

Thd exact equation of ε is:

$$[\Phi_1 U_\ell\varepsilon_{,\ell}] = [-2\nu_1\overline{u_{i,j}u_{i,\ell}}(\Phi_1 U_\ell)_{,j} - 2\nu_1\overline{u_{i,j}}u_{\ell,j}\Phi_1 U_{i,\ell} - 2\nu_1\overline{(\phi_1 u_\ell)_{,j}u_{i,j}}U_{i,\ell}$$

Convection =   (I) Production by the Mean Motion

$$- 2\nu_1\overline{u_{i,j}u_{i,\ell}(\phi_1 U_\ell)_{,j}} - 2\nu_1\overline{\phi_1 u_\ell u_{i,j}}U_{i,\ell j} - 2\nu_1\overline{u_{i,j}u_\ell}(\Phi_1 U_{i,\ell})_{,j}]$$

$$+ [-2\nu_1\overline{u_{i,j}u_{i,\ell}(u_\ell\Phi_1)_{,j}} - 2\nu_1\overline{u_{i,j}u_{i,\ell}(u_\ell\phi_1)_{,j}}]$$

(II) Production by Self-Stretching of
Vortex Tubes

$$+ [-2\nu_1\Phi_1\overline{u_{i,j}u_{i,\ell j}u_\ell} - 2\nu_1\overline{\phi_1 u_{i,j}u_{i,\ell j}u_\ell}]$$

(III) Turbulent Diffusion

$$+ [-2\nu_1\overline{\phi_1 u_{i,j}}(U_\ell U_{i,\ell})_{,j} - 2\nu_1\overline{u_{i,j}\phi_{1,j}}U_\ell U_{i,\ell} - 2\nu_1 U_\ell\overline{\phi_1 u_{i,j}u_{i,\ell j}}]$$

(IV) Production and Transfer

$$+ [-2\mu_1\overline{u_{i,j}(p_{,1}\phi_1)_{,j}} - 2\mu_1\overline{u_{i,j}(\phi_1 P_{,i})_{,j}} - 2\mu_1\overline{u_{i,j}(\phi_1 P_{,i})_{,j}}]$$

(V) Spatial Transport by Pressure (Fluctuation and Mean)

$$+ \left[-2\nu_1\sum_k (F^k + \dot{m}^k)(u_{i,j}[\phi^k(U_i - V_i^k)]_{,j} + u_{i,j}[u_i - v_i^k]\Phi^k]_{,j} - \overline{u_{i,j}[\phi^k(u_i - v_i^k)_{,j}}]\right]$$

(VI) Extra Dissipation

$$+ [2\nu_1^2\overline{u_{i,j}[u_{i,\ell} + u_{\ell,i})\Phi_1}]_{,j\ell}]$$

(VII) Viscous Diffusion
and Destruction

$$+ [2\nu_1^2\overline{u_{i,j}[\phi_1(U_{i,\ell} + U_{\ell,i})}]_{,j\ell} + 2\nu_1^2\overline{u_{i,j}\phi_1[u_{i,\ell} + u_{\ell,i})}]_{,j\ell}]$$

(VIII) Extra Viscous Diffusion and Destruction

APPENDIX C: TRANSPORT EQUATION OF MIXED WEIGHTED TURBULENT STRESS CORRELATIONS.

Transport Equation of $\overline{g_j u_i}$:

$$
\begin{aligned}
(G_k \overline{g_j u_i})_{,k} =\ & -\{\overline{g_j g_k} U_{i,k} + \overline{u_i g_k} G_{j,k} + G_j \overline{u_i g_{k,k}}\} \\
& -\{\overline{u_i g_j g_k} + (1 - K\Phi_2)\overline{g_j p}\delta_{ik} + \{\rho_1 \Phi_1 (1 - K\Phi_2)\overline{u_i p} + \overline{\rho_1' u_i p}\Phi_1 (1 - K\Phi_2)\}\delta_{jk}\}_{,k} \\
& + [G_k U_j \overline{u_i (\rho_1' \phi_1)}_{,k} + G_k \overline{u_i u_j}(\rho_1 \Phi_1)_{,k} + U_j \overline{g_k u_i}(\rho_1 \Phi_1)_{,k} \\
& + G_k \overline{u_i u_j (\Phi_1 \rho_1')}_{,k} + \overline{g_k u_i u_j}(\rho_1 \Phi_1)_{,k} U_j \overline{g_k u^i(\rho_1' \Phi_1)}_{,k} \\
& + \overline{g_k u_i u_j (\rho_1' \Phi_1)}_{,k} + G_k U_j \overline{(\rho_1 \phi_1)}_{,k} u_i + G_k \overline{u_i u_j (\rho_1 \Phi_1)}_{,k} \\
& + U_j \overline{g_k u_i (\rho_1 \phi_1)}_{,k} \overline{g_k u_i u_j (\rho_1 \phi_1)}_{,k} + G_k U_j \overline{(\rho_1' \phi_1)}_{,k} u_i \\
& + G_k \overline{u_i u_j (\rho_1' \phi_1)}_{,k} + U_j \overline{g_k u_i (\rho_1' \phi_1)}_{,k} + \overline{g_k u_i u_j (\rho_1' \phi_1)}_{,k}] \\
& - K\overline{\phi_1 g_j} P_{,i} - K\overline{\phi_1 g_j p}_{,i} - \rho_1 \Phi_1 K\overline{\phi_2 u_i} P_{,j} \\
& - \overline{\rho_1' u_i}(1 - K\Phi_2)\Phi_1 P_{,j} - \rho_1 (1 - K\Phi_2)\overline{\phi_1 u_i} P_{,j} \\
& + K\overline{\phi_1 \phi_2 u_i}, P_{,j} - (1 - K\Phi_2) P_{,j}\overline{\rho_1' \phi_1 u_i} + K\overline{\rho_1' \phi_1 \phi_2 u_i} P_{,j} \\
& + K\rho_1 \Phi_1 \overline{\phi_2 u_i p}_{,j} - (1 - K\Phi_2)\Phi_1 \overline{\rho_1' u_i p}_{,j} + K\Phi_1 \overline{\rho_1' \phi_2 u_i} P_{,j} \\
& - \rho_1 (1 - K\Phi_2)\overline{\phi_1 u_i p}_{,j} + K\rho_1 \overline{\phi_1 \phi_2 u_i p}_{,j} - (1 - K\Phi_2)\overline{\rho_1' \phi_1 u_i p}_{,j} \\
& + K\overline{\rho_1' \phi_1 \phi_2 u_i p}_{,j}. \\
& + \overline{p\{(1 - K\Phi_2)g_{j,i} + (\rho_1' u_{i,j} + u_i \rho_{1,j}')(1 - K\Phi_2)\Phi_1} \\
& \overline{+ [\rho_1 \Phi_1 (1 - K\Phi_2)u_i]_{,j}\}} \\
& + \Phi_1 \overline{g_j \tau_{jk,k}} + \rho_1 \Phi_1 \overline{u_i (\Phi_1 \tau_{jk})}_{,k} + \phi_1 \overline{\rho_1' u_i (\tau_{jk}' \Phi_1)}_{,k} \\
& + \Phi_1 \overline{\rho_1' u_i (\tau_{jk} \Phi_1)}_{,k} \\
& + \Phi_{1,k} \overline{g_j \tau_{jk}'} + \overline{g_j (\phi_1 \tau_{ik})}_{,k} + \overline{g_j (\phi_1 \tau_{ik}')}_{,k} + \rho_1 \Phi_1 \overline{u_i (\phi_1 \tau_{jk})}_{,k} \\
& + \rho_1 \Phi_1 \overline{u_i (\phi \tau_{jk})}_{,k} + \Phi_1 \overline{\rho_1' u_i (\tau_{jk})\phi_1)}_{,k} + \Phi_1 \overline{\rho_1' u_i (\tau_{jk}' \phi_1)}_{,k} \\
& + \rho_1 \overline{\phi_1 u_i (\tau_{jk} \Phi_1)}_{,k} + \rho_1 \overline{\phi_1 u_i (\tau_{jk}' \Phi_1)}_{,k} + \rho_1 \overline{\phi_1 u_i (\tau_{jk} \phi_1)}_{,k} \\
& + \rho_1 \overline{\phi_1 u_i (\tau_{jk}' \phi_1)}_{,k} + \overline{\rho_1' \phi_1 u_i (\tau_{jk} \Phi_1)}_{,k} + \rho_1' \overline{\phi_1 u_i (\tau_{jk}' \phi_1)}_{,k} \\
& + \overline{\rho_1 \phi_1 u_i (\tau_{jk} \phi_1)}_{,k} + \overline{\rho_1' \phi_1 u_i (\tau_{jk}' \phi_1)}_{,k} \\
& - \overline{g_i [\frac{2}{3}\delta_{ik}\mu_1 (\Phi_1 u_{\ell,\ell} + \phi_1 U_{\ell,\ell} + \phi_1 u_{\ell,\ell})]}_{,k} \\
& - \rho_1 \Phi_1 \overline{u_i [\frac{2}{3}\delta_{jk}\mu_1 (\Phi_1 u_{\ell,\ell} + \phi_1 U_{\ell,\ell} + \phi_1 u_{\ell,\ell})]}_{,k} \\
& - \rho_1 \overline{\phi_1 u_i [\frac{2}{3}\delta_{jk}\mu_1 (\Phi_1 U_{\ell,\ell} + \Phi_1 u_{\ell,\ell} + \phi_1 U_{\ell,\ell} + \phi_1 u_{\ell,\ell})]}_{,k} \\
& - \Phi_1 \rho_1 \overline{u_i [\frac{2}{3}\delta_{jk}\mu_1 (\Phi_1 U_{\ell,\ell}\Phi_1 u_{\ell,\ell} + \phi_1 U_{\ell,\ell} + \phi_1 u_{\ell,\ell})]}_{,k} \\
& - \overline{\rho_1' \phi_1 u_i [\frac{2}{3}\delta_{jk}\mu_1 (\phi_1 U_{\ell,\ell} + \phi_1 U_{\ell,\ell} + \phi_1 U_{\ell,\ell} + \phi_1 u_{\ell,\ell})]}_{,k} \\
& - KF_D [\Phi_2 \overline{g_j (u_i - v_i)} + \overline{\phi_2 g_j (U_i - V_i)} + \overline{\phi_2 g_j (u_i - v_i)}] \\
& - KF_D [\rho_1 \Phi_1 \Phi_2 \overline{u_i (u_j - v_j)} + \rho_1 \Phi_2 \overline{\phi_1 u_i}(U_j - V_j) + \rho_1 \Phi_2 \overline{\phi_1 u_i (u_j - v_j)} \\
& + \Phi_1 \Phi_2 \overline{\rho_1' u_i}(U_j - V_j) + \Phi_1 \Phi_2 \overline{\rho_1' u_i (u_j - v_j)} + \Phi_2 \overline{\rho_1' \phi_1 u_i}(U_j - V_j) \\
& + \Phi_2 \overline{\rho_1' \phi_1 u_i (u_j - v_j)} + \rho_1 \Phi_1 \overline{\phi_2 u_i}(U_j - V_j) + \rho_1 \Phi_1 \overline{\phi_2 u_i (u_j - v_j)} \\
& + \rho_1 \overline{\phi_1 \phi_2 u_i}(U_j - V_j) + \rho_1 \overline{\phi_1 \phi_2 u_i (u_j - v_j)} + \Phi_1 \overline{\rho_1' \phi_2 u_i}(U_j - V_j) \\
& + \Phi_1 \overline{\rho_1' \phi_2 u_i (u_j - v_j)} + \overline{\rho_1' \phi_1 \phi_2 u_i}(U_j - V_j) + \overline{\rho_1' \phi_1 \phi_2 u_i (u_j - v_j)}
\end{aligned}
$$

REFERENCES

1. Abou-Arab, T. W., "Towards a Novel Form for Multiphase Flow Equation for Vertical Motion," *Scientific Engineering Bulletin*, Vol. 3 (1984).
2. Al Taweel, A. M., and Landau, J., "Turbulence Modulation in Two-Phase Jets," *Int. J. Multiphase flow*, Vol. 3 (1979), pp. 341–351.

3. Depew, C. A., and Cramer, E. R., "Heat Transfer to Horizontal Gas-Solid Systems Flows," *Trans. ASME, J. Heat Transfer,* Vol. 92, Series G., 1970.
4. Gutfinger, C., and Abuaf, N., "Heat Transfer in Fluidized Beds," in *Advances in Heat Transfer,* Vol. 10, J. Hartnett and J. Irvine (Eds.), New York: Academic Press, 1974, pp. 167–218.
5. Mastanaiah, K., and Ganic, E. N., "Heat Transfer in Two-Component Dispersed Flow," *Trans. of the ASME. J. Heat Transfer,* Vol. 103 (May 1981), pp. 300–306.
6. Abou-Ellail, M. M. M., and Abou-Arab, T. W., *Heat Transfer in Gas-Solid Turbulent Pipe Flow,* Proc. of Int. Conf. on Numerical Methods for Transient and Coupled Problems, Venice, Italy, 1984, pp. 120.
7. Lee, J., and Growe, C. T., "Scaling Laws for Metering the Flow of Gas-Particle Suspensions Through Venturis," in *Polyphase Flow and Transport Technology,* R. A. Bajura (Ed.), New York: The ASME, 1980, pp. 245–249.
8. Digiacinto, M., Sabetta, F., and Pira, R. "Two-Way Coupling Effects in Dilute Gas-Particle Flows," *ASME-J. Fluids Engineering,* Vol. 104 (1982), pp. 304–317.
9. Lumley, J. L., "Two-Phase and Non-Newtonian Flows," in *Topics in Applied Physics,* Vol. 12, P. Bradshaw (Ed.), New York: Springer-Verlag 1978, pp. 289–324.
10. Brodky, R., *The Phenomena of Fluid Motion,* London: Addison-Wesley Publishing Company, 1967.
11. Danon, H., Wolfshtein, M., and Hetsroni, G., "Numerical Calculations of Two-Phase Turbulent Round Jet," *Int. J. Multiphase Flow,* Vol. 3 (1977), pp. 223.
12. Lee, S. L., and Durst, F., *On the Motion of Particles in Turbulent Flows,* Division of Reactor Safety Research Office of Nuclear Regulatory Research—U.S. Nuclear Regulatory Commission, Washington, NRC FIN No. B6 11, 1980.
13. Elghobashi, S. E., and Abou-Arab, T. W., *A Second-Order Turbulence Model for Two-Phase Flows,* Proc. of the 7th Int. Heat Transfer Conference, Vol. 5, Munich, West Germany, 1982, pp. 219.
14. Elghobashi, S. E., and Abou-Arab, T. W., "A Two-Equation Turbulence Closure for Two-Phase Flows," *Phys. Fluids,* Vol. 26, No. 4 (1983), pp. 931–938.
15. Abou-Arab, T. W. and Abou-Ellail, M. M. M. "*A Mathematical Model of the Two-Phase Turbulent Pipe Flow,*" Proc. of the Int. Conference on Engineering Software for Microcomputers, Venice, Italy, 1984.
16. Soo, S. L., *Fluid Dynamics of Multiphase Systems,* Waltham, Masschusetts: Blaisdell Publishing Company, 1978.
17. Hinze, J. O., *Turbulence,* McGraw-Hill, N.Y, 1975.
18. Rudinger, G., *Flow of Solid Particles in Gases,* AGARDograph No. 22, Sept. 1976.
19. Buyevich, Yu. A., "Diffusion of Suspended Particles in an Isentropic Turbulence," *Izv. AN SSSR. Mekhanika Zhidkosti i Gaza,* Vol. 3, No. 5, 1968, pp. 89–99.
20. Rudinger, G., "Reply to Comments by S. L. Soo," *Phys. Fluids,* Vol. 7, 1964, pp. 1885.
21. Buyevich, Yu. A, and Safari, V. M., "On the Theory of Early Turbulization of Disperse Systems," *PMTF (Journal of Applied Mechanic and Technical Physics,* Vol. 3 (1968).
22. Buyevich, Yu. A., "Statistical Hydrodynamics of Disperse Systems—Part 1. Physical Background and General Equations," *J. Fluid Mech.,* Vol. 49, No. 3 (1971), pp. 480–507.
23. Buyevich, Yu. A., "Statistical Hydrodynamics of Disperse Systems—Part 2. Solution of the Kinetic Equation for Suspended Particles," *J. Fluid Mech.,* Vol. 52, No. 2 (1972), pp. 345–355.
24. Buyevich, Yu. A., "Statistical Hydrodynamics of Disperse Systems—Part 3. Pseudo-Turbulent Structure of Homogeneous Suspensions," *J. Fluid Mech.,* Vol. 56, No. 2, pp. 313–336.
25. Sato, Y., Sadatomi, M., and Sekoguchi, K., "Momentum and Heat Transfer in Two-Phase Bubble Flow-1," *Int. Jour. Multiphase Flow,* Vol. 7 (1981), pp. 167–177.
26. Abou-Arab, T. W., Elkotb M. M., and Elshenawy, E. A., *Mutual Interaction in Multiphase Flows,* submitted for publication.
27. Elghobashi, S., et al., *Prediction of a Two-Phase Turbulent Round Jet,* Proc. 4th Symp. of Turbulent Shear Flows, Karlsruhe-West-Germany, Sept., 1983, pp. 12.9–12.14.
28. Mostafa, A., and Elghobashi, S., *A Study of the Motion of Vaporizing Droplets in a Turbulent Flow,* Proceeding of Int. Colloquium on Dynamics of Explosions and Reactive Systems, Poitiers-France, 1983.

29. Abou-Ellail, M. M., and Abou-Arab, T. W., *Modulation of Heat Transfer in Dusty Gas Pipe Flows*, submitted for publication, 1984.

30. Genchev, Zh. D., and Karpuzov, D. S., "Effects of the Motion of Dust Particles on Turbulence Transport Equations," *J. Fluid Mech.*, Vol. 101, No. 4 (1980), pp. 833–4842.

31. Brag, K. N. C., "*Kinetic Energy of Turbulence in Flames*," AGARD conference, No. 16, AGARD Paris, 1975, pp. 112–120.

32. DuPont-Donaldson, C., Sullivan, R. C., and Rosenbaum, H., *AIAA J.*, Vol. 10 (1972), pp. 162.

33. Janicka, J., and Kollmann, W., "*A Prediction Model for Turbulent Diffusion Flames Including No-Formation*," AGARD-PEP 54th Meeting, Cologne, 1979.

34. Favre, A., "Statistical Equations of Turbulent Gases," in *Problems of Hydrodynamics and Continuum Mechanics*, Society for Industrial and Applied Mechanics, Philadelphia: PA, 1969, pp. 237–266.

35. Kent, J. H., and Bilger, R. W., *The Prediction of Turbulent Flame Fields and Nitric Oxide Formation*, Proc. 16th Int. Symp. of Combustion-The Combustion Institute, 1976, pp. 1643.

36. Jones, W. P., "Models for Turbulent Flows with Variable Density and Combustion," in *Prediction Methods for Turbulent Flows*, W. Kollmann (Ed.) New York, 1980, pp. 379–421.

37. Ha Minh, H., Launder, B. E., and Mac Innes, J., "*A New Approach to the Analysis of Turbulent Mixing in Variable Density Flows*," Proc. 3rd Symp. Turbulent Shear Flows, University of California—Davis, 1981, pp. 19.19–19.25.

38. Prandtl, L. "Bemerkung zur Theorie der freien Turbulenz," *ZAMM*, Vol. 22 (1942), pp. 241–243.

39. Crowe, C. T., "On the Dispersed Flow Equations," in Two-Phase Momentum, *Heat and Mass Transfer*, Vol. 1, F. Durst and Afgan (Eds.) London, 1980, pp. 25.

40. Reynolds, W. C., and Cebeci, T., "Calculation of Turbulent Flows," *in Turbulence*, Vol. 12, P. Bradshaw (Ed.), New York: Springer Verlag, 1978, pp. 193–229.

41. Corrsin, S., "Limitations of Gradient Transport Models in Random Walks and in Turbulence," in *Advances in Geophysics*, Vol. 18A, H. E. Landesberg and J. Van Mieghem (Eds.), New York: Academic Press, 1974, pp. 25–60.

42. Lumely, J. L., "Modeling Turbulent Flux of Passive Scalar Quantities in Inhomogeneous Flows," *Phys. Fluids*, Vol. 18, No. 6 (June 1975), pp. 619–621.

43. Lumely, J. L., "*Turbulent Transport of Passive Contaminants and Particles—Fundamentals and Advanced Methods of Numerical Modeling*," Von Karaman Institute for Fluid Dynamics Lecture Series on Pollutant Dispersal, Belgium, 1978.

44. Launder, B. E., "Heat and Mass Transport," in *Turbulence*, P. Bradshaw (Ed.) New York: Springer Verlag, 1978, pp. 231–286.

45. Smaraweera, D. S. A., "Turbulent Heat Transport in 2- and 3-Dimensional Temperature Fields," Ph.D. Thesis, University of London, 1978.

46. Elghobashi, S., and Launder, B. E., "*Modeling the Dissipation Rate of Temperature Variance in a Thermal Mixing Layer*," Proc. 3rd Symp. Turbulent Shear Flows, University of California-Davis, 1981, pp. 15.13–15.17.

47. Hanjalic', K., and Launder, B. E. "A Reynolds Stress Model of Turbulence and Its Application to Asymmetric Shear Flows," *J. Fluid Mech.*, Vol. 52 (1972), pp. 609.

48. Launder, B. E., Reece, G., and Rodi, W., "Progress in the Development of a Reynolds Stress Closure," *J. Fluid Mech.*, Vol. 68 (1975), pp. 537–566.

49. Harlow, F. H., and Nakayama, P. I., *Transport of Turbulence Energy Decay Rate*, Los Alamos National Laboratory Report No. LA-38 54, University of California, 1968.

50. Chao, B. T., "Turbulent Transport Behavior of Small Particles in Dilute Suspension," *Österreichisches Ingnieur Archiv*, Vol. 18 (1964), pp. 7–21.

51. Tennekes, H., and Lumley, J. L., *A First Course in Turbulence*, MIT Cambridge: Massachussettes, 1972.

52. Lin, T. C., and Bywater, R. J., "Turbulence Models for High Speed, Rough Wall Boundary Layers, *AIAA J.*, Vol. 20, No. 3 (1982), pp. 325–3333.

53. Crowe, C. T., *Vapor-Droplet Flow Equations*, University of California Lawrence Livermore Laboratory UCRL-51877, August 1975.

54. Gitterman, M., and Steinberg, V., "Memory Effects in the Motion of a Suspended Particle in a Turbulent Fluid," *Phys. Fluids*, Vol. 23, No. 11 (1980), pp. 154–2160.

55. Gitterman, M. S., and Gertsenshtein, G. E., "Theory of the Brownian Motion Possibilities of Using it for the Study of the Critical State of a Pure Substance," *Zh. Eksp. Theor. Fiz. 50 (Sov. Phys. JETP 23 722 1966))*, 1966, pp. 1084.

56. Schlichting, H., *Boundary Layer Theory*, New York: McGraw-Hill Book Co. 1961.

57. Wilcox, D. C., and Alber, I. E., *A Turbulence Model for High Speed Flows*, Proc. of the 1972 Heat transfer and fluid Mechanics Institute, 1972, pp. 231–252.

58. Householder, M. K., and Goldschmidt, V. W., "Turbulent Diffusion and Schmidt Number of Particles," *J. Engineering Mechanics Division-Proc. ASCE*, Vol. 95, No. EM6 (1968), pp. 1345–1367.

59. Sreenivasan, K. R., Tavoularis, S., and Corrsin, S., *Turbulent Transport in Passively Heated Homogeneous Flows*, Proc. 3rd Symp. Turbulent Shear Flows, Univ. of Calif.—Davis, 1981, pp. 15.28–15.33.

60. Kronenburg., C., "On the Extension of Gradient-Type Transport to Turbulent Diffusion in Inhomogeneous Flows," *Applied Science Research*, Vol. 33 (1977), pp. 163–175.

61. Pope S. B., *Calculation of Velocity-Scalar Joint PDF'S*, Proc. 3rd Symp. Turbulent Shear Flows, Univ. of Calif.—Davis, 1981, pp. 3.32–3.37.

62. Hutchinson, P., Hewitt, G. F., and Dukler, A. E., *Deposition of Liquid or Solid Dispersions from Turbulent Gas Streams: A Stochastic Model*, U.K.A.E.A, Report No. AERE 6637, Harwell, 1970.

63. Reynolds, W. C., "Computation of Turbulent Flows," *Annual Review of Fluid Mechanics*, Vol. 8, 1976, pp. 184–208.

64. Chandrasekhar, S., "Stochastic Problems in Physics and Astronomy," *Reviews of Modern Physics*, Vol. 15, No. 1 (1943), pp. 1–89.

65. Davidson, G. A., and McComb, W. D., "Turbulent Diffusion in an Aerosol Jet," *J. Aerosol Sci*, Vol. 6 (1975), pp. 27–247.

66. Meek, C. C., and Jones, B. G., "Studies of the Behavior of Heavy Particles in Turbulent Fluid Flows," *J. Atmospheric Sci.*, Vol. 30 (1973), pp. 239–244.

67. Batchelor, G. K., *The Motion of Small Particles in Turbulent Flow*, Proc. of the 2nd Australasian Conference on Hydraulics and Fluid Mechanics, Univ. of Auckland, N.Z., 1966.

68. Yuu, S., Yasukoucki, N., and Tomosada, J., "Particle Turbulent Diffusion in a Dust-Laden Round Jet," *AIChE J.*, Vol. 24, No. 3 (1978), pp. 508.

69. Peskin, R. L., "Stochastic Application to Turbulent Diffusion," in *Int. Symp. on Stochastic Hydraulics*, C. L. Chiu. (Ed.) University of Pittsburg: Pittsburg, Pa., 1971, pp. 251–267.

70. Monin, A. S., and Yaglom, A. M., *Statistical Fluid Mechanics: Mechanics of Turbulence*, Vol. 1, Cambridge-Mass.: The MIT Press, 1971.

71. Reek, M. W., *The Transport of Discrete Particles in Turbulent Shear Flow*, Paper C71/82 Conference on gas-borne particles, Inst. of Mech. Engr., Oxford-England, 1981, pp. 87–92.

72. Nir, A., and Pismen L. M., "The Effect of a Steady Drift on the Dispersion of a Particle in Turbulent Fluid," *J. Fluid Mech.*, Vol. 94 (1979), pp. 364–381.

73. Tchen, C., "*Mean Value and Correlation Problems Connected with the Motion of Small Particles Suspended in a Turbulent Fluid*," Publication 51, Laboratory for Aero- and Hydrodynamics, Technical University, Delft, 1947.

74. Kuboi, R., Komasawa, I., and Otake, T., "Fluid and Particle Motion in Turbulent Dispersion—II. Influence of Turbulence of Liquid on the Motion of Suspended Particles," *Chemical Engineering Science*, Vol. 29 (1974), pp. 651–657.

75. Levins, D. M, and Glastonbury, J. R., "Particle-Liquid Hydrodynamics and Mass Transfer in a Stirred Vessel," *Trans. Instn. Chem. Engrs.*, Vol. 50 (1972), pp. 32.

76. Yudine, M. I., "Physical Considerations of Heavy-Particle Diffusion," in *Advances in Geophysics*, Vol. 6, 1959, pp. 185–191.

77. Csanady, G. T., "Turbulent Diffusion of Heavy Particles in the Atmosphere," *Journal of Atmospheric Sciences*, Vol. 20 (1963), pp. 201–208.

78. Friedlander, S. K., "Behaviour of Suspended Particles in a Turbulent Fluid," *AIChE J.*, Vol. 3 (1957), pp. 381–385.

79. Davis, C. N., "Deposition of Aerosols through Pipes," *Proc. of the Royal Society*, London, Vol. 289, Series A, 1966, pp. 235.

80. Rouhiainen, P. O., and Stachiewicz, J. W., "On the Deposition of Small Particles from Turbulent Streams, "*Journal of Heat Transfer,* Vol. 92 (1970), pp. 169–177.

81. Friedlander, S. K., and Johnstone, H. F., "Deposition of Suspended Particles from Turbulent Gas Streams," *Industrial and Engineering Chemistry,* Vol. 49 (1951), pp. 1151.

82. Ganic, E. N., and Rohsenow, W. M., "On the Mechanism of Liquid Drop Deposition in Two-Phase Dispersed Flow," *Journal of Heat Transfer,* Vol. 101 (1979), pp. 288–294.

83. Saffman, P. Q., "The Lift on a Small Sphere in a Slow Shear Flow," *J. Fluid Mech.,* Vol. 22 (1965), pp. 385.

84. Otterman, B., and Lee, S. L., "Particle Migrations in Laminar Mixing of a Suspension with a Clear Fluid," *Zeitschrift für angewandete mathematik und physik (ZAMP),* Vol. 20, Fasc. 5, 1969, pp. 730.

85. Hjelmfelt, A. T., Jr., and Morkos, L. F., "Motion of Discrete Particles in a Turbulent Fluid," *Applied Scientific Research,* Vol. 16 (1966), pp. 149–161.

86. Townsend, A. A., *The Structure of Turbulent Shear Flow,* Cambridge: Cambridge University Press, 1956.

87. Laufer, J., *The Structure of Turbulence in Fully Developed Pipe Flow,* NACA Technical note No. 2954, 1953.

88. Drew, D. A., and Lahey, R. T., "Phase-Distribution Mechanisms in Turbulent Low-Quality Two-Phase Flow in a Circular Pipe," *J. Fluid Mech.,* Vol. 117 (1982), pp. 91–106.

89. Clift, R., Grace, J. R., and Weber, M. E., *Bubbles, Drops, and Particles,* New York: Academic Press, 1978.

90. Alonso, C. V., "Stochastic Models of Suspended Sediment Dispersion," *J. of the Hydraulics Division-Proc. ASCE,* Vol. 107, No. HY6 (1981), pp. 733–757.

91. Launder, B. E., et al., *The Prediction of Free Shear Flows—A Comparison of the Performance of Six Turbulence Models,* Imperial College, TM/TN/19, 1972.

92. Modarress, D., Wuerer, J., and Elghobashi, S., *An Experimental Study of a Turbulent Round Two-Phase Jet,* AIAA/ASME 3rd Joint Thermophysics, Fluids, Plasma and Heat Transfer Conference, St. Louis-Missouri, 1982.

93. Modarress, D., Tan, H., and Elghobashi, S. *Two-Component LDA Measurement in a Two-Phase Jet,* AIAA 21st Aerospace Science Meeting, Reno-Nevada, 1983.

94. Spalding, D. B., *Numerical Computation of Multiphase Flows,* Lecture Notes, Thermal Sciences and Propulsion Centre, Purdue University, Indiana, 1979.

95. Tien, C. L., and Quan, V., *Local Heat Transfer Characteristics of Air Glass-Lead in Turbulent Pipe Flow,* ASME-Paper No. 62-HT-15, 1962.

96. Depew, C. A., and Kramer, T. J., "Heat Transfer to Flowing Gas-Solid Mixture," in *Advances in Heat Transfer,* Vol. 9, T. F. Irvine, Jr. and James P. Hartnett (Eds.), New York: Academic Press, 1973, pp. 113–180.

CHAPTER 31

MODELING TECHNIQUES FOR DISPERSED MULTIPHASE FLOWS

Stephen W. Webb*

Gilbert Associates, Inc.
Reading, Pennsylvania, USA

and

Donald S. Rowe
Rowe and Associates
Bellevue, Washington, USA

CONTENTS

INTRODUCTION

Dispersed multiphase flows are important in a number of applications such as nuclear reactors, steam generators, and chemical plants. Prediction of the behavior of the various phases is obviously important in the design of these facilities. This chapter is concerned with a discussion of the major modeling techniques used for dispersed multiphase flows. The multiphase flow under consideration may undergo a phase change from the variation in thermodynamic conditions due to heat addition, pressure changes, etc.; however, chemical reactions are not discussed in this chapter. Modeling techniques are evaluated from a practical point of view for application to dispersed-flow conditions, and a preferred modeling method is discussed in detail. In addition, a versatile numerical method is presented to solve the resulting equations. Thus, the material in this chapter is self-contained and allows the reader to formulate and solve problems. Due to space limitations, the

---

* Presently at Sandia National Laboratories, Thermal Hydraulic Analysis Division, Albuquerque
New Mexcio, USA.

chapter will only introduce the reader to some of the basic concepts of the field. References will be cited to direct the interested reader to appropriate material for more detail.

This chapter concentrates on one-component two-phase flows and steam-water in particular. This fluid has been extensively studied in the nuclear reactor and power conversion industries, and a wealth of material is available. The concepts presented for a steam-water mixture should be applicable to most one-component two-phase mixtures. Two-component two-phase flows, such as a solid-gas mixture, will only be discussed briefly. The interested reader is referred to recent articles by Wallis [1] and Crowe [2] for a review and discussion of gas-liquid and gas-particle models, respectively. In addition, the book edited by Meyer [3] discusses some specialized topics in dispersed multiphase flows including multicomponent situations.

MODELING TECHNIQUES

Many different modeling techniques have been used for two-phase steam-water flows. The most common techniques are the homogeneous, drift flux, and two-fluid models. General conservation equations for all three models have been derived from first principles by Ishii [4]. The two-fluid model is the most general of the three approaches. Partial differential equations for conservation of mass, momentum, and energy are written for each phase. Constitutive relationships are needed for the fluid properties and to specify interactions between the two phases. The two-fluid model is complex with six conservation equations (three for each phase) and a number of problematic interfacial relationships. While the two-fluid model may be appealing from a fundamentalist viewpoint, the complexity of the formulation and specification of the inter-facial conditions makes the full two-fluid model difficult to use. In practice, a number of the interfacial relationships are roughly approximated and may only be appropriate for a limited number of situations. Research is currently underway to more adequately define these interfacial relationships. At the present time, however, the specification of the interfacial conditions remains a significant problem in the two-fluid model. The formulation and solution of a full six-equation two-fluid model is exemplified by the TRAC-PD2[5] computer code.

If the motion of the two phases is strongly coupled, as is usually the case with dispersed flows, a major simplification to the two-fluid model can be made. Instead of writing two momentum conservation equations (one for each phase), a single momentum equation can be written for the mixture as a whole resulting in the drift-flux model. The relative velocity between the phases is specified through constitutive relationships, or algebraic relationships. Most of the troublesome interfacial equations in the two-fluid model are eliminated in this approach. The idea of the drift-flux model is to concentrate on the mixture as a whole rather than the individual phases. A five-equation drift-flux model is currently employed in certain situations by the TRAC-PD2[5] computer program, although future versions of the program will reportedly drop the drift-flux model. An independent assessment of the two-fluid and drift-flux models and the constitutive packages used in the TRAC-PD2[5] computer program has been performed by Rohatgi and Saha [6], and Rohatgi, Jo, and Neymotin [7].

The drift-flux model can be further simplified to give the homogeneous model. The homogeneous model assumes that each phase flows at the same velocity, or that the relative velocity between the two phases is zero. The same number of conservation equations is required for the homogeneous model as for the drift-flux model. The advantage in this approach is the simplification of the constitutive relationship for the relative velocity between the two phases. In general, the applicability of the homogeneous model is limited to high mass flux situations where the relative velocity is a small fraction of the individual phasic velocities.

Simplifications can also be made to the various models regarding the thermodynamic state of the phases. For any of the models, the specification of a particular phase at saturation reduces the number of conservation equations by one by requiring the use of only one energy equation. The determination of the particular phase at saturation is made by a constitutive relationship. This philosophy is currently employed in the five-equation two-fluid model used in the RELAP5/MOD1 [8] computer program, although the MOD2 version will reportedly revert to a full six-equation two-fluid model. An additional assumption of both phases at saturation, or thermodynamic equilibrium, further reduces the number of conservation equations by one by requiring only one continuity

Table 1
Conservation Equation Summary

Model	Assumptions	Number of required conservation equations
Two-fluid	General model	6(2C, 2M, 2E)
	One phase at saturation	5(2C, 2M, 1E)
	Both phases at saturation	4(1C, 2M, 1E)
Drift flux or homogeneous	Phases strongly coupled	5(2C, 1M, 2E)
	One phase at saturation	4(2C, 1M, 1E)
	Both phases at saturation	3(1C, 1M, 1E)

nC—number of continuity equations
nM—number of momentum equations
nE—number of energy equations

equation. An example of a three-equation homogeneous thermodynamic equilibrium model is the RELAP4/MOD5 [9] computer program. A summary of the number of conservation equations for all three models based on different velocity and thermodynamic assumptions is summarized in Table 1.

The choice of any particular model depends on the problem being considered. According to Ishii [4], the two-fluid model is most appropriate if the two phases are weakly coupled or if the dynamic interactions between the phases is important. An example of this situation is stratified flow where the phases are weakly coupled and interfacial conditions are important. The drift-flux model is appropriate if the phases are strongly coupled and for studies of system dynamics and instabilities. The homogeneous model is further limited to high mass flux situations where the phasic velocities are approximately equal.

Of the three modeling techniques just discussed, the drift-flux model is the obvious choice for dispersed flows since, in general, the flow of the two phases is strongly coupled. The homogeneous model does not offer any fundamental advantages and has the obvious drawback of equal phase velocities. The two-fluid model, while fundamentally appealing, uses six conservation equations and a number of problematic interfacial constitutive relationships. While the two-fluid model is some-times necessary and has been successfully applied in a number of situations, the drift-flux model will often suffice for many engineering applications and is the model that will be presented in detail in this chapter.

DRIFT-FLUX MODEL

The drift-flux model is based upon the velocity difference between the phases or between a phase and the average volumetric velocity of the mixture. Allowance for nonuniform velocity and void fraction profiles normal to the flow direction can also be included in the method. Consideration of nonuniform velocity and void fraction profiles in two-phase flow was presented by Bankoff [10] for homogeneous flow conditions. Zuber [11] discusses the Bankoff model and similarities with previous Russian works. An early version of the drift-flux model was presented by Wallis [12, 13] which concentrated on the relative velocity between the two phases for uniform velocity and void profiles. Wallis showed that the method is applicable to fluid-particle systems including unsteady situations and can also be used to evaluate the flooding limits of countercurrent flow. The first complete presentation of the drift-flux concepts is generally considered to be by Zuber and Findlay [14]. Zuber and Findlay presented the general theory for the drift-flux approach with nonuniform velocity and void profiles applicable to a gas-liquid or vapor-liquid system. Many of their expres-sions for the drift flux and concentration parameters are still in use today. In a recent reflection on his original work, Bankoff [15] contends that an extension of his work similar to that of Zuber and Findlay [14] was made by Neal [16] before the Zuber and Findlay paper. However, due to the obscurity of the report, the Zuber and Findlay [14] paper is generally regarded as the first complete presentation of the drift-flux concept. Some of the applications of the drift-flux theory will be presented later in the chapter. First, however, the conservation equations and necessary constitutive relationships will be discussed.

Conservation Equations

General Formulation

As summarized in Table 1, the most general drift-flux model consists of five conservation equations. In practice, however, one phase is usually assumed to be at saturation, and the four-equation drift-flux model is used. The full three-dimensional four-equation drift-flux model is presented by Ishii [4, 17]. This amount of detail is not necessary in most engineering problems, and a one-dimensional three- or four-equation drift-flux model is sufficient. The one-dimensional form of the four-equation drift-flux model was derived by Ishii [17] from the full three-dimensional equation set using averaging techniques. Averaging techniques, which are a complex subject by themselves, are discussed in detail by Ishii [4] and by Delhaye and Achard [18, 19]. The general one-dimensional four-equation drift-flux model conservation equations as presented by Ishii [17] are:

Mixture continuity equation

$$\frac{\partial \langle \rho_m \rangle}{\partial t} + \frac{\partial}{\partial z}(\langle \rho_m \rangle \bar{V}_m) = 0$$

Continuity equation for dispersed phase

$$\frac{\partial \langle \alpha_d \rangle \rho_d}{\partial t} + \frac{\partial}{\partial z}(\langle \alpha_d \rangle \rho_d \bar{V}_m) = \langle \Gamma_d \rangle - \frac{\partial}{\partial z}\left(\frac{\langle \alpha_d \rangle \rho_d \rho_c}{\langle \rho_m \rangle} \bar{V}_{dj}\right)$$

Mixture momentum equation

$$\frac{\partial \langle \rho_m \rangle \bar{V}_m}{\partial t} + \frac{\partial}{\partial z}(\langle \rho_m \rangle \bar{V}_m^2) = -\frac{\partial}{\partial z}\langle P_m \rangle + \frac{\partial}{\partial z}\langle \tau_{zz} + \tau_{zz}^T \rangle - \langle \rho_m \rangle g_z - \frac{f_m}{2D}\langle \rho_m \rangle \bar{V}_m |\bar{V}_m|$$

$$- \frac{\partial}{\partial z}\left[\frac{\langle \alpha_d \rangle \rho_d \rho_c}{(1 - \langle \alpha_d \rangle)\langle \rho_m \rangle} \bar{V}_{dj}^2\right] - \frac{\partial}{\partial z}\sum_k \text{COV}(\alpha_k \rho_k V_k V_k)$$

Mixture enthalpy-energy equation

$$\frac{\partial \langle \rho_m \rangle \bar{h}_m}{\partial t} + \frac{\partial}{\partial z}(\langle \rho_m \rangle \bar{h}_m \bar{V}_m) = -\frac{\partial}{\partial z}\langle q + qT \rangle + \frac{q_w'' \xi_h}{A} - \frac{\partial}{\partial z}\left[\frac{\langle \alpha_d \rangle \rho_d \rho_c}{\langle \rho_m \rangle} \Delta h_{dc} \bar{V}_{dj}\right]$$

$$- \frac{\partial}{\partial z}\sum_k \text{COV}(\alpha_k \rho_k h_k V_k) + \frac{\partial \langle P_m \rangle}{\partial t}$$

$$+ \left[\bar{V}_m + \frac{\langle \alpha_d \rangle (\rho_c - \rho_d)}{\langle \rho_m \rangle} \bar{V}_{dj}\right]\frac{\partial \langle P_m \rangle}{\partial z} + \langle \Phi_m^\mu \rangle$$

Terms with single brackets, $\langle \ \rangle$, are area average values of that parameter over the flow area normal to the flow direction, or

$$\langle F \rangle = \frac{1}{A}\int_A F \, dA$$

For flow in a pipe, the area A is simply the pipe flow area.

In addition to simple area averages, void-fraction-weighted area averages are used and are denoted by double brackets, $\langle\!\langle \ \rangle\!\rangle$, or

$$\langle\!\langle F_k \rangle\!\rangle = \langle \alpha_k F_k \rangle / \langle \alpha_k \rangle$$

where the subscript k refers to a particular phase. In the present discussion, the subscripts d and c will be used to designate the dispersed and continuous phases, respectively.

For convenience, the mixture thermal energy equation is used. In single-phase flow, the thermal energy equation is easily obtained by subtracting the mechanical energy contribution, or the momentum equation times the velocity, from the total energy equation. In the drift-flux model, however, a problem arises due to the diffusion transport terms. For low-speed two-phase flows, the mechanical energy contribution is negligible, and the use of a simplified mixture thermal energy conservation equation is acceptable. The interested reader is referred to Ishii [4] for more details on this subject.

The preceding conservation equations were derived under the assumptions of

● Uniform fluid density of each phase over the flow area A
● Equal phasic pressures.

These assumptions also imply that the phasic enthalpy is also uniform over the flow area A. In most practical situations, these assumptions are acceptable. Problems may arise with the uniform density assumption in situations such as in film boiling where the vapor temperature is not uniform across the flow area. However, film boiling is not a normal operational mode of most equipment, and this case will not usually be encountreted in practice. Film boiling is discussed briefly later in this chapter.

Based on the uniform phasic density assumption, the area average mixture density, $\langle \rho_m \rangle$, is defined by

$$\langle \rho_m \rangle \equiv \langle \alpha_d \rangle \rho_d + \langle \alpha_c \rangle \rho_c$$

where

$$\rho_k \equiv \langle\!\langle \rho_k \rangle\!\rangle = \frac{\langle \rho_k \alpha_k \rangle}{\langle \alpha_k \rangle}$$

In the case of only two phases present,

$$\langle \alpha_d \rangle + \langle \alpha_c \rangle = 1$$

The mean mixture enthalpy is given by

$$\bar{h}_m = \frac{\langle \rho_m h_m \rangle}{\langle \rho_m \rangle} = [\langle \alpha_d \rangle \rho_d \langle\!\langle h_d \rangle\!\rangle + \langle \alpha_c \rangle \rho_c \langle\!\langle h_c \rangle\!\rangle] / \langle \rho_m \rangle$$

Note that this mixture enthalpy is a static quantity, i.e., the value is dependent on static, not flowing, conditions. From this definition, a static quality can also be defined as the mass fraction of phase k, or

$$\langle X_{s,k} \rangle = \frac{\langle \rho_k \alpha_k \rangle}{\langle \rho_m \rangle}$$

or

$$\langle X_{s,c} \rangle = \frac{\bar{h}_m - \langle h_d \rangle}{\Delta h_{cd}}$$

$$\langle X_{s,d} \rangle = 1 - \langle X_{s,c} \rangle$$

Several other qualities are also important in two-phase flow analysis. In addition to the static quality, a thermodynamic equilibrium quality and a flowing quality are also used. The thermodynamic equilibrium quality is defined in terms of a flowing enthalpy for the mixture. These terms based on the continuous phase are

$$\langle X_{c,c} \rangle = \frac{\langle h_m \rangle - \langle h_d \rangle}{\Delta h_{cd}}$$

where

$$\langle h_m \rangle = \frac{\langle \rho_m V_m h_m \rangle}{\langle \rho_m V_m \rangle}$$

Since this term is based on the flowing enthalpy of the mixture, thermodynamic nonequilibrium effects will not affect the value.

The flowing quality, or actual quality, is defined as the mass fraction of phase k flowing, or

$$\langle X_{a,k} \rangle = \frac{\langle \rho_k V_k \alpha_k \rangle}{\langle \rho_m V_m \rangle} = \frac{\langle \alpha_k \rangle \rho_k \langle\!\langle V_k \rangle\!\rangle}{\langle \alpha_d \rangle \rho_d \langle\!\langle V_d \rangle\!\rangle + \langle \alpha_c \rangle \rho_c \langle\!\langle V_c \rangle\!\rangle}$$

Thermodynamic nonequilibrium is reflected in this variable.

Of course, the various qualities and enthalpies are easily related to each other. From an energy balance, the ratio of the flowing and equilibrium qualities based on the continuous phase is

$$\frac{\langle X_{a,k} \rangle}{\langle X_{e,k} \rangle} = \frac{\langle h_c \rangle - \langle h_d \rangle}{\Delta h_{cd,s}}$$

If thermodynamic equilibrium exists, the two quality values are equal. The flowing and static quality relationship is

$$\frac{X_k}{X_{s,k}} = \frac{\langle\!\langle V_k \rangle\!\rangle}{\bar{V}_m}$$

or, based on the continuous phase

$$\frac{\langle X_c \rangle}{1 - \langle X_c \rangle} = \frac{\langle\!\langle V_c \rangle\!\rangle}{\langle\!\langle V_d \rangle\!\rangle} \frac{\langle X_{s,c} \rangle}{1 - \langle X_{s,c} \rangle}$$

For homogeneous flow, the flowing and static qualities are the same. Finally, the static and flowing mixture enthalpies are related as

$$\langle h_m \rangle = \bar{h}_m + \Delta h_{dc} \frac{\rho_d \rho_c}{\langle \rho_m \rangle^2} \langle \alpha_d \rangle \langle \alpha_c \rangle \frac{\langle V_r \rangle}{\bar{V}_m}$$

$$\langle V_r \rangle = \langle\!\langle V_d \rangle\!\rangle - \langle\!\langle V_c \rangle\!\rangle$$

Note that for homogeneous flow, the two values are equal.

Problems with the definition and the use of the flowing quality occur in stagnant or countercurrent flow situations with the definition and sign of the phasic velocities. Therefore, the static quality is often preferred in a general formulation. The void-fraction-weighted value of the phasic velocities, which is also the center of mass velocity, is defined as

$$\langle\!\langle V_k \rangle\!\rangle = \frac{\langle \alpha_k V_k \rangle}{\langle \alpha_k \rangle} = \frac{\langle j_k \rangle}{\langle \alpha_k \rangle}$$

and the volumetric flux is

$$\langle j \rangle = \langle j_d \rangle + \langle j_c \rangle = \langle \alpha_d \rangle \langle\!\langle V_d \rangle\!\rangle + \langle \alpha_c \rangle \langle\!\langle V_c \rangle\!\rangle$$

The volumetric fluxes are simply the fluid velocities based on the entire flow area. These fluxes are easily evaluated from the following relationships if the flowing quality and total mass flux are known

$$\langle j_d \rangle = \frac{G \langle X_d \rangle}{\rho_d}$$

$$\langle j_c \rangle = \frac{G \langle X_c \rangle}{\rho_c}$$

The mixture velocity based on the center of mass is given by

$$\bar{V}_m \equiv \frac{\langle \rho_m V_m \rangle}{\langle \rho_m \rangle} = [\langle \alpha_d \rangle \rho_d \langle\!\langle V_d \rangle\!\rangle + \langle \alpha_c \rangle \rho_c \langle\!\langle V_c \rangle\!\rangle] / \langle \rho_m \rangle$$

The mean drift velocity is the velocity of the dispersed phase relative to the volumetric flux of the two-phase mixture, or

$$\bar{V}_{dj} = \langle\!\langle V_d \rangle\!\rangle - \langle j \rangle$$

Transforming the equation based on the center of mass velocities results in

$$\bar{V}_{dj} = \langle \alpha_c \rangle [\langle\!\langle V_d \rangle\!\rangle - \langle\!\langle V_c \rangle\!\rangle] = \frac{\langle j_d \rangle}{\langle \alpha_d \rangle} - \langle j \rangle$$

Using the fact that

$$V_d = V_{dj} + j$$

the mean drift velocity can be expressed as

$$\bar{V}_{dj} = \left\langle \frac{\alpha_d (j + V_{dj})}{\langle \alpha_d \rangle} - j \right\rangle$$

or, in a somewhat more conventional form,

$$\bar{V}_{dj} = \langle\!\langle V_{dj} \rangle\!\rangle + (C_o - 1)\langle j \rangle$$

where

$$\langle\!\langle V_{dj} \rangle\!\rangle = \frac{\langle \alpha_d V_{dj} \rangle}{\langle \alpha_d \rangle} = \langle\!\langle V_d \rangle\!\rangle - C_o \langle j \rangle$$

$$C_o = \frac{\langle \alpha_d j \rangle}{\langle \alpha_d \rangle \langle j \rangle}$$

The C_o parameter is known as the distribution parameter which relates the velocity and void fraction profiles. Typical values of the distribution parameter in different heat transfer regimes are depicted in Figure 1 from Lahey and Moody [25]. In addition, Zuber and Findlay [14] have studied the variation of C_o for various assumed velocity and void profiles.

The $\bar{V}_{dj}$ term on the LHS represents the total mean drift velocity which consists of the $\langle\!\langle V_{dj} \rangle\!\rangle$ term, or the average of the local drift velocity, plus the $(C_o - 1)\langle j \rangle$ term, which represents the convective effects. The V_{dj} term is the local drift velocity which is caused by buoyancy forces. Since the two phases have different densities, the lighter phase will rise upward relative to the heavier phase. The double brackets, $\langle\!\langle \; \rangle\!\rangle$, average the local drift velocity over the total flow area. The

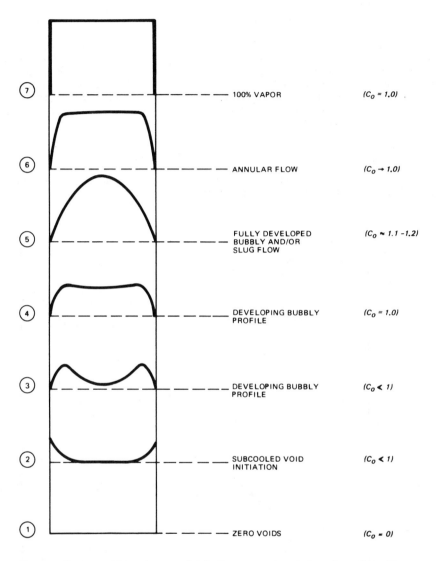

- (7) —— 100% VAPOR   *(C₀ = 1.0)*
- (6) —— ANNULAR FLOW   *(C₀ → 1.0)*
- (5) —— FULLY DEVELOPED BUBBLY AND/OR SLUG FLOW   *(C₀ ≈ 1.1 –1.2)*
- (4) —— DEVELOPING BUBBLY PROFILE   *(C₀ = 1.0)*
- (3) —— DEVELOPING BUBBLY PROFILE   *(C₀ < 1)*
- (2) —— SUBCOOLED VOID INITIATION   *(C₀ < 1)*
- (1) —— ZERO VOIDS   *(C₀ = 0)*

Figure 1. Typical void fraction can distribution parameters in two-phase flow. (Reproduced from Lahey and Moody [25] by permission.)

convective transport of the dispersed phase is due to differences in the velocity and void profiles. For example, in bubbly flow, the gas phase tends to migrate toward the center of a vertical pipe. In this case, the higher velocity and void fraction occur in the center of the pipe, so more gas is convectively transported than with a uniform distribution. Thus, the mean drift velocity, $\bar{V}_{dj}$, is the sum of the average buoyancy effect and the convective transport effect due to nonuniform profiles.

The equation for $\langle\!\langle V_{dj} \rangle\!\rangle$ can be rearranged resulting in

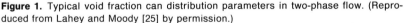

$$\langle\!\langle V_d \rangle\!\rangle = \frac{\langle j_d \rangle}{\langle \alpha_d \rangle} = C_o \langle j \rangle + \langle\!\langle V_{dj} \rangle\!\rangle$$

As mentioned by Zuber and Findlay [14], the value of C_o and $\langle\!\langle V_{dj}\rangle\!\rangle$ can be easily determined from experiments if the volumetric flow rates of each component is known, and the void fraction of either phase is measured. The dispersed-phase velocity can then be plotted as a function of the total volumetric flux, $\langle j \rangle$. From this plot, C_o is equal to the slope of the line while the intercept of the dispersed-phase velocity is equal to $\langle\!\langle V_{dj}\rangle\!\rangle$. Figure 2 shows a typical plot for a steam-water mixture where steam is the dispersed phase. Also shown on the figure is a line representing a homogeneous flow condition and regions of concurrent and countercurrent flow. The experimental data will usually lie on a straight line for a given flow pattern so the values of C_o and $\langle\!\langle V_{dj}\rangle\!\rangle$ are easily evaluated. The determination of $\bar{V}_{dj}$ from these terms is given by the expression

$$\bar{V}_{dj} = \langle\!\langle V_{dj}\rangle\!\rangle + (C_o - 1)\langle j \rangle$$

The void fraction and flowing quality in two-phase flow are related through the phasic densities and the ratio of phasic velocities. In the case of the drift flux model, the drift velocity is known,

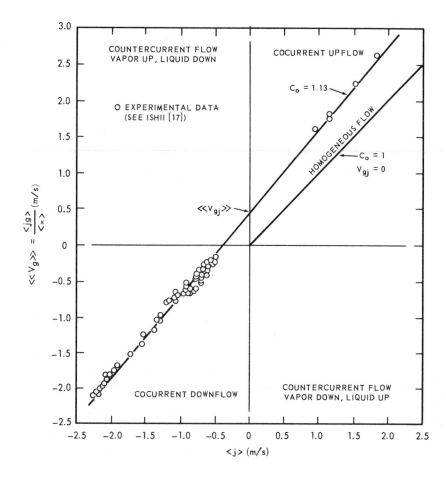

Figure 2. Typical experimental data on drift flux plot.

and the void-fraction/flowing-quality relationship is

$$\langle \alpha_d \rangle = \cfrac{\langle X_d \rangle}{\left\{ C_o \left[\langle X_d \rangle + \cfrac{\rho_d}{\rho_c} \langle X_c \rangle \right] + \cfrac{\rho_d \langle\!\langle V_{dj} \rangle\!\rangle}{G} \right\}}$$

A similar expression relating the void fraction and the static quality is

$$\langle \alpha_d \rangle = \cfrac{\langle X_{s,d} \rangle}{\left[\langle X_{s,d} \rangle + \cfrac{\rho_d}{\rho_c} \langle X_{s,c} \rangle \right]}$$

Convenient relationships between the various velocities follow:

$$\langle\!\langle V_d \rangle\!\rangle = \bar{V}_m + \frac{\rho_c}{\langle \rho_m \rangle} \bar{V}_{dj}$$

$$\langle\!\langle V_c \rangle\!\rangle = \bar{V}_m - \frac{\langle \alpha_d \rangle}{\langle \alpha_c \rangle} \frac{\rho_d}{\langle \rho_m \rangle} \bar{V}_{dj}$$

$$\langle j \rangle = \bar{V}_m + \frac{\langle \alpha_d \rangle (\rho_c - \rho_d)}{\langle \rho_m \rangle} \bar{V}_{dj}$$

$$\langle V_r \rangle = \langle\!\langle V_d \rangle\!\rangle - \langle\!\langle V_c \rangle\!\rangle = \frac{\bar{V}_{dj}}{\langle \alpha_d \rangle}$$

The covariance terms in the one-dimensional conservation equations, designated by the term COV, arise from the differences in the void fraction and the velocity profiles. In the derivation of the area averaged one-dimensional conservation equations, the convective flux is broken down into mixture contribution, the drift portion, and the covariance term, or

$$\frac{\partial}{\partial z} \left(\sum_k \langle \alpha_k \rho_k \psi_k V_k \rangle \right) = \frac{\partial}{\partial z} (\rho_m \bar{\psi}_m \bar{V}_m) + \frac{\partial}{\partial z} \left(\frac{\langle \alpha_d \rangle \rho_d \rho_c}{\langle \rho_m \rangle} \Delta\psi_{dc} \bar{V}_{dj} \right) + \frac{\partial}{\partial z} \sum_k COV(\alpha_k \rho_k \psi_k V_k)$$

where

$$\Delta\psi_{dc} \equiv \langle\!\langle \psi_d \rangle\!\rangle - \langle\!\langle \psi_c \rangle\!\rangle$$

and

$$COV(\alpha_k \rho_k \psi_k V_k) \equiv \langle \alpha_k \rho_k \psi_k (V_k - \langle\!\langle V_k \rangle\!\rangle) \rangle$$

Ishii [17] has demonstrated that the covariance term in the momentum equation is negligible for all practical situations. The covariance term in the energy equation is only important in highly thermodynamic nonequilibrium situations and may also be neglected in most practical applications. For more information on these terms, including a detailed evaluation, see Ishii [17].

Simplified Formulation

For most engineering problems, the preceding general conservation equations can be greatly simplified. For example, the normal stress term in the momentum equation, τ_{zz}, may be neglected as discussed by White [20] for single-phase flow. In the energy equation, the axial conduction term, q, is only important for high thermal conductivity, or low Prandtl number, fluids such as liquid metals and is negligible for a steam-water mixture. Viscous dissipation may be neglected for a steam-water mixture; this term is only significant for highly viscous fluids such as oil. The phases can also be assumed to be in thermodynamic equilibrium; this subject will be discussed in more detail later in this chapter.

Summarizing the assumptions, they are

1. Equal phasic pressures.
2. Uniform phasic densities normal to the flow direction.
3. Neglect axial conduction.
4. Neglect viscous dissipation.
5. Thermodynamic equilibrium.

Due to the assumption of thermodynamic equilibrium, the one-dimensional three-equation drift-flux model can be used. This set of equations is simply the four-equation model previously given without the dispersed-phase continuity equation. Further simplifications can be made in accordance with the stated assumptions, and the resulting one-dimensional three-dimensional drift flux model is summarized in the following:

Mixture continuity equation

$$\frac{\partial}{\partial t}\langle\rho_m\rangle + \frac{\partial}{\partial t}(\langle\rho_m\rangle\bar{V}_m) = 0$$

Mixture momentum equation

$$\frac{\partial}{\partial t}(\langle\rho_m\rangle\bar{V}_m) + \frac{\partial}{\partial z}(\langle\rho_m\rangle\bar{V}_m^2) = -\frac{\partial}{\partial z}\langle P_m\rangle\rangle - \langle\rho_m\rangle g - \frac{f_m}{2D}\langle\rho_m\rangle\bar{V}_m|\bar{V}_m|$$

$$-\frac{\partial}{\partial z}\left[\frac{\langle\alpha_d\rangle\rho_d\rho_c}{\langle\alpha_c\rangle\langle\rho_m\rangle}\bar{V}_{dj}^2\right]$$

Mixture thermal energy equation

$$\frac{\partial}{\partial t}(\langle\rho_m\rangle\bar{h}_m) + \frac{\partial}{\partial z}(\langle\rho_m\rangle\bar{h}_m\bar{V}_m) = \frac{q_w''\xi_h}{A} - \frac{\partial}{\partial z}\left[\frac{\langle\rho_d\rangle\rho_d\rho_c}{\langle\alpha_c\rangle\langle\rho_m\rangle}\Delta h_{dc}\bar{V}_{dj}\right] + \frac{\partial}{\partial t}\langle P_m\rangle$$

$$+ \left[\bar{V}_m + \frac{\langle\alpha_d\rangle(\rho_c - \rho_d)}{\langle\rho_m\rangle}\bar{V}_{dj}\right]\frac{\partial}{\partial z}\langle P_m\rangle$$

Constitutive Relationships

In addition to the conservation equations, constitutive relationships are needed to complete the equation set. The mean drift velocity, $\bar{V}_{dj}$, the fluid friction factor, f_m, and the heat flux to the fluid, q_w'', must be algebraically specified. In addition, the maximum two-phase flow rate, or critical flow rate, must be considered. Unfortunately, many of these constitutive relationships are a function of the two-phase flow pattern. For example, the mean drift velocity is much different for bubbly flow than for slug flow. Therefore, the prediction of two-phase flow patterns will be presented before the detailed discussions of the constitutive relationships.

Flow Patterns

The distribution of the phases in two-phase flow is generally described by the term flow pattern. Prediction of the flow pattern may be accomplished by a flow-pattern map, which graphically present the flow patterns as a function of two variables, and flow-pattern theory, which attempts to describe the phenomenological processes of phase distribution. Unfortunately, the theory of flow patterns is still in the development stages, although significant advances have been made in the last few years. Simple flow-pattern maps are heavily relied upon even in such advanced computer codes such as RELAP5/MOD 1 [8] and TRAC-PD2 [5].

Typical flow patterns for cocurrent upward vertical flow and for horizontal flow are depicted in Figure 3. Flow-pattern descriptions are also given in any number of two-phase flow references such as Tong [21], Collier [22, 23], Bergles et al. [24], Lahey and Moody [25], Hsu and Graham [26], and Wallis [13]. A comprehensive review of two-phase flow patterns is given by Rouhani and

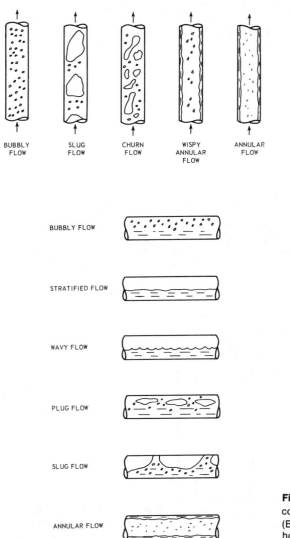

A

BUBBLY FLOW   SLUG FLOW   CHURN FLOW   WISPY ANNULAR FLOW   ANNULAR FLOW

BUBBLY FLOW

STRATIFIED FLOW

WAVY FLOW   B

PLUG FLOW

SLUG FLOW

ANNULAR FLOW

Figure 3. (A) Flow patterns for cocurrent vertical upward flow; (B) flow patterns for cocurrent horizontal flow.

Sohal [27]. In addition, Bornea and Taitel [28] present a discussion of two-phase flow patterns in Volume 6 of this series.

Flow pattern maps. A large number of flow-pattern maps have been generated from experimental data to try to correlate the flow pattern in a simple graphical form. The variety and inconsistency of flow-pattern mapping parameters is exemplified by the summary presented by Spedding and Nguyen [29]. Unfortunately, most of the flow-pattern maps have little or no sound theoretical basis for the flow-pattern transitions, so extrapolation to other fluids, pipe sizes, and conditions can be dangerous. Even so, flow-pattern maps are used regularly due to their ease of application and the lack of a comprehensive flow-pattern theory until recently.

The best known and most widely accepted flow-pattern maps for steam-water two-phase flow are by Baker [30] and by Mandhane et al. [31] for horizontal flow, and by Hewitt and Roberts [32] for cocurrent upward vertical flow. The flow-pattern map of Baker [30] as modified by Collier [23] is shown in Figure 4. This flow-pattern map uses the mass fluxes of the gas and liquid as flow mapping parameters as modified by the terms λ and ψ. These parameters are introduced to account for fluids and conditions which are different than those used in the flow-pattern map database. The parameters λ and ψ are defined as

$$\lambda = \left[\left(\frac{\rho_g}{\rho_a} \right) \left(\frac{\rho_f}{\rho_w} \right) \right]^{1/2}$$

and

$$\psi = \left(\frac{\sigma_w}{\sigma_f} \right) \left[\left(\frac{\mu_f}{\mu_w} \right) \left(\frac{\rho_w}{\rho_f} \right)^2 \right]^{1/3}$$

where the subscripts a and w refer to air and water properties at atmospheric pressure. The appropriate values used by Baker are 0.075 lb_m/ft^3, 62.3 lb_m/ft^3, 73 dynes/cm, and 1 centipoise for ρ_a, ρ_w, σ_w, and μ_w, respectively. The variation of λ and ψ with pressure for a steam-water mixture is shown in Figure 5 after the presentation by Collier [22]. While the flow-pattern map borders are given as discrete lines, the transition lines should be treated as only approximate locations of a flow-pattern change. Flow patterns for steam-water based on the Baker flow map

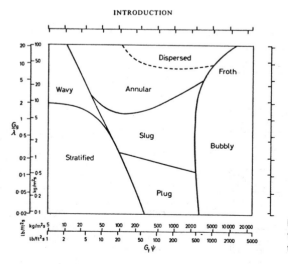

Figure 4. Baker flow pattern map for horizontal flow (reproduced from Collier [23] with permission).

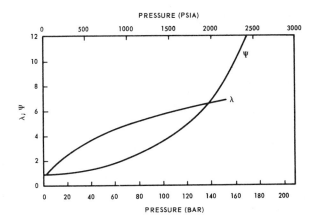

Figure 5. Variation of λ and ψ for a steam-water mixture.

are shown in Figure 6 for three different pressures as given by Tong [21] after the presentation of Goldmann et al. [33]. According to Hsu and Graham [26], Baker's map has also been found to be reasonably successful for vertical flow.

Mandhane, Gregory, and Aziz [31] have developed another horizontal flow map using superficial phasic velocities as the mapping parameters. Their flow map is based on almost 6,000 data points using air-water and other fluid combinations. The flow-pattern map for air-water is depicted in Figure 7. Physical property parameters, which were developed to try to account for the different fluid combinations, have a surprisingly small effect on the flow-pattern transitions and can be ignored in most situations. Of practical interest is the inclusion of a Fortran computer program in the paper which numerically describes the flow map including the property parameter effects.

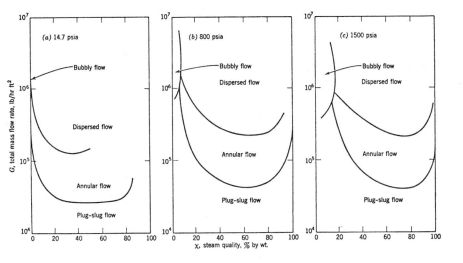

Figure 6. Two-phase flow patterns from Baker flow map (reproduced from Tong [21] with permission).

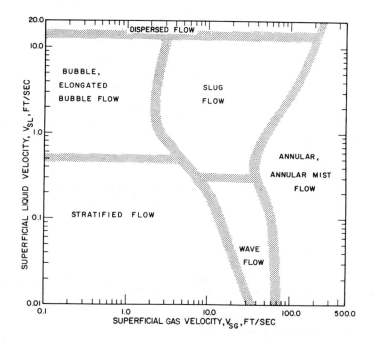

Figure 7. Mandhane et al. Flow pattern map for horizontal flow (reproduced from Mandhane et al. [31] with permission).

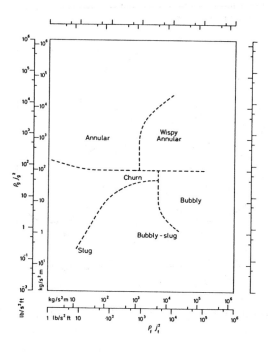

Figure 8. Hewitt and Roberts flow pattern map for vertical flow (reproduced from Collier [23] with permission).

For cocurrent upward vertical flow, Hewitt and Roberts [32] developed a flow-pattern map based on the superficial momentum fluxes of each phase. This map, which is based on limited low-pressures air-water and high-pressure steam-water data, is presented in Figure 8. The axes can also be expressed in terms of the flowing quality and total mass flux as follows

$$\rho_f \langle j + \rangle^2 = \frac{G^2 \langle 1 - X \rangle^2}{\rho_f}$$

$$\rho_g \langle j_g \rangle^2 = \frac{G^2 \langle x \rangle^2}{\rho_g}$$

According to Collier [22, 23], this flow-pattern map should only serve as a rough guide for vertical flow since their mapping parameters are not expected to be governing under all conditions.

Flow pattern theory. Until recently, no comprehensive flow-pattern theory had been developed, and flow-pattern maps were heavily relied upon. This gap has been partially filled by Dukler and Taitel and their coworkers who have published theoretical flow-pattern transitions for horizontal (Taitel and Dukler [34]) and vertical (Dukler and Taitel [35] and Taitel, Bornea, and Dukler [36]) flow situations. Comparison of their horizontal flow-pattern theory to the Mandhane et al. [31] flow map is shown in Figure 9 with good agreement. Ishii and his coworkers (Ishii and Mishima [37], Kataoka and Ishii [38], and Mishima and Ishii [39]) have also developed theoretical flow-pattern transitions for vertical flow. The map of Mishima and Ishii [39] compares favorably with the Dukler [35, 36] maps for vertical flow. Due to the theoretical nature of the flow pattern transitions previously discussed, extension to other fluids and conditions should be more reliable than using flow-pattern maps. The interested reader is referred to the original references for more details.

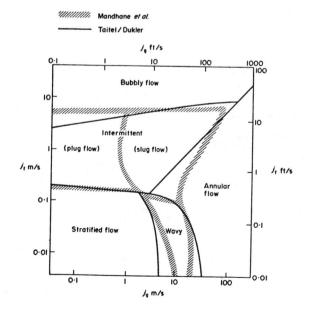

Figure 9. Comparison of prediction of Taitel and Dukler model with Mandhane et al. flow pattern map (reproduced from Collier [23] with permission).

General comments. The flow-pattern maps and flow-pattern theory just discussed are only directly applicable to adiabatic flow conditions, i.e., flow without heat transfer. Flow patterns with heat transfer, or diabatic flow, can result in significantly different flow patterns as noted, for example, by Nicholson et al. [40, 41]. The qualitative trends for the flow patterns with heat transfer are discussed by Hsu and Graham [26]. However, no flow pattern maps or theory are available at the present time that consider the effect of heat transfer.

The drift-flux model described in this chapter is generally not applicable to situations where the phases are not strongly coupled. This situation occurs in horizontal flow when a stratified or wave flow pattern is encountered. Under these conditions, the phases are not dispersed, and different analytical methods such as the two-fluid model should be considered.

Mean Drift Velocity

Predictive methods for the determination of $\bar{V}_{dj}$ will be discussed in the following sections.

Bubbly, slug, and churn flow. The general form of $\bar{V}_{dj}$ used for the bubbly, slug, and churn flow regimes is

$$\bar{V}_{dj} = \langle\!\langle V_{dj} \rangle\!\rangle + (C_o - 1)\langle j \rangle$$

The value of the distribution parameter, C_o, has been studied in detail by Ishii [17]. Using an extension of single-phase flow and the value of C_0 for a fully developed turbulent-flow situation the following expression is obtained

$$C_0 = C_\infty - (C_\infty - 1)(\rho_g/\rho_f)^{1/2}$$

where C_∞ is equal to 1.2 for a round tube and 1.35 for a rectangular channel. Figure 10 shows the comparison of the correlation with data. Each point is the average value of C_0 for anywhere from 5 to 150 separate data points.

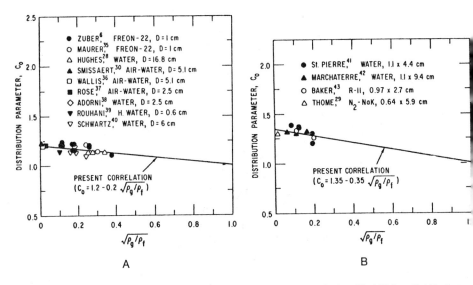

Figure 10. (A) Drift flux distribution parameter for flow in a round tube; (B) drift flux distribution parameter for flow in a rectangular channel. (reproduced from Ishii [17] with permission).

For heat transfer situations, the correlation has been modified slightly to account for the generation of voids near the wall which will decrease the value of C_o. In this case, the expression for C_o is

$$C_o = [C_\infty - (C_\infty - 1)(\rho_g/\rho_f)^{1/2}](1 - e^{-18\langle\alpha\rangle})$$

Figure 11 shows the comparison of the above correlation with experimental data. The rectangular channel data has been modified by the factor 1.2/1.35 to simplify the comparison. The above correlations for C_o are applicable to the bubbly, slug, and churn turbulent flow patterns.

In addition to the value of C_o $\langle\!\langle V_{dj}\rangle\!\rangle$ must bee specified. In general, the value of $\langle\!\langle V_{dj}\rangle\!\rangle$ is a function of the flow pattern. For the bubbly-flow regime, the influence of other bubbles on the drift velocity must be considered. Ishii [17] and Ishii and Zuber [42] have presented correlations for the drift velocity of bubbles in the distorted and undistorted fluid-particle regimes. These drift velocities are for a multiparticle system in an infinite media. The extension of these expressions to particles in a confined channel requires information on the turbulent structure of each phase. In practice, however, the infinite media expressions can be successfully used in a confined flow situation, or

$$\langle\!\langle V_{dj}\rangle\!\rangle \simeq V_{dj}$$

For undistorted particles, the appropriate dispersed-phase drift velocity is given by

$$V_{dj} = \frac{10.8\mu_c}{\rho_c r_d}\frac{\mu_c}{\mu_m}(1 - \alpha_d)^2 \frac{\psi^{4/3}(1 + \psi)}{1 + \psi\left[\dfrac{\mu_c}{\mu_m}(1 + \alpha_d)^{1/2}\right]^{6/7}}\frac{\rho_c - \rho_d}{\Delta\rho}$$

where the functions ψ and r_d^* are given by

$$\psi = 0.55[(1 + 0.08r_d^{*3})^{4/7} - 1]^{3/4}$$

$$r_d^* = r_d(\rho_c g\Delta\rho U/\mu_c)^{1/3}$$

and the value of r_d must be known.

The undistorted particle regime is applicable when the viscosity number, N_{μ_c},

$$N_{\mu_c} = \frac{\mu_c}{(\rho_c\sigma(\sigma/g\,\Delta\rho)^{1/2})^{1/2}}$$

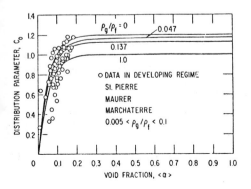

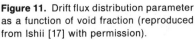

Figure 11. Drift flux distribution parameter as a function of void fraction (reproduced from Ishii [17] with permission).

satisfies the inequality

$$N_{\mu_c} \leq 0.11(1 + \psi)/\psi^{8/3}$$

The ratio of the continuous phase viscosity to the mixture viscosity for the undistorted particle regime can be estimated by the following relationship

$$\frac{\mu_c}{\mu_m} \cong 1 - \langle \alpha_d \rangle = \langle \alpha_c \rangle$$

For the distorted particle situation, or when the inequality is not satisfied, the relationships are more straightforward. The dispersed-phase drift velocity is given by the equation

$$V_{dj} = \sqrt{2} \left(\frac{\sigma g \, \Delta \rho}{\rho_c^2} \right)^{1/4} \langle \alpha_c \rangle^n \frac{\rho_c - \rho_d}{\Delta \rho}$$

where n is equal to 1.75 for a bubble-in-liquid situation.

The formulae for the drift velocities are summarized in Table 2. Also included in this table are the relationships for droplet and particle flows as well as for the churn turbulent regime.

Determination of the bubble size in order to determine the appropriate regime is difficult as discussed by Wallis [13]. If bubble sizes are known, then the undistorted particle expressions can be used. However, if the bubble sizes are not known, which is usually the case, a generally acceptable procedure is to calculate the bubble drift velocity from the distorted particle formula, which is independent of the bubble size.

With an increasing dispersed-phase void fraction, bubbly flow often changes to churn-turbulent flow. In this case, as noted in Table 2, the churn-turbulent drift-velocity expression is similar to the distorted-particle relationship, or

$$V_{dj} = \sqrt{2} \left(\frac{\sigma g \, \Delta \rho}{\rho_c^2} \right)^{1/4} \frac{\rho_c - \rho_d}{\Delta \rho}$$

For bubbles in liquid, the drift velocity becomes

$$V_{dj} = \sqrt{2} \left(\frac{\sigma g \, \Delta \rho}{\rho_f^2} \right)^{1/4}$$

This expression is consistent with the original work of Zuber and Findlay [14] and the recent work of Wallis [43], who recommends a coefficient between 1.41 and 1.56. In earlier work summarized by Wallis [13], the relative velocity of a large bubble has also been given by the equation

$$V_r = K \left(\frac{\sigma g}{\rho_f} \right)^{1/4}$$

where K values of 1.18 and 1.53 have been proposed by Peebles and Gardner [44] and by Harmathy [45], respectively. For many situations, the fluid density is much greater than the gas situations, the fluid density is much greater than the gas density, and the two expressions are essentially equivalent.

For slug flow, Ishii [17] recommends the drift velocity given by

$$V_{dj} = 0.35 \left(\frac{gD \, \Delta \rho}{\rho_c} \right)^{1/2}$$

which is the rise velocity of a slug in a stagnant fluid. Again, this expression agrees with the work of Zuber and Findlay [14].

Table 2
Summary of Drift Velocity V_{dj} in Infinite Media

	Bubble in liquid	Droplet in liquid	Droplet in gas	Solid particle
μ_c/μ_m	$(1-\alpha_d)$	$\sim(1-\alpha_d)^2$	$\sim(1-\alpha_d)^{2.6}$	$\sim(1-\alpha_d)^{2.6}$
Stokes regime	$\dfrac{2}{9}\dfrac{g\,\Delta\rho\,r_d^2}{\mu_f}(1-\alpha_d)^3$		$\dfrac{2}{9}\dfrac{g(\rho_c-\rho_d)}{\mu_c}\,r_d^2(1-\alpha_d)^2\,\dfrac{\mu_c}{\mu_m}$	
Undistorted-particle regime	$\dfrac{10.8\mu_c}{\rho_c r_d}\,\dfrac{\mu_c}{\mu_m}(1-\alpha_d)^2\,\dfrac{\psi^{4/3}(1+\psi)}{1\div\psi\left[\dfrac{\mu_c}{\mu_m}(1-\alpha_d)^{0.5}\right]^{6/7}}$			
$N_{\mu_c}\lesssim 0.11\dfrac{1+\psi}{\psi^{8/3}}$		where $\psi = 0.55[(1+0.08\,r_d^{*3})^{4/7}-1]^{0.75}$		For Newton's regime ($r_d^*\geq 34.67$),
Distorted-particle regime		$\sqrt{2}\left(\dfrac{\sigma g\Delta\rho}{\rho_c^2}\right)^{1/4}(1-\alpha_d)^n\,\dfrac{\rho_c-\rho_d}{\Delta\rho}$		
	$n = 1.75$	$n \simeq 2.0$	$n = 2.25$	$\psi = 17.67$
Churn-turbulent regime	$\sqrt{2}\left(\dfrac{\sigma g\,\Delta\rho}{\rho_f^2}\right)^{1/4}$	$\sqrt{2}\left(\dfrac{\sigma g\Delta\rho}{\rho_c^2}\right)^{1/4}\dfrac{\rho_c-\rho_d}{\Delta\rho}$		

All of the preceding expressions are for vertical flow situations. For horizontal flow, the drift-flux concept is less important since buoyancy effects are not as significant. According to Ishii [17], the value of $\langle\!\langle V_{dj}\rangle\!\rangle$ can be set equal to zero for horizontal flow. The correlations for C_o already given can be used for horizontal slug-flow conditions to account for the convective drift-flux effect.

Annular flow. In annular two-phase flow, the liquid phase appears on the wall and may also occur in the central core of the gas phase. Therefore, situations such as pure annular flow, which assumes a fluid film on the wall and a pure gas central core, and annular-mist flow, which has entrained fluid in the central core, must be addressed separately.

In the models used for annular flow, the drift velocity is given for the gas phase relative to the average two-phase velocity. Whether the gas phase is designated the discontinuous or continuous phase in the conservation equations is irrelevant as long as the notation is consistent. For simplicity, the use of gas as the discontinuous phase is suggested. However, the liquid phase could also be designated as the discontinuous phase, and after some algebra, the same equations would result.

According to Ishii [17], the average-drift-velocity model of Ishii, Chawla, and Zuber [46] is appropriate for pure annular flow. Their model expresses the drift velocity in terms of the fluid volumetric velocity, $\langle j_f\rangle$, with the concentration parameter, C_o, assumed equal to 1. The complete model is quite complicated and will only be summarized here. The interested reader should consult the original reference for more detail.

The drift-flux conservation equations presented earlier are based on the mixture velocity, $\bar{V}_m$. Therefore, in order to be consistent, the average-drift-velocity expressions must be reformulated in terms of the mixture velocity, $\bar{V}_m$. This change in the velocity variable accounts for most of the complexity of the final equations. For steady-state conditions in thermodynamic equilibrium, the equations in terms of $\langle j_f\rangle$ are more convenient since $\langle j_f\rangle$ can easily be determined.

Separate relationships are given for laminar and turbulent film flow. The transition between laminar and turbulent film flow is given in terms of the fluid volumetric flux, or

$$\langle j_f\rangle_{tr} = 3{,}200\mu_f/\rho_f D$$

This laminar-turbulent transition can be transformed into an expression relating the average drift velocity to the mixture velocity. Laminar film flow occurs in cocurrent or countercurrent conditions over the range

$$\frac{(1 - \langle\alpha\rangle)\langle\rho_m\rangle\bar{V}_m - \langle\rho_m\rangle\langle j_f\rangle_{tr}}{\langle\alpha\rangle\rho_g} \leq \bar{V}_{gj} \leq \frac{(1 - \langle\alpha\rangle)\langle\rho_m\rangle\bar{V}_m + \langle\rho_m\rangle\langle j_f\rangle_{tr}}{\langle\alpha\rangle\rho_g}$$

For laminar film flow, the average drift velocity in terms of the fluid flux is

$$\bar{V}_{gj} = \pm\left[\frac{16\langle\alpha\rangle}{\rho_g f_i \xi}\left|\frac{\mu_f\langle j_f\rangle}{D} + \frac{\Delta\rho g_z D(1 - \langle\alpha\rangle)^3}{48}\right|\right]^{1/2}$$

Recasting the expression in terms of the mixture velocity results in

$$\bar{V}_{gj} = \pm\frac{8\mu_f\langle\alpha\rangle^2}{\langle\rho_m\rangle D f_i \xi}\left\{-1 + \left(1 + \frac{f_i D\langle\rho_m\rangle^2(1 - \langle\alpha\rangle)\xi}{4\mu_f\langle\alpha\rangle^3\rho_g}\left|\bar{V}_m + \frac{\Delta\rho g_z D^2(1 - \langle\alpha\rangle)^2}{48\mu_f}\right|\right)^{1/2}\right\}$$

The negative root is used when the term inside the absolute value sign is negative. The interfacial friction factor f_i is given by the formula from Wallis [13, 47]

$$f_i = 0.005[1 + 75(1 - \langle\alpha\rangle)]$$

and ξ is ratio of the interface perimeter to the wall perimeter, which for annular flow in a pipe is equal to

$$\xi = \langle\alpha\rangle^{1/2}$$

For turbulent film flow, or when the vapor drift velocity is outside of the laminar limits, the expression as a function of the fluid volumetric flux is

$$\bar{V}_{gj} = \pm \left[\frac{\langle\alpha\rangle(1 - \langle\alpha\rangle)^3 D}{\rho_g f_i \xi} \left| \frac{0.005\rho_f\langle j_r\rangle|\langle j_r\rangle|}{D(1 - \langle\alpha\rangle)^3} + \frac{1}{3}\Delta\rho g_z \right| \right]^{1/2}$$

where, as in the case of laminar film flow, the negative root is used when the term in the absolute value signs is negative.

In terms of the average mixture velocity, this equation is much more complicated. The following parameters are introduced for convenience

$$a \equiv \frac{f_i \xi \rho_g}{0.005\langle\alpha\rangle\rho_f(1 - \langle\alpha\rangle)^2}$$

$$b \equiv \frac{\langle\alpha\rangle\rho_g}{\langle\rho_m\rangle(1 - \langle\alpha\rangle)}$$

$$c \equiv \frac{\Delta\rho g D(1 - \langle\alpha\rangle)}{0.015\rho_f}$$

Upward flow of the liquid phase is indicated by satisfying the inequality

$$\bar{V}_m \geq (cb^2/a)^{1/2} = \left\{ \frac{\Delta\rho g D(1 - \langle\alpha\rangle)\langle\alpha\rangle^3\rho_g}{3\langle\rho_m\rangle^2 f_i \xi} \right\}^{1/2}$$

and the vapor drift velocity is given by

$$\bar{V}_{gj} = \begin{cases} \dfrac{-b\bar{V}_m + [a\bar{V}_m^2 + (a - b^2)c]^{1/2}}{(a - b^2)} & \text{if } a - b^2 \neq 0 \\[2ex] (\bar{V}_m^2 + c)/2b\bar{V}_m & \text{if } a - b^2 = 0 \end{cases}$$

The transition region of countercurrent flow with the liquid film flowing downward and the vapor flowing upward is indicated by

$$-\sqrt{c} \leq \bar{V}_m < \sqrt{cb^2/a}$$

In this case, the vapor drift velocity is

$$\bar{V}_{gj} = \frac{b\bar{V}_m + [-a\bar{V}_m^2 + (a + b^2)c]^{1/2}}{a + b^2}$$

For cocurrent downward flow, or when

$$\bar{V}_m \leq -\sqrt{c}$$

the vapor drift velocity is

$$\bar{V}_{gj} = \frac{-b\bar{V}_m - [a\bar{V}_m^2 - c(a - b^2)]^{1/2}}{a - b^2}$$

A simplified relationship for the drift velocity applicable to cocurrent situations with large mixture velocities and a small effect of gravity is

$$\bar{V}_{gj} = \frac{(1 - \langle\alpha\rangle)\bar{V}_m}{\dfrac{\langle\alpha\rangle\rho_g}{\langle\rho_m\rangle} + \left\{\dfrac{\xi\rho_g[1 + 75(1 - \langle\alpha\rangle)]}{\langle\alpha\rangle\rho_f}\right\}^{1/2}}$$

Comparison of the drift velocity predicted by the complete model of Ishii, Chawla, and Zuber [46] with experimental data is shown in Figure 12. Good agreement is noted. Much of the scatter is attributed by the authors to experimental uncertainties in measurement of the void fraction.

The transition from pure annular flow to annular-mist flow, or dispersed annular flow, occurs when some of the fluid in the annular film is entrained into the central core of the flow. According to Kataoka and Ishii [38], the inception of liquid entrainment in annular flow, and therefore the inception of annular-mist flow, is given by the correlation of Ishii and Grolmes [48], which is

$$\frac{\mu_f j_{gc}}{\sigma}\sqrt{\frac{\rho_g}{\rho_f}} = \begin{cases} 11.78 N_{\mu f}^{0.8} Re_f^{-1/3} & Re_f < 1,635 \\ N_{\mu f}^{0.8} & Re_f \geq 1,635 \end{cases}$$

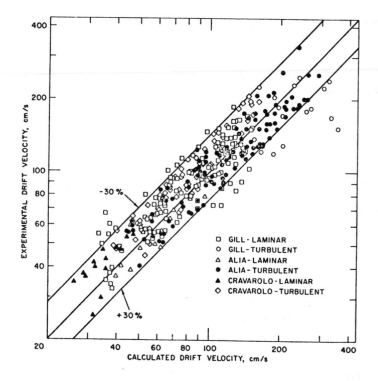

Figure 12. Data-model comparison for annular flow model (reproduced from Ishii [17] with permission).

where the liquid viscosity number and liquid Reynolds number are

$$N_{\mu f} = \mu_f/(\rho_f \sigma \sqrt{\sigma/g\,\Delta\rho})^{1/2}$$

$$Re_f = \frac{\rho_f j_f D}{\mu_f}$$

The amount of liquid entrained in the central core has been correlated by Ishii and Mishima [37]. The entrainment fraction is defined as the droplet flux over the total liquid flux, or

$$E = \frac{\text{droplet flux}}{\text{total liquid flux}} = \frac{j_{fe}}{j_f}$$

The expression for the entrainment in the fully developed situation is

$$E = \tanh(7.25 \times 10^{-7} We^{1.25} Re_f^{0.25})$$

where

$$We = \frac{\rho_g j_g^2 D}{\sigma} \left(\frac{\Delta\rho}{\rho_g}\right)^{1/3}$$

The preceding correlation is recommended by Kataoka and Ishii [38] for diabatic, or boiling, situations. Details on the model for entrance effects in adiabatic flow are given by Kataoka and Ishii [38].
   The relative velocity of the entrained fluid to the gas velocity is given by

$$V_{fe} - V_g = -\frac{r_d}{2}\left[\frac{(g\,\Delta\rho)^2}{\mu_g \rho_g}\right]^{1/3} (1 - \alpha_d)^{1.5}$$

and the drift velocity for the entire dispersed annular flow is

$$\bar{V}_{gj} = V_g - j = \frac{1 - \alpha_{core}}{\alpha_{core} + \left[\dfrac{1 + 75(1 - \alpha_{core})}{\sqrt{\alpha_{core}}}\dfrac{\rho_g}{\rho_f}\right]^{1/2}} \left\{ j + \sqrt{\frac{\Delta\rho g_z D(1 - \alpha_{core})}{0.015\rho_f}} \right\}$$

$$+ \frac{r_g}{2}\left[\frac{(g\,\Delta\rho)^2}{\mu_g \rho_g}\right]^{1/3} \alpha_d(1 - \alpha_d)^{1.5}$$

where

$$\alpha_d \equiv \frac{\text{droplet area}}{\text{gas core area}} \simeq E\frac{j_f}{j_g} = \frac{j_f}{j_g}\tanh(7.25 \times 10^{-7} We^{1.25} Re_f^{0.25})$$

$$\alpha_{core} \equiv \frac{\text{core area}}{\text{flow area}} = \frac{\alpha}{1 - \alpha_d}$$

The entrained droplet size, according to Kataoka, Ishii, and Mishima [49] is

$$r_d \simeq r_{vm} = 0.005 \frac{\sigma}{\rho_g j_g^2} Re_g^{2/3}\left(\frac{\rho_g}{\rho_f}\right)^{-1/3}\left(\frac{\mu_g}{\mu_f}\right)^{2/3}$$

Dispersed droplet or particle flow. For turbulent dispersed droplet or particulate flows, the distribution of the phases tends to become uniform, and according to Ishii [17], a value of C_o in the range of 1.0 to 1.1 is expected. For practical purposes, a value of 1.0 can be used in this regime.

For droplet or particle flows, the equations for V_{gj} are similar to bubbly flow. Ishii [17] and Ishii and Zuber [42] present applicable relationships for the local drift velocity in undistorted and distorted particle regimes. These relationships were previously discussed in the bubble, churn, and slug flow section, and the drift velocity expressions are summarized in Table 2.

As in the case of bubbly flow, the droplet size must be known for the undistorted droplet regime. As discussed by Wallis[13], a number of equations based on the Weber number are available to predict droplet sizes as well as the size spectrum. However, prediction of droplet sizes is usually not very accurate in practice due to a number of variables such as turbulence and impurities in the fluid. Therefore, consistent with the recommendations given in the bubbly flow section, the drift velocity for the distorted particles, which is independent of droplet size, is recommended unless the droplet size is known.

Fluid Friction Factor

The frictional pressure drop in two-phase flow has been and continues to be the subject of much research. Many different correlations have been developed over the years, and a number are given in standard two-phase books such as Bergles, et al. [24], Collier [22, 23], Hsu and Graham [26], Lahey and Moody [25], and Wallis[13]. Therefore, only a limited discussion of frictional pressure drop in two-phase flow will be presented in this section. In addition, Chisholm [50] presents a detailed discussion of two-phase pressure drop in Volume 6 of this series. The interested reader can consult the previous references for more information.

Many different approaches have been taken. The two most common techniques have been to

1. Use a friction factor based on homogeneous flow conditions.
2. Correlate the ratio of two-phase and single-phase pressure drops.

Some of the correlations using the two methods will be discussed in more detail. However, the reader should keep in mind that many more correlations and approaches exist than are mentioned in this section.

Friction factor. In the friction-factor approach, homogeneous flow conditions (no slip or no velocity difference between the phases) are often assumed, so the pressure drop is given by

$$\frac{dP}{dz}\bigg|_F = -\frac{f}{2D}\,\rho_{mh}V_{mh}^2$$

where the homogeneous mixture density and velocity are

$$\frac{1}{\rho_{mh}} = \frac{X}{\rho_g} + \frac{1-X}{\rho_f}$$

$$V_{mh} = \frac{G}{\rho_{mh}}$$

The homogeneous friction factor is assumed to be the same as the single-phase value for an appropriate Reynolds number. The total mass flux is used along with an appropriate two-phase viscosity, or

$$Re = \frac{GD}{\mu_{tp}}$$

Most methods of evaluating the two-phase viscosity are only directly applicable to homogeneous flow conditions. For example, the methods presented by Wallis [13] and Weisman and Choe [51]* are only for homogeneous flow conditions. However, Beattie and Whalley [53] have presented a hybrid viscosity model which seems to predict the frictional pressure drop over a wide range of fluids and conditions and is not restricted to homogeneous conditions. Their hybrid two-phase viscosity relationship combines bubbly flow and annular flow limits resulting in

$$\mu_{tp} = \mu_f(1 - \alpha_h)(1 + 2.5\alpha_h) + \mu_g\alpha_h$$

where the homogeneous void fraction, α_h, is given by

$$\alpha_h = \frac{X}{X + \dfrac{\rho_g}{\rho_f}(1 - X)}$$

The friction factor is calculated by the Colebrook-White single-phase friction-factor equation

$$\frac{1}{\sqrt{f'}} = 3.48 - 4\log_{10}\left[\frac{2\varepsilon}{D} + 9.35/(Re\sqrt{f'})\right]$$

and $f = 4f'$.

This approach was compared to other frictional pressure-drop methods using the HTFS [54] data bank. This comparison shows that this simplistic correlation is generally more accurate than most other popular methods such as Baroczy [55], Thom [56], and others.

Relating this expression to the term in the drift-flux momentum conservation equation presented earlier, the mixture friction factor is related to the homogeneous friction factor by the equation

$$f_m = f\frac{\rho_{mh}}{\langle\rho_m\rangle}\frac{V_{mh}^2}{V_m^2} = f\frac{V_{mh}}{V_m}$$

Pressure-drop ratio. Another popular method of predicting two-phase frictional pressure drop is through the ratio of two-phase to single-phase pressure drop. This method was originated by Lockhart and Martinelli [57] and Martinelli and Nelson [58]. These original methods are still frequently used, and the general approach of relating the two-phase pressure drop to the single-phase value is common.

The work of Lockhart and Martinelli [57] is based on a correlation of the frictional pressure ratio given by

$$\phi_g^2 = \frac{(dP/dz)_{F,tp}}{(dP/dz)_{F,g}}$$

where the numerator is the two-phase frictional pressure drop and the denominator is the frictional pressure drop for the gas phase if the gas is flowing alone in the entire pipe. This ratio has been correlated as a function of the Martinelli parameter, which is the ratio of the liquid-to-gas-phase

---

* The correct expression for the low void two-phase viscosity in the Weisman and Choe [51] model according to Weisman [52] is

$$\mu_{tp} = \mu_f \exp\left\{\frac{2.5\alpha}{1 - 39\alpha/64}\right\}$$

The void fraction in the numerator was inadvertently omitted in the original reference.

pressure drop if each phase is flowing alone in the pipe, or

$$X_{tt}^2 = \frac{(dP/dz)_{F,f}}{(dP/dz)_{F,g}}$$

If both phases are in turbulent flow, the Martinelli parameter is simply given by

$$X_{tt}^2 = \left(\frac{1-X}{X}\right)^{2-n}\left(\frac{\rho_g}{\rho_f}\right)\left(\frac{\mu_f}{\mu_g}\right)^n$$

The value of n is related to the friction factor variation with the Reynolds number, or

$$f \sim cRe^{-n}$$

For most practical purposes, a value of 0.2 for n can be used.

The correlation of ϕ_g with X_{tt} is shown in Figure 13. Once the value of ϕ_g^2 is known, the effective friction factor for use in the drift flux momentum equation can be evaluated by the expression

$$f_m = f_g \frac{\langle \rho_m \rangle}{\rho_g} X^2 \phi_g^2$$

Empirical fits to the Lockhart and Martinelli two-phase friction factor correlation have been presented by Wallis [12] and Chisholm [59, 60].

Critical Flow

The maximum flow rate of a fluid is defined by the critical flow rate. For a single-phase fluid, such as water or a gas, the prediction of the maximum flow rate is straightforward. However, for a two-phase mixture, the situation is considerably more complicated. The additional complexity is due to the presence of two phases which can have widely different velocities and thermodynamic conditions due to the interfacial phenomena involved.

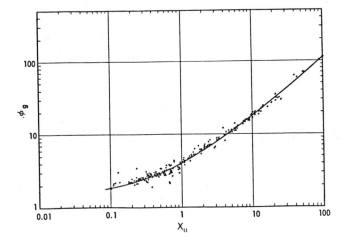

Figure 13. Correlation of Lockhart and Martinelli [57].

The critical flow rate can be determined by the momentum conservation equation given earlier. However, in order to calculate the critical flow rate accurately, small computational cells are required at the point of critical flow. The addition of these mesh points considerably increases the computational cost of the analysis. In addition, the drift-flux thermal energy equation and constitutive relationships presented in this chapter are only suitable for low speed flows as discussed earlier. Therefore, the critical flow is often calculated separately and imposed as a limit on the flow rate calculated by the momentum equation or as a boundary condition in the problem.

A number of theories have been proposed to calculate the critical flow rate of a two-phase mixture, although with limited success. Hsu and Graham [26] present a thorough discussion of the critical flow rate of a two-phase mixture. The interested reader is also referred to a recent article by Wallis [61] and a recent CSNI report [62] on the subject.

The most common critical flow models used for steam-water flow are the homogeneous equilibrium model (HEM) [63], the Moody models [64, 65], and the Henry-Fauske model [63]. In addition, some computer programs have their own detailed critical flow rate method such as the model given by Ransom and Trapp [66] for RELAP5/MOD1 [8]. A number of critical flow models have been compared to experimental data by Ardron and Furness [67], including the HEM, Moody [64], and Henry-Fauske models. A significant conclusion of their comparison is that the HEM model provides a lower bound to the data. Therefore, the HEM critical flow rate can be expected to be a minimum value in practice.

For application to dispersed flows, the assumptions of the HEM model, i.e., equal phasic velocities and thermodynamic equilibrium, are reasonable due to the strong phasic coupling. Therefore, the HEM model is tentatively recommended for dispersed-flow analysis unless more specific information is available. The HEM critical flow rate is based on isentropic flow conditions from the stagnation conditions to the exit plane. Relating the stagnation and static enthalpies through the velocity, the critical flow rate is given by

$$G_c = \frac{\{2(h_o - (1 - X_e)h_{fe} - X_e h_{ge})\}^{1/2}}{(1 - X_e)v_{fe} + X_e v_{ge}}$$

$$X_e = \frac{S_o - S_{fe}}{S_{fge}}$$

Calculations proceed by choosing different exit pressures for the fixed stagnation pressure until the flow rate exhibits a maximum value. Typical ratios of the exit static pressure to the upstream stagnation pressure are 0.5 to 0.7. The HEM critical flow rate for steam-water is depicted in Figure 14.

The critical flow rate presented in Figure 14 is a function of the two-phase stagnation pressure and enthalpy. Stagnation conditions can be related to the static properties available in the calculation by integration along an isentropic path. For the pressure, the stagnation value is obtained by evaluating the following integral

$$P_o = P + \int_h^{h_o} \frac{dh}{v}$$

$$v = f(h, P)$$

For the stagnation enthalpy, the stagnation value is simply the static value plus the velocity term, or

$$h_o = (1 - X)h_f + (1 - X)\frac{V_f^2}{2} + Xh_g + X\frac{V_g^2}{2}$$

where uniform flowing quality and velocity profiles have been assumed.

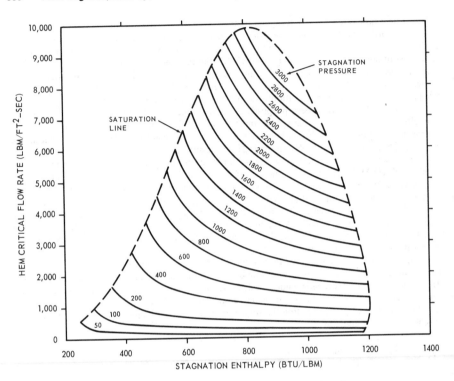

Figure 14. HEM critical flow rate for steam-water as a function of stagnation conditions.

In practice, the critical flow values are often calculated and stored in a data table in the program as a function of stagnation conditions. Stagnation values are then calculated during the transient, and the appropriate critical flow value is evaluated through table lookup.

Heat Transfer

The various two-phase heat transfer regimes in convective boiling are depicted in Figure 15. Five distinct regions can be noted which are

1. Single-Phase Convection
2. Subcooled Convection
3. Nucleate Boiling
4. Transition Boiling
5. Film Boiling

Condensation heat transfer, which is important in a number of applications, will not be discussed. The interested reader is referred to Collier [22, 23] for further details. The first three heat transfer regions will be discussed briefly. The last two regions, transition boiling and film boiling, are not usually encountered in normal operation. For some background on the subject including a summary of models, the reader is referred to Groeneveld [68], Groeneveld and Gardiner [69], Chen, Sundaram, and Ozkaynak [70], and Webb and Chen [71] as well as, of course, the many two-phase heat transfer books.

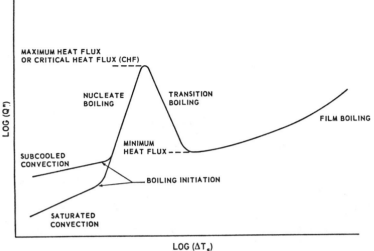

Figure 15. Two-phase heat transfer regimes.

Single-phase convection. Heat transfer in this region can be predicted by standard single-phase correlations which are available in a number of standard heat transfer textbooks such as Holman [72], Kreith [73], and Lienhart [74]. An example of a single-phase correlation is Dittus-Boelter [75], which is

$$Nu_D = \frac{hD}{k} = 0.023 Re_D^{0.8} Pr^{0.4}$$

where the properties are evaluated at the bulk, or average, fluid temperature.

The wall heat flux is equal to the product of the heat transfer coefficient and the temperature difference between the wall and the bulk fluid temperature, or

$$q_w'' = h(T_w - T_b)$$

Subcooled convection. Subcooled boiling occurs when vapor is generated on the heated surface even though the thermodynamic quality of the mixture is less than zero. In this situation, bubbles appear on the wall while the central part of the flow is still subcooled. Thus, the vapor is confined to the wall region, and the distribution parameter, C_o, is less than one. This behavior of the distribution parameter has been taken into account by the form of the correlation for C_o for heat transfer situations as discussed earlier. Ishii, Jones, and Zuber [76] have presented a relaxation method for predicting the vapor generation rate in subcooled boiling. A number of other models have been proposed, and further discussions on the subject may be found in the paper by Jones and Saha [77] and in Collier [22, 23]. However, the present form of the drift flux conservation equations assumes thermodynamic equilibrium, so a separate specification of the vapor generation rate is not necessary.

For the heat flux to the fluid in subcooled boiling, Butterworth [78] suggested that the Chen correlation, which is discussed in the next section, can be used. With reference to the next section, Butterworth modified the Chen correlation for subcooled boiling by setting the Reynolds number factor, F, equal to 1.0 consistent with the trends of the correlation, and evaluating the suppression factor, S, based on the liquid Reynolds number, or

$$Re_f = \frac{GD}{\mu_f}$$

The heat flux is then calculated by the following formula

$$q_w'' = h_{mic}(T_w - T_s) + h_{mac}(T_w - T_b)$$

where the microconvection and macroconvection heat transfer coefficients are given in the next section. Comparison to subcooled heat transfer data for a number of fluids showed reasonable results as discussed by Collier [22, 23].

Nucleate boiling. For heat transfer in nucleate boiling, the Chen correlation is widely accepted as the best method presently available. Chen [79] used a superposition technique by adding together the heat transfer contributions for microconvection due to boiling and macroconvection due to flow effects. The two terms are modified by the suppression factor, S, on the microconvection and the Reynolds number factor, F, on the macroconvection term. The heat transfer coefficient based on saturated two-phase conditions is given by

$$h = h_{mic} + h_{mac}$$

where

$$h_{mic} = 0.00122 \left[\frac{k_f^{0.79} C_{pf}^{0.45} \rho_f^{0.49} g_c^{0.25}}{\sigma^{0.5} \mu_f^{0.29} h_{fg}^{0.24} \rho_g^{0.24}} \right] \Delta T^{0.24} \Delta \rho^{0.75} S$$

$$h_{mac} = 0.023 Re_f^{0.8} Pr^{0.4} \frac{k_f}{D} F$$

$$Re_f = \frac{G(1 - X)D}{\mu_f}$$

$$\Delta T = T_w - T_s$$

$$\Delta P = P_s(T_w) - P_s(T_s)$$

$$X_{tt}^{-1} = \left(\frac{X}{1 - X} \right)^{0.9} \left(\frac{\rho_f}{\rho_g} \right)^{0.5} \left(\frac{\mu_g}{\mu_f} \right)^{0.1}$$

The Reynolds number factor, F, and the suppression factor, S, are shown in Figures 16 and 17, respectively. The Chen correlation was extended to binary mixtures and higher Prandtl number fluids by Bennett and Chen [80].

For convenience, the above curves for F and S can be represented by the following expressions as determined by Edelstein, Perez, and Chen [81]

$$F = (1 + X_{tt}^{-0.5})^{1.78}$$

$$S = 0.9622 - 0.5822(\tan^{-1}(Re/6.18 \times 10^4))$$

$$Re = Re_f F^{1.25}$$

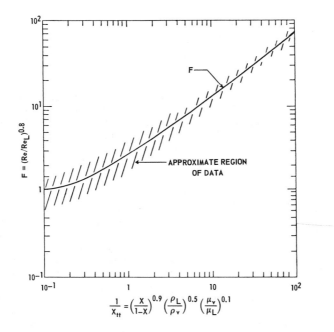

Figure 16. Chen-Reynolds number factor F (reproduced from Chen [79] with permission).

A fit to the F and S curves has also been presented by Bjornard and Griffith [82] as developed by Butterworth [83]. The expressions are

$$F = \begin{cases} 1.0 & X_{tt} \leq 0.10 \\ 2.35(X_{tt}^{-1} + 0.213)^{0.736} & X_{tt} > 0.10 \end{cases}$$

$$S = \begin{cases} (1 + 0.12Re_{tp}'^{1.14})^{-1} & Re_{tp}' < 32.5 \\ (1 + 0.42Re_{tp}'^{0.78})^{-1} & 32.5 \leq Re_{tp}' < 70 \\ 0.1 & Re_{tp}' \geq 70 \end{cases}$$

$$Re_{tp}' = \frac{G(1 - X)D}{\mu_f} F^{1.25}(10^{-4})$$

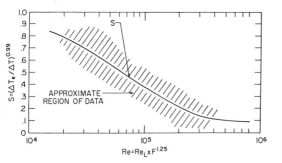

Figure 17. Chen suppression factor S (reproduced from Chen [79] with permission).

Note that the preceding expressions attributed to Butterworth are presently used in the TRAC-PD2[5] computer program. The heat flux is based on the Chen heat transfer coefficient times the wall superheat, or

$$q_w'' = h(T_w - T_s)$$

The maximum heat transfer rate in two-phase flow is determined by the critical heat flux (CHF) for the appropriate conditions. Determination of CHF and calculation of heat transfer in the post-CHF heat transfer modes of transition and film boiling will not be discussed. The interested reader should consult the book by Tong [84] on the subject or a general two-phase heat transfer book such as Collier [22, 23] and Hsu and Graham [26].

NUMERICAL SOLUTION

It is generally not possible to obtain analytical solutions for most practical problems in transient two-phase flow. Numerical methods based upon finite-difference concepts provide an alternate and powerful solution approach.

The "pressure-velocity" or P-V methods [85, 87] originally developed for single-phase flows have had an important role in the development of computational methods for two-phase flow. Those methods solve for primary variables (P, V) rather than for derived variables such as vorticity or stream function [86]. Patankar [87] provides a very good presentation of the P-V method for steady-state single-phase flow. Of particular significance to transient computational fluid mechanics is the implicit continuous Eulerian (ICE) developed by Harlow and Amsden [85]. The ICE method for single-phase flow is able to consider flow speeds ranging from incompressible subsonic to compressible supersonic. The basic idea of their method has had an important impact on the development of computational methods for transient two-phase flow. This is because the mixture two-phase flow equations are similar in form to the equations for compressible single-phase flow. They are complicated by the additional nonlinear terms for the mixture equation of state and the relative velocity of the liquid and vapor phases.

The following discussion presents a computational procedure based on standard finite difference methods for fluid mechanics and is strongly based in Newton's method for solving nonlinear equations. The methods to be presented are limited to one-dimensional two-phase flow in a uniform area channel; however, the basic ideas can be extended to variable area channels and to multidimensional flows.

Finite-Difference Principles

This section is concerned with transforming the mass, energy, and momentum equations into a form that is suitable for numerical solution. This is done by replacing the differential equations with difference equations. The difference equations are solved for a finite number of computational cells that represent the flow channel.

The three-equation thermal-equilibrium drift-flux formulation is use to illustrate a specific solution approach. The three equations to be solved are of the form:

$$\frac{\partial \rho}{\partial t} + \frac{\partial (\rho V)}{\partial z} = 0$$

$$\frac{\partial(\rho h)}{\partial t} + \frac{\partial(\rho V h)}{\partial z} - \frac{\partial P}{\partial t} - V\frac{\partial P}{\partial z} - Q + R_E = 0$$

$$\frac{\partial(\rho V)}{\partial t} + \frac{\partial(\rho V^2)}{\partial z} + \frac{\partial P}{\partial z} + F + G + R_M = 0$$

where $F = \dfrac{f}{2D}\, \rho |V| V$

$G = \rho g_z$

$Q = \dfrac{q''_w \xi_h}{A}$

$R_E = \dfrac{\partial}{\partial z}\left(\dfrac{(\alpha\rho)_d (\alpha\rho)_c}{\rho}\, \Delta h_{dc} V_r\right) - \dfrac{\alpha_d \alpha_c (\rho_c - \rho_d)}{\rho}\, V_r\, \dfrac{\partial P}{\partial z}$

$R_m = \dfrac{\partial}{\partial z}\left(\dfrac{(\alpha\rho)_d (\alpha\rho)_c}{\rho}\, V_r^2\right)$

The average and mixture notation has been dropped to simplify the discussion. These equations have the same form as those for one-dimensional single-phase flow except for the added relative velocity terms in the energy and momentum equations. Note that relative velocity has been introduced where

$V_r = V_d - V_c$

and $\bar{V}_{dj}$ is related to V_r by

$V_r = \dfrac{\bar{V}_{dj}}{\alpha_c}$

Computational Cell

The finite difference solution represents the flow channel by a series of connected control volumes or computational cells. The basic concept can best be shown by example. Figure 18 shows a one-dimensional channel that has been subdivided into computational cells. The cell location is denoted by the index i and the cell center is denoted by the physical distances z_i. Each cell has a length Δz_i.

The index notation $i + \frac{1}{2}$ indicates the boundary location $z_i + \Delta z_i/2$ between cells i and i + 1. Similarly, $i - \frac{1}{2}$ is the location $z_i - \Delta z_i/2$ between i − 1 and i.

The dashed cells at the end of the channel are used to define boundary conditions.

It has become customary for most contemporary computational methods to use a staggered placement of variables on the computational cell as shown in Figure 19. The convention is to place scalars such as pressure, enthalpy, density, void-fraction, and temperature at cell centers. The variables are subscripted by i to denote the cell centered location. The velocities and mass fluxes are placed at cell faces and are denoted by full and one-half indices to identify the cell face. For example, in Figure 19 the velocity out the right side of the cell is $V_{i+1/2}$. For computer programming the $\frac{1}{2}$ is not used and integer values are used by shifting the velocity index by $\frac{1}{2}$.

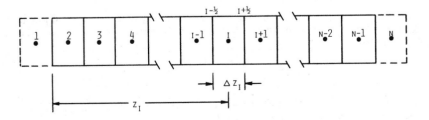

Figure 18. Computational cells for one-dimensional channel.

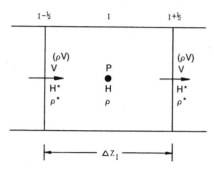

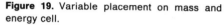

Figure 19. Variable placement on mass and energy cell.

Finite Difference Analogs

Finite difference analogs are used to approximate the time and space derivatives of the differential equations. They can be derived directly for the control volume by using the integral balance laws for a control volume [86, 87]. They can also be derived by formal mathematical statements involving Taylor's series [89, 91]. For purposes of this discussion the details of the derivations are bypassed and difference analogs are presented directly. The discussion is also limited to first-order differences since they are in widest use. They are also those that would be derived by using the control volume approach.

Mass equation. The finite difference analog for the mass equation is written as

$$\frac{\Delta\rho}{\Delta t} + \frac{\Delta(\rho V)}{\Delta z} = 0$$

The specific definition of the derivatives for a computational cell are:

$$\frac{\Delta\rho}{\Delta t} = \frac{\rho_i^{n+1} - \rho_i^n}{\Delta t}$$

$$\frac{\Delta(\rho V)}{\Delta z_i} = \frac{(\rho V)_{i+1/2} - (\rho V)_{i-1/2}}{\Delta z_i}$$

The superscripts n and n + 1 represent time levels t and t + Δt, respectively. Time levels are assigned to the spatial derivatives according to the level of implicitness, presented later in the discussion.

The mass flux (ρV) is defined as

$$(\rho V) = \rho^* V$$

where ρ^* is the density defined at the cell boundary. A variety of methods [85, 88] have been suggested to define density at the cell boundary. An attractive form is a weighted donor-cell definition [88] given by

$$\rho_{i+1/2}^* = \frac{1+\beta}{2}\rho_i + \frac{1-\beta}{2}\rho_{i+1}$$

where β can vary between -1 and $+1$. Choice of $\beta = 0$ produces a mathematically more accurate but less stable central difference. If β is defined by

$$\beta = \text{sign}(V_{i+1/2})$$

then full-donor differencing is obtained where density is assigned from the upstream density. Donor assignment produces very stable results but introduces second-order errors that produce numerical diffusion [86, 87]. In spite of this difficulty donor assignment is in wide use for numerical calculations. An assigned value is denoted by superscript * in the following discussion.

The previous donor definition is satisfactory for cocurrent flow; however, for countercurrent flow the definition can be modified as

$$\rho^* = (\alpha\rho)^*_d + (\alpha\rho)^*_c/(\alpha^*_d + \alpha^*_c)$$

where donor values are assigned based on phasic velocities V_d and V_c defined by

$$V_d = V + \frac{(\alpha\rho)^*_c}{\rho^*} V_r$$

and

$$V_c = V - \frac{(\alpha\rho)^*_d}{\rho^*} V_r$$

The same logic applies to the definition of all scalars required at cell boundaries.

Energy equation. The finite difference analog for the energy equation is written as

$$\frac{\Delta(\rho h)}{\Delta t} + \frac{\Delta(\rho V)h^*}{\Delta z} - \frac{\Delta P}{\Delta t} - V\frac{\Delta P}{\Delta z} - Q + R_E = 0$$

Consider the specific definitions for a computational cell.
The enthalpy terms are defined by

$$\frac{\Delta(\rho h)_i}{\Delta t} = \frac{(\rho h)^{n+1}_i - (\rho h)^n_i}{\Delta t}$$

and

$$\frac{\Delta(\rho V)h^*}{\Delta z_i} = \frac{((\rho V)h^*)_{i+1/2} - ((\rho V)h^*)_{i-1/2}}{\Delta z_i}$$

The assignment of h* at the cell boundary follows the previous definition and where $h^* = (\rho h)^*/\rho^*$.
The pressure terms are defined by

$$\frac{\Delta P_i}{\Delta t} = \frac{P^{n+1}_i - P^n_i}{\Delta t}$$

and

$$V\frac{\Delta P}{\Delta z} = \frac{\Delta(VP^*)}{\Delta z} - P\frac{\Delta V}{\Delta z}$$

or

$$V\frac{\Delta P}{\Delta z} = \frac{(VP^*)_{i+1/2} - (VP^*)_{i-1/2}}{\Delta z_i} - P_i\left(\frac{V_{i+1/2} - V_{i-1/2}}{\Delta z_i}\right)$$

Note that the definition for V $\Delta P/\Delta z$ consists of analogs of the terms that define V $\partial P/\partial z$. This is useful form because it is defined in terms of fluxes through the cell boundary.

Treatment of the relative velocity terms is not well developed in the literature. One possible treatment for cocurrent flow is to use

$$R_E = \frac{\Delta(a^*V_r)}{\Delta z} - bV_r \frac{\Delta P}{\Delta z}$$

where

$$a = \frac{(\alpha\rho)_d(\alpha\rho)_c}{\rho}(h_d - h_c)$$

$$b = \frac{\alpha_d\alpha_c(\rho_c - \rho_d)}{\rho}$$

For countercurrent flow it can be useful to define convective terms by their phasic components using donor assignment for each phase.

Momentum equation. The momentum equation has additional considerations because of the staggered variables. The momentum equation is shifted by one-half cell from the cell used by the mass and energy equations. This shift forms the staggered momentum cell illustrated in Figure 20. The momentum cell is centered at $i + \frac{1}{2}$ and spans the distance from i to i + 1.

The finite difference analog of the momentum equation can be written as

$$\frac{\Delta(\rho V)}{\Delta t} + \frac{\Delta(\rho V^2)}{\overline{\Delta z}} + \frac{\Delta P}{\overline{\Delta z}} + F + G + R_M = 0$$

The time derivative for the mass flux is represented by

$$\frac{\Delta(\rho V)_{i+1/2}}{\Delta t} = \frac{(\bar{\rho}V)_{i+1/2}^{n+1} - (\bar{\rho}V)_{i+1/2}^{n}}{\Delta t}$$

where the mass flux for momentum is defined as the product of velocity and average density defined by

$$\bar{\rho}_{i+1/2} = \frac{(\rho \,\Delta z)_i + (\rho \,\Delta z)_{i+1}}{\Delta z_i + \Delta z_{i+1}}$$

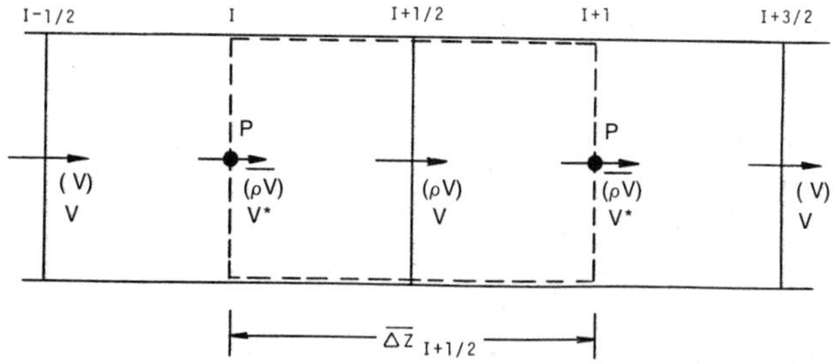

Figure 20. Variable placement on staggered momentum cell.

The momentum flux term is defined by

$$\frac{\Delta(\rho V^2)}{\overline{\Delta z}_{i+1/2}} = \frac{(\rho V^2)_{i+1} - (\rho V^2)_i}{\overline{\Delta z}_{i+1/2}}$$

where

$$\overline{\Delta z}_{i+1/2} = \tfrac{1}{2}(\Delta z_i + \Delta z_{i+1})$$

This derivative requires assignment of the velocity at the momentum cell boundary in a way that is similar to the assignment of a scalar at a cell boundary. This case, however, is not as simple and several methods of assignment are possible. A combination of averaging and donor assignment is typically used to make the definitions. A common approach is to define an average flow (mass flux) that transport a velocity to the edge of the momentum cell as shown in Figure 20. The average flow (mass flux) at i is defined to be the average of the adjacent flows at $i - \tfrac{1}{2}$ and $i + \tfrac{1}{2}$, thus,

$$\overline{\rho V}_i = \tfrac{1}{2}((\rho V)_{i+1/2} + (\rho V)_{i-1/2})$$

and a similar definition applies at i + 1. This definition for average velocity satisfies a mass balance for the momentum cell where the mass balance is the average of the two cells forming the staggered cell. The velocity V* is assigned based on the average mass flux. The derivative can now be more specifically written as

$$\frac{\Delta(\rho V^2)}{\Delta z} = \frac{\Delta(\overline{\rho V}V^*)}{\Delta z}$$

and

$$\frac{\Delta(\overline{\rho V}V^*)}{\overline{\Delta z}_{i+1/2}} = \frac{(\overline{\rho V}V^*)_{i+1} - (\overline{\rho V}V^*)_i}{\overline{\Delta z}_{i+1/2}}$$

The pressure gradient is defined as

$$\frac{\Delta P}{\overline{\Delta z}_{i+1/2}} = \frac{P_{i+1} - P_i}{\overline{\Delta z}_{i+1/2}}$$

The friction term for turbulent flow is defined as

$$F_{i+1/2} = \left(\frac{f}{2D} \, \bar{\rho}|V|V \right)_{i+1/2}$$

The gravity term is defined as

$$G_{i+1/2} = (\bar{\rho} g_z)_{i+1/2}$$

The relative velocity term is an extension of the momentum flux term and suffers similar difficulties when making definitions of velocity at the edge of the momentum cell. Liles and Reed [88] define the term as

$$R_{M_{i+1/2}} = \frac{1}{\overline{\Delta z}_{i+1/2}} \left[\left(\frac{(\alpha\rho)_c(\alpha\rho)_d}{\rho} \, V_r^{*2} \right)_{i+1} - \left(\frac{(\alpha\rho)_c(\alpha\rho)_d}{\rho} \, V_r^{*2} \right)_i \right]$$

where V_r^* is defined by using donor assignment. Using average phasic flows and donor velocities for the momentum flux offers an alternative and more general definition that is more applicable for countercurrent flow.

Difference analogs for the momentum flux terms are not universally accurate for all situations. The difference forms used for numerical analysis should be checked for their correctness in a particular application. This can usually be done by using simple conceptual cases with known analytical results (e.g., calculation of acceleration pressure drop with heat addition during steady state).

Conservative Versus Transportive Equations

The energy equation presented in the previous discussion can be called a conservative form. This is because it conserves energy (enthalpy) when globally integrated over the length of the channel. With the introduction of the mass balance it becomes

$$\rho \frac{\partial h}{\partial t} + \rho V \frac{\partial h}{\partial z} - \frac{\partial P}{\partial t} - V \frac{\partial P}{\partial z} - Q + R_E = 0$$

This is called the transportive form because it defines the transport of h along a streamline. In the absence of the source term, h would translate through the channel at velocity V. It is not always possible to integrate a finite difference form of the transportive equation and obtain conservation of energy, whereas it can be assured with the conservative form. The difficulty occurs when there is a local flow reversal. This situation is discussed by Roache [86], in the context of seeking a finite difference form that is both conservative and transportive.

It is possible to achieve the transportive property by combining the mass and energy equation numerically. The temporal term of the energy equation can be factored as

$$\frac{\Delta \rho h}{\Delta t} = \rho \frac{\Delta h}{\Delta t} + h \frac{\Delta \rho}{\Delta t}$$

and that factoring can be made exact by an appropriate time-level assignment of ρ and h. By combining the factored energy equation and the mass equation, the energy equation can be written as

$$\rho \frac{\Delta h}{\Delta t} + \frac{\Delta(\rho V)h^*}{\Delta z} - h \frac{\Delta(\rho V)}{\Delta z} - \frac{\Delta P}{\Delta t} - V \frac{\Delta P}{\Delta z} - Q + R_E$$

This equation has the desired transportive property. Note that the two spatial differences give an analog for a term of the form $\rho V \, \partial h/\partial z$ as presented previously. If the temporal factoring is not exact, the equation is still transportive but some of the temporal conservative properties may be lost.

Patankar [87] develops the transportive form but from the point of view of preserving fluxes through a cell boundary. The transportive form is valuable for numerical solutions because the energy equation is more tolerant of mass balance errors at intermediate stages of iterative solutions.

The transportive spatial difference term includes three possible values of enthalpy to define the energy balance for each computational cell. This term can be compactly represented and computed for donor assignment by using the definition

$$\frac{\Delta(\rho V)h^*}{\Delta z_i} - h_i \frac{\Delta(\rho V)}{\Delta z_i} = -a_i h_{i-1} + b_i h_i - c_i h_{i+1}$$

where $a_i = \max(0, (\rho V)_{i-1/2})/\Delta z_i$
$c_i = \max(0, -(\rho V)_{i+1/2})/\Delta z_i$
$b_i = a_i + c_i$

The same form applies to other transportive terms.

The momentum equation presented previously is also of conservative form and can be converted to transportive form. The momentum cell mass balance written as the average of two adjacent cells is

$$\frac{\Delta \bar{\rho}}{\Delta t} + \frac{\Delta \overline{(\rho V)}}{\overline{\Delta z}} = 0$$

By factoring the temporal term of the momentum equation and introducing the mass balance, the transportive form is

$$\bar{\rho}\frac{\Delta V}{\Delta t} + \frac{\Delta(\overline{\rho V}V^*)}{\overline{\Delta z}} - V\frac{\Delta(\overline{\rho V})}{\overline{\Delta z}} + \frac{\Delta P}{\overline{\Delta z}} + F + G + R_M = 0$$

The use of the average mass flux and donor-assigned velocity in the momentum flux terms produces correct steady-state pressure changes for several simple conditions in the absence of gravity, friction, and relative velocity. A zero-pressure gradient is correctly produced as a density change moves from cell to cell at a constant velocity. The spatial acceleration pressure drop under conditions of uniform and constant mass flux is correctly given but is shifted downstream one cell when the donor-velocity assignment is used. The use of a donor flow divided by the cell center density to define the donor velocity can eliminate the shift but does not produce correct results for the previous case.

Levels of Implicitness

The previous discussion has presented finite-difference equations without specific reference to the time level of the spatial difference terms or the source terms. The level of implicitness (or explicitness) is concerned with making those time specifications. This has an important affect on the time-step limits and stability of the numerical solution.

Explicit. The fully explicit equations are written in conservative form as:

$$\frac{\Delta\rho}{\Delta t} + \frac{\Delta(\rho V)^n}{\Delta z} = 0$$

$$\frac{\Delta(\rho h)}{\Delta t} + \frac{\Delta(\rho V)^n h^{*n}}{\Delta z} - \frac{\Delta P}{\Delta t} - V^n\frac{\Delta P^n}{\Delta z} - Q^n + R_E^n = 0$$

$$\frac{\Delta(\bar{\rho}V)}{\Delta t} + \frac{\Delta(\overline{\rho V}V^*)^n}{\overline{\Delta z}} + \frac{\Delta P^n}{\overline{\Delta z}} + F^n + G^n + R_M^n = 0$$

where all source and derivative terms are at time n.

Explicit methods are simple because the temporal derivatives are evaluated directly to advance the solution from n to n + 1. The equation of state is inverted in this case to define pressure in terms of density and enthalpy. The explicit treatment of the mass and momentum equation limits the time step to be on the order of a sonic transit time through the most limiting computational cell. This produces time steps that are on the order of 10^{-6} seconds for many steam-water flow applications. This limit is usually severe enough that the explicit method is not used for most practical two-phase flow numerical solutions. This level of implicitness was used in the early versions of FLASH [92].

Implicit. The fully implicit equations can be written in the form

$$\frac{\Delta\rho}{\Delta t} + \frac{\Delta(\rho V)^{n+1}}{\Delta z} = 0$$

$$\frac{\Delta(\rho h)}{\Delta t} + \frac{\Delta((\rho V)h^*)^{n+1}}{\Delta z} - \frac{\Delta P}{\Delta t} - V^{n+1}\frac{\Delta P^{n+1}}{\Delta z} - Q^{n+1} + R_E^{n+1} = 0$$

$$\frac{\Delta(\bar{\rho}V)}{\Delta t} + \frac{\Delta(\overline{\rho V}V^*)^{n+1}}{\overline{\Delta z}} + \frac{\Delta P^{n+1}}{\overline{\Delta z}} + F^{n+1} + G^{n+1} + R_M^{n+1} = 0$$

where all spatial derivatives and source terms are now at time n + 1.

Fully implicit equations can substantially reduce or eliminate time step restrictions at the expense of a simultaneous solution of all variables. For an arbitrary flow direction this can require a rather complex solution. The complexity is great enough that fully implicit methods are not generally available for transient two-phase flow. If flows are restricted to being in one direction, the numerical solution is simplified considerably and fully implicit methods are more practical. The use of an inlet flow rather than an inlet pressure boundary condition also greatly simplifies the fully-implicit solution.

Semi-implicit. Between the extremes of explicit and implicit are the semi-implicit equations. An important semi-implicit selection is:

$$\frac{\Delta\rho}{\Delta t} + \frac{\Delta(\rho^{*n}V^{n+1})}{\Delta z} = 0$$

$$\frac{\Delta(\rho h)}{\Delta t} + \frac{\Delta((\rho V)h^*)^n}{\Delta z} - \frac{\Delta P}{\Delta t} - V\frac{\Delta P^n}{\Delta z} - Q^n + R_E^n = 0$$

$$\frac{\Delta(\bar{\rho}V)}{\Delta t} + \frac{\Delta(\overline{\rho V}V^*)^n}{\overline{\Delta z}} + \frac{\Delta P^{n+1}}{\overline{\Delta z}} + F^n + G^n + R_M^n = 0$$

Note that the energy equation is explicit but the mass equation is implicit in velocity and the momentum equation is implicit in pressure. The implicitness of the mass and momentum equations removes the sonic time-step limitation provided the flow is subsonic. This is a fundamental feature of the ICE algorithm. The energy and momentum equations are still explicit in the spatial difference terms and this limits the time step to be on the order of the fluid transit time through a computational cell rather than the sonic transit time through a cell as for the fully explicit equations. This usually results in time steps that are several orders of magnitude larger than the time step for a typical application of the explicit solution method. As flow speeds approach sonic conditions, both methods require short time steps.

The functional form of the explicit source terms can also impose additional time-step restrictions. Making them implicit eliminates their contribution to the time-step limit, but can add to the complexity of the numerical solution.

The use of split time levels to define the mass flux in the mass equation has become common in the development of TRAC [5]. Split time levels are also used in other derivative and source terms.

Semi-implicit transportive forms of the energy and momentum equations can be written by factoring the temporal terms and substituting the mass balance:

$$\rho^n\frac{\Delta h}{\Delta t} + \frac{\Delta(\rho V)^n h^{*n}}{\Delta z} - h^n\frac{\Delta(\rho V)^n}{\Delta z} - \frac{\Delta P}{\Delta t} - V^n\frac{\Delta P^n}{\Delta z} - Q^n + R_E^n = 0$$

and

$$\bar{\rho}^n\frac{\Delta V}{\Delta t} + \frac{\Delta\overline{\rho V}^n V^{*n}}{\overline{\Delta z}} - V^n\frac{\Delta\overline{\rho V}^n}{\overline{\Delta z}} + \frac{\Delta P^{n+1}}{\Delta z} + F^n + G^n + R_M^n = 0$$

The factoring process produces spatially conservative equations at steady state; however, the temporal terms may not be exact depending upon the factoring approximations and level of implicitness used in the equations. If the mass flux $(\rho V)^{n+1}$ is defined by using the split time level definition $\rho^{*n}V^{n+1}$ with a corresponding definition for $(\rho V)^n$, exact factoring is achieved for the momentum equation by using an implicit mass equation shifted back one time step; however, this could be interpreted as not being totally conservative. Nonconservative forms of the momentum equations are often used because of their desirable numerical properties.

Similar reasoning can be used for the energy equation if the term $(\rho h)^{n+1}$ is defined as $\rho^n h^{n+1}$ with a corresponding definition for $(\rho h)^n$. In that case the preceding explicit transportive energy equation is obtained.

If the time level of velocity is raised to V^{n+1} in the energy flux term, exact temporal factoring and the implicit mass equation produce the conservative and transportive energy equation.

$$\rho^n \frac{\Delta h}{\Delta t} + \frac{\Delta(\rho^{*n}h^{*n}V^{n+1})}{\Delta z} - h^{n+1}\frac{\Delta(\rho^{*n}V^{n+1})}{\Delta z} - \frac{\Delta P}{\Delta t} - V^n\frac{\Delta P^n}{\Delta z} - Q^n + R_E = 0$$

Equation of state. The equation of state does not require a finite difference representation; however, the numerical solutions to be presented require the derivatives $\partial\rho/\partial P$ and $\partial\rho/\partial h$. These are fundamental to the numerical solution because the equation of state provides the distinguishing feature of the fluid mixture being considered.

This chapter has focused on liquid vapor flows so the equation of state and associated derivatives are presented here as they would apply to steam-water flow in thermal equilibrium. Let the continuous phase be the liquid and the dispersed phase be the vapor.

For subcooled liquid $(h < h_f)$

$$\rho = \rho_\ell(h, P)$$

is defined directly from the properties of the subcooled liquid. The derivatives $\partial\rho/\partial h$ and $\partial\rho/\partial P$ are also obtained directly.

Similarly, for a superheated vapor $(h > h_g)$

$$\rho = \rho_V(h, P)$$

and the derivatives $\partial\rho/\partial h$ and $\partial\rho/\partial P$ are obtained directly.

For two-phase mixture at saturation conditions, the density is defined by

$$\rho = \alpha\rho_g + (1 - \alpha)\rho_f$$

where the void fraction is defined by

$$\frac{\alpha\rho_g}{X_s} = \frac{(1 - \alpha)\rho_f}{1 - X_s}$$

and the static quality (vapor mass fraction) is defined by

$$X_s = \frac{h - h_f}{h_g - h_f}$$

The saturation properties ρ_r, ρ_g, h_f, and h_g are all functions of pressure when $h_f < h < h_g$. By using the preceding definitions and the chain rule

$$\frac{\partial\rho}{\partial h} = -\left(\frac{\rho_f - \rho_g}{h_g - h_f}\right)\frac{\rho^2}{\rho_g\rho_f}$$

and

$$\frac{\partial\rho}{\partial P} = X_s\frac{\partial\rho_g}{\partial P} + (1 - X_s)\frac{\partial\rho_f}{\partial P} + \left(\frac{\rho_f - \rho_g}{h_g - h_f}\right)\left(\frac{\rho^2}{\rho_g\rho_f}\right)\left(X_s\frac{\partial h_g}{\partial P} + (1 - X_s)\frac{\partial h_f}{\partial P}\right)$$

The derivatives $\partial h_f/\partial P$, $\partial h_g/\partial P$, $\partial\rho_f/\partial P$, and $\partial\rho_g/P$ are calculated along the saturation line.

The equation of state is discontinuous at $h = h_f$ and this can cause numerical difficulty. This i especially true when the density ratio ρ_f/ρ_g is large as in low pressure steam-water mixtures. I that case $\partial\rho/\partial h$ is very large and negative. The dependence of h_f on pressure is also troublesom because this is the switch that causes the solution to cross the discontinuity. Mathematical smooth ing of the discontinuity is sometimes required to obtain convergent solutions when the density ratio is large or when pressure changes are comparable to the absolute pressure.

Boundary Conditions

There are various ways that boundary conditions can be specified. One of the simplest and straightforward methods is to use a zero thickness phantom boundary cell. Figure 21 shows ar example of boundary cells and boundary conditions specified for pressure, enthalpy, and mass flux A pressure or enthalpy boundary condition is set by specifying the pressure in the boundary cell The velocity across the adjacent cell boundary is computed automatically by the numerical solution The use of a zero-thickness boundary cell produce the proper pressure gradient to the boundary because only one-half of the cell distance is used.

A velocity boundary condition is set by defining the velocity through a cell face and appropriately modifying the pressure gradient at the boundary. The velocity can be an arbitrarily specified value, including zero for a no-flow boundary. The averaging used in the momentum flux term requires

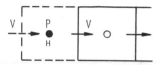

P,H GIVEN; V CALCULATED

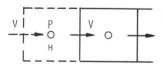

V,H GIVEN; P CALCULATED

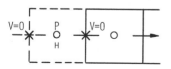

V = 0; P CALCULATED

○ CALCULATED PRESSURE
● SPECIFIED PRESSURE

Figure 21. Examples of boundary conditions in bound-ary cells.

that the velocity be defined for both sides of the phantom boundary cell. This is most easily done in a computer program by using index logic to assign velocity as needed.

Numerical Diffusion

The energy equation transports h along a stream line at velocity V. The equation can be classified as hyperbolic in the absence of diffusive terms. Unfortunately the errors from first-order spatial differencing are second order and introduce numerical diffusion into the solutions. While the errors are bothersome when propagating discontinuities, they can be relatively minor when transporting a gradual change. Numerical analysts currently live with numerical diffusion and attempt to reduce it by using partial-donor differencing and a sufficient number of computational cells. Higher-order methods are possible but are not currently being used for two-phase flows.

Newton's Method for Solving Nonlinear Equations

Newton's method can be effectively used to solve the difference equation for two-phase flow. It is a successive correction procedure that updates a tentative solution such that a residual error is driven to zero. The method is useful for both linear and nonlinear equations [90].
Consider the equation

$$F(x) = 0$$

where x is a solution to the equation. Let $\tilde{x}$ be an initial estimate close to the true solution and let δx be a correction such that the true solution is

$$x = \tilde{x} + \Delta x$$

and

$$F(\tilde{x} + \Delta x) = 0$$

Expanding the function gives

$$F(\tilde{x}) + \frac{\partial F}{\partial x} \delta x = 0$$

or

$$\frac{\partial F}{\partial x} \delta x = -F(\tilde{x})$$

The right side is the residual error from the initial estimate and the left side contains the coefficient of δx. Solving for δx gives

$$\delta x = -\left(\frac{\partial F}{\partial x}\right)^{-1} F(\tilde{x})$$

When $\partial F / \partial x$ is a single value, simple division provides the solution for δx. Given the solution for δx, the tentative value is updated and that value is used as the next tentative solution. The process is repeated until the residual is reduced to an acceptably small value. The Jacobian derivatives can be updated for each iteration to improve convergence although this is not always necessary.

The function can also be a vector function $F(x)$ and then x is the solution vector. In that case $\partial F/\partial x$ is a matrix and the vector ∂x is obtained by solution of simultaneous equations.

Newton's method is also a useful approach for solving linear equations. In that case a single update provides the correct solution and iteration is not necessary.

The Jacobian derivatives provide the "intelligence" to the numerical solution. Perfect derivatives can produce the correct solution in one update. In practice the derivatives are quite approximate and that has an impact on the rate of convergence. Iteration is most rapid when good derivatives are used.

Nonlinear equations can have highly nonlinear or discontinous Jacobian derivatives, and that can lead to numerical difficulties. Such a situation can occur at the start of boiling for a flow with a phase change where the mixture equation of state has discontinous derivatives $\partial \rho/\partial$ h and $\partial \rho/\partial P$. In such a case it is not possible to get good derivatives and compromise values must be used. It is usually important to use derivatives that change slowly during the iteration process. Derivatives that flip between two extremes may not produce a converged solution. Successful derivatives will drive the residual to zero.

Newton's method has several advantages over solving a "linearized" equation. The most important is that it solves the nonlinear equation. Solving a linearized equation does not necessarily assure that the nonlinear equation has been solved. Some nonlinear terms can be quite complex and, if errors are made when linearizing, they can be difficult to detect and can lead to erroneous solutions.

The residual is very useful for computation. It is really a statement of the equation being solved and can normally be written in a few lines of a computer program. This provides visibility of the equation and allows easier checking of the program. Monitoring the residual also provides assurance that the solution is actually converging. This is especially important to two-phase computation to assure conservation of mass and energy.

Newton's method allows use of a consistent numerical procedure as additional nonlinear terms are brought to a numerical solution. All that need be done is to include the added terms in the residual and Jacobian derivatives.

Newton's method is often used to find roots of equations. In that regard it is possible to obtain multiple solutions to multivalued functions, and the solution found depends on the initial $\tilde{x}$. Most two-phase applications do not experience difficulties here because $\tilde{x}$ is normally close to the desired solution which is single-valued. An exception to this could occur for situations involving flow instability.

Newton's method together with the ideas of the ICE algorithm are very useful for solution of the two-phase flow equations. Those concepts form the basis for much of the subsequent discussion.

Solution of the Two-Phase Equations

The transient numerical solution discussed here is concerned with advancement of the difference equations for energy, mass, and momentum through successive time steps as shown in Figure 22. Given that the calculation has been set up from input, the solution is started from a defined set of initial and boundary conditions. The difference equations are solved to advance the solution one time step. Time is then incremented, boundary conditions defined, and the process is repeated until the desired time is reached.

A variety of strategies are available and can be used to solve the equations of energy, mass, and momentum. For a wide class of problems it is possible and convenient to decouple the solution of the energy equation from the solution of the mass and momentum equations. This can occur by choice of the level of implicitness, or by terms that have been dropped by assumption. This allows advancement of enthalpy to new time by using existing values of pressure and velocity. Higher levels of coupling are possible and are discussed later.

Solving the Energy Equation

The energy equation contains coupling with the flow field through the terms containing pressure and velocity. For a wide class of applications it is possible to decouple the energy equation from the

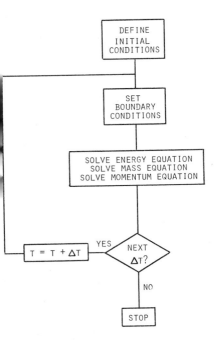

Figure 22. Flow diagram for transient computation.

momentum equation by using the explicit transportive forms of the energy equation. This applies to cases where velocity is at time n or at time n + 1. If velocity is used at time n + 1, iteration can be used to couple the energy and flow solution. In that case the previous iterate velocity is used. The use of the transportive form for a decoupled solution is important here because it simultaneously satisfies the mass balance. The use of the conservative form will not produce acceptable results when the energy equation is decoupled from the flow solution.

The explicit energy difference equation in transportive form is used here to illustrate the solution method:

$$\rho^n \frac{\Delta h}{\Delta t} + \frac{\Delta(\rho V)^n h^{*n}}{\Delta z} - h^n \frac{\Delta(\rho V)^n}{\Delta z} - \frac{\Delta P}{\Delta t} - V^n \frac{\Delta P^n}{\Delta z} - Q^n + R_E^n = 0$$

The temporal pressure derivative is updated through iteration with the solution of the mass and energy equation. If the velocity V is taken to be at time n + 1, it is updated through iteration.

The pressure terms are often small in many two-phase flow applications. This occurs when the pressure changes in space and time are small compared to the absolute pressure. When those terms are small enough to be dropped, the explicit energy equation is further decoupled from the flow solution.

The explicit energy equation can be solved directly for h at n + 1 at each computational cell to advance the solution one time step. The time step is limited by the Courant limit

$$\Delta t < \frac{\Delta z}{V}$$

when the relative velocity and source terms are independent of h. If they have strong dependence on h, the time-step limit for this explicit case would have to be decreased to maintain stability. The added time-step restriction caused by the source terms can be eliminated by making them implicit. The heat source term can become complicated by its dependence on void fraction and enthalpy. Consider the energy equation written functionally as

$$E_i(h_i) = 0$$

where the superscript $n + 1$ has been dropped to simplify notation and pressure is taken to be the previous iterate. Absence of the superscript is understood to imply time $n + 1$ in the following discussion. The Jacobian derivative is obtained by differentiation and is

$$\frac{\partial E_i}{\partial h_i} = \frac{\rho_i^n}{\Delta t}$$

The correction is calculated from

$$\delta h_i = -\frac{E_i(\tilde{h}_i)}{\partial E_i/\partial h_i}$$

and the updated solution is

$$h_i = \tilde{h}_i + \delta h_i$$

where $\tilde{h}_i$ is the tentative solution.

The implicit treatment of all terms containing enthalpy can use the same solution procedure but in this case the energy equation update solution must simultaneously consider h_{i-1} and h_i and h_{i+1} because of the donor assignment. The energy equation can be written functionally as

$$E_i(h_{i-1}, h_i, h_{i+1}) = 0$$

The Jacobian derivatives are expressed as

$$\frac{\partial E_i}{\partial h_{i-1}} = -a_i + \frac{\partial R_{E_1}}{\partial h_{i-1}}$$

$$\frac{\partial E_i}{\partial h_i} = \frac{\rho_i^n}{\Delta t} + b_i - \frac{\partial Q_i}{\partial h_i} + \frac{\partial R_{E_1}}{\partial h_i}$$

$$\frac{\partial E_i}{\partial h_{i+1}} = -c_i + \frac{\partial R_{E_1}}{\partial h_{i+1}}$$

where a_i, b_i and c_i are those defined previously. This leads to an equation of the form

$$\frac{\partial E_i}{\partial h_{i-1}} \delta h_{i-1} + \frac{\partial E_i}{\partial h_i} \delta h_i + \frac{\partial E}{\partial h_{i+1}} \delta h_{i+1} = -E_i(\tilde{h}_{i-1}, \tilde{h}_i, \tilde{h}_{i+1})$$

This is a tridiagonal linear system that can be solved simultaneously for all δh_i by using well-known methods [86, 87, 90, 91].

This level of implicitness has the advantage of removing the Courant time-step limit from the solution of the energy equation. The Courant time-step limit would still remain if the momentum equation is solved explicitly.

Note that the overall structure of the Newton solution remains the same in the preceding examples. The only difference is the definition of source terms and derivatives as the level of implicitness is increased.

The energy equation at its various levels of implicitness can be generally expressed as the vector function

$$E(h; V, P) = 0$$

where velocity and pressure are treated as a parameters. The Newton solution procedure requires calculation of the residual $E(h; V, P)$ and the derivatives $\partial E/\partial h$. The resulting linear system is solved for δh and $\tilde{h}$ is updated. The procedure can be iterated if necessary to drive the residual to zero.

Solving the Mass and Momentum Equations

Consider the case where the energy equation has been solved and it is now necessary to advance pressure and velocity to time n + 1. The semi-implicit equations used for the solution are:

$$\frac{\Delta\rho}{\Delta t} + \frac{\Delta(\rho^{*n}V)}{\Delta z} = 0$$

$$\bar{\rho}_n \frac{\Delta V}{\Delta t} + \frac{\Delta P}{\Delta z} + S^n = 0$$

where $\rho = \rho (P; h)$ and S^n is a collection of all terms at time n. The absence of superscripts is understood to imply time level n + 1 in this discussion.

The P-V solution method involves a simultaneous solution of the mass and momentum equation for pressure and velocity. The basic philosophy is to combine the mass and momentum equation to obtain an equation in terms of pressure and then to solve for the pressure field. With the pressure defined, velocity can be calculated from the momentum equation and density can be calculated from the equation of state.

The difference equations can be combined such that a Poisson equation for pressure is obtained for incompressible flow or a wave equation is obtained for compressible flow. The resulting second-order equation can be solved directly for pressure. Such an approach is used in RETRAN [93] and RELAP5 [8]. It is also possible to accomplish this by the Newton method where an incremental pressure correction is obtained to update pressure and velocity. This is the basic philosophy contained in the original ICE algorithm and it is used in TRAC [5, 88]. The Newton method has the advantage of being more easily extended to nonlinear problems. The Newton method is presented in the following discussion and follows the basic ideas presented for the energy equation.

The mass, momentum, and state equation can be written in the vector function form:

$$D(\rho, V) = 0$$

$$M(V, P) = 0$$

$$\rho = \rho(P; h)$$

where h is treated as a parameter in the state equation. Since changes in density at this point only depend on changes in pressure,

$$\delta\rho = \frac{\partial\rho}{\partial P} \delta P$$

By using this relationship, the mass and momentum equations for the Newton method can be written as:

$$\frac{\partial D}{\partial \rho} \frac{\partial \rho}{\partial P} \delta P + \frac{\partial D}{\partial V} \delta V = -D(\tilde{\rho}, \tilde{V})$$

$$\frac{\partial M}{\partial V} \delta V + \frac{\partial M}{\partial P} \delta P = -M(\tilde{V}, \tilde{P})$$

The derivatives are obtained by differentiating the mass and momentum equations and the result is

$$\frac{1}{\Delta t} \frac{\partial \rho}{\partial P} \delta P + \frac{\Delta(\rho^{*n} \delta V)}{\Delta z} = -D(\tilde{\rho}, \tilde{V})$$

$$\frac{\bar{\rho}^n}{\Delta t} \delta V + \frac{\Delta}{\Delta z} \delta P = -M(\tilde{V}, \tilde{P})$$

Note that Δz and Δt are given constants and, except for possibly $\partial \rho / \partial P$, this produces a linear system to be solved for δV and δP. These equations form a block matrix system that can be solved by standard matrix methods; however, it is possible to accomplish the solution in a simpler and more compact form. Following the basic ideas contained in ICE, the initial tentative pressure $\tilde{P}$ can be chosen to be P^n and the state equation solved for $\tilde{\rho}$ and the momentum equation solved for $\tilde{V}$. This step is often called the "tilde" phase of the solution. The result is that $M(\tilde{V}, \tilde{P}) = 0$ and

$$\frac{\bar{\rho}^n}{\Delta t} \delta V + \frac{\Delta}{\overline{\Delta z}} \delta P = 0$$

This is a linear relationship that defines the change in V for a change in P. Solving for δV and substituting into the mass equation gives

$$\frac{1}{\Delta t} \frac{\partial \rho}{\partial P} \delta P - \Delta t \frac{\Delta}{\Delta z} \left(\frac{\rho^{*n}}{\bar{\rho}^n} \frac{\Delta \delta P}{\Delta z} \right) = -D(\tilde{\rho}, \tilde{V})$$

Expanding this equation produces the tridiagonal system

$$\frac{1}{\Delta t} \frac{\partial \rho_i}{\partial P_i} \delta P_i - \frac{\Delta t}{\Delta z_i} \left[\left(\frac{\rho^*}{\bar{\rho}} \right)^n_{i+1/2} \left(\frac{\delta P_{i+1} - \delta P_i}{\Delta z_{i+1/2}} \right) - \left(\frac{\rho^*}{\bar{\rho}} \right)^n_{i-1/2} \left(\frac{\delta P_i - \delta P_{i-1}}{\Delta z_{i-1/2}} \right) \right] = -D_i(\tilde{\rho}, \tilde{V})$$

The right side is the residual mass error given by the tentative density and velocity. The equations are solved simultaneously for the pressure correction δP. The pressure correction is then used to calculate δV and to calculate $\delta \rho$. The final step is to update the solution by

$$P = \tilde{P} + \delta P$$

$$V = \tilde{V} + \delta V$$

$$\rho = \tilde{\rho} + \delta \rho$$

The update of the density by the incremental corrrection is optional. It is necessary in some cases to calculate density directly from the equation of state by using the updated pressure to prevent the density from going out of bounds for those cases where $\partial \rho / \partial p$ is large.

If ρ is linear or invariant with pressure, the preceding procedure produces the correct pressure, velocity, and density without iteration. A second iteration would produce zero residuals. This is especially useful when a reference pressure concept is used for those applications where pressure changes are very small compared to the absolute pressure.

If ρ is nonlinear with pressure, then the mass residual and pressure correction calculation would have to be repeated to drive the mass error to an acceptably small value. For low-pressure boiling where the density ratio ρ_f/ρ_g is large, the iteration procedure can encounter difficulties at the start of boiling. Pressure changes can take a cell into and out of boiling during the iteration process and inhibit convergence. Some form of mathematical smoothing or control of $\partial\rho/\partial P$ is necessary under those severe conditions.

A direct tridiagonal matrix solution is recommended over an iterative solution for the pressure correction. Iteration is too slow to converge and lack of convergence can produce unacceptable mass balance errors. The direct solution for δP produces a very good local and global mass balance.

The preceding tridiagonal equation for δP applies to the case of pressure boundary conditions defined in the phantom boundary cells. A velocity boundary condition is set by defining the velocity at the boundary and by breaking the pressure-velocity connection at the boundary. This is done by setting up the matrix with a zero coefficient to give $\delta V = 0$ at the boundary instead of the normal relationship between δV and δP.

The preceding solution procedure is equally valid for single-phase compressible and incompressible flow and two-phase flows. The derivative $\partial\rho/\partial P = 0$ for incompressible single-phase flow. The distinguishing feature between flows is the definition for density $\rho(h, P)$.

The time step in the preceding solution is defined by the Courant criterion for the most limiting momentum cell provided the source terms are weak functions of velocity. This limit is imposed by the explicit treatment of the momentum flux terms. If the momentum flux terms are dropped, that source of the time-step restriction is lost. If the other source terms have strong flow dependence they can impose additional restrictions on time step.

Time step limits can be relaxed by making the source terms implicit. The friction term is most easily made implicit. It can be included by adding its derivative to $\partial M/\partial V$; thus,

$$\frac{\partial M}{\partial V} = \frac{\tilde{\rho}^n}{\Delta t} + \frac{\partial F}{\partial V}$$

Since $\partial F/\partial V$ is normally a nonlinear function of velocity, the relationship between changes in pressure and velocity is no longer linear and the "tilde" phase solution would have to be included in the iteration. In that case $\tilde{P}$ is taken from the previous iteration. This is simple enough that it is usually done.

The relative velocity term is not easily implicit because of its complexity. In this case $\partial M/\partial V$ would be a tridiagonal matrix rather then just a diagonal matrix as in the preceding formulation. The same ideas presented above can be used; however, in this case a block tridiagonal system would have to be solved for δP and δV.

The overall procedure for the pressure and velocity solution is shown in Figure 23. The steps for one iteration cycle are as follows given the tentative pressure $\tilde{P}$:

1. Solve the momentum equation for $\tilde{V}$.
2. Solve the state equation for $\tilde{\rho}$ and $\partial\rho/\partial P$.
3. Solve the mass equation for δP.
4. Calculate δV.
5. Update P, V, and ρ.
6. Repeat cycle until converged.

Coupling the Energy and Flow Solution

The previous discussion presented a solution method that considered the energy equation solution to be decoupled from the flow field during an iteration cycle. The coupling that occurs through the pressure work terms and possibly by using V^{n+1} can be included by iteration where the energy equation is solved prior to each solution for pressure and velocity.

The energy and flow field can also be more closely coupled numerically for the case where V^{n+1} is used in the energy equation. This is the level implicitness used by Liles and Reed [88]. The result

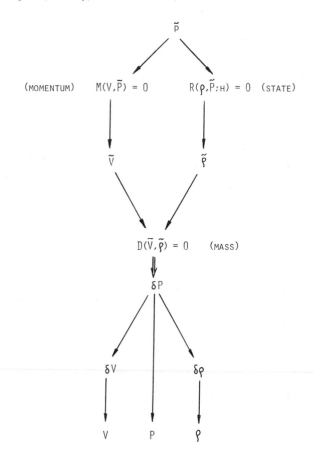

Figure 23. Solution diagram for semi-implicit P-V solution.

is that an additional Jacobian derivative enters the solution. The resulting matrix equation can be solved in block form or the incremental correction equations can be manipulated to obtain a pressure correction equation that can be solved as done in the previous discussion. The major difference is the additional contribution of the energy equation to the tridiagonal matrix coefficients. The pressure correction equation is solved in the same way for δP and is used to update the remainder of the solution.

To illustrate this method consider the incremental form of the difference equations written for the Newton method as:

$$\frac{\rho^n}{\Delta t}\delta h + \frac{\Delta((h\rho)^{*n}\,\delta V)}{\Delta z} - \tilde{h}\frac{\Delta(\rho^{*n}\delta V)}{\Delta z} = -E(\tilde{h},\,\tilde{V},\,\tilde{P})$$

$$\frac{\partial\rho}{\partial h}\frac{\delta h}{\Delta t} + \frac{\partial\rho}{\partial P}\frac{\delta P}{\Delta t} + \frac{\Delta(\rho^{*n}\,\delta V)}{\Delta z} = -D(\tilde{\rho},\,\tilde{V})$$

$$\frac{\Delta\,\delta P}{\overline{\Delta z}} + \frac{\bar{\rho}^n}{\Delta t}\delta V = -M(\tilde{V},\,\tilde{P})$$

This is a block system of equations that can be solved for δh, δP, and δV by using the previous solution philosophy. Given $\tilde{P}$ the momentum equation can be solved for $\tilde{V}$. The result as before is that $M(\tilde{V}, \tilde{P}) = 0$ and the linear relationship between δV and δP is

$$\frac{\bar{\rho}^n}{\Delta t} \delta V + \frac{\Delta \, \delta P}{\overline{\Delta z}} = 0$$

Now the energy equation is solved for $\tilde{h}$, by using $\tilde{P}$ and $\tilde{V}$. The result is $E(\tilde{h}, \tilde{V}, \tilde{P}) = 0$ and

$$\frac{\rho^n}{\Delta t} \delta h + \frac{\Delta((\rho h)^{*n} \, \delta V)}{\Delta z} - \tilde{h} \frac{\Delta(\rho^{*n} \, \delta V)}{\Delta z} = 0$$

The density $\tilde{\rho}$ is now calculated by using $\tilde{h}$ and $\tilde{P}$. The mass equation residual can now be calculated.
    The foregoing equations defining the increments of δP, δV, and δh can now be combined to produce an equation for δP that has the same form as that presented previously. Combining the momentum and energy increment equations gives

$$\frac{\rho^n}{\Delta t} \delta h - \Delta t \frac{\Delta}{\Delta z} \left(\frac{(\rho h)^{*n}}{\bar{\rho}^n} \frac{\Delta \, \delta \rho}{\overline{\Delta z}} \right) + \tilde{h} \frac{\Delta}{\Delta z} \left(\frac{\rho^{*n}}{\bar{\rho}^n} \frac{\Delta \, \delta P}{\overline{\Delta z}} \right) = 0$$

Substituting this into the incremental mass equation gives

$$-\frac{1}{\rho^n} \frac{\partial \rho}{\partial h} \left[\Delta t \frac{\Delta}{\Delta z} \left(\frac{(\rho h)^{*n}}{\bar{\rho}^n} \frac{\Delta \, \delta P}{\overline{\Delta z}} \right) - \Delta t \tilde{h} \frac{\Delta}{\Delta z} \left(\frac{\rho^{*n}}{\bar{\rho}^n} \frac{\Delta \, \delta P}{\overline{\Delta z}} \right) \right] + \frac{1}{\Delta t} \frac{\partial \rho}{\partial P} \delta P - \Delta t \frac{\Delta}{\Delta z} \left(\frac{\rho^{*n}}{\bar{\rho}^n} \frac{\Delta \, \delta P}{\overline{\Delta z}} \right)$$
$$= -D(\tilde{\rho}, \tilde{V})$$

Expanding the differences produces a tridiagonal equation for δP of the form:

$$\frac{\Delta t}{\rho_i^n} \left(\frac{\partial \rho}{\partial h} \right)_i \frac{1}{\Delta z_i} \left[(h_{i+1/2}^{*n} - \tilde{h}_i) \left(\frac{\rho^*}{\bar{\rho}} \right)_{it1/2}^n \left(\frac{\delta P_{i+1} - \delta P_i}{\Delta z_{i+1/2}} \right) - (h_{i-1/2}^{*n} - \tilde{h}_i) \left(\frac{\rho^*}{\bar{\rho}} \right)_{i-1/2}^n \left(\frac{\delta P_i - \delta P_{i-1}}{\Delta z_{i-1/2}} \right) \right]$$
$$+ \frac{1}{\Delta t} \left(\frac{\partial \rho}{\partial P} \right)_i \partial P_i - \frac{\Delta t}{\Delta_{zi}} \left[\left(\frac{\rho^*}{\bar{\rho}} \right)_{i+1/2}^n \left(\frac{\delta P_{i+1} - \delta P_i}{\Delta z_{i+1/2}} \right) - \left(\frac{\rho^*}{\bar{\rho}} \right)_{i-1/2}^n \left(\frac{\delta P_i - \delta P_{i-1}}{\Delta z_{i-1/2}} \right) \right] = -D(\tilde{\rho}, \tilde{V})$$

The first group of terms represents the Jacobian derivative coupling to the energy equation. The remaining terms are those of the decoupled solution. Notice that $(h^{*n} - \tilde{h})$ could be positive or negative and that $\partial \rho / \partial h$ can be a large negative term for boiling two-phase flows with large density ratios. If $(h^{*n} - \tilde{h})$ changes from positive to negative, there is the possibility of sign change in the coefficient matrix that would lead to a divergent solution. This can be prevented by limiting $(h^{*n} - \tilde{h}) > 0$ to assure positive contributions to the coefficient matrix. Inspection of the sign of each Jacobian coefficient is useful to check stability. The diagonal should be positive and dominant.
    The solution procedure for one iteration cycle is as follows given the tentative pressure $\tilde{P}$:

1. Solve the momentum equation for $\tilde{V}$.
2. Solve the energy equation for $\tilde{h}$.
3. Solve the state equation for $\tilde{\rho}$, $\partial \rho / \partial h$, and $\partial \rho / \partial P$.
4. Solve the mass equation for ∂P.
5. Calculate δV.
6. Calculate δh.
7. Update P, V, h, and ρ.
8. Repeat cycle until converged.

The rate of convergence with the explicit transportive energy equation using V^n is faster than when using V^{n+1} as already discussed. This is because the enthalpy is fixed at $n+1$ when using V^n, but it changes for each iteration cycle when using V^{n+1}. Personal experience is that the rate of convergence is similar for iterative or direct coupling when using V^{n+1}.

The basic ideas of the coupled approach can be extended to include two-fluid modeling such as additional energy equations for thermal nonequilibrium or additional momentum equations to calculate relative velocity. The interfacial heat transfer and friction terms are normally made implicit and only contribute to the diagonal of the matrices of interest. If the level of implicitness is extended such that the matrix structure is expanded beyond that presented above, block matrix methods would be necessary to accommodate the large system of equations.

Additional Remarks for Computational Methods

The numerical methods presented here can be extended beyond one-dimensional flow. Recognizing that the spatial discretization is a linear difference operation, it is possible to construct a linear operator that defines loops and multidimensional networks. Manipulation of those equations follows the same basic ideas as in the previous discussion. The key element is the formation and solution of the pressure correction equation. The matrix is no longer tridiagonal in those cases, and that complicates the solution. Loops are usually solved best by direct solution of the linear system for δP. Multidimensional analysis usually creates such a large linear system that a direct solution is not practical. In that case a combination of a direct solution and iteration can be used. An example for two-dimensional analysis is to use line-by-line iteration [87]. In this case a tridiagonal system is solved in one direction and that solution is successively swept in the other direction. The solve and sweep directions can also be switched to create an alternating direction sweep. Point iteration converges too slowly and is not recommended.

Fully implicit methods that remove time-step limits would be useful for general two-phase flow computation. Theoretically, the Newton method could be set up to accomplish this by using a very complete Jacobian matrix and solving the resulting linear system for the solution correction. That is a formidable task and is not normally practical. Some progress has been made to relax time-step limits for one-dimensional applications by using the SETS method [94]. It is being developed for TRAC and for multidimensional applications.

SUMMARY

The drift flux model for modeling dispersed multiphase flows has been discussed in this chapter including presentation of the applicable conservation equations, constitutive relationships, and a numerical solution technique. As mentioned in the earlier sections, the drift-flux model is most applicable to situations where the behavior of the two phases is strongly coupled, and the model has been extensively used to predict system dynamics and instabilities. Pioneering papers on the drift-flux model for steam-water application include Zuber and Staub [95, 96], Staub, Zuber, and Bijwaard [97], and Staub and Zuber [98]. The applicability of the drift flux model to Refrigerant-22 was established by Staub and Zuber [99]. Since that time, the drift-flux model has been extensively used. For example, Ishii, Saha, and Zuber [100–102] have studied flow instabilities with the model. Ohkawa and Lahey [103] have used the drift-flux model to analyze the countercurrent flooding limit. Other applications of the model include pipe blowdown and flashing predictions [104, 105] and two-phase flow analysis in piping networks [106, 107]. This list of applications is anything but complete. The authors hope that the foregoing discussion of the drift-flux model will be helpful and will encourage additional use of this powerful technique for the analysis of dispersed multiphase flows.

NOTATION

A	total flow area	C_o	distribution parameter
a, b, c	used as a variable in annular flow	C_∞	asymptotic value of C_o
	equations	C_p	constant-pressure specific heat

D	equivalent diameter	P	pressure
$D(\rho, V)$	functional form of the mass equation	Pr	Prandtl number
E	entrainment	Q	heat source term for energy equation
F	friction term for the momentum equation	q	axial conduction heat flux
F	Chen-Reynolds number factor; also friction term in the momentum equation	q^T	axial conduction heat flux due to turbulence
f	Moody friction factor	q''	wall heat flux
f'	Fanning friction factor	R	relative velocity term for the energy equation
G	total mass flow rate per unit area; also gravity term for the momentum equation	r	radius
		Re_D	Reynolds number based on diameter
g, g_c	gravitational constant	S	Chen suppression factor
g_z	axial component of gravity	t	time
h	heat transfer coefficient, enthalpy	T	temperature
h_k	enthalpy of phase k	v_s	specific volume
J	mixture volumetric flux	V_{dj}	local drift velocity
J_k	volumetric flux of phase k	$\bar{V}_{dj}$	mean drift velocity
k	thermal conductivity	$\langle\!\langle V_{dj} \rangle\!\rangle$	weighted mean value of V
$M(V, P)$	functional form of the momentum equation	V_r	relative velocity
		V	velocity
$\dot{m}$	mass flow rate	We	Weber number
Nu_D	Nusselt number, hD/k	X	flowing quality of vapor phase
$N\mu_k$	viscosity number based on phase k viscosity	X_k	flowing quality of phase k
		X_s	static quality of vapor phase
		z	axial coordinate

Greek Symbols

α	void fraction of vapor phase	μ_k	viscosity of phase k
α_k	void fraction of phase k	ζ_k	heated perimeter
α_{core}	area fraction of annular flow core region	ζ	ratio of interface perimeter to wall perimeter
α_{drop}	void fraction of droplets in annular flow core region	ρ	density
		σ	surface tension
β	donor assignment parameter	τ_{zz}	normal viscous stress
Γ_k	mass generation source function for phase k	τ_{zz}^T	normal turbulent stress
		ϕ_g^2	single-phase frictional pressure drop ratio
Δh_{dc}	enthalpy difference, hd − hc		
$\Delta\rho$	pressure difference	ϕ_m^u	mixture energy dissipation
ΔT	temperature difference	X	quality
Δt	time increment	X_{tt}	Martinelli parameter
$\Delta\rho$	absolute value of density difference	ψ	Baker flow map parameter, function of rd*
ε	pipe roughness		
λ	Baker flow map parameter		

Subscripts

a	air, actual	f	liquid or fluid phase
b	bulk	fg	phase change
c	continuous phase, critical value	g	gas or vapor phase
d	discontinuous phase, droplet	h	homogeneous
e	entrainment, exit, equilibrium	i	interfacial; also index for control volume
F	friction		

m	mixture	tp	two-phase
mic	microconvection	tr	transition
mac	macroconvection	tt	both phases in turbulent flow
o	stagnation	vm	volume mean
r	relative	w	water, wall
s	saturation, static		

Superscripts

~	tentative value	*	donor value
—	mean value		

Symbols

$\langle F \rangle$	area average value	*	nondimensional; also donor assign-
$\langle\langle f \rangle\rangle$	void fraction weighted average value	n	time t
COV	covariance	n + 1	time t + Δt

Operators

Δ	difference
δ	incremental correction

REFERENCES

1. Wallis, G. B., "Theoretical Models of Gas-Liquid Flows—Review," *Trans. ASME, J. Fluids Eng.*, Vol. 104, No. 3, pp. 279–283 (September 1982).
2. Crowe, C. T., "Numerical Models for Dilute Gas-Particle Flows—Review," *Trans. ASME, J. Fluids Eng.*, Vol. 104, No. 3, pp. 297–303 (September 1982).
3. Meyer, R. E., (Ed.) *Theory of Dispersed Multiphase Flow*, Academic Press, New York, 1983.
4. Ishii, M., *Thermo-Fluid Dynamic Theory of Two-Phase Flow*, Eyrolles, Paris, 1975.
5. TRAC-PD2—An Advanced Best-Estimate Computer Program for Pressurized Water Reactor Loss-of-Coolant Accident Analysis, NUREG/CR-2054, LA-8709-MS, Los Alamos Scientific Laboratory, 1981.
6. Rohatgi, U. S., and Saha, P. "Constitutive Relations in TRAC-PIA," NUREG/CR-1651, BNL-NUREG-51258, August 1980.
7. Rohatgi, U. S., Jo, J., and Neymotin, L., "Constitutive Relations in TRAC-PD2," NUREG/CR-3073, BNL-NUREG-51616, September 1982.
8. RELAP5/MOD1 Code Manual, NUREG/CR-1826, EGG-2070 DRAFT, Revision 2, September 1981.
9. RELAP4/MOD5—A Computer Program for Transient Thermal-Hydraulic Analysis of Nuclear Reactors and Related Systems, ANCR-NUREG-1355, Idaho National Engineering Laboratory, 1976.
10. Bankoff, S. G., "A Variable Density Single-Fluid Model for Two-Phase Flow with Particular Reference to Steam-Water Flow," *Trans. ASME, J. Heat Transfer*, Vol. 82, No. 4, pp. 265–272. (November 1960).
11. Zuber, N., "On the Variable-Density Single-Fluid Model for Two-Phase Flow," *Trans. ASME, J. Heat Transfer*, Vol. 82, No. 3, pp. 255–258 (August 1960).
12. Wallis, G. B., "Some Hydrodynamics Aspects of Two-Phase Flow and Boiling, Part I: The Rise of Bubbles Through a Liquid," Paper No. 38, Intern. Heat Transfer Conf, Boulder, Colo., pp. 319–325, 1961.

13. Wallis, G. B., *One-dimensional Two-phase Flow*, McGraw-Hill Book Company, New York, 1969.
14. Zuber N., and Findlay, J. A., "Average Volumetric Concentration in Two-Phase Systems," *Trans. ASME, J. of Heat Transfer*, Vol. 87, pp. 453–468 (November 1965).
15. Bankoff, S. G., Comments in the feature "This Week's Citation Classic," *Current Contents— Engineering, Technology & Applied Sciences*, Number 36, p. 18, (September 5, 1983).
16. Neal, L. G., "An Analysis of Slip in Gas-Liquid Flow Applicable to the Bubble and Slug Flow Regimes," Kjeller Research Establishment, Kjeller, Norway, Report KR-62, 1963.
17. Ishii, M., "One-Dimensional Drift-Flux Model and Constitutive Equations for Relative Motion Between Phases in Various Two-Phase Flow Regimes," ANL-77-47, October 1977.
18. Delhaye, J. M., and Achard, J. L., "On the Averaging Operators Introduced in Two-Phase Flow Modeling," *Transient Two-Phase Flow*, Proceedings of the CSNI Specialists Meeting, Toronto, Vol. 1, pp. 5–84 (August 1976).
19. Delhaye, J. M., and Achard, J. L., "On the Use of Averaging Operators in Two-Phase Flow Modeling," *Thermal and Hydraulic Aspects of Nuclear Reactor Safety, Vol. 1: Light Water Reactors*, pp. 289–332, ASME, 1977.
20. White, F. M., *Viscous Fluid Flow*, McGraw-Hill Book Company, Inc. 1974.
21. Tong, L. S., *Boiling Heat Transfer and Two-Phase Flow*, John Wiley & Sons, Inc., New York, 1965.
22. Collier, J. G., *Convective Boiling and Condensation*, McGraw-Hill Book Company, London, 1972.
23. Collier, J. G., *Convective Boiling and Condensation*, Second Edition, McGraw-Hill Book Company, New York, 1981.
24. Bergles, A. E., et al., *Two-Phase Flow and Heat Transfer in the Power and Process Industries*, Hemisphere Publishing Corporation, Washington, 1981.
25. Lahey, R. T., Jr., and Moody, F. J., *The Thermal Hydraulics of a Boiling Water Nuclear Reactor*, American Nuclear Society, LaGrange Park, Illinois, 1977.
26. Hsu, Y. Y., and Graham, R. W., *Transport Processes in Boiling and Two-Phase Systems*, Hemisphere Publishing Corporation, Washington, 1976.
27. Rouhani, S. Z., and Sohal, M. S., "Two-Phase Flow Patterns: A Review of Research Results," *Progress in Nuclear Energy*, Vol. 11, No. 3, pp. 219–259, 1983.
28. Barnea, D., and Taitel, Y., "Flow Pattern Transitions in Two-Phase Flows," *Encyclopedia of Fluid Mechanics*, Vol. 6, 1986.
29. Spedding, P. L., and Nguyen, V. T., "Regime Maps for Air Water Two Phase Flow," *Chem. Eng. Sci.*, Vol. 35, pp. 779–793 (1980).
30. Baker, D., "Simultaneous Flow of Oil and Gas," *The Oil and Gas Journal* (July 26, 1954), pp. 185–195.
31. Mandhane, J. M., Gregory, G. A., and Aziz, K., "A Flow Pattern Map for Gas-Liquid Flow in Horizontal Pipes," *Int. J. Multiphase Flow*, Vol. 1, pp. 537–553, 1974.
32. Hewitt, G. F., and Roberts, D. N., "Studies of Two-Phase Flow Patterns by Simultaneous X-Ray and Flash Photography," AERE-M-2159, HMSO, 1969, as referenced by Collier [22, 23].
33. Goldmann, K., Firstenberg, H., and Lombardi, C., "Burnout in Turbulent Flow—A Droplet Diffusion Model," *Trans. ASME, J. Heat Transfer*, Vol. 83, pp. 158–162 (1961).
34. Taitel, Y., and Dukler, A. E., "A Model for Predicting Flow Regime Transitions in Horizontal and Near Horizontal Gas-Liquid Flow," *AIChE J.*, Vol. 22, No. 1, pp. 47–55 (1976).
35. Dukler, A. E., and Taitel, Y., "Flow Regime Transitions for Vertical Upward Gas Liquid Flow: A Preliminary Approach Through Physical Modelling, Progress Report No. 1," NUREG-0162, January 1977.
36. Taitel, Y., Bornea, D., and Dukler, A. E., "Modelling Flow Pattern Transitions for Steady Upward Gas-Liquid Flow in Vertical Tubes," *AIChE J.*, Vol. 26, No. 3, pp. 345–354 (1980).
37. Ishii, M., and Mishima, K., "Study of Two-Fluid Model and Interfacial Area," NUREG/CR-1873, ANL-80-111 (December 1980).
38. Kataoka, I., and Ishii, M., "Mechanism and Correlation of Droplet Entrainment and Deposition in Annular Two-Phase Flow," ANL-82-44, NUREG/CR-2885, July 1982.

39. Mishima, K., and Ishii, M., "Flow Regime Transition Criteria Consistent with Two-Fluid Model for Vertical Two-Phase Flow," ANL-83-42, NUREG/CR-3338, April 1983.

40. Nicholson, M. K., et al., "A Comparison of Flow Regime and Pressure Drop Behavior in Adiabatic and Diabatic Two-Phase Simulations," Seventh Int. Heat Trans. Conf., Munich, Vol. 5, Paper TF 11, pp. 261–266, Hemisphere Publishing Corporation, Washington, 1982.

41. Nicholson, M. K., and Nickerson, J. R., "A Comparison of Flow Regime Behavior in Adiabatic and Diabatic Two-Phase Flow Trefoil Simulations," The Second International Topical Meeting on Nuclear Reactor Thermal-Hydraulics, Santa Barbara, Cal., pp. 153–160, ANS, La-Grange Park, Illinois, January 1983.

42. Ishii, M., and Zuber, N., "Drag Coefficient and Relative Velocity in Bubble, Droplet or Particulate Flows," *AIChE J.*, Vol. 25, No. 5, pp. 843–855 (1979).

43. Wallis, G. B., "The Terminal Speed of Single Drops or Bubbles in an Infinite Medium," *Int. J. Multiphase Flow*, Vol. 1, pp. 491–511 (1974).

44. Peebles, F. N., and Garber, H. J., "Studies on the Motion of Gas Bubbles in Liquid," *Chem. Eng. Progr.*, Vol. 49, pp. 88–97, 1953.

45. Harmathy, T. Z., "Velocity of Large Drops and Bubbles in Media of Infinite and Restricted Extent," *AIChE J.*, Vol. 6, pp. 281–288 (1960).

46. Ishii, M., Chawla, T. C., and Zuber, N., "Constitutive Equation for Vapor Drift Velocity in Two-Phase Annular Flow," *AIChE J.*, Vol. 22, No. 2, pp. 283–289 (1976).

47. Wallis, G. B., "Annular Two-Phase Flow, Part 1: Simple Theory," *Trans. ASME, J. Basic Eng.*, Vol. 59, No. 1, pp. 59–72 (1970).

48. Ishii, M., and Grolmes, M. A., "Inception Criteria for Droplet Entrainment in Two-Phase Concurrent Film Flow," *AIChE J.*, Vol. 21, pp. 308–318 (1975).

49. Kataoka, I., Ishii, M., and Mishima, K., "Generation and Size Distribution of Droplet in Annular Two-Phase Flow," *Trans. ASME, J. Fluid Eng.*, Vol. 105, No. 2, pp. 230–238 (1983).

50. Chisholm, D., "Predicting Two Phase Flow Pressure Drop," *Encyclopedia of Fluid Mechanics*, Vol. 6, 1986.

51. Weisman, J., and Choe, W. G., "Methods for Calculation of Pressure Drop in Cocurrent Gas-Liquid Flow," *Two-Phase Transport and Reactor Safety*, Hemisphere Publishing Corporation, Washington, 1978.

52. Weisman, J., private communication, 1980.

53. Beattie, D. R. H., and Whalley, P. B., "A Simple Two-Phase Frictional Pressure Drop Calculation Method," *Int. J. Multiphase Flow*, Vol. 8, No. 1, pp. 83–87 (1982).

54. HTFS (Heat Transfer and Fluid Flow Service), AERE Harwell and NEL East Kibride, unpublished information, 1981.

55. Baroczy, C. J., "A Systematic Correlation for Two-Phase Pressure-Drop," *Chem. Eng. Prog. Symp. Series*, Vol. 62, No. 64, pp. 232–249 (1966).

56. Thom, J. R. S., "Prediction of Pressure Drop During Forced Circulation Boiling of Water," *Int. J. Heat Mass Transfer*, Vol. 7, pp. 709–724 (1964).

57. Lockhart, R. W., and Martinelli, R. C., "Proposed Correlation of Data for Isothermal Two-Phase, Two-Component Flow in Pipes," *Chem. Eng. Prog.*, Vol. 45, No. 1, pp. 39–48 (1949).

58. Martinelli, R. C., and Nelson, D. B., "Prediction of Pressure Drop During Forced-Circulation Boiling of Water," *Trans. ASME*, Vol. 70, pp. 695–702, (1948).

59. Chisholm, D., "A Theoretical Basis for the Lockhart-Martinelli Correlation for Two-Phase Flow," *Int. J. Heat Mass Transfer*, Vol. 10, pp. 1767–1778 (1967).

60. Chisholm, D., "Pressure Gradients Due to Friction During the Flow of Evaporating Two-Phase Mixtures in Smooth Tubes and Channels," *Int. J. Heat Mass Transfer*, Vol. 16, pp. 347–358, (1973).

61. Wallis, G. B., "Critical Two-Phase Flow," *Int. J. Multiphase Flow*, Vol. 6, pp. 97–112 (1980).

62. *Critical Flow Modelling in Nuclear Safety*, Nuclear Energy Agency, CSNI Report No. 49, OECD, Paris, 1982.

63. Henry, R. E., and Fauske, H. K., "The Two-Phase Critical Flow of One-Component Mixtures in Nozzles, Orifices, and Short Tubes," *Trans. ASME, Heat J. Transfer*, Vol. 93, No. 2, pp. 179–187 (1971).

64. Moody, F. J., "Maximum Flow Rate of a Single Component, Two-Phase Mixture," *Trans. ASME, J. Heat Transfer*, Vol. 87, No. 1, pp. 134–142 (1965).

65. Moody, F. J., "Maximum Discharge Rate of Liquid-Vapor Mixtures from Vessels," *Non-Equilibrium Two-Phase Flows*, pp. 27–36, ASME, (1975).

66. Ransom, V. H., and Trapp, J. A., "The RELAP5 Choked Flow Model and Application to a Large Scale Flow Test," Proc. ANS/ASME/NRC International Topical Meeting on Nuc. Reactor Thermal/Hydraulics, NUREG/CP-0014, Vol. 2, pp. 799–819 (1980).

67. Ardron, K. H., and Furness, R. A., "A Study of the Critical Flow Models Used in Reactor Blowdown Analysis," *Nuc. Engng. Des.*, Vol. 39, pp. 257–266 (1976).

68. Groeneveld, D. C., "Post-Dryout Heat Transfer: Physical Mechanisms and a Survey of Prediction Methods," *Nucl. Engng Des.*, Vol. 32, pp. 283–294 (1975).

69. Groeneveld, D. C., and Gardiner, S. R. M., "Post-CHF Heat Transfer Under Forced Convective Conditions," *Thermal and Hydraulic Aspects of Nuclear Reactor Safety, Volume 1: Light Water Reactors*, pp. 43–73, ASME (1977).

70. Chen, J. C., Sundaram, R. K., and Ozkaynak, F. T., "A Phenomenological Correlation for Post-CHF Heat Transfer," NUREG-0237, June 1977.

71. Webb, S. W., and Chen, J. C., "A Numerical Model for Turbulent Non-Equilibrium Dispersed Flow Heat Transfer," *Int. J. Heat Mass Transfer*, Vol. 25, No. 3, pp. 325–335 (1982).

72. Holman, J. P., *Heat Transfer*, Fifth Edition, McGraw-Hill Book Company, New York, 1981.

73. Kreith, F., *Principles of Heat Transfer*, Second Edition, International Textbook Company, Scranton, PA, 1965.

74. Leinhard, J. H., *A Heat Transfer Textbook*, Prentice Hall, Inc., Englewood Cliffs, NJ, 1981.

75. Dittus, F. W., and Boelter, L. M. K., "Heat Transfer in Automobile Radiators of the Tubular Type," University of California, Publications in Engineering, Vol. 2, pp. 443–461, 1930.

76. Ishii, M., Jones, O., and Zuber, N., "Thermal Non-equilibrium Effects in Drift Flux Model of Two-Phase Flow," *Trans. ANS*, Vol. 22, p. 263, 1975.

77. Jones, O. C., Jr., and Saha, P., "Non-Equilibrium Aspects of Water Reactor Safety," *Thermal and Hydraulic Aspects of Nuclear Reactor Safety, Volume 1: Light Water Reactors*, pp. 249–288, ASME, 1977.

78. Butterworth, D., Private Communication as referenced in Collier [22, 23].

79. Chen, J. C., "Correlation for Boiling Heat Transfer to Saturated Fluids in Convective Flow," *Ind. Eng. Chem. Process Design Develop.*, Vol. 5, No. 3, pp. 322–329, 1966.

80. Bennett, D. L., and Chen, J. C., "Forced Convective Boiling in Vertical Tubes for Saturated Pure Components and Binary Mixtures," *AIChE J.*, Vol. 26, No. 3, pp. 454–461 (May 1980).

81. Edelstein, S., Perez, A. J., and Chen, J. C., "An Analytical Representation of Convective-Boiling Functions," to be published in AIChE J.

82. Bjornard, T. A., and Griffith, P., "PWR Blowdown Heat Transfer," *Thermal and Hydraulic Aspects of Nuclear Reactor Safety. Volume 1: Light Water Reactors*, pp. 17–41, ASME, 1977.

83. Butterworth, D., private communication as referenced by Bjornard and Griffith [82].

84. Tong, L. S., *Boiling Crisis and Critical Heat Flux*, AEC Critical Review Series, TID-25887, 1972.

85. Harlow, F. H., and Amsden, A. A., "A Numerical Fluid Dynamics Calculation Method for All Flow Speeds," *Journal of Computational Physics*, Vol. 8, No. 2 (October 1971).

86. Roache, P. J., *Computational Fluid Dynamics*, Hermosa Publishers, Albuquerque, NM, 1972.

87. Patankar, S. V., *Numerical Heat Transfer and Fluid Flow*, Hemisphere Publishing Corp, 1980.

88. Liles, D. R., and Reed, Wm. H., "A Semi-Implicit Method for Two-phase Fluid Dynamics," *Journal of Computational Physics* 26, pp. 390–407 (1978).

89. Forsythe, G. E., and Wasow, R. W., *Finite-Difference Methods for Partial Differential Equations*, John Wiley & Sons Inc, New York, 1960.

90. Forsynthe, G. E., and Moler, C. B., *Computer Solution of Linear Algebraic Systems*, Prentice-Hall Inc. Englewood Cliffs, NJ, 1967.

91. Richtmyer, R. D., and Morton, K. W., *Difference Methods for Initial Value Problems*, Second Edition, Interscience Publishers, New York, 1967.

92. Redfield, J. A., Murphy, J. H., and Davis, V. C., "FLASH-2: A FORTRAN IV Program for

the Digital Simulation of a Multinode Reactor Plant During Loss of Coolant," WAPD-TM-666, April, 1967.

93. "RETRAN—A Program for One-Dimensional Transient Thermal-Hydraulic Analysis of Complex Fluid Flow Systems Volume 1: Equations and Numerics," Prepared by Energy Incorporated, Idaho Falls ID for EPRI, EPRI NP-408, Projects 342-1-2 &889-2, Final Report, January 1977.

94. Mahaffy, J. H., "A Stability-Enhancing Two-Step Method for Fluid Flow Calculations," *Journal of Computational Physics*, Vol. 46, No. 3 (June 1982).

95. Zuber, N., and Staub, F. W., "The Propagation and the Wave Form of the Vapor Volumetric Concentration in Boiling, Forced Convection System Under Oscillatory Conditions," *Int. J. Heat Mass Transfer*, Vol. 9, pp. 871–895 (1966).

96. Zuber, N., and Staub, F. W., "An Analytical Investigation of the Transient Response of the Volumetric Concentration in a Boiling Forced Flow System," Nuc. Sci. Eng., Vol. 30, pp. 268–278 (1967).

97. Staub, F. W., Zuber, N., and Bijwaard, G., "Experimental Investigation of the Transient Response of the Volumetric Concentration in a Boiling Forced Flow System," *Nuc. Sci. Eng.*, Vol. 30, pp. 279–295, 1967.

98. Staub, F. W., and Zuber, N., "Void Response to Flow and Power Oscillations in a Forced-Convection Boiling System with Axially Nonuniform Power Input," *Nuc. Sci. Eng.*, Vol. 30, pp. 296–303, (1967).

99. Staub, F. W., and Zuber, N., "Void Fraction Profiles, Flow Mechanisms and Heat Transfer Coefficients for Refrigerant 22 Evaporating in a Vertical Tube," *ASHRAE Trans.*, Vol. 72, Part 1, pp. 130–146 (1966).

100. Ishii, M., and Zuber, N., "Thermally Induced Flow Instabilities in Two-Phase Mixtures," 4th Intern. Heat Transfer Conf., Paris, Vol. V, Paper B 5.11, 1970.

101. Saha, P., Ishii, M., and Zuber, N., "An Experimental Investigation of the Thermally Induced Flow Oscillations in Two-Phase Systems," *Trans. ASME, J. Heat Transfer*, Vol. 98, pp. 616–622 (1976).

102. Saha, P., and Zuber, N., "An Analytical Study of the Thermally Induced Two-Phase Flow Instabilities Including the Effect of Thermal Non-Equilibrium," *Int. J. Heat Mass Transfer*, Vol. 21, pp. 415–426 (1978).

103. Ohkawa, K., and Lahey, R. T., Jr., "The Analysis of CCFL Using Drift-Flux Models," *Nucl. Engng and Design*, Vol. 61, pp. 245–255, 1980.

104. Hirt, C. W., and Romero, N. C., "Application of a Drift-Flux Model to Flashing in Straight Pipes," NR-DRSR-001, LA-6005-MS, July 1976.

105. Kroeger, P. G., "Application of a Nonequilibrium Drift Flux Model to Two-Phase Blowdown Experiments," *Transient Two-Phase Flow*, Proceedings of the CSNI Specialists Meetings, Toronto, Vol. 1, pp. 112–155, August 1976.

106. Hirt, C. W., and Oliphant, T. A., "SOLA-PLOOP: A Non-Equilibrium, Drift-Flux Code for Two Phase Flow in Networks," *Transient Two-Phase Flow*, Proceedings of the CSNI Specialists Meeting, Toronto, Vol. 1, pp. 398–428, August 1976.

107. "SOLA-LOOP: A Nonequilibrium, Drift-Flux Code for Two-Phase Flow in Networks," NUREG/CR-0626, LA-7659, 1979.

SECTION III

REACTORS AND INDUSTRIAL APPLICATIONS

CHAPTER 32

CONTACTING AND HYDRODYNAMICS IN TRICKLE-BED REACTORS

Milorad P. Duduković

Department of Chemical Engineering
Washington University
St. Louis, Missouri, USA

and

Patrick L. Mills

Corporate Research Laboratories
Monsanto Company
St. Louis, Missouri, USA

CONTENTS

INTRODUCTION

Trickle-bed reactors are packed beds of catalyst with cocurrent downflow of gas and liquid reactants. Most of the hydrotreating of heavy residuals, hydrodesulfurization, denitrogenation, and demetallation of heavy fractions in petroleum processing are performed in trickle beds. Since oil refining is done on such a large scale, it is no surprise that based on total tonnage of material processed, trickle-beds are by far the most used reactor type. Besides oil refining, many chemical and petrochemical processes involve reactions between gases and liquids that are catalyzed by solids or solid-supported materials. Often, it is not economical to prevolatilize the liquid feed in order to conduct vapor-phase reactions, and hydrogen or oxygen, the usual gas phase reactants, cannot readily be liquified for conduction of reaction in the liquid phase. This results in the necessity for multiphase processing that can be conducted in a number of reactor types. Catalyst slurries, (i.e., finely powdered suspended catalyst particles (20 μm to 200 μm)) are used in mechanically agitated autoclaves, bubble columns, gas-lift reactors, while somewhat larger particles are employed in three-phase fluidized beds. Catalyst pellets (0.08 cm to 0.32 cm) are used in packed-beds with cocurrent flow, downflow, or upflow, and countercurrent gas-liquid flow. Germain et al. [1] compare the relative merits of packed beds and slurry reactors and conclude that, overall, packed beds are to be preferred due to their flow pattern that approaches plug flow, high catalyst loading per unit volume of the liquid, low energy dissipation rate (an order of magnitude lower than in slurry reactors), and much greater flexibility with respect to production rates and operating conditions used. The only marked disadvantages remain their intolerance of highly exothermic reactions and their impracticality for systems with rapidly deactivating catalysts.

In spite of their advantages, the potential of trickle-bed reactors has never been fully utilized in chemical processing in partial hydrogenations, partial oxidations, desulfurizations, hydroformylations or in pollution abatement, fermentations, and other biochemical reactions. The reason seems to lie in the difficulties associated with trickle-bed design which exceed those encountered with other reactor types [1]. While scale-up of trickle-bed reactors in petroleum processing for certain types of known feeds is well established as an art, a priori prediction of trickle-bed performance or scale-up from small laboratory units for feeds and processes for which previous know-how does not exist is still considered very risky and is simply not done [2]. This is because the phenomena in trickle-beds are incompletely understood and are not readily quantified. However, a qualitative picture has emerged over the years of what goes on and what one needs to know for proper reactor modeling and design.

Basically, we can divide the phenomena of interest into those that occur on reactor scale (macroscale) and those that happen on catalyst particle scale (microscale). On the macroscale, it is necessary to quantify the following:

- The state of macromixing of both flowing phases (i.e., residence time distributions for gas and liquid)
- Flow regimes
- Pressure drop
- The degree of liquid flashing
- Liquid holdup (dynamic and static)
- Gas-liquid and liquid-solid interfacial area and transport coefficients
- Radial distribution of fluids
- Macroscale catalyst contacting, (i.e., presence or absence of dry zones and their distribution)
- Heat transfer
- Energy dissipation.

On the microscale, it is important to quantify the following:

- Local texture of liquid (flowing film, stagnant pocket, or liquid rivulet)
- Local irrigation and external wetting of catalyst particles
- Liquid holdup within pores of catalyst particles
- Gas-flowing liquid interfacial area and mass transfer coefficients
- Flowing liquid-solid contacting area and mass transfer coefficients
- Contacting area and mass transfer coefficients between gas and stagnant liquid and solid
- Mass transfer coefficients between gas and vapor-filled pores of the solid catalyst
- Exchange coefficients between the stagnant and flowing liquid.

L' Homme [3] summarized in tabular form most of the preceding macroscale and microscale phenomena which are of importance in trickle-bed design. Progress in understanding and quantifying these phenomena, resulting from numerous investigations, has been summarized in a series of review articles [4–8] and in two monographs [9, 10]. The design and scale-up issues were particularly emphasized at the NATO Advanced Institute on Multiphase Reactors [11–13].

From the foregoing phenomenological description, it becomes apparent that liquid-solid contacting is one of the prime factors affecting trickle-bed reactor behavior. Processes conducted in trickle-bed reactors can be divided into two categories. In one of them, under operating conditions used, liquid reactant is nonvolatile and reaction can occur only on wetted catalyst particles since only there can liquid and gas reactant contact the catalyst. This would be typical of some high-pressure desulfurizations of heavy residuals. The other category consists of processes where the liquid reactant is partially vaporized and reaction occurs both on wetted and dry catalyst particles but at different rates due to different external and internal mass transfer effects. This can happen in partial hydrogenations or oxidations of chemicals. In either case, a knowledge of catalyst contacting with liquid is essential for proper reactor modeling and for the correct assessment of the catalyst effectiveness [14–16].

Liquid-solid contacting is determined by the hydrodynamics of two-phase flow through packed beds coupled with transport and reaction effects. In the first approximation, it can be assumed that the latter two cause negligible effects (an assumption not justified with exothermic reactions producing gaseous products) and that contacting is determined solely by the hydrodynamics of the two-phase flow.

Two-phase flow in packed beds can be approached either from the fundamental viewpoint (i.e., by writing the basic momentum equations for each phase including the necessary phase interaction terms) or from the mechanistic point of view which relies on formulation of an appropriate model which is used to determine the quantity of interest such as pressure drop, holdup, or flow regime. The first approach, while possible in principle with the advent of modern computers, is nevertheless excessively difficult since it requires proper characterization of the solid boundary and of the unknown gas-liquid interface which must also be computed. For this reason, this approach has not been pursued in describing the hydrodynamics of trickle-bed reactors. Instead, the mechanistic approach was utilized via postulated simplified models to determine the quantities of interest. These are:

- Flow regimes.
- Pressure drop.
- Liquid holdup.
- Liquid-solid contacting.

We will briefly describe the first three since these subjects are treated in detail by others, and will concentrate most of our discussion on the last item of liquid-solid contacting.

FLOW REGIMES

Packed beds with cocurrent downflow of gas and liquid are operated over a wide range of gas and liquid velocities. In small laboratory-scale reactors, liquid mass superficial velocities are of the order of 0.1 (kg/m^2 s) or lower and gas velocities are between 10^{-5} to 10^{-2} (kg/m^2 s). Large pilot and commercial-scale reactors have liquid superficial velocities in the range of 0.5 to 50 (kg/m^2 s) and gas superficial velocities in the range of 10^{-3} to 25 (kg/m^2 s). Depending on the gas and liquid velocities, physical properties of the liquid, wetting properties of the solid, and nature of the porous structure in the packed bed, various flow regimes may be observed. These flow regimes can be divided into two broad categories [17]: the low gas-liquid interaction regime and the high gas-liquid interaction regime. The low gas-liquid interaction regime can be further divided into the trickle-flow regime and the pulsing flow, spray flow, and dispersed bubble flow for nonfoaming systems. For foaming systems, the high gas-liquid interaction regime consists of pulsing flow without foaming, pulsing flow with foaming, foaming flow, and gas continuous or spray flow [18]. Alternatively, in the case of foaming liquids, a slightly different classification may be made by breaking the pulsing flow into foaming flow, foaming-pulsing, and pulsing flow [9]. In the low gas-liquid interaction regime, the shear at the gas-liquid interface does not affect the shape of the interface or the structure of the liquid films or rivulets. In the high gas-liquid interaction regime, the phase interaction term is important in determining the shape of the interface and of the flow pattern.

The phenomenological picture, based on experimental evidence, that emerges is as follows. At up to moderate gas velocities (G < 1 kg/m^2 s) and low liquid velocities (L < 5 kg/m^2 s) trickle-flow always persists. In this regime gas flows as a continuous phase through the bed as does the liquid which takes the form of films and rivulets and perhaps, a few stagnant zones. In this regime at a fixed gas velocity, as the liquid velocity is increased from transition to pulsing flow, (or a mode of pulsing-foaming flow as occurs in the case of foaming liquids), only at very low gas velocities $(G < 0.01 \text{ kg/m}^2 \text{ s})$ can a transition to a dispersed-bubble flow takes place. In dispersed-bubble flow the continuous liquid phase drags along the discrete gas bubbles. Pulsing flow is characterized by alternating flows of gas-rich and liquid-rich slugs which normally lead to noticeable pressure fluctuations in the bed and oscillations in the measured pressure drop. While visual observations have been largely used to determine the transition from trickle to pulse flow, a more indicative and objective criterion of sensing the transition has been to measure the sharp increase in the root mean square wall pressure fluctuations caused by a small increase in the gas or liquid flow rate. At a fixed liquid velocity in the trickle-flow regime, an increase in gas velocity also eventually leads from trickle to pulsing flow unless the liquid velocity is so low $(L < 5 \text{ kg/m}^2 \text{ s})$ that transition to spray flow occurs instead. In spray flow liquid droplets are carried by a continuous gas stream.

The preceding qualitative picture can be quantified based on experimental results and presented as a flow map. Such flow maps for foaming and nonfoaming liquids are given as Figures 1A and B, respectively. These are based on the extensive experimental work of Charpentier and Favier [19] with various hydrocarbons. These flow maps utilize the so-called Baker's coordinates [20] which were used originally to classify two-phase flow patterns of oil and gas in horizontal pipes. The flow maps of Charpentier and Favier [19] are by no means universally accepted. Chou et al. [21] demonstrated experimentally that the wetting characteristics of the packing and bed porosity, neither of which is included in Baker's coordinates, may affect the position of the transition line between trickle and pulsing flow. Nevertheless, if this transition is viewed as a zone rather than a sharp line, the Charpentier and Favier map is useful for the practitioner if bed porosity is included in the abscissa as done in Ramachandran and Chaudhari's text [10]. This leads to the following approximate criterion for maintaining trickle-flow conditions

$$L \leq L_{cr} \quad \text{and} \quad \frac{G}{\varepsilon_B \lambda} < 1 \tag{1}$$

where L_{cr} is the smaller of the two mass velocities evaluated in the following:

$$L_{cr} = \frac{10^3 \, G}{\lambda \psi} \tag{2a}$$

$$L_{cr} = 5.45 \left(\frac{\varepsilon_B \lambda}{G} \right)^{0.22} \frac{\varepsilon_B}{\psi} \tag{2b}$$

where

$$\lambda = \left(\frac{\rho_g}{\rho_{air}} \frac{\rho_L}{\rho_w} \right)^{1/2}$$

$$\psi = \frac{\sigma_w}{\sigma_L} \left[\frac{\mu_L}{\mu_w} \left(\frac{\rho_w}{\rho_L} \right)^2 \right]^{1/3}$$

and with SI units being used. When $L > L_{cr}$ and $G/\varepsilon_B \lambda < 1$, transition to pulsing flow occurs, while at $G/\varepsilon_B \lambda > 1$, transition to spray flow occurs.

Identifying the boundaries of the broad range of the trickle flow regime (see Figure 1) is important because many trickle-beds used for petrochemical processing are operated in this regime. This is due to the great flexibility of production rates (i.e., liquid and gas mass velocities that this flow regime allows), which is of greater advantage than the reported improved mass transfer coefficients and reduced dispersion effects in the pulsing regime [21–24]. The pulsing regime is often avoided in practice because of the undesirable and violent pressure oscillations.

Many additional flow maps have been proposed. Midoux et al. [25], Morsi et al. [26, 27], and Specchia and Baldi [17] provide data with a variety of liquids and packing in support of the use

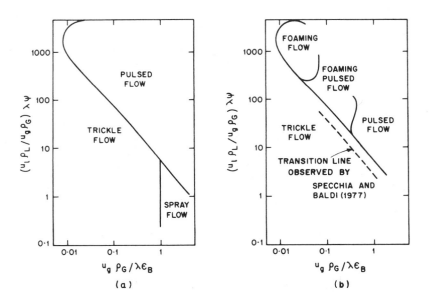

Figure 1. Flow regime map for two-phase flow through packed beds: (A) foaming liquids; (B) nonfoaming liquids. (After Charpentier and Favier [19].)

of Baker's coordinates and of the Charpentier and Favier map. Sato [28] presented an early flow map based on experiments with water which did not differ much from the results for nonfoaming hydrocarbons. Fukushima and Kusaka [29–31] presented a flow map in terms of gas- and liquid-phase Reynolds numbers consisting of trickle, wavy, pulse, spray, and dispersed-bubble regimes. The transition lines between the trickle to pulse regime and trickle to wavy regime are characterized by Equations 3a and 3b, respectively:

$$\phi_c^{-0.2} Re_L^{0.27} Re_G^{0.2} \left(\frac{d_p}{d_T}\right)^{-0.5} = 18 \tag{3a}$$

$$\phi_c^{-0.1} Re_L^{0.2} Re_G^{0.3} \left(\frac{d_p}{d_T}\right)^{-0.5} = 520 \tag{3b}$$

In Equations 3a and 3b the Reynolds numbers are based on the equivalent particle diameter, and the surface shape factor ϕ_c is defined as the ratio of the particle geometric external area to the square of packing diameter.

Talmor [18] presented his flow map for foaming and nonfoaming systems in terms of the ratio of liquid-to-gas superficial velocities and a parameter representing the ratio of inertia + gravity-to interface + viscous forces, i.e., $(1 + 1/Fr)/(We + 1/Re)$. This flow map and the various dimensionless groups used have been summarized in Ramachandran and Chaudhari's text [10]. Gianetto et al. [32] proposed that transition between trickle and pulsing flow occurs when the following liquid mass superficial critical velocity (in SI units) is exceeded:

$$L_{cr} = 10\left[\left(\frac{L_{cr}}{G}\right)^{0.2}\varepsilon_B - G\right] \tag{4}$$

Sicardi et al. [33] tried to develop a criterion for the trickle to pulse transition by modeling the flow as that in a bundle of parallel capillary tubes. They investigated the conditions that lead to formation of waves of such amplitude in the liquid film that the cross-section of the tube gets blocked, which results in the formation of the liquid slug. This led them to propose the following approximate transition criterion

$$\frac{\varepsilon_B}{H_{LE}} = 1.8 \text{ to } 4 \tag{5}$$

where H_{LE} is the external liquid holdup. The work of Drinkenburg [34], however, indicates that there is little resemblance between onset of pulsing in straight tubes and in packed beds. Drinkenburg and coworkers [24] have investigated extensively the pulsing flow regime and developed correlations for holdup and volumetric mass transfer coefficients in that regime. Blok and Drinkenburg [24] suggested, based on experimental evidence with air-water systems and packing of different sizes, shapes, and properties, the following criterion for transition between trickle and pulsing flow:

$$\frac{L}{\varepsilon d_p \rho_L} = 0.042 \left(\frac{a_t \rho_g}{G}\right)^{0.265} \tag{6}$$

where a_t is the specific area of the packing per unit volume of the bed. They also claim that the transition point is characterized by a constant Froude number

$$Fr = \frac{L^2}{H_L^2 \rho_L^2 g d_p} = 0.08 \text{ to } 0.09 \tag{7}$$

where H_L is the liquid holdup. It should be noted that the dependence of the critical liquid mass velocity on gas mass velocity in Equations 6 and 2b is very similar.

All the flow maps and transition lines presented have been, to a large extent, empirical and are based on experimental evidence. Recently, Ng [35] proposed some mechanistic models to interpret various flow transitions in packed beds. He took note of the "wavy" configuration of a typical pore in a packed bed which results in changes of cross-sectional area available for flow. Ng [35] further suggests that the transition to pulsing flow occurs at gas velocities at which the pressure difference between the widest cross section and the narrowest constriction in the pore, as computed by the Bernoulli equation, becomes equal to the capillary pressure rise in the liquid film computed from the balance of pressure, gravity, and surface-tension forces. This results in the following equation for the critical gas mass velocity required for transition to pulsing to occur:

$$G = \varepsilon_B \rho_g (1 - \alpha) \sqrt{\frac{2}{\rho_g}\left(\frac{4\sigma}{d_p} - \rho_L g \frac{d_p}{2}\right)} \tag{8}$$

Here, α is the fraction of the cross-sectional area of void space occupied by liquid which can be taken to be equal to external liquid holdup, H_{LE}, given by the correlation of Wijffels et al. [36]:

$$\frac{g d_p}{u_L^2} \frac{\varepsilon^3}{(1 - \varepsilon)^2} H_{LE}^4 = \frac{200}{Re_L} + \frac{1.75}{1 - \varepsilon} \tag{9}$$

Thus, the liquid velocity dependence in Equation 8 appears through its relationship to the liquid holdup. Preliminary comparison of data and Ng's proposed transition line seems satisfactory [37].

It should also be recognized that flow regime transition from trickle to pulsing may occur at a certain location in the bed. This is the case when pressure drop in the bed is substantial compared to the pressure of the inlet feed gas. This behavior can be qualitatively predicted from Equations 2b, 6, or 8 when one accounts for the decrease in gas density ρ_g with pressure. It is most pronounced in Equation 8. In this situation, the top of the bed is in the trickle-flow regime while pulsing starts in the bottom portion. Equation 8 is the only one to include the effect of packing size on the onset of pulsing.

In summary, we can say that a number of semi-empirical flow maps have been proposed for prediction of flow regimes. Potential users should rely on the flow map that is based on data obtained for systems that resemble the most, in physical properties and packing characteristics, the one of interest to them. The trickle-flow regime is widely encountered in practice and is of interest in this review because it is the only one that, besides spray flow, can lead to incomplete liquid-solid contacting. The boundaries of the trickle-flow regime can be broadly established from the equations for trickle-pulse transition and trickle-spray transition already presented. Predictions by these equations establish a transition zone. A more precise a priori location of the transition line is not possible at present. A more theoretical, mechanistic approach in describing the flow regime transitions is still in its infancy. A priori prediction of whether a liquid will foam or not is also not possible although the validity of some simple experiments for determination of foaming tendency has been documented by Charpentier [38].

PRESSURE DROP

Pressure drop calculations are important in the design of trickle-bed reactors not only in order to estimate the required feed pressures but also because the energy dissipated can be used to calculate other variables of interest such as liquid holdup, gas-liquid interfacial area, and mass transfer coefficients. The available correlations for pressure drop calculations for nonfoaming and foaming liquids have been summarized in a number of review papers and texts [7–10, 12]. For the convenience of the reader, the most frequently used ones are presented here in Table 1.

It is apparent from Table 1 that basically three approaches have been used by all investigators to develop pressure-drop correlations for two-phase flow in packed beds. The starting point is the Ergun equation which predicts the pressure drop for the flow of a single phase through a packed bed:

$$\delta = \frac{\Delta P}{L} = \frac{150(1 - \varepsilon_B)^2}{\varepsilon_B^3} \frac{u\mu}{d_{pe}^2} + \frac{1.75(1 - \varepsilon_B)}{\varepsilon_B^3} \frac{u^2\rho}{d_{pe}} \qquad (10)$$

Lockhart and Martinelli [44] established that the two-phase flow frictional pressure drop can be correlated with the parameter $\chi = (\delta_\ell/\delta_g)^{0.5}$. This approach has been used to obtain Equations 1-1 through 1-4 in Table 1. The frictional pressure drop can also be related to the two-phase friction factor, $f_{g\ell} = \delta_\ell d_{pe}/2u_g^2\rho_g$, which can be correlated with the dimensionless ratio of gas-phase and liquid-phase Reynolds numbers raised to appropriate powers, $Z = Re_g^{1.167}/Re_\ell^{0.767}$, as introduced by Turpin and Huntington [42] in obtaining Equation 1-6. A modification to account for liquid and gas properties through the additional parameter ψ was introduced by Specchia and Baldi [17] in order to get Equation 1-7 (Table 1). Charpentier and coworkers [25, 41] introduced the rate of frictional energy dissipation as a proper correlating parameter for high gas-liquid interaction and foaming systems and used it to develop Equations 1-3 and 1-5. For the low gas-liquid interaction regime, Specchia and Baldi [17] suggested that due to a lack of gas-liquid interaction, the two-phase pressure drop should be given by the Ergun equation for gas flow through a bed where the voidage available for gas flow is bed porosity minus liquid static and dynamic holdup. However, liquid holdup changes the configuration of the pores open to gas flow, and this causes the constants k_1 and k_2 in Equation 1-9 to deviate from those normally associated with the Ergun equation, i.e., $150/d_{pe}^2$ and $1.75/d_{pe}$, respectively. The coefficients k_1 and k_2 can be evaluated by measuring gas pressure drop in a prewetted and drained bed with residual saturation $\beta_r = H_{LS}/\varepsilon_{B_t}$, where H_{LS} is the static liquid holdup and ε_{B_t} is total bed porosity including particle porosity. This approach is an extension of the attempt by Hutton and Leong [45] to develop a theoretical foundation for pressure drop and holdup in structures packed with inclined surfaces. It should be noted that since the Ergun equation for single-phase flow has a firm theoretical foundation, the Specchia and Baldi [17] equation for the low gas-liquid interaction regime is the only one that is theoretically well-founded. This approach, however, still requires experimental determination of two constants which

Table 1
Pressure Drop Correlations

Number	Correlation	Reference	Comments
1-1	$$\log\left(\frac{\delta_{\ell g}}{\delta_\ell + \delta_g}\right) = \frac{0.146}{(\log \chi)^2 + 0.666}$$ $$0.0 < x = \left(\frac{\delta_\ell}{\delta_g}\right)^{0.5} < 30$$	[39]	All flow regimes
1-2	$$\log\left(\frac{\delta_{\ell g}}{\delta_\ell + \delta_g}\right) = \frac{0.70}{[\log(\chi/1.2)]^2 + 1} \quad 0.1 < \chi < 20$$	[40]	All flow regimes
1-3	$$\log\left(\frac{\xi_{\ell g}}{\xi_\ell + \xi_g}\right) = \frac{A}{(\log \chi')^2 + B}$$ A & B given for various packings	[41]	Tricke-Flow regime and pulsing regime
1-4	$$\left(\frac{\delta_{\ell g}}{\delta_\ell}\right)^{0.5} = 1 + \frac{1}{\chi} + \frac{1.14}{\chi^{0.54}} \quad 0.1 < \chi < 80$$	[25]	All flow regimes, non foaming liquid
1-5	$$\left(\frac{\xi_{\ell g}}{\xi_\ell}\right)^{0.5} = 1 + \frac{1}{\chi'} + \frac{6.55}{(\chi')^{0.42}}$$ $$\xi_\ell = L/\varepsilon_B; \qquad \xi_g = \left(\frac{1}{\rho_g}\delta_g + 1\right)\frac{G}{\varepsilon_B}$$ $$\xi_{\ell g} = \frac{1}{\varepsilon_B g}\left[\frac{L}{\rho_L} + \frac{G}{\rho_g}\right]\delta_{\ell g} + \frac{L + G}{\varepsilon_B}$$ $$0.05 < \chi' = (\xi_\ell/\xi_g)^{0.5} < 500$$	[25]	All flow regimes, foaming liquid
1-6	$$\ln f_{\ell g} = 7.96 - 1.34 \ln Z + 0.0021(\ln Z)^2 + 0.0078(\ln Z)^3$$ $$f_{\ell g} = \frac{\delta_{\ell g}d_{pe}}{2u_g^2\rho_g}; \qquad d_{pe} = \frac{2}{3}d_p\frac{\varepsilon_B}{1-\varepsilon_B}; \qquad d_p = \sqrt{S_{ex}/\pi}$$ $$0.2 < Z = \frac{Re_g^{1.167}}{Re_L^{0.767}} < 500$$	[42]	All flow regimes
1-7	$$\ln f_{g\ell} = 7.82 - 1.30\frac{Z}{\psi^{1.1}} - 0.0573\left(\ln\left(\frac{Z}{\psi^{1.1}}\right)\right)^2$$	[17]	High gas-liquid interaction regime
1-8	$$\frac{\delta_{g\ell}}{\delta_g} = 1507\mu_{Lp}^d\left(\frac{\varepsilon_B}{1-\varepsilon_B}\right)\left(\frac{Re_g We_g}{Re_L}\right)^{-1/3}$$ $$We_g = u_g^2\rho_g d_p/\sigma_L$$	[43]	Trickle and pulsing flow
1-9	$$\delta_{g\ell} = k_1\frac{[1 - \varepsilon_B(1 - \beta_r - \beta_f)]^2}{\varepsilon_B^2(1 - \beta_r - \beta_f)^3}\mu_g u_g$$ $$+ k_2\frac{1 - \varepsilon_B(1 - \beta_r - \beta_f)}{\varepsilon_B(1 - \beta_r - \beta_f)^3}\rho_g u_g^2$$ β_r—residual saturation (static holdup/porosity of the bed) β_f—dynamic saturation (dynamic holdup/porosity of the bed)	[17]	Low gas-liquid interaction regime

can be accomplished in a standard test apparatus. A priori prediction of two-phase pressure drop for design purposes relies then on the other correlations shown in Table 1, all of which are empirical.

From the viewpoint of pressure-drop predictions and modeling of reactor performance, it is of interest to note that multiple values for the two-phase pressure drop at fixed operating conditions have been reported and correlated by Kan and Greenfield [46, 47] for preflooded beds of small porous particles. The pressure drop was shown to be a function of the maximum gas flow rate to which the bed was exposed. The explanation of the phenomena is as follows. In a preflooded bed, the liquid forms bridges. As the gas flow rate is increased, some of these bridges are broken, first in the larger and then smaller pores, and converted into flowing liquid films. When the maximum specified gas rate is reached before spray flow occurs, and when the gas flow rate is reduced, there is no driving force for liquid bridges to reoccur. Hence, pressure drop at the same operating conditions, i.e., at the same gas and liquid flow rates, is now reduced. Moreover, multiple solutions for liquid film thickness are allowed in parallel pore arrangements at fixed values of pressure drop. Nevertheless, Kan's and Greenfield's [46, 47] results have not been observed by other investigators, including the authors of this review, and hence, until confirmed, have to be accepted with caution.

In summary, the available correlations for prediction of pressure drop in trickle-bed reactors, with a few exceptions, are empirical and need to be used judiciously by preferably comparing the results of various proposed applicable correlations. Caution is especially in order for foaming systems, systems with a large degree of flashing of the liquid, or systems with a high level of gas production by reaction. Multiple pressure drops at fixed operating conditions have been reported by one team of investigators but have not been confirmed by others, although theory allows the possibility of their existence.

LIQUID HOLDUP

Liquid holdup, H_L, is the fraction of the bed volume that is occupied by liquid. In the low gas-liquid interaction regime it is a function of liquid velocity, liquid properties, particle diameter, shape, and wettability. It also depends on gas velocity in the high gas-liquid interaction regime. Holdup is important for proper evaluation of the liquid residence time in the reactor and is related to liquid-solid contacting, average liquid-film thickness and gas-liquid-solid mass transfer. Since trickle beds are packed beds of porous catalyst particles, liquid holdup can be divided into two parts: external holdup and internal holdup as indicated in the following:

$$H_L = H_{LE} + H_{Li} \tag{11}$$

Normally, with hydrocarbon liquids of low surface tension, and even with water which has a higher surface tension, internal holdup equals the internal particle porosity of the bed [14, 48–51].

$$H_{Li} = \varepsilon_p(1 - \varepsilon_B) \tag{12}$$

That this is the case even when some of the particles are incompletely externally contacted by flowing liquid testifies to the highly interconnected pore structure of alumina-based catalysts employed in trickle-bed operation [49, 50]. The conclusion that the internal pore structure of the catalyst particles is always completely liquid filled is based on laboratory-scale tracer or isothermal reaction experiments. This should not be generalized to trickle-bed reactors operated adiabatically, or even close to isothermally, when the reaction is highly exothermic or when large amounts of product gas are evolved. It has been shown experimentally in hydrogenation of α-methylstyrene [52] and other hydrogenations [53, 54] that, under conditions of high volatilization, particles could dry out completely. This leads to different rates than on wetted particles due to different diffusional resistances and to apparent multiple steady states. The neglect of the preceding phenomena of dryout or partial condensation prevented complete interpretation of the experimental results for reduction of crotonaldehyde [55]. The basic mechanism of pore structure dryout in the presence of a temperature gradient or when product gas is evolved has not been fully clarified. Some preliminary attempts have been made by Kesten and Sangiovanni [131], Pismen [56], and Kim and Kim [57].

An approximate criterion for determining the critical pore radius above which all pores are vapor filled can be obtained based on the Kelvin and Clausius-Clapeyron equation assuming an ideal system and a single volatile (or condensible) species. The criterion is expressed in terms of the difference between the catalyst temperature, T_c, which can be assumed internally isothermal, and the surrounding bulk fluid temperature, T_b:

$$\frac{T_c - T_b}{T_b} = \frac{2\underline{V}\sigma_L}{\Delta\underline{H}_{vap}r^*_{pore}} \tag{13}$$

where $\underline{V}$ = the molar volume of the volatile (condensible) species
$\Delta\underline{H}_{vap}$ = its molar heat of vaporization
σ_L = the surface tension
r^*_{pore} = the critical pore radius

All pores with $r_{pore} > r^*_{pore}$ are then vapor filled. The temperature difference can be established from known reaction rates and estimated heat transfer coefficients:

$$\frac{T_c - T_b}{T_b} = \frac{(-\Delta H_R)R_w\eta\rho_p V_p}{hS_{ex}T_b} \tag{14}$$

where ΔH_R = the heat of reaction
R_w = the reaction rate of bulk conditions per unit mass of the catalyst
η = the effectiveness factor
ρ_p = catalyst density
V_p and S_{ex} = the particle volume and its external surface area
h = the film heat transfer coefficient

The external liquid holdup can also be divided into two parts—the dynamic and static holdup:

$$H_{LE} = H_{LD} + H_{LSE} \tag{15}$$

The dynamic holdup is the fraction of the reactor volume that is occupied by flowing liquid. It is this holdup that depends on the balance of gravity, viscous, and inertial forces in the low gas-liquid interaction regime and also on the gas-liquid-solid interaction forces in the high-interaction regime. Static holdup is the fraction of the reactor volume occupied by liquid external to the particles that is retained when the bed is drained of flowing liquid. The amount of this interparticle liquid is determined by the balance of gravity and surface-tension forces and is also a function of particle shape and wettability. It has been generally correlated with the Eötvos number [58, 59], Eö $= \rho_L g d_{pe}^2/\sigma_L$, or Bond number [60], Bn $= \rho_L g/\sigma_L a_p^2$. In the case of porous particles, total static holdup consists of internal holdup and external static holdup:

$$H_{LST} = H_{Li} + H_{LSE} = \eta_i\varepsilon_p(1 - \varepsilon_B) + H_{LSE} \tag{16}$$

Here, η_i is the fractional pore fillup which under certain conditions can be taken as unity.

While the above holdup definitions are customarily used in the United States, the use of relative holdup, called either holdup or liquid saturation, is frequently found in Europe and Japan. Liquid saturation (relative holdup) is holdup divided by bed porosity.

Low and Intermediate Gas-Liquid Interaction Regime

In the low gas-liquid interaction regime, the evaluation of liquid holdup has a firm theoretical basis. Based on the early attempts of Lynn et al. [61] and Davidson and Cullen [62], Davidson et al. [63] showed that the volume of the flowing liquid film per sphere on a string of spheres can be evaluated from first principles by balancing gravity and viscous forces and results in the following equation:

$$v_{LDS} = 2.02 \frac{\pi d_s^2}{2} \left(\frac{3Q_{LS}v_L}{\pi g d_s} \right)^{1/3} \tag{17}$$

where Q_{LS} is the liquid flow rate over a single string of spheres and d_s is sphere diameter. From the preceding equation we can establish that the dynamic liquid saturation in a bed of nonporous spheres, assuming that the bed behaves as a set of parallel strings, should be given by:

$$\omega_D = \frac{H_{LD}}{\varepsilon_B} = 5.51 \left(\frac{1 - \varepsilon_B}{\varepsilon_B} \right) \left(\frac{Re_L}{Ga_L} \right)^{1/3} = 5.08 \left(\frac{Re_L}{Ga_L} \right)^{1/3} \tag{18}$$

For a hexagonal packing of spheres, $\varepsilon_B = 0.52$. This results in the second equality just presented where $Re_L = L d_s/\mu$ and $Ga_L = g d_s^3/v_L^2$.

Davidson [64] also presented the theoretical expression for external liquid saturation (holdup) in a packed bed with random distribution of packing surfaces which takes the following form: the correlations from a power-law form to a form that asymptotically goes to unity. A similar form was used for correlation of dynamic contact angles [73]. Unfortunately, a dimensional parameter $a_v d_p^2/\varepsilon_B^2$ was inadvertently used which was later corrected by El-Hisnawi [71]. He showed that when the proper dimensionless group $a_t d_p/\varepsilon_B$ is used, the effect of surface tension forces vanishes, i.e., the exponent on the Weber number becomes almost zero. El-Hisnawi presented the correlation forms given by Equations 2.8 and 2.9 in Table 2 and demonstrated that the power law of Equation 2.9 provides the best fit of all available data for beds with small porous particles [16]. He also showed that for the systems studied, the group $a_t d_p/\varepsilon_B$ does not vary significantly so that its effect on holdup cannot be determined in a reliable manner.

It should be noted that incomplete external liquid-solid contacting has not been addressed by the correlations summarized in Table 2. In the theoretical approach of Davidson et al. [63, 64], complete external wetting of spheres was assumed. There has been no theoretical work that describes rivulet formation in a bed of spheres. An attempt with an inclined plane surface was made by Roberts and Yadwadkar [74] who tried to related dynamic holdup to the fraction of external surface wetting by flowing liquid, η_{CE}. They arrived at the following equation:

$$H_D = \frac{1.44}{\cos \beta} \eta_{CE}^{2/3} (Re_L/Ga_L)^{1/3} (a_v d_p)^{2/3} \tag{19}$$

where β is the average plane inclination with respect to the vertical axis which, if taken to be $45°$, leads to a leading coefficient in Equation 20 of 2.04. Crine and L'Homme [79] arrive essentially at

$$\omega_E = \frac{H_{LE}}{\varepsilon_B} = 1.217 \left(\frac{Re_L}{Ga_L} \right)^{1/3} \left(\frac{a_w d_p}{\varepsilon_B} \right) \tag{20}$$

Here, a_w is the external wetted packing area per unit volume which is assumed to be equal to the external geometric packing area per unit volume of the vessel a_t. The remaining parameters include the particle diameter, d_p, and the bed porosity, ε_B.

The work of Davidson et al. [63, 64] is significant in establishing that Re_L, Ga_L, and $a_w d_t/\varepsilon_B$ are the important dimensionless groups for correlating dynamic liquid holdup in low gas-liquid interaction regimes. Charpentier et al. [58, 65] also contributed significantly in expanding upon Davidson's theory and providing experimental confirmations of its basic form.

Holdup correlations have been summarized in recent review papers and texts [7–10]. For the convenience of the reader, some of the better known and recent ones for the low gas-liquid interaction regime are summarized in Table 2. Clearly, these correlations evolved from strictly empirical ones to those that utilized the proper dimensionless groups identified by Davidson et al. [63, 64]. Charpentier et al. [65] showed that in the trickle-flow regime liquid can take the form of laminar or turbulent films, laminar or turbulent rivulets, and stagnant pockets. They argued that the power dependence of the liquid holdup on liquid mass velocity (or Reynolds number) is $\frac{1}{3}$ and $\frac{2}{3}$ for laminar

Table 2
Liquid Holdup Correlations (Low Interaction Regime)

Number	Correlation	Reference
2-1	$H_{LE} \propto L^{0.52}$ to $L^{0.67}$	[66]
2-2	$H_{LE} \propto L^{0.33}$	[67]
2-3	$H_D = 0.00445 Re_L^{0.76}$	[68]
2-4	$H_D = A\,Re_L^{0.676} Ga_L^{-0.44}(a_v d_p)$ for spheres $\begin{cases} A = 1.294 \\ a = 1 \end{cases}$ for broken solids $\begin{cases} A = 15.1 \\ a = -0.6 \end{cases}$	[69]
2-5	$H_D = 0.68 Re_L^{0.8} Ga_L^{-0.44}(a_v d_p)$	[70]
2-6	$H_D = 3.86 Re_L^{0.545} Ga_L^{-0.42}(a_v d_p/\varepsilon_B)^{0.65}$	[17, 48]
2-7	$H_D = \varepsilon_B \tanh\left[0.731 Re_L^{-0.333} Fr_L^{0.708} We_L^{-0.346} \left(\dfrac{a_v d_p^2}{\varepsilon_B^2} \right)^{0.929} \right]$ $Fr_L = \dfrac{La_v}{\rho_{LB}^2 g}$; $\quad We_L = \dfrac{L}{\sigma_L \rho_L a_v}$	[49, 50]
2-8	$H_D = \varepsilon_B \tanh[1.658 Re_L^{0.429} Ga_L^{-0.279}(a_v d_p/\varepsilon_B)^{0.44}$	[71]
2-9	$H_D = 2.02\varepsilon_B Re_L^{0.344} Ga_L^{-0.197}$	[16, 71]
2-10	(All Regimes) $H_D = \varepsilon_B\{13.5(Re_L/Ga_L^*)^{1/3} + 1.2 Re_L(Ga_L^*)^{-0.5}\}$ $Ga_L^* = \dfrac{d_p^3 \rho_L}{\mu_L}(g\rho_L + \delta_{ge})$	[72]
2-11	$H_L = 0.185 a_v^{1/3} \chi^{0.22} \varepsilon_B$; $\quad \chi = (\delta_\ell/\delta_g)^{0.5}$	[40]
2-12	$H_L = \varepsilon_B \dfrac{0.66\chi^{0.81}}{1 + 0.66\chi^{0.81}}$	[25]

and turbulent films respectively, and $\frac{1}{2}$ and 0.8 for laminar and turbulent rivulets, respectively. This range indeed seems to be indicated by the correlations of Table 2.

An attempt was also made [49, 50] (see Equation 2-7, Table 2) to modify the same equation with a slightly different leading constant by using percolation theory and by appropriately averaging the holdup over various sections of the bed with different extents of local irrigation. Their result can be presented as:

$$H_D = 1.74 f_w^{2/3}(Re_L/Ga_L^*)^{1/3}(a_v d_p)^{2/3} \tag{21}$$

where the modified Galileo number also accounts for the pressure drop and is equal to the usual Galileo number in trickle-flow when $\delta_{\ell g}/\rho_L g \ll 1$. The modified Galileo number is defined by:

$$Ga_L^* = \frac{d_p^3 g}{v_L^2}\left(1 + \frac{\delta_{\ell g}}{\rho_L g}\right) = Ga_L\left(1 + \frac{\delta_{\ell g}}{\rho_L g}\right) \tag{22}$$

The average fraction of the external catalyst surface covered by flowing rivulets is f_w ($f_w = \eta_{CE}$) which was taken to be

$$f_w = \frac{L}{L + L_m} = \frac{L/L_m}{L/L_m + 1} \tag{23}$$

where L_m is the minimum liquid mass velocity required for complete contacting that must be determined by experiments. Thus, theoretical approaches attempted so far have not provided the means for a priori calculation of dynamic holdup and external contacting efficiency.

Holdup predictions based on correlations presented in Table 2 are on the average, well within 35% of each other. Attempts to introduce dimensionless numbers that contain surface-tension effects lead to no improvements in matching the available data [16, 38].

High Gas-Liquid Interaction Regime

It has been shown by a number of investigators [26, 66, 75] that liquid flow in trickle beds changes from being dominated by gravity-viscosity to gravity-inertia and finally gravity-surface tension and other interaction forces. For that reason, liquid holdup correlations suggested for the high gas-liquid interaction regime utilize either the Lockhart-Martinelli approach [44] and correlate holdup either in terms of pressure drop ratios for two-phase flow, χ, in terms of energy dissipation rates, or in terms of Re_L, Ga_L^*, and additional dimensionless groups that involve gas-liquid interaction and/or surface-tension forces. Some of the more recent correlations are shown in Table 3. A study by El-Hisnawi [71] indicates that there might be even a 50% or larger disparity between predictions based on various correlations. In the high gas-liquid interaction regime, liquid-solid contacting is assumed to be complete.

Experimental determination of various holdup components has relied on weighing the bed in operation and upon drainage [76], on measuring the liquid volume drained from the bed [69, 75], and on tracer studies with dyes, ionic solutions, and other tracers [36, 48, 49, 50, 77].

Table 3
Liquid Holdup Correlations (High Interaction Regime)

Number	Correlation	Reference
3-1	$H_D = \{0.132(L/G)^{0.24} - 0.017\}\varepsilon_B$	[42]
3-2	$H_D = A\varepsilon_B(Z/\psi^{1.1})^{-a}(a_v d_p/\varepsilon_B)^{0.65}$ $$Z = Re_g^{1.164}/Re_L^{0.767}; \quad \psi = \frac{\sigma_w}{\sigma_L}\left[\frac{\mu_L}{\mu_w}\left(\frac{\rho_w}{\rho_L}\right)^2\right]^{1/3}$$ foaming systems $\begin{cases} A = 0.0616 \\ a = 0.172 \end{cases}$ nonfoaming $\begin{cases} A = 0.125 \\ a = 0.312 \end{cases}$	[17]
3-3	$H_D = A\left(\dfrac{Re_g We_g}{Re_L}\right)^{-a}$ foaming $\begin{cases} A = 0.245 \\ a = 0.034 \end{cases}$ nonfoaming $\begin{cases} A = 0.111 \\ a = 0.15 \end{cases}$	[78]
3-4	$H_D = 1.6\varepsilon_B Re_g^{-0.153}Ga_L^{-0.054}Ca_L^{0.0615}$ $$Re_g = \frac{Gd_p}{\mu_g}; \quad Ca_L = \frac{Lv_L}{\sigma_L}$$	[71]

In summary, static external liquid holdup can be correlated with Eötvos or Bond number but represents a small fraction of total holdup. Theory suggests that in the low gas-liquid interaction regime, dynamic liquid holdup is a function of $(Re_L/Ga_L)^{1/3}$ and $a_t d_p/\varepsilon_B$, assuming complete external wetting of solid surfaces. Experimental results confirm that Re_L, Ga_L, and $a_t d_p/\varepsilon_B$ are the key dimensionless groups to be considered and differ somewhat in the best value of the particular exponents. Only a few studies [74, 76, 79] attempted to relate dynamic liquid holdup with the fraction of the external surface wetted by flowing liquid but were incomplete and inconclusive. Agreement among various correlations in the low gas-liquid interaction regime is better than in the high interaction regime. In this second regime, gas-liquid interaction forces have to be accounted for and various empirical approaches have been tried as shown in Table 3. The correlations presented give average holdup values. Liquid holdup can vary along the reactor length if the quantities that determine the pertinent dimensionless groups vary.

LIQUID-SOLID CONTACTING

Relationship to Catalyst Utilization and Reactor Performance

As mentioned already in the "Introduction", liquid-solid contacting is essential in determining the degree of catalyst utilization in trickle-bed reactors, since only wetted catalyst can contribute to the reaction in case of nonvolatile liquid reactants, and wetted and dry catalyst behave differently in case of volatile liquid reactants. Unfortunately, the concept of liquid-solid contacting is a rather broad one since it has been imprecisely defined and has meant different things to various people over the years. We attempt here to clarify this important concept and explain its relationship to reactor performance.

It is instructive to start with a simple example. If we consider a system with a nonvolatile liquid reactant B (a case frequently approached under operating conditions for heavy residuals hydro-desulfurization) which is also rate limiting (i.e., there is an excess of dissolved gaseous reactant such as a hydrogen) and assume a first-order reaction, plug flow of the liquid, complete external and internal wetting of catalyst particles, and isothermal conditions, then the equation for conversion of B can be written as:

$$\ln\left(\frac{1}{1 - X_B}\right) = Da_o \eta_o \tag{24}$$

or

$$X_B = 1 - e^{-Da_o \eta_o} \tag{25}$$

The Damkohler number is $Da_o = \rho_p(1 - \varepsilon_B)k_w L_R/u_L$ with k_w being the intrinsic rate constant per unit mass of catalyst and η_o is the overall catalyst-effectiveness factor

$$\frac{1}{\eta_o} = \frac{1}{\eta} + \frac{\Lambda^2}{Bi_w} \tag{26}$$

where η is the catalyst-effectiveness factor for a completely wetted catalyst particle which accounts only for internal diffusional effects. In the first approximation, it is given but the following shape-independent formula:

$$\eta = \frac{\tanh \Lambda}{\Lambda} \tag{27}$$

The generalized Thiele modulus is $\Lambda = (V_p/S_{ex})\sqrt{\rho_p k_w/D_e}$, and it expresses the ratio of the maximum kinetic to maximum diffusion rate into the particle. The generalized Biot number for liquid-solid transport is $Bi_w = k_{Ls}V_p/D_e S_{ex}$ and represents the ratio of diffusional and external mass transfer resistance. The overall effectiveness factor η_o accounts for both internal and external diffusional effects on the reaction rate. Cases where the liquid surrounds the catalyst particles and the catalyst pores are liquid filled usually lead to negligible internal and external temperature differences. The preceding is a summary of well-known chemical-reaction engineering formulas which can be found in any standard text on the subject [80].

To the practitioner any deviation from Equation 24 represented incomplete catalyst utilization. This was expressed by the introduction of an apparent rate constant k_{app} as shown:

$$\ln\left(\frac{1}{1-X_B}\right) = \frac{3,600(1-\varepsilon_B)k_{app}}{LHSV} \tag{28}$$

The liquid hourly space velocity is denoted by LHSV and is expressed in terms of liquid superficial velocity u_L (m/s) and packed reactor length L_R (m):

$$LHSV = \frac{3,600u_L}{L_R} \tag{29}$$

By comparing Equations 24 and 28, one can establish the relationship between the apparent rate constant observed in trickle-flow operation k_{app} with the actual rate constant per unit volume of catalyst $k_v = \rho_p k_w$:

$$k_{app} = k_v \frac{\eta}{1 + \dfrac{\Lambda^2 \eta}{Bi_w}} \tag{30}$$

Using the ratio of k_{app}/k_v (where k_{app} is measured in trickle-flow operation and k_v in a system with completely wetted catalyst particles,) as a measure of contacting effectiveness as suggested by Satterfield [4] may be misleading, since mass transfer resistances may be different in the two systems. If different particle sizes are used, even the catalyst-effectiveness factor for a totally wetted pellet denoted by η will differ.

The departure of actual reactor performance from the ideal one predicted by Equation 25 or the departure of k_{app} from $k_v\eta$ for the particles of the same size may be caused by a number of factors. Some of these factors are listed as follows:

• Liquid is distributed over a portion of the packing *only* and the rest of the catalyst is dry.
• Liquid is not a plug flow; there is little communication between various liquid rivulets resulting in a distribution of residence times, but all catalyst is wetted.
• Liquid is not in plug flow, but all catalyst is wetted, and there is extensive exchange between various liquid pathways.
• Some catalyst particles are externally only partly wetted by liquid.
• Some catalyst particles are internally only partly wetted by liquid.

All of the preceding items are certainly related to catalyst utilization or contacting effectiveness, but each of them represents a separate physical phenomenon. This diversity of effects that can change catalyst utilization in trickle-bed reactors has been the cause of the ambiguity that exists as to what is meant by liquid-solid contacting efficiency (effectiveness). The first three effects are determined by global (reactor scale) liquid distribution. The latter two are affected by local (particle scale) phenomena of liquid-solid wetting.

The effect of a dry catalyst zone on reactor performance, assuming that plug flow persists through the wetted fraction of the packing, is mainly to reduce the effective mean residence time. The effective Damkohler number becomes $f_w Da_o$ and conversion is given by:

$$X_B = 1 - e^{-f_w Da_o \eta_o} \tag{31}$$

Clearly, $f_w < 1$ leads to smaller conversions than those predicted by Equation 25 for an ideal reactor. The effect of liquid rivulets with no exchange between them is described by the segregated flow model:

$$X_B = 1 - \int_0^\infty E_\theta(\theta)e^{-Da_o\eta_o\theta}\, d\theta \tag{32}$$

where $E_\theta(\theta)$ is the dimensionless liquid-phase residence-time density function (often called residence-time distribution in chemical engineering literature) and $\theta = u_L t/H_L L_R$ is dimensionless time normalized with respect to the liquid mean residence time $H_L L_R/u_L$. It is not difficult to see that conversion is less than that predicted by Equation 25 for any $E_\theta(\theta)$ other than that of perfect plug flow $E_\theta(\theta) = \delta(\theta - 1)$ in which case Equation 25 is again obtained. For a plug flow occurring only in a fraction f_w of the bed, $E_\theta = \delta(\theta - f_w)$ and Equation 31 is recovered from Equation 32.

When the liquid distribution is somewhat nonuniform but the interaction between various flowing streams can be described by a random walk dispersion-type mechanism, the axial dispersion mode is often used to predict reactor performance [80]. The expression for the liquid reactant conversion in this case becomes

$$X_B = 1 - \frac{\left\{4\left(1 + \dfrac{Da_o n_o}{Pe_L}\right)^{1/2}\exp\left[\dfrac{Pe_L}{2}\right]\right\}}{\left\{\left(1 + \dfrac{Da_o\eta_o}{Pe_L}\right)^2\exp\left[\left(1 + \dfrac{Da_o\eta_o}{Pe_L}\right)^{1/2}\dfrac{Pe_L}{2}\right] - \left(1 - \dfrac{Da_o\eta_o}{Pe_L}\right)^2\exp\left[-\dfrac{Pe_L}{2}\left(1 + \dfrac{Da_o\eta_o}{Pe_L}\right)^{1/2}\right]\right\}} \tag{33a}$$

where the Peclet number is $Pe_L = u_L L_R/D_{LE}$ with D_{LE} being the axial liquid-dispersion coefficient. For large values of the Peclet number, Equation 33 can be presented in the first approximation as:

$$X_B = 1 - e^{-Da_o\eta_o}\left[1 + \frac{1}{Pe_L}Da_o^2\eta_o^2\right] \tag{33b}$$

Clearly, from Equation 33a, finite Peclet numbers (i.e., $Pe_L < \infty$) lead to lower conversion than plug flow. Of course, a nonuniform liquid distribution and liquid mixing can be described by a number of phenomenological models [68, 81–87] many of which seem to describe reality better than the axial dispersion model. However, the study of Schwartz and Roberts [88] established that, at least for an n-th-order liquid-reactant limiting reaction, the nature of the mixing model within the range of the dimensionless variances of residence times normally encountered in trickle-flow operation $\sigma_D^2 = 2/Pe_L$ does not much affect predicted conversion, which justifies the use of Equation 33a. This study [88] also confirmed previous assertions that liquid backmixing, (i.e, the departure of liquid residence time distribution from that expected in plug flow), is small and is generally insignificant for most laboratory and industrial reactors which operate at moderate conversion and high L_R/d_p ratio [86, 87]. However, an almost plug-flow liquid residence-time distribution does not guarantee perfect liquid-solid contacting on either reactor or particle scale as evident from the experimental work of Glaser and Lichtenstein [84].

The prior three causes of nonideal reactor operation are all related to liquid distribution and mixing on the reactor scale.

If, on the other hand, we consider the global liquid distribution to be uniform but that individual catalyst particles may have a fraction η_i of their pores occupied by liquid while only a fraction η_{CE} of their external surface is contacted by the flowing liquid, then the overall catalyst effectiveness factor for a liquid limiting reactant becomes a function of these two functions and takes the following approximate form [89]:

$$\eta(\eta_{CE}, \eta_i) = \eta_{TB} = \eta_{CE}\frac{\tanh\left(\dfrac{\eta_i}{\eta_{CE}}\Lambda\right)}{\Lambda} \tag{34}$$

This formula is only accurate at high values of the modulus, e.g., $\Lambda > 5$. At lower values of Λ, an appropriate model for an incompletely wetted catalyst pellet has to be solved numerically [15, 90, 91]. The overall effectiveness factor then becomes:

$$\eta_o(\eta_{CE}, \eta_i) = \eta_{TBo} = \frac{\eta_{TB}}{1 + \dfrac{\Lambda^2 \eta_{TB}}{\eta_{CE} Bi_w}} \tag{35}$$

Now, if the two-place density function of internal and external wetting efficiency is defined by

$$f(\eta_{CE}, \eta_i)\, d\eta_{CE}\, d\eta_i = \text{fraction of catalyst particles with the fraction of external area contacted by}$$
liquid between η_{CE} and $\eta_{CE} + d\eta_{CE}$ and internal pore fillup between η_i and $\eta_i + d\eta_i$ \hfill (36)

and there is no completely dry zone, reactor performance can be predicted from:

$$X_B = 1 - e^{-Dao} \int_0^1 \int_0^1 f(\eta_{CE}, \eta_i)\eta_{TBo}\, d\eta_{CE}\, d\eta_i \tag{37}$$

Equation 37 indicates that complete description of wetting on the particle scale is necessary. However since both $\partial\eta_{TBo}/\partial\eta_{CE} \geq 0$ and $\partial\eta_{TBo}/\partial\eta_i \geq 0$, and the second derivatives are negative (i.e., the overall effectiveness factor under trickle-flow conditions for a nonvolatile liquid limiting reactant is a monotonic, nondecreasing convex function of external wetting efficiency η_{CE}, and internal pore fill-up, η_i, then

$$\bar{\eta}_{TBo} = \eta_o(\bar{\eta}_{CE}, \bar{\eta}_i) \leq \int_0^1 \int_0^1 f(\eta_{CE}, \eta_i)\, \eta_o(\eta_{CE}, \eta_i)\, d\eta_{CE}\, d\eta_i \tag{38}$$

i.e., the effectiveness factor evaluated at average wetting efficiencies is less than the average effectiveness factor. This means that in order to establish a conservative estimate (lower bound) on reactor performance, only the mean wetting efficiencies $\bar{\eta}_{CE}$ and $\bar{\eta}_i$ need to be known. Reactant conversion is then:

$$X_B \geq 1 - e^{-Dao\bar{\eta}_{TBo}} \tag{39}$$

It is instructive to consider a few important limits. When internal pore fill-up is complete, i.e., internal holdup equals $\varepsilon_p(1 - \varepsilon_B)$ and external mass transfer effects limit the reaction rate

$$\eta_{TBo} \approx \eta_{CE} \frac{\tilde{Bi}_w}{\Lambda^2} \tag{40}$$

Substituting into Equation 37 gives that

$$X_B = 1 - e^{-\bar{\eta}_{CE} k_{Ls}(1 - \varepsilon_B)(L_R/u_L)a_p} \tag{41}$$

and the reactor performance depends directly on the mean external contacting efficiency so that $k_{app} \propto \bar{\eta}_{CE}$.

When external mass transfer effects are negligible, internal wetting is complete, and internal diffusional resistance is very pronouned, we find $\eta_{TBo} = \eta_{CE}\eta$ and reactor performance is

$$X_B = 1 - e^{-\bar{\eta}_{CE} Dao\eta} \tag{42}$$

so that k_{app} is proportional to the mean external contacting efficiency $\bar{\eta}_{CE}$. However, Equation 42 also results for the case of negligible external mass transfer effects when internal and external wetting efficiencies are equal, $\eta_{CE} = \eta_i$. Fortunately, this might not be realistic for usual catalyst particles with interconnected pore structure. However, this shows that it is difficult to determine the effects of internal and external particle-scale wetting from global conversion measurements.

When external mass transfer effects are not present and internal diffusional effects are negligible, then $\Lambda \ll 1$ and $\eta_{TBo} \approx \eta_i$. The reactor performance equation is then related to the mean internal pore fill-up $\bar{\eta}_i$ by the following expression for the conversion:

$$X_B = 1 - e^{-\bar{\eta}_i Da_0 \eta} \tag{43}$$

so that $k_{app} \propto \bar{\eta}_i$. Intuitively, the preceding limiting cases provide satisfactory answers. When external mass transfer controls the rate, or when strong internal diffusional limitations force the reaction to occur in a narrow zone close to the external catalyst surface, it is the surface fraction in contact with the liquid reactant supply $\bar{\eta}_{CE}$ that determines reactor performance. On the other hand, when neither external not internal diffusion affect the rate, it is the fraction of wetted catalyst volume available for reaction $\bar{\eta}_i$ that determines reactor performance. This shows that liquid mean residence time $H_L L_R / u_L$ is not a fundamental parameter in trickle-bed design since it is the mean liquid-catalyst contact time, not the residence time, that is important. Reactor performance then is not a direct function of liquid holdup as assumed by many industrial practitioners other than in a situation when kinetics limits the rate. For this case, the effectiveness factor η can approach unity so that internal holdup, as indicated by Equation 43, becomes a significant parameter. In almost all other cases, holdup affects reactor performance only inasmuch as it affects fractional bed irrigation f_w in Equation 31, liquid backmixing and the Peclet number in Equation 33, or external contacting efficiency in Equations 41 and 42. Unfortunately, firm relationships between holdup and these variables have not been established.

The preceding discussion is presented for the case of a nonvolatile, rate-limiting, liquid reactant *only* and first-order reaction. Its purpose is to familiarize the reader with five different effects which are all often disguised in the literature under the name of catalyst utilization and contacting efficiency. From the preceding discussion it is clear that one must distinguish between global effects of liquid maldistribution and backmixing and particle-scale incomplete external and internal wetting. Each of these effects can reduce conversion compared to that in an ideal reactor, and it is important to be able to assess which effect might be dominant.

Reactor performance equations for non-first-order reaction, gas limiting reactant, and volatile liquid reactant are beyond the scope of this chapter but could readily be derived for the various cases of nonideality already illustrated. It should be noted that the case of a gas limiting and of a volatile liquid reactant is much more complex to describe even for a simple first-order process. The same five effects of incomplete contacting just illustrated can occur. However, now both dry and wetted zones contribute to reaction at different rates. Design equations for various rate forms and liquid- or gas-limiting reactants that account for global liquid maldistribution are given in the text by Ramachandran and Chaudhari [10]. For the particle-scale incomplete contacting effects one should refer to a series of papers by Duduković and Mills [15, 90, 91] and Smith and coworkers [14, 92–94]. Some of these effects are summarized at the end of this chapter.

We review next the state of the art in understanding the global liquid distribution effects followed by the historical attempts to interpret incomplete catalyst utilization in trickle beds. Then we review the available methods for determination of particle-scale incomplete contacting and the possible theoretical tools for its a priori assesment. We conclude by summarizing the importance of this in trickle-bed reactor design.

Liquid Distribution and Backmixing

Liquid Distribution

Liquid distribution has been studied extensively in packed absorption towers [94–99]. These studies were performed mostly with large, nonporous particles and are not always relevant to trickle-bed operation with small, porous particles. A detailed account of studies pertinent to the trickle-flow and pulsing-flow regimes of packed-bed reactors [98, 100–108] is given in the reviews of Gianetto et al. [7] and Herskowitz and Smith [8] and in the text of Ramachandran and Chaudhari [10]. The reader is referred to these sources for details.

The topics that received the most attention are: the bed height required for achieving a fully developed liquid distribution (velocity profile), the shape of the fully developed liquid distribution, the wall flow, and the exchange coefficient between various liquid streams. The conclusions reached are often only relevant to the system studied. In addition, they are often expressed in terms of dimensional criteria, have been generally determined on nonreacting systems, and are frequently plagued by contradictions. It is fair to say that the understanding of the liquid distribution in packed beds of porous particles is not complete due to the lack of appropriate unifying theory that rests on first principles. A summary of the principal qualitative results follows:

Bed depths required to achieve a fully developed liquid distribution depend on initial liquid distribution, particle size and shape, column diameter, liquid physical properties, and liquid and gas velocities. Smaller depths are required for uniform liquid distribution when using smaller particles and higher liquid velocities. Fully developed liquid distribution in the trickle-flow regime was reported to be uniform [104], parabolic with the maximum at the center [98], parabolic with the minimum at the center [105] or to be unstable [108]. In either case, the nonuniformity was insignificant in terms of causing reactor malfunctioning. Increase in centerline velocities and uniform distribution [105, 108] as well as the fingering effect [109] were reported for the pulsing regime. Increasing gas flow rate seems to lead to a more uniform liquid distribution in both regimes. Wall flow was reported to be negligible for $d_t/d_p \geq 20$ in trickle-flow regime. It was also demonstrated that in laboratory reactors, addition of fines improves the uniformity of the liquid distribution [134].

Theoretically, two approaches have been taken to interpret liquid distribution. One relies on the random-walk concept which results in a diffusion-type equation for liquid axial velocity, u_z:

$$\frac{\partial u_z}{\partial z} = \frac{D_r}{r} \frac{\partial}{\partial r}\left(r \frac{\partial u_z}{\partial r}\right) \qquad (44)$$

The boundary conditions are

$$z = 0, \qquad u_z = u_{zi}(r) = \text{initial distribution} \qquad (45)$$

$$r = 0, \qquad \frac{\partial u_z}{\partial r} = 0 \qquad (46)$$

$$r = R, \qquad \frac{\partial u_z}{\partial r} = p_w(u_z - u_w) \qquad (47)$$

The spreading factor is defined as $s = 4D_r/d_p$, and it is found to be unity for granular-type packing. Equation 44 has been used by Herskowitz and Smith [103] to match various experimental results.

The other approach developed by Crine and coworkers [76, 79] is based on a percolation theory model for liquid distribution in packed beds. The model, while appealing from the theoretical standpoint, required characterization of the solid structure and its junction points and used excessive computational time. Its simplified version still required experimental results for determination of model parameters.

In summary, a significant amount of experimental information exists regarding liquid distribution in trickle-bed reactors. However, good correlations and a unifying theoretical approach are missing. The existing random-walk and percolation theory can fit the collected experimental data by proper selection of their parameters but fail to provide predictive ability. Nevertheless, the information collected thus far indicates that gross liquid maldistribution is unlikely to be the cause of poor reactor performance. This is usually true if one follows the industrial practice of carefully packing the bed in a uniform fashion and a good liquid distributor for uniform initial liquid distribution is designed. However, even a relatively uniform liquid distribution does not guarantee complete liquid-solid contacting on the particle scale [84]. The studies of Charpentier et al. [58, 65] on characterizing the texture of liquid flow consisting of films, rivulets, and stagnant zones are much more relevant to trickle-bed performance. Unfortunately, these studies have resulted in qualitative but not quantitative understanding of the liquid flow structure. This qualitative understanding gives rise to the following rules:

1. Fine particles dispersed among larger particles improve liquid distribution and reduce wall effects in laboratory reactors.
2. Better liquid distribution is achieved in prewetted beds.

However, even prewetted beds can exhibit zones of relatively stagnant liquid [36].

Caution should be exercised in interpreting the preceding remarks. It is a fact that liquid velocity profiles in the trickle-flow regime, which were measured extensively only for nonreacting systems and are summarized in detail in the work of Gianetto et al. [7] and Herskowitz and Smith [103, 104], do not exhibit reactor-scale incomplete contacting. Through their effect on liquid residence-time distribution alone, they are not able to cause significant reactor performance deviation from plug flow. However, particle-scale incomplete contacting is still possible and probable at low liquid mass velocities. This particle-scale incomplete contacting, as shown later, has been demonstrated on both nonreacting and reacting systems. Under reaction conditions, in the presence of volatile liquid reactants or when gaseous products are evolved, particle-scale incomplete contacting may give rise to reactor-scale incomplete contacting and dry-zone formation. Such dry zones have been experimentally observed under reaction conditions [52–55] on small laboratory reactors while they seem to be absent under identical operating but nonreacting conditions. This seems to indicate that the coupling between momentum, mass, and energy may be important in dry-zone formation on the reactor scale which sheds some doubts on the relevance of liquid-distribution studies under nonreacting conditions. However, designing distributors with uniform initial liquid distribution is important, as well as knowing the necessary calming depth to use in laboratory work when that is not the case. Some guidance on how to accomplish this can be found in the work of Herskowitz and Smith [103, 104], in the review of Gianetto et al. [7] and in an upcoming monograph of the authors of this review.

Liquid Backmixing

The axial dispersion model [86, 110], cross-flow model [68, 85], and time delay model [81] have been used to describe the exchange between flowing liquid and its semi-stagnant pockets caught at the particles' contact points. The analysis of Schwartz and Roberts [88] established that reactor performance for the various backmixing models is equivalent when the variance of the impulse response for each model is taken to be the same. Model parameters then can be related through this equality of the variance. This allows the determination of parameters for other models from the axial-dispersion Peclet numbers which are the only ones that have been correlated with appropriate dimensionless groups. The Peclet number correlations pertinent to the trickle-flow regime are summarized in Table 4. They have also been reviewed extensively by Gianetto et al. [7] and Shah [9].

The dispersion model has been predominantly used to interpret reactor performance even though this model does not have much merit on physical grounds. It predicts, for example, that a pulse of tracer injected into the liquid at a certain location would propagate upstream. Since liquid flows due to gravity and is the discontinuous phase, the impossibility of such upstream penetration of tracer is evident, and has never been detected experimentally. However, in the view of the Schwartz and Roberts [88] analysis, it does not matter which backmixing model is used from the viewpoint of reactor performance. Nevertheless, the cross-flow model, whose parameters can be estimated from holdup and Peclet number correlations, probably depicts physical reality better and computationally results in an initial value problem as opposed to the boundary value problem of the dispersion model and should therefore be used. The higher-order multiparameter models summarized by Gianetto et al. [7] and Calo [11] are not recommended due to our inability to evaluate their parameters either from available correlations or from first principles.

In summary, the backmixing problem of liquid in trickle beds has not been completely solved. However, its effect on reactor performance is negligible for most practical cases of moderate convesion and long reactor lengths in the trickle-flow regime and can always be neglected in the pulsing flow regime.

Table 4
Axial Peclet Number Correlations for Trickle Beds

Number	Correlation	Reference
4-1	$Pe_p = 0.042Re_L^{0.5}$ $Pe_p = u_Ld_p/D_L; \qquad Re_L = u_Ld_p\rho_L/\mu_L$	[68]
4-2	$Pe_p = 13Re_L^{0.4}Ga_L^{-0.333}$ $Ga_L = \dfrac{d_p^3g}{\nu_L^2}$	[83]
4-3	$Pe_p = 0.039Re_f^{0.5}$ $Re_f = 4\delta_f\rho_Lu_L/\mu_L$	[70]
4-4	$Pe_p = H_{LD}^{-0.7}Re_L^{0.7}Ga_L^{-0.32}$	[110]
4-5	$Pe_p = 0.2(a_vd_p)^{1.21}Re_L^{0.78}Ga_L^{-0.33}$	[111]
4-6	$Pe_p = 0.45Fr_L^{0.27}H_L^{1.54}$ $Fr_L = \dfrac{u_L^2}{d_pg}$	[112]
4-7	$Pe_p = 60(Re_L')^{0.63}(Ga_L')^{-0.73}$ $Pe_L' = Re_L/H_{LE}(1 + 4/a_vd_t)$ $Ga_L' = Ga_L(1 + \delta_{\ell g}/\rho_Lg)$	[113]
4-8	$(Pe_p)_g = 1.8Re_g^{-0.7}10^{-0.005Re_L}$ $Re_g = \dfrac{u_gd_p\rho_g}{\mu_g}; \qquad (Pe_p)_g = \dfrac{u_gd_p}{D_g}$	[68]

Particle-Scale Incomplete Contacting

Historical Developments

The deviations of trickle-bed performance from plug flow predictions were attributed at first to liquid maldistribution and dispersion effects until Ross [114] and Mears [115] singled out incomplete catalyst wetting as a primary culprit. The historical development of the models proposed to interpret reactor performance for nonvolatile liquid reactants is shown in Table 5. Bondi [116] used an empirical expression to relate the apparent rate constant under trickle-flow conditions to the one observed for a completely wetted catalyst which is shown as Equation 5-1 (Table 5). Ross [114] assumed that a good measure of wetting efficiency could be obtained by modeling k_{app} proportional to liquid holdup which resulted in Equation 5-2. Henry and Gilbert [117] followed up on this idea by substituting a correlation for liquid holdup (Equation 5-3) into Ross's equation. After first presenting the possibility of dispersion effects, Mears [86] concluded that the apparent rate constant is the product of catalyst external wetting efficiency η_{CE} and the true rate constant [115]. He proceeded to use the correlation of Puranik and Vogelpohl [118] for external contacting efficiency which resulted in Equation 5-4. Sylvester and Pitayagulsarn [119], by slightly modifying the model of Suzuki and Smith [120], accounted for internal diffusional limitations, external mass transfer limitations, and reactor-scale incomplete wetting (Equation 5-5). All of the preceding studies accounted for incomplete catalyst wetting either in an empirical way or by assuming that it occurs on a reactor scale so that its effects on a particle scale were neglected.

Table 5
Suggested Performance Models for Trickle-Bed Reactors
(Nonvolatile Liquid-Limiting Reactants)

Equation	Reference	Performance equation
5-1	Bondi [116]	$\dfrac{1}{k_{app}} = \dfrac{1}{k_v} + \dfrac{A}{u_L^b};\quad 0.5 < b < 0.7$
5-2	Ross [114]	$\ln\left(\dfrac{1}{1-X_B}\right) \alpha \dfrac{k_{app}H_{LE}}{LHSV}$
5-3	Henry and Gilbert [117]	$\ln\left(\dfrac{1}{1-X_B}\right) \alpha \dfrac{k_{app}L^{1/3}}{(LHSV)^{2/3}}$
5-4	Mears [115]	$\ln\left(\dfrac{1}{1-X_B}\right) \alpha L^{0.32}(LHSV)^{-0.68}d_p^{0.18}v_L^{-0.05}\left(\dfrac{\sigma_C}{\sigma_L}\right)^{0.21}\eta$
5-5	Sylvester and Pitayagulsarn [119]	$\ln\left(\dfrac{1}{1-X_B}\right) = \Lambda_3\omega$ where $\quad \Lambda_3 = \dfrac{N_{Bo}}{2}\left[1 + \dfrac{4\Lambda_2}{N_{Bo}-1}\right]$ $\Lambda_2 = \dfrac{1}{\Lambda_1^{-1} + N_{St}^{-1}}$ $\Lambda_1 = \dfrac{1}{f}\left[\phi\coth\phi - 1\right]$

The importance of particle-scale incomplete contacting was introduced by Schwartz and Roberts [88] and was fully explained in terms of its effects on the catalyst-effectiveness factor by Duduković and coworkers [2, 15, 16, 49, 50, 77, 89–91] and Smith and coworkers [14, 51, 92, 94]. Since then, it has been generally accepted that particle-scale phenomena are mainly responsible for deviations of reactor performance from the ideal. Numerous investigators attempted to interpret their experimental studies in this sense [14, 16, 51, 52, 55, 76, 79]. Due to our inability to predict catalyst contacting from a firmly established theory, this concept has not been that helpful for design purposes, although it has been useful in interpretation of experimental data.

Experimental Methods for Evaluation of Contacting Efficiency

As mentioned earlier in this section, several measures of incomplete contacting have been used. The three particle-scale contacting efficiencies that have been defined and used are: fraction of external catalyst area contacted by flowing liquid, η_{CE}, fraction of total (internal plus external) catalyst area contacted by liquid, η_C, and the fraction of internal catalyst pore structure filled with liquid, η_i. Clearly, for highly porous catalysts, η_C is the measure of internal pore area in contact with liquid. This would then equal η_i but neither could be determined from internal holdup unless the pore structure is known or uniform pore diameter is assumed.

The experimental techniques used to evaluate the preceding measures of incomplete contacting can be divided into destructive and non-destructive methods. Destructive methods either require a change in the nature of the bed or special choice of the flowing phase, or require dismantling of the beds. They have been mainly employed for evaluation of external contacting and consist of a nonreactive synthetic-packing dissolution method [121], dissolution of the synthetic packing with a reacting buffer solution [122], and direct measurement of the contacted area by permanent dye adsorption [123, 124]. In the former two, a comparison is made between mass transfer rates obtained in the column perfused by liquid only and the column with two-phase flow at the same liquid mass velocity. From this comparison, the contacted area is determined indirectly. The technique of Onda et al. [123] used dye injections, dismantling of the bed, and evaluation of the dyed area. A more elegant, indirect, and nondestructive method for evaluating external contacting is that of Wijffels et al. [36]. They saturated the liquid-full bed with a known concentration of nonadsorbing solute, drained it, operated it in trickle flow, and then expelled the stagnant pockets of remaining solution with a known volume of liquid. From the volume of stagnant liquid that they determined in this way, they inferred the external catalyst area contacted by liquid. Nondestructive methods relying on dynamic tracer testing were used to evaluate internal pore fill-up and liquid holdup [125, 126].

Schwartz et al. [77] and Colombo et al. [48] introduced the tracer-based methods for evaluation of both internal and external catalyst contacting. The validity of these techniques has been confirmed by Mills and Duduković [49, 50] and El-Hisnawi et al. [16, 71]. Evaluation of the fraction of total catalyst contacted by liquid relies on the use of a nonadsorbing and a linear, reversibly absorbing tracer. A pulse of each tracer is injected into the liquid at the inlet of the trickle-bed reactor, and the impulse response is monitored at the outlet. By the central volume principle [127, 128], the first moment for a nonvolatile tracer is model independent and equal to the equivalent volume of distribution of the tracer divided by liquid flow rate. For a column with two-phase flow, this can be represented by:

$$\mu_{1TP} = \frac{V_R H_L}{Q_L} + \eta_C \frac{S_g V_R \rho_p (1 - \varepsilon_B) K_A}{Q_L} \tag{48}$$

For a liquid-filled column operated under the same flow rate conditions, the same equation gives that

$$\mu_{1LF} = \frac{V_R(\varepsilon_B + \varepsilon_p(1 - \varepsilon_B))}{Q_L} + \frac{S_g V_R \rho_p (1 - \varepsilon_B) K_A}{Q_L} \tag{49}$$

For a nonadsorbing tracer, the adsorption equilibrium constant $K_A = 0$ and only the liquid volume is sensed by tracer. Hence, only the first term in Equations 48 and 49 remains. In two-phase flow, only a fraction η_C of catalyst total area which is dominated by internal area may be contacted by liquid while all of it is accessible in liquid-full operation. Mills and Duduković [49, 50] have shown that the total contacting efficiency η_C can then be obtained by

$$\eta_C = \frac{(\mu_{1TP})_{adsorbing} - (\mu_{1TP})_{nonadsorbing}}{(\mu_{1LF})_{adsorbing} - (\mu_{1LF})_{nonadsorbing}} \tag{50}$$

where the moments were obtained at identical liquid flow rates. This is the same as obtaining an apparent adsorption equilibrium constant in two-phase flow $K_{A, app}$ and dividing it by the value of the same parameter K_A obtained on the same packing in liquid-full flow operation. This method is to be preferred to an alternate approach which uses the value of the adsorption equilibrium constant K_A obtained from batch experiments, the known catalyst properties S_g, ε_p, and bed properties ε_B, V_R to extract η_C solely from two-phase flow runs. This may lead to systematic errors due to the fact that K_A is extremely sensitive to the state of activation of the packing which may be different in the batch and flow reactor. For example, Schwartz et al. [77] correctly determined contacting efficiency η_C to be independent of flow rate but systematically underestimated it below its value of unity due to the incorrect K_A value determined in batch experiments. Mills and Duduković [49, 50] and El-Hisnawi et al. [16] used Equation 50 successfully and obtained reproducible results.

Evaluation of external contacting efficiency is based on the interpretation of the variance of the impulse reponse and is not model independent. The usual approach is to employ the Suzuki and

Smith [120] and Sagara et al. [129] model for tracer transport in a packed bed since this includes axial dispersion, liquid-solid mass transfer, and diffusion. The following expression for the variance of the impulse response is obtained for the case of spherical particles:

$$\sigma_D^2 = \frac{2}{Pe_L} + \frac{2Q_L}{V_R H_L} \frac{\delta_1}{(1 + \delta_o)^2} \tag{51}$$

where:

$$\delta_1 = \delta_i + \delta_e \tag{52}$$

$$\delta_i = \frac{(1 - \varepsilon_B)\varepsilon_p}{H_{LE}} \left[1 + \frac{S_g K_A \rho_p^2}{\varepsilon_p} \right] \frac{R^2 \varepsilon_p}{15(D_{eo})_{app}} \tag{53}$$

$$\delta_e = \frac{(1 - \varepsilon_B)\varepsilon_p}{H_{LE}} \left[1 + \frac{S_g K_A \rho_p^2}{\varepsilon_p} \right] \frac{R \varepsilon_p}{3 k_{LS}} \tag{54}$$

$$\delta_o = \frac{(1 - \varepsilon_B)\varepsilon_p}{H_{LE}} \left[1 + \frac{S_g K_A \rho_p}{\varepsilon_p} \right] \tag{55}$$

In the case of liquid-full operation, bed porosity ε_B replaces external liquid holdup H_{LE}, and the effective diffusivity found in the liquid-full reactor $(D_{eo})_{LF}$ replaces the apparent diffusivity, observed in two-phase flow $(D_{eo})_{app}$. Experimental results of Colombo et al. [48], Mills and Duduković [49, 50] and El-Hisnawi [71] indicate that $(D_{eo})_{app} < (D_{eo})_{LF}$. The model is based on diffusion occurring through all of the external catalyst area, yet only a portion of it may be in contact with the liquid. The results with adsorbing tracers clearly indicate that total (internal) contacting efficiency η_C is unity (see Figure 2) which confirms the basic validity of the variance expression which is based on complete internal wetting. If only a portion of the external catalyst area is in contact with flowing liquid and all the internal area is accessible to the adsorbing tracer, then it can be concluded that the pore space is interconnected. The effective diffusional pathways are then lengthened on the average in two-phase flow conditions compared to the liquid-full case when all of the external area is accessible for diffusion. This results in an increase in the tortuosity factor for the two-phase flow case or a decrease in apparent effective diffusivity. The original asser-

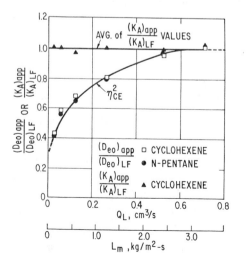

Figure 2. Comparison between total contacting efficiency η_C and external contacting efficiency η_{CE} determined by tracer methods. (After Mills and Duduković [49].)

tion of Colombo et al. [48] was that the ratio $(D_{eo})_{app}/(D_{eo})_{LF}$ should equal external contacting efficiency. This, however, was not in good agreement with other experimental evidence. To correct for that, Baldi and Gianetto [130] equated the Thiele modulus based on the calculated $(D_{eo})_{app}$ and on the actual V_p/S_{ex} ratio for the catalyst particle to that proposed by Duduković [89]. For conditions of complete internal wetting the following expression was obtained:

$$\eta_{CE} = \sqrt{\frac{(D_{eo})_{app}}{(D_{eo})_{LF}}} \tag{56}$$

The results obtained by the use of this equation were shown by Mills and Duduković [49, 50] to be in excellent agreement with the trends established for external contacting efficiency reported by Herskowitz et al. [14] and obtained by a completely different method of evaluating reaction rate data. This tracer method was used to obtain additional data on external contacting by El-Hisnawi [16, 71].

In summary, the tracer methods are the only ones that allow determination of contacting efficiency in actual trickle-beds under operating conditions using catalyst packings and liquids of interest. Evaluation of total (internal) catalyst area contacted and, by inference, fractional pore fill-up based on the method of Schwartz et al. [77] as perfected by Mills and Duduković [49, 50] seems reliable and has been proven to be reproducible. The method is powerful because the obtained result is model independent and is a consequence of the theoretical central volume principle [127, 128]. The evaluation of external contacting efficiency from the estimation of the apparent effective diffusivity as suggested by Colombo et al. [48] with the appropriate modification of Baldi and Gianetto [130] seems to agree well with trends established by other methods. However, the absolute values for external contacting obtained by this method should be subject to questioning because they lack a firm theoretical basis. Additional research in this area is needed. It should also be mentioned that incomplete contacting on the particle scale should not necessarily be envisioned as a single particle partly in contact with liquid as has been the practice so far. Another approach is to interpret the partial contacting phenomenon as a situation where, while liquid is well distributed on the reactor scale, islands of a few particles exist engulfed in a stagnant liquid pocket [13]. Interpretation of the tracer results based on such a model would be enlightening.

Empirical Correlations for Evaluation of Contacting Efficiency

Application of the various destructive and nondestructive methods for evaluation of various measures of incomplete liquid-solid contacting as outlined in the previous section has led to the development of empirical correlating equations for prediction of this parameter. Many of these correlations were developed during the late 1950s to the middle 1970s for absorber-column-type packings such as Raschig rings, Berl saddles, Intalox saddles, glass spheres, and other assorted nonporous materials whose physical characteristics are unlike those of smaller porous catalyst supports used in trickle-bed reactor applications. The lack of a suitable correlation for catalyst support packings until the early 1980s has probably forced many researchers and design engineers to use the nonporous packing correlations for trickle-bed reactor design and interpretation of performance. This practice is no longer necessary since tracer-based correlations are now available for prediction of external liquid-solid contacting efficiency η_{CE}. These correlations are valid for various trickle-bed catalyst packings over a fairly wide range of liquid physical and transport properties so that improved estimates of η_{CE} are now possible. It is expected that as better understanding of particle-scale phenomena is obtained, improved correlations will become available.

A summary of external contacting efficiency correlations for nonporous absorber columns is given in Table 6. Differences in the packing shape, size, and physical characteristics as well as differences in the flow regimes and mode of operation suggests that the application of these correlations to the prediction of external liquid-solid contacting efficiency in trickle beds is inappropriate. It is worth noting, however, that the correlation of Onda et al. [123] is based upon the most comprehensive set of data and has an equation form with a useful property. This form has the feature that proper limiting values for η_{CE} of zero and unity are obtained when proper assignment

Table 6

External Contacting Efficiency Correlations for Nonporous Packings

Reference	Correlation	Comments
Shulman et al. [75]	$\eta_{CE} = 0.24\left(\dfrac{L}{G}\right)^{0.25}$ $\eta_{CE} = 0.35\left(\dfrac{L}{G}\right)^{0.20}$	12.7, 25.4 & 38.1 mm Rashig rings 12.7 & 25.4 mm Berl saddles
Onda et al. [123]	$\eta_{CE} = 1.0 - \exp\left[-1.45Re_L^{0.1}Fr_L^{-0.05}We_L^{0.2}\left(\dfrac{\sigma_C}{\sigma_L}\right)^{0.75}\right]$	$0.04 < Re_L < 500$ $1.2 \times 10^{-3} < We_L < 0.27$ $2.5 \times 10^{-9} < Fr_L < 1.8 \times 10^{-2}$ $0.3 < \sigma_C/\sigma_L < 2.0$ $8.0 < d_P < 50.8$ mm $5.0 \times 10^2 \leq L \leq 3.0 \times 10^4$ kg/m²-hr 8, 17, 25 & 35 mm Rashig rings 12.7 & 25.4 mm spheres 12.7,25.4,38.1, & 50.8 mm Berl saddles
Krauze and Serwinski [124]	$\eta_{CE} = 0.655L^{0.36}$ –––––––––––––– $\eta_{CE} = 0.585L^{0.17}$	$2.88 \times 10^2 \leq L \leq 1.98 \times 10^3$ kg/m²-hr $1.98 \times 10^3 \leq L \leq 2.88 \times 10^4$ kg/m²-hr 5, 7, 10 & 17 mm rashig rings $0.75 \leq Re_L \leq 259.5$
Puranik and Vogelpohl [118]	$\eta_{CE} = 1.05Re_L^{0.047}We_L^{0.135}\left(\dfrac{\sigma_C}{\sigma_L}\right)^{0.206}$ (dynamic) $\eta_{CE} = 1.045Re_L^{0.041}We_L^{0.133}\left(\dfrac{\sigma_C}{\sigma_L}\right)^{0.182}$ (total)	$0.5 < Re_L < 85$ $2.1 \times 10^{-6} < We_L < 1.2 \times 10^{-2}$ $7.7 \times 10^{-7} < Fr_L < 4.7 \times 10^{-3}$ $0.3 < \sigma_L/\sigma_C < 1.05$ $10.0 < d_P < 37.5$ mm $9 \times 10^2 < L < 4.32 \times 10^4$ kg/m²-hr $0.08 < \eta_{CE}$ $0.5 < \mu_L < 13$ cp $25 < \sigma_L < 75$ dyness km

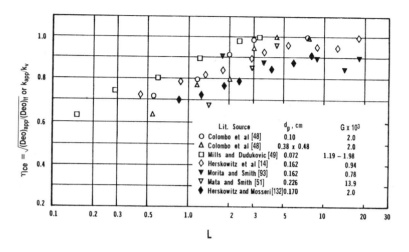

Figure 3. Effect of liquid rate on the external liquid-solid contacting efficiency from tracer and reaction studies. (After Herskowitz and Smith [8].)

of dimensionless groups is made, e.g., when $Re_L \rightarrow 0$ and $Re_L \rightarrow \infty$, respectively. Onda's correlation also incorporates the ratio of critical to normal liquid surface tensions σ_C/σ_L or, more generally, the ratio of critical to noncritical liquid capillary numbers. These particular parameters also occur in certain fundamental problems associated with the hydrodynamic flow of thin liquid films having a finite width. This suggests that these same parameters might also be important when correlating trickle-flow contacting data in randomly packed beds. Unfortunately, the critical surface tension, which is associated with stability of liquid rivulets, cannot be obtained from first principles and must be experimentally determined so that Onda's correlation is difficult to apply for packings and liquids other than those included in the original correlation. This fact suggests that another dimensionless group which is more readily evaluated than the σ_C/σ_L ratio should be considered as a substitute if an attempt is made to apply an Onda equation form to trickle-bed external contacting data. Otherwise, the use of the nonporous packing correlations for prediction of particle-scale external contacting efficiency is not recommended when dealing with small catalyst packings.

Figure 3 shows some of the available literature data for external liquid-solid contacting efficiency as a function of liquid mass velocity that was reported in the review paper of Herskowitz and Smith [8]. The data of Mills and Duduković [49] and Colombo et al. [48] are based upon impulse or step response tracer experiments and interpreted using the method of Baldi [12] as explained in the previous section. Thus, the tracer-based contacting efficiency is defined as

$$\eta_{CE} = \sqrt{(D_{eo})_{app}/(D_{eo})_{LF}} \tag{57}$$

where $(D_{eo})_{app}$ and $(D_{eo})_{LF}$ are the tracer-effective diffusivities in two-phase and liquid-filled operation, respectively. The remaining data of Herskowitz et al. [14], Morita and Smith [93], Mata and Smith [51], and Herskowitz and Mosseri [132] were extracted from trickle-bed reaction performance data using the hydrogenation of α-methylstyrene as a test reaction. Generally, these data show that external liquid-solid contacting efficiency is unity for $L \geq 5$ kg/m²-s with the smallest value being $\eta_{CE} = 0.6$ at $L = 0.15$ kg/m²-s.

Table 7 gives a summary of various correlations that have been developed for evaluation of external liquid-solid contacting efficiency for porous catalyst packings. Equations 7-1 and 7-2 (Table 7) proposed by Mills and Duduković [49] were developed using tracer-based values for η_{CE} as well as the reaction-based data of Herskowitz et al. [14]. When using this correlation, the packing factor group $a_v = a_t d_p^2/\varepsilon_B^2$ should have units of cm. A comparison between values of η_{CE}

Table 7

External Contacting Efficiency Correlations for Porous Packings

Equation number	Reference	Correlation	Range of validity
7-1	Mills and Dudukovic [49]	$\eta_{CE} = 1.0 - \exp\left[-0.634 Re_L^{-1/3} Fr_L^{0.842} We_L^{0.448}\left(\dfrac{a_t d_p^2}{\varepsilon_B^2}\right)^{1.086}\right]$	$0.3 \leq Re_L \leq 32$ $3.0 \times 10^{-5} \leq Fr_L \leq 2.2 \times 10^{-2}$
7-2		$\eta_{CE} = \tanh\left[0.731 Re_L^{-1/3} Fr_L^{0.708} We_L^{-0.346}\left(\dfrac{a_t d_p^2}{\varepsilon_B^2}\right)^{0.924}\right]$	$3.4 \times 10^{-7} \leq We_L \leq 9.1 \times 10^{-4}$ $0.87 \leq \dfrac{a_t d_p^2}{\varepsilon_B^2} \leq 8.1$
7-3	El-Hisnawi [71]	$\eta_{CE} = 1.617 Re_L^{0.1461} Ga_L^{-0.0711}$	$0.161 \leq Re_L \leq 32$
7-4		$\eta_{CE} = 1.021 \omega_D^{0.224}$	$1.06 \times 10^4 \leq Ga_L \leq 7.23 \times 10^5$

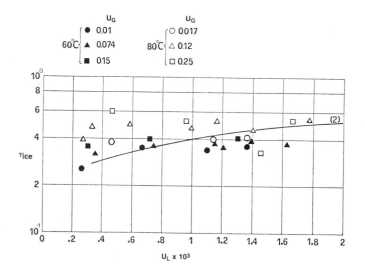

Figure 4. Comparison between reaction-based external liquid-solid contacting and Equation 7.2. (After Baldi et al. [133].)

calculated using this correlation to those obtained by Baldi et al. [133] from trickle-bed reaction experiments using the oxidation of ethanol is given in Figure 4, where the agreement is seen to be satisfactory. This correlation is valid in the trickle-flow regime.

The database used to develop the Mills and Duduković correlation was supplemented with additional tracer-based external liquid-solid contacting efficiency data by El-Hisnawi [71] on four hydrocarbon solvents to examine the role of liquid physical properties on η_{CE}. These data were used as the basis for testing various assumed correlating equation forms which ultimately resulted in Equations 7-3 and 7-4 in Table 7. Equations which had the same forms as Equations 7-1 and 7-2 given by Mills and Duduković [49] but with the dimensional group $a_t d_p^2/\varepsilon_B^2$ replaced by the dimensionless group $a_t d_p/\varepsilon_B$ yielded little improvement in reducing the error (not shown in Table 7). The power-law form of Equation 7-3 in terms of Reynolds and Galileo numbers is simpler and yields estimates for η_{CE} that are within $\pm 10\%$ of experimental values as shown in Figure 5. The

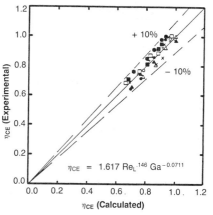

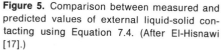

Figure 5. Comparison between measured and predicted values of external liquid-solid contacting using Equation 7.4. (After El-Hisnawi [17].)

effect of the Galileo number can be considered nearly insignificant which reduces Equation 7.3 to the form given by Equation 7.4 where external liquid-solid contacting efficiency is expressed in terms of dynamic liquid saturation of $\omega_D = H_D/\varepsilon_B$. Equation 7.3 does not include a dependence upon liquid surface tension which might be considered surprising in view of the nonporous packing correlations of Onda et al. [123] and Puranik and Vogelpohl [118] given in Table 6 where the ratio of critical to liquid surface tensions σ_C/σ_L appears. One possible explanation is that due to capillarity effects, wetting liquids, such as hydrocarbons or water which were used in all the experimental studies, always spread readily over small porous particles so that differences in surface tension have a lesser effect on contacting than in case of large nonporous particles. This observation remains to be quantitatively explained, however.

The preceding correlations for porous packings provide the basis for certain conclusions regarding the effects of key variables which were often qualitatively explained in previous investigations by analogy to the behavior of liquid holdup. One of these key variables is the effect of particle diameter on external liquid-solid contacting efficiency which is given in Figure 6 as a function of the liquid Reynolds number for the typical hydrodesulfurization catalysts labeled here as CHD 437 and CHD 492. Values of η_{CE} are seen to be inversely proportional to particle diameter, i.e., smaller particles have a greater actively wetted area when compared at the same value of Reynolds number. It is interesting to note that this behavior is consistent with the observation of Van Klinken [134] who found that addition of catalyst fines leads to improved reactor performance in the case of petroleum hydrotreating and dementallization systems due to better catalyst utilization. It should be reported, however, that El-Hisnawi [71], when working with a single solvent and different particle sizes, observed a much stronger inverse dependence of the external contacting efficiency on particle diameter than the one indicated by Equation 7-3 which is based on results for all solvents. This seems to indicate that the sensitivity with respect to particle diameter is lost to some extent in the generalized correlation due to unaccounted factors.

In summary, the porous packing correlations given in Table 7 should be used to obtain estimates of η_{CE} in trickle-bed reactor applications in lieu of the nonporous packing correlations given in Table 6. It should be remembered that the porous packing correlations are valid in the tricklingflow or low gas-liquid interaction regime and do not apply to high gas-liquid interaction regimes such as pulsing flow. Since these correlations are based upon an assumed model of liquid-solid wetting which has no real fundamental basis, absolute values of η_{CE} predicted from these correlations may be in error but can be expected to give correct trends. Since the correlations were developed under isothermal conditions, application to highly exothermic systems with appreciable vaporization of the liquid phase would represent an extrapolation of their range of validity. Further research is needed to answer these and related questions.

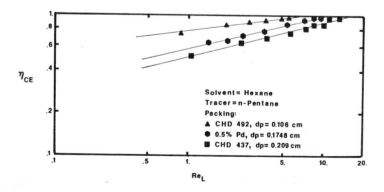

Figure 6. Effect of particle diameter on external liquid-solid contacting as a function of liquid Reynolds number. (After El-Hisnawi [71].)

Potential Applications of Fundamental Theory

The flow of gas and liquid phases through randomly packed beds in the trickling-flow regime is often qualitatively described as laminar, rivulet flow when referring to the liquid hydrodynamics. This leads to the suggestion that description of the liquid phase hydrodynamics on the particle scale, using the fundamental transport equations, might lead to better understanding of particle wetting processes and, ultimately, improved trickle-bed reactor scale-up and design methods. This section summarizes some recent literature dealing with the hydrodynamic theory of thin liquid films and porous capillary body transport phenomena since these areas are directly related to processes that determine catalyst wetting efficiency.

Hydrodynamic theory of thin liquid films. Quantitative description of liquid spreading and liquid flow on the exterior of small porous packings in randomly packed beds, taking into account the effect of chemical reaction and using fundamental transport theory to yield estimates of film thickness, film stability, and liquid evaporation rate, to name a few, has not yet been performed.

The flow of thin liquid films over smooth solid surfaces has received considerable attention from several aspects. The problem of defining criteria for which a smooth solid surface will remain completely wetted by an isothermal flowing liquid film has been studied by Hartley and Murgatroyd [135], Hobler [136, 137], Bankoff [138], and Mikielewicz and Moszynski [139]. One approach has been to define criteria based upon force balances at the leading edge of an assumed stable rivulet that precedes a dry patch. Another approach assumes that a stable film can occur only under such conditions where the energy or power of the moving liquid film is minimized. Both approaches yield expressions for the minimum film thickness, but they have a different functional form which cannot be readily discriminated due to lack of consistent data.

The above analysis for isothermal films has been extended to include:

1. The effects of shear and drag due to a flowing gas by Murgatroyd [140].
2. The effect of surface heating by Norman and McIntyre [141], Hsu et al. [142], Zuber and Staub [143], McPherson [144], Bankoff [145], Orell and Bankoff [146], Fujita and Ueda [147], and Sharon and Orell [148].
3. The effect of mass transfer by contact with a gas stream by Ponter et al. [149], Boyadiev [150], and Conder et al. [151].

Other various diverse problems such as the description of liquid rewetting a hot surface, description of laminar flow for films having a finite width that have a finite dynamic contact angle with the solid surface, and modeling of liquid movement at gas-liquid-solid (3-phase) contact lines, to name a few, have also been investigated but are too numerous to summarize here. It suffices to say that these and other related topics, although developed for applications other than trickle-flow over porous packings, have the potential for being extended to this problem, which remains a topic for future research.

Transport in capillary porous medium. Transport processes within porous materials have received considerable attention in connection with the design of heat pipes, development of equipment for energy transmission, supersonic wind tunnels with low gas throughputs, recovery of petroleum-derived products, and in the modeling of vapor-phase catalytic reactors. Despite this rather broad range of applications, very little attention has been given to the problem of describing gas-liquid distribution in porous catalytic bodies as applied to trickle-bed reactors. This conclusion is supported by the lack of such a treatment in the monographs of Scheidegger [152], Bear [153], Chizmadzhev et al. [154], Luikov [155], and Greenkorn [156]. This same topic is also not mentioned in the review papers of Dullien [157], Luikov [158], and Nikolaevskii and Somov [159] and references cited therein.

A variety of unsolved problems related to internal catalyst wetting as applied to trickle-bed reactors may be briefly outlined. These include:

1. Description of the rate at which liquid and gaseous reactant penetrate an initially dry catalyst pellet when the reaction products may be gases or liquids that exhibit a significant pressure.

2. Development and experimental verification of pseudo-homogeneous models for evaluation of gas-liquid distribution in porous catalyst structures.
3. Development of criterion for which a porous catalyst structure will remain liquid-filled under reaction conditions.
4. Investigation of the processes that occur when a wetted catalyst particle undergoes dryout and subsequent rewetting.
5. Application and extension of existing models for catalyst pore structure and gas transport to gas-liquid-solid catalyzed systems.

Some indication of preliminary research efforts in these areas can be obtained by consulting the papers of Wayner [160], Drobyshevich et al. [161], Saito and Seki [162], and Chen and Rinker [163] and the references cited therein. To summarize, many problems in this area as applied to trickle-bed reactors have not been solved and remain as potential research topics.

Effect of Contacting Efficiency on the Catalyst Effectiveness Factor

The catalyst effectiveness factor was introduced earlier in the development of a simplified performance equation for trickle-bed reactors for the case of a first-order, nonvolatile, liquid limiting reaction. Coverage of the external catalyst surface by actively flowing liquid, stagnant liquid films, and possibly dry areas will generally result in different mass transfer resistances over various parts

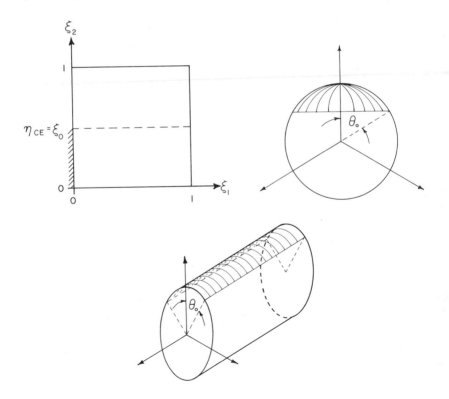

Figure 7. Representation of partial external wetting for various catalyst shapes: (A) slab geometry; (B) spherical geometry; (C) cylindrical geometry. (After Mills and Duduković [91].)

of the catalyst surface. Partial filling of the catalyst pore volume by liquid and gas will lead to differences in the characteristic diffusion time in both phases. Collectively, partial external, and internal catalyst wetting will yield different reactant concentration profiles in a catalyst pellet compared to the case of complete wetting and thus a different apparent reaction rate. The problem of obtaining a quantitative expression for the apparent reaction rate for partially wetted catalysts, from which the catalyst effectiveness factor can be obtained as the ratio of the apparent to intrinsic rate, has been the subject of various investigations. As shown below, an a priori knowledge of particle-scale incomplete contacting is necessary to obtain an estimate of the catalyst effectiveness factor for a partially wetted catalyst which is denoted here by η_{TB}.

A review of the literature on this subject up to 1982 has been given by Herskowitz and Smith [8]. To briefly summarize the literature, Duduković and coworkers performed a complete analysis of the problem for an isothermal pellet with first-order gas or liquid limiting kinetics in a series of papers [15, 89–91, 164]. Related cases were treated by Ramachandran and Smith [92], Tan and Smith [94], Herskowitz [14, 165–166], Martinez et al. [167], Goto et al. [168], Capra et al. [169], Sylvester and coworkers [170–171] and Lee and Smith [172].

All of the preceding models incorporate the concept of partial external wetting by subdividing the outer surface of the pellet into two or more subregions as illustrated in Figure 7 for slab, spherical, and cylindrical shapes. Each surface may have a different external mass transfer resistance depending upon whether the surface is covered by actively flowing liquid, a stagnant liquid film, or is dry and in direct contact with the gas. This leads to boundary conditions on each surface that have the same form but with different values for the mass transfer coefficients and surface concentrations. Although such a simplfied picture is somewhat removed from reality, it does provide a reasonable method for assessing the role of incomplete external wetting on catalyst performance. Additional explanation on the methodology and physical significance for various cases of interest are given by Mills and Duduković [15] to which the reader is referred for further details.

Table 8 gives a summary of the dimensionless material balance equations and associated boundary conditions for the case of diffusion and first-order reaction where the geometries corresponds to those given in Figure 7. The variable u denotes a dimensionless concentration for the limiting reactant which may be either dissolved gas or liquid. The Biot number for transport of limiting reactant to the actively wetted fraction of the external surface η_{CE} is denoted by Bi_w, while the Biot number for transport of limiting reactant to the remaining fraction of the surface $1 - \eta_{CE}$ is denoted by Bi_d. Liquid-to-solid mass transfer coefficients are used in Bi_w while either gas-to-inactively wetted solid or gas-to-dry solid mass transfer coefficients are used in Bi_d depending upon whether that surface is covered by a stagnant liquid film or is in direct contact with the gas or volatile liquid.

Solution of the partial differential equations given in Table 8 by separation of variables and applying the mixed boundary conditions leads to a set of dual-series equations which can be solved using various numerical techniques that are discussed elsewhere by Mills and Duduković [15, 91]. By assuming that the catalyst effectiveness factor for a partially wetted pellet can be expressed as the weighted sum of effectiveness factors for totally wetted and totally dry pellets [92], an approximate expression for the overall effectiveness factor of the partially wetted pellet can be obtained. This expression can be generally written as

$$\eta_{TB} = \eta_{CE}\eta_{o,aw} + (1 - \eta_{CE})\eta_{o,iw} \tag{58}$$

where $\eta_{o,aw}$ and $\eta_{o,iw}$ denote the overall catalyst effectiveness factors for the actively wetted and inactively wetted regions of the pellet. Table 9 gives a summary of the approximate forms reported by Mills and Duduković [15] for slab, cylindrical, and spherical catalyst shapes. Evaluation of the effectiveness factor η_{TB} can be performed by obtaining estimates of the external liquid-solid contacting given earlier by Equation 7-3, the various Biot numbers and either the Thiele ϕ or modified modulus Λ.

One question that arises when using the approximate formula given by Equation 58 is whether or not it has large errors when compared to the more exact but tedious numerical solution. The relative errors between effectiveness factors calculated by the approximate formula to those found by the numerical solution for the case of spherical geometry are given in Figure 8 for a fixed ratio

Table 8

Summary of Governing Equations and Boundary Conditions for Partially Wetted Catalyst Pellets

Geometry	Governing equation	Boundary conditions		Range of validity
Slab	$$\frac{\partial^2 u}{\partial x^2} + \frac{\partial^2 u}{\partial y^2} - \phi^2 u = 0$$	$x = 0$	$\begin{cases} -\dfrac{1}{Bi_w}\dfrac{\partial u}{\partial x} + u = 1 \\[2mm] -\dfrac{1}{Bi_d}\dfrac{\partial u}{\partial x} + u = 1 \text{ or } \varepsilon \end{cases}$	$0 \leq x \leq \xi_0$ $\xi_0 < x \leq 1$
		$x = 1$	$\dfrac{\partial u}{\partial x} = 0$	$0 \leq y \leq 1$
		$y = 0, 1$	$\dfrac{\partial u}{\partial y} = 0$	$0 \leq x \leq 1$
Cylinder	$$\frac{1}{\rho}\frac{\partial}{\partial \rho}\left(\rho \frac{\partial u}{\partial \rho}\right) + \frac{1}{\rho^2}\frac{\partial^2 u}{\partial \theta_2} - \phi^2 u = 0$$	$\rho = 1$	$\begin{cases} \dfrac{1}{Bi_w}\dfrac{\partial u}{\partial \rho} + u = 1 \\[2mm] \dfrac{1}{Bi_d}\dfrac{\partial u}{\partial \rho} + u = 1 \text{ or } \varepsilon \end{cases}$	$0 \leq \theta < \theta_0$ $\theta_0 < \theta \leq \pi$
Sphere	$$\frac{1}{\rho^2}\frac{\partial}{\partial \rho}\left(\rho^2 \frac{\partial u}{\partial \rho}\right) + \frac{1}{\rho^2 \sin \theta}\frac{\partial}{\partial \theta}\left(\sin \theta \frac{\partial}{\partial \theta}\right) - \phi^2 u = 0$$	$\rho = 0$	$\lim\limits_{\rho \to 0} \rho^\nu \dfrac{\partial u}{\partial \rho} = 0$ where $\quad \nu = 1$ for cylinders $\quad \nu = 2$ for spheres	$0 \leq \theta \leq \pi$
		$\theta = 0, \pi$	$\dfrac{\partial u}{\partial \theta} = 0$	$0 \leq \rho \leq 1$

Table 9
Approximate Equations for Evaluation of the Catalyst
Effectiveness Factor of Partially Wetted Pellets

Number	Geometry	Expression for η_{TB} (see note below)
9-1	Slab	$$\dfrac{\eta_{CE}}{\dfrac{\phi^2}{Bi_w}+\dfrac{\phi}{\tanh\phi}}+\dfrac{(1-\eta_{CE})\varepsilon}{\dfrac{\phi^2}{Bi_d}+\dfrac{\phi}{\tanh\phi}}$$
9-2	Cylinder	$$\dfrac{\eta_{CE}}{\dfrac{\phi^2}{2Bi_w}+\dfrac{\phi I_0(\phi)}{2I_1(\phi)}}+\dfrac{(1-\eta_{CE})\varepsilon}{\dfrac{\phi^2}{2Bi_d}+\dfrac{\phi I_0(\phi)}{2I_1(\phi)}}$$
9-3	Sphere	$$\dfrac{\eta_{CE}}{\dfrac{\phi^2}{3Bi_w}+\dfrac{\phi^2}{3[\phi\coth\phi-1]}}+\dfrac{(1-\eta_{CE})\varepsilon}{\dfrac{\phi^2}{3Bi_d}+\dfrac{\phi^2}{3[\phi\coth\phi-1]}}$$

Note: Alternate expressions for η_{TB} in terms of the modified (Aris) modulus are given by Mills and Duković [15].

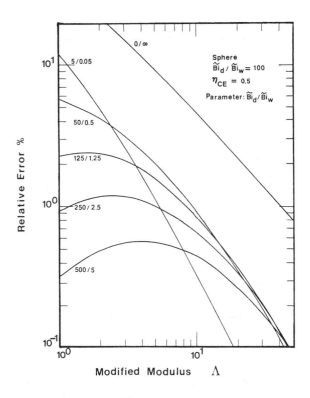

Figure 8. Relative error in the approximate formula for spherical geometry as a function of the modified modulus Λ. (After Mills and Duković [15].)

of the modified Biot numbers $\tilde{B}i_d/\tilde{B}i_w$. The largest error is 12.8% which occurs for $\phi = 1$ and $\tilde{B}i_d/\tilde{B}i_w = 5/0.05$ which is not excessive when compared to the 38% error found for the nonvolatile liquid reactant case, i.e., when $\tilde{B}i_w \to \infty$ and $\tilde{B}i_d \to 0$. Our detailed calculations for a variety of other cases that have not been reported in the open literature have shown that the approximate expression given in Table 9 generally underestimates the effectiveness factor which makes these safe to employ for reactor design estimates.

To explore two extremes of partially wetted catalyst performance, consider first the case where the intrinsic rate of reaction for a particular heterogeneous catalyzed gas-liquid system exhibits first-order dependence upon the nonvolatile liquid reactant. The effect of incomplete external liquid-solid contacting on the catalyst effectiveness factor with negligible mass transfer resistance on the actively wetted face ($\tilde{B}i_w \to \infty$) for this case is given in Figure 9A. The effectiveness factor increases with increasing values of external liquid-solid contacting due to the greater supply area for the reactant. The increase is less dramatic for the smaller value of the Thiele modulus, i.e., $\phi = 1$ since the demand for liquid reactant is not as great when compared to the larger value of the modulus.

Next, consider the case where the intrinsic rate of reaction exhibits first-order dependence upon the dissolved gaseous reactant such as that typically encountered in many chemical hydrogenations or oxidations, for example. The effect of incomplete external contacting on the catalyst effectiveness factor for $\tilde{B}i_d = 100$ and $\tilde{B}i_w = 5$ is shown in Figure 9B. In contrast to the liquid-limiting reactant situation given in Figure 9A, the effectiveness factor decreases with increased external catalyst

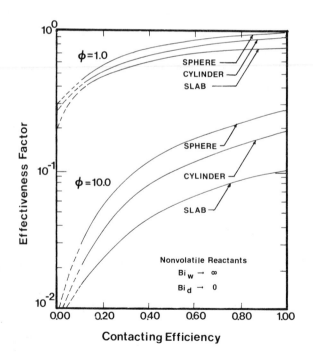

Figure 9. Catalyst effectiveness factor as a function of external contacting efficiency: (A) liquid reactant is limiting (after Mills and Duduković [91]); (B) gas reactant is limiting (after Mills and Duduković [15].)

wetting. This occurs because the inactively wetted surface acts as the major supply area for reactant so that a decrease in this area results in a lower net flux of reactant to the entire pellet surface.

From the preceding examples, it can be seen that external contacting efficiency can have a significant effect on the catalyst effectiveness factor for partially wetted catalyst pellets. With a few exceptions, most of the theoretical models that have been developed assume complete internal wetting. This latter assumption is reasonable for most applications where the liquid is relatively nonvolatile or if volatile, it remains as a condensed phase under capillary pressure in the catalyst pores. The major problem in applying the derived formulas for the catalyst effectiveness factor is in obtaining reliable values for the various mass transfer coefficients, Thiele modulus and, effective diffusivity of the reacting specie. This remains outside the scope of this chapter, but some appreciation of this problem can be obtained by referring to Reference 2.

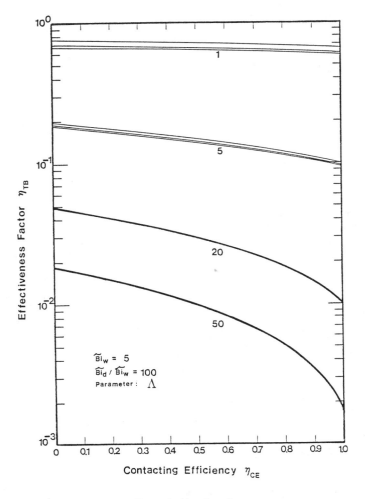

Figure 9. (Continued)

Use of Contacting Efficiency in Reactor Models

The role of liquid-solid contacting on reactor performance was introduced earlier by use of a simple but enlightening plug-flow reactor model for trickle-bed reactors with first-order, nonvolatile, liquid-limiting reaction kinetics. Various other reactor performance equations that have appeared in the literature for this type of reaction rate form were also summarized earlier in Table 5. Only the performance equations of Mears [115], Sylvester and Pitayagulsarn [119], and Duduković [89] account for particle-scale incomplete contacting. Detailed discussion of these various models is already available in several papers by Duduković and Mills [2, 89–90] and a review by Calo [11], to which the reader is referred. The role of liquid-solid contacting on reactor performance for systems where the gaseous reactant is the limiting reagent has received less attention in the literature. Since newer emerging chemical processes are expected to involve reactions where the gaseous reactant is limiting, such as chemical hydrogenations or oxidations, a brief summary of trickle-bed reactor models for these systems with a special emphasis upon the role of liquid-solid contacting is given here.

Most reactor models for gaseous-reactant limiting systems that have appeared in the literature generally assume that

1. Gas-to-liquid and liquid-to-solid external mass transfer as well as internal pore diffusion resistances may all be significant.
2. The intrinsic reaction is first-order with respect to the gaseous limiting reactant.
3. The axial dispersion model can be used to describe deviations from plug-flow.
4. Catalyst particles have complete internal wetting with either partial or complete external wetting.
5. Gas solubility can be accurately described by Henry's law.
6. The reactor operates isothermally.

The reactor models proposed by Goto et al. [173], Goto and Smith [174–176], and Levec and Smith [177] assume that the external liquid-solid contacting is complete, i.e., $\eta_{CE} = 1$. The models of Hartman and Coughlin [178], El-Hisnawi [71], Herskowitz and coworkers [14, 132, 179], Mata and Smith [51], and El-Hisnawi et al. [16], assume incomplete external liquid-solid contacting exists, although some noteworthy differences exist between the assumed physical situation at the inactively wetted catalyst surface. Some authors [16, 51, 71, 178] assume that the inactively wetted catalyst surface is covered by a thin stagnant liquid that can either be saturated with the bulk gas or subject to a finite mass transfer limitation. A few others [14, 93, 179] assume that this surface is dry so that the liquid-filled catalyst pore mouths are in direct contact with the flowing gas phase.

Turek and Lange [180–181] use the concept of a single, overall volumetric mass transfer coefficient $k_s a_s$ to lump the combined effects of finite gas-to-liquid mass transfer, liquid-to-actively wetted solid mass transfer, gas-to-inactively wetted solid transfer, and incomplete external liquid-solid contacting. This procedure allows the number of parameters to be reduced from four to one.

Crine and coworkers at the University of Liegé [76, 79] have developed a trickle-bed reactor model based upon percolation theory that couples both particle-scale and reactor-scale incomplete contacting with hydrodynamics and mass transfer. This model, although it has some fundamental basis, still contains a few adjustable parameters that must be identified using trickle-bed reactor performance data, which is a drawback. Reacting systems where it has yielded accurate predictions of trickle-bed reactor performance include: the hydrogenation of α-methylstyrene [76], hydrogenation of 2-butanone [182], hydrotreating of petroleum feedstocks [183], and the hydrogenation of maleic acid [184]. This model has not been widely accepted probably because of its complexity.

Stanek and coworkers [185–186] have coupled their model for calculation of liquid irrigation with additional mass and energy balances for predicting trickle-bed reactor performance. Besides the percolation theory approach, this represents one of the few attempts to relax the assumption of a uniform liquid velocity profile. Particle-scale contacting is assumed to be complete, however.

Mills et al. [2, 187] proposed a generalized dispersion model for isothermal trickle-beds that included incomplete external contacting and compared various limiting cases of the model to experimental trickle-bed performance data using the hydrogenation of α-methylstyrene as a test reaction. Some of the performance equations that were given included:

1. Completely wetted pellets with internal diffusion resistance controlling as typically encountered in basket reactors.
2. Completely wetted pellets with gas-to-liquid mass transfer resistance controlling.
3. Completely wetted pellets with liquid-to-solid mass transfer resistance controlling.
4. Partial externally wetted pellets with finite mass transfer resistance at the actively wetted catalyst surface and negligible mass transfer resistance at the inactively wetted catalyst surface.
5. Partial externally wetted pellets with unequal, finite mass transfer resistances at the actively and inactively wetted catalyst surfaces.

The detailed equations and methodology used are given in the previously cited references. The results can be summarized as follows: the model equation for case 1 always greatly overpredicted the measured trickle-bed reactor conversion, while the model predictions for cases 2 and 3 were substantially less than experimental values when the Goto and Smith [188], Turek and Lange [180], and Dwivedi and Upadhayay [189] gas-to-liquid and liquid-to-solid mass transfer coefficient correlations were used. The model predictions for case 4 underpredicted the experimental conversion for the smaller values of liquid space time $L/u_{s\ell}$ but gave significant overprediction at larger values of liquid space time. Good agreement between experimental and predicted values of the reactor conversion were obtained for case 5 by using the correlation for η_{CE} given in Table 7 and by using the following correlations for the liquid-to-actively-wetted solid mass transfer coefficient and gas-to-inactively-wetted solid mass transfer coefficient:

$$\frac{k_{\ell\text{-aws}}D_p}{D_m} = 9.72Re_L'^{0.274} Sc_L^{0.395} \tag{59}$$

$$\frac{k_{g\text{-iws}}D_p}{D_m} = 2850H_{LSE} \tag{60}$$

A comparison between the experimental and model-predicted results is given in Figure 10 for the different reaction solvents (hexane and cyclohexane) along with the external liquid-solid contacting results from the already cited correlation.

Several additional key questions related to the use of liquid-solid contacting efficiency in trickle-bed reactor models remain to be addressed. When incomplete external contacting is assumed in a reactor model and external mass transfer resistances are significant, evaluation of individual mass transfer coefficients on the actively and inactively wetted catalyst surfaces is difficult. Until now, the methodology used has been to first measure contacting by tracer methods in the absence of reaction. Then, the various mass transfer coefficients are obtained using trickle-bed reaction performance data assuming contacting under reaction conditions to be the same as that obtained in the absence of reaction. This latter condition has not been proven, nor has it been established that the various mass transfer coefficients are indeed independent. If the coefficients are not independent, additional questions can be raised regarding the well-posedness of the parameter estimation problem. Another question is whether a single, overall mass transfer coefficient can be used to fit reactor performance data either by assuming complete wetting ($\eta_{CE} = 1$) and using a correlation similar or possibly different than Equation 59, or assuming incomplete wetting ($\eta_{CE} \leq 1$) and using a correlation in terms of the overall volumetric mass transfer coefficient $k_s a_s$ where the effects of mass transfer and incomplete external contacting are lumped together.

Attempts to answer the previous questions up until now have led to inconclusive results when implemented using a limited amount of data for the α-methylstyrene to cumene hydrogenation in various organic solvents using palladium-on-alumina catalysts. The model predictions that assume incomplete external contacting are generally better than those obtained when using the available

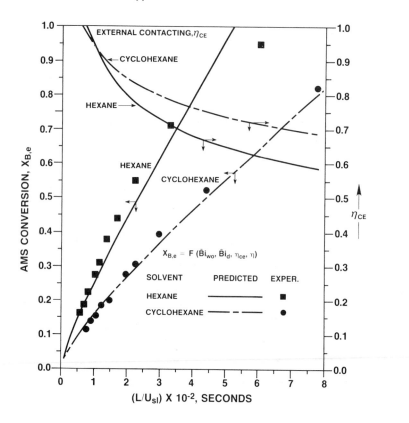

Figure 10. Experimental and model-predicted conversion for α-methylstyrene hydrogenation in a laboratory-scale trickle-bed reactor. (After Mills and Duduković [2].)

mass transfer correlations and assuming complete external contacting, but further research is needed before the results can be considered applicable to various systems with good reliability.

SUMMARY AND CONCLUSIONS

The hydrodynamics of cocurrent gas-liquid downflow through packed beds of catalysts as applied to trickle-bed reactors has been reviewed. This has included an overview of the basic transport processes associated with the characterization of the two-phase flow such as flow regimes, pressure drop or energy dissipation, liquid holdup and liquid-solid contacting effectiveness. Special emphasis has been given here to the role of liquid-solid contacting effectiveness since the degree to which the solid catalyst remains wetted can have a significant influence on overall trickle-bed reactor performance.

In the second section, a phenomenological description of the flow regimes encountered in two-phase downflow through a packed bed was given along with a summary of various flow maps that have been proposed for identification of these flow regimes. The trickling-flow regime corresponds to the low gas-liquid interaction regime while pulsing flow, spray flow, and dispersed bubble-flow correspond to the high gas-liquid interaction regime. The available information on pilot and commercial trickle-bed reactors suggests that these operate in either the trickle-flow or in an envelope between the trickle-flow and pulsing flow regime. Incomplete liquid-solid contacting was shown to be primarily associated with the low gas-liquid interaction regime. Theoretical models for prediction of flow regime and flow regime transition were shown to be generally lacking for both foaming and nonfoaming liquids so that correlations must presently be used for design purposes.

Methods for evaluation of two-phase flow pressure drop in trickle-beds were reviewed in the third section. It was shown that this parameter can be evaluated using various available correlations, most of which employ an empirical functional form in terms of the Lockhart-Martinelli parameter [44] for two-phase flow through empty conduits. Many of the available correlations, which were summarized in Table 1, are based upon large nonporous absorber column-type packings and may not give reliable results for small porous catalyst packings encountered in trickle-beds. The more reliable correlations are those based upon extension of the Ergun equation to two-phase flow where the free parameters have been identified using the packing and gas-liquid mixtures of interest. Multiple values of the two-phase pressure drop have also been reported at the same values of the gas and liquid flow rate but remain to be confirmed in future work.

A review of the various definitions for liquid holdup was given in the fourth section. The available correlations for evaluation of this parameter in both the low and high gas-liquid interaction regimes were summarized in Tables 2 and 3. It was shown that certain dimensionless groups should be used in correlations for the low gas-liquid interaction regime by analogy to fundamental results obtained on more well-defined packing geometry such as a string-of-spheres. The fraction of internal catalyst pore volume occupied by liquid was shown to be directly related to internal liquid holdup. This fraction has been shown to be unity in laboratory-scale tracer and isothermal trickle-bed reactor experiments, but has not been measured in larger-scale systems. A priori evaluation of internal catalyst wetting for systems involving volatile liquids, gas evolution, and non-isothermal conditions has not yet been performed.

Liquid-solid contacting in trickle-bed reactors and various factors that can be either directly or indirectly associated with it were reviewed in the fifth section. Some of the topics covered included:

1. The various definitions of liquid-solid contacting.
2. Phenomenological description.
3. Its effect on reactor performance.
4. The difference between particle- versus reactor-scale incomplete contacting.
5. Experimental methods for evaluation of liquid-solid contacting.
6. Empirical correlations for prediction of liquid-solid contacting.
7. The role of liquid-solid contacting on the catalyst effectiveness factor.
8. Use of liquid-solid contacting efficiency in trickle-bed reactor models.

In addition, a summary of recent fundamental studies related to the flow of thin liquid films and transport effects in capillary porous media which might be applicable to further fundamental studies on liquid-solid contacting was given. The fraction of internal catalyst pore volume occupied by liquid η_i, the fraction of external catalyst area that is contacted by actively flowing liquid η_{CE} and the fraction of total internal plus external catalyst area contacted by liquid η_C were reviewed and identified as being suitable measures of particle-scale contacting effectiveness. The fraction of the catalyst bed that is irrigated with flowing liquid and the uniformity of the liquid distribution across the bed cross-sectional area were shown to be important factors associated with reactor-scale contacting effectiveness. The fraction of external particle area that is contacted by actively flowing liquid η_{CE} has emerged thus far as perhaps the most useful parameter in trickle-bed reactor modeling design, scale-up, and interpretation of reactor performance. An example was given where this parameter was a fundamental part of modeling the reactor behavior in terms of assessing the role of internal and external transport effects.

NOTATION

a   exponent which appears in Equation 3-3 (Table 3)

a_p external packing surface area per unit volume of reactor, m^{-1}

a_t external packing surface area per unit volume of reactor, m^{-1}

a_v external packing surface area per unit volume of reactor, m^{-1}

A   correlation constant which appears in Table 1 and Table 2

Bi_d Biot number for the inactively wetted or dry catalyst surface; $k_{g\text{-}iws}L_s/D_e$ for slab geometry, $k_{g\text{-}iws}R/D_e$ for cylindrical or spherical geometry, dimensionless

$\tilde{Bi}_d$ generalized Biot number for the inactively wetted or dry catalyst surface, $V_p k_{g\text{-}iws}/(S_{ex}D_e)$, dimensionless

Bi_w Biot number for the actively wetted catalyst surface, $k_{\ell\text{-}aws}L_s/D_e$ for slab geometry, $k_{\ell\text{-}aws}R/D_e$ for cylindrical or spherical geometry, dimensionless

$\tilde{Bi}_w$ generalized Biot number for the actively wetted catalyst surface, $V_p k_{\ell\text{-}aws}/(S_{ex}D_e)$, dimensionless

B_n Bond number, $\rho_L g/(\sigma_L a_p^2)$, dimensionless

Ca_L Capillary number of the liquid phase first appearing in Table 3, $L\nu_L/\sigma_L$, dimensionless

d_p average diameter of the packing, m

d_{pe} equivalent diameter of the packing first appearing in Equation 10 given by $(2/3)d_p \varepsilon_B/(1 - \varepsilon_B)$, m

d_s average diameter of the sphere first appearing in Equation 17, m

d_T reactor inner diameter first appearing in Equations 3a and 3b, m

Da_0 Damkohler number first appearing in Equation 24, $k_w \rho_p (1 - \varepsilon_B)L_R/u_L$, dimensionless

D_e effective diffusivity of the gas or liquid reactant in the catalyst pores, $m^2 s^{-1}$

D_{eo} effective diffusivity of the tracer in the catalyst pores based upon total pellet cross-sectional area, $D_{eo} = D_m \varepsilon_p \tau^{-1}$, $m^2 s^{-1}$

D_{GE} axial dispersion coefficient of the gas phase based on total reactor cross sectional area appearing in Table 4, $m^2 s^{-1}$

D_{LE} axial dispersion coefficient of the liquid phase based on total reactor cross-sectional area first appearing below Equation 33, $m^2 s^{-1}$

D_m molecular diffusivity of the tracer or gas and liquid reactant in the catalyst pores, $m^2 s^{-1}$

D_p particle diameter based upon equivalent external surface area of a sphere, $(S_{ex}/\pi)^{-1/2}$, m

Eö   Eötvos number, $\rho_L g d_{pe}^2/\sigma_L$, dimensionless

$E_\theta(\theta)$ liquid phase residence time density function first appearing in Equation 32, dimensionless

$f_{\ell g}$ two-phase friction factor first appearing in Table 1, dimensionless

f_w average fraction of the external catalyst surface contacted by flowing liquid first appearing in Equation 21 and defined by Equation 23, dimensionless

Fr   Froude number for the flowing liquid phase defined by Equation 7, $L^2/(H_L^2 \rho_L^2 g d_p)$, dimensionless

Fr_L Froude number for the flowing liquid phased on a_v, first appearing in Table 2, $a_v L/(\rho_L^2 g)$, dimensionless

g   gravitational constant, 9.80665 $m s^{-2}$

G   superficial mass velocity of the gas phase first appearing in Equation 1, $kg\, m^{-2} s^{-1}$

Ga_L Galileo number of the liquid phase, $d_p^3 g/D_L$ or $d_s^3 g/D_L$, dimensionless

Ga_L^* modified Galileo number in terms of two-phase flow pressure drop appearing in Table 2 and defined by Equation 22, dimensionless

h   convective heat transfer coefficient to the particle first appearing in Equation 14, $J\, m^{-2} s^{-1} K^{-1}$

ΔH_{vap} heat of vaporization appearing in Equation 13, $J\, mol^{-1}$

H_D dynamic liquid external holdup (m^3 of flowing liquid)/(m^3 of bed volume), dimensionless

H_L total (internal + external) liquid holdup defined by Equation 11 (m^3

H_{Li} of total liquid)/(m³ of bed volume), dimensionless

H_{Li} internal catalyst liquid holdup defined by Equation 12 (m³ of liquid in the pores)/(m³ of bed volume), dimensionless

H_{LE} total (static + dynamic) external liquid holdup defined by Equation 15 (m³ of liquid static + dynamic liquid on the catalyst surface)/(m³ of bed volume), dimensionless

H_{LSE} external static liquid holdup (m³ of static liquid on the catalyst surface)/ (m³ of bed volume), dimensionless

H_{LD} dynamic liquid external holdup (m³ of flowing liquid)/(m³ of bed volume), dimensionless

k_{app} apparent first-order reaction rate constant appearing in Equation 28, hr^{-1}

k_1, k_2 empirical constants appearing in Table 1, Equation 1-9

$k_{g\text{-}iws}$ gas-to-inactively wetted solid mass transfer coefficient appearing in Equation 60, $m\,s^{-1}$

Pe_L Peclet number of the liquid phase based on reactor length first appearing in Equation 33, $u_L L_R/D_{LE}$, dimensionless

Pe_p Peclet number of the liquid phase based on particle diameter appearing in Table 4, $d_p u_L/D_{LE}$

$(Pe_p)_g$ Peclet number of the gas phase based on particle diameter appearing in Table 4, $d_p u_g/D_{GE}$

Q_L liquid volumetric flow rate appearing in Equation 48, $m^3\,s^{-1}$

Q_{LS} liquid volumetric flow rate over a string-of-spheres appearing in Equation 17, $m^3\,s^{-1}$

r radial coordinate appearing in Equation 44, m

Re_G Reynolds number of the gas phase based on the average particle diameter, $d_p u_G/v_G$, dimensionless

r^*_{pore} critical pore radius appearing in Equation 13, m

Re^*_G Reynolds number of the gas phase based on the equivalent particle diameter, $d_{pe} u_G/v_G$, dimensionless

Re_L Reynolds number of the liquid phase based on the average particle diameter, $d_p u_L/v_L$, dimensionless

Re^*_L Reynolds number of the liquid phase based on the equivalent particle diameter, $d_{pe} u_L/v_L$, dimensionnless

Re'_L Reynolds number of the liquid phase based on the equivalent sphere diameter, $D_{pe} u_L/v_L$, dimensionless

$k_{\ell\text{-}aws}$ liquid-to-actively wetted solid mass transfer coefficient appearing in Equation 59 ($= k_{LS}$), $m\,s^{-1}$

k_s overall gas-liquid-solid mass transfer coefficient, $m\,s^{-1}$

k_w first-order intrinsic reaction rate constant per unit catalyst weight, $m^3\,kg^{-1}\,s^{-1}$

k_v first-order intrinsic reaction rate constant per unit catalyst volume appearing in Equation 30, s^{-1}

K_A adsorption equilibrium constant appearing in Equation 48, m

L superficial mass velocity of the liquid phase first appearing in Equation 1, $kg\,m^{-2}\,s^{-1}$

L_{cr} superficial mass velocity of the liquid phase above which pulsing-flow occurs defined by Equation 2a, $kg\,m^{-2}\,s^{-1}$

L_m minimum superficial mass velocity of the liquid phase appearing in Equation 23, $kg\,m^{-2}\,s^{-1}$

L_R length of reactor-packed section appearing in Equation 29, m

LHSV   liquid hourly space velocity defined by Equation 29, hr^{-1}

L_s half-thickness of slab catalyst pellet, m

p_w wall exchange factor appearing in Equation 47, m^{-1}

R_w reaction rate based per unit weight of catalyst particle appearing in Equation 14, $mol\,kg^{-1}\,s^{-1}$

s spreading factor appearing below Equation 47, $4D_r/d_p$, $m\,s^{-1}$

S_{ex} external surface area of the catalyst pellet, m^2

S_g BET surface area of the catalyst pellet first appearing in Equation 48, $m^2\,kg^{-1}$

t denotes time first appearing below Equation 32, s

T_b temperature of the bulk fluid surrounding the catalyst first appearing in Equation 13, K

T_c mean temperature of the catalyst particle first appearing in Equation 13, K

u gas or liquid superficial velocity first appearing in Equation 10, m s^{-1}

u_G superficial gas velocity, m s^{-1}

u_L supeficial liquid velocity, m s^{-1}

u_w liquid velocity at the reactor wall appearing in Equation 47 m s^{-1}

u_z liquid velocity in the axial direction

$\underline{V}$ molar volume of the condensible species appearing in Equation 13, m^3 mol^{-1}

V_p pellet volume, m^3

V_R reactor volume appearing in Equation 48, m^3

We_g Weber number of the gas phase appearing in Table 1 Equation 1-8 $u_g^2 \rho_g d_p/\sigma_L$, dimensionless

We_L Weber number of the liquid phase appearing in Table 7 Equations 7-1 and 7-2, $L^2/\sigma_L^2 \rho_L a_t$, dimensionless

X_B conversion of liquid reactant B, dimensionless

Z two-phase flow pressure drop parameter defined in Table 1 by Equation 1-6, deimensionless

Greek Letters

α fraction of the cross-sectional area void space occupied by liquid first appearing in Equation 8, dimensionless

β average angle of inclination from the vertical appearing in Equation 20, radians

β_r residual liquid saturation appearing in Table 1 Equation 1-9, dimensionless

β_f dynamic liquid saturation appearing in Table 1 Equation 1-9, dimensionless

δ_g pressure drop per unit reactor length for gas only flowing through the packed bed, dynes m^{-3}

δ_ℓ pressure drop per unit reactor length for liquid only flowing through the packed bed, dynes m^{-3}

$\delta_i, \delta_e, \delta_o$ parameters defined by Equations 53–55, s

ε_B bed void fraction (m^3 of voids external to the catalyst pellets)/(m^3 of bed volume), dimensionless

ε_p porosity of the catalyst particles, dimensionless

η effectiveness factor for a totally wetted pellet defined by Equation 27, dimensionless

η_C liquid-solid contacting based on total catalyst area, dimensionless

η_{CE} liquid-solid contacting based on external catalyst area, dimensionless

$\bar{\eta}_{CE}$ average value of the liquid-solid contacting for the packed bed based on external catalyst area, dimensionless

η_i liquid-solid contacting based on internal catalyst area, dimensionless

$\bar{\eta}_i$ average value of the liquid-solid contacting for the packed bed based on internal catalyst are a, dimensionless

η_o overall catalyst effectiveness factor first appearing in Equation 26, dimensionless

η_{TB} effectiveness factor for a partially wetted catalyst in a trickle-bed first appearing in Equation 34, dimensionless

η_{TBo} overall effectiveness factor for a partially wetted catalyst in a trickle-bed first appearing in Equation 35, dimensionless

$\tilde{\eta}_{TBo}$ average value of the overall effectiveness factor for a partially wetted catalyst in a trickle-bed first appearing in Equation 38, dimensionless

θ residence time, $u_L t/H_L L_R$, dimensionless

λ flow-map parameter appearing after Equation 26, $(\rho_g \rho_L/\rho_{air}\rho_w)^{1/2}$, dimensionless

Λ generalized Thiele modulus or Aris modulus defined below Equation 27, $(V_p/S_{ex})\sqrt{k_w \rho_p/D_e}$, dimensionless

μ viscosity of gas or liquid appearing in Equation 10, kg m^{-1} s^{-1}

μ_g gas viscosity, kg m^{-1} s^{-1}

μ_L liquid viscosity, kg m^{-1} s^{-1}

μ_w water viscosity, kg m^{-1} s^{-1}

μ_{1LF} first absolute moment of a liquid-filled trickle bed, s

μ_{1TP} first absolute moment of a two-phase flow trickle bed, s

ν_L kinematic viscosity of the liquid phase, m^2 s^{-1}

ξ_ℓ liquid-phase pressure drop parameter appearing in Table 1 Equation 1-5, $kg\,m^{-2}\,s^{-1}$

ρ radial coordinate appearing in Table 8, r/R, dimensionless; gas or liquid density appearing in Equation 10, $kg\,m^{-3}$

ρ_{air} air density appearing below Equation 2b, $kg\,m^{-3}$

ρ_g gas density first appearing below Equation 2b, $kg\,m^{-3}$

ρ_L liquid density first appearing below Equation 2b, $kg\,m^{-3}$

ρ_p catalyst particle density, $kg\,m^{-3}$

ρ_w water density first appearing below Equation 2b, $kg\,m^{-3}$

σ_L liquid surface tension, $kg\,m^{-1}\,s^{-1}$

σ_w water surface tension, $kg\,m^{-1}\,s^{-1}$

v_{LDS} volume of flowing liquid per sphere defined by Equation 17, m^3

ϕ Thiele modulus, $L\sqrt{k_w\rho_p/D_e}$ for slab geometry, $R\sqrt{k_w\rho_p/D_e}$ for cylin-

drical or spherical geometry, dimensionless

ϕ_c catalyst shape factor appearing in Equations 3a and 3b, S_{ex}/d_p^2, dimensionless

χ Lockhart-Martinelli two-phase flow parameter appearing in Table 1, $\sqrt{\delta_\ell/\delta_g}$, dimensionless

χ' pseudo-Lockhart-Martinelli two-phase flow parameter appearing in Table 1, $\sqrt{\xi_\ell/\xi_g}$, dimensionless

ψ flow map parameter appearing after Equation 2b, $\sigma_w/\sigma_L[(\mu_L/\mu_w)\cdot(\rho_w/\rho_L)^2]^{1/3}$, dimensionless

ω_D dynamic liquid saturation for a parallel string of spheres defined by Equation 18, H_{LD}/ε_B, dimensionless

ω_E dynamic liquid saturation for a random distribution of spheres defined by Equation 19, H_{LE}/ε_B, dimensionless

Subscripts

app   denotes apparent

g   refers to the gas

L   refers to the liquid

LF   refers to liquid full operation

TP   refers to two-phase operation

w   denotes wetted or water

REFERENCES

1. Germain, A., L'Homme, G., and Lefebvre, A., in *Chemical Engineering of Gas-Liquid-Solid Catalyst Reactions*, G. L'Homme (Ed.), CEBEDOC, Liège, Belgium, 1979, p. 265.
2. Mills, P. L., and Duduković, M. P., *ACS Symposium Series*, P. L. Mills and M. P. Duduković (Eds.). 237:37 (1983)
3. L'Homme, G., in *Chemical Engineering of Gas-Liquid-Solid Catalyst Reactions*, G. L'Homme, (Ed.) CEBEDOC, Liège, Belgium, 1979, p. 1.
4. Satterfield, C. N., *AIChE J.*, 21:209 (1975).
5. Hoffman, H., *Int. Chem. Eng. J.*, 17:19 (1977).
6. Goto, S., Levec, J., and Smith, J. M., *Cat. Rev.-Sci. Eng.*, 15:187 (1977).
7. Gianetto, A., et al. *AIChE J.*, 24(6):1087 (1978).
8. Herskowitz, M., and Smith, J. M., *AIChE J.*, 29(1):1 (1983).
9. Shah, Y. T., *Gas-Liquid-Solid Reactor Design*, McGraw-Hill, N.Y., 1979.
10. Ramachandran, P. A., and Chaudhari, R. V., *Three-Phase Catalytic Reactors*, Gordon & Breach Science Publ., N.Y., 1983.
11. Calo, J., in *Multiphase Chemical Reactors Volume II—Design Methods*, A. E. Rodrigues et al., (Eds.), Series E—Applied Sciences No. 52, Sijthoff & Noordhoff, Alphen aan den Rijn, The Netherlands, 1981, p. 3.
12. Baldi, G., in *Multiphase Chemical Reactors Volume II—Design Methods, A. E. Rodrigues, et al., (Eds.), Series E—Applied Sciences No. 52, Sijthoff & Noordhoff, Alphen aan den Rijn, The Netherlands, 1981, p. 323.
13. Koros, R., in *Multiphase Chemical Reactors Volume II—Design Methods*. A. E. Rodrigues et al., (Eds.), Series E—Applied Sciences No. 52, Sijthoff & Noordhoff, Alphen aan den Rijn, The Netherlands, 1981, p. 429.

14. Herskowitz, M., Carbonell, R. G., and Smith, J. M., *AIChE J.*, 25:272 (1979).
15. Mills P. L., and Duduković, M. P., *Chem. Eng. Sci.*, 35:2267 (1980).
16. El-Hisnawi, A. A., Duduković, M. P., and Mills, P. L., *ACS Symposium Series*, J. Wei and C. Georgakis, (Eds.), 196:421 (1981).
17. Specchia, V., and Baldi, G., *Chem. Eng. Sci.*, 32:515 (1977).
18. Talmor, E., *AIChE J.*, 23:868 (1977).
19. Charpentier, J. C., and Favier, M., *AIChE J.*, 21:1213 (1975).
20. Baker, O., *Oil Gas J.*, 53:185 (1954).
21. Chou, T. S., Worley, F. L., Jr., and Luss, D., *I & EC Process Des. Develop.*, 16:424 (1977)
22. Lerou, J. J., Glaser, D., and Luss, D., *I & EC Fundamentals*, 19:66 (1980).
23. Gianetto, A., Specchia, V., and Baldi, G., *AIChE J.*, 19:916 (1973).
24. Blok, J. R., and Drinkenburg, A. A. H., *ACS Symposium Series*, J. Wei and C. Georgakis (Eds.) 196:353 (1981).
25. Midoux, N., Favier, M., and Charpentier, J. C., *J. Chem. Eng., Japan*, 9:350 (1976).
26. Morsi, B. I., Midoux, N., and Charpentier, J. C., *AIChE J.*, 24:357 (1978).
27. Morsi B. I., et al., *Entropie*, 91:38 (1980).
28. Sato, Y., *J. Chem. Eng., Japan*, 6:315 (1973).
29. Fukushima, S., and Kusaka, K., *J. Chem. Eng., Japan*, 10:461 (1977).
30. Fukushima, S., and Kusaka, K., *J. Chem. Eng. Japan.*, 10:468 (1977).
31. Fukushima, S., and Kusaka, K., *J. Chem. Eng. Japan.*, 11:241 (1978).
32. Gianetto, A., Baldi, G., and Specchia, V., *Ing, Chim. Ital.*, 6:125 (1970).
33. Sicardi, S., Gerhard, H., and Hofman, H., *Chem Eng. J.*, 18:173 (1979).
34. Drinkenburg, A. A. H., Rijksumversiteit Grömingen, Grömingen, The Netherlands, private communication (1982).
35. Ng, K. M., *I & EC Fundamentals*, (1984).
36. Wijffels, J. B., Verloop, J., and Zuiderweg, F. J., *Advances in Chemistry*, H. M. Hulburt, (Ed.), 133:151 (1974).
37. Dimenstein, D. M., Zimmerman, S. P., and Ng, K. M., *ACS Symposium Series*, M. P. Duduković and P. L. Mills (Eds.), 237:3 (1983).
38. Charpentier, J. C., in *Chemical Engineering of Gas-Liquid-Solid Catalyst Reactions*, G. A. L'Homme (Eds.), CEBEDOC, Liège, Belgium, 1979, p. 78.
39. Larkins, R. P., White, R. R., and Jeffrey, D. W., *AIChE J.*, 7:231 (1961).
40. Sato, Y. T., *J. Chem. Eng. (Japan)*, 6:147 (1973).
41. Charpentier, J. C., Prost, C., and LeGoff, P., *Chem. Eng. Sci.*, 24:774 (1969).
42. Turpin, J. L., and Huntington, R. L., *AIChE J.*, 13:1196 (1967).
43. Clements, L. D., and Schmidt, P. C., *AIChE J.*, 26:314 (1980).
44. Lockhart, R. W., and Martinelli, R. C., *Chem. Engr. Progress*, 45:39 (1949).
45. Hutton, B. E. G., and Leung, L. S., *Chem. Eng. Sci.*, 29:1681 (1974).
46. Kan, K. M., and Greenfield, P. F., *I & EC Process Des. Develop.*, 17:482 (1978).
47. Kan, K. M., and Greenfield, P. F., *I & EC Process Des. Develop.*, 18:740 (1979).
48. Colombo, A. J., Baldi, G., and Sicardi, S., *Chem. Eng. Sci.*, 31:1101 (1976).
49. Mills, P. L., and Duduković M. P., *AIChE J.*, 27:893 (1981).
50. Mills, P. L., and Duduković M. P., *AIChE J.*, 28:526 (1982).
51. Mata, A. R., and Smith, J. M., *Chem. Eng. J.*, 22:229 (1981).
52. Germain, A., Lefebvre, and L'Homme, G. A., *Advances in Chemistry*, H. Hulbert (Ed.), 133:164 (1974).
53. Hanika, J., et al., *Chem. Eng. Communications*, 2:19 (1975).
54. Hanika, J., *Chem. Eng. J.*, 12:193(1976).
55. Sedricks, W., and Kenney, C. N., *Chem. Eng. Sci.*, 28:559 (1973).
56. Pismen, L. M., *Chem. Eng. Sci.*, 31:693 (1976).
57. Kim, D. H., and Kim, Y. G., *J. Chem. Eng. Japan.*, 14:311 (1981).
58. Charpentier, J. C., et al., *Chem. Ind. Gemie Chim.*, 99:803 (1968).
59. Verhoeven, L., and Van Romray, P., *Proc. 7th European Symp. Compé. Appl. Chem. Ind.*, Erlangen, 1974, p. 90.
60. Mersmann, A., *Verfahrenstechmk*, 6:203 (1972).

61. Lynn, S., Straatemeier, J. R., and Kramers, H., *Chem. Eng. Sci.*, 4:63 (1955).
62. Davidson, J. F., and Cullen, E. J., *Trans, Instn. Chem. Engrs.*, 35:51 (1957).
63. Davidson, J. F., et al., *Trans. Instn. Chem. Engrs.*, 37:122 (1959).
64. Davidson, J. F., *Trans. Instn. Chem. Engrs.*, 37:131 (1959).
65. Charpentier, J. C., Prost, C., and LeGoff, P., *Chim. Ind. Gemie Chim.*, 100:653 (1968).
66. Jesser, B. W., and Elgin, J. C., *Trans. Am Inst. Chem. Engrs.*, 39:277 (1943).
67. Satterfield, C. N., and Way, P. E., *AIChE J.*, 18:305 (1972).
68. Hochman, J. M., and Effron, E., *I & EC Fundamentals*, 8:63 (1969).
69. Otake, T., and Okada, K., *Kagaku Kogaku*, 17:176 (1963).
70. Mitchell, R. W., and Furzer, I. A., *Trans. Instn. Chem. Engrs.*, 50:334 (1972).
71. El-Hisnawi, A. A., D.Sc. Thesis, Washington University, St. Louis, Missouri, August, 1981.
72. Matsuura, A., Akehata, T., and Shirai, T., *J. Chem. Eng. Japan*, 12:263 (1979).
73. Jiang, T. S., Oh, S. G., and Slattery, J. C., *J. Coll. Inter. Sci.*, 69:74 (1979).
74. Roberts, G. W., and Yadwadkar, S. R., *AIChE National Meeting*, Dallas, Texas, February, 1972.
75. Shulman, H. L., Ullrich, C. F., and Wells, N., *AIChE J.*, 1:247, (1955).
76. Crine, M., and Marchot, P., in *Chemical Engineering of Gas-Liquid-Solid Reactions*, G. A. L'Homme (Ed.), CEBEDOC, Liège, Belgium, 1979, p. 134.
77. Schwartz, J. G., Weger, E., and Duduković, M. P., *AIChE J.*, 22:953 (1976).
78. Clements L. D., and Schmidt, P. C., *69 Annual AIChE Meeting*, Chicago, November, 1976.
79. Crine, M. D., and L'Homme, G. A., *ACS Symposium Series*, J. Wei and C. Georgakis (Eds.), 196:407 (1981).
80. Levenspiel, O., *Chemical Reaction Engineering*, Wiley, 2nd ed., 1974.
81. Buffham, B. A., Gibilaro, L. G., and Rathor, M. N., *AIChE J.*, 16:218 (1970).
82. Deans. H. A., *Soc. Petrol. Engrs. J.*, 3:49 (1963).
83. Furzer, I. A., and Michell, R. W., *AIChE J.*, 16:380 (1970).
84. Glaser, M. B., and Lichtenstein, I., *AIChE J.*, 9:30 (1963).
85. Lips, J., and Hoogendoorn, C. J., *Can. J. Chem. Eng.*, 43:125 (1965).
86. Mears, D. E., *Chem. Eng. Sci.* 26:1361 (1971).
87. Schiesser, W. E., and Lapidus, L., *AIChE J.*, 7:163 (1961).
88. Schwartz, J. G., and Roberts, G. W., *I & EC Process Des. Develop.*, 12:262 (1973).
89. Duduković, M. P., *AIChE J.*, 23:940 (1977).
90. Duduković, M. P., and Mills, P. L., *ACS Symp, Series*, V. W. Weekman and D. Luss (Eds.) 65:387 (1978).
91. Mills, P. L., and Duduković, M. P., *I & EC Fundamentals*, 18:139 (1979).
92. Ramachandran, P. A., and Smith, J. M., *AIChE J.*, 25:538 (1979).
93. Morita, S., and Smith, J. M., *I & EC Fundamentals*, 17:113 (1978).
94. Tan, C. S., and Smith, J. M., *Chem. Eng. Sci.*, 35:1601 (1980).
95. Porter, K. E., *Trans. Instn. Chem. Engrs.*, 46:T69 (1968).
96. Porter, K. E., Barnett, V. D., and Templeman, J. J., *Trans. Instn. Chem. Engrs.*, 46:T74 (1968).
97. Porter., K. E., and Templeman, J. J., *Trans. Intn. Chem. Engrs.*, 46:T86 (1968).
98. Weekman, V. W., Myers, J. E., *AIChE J.*, 10:951 (1964).
99. Jameson, G. J., *Trans. Instn. Chem. Engrs.*, 44:T198 (1966).
100. Prchlik, J., et al., *Coll. Czech. Chem. Commun.*, 40:845 (1975).
101. Prchlik, J., *Coll. Czech. Chem. Commun.*, 40:3145 (1975).
102. Prchlik, J., et at., *Coll. Czech. Chem. Commun.*, 43:862 (1978).
103. Herskowitz, M., and Smith, J. M., *AIChE J.*, 24:439 (1978).
104. Herskowitz, M., and Smith, J. M., *AIChE J.*, 24:450 (1978.)
105. Specchia, V., Rossini, A., and Baldi, G., *Ing. Chim. Ital.*, 10:171 (1974).
106. Baldi, G., and Specchia, V., *Ing. Chim. Ital.*, 12:107 (1976).
107. Sicardi, S., Baldi, G., and Specchia, V., *Chem. Eng. Sci.*, 35:1775 (1980).
108. Sylvester, N. D., and Pitayagulsarn, P., *Can. J. Chem. Eng.*, 53:599 (1975).
109. Beimesch, W. E., and Kessler, D. P., *AIChE J.*, 17:1160 (1971).
110. Michell, R. W., and Furzer, I. A., *Chem. Eng. J.*, 4:53 (1972).
111. Elenkov, D., and Kolev, N., *Chem. Eng Technol.*, 44:845 (1972).

112. Buffham, B. A., and Rathor, M. N., *Trans. Instn. Chem. Engrs.*, 56:266 (1978).
113. Kobayashi, S., et al., *Kogaku Kagaku Ronbunshu*, 5:256 (1979).
114. Ross, L. D., *Chem. Engr. Progress*, 61:77 (1965).
115. Mears, D. E., *Adv. Chem. Ser.*, H. Hulburt (Ed.), 133:218 (1974).
116. Bondi, A., *Chem. Tech.*, 1:185 (1971).
117. Henry, H. C., and Gilbert, J. B., *I & EC Proc. Des. Develop.*, 12:328 (1973).
118. Puranik S. S., and Vogelpohl, A., *Chem. Eng. Sci.*, 29:501 (1974).
119. Sylvester, N, D., and Pitayagulsarn, P., *Can. J. Chem. Eng.*, 52:539 (1974).
120. Suzuki, M., and Smith, J. M., *AIChE J.*, 16:882 (1970).
121. Shulman, H. L., et al., *AIChE J.*, 1:253 (1955).
122. Specchia, V., Baldi, G., and Gianetto, A., *I & EC Proc. Des. Develop.*, 17:372 (1978).
123. Onda, K., Takeuchi, H., and Kayama, Y., *Kagaku Kogaku*, 31:126 (1967).
124. Krauze, R., and Serwinski, M., *Inzyn. Chemiczna*, 1:415 (1971).
125. Lapidus, L., *Ind. Eng. Chem.*, 49:1000 (1957).
126. Schiesser, W. E., and Lapidus, L., *AIChE J.*, 7:163 (1961).
127. Perl, W., *Circ. Res.*, 36:352 (1975).
128. Buffham, B. A., and Kropholler, H. W., *Chem. Eng. Sci.*, 28:1081 (1973).
129. Sagara, M., Schneider, P., and Smith, J. M., *Chem. Eng. J.*, 1:47 (1970).
130. Baldi, G., and Gianetto, A., in *Chemical Engineering of Gas-Liquid-Solid Catalyst Reactions*, G. L'Homme (Ed.), CEBEDOC, Liège, Belgium, 1979, p. 109.
131. Kesten, A. S., and Sangiovanni, J. J., *Chem. Eng. Sci.*, 26:533 (1971).
132. Herskowitz, M., and Mosseri, S., *I & EC Fundamentals*, 22(1):4 (1983).
133. Baldi, G., Gianetto, A., and Sicardi, S., "Oxidation of Ethyl Alcohol in Trickle-Bed Reactors: Analysis of the Conversion Rate," submitted to *Can. J. Chem. Eng.* (1984).
134. Van Klinken, J., in *Chemical Engineering of Gas-Liquid-Solid Catalyst Reactions*, G. L'Homme (Ed.), CEBEDOC, Liège, Belgium, 1979, p. 172.
135. Hartley, D. E., and Murgatroyd, W., *Int. Jnl. Heat and Mass Trans.*, 7:1003 (1964).
136. Hobler, T., *Chemia Stosow*, 213:145 (1964).
137. Hobler, T., *Chemia Stosow*, 213:265 (1968).
138. Bankoff, S. G., *Int. Jnl. Heat and Mass Trans.*, 14:2143 (1971).
139. Mikielewicz, J., and Moszynski, J. R., *Int. Jnl. Heat and Mass Trans.*, 19:771 (1976).
140. Murgatroyd, W., *Int, Jnl. Heat and Mass Trans.*, 8:297 (1965).
141. Norman, W. S., and McIntyre, V., *Trans. Instn. Chem. Engrs.*, 38:301 (1960).
142. Hsu, Y. Y., Simon, F. F., and Lad, J. F., *Chem. Eng. Progr. Symp. Ser.*, 61:139 (1965).
143. Zuber, N., and Staub F. W., *Int. Jnl. Heat and Mass Trans.*, 9:897 (1966).
144. McPherson, G. D., *Int. Jnl. Heat and Mass Trans.*, 13:1133 (1970).
145. Bankoff, S. G., *Int. Jnl. Heat and Mass Trans.*, 14:377 (1971).
146. Orell, A., and Bankoff, S. G., *Int. Jnl. Heat and Mass Trans.*, 14:1835 (1971).
147. Fujita, T., and Ueda, T., *Int. Jnl. Heat and Mass Trans.*, 21:97 (1978).
148. Sharon, A., and Orell, A., *Int. Jnl. Heat and Mass Trans.*, 23:547 (1980).
149. Ponter, A. B., et al., *Int. Jnl. Heat and Mass Trans.*, 10:349 (1967).
150. Boyadiev, C., *Int Jnl. Heat and Mass Trans.*, 25:535 (1982).
151. Conder J. R., Gunn, D. J., and Shaikh, A. S., *Int. Jnl. Heat and Mass Trans.*, 25:1113 (1982).
152. Scheidegger, A. E., *The Physics of Flow Through Porous Media*, University of Toronto Press, 1960.
153. Bear, J., *Dynamics of Fluids in Porous Media*, American Elsevier, 1972.
154. Chizmadzhev, Y. A., et al., *Makrokinetics of Processes in Porous Media* (in Russian), Nauka (Moscow), 1971.
155. Luikov, A. V., *Heat and Mass Transfer in Capillary Porous Bodies*, Pergamon Press, 1976.
156. Greenkorn, R. A., *Flow Phenomena in Porous Media*, Marcel Dekker (1983).
157. Dullien, F. A. L., *Chem. Eng. J.*, 10:1 (1975).
158. Luikov, A. V., *Int. Chem. Eng.*, 16(1):54 (1976).
159. Nikolaevskii, V. N., and Somov, B. E., *Int. J. Multiphase Flow*, 4:203 (1978).
160. Wayner, P. C., Jr., *Int. Jnl. Heat and Mass Transfer*, 25(5):707 (1982).
161. Drobyshevich, V. I., Kirilov V. A., and Kuzin, N. A., *Chem. Eng. Commun.* (1984).

162. Saito H., and Seki, N., *Trans. ASME Jnl. Heat Trans.*, 105 (1977).
163. Chen, O. T., and Rinker, R. G., *Chem. Eng. Sci.*, 34(1):51 (1979).
164. Mills, P. L., et al., *Chem. Eng. Sci.*, 36:947 (1981).
165. Herskowitz, M., *Chem. Eng. Sci.*, 36:1099 (1981).
166. Herskowitz, M., *Chem. Eng. Sci.*, 36:1665 (1981).
167. Martinez, O. M., Barreto, G. F., and Lemcoff, N. O., *Chem. Eng. Sci.*, 36:901 (1981).
168. Goto, S., Lakota, A., and Levec, J., *Chem. Eng. Sci.*, 36:157 (1981).
169. Capra, V., et al., paper presented at the *Second World Congress for Chemical Engineering*, Montreal, Canada, October 1981.
170. Sakornwimon, W., and Sylvester, N. D., *I & EC Process Des. Develop.*, 21:16 (1982).
171. Sylvester, N. D., Kulkarni, A. A., and Carberry, J. J., *Can. Jnl. Chem. Eng.*, 53:313 (1975).
172. Lee, H. H., and Smith J. M., *Chem. Eng. Sci.*, 37:223 (1982).
173. Goto, S., Watabe, S., and Matsubara, M., *Can. J. Chem. Eng.*, 54:551 (1976).
174. Goto, S., and Smith, J. M., *AIChE J.*, 21:714 (1975).
175. Goto, S., and Smith, J. M., *AIChE J.*, 24:286 (1978).
176. Goto, S., and Smith, J. M., *AIChE J.*, 24:294 (1978).
177. Levec, J., and Smith J. M., *AIChE J.*, 22:159 (1976).
178. Hartman, M., and Coughlin, R. W., *Chem. Eng. Sci.*, 27:867 (1972).
179. Herskowitz, M., *Chem. Eng. J.*, 22:167 (1981).
180. Turek, F., and Lange, R., *Chem. Eng. Sci.*, 36:569 (1981).
181. Turek, F., and Lange, R., *Chem. Eng. Sci.*, 38:275 (1983).
182. Germain, A., Lefebvre, A. G., and L'Homme, G. A., *ACS Symposium Series*, V. W. Weekman and D. Luss (Eds.), 65:411 (1978).
183. Crine, M., Marchot, P., and L'Homme, G. A., *Chem. Eng. Sci.*, 35:50 (1980).
184. Ruiz, P., et al., *ACS Symposium Series*, M. P. Duduković and P. L. Mills (Eds.), 237:15 (1984).
185. Stanek, V., et al., *Chem. Eng. Sci.*, 36:1045 (1981).
186. Stanek, V., and Hanika, J., *Chem. Eng. Sci.*, 37:1283 (1982).
187. Mills, P. L., Beaudry, E. G., and Duduković, M. P., *Trans. Instn. Chem. Engrs.* (ISCRE 8, Edinburgh, September, 1984, accepted).
188. Goto, S., and Smith, J. M., *AIChE J.*, 21:706 (1975).
189. Dwivedi, P. N., and Upadhayay, S. N., *I & EC Process Des. Develop.*, 16:157 (1977).

CHAPTER 33

RESIDENCE-TIME MODELING OF TRICKLE-FLOW REACTORS

P. F. Greenfield and D. Sudarmana

Department of Chemical Engineering
University of Queensland
St. Lucia, Australia

CONTENTS

INTRODUCTION

Knowing the macromixing characteristics of three-phase trickle-flow reactors not only provides the most reliable information on the gas- and liquid-phase residence times, but as with other systems, allows conclusions to be reached on the deviation of the flow behavior of these two phases from the ideal conditions of plug flow.

In trickle-flow systems, deviation from ideal behavior is caused by axial and radial dispersive effects, by short-circuiting and channeling, and importantly, by the existence of stagnant liquid zones. Because interphase, interparticle, and intraparticle heat and mass transfer depend on the mixing characteristics of each of the phases, knowledge of these characteristics is necessary in predicting reactor performance. Obtaining such knowledge involves measuring the residence-time distribution (RTD) of each phase within the trickle-flow system.

Trickle-flow reactors involve a column packed with catalyst particles over which the liquid flows in a thin film and through which the gas phase flows, usually as a continuous phase; the most common mode of operation of such systems is for both phases to flow cocurrently downwards. It is important to note that a number of flow regimes may exist in trickle-flow systems, the transition from one regime to another being governed by factors such as the gas and liquid flow rates, the fluid properties, the particle size, shape, and wetting properties and the packing density of these particles in the reactor. Significant differences in the macromixing behavior of the system have been noted for the different flow regimes.

For reactions in which the gas and liquid phases must be contacted with a solid catalyst, a trickle-flow reactor is often preferred over other three-phase systems, such as bubble-columns or slurry reactors, because high conversion and high selectivity can be achieved for relatively low capital and operating costs. Some past reactor performance studies for different reaction systems are listed in Table 1; the majority of these involve either hydrogen or oxygen as the gas phase. In the petroleum industry, trickle-flow reactors are used for hydrodesulphurization, hydrodenitrogenation, hydrocracking, hydrotreating, and various other hydrogenation reactions. Other applications have included the reaction of sulphur dioxide on wetted carbon, the oxidation of glucose to gluconic acid, the hydrogenation of glucose to sorbitol, and the synthesis of butynediol. Some useful reviews on trickle-flow reactors may be found in the literature [14, 28, 38, 41, 78, 81, 93].

As mentioned earlier, the performance of a multiphase chemical reactor depends both on the intrinsic kinetics of the reaction(s) and on the mixing processes occurring in the reactor. The residence time distribution (RTD) characterizes the macromixing phenomena in such systems by measuring the age distribution of various fluid elements inside the reactor. Numerous reviews on residence-time distribution theory are found in the literature [28, 40, 41, 51, 66, 71, 78, 81, 82, 96].

There are two extreme (ideal) cases of mixing in a flow reactor; these are plug flow and complete mixing. Plugflow is achieved when all the fluid elements have the same velocity and spend exactly the same amount of time inside the reactor; this implies complete radial mixing and a total absence of longitudinal mixing. The latter case is achieved when the composition of the exit stream is identical to the composition everywhere inside the reactor, i.e., a fluid element entering the system can

Table 1
Reactor Performance Studies in Trickle-Flow Systems

Reaction	Reference
Deuterium exchange between hydrogen and water	Enright and Chuang [20]
Hydrocracking of heavy gas oil	Henry and Gilbert [35]
Hydrodenitrogenation	Flinn et al. [24]
Hydrodesulfurization	Montagna and Shah [60]
Hydrogenation of α-methylstyrene	Babcock et al. [7]
	Satterfield et al. [78]
	Germain et al. [27]
Hydrogenation of benzene	Satterfield and Ozel [77]
Hydrogenation of crotonaldehyde	Sedricks and Kenney [80]
Hydrogenation of glucose to sorbitol	Bondi [10]
Hydrotreating	Mears [54]
	Paraskos et al. [64]
Isomerization of cyclopropane	Satterfield and Way [76]
Oxidation of formic acid in water	Goto and Smith [30, 31]
Oxidation of glucose to gluconic acid	Tsukamoto et al. [91]
Oxidation of SO_2 on wetted carbon	Hartman and Coughlin [34]
	Goto and Smith [32]
	Mata and Smith [52]

spend anywhere between zero and an infinite amount of time inside the reactor. Most real reactors fall in between these two extreme cases.

In trickle-flow systems, plug flow of the two fluids is desired. Deviations, however, from plug flow are commonly observed, especially with the liquid phase. Insignificant deviation from plug flow behavior has been observed for the gas phase, except in the bubble flow regime. Studies on the gas phase RTD can be found in works by DeMaria and White [18], Sater and Levenspiel [73], and Hochman and Effron [39]. The residence-time modeling of trickle-flow reactors, in particular the liquid phase, is centered around explaining deviations from plug flow. This work reviews liquid-phase residence-time distribution techniques and models and the estimation techniques used in obtaining model parameters. A brief description of the possible flow regimes in trickle-flow systems is provided to allow proper classification of the RTD work reported in the literature.

FLOW REGIMES IN TRICKLE-FLOW REACTORS

The existence of different flow regimes for the cocurrent downflow of gas and liquid in a packed bed is well known, and several workers have presented flow maps for the easy identification of the various regimes [13, 28, 41, 53, 74, 78, 89, 95]. The flow regime transition is generally defined as the condition at which a slight increase in gas or liquid flow rate causes a sharp increase in the root mean square wall pressure fluctuations [82].

Results indicate that there are four distinct flow regimes which depend on the gas and liquid flow rates, the nature and properties of the liquid, the nature and size of the packing, and the packing density:

- Trickling-flow regime (gas continuous)
- Pulsing-flow regime
- Spray-flow regime
- Bubble-flow regime (liquid continuous)

The transition between trickling and pulsing flow is sometimes referred to as rippling flow. Figure 1 shows these flow regimes and the flow-regime boundaries. This flow map is based on the work of Charpentier and Favier [13] and Gianetto et al. [28]. The flow-regime boundaries are by no means rigid and are intended only as rough guides, especially for packing sizes smaller than 3 mm, since the flow map was obtained from packed beds with packing size between 3 and 8 mm. With smaller packings, the transition between flow regimes is not as sharp as with the larger packings [53]. The parameters λ and ψ, appearing on the axes of the flow map, are corrections to be applied if the fluids in the system are not air and water.

At low gas and liquid rates, the liquid trickles over the packing as a laminar film, or as rivulets or drops, while the gas flows continuously through the external voids in the bed. This flow regime is usually encountered in laboratory- and pilot-scale operations. As the gas rate is increased, the drag force becomes sufficient to cause turbulence in the liquid phase, particularly at channel restrictions. Some liquid elements may also become separated from the film and move as slugs or droplets through the channels. This type of flow is typical of rippling or the transition between the trickling- and pulsing-flow regimes. Further increases in the gas rate increase the size of the slugs and drops which ultimately become large enough to block the channels. In turn, this leads to pulsing flow where alternate gas-rich and liquid-rich slugs pass through the column. The pulsing flow regime is often encountered in commercial petroleum processing. In packed beds with small packings, the size of the flow channels is correspondingly reduced, and this combined with surface tension effects, can cause early bridging or blocking of some of the flow paths, explaining the more gradual change from the trickling-flow regime to the pulsing flow regime.

Blok and Drinkenburg [9] studied several properties of these pulses. They concluded that pulse frequency is linearly controlled by the difference between the real liquid velocity and the real liquid velocity at the onset of pulsing; that the pulse holdup is determined by the gas flow, increasing slightly at higher liquid rates; that the holdup at the front of a pulse is generally 60% higher than the holdup between pulses and that this value is independent of gas and liquid rates; and that pulse

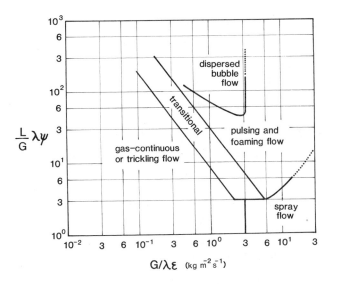

Figure 1. Flow regimes in cocurrent gas-liquid downflow through packed beds [13, 28].

velocity and height are independent of liquid rate and depend on the gas rate only, at low gas velocities.

If the gas rate is increased further, the liquid bridges are formed and destroyed more rapidly and the liquid is transported in the form of small droplets or as a fine mist. This type of flow, where the gas phase is continuous and the liquid phase partly covers the packing surface as a film and is partly in the form of a fine mist, is termed spray flow. Again with small packings, the void spaces between the packings are relatively smaller and, therefore, the small droplets of liquid have a higher chance of combining with each other. This makes the change from pulsing to spray flow more difficult to pinpoint.

At very low liquid flow rates, pulsing flow is not observed since liquid bridges do not form. As a result, the flow regime changes directly from trickling flow to spray flow.

For a sufficiently high gas flow rate, increasing the liquid flow rate will lead to a transition from trickling flow to pulsing flow for reasons similar to those already mentioned. The increase in liquid flow rate is accommodated by an increasing film thickness or by an increase in the number of rivulets, which will then block the flow channels causing alternate gas-rich and liquid-rich regions to form (pulsing flow). As the liquid flow rate is further increased, the liquid phase tends to fill all the voids in the system; the gas phase then moves as large bubbles through the reactor (known as bubble-flow regime). Further increases in the liquid flow rate result in the formation of smaller bubbles. This flow regime is called the dispersed-bubble flow regime. The two flow regimes are usually not differentiated.

For very high gas flow rates, the bubble-flow regime is generally not observed since the pressure gradient is large enough to push through any additional liquid which would otherwise accumulate in the void spaces around the packing. At still higher gas flow rates, only the spray flow regime is observed.

Several factors are found to affect the transition from trickling to pulsing flow. Chou et al. [15] noted that, for a constant gas flow rate, this transition occurred at higher liquid flow rates as the bed void fraction is increased. This can be explained in terms of the earlier discussion. The inclusion of a bed voidage term in the flow map was suggested by Gianetto et al. [28]. Packing wettability is another factor which can shift the regime transition boundary. The experimental data of Chou et al. [15] indicate that the flow transition from trickling to pulsing flow occurs at higher gas and liquid flow rates for nonwettable solids compared to wettable solids. The foaming properties of the liquid also affect this transition, especially with small packings, where capillary and surface tension effects become significant.

Kan and Greenfield [45] noted the existence of multiple pressure-drop and liquid-holdup values for the same operating conditions for packed beds with small preflooded packings. The actual steady-state value depended on the maximum gas velocity which had been achieved in the column. As this maximum gas velocity increased, the steady-state pressure drop for any set of operating conditions was found to decrease (see Figure 2). All experimental data were collected in the gas-continuous regime.

Specchia and Baldi [86] simplified the flow regime classification by defining two flow regimes— a low interaction regime, which covers the trickling flow regime, and a high interaction regime which includes the three other flow regimes defined earlier. While such a classification is correct, it ignores the unique characteristics of each phase in particular regimes; hence, while it may be suitable for the determination of pressure drop, it is not adequate from an RTD standpoint.

Because the behavior of each phase differs in the various flow regimes, any proposed RTD model should be based on the actual flow patterns which characterize a particular regime. Most of the RTD work reported in the literature and discussed in this review fails to specify the flow regime in which the data were collected. This, however, is not such a limitation as might be thought, since the fact that most data have been collected on small- and pilot-scale systems implies that the trickling-flow regime is the normal regime in which the reactor has been operated. In light of the advances in quantifying two-phase flow regimes, however, it is recommended that future work characterize the particular flow patterns experimentally. Additionally, it will become apparent to the reader that the trickle-flow regime is the only operating regime in which the liquid phase RTD has been characterized adequately. The pulsing regime, in view of its industrial significance, has not been investigated in a thorough fashion.

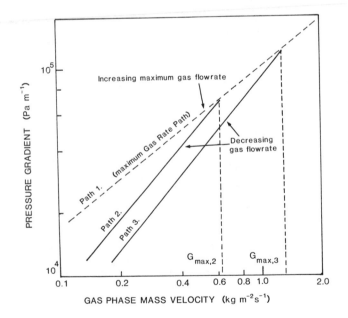

Figure 2. Multiple hydrodynamic states: effect of gas flow rate on pressure gradient in trickle-flow reactor. The solid lines indicate the pressure gradients found in the system at gas flow rates below the maximum gas flow rate applied to the system [43].

THEORETICAL ASPECTS OF RESIDENCE-TIME DISTRIBUTIONS

For any element of fluid flowing through a reactor, the time spent in the reactor can vary from 0 to ∞. A fluid element inside the reactor can be characterized by its *internal age*, t_I (i.e., by the time it has spent in the reactor) and by its life expectation, t_L (i.e., by the additional time it will spend in the reactor before leaving it). A fluid element leaving the system can be characterized by its residence time, t_R (i.e., by the time it spent in the reactor from the moment it entered until it left). For any particular element of fluid:

$$t_R = t_I + t_L \tag{1}$$

For all fluid elements entering and leaving the system, density functions can be defined which reflect the particular mixing patterns in any system [51, 71, 96]. These functions are summarized in Table 2.

The Dirac impulse function and the Heaviside step function are idealized forms of the most common tracer injection strategies for flow reactor systems. Originally analyzed by Danckwerts [17], the responses to these two inputs represent a starting point for RTD analysis of reactors.

Dirac Impulse Function

A hypothetical concentration C_o is defined which reflects the concentration that would exist in the reactor if the tracer were instantaneously and uniformly distributed in the available volume.

$$C_o \equiv M/V \tag{2}$$

Conditions at the tracer inlet position are given by:

$$C_E = C_o \tau_s \, \delta(t) = M/Q \, \Delta t \tag{3}$$

$$\text{where} \quad \delta(t) = \begin{bmatrix} 0 & t \neq 0 \\ \infty & t = 0 \end{bmatrix} \tag{4}$$

τ_s = space time = V/Q

$$\int_0^\infty \delta(t) \, dt = 1 \tag{5}$$

(Note: $\int_0^\infty \delta(t - t_o) f(t) \, dt = f(t_o)$)

At some output position removed from the inlet, the tracer concentration is followed as a function of time, $C(t)$. The following relationships hold:

$$M = \int_0^\infty QC(t) \, dt \tag{6}$$

$$C^*(t) = \frac{C(t)}{C_o} \equiv \text{C-curve} \tag{7}$$

$$\int_0^\infty C^*(t) \, dt = \tau_s \tag{8}$$

$$\int_0^\infty \bar{C}^*(\theta') \, d\theta' = 1 \tag{9}$$

where $\quad \theta' = t/\tau_s$
$\qquad \tau_s$ = space time = V/Q

A schematic plot of the C-curve is found in Figure 3.

Table 2
Density Functions that Characterize Fluid Mixing in Reactors

Name	Definition	Dimensionless Form	Mean Value	Diagrammatic Representation
Internal age distribution $I(t)$	$I(t)\, dt \equiv$ fraction of fluid elements within the reactor which have ages between t and t + dt $\int_0^\infty I(t)\, dt = 1$ $\int_0^\infty I(t)\, dt \equiv$ fraction of fluid elements within the reactor which have an age less than t_1	$\bar{I}(\theta') = \tau_s I(t)$ $\theta' = t/\tau_s$ $\tau_s =$ space time	$\bar{t}_I = \int_0^\infty t I(t)\, dt$ $\bar{\theta}_I = \bar{t}_I/\tau_s$	
Residence-time distribution $E(t)$	$E(t)\, dt \equiv$ fraction of fluid elements which remained in the reactor for a time between t and t + dt $\int_0^\infty E(t)\, dt = 1$	$\bar{E}(\theta') = \tau_s E(t)$ $\theta' = t/\tau_s$ $\tau_s =$ space time	$\bar{t}_R = \int_0^\infty t E(t)\, dt$ $\bar{\theta}_R = \bar{t}_R/\tau_s$	

	$\int_{t_1}^{\infty} E(t)\, dt \equiv$ fraction of fluid elements older than t_1 $E(t) = -\dfrac{dI(t)}{dt}$		
Cumulative exit-age distribution $F(t)$	$F(t) = \int E(t)\, dt$ $\equiv$ fraction of fluid elements in the outlet stream which have spent less than time t in the reactor	$\overline{F}(\theta') = F(t)$ —	
Life-expectation distribution $L(t)$	$L(t)\, dt \equiv$ fraction of fluid elements which are inside the reactor at time t and which will leave between t and $t + dt$ $L(t) = \dfrac{1}{\tau_s} \cdot \dfrac{E(t)}{I(t)}$	$\overline{L}(\theta') = \tau_s L(t)$ $\theta' = t/\tau_s$ $\tau_s =$ space time	$\bar{t}_L = \int_0^{\infty} t L(t)\, dt$ $\overline{\theta}_L = \bar{t}_L/\tau_s$

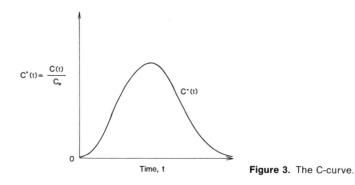

$$C^*(t) = \frac{C(t)}{C_o}$$

$C^*(t)$

Time, t

Figure 3. The C-curve.

Heaviside Step Function

The term C_o is defined as the size of the step change in concentration, i.e.

$$C_o \equiv C_f - C_i \tag{10}$$

where C_i, C_f = initial and final concentrations, respectively, of tracer in the inlet stream. Conditions at the tracer inlet are given by:

$$C_E = C_o H(t)$$

$$\text{where} \quad H(t) = \begin{bmatrix} 0 & t < 0 \\ 1 & t > 0 \end{bmatrix} \tag{11}$$

At some output point removed from the inlet, the concentration of tracer is followed as a function of time, $C(t)$. The following relationships hold.

$$F(t) = \frac{C(t) - C_i}{C_o}$$

$$= \frac{C(t) - C_i}{C_f - C_i} \equiv \text{F-curve} \tag{12}$$

A schematic plot of the F-curve is found in Figure 4.

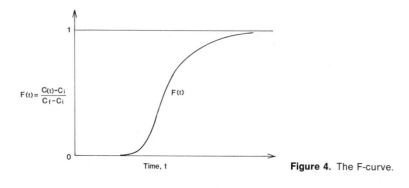

$$F(t) = \frac{C(t) - C_i}{C_f - C_i}$$

$F(t)$

Time, t

Figure 4. The F-curve.

Table 3
Relationships Between Theoretical
and Experimental Density Functions

Time Domain	Dimensionless
$F(t) + \tau_s I(t) = 1$	$\bar{F}(\theta') + \bar{I}(\theta') = 1$
$C^*(t) = \tau_s E(t) = \dfrac{\tau_s dF(t)}{dt}$	$\bar{C}^*(\theta') = \bar{E}(\theta') = \dfrac{d\bar{F}(\theta')}{d\theta'}$
$L(t) = \dfrac{1}{\tau_s} \cdot \dfrac{E(t)}{I(t)} = \dfrac{1}{\tau_s} \cdot \dfrac{C^*(t)}{(1 - F(t))}$	$\bar{L}(\theta') = \dfrac{\bar{E}(\theta')}{\bar{I}(\theta')} = \dfrac{\bar{C}^*(\theta')}{1 - \bar{F}(\theta')}$
$\theta' = t/\tau_s$	$\bar{I}(\theta') = \tau_s I(t)$
	$\bar{E}(\theta') = \tau_s E(t)$
$\tau_s = $ space time	$\bar{L}(\theta') = \tau_s L(t)$
$= V/Q$	$\bar{C}^*(\theta') = C^*(t)$
	$\bar{F}(\theta') = F(t)$

The relationships shown in Table 3 can be derived relating the theoretical density functions I, E, and L to the experimentally determined functions C* and F.

For the extreme reactor conditions of plug flow and perfect mixing, respectively, the theoretical and experimental age distribution functions are plotted in Figure 5. An additional measure, the holdback, is sometimes used to quantify the deviation from plug flow behavior. It is defined as follows:

Holdback ≡ fraction of fluid elements which stay in the reactor longer than the space time τ_s

$$= \int_1^\infty \bar{I}(\theta')\, d\theta' = \int_0^1 \bar{F}(\theta')\, d\theta' \tag{13}$$

$$= \begin{bmatrix} 0 & \text{for plug flow system} \\ 1/e & \text{for perfectly mixed system} \end{bmatrix} \tag{14}$$

PRACTICAL ASPECTS

The RTD function is usually obtained by injecting a tracer at the inlet or somewhere inside the reactor and observing the corresponding response at the exit or some point downstream from the injection point. The tracer input can take various forms, viz. pulse, step up or down, ramp, sinusoidal, or even a random input. These various input functions are shown in Figure 6. The response curve can then be compared to the theoretical curves obtained from the residence-time models.

Since the tracer flow path is supposed to represent closely the actual flow path of the reactants in the reactor, the choice of the tracer material is important. Shah [82] listed the basic requirements for a satisfactory tracer and tracer experiment. These are as follows:

• The tracer should be miscible with and have physical properties closely resembling the fluid stream under investigation.
• The tracer should be accurately detectable in small concentrations, so that the introduction of a tracer does not affect the flow pattern of the main fluid stream. Using small concentrations of tracer will often produce an approximately linear response in the detection device, so that prior calibration can be kept to a minimum.

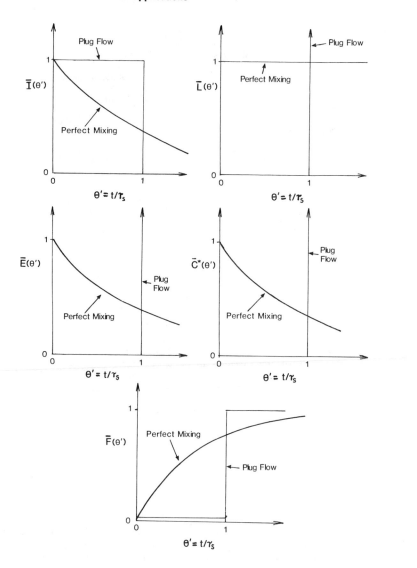

Figure 5. Comparison of theoretical age density functions I, E, and L with experimentally determined functions C* and F for the extreme conditions of plugflow and perfect mixing.

- The tracer should be nonreacting (inert) to keep the analysis simple.
- The tracer should not be transferrable from one phase to the other.
- The tracer detection device should cause the least amount of disturbance in the flow pattern. In this respect, a radioactive tracer has a distinct advantage over other chemical tracers in that the detection device can be placed externally.
- If heat is used as a tracer, the heat balance on the system should be properly checked.
- The sensitivity and response time of the tracer concentration recording equipment should be higher than the detection device.

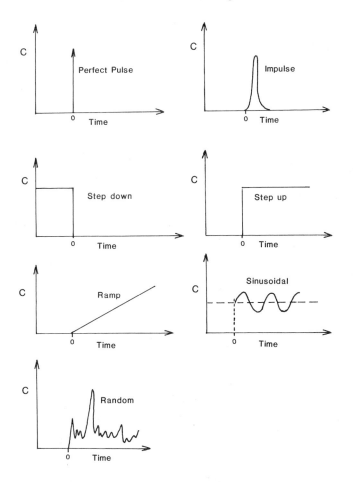

Figure 6. Schematic representation of various tracer input functions.

- The tracer itself and its detection device and other auxilliary equipment should be relatively cheap.
- In addition to the preceding list, it is preferable that the tracer molecules be of approximately the same size as and have similar properties to the reactant with the exception that it should be inert.

The most commonly used liquid-phase tracers are ionic salts and dyes, the reason being that the detection device is relatively cheap and capable of detecting low concentrations of tracer. Radio-active tracers have also been used [73]. Table 4 list some tracers used for determining the RTD function of the liquid and gas phases in gas-liquid-solid columns.

Although most tracer experiments employ inert tracers, some theoretical and experimental studies using reacting tracers have been reported [2, 19, 21, 23, 29, 58, 65, 68]. Parimi and Harris [65] showed that by using a reacting tracer exhibiting nonlinear kinetics, the most appropriate residence-time model can be chosen from a number of models which would have given identical response curves using nonreacting tracers.

Table 4
Tracers Used for Gas-Liquid Flow in Packed Columns

System	Tracers	Detection Device	Reference
Gas Phase			
Air-water	Helium	Sargent oscillometer	Lapidus [48]
Air-water	Argon 41	Baird Atomic Model 812B scintillation detector	Sater and Levenspiel [73]
N$_2$-Methanol	Helium	Gow Mac thermal conductivity detector	Hochman and Effron [39]
Liquid Phase			
Air-water	MgSO$_4$, KCl, HCl	Titration	Lapidus [48]
Air-water	HCl	Electrical conductivity	Kunigita et al. [47]
Air-water	H$_2$SO$_4$	Electrical conductivity	Stiegel and Shah [87, 88]
Air-water	NH$_4$Cl	Electrical conductivity	Hoogendoorn and Lips [42]
Air-water	NaCl	Electrical conductivity	Charpentier and Favier [13] Furzer and Michell [25] Van Swaaij et al [94]
Air-water	Methylene blue dye	FEK-M photoelectric colorimeter	Shestopalov et al. [83]
Air-water	Methylene blue dye	Spectrophotometer	Anderson et al. [4]
Air-water	Iodine 131	Baird atomic Model 812B scintillation detector	Sater and Levenspiel [73]
N$_2$-Methanol	KSCN	Electrical conductivity	Hochman and Effron [39]
Air-water	KCl	Electrical conductivity	Matsuura et al. [53]
Air-water	KCl, ZnSO$_4$	Electrical conductivity	Sicardi et al. [85]

Mathematically, ideal input signals are the easiest to treat; they are essentially impossible to achieve experimentally, however. For a nonideal or arbitrary input signal, the theoretical output signal can be calculated using the convolution theorem. Thus, for an arbitrary input function $C(t, 0)$ or $C(0, z)$, the response curve, $C(t, z)$, can be calculated from:

$$C(t, z) = \int_0^t G(\tau)C(t - \tau, 0) \, d\tau \tag{15}$$

$$= \int_0^z G(\zeta)C(0, z - \zeta) \, d\zeta \tag{16}$$

where $G(\tau)$ or $G(\zeta)$ is the response of the system to a perfect pulse input and $\tau(\zeta)$ is a dummy-time (distance) variable. The two forms of input functions are related by a simple mass balance equation provided that there is negligible dispersion or concentration gradient. For the liquid phase of a trickle-flow system this relationship may be written as:

$$Av_{sl} \int_0^\infty C(t, 0) \, dt = M = Ah_t \int_0^\infty C(0, z) \, dz \tag{17}$$

where A = the cross sectional area of the column
v_{sl} = the superficial liquid velocity
M = the total amount of tracer used
h_t = the total liquid holdup in the column

If the dispersion or concentration gradient is significant, then the first equality sign is not valid since a tracer injected at a particular position can disperse upstream and appear at a later time. The question of the appropriate boundary conditions to be used has been the subject of much discussion [71]. Discussion of these conditions and the effect they have on the solution of the model equations, describing the passage of a species through a flow reactor, may be found in Wen and Fan [96].

For nonradioactive tracers, the injection of an input pulse or step is generally achieved using either a hypodermic needle (pulse) or solenoid injection valve. In the case of radioactive tracers, the input pulse is produced by smashing an ampoule containing the radioactive tracer [73] in the path of the flowing fluid.

Levenspiel [51] pointed out that there are two ways of measuring/detecting the tracer concentration; these are the mixing-cup and the through-the-wall method. The former involves collecting small samples from the flowing fluid while the latter involves direct measurement within the reactor tube. Two different RTD curves are obtained from these methods. In practice, ionic salts are used for through-the-wall measurement in trickle-flow reactors; the conductivity cell can be made from two layers of conducting packing [94] or from a pair of parallel platinum wires woven into nylon netting [53]. To take care of the imperfect input signal, two detectors may be placed downstream from the injection point. The location of these detectors is important in determining the most appropriate boundary conditions for the axial-dispersion-type models.

Midoux and Charpentier [57] suggested an alternative method whereby two similar injections are made at two different positions upstream of the detector. This method eliminates the need of having two detectors.

The majority of literature studies have used either a pulse input or step input alone. For trickle-flow reactors packed with large (> 3 mm) nonporous packing, the two should give identical information about the reactor. When the packing is porous or small and nonporous, however, the use of only a pulse injection for the study of the RTD of the reactor could yield misleading information, especially when the experiment is conducted at relatively high liquid flow rates. This was pointed out by Lapidus [48] who performed tracer experiments using both porous and nonporous particles. The problem with a pulse input is that there may not be enough time for the tracer to diffuse in and out of the packing. With a step input this is not a problem, since before the introduction of the step change, the concentration of tracer inside the reactor would be everywhere the same. Residence time studies using step inputs are, therefore, superior to those using a pulse input, but the former are more expensive since they use more tracer and take longer to carry out. The equivalence between step and pulse inputs at low liquid flow rates is shown by Rothfield and Ralph [72].

Radial variations in the concentration of the tracer are usually neglected in residence-time studies of trickle-flow systems. This is justified when the ratio of column to particle diameter is greater than 20 or when the packing diameter is less than 5 mm [36, 37]. When radial variations are important, they will appear as flow maldistributions in an RTD study.

ANALYSIS OF TRACER EXPERIMENTS IN TRICKLE-FLOW REACTORS

As for all residence-time studies, the output from tracer injections into trickle-flow systems can be used to diagnose deviations from the ideal reactor behavior described earlier. Additionally, the resulting age distribution curve can be used to identify and test appropriate models for the reactor system and to estimate the parameters of these models. When the relevant kinetic functions are inserted, these models, in turn, will predict the reaction performance of the trickle-flow system.

A significant difference of trickle-flow reactors from other column reactors is that the available volume occupied by each of the flowing phases (i.e., gas and liquid) may not be known a priori (i.e., the theoretical liquid space time may not be able to be calculated). While various correlations exist for predicting liquid holdup in trickle-flow systems, tracer studies constitute the most reliable means of estimating the liquid-phase residence time. If used in this manner, the mean residence time calculated from the tracer output curve cannot, of itself, indicate flow nonidealities. The full curve, however, does contain this information.

The liquid-phase residence time is readily calculated for a pulse injection as long as the output device records some property of the tracer, which is concentration dependent, i.e., the output measurement device does not have to be calibrated absolutely. The mean residence time is then given by:

$$\bar{t}_R = \frac{\int_0^\infty ty(t)\,dt}{\int_0^\infty y(t)\,dt} \tag{18}$$

where $y(t)$ = output from measuring device

If the quantity of tracer injected is known (i.e., M) and if the output device is calibrated in concentration units $C(t)$, then the liquid flow rate, Q, the fractional liquid holdup, h_T, and the mean liquid phase residence time, $\bar{t}_R$, can be calculated as follows:

$$\bar{t}_R = \frac{\int_0^\infty tC(t)\,dt}{\int_0^\infty C(t)\,dt} \tag{19}$$

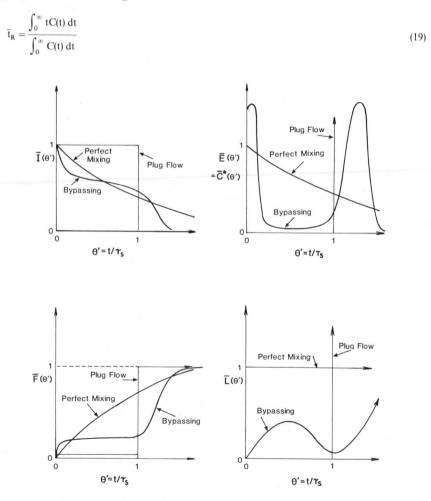

Figure 7. Schematic representation of theoretical and experimental density functions for a flow reactor with significant by-passing.

$$Q = \frac{M}{\int_0^\infty C(t)\, dt} \quad \text{(valid for small or moderate dispersion)} \tag{20}$$

$$h_T = \frac{Q \int_0^\infty t C(t)\, dt}{V_R \int_0^\infty C(t)\, dt} = \frac{Q \cdot \bar{t}_R}{V_R} \tag{21}$$

As mentioned, it is common in single-phase flow reactors to compare the experimentally determined mean residence time $\bar{t}_R$ against the calculated space time $\tau_s\,(= V/Q)$. If $\bar{t}_R < \tau_s$, then a dead zone is indicated (since the tail is not measured correctly) while, if $\bar{t}_R > \tau_s$, some form of bypassing may be indicated (since the initial peak is not properly considered). Provided a reliable, independent estimate of h_T can be obtained from hydrodynamic considerations, similar conclusions can be reached for trickle-flow systems.

It is preferable, however, in trickle-flow systems to utilize the additional information contained in the full output curve. The shapes of the expected age density functions for bypassing or channeling or for the existence of dead zones in a trickle-flow system are depicted in Figures 7–9.

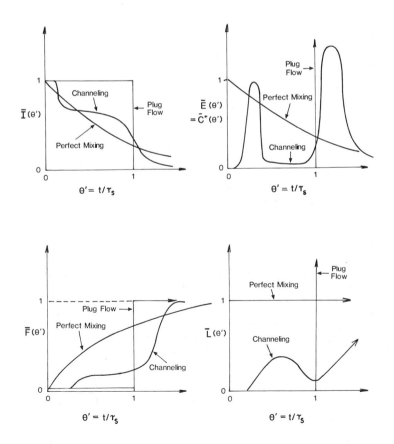

Figure 8. Schematic representation of theoretical and experimental density functions for a flow reactor with significant channeling.

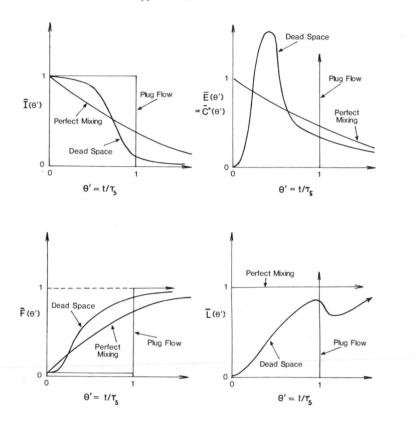

Figure 9. Schematic representation of theoretical and experimental density functions for a flow reactor with a large dead space.

PARAMETER ESTIMATION TECHNIQUES FOR RTD MODELING OF TRICKLE-FLOW REACTORS

While casual observation of the tracer output signal is useful for determining flow behavior which differs significantly from ideal conditions, the RTD curve contains significantly more information on the mixing processes within the reactor system. As mentioned, it can be used to identify and verify particular RTD models which can then be extended to the actual reaction situation. More sophisticated analysis and parameter estimation techniques are required, however, to delineate the particular contributions to the overall mixing behavior.

In modeling the residence-time distribution of a reactor, two types of problems are faced [5]:

- Representation problem, whereby a model incorporating particular features is chosen and typically fitted to the response curve generated for an idealized input.
- Identification problem, which involves choosing a set of parameters for the particular model which best relates the output to the input function.

Of course, the problems are linked in practice since ultimate acceptance or rejection of a proposed model depends both on its incorporating the key mixing mechanisms within its framework and on the model parameters having appropriate values.

Many different parameter estimation techniques are currently available. Those used in residence-time studies can be classified into four types:

1. Indirect methods which utilize cumulative properties of the experimental data such as moments, weighted moments, or weighted cumulants, or use Fourier analysis, frequency response fitting, or transfer function fitting.
2. Methods utilizing known properties of the experimental data/model.
3. Methods using combinations of 1 and 2.
4. Direct fitting of the model prediction to the experimental data. This method is the most accurate, but can only be used when the time-domain solution is available.

Parameter Estimation Using Indirect Methods

Indirect methods are used for those cases when the time domain solution is not known or, even if such a solution is possible, when the required computational time is excessive.

Moments analysis is a well-documented technique for parameter estimation in residence time studies [5, 22, 62, 92]. The n-th moment (n = 0, 1, 2 . . .) of a response curve is defined as:

$$m_n = \int_0^\infty t^n C(t)\, dt \tag{22}$$

$$= (-1)^n \lim_{s \to 0} \frac{d^n \bar{C}(s)}{ds^n} \tag{23}$$

where $\bar{C}(s)$ is the Laplace transformation of the concentration $C(t)$ with respect to time, t, and is defined as:

$$\bar{C}(s) = \int_0^\infty e^{-st} C(t)\, dt \tag{24}$$

Thus, if the solution of the proposed RTD model in the Laplace domain $\bar{C}(s)$ is known in terms of n different parameters, and $C(t)$ is known from experiments, then the n parameters can be determined by solving n simultaneous equations:

$$m_{i,\text{model (Equation 23)}} = m_{i,\text{expt (Equation 22)}} \tag{25}$$

$$i = 0 \text{ to } n - 1 \text{ or } i = 1 \text{ to } n$$

For the identification problem (i.e., with variable input and output distributions) it can be shown that:

$$\left[\frac{m_i}{m_0}\right]_{\text{model}} = \left[\frac{m_i}{m_0}\right]_{\text{output}} - \left[\frac{m_i}{m_0}\right]_{\text{input}} \tag{26}$$

$$i = 1 \text{ to } n$$

In practice, evaluation of the higher moments becomes increasingly inaccurate since calculation of the n-th moment involves the term t^n which becomes very large at high t and high n values; on the other hand, $C(t)$ at large t becomes very small and typically determined with less accuracy. To overcome this, Ostergaard and Michelsen [62] suggested the use of weighted moments, defined as:

$$w_k = \int_0^\infty t^k e^{-st} C(t)\, dt \tag{27}$$

$$= (-1)^k \frac{d^k \bar{C}(s)}{ds^k} \tag{28}$$

The preceding equations reduce to the ordinary moments when $s = 0$. Anderssen and White [5] pointed out, however, that no simple relationship exists for the input, output, and system-weighted moments for a linear-flow system. For the k-th weighted moment, the relationship is:

$$\left[\frac{w_k(s)}{w_0(s)}\right]_{output} = \sum_{i=0}^{k}\begin{bmatrix}k\\i\end{bmatrix}\left[\frac{w_{k-1}(s)}{w_0(s)}\right]_{system}\left[\frac{w_i(s)}{w_0(s)}\right]_{input} \tag{29}$$

The parameter estimation problem thus becomes more complicated for real systems with nonideal inputs.

Anderssen and White [5] proposed an alternative technique—the weighted cumulants method—by defining:

$$K_0(s) = \ln w_0(s) \tag{30}$$

and the recurrence relation

$$K_{k+1}(s) = -\frac{dK_k(s)}{ds} \tag{31}$$

A simple relationship between the input, output, and system-weighted cumulants for a linear-flow system is given by:

$$K_{k,system} = K_{k,output} - K_{k,input} \tag{32}$$

The cumulants can be easily computed from the weighted moments about the mean, which are defined as:

$$w'_k = \int_0^\infty \left(t - \frac{w_1}{w_0}\right)^k e^{-st}C(t)\,dt \tag{33}$$

Anderssen and White showed that:

$$K_1 = w_1/w_0 \tag{34}$$

$$K_2 = w'_2/w_0 \tag{35}$$

$$K_3 = w'_3/w_0 \tag{36}$$

$$K_4 = w'_4/w_0 - 3(w'_2/w_0)^2 \tag{37}$$

A useful property of the weighted cumulants lies in the shifting theorem. It can be shown that, if the weighted cumulant K'_k is the k-th weighted cumulant calculated from a new time scale for which a constant period t_D (such as a lag, breakthrough time) has been deducted, then:

$$K'_0 = K_0 + t_D s \tag{38}$$

$$K'_1 = K_1 - t_D \tag{39}$$

and

$$K'_i = K_i \qquad \text{for all } i \geq 2 \tag{40}$$

In using either the weighted-moments or the weighted-cumulants technique, a value for s must be specified. Anderssen and White [5] suggested the following equations for evaluating the optimum value of s:

$$s_{opt} = k/t_{mode} \tag{41}$$

for the representation problem, and

$$s_{opt} = k_{max}/(t_{mode,in} + t_{mode,out} - \Delta t_D) \tag{42}$$

for the identification problem, where t_{mode} is the time at which the signal is maximum (the peak of the signal), k_{max} is the highest-order cumulant/moment used for parameter estimation, and Δt_D is the difference in the time delays between the input and output signals. Again, the parameters for the model can be estimated by equating the analytical expressions for the cumulants or weighted moments to the numerically obtained values from Equations 32 to 37 or 27.

Sometimes, the mean and standard deviation of the RTD are used for the estimation of parameters (e.g., calculation of $\bar{t}_R$). This is an extension of the ordinary moments method with the mean, μ and standard deviation, σ defined as:

$$\mu = m_1/m_0 \tag{43}$$

$$\sigma^2 = m_2/m_0 - (m_1/m_0)^2 \tag{44}$$

For the identification problem:

$$\mu_{syst} = \mu_{output} - \mu_{input} \tag{45}$$

and

$$\sigma^2_{syst} = \sigma^2_{output} - \sigma^2_{input} \tag{46}$$

Fourier analysis and transfer-function fitting techniques have not been commonly used in residence-time studies of trickle-flow reactors and, hence, will not be discussed further. Some useful references on Fourier analysis may be found in Clements [16], Gangwal et al. [26], Fahim and Wakao [22], and on transfer function fitting in Ostergaard and Michelsen [62], Anderssen and White [5], and Fahim and Wakao [22].

Methods Utilizing Known Properties of the Experimental Data/Model

These methods involve deductions resulting from a comparison of various portions of the actual RTD curve with theoretical predictions. Generally, only one or two parameters can be determined in this way. This may produce, however, a significant reduction in the total amount of computation required when combined with Type 1 methods for determining the remaining parameters.

Hoogendoorn and Lips [42] suggested the use of the breakthrough time for estimating the value of ϕ, the ratio of the dynamic holdup to the total holdup, a parameter in the plug flow stagnancy model which is discussed later. They combined this approximation with the moments method to evaluate the other parameters. Since one parameter is known, one fewer moments expression needs to be evaluated (i.e., the n-th moment is not utilized), which reduces the computation time as well as improves the confidence limits of the parameters determined. Hochman and Effron [39] used a similar method in estimating parameters for their RTD model.

Bennett and Goodridge [8] used a step-decrease input and argued that the tail end of the RTD curve represents the removal of tracer from the stagnant pockets, after essentially all the tracer in the dynamic region has been removed. As such, the tail end of the RTD can be represented by an exponential decay, with the decay coefficient being numerically equal to the mass transfer coefficient. They also suggested a completely graphical method for estimating their model parameters, which will be discussed later.

Van Swaaij et al. [94] noted that the Bodenstein number for nonwettable and wettable packings differed considerably. The Bodenstein numbers obtained from the nonwettable packing experiments were considered to be free of stagnancy effects. Using this argument they claimed that the

Bodenstein number of a RTD model, which takes into account the stagnancy effects for a wettable packing can be independently determined from experiments with nonwettable packing of the same size.

Parameter Estimation Using Direct-Fitting Methods

The methods described so far will yield estimates of the model parameters which are very useful for cases in which RTD model solutions in the time domain are not available. For cases where the model solution is available, better estimates of the parameter values can be obtained by direct fitting to the time-domain response; "better" implies that there is less error area between the predicted and the experimental curves.

The "best" estimate of the parameters can be obtained by fitting the model to the experimental data using an optimization technique, for which a fitting criterion or an objective function needs to be defined.

The most commonly used criteria are:

1. Least squares deviation.
2. Least squares relative deviation.
3. Least absolute deviation.

Parameter values obtained by previously discussed methods can be used as starting values for the optimization routine to reduce the number of iterations needed. It is important to ensure that the optimum value obtained does not represent a local optimum.

Deviation of the predicted from the experimental curve can be caused either by an inadequacy in the model formulation or by a general lack of fit. In the former case, the model should be rejected for an alternative. In the latter case, a change in parameter value(s) may give a better fit. The question of "best" fit is open to debate; some researchers argue for the least-squares-deviation criterion since it weights the result towards the peak of the distribution where concentration can be measured with the greatest–accuracy. Others, such as Sicardi et al. [85], argue for the least-squares relative deviation criterion since it gives equal importance to the entire output curve. The answer lies in considering the accuracy of the measured experimental data and the distribution of the experimental errors associated with this measured data. If, as in most residence-time experiments, the sensitivity and accuracy of the detecting and recording devices remain approximately the same for the duration of the experiment, then, all data points (concentration of tracer) will have approximately the same absolute error associated with them. If this error is much smaller than the smallest data detected, then the least absolute deviation criterion can be used, since this criterion does not favor a better fitting of any particular part of the experimental curve. If, however, this error is of the same magnitude as or larger than the smallest data detected, then the least-squares deviation criterion should be used, since this criterion favors a better fitting of the peak of the distribution (i.e., the data with lowest relative error). If the sensitivity of the detecting and recording devices can be increased according to need (e.g., Bennett and Goodridge [8]), the least-squares relative deviation criterion should be used. This criterion favors a better fitting of the lower range data on linear coordinates, but is neutral on semilogarithmic coordinates.

An important point in considering possible parameter estimation techniques is that the parameter values obtained are sensitive to the estimation technique used. The work of Michell and Furzer [56], Sicardi et al. [85], and Kan [44] has shown this conclusively. Thus, in comparing the parameter values or correlations obtained by previous workers, it is recommended that the parameter estimation technique as well as the range of variables used be taken into consideration.

RESIDENCE-TIME MODELING OF TRICKLE-FLOW REACTORS

In this review, the term residence-time modeling will refer almost exclusively to the modeling of the liquid phase. As depicted in Figure 10, the trickle-flow reactor volume can be divided into three segments—the packing volume, the gas volumetric holdup, and the liquid volumetric holdup. The

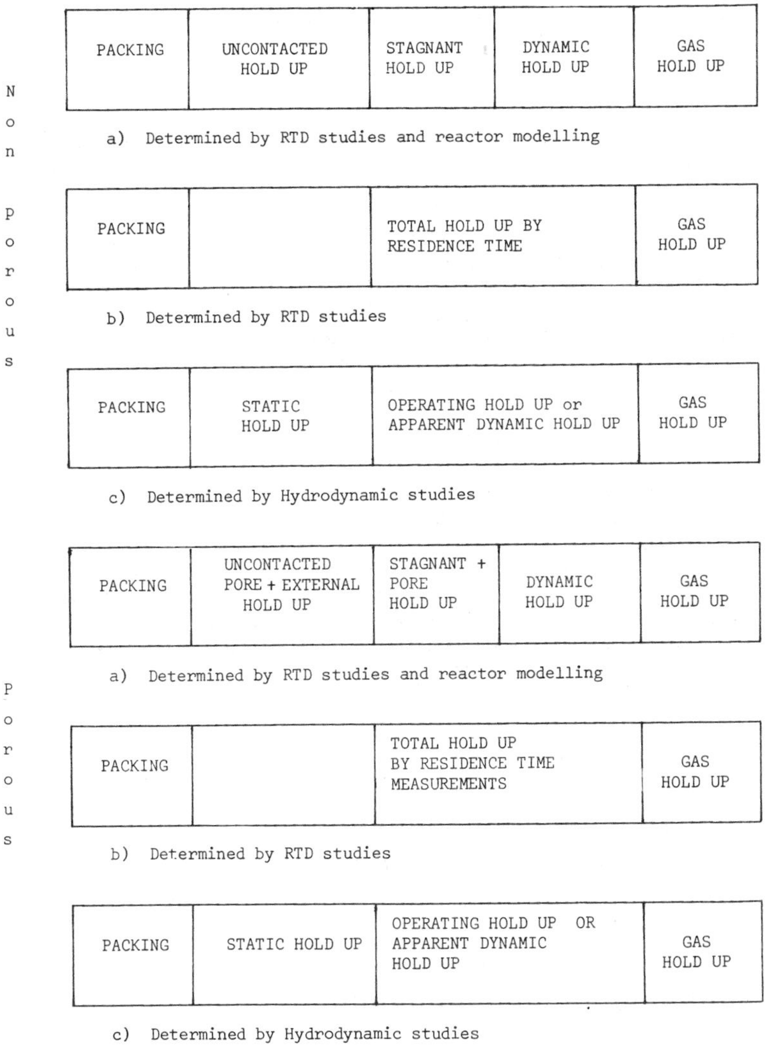

Nonporous

PACKING	UNCONTACTED HOLD UP	STAGNANT HOLD UP	DYNAMIC HOLD UP	GAS HOLD UP

a) Determined by RTD studies and reactor modelling

PACKING		TOTAL HOLD UP BY RESIDENCE TIME	GAS HOLD UP

b) Determined by RTD studies

PACKING	STATIC HOLD UP	OPERATING HOLD UP or APPARENT DYNAMIC HOLD UP	GAS HOLD UP

c) Determined by Hydrodynamic studies

Porous

PACKING	UNCONTACTED PORE + EXTERNAL HOLD UP	STAGNANT + PORE HOLD UP	DYNAMIC HOLD UP	GAS HOLD UP

a) Determined by RTD studies and reactor modelling

PACKING		TOTAL HOLD UP BY RESIDENCE TIME MEASUREMENTS	GAS HOLD UP

b) Determined by RTD studies

PACKING	STATIC HOLD UP	OPERATING HOLD UP OR APPARENT DYNAMIC HOLD UP	GAS HOLD UP

c) Determined by Hydrodynamic studies

Figure 10. Classification of liquid holdup in trickle-flow reactors for porous and nonporous packing.

liquid holdup can be obtained either by direct measurement (e.g., by weighing) or by residence-time methods. When direct measurement is used, two holdups can be defined, the operating holdup (apparent dynamic holdup) and the static holdup. The operating holdup is obtained by free draining of the reactor after both the gas and liquid flow rates have been halted, while the static holdup represents the amount of the liquid still remaining in the reactor. If residence-time or tracer methods are used, then three holdups can be envisaged. These are the dynamic holdup, the stagnant holdup and the uncontacted holdup. Both the dynamic and stagnant holdups can be estimated from residence-time studies, while the uncontacted holdup can be determined by subtracting the total holdup determined from residence-time studies from that measured physically or by the method detailed in Kan [44]. It should be noted that the operating holdup determined from hydrodynamic experiments is not necessarily equivalent to the dynamic holdup [44].

The degree of contacting between the liquid and solid phases is generally expressed as the wetting efficiency of the reactor. An alternative measurement of the wetting efficiency is found from reaction studies on the trickle-flow reactor where the global rate of reaction is compared with the performance of a liquid-full reactor operated at the same liquid rate. Reactor conditions should be chosen so that the reaction is not mass-transfer limited.

Since the liquid-phase flow pattern inside a trickle-flow reactor operated in the trickling-flow regime is essentially the same as the liquid-phase flow pattern inside a packed absorption column, many of the residence-time models originally proposed for absorption columns have been adapted to trickle-flow systems. It should be noted, however, that trickle-flow reactors generally involve smaller packing sizes than absorption columns while the packing (catalyst) is most often porous.

Most residence-time studies reported in the literature are performed in the trickling-flow regime. Data in the pulsing-flow regime are lacking, although many commercial trickle-flow reactors are operated around the transition between the trickling- and pulsing-flow regimes.

Classification of Residence-Time Models

There are several ways of classifying available trickle-flow reactor residence-time models. Gianetto et al. [28] classified the models according to the number of unknown parameters used in the model. Models with a larger number of parameters theoretically should describe the observed RTD better, but the determination of the additional parameters becomes more complex and their reliability is doubtful. As pointed out by Sicardi et al. [85], the definition of the best model is a questionable matter. A suitable model should not contain too many characteristic parameters and should describe the observed RTD even at long response times, and the parameters should have realistic physical meanings. Models involving the determination of more than four parameters from RTD curves are considered impractical.

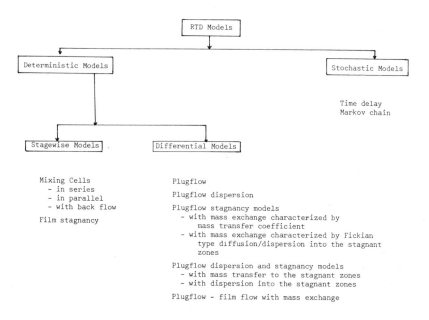

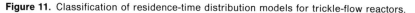

Figure 11. Classification of residence-time distribution models for trickle-flow reactors.

Shinnar [84] classified mathematical models into predictive and learning models. Predictive models are simple models with few parameters which can be correlated over a wide range of operating conditions, while learning models are usually more complicated, may have a more narrow range of applicability, and are designed to test specific hypotheses on mechanisms or indicate the direction of potential process improvements. In trickle-flow reactor systems, this dichotomy is very obvious, with almost all models used for design purposes being of a relatively simple, lumped nature, while the more complicated models have been used to test specific hypotheses on the nature and causes of the observed mixing in the liquid phase.

The classification used in this review is shown in Figure 11. The RTD models are classified into two categories—deterministic models and stochastic models. The deterministic models are the most widely used and studied, because the mathematics for solving these models are well understood. In turn, the deterministic models are classified into stagewise (lumped parameter) models and differential (distributed parameter) models. The stagewise models divide the trickle-flow reactor into a finite number of stages; in the limit of a very large number of stages the stagewise model becomes identical to one of the differential models. The differential models are generally preferred since they are more easily solved.

Stochastic models are models which, as the name suggests, involve elements of uncertainty or probability. The reactor is considered as a space where a number of possible events are occurring, with each event having its own probability density function. Thus, the parameters of this type of model represent the most probable number of times certain events will occur. Although the physical flow processes occurring in trickle-flow reactors are basically random in nature, stochastic models developed for such systems have not found much application to date.

Deterministic Models

There are two types of deterministic models, differential and stagewise. In deriving the differential models, a small (differential) element of the reactor is defined and material and energy balances derived over the element. In the limit that the element becomes negligibly small, a series of partial differential equations is obtained. Generally, Laplace transformation with respect to the time variable is used to transform the partial differential equations into ordinary differential equations. The ordinary differential equations are then solved and the Laplace domain solution inverted to the time domain solution. This inversion process is sometimes very tedious and may, in fact, not be possible; in such cases a numerical inversion technique, such as the Zakian inversion technique, is needed. The Zakian inversion technique, although quite accurate, is subject to instabilities, especially at or near discontinuities [97]. This method of solving the model leads to a solution in which the input function is considered to be of the form $C(t, 0)$.

A similar approach is used for the stagewise models, the principal difference being that, instead of modeling the differential element, a finite number of stages (usually identical stages) are defined and the modeling carried out on one typical stage. The solution for this stage is then generalized using the method of induction to obtain the overall solution. One of main drawbacks of stagewise models is that the number of stages carries no physical significance, and so, the models are not particularly suitable for scale-up purposes.

Differential Models

The differential models are summarized in Table 5. The simplest of these is the one-parameter plug-flow model (PF). In this model, all the liquid elements in the reactor are assumed to flow at the same velocity. The only parameter is the residence time of the liquid, $\bar{t}_R$, which is related to the total liquid holdup, h_t, by the following equation:

$$\bar{t}_R = h_t Z / v_{s1} \tag{47}$$

where $Z =$ the length of the reactor section
 $v_{s1} =$ the superficial liquid velocity

Table 5
Summary of Differential Models

Model	Schematic	Governing Equations	Moments of Normalized RTD	References
(a) Plugflow (PF) One parameter, h_t		$h_t \dfrac{\partial C_d}{\partial t} + v_{sl}\dfrac{\partial C_d}{\partial z} = 0$	$m_1 = \dfrac{h_t Z}{v_{sl}} = \bar{t}_R$	Otake and Kunigita [63], Sater and Levenspiel [73], Van Swaaij et al. [94], Hochman and Effron [39], Furzer and Michell [25]
(b) Plugflow dispersion (PD) Two parameters, h_t, D		$h_t \dfrac{\partial C_d}{\partial t} = Dh_t \dfrac{\partial^2 C_d}{\partial z^2} - v_{sl}\dfrac{\partial C_d}{\partial z}$	$m_1 = \dfrac{h_t Z}{v_{sl}} = \bar{t}_R$ $m_2 = m_1^2\left[\dfrac{2\mathscr{D}m_1}{Z^2} + 1\right]$	
(c) Plugflow stagnancy with mass exchange characterized by mass transfer coef. (PE1) Three parameters, $\phi = \dfrac{h_d}{h_s + h_d}$, h_t, $k_{sd}a_s$		$\phi h_t \dfrac{\partial C_d}{\partial t} = k_{sd}a_s(C_s - C_d) - v_{sl}\dfrac{\partial C_d}{\partial z}$ $(1-\phi)h_t\dfrac{\partial C_s}{\partial t} = k_{sd}a_s(C_d - C_s)$	$m_1 = \dfrac{h_t Z}{v_{sl}} = \bar{t}_R$ $m_2 = \dfrac{2(1-\phi)^2 v_{sl}m_1^2}{k_{sd}a_s Z} + m_1^2$	Hoogendoorn and Lips [42], Hochman and Effron [39], Sicardi et al. [85]
(d) Plugflow stagnancy with mass exchange characterized by Fickian-type dispersion into the stagnant zones (PE2) Three parameters, ϕ, h_t, $E'_s a_s(S_g)$		$\phi h_t \dfrac{\partial C_d}{\partial t} = E'_s a_s \left.\dfrac{\partial C_s}{\partial y}\right|_{y=0} - v_{sl}\dfrac{\partial C_d}{\partial z}$ $\dfrac{\partial C_s}{\partial t} = E'_s \dfrac{\partial^2 C_s}{\partial y^2}$	$m_1 = \dfrac{h_t Z}{v_{sl}} = \bar{t}_R$ $m_2 = m_1^2 + \dfrac{(1 - \phi)m_1 S_g^2 Z}{v_{sl}}$	Kan [44], Kan and Greenfield [45]

(e) Plugflow dispersion with mass exchange characterized by mass transfer coef. (PDE1) 4 parameters, $\phi, h_t, D, k_{sd}a_s$

$$\phi h_t \frac{\partial C_d}{\partial t}$$

$$= h_d \frac{\partial^2 C_d}{\partial z^2} - v_{sl}\frac{\partial C_d}{\partial z} + k_{sd}a_s(C_s - C_d)$$

$$(1-\phi)h_t \frac{\partial C_s}{\partial t} = k_{sd}a_s(C_d - C_s)$$

$$m_1 = \frac{h_t Z}{v_{sl}} = \bar{t}_R$$

$$m_2 = \frac{2m_1^3 D\phi}{Z^2} + \frac{2m_1^2(1-\phi)^2 v_{sl}}{Z k_{sd}a_s} + m_1^2$$

Van Swaaij et al. [94], Bennett and Goodridge [8], Matsuura et al. [53], Sicardi et al. [85]

(f) Plugflow dispersion with mass exchange characterized by Fickian-type diffusion into the stagnant zones (PDE2) 4 parameters, $\phi, h_t, D, E'_s a_s$

$$\phi h_t \frac{\partial C_d}{\partial t} = h_t\phi\frac{\partial^2 C_d}{\partial z^2} - v_{sl}\frac{\partial C_d}{\partial z}$$

$$\phi h_t \frac{\partial C_d}{\partial t} = h_t\phi\frac{\partial^2 C_d}{\partial z^2} - v_{sl}\frac{\partial C_d}{\partial z}$$

$$+ E'_s a_s \frac{\partial C_s}{\partial y}\Big|_{y=0}$$

$$\frac{\partial C_s}{\partial y} = E'_s\frac{\partial^2 C_s}{\partial y^2}$$

$$m_1 = \frac{h_t Z}{v_{sl}} = \bar{t}_R$$

$$m_2 = \frac{2m_1^3 D\phi}{Z^2} + \frac{(1-\phi)m_1 S^2 g Z}{v_{sl}} + m_1^2$$

Kan [44], Kan and Greenfield [45]

(g) Plugflow film flow with mass exchange

$$v_{s1}\frac{\partial C_1}{\partial z} + h_1\frac{\partial C_1}{\partial t} = k_{sf}a_f(C_2 - C_1)$$

$$v_{s2}\frac{\partial C_2}{\partial z} + h_2\frac{\partial C_2}{\partial t} = k_{sf}a_f(C_1 - C_2)$$

$$m_1 = \frac{(h_1 + h_2)Z}{v_{s1} + v_{s2}}$$

Lerou et al. [49]

This model represents an extreme condition and the response of the model for different inputs has been given earlier.

If the PF model is to give a good description of the residence-time distribution inside the trickle-flow reactor, then the input function $[C(t, 0)$ or $C(0, z)]$ should be almost identical to the response curve $[C(t, Z)$ or $C(T, z)]$ when they are superimposed. This is not the case, since a longer tail in the response curve is typically found. Despite this feature, the PF model is used in some design correlations.

Another extensively studied model is the plug-flow dispersion model or, more correctly, the plug-flow axial-dispersion model (PD). This two-parameter model lumps all the dispersive effects in the trickle-flow reactor into a single parameter, D, known as the axial dispersion coefficient. In essence, the model considers the bulk of the liquid as flowing in a plug-flow manner while at the same time a Fickian-type diffusion process, characterized by the dispersion coefficient D, is superimposed on the liquid flow. The governing equation for this model is:

$$h_t \frac{\partial C_d}{\partial t} = Dh_t \frac{\partial^2 C_d}{\partial z^2} - v_{s1} \frac{\partial C_d}{\partial z} \tag{48}$$

with the following boundary and initial conditions:

$$C_d(0, Z) = 0 \tag{49a}$$

$$C_d(t, 0) = C_{di}(t, 0) \tag{49b}$$

$$C_d(t, \infty) = \text{finite} \tag{49c}$$

If the preceding equations are solved using Laplace transformations, the following is obtained:

$$\bar{C}_d(s, Z) = \bar{C}_{di}(s, 0) \exp\left[\frac{v_{s1}Z}{2Dh_t}\left(1 - \left(1 + \frac{4h_t^2 Ds}{v_{s1}^2}\right)^{0.5}\right)\right] \tag{50}$$

The response to a perfect pulse input, $\delta(t, 0)$, such that $Av_{s1} \int_0^\infty \delta(t, 0)\, dt = M$, can be obtained by setting $\bar{C}_{di}(s, 0) = M/Av_{s1}$ and inverting the resulting equation, which yields:

$$C_d(t, Z) = \frac{ZM}{2Av_{s1}\sqrt{\pi Dt^3}} \exp\left[\frac{-Z^2(1 - t/\bar{t}_R)^2}{4Dt}\right] \tag{51}$$

For an imperfect pulse or arbitrary input signal, the convolution theorem given by Equation 15 can be used to obtain the response.

Another solution to Equations 48 and 49 was proposed by Levenspiel and Smith [50], which considers a perfect input pulse with respect to distance, $\delta(0, z)$, such that $Ah_t \int_0^\infty \delta(0, z)\, dz = M$. Their solution is:

$$C_d(t, Z) = \frac{M}{2Ah_t\sqrt{\pi Dt}} \exp\left[\frac{-Z^2(1 - t/\bar{t}_R)^2}{4Dt}\right] \tag{52}$$

which must be used in conjunction with Equation 16 for an imperfect input signal. It should be noted that both solutions satisfy Equation 48, the difference lying in the assumptions made concerning the form of the input pulse function. The two solutions agree with each other when the dispersion coefficient is small (large Pe), which is often the case with flow in trickle-bed reactors. As the dispersion coefficient increases, however, the divergence between the two solutions becomes more significant (see Figures 12 and 13). The parameters for this model may be estimated either by the moments method or by time-domain curve fitting. In light of Figures 12 and 13, it is clear that if dispersion is considered significant, care needs to be exercised in achieving a specified set of initial and boundary conditions if the parameters obtained from real time fitting are to be given

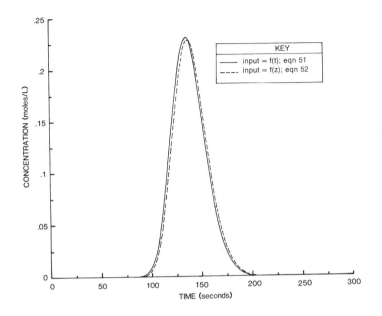

Figure 12. Tracer response curve as predicted by plugflow dispersion model (PD) for a perfect input pulse (Bo = 0.185, Pe = 14.2).

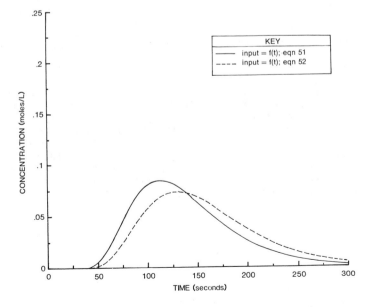

Figure 13. Tracer response curve as predicted by plugflow dispersion model (PD) for a perfect input pulse (Bo = 0.0185, Pe = 1.42).

physical significance. Such problems are avoided if the moments or cumulants methods are used for parameter estimation.

In general, a dimensionless group defined as:

$$Pe = v_{sl}Z/Dh_t \tag{53}$$

and known as the Peclet number is used to characterize the dispersion in the reactor. In packed beds, the packing size is a more important parameter in determining the degree of dispersion than the length/depth of the bed. A modified Peclet number known as the particle Peclet number or the Bodenstein number is therefore used to report dispersion in trickle-flow reactors:

$$Pe_p = Bo = v_{sl}d_p/Dh_t \tag{54}$$

Correlations for the plug-flow dispersion model parameters are shown in Table 6. Care should be exercised when comparing these correlations, especially with regard to the parameter estimation technique, definitions of the dimensionless numbers, and range of validity. Several correlation obtained from the countercurrent mode of operation are included in the table for comparison. It is interesting to note that gas flow rate (gas-phase Reynolds number) does not appear in any of the correlations. Most investigators have found that the gas flow rate has very little effect on either dispersion parameter. Tosun [89] studied the effect of gas flow rate on the Bodenstein number, but his results were inconclusive. It is expected that the gas flow rate would have some effect on the total liquid holdup for beds of small packings [44].

Instead of the total holdup, the operating holdup (h_{op}) is often reported. The dispersion coefficient has been correlated against various definitions of the liquid Reynolds number. In general, it can be concluded that both the total holdup and the Bodenstein number increase with increasing liquid flow rate, and that the Bodenstein number is proportional to L^β, where β ranges from 0.4 to 0.7

Relatively little work using the plug flow dispersion model has been reported for cocurrent downflow operation as compared with the countercurrent flow mode; most work has been performed with particles larger than 3 mm. To date, the validity of the PD model in representing the liquid-phase flow in trickle-flow reactors has been mainly restricted to the trickling-flow regime. The model has been found to describe inadequately the long tailing generally observed in the RTD of trickling flow through packed beds [42, 55, 56, 73]. Because of its relative simplicity, however it is frequently used in reactor design.

The pronounced tailing of trickle-flow RTD curves has been attributed to the existence of stagnant regions in the bed. This line of thinking has resulted in the development of so-called stagnancy models, which divide the liquid in the reactor into two parts—stagnant pockets and flowing liquid—which continuously exchange mass with each other. The flowing liquid can move either in plug flow or in dispersed plug flow, while the stagnant pockets can be perfectly mixed or quiescent. If the stagnant regions are assumed to be perfectly mixed, then the exchange of mass/solute with the flowing liquid is characterized by a mass transfer coefficient (models c and e in Table 5). If, instead, a quiescent stagnant region is assumed, then the mass transfer process is characterized by a Fickian-type diffusion into and out of the stagnant regions (models d and f in Table 5).

In the plug flow stagnancy model with mass exchange characterized by a mass transfer coefficient (PE1 model, also known as the crossflow model or the side-mixing model), the governing equations are:

$$\phi h_t \frac{\partial C_d}{\partial t} = k_{sd}a_s(C_s - C_d) - v_{sl}\frac{\partial C_d}{\partial z} \tag{55}$$

for the flowing (dynamic) liquid, and

$$(1 - \phi)h_t \frac{\partial C_s}{\partial t} = k_{sd}a_s(C_d - C_s) \tag{56}$$

for the stagnant liquid.

Table 6
Plugflow Dispersion Model Parameters

Holdup	Dispersion Coefficient	Range/Regime	Remarks	References
	$$\left(\frac{v_{sl}d_p}{D}\right) = 0.042\left(\frac{d_p L}{\mu_L(1-\varepsilon)}\right)^{0.5}$$	Trickle flow $L \leq 6.85 \text{ kg/m}^2 \text{ s}$ $G \leq 0.1 \text{ kg/m}^2 \text{ s}$	Cocurrent downflow of methanol and nitrogen. 4.8 mm glass spheres. Moments method, imperfect pulse.	Hochman and Effron [39]
	$$\left(\frac{v_{sl}d_p}{Dh_t}\right) = 7.58 \times 10^{-3}\left(\frac{d_p L}{\mu_L}\right)^{0.703}$$	$L \leq 40.8 \text{ kg/m}^2 \text{ s}$ G not available	Countercurrent air water. 12.7 mm Rachig rings and Berl saddles moments method, imperfect pulse.	Sater and Levenspiel [73]
	$$\left(\frac{v_{sl}d_p}{Dh_t}\right) = 13\left(\frac{d_p L}{\mu_L h_t}\right)^{0.4}\left(\frac{d_p^3 \rho_L^2 g}{\mu_L^2}\right)^{-0.33}$$	$0.134 \leq L \leq 9.1 \text{ kg/m}^2 \text{ s}$ $G \leq 0.765 \text{ kg/m}^2 \text{ s}$	Countercurrent water-air 6.35 mm Raschig rings. Time domain curve fitting, perfect pulse.	Furzer and Michell [25]
	$$\left(\frac{v_{sl}d_p}{Dh_t}\right) = 1.0\left(\frac{d_p L}{\mu_L h_t}\right)^{0.7}\left(\frac{d_p^3 \rho_L^2 g}{\mu_L^2}\right)^{-0.32}$$	As above	Countercurrent water air 6.35, 25.4, and 50.8 mm Raschig rings and lessing rings. Time domain curve fitting, perfect pulse.	Michell and Furzer [55]

(Continued)

Table 6 (Continued)

Holdup	Dispersion Coefficient	Range/Regime	Remarks	References
	$\left(\dfrac{v_{sl}d_p}{Dh_t}\right) = 0.039\left(\dfrac{2\pi L}{a_w\mu_L}\right)^{0.5}$	As above	As above	Michell and Furzer [56]
	$\left(\dfrac{v_{sl}d_p}{Dh_t}\right) \propto \left(\dfrac{d_pL}{\mu_Lh_t}\right)^{0.5}$	Trickling, pulsing, bubbling flow. $2 \leq L \leq 100$ kg/m² s $0.024 \leq G \leq 0.24$ kg/m² s $0.1 < (\Delta P_L/\Delta P_G)^{0.5} < 20$	Cocurrent downflow water-air 1.2, 2.6, and 4.3 mm glass spheres Parameter estimation technique not mentioned.	Matsuura et al. [53]
	$\left(\dfrac{v_{sl}d_p}{D}\right) \propto \left(\dfrac{d_pL}{\mu_L}\right)^{0.37}$* $0.04 \leq \left(\dfrac{v_{sl}d_p}{D}\right) \leq 0.4$	Trickle flow $0.3 < L < 5$ kg/m² s $0.0001 < G < 0.002$ kg/m² s	Cocurrent downflow hexane-helium 0.6-mm alumina pellets moments method, imperfect pulse.	Schwartz et al. [79]

$$h_t = 0.19\frac{6(1-\varepsilon)}{d_p} \times \left[\left[1 + \frac{4d_p}{6D_l(1-\varepsilon)}\right]^{1/3}\right]\left(\frac{\Delta P_L}{\Delta P_G}\right)^{0.11}$$

* *Approximated regression*

This is a three-parameter model, the parameters being ϕ, the ratio of the dynamic to the total hold-up, the total hold-up, h_t, and the mass transfer coefficient between the stagnant and dynamic regions, $k_{sd}a_s$. Applying the appropriate initial and boundary conditions, taking Laplace transforms, integrating, and rearranging, the following Laplace domain solution is obtained:

$$\bar{C}_d(s, Z) = \bar{C}_d(s, 0) \exp\left[-\phi\bar{t}_R s - \frac{k_{sd}a_s(1 - \phi)\bar{t}_R s}{(1 - \phi)h_t s + k_{sd}a_s} \right] \tag{57}$$

The response to a perfect-pulse input signal for this model is given by:

$$C_d(t, Z) = 0 \quad \text{for} \quad t < \phi\bar{t}_R \tag{58}$$

$$C_d(t, Z) = \frac{M_1}{Av_{s1}} \left\{ \frac{k_{sd}a_s}{h_t} \sqrt{\frac{\bar{t}_R}{(1 - \phi)(t - \phi\bar{t}_R)}} \right.$$

$$\left. I_1\left[\frac{2k_{sd}a_s}{h_t} \sqrt{\frac{\bar{t}_R(t - \phi\bar{t}_R)}{(1 - \phi)}} \right] \right\} \exp\left[-\frac{k_{sd}a_s(t - \phi\bar{t}_R)}{(1 - \phi)h_t} - \frac{\bar{t}_R k_{sd}a_s}{h_t} \right] \quad \text{for} \quad t \geq \phi\bar{t}_R \tag{59}$$

where I_1 is a Bessel function of the first order. Other approximate time-domain solutions have also been used [39, 85]. The solution given by Sicardi et al. [85] is for a step-decrease input, and in dimensionless form becomes:

$$C_{sd} = 1 - \exp\left\{ -[\theta(1 - \alpha) - 1]\frac{N}{\alpha} - N \right\} \left[1 + \sum_{m=1}^{\infty} \left(\frac{\{[\theta(1 + \alpha) - 1]N/\alpha\}^m}{m} \sum_{r=0}^{m} \frac{N^{(m-r)}}{(m - r)} \right) \right] \tag{60}$$

where $\theta = t/\bar{t}_R$
$\alpha = h_s/h_d = (1 - \phi)/\phi$
$N = k_{sd}a_s Z/v_{s1}$

The other plug flow stagnancy model was first proposed by Kan and Greenfield [43]. The main difference between this model (PE2) and the previous model is in the concept of the stagnant region. In the PE1 model, the transfer of materials between the stagnant and dynamic regions is characterized by a mass transfer coefficient, which implies that the concentration of the reactants or tracer in the stagnant region is everywhere the same (i.e., a completely mixed stagnant region or it can be represented by a single mean value). Gottschlich [33] suggested that mixing in the stagnant region occurs incompletely by molecular diffusion. Kan and Greenfield [43] extended this idea and proposed the incomplete mixing process occurring by dispersion in the stagnant regions, which can be described by a Fickian-type relationship:

$$\frac{\partial C_s}{\partial t} = E_s' \frac{\partial^2 C_s}{\partial y^2} \tag{61}$$

The mass balance equation for the dynamic region is given by:

$$\phi h_t \frac{\partial C_d}{\partial t} = -v_{s1} \frac{\partial C_d}{\partial z} + a_s E_s' \frac{\partial C_s}{\partial y}\bigg|_{y=0} \tag{62}$$

With the assumption of a simple geometry for the stagnant regions, namely,

$$a_s \bar{\Delta} = (1 - \phi)h_t \tag{63}$$

where $\bar{\Delta}$ is the average thickness of the stagnant layer, and by applying the appropriate boundary and initial conditions,

$$\frac{\partial C_s}{\partial y}\bigg|_{y=\bar{\Delta}} = 0 \tag{64a}$$

$$C_s(t, z) = C_d(t, z) \qquad \text{at } y = 0 \tag{64b}$$

$$C_d(t, 0) = C_{di}(t, 0) \tag{64c}$$

$$C_d(0, z) = C_s(0, z) = 0 \qquad \text{at all } y, \tag{64d}$$

the preceding equations can be solved using Laplace transformation, to yield:

$$\bar{C}_d(s, Z) = \bar{C}_d(s, 0) \exp\left[\frac{\phi h_t Z}{v_{s1}}\left\{s + \frac{(1 - \phi)}{\phi\bar{\Delta}}\sqrt{sE_s'}\tanh\bar{\Delta}\sqrt{\frac{s}{E_s'}}\right\}\right]\cdots \tag{65}$$

The stagnancy number S_g is defined as:

$$S_g = \bar{\Delta}\left[\frac{v_{s1}}{E_s'Z}\right]^{0.5} \tag{66}$$

Substitution of Equation 66 into Equation 65 leads to:

$$\bar{C}_d(s, Z) = \bar{C}_d(s, 0)\exp(-\phi\bar{t}_R s)\exp\left[\frac{(1 - \phi)\bar{t}_R}{S_g}\left[\frac{sv_{s1}}{Z}\right]^{0.5}\tanh S_g\left[\frac{sZ}{v_{s1}}\right]^{0.5}\right] \tag{67}$$

Equation 67 is difficult to invert analytically and a numerical inversion method, such as the Zakian method [97], is necessary.

Both of the preceding stagnancy models have been tested only for the trickling-flow regime. The parameter ϕ in both models carries the same meaning and can be estimated roughly by graphical methods as suggested by Hoogendoorn and Lips [42]. Since ϕ represents the ratio of the dynamic to total holdup, it follows that the first breakthrough of tracer material occurs at time, $t_D = \phi\bar{t}_R$. For a better estimate of ϕ, the time-domain curve-fitting method is recommended. ϕ values obtained from graphical methods are generally lower than those values obtained by fitting the time-domain solution. In either case, reported values of ϕ range from 0.5 to 0.9. The parameter has been generally found to be a weak function of the liquid Reynolds number, although Kan and Greenfield [45] found that it was constant over the range of liquid flow rates tested ($\phi = 0.73$).

As in the case of the PD model, the parameter h_t (or $\bar{t}_R$) is generally not reported. In all the models, h_t has the same physical meaning—it is the fraction of the reactor occupied by the liquid phase. Kan and Greenfield [45] correlated their total holdup data, obtained from fitting the time-domain curve, by:

$$h_t = \frac{1}{3.5} \text{Re}_L^{0.15} \text{Re}_G^{-0.25} \text{Re}_{G,\max}^{0.014} \tag{68}$$

There is a misprint in the original paper, 8.5 was printed instead of 1/3.5. The term $\text{Re}_{G,\max}$ is the maximum gas-phase Reynolds number reached prior to the existing operating conditions. This was found to be important for trickle-flow systems with small packing sizes ($d_p < 3$ mm).

The mass transfer coefficient for the PE1 model has been estimated using the moments method by Hoogendoorn and Lips [42] in a countercurrent system and by Hochman and Effron [39] in a cocurrent system. Sicardi et al. [85] evaluated the mass transfer coefficient for the PE1 model using the moments method and the best fit method, obtaining different estimates with each method.

The stagnancy number of the PE2 model was found to be constant, 0.13 [45]. These authors argued that E_s' is not equal to the molecular diffusivity since the stagnancy numbers for identical experiments, performed using two different tracers with different molecular diffusivities, were almost identical when they should have differed by a factor of 2.

The plug-flow stagnancy models describe the RTD of the liquid phase in trickle-flow reactors better than does the plug-flow dispersion model [39]. A comparison between the two plug-flow stagnancy models has not been reported and certainly deserves investigation. Table 7 summarizes the results obtained with the plug-flow stagnancy model.

Table 7
Plugflow Stagnancy Model Parameters

Total Holdup	$\phi = h_d/h_t$	$k_{sd}a_s$	S_g	Range/Regime	Remarks	References
	$\phi = 0.335\left(\dfrac{d_pL}{\mu_L}\right)^{0.14}$ * $0.52 \leq \phi \leq 0.63$	$\dfrac{k_{sd}a_s}{h_t} \propto \left(\dfrac{d_pL}{\mu_L}\right)^{0.86}$ *	—	$2.1 \leq L \leq 5.2$ kg/m²s G-unknown	Countercurrent water-air 12.7-mm Raschig rings, moments method, perfect pulse $\phi = t_D/\overline{\tau}_R$.	Hoogendoorn and Lips [42]
	$\phi = 0.52\dfrac{\left(\dfrac{d_pL}{\mu_L(1-\varepsilon)}\right)^{0.08}}{10^{0.001}\left(\dfrac{d_pG}{\mu_G(1-\varepsilon)}\right)}$ $0.65 \leq \phi \leq 0.85$	$\dfrac{k_{sd}a_s}{h_t} = 0.010\left(\dfrac{d_pL}{\mu_L(1-\varepsilon)}\right)^{0.60}$	—	Trickle flow $L \leq 6.85$ kg/m²s $G \leq 0.1$ kg/m²s	Cocurrent downflow methanol-nitrogen, 4.8-mm glass spheres, moments method, imperfect pulse $\phi = t_D/\overline{\tau}_R$.	Hochman and Effron [39]
	$\phi = 0.587\left(\dfrac{d_pL}{\mu_Lh_L}\right)^{0.089}$ * $0.77 \leq \phi \leq 0.87$	$\dfrac{k_{sd}a_sd_p}{\phi h_L} \propto \left(\dfrac{d_pL}{\mu_Lh_L}\right)^{1.63}$ *	—	Trickle flow $0.55 \leq L \leq 7.29$ kg/m²s $0 \leq G \leq 0.73$ kg/m²s	Cocurrent downflow, water-air 2.7-mm glass spheres (nonporous). Time-domain fitting, minimum sum of square error, perfect step down.	Sicardi et al. [85]
$h_t = \dfrac{1}{3.5}\left(\dfrac{d_pL}{\mu_L}\right)^{0.15}\left(\dfrac{d_pG}{\mu_G}\right)$ $\times \left(\dfrac{d_pG_{max}}{\mu_G}\right)^{0.014}$	$\phi = \text{const} = 0.73$		$S_g = 0.13$	Trickle and pulsing flow $1 \leq L \leq 10$ kg/m²s $0.01 \leq G \leq 1.85$ kg/m²s	Cocurrent downflow, water-air. 0.5–1.0-mm nonporous glass spheres. Time-domain fitting, minimum sum of square error, imperfect pulse.	Kan and Greenfield [45]

* Approximated regression

An additional parameter to account for the axial dispersion in the dynamic region was independently proposed by Van Swaaij et al. [94] and Bennett and Goodridge [8]. The four-parameter dispersed plug-flow stagnancy model (PDE-1) is given by:

$$\phi h_t \frac{\partial C_d}{\partial t} = D\phi h_t \frac{\partial^2 C_d}{\partial z^2} - v_{s1} \frac{\partial C_d}{\partial z} + k_{sd}a_s(C_s - C_d) \tag{69}$$

for the dynamic liquid, and by Equation 56 for the stagnant liquid.

Van Swaaij et al. [94] performed experiments using wettable and nonwettable packings. They found that the Bodenstein number for the nonwettable packing, calculated from the moments method using the PD model, is constant at high liquid velocities or high h_d/h_s. For the wettable packing, where h_s is greater than the h_s of the nonwettable packing, the Bodenstein number is smaller, indicating some additional mechanism which increases the spread in the residence-time distribution. They attributed the additional mechanism to a slow mass exchange between the stagnant and dynamic regions. Van Swaaij et al. [94] provide expressions for the first three moments of this model with a pulse input.

Bennett and Goodridge [8] proposed the same model but used a step decrease as input. They solved the dimensionless forms of Equations 69 and 56 by applying Laplace transformations and inverting the Laplace domain solution using the method of residues. However, the solution obtained converged too slowly and they suggested the use of a Crank-Nicholson procedure. Instead, Bennett and Goodridge used a completely graphical method for determining the model parameters. The dimensionless concentration-time response curve, when plotted on semilogarithmic paper, shows two linear sections. The first linear section can be ascribed to dispersion taking place in the bulk of the liquid, which is the dynamic portion. In this section, the effect of the stagnant region is negligible. The second linear portion is due mainly to mass transfer from the stagnant regions to the relatively tracer-free dynamic regions. Noting this fact, the mass transfer coefficient, $k_{sd}a_s$, can be obtained from the slope of the second linear portion. By simulating the model using various parameter values, it was noted that the intercept of the second linear portion depends only on the values of the mass transfer coefficient and the ratio of the stagnant to dynamic holdup ($\alpha = (1 - \phi)/\phi$). A graph of this intercept versus α for various values of the mass transfer coefficient was produced, and from this graph and a knowledge of the mass transfer coefficient, α was determined. The slope of the first linear portion, g_1, was found to be dependent on the Peclet number, α and N ($= k_{sd}a_s Z/v_{s1}$). By plotting g_1 versus α at various Peclet numbers and recognizing that the value of N can be determined from the previous analysis, the Peclet number can be found. The parameter estimation technique proposed by Bennett and Goodridge appears to be quite simple, however, a large number of computations must be performed to produce the graphs. Correlations of the parameters obtained are shown in Table 8. The original paper appears to have some misprints in the quoted values of the coefficients used in the correlations for Pe and $k_{sd}a_s d_p$.

Matsuura et al. [53] used the PDE1 model to investigate the liquid phase RTD of a trickle-flow reactor operated in the trickling-, pulsing-, and bubbling-flow regimes. They also solved the PDE 1 model for the case of a perfect-pulse input. The dimensionless solution is given by:

$$C_d(\theta, 1) = \int_0^\theta \frac{N}{2x} \sqrt{\frac{P}{\pi(1 - \phi)(\theta - x)}} I_1 \left[2N \sqrt{\frac{x(\theta - x)}{\phi(1 - \phi)}} \right]$$

$$\times \exp\left[-\frac{P(x - \phi)^2}{4\phi x} - N \frac{x - 2\phi x + \theta\phi}{\phi(1 - \phi)} \right] dx$$

$$+ \frac{1}{2} \sqrt{\frac{P\phi}{\pi\theta^3}} \exp\left[-\frac{P(\theta - x)^2}{4\theta\phi} - N \frac{\theta}{\phi} \right] \tag{70}$$

where

$$C_d(\theta, 1) = C_d/C_{do} \tag{71}$$

C_{do} is such that $\int_0^\infty C_d(\theta, 1)\, d\theta = 1$

Table 8
Dispersed Plugflow Stagnancy Model Parameters

Total Holdup	$\phi = h_d/h_t$	D	$k_{sd}a_s$	Range/Regime	Remarks	References
	$0.605 \leq \phi \leq 0.816$		$\dfrac{v_{sl}}{k_{sd}a_s} \simeq 0.41$ m	Trickle flow $1.8 < L < 11.1$ kg/m^2 s $G \leq 0.9$ kg/m^2 s	Counter current/cocurrent air-water. 6.4, 10.3, and 22-mm Raschig rings, moments method, perfect pulse, combined with determination of B_o using nonwettable packing.	Van Swaaij et al. [94]
$h_t = 0.04 + 0.479\, Q_L^{0.635}$	$(1 - \phi)h_t$ is independent of G and L, depends on d_p	$\left(\dfrac{d_p v_{sl}}{D\phi h_t}\right) = 0.0095 \left(\dfrac{d_p L}{\phi h_t \mu_L}\right)^{0.51}$	$k_{sd}a_s d_p = 1.95 \times 10^{-5}\left(\dfrac{d_p L}{\phi h_t \mu_L}\right)^{0.58}$	$3.4 < L < 20.6$ kg/m^2 s $G <$ loading point	Countercurrent air water 9.5 and 6.4-mm Raschig rings, perfect step down. Graphical method of parameter estimation.	Bennett and Goodridge [8]

(Continued)

Table 8 (Continued)

Total Holdup	$\phi = h_d/h_t$	D	$k_{sd}a_s$	Range/Regime	Remarks	References
$h_t = 0.19 \, a_1^{1/3} \chi^{0.22}$ $a_1 = \dfrac{6(1-\varepsilon)}{d_p}\left[1 + \dfrac{4d_p}{6D_t(1-\varepsilon)}\right]$ bubble and pulse flow regime	$\phi h_t \alpha \, (v_{sl}/d_p^{0.82})^{0.67}$ in trickle flow ϕh_t = constant depending on v_{sg} in pulsing and bubbles flow regime ϕ is a weak function of v_{sl} in trickle flow, approach const value of 0.95 at high v_{sl}	$\left(\dfrac{d_p v_{sl}}{D \phi h_t}\right) = 0.43 \; Re < 150$ in trickle flow increase with Re $150 < Re < 400$ $Re = \dfrac{d_p L}{\phi h_t \mu_L}$	$k_{sd}a_s = 4.2 \times 10^{-4} d_p^{-1.25} v_{sl}^{1.2} v_{sg}^{0.64}$ $v_{sg} > 5$ cm/s d_p in cm v_{sl}, v_{sg} in cm/s	trickle, pulse, bubble flow $2 < L < 100$ kg/m² sec $0.024 < G < 0.24$ kg/m²s $0.1 < x < 20$	Cocurrent air water 1.2, 2.6 and 4.3-mm glass spheres, imperfect pulse. Time-domain fitting and moment method (for h_t).	Mastuura et al. [55]
	$\dfrac{(1-\phi)}{\phi} \alpha \left(\dfrac{v_{sl}}{\phi h_t}\right)^{-0.715*}$	$\left(\dfrac{Z v_{sl}}{D}\right) \alpha \left(\dfrac{v_{sl}}{\phi h_t}\right)^{0.866*}$	$\dfrac{k_{sd}a_s}{(1-\phi)h_t} \alpha \left(\dfrac{v_{sl}}{\phi h_t}\right)^{1.66*}$	Trickle flow $0.55 < L < 7.29$ kg/m²s $G < 0.73$ kg/m²s	Cocurrent air water 2.7 mm nonporous glass cylinders, perfect step down. Minimum sum of squares relative error.	Sicardi et al. [85]

Approximated regression

$$N = k_{sd}a_s Z/v_{s1} \qquad (72)$$

$$x = z/Z \qquad (73)$$

$$P = v_{s1}Z/D\phi h_t \qquad (74)$$

$$\theta = t/\bar{\tau}_R = t v_{s1}/Zh_t \qquad (75)$$

The preceding solution reduces to the PD model solution when $N = 0$ and $\phi = 1$. By equating the second central moments of the PDE1 and the PD models, it was shown that the Bodenstein numbers from the two models are related by:

$$\frac{1}{Bo(PD)} = \frac{1}{Bo(PDE1)} + \frac{1}{d_p N/(1 - \phi)^2 Z} \qquad (76)$$

On comparing the Bodenstein numbers, Matsuura et al. [53] found that the contribution of the mass transfer term is very much larger than the axial dispersion term, even in the pulsing- and bubble-flow regimes. They also found that the Bodenstein number obtained using the PDE1 model with their two-phase flow data compared well with published correlations for single-phase flows through packed beds using the PD model. The axial dispersion in single-phase flow is governed mainly by a convective term or by dispersion due to hydrodynamic mixing [59]. The mass transfer coefficient was correlated against particle size, gas, and liquid superficial velocities; the correlation is shown in Table 8. ϕ values showed a weak dependency on liquid flow rate in the trickling-flow regime and approached a constant value of 0.95 at high liquid flow rates.

Sicardi et al. [85] investigated the influence of the parameter estimation method used on the parameter values obtained. Both the PE1 and PDE1 models were examined. Three different parameter estimation methods were used for the PDE1 model—time-domain curve fitting with minimum sum of square error criterion, time-domain curve fitting with minimum sum of squares relative error criterion, and a combined graphic and moments method. Sicardi et al. [85] claim that the second method assigns equal importance to the entire response curve. This is only true when the response curve is plotted on semilogarithmic coordinates and if the relative error of the experimental data remain constant. They concluded that, with the exception of the total liquid holdup, the values of the other parameters were very sensitive to the parameter estimation methods, especially at low liquid flow rates. They further warned that care must be taken in comparing literature results. Sicardi et al. [85] also performed experiments using two tracers of different molecular diffusivities but found that this had a negligible effect on the parameters of the models. From this result, they concluded that mass transfer between the dynamic and stagnant regions was mainly attributable to the movement of fluid streams between them. The failure to detect any significant effects of the tracers on the model parameters is possibly due to the fact that the tracer measurements were stopped just when some difference in the response curve would be expected to show (Figure 14).

The influence of tracer diffusivity on the Bodenstein number and on the total holdup should be insignificant (PDE models). It should only affect the values of ϕ and $k_{sd}a_s$ (or S_g) if the mode of mass transfer between the stagnant and dynamic regions is governed by molecular diffusion, the value of ϕ being smaller and/or $k_{sd}a_s$ larger for tracers with high molecular diffusivity. The results of Sicardi et al. [85] and Kan and Greenfield [45] show that molecular diffusion is not the sole transfer mechanism; neither results are conclusive in disproving that under some conditions molecular diffusion may be important.

In their paper, Kan and Greenfield [45] also proposed a model similar to the PDE2 model but with the addition of an axial dispersion term. The model equations are:

$$\phi h_t \frac{\partial C_d}{\partial t} = D\phi h_t \frac{\partial^2 C_d}{\partial z^2} - v_{s1} \frac{\partial C_d}{\partial z} + E'_s a_s \frac{\partial C_s}{\partial y}\bigg|_{y=0} \qquad (77)$$

for the dynamic liquid fraction and Equation 61 for the stagnant zone. They did not investigate this model further.

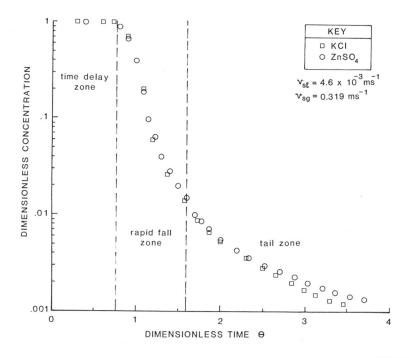

Figure 14. Response curve to a step decrease in tracer concentration [85].

Lerou et al. [49] proposed a residence-time model for pulsing flow in trickle-flow reactors. The model is basically similar to the plug-flow stagnancy model (PE1), with the stagnant region replaced by a continuous liquid film moving in plug flow at a much slower velocity than the main stream. The governing equations are:

$$v_1 \frac{\partial C_1}{\partial z} + \frac{\partial C_1}{\partial t} = k_1(C_2 - C_1) \tag{78}$$

and

$$v_2 \frac{\partial C_2}{\partial z} + \frac{\partial C_2}{\partial t} = k_2(C_1 - C_2) \tag{79}$$

where $v_i = v_{si}/h_i$, is the linear velocity of the i-phase, $k_i = k_{sf}a_f/h_i$, is the mass transfer coefficient, a_f is the surface area of free liquid taken up by the pulses per unit reactor volume, v_{si} is the volumetric flow rate of the i-phase per column cross-sectional area, and h_i is the volumetric holdup of the i-phase per reactor volume. The exit stream concentration is obtained by averaging the concentrations of the two streams:

$$C(t, z) = \frac{v_{s1}C_1 + v_{s2}C_2}{v_{s1} + v_{s2}} = \frac{k_2v_1C_1 + k_1v_2C_2}{k_2v_1 + k_1v_2} \tag{80}$$

The first moment and standard deviation of this model are as follows:

$$m_1 = \frac{(h_1 + h_2)Z}{v_{s1} + v_{s2}} = \frac{(k_1 + k_2)Z}{k_1v_2 + k_2v_1} \tag{81}$$

and

$$\sigma^2 = \frac{2k_1k_2(v_2 - v_1)^2 Z}{(k_1v_2 + k_2v_1)^3} \left\{ 1 + \frac{\exp\left[-\left[\dfrac{k_1}{v_1} + \dfrac{k_2}{v_2}\right]Z\right] - 1}{\left[\dfrac{k_1}{v_1} + \dfrac{k_2}{v_2}\right]Z} \right\} \tag{82}$$

By making a number of assumptions about the order of magnitude of v_{s2}/v_{s1} and h_2/h_1 in the pulsing-flow regime, the authors arrived at the following simple relationship:

$$\frac{\sigma^2}{m_1} = \frac{2}{k_1} \tag{83}$$

Comparing the preceding with the expression for σ^2/m_1^2 from the axial-dispersion (PD) model, the axial-dispersion coefficient can be related to k_1 by:

$$D = (v_{sl}/h_l)^2/k_1 \tag{84}$$

In other words, the axial-dispersion coefficient of the PD model is inversely proportional to the mixing intensity between the slug and the film. From their tracer experiments, Lerou et al. [49] plotted the values of σ^2/m_1 versus superficial gas velocity at various liquid velocities and found that σ^2/m_1 (hence $2/k_1$ or D) reaches a minimum value at a gas velocity close to the transition from trickling to pulsing flow, and approached asymptotically a constant value at very high gas rates. These asymptotic values decrease hyperbolically with increasing liquid rate. From this, it can be deduced that, at the transition of or in the pulsing-flow regime, axial dispersion (PD model) is less than that in the trickling-flow regime, or alternatively, the liquid flow in the transitional- and pulsed-flow regime is closer to plug flow when compared to the trickling-flow regime.

The phenomenon of tailing so commonly observed in the trickling-flow regime has not been mentioned in papers covering the pulsing-flow regimes. Typical response curves for the pulsing-flow regime have not been shown either. The work of Lerou et al. [49] and Matsuura et al. [53] have shown that less dispersion is observed in the pulsing-flow regime. Other advantages of operating in the pulsing-flow regime are increased catalyst wetting, enhanced transport coefficients, and improved uniformity of flow through the bed [49]. It is thus surprising that very few residence-time studies in this flow regime have been reported.

Trickle-flow reactors with small (<2 mm) packings have had only limited investigation, as well. The use of smaller particles has the following advantages:

- Decreased backmixing or dispersion.
- Increased catalyst activity per unit volume of reactor.
- Increased surface area per unit volume of reactor.
- Increased pressure drop and hence gas-liquid interaction.
- Increased transfer coefficients.
- Increased wetted areas (wetting efficiency).
- Increased flow uniformity (reduced flow maldistribution).
- Increased liquid holdup and hence mean residence time.

The increased pressure drop, however, implies an increase in operating costs. The optimal catalyst size is a function of the catalyst cost, expected life, and poisoning or deactivation mechanism (if applicable).

Table 9 summarizes the flow regimes in trickle-flow systems for which RTD studies have been reported.

Table 9
RTD Models and Flow Regimes in Which Various Types of Flow Been Used

Flow Regimes	Trickle Flow	Pulsing Flow	Bubble Flow	Spray Flow
Plugflow	✓	—	—	—
Plugflow dispersion	✓	✓	✓	—
Plugflow stagnancy PE1	✓	—	—	—
Plugflow stagnancy PE2	✓	—	—	—
Plug and Film flow and mass exchange	—	✓	—	—
Plugflow dispersion stagnancy PDE1	✓	✓	✓	—
Plugflow dispersion stagnancy PDE2	—	—	—	—

Stagewise Models

A summary of stagewise models of trickle-flow systems is provided in Table 10. The simplest of the stagewise models is the stirred-tanks-in-series model. In this model, the reactor is represented by a series of perfectly mixed identical stages, the output from one stage being the input to the next. This model has been discussed at great length in many chemical reaction engineering text books [51]. The degree of backmixing in the reactor is characterized by the volume of a single stage and the number of such stages; the larger the number of stages, the less the overall degree of backmixing. This model was used by Ramachandran and Smith [69] to analyze the performance of a trickle-flow reactor. Although the model is simple, it gives little insight into the physical processes actually occurring in the reactor.

With the acceptance of the concept of stagnant zones existency in packed beds, both the differential models and stagewise models were developed to take this into account. Van Swaaij et al. [94] proposed the parallel mixed-cell model. The liquid flow in the reactor is divided into two streams; a small quantity q_1 passes through the stagnant zone of volume V_1. The parameters for this model are the total holdup, h_t; the stagnant volume, V_1; the fraction of fluid entering the stagnant zone, q_1; and the number of such cascades, n. The transfer function for the model was shown to be:

$$\frac{\bar{C}(j)}{\bar{C}(0)} = G(j) = \left[\frac{1 + (q_1\bar{t}_{R2}/\bar{t}_R + (1 - q_1)\bar{t}_{R1}/\bar{t}_R)s}{(1 + \bar{t}_{R1}s/\bar{t}_R)(1 + \bar{t}_{R2}s/\bar{t}_R)} \right]^j \tag{85}$$

The number of stages, j, can be evaluated from experiments using a nonwettable packing (i.e., $V_1 = 0$), for which it can be shown that $\sigma^2 = 1/j$.

Michell and Furzer [55, 56] modeled the liquid flow through packed beds by considering the liquid flow as flowing in a laminar film between the packings with partial mixing occurring at the packing junctions. The partial mixing is modeled as a perfectly mixed stagnant zone with a bypass stream. The model parameters are the total and dynamic holdups, the fraction of fluid entering the stagnant zone, q_1, and the number of cascades. The model was shown to give a good fit to the experimental RTD. The authors prematurely concluded that the mixing at the packing junction is achieved mainly by hydrodynamic effects. Since their experiments were conducted at quite high liquid flow rates and a pulse input was used, the tracer may not have diffused completely into the stagnant zones. This is reflected by the fact that their model predicted 90% to 94% instantaneous bypass at the packing junction. The increase in q_1 as the liquid flow rate is increased may have been caused by increased mass transfer rate between the stagnant and dynamic regions or by incomplete catalyst wetting at the lower liquid rates. Under this condition, the increase in liquid flow rate would be accommodated by an increasing surface area of catalyst being wetted and hence by an increasing number of contact points.

Rao and Varma [70] proposed a more complex model, which takes into account dispersion in the laminar film. They modeled the incomplete mixing at the packing junction by two perfectly mixed tanks which exchange mass with each other. The model contains six parameters, the total

Table 10
Summary of Stagewise Model

Model	Schematic Representation	Reference
Series of mixed-cell model		Ramachandran and Smith [68, 69]
Parallel mixed-cell model		Van Swaaij et al. [94]
Michell-Furzer model (laminar film-mixing cell with bypass model)		Michell and Furzer [55, 56]
Rao-Varma model		Rao and Varma [70]
Modified mixed-cell model		Popovic and Deckwer [67]

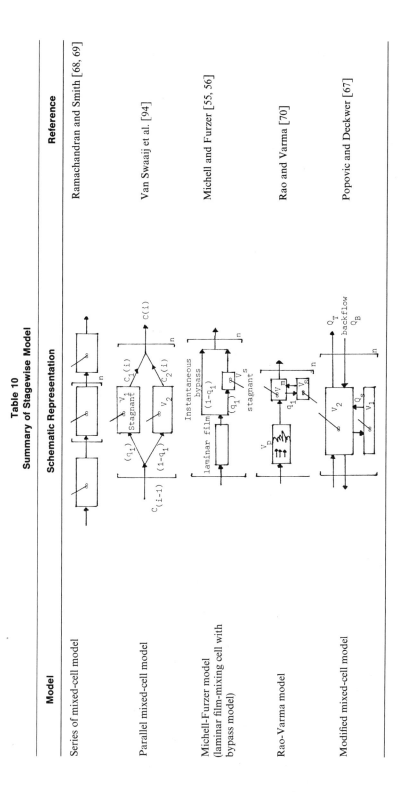

Table 11

Comparison between Differential and Stagewise Models

Differential Models	Stagewise Models
Difficult to solve, consist of partial differential equations.	Simple to solve. Consist of algebraic equations.
Boundary conditions can be complicated.	Uncomplicated boundary conditions.
Contain one less parameter than the corresponding stagewise model.	Contain one more parameter than the corresponding differential model.
Parameter estimation is easier and more accurate, especially when an analytical solution is available	Parameter estimation is more difficult and less accurate, since the number of cascades can only take integer values.
Relatively easy to use for scale-up purposes.	Difficult to use for scale-up purposes.

holdup, dynamic holdup, stagnant holdup, the fraction of the feed which exchanges mass with the stagnant region, q_1, the dispersion coefficient, D, and the total number of such cascades, n. The model predicted that an element of liquid would spend on average half of its time on the packing surface and the remaining period in the interstices between the packings. The number of parameters which need to be determined was reduced by taking n as the ratio of bed height to particle size, the fractional dispersed film volume as 0.5, and the fraction of feed which exchanges mass with the stagnant zones as $q_1 = 10^{-5}$. The last two values were determined from simulated response observations. The other three parameters were obtained by curve fitting using the least-squares deviation criterion. The low value of q_1 indicates that the authors used data from pulse input experiments.

Popovic and Deckwer [67] proposed a modified version of the mixed-cell-in-series model by adding two additional features: mass exchange with a stagnant region and a backflow of fluid from the next cascade. This model has five parameters: the total holdup, the stagnant holdup, the backflow rate, the mass exchange rate, and the total number of cascades. If the number of cascades is very large, this model approaches the PDE1 model; similarly, if backflow is negligible, the stagewise model approaches the PE1 model. Table 11 gives a general comparison between stagewise models and differential models.

Very little has been done in correlating the parameters of the stagewise models with the operating conditions, packing, and column geometry, etc. Generally, these models have only been tested with countercurrent flow in packed beds.

Stochastic Models

Only two types of stochastic models will be discussed in this section; these are models based on the time delay concept and models based on the Markov chain concept.

Buffham et al. [11, 12] proposed the probabilistic time-delay model for the description of flow in packed beds. The model is based on the probability of an element of fluid being delayed (the stopping process), and on the nature of the delay process itself. While the stopping process is described by a Poisson distribution, two types of delays are considered. The first one is a fixed time delay, in which it is assumed that the same length of time is spent at each stop by the delayed elements. This corresponds to the delay process being made up of a number of plug-flow pores. The second delay process is an exponentially distributed time delay which corresponds to entering perfectly mixed regions. This second model is conceptually similar to the PE1 model. The parameters for the model are the number of stops, which is numerically equal to the Poisson Distribution parameter θ, the average delay time, and the mean residence time or total holdup. The parameters of the model were estimated using a graphical method.

Oorts and Hellinckx [61] proposed a modified time-delay model, in which an additional parameter is added to take into account the imperfect mixing during the stop (delay). The parameters of the model were obtained by curve fitting using the least-squares deviation criterion. The model gave a better fit than did the PD model. Unfortunately, the validity of the model at high response time was not investigated and the physical meaning of the additional parameter is not known.

Achwal and Stepanek [1] proposed a stochastic residence-time model based on the Markov chain concept. The model assumes that the moving liquid can be divided into small elements that retain their identity during passage through the reactor. These elements can alternate between several velocity states and the transition from one velocity state to another is a completely random event. Their model is the simplest of the Markov chain-type models and considers only two velocity states. The introduction of additional velocity states is accompanied by a rather dramatic increase in the number of adjustable parameters; this is considered undesirable. The parameters of the model are the total holdup and the number of times the velocity state changes from positive to negative, p, and from negative to positive, q. Although the system studied by Achwal and Stepanek was two-phase cocurrent upflow through a packed bed, the same model can be used for the downflow case. Upon comparing their model with the PD model, they concluded that the two models were in contradiction with each other. They reasoned that the PD model predicts an intensification of mixing (higher dispersion coefficients) at higher gas and liquid flow rates, while for the same condition their model predicts longer distances between transitions of the velocity states and hence, less intense mixing. To interpret this situation correctly, however, it is necessary to distinguish between the overall extent of mixing (a measure which is given by the value of the dispersion coefficient) and the intensity of a local mixing process. It is quite feasible to have very few transitions between velocity states (e.g., exchange with stagnant zones) and yet, still have a high, effective level of mixing as shown by an RTD curve with greater spreading.

CONCLUSIONS

Among the different types of models discussed, the differential models are the most widely used. Table 9 summarizes the differential models and the flow regimes in which they have been investigated. Although operation in the pulsing- and bubbling-flow regimes offers certain advantages, very few residence-time studies in these regimes have been reported. No RTD work has been reported in the spray-flow regime. There is a need for further work in these areas.

Trickle-flow reactors with small (<2 mm) packings are also another area that needs further investigation. The significance of interfacial tension effects is not well understood, although studies of unsaturated flow in soils and in oil-bearing rocks provide an excellent starting point. As catalysts become more active and more expensive the optimal particle size for trickle-flow operation will decrease.

The major sources of dispersion in flow systems are summarized in Table 12. The works of Matsuura et al. [53] and Lerou et al. [49] showed that the main source of dispersion in trickle-flow reactors is the relatively slow mass transfer between the stagnant and the flowing liquid, this

Table 12
Major Sources of Dispersion in Flow Systems

Sources	Single-Phase Flow in Pipes	Single-Phase Flow in Packed Beds	Two-Phase Flow in Packed Beds
1. Velocity profile	X	X	X
2. Molecular diffusion	X	X	X
3. Eddy mixing	X	X	X
4. Fluid maldistribution			X
5. Flow path variation			X
6. Stagnancy		Y	X
7. Fluid-fluid interaction			X

X Present
Y Probably present

being proportionately larger in the pulsing- and bubbling-flow regimes. This suggests that the simple plug-flow stagnancy models or even the plug-flow dispersion model may be adequate for modeling the residence time of the liquid in these higher interaction regimes.

A reactor model can be obtained by combining the most appropriate residence-time model with the kinetic, heat, and mass transfer expressions. However, there may be several residence-time models which will fit the RTD of the reactor with the same goodness of fit. In such cases, the ultimate test of the residence-time model is to predict the reactor performance under various conditions when converted into a reactor model.

NOTATION

a	specific surface area of packing (L^{-1})
a_f	surface area of free liquid taken up by pulses per unit reactor volume (L^{-1})
a_s	interregional area between dynamic and stagnant zones per unit volume of reactor (L^{-1})
a_w	surface area of wetted packing per reactor volume (L^{-1})
A	cross-sectional area of column (L^2)
Bo	Bodenstein number, $d_p v_{s1}/Dh_t$ $(-)$
C, C_s, C_d	concentration of tracer $(M\ L^{-3})$
C_{sd}	response to step decrease input $(-)$
C_1, C_2	concentration in phase 1 and 2 $(M\ L^{-3})$
$\bar{C}(s)$	Laplace transform of C, as defined in Equation 24 $(M\ T\ L^{-3})$
$C^*(t)$	C-curve, dimensionless concentration of tracer, $C(t)/C_o$ where C_o is defined by Equation 2 $(-)$
$\bar{C}^*(\theta')$	Normalized C-curve as defined by Equation 9 $\equiv \bar{E}(\theta')$ $(-)$
d_p	particle diameter (L)
D	axial dispersion coefficient $(L^2\ T^{-1})$
D_t	diameter of reactor tube (L)
$E(t)$	normalized residence-time distribution (T^{-1})
E_s'	dispersion coefficient in the stagnant region $(L^2\ T^{-1})$
$\bar{E}(\theta')$	dimensionless form of E(t) $(-)$
$F(t)$	cumulative exit age distribution $(-)$
$\bar{F}(\theta')$	dimensionless form of F(t) $(-)$
g_1	slope of the first linear section of the response to a step decrease plotted on semilogarithmic paper (T^{-1})

G	gas-phase mass velocity $(M\ L^{-2}\ T^{-1})$
$G(\ )$	transfer function $(-)$
h_d, h_{op}, h_s, h_t	dynamic, operating, stagnant, and total liquid holdup, liquid volume/reactor volume $(-)$
h_1, h_2	liquid holdup of phase 1 and 2 $(-)$
$H(t)$	heavyside step function $(-)$
$I(t)$	internal age distribution (T^{-1})
I_0, I_1	Bessel function of zero-th and first order, respectively
$\bar{I}(\theta')$	dimensionless form of I(t) $(-)$
k_1, k_2	mass transfer coefficients of phase 1 and 2 (T^{-1})
k_{max}	highest-order cumulant used for parameter estimation $(-)$
$k_{sd}a_s$	mass transfer coefficient between stagnant and dynamic regions (T^{-1})
K_i	i-th cumulant as defined by Equations 30 and 31
K_i'	i-th cumulant with a time lag deducted
L	liquid-phase mass velocity $(M\ L^{-2}\ T^{-1})$
$L(t)$	life expectation distribution (T^{-1})
$\bar{L}(\theta')$	dimensionless form of L(t) $(-)$
m_i	i-th moment as defined in Equations 22 and 23 $(M\ T^{i+1}\ L^{-3})$
M, M_1	total amount of tracer injected (M)
n	number of cascades in stagewise models $(-)$
N	number of mass transfer units, $k_{sd}a_s Z/v_{s1}$ $(-)$
p	number of times the velocity state changes from positive to negative $(-)$
P	Peclet number for the PDE models, $v_{s1}Z/D\phi h_t$ $(-)$

ΔP_G pressure drop of gas flow $(M\,T^{-2}\,L^{-1})$

ΔP_L pressure drop of liquid flow $(M\,T^{-2}\,L^{-1})$

Pe Peclet number for the PD model, $v_{s1}Z/Dh_t$ (–)

Pe_p particle Peclet number $\equiv$ Bodenstein number (–)

q number of times the velocity state changes from negative to positive (–)

q_1 fraction of liquid flowing through the stagnant region (–)

Q volumetric flow rate $(L^3\,T^{-1})$

Q_B, Q_T volumetric backflow and throughflow rates $(L^3\,T^{-1})$

Re_L liquid Reynolds number, $d_p\rho_L v_{s1}/\mu_L$ (–)

s Laplace transform variable (T^{-1})

s_{opt} optimum value of s (T^{-1})

S_g stagnancy number defined by Equation 56 (–)

t time variable (T)

t_D time lag, breakthrough time (T)

Δt_D difference in time lag between output and input signals (T)

t_{mode} time at which signal is maximum (T)

t_I internal age, the time a fluid element inside the reactor has been in the reactor (T)

t_L life expectation, the additional time a fluid element will spend in the reactor before leaving (T)

t_R residence time, the time a fluid

element spent inside the reactor, i.e., the time from when it enters until it leaves (T)

$\bar{t}_I$ mean (average) internal age (T)

$\bar{t}_L$ mean (average) life expectation (T)

$\bar{t}_R$ mean (average) residence time (T)

v_1, v_2 velocities of phases 1 and 2, v_{si}/h_i $(L\,T^{-1})$

v_{s1}, v_{s2} superficial velocities of phase 1 and 2 $(L\,T^{-1})$

v_{sl}, v_{sg} superficial liquid and gas velocity $(L\,T^{-1})$

V_1, V_2 volume of stagnant and dynamic compartments (L^3)

V_m volume of the mixing compartments at the packing junction (L^3)

V_p volume of the dispersed film in Rao and Varma's model (L^3)

V_R volume of reactor (L^3)

V_s volume of the stagnant region (L^3)

w_i i-th weighted moment $(M\,T^{i+1}\,L^{-3})$

w_i' i-th weighted moment about the mean $(M\,T^{i+1}\,L^{-3})$

x dimensionless distance, z/Z (–)

y distance from dynamic/stagnant interregional boundary into the stagnant regions (L)

z distance from the reactor inlet (L)

Z reactor length (L)

Greek Symbols

α ratio of stagnant to dynamic holdups, h_s/h_d (–)

$\delta(\ )$ Dirac δ function (T^{-1})

$\bar{\Delta}$ average stagnant film thickness (L)

ε external bed voidage (–)

λ correction factor for flowmap, $(\rho_G\rho_L/\rho_{air}\rho_{water})^{1/2}$, (–)

μ mean of residence-time distribution (T)

μ_L, μ_G liquid and gas viscosity $(M\,L^{-1}\,T^{-1})$

ϕ ratio of dynamic to total holdup, h_d/h_t (–)

ψ correction factor for flowmap, $\dfrac{\sigma_{water}}{\sigma_L}\left[\dfrac{\mu_L}{\mu_{water}}\left[\dfrac{\rho_{water}}{\rho_L}\right]^2\right]^{1/3}$, (–)

ρ_L, ρ_G liquid and gas density $(M\,L^{-3})$

σ standard deviation of residence time distribution (T)

τ dummy time variable (T)

τ_s mean residence time, residence time of system with no short circuiting and dead zones (T)

θ dimensionless time variable, $t/\bar{t}_R$ (–)

θ' dimensionless time variable, t/τ_s (–)

$\bar{\theta}_I$ dimensionless mean internal age, $\bar{t}_I/\tau_s$ (–)

$\bar{\theta}_L$ dimensionless mean life expectation, $\bar{t}_L/\tau_s$ (–)

$\bar{\theta}_R$ dimensionless mean residence time, $\bar{t}_R/\tau_s$ (–)

ζ dummy distance variable (L)

Subscripts

d	dynamic region	G, max	maximum gas flow condition
di	dynamic input	L	liquid
G	gas	s	stagnant region

REFERENCES

1. Achwal, S. K., and Stepanek, J. B., "Residence-Time Distribution in a Liquid Flowing Cocurrently with a Gas Through a Packed Bed," *Can. J. Chem. Eng.*, 57:409 (1979).
2. Adachi, S., et al., "Pulse Response in an Immobilized Enzyme Column: Theoretical Method for Predicting Elution Curves," *Biotech. Bioeng.*, 22:779 (1980).
3. Adachi, S., et al., "Pulse Response in an Immobilized Enzyme Column: Elution Profiles in Reversible and Consecutive Reactions," *Biotech. Bioeng.*, 23:1961 (1981).
4. Anderson, K. L., Stokke, O. M., and Gilbert, R. E., "Radial Mixing During Two-Phase Countercurrent Flow through a Packed Column," *Ind. Eng. Chem. Fundam.*, 5(3):430 (1966).
5. Anderssen, A. S., and White, E. T., "Parameter Estimation by the Transfer Function Method," *Chem. Eng. Sci.*, 25:1015 (1970).
6. Anderssen, A. S., and White, E. T., "Parameter Estimation by the Weighted Moments Method," *Chem. Eng. Sci.*, 26:1203 (1971).
7. Babcock, B. D., Mejdell, G. T., and Hougen, O. A., "Catalysed Gas Liquid Reaction in Trickling Bed Reactors: Part I. Hydrogenation of α-methylstyrene Catalysed by Palladium," *AIChE J.*, 3(3):366 (1957).
8. Bennett, A., and Goodridge, F., "Hydrodynamic and Mass Transfer Studies in Packed Absorption Columns—Part I: Axial Liquid Dispersion," *Trans. Instn. Chem. Eng.*, 48:T232 (1970).
9. Blok, J. R., and Drinkenburg, A. H., "Hydrodynamic Properties of Pulses in Two-Phase Downflow Operated Packed Columns," *Chem. Eng. J.*, 25:89 (1982).
10. Bondi, A., "Handling Kinetics from Trickle-Phase Reactors," *Chem. Tech.*, 186 (March 1971).
11. Buffham, B. A., Gibilaro, L. G., and Rathor, M. N., "A Probabilistic Time Delay Description of Flow in Packed Beds," *AIChE J.*, 16:218 (1970a).
12. Buffham, B. A., and Gibilaro, L. G., "A Unified Time Delay Model for Dispersion in Flowing Media," *Chem. Eng. J.*, 1:31 (1970b).
13. Charpentier, J. C., and Favier, M., "Some Liquid Hold-Up Experimental Data in Trickle-Bed Reactors for Foaming and Non foaming Hydrocarbons," *AIChE J.*, 21(6):1213, (1975).
14. Charpentier, J. C., "Recent Progress in Two-Phase Gas-Liquid Mass Transfer in Packed Beds," *Chem. Eng. J.*, 11:161 (1976).
15. Chou, T. S., Worley, F. L., Jr., and Luss, D., "Transition to Pulsed Flow in Mixed Phase Cocurrent Downflow through a Fixed Bed," *Ind. Eng. Chem. Process Des. Dev.*, 16(3):242 (1977).
16. Clements, W. C., Jr., "A Note on Determination of the Parameters of the Longitudinal Dispersion Model from Experimental Data," *Chem. Eng. Sci.*, 24:957 (1969).
17. Danckwerts, P. V., "Continuous Flow Systems. Distribution of Residence Times," *Chem. Eng. Sci.*, 2:1 (1953).
18. DeMaria, F., and White, R. R., "Transient Response Study of Gas Flowing through Irrigated Packing," *AIChE J.*, 6(3):473 (1970).
19. Domnesteanu, R., "Evaluating both Macro and Micromixing in a Chemical Reactor by Means of Reactant Tracers," *Chem. Eng. Sci.*, 28:2260 (1973).
20. Enright, J. T., and Chuang, T. T., "Deuterium Exchange Between Hydrogen and Water in a Trickle-Bed Reactor," *Can. J. Chem. Eng.*, 56:246 (1978).

21. Eroglu, I., and Dogu, T., "Dynamic Analysis of a Trickle Bed Reactor by Moment Technique," *Chem. Eng. Sci.*, 38(5):801 (1983).
22. Fahim, M. A., and Wakao, N., "Parameter Estimation from Tracer Response Measurements," *Chem. Eng. J.*, 25:1 (1982).
23. Farid, M. M., and Gunn, D. J., "Dispersion in Trickle and Two-Phase Flow in Packed Columns," *Chem. Eng. Sci.*, 34:579 (1979).
24. Flinn, R. A., Larson, O. A., and Beuther, H., *Hydrocarbon Proc. Petr. Refiner*, 42(9):129 (1963).
25. Furzer, I. A., and Michell, R. W., "Liquid Phase Dispersion in Packed Beds with Two-Phase Flow," *AIChE J.*, 16(3):380 (1970).
26. Gangwal, S. K., et al., "Interpretation of Chromatographic Peaks by Fourier Analysis," *Can J. Chem. Eng.*, 49:113 (1971).
27. Germain, A. H., Lefebvre, A. G., and L'Homme, G. A., "Experimental Study of a Catalytic Trickle-Bed Reactor," *Adv. Chem. Series No.*, 133:164 (1974).
28. Gianetto, A., et al., "Hydrodynamics and Solid Liquid Contacting Effectiveness in Trickle Bed Reactors," *AIChE J.*, 24(6):1087 (1978).
29. Goldfish, L. H., Koutsky, J. A., and Adler, R. J., "Tracer Introduction by Flash Photolysis," *Chem. Eng. Sci.*, 20:1011 (1965).
30. Goto, S., and Smith, J. M., "Trickle-Bed Reactor Performance: Part I. Hold-up and Mass Transfer Effects," *AIChE J.*, 21(4):706 (1975a).
31. Goto, S., and Smith, J. M., "Trickle-Bed Reactor Performance: Part II. Reaction Studies," *AIChE J.*, 21(4):714 (1975b).
32. Goto, S., and Smith, J. M., "Performance of Slurry and Trickle-Bed Reactors: Application to Sulfur Dioxide Removal," *AIChE J.*, 24(2):286 (1978).
33. Gottschlich, C. F., "Axial Dispersion in a Packed Bed," *AIChE J.*, 9(1):88 (1963).
34. Hartman, M., and Coughlin, R. W., "Oxidation of SO_2 in a Trickle-Bed Reactor Packed with Carbon," *Chem. Eng. Sci.*, 27:867 (1972).
35. Henry, C. H., and Gilbert, J. B., "Scale up of Pilot Plant Data for Catalytic Hydroprocessing," *Ind. Eng. Chem. Process Des. Dev.*, 12(3):328 (1973).
36. Herskowitz, M., and Smith, J. M., "Liquid Distribution in Trickle-Bed Reactors: Part I. Flow Measurements," *AIChE J.*, 24(3):439 (1978a).
37. Herskowitz, M., and Smith, J. M., "Liquid Distribution in Trickle-Bed Reactors: Part II. Tracer Studies," *AIChE J.*, 24(3):450 (1978b).
38. Herskowitz, M., and Smith, J. M., "Trickle-Bed Reactors: A Review," *AIChE J.*, 29(1):1 (1983).
39. Hochman, J. M., and Effron, E., "Two-Phase Cocurrent Downflow in Packed Beds," *Ind. Eng. Chem. Fundam.*, 8(1):63, (1969).
40. Hofmann, H., "Hydrodynamics, Transport Phenomena, and Mathematical Models in Trickle-Bed Reactors," *Int. Chem. Eng.*, 17(1):19 (1977).
41. Hofmann, H., "Multiphase Catalytic Packed-Bed Reactors," *Cat. Rev. Sci. Eng.*, 17:71 (1978).
42. Hoogendoorn, C. J., and Lips, J., "Axial Mixing of Liquid in Gas-Liquid Flow through Packed Beds," *Can. J. Chem. Eng.*, 43:125 (1965).
43. Kan, K. M., and Greenfield, P. F., "Multiple Hydrodynamic States in Cocurrent Two-Phase Downflow Through Packed Beds," *Ind. Eng. Chem. Process. Des. Develop.*, 17(4):482 (1978).
44. Kan, K. M., "Modelling of Trickle Bed Reactors with Small Packings—Hydrodynamics, Residence Time Distribution and Reactor Design," University of Queensland, Ph.D. Thesis, Australia, (1981).
45. Kan, K. M., and Greenfield, P. F., "Residence Time Model for Trickle Flow Reactors Incorporating Incomplete Mixing in Stagnant Regions," *AIChE J.*, 29(1):123 (1983).
46. Klinkenberg, A., "Numerical Evaluation of Equations Describing Transient Heat and Mass Transfer in Packed Solids," *Ind. Eng. Chem.*, 40:1992 (1948).
47. Kunigita, E., Otake, T., and Yamanishi, T., *J. Chem. Eng. Japan*, 26:800 (1962).
48. Lapidus, L., "Flow Distribution and Diffusion in Fixed-Bed two-phase reactors," *Ind. Eng. Chem.*, 49(6):1000 (1957).
49. Lerou, J. J., Glasser, D., and Luss, D., "Packed-Bed Liquid Phase Dispersion in Pulsed Gas Liquid Downflow," *Ind. Eng. Chem. Fundam.*, 19(1):66 (1980).

50. Levenspiel, O., and Smith, W. K., "Notes on the Diffusion-Type Model for the Longitudinal Mixing of Fluids in Flow," *Chem. Eng. Sci.*, 6:227 (1957).

51. Levenspiel, O., Chemical Reaction Engineering, 2nd Edn., Chapter 9, Wiley International Edition, John Wiley and Sons, N. Y. (1972).

52. Mata, A. R., and Smith, J. M., "Oxidation of Sulfur Dioxide in a Trickle-Bed Reactor," *Chem. Eng. J.*, 22:229 (1981).

53. Matsuura, A., Akeheta, T., and Shirai, T., "Axial Dispersion of Liquid in Cocurrent Gas-Liquid Downflow in Packed Beds," *J. Chem. Eng. Japan*, 9(4):294 (1976).

54. Mears, D. E., "The Role of Liquid Hold-Up and Effective Wetting on the Performance of Trickle-Bed Reactors," *Adv. Chem. Ser.*, 133:218 (1974).

55. Michell, R. W., and Furzer, I. A., "Trickle-Flow in Packed Beds," *Trans. Instn. Chem. Eng.*, 50:334 (1972a).

56. Michell, R. W., and Furzer, I. A., "Mixing in Trickle-Flow through Packed Beds," *Chem. Eng. J.*, 4:53 (1972b).

57. Midoux, N., and Charpentier, J. C., "On an Experimental Method of Residence-Time Distribution Measurement in the Fast Flowing Phase on a Two-Phase Apparatus. Application to Gas Flow in Gas Liquid Packed Column," *Chem. Eng. J.*, 4:287 (1972).

58. Mills, P. L., Wu, W. P., and Dudukovic, M. P., "Tracer Analysis in Systems with Two-Phase Flow," *AIChE J.*, 25(5):885 (1979).

59. Miyauchi, T., and Kikuchi, T., "Axial Dispersion in Packed Beds," *Chem. Eng. Sci.*, 30:343 (1975).

60. Montagna, A. A., and Shah, Y. T., "The Role of Liquid Hold-Up, Effective Catalyst Wetting, and Backmixing on the performance of a Trickle-Bed Reactor for Residue Hydrodesulfurization," *Ind. Eng. Chem. Process Des. Dev.*, 14(4):479 (1975).

61. Oorts, A. J., and Hellinckx, L. J., "A Modified Time Delay Model for Flow in Packed Columns," *Chem. Eng. J.*, 7:147 (1974).

62. Ostergaard, K., and Michelsen, M. L., "On the Use of the Imperfect Tracer Pulse Method for Determination of Hold-Up and Axial Mixing," *Can. J. Chem. Eng.*, 47:107 (1969).

63. Otake, T., and Kunigita, E., *J. Chem. Eng. Japan*, 22:144 (1958).

64. Paraskos, J. A., Frayer, J. A., and Shah, Y. T., "Effect of Hold-Up, Incomplete Catalyst Wetting and Backmixing During Hydroprocessing in Trickle-Bed Reactors," *Ind. Eng. Chem. Process Des. Dev.*, 14(3):315 (1975).

65. Parimi, K., and Harris, T. R., "The Identification of Residence-Time Models by Reacting Tracer Experiments," *Can J. Chem. Eng.*, 53:175 (1975).

66. Petho, A., and Noble, R. D. (Eds.), *Residence-Time Distribution Theory in Chemical Engineering*, Weinheim, Deerfield Beach, Fla., Basel: Verlag Chemie (1982).

67. Popovic, M., and Deckwer, W. D., "Transient Behaviour of Reactors with Dispersion and Stagnant Zones," *Chem. Eng. J.*, 11:67 (1976).

68. Ramachandran, P. A., and Smith, J. M., "Dynamic Behaviour of Trickle-Bed Reactors," *Chem. Eng. Sci.*, 34:75 (1979a).

69. Ramachandran, P. A., and Smith, J. M., "Mixing Cell Method for the Design of Trickle-Bed Reactors," *Chem. Eng. J.*, 17:91 (1979b).

70. Rao, V. G., and Varma, Y. B. G., "A Model for the Residence-Time Distribution of Liquid Phase in Trickle Beds," *AIChE J.*, 22(3):612 (1976).

71. Rodrigues, A. E., Calo, J. M., and Sweed, N. H. (Eds), *Multiphase Chemical Reactors*, Vols. 1 and 2, Nato Advanced Study Institute Series, Sijthoff & Noordhoff, Maryland, U.S.A. (1981).

72. Rothfield, L. B., and Ralph, J. L., "Equivalence of Pulse and Step Residence-Time Measurements in a Trickle Bed," *AIChE J.*, 9(6):852 (1963).

73. Sater, V. E., and Levenspiel, O., "Two-Phase Flow in Packed Beds," *Ind. Eng. Chem. Fundam.*, 5(1):86 (1966).

74. Sato, Y., et al., "Flow Pattern and Pulsation Properties of Cocurrent Gas Liquid Downflow in Packed Beds," *J. Chem. Eng. Japan*, 6(4):315 (1973).

75. Satterfield, C. N., Pelossof, A. A., and Sherwood, T. K., "Mass Transfer Limitation in a Trickle-Bed Reactor," *AIChE J.*, 15(2):226 (1969).

76. Satterfield, C. N., and Way, P. R., "The Role of the Liquid Phase in the Performance of a Trickle-Bed Reactor," *AIChE J.*, 19(2):305 (1972).

77. Satterfield, C. N., and Ozel, F., "Direct Solid Catalyzed Reaction of a Vapor in an Apparently Completely Wetted Trickle Bed Reactor," *AIChE J.*, 19(6):1259 (1973).

78. Satterfield, C. N., "Trickle-Bed Reactors." *AIChE J.*, 21(2):209 (1975).

79. Schwartz, J. G., Weger, E., and Dudukovic, M. P., "Liquid Holdup and Dispersion in Trickle Bed Reactors" *AIChE J.*, 22(5):953 (1976).

80. Sedriks, W., and Kenney, C. N., "Partial Wetting in Trickle-Bed Reactors—the Reduction of Crotonaldehyde over a Palladium Catalyst," *Chem. Eng. Sci.*, 28:559 (1973).

81. Shah, Y. T., Stiegel, G. J., and Sharma, M. M., "Backmixing in Gas Liquid Reactors," *AIChE J.*, 24(3):369 (1978).

82. Shah, Y. T., *Gas-Liquid-Solid Reactor Design*, McGraw Hill International Book Company, N.Y. (1979).

83. Shestopalov, V. V., Kagarov, V. V., and Blyakham, L. I., "Longitudinal Mixing in Packed Columns," *Int. Chem. Eng.*, 4(1):17 (1964).

84. Shinnar, R., *Chem. Reaction Eng. Reviews*—Houston, ACS Symp. Series, 72:1 (1978).

85. Sicardi, S., Baldi, G., and Specchia, V., "Hydrodynamic Models for the Interpretation of the Liquid Flow in Trickle-Bed Reactors," *Chem. Eng. Sci.*, 35:1775 (1980).

86. Specchia, V., and Baldi, G., "Pressure Drop and Liquid Hold-Up for Two-Phase Cocurrent Flow in Packed Beds," *Chem. Eng. Sci.*, 32:515 (1977).

87. Stiegel, G. J., and Shah, Y. T., "Axial Dispersion in a Rectangular Bubble Column," *Can. J. Chem. Eng.*, 55:3 (1977a).

88. Stiegel, G. J., and Shah, Y. T., "Backmixing and Liquid Hold-Up in a Gas Liquid Cocurrent Upflow Packed Column," *Ind. Eng. Chem. Process Des. Dev.*, 16(1):37 (1977b).

89 Talmor, E., "Two-Phase Downflow Through Catalyst Beds: Part I. Flowmaps," *AIChE J.*, 23(6):868 (1977).

90. Tosun, G., "Axial Dispersion in Trickle-Bed Reactors. Influence of the Gas Rate," *Ind. Eng. Chem. Fundam.*, 21:184 (1982).

91. Tsukamoto, T., Morita, S., and Okada, J., "Liquid-Solid Contacting Efficiency in Trickle-Bed Reactors," *Chem. Pharm. Bull.*, 28(7):2188 (1980).

92. Van der Laan, E. Th., "Notes on the Diffusion-Type Model for the Longitudinal Mixing in Flow," *Chem. Eng. Sci.*, 7:187 (1958).

93. Van Landeghem, H., "Multiphase Reactors: Mass Transfer and Modeling," *Chem. Eng. Sci.*, 35:1912 (1980).

94. Van Swaaij, W. P. M., Charpentier, J. C., and Villermaux, J., "Residence Time Distribution in the Liquid Phase of Trickle Flow in Packed Columns," *Chem. Eng. Sci.*, 24:1083 (1969).

95. Weekman, V. W., Jr., and Myers, J. E., "Fluid Flow Characteristics of Cocurrent Gas Liquid Flow in Packed Beds," *AIChE J.*, 10(6):951 (1964).

96. Wen, C. Y., and Fan, L. T., *Models for Flow Systems and Chemical Reactors*, Marcel Dekker, N.Y., (1975).

97. White, E. T., Automation 77 Conference, Auckland, N.Z., (1975).

CHAPTER 34

ANALYSIS OF GAS DISCHARGE FROM PACKED BEDS

J. Drahos and J. Cermak

Institute of Chemical Process Fundamentals
Czechoslovak Acadamy of Science
Prague, Czechoslovakia

CONTENTS

INTRODUCTION

Gas flow through packed beds having a spatially nonuniform resistance to flow has been studied for over thirty years due to its considerable importance in chemical, metallurgical, and nuclear reactor engineering. Typical examples of packed beds are catalytic reactors, oil shale reactors, heat exchangers, stack region of blast furnaces, and pebble bed nuclear reactors. A spatial nonuniformity of bed resistance to flow results from variations of porosity caused by wall effect, nonuniform packing or variable size of packing particles. Because of its primary importance, the problem of porosity variations in packed beds is first briefly reviewed. A direct consequence of bed resistance nonuniformity is a gas flow maldistribution that may cause many undesirable effects, e.g. formation of hot spots, a loss of gas-solid contacting efficiency, etc. Experimental determination of flow maldistribution in packed beds has been investigated by many authors and the most important method used has been a determination of gas velocity field using hot wire anemometry. This experimental technique is described in the second section. The third section discusses results of experimental determination of gas flow maldistribution for one- and multidimensional approaches. Recently there has also been a growing interest in developing the adequate modeling equations to represent flow maldistribution. Several methods for computing the velocity profiles across the bed are given in the last section of this chapter.

POROSITY VARIATIONS IN PACKED BEDS

Having a volume filled with solid particles, a point porosity, ε_p, can be defined as $\varepsilon_p = 1$ inside a particle, and $\varepsilon_p = 0$ outside a particle. Using the point porosity, an area porosity, ε_A, or a volume porosity, ε_V, are defined by [1]

$$\varepsilon_A = \frac{1}{A} \int_A \varepsilon_p \, dA \tag{1}$$

$$\varepsilon_V = \frac{1}{V} \int_V \varepsilon_p \, dV \tag{2}$$

For cylindrical packed beds where the porosity variations are mainly due to bed wall, the area porosity ε_A will be defined for the area A concentric with the wall. When speaking about porosity in this study we always mean the area porosity and we let $\varepsilon_A = \varepsilon$.

The radial variation of porosity in packed beds has been studied by many authors, e.g., [2]. It has been found for spherical particles that porosity close to the bed wall is substantially higher than in the bulk, because a spherical particle contacts the wall in only one point, in contrast to contacting many other particles in the bulk of the bed. The radial profiles of porosity generally depend on the column to particle diameter ratio and the particle size and shape; several illustrative porosity profiles are given in Figure 1 both for commercial packing Raschig rings, Berl saddles) and for regularly shaped particles (spheres and cylinders). To characterize the nonspherical particles (approximately equidimensional), an equivalent diameter and sphericity can be used. The equivalent diameter, d_P, is defined as the diameter of a sphere having the same volume, V_P, as the particle:

$$d_P = (6V_P/\pi)^{1/3} \tag{3}$$

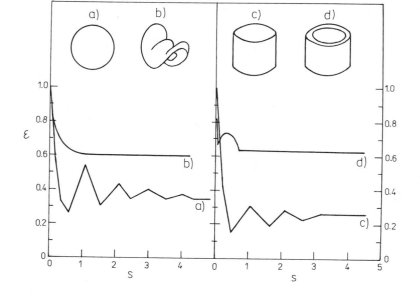

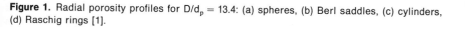

Figure 1. Radial porosity profiles for $D/d_p = 13.4$: (a) spheres, (b) Berl saddles, (c) cylinders, (d) Raschig rings [1].

The sphericity, ψ, is the ratio of the surface area of this sphere to the actual surface of the particle The dimensionless radial coordinate $s = (D/2 - r)/d_P$, where D is the column diameter.

It can be seen from Figure 1 that for highly irregular packing, such as Berl saddles, the porosity decreases from unity to a constant value about 1 particle diameter from the wall. For Raschig rings a single local maximum was observed at about 0.25 diameter from the wall followed by flat profile beginning about 0.6 diameter from the wall. For spheres and cylinders the local variations of porosity were found up to 4–5 particle diameters from the wall.

In studies [3] of the porosity in the bed consisting of particles of different sizes the overall bed porosity for the mixture was found to be less than for the individual components and the marked variations depending on the particle size ratio and the bed composition were observed. So, one can expect that radial porosity profile will have a great influence on spatial distribution of bed resistance to flow and thus on gas flow maldistribution, which is discussed in the following parts of this chapter.

HOT WIRE ANEMOMETRY

Although there are several methods for measuring gas flow velocity (e.g., pitot tube arrangements, electromagnetic induction measurements or Laser-Doppler anemometry), only the hot wire anemometry seems to provide reliable information about velocity distribution across the packed bed in both space and time domains.

Measuring Principles

Determining flow velocity using hot wire anemometry is based upon the heat exchange between a sensing element and surrounding medium. The sensing device, a thin electrically heated wire, is convectively cooled when placed in moving medium. The most common wire materials are tungsten, platinum, and platinum-iridium alloy.

There are two basic types of circuitry used in hot wire anemometry:

1. The constant current system in which the hot wire sensor is fed by a constant direct current that is independent of flow velocity. The changes in wire resistance due to the flow velocity changes cause the sensor voltage to vary.
2. The constant temperature system in which the wire temperature and hence its resistance are kept constant for all flow rates. The output of the constant temperature system is the voltage required to drive necessary current through the sensor.

When comparing both types of circuitry, the constant temperature system has several advantages (e.g., it prevents sensor burn-out when cooling velocity is suddenly decreased, allows linearizing and temperature compensation, and it is compatible with hot film types sensors) and therefore essentially replaced the constant current anemometer, which was used mainly because of electronic simplicity.

Directional Sensitivity of Hot Wire

The instantaneous response of the hot wire normal to the gas flow with velocity u_N can be described by a general form of King's law:

$$E^2 = [A' + B'(\rho u_N)^n](t_s - t_e) \tag{4}$$

where E is the wire bridge voltage, A' and B' are constants depending on fluid properties, ρ is fluid density, n is exponent that varies with velocity range and fluid used (n $\sim$ 0.5), t_s is sensor operating temperature, and t_e is environmental (fluid) temperature. In the original form of King's law [4] n = 0.5.

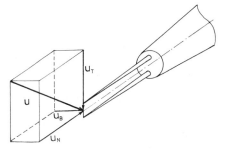

Figure 2. Velocity vector, U, and its normal, U_N, binormal, U_B, and tangential, U_T, components with respect to the hot wire.

If the flow direction is not normal to the sensor, a directional response of hot wire must be considered. It can be expressed using the effective cooling velocity, u_{eff}, and Equation 4 can be rewritten as

$$E^2 = A + Bu_{eff}^n \tag{5}$$

where A, B, and n can be determined by calibrating procedure. According to Jørgensen [5], the cooling velocity can be written as a function of the normal, u_N, binormal, u_B, and tangential, u_T, velocity components relative to the hot wire (Figure 2). Many papers dealing with the calculation of heat transfer at the hot wire use the simplified assumption that heat transfer depends only on the normal velocity component, u_N. The assumption:

$$u_{eff} = u_N \tag{6}$$

holds, however, exactly only for a laminar flow past an infinitely long cylinder in a uniform undisturbed velocity field [6], which is not the case of measuring the gas flow velocity inside or close above the packed bed. A better approach is to assume that the hot wire is equally sensitive along its entire length to u_N and make the same assumption for the second velocity component binormal to the wire, u_B, i.e.

$$u_{eff}^2 = u_N^2 + u_B^2 \tag{7}$$

An equation that considers an overall directional sensitivity of the hot wire can be written as [5]

$$u_{eff}^2 = u_N^2 + k_1^2 u_T^2 + k_2^2 u_B^2 \tag{8}$$

and the mean values for k_1 and k_2 were shown to be [5] 0.15 and 1.02, respectively, in the velocity range between 10 and 30 m/s. For velocities below 10 m/s, which occur in the case of gas flowing through packed beds, the tangential velocity component in Equation 8 can be neglected and holding $k_2 = 1$ we get Equation 7. The problem of the accuracy of hot wire signal determination with respect to the neglecting of u_T and u_B is discussed by Acrivlellis [7].

It follows from simple geometric considerations that it is possible to determine velocity components if the hot wire is made to assume as many angular positions to the time-averaged velocity vector as the number of unknowns to be determined. Several calculating procedures were suggested for both low- and high-turbulence regions using either a sensor consisting of three mutually perpendicular wires [8] or a rotated hot wire technique [9]. A practical example of the latter technique is discussed in the following section.

EXPERIMENTAL DETERMINATION OF FLOW MALDISTRIBUTION

The most important method for characterizing the flow maldistribution in packed beds is experimental determination of gas velocity field across the bed. The other methods are of limited practical significance and so only two of them are described to illustrate different ways to solve the problem.

Gas Velocity Distribution at the Exit from the Bed

From the papers dealing with the experimental determination of gas velocity field across the bed, two different approaches can be distinguished with respect to the velocity probe location: measurements inside the bed, and measurements at the exit from the bed. It is obvious that to describe the flow maldistribution in a packed bed it would be ideal to know the velocity field inside the bed. However, the flow of gas through the bed occurs along flow channels and can be characterized using a local pore velocity which is, in general, a vectorial quantity changing in both magnitude and direction. Thus, many local measurements inside the bed are necessary to representatively characterize the velocity profile. This poses a serious experimental problem. Another problem is that of disturbing the flow by the velocity probe itself. The use of a miniature hot wire probe [10, 11] is limited only to the ordered arrays of sufficiently large spherical particles and it is quite unrealistic in the case of randomly packed beds.

Because of these reasons most investigators have made their measurements at the exit from the bed using the hot wire anemometry technique. Two types of hot wire probe design have been used: a set of circular loops for determining integrated average velocities at given radial positions, and a miniature short-wire probe fixed on a traversing mechanism enabling both radial scanning and angular rotation of the probe. The first probe design, used mainly in the past, does not allow detailed study of the effects of irregularity of packing, channeling, etc. Moreover, only a limited number of loops can be used across the bed and so only a limited number of points can be obtained on the radial profile of averaged velocity. Another serious disadvantage of circular loops is discussed in the following, and therefore only the miniature short-wire probes have been used at present.

Optimal Probe Distance above the Bed

When measuring in the exit stream from the bed, an important question is that of proper distance of the probe above the bed to get a representative velocity profile. This problem is illustrated in Figure 3.

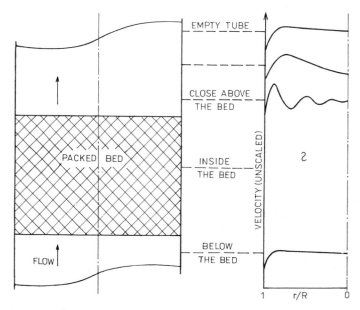

Figure 3. Illustration of radial velocity profiles measured at different axial positions.

If the velocity probe is close to the top of the bed, a velocity distribution is obtained that resembles a pore velocity distribution in a few last top layers of particles. However, as the flow exiting the bed is essentially three-dimensional and turbulent, at least normal and binormal (i.e., axial and radial) velocity components contribute to the cooling of the hot wire, and Equation 7 must be used for u_{eff}. When using the circular hot wire loops, rather long distance of the probe from the bed is necessary to eliminate the influence of both radial velocity component and turbulence. At such a long distance, Schwatz and Smith [12] used a distance of 51 mm, the velocity profile changes markedly toward the empty pipe velocity profile and is no longer representative for the bed itself.

If follows from these facts that only the short-wire miniature probe can be used to study the velocity field sufficiently close to the bed. To use this probe properly we have to consider two cases:

1. If we want to measure the velocity field very close to the bed (at the distance less than, say, 5 mm) a turbulent three-dimensional flow must be assumed. The problem of analyzing the anemometer output signal consists of finding the velocity components together with the fluctuating (turbulent) components using rather complicated procedure described e.g., by Acrivlellis [9].
2. A substantial simplification of this time-consuming technique can be achieved by shifting the probe up to the distance where effects of turbulence can be neglected; then, it is sufficient to consider only normal and binormal velocity components as contributing to the cooling of hot wire, i.e., to use Equation 7 for u_{eff}. In this case, it is possible for each point above the bed defined by cylindrical coordinates z, r, and θ to compute corresponding local velocity components u_z, u_r, and u_θ from three anemometer output signals corresponding to three different probe settings with respect to the z axis. As detailed by Ziolkowska et al. [13] and Drahoš et al. [14], the velocity components can be obtained from equations:

$$u_0^2 = u_r^2 + u_\theta^2 \tag{9}$$

$$u_{\pi/4}^2 = u_r^2 + \tfrac{1}{2}(u_z + u_\theta)^2 \tag{10}$$

$$u_{\pi/2}^2 = u_r^2 + u_z^2 \tag{11}$$

where u_0, $u_{\pi/4}$, and $u_{\pi/2}$ are the local velocities measured at probe settings of 0, $\pi/4$, and $\pi/2$, respectively, with respect to the column axis z.

An optimal probe distance from the bed can be determined by comparing the average superficial velocity, $\bar{u}_s$, and averaged axial velocity computed from experimentally determined radial profile of $\bar{u}_z$.

One-Dimensional Velocity Distribution

Despite the fact that a three-dimensional flow through the packed bed is to be assumed and thus at least the axial and radial velocity components should be determined, in many experimental studies the one-dimensional approach has been considered, i.e. only a radial dependence of the axial velocity averaged over a given circumference has been measured. A survey of the most important studies concerning one-dimensional velocity profiles above the bed is given in Table 1 (for more details see review paper by Lyczkowski [25]). Owing to a wide range of experimental conditions used—a hot wire probe design and its distance from the bed, method of evaluation of hot wire response, apparatus geometry, packing particles size and shape, flow conditions, etc.—a detailed critical comparison of results of different investigators is hardly possible. Some general conclusions can be, however, written for a cylindrical column packed with spherical on nearly spherical particles:

1. The radial profiles of velocity are nonuniform and exert local maxima near the wall.
2. The nonuniformity of velocity profiles increases when a radial temperature gradient oriented from column axis to the wall is present.

Table 1
A Survey of Experimental One-Dimensional Velocity Studies

Investigator	Experimental technique	Probe distance (mm)	Apparatus geometry				Maximal $\bar{u}_s$ (m/s)
			D_{max} (mm)	L_{max} (mm)	Packing	dp (mm)	
Morales et al. [15]	CLA[a]	9.5	52.5	460	cylinders	3.2–9.5	0.6
Schwartz, Smith [12]	CLA[a]	51	100.2	584	cylinders	3.2–6.4	1.1
Calderbank, Pogorski [16]	CLA[a]	?	128	1800	cylinders	3.2–6.4	1.0
Dorweiler, Fahien [17]	CLA[a]	25	102	?	spheres	6.4	?
Schertz, Bischoff [18]	CLA[a]	25	102	635	spheres	7.6	0.9
Price [19]	SWA-S[b]	203	305	460	spheres	6.4–25.4	6.4
Marivoet et al. [20]	TH[c]	5	75	1000	spheres	8.0	0.3
Szekely, Poveromo [21]	SWA[d]	10	153	600	spheres	1.0–6.0	0.46
Lerou, Froment [22]	SWA[d]	25	99	1000	cylinders	9.5	1.8
Stroh et al. [23]	SWA[d]	?	762	1350	spheres	38.1	3.5
Schuster, Vortmeyer [24]	LDA[e]	—	40 × 40	140	spheres	2.0	0.06

[a] *Circular loop anemometer*
[b] *Short-wire anemometer with splitter*
[c] *Thermistor*
[d] *Short-wire anemometer*
[e] *Laser-Doppler anemometer*

3. For $Re_p > 100$ there is no effect of flow rate on normalized (with respect to the average) velocity profiles.
4. Increasing the column to particle diameter ratio flattens velocity profiles.

The particle Reynolds number, Re_p, is defined by

$$Re_p = \frac{\bar{u}_s d_p \rho}{\mu} \tag{12}$$

where μ is the viscosity.

The use of one-dimensional approach restricts considerably the available amount of basic information about flow structure apart from a possible incorrectness of results when measuring too close to the bed surface. Owing to these facts, the concept of analysis of three-dimensional local velocity data is introduced in next section. Using a consistent set of three-dimensional experimental data, the effect of various experimental conditions on velocity field is discussed later.

Analysis of Three-Dimensional Local Velocities

It follows from the facts previously discussed that the three-dimensional flow approach must be considered in hot wire cooling when measuring at the exit from the bed. Using a short-wire anemometric probe it is possible to determine the velocity field across the whole exit area. After decomposing the velocity vector into its components in cylindrical coordinates and analyzing their local values, much important information can be obtained about flow structure as suggested by Drahoš et al. [14]. To illustrate the proposed approach some results of the statistical analysis of a set of experimental local velocity data are given in the following section:

Apparatus of experiment. A cylindrical column of D = 94 mm packed with spherical particles to the height L = 1,050 mm was employed. Various particle diameters were used corresponding to the values of D/d_p = 9.6, 10.8, 13.1 and 22.9, respectively. Air was passed through the column at superficial velocities up to 0.8 m/s. A short-wire probe was used at the distance of 15 mm above the bed. The circumferential profiles of velocity components, u_z, u_r, and u_θ were obtained from Equations 9–11 using a rotated hot wire technique described previously. For each circumference 128 velocity points were measured, and for analysis the local dimensionless values of velocity components, U_z, U_r, and U_θ, were used obtained by dividing by the corresponding average superficial velocity, $\bar{u}_s$:

$$U_i = \frac{u_i}{\bar{u}_s} \qquad i = z, r, \theta \tag{13}$$

Results. Figure 4 illustrates the circumferential profiles of the velocity components. The oscillating character of all profiles is clearly visible and the influence of the arrangement of particles in last layers of the bed can be discerned. For the U_z profile the number of peaks corresponded with the theoretical number of particles at a given circumference, n_t, which is given by

$$n_t = \frac{2\pi r}{d_p}(1 - \varepsilon) \tag{14}$$

It can be stated that the last bed layer representing approximately the structure of the lower ones has a decisive effect on the shape of the circumferential velocity profiles. The repacking of the bed caused a modification of all profiles, while the effect of $\bar{u}_s$ was on the whole negligible. It also follows from Figure 4 that the radial flow component that influences radial heat transfer is relatively stable when compared with the extremely fluctuating axial component (determining the gas residence time in the bed) and angular component.

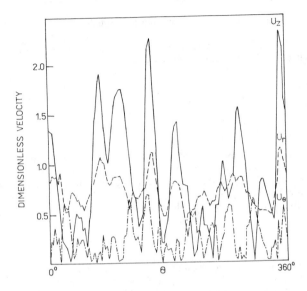

Figure 4. Examples of circumferential profiles of velocity components.

Circumferential profiles were arithmetically averaged for a given value of r to give the mean values $\bar{U}_z$, $\bar{U}_r$, and $\bar{U}_\theta$. The radial profiles of velocity components are given in Figure 5 for $D/d_p = 10.8$ together with the corresponding velocity component profiles measured 15 mm below the packed bed. It can be seen that, in contrast to apparently one-dimensional character of the flow below the bed, the flow at the exit from the bed is essentially three-dimensional at a variable ratio between the values of axial, radial, and angular components. While radial profile of $\bar{U}_z$ exerts

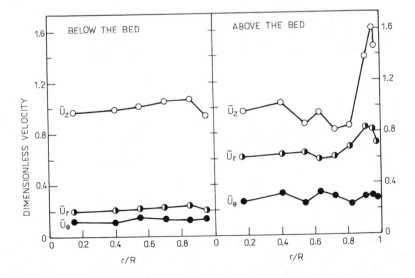

Figure 5. Radial profiles of velocity components measured below and above the bed: D = 94 mm, spheres, $d_p = 8.7$ mm.

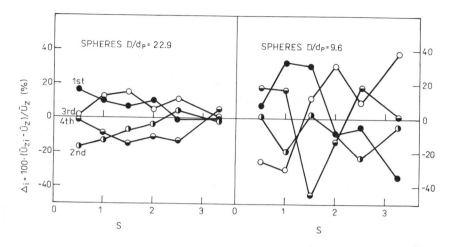

Figure 6. Illustration of angular nonuniformity of flow: ● 1st sector, ◑ 2nd sector, ○ 3rd sector, ◕ 4th sector.

a pronounced maximum near the wall (the value of maximal velocity being approximately twice that of minimal one), the profiles of $\bar{U}_r$ and $\bar{U}_\theta$ are substantially more flat. Comparing the radial profiles for different values of $\bar{u}_s$ it resulted that the effect of overall gas flow rate is negligible, which is consistent with results of previous investigators.

An attempt was made to check the axial symmetry of the flow for different values of D/d_P. The cross section of the column was divided into four sectors of equal area and mean values, $\bar{U}_{zi}$, were estimated for each sector i. The radial dependence of the relative deviations, Δ_i, of $\bar{U}_{zi}$ from the corresponding mean values $\bar{U}_z$ is given in Figure 6 for $D/d_P = 9.6$ and 22.9, respectively. It follows from Figure 6 that in addition to the radial nonuniformity of the flow there can exists also a significant angular nonuniformity, even in the case of the carefully packed bed. For low values of D/d_P the angular nonuniformity was caused mainly by individual particles themselves—the tendency of changing the sign of Δ_i with one particle diameter was observed. For higher D/d_P values the fluctuating characters of Δ_i profiles were less pronounced but slight systematic flow irregularities could be observed indicating possible packing nonuniformities.

To estimate the fluctuating component of circumferential velocity profiles the values of coefficient of variation were calculated for U_z, U_r, and U_θ. Table 2 gives the average values of the coefficient of variation for different values of D/d_P. The extremely fluctuating character of the axial and angular velocity components is clearly visible as compared with the radial one (Figure 4). It follows from Table 2 that with increasing D/d_P the fluctuating tendency of axial velocity component decreases. In Figure 7 the radial profiles of c_z are given for lower and higher values of D/d_P together with radial porosity profile for lower value of D/d_P. The pronounced correlation between the corresponding profiles of c_z and ε can be observed for low D/d_P value indicating the influence of

Table 2
Average Values of Variation Coefficients [14]

D/d_P	c_z	c_r	c_θ
22.9	0.38	0.30	0.80
13.1	0.42	0.28	0.80
10.8	0.45	0.30	0.76
9.6	0.45	0.30	0.74

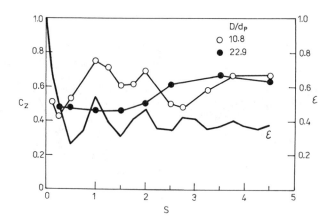

Figure 7. Radial profiles of variation coefficient, c_z, together with porosity profile for $D/d_p = 10.8$

bed microstructure on flow nonuniformity. It was found that for $D/d_P > 20$ this influence can be neglected.

To evaluate the interrelation between radial and axial velocity components the cross-correlation function was estimated along each circumference. It was ascertained that the cross-correlation function has a maximum for the zero lag, i.e., for the zero shift between velocity components with respect to the distance along the considered circumference. Thus, the normalized cross-correlation function, ρ_{rz}, can be estimated from

$$\rho_{rz} = \frac{R_{rz}}{(\sigma_r^2 \sigma_z^2)^{1/2}} \tag{15}$$

where σ_r^2, σ_s^2 are variance estimates and R_{rz} is defined by

$$R_{rz} = \frac{1}{N} \sum_{i=1}^{N} (U_{ri} - \bar{U}_r)(U_{zi} - \bar{U}_z) \tag{16}$$

with $N = 128$ being the number of samples along the given circumference.

Analyzing the radial profiles of ρ_{rz} it was found that in the wall region the strongest cross-correlation exists with ρ_{rz} being always positive. This implies that the increase of axial component in this region is not compensated by the decrease of radial component. As shown by Ziolkowska et al. [26], who used the proposed method for the analysis of a larger set of data, the values of ρ_{rz} in the central region of the bed are often highly negative, which means that the increase of axial component is associated with the decrease of radial component and vice versa.

Structure of Three-Dimensional Velocity Distribution

A three-dimensional approach by Ziolkowska et al. has been used for processing and analyzing experimental velocity data measured at the exit from the packed bed [26–29]. The influence of following parameters on the velocity field structure has been studied: packing particles size and shape together with repacking the bed; packed bed length; bed diameter; and nonisothermal conditions.

The Effect of Packing Particles Size and Shape. To study the influence of particles size and shape together with repacking the bed following parameters were used to characterize the deviation from the uniform flow profile:

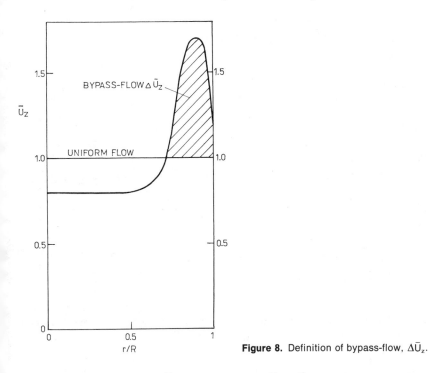

Figure 8. Definition of bypass-flow, $\Delta\bar{U}_z$.

1. The maximal axial velocity $\bar{U}_{z\,max}$ and the ratio of $\bar{U}_{z\,max}/\bar{U}_{z\,min}$; in the case of uniform flow profile both parameters are equal to 1.
2. The bypass-flow in wall region, $\Delta\bar{U}_z$, which expresses the percentage increase of axial velocity in wall region with respect to the uniform velocity profile (Figure 8) where the bypass-flow encompasses the shaded area. As the velocity increase in wall region is compensated by the corresponding decrease of velocity in the bulk of the bed, flow nonuniformity can be characterized using quantity $2\Delta\bar{U}_z$. For the uniform flow profile $\Delta\bar{U}_z = 0$.

To describe the effect of bed repacking on radial profiles of velocity components, $\bar{U}_z$, $\bar{U}_r$, and $\bar{U}_\theta$, the mean percentage deviation, Δ_X, was used between the corresponding values before and after repacking (Table 3):

$$\Delta_X = \frac{1}{K} \sum_{i=1}^{K} \left| \frac{X_i - X_{i(rep)}}{X_i + X_{i(rep)}} \right| \cdot 100, \qquad X = \bar{U}_z, \bar{U}_r, \bar{U}_\theta \qquad (17)$$

where K is the number of points on the radial profile.

Table 3
Effect of Bed Repacking [27]

Packing	d_p (mm)	ψ	$\bar{\varepsilon}$	Δ_z (%)	Δ_r (%)	Δ_θ (%)
Spheres	8.7	1	0.375	5	4	6
Spheres	5.5	1	0.395	11	10	17
Cylinders	11.5	0.882	0.343	4	4	7
Raschig rings	10.0	0.625	0.495	4	2	7

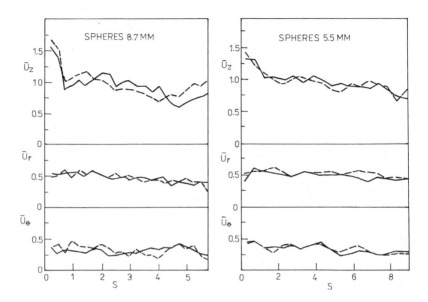

Figure 9. Effect of repacking on radial profiles of velocity components for spherical particles: (————) before repacking, (———————) after repacking [27].

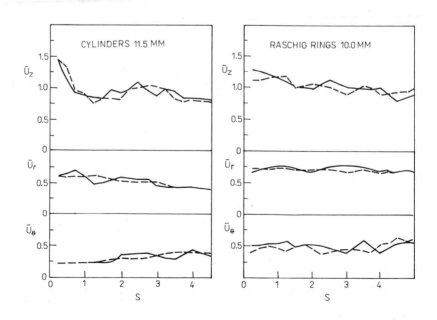

Figure 10. Effect of repacking on radial profiles of velocity components for nonspherical particles: (————) before repacking, (———————) after repacking [27].

The velocity field was measured at the exit from the cylindrical column of D = 100 mm packed with spheres, cylinders and Raschig rings [27]. The three-dimensional structure of velocity field together with the effect of bed repacking is illustrated in Figures 9 and 10 and in Table 4. It can be seen that the bed repacking influences radial profiles of all velocity components and its effect decreases with increasing value of D/d_p and with decreasing sphericity, ψ. The value of maximal axial velocity, $\bar{U}_{z\,max}$, and its radial coordinate remains unchanged within the range of experimental error even for lower values of D/d_p. It can be assumed that bed repacking will manifest itself for spherical particles in cases when $D/d_p < 10$ while for values of $D/d_p > 20$ it can be neglected entirely.

The effect of packing particles size and shape is summarized in Table 4. The nonuniformity of flow increases with decreasing value of D/d_p and with increasing sphericity. This can be explained from the equation for pressure drop in packed beds which expresses the bed resistance to flow [30]:

$$\frac{\Delta P}{L} = f_p \frac{\rho \bar{u}_z^2}{d_p} \frac{1 - \varepsilon}{\varepsilon^3} \tag{18}$$

where the friction factor, f_p, is generally function of ε, ψ, and Re_p. As in the wall region the porosity is higher than in the bulk, the local resistance in this region is relatively low and preferential flow can be suspected. The oscillating character of radial porosity profile increases with increasing values of d_p and ψ and thus the tendency to flow nonuniformity in the bulk increases with increasing d_p and ψ.

The Effect of Bed Length. The influence of bed length on the velocity field structure was studied by Ziolkowska et al. [28] using a column of D = 94 mm packed with spherical particles. Experimental configuration allowed to change the desired parameters in the following ranges: $0.53 \le L/D < 11.2$, $9.6 \le D/d_p \le 22.9$, $2,400 \le Re_D \le 6,010$, where $Re_D = \bar{u}_s D\rho/\mu$.

The dimensionless velocity components $\bar{U}_z$, $\bar{U}_r$, and $\bar{U}_\theta$ were determined both below and above the bed for different values of L and a tendency to stabilization of the velocity field was observed with increasing bed length. As a sufficient condition for the stabilized flow structure the change of velocity components was chosen, which was within the dispersion caused by repacking the bed. The length of the entrance section, L^*, corresponding to the developing velocity field was correlated with flow conditions and packing particle diameter, and the following empirical correlation was proposed [28]:

$$L^*/D = 7.32 . 10^{-3}(D/d_p)^{1.59} Re_D^{0.27} \tag{19}$$

The comparison of experimentally determined entrance section lengths with those computed from Equation 19 is given in Figure 11.

The Effect of Column Diameter. The knowledge of the influence of column diameter on the velocity field structure is of primary importance in process of industrial application of packed beds

Table 4
Effect of Packing Particles Size and Shape [27]

Packing	D/d_p	$\bar{U}_r/\bar{U}_z$ aver.	$\bar{U}_\theta/\bar{U}_z$ aver.	$\bar{U}_{z\,max}/\bar{U}_{z\,min}$	$\bar{U}_{z\,max}$	$2\Delta\bar{U}_z$ (%)
Spheres	18.2	0.50	0.39	1.9	1.4	13
Spheres	11.5	0.54	0.31	2.0	1.5	15
Spheres	10.0	0.56	0.37	2.2	1.6	18
Cylinders	8.7	0.57	-0.30	1.9	1.5	12
Raschig rings	10.0	0.59	0.47	1.6	1.3	9

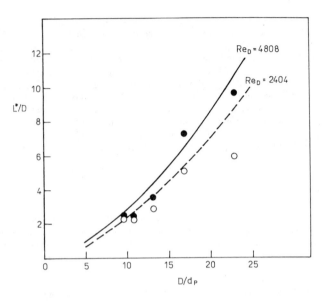

Figure 11. Effect of D/d_p on entrance section length: (— — — — —) and (—————) computed from Equation 19; ($\bigcirc$) and ($\bullet$) experimental for $Re_D = 2{,}404$ and $4{,}808$, respectively [28].

when scaling up is necessary. This problem was studied by Ziolkowska et al. [26] using two cylindrical columns of $D_1 = 100$ mm and $D_2 = 185$ mm, respectively. For different geometric and hydrodynamic conditions both velocity fields were compared using the same criterion of similarity as previously discussed, i.e. that the differences between the corresponding velocity field parameters have to be less than those caused by repacking the bed.

It follows from the previous discussion that the influence of packing particles shape on velocity field is so important that in process of scaling up it is strictly necessary to fulfill the condition:

$$\psi = \text{const.} \tag{20}$$

Owing to this fact the spherical packing was used in both columns investigated.

In Table 5 the parameters changed during experiments are given together with corresponding ranges, and their effect on similarity of both velocity field distributions is summarized in Table 6 for seven experimental sets examined. The mean percentage deviations, Δ_x, were computed from Equation 17 where instead of values before and after repacking, the values obtained for smaller and larger column were used.

Table 5
Parameters Changed [26]

Parameter	Range
$\bar{\varepsilon}$	0.370–0.413
D/d_p	7.4–18.9
L/d_p	40–115
L/D	4–10
Re_p	445–855

Table 6
Effect of Experimental Conditions on the Similarity of Velocity Field Distributions [26]

Set no.	Constant parameters for both columns	Δ_z (%)	Δ_r (%)	Δ_θ (%)
1	$\bar{\varepsilon}$	17	16	15
2	$\bar{\varepsilon}, Re_p$	19	12	15
3	$\bar{\varepsilon}, D/d_p$	15	21	18
4	$\bar{\varepsilon}, d_p$	9	22	12
5	$\bar{\varepsilon}, d_p, \bar{u}_s, Re_p$	10	3	23
6	$\bar{\varepsilon}, \bar{u}_s, D/d_p$	8	7	23
7	$\bar{\varepsilon}, D/d_p, Re_p$	7	4	15

The following conclusions were formulated concerning the conditions for similarity of velocity fields structure for both columns packed with particles having the same sphericity [26]:

1. The axial flow similarity:

$$(\bar{\varepsilon}, d_p)_1 = (\bar{\varepsilon}, d_p)_2 \tag{21}$$

2. The axial and radial flows similarity:

$$(\bar{\varepsilon}, d_p, \bar{u}_s)_1 = (\bar{\varepsilon}, d_p, \bar{u}_s)_2 \tag{22}$$

3. The similarity of all three velocity components:

$$(\bar{\varepsilon}, D/d_p, \bar{u}_s)_1 = (\bar{\varepsilon}, D/d_p, \bar{u}_s)_2 \tag{23}$$

or

$$(\bar{\varepsilon}, D/d_p, Re_p)_1 = (\bar{\varepsilon}, D/d_p, Re_p)_2 \tag{24}$$

As it can be seen from Figure 12, where the radial profiles of $\bar{U}_z$ are given for sets 6 and 7, there was no substantial difference between the results of both sets. This fact is important for experimental modeling of flow structure using the columns of smaller diameter because the condition of preserving $\bar{u}_s$ allows to carry out experiments at much higher flow velocities than in the case of preserving Re_p.

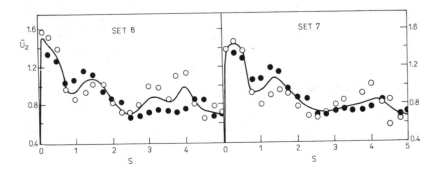

Figure 12. Effect of column diameter on radial profiles of $\bar{U}_z$ for sets 6 and 7 (see Table 6): ($\bigcirc$) $D = 185$ mm, ($\bullet$) $D = 100$ mm [26].

The Effect of Nonisothermal Conditions. It follows from Equation 18 that owing to the temperature dependence of density and viscosity (which appears in correlations of friction factor, f_p), the structure of the flow field will be influenced by the temperature of the flow. This effect was systematically investigated by Ziolkowska and Mieszkowski [27, 29] using two columns of $D = 100$ mm packed with regular particles. The former column was used for the heat transfer from the axis toward the wall, while the latter in the opposite heat flow direction. Temperature and velocity fields were measured using the hot wire anemometry and the nonisothermality was expressed by the temperature difference, Δt, between the axis and the wall, both measured at the exit from the bed:

$$\Delta t = t_a - t_w \tag{25}$$

Because of the presence of radial temperature profile, the mass flow velocity, G, was used to describe the flow field:

$$\bar{G}_i(r) = \bar{u}_i(r) \cdot \rho(r) \qquad i = z, r, \theta \tag{26}$$

To characterize the effect of temperature on the profile of axial velocity, similar parameters as described earlier were used, i.e. $\bar{G}_{z\,max}/\bar{G}_{z\,min}$ and $\Delta\bar{G}_z$.

1. Heat transfer oriented toward the wall, i.e. $\Delta t > 0$. The examples of radial profiles of the mass velocity components for different packing particles are compared in Figures 13 and 14 with the corresponding profiles for $\Delta t = 0$. The effect of temperature on the velocity field structure is summarized in Table 7 and Figure 15.

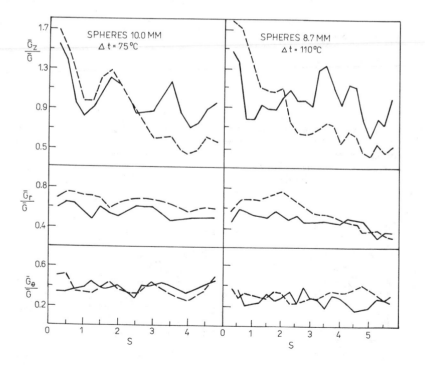

Figure 13. Effect of temperature gradient on velocity field structure for spherical particles: (————) $\Delta t = 0$, (– – – – – –) $\Delta t > 0$ [27].

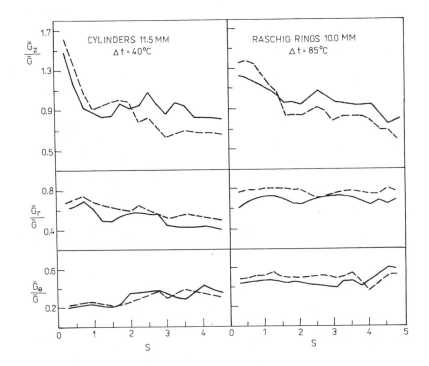

Figure 14. Effect of temperature gradient on velocity field structure for nonspherical particles:
(————) Δt = 0, (––––––) Δt > 0 [27].

Table 7
Effect of Temperature on Velocity Field [27]

Packing	d_p (mm)	Δt (°C)	$\bar{G}_r/\bar{G}_z$ aver.	$\bar{G}_e/\bar{G}_z/\bar{G}_\theta/\bar{G}_z$ aver.
Raschig rings	10	0	0.59	0.47
		50	0.60	0.46
		80	0.63	0.49
Cylinders	11.5	0	0.57	0.30
		40	0.66	0.29
Spheres	5.5	0	0.50	0.39
		80	0.62	0.42
Spheres	8.7	0	0.54	0.31
		40	0.57	0.30
		80	0.63	0.36
		110	0.65	0.38
Spheres	10	0	0.56	0.37
		75	0.65	0.40

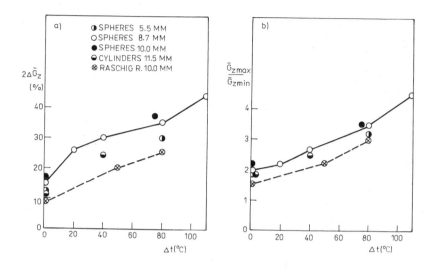

Figure 15. Effect of temperature gradient on flow nonuniformity [27].

2. The effect of heat transfer oriented from the wall to the axis, i.e. $\Delta t < 0$, is illustrated in Figure 16 for spherical particles.

It can be seen from presented material that flow of gas through the packed bed under nonisothermal conditions differs substantially from that for isothermal case. In the presence of temperature gradient oriented from the axis to the wall ($\Delta t > 0$) gas temperature in wall region is lower than in the bulk and thus the gas density is higher in this region. Equation 18 can be written for the

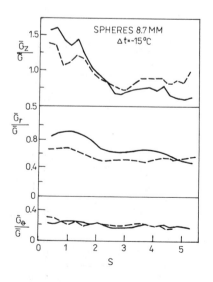

Figure 16. Effect of temperature gradient on velocity field structure: (———) $\Delta t = 0$, (– – – – –) $\Delta t < 0$ [29].

mass velocity:

$$\frac{\Delta P}{L} = f_p \frac{\bar{G}_z}{\rho d_p} \frac{1 - \varepsilon}{\varepsilon^3} \tag{27}$$

and it is obvious that with increasing density the resistance to flow decreases. This fact causes additional increasing of flow nonuniformity compared to the isothermal case, i.e. the increase of radial velocity component and the increase of axial component in the wall region, which must be compensated by the decrease of $\bar{G}_z$ in the bulk of the bed.

The opposite situation arises when $\Delta t < 0$. Both $\bar{G}_z$ in the wall region and $\bar{G}_r$ decrease, whereas $\bar{G}_z$ in the bulk increases, so that the velocity field becomes more uniform comparing with the isothermal case.

Other Methods

Arthur et al. [31] measured the flow distribution directly: the exit flow area was divided by the insertion of thin concentric rings at the top of the bed and the average flow rate was measured in each annuli formed by adjacent rings using a soap bubble technique to minimize pressure losses. The main experimental difficulty of this method was to maintain the same resistance in the separate flow paths and thus only a limited number of measurements was carried out. According to Lerou and Froment [22] each such device placed at the top of bed redistributes the flow in the top layers of the packing so that measured flow distribution should be viewed with caution.

Quite different approach to study the flow distribution in packed bed was suggested by Oliveros and Smith [32]. Authors tried to determine the extent of channeling from the response in the effluent gas to a tracer input. Experiments were carried out in cylindrical packed bed (D = 83.4 mm, L = 594 mm) purposely prepared with nonuniform void fraction by filling annular and core sections with spherical particles of different sizes. Data were obtained for both a noninteracting arrangement including a thin aluminium foil separating the core and annulus, and an interacting case where only the screen separated the two sections. The experimental response curves for nearly all cases of noninteracting arrangement showed two distinct peaks and it was possible to establish the flow rate and void area of the channel. The method failed completely in the case of interacting arrangement where the radial transport of tracer was sufficiently rapid to disguise most effects of channeling (perhaps because of small diameter of the apparatus used). It follows from this fact that practical application of the proposed method is limited for large-diameter bed with small superficial velocities, e.g. for oil-shale retorts.

MODELING OF FLOW MALDISTRIBUTION

The rigorous solution of the problem of fluid flow through packed beds is hardly possible because of the extremely complicated nature of the subject. Many variables must be considered characterizing flow type (laminar or turbulent), type of packing (porosity, sphericity, size distribution, manner of packing), and state (temperature distribution), which complicate even empirical models. As pointed out by Bird et al. [30] two fundamentally different approaches can be distinguished in packed bed modeling: (1) the conduit flow approach, which envisages the packed bed as consisting of a set of conduits; and (2) the discrete particle approach, which regards the bed as consisting of a collection of particles submerged in the flowing fluid. For both approaches the analytical solutions of the one-dimensional Navier-Stokes equations exist for the creeping flow range and are known respectively as Hagen-Poisseuille equation and Stokes' law. There also exist several attempts to solve the complete Navier-Stokes equations for creeping flow through porous media but the corresponding solution in the case of turbulent flow presents serious computational problems. To overcome these difficulties, some experimental results were incorporated in the analysis to correlate the gas flow behavior for geometrically similar systems. This approach was called phenomenological by Dullien [33] and its typical example is the Ergun equation [34] or its revised form proposed by Macdonald et al. [35].

All models describing the gas flow through the packed bed are based on some of the basic approaches previously given or on their combination (the detailed review of different modeling approaches is given by Dullien [33]). In the next two sections several models are briefly discussed for both one- and multi-dimensional velocity distribution.

One-Dimensional Velocity Profiles

Lyczkowski [25] proposed the model based on the conduit flow approach, which describes the slow inertialess flow through beds of particles having a wide size range. He defined the control volume j sufficiently large with respect to flow path size, containing a mixture of particle sizes. Neglecting the gas stream interactions between different particle size ranges, the equation between pressure, frictional and body forces for particle size range i can be written as [30]

$$\left(\frac{\partial p_i}{\partial z}\right)_j = -\left(\frac{f_{pi}\rho_i v_{zi}^2}{2D_{H_i}}\right)_j + (\rho_i g_z)_j \tag{28}$$

In Equation 28 p_i is the partial pressure, f_{pi} the friction factor, v_{zi} the average pore velocity, D_{Hi} the hydraulic diameter, ρ_i the gas density, and g_z gravitational force in z direction, all associated with the i-th particle size range.

The hydraulic diameter, D_{Hi}, is defined by means of the hydraulic radius, R_{Hi}:

$$D_{Hi} = 4R_{Hi} = 4\frac{\text{volume available for flow in size range i}}{\text{wetted surface of particles in size range i}} \tag{29}$$

or

$$D_{Hi} = 4\frac{\varepsilon_i V_c}{A_{wi}} \tag{30}$$

where V_c is the volume of control volume.

By substituting Equation 30 into 28 and summing over all particle sizes, the author obtained a general form of equation describing the laminar flow through a control volume having a range of particle sizes:

$$\left(\frac{\partial p}{\partial z}\right)_j = -\left[\sum_i \frac{f_{pi}\rho_i v_{zi}^2}{8\varepsilon_i}\frac{A_{wi}}{V_c} + \sum_i \rho_i g_z\right]_j \tag{31}$$

where the total gas pressure $p = \sum p_i$.

Rewriting Equation 31 for the case of all spherical particles in each size range Lyczkowski obtained:

$$\left(\frac{\partial p}{\partial z}\right)_j = \left[-\frac{9}{8}\sum_i \frac{k_i\mu_i(1-\varepsilon_i)^2 u_{zi}}{d_{pi}^2\varepsilon_i^3} + \sum_i \rho_i g_z\right]_j \tag{32}$$

where u_{zi} is the superficial velocity related to the pore velocity by Dupuit assumption

$$v_{zi} = \frac{u_{zi}}{\varepsilon_i} \tag{33}$$

and k_i is a constant in friction factor expression for laminar flow:

$$f_{pi} = \frac{k_i}{Re_i} \tag{34}$$

For the case of a single particle size Equation 32 reduces to the Carman-Kozeny equation [33]

$$\left(\frac{\partial p}{\partial z}\right)_j = \left[-\frac{k'\mu u_z}{d_p^2}\frac{(1-\varepsilon)^2}{\varepsilon^3} + \rho g_z\right]_j \tag{35}$$

where $k' = 9k/8$.

Equation 32 is recommended for beds with a wide size range of particles where the usual approach, i.e. the use of Equation 35 with some average particle diameter may lead to the large errors (see also Lyczkowski [36]).

To illustrate the effect of porosity on flow velocity a simple model based on phenomenological approach can be used, as proposed by Martin [37]. The author idealized the bed structure as consisting of two parallel nonuniform flow channels, one of high porosity near the wall and the other of lower porosity in the bulk of the bed. Assuming that the Ergun equation [34]

$$\frac{\Delta P}{L} = 150\frac{\mu\bar{u}_z(1-\bar{\varepsilon})^2}{d_p^2\bar{\varepsilon}^3} + 1.75\frac{\rho\bar{u}_z^2(1-\bar{\varepsilon})}{d_p\bar{\varepsilon}^3} \tag{36}$$

holds for each of two idealized regions, Martin proposed an expression for the ratio of the superficial velocity in the wall region, u_{z2}, to that in the bulk of the bed, u_{z1}:

$$\omega = \frac{u_{z2}}{u_{z1}} = \frac{\phi(1+\omega_o) - 1 + [(\phi(1+\omega_o)-1)^2 + 4\omega_o(\phi+MZ)(1-\phi+Z)]^{1/2}}{2(\phi+MZ)} \tag{37}$$

where

$$\omega_o = \lim_{Re_p\to 0}\omega = \frac{(1-\varepsilon_1)^2\,\varepsilon_2^3}{(1-\varepsilon_2)^2\,\varepsilon_1^3} \tag{38}$$

ε_2 and ε_1 are the porosities in the wall region and in the bulk of the bed, respectively, the ratio of the wall to bed area, ϕ, is given by

$$\phi = \frac{A_2}{A} \tag{39}$$

M and Z are defined by

$$M = \frac{1-\varepsilon_1}{1-\varepsilon_2} \tag{40}$$

$$Z = \frac{1.75Re_p}{150(1-\varepsilon_1)} \tag{41}$$

For the limiting value of high flow Equation 37 can be written:

$$\omega_\infty = \lim_{Re_p\to\infty}\omega = \frac{[\omega_o(1-\varepsilon_2)]^{1/2}}{(1-\varepsilon_1)^{1/2}} \tag{42}$$

In Figure 17 the effect of D/d_p ratio on u_{z2}/u_{z1} ratio computed from Equation 37 is given assuming that the wall region is defined as the area corresponding to the distance of $d_p/2$ from the wall. Two different values of porosity in the wall region are used: $\varepsilon_2 = 0.65$ and $\varepsilon_2 = 0.6$. The value of bulk porosity $\varepsilon_1 = 0.4$ for both cases. It can be seen that the ratio of superficial velocities is extremely sensitive to small changes of ε_2, especially at low values of Re_p. The dependence of ω on D/d_p (i.e. on changes of the ratio ϕ) is substantially smaller. It is to be expected that the nonuniformity of

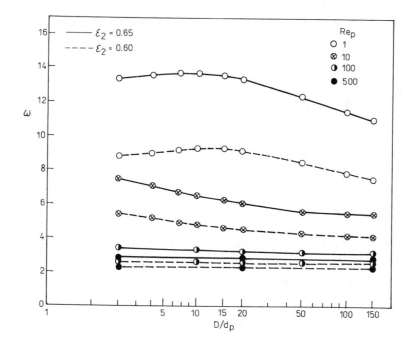

Figure 17. Illustration of flow maldistribution computed from Equation 37 for $\varepsilon_1 = 0.4$.

radial distribution of porosity will create a considerable flow maldistribution, especially at low flow rates.

Vortmeyer and Schuster [38] computed the velocity profiles in the bed packed with spherical particles using the Brinkman equation [39]

$$\nabla P = -\frac{\mu}{k} u + \mu \nabla^2 u \tag{43}$$

which was extended to higher flow rates by incorporating the Ergun equation (36). The resulting equation can be written in one-dimensional form as [38]

$$\frac{\partial P}{\partial z} = -u_z \frac{150\mu(1 - \varepsilon)^2}{d_p^2 \varepsilon^3} - u_z^2 \frac{1.75\rho(1 - \varepsilon)}{d_p \varepsilon^3} + \mu \left(\frac{\partial^2 u_z}{\partial r^2} + \frac{1}{r} \frac{\partial u_z}{\partial r} \right) \tag{44}$$

The original Brinkman equation (43), based on the discrete particle approach, is an extension of Darcy's law

$$\underline{\nabla} P = -\frac{\mu}{k} \underline{u} \tag{45}$$

and the term $\mu \underline{\nabla}^2 \underline{u}$ accounts for distortion of the velocity profiles near the wall.

Vortmeyer and Schuster solved Equation 44 by a variational method for both oscillating and smoothed exponentially decreasing radial profiles of porosity using the boundary condition of zero velocity at the wall. The calculated velocity profiles exhibited maxima located at the distance of about $d_p/4$ from the wall, which were substantially higher than those measured above the bed (Figure 18). The computed dependence of the ratio $u_{z\,max}/u_{z\,center}$ on the value of D/d_p for different values of Re_p, presented by authors, is very similar to that computed from Martin's model in Figure 17 for $\varepsilon_2 = 0.65$ and $\varepsilon_1 = 0.4$. The authors [38] also compared velocity profiles measured above the bed with those computed from the two-dimensional Navier-Stokes equations for the developing flow inside the empty tube, with the velocity profiles from Equation 44 as an inlet condition. The agreement between measured and computed velocity profiles above the bed was satisfactory, as shown in Figure 19. The velocity profile is markedly changed above the bed, especially for low values of Re_p. The effect of temperature on radial velocity profiles, as computed by Vortmeyer and Schuster, was similar, at least qualitatively, to that discussed earlier.

In all models previously given the velocity profile was determined solely by the radial porosity distribution. Ziolkowska [40] proposed a model that, in addition to the porosity effect, considers radial dispersion in the bed. The nonuniform dissipation of gas kinetic energy across the bed was expressed as the sum of drag force on packing elements, stress components, and radial dispersion. For drag force the expression proposed by Ranz [41] was used:

$$F = c_D A_p \rho \bar{v}_z^2 \frac{1 - \bar{\varepsilon}}{V_p} \tag{46}$$

where c_D is the drag coefficient, A_p is the mean projected area of a particle, $\bar{v}_z$ is the average pore velocity, and V_p is the volume of a particle.

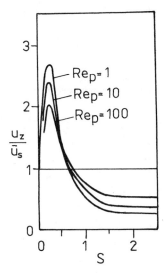

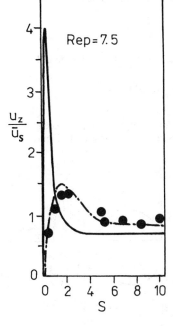

Figure 18. Velocity profiles computed from Equation 44: D = 40 mm, d_p = 8 mm [38].

Figure 19. Comparison of velocity profiles: ● experimental 10 mm above the bed, (————) computed from Equation 44 inside the bed, (– – – – –) computed from Navier-Stokes equation 10 mm above the bed [38].

The stress components are given by the sum of molecular and Reynolds stresses [30]:

$$\tau_{rz} + \tau_{rz}^{(t)} = (\mu + \mu^{(t)}) \frac{\partial v_z}{\partial r} \tag{47}$$

where $\mu^{(t)}$ is the turbulent coefficient of viscosity.

The pressure drop per unit length of packing was expressed using the friction factor (Equation 18), where for spherical and nearly spherical particles Ergun equation can be used for f_p:

$$f_p = 1.75 + 150 \frac{1 - \bar{\varepsilon}}{Re_p} \tag{48}$$

For low spherical particles ($\psi < 0.6$) the correlation proposed by Gauvin and Katta [42] is suitable:

$$f_p = 2.24\psi^{-1.62} \tag{49}$$

Dupuits assumption [33] was used as the relation between pore and superficial velocities. The equation of continuity containing the radial dispersion coefficient, D_r, was numerically integrated together with the equation of motion to give the dimensionless pore velocity, V_z, as a function of porosity, drag coefficient, and modified Reynolds number, Re_p^*:

$$V_z = f(\varepsilon, c_D, Re_p^*) \tag{50}$$

Drag coefficient can be computed from

$$c_D = \frac{2V_p}{A_p d_p} f_p \tag{51}$$

using Equation 48 or 49. Modified Reynolds number is defined as

$$Re_p^* = \frac{u_z d_p}{v_e} \tag{52}$$

and for the effective viscosity coefficient, v_e, the empirical correlations were proposed for different types of packing particles. In Figure 20 the computed radial profiles of pore velocity and modified

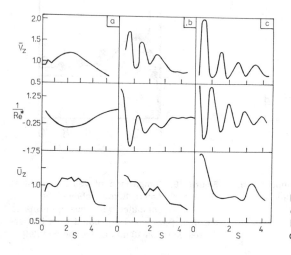

Figure 20. Effect of particle shape on radial profiles of $\bar{U}_z$, $\bar{V}_z$, and Re_p^*: (a) Raschig rings, (b) cylinders, (c) spheres [43].

Reynolds number are given together with experimentally determined velocity profiles above the bed for different types of packing [43].

Multi-dimensional Velocity Profiles

Most models describing the multi-dimensional gas flow through the packed bed is based on Forchheimer-type equation [44] relating the pressure and velocity:

$$\frac{\Delta P}{L} = f_1 \bar{v}_z + f_2 \bar{u}_z^2 \tag{53}$$

where the terms on the right-hand side represent the viscous and inertial loss terms, respectively. It is obvious that the Ergun equation (36) or its modifications are special forms of Equation 53 in which the parameters f_1 and f_2 are expressed in terms of μ, ρ, d_p, and ε. Staněk and Szekely [45] used the vectorial form of Equation 53,

$$-\underline{\nabla} P = \underline{u}(f_1 + f_2 u) \tag{54}$$

with parameters f_1 and f_2 expressed from the Ergun equation (36):

$$f_1 = 150 \frac{\mu(1-\varepsilon)^2}{d_p^2 \varepsilon^3} \tag{55}$$

$$f_2 = 1.75 \frac{\rho(1-\varepsilon)}{d_p \varepsilon^3} \tag{56}$$

For the case of compressible fluid or nonisothermal conditions Equation 54 can be written using the mass velocity, G:

$$-\underline{\nabla}(P^2) = \underline{G}(g_1 + g_2 G) \tag{57}$$

where

$$g_1 = \frac{2P}{\rho} f_1 \tag{58}$$

$$g_2 = \frac{2P}{\rho^2} f_2 \tag{59}$$

Staněk and Szekely applied Equations 54 and 57 to the analysis of flow in cylindrical packed bed consisting of intercommunicating annular and core sections with the different resistances to flow. They proposed a formal solution of Equations 54 and 57 for both laminar and turbulent flows together with the numerical solution of particular case of the turbulent two-dimensional axisymmetrical flow, when the viscous term was neglected. The computed results in the form of streamlines and isobars showed the preferential axial flow in the region of higher porosity. The radial velocity component was found to be significant only at the inlet part of the bed. The proposed method was verified by Szekely et al. [21, 46] by comparing computed velocity profiles with those measured at the exit from the bed packed with spherical particles. Different arrangements of bed resistance were used that appeared in the model as radial dependence of parameter f_2 in Equation 54 (again the turbulent flow was considered). The comparison of experimental and predicted profiles of velocity vector magnitude is given in Figure 21 for the bed packed with a high resistance core.

The first attempt to describe adequately the flow behavior in nonisothermal systems was proposed by Staněk and Szekely [47]. In their model based on the two-dimensional form of Equation 57 the authors assumed uniform porosity distribution across the bed and calculated local variations in the profiles of axial and radial velocity components as caused by the temperature nonuniformity.

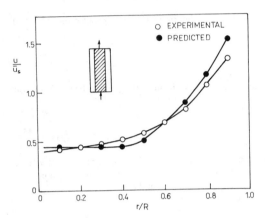

Figure 21. Comparison of experimental and predicted velocity profiles for parallel flow through a bed packed with high resistance core: $D = 100$ mm, core $d_p = 1$ mm, interface $d_p = 2$ mm, annulus $d_p = 3$ mm [46].

The nonuniformity of axial velocity component profiles increased with increasing temperature gradient oriented from center to wall, and vice versa, which is in agreement with the experimental results discussed earlier. The computed profiles of radial velocity component exhibited local maxima at radial coordinate $r/R \sim 0.65$.

Stroh et al. [48] applied Equation 57 in the case of flow at high Reynolds numbers, which is important in applications of high-temperature pebble bed nuclear reactors. Parameters g_1 and g_2 were expressed using the friction factor correlation for high Reynolds number flows. Using the equation of continuity and thermal energy balances on the solid and gas phases the system of nonlinear elliptic partial differential equations was obtained describing the nonisothermal axisymmetrical flow of gas through the bed. The proposed model was tested against the experimental velocity vector magnitude profiles obtained at the exit from the full scale mockup of a pebble bed reactor core [23] (see Table 1). The comparison between experimental and predicted isothermal velocity profiles is illustrated in Figure 22.

Ziolkowska [49] proposed the stochastic model of three-dimensional gas flow through the packing of regular elements. Following the formal approach used for describing the turbulent velocity distribution in pipes [30], she expressed the instanteous pore velocity components as the sum of mean and fluctuating component. The latter was characterized by the standard deviations, σ_z, σ_r, and σ_θ, corresponding to the given circumference. Considering the flow determined by axial pressure gradient, Equation 18 and 48, or 49 were used for pressure drop across the bed. Analogously

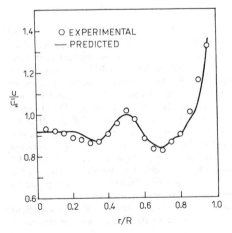

Figure 22. Comparison of experimental and predicted velocity profiles: $D = 762$ mm, spheres, $d_p = 38.1$ mm [48].

to the one-dimensional model given earlier, the dissipation of kinetic energy across the bed was expressed by the drag force and stress components and Equations 46 and 47 were adopted for each velocity component. Solving the equation of continuity together with the equations of motion in cylindrical coordinates (for details see the original paper [50]) the radial profiles of the following parameters characterizing the pore velocity field can be obtained: axial pore velocity, $\bar{V}_z$, together with its standard deviation, σ_z, standard deviations σ_r and σ_θ, normalized crosscorrelation functions, ρ_{rz} and $\rho_{r\theta}$ (Equation 15), drag coefficient together with Reynolds and molecular stresses. To compute these quantities the knowledge of circumferential profiles of the superficial velocity components, U_z, U_r, U_θ, measured at the exit from the bed is also necessary (considering Equation 33 between pore and superficial velocities). Comparing the computed pore velocity field with that determined experimentally at the exit from the bed packed with both spherical and nonspherical particles, the following conclusions can be drawn [50]:

1. Both pore and superficial velocity fields are three-dimensional and their characters depend on both ψ and d_p.
2. The contribution of axial component is comparable in both velocity fields; the contribution of angular and mainly of radial components is lower in the pore velocity field.
3. Increasing the average superficial velocity implies the increase of angular component of pore velocity and the change of structure of resistance to flow (the increase of Reynolds stresses and the decrease of drag coefficient).

The structure of both velocity fields for different types of packing is illustrated in Figure 23.

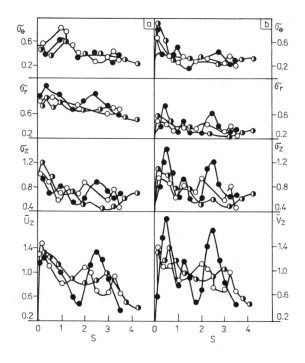

Figure 23. Comparison of velocity fields for different packing particles: (a) superficial velocity field, (b) pore velocity field; $D/d_p \sim 8$, ($\bullet$) spheres, $\psi = 1$, ($\bigcirc$) Raschig rings, $\psi = 0.48$, ($\circleddash$) Intalox rings, $\psi = 0.352$ [50].

CONCLUSIONS

It follows from the previous review that the nonuniform flow distribution must be considered in a packed bed. The experimental determination of flow velocity field inside the bed presents serious problems and thus the velocity field at the exit from the bed must be measured. As the velocity profile above the bed changes rapidly toward the empty tube velocity profile, it is necessary to measure sufficiently close to the bed surface. To account for the three-dimensional character of the flow, the rotated short-wire anemometry technique has to be used. Applying this technique properly, the representative velocity field suitable for reactor design purposes is obtained. As previously shown, the character of velocity field depends mainly on packing particle shape, column to particle diameter ratio, and temperature gradient across the bed.

For modeling purposes the Darcy, Brinkman and Ergun equations are mostly used. Several things must be considered when applying these equations:

1. All these equations are the macroscopic relations, i.e. they describe the pressure drop per unit length of the bed in terms of the superficial velocity averaged over some region of space. This region should be smaller than macroscopic dimensions of the bed but large enough with respect to the pore size. Thus, when solving the differential forms of the aforementioned equations one must specify the averaging space to avoid formal incorrectness [51].
2. The often accented problem is that the vectorial form of these equations holds only for the isotropic (nonoriented) packed beds. In general, to also include anisotropic packing, the proper tensorial forms of the considered equations should be used. This problem was studied by Yoshikawa [52] for the Ergun equation and he found that the truly tensorial form plays a minor role except in the vicinity of sharp boundary between particles of different sizes.
3. None of the equations considers the radial dispersion in the bed.

For practical use one-dimensional models can be easily adopted as the first necessary step in describing the radial nonuniformity of gas flow through the fixed-bed chemical reactors [22, 53]. While this approach may be sufficient when solving the mass transport problems, the radial velocity component must be considered in beds with heat transfer, i.e. the use of at least two-dimensional model is recommended [54].

Acknowledgment

The authors wish to thank to Dr V. Staněk from the same Institute for his helpful comments in preparation of the manuscript.

NOTATION

A	area; constant in Equation 5	E	anemometer bridge voltage
A'	constant in Equation 4	f_1, f_2	parameters in Equation 53
A_p	mean projected area of a particle	f_p	friction factor
A_w	wetted surface	F	drag force
B	constant in Equation 5	g	gravitational acceleration
B'	constant in Equation 4		
c	coefficient of variance	g_1, g_2	parameters in Equation 57
c_D	drag coefficient		
d_p	equivalent particle diameter	G, G, G_z, G_r, G_θ	mass velocity vector, its magnitude and components
D	column diameter		
$D_H = 4R_H$	hydraulic diameter	$\bar{G}$	mass velocity averaged

	over column cross-section	t_c	environmental temperature
$\Delta\bar{G}_z$	bypass flow	t_s	sensor operating temperature
k	specific permeability		
k_1, k_2	constants in Equation 8	t_w	temperature at column wall
k'	constant in Equation 35		
K	number of points on radial profile of velocity	$\underline{u}, u, u_z, u_r, u_\theta$	superficial velocity vector, its magnitude and components
L	bed length		
L^*	length of bed entrance section	$\bar{u}_s$	superficial velocity averaged over column cross section
M	parameter in Equation 37		
n	exponent in Equations 4 and 5	u_{eff}	effective cooling velocity
		u_N, u_B, u_T	normal, binormal, and tangential velocity components with respect to hot wire
n_t	theoretical number of particles along given circumference		
N	number of samples along given circumference	U_z, U_r, U_θ	normalized superficial velocity components—see Equation 13
p	gas pressure		
p_o	reference pressure	$\Delta\bar{U}_z$	bypass flow, Figure 8
$\Delta P = p - p_o + \rho\Phi$	pressure drop across bed	$\underline{v}, v, v_z, v_r, v_\theta$	average pore velocity vector, its magnitude and components
r	radial coordinate		
R	column radius	V	volume
R_H	hydraulic radius	V_p	particle volume
R_{ij}	cross correlation function for components i, j	V_z, V_r, V_θ	normalized pore velocity components
$s = (D/2 - r)/d_p$	dimensionless radial coordinate	z	axial coordinate
		Z	parameter in Equation 37
t	temperature		
t_a	temperature in column axis		

Greek Letters

Δ	deviation	σ	standard deviation
ε	local area porosity	σ^2	variance
$\bar{\varepsilon}$	average bed porosity	τ	stress component
θ	angular coordinate	ϕ	area ratio, Equation 39
μ	viscosity	Φ	gravitational potential function
ν_e	effective kinematic viscosity coefficient		
ρ	density	ψ	particle sphericity
ρ_{ij}	normalized crosscorrelation function for components i, j	ω	ratio of superficial velocities Equation 37

Special Symbols

| $\underline{\nabla}$ | nabla operator |
| $\underline{\nabla}^2$ | Laplacian operator |

Dimensionless Groups

$$Re_p = \frac{\bar{u}_s d_p \rho}{\mu}$$ particle Reynolds number

$$Re_D = \frac{\bar{u}_s D \rho}{\mu}$$ column Reynolds number

$$Re_p^* = \frac{\bar{u}_s d_p}{\nu_e}$$ modified particle Reynolds number

Subscripts

max maximal value
min minimal value

Overlines

— value averaged over $2\pi r$ circle

REFERENCES

1. Roblee, L. H. S., Baird, R. M., and Tierney, J. W. "Radial Porosity Variations in Packed Beds," *AIChE J.*, 4, 460 (1958).
2. Staněk, V., and Eckert, V. "A Study of Area Porosity Profiles in a Bed of Equal-Diameter Spheres Confined by a Plane," *Chem. Eng. Sci.*, 34, 933 (1979).
3. Furnas, C. C. "Flow of Gases Through Beds of Broken Solids," *Bull.* 307, U.S. Bureau of Mines (1929).
4. King, L. V. "On the Convection of Heat from Small Cylinders in a Stream of Fluid," *Phil. Trans. Soc.* (London), A214, 373 (1914).
5. Jørgensen, F. E. "Directional Sensitivity of Wire and Fiber-film Probes," *DISA Inform.*, 11, 31 (1971).
6. Corrsin, S. "Turbulence, Experimental Methods," in *Handbuch der Physik*, Vol. 8/2, Berlin: Springer Verlag, 1963, pp. 523–590.
7. Acrivlellis, M. "Flow Field Dependence on Hot-Wire Probe Cooling Law and Probe Adjustment," *DISA Inform.*, 23, 17 (1978).
8. Gaulier, C. "Measurement of Air Velocity by Means of a Triple Hot-Wire Probe," *DISA Inform.*, 21, 16 (1977).
9. Acrivlellis, M. "An Improved Method for Determining the Flow Field of Multidimensional Flow of Any Turbulence Intensity," *DISA Inform.*, 23, 11 (1978).
10. Mickley, H. S., Smith, K. A., and Korchak, E. I. "Fluid Flow in Packed Beds," *Chem. Eng. Sci.* 20, 237 (1965).
11. Van der Merve, D. F., and Gauvin, W. H. "Velocity and Turbulence Measurements of Air Flow Through a Packed Bed," *AIChE J.*, 17, 519 (1971).
12. Schwartz, C. E., and Smith, J. M. "Flow Distribution in Packed Beds," *Ind. Eng. Chem.*, 45, 1209 (1953).
13. Ziolkowska, I., Badowska, I., and Morawska, B. "Determination of Velocity Vector Components in Column with Granular Packing," (in Polish), *Inz. Chem.*, 6, 693 (1976).
14. Drahoš, J. et al. "Statistical Analysis of Local Gas Velocities at the Exit from a Packed Bed," *Chem. Eng. J.*, 24, 71 (1982).
15. Morales, M., Spinn, C. W., and Smith, J. M. "Velocities and Effective Thermal Conductivities in Packed Beds," *Ind. Eng. Chem.*, 43, 225 (1951).
16. Calderbank, P. H., and Pogorski, L. A. "Heat Transfer in Packed Beds," *Trans. Inst. Chem. Engrs.*, 35, 195 (1957).

17. Dorweiler, V. P., and Fahien, R. W. "Mass Transfer at Low Flow Rates in a Packed Column," *AIChE J.*, 5, 139 (1959).
18. Schertz, W. W., and Bischoff, K. B. "Thermal and Material Transport in Nonisothermal Packed Beds," *AIChE J.*, 15, 597 (1969).
19. Price, J. "The Distribution of Fluid Velocities for Randomly Packed Beds of Spheres," *Mech. Chem. Engng. Trans.* (Australia), 7 (May 1968).
20. Marivoet, J., Teodoroiu, P., and Wajc, S. J. "Porosity, Velocity and Temperature Profiles in Cylindrical Packed Beds," *Chem. Eng. Sci.*, 29, 1836 (1974).
21. Szekely, J., and Poveromo, J. J. "Flow Maldistribution in Packed Beds: A Comparison of Measurements with Predictions," *AIChE J.*, 21, 769 (1975).
22. Lerou, J. J., and Froment, G. F. "Velocity, Temperature, and Conversion Profiles in Fixed Bed Catalytic Reactors," *Chem. Eng. Sci.*, 32, 853 (1977).
23. Stroh, K. R., Olson, H. G., and Jiacoletti, R. J. "Comparison of Coolant Flow Predictions with Those Measured on a Full-Scale Mockup of a Pebble Bed Reactor Core," *Nuclear Eng. and Design*, 52, 349 (1979).
24. Schuster, J., and Vortmeyer, D. "Velocity Distribution of Gas Flowing Through Isothermal Packing of Spherical Particles," (in German), *Chem.-Ing.-Tech.*, 53, 806 (1981).
25. Lyczkowski, R. W. "Modeling of Flow Nonuniformities in Fissured Porous Media," *Can. J. Chem. Eng.*, 60, 61 (1982).
26. Ziolkowska, I. et al. "Effect of Column Diameter on Velocity Field Structure," (in polish), *Inz. Chem. Proc.*, 4, 209 (1983).
27. Ziolkowska, I., and Mieszkowski, Z. "Effect of Packing Particle Shape on Velocity Field Structure at Nonisothermal Conditions," (in polish), *Inz. Chem. Proc.*, 5 (1984) in print.
28. Ziolkowska, I., et al. "Effect of Bed Height on Velocity Profiles in Packed Column," (in polish), *Inz. Chem. Proc.*, 1, 393 (1980).
29. Ziolkowska, I., and Mieszkowski, Z. "Velocity Distribution in Column Packed with Spheres at Nonisothermal Conditions," (in polish), *Inz. Chem. Proc.*, 3, 413 (1982).
30. Bird, R. B., Stewart, W. E., and Lightfoot, E. N. *Transport Phenomena*. New York: Wiley and Sons, Inc., 1960.
31. Arthur, J. R. et al. "Flow of Air Stream Through Layer of Granules," *Trans. Faraday Soc.*, 46, 270 (1950).
32. Oliveros, G., and Smith, J. M. "Dynamic Studies of Dispersion and Channeling in Fixed Beds," *AIChE J.*, 28, 751 (1982).
33. Dullien, F. A. L. *Porous Media: Fluid Transport and Pore Structure*. New York: Academia Press, 1979, pp. 157–230.
34. Ergun, S. "Fluid Flow Through Packed Column," *Chem. Eng. Progr.*, 48, 89 (1952).
35. Macdonald, I. F. et al. "Flow Through Porous Media—The Ergun Equation Revisited," *Ind. Eng. Chem. Fundam.*, 18, 199 (1979).
36. Lyczkowski, R. W. "Multi-Dimensional Simulation of Flow Nonuniformities in Fissured Porous Media," *Chem. Eng. J.*, 24, 7 (1982).
37. Martin, H. "Low Peclet Number Particle-to-Fluid Heat and Mass Transfer in Packed Bed," *Chem. Eng. Sci.*, 33, 913 (1978).
38. Vortmeyer, D., and Schuster, J. "Evaluation of Steady Flow Profiles in Rectangular and Circular Packed Beds by a Variational Method," *Chem. Eng. Sci.* 38, 1691 (1983).
39. Brinkman, H. C. "Calculation of the Viscous Force Exerted by Flowing Fluid on a Dense Swarm of Particles," *Appl. Sci. Res.*, Al, 27, 81 (1949).
40. Ziolkowska, I. "Mathematical Model of Gas Flow Through a Bed of Randomly Packed Regular Elements," (in polish), *Inz. Chem. Proc.*, 1, 641 (1980).
41. Ranz, W. E. "Friction and Transfer Coefficient for Single Particles and Packed Beds," *Chem. Eng. Progr.* 48, 247 (1952).
42. Gauvin, W. H., and Katta, S. "Momentum Transfer Through Packed Beds of Various Particles in the Turbulent Flow Regime," *AIChE J.*, 19, 775 (1973).
43. Ziolkowska, I., Badowska, I., and Mieskowski, Z. "Mathematical Model of Gas Flow Through a Bed of Randomly Packed Regular Elements: Verification of the Model for Cylinders and Raschig Rings," (in polish), *Inz. Chem. Proc.*, 1, 889 (1980).

44. Scheidegger, A. E. *The Physics of Flow Through Porous Media.* Toronto: Toronto Univ. Press, 1957, p. 127

45. Staněk, V., Szekely, J. "Three-Dimensional Flow of Fluids Through Nonuniform Packed Beds," *AIChE J.*, 20, 974 (1974).

46. Choudhary, M., Propster, M., and Szekely, J. "On the Importance of the Inertial Terms in the Modeling of Flow Maldistribution in Packed Beds," *AIChE J.*, 22, 600 (1976).

47. Staněk, V., and Szekely, J. "Flow Maldistribution in Two-Dimensional Packed Beds: The Behavior of Nonisothermal Systems," *Can. J. Chem. Eng.*, 51, 22 (1973).

48. Stroh, K. R., Jiacoletti, R. J., and Olson, H. G. "Thermal-Hydraulic Analysis Techniques for Axisymmetric Pebble Bed Reactor Cores," *Nuclear Eng. and Design*, 52, 343 (1979).

49. Ziolkowska, I. "Stochastic Model of Gas Flow Through a Packed Bed," (in polish), *Inz. Chem. Proc.*, 3, 731 (1982).

50. Ziolkowska, I., Badowska, I., and Flejter, B. "Stochastic Model of Gas Flow Through a Packed Bed: Verification of the Model for Raschig and Intalox Rings," (in polish), *Inz. Chem. Proc.*, 5 (1984) in print.

51. Slattery, J. C. *Momentum, Energy and Mass Transfer in Continua.* New York: McGraw-Hill, 1972, pp. 191–215.

52. Yoshizawa, A. "A Proper Tensorial Form of Darcy-Ergun Equation," *Trans. Iron and Steel Inst.* (Japan) 19, 559 (1979).

53. Vortmeyer, D., and Winter, R. P. "Improvement of Analysis of Fixed Bed Reactors by Consideration of Porosity and Flow Distribution," (in german), *Chem.-Ing.-Tech.*, 55, 312 (1983).

54. Choudhary, M., Szekely, J., and Weller, S. W. "The Effect of Flow Madistribution on Conversion in a Catalytic Packed-Bed Reactor," *AIChE J.*, 22, 1021 (1976).

CHAPTER 35

DETERMINING LIQUID-SIDE MASS-TRANSFER COEFFICIENTS AND EFFECTIVE INTERFACIAL AREA IN GAS-LIQUID CONTACTORS

J. K. Gehlawat

Indian Institute of Technology
Kanpur, India

CONTENTS

INTRODUCTION

Gas-liquid contactors form an important class of equipment used in a variety of industrial applications. Typical gas-liquid contactors are schematically shown in Figures 1-6. Process applications include absorption, distillation, humidification, dehumidification, evaporation, and drying operations. Broad characteristics of gas-liquid contactors are given in Table 1.

An intimate contact between the gas and liquid phases must be provided by the contactor design. A proper understanding of the dynamics at the gas-liquid interface is important. Several physical models, namely film, penetration, surface renewal, film penetration etc., have been used to analyze the transport processes at the gas-liquid interface. These models have been described by Danckwerts [1]. The mechanism of transfer of a species A from the gas phase into the liquid phase containing a solvent or reactant B may be controlled by the resistance to transfer located either in the gas

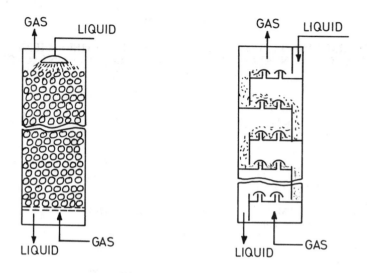

Figure 1. Packed column.   **Figure 2.** Bubble plate column.

phase or in the liquid phase. Generally, the absorption of a highly soluble gas, as for example ammonia into water, is gas-film controlled. On the other hand, for a sparingly soluble gas, such as absorption of oxygen into aqueous solutions of sodium sulfite, the resistance to transfer is confined entirely to the liquid phase. Intermediate cases also occur in practice. However, the discussions in this chapter will be limited essentially to liquid-film controlled gas-liquid operations.

The absorption of a gas into the liquid phase may be accompanied by a chemical reaction. Many reactive systems are used in practice for the absorption of a wide range of gaseous products.

Liquid-side mass transfer coefficients and effective interfacial areas are important parameters in the design of industrial contactors. Physical as well as chemical methods have been used for the

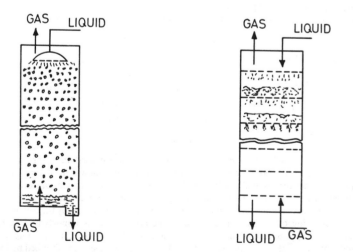

Figure 3. Spray column.   **Figure 4.** Sieve plate column.

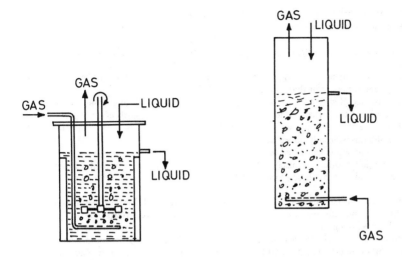

Figure 5. Agitate contactor.   Figure 6. Bubble column.

determination of mass transfer coefficients and effective interfacial area. There is much literature regarding volumetric liquid-film coefficients for physical absorption of gases in packed towers [2–6]. Sherwood and Holloway [2] developed empirical correlations for packed towers. Danckwerts [7] described the significance of liquid-film coefficients in gas-absorption. Vivian and King [8] discussed the mechanism of liquid-phase resistance to gas-absorption in packed columns. Sideman et al. [9] reviewed physical methods of determining mass transfer coefficients. It was noted that most of the reported data were specific to the apparatus used and were applicable only within the given experimental range.

The physical methods for determining effective interfacial area in gas-liquid dispersions are (1) photographic technique for determination of the dispersed phase volume-average droplet bubble size [10–13], (2) optical transmittance method [13–15], and (3) sedimentation method [16]. These

Table 1
Broad Characteristics of Gas-Liquid Systems

Equipment type	Mode of flow	Phase in turbulence	Process applications
Bubble column	Counter-current or current	Liquid	Absorption
Agitated vessel	Single stage	Liquid	Absorption
Packed tower	Counter-current or co-current	Gas	Absorption, distillation, humidification, dehumidification
Spray tower	Counter-current or co-current or cross-flow	Gas	Absorption, humidification, drying
Falling film, Wetted wall column	Counter current or co-current	Neither	Absorption, evaporation, stripping
Venturi	Co-current	Gas	Absorption

physical methods for determining interfacial area suffer from considerable disadvantages due to one or more of the following reasons:

1. Probes inserted into the gas-liquid dispersion for measurements disturb the system and thereby affect the area.
2. Photographs taken at the walls of the column give a picture of the bubbles that may not be truely representative of that in the bulk of the liquid.
3. The existence of small micro-sized ionic bubbles may not be brought out by these methods. It is very likely that the areas measured by this way are not necessarily effective for mass-transfer.
4. When more than two phases are present in the system such as in the following situations:
   a) gas-liquid-externally added solids
   b) gas-liquid-solids generated *in situ*
   c) gas-liquid-another immiscible liquid, it probably becomes impossible to find effective interfacial area by these physical techniques.

Chemical methods have definite advantage over physical methods for the determination of liquid-film coefficients and effective interfacial. The status reports of Westerterp et al. [17] and Sharma and Danckwerts [18] gave a new direction to this subject. Use of the absorption theory with chemical reaction was suggested as a more reliable method. Recently, Laurent and Charpentier [19], Figueiredo and Calderbank [20], and Charpentier [21] have reviewed various aspects of different methods of measuring mass transfer coefficients. Neelakantan and Gehlawat [22] described new chemical systems for determining liquid-side mass transfer coefficients and effective interfacial area in gas-liquid contactors.

Chemical methods of measuring liquid-side mass transfer coefficients and interfacial area in gas-liquid systems are discussed in the following. The A-phase is the gas and the B-phase is the liquid. A solute A is transferred from A-phase to the B-phase. The B-phase contains a reactant that reacts with A and is insoluble in the A-phase.

MEASUREMENTS OF MASS TRANSFER COEFFICIENTS

The mass transfer coefficient for the transfer of A between the phases is k_L. The resistance to transfer is entirely on the B-phase side of the interface and the rate of transfer per unit interfacial area (in the absence of chemical reaction) is $k_L(A^* - A_0)$, where $[A^*]$ is the concentration of A at the surface of B-phase and is in equilibrium with the bulk concentration of A in the A-phase. Numerically this value is equal to the saturation physical solubility of the solute A in B-phase at the given conditions for absorption. $[A_0]$ is the bulk concentration of A in the B-phase. The values of $[A^*]$, $[A_0]$ may vary from one part of the system to another. The area of interface between the two phases, per unit volume of the system, is a. If $[A^*]$ and $[A_0]$ were uniform the rate of transfer of A per unit volume of the system would be given by

$$R_a = k_L a[A^* - A_0] \tag{1}$$

Thus, in certain circumstances, the value of $k_L a$ may be determined by purely physical absorption experiments using Equation 1. For instance, the two phases may be well-stirred so that the values of $[A_0]$ and $[A^*]$ are the same at all the points. Alternatively, it may be a piston-like counter-current flow of the two-phases so that $[A_0]$ is a known function of $[A^*]$. In either case it is possible to infer $k_L a$ from the observed total rate of transfer as given by Equation 1. However, there are two possible difficulties about the determination of $k_L a$ by the physical method. One is that the flow-pattern and residence-time-distribution of the phases may be complicated and undetermined, so that the value of A_0 is not known as a function of A^* and hence the value of $k_L a$ cannot be deduced from the total rate of transfer. The other is that in a system consisting of an efficient contacting device (a bubble plate for example) the two phases may approach equilibrium quite closely. As noted from Equation 1, the determination of $k_L a$ depends on the difference between the actual $[A_0]$ and the equilibrium $[A^*]$ extent of transfer, that is, on the driving force. This then demands an extremely rapid and accurate measurement of the flow rates and composition of the various streams and may become impractical.

The chemical method for determining $k_L a$ avoids both these difficulties. Astarita [23] and Danckwerts [1, 24] have discussed the theory of mass transfer accompanied by chemical reaction. Consider the reaction

$$A + B \longrightarrow Products$$

which is irreversible and mth order with respect to A and nth order with respect to B.

Slow Reaction Regime

Under certain conditions the reaction is fast enough to keep the concentration of A in the bulk of B-phase equal to zero, while it is not fast enough for an appreciable amount of A to react in the diffusion film at the surface of B-phase. Under these conditions the rate of transfer is that for physical transfer with $A_0 = 0$, that is,

$$Ra = k_L a [A^*] \tag{2}$$

The condition to be satisfied if $A_0 = 0$ is

$$k_L a [A^*] \ll k_{mn} [A^*]^m [B_0]^n \tag{3}$$

where $[B_0]$ is the concentration of B in the bulk of the B-phase, l is the volume of B-phase per unit volume of the system and k_{mn} is the rate constant. The condition to be satisfied if no A is to react in the diffusion film is

$$\frac{\left[\dfrac{2}{m + 1} D_A k_{mn} [A^*]^{m-1} [B_0]^n \right]^{1/2}}{k_L} \ll 1 \tag{4}$$

where D_A is the diffusivity of A in the B-phase. Reliable methods of predicting $[A^*]$ in electrolyte solutions are available in literature [25].

From Equation 2 it is noted that if conditions are such that the concentration of A in the A-phase, and hence the value of $[A^*]$, is the same at all points, volumetric mass transfer coefficient $k_L a$ can be found from a measurement of the total rate of transfer of A. In other cases (eg., counter-current flow) the value of $[A^*]$ may vary with position in a known way, and then it is possible to derive an equation relating to the values of $[A^*]$ in the inflowing and outflowing streams to the rate of transfer and the value of $k_L a$. In either case, the residence-time distribution of the B-phase is irrelevant.

Consider an agitated absorber in which the A-phase consists of the solute gas A diluted with a carrier gas and the B-phase is an aqueous solution of a reagent. If the concentration of A in the gas varies little in its passage through the liquid, the value of $[A^*]$ may be taken to be the same at all points, and the value of $k_L a$ may be calculated from Equation 2. Further, at speeds of agitation greater than 800 rpm, the gas phase is completely back-mixed [26]. Under these conditions the effective concentration of A corresponds to its partial pressure in the exit stream. Thus, the value of $[A^*]$ is known and Equation 2 may be used to calculate values of $k_L a$.

If the contactor is a packed column with the gas-phase flowing up in it and if the concentration of A in the A-phase is small, the bulk concentration of A in the A-phase at any level being A_0, the following equations hold,

$$G \, dA_0 = -k_L a A^* \, dh \tag{5}$$

$$A^* = HA_0 \tag{6}$$

where h is the height measured from bottom of the column, G is the superficial velocity of the carrier gas, and H is the Henry's law constant relating equilibrium concentrations in the A- and B-phases. These equations can be integrated to relate the inflowing and outflowing values of $[A_0]$ to $k_L a$.

The following are some suitable chemical systems for the determination of $k_L a$. The absorption of CO_2 into carbonate-bi-carbonate buffer solution is very convenient. The reaction is second order ($m = 1, n = 1$) and may be described as

$$CO_2 + O\bar{H} \longrightarrow HC\bar{O}_3$$

Sharma and Danckwerts [18] have discussed pertinent details for the conditions to be satisfied as given by Inequalities 3 and 4 for this system.

Absorption of oxygen from air into sodium sulfite solution containing copper catalyst or very low concentrations of cobalt may be used. The reaction appears to be second order in O_2 and zero order in $S\bar{O}_3$ ($m = 2, n = 0$) under the usual conditions (Na_2SO_3 about 0.8 M; pH, 7.5–8.5). This system has been used for a long time for determining $k_L a$ in mechanically agitated and sparged contactors [27].

Oxygen may be absorbed from air into dilute acid solutions of CuCl, which is oxidized to $CuCl_2$. Jhaveri and Sharma [28] have reported the kinetics of this system.

Very limited information is available on the liquid-side mass transfer coefficients for molten systems. Recently Neelakantan and Gehlawat [22] used absorption of butadiene in molten maleic anhydride to determine $k_L a$ in a bubble column. The kinetics of absorption of butadiene in molten maleic anhydride was studied by Gehlawat [29]. It is a second order reaction with ($m = 1, n = 1$). In a bubble column, this system conforms to the slow reaction regime.

Intermediate Case Between Slow and Very Slow Reaction

It may not always be easy to satisfy both the conditions simultaneously for a slow reaction as given by inequalities 3 and 4. Thus, if $k_2[B_0]$ is made large enough to satisfy Condition 3 (i.e. $[A_0] = 0$), it may become too large for Condition 4 to be satisfied (i.e., no reaction in the film). When Condition 4 is satisfied, but Condition 3 is not satisfied, it is easily shown that

$$\frac{1}{k_{LR}a} = \frac{1}{k_L a} + \frac{1}{lk_2[B_0]} \tag{7}$$

where k_{LR} is defined by

$$Ra = k_{LR}a[A^*] \tag{8}$$

If $k_2[B_0]$ is varied, keeping $k_L a$ constant (at constant hydrodynamic conditions), a plot of $1/k_{LR}a$ against $1/k_2[B_0]$ will be a straight line of slope $1/l$ with intercept $1/k_L a$. This offers a method of determining $k_L a$ when it is not possible to satisfy Condition 3.

Instantaneous Reactions

The theory of absorption accompanied by instantaneous reaction can also be deployed for the measurements of $k_L a$. In case the solute is diluted with an inert gas, it is essential to ensure that the gas-side resistance is absent. The following rate expression holds:

$$Ra = k_L a \frac{[B_0]}{z} \sqrt{\frac{D_B}{D_A}} \tag{9}$$

The conditions to be satisfied for Equation 9 to be applicable are:

$$\frac{\left[\frac{2}{m+1} D_A k_{mn}[A^*]^{m-1}[B_0]^n\right]^{1/2}}{k_L} \gg \frac{[B_0]}{z[A^*]} \sqrt{\frac{D_B}{D_A}} \tag{10}$$

and $\quad \dfrac{[B_0]}{z[A^*]} \gg 1$ $\hfill (11)$

The absence of gas-side resistance when the solute gas is diluted with an inert gas can be checked through the following condition:

$$k_G P_G \gg k_L \frac{[B_0]}{z} \sqrt{\frac{D_B}{D_A}} \hspace{3cm} (12)$$

If pure gas is used and solvent is non-volatile, then the question of gas-side resistance does not arise.

The absorption of pure CO_2 in aqueous caustic alkaline solutions and solutions of alkanolamines, absorption of CO/olefins in cuprous amine complexes in aqueous and non-aqueous solutions etc., fall in this category. In packed column and trickle bed reactors this strategy has been successfully used [30–31]. Ranade and Ulbrecht [32] added polymeric substances to such cases to impart non-Newtonian behavior.

Danckwerts' plot

The following equation holds for a fast pseudo mth order reaction:

$$Ra = a[A^*]\left[\frac{2}{m+1} D_A k_{mn}[A^*]^{m-1}[B_0]^n\right]^{1/2} \hspace{2cm} (13)$$

provided

$$\frac{\left[\dfrac{2}{m+1} D_A k_{mn}[A^*]^{m-1}[B_0]^n\right]^{1/2}}{k_L} > 3 \hspace{2cm} (14)$$

and $\qquad\qquad\qquad\qquad\qquad < \dfrac{[B_0]}{z[A^*]} \sqrt{\dfrac{D_B}{D_A}}$ $\hfill (15)$

If the condition given by Inequality 15 is satisfied but the reaction is not fast enough to satisfy Inequality 14, the following rate expression holds for a second order reaction with m = 1 and n = 1

$$Ra = a[A^*] \sqrt{D_A k_2 [B_0] + k_L^2} \hspace{3cm} (16)$$

If Ra is measured with different values of $k_2[B_0]$, the hydrodynamic conditions being kept constant, a plot of $(Ra)^2$ against $k_2[B_0]$ gives a straight line with intercept $(k_L a[A^*])^2$ and slope $(a[A^*])^2 D_A$. This plot is referred to as Danckwerts' plot. If $[A^*]$ and D_A are known, both $k_L a$ and a can be determined. It is necessary to ensure that the physical properties of the system do not alter as $k_2[B_0]$ is changed. Danckwerts' plot is valid for any pseudo first-order reaction and the reaction can well be second order with respect to B. Danckwerts' plot cannot be made for any non-pseudo first-order reaction.

The absorption of CO_2 in carbonate/bicarbonate buffer with variation in catalytic concentration provides an ideal system without any change in the system properties as the catalyst concentration is changed [33–35]. Jhaveri and Sharma [36] used Danckwerts' plot for the absorption of oxygen in acidic aqueous solutions of CuCl in a packed column. Dewaal and Okeson [37] absorbed oxygen in aqueous solutions of sodium sulfite containing cobalt catalyst in an agitated contactor to obtain Danckwerts' plot.

Measurement of True Liquid-Side Mass Transfer Coefficient

Sometime it is essential to know the values of true liquid-side mass transfer coefficients obtainable in a contactor under given conditions. For systems where gas absorption is accompanied by a fast pseudo mth-order reaction and the value of m is other than one, then the following procedure can sometimes be employed to obtain true values of k_L and a from a set of experiments. The procedure involves changing the partial pressure of the solute gas and the concentration of species B. Consider the case of absorption of oxygen in aqueous alkaline solutions of dithionite (m = O, n = 1 for $[B_0] < 8 \times 10^{-5}$ mol cm^{-3}). Here, the enhancement factor given by $[2D_A k_1 [B_0]/[A^*]]^{1/2}$ is inversely proportional to the square root of the partial pressure of A and directly proportional to the square root of the concentration of B. Now suppose the value of enhancement factor is 5 for partial pressure of A of 0.05 atm and for concentration of B of 5×10^{-5} mol cm^{-3} then at a partial pressure of A of 1 atm and concentration of B of 3×10^{-6} mol cm^{-3}, under otherwise uniform conditions, the value of enhancement factor becomes 0.275. Experiments with the first set of conditions will give values of a and the second set will give values of $k_L a$. Juvekar and Sharma [38] have successfully used this method to obtain values of true k_L and a in a mechanically agitated contactor and a bubble column. Levec and Pavko [39] and Gopal and Sharma [40] have also utilized this strategy.

Fast Pseudo mth-Order Reaction When n = 0

For systems that conform to fast pseudo mth-order reaction regime, but are zero order with respect to species B (i.e. n = 0), it may be possible to adopt yet another method to measure a and $k_L a$ (and hence true k_L) with the same system. It is presumed that in the entire range of concentration of B under consideration the reaction is zero order in B. In a system of this type, the controlling regime changes sharply from the fast pseudo mth-order reaction regime to the instantaneous reaction regime.

For a case where m = 1 and n = 0, operating rate equations for fast pseudo first-order reaction regime and instantaneous reaction regime, respectively are.

$$Ra = a[A^*]\sqrt{D_A k_1} \tag{17}$$

$$Ra = \frac{k_L a[B_0]}{z}\sqrt{\frac{D_B}{D_A}} \tag{18}$$

The values of $[B_0]$ at which the abrupt transition will occur at a specified k_L and $[A^*]$ can be obtained by equating Equations 17 and 18:

$$[B_0]_{\text{(at transition point)}} = \frac{z[A^*]}{k_L}\left(\frac{D_A}{D_B}\right)^{1/2}(D_A k_1)^{1/2} \tag{19}$$

Thus, when the system conforms to the fast pseudo mth-order reaction regime we can measure a and when it conforms to instantaneous reaction regime we can obtain $k_L a$ (and hence true k_L as the switch over does not result in significantly changing the physical properties of the B phase).

MEASUREMENT OF INTERFACIAL AREA IN GAS-LIQUID SYSTEMS

Fast Reaction Regime

The theory of gas absorption accompanied by a fast pseudo mth-order reaction has been widely used for the determination of effective interfacial area in gas-liquid contactors. The operating rate expression is given by Equation 13. The pertinent conditions to be satisfied are given by Inequalities 14 and 15. A variety of chemical systems conforming to this fast reaction regime have been described in the literature for the measurements of interfacial areas [17, 18, 22, 25, 41]. For a second-order reaction (m = 1, n = 1), the rate expression (Equation 13) reduces to

$$Ra = a[A^*]\sqrt{D_A k_2[B_0]} \tag{20}$$

The conditions to be satisfied for Equation 20 to be applicable reduce to:

$$\frac{\sqrt{D_A k_2[B_0]}}{k_L} > 3 \tag{21}$$

$$< \frac{[B_0]}{z[A^*]}\sqrt{\frac{D_B}{D_A}} \tag{22}$$

It is noted from Equation 20 that the rate of absorption is independent of k_L, that is, it is independent of hydrodynamic conditions. Ra is the total rate of absorption in an apparatus having total effective interfacial area of a.

From Equation 20 it is evident that effective interfacial area a can be obtained from a knowledge of Ra (an experimental observation) and $[A^*]\sqrt{D_A k_2[B_0]}$. The value of the expression $[A^*]\sqrt{D_A k_2[B_0]}$ can be calculated for a system of known kinetics from the pertinent physicochemical data. It is not always necessary to know the kinetics of the reaction. The specific rate of absorption R may be determined by absorbing gas in the given reactive system in some laboratory apparatus with a known interfacial area. It is necessary to vary the flow rate, or stirring-speed to confirm that the rate of absorption R is really independent of k_L and liquid volume.

It is often possible to arrange (especially in model laboratory apparatus) that the change in $[B_0]$, while sufficient to determine analytically, is not large enough to cause a substantial change in R. In types of systems where the residence-time distribution of the gas-phase is unknown, it is sometimes possible to choose conditions such that there is practically no change in the partial pressure of the gas, e.g. by using high gas flow rates. The residence-time distribution of the gas-phase becomes irrelevant if a pure gas is used.

The absorption of lean CO_2 in a variety of aqueous alkaline solutions and solutions containing alkanolamines and amines has been used along with the absorption of O_2 in aqueous solutions of sodium sulfite containing cobalt catalyst. Westerterp et al. [17] provided a lead in utilizing chemical methods for measuring a. Jhaveri and Sharma [36] used absorption of O_2 in aqueous alkaline solutions of sodium hydrosulfite. Here the absorption of O_2 is accompanied by fast pseudo zero-order reaction. Neelakantan and Gehlawat [22] introduced a new system of absorption of O_2 in aqueous solutions of ammonium sulfite containing cobalt catalyst. This system was found to conform to fast pseudo mth-order reaction regime [42]. It was first-order with respect to oxygen and second-order with respect to ammonium sulfite.

Interfacial Area in Organic Liquids

Many industrially important systems involve polar and non-polar organic liquids. Sharma and Mashelkar [35] and Mehta and Sharma [26] absorbed CO_2 in alcohols such as methanol, isopropanol, etc. containing alkanolamines. Sridharan and Sharma [43] have shown that non-polar systems can be used through absorption of lean CO_2 in toluene/xylene containing cyclohexylamine and a small amount of (5 to 10%) isopropanol or cyclohexanol. Measurements of a have been made in mechanically agitated and bubble column contactors. Recently Alvarez-Fuster et al. [44, 45] and Carpentier [21] have utilized this system in different types of reactors. This system offers a number of advantages as it is simple and allows a wide range of viscosity and surface tension to be covered.

Under certain conditions absorption of H_2 in triglycerides with Ziegler-Natta type dissolved catalysts is accompanied by fast pseudo mth-order reaction. This system can be used to measure a. Ganguli and Van Denberg [46, 47] have used this system for measurements of a. It is quite likely that hydrogenation of α-olefins with Ziegler-Natta type catalysts would fall in the fast pseudo mth-order reaction regime and hence may be suitable for measuring effective interfacial area, a, with a wide variation in system properties.

Interfacial Area in Non-Newtonian Systems

There is real dearth of data on non-Newtonian systems. Most of the information has come out in the last about six years. The absorption of O_2 in aqueous alkaline dithionite solutions lends itself to extension to non-Newtonian systems by using polyvinyl alcohol, polyacrylamide, carboxy methyl cellulose (CMC) [48]. Onken and Schalk [49] have shown that even cobalt-catalyzed reaction between oxygen and sodium sulfite can be adopted by using CMC. There is need for further work in this area. It is very likely that absorption of lean O_2 in toluen/xylenes, etc. containing cyclohexylamine can be extended by using suitable polymeric materials such as polystyrene. A similar strategy can be adopted for alcoholic solutions where a suitable polymer can be amployed. However, it is doubtful if simulation with added materials as above can provide information of practical significance. The real need is to obtain data from industrial reactors.

Interfacial Area in Molten Systems/Salts

Holroyd and Kenney [50] have shown that the absorption of SO_2 into a melt of vanadium pentoxide in potassium pyrosulfate in the temperature range of 360 to 480°C conforms to the fast pseudo first-order reaction regime. Similarly, the absorption of O_2 in the melt containing vanadium in the reduced state also conforms to the regime and was found to be zero-order in oxygen. Both these systems can be employed to obtain a in contactors employed for melts.

The oxidation of cuprous benzoate in molten benzoic acid medium can also be used to determine a since the absorption of O_2 is accompanied by fast pseudo first-order reaction. Ghorpade et al. [51] used this system for measuring a in a bubble column and a mechanically agitated contactor. The values of a obtained for this molten system were found to be comparable to those found with aqueous solutions under otherwise similar conditions.

Comparison of Values Obtained from Different Systems and Different Methods

The published data clearly show that in packed columns, systems conforming to different kinetics give practically the same values of effective interfacial area for any packing, at any specified liquid velocity [36, 42, 43, 52–55]. Likewise for contactors where a gas is dispersed in the liquid, practically the same value of effective interfacial area has been obtained, under otherwise similar conditions, from systems obeying different kinetics [22, 26, 35, 38, 43].

Reith and Beck [56] obtained values of interfacial areas by both photographic as well as chemical method in a bubble column and a close agreement was found between the two sets of values. Radinov et al. [57] also determined values of effective interfacial area in grid columns with liquid viscosities varying from 1 to 37 cp by the chemical and the light transmission method and found a close agreement between the two sets of values. Allenbach et al. [58] have also made measurements of effective interfacial area in a bubble column by the chemical method as well as the photographic method and observed good agreement between the two sets of values. Similar observations have been made by Landau et al. [59] and Ostergaard [60]. However, some measurements have been made in jet contactors where a was measured by photographic as well as chemical methods and large differences between these two sets of values have been reported. [61] Kurten and Zehner [62] have shown that the photographic method gives excessively high values of a as only the smallest bubbles are detected at the reactor walls and large bubbles migrate from the wall boundary layer into the bulk of the liquid. Thus, the measured size distribution becomes un-representative. Schumpe and Deckever [63, 64] have recently reported measurements of a in two bubble columns by photographic and chemical methods. CMC was added to vary viscosity of O_2-sulfite system. It was noted that the values of a obtained by the photographic method always tend to be higher than those obtained by the chemical methods. This was attributed to the maldistribution of bubbles and systematic under estimation of the Sauter diameters for non-spherical bubbles.

Presence of Small Amounts of Solids in Gas-Liquid Systems

It is not uncommon in practice to find the presence of a solid phase (perhaps formed *in situ* as a result of reaction, etc.) in the conventional gas-liquid contactors. The slurry reactors form an important field of gas-liquid solid systems. Shah [65] has treated this subject in greater detail. Here the concern is about the effect of the presence of a solid phase on the effective interfacial area obtainable in gas-liquid systems.

The chemical method lends itself very well to the measurement of a in three-phase systems. The slurry can be considered as an absorbent. For instance, precipitated $CaCO_3$ may be added to alkaline solutions or alkanolamine solutions or in dithionite solutions to study the effect of the presence of added solids on the system properties like a. The effect of solids generated *in situ* may be noted. For instance, when lean CO_2 is absorbed in aqueous solutions of LiOH, the product of reaction $LiCO_3$ being sparingly soluble in water precipitates out [35]. Similarly absorption of CO_2 in sodium carbonate/bicarbonate buffer, with a catalyst, may lead to the precipitation of sodium carbonate under certain conditions. CO_2 may be absorbed in aqueous slurry of lime to produce precipitated calcium carbonate. Here lime is sparingly soluble in water and the reaction occurs between the dissolved CO_2 and OH ions. The effect of fine and coarse particles, at low and high loadings, on effective interfacial area a can be quite complex. Sharma and Mashelkar [35], Mehta and Sharma [26], Joosten et al. [66] have studied this problem. The presence of solid particles is found to reduce the effective interfacial area.

TYPICAL EXPERIMENTAL TECHNIQUES

Model apparatus, such as a stirred cell, a laminar jet or a wetted wall column, provide a well-defined interfacial geometry. They have been used to obtain specific rates of absorption for a given gas-liquid system and for evaluating reaction kinetics of relatively fast reactions. Figures 7–9

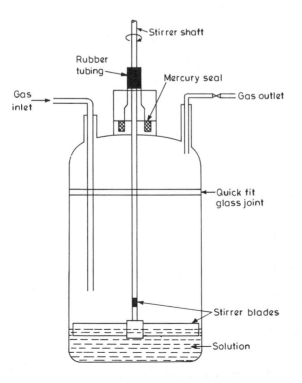

Figure 7. Stirred cell.

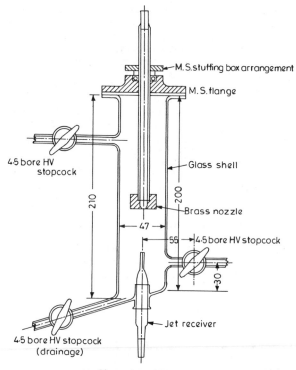

Dimensions in mm

Figure 8. Laminar jet apparatus.

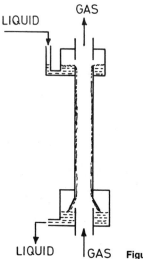

Figure 9. Wetted wall column.

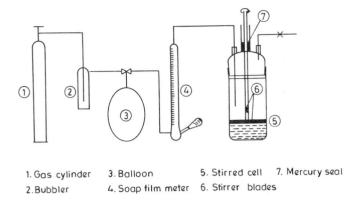

1. Gas cylinder   3. Balloon   5. Stirred cell   7. Mercury seal
2. Bubbler   4. Soap film meter 6. Stirrer blades

Figure 10. Experimental setup for a stirred cell.

show respectively typical stirred cell, laminar jet apparatus, and wetted wall column. An experimental setup using a stirred cell assembly is shown in Figure 10. The design features of stirred cells and the experimental procedure are described by Sharma and Danckwerts [67], Gehlawat and Sharma [68, 69], and Jhaveri and Sharma [28].

An experimental set-up for a laminar jet apparatus is shown in Figure 11. The design features of the apparatus are akin to those employed by Sharma and Danckwerts [67]. The rate of absorption of the gas stored in a balloon may be determined by the volumetric up-take method using a soap film meter. Neelakantan [70] has described the pertinent details. According to Danckwerts [1], model laboratory experiments may be carried out in apparatus of such design to obtain meaningful results for the design and simulation of the performance of industrial gas-liquid contactors.

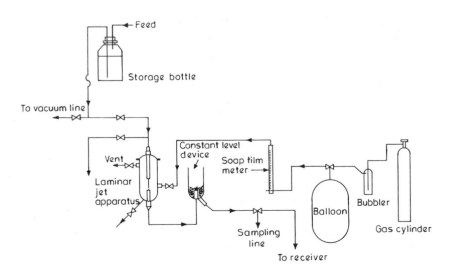

Figure 11. Experimental setup for a laminar jet apparatus.

Measurements of $k_L a$ in a Bubble Column

The absorption of butadiene in molten maleic anhydride in a bubble column is found to conform to the slow reaction regime [22]. It is a second-order reaction with m = 1 and n = 1. The operating rate expression given by Equation 2 is rewritten as

$$Ra = K_L a[A^*] \tag{23}$$

The conditions given by Inequalities 3 and 4 for this rate expression to be applicable are reduced to:

$$k_L a \ll lk_2[B_0] \tag{24}$$

$$\frac{\sqrt{D_A K_2[B_0]}}{k_L} \ll 1 \tag{25}$$

The apparatus used and the detailed experimental procedure are described by Neelakantan and Gehlawat [22]. A typical value of $lk_2[B_0]$ for the reaction between dissolved butadiene and molten maleic anhydride at 105°C (when l = 0.9, k_2 = 12 cm^3 mol^{-1} s^{-1} and $[B_0]$ = 10^{-2} mol cm^{-3}) is 0.11. The values of the liquid-side mass transfer coefficients, $k_L a$, in a bubble column are found to range between 2×10^{-2} to 6×10^{-2}. Therefore, the condition given by the Inequality 24 i.e. $k_L a <$ $lK_2[B_0]$ is satisfied. Further, the typical value of $\sqrt{D_A K_2[B_0]}/k_L$ is 0.2. Hence the condition given by Inequality 25 is also satisfied. Equation 23 may, therefore, be used to calculate the values of mass transfer coefficient from the observed rates of absorption of butadiene in molten maleic anhydride in a bubble column. The results obtained are given in Table 2. It is note worthy that the values of $k_L a$ obtained at the same superficial gas velocity for different column sizes are comparable

Table 2
Mass Transfer Coefficients in Jacketed Bubble Columns for the Butadiene-Molten Maleic Anhydride System at 102°C [22]

Run no.	Column diameter (cm)	Superficial gas velocity (cm s^{-1})	Mass transfer coefficient $k_L a \times 10^2$ (s^{-1})	Remarks
1	3.5	4.1	1.9	
2	3.5	8.2	3.8	
3	3.5	11.7	5.1	
4	3.5	15.2	5.7	
5	4.6	4.9	2.2	
6	4.6	10.3	4.6	
7	4.6	15.5	5.9	
8	4.6	10.3	5.7	9.0-mm diameter Rashing
9	4.6	19.4	7.8	rings used as column packings
10	7.5	3.5	1.5	Higher gas flow rates could not
11	7.5	7.0	2.5	be used
12	7.5	4.3	2.7	9.0-mm diameter Rasching rings used as column packings

Table 3
Typical Values of Mass Transfer Coefficients in Bubble Columns
for Aqueous Systems [22]

Superficial gas velocity (cm s^{-1})	$k_L a \times 10^2$ (s^{-1})
2	1.5
5	2.5
7	4.0
10	5.0
15	6.0
20	6.9

However, it may be seen from run numbers 8, 9, and 12 that the values of $k_L a$ are appreciably higher in the presence of packings. A similar effect was observed by Mashelkar and Sharma [35, 71] for aqueous systems. Table 3 gives the typical values of mass transfer coefficients in bubble columns for aqueous systems. The data in Tables 2 and 3 show that the values of $k_L a$ obtained for the molten system (of butadiene in maleic anhydride) are of comparable order of magnitude with the values of aqueous systems.

Effective Interfacial Area

Neelakantan and Gehlawat [22] absorbed oxygen in aqueous solutions of ammonium sulfite for determining effective interfacial area. For the O_2-ammonium sulfite system (m = 1, n = 2), the rate expression (Equation 13) reduces to:

$$R a = a[A^*]\sqrt{D_A k_3 [B_0]^2} \tag{26}$$

The physical conditions to be satisfied are:

$$\frac{\sqrt{D_A k_3 [B_0]^2}}{k_L} > 3 \tag{27}$$

$$< \frac{[B_0]}{z[A^*]} \tag{28}$$

It is noted from Equation 26 that a knowledge of the absorption rate, $R a$, in a contactor (an experimental observation) and a measure of the specific rate of absorption per unit area, R, in an apparatus of known interfacial area (such as stirred cell) would enable the values of effective interfacial area, a, to be calculated. Figure 12 shows an experimental set-up for determining effective interfacial area in a packed column. Pure O_2 was absorbed in aqueous solutions of ammonium sulfite in a 5-cm ID glass column packed randomly with 9-mm glass Raschig rings. The rate of absorption was measured using a soap film meter [22, 28]. Experiments were also conducted using a bubble column of 5-cm ID. Gas was introduced through a single bottom inlet tube of 4-mm diameter. The inlet and outlet of ammonium sulfite were analyzed for sulfite content iodometrically. The ratio of the height of dispersion to the column diameter (L/D) was kept constant at 10.0 by using a constant level device.

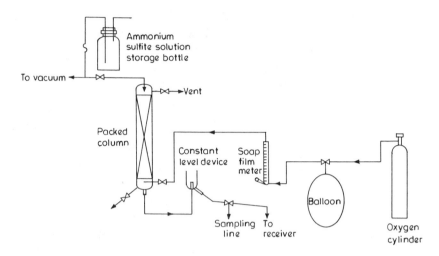

Figure 12. Experimental setup for a packed column.

Effective Interfacial Area in Packed Columns

For a typical run for the absorption of pure O_2 in aqueous solutions of ammonium sulfite in a packed column at 30°C the following values are applicable:

$$D_A = 2.2 \times 10^{-5} \, \text{cm}^2 \, \text{s}^{-1}$$

$$k_3 = 2.7 \times 10^4 \, (1/\text{mol})^2 \, \text{s}^{-1}$$

$$k_L = 5 \times 10^{-3} \, \text{cm} \, \text{s}^{-1}$$

$$[B_0] = 4 \times 10^{-4} \, \text{mol} \, \text{cm}^{-3}$$

$$[A^*] = 9.4 \times 10^{-7} \, \text{mol} \, \text{cm}^{-3}$$

$$z = 2$$

whence, the physical conditions are calculated as follows:

$$\frac{\sqrt{D_A k_3 [B_0]^2}}{k_L} = 63$$

$$\frac{[B_0]}{z[A^*]} = 213$$

It is noted that the conditions given by Expressions 27 and 28 are satisfied. The specific rates of absorption were determined using a stirred cell [70]. Hence, Equation 26 can be used to determine the values of effective interfacial area in packed columns. Figure 13 shows the effective interfacial area as a function of the liquid flow rate. The results have been compared with the data reported by Jhaveri and Sharma [28]. A close agreement is observed.

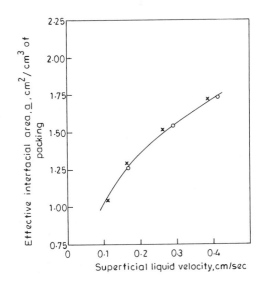

Figure 13. Effect of superficial liquid velocity on effective, interfacial area, *a*, in a packed column: x—ammonium sulfite-oxygen system [22]; o—acidic CuCl-oxygen system [36]. (Adopted from Neelakantan and Gehlawat [22].

Effective Interfacial Area in Bubble Columns

For a typical run for the absorption of O_2 from air in aqueous solutions of ammonium sulfite in a bubble column at 30°C the following data are representative:

$$D_A = 2.2 \times 10^{-5} \text{ cm}^2 \text{ s}^{-1}$$

$$k_3 = 2.7 \times 10^4 \text{ (1/mol)}^2 \text{ s}^{-1}$$

$$k_L = 2 \times 10^{-2} \text{ cm s}^{-1}$$

$$[B_0] = 4 \times 10^{-4} \text{ mol cm}^{-3}$$

$$[A^*] = 2 \times 10^{-7} \text{ mol cm}^{-3}; z = 2$$

whence the physical conditions may be calculated as follows:

$$\frac{\sqrt{D_A k_3 [B_0]^2}}{k_L} = 15; \quad \frac{[B_0]}{z[A^*]} = 1,000$$

It is observed that the conditions given by Expressions 27 and 28 are satisfied. Hence, Equation 26 may be used to determine the values of effective interfacial area in bubble columns. Figure 14 shows the effective interfacial area obtained in the bubble column as a function of the superficial gas velocity. The results have been compared with the data reported by Juvekar and Sharma [38]. A close agreement is noted.

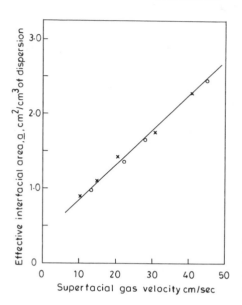

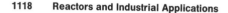

Figure 14. Effect on superficial gas velocity on effective interfacial area, a, in a bubble column: x—ammonium sulfite-oxygen system [22]; o—sodium dithionite-oxygen system [38]. (Adopted from Neelakantan and Gehlawat [22].)

CONCLUSION

The chemical methods of measuring volumetric mass-transfer coefficient, $k_L a$, true mass-transfer coefficient, k_L and effective interfacial area, a, are simple and very useful methods for making a systematic study of performance characteristics of gas-liquid contactors and providing basic data for a design. The main deficiency in measuring values of a by chemical methods is that only integral values are obtained. A distribution of bubble or drop sizes, when relevant, cannot be obtained by chemical methods.

Reliable data or methods of measurement of $k_L a$ and a are important for a rational design of industrial reactors. In most cases of practical importance a systematic approach, as discussed in this chapter, may be found useful to obtain relevant data and to arrive at procedures for the design of large-scale contactors. Danckwerts and Sharma [25], Mashelkar [72], and Juvekar and Sharma [73] have discussed design procedures for gas-liquid contactors.

NOTATION

a effective interfacial area for gas-liquid contactors/reactors, cm^2/cm^3 contactor volume, cm^2/cm^3 dispersion volume, cm^2/cm^3 of clear liquid volume

$[A^*]$ solubility of species A in B-phase, mol/cm^3

$[B_0]$ bulk concentration of species B in B-phase, mol/cm^3

D_A diffusivity of species A in B-phase, cm^2/s

D_B diffusivity of species B in B-phase, cm^2/s

G molar flow rate of inerts in the gas phase, mol/s

h height of the column/reactor, cm

H Henry's Law constant for the solute gas in liquid, mol/cm^3 atm

k_1 first-order rate constant, s^{-1}

k_2 second-order rate constant, $(cm^3/mol) s^{-1}$

k_3 third-order rate constant, $(cm^3/mol)^2 s^{-1}$

k_{mn} (m + n)th order rate constant, $(cm^3/mol)^{(m+n)-1} s^{-1}$

k_L true liquid-side mass-transfer coefficient, cm/s

$k_L a$ volumetric mass-transfer coefficient, s^{-1}

k_{LR} as defined by Equation 8, cm/s

k_G true gas-side mass-transfer coefficient, mol/cm^2 s atm

l fractional hold-up, cm^3/cm^3 dispersion,

L	liquid flow rate, cm^3/s	R	rate of transfer of A per unit area of
m	order of reaction with respect to A		interface, mol/cm^2 s
n	order of reaction with respect to B	z	number of moles of B reacting with one
P	operating pressure, atm		mol of A
P_G	partial pressure of gas, atm		

REFERENCES

1. Danckwerts, P. V. *Gas-Liquid Reactions*, McGraw-Hill Book Co., New York, 1970.
2. Sherwood, T. K. and Holloway, F. A. L. *Trans. Am. Inst. Chem. Engrs.* 36, 21, 39, 181, 1940.
3. Sherwood, T. K. and Pigford, R. L. *Absorption and Extraction*, 2nd Edition, McGraw-Hill Book Co., New York, 1952.
4. Norman, W. S. *Distillation, Absorption and Cooling Towers*, Longmans Green and Co. London, 1961.
5. van Krevelen, D. W. and Hoftyzer, P. J. *Chem. Eng. Prog.* 1948, 44, 529.
6. Davidson, J. F. *Trans. Instn. Chem. Engrs.* 37, 131, 1959.
7. Danckwerts, P. V. *Ind. Eng. Chem. Ind. Edn.* 43, 1460, 1951.
8. Vivian, J. E. and King, C. J. *A.I.Ch.E. J.*, 10, 221, 1964.
9. Sideman, S., Hortacsu, O. and Fulton, J. W. *Ind. Eng. Chem.* 58, 32, 1966.
10. Trice, V. G. J. and Rodger W. A. *A.I.Ch.E. J.*, 2, 205, 1956.
11. Marrucci G. and Nicodemo, L. *Chem. Eng. Sci.* 22, 1257, 1967.
12. Voyer, R. D. and Miller, A. I. *Cand. J. Chem. Eng.* 46, 335, 1968.
13. Burekhart, R. and Deckwer, W. D. *Chem. Eng. Sci.* 30, 354, 1975.
14. Calderbank, P. H. *Trans. Instn. Chem. Engrs.* 36, 443, 1958.
15. Lee, J. C. and Meyrick, D. L. *Trans. Instn. Chem. Engrs.* 48, T37, 1970.
16. Kafarov, V. V. and Babnov, B. M. *J. Appl. Chem.* (U.S.S.R), 32, 810, 1959.
17. Westerterp, K. R., Van Dierendonek, L. L. and deKraa, J. A. *Chem. Eng. Sci.* 18, 157, 1963.
18. Sharma, M. M. and Danckwerts, P. V. *Brit. Chem. Eng.* 15, 522, 1970.
19. Laurent, A. and Charpentier, J. C. *Chem. Eng. J.* 8, 85, 1974.
20. Figueiredo, M. and Calderbank, P. H. *Chem. Eng. Sci.* 34, 1333, 1979.
21. Charpentier, J. C. *Trans. Instn. Chem. Engrs.* 60, 131, 1982.
22. Neelakantan, K. and Gehlawat, J. K. *Chem. Eng. J.* 24, 1, 1982.
23. Astarita, G. *Mass Transfer with Chemical Reaction*, Elservier Scientific Publishing Co. Amsterdam, 1967.
24. Danckwerts, P. V. *Ind. Eng. Chem.* 43, 1460, 1951.
25. Danckwerts, P. V. and Sharma, M. M. *Chem. Engr.* Oct., C.E. 244, 1966.
26. Mehta, V. D. and Sharma, M. M. *Chem. Eng. Sci.* 26, 461, 1971.
27. Phillips, D. H. and Johnson, M. J. *Ind. Eng. Chem.* 51, 83, 1959.
28. Jhaveri, A. S. and Sharma, M. M. *Chem. Eng. Sci.* 22, 1, 1967.
29. Gehlawat, J. K. *Indian Chem. Engr.* 14, 1, 1972.
30. Mahajani, V. V. and Sharma, M. M. *Chem. Eng. Sci.* 34, 1425, 1979.
31. Mahajani, V. V. and Sharma, M. M. *Chem. Eng. Sci.* 35, 941, 1980.
32. Ranade, V. R. and Ulbrecht, J. J. *A.I.Ch.E. J.* 24, 796, 1978.
33. Richards, G. M., Ratcliff, G. A. and Danckwerts, P. V. *Chem. Eng. Sci.* 19, 325, 1964.
34. Danckwerts, P. V. and Gillham, A. J. *Trans. Instn. Chem. Engrs.* 44, T42, 1966.
35. Sharma, M. M. and Mashelkar, R. A., in Pirie J. M. (ed.) *Proceedings of a Symposium held at the Tripartite Chemical Engineering Conference*, Montreal, Sept. 1968. 1968, pp. 10.
36. Jhaveri, A. S. and Sharma, M. M. *Chem. Eng. Sci.* 23, 669, 1968.
37. DeWaal, K. J. A. and Okeson, J. C. *Chem. Eng. Sci.* 21, 559, 1966.
38. Juvekar, V. A. and Sharma, M. M. *Chem. Eng. Sci.* 28, 976, 1973.
39. Levec. J. and Pavko, S. *Chem. Eng. Sci.* 34, 1159, 1979.
40. Gopal, J. S. and Sharma, M. M. *Can. J. Chem. Eng.* 60, 353, 1982.
41. Robinson, C. W. and Wilke, C. R. *A.I.Ch.E. J.*, 20, 285, 1974.
42. Neelakantan, K. and Gehlawat, J. K. *Ind. Eng. Chem. Fundam.* 19, 36, 1980.

43. Sridharan, K. and Sharma, M. M. *Chem. Eng. Sci.* 31, 767, 1976.
44. Alvarez-Fuster, C, Midoux, N., Laurent, A., and Charpentier, J. C. *Chem. Eng. Sci.* 35, 1717, 1980.
45. Alvarez-Fuster, C, Midoux, N., Laurent, A. and Charpentier, J. C. *Chem. Eng. Sci.* 36, 1513, 1981.
46. Ganguli, K. L. and VanDenberg, H. J. *Chem. Eng. Sci.* 33, 27, 1978.
47. Ganguli, K. L. and VanDenberg, H. J. *Chem. Eng. J.* 16, 193, 1978.
48. Ravetkar, D. D. and Kale, D. D., *Chem. Eng. Sci.* 36, 399, 1981.
49. Onken, U. and Schalk, W., *Ger. Chem. Eng.* 1, 191, 1978.
50. Holroyd, F. P. B. and Kenny, C. N., *Chem. Eng. Sci.* 26, 1963, 1971.
51. Gorpade, A. K., Chipalkatti, S. V. and Sharma, M. M. *Chem. Eng. Sci.* 36, 1227, 1981.
52. Danckwerts, P. V. and Rizvi, S. F. *Trans. Instn. Chem. Engrs.* 49, 124, 1971.
53. Sahay, B. N. and Sharma, M. M. *Chem. Eng. Sci.* 28, 2245, 1973.
54. Joosten G. E. H. and Danckwerts, P. V. *Chem. Eng. Sci.* 28, 453, 1973.
55. Alper, E. *Trans. Instn. Chem. Engrs.* 57, 64, 1979.
56. Reith, T, and Beck, W. J., *Proceedings of the Fourth European Symposium on Chemical Reaction Engineering*, Brussels, 1968.
57. Radinov, A. I., Vinter, A. A., Ul'yanov, B. A. and Zenkov, V. V., *International Chem. Eng.* 10, 166, 1970.
58. Allenbach, U., Wirges, H. P. and Deckwer, W. D. *Verfahrenstechnik*, 11(12). 751, 1977.
59. Landan, J., Boyle, J., Gomra, H. G. and Al Taweel, A. M. *Can. J. Chem. Eng.* 13, 1977.
60. Ostergaard, K. *Three-phase Fluidization: Studies of Hold-up, Mass Transfer and Mixing*, Chemical Engineering with Per Soh-toft, Teknisk for lag a-s, Copenhagen, Denmark, 119, 1977.
61. Weisweiler, W. and Roschi, S. *Germ. Chem. Eng.* 1, 212, 1978.
62. Kurten, H. and Zehner, P. *Ger. Chem. Eng.* 1, 374, 1978.
63. Schumpe, A. and Deckwer, W. D. *Chem. Eng. Sci.* 35, 2221, 1980.
64. Schempe, A. and Deckwer, W. D., *Chem. Eng. Commun.* 17, 313, 1982.
65. Shah, Y. T., *Gas-Liquid-Solid Reactor Design*, McGraw-Hill Book Co. New York, 1979.
66. Joosten, G. E. H., Schilder, J. G. M. and Janssen, J. J. *Chem. Eng. Sci.* 32, 563, 1977.
67. Sharma, M. M. and Danckwerts, P. V. *Chem. Eng. Sci.* 19, 99, 1964.
68. Gehlawat, J. K. and Sharma, M. M. *Chem. Eng. Sci.* 23, 1173, 1968.
69. Gehlawat, J. K., Ph.D. dissertation Bombay Univ. 1969.
70. Neelakantan, K. Ph.D., dissertation, I. I. T. Kanpur, 1979.
71. Mashelkar, R. A. and Sharma, M. M. *Trans. Instn. Chem. Engrs.* 48, 162, 1970.
72. Mashelkar, R. A., *Brit. Chem. Eng.* 15, 1297, 1970.
73. Juvekar, V. A. and Sharma, M. M. *Trans. Instn. Chem. Engrs.* 55, 77, 1977.

CHAPTER 36

RADIAL LIQUID MIXING IN CO-CURRENT GAS-LIQUID UPFLOW PACKED BEDS

M. Nakamura

Department of Chemical Engineering
Nagoya University
Nagoya, Japan

CONTENTS

ASPECTS OF TRICKLE BED REACTOR

Packed beds with co-current gas-liquid downflow, "trickle bed," reactors, have been widely used in the chemical and petroleum refining industries. In the hydrodesulfurization process, for example, heavy or residual oil is fed with hydrogen at the top of the reactor and passes through the stationary catalyst bed in the downward direction while the desulfurized product is discharged from the bottom of the reactor. Commercial trickle bed reactors may vary from 1 to 6 m in diameter and have catalyst volumes of up to 200 m³ [1]. In consequence of such huge scales they are generally operated adiabatically in the case of an exothermal reaction, in which the subsequent marked temperature rise from the inlet to the outlet of the reactor requires that the catalyst bed be divided into successive multiple stages each of about 3- to 6-m depth and that the stream be quenched by cold recycle gas and/or liquid at each interspace between stages for temperature control—cold shot cooling [2]. On the other hand, evaporation of a part of the liquid in the reactor may contribute to decreased temperature. This may lead to approximately isothermal conditions because of the high latent heat of vaporization of liquid, if liquid loading and distribution are sufficient to effectively wet the surface of the catalyst. In packed bed reactors the catalyst may be poisoned or deactivated progressively by metal contaminants and coke-like materials deposited from heavy and residual oils. Deposition of metals and cokes causes the bed to plug, leads to the formation of channelling flow in the bed, and finally reduces the process efficiency. The exothermal reaction may also contribute indirectly to the bed plugging, possibly because lack of heat removal causes some localized hot spots to form which enhance metal and coke deposition on the catalyst surface.

Since it is certain that different reactor designs have advantages and disadvantages, various kinds of reactors are used competitively to manufacture the same product [3, 4]. Regarding the trickle bed reactor that has still some disadvantages in spite of the widespread use on a large scale as previously mentioned, the principal competing reactor is a 'slurry reactor,' or 'ebullating bed,' in which the catalyst particles are in motion. These are also sometimes termed "three-phase fluidized bed reactors" or "suspended bed reactors." Some advantages and disadvantages of those reactors were described by Satterfield [2].

ADVANTAGES OF THE FLOODED BED REACTOR

Recently the flooded bed reactors (or packed bubble columns) with co-current gas-liquid upflow were used on both laboratory and pilot plant scales as alternatives to the trickle bed reactor. Ohtsuka et al. [5], Kato et al. [6], Takematsu and Parsons [7], Takematsu [8], and Montagna and Shah [9] used this type of reactor for hydrodesulfurization of crude or heavy oil. Mochizuki and Matsui [10] used it for selective hydrogenation of phenylacetylene in styrene solution. All these studies showed superior performance—higher conversion, better selectivity, longer catalyst life, and better temperature control—with the co-current upflow mode compared to the performance with the co-current downflow mode. Although there should be many reasons why the upflow reactor is superior to the downflow reactor, the disadvantages of the latter as mentioned in the previous section have been fundamentally overcome by the former.

Figure 1 makes a comparison between the flow patterns of the downflow and the upflow reactors [11]. Although many definitions of flow regimes have been presented, they may be mainly summarized in the following four regimes: spray (or churn) flow, trickle flow, pulse (or plug) flow, and bubble flow. The great difference between the flow charts in Figure 1 is caused by trickle flow, which is very often observed in downflow operation but hardly at all in upflow operation. In the region of lower gas flow rates, only bubble flow is observed in the upflow reactor while both trickle and bubble flows are found in the downflow reactor. In trickle flow, the liquid trickles down over the catalyst surfaces in a thin film or in rivulets and the gas flows continuously through the voids in the bed, so that the interaction between both fluids may be weak. On the other hand, in bubble flow the gas disperses in the continuous liquid phase and rises as the dispersed phase. Consequently the gas and liquid in upflow reactors flow with strong interaction between each other. It is obvious that strong interaction between the different phases is essential to high reactor performance in multiphase reactions.

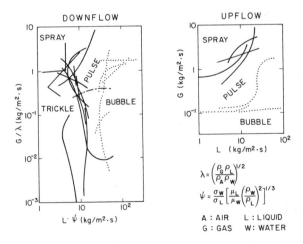

Figure 1. Flow patterns in the downflow and upflow reactors.

The upflow reactor has the following characteristics:

1. It is preferred to operate at low liquid flow rates where high liquid holdup, high liquid-to-solid ratio, and large liquid residence time are obtained.
2. The liquid residence time can be varied more easily than in the downflow reactor.
3. Due to the high liquid holdup, the catalyst surfaces are wetted and contacted very well by the liquid.
4. Contacting efficiencies not only between liquid and solid but also between gas and liquid are good.
5. Because of better sweeping over the catalyst surfaces and high heat capacity of the liquid, the heat removal from the catalyst particles is good and thus hot spots are dissipated.
6. It is possible to remove the deactivated catalysts and replace the activated ones during operation. In this case, the bed must be actually moved downward at a very slow speed [12].

This chapter highlights the radial liquid mixing and then the radial heat transfer in packed beds with co-current gas-liquid upflow. These two phenomena are quite different from those in the downflow mode. In addition, they provide a background for the superiority of the upflow reactor over the downflow one.

AXIAL LIQUID DISPERSION IN PACKED BEDS WITH CO-CURRENT FLOW

In general the main product in multiphase reactors exists in the liquid phase [3, 4]. Therefore, several studies have considered the fluid dynamics of the liquid in the trickle bed reactor. The one-dimensional plug-flow-dispersion model (PD model) is simple and has been widely applied to axial liquid mixing. According to this model, the unsteady state equation for mass balance of a tracer material can be derived as follows:

$$\partial C/\partial t = E_z(\partial^2 C/\partial Z^2) - U_\ell(\partial C/\partial Z) \tag{1}$$

where E_z is defined as the axial liquid dispersion coefficient and accounts for all the factors, such as turbulent diffusion, local channeling, and liquid exchange into and out of stagnant pockets, which cause liquid to mix in the axial direction. However, this model may be too simplified to explain the residence time distribution with a marked tail observed in unsteady tracer experiments, probably because a considerable amount of liquid exists in stagnant pockets. A model, in which the liquid phase is divided into free-flowing and stagnant regions and is allowed to exchange reversibly from one region into the other, has been proposed and is called the cross-flow model. To explain the marked tail of the residence time distribution a more sophisticated model has been proposed, called the cross-flow dispersion model or the PDE model, which combines the plug-flow-dispersion model with liquid exchange into and out of stagnant pockets.

With respect to the upflow reactor, Hofmann [13] summarized the axial liquid dispersion coefficients based on the PD model. It is generally shown that $Pe_z(= U_\ell d_p/E_z)$ decreases with increasing gas velocity and increases with increasing liquid velocity. On the other hand, some investigations showed an effect of bed height on Pe_z, probably because the gas hold-up may increase toward the top of the bed. Ohsasa et al. [14] showed that Pe_z for pulse flow should be correlated with interstitial (not apparent) liquid velocity and hence be independent of gas velocity. In addition, they found that Pe_z for pulse flow was independent of the flow direction whether it was upward or downward when the interstitial liquid velocity was used for correlation.

MODEL FOR DETERMINING RADIAL LIQUID DISPERSION

The radial concentration distribution of a tracer material is obtained by continuously injecting a liquid tracer from a point on the central axis of the packed bed. If it is assumed that (1) gas and liquid velocities are uniform in any sectional area and (2) the radial and axial liquid dispersion coefficients, E_r and E_z, are constant through the bed, then the mass balance equation of the tracer at the steady state is given as follows:

$$E_z(\partial^2 C/\partial Z^2) + (E_r/r)\partial(r\ \partial C/\partial r)/\partial r - U_d(\partial C/\partial Z) = 0 \tag{2}$$

with the boundary conditions

$$r = 0, \qquad C = \text{finite}$$

$$r = r_w, \qquad \partial C/\partial r = 0$$

$$Z = \infty, \qquad C = \bar{C}$$

The solution of Equation 2 has been given by Klinkenberg et al. [15]:

$$C/\bar{C} = 1 + (1/2) \sum_{i=1}^{\infty} J_0(\alpha_i R) \exp[(1/2 - \beta_i)Pe_r Z/nd_p]/\beta_i J_0^2(\alpha_i) \tag{3}$$

where α_i is the i-th positive root of $J_1(\alpha) = 0$, $\bar{C}$ is the mean tracer concentration, Pe_r is the radial Peclet number $(= U_d d_p/E_r)$, Pe_z is the axial Peclet number $(= U_d d_p/E_z)$, $n = Pe_r/Pe_z$ and $\beta_i = [1/4 + n(\alpha_i/Pe_r)^2(d_p/r_w)^2]^{1/2}$.

The least square method can be used to determine the values of Pe_r and n. For the trickle bed reactor Muroyama et al. [16] found that n varied in the range between 10 and 30 and had little influence on the calculated values of Pe_r. Nakamura et al. [17] also found that for the co-current upflow reactor n had very little effect on the calculated values of Pe_r over the range between 5 and 50. Hence, it may safely be assumed that n is almost 20 in application of the least square method to calculation of Pe_r with consideration of the axial dispersion coefficient Pe_z obtained by Ohsasa et al. [14]. On the basis of the assumption that the mean tracer concentration $\bar{C}$ at $Z = \infty$ was different from the cup-mixed tracer concentration C_{mix} at the bed outlet, Bernard and Wilhelm [18] introduced a correction factor $\Gamma (= \bar{C}/C_{mix})$. Therefore, the sum of the squares of difference between the measured tracer concentration C^* and the calculated concentration C from Equation 3 is obtained:

$$\Phi = \sum_{j=1}^{m} |C_j^*/C_{mix} - \Gamma \cdot (C_j/\bar{C})|^2 \tag{4}$$

where m is the number of measuring points of the tracer concentration at a distance Z from the tracer inlet. Since the unknown parameters are Pe_r and Γ, both $\partial\Phi/\partial Pe_r = 0$ and $\partial\Phi/\partial\Gamma = 0$ must be satisfied simultaneously when Φ is minimized. Hence

$$\sum_{j=1}^{m} |C_j^*/C_{mix} - \Gamma \cdot (C_j/\bar{C})|\partial(C_j/\bar{C})/\partial Pe_r = 0 \tag{5}$$

$$\sum_{j=1}^{m} |C_j^*/C_{mix} - \Gamma \cdot (C_j/\bar{C})|(C_j/\bar{C}) = 0 \tag{6}$$

so that

$$\Gamma = \bar{C}/C_{mix} = \sum_{j=1}^{m} (C_j^*/C_{mix})(C_j/\bar{C}) \bigg/ \sum_{j=1}^{m} (C_j/\bar{C}) \tag{7}$$

Finally, the unknown parameters Pe_r and Γ are calculated by solving Equations 5 and 6 simultaneously.

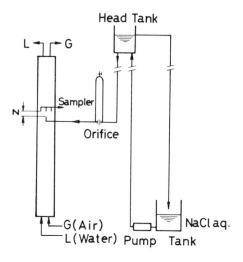

Figure 2. Apparatus for measurement of radial concentration distribution of tracer in co-current upflow system.

RADIAL CONCENTRATION DISTRIBUTION AND DISPERSION COEFFICIENT

Figure 2 shows schematically an experimental apparatus for measurement of the radial concentration distribution of the tracer material. A tracer injection tube of 1 mm internal diameter is positioned on the central axis of the bed close to its midpoint. The tracer, for example, an aqueous saturated solution of sodium chloride to which ethyl alcohol is added to adjust its specific gravity down to about 1, is injected continuously at a flow rate that is negligibly small in comparison with the liquid flow rate L in the main stream. Some syringes are radially located around the bed at a distance Z downstream from the tracer injection tube for collection of liquid samples. The tracer concentration C^* at each sampling tube and the cup-mixed concentration C_{mix} at the bed outlet are measured with a conductivity meter.

Figure 3 shows the tracer concentration profile for gas-liquid co-current upflow. In the single-phase flow of liquid most of the tracer flows through the middle of the bed and no part of the tracer

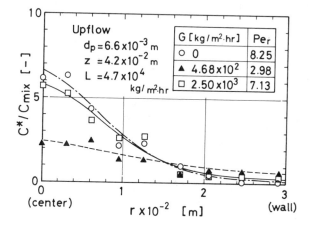

Figure 3. Radial concentration profiles of tracer in co-current upflow system.

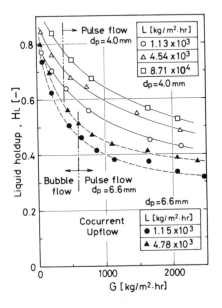

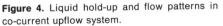

Figure 4. Liquid hold-up and flow patterns in co-current upflow system.

reaches the wall. At low gas flow rate the tracer is evenly distributed between the middle of the bed and the wall, while the concentration profile at higher gas flow rate is close to that of single-phase liquid flow. Figure 4 shows the flow pattern and the liquid hold-up H_ℓ, which is the fraction of liquid in the bed void. The flow pattern changes from bubble flow to pulse flow with increasing the gas flow rate at constant liquid flow rate. By comparison between Figures 3 and 4, it is suggested that the radial liquid mixing may be more appreciable in the bubble flow region than in the pulse flow region. In fact, as shown in Figures 3 and 5, the calculated radial Peclet number $Pe_r (= U_\ell d_p/E_r)$ is much lower in the bubble flow region than in the pulse flow region. In addition Pe_r is lower at low gas flow rates than for the single-phase liquid flow. That is, the radial Peclet number has a minimum value when the gas flow rate G is increased at any constant liquid flow rate L. The radial

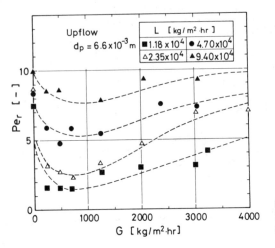

Figure 5. Radial Peclet numbers of liquid mixing in co-current upflow system.

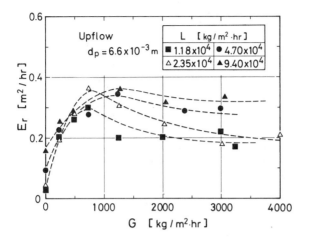

Figure 6. Radial liquid dispersion coefficients in co-current upflow system.

liquid dispersion coefficients E_r ($= U_\ell d_p/Pe_r$) in Figure 6 are calculated using the radial Peclet number in Figure 5. The mean liquid velocity U_ℓ in the bed is estimated from the liquid flow rate L and liquid holdup H_ℓ, for example, in Figure 4. As expected from Figure 5, the radial dispersion coefficient has a maximum value with increasing the gas flow rate at a given liquid flow rate and then is almost constant in the region of higher gas flow rate where the flow pattern is in pulse flow.

For comparison between the upflow mode and the downflow mode Figures 7 and 8 are shown. In Figure 7 the radial tracer concentration profiles are almost the same in spite of increasing the gas flow rate. The tracer concentration is still high in the center of the bed and low near the wall rather than being evenly distributed radially, so that the radial liquid mixing cannot be said to be very good as verified in Figure 8. Furthermore, the radial Peclet number for the downflow system does not have a minimum value while that for the upflow system does. The main reason for such a big difference between the upflow and downflow systems is due to the differences in flow patterns as shown in Figure 1.

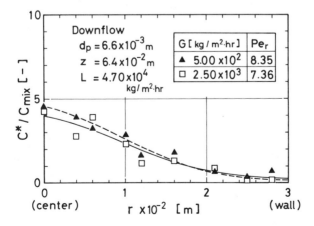

Figure 7. Radial concentration profiles of tracer in co-current downflow system.

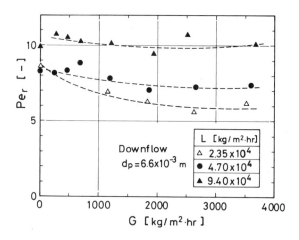

Figure 8. Radial Peclet numbers of liquid mixing in co-current downflow system.

RADIAL HEAT TRANSFER CHARACTERISTICS IN CO-CURRENT FLOW

When a packed bed with the co-current gas-liquid flow is heated from the outside of the bed wall, for example, with a steam jacket, the heat transfer equation at steady state is derived under the assumptions: (1) the axial heat conduction is negligible in comparison to the axial heat convection due to the gas and liquid flow, (2) gas, liquid, and solid temperatures are equal at any position in the bed, (3) both velocity and hold-up of gas and liquid are uniform in the bed, and (4) radial effective thermal conductivity k_{er} in the bed and apparent heat transfer coefficient h_w at the wall are uniform: Then

$$(k_{er}/r)\partial(r\,\partial t/\partial r)/\partial r - (LC_{p\ell} + GC_{pg}^*)\,\partial t/\partial Z = 0 \qquad (8)$$

where C_{pg}^* is defined as the rate of enthalpy change with respect to the temperature rise of the gas phase, because the latent heat transfer due to the evaporation of liquid must be considered. The necessary conditions are:

$$Z = 0, \qquad t = t_0$$

$$Z = \infty, \qquad t = t_w$$

$$r = 0, \qquad \partial t/\partial r = 0$$

$$r = r_w, \qquad -k_{er}(\partial t/\partial r) = h_w(t - t_w)$$

In single-phase flow of gas or liquid, the exact solution of Equation 8 was given by Hatta and Maeda [19] and Phillips et al. [20]. This solution has been extended to the two-phase flow of gas and liquid by Weekman and Meyers [21].

$$T = 2 \sum_{i=1}^{\infty} J_0(\zeta_i R)\exp[-\zeta_i^2 k_{er}Z/r_w^2(LC_{p\ell} + GC_{pg}^*)]/\zeta_i J_1(\zeta_i)[1 + (\zeta_i/H)^2] \qquad (9)$$

where $T = (t_w - t_0)/(t_w - t)$, $R = r/r_w$, $H = h_w r_w/k_{er}$, and ζ_i is the i-th root of $\zeta J_1(\zeta) = HJ_0(\zeta)$. Since Equation 9 is a rapidly converging series, it may be possible to approximate with only the first term, especially when $k_{er}Z/(LC_{p\ell} + GC_{pg}^*)r_w^2 > 0.2$ in the gas-liquid flow [22]. Then,

$$\log T = mZ + \log\{n/J_0(\zeta_1 R)\} \tag{10}$$

where $m = k_{er}\zeta^2/2.303(LC_{p\ell} + GC_{pg}^*)r_w^2$ and $n = \zeta_1 J_1(\zeta_1)\{1 + (\zeta_1/H)^2\}/2$. If $\log T$ is plotted against Z at $R = 0$ and another radius, R_1, the vertical distance ℓ between the two lines on the graph is $\ell = -\log J_0(\zeta_1 R_1)$, which gives the first positive root ζ_1. The parameter m is also obtained as the slope of the $\log T$ vs. Z line. Thus, when ℓ, m, and ζ_1 are experimentally obtained from the temperature profiles, the radial effective thermal conductivity and apparent heat transfer coefficient are determined:

$$k_{er} = 2.303 \, m \, (LC_{p\ell} + GC_{pg}^*)(r_w/\zeta_1)^2 \tag{11}$$

$$h_w = k_{er}\zeta_1 J_1(\zeta_1)/r_w J_0(\zeta_1) \tag{12}$$

Figures 9 and 10 show the radial effective thermal conductivity k_{er} and apparent heat transfer coefficient h_w, respectively, in the co-current gas-liquid upflow system [23]. As the gas flow rate increases at a given liquid flow rate, both k_{er} and h_w become larger in the bubble flow region than for single-phase liquid flow, reach a maximum value in the bubble flow region, and then decrease gradually or remain constant in the pulse flow region. This behavior of k_{er} and h_w in the upflow system is similar to that in Figure 6, which shows the radial liquid dispersion coefficient in the upflow system. Thus, both the radial liquid dispersion and the radial heat transfer follow the same trend and, apparently, result from similar mechanisms. Gas bubbles enhance the radial liquid mixing and heat transfer in the bubble flow region (positive effect). In the pulse flow region that appears in the range of higher gas flow rates, both the pulse frequency and pulse velocity increase (positive effect) [14], but the liquid hold-up as the main medium of heat transfer decreases as shown in Figure 4 (negative effect). In the pulse flow region at higher gas flow rates these opposing effects conflict and hence cause the heat transfer properties to decrease gradually or to remain constant.

On the other hand, in the co-current downflow system both k_{er} and h_w exhibit no maximum over the whole range of gas flow rates. In addition, the radial Peclet number has no minimum as shown in Figure 8 [22, 24, 25].

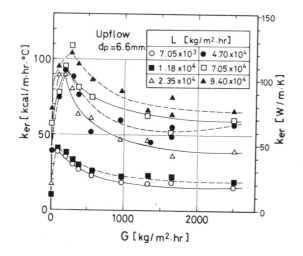

Figure 9. Radial effective thermal conductivity in co-current gas-liquid upflow system.

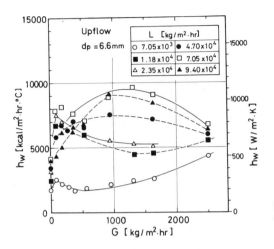

Figure 10. Apparent heat transfer coefficient in co-current gas-liquid upflow system.

ANALOGY BETWEEN LIQUID MIXING AND HEAT TRANSFER

Both the radial liquid mixing and heat transfer properties show similar trends when the gas flow rate increases at a given liquid flow rate. Therefore, it is certain that an analogy exists between them. However, heat transfer in packed beds is caused by various mechanisms, as Yagi and Kunii [26, 27] showed for packed beds with single-phase flow. Weekman and Meyers [21] extended Yagi and Kunii's concept to the co-current gas-liquid flow system and described the heat transfer coefficient as the sum of three terms:

$$k_{er} = (k_{er})_0 + (k_{er})_g + (k_{er})_\ell \tag{13}$$

or

$$k_{er}/k_\ell = (k_{er})_0/k_\ell + (\alpha\beta)_g(d_p GC^*_{pg}/k_g)(k_g/k_\ell) + (\alpha\beta)_\ell(d_p LC_{p\ell}/k_\ell) \tag{14}$$

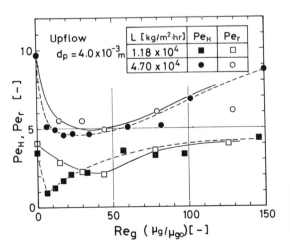

Figure 11. Comparison of radial liquid mixing with heat transfer in co-current gas-liquid upflow system.

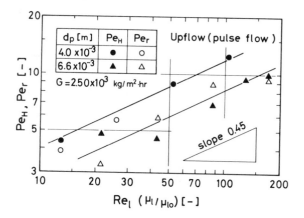

Figure 12. Comparison of radial liquid mixing with heat transfer for pulse-flow region in co-current gas-liquid upflow system.

where $(k_{er})_0$ is the contribution of heat transfer through the stagnant bed without any gas or liquid flow, that is, the effective thermal conductivity of the wet bed without gas and liquid flow. $(k_{er})_g$ and $(k_{er})_\ell$ are the heat transfer contributions due to gas and liquid flows, respectively. When only gas flows in the packed bed wetted by liquid, $(k_{er})_0 + (k_{er})_g$ is obtained and it is found that these terms contribute little to k_{er} of the two-phase flow. Finally, the contribution of the radial liquid mixing to the effective thermal conductivity is obtained as $(k_{er})_\ell = k_{er} - \{(k_{er})_0 + (k_{er})_g\}$.

Figure 11 shows the comparison between the radial liquid mixing and heat transfer in the co-current gas-liquid flow system. Pe_r for liquid mixing and Pe_H for heat transfer are defined as $U_\ell d_p/E_r$ and $LC_{p\ell}d_p/(k_{er})_\ell$, respectively. The abscissa variable is modified to remove the effect of the different experimental temperatures by multiplication by the viscosity ratio μ/μ_0, where μ_0 represents the viscosity at a certain standard temperature, for example, 20°C in this figure. The overall trend in the two Peclet numbers is similar. There is an especially close similarity at higher gas and liquid flow rates.

At low liquid and gas flow rates Pe_H changes rapidly while the change in Pe_r is more gradual. Figure 12 shows the relationship between Pe_r, Pe_H and the liquid flow rate for pulse flow in the co-current upflow system. Straight lines on the logarithmic graph are obtained with Pe_r and Pe_H proportional to $Re_\ell^{0.45}$.

COMPARISON BETWEEN CO-CURRENT UPFLOW AND DOWNFLOW SYSTEMS

Bischoff and Levenspiel [28] considered that the radial dispersion coefficient for single-phase flow in a packed bed can be correlated with Reynolds number using the equivalent diameter d_e of the packed bed and the mean interstitial velocity U_ℓ of liquid in the bed, thus:

$$d_e = \varepsilon D_t/\{1 + 1.5(D_t/d_p)(1 - \varepsilon)\} \tag{15}$$

$$d_e U_\ell/v_\ell = Ld_e/\varepsilon H_\ell \mu_\ell \tag{16}$$

Muroyama et al. [16] extended this concept for the co-current gas-liquid downflow system and obtained a correlating equation:

$$E_r/v_\ell = 0.148(Ld_e/\varepsilon H_\ell \mu_\ell) + [0.0217 + 2.54(Ld_e/\varepsilon H_\ell \mu_\ell)^{-1}]^{-1} \tag{17}$$

Figure 13 shows the relationship between the radial liquid dispersion coefficient E_r and liquid Reynolds number defined by Equation 16. The broken line represents the results given by Bischoff and Levenspiel [28] for single-phase flow, while the solid line represents the results given by Equation 17 for the co-current gas-liquid downflow. The experimental results tied with the dotted lines show the radial liquid dispersion coefficients of the bubble flow region in the cocurrent upflow system. These data are much higher than those for the single-phase liquid flow at low gas flow rates, whereas they converge with those for the liquid flow alone at high gas flow rates. In the pulse flow region at higher gas flow rates and/or lower liquid flow rates, the experimental results for the co-current upflow are satisfactorily correlated by Equation 17 for the co-current downflow. If the argument is restricted only to the well-developed pulse flow region, Pe_r for the co-current upflow is proportional to $Re_\ell^{0.45}$ at a given gas flow rate, that is, $E_r \propto L^{0.55}$, as shown in Figure 12.

Figure 14 shows the relationship between the radial effective thermal conductivity $(k_{er})_\ell$ and the liquid Reynolds number defined by Equation 16. The dot-dash line represents the correlation obtained for the co-current downflow by Hashimoto et al. [22], that is:

$$\{(k_{er})_\ell/\varepsilon H_\ell k_\ell Pr_\ell\}(\mu_\ell/\mu_{\ell 0}) = 0.197(Ld_e/\varepsilon H_\ell\mu_\ell)(\mu_\ell/\mu_{\ell 0})$$
$$+ [0.0264 + 1.90(Ld_e/\varepsilon H_\ell\mu_\ell)^{-1}(\mu_\ell/\mu_{\ell 0})^{-1}]^{-1} \qquad (18)$$

The solid and broken lines have the same significance as in Figure 13. Whereas in the pulse flow region the liquid dispersion coefficients are more or less the same for the co-current upflow as for the co-current downflow, the effective thermal conductivities for the co-current upflow are higher than for the co-current downflow given by Equation 18. The difference between the upflow and the downflow is large at low liquid flow rates but diminishes at higher liquid flow rates, because k_{er} and hence $(k_{er})_\ell$ are almost constant and independent of the gas flow rate for the co-current downflow while the gas flow rate exerts influence on k_{er} for the co-current upflow, especially at low gas flow

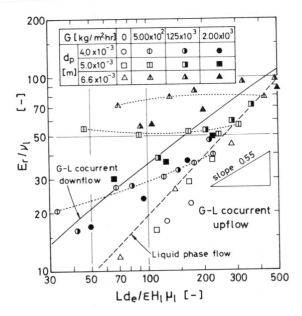

Figure 13. Comparison of radial liquid dispersion coefficient in co-current upflow with that in co-current downflow.

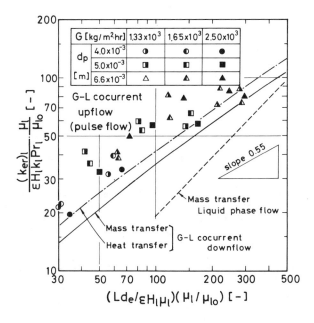

Figure 14. Comparison of radial effective thermal conductivity in co-current upflow with that in co-current downflow.

rate as shown in Figure 9. In the pulse flow region a correlation of the form $k_{er} \propto G^{-0.3}$ was obtained, and the higher the gas flow rate at a given liquid flow rate, the lower the effective thermal conductivity.

NOTATION

C	tracer concentration, $kg \cdot m^{-3}$	k_{er}	effective thermal conductivity with co-current gas-liquid flow, $W \cdot m^{-2} \cdot K^{-1}$
C*	measured concentration of tracer, $kg \cdot m^{-3}$	$(k_{er})_\ell$	effective thermal conductivity due to radical liquid mixing, $W \cdot m^{-2} \cdot K^{-1}$
C	mean of tracer concentration, $kg \cdot m^{-3}$	k_ℓ	thermal conductivity of liquid, $W \cdot m^{-2} \cdot K^{-1}$
C_{mix}	cup-mixed tracer concentration at the bed outlet, $kg \cdot m^{-3}$	L	liquid flow rate, $kg \cdot m^{-2} \cdot s^{-1}$
C_{pg}^*	specific heat of saturated gas, $J \cdot kg^{-1} \cdot K^{-1}$	P_r	Prandtl number, $C_{p\ell} \mu_\ell / k_\ell$ —
$C_{p\ell}$	specific heat of liquid, $J \cdot kg^{-1} \cdot K^{-1}$	Pe_H	Peclet number of heat transfer, $LC_{p\ell} d_p / (k_{er})_\ell$, —
D_t	bed diameter, m		
d_e	equivalent bed diameter, m	Pe_r	Peclet number of radial liquid mixing, $U_\ell d_p / E_r$, —
d_p	particle diameter, m		
E_r	radial dispersion coefficient of liquid $m^2 \cdot s^{-1}$	Pe_z	Peclet number of axial liquid mixing, $U_\ell d_p / E_z$, —
E_z	axial dispersion coefficient of liquid, $m^2 \cdot s^{-1}$	R	r/r_w , —
G	gas flow rate, $kg \cdot m^{-2} \cdot s^{-1}$	Re_g	gas Reynolds number, $G d_p / \mu_g$, —
H_ℓ	liquid hold-up, —	Re_ℓ	liquid Reynolds number, $L d_p / \mu_\ell$, —
h_w	apparent heat transfer coefficient at the wall, $W \cdot m^{-2} \cdot K^{-1}$	r	radial distance, m
		r_w	radius of the packed bed, m
		T	$(t_w - t_0)/(t_w - t)$, —

t	temperature, K	Z	axial distance, m
t_0	inlet temperature of the gas-liquid flow, K	Γ	$\bar{C}/C_{mix}$, —
		ε	bed voidage, —
t_w	wall temperature, K	μ	viscosity, Pa·s
U_ℓ	interstitial liquid velocity, m·s^{-1}	v	kinematic viscosity, m^2·s^{-1}

Subscripts

g   gas
ℓ liquid

REFERENCES

1. Hofmann, H. "Hydrodynamics, Transport Phenomena, and Mathematical Models in Trickle-Bed Reactors." *Int. Chem. Eng.*, vol. 17, no. 1, pp. 19–28, 1977.
2. Satterfield, C. N. "Trickle-Bed Reactors." *A.I.Ch. E. Journal*, vol. 21, no. 2, pp. 209–228, 1975.
3. Shah, Y. T. *Gas-Liquid-Solid Reactor Design*. New York: McGraw-Hill, 1979.
4. Nakamura, M. "Three-Phase Reactors Applied to Chemical Industry."*Kagaku Kogaku* (Japan), vol. 46, no. 4, pp. 199–202, 1982.
5. Ohtsuka, T. et al. "Hydrodesulfurization of Khafji Crude Oil—Part V. On the Effect of Flow Directions in a Fixed Catalyst Bed." Preprint of the 21st Annual Meeting of Chem. Soc. Japan, vol. 4, pp. 2364, 1968.
6. Kato, J. et al. "Hydrotreatment of the Heavy Fraction of Petroleum. 2.2 Kl/day Pilot Plant Test for a New Direct Desulfurization Process by Moving Bed Type Reactor." *Kogyo Kagaku Zasshi* (Japan), vol. 74, no. 6, pp. 1047–1051, 1971.
7. Takematsu, T. and Parsons, B. I. "A Comparison of Bottom-Feed and Top-Feed Reaction Systems for Hydrodesulphurization." *Fuels Res. Centre Tech. Bull.* (Dept. of Energy, Mines and Resources, Ottawa, Canada), TB-161, Sept. 1972.
8. Takematsu, T. "A Comparison of Bottom-Feed and Top-Feed Reaction Systems for Hydrodesulphurization of Coker Gas-Oil Derived from Tar-Sands." *Journal of the National Chem. Lab. for Ind.* (Tokyo Kogyo Shikensho Hokoku, Japan), vol. 69, no. 9, pp. 299–307, 1974.
9. Montagna, A. and Shah, Y. T. "Backmixing Effect in an Upflow Co-Current Hydrodesulfurization Reactor." *Chem. Eng. J.*, vol. 10, no. 2, pp. 99–105, 1975.
10. Mochizuki, S. and Matsui, T. "Selective Hydrogenation and Mass Transfer in a Fixed-Bed Catalytic Reactor with Gas-Liquid Concurrent Upflow." *A.I.Ch.E. Journal*, vol. 22, no. 5, pp. 904–909, 1976.
11. Kato, Y. and Hirose, T. "Types of Three-Phase Reactors and Flow Patterns." *Kagaku Kogaku* (Japan), vol. 46, no. 4, pp. 215–217, 1982.
12. Shimada, K. et al. "Hydrodesulfurization of Heavy-Oil in the Fixed-Bed Co-Current Upflow Reactor." *Kogyo Kagaku Zasshi* (Japan), vol. 74, no. 7, pp. 1308–1312, 1971.
13. Hofmann, H. "Co-Currrent Upflow in Fixed Beds." In *Handbook of Fluids in Motion*, N. P. Cheremisinoff and R. Gupta, eds. Ann Arbor: Ann Arbor Science, Chapter 20, pp. 539–560, 1983.
14. Ohsasa, K. et al. "Liquid Mixing and Pulsation Properties of Gas-Liquid Upward Co-Current Flow in Packed Beds." *Kagaku Kogaku Robunshu* (Japan), vol. 4, no. 3, pp. 314–317, 1978.
15. Klinkenberg, A. et al. "Diffusion in a Fluid Moving at Uniform Velocity in a Tube." *Ind. Eng. Chem.*, vol. 45, no. 6, pp. 1202–1208, 1953.
16. Muroyama, K. et al. *Kagaku Kogaku Ronbushu* (Japan), vol. 1, pp. 520, 1975.
17. Nakamura, M. et al. "Heat Transfer in a Packed Bed with Gas-Liquid Co-Current Upflow." *Kagaku Kogaku Ronbunshu* (Japan), vol. 7, no. 1, 1981, pp. 71–76. Translated into English: *Heat Transfer—Japanese Research*, vol. 10, no. 1, pp. 92–99, 1981.
18. Bernard, R. A. and Wilhelm, R. H. "Turbulent Diffusion in Fixed Beds of Packed Solids." *Chem. Eng. Prog.*, vol. 46, no. 5, pp. 233–244, 1950.
19. Hatta, S. and Maeda, S. "Heat Transfer in Granular Beds." *Kagaku Kogaku* (Japan), vol. 12, pp. 56–64, 1948.

20. Phillips, B. D. et al. "Heat Transfer with Molecular Sieve Adsorption: 1. Effective Thermal Conductivity." *Chem. Eng. Prog. Symp. Ser.*, vol. 56, no. 30, pp. 219–228, 1960.
21. Weekman, V. W. Jr. and Meyers, J. E. "Heat Transfer Characteristics of Concurrent Gas-Liquid Flow in Packed Beds." *A.I.Ch.E. Journal*, vol. 11, no. 1, pp. 13–17, 1965.
22. Hashimoto, K. et al. "Effective Radial Thermal Conductivity in Co-Current Flow of Gas and Liquid through a Packed Bed." *Kagaku Kogaku Ronbunshu* (Japan), vol. 2, no. 1, pp. 53–59, 1976. Translated into English: *Int. Chem. Eng.*, vol. 16, no. 4, pp. 720–727, 1976.
23. Nakamura, M. et al. "Radial Liquid Mixing in a Packed Bed with Gas-Liquid Co-Current Upflow." *Kagaku Kogaku Ronbunshu* (Japan), vol. 7, no. 2, pp. 151–156, 1981. Translated into English: *Int. Chem. Eng.*, vol. 23, no. 2, pp. 307–314, 1983.
24. Matsuura, A. et al. "Radial Effective Thermal Conductivity in Packed Beds with Co-Current Gas-Liquid Downflow." *Kagaku Kogaku Ronbunshu* (Japan), vol. 5, no. 3, pp. 263–268, 1979.
25. Specchia, V. and Baldi, G. "Heat Transfer in Trickle-Bed Reactors." *Chem. Eng. Commun.*, vol. 3, pp. 483–499, 1979.
26. Yagi, S. and Kunii, D. "Effective Thermal Conductivities in Packed Beds." *Kagaku Kogaku* (Japan), vol. 18, no. 12, pp. 576–585, 1954.
27. Yagi, S. and Kunii, D. "Studies on Effective Thermal Conductivities in Packed Beds." *A.I.Ch.E. Journal*, vol. 3, no. 3, pp. 373–381, 1957.
28. Bischoff, K. B. and Levenspiel, O. "Fluid Dispersion—Generalization and Comparison of Mathematical Models. II. Comparison of Models." *Chem. Eng. Sci.*, vol. 17, no. 4, pp. 257–264, 1962.

CHAPTER 37

AXIAL MIXING IN MULTIPHASE SPARGED CONTACTORS

J. B. Joshi, A. B. Pandit, and K. S. M. S. Raghav Rao

Department of Chemical Technology
University of Bombay
Bombay, India

CONTENTS

INTRODUCTION

Bubble columns, solid-liquid, gas-solid and gas-liquid-solid fluidized beds, and liquid-liquid spray extraction columns, collectively known as sparged contactors, are widely used in industry because of no moving parts and the continuous phase residence time can be varied. In the sparged contactors, the energy required for dispersion (of bubbles and drops) and mixing is provided by the introduction of the dispersed phase. For the rational design of these contactors, the knowledge of individual phase hold-ups, pressure drop, interface mass transfer coefficients, extent of mixing and heat transfer coefficient is desirable. During the past two decades, there has been much experimental investigation of these parameters. The results are available in empirical correlations that are presented either in the form of dimensionless numbers or in terms of power consumption per unit volume. Further, the case of each sparged contactor has been treated separately and efforts to find some unified approach for the design of the whole class of sparged contactors have been meager. In general, the design and scale-up of the multi-phase contactors have been very difficult because of their complicated hydrodynamic behavior.

Recently, investigators have analyzed the continuous phase flow pattern in bubble columns [2–14] gas-solid fluidized beds [2], gas-liquid-solid fluidized beds [2, 12], solid-liquid fluidized beds [5, 14, 15] and liquid-liquid spray columns [14, 15]. Joshi and Shah [9] have critically reviewed all the earlier published literature regarding the liquid phase flow pattern in bubble columns. On the basis of flow pattern Joshi [2] developed a unified correlation for the continuous phase axial dispersion coefficient (D_L). Axial dispersion coefficient is the model representation of the residence time distribution. Shah et al. [1] have given a systematic discussion on this subject. The first part of this chapter discusses the method of elucidating the hydrodynamic behavior of multiphase sparged contactors and examines a unique correlation based on average continuous phase circulation velocity.

ENERGY BALANCE FOR MULTIPHASE CONTACTORS

The continuous phase velocity profiles in the case of sparged contactors are found using energy balance [2, 6, 7].

The energy is supplied to the multiphase contactor because of the introduction of gas. The energy input rate is given by

$$E_i = \frac{\pi}{4} T^2 V_G(\rho_C - \rho_G)H(1 - \varepsilon_G)g \tag{1}$$

When the liquid phase (in bubble columns and three-phase fluidized beds) is also continuous the energy input rate for the co-current flow is given by

$$E_i = \frac{\pi}{4} T^2 (V_G + V_L)(\rho_C - \rho_G)H(1 - \varepsilon_G)g \tag{2}$$

The kinetic energy associated with input gas has been neglected for simplicity. The procedure for its evaluation is discussed by Joshi and Sharma [16], Joshi [17], Lehrer [18], and Field and Davidson [19]. The energy dissipation occurs because of the following factors:

1. Frictional energy dissipation in the vicinity of bubble-liquid and particle-liquid interfaces.
2. When the liquid phase is continuous co-current, some energy is required for pumping the liquid.
3. Turbulent energy dissipation in the liquid motion.
4. Frictional energy dissipation at the column wall.
5. Energy is required for the bubble break-up to create gas-liquid interfacial area.

An order of magnitude calculation indicates that the rate of energy dissipation due to factors 4 and 5 is negligible as compared to the energy input rate.

ESTIMATIONS OF ENERGY DISSIPATION

Gas-Liquid and Particle-Liquid Interfaces

Bubble rises at its terminal velocity when the net gravity force (buoyancy minus gravity) becomes equal to the frictional (form and skin) drag at the interface. The rate of energy dissipation for a single bubble (rising in a pool of liquid) is given by

$$e_B = \frac{\pi}{6} d_B^3 (\rho_L - \rho_G) g V_{b\infty} \tag{3}$$

the number of bubbles is given by

$$N_B = \frac{\pi}{4} T^2 H \varepsilon_G \bigg/ \frac{\pi}{6} d_B^3 \tag{4}$$

For gas-liquid dispersion (in the absence of solid particles) the continuous phase density is

$$\rho_C = \rho_L (1 - \varepsilon_G) + \varepsilon_G \rho_G \tag{5}$$

Substituting Equation 4 into 3, replacing ρ_L by ρ_C for dispersion in Equation 3, and neglecting $\rho_G \varepsilon_G$, gives

$$E_B = \frac{\pi}{4} T^2 H \varepsilon_G (1 - \varepsilon_G) \rho_L g V_{b\infty} \tag{6}$$

In the presence of solid particles Equation 6 takes the following form:

$$E_B = \frac{\pi}{4} T^2 H \varepsilon_G (\varepsilon_S \rho_S + \varepsilon_L \rho_L - \rho_G) g V_{b\infty} \tag{7}$$

The rate of energy dissipation at the particle-liquid interface can also be obtained by following the same procedure as Equations 3–6.

$$E_S = \frac{\pi}{4} T^2 H \varepsilon_S (\rho_S - \rho_C) g V_S \tag{8}$$

where $\quad \rho_C = \rho_S \varepsilon_S + \rho_L \varepsilon_L \tag{9}$

Pumping of the Liquid Phase (Bubble Columns and Three-Phase Sparged Contactors)

When the liquid phase is continuous co-current, the liquid is introduced against the static head (H) of dispersion, whereas, the outgoing liquid is available at a height H. As a result, the liquid is pumped by using some of the energy associated with the gas. The potential energy of liquid at height H is

$$E_L = \frac{\pi}{4} T^2 V_L \rho_L H g \tag{10}$$

The energy input for this case is given by Equation 2.

Continuous Phase Motion

Knowing the energy input rate and the rates of energy dissipation due to modes 1 and 2, one can obtain the rate of energy dissipation in the continuous phase motion by the energy balance. Each item of equipment will be considered separately.

Bubble Column

The energy balance gives

$$E = E_i - E_B - E_L \tag{11}$$

In the absence of any liquid flow ($E_L = 0$), substituting Equations 1 and 6 into 11 gives

$$E = \frac{\pi}{4} T^2 H \rho_L g (1 - \varepsilon_G)(V_G - \varepsilon_G V_{b\infty}) \tag{12}$$

For the case of continuous co-current liquid, substituting Equations 2, 6, and 10 into Equation 11 gives

$$E = \frac{\pi}{4} T^2 H \rho_L g (1 - \varepsilon_G) \left(V_G - \frac{\varepsilon_G V_L}{1 - \varepsilon_G} - \varepsilon_G V_{b\infty} \right) \tag{13}$$

Gas-Liquid-Solid Sparged Contactors

The energy balance gives

$$E = E_i - E_B - E_S - E_L \tag{14}$$

Substituting Equations 2, 7–10 into Equation 14 gives:

$$E = \frac{\pi}{4} T^2 H g \{ (V_G + V_L)(\varepsilon_S \rho_S + \varepsilon_L \rho_L) - \rho_L V_L - \varepsilon_S V_S (\rho_S - \varepsilon_S \rho_S - \varepsilon_L \rho_L)$$
$$- \varepsilon_G V_{b\infty} (\varepsilon_S \rho_S + \varepsilon_L \rho_L - \rho_G) \} \tag{15}$$

In the absence of any liquid flow ($V_L = 0$), Equation 15 simplifies to:

$$E = \frac{\pi}{4} T^2 H g \{ V_G (\varepsilon_S \rho_S + \varepsilon_L \rho_L) - \varepsilon_S V_S (\rho_S - \varepsilon_S \rho_S - \varepsilon_L \rho_L) - \varepsilon_G V_{b\infty} (\varepsilon_S \rho_S + \varepsilon_L \rho_L - \rho_G) \} \tag{16}$$

Gas-Solid Fluidized beds

In this case assume that the power required for the suspension of solid particles corresponds to the energy input rate at the condition of minimum fluidization. The rate of energy dissipation in the liquid motion is given by

$$E = \frac{\pi}{4} T^2 \rho_C g H (V_G - V_{mf} - \varepsilon_G V_{b\infty}) \tag{17}$$

Experimental observations of Toei and Matsumo (Joshi [2]) have shown that:

$$\varepsilon_G = \frac{V_G - V_{mf}}{1.2 V_{b\infty}} \tag{18}$$

Substituting Equation 18 into Equation 17 gives

$$E = \frac{0.167\pi}{4} T^2 \rho_C g H (V_G - V_{mf})$$ (19)

CONTINUOUS PHASE FLOW PATTERNS

The hydrodynamic behavior of all the sparged contactors is more or less similar. As a representative contactor, the hydrodynamic behavior of bubble column is discussed in this section.

At very low superficial gas velocities (approaching zero), the bubbles generated at the sparger rise as single entities. The bubbles hardly coalesce and in the case of a single point sparger the bubbles flow in the form of a chain. The bubble diameter at the nozzle remains practically constant except for the effect of the hydrostatic head of the liquid. When a single point sparger is replaced by a sieve plate or a sintered disk, bubble chains, equal to the number of holes, are formed. At superficial gas velocities greater than about 0.5 mm s^{-1}, the bubbles oscillate and the identity of the chains (one chain in the case of a single point sparger) is lost. Although the individual bubbles are unstable, they together form a centrally located plume. The diameter of the plume increases with an increase in the superficial gas velocity and the whole column fills with bubbles when the superficial gas velocity is about 10 mm s^{-1}. However, the bubbles hardly coalesce and most of the bubbles retain their diameter at the orifice. Under this condition the bubble size distribution is narrow. Most of the input energy ($>95\%$) is dissipated in the vicinity of the gas-liquid interface and the liquid recirculation is poor. This flow pattern is called homogeneous, ideal bubbly, or bubbly flow.

The variation of fractional gas hold-up (ε_G) with superficial gas velocity is shown in Figure 1. In the case of homogeneous flow, ε_G varies almost linearly with V_G. However, at a certain critical

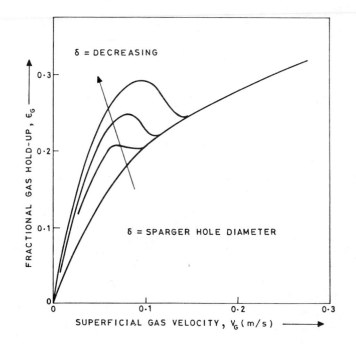

Figure 1. Effect of superficial gas velocity on fractional gas hold-up [3].

superficial gas velocity the onset of strong liquid circulation occurs, with upward flow at the center and downward flow at the wall. The bubbles coalesce and redispersion also begins and the homogeneous flow regime cannot be maintained. In the presence of liquid recirculation the bubbles rise faster than the terminal rise velocity. As a result of liquid recirculation, depending on its strength, the average residence time of a bubble remains constant or even decreases. The fractional gas hold-up, therefore, remains constant or decreases with an increase in V_G. The reduction in ε_G occurs over a small range of V_G and ε_G increases with an increase in V_G. The flow pattern above the gas velocity at which the minimum ε_G occurs is called churn turbulence or heterogeneous flow. The range of V_G in which the reduction in ε_G occurs may be called a transition regime. Joshi and Lali [15] have discussed in detail the aspects of transition from homogeneous to heterogeneous regime and vice versa. The roles of sparger design, column diameter and physical properties on the transition have been described. It has been shown that the variation of ε_G with V_G can also occur without any maxima or minima. In such cases, which are more common, the transition occurs when the liquid phase turbulence intensity exceeds the terminal rise velocity of a bubble.

In sparged contactors, the heterogeneous regime is more common particularly in the commercial size columns. In the heterogeneous regime, the contactor can be divided into three regions (Figure 2). In the first region, near the column bottom, the properties and behavior of bubbles are determined by the sparger design. The continuous phase flow pattern is developed in this region. The height of the first region extends in the range of 0.2 to 2 times the column diameter depending upon the sparger design. In the second region, which occupies most of the column volume, the properties and behavior of bubbles are determined by the continuous phase motion. The continuous phase motion is usually upward at the center and downward near the column wall. The third region is characterized by the coalescence of bubbles.

In the heterogeneous regime, the second region governs the performance of sparged contactors and it is desirable to understand the continuous phase flow patterns in this region.

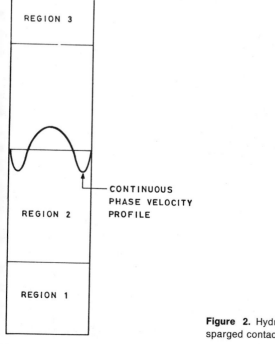

Figure 2. Hydrodynamic regions in multiphase sparged contactors.

For an axisymmetric case, Lamb [20] has given the following equation for the vorticity, ω, in inviscid fluids. The coordinates are explained in Figure 3.

$$\omega = -\frac{1}{r}\left(\frac{\partial^2 \psi}{\partial z^2} + \frac{\partial^2 \psi}{\partial r^2} - \frac{1}{r}\frac{\partial \psi}{\partial r}\right) \tag{20}$$

Further, Lamb [20] has shown that the vorticity divided by the radial distance from the axis of symmetry is dependent on the stream function only.

$$\frac{\omega}{r} = k_2 \psi \tag{21}$$

The boundary conditions are:

$$\psi = 0 \quad \text{at} \quad r = 0 \quad \text{and} \quad r = T/2 \tag{22}$$

$$\psi = 0 \quad \text{at} \quad z = 0 \quad \text{and} \quad z = H \tag{23}$$

The procedure for solving Equation 20 is given by Whalley and Davidson [6]. For this purpose, the second-order partial differential equation is first converted into two second-order ordinary differential equations by the method of separation of variables; the dependent variables being, respectively, the radial (R_1) and the axial (z) components of the dimensionless stream function. The values of k_2 and other integration constants (of the differential equations in R_1 and z) are evaluated from the boundary conditions given by Equations 22 and 23.

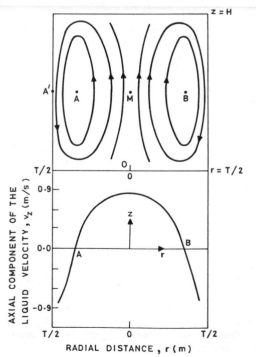

Figure 3. Axisymmetric flow [7].

The solution of Equation 20 gives the following velocity profile:

$$V_1 = \frac{2\psi_0}{T} \left\{ \left[\frac{\pi}{H} \frac{R_1}{r^*} \cos(\pi z^*) \right]^2 + \left[\frac{2}{Tr^*} \frac{dR_1}{dr^*} \sin\left(\frac{\pi}{z^*}\right) \right]^2 \right\}^{1/2} \tag{24}$$

where V_1 is the continuous phase velocity at any point. The axial component of the continuous phase velocity is given by

$$v_z = \frac{\psi_0}{(T/2)^2} \cdot \frac{1}{r^*} \frac{dR_1}{dr^*} \sin(\pi z^*) \tag{25}$$

where r^* and z^* are the dimensionless radial and axial coordinates, respectively. The radial component of the continuous phase velocity is given by

$$v_r = -\frac{2\pi\psi_0}{TH} \frac{R_1}{r^*} \cos(\pi z^*) \tag{26}$$

In Equations 25 and 26 ψ_0 is the unknown. Its value is calculated using the following procedure:

1. In the case of sparged contactors, the visual observations indicate the existence of multiple circulation cells (Figure 4). The height of each circulation cell was found on the basis of minimum continuous phase vorticity and was found to be equal to the column diameter [7]. Further, the height of each circulation cell was found to be independent of the column diameter and the superficial gas velocity. As a result, in the calculation of energy dissipation rate in the continuous phase motion of one circulation cell, H in the Equations 12, 13, 15, 16, 25, and 26 should be replaced by T.

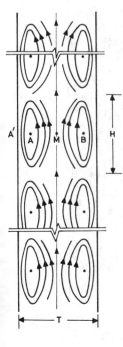

Figure 4. Multiple circulation cell model of Joshi and Sharma [7].

2. From Equation 25 it can be seen that the axial component of the liquid velocity (v_z) varies sinusoidally (Figure 5). This means that, in the case of first cell near the bottom, the value of v_z is zero at z^* equal to zero and v_z increases and reaches maximum at z^* equal to 0.5. Again v_z decreases as the value of z^* is increased from 0.5 to 1.0. In the next circulation cell ($1 < z^* < 2$), the value of v_z is negative and reaches a minimum value at z^* equal to 1.5. The flow pattern in the third cell ($2 < z^* < 3$) is identical to that in the first and so on. Such a type of flow pattern (with alternating flow directions in the consecutive cells) was observed by Van den Akker and Rietema [21] in the case of liquid-liquid spray columns. Perhaps this type of flow pattern occurs during the transition from the homogeneous to the heterogeneous regime.

In the heterogeneous regime, several experimental measurements [10–13, 22] have shown that the continuous phase flow is always upward near the center and downward near the column wall. At a given location there may be fluctuations in the values of velocity because of turbulence. However, there is no change in the flow direction either near the center or near the column wall. To accommodate this experimental observation, Joshi and Sharma [7] assumed that all the cells are identical with upflow near the center and downflow near the wall (Figure 4). This model, however, predicts zero axial velocity at the junction of two consecutive cells and thus avoids the possibility of interactions between the adjacent cells. In practice, the adjacent cells are strongly interacting and a considerable amount of intercell recirculation occurs. Therefore, Joshi [2] modified the multiple cell circulation model of Joshi and Sharma [7] and is shown in Figure 6. The height of each circulation cell was selected as 0.8 T and as a result a good agreement was found between the predicted and experimental values of fractional gas hold-up in bubble columns. Thus, in the multiple cell circulation model of Figure 6, the value of z^* is varying from 0.1 to 0.9 in all the cells and the

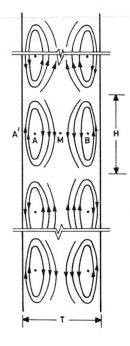

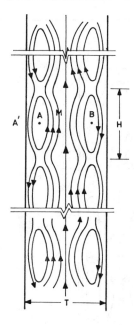

Figure 5. Multiple circulation cell model of Joshi and Sharma [8].

Figure 6. Mutliple circulation cell model with intercell recirculation [2].

axial and radial components of the continuous phase velocity can be obtained using Equations 25 and 26.

3. The continuous phase downflow near the column wall is against the static head. Therefore, the kinetic energy associated with the downward flowing continuous phase is dissipated in the turbulence. The rate of energy dissipation in the continuous phase motion (E) for each item of equipment was found in the previous section. The value of E was assumed to be equal to the kinetic energy associated with the downward flowing continuous phase. This gives the value of ψ_0 as:

$$\psi_0 = \frac{T^2}{12.3}\left\{\frac{E}{\frac{\pi}{4}T^2\rho_C}\right\}^{1/3} \tag{27}$$

The knowledge of ψ_0 (Equations 25 and 26) describes the axial and the radial velocity profiles completely. Figure 7 shows a comparison between the predicted and the experimental liquid velocity profiles in bubble columns. Similarly, a comparison of the liquid velocity at the center is shown in Table 1. An excellent agreement can be seen in the ranges of column diameter of 0.13 to 5.5 m and the superficial gas velocity of 20 to 1452 mm/s. In addition to the correct prediction of liquid velocity profiles, Joshi et al. [23] have shown that the model also successfully explains the wall heat transfer coefficient.

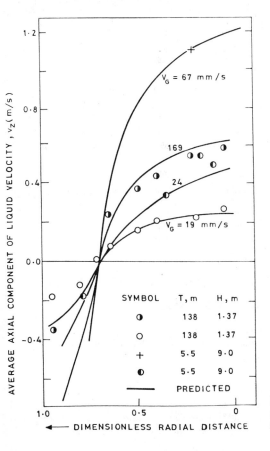

SYMBOL	T, m	H, m
◑	138	1·37
○	138	1·37
+	5·5	9·0
◐	5·5	9·0
——	PREDICTED	

Figure 7. Comparison between predicted and experimental velocity profiles in bubble columns [9].

Table 1
Comparison Between Predicted and Experimental Values of
Liquid Velocity at the Column Axis of Bubble Column

No.	T (m)	V_G (m s^{-1})	v_a (m s^{-1}) experimental	v_a (m s^{-1}) predicted (Equation 29a)	v_a (m s^{-1}) predicted (Equation 42)	Reference
1	0.138	0.019	0.223	0.238	0.212	Hills [22]
		0.038	0.335	0.322	0.283	
		0.064	0.410	0.400	0.357	
		0.095	0.484	0.478	0.420	
		0.165	0.620	0.614	0.544	
2	0.172	0.044	0.320	0.367	0.323	Pavlov [24]
		0.100	0.523	0.530	0.467	
		0.170	0.630	0.670	0.591	
		0.710	0.955	1.190	1.049	
3	0.300	0.020	0.266	0.315	0.274	Pozin et al. [25]
		0.060	0.440	0.507	0.444	
		0.100	0.560	0.646	0.569	
4	0.100	0.045	0.270	0.309	0.272	Miyauchi and Shyu [26]
		0.082	0.320	0.405	0.359	
		0.155	0.400	0.537	0.473	
		0.225	0.680	0.630	0.555	
		0.280	0.850	0.693	0.610	
		0.320	0.980	0.730	0.643	
		0.370	1.050	0.774	0.682	
5	0.600	0.350	1.800	1.370	1.200	Ueyama and Miyauchi [10]
		0.530	2.000	1.620	1.410	
		0.920	2.500	1.990	1.750	
6	0.250	0.052	0.430	0.448	0.400	Yamagohsi (From Ueyama and Miyauchi [10])
	0.150	0.075	0.400	0.444	0.390	
7	5.500	0.019	1.100	1.140	1.000	Kojima [11]
		0.069	1.210	1.230	1.090	
8	0.450	0.012	2.150	2.120	1.870	Nottenkamper et al. [13]
		0.053	1.400	1.720	1.520	
		0.105	0.750	1.200	1.070	
		0.105	0.750	1.200	1.070	
		0.324	0.620	0.730	0.660	
		0.823	0.500	0.470	0.410	
		1.452	0.250	0.230	0.200	

AVERAGE CONTINUOUS PHASE CIRCULATION VELOCITY

Knowing the velocity profiles (Equations 25 and 26) the average continuous phase velocity at any cross-section can be found out. For instance, at the plane AMB (Figure 6), it is given by

$$V_c = \frac{16\psi_0}{T^2} \tag{28}$$

where ψ_0 is given by Equation 27. Since, the energy dissipation pattern is different in different sparged contactors, each item of equipment will be considered separately. The rate of energy dissipation in the continuous phase motion (E) is given by Equations 12, 13, 15, 16, and 17.

Bubble Columns

Liquid phase continuous co-current:

$$V_C = 1.31 \left\{ gT \left(V_G - \frac{\varepsilon_G V_L}{1 - \varepsilon_G} - \varepsilon_G V_{b\infty} \right) \right\}^{1/3} \tag{29}$$

Liquid phase batch:

$$V_C = 1.31 \{ gT(V_G - \varepsilon_G V_{b\infty}) \}^{1/3} \tag{30}$$

Gas-Liquid-Solid Sparged Contactors

Liquid phase continuous co-current:

$$V_C = 1.31 \left\{ gT \left[V_G + V_L - \frac{\rho_L V_L}{\varepsilon_S \rho_S + \varepsilon_L \rho_L} - \varepsilon_S V_S \left(\frac{\rho_S}{\varepsilon_S \rho_S + \varepsilon_L \rho_L} - 1 \right) - \varepsilon_G V_{b\infty} \right] \right\}^{1/3} \tag{31}$$

Liquid phase batch:

$$V_C = 1.31 \left\{ gT \left[V_G - \varepsilon_S V_S \left(\frac{\rho_S}{\rho_S \varepsilon_S + \rho_L \varepsilon_L} - 1 \right) - \varepsilon_G V_{b\infty} \right] \right\}^{1/3} \tag{32}$$

Gas-Solid Fluidized Bed

$$V_C = 0.72 \{ gT(V_G - V_{mf}) \}^{1/3} \tag{33}$$

The liquid velocity at the column axis is given by Equations 29–32 with the coefficient as 1.18. Thus, for instance, in the case of semi-batch bubble column:

$$V_a = 1.18 \{ gT(V_G - \varepsilon_G V_{b\infty}) \}^{1/3} \tag{29a}$$

There are some experimental data available on the average continuous phase circulation velocity. These values agree favorably to those predicted by Equations 29–33. Thus it can be seen that the flow model represented by Figure 6 explains several performance characteristics that include fractional gas hold-up, continuous phase velocity profiles, and the wall heat transfer coefficient. However, the model has one limitation that, at the cell interface, the radial components of the liquid velocity in the adjacent cells are in the opposite direction. In order to overcome this limitation Joshi [5] developed a new model, and it is described in the following section.

OVERALL TURBULENCE MODEL FOR MULTIPHASE FLOWS

Turbulent shear stress is given by the following equation [13]:

$$\tau = -\rho_L \overline{v'_z v'_y} \tag{34}$$

where v'_z and v'_y are the fluctuating components of the liquid velocity in the axial and radial directions, respectively. In this case the bulk turbulence is perhaps isotropic. Therefore, it can be seen from Equation 34 that the value of τ/ρ_L is uniform throughout the bed. Assuming that the scale of turbulence is independent of the spatial coordinates, we get

$$\frac{dv_z}{dy} = \left(\frac{-\tau}{\rho_L} \right)^{1/2} \bigg/ 1 \tag{35}$$

where l is the mixing length. Substituting Equation 34 into 35 gives the velocity profile, if the value of l is known. For the aggregative solid-liquid fluidized beds the predicted velocity profile cannot be confirmed because of the lack of experimental data. Fortunately, for bubble columns the experimental measurements of the liquid velocity are available over a wide range of variables (0.13 < T < 5.5 m; 20 < V_G < 900 mm s^{-1}). Therefore, the liquid velocity profile will be predicted for a bubble column and compared with the experimental data. The power consumption per unit mass in bubble columns is given by

$$P_m = g(V_G - \varepsilon_G V_{b\infty}) \qquad (36)$$

It is reasonable to assume that the value of l is 0.08 T in bubble columns under turbulent conditions.

Turbulence intensity is given by

$$(U_y')^3 = P_m l \qquad (37)$$

$$= 0.08 Tg\{V_G - \varepsilon_G V_{b\infty}\} \qquad (38)$$

$$v_y' = 0.25 \{gT(V_G - \varepsilon_G V_{b\infty})\}^{1/3} \qquad (39)$$

The relationship between the velocity gradient and the turbulence intensity is obtained by substituting Equation 34 into Equation 35, we get

$$dy_z/dy = v_y'/l \qquad (40)$$

Equations 39 and 40 indicate that the velocity gradient is constant throughout the cross-section. (The velocity at the wall is zero and it may be assumed that the velocity increases from zero to the maximum downward velocity in a short distance from the wall). It is well known that the liquid flow is upward in the center and downward near the column wall. The liquid velocity will be zero at a point between the center and the column wall. This point can be obtained on the basis of Equation 40 and the material balance. In the case of no net liquid flow (liquid—batch; gas—continuous) the upward and downward flows are equal. Therefore, we write

$$\int_0^A 2\pi r \, dr \, v_z = \int_A^{T/2} 2\pi r \, dr \, v_z \qquad (41)$$

where $r = R - y$

Solving Equation 41 gives the value of A equal to 0.67R. The value of A equal to 0.71R was obtained by Joshi and Sharma [7] using the vorticity equation, which is close to that obtained in the present analysis. The liquid velocity at the column axis can now be obtained:

$$V_a = 1.04\{gT(V_G - \varepsilon_G V_{b\infty})\}^{1/3} \qquad (42)$$

The comparison between the experimental values of liquid velocity and those predicted by Equation 42 is given in Table 1. An excellent agreement can be seen from the table. However, in this model, the predicted velocity profile is triangular, basically because of the assumption of the constant value of l throughout the contactor and the assumption of isotropic turbulence. These turbulence parameters must be measured for further insight in the hydrodynamic behavior of multiphase contactors.

CONTINUOUS PHASE AXIAL MIXING

The performance of multiphase reactors depends upon the residence time distribution (RTD) and the micromixing behavior of all the phases. Brodkey [28] and Nauman [29] have discussed in detail the mechanisms of RTD and micromixing. Turner [30] and Bourne [31] have critically reviewed the published literature on RTD and micromixing, respectively.

For the representation of residence time distribution, one directional axial dispersion model is widely used [29, 32] where the axial dispersion coefficient is the model parameter. There are various experimental techniques by which the values of dispersion coefficient can be measured and much data have been published using a variety of equipment. In some cases, the data have been suitably correlated.

Heterogeneous Regime

Since the heterogeneous regime is more common particularly in the commercial size equipment, this regime will be analyzed in detail.

In the case of single-phase turbulent piple flow Taylor [33] has derived the following equation from first principles:

$$D_L = 0.05\sqrt{0.5f'}\,TV_L \tag{43}$$

where f' is the friction factor.

From Equation 43 it can be seen that the continuous phase axial dispersion coefficient is proportional to the contactor diameter and the average continuous phase velocity. On this basis the axial mixing in all the contactors will be examined.

Bubble Columns

The pertinent details regarding the equipment, the system used and procedure for the reported data on liquid phase backmixing have been summarized in Table 2. The reported data on liquid phase axial dispersion coefficient (D_L) are plotted against TV_C in Figure 8. The following correlation was found to hold with a standard deviation of 7%:

$$D_L = 0.33TV_C \tag{44}$$

In the range of variables given in Table 2, V_C was found to be much greater than V_L. When V_C and V_L are comparable the following equation is recommended:

$$D_L = 0.33(V_C + V_L)T \tag{45}$$

From Equations 43 and 44 it can be seen that the average recirculation velocity (V_C) is the characteristic velocity for the liquid phase in bubble columns. Further, Taylor's equation can probably be applied to the case of bubble columns if V_L (Equation 43) is replaced by V_C. The value of the friction factor can be calculated by the following procedure.

Reynolds numbers may be defined by

$$N_{Re} = \frac{D_0 V_C \rho_c (1 - \varepsilon_G)}{\mu_c} \tag{46}$$

where

$$D_0 = \frac{\pi(T^2 - 4A^2)}{\pi T}$$

$$= 0.5T \tag{47}$$

$$f' = 0.046(N_{Re})^{-0.2} \tag{48}$$

For the sake of comparison, Taylor's equation is also plotted in Figure 8. It can be seen from Figure 8 that the agreement between Taylor's equation and the correlation given by Equation 44 is within 10%.

Table 2

Experimental Details for Liquid-Phase Axial Mixing in Gas-Liquid Bubble Columns

Symbol in Figure 8	T (m)	H (m)	V_G (m/s)	V_L (mm/s)	Sparger	System	Tracer	Technique of measurement	Reference
▷	0.14	3.53	0.075–0.39	15.6	sieve plate	air-water	aqueous NaCl solution	Steady state	Reith et al. [36]
◁	0.29	3.8	0.08–0.45						
◐	0.1	2.02	0.02–0.07	1.8–3.4	porous plate and sieve plate	air-water	aqueous KCl solution and heat	Steady state	Aoyama et al. [37]
◑	0.2	1.0	0.003–0.065	1.8–6.2					
◕	0.122	2.0	0.04–0.2	5.15	sieve plate	air-water	aqueous KCl solution	transient, pulse	Kato and Nishiwaki [38]
◑	0.214	4.05	0.04–0.18	5.15					
◰	0.406	1.5	0.05–0.268	6–15	single tube	air-water	methylene blue dye	steady state, transient pulse	Towell and Ackerman [39]
◱		1.9							
■		2.84							
□									
●	1.067	5.11	0.017–0.035	3–7	eight point spider	air-water	methylene blue dye	steady state, transient pulse	Towell and Ackerman [39]
●	0.2	2.22	0.05–0.068	4.4–7.4	sintered porous plate	air-water	electrolyte dye and heat	steady state	Deckwer et al. [40]
●	0.102	2.56	0.05–0.12	7.07	56 nozzles of 1 mm i.d.	air-water	electrolyte dye and heat	steady state	Deckwer et al. [41]
○	0.2	7.23							
⚲	0.1	1.33	0.04–0.34	semi-batch	single tube	air-water	aqueous KCl solution	transient and steady state measurement	Hikita and Kikukawa [42]
⚲	0.19	1.33	0.04–0.34						
⚲	0.19	2.2	0.04–0.34						
+	0.214	7.0	0.01–0.3	0.07–0.12, m/s	wire screen	air-water	Bromine-82 (ammonium bromide solution)	transient, pulse	Ostergaard [43]
×	0.146	1.5	0.01–0.1	0.017–0.031, m/s	sieve plate, 2 mm holes	air-water	aqueous NaCl solution	steady state	Vail et al. [44]

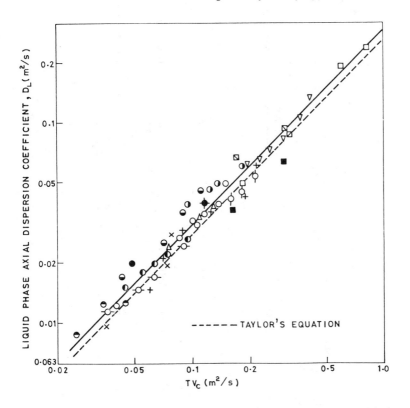

Figure 8. Effect of average liquid circulation velocity on liquid phase axial dispersion coefficient in bubble columns; for symbols refer to Table 2 [2].

Gas-Liquid-Solid Fluidized Beds

Kato et al [46], Michelson and Ostergaard [47], and Vail et al [44] have measured the liquid phase axial dispersion coefficient from 0.05 to 0.214 m I.D. contactors. The observations may be summarised as follows:

1. When the particles are very small and/or the difference between the densities of liquid and solid is small and/or the solid loading is relatively small, the extent of liquid-phase axial mixing in the three-phase systems is practically the same as that for gas-liquid systems. The value of D_L varies with T and V_G and under turbulent conditions ($N_{Re} > 2,100$) D_L is practically independent of V_L and particle diameter.

2. When the particle size is large and the density difference high, the dispersion coefficient depends upon the particle size and the superficial gas and liquid velocities. Michelson and Ostergaard [47] made the following observations:
   (a) For 6-mm glass beads and a 0.15-m I.D. column, at relatively low superficial gas velocities, the values of D_L were found to be practically equal to those for a liquid-solid fluidized bed. V_G was found to have nominal influence on D_L. At high V_G, however, substantial enhancement in D_L over those for a liquid-solid system was observed.
   (b) For 3-mm glass beads and a 0.15-m I.D. column, at low V_L, the introduction of gas increases D_L substantially. However, at relatively high V_L, the introduction of gas even

Table 3
Experimental Details for the Liquid-Phase Axial Mixing in Gas-Liquid-Solid Sparged Contactor

Symbol in Figure 9	T (m)	V_G (mm/s)	V_L (mm/s)	H_T (m)	d_p (mm)	ε_S	Solid and density (kg/m^3)	Tracer	Technique of measurement	Reference
+	0.066	20–200	6–20	2.01	0.149–0.177	0.1	glass beads, 2,600	aqueous KCl solution	transient, pulse	Kato et al. [46]
⊕	0.122	20–200	6–20	1.96	0.125–0.149	0.1				
○	0.214	20–200	6–20	4.05	0.149–0.177	0.1				
▷	0.15	0–300	100–260	11.0	6.0	0.18–0.4	glass beads, 2,600	Bromine-82 (Aqueous NH$_4$Br solution)	transient, imperfect pulse	Michelson and Ostergaard [47]
◁	0.15	0–120	66–160	11.0	3.0	0.23–0.44				
◀	0.15	0–150	30–90	11.0	1.0	0.23–0.5				
◪	0.214	0–200	68–106	7.0	6.0	0.35–0.45	glass beads, 2,600	Bromine-82 (Aqueous NH$_4$Br solution)	transient, imperfect pulse	Ostergaard [43]
□	0.214	0–200	30–90	7.0	1.0	0.2–0.44				
■	0.214	0–100	46–145	7.0	3.0	0.3–0.5				
●	0.146	15–100	17–30	1.5	0.87	0.47–0.54	2700	aqueous NaCl solution	Steady state	Vail et al. [44]

reduces D_L as compared to that for a liquid-solid system. Such a reduction was not observed in a 0.214-m I.D. column.

(c) For 1-mm glass beads, similar observations as previously discussed in (1) were made. In some cases, D_L in the presence of solids was found to be even higher than that for the gas-liquid system under otherwise identical conditions. These observations can be explained on the basis of average liquid circulation velocity given by Equation 31. Depending upon the particle diameter and the settling velocity, Equation 31 has the two limiting cases. The particle settling velocity in Equations 29 and 31 are practically the same in which case the same values of D_L are predicted for the gas-liquid and gas-liquid-solid systems. This situation corresponds to 1.

When the condition given by the following equation is satisfied

$$V_G + V_L - \left(\frac{\rho_L}{\varepsilon_S \rho_S + \varepsilon_L \rho_L}\right) V_L - \varepsilon_S V_S \left(\frac{\rho_S}{\varepsilon_S \rho_S + \varepsilon_L \rho_L} - 1\right) - \varepsilon_G V_{b\infty} = 0 \tag{49}$$

the liquid recirculation does not occur (Equation 31) and the extent of axial mixing is very poor and is comparable to that in liquid-solid fluidized bed. This situation corresponds to observation (a) at relatively low superficial gas velocities.

In between the two extremes just reported the value of the average liquid circulation velocity can be found from Equations 31 and 32. The pertinent details regarding the equipment and the range of operating variables are given in Table 3.

The reported data on liquid phase axial dispersion coefficient (D_L) are plotted against $T(V_C + V_L)$ in Figure 9. The following equation holds with a standard deviation of 16%:

$$D_L = 0.29(V_C + V_L)T \tag{50}$$

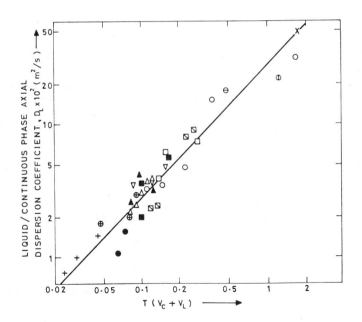

Figure 9. Effect of average continuous phase circulation velocity and column diameter on continuous phase axial dispersion coefficient in three-phase sparged contactors and gas-solid fluidized beds; for symbols refer to Tables 3 and 4 [2].

It may be noted that the coefficients in Equations 43 (f' ≃ 0.005), 45, and 50 are practically the same.

While using Equations 45 and 50, it is necessary to know the values of ε_G, $V_{b\infty}$, ε_S, and V_S. Under certain conditions most of the input energy is dissipated at the gas-liquid and solid-liquid interfaces and very little energy remains available to sustain the liquid circulation. Under these conditions we need very precise estimates of ε_G, $V_{b\infty}$, and V_S. These situations are faced in the presence of surface active agents. In such cases the fractional gas hold-up is likely to be very high as compared with air-water system under otherwise identical conditions. Further details regarding the effect of physical properties on the continuous phase axial mixing are discussed later in this chapter.

Gas-Solid Fluidized Beds

May [48] and deGroot [49] reported data on emulsion phase backmixing from 0.076, 0.1, 0.3, 0.381, 1.51, and 1.52-m I.D. fluidized beds. The pertinent details are summarized in Table 4.

When $V_G > 5V_{mf}$, Schugerl [50] has given the following equation for the viscosity of fluidized bed:

$$\frac{\mu_F}{\rho_F} = 0.12 \times 10^{-3} \tag{51}$$

where $\rho_F = \varepsilon_S \rho_S$ \hfill (52)

The Reynolds number may be defined by

$$N_{Re} = \frac{0.5 T V_C \rho_F}{\mu_F} \tag{53}$$

The data reported by May [48] and deGroot [49] was analyzed and only those points for which turbulent conditions prevail were considered for correlation. (Under laminar conditions it will be shown later that the correlation parameter is perhaps $V_C^2 T^2$ in place of $V_C T$ (Mashelkar and Ramchandran [51]). The laminar conditions were found to exist for column diameters up to about 0.3 m. It may be noted at this stage that most of the laboratory investigations have been reported from column diameters of less than 0.3 m. In small diameter columns the liquid recirculation is either very poor or absent. From Figure 9 it can be seen that the following equation holds ($V_L = 0$):

$$D_L = D_E = 0.29 T V_C \tag{54}$$

Table 4
Experimental Details of Gas-Solid Fluidized Beds [2]

Symbol in Figure 9	T (m)	H (m)	V_G (m/s)	Particle size (microns)	Tracer	Reference
⊖	0.6	2.23–2.25	0.1–0.2	50–150	Gold-198 particles	deGroot [49]
①	1.5	4.91	0.1–0.2			
×	1.525	9.60	0.24	20–150	Radioactive particles	May [48]

Homogeneous Regime

In the homogeneous regime, the bubbles generated at the sparger rise upward practically without dispersion and coalescence. The bubble rise velocity almost equals the terminal rise velocity and all the input energy is dissipated in the vicinity of the gas liquid interface. As a result, bulk liquid circulation cannot be sustained. Some amount of liquid is carried upward with wakes behind the bubbles and released at the top surface of dispersion. This liquid flows downward in the bubble free region.

Since at any cross-section there is no net liquid flow (in the case of semi-batch operation), the liquid downflow occurs everywhere except in the area occupied by the gas. A material balance with respect to liquid phase gives

$$\begin{pmatrix} \text{fractional} \\ \text{gas hold-up} \end{pmatrix} \begin{pmatrix} \text{ratio of wake volume} \\ \text{to the bubble volume} \end{pmatrix} \begin{pmatrix} \text{rise velocity} \\ \text{of bubbles} \end{pmatrix} = \begin{pmatrix} \text{1-fractional gas} \\ \text{hold-up-fractional} \\ \text{wake hold-up} \end{pmatrix} \begin{pmatrix} \text{downflow} \\ \text{velocity} \\ \text{of liquid} \end{pmatrix} \quad (55)$$

or $\quad \varepsilon_G \alpha V_{b\infty} = (1 - \varepsilon_G - \alpha\varepsilon_G)V_C \quad$ (56)

and $\quad V_C = \dfrac{\alpha\varepsilon_G}{1 - \varepsilon_G - \alpha\varepsilon_G} V_{b\infty} \quad$ (57)

Kumar and Kuloor [52] reported the value of α to be 11/16. The value of $V_{b\infty}$ may be taken as 0.23 m s^{-1} for air-water systems (The numerical values of α and $V_{b\infty}$ are not very important since they enter into the proportionality constant).

Continuous phase axial mixing in the homogeneous regime can be analyzed on the basis of laminar flow in a circular pipe.

In the case of single phase pipe flow, Taylor [53] has given the following equation for the axial dispersion coefficient in laminar flow:

$$D_L = \frac{T^2 V_L^2}{192D} \quad (58)$$

where D is the molecular diffusivity. For turbulent flow D_L is given by Equation 43. Equations 43 and 58 are plotted in Figure 10 (for simplicity it is assumed that ρ_L/μ_L is 100). It can be seen from Figure 10 that D_L decreases markedly during the transition from laminar to turbulent flow. This also results in a maxima and a minima in the values of the axial dispersion coefficient. A similar behavior is probably exhibited by multiphase contactors. For instance, we will analyze the case of a bubble column.

Ohki and Inoue [54] have reported data on axial dispersion in the low range of superficial gas velocity (Figure 11). The observations may be summarized as:

1. The values of D_L follow, in general, the pattern of Figure 10. Below a certain critical superficial gas velocity (V_{GC}) D_L increases faster with V_G. Further, D_L depends upon the sparger design. The value of V_{GC} depends upon the column diameter and the sparger design. The D_L data below V_{GC} has been correlated by

$$D_L = 0.3T^2 V_G^{1.2} + 170\delta \quad (59)$$

where δ is the diameter of the sparger hole.

2. An increase in V_G, beyond V_{GC} results in a decrease in D_L. As a consequence, a maximum D_L is obtained at V_{GC}. The reduction in D_L occurs over a small range of V_G, a minimum occurs in D_L, and again D_L increases with V_G. The range of V_G higher than that at which the minima occurs conforms to the turbulent regime. All the experimental data reported by

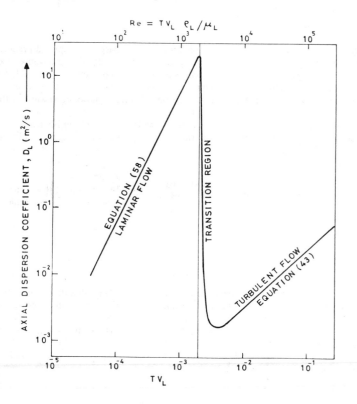

Figure 10. Axial dispersion in single phase pipe flow [3].

Ohki and Inoue [54] in the homogeneous as well as heterogeneous regime are plotted in Figure 11. For the homogeneous regime (data represented by Equation 59) Equation 57 was used, whereas for the heterogeneous regime the procedure discussed in the previous section was employed. It can be seen from Figure 11 that all the data in the homogeneous regime fall on a straight line irrespective of the column diameter and the number and diameter of sparger holes. The following correlation holds:

$$D_L = 326(TV_C)^{1.7} \tag{60}$$

The dependence on TV_C was found to be 1.7, which is close to the theoretical value of 2 (equation 58) for a laminar flow in circular pipes. Mashelkar and Ramchandran [51] have also shown that the values of D_L vary as $(TV_C)^2$ in the case of bubbles columns operated in the laminar regime. It may be emphasized that turbulent conditions can prevail in the homogeneous regime depending upon column diameter and the intensity of liquid circulation. Under turbulent conditions, D_L will perhaps vary as TV_C even in the homogeneous regime. For more understanding and for proper definition of Reynolds number, further experimentation in this region is required.

It may be emphasized that the experimental data in the homogeneous regime are scanty. Systematic investigations need to be undertaken covering a wide range of parameters and in all the sparged contactors. In particular, the transition from homogeneous to heterogeneous regime and its effect on axial mixing needs to be understood.

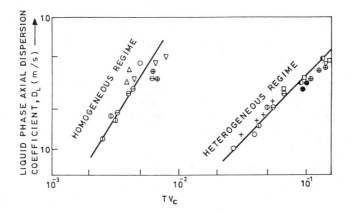

Figure 11. Axial dispersion coefficient in homogeneous and turbulent regimes for symbols refer to [3].

Liquid Phase Axial Mixing in Solid-Liquid Fluidized Beds (SLFB)

Chung and Wen [55] have critically reviewed the work on liquid phase axial mixing in SLFB. They have proposed the following correlation, which holds for fixed beds as well:

$$\frac{\varepsilon_L Pe}{(Re)_{mf}/Re} = 0.2 + 0.011 Re^{0.48} \tag{61}$$

Shemilt and co-workers [56] have extensively studied liquid phase axial mixing and have reported the following correlation [56]. For this purpose, all the published data have also been analyzed.

$$\left[1 - \left(\frac{2D_L}{V_SH}\right)^{1/2}\right]\varepsilon_L^{0.25} = 0.74 \tag{62}$$

Equation 62 perhaps suggests that the values of D_L depend upon the bed height, which is contrary to experimental observations.

Joshi [5] has developed the following correlation for turbulent regime ($d_p V_{s\infty}\rho_L/\mu_L > 500$):

$$D_L = 3.75 D_e V_s \tag{63}$$

From Figure 12 it can be seen that Equation 63 fits all the experimental data with a standard deviation of 17%. The value of the proportionality constant is larger in Equation 63 as compared to that in Equations 43, 44, and 50. This is probably for two reasons. First, the value 0.33 holds perhaps in the range of high Reynolds numbers. Tichacek and Barkelew [57] have shown, for the case of flow through circular pipes, that the value of the constant increases with a decrease in Re below 30,000. Second, the wall in the case of pipes, bubble column and gas-solid and gas-liquid-solid fluidized beds is stationary. In the case of solid-liquid fluidized beds the equivalent diameter is based on the wetted area of particles. The particles, however, are in turbulent motion.

In the laminar regime, it was discussed earlier that D_L varies as $(D_e V_L)^2$. This dependence cannot be checked for SLFB because of the lack of data in this region. A rational analysis of data in the transition region is very difficult and extensive experimentation is needed before a systematic analysis is possible.

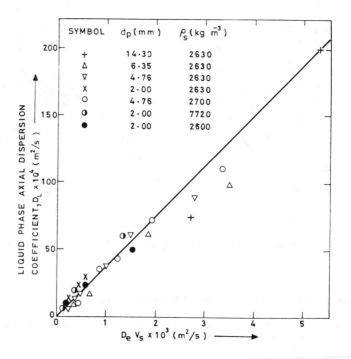

Figure 12. Correlation for liquid-phase axial dispersion coefficient in turbulent regime in solid-liquid fluidized beds [5].

Liquid Phase Axial Mixing in Packed Bubble Columns

Niranjan [58] has made extensive measurements of liquid phase axial mixing in 200- and 385-mm I.D. columns. He used 12.5-, 25-, and 38-mm ceramic Raschig rings; 19-, 25-, and 38-mm ceramic Intalox saddles; and 25-, 38-, and 50-mm polypropylene Pall rings. The height to diameter ratio was varied between 2 and 8 and the superficial gas velocity was varied in the range of 50–300 mm/s.

In order to correlate the data on D_L, it is desirable to know the flow pattern of liquid phase. Packings hinder the liquid phase circulatory flow to some extent. However, the extent of reduction depends upon the type and size of the packing. It was found that the liquid circulation was practically absent when the packing size was less than 25 mm. The strength of liquid circulation increases with an increase in the packing size. The average liquid circulation velocity can be found according to the procedure given earlier. As compared with bubble columns, there is an additional mode of energy dissipation at the solid-liquid (packing surface) interface and is given by the following equation:

$$E_{SL} = \frac{\pi}{4} T^2 H \rho_L (1 - \varepsilon_G) \frac{a_p f'}{6\varepsilon^3} V_C^3 \tag{64a}$$

Using the procedure previously described the following equation is obtained for the average liquid circulation velocity.

$$V_C = 1.817\varepsilon \left\{ \frac{g}{f'a_p} (V_G - \varepsilon_G V_{b\infty}) \right\}^{1/3} \tag{64b}$$

where f' is the frictional factor for packings, which depends upon the type but is independent of the size of the packing. The values of f' are as follows: ceramic Raschig rings, 3.76; metal Raschig rings, 5.07; stainless steel and polypropylene Pall rings, 2.17; and Intalox saddles, 2.03. a_p is the dry surface area per unit volume.

Niranjan [58] has developed the following correlation for D_L, which holds for the range of variables covered:

$$D_L = 2.5V_cD_e \qquad (64c)$$

where $D_e = 4\varepsilon/a_p$

Equation 64c is similar to Equation 63, which was developed for solid-liquid fluidized beds (SLFB) in the turbulent regime. The value of coefficient for SLFB is more than that for packed bubble columns. This is probably because the solid particles in SLFB undergo random motion, which gives rise to higher values of dispersion coefficient. The solid particles in the packed bubble column are stationary.

Another useful observation in packed bubble columns is that the value of D_L is practically independent of the superficial gas velocity (V_G) when the packing size is less than 25 mm. The dependence of D_L on V_G increases with an increase in the packing size. In general the value of D_L in packed bubble column was found to be 5 to 20 times lower than that in bubble column.

Liquid Phase Axial Mixing in Sectionalized Bubble Columns

In bubble columns the high values of liquid phase axial dispersion coefficient occur because of the intense liquid circulation. In packed bubble columns the packings provide resistance to the liquid circulation and the extent of axial mixing is considerably reduced.

Another way to reduce the liquid phase axial mixing is to provide radial baffles with a circular opening at the center. The baffles prevent the liquid flow near the column wall. Joshi and Sharma [59] have considered the problem of sectionalization and they have recommended that the baffle packing should be 0.81 times the column diameter and the diameter of central hole should be 0.71 times the column diameter. Using this suggested geometry, Pandit and Joshi [60] measured the liquid phase axial mixing in a 385-mm I.D. sectionalized bubble column. They have reported that the presence of baffles reduces the value of D_L (in bubble columns) by a factor of 3 to 4. In addition to the reduction in D_L sectionalized bubble columns and packed columns provide high values of fractional gas hold-up and effective interfacial area.

Liquid Phase Axial Mixing in Bubble Columns with Draft Tubes

Bubble columns with draft tubes are widely used as fermenters. The introduction of draft tubes increases the fractional gas hold-up and the effective gas-liquid interfacial area. Pandit and Joshi [60] measured the liquid phase mixing in a 385-mm I.D. bubble columns with 230-mm and 270-mm I.D. draft tubes. They have shown that the extent of mixing decreases by a factor of 4 to 6 by using draft tubes.

GAS PHASE AXIAL MIXING

There are many gas-liquid reactions of industrial importance carried out in bubble columns and for which the conversion with respect to the gas phase is high. For instance, chlorination of a variety of organic compounds, hydrochlorination of alcohols, ammination of fatty acids, oxidation with molecular oxygen, ozonolysis, and the removal of noxious gases for pollution abatement fall in this category. In order to design a bubble column for these cases, the knowledge of the degree of axial mixing in the gas phase is important. The experimental investigation for the gas phase axial mixing in bubble columns has been studied by Kolbel et al. [61], Carleton et al. [62], Towell and Ackerman

[39], Men'shchikov and Aerov [63], Pilhofer et al. [64], Seher and Schumacher [65], and Field and Davidsen [45]. The details pertaining to the experiments have been summarized in Table 5. In all the cases, a one-dimensional axial dispersion model has been used. A review of the published information indicates that the proposed correlations for the gas phase axial dispersion coefficient (D_G) fit a limited amount of the experimental data.

Pavlica and Olson [73] correlated the data reported by Kolbel et al. [61] by the following equation:

$$\frac{V_S T}{D_G} = 0.2 \tag{65a}$$

where $\quad V_S = \dfrac{V_G}{\varepsilon_G} - \dfrac{V_L}{1 - \varepsilon_G}$ \hfill (65b)

This correlation was developed for 0.092-m I.D. column. Carleton et al. [62] obtained the D_G data from 0.076, 0.153, and 0.305-m I.D. columns and these data cannot be correlated by Equation 65a. Men'shchikov and Aerov [63] studied the gas phase axial mixing in 0.3-m I.D. column using hydrogen pulse as a tracer. Superficial gas velocity (V_G) was varied in the range of 7.6–96 mm s^{-1} and the following correlation is proposed:

$$D_G = 1.47 V_G^{0.72} \tag{66}$$

Since the column diameter was not varied in this work, it does not appear in Equation 66.

Towell and Ackerman [39] studied the gas phase axial mixing in 0.406 and 1.07-m I.D. bubble columns using radioactive argon as a tracer. The authors could correlate their own data and those reported by Kolbel et al. [61] and Carleton et al. [62] by the following equation:

$$D_G = 19.7 T^2 V_G \tag{67}$$

Equation 67, however, cannot correlate the data reported by Men'shchikov and Aerov [63].

Pilhofer et al. [64] used a sinusoidal forcing function of CO, CO_2, and CH_4 tracers to investigate the gas-phase dispersion. Air-water, air-glycol and N_2-n-propanol systems were employed in the 0.1- and 0.14-m I.D. bubble columns. They correlated their own data and those reported by Kolbel et al. [61] by the following equation:

$$D_G = 50 T^{1.5} (V_G/\varepsilon_G)^3 \tag{68}$$

The predictions of Equation 68 deviate substantially from reported data [63, 65]. Further, the difference between the predicted and the experimental values of D_G increases markedly as the value of V_G/ε_G approaches the terminal rise velocity of a single bubble.

Correlation

The gas phase dispersion occurs mainly for the two reasons:

1. Because of liquid recirculation, the bubble rise velocity is maximum at the column axis and minimum near the column wall. Some bubbles move downward with the liquid. This results in a radial variation of the fractional gas hold-up. The variations in the terminal rise velocities because of the bubble size distribution also give radial variation in the gas hold-up. The existence of the radial hold-up profile gives, similar to the liquid velocity profile in bubble columns [2], the spread in residence time distribution.
2. Under turbulent conditions, it is known that the coalescence and the dispersion of bubbles prevail in bubble columns. The assessment of axial mixing because of the coalescence and dispersion patterns is difficult. Here we analyze the problem of dispersion on the basis of hold-up profile, which is mainly a result of the different rise velocities of bubbles.

Table 5
Summary of the Studies on Gas-Phase Axial Mixing [4]
System: Air-Water

No.	Symbol in Figure 13	T (mm)	H (mm)	V_G (mm s^{-1})	V_L (mm s^{-1})	Sparger	Tracer	Forcing function	Reference
1	□	92	700	40–70	—	—	—	—	Kolbel et al. [61]
2	△ ▷	153 305	1300	30–50	—	sieve-plate	H_2	pulse	Carleton et al. [62]
3	+ ⊕	406 1067	2840 5100	16.2–131.0 8.5–34.4	13.5 7.2	single tube eight point spider	freon	pulse and step	Towell and Ackerman [39]
4	●	300	5000	7.6–96.0	—	single tube	H_2 CH_4, CO_2 CO	pulse	Men'shchikov and Aerov [63]
5	◐ ◑	100 140	700, 1700 600, 900, 1200	15–60 10–130	0–60 0–60			sinusoidal	Pilhofer et al. [64]
6	◇ ◈	450 1000	4000 4000	22	11	sieve-plate	Ar-41	pulse	Seher and Schumacher [65]

Hills [22] and Ueyama and Miyauchi [10] have measured the radial variation in the gas hold-up and the following equation is proposed:

$$\varepsilon_G' = 2\varepsilon_G \left[1 - \left(\frac{r}{R} \right)^2 \right] \tag{69}$$

The average rise velocity of the gas phase with respect to the column wall is given by

$$V_0 = V_G/\varepsilon_G \tag{70}$$

The gas phase may be viewed to be moving with a parabolic velocity profile (Equation 69) and with the average velocity of V_0.

Since the gas phase occupies a fraction of the column, the effective diameter for the gas flow is:

$$d_G = \sqrt{\varepsilon_G} \, T \tag{71}$$

Taylor [53] has analyzed theoretically the case of laminar liquid flow with a parabolic velocity profile in a circular pipe. He has shown that the liquid phase axial dispersion coefficient varies as the square of the column diameter and the average liquid velocity:

$$D_L \propto V^2 T^2 \tag{72}$$

for the gas phase in bubble column, with a parabolic velocity profile, a similar relationship was assumed. It may be emphasized that the use of the Taylor model to explain the gas phase dispersion is provisional in nature. In particular, we note the following points:

1. The Taylor model assumes the diffusion in the laminar case to be constant because it is the molecular diffusion. The gas-phase radial dispersion coefficient will vary with superficial gas velocity and column diameter.
2. Coalescence between bubbles from different radial positions may even enhance radial mixing and therefore reduce axial dispersion as follows from the Taylor model.

However, because of simplicity, Taylor's model will be used. On the basis of Equation 72, we can write the following equation for the gas phase axial dispersion coefficient:

$$D_G \propto V_0^2 d_G^2 \tag{73}$$

Substituting Equations 70 and 71 into Equation 73 gives

$$D_G \propto \frac{V_G^2}{\varepsilon_G} T^2 \tag{74}$$

From Figure 13, it can be seen that the following equation holds with a standard deviation of 26%

$$D_G = 110 \frac{V_G^2}{\varepsilon_G} T^2 \tag{75}$$

For the case of turbulent conditions, it was shown that the liquid-phase axial dispersion data from bubble columns can be correlated by

$$D_L = 0.33 T V_C \tag{76}$$

The change from the square dependence of T and V on the dispersion coefficient to the linear dependence occurs as the flow conditions change from laminar to turbulent [3, 32]. Equation 75 was developed for the parabolic (laminar type) hold-up profile.

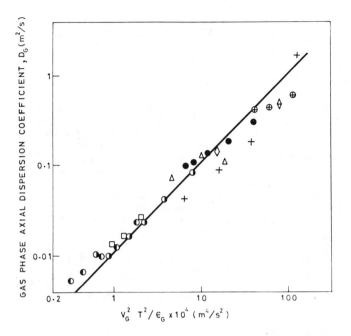

Figure 13. Correlation for gas phase axial dispersion coefficient in bubble columns; for symbols refer to Table 5 [4].

For the gas phase, however, it is difficult to define the Reynolds number because the radial variation in the hold-up occurs because of the liquid velocity profile. It is known that the gas hold-up profile is parabolic even if the liquid phase is highly turbulent $[(0.5TV_c\rho_L)/\mu_L] \geq 2 \times 10^5$. Based on the gas-phase dispersion data, the following definition for the Reynolds number is selected:

$$Re_G = (\sqrt{\varepsilon_G}TV_0\rho_G)/\mu_G \tag{77}$$

The gas phase will be considered laminar if $Re_G < 4,000$ and turbulent for larger values of Re_G. On the basis of Equation 77, all the reported data fall in the laminar region. For large industrial bubble columns, it is likely that $Re_G > 4,000$. For the development of a correlation in this region or for the extension of the correlation given by Equation 75, experimental investigations are needed for the case of large column diameters and/or large superficial gas velocities.

For gas-phase dispersion also, it is perhaps expected that the transition from laminar to turbulent region occurs according to the nature shown in Figure 10. Recently, Field and Davidson [45] have measured the values of D_G from 3.2-m I.D. bubble column. According to the definition of Equation 77, the data reported by Field and Davidson [45] falls in the transition regime. Since the liquid phase was continuous co-current, Equation 70 takes the following form:

$$V_0 = \frac{V_G}{\varepsilon_G} - \frac{V_L}{\varepsilon_L} \tag{78}$$

The D_G data reported by Field and Davidson [45] can be correlated by the following equation:

$$D_G = 2.1V_0d_G \tag{79}$$

The value of coefficient (Equation 79) in the transition regime is much higher than the value of 0.29 reported for the turbulent regime. This supports the case that the behavior of D_G is like that shown in Figure 10. In order to confirm this conjecture further experimental evidence is needed.

General Remarks

Joshi and Sharma [59] have shown that the liquid-phase backmixing can be considerably reduced by using radial baffles with a central hole of 0.7 T and the baffle spacing of 0.81 T. These baffles prohibit the downward liquid flow and it is expected that the backflow of bubbles will also be reduced. Since the backflow of bubbles occurs within a short distance from the wall, the diameter of the central hole can perhaps be increased if the axial mixing in the gas phase alone is to be reduced. Experimental work is needed to investigate the effect of baffle design on the gasphase axial dispersion coefficient.

The volumetric gas flow rate decreases along the length of the column because of the absorption of one or more components from the gas phase. On the contrary, the volumetric gas flow rate increases because of the reduction in pressure due to the hydrostatic head of liquid or by desorption of some component from the liquid phase. Because of these factors, the superficial gas velocity and the fractional gas hold-up will vary along the length of the column. Experimental work is needed to investigate the effects of V_G and ε_G on D_G. In the absence of any data, Equation 75 may be used where V_G, ε_G, and D_G will vary from bottom to top.

There is scanty information available in the literature regarding the effects of physical properties of the gas and liquid phases on gas-phase axial dispersion coefficient.

SOLID PHASE AXIAL MIXING

The axial dispersion model is used to describe behavior of solid phase as well with the difference that provision is made for the settling of particles. The resulting dispersion-sedimentation model gives the following equation for the solid phase concentration profile:

$$C = \left(C_0 + \frac{V_L}{V_S - V_L} \cdot C^* \right) \exp\left(-\frac{V_S - V_L}{D_S} \cdot z \right) - \frac{V_L}{V_S - V_L} \cdot C^* \tag{80a}$$

In the absence of liquid flow, Equation 80a takes the following form:

$$\frac{C}{C_0} = \exp\left(-\frac{V_S \cdot z}{D_S} \right) \tag{80b}$$

Very limited information is available in the literature regarding the solid phase axial mixing. Kato et al [38] used Equation 80a to find the values of solid phase axial dispersion coefficient. The authors used a 200-mm I.D. column and particle size in the range of 63 to 177 microns, and assumed that the value of D_S is independent of superficial liquid velocity. The particle settling velocity was found to increase in the presence of gas. The following correlation was proposed:

$$V'_S = 1.33 V_{S\infty} \left(\frac{V_G}{V_{S\infty}} \right)^{0.25} \left(\frac{\varepsilon_L}{1 - \varepsilon_G} \right) \tag{81}$$

Recently, Pandit and Joshi [66] measured the axial concentration profiles of particles in 200- and 385-mm I.D. three-phase sparged contactors, which were operated in a semi-batch manner ($V_L = 0$). Non-spherical particles were used and the size was varied in the range of 340 to 2,000 microns (see Figure 14 and Table 6). The following correlation has been proposed:

$$D_S = 0.33 T (V_C - 1.785 V_{SN\infty}) \tag{82}$$

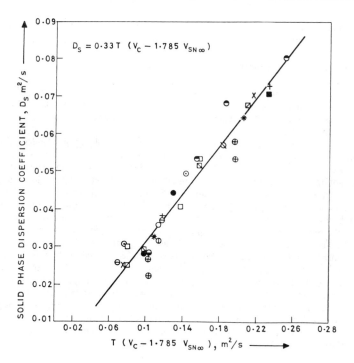

Figure 14. Correlation for solid-phase axial dispersion coefficient in three-phase sparged contactors; for symbols refer to Table 6 [66].

where $V_{SN\infty}$ is the terminal settling velocity of a non-spherical particle. On the basis of volumetric shape factors, the terminal settling velocities of equivalent spherical particles were estimated. Equation 82 takes the following form:

$$D_S = 0.33T(V_C - V_{S\infty}) \tag{83}$$

Table 6
Experimental Details for Solid Phase Axial Mixing
in Three-Phase Sparged Contactors [66]
Column Diameter = 200, 385 mm
System: Air-Water-Quartz Particles

Symbols in Figure 14 $0.0027 \leqslant \varepsilon_s \leqslant 0.05$	Average particle size (microns)	Density (kg/m³)	Terminal settling velocity	Volumetric shape factor
× ⊙ * ● +	340	2500	76	—
□ ▨ ▧	500	2500	104	—
◖ ⊘ ⊖ ◗ ①	850	2500	134	0.623
⊕	2000	2500	164	0.752

It is interesting to know that the solid-phase dispersion coefficient (D_S) tends to liquid phase axial dispersion coefficient (D_L) as the settling velocity of the particles tends to zero ($V_{s\infty} \to 0$).

EFFECT OF PHYSICAL PROPERTIES ON AXIAL MIXING

The extent of axial mixing in all the phases depend upon the physical properties of the different phases. The major influence of the physical properties occurs on the bubble size and rise velocity and on the settling velocity of the particle. As a result of these, the fractional phase hold-ups strongly depend upon the physical properties.

Earlier it was shown that the axial dispersion coefficients for liquid, gas, and solid phases in variety of equipment can be correlated with a unique parameter, namely average liquid (or continuous phase) circulation velocity, V_C. The value of V_C depends upon the net energy dissipated in the liquid motion. Therefore, for a given column diameter and superficial gas velocity if ε_G or $V_{b\infty}$ is increased, the value of V_C decreases (Equation 29). From Equation 44 it can be seen that the value of liquid phase axial dispersion coefficient decreases with a decrease in V_C. Such a observation was made by Field and Davidson [45]. Similarly, in the case of three-phase sparged reactors, an increase in the particle settling velocity (V_S) and the fractional solid phase hold-up (Equation 31) decreases V_C and hence D_L. Therefore, on the basis of Equations 29, 31, 44, 45, 50, the effect of physical properties on D_L can be explained. Similarly, the effect on the solid-phase axial dispersion coefficient (D_S) can be seen from Equations 31, 82a, and 82b. The physical properties influence the gas-phase dispersion directly as well as indirectly. Because of the changes in the gas hold-up and the rise velocity, the value of D_G varies directly (Equations 73 and 75). Indirectly, the physical properties govern the dispersion/coalescence phenomena and hence, the extent of mixing in the gas phase.

Hikita and Kikukawa [42, 67] have studied the effect of liquid viscosity and surface tension in 100- and 190-mm bubble columns. The liquid viscosity and surface tension were varied in the range of $1-20$ mPa·s and $38.2-72$ mN/m. They have proposed the following equation:

$$\left(\frac{D_L}{\sqrt{T^3 g}}\right)\left(\frac{\mu_L^4 g}{\rho_L \sigma^3}\right)^{0.03} = 0.037 + 0.188\left(\frac{V_G}{\sqrt{gT}}\right)^{0.72} \tag{83}$$

Aoyoma et al [37] and Alexander and Shah [68] have shown that the liquid-phase axial dispersion coefficient (D_L) is practically independent of the surface tension. Field and Davidsen [45] have reported that the value of D_L is about five times lower in the case of N_2-methanol system as compared with air-water system. Konig et al [69] have shown that the presence of coalescence-supressing agents reduce the value of D_L. Thus, the addition of 2% methanol and 0.5% ethanol was found to reduce D_L by a factor of 2 to 15 depending upon the value of V_G.

Recently, Kelkar et al [70] have studied the effect of addition of alcohols on axial mixing in 154- and 300-mm I.D. bubble columns. Methanol, ethanol, n-propanol, i-propanol, and n-butanol were added to water in the range of $0.5-2.4\%$ by weight. The surface tension was varied in the range of $45-72$ mN/m. The following correlation has been proposed:

$$D_L \varepsilon_L = 1.42 T^{1.33}\left\{V_G - \frac{\varepsilon_G V_L}{(1 - \varepsilon_L)}\right\}^{0.73} \tag{84}$$

All the published data previously reviewed [37, 42, 45, 67–70] can be analyzed on the basis of Equations 29, 44, and 45. Pandit and Joshi [60] made the mixing time and residence time distribution measurements in a 200-mm I.D. bubble column. They developed a mathematical model for the prediction of mixing time, and a simplified version is as follows:

$$\theta_{mix} = \frac{7.5T}{V_C}\left\{1 - 0.174\left(\frac{H}{T} - 1\right) + 0.179\left(\frac{H}{T} - 1\right)^2\right\} \tag{85}$$

where V_C is the average liquid circulation velocity given by Equation 30 in bubble columns. When the fraction of the input energy dissipated in the liquid motion given by the ratio $[(V_G - \varepsilon_G V_{b\infty})/ V_G]$ is less than 0.1, Equation 30 needs precise values of ε_G and $V_{b\infty}$. Under these conditions the following empirical equation may be used:

$$V_C = \frac{2V_G}{\varepsilon_G} T^{0.33} \tag{86}$$

Pandit and Joshi [60] have studied the effects of the presence of electrolyte, surface tension, liquid viscosity, non-Newtonian bahavior, and the presence of drag reducing agents on the values of mixing time. These effects will now be discussed systematically.

Presence of Electrolytes

Mixing time was found to increase in the presence of electrolytes. Experiments were performed using aqueous solutions of sodium sulphate (2.5 k moles/m³) and sodium chloride (5.0 k moles/ m³) in a 0.20-m I.D. bubble column with H_c/T equal to 4. Results are shown in Figure 15. As the

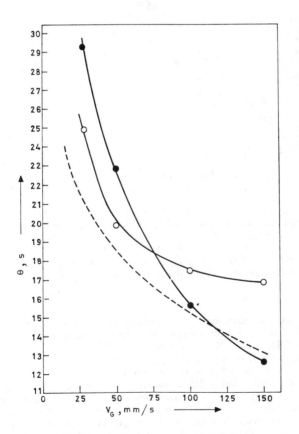

Figure 15. Effect of electrolytes on mixing time in the case of bubble columns [60].

Symbol	T, m	H_c/T	Electrolyte concentration, k ions/m³
○	0.20	6	2.5 Na_2SO_4
●	0.20	6	5.0 NaCl

Dotted line indicates the values of θ_{mix} for air-water system

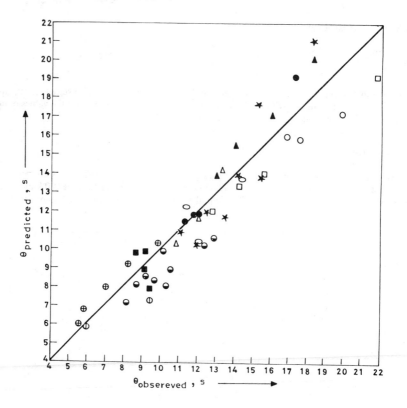

Figure 16. Comparison between the predicted (based on Equations 85 and 86) and observed values of mixing time for solutions having different physical properties [60]. $T = 0.20$ m, $H_c/T = 4$. ( ) glycerine, 50% aqueous solution; ($\oplus$) PVA, 6% aqueous solution ($T = 0.15$ m, $H_c/T = 4$); ($\blacktriangle$) PVA, 6% aqueous solution ($T = 0.15$ m, $H_c/T = 6$); ($\bullet$) butanol; ($\blacksquare$) ethanol; ($\circ$) CMC 1% by weight in water; ($\triangle$) CMC 2% by weight in water; ($\bigcirc$) Na_2SO_4, 2.5 k moles/m^3; ($\square$) NaCl, 5 k moles/m^3; ($\star$) polyethylene oxide, (PEO); ($\ominus$) glass fibers, dia $= 0.216$ mm; aspect ratio 40.

average bubble size in the electrolytes is very small, an increase in the gas-phase hold-up (ε_G) and a decrease in terminal rise velocity are expected. Further, the liquid viscosity of salt solution is higher than water. The overall effect of these factors is probably the decrease in the liquid circulation velocity, which results in an increase in the mixing time.

In order to quantify the effect of the presence of electrolytes, let us consider a case of 2.5 k moles/m^3 of Na_2SO_4 solution. The increase in the fractional gas hold-up decreases the average circulation velocity by about 18% (Equation 86). In addition, the height of dispersion also increases. The effect of a change in H and V_C on mixing time can be calculated by using Equation 85. For instance, at the superficial gas velocity of 150 mm/s, the predicted and experimental values were found to be 16.01 and 16.80 s, respectively. The corresponding values in the absence of electrolytes were found to be 13.4 and 12.89 s, respectively. A detailed comparison between the predicted (based on Equations 85 and 86) and experimental values of mixing time is given in Figure 16. A very good agreement can be seen over a wide range of the concentration of electrolytes and superficial gas velocities.

Table 7
Surface Tension of Alcohol Solution

Alcohol	Concentration % by volume	σ mN/m
Butanol	0.1	66
Butanol	1.0	57
Butanol	2.5	47
Ethanol	2.0	62

Effect of Surface Tension

To investigate the effect of surface tension ethyl and butyl alcohols were added to water. The alcohol concentration was varied in the range of 0.1 to 2.5% by volume. The changes in surface tension are given in Table 7. The experiments were performed in 0.20-m I.D. bubble column with H_c/T equal to 4. The results are shown in Figure 17. In general, it was observed that the mixing time is longer in the presence of alcohol.

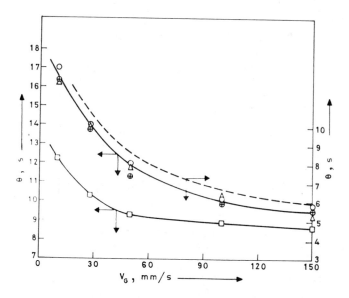

Figure 17. Effect of addition of alcohols on mixing time [60].

Symbol	T, m	H_c/T	Alcohol volume %	Type
⊕	0.2	4	0.1	Butanol
△	0.2	4	1.0	Butanol
○	0.2	4	2.5	Butanol
□	0.2	4	2.0	Ethanol

A large increase (by 100%) in the gas-phase hold-up was observed even with 0.1% butanol. The increase in fractional gas hold-up increases the total height of dispersion and probably decreases the average circulation velocity. The overall effect is that the mixing increases in the presence of alcohol.

Figure 17 indicates the concentration of alcohol has nominal effect on mixing time. Figure 16 gives a detailed comparison between observed and predicted values of mixing times based on Equations 85 and 86 in the case of alcohol/water-air system. Above the superficial gas velocity of 150 mm/s the system starts foaming and Equations 85 and 86 are not likely to hold under foaming conditions.

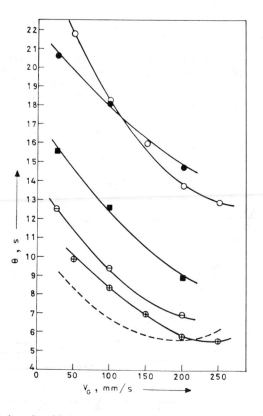

Figure 18. Effect of viscosity of fluid on mixing time [60].

Symbol	T, m	H_c/T	Solution	Viscosity, m Pa.s
●	0.20	4	90 % glycerine	121.54
○	0.15	6	6 % PVA	27.00
■	0.20	4	80 % glycerine	50.44
⊖	0.20	4	50 % glycerine	12.25
⊕	0.15	4	6 % PVA	27.00

Dotted line indicates values of θ_{mix} for air-water system (T = 0.20, H_c/T = 4)

Effect of Liquid Viscosity

The liquid viscosity was varied by using aqueous solutions of glycerine of various concentrations with viscosities 395, 121.5, 50.4, and 12.25 mPa·s, respectively. The experiments were performed in the 0.2-m I.D. column with H_c/T equal to 4 and in the range of superficial gas velocity of 28 to 200 mm/s. The results are shown in Figure 18. It can be seen that the mixing time increases with an increase in the liquid viscosity. At lower gas superficial velocities (V_G) the effect of viscosity was much more pronounced than that at higher superficial gas velocities. For viscosities greater than 100 mPa·s, gas-phase dispersion was very poor and large slugs were observed. The effect of liquid viscosity was also studied by using aqueous solutions of polyvinyl alcohol (PVA) (T = 0.15 m, H_c/T = 6). In the range of concentrations of PVA used in this work, the solutions showed New-tonian behavior. The viscosity of 6% PVA solution was found to be 27 mPa·s and surface tension 55 mN/m.

The overall effect of the changes in viscosity and surface tension leads to an increase in fractional gas hold-up (ε_G). On the basis of Equations 85 and 86 the predicted and observed values of mixing time are shown in Figure 16. Data on aqueous glycerine solutions having viscosities 395, 121.5, and 50.4 mPa·s could not be correlated on the basis of previous equations because of the slug flow behavior of gas phase. Equations 85 and 86 are not likely to be valid for slug flows. Similarly, in the case of viscosus systems the homogeneous (bubbly flow) regime may get extended to higher values of superficial gas velocities (28 to 30 mm/s). In the homogeneous bubbly flow regime, Equation 86 is not valid and hence data on mixing time for low superficial gas velocities could not be correlated.

Non-Newtonian Behavior of Liquid

Aqueous solutions of carboxy methyl cellulose (CMC) (6%, 3%, 2%, and 1%) and guar gum (0.5% and 1%) were used in the 0.20-m I.D. and 0.15-m I.D. columns, respectively. The details of the rehological properties are given in Table 8.

It has been observed in many cases that the change in pH of a non-Newtonian solution changes its rheological properties. However, in the range of pH covered in this work (3–9), the maximum change in the flow behavior index and consistency index was 10 and 15% respectively. The pertinent rheological properties are given in the same table. The change in mixing time because of this change in rheological behavior is expected to be less than 5%. Similar observations have been made by Ulbrecht and Baykara [71].

Table 8
Rheological Properties of Non-Newtonian Fluids [60]

Sr. no.	Material	Concentration % by weight	n B*	n A	$k\,Pa\cdot s^n$ B*	$k\,Pa\cdot s^n$ A
1	Carboxy methyl cellulose	6	0.58	0.62**	3.48	3.12**
2	Carboxy methyl cellulose	3	0.47	0.54**	1.202	1.02**
3	Carboxy methyl cellulose	2	0.86	0.96†	0.19	0.15†
4	Carboxy methyl cellulose	1	1.00	1.00	0.0485	0.0485
5	Guar Gum	0.5	0.60	0.68**	0.135	0.103**
6	Guar Gum	1	0.64	0.75†	0.225	0.182†

* *refers to pH value of 7.0*
† *refers to pH value of 3.0*
** *refers to pH value of 9.0 $\pm$ 0.2*

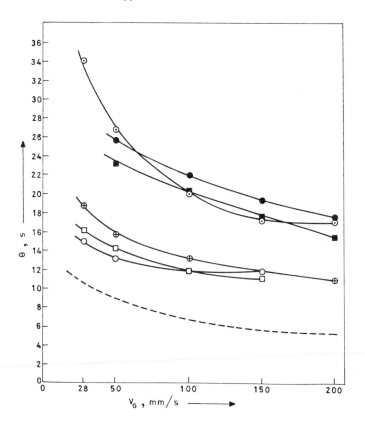

Figure 19. Effect of non-Newtonian behavior on mixing time [60].

Symbol	T, m	H_c/T	Solution
⊙	0.20	4	6 % CMC
●	0.15	6	1 % guar gum
■	0.15	6	0.5 % guar gum
⊕	0.20	4	3 % CMC
□	0.20	4	1 % CMC
○	0.20	4	2 % CMC

Dotted line indicates values of θ_{mix} for air-water system (T = 0.20 m, H_c/T = 4)

It can be seen from Figure 19 that the mixing time increases with an increase in k values. This conclusion is drawn when the results of mixing time at a shear rate of 750 s^{-1} (V_G = 150 mm/s, Nishikawa et al. [72])were compared with aqueous solutions of glycerine having equivalent viscosity. A detailed comparison is given in Table 9. As seen from this table, larger the deviation in k values more is the increase in mixing time. Data on mixing time for 2% and 1% CMC are compared with the predicted values (Equations 85 and 86) in Figure 16. Data for 6% and 3% CMC solutions could not be correlated as slugs and large bubbles were observed, respectively. The difference is substantial at low values of V_G and progressively reduces as V_G increases.

Table 9
Comparison of Mixing Times for Newtonian and
Non-Newtonian Behavior of Fluids with
Same Apparent Viscosity [60]

Sr. no.	Viscosity mPa·s	Newtonian, Aqueous glycerine		Non-Newtonian	
		Conc. %	θ_{mix}, s	CMC, %	θ_{mix}, s
1	23.7	70	10.8	6	18.6
2	12.9	50	8.32	3	12.35
3	10.2	47	7.75	2	10.80
4	4.85		—	1	11.28
				guar gum	
5	2.68		11.8*	1	16.5
6	1.18		11.8*	0.5	14.2

for air-water system

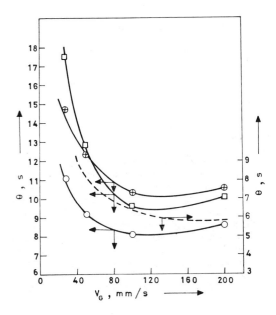

Figure 20. Effect of drag reducing agent on mixing time—glass fibres, aspect ratio 40 [60].

Symbol	T, m	H_c/T	Concentration, ppm
○	0.20	4	500
⊕	0.20	4	1000
□	0.20	4	1500

Dotted line indicates the values of θ_{mix} for air-water system

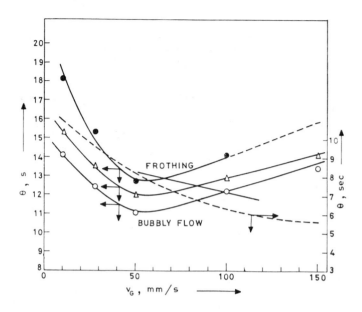

Figure 21. Effect of drag reducing agent on mixing time—polyethylene oxide (PEO) [60].

Symbol	T, m	H_c/T	Concentration, ppm
○	0.20	4	50
△	0.20	4	300
●	0.20	4	500

Dotted line indicates the values of θ_{mix} for air-water system.

Effect of Drag Reducing Agents

Glass fibres of 0.214-mm diameter and aspects ratio of 40 were used on 0.20-m I.D. bubble column. The level of concentration of fibre glass was 500, 1,000, and 1,500 ppm. Polyethylene oxide (PEO) was also used in the concentration range of 50—500 ppm. Experiments were performed in the 0.20-m I.D. bubble column with H_c/T ratio of four. The results are shown in Figures 20 and 21.

In the presence of drag reducing agents, the fractional gas hold-up increases. The mixing time data are analyzed on the basis of Equations 85 and 86 and a comparison between the predicted and experimental values of mixing time is shown in Figure 16, which illustrates very good agreement. It may be pointed out that substantial frothing occurred when the concentration of PEO was greater than a certain concentration that depends on V_G (Figure 21). Under these conditions, Equation 86 will not hold. The operation of bubble column will be unstable under frothing conditions, and it is essential that the amount of drag reducing agents be kept low. Figure 21 shows the bubbly and frothing regions.

CONCLUSION

☐ The extent of axial mixing of liquid, gas and solid phases can be correlated on the basis of continuous phase flow pattern. It has been shown that the relationship between continuous phase axial dispersion coefficient and the average circulation velocity is similar in a variety of equipment.
☐ The following equations are recommended to calculate the values of axial dispersion coefficient: Continuous Phase

1. *Bubble columns, three-phase sparged reactors and gas-solid fluidized beds*

$$D_L = (0.29 \pm 0.04)T(V_C + V_L)$$

2. *Solid-liquid fluidized beds*

$$D_L = 3.7D_e V_S$$

3. *Packed bubble column*

$$D_L = 2.5D_e V_c$$

Gas Phase (Bubble Column)

$$D_G = 110 \frac{V_G^2}{\varepsilon_G} T^2$$

Solid Phase (Three-Phase Sparged Contactor)

$$D_S = 0.33T(V_C - V_{S\infty})$$

The physical properties can change the extent of mixing dramatically. It is suggested that the experiments be performed on a small-scale apparatus using the desired system and the results be extrapolated to the large-size equipment using correlations presented here.
□ Very little information is available in the literature on the following aspects:

1. Liquid, gas, and solid-phase axial mixing in the homogeneous regime.
2. The mixing behavior during the transition from homogeneous to heterogeneous regime.
3. The extent of mixing, under the conditions of practical importance. For instance, sparged contactors are used at elevated temperatures and pressures.
4. For variety of gas-liquid and gas-liquid-solid systems, it is likely that for identical physical properties, the dispersion characteristics are different.
5. Gas-phase and solid-phase axial mixing need to be studied systematically.

□ Modeling of large-scale operating equipment enhances the confidence in the available prediction procedures for the degree of axial mixing in different phases.

NOTATION

a_p dry surface area of the solid packing per unit contactor volume, m^2/m^3

A distance between the column axis and the point of zero velocity where the change in flow direction occurs, m

C concentration of solids, kg/m^3

C^* concentration of solids in feed, kg/m^3

C_0 concentration of solids at the bottom $(z = 0)$, kg/m^3

d pipe diameter, m

d_B average bubble diameter, m

d_G equivalent column diameter for the gas phase, m

d_p average particle diameter, m

D molecular diffusivity, m^2/s

D_e equivalent diameter of the void area in solid-liquid fluidized beds and packed bubble columns, m

D_E emulsion phase or continuous phase axial dispersion coefficient, m^2/s

D_G gas-phase axial dispersion coefficient, m^2/s

D_L liquid phase axial dispersion coefficient, m^2/s

D_0 equivalent diameter of the downflow area in bubble column, m

D_S solid phase axial dispersion coefficient, m^2/s

e_B energy dissipation rate in the vicinity of a single bubble or particle, W

E	energy dissipation rate in the liquid motion, W		mum fluidization in solid-liquid fluidized beds
E_B	energy dissipation rate at the gas-liquid interface, W	T	column diameter, m
E_i	energy input rate, W	u_y'	turbulence intensity, m/s
E_L	energy recovery rate because of the pumping of liquid, W	v_r	radial component of the liquid velocity, m/s
E_S	energy dissipation rate in the vicinity of solid particles, W	v_y	component of the liquid velocity in y direction, m/s
E_{SL}	energy dissipation rate in the vicinity of packings in packed bubble columns, W	v_z	axial component of the liquid velocity, m/s
f'	friction factor	v_y'	turbulence intensity, m/s
g	acceleration due to gravity, m/s^2	v_z'	turbulence intensity, m/s
H	height of dispersion, m	V_a	vertical (axial) component of the liquid velocity at the column axis, m/s
H_c	clear height of the liquid, m	V_C	average continuous phase circulation velocity, m/s
H_T	total height of the contactor, m		
k_2	proportionality constant in Equation 21	V_G	superficial gas velocity, m/s
l	mixing length, m	V_{GC}	superficial gas velocity at which the transition form homogeneous to heterogeneous regime occurs, m/s
N_B	number of bubbles		
N_{Re}	Reynolds number, Equation 46	V_L	superficial liquid velocity, m/s
Pe	Peclet number, HV_S/D_L	V_0	average rise velocity of the gas phase with respect to the column wall, m/s
P_m	power consumption per unit mass, W/kg		
r	axisymmetric or radial coordinate, m	V_S	hindered settling velocity or interstitial fluidization velocity, m/s
r^*	dimensionless axisymmetric or radial coordinate	$V_{b\infty}$	terminal rise velocity of bubble, m/s
R	column radius, m	V_{mf}	minimum fluidization velocity, m/s
R_1	radial component of the dimensionless stream function	$V_{s\infty}$	terminal settling velocity of a particle, m/s
		V_1	local velocity, m/s
Re	particle Reynolds number, $d_p V_S \rho_L/\mu_L$	y	distance from the column wall, m
Re_G	Reynolds number for the gas phase, Equation 77	z	axial coordinate, m
		z^*	dimensionless axial coordinate
$(Re)_{mf}$	particle Reynolds number at mini-	Z	axial component of the dimensionless stream function

Greek Symbols

α	ratio of wake volume to bubble volume	ψ	stream function
δ	sparger hole diameter, m	ψ_0	maximum value of the stream function
ρ	density, kg/m^3	τ	turbulent shear stress, N/m^2
ε	fractional phase hold-up	σ	surface tension, N/m
μ	viscosity, Pa·s	ω	vorticity
θ_{mix}	mixing time, s		

Subscripts

C	continuous phase	G	gas
D	dispersed phase	L	liquid
F	fluidized emulsion phase	S	solid
SN	non-spherical		

Superscripts

°	local value

REFERENCES

1. Shah, Y. T., Stigel, G. J. and Sharma, M. M., "Backmixing in Gas-Liquid Reactors," *A.I.Ch.E.J.*, vol. 24, no. 3, pp. 369–400, 1978.
2. Joshi, J. B., "Axial Mixing in Multiphase Contactors—A Unified Correlation," *Trans. Instn. Chem. Engrs.*, vol. 58, no. 3, pp. 155–165, 1980.
3. Joshi, J. B., "Axial Mixing in Multiphase Contactors—A Unified Correlation," *Trans. Instn. Chem. Engrs.*, vol. 59, no. 1, pp. 139–143, 1981.
4. Joshi, J. B., "Gas Phase Dispersion in Bubble Columns," *Chem. Eng. J.*, vol. 24, no. 3, pp. 213–216, 1982.
5. Joshi, J. B., "Solid-Liquid Fluidized Beds—Some Design Aspects." *Chem. Eng. Res. Des.*, vol. 61, no. 3, pp. 143–161, 1983.
6. Whalley, P. B. and Davidsen, J. F., "Liquid Circulation in Bubble Columns," in *Proceedings of the Symposium on Multiphase Flow Systems, Symp. Ser. No. 38*, London: The Institution of Chemical Engineers, p. J5, 1974.
7. Joshi, J. B. and Sharma, M. M., "A Circulation Cell Model for Bubble Columns." *Trans. Instn. Chem. Engrs.*, vol. 57, no. 4, pp. 244–251, 1979.
8. Joshi, J. B. and Sharma, M. M., "Liquid Phase Flow Pattern in Bubble Columns." *Trans. Instn. Chem. Engrs.*, vol. 60, no. 4, pp. 255–256, 1982.
9. Joshi, J. B. and Shah, Y. T., "Hydrodynamic and Mixing Models for Bubble Column Reactors," *Chem. Eng. Communications*, vol. 11, pp. 156–199, 1981.
10. Ueyama, K. and Miyauchi, T., "Properties of Recirculating Turbulent Two-Phase Flow in Gas Bubble Columns," *A.I.Ch.E.J.*, vol. 25, no. 2, pp. 258–266, 1979.
11. Kojima, E. et al., "Liquid-Phase Velocity in a 5.5-m Diameter Column," *J. Chem. Eng. Japan*, vol. 13, no. 1, pp. 16–21, 1980.
12. Morooka, S., Uchida, K., and Kato, Y., "Recirculating Turbulent Flow of Liquid in Gas-Liquid-Solid Fluidized Bed," *J. Chem. Eng. Japan*, vol. 15, no. 1, pp. 29–34, 1982.
13. Nottenkamper, R., Steiff, A., and Weinspach, P. M., "Experimental Investigation of Hydrodynamics of Bubble Columns," *Ger. Chem. Eng.*, vol. 6, no. 3, pp. 147–155, 1983.
14. Rietema, K., "Science and Technology of Dispersed Two-Phase Systems—I and II," *Chem. Eng. Sci.*, vol. 37, no. 8, pp. 1125–1150, 1982.
15. Joshi, J. B. and Lali, A. M., "Velocity-Hold-up Relationships in Multiphase Reactors—A Unified Approach," In *Frontiers in Chemical Reaction Engineering*, vol. 1 L. K. Doraiswamy and R. A. Mashelkar, (eds.) New Delhi: Wiley Eastern, pp. 314–329, 1984.
16. Joshi, J. B. and Sharma, M. M., "Mass Transfer Characteristics of Horizontal Sparged Contactors," *Trans. Instn. Chem. Engrs.*, vol. 54, no. 1, pp. 42–53, 1976.
17. Joshi, J. B., "Energy Balance in Multiphase Contactors," *Trans. Instn. Chem. Engrs.*, vol. 60, no. 1, pp. 126, 1982.
18. Lehrer, I. H., "Energy Balance in Multiphase Contactors." *Trans. Instn. Chem. Engrs.*, vol. 60, no. 1, pp. 125–126, 1982.
19. Field, R. W. and Davidson, J. F., "Energy Balance in Multiphase Contactors." *Trans. Instn. Chem. Engrs.*, vol. 60, no. 1, pp. 126–127, 1982.
20. Lamb, H., *Hydrodynamics*. Sixth ed., Cambridge: University Press, p. 236, 1946.
21. Van den Akker, H. E. A. and Rietema, K., "Flow Patterns and Axial Mixing in Liquid-Liquid Spray Columns," *Trans. Instn. Chem. Engrs.*, vol. 57, no. 3, pp. 147–155, 1979.
22. Hills, J. H., "Radial Non-Uniformity of Velocity and Voidage in a Bubble Column." *Trans. Instn. Chem. Engrs.*, vol. 52, no. 1, pp. 1–9, 1974.
23. Joshi, J. B., et al., "Heat Transfer in Multiphase Contactors." *Chem. Eng. Communications*, vol. 6, pp. 257–271, 1980.
24. Pavlov, V. P., "Tsirkulyatsiya Zhidkosti V Barbotazhnom Apparate Periodicheskogo Deistviya." *Khim. Prom.*, no. 9, pp. 698, 1965.
25. Pozin, L. S., Aerov, M. E., and Bystrova, T. A., *Theoretical Foundations of Chemical Engineering* (English Translation), vol. 3, pp. 714, 1969.
26. Miyauchi, T. and Shyu, C. N., "Flow of Fluid in Gas Bubble Columns," *Kagaku Kogaku*, vol. 34, pp. 958, 1970.
27. Danckwerts, P. V., "Continuous Flow Systems." *Chem. Eng. Sci.*, vol. 2, no. 1, pp. 1, 1953.

28. Brodkey, R. S., "Fundamentals of Turbulent Motion: Mixing and Kinetics," *Chem. Eng. Communications*, vol. 8, pp. 1–23, 1981.

29. Nauman, E. B., "Residence Time Distributions and Micromixing," *Chem. Eng. Communications*, vol. 8, pp. 53–131, 1981.

30. Turner, J. C. R., "Perspectives in Residence—Time Distributions," *Chem. Eng. Sci.*, vol. 38, no. 1, pp. 1–4, 1983.

31. Bourne, J. R., "Mixing on the Molecular Scale—Micromixing," *Chem. Eng. Sci.*, vol. 38, no. 1, pp. 5–8, 1983.

32. Levenspiel, O., *Chemical Reaction Engineering* New York: John Wiley and Sons, Inc., pp. 253–346, 1972.

33. Taylor, G. I., "The Dispersion of Matter in Turbulent Flow through a Pipe," *Proc. Royal Soc. (London)*, vol. A223, pp. 446–468, 1954.

34. Baird, M. H. I. and Rice, R. G., "Axial Dispersion in Large Unbaffled Columns," *Chem. Eng. J.*, vol. 9, no. 2, pp. 171–174, 1975.

35. Argo, W. B. and Cova, D. R., "Longitudinal Mixing in Gas-Sparged Tubular Vessels," *Ind. Eng. Chem: Proc. Des. Develop.* vol. 4, no. 4, pp. 352–359, 1965.

36. Reith, T., Renken, S., and Israel, B. A., "Gas Hold-up and Axial Mixing in the Fluid Phase of Bubble Columns," *Chem. Eng. Sci.*, vol. 23, no. 6, pp. 619–629, 1968.

37. Aoyoma, Y. et al., "Liquid Mixing in Co-current Bubble Columns," *J. Chem. Eng. Japan*, vol. 1, no. 2, pp. 158–163, 1968.

38. Kato, Y. and Nishiwaki, A., "Longitudinal Dispersion Coefficient of a Liquid in a Bubble column." *Int. Chem. Eng.*, vol. 12, no. 1, pp. 182–187, 1972.

39. Towell, G. D. and Ackerman, G. H., "Axial Mixing of Liquid and Gas in Large Bubble Column Reactors," in *Proceedings of the fifth European/Second International Symposium on Chemical Reaction Engineering*, Amsterdam: Elsevier, pp. B3:1–13, 1972.

40. Deckwer, W. D., et al., "Zones of Different Mixing in the Liquid Phase of Bubble Columns." *Chem. Eng. Sci.*, vol. 28, no. 5, pp. 1223–1225, 1973.

41. Deckwer, W. D., Burckhart, R., and Zoll, G., "Mixing and Mass Transfer in Tall Bubble Columns." *Chem. Eng. Sci.*, vol. 29, no. 12, pp. 2177–2188, 1974.

42. Hikita, H. and Kikukawa, H., "Liquid Phase Mixing in Bubble Columns: Effect of Liquid Properties," *Chem. Eng. J.*, vol. 8, no. 3, pp. 191–197, 1974.

43. Ostergaard, K., "Hold-up, Mass Transfer, and Mixing in Three-Phase Fluidization," *A.I.Ch.E. Symp. Ser. No. 176*, vol. 74, pp. 82–86, 1978.

44. Vail, Yu. K., Manakov, N. Kh., and Manshilin, V. V., "Turbulent Mixing in a Three-Phase Fluidized Bed," *Int. Chem. Eng.*, vol. 8, no. 2, pp. 293–296, 1968.

45. Field, R. W. and Davidson, J. F., "Axial Dispersion in Bubble Columns." *Trans. Instn. Chem. Engrs.*, vol. 58, no. 4, pp. 228, 1980.

46. Kato, Y., Fukuda, T., and Tanaka, S., "The Behavior of Suspended Solid Particles and Liquid in Bubble Columns." *J. Chem. Eng. Japan*, vol. 5, no. 2, pp. 112, 1972.

47. Michelson, M. L. and Ostergaard, K., "Hold-up and Fluid Mixing in Gas-Liquid Fluidized Beds," *Chem. Eng. J.*, vol. 1, no. 1, pp. 37–46, 1970.

48. May, W. G., "Fluidized Bed Reactor Studies," *Chem. Eng. Progr.*, vol. 55, no. 12, pp. 49–52, 1959.

49. deGroot, G. H., In *Proc. Int. Symp. Fluidization*, Drinkenburgh, A.A.H., (ed.) Amsterdam: Netherland Univ. Press, pp. 348, 1967.

50. Schugerl, K., "Rhelogical Behavior of Fluidized Systems," in *Fluidization*, Davidson, J. F. and Harrison, D., (eds.) London: Academic Press, pp. 261–291, 1971.

51. Mashelkar, R. A. and Ramchandran, P. A., "Longitudinal Dispersion in Circulation-Dominated Bubble Columns." *Trans. Instn. Chem. Engrs.*, vol. 53, no. 4, pp. 274–277, 1975.

52. Kumar, R. and Kuloor, N. R., "Formation of Bubbles and Drops" In *Advances in Chemical Engineering*, vol. 8, T. B. Drew *et al.* Eds. New York: Academic Press, 1970, pp. 256-365.

53. Taylor, G. I., "Dispersion of Soluble Matter in Solvent Flowing Through a Pipe" *Proc. Roy. Soc. (London)*, vol. A219, 1953, pp. 186–203.

54. Ohki, Y. and Inoue, H., "Longitudinal Mixing of the Liquid Phase in Bubble Columns" *Chem. Eng. Sci.*, vol. 25, no. 1, Jan. 1970, pp. 1–16.

55. Chung, S. F. and Wen, C. Y., "Longitudinal Dispersion of Liquid Flowing Through Fixed and Fluidized Beds." *A.I.Ch.E.J.*, vol. 14, no. 6, Nov. 1968, pp. 857–866.
56. Krishnaswamy, P. R., Ganapathy, R. and Shemilt, L. W., "Correlating Parameters for Axial Dispersion in Liquid Fluidized Systems." *Can. J. Chem. Eng.*, vol. 56, no. 5, Oct. 1978, pp. 550–553.
57. Tichacek, L. J., Barkelew, C. H. and Baron, T. "Axial Mixing in Pipes." *A.I.Ch.E.J.* vol. 3, no. 4, Dec. 1957, pp. 439–442.
58. Niranjan, K., "Hydrodynamic and Mass Transfer Characteristics of Packed Columns." Ph.D. (Tech.) Thesis, Univ. of Bombay, 1983.
59. Joshi, J. B. and Sharma, M. M., "Some Design Features of Radial Baffles in Sectionalized Bubble Columns." *Can. J. Chem. Eng.* vol. 57, no. 3, June 1979. pp. 375–377.
60. Pandit, A. B. and Joshi, J. B., "Mixing in Mechanically Agitated Contactors, Bubble Columns and Modified Bubble Columns." *Chem. Eng. Sci.*, vol. 38, no. 8, Aug. 1983, pp. 1189–1215.
61. Kolbel, H., Langemann, H., and Platz, J., *Dechema Monographien*, vol. 41, pp. 225, 1962.
62. Carleton, A. J. et al., "Some Properties of Packed Bubble Column," *Chem. Eng. Sci.*, vol. 22, no. 12, pp. 1839–1845, 1967.
63. Men'shchikov, V. A. and Aerov, M. E., *Theor. Found. Chem. Eng.* (English translation), vol. 12, pp. 739, 1967.
64. Pilhofer, Th., Bach, H. F., and Mangartz, K. H., "Investigation of Gas-Phase Dispersion in Bubble Column Reactor," *5th Int. Symp. Chem. Reaction Engineering* 31, ACS Washington D.C., 1978.
65. Seher, A. and Schumacher, V., "Determination of Residence Times of Liquid and Gas Phases in Large Bubble Columns with the Aid of Radioactive Tracers," *Ger. Chem. Eng.*, vol. 2, no. 2, pp. 117–122, 1979.
66. Pandit, A. B. and Joshi, J. B., "Some Design Aspects of Three-Phase Sparged Reactors," *Reviews in Chemical Eng.*, 1984, Forwarded for publication.
67. Hikita, H. and Kikukawa, H., "Dimensionless Correlation of Liquid Phase Dispersion Coefficient in Bubble Columns," *J. Chem. Eng. Japan*, vol. 8, no. 5, pp. 412–413, 1975.
68. Alexander, B. F. and Shah, Y. T., "Axial Dispersion Coefficient in Bubble Columns." *Chem. Eng. J.*, vol. 11, no. 2, pp. 153–156, 1976.
69. Konig, B. R., et al., "Longitudinal Mixing of the Liquid Phase in Bubble Columns," *Ger. Chem. Eng.*, vol. 1, no. 4, pp. 199–205, 1978.
70. Kelkar, B. G., et al., "Effect of Addition of Alcohols in Gas Hold-up and Backmixing in Bubble Columns," *A.I.Ch.E.J.* vol. 29, no. 3, pp. 361–369, 1983.
71. Ulbrecht, J. J. and Baykara, L. S., "Significance of the Central Plume Velocity for the Correlation of Liquid Phase Mixing in Bubble Columns." *Chem. Eng. Communications*, vol. 10, no.1–3, pp. 165–185, 1981.
72. Nishikawa, M., Kato, H. and Hashimoto, K., "Heat Transfer in Aerated Tower Filled with Non-Newtonian Liquid," *Ind. Eng. Chem: Proc. Des. Develop.*, vol. 16, no. 1, pp. 133–137, 1977.
73. Pavlica, R. T. and Olson, J. H., "Unified Design Method for Continuous Contact Mass Transfer Operations," *Ind. Eng. Chem.*, vol. 62, no. 12, pp. 45–58, 1970.

CHAPTER 38

FLOW PATTERNS IN BUBBLE COLUMNS

K. Viswanathan

Particle Technology Consultants Research Centre
B-113/2, East of Kailash
New Delhi-110 065, INDIA

CONTENTS

INTRODUCTION

Bubble columns are gas-liquid contactors in which a relative motion exists between gas in the form of bubbles and the continuous liquid phase. Essentially in such columns, there is no net movement of the liquid, or the superficial liquid velocity is so small compared to the average liquid circulation velocity that it can be neglected. This chapter deals only with the case of no net movement of the liquid. However, the results can be extended easily to cases where the liquid moves co-currently or counter-currently to the rising gas bubbles. Further, only the case of bubbles rising due to free convection in the gravitational force field is treated here. Due to their simplicity and absence of moving parts, bubble columns are widely used in the process industry as absorbers, strippers, gas-liquid reactors, etc. High pressure drop, liquid back-mixing, and gas channeling due to bubble coalescence can be disadvantages in some cases. However, these can be overcome by

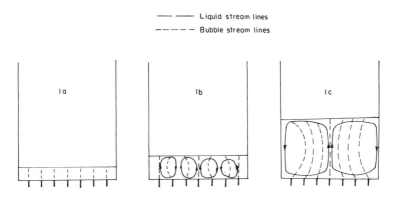

Figure 1. Illustration of liquid circulation induced by bubble movement in bubble columns.

using modified designs [1]. Bubbling of gas in a pool of liquid is illustrated in Figure 1. When the liquid depth is low (Figure 1A) the bubbles forming over each orifice rise in a straight path apparently without sensing the adjacent bubbles. When the liquid depth is increased (Figure 1B), bubbles from an orifice tend to bend toward bubbles from an adjacent orifice. The density difference between the bubble-lean and the bubble-rich zones causes the liquid to circulate as shown. When the liquid depth is further increased (Figure 1C) the interaction between adjacent bubbles is so strong that only a single axially symmetric circulation cell is formed; in the case of two-dimensional bubble columns, two circulation cells are formed side by side. The liquid circulation thus caused results in a high degree of backmixing. Further, due to circulation, the rise velocity of the bubbles is increased, which results in reduced gas hold-up and interfacial area. The performance of such gas-liquid contactors is greatly influenced by backmixing, gas hold-up and interfacial area, which are in turn interrelated with the liquid circulation. Thus, liquid flow patterns in bubble columns become of paramount importance.

Liquid circulation in bubble columns can be analyzed by considering the two extreme cases of the predominance of either viscous or inertial forces. In this chapter, an inviscid model and a viscous model are presented for circulation in axi-symmetric bubble columns. The results of the two models are combined to obtain the validity region of each of the two models. The theoretically interesting case of circulation in a two-dimensional bubble column has been treated elsewhere [3, 19].

LITERATURE REVIEW

Only a brief account of the available literature on the topic is presented here. For more detailed accounts the reader is referred to some recent reviews [1, 2]. Numerous investigators, as detailed elsewhere [3], have experimentally measured liquid circulation induced by bubble movement. The experimental techniques for determining the flow patterns in bubble columns are not reviewed here.

Flow Regimes

Three different flow regimes have been identified [4] to occur in bubble columns. These regimes are illustrated in Figure 2 [1, 4, 5]. They are

1. *Homogeneous bubbly flow regime*, which occurs generally for superficial gas velocity (U_G) less than 0.05 m/s. This regime is characterized by small uniformly sized bubbles with a rise velocity in the range 0.18 to 0.3 m/s [6].

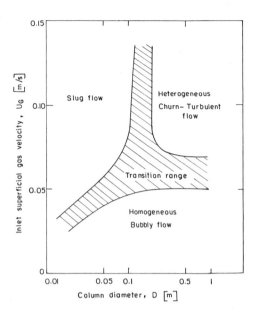

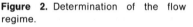

Figure 2. Determination of the flow regime.

2. *Heterogeneous or churn-turbulent regime*, which is characterized by the simultaneous presence of large and small bubbles [7]. The large bubbles can be of sizes about 0.08 to 0.15 m with rise velocities greater than about 0.8 m/s. The fraction of gas that bypasses through large bubbles with very short residence times can be roughly obtained [1] from Figure 3. It can be seen that for gas velocities greater than about 0.1 m/s, about three-fourths of the entering gas bypasses the column through large bubbles.
3. *Slug flow regime*, where large bubbles (called slugs) occupy the entire column cross-section. As can be seen from Figure 2 slug flow can occur only in small diameter laboratory bubble columns. Slug flow is not considered in this chapter.

In Figure 2, the transition between the different flow regimes is affected by the type of sparger and the physicochemical properties of the liquid. For example, slug flow can occur at lower veloc-

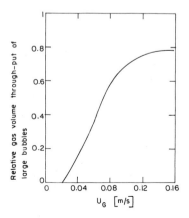

Figure 3. Fraction of inlet gas rising as large bubbles.

ities than shown in Figure 2 for highly viscous liquids [1]. Similarly, bubbly flow can be extended to higher gas velocities with porous distributors with pore sizes less than 150 microns [4] or with flexible spargers [8].

We are concerned here primarily with the flow patterns in the first two flow regimes, namely, the homogeneous bubbly flow and the heterogeneous churn-turbulent flow regimes.

Bubble Parameters

The important bubble parameters are bubble diameter, isolated bubble rise velocity, bubble hold-up, and the gas-liquid specific interfacial area.

In the bulk region of the bubble column, due to the shear fields present, bubble sizes greater than a maximum value are unstable and liable to rupture. The Weber number,

$$We = \rho_L \overline{u^2} d_b / \sigma \tag{1}$$

which is the ratio of the inertial forces deforming the bubble and the surface tension forces maintaining the shape of the bubble, determines the maximum stable bubble diameter, d_{bm} [9, 10]. In the Weber number, u^2 is the mean square velocity difference over a distance equal to the bubble diameter d_b, which is the diameter of the sphere having the same volume as the bubble. For isotropic turbulence it follows that [9–11]

$$u^2 = 2(Pd_b/V\rho_L)^{2/3} \tag{2}$$

where P/V is the energy dissipation rate per unit volume of dispersion. The critical Weber number has been obtained by Lewis and Davidson [12] to be 4.7. Letting $We_c = 4.7$ in Equation 1 and using Equation 2, Lewis and Davidson [12] obtained

$$d_{bm} = 1.67(\sigma^3 V^2/P^2 \rho_L)^{0.2} \tag{3}$$

In a bubble column the energy input rate, neglecting the kinetic energy of the entering gas, is

$$P_i = (\rho_L gL)(A_t U_G) \tag{4}$$

Equating P with P_i and substituting $A_t L$ for V in Equation 3 leads to

$$d_{bm} = 1.67(\sigma^3/\rho_L^3 g^2 U_G^2)^{0.2} \tag{5}$$

It may be noted that similar analyses have been made by many investigators [13–17] for similar or different systems. It must be pointed out that the validity of Equation 6 is yet to be checked with experimental data. In a bubble column, bubbles will be coalescing and rupturing continuously (Figure 3). A coalesced bubble of size greater than d_{bm} cannot rupture instantaneously. If the time for rupturing exceeds the residence time of the bubble in the column then there is no meaning in a d_{bm} value. How much time it takes for a coalesced bubble to rupture is not known. Strictly, Equation 5 is valid only for non-coalescing systems.

In any case, the bulk region of a bubble column will contain a distribution of bubble sizes. Such a distribution is often characterized by the volume-to-surface mean bubble diameter, also called the Sauter mean diameter, and is defined as

$$d_{vs} = \frac{6(\text{volume of bubbles})}{(\text{total gas-liquid interfacial area})} \tag{6}$$

Akita and Yoshida [18] have reported experimental d_{vs} values for several liquids. Assuming the form of the equation for d_{vs} to be the same as that for d_{bm} (Equation 5), the following equation is tested with their data in Figure 4.

$$d_{vs} = C(\sigma^3/\rho_{LG}^3 g^2 U_G^2)^{0.2} \tag{7}$$

A mean value of C for the dotted line is 1.02 with 60% mean deviation. However, it can be seen from Figure 4 that the C value shows a definite increasing trend with the inlet gas velocity. Hence, an empirical fit of the C value as shown by the full line results in the following expression for d_{vs}:

$$d_{vs} = \ln(7.768 U_G^{0.26})[\sigma^3/\rho_{LG}^3 g^2 U_G^2]^{0.2} \tag{7a}$$

with 25% mean deviation. Akita and Yoshida's empirical correlation indicated d_{vs} to be proportional to $D^{-0.3}$, whereas Equation 7a, which has some theoretical basis, does not show any effect of D on d_{vs}. Koide et al. [33] have reported bubble sizes in a 5.5-m diameter bubble column at $U_G = 0.024$ to 0.044 m/s to be about 15 mm. For this data, Akita and Yoshida's correlation (even with $D = 0.6$ m) predicts d_{vs} to be about 4 mm, whereas Equation 7a predicts d_{vs} to be about 6 mm. Though no general conclusions can be drawn from this limited comparison, it is evident that in large shallow bubble columns coalesced bubbles greater in size than the maximum stable size do not stay in the column for long enough time to get ruptured. This is an important point that must be clarified by further research. The estimation of bubble size in stagnant and flowing fluids is the detailed subject matter of Chapter 4 by Vogelpohl and Rabiger.

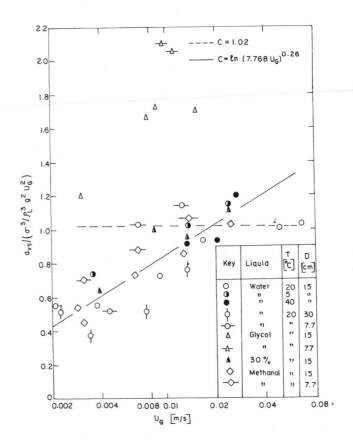

Figure 4. Determination of a relation for Sauter mean bubble diameter, d_{vs}.

More than the bubble diameter, it is the isolated bubble rise velocity (u_{br}) that influences (as will be shown) the flow patterns in bubble columns. For many liquids u_{br} is essentially a constant equal to 0.235 m/s for a bubble size range of 3 to 8 mm diameter [19, 20]. However, for bubbles not in this size range, Clift et al.'s [21] equation may be used:

$$u_{br} = \frac{\mu}{\rho_L d_{vs}} M^{-0.149}(J - 0.857) \tag{8}$$

where
$$M = g\mu^4(\rho_L - \rho)/\rho_L^2\sigma^3$$
$$J = \begin{array}{l} 0.94 H^{0.747} \quad 2 < H < 59.3 \\ 3.42 H^{0.441} \quad\quad H > 59.3 \end{array}$$
$$H = (\tfrac{4}{3}Eo)M^{-0.149}(\mu/\mu_{water})^{-0.14}$$
$$Eo = g(\rho_L - \rho)d_{vs}^2/\sigma$$

for the range $M < 10^{-3}$, $Eo < 40$, $Re > 0.1$ (where $Re = d_{vs}u_{br}\rho_L/\mu$). Typical predictions of Equation 8 are given in Figure 5 for ready estimation of u_{br}. The correlations for bubble rise is the detailed subject matter of Chapter 6 by Abou-El Hasan.

The specific interfacial area is related to gas hold-up' (δ) and volume-to-surface mean bubble diameter (d_{vs}) by the following relationship, which follows from Equation 6:

$$a = 6\delta/d_{vs} \tag{9}$$

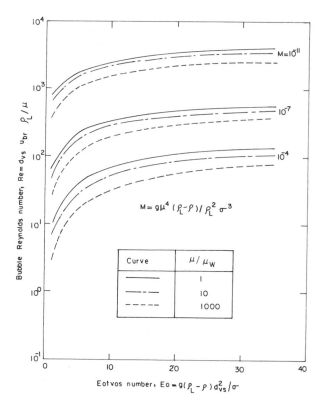

Figure 5. Determination of isolated bubble rise velocity.

Thus, prediction of the bubble parameters would be complete if an expression for bubble hold-up can be derived. It will be shown that the model for flow patterns to be presented below would automatically lead to a theoretical expression for bubble hold-up too.

Inviscid Models

The vector "vorticity" plays an important role in inviscid models and will be valid under highly turbulent conditions where viscous effects are negligible. Inviscid models describing liquid circulation in axi-symmetric bubble columns are those of Whalley and Davidson [20], Joshi and Sharma [22], and Field and Davidson [23]. The reader is referred to standard texts [24, 25] for basic background information.

The starting equation in all the inviscid models [20, 22, 23] describing circulation in axi-symmetric bubble columns is [20, 24, 25]

$$\frac{\partial^2 \psi}{\partial r^2} - \frac{1}{r}\frac{\partial \psi}{\partial r} + \frac{\partial^2 \psi}{\partial y^2} = -K_3^4 r^2 \psi \tag{10}$$

with the no-flow boundary conditions at the column axis and the vessel boundaries given by

$$\psi = 0 \quad \text{at } r = 0 \text{ and } R \text{ for all } y \tag{11}$$

$$\psi = 0 \quad \text{at } y = 0 \text{ and } L \text{ for all } r \tag{12}$$

where Ψ is the liquid stream function.

Equation 10 implies that the velocity divided by the radial distance from the axis of symmetry is proportional to the liquid stream function. It was originally used by Whalley and Davidson [20] along with a relation equating the energy input rate by the introduction of the bubbles at the base of the column with the sum of the energy dissipation rate in the wakes behind the bubbles and the energy dissipation rate in the hydraulic jump at the liquid surface. For a tall bubble column, Joshi and Sharma [22] argued that multiple circulation cells in the vertical direction would be formed. By minimizing the maximum vorticity, they found that the height of a circulation cell would be equal to the column diameter. The drawbacks of this model have been brought out elsewhere [26]. The main drawback is that the model requires accurate measurements of inlet gas velocity (U_G), isolated bubble rise velocity (u_{br}), and bubble hold-up (δ). Thus, it is not predictive a priori. Further, it requires highly numerical calculations.

Under essentially non-viscous conditions, some investigators [27, 28] have obtained the liquid velocity profile in cylindrical columns by solving the Navier-Stokes equation along with an empirical expression for radial variation of gas hold-up and with turbulent viscosity as a parameter. These models assume that the axial liquid velocity is independent of axial position, which will not be valid for shallow columns.

For circulation in two-dimensional bubble columns, the inviscid models are those of Freedman and Davidson [19] and Whalley and Davidson [20]. They realized that the vorticity must be a constant [24, 25] and obtained

$$w = \frac{\partial^2 \psi}{\partial x^2} + \frac{\partial^2 \psi}{\partial y^2} = \text{constant} \tag{13}$$

along with the no-flow boundary conditions at the circulation cell boundaries given by

$$\psi = 0 \quad \text{at } r = 0 \text{ and } a \text{ for all } y \tag{14}$$

$$\psi = 0 \quad \text{at } y = 0 \text{ and } b \text{ for all } x \tag{15}$$

However, they obtained solutions only for the case of sinusoidal variation of vorticity in both dimensions as

$$w = -w_0 \sin(\pi x/a) \sin(\pi y/b) \tag{16}$$

The pressure balance approach was used by Freedman and Davidson [19], whereas Whalley and Davidson [20] used the energy balance approach to obtain the circulation strength w_0. The relative merits of the two approaches have been examined elsewhere [3, 26] where the pressure balance approach was recommended. It was shown [3] that analytical solutions could be obtained even if the sinusoidal variation of vorticity was restricted to a single dimension, i.e.,

$$w = -w_0 \sin(\pi x/a) \qquad (16a)$$

which is more close to Equation 13 than Equation 16.

Viscous Models

Viscous models available for describing liquid circulation in cylindrical bubble columns are those of Crabtree and Bridgewater [29] and Rietema and Ottengraf [30]. Crabtree and Bridgewater [29] analyzed the ideal situation of a chain of bubbles issuing from a single orifice. The practically useful case of several orifices at the distributor producing bubbles has been analyzed only by Reitema and Ottengraf [30]. This model will be discussed in detail later.

There does not exist any viscous model to describe liquid circulation in two-dimensional bubble columns.

INVISCID MODEL FOR AXI-SYMMETRIC CIRCULATION

The inviscid model described here has been published elsewhere [3, 26]. This model has also been applied to describe circulation in fluidized beds [31].

The representation of a bubble column according to this model is illustrated in Figure 6. In a shallow bubble column, several circulation cells in the lateral direction are assumed to form; the number and the radius of each circulation cell being unknowns. In a tall bubble column, according to Joshi and Sharma [22], several circulation cells in the vertical direction are assumed to form; the number and the height of each circulation cell being unknowns in this case. It can be seen

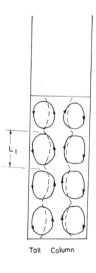

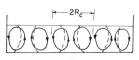

Shallow Column   Tall Column

——————— Liquid Stream lines

— — — — — Bubble Stream lines

Figure 6. Inviscid model representation of a bubble column.

that the direction of liquid movement (and hence the liquid velocity) at the cell boundaries is continuous in the shallow column, whereas it is discontinuous in the tall column. Such a discontinuity is permissible because the model treats the liquid to be inviscid (because of zero viscosity two adjacent liquid layers can move in opposite direction).

Two main assumptions of the model are

1. Circulation is axi-symmetric i.e., all the parameters are invariant in the θ-direction.
2. The isolated bubble rise velocity is a constant mean value every where in the column. This does not necessarily mean that the bubble size is constant everywhere.

Stream Function and Velocity Profiles

Equations 10–12 are the basic equations for the liquid stream function and the corresponding boundary conditions. The solution to these equations can be obtained by variable separable method [32] as

$$\psi = A' \sin(\pi y/L_1)\, F(r) \tag{17}$$

where L_1 is the height of a circulation cell. The solution $F(r)$ was obtained by Whalley and Davidson [20] who solved the following differential equation numerically

$$z\frac{d^2F}{dz^2} - \frac{dF}{dz} + (B^4 z^3 - \pi^2 z)F = 0 \tag{18}$$

where z and B equal r/L_1 and $K_3 L_1$ respectively. However, Viswanathan and Subba Rao [3, 26] obtained a truncated analytical solution for F as

$$F = z^2\left[1 + \frac{\pi^2}{8}z^2 + \frac{(\pi^4 - 8B^4)}{192}z^4 + \frac{\pi^2(\pi^4 - 32B^4)}{9216}z^6\right] \tag{19}$$

The deviation between the exact and the truncated solution has been shown [26] to be negligible for practical bubble columns. The parameter B^4 can be obtained by using the boundary condition, Equation 11 in Equation 19 as

$$B^4 = 24\pi^4\left[1 + \frac{\gamma^2}{8} + \frac{\gamma^4}{192} + \frac{\gamma^6}{9216}\right]\Big/\left[\gamma^4\left(1 + \frac{\gamma^2}{12}\right)\right] \tag{20}$$

where $\quad \gamma = \pi R/L_1 \tag{21}$

Substituting Equations 20 and 19 in Equation 17 the final equation for liquid stream function can be obtained [3, 26] to be

$$\psi = A\gamma^2 \sin\left(\frac{\pi y}{L_1}\right)\eta^2\left[1 + \frac{\gamma^2}{8}\eta^2 - \frac{\left(1 + \frac{\gamma^2}{8} - \frac{\gamma^6}{3072}\right)}{(1 + \gamma^2/12)}\eta^4 - \frac{\left(1 + \frac{\gamma^2}{8} + \frac{\gamma^4}{256}\right)}{(1 + 12/\gamma^2)}\eta^6\right] \tag{22}$$

where $\quad \eta = r/R \tag{23}$

The liquid velocity profiles in the axial and the radial directions are related to the stream function according to

$$u_r = -\frac{1}{r}\frac{\partial \psi}{\partial y} \tag{24}$$

$$u_y = \frac{1}{r}\frac{\partial \psi}{\partial r} \tag{25}$$

The stream function and the liquid velocity profiles can be predicted if the two parameters, A and L_1, in Equation 22 can be predicted.

Flow Strength

The constant A in Equation 22 is proportional to maximum flow $(2\pi\psi_{max})$. Hence, it is called flow strength, and can be obtained from a force balance as follows. Such a force balance was originally applied by Freedman and Davidson [19] for two-dimensional bubble columns.

The corner points (the entire circumference) in each circulation cell are stagnation points. Hence, the pressure at the corner points in any cell with respect to those of the cell immediately above is $\rho_L g L_1$. If u_{Base} is the liquid velocity at any point at the base of a cell, then the pressure from Bernoulli's principle becomes equal to

$$P_{Base} = \rho_L[gL_1 - \tfrac{1}{2}u_{Base}^2] \tag{26}$$

This P_{Base} acts over an area $2\pi r\,dr$ because u_{Base} depends on r. The total upward force on the base of a cell with respect to the cell above is

$$\int_0^R P_{Base}\,2\pi r\,dr = \int_0^R \rho_L[gL_1 - \tfrac{1}{2}u_{Base}^2]2\pi r\,dr \tag{27}$$

This force must balance the weight of the liquid in the circulation cell, i.e., $\pi R^2 L_1(1-\delta)\rho_L g$. Therefore, it follows that

$$\int_0^R \rho_L[gL_1 - \tfrac{1}{2}u_{Base}^2]2\pi r\,dr = \pi R^2 L_1(1-\delta)\rho_L g \tag{28}$$

which simplifies to

$$gR^2\delta L_1 = \int_0^R r u_{Base}^2\,dr \tag{29}$$

Now, u_{Base} can be obtained from Equations 24 and applied at y = 0. Substituting u_{Base} thus obtained into Equation 29, performing the integration, and subsequent rearrangement of terms yields [34]

$$\frac{L_1^7 g\delta}{A^2\pi^6 R^2} = b_3 \tag{30}$$

where $\quad b_3 = b_0 - b_1 B^4 + b_2 B^8 \tag{31}$

$$b_0 = \frac{1}{4} + \frac{\gamma^2}{24} + \frac{5\gamma^4}{1536} + \frac{7\gamma^6}{46080} + \frac{\gamma^8}{221184} + \frac{\gamma^{10}}{12386304} \tag{32}$$

$$b_1 = \frac{s^4}{96}\left[1 + \frac{\gamma^2}{6} + \frac{\gamma^4}{96} + \frac{5\gamma^6}{16128} + \frac{3\gamma^8}{694802}\right] \tag{33}$$

$$b_2 = s^8\left[\frac{1}{6912} + \frac{\gamma^2}{48384} + \frac{\gamma^4}{1389604}\right] \tag{34}$$

$$s = R/L_1 \tag{35}$$

Since only the value of b_3 is required to calculate the flow strength A from Equation 30, it is interesting to note from Equations 20 and 31–35 that b_3 is a function only of $\gamma(=\pi R/L_1)$. Hence,

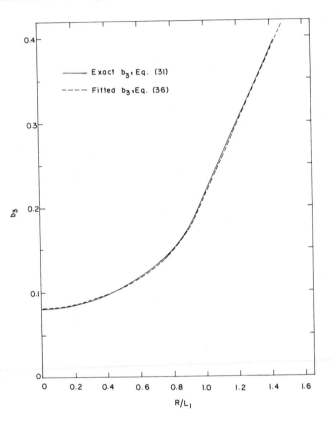

Figure 7. Variation of the parameter b_3 with R/L_1.

it is calculated from Equations 31–35 and given as a function of (R/L_1) in Figure 7. The theoretical function thus evaluated is also in close agreement with the following relationship

$$b_3 = \begin{cases} 0.088 + 0.111s^2 & 0 \le s \le 0.3 \\ 0.1 - 0.085s + 0.188s^2 & 0.3 \le s \le 0.9 \\ 0.424s - 0.21 & 0.9 \le s \le 1.6 \end{cases} \tag{36}$$

where s equals R/L_1 (Equation 35). The prediction of the mathematically approximate Equation 36 is given as a dotted line in Figure 7. It can be seen that Equation 36 compares well with the more cumbersome Equation 31. Application of Bernoulli's principle has thus yielded a relationship (Equation 30) between flow strength A and bubble hold-up δ. Another relationship to predict δ is therefore necessary.

Bubble Envelope

The central portion of the bubble column where bubbles rise with the liquid is called the bubble envelope. The bubble hold-up in this envelope (δ_e), which will be greater than δ, can be obtained

[34] from

$$\delta_e = \{R^2 U_G + r_0^2 u_{br} + 2\psi_0 + [(R^2 U_G - r_0^2 u_{br})^2 + (R^2 U_G + r_0^2 u_{br} + \psi_0)4\psi_0]^{1/2}\}/2r_0^2 u_{br} \qquad (37)$$

where ψ_0 is the ψ value evaluated at (r_0, y_0)—coordinates of the bubble injector farthest from the axis of the column. It can be shown that for either $Y_0 = 0$ (inlet nozzles flush with the base) or $r_0 = R$ (entire base aerated), Equation (37) reduces to

$$\delta_e = R^2 U_G / r_0^2 u_{br} \qquad (38)$$

The shape of the bubble envelope is given by [20]

$$r_e^2 = r_0^2 - 2\psi_e/(1 - \delta_e)U_{br} \qquad (39)$$

where ψ_e equals ψ evaluated at (r_e, y_e). The hold-up inside the bubble envelope is related to the overall bubble hold-up by

$$\delta = V_e \delta_e / V \qquad (40)$$

where V_e is the volume of the bubble envelope obtainable (by numerical integration) once the shape of the bubble envelope is obtained.

The exact method of calculation of A and δ is then as follows. Assuming a value of A, ψ_e can be calculated from Equation 39 and δ_e from Equation 37 or 38. Then δ can be obtained from Equation 40. The calculated δ can be used in Equation 30 to obtain A, which can be checked with the assumed value. The procedure of calculations can be continued until a desired convergence level is reached. Clearly, such a procedure of calculations is extremely laborious. A considerably simpler method yielding explicit expressions but involving a slight approximation is presented in the following section.

Direct Method of Calculation

Letting the ratio of minimum to mean residence time of bubble gas to be equal to f_r results in [26]

$$\int_0^R \frac{1}{u_{by}}\bigg|_{r=0} dy = \frac{f_r \delta L_1}{U_G} \qquad (41)$$

The bubbles move everywhere with a relative velocity of u_{br} with respect to the liquid. Since Equation 25 refers to the bubble free liquid region, the liquid velocity inside the bubble envelope, in order to satisfy continuity, must be

$$\frac{1}{(1 - \delta_e)} \frac{1}{r} \frac{\partial \psi}{\partial r}$$

Hence, the upward bubble velocity inside the envelope is

$$u_{by} = u_{br} + \frac{1}{(1 - \delta_e)} \frac{1}{r} \frac{\partial \psi}{\partial r} \qquad (42)$$

Substituting for ψ from Equation 22 in Equation 42, substituting the resultant u_{by} into Equation 41, and performing the integration leads to [34]

$$\frac{\pi f_r U_b \delta}{(1 - \delta_e)U_G} = 2\left[\frac{\cosh^{-1}C}{\sqrt{(C^2 - 1)}} \text{ or } \frac{\cos^{-1}C}{\sqrt{(1 - C^2)}}\right] \qquad (43)$$

where the relative rising velocity of bubble cloud is given by [35]

$$U_b = u_{br}(1 - \delta_e) \tag{44}$$

The parameter C in Equation 43 equals

$$C = 2A\pi^2/L_1^2U_b \tag{45}$$

The bubble hold-up is related to flow strength from Equation 30 by

$$\delta = A^2\pi^6R^2b_3/gL_1^7 \tag{46}$$

Substituting for δ from Equation 46 in Equation 43 leads to

$$C^2\left[\frac{\sqrt{(C^2 - 1)}}{\cos h^{-1}C} \text{ or } \frac{\sqrt{(1 - C^2)}}{\cos^{-1} C}\right] = \frac{8\mu_i}{\pi^3} \tag{47}$$

where $\mu_i = gL_1^3U_G(1 - \delta_e)/b_3fR^2U_b^3$ (48)

The function on the left-hand side of Equation 47 excellently approximates to a straight line on a log-log plot as shown in Figure 8. The resultant expression for the flow strength from Figure 8, and Equations 45 and 47 is [34]

$$A = d_1L_1^2u_{br}\left[\frac{gL_1^3U_G}{b_3R^2u_{br}^3}\right]^{1/d_2} \tag{49}$$

where the constants d_1 and d_2 are given by

Range	d_1	$d_2 = 1/d_3$	Equation
$0.03 \leq \mu_i \leq 3$	0.0271	2.25	(49a)
$3 \leq \mu_i \leq 300$	0.0285	2.50	(49b)
$300 \leq \mu_i \leq 3000$	0.0350	2.75	(49c)

All the data that has been published to date follows [3] the criterion of Equation 49b (see Table 1). Hence substituting Equation 35 into Equation 49 leads to

$$A = 0.0285R^2u_{br}(gRU_G/b_3s^8u_{br}^3)^{0.4} \tag{50}$$

The only unknown in Equation 50 for flow strength is the parameter $s(= R/L_1)$.

The principle of minimization of maximum vorticity (maximum $K_3^4r\psi$), originally proposed by Whalley and Davidson [20] for two-dimensional bubble columns, was used by Joshi and Sharma [22] to estimate the height of each circulation cell in an axi-symmetric bubble column. Following this procedure along with the present model it can be shown [3] that

$$\left.\begin{array}{l} L_1 = 1.25R \\ s = 0.8 \end{array}\right\} \tag{51}$$

For s = 0.8, b_3 from Equation 36 equals 0.1523. With these s and b_3 values, the flow strength from Equation 50 becomes

$$A = 0.127R^2u_{br}(gRU_G/u_{br}^3)^{0.4} \tag{52}$$

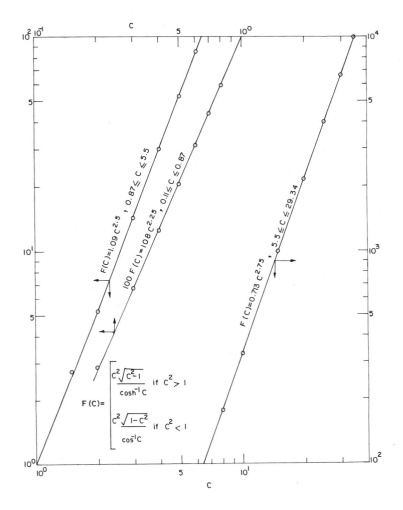

Figure 8. Determination of a simpler relation for the function F(C).

As was originally pointed out, it is u_{br} (and only indirectly d_{vs}) that affects the flow strength and liquid velocity profiles.

Liquid Velocity Profiles

Axial Variation

The axial liquid velocity can be expected to vary in the axial direction only for shallow columns (say up to $L/D \approx 1.5$). The only investigators who have experimentally measured the axial variation of axial liquid velocity are Whalley and Davidson [20]. Since they used a Pavlov tube [36] for measurements, they measured the liquid velocity only at the column axis. Since the axis is inside the bubble envelope, the liquid velocity given by Equation 25 should be divided by $(1 - \delta_e)$. Then

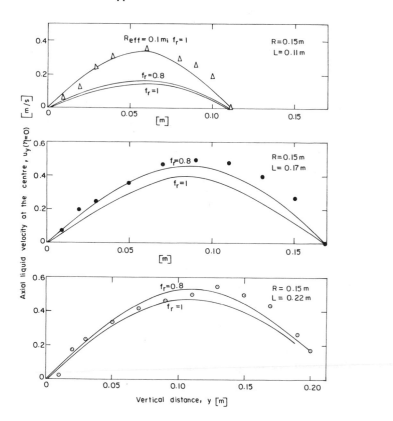

Figure 9. Comparison of experimental and predicted axial variation of axial liquid velocity at the column axis.

Equations 21–23 and 25 yield

$$u_y\big|_{r=0} = \frac{2A\pi^2}{L_1^2(1 - \delta_e)} \sin\left(\frac{\pi y}{L_1}\right) \tag{53}$$

The predictions of Equation 53 are compared with the experimental data [20] in Figure 9. The flow strength A, and δ_e are obtained from Equations 52 and 38, respectively. To indicate the effect of f_r (implying a distribution of bubble velocities) calculations are also shown for $f_r = 0.8$ for which the flow strength given by Equation 52 is multiplied by $f_r^{-0.4}$. It can be seen that a value of 0.8 to 1 for f_r predicts the experimental results quite satisfactorily though for the shallowest column studied (R/L = 1.4) the predicted values are too low. In this case, multiple circulation cells in the lateral direction may form as depicted in Figure 6 with the effective radius of a circulation cell being about 0.8L (Equation 51). This is confirmed by the predictions shown for $R_{eff} = 0.1$ m (even though R = 0.15 m), which show good agreement with the data.

Radial Variation

Most investigators who have measured radial variation of axial liquid velocity have used tall bubble columns. In such columns, an average radial velocity profile may be expected to exist except in the gas entrance (bottom) and disengaging (top) zones. The average radial velocity profile is then given from Equation 22, 25, and 51 to be

$$u_{y,avg} = \frac{1}{\lambda} \frac{2A\pi^2}{(1.25R)^2} [1 + 1.58\eta^2 - 3.36\eta^4 - 2.68\eta^6] \tag{54}$$

where $\lambda = u_{y,max}/u_{y,avg}$ $\tag{55}$

$$u_{y,max} = \frac{1}{(1 - \delta_e)} \frac{2A\pi^2}{(1.25R)^2} \tag{56}$$

The parameter λ represents the average value of $[1/\sin(\pi y/L_1)]$. It has been proved [3] that

$$\lambda = 2 \tag{57}$$

From Equations 54 and 57, it follows that

$$u_{y,avg} = 6.32 \frac{A}{R^2} [1 + 1.58\eta^2 - 3.36\eta^4 - 2.68\eta^6] \tag{58}$$

The experimental data [27, 37] are compared with the model predictions obtained from Equations 58 and 52 in Figure 10. It can be seen that the predictions compare extremely well with the experimental data. It may be noted that the model predicts (in accord with data) the liquid velocity to be almost uniform in the upflow liquid zone and highly non-uniform in the downflow liquid zone. Since most bubbles travel in the upflow liquid zone this implies that most bubbles travel at the same velocity. This leads to an f_r value of nearly 1 (Equation 41) thereby confirming the value (0.8 to 1) that predicted the data [20] of axial variation of axial liquid velocity correctly.

It may be noted from Equation 58 that the downward liquid velocity is predicted to be maximum at the wall, $\eta = 1$. In the inviscid model, the liquid is not assumed to stick to the wall of the bubble column. For air-water like systems, this is an unrealistic assumption only for a very small boundary layer near the wall. Many investigators [38, 39] have indeed experimentally found the downward liquid velocity to be a maximum just a few millimeters away from the column wall. Hence, for the bulk of the bubble column the velocity profile predicted by Equation 58 would be realistic.

Many investigators [27, 36, 37, 40–44] have measured only $u_{y,avg}$ ($\eta = 0$) given by

$$u_{y,avg} (\eta = 0) = 6.32 \, A/R^2 \tag{59}$$

The prediction of Equation 59 along with Equation 52 are compared with the data in Table 1. The comparison shows an average absolute error of only 10%, which is quite remarkable in view of the wide variation in the experimental conditions of the various investigators. It may be noted that the μ_i value for all the data lies between 3 and 300 (i.e., Equation 49b holds).

Average Liquid Circulation Velocity

The maximum quantum of liquid circulation equals

$$Q_{max} = 2\pi\psi|_{y=L_1/2, u_y=0} \tag{60}$$

The axial liquid velocity u_y is predicted to be equal to 0 by Equation 58 at $\eta = 0.79$. At $\eta = 0.79$, $y = L_1/2$, and $\gamma = 0.8\pi$, Equation 22 yields

$$\psi_{max} = 3.97A \tag{61}$$

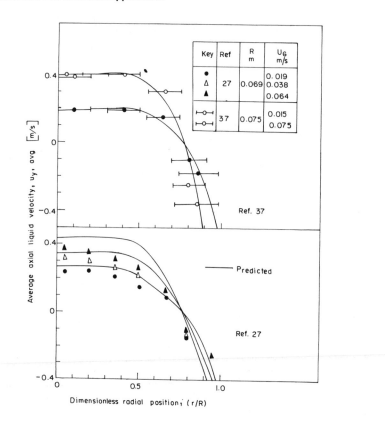

Figure 10. Comparison of experimental and predicted radial variation of average axial liquid velocity.

Average quantum of liquid circulation is

$$Q = Q_{max}/\lambda \tag{62}$$

Average liquid circulation velocity is defined by

$$U_c = Q/(\pi R^2/2) \tag{63}$$

From Equations 52, 57, and 60–63 it can be shown [34] that

$$U_{oi} = u_{br}(gRU_G/u_{br}^3)^{0.4} \tag{64}$$

where the additional subscript i to U_c indicates that it is obtained from the inviscid model. The average liquid circulation velocity can be used as a useful correlating parameter in many instances, such as liquid mixing characterized by the dispersion coefficient, heat transfer in bubble columns etc.

Table 1
Summary of Available Experimental Data and Theoretical Calculations of Axial
Liquid Velocity at the Center of Cylindrical Bubble Columns
(System: Air-Water*)

Ref.	R m	U_G m/s	u_{br} m/s	μ_i†	10^6 A from Equation 52 m^3/s	$\delta_e = U_G/u_{br}$ Equation 38	$u_{y,max}$ m/s	$u_{y,exp}$ m/s	$u_{y,pred}$ m/s
1	2	3	4	5	6	7	8	9	10
[27]	0.069	0.019	0.235	12.7	142	0.081	0.4100	0.223	0.205
		0.038	0.235	25.4	187	0.162	0.5921	0.335	0.296
		0.064	0.300	20.6	219	0.213	0.7384	0.410	0.369
		0.095	0.390	13.9	244	0.244	0.8564	0.484	0.428
		0.165	0.540	9.1	285	0.306	1.0897	0.630	0.545
[36]	0.086	0.044	0.280	21.7	325	0.157	0.6585	0.320	0.329
		0.100	0.360	23.2	429	0.278	1.0149	0.523	0.508
		0.170	0.500	14.5	496	0.340	1.2837	0.630	0.542
		0.257	0.620	11.7	561	0.415	1.6380	0.690	0.819
[37]	0.075	0.008	0.235	5.8	122	0.034	0.2836	0.150	0.142
		0.015	0.235	10.9	157	0.064	0.3767	0.190	0.188
		0.020	0.235	14.5	177	0.085	0.4344	0.220	0.217
[40]	0.150	0.020	0.235**	29.1	932	0.085	0.5719	0.266	0.286
		0.060	0.235	87.3	1446	0.255	1.0898	0.440	0.545
[41]	0.075	0.015	0.235	10.9	157	0.064	0.3767	0.180	0.188
		0.075	0.320	21.6	282	0.234	0.8268	0.400	0.413
[42]	0.125	0.052	0.210	88.3	902	0.248	0.9798	0.430	0.490
[43]	0.050	0.045	0.300	10.5	88	0.150	0.5232	0.270	0.261
		0.082	0.420	7.0	104	0.195	0.6528	0.320	0.326
		0.155	0.570	5.3	127	0.272	0.8815	0.400	0.441
		0.225	0.600	6.6	146	0.375	1.1804	0.680	0.590
		0.280	0.610	7.8	158	0.459	1.4758	0.850	0.738
		0.320	0.610	8.9	167	0.525	1.7766	0.980	0.888
		0.370	0.610	10.3	177	0.607	2.2759	1.050	1.138
[44]	2.750	0.036	0.700**	35.3	1,019,462	0.051	1.7945	0.750	0.897
		0.044	0.800	29.7	1,075,556	0.055	1.9013	0.880	0.951
		0.067	0.900	31.8	1,242,943	0.074	2.2423	1.100	1.121
		0.085	1.000	29.4	1,338,559	0.085	2.4438	1.280	1.222

* It is assumed that whole base is aerated i.e., $r_0 = R$
** These are assumed values
† Note that μ_i is always between 3 and 300.

Liquid Axial Dispersion Coefficient

Many investigators have characterized the liquid mixing in terms of liquid axial dispersion coefficient, D_L. It has been suggested [22] that D_L might be proportional to RU_{ci}. From Equation 64 this means

$$D_L = KRu_{br}(gRU_G/u_{br}^3)^{0.4} \tag{65}$$

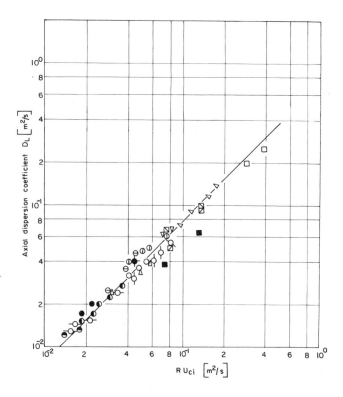

Figure 11. Effect of average liquid circulation velocity on axial dispersion coefficient. For legend see Table 2.

Table 2
Summary of Available Experimental Data on Liquid Axial Dispersion Coefficient in Cylindrical Bubble Columns
(System: Air-Water)

R m	L m	Sparger	Tracer	Technique of Measurement	Ref.
0.050 0.100	2.02 1.00	Porous and sieve plates	Aq. KCl and heat	Backmixing	[45]
0.100	7.23	Nozzles	Electrolyte dye and heat	Backmixing	[46]
0.100 0.051	2.22 2.56	Porous plate		Backmixing	[47]
0.050 0.095 0.095	1.33 1.33 0.22	Single; tube	Aq. KCl	Transient	[48]
0.061 0.107	2.00 4.05	Sieve plate	Aq. KCl	Pulse	[49]
0.070 0.145	3.53 3.80	Sieve plate	Aq. NaCl	Backmixing	[50]
0.203	1.50 1.90 2.84	Single tube	Methylene blue dye	Backmixing and pulse	[51]
0.534	5.11	Eight-point spider			

The experimental data of a large number of investigators [45–51] are tested for the relationship, Equation 65, in Figure 11. Here it is assumed that $u_{br} = 0.235$ m/s. The legend for Figure 11 and the details of the operating conditions are summarized in Table 2. The final relationship obtained from Figure 11 is

$$D_L = 0.77Ru_{br}(gRU_G/u_{br}^3)^{0.4} \tag{66}$$

It can be seen in Figure 11 that Equation 66 fits the data extremely well.

Gas Hold-Up

The gas hold-up is obtained by substituting Equations 51 and 52 in Equation 46 as

$$\delta = 0.5\left(\frac{u_{br}}{\sqrt{gR}}\right)^{0.4}\left(\frac{U_G}{u_{br}}\right)^{0.8} \tag{67}$$

For shallow columns (like say distillation plates) the radius to be used in Equation 67 from Equation 51 is 0.8L, where L is the liquid depth.

The predictions of Equation 67 are compared with the experimental gas hold-up data of a large number of investigators [46, 50, 52–55] in Figure 12. The predictions are given for $u_{br} = 0.15$ and

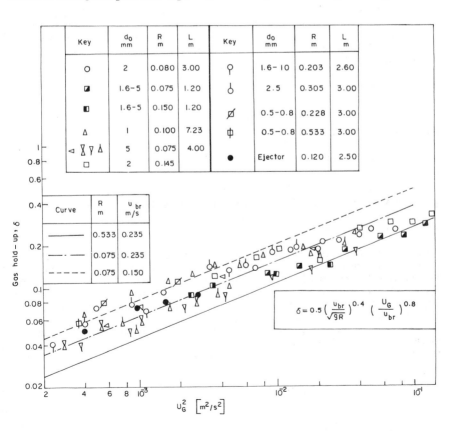

Figure 12. Comparison of experimental and predicted gas hold-up.

Table 3
Comparison of Experimental and Predicted Gas Hold-up
(System: Air-Water at NTP)

Ref.	R m	Sparger	U_G m/s	u_{br} m/s	δ exp	δ cal
[42]	0.125	Single nozzle	0.052	0.180	0.15	0.09
[43]	0.050	Single nozzle	0.045	0.300	0.12	0.08
			0.082	0.420	0.15	0.11
			0.155	0.570	0.21	0.16
			0.225	0.600	0.26	0.21
			0.280	0.610	0.29	0.25
			0.320	0.610	0.31	0.28
			0.370	0.610	0.34	0.32
[56]	0.300	Single nozzle	0.350	0.490	0.32	0.23
			0.530	0.510	0.38	0.32
			0.930	0.520	0.52	0.49

0.235 m/s. It can be seen that as U_G increases, the u_{br} value that explains the data correctly also increases from 0.15 to 0.235 m/s. Since this is reasonable, it confirms adequately the validity of Equation 67. Additional data of gas hold-up [42, 43, 56] are compared with the predictions of Equation 67 in Table 3. Here, observed u_{br} values are used in the predictions. The good comparison therefore substantiates the validity of the theoretically derived gas hold-up relationship.

Since all the gas that enters passes through the column as bubbles, the average bubble rise velocity is given by

$$\bar{u}_{by} = u_b = U_G/\delta \tag{68}$$

Substituting for δ from Equation 67 into Equation 68 yields

$$u_b = 2u_{br}\left(\frac{U_G}{u_{br}}\right)^{0.2}\left(\frac{u_{br}}{\sqrt{gR}}\right)^{-0.4} \tag{69}$$

VISCOUS MODEL FOR AXI-SYMMETRIC CIRCULATION

Rietema and Ottengraf's Model

The viscous model described here has Rietema and Ottengraf's model [30] as the basis. The bubble column is supposed to be divided into a bubble envelope of diameter d with a constant bubble fraction δ_e (which is independent of position in the envelope), and an annular bubble free region. Such a physical picture is illustrated in Figure 13. Radial pressure gradients and end effects are neglected here. We are concerned mainly with what happens in the bulk of the bubble column where the bubble envelope is cylindrical. In such a column, liquid circulation sets in with liquid moving up in the bubble envelope and down near the walls. Circulation in the angular (θ) direction is assumed to be absent. With these assumptions, the momentum balance equations for the bubble envelope and the annulus regions are respectively [30]

$$-\frac{dP}{dy} - \rho_D g = \frac{1}{r}\frac{d}{dr}\left[(1 - \delta_e)r\tau_1\right] \tag{70}$$

$$-\frac{dP}{dy} - \rho_L g = \frac{1}{r}\frac{d}{dr}\left[r\tau_2\right] \tag{71}$$

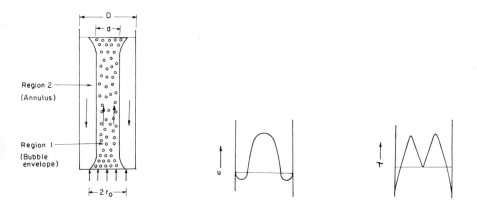

Figure 13. Viscous model representation of a bubble column.

The dispersion density in Equation 70 is given by

$$\rho_D = \delta_e \rho + (1 - \delta_e)\rho_L \approx (1 - \delta_e)\rho_L \qquad (72)$$

The boundary conditions are

$$r = 0 \qquad\qquad \tau_1 = 0 \qquad\qquad (73)$$

$$r = \tfrac{1}{2}d \qquad (1 - \delta_e)\tau_1 = \tau_2 \qquad\qquad (74)$$

The shear stress profile is obtained by solving Equations 70–74 as

$$\tau_1 = -r\frac{\left(\dfrac{dP}{dy} + \rho_D g\right)}{12(1 - \delta_e)} \qquad\qquad (75)$$

$$\tau_2 = -\frac{r}{2}\left(\frac{dP}{dy} + \rho_L g\right) + \frac{gd^2(\rho_L - \rho_D)}{8r} \qquad (76)$$

Velocity profiles can be calculated from Equations 75 and 76 by assuming Newtonian liquid behavior

$$\tau = -\mu\frac{du}{dr} \qquad\qquad (77)$$

and using the boundary conditions

$$r = \tfrac{1}{2}d \qquad u_1 = u_2 \qquad\qquad (78)$$

$$r = R \qquad u_2 = 0 \qquad\qquad (79)$$

The liquid velocity profile thus derived by Rietema and Ottengraf [30] can be expressed as

$$u_1 = \frac{\rho_L g R^2}{4\mu}\left[\frac{(-p' + 1 - \delta_e)}{(1 - \delta_e)}(\eta^2 - K) - (-p' + 1)(1 - K) + \delta_e K \ln(1/K)\right] \qquad (80)$$

$$u_2 = \frac{\rho_L g R^2}{4\mu} \left[(-p' + 1)(\eta^2 - 1) + \delta_e K \ln(1/\eta^2) \right] \tag{81}$$

where

$$p' = -\frac{dP/dy}{\rho_L g} = \frac{1 - 4\delta_e K + 3\delta_e K^2 - 2\delta_e^2 K^2 \ln K}{1 - 2\delta_e K(1 - K)} \tag{82}$$

$$K = (d/D)^2 \tag{83}$$

The velocity profiles can be predicted from Equations 80 and 81 if the parameters K and δ_e can be predicted. For predicting K and δ_e Rietema and Ottengraf [30] derived the following expressions:

$$\frac{8\mu}{\pi \rho_L g D^4} \frac{\pi D^2}{4} U_G = \frac{\delta_e}{(1 - \delta_e)} q_c + 2K\delta_e \frac{\mu}{\rho_L g D^2} u_{br} \tag{84}$$

$$q_c = (K^2 \delta_e / 16) G(K, \delta_e) \tag{85}$$

$$G(K, \delta_e) = \frac{-3 + 4\delta_e + 4K - 8K\delta_e - K^2 + 4K^2\delta_e - 2(1 - \delta_e + K^2\delta_e) \ln K}{1 - 2\delta_e K(1 - K)} \tag{86}$$

The term q_c represents the dimensionless liquid turn-over rate and is related to Q by [30]

$$Q = \left(\frac{\pi \rho_L g D^4}{8\mu} \right) q_c \tag{87}$$

Introducing a factor

$$f = K\delta_e u_{br}/U_G \tag{88}$$

in Equation 84 and using Equation 85 leads to

$$\frac{2\mu U_G}{\rho_L g D^2} (1 - f) = \frac{f^2 U_G^2}{16(1 - \delta_e) u_{br}^2} G(K, \delta_e) \tag{89}$$

In compact form, Equation 89 can be expressed as

$$32 \frac{(1 - f)}{f^2} = \frac{Re_G}{(1 - \delta_e) Fr^2} G(K, \delta_e) \tag{90}$$

where

$$Re_G = DU_G \rho_L / \mu \tag{91}$$

$$Fr = u_{br}/\sqrt{gD} \tag{92}$$

In Equation 90, the unknowns are K, δ_e, and f. Another relationship relating K, δ_e, and f is Equation 88. Thus, we have three unknowns and two equations, Equations 88 and 90. The required additional relationship was obtained by Rietema and Ottengraf [30] by utilizing the principle of minimum energy dissipation. According to this principle, they showed that the other relationship is obtained by minimizing e_t, where e_t is given by

$$e_t = \frac{1 - 4K\delta_e + 3K^2\delta_e - 2K^2\delta_e^2 \ln K}{(1 - 2\delta_e K(1 - K))(1 - K\delta_e)} \tag{93}$$

The procedure of calculations is then as follows:

1. Calculate Re_G and Fr from known U_G and u_{br} values from Equations 91 and 92.
2. Assuming a K value, calculate δ_e from Equation 90 after substituting for f from Equation 88.
3. Calculate e_t from Equation 93 using the assumed K value and the calculated δ_e in Step 2.
4. Repeat the procedure for different K values, and plot e_t versus K.
5. The solution is obtained by the minimum in the curve obtained in Step 4.

Once K and δ_e are thus obtained, the liquid velocity profile and the circulation rate of liquid can be calculated.

Clearly, the procedure is extremely tedious. Because many simplifying assumptions are involved in the model, a simplified model would be extremely useful for engineering applications even if it is based on some mathematical approximations.

The Present Model

Simpler form for the Function $G(K, \delta_e)$

The function in Equation 86 can be expressed as

$$G(K, \delta_e) = \frac{f_1(K) - \delta_e f_2(K)}{1 - \delta_e f_3(K)} \tag{94}$$

where $f_1(K) = 2\ln(1/K) - (3 - K)(1 - K)$ (95)

$$f_2(K) = 2(1 - K)[(1 + K)\ln(1/K) - 2(1 - K)] \tag{96}$$

$$f_3(K) = 2K(1 - K) \tag{97}$$

It can be shown [57] that for most practical purposes, Equation 94 reduces to

$$G(K, \delta_e) = f_1(K) = 2\ln(1/K) - (3 - K)(1 - K) \tag{98}$$

The maximum error in this approximation, for most practical systems, is about 5%. The main advantage in such an approximation is that $G(K, \delta_e)$ is now independent of δ_e. Substituting Equation 98 in Equation 90 leads to

$$\frac{Re_G}{(1 - \delta_e)Fr^2} = \frac{32}{(f/K)^2} \frac{(1 - f)}{K^2 f_1(K)} \tag{99}$$

Up until now, no physical assumption has been used apart from Rietema and Ottengraf's basic assumptions themselves. However, in Equation 99 there still exist two unknowns, K and F, δ_e being already related to these through Equation 88. The additional equation required to complete the model is given in the next section.

Bubble Hold-Up Inside the Envelope

Instead of the principle of minimum energy dissipation, the following postulate is used without proof: "The gas hold-up inside the bubble envelope δ_e is given in the case of viscous liquid circulation by the same expression as in the case of inviscid liquid circulation", namely

$$\delta_e = R^2 U_G / r_0^2 u_{br} \tag{38}$$

For viscous liquid circulation, we are unable to give a theoretical proof of Equation 38. However, as will be shown, its use simplifies calculations considerably. Further, it is shown below that its predictions match well the experimental data of Rietema and Ottengraf [30]. Hence, its use is justified. From Equations 83, 88, and 38, f and K become related as

$$f = K(R/r_0)^2 = (d/2\,r_0)^2 \tag{100}$$

The only investigators who have experimentally measured δ_e are again Rietema and Ottengraf [30]. From the photograph given in their paper, the radial coordinate of the bubble injector farthest from the column axis appears to be about $r_0 = 0.08$ m. Their column diameter was $D = 0.22$ m. Then, Equation 38 becomes

$$\delta_e = 1.89 U_G/u_{br} \tag{38a}$$

The predictions of Equation 38a are compared with their data in Table 4. The predicted values by Rietema and Ottengraf's numerical method are also included in Table 4 for comparison. It can be seen that not only the average absolute error but also the standard deviation of the absolute error is significantly smaller for the present model than that for Rietema and Ottengraf's model. Thus the validity of the postulated Equation 38 is established for viscous systems. The effect of liquid viscosity is felt through its dependence on the isolated bubble rise velocity, u_{br} ($=$ slip velocity). Thus, the model requires that u_{br} be known before hand.

Simpler Relation for $1/K^2 f_1(K)$

The function $1/K^2 f_1(K)$ in Equation 99 is calculated for various K values and plotted against $(1 - f)$ in Figure 14. For a given K, f is calculated from Equation 100. In large-scale industrial

Table 4
Comparison of Experimental and Predicted Values of Bubble Hold-up Inside the Bubble Envelope [30]

| | | | | | | δ_e | δ_e | Absolute error, % | |
Run	μ Pas	$10^6\,Q_G$ m³/s	$10^3\,U_G$ m/s	$10^3\,U_{br}$ m/s	Exp.	Equation 38	R and 0	Equation 38	R and 0
1	1.080	11.4	0.30	24.0	0.0290	0.0236	0.0151	18.6	47.9
2		7.1	0.19	19.8	0.0210	0.0181	0.0117	13.8	44.3
3		4.8	0.13	18.5	0.0150	0.0133	0.0083	11.1	44.0
4	0.622	11.4	0.30	45.4	0.0200	0.0125	0.0099	37.5	50.5
5		7.1	0.19	45.4	0.0115	0.0079	0.0071	31.3	38.3
6		4.8	0.13	45.4	0.0053	0.0054	0.0055	1.9	3.8
7	0.350	11.4	0.30	66.7	0.0118	0.0085	0.0071	28.0	39.8
8		7.1	0.19	66.7	0.0056	0.0054	0.0053	3.6	5.4
9		4.8	0.13	66.7	0.0037	0.0037	0.0041	0	10.8
10	0.164	11.4	0.30	83.3	0.0097	0.0068	0.0052	29.9	46.4
11		7.1	0.19	83.3	0.0040	0.0043	0.0038	7.5	5.0
12		4.8	0.13	83.3	0.0027	0.0029	0.0030	7.4	11.1
13	0.097	11.4	0.30	105.3	0.0050	0.0054	0.0040	8.0	20.0
14		7.1	0.19	105.3	0.0036	0.0034	0.0030	5.6	16.7
15		4.8	0.13	105.3	0.0024	0.0023	0.0024	4.2	0
							$\bar{E} =$	13.9	25.6
							$\sigma_E =$	11.7	18.4

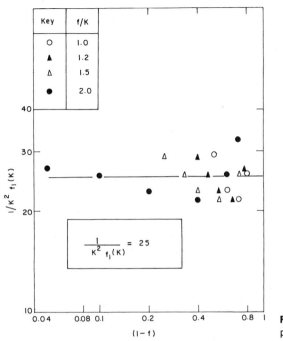

Figure 14. Illustration of the independence of $1/K^2f_1(K)$ on $(1 - f)$.

columns, though gas distribution will be through discrete holes, the ratio of r_0 to R will be close to unity. Similarly, in small-scale laboratory-size columns, if the distributor is a porous plate, r_0 will be equal to R. In such cases, $f = K$. On the other hand, in small-scale laboratory-size columns where gas enters through a discrete number of holes (r_0/R) may be much smaller than unity, and (f/K) from Equation 100 will be greater than unity. Hence, calculations are shown for (f/K) from 1.0 to 2.0 in Figure 14. The calculations in Figure 14 indicate that to a good approximation ($< 20\%$) the following is valid

$$1/K^2f_1(K) \approx 25 \tag{101}$$

The validity region of Equation 101 is given in Table 5. The validity region is such that practically all the operating conditions are covered. For example, for Rietema and Ottengraf's data [30], $f/K \approx 2.0$ and 14 out of 15 (d/D) values fell within 0.37 and 0.70, i.e., within the validity region of Equation 101.

Table 5
Validity Region of the Approximate Equation 101*

f/K	(1 − f) Min.	(1 − f) Max.	Range of Min.	(d/D) Max.
1.0	0.50	0.8	0.70	0.45
1.2	0.40	0.8	0.70	0.41
1.5	0.25	0.8	0.70	0.36
2.0	0.00	0.7	0.70	0.37

* For a maximum deviation of 20%.

Substituting Equation 101 in Equation 99 leads to

$$\frac{Re_G}{(1 - \delta_e)Fr^2} = \frac{800}{(f/K)^2}(1 - f) \tag{102}$$

Bubble Parameters

Bubble envelope diameter. The bubble envelope diameter can be obtained from Equations 100 and 102 as

$$\sqrt{K} = \frac{d}{D} = \frac{r_0}{R}\left[1 - \frac{Re_G(R/r_0)^4}{800(1 - \delta_e)Fr^2}\right]^{1/2} \tag{103}$$

which reduces for Rietema and Ottengraf's data [30] to (in S.I. units)

$$\sqrt{K} = \frac{d}{D} = 0.727\left[1 - \frac{2.137}{(1 - \delta_e)}\left(\frac{U_G}{\mu u_{br}^2}\right)\right]^{1/2} \tag{103a}$$

The predictions of Equation 103a are compared with their experimental data in Table 6. The predictions obtained by the highly numerical method of Rietema and Ottengraf [30] are also included in Table 6 for comparison. It can be seen that both the mean and the standard deviation of the absolute error are significantly smaller for the present model than those for their model. Another important point to be noted in Table 6 is that for all the five sets, each with different μ, experimental (d/D) decreases with increasing U_G which is in accord with the trend predicted by the present model whereas it is contrary to the trend predicted by Rietema and Ottengraf's [30] model. This is a serious limitation of their model and is a significant positive support of the present model. This

Table 6
Comparison of Experimental and Predicted d/D Values [30]

Run*	$10^3 U_G$ m/s	$\sqrt{K} = d/D$ exp.	Equation 103	R and 0	Absolute error, % Equation 103	R and 0
1	0.30	0.32	—	0.71	—	122
2	0.19	0.37	0.17	0.70	54	89
3	0.13	0.37	0.37	0.73	0	97
4	0.30	0.41	0.51	0.66	25	61
5	0.19	0.55	0.60	0.64	10	16
6	0.13	0.59	0.65	0.60	10	2
7	0.30	0.46	0.56	0.66	21	43
8	0.19	0.59	0.63	0.60	6	2
9	0.13	0.64	0.66	0.57	3	11
10	0.30	0.46	0.48	0.68	4	48
11	0.19	0.59	0.59	0.63	1	7
12	0.13	0.64	0.64	0.58	1	9
13	0.30	0.55	0.46	0.72	16	31
14	0.19	0.55	0.58	0.62	5	13
15	0.13	0.59	0.63	0.60	7	2
					$\bar{E} = 12$	37
					$\sigma_E = 14$	38

* *Operating conditions are the same as in Table 4.*

indicates that the somewhat heuristic postulate for δ_e used in the present model is more practically sound than the principle of minimum energy dissipation used by Rietema and Ottengraf [30].

Gas hold-up. In the bulk portion where the bubble envelope is cylindrical the overall gas hold-up is related to gas hold-up inside the bubble envelope according to

$$\delta = (d/D)^2 \delta_e \tag{104}$$

From Equations 83, 103, and 104, one obtains

$$\delta = \delta_e \left(\frac{r_0}{R}\right)^2 \left[1 - \frac{Re_G(R/r_0)^4}{800(1 - \delta_e)Fr^2}\right] \tag{105}$$

Substituting for δ_e from Equation 38 in Equation 105 leads to

$$\delta = \frac{U_G}{u_{br}} \left[1 - \frac{Re_G(R/r_0)^4}{800(1 - \delta_e)Fr^2}\right] \tag{106}$$

In a rather thorough experimental study, Franz et al. [58] showed that in highly viscous systems bubbles of a very wide size distribution coexist in the column. They measured the gas hold-up contributions of "small" and "intermediate to large" bubbles separately. The different bubble sizes may be assumed to be non-interfering and the gas hold-up due to each bubble size may then be obtained from Equation 106. The superficial gas velocity due to large and small bubbles may be taken as $f_e U_G$ and $(1 - f_e)U_G$, where f_e can be obtained from Figure 3. (The validity of Figure 3 for viscous systems is, however, a speculation). The reasonableness of this method must be tested by further research.

Applications involving gas-liquid mass transfer in bubble columns do not require the presence of very small bubbles that might stay in the column even after achieving mass transfer equilibrium. In such cases, it is probable that only the "intermediate to large" bubbles of Franz et al. [58] may be in the desired size range. This desired bubble size range would however depend on the specific mass transfer application. This is again a useful area for further work.

Liquid Velocity Profile

Neglecting second and higher order terms of δ_e it can be shown [57] that p' in Equation 82 approximates to the simple expression

$$p' = 1 - K\delta_e(2 - K) \tag{107}$$

Using Equation 107 in Equations 80 and 81, it can be shown [57] that

$$\frac{u_1}{\sqrt{gD}} = \frac{\delta_e Re_{br}}{16Fr} \left[K \ln(1/K) - K(1 - K)(2 - K) - (1 - K)^2(\eta^2 - K)\right] \tag{108}$$

$$\frac{u_2}{\sqrt{gD}} = \frac{\delta_e Re_{br}}{16Fr} \left[K \ln(1/\eta^2) - K(2 - K)(1 - \eta^2)\right] \tag{109}$$

where $\quad Re_{br} = Du_{br}\rho_L/\mu \tag{110}$

$$Fr = u_{br}/\sqrt{gD} \tag{92}$$

Rietema and Ottengraf [30] have reported experimental liquid velocity profile for one of their runs. Their experimental data is compared with the predictions of Equations 108 and 109 in Figure 15. In the predictions, δ_e and K were obtained from Equations 38a and 103a, respectively. The good comparison is sufficient proof of the validity of the various physical assumptions and the mathematical approximations used in the model.

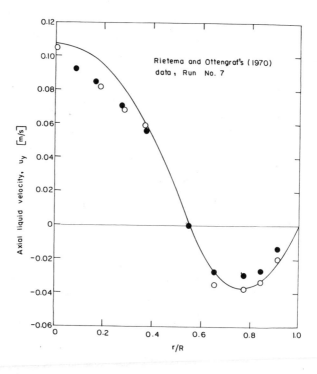

Figure 15. Comparison of experimental and predicted viscous liquid velocity profile.

WHICH MODEL TO USE AND WHEN

So far, an inviscid model and a viscous model have been presented to estimate liquid circulation in bubble columns. What is required now is a criterion to tell whether the inviscid model or the viscous model should be used under a given set of operating conditions. In other words, we need to explain why the inviscid model is overwhelmingly valid for air-water like systems, whereas for air-glycerol like systems only the viscous model is able to explain the experimental results. Such a criterion is developed here.

The Criterion

The average viscous liquid circulation velocity can be obtained from Equations 63, 85, 87, 98, 100, and 101 as [57]

$$U_{cv} = \frac{(R/r_0)^2}{400} u_{br} \frac{Re_G}{Fr^2}$$

(111)

The average inviscid liquid circulation velocity is given by Equation 64 as

$$U_{cl} = 0.76 u_{br}(gDU_G/u_{br}^3)^{0.4}$$

(112)

With Equations 91, 92, and 110, Equation 112 becomes

$$U_{ci} = 0.76u_{br}(Re_G/Re_{br}Fr^2)^{0.4} \tag{113}$$

Dividing U_{ci} in Equation 113 by U_{cv} in Equation 111 leads to

$$\frac{U_{ci}}{U_{cv}} = 304\left(\frac{r_0}{R}\right)^2\left[\frac{Re_G Re_{br}^{2/3}}{Fr^2}\right]^{-0.6} \tag{114}$$

The actual rate of circulation will be determined by viscous or inertial (inviscid) conditions depending on whichever is smaller. That is

$$\begin{aligned}U_{ci}/U_{cv} &< 1 \quad \text{inertial control} \\ U_{ci}/U_{cv} &> 1 \quad \text{viscous control}\end{aligned} \tag{115}$$

The critical condition is obtained by letting $U_{ci}/U_{cv} = 1$. The predictions of Equation 114 are shown in Figure 16. The critical condition is obtained as

$$\chi_c = \left\{\frac{Re_G Re_{br}^{2/3}}{Fr^2(r_0/R)^{10/3}}\right\} = 13744 \tag{116}$$

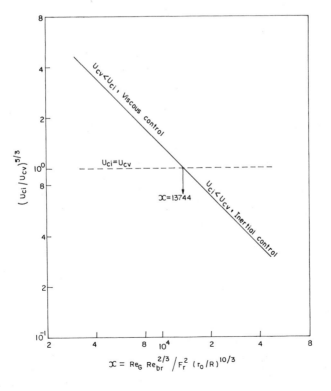

Figure 16. Determination of the controlling regime.

From Figure 16, it can be concluded that if $\chi > \chi_c$ use the inviscid model, and if $\chi < \chi_c$ use the viscous model, where

$$\chi = \frac{D^{8/3}U_G\rho_L^{5/3}g}{u_{br}^{2/3}\mu^{5/3}} \left(\frac{r_0}{R}\right)^{-10/3} \tag{117}$$

It can be seen from Equation 117 that the inviscid theory is more likely to be applicable in larger columns, higher inlet superficial gas velocities, denser liquids, and/or less viscous liquids. It can also be seen that if the same amount of gas is sparged through a lesser distributor area ($r_0 < R$), the number χ will be greater and hence inviscid theory is more likely to be valid. It can be seen from Equations 111 and 113 that the viscous liquid circulation velocity is greater for a lesser (r_0/R), whereas the inviscid liquid circulation velocity is independent of (r_0/R). Consider a bubble column consisting of a viscous liquid. Let a certain amount of gas be sparged through the entire base area ($r_0 = R$) such that $\chi < \chi_c$. Now consider different gas distributers having different r_0 values. Let the same amount of gas as before be sparged through the distributors having progressively smaller r_0 values. Up to a certain r_0 value, as long as $\chi < \chi_c$, U_c will increase with decreasing r_0. But once $\chi > \chi_c$, for any further reduction in the r_0 value U_c will remain constant. These are some of the interesting predicted consequences of the model that must be tested experimentally.

Examples

Air-Water System

Typical data: $D = 0.3$ m, $r_0 = R$, $U_G = 0.01$ m/s, $\rho_L = 1000$ kg/m³, $\mu = 10^{-3}$ Pas, $u_{br} = 0.235$ m/s.
For this data, $Re_G = 3000$, $Fr = 0.137$, $Re_{br} = 70500$, $\chi = 2.73 \times 10^8$.
Thus χ is much greater than χ_c. This explains why inviscid theory is valid to a good degree for such systems.

Air-Glycerol System

Typical data: $D = 0.22$ m, $r_0 = R$, $U_G = 0.003$ m/s, $\rho_L = 1000$ kg/m³, $\mu = 1$ Pas, $u_{br} = 0.05$ m/s.
For this data, $Re_G = 0.66$, $Fr = 0.034$, $Re_{br} = 11$, $\chi = 2824$.
Thus, χ is much smaller than χ_c. This explains why viscous model is valid to a good degree for such systems.

Fluidized Beds

Since fluidized beds are similar to bubble columns in that the circulation of the dense phase is affected by the movement of bubbles, it may be worthwhile to evaluate χ for them and see if it is greater or less than χ_c. The superficial bubble velocity ($\equiv U_G$) equals approximately the flow in excess over minimum fluidization [59–61]. Consider the following typical data [62, 63].
Typical data: $u_{mf} = 0.035$ m/s, $u_0 = 3 u_{mf}$, $U_G = 0.07$ m/s, $\rho_L = 1325$ kg/m³, $\mu = 0.6$ Pa·s, $u_{br} = 0.5$ m/s.
In a small-scale laboratory bed ($D = 0.1$ m), for the above data $\chi = 1,400$, whereas in a large scale bed ($D = 1$ m) $\chi = 6.5 \times 10^5$. Thus, $\chi < \chi_c$ for the laboratory bed and $\chi > \chi_c$ for the large-scale bed. This means that a viscous model is more appropriate for the laboratory bed, whereas an inviscid model is necessary for a large-scale bed. It may be mentioned that only very little effort has gone into developing models to describe gross solid circulation in fluidized beds [31, 34]. The models presented here for liquid circulation in bubble columns have considerable potential to be extended to fluidized beds as well.

CONCLUSION

In bubble columns, inertial forces predominate over viscous forces if the dimensionless number

$$\chi = Re_G Re_{br}^{2/3}/Fr^2(r_0/R)^{10/3}$$

is greater than 13,744. In such situations, a model based on the inviscid theory is appropriate. According to the inviscid model,

1. The axial variation of axial liquid velocity in shallow bubble columns is given by

$$u_y = 12.64 \frac{A}{R^2} \sin\left(\frac{\pi y}{L_1}\right)[1 + 1.58\eta^2 - 3.36\eta^4 - 2.68\eta^6]$$

2. The radial variation of average axial liquid velocity in tall bubble columns is given by

$$u_{y,avg} = 6.32 \frac{A}{R^2} [1 + 1.58\eta^2 - 3.36\eta^4 - 2.68\eta^6]$$

3. The flow strength is given by

$$A = 0.127R^2 u_{br}(gRU_G/u_{br}^3)^{0.4}$$

4. The average liquid circulation velocity and the liquid axial dispersion coefficient are given, respectively, by

$$U_{ci} = u_{br}(gRU_G/u_{br}^3)^{0.4}$$

$$D_L = 0.77 Ru_{br}(gRU_G/u_{br}^3)^{0.4}$$

5. The gas hold-up is given by

$$\delta = 0.5\left(\frac{u_{br}}{\sqrt{gR}}\right)^{0.4}\left(\frac{U_G}{u_{br}}\right)^{0.8}$$

6. The average absolute bubble rise velocity is given by

$$u_b = 2u_{br}\left(\frac{U_G}{u_{br}}\right)^{0.2}\left(\frac{u_{br}}{\sqrt{gR}}\right)^{-0.4}$$

In these expressions, the radius R to be used is given by

$$R = \begin{array}{ll} = R & \text{if } R < 0.8L \\ = 0.8L & \text{if } R > 0.8L \end{array}$$

If the dimensionless number χ is less than 13,744, then a viscous model should be used to describe flow patterns in bubble columns. According to the viscous model

1. The radial variation of axial liquid velocity is given in the bubble envelope and in the annulus, respectively, by

$$\frac{u_1}{\sqrt{gD}} = \frac{\delta_e Re_{br}}{16Fr}[K \ln(1/K) - K(1 - K)(2 - K) - (1 - K)^2(\eta^2 - K)]$$

$$\frac{u_2}{\sqrt{gD}} = \frac{\delta_e Re_{br}}{16Fr}[K \ln(1/\eta^2) - K(2 - K)(1 - \eta^2)]$$

2. The bubble hold-up inside the bubble envelope and the overall bubble hold-up are respectively given by

$$\delta_e = R^2 U_G / r_0^2 u_{br}$$

$$\delta = \frac{U_G}{u_{br}} \left[1 - \frac{Re_G(R/r_0)^4}{800(1 - \delta_e)Fr^2} \right]$$

3. The dimensionless bubble envelope diameter is given by

$$\sqrt{K} = \frac{d}{D} = \frac{r_0}{R} \left[1 - \frac{Re_G(R/r_0)^4}{800(1 - \delta_e)Fr^2} \right]^{1/2}$$

4. The absolute bubble rise velocity and the viscous liquid circulation velocity are respectively given by

$$u_b = u_{br} \bigg/ \left[1 - \frac{Re_G(R/r_0)^4}{800(1 - \delta_e)Fr^2} \right]$$

$$U_{cv} = \frac{(R/r_0)^2}{400} u_{br} \frac{Re_G}{Fr^2}$$

Although the predictions of the inviscid model have been adequately compared with available experimental data, the predictions of the viscous model have been checked only against limited data. There is a need for comfirming/rejecting/modifying the viscous model by comparing its predictions more comprehensively with experimental data. Similarly, the criterion developed to determine the validity region of the inviscid and the viscous models, though found to explain adequately the data for air-water and air-glycerol systems, must be checked more critically. For example, if the function $1/K^2 f_1(K)$ in Equation 101 is assumed to vary between 20 to 30 (refer Figure 14), the cirtical number χ_c in Equation 116 varies from about 10,000 to 18,000. In any case, there will be a gradual transition from viscous to inviscid conditions (as χ is increased). It should be interesting and worthwhile to explore this transition region. However, the number χ (Equation 117) does reveal certain interesting features that may be crucial in scaling up bubble column reactors. For example, it shows that the column diameter critically determines the flow conditions; systems controlled by viscous forces in small laboratory columns may be controlled by inertial forces in large-scale industrial columns at the same operating gas velocity. Another interesting projection of the model regarding the effect of the gas distributor (r_0/R) discussed earlier is also worthy of experimental verification. The number χ also enables one to choose the design and operating parameters so as to achieve inertial or viscous conditions as may be desired.

The predictions of the inviscid and the viscous models indicate that the isolated bubble rise velocity u_{br} directly affects the flow patterns. Hence, it is recommended that this parameter be obtained experimentally for the particular system. In the absence of experimental u_{br} values, however, Equation 8 may be used to predict it. The Sauter mean bubble diameter required to obtain u_{br} from Equation 8 may be obtained from Equation 7a. From limited data on bubble sizes in large columns [33] it was found that the observed bubble sizes were nearly double those predicted by Equation 7a. The discrepancy was attributed to bubble coalescence and the insufficient time available for coaelesced bubbles, greater in size than the maximum stable size, to rupture within the time they stay in the bubble column. Bubble splitting in the presence of bubble coalescence in bubble columns is another important area for further research.

Acknowledgments

The author is grateful to Professor D. Subba Rao for having introduced the field bubble columns to him and for the many fruitful discussions he has had with him. Mr. V. P. Gulati deserves warmest thanks for his tireless efforts in typing this manuscript.

The author is grateful to Gordon and Breach Science Publishers and Pergamon Press for permission to include most of the material from his two papers ([3], and [26], respectively).

NOTATION

a	specific gas-liquid interfacial area, m^2/m^3	q_c	$(8\mu/\pi\rho_L g D^4)Q$, dimensionless
A	flow strength, m^3/s	Q	liquid volumetric turnover rate, m^3/s
A_t	area of cross-section of the bubble column, m^2	r	radial coordinate, m
		r_e	coordinate of bubble envelope, m
b_3	a constant given by Equation 31, dimensionless	r_0	coordinate of bubble injector farthest from the axis (nearest to the wall), m
B	K_3L_1, dimensionless	R	radius of the column, in shallow columns equals 0.8 L, m
C	$2A\pi^2/L_1^2U_b$, dimensionless	Re_{br}	$Du_{br}\rho_L/\mu$, dimensionless
d	bubble envelope diameter, m	Re_G	$DU_G\rho_L/\mu$, dimensionless
d_b	bubble diameter, m	s	R/L_1, dimensionless
d_{bm}	maximum stable bubble diameter, m	u_b	absolute bubble rise velocity, m/s
d_{vs}	Sauter mean bubble diameter, m	u_{br}	isolated bubble rise velocity, m/s
D	diameter of the bubble column, m	u_{Base}	lateral liquid velocity at the base of a circulation cell, m/s
D_L	liquid axial dispersion coefficient, m^2/s		
f	$K\delta_e u_{br}/U_G$, dimensionless	U_b	relative rising velocity of bubble cloud, m/s
f_r	ratio of minimum to mean residence time of bubbles, dimensionless	U_{ci}	average liquid circulation velocity predicted by the inviscid model, m/s
$f_1(K)$	function given by Equation 95, dimensionless	U_{cv}	average liquid circulation velocity predicted by the viscous model, m/s
Fr	$u_{br}/\sqrt{gD}$, dimensionless	U_G	inlet superficial gas velocity forming bubbles, m/s
F(r)	radial component of stream function, dimensionless		
g	acceleration due to gravity, m^2/s	w	vorticity, 1/s
K	$(d/D)^2$, dimensionless	w_0	maximum vorticity or circulation strength, 1/s
L	liquid depth in bubble column, m		
L_1	height of a circulation cell, Equation 51, m	x	Cartesian coordinate, m
		y	vertical coordinate, m
p'	pressure gradient, Equation 82, dimensionless	y_e	coordinate of bubble envelope, m
		Y_0	coordinate of bubble injector nearest to wall, m
P	pressure, Pa; also power, W	z	r/L_1, dimensionless
P_{Base}	pressure at the base of a circulation cell with respect to the cell above, Pa		

Greek Symbols

δ	bubble fraction or gas hold-up, dimensionless	ρ_D	dispersion density, kg/m^3
		ρ_L	liquid density, kg/m^3
δ_e	bubble hold-up inside the bubble envelope, dimensionless	σ	interfacial tension, kg/s^2
η	r/R, dimensionless	ψ	liquid stream function, m^3/s
λ	ratio of maximum to average liquid velocity, dimensionless	ψ_e	stream function evaluated at the bubble envelope, m^3/s
μ	liquid viscosity, Pas	ψ_0	stream function evaluated at (r_0, Y_0), m^3/s
μ_i	$gL_1^3U_G(1-\delta_e)/b_3fR^2U_b^3 \approx$ $gL_1^3U_G b_3R^2u_{br}^3$, dimensionless	χ	$Re_GRe_{br}^{2/3}/Fr^2(r_0/R)^{10/3}$, dimensionless
ρ	gas density, kg/m^3	χ_c	critical $\chi(=13,744)$ at which $U_{ci}=U_{cv}$, dimensionless

REFERENCES

1. Shah, Y. T., Kelkar, B. G., Godbole, S. P., and Deckwer, W. C., *AIChE J*, 28:353 (1982).
2. Rietema, K., *Chem. Eng. Sci.*, 37:1125 (1981).
3. Viswanathan, K. and Subba Rao, D., *Chem. Eng. Commun.*, 25:133 (1983).
4. Wallis, G. B., *One-Dimensional Two-Phase Flow*, McGraw Hill, New York, 1969.
5. Deckwer, W. D., ACS Symposium Series, No. 168, pp. 213–241 (1981).
6. Levich, V. G., *Physicochemical Hydrodynamics*, Prentice-Hall, Englewood Cliff, NJ, 1962.
7. Hills, J. H. and Darton, R. C., *Trans. Inst. Chem. Engrs.*, 54:258 (1976).
8. Rice, R. G., Tupperainen J. M. I., and Hedge, R. M., *Can. J. Chem. Eng.*, 59:677 (1981).
9. Hinze, J. O., *AIChE J*, 1:289 (1955).
10. Kolmogorov, A. N., Doklady Akad. Nauk. *SSSR*, 66:825 (1949).
11. Batchelor, G. K., *Proc. Camb. Phil. Soc.*, 47:359 (1951).
12. Lewis, D. A. and Davidson, J. F., *Trans. Inst. Chem. Engrs.*, 60:283 (1982).
13. Calderbank, P. H., *The Chem. Engr.*, 45:CE209 (1967).
14. Nagel, O., Kurten, H. and Sinn, R., *Chem. Ing. Techn.*, 44:367 (1972).
15. Nagel, O., Hegner, B. and Kurten, H., *Chem. Ing. Techn.*, 50:934 (1978).
16. Berghmans, J., *Chem. Eng. Sci.*, 28:2005 (1973).
17. Kubie, J., *Chem. Eng. Sci.*, 36:234 (1981).
18. Akita, K. and Yoshida, F., *Ind. Eng. Chem. Process Des. and Dev.*, 13:84 (1974).
19. Freedman, W. and Davidson, J. F., *Trans. Inst. Chem. Engrs.* 47:T251 (1969).
20. Whalley, P. B. and Davidson, J. F., *Inst. Chem. Engrs. Symp. Ser. No. 36*, Paper J5 (1974).
21. Clift, R., Grace J. R., and Weber, M. E., *Bubbles, Drops, and Particles*, Ch. 7, Academic Press, New York, 1978.
22. Joshi, J. B. and Sharma, M. M., *Trans. Inst. Chem. Engrs.*, 57:42 (1979).
23. Field, R. W. and Davidson, J. F., *Trans. Inst. Chem. Engrs.*, 58:228 (1980).
24. Lamb, H., *Hydrodynamics*, Cambridge University Press, Cambridge, 1932.
25. Batchelor, G. K., *An Introduction to Fluid Dynamics*, Cambridge University Press, Cambridge, 1967.
26. Viswanathan, K. and Subba Rao, D., *Chem. Eng. Sci.*, 38:474 (1983).
27. Hills, J. H., *Trans. Inst. Chem. Engrs.*, 52:1 (1974).
28. Ueyama, K. and Miyauchi, T., *AIChE J*, 25:258 (1979).
29. Crabtree, J. R. and Bridgewater, J., *Chem. Eng. Sci.*, 24:1755 (1969).
30. Rietema, K. and Ottengraf, S. P. P., *Trans. Inst. Chem. Engrs.*, 48:T54 (1970).
31. Viswanathan, K. and Subba Rao, D., Paper presented at the IVth International Fluidization Conference, Tokyo, Japan, May 29–June 3, 1983.
32. Kreyszig, E., *Advanced Engineering Mathematics*, Wiley Eastern Ltd., New Delhi, 1970.
33. Koide, K. et al., *J. Chem. Eng. Japan*, 12:98 (1979).
34. Viswanathan, K., Ph.D. thesis, Indian Institute of Technology, Delhi, 1983.
35. Turner, J. C. R., *Chem. Eng. Sci.*, 21:971 (1966).
36. Pavlov, V. P., *Khim Prom.*, 9:698 (1965).
37. Yoshitome, H. and Shirai, T., *J. Chem. Eng. Japan*, 3, 29 (1970).
38. Ulbrecht, J. J. and Baykara, Z. S., *Chem. Eng. Commun.*, 10, 165 (1981).
39. Walter, J. F. and Blanch, H. W., *Chem. Eng. Commun.*, 19:243 (1983).
40. Pozin, L. S., Aeroy, M. E. and Bystrova, T. P., *Theor. Found. Chem. Eng.*, 3:714 (1969).
41. Yoshitome, H., Dr. Eng. dissertation, Tokyo Institute of Technology, 1967.
42. Yamagoshi, T., Thesis, B. S., University of Tokyo, 1969.
43. Miyauchi, T. and Shyu, C. N., *Kagaku Kogaku*, 34:958 (1970).
44. Kojima, E. et al., *J. Chem. Eng. Japan*, 13:16 (1980).
45. Aoyama, Y., Ogushi, K., Koide, K. and Kubota, H., *J. Chem. Eng. Japan*, 1:158 (1968).
46. Deckwer, W. D., Burchhart, R. and Zoll, G., *Chem. Eng. Sci.*, 29:2177 (1974).
47. Deckwer, W. D., Graeser, U., Serpemen, Y. and Langemann, H., *Chem. Eng. Sci.*, 28:1223 (1973).
48. Hikita, H. and Kikukawa, H., *Chem. Eng. J.*, 8:191 (1974).
49. Kato, Y. and Nishiwaki, A. *Int. Chem. Eng.*, 12:182 (1972).

50. Reith, T. S., Renken, S. and Israel, B. A., *Chem. Eng. Sci.*, 23:619 (1968).
51. Towell, G. D. and Ackermann, G. H., *Proc. Fifth European/Second Int. Symp. on Chem. Reaction Eng.*, Elsevier, Amsterdam, Paper B-1 (1972).
52. Towell, G. D., Strand C. P., and Ackermann, G. H., in *Mixing-Theory Related to Practice*, P. A. Rottenberg (ed.), Inst. Chem. Engrs., London, pp. 90 (1965).
53. Akita, K., and Yoshida, F., *Ind. Eng. Chem. Process Des. and Dev.*, 12:76 (1973).
54. Fair, J. R., Lambright, A. J. and Anderson, J. W., *Ind. Eng. Chem. Process Des. and Dev.*, 1:33 (1962).
55. Ohki, Y. and Inoue, H., *Chem. Eng. Sci.*, 25:1 (1970).
56. Ueyama, K. and Miyauchi, T., *Kagaku Kogaku Ronbunshu*, 3:17 (1977).
57. Viswanathan, K., Unpublished work, 1983.
58. Franz, K., Buchholz R., and Schugerl, K., *Chem. Eng. Commun.*, 5:165 (1980).
59. Davidson, J. F. and Harrison, D., *Fluidized Particles*, Cambridge University Press, Cambridge, 1963.
60. Kunii, D. and Levenspiel, O., *Fluidization Engineering*, John Wiley and Sons, New York, 1969.
61. Viswanathan, K. and Subba Rao, D., *Int. J. Multiphase Flow*, 9:219 (1982).
62. Botterill, J. S. M. and Kolk, M. V., *AIChE Symp. Ser. No. 116*, 67:70 (1971).
63. Botterill, J. S. M. and Bessant, D. J., in *Fluidization Technology*, D. L., Keairns, (ed.) vol. 2, pp. 7, (1976).

CHAPTER 39

DESIGN AND OPERATION OF BUBBLE COLUMN REACTORS

S. P. Godbole

Petroleum Engineering Department
University of Alaska
Fairbanks, Alaska, USA

and

Y. T. Shah

Department of Chemical and Petroleum Engineering
University of Pittsburgh
Pittsburgh, Pennsylvania, USA

CONTENTS

INTRODUCTION

A bubble column is a contactor in which a discontinuous gas phase, in the form of bubbles, moves relative to a continuous phase, which can either be a liquid or a homogeneous slurry. Bubble columns are widely used in the industry as absorbers, strippers, reactors, and fermenters because of the absence of moving parts, less cost, ease of solid handling, higher heat transfer rates, and the ease with which liquid residence time can be varied. Bubble coalescence, high pressure drop, considerable backmixing in both phases, short residence time of gas, and complex hydrodynamic flow patterns are the major disadvantages in the use of bubble columns.

Bubble columns can be batch or continuous, single staged or multistaged, and can be operated co-currently or countercurrently. Various types of bubble columns and their modifications are described by Shah et al. [1]. Modifications of bubble columns include loop reactors [2], horizontally sparged bubble column [3], downflow bubble column [4], and sectionalized bubble column [5]. Vertically sparged bubble columns are most commonly used in the industry. Table 1 gives the practical examples of the use of bubble columns in the industry.

Bubble columns are difficult to design because of the complexity of flow characteristics, and their unknown behavior under different sets of design parameters such as height, diameter, and distributor design. The proper design and scale-up of a bubble column reactor requires a good mathematical model. Deckwer [50] has outlined a design procedure for modeling a reactor. Application of this procedure requires an exact definition of the requirements, i.e. the required production level, the nature of the reaction system, and the type of product yield structure. These quantities permit an initial choice of the adjustable operational conditions that include phase velocities, temperature, pressure, and the directions of flow. In addition, data on physical properties of the reaction mixture and its components, and phase equilibrium data as well as kinetic parameters are needed. Based on these data, non-adjustable parameters such as phase hold-ups, mixing, and transport parameters are estimated using the available literature correlations. Knowing these parameters, one can solve the mass, momentum and heat balance equations to calculate product yield, productivity, concentration, and temperature profiles. If possible, experimental verification is provided from collecting the relevant data in the pilot plant. The procedure is iterative so that both model and model parameters can be constantly updated with the availability of new data.

Table 1
Practical Examples of Use of Bubble Columns

Systems	References
1. Carbonylation of methanol to acetic acid	[6, 7]
2. Catalytic desulfurization of petroleum fractions	[8, 9]
3. Coal liquefaction	[10–14]
4. Fischer-Tropsch synthesis	[15–18]
5. Hydrogenation of benzene to cyclohexane	[19, 20]
6. Methanol from synthesis gas	[21]
7. Methanation of CO	[22, 23]
8. Oxidation of acetaldehyde to acetic acid	[24, 25]
9. Oxidation of acetaldehyde to acetic anhydride	[26]
10. Oxidation of butanes to acetic acid and methyl ethyl ketone	[27–29]
11. Oxidation of ethylene in acetic acid solutions to vinyl acetate	[30]
12. Oxidation of cumene to phenol and acetone	[31]
13. Oxidation of toluene to benzoic acid	[32]
14. Oxidation of cyclohexane to adipic acid	[33]
15. Oxidations of n-parrafins to sec-alcohols	[34]
16. Oxydesulfurization of coal	[35]
17. Partial oxidation of ethylene to acetaldehyde	[36]
18. Polymerization of olefins	[37–38]
19. Production of hydrocarbons from CO and steam	[39–40]
20. Production of single cell protein	[5, 41, 42]
21. Upgrading of coal oils and heavy oil fractions by hydrogenations	[43, 44]
22. Waste water treatment	[45]
23. Wet oxidation of waste water	[46, 47]
24. Wet oxidation of waste sludge	[48, 49]

Table 2
Hydrodynamic Models

Model name	Comments
1. Laminar liquid circulation and bubble street model of Rietema and Ottengraph [51, 52]	• Valid for highly viscous solutions at very low superficial gas velocity in small diameter columns. • Model used the method of energy balance for discerning the liquid flow pattern.
2. Laminar liquid circulation and bubble chain model of Crabtree and Bridgewater [53]	• Limited to chain bubbling for highly viscous solutions at low superficial gas velocities. • Use is limited to give basic understanding of liquid circulation in bubble columns.
3. Gulf stream model of Freedman and Davidson [54].	• Applicable to shallow two dimensional bubble columns to be operated at low superficial gas velocities. • Use of pressure balance method.
4. Circulating cell model of Miyauchi and co-workers [55, 56].	• Applicable for turbulent liquid flow with radial variation in gas holdup. • A priori determination of liquid velocity profile is not possible for new gas-liquid system.
5. Liquid circulation model of Bhavraju et al. [57].	• Although applicable for turbulent liquid flow, use is limited to shallow bubble columns where the multiple circulation cells in traverse direction can exist. • Does not account for the energy dissipation at the gas-liquid interface and is unable to predict the circulation velocity.
6. Energy balance method of Whalley and Davidson [58].	• Application of energy balance method to turbulent liquid velocity profile. For $L/D_C < 1$, the liquid velocity predictions were erroneous. • Liquid velocity profile can be calculated with knowledge of average fractional gas-holdup and bubble rise velocity.
7. A circulation cell model of Joshi and Sharma [59].	• This model removed the drawbacks of Whalley and Davidson's energy balance by introducing a multiple-cell circulation model. • The liquid phase velocity distribution and average velocities could be successfully predicted.
8. Hydrodynamic model for three-phase fluidized beds and slurry reactors, Joshi [60].	• Height of each circulation cell is adjusted for the condition of minimum liquid phase vorticity. Intercell recirculation is allowed. • Most suitable model for calculation of liquid velocity profile, etc.
9. Churn turbulent flow model of Zuber and Findlay [61].	• Continuity equations for the dispersed flow, drift flux and slip velocity relations are used. • Can be applied for churn turbulent flow where high superficial liquid velocities are employed.
10. Application of Kolmogoroff's theory of isotropic turbulence by Nagel et al. [62–65].	• Assumes stochastic turbulent mixing process in the gas-liquid dispersion.

HYDRODYNAMICS AND MIXING

It is essential to understand the hydrodynamics and mixing in bubble columns before developing the appropriate design equations for the bubble column reactor. The hydrodynamics of bubble columns can be divided into three separate axial regions. In the first region, near the gas sparger, characteristic bubble behavior depends on the sparger design and the gas flow rate. In the second region, which occupies most of the column volume, the bubble behavior is solely controlled by the liquid flow pattern. Coalescence occurs in the third region. Theoretical and experimental investigations of liquid phase flow pattern are reported in the literature. It has been shown that a strong liquid circulation pattern is developed because of the introduction of gas. Tables 2 and 3

Table 3
Mixing Models Used For Describing Liquid Phase
Dispersion in Bubble Column Reactors

Model Name	Comments
1. Backflow model by Miyauchi and Vermeulen [66] and Nishikawi and Kato [67, 68]	• Stagewise model assumes backflow superimposed on the net flow through a column with perfectly mixed stages in cascade. • In two limiting cases it is reduced to a perfectly mixed model and an axial dispersion model.
2. Backflow model with imperfectly mixed stages by Nishikawi et al. [68]	• Simple extension of the above backflow model.
3. Interstage recirculation model by Mecklenburgh [69]	• It assumes a backmix reactor with a series of perfectly mixed stages with recirculation between stages.
4. Axial mixing model of Deckwer et al. [70]	• Estimates the axial liquid phase dispersion coefficient by fitting the concentration profiles to the axial dispersion equation.
5. Axial dispersion model of Baird and Rice [71]	• Uses the dimensional analysis and Kolmogoroff's theory of isotropic turbulence. • Dimensionally consistent expression for axial dispersion coefficient is applicable to both cocurrent and countercurrent systems
6. Recirculation model of Joshi [60]	• Assumes multiple recirculation cells in the axial direction with liquid upflow at center and downflow near the wall • For the turbulent liquid flow, axial dispersion coefficient data compares very well with predictions of this model.
7. Tank in series with recirculation model of Joshi [60]	• Assumes N tanks in series with the height of each tank equal to the height of circulation cell with interstage circulation prevailing between the consecutive cells.
8. Dispersion coefficients in different flow regimes by Rice et al. [72]	• This study proposes the dependence of the dispersion coefficient on superficial gas velocity in chain bubbling, bubbly flow, churn-turbulent flow and slug flow.
9. The dispersion model of Riquarts [73]	• Assumes Peclet number equals 2 for bubble columns.

summarize the hydrodynamic and mixing models that can be applied to describe a bubble column reactor. Joshi and Shah [74] have critically reviewed the hydrodynamic and mixing models for bubble column reactors. They have recommended the multiple cell circulation model with intercell circulation [60, 75] for the estimations of average liquid velocity and liquid velocity profile. Deckwer et al. [76] have tested the applicability of the axial dispersion model over a wide range of operating conditions.

In bubble columns the hydrodynamic, mixing, and transport characteristics depend strongly on the flow regime. Therefore, it is necessary to define the possible flow regimes in bubble columns before presenting the model equations. Wallis [77] has defined the upward movement of bubbles into three separate flow regimes, namely bubble, slug, and churn turbulent. In an air-water system for a superficial gas velocity less than 0.05 m/s, a bubble flow region is generally present. This regime is characterized by almost uniformly sized bubbles that rise approximately with the same rise velocity. In the bubbly flow regime, a maximum amount of gas is transported through the column.

At higher gas velocities, the homogeneous gas-in-liquid dispersion cannot be maintained and an unsteady flow pattern with channeling occurs. This is defined as heterogeneous or churn turbulent flow regime, and is characterized by large bubbles moving with high rise velocities in the presence of small bubbles [78–84].

In small diameter columns, at high gas flow rates, large bubbles are stabilized by the column wall leading to the formation of bubble slugs. For highly viscous solutions with an apparent viscosity of 0.15 Pa.s, Godbole et al. [79] have reported the presence of slugs even in a 0.304-m diameter column.

Various flow regimes are schematically represented in Figure 1. The dependence of the flow regime on column diameter and superficial gas velocity can be seen from Figure 2. The transition between the flow regimes can be strongly affected by the physico-chemical properties of liquid, the liquid velocity, and the type of sparger used [85]. For example, (a) porous spargers, with mean pore sizes less than 150 μm, generally produce bubbly flow up to 0.05–0.08 m/s, whereas, perforated plates with an orifice diameter larger than 1 μm, produce bubbly flow only at small velocities; (b) Kelkar et al. [81] have reported that for dilute alcohol solutions, bubbly flow regime is present up to gas hold-up values of 50%; (c) Schumpe [83] has reported the presence of slug flow regime in a 0.150-m diameter column for highly viscous solutions even at a superficial gas velocity of 0.02 m/s.

Besides these factors, the foaming nature of liquids can significantly affect the hydrodynamics in a bubble column. Many liquid mixtures have foaming tendencies, whereas pure liquids do not foam and saturated solutions might foam very slightly if at all. Some examples of foaming liquids are

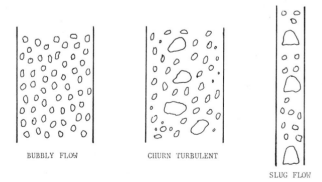

BUBBLY FLOW   CHURN TURBULENT   SLUG FLOW

Figure 1. Flow regimes in bubble columns.

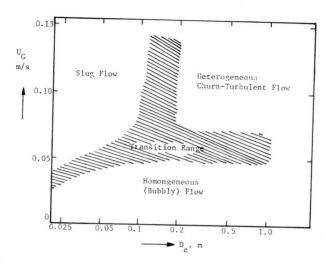

Figure 2. Dependency of flow regime on gas velocity and column diameter for aqueous solutions.

given in Table 4. Shah et al. [86] derived the condition for foaming in the absence of liquid flow based on the works of Marrucci [87] and Joshi [60] as:

$$Fr_{gc} = \frac{U_{gc}}{\sqrt{gD_c}} = \frac{0.25\varepsilon_G^2}{(1 - \varepsilon_G)^{3/2}} \tag{1}$$

The foaming would occur for $Fr < Fr_{gc}$. Equation 1 can be used as a first approximation for predicting the onset of foaming in bubble columns.

REACTOR MODELS

Most of the bubble column reactor models proposed in the literature invariably assume a bubble class with a uniform bubble size. For approximately uniform sized bubbles such a model would be suitable. As pointed out earlier, the churn turbulent regime is characterized by the fast rising large bubbles moving through a swarm of small bubbles. The concept of a mean gas phase residence time in this regime is somewhat meaningless. The two bubble classes move at different speeds within the column. It can be assumed that the fast rising large bubbles rise in plug flow, whereas the backmixing of small bubbles is more difficult to quantify. A realistic model should consider the axial dispersion of small bubbles. Plug flow for small bubbles is only realizable at very low gas velocities when bubbly flow regime is present. In a limiting case of large diameter columns, the small bubbles are completely mixed. The mean residence time of large bubbles is smaller than that of small bubbles.

Readers are referred to the development of the bubble column reactor models for uniform sized bubbles by Deckwer [50]. Generally, the scale-up of a bubble column is accompanied by the change in flow regime and under this situation, the two-bubble class model will give a more reliable scale-up than conventional single-bubble class models. In addition, the churn turbulent regime is the most commonly encountered flow regime in industrial bubble columns. Hence, a two-bubble class model developed by Godbole [88] and Shah et al. [89] is outlined here.

Table 4
Practical Examples of Foaming Liquids

Aqueous Systems
- Teepol/water, glycol/water, glycerol/water, m-cresol/water.
- Alcohol (e.g. methanol, ethanol, propanol, 2-methyl propanol, 3-methyl butanol, 2,2-dimethyl propanol, 1-pentanol, 1-hexanol, 1-octanol, butanol, n-heptyl, n-amyl etc.)/water, alcohol/glycerol/water, phenol/water, benzyl alcohol/water.
- Acid (acetic, formic, propionic, butyric, valeric, heptanoic, lactic, octanoic, adipic, glutaric, succinic, malonic, oxalic, decanoic, caproic etc.)/water mixtures
- Inorganic compounds such as KSCN, NaOH, Na_2SO_4, Na_2CO_3, KBr, KCl, $K_3Fe(CN)_6$, K_2SO_4 and $AlCl_3$ in water
- Aqueous solutions of the following organic substances:

Sucrose	Nitrobenzene
Acetone	Ethylamine
2-Pentanone	Ether
Acetaldoxime	Aniline
Paraldehyde	p-toluidine
Ethyl acetate	α-naphthylamine

- Aqueous solutions of soaps (e.g. sodium, calcium and potassium laurate, sodium myristate, oleate, palmitate decanoate, stearate, caprate, ricinoleate, abietate)
- Aqueous solutions of synthetic detergents
- Aqueous solutions of poorly identified organic substances such as pine oil (α- and β-terpineol), peptone, gelatin, albumin, pectin, casein, bile acids and their salts, sodium glycocholate and its mixture with sodium hexamoate, and sodium undecylenate
- Aqueous solutions of proteins, gelatin and egg albumin

Organic Systems
- Concentrated solutions of diphenyl in benzene and naphthalene in gasoline
- Medicinal paraffin oil
- Monohydrocarbons in hydrocarbons, e.g. stearic acid in heptane
- Mixture of n-hexane, n-octane and nitorbenzene
- Methanol-p-cymene, methanol-m-xylene and methanol-mesitylene mixtures (also similar mixtures with ethanol, propanol etc.)
- Commercial detergents in various organic liquids
- Industrial oils particularly at high temperature and pressure
- Polyethylene glycols in methanol or acetone
- Sodium diamyl sulfosuccinate in benzene and other aromatic hydrocarbons including nitrobenzene
- Sodium dioctyl sulfosuccinate in triethanol amine
- Mixture of oxtene (e.g. linseed oil) and inactive (e.g. olive, peanut) oils
- Variety of industrial ternary and multi-component mixtures

Consider a bubble column reactor operating in the churn turbulent flow regime (see Figure 3). As previously discussed, in the churn turbulent flow regime the gas flow can be approximately broken down in terms of transport flow (i.e. flow by large bubbles) and entrained flow (i.e., flow by small bubbles) [84]. The large bubbles rise much faster through a swarm of small bubbles and can be assumed to rise in a plug flow manner. The small bubbles are assumed to be completely backmixed. No interaction between the two bubble classes is considered. Assume a gas-liquid reaction

$$A_{(gas)} + UB_{(liquid)} \rightarrow products \tag{2}$$

If the reaction is non catalytic, it is assumed to be slow so that it occurs in the bulk liquid. If the reaction is catalytic, the reaction occurs at the catalyst surface in the liquid phase and the catalyst is assumed to be uniformly distributed in the liquid phase. The rate of the reaction is dependent only on the liquid phase concentration of component A (i.e., the concentration of species B is in excess) and it is assumed to be first order. The pressure in the reactor is assumed to be constant. With these assumptions, a mass balance for the reactant A in large bubbles yields

$$-\frac{d}{dx}\left(U_G^L \frac{Y_{AG}^L P}{RT}\right) = (k_L a)^L ((C_{AL}^*)^L - C_{AL}) \tag{3}$$

The mass balance for the reactant A in small bubbles can be expressed as

$$U_G^S(Y_{AG,0}^S - Y_{AG,1}^S) = (k_L a)^S \frac{RT}{P}((C_{AL}^*)^S - C_{AL}) \tag{4}$$

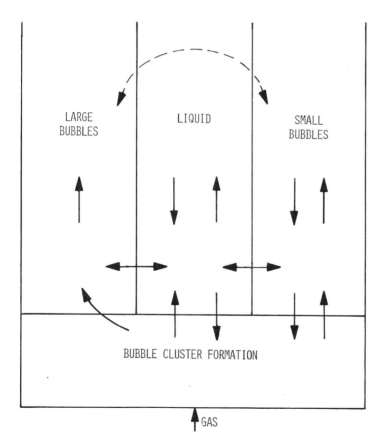

Figure 3. Schematic of bubble column in churn turbulent flow regime.

We assume the batch (no flow) liquid phase to be completely backmixed. Thus, the material balance for the reactant A in the liquid phase can be expressed as

$$(k_L a)^L \int_0^L ((C_{AL}^*)^L - C_{AL})\, dx + (k_L a)^S ((C_{AL}^*)^S - C_{AL}) - k_A C_{AL} \varepsilon_L = 0 \tag{5}$$

If the reaction is catalytic, the liquid-solid mass transfer resistance is assumed to be negligible, and the kinetic constant k_A includes the catalyst concentration in the slurry phase. The equilibrium liquid phase concentration of component A for small and large bubbles will be assumed to follow Henry's law. Thus,

$$(C_{AL}^*)^S = \frac{P Y_{AG}^S}{H}, (C_{AL}^*)^L = \frac{P Y_{AG}^L}{H} \tag{6}$$

The gas velocity of the reactant is reduced due to the chemical reaction. This variation in gas velocity can be related to the conversion by Equation 7.

$$U_G = U_{G,0}(1 + \alpha X_A) \tag{7}$$

$$\text{where} \quad \alpha = \frac{U_G (X_A = 1) - U_G (X_A = 0)}{U_G (X_A = 0)} \tag{8}$$

$$X_A = \frac{U_{G,0} Y_{AG,0} - U_G Y_{AG}}{U_{G,0} Y_{AG,0}} \tag{9}$$

From Equations 8 and 9 we obtain

$$U_G = \frac{U_{G,0}(Y_{AG,0} + \alpha Y_{AG,0})}{(Y_{AG,0} + \alpha Y_{AG})} \tag{10}$$

The flux of A through large bubbles and small bubbles is given by

$$U_G^L = U_{br}^L \varepsilon_G^L \tag{11}$$

$$U_G^S = U_{br}^S \varepsilon_G^S$$

Equations 3, 4, and 5 will simplify as:

$$-\frac{d}{dz} (U_{br}^L \varepsilon_G^L Y_{AG}^L) = \frac{L(k_L a)^L RT}{P} \left(\frac{P Y_{AG}^L}{H} - C_{AL} \right) \tag{12}$$

$$L(k_L a)^S \left(\frac{P Y_{AG}^S}{H} - C_{AL} \right) = \frac{P}{RT} U_{br,0}^S \varepsilon_{G,0}^S Y_{AG,0}^S - \frac{P}{RT} U_{br,1}^S \varepsilon_{G,1}^S Y_{AG,1}^S \tag{13}$$

$$(k_L a)^S \left(\frac{P Y_{AG}^S}{H} - C_{AL} \right) + \int_0^1 (k_L a)^L \left(\frac{P Y_{AG}^L}{H} - C_{AL} \right) dz = k_A C_{AL} \varepsilon_L \tag{14}$$

Since the concentration of A in the large bubbles varies along the length of the column, an average value of the driving force is used in the balance for well mixed liquid phase. Using the variation of gas velocity along the column given by Equation 10, we get a mass balance for the reactant A in large bubbles as:

$$-U_{br,0}^L \varepsilon_{G,0}^L Y_{AG,0}^L (1 + \alpha) \frac{d}{dz} \left(\frac{Y_{AG}^L}{Y_{AG,0}^L + \alpha Y_{AG}^L} \right) = \frac{L(k_L a)^L RT}{P} \left(\frac{P Y_{AG}^L}{H} - C_{AL} \right) \tag{15}$$

The mass balance for the reactant A in small bubbles can be related to the liquid phase concentration as:

$$C_{AL} = -\frac{PU_{br,0}^S \varepsilon_{G,0}^S Y_{AG,0}^S}{LRT(k_L a)^S}\left(\frac{Y_{AG,0}^S - Y_{AG}^S}{Y_{AG,0}^S + \alpha Y_{AG}^S}\right) + \frac{PY_{AG}^S}{H} \tag{16}$$

Thus, Equation 15 can be rewritten as:

$$\frac{dY_{AG}^L}{dz} = \frac{(Y_{AG,0}^L + \alpha Y_{AG}^L)^2 L(k_L a)^L RT}{U_{br,0}^L \varepsilon_{G,0}^L Y_{AG,0}^L(1+\alpha)P}\left(C_{AL} - \frac{PY_{AG}^L}{H}\right) \tag{17}$$

Boundary conditions for Equation 17 are:

$$Y_{AG}^L = Y_{AG,0}^L \quad \text{at } z = 0 \tag{18}$$

and

$$Y_{AG}^L = Y_{AG,1}^L \quad \text{at } z = 1 \tag{19}$$

The liquid phase concentration of the reactant A is constant throughout the reactor and hence Equation 17 can be integrated analytically as:

$$z = \frac{A'(Y_{AG}^L - Y_{AG,0}^L)}{(1+\alpha)Y_{AG,0}^L(Y_{AG,0}^L + \alpha Y_{AG}^L)} + \frac{B'}{\alpha}\ln\frac{Y_{AG,0}^L + \alpha Y_{AG}^L}{Y_{AG,0}^L(1+\alpha)} + \frac{C'}{b}\ln\frac{C_{AL} - bY_{AG,0}^L}{C_{AL} - bY_{AG}^L} \tag{20}$$

where
$$A' = \frac{B'[a\alpha - bY_{AG,0}^L + 2bY_{AG,0}^L]}{b}$$

$$B' = \frac{1}{\left(\dfrac{a}{b}(a\alpha + bY_{AG,0}^L) + \dfrac{b}{\alpha}(Y_{AG,0}^L)^2\right)}$$

$$C' = \frac{bB'}{\alpha}$$

$$a = \frac{C_{AL}L(k_L a)^L RT}{U_{br,0}^L \varepsilon_{G,0}^L(Y_{AG,0}^L)^2(1+\alpha)P}$$

$$b = \frac{L(k_L a)^L RT}{U_{br,0}^L \varepsilon_{G,0}^L(Y_{AG,0}^L)^2(1+\alpha)H}$$

From the liquid phase balance, we get

$$C_{AL} = \frac{\dfrac{(k_L a)^S PY_{AG}^S}{H} + \displaystyle\int_0^1 \dfrac{(k_L a)^L PY_{AG}^L}{H}dz}{(k_L a)^S + (k_L a)^L + k_A \varepsilon_L} \tag{21}$$

Equations 16, 20, and 21 must be solved simultaneously to obtain the values for Y_{AG}^S and profile for Y_{AG}^L. In order to calculate the gas phase conversions for the component A, the mass balance for the gas phase at the outlet of the reactor can be written as

$$U_{br}^S \varepsilon_G^S Y_{AG,1}^S + U_{br}^L \varepsilon_G^L Y_{AG,1}^L = U_G Y_{AG,1} \tag{22}$$

or

$$\frac{U_{br,0}^S \varepsilon_{G,0}^S Y_{AG,0}^S Y_{AG,1}^S}{(Y_{AG,0}^S + \alpha Y_{AG,1}^S)} + \frac{U_{br,0}^L \varepsilon_{G,0}^L Y_{AG,0}^L Y_{AG,1}^L}{(Y_{AG,0}^L + \alpha Y_{AG,1}^L)} = \frac{U_{G,0} Y_{AG,0} Y_{AG,1}}{(Y_{AG,0} + \alpha Y_{AG,1})} \tag{23}$$

and $\quad X_A = \dfrac{Y_{AG,0} - Y_{AG,1}}{Y_{AG,0} + \alpha Y_{AG,1}}$ \hfill (24)

Thus, the overall conversion for a first order reaction in the churn turbulent regime can be calculated if fractional gas hold-ups, rise velocities, and volumetric mass transfer coefficients for two-bubble classes and the kinetic data are known.

For uniform sized bubbles, with the assumption of plug flow in the gas phase and well mixed liquid phase, the conversion of the reactant A can be calculated from:

$$-\frac{d}{dz}(U_G Y_{AG}) = L(k_L a) \frac{RT}{P} (C_{AL}^* - C_{AL}) \tag{25}$$

where $\quad C_{AL} = \dfrac{\dfrac{P(k_L a)}{H} \int_0^1 Y_{AG}\, dz}{k_L a + k_A \varepsilon_L}$ \hfill (26)

The conversion, X_A, as functions of $k_L a$, k_A and ε_G (i.e. $1 - \varepsilon_L$) can be obtained by integrating Equation 25 with the boundary condition $Y_{AG} = Y_{AG,0}$ at $z = 0$. The integration procedure is the same as before and uses Equation 7, 25, and 26. The final calculation requires a trial and error procedure for C_{AL} so that Equations 25 and 26 are simultaneously satisfied.

These equations were evaluated by Shah et al. [89] and Joseph et al. [90]. The important conclusions of these studies are as follows:

1. In churn turbulent flow regime a two-bubble class model is more realistic and gives results close to those predicted by a single-bubble class model as long as k_A is small ($< 0.15 \text{ s}^{-1}$) and $(k_L a)^S$ is negligible. The mass transfer coefficient for large bubbles $(k_L a)^L$ can be easily obtained for a variety of bubble column operations (i.e., bubble columns with and without internals).
2. The mass transfer from small bubbles can be neglected at very high gas velocities ($U_G > 0.3$ m/s). For $U_G < 0.3$ m/s, $(k_L a)^S$ must be determined. $(k_L a)^S$ can be obtained from bubble size distribution measurements as well as from the use of the correlation of Calderbank and Moo Young [91] for k_L. If $(k_L a)^S$ is large at low gas velocities ($U_G < 0.3$ m/s) a two-bubble class model predicts significantly higher conversion than a single-bubble class model. Some details on ε_G^S, ε_G^L, and $(k_L a)^L$ are given in the next section on the design parameter estimations. Joseph and Shah [92] applied a two-bubble class model to a pseudo first-order and fast gas-liquid reaction and showed that in this case the conversion strongly depends on the diameter of the large bubbles since both k_L^L and a^L appear separately in the analysis.

DESIGN PARAMETERS ESTIMATIONS

Design parameters for a bubble column reactor can be broadly divided into two categories; adjustable operating parameters and non-adjustable parameters. Adjustable operating conditions include temperature, pressure, superficial gas and liquid velocities, nature of flow, i.e. co-current or countercurrent operation, etc. Non-adjustable design parameters include phase hold-ups, bubble size distribution, fluid-fluid interfacial areas, interphase transfer coefficients, dispersion coefficients for various processes, etc. These non-adjustable parameters have complex dependencies on adjustable parameters. Flow regimes strongly dictate the non-adjustable parameters. Numerous empirical correlations have been proposed in the literature for the estimation of non-adjustable parameters. Only those correlations with broader applicability are reported here. In addition, the emphasis is given to those correlations that are based on sound theoretical basis.

Gas Hold-up

Gas hold-up (ε_G) is one of the most important parameters characterizing the hydrodynamics of bubble columns. It depends primarily on the superficial gas velocity and to a certain extent, on the sparger design, physico-chemical properties, and column diameter. For large values of the ratio of column diameter to bubble diameter (≥ 40), the ε_G is independent of column diameter. This condition is usually satisfied for a column diameter greater than 0.15 m.

The dependency of the gas hold-up on the superficial gas velocity is generally of the form:

$$\varepsilon_G \propto U_G^n \tag{27}$$

where the value of the exponent n depends on the flow regime. For the bubbly flow regime n varies from 0.7 to 1.2, while for the churn turbulent or transition regime, the effect of U_G is less pronounced and the exponent n takes values of 0.4 to 0.7.

Large numbers of gas hold-up correlations in the literature indicate that a unique equation is not available. For less viscous and coalescing liquids ($\mu_L \leq 0.02$ pa·s), gas hold-up equations by Akita and Yoshida [93] and Hikita et al. [94] are recommended. Akita and Yoshida [93] have correlated their gas hold-up data for water and aqueous solutions of glycerine, glycol, methanol, and salts like sodium chloride by:

$$\frac{\varepsilon_G}{(1 - \varepsilon_G)^4} = 0.2 \left(\frac{gD_C^2 \rho_L}{\sigma} \right)^{1/8} \left(\frac{gD_C^3}{v_L^2} \right)^{1/12} \left(\frac{U_G}{\sqrt{gD_C}} \right) \tag{28}$$

Conservative estimates are obtained when the gas hold-up correlation of Akita and Yoshida [93] is used. Only the correlation of Hikita et al. [94] considers the gas phase properties. It is based on the gas hold-up data in water, organic liquids, and electrolyte solutions. Hikita et al. [94] have proposed the following relation:

$$\varepsilon_G = 0.672f \left(\frac{U_G \mu_L}{\sigma} \right)^{0.578} \left(\frac{\mu_L^4 g}{\rho_L \sigma^3} \right)^{-0.131} \left(\frac{\rho_G}{\rho_L} \right)^{0.062} \left(\frac{\mu_G}{\mu_L} \right)^{0.017} \tag{29}$$

$f = 1.0$ for non-electrolyte solutions

$f = 10^{0.0414I}$ $I < 1.0$ kg ion/m^3

$f = 1.1$ $I > 1.0$ kg ion/m^3

$I = $ Ionic strength of the solutions

In many practical applications, these correlations as well as other literature correlations fail [79–81, 95]. For gas hold-up in highly viscous psuedoplastic solutions in large diameter columns, the correlation of Godbole et al. [79] is recommended. For cases of liquid mixtures, measurement of the gas hold-up in a lab-scale column with diameter of 0.15 m or larger is recommended.

Gas hold-up in foaming ethanol-water mixtures are reported by Shah et al. [86]. This study has shown that foaming liquids generally gave a much higher gas hold-up than for non-foaming liquids. A theoretical model or gas hold-up in surfactant solutions is outlined by Kulkarni et al. [96].

Bubble Dynamics

Bubble size, bubble rise velocity, distribution, and liquid and bubble velocity profiles are the basic factors deciding the bubble column performance. For estimating bubble diameters in bubble columns, the general equation of Calderbank [97] is recommended. Calderbank [97] proposed the following relation based on the Kolmogoroff's isotropic turbulence theory:

$$d_{vs} = C \frac{\sigma^{0.6}}{(P'/V_D)^{0.4} \rho_L^{0.2}} \varepsilon_G^n \left(\frac{\mu_G}{\mu_L}\right)^{0.25} \tag{30}$$

Where the constant C and exponent n depend on the liquid phase properties and stirrer type. (P'/V_D) is the rate of energy dissipation per unit dispersion volume.

Akita and Yoshida [98] measured the bubble size using perforated plates and single orifices, and water, aqueous and pure glycol, methanol and carbon tetrachloride. Their correlation is recommended in the churn turbulent regime for less effective spargers. Akita and Yoshida's correlation is as follows:

$$\frac{d_{vs}}{D_C} = 26 \left(\frac{D_C^2 g \rho_L}{\sigma}\right)^{-0.5} \left(\frac{g D_C^3}{v_L^2}\right)^{-.012} \left(\frac{U_G}{\sqrt{g D_C}}\right)^{-0.12} \tag{31}$$

Most recently Shah et al. [86] reported bubble size in an ethanol-water mixture under both foaming and non-foaming conditions. These bubble sizes were always smaller than the ones observed in water. Similar conclusions for other foaming liquids were also drawn by Zieminski et al. [99].

For the calculation of terminal bubble rise velocity of single bubbles, the correlation by Clift et al. [100] is recommended.

$$U_{b\infty} = \frac{\mu_L}{\rho_L d_{vs}} M^{-0.149} (J - 0.857) \tag{32}$$

where, $M = \dfrac{g \mu_L^4 (\rho_L - \rho_G)}{\rho_L^2 \sigma^3}$,

$$Re = \frac{d_{vs} U_{b\infty} \rho_L}{\mu_L}$$

$$Eo = \frac{(g(\rho_L - \rho_G) d_{vs}^2)}{\sigma}$$

$$J = 0.94 H^{0.747} \ (2 < H \leq 59.3)$$

and $J = 3.42 H^{0.441} \ (H > 59.3)$

where, $H = \dfrac{4}{3} (Eo) M^{-0.149} \left(\dfrac{\mu_L}{\mu_\omega}\right)^{-0.14}$

for the range $M < 10^{-3}$, $Eo < 40$, and $Re > 0.1$.

It should be noted that d_{vs} is the Sauter mean bubble diameter. d_{vs} will be a true representation of the bubble size in the homogeneous or bubbly flow regime. In the churn turbulent regime, large bubbles rise through a swarm of uniformly sized small bubbles. Approximate bimodal size distribution for the churn turbulent regime in a bubble column reactor is proposed by Sriram and Mann [101], Vermeer and Krishna [84], Kelkar et al. [81], Godbole et al. [78–80]. The measurements of sauter mean diameters of large and small bubbles for nitrogen-water system are reported by Shah et al. [89].

Gas-Liquid Interfacial Area

The gas-liquid interfacial area is an important non-adjustable design parameter that can easily influence the volumetric mass transfer coefficient. The gas-liquid interfacial area is the main design criteria for absorption with a chemical reaction in a fast reaction regime. Specific interfacial areas can be calculated with the knowledge of sauter mean bubble diameter, d_{vs}, and gas hold-up ε_G.

$$a = \frac{6\varepsilon_G}{d_{vs}} \tag{33}$$

$$\text{with} \quad d_{vs} = \frac{\sum N_i d_{bi}^3}{\sum N_i d_{bi}^2} \tag{34}$$

Akita and Yoshida's [98] correlation can be used to estimate a conservative value of gas-liquid interfacial area a for less effective spargers.

$$aD_C = \frac{1}{3}\left(\frac{gD_C^2\rho_L}{\sigma}\right)^{0.5}\left(\frac{gD_C^3}{v_L^2}\right)^{0.1}\varepsilon_G^{1.13} \tag{35}$$

The correlation given in the Equation 33 is based on data with water, glycol solutions, and carbon tetrachloride. In general, the equation of Nagel et al. [65] can be recommended for bubble columns aerated by two-phase nozzle spargers and other kinds of gas-liquid contactors. They derived the following expression for "a" based on the Kolmogoroff's theory of isotropic turbulence.

$$a = K\left(\frac{e'}{V_R}\right)^{0.4}\varepsilon_G^n \tag{36}$$

The exponent of the energy dissipation density varies between 0.4 and 1.0.

Recently, Godbole et al. [79] used a sulfite oxidation technique to measure "a" in carboxy methyl cellulose solutions in a 0.304-m diameter bubble column, and their correlation is:

$$a = 19.2(U_G)^{0.47}(\mu_{eff})^{-0.76} \tag{37}$$

The effective viscosity μ_{eff} of the liquid phase was obtained from the measured shear rate against shear stress using the correlation of Nishikawa et al. [102]. The previous correlations are not adequately tested for foaming liquids such as alcohol-water and acid-water mixtures [99].

Volumetric Gas-Liquid Mass Transfer Coefficients

The knowledge of the residence time distribution of phases is necessary to determine the volumetric mass transfer coefficient, k_La. The assumption of complete mixing is only justified in large diameter columns, say $D_C \geq 1.0$ m. The measurement of axial concentration profiles and the use of an axial dispersion model for measuring k_La is recommended for small diameter tall bubble columns.

Shah et al. [1] have correlated literature data on the volumetric mass transfer coefficients in tap water and salt solutions and they proposed the following relation:

$$k_La = bU_G^{0.82} \tag{38}$$

where b is 0.0107 for nozzle spargers and 0.0296 for sintered plates. The value of b is not only influenced by the sparger design but also by the physico-chemical properties of liquid phase. The exponent of U_G in Equation 36 is in full agreement with the theoretical relation developed by Kastanek [103].

For the case of the less effective spargers, the correlation of Akita and Yoshida [93] is recommended for conservative estimates. Their correlation is given by:

$$\frac{k_LaD_C^2}{D_i} = 0.6\left(\frac{v_L}{D_i}\right)^{0.5}\left(\frac{gD_C^2\rho_L}{\sigma}\right)^{0.62}\left(\frac{gD_C^3}{v_L2}\right)^{0.31}\varepsilon_G^{1.1} \tag{39}$$

Schugerl and co-workers [5, 104, 105] have presented comprehensive k_La data for oxygen mass transfer in aqueous solutions of alcohols and glucose, with and without presence of inhibitors. They explained their experimental findings by means of coalescence promoting and hindering properties of the liquid medium.

For prediction of k_La in highly viscous pseudoplastic solution, use of the following correlation by Godbole et al. [79] is recommended.

$$k_La = 8.35 \times 10^{-4}U_G^{0.44}\mu_{eff}^{-1.01} \tag{40}$$

The reported studies on volumetric mass transfer coefficients for organic liquids and surfactant solutions are relatively scarce. Recently, Godbole et al. [80] have shown the failure of the literature correlation for predicting k_La in a C_{9+} isoparaffin mixture. In addition, the literature correlations have not been verified for foaming systems, such as alcohol-water and acid-water mixtures. Zieminski et al. [99] reported significantly larger k_La in these systems compared to water.

Liquid Side Mass Transfer Coefficient k_L

A knowledge of k_La is sufficient for the mass transfer processes accompanied by a slow chemical reaction. For fast and instantaneous reactions within the liquid film, a knowledge of k_L is required to calculate the enhancement factors. The correlations of Calderbank and Moo-Young [91] are recommended for the estimation of k_L.

Calderbank and Moo-Young's correlation [91] is as follows:

For $d_{vs} > 2.5$ mm

$$k_L = 0.0042\left(\frac{(\rho_L - \rho_G)\mu_L g}{\rho_L^2}\right)^{1/3} * \left(\frac{\mu_L}{\rho_L D_i}\right)^{-1/2} \tag{41}$$

For $d_{vs} < 2.5$ mm

$$k_L = 0.0031\left(\frac{(\rho_L - \rho_G)\mu_L g}{\rho_L^2}\right)^{1/3} * \left(\frac{\mu_L}{\rho_L D_i}\right)^{-1/3} \tag{42}$$

where, all the quantities should be in C.G.S. units. These correlations are not adequately tested for foaming liquids, such as alcohol-water and acid-water mixtures [99].

Gas-Side Mass Transfer Coefficient k_G

During the absorption of highly soluble lean gas accompanied by instantaneous and irreversible chemical reaction, gas transfer resistance becomes important. No correlation is available for k_G and, hence, no recommendation can be given.

Liquid-Solid Mass Transfer Coefficient k_s

The mass transfer from the bulk liquid to the solid surface can play an important role in the overall apparent reaction rate for three-phase bubble column slurry reactors. Shah [9] has reviewed earlier studies on the liquid-solid mass transfer. The following correlation developed by Sanger and Deckwer [106] is recommended for the determination of k_s.

$$\frac{k_s d_p}{D_i} = 2.0 + 0.545\left(\frac{\mu_L}{\rho_L D_i}\right)^{1/3}\left(\frac{e d_p^4}{v_L^3}\right)^{0.264} \tag{43}$$

This correlation is based on the wide range of Reynolds and Schmidt numbers.

Backmixing

As outlined in the summary of mixing models, there are many different approaches to characterize the mixing in bubble columns. The axial dispersion model is quite sufficient to describe the mixing in bubble columns. Axial dispersion coefficients D_L, D_G, and D_s for liquid, gas and solid phases are generally sufficient to characterize the mixing in bubble column. Shah et al. [107] have critically reviewed the backmixing in gas-liquid reactors.

Axial Dispersion Coefficient for Liquid Phase D_L

Literature data on the liquid phase dispersion coefficient indicate that D_L depends on the superficial gas velocity and column diameter. The liquid flow, the type of gas sparger and physicochemical properties of gas are of minor importance. D_L can be estimated with the help of correlations of Deckwer et al. [70] or Joshi [60]. These correlations describe the measured data in waterlike low viscosity media. Equations 44 and 45 give the correlations of Deckwer et al. [70] and Joshi [60], respectively

$$D_L = 0.678 D_C^{1.4} U_G^{0.3} \tag{44}$$

$$D_L = 0.33(V_C + U_L)D_C \tag{45}$$

where the circulation velocity is calculated from

$$V_C = 1.31 \left[gD_C \left(U_G - \frac{\varepsilon_G}{1 - \varepsilon_G} U_L - \varepsilon_G U_{b\infty} \right) \right] \tag{46}$$

Axial Dispersion Coefficient for Gas Phase D_G

Literature data on D_G are relatively scarce, the data reveal considerable scatter. For the prediction of D_G, the correlation of Mangartz and Pilhofer [108] is recommended. Equation 47 represents their correlation and is based on all the available literature data. They concluded that the bubble rise velocity in the swarm (U_G/ε_G) is a characteristic variable influencing gas phase dispersion.

$$D_G = 50 D_C^{1.5} (U_G/\varepsilon_G)^{3.0} \tag{47}$$

Another useful correlation is that of Joshi [109] which is of the form:

$$D_G = 100 \frac{U_G^2}{\varepsilon_G} D_C^2 \tag{48}$$

Shah et al. [86] showed that this correlation fails for a foaming system such as an ethanol-water mixture, except when pronounced foaming occurs at low gas velocities.

Axial Dispersion Coefficient for Solid Phase D_s

Solid dispersion coefficients can be calculated from the equation proposed by Kato et al. [110, 111]. They measured the solids concentration profiles under co-current and batch situations and proposed the following relations:

$$\frac{U_G D_C}{D_s} = \frac{13(U_G/\sqrt{gD_C})}{1 + 8(U_G/\sqrt{gD_C})^{0.85}} \tag{49}$$

Heat Transfer Coefficient

Bubble column reactors are particularly used to carry out highly exothermic gas-liquid reactions, such as chlorinations, hydrogenations, and oxygenations. One reason for this use is very high heat transfer coefficients achieved in bubble columns compared to single phase flow. For the calculation of the heat transfer coefficients in bubble columns, a correlation of Deckwer [112] is recommended and is given in the equation

$$\frac{h_w}{\rho_L C_p U_G} = 0.1 \left(\frac{U_G^3 \rho_L}{g\mu_L}\right)^{-0.25} \left(\frac{C_p \mu_L}{k'}\right)^{-0.5} \tag{50}$$

Effect of Solids on Various Design Parameters

Bubble columns are widely used to carry out three-phase reactions, such as Fischer-Tropsch synthesis, desulfurization, polymerization, coal liquefaction, and waste water treatment. It is therefore necessary to know the effect of solids on the non-adjustable design parameters.

The presence of solids does not affect the gas hold-up significantly. Begovich and Watson [113] have proposed an empirical correlation for phase hold-up in three-phase systems with batch liquid and solid phases. If the solids are completely suspended in the solution, the correlation proposed by Akita and Yoshida [93] is adequate. In the three-phase bubble column reactor, the volumetric mass transfer coefficients can be affected by the presence of solids. This effect of solids on $k_L a$ depends on the particle concentration, the particle size, the liquid-solid density difference, the geometrical sizes, and the operating conditions of the reactor. The effect is, however, not yet fully studied. For solids with a particle diameter of less than 50 μm and solids concentration less than 16% weight, Deckwer et al. [114] have shown that the solids have a negligible effect on $k_L a$. This discussion is valid only for non-porous particles. Chandrasekaran and Sharma [115, 116], Kars et al. [117], and Alper et al. [118] have shown a significant increase in $k_L a$ for particles of small size and high porosity.

The effect of solid particles on the liquid dispersion coefficients has also been recently examined. Ying et al. [119] observed large discrepancies between the dispersion coefficient calculated from the literature correlations, and the liquid-phase dispersion coefficient measured in the presence of solids. Most recently, Kelkar et al. [120] reported a strong dependence of the axial dispersion coefficient on the wetting characteristics of solids. Kelkar et al. [120] examined the axial dispersion coefficient in slurries containing polystyrene beads and oil shale particles.

Estimations of Additional Parameters Involved in the Two-bubble Class Model

The additional parameters involved in the two-bubble class model are the fractional gas hold-ups due to large and small bubbles, their bubble rise velocities and the volumetric mass transfer coefficients for small and large bubbles. The fractional gas hold-up structure due to small and large bubbles has been investigated by Vermeer and Krishna [84], Schumpe [83], Kelkar et al. [81], and Godbole et al. [78, 80] using the dynamic gas disengagement technique. Joseph and Shah [92] have correlated the gas hold-up due to small bubbles in various systems with a maximum deviation of $\pm 6.0\%$

$$\varepsilon_G^S = 1.156 \left(\frac{U_G \mu_L}{\sigma}\right)^{0.321} \tag{51}$$

Using the correlations for overall gas hold-up and fractional gas hold-up due to small bubbles, the fractional gas hold-up due to large bubbles can be determined. To determine bubble rise velocity due to small and large bubbles simple dynamic gas disengagement experiments should be carried out. A brief summary of ε_G^S and ε_G^L is given in Table 5.

Table 5
Large and Small Bubble Gas Hold-ups as a function of Gas Velocity for Various Systems [113]

System	U_G, m/s	ε_G	ε_G^S	ε_G^L	$\varepsilon_G^L/\varepsilon_G$
Air-Water	0.0787	0.1534	0.1135	0.0399	0.2601
	0.118	0.1881	0.1333	0.0548	0.2913
	0.154	0.2241	0.158	0.0661	0.295
	0.193	0.2474	0.170	0.074	0.3128
Air-Soltrol-130	0.111	0.280	0.234	0.046	0.1643
	0.137	0.298	0.251	0.047	0.1577
	0.164	0.318	0.262	0.056	0.1761
	0.201	0.338	0.274	0.064	0.1893
	0.235	0.354	0.280	0.074	0.2090
N_2-Turpentine-5	0.110	0.277	0.197	0.108	0.390
	0.165	0.336	0.228	0.108	0.321
	0.218	0.382	0.248	0.134	0.351
	0.272	0.418	0.260	0.158	0.378
	0.324	0.45	0.271	0.179	0.398
Air-0.5 wt % CMC	0.0484	0.0658	0.0398	0.026	0.395
solution	0.0933	0.0976	0.0516	0.046	0.471
	0.140	0.1345	0.0625	0.072	0.535
	0.186	0.1692	0.0802	0.089	0.526
	0.237	0.1798	0.0797	0.1001	0.556
	0.280	0.1979	0.0819	0.116	0.586
Air-Water & 10 wt %	0.0478	0.1172	0.0882	0.029	0.247
polystyrene	0.0918	0.1614	0.1164	0.045	0.279
	0.14	0.1912	0.1192	0.072	0.376
	0.187	0.2172	0.1422	0.075	0.345
	0.230	0.2372	0.1532	0.084	0.354
	0.246	0.2533	0.1603	0.093	0.367
Air-Water + 20 wt %	0.0499	0.1131	0.0761	0.037	0.333
polystyrene	0.140	0.1844	0.1204	0.064	0.347
	0.186	0.1951	0.1141	0.081	0.415
	0.233	0.2368	0.1388	0.098	0.414
	0.258	0.2570	0.133	0.124	0.482
Air-Water + 30 wt %	0.0483	0.1070	0.066	0.034	0.317
polystyrene	0.0943	0.1364	0.082	0.054	0.396
	0.186	0.2074	0.1084	0.099	0.477
	0.233	0.2131	0.106	0.107	0.502
	0.258	0.2409	0.111	0.130	0.539

Vermeer and Krishna [84] and Godbole et al. [80] have concluded that for churn turbulent regime, $k^L a/\varepsilon_G^L$ does not depend on the superficial gas velocity. $k_L a/\varepsilon_G^L$ represents the volumetric mass transfer coefficients per unit volume of large bubbles. This observation was based on their data in water, Soltrol-130 [80] and turpentine-5 [84]. A summary of $k_L a/\varepsilon_G^L$ for a variety of systems is outlined in Table 6. Thus, volumetric mass transfer coefficients for large bubbles in a variety of systems can be evaluated. For determining volumetric mass transfer coefficients for small bubbles, it is necessary to know the sauter mean diameter for small bubbles. The liquid-side mass transfer coefficient can be found out using Calderbank and Moo Young's correlation [91] for k_L, and "a" can be calculated as $a = 6\varepsilon_G^S/d_{vs}^s$. Additional data for d_{vs}^s are reported by Shah et al. [89].

Table 6
Comparison of the Volumetric Mass Transfer Coefficients for Large Bubbles with the
Assumption of Gas Transport Occurring Through Large Bubbles Only [113]

System	U_G m/s	$(k_L a)$ s^{-1}	$(k_L a)/\varepsilon_G^L$ s^{-1}
Air-Water	0.0787	0.0578	1.45
	0.118	0.0774	1.41
	0.154	0.951	1.44
	0.193	0.1103	1.43
	0.229	0.1176	1.22
Air-Soltrol-130	0.106	0.08	1.74
	0.130	0.0906	1.93
	0.156	0.1011	1.80
	0.191	0.1142	1.78
	0.223	0.1254	1.69
N_2-Turpentine-5	0.110	0.0424	0.53
	0.165	0.0594	0.55
	0.218	0.0737	0.55
	0.272	0.0866	0.55
	0.324	0.10	0.56
Air-0.5 wt % CMC Solution	0.0484	0.00289	0.111
	0.0933	0.00531	0.115
	0.14	0.00773	0.107
	0.186	0.01	0.112
	0.237	0.0126	0.126
	0.280	0.0147	0.126
Air-Water + 10 wt %* Polystyrene	0.0478	0.029	1.0
	0.0918	0.050	1.11
	0.14	0.069	0.96
	0.187	0.074	1.0

* $k_L a$ *values estimated.*

SCALE-UP CONSIDERATIONS

Laboratory reactors are often 70 to 150 mm in diameter and in the case of gas-sparged reactors the height to diameter ratio may be 3 to 10. Commercial reactors can be 5 m in diameter, and height to diameter ratio may vary significantly with application. The gas distributor used in small reactors is often not useful for large reactors. Therefore, the effect of gas distributors on the column hydrodynamics, particularly for small height to diameter ratio columns, must be properly evaluated.

In commercial reactors, if large height to diameter ratio is used, the axial variations in hydrodynamic and transport characteristics also need to be examined. Such axial variations can cause dramatic changes in the reactor performance. Also, when a solid phase is present in the bubble column, the effects of scale-up variables, such as gas velocity, distributor design, and column diameter on the distribution (both axial and radial) of the solid phase, need careful consideration.

Finally, in small diameter columns, radial variations in hydrodynamic and transport parameters are generally neglected. In large diameter columns such variations may become significantly important.

RECOMMENDATIONS FOR THE DESIGN AND SCALE-UP

As mentioned at the onset of this chapter, the design and scale-up of a bubble column requires several considerations. Some important guidelines and recommendations are as follows:

1. The prevailing flow regime must be known. If the scale-up changes the flow regime, this must be considered in the reactor model and in the model parameter estimations. Since the flow characteristics depend very significantly upon the gas distributor design, careful attention must be given to the design of the distributor. Flow maldistribution can be a problem in the large diameter column.
2. If the flow regime is churn turbulent, the two-bubble class model outlined in this chapter should be used.
3. The gas phase axial dispersion can be generally neglected as long as the gas-phase conversion requirement is not high. The solid phase axial dispersion can be assumed to be the same as that of liquid phase as long as particles are 100 to 300 micron size or less.
4. The gas-side resistance to the gas-liquid mass transfer can be neglected as long as the solubility of the gaseous reactant in liquid is low and the concentration of the gaseous reactant in the gas phase is not very small.
5. For tall bubble columns, the axial variations in gas hold-up and gas-liquid mass transfer coefficient should be carefully evaluated.
6. Models for the bubble column reactor can be significantly facilitated by the knowledge of the reaction regime i.e. mass transfer controlled, kinetic controlled, etc. If a number of reactions occur simultaneously, the reaction regime for each reaction should be separately known.

NOTATION

a	gas-liquid interfacial area, m^{-1}	I	inlet ratio of component A to B, Equation 1
A	gas phase reactant, Equation 2		
B	liquid phase reactant, Equation 2	k'	thermal conductivity of liquid phase, $J/m\,s\,k$
C_{AL}	liquid phase concentration of component A, kg mole/m^3	k_A	kinetic constant for the first order reaction, s^{-1}
C_{AL}^*	equilibrium concentration of component A in the liquid phase, kg mole/m^3	k_G	gas-side mass transfer coefficient, m/s
d_b, d_{vs}	bubble size, m	k_L	liquid-side mass transfer coefficient, m/s
D_C	column diameter, m	k_La	volumetric mass transfer coefficient based on the dispersion volume, s^{-1}
d_p	diameter of the particle, m		
D_i	diffusion coefficient for component i, m^2/s	k_s	liquid-solid mass transfer coefficient, m/s
D_G	dispersion coefficient of the gas phase, m^2/s	k_La'	volumetric mass transfer coefficient per unit clear liquid volume, s^{-1}
D_L	liquid phase dispersion coefficient, m^2/s	K_A	overall absorption reaction coefficient, s^{-1}
D_S	solid phase dispersion coefficient, m^2/s	L	length of the reactor, m
e	local energy dissipation per unit mass, $J/kg\,s$	N_i	number of bubbles with a size d_{bi}
e'	energy dissipation rate, J	P	pressure, Pa
Fr	Froude number ($U_G/\sqrt{gD_c}$), dimensionless	P'	energy input, J
		P_T	pressure at the top of the column, Pa
g	acceleration due to gravity, $m\,s^{-2}$	R	gas constant, $\dfrac{Pa\,m^3}{kg\,mole\,K}$
h_w	wall bed heat transfer coefficient, $J/m^2\,s\,k$		
H	Henry's constant, Pa m^3/kg mole	t	time, s
H_i	dispersion height, m	T	temperature, K

$U_{b\infty}$ terminal bubble rise velocity of a single bubble, m/s
U_{br} bubble rise velocity, m/s
U_G superficial gas phase velocity, m/s
U_L superficial liquid phase velocity, m/s
U usage ratio of reactant A to B, Equation 1
V_C circulation velocity, m/s

V_D dispersion volume, m^3
V_R reactor volume, m^3
X_A gas-phase conversion of reactant A
X_{ov} overall conversion,
x reactor distance, m
Y_{AG} gas-phase mole fraction of component A
z dimensionless reactor distance

Greek Letters

α ratio of hydrostatic head to the total pressure at the top
ρ phase density, Kg/m^3
σ interfacial tension, N/m

ν kinematic viscosity, m^2/s
ε phase hold-up, dimensionless
μ, μ_{eff} dynamic viscosity, Pa·s

Subscripts

G   gas phase
L   liquid phase
S   solid phase

O   inlet
1   outlet

Superscripts

L   Large bubbles
S   Small bubbles

REFERENCES

1. Shah, Y. T., Kelkar, B. G., Godbole, S. P., and Deckwer, W. D., *AIChE Journal*, 28, 374 (1982).
2. Hines, D. A., Proc. 1st Eur. Congr. Biotechn. CH-Interlaken, Sept. 1978, *Dechema Monographs*, 82, p. 55, Verlag Chemie, Weinheim (1978).
3. Joshi, J. B., and Sharma, M. M., *Trans. Inst. Chem. Engrs.*, 54, 42 (1976).
4. Herbrechtsmeier, P., and Steiner, R., *Chem. Ing. Tech.*, 50, 944 (1978).
5. Schugerl, K., Lucke, J., Lehmann, I., and Wagner, F., *Adv. Biochem Eng.*, 8, 63 (1978).
6. von Kutepow, Himmele, N. W., and Hohnschutz, H., *Chem. Ing.Tech.*, 37, 383 (1965).
7. Hjortkjaer, J. and Jensen, V. W., *Ind. Eng. Chem. Proc. Des. Dev.*, 15, 46 (1976).
8. Karolyi, J., Zulai, A., Birthler, R., and Spitzner, H., *Int. Chem. Eng.*, 3, 597 (1963).
9. Shah, Y. T., *Gas-Liquid-Solid Reactor Design*, McGraw-Hill Publ. Co., New York (1979).
10. Wu, W. R. K., and Storch, H. H., U.S. Bureau of Mines Bulletin, 633 (1968).
11. Konig, B., "Untersuchungen zur Penicillinproduktion in Blasensaulen," Dr. Thesis, Universitat Hannover (1980).
12. Shah, Y. T., Cronauer, D. C., McIlvried, H. G., and Paraskos, J. A., *Ind. Eng. Chem. Proc. Des. Dev.*, 17, 288 (1978a).
13. Franck, H. G., and Knop, A., *Kohleveredelung-Chemie and Technologie*, Springer Verlag, Berlin, New York (1979).
14. Shah, Y. T., *Reaction Engineering in Direct Coal Liquefaction*, Addison-Wesley Publ. Co., Reading, MA (1981).
15. Kolbel, H., and Ackermann, P., *Chem. Ing. Tech.*, 28, 381 (1956).
16. Kolbel, H., Ralek, M., Falbe, J., and Thieme Verlag, G., Stuttgart (1977).
17. Kolbel, H., and Ralek, M., *Catal. Rev. Sci. Eng.*, 27 (2), 225 (1980).

18. Deckwer, W. D., Serpemen, Y., Ralek, M., and Schmidt, B., *Ind. Eng. Chem. Proc. Des. Dev.*, 21, (No. 2), 231 (1982).
19. Dufau, F. A., Eschard, F., Haddad, A. C., and Thonon, C. H., *Chem. Eng. Prog.*, 60, (No. 9), 43 (1964).
20. Bernard, M., *Ullmanns Encyklopadie der Technischen Chemie*, 9, p. 680, Verlag Chemie, Weinheim (1975).
21. Sherwin, M. B., and Frank, M. E., *Hydrocarbon Process.*, 55, No. 11, 122 (1976).
22. Blum, D. B., Sherwin, M. B., and Frank, M. E., Adv. Chem. Series, No. 146, ed., L. Seglin, ACS, Washington, DC (1975).
23. Frank, M. E., *Hydrocarbon Proc.*, 56 (7), 167 (1977).
24. Sittig, M., *Organic Chemical Process Encyclopedia*, Noyes Develop. Corp. U.S.A. (1967).
25. Kostyak, N. G., L'ov, S. V., Falkovski, V. B., Starkov, A. V., and Levina, N. M., *J. Appl. Chem. USSR*, 35, 1939 (1962).
26. Yau, A. V., Hemielec, A. E., and Johnson, A. I., paper presented at International Symp. On Research in Co-current Gas-Liquid Flow, Waterloo (September, 1968).
27. Broich, F., *Chem. Ing. Tech.* 36, 417 (1964).
28. Hofermann, H., *Chem. Ing. Tech.*, 36, 422 (1964).
29. Saunby, J. B., and Kiff, B. W., *Hydrocarbon Process*, 247 (Nov. 1976).
30. Krekeler, H., and Schmitz, H., *Chem. Ing. Tech.*, 40, 785 (1968).
31. Hattori, K., Tanaka, Y., Suzulo, H., Ikawa, T., and Kubota, H., *J. Chem. Eng.* Japan, 3, 72 (1970).
32. Kaeding, W. W., Lindblom, R. O., Temple, R. G., and Mahon, H. I., *Ind. Eng. Chem. Proc. Des. Dev.* 4, 97 (1963).
33. Berezin, I. V., Denisov, E. T., and Emanuel, N. M., *The Oxidation of Cyclohexane*, Pergamon Press, Oxford (1966).
34. Kurata, N., and Koshida, K., *Hydrocarbon Processing*, 145 (Jan., 1978).
35. Joshi, J. B., Abichandani, J., Shah, Y. T., Ritz, M., and Ruether, J. A., *AIChE J.*, 27, 937 (1981).
36. Jira, R., Blau, W., and Grimm, D., *Hydrocarbon Process.*, 97 (March, 1976).
37. Albright, L. F., *Chem. Eng.*, 169 (Jan. 16, 1967a).
38. Gates, B. C., Katzer, J. R., and Schuit, C. G. A., *Chemistry of Catalytic Processes*, McGraw-Hill, New York (1979).
39. Kolbel, H., and Engelhardt, F., *Erdol und Kohle*, 5, 1 (1952).
40. Kolbel, H., Ackermann P., and Engelhardt, F., *Erdol und Kohle*, 9, 303 (1956).
41. McLaren, D. D., *Chemtech.*, 594 (Oct., 1975).
42. Moo-Young, M., *Can J. Chem. Eng.*, 53, 113 (1975).
43. van Driesen, R. P., and Stewart, N. C., *Oil Gas J.*, 101 (May 18, 1964).
44. Ostergaard, K., *Society for the Chemical Industry*, London, 50 (1964).
45. Bayer, Turmbiologie, Bayer Prospects D. 991-7127/89 77797 and E589-777/68619 (1977).
46. Beyrich, J., Gautschi, W., Regenass, W., and Weidmann, W., *Proceed. 13th Symp. Comp. Appl. Chem. Eng.*, Montreux (Switzerland) (April, 1979).
47. Perkow, H., Steiner, R., and Vollmuller, H., *Chem. Ing. Tech.*, 52, 943 (1980).
48. Ploos van Amstel, J. J. A., and Rietma, K., *Chem. Ing. Tech.*, 42, 981 (1970).
49. Ploos van Amstel, J. J. A., and Rietma, K., ibid., 45, 1205 (1973).
50. Deckwer, W. D., International Chem. Eng., 19, 21 (1979).
51. Rietema, J., and Ottengraph, S. P. P., paper presented at the North Western Branch of the I. Chem., January (1969).
52. Rietema, J., and Ottengraph, S. P. P., *Trans. Inst. Chem. Engrs.*, 48, T54 (1970).
53. Crabtree, J. R., and Bridgwater, J., *Chem. Eng. Sci.*, 24, 1755 (1969).
54. Freedman, W., and Davidson, J. F., *Trans. Instn. Chem. Engrs.*, 47, T251 (1969).
55. Miyauchi, T., and Shyu, C. N., *Kagaku Kogaku*, 34, 958 (1970).
56. Ueyama, K., and Miyauchi, T., *AIChE J.*, 25, 258 (1979).
57. Bhavraju, S. M., Russel, T. W. F., and Blanch, H. W., *AIChE J.*, 24, 454 (1978).
58. Whalley, P. B., and Davidson, J. F., *Inst. Chem. Engrs., Symp. Series No. 38*, 55 (1974).
59. Joshi, J. B., and Sharma, M. M., *Trans. Instn. Chem. Engrs.*, 57, 244 (1979).

60. Joshi, J. B., *Trans. Instn. Chem. Engrs.*, 58, 155 (1980).
61. Zuber, N., and Findlay, J. A., *Trans. ASME, J. of Heat Transfer*, 87, 453 (1965).
62. Nagel, O., Kurten, H., and Hegner, B., *Chem. Ing. Tech.*, 45, 913 (1973).
63. Nagel, O., and Kurten, H., *Chem. Ing. Tech.*, 48, 513 (1976).
64. Nagel, O., Hegner, B., and Kurten, H., *Chem. Ing. Tech.*, 50, 934 (1978).
65. Nagel, O., Kurten, H., and Hegner, B., "Design of Gas/Liquid Reactors: Mass Transfer Area and Input of Energy," *Two-Phase Momentum Heat and Mass Transfer in Chemical Process and Engineering Systems*, ed., Durst, F., Tsiklauri, G. V., and Afgan, N. H., 2, 835, Hemisphere Publ. Corp., Washington, D. C. (1979).
66. Miyauchi, T., and Vermeulen, *Ind. Eng. Chem. Fundamentals*, 2, 304 (1963).
67. Nishikawi, A., and Kato, Y., *Kagaku Kogaku*, 36, 1112 (1972).
68. Nishikawi, A., and Kato, Y. *Can J. Chem. Eng.*, 52, 276 (1974).
69. Mecklenburgh, J. C., *Trans. Inst. Chem. Engrs.*, 52, 180 (1974).
70. Deckwer, W. D., Burckhart, R., and Zoll, G., *Chem. Eng. Sci.*, 29, 2177 (1974).
71. Baird, M. H. I., and Rice, R. G., *Chem. Eng. J.*, 9, 171 (1975).
72. Rice, P., Tuppurainen, J. H. I., and Hedge, R. M., "Dispersion and Holdup in Bubble Columns," paper presented at ACS Meeting, Las Vegas (August, 1980).
73. Riquarts, H. P., *Ger. Chem. Eng.*, 4, 18 (1981).
74. Joshi, J. B., and Shah, Y. T., *Chem. Eng. Commun.*, 11, 165 (1981).
75. Joshi, J. B., *Trans. Inst. of Chem. Engrs.*, 59, 139 (1981).
76. Deckwer, W. D., Nguyen-tien, K., Kelkar, B. G., and Shah, Y. T., *AIChE J.*, 29, 915 (1983).
77. Wallis, G. B., *Instn. Chem. Engrs.*, London, 9 (1962).
78. Godbole, S. P., Honath, M. F., and Shah, Y. T., *Chem. Eng. Commun.*, 16, 119 (1982).
79. Godbole, S. P., Schumpe, A., Shah, Y. T., and Carr, N. L., *AIChE J.*, 30, 213 (1984).
80. Godbole, S. P., Joseph, S., Shah, Y. T., and Carr, N. L., *Can. J. Chem. Eng.*, 62, 440 (1984).
81. Kelkar, B. G., Godbole, S. P., Honath, M. F., Shah, Y. T., Deckwer, W. D., and Carr, N. L., *AIChE J.*, 29, 361 (1983).
82. Hills, J. H., and Darton, R. C., *Trans. Inst. Chem. Engrs.*, 54, 258 (1976).
83. Schumpe, A., "Die Chemische Bestimmung von Phasengrenzflachen in Blasensaulen bi uneinheitlichen Blasengrao β," Dr. Thesis, Universitat Hanover (1981).
84. Vermeer, D. J., and Krishna, R., *Ind. Eng. Chem. Process Des. Dev.*, 20, 475 (1981).
85. Shah, Y. T., and Deckwer, W. D., "Scale-Up Aspects of Fluid-Fluid Reaction," *Scale-Up in Chemical Process Industries*, ed., Kabel, R., and Bisio, A., John Wiley (1981).
86. Shah, Y. T., Joseph, S., Smith, D. N., and Ruether, J. A., "On the Behavior of Gas Phase in a Bubble Column with Ethanol-Water Mixtures," accepted, *Ind. Eng. Chem. Process Design & Develop.* (1984).
87. Marrucci, G., *I&EC Fundamentals* 4, 224 (1965).
88. Godbole, S. P., Ph.D. Thesis, University of Pittsburgh, Pittsburgh, PA 15260.
89. Shah, Y. T., Joseph, S., Smith, D. N., and Ruether, J. A., "Two-Bubble Class Model for Churn Turbulent Bubble Column Reactor," accepted, I&EC Process Design & Dev. (1984).
90. Joseph, S., Shah, Y. T., and Carr, N. L., "A New Model for Hydrodynamics and Mass Transfer in Bubble Column," a paper submitted to ISCRE 8, Editiburgh, U.K. (Sept., 1984).
91. Calderbank, P. H., and Moo-Young, M. B., *Chem. Eng. Sci.*, 16, 39 (1961).
92. Joseph, S. and Shah, Y. T., *ACS Symposium Series* 237, ed. Dudkovik, M. P., and Mill, P. L., p. 149 (1984).
93. Akita, K., and Yoshida, F., *Ind. Eng. Chem. Proc. Des. Dev.*, 12, 76 (1973).
94. Hikita, H., Asai, S., Tanigawa, K., Segawa, K., and Kitao, M., *Chem. Eng. J.*, 20, 59 (1980).
95. Quicker, G., and Deckwer, W. D., *Chem. Eng. Sci.*, 36, 1577 (1981b).
96. Kulkarni, A., Shah, Y. T., and Kelkar, B. G., "Gas Hold-up in Bubble Column with Surface Active Agents—A Theoretical Model," a paper submitted to The Chem. Eng. J. (1984).
97. Calderbank, P. H., *The Chem. Engr.*, 45, E209 (1967).
98. Akita, K., and Yoshida, F., *Ind. Eng. Chem. Proc. Des. Dev.*, 13, 84 (1974).
99. Zieminski, S. A., Carron, M. M., and Blackmore, R. B., *I&EC Fund.* 6 (2), 233 (May, 1967).
100. Clift, R., Grace, J. R., and Weber, M. E., *Bubbles, Drops, and Particles*, Chapter 7, Academic Press, New York (1978).

101. Sriram, K., and Mann, R., *Chem. Eng. Sci.*, 32, 571 (1976).
102. Nishikawa, M., Kato, H., and Hashimoto, K., *Ind. Eng. Chem. Prog. Des. Dev.*, 16, 133 (1977).
103. Kastanek, F., *Coll. Czechoslov. Chem. Commun.*, 42, 2491 (1977).
104. Schugerl, K., Lucke, J., and Oels, U., *Adv. Biochem. Eng.*, ed., T. K. Ghose, A. Fiechter, and N. Blakeborogh, 7, 1 (1977).
105. Oels, U., Lucke, J., Buchholz, R., and Schugerl, K., *Germ. Chem. Eng.*, 1, 115 (1978).
106. Sanger, P., and Deckwer, W. D., *Chem. Eng. J.*, 22, 179 (1981).
107. Shah, Y. T., Stiegel, G. J., and Sharma, M. M., *AIChE J.*, 24, 369 (1978b).
108. Mangartz, K. H., and Pilhofer, T. H., Verfahrenstechnik (Mainz), 14, 40 (1980).
109. Joshi, J. B., *Chem. Eng. J.*, 24, 213 (1982).
110. Kato, Y., Nishiwaki, A., Takashi, F., and Tanaka, S., *J. Chem. Eng.* Japan, 5, 112 (1972a).
111. Kato, Y., Nishiwaki, A., Takashi, F., and Tanaka, S., *Int. Chem. Eng.*, 12, 182 (1972b).
112. Deckwer, W. D., *Chem. Eng. Sci.*, 35, 1341 (1980).
113. Begovich, J. M., and Watson, J. S., *Fluidization Proc. 2nd Eng. Found. Conf.*, ed., J. F., Davidson, and D. L., Keairns, 190, (1978).
114. Deckwer, W. D., Louisi, U., Zaidi, A., and Ralek, M., *Ind. Eng. Chem. Proc. Des. Dev.*, 19, 699 (1980a).
115. Chandrasekaran, K., and Sharma, M. M., *Chem. Eng. Sci.*, 29, 2130 (1974).
116. Chandrasekaran, K., and Sharma, M. M., *Chem. Eng. Sci.*, 32, 669 (1977).
117. Kars, R. L., Best, R. J., and Drinkenburg, A. A., *Chem. Eng. J.*, 17, 201 (1979).
118. Alper, E., Wichtendahl, B., Deckwer, W. D., *Chem. Eng. Sci.*, 35, 217 (1980).
119. Ying, D. H., Sivasubramanian, R., and Givens, E. N., "Gas/Slurry Flow in Coal Liquefaction Process," DOE Report FE-14801-3 (Jan., 1980b).
120. Kelkar, B. G., Shah, Y. T., and Carr, N. L., "Hydrodynamics and Axial Mixing in a Three Phase Bubble Column. Effect of Slurry Properties," *I&EC Process Design & Dev.*, 23, 308 (1984).

CHAPTER 40

MODELING BUBBLE COLUMN REACTORS

W. Krug and K. Hertwig

Engineering College

Koethen, German Democratic Republic

CONTENTS

INTRODUCTION

The bubble column is the most common reactor for gas-liquid reactions. Normally, it consists of
a liquid layer as the continuous phase into which the gas is dispersed in the form of bubbles. The
advantages of the bubble column reactor are its relatively simple and, therefore, economical design and its favorable thermal stability contributing to a secure conduct of reaction. Within the
reactor, in most cases, only slight temperature differences occur as the heat transfer between the
phases and from the gas-liquid phase mixture to the reactor walls is characterized by high heat
transfer coefficients, and there is often a good thorough mixing.

Bubble column reactors have frequently proven satisfactory in carrying out industrial reaction
processes. They are used, for example, for urea synthesis, acetic acid synthesis, oxosynthesis, and
many processes of waste-water purification and biotechnology.

The design of the reactor and, above all, the phase conditions of gas and liquid depend on the
required residence time and the velocities of mass transfer between the phases and the chemical
reaction. In the case of upwardflow bubble columns there is either a cocurrent flow or counter-

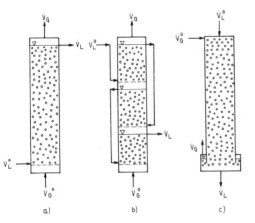

Figure 1. Bubble columns. Phase conduct is effected in the co-current flow or in the countercurrent flow (a), as a cascade (b) or in a co-current flow directed downwards (c).

flow of the liquid (Figure 1a). A step-by-step operation can be realized in a bubble column cascade (Figure 1b). If the co-current flow of the two phases is directed downwards (Figure 1C), there is a possibility of obtaining very long residence times of the gas phase. In this case high liquid through-put rates are required.

In designing industrial bubble column reactors and in rationalizing equipment being in operation it is of great importance that the preliminary calculation of the concentration fields, flow rate, and temperature fields be as exact as possible.

Considering the present state of knowledge, mathematical modeling offers the possibility of determining the main dimensions of such reactors or of characterizing the operating behavior for given reactors provided that there are certain simplifications. Of paramount importance is the determination of the hydrodynamics of the two phases influencing mass and heat transport and also chemical reaction.

HYDRODYNAMIC PROBLEMS IN THE MODELING OF BUBBLE COLUMN REACTORS

In bubble columns a mutual influencing of the flow conditions of gas and liquid occurs and, consequently, of the residence time distribution of both phases. At low superficial velocities of the gas ($w_{sG} < 0.03$–0.06 m/s) the homogeneous range presents bubbles uniformly flowing upward and the gas hold-up and flow rates largely independent of the radial position, whereas at higher gas loads heterogeneous flow rates occur that are characterized by vortices unsteady with regard to space and time. This results in the development of marked radial profiles of the gas hold-up and liquid phase velocity. For the system of air-water, corresponding measurement results are represented in Figures 2 and 3. The transition from the homogeneous to the heterogeneous state of flow is also shown by the dependence of the gas hold-up on gas velocity (Figures 4).

It stands to reason that unsteady liquid vortices or circulatory flows may lead to a reduction of the concentration and temperature differences in the bubble column. In many cases, for this reason and because of the favorable heat transfer, isothermal conditions can be supposed to exist. Concerning the material mixing of the two phases, in accordance with reactor geometry and gas and liquid load, all the variants ranging from ideal plug flow to complete mixing may exist.

Therefore, in the last two decades many attempts were made to describe both phases of the bubble column reactor by means of the dispersion model and to determine effective axial diffusion coefficients (dispersion coefficients D_{zL} and D_{zG}). For this, numerous measurement results are available that provide the basis for formulating empirical equations or equations derived from models. A comparison of such correlations with comprehensive data was made by Zehner [2, 3], who also developed a cell model for describing the axial vortical flow leading to the dispersion

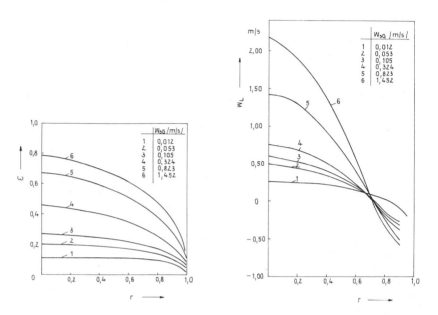

Figure 2. Local gas hold-up. The mean local gas contents depends on the dimensionless column radius and on the superficial gas velocity.

Figure 3. Liquid velocity. Direction and velocity of the liquid flow depend on the dimensionless column radius and on the superficial gas velocity.

coefficients:

$$D_{zL} = 0.5\, d_R \left(\frac{1}{\zeta}\frac{\rho_L - \rho_G}{\rho_L}\, g d_R w_{sG}\right)^{1/3} \tag{1}$$

with $\zeta = 2.5$ this relation can satisfactorily reproduce the measured values if there are aqueous liquids in the range $d_R = 0.04$ to 1.07 m, and $w_{sG} = 0.02$ to 0.45 m/s. The existence of many circulation cells is also assumed by Joshi and Sharma [4]. For the mixing time of such a cell according to

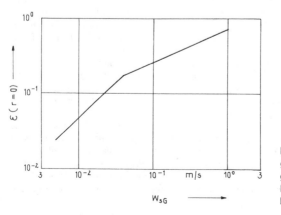

Figure 4. Gas hold-up at $r = 0$. The gas hold-up in the column axis grows with the superficial gas velocity. The homogeneous and the heterogeneous range are shown.

Pandit and Joshi [5]

$$\theta_{cell} = 5 \frac{1.5 \, d_R}{w_c} \tag{2}$$

whereas for the entire mixing time of the column the following value was determined:

$$\theta_{mix} = \theta_{cell}\left[1 - 0.174\left(\frac{L_R}{d_R} - 1\right) + 0.179\left(\frac{L_R}{d_R} - 1\right)^2\right] \tag{3}$$

(0.01 m/s $< w_{sG} <$ 0.25 m/s; 0.15 m $< d_R <$ 0.385 m; system of air-water)
A correlation between the circulation rate w_c and the dispersion coefficient of the liquid phase exists in [4]:

$$D_{zF} = 0.31 \, d_R w_c \tag{4}$$

with $w_c = 1.31[gd_R(w_{sG} - w_B)]^{1/3}$ \hfill (5)

or in a simplified form for a wide working range:

$$w_c = 2(w_{sG}/\varepsilon)d_R^{1/3} \tag{6}$$

By an empirical equation Wendt et al. [6] describe the experimental value of many authors:

$$D_{zF} = Cd_R^{1.4}(0.219 \, w_{sG}^{0.77} + 0.122 \, w_{sG}^{0.1}) \tag{7}$$

with   C = 2.7 at $d_R \geq$ 0.1 m
       C = 3.78 at $d_R <$ 0.1 m

at   0.01 m/s $< w_{sG} <$ 0.85 m/s
      0.002 m/s $< w_{sL} <$ 0.045 m/s
      0.04 m $\leq d_R \leq$ 1.07 m

A comparison of the correlations according to Equations 1 and 7 shows a good agreement in wide load ranges (Figure 5). The linear dependence of the dispersion coefficient on the reactor diameter

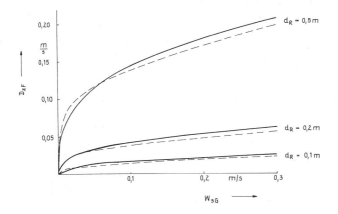

Figure 5. Dispersion coefficient of the liquid phase. The coefficients determined according to Equation 1 (————) and Equation 7 (------) differ only slightly from each other.

in the form of

$$D_{zL} = 0.33 \, d_R \frac{w_{sG}}{\varepsilon} \tag{8}$$

given by Reith et al. [7] however, leads to greater deviations. For the gas phase dispersion coefficient in the bubble columns Pavlica and Olson [8] have determined the following relation for the range $0 < w_{sG} < 0.5$ m/s:

$$D_{zG} = 5 \, d_R \frac{w_{sG}}{\varepsilon} \tag{9}$$

According to this relation a relatively intense mixing of the gas phase is obtained that might be less for bubble columns of a smaller diameter. Decker [9] points out that for reactors with $d_R <$ 0.4 m backmixing is reduced and can be neglected. For industrial bubble columns, Bodenstein numbers of 1 to 10 for the gas phase should be used where for L_R/d_R ratios of 5 the lower value and for $L_R/d_R \approx 50$ the upper value should be applied.

A checking and evaluation of experimental data obtained by different authors was carried out by Joshi [9] giving

$$D_{zG} = 110 \frac{w_{sG}}{\varepsilon} d_R^2 \tag{10}$$

However, the analysis also showed that the measurement results received by different authors differ from each other in some cases considerably.

PARAMETERS OF MASS AND HEAT TRANSPORT

The velocity of mass transport between gas and liquid phase depends on the interfacial area and on the mass transfer coefficient. Both quantities are influenced by the gas hold-up that can be computed [11]:

$$\frac{\varepsilon}{(1 - \varepsilon)^4} = K \left(\frac{w_{sG}\mu_L}{\sigma} \right) \left(\frac{\rho_L \sigma^3}{g\mu_L^4} \right)^{7/24} \tag{11}$$

with $K = 0.2$ for pure liquids
$K = 0.25$ for electrolytes

Provided there is an averaged bubble diameter the interfacial area can be calculated by

$$a = \frac{6\varepsilon}{d_B} \tag{12}$$

The bubble diameter $\bar{d}_B$ corresponds to a representative mean value of bubble size distribution (Sauter diameter):

$$\bar{d}_B = \frac{\sum_i n_i d_i^3}{\sum_i n_i d_i^2} \tag{13}$$

(n_i = number of a bubble fraction with the diameter d_i) Akita and Yoshida [12] give the following equation for calculating the bubble diameter:

$$\bar{d}_B = 26 \sqrt{\frac{\sigma}{\rho_L g}} \left[\frac{v_L^4}{w_{sG}^2 d_R^5 g} \right]^{0.06} \tag{14}$$

In bubble swarms often a coalescence of bubbles and, consequently, a reduction of the interfacial area occurs. An inhibition of the coalescence is achieved by electrolytes in the liquid phase with this effect being proportional to ionic strength. But also the addition of organic admixtures was found to produce a marked coalescence inhibition [13] which presents a group-specific behavior. The highest efficiency is achieved by organic acids and alcohols. In the calculation of mass transfer coefficients in bubble columns it can often be supposed that the transport resistance on the liquid side is considerably higher than that on the gas side, so that the molar flow transported between the phases only depends on the k_L value. Akita and Yoshida [11] give the following equation:

$$\frac{k_L d_B}{D_L} = 0.5 \left(\frac{\mu_L}{\rho_L D_L}\right)^{0.5} \left(\frac{g d_B^3 \rho_L^2}{\mu^2 L}\right)^{0.25} \left(\frac{g d_B^2 \rho_L}{\sigma}\right)^{0.375} \tag{15}$$

Numerous experiments have also confirmed the correlations by Calderbank and Moo Young [14], which apply to different ranges of the bubble diameter:

$$k_L = 0.31 \left(\frac{g \mu_L}{\rho_L}\right)^{1/3} \left(\frac{D_L \rho_L}{\mu_L}\right)^{2/3} \qquad \text{for } d_B < 2.5 \text{ mm} \tag{16}$$

$$k_L = 0.42 \left(\frac{g \mu_L}{\rho_L}\right)^{1/3} \left(\frac{D_L \rho_L}{\mu_L}\right)^{1/2} \qquad \text{for } d_B > 2.5 \text{ mm} \tag{17}$$

An equation for calculating the product of mass transfer coefficient and interfacial area is given by Akita and Yoshida [11]:

$$\frac{k_L a d_R^2}{D_L} = 0.6 \left(\frac{\mu_L}{\rho_L D_L}\right)^{0.5} \left(\frac{g d_R^2 \rho_L}{\sigma}\right)^{0.62} \left(\frac{g d_R^3 \rho_L^2}{\mu_L 2}\right)^{0.31} \varepsilon^{1.1} \tag{18}$$

According to Laurant and Charpentier [15], the following ranges can be realized in bubble columns:

$$a = 50 \text{ to } 600 \text{ m}^2/\text{m}^3$$

$$k_L = 1 \times 10^{-4} \text{ to } 4 \times 10^{-4} \text{ m/s}$$

$$\varepsilon = 0.02 \text{ to } 0.40$$

Concerning the heat transport processes in bubble columns the transition between the fluid system of gas-liquid and the reactor wall is the most important step because it influences the cooling or heating of the reactor. When calculating the transfer coefficient one should proceed from two different ranges of the superficial velocity of the gas. Up to about $w_{sG} = 0.1$ m/s the heat transfer coefficient increases as the increasing turbulence leads to a more and more intensive penetration of the boundary layer by bubbles at the reactor wall. In the second range this effect is nearly compensated by the gas bubbles going on penetrating the liquid boundary layer but at the same time causing a partial and temporary covering of the wall that does not permit any increase in the transfer coefficient on account of the low thermal conductivity of the gas.

Up to a gas velocity of $w_{sG} = 0.12$ m/s, according to Fair [16] the following is obtained:

$$\alpha_w = 1610 \, w_{sG}^{0.22} \, Pr_L^{-0.5} \text{ in W m}^{-2} \text{ K}^{-1} \tag{19}$$
$$(w_{sG} \text{ in m/s})$$

For the range of higher gas loads ($w_{sG}/w_{Bmax} > 0.2$) Mersmann [17] found the following correlation no longer depending on gas velocity:

$$\alpha_w = 0.12 \left(\frac{g^2}{v_L}\right)^{1/6} \left(\frac{\rho_L - \rho_G}{\rho_L}\right)^{1/3} (\lambda_L \rho_L c_{pL})^{1/2} \tag{20}$$

Zehner [3] proceeds from the fact that the heat transfer is considerably influenced by the velocity w_F of the liquid vortex and by the mean bubble distance l_B. With satisfactory accuracy for the range

$$0.4 \text{ mPa s} \leq \nu_L \leq 100 \text{ mPa s}$$

$$0.14 \text{ W/mK} \leq \lambda_L \leq 0.6 \text{ W/mK}$$

$$0.005 \text{ m/s} \leq w_{sG} \leq 0.5 \text{ m/s}$$

the experimental results obtained by several authors can be described by the following modified model of the plate hit by a free flow:

$$\alpha_w = 0.18(1 - \varepsilon)\sqrt[3]{\lambda_L^2 \rho_L c_{pL} \frac{w_F^2}{l_B \nu_L}} \tag{21}$$

In this connection

$$l_B = d_B \sqrt[3]{\frac{\pi}{6}} \quad \text{and} \tag{22}$$

$$w_F = \sqrt[3]{\frac{1}{\zeta} \frac{\rho_L - \rho_G}{\rho_L} g d_R w_{sG}} \tag{23}$$

The heat transfer coefficients between gas and liquid phase are of little importance for the modeling of industrial reactors. It is possible to estimate these quantities considering the analogy of heat and mass transfer in accordance with the relations of Calderbank [14].

MATHEMATICAL MODELS FOR BUBBLE COLUMNS

Strategy of the Modeling of Industrial Reactors

The basis for the mathematical modeling of bubble column reactors is the system of material, energy, and impulse balance equations. The specific character of the gas-liquid system involves some special features in determining the main influences. In many cases an energy balance for calculating the temperature fields in both phases will not be necessary, because as already mentioned the temperature differences in the whole reactor are small. For determining the reaction temperature, a global heat balance as is formulated for ideally mixed systems will be sufficient. The influence of the flow rate fields was already discussed. In reactor modeling it is usually unnecessary to include impulse balance and attempts are made to consider the hydrodynamic conditions in the parameters of axial dispersion and of mass and heat transfer. Pressure distribution in the reactor is required for determining the molar volumes of the gaseous components. It is often represented by means of a simplified linear function.

$$P(z) = P_1 + \rho_L g(1 - \varepsilon)L_R(1 - z) \tag{24}$$

$(P_1 = \text{top pressure of the column})$

In formulating the material balances it is necessary to consider the influences of convection, mass transfer between phases, axial dispersion, and chemical reactions. It is supposed that radial concentration profiles are not important and that considering the effective axial mixing a unidimensional approach can be made.

Some special model variants result from the fact that one of the successive steps of mass transport and liquid phase reaction may be considerably slower than the other and that, therefore, it determines the total velocity. If then you assume the reaching of the phase equilibrium (in material transport) or of the chemical equilibrium (in the reaction), respectively, then simplified material balances are often obtained.

Models Without Supposing a Velocity-Determining Step

Under the conditions mentioned, an isothermal model is formulated that consists of the material balances for the gas and liquid phase. The gas input occurs at $z = 0$ where z is the dimensionless reactor length coordinate (Figure 6).

Gas phase:

$$-\frac{\partial \dot{n}_{iG}}{\partial z} - k_L a L_R \left(\alpha_i \frac{\dot{n}_{iG}}{w_{sG}} - \frac{\dot{n}_{iL}}{w_{sL}} \right) + \frac{1}{L_R} \frac{\partial}{\partial z} \left[\varepsilon D_{zG} \frac{\partial \left(\frac{\dot{n}_{iG}}{w_{sG}} \right)}{\partial z} \right] + V_R \varepsilon \sum_k \nu_{ik} r_k = \left[\varepsilon L_R \frac{\partial \left(\frac{\dot{n}_{iG}}{w_{aG}} \right)}{\partial t} \right] \quad (25)$$

Liquid phase:

$$(\mp)\frac{\partial \dot{n}_{iL}}{\partial z} + k_L a L_R \left(\alpha_i \frac{\dot{n}_{iG}}{w_{sG}} - \frac{\dot{n}_{iL}}{w_{sL}} \right) + \frac{1}{L_R} \frac{\partial}{\partial z} \left[D_{zL}(1 - \varepsilon) \frac{\partial \left(\frac{\dot{n}_{iL}}{w_{sL}} \right)}{\partial z} \right]$$

$$+ V_R(1 - \varepsilon) \sum_j \nu_{ij} r_j = (1 - \varepsilon)L_R \frac{\partial \left(\frac{\dot{n}_{iL}}{w_{sL}} \right)}{\partial t} \quad (26)$$

This balance equation system is to be formulated for all the main components $i = 1$ to N; k and j are the indices for the reactions occurring in the gas or liquid phase. In most cases of industrial application only liquid phase reactions are important. The sign in brackets refers to the case of counterflow of the liquid. From the molar flows of the components the flow rates and molar concentrations in both phases can be determined as follows:

Total molar flow of all components in the gas phase:

$$\dot{n}_G = \sum_{i=1}^{N'} \dot{n}_{iG} \qquad (N' = \text{total number of all components}) \quad (27)$$

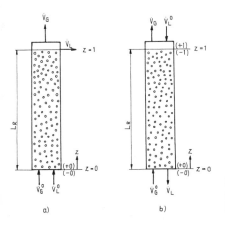

Figure 6. Scheme of bubble column. For cocurrent flow of the phases the liquid is added from below (a), for counter-flow from above (b).

Superficial velocity of the gas phase:

$$w_{sG} = \frac{\dot{n}_G V_{Mol}}{A_R} \tag{28}$$

$$w_{sG} = \varepsilon w_G \tag{29}$$

Gas phase concentration:

$$c_{iG} = \frac{\dot{n}_{iG}}{w_{sG} A_R} \tag{30}$$

Flow rate of the liquid phase:

$$w_{sL} = \frac{1}{A_R} \sum_{i=1}^{N'} \dot{n}_{iL} \frac{M_i}{\rho_{iL}} \tag{31}$$

$$w_{sL} = (1 - \varepsilon) w_L \tag{32}$$

Liquid phase concentration:

$$c_{iL} = \frac{\dot{n}_{iL}}{w_{sL} A_R} \tag{33}$$

As a driving force of mass transfer the deviation from phase equilibrium expressed by the molar concentrations in both phases is used here. In the case of equilibrium we have

$$c_{iL} = \alpha_i c_{iG}$$

This equation is a modified form of Henry's law, which is supposed to be valid.

In the general material balances according to the Equations 25 and 26 the unsteady term was also considered.

Most technical problems occur in the preliminary calculation of bubble columns (determination of the main dimensions) or in the rationalization of the process. In these cases the application of steady models is sufficient, and the following boundary values are formulated:

□ Co-current flow of the phases:

Gas phase:

$$z = 0 \rightarrow \dot{n}_{iG}(-0) = \dot{n}_{iG}(+0) - \frac{D_{zG}\varepsilon}{L_R} \frac{d\left(\dfrac{\dot{n}_{iG}(+0)}{w_{sG}}\right)}{dz} \tag{34}$$

$$z = 1 \rightarrow \frac{dn_{iG}}{dz} = 0 \tag{35}$$

Liquid phase:

$$z = 0 \rightarrow \dot{n}_{iL}(-0) = \dot{n}_{iL}(+0) - \frac{D_{zL}(1 - \varepsilon)}{L_R} \frac{d\left(\dfrac{\dot{n}_{iL}(+0)}{w_{sL}}\right)}{dz} \tag{36}$$

$$z = 1 \rightarrow \frac{d\dot{n}_{iL}}{dz} = 0 \tag{37}$$

□ Countercurrent flow of the phases:

Gas phase: See Equations 34 and 35.

Liquid phase:

$$z = 0 \rightarrow \frac{d\dot{n}_{iL}}{dz} = 0 \tag{38}$$

$$z = 1 \rightarrow \dot{n}_{iL}(+1) = \dot{n}_{iL}(-1) + \frac{D_{zL}(1 - \varepsilon)}{L_R} \frac{d\left(\frac{\dot{n}_{iL}(-1)}{w_{sL}}\right)}{dz} \tag{39}$$

According to the designations chosen here the input molar flows of gas and liquid phase correspond to the following quantities:

$$\dot{n}_{iG}^0 = \dot{n}_{iG}(-0)$$

$$\dot{n}_{iL}^0 = \dot{n}_{iL}(+1)$$

The special case of the ideal plug flow in one or two phases is a borderline case of the dispersion model. The boundary values are then to be modified in the following way:

□ Gas phase with ideal plug flow ($D_{zG} = 0$):

$$z = 0 \rightarrow \dot{n}_{iG} = \dot{n}_{iG}^0 \quad \text{(for unidirectional flow and counterflow)} \tag{40}$$

□ Liquid phase with ideal plug flow ($D_{zL} = 0$):

$$z = 0 \rightarrow \dot{n}_{iL} = \dot{n}_{iL}^0 \quad \text{(unidirectional flow)} \tag{41}$$

$$z = 1 \rightarrow \dot{n}_{iL} = \dot{n}_{iL}^0 \quad \text{(counterflow)} \tag{42}$$

In many cases it is possible to start from constant volume flows of the gas and liquid phase. Using the molar concentrations the steady material balances for the co-current flow of the phases can be transformed in the following way:

Gas phase:

$$\frac{w_{sG}}{L_R} \frac{dc_{iG}}{dz} - k_L a(\alpha_i c_{iG} - c_{iL}) + \frac{1}{L_R^2} \frac{d}{dz}\left(D_{zG}\varepsilon \frac{dc_{iG}}{dz}\right) + \varepsilon \sum_k \nu_{ik} r_k = 0 \tag{43}$$

Liquid phase:

$$\frac{w_{sL}}{L_R} \frac{dc_{iL}}{dz} + k_L a(\alpha_i c_{iG} - c_{iL}) + \frac{1}{L_R^2} \frac{d}{dz}\left[D_{zL}(1 - \varepsilon) \frac{dc_{iL}}{dz}\right] + (1 - \varepsilon) \sum_j \nu_{ij} r_j = 0 \tag{44}$$

The following boundary values are available:

Gas phase:

$$z = 0 \rightarrow c_{iG}(-0) = c_{iG}(+0) - \frac{D_{zG}\varepsilon}{w_{sG}L_R} \frac{dc_{iG}(+0)}{dz} \tag{45}$$

$$z = 1 \rightarrow \frac{dc_{iG}}{dz} = 0 \tag{46}$$

Liquid phase:

$$z = 0 \rightarrow c_{iL}(-0) = c_{iL}(+0) - \frac{D_{zL}(1 - \varepsilon)dc_{iL}(+0)}{w_{sL}L_R \quad dz} \tag{47}$$

$$z = 1 \rightarrow \frac{dc_{iL}}{dz} = 0 \tag{48}$$

For very low liquid throughput rates and relatively slender bubble columns, an ideal plug flow in the gas phase and an ideal mixing of the liquid phase may sometimes be supposed approximately. In this case the following mass balances exist if gas phase reactions are neglected.

$$-\frac{w_{sG}}{L_R}\frac{dc_{iG}}{dz} - k_L a(\alpha_i c_{iG} - c_{iL}) = 0 \tag{49}$$

Boundary value:

$$z = 0 \rightarrow c_{iG} = c_{iG}^0 \tag{50}$$

Liquid phase:

$$-\frac{w_{sL}}{L_R}(c_{iL} - c_{iL}^0) + k_L a(\alpha_i \bar{c}_{iG} - c_{iL}) + (1 - \varepsilon)\sum_j v_{ij}r_j = 0 \tag{51}$$

The gas phase balance can be solved here for each component analytically if, in addition to the flow rate, the mass transport parameters and the coefficients of the phase equilibrium are constant, too. The integration gives:

$$c_{iG} = \frac{1}{\alpha_i}\left[c_{iL} + (\alpha_i c_{iG}^0 - c_{iL})\exp\left(-\frac{\alpha_i k_L a L_R}{w_{sG}}z \right) \right] \tag{52}$$

The mean gas phase concentration of the component i is obtained by integral averaging between reactor input and output:

$$c_{iG} = \frac{1}{\alpha_i}\left\{ c_{iL} + \frac{(\alpha_i c_{iG}^0 - c_{iL})w_{sG}}{\alpha_i k_L a L_R}\left[1 - \exp\left(-\frac{\alpha_i k_L a L_R}{w_{sG}} \right) \right] \right\} \tag{53}$$

Thus, a system of $(2 \cdot N)$ algebraic equations (51 and 53) is available, which is to be solved by suitable approximation methods. Analytical solutions result in the case of simple reactions in which the balanced component is dosed only in a gaseous form and after a reaction of zeroth, first, or second order reacts in the liquid phase [18].

Models Supposing a Velocity-Determining Step

Chemical reactions in the liquid phase of bubble column reactors can sometimes be considerably slower, in other cases, however, much quicker than the mass transport between the phases. For the classification of the models the following ranges are distinguished:

1. Slow reactions with the partial ranges of the kinetic and the diffusion regime.
2. Rapid reactions.
3. Instantaneous reactions.

In *slow reactions* the part of the quantity of the reacting component transformed already within the boundary layer is supposed to be negligible in comparison with the component in the bulk of the liquid phase (i.e., outside the boundary layer).

In the kinetic regime (slow and, therefore, velocity-determining reaction, rapid mass transfer) this condition can be regarded as given from the very beginning. But also in the diffusion regime that is characterized by a very slow mass transfer as compared to reaction, the previous condition of slow reaction (negligible conversion in phase boundary layer) may be given. For characterizing the individual regimes the Hatta number, Ha, and the degree of saturation, f, are used.

$$Ha = \frac{1}{k_L} \sqrt{kD_{AL}} \tag{54}$$

where k = kinetic constant of a liquid phase reaction of first order ($r = kc_{AL}$). For the reaction orders deviating from one, concentration-depending Hatta numbers result.

$$f = \frac{c_{AL}}{\alpha_A c_{AG}}; 0 < f < 1 \tag{55}$$

Slow reactions exist for Ha < 0.3. In the kinetic regime we have $f \approx 1$, whereas $f \approx 0$ refers to the diffusion regime.

Balance Equations for the Kinetic Regime

☐ Mass balance of gas phase

The gas-phase balance:

$$-\frac{d\dot{n}_{iG}}{dz} - k_L a L_R \left(\alpha_i \frac{\dot{n}_{iG}}{w_{sG}} - \frac{\dot{n}_{iL}}{w_{sL}} \right) = 0 \tag{56}$$

existing on the assumption that the axial dispersion is negligible ($D_{zG} = 0$) need not be solved because the relation correlation between the gas and liquid phase concentrations is given approximately by the condition of the phase equilibrium according to the modified Henry law:

$$\alpha_i \frac{\dot{n}_{iG}}{w_{sG}} = \frac{\dot{n}_{iL}}{w_{sL}} \tag{57}$$

☐ Mass balance of liquid phase

The liquid-phase balance corresponds to the general model according to Equation 26. However, in accordance with Equation 56 the term of mass transport can be eliminated here so that the following balance equation for the steady case is obtained:

$$(\pm)\frac{d\dot{n}_{iL}}{dz} - \frac{d\dot{n}_{iG}}{dz} + \frac{1}{L_R} \frac{d}{dz} \left[D_{zL}(1 - \varepsilon) \frac{d\left(\frac{\dot{n}_{iL}}{w_{sL}}\right)}{dz} \right] + V_R(1 - \varepsilon) \sum_j v_{ij} r_j = 0 \tag{58}$$

Here the sign put in brackets refers to the countercurrent flow of the liquid phase (input of liquid at z = 1), too. If Equation 57 is inserted in Equation 58, the following mass balance is obtained in which only the molar flow rate of the component i is contained yet in the liquid phase:

$$-\frac{d\left[\left((\pm)1 + \frac{w_{sG}}{\alpha_i w_{sL}} \right) \dot{n}_{iL} \right]}{dz} + \frac{1}{L_R} \frac{d}{dz} \left[D_{zL}(1 - \varepsilon) \frac{d\left(\frac{\dot{n}_{iL}}{w_{sL}}\right)}{dz} \right] + V_R(1 - \varepsilon) \sum_j v_{ij} r_j = 0 \tag{59}$$

The boundary values are to be formulated according to Equations 36 to 39. However, remember that the molar flow rates $\dot{n}_{iL}$ (-0) and $\dot{n}_{iL}$ ($+1$) do not correspond here to the liquid quantities dosed as the establishment of the phase equilibrium for these positions is already supposed. According to the dosage conditions represented in Figure 7 the following input and output values are obtained:

□ Co-current flow (Figure 7A)

Total dosed molar flow of the component i:

$$\dot{n}_i^0 = \dot{n}_{iG}^0 + \dot{n}_{iL}^0 = \dot{n}_{iG}(-0) + \dot{n}_{iL}(-0) \tag{60}$$

Phase equilibrium at $z = -0$:

$$\dot{n}_{iL}(-0) = \alpha_i \frac{w_{sL}}{w_{sG}} \dot{n}_{iG}(-0) \tag{61}$$

$$\dot{n}_{iL}(-0) = \frac{\dot{n}_i^0}{1 + \dfrac{w_{sG}}{\alpha_i w_{sL}}} \tag{62}$$

□ Countercurrent flow (Figure 7B)

Input molar flows at $z = 0$:

$$\dot{n}_{iG}^0 - \dot{n}_{iL}^{Aus} = \dot{n}_{iG}(0) - \dot{n}_{iL}(0) \tag{63}$$

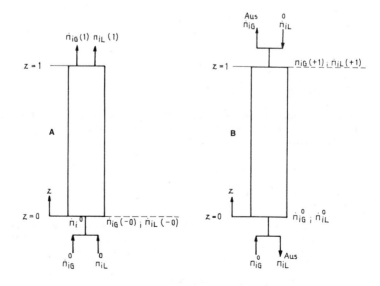

Figure 7. Input and output flows if phase equilibrium is supposed: (a) represents the conditions for co-current flow; (b) for countercurrent flow.

Phase equilibrium at $z = 0$:

$$\dot{n}_{iL}(0) = \alpha_i \frac{w_{sL}}{w_{sG}} \dot{n}_{iG}(0) \tag{64}$$

$$\dot{n}_{iL}(0) = \frac{\dot{n}_{iL}^{Aus} - \dot{n}_{iG}^0}{1 - \dfrac{w_{sG}}{\alpha_i w_{sL}}} \tag{65}$$

Output molar flows at $z = 1$:

$$\dot{n}_{iG}^{Aus} - \dot{n}_{iL}^0 = \dot{n}_{iG}(+1) - \dot{n}_{iL}(+1) \tag{66}$$

Phase equilibrium at $z = +1$:

$$\dot{n}_{iL}(+1) = \alpha_i \frac{w_{sL}}{w_{sG}} \dot{n}_{iG}(+1) \tag{67}$$

$$\dot{n}_{iL}(+1) = \frac{\dot{n}_{iL}^0 - \dot{n}_{iG}^0}{1 - \dfrac{w_{sG}}{\alpha_i w_{sL}}} \tag{68}$$

As concerns Equations 63 to 68, the most general case of the dosing of one component within both phases in the countercurrent flow was considered. Substantial simplifications result for the practically usual case of dosage in one phase

$$(\dot{n}_{iL}^0 = 0 \quad \text{or} \quad \dot{n}_{iG}^0 = 0).$$

Balance Equations for the Diffusion Regime

In this case the velocity of mass transport between the phases is much lower than the reaction rate so that within the liquid phase the establishment of the chemical equilibrium can be supposed. However, it must be pointed out again that, nevertheless, the region of slow reactions exists because the reaction does not develop so quickly that a considerable part of the conversion may occur already in the phase boundary layer on the liquid side. For the diffusion regime the following quantities are characteristic:

$$\text{Ha} < 0.3; \quad f \approx 0$$

Mass balance of gas phase (steady state, without axial dispersion, no gas phase reactions):

$$-\frac{d\dot{n}_{iG}}{dz} - k_L a L_R \left(\alpha_i \frac{\dot{n}_{iG}}{w_{sG}} - \left[\frac{\dot{n}_{iL}}{w_{sL}} \right]^* \right) = 0 \tag{69}$$

Mass balance of liquid phase: With the supposition of the velocity-determining mass transfer, for all components in the liquid phase the establishment of the chemical equilibrium is given:

$$c_{iL} = c_{iL}^*$$

$$\text{mit } c_{iL}^* = \frac{L_R}{V_R} \left[\frac{n_{iL}}{w_{sL}} \right]^*$$

If the limiting mass transport of a reference component k (reactant of a simple reaction) from the gas phase into the liquid phase is considered,

$$-\frac{d\dot{n}_{kG}}{dz} = k_L a\, L_R \left(\alpha_k \frac{\dot{n}_{kG}}{w_{sG}} - \left[\frac{\dot{n}_{kL}}{w_{sL}} \right]^* \right) \tag{71}$$

then the following liquid-phase balance for all the other reactants and reaction products i (without axial dispersion) is obtained:

$$-w_{sL}\frac{d\left[\frac{\dot{n}_{iL}}{w_{sL}}\right]^*}{dz} + k_L a L_R \left(\alpha_i \frac{\dot{n}_{iG}}{w_{sL}} - \left[\frac{\dot{n}_{iL}}{w_{sL}} \right]^* \right) + \frac{v_i}{v_k}\left(\frac{d\dot{n}_{kG}}{dz} + w_{sL}\frac{d\left[\frac{\dot{n}_{kL}}{w_{sL}}\right]^*}{dz} \right) = 0 \tag{72}$$

From the equilibrium constant of the chemical reaction the concentration of the reference component in the liquid phase is calculated.

☐ Boundary values:

Gas phase:

$$z = 0 \rightarrow \dot{n}_{kG} = \dot{n}_{kG}^0,\ \dot{n}_{iG} = \dot{n}_{iG}^0$$

Liquid phase:

$$z = 0 \rightarrow \dot{n}_{kL} = \dot{n}_{kL}^0,\ \dot{n}_{iL} = \dot{n}_{iL}^0$$

Balance Equations for Rapid and Instantaneous Reactions in the Liquid Phase

Just as in the case of the diffusion regime, mass transfer is the velocity-determining step. However, this step is influenced by the chemical reaction, because to a large extent, it occurs in the boundary layer and, therefore, reduces the effective boundary layer thickness. This is determined quantitatively by means of the chemical acceleration factor σ_R, which represents the relation of mass transfer coefficient with chemical reaction and mass transfer coefficient without chemical reaction.

$$\sigma_R = \frac{k_{LR}}{k_L} \tag{73}$$

Rapid reactions occur at Ha > 0.3. In literature, possibilities of calculating the chemical acceleration factor are given for different reaction types. On the basis of the film theory [19] for a reaction of first order with

$$r = k_1 c_{AL} \quad \text{(A = co-reactant passing from the gas phase into the liquid phase)}$$

$$\text{and} \quad Ha = \frac{\sqrt{K_1 D_{AL}}}{k_L} \tag{74}$$

have determined the following acceleration factor:

$$\sigma_R = \sqrt{1 + Ha^2} \tag{75}$$

For a reaction of nth order with

$$r = k_n c_{AL}^n$$

according to Hikita and Asai [20] with

$$Ha = \frac{\sqrt{[2/(n+1)]k_n(\alpha_A c_{AG})^{n-1}D_{AL}}}{k_L}$$

(76)

the following approximate solutions for the chemical acceleration factor are obtained:

$$\sigma_R = \frac{Ha}{\tanh Ha} \qquad \text{for } n = 0, 1, 3 \text{ (error } \pm 6\%)$$

(77)

$$\sigma_R = \sqrt{1 + Ha} \qquad \text{for } n > 1 \qquad \text{(error } \pm 8\%)$$

(78)

For a reaction of $(m + n)$th order

$$r = k_{m+n}c_{AL}^m c_{BL}^n \qquad \text{(component A: reactant that passes from the gas phase into the liquid phase with)}$$

$$f_A = \frac{c_{AL}}{\alpha_A c_{AG}} \approx 0$$

(component B: reactant that abounds in the liquid phase)

with $\quad Ha = \dfrac{\sqrt{[2/m+1)]k_{m+n}D_{AL}[\alpha_A c_{AG}]^{m-1}c_{BL}^n}}{k_L}$

(79)

the same authors give the following acceleration factor:

$$\sigma_R = \frac{Ha\sqrt{c_{BL}/(\alpha_A c_{AG})}}{\tanh(Ha\sqrt{c_{BL}/(\alpha_A c_{AG})})}$$

(80)

Further references to literature concerning the chemical acceleration factor were compiled by Hertwig [18].

In instantaneous reactions the reaction rate is so high that the conversion already occurs completely in the liquid boundary layer. Thus the concentration of a gaseous dosed reactant in the case of simple reactions in the boundary layer is reduced to the value

$$c_{iL} = 0$$

This region is characterized by

$$Ha > 3$$

For the chemical acceleration factor, in reactions of first order, we have

$$\sigma_R = Ha$$

(81)

At a high acceleration of the mass transfer on the liquid side due to chemical reaction, the reaction plane can lie immediately at the phase boundary surface. Then it is possible that mass transport resistances occur on the gas side. In this case the possibility of replacing the whole mass transfer coefficient by the transport coefficient on the gas side or the possibility of its being influences considerably at least by k_G is to be checked.

MATHEMATICAL SOLUTION METHODS

Typical Model Equations

Under certain technical and physical conditions for the modeling of bubble column reactors, typical mathematical setups of equations are to be seen. Equations 25 and 26 are parabolic partial differential equations that can be written in a general form as follows:

$$A_1 \frac{\partial^2 G}{\partial z^2} + A_2 \frac{\partial G}{\partial z} + A_3 \cdot G + A_4 = \frac{\partial G}{\partial t} \tag{82}$$

In this connection, G is a vector and contains the molar flows for the gas and liquid phase and for all the main components $i = 1$ to N.

The coefficients A_1 to A_4 are in the general case vectors, too, which depend in a linear or non-linear way on the chemical and physical data, flow rates, etc., as is shown by Equations 25 to 33. Equations 30 and 33 are auxiliary equations for calculating the concentrations. Furthermore, Equation 82 always includes initial and boundary conditions that are to be described.

As an initial condition there is the vector equation

$$G(z, 0) = G_A \tag{83}$$

and for the boundary conditions three types H_1 to H_2 are responsible:

$$\text{1st type: } G(z, t) = H_1 \tag{84}$$

$$\text{2nd type: } \frac{\partial G}{\partial z}(z, t) = H_2 \tag{85}$$

$$\text{3rd type: } E \cdot G(z, t) + F \cdot \frac{\partial G}{\partial z}(z, t) = H_3 \tag{86}$$

E and F are also coefficients. Equation 82 with $\partial G/\partial t$ also the unsteady process of a bubble column reactor is considered. For $\partial G/\partial t = 0$ only steady solutions are possible. Thus the boundary conditions are independent of time ($t = 0$).

This is also demonstrated by the boundary conditions formulated in Equations 34 to 48 for co-current flow and counter-current flow of the phases. Equations 43 and 44 and Equation 49 are boundary value differential equations for computing the concentrations of the gas and liquid phase for constant volume flows and steady mass balances. It can be seen that the boundary value differential equations results from Equation 82, which means

$$A_1 \frac{\partial^2 G}{\partial z^2} + A_2 \frac{\partial G}{\partial z} + A_3 \cdot G + A_4 = 0 \tag{87}$$

and for the boundary conditions the following is obtained at:

$$\text{1st type: } G(z) = H_1 \tag{88}$$

$$\text{2nd type: } \frac{\partial G}{\partial z}(z) = H_2 \tag{89}$$

$$\text{3rd type: } E \cdot G(z) + F \cdot \frac{\partial G}{\partial z}(z) = H_3 \tag{90}$$

in comparison with the unsteady problem according to Equations 84 to 86. Under certain conditions from A_1 to A_4 and for boundary conditions of the first type (linear), an analytical solution of

Equation 87 is possible and a linear or non-linear set of equations of the dimension (2 · N) is obtained according to Equation 52 and 53. This set of equations can generally be written as a vector and reads

$$F(X) = 0 \tag{91}$$

where F describes, for example, the functional dependences of the concentrations, and X is the variable vector.

The modeling of the bubble column reactors considers the kinetic regime according to Equations 56 to 72 and leads in the unsteady cases to the typical mathematical model equations too; i.e. partial differential equation sets of the form of equations 82 to 86, and in the unsteady case to the boundary value differential equation sets according to Equations 87 to 90, and in special cases to sets of equations according to Equation 91.

Solution Methods

Solution of Partial Differential Equation Sets

The solution of partial differential equation sets of the parabolic type according to Equation 82 with the initial and boundary conditions of Equations 83 to 86, and the special cases of the steady process of bubble column reactors according to Equation 87 and its boundary conditions according to Equations 88 to 90, which can be derived from them, can only be achieved by modern numerical mathematical methods. Moreover, computer programs tailored to the user's needs are required that assist the modeling of the bubble column reactor and the numerical solution of the mathematical model developed. Such a program system was developed and tested at the Engineering College of Köthen in several years of research work and provides a solution of the mentioned typical model equations for bubble column reactors. The program system is called DISIP and means DIgital SImulation Partial differential equation sets. It has the general program structure shown in Fig. 8.

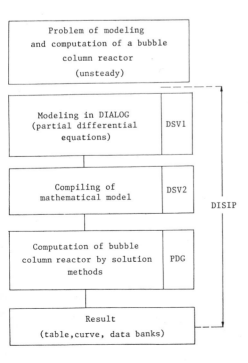

Figure 8. Running of the DISIP program system. This program permits the modeling and numerical solution of unsteady model equations for bubble column reactors.

For the application of DISIP the user requires only little knowledge of the programming language PL1 and can receive the model development and solution both as a dialog and as closed job. The simulation system DISIP is of modular construction. It consists of the program parts:

DSV—Model development in dialog
DSV 2—Compiling of the model
PDG—Numerical solution methods

In the normal case these program parts are worked off successively. However, it is possible for the experienced user to work with part PDG separately. For DISIP there is a display version and a punched card version.

DSV 1

The program part DSV 1 consists of 10 modules:

DSV 11—Preparatory actions, introduction dialog
DSV 12—Selection of the type of model equations
DSV 13—Model parameters
DSV 14—Initial conditions
DSV 15—Boundary conditions
DSV 16—Selection of solution methods, data selected especially to meet the user's requirement
DSV 17—Treatment of errors
DSV 18—Coordinate system, dimension, number of phases
DSV 19—Dialog organization
DSV 1A—Number of balance spaces, information about balance spaces

In the display version the user gives the following information:

1. Number of balance spaces
2. Coordinate form and vector
3. Number of phases in the balance room
4. Type of balance and result conversion
5. Parameter values for partial differential equation
6. Initial condition
7. Boundary condition type
8. Coefficients for boundary conditions
9. Solution method desired
10. Comments

All the display input data are recorded and the system displays the following information:

1. Types of model equations selected for the corresponding reactor
2. Selection of parameter sets
3. Error printing

All user's information fed and the information produced by the system are made available in the data banks for the program part DSV 2. All the user's inputs and system outputs are made in the language PL 1. Analogous is the work with the punched card version. All the user's input data are checked with regard to their correctness. In the display version the user directly receives indications for error elimination, in the punched card version errors are printed only subsequently.

DSV 2

This is the compiler program between DSV 1 and PDG. The instructions for the user produced by DSV 1 are transformed and classified. They form a data input flow for the MAKRO PL 1 compiler at the moment of the generation of PDG. The PDG program produced in this way is then a real image of the specific model of a bubble column reactor to be simulated by the computer. The solution method PDG is based on the line method. It is to be regarded as a construction methodology for the development of numerical methods for the solution of parabolic differential equations. A stability investigation of this method is given by Breitschuh [21].

The basic idea of the line method is the separation of the approximation of the place variables and time variables. It is subdivided into two discretization steps according to Figure 9:

1. By approximating the place derivatives the parabolic differential equations are transferred into a system of ordinary differential equations for which the initial value problem is to be solved.
2. These differential equations are solved by suitable numerical integration methods.

In the present stage of extension of the simulation system DISIP the program part PDG contains the following place discretizations:

☐ Three-point difference formulas:

$$U_x = \frac{1}{2h}(U_{n+1} - U_{n-1}) \tag{92}$$

$$U_{xx} = \frac{1}{h^2}(U_{n+1} - 2U_n + U_{n-1}) \tag{93}$$

☐ Five-point difference formulas:

$$U_x = \frac{1}{12h}(-U_{n+2} + 8U_{n+1} - 8U_{n-1} + U_{n-2}) \tag{94}$$

$$U_{xx} = \frac{1}{12h^2}(-U_{n+2} + 16U_{n+1} - 30U_n + 16U_{n-1} - U_{n-2}) \tag{95}$$

Figure 9. Approximation scheme for the line method. The operator equation Ax = y, A:E → F BANACH spaces is discretized by a sequence of substitution problems: $A_n x_n = y_n$ (n ∈ N), $A_N:E_n → F_n$, where p_n and q_n are discretization operators for the spatial coordinates. In an analogous way this applies to $p_{n,m}$ and $q_{n,m}$ in the time range. Stability is reached if

$$A_n \xrightarrow[(\alpha)]{p_n, q_n} A \qquad \text{with } \alpha > 0$$

$$A_{n,m} \xrightarrow[(\beta)]{p_{n,m}q_{n,m}} A_n \qquad \text{with } \beta > 0$$

and

$$A_{n,mn} \xrightarrow[(\gamma)]{p_{n,m}q_{n,m}} A \qquad \text{with}$$

$$\gamma = \min(\alpha, \beta)$$

□ Upwind difference formulas:

This form of difference formulas depends on the coefficients of the differential equation set. For example, they assume, for the differential equation

$$U_t = aU_{xx} + bU_x + cU \tag{96}$$

the following form:

$$bU_x = \frac{b}{2h}(U_{n+1} - 2U_n + U_{n-1}) + \frac{|b|}{2h}(U_{n+1} - U_{n-1}) \tag{97}$$

$$U_{xx} = \frac{1}{h^2}(U_{n+1} - 2U_n + U_{n-1}) \tag{98}$$

This form of difference approximation has the advantage that it is stable for any place step width. For numerical integration the following integration methods are employed:

□ Euler method (RKV 1):

$$
\begin{aligned}
k_1 &= \tau \cdot f(t_n, y_n) \\
y_{n+1} &= y_n + k_1
\end{aligned}
\tag{99}
$$

□ Heun method (RKV 2):

$$
\begin{aligned}
k_1 &= \tau \cdot f(t_n, y_n) \\
k_2 &= \tau \cdot f(t_n + \tau, y_n + k_1) \\
y_{n+1} &= y_n + \tfrac{1}{2}(k_1 + k_2)
\end{aligned}
\tag{100}
$$

□ Runge-Kutta method (RKV 4):

$$
\begin{aligned}
k_1 &= \tau \cdot f(t_n, y_n) \\
k_2 &= \tau \cdot f\left(t_n + \frac{\tau}{2}, y_n + \frac{k_1}{2}\right) \\
k_3 &= \tau \cdot f\left(t_n + \frac{\tau}{2}, y_n + \frac{k_2}{2}\right) \\
k_4 &= \tau \cdot f(t_n + \tau, y_n + k_3) \\
y_{n+1} &= y_n + \tfrac{1}{6}(k_1 + 2k_2 + 2k_3 + 2k_4)
\end{aligned}
\tag{101}
$$

□ Rational Runge-Kutta method:

$$
\begin{aligned}
k_1 &= \tau \cdot f(t_n, y_n) \\
k_2 &= \tau \cdot f\left(t_n + \frac{\tau}{2}, y_n + \frac{k_1}{2}\right) \\
k_3 &= 2k_1 - k_2 \\
y_{n+1} &= y_n + \frac{2(k_1, k_3)k_1 - (k_1, k_1)k_3}{(k_3, k_3)}
\end{aligned}
\tag{102}
$$

The rational Runge-Kutta method is absolutely stable as an explicit integration procedure. Its errors are of the second order. In this way the user of the PDG program has twelve numerical methods. A method advantageous for newly developed models is the coupling of the rational Runge-Kutta method with the upwind difference formulas. This method is absolutely stable.

Further details relating to the program structure and the algorithms and practical applications are given by Krug [22].

Solution of Boundary Value Differential Equation Sets

The solutions of boundary value differential equations such as of the Equation 87 with the boundary conditions according to Equations 88 to 90 describe the steady process of the bubble column reactor, whereas Equations 82 to 86 represent the unsteady process. Therefore, in general the program system DISIP also lends itself to solving the steady problem as was described in the preceding paragraph. Consequently, the partial differential equation set is computed numerically and for the time $t \to \infty$ the steady solution is obtained. But this corresponds to the solution of the boundary value problem according to Equations 87 to 90.

This procedure is ineffective, because non-linear behavior of the partial differential equation sets the place and the time discretizations chosen must be different in size, resulting in long computer times. On the other hand, special measures for suppressing the numerical errors in place and time are necessary. For this reason, the numerical solution of the boundary value differential equation set according to Equations 87 to 90 by means of the program system BORIS1-DIALOG applied by Hertwig and Werner [23] was recommended.

Figure 10 shows the general structure of this program system. The program systems described by Schwarze [24] and Jentsch [25] are suitable for the simulation of linear block-oriented control systems; whereas BORIS1, in addition, lends itself to the solution of non-linear differential equation sets with initial and boundary conditions.

The user can write the special mathematical model for the steady calculation of a bubble column reactor in the modeling part of BORIS1 according to Figure 10.

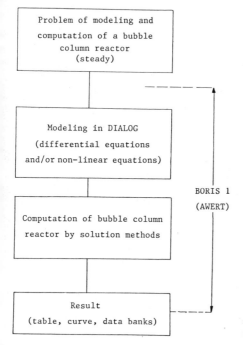

Figure 10. Sequence plan of the program system BORIS 1(AWERT). This program permits the modeling and numerical solution of steady model equations for bubble column reactors.

In the organizational part the notation of parameters for the model and the initial and boundary conditions occurs. By compiling the model the solution algorithm is activated and the result can be represented in tables or printed as a discrete curve. All the activities ranging from modeling to the solution and representation of the results can occur as a dialog, However, on the other hand a closed job procedure is possible too. The program system BORIS1 can be applied in FORTRAN IV on computers with a memory capacity of more than 256 K byte [26, 27].

For numerical integration a solution algorithm RK2DSS is available, which uses a modified Runge-Kutta method according to Equations 101 and 102 and an automatic step width control.

Furthermore, for the numerical computation of the boundary value problem a solution algorithm AWERT is available that can solve a non-linear equation set of the type of Equation 91.

Methods of Solution

The solution of the vector function

$$F(X) = (F_1(X), \ldots F_m(X))^T \tag{103}$$

with $\quad X^T = (X_1, \ldots, X_n)$

is effected in $F/R^n \rightarrow R^m$ for $m \geq n$ by a discretized regularized Gauss-Newton method, where the function

$$g(X) = 0.5 \sum_{i=1}^{m} (F_i(X))^2 \tag{104}$$

is minimized. The step sequence with k as a step counter is calculated as follows:

$$X^{k+1} = X^k - \gamma_k \cdot p^k(X^{k,} \lambda_k) \tag{105}$$

$$p^k(X^k, \lambda_k) = ((1 - \lambda_k) \cdot I + \lambda_k \delta F_k^T \cdot \delta F_k)^{-1} \cdot \delta g^k \tag{106}$$

and $\quad \delta g^k = \delta F_k^T \cdot F(X^k) \tag{107}$

where $\quad \lambda_k$ = regulating parameter
$\quad\quad\quad \gamma_k$ = damping factor
$\quad\quad\quad I$ = unit matrix
$\quad\quad\quad F_k$ = approximation for the Jacobi matrix $F'(X^k)$, and is calculated in the following way:

$$\delta F_k \cdot e^i = (F(X^{k-1} + h_j \cdot e^i) - F(X^{k-1}))/h \tag{108}$$

with $\quad e^i$ = unit vector of the jth component
$\quad\quad\quad h_j$ = discretization step width calculated by

$$h_j = 10^{-4}(|X_j^k| + 10^{-3}) \tag{109}$$

For the computation of X^{k+1} from X^k the sequences λ_k and γ_k are varied in a suitable way until the Goldstein inequality

$$\eta \cdot (X^k - \gamma_k \cdot p^k(X^k, \lambda_k)) \leq \eta \cdot X^k - \eta \cdot \gamma_k \cdot (\delta g^k)^T \cdot p^k(X^k, \lambda_k) \tag{110}$$

with $\eta = 0.01$ is met. The direction of descent p^k is not determined from the regularized normal equation set generally badly conditioned

$$(\alpha_k^2 \cdot I + (\delta F_k)^T \delta F_k) \cdot q^k = (\delta F_k)^T F(X^k) \tag{111}$$

but by means of a Householder orthogonal transformation as a root mean square solution of the inconsistent linearized equation set

$$\left[\begin{matrix} \delta F_k \\ \alpha_k^l \end{matrix}\right] \frac{q^k}{1} - \left[\begin{matrix} F(X^k) \\ 0 \end{matrix}\right] = \left[\begin{matrix} 0 \\ 0 \end{matrix}\right] \qquad (112)$$

with $q^k = \lambda_k \cdot p^k$ and $\alpha_k = (1 - \lambda_k)/\lambda_k$. The method is globally convergent.

Program Realization [28]

Within BORIS1 the SUBROUTINE

CALL AWERT (N, X, M, F, EPSREL, EFX, EGST, ITMAX, IPRINT, IE, HELP)

is used. The user has to write the non-linear equation set $F(X)$ as follows:

SUBROUTINE F(N, XA, M, FX, IEX)
DIMENSION X(N), FX(M)
FX = ...
RETURN
END

In the connecting lines we have:

$\quad$ N = length of the variable vector X
$\quad$ XA = starting vector
$\quad$ M = number of equations $F(X)$
$\quad$ F = name of the subroutine for computing $F(X)$
EPSREL = truncation bound for the relative change of the arguments
$\quad$ EFX = truncation bound for $g(X)$
$\quad$ EGST = truncation bound for $\|\delta g^k\|$
ITMAX = maximum number of iteration steps
IPRINT = printing parameter
$\quad$ IEX = $\{^0_1$ if FX can be calculated with X,
$\quad$ HELP = auxiliary field, two-dimensional in N $\times$ M that can be determined by the user.

If the starting value XA is sufficiently good the method requires only two calls of F per k step. The Jacobi matrix of $F(x)$ is updated for each step in one column. If the solution is achieved with an unfavorable starting value the direction of descent computed by the Jacobi matrix no longer provides any success after some steps. Therefore, AWERT carries out a partial renewal of the matrix and continues the solution until the dominant truncation bound EFX interrupts the procedure.

$\quad$ By means of EPSREL a high accuracy of iteration can be reached. From experience endeavors are made to obtain EGST < EFX in order to prevent a possible truncation at a "flat" location of $g(x)$. The number of iteration steps ITMAX essentially depends on the dimension and non-linearity of $F(X)$. As a reference number, ITMAX = 20 is used. The user receives extensive information on the solution process if he desires. For IPRINT = 4 the following are printed:

NORM (FX)	$= \|F(X^k)\|_2$
NORMGRAD	$= \|\delta g^k\|_2$
CORRECTION	$= \|X^k - X^{k-1}\|_2$
LAMDA	$= \lambda_k$
GAMMA	$= \gamma_k$
GOLDST	= checking function for γ determination
LAMZ	= number of the γ values required for γ_k determination
FZ	= calls of F required
HMAX	= discretization step width for the approximation of $F'(X)$

X(EPSREL)   = solution vector
IE   = cause of truncation
    0 if $\|F(X^k)\|_2 < EFX$
    1 if $\|\delta g^k\|_2 < EGST$
    2 if EPSREL is reached
    3 if ITMAX is reached
    4 if no descent is possible any more
    5 if there is an unsuitable starting vector
    6 if δF_k cannot be calculated
    7 if $M < N$

Example of Application

The following is to be calculated: model III bubble column reactor with ideally mixed liquid phase and partial axial return mixing in the gas phase and place dependence of the following parameters

1. Mass transfer coefficient k_L
2. Interfacial area a
3. Gas hold-up ε
4. Equilibrium coefficient α_i
5. Superficial velocity of the gas phase and liquid phase w_{sG}, w_{sL}

Model Equations for the Simulation Dependent Variables

Variable	No.
P	I
$\dot{n}_G$	II
w_{sG}	III
D_{zG}	IV
$\dfrac{d\dot{n}_{AG}}{dz}$	V
U	VI
$\dot{n}_{WG}$	VII
$\dot{n}_{EG}$	VIII
$\bar{\dot{n}}_{AG}$	IX
$\bar{\dot{n}}_{EL}$	

Model Equations for the Simulation Independent Variables

Variable	No.	Variable	No.	Variable	No.
$\bar{a}$	X				
q_R	XI	w_B	XV	α_A	XXI
D_{AL}	XII	Re	XVI	r	XXII
D_{EL}		Sh_A	XVII	$\dot{n}_{AL}^A$	XXIII
Sc_A	XIII	Sh_W	XVIII	c_{AL}^A	XXIV
Sc_W		Sh_E	XIX	α_W	
Sc_E		k_{LA}	XX	c_{WL}^A	
c_{SL}	XIV	k_{LW}		α_E	XXV
		k_{LE}		$\dot{n}_{EL}^A$	
				c_{EL}^A	

Boundary Conditions

$$z = 0: \dot{n}_{AG}(-0) = \dot{n}_{AG}(0) - \frac{D_{zG}\varepsilon}{L_R w_{sG}} \frac{d\dot{n}_{AG}(0)}{dz} \quad XXVI$$

$$\dot{n}_{AG}(-0) = \dot{n}_{AG}$$

$$z = 1: \frac{d\dot{n}_{AG}}{dz} = 0$$

Model Parameters

$$\rho_L, d_B, w_{sL}, \mu_L, V_{mol}, L_R$$

$$d_R, T, p^0, \dot{n}_{SL}^0, \dot{n}_{WG}^0, \dot{n}_{WL}^0, \dot{n}_{AG}^0$$

Solution Process in the Program System BORIS1 (AWERT)

PROGRAM REAK BORIS1

1. Reading in of the starting values for w_{sG}, ε, $\dot{n}_{AG}$, $\dot{n}_{WG}$, $\dot{n}_{EG}$ on COMMON for the computation of the agitating vessel balances for the reactor computation and the boundary values $\dot{n}_{AG}(0)$, $w_{sG}(0)$, $D_{zG}(0)$, $\dot{n}_G(0)$.
2. Computation of the model equations for the simulation independent variables Equation X to XXV.
3. CALL AWERT (. . .) for the solution of the model equations (Equation 24).
4. CALL AWERT (. . .) for the solution of the model equations (Equation 25).
5. CALL AWERT (. . .) for the computation of the boundary conditions according to Equations XXVI.
6. CALL ANFANG BORIS1-SUBROUTINE for initial value determination.
7. CALL DATEN1 BORIS1-SUBROUTINE for reading-in of control data for the numerical integration of the boundary value differential equations.
8. CALL BEGZYK BORIS1-SUBROUTINE for the organization of the numerical integration process—beginning.
9. Notation of the model equations for the simulation dependent variables according to Equations I to IX.
10. CALL RK 2d SS (. . .) for the numerical integration of Equation V.
11. CALL INTGA BORIS1-SUBROUTINE for the computation of the mean values according to Equation IX.
12. CALL TAB BORIS1-SUBROUTINE for the tabular output of the simulation dependent variables according to Equations I to IX.
13. CALL KURVA BORIS1-SUBROUTINE for the curve output of $\dot{n}_{AG} = f(z)$
14. CALL ENDZYK BORIS1-SUBROUTINE for the organization of the numerical integration process—end.
15. Printing of the mean values computed

$$E(I) = (\bar{w}_{sG}, \bar{\varepsilon}, \bar{\dot{n}}_{AG}, \bar{\dot{n}}_{WG}, \bar{\dot{n}}_{LG})$$

16. CALL ITER BORIS1-SUBROUTINE
    GOTO 2 if
    $/E(I\text{-}1) - E(I)/ > $ FEHLER
    otherwise GOTO 17

17. END REAK BORIS1

The results are represented in Figure 13. The molar flow of the ethine in the gas phase shows approximately the same distribution as for the results according to Figure 14.

MODELING OF AN INDUSTRIAL BUBBLE COLUMN REACTOR

Problems to be Solved

The preparation of ethanal as an important intermediate product of chemical industry can be made by catalytic water addition to dissolved ethine. In the presence of Hg^{2+} ions in a sulphuric solution the reaction

$$C_2H_2 + H_2O \xrightarrow{S} CH_3CHO$$

$$(A + W \xrightarrow{S} E)$$

occurs only in the direction given and without an essential by-product formation. In the industrial reactor at temperatures of between 90 and 98°C ethine conversion of about 85% is obtained. By recirculating and regeneration of the liquid phase (contact acid) its catalytic activity is largely kept constant. The dosage of ethine and water vapor and the feeding of regenerated contact acid including the water required additionally are effected at the bottom of the reactor ($d_R = 1.6$ m; $L_R = 17$ m).

In the present case the problem to be solved consists in determining possible variants of the capacity increase of the bubble column by the application of mathematical modeling [23]. In developing intensive and extensive methods of capacity increase the relation of the velocities of mass transfer between the phases and chemical kinetics plays a decisive role. If mass transfer is the slowest step and, therefore, velocity-determining, the primary task is to find possibilities of increasing the mass transfer coefficient or the specific phase boundary surface.

Such measures can be the reduction of primary bubble size by the corresponding dispersing systems, coalescence inhibition, or an increase of the turbulence in the reactor.

If, however, the chemical liquid phase reaction is much slower than the mass transfer between the phases, then an increase in the liquid phase volume (greater reactor height or diameter) is necessary. Another possibility is the raising of reaction temperature or of the liquid phase concentration of the components influencing kinetics. In addition to an intenser catalyst activity, an increase in pressure may be advantageous as far as this does not accelerate secondary reactions.

In the present case parameter studies on the basis of an unchanged reaction temperature and catalyst activity are carried out.

Model Variants

In choosing a definite strategy of mathematical modeling, on the one hand, the reactor model must be supposed to describe the real conditions in the whole reactor and the influence of all the partial processes with a technically interesting accuracy. On the other hand, it must be considered that models describing gas-liquid reactors are complicated differential equation systems whose numerical solution often requires an extensive programming amount and high computing cost. For economical reasons one must consider whether for the solution of definite problems simplified model variants are applicable without a considerable loss in information. In such considerations one should especially answer the question whether one of the phases can be assumed to be ideally mixed. In such a case the mass balances for this phase would be a system of algebraic equations. The time required for solution would be much shorter than for a phase with ideal plug flow (differential equation system of first order) or a phase with partial backmixing (differential equation system of second order). From this point of view, in the present case three general model variants were formulated and solved:

Model I: Bubble column reactor with ideally mixed liquid phase and plug flow in the gas phase.

Model II: Bubble column reactor with partial axial backmixing in the liquid phase and plug flow in the gas phase.

Model III: Bubble column reactor with ideally mixed liquid phase and partial axial backmixing in the gas phase.

Moreover, in these models two variants of mathematical solution are applicable that are associated with the dependence of the model parameters on the axial coordinate in the reactor.

Variant a

The parameters:

1. Mass transfer coefficient k_L
2. Interfacial area a
3. Gas hold-up ε
4. Equilibrium coefficient α_i
5. Superficial velocity of the gas phase and the liquid phase w_{sG} and w_{sL}

can be supposed to be constant. In this case it is assumed that the mean values of these quantities exist over the whole reactor volume. This simplification is often possible without major errors. In this connection, special attention should be paid to the flow rate of the gas phase. The advantage of variant a is the possibility of an analytical solution of the balance equations for simple first-order reactions.

Variant b

The previous parameters are considered in their space dependence. This model variant brings more accurate results and at the same time permits the checking of the deviations occurring in variant a. The mathematical solution of the balance equations must be performed numerically. By comparing the results obtained with the individual model variants it is possible to check the reliability of definite model simplifications. Finally, parameter studies provide information about the influence of essential partial processes and the operational behaviour of the reactor.

In formulating the balance equations in the present case isothermal conditions may be supposed to exist so that the heat balance is not necessary. In the model the influences of convection, axial dispersion, mass transfer, and liquid-phase reaction are considered. According to Equations 25 and 26 the following mass balances result:

Gas phase:

$$-\frac{d\dot{n}_{iG}}{dz} - k_L a L_R \left(\alpha_i \frac{\dot{n}_{iG}}{w_{sL}} - \frac{\dot{n}_{iL}}{w_{sL}} \right) + \frac{\varepsilon D_{zG}}{L_R w_{sG}} \frac{d^2 \dot{n}_{iG}}{dz^2} = 0$$

Liquid phase:

$$-\frac{d\dot{n}_{iL}}{dz} + k_L a L_R \left(\alpha_i \frac{\dot{n}_{iG}}{w_{sG}} - \frac{\dot{n}_{iL}}{w_{sL}} \right) + \frac{D_{zL}(1 - \varepsilon)}{L_R w_{sL}} \frac{d^2 \dot{n}_{iL}}{dz^2} + v_i(1 - \varepsilon) V_R r = 0$$

The boundary values are to be formulated according to the conditions of the dispersion model. For the case of ideal plug flow of the gas phase (models I and II) we have $D_{zG} = 0$. In the perfect mixing of the liquid phase supposed in models I and III, the balance of the continuous tank reactor is to be used (see Equation 51).

Determination of Model Parameters

The reaction kinetics of catalytic water addition to ethine can be described at constant catalyst activity by a velocity equation of first order. The kinetic constant was adapted on the basis of the measurement results obtained in the technical reactor. According to the relation of Akita and Yoshida [11] the gas hold-up approximately gave the value of $\varepsilon = 0.30$ measured for the standard operational condition. The mean bubble diameter was computed from the energy dissipation according to Liepe [29].

Accordingly, one obtains

$$\bar{d}_B = 0.0018 \text{ m}$$

and, consequently,

$$a = 1,000 \text{ m}^2/\text{m}^3$$

In determining the mass transfer coefficient the author's measurement results were compared with the data mentioned by several other authors in literature. In accordance with the relation given by Calderbank et al. [30] the measured values are reproduced satisfactorily whereas the equation of Hughmark [31] frequently employed provides values reduced by 50%.

In order to determine the equilibrium coefficients, because of the low liquid-phase concentrations for ethine and ethanal, only solubility data were used, whereas the activity coefficients for water and contact acid were correlated by the Wilson equation.

The computation of the axial diffusion coefficients was made for the gas phase according to Pavlica and Olson [8]

$$Pe_G = \frac{d_R w_{sG}}{D_{zG}} \approx 0.2$$

and for the liquid phase according to Reith et al. [7]

$$Pe_L = \frac{d_R w_{sG}}{D_{zL}} \approx 3$$

Mathematical Solution and Selected Computation Results

For model Ia (ideally mixed liquid phase, plug flow in the gas phase, preselection of an averaged gas phase velocity), an analytical solution can be determined by integration of the gas phase balance. The parameter studies were made by means of these simplified model variants with the aim of

Table 1
Parameter Studies with Model Ia ($d_R = 1.6$ m)

Variant	L_R in m	$\dot{n}_{AG}^0$ in kmol/h	k in 1/s	a in m²/m³	P in MPa	U_A —
I a/1	17	76.1	0.41	1000	0.20	0.85
2	20	76.1	0.41	1000	0.20	0.87
3	25	76.1	0.41	1000	0.20	0.89
4	25	112.0	0.41	1000	0.20	0.85
5	17	76.1	0.41	2000	0.20	0.85
6	17	76.1	0.82	1000	0.20	0.92
7	14	76.1	0.41	1000	0.22	0.85

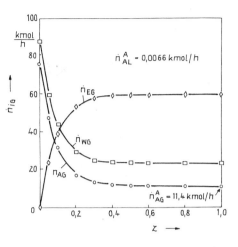

Figure 11. Axial distribution of the molar flows of ethine, ethanal, and water in the gas phase (standard operational condition—model Ia).

obtaining information on the velocity-determining step and on general possibilities of solving the scale up problem. The computing variants given in Table 1 provide the following information:

1. The standard operational condition (variant 1) is the adaptation variant with respect to the molar flows of ethine and ethanal (Figure 11).
2. By extending the reactor height by 3 or 8 m, respectively (variants 2 and 3), the conversion is increased by 2% in each case at constant input molar flows.
3. If at the same time the input molar flows and the reactor height increase (in variant 4 by 47% in each case), the ethine conversion remains constant. Thus the capacity increase corresponds to the same percentage. A rise of the input pressure was not considered here.
4. In variants 5 and 6 characteristic parameters of mass transport (interfacial area) and reaction kinetics (velocity constant) were changed arbitrarily. While there is no effect on the ethine conversion in the doubling the mass transport velocity, an increase in the kinetic constants has a great influence. Therefore, it can be regarded as sure that the chemical liquid phase reaction is the velocity-determining step of this process. In Figure 12 these variants are compared with the standard variant.
5. Another interesting possibility of rationalization is an increase in the liquid-phase concentration of ethine and, therefore, in reaction rate by a rise in pressure. Variant 7 shows that a shortening of the reactor by 3 m gives the same final conversion if the mean pressure is raised

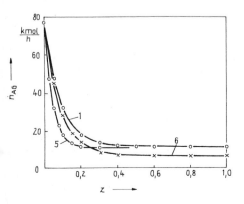

Figure 12. Axial distribution of the molar flow of ethine in the gas phase (model Ia). 1—Standard operational condition: $n_{AL}^A = 0.0066$ kmol/h. 5—Increase of the specific phase boundary surface by 100%: $n_{AL}^A = 0.0066$ kmol/h. 6—Increase of the kinetic constant by 100%: $n_{AL}^A = 0.0036$ kmol/h.

Table 2
Comparison of the Model Ia with More Comprehensive Model Variants

Variant	L_R in m	d_R in m	$\dot{n}_{AG}^0$ in kmol/h	P in MPa	D_{zL} in m²/s	k in 1/s	a in m²/m³	U_A	note
I a/1	17	1.6	76.1	0.20	∞	0.41	1000	0.85	w_{sG} = const.
I b/1	17	1.6	76.1	0.20	∞	0.41	1000	0.80	w_{sG} = f(z)
II a/1	17	1.6	76.1	0.20	0.422	0.41	1000	0.97	w_{sG} = const.
II a/2	17	3.2	304.4	0.20	0.844	0.41	1000	0.96	
II a/3	14	1.6	76.1	0.22	0.422	0.41	1000	0.97	
II a/4	17	1.6	76.1	0.20	0.422	0.41	2000	0.98	
II a/5	17	1.6	76.1	0.20	0.422	0.41	500	0.94	
II a/6	17	1.6	76.1	0.20	0.422	0.205	1000	0.89	
III b/1	17	1.6	76.1	0.20	∞	0.41	1000	0.83	w_{sG} = f(z)

by 10%. This variant can be realized even at unchanged input pressure if the pressure at the top is increased. Unintentional side effects that might result from the higher liquid-phase concentration of ethanal (e.g., consequent reactions) have not been considered so far.

In checking detailed model variants (Table 2), by means of the standard variant the axial dependence of the superficial gas velocity was considered (variant I b/1). Here the gas-phase balance of ethine is solved by means of RK2 DSS and AWERT (preselection and subsequent checking of the mean values in the liquid-phase balances). By means of the program system BORIS1-dialog the numerical and computational solution of the problem was made. The results are shown in Figure 13. The molar flow of ethine in the gas phase has approximately the same distribution as in variant I a/1 (Figure 14). The occurrence of a minimum of this function is interesting. The cause is that, on the one hand, on account of the ideal mixing of the liquid phase supposed a constant ethine concentration exists in this phase, but, on the other, the gas-phase concentration in the upper part of the reactor greatly decreases because of the increase in gas velocity as a result of the pressure drop. Because of the very quick mass transfer, the desorption of ethine and, consequently, an increase in molar flow occurs there.

If this variant is compared with the corresponding result according to model variant III b (ideal mixing of the liquid phase, partial mixing of the gas phase), then in spite of the mixing conditions that are to be regarded at first as more unfavorable, a slightly increased ethine conversion at the output is obtained. The cause is that the partial backmixing of the gas phase slightly reduces the noticeable rise of gas phase velocity in the upper part of the reactor as compared to variant I b/1 and, therefore, also reduces the desorption of ethine in this region (Figure 15).

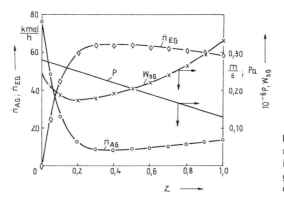

Figure 13. Axial distribution of the molar flows of ethine and ethanal in the gas phase and of superficial gas velocity and pressure (standard operation condition—model Ib).

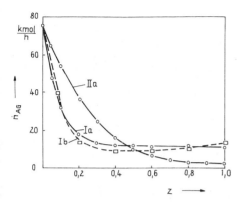

Figure 14. Comparison of the computed axial distribution of the ethine molar flow in the gas phase for different model variants (standard operational condition).

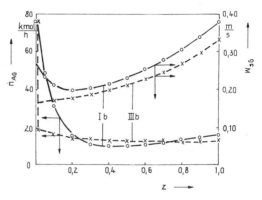

Figure 15. Axial distribution of the molar flows of ethine in the gas phase and superficial gas velocity in model Ib/1 and IIIb/1 (standard operational condition).

At this moment it is necessary to check whether the supposition of the ideally and, consequently, infinitely rapid mixing of the liquid phase in the presence of another quickly developing partial process (mass transfer) is admissible. The computations with the model variant II a (consideration of the partial axial backmixing in the liquid phase according to the dispersion model) show that in spite of high mixing coefficients and Bodenstein numbers that are considerably less than one marked concentration profiles exist in the liquid phase (Figure 16). In this way the increased conversions computed can be justified too.

By means of this improved model variant substantial possibilities of capacity increase were com-

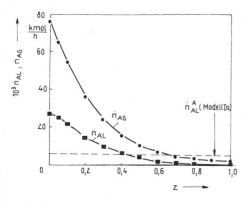

Figure 16. Axial distribution of the ethine molar flows in the gas and liquid phases (standard operational condition—model IIa).

puted in advance. If the reactor diameter doubles and the input molar flow of ethine and water increases by 400%, the conversion obtained is reduced only slightly in comparison with that of the standard variant. Thus, the doubling of the axial dispersion coefficient has hardly any effect.

The shortening of the reactor and the simultaneous increase in mean pressure (variant II a/3) lead to the same conclusions as in model Ia (variant 7). The additional test calculations for checking the velocity-determining step (variants II a/4 and 5 or II a/6), even if a partial mixing of the liquid phase is considered, show the great influence of reaction kinetics, whereas an arbitrary variation of the mass transfer parameter results in comparatively small changes of the conversion.

In summary, a rise in the ethanal production is only possible by increasing the liquid-phase volume if temperature and catalyst activity remain constant. Because of the limitation of initial pressure it will hardly be possible to extend reactor height, whereas the reactor diameter can be widened considerably. The results of computation show that an increase in axial backmixing causes only slight reductions of conversion even if the diameter doubles. The constancy of the relative gas phase component can be supposed in both cases.

Another variant favorable with regard to the ethine conversion is the reduction of the reactor height, simultaneously increasing top pressure as far as this does not speed up unintentional consequent reactions.

NOTATION

A_R	cross-sectional area of the reactor, m^2	M	molar weight, $g\,mol^{-1}$
a	interfacial area, $m^2\,m^{-3}$	m, n	reaction order
c_i	molar concentration of the component i, $mol\,m^{-3}$	N	number of main components
		N'	total number of components
D_L, D_{iL}	diffusion coefficient in the liquid phase, $m^2\,s^{-1}$	$\dot{n}_i$	molar flow of component i, $mol\,s^{-1}$
D_{zG}, D_{zL}	axial dispersion coefficients of the gas phase or liquid phase, $m^2\,s^{-1}$	$\dot{n}$	total molar flow, $mol\,s^{-1}$
		P	pressure, Pa
d_B	bubble diameter, m	P_1	top pressure of the column, Pa
d_R	reactor diameter, m	Pe	Peclet number
f	degree of saturation	r	dimensionless radial coordinate
g	gravitational acceleration, $m\,s^{-2}$	r	reaction velocity, $mol\,m^{-3}\,s^{-1}$
Ha	Hatta number	t	time, s
k, k_1, k_n	kinetic constant, $mol^{1-n}\,m^{3(n-1)}\,s^{-1}$	U	conversion
		V_{mol}	molar volume, $m^3\,mol^{-1}$
k_L	mass transfer coefficient on the liquid side, $m\,s^{-1}$	V_R	reactor volume, m^3
		w_B	bubble rise velocity, $m\,s^{-1}$
k_{LR}	mass transfer coefficient influenced by chemical reaction, $m\,s^{-1}$	w_c	circulation rate, $m\,s^{-1}$
		w_G, w_L	gas or liquid velocity, $m\,s^{-1}$
L_R	reactor height, m	w_F	velocity of liquid vortex, $m\,s^{-1}$
l_B	mean bubble distance, m	w_{sG}, w_{sL}	superficial velocity of gas or liquid phase, $m\,s^{-1}$
		z	dimensionless axial coordinate

Greek Symbols

α_i	coefficient of the phase equilibrium gas-liquid	θ_{Cell}	mixing time of a cell, s
		θ_{mix}	mixing time of column, s
α_w	wall heat transfer coefficient, $W\,m^{-2}\,K^{-1}$	λ	coefficient of thermal conductivity, $W\,m^{-1}\,K^{-1}$
ε	gas hold-up	μ	dynamic viscosity, Pa s
ζ	flow loss coefficient	ν	kinematic viscosity, $m^2\,s^{-1}$

ν_i stoichiometric coefficient of the component i

ρ specific weight, $kg\,m^{-3}$

σ boundary surface tension, $N\,m^{-1}$

σ_R chemical acceleration factor

Subscripts

A ethine
E ethanal
G gas phase
i component

j liquid-phase reaction
k gas-phase reaction
L liquid phase
W water

Superscripts

A, Aus output
0 input

* chemical equilibrium

REFERENCES

1. Nottenkaemper, R., Steiff, A. and Weinspach, P. M. "Zur Hydrodynamik in Blasensäulen-Reaktoren," *Chemie-Ingenieur-Technik*, v. 54, no. 10, Oct. 1982, pp. 918–919.
2. Zehner, P. "Impuls-, Stoff- und Wärmetransport in Blasensäulen Teil 1: Strömungsmodell der Blasensäule und Flüssig-keitsgeschwindigkeiten," *Verfahrenstechnik*, v. 16, no. 5, May 1982, pp. 347–351.
3. Zehner, P. "Impuls-, Stoff- und Wärmetransport in Blasensäulen Teil 2: Axiale Durchmischung und Wärmeübergang," *Verfahrenstechnik*, v. 16, no. 6, June 1982, pp. 514–518.
4. Joshi, J. B. and Sharma, M. M. "A Circulation Cell Model for Bubble Columns," *Transactions of the Institution of Chemical Engineers*, v. 57, no. 4, April 1979, pp. 244–251.
5. Pandit, A. B. and Joshi, J. B. "Mixing in Mechanically Agitated Gas-Liquid Contactors, Bubble Columns, and Modified Bubble Columns," *Chemical Engineering Science*, v. 38, no. 8, August 1983, pp. 1189–1215.
6. Wendt, R., Steiff, A. and Weinspach, P. M. "Flüssigphasenrückvermischung in Blasensäulen-reaktoren," *Chemie-Ingenieur-Technik*, v. 55, no. 10, Oct. 1983, pp. 796–797.
7. Reith, T., Renken, S. and Israel, B. A. "Liquid Phase Dispersion in Bubble Columns," *Chemical Engineering Science*, v. 23, no. 6, June 1968, pp. 619–629.
8. Pavlica, R. T. and Olson, J. H. "Unified Design Method for Continuous-Contact Mass Transfer. Operations," *Industrial and Engineering Chemistry*, v. 62, no. 12, 1970, pp. 45–58.
9. Deckwer, W. D. "Blasensäulen-Reaktoren-ihre modellmäßige Erfassung und Berechnung," *Chemie-Ingenieur-Technik*, v. 49, no. 3, March 1977, pp. 213–223.
10. Joshi, J. B. "Gas-Phase-Dispersion in Bubble Columns," *The Chemical Engineering Journal*, v. 24, no. 2, Sept. 1982, pp. 213–216.
11. Akita, K. and Yoshida, F. "Gas Hold-up and Volumetric Mass Transfer Coefficient in Bubble Columns" *Industrial and Engineering Chemistry Process Design and Development*, v. 12, no. 1, January 1973, pp. 76–80.
12. Akita, K. and Yoshida, F. "Bubble Size, Interfacial Area, and Liquid-Phase Mass Transfer Coefficient in Bubble Columns," *Industrial and Engineering Chemistry Process Design and Development*, v. 12, no. 1, January 1974, pp. 84–91.
13. Keitel, G. and Onken, V. "Zur Koaleszenzhemmung durch Elektrolyte und organische Verbindungen in wässrigen Gas-Flüssigkeits-Dispersionen," *Chemie-Ingenieur-Technik*, v. 54, no. 3, March 1982, pp. 262–263.
14. Calderbank, P. H. and Moo Young, M. B. "The Continous Phase Heat and Mass-Transfer Properties of Dispersions," *Chemical Engineering Science*, v. 16, no. 1/2, 1962, pp. 39–54.

15. Laurent, A. and Charpentier, J. C. "Anwendung experimenteller Labormodelle bei der Voraussage der Leistung von Gas-Flüssigkeits-Reaktoren," *Chemie-Ingenieur-Technik*, v. 53, no. 4, April 1981 pp. 244–251.
16. Fair, J. R. "Designing Gas-Sparged-Reactors," *Chemical Engineering*, v. 74, July 17, 1967, pp. 207, 214.
17. Mersmann, A. "Zum Wärmeübergang zwischen dispersen Zweiphasensystemen und senkrechten Heizflächen im Erdschwerefeld," *Verfahrenstechnik*, v. 10, no. 10, Oct. 1976, pp. 641–645.
18. Hertwig, K. "Gas-Flüssigphase-Reaktoren," *Handbuch Verfahrenstechnische Berechnungsmethoden*, v. 5 Chemische Reaktoren, Leipzig: VEB Deutscher Verlag für Grundstoffindustrie, 1981, pp. 245–269.
19. Beek, W. J. and Muttzall, K. M. K. *Transport Phenomena*, New York, John Wiley and Sons, Inc., 1975.
20. Hikita, H. and Asai, S. "Gas Absorption with (m, n)-th Order Irreversible Chemical Reaction," *International Chemical Engineering*, v. 4, no. 2, Febr. 1974, pp. 332–340.
21. Breitschuh, U. "Zur numerischen Lösung partieller Differentialgleichungen mit dem Linienverfahren." *Dissertation A*, Technische Hochschule Ilmenau, DDR, 1980.
22. Krug, W. "Digital Simulation of Partial Differential Equations of Chemical Engineering Systems," *Systems Analysis Modeling Simulation*, v. 1, no. 1, Jan. 1984, pp. 205–213.
23. Hertwig, K. und Werner, H. "Anwendung der mathematischen Modellierung bei der Kapazitätssteigerung industrieller Blasensäulenreaktoren," *Chemische Technik*, v. 34, no. 1, Jan. 1982, pp. 3–6.
24. Schwarze, G. "Simulation kontinuierlicher Systeme," *Reihe Automatisierungstechnik*, Bd. 177, Berlin, VEB Verlag Technik, 1976, pp. 40–60.
25. Jentsch, W. *Digitale Simulation*, Münschen, Wien, Oldenbourg Verlag GmbH, 1969, pp. 70–110.
26. Heinrich, G. und Krug, W. Modellierung Luft-und kältetechnischer Systeme, *Reihe Luft-und Kältetechnik*, Berlin, Verlag Technik, 1978, pp. 11–139.
27. Krug, W. "Ein Modularsystem zur digitalen Simulation und Optimierung kontinuierlicher Systeme," *Messen-Steuern-Regeln*, v. 19, no. 10, Oct. 1976, pp. 347–350.
28. Krug, W. "Zur nichtlinearen Optimierung im interaktiven Dialog mit LAMAIN," *Messen-Steuern-Regeln*, v. 24, no. 1, Jan. 1981, pp. 6–9.
29. Liepe, F. and Weissgaerber, H. "Verfahrenstechnische Berechnungsmethoden," *Stoffvereinigen in fluiden Phasen*, v. 4/2, Leipzig, VEB Deutscher Verlag für Grundstoffindustrie, 1979, p. 177.
30. Calderbank, P. H., Johnson, D. S. L., and Loudon, J. "Mechanics and Mass Transfer of Single Bubbles in Free Rise through Some Newtonian and Non-Newtonian Liquids," *Chemical Engineering Science*, v. 25, no. 2, Febr. 1970, pp. 235–236.
31. Hughmark, G. A. "Hold-up and Mass Transfer in Bubble Columns," *Industrial and Engineering Chemistry Process Design and Development*, v. 6, no. 2, Febr. 1967, pp. 218–220.

CHAPTER 41

HOLD-UP AND INTERFACIAL AREAS IN PULSED LIQUID-LIQUID SIEVE PLATE COLUMNS

J. A. Golding

Department of Chemical Engineering
University of Ottawa
Ottawa, Canada

CONTENTS

INTRODUCTION

The pulsed sieve-plate column is a type of contractor frequently used in solvent extraction (liquid-liquid extraction) operations. It has the advantage that there are no internal moving parts making the column very suitable for handling both corrosive and radioactive solutions. The column operates under countercurrent flow conditions and finds applications where extraction rates are mass transfer (diffusion) controlled. A pulsed column is considered to have the following advantages:

1. Differential type of contactor so that it can be employed for operations requiring many theoretical stages.
2. Good dispersion characteristics that enhance mass transfer rates.
3. moderate cost.
4. Relatively low solution inventory.
5. Availability of correlations for predicting throughputs and mass transfer efficiencies.

Also in applications requiring many theoretical stages the use of concatenated column has been proposed by Jealous and Lieberman [21] so as to avoid excessive column heights or where head room is limited.

The concept of using a pulsed continuous phase to increase interphase mass transfer was first presented by Van Dijk [53] in 1935 and as presently used comprises a column containing a series of perforated plates. These plates, depending on the column diameter, can then be assembled either in the form of a plate cartridge inserted into the column or the plates can be mounted on a shaft suspended down the center of the column (Figure 1). Agitation inside the column is achieved by pulsing the continuous phase either by mechanical means as originally proposed by Van Dijk, or through the use of an air pulse as described by Thornton [50] (see also work of Baird [2]). Power requirements for pulse generators were studied by Jealous and Johnson [20] who developed an equation in terms of the column and pulse leg heights, effective fluid densities in the column and pulse leg, cross-sectional areas of the column and pulse leg, plate free area, as well as the rate of fluid displacement. A more complete description of pulse generators in current use is given by

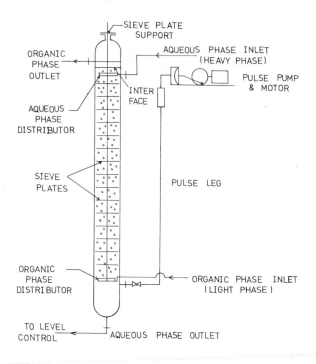

Figure 1. Pulsed sieve plate column.

Logsdail and Slater [30]. These authors also discuss the design of the plate cartridge which has also been shown to affect column performance [16, 49]. Actual plate hole size and plate spacing depends on system physical characteristics, desired throughputs, and the required extraction efficiency. Although sieve plate holes are usually sharp-edged orifices nozzle orifices, i.e. sieve plates with indented holes, they can improve dispersion characteristics [16]. Louver plate redistributors for large diameter columns have been suggested by Woodfield and Sege [55].

OPERATING CHARACTERISTICS

A pulse sieve-plate column operates as follows; the liquids are fed continuously into the column (Figure 1) and flow countercurrently along the column. The pulsing action required to disperse either the light or the heavy phase is applied to the base of the column. Thus, in the former case the light phase is forced through the sieve plate holes on the up-stroke of the pulse while in the latter case the heavy phase is forced through the holes on the down stroke.

In the actual operation of a pulsed column three distinct regions have been noted [15, 44]; namely the mixer settler region, the emulsion region, and an unstable region depending on the total flow rate, pulse frequency and pulse amplitude (Figure 2). Initially at low flow rates, frequencies, and amplitudes the two phases separate between pulses. Thus, when the light phase is dispersed, it is first forced through the sieve plate, droplets then rise through the continuous phase, and coalesce under the next plate at the end of the pulse. When the heavy phase is dispersed the process is similar, however, the dispersed phase flow is from the upper to the lower plate, i.e. the dispersed phase coalesces on the top of the lower plate. This region is called the mixer settler region. Increase in either the flow rate or the pulsation intensity ($f \cdot A_p$) results in a decrease in coalescence and stable drops are formed. This region is called the emulsion region and is one where overall mass transfer rates are considered to be the highest, however, longitudinal mixing

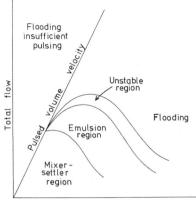

Figure 2. Flow regimes in a pulsed column.

does occur. Further increase in flow rate or pulsation intensity will eventually cause flooding in the column. Flooding under these conditions is due to the formation of small droplets with the droplet settling (or rise) velocity being smaller than the superficial velocity of the continuous phase. Flooding also occurs when the pulsation is insufficient to force the dispersed phase through the holes in the sieve plate. The effect of increasing flow rate and amplitude on column hold-up is shown in Figure 3.

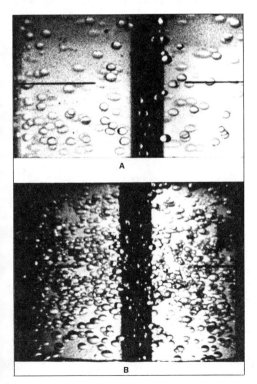

Figure 3. Effect of flow rate and pulse amplitude on dispersed phase hold-up. System: Di2 ethyl hexyl phosphoric acid; kerosene – TBP – water; nickel loading in organic phase = 7.0 g/l; pulse frequency 0.667 s^{-1}; (a) $A_P = 0.5$ cm $V_D = 5.04$ cm/s; (b) $A_P = 1.0$ cm, $V_D = 9.36$ cm/s.

HOLD-UP AND FLOODING

Most hold-up data reported in the literature refer to an average value of the hold-up for the entire length of the column. These values are obtained by shutting off the flow of both phases to the column and allowing the two phases to settle. Solenoid shut-off values are used in the inlet and outlet lines for both phases to prevent any drainage from the column. However, studies carried out by Jiricny and Prochazka [22] using pulsed-plate columns and by Kagan et al. [23] on pulsed sieve plate show that the actual plate hold-up varies from plate to plate. Jiricny and Prochazka used differential pressure measurements to measure the hold-up, while Kagan et al. used photographic techniques. Other techniques used for the measurement of hold-up are discussed by Bell and Babb [4].

Flooding Characteristics

An estimate of the flooding characteristics in pulsed column is needed to determine maximum column throughputs and hence the required column diameter. Variables considered to affect flooding are related to:

1. Column dimensions, i.e., column diameter, plate spacing, number of plates, hole diameter and plate free space expressed as a fraction of the plate area.
2. Fluid flows and agitation intensity, i.e. individual phase superficial velocities, slip velocity, pulse frequency and pulse amplitude.
3. Individual phase physical properties, i.e. density, density difference, interfacial tension, and viscosity [46].

The most comprehensive studies have been carried out by Thornton [51] and by McAllister et al. [34]. Thornton correlated flooding data in terms of a characteristic velocity V_0 related to the slip velocity and the superficial phase velocities V_d and V_c. This approach was also used by Logsdail et al. [32] for studying the performance of rotary disc contactors.

$$V_{slip} = V_0(1 - x) = Vd/x + V_c/(1 - x) \tag{1}$$

where x is the dispersed phase hold-up.

Data were reported for the following systems under the conditions where no mass transfer was occurring: water/toluene, water/butyl acetate, water/ethyl acetate, water/MIK, water/iso-octane, and water/white spirit. The reported correlation is:

$$\frac{V_0\mu_c}{\sigma} = 0.6\left[\frac{\psi_f\mu_c^5}{\rho_c\sigma^4}\right]^{-0.24} \cdot \left[\frac{d_0\rho_c\sigma}{\mu_c^2}\right]^{0.9} \cdot \left[\frac{\mu_c^4 g}{\Delta\rho\sigma^3}\right]^{1.01} \cdot \left[\frac{\Delta\rho}{\rho_c}\right]^{1.8}\left[\frac{\mu_d}{\mu_c}\right]^{0.3} \tag{2}$$

where $\quad \psi_f = \pi^2 N(1 - S^2)(fA_p)^3/2\ S^2 C_0^2 H_c$

$C_0 = 0.6$

McAllister et al. [33] carried out a detailed survey of flooding data in the literature. The flow capacity at flooding $(V_c + V_d)_f$ was correlated in terms of the drag coefficient, C_d the capillary number, N_c the flow ratio, pulse amplitude, and the plate spacing. The equation developed is

$$\ln\frac{V_c + V_d}{\Delta_c + \Delta_d} = -3.471 + 0.2568\ \ln C_d - 0.07194(\ln C_d)^2$$

$$+ 0.006191(\ln C_d)^3 - \ln N_c$$

$$- 0.09096(\ln N_c)^2 + 0.1424\ \ln V_c/V_D$$

$$- 0.1807(\ln A_p/H_c) + 0.07198\ \ln C_d/\ln N_c \tag{3}$$

where $C_d = (\Delta\rho \cdot d_0 \cdot S^2 \cdot g/\rho_c \pi_m^2)$

$N_c = (\mu_c \pi_v/S \cdot \sigma)$

A trial and error procedure is required. Another equation proposed in the literature was developed by Smoot et al. [48] and is reported to give similar results to the Thornton. The equation is

$$\frac{(V_c + V_d)\mu}{\sigma} = 0.527[V_c/V_d]^{-0.014} \cdot [\Delta\rho/\rho_c]^{0.63} \cdot [\psi_f \mu_c^5/\rho_c \sigma^4]^{-0.207} \cdot [d_0 \sigma \rho_c/\mu_c^2]^{0.458}$$

$$\cdot [D/d_0]^{0.0}[g\mu_c^4/\rho_c \sigma]^{0.81} \cdot [\mu_d/\mu_c]^{-0.2} \tag{4}$$

It should be noted mass transfer affects droplet coalescence and, consequently, care must be taken when using these equations [31, 34]. Other investigations of interest concerned with flooding, hold-up, and axial dispersion include those of Batey et al. [3], Bell and Babb [4], Coggan [6], Cohen and Beyer [7]. Foster et al. [12] (who considered transient behavior), Geier [15], Li and Newton [28], Logsdail and Larner [29, 30], Miyauchi and Oya [37]. Niebuhr and Vogelpohl [39], and Schmidt [43], and Sehmel and Babb [45].

Hold-up

There is no general overall correlation for predicting column hold-up. In addition to the effects or agitation intensity, individual phase flow velocities and system physical properties, hold-up can also depend on the presence or absence of mass transfer if droplet coalescence is affected [6, 33]. At low agitation intensities when the column is operating in the mixer settler zone, hold-up decreases with increase in agitation intensity. Griffith et al. [19], suggested in this region that hold-up in any section can be related to the volumetric flow rate and the pulse frequency hence,

$$x = V_d/fH_c \tag{5}$$

Sehmel and Babb [45] developed an equation for determining the transition frequency at minimum hold-up. They found the transition frequency depended on pulse amplitude, density difference, dispersed phase viscosity, and interfacial tension. Golding et al. [17] observed that under the same agitation and flow conditions in the presence of mass transfer, contacting behavior changed from the mixer settler region to the emulsion region.

In the emulsion region hold-up can be evaluated from the correlation proposed by Thornton [50] relating individual phase velocities and hold-up to the characteristic velocity V_0. This approach has also been used by Rouyer et al. [42] and by Misek [35] in his studies on mechanically agitated contactors. Misek noted that the previous equation would only apply under the limiting condition of zero dispersed phase hold-up and a coalescence coefficient should be included to consider the variation of hold-up along the column. Logsdail and Thornton [33] reported on the effect of mass transfer on hold-up when V_0 values were increased by a factor of 2.6 when compared to values predicted by Thornton's original equation.

Miyauchi and Oya [37] studied the methyl isobutyl ketone 0.1 N aqueous potassium chloride system. The authors correlated their hold-up data and data reported in the literature by Cohen and Beyer [7], Li and Newton [28]. Sehmel and Babb [45], and Shirotsuka et al. [46]. The correlation was proposed in terms of a parameter ψ,

where $\psi = [f \cdot A_\rho/(\beta \cdot H_c)^{1/3} \cdot [\mu_d^{1/2}/(\Delta\rho \cdot \sigma)^{1/4}]$ \hfill (6)

and $\beta = S^2/(1 - S)(1 - S^2)$ \hfill (7)

Hence, $x = 0.66\psi^{0.84}V_d^{2/3} \cdot \psi < 0.21$ \hfill (8)

$x = 6.32\psi^{2.4}V_d^{2/3} \cdot \psi > 0.21$ \hfill (9)

Khemangkorn et al. [23], also found a similar dependence of the hold-up on the dispersed phase velocity at high pulsation intensities. Hold-up data were correlated in the following form:

$$x = C(Ap \cdot f^{1.24})^a V_d^b \tag{10}$$

when for $Ap \cdot f^{1.24} \geq 5.5$, $b = 2/3$ while for $Ap \cdot f^{1.24} < 5.5$, $b = 1.0$. The constant C and the exponent a can be expected to vary with column dimensions and system physical properties. The authors also reported an effect of the direction of mass transfer on the values of a, b, and c. The system studied was carbon tetrachloride/water/iodine. Other studies include those of Bell and Babb [4] who studied the variation of individual plate hold-up with column height and Foster et al. [12], who reported on transient hold-up changes in a pulsed column.

Drop Diameter, Distributions, and Interfacial Areas

The method most commonly used is direct photography using conventional methods [37] or employing high-speed cameras typically [17, 18].

Photographic techniques have the disadvantage that analysis of the photographic data is tedious and time consuming. Counting methods using Zeiss particle analyzers can be empolyed, but there is a tendency to underrepresent the small drops. More recent techniques involve the use of a data tablet digitizers or graphic tablets together with a tracing stylus. Individual droplets are then out-lined and the diameter of major and minor axes determined [18, 27]. These latter methods have the greater advantage that droplet size adata is inputed directly into a computer so that drop sizes, drop distributions, and Sauter mean diameters can be computed directly.

Techniques involving the withdrawal of drops with the work of Philhofer and of Miller a photo-electric suction probe have also been used [41]. See also the studies of Mylnek and Resnick [38]. Several other techniques have been used in measuring drop diameter and distributions in agitated liquid-liquid dispersions. These methods could be applied to pulse columns, e.g. the combination of fiber optical probes with high-speed photography [40, 52]. In addition the transmission of light in dispersion has been employed, with Calderbank [5] showing that for spherical droplets the mean diameter can be determined directly from light absorbance measurements.

Indirect methods have also been employed. Generally, authors have assumed droplets would act as rigid spheres while for several limited systems total areas can be determined based on a chemically reacting system. Thus, Fernandes [11] studied the alkaline hydrolysis of formate esters to determine the total effective area for mass transfer, i.e. including droplet formation and coalescence.. Agitation intensity and dispersed phase frequency was found to influence the effective area with distinct mini-mums and maximums being observed with respect to these variables.

When droplets are assumed to act as rigid spheres, i.e. no internal circulation, the characteristic or slip velocity is the terminal velocity of the mean drop size, i.e.

$$V_T = (4d_m \, \Delta\rho g/3C_d\rho_c)^{0.5} \tag{11}$$

Miyauchi and Oya [37] used this equation with $C_d = 24/Re$ when comparing the results of their studies. Misek [36] also used this approach to measure average drop sizes and developed an equation for predicting drop sizes for reciprocating plate columns where plate hole sizes were large compared to drop sizes. In addition Logsdail and Slater [30] employed Thornton's equation to predict V_t and suggest the use of the following relationship for the drop coefficient C_d in Equation 11 to account for viscous effects:

$$C_d = 24/Re\{1.0 + 0.15 \, Re^{0.687}\}, 0.2 \leq Re \leq 700 \tag{12}$$

where Re is the Reynolds number based on the mean drop diameter and is equal to $Re = \rho_c d_m V_t/\mu_c$.

Khemangkorn et al. [25], considered the applicability of equations that have been developed for predicting droplet diameters in agitated dispersions, i.e. $d_m \simeq (A_p f)^{1.2}$. Experimentally the authors found that interfacial areas increased rapidly with increase in agitation intensity and that amplitude

Table 1
Mean Drop Diameter Correlations

Investigators	Column Dimensions	System	d_m
Assenov and Penchev [1] d_m in mm	$D = 4.9$ cm $H_c = 5$ cm $h = 1.022$ m $d_0 = 2.25$ mm	water CCl_4	$d_m = .01 \times \left(\dfrac{\sigma}{\Delta\sigma g}\right)^{0.5} \left(\dfrac{Ap \cdot f \cdot \mu_c}{\sigma}\right)^{-0.5} \times N_b^{-0.1}$
Kagen, Aerov [23] Lonik, and Volkova d_m in mm	$D = 5.6$ cm $H_c = 5$ cm $h = 4.0$ m $d_0 = 2.0$ mm	kerosene-water CCl_4-water	$d_m = 0.92(\sigma/\rho_c g)^{0.5} \times Re^{-0.1}Fr^{-0.1}N^{-0.11}$
Khemangkorn, Muratet, and Angelino [25] d_m in cm	$D = 5.0$ cm $H_c = 5$ cm $h = 1.0$ m $d_0 = 2.0$ mm	CCl_4-water	$d_m = 0.38\, Ap^{-1.0}f^{-1.24} \times N_b^{-0.21}V_d^{-0.083\,(1)}$ $d_m = 0.49\, Ap^{-1.0}f^{-1.24} \times N_b^{-0.21}V_d^{-0.0002\,(2)}$
Kubica and Zdunkiewicz [26] d_m in m	$D = 6.1$ cm $H_c = 5.0$ cm $h = 1.0$ m $d_0 = 2.0$ mm	dichloroethane 20% glycerol xylene-water butyl acetate water	$\dfrac{d_m}{D} = 0.0135(f^2 \cdot Ap^2 \cdot \rho_c d_0)^{-0.225}$ $\times (\mu_c/\mu_D)^{-0.0163}$
Logsdail and Slater [31] d_m in m	V_T evaluated from Thornton's [50] correlation of characteristic droplet velocity		$d_m = [18\, V_T \cdot \mu_c(1 + 0.15\, Re^{0.687})/g\,\Delta\rho]^{0.5}$
Misek [36] Reciprocating plate column d_m, d_0 in cm	$D = 25$ cm $H_c = 12.5,\ 25$ cm $h = 1.0$ and 2.0 cm $d_0 = 0.5$–3.0 cm	kerosene-water water-amly alcohol water-butyl acetate water-cyclo-hexanol	$\dfrac{d_m}{d_0} = 0.439[\sigma S^{0.5}/(d_0\rho_c \times (\pi f A_p + V_c)^2)]^{0.6}$
Miyauchi and Oya [37] d_m in cm	$D = 3.2\ \&\ 5.4$ cm $H_c = 1.0$–10 cm $h = 37,78,$ and 86 cm $d_0 = 1.5\ \&\ 3.0$ mm	MIBK water	$d_m = 0.081(fA_pH_c^{0.333})^{-1.2}$

(1) *Mass transfer from continuous phase to dispersed phase*
(2) *Mass transfer from dispersed to continuous phase*

and frequency have different effects on drop size. Effects of dispersed phase flow rate and position in the column were noted as well as the direction of mass transfer. Golding et al. [18], also reported effects of extractant loading on drop size.

In equations developed to correlate mean drop size date the following variables have been considered; pulsation intensity, continuous phase density, density difference, interfacial tension, plate hole diameter and viscosity ratio. The equations proposed by several investigators are given in Table 1.

There is no general agreement on the acceptability of any one of these equations over a wide range of conditions. Logsdail and Slater [31] compared values predicted by several of the equations and noted that there were considerable differences between the predicted d_m values. In addition, both Golding et al. [18] and Klemangkorn et al. [24, 25] report mass transfer effects on drop sizes. However, if hold-up data are available equations based on the assumption that the slip velocity equals the drop terminal velocity can be expected to give reasonable results.

Klemangkorn et al. [24] studied drop size distributions and found that they were best represented by a Weibull distribution. Garg and Pratt [12] also reported similar findings, and in further work they examined droplet break up and coalescence in both the mixer settler range and the emulsion region. They reported that though droplet interactions are beneficial to mass transfer, their effect was not highly significant [13]. This means, that calculations of column height based on the Sauter mean diameter can be expected to give reasonable results. It should be noted that differs from the work of Cruz-Pinto and Korchinsky [8] who found that for a rotating disk contactor increase in drop size distributions substantially affected column performance. In other work on droplet distributions Batey et al. [3] noted an approximately Gaussian distribution, however, Vassallo et al. [53] reported that the form of droplet distributions are a function of the pulse velocity. It has also been suggested that the approach to equilibrium will also influence drop distributions [9]. The actual mass transfer performance has been considered in several ways, generally in terms of the height of a transfer unit [33, 48] or occassionally in terms of an overall mass transfer unit [17, 24] as well as the use of rate equations considering mass transfer during droplet formation, droplet rise or fall, and during coalescence [47]. Back-mixing can also significantly affect column performance and must be considered, for a discussion of mass transfer in a pulsed column see the article by Logsdail and Slater [31].

NOTATION

a	constant, Equation 10	h	effective column height
A_p	pulse amplitude	N	number of plates in column
b	constant, Equation 10	N_b	compartment number
C	constant, Equation 10	S	plate free area
C_0	orifice coefficient	V	superficial liquid flow rate in column
d_m	mean drop diameter	V_0	characteristic drop velocity
d_0	plate hole diameter	V_{slip}	mean drop velocity relative to continuous phase
f	pulse frequency		
g	acceleration due to gravity	V_T	terminal drop velocity
H_c	axial distance between adjacent plates	x	dispersed phase hold-up (fractional)

Greek Letters

β factor as defined by Equation 7

Δ_c average flow of all material past the pulse plate in the direction of the continuous phase flow averaged over the pulse cycle,

$$= f \cdot A_p \left[\sqrt{1 - \lambda^2} - \lambda \left(\frac{\pi}{2} - \arcsin \lambda \right) \right]$$

Δ_d average flow of all material past the pulse plate in the direction of the dispersed phase flow averaged over the pulse cycle,

$$= f \cdot A_p \left[\sqrt{1 - \lambda^2} + \lambda \left(\frac{\pi}{2} + \arcsin \lambda \right) \right]$$

Δ_ρ density difference

λ_c velocity difference divided by pulse velocity

$$= (V_C - V_D)/(\pi \cdot f \cdot A_p)$$

μ viscosity

π_c average flow of all material past the pulse plate in the direction of the continuous phase flow, averaged over the actual time for flow in that direction,

$$= \pi f A_p \left[\frac{\sqrt{1 - \lambda^2}}{\dfrac{\pi}{2} + \arcsin \lambda} + \lambda \right]$$

π_d average flow of all material past the

pulse plate in the direction of the dispersed phase flow, averaged over the actual time for flow in that direction,

$$= \pi f \cdot A_p \left[\frac{\sqrt{1 - \lambda^2}}{\dfrac{\pi}{2} - \arcsin \lambda} - \lambda \right]$$

π_m mean of π_c^2 and π_d^2

π_v average of π_c and π_d

ψ correlation parameter, Equation 6

ψ_f maximum frictional power absorbed per unit mass of fluid, Equation 2

ρ density

σ interfacial tension

Subscripts

c   continuous phase
d   dispersed phase
f   refers to flooding conditions
* Any consistent set of units may be used.

REFERENCES

1. Assenov, A., and Penchev, I., "The Effect of Pulsing Intensity Upon Droplet Size in a Plate-Pulsed Extraction Column," Comptes Rendus de l'Academie Bulgare des Sciences 24, 1381 (1971).
2. Baird, M. H. I., "A Self Triggered Resonant Pulse Column," A.I.Ch.E. Inst. Chem. Eng. Symposium Series 6, 53 (1965).
3. Batey, W., Arthur, T., Thompson, P. J., and Thornton, J. D., "The Dynamics of Pulsed Plate Columns Part 1: Dispersed Phase Hold-up, Droplet Size and Flooding Rates in a 3 inch Diameter Pulsed Plate Column." Proceedings International Solvent Extraction Conference ISEC-83, A.I.Ch.E., 166 (1983).
4. Bell, R. L., and Babb, A. L., "Hold-up and Axial Distribution of Hold-up in a Pulsed Sieve-Plate Solvent Extraction Column," Ind. & Eng. Chem. Process Design & Development 8, 392 (1969).
5. Calderbank, P. H., "Physical Rate Processes in Industrial Fermentation Part I: The Interfacial Area in Gas Liquid Contacting with Mechanical Agitation," Trans. Inst. Chem. Engrs. 36, 443 (1958).
6. Coggan, G. C., "The Scaling-up of Pulsed Extraction Columns Part I: Limiting Throughputs," Inst. Chem. Engrs. Symp. Series, No. (26), 138 (1967).
7. Cohen, R.M., and Beyer, G. H., "Performance of a Pulse Extraction Column," Chem. Eng. Progress 49, 279 (1953).
8. Cruz-Pinto, J. J. C., and Korchinsky, W. J., "Experimental Confirmation of the Influence of Drop Size Distribution on Liquid-Liquid Extraction Column Performance," Chem. Eng. Sci. 35, 2213 (1980).
9. Dollfus, J., "Influencial Parameters of Size Distribution in Various Dispersion Processes," Proceedings International Solvent Extraction Conference, ISEC-83, A.I.Ch.E., 159 (1983).
10. Edwards, R. B., and Beyer, G. H., "Flooding Characteristics of a Pulse Extraction Column," A.I.Ch.E. J. 2, 147 (1956).
11. Fernandes, J. B. Effective Areas and Hold-up in Pulsed Extraction Column" Recent Advances in Separation Techniques, A.I.Ch.E. Symposium Series No. 120 68, 124 (1968).

12. Foster H. R., McKee, R. E., and Babb, A. L., "Transient Hold-up Behavior of a Pulsed Sieve Plate Solvent Extraction Column," *Ind. & Eng. Chem. Process Des. Develop.* 9, 272 (1970).

Garg, M. O., and Pratt, H. R. C., "Steady-State Droplet Size Distribution in a Pulsed Plate
13. Extraction Column," *Proceedings International Solvent Extraction Conference*, ISEC-83, A.I.Ch.E., 157 (1983).

14. Garg, M. O., and Pratt, H. R. C., "Measurement and Modeling of Droplet Coalescence and Breakage in a Pulsed-Plate Extraction Column," *A.I.Ch.E. J.* 30, 432 (1984).

15. Geier, R. G., "Application of the Pulse Column to the Purex Process" *USAEC Report* T1D-7534 Book 1, 107 (1957).

16. Geier, R. G., "Improved Pulse Extraction Column Cartridges," *Proceedings of the Second Conference on Peaceful Uses of Atomic Energy*, Geneva 17, 192 (1958).

17. Golding, J. A., and Lee, J., "Recovery and Separation of Cobalt and Nickel in a Pulsed Sieve-Plate Extraction Column," *Ind. & Eng. Chem. Process Design and Development* 20, 256 (1981).

18. Golding, J. A., Gorowski, D., and Kasvand, T., "Hold-up and Interfacial Areas in a Pulsed Sieve Plate Column," *Proceedings 2nd World Congress of Chemical Engineering*, vol. IV, 427 (1981).

19. Griffith, W. L., Jasny, G. R., and Tupper, H. T., "The Extraction of Cobalt From Nickel in a Pulse Column," *USAEC Report* T1D 4500 July 15th (1952).

20. Jealous, A. C., and Johnson, A. F., "Power Requirements for Pulse Generation in Pulse Columns," *Ind. & Eng. Chem.* 47, 1159 (1955).

21. Jealous, A. C., and Lieberman, E., "The Concatenated Pulse Column," *Chem. Eng. Progress* 52, 366 (1956).

22. Jiricny, V., and Prochazka, J., "Counter-Current Flow of Dispersed and Continuous Phase-III Measurements of Hold-up Profiles and Particle Size Distributions in a Vibrating Plate Contactor," *Chem. Eng. Sci.* 35, 2237 (1980).

23. Kagen; S. Z., Aerov, M. E., Lonik, V., and Volkova, T. S., "Some Hydrodynamic and Mass Transfer Problems in Pulsed Sieve Plate Extractors," *International Chem. Eng.* 5, 656 (1965).

24. Khemangkorn, V., Molinier, J., and Angelino, H., "Influence of Mass Transfer Direction of the Efficiency of a Pulsed Perforated Plate Column," *Chem. Eng. Science* 33, 501 (1978).

25. Khemangkorn, V., Muratet, G., and Angelino, H., "Study of Dispersion in a Pulsed Sieve Plate Column," *Proceedings International Solvent Extract Conference*, ISEC-77 CIM Special Vol. 21, 1, 429 (1979).

26. Kubica, J., and Zdunkiewicz, K., "The Average Drop-size Diameter of the Dispersed Phase in a Pulsed Extraction Column with Louvre and Sieve Plates," *Inz. Chem.*, 7, 903 (1977).

27. Landau, J., Boyle, J., Gorman, H. G., and Al Taweel, A. M., "Comparison of Methods for Measuring Interfacial Areas in Gas-Liquid Dispersions," *Can. J. Chem. Eng.* 55, 13 (1977).

28. Li, W. H., and Newton, W. M., "Liquid-Liquid Extraction in a Pulsed Perforated-Plate Column," *A.I.Ch.E. Journal* 3, 56 (1957).

29. Logsdail, D. H., and Larner, G. S., "Processing in Limited Geometry, Part VII: High Throughputs in Pulsed Plate Columns for Uranium-Tri-butyl Phosphate Systems," UKAERE Report No. R4408 (1964).

30. *Ibid*, "Part VIII: The Influence of Organic Phase Diluent and Plate Material on the Performance of Pulsed Plate Columns for Uranium TBP Systems," UKAERE No. RR4409 (1964).

31. Logsdail, D. H., and Slater M. J., "Pulsed Perforated Plate Columns," in *Handbook of Solvent Extraction*, Lo, Baird, and Hanson (eds.), J. Wiley Interscience p. 355 (1983).

Logsdail, D. H., Thornton, J. D., and Pratt, H. R. C., "Liquid-Liquid Extraction Part XII: Flooding Rates and Performance Data for a Rotary Disc Contactor," *Trans. Inst. Chem. Eng.* 35, 301 (1957).

33. Logsdail, D. H., and Thornton, J. D., "Liquid-Liquid Extraction Part XIV: The Effect of Column Diameter Upon the Performance and Throughput of Pulsed Plate Columns," *Trans. Inst. Chem. Eng.* 35, 331 (1957).

34. McAllister, R. A., Groenier, W. S., and Ryon, A. D., "Correlation of Flooding in Pulsed, Perforated Plate Extraction Columns," *Chem. Eng. Sci.* 22, 931 (1967).

35. Misek, T., "Vertical Motion of Drop in Agitated System," *Coll. Czech. Chem. Commun.* 28, 570 (1963).

36. Misek, J., "The Hydrodynamic Behavior of Pulsed Liquid-Liquid Extractors," *Coll. Czech. Chem. Commin.* 29, 1755 (1964).

37. Miyauchi, T., and Oya, H., "Longitudinal Dispersion in Pulsed Perforated-Plate Columns," *A.I.Ch.E. J.* 11, 395 (1965).

38. Mylnek and Resnick, "Drop Sizes in an Agitated Liquid-Liquid System," *A.I.Ch.E.. J.* 18, 122 (1972).

39. Niebuhr, D., and Vogelpohl, A., "Fluid Dynamics in Pulsed Sieve-Plate Extraction Column," *Proceedings 2nd World Congress Chem. Eng.*, IV, 422 (1981).

40. Park, J. Y., and Blair, L. M., "The Effect of Coalescence on Drop Size Distribution in an Agitated Liquid-Liquid Dispersion," *Chem. Eng. Sci.* 30, 1057 (1975).

41. Pilhofer, T., and Miller, H. D., "Photoelektrische MeBmethod Zur Bestimmung der GroBenverteilung mitteldisperser Tropfen in linen nicht mischbaren flussigen Zweistoffsystem," *Chemie. Ing., Techn.*, 44, 295 (1972).

42. Rouyer, H., Lebouhellec, J., Henry, E., and Michel, P., "Present Study and Development of Extraction Pulsed Columns," *Proceedings International Solvent Extraction Conference*, ISEC-74 Soc. Chem. Ind. London, 2339 (1974).

43. Schmidt, H., "Hold-up, Drop Size, and Axial Mixing of Pulsed Extraction Columns," *Proc. Int. Solvent Extraction Conference*, ISEC-83, A.I.Ch.E. 164 (1983).

44. Sege, G., and Woodfield, F. W., "Pulse Column Variables," *Chem. Eng. Progress* 50, 396 (1954). See also *Chem. Eng. Process Symposium Series*, No. 13, 179 (1954).

45. Sehmel, G. A., and Babb, A. L., "Hold-up Studies in a Pulsed Sieve-Plate Solvent Extraction Column," *Ind. & Eng. Chem. Proc. Design and Development* 2, 38 (1963).

46. Shirotuka, M., Honda, S., and Oya, H., "Extraction Characteristics of and Flow Properties with Pulsed Extraction Columns Either Packed or Perforated," *Chem. Eng.* (Japan) 22, 687 (1958).

47. Skelland, A. H. P., and Cornish, A. R.H., "Design of Perforated-Plate Extraction Columns from Rate Equations," *Can. J. Chem. Eng.* 43, 302 (1965).

48. Smoot, L. D., Mar, B. W., and Babb, A. L., "Flooding Characteristics and Separation Efficiencies of Pulsed Sieve-Plate Extraction Columns," *Ind. & Eng. Chem.* 51, 1005 (1959).

49. Thornton, J. D., and Pratt, H. R. C., "Liquid-Liquid Extraction: Part VII. Flooding Rates and Mass Transfer Data for Rotary Annular Columns," *Trans. Inst. Chem. Engrs.* 31, 289 (1953).

50. Thornton, J. D., "Recent Developments in Pulsed Column Techniques," *Chem. Eng. Progress Symposium Series*, No. 13, 39 (1954).

51. Thornton, J. D., "Liquid-Liquid Extraction Part XIII: The Effect of Pulse Wave-Form and Plate Geometry on the Performance and Throughput of a Pulsed Column," *Trans. Inst. Chem. Engrs.* 35, 316 (1957).

52. Topaz, H., "Development of a Novel Photographic Design for Drop Size Measurement in Agitated Vessels," *Proceedings International Solvent Extraction Conference*, ISEC-83, A.I.Ch.E., 161 (1983).

53. Van Dijk, "Process and Apparatus for Intimately Contacting Fluids," U.S. Patent 201, 186 (1935).

54. Vassalo, G., Thornton, J. D., and Dworschak, H., "The Hydrodynamic Behavior of a Pulsed Perforated-Plate Column," *Proceeding International Solvent Extraction Conference*, ISEC 83, A.I.Ch.E., 168 (1983).

55. Woodfield, F.W., and Sege, G., "Louver-Plate Redistributor for Large-Diameter Pulse Columns," *Chem. Eng. Progress, Symposium Series*, No., 13, 14 (1954).

CHAPTER 42

HYDRODYNAMICS OF PULSED SIEVE PLATE EXTRACTION COLUMNS

D. Niebuhr

Institut fur Thermische Verfahrenstechnik
Technische Universitat Clausthal
German Democratic Republic

CONTENTS

INTRODUCTION

A special feature of the two-phase flow in PSE (pulsed sieve plate extraction columns) is the essential change of flow pattern depending on the pulsation intensity. Therefore, the following section presents some ideas concerning the so-called "operating regimes" of PSE.

Most of the experimental investigations of fluid dynamics in extraction columns concentrate on the three phenomena: flooding, hold-up of the dispersed phase, and mixing of both, the continuous and dispersed phase. This chapter is divided according to these keywords, although most of the publications cited deal with more than one of the subjects.

In recent years much effort was spent on a generalized treatment of all three phenomena by the investigation of the movement of the drops. Therefore, a later section deals with correlations of drop sizes and their movement in swarms.

Within this outline, emphasis is given to the experimental results, whereas publications on theoretical models will not be reported comprehensively but only when necessary for the understanding of the phenomena.

The coupling of flooding, hold-up and axial mixing effects is demonstrated in Figure 1, which, as an example, shows some experimental data of Niebuhr [1]. The maxima and minima of the

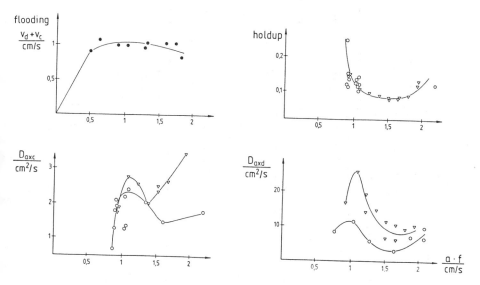

Figure 1. Experimental results of Niebuhr [1] for flooding points, hold-up of the dispersed phase and dispersion coefficients of both phases. Toluene (disp.) − water systems; $h_s = 5$ cm; $d_h = 0.2$ cm, $m = 0.22$, $v_d = v_c = 0.42$ cm/s. (O)$d_k = 7.2$ cm, (∇)$_k = 21.5$ cm.

experimental curves in some way correspond to each other. This interaction will be explained in the respective sections of this distribution.

Table 1 shows the characteristic data of the published experimental works on fluid dynamics in PSE. It contains the most important column layout data as well as the operating conditions and two-phase systems used. All publications listed in Table 1 deal with the type of column equipped with fixed trays and pulsation of the liquid. Reciprocating plate columns are not covered although their fluid dynamic behavior is not essentially different when the column geometry is similar.

OPERATING REGIMES OF A PSE

A characteristic of this type of extraction column is the formation of basically different patterns of the two-phase flow depending on pulsation and the flow rates. The phenomena have frequently been described [2]. Normally a distinction is made between two operating regimes, the mixer-settler regime, when the dispersed phase settles between two pulsation strokes, and the emulsion regime (in European literature often called "dispersion" regime), when (except for the overlay of pulsation) a quasi-steady countercurrent flow of both phases is established.

Both kinds of flow pattern change into each other very slightly. This is why some authors defined a third operating regime, the "transition" [3] or "dispersion" regime [4].

Based on the experimental results of Niebuhr and Vogelpohl [5] and Aufderheide and Vogelpohl [6] one can say that for the interpretation of flooding and hold-up the distinction between three operating regimes is not necessary, whereas it is very useful for the analysis of axial mixing.

Some of the investigators suggested equations for the calculation of the boundary between the operation regimes. Equation 1 is the first attempt to fix the transition frequency between MS and E regimes:

$$f_t = 0.67 \, (1.23 + 38.2\eta_d\sigma \, \Delta\zeta - \ln a) \tag{1}$$

Table 1

Experimental Investigations on Fluid Dynamics in PSE

Ref.	fl hu mx	d_K cm	d_h cm	h_s cm	m 1	a (a*f) f cm /s	v_d cm/s	v_c cm/s	v_d/v_c 1	$v_d + v_c$ cm/s	System Cont. (Transf.) Disp. Tracer and remarks
[1]	fl hu cd	7.2 -21.5	0.2	5	0.22	0.56 -1.13 / 0.89 -1.83	0.11 -1.0	0.11 -1.1	0.13 -5	0.22 -1.2	H₂O—toluene fluoresceine(c), anthracene(d)
[2]	fl	7.62	0.16 -0.48	3.5 -10.1	0.1 -0.4	1.27 -3.81 / 0 -10			0.5 -2	0.12 2.9	H₂O—TBP/"Hydrocarbon"
[3]	hu	3.5	0.1 -0.49	2.5 -7	0.081	0.6 -2 / 0.33 -3.3	0.1 -0.5	0.1 -1.0	1 -5		H₂O-acetic acid-MIBK
[4]	hu	5	0.25 -0.35	5 -15	0.04 -0.19	0.15 -0.45 / 0.4 -10	0 -0.45	0.3 -0.5			H₂O-trichlorethylene
[6]	fl hu cd	7.2 -21.5	0.2 0.4	5 10	0.22 0.39	0.8 1.0 / 0.5 -2.5	0.2 -1.0	0.2 -1.0	0.2 -5	0.8 -1.8	H₂O-toluene/butylacetate NaCl(c), anthracene(d)
[9]	fl	7.62 -30.5	0.32	1.27 -5.08	0.13 -0.62	0.64 -2.21 / 1.5 -7					6 two-phase systems
[10]	hu	7.5	0.3 -0.65		0.23 -0.6						H₂O-acetone/acet.acid-toluene ethylhexanol/n-butane
[12]	fl	4	0.2	5	0.23	2.8 -8 / 0 -3.3	0.29	0.22			H₂O-heptane
[13]	fl	4	0.2	5	0.23	2.8 8 / 0 -3.3	0.29	0.22			H₂O-heptane

Ref										System / Notes
[14]	fl	2.54	0.07	5.08	0.25	0.32 / -2.72	0.29 / -1.21	0.99		H$_2$O-hexane lower flooding point
[20]	fl	25	0.15	25	0.46	2 / -5	0.75 / -1.5	0.339 / -0.60		H$_2$O-kerosene
[21]	fl	5.6	0.2	5	0.082	0.5 / -1.5	0.8 / -1.7		0.1 / -0.5	H$_2$O-kerosene/CCl$_4$
[25]	fl	0.6 / -5.08	0.3	5.08	0.25	0.5 / -5	0.3 / -3		1	H$_2$O/TBPH$_2$O/TBP interface phenomena, wetting
[26]	fl	6	0.15	5	0.06 / -0.23	0.42 / -0.84			0.5 / -0.62	H$_2$O-TBP
[28]	fl	30		5 / -20	0.23 / -0.5				0.8 / 1.8	H$_2$O-TBP
[32]	hu	2.54	0.1	5.08	0.09	0.25 / -5.08	0.28 / -1.1	0.03 / -0.45	0.03 / -0.15	H$_2$O-boric acid-isoamylalkohol
[33]	hu	5.08	0.16	5.72	0.085	5.72	0.16 / -0.62	0.08 / -0.58	0.15 / -0.49	
[36]	hu	5.08	0.32	5.08	0.23	0.64 / -5.2	0.33 / -3.3	0 / -0.43	0.174 / -0.43	H$_2$O-hexane/benzene/MIBK

Numerical values with "," = range of operating variables
without "," = single values of operating parameters

Abbreviations: fl = flooding measurements
hu = hold-up measurements
mx = measurements of axial mixing
c = continuous phase
d = dispersed phase
MIBK = methyl-iso-butyl-ketone
TBP = tri-n-butyl-phosphate

(*Continued*)

Table 1 (Continued)

Ref.	fl hu mx	d_k cm	d_h cm	h_s cm	m 1	a (a*f) cm	f /s	v_d cm/s	v_c cm/s	v_d/v_c 1	$v_d + v_c$ cm/s	System Cont. (Transf.) Disp. Tracer and remarks
[37]	fl											
[38]	hu	-5.08	0.3	5.86	0.23	3			0 / 0.54			H₂O-MIBK dynamic response
[39]	d		0.32 / -0.16	4.06 / -5.59		2.54 / -3.31	1.33 / -3.33	0.17 / -0.37	0.20 / -0.37			H₂O-MIBK/kerosene/n-hexane
[40]	hu	3.2 / -5.4	0.15 / -0.3	1 / -10	0.095	21.5	0.4 / -3	0.043	0.05 / -0.59			H₂O-MIBK
[41]	hu					0.25 / -0.3	0.83 / -2.33			0.3 / -1		H₂O-o-nitrophenol-CCl₄
[42]	hu	5.08	0.32	5.59	0.23	0.72 / -4.45	0.33 / -3.3					H₂O-n-hexane
[43]	fl hu	7.62	0.48 / -0.64	5 / -10	0.23 / -0.36	0.79 / -1.7	0.42 / -2	0.08 / -0.25	0.08 / -0.27			H₂O-toluene
[45]	hu	7.62	0.16	5.75	0.23	0.5 / -4	0.32 / -3.3	0.44	0.44			2N NaOH-ester (2-ethyl-hexyl-formate)
[46]	fl'hu c	10	0.2	10	0.22	0.83 / -1.84	1.0 / -1.93	0.14 / -0.44	0.13 / -0.69	0.25 / -1.1	0.28 / -0.86	H₂O-acetone-o-oxylene K Cl solution
[55]	cd	5.08	0.32 / -1.02	5.08	0.23	1 / -2	1.0 / -1.33	0.56	1.13	0.5	1.7	H₂O-"Supersol"
[56]	c	5.08	0.15 / -0.31	7.62 / -15.24	0.23	1.27 / -2.54	1 / -2	0.24 / -0.41	0.16 / -0.58	0.4 / -0.8		H₂O-hexane/benzene/CCl₄ 48 experimental runs

Ref											Description
[58]	c	5.08	0.22		0.2	0.55	0.75 / -7.47			0.11 / -9	0.12 / 0.82	H$_2$O-toluene/MIBK manganese sulfate. steady state
[61]	c	5.6	1.5 / -3	0.25 / -15	0.03 / -0.15	0 / -0.2	1.67 / -1.67	0.28 / -1.5			0.28 / -1.5	H$_2$O/glycerol-H$_2$O/glycerol single phase
[62]	cd	10	0.15 / -0.45	5 / -30	0.1 / 0.6							H$_2$O-kerosene
[63]	c	56 / -30	0.21	5 / -15	0.87	0.3 / -5	0.83 / -2.5					H$_2$O-CCl$_4$ single phase
[64]	cd	5.6	0.2	5	0.081	0.3 / -4.3	1 / -2	0 / -0.26	0.12 / -0.42	0 / -1		H$_2$O-CCl$_4$ methylene blue
[65]	c	5.8	0.2	4		1.8	0.33					H$_2$O-acetic acid-benzene
[66]	c	5.08	0.3	5 / -10	0.23	0.1 / -2	0.5	0.016 / -0.2	0.1 / -0.6			H$_2$O-TBP
[67]	d	5	0.2	5	0.2	2 / -4.1		0.05 / -0.15	2.03	1/40 / -3/40		H$_2$O-CCl$_4$
[75]	fl	5	0.1	4 / -6	0.15 / -0.25	0.1 / -1.7	1.86 / -6.5			0.2 / -5		H$_2$O/petroleum-petroleum/H$_2$O

Sato et al. [3] gave correlations for the boundaries between MS and D regimes as well as D and E regimes. McAllister et al. [7], for the classification of experimental results, used the very simple but also very wrong condition of all throughputs below 50% of the lower flooding point representing the emulsion regime. If this condition is used, those flooding points close to the maximum of the flooding curve, which are very interesting for the industrial application of PSE, are classified into the wrong operating regime.

Mersmann [8] suggested Equation 2 as the definition of the E regime.

$$\frac{af}{w_0} > 0.22 + 0.75 \frac{v_c}{w_0} \tag{2}$$

with w_0, the rising or falling velocity of a single drop. Mersmann [8] was the first to present w_0 as a system specific variable in a calculation of this kind, but gave no information about the deduction of his formulation.

Niebuhr [1], based on a theoretical analysis, gave

$$\frac{h_s}{a}\left(1 - \frac{x}{2}\right) > \left(w_s - \frac{v_c}{1-x}\right)\frac{1}{af} > 2 \tag{3}$$

for the lower and upper boundary of the dispersion regime, with w_s, the mean rising or falling velocity of the drop swarm.

FLOODING IN PSE

Flooding means the collapse of the two-phase countercurrent flow due to increasing feed flow of one or both phases. In the case of PSE there are two phenomena limiting the maximum throughput:

☐ At low pulsation velocities the column operates like a reciprocating pump alternatively forcing the lighter and heavier phase through the perforations of the plates. During the upward stroke of pulsation the lighter phase is dispersed into the heavier phase, and vice versa, so that none of them can be said to be the "dispersed" phase. This mode of operation is well known as the mixer-settler regime. If the total flow rate exceeds the flow capacity of the reciprocating "pump", flooding due to insufficient pulsation occurs, and is called the lower flooding point.

☐ At higher pulsation intensity one of the two phases is dispersed permanently, because there is no time for the drops to form a layer close to the plates within one pulsation cycle. In contrast to the mixer settler regime the drops are not only formed by the plate orifices but also by turbulent shear flow. There by the plates work only as an agitation equipment that is penetrated by both phases in both directions. The throughput then is limited by the relation of the actual velocity of the continuous phase to the countercurrent rising or falling velocity of the drops, which is mainly dependent on their size.

The mean drop size decreases with increasing pulsation, which decreases the flow rate of the dispersed phase within the column.

If the flow rate of the dispersed phase is less than the feed flow rate, the column is operated beyond the upper flooding point, which is known as emulsion flooding.

Both kinds of flooding cause the dispersed phase to short cut and leave the column at the continuous phase outlet.

Although the definition of flooding presented has never been a matter of discussion, the problem of exact measurement of flooding points has been solved in different ways by various authors. Therefore, the experimental results also deviate from each other. It seems strange that there is no standard measuring routine up to now and the exact descriptions of the method applied are rare.

Most of the difficulties in flooding point measurement arise from the fact that flooding is no stable point of operation, so the experiments can only approximate to flooding conditions with an error. Due to the large time constants of the transient behavior of the dispersed phase hold-up, the process of flooding can last for hours until being detected. Most of the investigators obviously "measure" flooding by observing the column content [9], which shows an increase of the dispersed phase during flooding. The entrainment of small drops through the continuous phase outlet, however, is not significant for flooding but was also found at stable operation. Berger et al. [10] measured the pressure drop across the column, combined with a balance of measured inlet and outlet flow rates.

Sege and Woodfield [2] presented the characteristic diagram to show the fluid dynamic operating regimes of PSE and the corresponding flooding curves in the form of $(v_d + v_c)_F = f(af)$. The authors defined the mixer-settler and the emulsion regime as previously mentioned and suggested a column geometry $(d_h = 3$ mm, $h_s = 5.08$ cm) that remained a standard over several years of application of PSE.

Their main intention and that of several other authors [9, 11–16] was the application of PSE for the purification of uranium. With one exception [14] only emulsion flooding was investigated. Gayler et al. [11] derived the fundamental correlation between the flow rates and the hold-up of both phases in the form of a characteristic velocity that can be interpreted as the rising or falling velocity of a single drop:

$$\frac{v_d}{x} + \frac{v_c}{1-x} = w_0(1-x) \tag{4}$$

The factor $(1-x)$ describes the slowdown of the drop swarm movement because of the smaller density difference in the two-phase system compared to the pure continuous phase.

Thornton [9] calculates the hold-up in the vicinity of the flooding point by setting the derivatives $(dv_d/dx)_F$ and $(dv_c/dx)_F$ equal to zero

$$x_F = \frac{(s^2 + 8s)^{1/2} - 3s}{4(1-s)}, \quad \text{with} \quad s = v_d/v_c \tag{5}$$

Equations 4 and 5 are in principle valid for any type of two-phase countercurrent flow. For the application on a certain type of column the characteristic velocity w_0 must be known. w_0 only depends on system properties and the size of the drops. Thornton [9] found a correlation between w_0 and p_F, the specific power input per unit volume, based on the theory of local isotropic turbulence of Kolmogoroff. For the calculation of p_F an equation derived by Jealous and Johnson [17] was used:

$$p_F = \left(\frac{N(1-m^2)}{2gm^2k_0^2h_s}\left(\frac{da}{dt}\right)^2\right)\left|\frac{da}{dt}\right| \tag{6}$$

taking the form of

$$p_F = \frac{\pi^2 N(1-m^2)}{2gm^2k_0^2h_s}(af)^3, \quad \text{with} \quad k_0 = 0.6 \tag{7}$$

for sinusoidal pulsation.

Experimental results using six different two-phase systems were correlated by:

$$\left(\frac{w_0\eta_c}{\sigma}\right) = 0.6\left(\frac{p_F\eta_c^5 g}{\zeta_c\sigma^4}\right)^{-0.24}\left(\frac{d_h\zeta_c\sigma}{\eta_c^2}\right)^{0.9}\left(\frac{\eta_c^4 g}{\Delta\zeta\sigma^3}\right)^{1.01} \cdot \left(\frac{\Delta\zeta}{\zeta_c}\right)^{1.8}\left(\frac{\eta_d}{\eta_c}\right)^{0.3} \tag{8}$$

Logsdail and Thornton [15] tested this equation experimentally using two PSE of different diameters finding that w_0 was independent from d_K.

Investigators [9, 11, 17] propose two fundamental concepts:

1. The correlation of the maximum throughput of a PSE to a characteristic velocity of the drops.
2. The description of the drop size distribution as a function of the specific power input by pulsation.

The simplifications implied in this model restrict the range of operating conditions under which it is valid. Only in the emulsion regime a quasi stationary movement of the drops without a strong influence of the sieve plates can be assumed, though the formation of vortices is still not considered. Neglecting the coalescence of the drops means another simplification, which is only possible with high pulsation intensity and small hold-up of the dispersed phase, as given in the authors' [9] experiments.

The movement of the drops was described by the term $w_0(1 - x)$. This means that an important element of this concept cannot be directly investigated by experiments. In this context one should consider that the first experimental investigations on the interaction of particles moving in a swarm were published at the same time [19].

The setbacks in Thornton's theory previously mentioned may be why later correlations did not contain the term w_0. These authors [16, 22, 75] concentrated on dimensional analysis of the parameters influencing flooding. The dimensionless groups were correlated by power product formulations.

Misek [20] succeeded in improving the concept of Thornton and Logsdail by investigating the drop formation in an orifice of a sieve plate under the influence of pulsation. In the model equation

$$\frac{v_d}{x} + \frac{v_c}{1 - x} = w_0(1 - x)\exp((z - 4.1)x) \tag{9}$$

which was also applied by Misek to other types of extractors, coalescence was considered by the term $\exp((z - 4.1)x)$. Drop size distributions were not measured, but w_0 was determined indirectly, as shown by Thornton [9].

Kagan et al. [21] continued a series of interpretations by dimensional analysis, based on the theoretical work of Konovalov et al. [22].

Groenier et al. [23] and McAllister et al. [7] presented the most comprehensive study of this kind up to the present time, finding the following equation as the best correlation for more than 1,000 experimental results of other authors:

$$\ln\frac{v_d + v_c}{\Delta c + \Delta d} = -3.741 + 0.2568 \ln W - 0.07194(\ln W)^2$$

$$+ 0.006191(\ln W)^3 - 1.034 \ln K$$

$$- 0.09096(\ln K)^2 - 0.0008898(\ln K)^3$$

$$+ 0.1424 \ln(v_c/v_d) - 0.1807 \ln(a/h_s)$$

$$+ 0.07198 \ln W/\ln K \tag{10}$$

($-0.0008898(\ln K)^3$ missing in [7, 23])

Equation 10 describes both the mixer-settler and emulsion flooding qualitatively correct. Its advantage is the broadest basis of experimental results of all the correlations published. The dimensionless groups in Equation 10 are

v_c/v_d and a/h_s

$$W = \frac{\Delta\zeta d_h m^2 g}{\zeta_c p_M^2}, \text{ a drag coefficient}$$

of the pulsating flow through a sieve plate and

$$K = \frac{\eta_c p_V}{m\sigma},$$

a capillary number, which is equivalent to We/Re.

The terms Δ_c, Δ_d, p_M^2, and p_V describe the influence of pulsation on the transport of both phases and are necessary to determine the operating regime of the column. Their dimensions are those of a velocity and they are inserted into W and K in place of a velocity.

Both publications [7, 23], however, contained several errors, the correction of which was not published before 1979. It seems strange that the missing term, $-8*10^{-4}(\ln K)^3$, was found by Berger [18] and Miller [24] independently by fitting Equation 10 to the calculated flooding curves presented in [23] and to experimental results of their own.

Coggan [25] investigated the influence of wetting properties on the maximum throughput in PSE, but gave no correlation for the experimental results.

Klicka and Cermak [26] and Pilhofer [27], who were the first to consider the size distribution of the drops, developed the model of drop swarm movement, both using own experimental results. Flooding points, however, were not measured. They succeeded in calculating the characteristic velocity of a swarm of drops with higher accuracy than Thornton using the results of other authors of recent experimental investigations on the movement of drop swarms.

Pilhofer [27] further improved the model of a swarm of drops by leaving off the assumption of drops being rigid spheres and introducing criteria for the distinction between quasi rigid, rotating, and oscillating drops. An equation for the mean drop diameter was also given. Appendix A (at the end of this chapter) contains details of Pilhofer's model.

Rouyer et al. [28] reported their experimental results and compared them with the equation of Smoot et al. [16] and Equation 10.

A comprehensive study on flooding in extraction columns was published by Mersmann [8]. In this paper the dependence of the relative velocity of a drop swarm with a certain mean diameter from the velocity of a single drop of same diameter, determined experimentally by several authors, was used to write the right hand side of Equation 4 in the form $w_0 (1 - x)^k$.

Mersmann's formulation, which had been adapted from the theory of sedimentation of particles, erroneously contains the exponent $k - 1$, which is only correct when the movement of the particles takes place in a vessel closed at the bottom. In the case of countercurrent flow through a column the exponent must be k. But, due to the lack of accuracy in determining k, this error is of little influence on the results derived from the model.

Mersmann [8] presented the maximum troughput as a function of the relative velocity of a characteristic single drop. This velocity was given by a new experimental correlation, which has the advantage of easy treatment in calculations and of dimensionless but expressive terms.

For PSE Mersmann combined the equation for the lower flooding point:

$$(v_d + v_c)_F = 2 \, af \tag{11}$$

and the modified Equation 4 describing the upper flooding point, in a simple way:

$$(v_d + v_c)_F^{-1} = \left((2af)^{-r} + \left(x_F(1 - x_F)^{k-1} w_S + \frac{1 - 2x_F}{1 - x_F} v_c \right)^{-r} \right)^{1/r} \tag{12}$$

x_F may be calculated by differentiation similar to Equation 5, w_S comes from the empirical equation just mentioned. w_S in the last analysis depends on the drop diameter, which was calculated by Pilhofer's equation. k must be estimated from experimental results of other authors [19, 29, 30, 31] and for r the values of 1, 2, and 3 dependent on the two-phase system, were recommended.

Niebuhr [1] measured flooding points by visual observation in two PSE of different diameter and found his results to agree well with Equation 10.

Aufderheide and Vogelpohl [6] recently presented a new model for the determination of hold-up and flooding points in both the mixer-settler and the emulsion regime. Based on Pilhofer's theory for the calculation of the relative velocity of the drops, the movement of the drop swarm from one sieve tray to another is described by the model, including the limiting condition of no drops passing the holes of a tray during the backward stroke of pulsation. The model equations, details of which are given in Appendix A, were solved numerically on a computer. The results were found to be in good agreement with experiments in two PSE of different diameter using two different two-phase systems with variation of the operating parameters, the plate spacing and the free cross sectional area (see Table 1).

In summary, one can state that Equation 10 still gives the most reliable information on flooding in PSE, but only within the range of parameters covered by this empirical correlation. Any extrapolations beyond these limits yield wrong results, because there is no consistent physical model implied in the equation.

The model of drop swarm movement as an alternative does not have this disadvantage. Until 1984, however, it could only be applied to the emulsion type of operation. In their very recent publication Aufderheide and Vogelpohl [6] presented a substantial improvement of this model, by which both the MS and E regimes are now covered. Due to the increased complexity of the model equations, however, they have to be solved by an iteration procedure on a computer. Concerning the precision of the results, there is only experience with experimental data of Aufderheide and Vogelpohl [6] and Niebuhr [1].

HOLD-UP OF THE DISPERSED PHASE IN PSE

In the early investigations measuring methods were presented with same emphasis as the results, due to the various methods applicable for the measurement of hold-up.

Cohen and Beyer [32], one of the first investigators on PSE, measured the hold-up by draining the column into a graduated cylinder. Naturally this method is applicable only to laboratory columns of very small scale. In addition, as the authors state, the error caused by the liquid in the end sections of the column can only be estimated.

Li and Newton [33] measured the hold-up by closing all inlet and outlet valves simultaneously and stopping the pulsation. The thickness of the layers of dispersed phase close to the plates was then measured. This method allows the determination of an axial hold-up profile. The overall hold-up, which is the sum of the volumes in each column compartment, was then checked by a method similar to Cohen and Beyer [32]. The authors found an increase of the hold-up with increasing v_d and af, but no dependence of v_c. The range of operating variables used in their investigations (large amplitudes, small frequencies) from today's point of view seems untypical for PSE.

Logsdail and Thornton [15] checked Equation 5 by the measurement of the hold-ups at the flooding point. They used the method of simultaneously closing all inlet and outlet valves and measuring the displacement of the phase interface with continued pulsation. This method was described earlier by Gayler et al. [11].

Defives et al. [34] presented a method of measuring the electric conductivity of the two-phase mixture between two sieve plates. With this technique the axial hold-up profile within a PSE was determined in absence of continuous phase flow.

Sehmel and Babb [35, 36] used the technique of simultaneously closing the feed and outlet valves to determine the overall hold-up in a PSE. They found that the hold-up as a function of pulsation intensity showed a minimum corresponding to the maximum of the flooding curve and marking the transition from the mixer-settler to the emulsion regime. The transition frequency was given by Equation 1.

Sato et al. [3] defined a transition region instead of the transition point as given by Sehmel and Babb [36] as a result of their experiments and gave correlations for the limiting pulsation frequencies at the two boundary points as well as for the hold-up in the three operating regions.

Jones [37] used a method of measuring the pressure drop along the column. The dynamic fraction of the pressure drop, however, which is dependent on the throughput of both phases, must be eliminated by calibration measurements.

Misek [20] was the first investigator to try to verify the theory of Logsdail and Thornton at operating conditions below the flooding point. The hold-up was measured by taking samples of the two phase dispersion. Equation 9 was found to be valid and a correlation for w_0 was developed.

Foster [38] investigated the transient hold-up response to a change in the operating parameters using a method developed by Bell [39] for the investigation of axial mixing. The dispersed phase was marked by a luminescent dye. At constant concentration of the dye the intensity of luminescence was used to determine the hold-up of the dispersed phase. No correlation of the results was given.

Kagan et al. [21] gave some measuring results for the hold-up as a function of overall throughput with af, v_d and v_c = const.

Miyauchi and Oya [40] used the well known method of simultaneously closing the inlet and outlet valves. They succeeded in interpreting their results by the model of drop swarm movement (Equation 4). The term $w_0(1 - x)$ was represented by the relative velocity of a solid particle. Their results and those of other authors can be correlated by the following equations:

$$x = 0.66 \, p_M^{0.84} v_d^{2/3}, \quad \text{for} \quad p_M \leq 0.21$$
$$x = 6.32 \, p_M^{2.4} v_d^{2/3}, \quad \text{for} \quad p_M > 0.21 \tag{13}$$

with $\quad p_M = \dfrac{af}{(Rh_s)^{1/3}} \left(\dfrac{\eta_d^2}{\sigma \, \Delta \zeta} \right)^{1/4}$

and $\quad R = \dfrac{m^2}{(1 - m)(1 - m^2)}$

Tutaeva and Kagan [41] described the hold-up as a function of pulsation by a parabolic formula, with empirical coefficients:

$$x = x_0 + x_1(a - a_1)^2 \tag{14}$$

with $\quad x_0 = 1 - 1.03^{-(s+1)}; \quad x_1 = k \, s^{0.0456f}$
$\quad\quad\ a_1 = 1.18 \, f^{-1.2}; \quad\quad k = ((0.128 \, f)^2 - 0.01)^{1/2}$
$\quad\quad\ s = v_d/v_c$

Their paper, however, does not contain any information about the total flow rate, which was obviously constant, so Equation 14 cannot be checked.

Bell and Babb [42] used two shutter plates for the measurement of the hold-up. This method, described earlier by Foster [38], allows the determination of an axial hold-up profile if the axial position of the shutter plates is varied. The authors gave Equation 15 for the mean hold-up in the column:

$$x = v_d(k_1 + (0.0292 + 0.0667 \, v_c)(af - k_2)^2) \tag{15}$$

k_1 and k_2 depend upon the two phase system:

water-n-hexane: $k_1 = 0.126$, $\quad k_2 = 2.71$
water-MIBk: $\quad k_1 = 0.21$, $\quad k_2 = 1.61$

k_2 is equivalent to the transition frequency as given by Sehmel and Babb [36]. The results for f_t calculated by Equation 1, however, do not correspond to the minima of the measured hold-up curves in [42].

Example: $a = 1$ cm, water-n-Hexane: $f_t = 2.39$,
water-MIBK: $f_t = 1.12$

This contradiction was not explained in [42].

Mishra and Dutt [43] used a method similar to that of Li and Newton [33] for the hold-up measurement. Their experimental data, mainly measured in the emulsion regime, proved the applicability of Thornton's model, but no correlation for w_0 in Equation 4 was given. The results were correlated by

$$x = kp^{0.81}v_d^{0.89}d_h^{-0.924} \tag{16}$$

with $\quad p = \dfrac{af}{(Rh_s)^{1/3}}$

and with the mass specific power input p as given by Miyauchi and Oya (Equation 13), without the correction term $(\eta_d^2/(\sigma\,\Delta\zeta))^{1/4}$. For the water-Toluene system k is equal to 3.66. If p_M instead of p is used in Equation 16, k assumes the value 0.325.

Klicka and Cermak [44] developed the model of the movement of drop swarms (Equation 4) by a theoretical contribution. As a result of the hold-up measurements the authors found that the expression $w_0(1 - x)$ on the right-hand side of Equation 4 must be replaced either by w_s (static relative velocity of a sphere representing the relative velocity of the two phases) for $x < 0.09$, or

$$0.24w_s\left(\frac{1-x}{x}\right)^{0.61}, \quad \text{for} \quad x > 0.09 \tag{17}$$

This means that the drops do not influence each other at hold-ups less than 9%.

Fernandes [45] empirically found an increase of the hold-up with increasing v_d and f, and a minimum with variation of the amplitude, whereas there was no influence of v_c. The range of pulsation intensity covered was very broad (see Table 1). No correlation was given.

Nemecek and Prochazka [4] investigated a column equipped with reciprocating plates and operated in the emulsion regime (uniform axial hold-up distribution between two sieve plates). They found the empirical correlation

$$x = 3.5*10^{-5}v_d^{1.5}\left(\frac{af}{m^{0.66}}\right)^{3.6} \tag{18}$$

which is valid for $(af/m^{0.66}) > 13$

The works of Pilhofer [27] and Aufderheide and Vogelpohl [6] have already been discussed. These models are applicable to the interpretation of both flooding points and the hold-up. (See Appendix A for details).

Ugarcic [46] determined the hold-up in a PSE by the measurement of the pressure drop and additionally using a radioactive source and receiver. Some of the results were checked by a volumetric method. The author suggested the expression

$$16.76\,\frac{\Delta\zeta^{0.58}\sigma^{0.42}}{\zeta_c^{0.87}\eta_c^{0.11}}\,k^{-0.28}\,af^{-0.84} \tag{19}$$

with $\quad k = \dfrac{\pi^2}{2}\dfrac{1-m^2}{2h_sC_0^2m^2}$

for the right-hand side of Equation 4.

Niebuhr [1] measured the hold-up in PSE using the method of simultaneously closing the inlet and outlet valves and letting the dispersed phase settle at the top of the column. The results were correlated by Equation 15 with the modified coefficients $k_1 = 0.287$, $k_2 = 1.84$, $k_3 = 0$, $k_4 = 0.38$.

The survey given in this section not only shows a variety of measuring methods, but many mathematical formulations for the interpretation of the experimental results as well. The latter may be basically classified into three different kinds of models:

1. The parabolic formulations, for the first time presented by Sehmel and Babb [36], which are useful for describing the hold-up curve over the whole range of pulsation, with the minimum of the function marking the transition point from the mixer-settler to the emulsion regime. The works of Tutaeva and Kagan [41] and Bell and Babb [42] belong into this category.
2. The power product formulations describing the hold-up as a function of the specific power input and the flow rate of the dispersed phase [40, 43].
3. The model of the movement of drop swarms, established by Logsdail and Thornton [15], improved and developed by some authors [6, 20, 27, 40, 44].

The flow rate of the continuous phase is in general considered unimportant, so the formulations only contain the operating variables af and v_d, system properties and geometrical data. Correlations of this kind were published by Sato et al. [3] (MS, D, and E regimes), and others [4, 40, 43] (only D and E regimes).

MIXING IN PSE

Mixing in this context means the non-ideal flow of both the continuous and dispersed phase within the column, which causes a residence time distribution of the fluid elements. Mixing effects in the continuous phase are caused by

1. Molecular diffusion in axial and radial direction.
2. Convective flow in axial and radial direction.
3. Taylor diffusion.
4. Entrainment of continuous phase by the drops.

and in the dispersed phase by

1. Entrainment of drops by the continuous phase
2. Distribution of sizes and relative velocities of the drops.

If the axial mixing causes a backward flow relative to a fixed position, the effect is called backmixing [47, 48].

The experimental analysis of mixing was already part of the first investigations on PSE and has remained an important subject of interest until today. But due to the immense experimental and computational requirements all the works published up to now consider only axial mixing, whereas radial mixing is not investigated.

As a tracer substance is necessary for any experimental investigation of mixing, care must be taken in selecting a suitable tracer and measuring its concentration.

Regarding the method of tracer injection and measurement, one can differentiate the dynamic methods [49] of injecting a time-variant tracer signal and recording the function of tracer concentration vs. time at a fixed position downstream, from the steady state experiments [50] of continuously feeding a tracer flow into the column near the outlet and withdrawing samples of the respective phase at several places upstream. The latter method is only applicable in the presence of backmixing.

Mixing Models

The interpretation of the experimental results requires a suitable mathematical model of mixing, the parameters of which are fitted to the measured curves. There is a variety of mixing models differing from each other by the assumption of lumped or distributed parameters and the number of parameters.

The dispersion model is based on a material balance around an infinitely small fluid element thus belonging to the class of models with distributed parameters. It describes mixing in analogy to Fick's law of diffusion. Assuming total radial mixing, the axial dispersion model takes the mathematical form of

$$t_R \frac{\partial C}{\partial t} = \frac{1}{Pe} \frac{\partial^2 C}{\partial Z^2} - \frac{\partial C}{\partial Z} \qquad (20)$$

where   C = dimensionless concentration

       Z = dimensionless coordinate of flow direction

$$t_R = \text{residence time} = \frac{H}{v_i x_i}$$

       Pe = Peclet Number

       H = height of the column or part of the column in which mixing is investigated

       V_i = specific flow rate of phase i

       x_i = hold-up of phase i

$$Pe_i = \frac{v_i H}{D_{axi}} \qquad (21)$$

Pe_i is the dimensionless formulation of the dispersion coefficient D_{ax}, the main parameter of the dispersion model. Pe may also be defined with the "true" velocity of the respective phase, w_i, instead of v_i, as expressed by

$$Pe_i^* = \frac{w_i H}{D_{axi}} = \frac{H^2}{D_{axi} t_R} \qquad (22)$$

Both are related by

$$Pe_i^* = \frac{Pe_i}{x_i} \qquad (23)$$

Therefore, care must be taken in comparing the experimental results of different authors with respect to the definition of Pe and D_{ax}, when two phase flow is dealt with.

The various models of mixing cells are based on the assumption of a series of ideal mixers of finite size within each of the two countercurrent phases. They represent the class of models with locally lumped parameters. The model of a cascade of mixers with no backflow is the simplest of them. The material balance across a single mixing cell is given by

$$\frac{t_R}{n} \frac{\partial C_i}{\partial t} + C_i = C_{i-1} \qquad (24)$$

where   n = number of mixing cells

       C = dimensionless concentration within the i th mixing cell

Introducing a backflow coefficient, as done by Miyauchi and Vermeulen [51], makes this model more versatile, but on the other hand the additional model parameter requires more experiments for its identification.

Most of the authors used the axial dispersion model for the interpretation of their experimental data, knowing well that the main pre-assumption of this model, the random nature of the motion of the fluid particles, in most cases is not fulfilled.

As previously stated, details of the various mixing models shall not be discussed here. In general, mixing models are not restricted to a certain type of column, so a variety of publications beyond the scope of liquid-liquid extraction deal with this subject. They are discussed comprehensively by Himmelblau and Bischoff [52]. The same is valid for the various methods of parameter identification from experimental mixing data. Boexkes and Hofmann [49] gave a summary of the identification methods for the dispersion model, whereas Kardos et al. [53] and Pulz [54] in a similar way treated some models of mixing cells.

The line of experimental investigations in the following sections are divided into those dealing with the continuous phase, about which the majority of the publications are available, and those treating the dispersed phase.

Mixing in the Continuous Phase

The first authors to investigate the axial mixing in PSE were Burger and Swift [55]. They marked both the continuous and the dispersed phase of a laboratory scale column by a tracer dye and qualitatively observed its spreading. They found a considerable amount of axial mixing in both phases.

Mar and Babb [56, 57] published the first quantitative results on mixing in PSE. They used both the steady state technique and an instationary method of injecting a pulse shaped tracer signal. The tracer was ferric nitrate. The values of the dispersion coefficient determined from 48 experimental runs were correlated by the equation

$$D_{axc} = kh_s^{0.68}v_d^{0.3}f^{0.36}a^{0.07}d_h^{0.3}\sigma^{0.42}v_c^{-0.45}s^{0.05} \tag{25}$$

s = plate thickness

Claybaugh [58] investigated the backmixing in a PSE using the steady state method with manganese sulfate as tracer. His results, which were not correlated by an equation, show a strong dependence of the axial mixing on pulsation intensity and overall throughput. The function $D_{axc} = f(af)$ shows a relative maximum at af = 2.5 to 3.3 cm/s.

Sehmel and Babb [35, 59] analyzed the backmixing using the steady state technique with copper sulfate as tracer. The authors found a minimum of axial mixing in the transition region from the mixer settler to the emulsion regime. From visual observations two different mechanisms were found to be the cause of the axial mixing: the mixing effect of the sieve plates and the entrainment of continuous phase by the drops. One section between two trays, according to Sehmel and Babb [59] can be divided into two regions close to the plates, where the first effect prevails, and a zone in between, where the second mechanism is dominant.

The presence of a maximum could be interpreted, stating that with increasing pulsation the mixing effect of the trays increases, whereas the entrainment of continuous phase decreases due to a decrease of the mean drop size. For each of the two operating regimes an experimental correlation was given. For the mixer-settler regime:

$$D_{axc}(1 - x) = 1.08 - 1.81v_c(f - f_t)^2 + 3.07 \Delta\zeta$$

and for the emulsion regime:

$$D_{axc}(1 - x) = 1.8 - 0.231v_c^3(f - f_t)^2 + 2.68 \Delta\zeta - 0.487a + 0.0995a^2 \tag{26}$$

The transition frequency was given by Equation 4.

Gelperin and Neustroev [60] visually observed the spreading of a tracer dye pulse injected at the middle of the column. The spreading velocity was measured by a stop watch.

Kagan et al. [21] determined the dispersion coefficients with single and two-phase flow, both by steady state feed of methylene blue and by pulse shaped injection. They found larger values for the dispersion coefficient with single-phase than with two-phase operation. This result, which is surprising at first sight, was explained by the effect of phase separation at the upper and the lower turning point of the pulsation cycle. This statement and the relatively low af values indicate that most of the experiments were carried out in the mixer-settler regime. The authors gave Equation 27 for a water-kerosene system.

$$D_{axc} = k \frac{a^{1.2} f^{1.35}}{(v_d + v_c)^{1.4}}$$ (27)

Miyauchi and Oya[40] used a pulse shaped signal of potassium chloride tracer at the inlet of the continuous phase. The tracer concentration was measured by a conductivity cell at a single position within the column. The measured response functions of concentration vs. time were interpreted with the help of a model developed by Miyauchi and Vermeulen [51], which is based on the assumption of each stage in the PSE being equivalent to n ideal mixers. The model equation is

$$\frac{D_{axi}}{x_i a f h_s} = \frac{v_i/(a f x_i)}{2n - 1/ns} + \frac{1}{n}$$ (28)

An empirical correlation was given for n

$$n = 0.57 \left(\frac{d_k^2}{h_s}\right)^{1/3} \frac{m}{d_h}$$ (29)

The index i indicates that the model was also applied to the dispersed phase without modification (i = c, d). No substantial difference was found between single and two phase flow.

Novotny et al. [61] measured the steady-state concentration profile of two different tracers for the continuous and dispersed phases (potassium chloride and fuchsin resply). Their results were interpreted with the help of a model of two ideal mixers close to the plates, separated by a zone of diffusion-type mixing for each stage of the PSE. This means that Novotny et al. [61] presented the first mathematical formulation of the ideas of Sehmel and Babb [59]. A backflow coefficient for each ideal mixer was derived;

$$q = \frac{\Phi}{\pi} - \frac{1}{2} + \frac{af}{v_c} \cos \Phi$$ (30)

where $\quad \Phi = \arcsin\left(\frac{v_c}{\pi a f}\right)$

For the regions of diffusion-type mixing a Pe-number was defined as

$$Pe_M = k \frac{(h_s - h_M) v_c m^{3/2}}{a f d_h}$$ (31)

with a multiple of the hole spacing $d_h * m^{-1/2}$ as the characteristic length. Thus, the model equation is

$$q_e = \left(\left(1 + \frac{1}{q}\right) \exp(Pe_M) - 1\right)^{-1}$$ (32)

The constants k and h_M (length of a region with diffusion type mixing) were determined from about 180 measuring points by regression analysis, taking the values of k = 6.6 and h_M = 4.5. It is self-evident that the condition $h_s > 4.5$ must be fulfilled. A comparison with the model of Miyauchi and Oya[40] via the transformation equation:

$$\frac{v_c h_s}{D_{axc}} = Pe_e = \ln \frac{1 + q_e}{q_e}$$ (33)

carried out by the authors, yields large deviations for $h_s > 4.5$, Novotny et al. [61] explained this by the different experimental range of the plate spacing (<4.5 with [40], >4.5 with [61]).

Rozen et al. [62] investigated the axial mixing in PSE using a pulse-shaped injection of methylene blue. The concentration was measured colorimetrically at the outlet of the continuous phase. The dispersion coefficient of the axial dispersion model used in their investigations was given as a function of an effective velocity w_{ef} and an effective length l_{ef}. The equations are

$$\left.\begin{array}{l} D_{axc} = kl_{ef}w_{ef} \\[2ex] l_{ef} = \left(\dfrac{mh_s}{1 + h_B/d_K}\right)^{2/3} d_h^{1/3} \\[2ex] w_{ef} = v_c + 0.5v_d + af \end{array}\right\} \tag{34}$$

k was found to be 3.0.

Kagan et al. [63] measured dispersion coefficients using the pulse injection technique of methylene blue or potassium chloride. They found little influence of the column diameter on axial mixing. Their measuring results were correlated by

$$D_{axc} = 0.49h_s^{0.75}(af + v_c) \tag{35}$$

In spite of the similar structure of this equation to Equations 34 and 28 the authors found large differences in the results calculated from the equations, requiring an improvement of the concept.

Veisbain et al. [64] investigated the axial mixing in the continuous phase by pulse injection of a dye and discontinuous sampling at the outlet. They found an almost linear increase of the dispersion coefficient with pulsation intensity and dispersed phase flow rate. No correlation was given.

Rouyer et al. [28] reported some measuring results for the dispersion coefficient, which was found to be linearly dependent on af and to increase with increasing plate spacing.

Nemecek and Prochazka [4] continued the work of Novotny et al. [61] for single-and two-phase flow. They succeeded in measuring the height of an ideal mixer by visual observation. As a result, the constant $h_M = 4.5$ in Equation 31, under single-phase flow conditions, was replaced by

$$h_{M1} = 1.05\left(\frac{af}{m^2}\right)^{0.29} \quad \text{for} \quad h_{M1} < 0.65(h_s + 2.35)$$

$$h_{M1} = 0.65(h_s + 2.35) \quad \text{otherwise.} \tag{36}$$

For two-phase flow they found

$$h_{M2} = 1.0 \quad \text{for} \quad \frac{af}{m} < 13$$

$$h_{M2} = 0.21\frac{af}{m} \quad \text{for} \quad \frac{af}{m} > 13 \text{ and } h_{M2} < 0.54(h_s + 3.6) \tag{37}$$

$$h_{M2} = 0.54(h_s + 3.6) \quad \text{otherwise}$$

Also by visual observation a distinction was made between three operating regimes:

1. The mixer-settler (MS) regime, which is marked by the presence of coalescing layers of dispersed phase.
2. The dispersion (D) regime with no coalescence but regions of high hold-up separated by regions of very low hold-up alternatively moving through the column. There is no backflow of drops through the plates.

3. The emulsion (E) regime, characterized by a totally even hold-up distribution across a stage. The two phases behave like an emulsion, including backflow of drops through the plates.

The theoretical derivation of the backflow coefficient of the continuous phase for the ideally mixed zone close to the plates yields Equation 38 for two-phase flow instead of Equation 30 for single-phase flow.

$$q_c = \frac{1-s}{\pi}\left(k + \cotg k - \frac{\pi}{2}\right) - s(1 + q_d) \tag{38}$$

which, is to be preferred in the MS and D regimes due to the presence of the backflow coefficient q_d of the dispersed phase. Introducing the hold-up x and rearrangement gives

$$q_c = \frac{1}{\pi}\left(k + (1-s)(1-x)\cotg k - \frac{\pi}{2}\right) \tag{39}$$

where $\quad k = \arcsin\left(\dfrac{v_c - v_d}{\pi af}\right)$

for the E regime. In Equation 40 q_d has been eliminated, but x must be known.

Instead of the semi-empirical Equation 31, the empirical correlation (Equation 40) was given, describing the single phase measuring results more exact:

$$D_{M1} = 0.3\frac{h_B - h_{M1}afd_h^2}{h_B - 4.5m} \tag{40}$$

The function $D_{ax2} = f(af)$, taking a positive parabolic form, was described separately for the three operating regimes. The dispersion coefficient of the zone with diffusion type mixing was given by

$$D_{M2} = D_{M1} + \Delta D \tag{41}$$

with ΔD as an increment for two-phase flow. ΔD, in the three operating regimes, was described as follows:

In the MS regime $(af/m^{0.66} < 6)$ with

$$\Delta D = 55(h_s - h_{M2})d_{32}^3$$

In the D regime $(6 \leq af/m^{0.66} \leq 13)$ with

$$\Delta D = 55(h_s - h_{M2})d_{32}^3 - 0.3$$

In the E regime $(13 < af/m^{0.66})$ with

$$\Delta D = 0.4\frac{x}{m^{1.2}} - 1.01 \tag{42}$$

The Sauter mean drop diameter, which determines the mixing in the MS and D regimes, was calculated from

$$\left.\begin{array}{ll} d_{32} = 0.28h_s^{0.11}\left(\dfrac{af}{m^{0.66}}\right)^{-0.34} & \text{for} \quad \dfrac{af}{m^{0.66}} < 9 \\[4mm] d_{32} = 2.3\left(\dfrac{af}{m^{0.66}}\right)^{-1.2} & \text{for} \quad \dfrac{af}{m^{0.66}} \geq 9 \end{array}\right\} \tag{43}$$

The hold-up, which determines the mixing in the E regime, was given by

$$x = 3.5*10^{-5} v_d^{1.5} \left(\frac{af}{m^{0.66}} \right)^{3.6} \tag{44}$$

The effective Pe-number (according to the "general" axial dispersion model) was calculated from Equations 32 and 33, already derived for single-phase flow. (See Appendix B for details.)

Zheleznyak [65] presented a four-stroke-model for the MS- operating conditions of a PSE, describing the mixing in both phases within a pulsation cycle. Good agreement with experimental results using a laboratory scale column was found.

Kasipathi Rao [66] investigated axial mixing of the continuous phase using the pulse injection technique of fluoresceine and a photometric method of concentration measurement. All experiments were carried out in the emulsion regime. The authors found a decrease of axial mixing with increasing af until a minimum was reached. The small increase with high af values recognizable in their diagrams was not interpreted. The model of Sehmel and Babb [59] cited by the authors offers no way of describing a relative minimum of the function $D_{axc} = f(af)$. The influence of v_d on D_{axc} was not definite. With small plate spacing (5 cm) a maximum was observed, which was explained as a result of hydraulic irregularities. With high plate spacing both the amplitude of the maximum of the function $D_{axc} = f(v_d)$ and, in general, the amount of two-phase axial mixing was reduced, whereas mixing with single phase flow increased.

Ugarcic [46] used the steady state technique for the determination of the axial mixing in the continuous phase. The tracer was a solution of KCl. The author correlated his results by the equation

$$D_{axc} = (8.06/N_s)v_c h_s + (3.77/N_s)af\,h_s \tag{45}$$

Niebuhr [1] measured the axial mixing in PSE using a pulse shaped injection of a fluoresceine tracer. The function of D_{axc} plotted against af showed a relative maximum at the transition from MS to D regime and a relative minimum at the transition from D to E regime (see Figure 1). His results could be correlated using a modified version of the model of Nemecek and Prochazka [4], details of which are given in Appendix B.

Summarizing the state of knowledge about mixing in the continuous phase, one can say that the mathematical models published are inconsistent. In fact, the experimental results so far make a homogeneous interpretation extremely difficult. The influence of the four operating parameters, for example, in several publications is given in an opposing way. Table 2 contains information about the direction of change of the dispersion coefficient when one of the operating parameters is increased.

The structure of the correlations covers the range from a simple power product formulation [56], through polynomials [35, 59], semi-empirical correlations with correct dimensions [21, 62, 63], in

Table 2
Effect of the Increase of Operating Parameters on the Axial Dispersion Coefficient of the Continuous Phase
I = increase, D = decrease of D_{axc} — = no effect,
*** (depending on pulsation intensity)**

Ref.	a	f	v_d	v_c
[4]	*I (D)	*I (D)	* — (I)	* —
[40]	I	I	—	I
[56]	I	I	I	D
[21]	I	I	D	D
[62]	I	I	I	I
[63]	I	I	—	I

which the dispersion coefficient is assumed to be dependent on variables of type length and velocity, to physically sound models [4, 40, 61]. In the last group of models the space between two sieve trays is divided into two ideal mixers close to the plates and a zone of diffusion type mixing in between. They are relatively complicated, but are the only models giving the possibility of interpreting the partially opposing effects of variations of the operating parameters. The influence of the column diameter up to now, has only been investigated by two authors [1, 40], but no clear results were found. The model equation (Equations 28 and 29) contradicts the experience of most of the industrial users of PSE who observe an increase of axial mixing with larger column diameters.

Mixing in the Dispersed Phase

Mixing in the dispersed phase of PSE has been investigated very rarely up to now. Bell [39] presented a technique of injecting a pulse signal of a luminescent dye into the dispersed phase inlet and measuring the intensity of luminescence downstream in the column. The luminescence was incited by an ultraviolet lamp, the emitted visual light received by a photomultiplier through the wall of the glass column. Additonally, steady state experiments with sampling were carried out.

Bell gave the reduced variance of the residence time distribution as representative quantity for the axial mixing. This variance as a function of pulsation intensity showed one or two extremes. Bell interpreted the mechanism of mixing by the distinction of four operating regimes:

1. Mixer-settler regime, complete coalescence within each pulsation cycle with the result of theoretically no axial mixing.
2. Transition from MS to emulsion regime, no complete coalescence but irregular distribution of the dispersed phase across the cross section of a tray, broad ranged drop size distribution with the result of an increase in axial mixing.
3. More uniform drop size distribution and the beginning of the influence of eddies in the continuous phase, resulting in a decrease of the axial mixing down to a relative minimum.
4. Prevailing influence of turbulence in the continuous phase, causing an increase of axial mixing up to the flooding point.

Bell [39] gave no correlation for his results of axial mixing.

Miyauchi and Oya [40] measured axial mixing in the dispersed organic phase by the injection of a pulse of red dye, the intensity of which was measured colorimetrically in the coalescence layer close to the phase interphase at the top of the column. The whole column cross section was illuminated similar to Bell [39]. The dispersion coefficients measured by them, plotted as a function of pulsation intensity, showed a relative minimum but approximated Equations 28 and 29 for large af values. The authors conclude from this result that with high af values the axial mixing of the dispersed phase may be interpreted by the same model as that of the continuous phase.

Rozen et al. [62] marked the dispersed phase by a pulse injection of sudan brown, the intensity of which was registrated by a photocolorimeter placed at the outlet. The curves of the dispersion coefficient, plotted against an effective velocity, are given by the equation

$$w_{ef} = 1.4v_c + 0.8v_d + af \tag{46}$$

all showed a relative minimum. The authors interpreted this result by assuming two mixing mechanisms:

1. With low pulsation intensity an irregular distribution of the partially coalesced dispersed phase over the sieve plate cross section and a broad drop size distribution with two maxima.
2. With high pulsation intensity an entrainment of the drops by the continuous phase.

According to this interpretation Rozen et al. [62] formulated the equation

$$D_{axd} = \frac{k_1}{w_{ef}} + \frac{k_2}{w_{ef}^{k_3}} + k_4 l_{ef} w_{ef} \tag{47}$$

with l_{ef} taken from Equation 34. k_3 was found to be constant and equal to 1.5 in all cases investigated by the authors, whereas the other constants depended on the tray geometry.

Veisbain et al. [64] measured the axial mixing in the dispersed phase in a similar way as in the continuous phase. They found a maximum of the dispersion coefficient plotted against af at the point of the minimal hold-up. With high pulsation intensity the values approximate those of the continuous phase. The authors explained that with small pulsation intensity, large and fast rising drops dominate the residence time function, which, at the minimum of the hold-up, show a nonuniform size distribution. The growing uniformity of the drop size distribution and the small mean drop size cause the approximation to the values of the continuous phase with high af.

Arthayukti [67] measured the axial mixing of the dispersed phase by pulse injection of a radioactive tracer, which was registrated at two positions in the column. The Pe number as a function of pulsation intensity showed a continued decrease, which meant an increase of the axial mixing with increasing af. No relative extremes were found. The authors did not give a correlation. Remarkable are the extremely low phase ratios and the high pulsation intensities coming from the process of recycling nuclear fuel. Probably the transition regime from MS to D was not covered in their measurements. Therefore only one mechanism, turbulence in the continuous phase, is supposed to prevail.

Niebuhr and Vogelpohl [68] measured axial mixing in the dispersed phase of two PSE of different diameter using a similar technique as Bell [39]. The results, shown in Figure 1, also showed a relative maximum of the dispersion coefficient at the transition from MS to D regime, a decrease of D_{axd} with increasing af until a minimum was reached. With high af values the axial mixing again increased. The results were interpreted in a similar way as those of Bell [39]. No correlation was given.

The results published up to now may be summarized as follows. Most of the authors [39, 62, 64, 68] found two main mechanisms influencing axial mixing in the dispersed phase:

1. The nonuniform drop size distribution with low pulsation intensity that causes a broad residence time distribution.
2. The mixing effect of the trays with high pulsation intensity causing turbulence in the continuous phase and entrainment of drops.

Two correlations were given [40, 62], but both are only valid within a narrow range of experimentally verified data.

DROP SIZES IN PSE

The dominating influence of the drop size distribution on the whole fluid dynamic behavior of PSE was recognized very soon. Thornton [9], based on theoretical considerations, gave the parameters influencing the mean drop size

$$d_p \sim \left(\frac{\eta_c^2}{g\zeta_c}\right)^{1/3}\left(\frac{\zeta_c}{\Delta\zeta}\right)^{2/3}\left(\frac{w_0^3(1-x)^3\zeta_c}{g\eta_c}\right)^{1/3} \tag{48}$$

Misek [20] calculated the mean drop size on the basis of hold-up measurements assuming that the drops behave like solid particles. He set up the formulation

$$\frac{d_p}{d_h} = k_1\left(\frac{\sigma m^2(1-k_3)}{\zeta_c d_h(k_2 af + v_c)^2}\right)^{0.6} \tag{49}$$

and determined the coefficients $k_1 = 0.439$, $k_2 = 5.1$, $k_3 = 0.75$.
Kagan et al. [21] got the correlation

$$d_{32} = 0.234(af)^{-0.3}\sigma^{0.5}\zeta_c^{-0.4}\eta_c^{-0.1} \tag{50}$$

from photographical measurements.

Miyauchi and Oya [40] also measured photographically and correlated their results by the equation

$$d_{32} = 0.081 \left(\frac{af}{h_s^{1/3}} \right)^k \tag{51}$$

where $k = -1.2$ for $\left(\dfrac{af}{h_s^{1/3}} \right) > 1.2$

and $k = -0.6$ for $\left(\dfrac{af}{h_s^{1/3}} \right) \le 1.2$

Assenov and Penchev [69], on the basis of investigations on PSE with low and medium pulsation intensities (0.5 to 2.5 cm/s) gave Equation 52 for the calculation of drop sizes:

$$d_{32} = 10^{-2} \left(\frac{\sigma}{\Delta \zeta g} \right)^{0.5} \left(\frac{af\eta}{\sigma} \right)^{-0.5} N^{-0.1} \tag{52}$$

Assenov et al. [70] determined size distributions photographically in a reciprocating plate column. They found that the distributions could be described by Johnson's [71] formulation of logarithmic normal distribution. Increasing af caused a more uniform drop size distribution with smaller mean drop size. A better correlation resulted when the pulsation intensity af was replaced by the pulsation acceleration af^2. No correlation was given.

Nemecek and Prochazka [4] determined the correlations for the Sauter mean diameter

$$d_{32} = 0.28 h_s^{0.11} \left(\frac{af}{m^{0.66}} \right)^{-0.34} \quad \text{for} \quad \frac{af}{m^{0.66}} < 9$$

$$d_{32} = 2.3 \left(\frac{af}{m^{0.66}} \right)^{-1.2} \quad \text{for} \quad \frac{af}{m^{0.66}} \ge 9 \tag{53}$$

Khemangkorn et al. [72], on the basis of investigations on PSE with the water-CCl_4 system gave equation

$$d_{32} = 0.38 a^{-1.0} f^{-1.24} N^{-0.21} v_d^{-0.083} \tag{54}$$

for the direction of mass transfer from the continuous into the dispersed phase and

$$d_{32} = 0.49 a^{-1.0} f^{-1.24} N^{-0.21} v_d^{-0.0002} \tag{55}$$

for the reverse direction. Their experiments were carried out with very low phase ratios and very high pulsation intensities.

Pilhofer [27] gave a formula derived from Kolmogoroff's theory of local isotropic turbulence.

$$d_p = k \sigma^{0.6} \zeta_c^{-0.6} p^{-0.4} \tag{56}$$

Pilhofer and Goedl [73] gave $k = 0.81$ for PSE.

Ugarcic [46] improved Equation 56 by the introduction of k as a function of pulsation:

$$k = 0.0434(af)^{1.2} - 0.00574(af)^{2.2} \tag{57}$$

A comparison between the correlations is only possible for Equations 49–57, because Equation 48 contains w_0, which cannot be determined directly. Concerning the effect of the operating parameters on the mean drop size one can summarize that the exponent of the pulsation intensity varies between -0.3 and -1.2. The latter value corresponds to the theory of Kolmogoroff and is only verified with high pulsation intensities. Low af values result in smaller absolute values of the exponent, indicating that turbulence in the continuous phase is no more the prevailing mechanism of drop formation.

The effect of flow rates on the drop diameter is considered small in most of the publications. None of the correlations represents the effect of hold-up, although it influences the rate of coalescence. Another effect of hold-up on drop formation in turbulent flow, disregarding coalescence, was discussed by Doulah [74] in a theoretical paper. A change in the specific power input is caused by a modified effective viscosity of the two-phase dispersion. Doulah derived the equation

$$d_{32} = d_{32}^{\phi} (1 + 3x) \tag{58}$$

with d_{32}^{ϕ}, the Sauter mean diameter of an "infinitely diluted" dispersion.

CONCLUSION

Considering the papers published up until now in the field of fluid dynamics in PSE, one can notice a very different state of knowledge about the main sections flooding, hold-up, and axial mixing. Both, the number of measured data and the consistency of the models for the interpretation of the phenomena differ from one section to another.

Flooding was investigated very intensively, because a column can hardly be operated without the knowledge about its limiting throughput. The immense requirement of time, however, limited the number of measuring points available, so that the most comprehensive correlation (Equation 10) is based on not more than 1,000 measuring points.

Hold-up values are to be measured relatively easy by a variety of methods. Therefore, the number of hold-up data is supposed to be much larger than that of the flooding points. But a generalized theory is still missing, because more informations about drop sizes are needed to establish a model of drop swarm movement. These informations require immense experimental and computational efforts, therefore this section has been cleared up with little success till today. The works of Pilhofer [27] and Aufderheide and Vogelpohl [6] give a good promise but are not yet widely accepted (see Appendix A).

Similar problems arise with the investigation of axial mixing, especially in the dispersed phase. In the case of dynamic measurements partially automated experimental set-ups are required. These problems and the interest in mixing data arising relatively late were the reasons why investigations on axial mixing started later than on the other fluid dynamic phenomena. The results that are known now partially contradict each other, as shown in Table 2, so that a generalized model could not yet be developed. For the continuous phase Nemecek and Prochazka [4] presented the most interesting model, which was improved by Niebuhr [1] (see Appendix B).

APPENDIX: MATHEMATICAL MODELS OF FLUID DYNAMICS IN PSE

This contains some of the most interesting mathematical models available for the calculation of flooding, hold-up of the dispersed phase, and axial mixing of the continuous phase. The models were taken from the publications previously cited and in some cases modified by the author, in order to facilitate the numerical evaluation or to improve the precision of the results.

Appendix A: Model of Drop Swarm Movement for Calculating Hold-Up and Flooding Points

Starting point of the calculation is the evaluation of a mean drop size. Pilhofer [27] inserted the energy dissipation

$$p = \frac{\pi^2 (1 - m^2)(af)^3}{2C_0^2 m^2 h_s} \tag{59}$$

$(C_0 = 0.6)$

into an equation derived from Kolmogoroff's theory of isotropic turbulence

$$d_p = 0.18 \left(\frac{\sigma}{\zeta_c}\right)^{0.6} p^{-0.4} \tag{60}$$

This equation was found to be in good agreement with experimental data of Aufderheide and Vogelpohl [6], but only with high pulsation intensities. Therefore, Aufderheide and Vogelpohl [6] proposed a modification for af products less than 2.5 cm/s:

$$d_p = d_{p0}(af/(af)_0)^{-0.5} \tag{61}$$

with d_{p0}, the drop diameter calculated with af $= (af)_0 = 2.5$ cm/s.
With d_p the Archimedes number may be calculated from its defining equation:

$$Ar = \frac{\Delta \zeta d_p^3 g \zeta_c}{\eta_c^2} \tag{62}$$

The modified fluid constant of Brauer [68]

$$K_F' = \frac{\zeta_c^2 \sigma^3}{\Delta \zeta_g \eta_c^4} \tag{63}$$

is used to determine the limiting value of the Archimedes number for the transition from rotating to oscillating drops.

$$Ar_1 = 371.90 \; K_F'^{0.275} \tag{64}$$

In the regime of oscillating drops (Ar $>$ Ar$_1$) the Reynolds number of a single drop moving in unlimited continuous phase is given by

$$Re_\infty = K_F'^{0.15}(4.18Ar^{0.281}K_F'^{-0.0774} - 0.75) \tag{65}$$

Correspondingly for rotating drops (Ar $<$ Ar$_1$) Equation 66 is valid.

$$Re_\infty = K_F'^{0.15}(Ar^{0.523}K_F'^{-0.1438} - 0.75) \tag{66}$$

With hold-up values less than 6% there is no influence of the drops on each other, thus

$$Re_r = Re_\infty \quad \text{for} \quad x < 0.06 \tag{67}$$

With higher hold-up the decrease of the Reynolds-number must be calculated. Taking the correction factor of Hadamard and Rybczynski for a mobile drop surface into account

$$Ha = \frac{3\eta_d + 3\eta_c}{3\eta_d + 2\eta_c} \tag{68}$$

one may determine the inertial fraction of the drag coefficient of a single particle

$$C_I = \left(\frac{1}{6}\frac{Ar}{Re_\infty} - \frac{3}{Ha}\right)\frac{1}{Re_\infty} \tag{69}$$

Pilhofer suggested two combinations of the cross section coefficient z and the convolution factor q, as given in Equation 70–72:

$$q^3 = 5Ha^{-3/2}\left(\frac{x}{1-x}\right)^{0.45} \tag{70}$$

$$zq^2 = \exp\left(\frac{2.5}{1 - 0.61x}\right)^{\frac{1-x}{2x}} \frac{1}{Ha} \quad \text{for} \quad 0.06 < x < 0.55 \tag{71}$$

$$zq^2 = 2.2 \exp\left(\frac{0.44x}{1 - 0.61x}\right)^{\frac{1-x}{x}} \quad \text{for} \quad 0.55 < x < 0.74 \tag{72}$$

The Reynolds number of the drops in the swarm may then be calculated by

$$Re_r = \frac{3zq^2x}{(1-x)q^3C_I}\left(\left(\frac{(1-x)^3q^3ArC_I}{54(zq^2)^2x^2} + 1\right)^{1/2} - 1\right) \tag{73}$$

With Re_r, the relative velocity of the drops is defined as

$$w_r = \frac{Re_r\eta_c}{\zeta_c d_p} \tag{74}$$

and the overall throughput in the emulsion regime as

$$v_g = v_d + v_c = \frac{w_r}{y} \tag{75}$$

with the auxiliary factors

$$y = \frac{k}{x} + \frac{k}{(1-x)v_d/v_c} \tag{76}$$

and

$$k = \frac{v_d/v_c}{1 + v_d/v_c} \tag{77}$$

The algorithm of evaluation of the model equations depends on the desired result. If the hold-up is to be determined, Equations 67–77 must be solved by an iteration procedure. If the flooding throughput is desired, in each iteration the overall throughput has to be differentiated with respect to the hold-up

$$\frac{dv_g}{dx} = 0 \tag{78}$$

At the flooding point this derivation must be equal to zero. Due to the limited range of validity of some of the model equations this iteration should be carried out on a computer.

The model presented recently by Aufderheide and Vogelpohl [6] is more complex but more powerful for the calculation of both mixer-settler and emulsion flooding and hold-up, respectively. Figure 2 shows the boundary, across which the material balance of the dispersed and continuous phase is established for the case of rising drops. The balance equation is

$$v_c = v_d + v_{c0} - v_{d0} - v_p \tag{79}$$

with v_c and v_d, the local flow rates of the continuous and dispersed phase at a certain cross section of the column, and v_{c0} and v_{d0}, the respective feed flow rates. The pulsation flow rate is given by

$$v_p = \pi af \sin(2\pi ft) \tag{80}$$

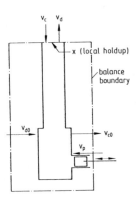

Figure 2. Model of drop swarm movement taken from Aufderheide and Vogelpohl [6].

The required rising velocity of the drop swarm relative to the continuous phase is given by the well known model equation

$$\frac{v_d}{x} + \frac{v_c}{1 - x} = w_r \tag{81}$$

which is equivalent to Equation 75.

w_r may be calculated using Equations 59–74. The true momentary rising or falling velocity relative to a fixed position is then given by

$$w_t = \frac{v_d}{x} = w_r(1 - x) - v_{c0} + v_{d0} + v_p \tag{82}$$

w_t is needed for the calculation of the momentary flow of dispersed phase through any column cross section.

In order to solve the balance equations numerically the authors [6] divided each stage of the PSE into several cells with locally lumped parameters. In the ith cell the number of entering drops is given by

$$N_{in} = v_{d, i-1} A \left/ \left(\frac{\pi}{6} d_p^3 \right) \right. \tag{83}$$

and the number of leaving drops by

$$N_{out} = v_{d,i} A \left/ \left(\frac{\pi}{6} d_p^3 \right) \right. \tag{84}$$

The increase or decrease of the hold-up within a certain time interval is then given as

$$\Delta x = (N_{in} - N_{out}) \, \Delta t \left(\frac{\pi}{6} d_p^3 \right) \left/ (Ah_c) \right. \tag{85}$$

with h_c, the height of a cell and x_c, the local hold-up in that cell.

For the cell located nearest to the sieve tray the authors [6] made a special assumption that during the downward stroke of pulsation no drop passes the tray, but the drops accumulate beneath the tray. This accumulation is described using an exponential function of time. The number of drops leaving this cell is given by

$$N_{out} = (v_p + v_{d0} + v_{c0}) x_c A \left/ \left(\frac{\pi}{6} d_p^3 \right) \right. \tag{86}$$

The model equations were solved numerically on a computer by an iteration procedure.

Appendix B: Model Describing Axial Mixing in The Continuous Phase of PSE

Nemecek and Prochazka [4] assumed that axial mixing in the MS and D regimes is mainly dependent on the drop size, whereas in the E regime the effect of hold-up is most important. Consequently, the mean drop size and the hold-up must be known either by measurement or by any of the model equations previously presented (Appendix A). Knowledge about the operating regime is also required, for which Equation 3 may be used.

According to the model, each stage of a PSE represents two ideal mixers close to the plates and a zone of diffusion type axial mixing in between. For twice the height of an ideal mixing cell Niebuhr [1] proposed a formulation incorporating the geometrical restrictions and describing the expansion of the ideal mixers with increasing pulsation intensity in a steady way.

$$2h_M = a + (h_s - a)(1 - \exp(-k_1 af)) \tag{87}$$

The lower limit of $2h_M$ is the pulsation amplitude whereas the upper limit is given by the plate spacing with $h_M = h_{M1}$, $k_1 = k_{11} = 0.038$ for single-phase and $h_M = h_{M2}$, $k_1 = k_{21} = 1.4*10^{-7}$ for two-phase operation. The dispersion coefficient of the diffusion zone may be calculated by

$$D_{M1} = k_{12} \frac{h_s - 2h_{M1}}{h_s - k_{13}} af^{k_{14}} \tag{88}$$

which is Equation 41 modified by Niebuhr and Vogelpohl [5], who determined the coefficients as

$$k_{12} = 0.24, k_{13} = 4.4, k_{14} = 0.98$$

Nemecek and Prochazka [4] assumed that the dispersion coefficient with two-phase operation is the sum of D_{M1} and ΔD, an increment for two phase operation, which may be positive or negative.

$$D_{M2} = D_{M1} + \Delta D \tag{89}$$

Niebuhr [1] adapted two equations of Nemecek and Prochazka [4] for ΔD and determined new coefficients fitting them to his own experimental results. For the MS and D regime

$$\Delta D = k_{22}(h_s - 2h_{M2}) d_{32}^{k_{23}} - k_{24} \tag{90}$$

and for the E regime

$$\Delta D = k_{25} \left(\frac{x}{m} \right)^{k_{26}} - k_{27} \tag{91}$$

The coefficients are:

$$k_{22} = 55, \qquad k_{23} = 3, \qquad k_{24} = 3, \qquad k_{25} = 1.7, \qquad k_{26} = 1, \qquad k_{27} = 2$$

For the zone of diffusion type mixing a Pe number may be defined as

$$Pe_M = \frac{v_c(h_s - 2h_M)}{D_M} \tag{92}$$

where $\quad h_M = h_{M1}$ for single-phase flow
$\qquad h_M = h_{M2}$ for two-phase flow

The same is valid for D_M.

Nemecek and Prochazka [4] derived analytically the backflow coefficient for the ideal mixers according to the backflow model, i.e. for the MS and D regimes

$$q_c = \frac{1 - v_d/v_c}{\pi} \left(k + \cotg k - \frac{\pi}{2} \right) - \frac{v_d}{v_c} (1 + q_d) \tag{93}$$

with $q_d = 0$, this means, the dispersed phase does not move back through a plate.

For the E regime, Equation 94 was given, which contains the hold-up x instead of the unknown backflow coefficient q_d:

$$q_e = \frac{1}{\pi}\left(k + \left(1 - \frac{v_d}{v_c}\right)(1 - x)\cot g\, k - \frac{\pi}{2}\right)$$ (94)

The auxiliary variable k is given by

$$k = \arcsin\left(\frac{v_c - v_d}{\pi a f}\right)$$ (95)

The coupling of an ideal mixing cell and a diffusion zone is carried out by a transformation of the dispersion model with its parameter Pe_M into the more universal model of a series of mixers with backflow, which is known to include the dispersion model as the special case of infinitely small size of a mixing cell. Then the effective backflow coefficient for a whole stage may be calculated by

$$q_e = \left(\left(1 + \frac{1}{q_c}\right)\exp(Pe_M) - 1\right)^{-1}$$ (96)

By the reverse transformation an effective Pe number per stage may be calculated from q_e

$$Pe_e = \ln\frac{1 + q_e}{q_e}$$ (97)

Then the dispersion coefficient is defined as

$$D_{axe} = \frac{v_c h_s}{Pe_e}$$ (98)

It should be noted that Pe_e is formed with the superficial velocity of the continuous phase.

NOTATION

a	pulsation amplitude = space between upper and lower turning point, cm	k	constant (general)
a_1	amplitude with minimum of hold-up, Equation 14, cm	K_F'	fluid constant, Equation 63
		l	length, cm
A	cross-sectional area	m	free cross-sectional area of a sieve plate
Ar	Archimedes number, Equation 62	n	number of ideal mixers per stage, Equation 29
C	dimensionless concentration, Equation 20	N	number of stages (Equation 28), number of drops (Equations 83 and 84)
C_I	drag coefficient, Equation 69	p	specif. power input, energy dissipation, $cm^2 s^{-3}$
d	diameter, cm		
d_{32}^0	Sauter mean diameter, Equation 58, cm	Pe	Peclet number
D	Dispersion coefficient, $cm^2 s^{-1}$	q	backflow coefficient, convolution factor (Equation 73)
f	pulsation frequency, s^{-1}		
g	gravity acceleration, $cm s^{-2}$	r	constant, Equation 11
h	height, cm	R	geometr. constant, Equation 13
H	height of measuring section, cm	Re	Reynolds number, l
Ha	Hadamard and Rybczynski correction factor, Equation 68	s	phase ratio dispersed/contin., l
		t	time, s
		v	superficial velocity, $cm s^{-1}$

w	velocity, cms^{-1}	z	cross section coefficient, Equation 71
x	hold-up of dispersed phase	Z	dimensionless coordinate of flow,
x_0, x_1	constants, Equation 14		Equation 20
y	constant, Equation 76		

Greek Letters

η	dyn, viscosity, $g\,cm^{-1}s^{-1}$	σ	interfacial tension, $g\,s^{-2}$
ζ	density, $g\,cm^{-3}$	Δ	difference of two quantities

Sub/superscripts

ax	axial	out	output, flow out
s	stage	P	particle, pulsation (Equations 79–82)
c	continuous phase	r	relative
d	dispersed phase	R	residence (time)
e, ef	effective	S	rising or falling (velocity)
F	fluid or flooding	t	transition state
g	general, overall	0	normal or initial state, single drop
h	hole, perforation of a plate		condition
i	ith stage, ith measuring point	∞	infinite cross section of flow
in	input, feed	1	single-phase
K	column	2	two-phase
l	limiting	32	Sauter (mean diameter)
M	referring to a mixing cell		

REFERENCES

1. Niebuhr, D. *Untersuchungen zur Fluiddynamik in pulsierten Siebbodenextraktionskolonnen*, Diss. TU Clausthal 1982.
2. Sege, G. and Woodfield, F. W. "Pulse Column Variables." In *Chem. Eng. Progr.* vol. 50, no. 8, 1954, pp. 396–402.
3. Sato, T. and Sugihara, K. and Taniyama, I. "The Performance Characteristics of Pulsed Perforated Plate Columns." In *Kagaku Kogaku (Chem. Eng. Japan)*, vol. 27, no. 8, 1963, pp. 583–586.
4. Nemecek, M. and Prochazka, J. "Longitudinal Mixing in a Vibrating Sieve-Plate Column— Two-phase Flow." In *Can. J. Chem. Eng.* vol. 52, 1974, pp. 739–749.
5. Niebuhr, D. and Vogelpohl, A. "Axial Mixing in Pulsed Sieve-Plate Extraction Columns." In *Ger. Chem. Eng.* vol. 3, no. 4, 1980, pp. 264–268.
6. Aufderheide, E. and Vogelpohl, A. "Zum Flutpunkt in pulsierten Siebboden-Extraktionsko-lonnen unter Einbeziehung experimenteller Tropfengroessendaten." *Chem. Ing. Tech.* 1984 (to be published).
7. McAllister, R. A. and Groenier, W. S. and Ryon, A. D. "Correlation of Flooding in Pulsed, Perforated-Plate Extraction Columns." In *Chem. Eng. Sci.* vol. 22, 1967, pp. 931–944.
8. Mersmann, A. "Zum Flutpunkt in Fluessig/Fluessig-Gegenstromkolonnen." *In Chem.-Ing.-Tech.*, vol. 52, no. 12, 1980, pp. 933–942.
9. Thornton, J. D. "The Effect of Pulse Wave-Form and Plate Geometry on the Performance and Throughput of a Pulsed Column." In *Trans. Instn. Chem. Engrs.* vol. 35, 1957, pp. 316–330.
10. Berger, R. and Leuckel, W. and Wolff, D. "Untersuchungen zur Betriebscharakteristik von pulsierten Siebbodenkolonnen fuer Fluessig/Fluessig-Extraktion." In *Chem.-Ing.-Tech.* vol. 50, no. 7, 1978, pp. 544–545, (Synopse 602).

11. Gayler, R. and Roberts, N. W. and Pratt, H. R. C. "Liquid-Liquid Extraction: Part IV. A Further Study of Hold-up in Packed Columns." In *Trans. Instn. Chem. Engrs.* vol. 31, 1953, pp. 57–68.

12. Thornton, J. D. "Recent Developments in Pulsed-Column Techniques." In *Chem. Eng. Prog. Symposium Series*, vol. 50, no. 13, 1954, pp. 39–52.

13. Defives, D. and Durandet, J. and Gladel, Y. L. "Etude d'une colonne à pulsations pour l'extraction liquide-liquide." In *Revue de l'Institut Francais du Petrole*, vol. 11, no. 2, 1956, pp. 231–246.

14. Edwards, R. B. and Beyer, G. H. "Flooding Characteristics of a Pulse Extraction Column." In *AIChE J.* vol. 2, no. 2, 1956, pp. 148–152.

15. Logsdail, D. H. and Thornton, J. D. "The Effect of Column Diameter Upon the Performance and Throughput of Pulsed Plate Columns." In *Trans. Instn. Chem. Engrs.* vol. 35, 1957, pp. 331–342.

16. Smoot, L. D. and Mar, B. W. and Babb, A. L. "Flooding Characteristics and Separation Efficiencies of Pulsed Sieve-Plate Extraction Columns." In *Ind. Eng. Chem.* vol. 51, no. 9, 1959, pp. 1005–1010.

17. Jealous, A. C. and Johnson, H. F. "Power Requirements for Pulsed Columns." In *Ind. Eng. Chem.* vol. 47, no. 6, 1955, pp. 1159–1166.

18. Berger, R. Paper presented at the internal session of the GVC-committee, "Thermal Separation of Gases and Liquids," 5 May 1979 in Muenstereifel.

19. Richardson, J. F. and Zaki, W. N. "Sedimentation and Fluidization: Part I." In *Trans. Instn. Chem. Engrs.* vol. 32, 1954, pp. 35–53.

20. Misek, T. "The Hydrodynamic Behavior of Pulsed Liquid-Liquid Extractors." In *Coll. Czechoslov. Chem. Comm.* vol. 29, 1964, pp. 1755–1766.

21. Kagan, S. Z. et al. "Some Hydrodynamic and Mass Transfer Problems in Pulsed Sieve-Plate Extractors." In *Int. Chem. Eng.* vol. 5, no. 4, 1965, pp. 656–661.

22. Konovalov, V. I. and Shtrobel, V. O. and Romankov, P. G. "Criterial Equations for Flooding in Countercurrent Extraction Columns." In *Zh. Prikl. Khim.* vol. 34, no. 9, 1961, pp. 1966–1971, translation in *Int. Chem. Eng.*

23. Groenier, W. S. and McAllister, R. A. and Ryon, A. D. "Flooding in Perforated-Plate Pulsed Extraction Columns." In *US Atom. Ener. Comm. Report ORNL-3890 Oak Ridge (Tenn.)*, 1966.

24. Miller, Paper presented at the workshop for the coordination of extraction research, 26 Oct 1979 in Karlsruhe.

25. Coggan, G. C. "The Scaling-Up of Pulsed Extraction Columns, Part I: Limiting Throughputs." In *Instn. Chem. Engrs. Symposium Series*, vol. 26, 1967, pp. 138–144.

26. Klicka, V. and Cermak, J. "Zweiphasenstroemung in der Pulsier-Extraktionskolonne." In *Verfahrenstechnik*, vol. 5, no. 8, 1971, pp. 320–327, (1.Teil).

27. Pilhofer, T. "Grenzbelastungen verschiedener Gegenstrom-Extraktionskolonnen." In *Chem.-Ing.-Tech.* vol. 51, no. 3, 1979, Synopse pp. 667–679.

28. Rouyer, H. and Lebouhellec, J., and Henry, E. "Elements pour l'etude et le development de l'utilisation des colonnes pulsees." In *Bull. Inform. Sci. Tech. Commiss. Energ. At. (Fr.)* no. 184, 1973, pp. 29–34.

29. Lewis, W. K. and Gilliland, E. R., and Bauer, W. C. "Characteristics of Fluidized Particles." In *Ind. Eng. Chem.* vol. 41, 1949, pp. 1104–1117.

30. Anderssen, A. S. and White, E. T. "Parameter Estimation by the Weighted Moments Method." In *Chem. Eng. Sci.* vol. 26, 1971, pp. 1203–1221.

31. Molerus, O. "Das Widerstandsverhalten von Partikeln in Packungen und in homogenen Fluessigkeit/Feststoff-Wirbelschichten." In *Verfahrenstechnik*, vol. 12, no. 8, 1978, pp. 493–499.

32. Cohen, R. M. and Beyer, G. H. "Performance of a Pulse Extraction Column." In *Chem. Eng. Prog.* vol. 49, no. 6, 1953, pp. 279–286.

33. Li, W. H. and Newton, W. M. "Liquid-Liquid Extraction in a Pulsed Perforated Plate Column." In *AIChE J.* vol. 3, no. 1, 1957, pp. 56–62.

34. Defives, D. and Reed, C., and Schneider, A. "Mesure de la 'fraction volumique' d'une dispersion liquide-liquide par conductometrie." In *Genie Chimique*, vol. 84, no. 4, 1960, pp. 120–129.

35. Sehmel, G. A. "Longitudinal Mixing and Hold-Up Studies in a Pulsed Sieve-Plate Solvent Extraction Column," Ph.D.diss. Univ. of Washington, Seattle (Wash.) 1967.
36. Sehmel, G. A. and Babb, A. L. "Hold-Up Studies in a Pulsed Sieve-Plate Solvent Extraction Column." In *Ind. Eng. Chem. Proc. Des. Develop.* vol. 2, no. 1, 1963, pp. 38–42.
37. Jones, S. C. "On the behavior of a Pulsed Extraction Column," Ph.D.diss. University of Michigan, Ann Arbor (Mich.) 1963.
38. Foster, H. R. *The Transient Hold-Up Response of a Pulsed Sieve-Plate Extraction Column,* Ph.D.diss. University of Washington, Seattle (Wash.) 1964.
39. Bell. R. L. "A Theoretical and Experimental Study of the Dispersed Phase Axial Mixing in Sieve-Plate Pulsed Solvent Extraction Columns," Ph.D.diss. Univ. Washington, Seattle (Wash.) 1964.
40. Michauchi, T. and Oya, H. "Longitudinal Dispersion in Pulsed Perforated-Plate Columns." In *AIChE J.* vol. 11, no. 3, 1965, pp. 395–402.
41. Tutaeva, A. N. and Kagan, S. Z. "Some Problems of Hydrodynamics of Pulsed Sieve-Plate Extraction Columns for Liquid-Liquid Systems. Part 2: Hold-Up of the Dispersed Phase" (russ.) *Trudy instituta. Moskovskij chimiko-technologiceskij institut im D. I. Mendeleeva,* vol. 54, 1967, pp. 248–250.
42. Bell, R. L. and Babb, A. L. "Hold-Up and Axial Distribution of Hold-Up in a Pulsed Sieve-Plate Solvent Extraction Column." In *Ind. Eng. Chem. Process Des. Develop.* vol. 8, no. 3, 1969, pp. 392–400.
43. Mishra, J. C. and Dutt, D. K. "Engineering Study of Hold-Up in a Perforated Plate Pulse Column for the Countercurrent Flow of Two Immiscible Liquids." *Chemical Age of India,* vol. 20, no. 10, 1969, pp. 845–852.
44. Klicka, V. and Cermak, J. "Zweiphasenstroemung in der Pulsier-Extraktionskolonne." In *Verfahrenstechnik,* vol. 6, No. 3, 1972, pp. 96–105, (2. Teil).
45. Fernandes, J. B. "Effective Interfacial Area and Hold-Up in Pulsed Extraction Column." In *AIChE Symposium Series,* vol. 68, no. 120, pp. 124–129.
46. Ugarcic, M. *Hydrodynamik und Stoffaustausch in Spgrueh- und gepulsten Siebbodenkolonnen,* Diss. ETH Zuerich 1981.
47. Klinkenberg, A. "The Concept of Backmixing." In *Chem. Eng. Sci.* vol. 23, 1968, p. 92.
48. Hartland, S. and Mecklenbourgh, I. C. "The Concept of Backmixing." In *Chem. Eng. Sci.* vol. 23, 1968, pp. 186–187.
49. Boexkes, W. and Hofmann, H. "Vor- und Nachteile verschiedner Befragungstechniken zur Analyse des Mischverhaltens in chemischen Reaktoren." In *Chem.-Ing.-Tech.* vol. 44, no. 14, 1972, pp. 882–889.
50. Gilliland, E. R. and Mason, E. A. "Gas and Solid Mixing in Fluidized Beds." In *Ind. Eng. Chem.* vol. 41, no. 6, 1949, pp. 1191–1196.
51. Miyauchi, T. and Vermeulen, T. "Longitudinal Dispersion in Two-Phase Continuous-Flow Operations" (pp. 113–125) and "Diffusion and Back-Flow Models for Two-Phase Axial Dispersion (pp. 304/309)." In *Ind. Eng. Chem. Fundamentals,* vol. 2, 1963.
52. Himmelblau, D. M. and Bischoff, K. B. *Process Analysis and Simulation, Deterministic Systems,* Chapter 4.5: "Interpretation of age Distribution Functions," New York: Wiley, 1968.
53. Kardos, J. and Pulz, A. and Schubert, P. "Darstellung und Auswertung von Verweilzeitvertei-lungen nach dem Zellenmodell." In *Chem. Techn.* vol. 28, no. 6, 1976, pp. 329–332.
54. Pulz, A. "Mathematische Modelle zur Analyse von Verweilzeitverteilungen." In *Chem. Techn.* vol. 26, no. 10, 1974, pp. 652–654.
55. Burger, L. L. and Swift, W. H. "Backmixing in Pulse Columns with Particular Reference to Scale-Up." In *US Atom. Ener. Comm. Report HW 28867, Oak Ridge (Tenn.),* 1953.
56. Mar, B. W. "Longitudinal mixing in pulsed extraction columns, Ph.D.diss. University of Washington, Seattle (Wash.) 1958.
57. Mar, B. W. and Babb, A. L. "Longitudinal Mixing in a Pulsed Sieve-Plate Extraction Column." In *Ind. Eng. Chem.* vol. 51, no. 9, 1959, pp. 1011–1014.
58. Claybaugh, B. E. "Effects of Backmixing on concentration Profiles in a Pulse Column, Ph.D.diss. Oklahoma State University 1961.

59. Sehmel, G. A. and Babb, A. L. "Longitudinal Mixing Studies in a Pulsed Extraction Column." In *Ind. Eng. Chem. Proc. Des. Develop.* vol. 3, no. 3, 1964, pp. 210–214.

60. Gelperin, N. I. and Neustroev S. A. "Longitudinal Mixing in a Pulsed Sive-Plate Extraction Column," (Russ.), *Khim. Prom.*, vol. 5, 1964, pp. 360–364.

61. Novotny, P. and Prochazka, J. and Landau, J. "Longitudinal Mixing in Reciprocating and Pulsed Sieve-Plate Column—Single-Phase Flow." In *Can. J. Chem. Eng.* vol. 48, 1970, pp. 405–410.

62. Rozen, A. M. and Rubezhnyy, Y. G. and Martynov, B. V. "Longitudinal Mixing in Pulsating Extraction Columns." In *Sov. Chem. Ind.* no. 2, 1970, pp. 66–73.

63. Kagan, S. Z. et al. "Longitudinal Mixing and Its Effect on Mass Transfer in Pulsating Sieve-Type Extractors." In *Soviet Chemical Industry*, vol. 4, no. 4, 1972, pp. 256–259.

64. Veisbain, D. A., Kagan, S. Z. Trukhanov, V. G. *Trudy instituta. Moskovskij chimiko-technologiceskij institut im D. I. Mendeleeva*, vol. 65, 1970, pp. 202–209.

65. Zheleznyak, A. S. "Four-Stroke Model of the Action of a Pulsed Plate Column." In *Zhurnal Prikladnoi Khimii*, vol. 51, no. 11, 1978, pp. 2514–2519. (Translation in *Int. Chem. Engng.*)

66. Kasipathi Rao, K. V. and Jeelani, S. A. K., and Balasubramanian, G. R. "Backmixing in Pulsed Perforated Plate Columns." In *Can. J. Chem. Engng.* vol. 56, 1978, pp. 120–123.

67. Arthayukti, W. and Muratet, G. and Angelino, H. "Longitudinal Mixing in the Dispersed Phase in Pulsed Perforated Plate Columns." In *Chem. Eng. Sci.* vol. 31, 1976, pp. 1193–1197.

68. Brauer, H. *Grundlagen der Einphasen- und Mehrphasenstroemungen*, first ed. Aarau: Sauerlaender Publ. Comp., 1971, p. 297.

69. Assenov, A. and Penchev, I. "Effect of Pulsing Intensity Upon Droplet Size in a Plate-Pulsed Extraction Column." In *Compte Rendu de l'Academie Bulgare des Sciences*, vol. 24, no. 10, 1971, p. 1381.

70. Assenov, A. et al. "Drop Size Determination in a Vibrating Extractor." In *Verfahrenstechnik (Mainz)*, vol. 7, no. 8, 1973, pp. 242–244.

71. Johnson, N. L. *Biometrica*, vol. 36, no. 149, 1949.

72. Khemangkorn, V. and Muratet, G. and Angelino, H. "Study of Dispersion in a Pulsed Perforated Plate Column." In *ISEC 77 CIM Special*, vol. 21, pp. 429–435.

73. Pilhofer, T. Habilitation thesis, TU Muenchen 1979.

74. Doulah, M. S. "An Effect of Hold-Up on Drop sizes in Liquid-Liquid Dispersions." In *Ind. Eng. Chem. Fundam.* vol. 14, no. 2, 1975, pp. 137–138.

75. Doronin, V. N. and Niklaev, A. M. "Maximum Throughput of a Pulsed Extraction Column." (Russ.) In *Chimija i chimiceskaja technologija* vol. 7, no. 3, 1964, pp. 497–500.

CHAPTER 43

PREDICTING TRANSIENT SUBCOOLED TWO-PHASE FLOWS

H. A. Khater

Nuclear Products Department
Westinghouse Canada Inc.
Hamilton, Ontario, Canada

CONTENTS

INTRODUCTION

The advent of nuclear power reactors, and the stringent requirements for the safety analysis of such devices, has made it necessary to develop accurate prediction techniques capable of treating a variety of transient two-phase flows. In general, the requirement makes it necessary to include phenomena that arise from departures from cross-sectionally uniform void and velocity profiles, and departures from thermal equilibrium.

In many situations, where heat is transferred to a liquid, vapor is generated despite the fact that the mixed-mean fluid temperature is below saturation. This phenomenon, called sub-cooled boiling, is simply a consequence of the non-uniformity of the temperature distribution across the flow cross-section. Thus, while the average liquid temperature is below saturation, the liquid near the wall is not. Whether or not significant vapor generation occurs is then determined by the balance between the rate at which vapor is created in the wall region and is condensed in the subcooled liquid core, and the rate at which this vapor is transferred to, and condensed by, the sub-cooled liquid in the regions of the flow remote from the walls. Figure 1 illustrates a schematic of a typical subcooled boiling void, liquid bulk temperature and wall temperature profiles in a uniformly heated tube. In the initial regions of such a flow, as suggested by Griffith, Clark and Rohsenow [1], the condensation process dominates and the void is confined to the near wall region; this is called the region of attached void. Because the cross-section average void in this region is very small, say of the order of one percent, it is usually neglected. At some point the capacity of the subcooled liquid

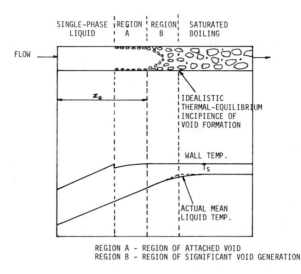

REGION A - REGION OF ATTACHED VOID
REGION B - REGION OF SIGNIFICANT VOID GENERATION

Figure 1. Schematic of typical subcooled boiling, liquid bulk temperature and wall temperature profiles in a uniformly heated channel.

to condense the vapor generated in the wall region ceases to be sufficient to confine the vapor to the near wall region and an appreciable rate of change of cross-section average void commences. The location of this point is determined by the capacity of the liquid core to absorb the heat released by the vapor condensation process. In the literature it is often referred to as the point of incipient void formation or boiling boundary, given the symbol Z_0 by Zuber and Kroeger [2]. This location is usually determined using empirical or semi-empirical relations. Since, in this work, unsteady flows in which the heat flux may vary with time and space are of interest, this location is not a convenient representation. Noting that Z_0 is the location where the thermal capacity of the subcooled liquid core balances the wall heat flux, it is clear that the relations for Z_0 implicitly contain an expression for the heat transfer rate to the subcooled liquid q_b''. The expression, as derived by Hancox and Nicoll [3] is

$$q_b'' = \frac{h_0}{c_{p_\ell}} (i_f - \langle i_\ell \rangle) \tag{1}$$

where h_0 is a suitable heat transfer coefficient to the liquid core corresponding to Z_0, i_f is the liquid saturation enthalpy, and $\langle i_\ell \rangle$ is the cross-sectional average liquid enthalpy. The cross-sectional averaging operator $\langle \Delta \rangle$ is defined as

$$\langle \Delta \rangle \triangleq \frac{1}{A_c} \int_{A_c} (\Delta) \, dA_c \tag{2}$$

where A_c is the flow cross-sectional area. The liquid average specific heat c_{p_ℓ} is defined as

$$c_{p_\ell} = (i_f - \langle i_\ell \rangle)/(T_s - \langle T_\ell \rangle) \tag{3}$$

where T_s is the saturation temperature, and $\langle T_\ell \rangle$ is the cross-sectional average liquid temperature.

In the form given by Equation 1 the heat transfer model can be used for the prediction of condensation as well as vapor generation. The latter occurs when the wall heat flux $q_w'' > q_b''$, and the former when $q_w'' < q_b''$. This is an important formulation since it permits the prediction of condensation driven flow reversal. In order to obtain an effective subcooled boiling model, the point of incipient void formation has to be accurately predicted. Several criteria are available in the literature; the most common ones are listed below.

Griffith, Clark and Rohsenow [1] used a heat transfer model to find

$$h_0 = 5.0 \, h_{sp} \tag{4}$$

where h_{sp} refers to the heat transfer coefficient to single-phase liquid.

Bowring [4] empirically obtained the following equation, which is valid for the pressure range 1.08 to 13.89 MPa

$$h_0 = \frac{G\eta}{\rho_\ell} \tag{5}$$

where G is the mass flux and ρ_ℓ is the liquid density. The parameter η accounts for the effect of pressure. Expressing the variables in SI units, and the pressure p in MPa; η becomes

$$\eta = 0.94 + 0.667 \times 10^{-1} p$$

Levy [5] used a force balance model to obtain

$$h_0 = \left[\frac{1}{h_{sp}} - \frac{\text{Pr} \, y_b^+}{c_{p_\ell} G(f/8)^{1/2}} \right]^{-1}, \, 0 \le y_b^+ \le 5.0$$

$$h_0 = \left[\frac{1}{h_{sp}} - \frac{5.0 \left\{ \text{Pr} + \ln \left[1 + \text{Pr} \left(\frac{y_b^+}{5.0} - 1 \right) \right] \right\}}{c_{p_\ell} G(f/8)^{1/2}} \right]^{-1}, \, 5.0 \le y_b^+ \le 30.0 \tag{6}$$

$$h_0 = \left[\frac{1}{h_{sp}} - \frac{5.0 \left\{ \text{Pr} + \ln \left(1 + 5.0 \, \text{Pr} \right) + 0.5 \ln \left(\frac{y_b^+}{30} \right) \right\}}{c_{p_\ell} G(f/8)^{1/2}} \right]^{-1}, \, y_b^+ \ge 30.0$$

In Equation 6 $\text{Pr} \triangleq \mu c_{p_\ell}/k_\ell$ is the liquid Prandtl number, and f is the friction factor. The parameter y_b^+ is a function of the coefficient of surface tension σ, the equivalent hydraulic diameter D_h, the viscosity μ_ℓ and the density ρ_ℓ; y_b^+ is equal to

$$y_b^+ = 0.01 \left(\frac{\sigma g_c D_h \rho_\ell}{\mu_\ell} \right)^{1/2}$$

Hancox and Nicoll [3] used a semi-empirical model to obtain

$$h_0 = 0.40 \frac{k_f}{D_h} (\text{Re})^{0.662} \, \text{Pr} \tag{7}$$

where k_f is the liquid saturation thermal conductivity, and Re is the Reynolds number.

Saha and Zuber [6] empirically found

$$h_0 = 445 \frac{k_\ell}{D_h}, \, \text{Pe} < 70,000 \tag{8}$$

$$h_0 = (G c_{p_\ell})/154, \, \text{Pe} \ge 70,000$$

where k_ℓ is the bulk liquid thermal conductivity, and Pe is Peclet number.

Other criteria for the prediction of the point of incipient void generation which are on the same line as Levy's [5] analysis were developed by Staub [7], Madejski [8] and Betten and Paul [9].

Because of the extensive data base used to develop Equation 8, it is likely to be the most accurate available to date.

It should be observed here that, in the derivation of the previous formulas, the authors concentrated on steady low void flows such as the data reported by Maurer [10], Egen et al. [11], Marchaterre et al. [12], Christensen [13], Foglia et al. [14], Rouhani [15] and Bartolomei and Chanturiya [16]. Thus, it is quite possible that the expression derived for q_b'' is not correct when either of these conditions is violated. In fact, Roy and Yadigaroglu [17] have indicated that the velocity and temperature profiles near the heated wall may be quite different from those of the quasi steady profiles, even for relatively slow transients. Two comments concerning this question are appropriate. First, while at higher voids the physical arguments that led to the previous equations are poor approximations to reality, this matters little since the driving temperature difference is small and so therefore is the heat transfer rate to the liquid. Second, in transient flows little is known about the detailed heat transfer processes. Further, direct experimental verification is difficult, with the results that the adequacy of a model can only be judged within the framework of how the final predictions agree with quantities that are measureable.

THE ENERGY FLOW INVENTORY

The major features of thermal non-equilibrium two-phase flows can be best understood in terms of energy inventory as described by Khater, Nicoll and Raithby [18]. A schematic representation of the energy inventory is displayed in Figure 2. The essential physical inputs, for specified wall heat flux, include the fraction of the total heat transfer, which goes directly to each phase and the heat transfer from each phase to the interface where, it is assumed, the phase change process (vaporization or condensation) occurs.

For the sake of convenience assume that the flow is described by one-dimensional cross-sectionally averaged conservation equations. Hence, the phase-interface heat transfer coefficients are defined on the basis of the average phase temperature and the interface temperature which in all cases is assumed to be at the saturation temperature corresponding to the instantaneous pressure. Thus,

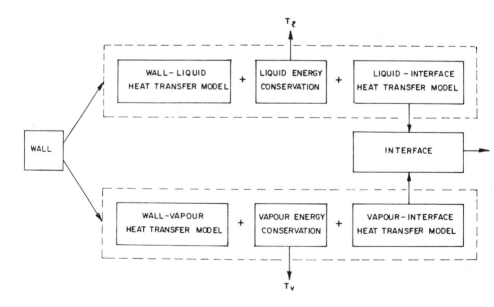

Figure 2. Schematic representation of the energy flow inventory.

when one or both phases are assumed to be at equilibrium, it is equivalent to the assumption of an infinite heat transfer coefficient between the equilibrium phase (or phases) and the interface. When these coefficients are finite the product of the interface area and the heat transfer coefficients must be specified. Quite obviously, the specification must be flow regime (or, preferably, phase distribution) dependent.

When the wall heat flux is not specified, then the heat transfer between the wall and either phase must be modeled in the same way. It is the combination of the two heat transfer models (wall to phase, and phase to interface) and the energy conservation equation that constitute the model for each phase, as indicated in Figure 2.

From this discussion it is seen that the various models can be classified in terms of the heat transfer models. It should be observed that, while it is useful to have a mental image of the phase distribution across the flow cross-section when constructing the heat transfer models, there is no need to do so. Thus, there is no necessity that the mental model corresponds in detail to the actual phase distribution but only that the various heat transfer rates be adequately determined. This is mentioned because in many real situations almost nothing is known about the phase distribution; this is particularly true for depressurization transients.

THERMAL NON-EQUILIBRIUM TWO-PHASE FLOW MODELS

A Review

The equations describing the local instantaneous motion of the fluids and interfaces in multiphase flow are described by Delhaye [19] and Ishii [20]. These equations form the basis for most of two-phase flow modeling techniques. The conservation laws for each phase are expressed in terms of partial differential equations; whereas on the interface conservation laws are formulated in terms of jump conditions.

Much more tractable equations can be obtained by performing certain averages over time and/or space, by introducing idealizations, and by supplying information (e.g. through correlations) that has been lost in the averaging process. Bouré, [21] presents a discussion on many of the widely used idealization and averaging techniques in two-phase constitutive equations.

The most accurate description of thermal non-equilibrium two-phase flows is achieved using two fluid models. For transient one-dimensional problems, instantaneous space averaged equations are used. These equations were developed by Delhaye [22], and Vernier and Delhaye [23]. A detailed study of these equations is given by Kocamustafaaogullari [24]. For transient three-dimensional problems, local time averaged equations are usually used. These equations were proposed by Teletov [25]. Ishii [20] presents an excellent review of such formulation, and compares the different types of averages used.

One of the interesting and relatively simple two-phase flow formulation methods is the drift-flux formulation that has its origins in the papers by Zuber and Findlay [26], Zuber and Staub [27], Zuber et al. [28] and Zuber and Kroeger [2]. This is a one-dimensional model that accounts for the variation of the velocity and void profiles across the flow cross-section, and for the velocity difference between the phases through cross-sectional averaged parameters. The drift-flux formulation was later generalized by Hancox and Nicoll [3], and Yadigaroglu and Lahey [29].

Solution procedures, for the prediction of transient subcooled two-phase flow problems, which are based on the generalization of the drift-flux formulation were developed by several authors. Hancox and Nicoll [3, 30] used an implicit finite difference calculation procedure for flow transients and stability analysis problems. Shiraklar, Schnebly, and Lahey [31] developed a solution technique for the analysis of two-phase stability problems. Khater, Nicoll, and Raithby [32] used a Lagrangian semi-analytical solution procedure for the prediction of transient subcooled two-phase flows.

Many of the solution procedures that account for the velocity and temperature differences between the phases are designed primarily for the prediction of transients resulting from hypothetical accidents in nuclear power reactors, such as the solution procedures in the computer codes RELAP 5 [33], and TRAC [34]. A model based on the method of characteristics was developed by Ferch [35]. Other models were developed by Hughes, Lyzkowski, and McFadden [36], and Hancox et. al. [37].

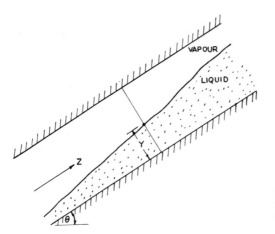

Figure 3. Schematic of the flow channel and geometry considered when deriving the conservation equations.

One-Dimensional Conservation Laws

In this section the one-dimensional cross-sectional average conservation equations describing transient thermal non-equilibrium two-phase flows are presented. However, extension to three-dimensions is straightforward. The equations discussed are similar to those proposed by Yadigaroglu and Lahey [29]. Figure 3 illustrates a schematic of the flow channel and geometry considered when deriving the following equations.

Conservation of Mass

The equation of conservation of mass for the vapor phase is

$$\frac{\partial}{\partial t}\langle \alpha\rho_v \rangle + \frac{\partial}{\partial z}\langle \alpha\rho_v V_v \rangle = \langle \Gamma \rangle \tag{9}$$

Similarly, the equation of conservation of mass for the liquid phase is

$$\frac{\partial}{\partial t}\langle (1-\alpha)\rho_\ell \rangle + \frac{\partial}{\partial z}\langle (1-\alpha)\rho_\ell V_\ell \rangle = -\langle \Gamma \rangle \tag{10}$$

In Equations 9 and 10 t is the time, z is the space coordinate, α is the void fraction, ρ_v and ρ_ℓ are the vapor and liquid densities, respectively, V_v and V_ℓ are the vapor and liquid velocities, respectively, and Γ is the volumetric rate of vapor generation.

Conservation of Energy

In the absence of significant conversion of potential and kinetic energy to internal energy, the equation of conservation of energy for the vapor phase may be written as

$$\frac{\partial}{\partial t}\left\langle \alpha\rho_v\left(i_v - \frac{P_v}{\rho_v}\right)\right\rangle + \frac{\partial}{\partial z}\langle \alpha\rho_v V_v i_v \rangle = \langle \Gamma_{uv} \rangle \tag{11}$$

Similarly, the energy equation for the liquid phase is

$$\frac{\partial}{\partial t}\left\langle (1-\alpha)\rho_\ell\left(i_\ell - \frac{P_\ell}{\rho_\ell}\right)\right\rangle + \frac{\partial}{\partial z}\left\langle (1-\alpha)\rho_\ell V_\ell i_\ell \right\rangle = \langle \Gamma_{u\ell} \rangle \tag{12}$$

where in Equations 11 and 12 i_v and i_ℓ are the specific enthalpies for the vapor and liquid, respectively, and P_v and P_ℓ are the pressures of the vapor and liquid respectively. For most cases of interest it is not necessary to distinguish between P_ℓ and P_v in the energy equations (i.e., $P_v = P_\ell = P_i$). The quantities Γ_{uv} and $\Gamma_{u\ell}$ are the volumetric rate at which the vapor and the liquid, internal energies are increased respectively, either through heat transfer or shear work or through the creation of vapor by phase change. Assuming that no work transfers across the boundaries of the system other than the flow work, Γ_{uv} and $\Gamma_{u\ell}$ are related through the expression:

$$\langle \Gamma_{uv} \rangle + \langle \Gamma_{u\ell} \rangle = \frac{q''_w P_h}{A_c} \tag{13}$$

where q''_w is the wall heat flux, P_h is the heated perimeter, and A_c is the flow cross-sectional area (assumed to be constant).

The general expressions for $\langle \Gamma_{uv} \rangle$ and $\langle \Gamma_{u\ell} \rangle$, as discussed by Yadigaroglu and Lahey [29] are

$$\langle \Gamma_{uv} \rangle = \frac{q''_w P_{hv}}{A_c} - \frac{q''_{vi} P_i}{A_c} + \langle \Gamma \rangle i_{vi} + q'''_v \langle \alpha \rangle - p_v \frac{\partial \langle \alpha \rangle}{\partial t} + \frac{\tau_i V_i \varepsilon P_i}{A_c} \tag{14}$$

$$\langle \Gamma_{u\ell} \rangle = \frac{q''_w P_{h\ell}}{A_c} + \frac{q''_{\ell i} P_i}{A_c} - \langle \Gamma \rangle i_{\ell i} + q'''_\ell \langle 1 - \alpha \rangle - p_\ell \frac{\partial \langle 1 - \alpha \rangle}{\partial t} - \frac{\tau_i V_i (1 - \varepsilon) P_i}{A_c} \tag{15}$$

where P_{hv} and $P_{h\ell}$ are the portions of the heated perimeter in contact with the vapor and liquid phases, respectively; q''_{vi} and $q''_{\ell i}$ are the heat fluxes from the vapor to the interface and from the interface to the liquid, respectively; i_{vi} and $i_{\ell i}$ are the enthalpies of the vapor and liquid, respectively, generated at the interface. q'''_v and q'''_ℓ are the volumetric rates of internal heat generation within the vapor and liquid phase respectively; τ_i is the interface shear stress; ε is the fraction of the interfacial shear work that is transported to the vapor phase; P_i is the interface area per unit length of channel; and V_i is the interface velocity given by

$$V_i = \beta V_v + (1 - \beta) V_\ell \tag{16}$$

In most practical cases of interest, β is assumed equal to zero (see for example Wallis [38]).

Thus, in Equation 14 the first term represents the rate at which heat transfer from the wall increases the vapor internal energy, the second term the volumetric rate of decrease due to heat transfer from the vapor to the interface, and the third term the volumetric rate of increase due to vapor creation, the fourth the increase due to internal heat generation, the fifth the decrease due to the expansion work done by the vapor on the interface, and the final term the rate of dissipation at the interface, which results in an increase of the vapor internal energy.

Conservation of Momentum

The equations of conservation of momentum for the vapor and liquid may be written as

$$\frac{\partial}{\partial t} \langle \alpha \rho_v V_v \rangle + \frac{\partial}{\partial z} \langle \alpha \rho_v V_v^2 \rangle = F_v + \langle \Gamma \rangle v_i - \frac{\tau_i P_i}{A_c} - \frac{\tau_{wv} P_{wv}}{A_c} \tag{17}$$

$$\frac{\partial}{\partial t} \langle (1 - \alpha) \rho_\ell V_\ell \rangle + \frac{\partial}{\partial z} \langle (1 - \alpha) \rho_\ell V_\ell^2 \rangle = F_\ell - \langle \Gamma \rangle v_i + \frac{\tau_i P_i}{A_c} - \frac{\tau_{w\ell} P_{w\ell}}{A_c} \tag{18}$$

The equations for F_v and F_ℓ as mentioned in Khater and Raithby [39] are given by

$$F_v = -\langle \alpha \rangle \frac{\partial P_i}{\partial z} - \langle \alpha \rho_v \rangle g \sin \theta - a_f \left\langle \alpha \rho_v \frac{\partial y}{\partial z} \right\rangle g \cos \theta \tag{19}$$

$$F_{\ell} = -\left\langle 1 - \alpha \right\rangle \frac{\partial P_i}{\partial z} - \left\langle (1 - \alpha)\rho_{\ell} \right\rangle g \sin \theta - a_f \left\langle (1 - \alpha)\rho_{\ell} \frac{\partial y}{\partial z} \right\rangle g \cos \theta \qquad (20)$$

$$\text{where} \quad a_f = \begin{cases} 1 & \text{for stratified flows (not annular)} \\ 0 & \text{for other flows} \end{cases} \qquad (21)$$

In Equations 17 through 21 τ_{wv} and $\tau_{w\ell}$ are the wall-vapor and wall-liquid shear stresses, respectively; P_{wv} and $P_{w\ell}$ are the vapor and liquid wetted perimeters; θ is the inclination of the channel to the horizontal axis; y is the height of the interface above the channel bottom; and P_i is the average cross-sectional pressure when $a_f = 0$, and is the pressure of the liquid-vapor interface when $a_f = 1$.

Closing Remarks

To close the previous equation set, models are required to describe ε, β, y, $q''_{\ell i}$, q''_{vi}, τ_i, τ_{wv}, $\tau_{w\ell}$, P_i, $P_{h\ell}$, and P_{hv}. All these quantities are flow regime (or more precisely, phase distribution) dependent. In addition, models, either empirical or analytical, are required to describe the relation between the cross-sectional average of the product of two quantities, say $\langle xy \rangle$, and the product of the cross-sectional average of the two quantities $\langle x \rangle \langle y \rangle$. Many authors consider both quantities to be identical (uniform cross-sectional distribution); others (drift-flux formulation) use models or expressions to describe the relations. An equation of state for each fluid (phase) is also required. The equations of state are usually found in the form of tables, or functional fits, to the properties (such as the functional fits suggested by Agee, Paulsen and Hughes [40] for steam-water properties). The latter form is useful in computer programs because of its ease of implementation and algebraic manipulation.

In the following section a relatively simple solution technique, using Lagrangian drift-flux formulation, for the prediction of transient subcooled two-phase flows is presented.

A Semi-Analytical Solution Procedure for Predicting Transient Subcooled Two-Phase Flows

The following presents a semi-analytical method for solving many transient subcooled two-phase flow problems of interest. The method is due to Khater, Nicoll, and Raithby [18, 32], and is extremely attractive in terms of accuracy, economy, and stability, and yet sufficiently general to handle many of the problems of practical interest such as the analysis and interpretation of experiments, application of out-of-pile data to reactor flow conditions, and calculation of core behavior in reactor transients.

The method is based on the cross-sectionally averaged equations of mass (Equations 9 and 10), and energy (Equations 11 and 12). The two conservation of momentum equations (Equations 17 and 18) are replaced by a prescription of the vapor drift velocity, which will be defined later, and by an assumption that the pressure drop along the channel is not significant. The latter assumption makes the method unsuitable for the prediction of pressure-wave propagation. On the positive side, the method treats temporally and spatially variable wall heat flux, as well as pressure and flow transients.

The Liquid Phase-Interface Heat Transfer Model

As mentioned earlier, a model that describes the rate of heat transfer from the interface to the liquid phase, $q''_{\ell i}$, is required. In subcooled boiling, it is plausible to assume that the vapor that is generated at the interface remains at saturation conditions. In fact, measurements of temperature profiles in forced convection boiling in channel flows by Jiji and Clark [41] support this assumption. According to the discussion presented earlier this, combined with the assumption that the interface remains at saturation, corresponds to an infinite coefficient of heat transfer between the vapor phase and the interface, h_{vi}. As for the liquid phase, there must be a finite value for the coefficient of heat transfer between the liquid phase and the interface, $h_{\ell i}$. It is plausible to assume that the amount of heat transferred from the interface to the liquid-phase to reduce its subcooling $q''_{\ell i}$, is proportional to the temperature difference between the interface and the bulk liquid, i.e.,

$$q''_{\ell i} = h_{\ell i}(T_s - \langle T_\ell \rangle) \tag{22}$$

If the mean liquid specific heat $c_{p\ell}$, defined in Equation 3, is used, the above equation reduces to

$$q''_{\ell i} = h_{\ell i}(i_f - \langle i_\ell \rangle)/c_{p\ell} \tag{23}$$

Several authors have assumed that the coefficient of heat transfer $h_{\ell i}$ is equal to h_0 (defined in Equation 1). This assumption has been successfully used by Ahmad [42], and Hancox and Nicoll [30].

The Drift-Flux Formulation

The solution method uses analytical solutions to the equations of interest. These solutions are only valid within discrete time intervals. The total time domain of interest is divided into discrete intervals of appropriate size, and the analytic solutions that are valid within each of these sub-domains are used to construct the solution over the whole domain. The formulation used is a generalization of the drift-flux formulation. This formulation contains the distribution parameter C_0, which accounts for void and velocity variations across the cross-section, and the vapor drift velocity V_{vj}, where

$$C_0 \triangleq \langle \alpha j \rangle / \langle \alpha \rangle \langle j \rangle \tag{22}$$

$$V_{vj} \triangleq V_v - j; \quad j \triangleq \langle \alpha V_v \rangle + \langle (1 - \alpha) V_\ell \rangle \tag{23}$$

where j is the superficial velocity. In addition, many other parameters as indicated by Khater, Nicoll, and Raithby [18] arise when Equations 9–15 are converted to the drift-flux formulation. To obtain a tractable set of equations, the following approximations are introduced within a particular interval, or subdomain, in time and space:

Approximation 1. Internal heating, the work done by interfacial shear stresses and, as already stated, the conversion of kinetic and potential energy to internal energy are all ignored.
Approximation 2. The enthalpies of the two phases are uniform over the cross-sections.
Approximation 3. The density of the two phases, the latent heat of vaporization, C_0, and V_{vj} are all constant (over the subdomain). The values of the latter two are obtained from correlation equations, as functions of α alone.
Approximation 4. The interface between vapor and liquid remains at saturation.
Approximation 5. All averages of products (except for $\langle \alpha j \rangle$ in Equation 22) are approximated as the product of the averages. Thus, for example, $\langle \alpha i_v \rangle$ is approximated as $\langle \alpha \rangle \langle i_v \rangle$.

Even with Approximation 5, there are three propagation velocities, V_x, in equations of the form $\partial x / \partial t + V_x \partial x / \partial z = \Gamma_x$. The liquid and vapor enthalpies are propagated at velocities V_ℓ and V_v respectively, and void is propagated at V_α, where

$$V_\alpha = C_0 \langle j \rangle + V_{vj} \tag{24}$$

Although not an essential approximation, the propagation velocities for i_v and i_ℓ have, for simplicity, been both approximated by V_α. While this is not true in general, for problems in which the drift-flux formulation is generally satisfactory V_{vj} will be small so that little error is introduced. There are situations, however (e.g. countercurrent or stratified flows) where this approximation will not be adequate. Further discussion of the validity of the drift flux formulation and the assumed equality of the propagation velocities may be found in Khater, Nicoll and Raithby [18], and Khater and Raithby [39].

As pointed out in the Introduction, the effects of pressure gradients along the channel have been ignored. Pressure would normally be specified as a boundary condition at the inlet or outlet and this pressure is then taken as the system pressure. Such a treatment implies that the pressure popagates at infinite velocity.

Equations 9–15 can be transformed to a set of drift-flux equations, which become greatly simplified when the previous approximations are introduced. Only the resulting equations will be reported here in terms of the following non-dimensional parameters:

$$z^* = \frac{z}{L}; \quad \tau^* = \frac{tV_a}{L}; \quad i_\ell^* = \frac{\langle i_\ell \rangle}{\lambda_0}; \quad i_g^* = \frac{\langle i_g \rangle}{\lambda_0}$$

$$\alpha^* = \frac{C_0 \, \Delta\rho \langle \alpha \rangle}{\rho_\ell}; \quad \Gamma^* = \frac{C_0 \, \Delta\rho L}{\rho_\ell \rho_g V_a} \langle \Gamma \rangle; \quad V_a^* = \frac{V_a}{V_a} \tag{25}$$

where V_a is a reference velocity, λ_0 is a reference latent heat of vaporization and L is a reference length (usually the channel length). The equations resulting from combining Equations 9 and 10 are

$$\frac{D\alpha^*}{D\tau^*} = (1 - \alpha^*)\Gamma^* \tag{26}$$

$$V_a^* = \frac{Dz^*}{D\tau^*} = (V_a^*)_0 + C_0 \int_0^{z^*} \left(\frac{\Gamma^*}{C_0}\right) dz^* \tag{27}$$

where $(V_a^*)_0$ is the specified instantaneous value of V_a^* at $z^* = 0$. The following vapor generation equation is obtained by adding Equations 11 and 12 and combining the result with Equations 9 and 10, assuming that any vapor produced remains at saturation conditions:

$$\Gamma^* = \frac{1}{(i_g^* - i_\ell^*)} \cdot \frac{C_0 \, \Delta\rho L}{\rho_\ell \rho_g V_a} \cdot \left\{ \frac{q_w'' P_h}{A_c \lambda_0} + \frac{\dot{P}}{\lambda_0} - \frac{\rho_\ell \rho_g \dot{P} C_g}{\lambda_0 C_0 \, \Delta\rho} \alpha^* - \frac{\rho_\ell V_a}{L} \left(1 - \frac{\rho_\ell \alpha^*}{C_0 \, \Delta\rho}\right) \frac{Di_\ell^*}{D\tau^*} \right\} \tag{28}$$

where $\quad \dot{P} \triangleq \dfrac{\partial p}{\partial t}$

and $\quad C_g \triangleq \dfrac{di_g}{dp}$

The propagation equation for the liquid enthalpy, obtained from Equations 12 and 15 is

$$\frac{Di_\ell^*}{D\tau^*} = \frac{L}{\rho_\ell V_a} \cdot \frac{1}{\left(1 - \dfrac{\rho_\ell \alpha^*}{C_0 \, \Delta\rho}\right)} \cdot \left\{ \frac{q_w'' P_{h\ell}}{A_c \lambda_0} + \frac{q_{\ell i}'' P_i}{A_c \lambda_0} - \frac{\rho_\ell \rho_g V_a}{C_0 \, \Delta\rho L} \Gamma^*(i_f^* - i_\ell^*) + \left(1 - \frac{\rho_\ell \alpha^*}{C_0 \, \Delta\rho}\right) \frac{\dot{P}}{\lambda_0} \right\} \tag{29}$$

Under the conditions just mentioned, (the vapor produced remains at saturation conditions) the propagation equation for vapor enthalpy becomes

$$\frac{Di_g^*}{D\tau^*} = C_g \dot{P} L / (V_a \lambda_0) \tag{30}$$

Solution Procedure

The fluid in the channel is initially divided into NELM elements, and a time step $\Delta\tau^*$ is chosen. The procedure uses analytical solutions to the previous equations, which are valid over the spatial subdomain occupied by the element and over the time $\Delta\tau^*$, to find the liquid enthalpy, the void, and the position of each element at the end of the time step. Some iteration is required because the analytical solutions used for different variables are coupled. The element, or some elements, near outflow boundaries may leave during the $\Delta\tau^*$ time interval. In addition, one or more elements are made to enter at the inflow boundary, or boundaries, during $\Delta\tau^*$. The final position and properties of each element at the end of the time step are the initial conditions for the next time step. The number of elements that are required, and the allowable time step, are dictated by the extent of the spatial and temporal domains over which the analytical solutions are valid. For the analytical solutions used, often very few elements and very large $\Delta\tau^*$'s are sufficient to make the global solution independent of NELM and $\Delta\tau^*$.

Before deriving the analytical solutions, it is necessary to describe the subscripting used. The time-vs-displacement trajectories of fluid elements in the channel are sketched in Figure 4. At time level i the centers of the elements in the channel are shown ((i, 1), (i, 2), . . ., (i, j), . . . (i, NELM)). At τ_{i+1}^*, $\Delta\tau^*$ later, their positions have changed as shown; one element has been "lost" through the $z^* = 1$ boundary and two have been added through $z^* = 0$. Attention is focussed on the jth element in the time interval $\tau_i^* \leq \tau^* \leq \tau_{i+1}^*$. A doubly subscripted variable (e.g. α_{ij}^*) refers to its value at the point (i, j); a single subscript (e.g. α_j^*) refers to the value of the variable at a general time τ^* within the time interval under consideration.

Some additional simplifications are introduced into Equations 27–29, which are valid over restricted subdomains of τ^* and z^*, in order to obtain the required analytical solutions. For a particular element over the $\Delta\tau^*$ interval, these are:

Approximation 6. The inlet velocity is a linear function of time over the τ^* interval, i.e. $(V_z^*)_0 = (V_z^*)_{0i} + (\dot{V}_z^*)_0(\tau^* - \tau_i^*)$, where $(V_z^*)_{0i}$ is the inlet velocity at τ_i^* and $(\dot{V}_z^*)_0$ is the average rate of change of $(V_z^*)_0$ with τ^* over the $\Delta\tau^*$ interval.

Approximation 7. The saturation enthalpies of both phases are linear functions of pressure (over the subdomain).

Approximation 8. The wall heat flux is constant (over the subdomain).

Approximation 9. In calculating Γ^* from Equation 28, $i_g^* - i_\ell^*$ is replaced by the average value for the jth element over the time interval (i.e. $(\overline{i_g^* - i_\ell^*})$) and $Di_\ell^*/D\tau^*$ is replaced by $((i_\ell^*)_{i+1j} - (i_\ell^*)_{ij})/\Delta\tau^*$.

With these approximations, Equations 26 and 28 can be combined to give, for the jth element,

$$\frac{D\alpha_j^*}{D\tau^*} = a_\alpha + b_\alpha\alpha_j^* + c_\alpha(\alpha_j^*)^2 \qquad (31)$$

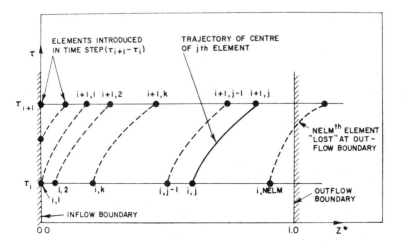

Figure 4. Schematic of the time versus displacement trajectories of the fluid elements in the flow channel.

where a_α, b_α, and c_α are constants over a particular subdomain (see Appendix). The initial conditions are $\alpha_j^* = \alpha_{ij}^*$ at $\tau^* = \tau_i^*$. The solution to Equation 31, which depends on the sign of $\Delta_\alpha \triangleq 4a_\alpha c_\alpha - b_\alpha^2$, is [43]

$$
\alpha_j^* = \begin{cases}
\dfrac{b_\alpha - \sqrt{-\Delta_\alpha} - (b_\alpha + \sqrt{-\Delta_\alpha}\,\exp[\sqrt{-\Delta_\alpha}\,(\tau^* + c_1)]}{2c_\alpha(\exp[\sqrt{-\Delta_\alpha}\,(\tau^* + c_1)] - 1)}; & \Delta_\alpha < 0 \\[4ex]
-\dfrac{1}{2c}\left(b + \dfrac{2}{\tau^* + c_2}\right); & \Delta_\alpha = 0 \\[4ex]
\dfrac{1}{2c_\alpha}\left\{\sqrt{\Delta_\alpha}\,\tan\left[\dfrac{\sqrt{\Delta_\alpha}\,(\tau^* + c_3)}{2}\right] - b_\alpha\right\}; & \Delta_\alpha > 0
\end{cases}
\tag{32}
$$

The details appear in the Appendix.

The position of this element at $\tau^* > \tau_i^*$ is obtained from Equation 27. The integral is approximated as

$$
\int_0^{z_j^*}\left(\frac{\Gamma^*}{C_0}\right)dz^* = \sum_{k=1}^{j-1}\left(\frac{\tilde{\Gamma}^*}{C_0}\right)_k (z_{ik+1}^* - z_{ik}^*) + \left(\frac{\tilde{\Gamma}^*}{C_0}\right)_j (z_j^* - z_{ij}^*)
$$

where $(\tilde{\Gamma}^*/C_0)_k$ is the value of $(\tilde{\Gamma}^*/C_0)$ at $\tau_i^* + \Delta\tau^*/2$ averaged over the range $z_{ik}^* \leq z^* \leq z_{ik+1}^*$. Introducing Approximation 6 and carrying out the integration yields the following position of the jth element as a function a τ^*:

$$
z_j^* = z_{ij}^* + \frac{\exp[\tilde{\Gamma}_j^*(\tau^* - \tau_i^*)] - 1}{\Gamma_j^*}\left\{(V_\alpha^*)_0 + \frac{(\dot{V}_\alpha^*)_0}{\Gamma_j^*} + C_{0j}\sum_{k=1}^{j-1}\left(\frac{\tilde{\Gamma}^*}{C_0}\right)_k (z_{ik+1}^* - z_{ik}^*)\right\}
$$
$$
- \frac{(\dot{V}_\alpha^*)_0}{\Gamma_j^*}\{\tau^* - \tau_i^*\exp(\tilde{\Gamma}_j^*(\tau^* - \tau_i^*))\}
\tag{33}
$$

When $\tilde{\Gamma}_j^*$ approaches zero, the exponentials in Equation 33 are replaced by their Taylor series expansion. Some details related to the derivation of Equation 33 are contained in the Appendix.

The solution to the liquid enthalpy equation (Equation 29) for the jth fluid element is now described. Substituting Equation 28 for Γ^* into Equation 29, replacing α^* over the jth element during the interval $\Delta\tau^*$ by $\overline{\alpha_j^*}$, and using Approximation 7, the liquid enthalpy equation becomes

$$
\frac{Di_{\ell j}^*}{D\tau^*} = k_1 + k_2\tau^* + k_3 i_{\ell j}^* + k_4\tau^{*2} + k_5\tau^* i_{\ell j}^* + k_6(i_{\ell j}^*)^2
\tag{34}
$$

The values of k_1 to k_6 are constants over the jth element and over $\Delta\tau^*$. The series solution to this equation is

$$
i_{\ell j}^* = \sum_{n=1}^\infty nA_n\tau^{*n-1}\Big/\left\{-k_6\left(1 + \sum_{n=1}^\infty A_n\tau^{*n}\right)\right\}
\tag{35}
$$

Again, the details related to Equations 34 and 35 are contained in the Appendix.

For the element closest to $z^* = 0$, and starting at τ_i^*, the closed-form solutions are used to determine the position and properties of the element at τ_{i+1}^*. This process is then repeated for each element in the channel. Presuming that solutions have already been obtained for the first $j - 1$ elements, the solution for the jth element is established as follows:

Step 1. The enthalpy of the liquid in the jth element is found from Equation 35. The constants contain the average void α_j^*, which is not yet known. It was found that $\overline{\alpha_j^*}$ could be replaced, without appreciable error, by α_{ij}^*. This avoids the need for iteration.

Step 2. With $Di_\ell^*/D\tau^*$ known (see Approximation 9), the constants in Equation 32 can be evaluated and α_{i+1j}^* found.

Step 3. The values of $(i_\ell^*)_{i+1j}$, Γ_{i+1j}^* and α_{i+1j}^* (i.e., at τ_{i+1}^*) are now known and the position of the element at τ_{i+1}^* is sought. This is found from Equation 33. Iteration is needed because the averaged quantities denoted by (~) depend on the final position of the element (i.e. on z_{i+1j}^*).

These solutions then serve as initial conditions for the advancement of the solution over the next time step.

In order to use this method, care is needed in the selection of expressions for C_0, V_{vj}, P_i, $h_{\ell i}$, h_0, etc., since the accuracy of the predictions depends on the expressions chosen. The predictions of the aforementioned model were compared with both steady and transient subcooled boiling experimental data, and with contrived problems where no experimental data were available [18, 32, 44].

Figure 5 displays the comparisons between the predictions of the method, and experimental mass hold-up data reported by Primoli and Hancox [45]. The measurements were done for blow down from a system consisting of an unheated feeder section, a heated section of larger diameter, and an

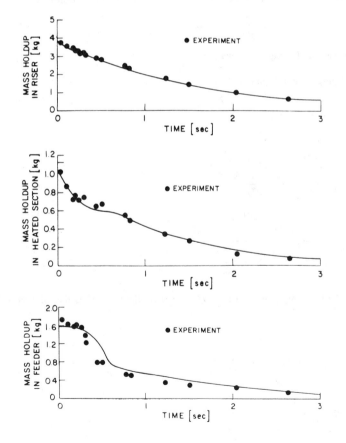

Figure 5. Comparisons between the predicted mass hold-up and the experimental data of Primoli and Hancox [45] for a subcooled boiling blowdown test.

unheated riser of still larger diameter. At the high initial pressure the feeder flow was highly subcooled, while fluid in the riser was near saturation. At the start of the transient the riser outlet was
blocked, the feeder was opened to atmosphere, and the wall heat flux was maintained constant in
the middle section, resulting in flow reversal and discharge back through the feeder. Because of the
higher fluid temperature in the riser, flashing may be expected to occur first in the riser as well as
at the open end of the feeder. As the system pressure becomes lower, the region of flashing may be
expected to move into the heated section. The data reported included the mass hold-up in the three
sections and pressures at various locations in the system.

The boundary conditions applied in the model were zero velocity at the riser exit, and a system
pressure equal to the average pressure in the riser section. Because of the rapid depressurization,
the flow will tend to be homogeneous and thus a value of unity has been assigned to C_0, and a
value of zero to V_{vj}. The heat transfer coefficient $h_{\ell i}$ was assumed equal to h_0. Equation 8 was
used for h_0. Other details may be found in Khater, Nicoll, and Raithby [32].

With reference to Figure 5, it is seen that in general the agreement is good. The only significant
discrepancy occurs in the feeder mass hold-up at approximately 0.4 second, where the experimental
values are lower than the predicted values. This is likely a consequence of the assumption of spatially
uniform pressure, which underestimates flashing in the feeder. Mass balances on the system showed
that the procedure conserved mass closely (within 1%) throughout the transient.

APPENDIX

Solution of the Void Propagation Equation

The void propagation, Equation 31, is

$$\frac{D\alpha_j^*}{D\tau} = a_\alpha + b_\alpha \alpha_j^* + C_\alpha (\alpha_j^*)^2 \tag{36}$$

where

$$a_\alpha = \frac{C_0 \Delta\rho L}{\rho_\ell \rho_g V_a} \frac{\dfrac{q_w'' P_h}{A_c} + \dfrac{\dot{P}}{\lambda_0} - \dfrac{\rho_\ell V_a}{L}\left(\dfrac{\Delta i_\ell^*}{\Delta\tau^*}\right)}{(i_g^* - i_\ell^*)}$$

$$c_\alpha = -\frac{1}{\rho_g} \frac{\left[\rho_\ell\left(\dfrac{\Delta i_\ell^*}{\Delta\tau^*}\right) - \rho_g \dfrac{C_g \dot{P} L}{V_a \lambda_0}\right]}{(i_g^* - i_\ell^*)} \tag{37}$$

$$b_\alpha = -(a_\alpha + c_\alpha)$$

Subject to the boundary condition $\alpha^* = \alpha_{ij}^*$ at $\tau^* = \tau_i^*$, Equation 32 is the solution to Equation
36 where

$$\Delta_\alpha = 4a_\alpha c_\alpha - b_\alpha^2$$

$$c_1 = \frac{1}{\sqrt{-\Delta_\alpha}} \ln\frac{b_\alpha + 2c_\alpha\alpha_{ij}^* - \sqrt{-\Delta_\alpha}}{b_\alpha + 2c_\alpha\alpha_{ij}^* + \sqrt{-\Delta_\alpha}} - \tau_i^* \tag{38}$$

$$c_2 = -\left(\tau_i^* + \frac{2}{b_\alpha + 2c_\alpha\alpha_{ij}^*}\right)$$

$$c_3 = \frac{2}{\sqrt{\Delta_\alpha}} \tan^{-1}\left(\frac{b_\alpha + 2c_\alpha\alpha_{ij}^*}{\sqrt{\Delta_\alpha}}\right) - \tau_i^*$$

Solution of the Space-Time Differential Equation

Equation 27 establishes the position of each element at the end of the time step. Rewriting this equation for the jth element

$$\frac{dz_j^*}{d\tau^*} = V_{\alpha j}^* = (V_\alpha^*)_0 + C_{0j} \int_0^{z_j^*} \left(\frac{\Gamma^*}{C_0}\right) dz^* \tag{39}$$

As discussed in the text, the integral can be approximated by

$$\int_0^{z_j^*} \left(\frac{\Gamma^*}{C_0}\right) dz^* = \sum_{k=1}^{j-1} \left(\frac{\tilde{\Gamma}^*}{C_0}\right)_k (z_{ik+1}^* - z_{ik}^*) + \left(\frac{\tilde{\Gamma}^*}{C_0}\right)_j (z_j^* - z_{ij}^*)$$

Equation 39 thus becomes, using Approximation 6 in the text,

$$\frac{dz_j^*}{d\tau^*} - \tilde{\Gamma}_j^* z_j^* = (V_\alpha^*)_{0i} + (V_\alpha^*)_0 (\tau^* - \tau_i^*) + C_j \tag{40}$$

where

$$c_j = c_{0j} \sum_{k=1}^{j-1} \left(\frac{\tilde{\Gamma}^*}{C_0}\right)_k (z_{ik+1}^* - z_{ik}^*) - (\tilde{\Gamma}^*) z_{ij}^*$$

Equation 40 is a first order, linear, non-homogeneous ordinary differential equation; its solution given by

$$z_j^* e^{\int -(\Gamma_j^*) d\tau^*} = \int e^{\int -(\Gamma_j^*) d\tau^*} ((V_\alpha^*)_{0i} + (\dot{V}_\alpha^*)_0 (\tau^* - \tau_i^*) + c_j) d\tau^* + c_4$$

Subject to the boundary condition $z^* = z_{ij}^*$ at $\tau^* = \tau_i^*$, the above integration yields Equation 33 in the text.

Solution of the Liquid Enthalpy Propagation Equation

Equation 34 is the liquid enthalpy propagation equation

$$\frac{Di_{\ell j}^*}{D\tau^*} = k_1 + k_2\tau^* + k_3 i_{\ell j}^* + k_4\tau^{*2} + k_5\tau^* i_{\ell j}^* + k_6(i_{\ell j}^*)^2 \tag{41}$$

Defining the constants

$$A_\ell = \left(\frac{q_w'' P_h}{A_c} + \dot{P}\left(1 - \frac{\rho_g \rho_\ell}{\Delta\rho C_0} C_g \tilde{\alpha}^*\right)\right)\Big/ \lambda$$

$$B_\ell = \left(\frac{q_w'' P_{h\ell}}{A_c} + \left(1 - \frac{\rho_\ell}{C_0 \Delta\rho} \tilde{\alpha}^*\right)\dot{P}\right)\Big/ \lambda$$

$$C_\ell = \frac{h_{\ell i} P_i \lambda_0}{A_c C p_\ell \lambda} \tag{42}$$

$$D_\ell = -C_f \dot{P} \frac{L}{V_\alpha \lambda_0}$$

$$E_\ell = -C_g \dot{P} \frac{L}{V_a \lambda_0}; F_\ell = \frac{L}{V_a \rho_\ell \left(1 - \dfrac{\rho_\ell}{C_0 \Delta \rho} \tilde{\alpha}^*\right)} \tag{43}$$

the constants k_1 through k_6 are

$$k_1 = (-A_\ell i_{fi}^* + B_\ell i_{gi}^* + C_\ell i_{fi}^* i_{gi}^*)F_\ell$$

$$k_2 = (D_\ell A_\ell - E_\ell B_\ell - C_\ell D_\ell i_{fi}^* - C_\ell E_\ell i_{gi}^*)F_\ell$$

$$k_3 = (A_\ell - B_\ell - C_\ell(i_{fi}^* + i_{gi}^*))F_\ell$$

$$k_4 = C_\ell D_\ell E_\ell F_\ell$$

$$k_5 = (D_\ell + E_\ell)C_\ell F_\ell$$

$$k_6 = C_\ell F_\ell \tag{44}$$

Equation 41 has the form

$$(i_\ell^*)' + P(\tau^*)i_\ell^* + Q(\tau^*)(i_\ell^*)^2 = R(\tau^*)$$

which is a Ricatti equation [43]. Introducing the transformation $i_\ell^* = \dfrac{u'}{uQ}$, Equation 41 becomes

$$u'' + (b_0 + b_1\tau^*)u' + (b_2 + b_3\tau^* + b_4(\tau^*)^2)u = 0 \tag{45}$$

where

$$b_0 = -k_3; \qquad b_1 = -k_5; \qquad b_2 = k_1 k_6;$$
$$b_3 = k_2 k_6; \qquad b_4 = k_4 k_6 \tag{46}$$

To solve Equation 45 assume a series solution of the form

$$u = \sum_{n=0}^{\infty} a_n(\tau^*)^{m+n} \tag{47}$$

Differentiating twice, and substituting into Equation 45 yields

$$\sum_{n=0}^{\infty} a_n(n + m)(n + m - 1)(\tau^*)^{n+m-2} + b_0 \sum_{n=1}^{\infty} a_{n-1}(n + m - 1)(\tau^*)^{n+m-2}$$
$$+ \sum_{n=2}^{\infty} [b_2 + (n + c - 2)b_1]a_{n-2}(\tau^*)^{n+m-2} + b_3 \sum_{n=3}^{\infty} (\tau^*)^{n+m-2} + \sum_{n=4}^{\infty} a_{n-4}(\tau^*)^{n+m-2} = 0 \tag{48}$$

Equating the sum of the coefficients of the different powers of τ to zero starting with the lowest power ($n = 0$) we find, from the $n = 0$ and $n = 1$ equations, that $m = 0$ and that both a_0 and a_1 are arbitrary constants. The remainder of the coefficients in the series are found in the same manner and are listed below. To find i_ℓ^* substitute Equation 47 into the transformation used. This yields

$$i_\ell^* = \frac{\displaystyle\sum_{n=1}^{\infty} n a_n \tau^{*n-1}}{-k_6 \displaystyle\sum_{n=0}^{\infty} a_n \tau^{*n}} \tag{49}$$

Dividing by a_0, and defining the coefficients $A_n \triangleq \dfrac{a_n}{a_0}$ yields Equation 35 in the text where A_1 is an arbitrary constant and can be found from the boundary condition $i_{\ell j}^* = i_{\ell ij}^*$ at $\tau^* = \tau_0^*$. In the case where $\tau_0^* = 0$, $A_1 = -k_6 i_{\ell ij}^*$. The other coefficients are

$$A_2 = -(b_0 A_1 + b_2)/2$$

$$A_3 = -(2b_0 A_2 + (b_2 + b_1)A_1 + b_3)/6 \tag{50}$$

$$A_n = -((n-1)b_0 A_{n-1} + (b_2 + (n-2)b_1)A_{n-2} + b_3 A_{n-3} + b_4 A_{n-4})/(n(n-1)); \quad n \geq 4$$

NOTATION

A_c	cross-sectional area, m²	$\dot{p}$	$\partial p/\partial t$, MPa/s
C_f	di_f/dp, J/Kg MPa	q''	heat flux, W/m²
C_g	di_g/dp, J/kg MPa	Re	$(\rho_\ell j D_h)/\mu_f$, Reynolds number, dimensionless
C_0	$\langle \alpha j \rangle/\langle \alpha \rangle \langle j \rangle$; Zuber's distribution parameter, dimensionless	T	temperature, K
C_p	specific heat, J/kg K	ΔT_i	inlet subcooling, K
D_h	hydraulic diameter, m	t	time, sec
f	friction factor	V	velocity, m/s
G	mass flux, kg/m² s	V_{vj}	$V_v - j$, m/s
h	coefficient of heat transfer, W/m²K	V_α	$C_0 \langle j \rangle + V_{vj}$, m/s
i	enthalpy, J/kg	V_α^*	V_α/V_a, dimensionless
i*	i/λ_0, (dimensionless)	$\dot{V}_\alpha^*$	average rate of change of $(V_\alpha^*)_0$ with τ^*
j	superficial velocity, m/s	y	height of interface above channel bottom, m
k	thermal conductivity, W/m K		
L	length, m	z	axial position, m
P	perimeter, m	z_0	boiling boundary, m
Pr	Prandtl number	z*	z/L, dimensionless
p	pressure, MPa		

Greek Symbols

α	void fraction, dimensionless	ρ	density, kg/m³
α^*	$C_0 \Delta\rho \langle \alpha \rangle/\rho_\ell$, dimensionless	$\Delta\rho$	$\rho_\ell - \rho_g$, kg/m³
Γ	rate of vapor generation, kg/m³	τ_i	shear stress, MPa
Γ^*	$(C_0 \Delta\rho_\ell/\rho_\ell \rho_g V_\alpha)$, dimensionless	τ^*	tV_α/L, dimensionless
λ	latent heat of vaporization, J/kg	$\Delta\tau^*$	$\tau^* - \tau_i^*$, dimensionless
λ_0	reference latent heat of vaporization, J/kg	θ	channel inclination to the horizontal, deg

Subscripts

a	arbitrary value	hv	heated vapor
b	boiling boundary	i	initial or interface
f	saturated liquid	ij	initial for the jth element
g	saturated vapor	j	the jth element
h	heated	ℓ	liquid
hℓ	heated liquid	ℓi	liquid interface

vi	vapor interface	v	vapor
o	channel inlet	w	wall
oi	initial value at the channel inlet	wℓ	wetted liquid
s	saturation	wv	wetted vapor
sp	single phase		

Superscripts

n   new time level
0   old time level

REFERENCES

1. Griffith, P., Clark, J. A., and Rohsenow, M. W., "Void Volumes in Subcooled Boiling Systems," paper 58-HT-19, American Society of Mechanical Engineers, 1958.
2. Zuber, N., and Kroeger, P. G., "An Analysis of the Effects of Various Parameters on the Average Void Fractions in Subcooled Boiling," *International Journal of Heat and Mass Transfer*, vol. 11, Feb. 1968, pp. 211–233.
3. Hancox, W. T., and Nicoll, W. B., "A General Technique for the Prediction of Void Distributions in Non-Steady Two-Phase Forced Convection," *International Journal of Heat and Mass Transfer*, vol. 14, 1971, pp. 1377–1394.
4. Bowring, R. W., "Physical Model Based on Bubble Detachment and Calculations of Steam Voidages in the Subcooled Region of a Heated Channel," OECD Halden Reactor Project, Report HPR-10, 1963.
5. Levy S., "Forced Convection Subcooled Boiling: Prediction of Vapor Volumetric Fraction," General Electric Company, Report GEAP-5157, 1966.
6. Saha, P., and Zuber, N., "Point of Net Vapor Generation and Vapor Void Fraction in Subcooled Boiling," Fifth International Heat Transfer Conference, Paris, vol. 4, Sept. 1974, pp. 175–179.
7. Staub, R. W., "The Void Fraction in Subcooled Boiling—Prediction of the Initial Point of Net Vapor Generation," *Journal of Heat Transfer, Trans. ASME*, vol. 90, no. 1, 1968, pp. 151–158.
8. Madejski, J., "Vapor Bubble Departure Conditions in Flow Boiling," *Trans. Inst. Fluid Flow Machining*, Polish Acad. Sciences, vol. 49, 1970, pp. 3–22.
9. Betten, P. R., and Paul, F. W., "Determination of the Point of Net Vapor Generation in Forced Convection Subcooled Boiling," ASME paper 76-WA/HT-86, 1976.
10. Maurer, G. W., "A Method of Predicting Steady-State Boiling Fractions in Reactor Channels," WAPD-BT-19, 1956.
11. Egen, R. A., et al., "Vapor Formation and Behavior in Boiling Transfer," Battle Memorial Institute Report, BMI-1168, 1957.
12. Marchaterre, J. F., et al., "Natural and Forced Circulation Boiling Studies," ANL-5735, 1960.
13. Christensen, H., "Power to Void Transfer Function," ANL-6385, 1961.
14. Foglia, J. J., et al., "Boiling Water Void Distribution and Slip Ratio in Heated Channels," Battle Memorial Institute Report BMI-1517, 1961.
15. Rouhani, S. Z., "Void Measurements in the Region of Subcooled and Low Quality Boiling," Paper #5 presented at the Symposium on Two-Phase Flow held at Exeter University, 21–21 June 1965.
16. Bartolomei, C. C., and Chanturiya, V. M., "Experimental Study of True Void Fraction when Boiling Subcooled Water in Vertical Tubes," *Thermal Engineering*, Vol. 14, No. 2, 1967, pp. 123–128.
17. Roy, R. P., and Yadigaroglu, C., "An Investigation of Heat Transport in Oscillatory Subcooled Flow," *Journal of Heat Transfer, Trans. ASME*, vol. 98, 1976, pp. 630–637.
18. Khater, H. A., Nicoll, W. B., and Raithby, G. D., "Prediction of Transient Non-equilibrium Two-Phase Flows: An Extension to the FAST Technique," Electric Power Research Institute, Report EPRI-NP-1339, vols. 1 & 2, 1980.

19. Delhaye, J. M., "Jump Conditions and Entropy Sources in Two-Phase Systems, Local Instant Formulation," *International Journal of Multiphase Flow*, vol. 1, 1974, pp. 395–409.
20. Ishii, M., "Thermo-Fluid Dynamic Theory of Two-Phase Flow," Eyrolles, Paris, 1975.
21. Bouré, J. A., "Mathematical Modeling and the Two-Phase Constitutive Equations," European Two-Phase Flow Group Meeting, Haifa, Israel, 1975.
22. Delhaye, J. M., "Equations Fondamentals des Ecoulements Diphasiques," CEA-R-3429, 1968.
23. Vernier, Ph., and Delhaye, J. M., "General Two-Phase Flow Equations Applied to the Thermohydrodynamics of Boiling Water Nuclear Reactors," *Energie Primaire*, vol. 4, no. 1–2, 1968, pp. 5–46.
24. Kocamustafaaogullari, G., "Thermo-Fluid Dynamics of Separated Two-Phase Flow," Ph.D. thesis, School of Mechanical Engineering, Georgia Institute of Technology, Atlanta, Georgia, 1971.
25. Teletov, S. G., "Two-Phase Flow Hydrodynamics. 1. Hydrodynamics and Energy Equations," Bull. Moscow University, vol. 2, 1958 (in Russian).
26. Zuber, N., and Findlay, J. A., "Average Volumetric Concentration in Two-Phase Flow Systems," *Journal of Heat Transfer, Trans, ASME*, vol. 87, 1966, pp. 871–895.
27. Zuber, N., and Staub, F. W., "The Propagation and the Wave Form of the Vapor Volumetric Concentration in Boiling, Forced Convection System Under Oscillatory Conditions," *International Journal of Heat and Mass Transfer*, vol. 9, 1966, pp. 871–895.
28. Zuber, N., Staub, F. W., Bijwaard, G., and Kroeger, P. G., "Steady State and Transient Void Fraction in Two-Phase Flow Systems," GEAP-5417, 1967.
29. Yadigaroglu, G., and Lahey, R. T., "On Various Forms of the Conservation Equations in Two-Phase Flow," *International Journal of Multiphase Flow*, vol. 2, April 1976.
30. Hancox, W. T., and Nicoll, W. B., "Prediction of Time-Dependent Diabatic Two-Phase Water Flows," *Progress in Heat and Mass Transfer*, vol. 6, Pergamon Press, 1972.
31. Shiralkar, B. S., Schnebly, L. E., Lahey, R. T., Jr., "Variation of the Vapor Volumetric Fraction During Flow and Power Transient," *Nuclear Engineering and Design*, vol. 25, 1973, pp. 350–368.
32. Khater, H. A., Nicoll, W. B., and Raithby, G. D., "The FAST Procedure for Predicting Transient Subcooled Two-Phase Flows," *International Journal of Multiphase Flow*, vol. 8, no. 1, 1982, pp. 261–278.
33. Ransom, V. H., et al., "RELAP5/MOD '0' Code Description," CDAP-TR-057, 1979.
34. Safety Code Development Group, "TRAC-PIA: An advanced Best-Estimate Computer Program for PWR LOCA Analysis," LA-777-MS, 1979.
35. Ferch, R. L., "Method of Characteristics Solutions for Nonequilibrium Transient Flow Boiling," *International Journal of Multiphase Flow*, vol. 5, 1979, pp. 265–279.
36. Hughes, E. D., Lyzkowski, R. W., and McFadden, J. H., "An Evaluation of State-of-the-Art Two-Velocity, Two-Phase Flow Models and Their Applicability to Nuclear Reactor Transient Analysis," Electric Power Research Institute, Report No. EPRI-NP-143, 1976.
37. Hancox, W. T., Ferch, R. L., Liu, W. S., and Nieman, R. E., "One-Dimensional Models for Transient Gas-Liquid Flows in Ducts," *International Journal of Multiphase Flow*, vol. 6, 1980, pp. 25–40.
38. Wallis, G. B., *One-Dimensional Two-Phase Flow*, McGraw-Hill Book Company, New York, 1969.
39. Khater, H. A., and Raithby, G. D., "Development of a Two-Velocity Model for Transient Nonequilibrium Two-Phase Flow Based on the FAST Approach," Electric Power Research Institute, Report No. EPRI-NP-1732, March 1981.
40. Agee, L. J., Paulsen, M. P., and Hughes, E. D., "Equations of State for Nonequilibrium Two-Phase Flow Models," *Proceedings of the Third CSNI Specialist Meeting*, Pasadena, California, 1981, pp. 287–306.
41. Jiji, L. M., and Clark, J. A., "Bubble Boundary Layer and Temperature Profiles for Forced Convection Boiling in Channel Flow," *ASME Journal of Heat Transfer*, February 1964, pp. 50–58.
42. Ahmad, S. Y., "Axial Distribution of Bulk Temperature and Void Fraction in a Heated Channel with Inlet Subcooling," *ASME Journal of Heat Transfer*, November 1970, pp. 595–609.

43. Gradshteyn, I. S., and Ryzhik, I. M., *Tables of Integrals Series and Products*, Academic Press Inc., New York, San Francisco, London, 1965.
44. Khater, H. A., Raithby, G. D., and Merilo, M., "Analysis of Westinghouse Controlled Transient Heat Transfer Tests Using the FAST Code," *Proceedings of the Second International Topical Meeting on Nuclear Reactor Thermal Hydraulics*, Santa Barbara, California, vol. 1, January 11–14, 1983, pp. 519–527.
45. Primoli, A., and Hancox, W. T., "An Experimental Investigation of Subcooled Blowdown with Heat Addition," *Proceedings OECD Committee for Safety of Nuclear Installations Specialist Meeting in Two-Phase Flow*, Toronto, 1976.

CHAPTER 44

PREDICTING QUENCH FRONT VELOCITY IN THE REWETTING OF HOT SURFACES

E. Oliveri, F. Castiglia, S. Taibi, and G. Vella

Istituto di Applicazioni e Impianti Nucleari
Facoltà di Ingegneria
Università di Palermo, Viale delle Scienze
Palermo, Italy

CONTENTS

INTRODUCTION

Rewetting is the re-establishment of liquid in contact with a dryed surface, the initial temperature of which is higher than the so-called *rewet temperature*. Consequently, the hot surface experiences a rapid cooling. It is worth noting, however, that an effective cooling is attained, before the liquid-solid contact is made, by a process that entails complex heat transfer phenomena between the surface and the coolant as well conduction into the solid. Such a process, which precedes rewetting, is often termed "quenching" and initiates at a temperature higher than the rewetting.

It should be noted, however, that since both the "rewet temperature" and the "quench temperature" are not precisely known, most authors consider the two phases as indistinct and characterized by only one temperature. This assumption is maintained in this chapter. The rewetting or quenching of hot surfaces has been a subject of great importance in many engineering branches (for example, in the quenching of the steels or in the drying out of boiler tubes) and has gained considerable interest in recent years due to its fundamental importance in the emergency core cooling of nuclear water reactors following a postulated loss-of-coolant accident (LOCA).

In vertical tube, slab, annulus, or rod bundle fuel element, the coolant may be admitted either from above (top flooding—rewetting by a falling liquid film, relevant to BWR spray cooling) or from the base of the channel (bottom flooding—rewetting by an upflow of water relevant to BWR and PWR core reflooding).

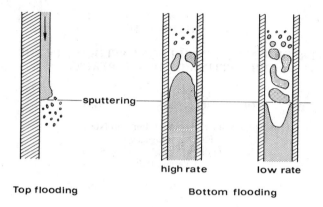

Figure 1. Physical phenomena in rewetting.

Figure 1 depicts the physical processes that occur in the case of top flooding and in that of bottom flooding. In the first case, initial cooling at the top of the channel allows a liquid film to form. The liquid front advances into a high-temperature region by cooling the preceding solid surface via axial heat conduction to the wet-wall region. At the front, the film is violently thrown off the surface. The ejection of the film from the wall has been termed "sputtering". The sputtering region (or quench front) is typically very narrow and, staying at a constant temperature*, proceeds down the surface at a nearly uniform velocity that is, among other factors, a function of the initial surface temperature.

The physical processes that occur with bottom flooding are different, depending on whether the rate of admission of coolant to the channel is high or low. At *low* flooding rates an annular flow region is formed, with the quench front being marked by the burnout transition between the hot wall, liquid-deficient region, and the climbing liquid film. At *high* flooding rates the liquid level in the channel rises more rapidly than the quench front and a region of film boiling (inverted annular region) is formed. The quench front is marked in this instance by the point of collapse of the thin vapor film.

While the falling-film rewetting is conduction-controlled, the bottom flooding rewetting may be partially inertia-controlled.

In the following we will deal especially with the rewetting by falling film, the bottom flooding having been investigated to a lesser extent. It should be stressed that, in any case, the main questions to be answered concern the evaluation of the front velocity, v, and the evaluation of the temperature distribution. In fact, the knowing v allows one to estimate the time required for an effective cooling of the hot surface(s); on the other hand, the temperature distribution allows the evaluation of the heat removed.

ANALYTICAL MODELS OF THE REWETTING BY FALLING FILM

The analytical models of the rewetting by falling film all involve solution of the Fourier heat conduction equation for specified boundary conditions representative of the heat transfer process at the surface of the solid. To make the problem tractable, it is necessary to introduce some simplifications.

A simplifying assumption, common to most of the proposed models, is to consider the solid to be an infinitely extended vertical slab of uniform thickness ε and with temperature-independent

---

* This temperature is termed "sputtering temperature" and for design purposes is often assumed to be the Leidenfrost temperature which, strictly speaking, is only an upper limit for the rewet temperature.

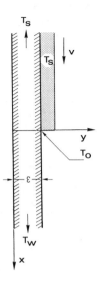

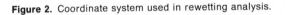

Figure 2. Coordinate system used in rewetting analysis.

physical properties. Other usual assumptions are

1. There is no heat generation within the slab.
2. The slab is initially at a constant temperature T_w.
3. The falling liquid film wets the front face of the slab up to the axial location where the surface temperature equals the sputtering temperature T_0, while the back face is thermally insulated.
4. The cooling water is at the saturation temperature T_s.
5. The heat transfer coefficient h is a known function of either the temperature difference between the surface and the coolant or the location with respect to the quench front.

On the basis of the previous assumptions *, when the initial transients have died out, one may assume the rate of the quench front progression to be a constant [1]; consequently, the temperature distribution viewed from a coordinate system moving along with the wet front is invariant with respect to such a system. Thus, the heat conduction equation for this two-dimensional problem, written in a time-independent form, results:

$$\frac{\partial^2 T}{\partial x^2} + \frac{\partial^2 T}{\partial y^2} + \frac{\rho c \varepsilon v}{k} \frac{\partial T}{\partial x} = 0 \tag{1}$$

where T is the local temperature, y is the coordinate measured into the slab from the back face, x is the coordinate along the direction of the advancing film, measured from the quench front (see Figure 2) and k, ρ, and c are the thermal conductivity, density, and specific heat, respectively.

In a non dimensional form Equation 1 becomes

$$\frac{\partial^2 \theta}{\partial \xi^2} + \frac{\partial^2 \theta}{\partial \eta^2} + u \frac{\partial \theta}{\partial \xi} = 0 \tag{2}$$

where $\theta = \dfrac{T - T_s}{T_w - T_s}; u = \dfrac{\rho c \varepsilon v}{k}; \xi = \dfrac{x}{\varepsilon}; \eta = \dfrac{y}{\varepsilon}$

---

* It is worth to note that a more realistic modeling requires the modification of some of these assumptions. For instance, it might be necessary to consider the internal heat source or the heat flux at the back face of the slab.

It is readily seen that, owing to the previous assumptions, the boundary conditions for Equation 2 are

$$
\left.
\begin{aligned}
&\text{a)} \quad \theta \to 0 \qquad && \text{for} \quad \xi \to -\infty \\[4pt]
&\text{b)} \quad \theta \to 1 \qquad && \text{for} \quad \xi \to +\infty \\[4pt]
&\text{c)} \quad \frac{\partial \theta}{\partial \eta} = 0 \qquad && \text{for} \quad \eta = 0 \\[4pt]
&\text{d)} \quad \frac{\partial \theta}{\partial \eta} = -B\theta \qquad && \text{for} \quad \eta = 1 \\[4pt]
&\text{e)} \quad \theta = \theta_0 \qquad && \text{for} \quad \eta = 1;\, \xi = 0
\end{aligned}
\right\}
\tag{3}
$$

where

$$
B = \frac{h\varepsilon}{k} = \text{the Biot number}
$$

$$
\theta_0 = \frac{T_0 - T_s}{T_w - T_s} = \text{the dimensionless sputtering temperature}
$$

A further simplification can be made if the slab is thin and the rewetting rate is low enough so that the temperature in the η-direction will remain nearly uniform. In this case the problem will be essentially one-dimensional and Equation 2 reduces to

$$
\frac{d^2\theta}{d\xi^2} + u\frac{d\theta}{d\xi} = B\theta
\tag{4}
$$

with the appropriate boundary conditions 3a, 3b, 3e. At this point, in order to carry out the integration of either the Equation 2 or 4, only the knowledge of the Biot number, as function of either θ or ξ is required, at least in principle.

However, the specification of such a function is a crucial question because the mechanism of boiling behind the quench front as well as that of the *precursory cooling* ahead the quench front, due to droplets flung off, are not fully understood. As a matter of fact, this lack of knowledge has led to various formulations for the heat transfer coefficient. In general, these formulations are given by various authors dividing the slab into a suitable number of axial regions and specifying the heat transfer coefficient for each region as a constant, as a function of the temperature difference between the surface and the coolant, and as a function of the location with respect to the quench front. Each author also gives the value of T_0 or of $(T_0 - T_s)$ to be used in connection with the pattern of h proposed.

ONE-DIMENSIONAL MODELS

A survey of the various one-dimensional models was made by Elias and Yadigaroglu [2] (see Table 1). In the following we shall briefly highlight some of these models. In the models of Semeria and Martinet [3] and Yamanouchi [4], only two regions are assumed: a dry region, ahead of the quench front, where B equals zero and a wet region, behind the quench front, where B is constant. For these assumptions the solution of Equation 4 results:

In the wet region ($\xi \leq 0$)

$$
\theta^-(\xi) = \theta_0 \exp(+\lambda\xi)
\tag{5a}
$$

Table 1
One-Dimensional Models for Top Flooding

Authors	Heat Transfer Coefficient Profile h (W/m²°C)	Sputtering Temperature $(T_0)(°C)$
Semeria & Martinet (1966) Yamanouchi (1968)	$h_2 = 2 \cdot 10^5 \div 10^6$, $h_3 = 0$	150
Thompson (1972)	$h_2 \cap \Delta T_s^3$, $h_3 = 0$	$T_s + 100$
Sun et al. (1974)	$h_2 = 1.7 \cdot 10^4$, $h_1 = 570$, $h_3 = 0$	260
Ishii (1975)	$h_2 = 4 \cdot 10^5$, $h_1 = h_{chf}$, $h_3 = 0$	$260 \div 390$
Sun et al. (1975)	$h_2 = 1.7 \cdot 10^4$, $h_3 = \dfrac{h_2}{N} \exp[-0.05 \cdot x]$	260
Chun & Chon (1975)	$h_2 = 2.56 \cdot 10^4$, $h_3 = 170$, $h_4 = 0$	260
Elias & Yadigaroglu (1977)	h_3, h_2, $h_2,... =$ boiling curve approximation, $h_1 = 170$	260

where

$$\lambda = -\frac{u}{2} + \left[\left(\frac{u}{2} \right)^2 + B \right]^{1/2}$$

In the dry region ($\xi > 0$)

$$\theta^+(\xi) = 1 - (1 - \theta_0) \exp(-u\xi) \qquad \text{(5b)}$$

The expression for u can be obtained by matching the two temperature gradients at $\xi = 0$:

$$u = \left[\frac{B\theta_0^2}{1 - \theta_0} \right]^{1/2} \tag{6}$$

The same expression for u was obtained by Duffey and Porthouse [1] carrying out, alternatively, a heat balance since the heat flowing across the surface to the water per unit time equals the enthalpy loss in slab per unit time.

Sun et al. [5] assumed a constant heat transfer coefficient in the wet region and an exponentially decaying one in the dry region. An implicit equation for the dimensionless wet front velocity was obtained by the condition of heat flux continuity at the quench front.

Thompson [6] assumed the heat transfer coefficient to be proportional to the temperature difference $(T - T_s)$ raised to the third power. The solution of the energy equation with the respective boundary conditions was obtained by applying a finite difference technique.

Elias and Yadigaroglu [7] carried out a computer oriented analysis by axially subdividing the slab in a number (as many as 12) of segments each with a constant h, accounting also for the precursory cooling. It should be noted that, in each segment, heat generation and heat flux at inner surface is considered. The aforementioned models are the most quoted. Note that none of them, except the Yamanouchi's one, furnishes an explicit formulation for the rewetting velocity.

REMARKS ON ONE-DIMENSIONAL MODELING

If one assumes $B = B(\xi)$, Equation 4 results in a second-order linear differential equation with non-constant coefficients which, with a fairly good approximation, can be integrated by the WKBJ [8] method.

If, on the contrary, one assumes $B = B(\theta)$, Equation 4 is non-linear and its integration by either analytical or numerical methods might result difficult.

However, when the main goal is to evaluate the rewetting velocity, it is possible to lower the difficulties inherent to such integration by resorting to a different formulation of Equation 4. In fact, if we use $D = d\theta/d\xi$ as the dependent variable, Equation 4 becomes [9]:

$$D \frac{dD}{d\theta} + uD = \theta \cdot B(\theta) = F(\theta) \tag{7}$$

i.e. a non-linear first-order differential equation.

It should be noted that for $F = 0$, Equation 7 exhibits a singularity, in that it furnishes two solutions:

$$D = 0 \quad \text{for} \quad \theta = 0 \tag{8}$$

$$\frac{dD}{d\theta} = -u \quad \text{for} \quad B = 0 \tag{9}$$

Moreover, one must put

$$D = 0 \quad \text{for} \quad \theta = 1 \tag{10}$$

Finally, if one assumes that the sputtering temperature θ_0 occurs at the point of the wet region where D is maximum, in this point it gives

$$uD(\theta_0) = \theta_0 \cdot B(\theta_0) = F(\theta_0) \tag{11}$$

This situation is qualitatively represented in Figure 3. One can utilize Equation 7 in various ways [10]. For instance, by the Picard-Peano method stopped at the first approximation one obtains

$$u = \frac{I^{1/2}}{1 - \theta_n} \tag{12}$$

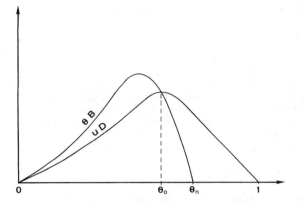

Figure 3. A qualitative representation of $\theta \cdot B(\theta)$ and uD versus θ, with reference to Equation 7.

whereas the second approximation provides

$$u = \frac{[J^2 - I(1 - \theta_n)^2]^{1/2} - J}{(1 - \theta_n)^2} \tag{13}$$

In Equations 12 and 13 θ_n is the dimensionless temperature above of which $B = 0$; furthermore,

$$I = 2 \int_0^{\theta_n} \theta B(\theta)\, d\theta$$

$$J = 2 \int_0^{\theta_n} \left[\int_0^{\theta} \theta' \cdot B(\theta')\, d\theta' \right]^{1/2} d\theta$$

As a further example, consider, like in the model proposed by Elias and Yadigaroglu, the B pattern represented in Figure 4.

The integration of Equations 7 and 9 gives

$$D = \alpha_1 \theta \qquad \text{for} \quad 0 \le \theta \le \theta_1$$

$$\frac{(D - \alpha_i \theta)^{\alpha_i}}{(D - \beta_i \theta)^{\beta_i}} = C \qquad \text{for} \quad \theta_{i-1} \le \theta \le \theta_i; i = 2, 3, \ldots n \tag{14}$$

$$D = u(1 - \theta) \quad \text{for} \quad \theta_n \le \theta \le 1$$

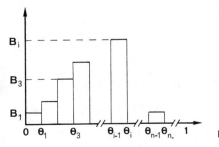

Figure 4. Schematic histogram of B pattern.

where $\alpha_i > 0$; $\beta_i < 0$ are the roots of the characteristic equation of Equation 4:

$$Z^2 + uZ - B_i = 0 \tag{15}$$

and C is a constant.

By the previous equations one can calculate C and, sequentially, $D(\theta_n)$, $D(\theta_{n-1})$, $D(\theta_{n-2})$, etc. in order to individuate the interval in which the maximum of D occurs; the sputtering temperature θ_0 is evaluated by solving, in this interval, simultaneous Equations 11 and 14. Obviously, this procedure allows one to generate tables that give u versus B and θ_0.

In conclusion, it is to be noted that the main advantage of Equation 7 consists in the elimination of the spatial coordinate.

TWO-DIMENSIONAL MODELS

The one-dimensional approximation is only valid for very small Biot number B and quench front dimensionless velocity u. However, since many cases of practical interest lie outside those limits, several efforts have been devoted to solve the two-dimensional problem [1, 11–16]. The B patterns considered are in practice those reported in Table 1.

In the following we shall consider in some detail only the case B = const. in the wet region and zero in the dry one. It should be stressed, however, that even with this simplifying assumption a complete solution of Equation 2 is not yet available. A general solution, obtained by the method of separation of variables, is expressed in terms of the two following infinite series:

$$\theta^- = \sum_{n=1}^{\infty} A_n \exp(\lambda_n \xi) \cos(\omega_n \eta) \qquad \text{for} \quad -\infty \le \xi \le 0 \tag{16a}$$

$$\theta^+ = 1 + \sum_{n=1}^{\infty} C_n \exp(\mu_n \xi) \cos(n-1)\pi\eta \quad \text{for} \quad 0 \le \xi \le +\infty \tag{16b}$$

where

$$\lambda_n = -\frac{u}{2} + \left[\left(\frac{u}{2} \right)^2 + \omega_n^2 \right]^{1/2} \tag{17a}$$

$$\mu_n = -\frac{u}{2} - \left[\left(\frac{u}{2} \right)^2 + \pi^2(n-1)^2 \right]^{1/2} \tag{17b}$$

and the eigenvalues ω_n are the solutions of the following trascendental equation:

$$\omega \tan \omega = B \tag{18}$$

In principle, the constants A_n and C_n in Equations 16a and b might be obtained by the continuity conditions for the temperature and its axial derivative at $\xi = 0$, i.e.:

$$\theta^-(0, \eta) = \theta^+(0, \eta); \frac{\partial \theta^-}{\partial \xi} \bigg|_{0,\eta} = \frac{\partial \theta^+}{\partial \xi} \bigg|_{0,\eta} \tag{19}$$

This process, clearly, generates an infinite system of linear equation in an infinite number of unknowns.

An approximate numerical solution of such a system can be found by neglecting all but the first N coefficients and solving the resulting reduced system obtained by satisfying Equation 19 only in N suitably selected points. That, for example, was the way followed by Coney [11].

Table 2
Numerical Values of θ_0 Obtained From RISET Code

B \ u	0.10	0.50	1.00	2.00	3.00	5.00	10.00	15.00	20.00	25.00
0.10	0.2696	0.7588	0.9054	0.9647	0.9787	0.9877	0.9939	0.9959	0.9969	0.9975
0.50	0.1311	0.4890	0.7053	0.8575	0.9069	0.9434	0.9706	0.9801	0.9849	0.9879
1	0.0945	0.3788	0.5856	0.7670	0.8380	0.8964	0.9440	0.9614	0.9706	0.9762
2	0.0677	0.2850	0.4646	0.6524	0.7401	0.8219	0.8973	0.9275	0.9439	0.9543
5	0.0432	0.1896	0.3238	0.4880	0.5798	0.6805	0.7930	0.8456	0.8766	0.8972
10	0.0307	0.1370	0.2390	0.3733	0.4557	0.5550	0.6821	0.7496	0.7927	0.8228
15	0.0251	0.1128	0.1985	0.3146	0.3886	0.4818	0.6092	0.6817	0.7303	0.7654
20	0.0217	0.0981	0.1734	0.2772	0.3448	0.4320	0.5563	0.6303	0.6813	0.7192
30	0.0177	0.0804	0.1429	0.2306	0.2890	0.3667	0.5827	0.5557	0.6081	0.6484
50	0.0137	0.0624	0.1115	0.1814	0.2290	0.2940	0.3957	0.4641	0.5140	0.5543
100	0.0097	0.0442	0.0792	0.1298	0.1648	0.2139	0.2942	0.3509	0.3944	0.4308
150	0.0079	0.0360	0.0647	0.1063	0.1354	0.1766	0.2451	0.2941	0.3327	0.3655
200	0.0068	0.0312	0.0561	0.0923	0.1177	0.1537	0.2144	0.2583	0.2934	0.3234
500	0.0043	0.0197	0.0355	0.0586	0.0750	0.0984	0.1386	0.1685	0.1928	0.2140
1000	0.0030	0.0140	0.0252	0.0416	0.0532	0.0699	0.0989	0.1206	0.1385	0.1542

As alternatives to the method of separation of variables, various other analytical and numerical studies have been performed in order to obtain an approximate solution to Equation 2. These studies include the work of Tien and Yao [14] based on the Wiener-Hopf technique, and that of Oliveri et al. [16] based on the finite difference method.

It should be stressed that, by the aforementioned methods one obtains the distribution of θ, and in particular the dimensionless sputtering temperature θ_0, by furnishing as input both the Biot number and the dimensionless rewetting velocity. See for example Table 2, which reports some results obtained from RISET code [16].

Other numerical results obtained by different procedures can be found in [11, 12]. Many authors, however, have preferred to look for approximate relations that are easier. Some of the most quoted formulae are reported below.

Duffey and Porthouse [1]

$$u = \frac{2}{\pi} B \frac{\theta_0}{1 - \theta_0} \left[1 - \left(\frac{2}{\pi}\right)^2 B \frac{\theta_0}{1 - \theta_0} \right]^{1/2} \tag{20}$$

This formula, which is the early one for the two-dimensional problems, was derived by neglecting all but the first term in Equation 16a and by applying an energy balance instead of using the downstream expansion (Equation 16b). However, Equation 20, which was presented as valid only for $B \gg 1$, furnishes non-real quench front velocities for realistic values of θ_0 and B. The authors themselves show that for $\theta_0 \simeq 0.25$ the limiting value for the Biot number is $B \simeq 7$.

Andersen [12]

$$u = 2^{-0.25\pi^{1/2}} \cdot B \cdot \left[\frac{\theta_0^2}{1 - \theta_0} \right]^{(0.5 + 0.25\pi^{1/2})} \tag{21}$$

This formula, which is valid for large B, was deduced from numerical calculations.

Table 3
Variation of the Coefficient K for Coney's Correlation

θ_0	1.000	0.833	0.667	0.500	0.400	0.333	0.250	0.200	0.167	0.143
K	1.570	1.478	1.395	1.315	1.256	1.220	1.172	1.139	1.117	1.094

Coney [17]

$$u = \frac{B}{K(\theta_0)}\left[\frac{\theta_0^2}{1 - \theta_0}\right] \tag{22}$$

This equation, which is a convenient correlation of the numerical results of Coney, may be used over the full range of Biot numbers, provided the value of u predicted by it is higher than about 4. Table 3 supplements Equation 22.

We have previously reported an equation similar to Equation 22 but K was given by

$$K(\theta_0) = 1.04 + 0.60\theta_0 \tag{23}$$

This correlation, which provides good results for $u \geq 3$, was deduced from the RISET code results [16].

Tien and Yao [14]

$$\frac{B}{u} = 1.707\left[\frac{1 - \theta_0}{\theta_0}\right] + 1.457\left[\frac{1 - \theta_0}{\theta_0}\right]^2 \tag{24}$$

This expression is a two-dimensional asymptotic solution valid only for large values of u.

Dua and Tien [18]

$$u^2 = \left[\frac{B\theta_0^2}{1 - \theta_0}\right]\left[1 + \frac{0.4B\theta_0^2}{1 - \theta_0}\right] \tag{25}$$

This correlation is presented as valid in the full range of B and θ_0.

Oliveri et al. [19]

$$\frac{w^2 u^4}{w^2 + u^2} = \left[\frac{B\theta_0^2}{1 - \theta_0}\right]^2 \tag{26}$$

where

$$w^2 = 1.018 + 1.598\theta_0 \tag{27}$$

This correlation is valid in the full range of the operating parameters, where it proves very successful, providing a root mean square error of about 2.5% with respect to the numerical results of Coney [11, 17] and of the RISET code [16]. Moreover, it is readily seen that Equation 26 presents some interesting features:

1. For $u \ll w$ it reduces to Equation 6.

2. For $u \gg w$ it reduces to Equation 22.
3. The dimensionless rewetting velocity can be easily obtained in an explicit form.

Before we conclude this section let us note that, assuming $B = \text{const.}$ in the wet region and $B = 0$ in the dry one, in the one-dimensional approximation it results $u \cap B^{1/2}$, whereas in the two-dimensional ones the dependence of u on B always tends to become linear as B becomes large. Consequently, the quench front velocity v tends to be independent of the slab thickness.

THE PROBLEM OF THE RIVULETS

All the previously mentioned studies assume a water falling film uniform in the direction normal to both ξ and η. Some authors [17, 20–21], however, have observed that, depending on flow rates and subcoolings of the injected water, even if this one is sprayed uniformly at the top of the hot vertical surface, the front of the film is far from uniform since the flow tends to canalize in rivulets.

Indeed, experiments performed with subcooled water and/or low flow rates show the onset of rivulets straight and isolated, and winding with branches and/or coalescences [22]. Obviously a theoretical study of such a phenomenon is far from practical.

In order to gain some information about the rivulet front advance, Oliveri et al. [23–24] have developed a very simplified model that supposes an array of identical rivulets descending along an infinitely extended vertical slab (Figure 5) with a constant heat transfer coefficient in the regions wetted by the rivulets and zero elsewhere. One readily recognizes that, generally, such a model requires a three-dimensional analysis; moreover three distinct regions must be considered:

1. The rewetted region 1, with $B = \text{const}$
2. The side dry region 2, with $B = 0$
3. The front dry region 3, with $B = 0$

The heat conduction equation in each of these regions, written in a time independent form, is

$$\frac{\partial^2 \theta_i}{\partial \xi^2} + \frac{\partial^2 \theta_i}{\partial \eta^2} + \frac{\partial^2 \theta_i}{\partial \zeta^2} + u_r \frac{\partial \theta_i}{\partial \xi} = 0; \quad i = 1, 2, 3 \tag{28}$$

where u_r is the dimensionless rewetting velocity of the rivulet front.

Numerical solutions of the differential system (Equation 28) with the appropriate boundary conditions, here omitted for the sake of brevity, were obtained by the finite difference code RIVOLI-3

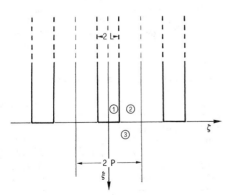

Figure 5. Coordinate system used in analysis of rewetting by rivulets flow.

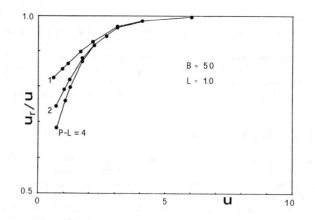

Figure 6. Variation of the ratio u_r/u with u and (P-L), for assigned values of B and L.

[24]. The analysis has shown that:

1. For given values of B and θ_0 it is always $u_r < u$, being u the front velocity of the continuous film as deduced by the RISET code.
2. For either $L \gg 1$ or $u \gg 1$, as one can expect, u_r results very close to u; the same obviously happens as well for $P \ll 2L$.

Examples of this are shown in Figure 6 and in Table 4.

Table 4
Values of u_r and the Ratio u_r/u, as Functions of θ_0

	B = 0.5, L = 1, P − L = 4				B = 0.5, L = 5, P − L = 4		
u_r	θ_0	u	$S = u_r/u$	u_r	θ_0	u	$S = u_r/u$
0.5	0.665000	0.8821	0.5668	0.5	0.518138	0.5536	0.9032
1.0	0.790739	1.4132	0.7076	1.0	0.713641	1.0415	0.9602
2.0	0.878663	2.3443	0.8531	2.0	0.858638	2.0319	0.9843
3.0	0.912734	3.2286	0.9292	2.5	0.886971	2.5080	0.9968

	B = 50, L = 1, P − L = 4				B = 50, L = 5, P − L = 4		
u_r	θ_0	u	$S = u_r/u$	u_r	θ_0	u	$S = u_r/u$
0.5	0.085428	0.7325	0.6826	0.5	0.062495	0.5096	0.9812
0.8	0.114998	1.0579	0.7562	0.8	0.092863	0.8091	0.9888
1.0	0.130925	1.2566	0.7958	1.0	0.110833	1.0087	0.9914
1.5	0.163716	1.7265	0.8688	1.5	0.149144	1.5066	0.9956
2.0	0.189970	2.1856	0.9151	2.0	0.180066	2.0014	0.9993

EXPERIMENTAL STUDIES ON THE REWETTING AND CORRELATIONS

In order to predict the wet front velocity by the formulas reported in the previous sections, the knowledge of the sputtering temperature T_0 and the heat transfer coefficient h is a prerequisite. However, the physical mechanisms controlling such parameters are not fully understood; on the other hand, the experimental data [1, 4, 25–30] show complex and sometime disagreeing relations between quench front velocity and system variables such as initial wall temperature, material and surface conditions, coolant flow rate and subcooling, and environmental pressure. For instance, as for the effect of the flow rate, Yamanouchi [4], Yoshioka and Hasegawa [26], and Duffey and Porthouse [29], who had performed their experiment at atmospheric pressure using subcooled water, observed that the rewetting velocity increases with increasing of the mass flow per unit perimeter of surface. On the contrary, Bennett et al. [25] and Elliott and Rose [27–28], whose experiments were carried out with saturated water and covered a pressure range from 1 to 69 bar, found a very weak dependence from the flow mass but pointed out a significant dependence from the working pressure.

Yu and al [17] performed experiments at various pressures and flow rates using either saturated or subcooled water and settled the controversy by asserting that some effect of flow rate on the rewetting velocity is detected only in the low-pressure tests; such an effect is appreciable if subcooled water is used as in the experiments performed by Yamanouchi [4], Yoshioka and Hasegawa [26], and Duffey and Porthouse [29]. On the contrary it becomes very small as the water at the quench front becomes saturated [17].

Before we present some correlations of the experimental results versus the main system parameters, let us recall that, by using explicit variables, Equation 26 gives

$$v(T_w - T_s)\rho c \sqrt{\frac{\varepsilon}{k}} = \sqrt{h}(T_0 - T_s)\left[\frac{T_w - T_s}{T_w - T_0}\right]^{1/2} \tag{29}$$

for $u^2 \ll w^2$;

$$v(T_w - T_s)^2 \rho c = h(T_0 - T_s)^2 \frac{\left[\dfrac{T_w - T_s}{T_w - T_0}\right]}{\left[1.018 + 1.598\,\dfrac{T_0 - T_s}{T_w - T_s}\right]^{1/2}} \tag{30}$$

for $u^2 \gg w^2$.

It is to be noted that the left side of these equations is given by the experimental conditions and measurements. As for the right side, it is to be observed that the terms in the square brackets are of minor importance and, in practice, rather constant.

This suggests looking for correlations in the form:

$$\sqrt{h}(T_0 - T_s) = F(G, p, T_w) \tag{31}$$

where G is the flow rate per unit perimeter of heated surface and p is the environmental pressure.

Yu, Farmer, and Coney [17] suggested the following parameter:

$$F_q = \sqrt{h}(T_0 - T_q) \tag{32}$$

where T_q is the temperature of the water in the region of the quench front ($T_q = T_s$ for a saturated liquid).

These authors determined a correlation for F_q from a variety of different experimental results and proposed, for rewetting by falling film, the following expression:

$$F_q = 4.52{\cdot}10^4(1 + 0.036\Delta T_q \cdot G)(2.216 + 1.216\log_{10}p)^{1/2}G^{0.00765/p} \tag{33}$$

where $\Delta T_q = T_s - T_q$ is the local subcooling in °C at the quench front, G is expressed in Kg/ms, and p is expressed in MPa. The sputtering temperature T_0 was found to be approximately given by:

$$T_0 = T_s + 80°C \tag{34}$$

In the case of bottom flooding at atmospheric pressure, for saturated liquid, the authors [17] proposed the following correlation:

$$F_s = \sqrt{h}(T_0 - T_s) = 4.24 \cdot 10^4 V^{0.15} \tag{35}$$

where V is the flooding rate in m/s; on the contrary, for subcooled liquid they suggested:

$$F_q = \gamma F_s \tag{36}$$

where

$$\gamma = 0.4839(1 + V\Delta T_q^2)^{0.346} \quad \text{for} \quad (1 + V\Delta T_q^2) \geq 40 \tag{37}$$

$$\gamma = (1 + V\Delta T_q^2)^{0.13} \qquad \text{for} \quad (1 + V\Delta T_q^2) < 40 \tag{38}$$

In order to draw correlations for h and T_0, other authors have suggested grouping the two above parameters in a manner different from that suggested by Equation 31. Thompson [31], who used Blair's [13] analytic solution, found

$$h(T_0 - T_s) = 21 \text{ MW/m}^2 \tag{39}$$

valid for top flooding at pressures greater than 0.35 MPa,

$$h(T_0 - T_s) = 3.4 \text{ MW/m}^2 \tag{40}$$

valid for bottom flooding at less than 0.34 MPa

An attempt [32] has been made to determine separately the sputtering temperature T_0 and the heat transfer coefficient h. The approach is based on the following assumptions:

1. The sputtering temperature is given by [17]

$$T_0 = T_s + \text{const} \tag{41}$$

2. The heat transfer coefficient, whose dependence on the mass flow rate [25, 27–28] is of minor consequence, can be expressed:

$$h = f(p)(T_w - T_0)^m \tag{42}$$

3. The quench front velocity v is furnished by Equation 26, where B and θ_0 are evaluated by means of Equations 41 and 42.

Assuming m = 0.5 in Equation 42, on the basis of the experimental data obtained by Bennett et al. [25], one obtains

$$T_0 = T_s + 98.9°C \tag{43a}$$

$$f(p) = 37,100 + 289p \tag{43b}$$

whereas on the basis of results of Elliot and Rose [27] (1st series st. steel and inconel and 2nd series st. steel considered as a whole), it results:

$$T_0 = T_s + 71.5°C \tag{44a}$$

$$f(p) = 56,160 + 1,305p \tag{44b}$$

In Equations 43b and 44b p is expressed in bar. Figures 7 and 8 show comparisons between some experimental data and the preliminary theoretical curves as deduced by the previous correlations

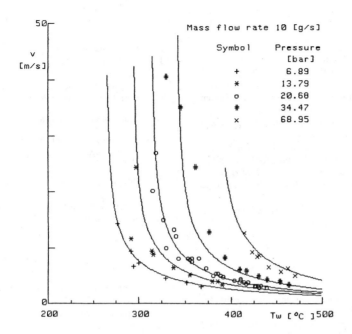

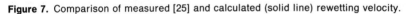

Figure 7. Comparison of measured [25] and calculated (solid line) rewetting velocity.

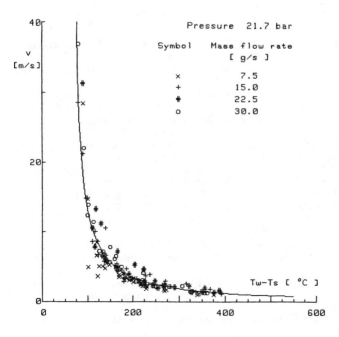

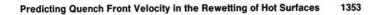

Figure 8. Comparison of measured [27] and calculated (solid line) rewetting velocity.

NOTATION

A_n, C_n	integration constants	T_0	sputtering temperature, °C
B	Biot number, $h\varepsilon/k$	T_q	temperature of the subcooled water at
c	solid specific heat, J/kg K		the quench front, °C
D	derivative of the dimensionless temperature with respect to the dimensionless coordinate ξ	T_s	saturation temperature, °C
		T_w	initial dry wall temperature, °C
G	mass flow rate per unit perimeter, kg/m s	u	dimensionless rewetting velocity, $\dfrac{\rho c \varepsilon v}{k}$
h	heat transfer coefficient, W/m² K	u_r	dimensionless rewetting velocity of rivulets, $\dfrac{\rho c \varepsilon v_r}{k}$
k	solid thermal conductivity, W/m K		
L	dimensionless half-width of rivulets	V	flooding rate, m/s
P	dimensionless half-pitch between rivulets	v	rewetting velocity, m/s
p	environmental pressure, Pa	v_r	rewetting velocity of rivulets, m/s
T	solid temperature, °C	x, y, z	spatial Cartesian coordinates

Greek Symbols

ε	solid thickness, m	θ_0	dimensionless sputtering temperature $(T_0 - T_s)/(T_w - T_s)$
ξ, η, ζ	dimensionless Cartesian coordinates, x/ε, y/ε, z/ε	λ_n, μ_n	separation constants
θ	dimensionless solid temperature, $(T - T_s)/(T_w - T_s)$	ρ	solid density, kg/m³
		ω_n	eigenvalues, solutions of Equation 18.

REFERENCES

1. Duffey, R. B., and Porthouse, D. T. C. "The Physics of Rewetting in Water Reactor Emergency Core Cooling," *Nucl. Engng. Des.*, vol. 25, 1973, pp. 379–394.
2. Elias, E., and Yadigaroglu, G. "Rewetting and Liquid Entrainment During Reflooding. State of the Art," EPRI, Report NP-435, May 1977.
3. Semeria, R., and Martinet, B. "Calefaction Spots on a Heating Wall: Temperature Distribution and Resorption," *Proc. Inst. Mech. Eng. London*, vol. 180, 1966, pp. 192–205.
4. Yamanouchi, A. "Effect of Core Spray Cooling in Transient State after Loss of Coolant Accident," *J. Nucl. Sci. Technol.*, vol. 5, no. 11, Nov. 1968, pp. 547–558.
5. Sun, K. H., Dix, G. E., and Tien, C. L. "Effect of Precursory Cooling on Falling-Film Rewetting," *J. Heat Transfer, Trans. ASME*, vol. 97, August 1975, pp. 360–365.
6. Thompson, T. S. "An Analysis of the Wet-Side Heat-Transfer Coefficient During Rewetting of a Hot Dry Patch," *Nuclear Engng. Des.*, vol. 22, 1972, pp. 212–224.
7. Elias, E., and Yadigaroglu, G. "A General One-Dimensional Model for Conduction-Controlled Rewetting of a Surface," *Nucl. Engng. Des.*, vol. 2, 1977, pp. 185–194.
8. Morse, P. M., and Feshbach, H. *Methods of Theoretical Physics*, vol. 2, New York, McGraw-Hill Book Company, 1953, pp. 1092–1106.
9. Castiglia, F., Oliveri, E., Taibi, S., and Vella, G. "Sulla Valutazione della Velocità di Ribagnamento di Superfici ad Elevata Temperatura," paper presented at *XXXIV Congresso Nazionale A. T. I.*, Palermo, Oct. 1979.
10. Oliveri, E., Castiglia, F., Taibi, S., and Vella, G. "Sul Ribagnamento di Superfici ad Elevata Temperatura-Parte I," *Instituto di Applicazioni e Impianti Nuclear, Università di Palermo*. Quaderni 5/83, Aprile 1984.
11. Coney, M. W. E. "Calculations on the Rewetting of Hot Surfaces," *Nucl. Engng. Des.*, vol. 31, 1974, pp. 246–259.

12. Andersen, J. G. M., and Hansen, P. "Two-Dimensional Heat Conduction in Rewetting Phenomenon," Report No. Norhav-D-6 Danish Atomic Energy Commission Research Establishment, RISØ, Denmark, June 1974.
13. Blair, J. M. "An Analytical Solution to a Two-Dimensional Model of the Rewetting of a Hot Dry Rod," *Nucl. Engng. Des.*, vol. 32, 1975, pp. 159–170.
14. Tien, C. L., and Yao, L. S. "Analysis of Conduction-Controlled Rewetting of a Vertical Surface," *J. Heat Transfer*, vol. 97, 1975, pp. 161–165.
15. Dua, S. S., and Tien, C. L. "Two-Dimensional Analysis of Conduction Controlled Rewetting with Precursory Cooling," *J. Heat Transfer*, vol. 98, 1976, p. 407.
16. Oliveri, E., Taibi, S. R., Vella, G., and Castiglia, F. "Un'Analisi Numerica Bidimensionale del Ribagnamento di Superfici Calde," *Ingegneria Nucleare*, vol. 1, 1981, pp. 21–30.
17. Yu, S. K. W., Farmer, P. R., and Coney, M. W. E. "Methods and Correlations for the Prediction of Quenching Rates on Hot Surfaces," *Int. J. Multiphase Flow*, vol. 3, no. 5, 1977, pp. 415–443.
18. Dua, S. S., and Tien, C. L. "A Generalized Two-Parameter Relation for Conduction-Controlled Rewetting of a Hot Vertical Surface," *Int. J. Heat Mass Transfer*, vol. 20, 1977, pp. 174–176.
19. Oliveri, E., Castiglia, F., Taibi, S., and Vella, G. "A New Correlation for Quench Front Velocity," *Int. J. Heat Mass Transfer*, vol. 25, no. 10, 1982, pp. 1589–1593.
20. Agricola, B., Cioffi, M., Cumo, M., Farello, G. E., and Ferrari, G. "Sulla Refrigerazione di Emergenza in LWR," *CNEN-RT/ING* (79) 34, 1979.
21. Cumo, M., Farello, G. E., and Furrer, M. "Experimental Remarks on Sputtering Phenomena and Droplets Generation in Falling Film Rewetting," *CNEN-RT/ING* (80) 2, 1980.
22. Oliveri, E., Castiglia, F., Taibi, S., and Vella, G. "Sul Ribagnamento di Superfici ad Elevata Temperatura. Parte III," *Ìstituto di Applicazioni e Impianti Nuclear, Universiti di Palermo*, Quaderni-7/83, Aprile 1984.
23. Taibi, S., Vella, G., Castiglia, F., and Oliveri, E. "Un Modello Bidimensionale per lo Studio del Ribagnamento di Superfici Calde mediante una Schiera di Rivoli di Refrigerante," paper presented at *XXXVII Congresso Nazionale A. T. I.*, Padova, Oct. 1982.
24. Castiglia, F., Oliveri, E., Taibi, S., and Vella, G. "Sviluppo di un Modello Tridimensionale per lo Studio del Ribagnamento di una Lastra Piana Simulante un Fodero di BWR Refrigerato mediante una Schiera di Rivoli." *Istituto di Applicazioni e Impianti Nucleari, Università di Palermo*, Quaderni-8/83, Aprile 1984.
25. Bennett, A. W., Hewitt, G. F., Kearsey, H. A., and Keeys, R. K. "The Wetting of Hot Surfaces by Water in a Steam Environment at High Pressure," *Report AERE-R5146*, UKAEA, Harwell, May 1966.
26. Yoshioka, K., and Hasegawa, S. "A Correlation in Displacement Velocity of Liquid Film Boundary Formed on a Heated Vertical Surface in Emergency Cooling," *J. Nucl. Sci. Tech.*, vol. 7, 1970, pp. 418–425.
27. Elliott, D. F., and Rose, P. W. "The Quenching of a Heated Surface by a Film of Water in a Steam Environment at Pressures up to 53 bar," *Report* AEEW-M976, UKAEA, Winfrith, July 1970.
28. Elliott, D. F., and Rose, P. W. "The Quenching of a Heated Zircaloy Surface by a Film of Water in a Steam Environment at Pressures up to 53 bar," *Report* AEEW-M1027, UKAEA, Winfrith, August 1971.
29. Duffey, R. B., and Porthouse, D. T. C. "Experiments on the Cooling of High-Temperature Surfaces by Water Jets and Drops," *Proc. of the CREST specialist meeting on emergency core cooling for light water* reactors, Technische Universität Munchen, Oct. 1972.
30. Piggot, B. D. G., and Porthouse, D. T. C. "A Correlation of Rewetting Data," *Nuclear Engng. Des.*, vol. 32, 1975, pp. 171–181.
31. Thompson, T. S. "Rewetting of a Hot Surface," *Proc. 5th Int. Heat Transfer Conf.*, Tokjo, paper B3.13, Vol. 4, 1974, pp. 139–143.
32. Castiglia, F., Oliveri, E., Taibi, S., and Vella, G. "Determination of the Sputtering Temperature and Heat Transfer Coefficient in the Rewetting Phenomenon," *Istituto di Applicazioni e Impianti Nucleari, Università di Palermo*, work in progress.

CHAPTER 45

HEAT TRANSFER AND HYDRODYNAMICS OF TWO-PHASE ANNULAR FLOW

K. Suzuki

Department of Mechanical Engineering
Kyoto University
Kyoto, Japan

CONTENTS

INTRODUCTION

This chapter discusses the heat transfer and the hydrodynamics of two-phase annular flow. The annular flow is one of the various flow patterns appearing in the gas-liquid two-phase flows in pipes and it is encountered when the gas-to-liquid mass flow rate ratio is high. In annular two-phase flow, liquid flows wet the inner surface of the pipe and the gas-phase fluid flows occupy the central part of the pipe. Instability occuring at the interface of the two phases leads to the incipience of interfacial waves, and the large amplitude waves called disturbance waves are nonlinear in nature. Sometimes, the problem becomes more complicated by the large amount of droplets entrained from the waves. Gas-phase flow is turbulent in usual practical situations and the liquid flow also becomes turbulent when the liquid film Reynolds number is brought high enough.

The combined effects of these complicated aspects have prevented us so far from developing a good picture of the two-phase annular flow. Therefore, a large part of this chapter will be spent describing empirical relationships for the heat transfer and the hydrodynamics of the two-phase annular flow. The hydrodynamics will be discussed first in the following since it is the basis of understanding the heat transfer characteristics. In the sections for heat transfer, single-component boiling and condensation heat transfers and two-component evaporative heat transfer will be discussed.

GENERAL DESCRIPTION OF TWO-PHASE ANNULAR FLOW

Two-phase flow is characterized by the existence of the interface between the phases. The density difference between the two phases in gas-liquid two-phase flow is similar to that in gas-solid two-phase flow; in all other respects the flow are quite different (except for dispersed flows). In the case of gas-liquid two-phase flow, the interface can be deformed in various ways but not at all in the case of gas-solid two-phase flow. This deformability of the interface leads to the possible appearance of different flow patterns of gas-liquid two-phase flows in tubes and they are classified into several typical ones: bubbly flow, slug flow, annular flow, etc. Transition from one flow pattern to another is observed when the mass flow rates of the phases are changed. The observed flow pattern data are presented usually in terms of flow pattern maps. Detailed specification of each flow pattern and discussions of some typical flow pattern maps have been given by Delhaye [1] and Hewitt [2–4].

A schematic illustration of annular flow in a vertical tube is given in Figure 1. It is characterized by a gas flow in the core region of higher velocity than that of liquid film which flows clinging annularly to the inner surface of the tube. In downward vertical flows, the annular flow can be formed even at a rather low gas-to-liquid mass-flow-rate ratio, either artificially or in a tubular condensation device in practice. An important parameter of the flow in the liquid film is the liquid film Reynolds number defined by

$$Re_f = \frac{4M_f}{\pi D \mu_l} = \frac{m_f D}{\mu_l} \left(\cong \frac{4\rho_l \bar{U}_f \delta}{\mu_l} \text{ for } \delta \ll D \right) \tag{1}$$

where M_f and $\bar{U}_f$ = the liquid film mass flow rate and the liquid averaged velocity in a film, respectively

m_f = the mass flux of liquid flowing in the film

D = the tube diameter

δ = the liquid film thickness

ρ_l and μ_l = the density and the viscosity of the liquid, respectively

Other important parameters to be used later follow:
Denoting the total mass flux by m, the liquid mass flux by m_l and the gas mass flux by m_g, the quality x is defined as follows:

$$x = \frac{m_g}{m} = \frac{m - m_l}{m} \tag{2}$$

The void fraction α is the ratio of the cross-sectional area A_g occupied by gas-phase flow to the total tube cross-sectional area $A = (\pi/4)D^2$. Thus

$$\alpha = \frac{A_g}{A} = \frac{A - A_l}{A} \tag{3}$$

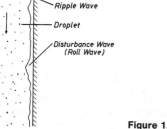

Ripple Wave

Droplet

Disturbance Wave (Roll Wave)

Figure 1. Schematic of two-phase annular flow in a tube.

where A_l is the area occupied by the liquid flow. Introducing the averaged velocities of liquid and gas phases by $\bar{U}_l$ and $\bar{U}_g$,

$$M_l = m_l A = \rho_l A_l \bar{U}_l \tag{4}$$

$$M_g = m_g A = \rho_g A_g \bar{U}_g \tag{5}$$

$\bar{U}_l$ becomes equal to $\bar{U}_f$ when no dispersed phase exists so that $m_l = m_f$. In terms of $\bar{U}_l$ and $\bar{U}_g$,

$$\alpha = \frac{\dfrac{m_g}{\rho_g \bar{U}_g}}{\dfrac{m_l}{\rho_l \bar{U}_l} + \dfrac{m_g}{\rho_g \bar{U}_g}} \tag{6}$$

or with the slip ratio $S = \bar{U}_g / \bar{U}_l$,

$$\alpha = \frac{\dfrac{m_g}{\rho_g}}{S\dfrac{m_l}{\rho_l} + \dfrac{m_g}{\rho_g}} = \frac{\rho_l x}{S\rho_g(1 - x) + \rho_l x} \tag{7}$$

Superficial velocities W_l and W_g of liquid and gas phases are also widely used. They are defined by:

$$W_l = \frac{m_l}{\rho_l} \tag{8}$$

$$W_g = \frac{m_g}{\rho_g} \tag{9}$$

and correspond to the phase-averaged velocities if each phase flows alone filling the entire tube. In terms of W_l and W_g, the quality x is expressed as follows:

$$x = \frac{\rho_g W_g}{\rho_g W_g + \rho_l W_l} \tag{10}$$

Assuming thermodynamic equilibrium between the phases, x can also be expressed for single-component flow in terms of enthalpies i_g, i and i_l:

$$x = \frac{i - i_l}{i_g - i_l} \tag{11}$$

where i_g = the enthalpy of the saturated vapor
i_l = the enthalpy of the saturated liquid
i = the local enthalpy of two-phase flow

However, difficulties often arise because the departure from the thermodynamic equilibrium exists actually. An example of this includes the supersaturation of vapor, subcooled boiling, superheated liquid, and the existence of droplets in superheated vapor.

Except at a low liquid-film Reynolds number, the surface of the liquid film is unstable and wavy in nature. Two different types of waves are observed, namely ripple waves and disturbance waves or roll waves. The former waves are of a 3-dimensional structure in contrast to the 2-dimensional

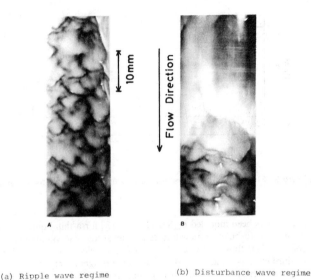

(a) Ripple wave regime   (b) Disturbance wave regime

Figure 2. Wave pattern visualized in an air-water downward annular flow [5].

structure of the disturbance waves. These are demonstrated in the two photographs of Figure 2A, B [5]. These photographs of scattered light from the T_1O_2 fine particles dispersed in the liquid film of annular flow in a vertical tube were taken by a camera located outside the transparent tube. Therefore, the dark parts correspond to the troughs of the waves and the bright parts to the crests of the waves. While ripple waves are shaped like fish scales whose center is the crest as found in Figure 2A, the disturbance waves are almost peripherally uniform and much larger in size as seen in Figure 2B.

From the viewpoint of their effects on momentum, heat and mass transfer, the ripple waves are not so important but the disturbance waves play an important role. In the experiments on air-water annular flow heat transfer, the heat transfer coefficient is found to increase steeply with an increase of the air flow rate above its critical value for the inception of disturbance waves [6]. In other words, the disturbance waves cause the enhancement of heat transfer.

Figure 3 shows an example of simultaneous records of the wave height and the tube wall shear stress obtained in an air-water downward annular flow in a circular tube [7]. In this experiment, the appearance of disturbance waves was detected by a method paying attention to a fact that the wave height record shows a rapid increase for the disturbance waves. In Figure 3, two disturbance waves are detected and it is found that the wall shear stress can increase at the time of the detection of disturbance waves. This is the indication of enhanced momentum transfer due to the appearance of the disturbance waves. There may be several mechanisms for wave-induced enhancement of momentum and heat transfer including:

1. Non-linear wave effect.
2. Turbulence caused by the waves.
3. The alternate contraction and expansion of gas-phase flow cross-sectional area.

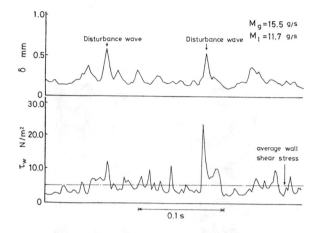

Figure 3. Fluctuation of wall shear stress and liquid film thickness [7].

The non-linear effect has been modeled by Suzuki et al. [8] for a thin liquid film. It is common accepted that laminar-to-turbulence transition can occur at lower Reynolds numbers in the liqu film but some of the effects thought to have been turbulence effects might have been the nonline wave effect. The third effect is sometimes referred to as the roughness effect and the sinuous motie of gas-phase flow causes the momentum loss [7]. Sometimes, it is expected that the gas-phase fle separates at the crests of waves and recirculates at the front side of the waves. This has been d cussed by Friedel [9].

Another important feature of the waves is the entrainment of droplets from the crests of t waves. Acceleration of the entrained droplets causes an additional pressure drop and the depos tion of the entrained droplets plays an important role on heat transfer, especially, in postburno heat transfer. Annular flow dispersed with a significant amount of liquid droplets is called annula mist flow. The inception criterion for the droplet entrainment and the droplet entrainment fractie will be discussed later.

PRESSURE DROP

Pressure gradient (dp/dz) in two-phase flow may be divided into three parts corresponding the gravitational term $(dp/dz)_g$, the acceleration term $(dp/dz)_a$ and the frictional term $(dp/dz$ respectively. Thus,

$$\frac{dp}{dz} = \left(\frac{dp}{dz}\right)_g + \left(\frac{dp}{dz}\right)_a + \left(\frac{dp}{dz}\right)_f \tag{1}$$

In terms of the void fraction α, the first term can be written down as follows:

$$\left(\frac{dp}{dz}\right)_g = -[\rho_1(1 - \alpha) + \rho_g\alpha]g \sin \gamma \tag{1}$$

where z is the axial distance measured upward, and γ the inclination angle of tube raised from the horizontal plane. To evaluate the gravitational term, the local void fraction is required to b known and this will be discussed in the next section. Friedel [9] presented an expression for th acceleration pressure drop Δp_a due to the change in quality x as follows:

$$\Delta p_a = \frac{\Delta J}{A} \tag{14}$$

where J is the total momentum flux defined by

$$J = \left(\frac{M_g^2}{\rho_g A_g} + \frac{M_l^2}{\rho_l A_l}\right) = \frac{M^2}{A}\left[\frac{x^2}{\alpha \rho_g} + \frac{(1-x)^2}{(1-\alpha)\rho_l}\right] \tag{15}$$

where M is the total mass flow rate. Therefore, the acceleration pressure gradient is given by

$$\left(\frac{dp}{dz}\right)_a = \frac{-1}{A}\frac{dJ}{dz} \tag{16}$$

The frictional pressure gradient is most difficult to evaluate and has been discussed by many papers. It has been found convenient to use the following two-phase flow friction multipliers ϕ_g, ϕ_l, ϕ_{g0}, ϕ_{l0}

$$\phi_g^2 = \frac{\left(\dfrac{dp}{dz}\right)_f}{\left(\dfrac{dp}{dz}\right)_{fg}}, \qquad \phi_l^2 = \frac{\left(\dfrac{dp}{dz}\right)_f}{\left(\dfrac{dp}{dz}\right)_{fl}}, \qquad \phi_{g0}^2 = \frac{\left(\dfrac{dp}{dz}\right)_f}{\left(\dfrac{dp}{dz}\right)_{fg0}}, \qquad \phi_{l0}^2 = \frac{\left(\dfrac{dp}{dz}\right)_f}{\left(\dfrac{dp}{dz}\right)_{fl0}} \tag{17--20}$$

where $(dp/dz)_f$ is the two-phase frictional pressure gradient appearing in Equation 12. $(dp/dz)_{fg}$ is the single-phase flow frictional pressure gradient to be attained if the gas-phase fluid flows alone filling the entire tube at the actual flow rate M_g and $(dp/dz)_{fl}$ is the counterpart for liquid-phase flow at the flow rate M_l or $(M - M_g)$. $(dp/dz)_{fg0}$ and $(dp/dz)_{fl0}$ are the fictitious frictional pressure gradients for the gas-phase flow and for the liquid-phase flow, respectively, both flowing at the same flow rate equivalent to the total mass flow rate M. Introducing the Fanning friction factors f_g, f_l, f_{g0} and f_{l0}, the preceding single-phase pressure gradients can be expressed as follows:

$$-\left(\frac{dp}{dz}\right)_{fg} = f_g \frac{2\rho_g W_g^2}{D} = f_g \frac{2m_g^2}{\rho_g D} = f_g \frac{2m^2 x^2}{\rho_g D} \tag{21}$$

$$-\left(\frac{dp}{dz}\right)_{fl} = f_l \frac{2\rho_l W_l^2}{D} = f_l \frac{2m_l^2}{\rho_l D} = f_l \frac{2m^2(1-x)^2}{\rho_l D} \tag{22}$$

$$-\left(\frac{dp}{dz}\right)_{fg0} = f_{g0}\frac{2m^2}{\rho_g D} \tag{23}$$

$$-\left(\frac{dp}{dz}\right)_{fl0} = f_{l0}\frac{2m^2}{\rho_l D} \tag{24}$$

The values of friction factors are obtained with the aid of usual friction formulae related to the Reynolds number. For example,

$$\text{Re} < 2{,}000; \qquad f = \frac{16}{\text{Re}} \tag{25}$$

$$\text{Re} > 2{,}000; \qquad f = 0.079\text{Re}^{-1/4} \tag{26}$$

The Reynolds number for each of Equation 21 through 24 can be defined as follows:

$$Re_g = \frac{\rho_g W_g D}{\mu_g} = \frac{m_g D}{\mu_g} \tag{27}$$

$$Re_l = \frac{\rho_l W_l D}{\mu_l} = \frac{m_l D}{\mu_l} \tag{28}$$

$$Re_{g0} = \frac{mD}{\mu_g} = \frac{1}{x} Re_g \tag{29}$$

$$Re_{l0} = \frac{mD}{\mu_l} = \frac{1}{1-x} Re_l \tag{30}$$

where μ_g and μ_l are the viscosities for the gas and liquid phases, respectively. In the homogeneous model to be mentioned later, the two-phase Reynolds number Re_{tp} is used.

$$Re_{tp} = \frac{mD}{\mu_{tp}} \tag{31}$$

where the two-phase viscosity is defined, for example, as follows:

$$\frac{1}{\mu_{tp}} = \frac{x}{\mu_g} + \frac{1-x}{\mu_l} \tag{32}$$

This is usually cited as suggested by McAdams et al. [10]. Except for some works including Beatty [11], the correlations for the frictional pressure gradient have been studied without specifying the flow pattern. Therefore, the discussions that follow may be used for the flow patterns other than the annular flow.

With the homogeneous model, the two-phase friction coefficient f_{tp} is introduced and the friction pressure gradient is expressed as follows:

$$-\left(\frac{dp}{dx}\right)_f = f_{tp} \frac{2m^2}{\rho_{tp} D} \tag{33}$$

where the homogeneous density ρ_{tp} is [10]:

$$\rho_{tp} = \frac{\rho_g \rho_l}{\rho_l x + (1-x)\rho_g} \tag{34}$$

and f_{tp} is evaluated using the two-phase Reynolds number Re_{tp} given by Equation 31 for Re in Equation 25 or 26. When Equation 26 is used for f_{tp} and f_{l0}, the value of ϕ_{l0}^2 may become:

$$\phi_{l0}^2 = \left(1 + x\frac{\rho_l - \rho_g}{\rho_g}\right)\left(1 + x\frac{\mu_l - \mu_g}{\mu_g}\right)^{-1/4} \tag{35}$$

The homogeneous model is simple to use but tends to underestimate the two-phase friction pressure gradient.

The most widely used method for the evaluation of the friction multipliers defined by Equations 17 through 20 originated from the works by Lockhart and Martinelli [12]. They introduced a

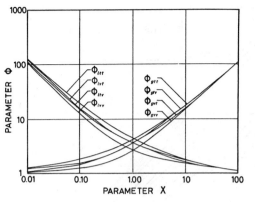

Figure 4. Correlation for pressure drop multiplier [12].

parameter X defined as follows:

$$X^2 = \frac{\left(\dfrac{dp}{dz}\right)_{f_1}}{\left(\dfrac{dp}{dz}\right)_{f_g}} \tag{36}$$

Their results for the correlation curve of multipliers ϕ_g and ϕ_1 are indicated in graphical form and are reproduced in Figure 4. The correlation curve differs from one case to another depending on whether each phase flow is laminar (Re$_1 <$ 2,000 or Re$_g <$ 2,000) or not. The first suffix of ϕ_g and ϕ_1 designates the flow state (v for laminar (viscous) and t for turbulent) of the liquid having the frictional pressure gradient $(dp/dz)_{f_1}$ and the second suffix denotes the same for the gas-phase flow of the frictional pressure gradient $(dp/dz)_{f_g}$. Turbulent-turbulent is the most important flow regime and an approximate form of X_{tt} used by Lockhart and Martinelli is:

$$X_{tt} = \left(\frac{\mu_1}{\mu_g}\right)^{0.1} \left(\frac{\rho_g}{\rho_1}\right)^{0.5} \left(\frac{1-x}{x}\right)^{0.9} \tag{37}$$

In this relation, $f \sim \text{Re}^{-0.2}$ has been used instead of Equation 26. As seen from Equation 37, X_{tt} is small for high quality or for annular flow and X_{tt} is large for low quality two-phase flow. Martinelli and Nelson [13] presented a correction factor of the multiplier curve for pressure variation.

Chisholm and Laird [14] and Chisholm [15] suggested that the Lockhart-Martinelli correlation curves can approximately be expressed by the following type of simple equations.

$$\phi_g^2 = 1 + CX + X^2 \tag{38}$$

$$\phi_g^2 = 1 + \frac{C}{X} + X^2 \tag{39}$$

where C takes the following value:

$$
\begin{aligned}
C &= 20 \quad \text{for} \quad X_{tt} \\
C &= 12 \quad \text{for} \quad X_{vt} \\
C &= 10 \quad \text{for} \quad X_{tv} \\
C &= 5 \quad \text{for} \quad X_{vv}
\end{aligned}
\tag{40}
$$

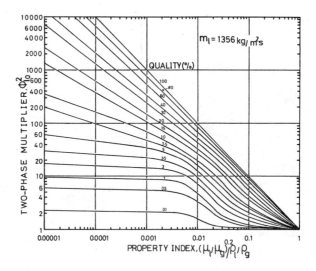

Figure 5. Friction multiplier ϕ_{10}^2 versus property index [16].

One of the deficiencies of the Lockhart-Martinelli method is that it does not include the known effect of mass flux on the friction multipliers. Baroczy [16] first succeeded in correlating the dependence of the friction multiplier ϕ_{10}^2 on the mass flux. He has established the ϕ_{10}^2 curve-versus-property index $(\mu_1/\mu_g)^{0.2}(\rho_g/\rho_1)$ for a standard mass flux $= 1{,}356 \ kg/m^2$ as shown in Figure 5. For the previously mentioned property index, we have

$$\left(\frac{\mu_1}{\mu_g}\right)^{0.2} \frac{\rho_g}{\rho_1} = \frac{\left(\dfrac{dp}{dz}\right)_{f10}}{\left(\dfrac{dp}{dz}\right)_{fg0}} \tag{41}$$

if the friction law of $f \sim Re^{-0.2}$ is used again for each phase. This property index, therefore, corresponds to the Chisholm parameter Y to be referred to later:

$$Y^2 = \frac{\left(\dfrac{dp}{dz}\right)_{f10}}{\left(\dfrac{dp}{dz}\right)_{fg0}} \tag{42}$$

Baroczy then deduced a mass velocity correction factor Ω which is graphically given as reproduced in Figure 6. The value of Ω must be multiplied by ϕ_{10}^2 shown in Figure 5.

Chisholm [17] showed that the mass velocity effect can be expressed by the following relationship:

$$\phi_{10}^2 = 1 + (Y^2 - 1)[Bx^{2-n/2}(1-x)^{2-n} + x^{2-n}] \tag{43}$$

where $n = 0.2$ and B is a parameter given by:

$$0 < Y < 9.5$$

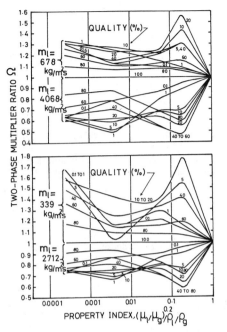

Figure 6. Correction factor for pressure drop multiplier accounting mass flux effect [16].

$$B = \frac{55}{m^{1/2}} \quad \text{for} \quad m > 1,900 \text{ kg/m}^2\text{s}$$

$$= \frac{2,400}{m} \quad \text{for} \quad 500 < m < 1,900 \text{ kg/m}^2\text{s}$$

$$= 4.8 \quad \text{for} \quad m < 500 \text{ kg/m}^2\text{s}$$

$$9.5 < Y < 28$$

$$B = \frac{520}{Ym^{1/2}} \quad \text{for} \quad m \leq 600 \text{ kg/m}^2\text{s}$$

$$= \frac{21}{Y} \quad \text{for} \quad m > 600 \text{ kg/m}^2\text{s}$$

$$28 < Y$$

$$B = \frac{15,000}{Y^2 m^{1/2}}$$

Friedel [9, 18] proposed the following relationship for ϕ_{lo}^2:

$$\phi_{lo}^2 = 8.59 \frac{x^{0.69}}{m^{0.29} D^{0.086}} \left(\frac{\rho_l}{\rho_g} \right)^{0.84} \tag{44}$$

This can be applied to the steam-water data in the range of the parameters,

$344 \, \text{kg/m}^2\text{s} < m < 4,661 \, \text{kg/m}^2\text{s}$

$12.7 < (\rho_l/\rho_g) \text{ water} < 86.4$

$0.0032(\text{m}) < d_h < 0.0249(\text{m})$

$0.0001 < x < 0.999$

where d_h is the hydraulic diameter of the tube. Another form of the correlation proposed by Friedel has been discussed by Hewitt [19, 20].

Another empirical approach rather widely used is to correlate the interfacial friction factor f_i defined below as a function of film thickness. The interfacial friction factor is given by:

$$f_i = \frac{\tau_i}{\frac{1}{2} \rho_c W_g^2} \tag{45}$$

where τ_i is the shear stress acting on the interface and ρ_c is the mean density of the fluid flowing in the core region. The latter is given by:

$$\rho_c = \frac{m_1 - m_f + m_g}{\dfrac{(m_1 - m_f)}{\rho_1} + \dfrac{m_g}{\rho_g}} \tag{46}$$

where $(m_1 - m_f)$ is the liquid mass flux entrained in the gas core. Empirical relationships for f_i are usually recommended in the following form:

$$f_i = f_{is} \cdot f\left(\frac{\delta}{D}\right) \tag{47}$$

where f_{is} is the friction factor for single-phase flow in a smooth tube like that given by Equation 26. The underlying concept for the above expression of f_i is that the interfacial wave whose height relates to the film thickness may act as the roughness element for the gas-phase flow in the core region [21, 22]. The functional form of $f(\delta/D)$ has been discussed by many papers including those by Wallis [23] and Martindale and Smith [24]. One of the inconveniences of this approach is that the relationship between τ_i and $(dp/dz)_f$ is not simple unless the void fraction is known separately as will be discussed in the next section.

For practical purposes, the previously mentioned empirical formulae are used commonly but their physical background is not known well. Furthermore, we must admit that still discrepancies, which are sometimes quite large, exists between those formulae and the experimental data.

Apart from the empirical approaches already mentioned, there exist some analytical approaches. Connected with the present insufficient knowledge of two-phase annular flow, any of these analyses need the incorporation of some experimental information. Levy and Healzer [25] carried out an analysis for two-phase annular flow assuming a transition layer between the crest and trough of waves. Within this transition layer ($\delta_{\min} \leq y \leq \delta_{\max}$), it is assumed that

$$\frac{\rho}{\rho_1} = \left(\frac{y}{\delta_{\min}}\right)^{-\xi} \tag{48}$$

$$u = U_w \tag{49}$$

where y = the distance from the tube wall surface

      $\delta_{\min}$ = the minimum thickness of the liquid film or the value of y at the trough of waves

δ_{max} = the value of y at the crest of waves

ρ = the local apparent density of two-phase flow

U_w = the wave velocity

It is also assumed that the liquid flowing within this transition layer is the portion of liquid flow entrained into the core. The parameters ξ and U_w are chosen by comparing the computed wave velocity and entrainment rate with respective experimental counterparts. Inside the liquid film ($y \leq \delta_{min}$), the velocity distribution is taken to be equal to that for the single-phase turbulent flow. Also in the core region ($y \geq \delta_{max}$), the gas-phase velocity is assumed to yield to the logarithmic law of the wall, and its value at the position of the crest of the waves ($y = \delta_{max}$) is set by the following relationship. Denoting the wall shear stress by τ_w, that is

$$U^+ = \frac{U}{\sqrt{\tau_w/\rho}} = 5.5 \tag{50}$$

which corresponds to assume that the roughness at the interface is 3.32 times the minimum film thickness δ_{min}. They showed that the calculated values of the two-phase friction multiplier and minimum film thickness generally agree with existing empirical correlations and experimental data for annular flow regime.

Suzuki et al. [8] proposed a theoretical approach to a thin film two-phase annular flow based on a model for the effect of waves on interfacial momentum transfer. Their model introduces the apparent viscosities accounting for the wave effect, $\tilde{\mu}_l$ and $\tilde{\mu}_g$, for the liquid film and for the gas-phase flow near the interface, respectively. The final forms of the proposed expressions for the viscosities are as follows:

$$\tilde{\mu}_l = C\rho_l L^2 \omega \tag{51}$$

$$\tilde{\mu}_g = C\rho_g L^2 \omega \tag{52}$$

where L is the wave amplitude and ω the average number rate of waves passing a cross-sectional plane. Since the apparent viscosities are put proportional to L^2, the ripple waves contribute almost nothing to the interfacial momentum transfer, but the disturbance waves do significantly. With this model, they calculated the pressure gradient and the averaged film thickness for annular flow with thin liquid film. The computation of the averaged liquid-film thickness enables calculation of the void fraction as will be discussed in the next section. The computed film thickness is found to be larger for the flow rate conditions with the appearance of disturbance waves. In connection with this, the computed values of the pressure gradient for such conditions are smaller than the observed data, but are not so bad on the whole. The model proposed is equivalent to the empirical approach accounting for the roughness effect just mentioned, in the sense that the viscous sublayer of the gas-phase flow has been assumed broken up intermittently by the appearance of waves. As discussed by Friedel [9] and suggested from experimental work by Hagiwara et al. [7], the sinuous motion of gas-phase flow or the alternate contraction and expansion of the gas-phase flow area occurs when the gas flows over the crest of waves and causes additional momentum loss. Thus, the incorporation of this source of momentum loss into their model should be promising. This may become important for flows with thicker liquid film. In their theoretical treatment, the actually observed data were used for the values of L and ω so that their treatment is not still completely analytical. To devise a general means for the determination of such wave parameters is required.

VOID FRACTION AND FILM THICKNESS

Void fraction α is defined as the fraction of the tube cross-sectional area which is occupied by the gas-phase on an average and is an important parameter for the calculation of various two-phase quantities, as already seen by the inclusion of α in Equations 13 and 15. It is sometimes called the hold-up.

The homogeneous model assumes the local slip ratio to be unity everywhere (S = 1) so that for the void fraction it gives.

$$\alpha = \frac{\rho_l x}{\rho_g(1 - x) + \rho_l x} \tag{53}$$

Sometimes, the drift flux model developed by Zuber and Findlay [26] is used as a tool for the determination of the void fraction. It is called a "model" but is actually a frame of generalized theory paying attention both to the relative velocity between the phases and to the nonuniformity of the flow and the local void fraction. The usual average of a quantity Q is defined as follows:

$$\langle Q \rangle = \frac{1}{A} \int_A Q \, dA \tag{54}$$

Against this, a weighted average of Q can also be introduced:

$$\bar{Q} = \frac{\dfrac{1}{A} \int_A \tilde{\alpha} Q \, dA}{\dfrac{1}{A} \int_A \tilde{\alpha} \, dA} \tag{55}$$

where $\tilde{\alpha}$ is the local void fraction. For simplicity, the averaged quantities in the numerator and denominator are expressed respectively as $\langle \tilde{\alpha} Q \rangle$ and $\langle \tilde{\alpha} \rangle$ in the following. The actual average velocities $\bar{U}_g$ for the gas phase introduced before have already been defined following the above general definition of $\bar{Q}$.

The drift velocities w_g and w_l are defined as the differences between the actual local velocities of the phases and the volumetric flux density of the mixture j by the relationships:

$$w_g = U_g - j \tag{56}$$

$$w_l = U_l - j \tag{57}$$

where

$$j = j_g + j_l \tag{58}$$

and

$$j_g = \tilde{\alpha} U_g \tag{59}$$

$$j_l = (1 - \tilde{\alpha}) U_l \tag{60}$$

Defining the distribution parameter C_0 by:

$$C_0 = \frac{\langle \tilde{\alpha} j \rangle}{\langle \tilde{\alpha} \rangle \langle j \rangle} \tag{61}$$

the slip ratio S is described as follows:

$$S = \frac{\bar{U}_g}{U_l} = \frac{1 - \langle \tilde{\alpha} \rangle}{\dfrac{1}{C_0 + \dfrac{\langle \tilde{\alpha} w_g \rangle}{\langle \tilde{\alpha} \rangle \langle j \rangle}} - \langle \tilde{\alpha} \rangle} = \frac{1 - \alpha}{\dfrac{1}{C_0 + \dfrac{\langle \tilde{\alpha} w_g \rangle}{\alpha \langle j \rangle}} - \alpha} \tag{62}$$

where $\alpha = \langle \tilde{\alpha} \rangle$ has been used. Incidentally, when $w_g = 0$ everywhere, the previous relationship reduces to:

$$S = \frac{1 - \alpha}{1/C_0 - \alpha} \tag{63}$$

which corresponds to the equation for the velocity slip ratio given originally by Bankoff [27]. Furthermore, the following relationship holds.

$$\langle j \rangle = \frac{m}{\rho_g \rho_1} [\rho_1 x + \rho_g(1 - x)] \tag{64}$$

Combining Equations 62 and 64 and using another form of the slip ratio definition by

$$S = \frac{\rho_1 x(1 - \alpha)}{\rho_g(1 - x)\alpha} \tag{65}$$

the void fraction may be written as follows for the case of uniform distribution of w_g:

$$\alpha = \frac{\rho_1 x}{C_0[\rho_1 x + \rho_g(1 - x)] + \rho_g \rho_1 w_g/m} \tag{66}$$

The distribution parameter C_0 and the gas-phase drift velocity w_g are functions of flow pattern and other flow situation parameters. But their general expressions have been studied rather scarcely. For annular flow, C_0 takes a value close to unity [25] and w_g is not so large, at least, in the core region. Thus, for the annular flow, the value of α given by Equation 66 may roughly be estimated from Equation 53. Further discussion of this drift flux model has been made by a number of authors including Hewitt [4], Ishii [28, 29], and Rouhani [30].

An empirical relationship for the void fraction has also been presented in a graphical form by Lockhart and Martinelli in terms of their parameter X defined by Equation 36. Their result is reproduced in Figure 7. From a similar view point for the frictional pressure gradient, Martinelli and Nelson [13] introduce a pressure correction factor to the graphical relationship by Lockhart and Martinelli. Although this relationship was derived for steam-water two-phase flow, it has also been applied to the two-phase flow of other fluids. This correlation is widely used but, as already mentioned, it cannot account for the effect of mass flux in an adequate way.

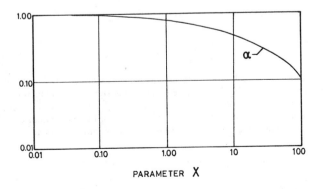

Figure 7. Void fraction [12].

Some alternative methods have been researched, and Premoli et al. [31] present the correlation for the slip ratio taking account of the mass flux effect for wide range of data. Their correlation is

$$S = 1 + E_1 \left(\frac{\eta}{1 + \eta E_2} - \eta E_2 \right)^{1/2} \tag{67}$$

where η is a function of volumetric flow rate ratio ζ and is defined by:

$$\eta = \frac{\zeta}{1 - \zeta}$$

$$\zeta = \frac{\dfrac{m_g}{\rho_g}}{\dfrac{m_g}{\rho_g} + \dfrac{m_l}{\rho_l}} = \frac{\alpha S}{\alpha S + (1 - \alpha)}$$

and

$$E_1 = 1.578 Re_{l0}^{-0.19} \left(\frac{\rho_l}{\rho_g} \right)^{0.22}$$

$$E_2 = 0.0273 We\ Re_{l0}^{-0.51} \left(\frac{\rho_l}{\rho_g} \right)^{-0.08}$$

The Weber number We is defined by:

$$We = \frac{Dm^2}{\sigma \rho_l} \tag{68}$$

For annular flow without a significant amount of entrained droplets, the contribution from droplets flowing in the gas-phase core to the void fraction may be ignored with reasonable accuracy. Under this treatment, the void fraction can be related to the averaged film thickness δ as follows:

$$\alpha = \frac{(D - 2\delta)^2}{D^2} \tag{69}$$

For thin film of $\delta/D \ll 1$, this may be approximated by

$$\alpha = \frac{D - 4\delta}{D}$$

Thus, the methods for the calculation of film thickness are basically equivalent to the method for the evaluation of α. If the local liquid flow rate in the film is known, several methods are available for the calculation of δ [2, 3, 4, 19].

If the effects of flow acceleration in a tube can be ignored, the momentum equations for the liquid flow in the film and the gas-phase flow in the tube core may be written as follows:

$$D/2 \geq r \geq r_i;$$

$$0 = -\frac{dp}{dz} + \frac{1}{r} \frac{\partial}{\partial r} (r\tau_l) - \rho_l g \sin \gamma \tag{70}$$

$r_i \geqq r \geqq 0;$

$$0 = -\frac{dp}{dz} + \frac{1}{r}\frac{\partial}{\partial r}(r\tau_g) - \rho_g g \sin \gamma \tag{71}$$

where r is the radial coordinate, τ the local shear stress acting on the fluid element, and z is measured upward. Integration of Equation 70 once with respect to r gives the following differential equation for U_l:

$$r\mu_e \frac{dU_l}{dr} = -\frac{1}{2}\left(\frac{D^2}{4} - r^2\right)\frac{dp}{dz} + \frac{D}{2}\tau_w - \frac{1}{2}\left(\frac{D^2}{4} - r^2\right)\rho_l g \sin \gamma \tag{72}$$

where τ_w is the wall shear stress acting on the tube surface and the effective viscosity μ_e has been introduced:

$$\tau_l = \mu_e \frac{dU_l}{dr} \tag{73}$$

When the liquid film remains to be in laminar state, μ_e is just equal to the liquid viscosity μ_l. When the liquid film flow is turbulent, μ_e can be related to the local velocity distribution or its parameter following Dukler [32] as follows:

For $\dfrac{\rho_l u_\tau y}{\mu_l} < 20$

$$\mu_e = \mu_l + \rho_l n^2 U_l y \left[1 - \exp\left(-\frac{\rho_l n^2 U_l y}{\mu_l}\right)\right] \tag{74}$$

For $\dfrac{\rho_l u_\tau y}{\mu_l} > 20$

$$\mu_e = \frac{\kappa(dU_l/dy)^3}{(d^2U_l/dy^2)} \tag{75}$$

where u_τ is the friction velocity ($\sqrt{\tau_w/\rho_l}$), y the distance from the tube wall, and n and κ the constants.

Equations 74 and 75 are respectively the Deissler expression and the von Kármán expression. They may be replaced by other alternative expressions of μ_e found in textbooks on fluid mechanics (e.g., Schlichting [33]).

Combining the integrated forms of Equations 70 and 71 and taking account of the interfacial shear stress matching condition $\tau_l = \tau_g = \tau_i$ at $r = D/2 - \delta$, the following relationship is obtained.

$$\frac{dp}{dz} = \frac{4\tau_w}{D} - [(1 - \alpha)\rho_l + \alpha\rho_g]g \sin \gamma \tag{76}$$

The second term on the right-hand side of Equation 76 is the gravitational pressure gradient as seen from Equation 13. Then, it follows:

$$\frac{4\tau_w}{dz} = \left(\frac{dp}{dz}\right)_f \tag{77}$$

which can be calculated with a method mentioned earlier. Using this as a boundary condition for the velocity gradient at $r = D/2$, the velocity distribution inside the liquid film can be calculated.

The liquid flow rate inside the film m_f is related to the integrated value of U_1 as follows:

$$m_f = \int_{D/2 - \delta}^{D/2} 2\pi\rho_1 U_1 r \, dr \tag{78}$$

If m_f is known, Equation 78 is used as a relationship to determine the liquid film thickness δ.
There is an alternative method using τ_i as a boundary condition for determining U_1. Integrating
Equation 70 with respect to r from $D/2 - \delta$ to D, the following relationship results in:

$$(1 - \alpha) \frac{dp}{dz} = \frac{4\tau_w}{D} - \frac{4(D - 2\delta)}{D^2} \tau_i - \rho_1 g(1 - \alpha) \sin \gamma \tag{79}$$

Combining this and Equation 76, the following result is obtained:

$$\frac{4\tau_i}{D} = \sqrt{\alpha} \left(\frac{dp}{dz}\right)_f - \sqrt{\alpha} (1 - \alpha)(\rho_1 - \rho_g)g \sin \gamma \tag{80}$$

For very thin film, the value of α on the right-hand side of the equation can be approximated by
unity. Then, it follows

$$\frac{4\tau_i}{D} \cong \left(\frac{dp}{dz}\right)_f \tag{81}$$

If this relationship is used for determining the velocity gradient at the interface instead of giving
the velocity gradient at r = D/2, the liquid velocity can also be calculated with a method similar
to the preceding. However, if the approximation $\alpha \cong 1$ is not good, Equation 80 must be used. In
that case, the calculation must be done with an iterative procedure because Equation 80 includes
α which becomes known only after the value of δ has been determined.

Suzuki et al. [8] claims that the interfacial momentum transfer due to wave-induced motion of
the fluids may be important for a thin liquid film. This leads them to add the wave effect viscosity
$\bar{\mu}_1$ given by Equation 51 into the expression of μ_c. The calculated results of δ for a wavy laminar
liquid film are a little overestimated but are generally reasonable.

As already mentioned some portion of liquid flow is entrained into the gas-phase flow in the
form of droplets. Therefore, even if the local liquid flow rate m_1 is known, the value of m_f in
Equation 78 is still unknown. To make this known, we have to discuss the entrainment of droplets.

The entrainment of droplets can occur through several different mechanisms and causes a larger
pressure loss in a tube. Ishii and Grolmes [34] studied a model for the shearing-off entrainment from
role waves by the high-velocity gas-phase flow and presented a criterion for the inception of droplet
entrainment. Unknown coefficients introduced into the criterion were determined referring to the
data reported for different geometries of the tube and different flow direction, including their own
data, and those by van Rossum [35], Ueda and Tanaka [36], Yablonik and Khaimov [37] and
Zhivaikin [38]. Their final comparison is cited in Figure 8. $Re_f > 1,635$, the critical gas velocity, is
proposed to be independent of the value of Re_f. The criterion for $Re_f < 1,635$ shown by the solid line
can be expressed as follows:

$$\frac{\mu_1 W_g}{\sigma} \sqrt{\frac{\rho_g}{\rho_1}} = 11.78 \, N_\mu^{0.8} Re_1^{-1/3} \tag{82}$$

where N_μ is the viscosity number

$$N_\mu = \frac{\mu_1}{\left(\rho_1 \sigma \sqrt{\frac{\sigma}{g \, \Delta\rho}}\right)^{1/2}} \tag{83}$$

and $\Delta\rho$ is the density difference between the phases and σ the surface tension. The inception criterion
by Ishii and Grolmes are discussed also by Ishii and Kataoka [39] and Ishii [28].

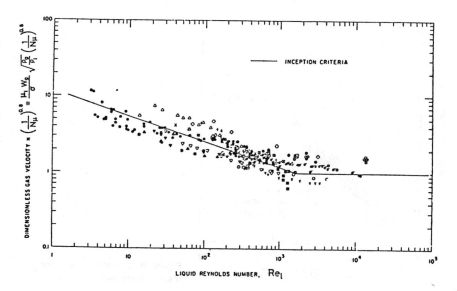

Figure 8. Inception criterion for droplet entrainment [34].

The entrainment rate of droplets is also discussed by Ishii and Mishima [40], and they proposed the following correlation function for the droplet entrainment fraction E in the region far from the tube entrance.

$$E = \tanh(7.25 \times 10^{-7} j_g^{*5/2} D^{*5/4} Re_l^{1/4}) \tag{84}$$

where

$$E = (1 - m_f/m_j) \tag{84}$$

$$j_g^* = \frac{W_g}{\left[\dfrac{\sigma g \Delta\rho}{\rho_g^2} \left(\dfrac{\rho_g}{\Delta\rho} \right)^{2/3} \right]^{1/4}} \tag{85}$$

$$D^* = d_h \sqrt{\frac{g\,\Delta\rho}{\sigma}} \tag{86}$$

and d_h is the hydraulic diameter of the tube. Equation 4 holds for the axial region of nondimensional distance Z^* from the tube entrance

$$Z^* = 600 d_h \sqrt{\frac{j_g^*}{Re_l}} \tag{87}$$

Equation 84 is compared with some experimental data in Figure 9. Incidentally, from the definition of the entrainment fraction E, the following relationship holds between Re_l, introduced in Equations 84 and 87 and defined by Equation 28, and Re_f defined by Equation 1.

$$Re_f = (1 - E)Re_l \tag{88}$$

Discussions about the void fraction and the entrainment rate are also given by Hewitt [19, 41].

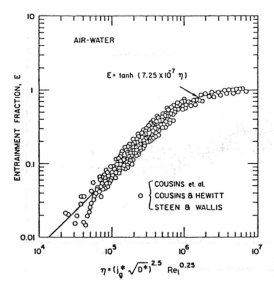

$$\eta = (j_g^* \sqrt{D^*})^{2.5} \, \text{Re}_l^{0.25}$$

Figure 9. Correlation for entrainment fraction [40].

SINGLE-COMPONENT HEAT TRANSFER

In single-component two-phase flow heat transfer, interfacial heat transfer resistance may be negligibly small in usual circumstances. Thus, the heat transfer resistance in the liquid film is an important factor in that case.

Boiling Heat Transfer

For boiling heat transfer, the total tube wall heat flux q_w may be separated into two parts, the nucleate boiling heat flux q_{NB} and the convective heat flux q_c:

$$q_w = q_{NB} + q_c = h_{NB} \Delta T_{sat} + h_c \Delta T_b \tag{89}$$

where h_{NB} and h_c = the nucleate boiling heat transfer coefficient and the convective heat transfer coefficient, respectively and ΔT_{sat} the wall superheat or the temperature difference between the wall temperature T_w and the saturation temperature T_s given by:

$$\Delta T_{sat} = T_w - T_s \tag{90}$$

and ΔT_b is the difference between T_w and the fluid bulk mean temperature T_b defined by:

$$\Delta T_b = T_w - T_b \tag{91}$$

Except for subcooled boiling, $\Delta T_{sat} = \Delta T_b$, so that Chen [42] reduced the following relationship:

$$h = h_{NB} + h_c \tag{92}$$

where h is the coefficient of two-phase heat transfer with boiling for a high quality flow or for the annular two-phase flow. Heat transfer characteristics generally depend on the tube position (horizontal or vertical). In the following, the forced-convective boiling heat transfer in a vertical tube is mentioned first.

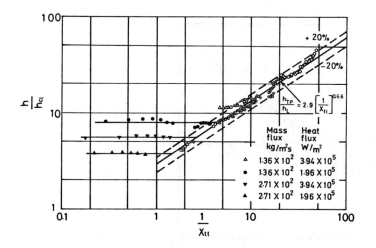

Figure 10. Variation of heat transfer coefficient ratio with Martinelli parameter [43].

Figure 10 shows the two-phase heat transfer coefficient for steam-water annular flow given by Collier et al. [43]. The abscissa of the figure is the reciprocal of the Martinelli parameter X_{tt} for a turbulent-turbulent case, and from the left to the right, the quality increases. At low quality, the two-phase heat transfer coefficient depends on the heat flux q_w. This suggests that boiling is the important mechanism of heat transfer at low quality. At high quality, however, the two-phase transfer coefficient solely depends on the Martinelli parameter and not on the heat flux. In this high quality condition, therefore, the convective heat transfer is believed to be predominant. This is because, on one hand, the higher vapor velocity brings the liquid velocity higher and the film thickness thinner so that the convective heat transfer resistance inside the film is brought smaller, and on the other hand the lower wall temperature caused by a higher convective heat transfer rate reduces the effective number of bubble nucleation sites.

The convective heat transfer coefficient h_c is usually expressed in the following form:

$$\frac{h_c}{h_{cl}} = F \tag{93}$$

where h_{cl} is the heat transfer coefficient to be obtained of the liquid is flowing alone in the tube and F accounts for the effect of the existing vapor flow. The correlation shown by the solid line running from the left bottom to the right top in Figure 10 for high quality region actually corresponds to F, so that the result of Collier et al. [43] shows

$$F = 2.9\left(\frac{1}{X_{tt}}\right)^{0.66} \tag{94}$$

at high quality. Chen suggested that F should be a flow parameter so that it is a function of the Martinelli parameter [42]. His correlation for F in a graphical form is reproduced in Figure 11. In his correlation, h_{cl} was evaluated with the Dittus–Boelter equation:

$$h_{cl} = 0.023 Pr_l^{0.4} Re_l^{0.8} \frac{\lambda_l}{D} \tag{95}$$

where λ_l and Pr_l are the thermal conductivity and the Prandtl number of liquid, respectively.

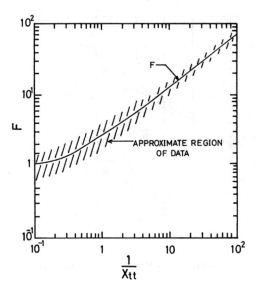

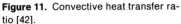

Figure 11. Convective heat transfer ratio [42].

Bennett and Chen [44] extended the expressions of F to take into account the effect of the fluid Prandtl number. One of their correlation is:

$$F = Pr_1^{0.296}\phi_1^{0.888} \tag{96}$$

which may be valid for the range of the Prandtl number from 1 to 6.

Chen [42] introduced a suppression factor S_n of nucleate boiling in the expression of h_{NB} which is given by:

$$h_{NB} = S_n h_p \tag{97}$$

where h_p is the nucleate pool boiling heat transfer coefficient. Chen himself used the modified form of the Forster–Zuber equation [45] for h_p. But other correlations may be used as well. Chen also presented a correlation for the S_n factor in a graphical form which is shown in Figure 12. The abscissa of the figure is the two-phase Reynolds number. Inclusion of F in Re indicates that the suppression of nucleation is remarkable at high-quality at thin-liquid film.

Bennett et al. [46] derived the expression for S_n analytically, and it is given by:

$$S_n = \frac{\lambda_1}{h_{cl}F\delta_b}\left[1 - \exp\left(-\frac{h_{cl}F\delta_b}{\lambda_1}\right)\right] \tag{98}$$

where

$$\delta_b = 0.041\left[\frac{\sigma}{g(\rho_1 - \rho_g)}\right]^{1/2}$$

They found that Equation 98 agrees well with the graphical presentation of S_n given by Chen. Their results are shown in Figure 13.

Other forms of the h correlation were proposed in many papers including those by Dengler and Addoms [47] and Guerrieri and Talty [48]. These are tabulated and reviewed by Rohsenow [49].

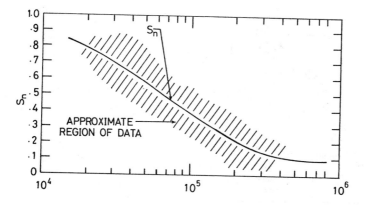

Figure 12. Suppression factor of nucleate boiling S [42].

However, Chen's correlation is often used and may be best. Kihara et al. [50] checked the validity of his correlation and found very good agreement with their own experimental data of Freon-11.

In a horizontal tube, stratification of the flow is likely to occur at a low mass flow rate and, even at a high mass flow rate condition corresponding to the annular flow regime, peripheral non-uniformity of film thickness is often observed. Although the latter effect has not been clarified well enough, many correlations for heat transfer are proposed.

For refrigerant flows in horizontal tubes, many correlations of the following simple form have been proposed.

$$h = A m^{\alpha} q_w^{\beta} D^{\gamma} \tag{99}$$

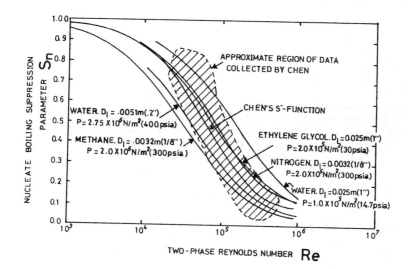

TWO-PHASE REYNOLDS NUMBER Re

Figure 13. Suppression factor of nucleate boiling S [46].

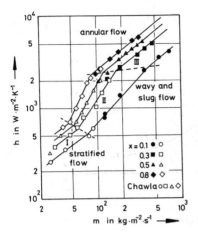

Figure 14. Two-phase heat transfer coefficient [53].

Comparison of the values of α, β, and γ proposed by different authors are made by Butterworth and Shock [51] and large discrepancies can be found among the tabulated values. Slipcevic [52] proposed two sets of values for exponents α, β, and γ; one for a low mass flux condition and another for a high mass flux condition. For the low mass flux condition, $\beta = 0.7$ so that nucleate boiling was believed to be dominant. For the high mass flux condition, $\beta = 0$ so that the convective heat transfer must have been predominant. No explanation is given explicitly for flow pattern or even for stratification. Moreover, the proposed value 1.4 for α may be unreasonably large.

Figure 14 shows the experimental data of the two-phase heat transfer coefficient obtained by Bandel and Schlünder [53] for horizontal tube flow. Their results in the annular flow regime show that $h \propto m^{0.8}$ and the dependency of h on m is equivalent to that for single-phase turbulent flow heat transfer. They correlated the heat transfer data including some with boiling in the following form:

$$\frac{h}{h_{cl}} = C \left[\frac{\left(\dfrac{dp}{dz}\right)_f}{\left(\dfrac{dp}{dz}\right)_{f_1}} \right]^{0.429} \tag{100}$$

Dembi et al. [54] compared several correlations including those of Chen [42] for vertical flows [55, 56]. They claim that inclusion of the Weber number in the correlation is important for horizontal flow heat transfer. They also concluded that the correlation by Bandel and Schlünder [53] and the graphic chart given by Shah [56] are good. Figure 15 shows the chart given by Shah. Abscissa C_0' is the convection number defined as:

$$C_0' = \left(\frac{1-x}{x}\right)^{0.8} \left(\frac{\rho_g}{\rho_1}\right)^{0.5} \tag{101}$$

and the parameter B_0 in the figure is the boiling number:

$$B_0 = \frac{q_w}{H_m} \tag{102}$$

where H is the latent heat of vaporization. Another parameter Fr appearing for horizontal tube heat transfer is the Froude number $Fr = m^2/\rho^2 gD$.

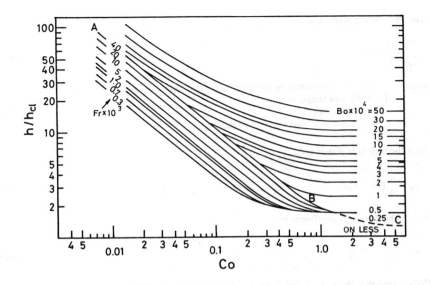

Figure 15. The chart correlation of two-phase heat transfer coefficient for annular flow [56].

CONDENSATION HEAT TRANSFER

Since it is impossible to maintain cooling surfaces in a state that maintains dropwise condensation for long periods of time, film condensation is of practical importance. This means the flow pattern more or less like the annular flow is formed in a case of vapor condensation inside a tube. The basis of theoretical approaches of film condensation has been established by Nusselt [57].

For film condensation on a vertical flat plate, the film thickness of condensate increases downward as shown in Figure 16. Ignoring the interfacial heat transfer resistance mentioned already and the convective transport of heat inside the film, the temperature distribution inside the film is

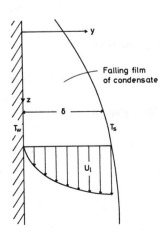

Figure 16. Film condensation on a vertical flat plate.

given by a linear relationship:

$$\frac{T_s - T}{T_s - T_w} = 1 - \frac{y}{\delta} \tag{103}$$

where T_s = the vapor saturation temperature or the temperature of the film surface
 T_w = the wall temperature
 δ = the film thickness
 y = the distance from the wall surface

Then the wall heat flux is given by:

$$q_w = \frac{\lambda_1}{\delta}(T_s - T_w) \tag{104}$$

and the heat transfer coefficient by

$$h = \frac{\lambda_1}{\delta} \tag{105}$$

Considering that the vapor is stagnant, the static pressure gradient becomes:

$$\frac{dp}{dz} = \rho_v g \tag{106}$$

where ρ_v is the vapor density and z is measured downward. Thus, the equation of motion for condensate can be written as follows:

$$0 = \frac{d\tau_1}{dy} + (\rho_1 - \rho_v)g \tag{107}$$

Assuming the laminar flow of condensate and the zero shear stress at the interface, the following relationship can be derived:

$$\mu_1 \frac{dU_1}{dy} = g(\rho_1 - \rho_v)(\delta - y) \tag{108}$$

With the boundary condition $U_1 = 0$ at $y = 0$, the prior equation integrates to:

$$U_1 = \frac{g(\rho_1 - \rho_v)}{\mu_1}\left(\delta y - \frac{y^2}{2}\right) \tag{109}$$

Then, the condensate mass flow rate per unit spanwise width of film is given by:

$$\Gamma = \int_0^\delta \rho_1 U_1 \, dy = \frac{g\rho_1(\rho_1 - \rho_v)\delta^3}{3\mu_1} \tag{110}$$

or

$$\frac{d\Gamma}{dz} = \frac{g\rho_1(\rho_1 - \rho_v)\delta^2}{\mu_1}\frac{d\delta}{dz}$$

The wall heat flux q_w is related to $d\Gamma/dz$ as follows:

$$\frac{\lambda_l}{\delta}(T_s - T_w) = \frac{d\Gamma}{dz}\left[H + \frac{1}{\Gamma}\int_0^\delta \rho_l U_l C_l (T_s - T)\, dy\right] \tag{111}$$

where C_l is the specific heat of condensate. Substituting Equations 103 and 109 into the integral of Equation 111 and Equation 110 into $d\Gamma/dz$, the following relationship is obtained:

$$\delta^3 d\delta = \frac{\lambda_l \mu_l (T_s - T_w)}{g\rho_l(\rho_l - \rho_v)H'}\, dz \tag{112}$$

where

$$H' = H + \frac{3}{8}C_l(T_s - T_w) \tag{113}$$

Rohsenow [58] refined this expression taking into account nonlinear temperature distribution:

$$H' = H + 0.68C_l(T_s - T_w) \tag{114}$$

Solving Equation 112 with a condition $\delta = 0$ at $z = 0$, δ can be obtained:

$$\delta = \sqrt[4]{\frac{4\lambda_l \mu_l z(T_s - T_w)}{g\rho_l(\rho_l - \rho_v)H'}} \tag{115}$$

Thus, the local heat transfer coefficient becomes:

$$h = \sqrt[4]{\frac{g\rho_l(\rho_l - \rho_v)\lambda_l^3 H'}{4z\mu_l(T_s - T_w)}} \tag{116}$$

and the averaged heat transfer coefficient $\bar{h}$ between $z = 0$ and l is:

$$\bar{h} = 0.943 \sqrt[4]{\frac{g\rho_l(\rho_l - \rho_v)\lambda_l^3 H'}{\mu_l(T_s - T_w)l}} \tag{117}$$

Equations 116 and 117 can be written in the following alternative forms:

$$\frac{h}{\lambda_l}\left[\frac{\mu_l^2}{\rho_l g(\rho_l - \rho_v)}\right]^{1/3} = 1.10 Re_f^{-1/3} \tag{118}$$

$$\frac{\bar{h}}{\lambda_l}\left[\frac{\mu_l^2}{\rho_l g(\rho_l - \rho_v)}\right]^{1/3} = 1.47 Re^{-1/3} \tag{119}$$

where the condensate film Reynolds number Re_f is given by:

$$Re_f = \frac{4\Gamma}{\mu_l} \tag{120}$$

When the subcooling of the condensate is considered to have been taken into account already in Equation 111, the influence of variable fluid properties must be accounted for. This is usually done by introducing an effective film temperature T_{fm}:

$$T_{fm} = T_w + \chi(T_s - T_w) \tag{121}$$

Mincowycz and Sparrow [59] proposed 0.31 for χ.

The preceding simple analysis originating from Nusselt agrees well with the experimentally observed value of the heat transfer coefficient only at low Reynolds numbers, $Re_f < 10$. At higher

Reynolds numbers, the assumption that the film flow is in laminar state may not be accurate enough. Colburn [60] attempted to take into account the effect of turbulence. His result reads:

$$\frac{h}{\lambda_l}\left[\frac{\mu_l^2}{\rho_l g(\rho_l - \rho_v)}\right]^{1/3} = 0.056 Re_f^{0.2} Pr_l^{1/3} \tag{122}$$

He assumed that the film flow becomes turbulent when $Re_f > 2,000$. However, it is well known that the observed value of h is remarkably larger than the predicted value with a Nusselt-type analysis in the middle range of Reynolds numbers $10 < Re_f < 2,000$. This may be attributed partially to the effect of waves appearing on the interface [61]. Hirshburg and Florschuetz [61] treated this effect basically with a linear theory for waves and Suzuki et al. [63] with a wave effect model proposed in [8].

Condensation occurring in a tube differs from that on a vertical flat plate mentioned previously in a point that the vapor comes into the tube with some magnitude of velocity. This exerts the shear stress τ_i at the vapor-condensate interface. Due to Rohsenow et al. [64], the following relationship holds for laminar condensate film in downward flow instead of Equation 114 for $\tau_i = 0$.

$$\left[\frac{4\mu_l \lambda_l z(T_s - T_w)}{g\rho_l(\rho_l - \rho_v^*)H'}\right] = \delta^4 + \frac{4}{3}\left[\frac{\tau_i \delta^3}{(\rho_l - \rho_v^*)g}\right] \tag{123}$$

where ρ_v^* is the fictitious density of vapor defined by:

$$\left(\frac{dp}{dz}\right) = \rho_v^* g \tag{124}$$

ρ_v^* is equal to the actual vapor density ρ_v only when the vapor flow is stagnant. Otherwise, the pressure gradient is not solely determined from the vapor static head. Equation 124 clearly shows that δ becomes smaller at a higher shear rate. This leads to lower heat transfer resistance inside the film and hence to a higher heat transfer coefficient.

Figure 17 shows the theoretical results obtained by Dukler [32]. He assumed that the condensate velocity profile in the film is equal to that of single-phase flow at the same Reynolds number in a

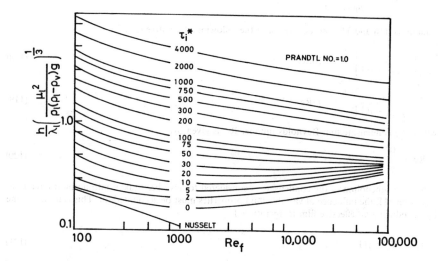

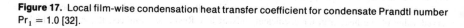

Figure 17. Local film-wise condensation heat transfer coefficient for condensate Prandtl number $Pr_l = 1.0$ [32].

tube, and introduced the eddy viscosity defined by Equations 74 and 75. The parameter τ_i^* in the figure is the nondimensional magnitude of the interfacial shear stress τ_i. Rohsenow et al. [64] executed similar analysis before. They also derived a relationship for the dependency of the critical Reynolds number on the interfacial shear stress.

Recently, Blangetti [65] and Blangetti and Schlünder [66] carried out experimental and analytical works on condensation in a vertical tube. They took into account the suppression of turbulence in the liquid at the interface [67]. Their analytical results show the dependence

$$h \propto Re_f^{0.4} \tag{125}$$

They agree with their experimental data in the Reynolds number range of $Re_f > 900$ and equivalent in form to the recommended curve by McAdams [68] for $\bar{h}$. They also suggests that the heat transfer at a lower value of Re_f may occur under the effect of interfacial waves.

As mentioned in the first part of this section, film condensation is important in a practical sense. This may also be applied to the condensation in horizontal tubes. This is different from the boiling heat transfer so dry-patches are unlikely to occur on the upper inner surface of a horizontal tube in the case of condensation. A part of the film formed there is likely to run down toward the lower part of the tube inner surface. Therefore, at a small vapor velocity or at a low interfacial shear stress, stratification of the flow may certainly occur. However, at a large vapor velocity or at a high interfacial shear stress, the effect of flow stratification on condensation heat transfer may be neglected. Thus, the relationships mentioned previously for the vertical tube may approximately be used for condensation in horizontal tubes at high vapor velocity.

TWO-COMPONENT HEAT TRANSFER

In single-component heat transfer, the interfacial heat transfer resistance is not important is usual situations as already mentioned. Against this, the gas-side heat transfer resistance is crucial in two-component heat transfer problems. Therefore, in two-component heat transfer problems, it is not enough to treat the flow and heat transport inside the liquid film only, but is required to treat the flow, heat, and mass transport in gas-phase flow simultaneously. In this section, attention will be paid only to a case when evaporation proceeds at the interface at moderate heat flux. More detailed discussions of the same matter are given by Michiyoshi [68]. For condensation of a vapor mixture and boiling of a binary or multicomponent mixture, see References 69, 70, and 71.

For evaporative heat transfer in a two-phase two-component annular flow, several experiments have been conducted by Groothuis and Hendal [72], Kudirka et al. [73], Fried [74], Johnson and Abou-Sabe [75], and Pletcher and McManus [76]. Pletcher and McManus introduced an equilibrium temperature T_F to correlate the heat transfer data obtained within a horizontal tube. The local heat transfer coefficient defined by them is given by:

$$h = \frac{q_w}{T_w - T_m} \tag{126}$$

where the equilibrium temperature T_m may be calculated from the following heat balance equation if the change in flow kinetic energy is neglected:

$$\frac{4zq_w}{D} = m_{lz}(i_{lz} - i_{l0}) + m_a(i_{az} - i_{a0}) + m_{v0}(i_{vz} - i_{v0}) + \Delta m_v(i_{vz} - i_{l0}) \tag{127}$$

i_{lz}, i_{az}, and i_{vz} in the preceding equation are the enthalpy at the temperature T_m to be defined at a position z for liquid, noncondensable gas, and vapour, respectively. m_a is the mass flux of noncondensable gas, m_{lz} the local mass flux of liquid, m_{v0} the initial mass flux of vapor at the inlet to the tube $z = 0$, and Δm_v is the mean evaporating flux averaged between the position z and the inlet. i_{l0}, i_{a0}, and i_{v0} are the enthalpy at the inlet for the liquid, noncondensable gas, and vapor, respectively. Pletcher and McManus correlated the local heat transfer coefficient h and the averaged heat transfer coefficient $\bar{h}$ in the form divided by ϕ_l defined by Equation 18 against the Lockhart-Martinelli parameter X. They also show that the data by Johnson and Abou-Sabe [75] and Fried [74] group near the extended line of their correlation, although the data given by themselves are for the annular flow and the latter for the flow with lower quality.

A theoretical treatment for the same problem has been given by another paper by Pletcher and McManus [77]. Their analysis did not take into account the effect of gravity force so that it can also be applied to vertical annular flow at high shear rate. Their analysis assumes that the vapor is in saturated condition both at the interface and in the core region of a tube. They also uses the similarity between the heat transport and mass transport in gas-phase flow. The computed value of h/ϕ_l shows the same dependency on the parameter X as their experimental data but is higher than the latter by about 50%.

Recently, Vijay et al, [78] applied the Fried correlation of the heat transfer coefficient [74] to a vertical two-phase, two-component annular flow and proposed the following relationship for the annular flow regime:

$$\frac{h}{h_{cl}} = (\phi_l^2)^{0.455} \tag{128}$$

Their correlation agrees rather well with the experimental data.

The previous forms of correlations are simple in form and convenient to use. However, a caution has been given by Suzuki et al. [8] about the usage of such correlations because they do not include the effect of temperature level. It is well established that the total heat flux at the interface q_i is given by the sum of the interfacial conduction heat flux q_{ci} and the removal rate of the latent heat of vaporization. The latter is given by the product of the latent heat of vaporization H and the evaporation flux $\dot{m}_v$. Thus,

$$q_i = q_{ci} + H\dot{m}_v \tag{129}$$

where the inward heat transport is taken to be positive. Dividing Equation 129 by a representative temperature difference ΔT, we have

$$\frac{q_i}{\Delta T} = \frac{q_{ci}}{\Delta T} + \frac{H\dot{m}_v}{\Delta T} \tag{130}$$

The left-hand side corresponds to the interfacial heat transfer coefficient. In a case when the heat transfer resistance inside the liquid film can be ignored, $q_i = q_w$. Then, the left-hand side of the preceding equation becomes identical with the overall heat transfer coefficient h. The first term on the right-hand side is the pure convective heat transfer coefficient h_c and the second term the heat transfer coefficient relating to the latent heat removal h_m. Then, in alternative form,

$$h = h_c + h_m \tag{131}$$

The value of $\dot{m}_v$ depends on the mass transfer rate of vapor, therefore, on the vapor pressure at the interface. The vapor saturation pressure is a nonlinear function of temperature so that the ratio between the first term and the second term of Equation 131 can vary with temperature. This indicates that the value of h depends not only on hydrodynamic parameters but also on thermodynamic parameters. The same argument can be applied to the cases when q_i differs from q_w. Suzuki et al. [8] proposed a nondimensional thermodynamic parameter β. It is given by:

$$\beta = \frac{H^2 \tilde{M}_v}{\tilde{M}_a C_{pg} P T_m V_{vm}} \tag{132}$$

where $\tilde{M}_v$ = the molecular weight of vapor,
$\tilde{M}_a$ = the molecular weight of noncondensable gas.
C_{pg} = the specific heat of a mixture at constant pressure,
P = the total pressure,

T_m = the equilibrium temperature introduced by Pletcher and McManus [76],
V_{vm} = the specific volume of vapor at the temperature T_m.

V_{vm} is a sensitive function of temperature so that this parameter may be available for evaluating how the heat transfer coefficient depends on the temperature level. The higher the temperature level, the larger the evaporation effect or the heat transfer coefficient will be. The interfacial heat flux q_i is related to the interfacial conductive heat flux q_{ci} by the following equation with the above parameter β:

$$q_i = (1 + \beta)q_{ci} \tag{133}$$

In the light of this equation, the overall heat transfer coefficient h may be expressed by:

$$h = (1 + \beta)h_c \tag{134}$$

for such a thin liquid film whose heat transfer resistance can be ignored. Equation 134 may be used as a rule of thumb for the two-component annular flow heat transfer coefficient.

Suzuki et al. conducted a theoretical study of the evaporative heat transfer in a downward annular flow in a vertical tube. They showed that the evaporative heat transfer can rather easily be treated if the assumption that the vapor is in a saturated condition everywhere is adopted. They also showed that the energy and vapor mass transfer equations can be combined into a single equation for the gas temperature, which has the same form as the energy equation for single-phase flow. The parameter β has been introduced in the course of this derivation of the combined equation. The combined equation has been solved for the fully developed condition which is expected to exist at the low wall heat flux. Equation 133 was used as a matching condition for the energy equation at the interface between the liquid film and the gas-phase flow dispersed with droplets. They took into account the wave effect on the heat, mass, and momentum transfer by Equations 51 and 52. Their results are shown in Figure 18 in comparison with their experimental data obtained for air-water flow in a vertical tube of 26.4-mm ID [6]. The symbols specified as "Ripple" are for the flow conditions when only the ripple waves are observed on the interface and the symbols

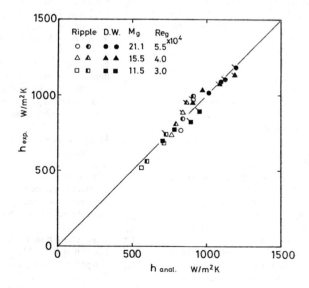

Figure 18. Comparison of heat transfer coefficient for two-component annular flow [8].

specified as "D.W." are for the conditions when the disturbance waves are observed as well. Their method would be used for the cases at low wall heat flux which was assumed in their calculation. Their experimental conditions compared in Figure 18 cover the ranges of the wall heat flux 0.93×10^4 W/m$^2 \leqq q_w \leqq 2.87 \times 10^4$ W/m^2, the tube wall temperature 313K $\leqq T_w \leqq$ 343K, and the film Reynolds number 140 $\leqq Re_f \leqq$ 500.

NOTATION

A	flow cross-sectional area
A_g	cross-sectional area occupied by gas flow
A_t	cross-sectional area occupied by liquid flow
A_l	cross-sectional area occupied by liquid flow
B_0	boiling number defined by Equation 102
C_l	specific heat of condensate
C_0'	convection number defined by Equation 101
C_0	coefficient introduced into Equation 61
D	tube diameter
D*	non-dimensionalized tube hydraulic diameter defined by Equation 86
d_h	tube hydraulic diameter
E	droplet entrainment fraction ($= m_l - m_f/m$)
F	heat transfer coefficient factor defined by Equation 93
Fr	Froude number ($= m^2/\rho^2 gD$)
f	Fanning factor of single-phase flow
f_g	two-phase flow Fanning factor introduced in Equation 21
f_{g0}	two-phase flow Fanning factor introduced in Equation 23
f_i	interfacial friction factor introduced in Equation 33
f_{is}	single-phase flow friction factor
f_l	two-phase flow Fanning factor introduced in Equation 22
f_{l0}	two-phase flow Fanning factor introduced in Equation 24
f_{tp}	two-phase flow friction factor used in the homogeneous model and defined by Equation 33
g	gravitational acceleration
H	latent heat of vaporization
H'	apparent latent heat of vaporization defined by Equation 114
h	two-phase flow heat transfer coefficient
$\bar{h}$	averaged heat transfer coefficient
h_c	convective heat transfer coefficient
h_{c1}	single-phase flow convective heat transfer coefficient

h_{NB}	nucleate boiling heat transfer coefficient
h_p	nucleate pool boiling heat transfer coefficient
h_m	equivalent heat transfer coefficient relating to latent heat removal from the interface ($= H\dot{m}_v/\Delta T$)
i	local two-phase flow enthalpy
i_a	enthalpy of noncondensable gas
i_g	saturated gas-phase enthalpy
i_l	saturated liquid-phase enthalpy
i_v	condensable gas enthalpy
J	total momentum flux
j	local volumetric flux density of two-phase mixture
j_g	gas phase volumetric flux density
j_g^*	nondimensional gas-phase volumetric flux density defined by Equation 85
j_l	liquid-phase volumetric flux density
L	averaged wave amplitude
M_f	liquid film mass flow rate
M_g	gas-phase mass flow rate
M_l	liquid-phase mass flow rate
m	total mass flux ($= m_l + m_g$)
m_a	mass flux of noncondensable gas
m_f	mass flux of liquid flowing inside film ($= M_f/A$)
m_g	gas-phase mass flux ($= M_g/A$)
m_l	liquid-phase mass flux ($= M_l/A$)
m_v	mass flux of condensable gas
$\dot{m}_v$	evaporation flux at the interface
N_μ	viscosity number defined by Equation 83
P_{r_l}	Prandtl number of liquid
p	pressure
Q	arbitrary quantity
q_c	conductive heat flux
q_{ci}	interfacial conductive heat flux
q_i	interfacial total heat flux
q_{NB}	nucleate boiling heat flux
q_w	wall heat flux
Re	single-phase flow Reynolds number
Re_f	liquid film Reynolds number
Re_g	gas-phase flow Reynolds number defined by Equation 27
Re_{g0}	gas-phase flow Reynolds number defined by Equation 29

Re_l	liquid-phase flow Reynolds number defined by Equation 28	$\bar{U}_l$	averaged liquid-phase velocity ($= M_l/\rho_l A_l$)
Re_{l0}	liquid-phase flow Reynolds number defined by Equation 30	U_w	wave velocity
Re_{tp}	two-phase flow Reynolds number defined by Equation 31	U_τ	friction velocity
		V_{vm}	specific volume of saturated vapor at temperature T_m
τ_i	radial position of interface	We	Weber number defined by Equation 68
S	slip ratio		
S_n	suppression factor of nucleate boiling	W_g	superficial gas velocity
T_b	bulk mean fluid temperature	W_l	superficial liquid velocity
T_{fm}	effective film temperature	w_g	gas-phase drift velocity
T_m	equilibrium temperature defined by Equation 127	w_l	liquid-phase drift velocity
		x	vapor quality
T_s	vapor saturation temperature	X	Lockhart-Martinelli parameter defined by Equation 36
T_w	wall temperature		
U	streamwise velocity	Y	Chisholm parameter defined by Equation 42
U^+	universal velocity defined by Equation 50	y	distance from the wall
		Z^*	nondimensional streamwise distance defined by Equation 87
$\bar{U}_f$	averaged liquid film velocity ($= M_f/\pi\rho_l D\delta$)	z	Streamwise distance
$\bar{U}_g$	averaged gas-phase velocity ($= M_g/\rho_g A_g$)		

Greek Symbols

α	mean void fraction	μ_{tp}	two-phase flow viscosity defined by Equation 32
$\tilde{\alpha}$	local void fraction		
β	nondimensional mass transfer effect parameter defined by Equation 132	ρ_c	mean density of the fluid flowing in the tube core region defined by Equation 46
Γ	condensate mass flow rate per unit film spanwise width	ρ_g	density of gas
γ	inclination angle of tube raised from the horizontal plane	ρ_l	density of liquid
		ρ_{tp}	two-phase flow density defined by Equation 34
ΔJ	change of J		
Δm_v	change of m_v	ρ_v^*	Fictitious density of vapor defined by Equation 24
ΔP_a	pressure drop due to flow acceleration	σ	surface tension
ΔT	representative temperature difference	τ_g	shear stress in gas-phase flow
ΔT_b	temperature difference ($= T_w - T_b$)	τ_l	shear stress i liquid-phase flow
ΔT_{sat}	wall superheat ($= T_w - T_s$)	τ_i	interfacial shear stress
$\Delta\rho$	density difference between two phases	τ_l^*	Nondimensionalized interfacial shear stress
δ	liquid film thickness		
δ_b	thickness of bubble growth region introduced in Equation 98	τ_w	wall shear stress
		ϕ_g	two-phase flow friction multiplier defined by Equation 17
δ_{max}	maximum film thickness		
δ_{min}	minimum film thickness	ϕ_{g0}	two-phase flow friction multiplier defined by Equation 19
ζ	volumetric flow rate ratio		
η	function of $\zeta(=\zeta/1-\zeta)$	ϕ_l	two-phase flow friction multiplier defined by Equation 18
λ_l	liquid thermal conductivity		
μ_e	effective viscosity	ϕ_{l0}	two-phase flow friction multiplier defined by Equation 20
μ_g	effective viscosity		
μ_g	gas viscosity	Ω	mass velocity correction factor for ϕ_{l0}^2
$\tilde{\mu}_g$	gas-phase apparent wave viscosity	ω	averaged wave frequency
μ_l	liquid viscosity		
$\tilde{\mu}_l$	liquid-phase apparent wave viscosity		

REFERENCES

1. Delhaye, J. M., "Two-Phase Flow Patterns," in *Two-Phase Flow and Heat Transfer in the Power and Process Industries* by A. E. Bergles et al., Washington D.C.: Hemisphere, 1981, pp. 1–36.
2. Hewitt, G. F., "Two-Phase Flow Patterns and Their Relationship to Two-Phase Heat Transfer," *Two-Phase Flows and Heat Transfer*, Volume 1, S. Kakaç and F. Mayinger (eds.), Washington D.C.: Hemisphere, 1977, pp. 11–35.
3. Hewitt, G. F., "Flow Patterns," in *Two-Phase Flow and Heat Transfer*, D. Butterworth and G. F. Hewitt (eds.), Oxford: Oxford University Press, 1977, pp. 18–36.
4. Hewitt, G. F., "Flow Regimes," in *Handbook of Multiphase Systems*, G. Hetsroni (ed.), Washington D. C.: Hemisphere, 1981, pp. 2.3–2.43.
5. Hagiwara, Y., et al., "A Study on Liquid Film Flow Characteristics in Annular Two-Phase Flow," in *Proc. 3rd Multiphase Flow and Heat Transfer Symposium-Workshop*, T. N. Veziroglu (ed.), 1983, pp. 43–46.
6. Hagiwara, Y., et al., "Studies on Thin Liquid Film of Annular-mist Two-Phase Flow. I. Wave Characteristics and Heat Transfer," *Mem. Faculty Engng Kyoto Univ.*, vol. 44, no. 2 (April 1982), pp. 309–328.
7. Hagiwara, Y., et al., "Simultaneous Measurements of Wall Shear Stress and Liquid Film Thickness in an Annular Mist Two-Phase Flow in a Vertical Circular Tube," in *ASME/JSME Thermal Engineering Joint Conference Proceedings*, Volume 1, Y. Mori and W. J. Yang (eds.), New York. The American Society of Mechanical Engineers, 1983, pp. 55–62.
8. Suzuki, K., Hagiwara, Y., and Sato, T., "Heat Transfer and Flow Characteristics of Two-Phase Two-Component Annular Flow," *Int. J. Heat Mass Transfer*, vol. 26, no. 4 (1983), pp. 597–605.
9. Friedel, L., "Momentum Exchange and Pressure Drop in Two-Phase Flow," in *Two-Phase Flows and Heat Transfer*, Volume 1, S. Kakaç and F. Mayinger (eds.) Washington D.C.: Hemisphere, 1977, pp. 239–312.
10. McAdams, W. H., "Vaporization Inside Horizontal Tubes. Part 2: Benzine-Oil Mixtures," *Trans. ASME*, vol. 64 (1942), pp. 193–200.
11. Beattie, D. R. H., "A Note on The Calculation of Two-Phase Pressure Losses," *Nuclear Engineering and Design*, vol. 25 (1973), pp. 395–402.
12. Lockhart, R. W., and Martinelli, R. C., "Proposed Correlation of Data for Isothermal Two-Phase, Two-Component Flow in Pipes," *Chemical Engineering Progress*, vol. 45, no. 1 (1949), pp. 39–48.
13. Martinelli, R. C., and Nelson, D. B., "Prediction of Pressure Drop during Forced-Circulation Boiling of Water," *Trans. ASME*, vol. 70 (1948), pp. 695–702.
14. Chisholm, D., and Laird, A. D. K., "Two-Phase Flow in Rough Tubes," *Trans. ASME*, vol. 80, no. 2 (1958), pp. 276–283.
15. Chisholm, D., "A Theoretical Basis for The Lockhart-Martinelli Correlation of Data for Isothermal Two-Phase, Two-Component Flow in Pipes," *Int. J. Heat Mass Transfer*, vol. 10 (1967), pp. 1767–1778.
16. Baroczy, C. J., "A Systematic Correlation for Two-Phase Pressure Drop," *Chem. Engng. Prog. Symp. Ser.*, No. 44, vol. 62 (1966), pp. 232–249.
17. Chisholm, D., "Pressure Gradients Due to Friction during the flow of Evaporating Two-Phase Mixtures in Smooth Tubes and Channels," *Int. J. Heat Mass Transfer*, vol. 16 (1973), pp. 347–358.
18. Friedel, L., "Modellgesetz für Den Reibungs-druckverlust in Der Zweiphasenströmung," *VDI-Forschungs Heft* 572, 1975.
19. Hewitt, G. F., "Pressure Drop," *Handbook of Multiphase System*, G. Hetsroni (ed.), Washington D.C.: Hemisphere, 1981, pp. 2.44–2.75.
20. Hewitt, G. F., "Multiphase Fluid Flow and Pressure Drop," *Heat Exchanger Hand Book*, E. U. Schlünder et al. (eds.), Washington D.C.: Hemisphere, 1983, pp. 2.3.1.1–2.3.2.34.
21. Gill, L. E., et al., "Sampling Probe Studies of The Gas Core in Annular Two-Phase Flow—I. The Effect of Length on Phase and Velocity Distribution," *Chem. Engng Sci.*, Vol. 18 (1963), pp. 525–535.

22. Hewitt, G. F., and Lacey, P. M. C., "The Breakdown of The Liquid Film in Annular Two-Phase Flow," *Int. J. Heat Mass Transfer*, vol. 8 (1965), pp. 781–791.

23. Wallis, G. B., "Annular Two-Phase Flow," *Trans. ASME, J. Basic Engng*, vol. 92–93 (1970), pp. 59–82.

24. Martindale, W. R., and Smith, R. V., "Two-Phase Two-Component Interface Drag Coefficients in Separated Phase Flows," *Int. J. Multiphase Flow*, vol. 7 (1981), pp. 211–219.

25. Levy, S., and Healzer, J. M., "Application of Mixing Length Theory to Wavy Turbulent Liquid-Gas Interface," *J. Heat Transfer*, vol. 103 (1981), pp. 492–500.

26. Zuber, N., and Findlay, J. A., "Average Volumetric Concentration in Two-Phase Flow Systems," *J. Heat Transfer*, vol. 87 (1965), pp. 453–468.

27. Bankoff, S. G., "A Variable Density Single-Fluid Model for Two-Phase Flow with Particular Reference to Steam-Water Flow," *J. Heat Transfer*, vol. 82 (1960), pp. 265–272.

28. Ishii, M., "Wave Phenomena and Two-Phase Flow Instabilities," in *Handbook of Multiphase Systems*, G. Hetsroni (ed.), Washington D.C.: Hemisphere, 1982, pp. 2-95–2-128.

29. Ishii, M., "Drift Flux Model and Derivation of Kinematic Constitutive Laws," in *Two-Phase Flows and Heat Transfer*, Volume 1, S. Kakac and F. Mayinger (eds.), Washington D.C.: Hemisphere, 1977, pp. 187–208.

30. Rouhani, Z., "Steady-State Void Fraction and Pressure Drop in Watercooled Reactors," in *Two-Phase Flows and Heat Transfer*, J. J. Ginoux (ed.), Washington D.C.: Hemisphere, 1978, pp. 241–273.

31. Premoli, A., et al., "Una Correlazionne Adimensionale per La Determinazione Della Densità di Miscele Bifasiche," *La Termotecnica*, vol. 25, 1971, pp. 17–26.

32. Dukler, A. E., "Fluid Mechanics and Heat Transfer in Vertical Falling-Film Systems," *Chem. Engng. Prog. Symp. Ser.*, No. 30, vol. 56 (1960), pp. 1–10.

33. Schlichting, H., *Boundary Layer Theory*, 7th ed., New York: McGraw-Hill, 1979, pp. 578–594.

34. Ishii, M., and Grolmes, M. A., "Inception Criteria for Droplet Entrainment in Two-Phase Concurrent Film Flow," *AIChE Journal*, vol. 21, no. 2 (March 1975), pp. 308–318.

35. van Rossum, J. J., "Experimental Investigation of Horizontal Liquid Films," *Chem. Engng Sci.*, vol. 11 (1959), pp. 35–52.

36. Ueda, T., and Tanaka, T., "Studies of Liquid Film Flow in Two-Phase Annular and Annular-Mist Flow Regions, Part 1 and 2," *Trans. JSME*, vol. 39, no. 325 (1973), pp. 2842–2862.

37. Yablonik, R. M., and Khaimov, V. A., "Determination of The Velocity of Inception of Droplet Entrainment," *Fluid Mechanics Soviet Research*, vol. 1, no. 1 (1972), pp. 130–134.

38. Zhivaikin, L. Ya., "Liquid Film Thickness in Film-Type Units," *International Chem. Eng.*, vol. 2, no. 3 (1962), pp. 337–341.

39. Ishii, M., and Kataoka, I., "Interfacial Transfer in Annular Dispersed Flow," in *Advances in Two-Phase Flow and Heat Transfer*, Volume 1, S. Kakac and M. Ishii (eds.), Boston: Martinus Nijhof, 1983, pp. 91–118.

40. Ishii, M., and Mishima, K., "Liquid Transfer and Entrainment Correlation for Droplet-Annular Flow," *Heat Transfer 1982, Proc. Seventh International Heat Transfer Conf.*, Volume 5, U. Grigull et al. (eds.), Washington D.C.: Hemisphere, 1982, pp. 307–312.

41. Hewitt, G. F., "Void Fraction," in *Handbook of Multiphase Systems*, G. Hetsroni (ed.), Washington D.C.: Hemisphere, 1982, pp. 2.76–2.94.

42. Chen, J. C., "Correlation for Boiling Heat Transfer to Saturated Fluids in Convective Flow," *Ind. Eng. Chem. Process Des. Development.*, vol. 5, no. 3 (1966), pp. 322–329.

43. Collier, J. G., et al., "Heat Transfer to Two-Phase Gas-Liquid Systems Part II. Further Data on Steam/Water Mixtures in the Liquid Dispersed Region in An Annulus." *Trans. Instn. Chem. Engrs*, vol. 42 (1964), pp. 127–139.

44. Bennett, D. L., and Chen, J. C., "Forced Convective Boiling in Vertical Tubes for Saturated Pure Components and Binary Mixtures," *AIChE Journal*, vol. 26, no. 3 (1980), pp. 454–461.

45. Forster, H. K., and Zuber, N., "Dynamics of Vapor Bubbles and Boiling Heat Transfer," *AIChE Journal*, vol. 1. no. 4 (1955), pp. 531–535.

46. Bennett, D. L., et al., "The Suppression of Saturated Nucleate Boiling by Forced Convective Flow," *AIChE Symp. Ser.*, no. 199, vol. 76 (1980), pp. 91–103.

47. Dengler, C. E., and Addoms, J. N., "Heat Transfer Mechanism for Vaporization of Water in A Vertical Tube," *AIChE Symp. Ser.*, no. 18, vol. 52 (1956), pp. 95–103.

48. Guerrieri, S. A., and Talty, R. D., "A Study of Heat Transfer to Organic Liquids in Single-Tube, Natural-Circulation, Vertical-Tube Boilers," *Chem. Engng. Prog. Symp. Ser.*, no. 18, vol. 52 (1956), pp. 69–77.

49. Rohsenow, W. M., "Boiling," in *Handbook of Heat Transfer*, W. M. Rohsenow and J. P. Harnett (eds.), New York: McGraw-Hill, pp. 13-1–13-75.

50. Kihara, D. H., et al., "Forced Convection Boiling Heat Transfer of Freon–11 in A Vertical Annular Passage," *Letters in Heat Mass Transfer*, Vol. 6 (1979), pp. 13–21.

51. Butterworth, D., and Shock, R. A. W., "Flow Boiling," *Heat Transfer 1982, Proc. Seventh International Heat Transfer Conf.*, Volume 1, U. Grigull et al. (eds.) Washington D.C.: Hemisphere, 1982, pp. 11–30.

52. Slipcevic, B., "Heat Transfer to Boiling Fluorocarbon Refrigerants," *ASHRAE Journal*, vol. 12 (June 1970), pp. 65–68.

53. Bandel, J., and Schlünder, E. U., "Frictional Pressure Drop and Convective Heat Transfer of Gas-Liquid Flow in Horizontal Tubes," *Heat Transfer 1974, Proc. 5th International Heat Transfer Conf.*, Volume 4, 1974, pp. 190–194.

54. Dembi, N. J., et al., "Statistical Analysis of Heat Transfer Data for Convective Boiling of Refrigerants in A Horizontal Tube," *Letters in Heat Mass Transfer*, vol. 5 (1978), pp. 287–296.

55. Chawla, J. M., "Wärmeübergang und Druckabfall in Waagerechten Rohren bei Der Strömung von Verdampfenden," *VDI-Forschungs Heft* 523, 1967.

56. Shah, M. M., "A New Correlation for Heat Transfer during Boiling Flow through Pipes," *ASHRAE Trans.*, vol. 82, no. 2 (1976), pp. 66–86.

57. Nusselt, W., "Die Oberflachenkondensation des Wasserdampfes." *VDI Zeitschrift*, Vol. 60 (1916), pp. 541–546 and pp. 569–575.

58. Rohsenow, W. M., "Heat Transfer and Temperature Distribution in Laminar-Film Condensation," *Trans. ASME*, Vol. 78 (1956), pp. 1645–1648.

59. Minkowycz, W. J., and Sparrow, E. M., "Condensation Heat Transfer in the Presence of Non-Condensables, Interfacial Resistance, Superheating, Variable Properties and Diffusion," *Int. J. Heat Mass Transfer*, vol. 9 (1966), pp. 1125–1144.

60. Colburn, A. P., "The Calculation of Condensation Where a Portion of the Condensate Layer Is in Turbulent Motion," *Trans. AIChE*, vol. 30 (1933–34), pp. 187–193.

61. Kutatelatze, S. S., "Semi-empirical Theory of Film Condensation of Pure Vapors," *Int. J. Heat Mass Transfer*, vol. 25, no. 2 (1982), pp. 653–660.

62. Hirshburg, R. I., and Florschuetz, L. W., "Laminar Wavy-Film Flow: Part II, Condensation and Evaporation," *J. Heat Transfer*, vol. 104 (1982), pp. 459–464.

63. Suzuki, K., et al., "An Analysis on Film Condensation Heat Transfer Taking Account of Interfacial Wave Effect," *Proc. 20th National Heat Transfer Symposium of Japan*, 1982. pp. 253–255.

64. Rohsenow, W. M., et al., "Effect of Vapor Velocity on Laminar and Turbulent-Film Condensation," *Trans. ASME.*, vol. 78 (1956), pp. 1637–1643.

65. Blangetti, F., "Lokaler Wärmeübergang bei Der Kondensation mit Überlagerter Konvektion im Vertikalen Rohr," Dr. Dissertation Universität Karlsruhe, 1979.

66. Blangetti, F., and Schlünder, E. U., "Local Heat Transfer Coefficients on Condensation in A Vertical Tube," *Heat Transfer Proc. Sixth International Heat Transfer Conf.*, Volume 2, Washington D.C.: Hemisphere, 1978, pp. 437–442.

67. Ueda, H., et al., "Eddy Diffusivity Near the Free Surface of Open Channel Flow," *Int. J. Heat Mass Transfer*, vol. 20 (1977), pp. 1127–1136.

68. Michiyoshi, I., "Two-Phase Two-Component Heat Transfer," *Heat Transfer 1978, Proc. Sixth International Heat Transfer Conf.*, Volume 6, Washington D.C.: Hemisphere, 1978, pp. 219–233.

69. Butterworth, D., "Condensation of Vapor Mixtures," in *Heat Exchangers Hand Book*, Volume 1, E. U. Schlünder et al. (eds.) Washington D.C.: Hemisphere, 1983, pp. 2.6.3.1–2.6.3.10.

70. Collier, J. G., "Boiling of Binary and Multicomponent Mixtures." In *Heat Exchangers Hand Book*, Volume 1, E. U. Schlünder et al. (eds.) Washington D.C.: Hemisphere, 1983, pp. 2.7.8.1–2.7.8.10.

71. Collier, J. G., *Convective Boiling and Condensation*, 2nd ed., New York: McGraw-Hill, 1981, pp. 394–426.

72. Groothuis, H., and Hendal, W. P., "Heat Transfer in Two-Phase Flow," *Chem. Eng. Sci.*, Vol. 11, 1959, pp. 212–220.

73. Kudirka, A. A., et al., "Heat Transfer in Two-Phase Flow of Gas-Liquid Mixtures," *Ind. Engng. Chem. Fundamentals*, vol. 4 (1965), pp. 339–344.

74. Fried, L., "Pressure Drop and Heat Transfer for Two-Phase Two-Component Flow," *Chem. Engng. Prog. Symp. Ser.*, vol. 50 (1954), pp. 47–51.

75. Johnson, H. A., and Abou–Sabe, A. H., "Heat Transfer and Pressure Drop for Turbulent Flow of Air-Water Mixtures in a Horizontal Pipe," *Trans. ASME*, vol. 74 (1952), pp. 977–987.

76. Pletcher. R. H., and McManus, H. N., "Heat Transfer and Pressure Drop in Horizontal Annular Two-Phase Two-Component Flow," *Int. J. Heat Mass Transfer*, vol. 11 (1968), pp. 1087–1104.

77. Pletcher. R. H., and McManus, H. N., "A Theory for Heat Transfer to Annular Two-Phase Two-Component Flow," *Int. J. Heat Mass Transfer*, vol. 15 (1972), pp. 2091–2096.

78. Vijay, et al., "A Correlation of Mean Heat-Transfer Coefficient for Two-Phase Two-Component Flow in A Vertical Tube," *Heat Transfer 1982, Proc. Seventh International Heat Transfer Conf.*, Volume 5, Washington D.C.: Hemisphere, pp. 367–372.

CHAPTER 46

HEAT TRANSPORT IN NUCLEAR REACTOR CHANNELS

Jan Lach

Institute of Atomic Energy
Department of Reactor Engineering
Otwock-Swierk, Poland

Marian Kielkiewicz and Marek Kosinski

Warsaw Technical University
Institute of Heat Engineering
Warsaw, Poland

CONTENTS

INTRODUCTION

This chapter examines basic problems of heat transport and fluid flow dynamics in nuclear reactor channels during normal full-power reactor operation. Heat removal from the reactor core is the same as in conventional thermal installations. However, the requirements concerning reactor calculations are critical because of safety issues concerning both fuel elements and the surrounding environment. The complexity of nuclear reactor systems must be emphasized, particularly in relation to safety along with the need for nonlinear coupling of neutronic and thermal reactor behavior.

The basic topics discussed below include: thermal energy generation, special power distribution, heat transfer with single-phase forced convection, heat transfer with boiling and boiling crisis. Since this is presented as an overview chapter, the reader is liberally referred to the literature for more in depth coverage.

NUCLEAR REACTORS

A neutron hitting a heavy nucleus may cause a fission reaction, i.e., disintegration of the original nucleus into new ones with the release of an enormous amount of energy and simultaneous emission of a few neutrons and gamma photons. Two new nuclei, called fission fragments, usually have unequal masses and are left in an excited state. Neutrons emitted in fission are called prompt neutrons and have an average kinetic energy about 2 MeV.

The average number of prompt neutrons per fission is about 2.5. The average energy released in fission is about 200 MeV. Most of it appears as a kinetic energy of fission fragments and prompt neutrons. This energy, appearing as heat, is millions of times greater than the energy released in most energetic chemical reactions.

Because more than one prompt neutron is emitted per fission, the possibility of achieving self-sustaining fission chain reaction in a device called a nuclear reactor is possible. In a nuclear reactor some of the neutrons emitted in fission are absorbed in different materials white some of them escape from the reactor.

A nuclear reactor is in the critical state when the number of neutrons produced in it in a unit of time is equal to the number of neutrons lost due to absorption and leakage in a unit of time. In other words, the critical state of a nuclear reactor is a state of balance between production and destruction of neutrons.

Obviously, this balance can be attained at different power levels. Note, however that, certain conditions have to be met in order to achieve a critical state.

For given reactor composition, the size of a reactor should not be too small, otherwise it would be impossible to account for the large leakage of neutrons. The minimal size of a nuclear reactor at which the critical state can be attained is called the critical size. The mass of nuclear fuel corresponding to it is called a critical mass.

Nuclear fuel is a composition of one fissile isotopes with fertile isotopes and other materials. Fissile isotopes are those which quite easily undergoe fission when bombarded by low energy neutrons. To them belong U^{235}, U^{233}, and Pu^{239}. Only U^{235} can be found in nature. In natural uranium there is only 0.7% by weight of U^{235}; the others, U^{238}. U^{233} and Pu^{239}, are not found in nature. These are produced in nuclear reactors due to irradiation of so called fertile isotopes, namely U^{238} and Th^{232}. In most operating reactors, enriched uranium is used in which the content of U^{235} is higher than 0.7%.

Fission of fissile isotopes may be induced by neutrons having different energies. Reactors in which the majority of fissions is caused by low energy neutrons (~ 0.025 eV) are called thermal reactors. Reactors in which the majority of fissions is caused by fast neutrons ($\sim$ tenths of MeV) are called fast reactors.

In thermal reactors neutrons must be slowed down from a high energy state (2 MeV) to a thermal energy state (~ 0.025 eV). Therefore a material of a low atomic mass, called a moderator, must be used. Neutrons loose their energy by collisions with moderator nuclei. The most frequently used moderators are: water, heavy water, and graphite (rarely beryllium).

A nuclear reactor in which nuclear fuel and other materials form a homogeneous mixture is called a homogeneous reactor. A nuclear reactor in which nuclear fuel is distinctly separated from other materials is called a heterogeneous reactor. Nearly all operating nuclear reactors are of the heterogeneous type. Hence subsequent considerations will be limited to these.

In a heterogeneous reactor, nuclear fuel is contained in the fuel elements. These are usually in the form of cylindrical rods, although other geometries can be used. A cylindrical fuel element consists of a thin walled tube called cladding, inside which are stacked fuel pellets. The cladding must be tight to prevent the release of fission products.

Fuel elements are long and have a small diameter; hence they are susceptible to bending. In order to increase their stiffness and to ease handling, fuel elements are grouped into fuel assemblies. Some of fuel elements and fuel assemblies are shown in Figure 1. Fuel assemblies form the reactor core, which usually has an approximately cylindrical shape.

Heat generated in fuel elements by fissions is removed by coolant flowing through the core. Coolants may be gaseous or liquid. The most popular coolants are water, heavy water, carbon dioxide, helium and liquid sodium. In many cases the coolant also serves as a moderator.

a) fuel elements

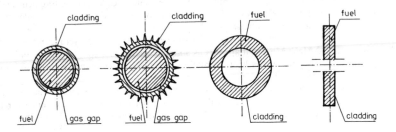

b) fuel assemblies

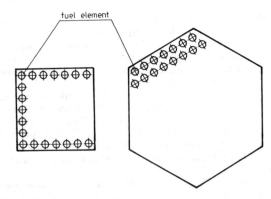

Figure 1. Some typical fuel elements and fuel assemblies.

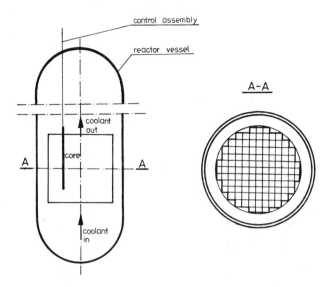

Figure 2. Vessel type reactor.

Pressure in the cooling circuits of nuclear reactors usually falls in the range from a few tenths of MPa to about 16 MPa. Hence a reactor core must be housed in a pressure vessel. Reactors where the entire core is placed in a pressure vessel are called vessel-type reactors and are the most popular in contemporary design.

Reactors whose core is divided into clusters of fuel elements positioned in separate pressure tubes are called channel-type reactors. This design is much less popular than the previous one. Therefore attention is restricted to vessel type reactors.

Other main components of a nuclear reactors are the control assemblies. These are usually clusters of rods or single rods (with circular, annular, and possibly other cross sections) made from material that can strongly absorbi neutrons. Absorption of neutrons changes when control assemblies are inserted into a reactor core or removed from it. In this way a nuclear reactor can be controlled. A schematic of a vessel-type reactor is shown in Figure 2.

Coolant leaving a reactor in most cases passes through a heat exchanger (steam generator), where steam is generated to drive a steam turbine. Hence there are two circuits—primary and secondary (sodium cooled reactors have three circuits: primary, intermediate, and secondary).

There are also reactors whose coolant also serves as the working fluid passing through the turbine (steam or gaseous). There are several types of nuclear power reactors. The principal features and typical parameters of these are shown in Table 1. Basic information on nuclear power reactors can be found in the literature (e.g., [1–4]).

NEUTRON BALANCE EQUATIONS

The theory of nuclear reactors is based on neutron transport. Generally transport theory raters to the mathematical description of the transport of large numbers of identical particles like gas molecules, ions, neutrons, photons, electrons, etc. Therefore one can encounter transport equations in many fields of physics and engineering, for example in nuclear reactor theory, rarefied gas dynamics, plasma physics, and astrophysics.

Table 1
Typical Average Parameters of Nuclear Reactors

	PWR	BWR	PHWR	GCR	AGR	HTGR	FBR
1 Fuel	UO_2	UO_2	UO_2	U	UO_2	UO_2, UC_2	$UO_2 + PuO_2$
2 Fuel enrichment (%)	1.8–3.2	2–2.7	Nat.	Nat.	2–4	93	15–75
3 Cladding	Zircaloy	Zircaloy	Zircaloy	Magnox	SS	Graphite	SS
4 Moderator	H_2O	H_2O	D_2O	Graphite	Graphite	Graphite	—
5 Coolant	H_2O	H_2O	D_2O	CO_2	CO_2	He	Na
6 Core heat transfer area (m^2)	5,000	6,000	4,000	5,000	8,000	Not app.	500
7 Core power density (kW/dm^3)	100	50	10	1	2.5	10	500
8 Fuel power density (kW/kg)	30	20	20	3	10	600	1,000
9 Heat flux (MW/m^2)	0.7	0.5	0.5	0.2	0.1	Not app.	2
10 Cooling circuit pressure (MPa)	16	7	10	2.5	4	5	0.8
11 Coolant temperature rise in core (°C)	35	15	50	200	300	400	200
12 Coolant velocity (m/s)	4.5	2	4.5	25	25	30	7
13 Coolant mass flow rate (kg/s)	$2 \cdot 10^4$	$1.3 \cdot 10^4$	$1 \cdot 10^4$	$1 \cdot 10^4$	$5 \cdot 10^3$	$4 \cdot 10^2$	$6 \cdot 10^3$
14 Heat transfer coefficient ($W/m^{2}°K$)	$4 \cdot 10^4$	$8 \cdot 10^4$	$4 \cdot 10^4$	$6 \cdot 10^3$	$3 \cdot 10^3$	Not app.	$1 \cdot 10^5$

PWR—pressurized water reactor; BWR—boiling water reactor; PHWR—pressurized heavy water reactor; GCR—gas cooled reactor; AGR—advanced gas-cooled reactor; HTGR—high temperature gas-cooled reactor; FBR—fast breeder reactor.

Neutron Transport Equation

The dependent variable in the neutron transport equation is the neutron angular flux Φ, which in the most general case is a function of coordinates $\mathbf{r}$, direction unit vector $\mathbf{\Omega}$, energy E, and time t. The neutron angular flux is defined as:

$$\Phi(\mathbf{r}, \mathbf{\Omega}, E, t) \overset{df}{=} vn(\mathbf{r}, \mathbf{\Omega}, E, t)$$

where
$$\mathbf{v} = \text{neutron speed} = v\mathbf{\Omega}$$
$$n = \text{neutron angular density}$$
$n(\mathbf{r}, \mathbf{\Omega}, E, t) \, dV \, d\Omega \, dE = $ the expected number of neutrons in volume dV about $\mathbf{r}$ with kinetic energy E in dE moving in direction $\mathbf{\Omega}$ in solid angle $d\Omega$

The neutron transport equation has the form:

$$\frac{1}{v}\frac{\partial}{\partial t}\Phi(\mathbf{r}, \mathbf{\Omega}, E, t) = -\mathbf{\Omega}\nabla\Phi(\mathbf{r}, \mathbf{\Omega}, E, t) - \sum(\mathbf{r}, E, t)\Phi(\mathbf{r}, \mathbf{\Omega}, E, t)$$

$$+ \int \Phi(\mathbf{r}, \mathbf{\Omega}, E, t)\sum_s(\mathbf{r}, \mathbf{\Omega}' \to \mathbf{\Omega}, E' \to E)\,d\Omega\,dE + S(\mathbf{r}, \mathbf{\Omega}, E, t) \qquad (1)$$

where
$\nabla = $ nabla operator
$\sum = $ total macroscopic cross section
$\sum_s = $ macroscopic differential scattering cross section
$S = $ neutron source

The initial condition is

$$\Phi(\mathbf{r}, \mathbf{\Omega}, E, t) = \psi(\mathbf{r}, \mathbf{\Omega}, E) = \text{given function}$$

The boundary conditions are more complicated and depend on the specific problem of interest. For example, the boundary condition for a free surface follows. A free surface is defined such that neutrons can only escape a body through the surface; they cannot reenter it. Hence we would require that the angular neutron flux vanish on the surface for all inward directions:

$$\Phi(\mathbf{r}, \mathbf{\Omega}, E, t) = 0 \qquad \text{on a free surface for all } \mathbf{\Omega} \text{ such that } \mathbf{\Omega} \cdot \mathbf{N} < 0, \text{ where } \mathbf{N} = \text{outwardbound unit vector normal to the surface.}$$

The neutron transport equation is an integral-differential equation. The theory of it may be found for example in References 5 and 6.

Neutron Diffusion Equation

The solution of the neutron transport equation poses severe mathematical difficulties. Hence, there is a need for a development of a far simpler equation, which would be more amenable to mathematical treatment.

Such an expression, called the neutron diffusion equation, can be derived from transport theory. It has the form:

$$\frac{1}{v}\frac{\partial}{\partial t}\Phi(\mathbf{r}, E, t) = \nabla D(\mathbf{r}, E, t)\nabla\Phi(\mathbf{r}, E, t) - \sum(\mathbf{r}, E, t)\Phi(\mathbf{r}, E, t)$$

$$+ \int \Phi(\mathbf{r}, E', t)\sum_s(\mathbf{r}, E' \to E)\,dE' + S(\mathbf{r}, E, t) \qquad (2)$$

where $\quad \Phi(r, E, t) = \int \Phi(r, \Omega, E, t) \, d\Omega$

$\quad\quad D = $ diffusion coefficient.

The initial condition has the form:

$\Phi(r, E, 0) = \psi(r, E) = $ given function

The boundary conditions depend on the problem of interest. For a free surface it has the form:

$\Phi(r, E, t) + 2D(r, E, t)NV\Phi(r, E, t) = 0$

The Multigroup Form of Neutron Balance Equations

Before application of any approximate method of solution, the neutron balance equations must be recast in the so-called multigroup form. This consists of dividing the entire neutron energy range into a number of intervals which are called energy groups. Energy E belongs to the g-th energy group, if $E \in [E_{g-1}, E_g]$, $g = 1, 2, \ldots, G$, where $G = $ total number of energy groups. One gets the set of G-coupled neutron balance equations. For example, from Equation 2 one obtains a set of equations for steady state in the form:

$$-\nabla D_g(r)\nabla\Phi_g(r) + \sum_g (r)\Phi_g(r) = \sum_{i \neq g}^{G} \Phi_g(r) \sum_{ig}^{sl} (r) + S_g(r) \quad\quad g = 1, 2, \ldots, G \quad\quad (3)$$

$\sum\limits_{ig}^{sl}$ is the macroscopic slowing down cross section from i-th to the g-th group. All other symbols are the same as before, and subscript g denotes that the quantity of interest is suitably averaged over the g-th energy group.

Computer-Based Approximate Methods in Neutron Transport Theory

The complexity of the neutron balance equations usually forces one to use computer-based approximate methods to obtain a solution. These are applied to the multigroup form of transport or diffusion equations.

There are many methods of approximate solution of the neutron transport equation, among the most popular are the method of discrete ordinates and the Monte Carlo method. Finite element methods have also gained popularity over the past few years.

The most popular methods of approximate solution of the diffusion equation are the finite difference method, the finite element method, and different coarse mesh methods. More information on approximate methods and computer codes can be found in the literature sus as References 7 and 8.

Nuclear Data in Reactor Calculations

Nuclear reactor calculations require a knowledge of cross sections for different nuclear reactions induced by neutrons. Because of the enormous amount of nuclear data, storage on magnetic tapes is necessary. There exist many libraries of evaluated neutron cross sections. A good example is the ENDF library (Evaluated Nuclear Data File) developed in the United States and used in many countries around the world. Multigroup equations are used in reactor calculations, therefore it is necessary to generate group cross sections using libraries of evaluated neutron cross sections. Special computer codes are used for this purpose.

The group cross sections generated by these codes form multigroup cross-sections libraries in which a number of energy groups may extend up to several hundred. The basic information on these problems may be found for example in Reference 9.

Critical State of a Nuclear Reactor

The critical state is the normal operating state of a nuclear reactor. For the analysis of this state, in principle any of the neutron balance equations just described may be used with the source term to express the contribution from neutrons born in fissions. For example, the source term used in Equation 3 has the form:

$$S_g(\mathbf{r}) = X_g \sum_{g=1}^{G} v_g(\mathbf{r}) \sum_g^f (\mathbf{r}) \Phi_g(\mathbf{r})$$

where X_g = fraction of prompt neutrons belonging to g-th group

v_g = average number of neutrons emitted per fission for g-th group

$\sum_g^f$ = macroscopic fission cross section for g-th group

The neutron balance equation for a critical state is a homogeneous equation, hence its solution gives only relative values of the neutron flux. The absolute value of the neutron flux can be determined when the power of the reactor is known.

A balance of neutrons in a reactor may be characterized by a neutron effective multiplication factor k. [10]. This is defined as the ratio of the number of neutrons produced in a reactor per unit time to the number of neutrons lost per unit time due to absorption and leakage. Hence for a critical state k = 1. When the number of neutrons produced exceeds the number of neutrons lost per unit time, then k > 1, and the reactor is supercritical. In the opposite case k < 1 and a reactor is subcritical. In normal operating conditions k does not differ too much from unity.

In many cases it is convenient to use related quantity called the reactivity ρ, defined below:

$$\rho = \frac{k-1}{k}$$

Obviously $\rho = 0$ for a critical state, $\rho > 0$ for a supercritical state, and $\rho < 0$ for a subcritical state.

HEAT GENERATION IN A REACTOR CORE

The energy of neutrons deposited in matter due to nuclear reactions caused by them appears as a heat. The main source of heat in nuclear reactors is a fission reaction taking place in the fuel elements, i.e., strictly speaking, in the fuel pellets. Heat sources in cladding, coolant, and other materials in a nuclear reactor result from other neutron-induced reactions such as scattering and absorption. There is also heating by gamma (γ) photons emitted by fission products and resulting from radiative capture of neutrons. In a nuclear reactor core a contribution from other than fission sources does not exceed a few percent and usually may be neglected. Obviously this contribution cannot be neglected in nonmultiplying media, e.g., in a biological shield of a nuclear reactor.

Heat Generation by Neutrons

Heating by neutrons at any spatial point can be expressed as:

$$q_v(\mathbf{r}) = \sum_{j=1}^{J} \int \Phi(\mathbf{r}, E) k_j(E) N_j(\mathbf{r}) \, dE$$

where $q_v(\mathbf{r}) \, dV$ = thermal power released in volume dV about $\mathbf{r}$

$N_j(\mathbf{r})$ = number density of isotope j at point $\mathbf{r}$

$k_j(E)$ = microscopic kerma factor for isotope j

J = number of isotopes

The term "kerma" is an acronym for kinetic energy released in material.

$$k_j(E) = \sum_i \sigma_{ij}(E) E_{ij}(E)$$

where $\sigma_{ij}(E)$ = microscopic neutron cross section for isotope j for reaction i at neutron energy E
         $E_{ij}(E)$ = energy deposited per reaction i for isotope j at neutron energy E

In nuclear fuel the main heat source stems from the fission reaction, contributions from other reactions are negligible. Then

$$k_j(E) = \sigma_{fj}(E) E_{fj}$$

where σ_{fj} = microscopic fission cross section for isotope j
        E_{fj} = fission energy released in isotope j

In fact $E_{fj} \approx E_f$ = const.; E_f is usually taken as equal about 180 MeV.
Hence in fuel

$$q_v(\mathbf{r}) = E_f \sum_j N_j(\mathbf{r}) \int \Phi(\mathbf{r}, E) \sigma_{fj}(E) \, dE \tag{4}$$

In thermal reactors, in which the majority of fissions is caused by thermal neutrons the preceding expression greatly simplifies to:

$$q_v(\mathbf{r}) = E_f \Phi_{th}(\mathbf{r}) \sum_j N_j(\mathbf{r}) \sigma_{fj}^{th} \, g_{fj} \tag{5}$$

where Φ_{th} = thermal neutron flux
       σ_{fj}^{th} = microscopic fission cross section for thermal neutrons for isotope j
       g_{fj} = Westcott coefficient for fission of isotope j

Hence, in thermal reactors heat generated in the fuel by fissions is proportional to the thermal neutron flux.

Heat Generation by Gamma Photons

Heating by gamma (γ) photons can be described by an expression similar to Equation 4. The microscopic kerma factor for photons takes into account three main effects: photoelectric, Compton, and pair production.

Heating by γ photons is important when decay heat is calculated in a reactor core after reactor shutdown or in nonmultiplying media (e.g., reactor shield).

Typical Heat Source Distributions in a Reactor Core

Heat source in a reactor core are functionals of neutron flux as is seen from Equation 4. In thermal reactors heat sources are proportional to the thermal neutron flux.

Typical heat source distributions in a reactor core are shown in Figure 3.

The axial distribution is symmetrical with respect to half the core height where it reaches maximum value.

It can be approximated by a chopped cosine distribution:

$$q_v(z) = q_{v_{max}} \cos \frac{\pi z}{H_e} \tag{6}$$

where H_e = extrapolated height of a reactor core, $H_e = H + 2\delta$. The extrapolation length δ can be determined from reactor physics calculations.

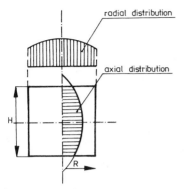

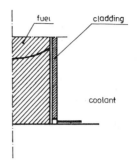

Figure 3. Typical heat source distribution in a cylindrical reactor core.

Figure 4. Heat source distribution in an elementary cell.

The radial distribution cannot be described so simply. It would be well to have this as uniform as possible to attain uniform heat removal and fuel burnup throughout a core. It can be approximately achieved by a suitable distribution of fuel assemblies with different enrichments.

In physical calculations one considers a single fuel element with a coolant. This is referred to as an elementary cell. The local heat source distribution in an elementary cell is shown in Figure 4.

The heat source in fuel attains its minimal value at the center. The difference between the minimal and maximal value usually does not exceed 3%–4%. Hence it is customary to assume a constant radial heat source in the fuel. Heat sources in the gas gap, cladding, and coolant are usually neglected.

Decay Heat in a Nuclear Reactor Core

After shutdown of a nuclear reactor heat continues to be generated in the core. This heat, called decay or shutdown heat, is a result of radioactive decay of fission products.

The amount of decay heat depends on the time after shutdown and also on the operating time and power before shutdown. Results of calculations or measurements are presented in the form:

$$P/P_0 = f(t_0, t) \tag{7a}$$

where P = reactor decay power
  P_0 = reactor power before shutdown
  t_0 = reactor operating time at power P_0
  t = time after reactor shutdown

When the operating time t_0 is sufficiently long (e.g. one year), then

$$P/P_0 = f(t) \tag{7b}$$

There are many expressions of the form of Equations 7a and b. For example

$$P/P_0 = 0.095 \, t^{-0.26} \quad \text{for} \quad t > 200 \, s$$

where t is in seconds.

Just after reactor shutdown P/P_0 is equal approximately 3% and later slowly decreases. Hence it is necessary to provide for suitable cooling of a reactor core after its shutdown.

HEAT REMOVAL FROM A REACTOR CORE

The maximum allowable thermal power of a nuclear reactor is established by the ability to effective remove heat from its core. The heat removal system should assure that the values of fuel temperatures, cladding temperatures, and heat fluxes in steady and transient states will be less than the maximal permissible levels.

Heat generated in fuel is transferred through fuel element components (fuel pellet, gas gap, cladding) to an external surface of cladding by conduction. From an external surface of cladding heat is transferred to the coolant by one- or two-phase forced convection.

In normal operating conditions the flow of coolant is turbulent. This results in high heat transfer coefficients and hence, enables effective heat transfer from fuel to coolant. Laminar flow takes place only in special cases (for example, removal of decay heat after reactor shut-down).

The choice of a suitable coolant is an important problem and depends on reactor type and the nuclear power plant thermal system. Values of thermal and hydraulic parameters encountered in nuclear reactor cores (see Table 1) clearly illustrate the complexity of the heat transfer analysis.

It is well known that analytical solutions of heat transfer problems for turbulent coolant flow through channels of complex geometries are impossible. Therefore, analysis of the heat removal from the core must rely strongly on experiments and requires the use of computer-based approximation methods.

Conservation Laws for Convective Heat Transfer in a Nuclear Reactor Core

The convective heat transfer from fuel elements to coolant is described by a set of equations based on the general laws of mechanics and thermodynamics. These equations express the principles of conservation of mass, momentum, and energy and are derived for an arbitrary control volume Ω with boundary Γ filled with flowing fluid.

These have the form [11–17]:

$$\iiint_\Omega (\partial \rho_c / \partial t) \cdot d\Omega + \iint_\Gamma \rho_c \cdot \mathbf{V} \cdot \mathbf{n} \cdot d\Gamma = 0$$

$$\frac{D}{Dt} \iiint_\Omega \rho_c \cdot \mathbf{V} \cdot d\Omega = \iint_\Gamma \mathbf{n} \cdot T_s \cdot d\Gamma + \iiint_\Omega \rho_c \cdot \mathbf{f} \cdot d\Omega$$

$$\iiint_\Omega [\partial(\rho_c e)/\partial t] \cdot d\Omega + \iint_\Gamma \rho_c \cdot e \cdot \mathbf{V} \cdot \mathbf{n} \cdot d\Gamma = \iint_\Gamma \lambda_c \cdot \text{grad } T_c \cdot \mathbf{n} \cdot d\Gamma + \iiint_\Omega q_{v_c} \cdot d\Omega \qquad (8)$$

$$+ \iiint_\Omega \rho_c \cdot \mathbf{f} \cdot \mathbf{V} \cdot d\Omega + \iint_\Gamma \mathbf{V} \cdot (T_s \cdot \mathbf{n}) \cdot d\Gamma$$

The preceding integral equations may be transformed into partial differential equations by use of vector calculus (Gauss, Green, Stokes) and transport theorems. The following assumptions are applied: Newtonian fluid, Stokes' hypothesis, zero dilatational viscosity coefficient, and differentiability of parameters. These allow the counterpart of Equation 8 in a differential form:

$$\partial \rho_c / \partial t + \text{div} (\rho_c \cdot \mathbf{V}) = 0$$

$$\rho_c \cdot D\mathbf{V}/Dt = \rho_c \cdot \mathbf{f} + \text{Div}[2\mu \cdot T_d - (p + 2/3\mu \cdot \text{div } \mathbf{V})\varepsilon] \qquad (9)$$

$$\rho_c \cdot Du/Dt = \text{div}(\lambda_c \text{ grad } T_c) - p \cdot \text{div } \mathbf{V} + q_{v_c} + \mu \cdot \Phi$$

or in terms of enthalpy

$$\rho_c \cdot Dh/Dt = \text{div}(\lambda_c \text{ grad } T_c) + Dp/Dt + q_{v_c} + \mu \cdot \Phi$$

The preceding equations are supplemented by additional equations and data such as:

- Equation of state $f(\rho_c, T, p) = 0$
- Properties of fluid e.g. $\mu = \mu(T, p)$, $\lambda_c = \lambda_c(T, p)$
- Mass force field $\mathbf{f} = \mathbf{f}(\mathbf{r}, t)$
- Heat source q_{v_c}

Fourier's law and Newton–Stokes hypothesis have been taken into account in Equations 8 and 9.
Obviously it is necessary to formulate suitable initial and boundary conditions. The preceding equations are extremely complex, therefore simplifying assumptions must be introduced.

Usually in reactor channels one considers fully-developed flows where by the heat transfer intensity is the lowest. Assuming: $Dp/Dt = \Phi = \mathbf{f} = q_{v_c} = 0$, $\lambda_c = $ const, $\rho_c = $ const, $v = $ const and neglecting axial heat conduction (usually $Pe \gg 10$) we obtain for turbulent single-phase, two-dimensional coolant flow the following momentum and energy conservation equations:

$$\partial/\partial x[(v + \varepsilon_m)\partial w/\partial x] + \partial/\partial_y[(v + \varepsilon_m)\partial w/\partial y] = -1/\rho \cdot \partial p/\partial z$$

$$\partial/\partial x[(\kappa + \varepsilon_h)\partial T_c/\partial x] + \partial/\partial y[(\kappa + \varepsilon_h)\partial T_c/\partial y] = w \cdot \partial T_c/\partial z$$

(10)

For laminar flow $\varepsilon_m = \varepsilon_h = 0$.

A simple solution to this set of equations is possible only in the case of laminar coolant flow through channels of simple geometry with classic boundary conditions ($T_w = $ const, $q_w = $ const). For the case of turbulent flow which is typical for reactor channels, only approximate solutions are possible.

Useful and effective one-dimensional mass, momentum, and energy equations have been derived by J. E. Meyer [18], by suitable averaging on planes perpendicular to the coolant flow. Introducing:

- Average density

$$\bar{\rho}_c = \frac{1}{A} \iint_A \rho_c \cdot dA$$

- Mass velocity

$$G = \frac{1}{A} \iint_A \rho_c \cdot w \cdot dA$$

- Effective specific volume

$$v_{ef} = 1/G^2 \left[\frac{1}{A} \iint_A \rho_c \cdot w^2 \cdot dA \right]$$

- Average enthalpy over the channel cross section

$$\bar{h} = \frac{1}{\bar{\rho}_c A} \iint_A \rho_c \cdot h \cdot dA$$

- "Mixing cup" enthalpy

$$\tilde{h} = \frac{1}{G \cdot A} \iint_A \rho_c \cdot w \cdot h \cdot dA$$

Meyer obtained the following one-dimensional slice equations:

- Continuity equation

$$\partial(\bar{\rho}_c A)/\partial t + \partial(GA)/\partial z = 0 \tag{11}$$

- Momentum equation

$$\partial(GA)/\partial t + \partial(v_{ef}G^2A)/\partial z = -A \cdot \partial p/\partial z - \zeta \cdot G \, |G| \, A/(2 \, \rho_c D_e) - g\bar{\rho}_c A \tag{12}$$

- Energy equation

$$\partial(\bar{\rho}_c \bar{h} A)/\partial t + \partial(G\tilde{h}A)/\partial z = \int_{\Pi_q} q_w \cdot d\Pi_q + \iint_A q_{v_c} \cdot dA \tag{13}$$

Meyer's approach has found numerous and successful applications in many so called "channel codes" used in an analysis of a reactor core and primary cooling circuit.

Temperature fields in fuel elements are described by the heat conduction equation:

$$\text{div}(\lambda_f \, \text{grad} \, T_f) + q_v(\mathbf{r}, t) = \rho_f c_{p_j} \cdot \partial T_f/\partial t \tag{14}$$

supplemented by suitable initial and boundary conditions. This is a quasilinear equation, since in general λ_f depends on temperature. The methods of solution of Equation 14 are presented in numerous publications [19–24].

Equations 11 through 13 for coolant, and Equation 14 for fuel elements are mutually connected since on cladding surface $q_w \neq$ const and $T_w \neq$ const. Simultaneous solution of the all differential equations is very complicated. Hence, in practice, these equations are separated.

Usually the rate of heat transferred by convection between a cladding surface and coolant is evaluated by means of the Newton cooling law:

$$q_w = \alpha(T_w - T_b) \tag{15}$$

where T_w, q_w, α are averaged quantities on the external surface of the cladding and T_b may be determined from Equation 13.

The simplicity of Equation 15 is a consequence of introducing the convective heat transfer coefficient which, unfortunately, is difficult to determine since the convective heat transfer is strictly related to the system hydrodynamics.

The nonuniform circumferential temperature distribution may be taken into account by means of the so-called conduction parameter ε [25, 26]. This parameter links geometrical and thermal parameters of a fuel element with the intensity of heat transfer on cladding surface. It is a measure of the ratio of heat flow along a fuel element and in coolant for the same temperature difference (if $T_w =$ const then $\varepsilon \to \infty$ and if $q_w =$ const then $\varepsilon \to 0$).

For the determination of temperatures, mass flow rates and pressures in the core, information on the heat transfer coefficient α and the friction factor ζ are needed. In practice, these can be determined using dimensional analysis and the theory of similarity combined with experiments.

Geometry of Cooling Channels

Geometry of cooling channels is strictly connected with geometry of fuel elements and different additional elements and their layout in a nuclear reactor core. It is convenient to divide cooling channels into closed and open channels. Closed channels are bounded by a real wall. The open channel are partly bounded by a hypothetical wall.

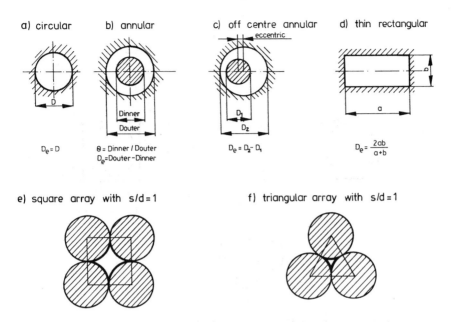

a) circular   b) annular   c) off centre annular   d) thin rectangular

$D_e = D$

$\theta = D_{inner} / D_{outer}$
$D_e = D_{outer} - D_{inner}$

$D_e = D_2 - D_1$

$D_e = \dfrac{2ab}{a+b}$

e) square array with s/d = 1   f) triangular array with s/d = 1

Figure 5. Various closed channel geometries.

Possible shapes of the closed and open channels are shown in Figure 5 and Figure 6. Open channels are also called subchannels. Hence, fuel assemblies are sets ("i"–"1" Figure 6) of parallel subchannels with mass, momentum, and energy transfer between them.

The complexity of subchannel cross-sectional shapes results from the presence of distancing elements, finned cladding (gas cooling), and special elements for increasing flow turbulence. These elements increase both intensity heat removal from fuel elements and, on the other hand, local friction factors.

Complex geometry of cooling channels and nonuniform axial and radial heat source distribution cause nonuniform heat loading of subchannels (particularly, the peripheral subchannels—"k," "1"

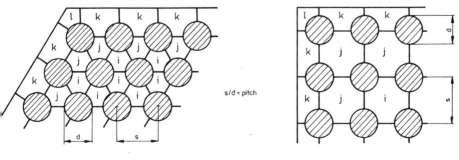

s/d = pitch

Triangular – lattice rod bundles

Square-lattice rod bundles

Figure 6. Non-circular open channels (subchannels) in two different fuel assemblies.

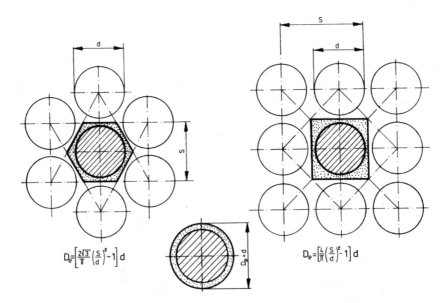

Figure 7. Isolated channel in triangular and in square lattices and equivalent annulus model.

(Figure 6)), nonuniform distribution of tangential stress, heat transfer coefficient, and temperature. For this reason, the behavior of peripheral subchannels has the significant influence (fast reactors) on permissible power of a fuel assembly.

In principle, it would be desirable to perform heat and mass transfer calculations for all subchannels in a fuel assembly. However, it is not always practical, possible, or suitable.

In practice, one can define (Figure 7) thermally and hydraulically isolated channels connected with a particular fuel element by neglecting interchannel influences and considering a cluster with an infinite number of fuel elements. This channel may be approximated by an equivalent annular channel (so-called the equivalent annulus model) with the hypothetical external wall, particularly when s/d ≧ 1.3 (thermal reactors). Such an approximation is not advisable in fast reactors, where s/d ≈ 1.1–1.2. The isolated channel approach is also used in an analysis of a reactor primary circuit, particularly in transient states.

Nuclear Reactor Coolants

Nuclear reactor coolants should satisfy many, in general contradictory, thermal, nuclear, and economic requirements.

Thermal and economic requirements are the same as for coolants used in other applications. From the point of view of nuclear requirements, coolants should have small absorption and activation cross sections and high resistance to radiation damage.

If the coolant serves also as a moderator it should have a small mass number and high neutron scattering cross section. Therefore in selecting a reactor coolant certain criteria must be met. This problem is considered for example in References 22–29.

Actually used coolants in nuclear power reactors are: water, heavy water, carbon dioxide, helium, and liquid sodium (in fast reactors). Thermal and physical properties of coolants depend on temperature and pressure and can be found in References 28–40.

Heat Transfer Through Fuel Element to Coolant

In general, cooling of fuel elements is described by the system of equations presented in the previous subsection. To determine the solution, a computer is needed. One may perform approximate analysis of heat transfer through an individual fuel element to coolant. The analysis enables an estimate of the maximum fuel and cladding temperatures both in "hot" and "average" channels, and provides functional relationships between parameters of fuel element components and coolant. In practice, these calculations are performed for the most thermally loaded fuel element in the most thermally loaded cluster ("hot" cluster). One of the simplest examples is heat flow through a cylindrical fuel rod of radius r_f surrounded by cladding of thickness δ_{c1} and cooled by constant mass-flow rate W of a single-phase coolant having bulk temperature $T_b(z)$ (27–29).

Making the following simplifying assumptions:

1. Steady state, $\partial/\partial t = 0$.
2. Distribution of heat generation is such as in reactor core without reflector, i.e., $q_v(r, z) = q_{v_0} \cdot \cos(\pi \cdot z/H_c)$, where q_{v_0} is the maximal value in a given fuel rod.
3. There is no heat generation in cladding and coolant.
4. Constant thermal conductivities λ_f and λ_{c1}.
5. Axial heat conduction in fuel, cladding, and coolant an negligible.
6. Lack of gas gap between fuel rod and cladding, perfect contact on the fuel-rod cladding interface.
7. Slug flow of coolant ($\tilde{h} = \bar{h} = h$), constant coolant properties.
8. Constant heat transfer coefficient.

One obtains the conservation equations in the form:

$$\lambda_f/r \cdot \partial/\partial r(r \cdot \partial T_f/\partial r) + q_{v_0} \cdot \cos(\pi z/H_c) = 0$$

$$1/r \cdot \partial/\partial r(r \cdot \partial T_{c1}/\partial r) = 0$$

$$dh/dz = \pi_{\text{heated}} q_w/W \quad \text{where} \quad q_w = r_f^2 \cdot q_v/[2(r_f + \delta_{c1})]$$

with boundary conditions:

$$\partial T_f/\partial r|_{r=0} = 0, \qquad -\lambda_f \cdot \partial T_f/\partial r|_{r=r_f} = -\lambda_{c1} \cdot \partial T_{c1}/\partial r|_{r=r_f}$$

$$T_f|_{r=r_f} = T_{c1}|_{r=r_f}, \qquad -\lambda_{c1} \cdot \partial T_{c1}/\partial r|_{r=r_f+\delta_{c1}} = \alpha(T_{c1}|_{r=r_f} - T_b)$$

$$h|_{z=-H/2} = h_{in}$$

An analytical solution is shown in Figures 8 and 9. This treatment is useful in some preliminary calculations. In practice, most of the preceding assumptions do not hold. Physical properties (first of all, conductivities) of fuel element components depend on temperature and vary during irradiation [41–42]. Thus the heat conduction equations are quasi-linear, and consequently approximate solutions are available only. In addition, the distribution of heat generation differs largely from that of reactors without reflectors. A gas gap containing a gaseous mixture occurs usually between the fuel rod and cladding. Description of heat flow through the gap is complex since there are simultaneous processes of conduction, convection, and thermal radiation. The composition of the gas mixture varies continuously in view of diffusion of gaseous fission products. The problem of heat transfer through the fuel element to coolant is usually solved by use of computer codes (e.g. [50, 51]). A special code used to estimate heat flow through the gas gap [52] has lately been submitted for critical examination [53, 54]. Detailed description of the problems just discussed are given in Reference 49.

In thermal and hydraulic calculations a large number of simplifications are usually made, although their experimental verification is often difficult. Hence all unknowns and uncertainties are estimated by the use of so-called hot-spot and hot-channel factors [15, 28, 49, 55].

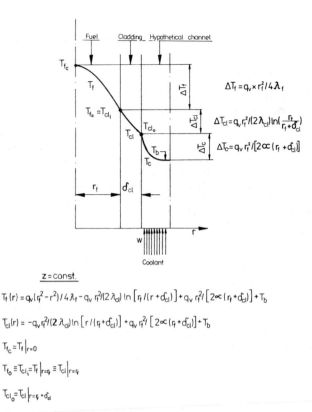

$\underline{z = \text{const.}}$

$$T_f(r) = q_v(r_f^2 - r^2)/4\lambda_f - q_v\, r_f^2/(2\lambda_{cl})\ln\left[r_f/(r+d_{cl})\right] + q_v\, r_f^2/\left[2\alpha(r_f+d_{cl})\right] + T_b$$

$$T_{cl}(r) = -q_v\, r_f^2/(2\lambda_{cl})\ln\left[r/(r_f+d_{cl})\right] + q_v\, r_f^2/\left[2\alpha(r_f+d_{cl})\right] + T_b$$

$$T_{f_c} = T_f\big|_{r=0}$$

$$T_{f_0} \equiv T_{cl_i} = T_f\big|_{r=r_f} \equiv T_{cl}\big|_{r=r_f}$$

$$T_{cl_0} = T_{cl}\big|_{r=r_f+d_{cl}}$$

Figure 8. Temperature radial distribution in an elementary cell.

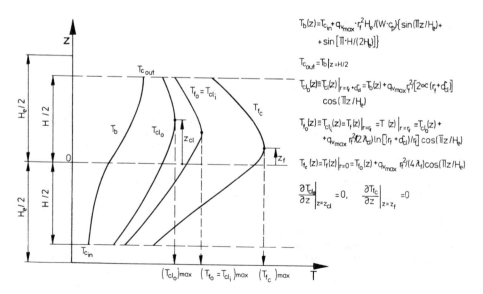

$$T_b(z) = T_{c_{in}} + q_{v_{max}} \cdot r_f^2\, H_e/(W\cdot c_p)\left\{\sin(\Pi z/H_e) + \sin\left[\Pi\cdot H/(2H_e)\right]\right\}$$

$$T_{c_{out}} = T_b\big|_{z=H/2}$$

$$T_{cl_b}(z) \equiv T_{cl}(z)\big|_{r=r_f+d_{cl}} = T_b(z) + q_{v_{max}}\, r_f^2/\left[2\alpha(r_f+d_{cl})\right]\cos(\Pi z/H_e)$$

$$T_{f_0}(z) \equiv T_{cl_i}(z) = T_f(z)\big|_{r=r_f} = T(z)\big|_{r=r_f} = T_{cl_b}(z) + q_{v_{max}}\, r_f^2/(2\lambda_{cl})\ln\left[(r_f+d_{cl})/r_f\right]\cos(\Pi z/H_e)$$

$$T_{f_c}(z) = T_f(z)\big|_{r=0} = T_{f_0}(z) + q_{v_{max}}\, r_f^2/(4\lambda_f)\cos(\Pi z/H_e)$$

$$\frac{\partial T_{cl_0}}{\partial z}\bigg|_{z=z_{cl}} = 0, \qquad \frac{\partial T_{f_c}}{\partial z}\bigg|_{z=z_f} = 0$$

Figure 9. Temperature axial distribution in fuel element and coolant.

Heat Transfer in Flow Through Rod Bundles

Analysis of thermal and hydraulic phenomena in both thermal and fast reactors requires consideration of thermal and hydraulic channel-interactions and possible cluster-interactions. Mass, momentum, and energy exchanges between subchannels and adjacent channels take place. The transverse flow is caused by flow distribution and rod spacers. Coolant flowing in intercluster spaces also takes place at part of the heat transfer between adjacent clusters. If cluster walls are perforated then intercluster hydrodynamic interactions occur.

Mathematical modeling of the preceding phenomena is based on mass, energy, and momentum (axial and transverse components) equations which are written for all subchannels in the rod bundle. In each fuel assembly, apart from a kind of lattice, four types of subchannels may be distinguish: central, side, adjacent to them, and corner ones (see Figure 6). Conservation equations are also formulated for the flow between clusters, or cluster interactions are considered vie boundary conditions. Adding a heat transfer model to fuel elements gives the possibility of total analysis of rod bundles. The form of the equations depends on whether the coolant flow is single- or two-phase, and whether the state is steady or unsteady.

Heat transfer modeling in the flow through bundles was initiated by Rowe [56]. His work as well as that of other investigators [57–65] has greatly enhanced design capabilities, however further studies are necessary, particularly in the case of unsteady and two-phase flows. Thus, different versions of bundle codes, being the computer realization of the conservation equations, are still improved. The simplest system of mass, energy, and momentum equations for single-phase flow which served as the basis of COBRA [56] is given in the following (two-phase flow terms are neglected):

- Continuity equation

$$dm_m/dz = -\sum_{n=1}^{N} W_{mn}$$

- Energy equation

$$m_m \cdot dh_m/dz = (q_1)_m - \sum_{n=1}^{N} \begin{bmatrix} 0, & \text{if } W_{mn} \geqq 0 \\ W_{mn} \cdot (h_n - h_m), & \text{if } W_{mn} < 0 \end{bmatrix} + \sum_{n=1}^{N} W'_{mn} \cdot (h_n - h_m)$$

- Axial momentum equation

$$-dp/dz = (m_m/A_m)^2 \cdot \zeta_m/[2\rho_m(D_e)_m] + 1/A_m \cdot \sum_{n=1}^{N} f_T \cdot W'_{mn}(\bar{w}_m - \bar{w}_n)$$

$$+ 1/A_m \cdot \sum_{n=1}^{N} \begin{bmatrix} W_{mn} \cdot \bar{w}_m \cdot (f_D - 2), & W_{mn} \geqq 0 \\ W_{mn} \cdot (f_D \cdot \bar{w}_n - 2 \cdot \bar{w}_m), & W_{mn} < 0 \end{bmatrix}$$

- Transverse momentum equation

$$p_m - p_n = C_{mn} \cdot W_{mn} \cdot |W_{mn}|$$

where $W'_{mn} = 1/2 \cdot \beta \cdot S_{mn} \cdot (m_m/A_m + m_n/A_m)$
$m = 1, 2, \ldots, N_t$.

The coolant parameters are averaged over the channel cross section. Two-phase flow problems are described later in this chapter. Bundle code details are presented e.g. in References 66–73. Many of the mentioned codes require choosing from available correlations of the heat transfer coefficient, friction factor, and transverse flow parameters describing as two-phase flow. In bundle codes the complex problems such as heat transfer in fuel rods, coolant flow distribution, form of the momentum equation, influence of rod spacers on transverse flow, accustic effects, heat transfer in two-phase flow, using steady-state empirical correlations in unsteady state should be solved. A large number of clusters in the core and subchannels in a cluster makes it impossible to use bundle programmes for computation of the entire reactor core. Therefore, as a first step, it is necessary to resign from a detailed heat transfer analysis by replacing each cluster by a single channel. Such calculations allow one to select the most heat overloaded cluster ("hot" cluster). A detail analysis of this cluster by use of a bundle programme constitutes the second step of calculations. If cluster walls are not perforated and the flow distribution to particular clusters is uniform, then the "hot" cluster is chosen according to the radial power distribution in the reactor core. In this case the first step in the calculation is superfluous. The second step allows one to determine the "hot" subchannel, which is next investigated as an individual fuel element (see the previous subsection).

SINGLE-PHASE FORCED CONVECTION IN REACTOR CHANNELS

Single-phase flow of different coolants takes place during normal full-power operation (steady state) of all nonhomogeneous reactors, except of BWR. In practice, the most important coolants are water (PWR) and liquid sodium (FBR).

Since the intensity of heat removal determines the temperature distribution in fuel elements and the latter establishes the maximum reactor power level, the coolant flow is highly turbulent and heat removal occurs under forced-convection conditions.

The analysis of single-phase forced convection leads to theoretical and experimental studies of nonisothermal, fully or nonfully developed turbulent or rare laminar flows through straight closed channels with complex geometry and, first of all, along rod bundles triangular or square spacings (see Figures 5 through 7).

Additional difficulties are caused by: nonuniform heat flux distribution on channel walls, dependence of channel thermal load on its location in the reactor core as well as by dependence of coolant physical properties and various reactor materials on the temperature and, if need be, the pressure.

In this subsection, the analysis is confined to the steady state and includes determination of basic parameters (the heat transfer coefficient, the friction factor, the pressure drop) whose influence on the heat transport in nuclear reactor channels is decisive.

Convective Heat Transfer Coefficient

Heat removal from fuel elements by means of different cooling agents is a very complex phenomenon. Neglecting the usually small influence of radiation, heat flow between a cladding surface, and coolant take place by conduction and mass transfer. In laminar flow, heat is transferred from fuel elements only by molecular conduction. A small effect of free convection may be neglected.

In turbulent flow, molecular conduction plays an unimportant role but there exist turbulent mixing currents and eddies which transport energy across streamlines. In addition, for a given fluid motion, the contribution of both of these heat transfer mechanisms depends on the type of coolant (ordinary fluids or liquid metals). The influence of cooling medium properties (in particular the Prandtl number) on the process of heat removal is essential in turbulent flow.

It is useful to distinguish between correlations used to calculate the heat transfer coefficient. Moreover, it should be taken into account the variety of reactor channel geometries.

Turbulent Flow

Turbulent flow is characteristic of a normal full-power reactor operation. It enables high values of the heat transfer coefficient, to be attained. In the case of fully-developed turbulent flow through straight channels with constant cross section, these coefficients to a small degree depend on boundary conditions (T_w = const, or g_w = const) given on the channel wall. Their variations in fluid flow direction are connected with dependence of coolant physical properties (mainly viscosity) on the temperature.

Difficulties relating to the theoretical approach of heat transfer in turbulent flow are commonly known. Assuming that the channel has a simple geometry (circular tube), q_w = const, the flow is fully-developed, the fluid is incompressible with constant physical properties and neglecting the influence of conduction and turbulent heat transfer in the axial direction, one may obtain [74] an analytical solution of the energy Equation 10 in a form of the so-called Lyon integral [75]:

$$1/\text{Nu} = 2\int_0^1 \left\{ \left[\int_0^{\rho*} (w/\bar{w}) \cdot \rho* \cdot d\rho* \right]^2 / \{ \rho*[1 + (\text{Pr}/\text{Pr}_t) \cdot (\varepsilon_m/\nu)] \} \right\} d\rho* \qquad (16)$$

where $\rho* = r/R$

In order to integrate Equation 16, one must know, the velocity profile and the relations of the turbulent eddy viscosity and the eddy diffusivity with physical and hydrodynamic fluid parameters. Although hydrodynamic heat transfer theory has a number of remarkable achievements, in practice the heat transfer coefficients are calculated with the use of empirical correlations based on the similarity theory, the dimensional analysis, and generalization of many experimental data. The determination of quantities occurring in Equation 16 is difficult, especially in flows through complex shape channels commonly appearing in reactor cores.

Ordinary fluids. Determination of the forced-convection heat transfer coefficients is first of all based on empirical correlations obtained for flows through straight circular tubes with either q_w = const. or T_w = const. The same correlations may be used for noncircular closed-channels if the pipe diameter D_p is replaced by the equivalent (hydraulic) diameter D_e. This procedure sometimes leads to not so sufficiently correct results. The reason is underlined in the specific character of flow dynamics through some noncircular closed channels and in large temperature gradients occurring in reactor channel cross sections. Various correlations for different channel geometries are alluded to in the following.

Table 2 gives correlations which are usually recommended for the evaluation of the heat transfer coefficients in flow through circular closed channels with smooth walls.

The physical properties of coolants depend more or less on the temperature. Therefore there exists feedback between the velocity and temperature profiles. The viscosity variation is of most importance. This fact is taken into account either by an appropriate selection of a fluid reference temperature T_{ref} or by introducing the multiplier $(\mu_b/\mu_w)^n$ into the correlations. In selecting T_{ref} one should take into consideration the influence of the wall temperature T_w. This requirement is best satisfied by the temperature T_{ref} used in the Colburn correlation. However, application of the correlation requires a trial-and-error solution, because in practical problems both temperatures T_w and T_b are not known in advance. Two different types of corrections already discussed were suggested by Sieder-Tate and Mikheiev (see Table 2). Moreover, it is recommended in Reference 83 to set n = 0.11 for nonmetallic liquid coolants. This problem is more complicated as far as gases are concerned. The reguned data are available for example in References 84–89.

Apart from the prior empirical correlations, it is also known that the Petukhov formula 83, evaluated by use of the Lyon integral gives:

$$\alpha = \lambda_c/D_p \cdot (\zeta/8) \cdot \text{Re} \cdot \text{Pr}/[(1 + 900/\text{Re}) + 12.7(\zeta/8)^{1/2} \cdot (\text{Pr}^{2/3} - 1)]$$

$$10^4 < \text{Re} < 5 \cdot 10^6$$

$$0.5 < \text{Pr } 2,000 \qquad (17)$$

The friction factor ζ is calculated from the Filonenko formula given in the next subsection.

One of the basic noncircular closed-channel geometries is an annular channel. Flows through a circular tube and between parallel plates constitute two extreme cases. In addition, there exists a strict relationship between the annular channels and the in-line cooled fuel rod bundles. This fact was mentioned when constructing isolated (equivalent) channels (see Figure 7).

Table 2

Empirical Forced Convection Correlations for Turbulent Flows through Circular Channels ($Nu = \alpha \cdot D_e/(\lambda_c, D_e = D_p)$)

Author(s)	Correlations	Range of Applications	References
Dittus-Boelter	$Nu \equiv Nu_{D-B} = C \cdot Re^{0.8} \cdot Pr^{0.4}$ $C = \begin{cases} 0.023 - \text{Dittus-Boelter} \\ 0.019 - \text{Rohsenow-Clark} \end{cases}$	$Re > 10^4$, $0.7 < Pr < 100$, $L/D_e > 60$ $T_{ref} = (T_{b|z=z1} - T_{b|z=z2})/2$	[76], [77]
Sieder-Tate	$Nu = Nu_{D-B} \cdot (\mu_b/\mu_w)^{0.14}$	$Re > 10^4$, $0.7 < Pr < 16{,}700$, $L/D_e > 60$ $\mu_b = \mu(T_b)$, $\mu_w = \mu = \mu(T_w)$	[78]
Colburn	$Nu = 0.023 \cdot Re^{0.8} \cdot Pr^{1/3}$	$Re > 10^4$, $0.7 < Pr < 16{,}700$, $L/D_e > 60$ $T_{ref} = (T_w + T_b)/2$ except for $c_p = c_p(T_b)$	[79], [80]
Mikheiev	$Nu \equiv Nu_M = 0.021 \cdot Re^{0.8} \cdot Pr^{0.43}$ $Nu = Nu_M \cdot (Pr_b/Pr_w)^{0.25}$	$10^4 < Re < 5 \cdot 10^6$, $0.6 < Pr < 2{,}500$ $T_{ref} = T_b$ except for $Pr_w = Pr(T_w)$	[81], [82]
Zhukauskas	$Nu = 0.0225 \cdot Re^{0.8} \cdot Pr^{0.6}$ (for gases only)	The same as in the Mikheiev correlation with $T_{ref} = T_b$	[74]

The most frequently cited empirical correlations are based on the following rule founded by Kays [90]. If both walls of an annular channel are heated independent of each other (i.e., with varied heat fluxes at the walls and along the axis, the Nusselt numbers (Nu_{inner} and Nu_{outer} may be evaluated by the superposition principle). First, one should determine the Nusselt numbers (Nu_{inner}^* and Nu_{outer}^*) in two cases: heat transfer from the inner wall and outer wall. When heat is removed from one wall, the second one is considered as an adiabatic wall. In such a case, under the additional assumption that the q_{inner} and q_{outer} are constant, the Petukhov–Roizen correlation [84–86] is recommended in References 26 and 74:

$$Nu_{inner}^*/Nu = [1 - \varphi(Pr)] \cdot (1/\Theta)^{n(Pr)} \cdot \delta, \qquad 0.03 \leq \Theta \leq 1$$

$$Nu_{outer}^*/Nu = 1 - \varphi(Pr) \cdot \Theta^{0.6}, \qquad 0 \leq \Theta \leq 1$$

(18)

where $\quad \varphi(Pr) = 0.45/(2.4 + Pr)$

$\qquad n(Pr) = 0.16 \cdot Pr^{-0.15}$

$$\delta = \begin{cases} 1 + 7.5[(1/\Theta - 5)/Re]^{0.6}, & \Theta < 0.2 \\ 1, & \Theta \geq 0.2 \end{cases}$$

$$0.7 \leq Pr \leq 100, \qquad 10^4 \leq Re \leq 10^6, \qquad \Theta = D_{inner}/D_{outer}$$

an Nu is the Nusselt number for a circular tube ($D_e = D_{outer} - D_{inner}$) evaluated from either Equation 17 or its more general version:

$$Nu = (\zeta/8) \cdot Re \cdot Pr/[1.07 + 900/Re - 0.63/(1 + 10 \cdot Pr) + 12.7 \cdot (\zeta/8)^{1/2} \cdot (Pr^{2/3} - 1)]$$

The so-called adiabatic temperatures of nonheated walls T^{ad} are calculated using the formulas:

$$T_{inner}^{ad} = 22 \cdot (0.27 \cdot \Theta^2 - 1) \cdot Re^{-0.87} \cdot Pr^{-0.18}$$

$$T_{outer}^{ad} = \Theta \cdot T_{inner}^{ad}$$

Finally, the correlation takes the form:

$$Nu_{inner} = Nu_{inner}^*[1 + (q_{outer}/q_{inner}) \cdot T_{inner}^{ad} \cdot Nu_{inner}^*]$$

$$Nu_{outer} = Nu_{outer}^*[1 + (q_{inner}/q_{outer}) \cdot T_{outer}^{ad} \cdot Nu_{outer}^*]$$

(19)

In the case of gaseous coolants one may set $Pr \approx 0.7$ which simplifies the expressions adduced. Additional correlations are available in Reference 91. Heat transfer in a thin rectangular, square or triangular channels may be performed using the circular channel correlations given in Table 2. The reader should consult the literature for examples [92] since, in some cases, there exist more precise equations.

Heat transfer in in-line cooled rod bundles is far more complicated than in a circular channel or other closed channel cases. For s/d < 1.15 [74] circumferential variations of the heat transfer coefficient should be accounted for. One must then solve the differential equation conjugate system (10) and (14) with proper boundary conditions, which is extremely difficult. Difficulties are of a similar type when attempting to integrate Equation 16, although their scope is far larger because of the multidimensionality of the problem. For s/d > 1.15 [74] the circumferential walltemperature variations are insignificant and may be neglected. In such a case, the system of Equations 10 and 14 is separable. It suffices then to solve the conservation equations on the fluid, which, however, is still a nontrivial problem.

In practice, the heat transfer coefficient is calculated by using empirical correlations. Zhukauskas [74] recommends the following formula for nonmetallic coolants [93]:

$$Nu/Nu_p = 1 + 0.91 \cdot Re^{-0.1} \cdot Pr^{0.4} \cdot [1 - 2 \cdot \exp(-B)]$$

(20)

$$3 \cdot 10^3 < Re < 10^6, \, 0.66 < Pr < 5.0, \, 0.103 \leq B \leq 3.5, \, 1.02 < s/d < 2.5$$

where Nu_p is calculated based on the Dittus–Boelter correlation (see Table 2) and using an equivalent diameter $D_e = B \cdot d$ (see Figure 7). Hence, the coefficient B is given by

$$B = \begin{cases} 2\sqrt{3}/\pi \cdot (s/d)^2 - 1, & \text{for triangular array} \\ 4/\pi \cdot (s/d)^2 - 1, & \text{for square array} \end{cases}$$

In addition, there exists a number of correlations of the form

$$Nu = C(s/d) \cdot Re^m \cdot Pr^n \tag{21}$$

According to Weisman [94]:

$$C = \begin{cases} 0.026(s/d) - 0.006, 1.1 \leq s/d \leq 1.5, \text{for triangular array} \\ 0.042(s/d) - 0.024, 1.1 \leq s/d \leq 1.3, \text{for square array} \end{cases}$$

and $m = 0.8, n = 1/3, T_{ref} = T_b$

The correlation [26]:

$$C = 0.032 \cdot (s/d) - 0.0144$$

where $Re > 1.3 \cdot 10^4$ for $s/d = 1.1 \div 1.2$
    $Re > 2 \cdot 10^4$ for $s/d = 1.2 \div 1.4$
    $Re > 3 \cdot 10^4$ for $s/d = 1.4 \div 1.5$

and $m = 0.8,$ $n = 1/3,$ $T_{ref} = (T_b + T_w)/2$

verges upon the correlation above.
However, for a triangular array and liquid coolants, Subbotion–Ibragimov [91] recommend:

$$C = 0.0165 + 0.02 \cdot [1 - 0.91/(s/d)^2] \cdot (s/d)^{0.15}$$

where $5 \cdot 10^3 < Re < 5 \cdot 10^5,$ $1.0 < Pr \leq 20,$ $1.1 \leq s/d \leq 1.8$

and $m = 0.8,$ $n = 0.4,$ $T_{ref} = T_b$

For gaseous coolants one may apply the correlation [95]:

$$Nu/Nu_p = 0.351 \cdot \lg (s/d - 1) + 0.0272, \qquad 1.03 \leq s/d \leq 2.4 \tag{22}$$

where Nu_p is calculated with the help of the Dittus–Boelter formula (see Table 2).
    The preceding adduced correlations (Equations 20 through 22) contain the characteristic array pitch s/d, the influence of which on heat transfer decreases together with its increase. Moreover, this parameter plays more of a role in liquid than gaseous coolants. The preceding correlations do not take into consideration the influence of disturbances caused by

- Rod spacers with a given geometry.
- Clad-finning.
- Special elements for increasing flow turbulence [96].

    Liquid metals. Determination of the heat transfer coefficient in turbulent flow of liquid metals through closed or open channels is based on correlations different from those of ordinary fluids. It results from low values of Prandtl numbers for liquid metals ($Pr \sim 10^{-2}$). The turbulent eddy diffusivity is much less than molecular diffusivity. Therefore, the heat transfer correlations resemble those of laminar flow.

A classical correlation in the flow through pipes with $q_w = $ const. is the Lyon–Martinelli Equations 75, 97.

$$Nu = 7.0 + 0.025 \cdot Pe^{0.8}, \qquad Pe > 300 \tag{23}$$

obtained either by the use of the Lyon integral [75] with $\Psi \equiv \varepsilon_h/\varepsilon_m = 1$ or by an analogy between heat and momentum transfer [97]. Lyon suggested [98] the following extended form of Equation 23:

$$Nu = 7.0 + 0.025 \cdot (Pe \cdot \bar{\Psi})^{0.8} \tag{24}$$

and Dwyer [99, 100] recommended the average ratio of eddy diffusivities

$$\bar{\Psi} = 1 - 1.82/[Pr(\varepsilon_m/v)_{max}^{1.4}] \tag{25}$$

where $(\varepsilon_m/v)_{max}$ is a function of the Reynolds number given graphically. Additional correlations may be found in numerous literature cited in review papers [40, 49, 101].

Dwyer [102–105] addressed himself to the problem of heat transfer in flows through annuli and between parallel plates. He generalized Equation 24 postulating:

$$Nu = \alpha + \beta(\bar{\Psi} \cdot Pe)^\gamma, \qquad 10^2 \leq Pe \leq 10^4 \tag{26}$$

where

- $\bar{\Psi}$ is given by (5.10).
- $(\varepsilon_m/v)_{max}$ is given graphically for the mentioned channel geometries as a function of Reynolds number.
- α, β, γ are constants for flows through pipes (see Equation 24) and between parallel plates (if heat fluxes from both plates are equal then $\alpha = 0.49$, $\beta = 0.0596$, $\gamma = 0.688$ [106]), and functions of the ratio of inner-to-outer diameters Θ for flows through annuli (and function of

$$\xi = \{(q_{w, inner}/q_{w, outer})/[(q_{w, inner}/q_{w, outer}) + 1/\Theta]\}$$

for heat transfer from both walls).
- Pe and Nu are calculated using the channel equivalent diameter D_e

The values of the parameters α, β and γ for different geometries and heat transfer conditions are presented in above cited Dwyer's papers [102–106]. Some additional correlations for heat transfer in flows through annuli and between parallel plates are also presented in Reference 101. However, certain particular cases of heat transfer to liquid metals flowing in eccentric annuli are considered in References 107 and 108.

Equation 26 can be also applied for in-line flow between rod bundles with equilateral triangular or square spacing. The values of $(\varepsilon_m/v)_{max}$ are given, similarly as for the preceding geometries in Reference 100. However, the values of α, β, γ are functions of the pitch-to-diameter ratio (s/d). Assuming that the equivalent annulus model can be applied, Dwyer-Lyon-Maresca recommend [106, 109], $\alpha = 6.66 + 3.126 \cdot (s/d) + 1.184 \cdot (s/d)^2$, $\beta = 0.0155$, $\gamma = 0.86$ for triangular array with s/d = 1.3–3.0, $\alpha = 7.0 + 4.24 \cdot (s/d)^{1.52}$, $\beta = 0.0275 \cdot (s/d)^{0.27}$, $\gamma = 0.8$ for square array with s/d = 1.7–10.0.

In reactor cores cooled by liquid metals (first of all, Na), in view of the neutron balance, the pitch s/d is usually less than 1.3. In such a case, there occurs circumferential variations of the outside surface cladding temperature and heat transfer coefficient. Hence, it is necessary to calculate the local and average heat transfer coefficients. The equivalent annulus model cannot be applied. One should consider heat transfer in the real geometry (see Figure 7).

Dwyer–Berry and Subbotin–Ushakov [110–113] showed that for s/d < 1.3 the crucial influence on circumferential temperature and heat transfer coefficient distributions has the pitch s/d. If s/d tends to 1 then temperature variations rapidly increase and average heat transfer coefficients rapidly decrease. Moreover, some influence is also due to

• Fuel element geometrical parameters.
• Thermal conductivies of fuel element components and coolant.
• Low value of the Prandtl number.

In the Soviet literature, this influence is given by so-called thermal modeling of fuel elements [25–36, 114] by the help of the conduction parameter ε. Analysis of comprehensive experimental data obtained in the recent years in the Soviet Union and Czechoslovakia is presented in Reference 114, where the reader may also find a number of formulas concerning thermal and hydrodynamic calculations related to fast reactor cores cooled by liquid sodium. In addition, there is also given a comprehensive literature review. Special attention should be directed to reports of the FEI–Obninsk [115–124].

A few correlations recommended in [114] are given below. The following formula deals with triangular arrays with an infinite number of fuel elements:

$$Nu = Nu_{lam}^{*} + \Psi(\varepsilon, s/d) \cdot Pe^{\gamma(s/d)}$$
$$1 \leq Pe \leq 4{,}000, \qquad 1.0 < s/d < 2.0, \qquad \varepsilon \geq 0.01 \qquad (27)$$

where $\Psi = 0.041/(s/d)^2 \cdot \{1 - \{[(s/d)^{30} - 1]/6 + (1.24\,\varepsilon + 1.15)^{1/2}\}^{-1}\}$
$\gamma = 0.56 + 0.19 \cdot (s/d) - 0.1/(s/d)^{80}$

The Nusselt number Nu_{lam}^{*} corresponding to laminar flow will be defined in the next section; similarly as Nu_{lam}^{**} and Nu_{lam}^{***}. If $(s/d) = 1$ then

$$Nu = Nu_{lam}^{**} + 0.041 \cdot \{1 - [(1.24\,\varepsilon + 1.15)^{1/2}]^{-1}\} \cdot Pe^{0.65} \qquad (28)$$

However, for $1.20 < s/d < 2.0$ the formula holds:

$$Nu = Nu_{lam}^{***} + 0.041/(s/d)^2 \cdot Pe^{0.56 + 0.19(s/d)} \qquad (29)$$

The accuracy of Equations 27 through 29 is about $\pm 15\%$.

In Reference 114, one may find formulas for the heat transfer coefficient in the subchannels of types "k" or "l" (see Figure 6). The average values of these coefficients on the peripheral element circumference are essentially less than those in the channels of types "i" and "j" (see Figure 6).

The maximal dimensionless circumferential temperature variation ΔT may be evaluated from the formula given in Reference 114:

$$\Delta T = \Delta T_{lam}/[1 + \gamma(\varepsilon) \cdot Pe^{\beta(s/d)}]$$

$$1.0 \leq s/d \leq 1.15, \qquad 1 \leq Pe \leq 2{,}000, \qquad \varepsilon \geq 0.2 \qquad (30)$$

where $\gamma(\varepsilon) = 0.008(1 + 0.03\varepsilon)$
$\beta(s/d) = 0.65 + 51 \cdot \lg(s/d)/(s/d)^{20}$

and ΔT_{lam} corresponds to laminar flow (see next section). In the real cluster this variation is greater; in particularly, in case of peripheral rods, if $s/d \to 1$ then the maximum power cluster can be determined. The preceding equations refer to smooth rod-bundle heat transfer in an equilateral triangular array. In practice, it is necessary to take into consideration the influence of different types of rod spacers on the local and average heat transfer coefficients. A number of these correlations is demonstrated in Reference 114. Additional information with reference to heat transfer to liquid metals are discussed in References 125 through 132.

Laminar Flow

In principle, the controlling heat transfer mechanism in laminar flow is conduction. Therefore it is not possible to obtain a high heat transfer coefficient α, although this coefficient is relatively high in most liquid metals. The result is that laminar flow of coolants cannot occur in reactor cores during normal full-power operation. This flow can occur in various failures leading to reactor shut-downs. The removal of the residual heat should be intensive enough in order not to exceed admissible temperatures in all reactor core elements.

Ordinary fluids. If the coolant physical properties are constant then the fully developed laminar flow is described by the energy equation:

$$\lambda_c(\partial^2 T_c/\partial x^2 + \partial^2 T_c/\partial y^2) = w \cdot p_c \cdot c_{p_c} \cdot \partial T_c/\partial z \tag{31}$$

Graetz [133] gave its solution for the case of flow through a straight circular tube with a uniform wall temperature T_w. The Nusselt number takes its minimal value $Nu_\infty = 3.656$ and the thermal entrance region length is differently estimated (e.g. $\delta_T = 0.055 \cdot D \cdot Re \cdot Pr$ [134]). In practical calculations Zhukauskas [74] recommends the empirical correlations given in References 83 and 135. In the case of uniform heat flux on the channel wall one has $Nu_\infty = 4.364$ and the appropriate convective correlations are listed in Reference 136. In addition, one may set $\delta_T = 0.07 \cdot D \cdot Pe$.

In laminar flow the equivalent-diameter concept may not be applied. Evaluating Nusselt numbers for noncircular closed channels is therefore based on correlations different than those of a circular tube. The determination of heat transfer between the wall and fluid is difficult in view of the complicated form of the velocity profile. Both for uniform wall temperature and uniform heat flux, Nu_∞ can be evaluated using by approximate methods only [134, 137]. For flows through annular channels with a uniform temperature of the heated wall, Nu_∞ may be estimated as follows

- $Nu_\infty = 3.96 + 0.9 \cdot \Theta^{-0.95}$ ($\Theta \geq 0.2$) for heat flow between the inner wall and coolant.
- $Nu_\infty = 4.03 \cdot \exp(0.185 \cdot \Theta)$, where $\Theta \geq 0.15$ for heat flow between the outer wall and coolant.

If both channel walls are cooled then the corresponding expressions may be found in [26, 91, 138]. In the cited literature, the values of Nu_∞ for uniform wall temperature and uniform heat flux are also adduced for the flow between parallel plates and through triangular and rectangular channels. The relation $Nu_\infty|_{T_w = const} < Nu_\infty|_{q_w = const}$ is independent on the closed-channel geometry.

Heat transfer in laminar flow through rod bundles differs to some extent from that in closed channels. This is a result of a lack of axial symmetry in different subchannels. If the pitch-to-diameter ratio $s/d < 1.3$, then the circumferential temperature and heat flux distributions are not uniform. These variations decrease when s/d increases. The values of Nu_∞ for in-line flow between rod bundle triangular and square spacings corresponding to uniform circumferential wall temperature and heat flux distributions are given in Tables 3 and 4. These results concerning both triangular- and square-lattice rod bundles have the following specific properties:

- $Nu_T > Nu_q$ with $\Delta Nu = Nu_T - Nu_q$ being essential when s/d tending to 1 [91]
- Both Nu_T and Nu_q increase when s/d does

To evaluate of Nu_∞ corresponding to a given value of the parameter ε the following relation in recommended [26]:

$$Nu(\varepsilon, s/d) = Nu_q(s/d) + f(\varepsilon, s/d) \cdot [Nu_T(s/d) - Nu_q(s/d)]$$

The function $f(\varepsilon, s/d)$ is given graphically and practically depends on ε only.

In the formulas-above there is not taken into account the dependence of coolant physical properties (first of all, viscosity) on temperature. In the contrary, the equations of energy (Equation 31) and motion (Equation 10) should be solved simultaneously. For flow between rod bundles with $s/d < 1.3$ the preceding system of equations should be completed by the heat conduction equation

Table 3
Values of Nu_∞ for Laminar Flow of Water through Fuel Rod Bundles with Equilateral Triangular Spacing

s/d	$Nu_\infty = Nu_T$ (T_w = const.)	$Nu_\infty = Nu_q$ (q_w = const.)	$Nu_T - Nu_q$	s/d	Nu_T	Nu_q	$Nu_T - Nu_q$
1.00	1.26	0.15	1.11	1.12	5.19	3.75	1.14
1.02	1.80	0.40	1.40	1.16	6.40	5.40	1.00
1.04	2.43	0.83	1.60	1.20	7.44	6.90	0.54
1.06	3.13	1.38	1.75	1.24	8.27	7.92	0.35
1.08	3.88	2.07	1.81	1.28	8.94	8.70	0.24
1.10	4.57	2.90	1.67	1.30	9.20	9.05	0.15

From Emelianov [26].

for the fuel element. The influence of the variation of physical properties due to the temperature gradient on heat-transfer correlations may be taken into consideration (multipliers: $(\mu_w/\mu_b)^n$ [134], $(Pr_w/Pr_b)^m$ [139]. One may also solve the system of conservation equations assuming some form of the function $\mu = \mu(T)$ 140–142. Moreover, there are known relations that account for the effect of free convection.

Liquid metals. In principle, in laminar flow through closed channels the heat-transfer correlations for nonmetallic coolants may be used. The only obstacle is the range of the Prandtl number values. The axial heat conduction in metal is usually neglected when $Pe > 10$ [40]; i.e., $Re > \sim 10^3$. Otherwise, it should be taken into account. Empirical heat transfer correlations for closely packed rod bundles in equilateral triangular pitch only are given in the following.

For liquid-metal heat transfer in rod bundles (with an infinite number of fuel elements), the correlated result is [114]:

$$Nu = Nu_{lam}^* = \{7.55 - 6.3/(s/d)^{17(s/d) \cdot [(s/d) - 0.81]}\} \cdot \{1 - 3.6/[(s/d)^{20} \cdot (1 + 2.5 \cdot \varepsilon^{0.86}) + 3.2]\}$$

for $\quad 1.0 \leq s/d \leq 2.0, \quad Pe \geq 1, \quad \varepsilon \geq 0.01$

In the case of tightly packed rod bundles, i.e. where $s/d = 1$, the preceding equation reduces to

$$Nu = Nu_{lam}^{**} = 1.25 \cdot [1 - 3.6/(4.2 + 2.5 \cdot \varepsilon^{0.86})]$$

Table 4
Values of Nu_∞ for Laminar Flow of Water through Fuel Rod Bundles with Square Spacing

s/d	$Nu_\infty = Nu_T$ (T_w = const.)	$Nu_\infty - Nu_q$ (q_w = const.)	$Nu_T - Nu_q$	s/d	Nu_T	Nu_q	$Nu_T - Nu_q$
1.00	1.30	—	—	1.2	4.58	3.70	0.88
1.02	1.61	0.52	1.09	1.3	6.40	5.82	0.58
1.05	2.05	0.84	1.21	1.4	9.43	9.35	0.08
1.10	2.83	1.72	1.11	1.5	15.05	15.05	0

From Polanin, Ibragimov, and Sabelev [138].

If $1.2 \leq s/d \leq 2.0$ then the corresponding equation is

$$Nu = Nu_{lam}^{***} = 7.55 \cdot (s/d) - 20 \cdot (s/d)^{-13}$$

The circumferential variation of cladding surface temperature is correlated with the following equation [114]:

$$\Delta T_{lam} = 0.022\{(s/d)^3[(s/d) - 1]^{0.4} - 0.99\} \cdot [1 - \tanh \cdot \{\{1.2 \exp\{-26.4[(s/d) - 1]\} + \ln \varepsilon\}\{0.84 + 0.2\{[(s/d) - 1.06]0.06\}^2\}\}]$$

In clusters, these variations are somewhat more significant, first of all, on the surfaces of peripheral elements "k" and "l" (see Figure 6). Suitable correlations are reported in reference [114]. Some additional relevent information can be found in References 40, 105, 112–114, 132, 142–146.

Hydraulic Calculations of Reactor Channels

The goal of hydraulic calculations of a reactor core is the determination of pressure drop in reactor channels, pumping power, and flow distribution.

In the case of thermal reactors, where $s/d \sim 1.3$, it would be sufficient to use in these calculations a coolant velocity $\bar{w}$ averaged over the fuel assembly is cross section area.

More complicated situations arise in fast reactors, where $s/d \sim 1.1$–1.2 and detailed analysis of local hydrodynamic characteristics is necessary. This is mainly caused by specific interchannel interactions especially in peripheral channels.

Reactor Core Pressure Drop

The total pressure drop in a reactor core is the sum:

$$\Delta p_{total} = \Delta p_f + \Delta p_g + \Delta p_a + \sum \Delta p_{local} \tag{32}$$

In a case of liquid coolants, Δp_a may be neglected because of its low compressibility. Also Δp_g may be neglected because $\Delta p_g \ll \Delta p_f$. Changes of coolant density have to be taken into account for gaseous coolants since Δp_a is about 10% of Δp_{total}.

Friction loss. For laminar or turbulent flow through a circular tube, the frictional loss is defined as follows

$$\Delta p_f = \zeta \cdot (L/D_p) \cdot (\rho_c \cdot \bar{w}^2/2) \tag{33}$$

where ζ is the Darcy–Weisbach friction factor.

It can be determined theoretically only for the case of fully-developed isothermal laminar flow. For turbulent flow empirical and semi-empirical correlations exist. Some formulas for incompressible fully-developed isothermal laminar flow are given below 26, 138:

- Circular tube

$$\zeta = \zeta_p = 64/Re.$$

- Plane gap

$$\zeta = 1.5 \cdot \zeta_p.$$

- Annular channel

$$\zeta = (1 - \Theta^2)/[1 + \Theta^2 + (1 - \Theta^2)/\ln \Theta]\zeta_p.$$

For laminar coolant flow along a cluster of smooth fuel elements the friction factor ζ can be determined [114, 146, 147] from the empirical formula

$$\zeta = f(s/d) \cdot \zeta_p$$

where

$$
f(s/d) = \begin{cases}
0.41 + 1.9[(s/d) - 1]^{1/3}, & [146] \\
1.369 - 0.709 \cdot (s/d)^{-10.7}, & [114, 147]
\end{cases} \text{triangular lattice} \\
\begin{cases}
0.41 + 1.9[(s/d) - 1]^{1/2}, & [146] \\
1.436 - 0.791 \cdot (s/d)^{-5.3}, & [114, 147]
\end{cases} \text{square lattice}
$$

For noncircular channels the Reynolds number calculation is based on equivalent (hydraulic) diameter D_e. The average fluid velocity is calculated from the theoretical velocity distribution [74, 148, 149].

In the case of turbulent flow, which is typical for nuclear reactors, the friction factor can be determined from the formulas given below.

Friction factor ζ for fully-developed isothermal turbulent flow of incompressible fluid in circular tube (smooth or almost smooth):

$$
\zeta = \zeta_p = \begin{cases}
0.3164 \cdot Re^{-0.25}, Re \leq 10^5, [150] \\
(1.82 \cdot \lg Re - 1.64)^{-2}, 10^4 \leq Re \leq 5 \cdot 10^6, [151] \\
0.032 + 0.221 \cdot Re^{-0.237}, 10^5 \leq Re \leq 4 \cdot 10^6, [26]
\end{cases} \tag{34}
$$

and

$$
\zeta_p^{-1/2} = \begin{cases}
2.0 \cdot \ln (Re \cdot \zeta_p^{1/2}) - 0.8, 10^4 \leq Re \leq 5 \cdot 10^6, [152] \\
-2 \cdot \lg [\delta/3.7 + 2.51/(Re \cdot \zeta_p^{1/2})], \text{turbulent flow}, [153] \\
2 \cdot \lg (1/\delta) + 1.74, Re > 500/\delta, [138]
\end{cases} \tag{35}
$$

Colebrook's correlation [153] is the most popular one in the western technical literature. It is plotted in Figure 10. This plot is known as Moody diagram [154] and is widely used in the whole range of turbulent flows.

The preceding formulas can be also used for noncircular channels when hydraulic diameter D_e is used instead of pipe diameter D_p. There exist also correlations for channels of different geometry [26, 91, 138]. For example, in a case of annular channel:

$$\zeta = (1 + 0.04 \cdot \Theta) \cdot \{(1 - \Theta)/[1 + (1 - \Theta^2) \ln \Theta^2]\}^{0.62} \cdot \zeta_p$$

where ζ_p is given by Equations 34 or 35.

The above formula is particularly recommended for large Θ values.

Determination of the friction factor in flow along closely packed rod bundles is more complicated. In this case, a certain role is played by anisotrope of flow. In addition, the transition region is much greater than that of closed channels.

The corresponding formulas containing the pitch-to-diameter ratio s/d can be found in References 26, 74, 91, 138, and 158. For example, the formula

$$
\zeta/\zeta_p = \begin{cases}
0.57 + 0.18[(s/d) - 1] + 0.53[1 - \exp(-a)], \\
a = 0.58\{1 - \exp\{-70[(s/d) - 1]\}\} + 9.2[(s/d) - 1] & \text{for triangular lattice,} \\
0.59 + 0.19[(s/d) - 1] + 0.52\{1 - \exp\{-10[(s/d) - 1]\}\} & \text{for square lattice,}
\end{cases}
$$

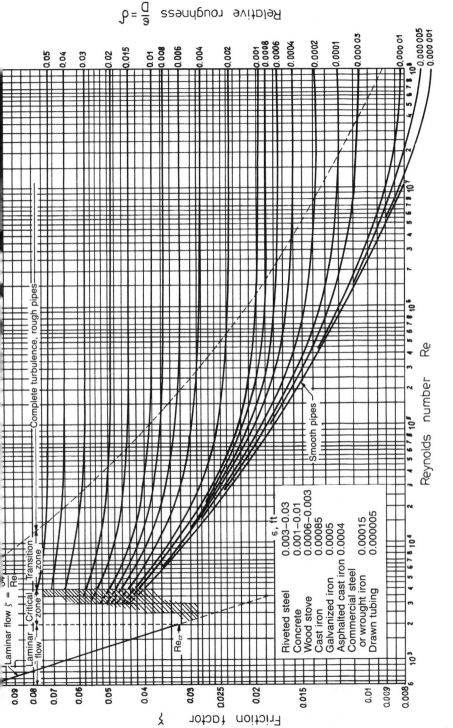

Figure 10. Moody friction factor chart, (Reprinted with permission from *Trans. ASME*, vol. 66, Moody L.F., "Friction factors for pipe flows," Copyright 1944, ASME, pp. 671–684.)

Relative roughness $\dfrac{\varepsilon}{D} = \zeta$

Friction factor ζ

Reynolds number Re

Laminar flow $\zeta = \dfrac{}{Re}$

Laminar flow

Critical zone

Transition zone

Complete turbulence, rough pipes

Re_{cr}

Smooth pipes

	ε, ft
Riveted steel	0.003–0.03
Concrete	0.001–0.01
Wood stove	0.0006–0.003
Cast iron	0.00085
Galvanized iron	0.0005
Asphalted cast iron	0.0004
Commercial steel or wrought iron	0.00015
Drawn tubing	0.000005

for $1 < s/d < 10, 2 \cdot 10^4 < Re < 5 \cdot 10^5$ (ζ_p is calculated from Equation 34 [150], is given in Reference 91. The correlation below

$$\zeta = C \cdot (\Pi_w/\Pi_f) \cdot (A_{ch}/A_f)^m \cdot Re^{-0.25}, 4 \cdot 10^3 < Re < 5 \cdot 10^4$$

where

$C = 0.47, m = 0.35, 4 \cdot 10^3 \leq Re \leq 10^5$; triangular lattice

$C = 0.38, m = 0.45, 10^3 \leq Re \leq 5 \cdot 10^4$; square lattice

is recommended in [138]. The following correlations are also useful:

- [114]: $(K/\zeta)^{1/2} = 2 \cdot \lg (Re \cdot \zeta^{1/2}/K^{1.5}) - 0.8$ with K being approximated for $1.0 \leq s/d \leq 1.4$ as follows:

$$K = \begin{cases} 1.277 - 0.532 \cdot (s/d)^{-10.7}; \text{ triangular lattice,} \\ 1.327 - 0.593 \cdot (s/d)^{-5.3}; \text{ square lattice,} \end{cases}$$

remembering that, for $Re > 10^4$, one has

$$\zeta = 0.184 \cdot K^{1.2} \cdot Re^{-0.2};$$

- [147]: $\zeta = C \cdot a \cdot Re^{-m}, 1 \leq s/d \leq 2$

where

$$C = 1 + 0.316[1 + 2.83 \cdot \exp(-2 \cdot 10^3 \cdot Re)] \cdot [(s/d) - 1]$$
$$+ 0.93[1 + 2.95 \cdot \exp(-2 \cdot 10^{-3} \cdot Re)] \cdot \{1 - \exp\{-9.2[(s/d) - 1]\}\}$$

$$a = 0.19 + 20 \cdot \exp(-4 \cdot 10^3 \cdot Re) + 5.81 \cdot \exp(-1.6 \cdot 10^{-3} \cdot Re),$$

$$m = 0.25 + 0.75 \cdot \exp(-1.1 \cdot 10^{-3} \cdot Re).$$

The latter correlation is recommended both for turbulent flow and the transition region.

There are also a number of similar formulas for different subchannel-shapes occurring in a fuel assembly.

In the preceding correlations, isothermal flow of coolants was assumed. However, intensive heat transfer processes leading to considerable temperature gradients occur between reactor channel walls and the cooling medium. The Darcy–Weisbach friction factor in nonisothermal flow $\zeta_{n\text{-iso}}$ may be evaluated by means of one of the correlations below:

- Rohsenow–Clark [77]

$$\zeta_{n\text{-iso}} = \zeta[\mu(T_w)/\mu(T_b)]^{0.60}$$

recommended first of all for water.
- Taylor [156]

$$\zeta_{n\text{-iso}} = (0.0028 + 0.25/Re_m^{0.32}) \cdot (T_b/T_w)^{0.5}$$

where the Reynolds number Re_m is calculated based on $\rho_c(T_b)$ and $\mu(T_w)$ and temperatures are absolute.

- $[83, 138]$

$$\zeta_{n\text{-iso}} = \zeta \cdot [1 - 0.5(1 + M)^n \cdot \lg(1 + M)]$$

where

$$M = [\mu(T_b)/\mu(T_w) - 1] \cdot [\mu(T_b)/\mu(T_w)]^{0.17}$$

$$n = 0.17 - 2 \cdot 10^{-6} \cdot Re + 180/Re$$

and $10^4 < Re < 3 \cdot 10^5$, $1.3 < Pr < 10$.

- $[157]$

$$\zeta_{n\text{-iso}} = \zeta\{1 + \Pi_q/\Pi_w\{[\mu(T_w)/\mu(T_b)]^{0.6} - 1\}\}.$$

Zhukauskas [74] suggests more general expressions. However, a unique estimation of the influence of temperature gradient in the fluid on the friction factor value is not known. In the case of gaseous coolants, it is useful to account for the term Δp_a. Then Δp_{total} may be calculated from the following simplified formula [28, 29]:

$$\Delta p_{total} = \Delta p_f + \Delta p_a = (1/\bar{\rho}_c) \cdot G[\zeta \cdot L/D_e + (T_{c,\,out} - T_{c,\,in})/\bar{T}_c]$$

More detailed procedures are given in References 55 and 158.

Local losses. Additional pressure losses in straight reactor channels are caused by:

- Changes of channel cross-section, e.g., at inlet and outlet of reactor core.
- Rod spacers and finning of fuel elements.

The contraction and expansion coefficients may be found, e.g., in References 155 and 159. They depend on the Reynolds number and the ratio of channel cross-sectional areas. A variety of distancing elements and fuel element fins have produced the correlations cited, for example in References 26, 114, and 116, which are not sufficiently general. In each particular case, it is reasonable to examine the literature.

Pumping Power

The reactor is the basic element of the primary circuit. To ensure the required coolant flow through the reactor core, pumps (for liquid coolants) and gas-blowers are used. Maintenance of continuous coolant circulation is due to the fact that the pumping power is equalized with the total pressure drop. If the pressure drop over reactor is taken into account only, then the pumping power $P_{pumping}$ is defined as follows:

$P_{pumping} = \Delta p_{total} \times$ total area of coolant flow $\times$ average coolant speed/pump efficiency.

In a reactor circuit this power is considerably greater since the total pressure drop is the sum of pressure drops in all elements of this circuit.

Flow Distribution

The spatial distribution of the heat generation requires readjustment of the mass flow rate to local power of fuel element. There exist a number of possibilities of realization of this postulate, which is often called the flow distribution [26–29 and 55]. One may assume a constant static pressure (or pressure gradient) in the channel cross-section. This method is usually termed as the equivalent diameter method. In more detailed calculations other methods are applied in which the reactor core is divided into a number of so-called hydraulic zones consisting of channels with similar thermal parameters (see e.g. [26]). For example, flow distribution is assumed to be proportional to the power of the most thermally loaded channel ("hot" channel) in a zone or such that the maximal fuel element temperature is the same in the all zones. Independent of the method, cooling of all fuel elements should be such that their maximal temperature values are less than the maximal permissible levels.

TWO-PHASE FLOW AND HEAT TRANSFER WITH BOILING

The thermal and hydraulic calculations of BWR and PWR reactor cores in steady and unsteady states require thorough analysis of coolant (mainly water) boiling.

In the case of two-phase flow, different nonhomogeneous phases may occur. The flow patterns for vertical circular tubes are shown in Figures 11 and 12 [161]. In the situation demonstrated in Figure 12 critical heat flux takes place (the fast increase of wall temperature and burnout).

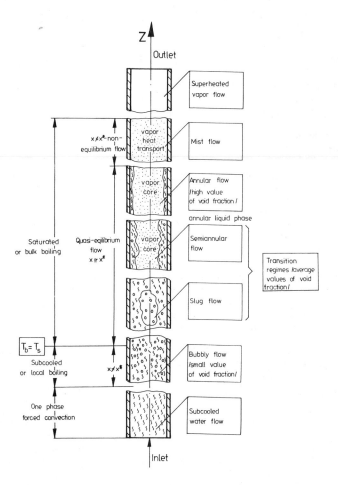

Figure 11. Flow regimes in a vertical heated pipe with up-flow of coolant.

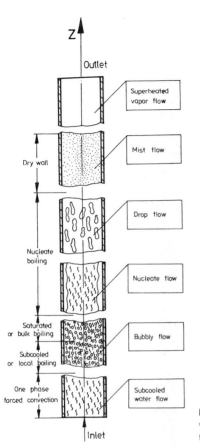

Figure 12. Flow regimes in a vertical heated pipe with up-flow of coolant—case of the critical condition.

In a case of complex geometry channels the following flow patterns can exist: bubble flow, slug flow, inverse annular flow (in the critical heat transfer conditions) and next when quality increases, complicated structures being the composition of the main flow patterns can occur.

More details about two-phase flow modes are described for example in References 162–166. Theoretical and experimental investigations of two-phase flow through reactor core are extremely complicated. It is connected with the presence of turbulent (in transient states also nonequilibrium) flow and nonuniform heat flux distribution.

In practice, correlations based on similarity theory and dimensional analysis for the case of q = constant are used, although correlations taking into account attributes of boiling in core channels exist (e.g. [166–170]).

Basic heat transfer phenomena and the predictive techniques which are particularly important in nuclear water reactor safety are described in [171–172].

In spite of great progress in numerical hydromechanics [64, 173–178] and in computer technology further experiments on boiling mechanisms during the flow are necessary. It results from the fact that reactor technology demands precise treatment of flow and heat transfer problems.

Void Fraction, Quality and Slip Relations

The description of two-phase flow requires three new parameters, not used in the single-phase case: void fraction φ, quality x, and slip ratio S.
These are defined as follows:

$$\varphi = A_v/(A_v + A_1)$$

$$x = W_v/(W_v + W_1) = A_vG_v/(A_vG_v + A_1G_1)$$

$$S = w_v/w_1$$

These are quantities averaged over the channel cross section. It is possible to define average values of these parameters for the flow channel (A → V) as well as their local values for a given z.

Since φ can be measured [163, 179–181] then the average density of liquid-vapor mixture can be determined from the following relationship:

$$\rho_m = \rho_v \cdot \varphi + \rho_1 \cdot (1 - \varphi)$$

The fundamental relationship between above parameters φ, x, S is:

$$(1 - \varphi)/\varphi = (1 - x) \cdot \rho_v \cdot S/(x \cdot \rho_1)$$

In homogeneous flow, $w_v = w_1$ and one has S = 1. Figure 13 shows φ versus x for liquid water at 6.89 MPa (1,000 psia) and several slip ratios.

Difficulties in the experimental and theoretical establishing of φ, x, S resulted in numerous correlations, most of which do not depend on two-phase flow patterns. Some useful correlations which can be used in reactor channel calculations are available (e.g. [55, 138, 182–191]). The most frequently used formula is that of Martinelli–Nelson (Figure 14 [182]).

More general definition of quality based on thermodynamic enthalpy is also used

$$x^* = (h_m - h_1)/\Delta h_{vl}$$

However, for complete thermodynamic equilibrium one has x = x*. In reactor conditions, certain divergences between measured and calculated results must be taken into account.

For the typical boiling reactor channel the $\varphi(z)$ curve is shown in Figure 15. The vapor amount in the channel during subcooled boiling (region L_1L_2) has an effect on the pressure gradient. For

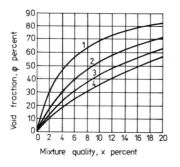

1- S =1 (no slip)
2- S = 2
3- S = 3
4- S = 4

Figure 13. φ vs. x for water at 1,000 psia and various slip ratios in a flow system. (Reprinted with permission from EL Wakil M. M., *Nuclear Power Engineering*, Copyright 1962. Mc-Graw-Hill p. 280.)

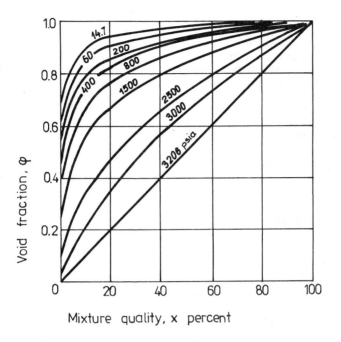

Figure 14. Martinelli-Nelson void fraction correlation (φ vs. x for steam-water mixture). (Reprinted with permission from *Trans.ASME*, vol. 70, Martnelli R. C. and Nelson D. B., "Prediction of pressure drop during forced circulation boiling of water," Copyright 1948, ASME, pp. 695–702.)

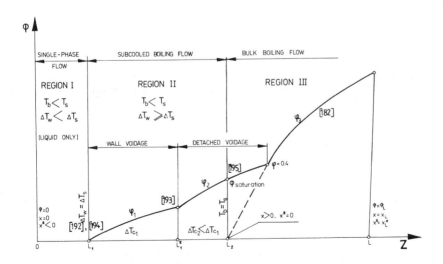

Figure 15. Characteristic regions of void fraction φ formation in boiling channels [$q_w < q_{w,crit}$ and $\Delta T_w = (T_b + q_w/\alpha_{convection}) - T_S$].

high subcoolings, after the onset of nucleation (region $L_1 L_1^*$) bubbles are attached to the heating surface and growing and collapsing take place. Voidage in this region is a wall effect. For lower subcoolings, bubbles detach from the heating surface and condense as they are in motion through the slightly subcooled liquid core. Voidage in this region is a bulk fluid effect. Over the region $L_1 L_1^*$ the void fraction remains low and its influence on the pressure gradient may be neglected. Saha and Zuber [193] have proposed a method which is recommended to calculate the point of net vapor generation. This point may be considered the point of bubble detachement (L_1^*). If $Pe_1 \leqq 70{,}000$, then the value of $\Delta T_1^* = T_{sat} - T_c(L_1^*)$ is given by relationship

$$\Delta T_{L_1^*} = q_w \cdot D_e/(455 \cdot \lambda_1)$$

and if $Pe_1 > 70{,}000$ then the value of $\Delta T_{L_1^*}$ is evaluated from the equation

$$\Delta T_{L_1^*} = q_w/(0.0065 \cdot G \cdot c_{pl})$$

For the region of detached voidage, Levy [195] assumed that the actual vapor mass fraction $x(z)$ and the thermodynamic vapor mass fraction $x^*(z)$ are connected by formula

$$x(z) = x^*(z) - x^*(L_1^*) \cdot \exp\left[x^*(z)/x^*(L_1^*) - 1 \right]$$

where $x^*(L_1^*)$ is thermodynamic vapor mass fraction at the point of bubble detachment, formed as

$$x^*(L_1^*) = -c_{pl} \cdot \Delta T_{sub}(L^*)/h$$

In the preceding formula the following boundary conditions are fulfiled:

- If $x^*(z) = x^*(L_1)$ then $x(z) = 0$.
- $(dx/dz)|_{z=L_1^*} = 0$.
- $x(z) \rightarrow x^*(z)$ for $x^*(z) \gg |x^*(L_1^*)|$.

Two-Phase Pressure Drop

The total pressure drop in two-phase flow is expressed by the same formula (Equation 32) as in the case of single-phase flow. When determining the particular terms, various methods taking into consideration the two-phase flow specificity may be applied, for example, the homogeneous method, the Martinelli–Nelson method, the Thom method.

In the homogeneous method, the following relations are used:

$$\Delta p_f = \zeta(L/D) \cdot (G^2 v_m/2)$$

$$\Delta p_g = \rho_m \cdot g \cdot L \cdot \sin \omega$$

$$\Delta p_a = G^2 \cdot (v_{out} - v_{in})$$

where $v_m = 1/\rho_m = v_1 + x \cdot \Delta v_{vl}$
        $G = W/A$
        ζ = the friction factor from Moody diagram (see Figure 10) for liquid single-phase
              phase flow of mass flow rate equal to the total mass flow rate
        ω = the angle measured from horizontal

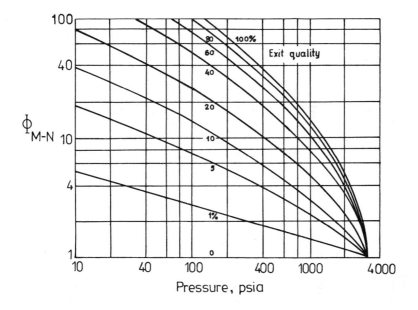

Figure 16. Martinelli-Nelson friction-multiplier as a function of pressure and exit quality. (Reprinted with permission from *Trans.ASME*, vol. 70, Martinelli R. C. and Nelson D. B., "Prediction of pressure drop during forced circulation boiling of water," Copyright 1948, ASME, pp. 695–702.)

Other methods that follow represent improvement, over the homogeneous method. In the Martinelli–Nelson method [182] the pressure drop is calculated according to:

$$(\Delta p_f)_{TP} = \Delta p_f \cdot \Phi_{M-N}$$

where Φ_{M-N} is the Martinelli–Nelson two-phase multiplier shown in Figure 16.

Although the friction multiplier Φ_{M-N} was evaluated for horizontal flow it is never the less often used for vertical reactor channel calculations.

Similar correlations are found by Thom [196]. They are based on experimental data obtained for vertical water-steam mixture flow through a pipe with uniform heat flux on its wall. The range of parameters examined by Thom is the nearest those occuring in reactor channels (see Table 5). The Thom multiplier Φ_T^f given in Figure 17 is also a function of quality and pressure. The gravity contribution is evaluated assuming flow of saturated water at water-steam mixture mass velocity and using the multiplier Φ_T^g given in Figure 18, so

$$\Delta p_g = \rho_1 \cdot g \cdot L \cdot \sin \omega \cdot \Phi_T^g$$

It is also known as the correlation developed by Baroczy in which the two-phase multiplier is a function of quality and so-called property index [197].

The method of the friction pressure drop evaluation was also elaborated by Armand [198].

More general treatment of the problem may be found in numerous references (e.g. [28, 29, 55, 92, 164, 166, and 190]).

Table 5

Correlations for Heat Transfer in Two-Phase Forced Convection and Nucleate Boiling Regions

Author(s)	Correlations	Range of Application
Jens, Lottes [201]	$T_w - T_{sat} = 25.012(q_w/10^6)^{0.25} \exp(-0.016p)$	Subcooled boiling $p = 0.7–17.2$ [MPa] $G = 11–10{,}500$ [kg/m^2/s^1] $q_w < 12.5 \cdot 10^6$ [W/m^2]
Thom [189]	$T_w - T_{sat} = 22.52(q_w/10^6)^{0.25} \exp(-0.0115p)$	Subcooled boiling $p = 5.2–13.8$ [MPa] $G = 1{,}000–38{,}000$ [kg/m^2/s^1] $q_w < 1.577 \cdot 10^6$ [W/m^2] $x < 0.8$
Rasohin [138]	$\alpha_{NB} = 5.513p^{0.25}q_w^{2/3}$ $\alpha_{NB} = 0.048p^{4.33}q_w^{2/3}$	$p = 0.1–8$ [MPa] $p = 8–20$ [MPa]
Borishanski [138]	$\alpha_{NB} = 9q_w^{0.7}[3.3 - 0.0113(T_{sat} - 100)]$	$p = 3–20$ [MPa] $G = 100–4{,}000$ [kg/m^2/s^1] $q_w < 2.3 \cdot 10^6$ [W/m^2]
Labuncov [138]	$\alpha_{NB} = 3.4(10p)^{0.18}q_w^{2/3}/(1 - 0.045p)$ $\alpha_{TP}/\alpha_1 = Bq_w/(Gh_{vl}) + A(1/X_{tt})^n$ where $B = 7.39 \cdot 10^3 \quad A = 1.54 \cdot 10^{-4} \quad n = 0.66$	$p = 0.1–20$ [MPa] Two-phase forced convection and nucleate boiling $p = 0.3–3.5$ [MPa] $G = 240–4{,}430$ [kg m^{-2} s^{-1}]

Schrock–Grossman [202], [203]

or

$B = 6.7 \cdot 10^3$ $A = 3.5 \cdot 10^{-4}$ $n = 0.66$

from [166] p. 248

$\alpha_{TP} = \alpha_{mic} + \alpha_{mac}; \quad \alpha_{mac} = \alpha_l F$

$\alpha_{mic} = 0.00122 \left[\dfrac{\lambda_l^{0.79} \cdot c_{pl}^{0.45} \cdot \rho_l^{0.49}}{\sigma^{0.5} \cdot \mu_l^{0.29} \cdot \Delta h_{vl}^{0.24} \cdot \rho_v^{0.24}} \right] \cdot$

$(\Delta T_{sat})^{0.24} \cdot (\Delta p_{sat})^{0.75} \cdot S$

x = 0.05–0.57

$q_w = (0.19–4.57) \cdot 10^6$ [W m^{-2}]

Chen [204]

with

$\Delta p_{sat} = \dfrac{\Delta T_{sat} \Delta h_{vl}}{T_{sat} \Delta v_{vl}}; \quad \Delta T_{sat} = T_w - T_{sat}$

$F = f(1/X_{tt})$ and $S = f(Re_l F^{1.25})$

are given in Figures 20 and 21

Two-phase forced convection and nucleate boiling

p = 0.06–3.5 [MPa]

x = 0–0.71

$q_w = (0.0063–2.4) \cdot 10^6$ [W m^{-2}]

Note: α in [W/m$^2 \cdot$ °C^1]; q_w in [W/m^2]; p in [bars]; T_{sat} in [°C]; σ in [N/m^1]; $\alpha_l = 0.0023(\lambda_l/D_e) \cdot [G(1-x)D_e/\mu_l]^{0.8}(Pr_l)^{0.4}$

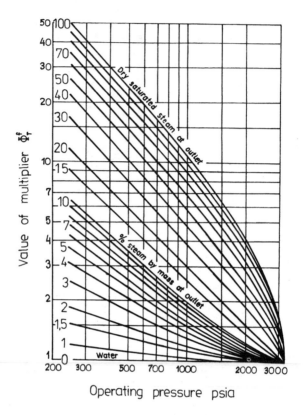

Operating pressure psia

Figure 17. Thom frictional pressure drop multiplier for boiling flow of water and steam. (Reprinted with permission from *Int. J. Heat Mass Transfer*, vol. 7, Thom J. R. S., "Prediction of pressure drop during forced convection circulation boiling of water," Copyright 1964, Pergamon Press Ltd., pp. 709–724.

Heat Transfer with Boiling

When the wall temperature remains below that necessary for nucleation, the mode of heat transfer is single-phase (liquid) convection. Nucleate boiling occurs when the wall temperature is greater than the saturation temperature. This mode of heat transfer takes place in the presence of sub-cooled liquid in the liquid core. Qualitative transient from forced convection to nucleate boiling is shown in Figure 19. In reactor practice, the onset of subcooled boiling may be estimated from the intersection of the forced convection curve ABD' with fully developed boiling curve C'EF (e.g. [199]). Other methods of onset subcooled boiling determination in flow through the tube are listed in References 163 and 166. For determination of the onset point in flow through rod bundles, Barulin et al. [170] suggest the following equation

$$\Delta h_{ONB} = (h_c - h_l)_{ONB} = -1.23 \cdot 10^6 \cdot q_w^{1.15} \cdot D^{0.3} \cdot (\rho_l/\rho_v)^2/(3{,}600 \cdot G)$$

where $h = [J/kg]$
$q_w = [W/m^2]$
$D = [m]$
$G = [kg \, m^{-2} s^{-1}]$

which is based on the experimental data.

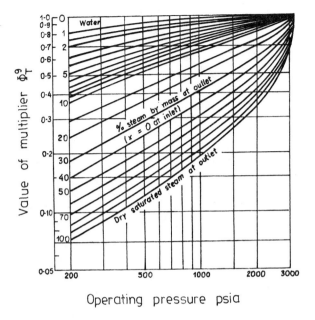

Figure 18. Thom gravitational pressure drop multiplier for boiling flow of water and steam. (Reprinted with permission from *Int. J. Heat Mass Transfer*, vol. 7, Thom J. R. S., "Prediction of pressure drop during forced convection circulation boiling of water," Copyright 1964, Pergamon Press Ltd., pp. 709–724.)

At the same temperatures, the value of Δh_{ONB} is less than that for a tube. The difference results from the fact that the fluid bulk temperature in flow through rod bundles is greater than that one in flow through a tube. An appropriate correlation is given in Reference 200. From the point where the coolant temperature reaches the saturation temperature (x = 0) the saturated nucleate boiling mode appears. As the quality is increased through the saturated nucleate boiling region the process of "boiling" is replaced by the process of "evaporation." This transient is preceded by the flow pattern change from bubbly or slug flow to annular flow. Thus, in this region heat is mostly carried away from the wall by forced convection in the film to the liquid-vapor interface where evaporation takes place. In reactor technology, the correlations used to determine the heat transfer rates in subcooled

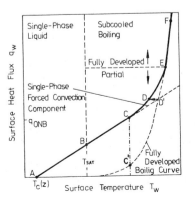

Figure 19. Subcooled boiling curve. (Reprinted with perimission from Bergles A. E., Collier J. G., Delhaye J. M., Hewitt G. F., Mayinger F., *Two-Phase Flow and Heat Transfer in the Power and Process Industries*", Copyright 1981. Hemisphere Publishing Corporation, p. 235.)

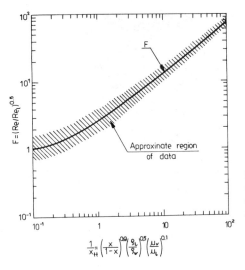

$$\frac{1}{X_H} = \left(\frac{x}{1-x}\right)^{0.9} \left(\frac{\varrho_l}{\varrho_v}\right)^{0.5} \left(\frac{\mu_v}{\mu_l}\right)^{0.1}$$

Figure 20. Reynolds number factor F for Chen correlation. (Reprinted with permission from *Ind. Eng. Chem. Process Design and Developments*, vol. 5, Chen, J. C., "Correlation for boiling heat transfer to saturated liquids in convective flow," Copyright 1966, p. 322)

Figure 21. Suppression factor S for Chen correlation. (Reprinted with permission from *Ind. Eng. Chem. Process Design and Developments*, vol. 5, Chen, J. C., "Correlation for boiling heat transfer to saturated liquids in convective flow," Copyright 1966, p. 322.)

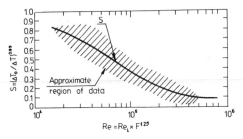

and saturated nucleate boiling and forced convection vaporization are summarized in Table 5. Chen's correlation is generally accepted as one of the best available for saturated forced convective boiling region. Colier [166] gives approximative formulas to the functions shown in Figures 20 and 21 for F and S, respectively, as:

$$F = \begin{cases} 1 & \text{for} \quad 1/X_{tt} \leq 0.1 \\ 2.35 \cdot (1/X_{tt} + 0.213)^{0.736} & \text{for} \quad 1/X_{tt} > 0.1 \end{cases}$$

$$S = 1/(1 + 2.53 \cdot 10^{-6} \cdot Re_l)^{1.17}$$

where $\quad Re_l = G \cdot (1 - x) \cdot D_e/\mu_l$

These correlations are very useful and recommended for rapid calculations. Recently the correlation developed by Chen is used in the transient reactor analysis code TRAC [173].

Boiling Crisis

In forced convective boiling the boiling crisis occurs when the heat flux attains such a high level that the heat surface can no longer support continuous liquid contact. The peak heat flux is called critical heat flux (CHF).

The temperature difference between surface temperature and bulk temperature corresponding to point CHF is likewise called the maximum nucleate or the critical temperature difference.

The CHF is characterized by a sudden rise of surface temperature when the heated surface is covered by a stable vapor blanket or by small surface temperature spikes when dry spots appear and disappear.

A rapid increase of surface temperature of fuel elements during the boiling crisis is often sufficient to cause melting of the cladding, and releasing of considerable amount of fission product into the coolant flow.

Consequently, in water-cooled reactors CHF may be the most restrictive limit on the reactor power level.

CHF can occur either in a subcooled (low quality) bubbly flow or in saturated annular flow. The former is called departure from nucleate boiling (DNB) and the latter is called dryout. In general, the subject of boiling crisis and critical heat flux has been reviewed by Hewitt [205] and Tong [206].

In reactor practice, a minimum of the DNB ratio, which is defined by

$$DNBR = \frac{DNB \text{ heat flux predicted by applicable correlation}}{\text{local reactor operating heat flux}}$$

is usually applied as a design criterion 49, 55, 190. Experiments have shown that CHF is a function of the local coolant enthalpy, inlet subcooling, pressure, mass velocity, geometry, i.e.

$$q_{CHF} = q_{CHF}(h, h_{in}, p, G, D, L, \ldots)$$

Since CHF is affected by a large number of variables, it is difficult to obtain such CHF data which cover the range of all variables appearing in reactor design. The most interesting is CHF in rod bundle geometries, because fuel assemblies are widely used at present nuclear reactors. In particular, the annulus can be regarded as a single rod bundle (see Fig. 7).

It was confirmed that the critical heat flux value in rod bundles decreases as the vapor quality increases. This relation is approximately linear. The pressure in the case of G = constant, results generally in the decrease of the CHF value. Boiling crisis in cluster where rods are distributed compactly occurs usually in outside subchannels. The grids cause the flow redistribution and an increase of the critical heat flux. More details concerning the influence of different factors on the critical heat flux can be found for example, in References 168, 206 and 207.

In reactor technology, there are two methods which can be used for the calculation of the critical heat flux. In the first, different correlations based on experimental data of a given fuel cluster are used (e.g. Bezorukov correlation [208]):

$$q_{CHF} = 190 \cdot (1 - x)^{-0.5 + 0.103 \cdot p} \cdot G^{-0.127 + 0.311(1 - x)} \cdot (1 - 0.00182 \cdot p)$$

where $p = 75.5{-}167$ [bar]
$x = 0.07{-}0.4$
$G = 700{-}3800$ [$kgm^{-2}s^{-1}$]

used in the thermo-hydraulic calculation of VVER–1000

The second method is based on subchannels analysis. That is, the rod bundle is divided into subchannels. The thermo-hydraulic conditions are estimated for these subchannels, taking into consideration cross-flows generated by the pressure differences between subchannels and cross-mixing between adjacent channels. Therefore, the local value of critical heat flux may be calculated using these local channel parameters in appropriate correlations. Application of the latter method is discussed by Weisman and Bowring [71] and Gaspari [209]. Numerous correlations are currently available for the steady-state case. Reference to some of them are given in Table 6.

Many of the various correlations are adduced in Reference [206]. It is worth noting that some of these correlations describe DNB, some are valid for dryout and others deal with both kinds of boiling crisis. Recently, the necessity of verification of these correlations under depressurization transients (major LOCA and small breaks) has arisen. Comparison of experimental data obtained during LOCA simulations with those obtained by use of various correlations was made by Leung [220, 221].

Table 6
Critical Heat Flux Data

| | | Range of Application | | |
Name	Geometry	p[MPa]	G[kg/m²s¹]	x
Miropolski [210], [170]	Rod bundle	2.9–16.7	400–5,000	−0.1–0.3
Smolin-Poliakov [211]	Rod bundle	2.9–9.81	380–4,000	−0.2–0.25
Bezorukov [208]	Rod bundle	7.55–16.7	700–3,800	−0.07–0.4
Osmachkin [169]	Rod bundle	5–17	500–4,000	$\hat{x} = -1$–3
Babcock–Wilcox [212]	Rod bundle	1.66–13.8	1,020–5,400	−0.03–0.2
W-3 [213], [206]	Rod bundle Pipe	7–14	1,350–6,750	−0.25–0.15
Biasi [214]	Pipe	2.7–14	100–6,000	0–1
Bowring [215]	Pipe	2–19	136–18,600	0–1
Barnett [216]	Annulus	3–10	190–8,400	0–1
CISE-4 [209]	Pipe	4.5–15	1,000–4,000	0–1
Macbeth [217], [218]	Pipe	0.1–13.8	27–15,730	0–1
Griffith-Zuber [206], [219]	Short annulus	All range	Low	0–1

Up to now, there are no correlations totally describing the problem of boiling crisis in reactor channels in steady- and unsteady-states. Therefore, in addition to reviewing existing correlations, further efforts for adopting recommended correlations must proceed.

FINAL REMARKS

This chapter is abbreviated and consequently does not include all problems connected with heat transfer in reactor channels. In reactors, feedbacks occur due to both thermal-hydraulic phenomena and nuclear processes. Unstable conditions arise from:

1. Variations in neutron flux generation over the volumetric thermal source strength distribution.
2. Distribution of temperatures followed by condition 1, which causes changes of properties of nuclear structural materials, temperature fields in the fuel elements, and heat transfer to coolants.
3. Coolant parameters resulting from condition 2 or other extraneous phenomena which affect the neutron balance.

In view of the complexity of these phenomena, experiments together with often subtle numerical methods have become a basic cognizance tool. Experiments are necessary as far as an analysis and modeling of two-phase flow and unsteady states is concerned. In recent years, experiments were related to reactor safety research in connection with LOCA (the loss-of-coolant accident) resulting from the rupture of the main pipe in a primary coolant circuit. When LOCA occurs almost all known heat transfer modes may appear in the reactor channel. The reader is referred to Reference 222 for detailed discussions.

In the first period of LOCA (5–100 ms) a rapid depressurization in the cooling system occurs as a result of subcooled water loss. In addition large dynamic loads inside the reactor core take place. As a rule, during the first second, the reactor is shutdown. The heat power decreases to the level of 6%–7% of the initial power. The energy released depends on the rate of fission product decay. After about 5 hours the power of the shutdown reactor is about 1% of the initial power (see the third section of this chapter). In the second period of blowdown the rate of depressurization decreases. A consequence of the heat generation and flashing process are large bubbles resulting in a fast growth of the void fraction. Reversal flow in the core may occur in the case of a break of the cold leg. Critical heat flux appears in reactor cooling channels. Leung [220] confirmed that it is dryout. Conditions of heat removal from fuel elements worsens considerably. There appears a transition regime and film boiling. An overview of various correlations and comparison with experimental works may be found in Groeneveld [223], Mayinger [224], and Tong [171]. One of the most important parameters, the cladding temperature, increases during the accident and therefore each analysis must take into consideration unsteady convection problems, boiling crisis and post-dryout heat transfer as well as problems of fuel rods rewetting. Water is injected to cold legs causing a refill of the lower plenum and then the entire core. It is characterized by steam-water interaction and quenching processes leading to pressure and flow oscillation [225, 226]. The processes are severely complicated, mainly nonequilibrium. In principle, the resulting correlations are based on experiments. Research is conducted in many countries (the U. S., FRG, Japan, Soviet Union) in connection with the development of computer codes applying to numerical simulations of LOCA. The aim of this work is

- Development of needed correlations useful in blowdown analysis, transient heat transfer, behavior of fuel and fission products.
- Development of theoretical methods such as two-phase flow models [227] and nonequilibrium processes [228].
- Development of multidimensional hydraulic models and appropriate numerical methods [229, 176].
- Verification of codes by comparison with other ones and experimental tests.

One should underline that the research work is aimed to provide knowledge about secure and failure-free reactor operation.

NOTATION

A	coolant flow area, channel cross section area		momentum exchange between subchannels on coolant enthalpy and mass flow rate distributions in subchannels
A_{ch}	wetted perimeter of channels in rod cluster		
A_f	perimeter of fuel elements in rod cluster	f_T	dimensionless coefficient used in the estimation of influence of turbulent momentum exchange between subchannels on coolant enthalpy and mass flow rate distributions in subchannels
A_m	cross section area of the sub-channel "m"		
c_p	specific heat		
C_{mn}	empirical function of pressure losses		
d	fuel element diameter	F	Chen factor
D	diffusion coefficient, diameter	g	Westcott coefficient; gravitational acceleration
D_e	equivalent (hydraulic) diameter of non-circular channel, ($= 4*$ flow area/wetted perimeter)	G	number of energy groups; mass velocity
D/Dt	total derivative	h	specific enthalpy
Div	dyadic (tensor) divergence	h_m, h_n	coolant enthalpies in the subchannels "m" and "n" (averaged over the subchannel cross section)
e	specific total internal energy		
E	energy	H	height of a reactor core
f	unit mass force vector independent of flow motion	k	neutron effective multiplication factor; kerma factor
f_D	dimensionless coefficient used in the estimation of influence of molecular	L	channel length

m_m coolant flow through the subchannel "m"

n   angular neutron density; neutron density

n or **N**   outward-bound unit vector normal to a surface

N   number density of isotope, total number of subchannels adjacent to the subchannel "m"

N_t total number of subchannels in a rod cluster

Nu   Nusselt number

p   pressure

P   reactor power

Pe   Peclet number

Pr   Prandtl number

Pr_t turbulent Prandtl number

q   heat flux at surface of channel

$(q_l)_m$ heat transferred to coolant per unit length of the subchannel "m"

q_v volumetric heat internal generation, volumetric thermal source strength

$\left.\begin{array}{l} q_{w,crit} \\ q_{crit} \\ q_{CHF} \end{array}\right\}$ critical heat flux

r   radial coordinate

r   position vector with respect to the fixed coordinate system

R   pipe radius

Re   Reynolds number

s   center-to-center distance (pitch)

S   neutron source, slip ratio, Chen suppression factor

S_{ij} gap between adjacent fuel elements; gap through which cross-flow may occur

St   Stanton number

t   time

T   temperature

T_b fluid-bulk temperature

$\bar{T}_c$ average coolant temperature in a channel

$T_{c,\,in}$ coolant temperature at the channel inlet

$T_{c,\,out}$ coolant temperature at the channel outlet

T_d deformation velocity dyadic (tensor)

T_{ref} some fluid reference temperature

T_s symmetric stress dyadic (tensor)

u   internal energy per unit mass

v   neutron velocity, specific volume

V   volume

$\underline{V}$ coolant velocity vector

w   coolant velocity component in the axial direction

$\bar{w}$ average coolant velocity in the channel cross section

W   mass flow rate, coolant flow through channel

W_{mn} coolant cross flow between the subchannel "m" and adjacent subchannel "n"

W'_{mn} turbulent cross flow between the subchannel "m" and adjacent subchannel "n"

x   coordinate in channel cross section; mass quality

$\hat{x}$ generalized quality

X   fraction of prompt neutrons

X_{tt} Lockhart–Martinelli factor

y   coordinate in channel cross-section

z   axial coordinate

Greek Symbols

α heat transfer coefficient

β empirical turbulent mixing parameter

Γ boundary-surface enclosing Ω

δ extrapolation length; relative roughness of the pipe inner surface

ε conduction parameter

ε_h turbulent, or eddy, diffusivity

ε_m turbulent, or eddy, diffusivity of momentum (turbulent kinematic viscosity)

$\underline{\varepsilon}$ unit dyadic (tensor)

ζ Darcy–Weisbach friction factor

Θ relationship between inner and outer diameters of annular channel

κ thermal diffusivity

λ thermal conductivity

μ dynamic viscosity

ν kinematic viscosity; average number of neutrons emitted per fission

$\left.\begin{array}{l} \Pi_q \\ \Pi_{heated} \end{array}\right\}$ heated perimeter of channel

Π_w wetted perimeter of channel

Π_f perimeter of fuel element

ρ reactivity, mass density

$\bar{\rho}c$ average coolant density in the channel

σ microscopic cross-section, surface tension

Σ	macroscopic cross-section	Φ_T^g	Thom gravitational multiplier
Φ	angular neutron flux; neutron flux; Rayleigh dissipation function	φ	void fraction
		Ω	direction unit vector
Φ_{M-N}	Martinelli–Nelson multiplier	$\bar{\Omega}$	control volume
Φ_T^f	Thom frictional multiplier		

Delta Quantities

Δh_{ONB}	subcooling enthalpy at the onset point	Δp_{total}	total pressure drop
		Δp_{TP}	two-phase pressure drop
Δh_{vl}	latent heat of vaporization	ΔT	maximal circumferential tempera-
Δp_a	acceleration (or momentum) pres-		ture variation, dimensionless
	sure drop	ΔT_l^*	subcooling at the point of net vapor
Δp_f	friction pressure drop		generation
Δp_g	gravity pressure drop	Δv_{vl}	specific volume change for vapor-
Δp_{local}	local losses		ization

Superscripts

ad	adiabatic	sl	slowing down
f	fission		

Subscripts

b	at the fluid bulk temperature	p	pipe
c	coolant	q	at constant heat flux on channel wall
cl	cladding		
e	extrapolated; equivalent	s	scattering
f	fission; fuel	sat	saturation
g	number of energy group	sub	subcooling
i	reaction	th	thermal
in	inlet channel cross section	T	at constant wall temperature
j	number of isotope	TP	two-phase
l	liquid	tt	turbulent-turbulent; turbulent flow of both phases
lv	liquid-vapor mixture		
m	index of subchannel in rod cluster	v	vapor
max	maximal	w	wall; channel wall; at constant wall temperature
n	index of subchannel adjacent to the subchannel "m"	w, inner⎱ inner⎰	on the inner wall of annular channel
noniso	nonisothermal flow		
0	before reactor shutdown	w, outer⎱ outer⎰	on the outer wall of annular channel
out	outlet channel cross section		
ONB	onset of boiling		

REFERENCES

1. Glasstone S., and Sesonske A., *Nuclear Reactor Engineering*, 3rd ed., Van Nostrand Reinhold Company, Princeton, 1981.
2. Connolly, T. J., *Foundations of Nuclear Engineering*, John Wiley § Sons, New York, 1978.
3. Smidt, D., *Reaktortechnik*, G. Braun, Karlsruhe, 1971.
4. "Directory of Nuclear Reactors," International Atomic Energy Agency, Vienna, 1959.

5. Duderstadt, J. J., and Martin, W. R., *Transport Theory*, John Wiley § Sons, New York, Chichester, Brisbane, London, 1979.
6. Bell, G. I., and Glasstone, S., *Nuclear Reactor Theory*, Van Nostrand Reinhold Company, Princeton, 1971.
7. Greenspan, M., Kelber, C. N., and Okrent, D., *Computing Methods in Reactor Physics*, Gordon and Breach, Science Publishers, Inc., New York, 1968.
8. Henry, A. F., *Nuclear Reactor Analysis*, M. I. T. Press, Cambridge, Mass., 1975.
9. Massimo, L., *Physics of High-Temperature Reactors*, Pergamon Press, Oxford, New York, Toronto, Sydney, Paris, Braunschweig, 1976.
10. Duderstadt, J. J., and Hamilton, L. J., *Nuclear Reactor Analysis*, John Wiley § Sons, Inc., New York, London, 1976.
11. Bird, R. B., Steward, W. E., and Lightfoot, E. N., *Transport Phenomena*, John Wiley § Sons, Inc., New York, 1960.
12. Loitsiansky, L. G., *Liquid and Gas Mechanics* (in Russian), 4th ed. Nauka, Moskva, 1973.
13. Landau, L. D., and Lifshits, E. M., *Fluid Mechanics* (in Russian), Gostekhizdat, Moskva, 1953.
14. Prosnak, W. J., *Fluid Mechanics* (in Polish), Vol. 1., PWN, Warsaw, 1970.
15. Phennigwerth, P. L., and Minkler, B., "Heat Transfer and Fluid Flow with Applications to Pressurized Water Reactors," WAPD–TM–1,000, Bettis Atomic Power Laboratory, Pittsburgh, Penn., January, 1971.
16. Staniszewski, B., "Heat Transfer–Theoretical Foundations," in Polish, PWN, Warsaw, 1963.
17. Madejski, J., *Theory of Heat Transfer*, (in Polish), PWN, Warsaw, Poznań, 1963.
18. Meyer, J. E., "Conservation Laws in One-Dimensional Hydrodynamics," Bettis Technical Review, Reactor Technology, WAPD–BT–20, September 1960, pp. 61–72.
19. Carslaw, H. S., and Jaeger, J. C., "Conduction of Heat in Solids," 2nd ed., Oxford University Press, Oxford, 1959.
20. Eckert, E. R. G., and Drake, R. M., "*Heat and Mass Transfer*" 2nd ed., McGraw Hill, New York, Toronto, London, 1959.
21. Jacob, M., *Heat Transfer*, Vol. I, John Wiley § Sons, New York, 1949.
22. Schneider, P. J., "Conduction Heat Transfer," Addison–Wesley Publishing Co., Reading, Mass., 1955.
23. Luikov, A. V., "*Analytical Heat Diffusion Theory*" Academic Press, New York, 1968.
24. Özisik, M. N., *Heat Conduction*, Wiley Interscience Publication, John Wiley § Sons, New York, Chichester, Brisbane, Toronto, 1980.
25. Ushakov, P. A., "Approximate Thermal Modeling of Cylindrical Fuel Elements," (in Russian), in *Liquid metals*, Atomizdat, Moskva, 1967.
26. Emelianov, I. Ia., et al., *Design of Nuclear Reactors* (in Russian), Energoizdat, Moskva, 1982.
27. Glasstone, S., *Principles of Nuclear Reactor Engineering*, D. Van Nostrand Company, Inc., Toronto, New York, London, 1955.
28. El Wakil, M. M., *Nuclear Power Engineering*, McGraw-Hill, New York, Toronto, London, 1962.
29. El Wakil, M. M., *Nuclear Heat Transport*, International Textbook Company, Scranton, Toronto, London, 1971.
30. Cohen, P., *Water Coolant Technology of Power Reactors*, Gordon and Breach Science Publishers, Inc., New York, 1970.
31. Gebhardt, E., Thümmler, F., and Seghezzi, H. D., "Reaktorwerkstoffe. Teil 1. Metallische Werkstoffe 1964. Teil 2. Nichtmetallische Werkstoffe 1967," Teubner, Stuttgart.
32. Golden, G. H., and Tokar, J. V., "Thermophysical Properties of Sodium," USAEC Report ANL–7323, Lemont, Illinois, August 1967.
33. Hilsenrath, J., et al., *Tables of Thermodynamic and Transport Properties of Air, Argon, Carbon Dioxide, Carbon Monoxide, Hydrogen, Nitrogen, Oxygen, and Steam*, Pergamon Press, London, New York, Paris, Los Angeles, 1960.
34. Meyer, B., et al., *Thermodynamic and Transport Properties of Steam*, The American Society of Mechanical Engineers, New York, 1967.
35. Tipton, C. R. (Ed.), *Reactor Handbook*, vol. 1: Materials, Interscience Publishers Inc., New York, 1960.
36. Ulybin, S. A., *Coolants of Nuclear Power Reactors* (in Russian), Energia, Moskva, 1966.

37. Vukalovich, M. P. et al., *Tables of Thermophysical Properties of Water and Water Steam* (in Russian), Izdatelstvo Standardov, Moskva, 1969.
38. Chirkin, V. S., *Thermophysical Properties of Materials in Nuclear Technology* (in Russian), Atomizdat, Moskva, 1968.
39. Vargaftik, N. B., *Handbook on Thermophysical Properties of Gases and Liquids* (in Russian), Nauka, Moskva, 1972.
40. Borishanski, B. M. et al., *Liquid Metal Coolants*, 2nd ed., (in Russian), Atomizdat, Moskva, 1967.
41. Seddon, B. T., "Uranium Ceramics Data Manual: Properties of Interest in Reactor Design" British DEG-Report 120 and Addendum, March 7, 1960.
42. McIntosh, A., Heal, T. J. (eds.), *Materials for Nuclear Engineers*, Temple Press Ltd., London, 1960.
43. Powers, A. E., "Fundamentals of Thermal Conductivity at High Temperatures," Rep. KAPL–2143, Knolls At. P. Lab., 1961.
44. Powers, A. E., "Conductivity in Aggregates," Report KAPL–2145, Knolls Atomic Power Laboratory, 1961.
45. Goldsmith, A., et al., *Handbook of Thermophysical Properties of Solid Materials*, Armour Research Foundation, The MacMillan Co., New York, 1961.
46. Smith, C. O., *Nuclear Reactor Materials*, Addison–Wesley Publishing Company, Reading, Palo Alto, London, 1967.
47. *Fundamental Properties of Materials in Nuclear Fuel Assemblies*, North-Holland Publishing Co., Amsterdam, 1969.
48. Christensen, J. A., et al., "Uranium Dioxide Thermal Conductivity," *Trans. Am. Nucl. Soc.*, 7:2 (1964), p. 391.
49. Thompson, T. J., Beckerley, J. G. (eds.), *The Technology of Nuclear Reactor Safety, Vol. 2: Reactor Materials and Engineering*, Chapter 16—"Heat Transfer" by H. Fenech, W. M. Rohsenow, MIT Press, Cambridge, Massachusetts, 1973.
50. Wagner, R. J., "HEAT 1–A One-Dimensional Time Dependent or Steady-State Heat Conduction Code for the IBM–650, IDO–16867, April 1963.
51. Hocevar, C. J., Wineinger, T. W., "THETA 1–B, A computer code for nuclear reactor core thermal analysis," IN–1445, February 1971.
52. Hann, C. R., et al., "GAPCON THERMAL–1: A Computer Program for Calculating the Gap Conductance in Oxide Fuel Pins," BNWL–1778 (UC–78), September 1973.
53. Loyalka, S. K., "A Model for Gap Conductance in Nuclear Fuel Rods," *Nuclear Technology*, vol. 57, no. 2, 1982.
54. Chandola, V. K., and Loyalka, S. K., "Gap Conductance and Temperature Transients in Modified Pulse Design Experiments," *Nuclear Technology*, vol. 56, no. 1, 1982.
55. Weisman, J. (ed.), *Elements of Nuclear Reactor Design*, Elsevier Scientific Publishing Company, Amsterdam, Oxford, New York, 1977.
56. Rowe, D. S., "Cross-Flow Mixing Between Parallel Flow Channels During Boiling–Part 1–COBRA–Computer program for coolant boiling in rod arrays," BNWL–371, Pt. 1, UC–80, 1967.
57. Fajeau, M., "Programme FLICA–étude thermodynamique d'un reacteur ou d'une boucle d'essai," Rapport CEA–R–3716, CEN–Saclay, 1969.
58. Rowe, D. S., "COBRA–II: A Digital Computer Program for Thermal Hydraulic Subchannel Analysis of Rod Bundle Nuclear Fuel Elements," BNWL–1229, Pacific Northwest Laboratory, Richland, Washington, February 1970.
59. Vigassy, J., "COBRA–Computer Program for Coolant Boiling in Rod Arrays," KFKI–70–20 RPT, Hungarian Academy of Sciences, Central Research Institute for Physics, Budapest, June 1970.
60. Rowe, D. S., "Interim Report COBRA–III: A Digital Computer Program for Steady and Transient Thermal-Hydraulic Analysis of Rod Bundle Nuclear Fuel Elements," BNWL–B–82, Pacific Northwest Laboratory, Richland, Washington, 1971.
61. Rowe, D. S., "COBRA–IIIC: A Digital Computer Program for Steady State and Transient Thermal-Hydraulic Analysis of Rod Bundle Nuclear Fuel Elements," BNWL–1695, 1973.

62. Gosman, A., et al., "The SABRE–Code for Prediction of Coolant Flows and Temperatures in Pin Bundles Containing Blockages," AEEW–R–905, AEE Winfrith, October 1973.

63. Marr, W. W., "COBRA–3M: A Digital Computer Program for Analyzing Thermal-Hydraulic Behavior in Pin Bundles," ANL–8131, 1975.

64. Wnek, W. J., et al., "Transient Three-Dimensional Thermal-Hydraulic Analysis of Nuclear Reactor Fuel Rod Arrays: General Equations and Numerical Scheme (SCO-RE–EVET)," ANCR–1207, Aerojet Nuclear Company, Idaho Nat. Lab., Nov. 1975.

65. Stewart, C. W., et al., "COBRA–IV: The Model and the Method," BNWL–2214, Batelle Pacific Northwest Laboratories, Richland, Washington, July 1977.

66. Rogers, J. T., and Todreas, N. E., "Coolant Mixing in Reactore Fuel Rod Bundles–Single-Phase Coolants," *Heat Transfer in Rod Bundles, ASME*, 1968, pp. 1–56.

67. Ingesson, L. and Hedberg, S., "Heat Transfer Between Subchannels in a Rod Bundle," Paper No. FC 7.11, 4-th Int. Heat Transfer Conf., Versailles, France, 1970.

68. Stein, R. P., "Engineering Relationships for Turbulent Forced-Convection Heat Transfer in Duct with Flux Transient," ANL–7754, Argonne National Laboratory, Argonne, Illinois, June 1971.

69. Rogers, J. T., and Rosehart, R. G., "Mixing by Turbulent Inter-Change in Fuel Bundles. Correlations and Interferences," ASME Paper No. 72–HT–53, 1972.

70. Brown, W. D., et al., "Prediction of Cross Flow due to Coolant Channel Blockages," *Nucl. Sci. Engng.*, vol. 57, no. 2, 1975, pp. 164–168.

71. Weisman, J., and Bowring, R. W., "Methods for Detailed Thermal and Hydraulic Analysis of Water Cooled Reactors," *Nucl. Sci. Engng.*, vol. 57, no. 4, 1975, pp. 255–276.

72. Rowe, D. S., and Stewart, C. W., "Transient Hydraulic Analysis for Reactor Codes," ERDA Report CONF–750413, 1975, pp. II/17–II/26.

73. Wulf, W., "Development of a Computer Code for Thermal Hydraulic Analysis of Reactors," USAEC Report BNL–19978, Brookhaven National Laboratory, January 1975.

74. Zhukauskas, A. A., "Convective Heat Transfer in Heat Exchangers," (in Russian), Nauka, Moskva, 1982.

75. Lyon, R. N., "Forced Convection Heat Transfer Theory and Experiments with Liquid Metals," AECU–419, June 1949 and ORNL–361, August 1949.

76. Dittus, F. W., and Boelter, L. M. K., "Heat Transfer in Automobile Radiators of the Tabular Type," Univ. of California Publications, 2, 1930, pp. 443–461.

77. Rohsenow, W. M., and Clark J. A., "Heat Transfer and Pressure Drop Data for High Heat Flux Densities to Water and High Sub-critical Pressures," Heat Transfer and Fluid Mech. Inst., Stanford Univ. Press, Stanford, California, 1951.

78. Sieder, E. N., and Tate, C. E., "Heat Transfer and Pressure Drop of Liquids in Tubes," *Ind. Eng. Chem.* vol. 28 (1936), pp. 1429–1435.

79. Colburn, A. P., "A Method for Correlating Forced Convection Heat Transfer Data and a Comparison with Fluid Friction," *Trans. Am. Inst. Chem. Engrs.*, vol. 29 (1933), pp. 174–210.

80. Colburn, A. P., "A Method of Correlating Forced Convection Heat Transfer Data and a Comparison with Fluid Friction," *Trans. A. I. Ch. E.*, Vol. 29, 1933, p. 174.

81. Mikheiev, M. A., "Foundations of Heat Transfer for Turbulent Liquid Flow in Pipes" (in Russian), *Izv. AN SSSR*, OTN, no. 10 (1952), pp. 1448–1454.

82. Mikheiev, M. A., *Fundamentals of Heat Transfer*, 2nd ed. (in Russian), Gosenergoizdat, Moskva, Leningrad, 1956.

83. Petukhov, B. S., *Heat Transfer in Nuclear Power Plants* (in Russian), Atomizdat, Moskva, 1974.

84. Petukhov, B. S., and Roizen, L. I., "Heat Transfer in Annular Pipes," (in Russian), *Inzh.-Fiz. Zhurn.*, vol. 6, no. 3 (1963), pp. 3–11.

85. Petukhov, B. S., and Roizen, L. I., "Experimental Investigations of Heat Transfer in Turbulent Gas flow in Annular Pipes," (in Russian), *Teplofizika Vysokhikh Temperatur*, vol. 1, no. 3 (1963), pp. 416–424.

86. Petukhov, B. S., and Roizen L. I., "Generalized Relationships for Heat Transfer in Annular Pipes," (in Russian), *Teplofizika Vysokikh Temperatur*, vol. 12, no. 3 (1974), pp. 565–569.

87. Perkins, H. C., and Vorsce-Schmidt P., "Turbulent Heat and Momentum Transfer for

Gases in a Circular Tube at Wall to Bulk Temperature Ratios to Seven," *Int. J. Heat and Mass Transfer*, vol. 8, no. 7, 1965, pp. 1011–1031.

88. Taylor, M. F., "Correlation of Local Heat Transfer Coefficients for Single Phase Turbulent Flow of Hydrogen in Tubes with Temperatures Ratios to 23," NASA TND–4332, 1968.

89. Kurganov, V. A., and Petukhov, B. S., "Analysis and Generalization of Experimental Data on Heat Transfer in Pipes for Turbulent Flow of Gases with Variable Physical Properties," (in Russian), *Teplofizika Vysokikh Temperatur*, vol. 12, no. 2, 1974, pp. 304–315.

90. Kays, W. M., *Convective Heat and Mass Transfer*, (Russian transl.), Energia, Moskva, 1972.

91. Subbotin, V. I., et al., *Hydrodynamics and Heat Transfer in Nuclear Power Plants*, (in Russian), Atomizdat, Moskva, 1975.

92. Rohsenow, W. M., and Hartnett, J. P. (eds.), "Handbook of Heat Transfer," McGraw Hill Book Company, Inc., New York, 1973.

93. Markoczy, G., "Konvektive Wärmeübertragung in längsangeströmten Stabbündeln bei turbulenter Strömung," *Wärme und Stoffübertrag*, vol. 5, no. 4 (1972), pp. 204–212.

94. Weisman, J., "Heat Transfer to Water Flowing Parallel to Tube Bundles," *Nucl. Sci. Engng.*, vol. 6, no. 1 (July 1959), pp. 78–79.

95. Ain, E. M., and Puchkov, P. I., "Heat Transfer and Hydraulic Resistance in Gas-cooled Clusters of Smooth Rods," (in Russian), *Energomashinostroenie*, no. 11 (1964), pp. 21–22.

96. Sutherland, W. A., "Experimental Heat Transfer in Rod Bundles," *ASME*, New York, 1968, pp. 104–138.

97. Martinelli, R. C., "Heat Transfer to Molten Metals," *Trans. ASME*, vol. 69, no. 8 (1947), pp. 947–959.

98. Lyon, R. N., "Liquid Metal Heat Transfer Coefficients," *Chem. Eng. Progr.*, vol. 47, no. 2, 1951, p. 75.

99. Dwyer, O. E., "Eddy Transport in liquid-metal heat transfer," USAEC Report BNL–6149, Brookhaven National Laboratory, 1962.

100. Dwyer, O. E., "Eddy Transport in Liquid Metal Heat Transfer," *A. I. Ch. E. J.*, vol. 9 (March 1963), pp. 261–268.

101. Dwyer, O. E., "Recent Developments in Liquid Metal Heat Transfer," *Atomic Energy Review* 4, no. 1 (1966), pp. 3–92.

102. Dwyer, O. E., "Equations for Bilateral Heat Transfer to a Fluid Flowing in a Concentric Annulus," *Nucl. Sci. Engng.*, 15 (1963), pp. 52–57.

103. Dwyer O. E., and Tu, P. S., "Unilateral Heat Transfer to Liquid Metals Flowing in Annuli, *Nucl. Sci. Engng.*, vol. 15 (1963), pp. 58–68.

104. Dwyer, O. E., "On the Transfer of Heat to Fluids Flowing through Pipes, Annuli and Parallel Plates," *Nucl. Sci. Engng.*, 17 (1963), pp. 336–344.

105. Dwyer, O. E., "Bilateral Heat Transfer in Annuli for Slug and Laminar Flows," *Nucl. Sci. Engng.* vol. 19 (1964), pp. 48–57.

106. Dwyer, O. E., and Lyon, R. L., "Liquid Metal Heat Transfer," Proc. 3rd U. N. Int. Conf. PUAE, Geneva, vol. 8, 1965, pp. 182–189.

107. Yu, W. S., and Dwyer, O. E., "Heat Transfer to Liquid Metals Flowing Turbulently in Eccentric Annuli," *Nucl. Sci. Engng.* 24 (1966), pp. 105–117.

108. Yu, W. S., and Dwyer, O. E., "Heat Transfer to Liquid Metals Flowing Turbulently in Eccentric Annuli," *Nucl. Sci. Engng.* 27 (1967), pp. 1–9.

109. Maresca, M. W., and Dwyer, O. E., "Heat Transfer to Mercury Flowing in Line Through a Bundle of Circular Rods," *J. Heat Transfer*, Ser. C, vol. 86 (1964), p. 180.

110. Dwyer, O. E., "Analytical Study of Heat Transfer to Liquid Metals Flowing In-line Through Closely Packed Rod Bundles," *Nucl. Sci. Engng.* vol. 25 (1966), pp. 343–358.

111. Dwyer, O. E., and Berry, H. C., "Effects of Cladding Thickness and Thermal Conductivity on Heat Transfer to Liquid Metals Flowing In-line Through Bundles of Closely Spaced Reactor Fuel Rods," *Nucl. Sci. Engng.*, 40 (1970), pp. 317–330.

112. Subbotin, W. I., et al., "Experimental Investigations on Models of Thermal Behavior of Reactor BOR–60 Fuel Elements," (in Russian), Rep. FEI–137, Obninsk, 1969.

113. Ushakov, P. A., et al., "Generalized Method of Determination of Temperature and Heat

Removal in Triangular and Quadrangular Lattices of Cylindrical Fuel Elements," (in Russian), Rep. FEI–163, Obninsk, 1969.

114. "Recommendations on Thermal and Hydraulic Calculations of Fuel Assemblies in Fast Reactors," (in Russian), Sovet Ekonomicheskoi Vzaimopomoshchi, Postoianna Komisia po sotrudnichestvu v oblasti ispolzovania atomnoi energii v mirnykh celakh, Nauch-no-tekhnicheski sovet po bystrym reaktoram, Moskva, 1981.

115. Zhukov, A. V., et al., "Calculation Method of Determination of Interchannel Mixing Influence on Temperature Field in Coolant Flowing Through Fuel Assemblies with Wire Spacers," (in Russian), Preprint FEI–512, Obninsk, 1974.

116. Zhukov, A. V., et al., "Experimental Investigation of Temperature Fields and Heat Removal in Triangular Lattices of Fuel Rod Simulators with Liquid Metal Cooling," (in Russian), Preprint FEI–800, Obninsk, 1978.

117. Zhukov, A. V., et al., "Temperature Fields in Deformed Fast Reactor Fuel Lattices for Uniform and Nonuniform Thermal Loads," (in Russian), Preprint FEI–909, Obninsk, 1979.

118. Zhukov, A. V., et al., "Influence of Lattice Deformation on Temperature Fields and Heat Removal for Fuel Elements in Characteristic Zones of Fast Reactor Fuel Assembly Model," (in Russian), Preprint FEI–979, Obninsk, 1980.

119. Zhukov, A. V., Kirillova, G. P., "Calculation of Temperature Fields in Inlet Part of Fuel Lattices in the Case of Turbulent Flow of Liquid Metal Coolant," (in Russian), Preprint FEI–715, Obninsk, 1976.

120. Sidelnikov, V. N., and Zhukov, A. V., "Calculations of Temperature Fields in Inlet Part of Fuel Lattices and Analysis of Influence of Variable Power (Flat Coolant Flow)," (in Russian), Preprint FEI–414, Obninsk, 1973.

121. Zhukov, A. V., et al., "Experimental Investigation of Temperature Fields in Inlet Part of Fuel Lattices in the Case of Turbulent Flow of Liquid Metal Coolant (for Simultaneous Hydrodynamic and Thermal Stabilization)," (in Russian), Preprint FEI–781, Obninsk, 1977.

122. Zhukov, A. V., et al., "Temperature Fields in Inlet Part and in Stabilized Heat Transfer Zone of Fuel Lattices for Simultaneous Hydrodynamic and Thermal Stabilization (liquid metal cooling)," (in Russian), Preprint FEI–883, Obninsk, 1978.

123. Vladimirov, M. A., et al., "Method of Calculation of Temperature Decrease of "Hot" Channels due to Heat Dissipation," (in Russian), Preprint FEI–437, Obninsk, 1973.

124. Kurbatov, I. M., "Calculation of Random Temperature Fluctuations in Reactor Core," (in Russian), Preprint FEI–1090, Obninsk, 1980.

125. Johannsen, K., "Analytical Investigation of the Effect of Variable Wall Heat Flux on Turbulent Liquid-Metal Heat Transfer Coefficients in Reactor Coolant Channels," *Atomkernenergie*, vol. 1, 1968, pp. 21–24.

126. Nijsing, R., and Eifler, W., "Analysis of Liquid Metal Heat Transfer in Assemblies of Closely Spaced Fuel Rods," *Nucl. Engng. and Design*, vol. 10 (1969), pp. 21–54.

127. Marchese, A. R., "Analytical Study of Heat Transfer to Liquid Metals Flowing Parallel Through Tightly Packed Fuel Rod Bundles," Proc. of the Symp. sponsored by the Nucleonic Heat Transfer Committee (K–13) of the ASME Transfer Division, 1970, pp. 15–29.

128. Oberjohn, W. J., "Turbulent Flow Thermal-Hydraulic Charateristics of Hexagonal Pitch Fuel Assemblies," Proc. of the Symp. sponsored by the Nucleonic Heat Transfer Committee (K–13) of the ASME Heat Transfer Division, 1970, pp. 30–40.

129. Ushakov, P. A., et al., "Heat Transfer to Liquid Metals in Regular Fuel Element Lattices," *Teplofizika Vysokikh Temperatur*, (in Russian), vol. 15, no. 5 (1977), pp. 1027–1033.

130. Ushakov, P. A., et al., "Azimuthally Nonuniform Fuel Element Temperature Distributions for Regular Lattices and Turbulent Flow of Liquid Metals," (in Russian), *Teplofizika Vysokikh Temperatur*, vol. 15, no. 1 (1977), pp. 76–83.

131. Minashik V. E., et al., "Temperature Calculation in Reactor core for Arbitrary Axial Thermal Power Distribution," (in Russian), *Atomnaia Energia*, vol. 22, no. 5 (1967), pp. 362–366.

132. Proceedings of the ANS/ASME/NRC International Topical Meeting on Nuclear Reactor Thermal-Hydraulics, NUREG/CP–0014, Washington, D. C., 1980.

133. Graetz, L., "Über Wärmeleitungsfähigkeit von Flussigkeiten," *Ann. Phys. u. Chem.*, Bd. 25, 1885, pp. 773–778.

134. Petukhov, B. S., *Heat Transfer and Friction Losses for Laminar Liquid Flow in Pipes*, (in Russian), Energia, Moskva, 1967.

135. Grigull, U., and Tratz, H., "Thermischer Einlauf in ausgebildeter laminarer Röhrströmung," *Int. J. Heat and Mass Transfer*, vol. 8, no. 5 (1965), pp. 669–678.

136. Sellers, J. R., Tribus M., and Klein J. S., "Heat Transfer to Laminar Flow in a Round Tube or Flat Conduit—the Graetz Problem Extended," *Trans. ASME*, vol. 78, no. 2, (1956), pp. 441–448.

137. Clark, S. W., and Kays, W. M., "Laminar-Flow Forced Convection in Rectangular Tubesm," *Trans. ASME*, vol. 75, no. 7 (1953), pp. 859–866.

138. Polanin, L. N., Ibragimov, M. Kh., and Sabelev, G. I., "Heat Transfer in Nuclear Reactors," (in Russian), Energoizdat, Moskva, 1982.

139. Mikheev, M. A., and Mikheeva, I. M., "Foundations of Heat Transfer," (in Russian), Energia, Moskva, 1977.

140. Levêque, M. A., "Transmission de chaleur par convection," *Ann. des Mines*, vol. 13 (1928), pp. 201–239.

141. Zhukauskas, A. A., and Zhiugzhda, I. I., "Heat Transfer in Laminar Liquid Flow," (in Russian), Mintis, Vilnius, 1969, pp. 261.

142. Liutikas, N. S., and Zhukauskas, A. A., "Investigation of Influence of Variable Viscosity on Laminar Heat Transfer in Flat Channel," (in Russian), *Tr. AN Lit. SSR, Ser. B*, no. 2 (49) (1967), pp. 97–114.

143. Dwyer, O. E., and Berry, H. C., "Laminar-Flow Heat Transfer for In-Line Flow Through Unbaffled Rod Bundles," *Nucl. Sci. Engng.*, vol. 42 (1970), pp. 81–88.

144. Chia-Jung, Hsu, "Theoretical Solutions for Low Peclet Number Thermal Entry Region Heat Transfer in Laminar Flow Through Concentric Annuli," *Int. J. Heat and Mass Transfer*, vol. 13, 1970, pp. 1907–1924.

145. Dwyer, O. E., and Berry, H. C., "Effects of Cladding Thickness and Thermal Conductivity on Heat Transfer for Laminar In-line Flow Through Rod Bundles," *Nucl. Sci. Engng.*, 42 (1970), pp. 69–80.

146. Subbotin, V. I., et al., "Heat Transfer and Hydrodynamics Calculations for Slug and Laminar Coolant Flow Through Regular Fuel Element Bundles," *Atomnaia Energia*, vol. 33, no. 4 (1972), pp. 840–841, (in Russian).

147. Morozova, S. I., and Novofiliov, E. V., "Hydraulic Friction Coefficient in Transient Domain for Liquid Flow in Triangular Cell of Fuel Element Bundle," in *Heat Transfer and Hydrodynamics of One-Phase Flow in Fuel Element Bundles* (in Russian), Nauka, Leningrad, 1977, pp. 129–135.

148. Targ, S. M., *Main Problems of Laminar Flow Theory* (in Russian), Gostekhizdat, Moskva, 1948.

149. Minashin, V. E., et al., *Heat Transfer in Liquid Metal Cooled Reactors* (in Russian), Atomizdat, Moskva, 1971.

150. Blasius, H., "Das Ahnlichkeitsgesetz bei Reibungsvorgängen in Flussigkeiten," *Forschg. Arb. Ing.-Wes.*, 131 (1913), pp. 1–34.

151. Filonenko, G. K., "Pipe Hydraulic Resistance" (in Russian), *Teploenergetika*, vol. 4 (1954), pp. 40–44.

152. Prandtl, L., "Neuere Ergebnisse der Turbulenzforschung," *Zeitschrift VDI*, vol. 77 (1933), pp. 105–114.

153. Colebrook, C. F., "Turbulent Flow in Pipes with Particular Reference to the Transition Region Between the Smooth and Rough Pipe Laws," *Proc. Inst. Civ. Eng.*, Vol. 11 (1939), p. 133.

154. Moody, L. F., "Friction Factors for Pipe Flows," *Trans. ASME*, vol. 66 (1944), pp. 671–684.

155. Idelchik, I. E., *Handbook on Hydraulic Resistances* (in Russian), Mashinostrenie, 1975.

156. Taylor, M. F., "Correlation of Friction Coefficients for Laminar and Turbulent Flow with Ratios of Surface to Bulk Temperature From 0.35 to 7.35," NASA-TR-R-267, September 1967.

157. Tong, L. S., "Pressure Drop Performance of a Rod Bundle," *Heat Transfer in Rod Bundles*, ASME, 1968, pp. 57–69.

158. Waggener, J. P., "Friction Factors for Pressure-Drop Calculations," *Nucleonics*, vol. 19, no. 11 (November 1961), pp. 145–147.

159. Kays, W. M., and London A. L., "Compact Heat Exchangers," 2nd ed., McGraw-Hill, New York, 1964.

160. Nowendstern, E. H., "Turbulent Flow Pressure Drop Model for Fuel Rod Assemblies Utilizing a Helical Wire-wrap Spacer System," *Nuclear Eng. and Design*, vol. 22, 1972, pp. 19–27.

161. Madejski, J., "Boiling Heat Transfer and Two-Phase Flow," (in Polish), Part 2, Nuclear Energy Information Center, Warsaw, 1973.

162. Tippets, F. E., "Critical Heat Fluxes and Flow Patterns in High Pressure Boiling Water Flows," ASME Paper 62-WA-162, 1962.

163. Bennet, A. W., et al., "Flow Visualisation Studies of Boiling at High Pressure," AERE R-4874, Harwell, England, 1965.

164. Wallis, G. B., "One-Dimensional Two-Phase Flow," McGraw-Hill Book Company, New York, 1969.

165. Butterworth, D., Hewitt, G. F. (eds.), *Two-Phase Flow and Heat Transfer*, Oxford University Press, Oxford, 1977.

166. Bergles A. E., et al., *Two-Phase Flow and Heat Transfer in the Power and Process Industries*, Hemisphere Publishing Corporation, Washington, D.C., 1981.

167. Aden, V. G., et al., "The Study of Heat Exchange Enhancement in Models of Fuel Elements Bundles at the Coolant Boiling," paper presented at the 6th International Heat Transfer Conference, Toronto (August 7–11, 1978), vol. 5, pp. 41–45.

168. Smolin, V. N., Poliakov, V. K., "Coolant Boiling Crisis in Rod Assemblies," paper presented at the 6th International Heat Transfer Conference, Toronto (August 7–11, 1978), vol. 5, pp. 47–52.

169. Osmachkin V. S., "Problems of transient critical heat flux in rod bundles," paper presented at the 6th International Heat Transfer Conference, Toronto (August 7–11, 1978), vol. 5, pp. 59–64.

170. Barulin Iu. D., et al., "Experimental Investigations of Heat Transfer and Hydrodynamics on Models of Fuel Assemblies of VVER Reactor," (in Russian), *Trudy VTI*, No. 11 (1977), pp. 214–220.

171. Tong, L. S., "Heat Transfer in Reactor Safety," paper presented at the 6th International Heat Transfer Conference, Toronto (August 7–11, 1978), vol. 6, pp. 285–309.

172. Hsu, Y. Y., "Thermal Hydraulics Related to Reactor Safety," Nuclear Reactor Thermal-Hydraulic Topical Meeting, Saratoga, New York, October 6–8, 1980.

173. Vigil, J. C., and Pryor R. J., "Development and Assessment of the Transient Reactor Analysis Code (TRAC)," *Nuclear Safety*, vol. 21, no. 2 (1980), pp. 171–183.

174. Burwell, H., "DRUFAN—An Advanced Best-Estimate Code for LWR Blowdown Analysis," Newsletter of the NEA, Bank Data Bulletin, no. 28, (Sept. 1982), pp. 103–142.

175. Pryor, R. J., "Computational Methods in Thermal Reactor Safety," NUREG/CR-0851, LA-7856-MS, Los Alamos Scientific Laboratory, Los Alamos, 1979.

176. Lyczkowski, R. W., "Numerical Techniques for the Computation of Transient Unequal Phase Velocity, Unequal Phase Temperature, Two-Phase Flow and Heat Transfer," paper presented at the Two-Phase Flow and Heat Transfer Symposium-Work-shop, Florida, 1976.

177. Ranson, V. H., et al., "RELAP 5/MOD1 Code manual. Volume 1: System Models and Numerical Methods (draft)," NUREG/CR-1826, Idaho National Engineering Laboratory, Idaho Falls, Nov. 1980.

178. Agee, L. J., "RETRAN overview," *Nuclear Technology*, vol. 61, no. 2 (May 1983), pp. 143–152.

179. Spigt, C. L., "The Hydraulic Characteristics of a Naturally Circulating Boiling Water System," *Atoomenergie Haar Toepass.*, vol. 9, no. 1 (Jan. 1967), pp. 1–18.

180. Foglia, J. J., et al., "Boiling-Water Void Distribution and Slip Ratio in Heated Channels," USAEC Report BMI-1517, 1961.

181. Christensen, H., "Power-to-Void Transfer Functions," USAEC Report ANL-6385, 1961.

182. Martinelli, R. C., and Nelson, D. B., "Prediction of Pressure Drop During Forced Circulation Boiling of Water," *Trans. ASME*, vol. 70, (August 1948), pp. 695–702.

183. Levy, S., "Steam Slip—Theoretical Prediction from Momentum Model," *Trans. ASME, J. Heat Transfer*, vol. 82 (1960), pp. 113–124.

184. Zivi, S. M., "Estimation of Steady-State Steam-Void-Fraction by Means of the Principle of Minimum Entropy Production," *Trans. ASME, J. Heat Transfer*, vol. 86 (May 1964), p. 247.

185. Polomik, E. E., "Phase Velocities in Boiling Flow Systems by Total Energy and by Diffusion," ASME Paper No. 65-HT-34, 1965.

186. Kholodovski, G. E., "New Method of Experimental Data Generalization for Steam-Water Flow in Vertical Tubes," (in Russian), *Teploenergetika*, vol. 4, no. 7 (1957), p. 68.

187. Bankoff, S. G., "A Variable Density Single-Fluid Model for Two-Phase Flow with Particular Reference to Steam-Water Flow," *Trans. ASME, J. Heat Transfer*, vol. 82 (1960), pp. 265–272.

188. Hughmark, G. A., "Holdup in Gas-Liquid Flow," *Chem. Eng. Progr.*, vol. 58 (1962), p.62.

189. Thom, J. R. S., et al., "Boiling in Subcooled Water During Flow Up in Heated Tubes or Annuli," *Proc. Inst. Mech. Eng.*, 3C (1968), pp. 226–246.

190. Tong, L. S., and Weisman, J., "Thermal Analysis of Pressurized Water Reactors," *American Nuclear Society*, Hinsdale, Ill., 1970.

191. Osmachkin, V.S., and Borisov V. D., "Pressure Drop and Heat Transfer for Flow of Boiling Water in Vertical Rod Bundles," 4th Int. Heat Transfer Conf., Paper B 4.9, Paris–Versailles, 1970.

192. Bergles A. E., and Rohsenow W. M., "The Determination of Forced Convection Surface Boiling Heat Transfer," *Trans. ASME, J. Heat Transfer*, vol. 86 (1964), p. 365.

193. Saha P., and Zuber N., "Point of Net Vapor Generation and Vapor Void Fraction in Subcooled Boiling," 5th Int. Heat Transfer Conf., Paper B 4.7, Tokyo, 1974.

194. Bowring, R. W., "Physical Model Based on Bubble Detachment and Calculation of Steam Voidage in the Subcooled Region of a Heated Channel," OECD Halden Reactor Project Report HPR–10, Halden, Norway, 1962.

195. Levy, S., "Forced Convection Subcooled Boiling Prediction of Vapor Volumetric Fraction," *Int. J. Heat Mass Transfer*, vol. 10, 1967, pp. 951–965.

196. Thom, J. R. S., "Prediction of Pressure Drop During Forced Convection Circulation Boiling of Water," *Int. J. Heat Mass Transfer*, vol. 7 (1964), pp. 709–724.

197. Baroczy, C. J., "A Systematic Correlation for Two-Phase Pressure Drop," NAA–SR–Memo–11858, North American Aviation, March 1966.

198. Armand, A. A., "The Resistance During the Movement of a Two-Phase System in Horizontal Pipes," trans. by V. Beak, AERE Trans. 828. Izvestia Vsesoiuznogo Teplotekhnicheskogo Instituta (1), 1946, pp. 16–23.

199. Katama K. R., et al., "RELAP4/Mod5–A Computer Program for Transient-Hydraulic Analysis of Nuclear Reactors and Related Systems," Aerojet Nuclear Company, Report ANCR–NUREG–1335, September 1976.

200. Tarasova, N. V., and Orlov, V. M., Investigation of Hydraulic Resistance During Nucleate Boiling of Water in Pipe," (in Russian), *Teploenergetika*, vol. 9, no. 6 (1962), pp. 48–51.

201. Jens W. H., and Lottes P. A., "Analysis of Heat Transfer Burnout, Pressure Drop and Density Data for High Pressure Water," Argonne National Laboratory, Ill., Report ANL–4627, 1951.

202. Schrock, V. E., and Grossman, L. M., "Forced Convection Boiling Studies-Forced Convection Vaporization Project," USAEC Rep. TID–14632, 1959.

203. Schrock, V. E., and Grossman, L. M., "Forced Convection Boiling in Tubes," *Nucl. Sci. Engng.*, vol. 12 (1962), pp. 474–480.

204. Chen, J. C., "Correlation for Boiling Heat Transfer to Saturated Liquids in Convective Flow," *Ind. Eng. Chem. Process Design and Development*, vol. 5 (1966), p. 322.

205. Hewitt, G. F., "Critical Heat Flux in Flow Boiling," 6th International Heat Transfer Conference, vol. 6, Toronto, Canada, 1978, pp. 143–171.

206. Tong, L. S., "Boiling Crisis and Critical Heat Flux," U.S. Atomic Energy Commission, Office of Information Services, Oak Ridge, Tennessee, 1972.

207. Remizov, O. V., et al., "Some Features of Heat Transfer Burnout in Tubes with Non-uniform Axial Heat Flux Distribution," 6th International Heat Transfer Conference, vol. 5, Toronto, Canada, 1978, pp. 53–58.

208. Bezorukov J. A., "Experimental Investigation and Statistical Analysis of Data Related to Critical Heat Flux in VVER–1000 Rod Bundles," (in Russian), *Teploenergetika*, no. 2 (1976), pp. 80–82.

209. Gaspari G. P., et al., "A Rod Centered Sub-channel Analysis With Turbulent (Enthalpy) Mixing for Critical Heat Flux Prediction in Rod Clusters Cooled by Boiling Water," 5th International Heat Transfer Conference, vol. 44, Tokyo, Japan, 1974, pp. 295–299, CONF–740925 (1975).

210. Miropolski, Z. L., et al., "Statistical Correctness of the Critical Heat Flux Investigation," (in Russian), *Teploenergetika*, no. 4 (1969), pp. 49–52.

211. Smolin, V. N., and Poliakov, V. K., "Critical Heat Flux in Flow Through Rod Bundle," (in Russian), *Teploenergetika*, no. 7 (1967), pp. 54–58.

212. Gellerstedt, J. S., et al., "Correlation of Critical Heat Flux in a Bundle Cooled by Pressurized Water," The Winter Annual Meeting of the ASME, Los Angeles, 1969, p. 63.

213. Tong, L. S., "Prediction of Departure from Nucleate Boiling for an Axially Non-uniform Heat Distribution," *J. Nucl. Energy*, vol. 6 (1967), p. 21.

214. Biasi, L., et al., "Studies on Burnout, Part 3," *Energ. Nucl.*, vol. 14 (No. 9), 1967, p. 530.

215. Bowring, R. W., 'Simple but Accurate Round Tube, Uniform Heat Flux Dryout Correlation over the Pressure Range 0.7 to 17 MPa," AEEW-R-789, U.K. Atomic Energy Authority, 1972.

216. Barnett, P. G., "A Correlation of Burnout Data for Uniformly Heated Annuli and Its Use for Predicting Burnout in Uniformly Heated Rod Bundles," AEEW–R–463, U.K. Atomic Energy Authority, 1966.

217. Macbeth, R. V., "Application of a Local Condition Hypothesis to World Data of Uniformly Heated Round Tubes and Rectangular Channels," AEEW–R–267, U.K. Atomic Energy Authority, 1963.

218. Thompson, B., and Macbeth, R. V., "Boiling Water Heat Transfer Burnout in Uniformly Heated Round Tubes: A Compilation of World Data with Accurate Correlations," AEEW–R–356, U.K. Atomic Energy Authority, 1964.

219. Griffith, P., and Smith, R. A., "A Simple Model for Estimating Time to CHF in a PWR LOCA," ASME Paper 76–HT–9, American Society of Mechanical Engineers, 1976.

220. Leung, J. C. M., "Critical Heat Flux Under Transient Conditions: a Literature Survey," Argonne National Laboratory, Argonne, Illinois, NUREG/CR–0056, ANIL–78–39, 1978.

221. Leung, J. C. M., "Occurrence of Critical Heat Flux During Blowdown with Flow Reversal," Argonne National Laboratory, Argonne, Illinois, ANL–77–4, 1977.

222. Ybarrondo, L. J., et al., "The 'Calculated' Loss-of-Coolant Accident: a Review," AIChE Monograph Series, vol. 68, no. 7, 1972.

223. Groeneveld, D. C., "Post-Dryout Heat Transfer: Physical Mechanisms and a Survey of Prediction Methods," *Nucl. Engng. Design*, vol. 32 (1975), pp. 283–294.

224. Mayinger, F., and Longner, H., "Post-Dryout Heat Transfer," paper presented at the 6th International Heat Transfer Conference, Toronto (August 7–11, 1978), vol. 6, pp. 181–198.

225. Yadigaroglu, G., "The Reflooding Phase of the LOCA in PWRs. Part I: Core Heat Transfer and Fluid Flow," *Nuclear Safety*, vol. 19, no 1 (1978), pp. 20–36.

226. Elias, E., and Yadigaroglu, G., "The Reflooding Phase of the LOCA in PWRs. Part II: Rewetting and Liquid Entrainment," *Nuclear Safety*, vol. 19, no. 2 (1978), pp. 160–175.

227. Solbrig, C. W., et al., "Heat Transfer and Friction Correlations Required to Describe Steam-water Behavior in Nuclear Safety Studies," 15th National Heat Transfer Conference, San Francisco, California, August, 1975, CONF–750804–3.

228. Saha, P., "Review of Two-Phase Steam-Water Critical Flow Models with Emphasis on Thermal Nonequilibrium," NUREG/CR–0417, BNL–NUREG–50907, 1978.

229. Banerjee, S., and Hancox, W. T., "Transient Thermohydraulic Analysis for Nuclear Reactors," 6th International Heat Transfer Conference, Toronto, Canada, vol. 6, 1978. pp. 311–337.

CHAPTER 47

FLOW IN THIN-FILM EVAPORATORS

Katsutaka Nakamura

Anan Technical College
Minobayashi-Cho,
Anan City, Japan

Takashi Watanabe

Faculty of Engineering
Tokushima University
Minamijosanjima-Cho,
Tokushima City, Japan

CONTENTS

INTRODUCTION

Agitated thin-film evaporators are suitable for evaporating or concentrating heat-sensitive materials or highly viscous materials. In these evaporators the characteristics of heat transfer or evaporation [1–9] are seriously affected by flow.

For the flow in agitated falling-thin-film evaporators, many investigations have been reported [3, 6, 10–16]. However, research data on the flow in horizontal, agitated thin-film evaporators are insufficient, and there still remains a wide unexplored domain.

In the case of these horizontal evaporators, it is possible to control the residence time by selecting the rotational speed of the wiping blade. (By "residence time" we mean the time required for the working liquid to flow from the inlet to the outlet of an evaporator.) It is very significant that we investigate the flow in horizontal evaporators.

This chapter consists of the following sections.

In the following section an outline of agitated thin-film evaporators is given. Then the characteristics of these evaporators are described.

In the third section the effects of flow patterns on heat transfer are reviewed, and then the details of the flow patterns are surveyed. In this section, the authors distinguish between unsolved questions and solved problems.

In the next section the authors discuss their investigation of the flow in a horizontal agitated thin film evaporator [17-19], and in the final section, conclusions and recommendations for future work are given.

OUTLINE OF AGITATED THIN-FILM EVAPORATORS

Evolution

Agitated thin-film evaporators were developed in order to evaporate heat-sensitive materials or highly viscous materials. These evaporators were first used by the Luwa Corp. in 1946 [20] and research about these evaporators has been ongoing [21].

Treatment of Heat-Sensitive Materials

In order to evaporate or condense heat-sensitive materials such as natural vitamin D, it is necessary to decrease the residence time. For decreasing the residence time, it is desirable to make the liquid film thin.

Centrifugal molecular evaporators, centri-thermo evaporators, plate-and-frame evaporators [22], modified falling-film evaporators [23] and agitated thin-film evaporators are commonly used to make the liquid-film thin. Among these evaporators, agitated thin-film evaporators with several blades in the cylinder ensure the highest heat transfer coefficient, because the blades reliquidize the film.

Treatment of Highly Viscous Materials

In order to evaporate or condense highly viscous materials, it is necessary not only to make the liquid-film thin, but also to make it stable. To attain these ends, agitated thin-film evaporators are useful, because the blades repress the breakdown of liquid film.

Characteristics

The construction of agitated thin-film evaporators is as follows. In a concentric double cylinder several blades are attached onto a rotor, which is driven by an electric motor. The working liquid fed continuously from an inlet is spread on the inside of the inner cylinder by the action of the rotating blades. The steam in the annular cylinder heats and evaporates the working liquid. The working liquid evaporated is gathered by a mist-separator. The residuum is exhausted from an outlet of the inner cylinder.

These evaporators are classified differently according to the flow direction, the shape of the cylinder and the type of blade as shown in Table 1.

Flow Direction

Agitated climbing-film evaporators need a minimum rotational speed of the wiping blade for the liquid film to spread the whole length of cylinder. Then it is necessary to rotate the blades at a high speed. The power consumption of these evaporators is larger than that of agitated falling-thin-film evaporators (Figure 1). However, in the case of the former, there is an advantage in that the residence time is able to be controlled by selecting the rotational speed of the wiping blade.

Table 1
Classification of Agitated Thin-Film Evaporator

Flow Direction	Shape of Cylinder	Type of Blade
Agitated falling-thin-film evaporator	Straight cylinder [24] (Figure 1)	Fixed-clearance Blade (Figure 3A:Luwa rotor) Wiper (Figure 3B:Sambay rotor) (Figure 3C:Smith rotor)
Agitated climbing-film evaporator	Taper cylinder [25, 26]	Fixed-clearance blade
	Straight cylinder [27]	Fixed-clearance blade
Horizontal, agitated thin-film evaporator	Straight cylinder [26] (Figure 7) Forward-taper cylinder [28] (Figure 2) Reverse-taper cylinder [28]	Fixed-clearance blade

The superior characteristics of horizontal evaporators are as follows:

1. In the case of horizontal evaporators, the axial flow of the working liquid is scarcely affected by gravity, and a breakdown of liquid film does not occur even when the volumetric flow rate is small. Therefore, we can more effectively utilize the heating wall.
2. It is mechanically stable and the power consumption is small because the rotational speed of the wiping blade is low.
3. It is possible to control the residence time by selecting the rotational speed of the wiping blade.

However, there is a disadvantage in that we cannot as yet construct large units [20].

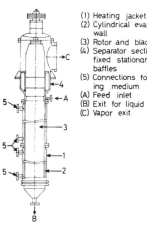

(1) Heating jacket
(2) Cylindrical evaporator wall
(3) Rotor and blades
(4) Separator section with fixed stationary baffles
(5) Connections for heating medium
(A) Feed inlet
(B) Exit for liquid product
(C) Vapor exit

Figure 1. Schematic section of the Luwa evaporator.

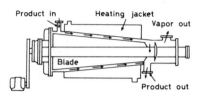

Figure 2. Forward-taper cylinder.

Shape of Cylinders

In this section, differences in characteristics between the horizontal, straight cylinder (Figure 7) and the horizontal, forward-taper cylinder (Figure 2) are described. The diameter at the outlet of the forward-taper cylinder is smaller than that at the inlet as shown in Figure 2.

The superior characteristics of horizontal, straight cylinders are as follows:

1. The straight cylinders are suitable for treating heat-sensitive materials because the residence time is small.
2. The straight cylinders promote heat transfer because the axial diffusion is small.
3. We can exhaust slurries if we incline the straight cylinder.
4. We can take it apart and clean it easily.

The superior characteristics of horizontal, forward-taper cylinders are as follows [20]:

1. There is no breakdown of liquid-film because the anti-flow-direction component of the centrifugal force acts on the liquid-film [28].
2. We can adjust the clearance by pulling the rotor in and out in the axial direction.

Types of Blades

There are three typical blades [11, 15, 17–19]. The first is arranged to give a fixed-clearance of 1 to 2 mm between the inner cylinder wall and the wiping blade tip (Figure 3A). The second blade is hinged so as to press on the inner cylinder wall by centrifugal force (Figure 3B). The third is swung to give a minimum clearance of 0.5 mm (Figure 3C).

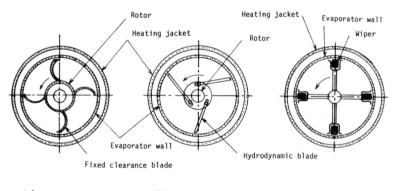

(a) Luwa rotor   (b) Sambay rotor   (c) Smith rotor

Figure 3. Typical blades.

Differences between the fixed-clearance blade and the wipers are as follows:

1. The construction of the fixed-clearance blade is simple, but the regulation of clearance must be accurate.
2. The wipers wear down and these materials mingle with the working liquid when the wipers contact with the cylinder wall.

In the case of the Smith rotor, we can control the axial flow by cutting grooves at the tip of the wiper [16, 30].

LITERATURE SURVEY

Effects of Flow Patterns on Heat Transfer

Effects of Wiping Interval on Heat Transfer

In Figure 4 experimental values and an empirical formula by Azoory [6] and Azoory and Bott [9] as shown.
The empirical formula

$$(u_c)_{pred} = \frac{8.74(c_p \rho n 2\pi NK/60)^{1/2}}{(Pr/500) + 3.5} \tag{1}$$

shows that u_c is in proportion to $\sqrt{nN}$. The correction factor f depends on Prandtl number $Pr = \rho c_p v/K$ as shown in Figure 4.
The wiping interval, which is defined as the time between successive blade passes, is

$$t_a = \frac{D/n}{R2\pi N/60} \doteq \frac{60}{nN} \tag{2}$$

Then

$$u_c \propto (t_a)^{-1/2} \tag{3}$$

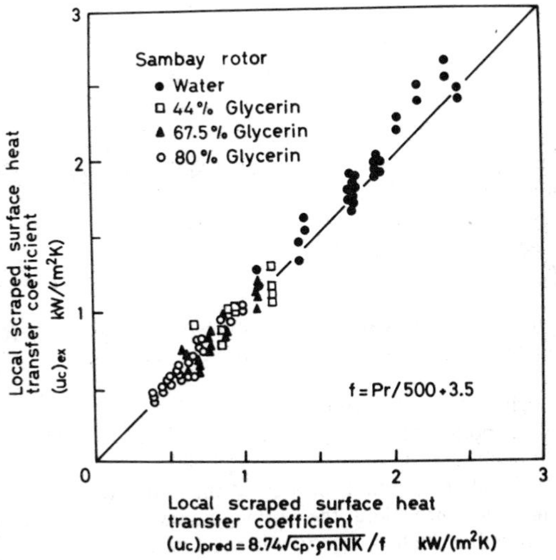

Figure 4. Correlation between experimental heat transfer coefficient $(u_c)_{ex}$ and predicted one $(u_c)_{pred}$.

Therefore, u_c increases with the increasing blade number n and the increasing rotational speed of the wiping blade N.

This result (Equation 3) is also derived from the heat penetration theory [1, 2, 4, 5, 7]. In this theory, it is assumed that the heat transfer coefficient depends on the rate of transitional conduction in the layer renewed each time the wiping blade passes. Namely the liquid layer at the wall is nearly completely removed by the shearing action each time the wiping blade passes. Then a fresh liquid layer comes back to the wall surface at its bulk temperature. Heat transfer occurs by conduction until the wiping blade passes again, thus repeating the process. Since the depth of conductive heat penetration per pass [31] is smaller than 0.2 mm in the range of the rotational speed of the wiping blade usually encountered, the small variation in circumferential fluid velocities within the thin heat transfer layer does not need to be considered. If it is also assumed that entrance and longitudinal flow effects are rendered unimportant by the intensity of cross-sectional mixing, then the heat transfer mechanism is identical to the molecular condition [31] in a semi-infinite solid [6]. The solution of Fourier's equation [31] is

$$q_r|_{r=D/2} = -K \left.\frac{\partial T}{\partial r}\right|_{r=D/2} = \frac{K}{\sqrt{\pi \alpha t}}(T_w - T_0) \tag{4}$$

where q_r = wall heat flux
T_0 = bulk temperature
T_w = wall temperature
K = thermal conductivity of working liquid
α = thermal diffusivity of working liquid

Heat flow Q_r per unit area and time t_a is given by

$$Q_r = \int_0^{t_a} q_r|_{r=D/2}\, dt = \frac{2K}{\sqrt{\pi \alpha}}(T_w - T_0)\sqrt{t_a} \tag{5}$$

Time average Q_m of Q_r is

$$Q_m = \frac{Q_r}{t_a} = \frac{2K(T_w - T_0)}{\sqrt{\pi \alpha t_a}} \tag{6}$$

Then

$$u_c = 2K/\sqrt{\pi \alpha t_a} \tag{7}$$

The heat transfer coefficient is smaller than that of Equation 7, because the cross-sectional mixing is weak when the rotational Reynolds number is small.

Effect of Axial Diffusion on Heat Transfer

The problem of the influence of axial diffusion on heat transfer was analyzed by Azoory [6] and Bott, Azoory, and Porter [8]. The following assumptions are made in these analyses:

1 The wall temperature is constant throughout the evaporator.
2 The local heat transfer coefficient is uniform both around the circumference and along the length of the evaporator.
3 The physical properties of the working liquid are constant throughout the evaporator.
4 The axial diffusion process operates uniformly throughout the working liquid at any section.
5 The thermal diffusivity of the working liquid in the flow direction is negligible.

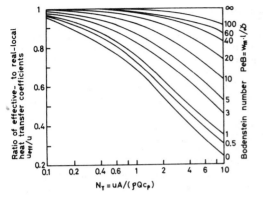

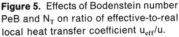

Figure 5. Effects of Bodenstein number PeB and N_T on ratio of effective-to-real local heat transfer coefficient u_{eff}/u.

By using

$$N_T = \frac{uA}{\rho Q c_p} \tag{8}$$

and Bodenstein number

$$PeB = w_m l / \mathcal{D} \tag{9}$$

the ratio of the real heat transfer coefficient u_{eff} to the heat transfer coefficient of plug flow u is deduced as follows:

$$\frac{u_{eff}}{u} = \frac{N_{T,eff}}{N_T} = \frac{-\ln\{f(PeB, N_T)\}}{N_T} \tag{10}$$

In Figure 5, u_{eff}/u is plotted against N_T for different values of PeB. Figure 5 shows that u_{eff}/u decreases with the increasing N_T and the decreasing PeB.

The values of the Bodenstein number obtained by Azoory [6] ranged from 30 to 100. From Figure 5, it is seen that the effects of axial diffusion reduce the ratio of heat transfer predicted on the assumption of plug flow by only 5% for an evaporator corresponding to a value of $N_T = 2$. Then Azoory [6] proposed that axial diffusion effects may be ignored.

Flow Patterns

Agitated, Falling Thin-Film Evaporator

There are many investigations [3, 6, 10–16] on the flow in agitated, falling thin-film evaporators. The flow affects not only heat transfer but also the breakdown of liquid-film. Among the investigators, Schneider [10] concluded that the residence time was independent of the rotational speed of the wiping blade because the axial flow was seriously affected by gravity.

In this section, some theoretical investigations on flow in the straight cylinder with fixed-clearance blades are mainly surveyed as follows:

Kern and Karakas [3] carried out excellent theoretical research work, and laid the ground work of this field. They derived the liquid hold-up and the power consumption under both conditions of heating and nonheating. In this theory, they assumed that the axial flow of the liquid fillet was laminar and the cross section of the liquid fillet was a right-angled isosceles triangle. (Liquid fillet is defined as the working liquid collected in front of the wiping blades.) They did not compare the theory with experimental data.

By using the turbulent theory, Domanskii, Avdonkin, and Sokolov [32] derived the liquid hold-up under the conditions of nonheating. They introduced the coefficient of contraction. However, there is a defect, namely, the power consumption is included in this theoretical liquid hold-up.

By using the Navier-Stokes equations and the boundary-layer theory, Reineman, Comel, and Dietz [33] calculate the liquid hold-up under the conditions of nonheating. The axial velocity and the circumferential velocity of the liquid film were derived. However, this theory is useful only when the liquid film thickness is less than the clearance regulated between the cylinder wall and the blade tip. Moreover, the effects of the rotational speed of the wiping blade on the flow are not considered in this theory.

Nakamura and Watanabe [34] further developed the theory by Kern and Karakas [3] and compared the theory with the experimental data under the conditions of nonheating. But there is a defect here too, namely, this theory is useful only when the ratio L_θ/h_2 of the circumferential length of the liquid fillet to the thickness of the liquid fillet is known.

Murakami et al. [35] and Murakami et al. [36] expressed the dimensionless liquid holdup under the condition of nonheating. Their dimensionless numbers were derived by the dimensional analysis.

Schweizer and Widmer [37] derived the residence time theoretically. Their theory agrees with the experimental data within the limit of 0.08 Pa.s to 10.0 Pa.s of viscosity. That is, the residence time increases with the increasing rotational speed of the wiping blade, clearance, number of wiping blades, and viscosity of the working liquid; however, the residence time decreases with the increasing volumetric flow rate. They measured both the vertical velocity and the circumferential velocity of the liquid film and the liquid fillet by using a Laser-Doppler anemometer.

Agitated Climbing-Film Evaporator

Hadley and Thomas [27] investigated the flow in an agitated climbing-film evaporator with the fixed-clearance of 1.5 mm both theoretically and experimentally. They calculated the liquid hold-up, the residence time, and the power consumption when the dimensions of the apparatus, the rotational speed of the wiping blade, and the properties of the working liquid were given. To compute film thickness, it was assumed that both the force balance for laminar flow and the Navier-Stokes equations applied. A critical angular velocity to spread the working liquid on the whole length of the cylinder.

$$\omega = \{2gL/(R^2 - R_0^2)\}^{1/2} \tag{11}$$

and the volume of the liquid fillet built by the action of the rotating blades

$$W_f = \pi gL^2/\omega^2 \tag{12}$$

were given. In Equation 12, it is assumed that the liquid fillet is built up all over the cylinder.

By assuming that the liquid fillet was moving at the same angular velocity as the blade, the power consumption was found as follows:

$$P \propto (LR^3/\delta)N^2\rho v \tag{13}$$

These theoretical values were in good accord with the experimental ones. Their conclusions are as follows:

1. It is desirable to operate at high speed in order to get high overall heat transfer, but it requires high power consumption.
2. A minimum radius and maximum height are desirable, because the power consumption depends on the radius cubed and on the height directly.

Horizontal, Agitated Thin-Film Evaporator

Horizontal, agitated thin-film evaporators have been used in some factories [21, 23, 28, 38]. However, there are very few investigations concerning the flow in horizontal evaporators, and as a result there are little data for determining the most suited dimensions to the operating conditions.

In this section, the flow in horizontal types with a fixed clearance is discussed as follows:

Flow in straight cylinder. Several reviews [23, 28] of the flow are reported. In one manufacturer's catalogue the differences between the liquid film and the liquid fillet are not clear. A new method of controlling the liquid hold-up by twisting the wiping blade both at the inlet and at the outlet of the cylinder is shown in a patent announcement [21].

Flow in reverse-taper cylinder. The diameter at the outlet of the reverse-taper cylinder is larger than that at the inlet. Some reviews by Atsumi and Horigichi [38], Gudheim and Donovan [28], and King [29] are reported. They described that the highly viscous materials could be exhausted easily because the additional thrust was produced by the flow directional component of the centrifugal force.

Flow in forward-taper cylinder. A new method of controlling the liquid hold-up by mounting wedges on the outlet parts of the wiping blades has been developed [21].

FLOW IN A HORIZONTAL, AGITATED THIN-FILM EVAPORATOR

Introduction

The performance of agitated thin-film evaporators is determined by the characteristics of heat transfer, the construction cost, and the operating cost.

The flow of working liquids in these agitated thin-film evaporators seriously affects the undesirable heat transfer conditions such as the breakdown of liquid film or its passing through. (Passing through is when the liquid fillet flows rapidly without cross-sectional mixing with the liquid film.) Moreover, the flow of working liquids affects the residence time, the effective area for evaporation, the axial diffusion, and the power consumption. Therefore, it is most important to make clear the flow of working liquids in these evaporators.

The purpose of the present investigation is to reveal the performance of horizontal, agitated thin-film evaporators and to furnish design data.

The authors have investigated the flow, disregarding thermal effects, because it is very difficult to resolve the thermal problems and the flow problems simultaneously.

Theoretical Analysis

This work is based on a theoretical analysis for axial flow in horizontal evaporators with a fixed-clearance when the working liquid viscosity is low.

Liquid-Fillet Model

Assuming that the viscosity of the working liquid is so low that the hydraulic jump theory [39, 40] can be applied to explain the thickness of the liquid fillet, we theoretically analyzed the axial flow in a horizontal, agitated thin-film evaporator. The liquid fillet model shown in Figure 6 was used.

For simplification, the following assumptions are made in the liquid-fillet model.

1. The centrifugal acceleration, which acts on the liquid fillet, is so large that the acceleration due to gravity is negligible.
2. The working liquid properties do not change in the axial direction.
3. The liquid film thickness h_{1m} depends on Q and N. The variation of h_{1m} in the axial direction is negligible. The liquid-film thickness in the outlet region ($z_e < z \leq L$) decreases from h_{1m} to h_e which is the thickness at the outlet of the evaporator.

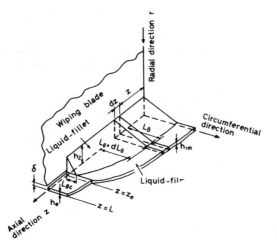

Figure 6. Liquid-fillet model.

4. In the outlet region, the working liquid flows in the liquid-film. When the volumetric flow rate Q is less than the critical flow rate Q_c, the liquid fillet disappears at the position z_e in the evaporator. In the case of $Q > Q_c$, the critical flow rate Q_c flows in the liquid film and $(Q - Q_c)$ flows in the liquid fillet.

In the main region ($z \leqq z_e$), all the working liquid flows in the liquid fillet.

5. The liquid fillet cross-section is a right-angled triangle [3, 18, 19, 41, 42]. Its radial thickness and circumferential length are expressed as h_2 and L_θ, respectively.

The Momentum Equation in the Main Region

From the experimental results [43] in the main region ($z \leqq z_e$), h_{1m} is given as follows:

$$h_{1m} = 1.67 \times \delta Q^{0.081} \, (N/60)^{-0.111} \quad \text{(N/60)} \tag{14}$$

where Q (m³/s) is the volumetric flow rate and N (rpm) is the rotational speed of the wiping blades. The thickness of the liquid fillet h_2 is given by the hydraulic jump theory [39, 40]:

$$\frac{h_2}{h_{1m}} = \frac{1}{2}(\sqrt{1 + 8Fr^2} - 1) \tag{15}$$

where the Froude number Fr is [43]

$$Fr = R\omega/\sqrt{R\omega^2 h_{1m}} = \sqrt{R/h_{1m}} \tag{16}$$

where R is the radius of the wiping blade and h_{1m} is the average liquid-film thickness excluding the liquid fillet in the main region.

The liquid fillet plays an important role by inducing such effects as cross-sectional mixing with the liquid film, forming a uniform liquid film, and thrusting the working liquid axially. The momentum equations for the axial flow in the liquid fillet (Figure 6) are able to be derived from the balance of the forces acting on the liquid in the axial direction.

Pressure forces caused by the centrifugal acceleration act on the liquid fillet at the axial position z and z + dz. Shearing forces act on the liquid fillet at the surfaces of both the wiping blade and the inner cylinder wall. A difference between the pressure forces and the shearing force acting on the liquid fillet causes the working liquid to flow in the axial direction. Using the distance c_g from the inner-cylinder wall to the center of gravity of the liquid fillet and the area of the liquid fillet cross section S, the momentum equation for the axial flow of the liquid fillet is deduced as follows:

$$\rho \frac{Q}{n}(w_{z+dz} - w_z) = \rho(D/2 - c_g)\omega^2 c_g\, dS - \left(\tau_{fb} h_2 + \tau_{fw} \frac{L_{\theta,z} + L_{\theta,z+dz}}{2}\right) dz \tag{17}$$

where

$$\tau_{fb} = \lambda_f \rho w_f^2/8 \tag{18}$$

$$\tau_{fw} = (\lambda_f'/8)\rho \cdot (V^2 + w_f^2)\sin(w_f/V) \tag{19}$$

The hydraulic radius of the liquid fillet r_h is defined [44] as the area of the liquid-fillet cross section S divided by its wetted perimeter $(h_2 + L_\theta)$. That is, $r_h = S/(h_2 + L_\theta)$, where h_2 is the thickness of the liquid-fillet and L_θ is the circumferential length of the liquid fillet. The equivalent diameter of the liquid fillet is defined [41, 44] as four times r_h.

Reynolds number Ref and Ref', based on the equivalent diameter of the liquid fillet $4r_h = 4S/(h_2 + L_\theta)$, the average axial velocity of the liquid-fillet w_f, and absolute velocity of the liquid-fillet $(V^2 + w_f^2)^{1/2}$ are

$$Ref = 4 \cdot w_f \cdot r_h/\nu \tag{20}$$

$$Ref' = 4\sqrt{V^2 + w_f^2}\, r_h/\nu \tag{21}$$

respectively. In Equation 21, V is the circumferential velocity of the wiping blade tip and ν is the kinetic viscosity. By using the Boussinesq coefficient [45] B listed in Table 2, the friction factor in Equation 18 and Equation 19 is given by

$$\lambda_f = B \cdot 64/Ref \tag{22}$$

$$\lambda_f' = B \cdot 64/Ref' \tag{23}$$

for Ref $\leq$ 2,320 and Ref' $\leq$ 2,320, respectively. If 2,320 < Ref < 10^5 and 2,320 < Ref' < 10^5, Blasius' equation [46]

$$\lambda_f = 0.3164\, Ref^{-1/4} \tag{24}$$

$$\lambda_f' = 0.3164\, (Ref')^{-1/4} \tag{25}$$

are used.

Axial Flow in the Outlet Region

Assuming that the centrifugal acceleration $R(k\omega)^2$ acts on the liquid film at the outlet region $(z_e < z \leq L)$, the critical axial velocity of the liquid film w_c at the outlet is given by

$$\omega_c = \sqrt{R(k\omega)^2 h_e}$$

Table 2
Boussinesq Coefficient

h_2/L_θ or L_θ/h_2	1	2	3	4	5	∞
B	0.895	0.973	1.07	1.14	1.19	1.50

The equation of w_c is derived from the assumption that the flow is the supercritical flow [44] in the vicinity of the outlet of the cylinder. The constance k is the ratio of the circumferential velocity of the liquid film in the outlet region to that of the wiping blade tip.

The volumetric flow rate Q in the outlet region is given by

$$Q_e = \pi D h_e \sqrt{R(k\omega)^2 h_e} \tag{26}$$

when h_e is formed circumferentially at the outlet. From Equation 26, we obtain $h_e = \{Q_e/[\pi D\sqrt{R(k\omega)^2}]\}^{2/3}$. When $h_e = h_{1m}$, the volumetric flow rate Q_e is equal to Q_c. The critical volumetric flow rate Q_c increases with the increasing ω and h_{1m}. The disappearance point of the liquid-fillet z_e is given by Oki's equation [46] for a back water curve

$$L - z_e = \frac{(\pi D)^2 R(k\omega)^2 (h_{1m}^4 - h_e^4)}{(\lambda/2)Q^2} - \frac{2(h_{1m} - h_e)}{\lambda/4} \tag{27}$$

which is derived from integrating the energy equation from z_e to L.

In the outlet region where the liquid fillet does not exist, the Reynolds number for an axial flow in the liquid-film is $Rel = (4Q/\pi D)/v$, where Q is the volumetric flow rate and D is the cylinder inner diameter. Then the friction factor λ in Equation 27 is given by $\lambda = 1.5 \times 64/Rel$ and the Blasius' equation $\lambda = 0.3164 Rel^{-1/4}$, when $Rel \leq 2,320$ and $2,320 < Rel < 10^5$, respectively.

Liquid Hold-up, Average Residence Time, and Power Consumption

The liquid hold-up is calculated by the equation

$$W = \int_0^{z_e} \{(\pi D - nL_\theta)h_{1m} + nS\} \cdot dz + \int_{z_e}^L \pi D \frac{h_{1m} + h_e}{2} dz \tag{28}$$

The effective area of evaporation $(\pi D - nL_{\theta m})L$, which is defined as the area occupied by the liquid film, increases with the decreasing average circumferential length of the liquid-fillet $L_{\theta m}$. The average residence time is defined [47, 48] as W/Q.

For vertical power consumption, a theoretical equation

$$P = \frac{s\rho W(R \cdot 2\pi N/60)^3}{4\pi R} \tag{29}$$

has been proposed by Kern and Karakas [3]. Their theory requires that there be a liquid hold-up W and the correcting coefficient s. We calculate the power consumption using Equation 29.

Experimental Apparatus

We made the horizontal, straight-cylinder model as shown in Figure 7. The cylinder and four wiping blades are made of transparent acrylic resin. The distance from the inlet to the outlet of the evaporator cylinder is L = 380 mm. In the cylinder, four wiping blades are attached on a rotor driven by a DC electric motor. The clearance between the inner cylinder wall and the wiping wall tip is kept at 1 mm in the axial direction.

When the rotational speed of the four wiping blades measured by means of the stroboscope is in the range of 400 rpm to 1,200 rpm, the centrifugal acceleration is sufficiently greater than the gravitational acceleration. The working liquids are fed by a Westco pump of 80 watts. A rotary piston flowmeter and a cock are installed at the inlet, and a measuring tank at the outlet. For distributing the working liquid in the cylinder evenly, a disk of 70 mm in diameter is installed 50 mm from the inlet.

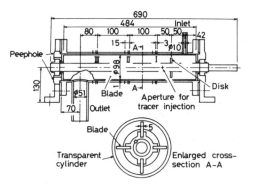

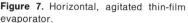

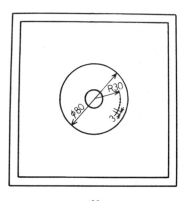

Figure 7. Horizontal, agitated thin-film evaporator.

Electrodes, which consist of a pair of platinum rods 1 mm in diameter with a gap of 3 mm between them, were (Figure 12) installed at positions I, II, and III, as shown in Figure 7 for measuring the liquid-film thickness. The tips of the electrodes are polished by sand paper and made flush with the inner cylinder wall. Two peepholes of 36 mm in diameter are installed at the outlet side flange for looking at the cross-section of the liquid fillet.

A liquid-film thickness calibrator (Figure 8) was devised to find the effect of the liquid-film thickness on the electric resistance. Two acrylic discs 80 mm in diameter face each other in the calibrator containing the working liquid. The upper disc moves up and down to adjust precisely to the liquid-film thickness between the two discs. As shown in Figure 8, six rods of platinum electrodes of 1 mm in diameter are mounted at positions that are 30 mm away from the center of the upper disc, and the gap between them is 3 mm in the circumferential direction. Each end of these electrodes is polished by sand paper and is made flush with the underside surface of the upper disc.

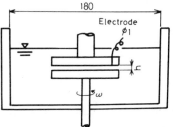

Figure 8. Liquid-film thickness calibrator.

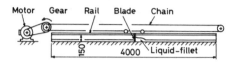

Figure 9. Two-dimensional shallow-water tunnel.

We conducted experiments in a two-dimensional shallow-water tunnel shown in Figure 9 for the purpose of finding out clearly how to determine the thickness of the liquid fillet and the cross-sectional mixing between the liquid fillet and the liquid film.

The overall length of the tunnel is 4,000 mm, the width is 500 mm, and the height is 150 mm. In the middle of the tunnel, a test section of 1,000 mm in length is installed. In the tunnel, the film thickness is measurable at any point by means of a micrometer. The accuracy of the measurement is within 1/20 mm in the range of the film thickness from 0 mm to 25 mm. The bottom plate of the tunnel is adjustable precisely in the vertical direction. A wiping blade is towed on two rails above the tunnel parallel to the bottom by a DC motor to which are attached a gear change apparatus and two chains (Figure 9). The blade speed is changed over a range from 0.32 m/s to 1.54 m/s. The clearance between the blade tip and the bottom of the tunnel has a constant value of 2.55 mm.

Experimental Method

Photographs of the liquid fillet were taken from the top of the transparent cylinder looking down and also from the peephole under the condition of the stroboscopic synchronized with the rotational speed of the wiping blade. The procedure for measuring liquid hold-up is as follows.

We shut the valve of the measuring tank at the outlet. When the liquid level in the measuring tank reaches a prescribed level, we shut the cock at the inlet. The liquid hold-up is defined as the liquid volume that flows into the measuring tank after closing the cock at the inlet.

We measured electric resistances of the working liquid in the calibrator (Figure 8) using an alternating current of 60 Hz and 12 V. The results show that the electric resistance increases linearly with the decreasing liquid-film thickness when the liquid-film thickness is less than 1 mm (Figure 10). These results indicate that we can measure the liquid-film thickness using the electrode method.

Next, the electric resistance of the liquid film in our calibrator was recorded on the electromagnetic oscillograph paper to make a correlation curve between the liquid-film thickness and the displacement on the oscillograph paper. In order to decrease electrolysis, a constant, alternating current of 5 kHz and 6 V was supplied to the Wheatstone bridge. The dynamic strain meter was set at zero balance, which corresponded to the condition that the liquid-film thickness in the calibrator was equal to the clearance between the inner cylinder wall and the wiping blade tip.

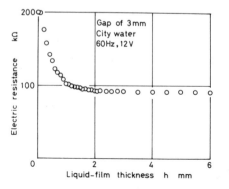

Figure 10. Effect of liquid-film thickness on electric resistance.

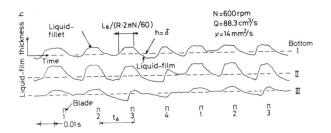

Figure 11. Typical example of observed liquid-film thickness.

A typical example of the observed curves in our agitated thin-film evaporator is shown in Figure 11. As the liquid fillet approaches the electrode, the electric resistance decreases and the curves in Figure 11 move upward. In Figure 11, the thickness level of δ is also shown in three curves.

We evaluated the liquid-film thickness as follows.

We measured the area under the line of thickness level of δ by using a planimeter. From the area divided by $(\pi D/n - L_\theta)$, we evaluated the average liquid-film thickness by using the correlation curve just mentioned. The average liquid-film thickness is defined as the average of the liquid-film thickness excluding the liquid-fillet.

These electrodes are used not only for measuring the film thickness and the time-average circumferential length of the liquid fillet, but also for measuring the residence-time distribution, because the electric resistance of liquid is more affected by the change of the tracer concentration than by that of the liquid-film thickness.

To obtain the residence-time distribution, the electrically conducting solution of salt (0.428 mol/kg, 0.5 cm³) was injected quickly at the aperture for tracer injection by using a syringe.

The residence time is calculated from the measured residence-time distribution shown in Figure 12.

$$t_2^* - t_1^* = \frac{\int_0^\infty t c_2 \, dt}{\int_0^\infty c_2 \cdot dt} - \frac{\int_0^\infty t c_1 \, dt}{\int_0^\infty c_1 \cdot dt} \tag{30}$$

Here, the concentration curve is replaced by a smooth one. c_1 and c_2 are concentrations of the first component and the output of the tracer, respectively. We could also detect the difference in the

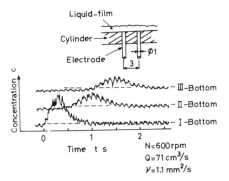

Figure 12. Typical example of observed residence-time distribution.

axial velocity along the axial direction, because we measured the tracer concentration at three positions (I, II, and III as shown in Figure 7).

To explain the axial diffusion we used "the degree of mixing" proposed by Inoue and Tonooka [49] as follows:

$$M = (\mu_{22} - \mu_{21})^{1/2}/(t_2^* - t_1^*) \tag{31}$$

where the values are normalized. μ_2 is the variance of the measured residence-time distribution and t is time. Using the Bishoff's equation [50], M is shown as follows,

$$M = \{2\mathscr{D}/(w_m l)\}^{1/2} = (2/PeB)^{1/2} \tag{32}$$

where l is the space between the electrodes, $w_m = l/(t_2^* - t_1^*)$ is the average axial velocity of the working liquid and PeB is the Peclet number. When $M = 0$, the flow is called "piston flow," and M increases with the increasing axial diffusion.

Results and Discussion

Liquid-Fillet Geometry and Turbulence in Liquid Film

The liquid-fillet geometry and turbulence in liquid film are sketched in Figure 13. From Figure 13, it can be said that L_θ decreases with the increasing of z.

Turbulence is observed in the liquid film of water (Figure 13A). On the other hand, only streaks are observed in the liquid film of viscous glycerine (Figure 13B).

The difference in turbulence between the two liquid films is caused by the working liquid viscosity. In case of water, the rotational film Reynolds number

$$Rew = 4Vh_{1m}/\nu \tag{33}$$

ranges from 1,980 to 5,940 as N varies from 400 too 1,200 rpm. V, h_{1m} and ν are the circumferential velocity of the wiping-blade tip, the average liquid-film thickness in the main region, and the kinetic viscosity, respectively. It can be said that the circumferential flow in the liquid-film is turbulent when Rel is larger than 1,980. It is unlikely that both the turbulence and the axial-flow component in the liquid fillet decay sufficiently in the liquid film left behind the wiping blade.

The viscosity of aqueous glycerine is about 30 times as large as that of water. In case of aqueous glycerine, Rew ranges from 53.7 to 161 as N varies from 400 to 1,200 rpm. It can be said that the circumferential flow in the liquid film is laminar when Rew is smaller than 161. They are qualitatively the same as the vertical ones [6].

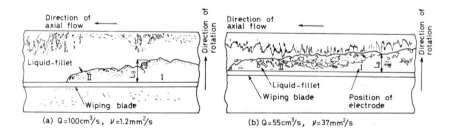

(a) Q=100cm³/s, ν=1.2mm²/s   (b) Q=55cm³/s, ν=37mm²/s

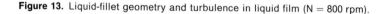

Figure 13. Liquid-fillet geometry and turbulence in liquid film (N = 800 rpm).

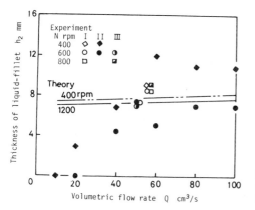

Figure 14. Effects of volumetric flow rate and rotational speed of wiping blades on thickness of liquid fillet.

Thickness of Liquid Fillet

The thickness of the liquid fillet h_2, calculated from Equation 15, is shown with the experimental data in Figure 14. It can be said that h_2 increases slightly with the increasing Q and with the decreasing N. When highly viscous working liquid is used, the thickness of the liquid fillet is different from that in water. Then the hydraulic jump theory is not applicable to the highly viscous working liquid.

From the following flow visualization study in a two-dimensional shallow-water tunnel (Figure 9), it was recognized that the cross-sectional mixing between the liquid-fillet and the liquid-film was affected by the working liquid viscosity. That is, in order to visualize the cross-sectional mixing pattern of water, the hydrogen-bubble method (probe diameter of 150 μm) was used. On the other hand, in the case of viscous glycerine, the flow visualization was not difficult because very small air bubbles on the surface of the liquid-film appeared on the liquid fillet in a line that showed the path line by the reflection of backlight (as shown in Figure 15B).

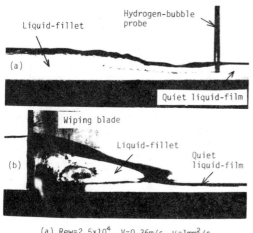

(a) Rew=2.5×10^4, V=0.36m/s, ν=1mm^2/s
(b) Rew=22, V=0.66m/s, ν=899mm^2/s

Figure 15. Flow pattern of liquid fillet in two-dimensional shallow-water tunnel.

One of the photographs of the liquid fillet of water (Figure 15A) shows that the quiet liquid film diffuses into the liquid fillet completely and a bore is formed in front of the wiping blade. Therefore, the thickness of the liquid fillet agrees with that given by the hydraulic jump theory. In Figure 15A, the wiping blade lies to the left and so it is invisible on this photograph.

In the case of such highly viscous liquid as glycerine, a shearing force acts on the interface between the lower quiet liquid and the upper moving liquid in the liquid fillet. The liquid film is rolled up into the liquid fillet. The liquid fillet geometry expresses the accumulation of a liquid-film sheet. The hydraulic jump theory, therefore, cannot be simply applied to these phenomena. The cross-sectional mixing between the liquid-fillet and the liquid-film is insufficient. It tends to cause, sometimes, deterioration in quality of products during the evaporating process or concentrating process.

Variation of Circumferential Length of Liquid Fillet in the Axial Direction

The theoretical results are obtained under $k = 0.4$. The effects of Q on the variation of L_θ in the axial direction are shown in Figure 16A. It can be said that L_θ decreases with the increasing of z, and the liquid fillet disappears in the evaporator when $Q \leqq 40$ cm^3/s. L_θ increases with the increasing Q and with decreasing N (Figure 16B). The effects of Q and N on the variation of L_θ in the axial direction are at least analyzed qualitatively. It seems that the qualitative differences between the theoretical values and the experimental ones may be explained by the fact that in our theory the axial flow of the liquid film in the main region is not equated.

When Q and N are constant, L_θ increases with the increasing kinetic viscosity ν of the working liquid. The effects of Q and ν on L_θ are the same as the vertical ones [6]. However, it is not necessary in the vertical apparatus that L_θ decrease in the axial direction if the gravitational force equals to the shearing force of the liquid fillet.

Next discussed is the effect of the differences in the clearances between each blade on the circumferential length of the liquid fillet.

If the rotor axis is eccentric with the cylinder axis, there is a difference in the disappearance point of the liquid fillet between each blade. This difference affects the liquid hold-up, the effective area for evaporation, the axial diffusion, and the power consumption. In order to calculate the performance of these evaporators exactly, we must regulate the rotor axis and the cylinder axis to be concentric with each other.

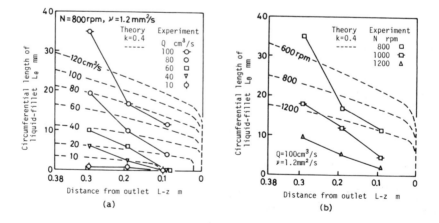

Figure 16. Effects of distance from outlet, volumetric flow rate, and rotational speed of wiping blades on circumferential length of liquid fillet.

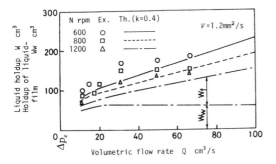

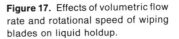

Figure 17. Effects of volumetric flow rate and rotational speed of wiping blades on liquid holdup.

Liquid Hold-up

The liquid hold-up W increases with the increasing Q and with the decreasing N as shown in Figure 17. The hold-up of the liquid film W_w is scarcely affected by Q and N. From the definition, $W - W_w$ shows the hold-up of the liquid fillet W_f. Figure 17 shows that the ratio of the hold-up of the liquid fillet to the total hold-up W_f/W increases with increasing Q. Figure 17 shows that the theoretical values are slightly less than the experimental data.

The liquid hold-up increases with the increasing kinetic viscosity v. The effects of Q and v on W are the same as the vertical effects [6]. The effects of N on W are, however, quite different from those of the vertical apparatus [15, 47]. The reason these differences occur between the horizontal apparatus and the vertical one are as follows.

The shearing force of the liquid fillet increases slightly with the increasing rotational speed of the wiping blade. The liquid hold-up, therefore, increases slightly with the increasing rotational speed of the wiping blade in the vertical apparatus [15, 47].

In the case of the horizontal apparatus, there is the variation of the circumferential length of the liquid fillet in the axial direction. Then, the axial thrust (and hence the axial velocity of the liquid fillet) caused by the centrifugal acceleration increases highly with the increasing rotational speed of the wiping blade. The liquid hold-up, therefore, decreases with the increasing rotational speed of the wiping blade in the horizontal apparatus. This is the most significant difference of the horizontal apparatus from the vertical one.

Characteristic of Axial Diffusion

We can say positively that the piston flow is a desirable condition for promoting heat transfer [8, 51] and for preventing the quality of products from deterioration. Figure 18 shows M, which is obtained from the residence-time distributions at the positions I (upsteam point) and III (downstream point). When Q is so large that a liquid fillet is built up, M is independent of Q and v and is about 0.2.

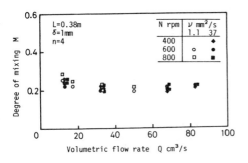

Figure 18. Effects of volumetric flow rate, rotational speed of wiping blades, and viscosity of working liquid on the degree of mixing.

The axial diffusion coefficient $\mathscr{D}$ increases with the increasing Q and with the decreasing v, because the average axial velocity w_m increases with increasing Q and decreasing v.

We can calculate the values of $\mathscr{D}$ by substituting the experimental values of M, w_m, and 1 into Equation 32. As a result, it is known that the values of the axial diffusion coefficient $\mathscr{D}$ are about 10^5 times as large as those of the molecular diffusion coefficient [52].

The values of the Bodenstein number PeB are within the range of $30 \leqq PeB \leqq 50$. These values are scarcely different from the values of the Sambay type [10, 53]. From Azoory's theory shown in Figure 5, u_{eff}/u is 0.95 when $N_T = 2$. Then, we can ignore the effects of the axial diffusion on u_{eff}.

When the volumetric flow rate Q is small, M is somewhat larger than 0.2.

Power Consumption

From our experiments on the horizontal apparatus, we obtain the results that the power consumption increases with the increasing volumetric flow rate, the increasing rotational speed of the wiping blade, and the increasing kinetic viscosity of the working liquid.

The effects of Q and N on P are qualitatively the same as the vertical ones [36]. The theoretical values by Kern and Karakas [3] are in proper accord with the experimental ones (Figure 19).

Conclusions

☐ The liquid-film thickness increases with the increasing volumetric flow rate and with the decreasing rotational speed of the wiping blade. The maximum liquid-film thickness is the value of the clearance between the inner cylinder wall and the wiping-blade tip.

☐ The thickness of the liquid fillet is almost independent of the volumetric flow rate, the rotational speed of the wiping blade, and the axial position. In the case of water, the thickness of the liquid fillet agrees with that given by the hydraulic jump theory. The cross-sectional mixing of water is sufficient.

When the kinetic viscosity of aqueous glycerine is large, the thickness of the liquid fillet is greater than that given by the hydraulic jump theory, and the cross-sectional mixing of viscous glycerine is completely different from that of water.

☐ When the thickness of the liquid-fillet agrees with that given by the hydraulic jump theory, the variation of L_θ in the axial direction is able to be determined theoretically. The circumferential length of the liquid fillet decreases with the increasing axial distance from the inlet of the cylinder and also with the increasing rotational speed of the wiping blade.

We conclude, therefore, that we can control the effective area for evaporation by selecting the rotational speed of the wiping blade.

☐ The liquid hold-up increases with the decreasing rotational speed of the wiping blade. This fact is the most significant difference of the horizontal apparatus from the vertical one. We conclude, therefore, that we can control the residence time, which is the most important factor, by selecting the rotational speed of the wiping blade.

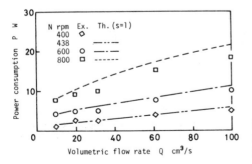

Figure 19. Effects of volumetric of flow rate and rotational of wiping blades on power consumption.

□ The degree of mixing, which expresses the characteristic of the axial diffusion, is about 0.2 except for a small volumetric flow rate. Then we can ignore the effects of the axial diffusion on the heat transfer coefficient.

□ The theory on power consumption by Kern and Karakas agrees with the experimental data.

CONCLUSION AND RECOMMENDATIONS FOR FUTURE WORK

Disregarding thermal effects, the authors investigated the flow in a horizontal, agitated thin-film evaporator both theoretically and experimentally. Their theory agrees with the experimental data.

The authors are very interested in comparing their theory with experimental data of different sizes and also in regarding the axial flow of the liquid-film in their theory.

With modification, the apparatus can also be used to study the cross-sectional mixing between the liquid fillet and the liquid film in the evaporator. Unfortunately, a lack of time made it impossible to carry out this part of the investigation.

Moreover, the technique of using a hot-film anemometer will be able to be used to measure the circumferential velocity of both the liquid film and the liquid fillet.

Not only the liquid-film thickness, but also the liquid fillet geometry is affected by gravity when the rotational speed of the wiping blade is low. The authors are planning an experimental investigation of these gravitational effects.

Acknowledgment

The authors wish to express their thanks for the guidance and encouragement received from Professor Yasutoshi Senoo of The Kyūsyū University. A part of this paper first appeared in *The Proceedings of The 2nd World Congress of Chemical Engineering.* Volume 5 (Montréal, Canada, October 4–9, 1981), p. 164.

NOTATION

B	Boussinesq coefficient, Table 1	N	rotational speed of wiping blades, rpm
c	concentration	N_T	$= uA/(\rho Q c_p)$, Equation 8
c_g	distance from cylinder wall to the center of gravity	P	power consumption
c_p	specific heat at constant pressure	q_r	wall heat flux
D	cylinder inner diameter	Q	volumetric flow rate, m^3/s
$\mathscr{D}$	axial diffusion coefficient	Q_m	time average of Q_r, Equation 6
f	correction factor	Q_r	heat flow per unit area and time t_a, Equation 5
g	acceleration due to gravity	r	radius
h	liquid-film thickness excluded liquid fillet	r_h	hydraulic radius of liquid fillet
h_{1m}	average liquid-film thickness excluded liquid fillet in main region	R	radius of wiping blades
		R_0	radius of shaft
h_2	thickness of liquid fillet	s_s	correction coefficient, Equation 29
k	ratio of circumferential velocity of liquid film to that of wiping blade tip in outlet region	S	area of liquid-fillet cross section
		t	time
		t_a	wiping interval
K	thermal conductivity of working liquid	T	temperature
l	space between electrodes	u_c	local heat transfer coefficient
L	distance from inlet to outlet of evaporator cylinder	V	circumferential velocity of wiping blade tip
L_θ	circumferential length of liquid fillet	w	average axial velocity
		W	liquid hold-up
n	number of wiping blades	z	axial coordinate

Greek Symbols

α	thermal diffusivity of working liquid	ω	angular velocity of wiping blade
δ	clearance between inner cylinder wall and wiping blade tip	λ	friction factor, $\tau/(\rho w^2/8)$
		μ_2	variance, Equation 31
ρ	density	ν	kinetic viscosity
τ	shearing stress		

Dimensionless Groups

Fr	Froude number, $\sqrt{R/h_{1m}}$	Ref'	Reynolds number for absolute velocity of liquid fillet, $4\sqrt{V^2 + w_f^2} \cdot r_h/\nu$
M	degree of mixing, $\sqrt{2\mathscr{D}/(w_m l)}$		
PeB	Peclet number, $w_m l/\mathscr{D}$	Rel	film Reynolds number, $4Q/(\pi D)/\nu$
Pr	Prandtl number, $\rho c_p \nu/K$	Rew	rotational film Reynolds number, $4Vh_{1m}/\nu$
Ref	Reynolds number for axial velocity of liquid fillet, $4w_f r_h/\nu$		

Subscripts

1	first output of tracer, Equation 31	f	in liquid fillet
2	second output of tracer, Equation 31	m	average
b	on blade	0	bulk
c	critical value	pred	predicted value
e	in outlet region	w	on wall
eff	real value	z	in axial direction
ex	experimental value	θ	in circumferential direction

Superscripts

'	absolute velocity
*	normalized value

REFERENCES

1. Latinen, G. A., *Chem. Engng. Sci.*, 9:263 (1958).
2. Harriot, P., *Chem. Engng. Prog., Symp. Ser.*, 55:137 (1959).
3. Kern, D. Q. and Karakas, H. J., *Chem. Engng. Prog., Symp. Ser.*, 55:141 (1959).
4. Ohara, S., *Kagaku Kōgaku*, 25:388 (1961).
5. Ohara, S., *Puranto Sekkei*, 58 (1965).
6. Azoory, S., *Heat Transfer and Mixing at Scraped Surface*, Ph.D. Thesis, Univ. of Birmingham, 1967.
7. Hensyūbu, Kagaku Sōchi, *Kagaku Sōchi*, 44 (1967).
8. Bott, T. R., Azoory, S., and Porter, K. E., *Trans. Inst. Chem. Engrs.*, 46:T37 (1968).
9. Azoory, S., and Bott, T. R. *Can. J. Chem. Eng.*, 48:373 (1970).
10. Schneider, R., *Chem.-Ing.-Tech.*, 27:275 (1955).
11. Dieter, V. K., *Chem.-Ing.-Tech.*, 32:521 (1960).
12. Ujhidy, A., Babos, B., and Heil, B., *Chem. Tech.*, 15:554 (1963).
13. Bott, T. R., and Romero, J. J. B., *Can. J. Chem. Eng.*, 213 (1963).
14. Fisher, R., *Chem. Engng.*, 175 (1965).
15. Dieter, V. K., and Hübner, W., *Chemiker-Z.*, 94:319 (1970).
16. Burrows, M. J., and Beveridge, G. S. G., *The Chemical Engineer*, 229 (1979).
17. Nakamura, K., *Research Reports of The Anan Technical College*, 19 (1981).

18. Nakamura, K., and Watanabe, T., *Proceedings of The 2nd World Congress of Chemical Engineering* (Montréal, Canada), 5:164 (1981).
19. Nakamura, K., and Watanabe, T., *Chem. Eng. Commun.*, 18:173 (1982).
20. Komatsu, Y., *Kemikaru Enjiniyaringu*, 228 (1965).
21. Watanabe, N., *Kagaku Sōchi*, 21:60 (1975).
22. Carter, A. L., and Kraybill, R. R. *Chem. Eng. Prog.*, 62:99 (1966).
23. Hensyūbu, Kagaku Sōchi, *Kagaku Sōchi*, 48 (1967).
24. Reay, W. H., *The Ind. Chemist.*, 3 (1963).
25. Babos, B., and Ujhidy, A., *Chem. Techn.*, 15:649 (1963).
26. Sano, H., *Kagaku Kōjō*, 10:66 (1966).
27. Hadley, G. F., and Thomas, A. L., *Ind. Eng. Chem.*, 52:71 (1960).
28. Gudheim, A. R., and Donovan, J., *Chem. Eng. Progr.*, 53:476 (1957).
29. King, P. J., *Chemical & Process Engineering*, 75 (1961).
30. Tozaki, Y., *Kemikaru Enjiniyaringu*, 40 (1969).
31. Bird, R. B., Stewart, W. E., and Lightfoot, E. N., *Transport Phenomena*, Toppan Company, 1960.
32. Domanskii, I. V., Avdonkin, A. F., and Sokolov, V. N., *Z. Prikl. Khim.*, 2009 (1971).
33. Reineman, G., Comel, M., and Dietz, H., *Chem. Techn.*, 25:143 (1973).
34. Nakamura, K., and Watanabe, T., *Kagaku Kōgaku Ronbunsyū*, 4:350 (1978).
35. Murakami, Y., et al., *Proceedings of The Society of Chemical Engineers*, Japan, Ooita Taikai, 35 (1979).
36. Murakami, Y., et. al., *Proceedings of The Society of Chemical Engineers, Japan*, Dai 46 Nen-Kai, 670 (1981).
37. Schweizer, P., and Widmer, F., *Verfahrenstechnik*, 15:29 (1981).
38. Atsumi, H., and Horiguchi, T., *Kagaku Sōchi*, 37 (1964).
39. Tsubaki, T., *Reports of RYŪTAI-KŌGAKU KENKYŪSHO, KYŪSYU University*, 5:16 (1949).
40. Ogris, H., *Wasserwirtsch.*, 54:157 (1964).
41. Bott, T. R., and Romero, J. J. B., *Can. J. Chem. Eng.*, 44:226 (1966).
42. Nakamura, K., and Watanabe, T., *Bulletin of the JSME*, 23:1483 (1980).
43. Watanabe, T., Toyama, M., and Nakamura, K., *Bulletin of the JSME*, 19:1047 (1976).
44. Vennard, J. K., *Elementary Fluid Mechanics*, Toppan Company, 1961.
45. Boussinesq, J., *J. Mathe., Pures et Appliquees*, 13:377 (1968).
46. Oki, I., *Suirikigaku*, Iwanami Shoten, 1944.
47. Bott, T. R., Azoory, S., and Porter, K. E. *Trans Instn. Chem. Engrs.*, 46:T33 (1968).
48. Unno, H., *Kagaku Sōchi*, 18:95 (1976).
49. Inoue, I., and Tonooka, Y., *Rika Gaku Kenkyūsho Hōkoku*, 40:317 (1964).
50. Bishoff, K. B., *Chem. Eng. Sci.*, 12:69 (1960).
51. Nakamura, K., and Watanabe, T., *Bulletin of the JSME*, 22:375 (1979).
52. Kunii, T, *Idō Sokudo Ron* (I), Iwanami Shoten, 1968.
53. Latinen, G. A., *Chem. Engng. Sci.*, 9:263 (1958).

CHAPTER 48

HYDRAULICS OF DISTILLATION COLUMN PIPING

Robert Kern

Hoffmann-La Roche Inc.
Nutley, NJ, USA

CONTENTS

INTRODUCTION

This chapter deals with the hydraulic system design of distillation columns: pump circuits, overhead condenser lines, and reboiler systems. A typical arrangement is shown on Figure 1.

On a distillation column, the largest lines are the overhead vapor line, reboiler downcomer and return, and the bottom pump suction line. These lines should have the simplest and most direct configurations to minimize pressure loss and cost.

Pump Circuits, Reboilers, and Condensers

During normal operation, the pumps in Figure 1 transport liquid at equilibrium. This means that the distillation column and reflux drum are evaluated to satisfy NPSH (net positive suction head) requirements. The discharge lines often have two destinations. Total-head requirements should be designed and calculated so that operating points fall on the pumps' head-capacity curves when pumping to an alternative destination. Alternative discharge lines can have equal capacity and alternative operation, or partial capacity with simultaneous operation. All alternatives should be investigated for the process pumps.

The design for a pumped reboiler circuit is similar to that of a reflux pump system. A bottom pump transports the liquid through an exchanger or fired heater and returns it to the distillation column. Close attention should be paid to possible two-phase flow in pipelines coming after the heater.

Inserted type reboilers have no process piping. Larger diameter towers can have one to four U-tube stub bundles inserted directly into the liquid space through tower nozzles, and extending across the tower diameter. Reboilers with small heat duties are usually designed as helical coils.

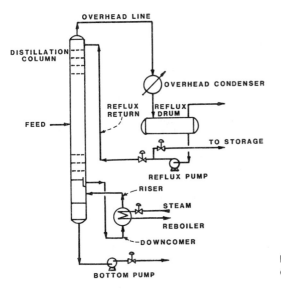

OVERHEAD LINE

DISTILLATION
COLUMN

OVERHEAD CONDENSER

REFLUX
RETURN

REFLUX
DRUM

FEED →

TO STORAGE

REFLUX PUMP

RISER

STEAM

REBOILER

DOWNCOMER

BOTTOM PUMP

Figure 1. Flow diagram of a typical distillation column.

REBOILER ARRANGEMENTS

In horizontal thermosyphon reboilers, liquid flows from an elevated drum or tower bottom or tower-trapout boot through a downcomer pipe to the bottom of exchanger shell. The liquid is heated, leaves the reboiler in the return piping as a vapor-liquid mixture, and flows back to the tower or drum.

In vertical reboilers, heating usually occurs on the shellside. In horizontal reboilers, heating is on the tubeside. For a large evaporation rate (for example, 90% of total flow), a kettle-type reboiler is used.

Piping to horizontal reboilers is designed as simply and directly as possible within the limitations of thermal-expansion forces.

Symmetrical arrangements between the drawoff and reboiler-inlet nozzles, as well as between the reboiler outlet and return connection on the tower, are preferred in order to have equal flow in the reboiler circuit. A nonsymmetrical piping configuration may also be accepted for a more-economical or more flexible piping design.

Reboilers often have two outlets and two parallel pipe segments. When sizing and arranging nonsymmetrical piping, an attempt should be made to equalize the resistance through both legs of the reboiler piping. More resistance in one leg produces a smaller flow than in the other. Hence, uneven heat distribution will occur in the reboiler—one segment of the riser will be hotter than the other.

At startup in reboilers having high, liquid drawoff nozzles, a gravity-flow bypass is usually provided from the tower's liquid space to a low point of the downcomer.

Valves are rarely included in reboiler piping, except when a standby reboiler is provided, or when two or three reboilers are used and operated at an extremely wide heat-capacity range. Some companies require line blinds to blank off the tower nozzles during shutdown, turnaround and maintenance.

The heating media (steam or a hot process stream) connect to the tubeside of horizontal reboilers. The inlet piping usually has a temperature-regulated control valve (with block valves and bypass globe valve, if required). This is normally arranged at grade near the reboiler's tubeside inlet.

Reboiler Elevations

Most reboilers are at grade next to the tower, with centerline elevations of about 3 to 5.5 ft above ground level for exchangers about 1 to 3 ft dia. Exchangers at grade provide economical arrangements—valves and instruments are accessible, tube-bundle handling is convenient, and maintenance is easy. In this arrangement, the static heads are well determined between the exchanger's centerline and the drawoff and return nozzles on the tower. Vertical reboilers are usually supported on the distillation column itself.

Some reboilers have a condensate or liquid-holding pot located after the tubeside outlet, as shown in Figure 2. In such cases, the centerline elevation of the reboiler is somewhat higher than units that do not have these control vessels.

The arrangement in Figure 2A is a high-capacity steam trap. The top of the condenser pot should not be higher than the bottom of the exchanger shell, to avoid flooding the tubes with condensate and adversely affecting the exchanger's heat-transfer duty.

The arrangement in Figure 2B maintains a required condensate level in the reboiler, to provide for a wide range of heat-transfer control. Process conditions determine the precise relationship between the exchanger and the vertical condensate-control pot.

In Figure 3, we show an example where a reboiler has been elevated to meet the NPSH requirement of the centrifugal pump. The elevated reboiler, in turn, raises the tower because the minimum liquid level in the bottom of the tower must be higher than the liquid level in the exchanger. The elevation difference (dimension H_1 in Figure 3) provides the positive static head for flow in the reboiler circuit, and overcomes friction losses in the exchanger, and downcomer and return lines.

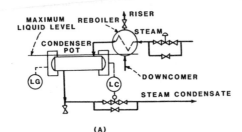

(A)

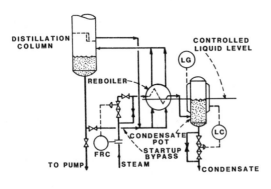

(B)

Figure 2. Process conditions determine equipment elevations: (A) bottom of reboiler should be elevated just above top of condensate pot; (B) condensate pot regulates liquid level in exchanger tubes. Physical relationship between liquid level in condensate and required liquid level in exchanger tubes is important.

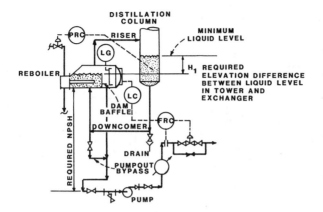

Figure 3. Reboiler elevated to meet pump's NPSH; in turn, top of dam in reboiler elevates minimum liquid level in tower.

Designing the Reboiler System

Typical reboiler arrangements are shown schematically in Figure 4. In all cases, the vessel pressure is the same at the tower's outlet and return nozzles. Circulation is forced by the static-head difference between the liquid column in the downcomer and the vapor-liquid column in the riser. For convenience, reference lines are chosen at the exchanger's centerline for horizontal reboilers, and at the bottom tubesheet for vertical reboilers.

If P_1 is liquid pressure in the downcomer at the reference line, and P_2 is backpressure in the riser's vapor-liquid column, the pressure difference ($\Delta P = P_1 - P_2$) must overcome the exchanger and piping friction losses. Therefore, P_1 must be greater than P_2. If $\rho_1 H_1/144 = P_1$, psi. The backpressure, P_2, can have two alternative expressions:

1. For horizontal exchangers (see Figure 4A and Figure 4C):

$$P_2 = \rho_2 H_2/144, \text{ psi} \tag{1}$$

where:

$$\rho_2 = \frac{W}{\dfrac{W_l}{\rho_1} + \dfrac{W_v}{\rho_v}} = \frac{100}{\dfrac{\% \text{ Liquid}}{\rho_1} + \dfrac{\% \text{ Vapor}}{\rho_v}} \tag{2}$$

2. For vertical exchangers (see Figure 4B and Figure 4D):

$$P_2' = (\rho_2 H_2 + \rho_3 H_3)/144, \text{ psi} \tag{3}$$

where ρ_2 is again the mixture's density, as expressed by Equation 2 for horizontal exchangers, and ρ_3 is the average density of liquid and liquid-vapor mixture in the reboiler:

$$\rho_3 = (\rho_1 + \rho_2)/2 \tag{4}$$

Equation 4 provides a conservative estimate of the density gradient in vertical reboilers. Actual density will be less than that expressed by Equation 4. In all equations, the units for ρ are lb/ft^3,

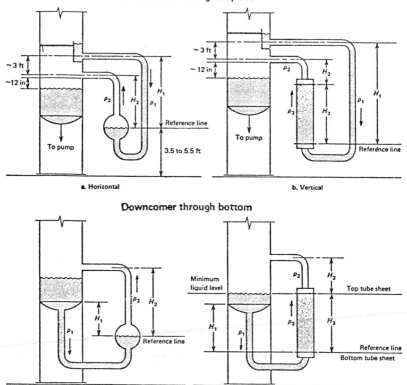

Downcomer through trapout

a. Horizontal

b. Vertical

Downcomer through bottom

c. Horizontal

d. Vertical

ρ_1, Liquid density in downcomer
ρ_2, Liquid-vapor mixture density in riser
$\rho_3 = (\rho_1 + \rho_2)/2$, Average density in vertical reboiler

Figure 4. Thermosyphon reboiler arrangements.

and for H, ft. The vertical reboiler should be flooded. The maximum elevation of the top tubesheet should not be higher than the minimum liquid level in the tower.

Hydraulics in Horizontal Reboilers

In the following discussion, the hydraulic conditions only in horizontal exchangers will be developed. (The derivations are the same for vertical exchangers, except that P_2' will replace P_2.) For horizontal exchangers:

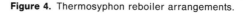

$$P_1 - P_2 = \Delta P = (1/144)(\rho_1 H_1 - \rho_2 H_2) \tag{5}$$

If a safety factor of 2 is introduced, then the available pressure difference for friction losses is halved, and:

$$\Delta P = (1/288)(\rho_1 H_1 - \rho_2 H_2) \tag{6}$$

The quantity $(H_1 - H_2)$ is usually 3 ft (see Figure 4A). Consequently, a minimum driving force of $\Delta P_{min} = (3/288)\rho_1 \approx 0.01\, \rho_1$ is always available at horizontal exchangers.

The maximum possible driving force depends on the elevation difference between the drawoff nozzle and exchanger centerline (dimension H_1) and on the total evaporation taking place in the reboiler. Neglecting the vapor-column backpressure in the return line, the maximum usable driving force is:

$$\Delta P_{max} = (H_1/288)\rho_1 \tag{7}$$

In most applications, the actual driving force is not much below this maximum. H_1 can range from 6 to 24 ft depending on the size of the arrangement and on NPSH for a pump taking suction at the bottom of the tower. For these H_1 values:

$$\Delta P_{max} = (6/288)\rho_1 \text{ to } (24/288)\rho_1 \tag{8}$$
$$\Delta P_{max} = 0.02\rho_1 \text{ to } 0.08\rho_1$$

Thus, the driving force is reduced to a function of the downcomer liquid density at operating temperature. For example, if the piping geometry produces $H_1 = 12$ ft, and $\rho_1 = 50$ lb/ft^3 for kerosene:

$$\Delta P_{max} = (12/288)50 \approx 2.0 \text{ psi}$$

These simple relationships are useful when the evaporation rate is not known and line sizes have to be estimated. The available driving force will be near but less than ΔP_{max}.

ΔP_{max} as evaluated here is, of course, an extreme value taken at total evaporation. In reboilers, partial evaporation usually takes place, which will reduce ΔP_{max}. However, even if the driving force is assumed at the maximum value, any inaccuracy is well compensated for by the safety factor of 2, and by the necessity to use commercially available pipe sizes that are normally larger than calculated pipe diameters.

Friction Losses in Reboilers

The total friction losses in a thermal-circulating reboiler system must be smaller than the available driving force. The pressure loss caused by friction takes place in two main locations: in the exchanger itself, Δp_e, and in the piping, Δp_p. Hence:

$$\Delta p_e + \Delta p_p < \Delta P$$

Friction losses in reboilers, Δp_e, are generally given as 0.25 to 0.5 psi. (A note should indicate whether entrance and exit losses are included.) Unit losses in downcomers and risers are in fractions of 1 psi/100 ft.

To avoid trial-and-error calculations, a selection chart for reboiler pipe size is presented in Figure 5. This chart is based on limiting velocities for flow in downcomers of 2 to 7 ft/s. We enter the graph with known liquid-flow quantities and obtain downcomer pipe sizes from the shaded portion of the graph, and also find the corresponding flow velocities for computing the Reynolds numbers. The riser can be assumed as one or two sizes larger than the downcomer pipe.

In vertical reboiler circuits, reboiler losses are greater, and pipe losses smaller, than in horizontal circuits. In this case, a safety factor of 1.25 applied to the driving force can be used. In kettle-type reboilers, evaporation rates are high. For these reboilers, a large-diameter return line is usually necessary.

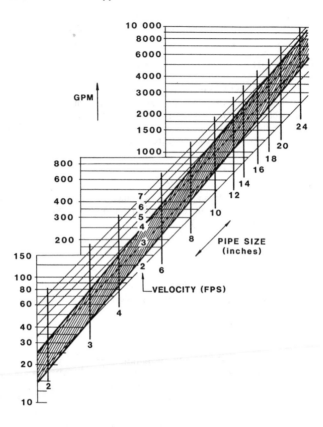

Figure 5. Chart for selecting downcomer pipe size.

Elevation of the Drawoff Nozzle

The minimum elevation, H_1, for the downcomer tower nozzle above that for the centerline of the horizontal reboiler may be found from Equation 6, where $H_2 = H_1 - 3$, ft:

$$H_1 = \frac{288\Delta p - 3\rho_2}{\rho_1 - \rho_2} \tag{9}$$

The downcomer nozzle cannot be lower than H_1. Δp replaces ΔP in Equation 6, and is the sum of the downcomer, riser and exchanger friction-losses:

$$\Delta p = \Delta p_d + \Delta p_r + \Delta p_e$$

The value of H_1 is useful when elevation adjustments are made to vessel heights during graphic piping design, or when the vessel can be located at a minimum elevation. The coefficient for ρ_2 in Equation 9 is the elevation difference between the downcomer and riser nozzles. If this is other than 3 ft, the correct dimension should be inserted.

Many towers have a bottom drawoff pump. NPSH requirements usually cause the process vessel and the reboiler drawoff nozzle to be raised higher than that of the reboiler's minimum elevation.

This increases the static head in the vertical legs, and also the driving force in the circuit. With increased tower height, it is worthwhile to check the reboiler circuit for a possible reduction in size of the liquid and return lines—especially where large-diameter lines are necessary.

OVERHEAD CONDENSER ARRANGEMENTS

The state of fluid in the pipelines, and the hydraulic and thermal conditions in condensing systems of distillation columns, are the reverse of those in reboiler circuits.

The inlet line to condensers can carry superheated or saturated vapor, or dispersed vapor-liquid mixtures. Fluid is cooled in the exchanger, and partial or full condensation takes place. The condenser's outlet line can have stratified and dispersed two-phase flow, saturated liquid, or subcooled liquid. In addition, the flowing fluid can be a mixture of two substances.

We will examine the hydraulics for the following:

1. Condensers with gravity-flow return lines.
2. Condensers with pumped-reflux lines.

Gravity-Flow Reflux

Horizontal Condensers

A condenser in gravity-flow arrangements is located above the level of the terminating point of the condenser's outlet line, as shown in Figure 6 and Figure 7. For the horizontal condenser in Figure 6B, vapor enters the exchanger at the top, and subcooled liquid leaves at the bottom. The looped-outlet pipe ensures a permanent liquid level in the condenser. The liquid flow is controlled through the reflux branch and through the takeoff line to storage.

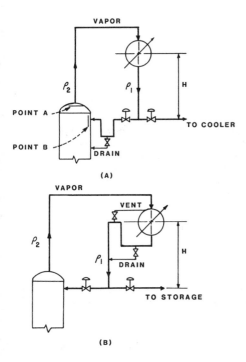

Figure 6. Horizontal condensers with gravity flow reflux: (A) saturated liquid (shell-side condensation); (B) subcooled liquid (shell-side condensation).

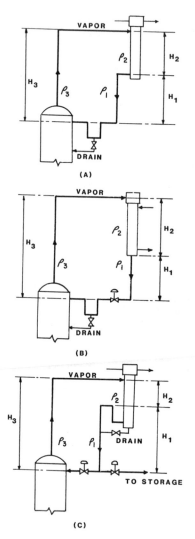

Figure 7. Vertical condensers with gravity flow reflux: (A) saturated liquid (shell-side condensation); (B) saturated liquid (tube-side condensation); (C) subcooled liquid (shell-side condensation).

The static-head pressure difference, ΔP_s, between the vertical overhead line and the condenser's outlet line for the arrangements in Figure 6 can be written as:

$$\Delta P_s = (H/144)(\rho_1 - \rho_2) \tag{11}$$

ΔP_s must be equal to or greater than the sum of (1) the pipe-system resistance, Δp_p, between reference points A and B; (2) exchanger pressure drop, Δp_e; and (3) required pressure difference across the control valve, Δp_{cv}:

$$\Delta P_s \geq \Delta p_p + \Delta p_e + \Delta p_{cv} \tag{12}$$

The required distance, H, between fractionator inlet and exchanger centerline can be calculated from Equation 1 as:

$$H = (144\Delta P_s)/(\rho_1 - \rho_2) \tag{13}$$

The vapor column can be neglected by assuming $\rho_2 = 0$ in Equations 11 and 13. All pressures are in psi; densities, ρ, in lb/ft³; and dimensions, H, in ft.

As Equation 13 shows, for a minimum of elevation difference between the top of the column and the exchanger centerline, the piping and components resistances must also be minimal.

Generally, in condensing systems, the unit loss in the piping is low—about a tenth or a hundredth of 1 psi/100 ft. Inlet and outlet resistances to process equipment usually take a considerable portion of the pipeline resistance and should not be ignored in the calculations. (Using three decimal places in the calculations is not unusual.)

In horizontal condensers, condensation takes place in the shell. This gives lower resistance than the tubeside. A baffle (or baffles) in the exchanger is in the horizontal plane through the exchanger's centerline. If necessary, two inlet and two outlet nozzles can halve the total flow, and reduce entrance and exit resistances considerably. In this case, the inlet and outlet piping should be symmetrical.

The subcooled liquid for the arrangement in Figure 6B can be drained or pumped directly to storage. The product stream for Figure 6A is usually directed through a cooler before storage.

Control valves in these systems should be located at a low point of the return line and product stream. Sufficient static head before the valve inlet will prevent vaporization across the valve. A product cooler should not receive a liquid-vapor mixture.

Vertical Condensers

Arrangements for these condensers with gravity-flow outlets are shown in Figure 7. Condensation can take place in the shell (Figure 7A), or tubes (Figure 7B). A single-pass vertical condenser is more suitable for liquid subcooling than a horizontal one. The seal-loop height can be adjusted with in a greater range than with horizontal condensers (Figure 7C). The required liquid level in the exchanger shell is determined by the exchanger's designer.

The hydraulic balance for the arrangements shown in Figure 7 is:

$$(1/144)(H_1\rho_1 + H_2\rho_2) \geq (1/144)H_3\rho_3 + \Delta P \tag{14}$$

where ΔP is the sum of piping, Δp_p, exchanger, Δp_e, and control-valve (if any), Δp_{cv}, resistances:

$$\Delta P = \Delta p_p + \Delta p_e + \Delta p_{cv} \tag{15}$$

The elevation difference, as expressed from Equation 14, between the condenser's outlet and the reflux inlet nozzle will be:

$$H_1 \geq (1/\rho_1)(H_3\rho_3 - H_2\rho_2 + 144\Delta P) \tag{16}$$

where ρ_1 is the density of condensate in the reflux line, ρ_3 is the vapor density in the overhead line, and ρ_2 is the average density in the vertical exchanger:

$$\rho_2 = 0.5(\rho_1 + \rho_2) \tag{17}$$

Seal Loops

In gravity-flow condensing systems, a seal loop is provided to prevent a reversed flow of vapor in the condenser's outlet line. This loop can be used for holding a liquid level in the condenser, as shown in Figure 6A and Figure 7C.

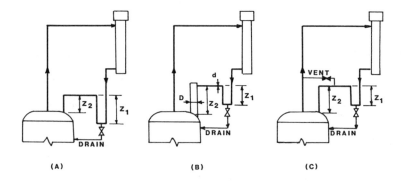

Figure 8. Seal loop arrangement to prevent reverse flow in downcomer: (A) $Z_1 > Z_2$; (B) $Z_1 < Z_2$; (C) $Z_1 < Z_2$.

If the gravity-flow reflux line terminates in a vertical leg (Z_2 dimension in Figure 8), the piping design should be such as to prevent siphoning that can empty the seal. If dimension Z_1 is smaller than Z_2, and the pressure just before the seal loop and at the terminating point after the seal loop is identical (for example, with greatly reduced flow), liquid can be siphoned out of the seal; and intermittently, the condenser will not operate well. This can be prevented if Z_1 is designed to be longer than Z_2 (see Figure 8A).

For the arrangement in Figure 8B, the final vertical leg has a larger diameter than the gravity-flow reflux line. Again, this can prevent the siphoning of liquid from the seal loop.

Another arrangement (Figure 8C) has a closed vent line. This can be opened at reduced condensate flow to keep the seal loop filled with liquid. With this type of venting, the pressure difference across the vent valve should be zero. Therefore, it is essential to connect the end-points of the vent line to locations where pressures are expected to be about equal.

Pumped-Reflux Arrangements

Typical overhead lines for hydrocarbon distillation columns are shown in Figure 9. Fluid circulation in the piping is the result of the thermosiphon effect in gravity-reflux condensation. For the systems shown in Figure 9 there is (and most of the time must be) a pressure difference between the top of the tower and reflux drum. The reflux drum has a pump, which returns the liquid to the top of the tower or sends it to storage.

In these arrangements (besides the sum of the static heads), actual pressure differences, ΔP_p, also enter into the calculations:

$$\Delta P_p = P_1 - P_2 \tag{18}$$

For the dimensions given in Figure 10, the static-head difference will be:

$$\Delta P_s = (1/144)(\rho_1 H_1 - \rho_2 H_2) \tag{19}$$

where ρ_1 is usually vapor density, and ρ_2 is vapor-liquid mixture (or liquid) density. The overall available ΔP is the sum of Equations 18 and 19, or:

$$\Delta P = \Delta P_s + \Delta P_p \tag{20}$$

If the right-hand side of Equation 20 becomes negative, the condenser must be placed at an elevation closer to, or above, the reflux drum. A negative value indicates that the static-head backpressure ($\rho_2 H_2$) in Equation 19 is greater than the sum of (1) pressure difference between the top of the tower

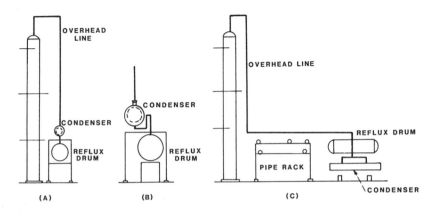

Figure 9. Overhead condenser piping: (A) simplest overhead line gives the smallest pipe size; (B) subcooled liquid in the gravity flow; (C) remote condenser location increases line length, number of fittings, and pipe diameter.

and the reflux drum plus (2) the vapor static head $(\rho_1 H_1)$ in the overhead line. The greater the condensation, the heavier the mixture becomes in the condenser's outlet line, which results in a greater backpressure. Of course, $\rho_2 H_2$ becomes positive when the line has a gravity-flow arrangement between the condenser outlet and the reflux-drum inlet, as shown in Figure 9A and Figure 9B.

Equation 20 shows the driving force in the overhead system. This must be greater than the sum of piping, inlet and exit losses, Δp_p, and exchanger resistance, Δp_e:

$$\Delta P > \Delta p_p + \Delta p_e \tag{21}$$

Δp_p usually is between 2 to 6 psi, and condenser Δp_s ranges from 0.5 to 5 psi.

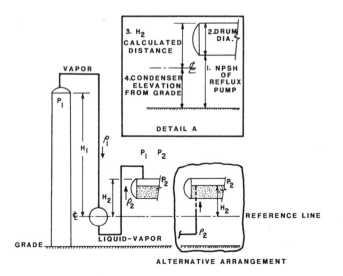

Figure 10. Piping for condenser at grade.

The maximum possible condenser-centerline location below the reflux drum (dimension H_2 in Figure 10) can be calculated from the combination of Equations 19, 20, and 21, to give:

$$(1/144)(\rho_1 H_1 - \rho_2 H_2) + \Delta P_p - (\Delta p_p + \Delta p_e) = 0 \tag{22}$$

As a safety factor, the positive static-head column pressure of the overhead vapor line can be neglected. Consider:

$\rho_1 H_1 = 0$.

Expressing H_2 from Equation 22 in feet, we get:

$$H_2 = (144/\rho_2)(\Delta P_p - \Delta p_p - \Delta p_e) \tag{23}$$

In layout design, usually the reflux drum is elevated first in accordance with the required NPSH (net positive suction head) of the reflux pump. The dimensions shown in Detail A of Figure 10 will establish the condenser elevation from grade.

Slug Flow

Slug flow can develop in the pocketed condenser-outlet line shown in Figure 10, depending on vapor-liquid proportion and fluid velocity. Slug flow should be avoided because it can cause undesirable pressure surges.

An empirical relation can be used to estimate the slug-flow region. If the velocity (calculated with two-phase desity) in the pipeline is smaller than $(5\rho_1/\rho_v)^{1/2}$, slug flow is possible.

The general criterion for selecting a suitable line size is that the pipe diameter must be sufficiently small to have the highest possible velocity, but large enough to stay within available pressure differential. The possibility of slug flow can be minimized by (a) increasing the pressure drop in the condenser's outlet line and reducing the resistance of the rest of the condensing system, (b) providing two parallel lines between condenser and reflux drum, (c) using valved alternative pipe runs for alternative flowrates, and (d) changing to a gravity-flow arrangement.

CHAPTER 49

HYDRODYNAMICS AND HOLD-UP IN AIR-LIFT REACTORS

Jose C. Merchuk

Department of Chemical Engineering
Ben-Gurion University of the Negev, Beer Sheva, Israel

INTRODUCTION

The name "air-lift reactor" denotes a wide range of gas-liquid contacting devices. Air lifts are distinguished by fluid circulation in a clear and defined cyclic pattern through channels built for this purpose. Fluid circulation and turbulence are generated by the injected gas. Usually, one of the gas-stream components is absorbed or desorbed into the liquid phase.

Generally, in biological processes oxygen and CO_2 are transferred between the gas and liquid phases. In fermentation or cell culture oxygen is the absorbed gas and CO_2 is desorbed. In the case of algal growth in photobio-reactors CO_2 is absorbed. Potentially, many chemical reactions can be carried out in air-lift reactors.

This chapter discusses the basic characteristics of air-lift reactors: gas hold-up and liquid velocity. These two parameters predominantly depend on the gas flow rate, reactor configuration and design, and the physical properties of the system. The gas hold-up and liquid velocity will determine process parameters such as interfacial area, mass transfer rate, heat dissipation rate, mean residence time of the gas, and process yield. All of these variables are interrelated and affect each other. However, a basic characteristic of air-lift reactors is that the main and easiest-to-manipulate variable is the gas flow rate.

Advantages of Air-Lift Reactors

Industrial-scale air-lift reactors have been designed and constructed for a few specific processes: waste-water treatment, single-cell protein production, and fuel ethanol production [1]. On the other hand, many experiments have been carried on a laboratory scale for a wide range of products. Some of them have been summarized by Onken and Weiland [1].

Air-lift devices offer several advantages over conventional bioreactors. The first advantage is simplicity: no moving mechanical parts are needed for agitation and this eliminates the danger of contamination through seals or the need for complicated magnetically-driven agitators. Additionally, all the energy required for agitation enters the system with the gas stream, which has a two-fold purpose: gas exchange and agitation. This promotes efficiency in the overall energy balance.

When compared to conventional bubble columns, air-lift reactors present the advantages of a loop reactor, which have been recognized in the chemical industry [2] and can be classified into three groups:

1. Increased heat and mass transfer capacity.
2. Reduction of energy consumption for mixing.
3. Easier scale-up from pilot-plant data.

In the case of biological processes, an additional advantage seems to be related to shear stress imposed by the turbulent field on cells or pellets suspended in the medium. This is especially important in plant and animal cells, which are very sensitive to stress [3–8]. In the case of microorganisms that are grown in the form of pellets, it has already been recognized [9–13] that turbulence is an important parameter in determining pellet size and density. Also in the case of bacterial cells, it has been reported that the mean cell volume is strongly affected by the agitation in the medium where they grow [14–15]. This emphasizes the need to understand the hydrodynamic behavior of an air-lift reactor. The main limitation of air-lift reactors is that they are not effective in handling high-viscosity fluids. This is due to high energy dissipation from wall friction leading to very low circulation velocity and inefficient mixing.

Morphology

When designing or interpreting data on air-lift reactors, it must be clearly recognized that the system is not a simple unit that can be scaled up as a whole. It is the sum of three connected elements: the riser, the gas separator, and the downcomer.

The Riser

The riser is the section where both gas and liquid flow upwards, the gas being injected at the bottom of this section. The type of gas sparger used may influence the hold-up of the gas and the recirculation rate [16, 17, 18]. The riser is in fact a bubble column and the main difference resides in the range of liquid velocities. Figure 1, adapted from Weiland and Onken [19], shows the respective ranges within which bubble columns and air-lift reactors are usually operated. An overlapping can be seen, and denotes the cases where the recirculation of the liquid is severely constrained by the design [20, 21] and the riser operates like a bubble column.

The Gas Separator

The gas separator is the section where the gas disenganges, totally or partially, from the liquid. The design of this section determines whether bubbles are recirculated or not, and is therefore crucial to liquid recirculation rate and total gas hold-up.

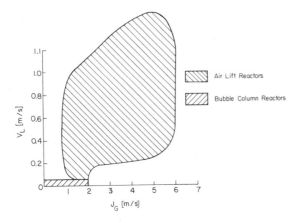

Figure 1. Typical operating ranges of air-lift reactors and bubble-column reactors.

The Downcomer

The downcomer is the section where the liquid flows down from the top to the bottom of the reactor. Depending on the specific process carried out, it may be desirable to prevent or increase bubble recirculation. In aerobic fermentations, to avoid recirculation of small bubbles with a low concentration of oxygen and a relatively high concentration of CO_2, it is desirable to prevent bubble recirculation. In systems that are not tall enough to assure satisfactory absorption of the gas component during a single pass, bubble recirculation is increased.

The general behavior of an air-lift reactor is due to the interaction of these three parts. The specific characteristics of each section should be taken into consideration in the design and scale-up of the reactor.

Classification

Several types of air lift design have been tested, and they may be classified by various criteria [1, 20]. Morphologically, there can be two classes, external loop [2, 16, 19, 20, 22–29], and baffled vessels or columns [29–47]. Figure 2 shows these classes schematically. In the first, the downcomer is a separate conduit, usually a round pipe, which runs parallel to the riser; this configuration is very convenient for heat dissipation, since it is very simple to insert a heat exchanger in the downcomer. These types of reactors can be operated at high gas throughput without much bubble recirculation.

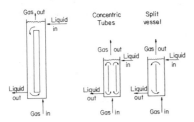

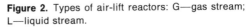

Figure 2. Types of air-lift reactors: G—gas stream; L—liquid stream.

In the second class of air-lift reactors, baffled vessels or columns, we have included several types of reactors that have been treated separately by other authors [1, 20]. They have in common that a single vessel is split by a vertical baffle, which can be a simple slab producing two sections in a tube [33, 35, 36, 39], or a rectangular vessel. Another common design is the use of a concentric tube as a baffle [15, 17, 18, 29, 32, 34, 37, 38, 41, 44]. Simplicity of construction is the most appealing characteristic of this type of air-lift reactor. The downcomer and the riser are simply connected at the end of the baffle. By changing the distance between the lower edge of the baffle and the bottom of the reactor, the hydraulic pressure drop in this region can be altered. Consequently, the liquid recirculation velocity, the gas holdup, and the mixing in the whole reactor is also changed. By varying the depth of submersion of the upper edge of the vertical baffle, the operation of the gas separator may be affected, especially if the level of the ungassed liquid is immediately below this edge [33]. The effectiveness of gas separation will also affect the gas holdup in the downcomer, and therefore the liquid recirculation rate and turbulence.

In the baffled vessel air-lift reactors, the gas separator is usually just the continuation of the vessel or column above the upper edge of the baffle. Consequently, the downcomer will remain ungassed only at very low liquid velocities. This usually corresponds to low gas flow rates, unless the circulation rate is severely restricted. This can be due to too small a distance between the lower edge of the baffle and the bottom, or by the presence of horizontal baffles. After a minimum liquid velocity is achieved, a considerable amount of bubbles are recirculated, and the total gas holdup is markly increased. In some cases [30, 31], a special design of the gas separator is provided to prevent this bubble recirculation.

MEASURING METHODS

Many experimental methods have been used for measurement of the parameters characterizing two-phase flow [49, 50, 51]. Much of this work has been done to obtain information about the safety and performance of pressurized-water- and boiling-water-type nuclear reactors and of boilers in general. This includes the whole range of gas-liquid flow configurations that may be present during boiling. Flow configurations that are easily attained in narrow tubes, such as slug flow, mist flow, or annular flow, are not present at the usual flow rate ranges in air-lift reactors, especially in full-scale reactors.

Liquid velocity can be easily measured by standard methods in the case of complete bubble disengagement in the gas separator, since bubble-free liquid flows in the downcomer. For the case of two-phase flow in the downcomer, Pitot tubes, photographic techniques, laser scattering, tracer particles, and many variations of these methods have been used [56].

The gas hold-up can be measured locally by many methods, such as manometric, conductance, and capacitance techniques. The manometric methods are the easiest and cheapest to implement, and have been used by most researchers reporting results on air-lift reactors.

The main problems in measuring two-phase pressure drops are [56]:

1. The ambiguity about which of the two fluids is actually in the lines connecting the manometers to the reactor. This can be solved by strategically located drains, and by using great care during the experiments to detect the penetration of bubbles into the lines.
2. The pressure fluctuations in time inherent to the bubbling regime make it difficult to average the pressure drop data. A simple method of overcoming this problem is the abatement of these fluctuations by inserting capillary sections in the lines, at the cost of a delay in the response of the manometers.
3. The total pressure drop between two points in a vertical tube are due to hydrostatic head, friction losses, and acceleration effects. The weight of these contributions decreases in this order and the last is usually negligible. Many researchers have completely neglected both acceleration and frictional pressure drop. This is probably due to the analogy to bubble columns, where the net liquid velocity is zero and frictional losses are difficult to evaluate. This assumption can lead to considerable errors, especially in tall equipment of small diameter.

Several researchers have carefully computed these effects [16, 19, 23]. Merchuk and Stein [16] presented the following model considering hydrostatic head, frictional losses, and acceleration effects. Assuming unidirectional isothermal flow, steady state, constant cross-section, negligible mass transfer effects between gas and liquid, and constant properties in a cross-section, the momentum balance equations for the liquid phase are given by Wallis [52] as:

$$-\rho_L A_L g dz - A_L dp + (\tau_{GL} C_{GL} - \tau_{wL} C_{wL}) dz = \overline{dm_L V_L} \tag{1}$$

Similarly, for the gas phase considered as a separate continuous phase:

$$-\rho_G A_G g dz - A_G dp + (\tau_{LG} C_{LG} - \tau_{wG} C_{wG}) dz = \overline{dm_G V_G} \tag{2}$$

In this case,

$$A_L + A_G = A \tag{3}$$

$$C_{LG} = C_{GL} \tag{4}$$

$$\tau_{LG} = -\tau_{GL} \tag{5}$$

$$C_{wL} = \pi D_c \tag{6}$$

Introducing the gas hold-up as:

$$A_G = \phi A \tag{7}$$

and considering that the gas-wall friction is negligible with respect to the liquid-wall friction, a single expression that relates ϕ and V_L to the energy losses in the tube is obtained. Relating the superficial liquid velocity, $J_L = Q_L/A$, to the liquid flux V_L by:

$$V_L = \frac{J_L}{1 - \phi} \tag{8}$$

we obtain:

$$-\frac{dp}{dz} = \frac{4\tau_{wL}}{D_c} + \rho_L J_L^2 \frac{d}{dz}\left(\frac{1}{1-\phi}\right) + \rho_L g(1 - \phi) \tag{9}$$

The terms in the right-hand side of Equation 9 represent, from left to right, the pressure drop due to friction, acceleration, and gravitation. If the total pressure drop is measured with a differential manometer, the height h observed is related to the pressure by:

$$(\rho_L - \rho_m)g\frac{dh}{dz} = \frac{dp}{dz} + \rho_L g \tag{10}$$

To express the frictional term, the following expression [52] was used:

$$\tau_{wL} = \frac{1}{2} C_{fM} \rho_M J_M^2 \tag{11}$$

where

$$J_M = J_L + J_G \tag{12}$$

$$J_G = Q_G/A \tag{13}$$

$$\rho_M = \rho_L(1 - \phi) + \rho_G\phi \tag{14}$$

Equation 11 can be approximated as:

$$\tau_{WL} = \frac{1}{2}C_{fM}\rho_L J_L J_M \tag{15}$$

The coefficient C_{fM} is given by Nassos and Bankoff [53] as:

$$C_{fM} = 0.046\,N_{Re}^{-0.2} \tag{16}$$

where the Reynolds number is given by:

$$N_{Re} = \frac{\rho_L J_L D_L}{(1 - \phi)\mu_L} \tag{17}$$

When Equations 10, 15, 16, and 17 are substituted into Equation 9, an implicit expression of the gas hold-up can be obtained as:

$$\phi = \frac{0.092\,J_L^{0.8}J_M}{g(v_L)^{-0.2}D_c^{1.2}}(1 - \phi)^{0.2} + \frac{J_L^2}{g(1 - \phi)^2}\frac{d\phi}{dz} + \frac{(\rho_m - \rho_L)}{\rho_L}\frac{dh}{dz} \tag{18}$$

The derivative of the manometer height h with respect to z, the height of the equipment, can be obtained measuring the pressure drop at a number of points along the column. A series of h-data points is obtained, which can be related to z by a polynomial equation, and the derivative can easily be evaluated.

The variation of hold-up along the height of the riser is evaluated from the second derivative of the experimental data, taking:

$$\frac{d\phi}{dz} = \frac{(\rho_m - \rho_L)}{\rho_L}\frac{d^2h}{dz^2} \tag{19}$$

Equation 19 is an approximation used to evaluate the hold-up derivative in Equation 18, and implies that the contribution of the variations of the frictional and accelerational terms to the changes in hold-up along the column are negligible. The lower the gas flow rates, the better this approximation. Equation 18 shows three terms representing, from left to right, friction, acceleration, and static head. Typically, the friction term will contribute less than 1/5 to the total hold-up ϕ, and the acceleration term less than 1%. With very high gas flow rates, the acceleration term will increase to 2% or 3% of ϕ. Therefore, the approximation given by Equation 19 is considered satisfactory.

The overall flux J_M is given by Equation 12. In Equation 12, J_L is constant along the column for given operational conditions, but J_G varies, increasing towards the top of the column. J_G can be calculated from the measurements in the rotameters and from the pressure and temperature at each height [54].

In the work reported by Merchuk and Stein [16], each experimental point was independently repeated several times and a fourth-order polynomial was fitted to them. An example of the dispersion of the experimental points and the polynomial fitting for a typical operational condition can be seen in Figure 3. With the exception of the zone of small values of z near the gas sparger, the deviation of the experimental points is about 1%.

Once the profile of hold-up along the equipment height has been obtained, the integral hold-up can be calculated as:

$$\phi = \frac{1}{L}\int_0^L \phi(z)dz \tag{20}$$

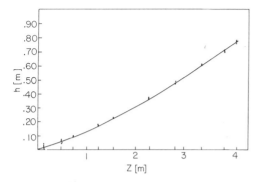

Figure 3. Manometer readings along the column and the corresponding polynomial fit for a typical operating condition [16].

FLOW PATTERNS

The flow pattern in the column helps to understand the variation of gas holdup with changes in the gas flow rate. A convenient device for the study of flow patterns is the two-dimensional column. It has been shown that the walls affect the ascending velocity of the bubbles, especially at low bubble-generation frequency [57]. However, Yamashita and Inoue [58] showed that the behavior of bubble swarms is similar in two- and three- dimensional columns. A two-dimensional air lift is easily transformed into a bubble column, by simply closing a valve in the downcomer [59].

When operating the two-dimensional air lift with the downcomer closed and with low gas velocities, bubbles ascend in straight lines, especially in the lower half of the column. In the top half of the column, they begin to oscillate (Figure 4A), apparently due to the increase in bubble diameter caused by the decrease of the hydrostatic pressure and some degree of coalescence. However, as the gas velocity increases, the oscillations of the bubbles increase in amplitude and a mainstream is generated, characterized by high local velocity and larger bubbles. Recirculation cells that oscillate in accordance to the mainstream line appear at the sides of the column, and small bubbles are trapped in these cells. With a further increase in gas velocity, the frequency of the oscillations increases sharply while the amplitude remains constant or increases slightly. This leads to a sharp increase in the turbulance. The recirculation flow rate in the side cells increases at the expense of the central path, which, under these conditions, consists of the largest bubbles present in the system (Figure 4C). A clear downstream pattern develops, bringing to the bottom of the column the smallest bubbles. At even higher values of superficial gas velocity, the weight of the main central path increases. The amplitude of the oscillation decreases and most of the gas passes rapidly through the center, while the loops at the sides become even more turbulent.

Flow configurations B and C correspond to the "transition regime" between uniform bubbling regime and the liquid recirculation regime. They exist in bubble columns having a sparger hole diameter of less than about 0.01 m [52]. One of the characteristics of this regime is a maximum in the gas hold-up. A critical superficial velocity has been defined [60, 61] as the superficial gas velocity at maximum hold-up, and is supposed to be the point where incipient regular recirculation begins.

The flow patterns observed when the value in the downcomer is completely open were substantially different from those just reported in bubble columns, especially at high gas velocities. In general, the bubbles ascend in straight lines and the oscillations observed in bubble columns appear only at high gas velocities, above the middle of the column. The movement of the liquid appears less turbulent. Two bubbles may ascend side by side for a long distance without touching each other, since the lateral components of the velocity vector are very small. Therefore, less coalescence is observed. The shape of the bubbles is rounder, probably due to a low gas-liquid relative velocity.

As the valve located in the downcomer is gradually closed, the flow pattern changes in the direction of higher liquid turbulence and a less-organized flow of bubbles and local recirculation.

A differentiation should be made between net and local liquid circulation. Net circulation refers to the net flow of liquid entering the bottom of the two-dimensional riser and leaving at the top

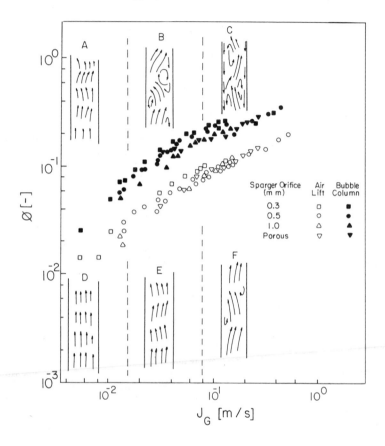

Figure 4. Gas holdup in a two-dimensional bubble column with and without external recirculation [59] and the flow patterns observed.

of the gas separator. Local circulation refers to recirculation within the riser. In other words, the local circulation loops inside the two-dimensional column itself.

In general, the net liquid circulation delays establishment of the so-called "transition regime" [52, 60]. Only at the higher superficial gas velocities does the bubble swarm begin to meander, but local recirculation is not detected. Ueyama and Miyauchi [62], who extended to the recirculation flow regime the relation originally derived by Nicklin [63] for the bubble regime, report that recirculation starts when the superficial gas velocity exceeds 0.05 m/s. The flow patterns observed in the two-dimensional air lift indicate that when net recirculation is not hindered, the transition regime, which is associated with local recirculation loops, does not appear even at much higher superficial gas velocities. This is in complete agreement with the observations of Weiland and Onken [1].

Figure 4 shows the change of air holdup in water in a two-dimensional air lift and bubble column obtained with four different gas spargers. The two distinctive differences are:

1. The gas content in the air lift is lower than in the bubble column.
2. A maximum in holdup, which characterizes the behavior of the two-dimensional bubble column near the critical superficial velocity, does not appear in the experimental data obtained

in the air-lift device. This is due to the effect of the liquid velocity, which retards the phenomenon of internal recirculation. This has been previously explained and shown in the observed recirculation patterns of Figure 4. The high velocity of the liquid increases the distance between bubbles, and therefore decreases the coalescence frequency. Also, due to a more uniform distribution of bubbles across the air-lift cross section, there is a further reduction in coalescence.

GAS HOLD-UP

The gas hold-up is very important not only because of its influence on the fluid dynamics in the reactor, but also because of its direct influence on the mass transfer between gas and liquid. The gas hold-up is a direct indication of the interfacial area. At a given throughput, the hold-up will be larger as the drift velocity, V_d, is smaller. This velocity is the difference between the velocity of the gas and the superficial velocity of the mixture [51].

$$V_d = V_g - J_M \tag{21}$$

The drift velocity is positive in the riser and negative in the downcomer. Since the gas flow rate in the downcomer is only a fraction of the gas flow rate in the riser, the hold-up in the downcomer will always remain lower, which is a necessary condition for circulation.

Local Gas Hold-up

The distribution of the gas hold-up along the column is also affected by the liquid recirculation. Figures 5 and 6 present the local value of gas hold-up in air-lift reactor with external downcomer [16]. Both riser and downcomer were round tubes 0.14 m in diameter and the total height of the tubes was 4.05 m. Figure 5 shows the local values of the hold-up along the riser for two different spargers: a 0.09-m-diameter copper tube bent to form a 0.10-m-diameter ring, in which fourteen 0.025-m-diameter holes were drilled (sparger A) and a single-orifice 0.09-m-diameter sparger (sparger B). Figure 6 is a similar plot for the case of partial obstruction of the downcomer. By increasing the resistance to liquid recirculation, the liquid velocity can be changed independently of the gas velocity.

Figures 5 and 6 show that the local values of the hold-up can increase up to 80% from the initial value at the bottom of the column in the range of variables studied. Figure 5 shows the gas hold-up at high values of superficial liquid velocities. A clear qualitative difference is seen between the data corresponding to an approximately even distribution of gas (sparger A) and the single-orifice sparger B. The data corresponding to sparger A increase almost linearly with z, while those corresponding to sparger B increase more sharply at low z, reach a maximum, and then decrease. The maximum tends to appear earlier as the superficial gas velocity increases. The same phenomenon is even more pronounced in Figure 6, where partial closure of the downcomer causes lower liquid velocities. In this case, sparger A also gives profiles of ϕ that show a local maximum.

The linear ϕ profiles for sparger A in Figure 5 indicate that coalescence is not important in this case. Bubbles ascend almost without interaction. The increase in hold-up indicates that the growth of bubbles due to the decrease of pressure prevails over the effect of the increase in ascending velocity.

An additional manifestation related to the same phenomenon is the generation of descending sidestreams near the walls. These appear in order to compensate for the high liquid velocity in the center with a given value of the net liquid flux [68]. This augments the overall hold-up and reaches an extreme at zero net liquid flow. Figure 6 shows the effect of partial closure of the downcomer, which reduces the liquid flow and consequently increases the internal recirculation. This leads not only to an increase in the hold-up, but also to an accentuation of the phenomenon of a maximum in local values of hold-up. The single-orifice sparger creates an uneven distribution of gas in the riser, and the bubbles generated are larger. This produces a higher mixture velocity in the center of the tube. The large differences in liquid velocity induce a migration of the larger bubbles toward the axis. Thus, a high concentration of bubbles is created around the axis, which increases the coalescence. This phenomenon of enrichment of large bubbles in the center of the column is well known

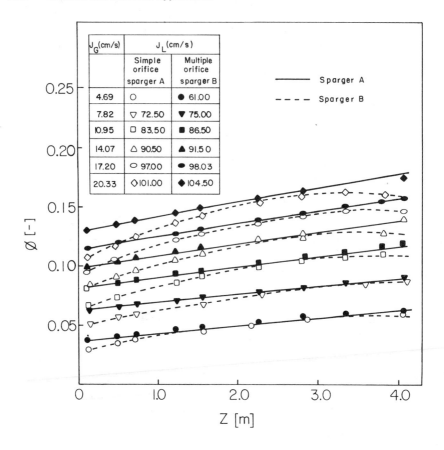

Figure 5. Dependence of gas hold-up ϕ on the distance from the sparger z for various gas velocities with the downcomer fully open [16].

[62, 66] and has been used to explain the existence of a maximum integral gas hold-up as a function of the superficial gas velocity. This is obtained with a single-orifice sparger and does not occur with a perforated plate or porous sparger [67].

Local values of the hold-up have also been reported for a baffled vessel air lift [33]. The experiments were performed using a split cylinder air lift, 1.5 m high, with equal cross-sections for riser and downcomer. The hold-up in the riser increased from the bottom to the top. The height of the ungassed liquid above the baffle exerted an influence on the hold-up, as expected. Thus, in this type of design the amount of liquid determines the effectiveness of the gas separator.

Integral Gas Hold-up

In the definition of the integral gas hold-up ϕ, Equation 20, L can be taken as the total length of the loop, or as the length of only one of the sections of the air-lift reactor. Therefore, the integral hold-up may refer to the riser, the downcomer, the separator, or all three sections together.

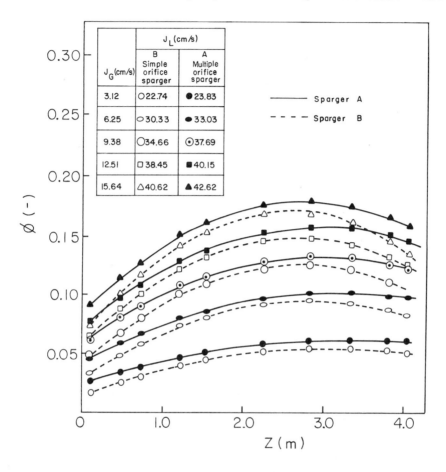

Figure 6. Dependence of gas hold-up ϕ on the distance from the sparger z for various gas velocities with 43% of the downcomer section open [16].

Riser

In external loop air-lift reactors, bubble recirculation can be avoided even at high gas throughput. In this case, the riser operates like a bubble column in the sense that the gas flow rate at any section is the same as that measured externally (no gas recirculation). Comparison between the hold-up in bubble columns and air-lift reactors is straightforward. However, it should be noted that hold-up in the air-lift reactor refers, in this case, to the riser that represents only a fraction of the total reactor volume.

Difficulty arises in the presentation of experimental data in a concise and general form. In addition to the influence of the column diameter, which has been studied and satisfactorily correlated for bubble columns [64, 65], the geometric design of the downcomer and the gas separator have a strong influence on the liquid circulation velocity. This, consequently, strongly affects the gas hold-up. This

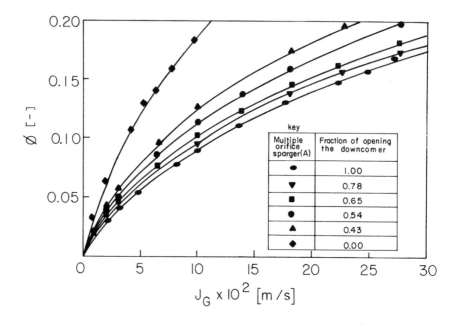

Figure 7. Gas hold-up in the riser of an external loop air-lift reactor for several different openings of the downcomer section, multiorifice sparger (sparger A) [16].

can be seen clearly in Figure 7 where the overall gas hold-up in the riser is plotted against the superficial gas velocity, J_G, for several degrees of obstruction in the downcomer [16]. The behavior agrees with the published data on bubble columns. It shows a sharp increase in the low range of superficial gas velocity, followed by a lower rate increase as J_G gets larger. No maxima such as those reported by Schugerl et al. [67], among many others, were found within the range of flows examined. The influence of closure of the downcomer, which decreases the superficial liquid velocity, is very strong, especially as the free section of the downcomer becomes smaller. The maximum values of ϕ always occur in a completely closed downcomer at zero superficial liquid velocity.

Figure 8 shows data on gas hold-up for single- and multiple-orifice spargers, plotted with J_L, the superficial liquid velocity, as a parameter. This form of graph is very common in reporting data on bubble columns where J_L is independent of J_G. Figure 8 shows that the mean hold-up, for all superficial liquid velocities, is higher in the case of the multiple-orifice sparger A. This is in agreement with data reported by Freedman and Davidson [69] and Schugerl et al. [67].

The influence of gas sparger configuration on hold-up has also been reported in baffled vessels with concentric tubes [17, 18]. Chakravarti et al. [45] reported that a single-orifice sparger gave higher gas hold-up, especially at low superficial gas velocities. The effect disappears at high superficial gas velocities. In analyzing Chakravarti's data, it should be noted that their air lift was only 0.73 m high. Thus, bypass or larger bubbles can be expected. Many of the experiments reported in this type of vessel have this same limitation.

Downcomer

The gas hold-up in the downcomer of air-lift reactors has been reported only for a few cases [22, 32, 42, 44]. All the bubbles disengage at the top and almost clear liquid circulates in the downcomer, up to a certain superficial gas velocity. As the gas flow rate increases, some bubbles

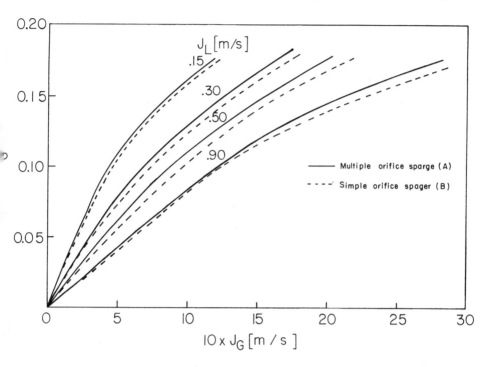

Figure 8. Gas hold-up in the riser for various liquid flow rates and two different spargers [16].

are trapped at the inlet of the downcomer. However, after the entrance zone, a front is formed separating bubbly liquid from bubble-free liquid.Distribution of bubbles according to size occurs, with larger bubbles escaping upwards. The front of the bubbly liquid consists of bubbles of almost equal size. As the flow rate increases, the front moves progressively downwards till it eventually reaches the bottom and gas recirculation begins. Chakravarti et al. [44, 45] reported measurements of gas hold-up in the annulus of a concentric tube air-lift reactor, where air was injected below the central tube. They proposed a model to predict the minimum velocity required for bubble recirculation. The reported data are consistent for the different types of air-lift reactors. The data show that the behavior of the hold-up in the downcomer is similar to that in the riser, but with lower absolute values, as expected.

If the gas hold-up in the downcomer rises above a critical value, the direction of flow may be reversed. This depends on the reactor configuration, the sparger location, and the physical properties of the system. An increase in the hold-up in the downcomer may be due to enhanced coalescence, which increases the upward velocity of the swarm and therefore reduces V_g. Presence of obstacles in the downcomer, due to poor design or the introduction of heat exchangers or bulky measuring devices, may lead to an increase in coalescence. In bubbly downward flow, every disturbance in the stream-lines becomes a center of coalescence. When a secondary stream of gas is injected into the downcomer, instability may arise. Under certain conditions, an inversion of the direction of flow may occur. Kubota et al. [31] proposed a model for the ICI deep-shaft aerator [30], based on mass and momentum balance and empirical relations between gas velocity, liquid velocity, and gas hold-up. The model predicted three zones on the J_L, J_G plane: one where the operation of the equipment is stable, one where the operation of the equipment is unstable, and one where the mathematical model gave no solution, implying inversion of the direction of flow.

Overall Gas Hold-up

Most of the reported data on gas hold-up in baffled vessels do not discriminate between different regions in the reactor. This is especially true when the data were not obtained from local pressure measurements, but by measuring the height of the clear liquid and evaluating the height of the bubbly liquid during operation. In such cases, within the range of clear liquid circulation in the downcomer, the measured gas content is about half of the real hold-up in the riser. Therefore, the onset of bubble recirculation should be clearly indicated in reports of hold-up data.

In an external loop device the hold-up depends strongly on the liquid velocity, and therefore on the geometric configuration (Figures 7 and 8). This has also been observed in baffled vessels. Optimal values for the diameter ratio have been proposed for concentric-tube air-lift reactors. Onken and Weiland [1] proposed an optimum diameter ratio of 0.8 for minimum mixing time. Wang and Cuevas [69] found that in the range 0.59 to 0.75 the diameter ratio was not very critical. However, the diameter ratio is not the only factor affecting the hold-up. Also, the height of the liquid above the baffle (which sets the size of the gas separator [33]) and the clearance at bottom of the reactor strongly influence the hold-up and hence the performance of air-lift fermentors. This makes it very difficult to establish a general correlation for hold-up. Figure 9 illustrates this difficulty. In the figure, some of the data reported on gas hold-up in air lifts are presented

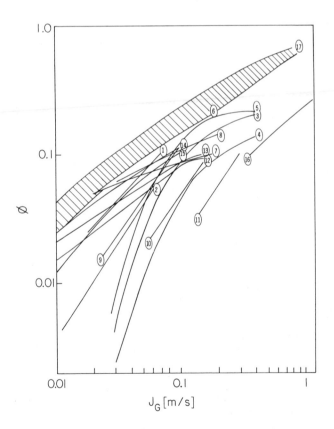

Figure 9. Experimental data on gas hold-up in air-lift reactors. See references in Table 1.

Table 1
Researchers and Experimental Data on Gas Hold-Up in Air-Life Reactors (Figure 9)

Reference	Type	D[m]	Dd[m]	System
1. Baker and Worgan [32]	Concentric tubes	0.1	0.07	Starch soln.
2. Baker and Worgan [32]	Concentric tubes	0.3	0.21	Starch soln.
3. Field-Slater [42]	Concentric tubes	0.152	0.095	Water
4. Field-Slater [42]	Concentric tubes	0.152	0.095	1% ethanol
5 Field-Slater [42]	Concentric tubes	0.152	0.095	Antifoam agent
6. Koide et al. [17]	Concentric tubes	0.140	0.094	Water
7. Koide et al. [17]	Concentric tubes	0.140	0.082	$270 \, mol/m^2 \, BaCl$
8. Koide et al. [17]	Concentric tubes	0.140	0.082	50% glycerol
9. Chakravarti et al. [45]	Concentric tubes	0.1	0.074	Water
10. Chakravarti et al. [45]	Concentric tubes	0.1	0.045	Water
11. Chakravarti et al. [45]	Concentric tubes	0.1	0.045	Water
12. Weiland and Onken [26]	External loop	0.1	0.05	Water
13. Weiland and Onken [26]	External loop	0.1	0.05	51% sacchrose
14. Akita and Kawasaki [25]	External loop	0.33	0.052	Water (riser)
15. Akita and Kawasaki [25]	External loop	0.33	0.052	Water (downcomer)
16. Hills [23]	External loop	0.149	0.149	Water
17. Shah et al. [56]	Bubble columns, various authors			

schematically. The dashed area (Figure 9) encloses the zone covered by several correlations for gas hold-up in bubble columns [56]. It is immediately seen that the dispersion is much wider for air-lift reactors.

The effect of liquid properties on gas hold-up has been studied by several authors [17, 18, 25, 26, 42, 45]. The effect of solutes that change the surface tension and coalescence has the same general trend in air-lift reactors as in bubble columns. However, the effect is much smaller, because bubble coalescence becomes less important as liquid velocity increases.

Some correlations have been proposed for specific types of air-lift reactors. Chakravarti et al. [45], and Koide et al. [17, 18] studied the influence of gas distribution, liquid properties, and some of the geometric characteristics of concentric-tube air-lift reactors. However, the ratio of gas separator volume to total reactor volume did not receive in those studies the importance that it deserves.

Akita and Kawasaki [25] performed a similar study on an external-loop air-lift reactor. They found that the gas hold-up depended on the same factors that appear in Akita-Yoshida's correlation for bubble columns [64]. Their data for six different liquids can be represented by the equation:

$$\phi/(1 - \phi)^4 = 0.31 \left(\frac{gD^2\rho_\ell}{\sigma}\right)^{1/5} \left(\frac{gD^3}{v_L^2}\right)^{1/30} \left(\frac{J_G}{\sqrt{gD}}\right) \tag{22}$$

This correlation holds for $J_G < 0.6$ m/s. In this range of low superficial gas velocities, the predicted hold-up is higher than the experimental results reported for the riser by Merchuk and Stein [16] or Onken and Weiland [26]. However, it must be recognized that the configuration of the reactors used by Merchuk and Weiland was different from Akita's. These authors obtained complete separation of the gas-liquid dispersion at the gas separator, which was a special section with a larger cross-sectional area than the riser. On the other hand, in Akita's air lift reactor, the gas separator was simply a continuation of the riser. This leads to recirculation of bubbles at low values of J_G. It is almost impossible to avoid trapping large quantities of gas in the entrance of the downcomer. In our laboratory we have also observed that with this type of downcomer, it is very difficult to avoid the formation of large bubbles in the lower part of the downcomer. These bubbles grow until eventually they rise against the current. This phenomenon appears in any downcomer with non-vertical sections, and diminishes the liquid recirculation velocity unless the system has very low coalescence or the downcomer is more than 0.10 m in diameter.

LIQUID VELOCITY

Liquid velocity is the main characteristic that differentiates bubble columns from air lift reactors (see Figure 1). Accordingly, it is one of the key parameters in design and scale-up. It affects the mixing characteristics of both gas and liquid phases, volumetric mass and heat transfer coefficients, suspension of solids, and uniformity of temperature and concentration, which determine the chemical reaction rates and therefore the performance of the reactor. In bubble columns that operate continuously, the liquid velocity is usually below 0.05 m/s, whereas in industrial-size air-lift reactors this velocity can be on the order of 1-2 m/s [30].

Since the circulation velocity of the liquid depends on the difference between the hydrostatic pressure in the riser and downcomer, the liquid velocity will depend on the height of the device. The experimental data from small equipment are therefore difficult to extrapolate since end effects may dominate. This is the case with most of the reported data on baffled vessels. The taller the experimental device, the easier to obtain meaningful data on liquid velocities.

In contrast to the data for hold-up ϕ shown in Figure 9, Figure 10 shows that there is a remarkable similarity between the data reported on superficial liquid velocity versus superficial gas velocity in different types of air-lift reactors. The similarity is not in the absolute value, but in the rate of change of J_L with J_G. The slope of all the lines, for both external-loop or baffled-vessel air-lift reactors, is approximately 0.4. The absolute value is determined by the pressure-drop-caused friction in the loop. Different frictional effects may be due to the different physical properties of the liquid [19] or to obstructions in the loop [16]. In the experiments of Merchuk and Stein [16] and Onken and Weiland [26] a series of parallel or almost-parallel lines were obtained, which are indicated as shaded zones in Figure 10. The superficial liquid velocity was higher the lower the viscosity of the liquid [26] and the smaller the obstruction to liquid flow in the circuit [16]. When mechanical obstruction of the conduit is too great with respect to the viscosity of the system, the slope of the V_L vs. J_G line changes, and the velocity tends toward an asymptotic value (Figure 11) [16]. This implies that the air-lift effect is less as we approach the slug-flow regime. The asymptotic zone indicates a situation where, due to frictional losses in the circuit, the energy introduced by the gas stream is dissipated more and more in internal recirculation loops within the riser. The lines are straight with a slope of approximately 0.4 up to a critical point where the velocity begins to tend asymptotically to a maximum value for a given system. Figure 11 shows that the liquid velocity

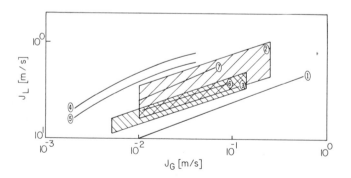

Figure 10. Superficial liquid velocity as function of superficial gas velocity for several air-lift reactors. See references in Table 2.

Table 2
Liquid Velocity as a Function of Gas Superficial Velocity (Figure 10)

Researcher	Type	D[m]	Dd[m]	System
1. Merchuk [59]	2-dimensional external loop	0.025*0.015	0.5	Water
2. Merchuk and Stein [16]	External loop	0.14	0.14	Water
3. Weiland and Onken [26]	External loop	0.10	0.05	Various liquids
4. Akita and Kawasaki [26]	External loop	0.33	0.075	Various liquids
5. Akita and Kawasaki [26]	External loop	0.33	0.075	Various liquids
6. Chakravarti et al. [45]	Concentric	0.1	0.074	Various liquids
7. Barker and Morgan [32]	Concentric	0.1	0.07	Starch solution

may be represented by the equation:

$$V_L = bJ_G^{0.4} \tag{23}$$

up to a critical point, as already indicated. The constant b depends on the physical properties of
the system and the geometric design of the reactor. The critical point seems to indicate a change
in the flow configuration from turbulent bubble flow to the regime defined by Zuber and Findley
[72] as "churn turbulent." This regime is a coalescing flow in which the tube is too wide to permit
its complete bridging by the gas that is defined in smaller tubes as slug flow.

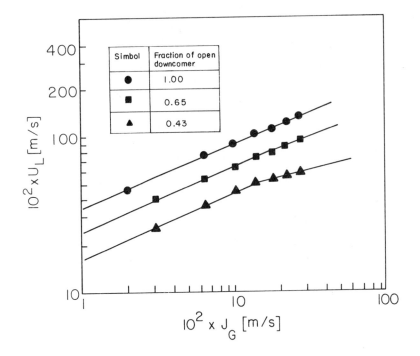

Figure 11. Liquid velocity versus superficial gas velocity in an external loop air-lift without gas
recirculation, for different degrees of obstruction of liquid flow in the downcomer [16].

If the liquid velocity cannot be directly measured and if no correlation of the type of Equation 23 is available, V_L can be obtained from the energy balance of the system if the hold-up is known. This approach will also make it possible to foresee the influence of the system geometry on V_L.

We have seen in Equation 9 that the pressure drop in the reactor can be considered to be generated by three components: gravity, friction, and acceleration. The last component will be neglected because calculations performed for our system have shown that the contribution of acceleration to the total pressure drop was in all cases less than 2%.

The pressure drop in the riser and the downcomer are given by Equations 24 and 25, respectively.

$$\Delta P_r = P_{1r} - P_{2r} = \Delta P_{Fr} + \Delta P_{Hr} \tag{24}$$

$$\Delta P_d = P_{1d} - P_{2d} = \Delta P_{Hd} - \Delta P_{Fd} \tag{25}$$

where the subscripts are

$\quad$ 1 = bottom of the tubes

$\quad$ 2 = top of the tubes

$\quad$ r = riser

$\quad$ d = downcomer

$\quad$ F = frictional loss

$\quad$ H = hydrostatic loss

Neglecting the pressure drop in the gas-liquid separator at the top of the equipment and indicating the pressure drop associated with the loop design as ΔP_B, Equations 24 and 25 give:

$$\Delta P_{Hd} - \Delta P_{Hr} = \Delta P_B + \Delta P_{Fr} + \Delta P_{Fd} \tag{26}$$

The left-hand term in Equation 26 is the difference in hydrostatic heads in the riser and downcomer and can be expressed as a function of the hold-up:

$$\Delta P_{Hd} - \Delta P_{Hr} = L\rho_L g(\phi - \phi_d) \tag{27}$$

Without loss of generality, we will assume here that there is no gas in the downcomer, i.e., that $\phi_d = 0$.

The frictional terms for the riser can be represented by an integrated form of Equation 15:

$$\Delta P_{Fr} = 2C_{fM}\rho_L J_L(J_L + J_G)\frac{L}{D_h} \tag{28}$$

with C_{fM} given by Equation 16.

For the downcomer and the additional term ΔP_B, the pressure drops can be written respectively as:

$$\Delta P_{Fd} = 2C_{fL}\rho_L L J_L^2/D_{hd} \tag{29}$$

$$\Delta P_B = 2C_{fL}\rho_L L_E J_L^2/D_{hB} \tag{30}$$

L_E being the length of an equivalent straight tube. The coefficient C_{fL} may be taken as the Blausius form:

$$C_{fL} = 0.0791\ Re^{-0.25} \tag{31}$$

Now Equation 26 can be written for round tubes as:

$$\phi = \frac{2J_L^2}{gD_r}\left[\left(1 + \frac{J_{Gr}}{J_L}\right)C_{fM} + C_{fL}\left(1 + \frac{L_E}{L}\right)\zeta\right]$$

(32)

where ζ is the ratio of the hydraulic diameters of the riser and the downcomer. Equation 32 is quite general and permits calculation of the superficial liquid velocity from direct measurements of the superficial gas velocity and the hold-up for a given geometric system. This method of calculation can be extended to the case of gas recirculation in the downcomer [31, 44]. Here, however, the increase in gas hold-up in the downcomer is an additional element, which eventually leads to an asymptotic value of the liquid velocity. If the geometric design of the air-lift allows the assumption that the frictional losses in the riser are negligible compared to the total energy losses in the loop, $\Delta P_{Fr} \ll \Delta P_{Fd} + \Delta P_{FB}$, Equation 32 predicts that J_L will be proportional to $J_G^{0.5}$, which is close to the observed values in Figures 10 and 11 and Equation 23.

GAS VELOCITY

The velocity of gas bubbles relative to the average velocity of the liquid surrounding them, is called the slip velocity and is one of the main elements that determines the gas content in the system. In Figure 12 the absolute and relative gas velocities are presented as a function of the superficial gas velocity J_G for an external-loop air-lift reactor without gas recirculation [16]. Since the gas velocity varies along the riser, the point $z = 2.25$ m, the middle of the column, was selected as representative.

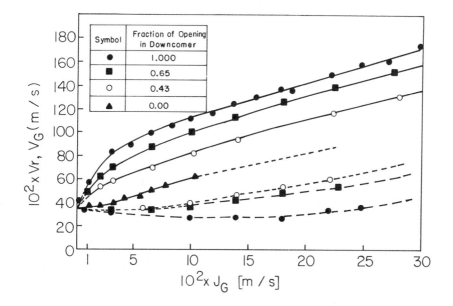

Figure 12. Gas absolute velocity (solid line) and relative velocity (broken line) as a function of the superficial gas velocity at a point in the middle of the riser ($z = 2.25$ m) in an external loop air-lift reactor [16].

Zuber and Findley [72] showed that in bubble flow the relative gas-liquid velocity is given by:

$$V_r = 1.53(\sigma g \Delta \rho / \rho_L^2)^{1/2} \tag{33}$$

This expression predicted, for the air-water system, a value of about 0.30 m/s, independent of the superficial gas velocity. On the other hand, for the bubble-slug region, they give:

$$V_r = 0.35 (g \Delta \rho D_c / \rho_L)^{1/2} \tag{34}$$

predicting for $D_c = 0.14$ m about 0.40 m/s.

Figure 12 shows that even if V_r remains in this range of values, the influence of J_G is present. The relative gas velocity obtained is in agreement with Zuber and Findley's predictions at low superficial gas velocities. As J_G increases a minimum appears, and after it, higher values of V_r are obtained, increasing as the obstruction in the downcomer is increased (i.e., the liquid velocity is decreased). A similar observation was made by Schugerl et al. [67] on an air-water system. They explained the phenomenon as due to coalescence of bubbles. In addition, they found that additives like alcohols, which hinder coalescence, produce curves of V_r vs. J_G that do not show a minimum, and that fit the expression given by Marucci [71]:

$$\frac{V_r}{J_G} = (1 - \phi)^2 / (1 - \phi^{5/3}) \tag{35}$$

deduced for a coalescence-free system. The data reported in Figure 12 seem to indicate that the bubbles rise almost without coalescence at low superficial gas velocity. At high values, the coalescence phenomenon becomes more and more important and the behavior departs from that predicted by Marrucci. An increase in coalescence will lead to a subsequent increase in the relative velocity.

The second influential factor is internal recirculation, which tends to increase the gas velocity at the axis, as noted before. This explains the higher values of V_r obtained as the downcomer is obstructed.

Curves of the absolute gas velocity show a quasi-exponential form in the range of net bubble flow (low J_G). After about 0.05 m/s they increase almost linearly with the superficial gas velocity J_G (Figure 12).

Zuber and Findley [72] derived the following expression for the case of two-phase, unidirectional flow:

$$V_G = \frac{J_G}{\phi} = C_o J_M + V_d \tag{36}$$

The drift velocity V_d is the gas velocity relative to the velocity of the gas-liquid mixture, and C_o, the distribution parameter, is a constant that depends on the radial profiles of velocity and hold-up in the column. The flatter these profiles, the closer C_o will be to unity. It was noted by Hills [23] that Equation 36 should be considered empirical, since the theoretical derivation was done for pure slug flow, where a control surface can be drawn ahead of the slug on a gas-free area [73, 74].

In Figure 13, the gas velocity V_G for a multiple-orifice sparger is presented as a function of the overall flux of the mixture J_M for various locations along the height of the tower and various openings of the downcomer. All data are fitted satisfactorily by a single straight line, giving $V_d = 0.33$ m/s, which is in agreement with the value calculated for V_r at a low superficial gas velocity.

The value obtained from the slope of the straight line in Figure 13 is $C_o = 1.03$. This indicates fairly flat velocity and hold-up radial profiles along the tower and for all experimental conditions with the same sparger. The correlation reported by Hatch [34] for two concentric-tube air-lift devices has a similar form as that reported here for separate tubes. Nassos and Bankoff [52] and Hills [23] reported similar results for separate tubes.

This homogeneity of gas hold-up profiles in the air-lift reactor contrasts with the parabolic profiles across the cross-section in bubble columns [19, 62]. They are a direct consequence of the circulation of liquid in the loop.

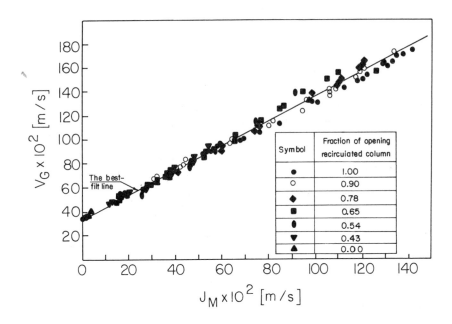

Figure 13. Gas velocity V_G vs. the overall flux of the mixture J_M in the riser of an external loop air-lift reactor without gas recirculation [16].

MIXING IN AIR-LIFT REACTORS

The phenomenon of mixing is important in the design of reactors, since the history of a fluid element (time spent in each of the environments that the reactor offers, age of other elements that it contacts) will be of crucial importance in evaluating conversion and yield. This has been shown by Bajpai and Reuss [75] in a simulation of the oxidative and fermentative growth of baker's yeast.

In continuous reactors, the mixing characteristics are usually expressed as residence-time distributions. In tubular reactors it is customary to adopt the axial or longitudinal dispersion model, which has the advantage of being a single parameter model. This parameter is the axial dispersion coefficient D_T, which can be expressed in dimensionless form as Peclet or Bodenstein numbers (Equations 37 and 38). In a batch system it is usual to report the mixing characteristics as the mixing time, which is the time to achieve some degree of homogeneity in concentration (usually 90% or 95%) after the injection of a pulse of tracer.

Consideration of the behavior of the fluid in the riser and downcomer of an air-lift reactor leads to the conclusion that it must share some of the characteristics of tubular reactors. On the other hand, if circulation around the loop is rapid, it will behave, as a whole, in a fashion similar to batch, backmixed reactors. It has been shown elsewhere [81, 82] that a higher superficial gas velocity leads to a higher liquid velocity, and therefore a lower recirculation time for the liquid. As the recirculation time becomes smaller, so does the change in concentration along the tubes. In other words, as J_G increases, the profiles of concentration become flatter, and therefore closer to the uniform concentration that characterizes an ideal continuous-stirred tank.

Because of this mixed behavior of air-lift reactors, data on mixing have been expressed both as mixing time and as axial dispersion coefficients.

In spite of the recognized need for knowledge of the mixing characteristics of air-lift reactors, not much data have been published yet. The liquid mixing in the riser can be compared with the mixing in bubble columns, especially when the recirculation ratio is low [20]. Data on the axial dispersion coefficient in bubble columns have been summarized by Shah et al. [76]. However, in the case of extensive recirculation, the liquid velocities are much larger and exceed the range of velocities usually used in bubble columns. Liquid velocity is an order of magnitude higher in air-lift reactors [1, 16] and influences gas hold-up and flow configuration [77]. Therefore, data obtained specifically in air-lift reactors are desirable. Some data have been published on the mixing characteristics of the liquid phase in outer-loop reactors [26, 27] and in concentric-tube air-lift reactors [41–43, 47, 79].

Blenke [47] developed an elegant solution for the response of a cyclic reactor to a pulse injection of tracer, by superimposing the responses expected in each successive cycle of the tracer in the reactor. By curve fitting, a single parameter is obtained that characterizes the behavior of the whole reactor. This method is especially suitable for systems with mean circulation time, which is the time spent by a liquid element in traveling around the loop, that is short with respect to the mixing time. If the circulation time is much shorter than the mixing time, the response to a pulse will be the sum of the effects of the successive passages of the traces in front of the detector. This will be essentially the case of short reactors. Many of the experimental data published on air-lift devices fall into this category, especially for baffled vessels. Since the gas-liquid separation zone can be approximately considered as perfectly mixed and the riser and downcomer as plug flow regions, it follows that an increase in the length of the latter zones will lead to a system whose response to a pulse injection will be peaks that can be easily separated, while a short device will yield peaks that are superimposed.

The model proposed by Blenke [47] permits handling such superimposed peaks and obtaining the corresponding Bodenstein numbers. However, the use in scale-up of the Bodenstein numbers, Bo, obtained by this method has a serious restriction. This parameter depends not only on the mixing in the three sections just defined, but also on the relation between them. This can be best explained intuitively. Consider as an example a concentric draft-tube air lift reactor. If we decide to increase the volume of the reactor by doubling the height but without changing the diameter of the tubes, it is obvious that the Bo obtained in the first configuration will not represent the system any longer. Furthermore, the Bo representing the second configuration cannot be derived from the first. It follows that, when possible, separate evaluation of the mixing in the different regions is desirable.

Many of the data on mixing in air-lift reactors have been presented as Bodenstein numbers:

$$Bo = V_L L/D_T \tag{37}$$

L being the length of the loop i. On the other hand, Joshi [79] has shown that most of the data on liquid-phase dispersion coefficients in bubble columns can be correlated as a simple function of the product of velocity times the column diameter D_c. Therefore, it seems more appropriate to present results as Peclet numbers:

$$Pe = V_L D_c/D_T \tag{38}$$

Data on Peclet numbers for several air-lift reactors are plotted against the superficial gas velocity in Figure 14. Lines 1 to 8 correspond to external-loop reactors. It can be seen that the higher Pe values correspond to the data by Mor and Nagar [80], which were obtained in a reactor where the downcomer and the riser had the same diameter. The lower value of Pe in some of the data of Lin et al. [27] can be explained by the presence of radial baffles in the riser, which increase the mixing. However, Lin's data for an unbaffled riser also are much lower than for all other unbaffled reactors. The data by Weiland and Onken [18] for several liquids are dispersed over a rather wide range of Peclet numbers. It becomes evident that there is no agreement between the reported data.

All the data on liquid dispersion in external loop reactors refer to the riser rather than to the total device. This is not the case for baffled reactors. The data plotted in Figure 14 (lines 9 to 12) correspond to concentric-tube air-lift reactors. In all these cases the Peclet numbers reflect to the overall performance of the device and were obtained by analysis of the global response of riser, gas separator, and downcomer. Therefore, great care should be taken in comparing these data with those corresponding only to the riser (lines 1 to 8). It seems reasonable to expect the Peclet numbers

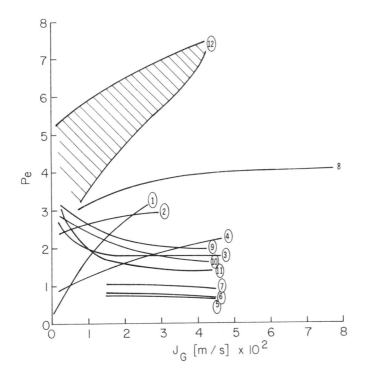

Figure 14. Peclet numbers for several air-lift reactors as a function of superficial gas velocity. See references in Table 3.

Table 3
Researchers and Data for Figure 14

Researcher	Type	D[m]	Di	Liquid
1. Weiland and Onken [19]	External loop	0.1	0.05	2-propanol 1.65%
2. Weiland and Onken [19]	External loop	0.1	0.05	2-propanol 1.65%
3. Weiland and Onken [19]	External loop	0.1	0.05	Water
4. Weiland and Onken [19]	External loop	0.1	0.05	CMC 50%
5. Lin et al. [27]	External loop Baffled	0.15	0.05	Water
6. Lin et al. [27]	External loop	0.075	0.025	Water
7. Lin et al. [27]	External loop unbaffled	0.15	0.05	Water
8. Mor and Nagar [1]	External loop unbaffled	0.14	0.14	Water
9. Fields and Slater [42]	Concentric tubes	0.152	0.095	Water antifoam
10. Fields and Slater [42]	Concentric tubes	0.152	0.095	Water
11. Fields and Slater [42]	Concentric tubes	0.152	0.095	1% ethanol
12. Blenke [47]	Concentric tubes	0.3	0.206	Various liquids

corresponding to the whole reactor to be lower (higher dispersion), but this is not so in Figure 14. It must be concluded that the experimental methods and data processing utilized by the different authors lead to results that are not comparable. The only safe conclusions are the qualitative conclusions that can be drawn from comparison of data obtained by the same researcher.

Weiland and Onken [18] concluded that the physical properties of the liquid phase and the gas velocity are the main parameters that determine the longitudinal dispersion in the liquid phase. Within the range of usual gas velocities, it decreases with increasing liquid viscosity and decreasing surface tension. They observed that longitudinal dispersion is smaller in alcoholic solutions because of more uniform liquid flow and the formation of smaller eddies by the narrower wakes resulting from smaller bubbles. This concurs with the observation of Fields and Slater [42] who found that addition of alcohols produced smaller bubbles that led to higher bubble recirculation, higher hold-up, and lower longitudinal dispersion. From the experiments run by the same authors [42], the shortcoming of Bo as a scale-up parameter are evident. They conducted two sets of experiments with an air-water system. In the first set, the total volume in the column was maintained constant, while in the second set the aerated volume was held constant. Therefore the volume acting as gas separator was kept constant. In this last case, they found that changes in the height of the concentric baffle led to substantial changes in the value of Bo. When the liquid volume was kept constant, the volume operating as the gas separator increased in proportion to the increase in the total holdup. This means that when the total hold-up in their experimental device increased from 10% to 15%, the volume of the gas separator increased by 100%. They found that in these experiments the Bodenstein number was the same for all baffle heights. This simply shows that the gas separator took the leading role in the system. Therefore the differences in mixing in the riser and downcomer become irrelevant. In this case, Bo is lower, indicating a higher degree of mixing. Fields and Slater [42] also present the only reported data on mixing in the gas separator (Figure 15). They show that as the gas flow increases, this section reaches a state of complete mixing, while at low flow rates little dispersion occurs. These data are very valuable since it is possible to extrapolate for other sizes of reactors, and they can be used in scale-up calculations. Such an extrapolation can only be made for data that refer to an individual reactor section, but not for data on overall mixing in the reactor. This applies also to the data on mixing time published by many researchers.

Mixing time is very important, particularly in fermentation processes, where acids or alkalis in high concentration are added for the purpose of pH control. If the system behavior is close to a plug-flow reactor, the acidity or alkalinity may locally exceed permissible values, and the micro-organisms can be damaged. Therefore, a short mixing time is desirable. However, the usefulness of the published values for mixing time is questionable because the mixing characteristics of the three sections of the air-lift are completely different. Therefore, the mixing time of the whole device cannot be used to extrapolate to other scales or designs. Obviously, the point of injection of an additive is very important. If rapid mixing is desirable the gas separator seems to be the obvious choice.

The mixing in the gas phase is very important for the design of an air-lift reactor. This is of particular interest in the gas separator. Indeed, appropriate design can lead to different degrees of recirculation of the gas bubbles, and even to entrapment of fresh gas from the top of the reactor. The degree in which each phenomenon contributes to gas recirculation in the downcomer is a most important element in the design and scale-up of air-lift reactors, and constitutes a point that must still be studied.

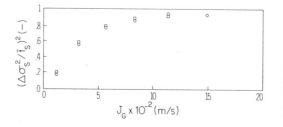

Figure 15. Change in dimensionless variance $\Delta\sigma_s^2/t^2$ of a pulse of tracer due to passage through the gas separator: 1.5-m drough tube ($\bullet$), 2-m draught tube ($\square$) [42].

CONCLUSIONS

Air-lift reactors have received much interest recently, both in basic research and industrial applications [1]. It is recognized that the fluid dynamic characteristics are the main point of difference between them and classical bubble columns. The co-current flow of gas and liquid produces a uniform distribution of both phases and also diminishes the collisions between bubbles, and hence coalescence. Therefore, the physical properties of the liquid, which determine whether two neighboring bubbles coalesce or not, are not as important in air lift reactors as in bubble columns. The gas hold-up is lower than in bubble columns, but the residence time of gas bubbles can be controlled better. This control may be done by design of the loop. The rate of liquid recirculation is determined by gas input, the frictional pressure drop in the loop and the degree of disengagement of the bubbles at the top of the reactor.

The homogeneity of the liquid and gas flow suggests that air-lift fermenters are suitable for cultivation of cells sensitive to shearing stress, in particular plant and animal cells. However, much work still remains to be done in studying the structure of the turbulence in air-lift reactors [20]. Even the macroscopic characteristics of the mixing have been only scantily studied, especially the analysis of the separate components of air-lift reactors. The same can be said to a lesser extent with respect to liquid velocity and gas hold-up, where some data are available but a unified way of presenting and correlating them is still needed.

NOTATION

A	cross section of the tube, m^2		g	gravitational acceleration, m/s^2
b	constant in Equation 24, $(m/s)^{1-n}$		h	manometric differential reading, m
C_f	friction coefficient, $(-)$		J	superficial velocity, m/s
C_{WG}	contact area between the gas phase and the wall, m^2		L	tube length, m
			L_e	equivalent tube length, m
C_{LW}	contact area between the liquid phase and the wall, m^2		$\dot{m}$	mass flow rate, kg/s
			N_{Re}	mixture Reynolds number, $(-)$
C_{LG}, C_{GL}	contact area between the liquid phase and the gas phase, m^2		n	constant in Equation 24, $(-)$
			P	pressure, Pa
C_o	distribution parameter, $(-)$		Q	volumetric flow rate, m^3/s
D_c	tube diameter, m		V	velocity, m/s
D_h	hydraulic diameter, m		z	axial coordinate, m
D_T	dispersion coefficient, m^2/hr			

Greek Symbols

μ	viscosity, poise		ρ	density, kg/m^3
v	dynamic viscosity, cm^2/s		σ	superficial tension, N/m
ζ	ratio of hydraulic diameter of riser and downcomer, $(-)$		τ	shear stress, Pa
			ϕ	hold-up

Indices

B	bottom		L	liquid
d	downcomer		m	manometer
F	friction		M	mixture
int	integral		W	wall of the pipe
G	gas		r	riser, relative
H	hydrostatic			

REFERENCES

1. Onken, U., and Weiland, P., in *Advances in Biotechnological Processes I*, A. Mizrahi and L. Van Wenzel (eds.) Alan R. Liss, Inc., N.Y. (1982).
2. Malone, R. J., *CEP*, June 1980, p. 53.
3. Vogelman, H., et al., in *Production of Natural Compounds by Cell Culture Methods*, A. W. Alferman and E. Reinert (Eds.) Muenchen: Gesellschaft fur Strahlen and Umweltforschung mbH, 1978.
4. Wagner, F., and Vogelman, H., in *Plant Tissue Culture and its Biotechnological Application*, W. Barz, E. Reinhart and M. H. Zend (eds.), p. 245, Berlin, Springer 1977.
5. Wilson, G., in *Advances in Biochemical Engineering*, A. Fiechter (Ed.) 16:1 (1980).
6. Mizrahi, A., *Advances in Fermentation*, Chelsea College, London (1983).
7. Mizrahi, A., and Moore, G. E., *Applied Microbiology*, 21:754 (1971).
8. Mizrahi, A., *J. Clin. Microbiol.* 2:11 (1976).
9. Choudary, A. G., and Pirt, S. J., *J. Gen. Microbiol*, 41:99 (1965).
10. Dion, W. H., et al., Rev. 1st. Super. Sanita. 1:177 (1961).
11. Elmayergi, H., Scharer, J. H., and Moo Young, M., *Biotechnol. Bioeng.*, 15:45 (1973).
12. Kobayashi, T., Van Dedem, G., and Moo Young, M., *Biotechnol. Bioeng.* 15:27 (1973).
13. Peppler, H. J., (Ed.), *Microbiol. Technology*, Reinhold, N.Y. (1967).
14. Vase, D. A. J., Patel, Y. R., and McManamoy, W. J., Proceedings of the Conference on Advances in Fermentation, Chelsea College, London (1983).
15. Flower, M. W., *Prog. Ind. Microbiol.*, 16:207 (1982).
16. Merchuk, J. C., and Stein, Y., *AIChE J.*: 27:377 (1981).
17. Koide, K., Sato, H., and Iwamoto, S., *J. Chem. Eng. Japan*, 16:407 (1983).
18. Koide, K., *J. Chem. Eng. Japan*, 16:413 (1983).
19. P. Weiland and U. Onken, *Ger. Chem. Eng.*, 4:174 (1981).
20. Schugerl, K., in *Advances in Biochemical Engineering*, (A. Fiechter, (ed.) 22:93 (1982).
21. Shah, Y. T., et al., *AIChE J.*: 28, 353 (1982).
22. Hsu, Y. C., and Dudukovic, M. P., *Chem. Eng. Sci.*, 35:135 (1980).
23. Hills, J. H., *The Chemical Engineering Journal*, 12:89 (1976).
24. Mercer, D. G., *Biotechnol. Bioeng.*, 23:2421 (1981).
25. K., Akita and Kawasaki, M., *Proceedings 48th Meeting of Chemical Engineers of Japan*, p. 122, Kyoto (1983).
26. Onken, U., and Weiland, P., *European J. Appl. Microbiol. Biotechnol.*, 10:31 (1980).
27. Lin, C. H., et al., *Biotechnol. Bioeng.* 18:1557 (1976)
28. Lewis, D. A., and Davidson, J. F., *Chem. Eng. Sci.*, 38:161 (1983).
29. Flower, M. W., and Stepan-Sarkissian, G., in *Advances in Biotechnological Processes* 2, A. Mizrahi and L. Van Wenzel (eds.), p. 135, Alan R. Liss, New York (1983).
30. Hines, D. A., et al., *Int. Chem. Eng. Symp. Ser.*, 41 (1975).
31. Kubota, H., Hasano, Y., and Fujie, K., *J. Chem. Eng. Japan*, 11:319 (1982).
32. Barker, T. W., and Worgan, J. T., *European J. Appl. Microbiol. Biotechnol.* 13:77 (1981).
33. Erickson, L. E., and Deshpande, V., in *Advances in Biotechnology I*, M. Moo Young, C. W. Robinson and C. Vezina (eds.), Oxford, England, Pergamon Press, p. 553 (1981).
34. Hatch, R. T., Ph. D. Dissertation, MIT (1973).
35. Ho, C. S., Erickson, L. E., and Fan, L. T., *Biotechnol. Bioeng.*, 19:1503 (1977).
36. Orazem, M., and Erickson, L. E., *Biotechnol. Bioeng.*, 21:69 (1979).
37. Bohner, K., and Blenke, H., *Verfahrenstechnik*, 6:50 (1972).
38. Fukuda, H., Sumino, Y., and Kanazaki, T., *J. Ferment. Technol.*, 46:829 (1978).
39. Wang, D. I. C., and Humphrey, A. E., *Chem. Eng.* 15:108 (1969).
40. Freedman, W., and Davidson, J. F., *Trans. Int. Chem. Engrs.*, 47:T251 (1969).
41. Hirner, W., and Blenke, H., *Verfahrenstechnik*, 11:279 (1977).
42. Field, P. R., and Slater, N. K. H., *Chem. Eng. Sci.*, 38:647 (1983).
43. Margaritis, A., and Sheppard, J. D., *Biotechnol. Bioeng.*, 23:2117 (1981).
44. Chakravarti, M., et al., *Indian Chem. Eng.*, 16:17 (1974).
45. Chakravarti, M., *Biotechnol. Bioeng. Symp. No.* 4:363 (1973).

46. Seipenbuch, R., and Blenke, H., in *Advances in Biochemical Engineering*, A. Feichter (ed.) 15:1 (1980).
47. Blenke, H., *Advances in Biochemical Engineering*, A. Fiechter (ed.) 13:121 (1979).
48. Gasner, L. L., *Biotechnol. Bioeng.*, 16:1179 (1974).
49. Hewitt, G. F., *Inl. Brit. Nucl. Energy Soc.*, 12:213 (1972).
50. Hewitt, G. F., and Lovegrove, P. C., *HITFS No. 21912*, EPRI NP-118 (1976).
51. Delhaye, J. M., Galaup, J. P., and Ricque, R., *C E N Grenoble*, Report CEA-R-4457 (1973).
52. Wallis, G. B., *One-Dimensional Two-Phase Flow*, McGraw-Hill Inc., N.Y. (1969).
53. Nassos, G. P., and Bankoff, B. G., *Chem. Eng. Sci.*, 22:661 (1967).
54. Stein, Y., *Gas Hold-up, Liquid Circulation and Mass Transfer Modeling in a Tower Cycling Reactor*, M.S. Thesis, Ben-Gurion University of the Negev, Israel (1979).
55. Bajpai, R. K., and Reuss, M., *The Canadian Journal of Chemical Engineering*, 60:384 (1982).
56. Shah, Y. T., et al., *AIChE J.*, 28:353 (1982).
57. Tsuge, H., and Hibino, S., *Int. Chem. Eng.*, 15:186 (1975).
58. Yamashita, F., and Inoue, H., *J. Chem. Eng. Japan*, 8:334 (1975).
59. Merchuk, J. C., *Chem. Eng. Sci.*, in press (1985).
60. Maruyama, T., Yoshida, S., and Misushina, T., *J. of Chem. Eng. Japan*, 14:352 (1981).
61. Sakata, M., and Miyauchi, T., *Kogaku Kogaku Ronbunshu*, 6:428 (1980).
62. Ueyama, K., and Miyauchi, T., *AIChE J.*, 25:258 (1979).
63. Nicklin, D. J., *Chem. Eng. Sci.*, 17:693 (1962).
64. Akita, K., and Yoshida, F., *Ind. Chem. Proc. Des. Dev.* 12:76 (1973).
65. Hikita, H., *Chem. Eng. J.*, 20:59 (1980).
66. Calderbank, P. H., Moo-Young, M. B., and Bibby, R., in *Third European Symposium on Chemical Reaction Engineering*, Pergamon Press (1964).
67. Schugerl, K., Lucke, J., and Oels, U., in *Advances in Biochemical Engineering*, A. Fiechter (ed.) 7:1 (1977).
68. Ueyama, K., and Miyauchi, T., *Kagaku Kogaku Ronbunshu*, 3:19 (1977).
69. Freedman, W., and Davidson, J. F., *Trans. Inst. Chem. Eng.*, 47:251 (1969).
70. Wang, D. I. C., Hatch, T. R., and Cuevas, C., *World Petroleum Congress*, Moscow, p. 149 (1971).
71. Marrucci, G., *Chem. Eng. Sci.*, 24:975 (1969).
72. Zuber, R. N., and Findlay, J. A., *J. Heat Transfer*, 87:453 (1965).
73. Davies, R. M., and Taylor, G., *Proc. R. Soc. Ser. A.*, 200:375 (1950).
74. Nicklin, D. J., Wilkes, J. O., and Davidson, J. F., *Trans. Inst. Chem. Eng.*, 40:61 (1962).
75. Bajpai, R. K., and Reuss, M., *The Canadian J. of Chem. Eng.*, 60:384 (1982).
76. Shah, Y. T., Stiegel, G. J., and Sharma, M. M., *AIChE Journal*, 24:369 (1978).
77. Walter, J. F., and Blanch, H. W., *Chem. Eng. Commun.* 19:213 (1983).
78. Kiese, S., Ebner, H. G., and Onken, U., *Biotechnol. Lett.*, 2:345 (1980).
79. Joshi, J. B., *Trans. I. Chem. E.*, 58:155 (1980).
80. Mor, G., and Nagar, H., *Senior Report, Dept. of Chemical Engineering, B.G. University of the Negev*, 1983.
81. Merchuk, J. C., Stein, Y., and Mateles, R., *Biotechnol. Bioeng.*, 22:1189 (1980).
82. Merchuk, J. C., and Stein, Y., *Biotechnol. Bioeng.*, 23:1309 (1981).

INDEX